ISBN 978-1-330-35306-6
PIBN 10037812

1 MONTH OF
FREE
READING

at
www.ForgottenBooks.com

By purchasing this book you are
eligible for one month membership to
ForgottenBooks.com, giving you
unlimited access to our entire
collection of over 700,000 titles via
our web site and mobile apps.

To claim your free month visit:

www.forgottenbooks.com/free37812

CATALOG OF COPYRIGHT ENTRIES

Third Series

VOLUME 1, PART 5A, NUMBER 1

Published Music

JANUARY–JUNE

1947

COPYRIGHT OFFICE

THE LIBRARY OF CONGRESS

WASHINGTON 25, D. C.

CONTENTS

PREFACE

THE Catalog of Copyright Entries for the year 1947 is issued in a new series and an enlarged format, a change designed to increase and extend the usefulness of the compilation. Inquiries, suggestions and comments on all details of the Catalog are solicited, and should be addressed to the Chief of the Cataloging Division, Copyright Office, Library of Congress, Washington 25, D. C.

CONTENTS. This part of the Catalog of Copyright Entries contains a list of published music registered in the Copyright Office from January 1, 1947, through June 30, 1947, in Class E, together with selected musical works registered in other classes. Renewal registrations of music made in this period are listed in Part 14 B of the Catalog.

ARRANGEMENT. The first section of this catalog consists of complete entries under main headings (composer, editor, arranger, or, in some cases, title). It is followed by an index by title for all registrations listed.

ENTRY. Under the main heading each entry includes the title, followed by the names of all authors. Name of publisher and place of publication are given when they differ from the name and address of the claimant. Filing titles are supplied in some entries to bring together all excerpts from one work, or to file works with non-distinctive titles under the name of the musical form. Filing titles are placed in curves in front of the title as taken from the work, for example:

> (Call me Mister) Going home train, from "Call me Mister."

> (Sonata, piano) 18th century theme from sonata in C major.

COPYRIGHT DATA. The statement giving the copyright facts is preceded by the copyright symbol ©. This is followed by the name and address of the claimant, the date of publication as defined in the Copyright Act, and the registration number. The registration number is preceded by one of the following symbols: EP (musical compositions published in the United States, registered in class E); EF (musical compositions published abroad, registered in class E); A (books proper, registered in class A); AA (selected pamphlets, registered in class A); B5 (contributions to periodicals, registered in class B); DP or D Pub. (published dramatic compositions, registered in class D). If the claim is based on new matter, a brief description of the new matter is given between the address and date.

DEPOSIT OF COPIES. In the case of every copyright entry listed in the catalog, the deposit of copies (or copy) as required by the Act of Congress of July 30, 1947 (Title 17, U.S.C., secs. 12, 13) has been made.

AUTHORITY. The Catalog of Copyright Entries is published pursuant to the authority given in the provisions of Sections 210 and 211 of the aforesaid Act.

Section 210 provides that the Catalog "shall be admitted in any court as prima facie evidence of the facts stated therein as regards any copyright registration."

ORGANIZATION OF THE CATALOG. This issue of the Catalog is part of Volume I of the new Third Series. The parts are numbered according to the alphabetical sequence of classes as listed in Section 5 of the aforesaid Act. Letters are used to designate subdivisions. The following is the plan of publication for 1947:

Part 1A - Books and Selected Pamphlets.
Part 1B - Pamphlets, Serials and Contributions to
          Periodical Literature.
Part 2 - Periodicals.
Parts 3 & 4 - Dramas and Works Prepared for Oral
          Delivery.
Part 5A - Published Music.
Part 5B - Unpublished Music.
Part 6 - Maps.
Parts 7-11A - Works of Art, Reproductions of Works of
          Art, Scientific and Technical Drawings, Photo-
          graphic Works, Prints and Pictorial Illustra-
          tions.
Part 11B- Commercial Prints and Labels.
Parts 12 & 13 - Motion Pictures.
Part 14A- Renewal Registrations - Literature, Art, Film.
Part 14B- Renewal Registrations - Music.

SUBSCRIPTION. The annual subscription price for the complete yearly Catalog of Copyright Entries is $10.00, payable in advance to the Superintendent of Documents, Government Printing Office, Washington 25, D. C., to whom inquiries and orders concerning the complete Catalog or any of its parts should be addressed.

A

AGREN, SIGURD.
Så kär som en flicka kan bli
... musik: Sigurd Agren,
text: E. Bohman. © Edition
Sylvain, a.b., Stockholm;
1Jan46; EF3732.

AHL, HELGA.
Jag blott tango dansa vill ...
av Curt Åkerlind, Compagna
[and] Helga Ahl; [arr. by
Sven Stiberg] © Skandinaviska
Odeon, a.b., Stockholm;
1Jan45; EF3746. Piano-conductor score (orchestra), and
parts.

AARON, MICHAEL.
Michael Aaron piano primer; [words
and music by Michael Aaron] ©
Mills Music, inc., New York;
7Jan47; EP6455.

AASTRUP, PER HOLMBERG- See
Holmberg-Aastrup, Per.

ACHESON, MARK W 1905-
The twenty-third psalm; for
mixed chorus with organ, by
Mark W. Acheson. © Composers
Press, inc., New York; 10May47;
EP14302.

ACHRON, ISIDOR.
Improvisation. [Op.11] [By]
Isidor Achron. © Carl Fischer,
inc., New York; 19Dec46;
EP11100. Score (violin and
piano) and part.

Sonnet, no. 2; [by] Isidor
Achron. Op. 6. © Carl Fischer,
inc., New York; on arrangement;
24Apr47; EP14066. For piano
solo.

ACKLEY, ALFRED H
Just leave it all with Jesus; [by]
A. H. Ackley, [words by] Oswald
J. Smith. © The Rodeheaver Co.,
Winona Lake, Ind.; 22Jul46;
EP10736. Close score: SATB.

ACKLEY, BENTLEY D 1872-
comp.
Easter helper, no. 47; comp.
by B. D. Ackley. Winona Lake,
Ind., Rodeheaver Hall-Mack Co.
© The Rodeheaver Co., Winona
Lake, Ind.; 10Feb47; EP12154.
Includes recitations, exercises
and hymns, with music.

A'DAIR, JEANNE, 1897-
(A hymn to) California; words by
Eleanor Roberts, music by
Jeanne A'Dair. © Jeanne A'Dair
& Eleanor Roberts, Los Angeles;
1Jan47; EP10924. For voice and
piano.

Idyll; lyric: Eleanor Roberts,
music: Jeanne A'Dair. © Jeanne
A'Dair and Eleanor Roberts, Los
Angeles; 28Apr47; EP14085.

Nothing but a dream? Words [by]
Eleanor Roberts, music [by]
Jeanne A'Dair. © Jeanne
A'Dair & Eleanor Roberts, Los
Angeles; 3Feb47; EP12050.

Pines; words by Eleanor Roberts, music
by Jeanne A'Dair. © Jeanne A'Dair
and Eleanor Roberts, Los Angeles;
8Jan47; EP11151. For voice and piano.

Vaquero Johnny; lyrics [by] Eleanor
Roberts, music [by] Jeanne A'Dair.
© Jeanne A'Dair and Eleanor
Roberts, Los Angeles; 19May47;
EP14539.

ADAM, ADOLPHE.
O holy night; [by] Adolphe Adam,
[arr. by H. P. Hopkins] ©
Century Music Publishing Co.,
New York; on arrangement;
12May47; EP14266. For piano
solo, with interlinear words.

ADAMS, CHARLES PERCIVAL, 1900-
You can't break a heart; words and
music by Charles Adams. © Charles
Percival Adams, Woodbury, N. J.;
13Dec46; EP11097.

ADAMS, STEPHEN.
The Holy City; for two choirs,
choir I, S.S.A. [and] choir
II S.A.T.B. [words by F. E.
Weatherly, music by Stephen
Adams] arr. by C. Albert
Scholin. © Belwin, inc., New
York; on arrangement; 3Apr47;
EP13194.

ADDINSELL, RICHARD, 1904-
Invocation; from the radio
feature "Journey to romance,"
by Richard Addinsell; for two
pianos. © Keith Prowse &
Co., ltd., London; on
arrangement; 31Dec46; EP4792.

Warsaw concerto; two pianos four
hand arrangement by Percy
Aldridge Grainger. New York,
Chappell. © Keith Prowse &
Co., ltd., London; on arrange-
ment; 30Dec46; EP11073.

ADRIAN, WALTER.
To music, to becalm his fever;
words by Robert Herrick, music
by Walter Adrian, arr. by Eric
H. Thiman. c1946. © Elkin
& Co., ltd., London; on
arrangement; 6Jun47; EP3831.
Score: SATB and piano re-
duction. Voice parts also in
tonic sol-fa notation.

AFRICAN METHODIST EPISCOPAL CHURCH.
Richard Allen hymnal.
The Richard Allen A.M.E. hymnal,
with responsive-Scripture
readings. Adapted ... by the
Committee on Revision of the
Hymnal. [c1946] © A.M.E.
Book Concern, Philadelphia; on
revision & compilation;
12Jan47; EP13546. With music.

AGOSTINI, FRANCOIS, 1898-
U vinu corsu. (Le vin corse)
... Paroles de Charles
Thibault, musique de François
Agostini. © Henry Lemoine
& Cie, Paris; 16Apr46;
EF3578. Melody and chord
symbols, with words.

AHDE, SVERKER.
Ska' man inte va' gla' ... Text
och musik: Sverker Ahde.
[c1946] © Edition Sylvain
a/b, Stockholm; 16Feb47;
EF5031.

AHLERT, FRED E
The moon was yellow. (El amor
llamé) Lyric by Edgar
Leslie, music by Fred E.
Ahlert. Standard ed. ©
Bregman, Vocco and Conn, inc.,
New York; on change in lyric;
7May47; EP14334.

ALARCÓN LEAL, EDUARDO.
Ay corazón; (Ora sí) ... letra
y música de Eduardo Alarcón
Leal. © Promotora Hispano
Americana de Música, s.a.,
México; 30Dec46; EF5456.

AHLSTRAND, DAVID, 1908-
Cheeriette; piano and accordion
novelty. © David Ahlstrand,
Port Orchard, Wash.; 31Dec46;
EP107060.

Kilroy boy; words by Louise
Parker, music by David Ahl-
strand. © Louise Parker,
Spartanburg, S. C.; 1Mar47;
EP12457.

Matrimony in disguise; words by
Arthur J. Pilon, music by
David Ahlstrand. © Arthur J.
Pilon, Dillon, Mont.; 1May47;
EP14512. Melody and chord
symbols, with words.

AKST, HARRY.
Say no more; words and music by
Benny Davis, Al Jolson [and]
Harry Akst. © Advanced Music
Corp., New York; 2Apr47;
EP13456.

The moon was yellow. (El amor llamé)
Lyric by Edgar Leslie, Spanish
lyric by Clotilde Arias, music
by Fred E. Ahlert ... © Bregman,
Vocco and Conn, inc., New York;
on Spanish words; 6Jan47;
EP10918. For voice and piano,
with chord symbols; English and
Spanish words.

Las golondrinas ... Letra y música
de Eduardo Alarcón Leal. © Promotora Hispano Americana de Música, s. a., México; 30Dec46;
EF5513.

Mala racha; y, Nomás porque sí;
letra y música de Eduardo
Alarcón Leal. © Promotora
Hispano Americana de Música, s.
a., México; 30Dec46; EF5519,
5518.

¡Viva mi suerte! ... Letra y
música de Eduardo Alarcón
Leal. © Promotora Hispano
Americana de Música, s.a.,
México; 17Dec45; EF5581.

ALBÉNIZ, ISAAC MANUEL FRANCISCO,
1860-1909.
Under the southern sky ... music
by I. Albéniz, arr. by Walling-
ford Riegger, words by Rhoda
Flammer, inc., New York; on
arrangement; 4Nov46; EP10836.
Under the southern sky; Tango in D;
music by I. Albéniz, arr. by Walling-
ford Riegger, words by Rhoda Newton
... S.A.B. © Harold Flammer, inc.,
New York; on arrangement; 31Dec46;
EP11421.
Under the southern sky; Tango in D;
music by I. Albéniz, arr. by
Wallingford Riegger, words by
Rhoda Newton ... S.A.T.B. ©
Harold Flammer, inc., New York; on
arrangement; 31Dec46; EP11420.

ALBERTI, SOLON.
A nation's prayer ... Poem by
Nita Gale, music by Solon
Alberti. © Elkan-Vogel Co.,
inc., Philadelphia; 25Mar47;
EP15931. Score: alto, chorus
(SSA) and piano.

ALBUM DE VILLANELLES; [words by
Pierre Bédat de Monlaur, music by
Robert Bernard, Francis Casa-
desus, Marcel Delannoy and
others] © Henry Lemoine et Cie,
Paris; 22Oct42; EF674.

ALCÁNTARA, RAÚL.
Estamos en paz; letra y música
de: Raúl Alcántara, arreglo de:
Evaristo Tafoya. © Promotora
Hispano Americana de Música,
s. a., Mexico; 30Dec46;
EF5278. Piano-conductor score
(orchestra, with words) and
parts.

ALDEN, JOHN.
La veeda; [by] John Alden, arr.
by Wm. C. Schoenfeld. New York,
Music Publishers Holding Corp.
© Remick Music Corp., New York;
on arrangement; 7May47; EP14406.
Parts: band.

ALDRICH, MARION, pseud. See
Mundlin, Lois.

ALEA, MARÍA MATILDE.
Te quiero y qué; letra y música
por María Matilde Alea. ©
Peer International Corp., New
York; 30Dec46; EF5553.

ALEWINE, ROBSON NEWMAN, 1898-
My Florida; words and music by
H. N. Alewine. © Hobson Newman Alewine, Hovona, Fla.;
1Dec46; EP14434.

ALEXANDER, JOSEF.
Three American episodes ... For
chorus of mixed voices, [by]
Josef Alexander, [words by]
Rosemary and Stephen Vincent
Benet. © The H. W. Gray Co.,
inc., New York; on 3 choruses;
28Feb47. Contents - [v.1].
Western wagons (© EP12397)-
[v.2] Negro spirituals (©
EP12396)- [v.3] Johnny Apple-
seed (© EP12399)

ALEXANDER, ROB ROY.
When the 13th comes on Friday ...
words and music by Rob Roy
Alexander. Cleveland, Music
Pub. Associates. © Rob Roy
Alexander, Cleveland; 17Apr47;
EP15677.

ALEXANDER, VAN.
First arrangement; by Van Alexander.
An introductory method of
arranging for the modern
orchestra. © Capitol Songs, inc.,
New York; 19Feb46; AA51817.

ALFORD, HARRY.
Imp ... by Harry Alford [ed. and
arr. by Karl Bradley] © Edwin H. Morris & Co., inc., New
York; on editing & arranging;
15May47; EP14527. Parts:
band.

ALKIRE, EDDIE. See
Alkire, Elbern H.

ALKIRE, ELBERN H   1907-
Eddie Alkire's Hawaiian hula
songs; arr. for piano accordion,
with words [and] steel guitar.
Easton, Pa., E. Alkire Publica-
tions. © Elbern H. "Eddie"
Alkire, Easton, Pa.; on arrange-
ment & 1 song (Malihini hula);
3Mar47; EP12624.
Eddie Alkire's Hawaiian waltz
songs; arr. for piano accordion,
with words [and] steel guitar.
Easton, Pa., E. Alkire Publica-
tions. © Elbern H. "Eddie"
Alkire, Easton, Pa.; on arrange-
ment; 3Mar47; EP12625.
Songs of my youth; [by Eddie
Alkire] Easton, Pa., E.
Alkire Publications. © Elbern
H. "Eddie" Alkire, Easton,
Pa.; 5Jun46; EP14151. For
guitar solo.
When you said goodbye; [by Eddie
Alkire] Easton, Pa., E. Alkire
Publications. © Elbern H.
"Eddie" Alkire, Easton, Pa.;
5Jun46; EP14152. For guitar
solo.

[ALLAN, GEORGE N   ]
Must Jesus bear the cross? [By
George N. Allan], arr. by John
Walter Davis & Johnnie Mae Norris.
Chicago, E. C. Davis. © John
Walter Davis, Chicago; on arrange-
ment; 8Jun46; EP12144.

ALLARD, JOSEPH A
Three octave scales and chords for
saxophone ... By Joe Allard.
© Joseph A. Allard, New York;
10May47; EP14307.

ALLEE, ERNEST E
A dream of reality; words;
Scott Taylor [pseud.], music;
Ernest E. Allee. © Lela
Taylor Burr, Houston, Tex.;
23Apr47; EP6858.

ALLEN, BOB.
Do a little bus'ness on the side;
[words] by Bob Hilliard and
[music by] Bob Allen. © Valiant
Music Co., inc., New York;
17Mar47; EP6663.

ALLEN, BUDD.
I know what you're puttin' down;
by Louis Jordan and Budd Allen.
© Preview Music Co., Chicago;
1Apr47; EP13586. For voice and
piano, with chord symbols.

ALLEN, C   F
The mun that I've got; words ...
by O. O. Bays & music [by]
C. F. Allen. © Melody Hour
Music Publishing Co., Washington,
D. C.; 5Apr47; EP14365.

ALLEN, REX.
Curtains of sorrow; by Arbie Gibson
and Rex Allen. © Preview Music Co.,
Chicago; 11Mar46; EP12076. For
voice and piano, with chord symbols.

ALLENDER, NICHOLAS DANIEL.
Staccato waltz; words and music
by N. D. Allender. © Bob
Wills Music, inc., Hollywood,
Calif.; 7Jan47; EP11201.

ALMA, MARIA.
Compréndeme ... de María Alma,
arreglo de Fernando Z.
Maldonado. © Promotora
Hispano Americana de Música,
s.a., Mexico, D.F.; 30Dec46;
EF4905. Piano-conductor score
(orchestra), condensed score
and parts.

ALONGI, FRANCIS. See
Alongi, François.

ALONGI, FRANÇOIS, 1899-
Laissons dormir nos souvenirs ...
paroles de Jean Rodor [pseud.],
musique de Francis Alongi.
© Éditions Musicales Nuances,
Paris; 15Jan47; EF3491.
Rosario ... paroles de Jean Rodor
[pseud.], musique de Francis
Alongi. © Éditions Musicales
Nuances, Paris; 15Jan47; EF3487.

ALONGI, MICHAEL, 1894-
When it's peach bloom time (Mary
Ann); words and music by Michael
Alongi. Chicago, Alongi's and
Ventre Publications. © Michael
Alongi, Chicago; 28Apr47;
EP15106.

ALPERT, HERMAN.
Mixup; by Herman Alpert and Barry
Galbraith. © Mutual Music
Society, inc., New York; 3Jan47;
EP11140. Parts: guitar and
double-bass.

ALSHIN, HARRY A   1909-
Tortillas; Chilean folk song,
four part mixed voices ...
Choral setting and English
text by Harry A. Alshin. ©
M. Witmark & Sons, New York;
30Apr47; EP14289.

ALVAREZ, JOSÉ GUADALUPE. See
Guadalupe Alvarez, José.

ALVAREZ MACISTE, MANUEL. See also
Maciste, Manuel Alvarez.
La vida castiga; letra y música
de Manuel Alvarez Maciste. ©
Promotora Hispano Americana
de Música, s. a., Mexico;
30Dec46; EF5529.

AMAME MUCHO. (Love me as I love you)
[English words adapted by Albert
Gamse] (In André, Julie, ed.
Songs from south of the border.
p. 44-45) © Edward B. Marks Music
Corp., New York; on English
adaptation; 28Dec46; EP10878.

AMAT, RUBEN.
Re guin tin pla ... letra y
música de Ruben Amat, arreglo
de A. Romay. © Peer International Corp., New York;
31Dec46; EF5429. Piano-
conductor score (orchestra)
and parts.

THE AMATEUR ORGANIST; [comp. by
Ellen Jane Lorenz] © Lorenz
Publishing Co., Dayton,
Ohio; no.4, 13Jan47; no.5,
9Jun47; EP12670, 16553.

AMERICA; [words by S. F. Smith,
music attributed to Henry Carey,
arr. by Victor Lakes Martin]
Easy piano arrangement with
keyboard charts. © Songs You
Remember Publishing Co.
(V. L. Martin, Proprietor),
Atlanta; on arrangement;
5Apr47; EP14746.

AMSTELL, BILLY.
Up and down the scale ... composed
and arr. by Billy Amstell. ©
Peter Maurice Music Co., ltd.,
New York; 31Dec46; EF4840. Piano-
conductor score (orchestra),
and parts.

ANASTASSIOU, SPARTAKOS GEORGE. See Spartakos, Giannēs.

ANCHETA, LAMBERTO L 1898-
Don't ever doubt my love for you ... Words and music by Lamberto L. Ancheta ... orchestration by Harold Potter. San Francisco, Ancheta Music Publications. © Lamberto L. Ancheta, San Francisco; 30Apr47; EP14546. Piano-conductor score (orchestra, with words) and parts.

ANCILLOTTI, GINO.
Mamma santa ... parole di E. Frati, musica di G. Ancillotti. © Abramo Allione, Milano; 1Jan46; EF3219.

ANDE, GEORGE.
Lay down your soul; words and music by George Ande. © Northern Music Corp., New York; 14Feb47; EP12151.

ANDERSEN, DEREK.
Shine on my silvery moon; words by Georgia Powell, music by Derek Andersen. © Cine-Mart Music Publishing Co., Hollywood, Calif.; 30Dec46; EP14117.

ANDERSEN, KAI NORMANN, 1900-
(Silkeborg) Sørgemarch, fra Kjeld Abell-Skuespillet "Silke-borg"; [by] K. Normann Andersen, [arr. by Peter Deutsch] © Wilhelm Hansen, Musik-Forlag, Copenhagen; 12Dec46; EF3440.

Sørgemarch. See his Silkeborg.

ANDERSON, LEROY
ANDERSON, ROBERT, 1918-
Let us wait upon the Lord ... choral arrangement, words by Elise Yancey, music by Robert Anderson. Gary, Ind., Robert Anderson's Good Shepherd Music House. © Robert Anderson & Elise Yancey, Gary, Ind.; 21May46; EP11277. Close score: SATB.

ANDERSSON, FRITHIOF STRÖMBERG- See Strömberg-Andersson, Frithiof.

ANDRÉ, JULIE, ed.
Songs from south of the border; comp. and ed. by Julie André, with original Spanish text, English adaptation by Albert Gamse. Supervised by Enric Madriguera. © Edward B. Marks Music Corp., New York; on adaptation, compiling & editing; 28Dec46; EP10884.

ANGEL, MIGUEL.
Compasión; by Miguel Angel, English lyric by Nora Weaver. © Miguel Angel Publications, New York; 20Mar47; EP6724. English and Spanish words.

ANGELIS, ALFREDO DE.
Pregonera ... letra de José Rótulo, música de Alfredo de Angelis. © Editorial Julio Korn, Buenos Aires; 12Jul45; EF5605.

ANGELO, LANI D' See D'Angelo, Lani.

ANGELONI, JOHN, 1909-
That's when my dreams all fade out; words and music by John Angeloni, arr. [by] Michaud. © John Angeloni, Gardena, Calif.; 10May47; EP14617.

ANGO, JACK, arr.
Santa's favorite carols; for boys and girls to play and sing. [For] B♭ trumpet solo or duet, arr. by Jack Ango. © Thomas Music Co., Detroit; on arrangement; 8Nov46; EP6750.

ANNUNZIATA, MICHELE R
Serenata; parole di Lorenzo Stecchetti, musica di Michele R. Annunziata. Complete vocal score and piano solo transcription. © The "A" & "Z" Music Publications, Utica, N. Y.; 26Nov46; EP11470.

ANSELL, ERIC NORMAN, 1900-
Vagabond heaven; words by David Davies, music by Eric Ansell. © Dix, ltd., London; 11Dec46; EF5325.

ANSON, BILL, 1907-
When I write my song; based on a theme from Saint Saëns' "Samson and Delilah"; words and music by Ted Mossman ... and Bill Anson. © Leon René Publications, Hollywood, Calif.; 20Jun47; EP15105.

ANSON, GEORGE.
In the desert; for the piano [by] George Anson. © Oliver Ditson Co., Philadelphia; 8Apr47; EP13486.

ANTES, JOHN, 1740-1811.
And Jesus said: It is finished, & bowed His head and gave up the ghost ... di John Antes. © The Board of Elders of the Northern Diocese of the Church of the United Brethren in the United States of America, Bethlehem, Pa.; on musical adaptation; 20Sep46; EP11783. Parts: soprano, violin 1, violin 2, viola, violoncello and organ.

ARASSICH.
La voce del violino ... di Giussani-Arassich. © Edizioni Leonardi, s.a.r.l., Milan; 8Sep45; EF4809. Piano-conductor score (orchestra) and parts.

ARCHANGELSKY, ALEXANDER. See Arkhangel'skii, Aleksandr Andreevich.

ARCOS, ERNEST.
Por la sierra. [On the mountain]; by Ernest Arcos, arr. by Joe Biviano, [for] accordion solo. [°1946] © Viccas Music Co., New York; 12May47; EP15097.

ARDEN, NEAL.
My dream came true; lyric by Neal Arden & Patrick Michael, music by Neal Arden. © Campbell, Connelly & Co., ltd., London; 19May47; EF3656.

ARDEN, NICK.
It's as simple as that; lyric by Portia Nelson, music by Nick Arden. [c1946] © Duchess Music Corp., New York; 14Feb47; EP12176.

It's as simple as that; lyric by Portia Nelson, music by Nick Arden ... arr. by Fred Weismantel. © Duchess Music Corp., New York; on arrangement; 14Apr47; EP13716. Piano-conductor score (orchestra, with words) and parts.

ARKHANGEL'SKII, ALEKSANDR ANDREEVICH, 1846-1924.
O light divine; motet for ... S.S.A.A. a cappella, [by] Alexander Archangelsky, arr. by Gwynn S. Bement. English text by E.P.P. and W.A.F. © Oliver Ditson Co., Philadelphia; on arrangement; 14Apr47; EP13628.

ARLEN, HAROLD, 1905-
After all; words by Ted Koehler, music by Harold Arlen. [New York, Chappell & Co.] © A-M Music Corp., New York; 13Mar47; EP2787.

ARMA, EDMÉE, pseud. See Weisshaus, Edmée Anne Léonie (Louin)

ARMA, PAUL, pseud. See Weisshaus, Imre.

ARMOND, EVERETT NORTON DE. See De Armond, Everett Norton.

ARNAUD, WILLIAM.
Cantilena; piano solo, by William Arnaud. Atlanta, American Music Publishers. © Wm. E. Arnaud, Atlanta; 29May47; EP6944.

Longing; piano solo, by William Arnaud. Atlanta, American Music Publishers. © Wm. E. Arnaud, Atlanta; 29May47; EP6943.

ARNDT, FELIX, d. 1918.
Nola; by Felix Arndt. Simplified teaching version for accordion by Charles Nunzio. © Sam Fox Publishing Co., New York; on arrangement; 30Apr47; EP14165.

ARNE, THOMAS AUGUSTINE.
(Alfred) Rule Britannia! From the masque of "Alfred" by Thomas Augustine Arne, arr. by Humphrey Searle. © Joseph Williams, ltd., London; on arrangement; 21May47; EF3572. Score: tenor, mixed chorus and piano or organ.

Rule Britannia! See his Alfred.

ARNELL, RICHARD.
Three childhood impressions; for four-part chorus of mixed voices. Words by Rose Fyleman, music by Richard Arnell. © The Boston Music Co., Boston; 1Apr47; EP13379.

ARRIEU, CLAUDE, pseud. See also Simon, Louise Marie.

ARNOLD, HARRY, pseud. See Person, Harry Arnold.

Quand verrai-je les fles? Poème de Francis Jammes, musique de Claude Arrieu. [c1946] © Enoch & Co., Paris; 25Feb47; EF5242.

(Sonatina, flute & piano) Sonatine; [by] Claude Arrieu. © Editions Amphion, Paris; 26Oct46; EF5231. Score and part.

ARTEGA, ALFONSO D' See D'Arteaga, Alfonso.

ARTHUR, BOBB, pseud. See Shaftel, Art.

ARTHUR, WILLIAM.
Although another separates us; words by Polly S. Clemons, music by William Arthur. © Nordyke Publishing Co., Los Angeles; 8Mar47; EP13278.

Blue Monday; words by G. Adeline Bell, music by William Arthur. © Nordyke Publishing Co., Los Angeles; 8Mar47; EP13237.

Coronado; words by Charles LeClair Mulligan, music by William Arthur. © Nordyke Publishing Co., Los Angeles; EP11050.

Do you remember? Words by Phil Strother, music by William Arthur. © Nordyke Publishing Co., Los Angeles; 7Mar47; EP13571.

Dreamboats; words by Bill Moore, music by William Arthur. © Nordyke Publishing Co., Los Angeles; 5Mar47; EP13267.

Drifting away from the day into the night; words by Jean S. Watson, music by William Arthur. [c1946] © Nordyke Publishing Co, Los Angeles; 13Jan47; EP14788.

*PROMENADE ... by LEROY ANDERSON.
CONDENSED SCORE (ORCHESTRA) AND PARTS.
© MILLS MUSIC, INC.*

3

Empty arms; words by Helen Cook,
music by William Arthur. ©
Nordyke Publishing Co., Los
Angeles; 5Mar47; EP13232.

Everlasting love; words by Bertha
May, music by William Arthur.
© Nordyke Publishing Co., Los
Angeles; 8Mar47; EP13572.

Hollywood stars; words by Thomas
Graham, music by William Arthur.
© Nordyke Publishing Co., Los
Angeles; 5Mar47; EP13252.

I couldn't forget you; words
by Ellen Boden, music by
William Arthur. © Nordyke
Publishing Co., Los Angeles;
8Mar47; EP13553.

I cried my last cry last night;
words by John W. Brown, music
by William Arthur. © Nordyke
Publishing Co., Los Angeles;
15Mar46; EP13533.

I like what you say; words by
Annalyle Raty, music by William
Arthur. © Nordyke Publishing
Co., Los Angeles; 5Mar47;
EP13255.

I think I'll shed a tear (and
go to sleep); words by William
J. Cramer, music by William
Arthur. © Nordyke Publishing
Co., Los Angeles; 5Mar47;
EP13241.

I'm dreaming of you; words by
Alberta Leaser, music by
William Arthur. © Nordyke
Publishing Co., Los Angeles;
8Mar47; EP13555.

I'm happier unhappy with you;
words by Betty Bratton, music
by William Arthur. © Nordyke
Publishing Co., Los Angeles;
5Mar47; EP13272.

I'm the romancing king; words by
Ammel Goodlett, music by William
Arthur. © Nordyke Publishing Co.,
Los Angeles; 8Mar47; EP13559.

In a little bungalow just built
for two; words by Mary Lyle,
music by William Arthur. ©
Nordyke Publishing Co., Los
Angeles; 5Mar47; EP13281.

In my heart; words by Hollis
Brown, music by William Arthur.
[c1946] © Nordyke Publishing
Co., Los Angeles; 15Feb47;
EP14778.

Just call me your love, love;
words by William Chernenkoff,
music by William Arthur.
© Nordyke Publishing Co., Los
Angeles; 8Mar47; EP13551.

Just suppose; words by Marie I.
Hill, music by William Arthur.
© Nordyke Publishing Co., Los
Angeles; 5Mar47; EP13251.

A longing; words by Cleo C. Owings,
music by William Arthur. © Nordyke Publishing Co., Los Angeles;
8Mar47; EP13553.

More precious to me; words by
Irene E. Zellers, music by
William Arthur. © Nordyke
Publishing Co., Los Angeles;
16Dec46; EP12718.

My thoughts seem to wander to
you; words by M. Bruce Edwards,
music by William Arthur. ©
Nordyke Publishing Co., Los
Angeles; 7Mar47; EP13249.

Oh, how can you do it? Words by
Stella J. Moore, music by
William Arthur. © Nordyke Publishing Co., Los Angeles;
5Mar47; EP13274.

Reminiscing; words by Teresa
Tibbets, music by William Arthur.
© Nordyke Publishing Co., Los
Angeles; 8Mar47; EP13556.

Since I have a sweetheart like
you; words by Hersel E.
Butka, music by William
Arthur. © Nordyke Publishing Co., Los Angeles;
5Mar47; EP13282.

Stars are kisses; words by Harold
Harris, music by William Arthur.
© Nordyke Publishing Co., Los
Angeles; 7Mar47; EP13553.

Take our love song into your
heart; words by Jule Ritchie,
music by William Arthur.
© Nordyke Publishing Co.,
Los Angeles; 8Mar47; EP13292.

There is someone new in town;
words by Bill O'Hara, music by
William Arthur. [c1946]
© Nordyke Publishing Co., Los
Angeles; 5Mar47; EP13256.

There will always be; words
by Alice Hoffman, music by
William Arthur. © Nordyke
Publishing Co., Los Angeles;
5Mar47; EP13279.

Till you came along; words by
Odell Newman, music by William
Arthur. © Nordyke Publishing
Co., Los Angeles; 5Mar47;
EP13560.

Underneath the tropic moon;
words by Beatrice Price,
music by William Arthur. ©
Nordyke Publishing Co.,
Los Angeles; 8Mar47; EP13286.

Walkin' on air; words by Cal
Hamlin, music by William
Arthur. © Nordyke Publishing
Co., Los Angeles; 8Mar47;
EP13234.

Why? Words by Isabel Clark,
music by William Arthur. ©
Nordyke Publishing Co., Los
Angeles; 5Mar47; EP13564.

Would you blame me? Words by
Frank McGee, music by William
Arthur. © Nordyke Publishing
Co., Los Angeles; 5Mar47;
EP13561.

You are everything in my life;
words by Charles R. Thomas,
music by William Arthur. ©
Nordyke Publishing Co., Los
Angeles; 8Mar47; EP13275.

You don't fall into love; words
by Harryett A. Shepherd, music
by William Arthur. © Nordyke
Publishing Co., Los Angeles;
7Mar47; EP13263.

ARTIGAS, HUGO CRUZ. See
Cruz Artigas, Hugo.

ASHE, JOHN.
Close dem pretty eyes; words and
music by John Ashe. © Nordyke
Publishing Co., Los Angeles;
8Mar47; EP13557.

ASHE, JOHN HAROLD.
Break, break, break; words by Lord
Tennyson, music by John Ashe.
© John Harold Ashe, Townsville,
Queensland, Australia; 11Apr47;
EF3525.

The night has a thousand eyes;
words by F. W. Bourdillon, music
by John Ashe. © John Harold
Ashe, Townsville, Queensland,
Australia; 11Apr47; EF3524.

Young and old; (When all the world
is young, lad); words by Charles
Kingsley, music by John Ashe.
© John Harold Ashe, Townsville,
Queensland, Australia; 11Apr47;
EF3525.

ASHFIELD, ROBERT.
Two introits; for men's voices and
organ, by Robert Ashfield.
© Novello & Co., ltd., London;
16Apr47. Contents.- To this
temple, where we call Thee
(© EF5635) - God be in my head
(© EF5636)

ASHLOCK, JESSE.
I'm gonna be boss; words and music
by Jesse Ashlock. © Bob Wills
Music, inc., Hollywood, Calif.;
28Mar47; EP13153.

ASHMALL, WILLIAM E   arr.
Palm Sunday and Easter organ
book; comp. and arr. by Wm.
E. Ashmall. © McLaughlin &
Reilly Co., Boston; on
compilation; 24May47; EP13013.

ASPELIN, SÖREN.
En sjöman till häst. © Edition
Sylvain a/b, Stockholm; on 3
songs; 1Jan41; EF5042-5044. For
voice and piano. Contents.-
Vi' har gungat uppå havet; text
och musik: Sören Aspelin - Jokern [pseud.]- Efter alla dessa
år; text och musik: Sören Aspelin -
Jokern [pseud.]- Lily.Christine;
text och musik: Sören Aspelin.

ATCHER, BOB.
Long gone, baby; words and music
by Bob Atcher. © Preview Music
Co., Chicago; 1Apr47; EP13565.

ATHERTON, ROBERT EDWIN.
All alone; words and music by
Robert Edwin Atherton. ©
Nordyke Publishing Co., Los
Angeles; 7Mar47; EP13247.

ATILLA, pseud. See
Quevido, Raymond.

ATKINSON, ALBERT BURNETT, 1926-
Daring; [words and music by] Bert
Atkinson, harmony by W. T.
Morris. Brownwood, Tex.? The
Freedom Gospel Press. © Albert
Burnett Atkinson, Brownwood,
Tex.; 21May47; EP14744.

AUBANEL, GEORGES.
Ave Maria; 4 voix mixtes a
cappella, [by] Georges Aubanel.
© Rouart, Lerolle et Cie.,
Paris; 31Dec46; EF3558.

Ave verum; 4 voix mixtes et
orgue (ou harmonium), [by]
Georges Aubanel. © Rouart,
Lerolle et Cie., Paris;
31Dec46; EF3557.

O salutaris; 4 voix mixtes, [by]
Georges Aubanel. © Rouart,
Lerolle et Cie., Paris;
31Dec46; EF3560.

Tantum ergo; 4 voix mixtes
a cappella, [by] Georges
Aubanel. © Rouart, Lerolle
et Cie., Paris; 31Dec46;
EF3470. Latin words.

Tower bells; for the piano, by
Francis E. Aulbach. © G. Schirmer,
inc., New York; 30Dec46; EP11600.

AULBACH, FRANCIS E
Playful pixies; for the piano, by
Francis E. Aulbach. © G. Schirmer,
inc., New York; 30Dec46; EP11599.

AUSTIN, GRACE LEADENHAM.
The silver dream ship; for two
equal voices, words and music
by Grace Leadenham Austin.
© McLaughlin & Reilly Co.,
Boston; 24May47; EP15008.

AUTRY, GENE.
When the snow-birds cross the
Rockies; words by Dick Howard,
music by Gene Autry and
Leonard Joy. © Shapiro,
Bernstein & Co., inc., New
York; 7May47; EP14335.

AVISON, CHARLES, 1710-1770.
Concerto in E minor; [by] Charles
Avison ... Transcribed and ed.
for string orchestra (piano
optional) by Paul Glass. ©
Broadcast Music, inc., New York;
on arrangement; 27Dec46; EP15242.

AXMAN, EMIL, 1887-
Kytice písní čuských; [by] Emil
Axman. © Hudební Matice Umělecke
Besedy, Prcha, Czechslovakia;
1Sep44; EF4941. For voice and
piano.

AYER, NAT D
Five keys to heaven; lyric by
Mark Heywond, music by Nat D.
Ayer. New York, Chappell.
© Chappell & Co., ltd., London;
22May47; EP14951.

AZZARO, AL.
Echo polka; arr. for piano or
accordion, by Al Azzaro.
© Peer International Corp.,
New York; 28Mar47; EP13650.

B

BABITZ, SOL.
Principles of extensions in violin
fingering. © Dolkas Music Publishing Co., Los Angeles; 20Jan47;
EP6547.

BACH, JOHANN CHRISTIAN, 1735-1782.
(Concerto, piano) Concerto in D
major, for the piano; by Johann
Christian Bach, freely transcribed by Karl Rechzeh, the
orchestra acc: arr. for a second
piano. © Clayton F. Summy Co.,
Chicago; on transcription; 2Jan47;
EP11220. Score: piano 1-2.

(Concerto, piano) Concerto in
D major for the piano; orchestral
score and parts. By Johann
Christian Bach, freely trans-
cribed by Karl Rechzeh. ©
Clayton F. Summy Co., Chicago;
on transcription; 10Feb47;
EP12058.

BACH, JOHANN SEBASTIAN, 1685-1750.
Adagio de la Toccate in ut majeur.
See his Toccata.

All glory, laud, and honor ...
[by] Melchior Teschner ...
harmonized by Johann Sebastian
Bach ... arr. by Gwynn S. Bement.
[Words by] St. Theodulph of
Orleans ... English version by
John M. Neale. © E. C.
Schirmer Music Co., Boston;
30Apr47; EP14472. Score:
chorus (TTBB) and piano
reduction.

The art of fugue; [by] John Sebastian
Bach, arr. for organ by E. Power
Biggs. © The H. W. Gray Co.,
inc., New York; on arrangement &
preface; 5Mar47; EP12436.

Bist du bei mir. If you are near
... Ed. by Ernst Naumann, English translation by Ermine Hunt-
ress. (In Swarthout, Gladys,
comp. Gladys Swarthout album of
concert songs and arias. p. 4-6)
© G. Schirmer, inc., New York;
on translation; 21Feb46; EP2413.

(Chorale preludes, organ) Two
choral preludes; [by] J. S.
Bach, arr. by R. Sterndale
Bennett ... [for] piano solo.
© J. & W. Chester, ltd., London;
on arrangement; 4Feb47; EF3302.

Commit thy ways to Jesus; [by] John
Sebastian Bach adapted by A.
Siegel. © McKinley Publishers,
inc., Chicago; on arrangement;
31Dec46; EP10848. For piano

(Die Elenden sollen essen)
Sinfonia from Cantata 75,
(Die Elenden sollen essen),
by J. S. Bach, arr. for two
pianos by Walter Emery. ©
Novello & Co., ltd., London;
on arrangement; 18Jun47;
EF3851.

Forty days and forty nights.
(Aus der Tiefe rufe ich) [By]
Bach, arr. by Harvey Gaul. ©
Volkwein Bros., inc., Pittsburgh; on arrangement;
9May47; EP14312. Score
(violin 1-2, viola, violoncello and double-bass) and
parts.

Herr Jesu Christ, Dich zu uns
wend'. (Lord Christ, reveal
Thy holy face), by J. S. Bach;
arr. for two pianos by W. H.
Harris. © Novello & Co., ltd.,
London; on arrangement; 6May47;
EF3327.

(Herz und Mund und That und Leben)
Jesu, joy of man's desiring,
choral from Cantata no. 147
(Herz und Mund und That und
Leben) ... [by] Johann Sebastian
Bach ... arr. by Victoria Glaser.
[Words by] Martin Jahn, English
version from The Church Music
Society, ed. by H. Clough
-Leightor. [c1946] © E. C.
Schirmer Music Co., Boston;
30Apr47; EP14473. Score:
chorus (SAB) and organ.

Jesu, joy of man's desiring; by J. S.
Bach, arranged by Wayne Howorth.
© Belwin, inc., New York; on arrange-
ment; 13Feb47; EP12071. Score;
SSA and piano.

Jesu, joy of man's desiring; from
cantata no. 147 [by] Joh. Seb.
Bach, concert arrangement by
A. Walter Kramer. [Words by
Robert Bridges] © Galaxy Music
Corp., New York; on concert
arrangement; 21Jan47; EP6485.

Jesu, joy of man's desiring. See also
his Herz und Mund und That und
Leben.

Jesus Christus, unser Heiland.
(Jesus Christ, our Saviour)
Chorale prelude by J. S. Bach,
arr. for 2 pianos by Walter
Emery. [c1946] © Novello
& Co., ltd., London; on
arrangement; 7Jun47; EF3804.

Jesus, fount of joy and peace;
(from Church cantata no. 190)
... words adapted from Catherine
Winkworth by Hugh Ross. (In Ross,
Hugh, arr. Sacred choruses for
women's or girls' voices.
p. 76-82) © G. Schirmer, inc.,
New York; on arrangement;
30Sep46; EP9787.

Jesus, Thou my heart's delight;
S.A.T.B., [by] J. S. Bach, arr.
[by] M. J. L., translation by
J. A. Rimbach. © Neil J. Kjos
Music Co., Chicago; on arrange-
ment and translation; 1Jul46;
EP10990.

(Lobt Ihn mit Herz und Munde)
I sing unto the Lord. Ich
freue mich im Herrn ... For
mixed voices. English text
adapted by Walter Wismar,
music by Joh. Seb. Bach] ©
Shattinger Piano & Music Co.,
St. Louis; on English translation; 31Dec46; EP11245.

Lord, grant us everlasting peace;
SATB a cappella, [by] J. S.
Bach, [words and] arr. by Milton
James. © Harold Flammer, inc.,
New York; on arrangement & words;
7May47; EP14370.

O Thou who camest; [melody by J.
Schein, harmonized by J. S. Bach]
... edited and arranged for mixed
chorus, SATB, by Milford Bren
[pseud. Words by Charles Wesley,
revised by Amy Randall, pseud.]
© Choral Press, Evanston, Ill.;
on arrangement and revision of
words; 10ct46; EP11705.

Our strength, O church of God,
thou art ... By Johann
Sebastian Bach, arr. by G. W.
Henninger, [words adapted from
Psalm 46] © Theodore Presser
Co., Philadelphia; 7May47;
EP14479. Score: chorus (SSAA)
and organ reduction.

Rest well, Beloved, sweetly
sleeping; for four-part
chorus of women's voices,
with piano or organ acc., from
the "St. John Passion,"
English translation by Henry
S. Drinker, [music by]
Johann Sebastian Bach, arr.
by Igor Buketoff. © G.
Schirmer, inc., New York; on
arrangement; 27Feb47; EP13191.

Sheep may safely graze. (Schafe
können sicher weiden) ... [By]
J. S. Bach, arr. by Percy
Jones, English words by Alfred
Wheeler. c1944. © Allan &
Co., pty. ltd., Melbourne,
Australia; on English words
and arrangement; 28Dec46;
EF3373.

Sinfonia from Cantata 75. See his
Die Elenden sollen essen.

(Toccata) Adagio de la Toccate en
ut majeur ... de J. S. Bach,
arr't ... par Rob't L. Bedell.
© Edition A. Fassio, Lachute,
Que., Can.; on arrangement;
1May47; EF5201. Score (violin
or flute and piano or organ) and
part.

Two choral preludes. See his
Chorale preludes, organ.

Tyve-fem lette klaverstykker i
urtekstutgave ... Utvalg &
kommentarer ved Arne Dørumsgaard.
[5th ed.] c1945. (Klaverets
mestere) © Musikk-Huset a/s,
Oslo, Norway; v.1, on commentaries
and illustrations; 16Sep46;
EF5018. For piano solo.

BACON, JOHN D 1900-
He that believes in Jesus; [words by]
T. O. Chisholm, [music by] John
D. Bacon. © John D. Bacon,
Dallas; 23Dec46; EP10948. Close
score: SATB, in shape-note
notation.

BACHER, ELMAN.
Spooks; piano solo, by Elman
Bacher. © Schroeder &
Gunther, inc., Rhinebeck,
N. Y.; 25Apr47; EP6839.

I cannot go beyond nor do less;
[words and music by] John D.
Bacon. © John D. Bacon, Dallas;
23Dec46; EP10949. Close score:
SATB, in shape-note notation.

The lights of home; [words by]
Katharyn Bacon, [music by] John
D. Bacon. © John D. Bacon,
Dallas; 23Dec46; EP10944. Close
score: SATB, in shape-note
notation.

Simple faith; [Londonderry air arr.
by John D. Bacon, words by J. D.
Bacon] © John D. Bacon, Dallas;
23Dec46; EP10947. Close score:
SATB, in shape-note notation.

Tune my heart ... [words by] Katharyn
Bacon, [music by] John D. Bacon.
© John D. Bacon, Dallas; 23Dec46;
EP10945. Close score: SATB, in
shape-note notation.

BAENA, FEDERICO.
Anoche platicamos ... Letra,
música y arreglo de Federico
Baena. © Promotora Hispano
Americana de Musica, s.a.,
Mexico; 30Dec46; EF3332.
Piano-conductor score (orchestra, with words) and parts.

BAGGETT, NITA.
Lay your head upon my shoulder (when
you cry); by Bill Nettles [and]
Nita Baggett. © Lee's Music Corp.,
New York; 24Jan47; EP11802. For
voice and piano, with guitar diagrams
and chord symbols.

BAILEY, A   SIDNEY, 1884-
Bluebonnets; words & music by A.
Sidney Bailey, [scored by Jay
F. Gilbuena] © Texas Song Shop
(A. Sidney Bailey, owner),
Houston, Tex.; on changes in
lyrics; 24Feb47; EP12235.

BAILEY, RALPH MARION, 1909-
High heaven ... song [by Ralph
M. Bailey] © Ralph M. Bailey,
sole owner, Songs of Service,
San Francisco; 28May47; EP14904.

Let those Christmas bells ring;
[by Ralph M. Bailey] © Ralph
M. Bailey, sole owner, Songs
of Service, Santa Fe, N. M.;
7Dec46; EP11196. For voice
and piano, with chord symbols.

BAIRD, WAYNE GORDON.
I want to concentrate on you; words
and music by Wayne G. Baird. ©
Wayne G. Baird, Houston, Tex.;
31Dec46; EP6453.

I'm a millionaire; words and music
by Wayne G. Baird. © Wayne G.
Baird, Houston, Tex.; 31Dec46;
EP6454.

BAJIĆ, I
Srpkinja kolo. (Serbian girl
kolo); music by I. Bajić, words
by J. Zivojnović, new matter &
arrangement by R. Cernkovich.
© Rudolph Cernkovich, Bradley,
Mich.; on introduction & arrangement; 27Jan47; EP11992.
Parts: string orchestra, with
words.

BAKER, DON.
Bless you for being an angel;
foxtrot, by Eddie Lane and Don
Baker ... arranged by Paul
Weirick and Bob Haring. ©
Shapiro, Bernstein & Co., inc.,
New York; on arrangement;
31Dec46; EP11069. Piano-conductor score (orchestra, with
words) and parts.

You're the only pebble on the
beach; words by Eddie Lane,
music by Don Baker. New York,
Shapiro, Bernstein & Co., inc.
© Skidmore Music Co., inc.,
New York; 25Jun47; EP15284.

BAKER, GENE.
Somewhere in Utah; words and music
by Gene Baker, arrangement by Joe
Leacsak. © Baker Bros. Publishing Co., Greensburg, Pa.; 23May47;
EP6916.

BAKER, HENRY W
O Jesus, Lord of heavenly grace;
anthem ... with alternative
text for national and patriotic
use (O God of love, O King of
peace) SATB with optional acc.;
on a tune by Henry W. Baker,
arr. by Ralph A. Harris.
[Text by Ambrose of Milan and
John Connick] © Harold Flammer,
inc., New York; on arrangement; 4Nov46; EP11162.

BAKER, KENNY.
First jump ... composed and arr.
by Kenny Baker. © Peter
Maurice Music Co., ltd., New
York; 31Dec46; EF4898.
Piano-conductor score (orchestra), condensed score and
parts.

BAKER, LYMAN MARTIN.
O soul, why in darkness? ... [by
L. M. Baker, words by Lyman M.
Baker] © Lyman Martin Baker,
McClure, Pa.; 26Feb47; EP6721.

BALDWIN, RALPH L
Little "Lorduen"; a Gaelic
Christmas fancy, [for] four
part women's voices, S.S.A.A.-
a cappella; poem by Sister M.
Charles Raymond, [music by]
Ralph L. Baldwin, choral setting
by F. Campbell-Watson. © M.
Witmark & Sons, New York; on
arrangement; 22May47; EP14707.

BALL, ERIC.
Free fantasia; for brass band, [by]
Eric Ball. Full score. © Besson
& Co., ltd., London; 14May47;
EF5417.

BALL, ERNEST R.   d. 1927.
A little bit of heaven; Shure
they call it Ireland; two part,
S.A. or T.B. Lyric by J.
Keirn Brennan, music by Ernest
R. Ball, arr. by Douglas
MacLean, [pseud.] © M. Witmark & Sons, New York; on
arrangement; 8May47; EP14405.

When Irish eyes are smiling; words
by Chauncey Olcott and Geo.
Graff, jr., music by Ernest R.
Ball, [arr. by Jerry Sears] ©
M. Witmark & Sons, New York; on
arrangement; 9Jun47; EP15166.
Piano-conductor score (orchestra,
with words) and parts.

BALLARD, ROBERT.
"I knew what I wanted;" music
by Bob Ballard, lyric by
Buddy Kaye, arr. by Lou
Halmy. © Martin Music,
Hollywood, Calif., 1Apr47;
Er13112.

BALLIF, SERGE CHADWICK, 1899-
Happy Utah; words and music by
Serge C. Ballif. © Serge Chadwick Ballif, Logan, Utah;
24Mar47; EP12922.

BALOGH, ERNO.
Pastorale at dawn; piano solo [by]
Ernö Balogh. New York, Marks Ed.
© Edward B. Marks Music Corp.,
New York; 30Apr47; EP14136.

BALTOR, HAROLD.
Two little crickets. Dos grillitos;
lyric by Gladys Flores, music by
Harold Baltor. © Peer International Corp., New York;
28Aug46; EP13988.

BAMPTON, RUTH, 1902-
I will lift up mine eyes; (S.S.A.
with soprano and alto solos)
[by] Ruth Bampton, Psalm CXXI.
© Neil A. Kjos Music Co., Chicago;
23Dec46; EP13348.

The little red hen; story and
characteristic music adapted
for children to read, play,
sing or dramatize. [Words] by
Lottie E. Coit and [music by]
Ruth Bampton. Illus. by
George Martin. © G. Schirmer,
inc., New York; 13May47;
EP14556.

BANBURY, GEORGE E
When I send white orchids; words and
music by George E. Banbury. New
York, Casey & Sisson Publishing
Co., inc. © George F. Briegel,
inc., New York; 30Dec46; EP10991.

BANKS, ESTELLE V   McKINLEY.
Let Jesus help you, He understands;
by Estelle V. McKinley Banks.
© Estelle V. McKinley Banks,
Atlanta; 3May47; EP6977. Close
score: SATB.

There'll be a happy time in heaven
one of these days; by Estelle
V. McKinley Banks. © Estelle
V. McKinley Banks, Atlanta;
3May47; EP6978. Close score:
SATB.

BARBERIS, A.
Tutto è leggero. Sangue blu ...
testi di M. Galdieri, musiche
di A. Barberis. © Edizioni
Leonardi, Milano; 15Jun46;
EF4909. Piano-conductor score
(orchestra, with words),
and parts.

BAREFIELD, EDDIE, 1909-
F'taint one thing it's another;
words by Buddy Payne, music by
Eddie Barefield. © Popular
Music Co., New York; 20Jun47;
EP15209.

It's a good day; by ... Dave
Barbour, arr. by Paul Yoder.
[c1946] © Capitol Songs, inc.,
New York; on arrangement;
10Mar47; EP12413. Condensed
score (band) and parts.

Just an old love of mine; words &
music by Peggy Lee [and] Dave
Barbour. © Campbell-Porgie
inc., New York; 16Jun47; EP6968.

BARCELATA, LORENZO, d. 1943.
Tuya es mi serenata ... Letra y
música de Lorenzo Barcelata.
© Peer International Corp.,
New York; 27Feb47; EP12763.

BARELLI, AIMÉ, 1917-
Embrasse-moi ... paroles de
Jacques Larue [pseud.], musique de Aimé Barelli. ©
Editions Musicales Nuances,
Paris; 28Nov46; EF5225.

Pour lui ... paroles de Henri
Contet, musique de Aimé
Barelli. © Editions Musicales
Nuances, Paris; 28Nov46; EF3150.

BARFELL, RALPH ALVIN.
The Ralph Barfell method for playing
Hawaiian Guitar. © Ralph A.
Barfell, Shawano, Wis.; bk.2,
9Apr47; AA49525.

BARILE, ENZO.
Dimme addó staie ... testo di E.
V. di Gianni, musica di Enzo
Barile. © Canzoni e Melodie,
Napoli, 7Dec42; EF3304.

Quattro successi; [by] Di Gianni -
Barilo. Napoli, Edizioni Musicali Di Gianni. [c1946-47]
© Italian Book Co., New York;
7Sep46; EF5507. For voice and
piano. Cover title: Raccolta di
successi Di Gianni - Barilo.

Raccolta di successi di Gianni-
Barile. See his Quattro successi.

BARBOUR, DAVE.
Everything's movin' too fast; by
Peggy Lee and Dave Barbour.
© Barbour-Lee Music Corp., New
York; 7May47; EP14162. For
voice and piano, with chord
symbols.

Right off the ice; words by Harry
Weinstein, music by Eddie Barefield. © Popular Music Co.,
New York; 13Jun47; EP15040.

6

BARILE, MICHAEL, 1895-
To love you forever; words and
music by Michael Barile.
© Michael Barile, New York;
7Apr47; EP13735.

BARLOW, HAROLD, 1915-
The best years of our lives; words
and music by Harold Barlow.
© Peer International Corp.,
New York; 13Feb47; EP12226.

[BARNBY, J   ]
Sweet and low; [words by Alfred
Tennyson, music by J. Barnby, arr.
by Victor Lakes Martin] Easy
piano arrangement with keyboard
charts. © Songs You Remember
Publishing Co., (V. L. Martin,
Proprietor) Atlanta; on arrangement; 5Apr47; EP14752.

BARNES, CLIFTON WELLESLEY, 1890-
Round-up lullaby; [by] Clifton W.
Barnes, poem by Badger Clark. Arr.
by Ralph H. Lyman ... ([for] S.A.T.B.
© Ralph Haine Lyman, Claremont,
Calif.; on arrangement; 8Mar47;
EP12917.

BARNES, EDWARD SHIPPEN.
Mother's Day hymn ... [for] S.S.A.,
[words by] Arthur L. Rice, [music
by] Edward Shippen Barnes. ©
L. Fischer & Bro., New York;
17Apr47; EP6906.

Mother's Day hymn ... [words by]
Arthur L. Rice, [music by]
Edward Shippen Barnes. © J.
Fischer & Bro., New York; 17Apr47;
EP6905. Score: chorus (TTBB) and
organ.

Responses for the church
service; composed and selected
by Edward Shippen Barnes. ©
J. Fischer & Bro., New York;
27Mar47; EP6804. Close score:
SATB.

BARNES, GEORGE.
G minor spin and Swoon of a goon
... Written and pub. by George
Barnes. © Milton G. Wolf
Publications, Chicago; 21Jun44;
EP6760. For 2 Spanish guitars.

BARNES, OWEN CORNELL, 1895-
Because I love you so; by Owen
Cornell Barnes. © Owen Cornell
Barnes, Chicago; 15Dec46; EP11444.
For voice and piano, with chord
symbols.

Remember when; by Owen Cornell
Barnes. [c1946] © Owen Cornell
Barnes, Chicago; 2Jan47; EP11443.
For voice and piano, with chord
symbols.

When good children sleep; by Owen
Cornell Barnes. © Owen Cornell
Barnes, Chicago; 20Nov46; EP11445.
For voice and piano, with chord
symbols.

BARNUM, KENNETH RAYMOND, 1884-
When the moonbeams come out tonight;
words and music by Kenneth R.
Barnum, [arr. by Charles Leslie
Johnson] Kansas City, Mo.,
Johnson-Barnum Co. © Kenneth
Raymond Barnum Kansas City,
Mo.; 15Jan47; EP11190.

BARON, VIC, 1910-
Echoes in the night; by Vic Baron,
[lyric by] Bert Mann.
© Adrienne Music Co., New York;
30May47; EP15068. Melody and
chord symbols, with words.

BARRAGAN, RAUL.
Evocacion Incaica; An Inca prayer.
[By] Raul Barragan, arr. by the
composer. © Broadcast Music,
inc., New York; 21May47; EP15211.
Condensed score (orchestra) and
parts.

BARRETO, JUSTI.
"Ñamboró" ... letra y música de
Justi Barreto, arreglo de
Eulogio Casteleiro (Yoyo) ©
Peer International Corp., New
York; 18Dec46; EP5588. Piano-
conductor score (orchestra),
and parts.

BARRETT, PAUL DAVIS, 1890-
Eileen, my colleen; words and
music by Paul Barrett. © Paul
Davis Barrett, San Francisco;
20Apr47; EP13969.

[BARRINGTON, JONAH] 1904-
Pathways to the proms; containing ... easy piano pieces on
themes from the orchestral
masterpieces of the great
composers ... comp. & arr. by
Cyril C. Dalmaine [pseud.] ©
Forsyth Brothers, ltd.,
London; on words & arrangement
in bk.1, 27Nov46; EF4858.

BARRIS, HARRY.
Then I met you; words by John Seely,
music by Harry Barris. © Mills
Music, inc., New York; 20Jan47;
EP6497.

Wrap your troubles in dreams
(and dream your troubles away);
by Ted Koehler, Billy Moll and
Harry Barris, [arr. by Charlie
Ventura] © Shapiro, Bernstein
& Co., inc., New York; on arrangement; 10Jun47; EP14981. Score
(B♭ tenor saxophone and piano)
and part.

BARROSO, ARY.
A batucada começou; música de Ary
Barroso, letra de Myrta Silva.
© Peer International Corp.,
New York; on words; 30Dec46;
EP13767.

BARSOTTI, ROGER.
Banners of victory ... [by] R.
Barsotti, arr. [by] Denis Wright.
c1945. © Bosworth & Co., ltd.,
London; on arrangement; 16Jul48;
EF5164. Cornet-conductor score
(band) and parts.

BARTH, JOHN F
Why don't you smile? ... By John F.
Barth, arr. by [Betty Glynn of]
the Oahu staff. [Oahu E-Z method,
lesson 50EZ]) © Oahu Publishing
Co., Cleveland; on arrangement;
26Aug46; EP6874. For voice and
2 guitars. Includes a musical
quiz and the discussion: Songs
of the people.

BARTLETT, FLOYD.
Dancing and dreaming; words by
Alice Strunk, music by Floyd
Bartlett. © Nordyke Publishing
Co., Los Angeles; 12Oct45;
EP6502.

Never more; words by Raymond Kiecker,
music by Floyd Bartlett. © Nordyke
Publishing Co., Los Angeles; 27Sep49;
EP12087.

Something to remember; words by
Carl Sorrell, music by Floyd
Bartlett. © Nordyke Publish-
ing Co., Los Angeles; 10Jan46;
EP13552.

BARTÓK, BÉLA, 1881-1945.
(Concerto, piano, no.3) 3rd piano
concerto, [by] Béla Bartok.
© Boosey & Hawkes, ltd., London;
13Feb47; EF4993. Miniature
score.

(Mikrokosmos) Seven pieces from
"Mikrokosmos"; for two pianos,
four hands, [by] Béla Bartók,
arr. by the composer. ©
Boosey & Hawkes, ltd., London;
on arrangement; 28Mar47;
EF5316.

BARTOŠ, JAN ZDENĚK, 1908-
Dvouhlasé invence. The inventions
for two voices ... [by] Jan Zd.
Bartoš. [Op. 5. c1947]
© Edition Continental Boh.
Leopold kom. spol., Praha,
Czechoslovakia; 15Dec46;
EF5412. For piano solo.

Maličkosti ... The bagatells.
[By] Jan Zd. Bartoš. [c1947]
© Edition Continental (Boh.
Leopold kom. spol.), Praha,
Czechoslovakia; 15Dec46;
EF5360. For piano solo.

BASIE, COUNT, 1906-
Bill's mill; by Count Basie and
Gene Roland ... Arr. by Will
Hudson. © Bregman, Vocco and
Conn, inc., New York; 18Apr47;
EP13873. Piano-conductor score
(orchestra) and parts.

Free eats [a free-bee]; lyric by
Harry Edison, Ted Donnelly,
Snookie Young and Freddy Green,
music by Count Basie ... Arr.
by Will Hudson. © Bregman,
Vocco and Conn, inc., New York;
18Apr47; EP13874. Piano-conductor score (orchestra, with
words) and parts.

The king; by Count Basie ... arr. by
Will Hudson. © Bregman, Vocco
and Conn, inc., New York; 2Jan47;
EP11847. Piano-conductor score
(orchestra) and parts.

Mutton leg; by Count Basie and
Harry Edison ... arranged by
Will Hudson. © Bregman, Vocco
and Conn, inc., New York;
10Feb47; EP12019. Piano-
conductor score (orchestra)
and parts.

BATTLE, EDGAR.
The red ball line; words by Noble
Sissle, music by Edgar Battle.
© Bob Miller, inc., New York;
2May47; EP14168.

Riding on a rainbow; by Edgar
Battle. © Rudine Music, inc.,
New York; 17Jun47; EP15072.
Piano-conductor score (orchestra)
and parts.

BAUDRIER, YVES MARIE, 1906-
La dame a la licorne; [for]
piano, [by] Yves Baudrier.
Grenoble, 1945. © Amphion,
Paris; 31Dec44; EF3592.

BAUER, EDWIN THOMAS, 1906-
Wanted: a place to live! Words
... by K. L. Bordner and music
[by] E. T. Bauer. © Edwin
Thomas Bauer & Kenneth Loroy
Bordner, St. Paul; 10Oct46;
EP11275.

BAUMANN, ERIK.
(Flickorna från gamla sta'n) Gamla
sta'n, (vals ur filmen: "Flickorna
från gamla sta'n"); text: Gideon
Wahlberg, musik: Erik Baumann. ©
Nordiska Musikförlaget, a/b,
Stockholm; 13Jan34; EF4827. For
voice and piano, with chord symbols.

Gamla sta'n. See his Flickorna från gamla sta'n.

BAUMER, CECIL.
Four keys: A minor, C, F, G;
album of sixteen short pieces
for pianoforte, by Cecil Baumer. © Alfred Lengnick & Co.,
ltd., London; 14Feb47; EF3356.

BAUMGART, GIL PRUEHER.
Bartender's ball; words and music
by Gil Prueher Baumgart. © American Academy of Music, inc.,
New York; 31Dec46; EP6458.

7

BAVA, JOHN, comp.
Songs of the hills and plains ...
comp. by John Bava. © Musical
Melody Publishers, Davis, W. Va.;
9Dec46; EP11283.

O dame, get up and bake your
pies; variations on a North
Country Christmas carol, for
piano solo, [by] Arnold Bax.
© Chappell & Co., ltd., London;
3Jun47; EF3798.

(Quartet, strings, no. 3)
Third string quartet, in F;
by Arnold Bax. © Murdoch,
Murdoch & Co., London;
17May41; EF3565.

(Quartet, strings, no. 3) Third
string quartet in F; by Arnold
Bax. Score. © Murdoch, Murdoch
& Co., London; 17May41; EF4138.

(Trio, piano & strings) Trio in
B flat ... by Arnold Bax.
© Chappell & Co., ltd., London;
31Dec46; EF5632. Score and parts.

Morning song; (Maytime in Sussex),
for piano & orchestra; by Arnold
Bax. © Chappell & Co., ltd.,
London; on arrangement; 7Nov46;
EF5909.

BAX, ARNOLD, 1883-
Five fantasies on Polish Christmas
carols; for voices in unison and
string orchestra ... English
translation by Jan Sliwinski.
© Chappell & Co., ltd., London;
27Mar46; EF4142.

BAXTER, JESSE R 1887-
comp.
Harmony gems; [comp. by] J. R.
Baxter, jr., [ed. by] V. O.
Fossett ... [and] B. B.
Edmiason. © Stamps-Baxter
Music and Printing Co.,
Dallas; 15Apr47; EP14319.
Close score: SATB; shape-note
notation.

Highest praise; [music ed. by
Vernie Fossett, words ed. by
Bernard Edmiaston, comp. by
Jesse R. Baxter] © Stamps-
Baxter Music and Printing Co.,
Dallas; 1Jun47; EP15139.
Hymns; shape-note notation.

Sunlit way; [comp. by] J. R.
Baxter, jr. ... [ed. by] V. O.
Fossett ... [and] B. B.
Edmiason. © Stamps-Baxter
Music and Printing Co.,
Dallas; 1Jun47; EP14318.
Close score: SATB; shape-note
notation.

BAY, ALBERT L
Upon the mountain side; and 'Till
my Saviour comes again; two ...
hymns by ... Albert L. Bay.
© Albert L. Bay, Mountain View,
Mo.; 23May47; EP14823-14824.

[BAYLY, T H]
Long, long ago; [words and music
by T. H. Bayly, arr. by Victor
Lakes Martin] Easy piano arrange-
ment with keyboard charts.
© Songs You Remember Publishing
Co., (V. L. Martin, Proprietor),
Atlanta; on arrangement; 5Apr47;
EP14745.

BAYNON, ARTHUR.
The Spanish Main; unison song,
words by E. V. Knox, music by
Arthur Baynon. © Novello &
Co., ltd., London; 19Feb47;
EF5162.

BEATON, JOHNNY.
All for you; words and music by
Johnny Beaton. © D. Davis &
Co., pty. ltd., Sydney; 11Dec46;
EP14846. For voice and piano,
with chord symbols.

BEATTY, BOB. See
Beatty, Robert James.

BEATTY, ROBERT JAMES, 1904-
Federal shield song; lyrics by
Mal Havens, music by Bob Beatty,
[arr. by Harold Potter] New York,
Edwards Music Co. © The Federal
Glass Co., Columbus, Ohio;
1Jul46; EP13857.

[BEAUREGARD, ABEL] 1902-
Nita corazón ... Paroles de
Bertal [pseud.], Maubon, & A.
Beauregard; musique de Flavia
[pseud.] & Rys. © Éditions
EIMEF-OPERA, Paris; 10Jan47;
EF3451. Piano-conductor score
(orchestra, with words), and
parts.

La rumba à Doudou; paroles de Ch.
Flavia [pseud.], musique de Ch.
Flavia et F. Burlet, arr. de
Francis Salabert ... Biguine à
Bikini; paroles de Ch. Flavia,
musique de Ch. Flavia et M. Thibault, arr. de Francis Salabert.
Paris, Éditions Salabert. © Salabert, inc., New York; on arrangement; 15Feb47; EP3461. Piano-conductor score (orchestra, with
words), and parts.

BECK, MARTHA.
At the ballet; piano solo by
Martha Beck. © The Boston
Music Co., Boston; 23Apr47;
EP13870.

BECK, THOMAS LUDVIGSEN, 1899-
Arnljot Gelline; [words by Bjørn-
stjerne Bjørnson] ... Op. 17.
© Musikkhuset a/s, Oslo; 7Oct44;
EF1873. Piano-vocal score.

Dansar fra Gudbrandsdal. Dances
from Gudbrandsdal. Op.24. [By]
Thomas Beck ... Piano duets.
© Musikk-Huset a/s, Oslo, Norway;
on arrangement of 3 pieces,
29Nov46. Contents.- Intrata
quasi springar (© EP5090) -
Brurleik frå Lesja (© EP5091) -
Halling fra Lom (© EP5092)

BECKER, JOHN J
Moments from the passion ... for
three part chorus, with soli
for high and medium voices,
the music by John J. Becker.
© Gamble Hinged Music Co.,
Chicago; 5Mar47; EP12311.

BECKER, RENÉ L
Mass in honor of St. Anthony of Padua
... [by] René L. Becker. © J.
Fischer & Bro., New York; 17Apr47;
EP6903. Score: chorus (SATB) and
organ.

BECKHELM, PAUL BLAIR, 1906-
Tragic march ... [by] Paul Beck-
helm. © Paul Beckhelm,
Frederick, Md.; 1Apr47;
EP14149. Score: brass instru-
ments and percussion.

BEDDIG, HARRY.
My first love affair; words and
music by Harry Beddig. ©
Cine-Mart Music Publishing Co.,
Hollywood, Calif.; 1Nov46;
EP11473.

BEDELL, ROBERT LEECH.
All Hollow's Eve; for organ,
by Robert Leech Bedell.
© Edward Schuberth & co.,
inc., New York; 25Mar47;
EP12876.

O Sacred Head surrounded; anthem
for mixed voices with sop.,
alto or ten. solo. Old Breton
melody, arr. by Robert L.
Bedell, [words by] St. Bernard
of Cluny. © Clayton F. Summy
Co., Chicago; on arrangement;
10Jan47; EP11328.

BEEKMAN, JACK.
Mahzel (means good luck); words and
music by Artie Wayne and Jack Beekman. © Leo Feist, inc., New York;
11Apr47; EP13748.

BEETHOVEN, LUDWIG VAN, 1770-1827.
Adagio from Sonate pathétique.
See his Sonata, piano.

Appassionata sonata. See his
Sonata, piano.

Beethoven; introducing all
Beethoven's greatest melodies,
[arr. by Victor Ambroise] ©
Lawrence Wright Music Co., ltd.,
London; on arrangement; 9Apr47;
EP5470. For piano solo.

Beethoven (simplified); ten
favorite compositions arr. for
piano solo by Richard Harding
[pseud.] © The Willis Music
Co., Cincinnati; on arrangement; 29Jan47; EP11795.

Cadence pour le concerto de L. van
Beethoven, op. 61, pour violon
seul [by Manuel Quiroga] © Éditions Salabert, Paris; 31Dec41;
EF70.

Fidelio overture; [by] Beethoven.
[Op.72b] Arr. for brass band
by Frank Wright. © Besson &
Co., ltd., London; on arrangement; 14May47; EF3285.

The Lord's prayer; musical setting
from L. van Beethoven's opus 27,
no. 2, adapted and arr. by Charles
E. Bodley. © Gordon V. Thompson,
ltd., Toronto; 26Feb47; EF3144.
For voice and piano.

March from "The ruins of Athens";
[by] L. v. Beethoven, in
adaptation for the piano by A.
Borovsky. © Wilhelm Hansen,
Musik-Forlag, Copenhagen; on
arrangement; 29Jan47; EF4439.

Minuet in G; [by] Beethoven, arr.
for easy piano solo by H. P.
Hopkins. © Century Music
Publishing Co., New York; on
arrangement; 31May47; EP14736.

Some of the happy melodies from
Beethoven's chamber music; arr.
for pianoforte by J. Michael
Diack. © Paterson's Publications, ltd., London; on arrangement; 14Apr47; EF3308.

(Sonata, piano) Adagio from
Sonata pathétique ... [by Beethoven. Arr. by Victor Ambroise]
© Lawrence Wright Music Co.,
ltd., London; on simplified arrangement; 11Apr47; EF3444.
For piano solo.

(Sonata, piano) Appassionata
sonata; (abbreviated version)
[By] Beethoven, [arr. by
Victor Ambroise] © Lawrence
Wright Music Co., ltd., London; on abbreviated version;
11Apr47; EF5572.

(Sonata, piano, no.14) Ludwig von
Beethoven's Moonlight sonata.
Piano solo arr. by Pietro
Ballatore. © J. & J. Kammen
Music Co., New York; on arrange-
ment; 6May47; EP6918.

(Symphony, no. 9) Themes-from
the 9th symphony; [choral section, by] Beethoven. For
brass band, arr. by Eric Ball.
© Besson & Co., ltd., London;
on arrangement; 14May47;
EF3284.

Themes from the 9th symphony. See
his Symphony, no. 9.

BEGLEY, MARJORY, 1904-
Silver; words by Walter De La
Mare, music by Marjory Begley.
© Wesley Webster, San Francisco;
24Dec46; EP10768.

8

BEHRENS, ESTELLE, 1910-
Life was meant to be a sweet ro-
mance; words and music by Estelle
Behrens, [arr. by Kurt Hintz]
New York, Cosmopolitan Music Co.
© Estelle Behrens d.b.a. Cosmo-
politan Music Co., New York;
21Apr47; EP15140.

BEITTEL, R   H
My theme of love; words and music
by R. H. Beittel. [c1946]
© Whitehouse Publishing Co.,
Hollywood, Calif.; 2Jan47;
EP11987.

BEKES, REMBERTO.
Bailadores ... letra y música de
Remberto Bokes, arreglo de
Pérez Prado. La Habana. ©
Peer International Corporation,
New York; 30Dec46; EF3310.
Parts: orchestra.

BELCHAMBER, EILEEN.
Two songs from De La Mare; music by
Eileen Belchamber, words by Walter
De La Mare. © Edward Arnold
& Co., London; 12Dec46; EP4760.
Contents.- The window.- Tired
Tim.

Two songs from Herrick; music by
Eileen Belchamber. 1. The bell-
man. 2. The night piece. ©
Edward Arnold & Co., London;
12Dec46; EP4761.

BELETZKY, VALENTIN.
Melody; for violin and piano,
[op.7, by] Valentin Beletzky,
[edited with special annotations by Arthur Hartmann]
Leeds Music Corp., New York; on
editing and foreword; 14Feb47;
EP12180.

BELL, ADOLPHUS, 1893-
My dainty little maid; words and
music by Adolphus Bell. ©
Adolphus Bell, Chicago; 1Apr47;
EP13914.

The rose; words and music by
Adolphus Bell. © Adolphus Bell,
Chicago; 1Apr47; EP13915.

BELL, E   W
Your love will linger (in my
heart); words and music by E.
W. Bell. © E. W. Bell, Wal-
halla, S. C.; 8May47; EP14503.

BELL, MILDRED, 1904-
Down that old moonlit trail;
[words] by Harry Glenn, and
[music by] Mildred and Harry
Bell. [c1946] © Gilbert Parmelee, Genoa, Ill.; on additional words; 10Feb47;
EP11978.

BELLAS, GIANNĒS GEORGIOS, 1910-
Esbyse enas megalos erōtas ...
etichoi Ch. Pyrpasou, mousikē
Giannē Bella. 2. ekdosis.
Athēnai, A. Charikiopoulou,
"Melody". © "S.O.P.E." Copy-
right Protection Society,
Athens; 11Dec45; EF3231.
Score: voice, violin & piano.

Tha se phileso ki'as mēn to
theleis; etichoi Ath. Tsonka,
mousikē Giannē Bella.
Athēnai, Ekdoseis Gaïtanou.
© Michel Gaetanos, Athens;
20Nov46; EF3125. For voice and
piano.

BELLEDNA, ALEX, pseud. See
Pinkard, Edna Belle Alexander.

BELLIN, BETTY.
Under the Texas moon; words by Wel-
lington F. Campbell, music by
Betty Bellin. © Ernest A.
Rock & Son, Memphis; 15Mar47;
EP6703.

BELLOVICH, THOMAS J
Stumbling home; words by Mary
Goohnour, music by Thomas J.
Bellovich. © Thomas J. Bello-
vich, Lorain, Ohio; 1Feb47;
EP6629.

BELMONT, ERIC, pseud. See
Nordman, Chester.

BELTON, JOHN.
Time marches on ... [by] John
Belton, arr. for military band
by W. J. Duthoit. Petite valse
de concert ... [by] R. Barsotti.
The way to the stars ... [by]
Nicholas Brodszky, arr. for
military band by W. J. Duthoit.
Time cannot change a faithful
heart; song, cornet solo ... [by]
Rex Burrows, [words by Bruce
Sievier], arr. for military band
by W. J. Duthoit ... Youth
triumphant ... [by] Capt. G. H.
Willcocks. (The Army journal
for full military band. No.731)
© Chappell & Co., ltd., London;
on 5 pieces (no.1, 3 & 4, on
arrangement); 3Feb47;
EF5093-5097. Condensed score
(band) and parts.

BEMENT, GWYNN S   1895-
When the Saviour Christ is born.
(Gdy sie Chrystus rodzi) ...
Polish Christmas carol arr. by
Gwynn S. Bement, English version
by Burges Johnson. © E. C.
Schirmer Music Co., Boston; on
arrangement; 24Apr47; EP14196.
Score: chorus (TTBB) and piano
reduction. English words.

BEMENT, GWYNN S   1895-   arr.
The golden day is dying; four-
part chorus for women's voices
with soprano solo (a cappella),
English version by Katherine K.
Davis, Finnish folk song arr.
by Gwynn S. Bement ... based
upon the arrangement ... by J.
A. Fitzgerald. © K. C. Schirmer
Music Co., Boston; on arrangement; 22 Apr47; EP13851.

BENDER, ALENE.
That rhythm; rhythm; by Alene
Bender. Columbus, Ohio, Langdon-
Fredericks Music Pub. Co. ©
Alene Bender, Columbus, Ohio;
7Nov46; EP6475. For voice and
piano.

BENEDETTI, L
Acquarello napoletano; versi di
E. Bonagura, musica di L. Bene-
detti. © Italian Book Co.,
New York; 18Jun47; EP15110.

BENES, JARO.
Alexander ... Text: J. Petrak,
Musik: J. Benes. © SIDEM,
Société Intercontinentale
d'Éditions Musicales, Vaduz,
Ginevra; 18Oct46; EF4933. For
voice and piano, with chord
symbols.

BENJAMIN, ARTHUR, 1893-
Jan; a Creole melody, song ...
set to music by Arthur Benjamin.
London, Boosey & Hawkes. ©
Boosey & Co., ltd., London;
11Jul47; EF5719.

(Sonata, viola & piano) Sonata
... [by] Arthur Benjamin. ©
Boosey & Hawkes, ltd., London;
15Apr47; EF5547. Score and
part.

BENNER, HUGH C
Happy, happy Easter! ... [Words by]
Mildred S. Edwards, [music by]
Hugh C. Benner. (In Beginner
teacher. v.1, no.3, p.[3] of
cover) © Nazarene Publishing
House, Kansas City, Mo.; 1Mar47;
EP6733. Close score: SATB.

I like the Bible book ... [Words
by] Mildred Speakes Edwards, [music
by] Hugh C. Benner. (In Beginner
teacher. v.1, no.3, p.[3] of
cover) © Nazarene Publishing
House, Kansas City, Mo.; 1Mar47;
EP6732.

My prayer for home ... [Words by]
Mildred Speakes Edwards, [music
by] Hugh C. Benner. (In Beginner
teacher. v.1, no.3, p.55) ©
Nazarene Publishing House, Kansas
City, Mo.; 1Mar47; EP6730. Close
score: SATB.

Spring is here ... [Words by]
Mildred Speakes Edwards, [music
by] Hugh C. Benner. (In Beginner
teacher. v.1, no.3, p.56) ©
Nazarene Publishing House, Kansas
City, Mo.; 1Mar47; EP6731.

BENNETT, DAVID.
Accordion to Hoyle ... By David
Bennett. © Carl Fischer, inc.,
New York; 31Mar47; EP13494.
Piano-conductor score (accordion
and band or piano) and parts.

Down by the old bayou ... music
by David Bennett, lyric by Stuart
Williams. © Carl Fischer, inc.,
New York; on arrangement; 19Dec46;
EP12143. Piano-conductor score
(tenor or baritone, mixed chorus
and band) and parts.

BENNETT, DONALD E   1894-
I'm on my way to heaven ... words
and music by Lou McDermott,
[pseud.] and Don Bennett.
© Donald E. Bennett, Larkspur,
Calif.; 8Mar47; EP14842.

BENNETT, ELLEN.
My dear one; words and music by
Josephine Clements and Ellen
Bennett. © Topik Tunes, New
York; 18Jun47; EP15204.

BENNETT, ELSIE M   1919-
ed. and arr.
Everybody's favorite Easy solos
for accordion; arr. and ed. by
E. M. Bennett. © Amsco Music
Publishing Co., New York; on
arrangement; 1Mar47; EP13381.

BENNETT, WILLIAM S
God is a Spirit; for ... S.S.A.;
[by] William S. Bennett, arr.
by Paul Fuller [pseud.] John
IV: 24. © Pro Art Publications,
New York; on arrangement;
21Apr47; EP13614.

BENSENBERG, NORMAN.
Cheri; by Norman Bensenberg. ©
Cino-Mart Music Publishing Co.,
Hollywood, Calif.; 1Dec46;
EP11497. For voice and piano,
with chord symbols.

BENTLEY, BERENICE BENSON.
The book of bells; for piano,
thirty-two pieces ... by
Berenice Benson Bentley.
© Clayton F. Summy Co.,
Chicago; 7Mar47; EP12622.

In a summer garden; piano solo by
Berenice Benson Bentley. ©
Clayton F. Summy Co., Chicago;
7Apr47; EP13422.

Sweet sleep ... For the piano
[by] Berenice Benson Bentley.
© Oliver Ditson Co., Philadelphia;
26May47; EP14697.

BENTZON, NIELS VIGGO.
(Partita, piano) Partita; [by]
Niels Viggo Bentzon. Op. 38.
© Wilhelm Hansen, Musik-Forlag,
Copenhagen; 19Dec46; EF3442.

[BERENDSOHN, BERNHARD] 1889-
I'm an eagle! (and I wanna fly
high); words and music by "Doc"
Brenson [pseud.] Fraternal
Order of Eagles, South
Chicago Aerie No. 1358. © Bern-
hard Berendsohn, Chicago; 3Feb47;
EP11933.

BEREZOWSKY, NICOLAI T
(Concerto, harp) Concerto for
harp and orchestra; [by] Nicolai
Berezowsky with original harp
cadenza by Carlos Salzedo, [harp
part ed. by Carlos Salzedo]
© Elkan-Vogel Co., inc., Philadelphia; 11Mar47; EP13922.
Score: harp and piano.
[BERG, CORNELIS JACOBUS VAN DEN]
1921-
Clownerie; solo voor accordeon
of piano, [by] Cor Monté
[pseud.] © Edition Heuwekemeijer (Firm Heuwekemeijer &
van Gaal), Amsterdam; 10Mar47;
EP3376.

Katjesspel; [by] Cor Monté
[pseud.] Solo voor piano of
accordeon. © Edition Heuwekemeijer (Firm Heuwekemeijer &
van Gaal), Amsterdam; 10Mar47;
EP3375.

Op en top; [by] Cor Monté [pseud.]
Solo voor accordeon. © Edition
Heuwekemeijer (Firm Heuwekemeijer
& van Gaal), Amsterdam; 28Aug45;
EP3386.

BERG, WAL- See
Wal-Berg.

BERGE, HERMAN VON. See
Von Berge, Herman.

BERGEN, ALFRED HILES.
Hymn to America ... S.A.T.B. ...
[by] Alfred Hiles Bergen, poem
by Eric Hoss. © Gamble Hinged
Music Co., Chicago; 25Apr47;
EP13825.

Put, put, put, went the Evinrude;
music and lyrics by Alfred Hiles
Bergen. © Outboard Marine and
Manufacturing Co., Milwaukee;
12May47; EP14598.

BERGEN, RALPH J. VON. See
Von Bergen, Ralph J.

BERGER, ARTHUR VICTOR, 1912-
(Quartet, wind) Quartet in C
major, for woodwinds [by]
Arthur Berger. © Arrow
Music Press, inc., New York;
24Dec46; EP12217. Miniature
score.

BERGERE, ROY.
I'm sorry to see Sunday go by; words
and music by Roy Bergere. ©
Sponsler-Bergere Songs, Baltimore
1Apr47; EP6743.

So weary; words and music by Roy
Bergere. © Sponsler-Bergere
Songs, Baltimore; 1Apr47;
EP6744.

BERGMAN, MARGUERITE.
Only in dreams; words and music
by Marguerite Bergman.
© Marguerite Bergman, Montgomery,
Ohio; 26Jun47; EP15217.

Weeping willow; words and music
by Marguerite Bergman. ©
Marguerite Bergman, Montgomery,
Ohio; 26Jun47; EP15216.

BERGSMA, WILLIAM LAURENCE, 1921-
In a glass of water before retiring
for four-part chorus of mixed
voices with soprano solo and
piano acc., poem by Stephen
Vincent Benét, music by William
Bergsma. © Carl Fischer, inc.,
New York; 11Mar47; EP13479.

Music on a quiet theme; [by]
William Bergsma. © Arrow
Music Press, inc., New York;
23Dec46; EP12218. Miniature
score: orchestra.

Paul Bunyan suite ... By William
Bergsma. © Carl Fischer,
inc., New York; 25Mar47;
EP13480. Score: orchestra.

Three fantasies, for piano solo;
[by] William Bergsma. (Contemporary
music series) © Hargail Music
Press, New York; 3Apr45; EP6490.

[BERGSTROM, GULLI]
Det Mr sa dMr nMr man Mr kMr
... musik: Kai Gullmar [pseud.],
arr.: GSata Haag. © Edition
Sylvain, a.b., Stockholm;
1Jan46; EP3759. Piano-conductor score (orchestra, with
words), and parts.

(Sonata, piano) Sonata for piano;
by Lennox Berkeley. © J. & W.
Chester, ltd., London; 15Feb47;
EP3303.

BERKELEY, LENNOX, 1903-
Divertimento in B flat for orchestra;
by Lennox Berkeley. © J. & W.
Chester, ltd., London; 12Dec46;
EP6645.

BERKMAN, VEDA M
The princess and the flute
player; piano solo, by Veda
M. Berkman. © Clayton F.
Summy Co., Chicago; 12May47;
EP14800.

BERLIN, IRVING, 1888-
Accordion transcriptions of Irving
Berlin melodies; arr. by Anthony
Galla-Rini. New York, Irving
Berlin Music Corp. © Irving Berlin,
New York; on arrangement of 9 songs;
26Aug46. Contents.- [v.1] A pretty
girl is like a melody (© EP11589) -
[v.2] Russian lullaby (© EP11587) -
[v.3] Marie (© EP11585) - [v.4] All
by myself (© EP11590) - [v.5] Always
(© EP11588) - [v.6] Blue skies
(© EP11584) - [v.7] Alexander's
ragtime band (© EP11591) - [v.8]
Easter parade (© EP11586) - [v.9]
White Christmas (© EP11592)

Alexander's ragtime band; [words
and music by Irving Berlin],
arranged by Dick Jacobs. New
York, Irving Berlin Music Corp.
© Irving Berlin, New York; on
arrangement; 7Oct46; EP11405.
Condensed score (band) and parts.

Always; [words and music by Irving
Berlin], arranged by Dick Jacobs.
New York, Irving Berlin Music
Corp. © Irving Berlin, New
York; on arrangement; 18Sep46;
EP11404. Condensed score (band)
and parts.

(Annie get your gun) Doin' what
comes natur'lly ... [from]
Annie get your gun; lyrics and
music by Irving Berlin, [arr.
by Paul Weirick] New York,
Irving Berlin Music Co. ©
Irving Berlin, New York; on
arrangement; 3Jun46; EP11579.
Piano-conductor score (orchestra, with words) and parts.

(Annie get your gun) Doin' what
comes natur'lly; from the Rodgers
and Hammerstein production "Annie
get your gun," [by Irving Berlin],
arranged by Erik W. G. Leidzén.
New York, Irving Berlin Music Co.
© Irving Berlin, New York; on
arrangement; 11Sep46; EP11410.
Condensed score (band) and parts.

(Annie get your gun) The girl that
I marry [from Annie get your gun]
by Irving Berlin; ... simplified
piano solo. Children's ed. New
York, Irving Berlin Music Corp.
© Irving Berlin, New York; on
simplified arrangement; 27Nov46;
EP11593.

(Annie get your gun) The girl that
I marry ... from] Annie get your
gun; lyrics and music by Irving
Berlin, [arr. by Paul Weirick]
New York, Irving Berlin Music Co.
© Irving Berlin, New York; on
arrangement; 24Jun46; EP11580.
Piano-conductor score (orchestra, with
words) and parts.

(Annie get your gun) The girl that
I marry; from the Rodgers and
Hammerstein production "Annie
get your gun," [by Irving Berlin],
arranged by Erik W. G. Leidzén.
New York, Irving Berlin Music
Co. © Irving Berlin, New York;
on arrangement; 6Sep46; EP11409.
Condensed score (band) and parts.

(Annie get your gun) I got lost
in his arms ... [from] Annie
get your gun; lyrics and music
by Irving Berlin, [arr. by
Jack Mason] New York, Irving
Berlin Music Co. © Irving
Berlin, New York; on arrangement; 5Apr46; EP11582. Piano-
conductor score (orchestra,
with words) and parts.

(Annie get your gun) I got the
sun in the morning ... [from]
Annie get your gun ... music
by Irving Berlin, [arr. by
Jack Mason] New York, Irving
Berlin Music Co. © Irving
Berlin, New York; on arrangement; 5Apr46; EP11581. Piano-
conductor score (orchestra)
and parts.

(Annie get your gun) I got the sun in
the morning, from ... "Annie get your
gun"; words and music by Irving Berlin,
arr. for ... S.A.T.B. by Charles
Boutelle. [New York, Irving Berlin
Music Corp.] © Irving Berlin, New York;
on arrangement; 17Sep46; EP11577.

(Annie get your gun) I got the sun
in the morning, from ... "Annie
get your gun"; words and music by
Irving Berlin, arr. for ... S.S.A.
by Charles Boutelle. [New York,
Irving Berlin Music Corp.] © Irving
Berlin, New York; on arrangement;
17Sep46; EP11572.

(Annie get your gun) I got the sun
in the morning, from ... "Annie get
your gun"; words and music by Irving
Berlin, arr. for ... T.T.B.B. by
Charles Boutelle. [New York, Irving
Berlin Music Corp.] © Irving Berlin,
New York; on arrangement; 17Sep46;
EP11576.

(Annie get your gun) I got the sun
in the morning; from the Rodgers
and Hammerstein production "Annie
get your gun" [by Irving Berlin],
arranged by Erik W. G. Leidzén.
New York, Irving Berlin Music Co.
© Irving Berlin, New York; on
arrangement; 6Sep46; EP11402.
Condensed score (band) and parts.

(Annie get your gun) Irving Berlin's
The girl that I marry from ...
"Annie get your gun" ... by
Jimmy Dale. New York, I. Berlin Music
Corp. © Irving Berlin, New York;
on arrangement; 8Aug46; EP11301.
Piano-conductor score (orchestra,
with words) and parts.

(Annie get your gun) Irving
Berlin's Who do you love, I
hope? From ... "Annie get your
gun" ... arr. by Jimmy Dale. New
York, Irving Berlin Music Corp. ©
Irving Berlin, New York; on arrangement; 5Aug46; EP11300. Piano-
conductor score (orchestra, with
words) and parts.

(Annie get your gun) They say
it's wonderful, from ... "Annie
get your gun" [by] Irving Berlin, arr. by Erik W. G. Leidzén. © Irving Berlin, New
York; on arrangement 12Aug46;
EP12350. Condensed score
(band) and parts.

(Annie get your gun) They say it's
wonderful ... [from] Annie get your
gun; lyrics and music by Irving
Berlin, [arr. by Jack Mason] New
York, Irving Berlin Music Co.
© Irving Berlin, New York; on
arrangement; 8Apr46; EP11583.
Piano-conductor score (orchestra,
with words) and parts.

BERLIN, IRVING. Cont'd.
(Annie get your gun) They say
it's wonderful, from ...
"Annie get your gun"; words
and music by Irving Berlin,
arr. for ... S.S.A. by Charles
Boutelle [New York, Irving
Berlin Music Co.] © Irving
Berlin, New York; on arrange-
ment; 17Sep46; EP11574.
(Annie get your gun) They say it's
wonderful, from ... "Annie get your
gun"; words and music by Irving
Berlin, arr. for ... S.A.T.B. by
Charles Boutelle. [New York, Irving
Berlin Music Co.] © Irving Berlin,
New York; on arrangement; 17Sep46;
EP11573.
(Annie get your gun) They say it's
wonderful, from ... "Annie get your
gun"; words and music by Irving Berlin,
arr. for ... T.T.B.B. by Charles
Boutelle. [New York, Irving Berlin
Music Co.] © Irving Berlin, New York;
on arrangement; 17Sep46; EP11575.
(Annie get your gun) Who do you love,
I hope? ... [From] Annie get your
gun; lyrics and music by Irving
Berlin, [arr. by Jack Mason] New
York, Irving Berlin Music Co. ©
Irving Berlin Music Co.; on arrange-
ment; 5Apr47; EP11578. Piano-
conductor score (orchestra, with
words) and parts.
(Blue skies) Heat wave; [by
Irving Berlin] arranged by Dick
Jacobs. New York, Irving
Berlin Music Corp. © Irving
Berlin Music Corp.; on arrange-
ment; 17Dec46; EP11407. Con-
densed score (band) and parts.
(Blue skies) Heat wave; lyrics
and music by Irving Berlin, from
... "Blue skies," [arranged by
Johnny Warrington] New York,
Irving Berlin Music Corp. ©
Irving Berlin, New York; on arrange-
ment; 7Oct46; EP11406. Piano-
conductor score (orchestra) and parts.
(Blue skies) A serenade to an old-
fashioned girl; words and music
by Irving Berlin, from Irving
Berlin's Blue skies ... A Johnny
Warrington arrangement. New
York, I. Berlin Music Corp. ©
Irving Berlin, New York; on
arrangement; 26Aug46; EP11303.
Piano-conductor score orchestra, with
words) and parts.
(Blue skies) You keep coming back
like a song [from Blue skies, by
Irving Berlin] ... Simplified piano
solo. Children's ed. New York,
Irving Berlin Music Corp. © Irving
Berlin, New York; on simplified
arrangement; 27Nov46; EP11594.
Doin' what comes natur'ally. See
his Annie get your gun.
The girl that I marry. See his
Annie get your gun.
Help me to help my neighbor; words
and music by Irving Berlin. ©
Irving Berlin, New York; 27Jan47;
EP11508.
I got lost in his arms. See his
Annie get your gun.
I got the sun in the morning.
See his Annie get your gun.
(The Jolson story) Let me sing,
and I'm happy; words and music
by Irving Berlin. Featured in
... The Jolson story. New York,
Irving Berlin Music Corp. ©
Irving Berlin, New York; on
arrangement; 13Dec46; EP11411.
For voice and piano, with chord
symbols.
Kate, have I come too early, too
late? Words and music by Irving
Berlin. © Irving Berlin, New
York; 3Jun47; EP14950.

Let me sing, and I'm happy. See
his The Jolson story.
Love and the weather; words and
music by Irving Berlin. ©
Irving Berlin, New York;
26May47; EP14729.
Mandy; [words and music by Irving
Berlin], arranged by Dick
Jacobs. New York, Irving Berlin
Music Corp. © Irving Berlin,
New York; on arrangement; 30Sep46;
EP11403. Condensed score (band)
and parts.
Marie; [by Irving Berlin], arranged
by Dick Jacobs. New York,
Irving Berlin Music Corp.,
[c1946] © Irving Berlin, New
York; on arrangement; 14Jan47;
EP11408. Condensed score (band)
and parts.
A serenade to an old-fashioned
girl. See his Blue skies.
They say it's wonderful. See his
Annie get your gun.
Who do you love I hope? See his
Annie get your gun.
You keep coming back like a song.
See his Blue skies.
BERLIOZ, HECTOR, 1803-1869.
Glory and triumph; choral hymn
from 3rd movement ("Apotheosis")
of Grand symphony for band ...
op. 15, [by] Berlioz. For mixed
chorus (SATB) with piano acc.
[arr. by Dorothy Cadzow] and
text in English [tr. by R. F.
Goldman] and French [by Antony
Deschamps] © Mercury Music
Corp., New York; on arrangement
and translation; 30Jun47;
EP15252.
Recitativo and prayer; (2nd movement of Grand symphony for band,
op. 15) [by] Berlioz ... with
piano acc. [arr. by Roger Smith]
© Mercury Music Corp., New York;
on editing and arrangement;
16Jun47; EP15249. Score (solo
instrument and piano) and part
for trombone or baritone.
(Symphony) Grand symphony for band
(funeral and triumphal); [by]
Hector Berlioz. Op.15. Rev. and
ed. for modern use by Richard
Franko Goldman. III. Apotheosis.
© Mercury Music Corp., New York;
on arrangement and scoring of
additional parts; 30Jun47;
EP15253.
BERMEJO, FELIPE.
Agua de limón ... Letra, música y
arreglo de Felipe Bermejo.
© Promotora Hispano Americana
de Música, s. a., Mexico;
30Dec46; EF5514.
Donde se la llaman brinco! ...
letra y música de Felipe Ber-
mejo. © Promotora Hispano
Americana de Música, s.a.,
Mexico; 29Jul47; EF5244.
Dos luceros; letra y música de
Felipe Bermejo. © Promotora
Hispano Americana de Música,
s. a., Mexico; 30Dec46;
EF5282. For voice and piano.
Los jaliscienses ... Letra y música
de Felipe Bermejo. © Promotora
Hispano Americana de Música, s.
a., Mexico; 29Oct46; EF5502.
BERMEJO, GUILLERMO.
La enredadora ... Letra y música
de Guillermo Bermejo. © Pro-
motora Hispano Americana de
Música, s.a., Mexico; 7May47;
EF3333.
BERMUDEZ, LUIS E
Buenos Aires ... letra y música
de Eugenio Nobile y Luis E.
Bermudez. Buenos Aires, Editorial
Argentina de Música Internacional.
© Peer International Corp., New
York; 24Mar47; EF5603. Parts:
orchestra.

BERNARD, BEN.
(The seventh veil) Seventh veil
waltz; by Ben Bernard, from
... The seventh veil, [arr.
by Len Stevens] © Southern
Music Publishing Co., ltd.,
London; 27May47; EF3587. For
piano solo.
Seventh veil waltz. See his
The seventh veil.
Waltz from Seventh veil. See his
The seventh veil.
BERNARD, FELIX.
Winter wonderland; two part
chorus, words by Dick Smith,
music by Felix Bernard, arr.
by William Stickles. © Breg-
man, Vocco and Conn, inc., New
York; on arrangement; 12Dec46;
EP12026.
BERNARD, PAUL JACQUES.
Christmas chimes; words & music by
Frank Ruhnau [and] Paul Jacques
Bernard. © Hollywood Music
Sales, Hollywood, Calif.; 12Dec46;
EP10943. For voice and piano.
BERNERS, GERALD HUGH TYRWHITT-WILSON,
baron, 1883-
(Nicholas Nickleby) Incidental
music from the ... film,
Nicholas Nickleby ... music by
Lord Berners. © Chappell & Co.,
ltd., London; 6Jun47; EF3913.
For piano solo.
BERNHARD, GÖSTA, pseud. See
Byhmar, Gösta.
BERNHARDT, CLYDE, 1905-
Lay your habits down; by Clyde
Bernhardt. © Popular Music
Co., New York; 23Jan47;
EP11534. For voice and piano,
with chord symbols.
My little dog got kittens; music
by Clyde Bernhardt, words by
Harry P. Stevenson [and]
Edgar L. Silvera. © Fowler
Music Co., New York; 18Apr47;
EP14236.
Triflin' woman blues; by Clyde
Bernhardt. © Popular Music
Co., New York; 23Jan47;
EP11535. For voice and
piano, with chord symbols.
Would you do me a favor? Music
by Clyde Bernhardt, words by
Walter Hilliard. © Popular
Music Co., New York; 23Jan47;
EP11536.
BERRY, PEARL L 1900-
Song of the gaucho; words and
music by Pearl Berry. © Pearl
L. Berry, Los Angeles; 1Mar47;
EP12307. Melody and chord
symbols, with words.
BERRY, MRS. WILLIE, 1896-
Trust God for everything ... words
and music by Mrs. Willie Berry,
arr. by Edward G. Mayo. © Mrs.
Willie Berry, Cleveland; 18Oct46;
EP13408.
BERT, HR., pseud. See
Wahlberg, Herbert.
BERWALD, WILLIAM.
When Silvia sings; for four-
part chorus of men's voices,
a cappella. [Words by]
Samuel Pitts Duffield,
[music by] William Berwald.
© G. Schirmer, inc., New
York; 24Mar47; EP13123.
BEST, WILLIAM.
(I love you) for sentimental reasons;
lyric by Deek Watson, music by
William Best, arr. by William
Teague. © Duchess Music Corp.,
New York; on arrangement; 31Dec46;
EP10839. Condensed score (band)
and parts.

BEST, WILLIAM. Cont'd.
(I love you) for sentimental
reasons ... Music by William
Best, concertina arr. by Joseph
P. Elsnic. [Chicago, Vitak-
Elsnic Co.] © Duchess Music
Corp., New York; on arrangement;
11Feb47; EP12008.

BESTHOFF, MABEL.
Dainty toes; duet for one piano,
four hands, by Mabel Besthoff.
© Mills Music, inc., New York;
23May47; EP6923.
Dancing Dolores; duet for one piano,
four hands, by Mabel Besthoff.
© Mills Music, inc., New York;
23May47; EP6922.
Tired hikers; duet for one piano,
four hands, by Mabel Besthoff.
© Mills Music, inc., New York;
23May47; EP6924.
The toy band parade; duet for one
piano, four hands, by Mabel
Besthoff. © Mills Music, inc.,
New York; 23May47; EP6925.
The young piano prodigy; duet for one
piano, four hands, by Mabel
Besthoff. © Mills Music, inc.,
New York; 23May47; EP6926.

BÉTOVE, pseud. See
Levy, Michel Maurice.

BETTI, HENRI.
Les rondondons ... paroles de
Maurice Vandair [pseud.] et
Maurice Chevalier, musique
de Henri Betti. © Éditions
E. M. U. L., Paris; 9Mar45;
EF3619.

BEUCKMANN, HENRY.
That's why I'm in love with you;
(novelty song ...) [Words and
music by] Hugh J. Wolfe and
Henry Beuckmann. © Hugh J.
Wolfe, Dayton, Ohio; 20Dec46;
EP10982.

BEYDTS, LOUIS, 1895-
Crépuscule; poème de Henri de
Régnier, musique de Louis Beydts.
© Durand et Cie., Paris; 15Mar47;
EF3888.
D'ombre et de soleil; huit
mélodies de Louis Beydts, sur
des poèmes extraits des
"Contrerimes" de P. J. Toulet.
© Éditions Durand & Cie.,
Paris; 31Oct46; EF5178. For
voice and piano.
Le présent; poème de Louise
Lalanne, musique de Louis
Beydts. © Durand & Cie.,
Paris; 15Mar47; EF3610.

BEYER, EMIL.
(Prelude, piano, no. 2) Prelude
in A minor, no. 2 ... for the
piano by Emil Beyer. Cincinnati, Beyer Music Studios.
© Emil Beyer, Cincinnati;
2May47; EP14505.

BEZDEK, JAN, 1896-
An introduction to Hanon; exercises
to precede and prepare for the
virtuoso pianist, [by] Jan
Bezdek. © Shattinger Piano &
Music Co., St. Louis; 31Dec46;
EP11247.

BIBO, IRVING.
Once upon a moonlight night;
lyric by Sidney Clare, music
by Irving Bibo. © Sinatra Songs,
inc., New York; 4Jun47; EP15118.

BICKEL, WILLIAM J
Hail Mary; by William J. Bickel.
South Bend, Ind., Imco Music
Publishing Co. © William J.
Bickel, South Bend, Ind.;
12Sep46; EP9211. For voice and
piano (or organ); version in
close score (SATB) at end.

[BIDERI, VALENTINA] comp.
'O solo mio! Raccolta delle
celebri canzoni dall'800 al 900;
[comp. by Valentina Bideri] Ed.
per canto e piano. © Casa
Editrice Ferdinando Bideri,
Napoli; ser, 1-2, 10Aug46; ser.
3-4, 22Aug46; EF3218, 3217,3221-
3222. Vol. 2-4 have title:
Canzoni celebri dall'800 al 900.
Piedigrotta Bideri 1946; [comp. by
Valentina Bideri] © Casa
Editrice Ferdinando Bideri,
Napoli; 31Aug46; EF3216. For
voice and piano.

BIENBAR, ARTHUR MICHAEL, 1868-1942.
Mass in honor of Padre Junipero
Serra ... for mixed voices, by
Arthur Michael Bienbar ... ed.
by ... Owen da Silva. Phoenix,
Ariz., St. Mary's choir. © The
Franciscan Fathers of California,
Los Angeles; 13Dec43; EP6754.

BIERMAN, BERNARD.
This is the inside story; words
and music by Jack Manus [and]
Bernard Bierman. © Stovens
Music Corp., New York; 11Jun47;
EP14978.

BIGGERS, LELA MACK WILLIAMS.
See Williams-Biggers, Lela Mack.

BILLINGS, WILLIAM, 1746-1800.
Compositions ... ed. by Oliver
Daniel. Ser. II. © C. C. Birchard and Co., Boston; v. 1-3,on
arrangement, notes & foreword,
laughs v. 4-5, 20Nov46;
EP6749, 8747, 8748, 10309, 9559.
For mixed chorus, with piano reduction. Contents.- [1] David's
lamentation.- [2] I heard a
great voice.- [3] Fare you well,
my friends.- [4] Emanuel.- [5]
Chester.

BILLSON, ADA. See
Grant, Ada (Billson)

BINDER, ABRAHAM WOLFE, 1895-
Shomor Yisroel. (Israel's keeper);
for voice and piano by A. W.
Binder. New York, Metro Music Co.
© A. W. Binder, New York; 16Jul47;
EP12260. Yiddish words (trans-
literated)

BINGE, RONALD, 1910-
Madrugado. (Daybreak) [By]
Ronald Binge; piano solo. ©
Ascherberg, Hopwood & Crew,
ltd., London; 12May47;
EF5777.

BINNEY, ALICE STEAD, 1887-
The gingham dog and the calico
cat; song for medium voice, to
the poem "The duel," by Eugene
Field; music by Alice Stead
Binney. © The Composers Press,
inc., New York; 16Jun47;
EP15108.

BIONDI, RAY.
Boogie blues; by Gene Krupa [and]
Ray Biondi. © Gene Krupa Music
Corp., New York; on arrangement
and changes in words; 29Aug46;
EP11009. For voice and piano,
with chord symbols.

BIRDSLEY, ASA EARLE, 1889-
Springtime in Nevada; words and
music by Asa E. Birdsley.
Hollywood, Calif., Nordyke
Music Publications, [c1945]
© Asa Earle Birdsley, Lovell,
Wyo., 20Dec46; EP14439.
Spring time in Nevada; words and
music by Asa E. Birdsley. ©
Nordyke Publishing Co., Los
Angeles; 28Nov45; EP6408. For
voice and piano, with chord
symbols.

BIRLEW, EUGENE CHATHAM, 1903-
Weiser? By Gene Birlew.
© Eugene Chatham Birlew,
Weiser, Idaho; 1Mar47;
EP13098. For voice and
piano.

BISIO, NANDO.
Melody swing ... Oblio ...
testi e musiche di Nando Bisio.
© Edizioni Leonardi, s.a.r.l.,
Milano; 2Jan47; EF5273.
Piano-conductor score (orches-
tra, with words), and parts.

BITGOOD, ROBERTA.
Be still, and know that I am
God; sacred song by Roberta
Bitgood. [Words from the
Psalms] © The H. W. Gray
Co., inc., New York; 9May47;
EP14380.

BIXBY, ALLENE K
In heavenly love abiding; two-part
hymn for treble voices, by
Allene K. Bixby, [words by Anna
L. Waring] © Theodore Presser
Co., Philadelphia; 5Feb47;
EP11879.

BIZET, GEORGES, 1838-1875.
(Carmen) Habaneras; [French words
by] H. Meilhac and L. Halevy,
English version by Frank Chap-
man. (In Swarthout, Gladys, comp
Gladys Swarthout album of con-
cert songs and arias. p. 33-39)
© G. Schirmer, inc., New York;
on English version; 21Feb46;
EP2416.
Habanera. See his Carmen.

BJÖRKLUND, NILS.
Prinsessans strumpeband; text:
Fritz-Gustaf [pseud.] musik:
Nils Björklund. © Nordiska
Musikförlaget, a.b., Stockholm;
1Jan42; EF5731.
Sveriges hemvärn; [by] Nils
Björklund, arrangör: Sam
Rydberg. © Nordiska
Musikförlaget, a.b., Stock-
holm; 1Jan44; EF5735. Piano-
conductor score (orchestra),
and parts.

BJORNSON, FREDA.
Lovely lady of lover's lane; words
and music by Freda Bjornson.
© Nordyke Publishing Co., Los
Angeles; 5Mar47; EP13269.

BLACKIE, pseud. See
Efrón, Taibe.

BLAKE, DOROTHY GAYNOR.
Huckleberry Finn; piano solo by
Dorothy Gaynor Blake. © The
Willis Music Co., Cincinnati;
2Apr47; EP13363.
The measuring-worm; piano solo,
by Dorothy Gaynor Blake.
© The Willis Music Co.,
Cincinnati; 18Mar47; EP12838.
With words.
On the lone prairee; cowboy tune
arr. for piano solo by Dorothy
Gaynor Blake. © The Willis
Music Co., Cincinnati; on
arrangement; 2Apr47; EP13364.

BLAKE, EUBIE.
Memories of you; by Andy Razaf and
Euble Blake, [arr. by Charlie
Ventura] © Shapiro, Bernstein
& Co., New York; on arrangement;
10Jun47; EP14980. Score (Bb
tenor saxophone and piano) and
part.

BLAKE, GEORGE.
The radiant morn hath passed
away ... for mixed voices, [by]
George Blake, [words by] God-
frey Thring. © Oliver Ditson
Co., Philadelphia; 16Apr47;
EP13891.

BLAKE, LEONARD.
Jubilate Deo; set to music in
the key of E flat by Leonard
Blake. © Novello & Co., ltd.,
London; 10Jun47; EF3802.
Score: SSATB and organ.
English words.

BLANC, JEAN ROBERT.
Vieille valse. © Jean Robert Blanc,
Paris; 1Mar45; EF479. For vio-
lin and piano.

BLANCHARD, CRAIG, 1918-
He can do abundantly; [words by]
Lois Blanchard, [music by]
Craig Blanchard. (In Church
of the Nazarene. Michigan
District. Nazarene Young
Peoples Society. Choruses
of the N. Y. P. S. p.52) ©
Michigan District, Nazarene
Young Peoples Society, Flint,
Mich.; 25Jul46; EP13072.
Close score: SATB.

BLANCHARD, LOIS F   1919-
Since at the Father's throne;
[by] Lois F. Blanchard, arr.
by W. M. T. (In Church of
the Nazarene. Michigan
District. Nazarene Young
Peoples Society. Choruses of
the N. Y. P. S. p. 58) ©
Michigan District, Nazarene
Young Peoples Society, Flint,
Mich.; 25Jul46; EP13078. Close
score: SATB.

[BLAND, JAMES A   ] 1854-1911.
Carry me back to old Virginny; [by
James A. Bland, and] Home on the
range. [Arr. by] Robert Whitford.
Erie, Pa., Robert Whitford Publi-
cations. © Robert H. Whitford,
Erie, Pa.; on arrangement; 10Dec46;
EP6488. For piano solo.

In the evening by the moonlight;
[words and music by James A.
Bland, arr. by Victor Lakes
Martin] Easy piano arrangement
with keyboard charts. © Songs
You Remember Publishing Co.,
(V. L. Martin, Proprietor),
Atlanta; on arrangement; 5Apr47;
EP14751.

BLANE, RALPH.
The bicycle song. See his
Jennie was a lady.

(Jennie was a lady) The bicycle
song; words and music by R.
Blane and George Bassman.
© Robbins Music Corp., New York;
1Jun46; EP4722.

BLANKENMORE, EARL.
I sure got it from you; words and
music by Dave Denney and Earl
Blankenhorn. © Bob Miller, inc.,
New York; 30Dec46; EP10743.

BLAREAU, RICHARD, 1910-
Dix-huit ans. See his L'ingénue de Londres.

(L'ingénue de Londres) Dix-huit
ans, de l'opérette "L'ingénue
de Londres" ... paroles de Maurice Vandair [pseud.], musique
de Richard Blareau & André
Muscat. © Éditions Musicales
Nuances, Paris; 28Nov46; EF5226.

(L'ingénue de Londres) L'ingénue
de mon coeur ... de l'opérette
L'ingénue de Londres ... paroles
de Maurice Vandair [pseud.],
musique d'André Muscat. © Éditions Musicales Nuances, Paris; 28Nov46;
EF5224.

(L'ingénue de Londres) J'ai tout
donné ... de l'opérette L'ingénue de Londres ... paroles de
Maurice Vandair [pseud.],
musique de Richard Blareau et
André Muscat. © Éditions Musicales Nuances, Paris; 28Nov46;
EF5223.

(L'ingénue de Londres) J'en ai
un p'tit bout, de l'opérette
"L'ingénue de Londres" ...
paroles de Maurice Vandair
[pseud.], musique de Richard
Blareau & André Muscat. ©
Éditions Musicales Nuances,
Paris; 28Nov46; EF5222.

(L'ingénue de Londres) La java
du champagne, de l'opérette
"L'ingénue de Londres" ...
paroles de Maurice Vandair
[pseud.], musique de Richard
Blareau & André Muscat. ©
Éditions Musicales Nuances,
Paris; 28Nov46; EF5221.

L'ingénue de mon coeur. See his
L'ingénue de Londres.

J'ai tout donné. See his L'ingénue de Londres.

J'en ai un p'tit bout. See his
L'ingénue de Londres.

La java du champagne. See his
L'ingénue de Londres.

Souviens-toi, (Remember me);
valse de l'opérette "L'ingénue
de Londres" ... Paroles de
Maurice Vandair [pseud.],
musique de Richard Blareau &
André Muscat. © Éditions
Musicales Nuances, Paris;
28Nov46; EF5171.

Le sport; de l'opérette "L'ingénue
de Londres" ... Paroles de
Maurice Vandair [pseud.],
musique de Richard Blareau &
André Muscat. © Éditions
Musicales Nuances, Paris;
28Nov46; EF5172.

Valse des coeurs; de l'operette
L'ingénue de Londres ...
Paroles de Maurice Vandair
[pseud.], musique de Richard
Blareau & André Muscat. ©
Éditions Musicales Nuances,
Paris; 28Nov46; EF5173.

La vie de printemps; valse de
l'opérette L'ingénue de Londres
... Paroles de Maurice Vandair
[pseud.], musique de Richard
Blareau & André Muscat. ©
Éditions Musicales Nuances,
Paris; 28Nov46; EF5174.

BLAUFUSS, WALTER, d.1945.
Your eyes have told me so; three
part women's voices, S.S.A.,
words by Gus Kahn and Egbert Van
Alstyne, music by Walter Blaufuss,
arr. by Douglas MacLean, [pseud.]
© Remick Music Corp., New York;
on arrangement; 5Jun47; EP15169.

Your eyes have told me so; two
part, S. A. or T. B., words by
Gus Kahn and Egbert Van Alstyne,
music by Walter Blaufuss, arr. by
Douglas MacLean [pseud.] ©
Remick Music Corp., New York; on
arrangement; 5Jun47; EP15171.

BLAŽEK, ZDENEK, 1905-
Klavírní variace na vlastní thema;
[by] Zdenek Blazek. [Op. 2]
Rev. [by] prof. Vilém Kurz. ©
Hudební Matice Umelecké Besedy,
Praha, Czechoslovakia; 1Dec43;
EF4949. For piano solo.

BLEKHMAN, J
My tones will tell. (Usta moi
molchat) For voice and piano
by J. Blekhman, English trans-
lation by Wladimir Lakond,
English adaptation by Olga Paul,
Russian lyric by F. Belozerov.
© Edward B. Marks Music Corp.,
New York; on adaptation of Eng-
lish lyrics; 4Apr47; EP13850.

BLEW, ETHEL MARGUERETTE.
You're breaking my heart (all
over again); lyrics and music
by Ethel Blew [arr. by Marshall
Near] © Ethel Marguerette
Blew, Kalamazoo, Mich.;
20Mar47; EP13143.

BLISS, ARTHUR.
(Memorial concert) Theme and
cadenza ... [by] Arthur Bliss,
from the play "Memorial
concert," by Trudy Bliss.
[Violin part ed. by Max Rostal]
© Keith, Prowse & Co., ltd.,
London; 18Jun47; EF3904.
Score (violin and piano) and
part.
Theme and cadenza. See his
Memorial concert.

BLITZ, LEONARD. See also
Towers, Leo, pseud.

Mia canzone d'amore. (My song
of love) ... [By] Don Pelosi
& Leo Towers [pseud.] Ukulele
arr. by R. S. Stoddon. ©
B. Feldman & Co., ltd., London;
28May47; EF3623. For voice
and piano, with ukulele diagrams and chord symbols;
melody also in tonic sol-fa
notation. English words.

BLOCH, ERNEST, 1880-
(Quartet, strings, no.2) Quatuor
à cordes (no.2) [by] Ernest
Bloch. © Boosey & Hawkes, ltd.,
London; 11Feb47; EF500G.
Miniature score.
Suite symphonique. [by] Ernest
Bloch. Full score. London,
Boosey & Hawkes. © Hawkes &
Son (London), ltd., London;
28Mar47; EF5317.

[BLOCH, PHILIPPE GÉRARD] 1924-
Boulevard; paroles de Gil-Renaud
[pseud.], musique de M. Philippe-
Gérard [pseud.], et P. Moslay
[pseud.] © Le Chant du Monde,
Paris; 20Dec46; EF5235.
Qu'il fait bon chanter! Paroles de
Gil-Renaud [pseud.] et A.
Farel [pseud.], musique de M.
Philippe-Gérard [pseud.] © Le
Chant du Monde, Paris; 25Nov46;
EF3298.

BLOOM, RUBE.
Maybe you'll be there; lyric by
Sammy Gallop, music by Rube
Bloom. © Triangle Music Corp.,
New York; 2Jan47; EP11850.
Same old blues; lyric by Rube
Bloom, music by Rube Bloom.
© Bregman, Vocco and Conn, inc., New York;
2Jan47; EP11850.

BLUE JAY SINGERS. See
Famous Blue Jay Singers.

BOATNER, EDWARD.
You're my heart's desire; words
by Hedley Dacon, music by Ed.
Boatner. © Hedley Clement
Dacon, Brooklyn; 4Mar46;
EP11112.

BOCHEROS, LOS.
Tiruliru; letra y música de Los
Bocheros. New York, Peer Inter-
national Corp. © Promotora
Hispano Americana de Música,
s. a., Mexico; 27Dec46;
EP14642.

BÖKE, JAN PIETER FREDERIK, 1907-
Valse simplice; voor piano, [by]
Jan Böke. © Edition Reuweke-
meyer (Firm A. J. Heuwekemeyer
& B. F. van Gaal), Amsterdam,
The Netherlands; 15Jul46; EF5115.
Vijftien melodische etudes. Op.
1. [For] piano, [by] Jan
Böke. © Edition Heuwekemeyer
(A. J. Heuwekemeyer & B. F.
van Gaal), Amsterdam, Nederland;
11Aug41; EF5116.

BØRDING, AXEL HOLM, 1885-
Danmark ... tekst af Elisabeth
Hansen-Møller, komponeret af
Axel Holm Børding. Copenhagen,
Kleinert. © Axel Holm Børding,
Hammond, Ind.; 20Jul47; EF6333.
Score: SAATTB and piano.

BOFFA, IMOLO.
Solo una lacrima ... versi e
musica di Imolo Boffa.
Napoli, Gesa. © Italian Book
Co. New York; 2Jan47; EF5420.

BOGERT, LILLIAN ESTELLA, 1880-
To Calvary; words and music by
Lillian E. Bogert, arr. by
Bertha C. Demarest. © Mrs.
Lillian E. Bogert, Wheelwright,
Ky.; 9Apr47; EP14261.

BOLADERES, GUILLERMO DE.
Escena clásica. Escena romántica.
Marcha. Para piano, por
Guillermo de Boladeres. Bar-
celona, A. Boileau y Bernasconi.
© Guillermo de Boladeres, Bar-
celona, Spain; 30Dec42; EF3248.
Escena oriental. Escena litúrgica.
Vals-romanza. Para Piano, por
Guillermo de Boladeres. Bar-
celona, A. Boileau y Bernasconi.
© Guillermo de Boladeres, Bar-
celona, Spain; 30Dec43; EF3247.
Estudio sobre la sonata "De la
aurora" de Beethoven; para piano,
por Guillermo de Boladeres.
Barcelona, A. Boileau y
Bernasconi [c1946] © Guillermo
de Boladeres, Barcelona, Spain;
30Dec40; EF3249.
Estudio sobre la sonata "Patética"
de Beethoven; para piano, por
Guillermo de Boladeres. Bar-
celona, A. Boileau y Bernasconi
[c1940] © Guillermo de Boladeres,
Barcelona, Spain, 30Dec46;
EF3250.

BOLAND, CLAY ALOYSIUS, 1903-
(Chris crosses) As ye sow shall ye
reap ... [From] University of
Pennsylvania ... 59th annual
production "Chris crosses" ...
Music by Clay Boland, lyrics by
Moe Jaffe and Darrell H. Smith.
[c1946] © General Music Publish-
ing Co., inc., New York; 15Feb47;
EP12025.
(Chris crosses) Interlude; from the
University of Pennsylvania production
"Chris Crosses" ... lyric by Moe
Jaffe & Nick Wells, music by Clay
Boland. © General Music Publishing
Co., inc., New York; 1Dec46; EP11547
(Chris crosses) It's the same the
whole world over, from the
University of Pennsylvania production
"Chris crosses" ... [music] by
Clay Boland, [words by] Moe
Jaffe [and] Dwight Latham. ©
General Music Publishing Co., inc.,
New York; 2Dec46; EP10939. For
voice and piano.
Interlude. See his Chris Crosses.

BOLICK, EARL.
I love her more (now mother's
old); by Bill and Earl Bolick.
© Acuff-Rose Publications,
Nashville; 28Apr47; EP14041.

BOLLMAN, BILL. See
Bollman, W. H.

BOLLMAN, W H
The Pass to the North; words and
music by Bill Bollman. © Cine-
Mart Music Publishing Co.,
Hollywood, Calif.; 30Dec46;
EP14031.

BONAVENA, ANTONIO.
¡Sigan tomando, muchachos! ... letra
de Rodolfo Scafidi y Montenieve,
música de Antonio Bonavena.
© Editorial Argentina de Música
Internacional, s. de r., ltd.,
Buenos Aires; 30Dec46; EF5601.

BOND, JASPER.
The lesser power; by Jasper
Bond. © Jasper Bond, San
Fernando, Calif.; 8Apr47;
EP13723. For voice and
piano, with chord symbols.

BONFILS, KJELD.
Swingin' in Sweden; [by] Kjeld
Bonfils, arrangemang; Gösta
Theselius. © Nordiska
Musikförlaget, a.b., Stock-
holm; 1Jan46; EF3736. Piano-
conductor score (orchestra),
and parts.

BONK, WALENTY, 1879-
Mass in honor of St. Frances X.
Cabrini, Mother Cabrini; for
2, 3 or 4 voices, soprano and
alto with tenor and bass ad lib.
with an accompaniment for the
organ, by Walenty Bonk. © X.
Jordan Publ. Co., Floral Park,
L.I., N.Y.; 31Dec46; EP10773.

BONNELL, WILLIAM CARL.
From out of heaven; music and
lyrics by Bill Bonnell.
[Seattle, Northwest Recording
Studios] © William Carl
Bonnell, Seattle; 10Sep46;
EP6887.
My dream girl; words and music
by Bill Bonnell. [Seattle,
Northwest Recording Studios]
© William Carl Bonnell,
Seattle; 1May46; EP6886.
You left me in September; music
and lyrics by Bill Bonnell.
[Seattle] Northwest Recording
Studios. © William Carl
Bonnell, Seattle; 10Sep46;
EP6885.

BONNER, RONNIE.
Lullaby of the trail; lyric by
Eddie Khoury, music by Ronnie
Bonner. © Topik Tunes, New
York; 5May47; EP15071.

BOOTHMAN, EDDIE, arr.
Santa's favorite carols; for boys
and-girls to play and sing,
piano solo with words, by
Eddie Boothman. [c1943] ©
Thomas Music Co., Detroit;
8Nov44; EP6765.

BORBÓN, ALFREDO NÚÑEZ DE. See
Núñez de Borbón, Alfredo.

BORDEAU, CÉLESTIN.
Cherubim song ... from the Russian
liturgy, tr. by Hugh Ross. (In
Ross, Hugh, arr. Sacred choruses
for women's or girls' voices.
p. 14-17) © G. Schirmer, inc.,
New York; on arrangement;
30Sep46; EP9779.

BORDINO, FRANCISCO.
Las Malvinas ... Woinendes Herz
... von Francisco Bordino.
Mailand, Leonardi Piero
Musikverlag. © Edizioni
Leonardi, Milan; 6Jun41; EF4805.
Piano-conductor score (orchestra)
and parts.

BORKOVEC, PAVEL, 1894-
Dve klavírní skladby; [by] Pavel
Borkovec. © Hudební Matice
Umelecke Besedy, Praha, Czecho-
slovakia; 6Oct44; EF4953. For
piano.
Krysar; baletní pantomime o dvou
obrazech na vlastní scénár podle
staroceské legendy. Der Ratten-
fänger ... [By] Pavel Borkovec.
Klavírní výtah. © Hudební
Matice Umelecke Besedy, Praha,
Czechoslovakie; 8Sep42; EF5007.
(Sonatina, violin & piano) Sonatina
[by] Pavel Borkovec. © Hudební
Matice Umelecké Besedy, Praha,
Czechoslovakia; 13Sep44; EF4954.
Score (violin and piano) and
part.

BORNE, HAL, 1911-
The brown Danube. See his
Carnegie Hall.

BORNSCHEIN, FRANZ.
Corn-tassel dance; for piano,
[by] Franz Bornschein. ©
McKinley Publishers, inc.,
Chicago; 28Feb47; EP12409.
Miniver Cheevy ... [words by]
Edwin Arlington Robinson, [music
by] Franz Bornschein. © R. D.
Row Music Co., Boston; 31Mar47;
EP13326. Score: (TTBB)
and piano.
Smoky Hollow tune; for piano,
by Franz Bornschein. ©
McKinley Publishers, inc.,
Chicago; 31Dec46; EP12190.

BORODIN, ALEKSANDR PORFIR'EVICH,
1833-1887.
Serenade; English lyric by Wladimir
Lakond, music by A. Borodin.
© Edward B. Marks Music Corp.,
New York; on English lyric;
18Dec46; EF12030. Score: TTBB
and piano.

BOROWSKI, FELIX.
Valsette; [by] Felix Borowski,
arr. by Galla-Rini. © Chart
Music Publishing House, inc.,
Chicago; on arrangement;
9May47; EP14561. For accordion solo.

BORTNIANSKY, DIMITRI STEPANOVITCH.
Arise, Lord ... tr. from the
Russian and adapted by Hugh Ross.
(In Ross, Hugh, arr. Sacred
choruses for women's or girls'
voices. p. 1-8) © G. Schirmer,
inc., New York; on arrangement,
translation & adaptation;
30Sep46; EP9777.
O, blessed is he; S.A.T.B., by
Bortniansky-Tkach, text from
Psalm 32 [adapted by] Hazel
Stageberg Tkach. © Neil A.
Kjos Music Co., Chicago; on
arrangement & adaptation of
words; 19Jun47; EP15189.

BORTOLI, FRANK, 1911-
Bortoli's Accordion method. ©
Frank Bortoli, Chicago; bk.2,
11Apr47; bk.3, 12Jul47;
EP15849-15850.

BOSCOVICH, ALEXANDER URIJAH, 1908-
Piano pieces for the youth; [by]
Boscovich. © Majer Joseph
Naidat, Tel-Aviv, Palestine;
11Sep45; EF5414.

BOSMANS, ARTHUR, 1908-
Two folk-songs from the planet
Mars ... for voice and piano
[by] Arthur Bosmans. Arbitrary
syllables as text. © Associated Music Publishers, inc.,
New York; 23Dec46; EF12303.

[BOSMANS, ROBERT] 1914-
Sentimental me; words by Ray
Martin, music by Robert Swing
[pseud. c1945] © Robert Bos-
mans d. b. a. Editions Ch.
Bens, Brussels; 1Feb46;
EF5356.
Vous et moi ... Musique de Robert
Bosmans, paroles de Raymond
Lefèbvre. © Robert Bosmans
d. b. a. Editions Ch. Bens,
Brussels; 5May41; EF5355.

BOSSI, M ENRICO.
Idylle; by M. Enrico Bossi, arr. by
Robert Leech Bedell ... [for]
organ solo. © Mills Music, inc.,
New York; on arrangement; 23May47;
EP6938.

BOSSI, RENZO, 1883-
Ricreazioni; [by] Renzo Bossi.
© Carisch, s.a., Milan; on ar-
rangement in ser. 4, 15Dec46;
EF5491. Score: string orchestra.

BOSTWICK, FRANCES JOHNSON.
I am satisfied with Jesus; [words by
F.J.B. and Mary Looney] and Go
gather in the grain; [words by
F. J. B. Music] by Frances John-
son Bostwick. © Frances Johnson
Bostwick, Venice, Calif.; 15Nov46;
EP6613, 6614. Close score:
SATB.
Praise ye the Lord ... [words
adapted from psalm 149 and
music] by Frances Johnson Bost-
wick. © Frances Johnson Bostwick,
Venice, Calif.; 1May47; EP6913.

BOTSFORD, TALITHA.
Carnival capers; for the piano, by
Talitha Botsford. © G. Schirmer,
inc., New York; 30Dec46; EP11598.

BOTTERO, SCHREIER-   See
Schreier-Bottero.

BOUGHTON, RUTLAND, arr.
The holly and the ivy; for three-
part chorus of women's voices
with pianoforte acc.; arr. by
Rutland Boughton, adapted by
Carl Deis. London, J. Curwen &
Sons. © Rutland Boughton, Newent,
England; on adaptation; 24Jan47;
EF5510.

BOUILLON, JO, 1905-
Mon triste coeur; paroles de
Lull Micaelli, musique de
Jo Bouillon et Pierre
Guillemin. © Éditions E.
M. U. L., Paris; 21Mar47;
EF3617.
Valse éternelle; paroles de Roland
Gerbeau et Georges Bérard,
musique de Jo Bouillon et André
Lodge [pseud.] © Éditions
Musicales Nuances, Paris;
15Feb47; EF3483.

BOURDON, ÉMILE.
Marche solennelle; pour grand
orgue, [by] Émile Bourdon. ©
S. Borrmann, Paris; 20Mar47;
EF3640.

BOURGEOIS, HÉLÈNE, 1911-
Sept complaintes pour les coeurs
serrés; [words by] Hélène
Bourgeois, [music by Hélène
Bourgeois & A. Ghirardini],
dessinateur Raphaël Ledoux.
© Éditions Ouvrières, Paris;
12Nov46; EF5182.

BOURGEOIS, LOUIS.
I greet Thee, my Redeemer ...
Melody by Louis Bourgeois
... harmonized by Claude
Goudimel ... arranged by
Clarence Dickinson. [Words
by] John Calvin. © The
H. W. Gray Co., inc., New
York; on arrangement;
14Mar47; EP12848. Score:
bass or alto, chorus (SATB)
and organ.

[BOWLBY, GEORGE WILLIAM] 1918-
comp.
Songs for the hour; fourteen
sacred compositions with words
and music [by R. Chester
Barger, Perry Everett Iverson,
and others. Comp. by George
William Bowlby] © Bowlby
Music Service, Geo. W. Bowlby,
owner, Coquille, Or.; folio
no.1, 12Aug46; EP13322.

BOWLES, PAUL.
Blue Mountain ballads; words by Tennes-
see Williams, music by Paul Bowles.
© G. Schirmer, inc., New York; on 4
songs; 30Dec46. Contents.- [v.1]
Heavenly grass (© EP11597)- [v.2]
Lonesome man (© EP11595)- [v.3] Cabin
(© EP11752)- [v.4] Sugar in the cane
(© EP11596)

Carretera de Estepona. (Highway
to Estepona); piano solo [by]
Paul Bowles. New York, Marks
Ed. © Edward B. Marks Music
Corp., New York; 30Apr47;
EP14135.
Letter to Freddy; for voice and
piano, words by Gertrude Stein,
music by Paul Bowles. © G.
Schirmer, inc., New York; on edit-
ing; 24Mar47; EP13133.
Once a lady was here; for voice
and piano, by Paul Bowles. ©
G. Schirmer, inc., New York;
16Nov46; EP12882.
Sonatina; for piano solo [by]
Paul Bowles. © Elkan-Vogel
Co., inc., Philadelphia;
11Mar47; EP13923.

BOWMAN, CARL B.
Noël pastoral; SATB accompanied,
words and music by Carl B.
Bowman. © Harold Flammer, inc.,
New York; 4Nov46; EP10828.

BOWMAN, WILLIAM L.
Dare to let you know; by William
L. Bowman. © Cine-Mart Music
Publishing Co., Hollywood,
Calif.; 1Nov46; EP11489. For
voice and piano, with chord
symbols.

BOWN, PEARL BOYCE.
The cronies and Pickaninny in the
dark; by Pearl Boyce Bown ...
Fingering, phrasing, and in-
structive annotations [by
Lillie-Mayes Dodd] (Art
Publication Society. Pro-
gressive series compositions,
catalog no. 290) © Art
Publication Society, Clayton,
Mo.; 22Nov46; EP11743.

BOYKIN, HELEN.
Ecstasy; piano solo, by Helen
Boykin. © Schroeder & Gunther,
inc., Rhinebeck, N. Y.;
25Apr47; EP6840.
Seafoam; piano solo, by Helen
Boykin. © Schroeder & Gunther,
inc., Rhinebeck, N. Y.; 16Jun47;
EP6984.

BOYT, EARL.
The veteran's friend; song
folio by Earl Boyt. © M. M.
Cole Publishing Co., Chicago;
folio no.1, 20Feb47; EP12233.

BOZZA, EUGÈNE, 1905-
Suite brève en trio; [by] Eugène
Bozza. [Op. 67] © Alphonse
Leduc et Cie., Paris; 11Feb47;
EF3445. Miniature score: oboe,
clarinet and bassoon.

BRACE, BLANCHE.
Loveliest night; two part (S. A.)
Christmas song ... [words by]
John Rudd, [music by] Blanche
Brace. © Blanche Brace,
Weston, Ont., Can.; 27Nov46;
EF4734.
O love divine; a wedding song.
Words by Eleanor Anderson,
music by Blanche Brace. Weston,
Ont., [Distributors, Draper
Music Co. © Blanche Brace,
Weston, Ont., Can.; 27Nov46;
EF4735.

BRADBURY, WILLIAM B
Even me, even me; by Mrs. Elizabeth Codner and Wm. B. Bradbury, special arrangement for
solo, quartette or choir by
Kenneth Morris. Chicago, Martin and Morris Music Studio.
© Kenneth Morris, Chicago; on
arrangement; 13Dec46; EP12465.

BRADFORD, MARVEL, 1908-
Take Thou my hand; [words by]
Marvel Bradford, [music by]
M. B. and Bernice Dodson, arr.
by W. M. Thorne. (In Church
of the Nazarene. Michigan
District. Nazarene Young
Peoples Society. Choruses of
the N. Y. P. S. p.4) ©
Michigan District, Nazarene
Young Peoples Society, Flint,
Mich.; 25Jul46; EP13030.
Close score: SATB.

BRADLEY, DOROTHY.
Sight-reading made easy; a complete
graded course for the pianoforte
[by] Dorothy Bradley & J. Raymond Tobin. © Joseph Williams,
ltd., London; on 3 vols.;
16Jul47. Contents.- bk. 1.
Primary (© EF5695) - bk. 2.
Elementary (© EF5842) - bk. 3.
Transitional (© EF5841)

BRADLEY, DOROTHY, arr.
Tuneful graded studies; arr. by
Dorothy Bradley. [c1945]
© Bosworth & Co., ltd., London;
on addition of fingering, phras-
ing, interpretive notes, metro-
nome rates, etc. to v.3; 7Aug46.
For piano solo. Contents.- 3.
Transitional & lower (© EF3176)

BRAGDON, SARAH COLEMAN.
Forest chimes; piano solo by
Sarah Coleman Bragdon. ©
The Willis Music Co., Cin-
cinnati; 14Mar47; EP13005.
Spring is coming; [by] Sarah Coleman
Bragdon. © Clayton F. Summy Co.,
Chicago; 10Feb47; EP12057. For
piano solo, with words.
Two playtime pieces; for piano
solo, by Sarah Coleman Brag-
don. © The Willis Music
Co., Cincinnati; 14Mar47;
EP13007, 13006. Contents.-
[v.1. At the seashore.-
[v.2. The paper chase.

BRAGERS, ACHILLE P
Missa in honorem Reginae Pacis; by
Achille P. Bragers. © McLaughlin
& Reilly Co., Boston; on arrange-
ment; 24May47; EP15010. Score:
chorus (SATB) and organ.

BRAHAM, PHILIP.
(Charlot's revue) Limehouse
blues, from "Charlot's revue"
... words by Douglas Furber,
music by Philip Braham, a
Johnny Sterling arrangement.
© Harms, inc., New York; on ar-
rangement; 5May47; EP13407.
Piano-conductor score (orches-
tra, with words) and parts.
Limehouse blues; [by] Philip Braham,
arr. by Johnny Sterling. ©
Harms, inc., New York; on arrange-
ment; 9Apr47; EP13751. Score
(Eb alto saxophone and piano)
and part.
Limehouse blues; [by] Philip
Braham, arr. by Johnny Sterling.
© Harms, inc., New York; on
arrangement; 11Apr47; EP13752.
Score (Bb trumpet (or cornet)
and piano) and part.
Limehouse blues. See also his
Charlot's revue.

BRAHMS, JOHANNES, 1833-1897.
Ave Maria; (S.S.A.A. with piano or
organ acc.) [by] Johannes Brahms.
Op. 12. Ed. by Ifor Jones. ©
Carl Fischer, inc., New York;
on reduction from orchestral
score; 17Feb47; EP12713. Latin
words.
Brahms at the piano; ed. by Felix
Guenther. © Heritage Music
Publications, inc., New York; on
arrangement & compilation; 24Mar47;
EP12772.

15

BRAHMS, JOHANNES. Cont'd.
Brahms' Lullaby (Cradle song);
piano accordion solo, arr.
by Lloyd Marvin. © Chart
Music Publishing House, inc.,
Chicago; on arrangement;
17Mar47; EP13166.
Four serious songs. (Vier ernste
gesänge) ... [by] Johannes
Brahms. Op.121. Arr. for
men's voices by N. Lindsay
Norden. © Broadcast Music,
inc., New York; on 4 songs;
8Feb47. English words. Contents.- [v.] 1. As with beasts.
(Denn es gehet dem menschen)
(© EP12696)- [v.] 2. So I returned. (Ich wandte mich und
sahe an) (© EP12691)- [v.] 3.
O death. (O tod, wie bitter
bist du.) (© EP12694)- [v.] 4.
Though I speak with the tongues
of men. (Wenn ich mit menschen-
und mit engelszungen) (© EP12690)
Lullaby; words by Karl Simrock,
music by Johannes Brahms.
[Easy piano arrangement with
keyboard charts by Victor
Lakes Martin] © Songs You
Remember Publishing Co. (V. L.
Martin, proprietor), Atlanta;
on arrangement and playing instructions; 20Dec46; EP11531.
Requiem; for soprano and baritone
soli, chorus and orchestra,
composed by Johannes Brahms.
Op. 45. Ed. by John E. West,
the English version adapted
from the Holy Scriptures by
Ivor Atkins. © Novello & Co.,
ltd., London; on English words;
21Apr47; EP5564. Piano-vocal
score.
(Sonata, clarinet & piano, no.1)
Slow movement; from Clarinet
and pianoforte sonata [Op. 120,
no.1] by Brahms, arr. for the
organ by John Forster.
© Stainer & Bell, ltd., London;
on arrangement; 12May47;
EP3341.
Song of destiny; by Johannes
Brahms, special organ part ...
with added harp part (ad lib.)
... made from woodwind and brass
parts for use with strings and
timpani, by N. Lindsay Norden.
© J. Fischer & bro., New York;
on organ & harp pts.; 17Apr47;
EP6907.
Souvenirs from the great masters,
Brahms; selected & arr. by
G. H. Clutsam, © Keith Prowse
& Co., ltd., London; on
arrangement; 30Dec46; EP4793.
For piano solo.
(Symphony, no. 3) Allegretto;
[from] Symphony no. 5. Op. 90.
By Johannes Brahms, for piano
solo. Arr. and ed. by Robert
Marden. © Edward Schuberth &
Co., inc., New York; 3Mar47;
EP12278.
(Symphony, no. 3, F major)
Brahms' Third symphony, 3rd
movement; [arr. by D. Savino]
© Hamilton S. Gordon, inc.,
New York; on arrangement;
14Apr47; EP13736. For piano
solo.
(Symphony, no. 3) Theme from
Brahms' third symphony
(third movement); for piano
solo, simplified, [by Chester
Wallis, pseud.] © The Boston
Music Co., Boston; on arrange-
ment; 28Feb47; EP12379.

BRANDT, ALAN.
Give me twenty nickels for a dol-
lar; words and music by Don Wolf
and Alan Brandt. © King Cole
Music, inc., New York; 7May47;
EP14163.

BRASLAVSKY, S   G   arr.
Hebrew chants; arr. for four part
mixed voices and organ [ad lib.]
by S. G. Braslavsky. © McLaughlin & Reilly Co., Boston; on
arrangement; 17Mar47; EP14879.
Transliterated Hebrew words.
Traditional Hebrew chants; arr.
for four part mixed voices and
organ by S. G. Braslavsky.
© McLaughlin & Reilly Co.,
Boston; on arrangement; 17Mar47;
EP14945. Words in Hebrew (transliterated)

BRATTEN, IRL F
Nocturne ... For violin and
piano, by Irl F. Bratten.
© Irl F. Bratten, Canton,
Ohio; 2May47; EP14155.

BRAZIER, ETHEL LEE, 1921-
Worthy is the Lamb who died to
set us free; words by Mariah
King, music and arrangement
by Ethel L. Brazier. Chicago,
Martin and Morris Music Studio.
© Mariah King, Cleveland;
2Jan47; EP13998. For alto,
bass and chorus (SATB)

BREAN, DENIS.
The bumble boogie samba. (Boogie-
woogie na Favela) Lyrics by
Mack David and Hal David, music
and Portuguese lyrics by Denis
Brean. © Remick Music Corp.,
New York; 23Apr47; EP13946.

BRECKER, DICK.
After a while; words and music
by Dick Brecker. © Peer
International Corp., New York;
27May47; EP14941.

BRENES CANDANEDO, GONZALO, 1907-
Arrullos de hamaca; (del libro:
"Tonadas del trópico niño");
música de Gonzalo Brenes.
Mexico, Editorial de Mexico.
© Gonzalo Brenes Candanedo,
San José, Costa Rica; 9Apr46;
EP5290. For voice and piano.
Rondás de niños; (Del libro:
"Tonadas del trópico niño");
música de Gonzalo Brenes,
letra de Gabriela Mistral.
Mexico, Editorial de Mexico.
© Gonzalo Brenes Candanedo,
San José, Costa Rica; 9Apr46;
EP5289.

BRENNAN, JAMES A
In the little red school house;
for four-part mixed voices ...
By Al Wilson [and] James A.
Brennan, arr. by Felix Guenther.
© Edward B. Marks Music Corp.,
New York; on arrangement;
23Apr47; EP13859.
Let's take it easy; words by
Pia Maurer, music by James
A. Brennan. © Nordyke
Publishing Co., Los Angeles;
8Mar47; EP13290.
Won't you come back to me;
words by Robert C. Molusky,
music by James A. Brennan.
© Nordyke Publishing Co.,
Los Angeles; 5Mar47; EP13285.

BRENNAN, JOHN R
I held a candle; a song for Christmas,
words & music by John R. Brennan.
© Allan & Co., pty. ltd., Mel-
bourne, Australia; 20Nov46;
EP3116.

BRENSON, DOC, pseud. See
Berendsohn, Bernhard.

BRENT, ROYAL.
Get up those stairs, mademoiselle;
by Clifford Jackson [and] Royal
Brent. © Duchess Music Corp.,
New York; 2Jun47; EP14972. For
voice and piano, with chord
symbols.

BREWER, JEWELL.
I'm in love with you; words and
music by Jewell Brewer. ©
Nordyke Publishing Co., Los
Angeles; 31Oct45; EP6451.

BREYDERT, F   M
Estote fortes. Be strong and
faithful; for four-part
chorus of mixed voices, a
cappella, [by] F. M. Breydert. © G. Schirmer, inc.,
New York; 24Mar47; EP13130.
Estote fortes. Be strong and
faithful; for three-part
chorus of women's voices,
a cappella, [by] F. M.
Breydert. © G. Schirmer,
inc., New York; 24Mar47;
EP13129.
Sanctus. For four-part chorus
of mixed voices, a cappella,
[by] F. M. Breydert, inc., New York;
24Mar47; EP13132. Latin and
English words.
Sanctus. For three-part chorus
of women's voices, with organ
acc., ad lib., [by] F. M.
Breydert. © G. Schirmer,
inc., New York; 24Mar47;
EP13131. Latin and English
words.
Vox in Rama. Lamentation for a
day of mourning; for four-
part chorus of mixed voices,
a cappella, [by] F. M.
Breydert. © G. Schirmer,
inc., New York; 24Mar47;
EP13127.
Vox in Rama. Lamentation for a day
of mourning; for three-part
chorus of women's voices, a cappella, [by] F. M. Breydert. © G.
Schirmer, inc., New York; 24Mar47;
EP13128.

BRIGADA, ANGELO.
Baby ... [by] Angelo Brigada.
© Edizioni Casiroli, s.a.r.l.,
Milano; 15Jun46; EP5792.
Piano-conductor score
(orchestra, with words), and
parts.

BRIGGS, EVERETT F   1908-
Anima Christi; translation and
music by Rev. E. F. Briggs.
© Everett F. Briggs, Clarks
Summit, Pa.; 8Jun47; EP14960.
Close score: SATB.

BRIGGS, FERD.
I fell for you; words by Edith M.
Briggs, music by Ferd Briggs,
jr. © Nordyke Publishing Co.,
Los Angeles; 5Mar47; EP13233.

BRIGGS, JOHN W., pseud. See
Ruckstuhl, Johnnie.

BRIGHT, ADA.
Waltz of the ladybugs; for the
piano, by Ada Bright. ©
G. Schirmer, inc., New
York; 16Nov46; EP12881.

BRISEÑO, SEVERIANO.
Los maizales ... Letra y música de
Severiano Briseño. © Promotora
Hispano Americana de Música, s.
a., Mexico; 30Dec46; EP5284.

BRITAIN, RADIE.
Heroic poem; [by] Radie Britain.
© American Music Center, inc.,
New York; 8Oct46; EP13102.
Score: orchestra.

BRITTEN, BENJAMIN, 1913-   arr.
Folk-song arrangements; [by]
Benjamin Britten. © Boosey &
Hawkes, ltd., London; on ar-
rangement & English text for
v.2, 31Dec46. Contents.- 2.
Franco; English translations
by Iris Rogers. (© EP4772)

16

BRITTEN, BENJAMIN. Cont'd.
The young person's guide to the
orchestra; variations and
fugue on a theme of Purcell,
[by] Benjamin Britten. Op.
34. Full score. [Commentary
by Eric Crozier] © Hawkes &
Son (London), ltd., London;
on arrangement, added original
music & commentary; 11Jun47;
EF3850.

The young person's guide to the
orchestra; (Variations and
fugue on a theme of Purcell);
[by] Benjamin Britten. Op. 34.
[London, Boosey & Hawkes] ©
Hawkes & Son (London) Ltd.,
London; on arrangement & added
original music; 11Jun47. Parts: orchestra.

BRIX, AAGE E
My heaven is where I find you ...
words and music by Aage E. Brix,
[arr. by Lou Halmy] © Cine-
Mart Music Publishing Co.,
Hollywood, Calif.; 12Apr47;
EP14146.

BROBST, HAROLD.
Blue as the night; by Harold
Brobst. Oakland, Calif.,
Golden Gate Publications. ©
Ray Meany, Golden Gate Publica-
tions, Oakland, Calif.; 1Apr47;
EP14141. For voice and 2
guitars; also diagrams and
chord symbols for ukelele.

Boogie beat Pete; words and music
by Harold Brobst. Oakland,
Calif., Golden Gate Publications. © Ray Meany, Golden Gate Publications, Oakland, Calif.; 22Apr47;
EP14119. For voice and 2
guitars; also diagrams and chord
symbols for ukelele.

BROCKMAN, JAMES. See also
Konbrovin, Jaan, pseud.

BROCKT, JOHANNES, 1901-
Piccoli pezzi kontrapuntistici.
Kleine kontrapunktische Stücke
... [by] Johannes Brockt. Op.
37. © Ludwig Doblingor (Bernhard Herzmansky), K. G., Vienna;
19Apr46; EF3401. For piano 4
hands.

BRODERSEN, MARTIN.
My bungalow dream girl; words
and music by Martin Brodersen.
© Nordyke Publishing Co., Los
Angeles; 21Feb47; EP12722.

BRODSKY, NICHOLAS, 1905-
(While the sun shines) While the
sun shines; words by Ian Grant,
music by Nicholas Brodsky;
from the film ... "While the
sun shines". © New World
Publishers, ltd., London;
31Jan47; EP5167.

BRODSKY, ROY.
Bagel and lox ... words and music
by Sid Topper and Roy Brodsky,
arr. by Will Hudson. © American
Academy of Music, inc.; on arrangement; 12Dec46; EP6632. Piano-
conductor score (orchestra, with
words) and parts.

Oshkosh, Wis.; words and music by
Sid Topper and Roy Brodsky. ©
Mills Music, inc., New York;
17Feb47; EP6604.

[BROECK, LEO VAN DEN] 1896-
My heart is yours. (Mon coeur
attend) Song, lyrics: Theo Al-
bert [pseud.], music: Léo
Panta [pseud.] © Prop, Gustave-
Marie-Louis-Norbert, sole
owner of Édition Metropolis,
Antwerp; 12May45; EF5570.

BROEKMAN, DAVID.
A la tzigane ... [By] David
Broekman ... For piano.
© Bregman, Vocco and Conn,
inc., New York; 18Apr47;
EP13875.

The beautiful blue Hudson ... for
piano [by] David Broekman.
© Bregman, Vocco & Conn, inc.,
New York; 20Jan47; EP11369.

The chant of the Amazon ... for
piano, [by] David Brockman. ©
Bregman, Vocco & Conn, inc., New
York; 17Jan47; EP11510.

Dialogue for lovers ... for piano,
[by] David Broekman. © Bregman,
Vocco & Conn, inc., New York;
17Jan47; EP11311.

Etude for violins and love; [by
David Broekman] © Bregman,
Vocco & Conn, inc., New York;
on arrangement; 20Jan47;
EP12761. Piano-conductor
score (orchestra) and parts.

Etude for violins and love ... for
piano [by] David Broekman.
© Bregman, Vocco & Conn, inc.,
New York; 20Jan47; EP11370.

(If your love goes away) the birds
will sing no more; lyrical setting
by Florence Tarr, music by David
Broekman. © Bregman, Vocco and
Conn, inc., New York; 20Jan47;
EP11849.

Intermezzo for a day in May; (on
a recurring theme) for piano,
[by] David Broekman. © Bregman,
Vocco & Conn, inc., New York;
17Jan47; EP11309.

Samba of the orchids ... for piano
[by] David Broekman. © Bregman,
Vocco & Conn, inc., New York;
20Jan47; EP11568.

BROENNEMULLER, ELIAS, c. 1700-
Sonata (in F major) ... [By]
Elias Broennemuller ... ed. ...
[and] acc. [arr.] by Erich Katz.
© E. C. Schirmer Music Co.,
Boston; on realization of figured
bass; 4Apr47; EP13574. Score
(alto recorder or flute, and
harpsichord or piano and viola
da gamba or violoncello, ad lib.)
and part.

BROMLEY, TED, pseud. See
Foldes, Andor.

BROOK, HARRY, 1893-
Fairy news; unison song, words by
John Smith ... music by Harry
Brook. © J. Curwen & Sons, ltd.,
London; 9Dec46; EF4763.

The orchard; two-part song for
equal voices with pianoforte
acc., words by Irene Gass,
music by Harry Brook. © J.
Curwen & Sons, ltd., London;
20Mar47; EF5464.

BROOKS, GEORGE CLARENCE, 1893-
I'm saving my kisses for you ...
words and music by George C.
Brooks. © Samuel Marko [and]
George Clarence Brooks, Phila-
delphia; 1May47; EP15069.

BROOKS, HARRY.
Ain't misbehavin'; by Andy
Razaf, Thomas Waller and Harry
Brooks ... arr. by "Zep"
Meissner. © Mills Music, inc.,
New York; on arrangement;
21Apr47; EP6846. Piano-con-
ductor score (orchestra) and
parts.

BROOKS, HARVEY O
Why is the sky so blue? Lyric
by Johnny Lake, music by Harvey O. Brooks ... and Opie
Cates. © Chi-Chi Music Publications, Encino, Calif.;
8Apr47; EP13727.

BROSE, EUGENE OLIN, 1897-
March chromatic; [by] E. O. Brose.
© Eugene O. Broso, Burlingame,
Calif.; 20May47; EP6919. Condensed
score (band) and parts.

Vagabond ... [by] E. O. Brose.
© Eugene O. Broso, Burlingame,
Calif.; 20Jun47; EP15292.
Condensed score (band) and
parts.

BROUGHTON, HAYDN.
The now moon is changing to gold;
[and Two bits in my pocket] words
and music by Haydn Broughton.
© Peer Inter-
national Corp., New York; 13Feb47;
EP12224, 12225.

BROUGHTON, WILLIAM FREDRICK,
1884-
[Supplement to Beginner's band
book, no. 2 & 3; by]
Broughton. © The Salvation
Army, San Francisco; 12Feb47;
EP14088. Part: cornet. Con-
tents.- The young soldier.-
The Lord's prayer, [by] L.
Slauson.- Encouragement.-
Joyful.

BROWN, ADRIA. See
Puscheck, Adria Brown.

BROWN, ALLANSON G Y arr.
Songs for worship; anthems and
other concerted music arr. for
medium voice. © Carl Fischer,
inc., New York; on arrangement;
23Jul46; EP14757.

BROWN, BILLIE.
Lullaby moon; (S.A.T.B.) text by
Anna Wolker Brown, music by Billie
Brown. © Leeds Music Corp., New
York; on arrangement; 24Jan47;
EP11811.

BROWN, G. A., pseud. See
Harden, John.

BROWN, JOHN W
I am digging at the end of the
rainbow; words, music by John W.
Brown, music by John W. Brown
and Louise Voyzey. © Nordyke
Publishing Co., Los Angeles;
13Jul46; EP13539.

BROWN, KEITH CROSBY.
The Lord is my Shepherd; sacred
song, music by Keith Crosby
Brown, words from the Bible,
twenty-third Psalm. © R. D.
Row Music Co., Boston; 8Mar47;
EP14813.

BROWN, LEON F
Hallelujah, Christ arose; Easter
anthem, SATB accompanied, words
and music by Leon F. Brown.
© Harold Flammer, inc., New York;
14Mar47; EP13469.

Holy Spirit, Truth Divine; for
four-part chorus of mixed voices
with piano or organ acc. [Words
by] S. Longfellow, music by Leon
F. Brown. © The Boston Music
Co., Boston; 22May47; EP14757.

BROWN, LEWIS.
Flitting butterflies; a piano
solo by Lewis Brown. ©
Theodore Presser Co.,
Philadelphia; 26May47;
EP14701.

BROWN, WILMER NILE, 1914-
Forward together with Christ;
words and music by Wilmer N.
Brown. © Wilmer Nilo Brown,
Salem, Or.; 1Apr47; EP14087.

BROWNE, LELAND B
Darling I love you; words by
Charlotte Roberts Wedin, music
by Lee B. Browne. © Cine-Mart
Music Publishing Co., Hollywood,
Calif.; 31Mar47; EP14656.

17

BROWNE, LELAND B. Cont'd.
If it's love you'll know it; words
by Charlotte R. Wedin, music by
Lee B. Browne. © Cine-Mart
Music Publishing Co., Hollywood,
Calif.; 1Nov46; EP11936.

[BROZA, ELLIOT LAWRENCE] 1925-
Baby boogie. (Dy-dee, dy-dee,
dy-dee) Lyric by Bickley
Reichner, music by Elliot
Lawrence [pseud.] New York,
Sole selling agent, Chas. H.
Hansen Music Co. © Elliot
Music Co., inc., Philadelphia;
9Jun47; EP14948.

BRUCE, ROBERT, 1905-
Bring the money in; [words by]
Buddy Feyne, [music by] Robert
Bruce [and] Milton Larkin.
© Popular Music Co., New York;
13Jun47; EP15039. For voice
and piano, with chord symbols.

BRUCKNER, ANTON.
Tota pulchra es Maria; for four-
part chorus of women's voices
with piano or organ acc. [by]
Anton Bruckner. English text
by C.A.O., arr. by C. A.
Garbedian. © G. Schirmer,
inc., New York; on arrangement; 30Dec46; EP11630.

BRUINSMA, HENRY ALLEN, 1916-
A Netherlands roundelay; for mixed
chorus, based on a Dutch rondedans
by J. J. Viotta ... Concert version
by Henry A. Bruinsma. © Wm. B.
Eerdmans Publishing Co., Grand
Rapids; 6Feb47; EP12097.

Psalm 25; based on Psalm 25 of the
Dutch Psalter, concert version
by Henry A. Bruinsma [for] so-
prano solo and S. A. T. B.
© Wm. B. Eerdmans Publishing
Co., Grand Rapids; 15Jan47;
EP11308.

Thy name is great (Psalm 8) ...
S.A.T.B., by Henry A. Bruinsma.
[text adapted by Grace H.
Bruinsma] © Wm. B. Eerdmans
Publishing Co., Grand Rapids;
17Nov46; EP11389.

BRUINSMA, HENRY ALLEN, ed.
Sacred songs for home and choir;
comp. and ed. by Henry A. Bruinsma.
© Wm. B. Eerdmans Publishing Co.,
Grand Rapids, Mich.; 28Jan47;
EP11791.

BRUNE, ALVINA.
From khaki to civics; words and
music by Alvina Brune. ©
Cine-mart Music Publishing Co.,
Hollywood, Calif.; 1Aug46;
EP10964. For voice and piano,
with chord symbols.

BRUNELLE, GENE, 1896-
Secret dreams; lyrics by Ginny
Johnson, music by Gene Brunelle,
arr. by Lindsay McPhail. ©
Scheuerle Bros. Music Publishers,
Mason, Pa.; 12Mar47; EP13446.

BRUNI, MARIO.
A letter from Stresa; words by
Wes Ross, music by Mario Bruni.
© Edizioni Leonardi, Milan;
1Jul43; EF4816. For voice and
piano.

BRUNO, DÉSIRÉ, 1909-
Simple rengaine; paroles de Chapus,
musique de Bruno. © Édition
Selection, Gentilly, France;
1Mar47; EF3513.

BRUNS, GEORGE.
Rainbow River; by George Bruns
... for piano. © Bregman,
Vocco and Conn, inc., New
York; 6Mar47; EP12437.

BRYAN, CHARLES F
The bell witch; secular folk
cantata for mixed chorus with
solos for altos and baritone,
by Charles F. Bryan. © J.
Fischer & Bro., New York;
27Mar47; EP6812.

BRYAN, CHARLES PAULKNER, arr.
American folk music; for high
school and other choral
groups, collected and [text]
ed. by George Pullen Jackson. [music] arr. by Charles
Faulkner Bryan. © C. C.
Birchard & Co., Boston; on
adaptation & arrangement;
18Mar47; EP13020. For 1-4
voices and piano.

BRYANS, ELLA.
Messenger star; by Odell Johnson
and Ella Bryans, North Hollywood, Calif., Huesco Music. ©
Odell Johnson, Bakersfield,
Calif.; 17Jan47; EP11523. For
voice and piano, with chord
symbols.

BRYANT, HOYT.
Eeny meeny Dixie deeny; (The hide
and go seek song); words and
music by Hoyt "Slim" Bryant.
© Peer International Corp.,
New York; 29Oct46; EP13624.

BRYANT, SLIM. See
Bryant, Hoyt.

BRYDSON, JOHN CALLIS, 1900- arr.
Two seventeenth century clavier
arias; [by Kuhnau and Telemann],
arr. for organ by John Brydson.
© Enoch & Sons (Proprietors,
Edwin Ashdown, ltd.), London;
on arrangement; 18Apr47;
EF5478.

BUCHANAN, MABEL.
All this to me; song, words
by Gerald Massey, music by
Mabel Buchanan. © Keith,
Prowse & Co., ltd., London;
14Feb47; EF5169.

BUCINO, MIGUEL.
Vine a verte ... letra y música
de Miguel Bucino. © Editorial
Argentina de Música Internacional, s. de r. ltd., Buenos
Aires; 24Jan47; EF3211. Piano-
conductor score (orchestra),
and parts.

BUCK, CARLTON C 1907-
Long ago; trio for ladies' voices
by Carlton C. Buck. © Carlton
C. Buck, Fullerton, Calif.;
25Apr47; EP14533.

Sing-a-while leaflet ... [by]
Carlton C. Buck. © Carlton
C. Buck, Fullerton, Calif.;
no.6, 31Dec46; EP6418.
Hymns, with music.

BUCK, DUDLEY.
Sing alleluia forth; for ...
S.S.A. (incidental soli: sop.I,
sop.II, alto) opt. [By] Dudley
Buck. Op.65,no.1. Arr. by Don
Ronaldson [pseud.] © Pro Art
Publications, New York; on ar-
rangement; 21Apr47; EP13605.

BUCK, RONALD, 1907-
That fascinating smile; words by
Cora Napier, music by Ronald
Buck. © Nordyke Publishing Co.,
Los Angeles; 8Mar47; EP13529.

BUCK, WOODROE, 1917-
Songs from the heart; words and
music by Woodroe Buck, [arr.
by Edward E. Menges] © Woodroe
Buck, St. Louis; 23Dec46;
EP11198.

BUGBEE, L A
Waltz of the willows; [by] L. A.
Bugbee [arr. by Rob Roy Peery]
© Theodore Presser Co., Phila-
delphia; on arrangement;
29Apr47; EP14467.

BUGBEE, MADGE, 1904-
He is with me; [by] Madge Bug-
bee, arr. by W. M. Thorne.
(In Church of the Nazarene.
Michigan District. Nazarene
Young Peoples Society.
Choruses of the N. Y. P. S.
p.14) © Michigan District,
Nazarene Young Peoples Society,
Flint, Mich.; 25Jul46; EP13040.
Close score: SATB.

Lord, let me shine! [By] Madge
Bugbee, arr. by W. M. Thorne.
(In Church of the Nazarene.
Michigan District. Nazarene
Young Peoples Society.
Choruses of the N. Y. P. S.
p.7) © Michigan District,
Nazarene Young Peoples Society,
Flint, Mich.; 25Jul46;
EP13033. For voice and piano.

Thou leadest me; [by] Madge
Bugbee, arr. by W. M. T.
(In Church of the Nazarene.
Michigan District. Nazarene
Young Peoples Society.
Choruses of the N. Y. P. S.
p.30) © Michigan District,
Nazarene Young Peoples Society,
Flint, Mich.; 25Jul46; EP13056.
For voice and piano.

BUKETOFF, IGOR.
We praise Thee; for full
chorus of mixed voices, a
cappella, [by] Igor Buke-
toff, tr. from the Russian
by the composer. © G.
Schirmer, inc., New York;
24Mar47; EP13120.

BULL, OLE BORNEMANN, 1810-1880.
Longing. (Saeter Jenten's Söndag)
[By] Ole Bull, arr. by Morten J.
Luvaas, [words by] Jane Lewis
McKnight. © Neil A. Kjos Music
Co., Chicago; on arrangement &
words; 19Jun47; EP15186. Score:
chorus (SAATBB) and piano re-
duction.

BULLER, BUDDY.
I'll say I do; words & music by
Murry Buller, Armon Buller
[and] Buddy Buller. © Puritan
Publishing Co. inc., Chicago;
10Ct46; EP11236.

BULLOCK, ERNEST.
O everlasting God; by Ernest
Bullock. © Novello & Co., ltd.,
London; 16Dec46; EF4791. Score:
chorus (SATB) and piano
reduction.

BULTERMAN, JACK.
Musique pour Mitzi ... [By]
Jack Bulterman. © Robert
Bosmans d. b. a. Editions Ch.
Bens, Brussels; 5Aug43;
EF5353. Piano-conductor score
(orchestra) and parts.

BUNKER, LOUISE.
Alone; [by] Louise Bunker, arr.
by W. M. T. (In Church of the
Nazarene. Michigan District.
Nazarene Young Peoples Society.
Choruses of the N. Y. P. S. p.
32) © Michigan District,
Nazarene Young Peoples Society,
Flint, Mich.; 25Jul46; EP13058.
Close score: SATB.

BUNN, ADELAIDE.
Belles of the Rio Grande; words
& music by Adelaide Bunn. ©
Laredo, Tex., Washington's
Birthday Assn. © Adelaide Bunn,
Laredo, Tex.; 9Apr47; EP13672.

18

BUNNER, G   G
Happy again; words and music by
G. G. Bunner. © Bunner
Publications, Lakewood, Ohio;
26Dec46; EP10718.

Memory of youth; words & music by
G. G. Bunner. © Bunner
Publications, Lakewood, Ohio;
26Dec46; EP10713.

BURGESS, ELMER.
A carol of the annunciation;
anthem for mixed voices ...
[Words by] Wanda J. Milbourne,
[music by] Elmer Burgess. ©
The H. W. Gray Co., inc., New
York; 23May47; EP14761.

BURGMULLER.
Burgmüller-Schaum for piano ...
[comp. and arr. by] John W.
Schaum. © Belwin, inc., New
York; on arrangement and compi-
lation; bk.1, 9May47; EP14464.

BURK, ARTHUR E
Jubilee cantata ... by Arthur E.
Burk. © Arthur E. Burk,
Chicago; 23Dec43; EP6749.
Score: solo voices, mixed
chorus and organ.

BURKE, JOE.
Rambling rose; lyric by Joseph
McCarthy, Jr., music by Joe
Burke. © Robbins Music Corp.,
New York; 7Jan47; EP11167. For
voice and piano, with chord symbols.

BURNAM, EDNA MAE.
Little Miss Muffet; for the piano,
by Edna-Mae Burnam. © Shattinger
Piano & Music Co., St. Louis;
31Dec46; EP11254. With words.

Stopping the hiccoughs; for the
piano [with storiette], by Edna-
Mae Burnam. © Shattinger Piano
& Music Co., St. Louis; 31Dec46;
EP11255.

BURNS, HAL.
Little you cared; by Hal Burns.
© Tex Ritter Music Publications,
inc., New York; 6Mar47; EP12306.
For voice and piano, with chord
symbols.

BURROWS, RAYMOND MURDOCK, 1905-
Young America at the piano ...
[by] Raymond Burrows ... [and]
Ella Mason Ahearn. © C. C.
Birchard & Co., Boston; bk. 2,
17Apr47; EP13939.

BURROWS, REX.
There is no end (to lovely things
like these); song, words by
Bruce Sievier, music by Rex
Burrows. © Chappell & Co., ltd.,
London; 25Apr47; EP3410.

BURT, JUSTIN G
He understands; [by] Justin G.
Burt. © Justin G. Burt,
Dallas; 12May47; EP6898.
Close score: SATB.

BURTON, ELDIN.
Hop-o'-my-thumb; for the piano,
[by] Eldin Burton. © Oliver
Ditson Co., Philadelphia;
12Mar47; EP12843.

BURY, WINIFRED, 1897-
The moon complaining; words by
Paul Heyse, English version by
Lily Henkel, music by Winifred
Bury. © Paterson's Publications,
ltd., London; 1Feb47; EP3306.

BUSH, GRACE, 1900-
I shall be near to you; text and
music by Grace Bush. © Wesley
Webster, San Francisco; 24Dec46;
EP10783.

BUSH, JOHN MELVIN, 1893-
The Beatitudes; by John Melvin
Bush. [n.p.] W. Dudley.
© John M. Bush, Portland,
Or.; 28Dec46; EP11018. Score:
chorus (SATB) and piano or
organ.

BUSHKIN, JOE.
Howdy! Have a coke! Music by Joe
Bushkin, words by Johnny De Vries.
© Harman Music, inc., New York;
6Feb47; EP12153.

BUTLER, MELVIN J
Where's my sweetie? By Melvin J.
Butler. © Cine-Mart Music Publishing Co., Hollywood, Calif.;
1Nov46; EP11719. For voice and
piano, with chord symbols.

BUTLER, THOMAS S
Reno town ... lyrics and music
by Thos. S. Butler, [arr. by
Lou Halmy] © Thos. S. Butler,
Topanga Canyon, Calif.;
19May47; EP14643.

[BUTTERFIELD, J   A   ]
When you and I were young,
Maggie; [words by George W.
Johnson, music by J. A. Butter-
field, arr. by Victor Lakes
Martin] Easy piano arrange-
ment with keyboard charts. ©
Songs You Remember Publishing
Co., (V.L. Martin, prop.),
Atlanta; on arrangement;
5Apr47; EP14744.

BUXTEHUDE, DIETRICH, 1637-1707.
Ciacona in E minor; for organ by
Dietrich Buxtehude, arr. ... by
William H. Harris. © Novello &
Co., ltd., London; on arrange-
ment; 30Apr47; EF5637. Score:
piano 1-2.

Klavervaerker; udgivet af Emilius
Bangert. 2den udgave. 1944.
© Wilhelm Hansen, Musik-Forlag,
Copenhagen; 20Jan42; EF5047.

BUYS, PETER.
All's well that ends well ... by
Peter Buys. © Belwin, inc.,
New York; 24Dec46; EP10700.
Condensed score (band) and parts.

BYERS, FRANK.
To you, sweetheart; words & music by
Frank Byers. © Nordyke Publishing
Co., Los Angeles; 9Aug46; EP12712.

[BYHMAR, GÖSTA]
(Casinorevyn, 1943) Tre gator, ur
Casinorevyn, 1943. Text o musik:
Stig Bergendorff [and] Gösta
Bernhard [pseud.] © Nordiska
Musikförlaget, a.b., Stockholm;
12Jan43; EF3739.

Tre gator. See his Casinorevyn,
1943.

BYLES, BLANCHE DOUGLAS.
Wood of the cross; an Easter song,
words by Violet Alleyn Storey,
music by Blanche Douglas Byles.
© Theodore Presser Co., Philadelphia; 3Jan47; EP11031. Edition
for low voice.

--- Edition for medium voice. ©
Theodore Presser Co., Philadelphia;
3Jan47; EP11033.

BYRNE, WILLIAM LAWRENCE, 1885-
Steppin' out tonight; words and
music by W. L. Byrne. ©
William Lawrence Byrne, Los
Angeles; 18Feb47; EP12147.

C

CABLE, HOWARD R
Jingles all the way ... Comp. and
arr. by Howard R. Cable. ©
Mills Music, inc., New York;
on compilation & arrangement;
29May47; EP6949. Condensed
score (orchestra) and parts.

CADENA RUBIN, ISAURO.
Por confiado ... letra y música
de Isauro Cadena Rubín. ©
Promotora Hispano Americana de
Música, s.a., Mexico; 24Apr47;
EF3206.

CADMAN, CHARLES WAKEFIELD, 1881-1946.
A red bird sang in a green, green
tree; for women's chorus (SSA)
Words by Helen Louise Shaffer,
music by Charles Wakefield
Cadman. © Edward Schuberth &
Co., inc., New York; 29Jun47;
EP12160.

Trees in the rain; S.S.A., [text
by Betty Davis, music by] Charles
W. Cadman. © J. Fischer & Bro.,
New York; 10Feb47; EP6615.

CADWALLADER, JOHN REECE, 1894-
Jesus Christ our Lord; Easter
hymn ... [by] J. R. Cadwallader.
© John Reece Cadwallader,
Meadville, Pa.; 1Mar47;
EP14416. Close score: SATB.

[CAFFOT, SYLVERE VICTOR JOSEPH]
1903-
(Les aventures de Casanova)
Chanson de Venise, barcarolle
chantée dans le film: "Les
aventures de Casanova" ...
paroles de René Rouzaud &
Maurice Vandair [pseud.],
musique de René Sylviano
[pseud.] © Éditions Regia,
Paris; 1Mar47; EF3608.

(Les aventures de Casanova)
Coraline; ou (La semaine
d'une courtisane) ...
paroles de René Rouzaud &
Maurice Vandair [pseud.],
musique de René Sylviano
[pseud.] © Éditions Regia,
Paris; 31Mar47; EF3609.

(Les aventures de Casanova)
La loi de l'amour, valse
chantée dans le film Les
aventures de Casanova ...
paroles de Jean Boyer, musique
de René Sylviano [pseud.] ©
Éditions Regia, Paris; 1Mar47;
EF3606.

(Les aventures de Casanova)
L'oiseau fiddle, menuet
chanté dans le film Les
aventures de Casanova ...
paroles de René Rouzaud [pseud.],
musique de René Sylviano
[pseud.] © Éditions Regia,
Paris; 1Mar47; EF3607.

(Les aventures de Casanova)
Rosa, Nina, Stella; sérénade
chantée dans le film: "Les
aventures de Casanova ...
paroles de René Rouzaud &
Maurice Vandair [pseud.],
musique de René Sylviano
[pseud.] © Éditions Regia,
Paris; 1Mar47; EF3644.

Chanson de Venise. See his Les
aventures de Casanova.

Chante, chante, mon coeur ...
paroles de Maurice Vandair
[pseud.,] & René Rouzaud, musique
de René Sylviano [pseud.]
© Éditions Regia, Paris; 1Mar47;
EF3883.

Coraline. See his Les aventures
de Casanova.

La loi de l'amour. See his Les
aventures de Casanova.

Rosa, Nina, Stella. See his Les
aventures de Casanova.

Souvenir d'un jour ... paroles
de Jean Boyer, musique de
René Sylviano [pseud.] ©
Éditions Regia, Paris; 1Mar47;
EF3646.

CAILLIET, LUCIEN, 1891-
Cailliet clarinet studies; by
Lucien Cailliet. © Belwin, inc.,
New York; on bk. 1; 11Mar47;
EP12576.

Campus chimes ... text by Bernard
Hamblen ... For ... symphonic
band. © Belwin, inc., New York;
on arrangement; 19Jan46; EP669.

CAIN, NOBLE, 1896-
Behold! I stand at the door;
mixed chorus with optional
acc., [by] Noble Cain, [words
from] Rev.3:20. © Harold
Flammer, inc., New York;
14Mar47; EP13466.

The bread of God; SATB with
optional acc., [by] Noble Cain
... [words from] John 6:32, 33,
51. © Harold Flammer, inc.,
New York; 14Mar47; EP13465.

Christ, whose glory fills the
skies; anthem ... SATB with
optional acc., [words by]
Charles Wesley, [music and
arrangement by] Noble Cain.
© Harold Flammer, inc., New
York; on arrangement; 14Mar47;
EP13470.

He that doeth truth; SSAATTBB
with optional acc., [by] Noble
Cain, the words ... [from]
St. John 3:21-20. © Harold
Flammer, inc., New York;
14Mar47; EP13467.

Keep your lamps trimmed; by Noble
Cain, arr. and ed. for women's
chorus, S.S.A. © Choral Art
Publications, New York; on arrangement; 14Feb47; EP12446.

Keep your lamps trimmed; [spiritual.
Music] by Noble Cain, arranged and
edited for mixed chorus, S.A.T.B.
© Choral Art Publications, New York;
on arrangement; 27Nov46; EP11185.

The King of love my Shepherd is;
by Noble Cain, arr. and ed.
for two-part chorus, S.A.
[Psalm 23 versified by Henry
Baker] © Choral Art Publications, New York; 8May47;
EP14587.

The Lord is my shepherd; SSA a
cappella or accompanied, [by]
Noble Cain, [words:] Psalm 23.
© Harold Flammer, inc., New
York; on arrangement; 4Nov46;
EP10835.

The music of life; for two-
part chorus of women's voices
with piano acc., [by] Noble
Cain. [Words by] Elizabeth
Evelyn Moore. © G. Schirmer,
inc., New York; on arrangement;
16Nov46; EP12880.

Oh, worship the King; by Noble
Cain, arr. and ed. for mixed
chorus. [Words by Robert
Grant] © Choral Art
Publications, New York; on
arrangement; 8May47; EP14395.

Religion is a fortune; SSA
accompanied, version of tune
and words by A. E. Carter;
traditional spiritual, concert
version by Noble Cain. ©
Harold Flammer, inc., New York;
on arrangement; 14Mar47;
EP13474.

Religion is a fortune; SSAATTBB
with optional acc., version of
tune and words by A. E. Carter;
traditional spiritual, concert
version by Noble Cain. © Harold
Flammer, inc., New York; on arrangement; 14Mar47; EP13473.

Welcome that star ... SATB accompanied, [by] Noble Cain, [words
by] Robert Hawker, metrical
version by Robert F. Hein. ©
Harold Flammer, inc., New York;
4Nov46; EP10747.

Welcome that star ... SSA accompanied,
[by] Noble Cain, words by] Robert
Hawker, metrical version by
Robert F. Hein. © Harold Flammer,
inc., New York; on arrangement;
4Nov46; EP10749.

CAIRO, PABLO.
Mi "lea" no baila ... letra y
música de Pablo Cairo. © Peer
International Corp., New York;
18Dec46; EP5587. Piano-conductor score (orchestra), and
parts.

CALDWELL, HANK, 1907-
What might have been; words and
music by Hank Caldwell. ©
Nordyke Publishing Co., Hollywood,
Calif.; 17Jan47; EP11528.

CALL, IDAHO.
Just hangin' on; words and music
by Idaho Call. [c1946] © Tim
Spencer Music, inc., Hollywood,
Calif.; 4Feb47; EP11960.

CALLA, NO LLORES. (Quiet, don't cry,
my heart) ... [English words adapted
by Albert Gamse] (In André,
Julio, ed. Songs from south of
the border, p.10-11) © Edward
B. Marks Music Corp., New York;
on English adaptation; 28Dec46;
EP10865.

CALLAWAY, PAUL.
O saving victim ... by Paul
Callaway. © The H. W. Gray
Co., inc., New York;
14Mar47; EP12847. Score:
chorus (SATB) and organ.

CAMACHO, JOHNNIE, 1916-
The girl with the Spanish drawl
... music and Spanish lyric by
Fausto Curbelo and Johnnie
Camacho, lyric by Mack David.
© Remick Music Corp., New York;
2Apr47; EP13360.

CAMARATA, M
My broadside gal ... Words by
Claybourne W. Hart, music and
arr. by M. Camarata. ©
Claybourne W. Hart, Chicago;
8Mar46; EP14250.

CAMERON, JOHN.
The song of home ... composed by
John Cameron, piano arrangement
by Gerald Shaw. © Dix, ltd,
London; 25Jan47; EF3152.

CAMPBELL, BILL, 1904-
The last man I'll ever lose; by
Bill Campbell. © Popular Music
Co., New York; 13Jun47; EP15036.
For voice and piano, with chord
symbols.

Social drag; by Bill Campbell.
© Popular Music Co., New York;
13Jun47; EP15038. For voice
and piano, with chord symbols.

You went too far and stayed too
long; by Bill Campbell. ©
Popular Music Co., New York;
4Jun47; EP14888. For voice
and piano, with chord symbols.

CAMPBELL, EDITH.
Paraphrase on "Jesus Christ is
risen today" (adapted from a
melody in "Lyra Davidica"
1718). © The H. W. Gray Co.,
inc., New York; 3Jan47; EP11061.
For organ solo.

CAMPBELL, EDITH L   1915-
When I speak your name; words by
James Ballister and Joseph
Failla, music by Edith L. Camp-
bell. © Modern Melodies
Publishing Co., New York;
3May40; EP12660.

CAMPBELL, JAMES.
Show me the way to go home; music
by Irving King (pseud.), arr.
by Jimmy Dale. © Harms, inc.,
New York; on arrangement;
29May47; EP14999. Piano-conductor score (orchestra) and
parts.

CAMPBELL, LUCIE E
Praise ye the Lord; [music] by
Lucie E. Campbell, [words: CL
psalm] Nashville, E. W. D.
Isaac. © National B. T. U.
Board, Nashville; 29Jul46;
EP10903. Score: soprano, chorus
(SATB) and piano or organ.

CAMPBELL, TED.
It's the twink, twink, twinkle in
your eye; [by] Harry Tavener
[and] Ted Campbell, [arr. by]
Al. Mcquin. © Stevens Music
Co., San Antonio; on arrangement; 19Apr47; EP14451. Piano-
conductor score (orchestra) and
parts.

CAMPBELL, WILBUR WATKINS, 1889-
Emperor Norton; a light comedy
opera, music by Wilbur Campbell. Partial score. 1st ed.
© Wilbur Campbell, Los Angeles;
2Jan47; EP10766.

CAMPO, M   V   Do.
Chiapanecas. (The Mexican hand-
clapping song) ... [By] M. V.
de Campo, Spanish lyric by Juan
Hernandez-Ribera, [English words
adapted by Albert Gamse] (In
André, Julio, ed. Songs from south
of the border. p.32-35) ©
Edward B. Marks Music Corp., New
York; on English adaptation; 28Dec46;
EP10873.

CANAAN ... words by Mr. A. B. Windom
... Scotch air. Solo or duett.
© A. B. Windom Studio (Aaron
Bash Windom, sole owner), St.
Louis; 5Jun40; EP11973.

CANARO, FRANCISCO.
Si tu me quisieras ... letra y
música de Francisco Canaro. ©
Corporación Musical Argentina-
Comar-s. a., Buenos Aires;
30Nov46; EF3143.

CANARO, MARIO.
Pena gris ... letra de Andrés
Chinarro, música de Mario
Canaro. © Editorial Argentina
de Música Internacional,s.
de r. ltd., Buenos Aires;
24Apr47; EF3207.

CANARY, MICHAEL THOMAS, 1878-
Back in the good old days; words &
music by M. T. Canary. [c1946]
© Canary Songs, Michael Thomas
Canary, sole owner, Chicago;
1Jan47; EP11887.

CANDANEDA, GONZALO BRENES. See
Brenes Candaneda, Gonzalo.

CANEVA, ERNEST O
Marimba capers; marimba or xylophone
solo with band accompaniment, by
Ernest O. Caneva, [arr. by Charles
S. Peters] © Remick Music Corp.,
New York; 30Dec46; EP11139.

CANNING, JAMES J   1897-
The magic city of the angels;
words and music by Jas. J.
Canning. © Shelby Music
Publishing Co., Detroit;
14Apr47; EP14326.

CANORO, LOUIS, 1888-
My dear, don't tell me "no"; words
and music by L. Canoro. © Louis
Canoro, Brooklyn; 1Feb47; EP12094.

Num me dicite "No"; versi e musica
di L. Canoro. © Louis Canoro,
Brooklyn; 1Feb47; EP11993.

CANOVA, JUDY.
Go to sleepy, little baby; lyric by Harry and Henry Tobias, music by Judy and Zeke Canova. © Mutual Music Society, inc., New York; on changes in words & music; 31Dec46; EP12124.

CANTWELL, NED.
I'm bringing a rose from old Ireland ... Words and music by Ned Cantwell. © Ned Cantwell, Joliet, Ill.; 3Feb47; EP11908.

CAPANNA MARIAROSA, ER SOR, pseud. See Finocchioli, Amedeo.

CAPEL, J   M
Love, could I only tell thee; music by J. M. Capel, words by Clifton Bingham, arr. for mixed voices S.A.T.B. by Clarence Lucas. © Chappell & Co., ltd., London; on arrangement; 18Mar47; EP5480.

CAPOCCI, FILIPPO.
Missa regina angelorum; by Filippo Capocci, arr. by Cyr De Brant [pseud.] © J. Fischer & Bro., New York; on arrangement; 23Jun47; EP6981. Score: chorus (SAB) and organ.

CAPRONNIER, M
Le bal des mariniers, du film "Le bal des mariniers" ... paroles de Carly, musique de M. Capronnier et R. de Buxeuil. © Productions Carly-Capronnier, Paris; 31Jan47; EF3857.

CARBO MENENDEZ, J   1925-
J'attends ton retour. (En tu ausencia) ... paroles de Lucien Thériault, letra y música de J. Carbo Menendez. Lachute, P. Q., Le Parnasse Musical. © Edition A. Fassio, Lachute, Que., Can.; 1May47; EF3200.

CARDENAS, GUTY.
Your love or no love; American adaptation of "Nunca" ... English lyric by Albert Gamso, Spanish lyric by Ricardo Lopez, music by Guty Cardenas. © Edward B. Marks Music Corp., New York; 4Dec46; EP11967.

CARENNE, LOUIS.
A la fin des vendanges ... paroles de Paul Gaissac, musique de Louis Carenne. (In Le Passe-Temps. no. 890, p. 14) © Les Editions du Passe-Temps, inc., Montreal; 20Sep45; EF3094. Melody and words.

CARENZIO, RENATO.
Amor, non mi lasciar ... testo e musica di Renato Carenzio. (In Un sorriso e 20 canzoni. p. 36-37) © Edizioni Leonardi, s.a.r.l., Milano; 22Nov45; EF4927. For voice and piano.

Quel tuo rosso ... testo e musica di Renato Carenzio. © Edizioni Leonardi, s.a.r.l.; Milan; 18Nov45; EF4813. For voice and piano.

CARGILL, IKE.
The clouds rained trouble down; words and music by Ike Cargill. © Hill and Range Songs, inc., Hollywood, Calif.; 28Mar47; EP13149.

CARISSIMI, GIACOMO, 1604-1674.
Plorate filii Israel, from "Jephtha" ... [By] Giacomo Carissimi ... ed. and arr. by O. C. C. © Neil A. Kjos Music Co., Chicago; on arrangement; 19Jun47; EP15185.

CARLE, ERIC, pseud. See Peterson, Karl Erik.

CARLE, FRANKIE, pseud. See Carlone, Francis N.

CARLETON, BOB. See Carleton, Robert L.

CARLETON, ROBERT L   1888-
After the round-up is over; words by Grace Walbridge, music by Bob Carleton. © Cine-Mart Music Publishing Co., Hollywood, Calif.; 31Mar47; EP14657.

The Army made a man out of Joe; words by Andrew C. Byran, music by Bob Carleton. © Cine-mart Music Publishing Co., Hollywood, Calif.; 1Aug46; EP10961. For voice and piano, with chord symbols.

Baby, the joke's on me; words by Charles E. Reyburn, music by Bob Carleton. © Cine-Mart Music Publishing Co., Hollywood, Calif.; 1Dec46; EP12103.

Bansi, you-all; words by Charles Dunlavy, music by Bob Carleton. © Cine-Mart Music Publishing Co., Hollywood, Calif.; 1Nov46; EP11727.

Because I'm already in love; words by Cynthia B. Landry, music by Bob Carleton. © Cine-Mart Music Publishing Co., Hollywood, Calif.; 1Dec46; EP12106.

Charmingly; words by Katherine Weisenberger, music by Bob Carleton. © Cine-Mart Music Publishing Co., Hollywood, Calif.; 30Dec46; EP14014.

Come in, Mister Santa; words by Gail W. Snyder, music by Bob Carleton. © Whitehouse Publishing Co., Hollywood, Calif.; 3Dec46; EP11990.

Crazy, lazy and in love; words by Stanley Belzak, music by Bob Carleton. © Cine-Mart Music Publishing Co., Hollywood, Calif.; 1Nov46; EP11480.

Cupid is love; words by Laurence J. Little, music by Bob Carleton. © Cine-Mart Music Publishing Co., Hollywood, Calif.; 30Dec46; EP14027.

Cute little dimples; words by Emil C. Hasenauer, music by Bob Carleton. © Cine-Mart Music Publishing Co., Hollywood, Calif.; 30Dec46; EP14209.

Darling little Irishman; words by Eva H. Lamothe, music by Bob Carleton. © Cine-Mart Music Publishing Co., Hollywood, Calif.; 1Nov46; EP11726.

Don't house me up; words by Dulah Mae Needham, music by Bob Carleton. © Cine-Mart Music Publishing Co., Hollywood, Calif.; 1Nov46; EP11716.

Don't keep her waiting; words by Dom Guarasci, music by Bob Carleton. © Cine-Mart Music Publishing Co., Hollywood, Calif.; 1Nov46; EP11486.

Don't let the moon get you; words by Joe Tarr, music by Bob Carleton. © Cine-Mart Music Publishing Co., Hollywood, Calif.; 1Dec46; EP12114.

The fault is all your own; words by Harry Van Liew, music by Bob Carleton. © Cine-Mart Music Publishing Co., Hollywood, Calif.; 1Dec46; EP12105.

Forever and after that; words by Will Venables, music by Bob Carleton. © Cine-Mart Music Publishing Co., Hollywood, Calif.; 30Dec46; EP14024.

Grieving my heart over you; words by Grace Stratton, music by Bob Carleton. © Cine-Mart Music Publishing Co., Hollywood, Calif.; 1Nov46; EP11715.

He has come home to stay; words by E. C. Barbee, music by Bob Carleton. © Cine-mart Music Publishing Co., Hollywood, Calif.; 1Aug46; EP10971. For voice and piano, with chord symbols.

He was a pal of mine; words by Marjorie E. Pamplona, music by Bob Carleton. © Cine-Mart Music Publishing Co., Hollywood, Calif.; 1Dec46; EP11413.

Hep step; words by Joseph Paul Koeppe, music by Bob Carleton. © Cine-Mart Music Publishing Co., Hollywood, Calif.; EP14652.

Honey doll; words by Gertrude Splitt, music by Bob Carleton. © Cine-mart Music Publishing Co., Hollywood, Calif.; 1Aug46; EP10972. For voice and piano, with chord symbols.

Honey, it's you; words by Helen Loftin, music by Bob Carleton. © Cine-Mart Music Publishing Co., Hollywood, Calif.; 30Dec46; EP11710.

How can I make you care? Words by Robert J. Taylor, music by Bob Carleton. © Cine-mart Music Publishing Co., Hollywood, Calif.; 1Aug46; EP10970. For voice and piano, with chord symbols.

I feel with my heart; words by Sylvester Jacura, music by Bob Carleton. © Cine-Mart Music Publishing Co., Hollywood, Calif.; 1Nov46; EP11937.

I love you still to-day; lyrics by Alice Tinsley, music by Bob Carleton, [arr. by Edward E. Monges] © Alice Tinsley, St. Louis; 1Nov46; EP11110.

I walk with my Master each day; words by Marion Malbon, music by Bob Carleton. © Cine-Mart Music Publishing Co., Hollywood, Calif.; 30Dec46; EP14057.

I want some love, baby; words by Alda Durk, music by Bob Carleton. © Cine-Mart Music Publishing Co., Hollywood, Calif.; 30Dec46; EP14032.

I wonder why I do not hear from you; words by Carlton Schalers, music by Bob Carleton. © Cine-Mart Music Publishing Co., Hollywood, Calif.; 1Dec46; EP11484.

I'd rather have a poor man than a rich man; words by Elmer League, music by Bob Carleton. © Cine-Mart Music Publishing Co., Hollywood, Calif.; 1Nov46; EP11939.

I'll remember that in the moonlight; words by Jimmy Morryman, music by Bob Carleton. © Cine-Mart Music Publishing Co., Hollywood, Calif.; 30Dec46; EP14026.

I'll tell the world I love you; words by Hazel McLeish, music by Bob Carleton. © Cine-Mart Music Publishing Co., Hollywood, Calif.; 31Mar47; EP14647.

The Golden Rule; words by Harry Craft, music by Bob Carleton. © Cine-Mart Music Publishing Co., Hollywood, Calif.; 1Nov46; EP11478.

Gotta make love; words by Alice F. Jones, music by Bob Carleton. © Cine-Mart Music Publishing Co., Hollywood, Calif.; 1Dec46; EP12117.

21

CARLETON, ROBERT L. Cont'd.

I'm all down in the dumps; words by Scuddy B. White, music by Bob Carleton. © Cine-Mart Music Publishing Co., Hollywood, Calif. 30Dec46; EP14023.

I'm like a raindrop; words by Carl A. Miller, music by Bob Carleton. © Cine-Mart Music Publishing Co., Hollywood, Calif.; 30Dec46; EP14022.

I'm longing for love 'cause it's springtime; words by Silas Qundrum, music by Bob Carleton. © Cine-Mart Music Publishing Co., Hollywood, Calif.; 31Mar47; EP14655.

I'm somebody's something today; words by Martha L. Henderson, music by Bob Carleton. © Cine-Mart Music Publishing Co., Hollywood, Calif.; 30Dec46; EP14019.

I'm under a cloud, dear; words by Blanche L. Jordan, music by Bob Carleton. © Cine-Mart Music Publishing Co., Hollywood, Calif.; 30Dec46; EP14022.

In my moonlit garden; words by John A. Krzyston, music by Bob Carleton. © Cine-Mart Music Publishing Co., Hollywood, Calif.; 1Nov46; EP11946.

In the depths of my heart; words by Kay Sue Davis, music by Bob Carleton. © Cine-Mart Music Publishing Co., Hollywood, Calif.; 30Dec46; EP14020.

Just a cabin in the mountains; words by Elvira Steffanson, music by Bob Carleton. Words and music revised by Tracy Knutson. © Elvira Steffanson, Roseland, Neb.; on revision of words & music; 22Apr47; EP14255.

Just a little tugboat; words by Carl K. Hageman, music by Bob Carleton. © Cine-Mart Music Publishing Co., Hollywood, Calif.; 30Dec46; EP14025.

Just lazin' around; words by Harland Vincent [pseud.], music by Bob Carleton. © Cine-Mart Music Publishing Co., Hollywood, Calif.; 1Dec46; EP12101.

Land of the Midnight Sun; words by Mabelle Burns, music by Bob Carleton. © Cine-Mart Music Publishing Co., Hollywood, Calif.; 1Nov46; EP11717.

Let's try it again; words by Van M. Worth, music by Bob Carleton. © Cine-Mart Music Publishing, Hollywood, Calif.; 1Nov46; EP11476.

The light of love; words by Lloyd J. Tyler, music by Bob Carleton. [c1946] © Whitehouse Publishing Co., Hollywood, Calif; 13Jan47; EP11989.

Lonely night; words by Vaughn C. Church, music by Bob Carleton. © Cine-Mart Music Publishing Co., Hollywood, Calif.; 31Mar47; EP14651.

Lost in love; words by Cora Luke, music by Bob Carleton. © Cine-Mart Music Publishing Co., Hollywood, Calif.; 1Nov46; EP11942.

The love star; words by Germaine Jolly, music by Bob Carleton. © Cine-Mart Music Publishing Co., Hollywood, Calif.; 30Dec46; EP14035.

Lovely sweetheart of mine; words by John Theo Bradberry, music by Bob Carleton. © Cine-Mart Music Pub. Co., Hollywood, Calif.; 1Nov46; EP11935.

Mabel, I'll tell the world; words by Gus Wager, music by Bob Carleton. © Cine-Mart Music Publishing Co., Hollywood, Calif.; 1Nov46; EP11714.

Moonbeams in your hair; words by Edna Bird, music by Bob Carleton. © Cine-Mart Music Publishing Co., Hollywood, Calif.; 30Dec46; EP14035.

Mother's fallen tears; words by John J. Murphy, music by Bob Carleton. © Cine-Mart Music Publishing Co., Hollywood, Calif.; 1Nov46; EP11479.

My beauty is you, Marilou; Words by W. Frank Brown, music by Bob Carleton. Keokuk, Iowa, Dr. Billie Song Shoppe. © W. Frank Brown, Keokuk, Iowa; 30Apr47; EP14507.

My dreamland sweetheart; words by Lylo Vernon Moore, music by Bob Carleton. © Cine-Mart Music Publishing Co., Hollywood, Calif.; 1Aug46; EP10973. For voice and piano, with chord symbols.

My fairy queen; words by Edna G. Small, music by Bob Carleton. © Cine-mart Music Publishing Co., Hollywood, Calif.; 1Aug46; EP10958. For voice and piano, with chord symbols.

My little dude ranch gal; words by Jesse Williams, music by Bob Carleton. © Cine-Mart Music Publishing Co., Hollywood, Calif.; 31Mar47; EP14650.

My old fashioned rose; words by Ray Shamley, music by Bob Carleton. © Cine-Mart Music Publishing Co., Hollywood, Calif.; 1Dec46; EP14110.

My picture of you; words by Anna Mae Huhta, music by Bob Carleton. © Cine-Mart Music Publishing Co., Hollywood, Calif.; 1Dec46; EP12115.

My sailor husband; words by Bertha Jonas, music by Bob Carleton. © Cine-Mart Music Publishing Co., Hollywood, Calif.; 1Dec46; EP14116.

My twilight rose; words by Orland Do Bord, music by Bob Carleton. © Cine-Mart Music Publishing Co., Hollywood, Calif.; 30Dec46; EP14021.

Oh how I loved you then; words by Peggie L. Lassiter, music by Bob Carleton. © Cine-Mart Music Publishing Co., Hollywood, Calif.; 1Dec46; EP12121.

Orange Blossom Bay; words by Frances R. Davis, music by Bob Carleton. © Cine-Mart Music Publishing Co., Hollywood, Calif.; 1Dec46; EP12107.

Pipe dreams; words by Edna Fillgrove, music by Bob Carleton. © Cine-Mart Music Publishing Co., Hollywood, Calif.; 1Nov46; EP11724.

The San Joaquin Valley blues; words by Lewis Chreman, music by Bob Carleton. © Cine-Mart Music Publishing Co., Hollywood, Calif.; 31Mar47; EP14648.

Sandy; words by Iris Ann Hall, music by Bob Carleton. © Cine-mart Music Publishing Co., Hollywood, Calif.; 1Aug46; EP10968. For voice and piano, with chord symbols.

Say "bye bye"... words by W. Frank Brown, [music by Bob Carleton] Keokuk, Iowa, Dr. Billie Song Shoppe. © W. Frank Brown, Keokuk, Iowa; 18Mar47; EP13689. Caption title: Say "bye bye" but never "good-night."

Shady lane; words by Marilyn Jenkins, music by Bob Carleton. © Cine-Mart Music Publishing Co., Hollywood, Calif.; 1Nov46; EP11712.

Skies of the west; words by Buster Rukel, music by Bob Carleton. © Cine-Mart Music Publishing Co., Hollywood, Calif.; 30Dec46; EP14017.

So jealous of you; words by Grace Robinson, music by Bob Carleton. © Cine-Mart Music Publishing Co., Hollywood, Calif.; 1Nov46; EP14475.

Sticky fingers; words by Henry R. McClelland, music by Bob Carleton. © Cine-Mart Music Publishing Co., Hollywood, Calif.; 1Dec46; EP12108.

Sweet memories of you; words by James E. Todd, music by Bob Carleton. © Cine-Mart Music Publishing Co., Hollywood, Calif.; 1Nov46; EP11723.

Swinging on your gate; words by Cooper P. Peacock, music by Bob Carleton. © Cine-Mart Music Publishing Co., Hollywood, Calif; 31Mar47; EP14658.

Tell me, what is love? Words by Wilfred R. Pobursky, music by Bob Carleton. © Cine-Mart Music Publishing Co., Hollywood, Calif.; 1Dec46; EP12118.

Thanks, soldier boy; words by Helen Cadile [pseud.], music by Bob Carleton. © Cine-Mart Music Publishing Co., Hollywood, Calif.; 30Dec46; EP14016.

There's fun out on the farm; words by Gona Stoeser, music by Bob Carleton. © Cine-Mart Music Publishing Co., Hollywood, Calif.; 30Dec46; EP14028.

The things I like about you; words by Virginia K. Oliver, music by Bob Carleton. © Cine-Mart Music Publishing Co., Hollywood, Calif.; 30Dec46; EP14036.

The things you do to me; words by Thomas Reilly, music by Bob Carleton. © Cine-Mart Music Publishing Co., Hollywood, Calif., 1Nov46; EP11944.

This is it! Words by William J. Cramer, music by Bob Carleton. © Cine-Mart Music Publishing Co., Hollywood, Calif.; 1Nov46; EP11947.

This is my dream; words by Grayce-Eva Carney Phillips, music by Bob Carleton. © Cine-Mart Music Publishing Co., Hollywood, Calif.; 30Dec46; EP11211.

Truck driving fever; words by Georgette Russell, music by Bob Carleton. © Cine-mart Music Publishing Co., Hollywood, Calif.; 1Aug46; EP10969. For voice and piano, with chord symbols.

Until you come home; words by Flora Toro, music by Bob Carleton. © Cine-Mart Music Publishing Co., Hollywood, Calif.; 1Nov46; EP11483.

The war is over; words by H. G. Frazier, music by Bob Carleton. © Cine-mart Music Publishing Co., Hollywood, Calif.; 1Aug46; EP10957. For voice and piano, with chord symbols.

We won't be strangers long; words by Robert R. Mac Gregor, music by Bob Carleton. © Cine-Mart Music Publishing Co., Hollywood, Calif.; 1Nov46; EP11487.

CARLETON, ROBERT L. Cont'd.
We're gonna catch up on romancing;
words by Gona Stoesor, music by
Bob Carleton. © Cine-Mart Music
Publishing Co.. Hollywood, Calif.;
1Nov46; EP11709.

When dreaming is through; words
by Laurel B. Cramer, music by
Bob Carleton. © Cine-mart
Music Publishing Co., Hollywood,
Calif.; 1Aug46; EP10959. For
voice and piano, with chord
symbols.

When the robins come again; words by
Britain Ogilvie, music by Bob Carle-
ton. © Cine-Mart Music Publishing
Co., Hollywood, Calif.; 1Nov46;
EP11725.

Why dream dreams of you; words by
Eduard A. Syganico, music by
Bob Carleton. © Cine-Mart
Music Publishing Co., Hollywood,
Calif.; 30Dec46; EP14029.

Why should I worry? Words by Billy
Carson, music by Bob Carleton. ©
Cine-Mart Music Publishing Co.,
Hollywood, Calif.; 1Nov46; EP11708.

You said it! Words by Neal
Hemer, music by Bob Carleton.
© Cine-Mart Music Publishing
Co., Hollywood, Calif.;
1Nov46; EP11474.

You're gonna miss your daddy (when
he's gone); words by Bessie
Denham, music by Bob Carleton.
© Cine-mart Music Publishing
Co., Hollywood, Calif.; 1Aug46;
EP10967. For voice and piano,
with chord symbols.

CARLISLE, CLIFFORD RAYMOND, 1910-
Just an old forgotten letter;
lyric by Sid Prosen, music by
Cliff Carlisle. © Hometown
Music Co., inc., New York;
4Apr47; EP13366.

A mean mama don't worry me; by
Cliff Carlisle. © Home-
town Music Co., inc., New
York; 26Feb47; EP12385. For
voice and piano, with chord
symbols.

Scars upon my heart; lyric by Sid
Prosen, music by Cliff Carlisle.
© Hometown Music Co., inc.,
New York; 19Mar47; EP12793.

CARLISLE, JEAN.
I've got you; words by Zella Gwynne,
pseud., music by Jean Carlisle.
© Cine-Mart Music Publishing Co.,
Hollywood, Calif.; 1Nov46; EP12100.

[CARLONE, FRANCIS N   ]
Roses in the rain; lyric by Al
Frisch [and] Fred Wise, music
by Frankie Carle [pseud.]
© Barton Music Corp., New York;
22Jan47; EP11386.

Roses in the rain; piano solo,
arr. by Frankie Carle, [pseud.]
© Barton Music Corp., New York;
on arrangement; 22Jan47;
EP13423.

You are there; by Dave Lieber,
Vic White & Frankie Carle
[pseud.] © Stept, inc., New
York; 7May47; EP14474. For
voice and piano, with chord
symbols.

CARLSON, ALEX.
Alex Carlson violin school,
elementary course. © Alex
Carlson, Portland, Or.; bk.2,
2Mar47; EP6770.

CARLSON, FRANCIS H
By His stripes ye are healed; [by]
Francis H. Carlson, [words by]
Selma J. Gagnon. © Selma J.
Gagnon, Los Angeles; 23Jun47;
EP6976. Close score: SATB.

CARMELO, ANTONIO, pseud. See
Renault, André.

CARMICHAEL, HOAGY, 1899-
Hoagy Carmichael's All-time
popular songs ... arr. for
piano, uke, guitar [and]
banjo, [comp. by Lyle K.
Engel] © Movie Songs, inc.,
New York; 28Dec46; EP11159.

Ivy, theme of the ... picture
"Ivy"; words and music by
Hoagy Carmichael. © Burke
and Van Heusen, inc., New
York; 4Apr47; EP13365.

CARNES, JOSEF R
I wish I had a pal. By Josef R.
Carnes. © Josef R. Carnes,
Hillsboro, Ind.; 19May47;
EP14687. For voice and key-
board instrument.

Lord, I adore Thee; sacred song
by Josef R. Carnes. © Josef R.
Carnes, Hillsboro, Ind.; 19May47;
EP14684. For voice and piano.

CARR, ARTHUR.
As on the night ... For voice and
piano, by Arthur Carr [words
adapted from George Wither's
"Hymns and songs of the church"]
© G. Schirmer, inc., New York;
13May47; EP14552.

Hosanna to the Son of David;
[words] adapted from the scriptures, [music by] Arthur Carr.
© G. Schirmer, inc., New York;
3Apr47; EP14052. For voice and
organ or piano.

[CARR, FRANK L   ]
It's the same old moon; [words and
music by Frank Carr] © Frank L.
Carr, Rochester, Minn.; 2Jun47;
EP15135.

Someone like you; words & music by
Frank L. Carr, Rochester, Minn.,
The Carr. Co. © Frank L. Carr,
Rochester, Minn.; 2Jun47;
EP15136.

CARR, LEON, 1910-
But no nickel; [words] by Leo Corday
... [music by] Leon Carr. ©
Ritchie Music Co., New York; 15Aug46;
EP12138.

Take a little off the top; [words] by
Leo Corday ... [music by] Leon Carr.
© Ritchie Music Co., New York;
15Aug46; EP12139.

CARR, MARGUERITE.
I'm looking for a Jack of all
trades; [by] Fannie West Light
[and] Marguerite Carr. © Song
Hit Publ. Co., Chicago; 12May47;
EP14597. For voice and piano,
with chord symbols.

CARRAGAN, MARTHA (BECK) See
Beck, Martha.

CARRIER, COTTON. See
Carrier, Joseph Aaron.

CARRIER, JOSEPH AARON.
Why should I worry now; words and
music by Cotton Carrier. ©
Carson-Carrier Publications,
Atlanta; 19May47; EP14682.

CARRIER, VIRGINIA, 1923-
Keep the faith; [by] Virginia
Carrier, arr. by W. M. T.
(In Church of the Nazarene.
Michigan District. Nazarene
Young Peoples Society.
Choruses of the N. Y. P. S.
p.22-23) © Michigan District,
Nazarene Young Peoples Society,
Flint, Mich.; 25Jul46;
EP13048. For voice and piano.

II Timothy 2:15; [by] Virginia
Carrier, arr. by W. M. Thorne.
(In Church of the Nazarene.
Michigan District. Nazarene
Young Peoples Society. Chorus-
es of the N. Y. P. S. p.6)
© Michigan District, Nazarene
Young Peoples Society, Flint,
Mich.; 25Jul46; EP13052. For
voice and piano.

CARROZZA, CARMELO ANGELO, 1921-
Nine bass boogie; [by] C. Carrozza.
© Accordion Music Publishing Co.,
New York; 21Apr47; EP14206. For
accordion solo.

CARSON, JAMES.
A broken vow will mean a broken
heart; words and music by James
Carson. © Carson-Carrier
Publications, Atlanta; 19May47;
EP14685.

You've had your way, now I'm having
mine; words and music by James
Carson. © Carson-Carrier Publications, Atlanta; 2Jun47; EP15137.

CARSON, JENNY LOU.
Ain't cha tired of makin' me
blue? Words and music by
Jenny Lou Carson. © Hill and
Range Songs, inc., Hollywood,
Calif.; 13May47; EP14423.

Gonna give you back to the Indians;
words and music by Jenny Lou
Carson. © Hill and Range Songs,
inc., Hollywood, Calif.; 7Jan47;
EP11203.

Honest injun (I love you);
words and music by Jenny Lou
Carson. © Hill and Range
Songs, inc., Hollywood, Calif.;
20Feb47; EP12196.

I'd trade all of my tomorrows
(for just one yesterday);
words and music by Jenny Lou
Carson. © Hill and Range
Songs, inc., Hollywood, Calif.;
7Jan47; EP11202.

A penny for your thoughts; words
and music by Jenny Lou Carson.
© Hill and Range Songs, inc.,
Hollywood, Calif.; 7Jan47;
EP11116.

You're laughing up your sleeve;
words and music by Jenny Lou
Carson. © Hill and Range Songs,
inc., Hollywood, Calif.;
10Jun47; EP15086.

You've gotta quit makin' me blue;
[words and music] by Jenny Lou
Carson. © Northern Music Corp.,
New York; 9Jan47; EP11169. For
voice and piano, with chord
symbols.

CARSON, SUNSET, 1920-   comp.
Sunset Carson mountain ballads
[and] cowboy songs ... [by
Atze Taconis and others, words
by Richard Coburn and others],
comp. by Sunset Carson, ed. by
Dave Gordon. © Sunshine Music
Co., Hollywood, Calif.;
10Sep46; EP12057.

CARTER, BUENTA.
The juggling clown; piano solo, by
Buenta Carter. © Clayton F.
Summy Co., Chicago; 19Dec46;
EP10754.

CARTER, ELLIOTT COOK, 1908-
Dust of snow; [words by] Robert Frost,
[music by] Elliott Carter. (Contemporary American songs for
medium voice and piano, 3d ser.)
© Associated Music Publishers, inc.,
New York; 18Feb47; EP12588.

Holiday overture; [by] Elliott
Carter. © Arrow Music Press,
inc., New York; 24Dec46;
EP12219. Miniature score:
orchestra.

CARTER, ELLIOTT COOK. Cont'd.
The rose family; [words by] Robert
Frost, [music by] Elliott Carter.
(Contemporary American songs for
medium voice and piano, 3d ser.)
© Associated Music Publishers,
inc., New York; 18Feb47; EP12587.

CARTWRIGHT, FRANCES, 1905-
I want to sing for Jesus; words
and music by Frances Cartwright, arr. by Odessa Steward.
© Frances Cartwright, Chicago;
19May47; EP14445.

CARTY, DALE.
Please play a dreamy waltz; by
Dale Carty. © La Mar Music
Publishers, inc., Canton, Ohio;
8May47; EP14506. For voice
and piano, with guitar diagrams
and chord symbols.

CARVER, ZEB.
Got a ring around Rosie's finger;
words and music by Jack Rollins,
Billy Hayes [and] Zeb Carver.
© Dawn Music, New York; 3Mar47;
EP13994.

I wish you could love me (like I
love you); by Billy Hayes,
Milton Leeds [and] Zeb Carver.
© Leeds Music Corp., New York;
14Feb47; EP12182. For voice
and piano, with guitar diagrams
and chord symbols.

CARVETH, WILLIAM, 1900-
His love for me; [by] William Carveth. © William Carveth, Turtle
Creek, Pa.; 10Jan47; EP11549. Close
score: SATB.

CASALINI, VITTORIO.
Allo fontane; [musica di] Vittorio
Casalini, testo di Nico-Bianchi.
Napoli, Edizioni musicali-M.
Gonnarelli. © Nario Gennarelli,
Naples; 10Sep46; EF5508. For
voice and piano.

CASAMOR, EUTIMIO.
Como visten las mujeres ... letra
de Evelio Matos Rodríguez,
música de Eutimio Casamor,
arreglo de Eulogio Casteleiro
(Yoyo) © Peer International
Corp., New York; 18Dec46;
EF5583. Piano-conductor score
(orchestra, with words), and
parts.

CASCIO, CARMELO.
Song without words; [for] piano-
forte, [by] Carmelo Cascio.
Schenectady, N. Y., House of
Music. © Carmelo Cascio,
Schenectady, N. Y.; 31Dec46;
EP10983.

CASEY, CLAUDE.
Look in the looking glass (at you);
words and music by Mel Foree and
Claude Casey. © Acuff-Rose Publi-
cations, Nashville; 21Jan47;
EP11438.

CASEY, CLAUDE, comp.
Claude Casey's caravan of songs;
[compiled by Claude Casey]
© Bourne, inc., New York;
25Feb47; EP12232.

CASEY, TONY, 1908-
Blueprint for two; words and music
by Tedd Lawrence & Tony Casey.
© Top Music Publishers, inc.,
New York; 30Jan47; EP11676.

CASIROLI, NINO.
Devi ricordare. See his Le sorprese del vagone letto.

Serenata ad un angelo; di
Rastelli-Casiroli. Milano,
Edizioni Musicali Irradio di
N. Casiroli. © Casa Editrice
"Nazionale" Musicale, Milano;
7Oct46; EF3226. For voice and
piano.

(Le sorprese del vagone letto)
Devi ricordare ... testo di N.
Rastelli, musica di Nino
Casiroli ... dal film: "Le
sorprese del vagone letto."
© Casa Editrice "Nazionale"
Musicale, Milano; 15Oct46;
EF3228.

CASSADY, EZRA EUGENE, 1916-
I'm always thinking of you; by
Ezra Eugene Cassady. © Shelby
Music Publishing Co., Detroit;
12Dec46; EP11123. For voice
and piano, with guitar diagrams
and chord symbols.

[CASSARD, EMMANUEL]
Vent du ciel ... paroles de René
Gonot, musique de Manuel del
Munte [pseud.] © Éditions
Musicales Nuances, Paris;
15Dec46; EF5482.

CASSEN, EDDIE.
How lucky you are; words by
Desmond O'Connor, music by
Eddie Cassen. © Edward
Kassner Music Co., ltd.,
London; 11Dec46; EF4693.

CASTELLANI, LEANDER, 1885-
Olenka ... Billy ... [by] L.
Castellani ... [for] piano
accordion solo. New York,
O. Di Bella Music Co. ©
Onofrio Di Bella, New York;
15Apr47; EP14306.

CASTELNUOVO-TEDESCO, MARIO.
Candide; six illustrations for
the novel by Voltaire. ©
Delkas Music Publishing Co.,
Los Angeles; 22Apr47; EP6842.
For piano solo.

Jock of Hazeldean; for chorus
of mixed voices with piano
acc., [by] Mario Castelnuovo-
Tedesco, [words by Sir Walter
Scott] © Galaxy Music Corp.,
New York; 12May47; EP6896.

CASTILLO, CATULO.
Organito de la tarde ... versos de
José González Castillo, música
de Catulo Castillo. © Editorial
Julio Korn, Buenos Aires; 7Feb39;
EF5606.

CASTILLO, JUAN P
No me jures ... letra y música
de José Servidio y Juan P.
Castillo. © Editorial Argentina
de Música Internacional, s. de
r., ltd., Buenos Aires; 30Dec46;
EF5215.

CASTILLO, NICANDRO.
El chichihua y La calandria ...
letra y música de Nicandro
Castillo. © Promotora Hispano
Americana de Música, s.a.,
Mexico; 24Apr47; EF3204-3205.

El cuerudo ... letra y música de
Nicandro Castillo. © Pro-
motora Hispano americana de
Música, s.a., Mexico; 24Apr47;
EF3213.

CASTLE, JERRY.
You're crying for the moon; words
by Ted Donofrio [and] Louis
Menaker, music by Jerry Castle.
© Grimes Music Publishers,
Philadelphia; 15Mar47; EP12918.

CASTRO, ARMANDO.
Cosó, cosó, cosó ... English words
by Joe Davis, Spanish words and
music by Armando Castro. ©
Caribbean Music, inc., New York;
28Apr47; EF3958.

Mary Ann ... English words by Joe
Davis, Spanish words by Jaime
Yamin, music by Armando Castro.
© Caribbean Music, inc., New
York; on English & Spanish
words; 28Oct46; EP11227.

El papylon. (Pretty butterfly)
... English words by Joe Davis,
Spanish words and music by
Armando Castro. © Caribbean
Music, inc., New York; 12May47;
EP14220.

Take me, take me! ... English
words by Joe Davis, Spanish
words by Jaime Yamin, music
by Armando Castro. © Caribbean Music, inc., New York;
23Jun47; EP15147.

CATALANO, ANGELA, 1933-
L'altalena della bambola ... per
pianoforte, [by] Angela
Catalano. © Angela Catalano,
Roma; 20Apr45; EF3771.

[CATSOS, NICHOLAS A]
You had your say (now I'll have
mine); words and music by
Tom Fowler and Garet Romero,
[pseud.] © Peer International
Corp., New York; 24Apr47;
EP14237.

CAYMMI, DORIVAL.
Marina ... De Dorival Caymmi.
© E. S. Mangione, Editor,
Sao Paulo, Brasil; 12Mar47;
EF4138. For piano solo, with
words. Portuguese words.

Soy bahiano. (Eu sou baiano)
... Letra en español de
Clotilde Arias, letra en
portugués y música de
Dorival Caymmi, [piano
arrangement by Domenico
Savino] © Robbins Music
Corp., New York; on Spanish
words and piano arrangement;
21Feb47; EP12389.

CEGLIE, COSIMO DI.
Oi Marf ... parole di Nisa, musica
di C. di Ceglie. Milano, Alfa
Leonardi. © Edizioni Leonardi,
Milan; 11Nov41; EF4810. Piano-
conductor score (orchestra, with
words) and parts.

Su con la vita ... testo di C.
Deani, musica di C. di Ceglie.
© Edizioni Casiroli, s.a.r.l.,
Milano; 15Jun46; EF3793.
Piano-conductor score
(orchestra, with words) and
parts.

CEGLIE-OLIVIERI, DI.
Boogie woogie ... testo e musica
di Di Ceglie-Olivieri. (In Un
sorriso e 20 canzoni. p. 6-7)
© Edizioni Leonardi, s.a.r.l.,
Milano; 15Jul45; EF4912. For
voice and piano.

CEIGA, GEORGE E
Life has loveliness to sell; [by]
George E. Ceiga, [words by]
Sara Teasdale. © Clayton F.
Summy Co., Chicago; 3Feb47;
EP11853. Score: SA and piano.

CEIGA, GEORGE E arr.
Pedal tunes for the Hammond student;
based on familiar melodies, by
George Ceiga. © Clayton F. Summy
Co., Chicago; 10Mar47; EP12549.

CEKOW, A. T., pseud. See
Travnicek, André.

CERNKOVICH, RUDOLPH, 1889-
Bouquet of Croatian folk songs.
(Strucak hrvatskih pukkih
pjesama) Combined & arr. by
Rudolph Cernkovich. © Rudolph
Cernkovich, Bradley, Mich.; on
arrangement; 7Mar47; EP12747.
Parts: string orchestra.

Golden waltz ... medley ... com-
bined & arr. by Rud. Cornkovich.
© Rudolph Cornkovich, Bradley,
Mich.; on arrangement; 3Feb47;
EP12651. Parts: string orhhestra.

24

CERNKOVICH, RUDOLPH. Cont'd.
Pjesmu ti pjevam. (I'm singing this song to you); new version & arrangement by Rud. Cernkovich. © Rudolph Cernkovich, Bradley, Mich.; on 3rd verse & arrangement; 1Feb47; EP11991. Parts: string orchestra.

CERNKOVICH, RUDOLPH, 1889- arr.
Famous sounds from the operas ... selected, combined & arr. by Rud. Cernkovich. © Rudolph Cernkovich, Bradley, Mich.; 30Apr47; EP14349. Parts: string orchestra.

Honolulu march ... arr. by Rud. Cernkovich. © Rudolph Cernkovich, Bradley, Mich.; on arrangement; 7Feb47; EP12649. Parts: string orchestra.

Od Naŧega rastanka. (Since we parted); words and arrangement by Rud. Cernkovich. © Rudolph Cernkovich, Bradley, Mich.; on words and arrangement; 7May47; EP14623. Parts: orchestra. Croatian words.

Oj, jesenske duge noŧi! (O, long autumn nights!) ... Mande, lijpa mande! [Pretty Magdalene!] [ed. & arr. by Rud. Cernkovich, Bradley, Mich.; on arrangement; 2May47; EP14624. Parts: orchestra. Croatian words.

CERNKOVICH, RUDOLPH, 1889- ed. and arr.
"Nene mlada oženiŧe" ... (They married me young) Ed. & arr. by Rud. Cernkovich. © Rudolph Cernkovich, Bradley, Mich.; on arrangement & 8th, 12th & 13th verses; 21Jan47; EP12469. Croatian words.

CHABRIER, EMMANUEL.
España; [by] Chabrier, themes from the rhapsody transcribed for the pianoforte by Henry Geehl. London, Enoch & Sons (Proprietors: E. Ashdown, ltd.) © Edwin Ashdown, ltd., London; on arrangement; 27Dec46; EP4980.

Prélude pastoral ... pour orchestre symphonique, [by] Emmanuel Chabrier, transcription pour piano à deux mains d'après l'orchestre par Gustave Samazeuilh. Paris, L. de Lacour, Editions Costallat. © Lucien de Lacour, Paris; on transcription; 30Nov46; EP3649.

CHADWICK, NORMA.
Song of the Armored division; arr. by Ruth L. Leathe, words and music by Norma Chadwick. © Cine-Mart Music Publishing Co., Hollywood, Calif.; 1Nov46; EP11938.

CHAIKOVSKIĬ, PETR IL'ICH, 1840-1893.
(Concerto, piano, no.1) Theme from Tschaikowsky's concerto no. 1. [Op. 23. Piano arrangement by Hugo Frey] © Hamilton S. Gordon, inc., New York; on arrangement; 27Jan47; EP13320. For piano solo.

Cossack's song; trepak from "The nut cracker suite," [by] P. I. Tschaikowsky. Arranged for chorus of men's voices by Lucy A. Alexander, English text by L. A. A. © The H. W. Gray Co., inc., New York; on arrangement & English words; 28Feb47; EP12401.

Fantasy overture, Romeo and Juliet; by Peter I. Tchaikovsky, adapted for piano solo by Albert Marland. © Chappell & Co., ltd., London; on adaptation; 14Mar47; EP5476.

Humoresque, by Tschaikowsky. [Op. 10, no. 2. Arr. by Victor Ambroise] © Lawrence Wright Music Co., ltd., London; on arrangement; 7May47; EP3259. For piano solo.

A legend; words by Alfred Wheeler, [music by] Tschaikowsky. Op. 54, no. 5. © Allan & Co., pty. ltd., Melbourne, Australia; on words; 16Sep46; EP3089. For voice and piano.

Legend (Long, long ago); S.A.T.B., [by] P. Tschaikowsky, anthem and concert version by Noble Cain, [text by N.C.] © Belwin, inc., New York; on arrangement; 31Dec46; EP11223.

The life of Tchaikovsky; first selection of famous Tchaikovsky melodies ... arr. by Victor Ambroise. © Lawrence Wright Music Co., ltd., London; on arrangement; 31Oct46; EP4859. For piano solo, with chord symbols.

Potito suite ... from Op. 39. By Peter Tschaikowsky, arr. ... by Robert Cray. © Edward B. Marks Music Corp., New York; on arrangement; 30Dec46; EP11316. Condensed score (band) and parts.

Pilgrim's song; poem by Tolstoi, English version by Arthur E. Ward; [music by] Peter Ilyitch Tchaikovsky, arr. by Arthur E. Ward. © Harold Flammer, inc., New York; on arrangement; 4Nov46; EP10833. Score: chorus (SA) and piano.

Romance; [by] Peter I. Tschaikowsky. Op. 5. Arr. by Sholom Secunda. © Broadcast Music, inc., New York; on orchestration; 16Dec46; EP11836. Piano-conductor score (orchestra) and parts.

Sleeping beauty; by Peter I. Tschaikowsky ... [words by Elsie Jean, pseud., arr. by Hugo Frey. © Hamilton S. Gordon, inc., New York; on arrangement and words; 11Jun47; EP15060. For piano solo, with words.

Song to the forest; words by Louis Lavater, music by Tschaikowsky. c1945. © Allan & Co., pty. ltd., Melbourne, Australia; on words; 1Dec46; EP3193.

(Symphony, no. 5) Themes from Tschaikowsky's Fifth; arr. by Frederic Fay Swift. © Pro Art Publications, New York; on arrangement; 3Feb47; EP11755. Piano-conductor score (orchestra) and parts.

(Symphony, no. 5) Valse from Symphony, no. 5 in E minor; by Tschaikowsky, arr. as piano solo by King Palmer. © William Paxton & Co., ltd., London; on arrangement; 27Dec46; EP3641.

Theme from Tschaikowsky's concerto no. 1. See his Concerto, piano, no. 1.

Themes from Tschaikowsky's Fifth. See his Symphony, no. 5.

Three pieces from "Album for children"; transcribed [by] Quinto Maganini] © Edition Musicus-New York, inc., New York; on transcription; 23Oct46; EP13722. Score (violin and piano) and part.

Tschaikowsky's Music you remomber; comp. and ed. by Harold Pottor and Eddy Dorr. © Manhattan Publications, Now York; 6Dec46; EP11759. In part for piano solo, in part for voice and piano, with chord symbols.

Valse from Symphony no. 5. See his Symphony, no. 5.

Waltz of the flowers, from the Nutcracker suite; by Tchaikovsky, arr. for piano by James Palmeri. © G. Schirmer, inc., New York; 16Nov46; EP12878.

CHAILLEY, JACQUES, 1910- ed.
Cinquante-huit canons; réunis, recueillis ou adaptés par Jacques Chailley. Paris, Rouart, Lerolle & Cie. © Salabert inc., New York; 31Dec46; on compilation & adaptation; EP3472. Melody and words.

CHAIROPOULOS, CHRISTOS KONSTANTINOS.
Den peirazei; [by] Chr. K. Chairopoulou, [Athens] Ekdoseis Ch. K. Chairopoulou. © "S.O.P.E." Copyright Protection Society, Athens; 5Mar44; EP3229. For voice and piano.

Je parsi (Tha phygo) ... Paroles et musique de Ch. C. Cheropoulos. Athenai, Ekdoseis Gaïtanou [c1947] © Michael Gaetanos, Athens; 20Nov46; EP3129. For voice and piano.

Opou ki'an pas ... mousikē; Chr. Chairopoulou, stichoi: Mimē Traïphorou. Athēnai, Ekdoseis Gaïtanou. © Michael Gaetanos, Athens; 15Feb47; EP5541. For voice and piano.

CHAJES, JULIUS.
Rejoice in Zion. Sim'chu b'tzion ... words by Ben Yehuda, music by Julius' Chajes, for mixed voices (S.A.T.B.) © Transcontinental Music Corp., New York; 2Dec46; EP13324. Hebrew words (transliterated)

CHAMPAGNE, PAUL, 1866-
Chant des jeunes mineurs; de France; poésie de François Delcourt, musique de Paul Champagne. © Rouart Lerolle et Cie., Paris; 15Nov46; EP5192.

CHANEY, WILBUR CLIFFORD, arr.
How to play Hawaiian guitar by note in different keys. © Norman Music Publishing Co., Wilbur Clifford Chaney, sole owner, Detroit; on compilation & arrangement; 28Dec46; EP6232.

CHANLER, THEODORE, 1902-
The second joyful mystery ... [by] Theodore Chanler. © Associated Music Publishers, inc., New York; 23Jun47; EP15263. Two scores for piano 1-2.

CHANSLOR, HAL, 1903-
Dreaming dreams; words by Helen Rotzell, music by Hal Chanslor. © Nordyke Publishing Co., Los Angeles; 5Mar47; EP13250.

Home, give me a home; words by Emil C. Hasenauer and William T. Farnsworth, music by Hal Chanslor. © Cine-Mart Music Publishing Co., Hollywood, Calif.; 30Dec46; EP14210.

Just to be with you tonight; words by Nora Butler, music by Hal Chanslor. © Nordyke Publishing Co., Los Angeles; 5Mar47; EP13266.

CHANSLOR, HAL. Cont'd.
Let me take a taste of your sweet
lips; words by John L. Adams,
music by Hal Chanslor. [c1946]
© Whitehouse Publishing Co.,
Hollywood, Calif.; 2Jan47;
EP11985.
Moonlight dreams; words by John
Hudson & Fred L. Pickard, music
by Hal Chanslor. © Nordyke
Publishing Co., Los Angeles;
15Jun46; EP11994.
My lesson learned; lyrics by
Jasper Bond, music by Hal
Chanslor. © Jasper Bond,
San Fernando, Calif.; 8Apr47;
EP13729.
Playing at love; words by Mrs.
Auburn Glover, music by Hal
Chanslor. [c1946] © White-
house Publishing Co., Hollywood,
Calif.; 2Jan47; EP11984.
So sez I, sez I, the moon;
words by Leslie Smith,
music by Hal Chanslor. ©
Nordyke Publishing Co.,
Los Angeles; 7Mar47; EP13294.

CHANTRIER, A
Il était une fois ... [by] A.
Chantrier. © Ste. ame. fse.
Chappell, Paris; 16May47;
EP3912. Piano-conductor score
(orchestra), and parts.

CHAPLIN, SAUL.
Anniversary song. See his The
Jolson story.
(The Jolson story) Anniversary
song, featured in ... "The
Jolson story" ... by Al Jolson
and Saul Chaplin, based on a
theme by Ivanovici. Piano
accordion arr. by Pietro Deiro.
© Mood Music Co., inc., New
York; on arrangement; 29May47;
EP14774.
(The Jolson story) Anniversary
song ... from the ... picture,
"The Jolson story," by Al
Jolson and Saul Chaplin, based
on a theme by Ivanovici, arr.
by Paul Yoder. © Mood Music
Co., inc., New York; on
arrangement; 19May47; EP14743. -
Condensed score (band) and
parts.
(The Jolson story) Anniversary
song ... from the ... picture
"The Jolson story," by Al
Jolson and Saul Chaplin.
Based on a theme by Ivanovici,
arr. by Jimmy Dale. © Mood
Music Co., inc., New York; on
arrangement; 16May47; EP14433.
Piano-conductor score (orches-
tra) and parts.

CHAPMAN, JACK.
Yes or no; by Jack Chapman. © Gate
Music Co., New York; 4Feb47;
EP12265. Piano-conductor score
(orchestra) and parts.

CHAPMAN, MARION CONKLIN.
O Lord, support us all the day
long ... for mixed voices, a
cappella, Cardinal Newman's
prayer, [music by] Marion
Conklin Chapman. © Oliver
Ditson Co., Philadelphia;
31Mar47; EP13206.

CHAPPELEAR, LEON.
I've learned my lesson; words and
music by Jimmie Davis and Leon
Chappelear, [and All I have is
love; words and music by Clyde
Coffey] © Peer International
Corp., New York; 13Feb47;
EP12228, 12230.

CHARDON, JULIEN, 1909-   See also
Lutèce, Jean, pseud.

Brumes; paroles de Louis
Hennevé, musique de Jean
Lutèce [pseud.] © Ste. ame.
Fse. Chappell, Paris; 28Feb47;
EP5419.
Madame de Sévigné; paroles de
Francis Blanche, musique de
Jean Lutèce [pseud.] ©
Éditions Vianelly, Paris;
27Dec46; EP3714.
Utrillo; paroles de Jacques Larue
[pseud.], musique de Jean Lutèce
[pseud.] Paris, Salabert.
© Salabert, inc., New York;
28Dec46; EP3509.

CHARETTE, WILFRID, 1895-   arr.
Corbleur, eh, marion! Mélodie
populaire avec harmonisation
de Wilfrid Charette, arr. pour
le sketch de folklore de L. de
Montigny (L'Epi rouge) Lachute,
P. Q., Parnasse Musical. ©
Éditions A. Passio, Lachute,
Qué., Can.; on arrangement;
1Apr47; EP5569. For voice and
piano, with violin obbligato.

CHARLES, HUGH.
A little bit more besides; words
and music by Desmond O'Connor &
Hugh Charles. © Noel Gay Music
Co., ltd., London; 6Mar47;
EP5459.

CHARLO.
Adios ... amor! ...Letra de Lito
Bayardo, música de Charlo. ©
Editorial Argentina de Música
Internacional, s. de r., ltd.,
Buenos Aires; 30Dec46; EF5549.

CHARNEY, LUCIEN, 1910-
Absent; paroles et musique de
Lucien Charney. © Lucien Charney
(Lucien Tchernaïa), Enghien-les-
Bains, France; 31Oct45; EF5511.
Près de la petite source; paroles
et musique de Lucien Charney.
© Lucien Charney (Lucien
Tchernaïa), Enghienles-Bains,
France; 31Oct45; EF5324.
For voice and piano.
Souvenir; paroles et musique de
Lucien Charney. © Lucien
Charney (Lucien Tchernaïa),
Enghien-Les-Bains, France;
31Oct45; EF5540.

CHARNOPH, CHARLES, 1878-
Old musician and his guitar; words
& music by Charles Charnoph.
© Charles Charnoph, Phillips,
Wis.; 14Jan47; EP11760.

CHARPENTIER, MARC ANTOINE.
Hail Thee. Ave Regina ... English
version by Hugh Ross (after Edward Caswall) [In Ross, Hugh,
arr. Sacred choruses for
women's or girls' voices.
p. 43-48] © G. Schirmer, inc.,
New York; on arrangement;
30Sep46; EP9784.
Panis angelicus ... words adapted
from the Catholic Encyclopaedia
by Hugh Ross. [In Ross, Hugh,
arr. Sacred choruses for
women's or girls' voices.
p. 136-140) © G. Schirmer, inc.,
New York; on arrangement;
30Sep46; EP9793.

CHATILLON, E
Le mystère de Lyon et de Notre
Dame; 7 choeurs à 4 voix mixtes
[and orchestra] Texte de J.
Folliet et J. Pallaix.
© Musique Erjac, Lyon, France;
31Oct40; EF599. Score: solo
voices and chorus, without the
accompaniment.

CHAULIAC, Léo.
Marie Marie; paroles de Charles
Trenet, musique de Léo Chauliac.
© Éditions Vianelly, Paris;
18Apr47; EF5640.

CHAUVET, PIERRE RENÉ.   See
Chauvet, René.

CHAUVET, RENÉ, 1879-
Confidences d'amour; pour piano,
[by] René Chauvet. © Éditions
Durand & Cie., Paris; 31Oct46;
EF5177.

CHAVEZ, CARLOS, 1899-
Al Fredome; for full chorus of
mixed voices, a cappella,
[words by] John Barbour ...
modern English by Willis
Wager, [music by] Carlos Chávez.
© G. Schirmer, inc., New
York; 24Mar47; EP13147.
A woman is a worthy thing; for
four-part chorus of mixed voices,
a cappella, [words] anonymous;
15th Century [modern English
by Willis Wager, music by]
Carlos Chávez. © G. Schirmer,
inc., New York; 24Mar47;
EP13146.

[CHEATHAM, ADOLPHUS ANTHONY] 1905-
Ad-lib chord reading; [by A. A.
Cheatham] © Adolphus Anthony
Cheatham, New York; pt. 2,
19Oct46; EP11545.

CHEKLER, EDWARD, 1917-
Tu dis, demain ... paroles de
Gisèle Reille [pseud.], musique
de Edward Chekler. © Éditions
Musicales Nuances; 15Dec46;
EF3485.

CHENETTE, ED.
The pioneer ... by Ed Chenette.
© Pro Art Publications, New
York; 3Feb47; EP11753. Con-
densed score (band) and parts.

CHENOWETH, WILBUR.
Puppets on parade; for full
chorus of mixed voices, with
piano acc., [words by] Alice
Grainger, [music by] Wilbur
Chenoweth. © G. Schirmer,
inc., New York; on words and
arrangement; 24Mar47; Er13121.

CHEREPNIN, ALEKSANDR NIKOLAEVICH, 1899-
Mouvement perpétuel ... [by] Alex-
andre Tcherepnine. © Durand et
Cie., Paris; 15Jun46; EF5142.
Score (violin and piano) and part.

CHEREPNIN, NIKOLAI NIKOLAEVICH,
1873-1945.
Praise ye the name of the Lord;
for four-part chorus of men's
voices (a cappella) [by]
Nikolai Nikolaievitch Tcherepnin
... Arranged by Gwynn S. Bemont.
[Words] from the liturgy of the
Russian Orthodox Church, tr.
and adapted by the Rev. Walter
Williams. © E. C. Schirmer
Music Co., Boston; on arrange-
ment; 22Apr47; EP13854.

CHERNIS, JAY.
Crying; lyric by Barney Ross,
music by Jay Chernis. © Green-
wich Music Co., inc., New York;
14May47; EP13858.

CHERUBINI, LUIGI.
Like as the Father ... S. A. B., by
Luigi Cherubini, arr. by the Krones,
Beatrice and Max. © Belwin, inc.,
New York; on arrangement; 21Jan47;
EP11357.

CHIAFFARELLI, ALBERTE, arr.
Go down, Moses; orchestral arrangement by Alberte Chiaffarelli, from
W. C. Handy's arrangement for
military band. New York, Handy
Brothers Music Co. inc. © William
C. Handy, New York, on orchestration;
27Feb46; EP12056. Piano-conductor
score (Orchestra) and parts.

26

CHILDE, ROBERT S   1899-   arr.
The first Noel; S.A.T.B., arr.
Robert Childe. © Neil A. Kjos
Music Co., Chicago; on arrange-
ment; 19Jun47; EP15190.

[CHILDERS, LEMUEL] 1899-   arr.
After dark; [arr. by Lemuel
Childers] © Society for the
Preservation and Encouragement
of Barber Shop Quartet Singing
in America, inc., Detroit; on
arrangement; 13Mar46; EP13595.
Close score: TTBB.

CHILDREN'S DAY HELPER. Winona Lake,
Ind., Rodeheaver Hall-Mack Co.
© The Rodeheaver Co., Winona
Lake, Ind.; no.47, 1Apr47;
EP13498. No.47 composed and
compiled by Bentley D. Ackley.

CHILENO, JORGE, pseud. See
Read, George.

CHIOCCHIO, UMBERTO.
Balla il boogie woogie ... testo
di R. Morbelli, musica di Umberto
Chiocchio. Cose da nulla ...
testo e musica di Clemse. ©
Edizioni Leonardi, s.a.r.l.,
Milano; 18Jun46; EP4908. Piano-
conductor score (orchestra, with
words), and parts.

CHITTENDEN, EDDIE.
I'm falling in love with you;
[by] Art Petivan and Eddie
Chittenden, [arr. by Jos C.
Schramm. c1947] © Sunset
Music Publishers, New Orleans;
26Dec46; EP11076. For voice
and piano, with guitar diagrams
and chord symbols.

Keep your mind on what you're
doin' (and let my boogie alone);
words and music by Art Petivan
& Eddie Chittenden, arr. by
Jos. C. Schramm. © Sunset
Music Publications, New Orleans;
7Apr47; EP13661.

CHITTISON, HERMAN.
Original piano solos; [by]
Herman Chitison. © Burke &
Van Heusen, inc., New York;
3Jan47; EP14283.

CHLUBNA, OSVALD, 1893-
Nokturno; [by] Osvald Chlubna.
Op. 36. © Hudební Matice
Umělecké Besedy, Praha, Czechoslo-
vakia; 3Nov43; EF4955. For piano
solo.

CHOBILLON, CHARLES.
(O.N.U.I) Prisonnier de l'amour;
paroles de Lucien Rimels, musique de Charles Chobillon ...
chanté dans la revue du concert
Mayol "O. N. U.I" © Ste. ame.
fse. Chappell, Paris; 22Jan47;
EF5100. Melody and chord
symbols, with words.

Prisonnier de l'amour ... paroles
de Lucien Rimels, musique de
Charles Chobillon. © Ste. ame.
fse. Chappell, Paris; 6May47;
EF3655.

[CHOISSER, JOSEPH DANIEL] 1925-
Pepito Santa Cruz; (Up in my
window) By Danny Hart [pseud.,
arr. by University Music Co.]
© University Music Co.,
Hollywood, Calif.; 9May47;
EP14470. For voice and
piano, with chord symbols.

Surely, I'm sure of Shirley;
by Danny Hart [pseud., arr.
by University Music Co.]
© University Music Co.,
Hollywood, Calif.; 9May47;
EP14467. For voice and piano,
with chord symbols.

A trip to Hollywood; by Danny Hart,
[pseud.] [arr. by University
Music Co.] © University Music
Co., Hollywood, Calif.; 9May47;
EP14469. For voice and piano,
with chord symbols.

CHOPIN, FRYDERYK FRANCISZEK, 1810-1849.
Chopin-Schaum; for piano ... bio-
graphical continuity by Nora
Schaum, musical adaptation by
John W. Schaum. © Belwin, inc.,
New York; on arrangement &
compilation; bk. 1, 28Jan47;
EP11682.

Etude in E major and Butterfly
study, by Chopin. [Op. 10,
no.3 & Op. 25, arr. by Victor
Ambroise] © Lawrence Wright
Music Co., ltd., London; on arrangement; 16May47; EF3321.

Everybody's favorite Chopin album
... ed. by Samuel Spivak. ©
Amsco Music Publishing Co.,
New York; 14Nov45; EP696. For
piano solo.

Nocturne; [by] Fr. Chopin.
Op. 9, no. 2 ... (arr't [by]
Robert L. Bedell) © Parnasse
Musical, Lachute, Que., Can.,
on arrangement; 1May46; EF4857.
Score (violoncello and piano)
and part.

Polonaise; [by Frederic Chopin,
arr. by] Robert Whitford. Erie,
Pa., Robert Whitford Publications.
© Robert H. Whitford, Erie, Pa.;
on arrangement; 28Feb47; EP6625.
For piano solo.

(Polonaise) Chopin's polonaise.
Op. 53. Simplified [arr. by
Hugo Frey] © Hamilton S. Gordon,
inc., New York; on arrangement;
27Jan47; EP13319. For piano
solo.

Polonaise in A flat; [by] Chopin,
arr. for easy piano solo by
Mark Ashley [pseud.] © Century
Music Publishing Co., New York;
on arrangement; 31May47;
EP14733.

Polonaise in A♭ ... transcribed
... by Henry Sopkin. © Mills
Music, inc., New York; on
arrangement; 28Dec45; EF716.
Piano-conductor score (orchestra)
and parts.

(Polonaise, piano, op. 53) Melody
from Polonaise (A flat major.
Op. 53) for piano solo, [by]
Frédéric Chopin, arr. by William
Priestley. © Theodore Presser Co.,
Philadelphia; on arrangement;
28Dec46; EP10888.

The raindrop; (Raindrop etude,
op. 28, no. 15) For chorus of
soprano I & II, and alto, [by]
Frederic Chopin, arr. by Robert
W. Gibb. [Words by] Mary B.
Austin. © The B. F. Wood Music
Co., Boston; on words & arrange-
ment; 21Apr47; EP13815.

Rondos; [by] Chopin. [Ed. de
travail par Alfred Cortot]
Paris, Salabert. © Salabert,
inc., New York; on arrangement;
31Oct46; EF5295. For piano
solo.

CHOVEAUX, NICHOLAS.
Three pieces ... by Nicholas
Choveaux. © Alfred Lengnick
& Co., ltd., London; 23Dec46;
EF3125. Score (violin and
piano) and part.

CHRISTENSEN, AXEL W   1881-
Axel Christensen's break studies...
associate arr., Anita Sampson.
© Axel W. Christensen, Chicago;
folio C, 18Nov46; EP12561. For
piano solo.

CHRISTIANSEN, ERIC.
(Fyrtøjet) Sangene til Eventyrfilmen
Fyrtøjet ... Tekst: Victor Skaarup,
Musik: Eric Christiansen og Vil-
fred Kjaer. [c1945] © Nyt
Dansk Musikforlag, Copenhagen;
15Apr46; EF3106-EF3112. Contents.-
En rask Soldat.- Paa min Faerden
gennem Verden.- Som Fuglen i'
Juret.- Skomagerdrengen.- Uh-Huh.-
Vi drikker, vi drikker.- Hjerternes
Vals.

CHRISTIE, CATHERINE ALLISON, 1896-
We thank Thee; two-part chorus
[by] Catherine Christie.
© The Raymond A. Hoffman Co.,
Chicago; 15Aug46; EP12658.

Axel Christensen's Break studies
for piano ... Anita Sampson,
associate & arr. © Axel W.
Christensen, Chicago; no.69,
7Sep46; no.70, 18Nov46; no.71,
1Feb47; no.72, 10Mar47;
EP12559-12560, 12557-12558.

CHRISTMAN, THEODORE L   1910-
Jesus, dear and precious Saviour;
[words by] Helen Mast, [music by]
Theodore L. Christman. (In Church
of the Nazarene. Michigan District.
Nazarene Young Peoples Society.
Choruses of the N. Y. P. S. p.68)
© Michigan District, Nazarene
Young Peoples Society, Flint,
Mich.; 25Jul46; EP13087. Close
score: SATB.

CHRISTY, BOB.
Me go where you go, amigo; words
and music by Andy Razaf, Chas.
S. Brower and Bob Christy. ©
Bob Miller, inc., New York;
30Dec46; EP10737.

CHURCHILL, SAVANNAH.
I want to be loved (but only by you);
by Savannah Churchill. © Record
Music Corp., New York; 14Feb47;
EP12137. For voice and piano, with
chord symbols.

CIESZYKOWSKI, L   A
Boga rodzica najświętsza panno;
[by L, A. Cieszykowski, and]
Bridal song ... arr. by L. A.
Cieszykowski. © Professional
Music Publishers, Chicago;
26Apr44; EP6758, 6757.

CILIBERTI, ANTHONY.
Brunilde ... testo italiano di
Arrigo, musica di Anthony
Ciliberti. (In Un sorriso e
20 canzoni. p. 34-35) ©
Edizioni Leonardi, s.a.r.l.,
Milano; 7Oct45; EP4926.
For voice and piano; Italian
and English words.

CIMAROSA, DOMENICO.
The impresario; [overture by]
Cimarosa, arr. and ed. by Adam
Carse. © Augener, ltd., London;
on arrangement & editing; 30Oct46;
EF3101. Score: orchestra.

CIOFFI, GIUSEPPE.
Chiomadoro ... musica di Giuseppe
Cioffi, arrang. di A. Giacomazzi.
Lontano ... (dagli occhi e dal
cuore) ... musica di Mario
Verrua. © Edizioni Leonardi,
Milano; 30Dec46; EP5270. Piano-
conductor score (orchestra,
with words), and parts.

Has anyone seen my beautiful Rosa?
Dove sta Zazà? ... English words
by "Petronius" [pseud.], original
version by R. Cutolo, music by G.
Cioffi. © Ascherberg, Hopwood &
Crew, ltd., London; on English
words; 31Dec46; EF4820. For voice
and piano, with chord symbols; melody
also in tonic sol-fa notation.

CIOFFI, GIUSEPPE. Cont'd.
Has anyone 'seen my beautiful
Rosa? "Dove sta Zaza?" ...
words by "Petronius" [pseud.],
music by Giuseppe Cioffi, arr.
by Ronald Binge [and Sing;
words by Clarkson Rose, music
by Charles Tovey, arr. by
Ronald Binge] © Ascherberg,
Hopwood & Crew, 1td., London;
on arrangement; 19May47;
EF3667-3668. Piano-conductor
score (orchestra, with English
words), and parts.

I nuovi successi del maestro
Cioffi; compilatore, G. Pisano,
poesie: di G. Pisano, N. de
Lutio, B. U. Canetti, L. Cioffi,
ecc. © Edizioni Musicali
Cioffi, Naples; 4Dec45; EF5509.

I nuovi successi del maestro Cioffi,
1946-47 ... testo di N. de Lutio,
G. Pisano [and others] ... musica
di G. Cioffi, A. Mazzucchi ...
[and] M. Coppola. Napoli,
Edizioni Musicali Cioffi. ©
Italian Book Co., New York;
2Dec46; EF4870. For voice and
piano.

One happy hour with you. ('N'
ora 'e felicita') Words by
Gigi Pisano, music by Giuseppe
Cioffi, English lyric by Jan
King [pseud.] © Keith, Prowse
& Co., 1td., London; on
English lyric; 22May47;
EF3348.

Se il grano potesse parlar;
versi di G. Pisano, musica di
G. Cioffi. © Italian Book Co.,
New York; 30Apr47; EF4680.

CIRELLI, LAZAR.
Fascinating polka; arr. by E.
Clinton Keithley, words and
music by Lazar Cirelli. ©
Puritan Publishing Co., inc.,
Chicago; 9Oct46; EP12250.

CLAPP, SUNNY.
Girl of my dreams; by Sunny Clapp.
Trio arrangement ... by Henry
Sopkin. © Mills Music, inc.,
New York; on arrangement;
24Jan47; EP6650. Score (violin,
violoncello and piano) and parts.

CLARK, AARON A   1907-
Alarm clock blues; words by Philip
A. Montroy, music by Aaron A.
Clark. © Philip Arthur Montroy,
Jennings, La.; 3Apr47; EP14107.

[CLARK, C   VAN NESS] 1894-
Filipino baby; by Billy Cox and
Clarke Van Ness, [pseud.] arr.
for Hawaiian, electric and
plectrum guitar (note and
diagram) [by the Oahu staff,
c1946] © Shapiro, Bernstein &
Co., inc., New York; on arrangement; 27Jan47; EP11827.

CLARK, COTTONSEED.
From now on; by Ike Cargill and
Cottonseed Clark. [c1946] ©
Tex Ritter Music Publications,
inc., New York; 8Jan47; EP11081.
For voice and piano with chord
symbols.

CLARK, JAMES.
Sage brush shuffle; by James
Clark ... piano arrangement by
Dick Kent. © Peer Inter-
national Corp., New York;
15May47; EP14574. For voice
and piano, with chord symbols.

CLARK, NELL.
Nobody but you; by Odell Johnson
and Noll Clark, North Hollywood, Calif., Musoco Music.
© Odell Johnson, Bakersfield,
Calif.; 17Jan47; EP11522. For
voice and piano, with chord
symbols.

CLARK, PALMER, 1893-
South American serenade; for three-
part chorus [by] Palmer Clark,
arr. by Don Wilson. © The
Raymond A. Hoffman Co., Chicago;
on arrangement; 10Aug46;
EP12656.

South American serenade; for two-
part chorus [by] Palmer Clark,
arr. by Don Wilson. © The
Raymond A. Hoffman Co., Chicago;
on arrangement; 10Aug46; EP12655.

CLARK, RAY.
A girl like you; by Ray Clark. ©
Ray Clark, Rayne, La.; 26Dec46;
EP10728. For voice and piano,
with chord symbols.

CLARKSON, FRED.
Yes, it's true what they say about
Dixie; words & music by Fred
Clarkson. © Nordyke Publishing
Co., Los Angeles; 10Mar45;
EP10860. For voice and piano.

CLARO FUMERO, J.
Machuquillo con puerco ...
música de J. Claro Fumero,
letra de Carlos Serrano.
© Peer International Corp.,
New York; 30Dec46; EF5434.
Parts: orchestra.

CLAYTON, BUCK, 1911-
A Brooklyn breeze ... by Buck
Clayton and Benny Goodman, arr.
by Buck Clayton. © Bregman,
Vocco and Conn, inc., New York;
14Feb47; EP12169. Piano-conductor score (orchestra) and
parts.

Celebrity hop ... by Buck Clayton and Benny Goodman, arr. by
Buck Clayton. © Bregman, Vocco
and Conn, inc., New York;
14Feb47; EP12168. Piano-conductor score (orchestra) and
parts.

Incognito ... by Buck Clayton
and Benny Goodman, arr. by
Buck Clayton. © Bregman,
Vocco and Conn, inc., New
York; 17Feb47; EP12156.
Piano-conductor score
(orchestra) and parts.

Subway squeeze ... by Buck Clayton and Benny Goodman, arr. by
Buck Clayton. © Bregman, Vocco
and Conn, inc., New York; 17Feb47;
EP12155. Piano-conductor score
(orchestra) and parts.

CLAYTON, NORMAN JOHN.
Heed now the voice; [by] Norman
J. Clayton. © Norman J. Clay-
ton, Malverne, N. Y.; 1Nov46;
EP11114. For 2 treble voices
and piano.

His love, like a sunbeam ... [words
and music by] Norman J. Clayton.
(In Moody Monthly. Chicago.
v.XLVII 1946/47, no.4, p. 309)
© Norman John Clayton, Malverne,
N. Y.; 9Dec46; EP6491. For 2
treble voices and piano.

CLAYTON, NORMAN JOHN, comp.
Low voice melodies ... comp. by
Norman J. Clayton. © Norman
J. Clayton, Malverne, N. Y.;
no.1, 31Dec46; EP10904.

Melodies of life; comp. by Norman
J. Clayton. Malverne, N. Y.,
Gospel Songs, inc. © Norman J.
Clayton, Malverne, N. Y.; 20Dec46;
EP11115. Hymns, with music.

CLERICI, ANTONIO, 1905-
[La par ona storia] Ti manderò
una cartolina di Milano, dalla
rivista "La par ona storia" ...
Parole di A. Clerici, musica di
A. Clerici e E. Storaci. ©
Carisch, s.a., Milan; 11Apr47;
EF3899. Melody and chord sym-
bols, with words.

Ti manderò una cartolina da Milano.
See his La par ona storia.

CLEVE, J   H   arr.
The Irwin Dash selection of serenades. © Irwin Dash Music Co.,
1td., London; on arrangement;
no. 1, 31Jan47; EF3153. For
piano solo.

CLOKEY, JOSEPH W
Agnus Dei; S.A., [by] Joseph W.
Clokey. © J. Fischer & Bro.,
New York; 27Mar47; EP6806.
English words:

God be in my head; S.A., [by]
Joseph W. Clokey. © J.
Fischer & Bro., New York;
27Mar47; EP6803.

Hail, Breath of Life; [by]
Joseph W. Clokey, [words by]
Venantius Fortunatus ... tr.
and freely adapted. © J.
Fischer, New York; 27Mar47;
EP6805. Score: chorus (SA)
and organ.

CLOSE, HARRY.
Au Tyrol; paroles de Teddy
Davis, musique de Harry
Close. © Teddy Davis, Paris;
1Mar47; EF3604.

CLYDE, TED.
Cupid on a shelf; words by
Gertrude Bales Qirdler, music
by Ted Clyde. © Nordyke Publishing Co., Los Angeles;
8Mar47; EP13244.

Fairest of the fair; words by
Hilton McCully, music by Ted
Clyde. © Nordyke Publishing
Co., Los Angeles; 5Mar47;
EP13548.

Home in Idaho; words by Mary
Edith Swinney, music by Ted
Clyde. [c1945] © Nordyke
Publishing Co., Los Angeles;
21Jun46; EP12721.

Just a sigh of love; words by
Frances Roth, [pseud.], music
by Ted Clyde. © Nordyke Publishing Co., Los Angeles;
5Mar47; EP13240.

Montana bound; words by Blanche
Barger, music by Ted Clyde.
© Nordyke Publishing Co., Los
Angeles; 7Mar47; EP13569.

Old fashion love; words by
Lyn Neal, music by Ted
Clyde. © Nordyke Publishing
Co., Los Angeles; 8Mar47;
EP13277.

One evening; words by Ann
Patereau, music by Ted
Clyde. © Nordyke Publish-
ing Co., Los Angeles; 8Mar47;
EP13276.

Sing a happy song and smile; words
by Christina B. Cheever, music
by Ted Clyde. © Nordyke Publishing Co., Los Angeles;
5Mar47; EP13265.

Sing a song of America; words by
Carl Ruppert, music by Ted
Clyde. © Nordyke Publishing
Co., Los Angeles; 21Mar47;
EP13538.

Two sweethearts; words by Mary
Coble, music by Ted Clyde.
© Nordyke Publishing Co.,
Los Angeles; 29Apr47; EP14793.

COATES, ERIC.
Sleepy lagoon; music by Eric
Coates, words by Jack Lawrence,
simplified teaching ed. for
piano, [arr. by Albert Sirmay]
© Chappell & Co., 1td., London;
on arrangement; 7Mar47; EP12679.

COBB, HAZEL.
My favorite tune; piano composition
with words, by Hazel Cobb. ©
Mills Music, inc., New York;
29May47; EP6947.

28

COBB, HAZEL. Cont'd.
Schoolmates; by Hazel Cobb. ©
Clayton F. Summy Co., Chicago;
26Dec46; EP11108. Two scores
for piano 1-2.

COBEN, CY.
How can I say I love you; by John
Jacob Loeb, Lewis Harris [and]
Cy Coben. © Mayfair Music
Corp., New York; 23Jun47; EP15248.
For voice and piano, with chord
symbols.

Why did I teach my girl to drive?
Words and music by John Jacob
Loeb and Cy Coben. © Mutual
Music Society, inc., New York;
14Apr47; EP13641.

COBLIN, KAY, 1915-
Hey! Mama, he's tryin' to kiss me
... Words ... by Nat Reich-
man, Nat Streeter [and] Kay
Coblin, [music by Joe Reichman
and Kay Coblin] © Royal Music
Corp., New York; 27Dec46;
EP15412.

COCCIARDI, FRANK, 1895-
Honeymoon; words and music by
Frank Cocciardi. © Frank
Cocciardi, Elmont, N. Y.;
23Apr47; EP13964.

COCHRANE, NICK.
Somebody stole my moustache cup;
words and music by Bernie
Williams and Nick Cochrane.
© Mills Music, inc., New
York; 19Apr45; EP6833.

COCKENPOT, FRANCINE.
Fleurs de mousse; 27 chansons
inédites de Francine Cockenpot; dessins de Guy Georget.
© Éditions du Seuil, Paris;
30Nov46; EF3633. For 1-4 voices.

Fleurs d'or; 30 chansons inédites de Francine Cockenpot;
dessins de G. Vallée. ©
Éditions du Seuil, Paris;
1Dec46; EF3632. For 1-3
voices.

CODEVILLA, PIERINO.
Tango habanera. Ramiro ... vom ...
komponisten P. Codevilla.
Mailand, Alfa Leonardi Musikverlag-
© Edizioni Leonardi, Milan;
10Jun46; EF4805. Piano-conductor
score (orchestra) and parts.

Uraguaya ... Tucuman ...vom
... komponisten P. Codevilla.
Mailand, Alfa Leonardi Musikverlag.
© Edizioni Leonardi, Milan;
10Jun46; EF4808. Piano-conductor
score (orchestra) and parts.

COEN, AUGUSTO.
Lagrimas de sangre. (Tears from
my heart) ... music and
Spanish lyrics by Augusto
Coen, English lyrics by
Roger Genger. © Bebe Music
Co., New York; 6May47; EF6889.

COFFIN, JANET ELIZABETH, 1926-
The rhubarb song; words by Francis
B. Coffin, music by Janet E.
Coffin. © Francis Burgess Coffin,
Newton Center, Mass.; 25Oct46;
EP11749.

COHEN, ETA, 1916-
The first-year violin method; by
Eta Cohen ... Pianoforte acc.
© William Paxton & Co., ltd.,
London; 27Dec46; EF3635.

COHN, ARTHUR.
Declamation and toccata ... [by]
Arthur Cohn. © Elkan-Vogel
Co., inc., Philadelphia;
6Dec46; EP11468. Score
(bassoon and piano) and part.

Hebraic study ... [by] Arthur
Cohn. © Elkan-Vogel Co.,
inc., Philadelphia; 6Dec46;
EF11469. Score (bassoon and
piano) and part.

COKE-JEPHCOTT, NORMAN.
Symphonic toccata; for organ by
Norman Coke-Jephcott. © The
H. W. Gray Co., inc., New
York; 30Apr47; EP14073.

COLDREY, ALBERT GEORGE JEFFERY, 1903-
Let us romance together. See his
Bandit prince.

COLE, A   L   1877-
Pathways in music; for the be-
ginning pianist, by A. L. Cole.
© Shattinger Piano & Music Co.,
St. Louis; 6May47; EP14231.

COLE, LOTTIE PITTMAN.
Beautiful Beckley; by Lottie
Pittman Cole. © Lottie Pittman Cole, Beckley, W. Va.;
26Dec46; EP10719. For voice
and piano, with chord symbols.

COLE (M.M.) PUBLISHING CO., comp.
Favorite songs; [words and music
by Billy Folger, Cliff Smith
and others, comp. by M. M.
Cole Publishing Co.] © M.
M. Cole Publishing Co., Chicago;
bk.2, 30Dec46; EP12925.

COLE, WILLIAM.
Harke, how the minstrils gin to
shrill aloud ... for six voices,
words from Epithalamion by
Edmund Spenser, music by William
Cole. © Novello & Co., ltd.,
London; 29Apr47; EP5634.

The rose-bud; part song for S. A.
T. B. (unaccompanied); words by
William Browne ... music by
William Cole. © Novello & Co.,
ltd., London; 15Feb47; EP5022.

COLEMAN, BYRON.
In quiet pastures; pastorale
for piano, by Byron Coleman.
© Theodore Presser Co., Philadelphia; 20Mar47; EP12885.

COLEMAN, EMIL.
Heaven above; words by Joseph Le
Roy [pseud.] & Harry Coleman,
music by Emil Coleman. ©
Domino Music Corp., New York;
19Dec46; EP11501.

COLEMAN, HENRIETTA, 1907-
Don't forget that you live in the
presence of the King; composed
by Henrietta Coleman, arr. by
D. Norman Tillman. Cleveland,
Coleman's Studio of Gospel
Music, [©19] © Henrietta
Coleman, Cleveland; 1Feb47;
EP13309. For voice and piano.

COLETTA, LORIS BERTHA STALIN, 1920-
Songs and choruses; by Loris Stalin
Colotta. © Vincent H. Coletta,
jr. & Loris Bertha Coletta,
Oakland, Calif.; 190ct46;
EP10905.

COLGIN, GEORGE L   1892-
No one knows our secret but the
moon; words and music by
George L. Colgin. © Bruce
Humphries, inc., Boston;
25Mar47; EP12456.

COLICCHIO, MICHAEL R
Louisiana hayride; by Howard
Dietz and Arthur Schwartz, para-
phrased for piano by Michael
Colicchio. © Harms, inc., New
York; on paraphrase; 11Apr47;
EP13750.

Swanee; by George Gershwin, para-
phrased for piano by Michael
Colicchio. © Harms, inc., New
York; on paraphrase; 14Apr47;
EP13749.

COLLAZO, BOBBY.
La última noche ... letra y
música de Bobby Collazo. ©
Peer International Corp., New
York; 30Dec46; EF5556.

COLLIN, JACK, 1912-
Figaro ... sur les motifs du
"Barbier de Séville" de Rossini;
paroles de O. Selluor [pseud.],
musique, arrt. et orchestration
de Jack Collin. Paris, Salabert.
© Salabert, inc., New York; on
arrangement; 31Oct46; EF3473.
Piano-conductor score (orchestra)
and parts.

COLMENERO, PEDRO M.
Te has de acordar de mí ... Letra
y música de Pedro M. Colmenero.
© Promotora Hispano Americana
de Musica, s. a., Mexico;
30Dec46; EF5522.

COLONNA, DON ROCCO.
By the Kea-la Ke-kua Bay; music
by Don R. Colonna ... lyric by
Sarah Willis. © Blue Bell Music
Pub. Co., inc., Birmingham, Ala.;
17Dec46; EP11085.

Manana. "To-morrow"... music by
Don R. Colonna ... lyric by
Sarah Willis. © Blue Bell
Music Pub. Co., inc., Birmingham,
Ala.; 17Dec46; EP11086. English
words.

"Memories of you dear"; music by
Don R. Colonna ... lyric by
Sarah Willis. © Blue Bell Music
Pub. Co., inc., Birmingham, Ala.;
17Dec46; EP11084.

[COMBE, RENÉ FRANCK] 1909-
Domain ... paroles de Jean Rodor
[pseud.], musique de René Frank
[pseud.] © Éditions Musicales
Nuances, Paris; 15Feb47; EF3493.

COMSTOCK, FRANK.
Nostalgia; [by] Frank Comstock,
piano solo, [transcription by
Edward White. London] Boosey &
Hawkes. © Hawkes & Son (London),
ltd.; on arrangement; 21Dec46;
EF4770.

CONCINA, CARLETTO.
Evviva l'allegria ... Musica di
Carletto Concina, testo di C.
Deani. Mocita ... Musica di
Carletto Concina, testo di C.
Deani. © Edizioni Casiroli s. a.
r. l., Milano; 2Jan47; EF5300.
Piano-conductor score (orchestra,
with words) and parts.

CONCINA, CARLO.
Don Pasquà ... Con la bella in
calessino ... musiche di C. Con-
cina, testi di C. Deani. Milano,
Alfa Leonardi. © Edizioni
Leonardi, Milan; 6Aug43; EF4807.
Piano-conductor score (orchestra,
with words) and parts.

CONDERCURI, ANGEL.
Con todo mi corazón ... letra de
Reinaldo Yiso, música de Angel
Condercuri. © Editorial
Argentina de Música Inter-
nacional, s. de r. ltd.,
Buenos Aires; 24Apr47; EF3212.

CONDON, LIONEL.
My heart was crying; words &
music by Lionel Condon. © Nordyke Pub. Co., Los Angeles;
9Nov46; EP11923.

CONFREY, EDWARD E
Some clay without a sculptor; by
Edward E. Confrey. © Robbins
Music Corp., New York; 29Nov46;
EP11006. For voice and piano.

CONKLIN, MARY H
Elfins' frolic ... by Mary H.
Conklin, for the piano.
© Harold Flammer, inc., New
York; 4Nov46; EP11379.

CONNELLY, REGINALD.
Beside the railroad; by Reg
Connelly. © Campbell, Connelly & Co., ltd., London;
on new words & changes in
music; 16Apr47; EF3324.
For voice & piano, with
chord symbols.

CONNOR, TOMMIE, 1904-
Serenade to no-one in particular;
words & music by Tommie Connor.
© Evans & Lowry, ltd., London;
21Mar47; EF5628.

CONSENTINO, ALBERT B   1898-
Songs by A. B. Consentino; The
toys in my room [and] Slumber
song. © Albert B. Consentino,
Haverhill, Mass.; 20Mar47;
EP14896.

CONSIGLIO, MARIO.
Gran premio ... musica di Mario
Consiglio, arrangiamento dell'
autore. Corsa ai milioni ...
musica di A. Puviani, arrangiamento di Fassino. © Edizioni
Leonardi, s.a.r.l., Milano;
2Jan47; EF5271. Piano-conductor
score (orchestra), and parts.

CONSTANTINI, ALESSANDRO.
O give thanks; (from a motet,
"Confitemini Domino") ... tr.
... by Hugh Ross. (In Ross,
Hugh, arr. Sacred choruses for
women's or girls' voices.
p. 117-128) © G. Schirmer, inc.,
New York; on arrangement;
30Sep46; EP9791.

COOK, SHORTY, pseud. See
Hinderer, Everett R.

COOK, WALTER, 1919-
Smoochin'; words and music by
Walter Cook. © Walter Cook,
Toledo; 14Jun47; EP15048.

COOKE, LaBELLE.
If you can't be held cow,
fall in behind; words and
music ... by Henry and LaBelle
Cooke. Tacoma, Henry and La-
Belle Cooke. © Henry Cooke,
Tacoma; 22Apr47; EP14248.

COOLEY, D   C
Crazy 'cause I love you; words and
music by Spade Cooley. © Hill
and Range Songs, inc., Hollywood, Calif.; 7Jan47; EP11204.

Minuet in swing; by Spade Cooley.
© Hill and Range Songs, inc.,
Hollywood, Calif.; 10Jun47;
EP15082. For piano solo, with
guitar diagrams and chord
symbols.

Oklahoma stomp; by Spade Cooley,
Lawrence De Paul and Andrew
Soldi. © Tune Towne Tunes,
Hollywood, Calif.; 16May47;
EP14642. Condensed score:
orchestra.

COOLEY, SPADE. See
Cooley, D. C.

COOPER, IRVIN, 1900-
Modern tunes for young violinists
... by Irvin Cooper. © Waterloo music Co., Waterloo, Ont.,
Can.; 23Dec46; EF4938. Score
(violin and piano) and part.

COOPER, WALTER B
Colorado's calling; words and
music by Walter B. Cooper.
Fort Collins, Colo., Cooper
Music Co. © Walter B.
Cooper, Fort Collins, Colo.;
29Apr47; EP14591.

She's just a wee tot (in the first
grade at school); words and
music by Walter B. Cooper. Fort
Collins, Colo., Cooper Music Co.
© Walter B. Cooper, Fort Collins,
Colo.; 12May47; EP14590.

COOTS, JOHN FREDERICK.
All suit! No man! ... lyric by
Alice D. Simms, music by J.
Fred Coots. © Kelton, inc.,
New York; 24Apr47; EP13849.

I can't believe it was all make-
believe (last night); lyric by
Sam M. Lewis, music by J. Fred
Coots. © Bregman, Vocco and Conn,
inc., New York; 2Jan47; EP11848.

Sippin' cider with my Ida (down
beside the Zuyder Zee); by J.
Fred Coots. © Emery Music, inc.,
New York; 18Feb47; EP12068. For
voice and piano, with chord symbols.

COPAS, COWBOY.
You live in a world all your own;
words and music by Cowboy
Copas. © Acuff-Rose Publica-
tions, Nashville; 12Mar47;
EP12627.

COPE, FOSTER.
Yosemite suite; by Foster Cope ...
for piano. © Bregman, Vocco and
Conn, inc., New York; 21Mar47;
EP13886.

COPELL, PHILIP.
My little pat of butter; words by
Emma Gladson, music by Philip
Copell. © Cine-Mart Music
Publishing Co., Hollywood, Calif.,
1Nov46; EP11945.

COPLAND, AARON, 1900-
Four dance episodes. See his
Rodeo.

(Rodeo) Four dance episodes from
Rodeo ... Full score. [New
York] Boosey and Hawkes. ©
Hawkes & Son (London) ltd., Lon-
don; 19Jun46; EF7171.

CORNELIUS, PETER, 1824-1874.
Once on a time Christ came to us
here; soprano solo and mixed
chorus (a capella) arr. by N.
Lindsay Norden. [Translation by N.
Lindsay Norden] © Broadcast
Music, inc., New York; on arrange-
ment & translation; 15May47;
EP15231.

The shepherds; soprano solo and
mixed chorus (with organ acc.)
by Peter Cornelius, arr. by N.
Lindsay Norden. [Translation
by N. Lindsay Norden] © Broadcast Music, inc., New York; on
arrangement & translation;
15May47; EP15229.

CORROYEZ, GEORGES.
Délivrance ... Four harmonie et
fanfare. © Georges Corroyez,
Versailles, France; 2May45;
EF618.

CORSI, G
Adoremus Te, Christe; by G.
Corsi, arr. and ed. for
women's chorus, S.S.A., by
Alfred Scott. © Choral Art
Publications, New York; on
arrangement; 8May47; EP14493.

COSGRAY, ORPHA.
Once a star shone bright. Floral
message; words and music by Orpha
Cosgray. © Orpha Cosgray, Eaton
Rapids, Mich.; 15Jan47; EP11394.

COSLOW, SAM, 1902-
(Copacabana) Je vous aime,
[from the picture "Copacabana"];
words and music by Sam Coslow.
[New York, Chappell] ©
Crawford Music Corp., New York;
29Apr47; EP14342.

(Copacabana) My heart was doing a
bolero, [from "Copacabana"]; words
and music by Sam Coslow. [New
York, Chappell & Co.] © Crawford
Music Corp., New York; 12May47;
EP14522.

(Copacabana) Stranger things
have happened; [from the
picture "Copacabana"], words
and music by Sam Coslow.
[New York, Chappell] ©
Crawford Music Corp., New
York; 5May47; EP14543.

Je vous aime. See his
Copacabana.

My heart was doing a bolero.
See his Copacabana.

Stranger things have happened.
See his Copacabana.

COSSELMON, ROBERT A   1910-
Jesus knows; [by] R. A. Cossel-
mon. (In Church of the
Nazarene. Michigan District.
Nazarene Young Peoples Society.
Choruses of the N. Y. P. S.
p.57) © Michigan District,
Nazarene Young Peoples Society,
Flint, Mich.; 25Jul46; EP13077.
Close score: SATB.

Love sets me free; [words by]
Iyla G. Crane, [music by]
Robert A. Cosselmon. (In
Church of the Nazarene.
Michigan District. Nazarene
Young Peoples Society.
Choruses of the N. Y. P. S.
p.36-37) © Michigan District,
Nazarene Young Peoples Society,
Flint, Mich.; 25Jul46; Er13062.
Close score: SATB.

The way of holiness; [words by]
Lois Blanchard, [music by]
R. A. Cosselmon. (In Church
of the Nazarene. Michigan
District. Nazarene Young
Peoples Society. Choruses of
the N. Y. P. S. p.59) ©
Michigan District, Nazarene
Young Peoples Society, Flint,
Mich.; 25Jul46; EP13079.
Close score: SATB.

You can count on me ... [by]
Robert A. Cosselmon. (In
Church of the Nazarene.
Michigan District. Nazarene
Young Peoples Society.
Choruses of the N. Y. P. S.
p.24-25) © Michigan District,
Nazarene Young Peoples Society,
Flint, Mich.; 25Jul46;
EP13051. Close score: SATB.

COSTA, J   S   DA.
Don't throw me over for somebody
else; words and music by Jesda
Costa. [c1946] © J. S. DaCosta,
Manila, P. I.; 1Mar47; EP12262.

COTTINGHAM, FRANK, 1884-
The Saviour is calling; [arr. by
Charles H. Gabriel] Why do you
say to Him nay? [Words by Don
Moon and] Since He took my sins
away, words and music by Frank
Cottingham, [arr. by Thoro
Harris] © Frank Cottingham,
Elgin, Ill.; on changes in music
in Why do you say to Him nay?;
14May47; EP15067.

COTTON, DORIS W
Bobby sox blues; words by Virgil
L. Cotton, music by Doris W.
Cotton. © Nordyke Publishing
Co., Los Angeles; 27Sep46;
EP14779.

COTTON, VIRGIL L
It's the color of my eyes; words
and music by Doris W. Cotton,
Margaret Gerrow [and] Virgil L.
Cotton. [c1946] © Nordyke Publishing Co., Los Angeles;
30Jan47; EP14780.

COUPLAND, LAURA HELEN.
Jumping rope rhyme ... by Laura H.
Coupland. © Clayton F. Summy Co.,
Chicago; 10Mar47; EP12548. For
piano solo, with interlinear words

30

COUPLAND, LAURA HELEN. Cont'd.
Rabbit jumps ... by Laura H. Coupland.
© Clayton F. Summy Co., Chicago;
10Mar47; EP12547. For piano solo.

COURTNEY, ALAN, 1911-
'Tis a privilege to live in
Colorado; words and music by
Alan Courtney. © Alan
Courtney Music Co., Denver;
1Jan47; EP13344.

COURTNEY, ARTHUR GERALD.
Wistful; words and music by
Arthur Courtney. San Pablo,
Calif., Courtney Publications.
© Arthur Gerald Courtney, San
Pablo, Calif.; 28Mar47; EP6740.

COUSIN LEE, pseud. See
Ellsworth, Arlie B.

COWAN, JOEL.
Just plain love; by Al Russell
[and] Joel Cowan. © Edwin H.
Morris & co., inc., New York;
2Jun47; EP14965. For voice and
piano, with chord symbols.

COWARD, NOËL.
(Bitter sweet) Zigouner, from
"Bitter sweet"; by Noël Coward
... arr. ... by Charles R.
Cronham. © Harms, inc., New
York; on arrangement; 17Jun47;
EP15280. For organ solo; in-
cludes registration for Hammond
organ.

Bright was the day. See his
Pacific 1860.

I saw no shadow. See his
Pacific 1860.

One, two, three. See his
Pacific 1860.

(Pacific 1860) Bright was the day,
from "Pacific 1860"; words and
music by Noël Coward. © Chappell
& Co., ltd., London; 17Dec46;
EP14778. For voice and piano.

(Pacific 1860) I saw no shadow,
from "Pacific 1860"; words and
music by Noël Coward. ©
Chappell & Co., ltd., London;
19Dec46; EP14780. For voice and
piano.

(Pacific 1860) One, two, three,
from "Pacific 1860"; words and
music by Noël Coward. © Chappell
& Co., ltd., London; 17Dec46;
EP14777. For voice and piano.

(Pacific 1860) Piano selection
[from] Pacific 1860; a musical
romance by Noël Coward [arranged
by Robb Stewart] © Chappell &
Co., ltd., London; on arrangement; 1Feb47; EP5164.

(Pacific 1860).Selection; [by]
Noël Coward, arr. for orchestra
by Geo. L. Zalva. © Chappell
& Co., ltd., London; on arrangement; 19Mar47; EP5505. Piano-
conductor score (orchestra) and
parts.

(Pacific 1860) This is a changing
world, from "Pacific 1860"; words
and music by Noël Coward. ©
Chappell & Co.,.ltd., London;
19Dec46; EP14779. For voice and
piano.

Someday I'll find you; three part
female chorus (S.S.A.), arr. by
William Stickles. Words and
music by Noël Coward. © Chappell
& Co., ltd., London; on arrangement; 13Jun47; EP15161.

Someday I'll find you; three part
mixed chorus (S.A.B.), arr. by
William Stickles. Words and
music by Noël Coward. © Chappell
& Co., ltd., London; on arrangement; 13Jun47; EP15160.

Someday I'll find you; two part
chorus, arr. by William Stickles.
Words and music by Noël Coward.
© Chappell & Co., ltd., London;
on arrangement; 13Jun47; EP15162.

This is a changing world. See his
Pacific 1860.

Zigeuner; [by] Noel Coward, arr.
by J. Louis Merkur, piano
duet. © Harms, inc., New
York; on arrangement; 1May47;
EP14410.

Zigeuner. See also his Bitter sweet.

COWLIN, RUPERT, ed. and arr.
Piano accordion album ... ed.
and arr. by Rupert Cowlin.
© Ascherberg, Hopwood &
Crew, ltd., London; on
arrangement in no.5, 9May47;
EF3778.

CRANE, HENRIETTA AYLSA G   1894-
Say it and play it ... A class
(or individual) method for
teaching violin in rhyme, by
Henrietta Aylsa Crane, illus.
by Helen M. Otto. [c1946] ©
Henrietta Aylsa G. Crane,
Pittsburg, Kan.; 15May47;
EP14809.

CRANE, J
Deep down in the heart of a rose;
words by Adiola Gray Taylor,
music by J. Crane. © Adiola
Gray Taylor, Forest, Va.;
22May47; EP14775.

Lonely; words by Nancy Hayes
[pseud.], music by J. Crane.
© Nordyke Publishing Co., Los
Angeles; 5Mar47; EP13550.

My darling Blue eyes; words by
Joseph Zielinski, music by J.
Crane. © Nordyke Publishing
Co., Los Angeles; 8Mar47
EP13523.

CRANTOCK, PETER.
Cockney capers; piano solo by
Peter Crantock. © Dix, ltd.,
London; 10Sep41; EF3543.

CRAWFORD, JOHN D
My old fashioned sweetheart;
by John D. Crawford. © John
D. Crawford, Canton, Ohio;
16May47; EP14639. For
voice and piano.

CRAWFORD, ROBERT LEE.
Hello Daddy; words and music by
Birdie Lee McFarland and Robert
Lee Crawford. [c1946] © White-
house Publishing Co., Hollywood,
Calif.; 2Jan47; EP11982.

CRAWFORD, ROBERT MACARTHUR, 1899-
My gal, my plane and I; by Robert
Crawford ... Official song of
Miami All American Air Maneuvers.
Miami, Fla., Blue Yonder. ©
Robert M. Crawford, South Miami,
Fla.; 12Jan47; EP11789.

CREMIEUX, OCTAVE, 1872-
Douze fables de La Fontaine; pré-
facées par Pierre Varenne, mises
en musique par Octave Crémieux,
illus. par Frédéric Delanglade.
(Agen, France, Distributeur,
Martin-Delbert) © Octave Crémieux, Paris; 1Dec46; EF5236.
For voice and piano.

CREMIN, ARTHUR T
Fun with violin technic; first
position. [By] Arthur T. Cremin.
New York, Art-I-So Music. ©
Arthur T. Cremin, New York;
29Apr47; AA52328.

CRESCENZO, V. DE, comp.
Raccolta di successi, Bottega di
Ritmi e Melodie ... versi di V.
de Crescenzo, F. Fiore [and
others] ... musica di G. Cioffi,
E. Barile [and others]. Comp.
by V. de Crescenzo] © Edizioni
Bottega di Ritmi e Melodie,
Naples; 31Dec45; EF4871. For
voice and piano.

CRISTALLI, OSCAR.
La serenata preferita ... testo e
musica di Oscar Cristalli. (In
Un sorriso e 20 canzoni. p. 32-33)
© Edizioni Leonardi, s.a.r.l.,
Milano; 12Nov45; EF4925. For
voice and piano.

CRITELLI, LOUIS.
Time-out for my heart and you;
words ... by L. Critelli. ©
Louis Critelli, Des Moines;
6Apr46; EP3114. For voice and
piano.

CROCKETT, ANNA BROY.
Crockett's spirituals; by Anna
Broy Crockett. © Anna Broy
Crockett, Chicago; on 2 hymns;
3Feb47. Close score; SATB.
Contents.- [v.] 1. Let Jesus
fix it for you. © EP11906)-
[v.] 2. Christ is real.
(© EP11905)

CRONHAM, CHARLES RAYMOND, 1896-
In the vale of Tempe ... for organ,
by Charles Raymond Cronham.
© The Boston Music Co., Boston;
24Mar47; EP13380. Includes
registration for Hammond organ.

Mary and-a Martha; Negro spiritual
for chorus of mixed voices with
piano acc. arr. by Charles Raymond Cronham. © The Boston
Music Co., Boston; on arrangement;
13Jan47; EP11304.

Ruth's entreaty; sacred song by
Charles Raymond Cronham, [text
from "Ruth"] © The Boston
Music Co., Boston; 13May47;
EP14414.

[CROOKHAM, DAISY DEAN]
Singing a song of love; words and
music by Daisy Dean. © W. E. Goldsberry & Co. (Daisy Dean Crookham,
sole owner), Los Angeles; 17Jan47;
EP6501.

We've found our Sioux City Sue; words
and music by Daisy Dean. © W. E.
Goldsberry & Co. (Daisy Dean Crookham, sole owner), Los Angeles;
17Jan47; EP6500.

CROSBY, ALPHEUS DIXI.
Save you nickela, save your
dimes   Words & music by
A. D. Crosby. © Alpheus
Dixi Crosby, Larchmont,
N. Y.; 10May47; EP6891.

CROSBY, VANDA MAE, 1926-
I am so happy; [by] Vanda Mae
Crosby, arr. by W. M. T.
(In Church of the Nazarene.
Michigan District. Nazarene
Young Peoples Society.
Choruses of the N. Y. P. S.
p.20) © Michigan District,
Nazarene Young Peoples Society,
Flint, Mich.; 25Jul46; EP13046.
Close score: SATB.

CROSLEY, EDNA JETT.
Give me the night so enchanting;
words & music by Edna Jett
Crosley. © Nordyke Publishing
Co., Los Angeles; 13Dec46;
EP13545.

CROSS, R   ARIEL, 1915-   arr.
Tympani passagos ... by R.
Ariol Cross. © Belwin, inc.,
New York; on compilation &
arrangement; bk. 1-2, 11Mar47;
bk.3 27Mar47; EP12572-12573,
13999.

CROSSMAN, ARTHUR GORDON, 1920-
Fight on ye Bruins; words and
music by Arthur G. Crossman.
[n.p.,] Crossman Publications,
[c1946] © Arthur Gordon Crossman, Los Angeles; 12May47;
EP14618.

31

CROUNSE, VALLEY VEDDER, 1886–
Moon over Easterland; lyric by
Elizabeth M. Snyder, music by
Valley V. Crounse. © Elizabet'
M. Snyder, Albany; 28Feb47;
EP13666.

CRUZ, ALEJANDRO SAENZ. See
Saenz Cruz, Alejandro.

CRUZ ARTIGAS, HUGO.
Falto de cariño ... Letra y música
de Hugo Cruz Artigas. Habana.
© Peer International Corp., New
York; 10Apr47; EF5512.

CRYOR, WALLACE MILTON, 1913–
He took my sins away ... [by]
Wallace M. Cryor. c1947.
© Cryor Publishing Co., Balti-
more; 22Dec46; EP11890. Close
score: SATB.

LOS CUATES CASTILLA (Musicians)
Corazón mexicano! ... Letra y
música de los cuates Castilla.
© Promotora Hispano Americana
de Música, s.a., México; 28Aug46;
EF5610.

Tal como fuiste ... De los
cuates Castilla, arr. de
Miguel A. Pazos. © Promotora
Hispano Americana de Música,
Mexico; 30Dec46; EF5286.
Piano-conductor score (orchestra,
with words) and parts.

CUGAT, XAVIER, 1904–
Illusion ... lyric by Bob Russell
and S. T. Gallagher, [pseud.]
music ... by Xavier Cugat and
José Morand, [pseud.] · © Pemora
Music Co., inc., New York;
31Mar47; EP15107.

CUI, CÉSAR, 1835–1918.
Orientale, from Kaleidoscope; by
César Cui. Op.50, no.9.
Arranged by Pietro Deiro. ©
Accordion Music Publishing Co.,
New York; on arrangement; 30Dec46;
EP10770. For accordion solo.

CULOTTA, ILLUMINATO.
A tu per tu! ... Di Illuminato
Culotta. © Edizioni Musicali
Cora, Milano; 25Jun42; EF5049.
Piano-conductor score
(orchestra)

L'esito da festa ... parole di
Tettoni, musica di Giannetto
[pseud.] © Edizioni Musicali
CORA, Milano; 1Nov45; EF3407.

Bozzetti montani (della Sicilia)
... [by] Illuminato Culotta.
... © Edizioni Musicali Cora,
Milano; 25Jun42; EF5048.
Piano-conductor score
(orchestra)

Festa di Vendemmia in Sicilia ···
[by] I. Culotta. © Edizioni
Musicali Cora, Milano; 30Apr42;
EF5052. Piano-conductor score:
orchestra.

Piccolo sentiero ... parole di
A. R. Borella [pseud.] musica
di Giannetto [pseud.] © Edizioni
Musicali CORA, Milano; 1Nov45;
EF5406.

Una serata al circo ··· One
evening at the circus-theatre.
... Musica di I. Culotta.
© Edizioni Musicale Cora,
Milano; 30Jul44; EF5050.
Piano-conductor score
(orchestra)

CUMA, ALOIS, 1903–
Hvězda a je'jí stin ... slova:
Alois Krnký, hudba: Alois
Cuma, [arr. by Vladimír Fuka]
Ak ti bude smutno ... slova:
Ant. Rakovský, hudba: Ant.
Závodný, [arr. by Antonín
Devátý] © Jaroslav Stožický,
Brno, Czechoslovakia; 9Jun46;
EF3361. Piano-conductor score
(orchestra, with words) and
parts.

CUMMING, JOHN W   W
Till He come; [by] John W. W.
Cumming. © John W. W.
Cumming, Portsmouth, Va.;
24Apr47; EP6837. Close
score: SATB.

CUMMINGS, MELVILLE HOMER, 1890–
'Tis safe to follow Him ... By
M. Homer Cummings, [words by]
M. H. C. © M. Homer Cummings,
Coalwood, W. Va.; 30Mar47;
EP14528. Close score: SATB.

CUMMINGS, RODNEY.
Saratoga ... by Rodney Cummings.
© Belwin, inc., New York; 3Mar47;
EP12755. Condensed score (band)
and parts.

CUNLIFFE, DICK.
¿Quién sabe? (Who knows?) Words
and music by Jimmy O'Keefe,
Jack Fulton and Dick Cunliffe.
© Harmony Music Corp., New York;
17Apr47; EP13668. English words.

CURBELO, JOSÉ.
Que no, que no! Letra y música de
José Curbelo. © Peer International Corp., New York;
13Dec46; EP13617.

CURIEL, GONZALO.
Solloso ... letra y música de
Gonzálo Curiel. © Promotora
Hispano Americana de Música,
s.a., Mexico, D. F.; 27Dec46;
EF4860. Piano-conductor
score (orchestra), condensed
score and parts.

CURIEL, NICOLÁS GARCÍA. See
García Curiel, Nicolás.

CURRY, W   LAWRENCE.
Choral Prelude on "Dundee"; by W.
Lawrence Curry. © The H. W.
Gray Co., inc., New York;
23May47; EP14764. For organ
solo.

[CURSAN, MARIE-LOUISE] 1894–
A coeur joie; [by] Tante Lou
[pseud.], illustrations de
Georges Grassiant. © Rouart,
Lerolle et Cie., Paris; 31Dec46;
EF3474. Melody and words.

CURTIS, KATHLEEN G. See
Starr, Kathleen Gerelda Curtis.

CZAJKOWSKI, FRANK T
I'll tell my lonely heart; by
Frank T. Czajkowski. ©
Frank T. Czajkowski, Morris-
ville, Pa.; 16May47; EP14638.
Piano-conductor score
(orchestra) and parts.

CZERNY, CARL, 1791–1857.
Czerny-Schaum; for piano, [arr. and
comp. by] John W. Schaum. ©
Belwin, inc., New York; on
arrangement & compilation; bk.1,
28Jan47; EP11683.

Etude de concert; for the pianoforte ... arr. ... by Carl
Richter. © Bach Music Co., Boston; on arrangement; 17Apr46;
EP3941.

D

DABNEY, FORD.
S-H-I-N-E; by Cecil Mack, Lew
Brown and Ford Dabney, [arr. by
Charlie Ventura] © Shapiro,
Bernstein & Co., inc., New York;
10Jun47; EP14984. Score (B♭
tenor saxophone and piano) and
part.

DACON, CLAUDIUS McALPIN, 1882–
Dear mother of mine ... words
and music by Claudius M.
Dacon. © Claudius Mcalpin
Dacon, Brooklyn; 11Jan47;
EP13116.

DACRE, HARRY.
A bicycle built for two; [for]
S.A. By Harry Dacre, arr. by
Frédéric Fay Swift. © Belwin,
inc., New York; on arrangement;
3Mar47; EP12753.

DAFFAN, TED.
Baby, you can't get me down;
words and music by Ted Daffan.
© Hill and Range Songs, inc.,
Hollywood, Calif.; 10Jun47;
EP15083.

Broken vows; words and music by
Ted Daffan. © Hill and Range
Songs, inc., Hollywood, Calif.;
7Jan47; EP11206.

You better change your ways;
words and music by Ted Daffan.
© Hill and Range Songs, inc.,
Hollywood, Calif.; 13May47;
EP14426.

DAHL, VIKING, 1895–1945.
Nocturne; pour violon et piano,
par Viking Dahl. © Nordiska
Musikförlaget, a/b, Stockholm;
1Jan21; EF5408.

[DAHLE, ALEXANDER A   ]
Hello Montana; lyrics and music by
Arizona Mulligan [pseud.], Eddie
Sosby [and] Spook McGlook [pseud.]
© Hillcrest Music Publications
(George Suomela, owner), Omaha;
14Mar47; EP6705.

I was born a hundred years too
late; lyrics and music by "Susie"
[pseud.], Edna Jean Hatfield
[and] Spook McGlook [pseud.]
© Hillcrest Music Publications,
Omaha; 10Jun47; EP15174.

DAHLQUIST, LARS ERIK.
Cream-cake-Charlie ... text och
musik: Lasse Dahlquist.
© Nils-Georgs Musikförlags,
a/b, Stockholm; 19Jun45;
EF4884. For voice and piano,
with chord symbols; Swedish
words.

Cuba, Havannah, Hawaii, Tahiti
och Florida; text och musik:
Lasse Dahlquist. © Nils-
Georgs Musik-förlags, a/b;
Stockholm; 1Jan46; EF4877.
Piano-conductor score
(orchestra), and parts.

Jolly Bob från Aberdeen ... text
och musik [by] Lasse Dahlquist.
© Nils-Georgs Musikförlags,
a/b, Stockholm; 1Jan38;
EF4880. For voice and piano,
with chord symbols.

En kväll pa Henriksberg ...
[words and music] av Lasse
Dahlquist, arr.: Peva Derwin.
© Skandinaviska Odeon, a.b.,
Stockholm; 1Jan44; EF3753.
Piano-conductor score
(orchestra), and parts.

"Lille Klumpedump" ... musik:
Lasse Dahlquist, arr.: W. Ring-
strand. © Nils-Georgs Musikförlags, a/b, Stockholm; 1Mar41;
EF4876. Piano-conductor score
(orchestra), and parts.

Oh boy, oh boy, oh boy ... text
och musik: Lasse Dahlquist.
© Nils-Georgs Musikförlags,
a/b, Stockholm; 1Jan46; EF4881.
For voice and piano, with chord
symbols; Swedish words.

Stuvnrevalsen; text och musik:
Lasse Dahlquist. © Nils-Georgs
Musikförlags, a/b, Stockholm;
1Jan44; EF4885. For voice
and piano.

Var lilla komedi; text och musik:
Lasse Dahlquist. © Nils-Georgs
Musikförlags, a/b, Stockholm;
6May45; EF4882. For voice and
piano, with chord symbols.

DAHLQUIST, LARS ERIK. Cont'd.
Very welcome home, Mr. Swanson;
text och musik av Lasse
Dahlquist. © Nils-Georgs
Musikförlngs, a/b, Stockholm;
1Jan39; EF4878. Caption title:
Very, very welcome hom, Mister
Swansson. For voice and piano,
with chord symbols; Swedish
words.

DAHLQUIST, LASSE. See
Dahlquist, Lars Erik.

DALE, JOHNNY.
Rendezvous with memory; words by
Lassie Moates, music by Johnny
Dale. © Cine-Mart Music Publish-
ing Co., Hollywood, Calif.;
1Nov46; EF11943.

DALE, RUTH, pseud. See
Wilson, Ira Bishop.

DALLAM, HELEN.
On a ferriswheel; for piano [by]
Helen Dallam. © McKinley
Publishers, inc., Chicago;
28Feb47; EP12408.

DALLAPICCIOLA, LUIGI, 1904-
Frammenti sinfonici dal balletto
"Marsia." See his Marsia.

DALLIN, LEON.
Concert rondo; by Leon Dallin
... arr. ... by Frederick
Westphal. © Mills Music,
inc., New York; 16Apr47;
EP6826. Score: (clarinet
1-4 and parts.

DALMAINE, CYRIL C., pseud. See
Barrington, Jonah.

DALMAU, JAIME TEXIDOR. See
Texidor Dalmau, Jaime.

DALMAU, JUAN.
Manhattan samba; English words by
Joe Davis, Spanish words and
music by Juan Dalmau. © Caribbean Music, inc., New York;
23Jun47; EP15143.

DALY, JOE.
The barnyard reel; [by] Joe
Daly, arr. by Geo. Chisholm.
© Keith, Prowse & Co., ltd.,
London; arr on arrangement;
19May47; EF3347. Piano-con-
ductor score (orchestra), and
parts.

DAMAIS, ÉMILE.
Cinq divertissements; pour
saxophone seul, [by] Emile
Damais. Paris, L. de Lacour,
Éditions Costallat. ©
Lucien de Lacour, Paris;
30Nov46; EF3621.

(Sonata, violin) Sonate pour
violon seul; [by] Émile Damais.
Paris, L. de Lacour, Éditions
Costallat. © Lucien de Lacour,
Paris; 30Nov46; EF3643.

DANBERGER, WILMA DOROTHY.
Lingering ... Words by Edwin W.
Kukkee, music by Wilma Dorothy
Danberger. © Edwin W. Kukkee,
Fort Williams, Ont., Can.;
28Dec45; EF5335.

D'ANGELO, LANI, 1913-
Conchitina; words and music by
Lani D'Angelo. © Lani D'Angelo,
Brooklyn; 10Apr47; EP14191.
English words.

I saw heaven in disguise; words
and music by Lani D'Angelo.
© Lani D'Angelo, Brooklyn;
10Apr47; EP14189.

It won't be long; words and
music by Lani D'Angelo. ©
Lani D'Angelo, Brooklyn;
5May47; EP14303.

Saddest gal in town; words and
music by Lani D'Angelo. © Lani
D'Angelo, Brooklyn; 10Apr47;
EP14190.

DANIELS, WANDA.
Blue, blue eyes; by Arthur Smith
[and] Wanda Daniels. © Fairway Music Co., Hollywood, Calif.;
31Dec46; EP11327. For voice
and piano, with chord symbols.

DARCY, THOMAS F arr.
National anthem of Afghanistan;
arr. by ... Thomas F. Darcy,
jr. © Bourne, inc., New York,
on arrangement; 3Jun47;
EP14797. Parts: band.

National anthem of Argentina; arr.
by ... Thomas F. Darcy, jr.
© Bourne, inc., New York; on arrangement; 3Jun47; EP14795.

National anthem of Denmark.
("King Christian stood by the
lofty mast"); arr. by Capt.
Thomas F. Darcy, jr. © Bourne,
inc., New York; on arrangement;
2Jun47; EP14856. Parts: band.

National anthem of Saudi Arabia;
arr. by Capt. Thomas F. Darcy,
Jr. © Bourne, inc., New York;
on arrangement; 2Jun47; EP14854.
Parts: band.

National anthem of Siam. Sansasoen
Barami; arr. by Capt. Thomas F.
Darcy, jr. © Bourne, inc.,
New York; on arrangement; 2Jun47;
EP14855. Parts: band.

National anthem of Sweden; arr. by
Thomas F. Darcy, jr. © Bourne,
inc., New York on arrangement;
3Jun47; EP14796. Parts: band.

DARRYS, RENÉ.
Dans le ciel de tes yeux ...
paroles de Chanty, musique de
René Darrys. © Éditions
Musicales René Darrys, Paris;
31Mar47; EF3650.

DARSEN, FREDERIC, pseud. See
Siegel, Arsene Frederic.

D'ARTEGA.
Dream concerto; by D'Artega [and]
Paul Reif. Piano solo.
© Bregman, Vocco and Conn, inc.,
New York; 17Apr47; EP13877.

(Dream concerto) Theme [from]
"Dream concerto," by D'Artega
[and] Paul Reif. Piano solo.
© Bregman, Vocco and Conn, inc.,
New York; 17Apr47; EP13876.

D'ARTEGA, ALFONSO.
(Carnegie Hall) Romance in the
picture "Carnegie Hall" ... by
Buddy Kaye ... and D'Artega.
© Shapiro, Bernstein & Co.,
inc., New York; on adaptation;
28Feb47; EP12377. For voice
and piano, with chord symbols.

Romance in Carnegie Hall. See his
Carnegie Hall.

DARWIN, LANIER.
I love my love; words and music
by Lanier Darwin. © Sun Music
Co., inc., New York; 24Sep46;
EP13378.

DASHER, JACKSON D
Just beyond my dreams; words and
music by Jackson D. Dasher.
Hebron, Ohio, Top Tunes. ©
Jackson D. Dasher, Hebron,
Ohio; 20Mar47; EP13140.

DASHER, JUNE LOWMAN, 1913-
For him; words & music by June
Lowman Dasher. © Katharine
C. Lowman Co., Willoughby,
Ohio; 17Aug46; EP11186. For
voice and piano; welcome speech
and gift presentation speech
laid in.

DA SILVA, OWEN.
Mass in honor of Our Lady, queen
of the Franciscan Order ... For
S.A.T.B. © J. Fischer & Bro.,
New York; on arrangement; 3Jun46;
EP4708.

DATIN, JACQUES, 1920-
Une femme a'en va ... paroles et
musique de Jacques Datin.
© Éditions Musicales Nuances,
Paris; 15Feb47; EF3484.

Histoire de fou ... paroles et
musique de Jacques Datin.
© Éditions Musicales Nuances,
Paris; 15Feb47; EF3492.

La nuit ... paroles et musique de
Jacques Datin. © Éditions
Musicales Nuances, Paris;
15Feb47; EF3489.

DAVICO, VINCENZO, 1889-
Cinque liriche romantiche; [by]
Vincenzo Davico. © Carisch,
s.a., Milan; on 5 songs; 15Apr47.
For voice and piano. Contents.-
[v.1] Ho il cuor così greve di
pianto (D. Valeri) (© EF3350)-
[v.2] Pioggia d'ottobre (G.
Covinini) (© EF3352)-[v.3]
Plenilunio (E. Turolla) (©
EF3354)-[v.4] Fiori (V.
Malpassuti) (© EF3351)- [v.5]
Rondini (D. Valeri) (© EF3353)

Fiori. See his Cinque liriche
romantiche.

Ho il cuor così greve di pianto.
See his Cinque liriche romantiche.

Pioggia d'ottobre. See his
Cinque liriche romantiche.

Plenilunio. See his Cinque liriche
romantiche.

Rondini. See his Cinque liriche
romantiche.

DAVID, LEE.
Moon river; (Down moon river
way), lyric by Benton Ley
[pseud.], music by Lee David.
© Forster Music Publisher,
inc., Chicago; 4Mar47;
EP12746.

DAVID, WILLIAM R
My darling little Peggy; words and
music by William R. David.
© Cine-Mart Music Publishing Co.,
Hollywood, Calif.; 1Nov46;
EP11950.

[DAVIDSON, HAROLD PRESCOTT] 1908-
Collection of California Polytechnic College school songs. ©
California Polytechnic College,
San Luis Obispo, Calif.;
12Oct46; EP11976. Parts: band;
word sheet laid in.

DAVIDSON, LOLA D
Pine Ridge mountain rendezvous;
lyrics and music by Spook
McGlook [pseud.], Arizona
Mulligan, [pseud. and] Lola D.
Davidson. © Hillcrest Music
Publications, Omaha; 10Jun47;
EP15175.

DAVIES, ALLAN, 1922-
Singing choruses; [words and
music by Gordon Davies and
Allan Davies] © Gordon
Davies, Los Angeles; 1Apr47;
EP13094.

DAVIES, HARRY PARR.
(The Shephard show) Counting sheep;
words by Harold Purcell. ©
Sterling Music Co., ltd., London; 21Oct46; EP9591. For voice
and piano.

DAVIES, IEUAN REES- See
Rees-Davies, Ieuan.

DAVIES, OWEN, pseud.
Who was old Zip Coon? by Owen
Davies [pseud., words by Robert
O. Lloyd, pseud.] Ed. and arr.
for men's chorus, TTBB. © Choral
Press, Evanston, Ill.; 15Jun47;
EP11699.

DAVIS, ANICE.
The Lambda Chi welcome song;
words and music by Anice Davis.
Marion, Ohio, D. G. Stephenson.
© Lambda Chi Omega National
Sorority, Marion, Ohio; 30Apr47;
EP14499.

33

DAVIS, DAVID.
Lullaby; unison song, melody by
David Davis, arr. by Sinclair
Logan, from "Folk song lyrics"
collected by S. Baring Gould.
London, J. Curwen, New York,
G. Schirmer, solo agents. ©
Sinclair Logan, Worcester, Eng.
& David Davis, Malvern, Eng.;
20Mar47; EF5465.

DAVIS, JAMES CLYDE, 1905-   comp.
Campaign specials ... [Comp.] by
Jimmie Davis. © James C. Davis,
Long Beach, Calif.; 5Jun47;
EP14946. Hymns.

DAVIS, JIMMIE.
I'm gonna write myself a letter;
[and Bang bang] words and music
by Jimmie Davis. © Peer International Corp., New York; 27Dec46;
EP11638,11639. Piano arrangement
of I'm gonna write a letter by
Larry Stanton.

DAVIS, JOE, 1896-
Confused; (song) words and music
by A. E. Swanson, D, K, Harri-
son and Joe Davis. © Joe
Davis Music Co., inc., New
York; 17Mar47; EP12640.

Ev'ryone like to rhumba. (Todos
gustan bailarlo) ... Spanish
words by Jaime Yamin, English
words and music by Joe Davis.
© Caribbean Music, inc., New
York; 12May47; EP14223.

DAVIS, KATHERINE K
The raising of Lazarus; sacred
song with piano or organ acc.,
text adapted from St. John XI,
music by Katherine K. Davis.
© Carl Fischer, inc., New York;
29May47; EP15015.

Three American folksongs; for a
medium (or low) voice, with
piano accompaniment, harmonized
and arr. by Katherine K. Davis.
© Galaxy Music Corp., New York;
on arrangements of 3 songs; 27Feb47.
Contents.- [v. 1] The deaf old
woman. (© EP6637)- [v. 2] Ho's
goin' away. (© EP6636)- [v. 3]
The soldier. (© EP6635).

DAVIS, LINK.
My pretty blonde; by Link Davis.
© Northern Music Corp., New
York; 10Mar47; EP12760. For
voice and piano, with chord
symbols.

DAVIS, NATHAN C
Don't you do that, what you want to
do, to do that to me; words by C.
Andrew Jacobs, music by Nathan
Davis ... arrangement ... by C.
Maurice King. © The Popular Song
Club, N.C. Davis, exclusive owner,
Hollywood, Calif.; 190ct46; EP6363.
For voice and piano, with guitar
diagrams and chord symbols.

If you talk just right to me;
words by Oussie L. Body, music
by Nathan Davis ... arrangement
... by C. Maurice King. © The
Popular Song Club, N.C. Davis,
exclusive owner, Hollywood,
Calif.; 190ct46; EP6364. For
voice and piano, with guitar diagrams and chord symbols.

Singing the boogie; words by Dennis
D. Fernando, music by Nathan
Davis ... arrangement ... by C.
Maurice King. © The Popular Song
Club, N.C.Davis, exclusive owner,
Hollywood, Calif.; 190ct46;
EP6365. For voice and piano, with
guitar diagrams and chord symbols.

DAVIS, STU.
Durlin', now I know the reason
why; by Stu Davis. © Bob
Miller, inc., New York; 2May47;
EP14174. For voice and piano,
with chord symbols.

DAVIS, TED.
Two fatal words; words and music
by Ted Davis. © Croxton Publishing Co., Los Angeles;
5May47; EP14822.

DAVIS, VIRGINIA.
I will move on up a little
higher ... (a spiritual) arr.
by Virginia Davis and Theodore
R. Frye. Chicago, The T. R. Frye
Publishers. © Theodore R. Frye
and Mahalia Jackson, Chicago; on
arrangement; 16Sep46; EP13385.

[DAVOL, RALPH] 1874-
Hands around the globe; [by Ralph
Davol, arr. by Preston Sandiford]
Taunton, Mass., Davol Publishing
Co. © Ralph Davol, Taunton,
Mass.; 1Feb46; EP11888. For
piano solo.

You,my friend me; [words and music by
Ralph Davol, arr. of Wally Taylor]
Taunton, Mass., Davol Publishing Co.,
[c1945] © Ralph Davol, Taunton, Mass.
1Feb46; EP11889.

DAWN, MURIEL.
Killyburn braes ... arr. by Muriel
& Douglas Dawn. © Novello &
Co., ltd., London; on arrange-
ment; 2May47; EF3241. For unison
chorus and piano.

DAWSON, ALICE E
I took a day to search for God ...
SATB with violin obbligato [by]
Alice E. Dawson, [words by]
Bliss Carman. © Harold Flammer,
inc., New York; 7May47; EP14376.

DAWSON, HERBERT.
The overlander's song; words and
music by Smoky Dawson. © Allan
& Co., pty. ltd., Melbourne,
Australia; 30ct46; EF3088.
For voice and piano, with guitar
diagrams and chord symbols.

DAWSON, SMOKY. See
Dawson, Herbert.

DAWSON, SYDNEY B
Toledo polka; by Sydney B. Dawson,
arr. by Calla-Rini. © Roma
Music Co., Cleveland; 20May47;
EP6909. Score; 2 accordions.

DAY, LAURI.
Although you've broken my heart;
words by Les Allen & Billy
Danvers, music by Lauri Day. ©
Irwin Dash Music Co., ltd.,
London; 1Jan47; EF3135. For
voice and piano, with chord
symbols; melody also in tonic
sol-fa notation.

DAY, RUTH E
Birdies' petite nocturne; piano
solo with words, by Ruth E.
Day. © The Willis Music Co.,
Cincinnati; 18Mar47; EP28539.

Message of the bells; piano solo
by Ruth E. Day. © The Willis Music
Co., Cincinnati; 18Dec46;
EP11560.

DAY, SONNY.
Let's sing a love song; words
& music by Jack Darrell and
Sonny Day. © Jack Darrell,
Ozone Park, N. Y.; 27May47;
EP6888.

DEAN, CHARLES W
Dreaming of the past at twilight;
by Charles W. Dean. Concord,
N.H., The DeFarreo Letter
Service. © Charles W. Dean,
Concord, N.H.; 8Mar46;
EP14249. For voice and piano,
with chord symbols.

DEAN, DAISY. See
Crookhan, Daisy Dean.

DEAN, EDITH B
On wings of melody; [by Edith B.
Dean] © Edith B. Dean, Colum-
bus, Ohio; 30Apr47; EP14407.
Hymns, with music.

DEAN, J   F   1909-
arr.
Army Catering Corps; "Sugar
and spice" ... arr. by J. F.
Dean. © Hawkes & Son (London),
ltd., London; on arrangement;
29Apr47; EF3780. Parts: band.

DEANE, BETTY.
It's a moonlight night; words and
music by Betty Deane, arr. by
Helo Dominici and Harold Brobst.
Oakland, Calif., Golden Gate
Publications. © Ray Moany,
Golden Gate Publications, Oak-
land, Calif.; 22Feb47; EP14122.
For voice and 2 guitars; also
diagrams and chord symbols for
ukolole.

Lazy buckaroo ... words and music
by Betty Deane. © Peer International Corp., New York; 24Feb47;
EP13648.

DE ANGELIS, ALFREDO. See
Angelis, Alfredo de.

DE ARMOND, EVERETT NORTON, 1925-
Take me back to Arizona; by Everett
DeArmond, [arr. by Lindsay Mc-
Phail] © Everett Norton DeArmond,
Mecca, Ind.; 16Nov46; EP10893.
For voice and piano, with chord
symbols.

DE BOLADERES, GUILLERMO. See
Boladeres, Guillermo de.

DE BORBÓN, ALFREDO NÚÑEZ. See
Núñez de Borbón, Alfredo.

DEBUSSY, CLAUDE, 1862-1918.
Beau soir; [by] Claude Debussy,
transcribed for piano solo by
Ralph Berkowitz. © Elkan-Vogel
Co., inc., Philadelphia; on
transcription; 24Dec46; EP11456.

Reverie; by Claude Debussy,
[arr. by Hugo Frey] ©
Hamilton S. Gordon, inc.,
New York; on simplified
arrangement; 26Feb47;
EP12868. For piano solo.

Reverie; by Claude Debussy. [Simpli-
fied; arr. by Hugo Frey] ©
Hamilton S. Gordon, inc., New
York; on arrangement; 26Feb47;
EP13739. For piano solo.

Reverie; by Claude Debussy.
[words by Elsie-Jean, pseud.]
arr. by Hugo Frey. © Hamilton
S. Gordon, inc., New York; on
arrangement and words; 6Jun47;
EP15063. For piano solo, with
words.

DECEICO, INEZ, 1902-
Tears in my heart; by Inez
Deceico. © Shelby Music
Publishing Co., Detroit;
2Apr47; EP14327. For voice
and piano, with chord
diagrams and chord symbols.

DECINA, LOUIS J   1912-
Alice; words and music by Louis
J. Decina. © The Chase-Santora
Studios, Philadelphia; 11Jan47;
EP11200.

DECKER, ARLAND ASA, 1890-
For you and me; words and music by
Arland Decker. [c1945] © Arland
A. Decker, Fresno, Calif.;
7Dec46; EP11537.

DECKER, HAROLD A   1914-   arr.
Bow low, elder; S.A.T.B. Version
collected by R. Emmett Kennedy
... arr. by Harold A. Decker. ©
C. C. Birchard & Co., Boston;
on arrangement; 27Aug46; EP10891.

DE CRESCENZO, V. See
Crescenzo, V. de.

DEERING, JIMMY.
That feeling of falling in love;
words & music by Jimmy Deering.
© Nordyke Publishing Co., Los
Angeles; 110ct46; EP11995.

34

DE FILLASTRE, GEORGETTE. See
Fillastre, Georgette de.
DE FLUITER, HENRY.
I could not live without Jesus;
[by] Henry de Fluiter. ©
Henry de Fluiter, Gardena,
Calif.; 1Jun47; EP6951. Close
score: SATB.
DE GOURNAY, ROGER. See
Gournay, Roger de.
DE HAAS, GEORGE.
Linked together. Lo nitka od.
[For] mixed voices (S.A.T.B.),
music by George de Haas, poem
by I. Lamdan. © Transcontinen-
tal Music Corp., New York;
12Mar47; EP12744. Hebrew text,
transliterated.
DE HELLEBRANTH, ELENA.
Give me tomorrow; words and
music by Elena de Hellebranth.
© Cine-Mart Music Publishing
Co., Hollywood, Calif.;
1Nov46; EP11496.
DEHETTE, MAURICE.
(Farandoles) Pour vous, madame
... de l'emission Radio-Lille,
"Farandoles"; paroles de
Edouard Rombeau et René
Bernoville, musique de
Maurice Dehette & Pierre
Drucbert. © Ste. ame. fse.
Chappell, Paris; 10May47;
EF3796. Melody and words.
DEIS, CARL.
Arise, all nations! Music by
Carl Deis, poem by Albert C.
Lisson. © Galaxy Music Corp.,
New York; 4Mar47; EP6641.
Loch Lomond; traditional Scottish
song. (In Swarthout, Gladys,
comp. Gladys Swarthout album of
concert songs and arias.
p. 69-72) © G. Schirmer, inc.,
New York; on arrangement;
21Feb46; EP2419.
DE JESUS MORALES, JOSE. See
Jesús Morales, José de.
DE KLERK, ALBERT. See
Klerk, Albert de.
Klerk, Albert Jozef de.
Klerk, Josef Albert de.
DEKNIGHT, JIMMY.
Cowboy deal ... music by Jimmy
DeKnight [and] R. G. Payne,
and [words by] Clyde Leighton.
© Jack Howard Publications,
inc., Philadelphia; 30Dec46;
EP10975. For voice and piano,
with chord symbols.
Dust on the trail; words and music
by Jimmy De Knight. (In Cousin
Lee book of original songs,
p.19-21) © Jack Howard Publica-
tions, inc., Philadelphia;
30Dec46; EP11735.
DEKOVEN, REGINALD, 1859-1920.
Oh promise me ... music by Reginald
DeKoven, vocal orchestration by
Dave Kaplan. © Broadcast Music,
inc., New York; on orchestration;
17Sep46; EP11024. Piano-
conductor score (orchestra) and
parts.
Oh, promise me; [words] by Clement
Scott and [music by] Reginald De
Koven. Choral version for women's
voices by Noble Cain. © Broadcast Music, inc., New York; on
arrangement; 21Apr47; EP15230.
R. DeKoven's Oh promise me ...
pianostyle by George Reynolds
[c1946] © Gamble Hinged
Music Co., Chicago; on arrangement; 10Jan47; EP11089.
R. De Koven's Oh promise me;
violin arrangement by Dorothy
Morriam, [piano acc. by Stanley
Bodnar. c1946] © Gamble
Hinged Music Co., Chicago; on
arrangement; 30Jan47; EP11498.
Score (violin and piano) and
part.

DELACHI, PAOLO, 1874-
(Sonata, violin & piano) Sonata
(appassionata) ... [by] Paolo
Delachi. © Carisch, società
anonima, Milan; 30Oct41;
EF5243. Score and part.
DE LALANDE, MICHEL RICHARD. See
Lalande, Michel Richard de.
DE LAMARTER, ERIC, 1880-
Break, new-born year; (with
piano or organ acc.) ... Text
by Thomas Hornblow Gill, music
by Eric De Lamarter. © M.
Witmark & Sons, New York;
14May47; EP14611.
Four eclogues ... For the organ
by Eric De Lamarter. © M.
Witmark & Sons, New York;
30Apr47; EP14295.
Overture; for the organ by Eric
De Lamarter. © M. Witmark &
Sons, New York; 23Apr47; EP13948.
DELAMATER, EUGENE, 1876-1943, arr.
Concert miniatures for orchestra;
selected and arranged by E. De-
Lamater. © Rubank, inc.,
Chicago; 1May47; EP13991.
Piano-conductor score (orchestra)
and parts.
DE LA ROSA, ORLANDO. See
Rosa, Orlando de la.
DE LA TORRE, HECTOR. See
Torre, Hector de la.
DE LEONE, FRANCESCO.
Spring in Donegal; words by
James Francis Cooke, music by
Francesco De Leone. © Theodore
Presser Co., Philadelphia;
8Apr47; EP13485.
DELETTRE, JEAN.
Un escargot sans coquille;
paroles de Pierre Dudan,
musique de Jean Delettre.
Paris, Paris-Monde. ©
Editions Paris-Broadway, Paris;
31Dec46; EF3815.
Il a le regard francais;
paroles de Francois Llenas,
musique de Jean Delettre. ©
Editions Paris-Broadway, Paris;
31Dec46; EF3818.
J'ai laissé mon coeur à Paris;
paroles de Georges et André
Tabet, musique de Jean
Delettre. © Editions Paris-
Broadway, Paris; 31Dec46;
EF3832.
Jimmy de Harlem; paroles de
Pierre Dudan, musique de Jean
Delettre. Paris, En vente aux
Editions R. Breton. ©
Editions Paris-Broadway, Paris;
31Dec46; EF3834.
Si vous vouliez, madame; paroles
[by] Roger Lucchesi, musique
[by] Jean Delettre. © Editions
Paris-Broadway, Paris; 31Dec46;
EF3880.
Trop tard; paroles de René
Baillié Duchateau, musique de
Jean Delettre & Ralph Carcel.
© Editions Paris-Broadway,
Paris; 31Mar46; EF3842.
Vous trouv'rez tout ça chez moi!
... paroles de Jean Boyer,
musique de Jean Delettre.
Paris, Paris-Monde. ©
Editions Paris-Broadway, Paris;
31Dec46; EF3816.
DELFAU, RENÉ, 1902-
Forgeons ... version pour quatre
voix mixtes, paroles de Emile
Ohlmann, musique de René Delfau.
© Rouart, Lerolle et Cie., Paris;
31Sep46; EF3468.

DELGADO, NARCISO, 1902-
Necesito de ti ... letra de
Gabriel Luna de la Fuente,
música de Narciso Delgado.
English lyric, Longing for
you, by Don Titman, version
française, J'ai besoin de toi,
de Lucien Thériault. ©
Editions A. Passio, Lachute,
Qué., Can.; 20Jun47; EF3933.
DELGADO, PEPÉ.
Champú de cariño ... letra y
música de: Pepé Delgado,
arreglo de: D. Pérez-Prado.
© Peer International Corp.,
New York; 16Dec46; EF3666.
Parts: orchestra.
Me voy pá Sibanicú ... letra y
música de Pepé Delgado,
arreglo del autor. © Peer
International Corp., New
York; 30Dec46; EF5431.
Piano-conductor score
(orchestra) and parts.
Oye; letra y musica de Pepé
Delgado. © Peer International
Corp., New York; 30Dec46;
EF5554.
DELIBES, LÉO, 1836-1891.
Chant of the Brahmans. See his
Lakmé.
(Lakmé) Chant of the Brahmans;
(from the opera Lakmé by
Delibes) S. A. T. B., adapted
and arr. by William A. Golds-
worthy. © Edwin H. Morris &
Co., inc., New York; 15May47;
EP14526.
Souvenirs from the great
masters, Delibes; selected &
arr. by G. H. Clutsam. ©
Keith Prowse & Co., ltd.,
London; on arrangement;
30Dec46; EF14794. For piano
solo.
DE LIMA, ALBERTO. See
Lima, Alberto de.
DELLO JOIO, NORMAN.
A fable; for four-part chorus of
mixed voices with tenor solo
and piano acc. ... [words] by
Vachel Lindsay, music by Norman
Dello Joio. © Carl Fischer,
inc., New York; 29Apr47; EP14090.
Madrigal; for four-part chorus
of mixed voices, with piano
acc., S.A.T.B., adapted from
the poem by Christina Rossetti,
music by Norman Dello Joio.
© Carl Fischer, inc., New
York; 18Mar47; EP13136.
DELLON, HAROLD.
Alone; words & music by Jack
Stanley, Geo. A. Little and
Harold Dellon. © Mills Music,
inc., New York, J.
Mills. (successors in interest to
Jack Mills), New York; 25May20;
EP6801.
DEL MUNTE, MANUEL, pseud. See
Cassard, Emmanuel.
DEL RIEGO, TERESA, 1876-
Homing; words by Arthur L. Salmon,
music by Teresa Del Riego, arr.
for ... S. A. T. B. by Clarence
Lucas. © Chappell & Co., ltd.,
London; on arrangement; 1May47;
EF3413.
The sunrise is coming; song, the
lyric by A. V. Broadhurst, the
music by Teresa Del Riego.
[c1945] © Albert Victor
Broadhurst, London; 25Sep46;
EF4799.

DELRIEU, GEORGES.
Trois noëls niçois; composés ou
recueillis par Georges Delrieu,
harmonisés ... par Paul
Berthier. © Georges Delrieu et
Cie., Nice, France; 15Nov46;
EF5207. Score: chorus (SSA)
and organ, and part for chorus.
Words in French dialect and
French.

DEL RIO, PEPE.
Lalo estuvo aqui; música de Pepe
Del Rio, letra de Alberto
Salinas [and] Castro Valencia.
© Peer International Corp.,
New York; 10Apr47; EF13696.

DELTOUR, EMILE, 1899-
Concerto-jazz; pour violon; [music
by] Emilo Doltour. © Robert
Bosmans d. b. a. Editions Ch.
Bens, Brussels; 25Sep46; EF5354.
Piano-conductor score (violin
and orchestra) and parts.

DELVOIE, JEAN CLAUDE, 1912-
Olé Maléna! ... [By] Jean Delvoie
& Raoul Laynez. © Éditions
Musicales Jean Delvoie, Paris;
15Jan47; EF3510. Piano-conductor
score (orchestra) and parts.

DEMAREST, CLIFFORD, 1874-1946.
Bo Thou exalted, O God; [by]
Clifford Demarest, arr. by
Hugh Gordon [pseud.] © The
Arthur P. Schmidt Co., Boston;
on arrangement; 14Jan47;
EP11208. Score: chorus (SSA)
and organ.

DE MARTINO, RODOLFO. See
Martino, Rodolfo de.

DE MENASCE, JACQUES. See
Menasce, Jacques de.

DE MOLIÈRE, ROGER. See
Molière, Roger de.

DEMUTH, NORMAN.
Mouvement perpetuel; for piano,
[by] Norman Demuth. © Augener,
ltd., London; 25Nov46; EF5113.

DEN BERG, CORNELIS JACOBUS VAN. See
Berg, Cornelis Jacobus van den.

DEN BROECK, LEO VAN. See
Broeck, Leo van den.

DENBY, JACK.
Daddy's little pin-up girl;
words & music by Muriel Watson
& Jack Denby. © Campbell,
Connelly & Co., ltd., London;
21Apr47; EF3326.
An empty chair and memories; words
and music by Muriel Watson & Jack
Denby. © Southern Music Publish-
ing Co., ltd., London; 16Dec41;
EF5623.

DENCHER, STAN.
My heart belongs to you; words by
Joel Dutton, music by Stan
Doncher. © Cine-Mart Music
Publishing Co., Hollywood, Calif.;
30Dec46; EP11212.

DENEKE, ERIK VICTOR MAX, 1904-
Giv mig dit Hjerte, Maria ...
Musik og Tekst; Erik Deneke.
© Jac. Boesens Musikforlag,
a/s, Copenhagen; 1Jun39; EF5158.

DE NIGRIS, NETTIE, ed.
Sing the mass ... Gregorian mass and
supplementary hymns edited and
simplified by Nettie De Nigris.
[Rev. and enl. ed.] © Herold
Flammer, inc., New York; on revision
and additions; 30Aug46; EP11166.

DENNEE, CHARLES, 1863-1946.
Echoes of the past; gavotte.
Op.27, no.2, [by] Charles
Donnée. © The Arthur P.
Schmidt Co., Boston; 5Nov46;
EP10756. Score: piano 1-2;
part for piano 1 also playable
as piano solo.

DENNEY, DAVE.
(He's my darlin') precious little
sonny boy; by Riley Shepard
[and] Dave Denney. © Leeds
Music Corp., New York; 15May47;
EP14420. For voice and piano,
with guitar diagrams and chord
symbols.

DENNY, DAVE.
That'll be the day; words and
music by Dave Denny. © Regent
Music Corp., New York; 20Mar47;
EP12765.

DE NOD, pseud. See
Donnaddu, A.

DENZA, LUIGI.
Funiculi funicula; by Luigi Denza,
arr. by Philip J. Lang. © Mills
Music, inc., New York; on arrangement; 18Mar47; EP6711. Condensed
score (band) and parts.

DE PACHMANN, LIONEL. See
Pachmann, Lionel de.

DePAUL, GENE.
Pig foot Pete; by Don Raye [and]
Gene DePaul, arr. by Van Alex-
ander. © Leeds Music Corp.,
New York; on arrangement; 14Apr47;
EP13714. Condensed score
(orchestra) and parts.

DE PAZ, RAFAEL. See
Paz, Rafael de.

DE RAAFF, ADRIANUS CORNELIS. See
Raaff, Adrianus Cornelis de.

DE RAAFF, ANDRÉ. See
Raaff, Adrianus Cornelis de.

DER MOLEN, ALBERT VAN. See
Van der Molen, Albert.

DE ROMNEY, pseud. See
Friebar, Louis.

DE ROSE, PETER.
As years go by. See his Song
of love.
(Earl Carroll vanities) A beauti-
ful girl (is lovely all the
time); lyric by Earl Carroll,
music by Peter De Rose, [from]
Earl Carroll vanities.
© Robbins Music Corp., New
York; 5Feb47; EP11866.
(Song of love) As years go by,
based on Brahms' Hungarian
dance, no. 4 ... [from] the
... picture, "Song of love"
by Charles Tobias and Peter
De Rose. © Miller Music
Corp., New York; 16May47;
EP14569. For voice and piano,
with chord symbols.
That's where I came in; lyric by
Charles Tobias, music by Peter
De Rose. © Robbins Music Corp.,
New York; 4Dec46; EP11000.

DE SANTIAGO MAJO, RODRIGO A. See
Santiago Majo, Rodrigo A. de.

DEUTSCH, ADOLPH.
The blaze of noon; words by
Charles Henderson, music by
Adolph Deutsch ... [from]
"Blaze of noon." © Famous
Music Corp., New York; 18Apr47;
EP13797.

DEVOL, FRANK, 1911-
Pinto Ben; poem by William S. Hart,
music arrangement by Frank
DeVol. © Ruval Music Co., Holly-
wood, Calif.; 24Dec46; EP10976.
For narrator and piano.

DEVONSHIRE, TED.
Labor ... words by Marie Young,
music by Ted Devonshire.
© Caribbean Music, inc., New
York; 7Apr47; EP13341.

DE VORE, GLADYS, 1909-
Down on Claiborne Avenue; words
and music by Gladys De Vore,
[arr. by Mrs. Alfred Farrell]
c1946. © Gladys De Vore, New
Orleans; 2Apr47; EP13804.

DE WITTE, ALFRED, 1908-
I can't forget your smile; by
Alfred De Witte. © Shelby
Music Publishing Co., Detroit;
3Dec46; EP11770. For voice
and piano, with guitar diagrams
and chord symbols.

DEXTER, AL.
I learned about love from you; words
and music by Al Dexter. Hollywood,
Calif., Hill and Range Songs. ©
Hill and Range Songs, inc. & Al
Dexter Music Publishing Co., Holly-
wood, Calif.; 21Feb47; EP12212.
That cute little girl down at the
roadside inn; words and music by
Al Dexter. Hollywood, Calif.,
Hill and Range Songs. © Hill
and Range Songs, inc. and Al
Dexter Music Publishing Co.,
Hollywood, Calif.; 10Jun47;
EP15085.

DEXTER, GLEN, pseud. See
Sanders, George H.

D'HARDELOT, GUY, pseud. See
Rhodes, Helen (Guy)

DIAL, HARRY, 1907-
Ev'ry day blues; by Harry Dial.
© Popular Music Co., New York;
15Jun47; EP15035. For voice
and piano, with chord symbols.

DIAMOND, DAVID.
Album for the young; for piano
solo, [by] David Diamond. ©
Elkan-Vogel Co., inc., Philadelphia; 11Mar47; EP13935.

DÍAZ, JESÚS.
"Cogiendo agua" ... letra y
música de Jesús Díaz, arreglo de
Eulogio Castelciro (Yoyo) ©
Peer International Corp., New
York; 18Dec46; EF5582. Parts:
orchestra.

DIAZ OVIEDO, IGNACIO. See
Diaz y Oviedo, Ignacio.

DIAZ Y OVIEDO, IGNACIO.
Belenciano soy ... letra y
música de Ignacio Díaz Oviedo
(Pelo) © Peer International
Corp., New York; 30Dec46;
EP5443. Parts: orchestra.

DI CEGLIE, COSIMO. See
Ceglie, Cosimo di.

DI CEGLIE-OLIVIERI. See
Ceglie-Olivieri, di.

DICKINSON, DOROTHY.
Black man's return; words & music
by Dorothy Dickinson. © Nordyke Pub. Co., Los Angeles;
27Sep46; EP11922.
My song is a threnody; words &
music by Dorothy Dickinson. ©
Nordyke Publishing Co., Los
Angeles; 16Dec46; EP11049.

DICKSON, ART.
Don't let the light burn low;
words and music by Art Dickson,
... piano arrangement by Dick
Kent. © Peer International
Corp., New York; 7May47;
EP14940.

DIESTELHORST, HULDA JEAN, 1904-
Santa, dear Santa; piano solo (with
words) by H. Jean Diestelhorst,
© Shattinger Piano & Music Co.,
St. Louis; 31Dec46; EP11253.

DIESTELHORST, HULDA JEAN, 1904-
arr.
Easter tidings; Easter melodies
arr. for piano by H. Jean
Diestelhorst. © Shattinger
Piano & Music Co., St. Louis;
on arrangement; 6May47;
EP14233.

36

DIETERICH, MILTON, 1900-
In deepest need; [by] Milton
Dieterich, SATB. © Clayton
F. Summy Co., Chicago;
20Jan47; EP11363.

Morning wind; [words by Lynn
Riggs, music by] Milton
Dieterich. SSA. © Clayton
F. Summy Co., Chicago;
10Jan47; EP11329.

When we lift our eyes to pray;
[words and music by] Milton
Dieterich. SATB. © Clayton
F. Summy Co., Chicago; 30Dec46;
EP10984.

DIÉVAL, JACK, 1920-
Jack's ideas; [by] Jack Diéval.
© Le Chant du Monde, Paris;
20Jan47; EF3511. Melody with
piano accompaniment.

DIGGLE, ROLAND.
Awake, my soul; [for] mixed voices,
[music by] Roland Diggle, [words
by] Bishop Ken. © Edward Schuberth
& Co., inc., New York; 21Jan47;
EP11414.

Concert piece on Forest green; [by]
Roland Diggle. © Edward Schuberth
& Co., inc., New York; 27Jan47;
EP11412. For organ solo; includes
registration for Hammond organ.

Down from the hills; by R. Diggle,
three part chorus for female
voices. © Edward Schuberth &
Co., inc., New York; 29Jan47;
EP11648.

Five responses; for chorus of
women's voices, S.S.A.A.,
a cappella, [by] Roland
Diggle. Adapted from Gloria
in excelsis (Episcopal prayer
book) © Carl Fischer, inc.,
New York; 10Feb47; EP12162.

I will extol Thee [by] Roland Diggle.
[words from the Psalms] (Anthem
for mixed voices) © Oliver Ditson
Co., Philadelphia; 29Jan47;
EP11883.

O be joyful in the Lord ... S.A.T.B.
[by] Roland Diggle. © Abbey
Music Co., Hollywood, Calif.;
17Dec46; EP10786.

O swallow, swallow; by R. Diggle,
three part chorus for female
voices, [words by A. Tennyson]
© Edward Schuberth & Co., inc.,
New York; 19Feb47; EP12159.

Oh Ninna and Anninia ... S.S.A.
[by] Roland Diggle. © Abbey
Music Co., Hollywood, Calif.;
17Dec46; EP10788.

Scherzo and fugue; for the organ,
by Roland Diggle. © M.Witmark
& Sons, New York; 14May47;
EP11612.

The short Te Deum ... [by] Roland
Diggle. © Abbey Music Co.,
Hollywood, Calif.; 17Dec46;
EP10787. Score: SATB and piano;
English words.

The spacious firmament; for
chorus of mixed voices [by]
Roland Diggle, [words by] J.
Addison. © The B. F. Wood
Music Co., Boston; 21Apr47;
EP13811.

DIHIGO H , ROGELIO.
A diez por kilo los hombres
... letra de Maria Bernal de
R., música de Rogelio Dihigo
H., arreglo de J. E. Lazaga.
© Peer International Corp.,
New York; 30Dec46; EF5436.
Parts: orchestra.

DILLER, ANGELA.
Second piano parts to First solo book
pieces; by Angela Diller. © G.
Schirmer, inc., New York; 30Dec46;
EP11629.

DILLER, MARTIN, pseud. See
Richards, Don.

DILLON, WILLIAM A comp.
Sunshine Mission melodies ...
written and comp. by William
and Mildred Dillon. Chicago,
Sunshine Gospel Mission, ©
William S. Dillon, Chicago;
no. 4, 18Feb46; EP2055.

DINICU.
Hora staccato; for piano (simpli-
fied version) [by] Dinicu-
Heifetz, [arranged by Maxwell
Eckstein] © Carl Fischer,
inc., New York; 23Dec46; EP11062.

DITMAR, WILLARD, 1910-
I knelt at Jesus' feet; [words
by] W. D. and Lois Blanchard,
[music by] Willard Ditmar.
(In Church of the Nazarene.
Michigan District. Nazarene
Young Peoples Society.
Choruses of the N. Y. P. S.
p.45) © Michigan District,
Nazarene Young Peoples Society,
Flint, Mich.; 2Jul46; Ep13067.
Close score: SATB.

DITTENHAVER, SARAH LOUISE.
Four piano compositions; by Sarah
L. Dittenhaver. © Clayton F.
Summy Co., Chicago; on 4 pieces;
29May47. Contents.- [v.1]
Among the daffodils (© EP11827)-
[v.2] Climbing up our apple
tree (© EP11828)- [v.3] My pet
squirrel (© EP11829)- [v.4]
My red wagon (© EP11830)

Let's play duets; for the piano
... by Sarah Louise Dittenhaver,
verses written or selected by
the composer. © Oliver Ditson
Co., Philadelphia; 25Mar47;
EP12995.

Once more, beloved; song by
Sarah Louise Dittenhaver.
© Oliver Ditson Co., Phila-
delphia; 29Apr47; EP14068.

DI VEROLI, DONATO. See
Veroli, Donato di.

DIXON, GEORGE.
We wish we had it but we ain't;
words and music by Gladys Patch,
Albert Patch and George Dixon,
... piano arrangement by Dick
Kent. © Peer International
Corp., New York; 27May47;
EP14959.

DJABADARY, HÉRACLIUS, 1891-1937.
[Concerto, violoncello, no. 1)
Concerto en ut majeur ...
"Souvenir de Hongrie," [by]
H. Djabadary. [Op. 11] Paris,
L. de Lacour, Éditions
Costallat. © Chotha Djabadary,
Paris; 7Apr43; EF3868. Score
(violoncello and piano) and
part.

La mélopée du serpent; pour
orchestre symphonique, (solo de
flûte) Op. 19. [By] Pce.
Héraclius Djabadary ... Piano
réduction de l'orchestre par
Paris,
L. de Lacour, Éditions Costallat.
© Chotha Djabadary, Paris;
7Apr43; EF3865.

Les moments vécus; [by] H.
Djabadary. Paris, Éditions
Costallat, L. de Lacour. ©
Chotha Djabadary, Paris;
7Apr43. For piano solo.
Contents.- [4] A. E. K.
(© EF3864) - [5] Sur la tombe
de Barczy Marguit (© EF3863)

Nocturne. Lied, Op. 18 ...
[By] Prince Héraclius Djabadary,
d'après la poésie de Marg.
Antoinette, princesse Héraclius
Djabadary. Paris, Scnart.
© Chotha Djabadary, Paris;
10Dec29; EF3870. Score (violoncello, speaker and piano) and
part for violoncello.

Nocturne en ut mineur; pour
piano et déclamation, paroles
de Barczy Marguit (Pocsse.
Héraclius Djabadary. Op. 14.
Paris, L. de Lacour, Éditions
Costallat. © Chotha Djabadary,
Paris; 16Mar43; EF3871.

Regrets ... Op. 24. Par H.
Djabadary. Nice, Delrieu Frères.
© Chotha Djabadary, Paris;
14Oct37; EF3867. Score (violoncello and piano) and part.

Rhapsodie géorgienne. Op.2.
Pour piano et orchestre,
[by] H. Djabadary, piano II
réduction de l'orchestre par
Chotha Djabadary. Paris,
Gallet et Fils. © Chotha
Djabadary, Paris; 4Jan42;
EF3872.

Variations sur un chant hongrois;
[by] H. Djabadary. Op. 23.
Paris, Gallot & Fils. © Chotha
Djabadary, Paris; 6Apr42; EF3866.
Score (violoncello and piano) and
part.

DOBIAS, VACLAV, 1909-
Tri toccaty; [by] Václav Dobiáš.
© Hudobní Matice Umělecké Besedy,
Praha, Czechoslovakia; 22Apr43;
EF4947. For piano solo.

DOCKING, LESTER.
I fell in love ... words and music
by Lester Docking. © Peer International Corp., New York;
24Feb47; EP13651.

I left my boots and saddle home
(just to make a little jeep go)
... words and music by Lester
Docking. © Peer International
Corp., New York; 24Feb47;
EP13647.

DODD, BONNIE.
Everyone knew it but me; by Bonnie
Dodd. © Tex Ritter Music
Publication, inc., New York;
1Apr47; EP13357. For voice and
piano, with chord symbols.

DODD, DOROTHY.
Once upon a time; words and
music by Amy Walton Lewis and
Dorothy Dodd. © D. Davis & Co.,
ltd., Sydney; 14Jan47; EF5156.

DOLAN, JAMES.
Good evening to you; words and
music by Jim Dolan. © Campbell, Connelly & Co., ltd.,
London; 21Apr47; EF3325.

DOLAN, ROBERT EMMETT, 1908-
(Dear Ruth) Fine thing; [From]
the ... picture "Dear Ruth,"
words by Johnny Mercer, music by
Robert Emmett Dolan. © Paramount
Music Corp., New York; 1May47;
EP14142.

DOMINGUEZ, ARMANDO.
Preferible es llorar; de
Armando Dominguez. © Promotora
Hispano Americana de Música,
s.a., Mexico, D. F.; 27Dec46;
EP14862. Piano conductor score
(orchestra), and parts.

DOMÍNGUEZ, ERNESTO.
Blanca luz ... de Ernesto
Domínguez. © Promotora Hispano
Americana de Música, s.a.,
México; 23Dec46; EF5073. For
piano solo.

DOMINGUEZ, PEPE.
Las suegras; letra y música de Pepe Dominguez. New York, Sole selling agent, Peer International Corp. © Promotora Hispano Americana de Música, s. a., Mexico; 13Dec46; EF11170. For voice and piano, with chord symbols.

DOMINICI, HELO, 1906-
Polynesian swing; words and music by Helo Dominici. Oakland, Calif., Golden Gate Publications. © Ray Meany, Golden Gate Publications, Oakland, Calif.; 1Apr47; EF13440. For voice and 2 guitars; also diagrams and chord symbols for ukelele.

Singing strings; words and music by Helo Dominici. Oakland, Calif., Golden Gate Publications. © Ray Meany, Golden Gate Publications, Oakland, Calif.; 1Apr47; EF13444. For voice and 2 guitars; also diagrams and chord symbols for ukelele.

DONADIO, LUIGI, 1885-
Senza pate, e' nnammarata! Versi e musica di Luigi Donadio. © Luigi Donadio, New York; 23Jun47; EF15254. For mandolin solo, with words.

DONALD, JANIE STEELE, 1913-
Along this way ... Lyrics by Mrs. Emma Davis Dorsey, music by Mrs. Janie Steele Donald. © Emma Davis Dorsey, New York; 26Apr47; EP14446.

DONALDSON, WALTER.
At ev'nin; words and music by Walter Donaldson, a Jack Mason arrangement. [c1947] © Leo Feist, Inc., New York; on arrangement; 16Dec46; EP11820. Piano-conductor score (orchestra, with words) and parts.

My mom ... By Walter Donaldson, (S.S.A.) arr. by William Stickles. © Bregman, Vocco and Conn, inc., New York; on arrangement; 9May47; EP14338.

DONATO, EDGARDO.
Julián porteño ... letra de Justo Ricardo Thompson, música de Edgardo Donato. Buenos Aires, Editorial Argentina de Música Internacional. © Peer International Corp., New York; 30Dec46; EF5555.

DONEDDU, A 1885-
Formosa ... [by] A. Doneddu (aud Niña, by De Nod, pseud.) © Editions A. Doneddu, Paris; 31Jan47; EF3517. Piano-conductor score (orchestra) and parts.

DONNELL, ROBERT.
This Canada of ours. Glorieux Canada. Words by Percy J. Philip, music by Robert Donnell, paroles françaises de Gustave Lacasse. © Gordon V. Thompson, ltd., Toronto; 4Feb47; EF3120. For voice and piano.

DONOVAN, RICHARD.
Down by the Sally gardens; traditional Irish air freely arr. for voice and piano by Richard Donovan, poem by W. B. Yeats. © Galaxy Music Corp., New York; on arrangement; 2May47; EP6971.

Good ale; for four-part chorus of men's voices with piano acc. T.T.B.B. Poem by John Still ... music by Richard Donovan. © Carl Fischer, inc., New York; 18Mar47; EP13161.

DORR, ALBERT I
"Apologies to Farmer MacDonald"; by Albert I. Dorr. © George F. Briegel, inc., New York; on arrangement; 2Dec46; EP10941. Condensed score (narrator and band) and parts.

March of the Twirling corps; [by] Albert I. Dorr. © George F. Briegel, inc., New York; 24Feb47; EP12435. Condensed score (band) and parts.

DORSETT, LARRY EUGENE, 1927-
The day you came along; words & music by Larry Dorsett. [c1946] © Larry Dorsett, Lubbock, Tex.; 1Feb47; EP13910.

DORSEY, JAMES ELMO, arr.
Two negro spirituals; arr. by James E. Dorsey. © G. Schirmer, inc., New York; on 2 songs, 3Apr47. Contents.-They led my Lord away (© EP14054)- Four and twenty elders (© EP14055)

DORSEY, JIMMY.
Dixieland detour [by] Jimmy Dorsey [and Toots Camarata, arr. by Murray Feldman] © Robbins Music Corp., New York; on arrangement; 27Nov46; EP11814. Score (saxophone and piano) and part.

Mood Hollywood [by] Jimmy Dorsey [and Lennie Hayton, arr. by Murray Feldman] © Robbins Music Corp., New York; on arrangement; 27Nov46; EP11819. Score (saxophone and piano) and part.

DORSEY, THOMAS A
Piano duet book of gospel hymns; by Thomas A. Dorsey, ed. and arr. by Rose Sattler Grimes. © Thomas A. Dorsey, Chicago; 30Dec44; EP6755.

DORSEY, TOMMY.
Tap dancer's nightmare [by] Jimmy Dorsey [and Larry Clinton, arr. by Murray Feldman] © Robbins Music Corp., New York; on arrangement; 27Nov46; EP11813. Score (saxophone and piano) and part.

DOSSEY, WARNER G.
I can't forget the day we met; words and music by Warner G. Dossey. © Cine-Mart Music Publishing Co., Hollywood, Calif.; 1Nov46; EP11477.

DOTEVSKY, ANDRE, pseud. See Row, Richard D.

DOWLE, FRED.
What was her name? Music by Fred Dowle, words by Larry Gondringer & Tommy Coley. © Unique Music Publishers, Detroit; 1Dec46; EP12027.

DOWNEY, C EARL.
Princely courtiers; march [by] C. Earl Downey, Arlington, Ind.; 17Jan47; EP13396. Piano-conductor score (orchestra) and parts.

DRAKE, GABE, 1918-
Where tho moonbeams kiss the river Rio Grande; by Leo Corday, Leon Carr [and] Gabe Drake. © Ritchie Music Co., inc., New York; 1Mar47; EP12920. For voice and piano, with chord symbols.

DREIER, MARIE.
Lord God Almighty; by Marie Dreier. [text arr. by Marie Dreier] © Marie Dreier, Chicago; 8Jun46; EP12146. Score: soprano, alto, chorus (SSAA) and piano.

DRONIOU, RENÉE.
Je cueille un bouquet; 12 chansons pour enfants, par R. Droniou avec la collaboration de Jacques Bernheim. © Éditions Bourrelier et Cie, Paris; 10Jul46; AF2984. For voice and piano.

DRUMM, GEORGE.
Ave Maria; adaptation from "Reverie," [by] George Drumm. © George F. Briegel, inc., New York; on adaptation; 2Dec46; EP10940. For voice and piano.

DRUMMOND-Wolff, S. See also Wolff, S. Drummond.

Christ the Lord is risen today; words from Michael Weisse ... [music by] S. Drummond Wolff. © Gordon V. Thompson, ltd., Toronto; 10Feb47; EF3151. Score: chorus (SATB) and organ.

DRUTTMAN, IRVING.
Advertising for a baby; by Jack Lawrence and Irving Druttman. © Whale Music Corp., New York; 14Apr47; EP13491. For voice and piano, with chord symbols.

DUANE, HARRY.
Right out of a dream; by Dudley Mecum and Harry Duane. © Dudley Mecum & Harry Duane, Hamilton, Ohio; 5May47; EP14601. For voice and piano.

[DUBARBIE, JEANNE] 1901-
Couli-couri; (Dernier rendez-vous], paroles de Jeanne Dumaine [pseud.], musique de Juanita Ferez [pseud.] © Publications Francis Day, Paris; 31Oct46; EF3580.

DUCHÁČ, MILOSLAV, 1924-
Rhythm. 21 special. [by] Miloslav Ducháč. © R. A. Dvorský, Praha, Czechoslovakia; 12Aug46; EF3357. Piano-conductor score (orchestra), condensed score and parts.

DUCLAYE, EDDY.
Romance au moulin; paroles et musique de Robert Duc et Eddy Duclaye. © Éditions Paris-Broadway, Paris; 31Dec45; EF3827.

DUFFY, JOHN JOSEPH, 1898- .
A cradle song; for voice and piano, by John Joseph Duffy, [words by William Butler Yeats] © G. Schirmer, inc., New York; 30Dec46; EP11635.

DUPOUR, BETTY.
Without you; words and music by Betty DuFour. © Nordyke Publishing Co., Los Angeles; 8Mar47; EF13291.

DUKE, JOHN.
Melody in E flat; [by] John Duke. © Elkan-Vogel Co., inc., Philadelphia; 24Dec46; EP11464. Score (violoncello and piano) and part.

Melody in E flat; [by] John Duke. © Elkan-Vogel Co., inc., Philadelphia; 24Dec46; EP11465. Score (viola and piano) and part.

DUKELSKY, VLADIMIR, 1903-April in Paris. See his Walk a little faster.

Nocturne ... [by] Vladimir Dukelsky. © Carl Fischer, inc., New York; 24Mar47; EP13003. Score (flute, oboe, clarinet, bassoon, horn and piano) and parts.

DUMAS, ROGER.
C'est toi le pays de mes rêves ... paroles de Jean Manse, musique de Roger Dumas. © Editions Royalty, Paris; 31Dec46; EF3612.
Faut pas bouder Bouddha ... paroles de Jean Manse, musique de Roger Dumas. © Editions Royalty, Paris; 31Dec46; EF3611.
J'ai un beau chapeau ... paroles de Jean Manse, musique de Roger Dumas. © Editions Royalty, Paris; 31Dec46; EF3885.
Je n'peux pas m'expliquer ... paroles de Jean Manse, musique de Roger Dumas. © Editions Royalty, Paris; 31Dec46; EF3886.
Savoir ce que l'on veut ... paroles de Jean Manse, musique de Roger Dumas. © Editions Royalty, Paris; 31Dec46; EF3893.
Un! deux! trois! ... Paroles de Jean Manse, musique de Roger Dumas. © Editions Royalty, Paris; 31Dec46; EF3894.

DUNAGAN, ESTHER, 1902-
Island paradise; words and music by Esther Dunagan. © Dunagan School of Music, Lubbock, Tex.; 21Aug46; EP11274.
My fair Hawaii; words and music by Esther Dunagan. © Dunagan School of Music, Lubbock, Tex.; 30Mar46; EP11241. For guitar solo, with words.

[DUNAGAN, I   D   ] arr.
The Red, White and Blue; [arr. by I. D. Dunagan] © Dunagan School of Music, Lubbock, Tex.; on arrangement; 30Mar46; EP11273. For guitar solo.

DUNCAN, CARLYLE, 1893-
Praise, my soul, the King of Heaven; for four-part chorus of mixed voices with contralto or baritone obbligato solo, and piano or organ acc. [By] Carlyle Duncan. [Words by] Henry Frances Lyte. © The Boston Music Co., Boston; on arrangement; 6Jun47; EP14990.
Shepherd's hymn; for four-part chorus of mixed voices with piano or organ acc. ad lib., a cappella. Words by W. Guernsey, music by Carlyle Duncan. © The Boston Music Co., Boston; on arrangement; 6Jun47; EP14989.

DUNCAN, THOMAS ELMER.
Stay a little longer (The hoe down fiddle song); words and music by Bob Wills and Tommy Duncan. © Peer International Corp., New York; 18Apr47; EP13986.

DUNCAN, TOMMY.
Cotton Eyed Joe; words and music by Bob Wills and Tommy Duncan. © Bob Wills Music, inc., Hollywood, Calif.; 28Mar47; EP13154.

DUNGAN, OLIVE. See also Pullen, Olive Dungan.
Fish seller; words by Florine Ashby, music by Olive Dungan. Low voice. © Carl Fischer, inc., New York; 21Apr47; EP13871.
Hurricane on de islan'; words by Florine Ashby, music by Olive Dungan. Low voice. © Carl Fischer, inc., New York; 21Apr47; EP13872.
Pale blue slippers; song, words by Vivian Yeisor Laramore, music by Olive Dungan. © The John Church Co., Philadelphia; 21Apr47; EP13944.

Rumba; for piano by Olive Dungan. © The Boston Music Co., Boston; 24Sep47; EP17727.
Vision; song, words by Vivian Yeisor Laramore, music by Olive Dungan. © The John Church Co., Philadelphia; 17May47; EP14608.

DUNHILL, THOMAS FREDERICK, 1877-1946.
By the river; [words by Kitty L. Beney], and Swallow-birds; [words by Margaret Rose] Unison songs, music by Thomas F. Dunhill. © Edward Arnold & Co., London; 12Dec46; EF4740.
Christmas eve; unison carol for trebles or mixed voices; music by Thomas F. Dunhill, words by Christina Rossetti. © Edward Arnold & Co., London; 12Dec46; EF4741.
King Winter; two-part song for treble voices with piano accompaniment; words by Irene Gass ... music by Thomas F. Dunhill. London, J. Curwen & Sons. © David Dunhill (executor of the late Thos. F. Dunhill) London; 16Nov46; EF4886.
Long ago at candle-light; unison carol, music by Thomas F. Dunhill, words by Margaret Rose. © Edward Arnold & Co., London; 12Dec46; EF4749.
The merry autumn days; unison song, music by Thomas F. Dunhill, words by Charles Dickens. © Edward Arnold & Co., London; 12Dec46; EF4750.
Mother Duck, and The pedlar; unison songs, music by Thomas F. Dunhill, words by Margaret Rose. © Edward Arnold & Co., London; 12Dec46; EF4751.
The rock pool; unison song, music by Thomas F. Dunhill, words by Dawson Freer. © Edward Arnold & Co., London; 12Dec46; EF4753.
Summer, the piper, and The little green elf; unison songs, music by Thomas F. Dunhill ... words by Margaret Rose. © Edward Arnold & Co., London; 12Dec46; EF4756.
Tommy Perkins, and The butterfly; unison songs, music by Thomas F. Dunhill, words by Margaret Rose. © Edward Arnold & Co., London; 12Dec46; EF4759.

DUNLAP, EDNA EARLE, 1888-
Mother beloved; arr. by Chester Nordman, words and music by Edna Earle Dunlap. © Shattinger Piano & Music Co., St. Louis; on arrangement; 6May47; EP14227. Score: SATB and piano.
Mother beloved; arr. by Chester Nordman, words and music by Edna Earle Dunlap. © Shattinger Piano & Music Co., St. Louis; on arrangement; 6May47; EP14228. Score: SSA and piano.
Mother beloved; words and music by Edna Earle Dunlap. © Shattinger Piano & Music Co., St. Louis; 6May47; EP14234.
Supplication; text from the Psalms, music by Edna Earle Dunlap. © Oliver Ditson Co., Philadelphia; 28May47; EP14696.

DUNLAP, FERN GLASGOW.
Wedding prayer; for voice and piano organ, by Fern Glasgow Dunlap. © G. Schirmer, inc., New York; 3Apr47; EP14056.

DUNLAP, MARY, 1897-
Why did we have to part, dear? by Mary Dunlap. Toronto; 10Dec46; EF4872. For voice and piano, with chord symbols.

DUNLOP, MERRILL.
New songs of Christian; [no.2] ... By Merrill Dunlop, Chicago, Van Kampen Press. © Merrill Dunlop, Oak Park, Ill.; 22May47; EP6967.

DUPONT, GABRIEL.
Mandoline. Mandolin. [Words by] Paul Verlaine, English version by Lorraine Noel Finley. (In Swarthout, Gladys, comp. Gladys Swarthout album of concert songs and arias. p. 40-49) © G. Schirmer, inc., New York; on English version; 21Feb46; EP2417.

DURAND, PAUL JULES, 1907-
L'amour! ... L'amour! ... paroles de Georgius; musique de Paul Durand, arr. [by] Raymond Legrand. © Editions Joubert, Paris; 31Mar47; EF3873. Piano-conductor score (orchestra), and parts.
Brouillard; paroles de Henri Contet, musique de Paul Durand. © Editions Musicales Nuances, Paris; 15Jan47; EF3496.
J'entends mon amour; paroles de Henri Contet, musique de Paul Durand. © Société d'Editions Musicales Internationales (S. E. M. I.), Paris; 15Dec46; EF3463.
Mon p'tit copain du cinéma ... paroles de Henri Contet, musique de Paul Durand, arr.: Raymond Legrand. © Editions Joubert, Paris; 31Mar47; EF3875. Piano-conductor score (orchestra), and parts.
Printemps ... paroles de Henri Contet, musique de Paul Durand. © Editions Feldman, Paris; 12Nov46; EF5213.

DURHAM, GEORGE H
The Lord of Hosts; for full chorus of mixed voices, a cappella; [words and music by] George H. Durham. © The Boston Music Co., Boston; 29Aug47; EP13373.

DURIEUX, GEORGES, 1888-
Men of the fenlands; by Georges Durieux. © B. Feldman & Co. ltd., London; 18Feb47; EF5078. For voice and piano; melody also in tonic sol-fa notation.

DUUREN, HENDRIK JOHANNES VAN, 1895-
Bloeiende ranken. Flowering shoots. 10 stukjes voor piano [by] H. J. v. Duuren. Op.6. © Edition Heuwekemeijer (A. J. Heuwekemeijer & B. F. van Gaal), Amsterdam, The Netherlands; 6May46; EF5112.
De speeldoos. The musical box. 10 voordrachtstukjes voor piano. Op.7. [By] H. J. v. Duuren. © Edition Heuwekemeijer (A. J. Heuwekemeijer & B. F. van Gaal), Amsterdam, The Netherlands; 11Feb46; EF5142.
Twintig melodische etuden; voor C blokfluit, [by] H. J. v. Duuren. Op. 8. © Edition Heuwekemeijer & B. F. van Gaal), Amsterdam, The Netherlands; 18Jun46; EF5140. For recorder solo.
Uit Leopold Mozart's notenboek; 20 stukjes bespeelbaar gemaakt voor 1 en 2 blokfluiten in C; door H. J. v. Duuren [opus 9] © Edition Heuwekemeijer, (firm A. J. Heuwekemeyer & B. F. van Gaal) Amsterdam; 25Jun46; EF5153.

DUUREN, HENDRIK JOHANNES VAN, 1895-
Cont'd.
Zonnige jeugd. Sunny youth. 10
stukjes pour piano. Op.5. [By]
H. J. v. Duuren. © Edition
Heuwekemeijer (A. J. Heuweke-
meyer & B. F. van Gaal), Amster-
dam, The Netherlands; 23Mar46;
EF5141.
DVOŘÁK, ANTONIN, 1841-1904.
By the waters of Babylon; (Bibli-
cal songs, no. 7) ... tr. by
Hugh Ross. (In Ross, Hugh, arr.
Sacred choruses for women's or
girls' voices. p. 9-13) © G.
Schirmer, inc., New York; on
arrangement; 30Sep46; EP9778.
By the waters of Babylon; [by]
(Anton Dvořák) arr. for S. A.
by J. Julius Baird. © Elkan-
Vogel Co., inc., Philadelphia;
on arrangement; 2May47;
EP14894.
Hear my crying; (Biblical songs,
no. 6) ... tr. by Hugh Ross.
(In Ross, Hugh, arr. Sacred
choruses for women's or girls'
voices. p. 49-52) © G. Schirmer,
inc., New York; on arrangement;
30Sep46; EP9785.
Hear my prayer, O Lord; [by]
(Anton Dvořák) arr. for S. A.
by J. Julius Baird. © Elkan-
Vogel Co., inc., Philadelphia;
on arrangement; 2May47;
EP14893.
Humoresque; by Anton Dvořák.
[Op.101, no.7] Arr. by Walter
L. Rosemont, piano solo, with
organ registration [and song,
lyric by Jack Edwards]
© Edwards Music Co., New York;
on new lyrics and arrangement;
17Feb47; EP14430.
Humoresque; lyric by William Nameiw,
music by Anton Dvořák, featured
in the Warner Bros. picture
"Humoresque." [adaptation by
Ken Macomber] © Remick Music
Corp., New York; on arrangement;
19Dec46; EP11067.
I will sing new songs of glad-
ness; [by] (Anton Dvořák) arr.
for S. A. by J. Julius Baird.
© Elkan-Vogel Co., inc.,
Philadelphia; on arrangement;
2May47; EP14892.
DYE, WILLIAM KAHLE
Moonlight over Manhattan; words
and music by William Kahle
Dye. © Nordyke Publishing Co.,
Los Angeles; 7Dec46; EP13821.
DYER, DEB.
The line on the highway; words &
music by Deb Dyer. © M. M. Cole
Publishing Co., Chicago; 24Jun47;
EP15289.
[DYKES, JOHN B
Lead, kindly light; [words by John
H. Newman, music by John B.
Dykes, arr. by Victor Lakes Mar-
tin] Easy piano arrangement with
keyboard charts. © Songs You
Remember Publishing Co., [V. L.
Martin, Proprietor], Atlanta; on
arrangement; 5Apr47; EP14749.
DYKES, JOHN BACCHUS, 1823-1876.
Jesus, the very thought of Thee;
anthem for soprano, alto and
baritones. [Words] ascribed to
Barnard of Clairvaux, tr. by
Edward Caswall. [Music by] John
B. Dykes, freely arr. by Kenneth
A. Runkel. © Oliver Ditson Co.,
Philadelphia; on arrangement;
26May47; EP14695.
DYSON, GEORGE, 1883-
High meadow; unison song, music by
George Dyson, words adapted from
John Dyer. © Edwards Arnold & Co.,
London; 12Dec46; EF4746.

E

EAKIN, VERA.
Wind and girl; for voice and piano
by Vera Eakin. [Words by Rosemary Cobham] © G. Schirmer, inc.,
New York; 28Apr47; EP14691.

EARLE, EDWARD, 1930-
The singing brook; by Edward Earle.
With biographical sketch, finger-
ing, phrasing, pedaling, and in-
structive annotations [by Lillie-
Mayes Dodd] © Art Publication
Society, Clayton, Mo.; 24Nov46;
EP10912. For piano solo.

EARLEE, PAUL.
Jolie blonde ... by Paul Earlee.
© Preview Music Co., Chicago;
15Apr47; EP13823. For voice
and piano, with chord symbols.

ECHEVARRIA, EFRAIN.
El amolador ... (Dan, the old grinder
man) ... English words by Al
Koppell, Spanish words and
music by Efrain Echevarria. ©
Caribbean Music, inc., New
York; 17Mar47; EP12644.

ECKHARDT, FANNY G
The bee and the buttercup; [by]
Fanny G. Eckhardt. © Century
Music Publishing Co., New York;
15Apr47; EP13225. For piano
solo.

ECKSTEIN, MAXWELL.
Fiesta time; piano solo by Max-
well Eckstein. © Carl Fischer,
inc., New York; 23Dec46; EP10917.
Romance arabesque ... Piano solo,
by Maxwell Eckstein. © Carl
Fischer, inc., New York;
29Mar47; EP15013.
Tribute to Chopin; [by] Maxwell
Eckstein. (In Eckstein, Maxwell.
A first duet book, p.16-17) ©
Carl Fischer, inc., New York;
3Apr47; EP13481. For piano 4
hands.

EDGAR, LA VERN.
Dreamland baby; words and music by
La Vern Edgar. © Cine-Mart Music
Publishing Co., Hollywood, Calif.;
1Dec46; EP12118.
I wasn't wanting to fall in love;
words and music by La Vern
Edgar. © Nordyke Publishing
Co., Los Angeles; 8Aug46;
EP13525.
I'd give a lot (for one of your
sweet kisses); words and music
by La Vern Edgar. © Nordyke
Publishing Co., Los Angeles;
11Oct46; EP13537.
Little madonna; words & music
by La Vern Edgar. © Nordyke
Publishing Co., Los Angeles;
11Oct46; EP13540.

EDMUNDSON, GARTH.
Alleluia! Christ is risen;
S.A.T.B. [by] Garth Edmundson.
© J. Fischer & Bro., New
York; 27Mar47; EP6810.

EDWARDS, BEN, comp.
Hoosier hop ... souvenir song
folio and photo album [comp.
by Ben Edwards] © Edwards
Music Co., New York; 15Nov46;
EP14956.
Songs of the gay '90's; a
collection of barber shop
ditties. © Edwards Music Co.,
New York; on compilation;
1May47; EP14673.

EDWARDS, CAMERON, pseud.
Oh, clap your hands; by Cameron
Edwards, [pseud. Psalm 47] Ed.
and arr. for mixed chorus, SATB.
© Choral Press, Evanston, Ill.;
15Jun46; EP11697.

Oh, clap your hands; by Cameron
Edwards, [pseud. Psalm 47] Ed.
and arr. for men's chorus, TTBB.
© Choral Press, Evanston, Ill.;
1Sep46; EP11698.

EDWARDS, GUS, d. 1945.
By the light of the silvery
moon; music by Gus Edwards,
arr. by Jimmy Dale. ©
Remick Music Corp., New York;
on arrangement; 9May47;
EP14402. Piano-conductor
score (orchestra) and parts.

EDWARDS, JACK.
Kilroy was here (who is this fellow
Kilroy?) By Jack Edwards, [words by]
Duke Leonard, Bill Thall and George
Skinner, arranged by Walter L. Rose-
mont. [c1946] © Edwards Music Co.,
New York; 24Jun47; EP11861.
Now I lay me down to sleep; [by
Jack Edwards, arr. by Walter
L. Rosemont] © Edwards Music
Co., New York; 15Mar47;
EP13397. For voice and organ.

EDWARDS, MICHAEL.
March modernistic ... by Michael
Edwards. [c1946] © Mills
Music, inc., New York; on
arrangement; 21Apr47; EP6853.
Piano-conductor score
(orchestra) and parts.

EFRÓN, TAIBE.
Mi Panama querido; letra y música
de Taibe Efrón (Blackie) © Peer
International Corp., New York;
13Feb47; EP12229.

EGGE, KLAUS, 1906-
Den dag kjem aldri at eg deg
gløymer. (Vinje) Tone fra Vinje
uppskriven etter Tjodvor
Flaaten. Klaus Egge, folketone
-arr. nr. 1. © Musikk-Huset
a/s, Oslo, Norway; 19Sep44;
on arrangement; EP5019. Score:
SSATB.
Fantasi i Halling. Tvørgyste
slatte-rytmer, nr. 1 ...
Phantasy in Halling. "Slatte"
-rhytms for two voices, nr. 1.
For piano av Klaus Egge. Verk
12a. © Musikk-Huset a/s, Oslo,
Norway; on arrangement;
22Nov41; EP5020.

EICHHORN, HERMENE WARLICK.
Mary Magdalene ... with text by
Rose Myra Phillips, music by
Hermene Warlick Eichhorn ...
(S.A.T.B.) © J. Fischer &
Bro., New York; 27Mar47;
EP6814.

EIDSON, ALONZO B 1908-
Brass bass method (tuba - sousaphone);
by Alonzo B. Eidson, ed. by Nilo
W. Hovey. © Belwin, inc., New York;
on bk. 1; 13Mar47; EP12565.
Brass bass method (tuba-sousaphone);
by Alonzo B. Eidson, ed. by
Nilo W. Hovey. © Belwin, inc.,
New York; bk.2, 27Mar47; EP14000.
Cornet method; [baritone treble
(baritone treble clef, Db
alto or mellophone); by Alonzo B.
Eidson, ed. by Nilo W. Hovey.
© Belwin, inc., New York; on bk. 1;
13Mar47; on bk. 2; 19Mar47; EP12566,
12809.
French horn method ... by Alonzo
D. Eidson, ed. by Nilo W. Hovey.
© Belwin, inc., New York; bk.1,
3Apr47; EP14012.
French horn method (double and
single); by Alonzo B. Eidson,
ed. by Nilo W. Hovey. ©
Belwin, inc., New York; bk.2,
13Mar47; EP12568.
Trombone method; (baritone and euphonium bass clef), by Alonzo B. Eidson,
ed. by Nilo W. Hovey. © Belwin,
inc., New York; on bk. 1; 13Mar47;
EP12567.

EIDSON, ALONZO B   1908-   Cont'd.
Trombone method (baritone and
euphonium bass clef); by
Alonzo B. Eidson, ed. by
Nilo W. Hovey. © Belwin,
inc., New York; bk.2, 27Mar47;
EP14001.

EISELE, FAITH W   1919-
Shelter of His wings; [by] Faith
Eisele, arr. by Phyllis Quisenberry
[Pasadena, Calif., C. M. Quisenberry]
© Phyllis W. Quisenberry, Pasadena,
Calif., 16Sep46; EP11566.

EISEN, NATHAN, 1890-
Dos versprochene land. The promised
land ... words and music by
Nathan Eisen. © Nathan Eisen,
Brooklyn; 6Jan47; EP11044.
Yiddish words (transliterated)

EISENSTEIN, JUDITH K
The seven golden buttons; a legend
with music by Judith K. and Ira
Eisenstein. New York, Jewish
Reconstructionist Foundation.
© Judith K. and Ira Eisenstein,
New York; 1Apr47; DP1182.

EITZEN, LEE.
A summer night; song with piano
acc., poem by Elizabeth Stoddard,
music by Lee Eitzen. © Carl
Fischer, inc., New York; 17May47;
EP14717.

ELAINE, sister.
Alleluia! ... For three-part chorus
of women's voices with piano acc.,
[by] Sister M. Elaine ... [Words]
adapted from the Scriptures. ©
G. Schirmer, inc., New York;
30Dec46; EP11620.

Jubilate Deo; (S.S.A.A.) [by]
Sister M. Elaine. © Broadcast
Music, inc., New York; 19Mar47;
EP13773.

Pledge to the flag; [by] Sister
M. Elaine. © Sister M. Elaine,
San Antonio; 7Apr47; EP13660.
For voice and piano.

ELAINE, Sister, arr.
Al nino Jesus. The Holy Child;
chorus for women's voices.
Spanish Christmas carol arr. by
Sister M. Elaine. © Broadcast
Music, inc., New York; on arrange-
ment; 31Mar47; EP15234.
Spanish and English words.

La noche esta serena. Serene
night; chorus for women's voices.
Traditional Spanish melody arr.
by Sister M. Elaine. © Broadcast Music, inc., New York; on
arrangement; 31Mar47; EP15233.
Spanish and English words.

ELAINE, MARY, sister. See
Elaine, sister

ELDRIDGE, ROY, 1911-
Yard dog ... By Roy Eldridge [and]
Buster Harding. © Little Jazz
Music Publications, inc., New
York; 31May47; EP14848. Piano-
conductor score (orchestra) and
parts.

ELENA, JULIA.
Espejismo ... Letra & musica
de Julia Elena. © Peer International Corp., New York; 30Dec46;
EP11872.

Que lindo es mi amor ... letra
y musica de Julia Elena. ©
Peer International Corp.,
New York; 30Dec46; EP11876.

ELER, pseud. See
Lambert, Rene.

ELERT, SIGFRID KARG- See
Karg-Elert, Sigfrid.

ELEY, L   CLINTON.
The healing leaves; for chorus of
mixed voices with alto solo
... [words by] L. G. Birch,
[music by] L. Clinton Eley.
© The H. W. Gray Co., inc.,
New York; 3Jan47; EP11057.

ELGAR, Sir EDWARD WILLIAM,
1857-1934.
As torrents in summer; for four-
part chorus of boys' voices
[by] Sir Edward Elgar, arr.
by Robert Gibb, [words by]
Henry W. Longfellow. © The
Boston Music Co., Boston; on
arrangement; 16May47; EP14615.

As torrents in summer. See also his
King Olaf.

(King Olaf) As torrents in
summer, from the cantata "King
Olaf"; chorus for three part
women's voices [by] Edward
Elgar, arr. by Harry L. Harts.
[Words by] Henry W. Longfellow.
© McLaughlin & Reilly Co.,
Boston; on arrangement;
10Apr47; EP13630.

Nimrod, from Variations on an
original theme [by] Edward
Elgar, arr. ... by Lucien
Cailliet. © Boosey & Hawkes,
inc., Lynbrook, L. I., N. Y.;
on arrangement; 29May47;
EP14688. Score (band) and
parts.

[ELIO, FRISIA] 1906-
La scuola dello jazz ... di Friel
[pseud.] e di Giaco Ricci.
© Carisch, s.a., Milan; v.1,
15Feb47; v.2, 28Apr47; EF5645,
3901. For accordion.

ELIZONDO, "EL CAMPESINO" R. See
Elizondo, Rafael.

ELIZONDO, RAFAEL, 1890-
Un canto al amor, folio no.1[-2]
... arreglos del gran "Chino"
Arturo Velasquez ... Musica y
letras de "El Campesino" R.
Elizondo. Alamo, Tex., Melodias
Campesinas. © R. Elizondo,
Alamo, Tex.; v.1-2, 20May47;
EP14840-14841. Folio no.2 has
title: Lo que siente el alma.

ELLINGTON, DUKE.
(Beggar's holiday) On the wrong side
of the railroad track ... [from]
Beggar's holiday; music by Duke
Ellington ... lyrics by John Latouche. © Mutual Music Society,
inc., New York; 13Feb47; EP12165.

(Beggar's holiday) Take love
easy ... [from] Beggar's holiday; music by Duke Ellington,
lyrics by John Latouche.
© Mutual Music Society, inc.,
New York; 7Feb47; EP11865.

(Beggar's holiday) Tomorrow Mountain
... [from] Beggar's holiday; music
by Duke Ellington ... lyrics by
John Latouche. © Mutual Music
Society, inc., New York; 13Feb47;
EP12166.

(Beggar's holiday) When I walk
with you ... [from] Beggar's
holiday, music by Duke Ellington, lyrics by John Latouche.
© Mutual Music Society, inc.,
New York; 7Feb47; EP11864.

On the wrong side of the railroad
track. See his Beggar's holiday.

Solitude ... words by Eddie
De Lange and Irving Mills,
music by Duke Ellington, arr.
by Van Alexander. © American
Academy of Music, inc., New
York; on arrangement; 21Apr47;
EP5845. Piano-conductor score
(orchestra, with words) and
parts.

Take love easy. See his
Beggar's holiday.

Tomorrow Mountain. See his
Beggar's holiday.

When I walk with you. See his
Beggar's holiday.

[ELLIOT, JAMES] 1882-
An evangel in song; [by James
Elliot] © James Elliot, Norfolk,
Va.; on 12 hymns; 15Apr47. Con-
tents.- A closer walk with Jesus
(© EP13835) - Ransomed forever
(© EP13836) - A faith that keeps
us (© EP13837) - Christian, in
a world below (© EP13838) - To
God all praise shall be (©
EP13839) - O, over I'll follow
the Lord (© EP13841) - O, tell me of
Jesus, my Saviour (© EP13842) -
Jesus is waiting to save you
(© EP13843) - Commit thy way unto
the Lord (© EP13844) - Thy grace
is sufficient for me (© EP13845)
- Cast your burden on the Lord
(© EP13846) - Can you hear the
call of the Saviour? (© EP13840)

ELLIOTT, MARJORIE, 1890-
Awake 'tis spring! Two-part
chorus [by] Marjorie Elliott,
© The Raymond A. Hoffman Co.,
Chicago; on arrangement;
15Aug46; EP12659.

The barn dance; an American
ruralette, two-part chorus,
[by] Marjorie Elliott. ©
The Raymond A. Hoffman Co.,
Chicago; on arrangement;
15Aug46; EP12657.

ELLIS, SAMUEL LEE, 1924-
If it's Thy will ... words and
music by Samuel Lee Ellis, sr.
[Chicago, Bowles Music House]
© Samuel Lee Ellis, sr.,
Chicago; 11Jan47; EP11118.

ELLIS, SEGER.
After you; words and music by
Seger Ellis. © Leslie
Music Corp., New York;
26Mar47; EP12889.

ELLIS, VESPEW BENTON, 1917-
ed.
SIng of Calvary; ed. by V. B.
(Vep) Ellis, [words and music
by Robert Bell, Fred Woodruff
and others] © Tenn. Music
& Printing Co., Cleveland,
Tenn.; 1Feb47; EP15023.
Hymns, in shape-note notation.

ELLIS, VIVIAN.
(Bless the bride) Ducky, from
"Bless the bride"; words by A.
P. Herbert, music by Vivian
Ellis. © Chappell & Co., ltd.,
London; 17Apr47; EF3264.

(Bless the bride) I was never
kissed before; and This is my
lovely day; both from the musical
play "Bless the bride." [Words
by A. P. Herbert, music by Vivian
Ellis, arr. by Phil Cardew]
© Chappell & Co., ltd., London;
on arrangement; 29Apr47; EF3412.
Piano-conductor score (orchestra,
with words), and parts.

(Bless the bride) I was never
kissed before, from "Bless the
bride"; words by A. P. Herbert,
music by Vivian Ellis. © Chappell & Co., ltd., London;
17Apr47; EF3266.

(Bless the bride) Ma belle
Marguerite, from "Bless the
bride"; words by A. P. Herbert, music by Vivian Ellis.
© Chappell & Co., ltd., London;
18Apr47; EF3268. English words.

41

ELLIS, VIVIAN. Cont'd.
(Bless the bride) Selection,
[from] Bless the bride; [by]
Vivian Ellis, arr. by Chris
Langdon. © Chappell & Co., ltd.,
London; on arrangement; 18Apr47;
EF3267. For piano solo.

Bless the bride; selection,
music by Vivian Ellis,
orchestrated by Geo. L. Zalva.
© Chappell & Co., ltd.,
London; 21May47; EF3800.
Piano-conductor score
(orchestra), and parts.

(Bless the bride) This is my
lovely day, from "Bless the
bride"; words by A. P. Herbert,
music by Vivian Ellis. © Chappell & Co., ltd., London;
17Apr47; EF3265.

Ducky. See his Bless the bride.

I dreamt I was back in Paris;
words and music by Vivian
Ellis. © Chappell & Co.,
ltd., London; 2May47; EF3630.

I was never kissed before. See his
Bless the bride.

Ma belle Marguerite. See his
Bless the bride.

This is my lovely day. See his
Bless the bride.

ELLISON, JESSE M
I've fallen in love with an angel;
words by Charles Cowgill, music
by Jesse Ellison. © Peer International Corp., New York;
18Apr47; EF13972.

Let's pretend we're in love; words
by Charles Cowgill, music by
Jesse M. Ellison. © Peer International Corp., New York;
18Apr47; EF13973.

ELLSTEIN, ABE.
"I have waited too long." Tsu lang
hob ich gevart oif dir ... words
by I. Lillian and J. Jacobs,
music by Abe Ellstein. © J. & J.
Kammen Music Co., New York; 22Jan47;
EP6667. Yiddish words (transliterated)

[ELLSWORTH, ARLIE B   ]
The angels are singing for mother;
words and music by Cousin Lee
[pseud.] (In Cousin Lee book
of original songs. p.16-17)
© Jack Howard Publications,
inc., Philadelphia; 30Dec46;
EP11734.

It seems I can't forget; words and
music by Cousin Lee [pseud.]
(In Cousin Lee book of original
songs. p.26-27) © Jack Howard
Publications, inc., Philadelphia;
30Dec46; EP11738.

Keep smiling; words and music by
Cousin Lee [pseud.] (In Cousin
Lee book of original songs.
p.8-9) © Jack Howard Publications, inc., Philadelphia;
30Dec46; EP11730.

The prairie trail; words and music
by Cousin Lee [pseud.] (In
Cousin Lee book of original
songs. p.32-33) © Jack Howard
Publications, inc., Philadelphia;
30Dec46; EP11741.

When Pa put the baby to bed; words
and music by Cousin Lee [pseud.]
(In Cousin Lee book of original
songs. p.12-13) © Jack Howard
Publications, inc., Philadelphia;
30Dec46; EP11732.

Why should I worry over you? Words
and music by Cousin Lee [pseud.]
(In Cousin Lee book of original
songs. p.22-23) © Jack
Howard Publications, inc., Philadelphia; 30Dec46; EP11736.

You keep going your way (I'll keep
going mine); words and music by
Cousin Lee [pseud.] (In Cousin
Lee book of original songs.
p.30-31) © Jack Howard Publications, inc., Philadelphia;
30Dec46; EP11740.

ELLY, JOSEPH.
You're what's the matter with
me; words and music by Lewis
Bollin and Joseph Elly. ©
Mills Music, inc., New York;
16Apr47; EP6831. For voice
and piano, with chord symbols.

ELMAN, ZIGGY.
Please, Mama; words by Don Reid,
music by Ziggy Elman. © Dorsey
Brothers' Music, inc., New York;
27Feb47; EP12237.

ELMORE, ROBERT.
He who would valiant be; anthem for
chorus of mixed voices, [by]
Robert Elmore, [words by] John
Bunyan. © Galaxy Music Corp.,
New York; 29May47; EP6970.

ELSNIC, JOSEPH PAUL, 1895-
Laendler no. 11; arr. by Joseph P.
Elsnic [for] concertina. ©
Vitak-Elsnic Co., Chicago; on
arrangement; 16Aug46; EP11564.

ELWELL, HERBERT.
Lincoln. Requiem aeternam; [for]
mixed chorus with baritone solo.
Poem by John Gould Fletcher, music
by Herbert Elwell. Vocal score.
© Broadcast Music, inc., New York;
16Dec46; EP11844.

EMBIL, JULIO R
When I look in your eyes ... by
Julio R. Embil. © Cine-Mart
Music Publishing Co., Holly-
wood, Calif.; 1Nov46; EP11494.
For voice and piano, with
chord symbols.

EMBURY, PHILIP W   arr.
After dark; [arr. by Philip W.
Embury] c1946. © Society for the
Preservation and Encouragement
of Barber Shop Quartet Singing in
America, Detroit; 15Oct44; EP10825.
Close score: TTBB.

EMER, MICHEL.
Je n'ai rien oublié; paroles de
Claude Gevel, musique de
Michel Emer. Paris, En vente
aux Éditions R. Breton. ©
Éditions Paris-Broadway, Paris;
30Sep45; EF3819.

Le petit poucet noir; paroles
de Michel Emer et Maurice
Yèpr, musique de Michel Emer.
© Éditions Paris-Broadway,
Paris; 31Dec45; EF3835.

EMERY, DOROTHY RADDE.
Sing unto the Lord; SAB accompanied,
[by] Dorothy Radde Emery, text
from Psalm 96. © Harold Flammer,
inc., New York; 7May47; EP14373.

EMERY, WALTER.
The lark; words by Talhaiarn (John
Jones), tr. from the Welsh by
Oliphant; music by Walter Emery.
© Novello & Co., ltd., London;
15May47; EF3405. Score: SATB
and piano reduction.

Song on May morning; words by John
Milton, music by Walter Emery.
© Novello & Co., ltd., London;
29Apr47; EF5633.

ENDERS, HARVEY, d. 1947.
The origin of valentines; for four-
part chorus of men's voices, a
cappella, [by] Harvey Enders,
[words by] Fairfax Downey. ©
G. Schirmer, inc., New York;
30Dec46; EP11631.

Russian picnic; for full chorus
of mixed voices (S.A.B.) and
piano, with incidental
soprano or tenor solo. Words
and music (based on Russian
folk tunes) by Harvey
Enders. © G. Schirmer, inc.,
New York; on arrangement;
24Mar47; EP13122.

[ENGEL, LYLE K   ] 1915-   comp.
Frank Luther's holiday music folio
of popular children's songs.
© Northern Music Corp., Sole
Selling Agent, Movie Songs, inc.,
New York; 22Nov46; EP10826.

Gene Autry's popular music folio
of Western songs; [comp. by
Lyle K. Engel] © Movie Songs,
inc., New York; 25Jan47;
EP11961.

ENGELEN, FRANK, 1912-
Crépuscule; [by] Frank Engelen.
© Robert Bosmans d. b. a.
Editions Ch. Bens, Brussels;
30Jun43; EF5352. Piano-
conductor score (orchestra)
and parts.

Studio 24 ... [By] Frank Engelen.
© Robert Bosmans d. b. a.
Editions Ch. Bens, Brussels;
15Jan42; EF5351. Piano-
conductor score (orchestra)
and parts.

ENGELMANN, H
Melody of love; by H. Engelmann.
[Op. 600] Simplified arrangement for piano by Bruce Carleton. © Theodore Presser Co.,
Philadelphia; on arrangement;
21Apr47; EP13942.

ENGLE, GENE, 1907-
Day after day; words and music by
Gene Engle. [c1945] © Gene
Engle, Business name, Gene
Engle Music Service, Indianapolis;
15Mar47; EP11543.

ENGLISH, BILLY.
Some time; [words and music by]
Billy English. © English
Tunes, Lancaster, Pa.; 27Dec46;
EP10979. For voice and piano,
with chord symbols.

ENGLISH, GRANVILLE, 1893-
Wings of a dove; for medium voice.
Music by Granville English,
verse by Henry Van Dyke. ©
The Composers Press, inc., New
York; 25Feb47; EP12243.

ENRISO, RAFAEL.
"Mi baile es así" ... letra
y música de Rafael Enriso
[Mená], arreglo de Pedro
Guida. © Peer International
Corp., New York; 30Dec46;
EF5433. Parts: orchestra.

ENTICKNAP, CLIFFORD G.
The London waltz; words by
Harold Crook, music by Clif-
ford G. Enticknap. © Rex
Music Co., London; 22Mar47;
EF5439.

Thanking you; words by Harold
Crook, music by Clifford G.
Enticknap. c1946. © Rex
Music Co., London; 18Jan47;
EF4895.

ERB, J   LAWRENCE, 1877-
Glory to God in the highest ...
S.A.T.B. [by] J. Lawrence Erb.
© M. Witmark & Sons, New York;
8Apr47; EP13487.

Nunc dimittis; three part
women's voices, S. S. A. [by]
J. Lawrence Erb. [Text from
Luke II: 29-32] © M. Witmark
& Sons, New York; 30Apr47;
EP14290.

ERB, J   LAWRENCE, 1877-
  O praise the Lord; four part
  mixed voices ... [By] J.
  Lawrence Erb. Paraphrase on
  Psalm XLVII. © M. Witmark &
  Sons, New York; 30Apr47;
  EP14288.
ERBY, JOHN.
  Love sick ... Words and music by
  John Costa, jr. and John Erby.
  Los Angeles, Unique Music Pub-
  lishers, [c1946] © John Erby,
  Los Angeles; 6Jun47; EP15176.
ERHARDT, SIEGFRIED.
  Czardas II; [by] Siegfried
  Erhardt. © Nordiska Musik-
  förlaget, a.b., Stockholm;
  1Jan44; EF3761. Piano-con-
  ductor score (orchestra), and
  parts.
ERIKSSON, JOSEF, 1872-
  Sång till Hälsingland; ord av
  A. Engberg, folkmelodi
  bearbetad för sång och piano
  av Josef Eriksson. ©
  Nordiska Musikförlaget, Stock-
  holm; on arrangement; 1Jan21;
  EF3672. Score (voice and
  piano) and voice part.
  Två dikter; [words by] (Per
  Lagerkvist] ... Komponerade
  för sång och piano av Josef
  Eriksson. Op. 41. © Nordiska
  Musikförlaget, a/b, Stockholm;
  on 2 songs; 1Jan23; EF5406-5407.
  Contents.- Jorden är blott du
  och jag och mull.- Ingenting
  får störa vår stund med
  varandra.
ERISMAN, FLORENCE, 1906-
  Just blue dolphinium and you; by
  Florence Erisman. © Richmond
  Melodies, Staten Island, N.Y.;
  17Mar47; EP12631. For voice
  and piano.
ERNIE, JOHN, pseud. See
  Krancher, Willy Carl.
ERSKINE, HELEN ELIZABETH RANDALL,
  1898-
  Out in Nevada; by Helen Elizabeth
  Randall Erskine. Boulder City,
  Nev., C. Erskine. © Helen
  Elizabeth Randall Erskine,
  Boulder City, Nev.; 22Apr47;
  EP14256. For voice and piano.
ESCARPENTER, JOSÉ.
  Guajirita mia. (My guajirita) ...
  [By] José Escarpenter, [English
  words adapted by Albert Gamse]
  (In André, Julie, ed. Songs from
  south of the border. p.22-25)
  © Edward B. Marks Music Corp., New
  York; on English adaptation;
  28Dec46; EP10869.
ESPARZA OTEO, ALFONSO.
  Canción del amor ... letra y
  música de Alfonso Esparza Oteo,
  arreglo de Jerry Castillo. ©
  Promotora Hispano Americana de
  Música, s.a., México; 22Dec42;
  EF5614. Piano-conductor score
  (orchestra), and parts.
ESPERÓN, MANUEL.
  (El ahijado de la muerte) No se
  por qué, canción de la película
  "El ahijado de la muerte."
  Música de Manuel Esperón, letra
  de Ernesto M. Cortázar. © Pro-
  motora Hispano Americana de
  Música, s.a., México; 23Dec46;
  EF5070.
  (Albur de amor) La mina de oro
  ... de la película "Albur de
  amor"; música de Manuel Esperón,
  letra de Ernesto M. Cortázar. ©
  Promotora Hispano Americana de
  Música, s.a., México; 30Dec46;
  EF5521.

Cont'd. Aunque lo quieran o nó ... Música
  de Manuel Esperón, letra de
  Ernesto M. Cortazar. © Promotora Hispano Americana de
  Música, s. a., Mexico; 30Dec46;
  EF5520.
  Chaparrita cuerpo de uva. See
  his No basta ser charro.
  Fiesta mexicana. See his No
  basta ser charro.
  Hasta que perdió Jalisco; de la
  película del mismo nombre,
  música de Manuel Esperón, letra
  de Ernesto M. Cortazar. ©
  Promotora Hispano Americana
  de Música, s.a., México;
  30Dec46; EF5287.
  La mina de oro. See his Albur
  de amor.
  (No basta ser charro) Chaparrita
  cuerpo de uva, de la película
  No basta ser charro ... música
  de Manuel Esperón, letra de
  Ernesto M. Cortázar. © Pro-
  motora Hispano Americana de
  Música, s.a., Mexico; 29Oct46;
  EF5497.
  No se por qué. See his El
  ahijado de la muerte.
  (El peñón de las ánimas) Sere-
  nata tapatía ... de la película
  El peñón de las animas! Música
  de Manuel Esperón, letra de
  Ernesto M. Cortázar. © Pro-
  motora Hispano Americana de
  Música, s.a., México; 29Oct46;
  EF5498.
  Serenata tapatía. See his El
  peñón de las ánimas!
  Y dicen por ahí ... Música de Manuel
  Esperón, letra de Ernesto M.
  Cortazar. New York, Peer Inter-
  national Corp. © Promotora Hispano
  Americana de Música, s. a., Mexico;
  30Dec46; EP11874.
ESSEX, KENNETH, arr.
  Naval patrol; a modern arrangement
  of traditional sea songs, by
  Kenneth Essex. © Bradbury Wood,
  ltd., London; on arrangement;
  8Feb47; EF5101. For piano solo,
  with chord symbols.
ESSEX, LEROY.
  You're heaven sent; words and
  music by Leroy (Teddy) Essex.
  © Nordyke Publishing Co., Los
  Angeles; 18Jul46; EP13151.
ESSEX, TEDDY. See
  Essex, Leroy.
ETOLL, GEORGE W   1911-
  Sing glory; words [and] music [by]
  G. W. Etoll. [2nd ed.] ©
  George W. Etoll, Bryan, Ohio;
  15Mar47; EP14838.
ETTEMA, THEO. See
  Ettema, Theodorus Antonius.
ETTEMA, THEODORUS ANTONIUS, 1906-
  Forest dreams; [by] Theo Ettema.
  For piano. © Edition Heuweke-
  meijer (Fa. A. J. Heuwekemeijer
  & B. F. van Gaal], Amsterdam;
  30Dec46; EF3379.
ETTORE, EUGENE, 1921-
  Polkatrinka; by Eugene Ettore and
  Joe Biviano, arr. by Joe Biviano
  [for] accordion solo. © Viccas
  Music Co., New York; 12May47;
  EP15098.
EVANGEL SPECIAL SACRED SONGS, no.1-
  © Evangel Publishers (T. J.
  Silva, owner) Boise, Idaho;
  on 10 songs; bk.1 5Apr47. Con-
  tents.- (Words and music by
  T. J. Silva unless stated)-
  After the storm (© EP5771)-
  Because He died on Calvary
  (© EP6772)- Christ will be
  your friend (© EP6773)- He
  knows the way I take (© EP6774)-

  I know Christ Jesus under-
  stands (© EP6775)- Man of
  sorrows (© EP6776)- Saviour,
  help me bear my cross (© EP6777)-
  That is why I love my Saviour;
  words by T. J. Silva, music
  by George F. Root (© EP6778)-
  The Saviour lives (© EP6779)-
  There's a story (© EP6780)-
  Jesus, only Saviour (© EP6781)-
  The world has lost all its
  attraction (© EP6782)
EVANS, DALE.
  My heart went that-a-way; words
  ... by Roy Rogers and music
  ... [by] Dale Evans. © Tim
  Spencer Music, inc., Hollywood,
  Calif.; 30Dec46; EP11022.
EVANS, DAVID M
  We come to worship Thee, O Lord ...
  [words by] John Calvin Slemp,
  [music by] David M. Evans. (In
  Young people's topic. v.7, no.3,
  p.[3] of cover) © The Judson
  Press, Philadelphia; 18Mar47;
  B5-259. Close score: SATB.
EVANS, DON.
  Without you; words and music by
  Johnny Gray and Don Evans. ©
  Nordyke Publishing Co., Holly-
  wood, Calif.; 30May46; EP11529.
EVANS, HAL. See
  Evans, Harold Percy.
EVANS, HAROLD PERCY, 1906-
  Jackanapes ... By Hal Evans.
  © Evans & Lowry ltd., London;
  30Dec46; EF5311. For piano
  solo.
EVANS, LOUISE, 1893-
  In an autumn garden; [by] Louise
  Evans ... S.A. [words by Edith
  Lovejoy Pierce] © The Raymond
  A. Hoffman Co., Chicago;
  29May47; EP15043.
  Velvet shoes; (S.A.) [by] Louise
  Evans, [words by Elinor Wylie]
  © The Raymond A. Hoffman Co.,
  Chicago; 29May47; EP15042.
EVANS, RAYMOND B   1915-
  Beside you. See his My favor-
  ite brunette.
  Don't change sweethearts (in the
  middle of a dream); music and
  words by Jay Livingston and
  Ray Evans. © Famous
  Music Corp., New York; 6Jan47;
  EP11051.
  Dreamboat; music and words by
  Jay Livingston and Ray Evans.
  [c1946] © Famous Music Corp.
  New York; 3Jan47; EP11052.
  Easy come, easy go; words and
  music by Jay Livingston and
  Ray Evans. © Famous Music
  Corp., New York; 18Apr47;
  EP13798.
  (My favorite brunette) Beside
  you [from] "My favorite
  brunette." Music and words
  by Jay Livingston and Ray
  Evans. [c1946] © Famous
  Music Corp., New York; 21Jan47;
  EP11367.
  My favorite brunette; words and
  music by Jay Livingston and
  Ray Evans. © Famous Music Corp.,
  New York; 3Apr47; EP13427.
EVANS, TOLCHARD.
  No more goodnight sweetheart; by
  Ralph Butler & Tolchard Evans.
  © Southern Music Publishing
  Co., ltd., London; 3Mar46;
  EF5579. For voice and piano,
  with chord symbols; melody also
  in tonic sol-fa notation.

EVERHART, LILLIAN.
Praise His holy name; words and
music by Lillian Everhart. ©
Lillian Everhart, Clearwater,
Fla.; 30Jan47; EP13968.

EVIS, FREDERICK.
Christmas time's the time for love;
words and music by Frederick
Evis. © Mills Music, inc.,
New York; 29May47; EP6948.

EWINS, WALTER WILLIAM JOHN, 1881-
Elizabeth waltz; by Walter Ewins.
© Walter Ewins, Montreal; 21Apr43;
EF5294. For piano solo.

F

FABER, BILLY.
The wedding waltz; by Nick
D'Amico, Gil Mills [and] Billy
Faber, arr. by Albert Kohn.
© Leeds Music Corp., New York;
16Jun47; EP15091. Piano-con-
ductor score (orchestra) and
parts.

FABIAN, DON.
Dos almas. (My lady of the roses)
... English lyric by Hal David,
Spanish lyric and music by Don
Fabian, arr. by Lewis Raymond,
New York, Leeds Music Corp.,
Aires; on arrangement; 31Dec46;
EP10840. Piano-conductor score
(orchestra, with words) and
parts.

FÁBREGA, RICARDO, 1905-
Santa Ana ... [by] Ricardo Fábrega.
© Ricardo Fábrega, Panama,
Republic of Panama; 28Jan47;
EF5104. For voice and piano.

FAGLIER, JIMMIE.
My turn; words by Raphael Kelley,
music by Jimmie Faglier. ©
Nordyke Publishing Co., Los
Angeles; 20Aug45; EP6503.

FAHSBENDER, R   1899-   ed. and comp.
String bass passages; selected, ed.,
and fingered by R. Fahsbender. ©
Belwin, inc., New York; on bk. 1;
15Mar47; EP12564.

FAIN, SAMMY.
Little Jim. See his Little
Mister Jim.
(Little Mister Jim) Little Jim;
lyric by Ralph Freed. © Robbins
Music Corp., New York; 29Jul46;
EP5399. For voice and piano,
with chord symbols.

FAIRMAN, BILLY.
I won't be home any more when you
call; by Dick Jurgens and Billy
Fairman. © Santly-Joy, inc.,
New York; 8Apr47; EP15436. For
voice and piano, with chord
symbols.

FALCOCCHIO, EDUARDO.
Serenata serena; versi di Enzo
Bonagura, musica di Eduardo
Falcocchio. © Italian Book
Co., New York; 18Jun47;
EP15109. Melody and words.

FAMOUS BLUE JAY SINGERS, arr.
Tho time is drawing near; spiritual,
arr. by Virginia Davis, new
arrangement by Famous Blue Jay
Singers. [Chicago, The Famous
Blue Jay Singers Studio of Gospel
Music, c1945] © The Famous Blue
Jay Singers, Charles Bridges,
manager, on arrangement;
30Nov46; EP10759. For voice and
piano.

FARMER, MISS WILLIE L   1914-
I don't dread this journey; words and
music by Rev. Miss W. L. Farmer,
[arranged by Odessa Steward] [c1946]
© Rev. Miss W. L. Farmer, Chicago;
6Jan47; EP11862.

I have made a promise and I can't
turn around; words & music by
... W. L. Farmer, [arr. by
Odessa Steward] © Rev. Miss
W. L. Farmer, Chicago; 6Dec46;
EP11243.
Wasn't it a pity how they did my
Lord? Words and music by ...
W. L. Farmer, [arr. by Odessa
Steward] © Rev. Miss W. L.
Farmer, Chicago; 6Dec46; EP11242.
Close score: SATB.

FARNES, ELLSWORTH, pseud.
All people that on earth ...
[Psalm 100. Early church melody]
ed. and arr. for mixed chorus,
SATB, by Ellsworth Fernes, [pseud.]
© Choral Press, Evanston, Ill.; on
arrangement; 10ct46; EP11693.
Praise, my soul, the King; [from
a melody by H. Smart] ... ed.
and arr. for junior choir, by
Ellsworth Farnes. [Words from
Psalm 103, adapted by Henry
Lyte] © Choral Press, Evanston,
Ill.; 10Oct46; EP11707.

FARR, HILDA BUTLER, 1892-
Red candles; a Christmas operetta
in two acts, book and lyrics by
Estelle Merrymon Clark, music by
Hilda Butler Farr and Don Wilson.
© The Raymond A. Hoffman Co.,
Chicago; 10Aug46; EP13997.

FARR, HUGH.
Farr-away blues; by Hugh and
Karl Farr. © Tim Spencer
Music, inc., Hollywood, Calif.,
13May47; EP14492. For piano
solo.
South in my soul; by Hugh and
Karl Farr. © Tim Spencer
Music, inc., Hollywood, Calif.;
13May47; EF14493. For piano
solo.

FARRANT, R   d. 1580.
Call to remembrance, O Lord; by
R. Farrant, arr. and ed. for
mixed chorus ... by Noble
Cain. © Choral Art Publications, New York; on arrangement; 8May47; EP14388.

FARRÉS, OSVALDO.
Quizas, quizas, quizas. (Per-
haps, perhaps, perhaps) ...
English words by Joe Davis,
Spanish words and music by
Osvaldo Farrés. © Caribbean
Music, inc., New York; 9Jun47;
EP14885.

FASSIO, A   1888-
Ton coeur est la forteresse ...
paroles de N. Bromand, musique
de A. Fassio. Lachute, Que.,
Parnasse Musical. © Edition A.
Fassio, Lachute, Que., Can.;
15Dec46; EF4855. For voice and
piano.

FASTOFSKY, STUART, 1927-
Reverie; by Stuart Fastofsky. ©
Queens Symphonic Society,
Jamaica, L. I., N. Y.; 20Feb47;
EP13827. For piano solo.
(Sonata, piano) Sonata (1945)
for piano; [by] Stuart Fastofsky.
© Queens Symphonic Society,
Jamaica, L. I., N. Y.; 20Feb47;
EP13828.

FAURÉ, GABRIEL URBAIN, 1845-1924.
Twenty-five selected songs; [by]
Gabriel Fauré, English trans-
lations by Marion Farquhar.
For high voice. © G. Schirmer,
inc., New York; on English
translation; 30Dec46; EP11602.
French and English words.

FAURE, JEAN BAPTISTE, 1830-1914.
O salutaris hostia. Come, ye that
weep for medium and high
voice. [By] J. Fauré, arr. by
James A. Reilly. © McLaughlin
& Reilly Co., Boston; on arrangement; 1May47; EP14880.

The palms; by Jean Baptiste Faure,
arranged by Wayne Howorth. ©
Belwin, inc., New York; on arrangement; 13Feb47; EP12072. Score:
baritone, chorus (SATB) and piano.
The palms ... For three-part
chorus of mixed voices (S.A.B.)
with organ acc. by Dudley Buck,
organ acc. by Dudley Buck,
choral arrangement by Kenneth
Downing [pseud.] English version by Frederick H. Martens.
© G. Schirmer, inc., New York;
on arrangement; 6Feb47;
EP12736.

FAVRE, GEORGES, 1905-
Solfège élémentaire; à deux voix.
25 leçons par Georges Favre.
© Editions Durand & Cie, Paris;
31Oct46; EF5175.

FEARS, WALTER ANTHONY, 1903-
Lovely California moon; words and
music by Walter A. Fears, arr.
by David Gussin. © Walter
Anthony Fears, Los Angeles;
5Feb47; EP15096.
The old Spanish trail; words and
music by Walter A. Fears, arr.
by David Gussin. © Walter
Anthony Fears, Los Angeles;
1Feb47; EP15095.

PEASEL, DICK.
Three brothers ... by Dick Peasel.
Cincinnati, Fillmore Music
House. © Fillmore Bros. Co.,
Cincinnati; 22Mar47; EP6737.
Score (cornet 1-3 and piano)
and parts.

FEAST, CHARLOTTE, 1901-
We two in a lean-to ... music by
Charlotte Feast and words by
Lee Hoffman. © Charlotte Feast
Hoffman and H. Lee Hoffman,
Cockeysville, Md.; 4Dec46; EP11551.

FEDERER, RALPH, comp.
Ralph Federer's piano solo album.
© Theodore Presser Co., Phila-
delphia; 29Apr46; EP3406.

FEDERICO, DOMINGO S
La noche y Marfil ... letra y
música de: Domingo S. Federico.
© Editorial Argentina de
Música Internacional, s. de r.,
ltd., Buenos Aires; 30Dec46;
EF5219.

FELDMAN, WILLIAM.
Plain Mary; words and music by
William Feldman. © William Feld-
man, Newark, N. J.; 28Jan47;
EP6493.

FELO, pseud. See
Diaz y Oviedo, Ignacio.

FELTON, GORDON.
If I fall in love again; words &
music by Gordon Felton. ©
Nordyke Publishing Co., Los
Angeles; 8Aug46; EP13822.

FEMAT, MIGUEL MACIAS. See
Macias Femat, Miguel.

FENBY, ERIC, 1906-
Rossini on Ilkla Moor ... military band score [arr. by Norman Richardson] London, Boosey & Hawkes. © Hawkes & Son
(London) ltd., London; on
arrangement; 14Feb46; EF324.

FENNER, BEATRICE, 1904-
Two little piano sonatas; after the
style of Scarlatti, by Beatrice
Fenner. Op. 38. © Shattinger
Piano & Music Co., St. Louis; on
2 pieces; 31Dec46. Contents.-
[v.1] Little sonata no. 1 in G
major (© EP11258) - [v.2] Little
sonata no.2 in G minor (© EP11248)

44

FERGUSON, FANNIE MARIA.
I love you so sincerely; by
Fannie Maria Ferguson. © Cine-
Mart Music Publishing Co., Holly-
wood, Calif.; 1Nov46; EP11948.
For voice and piano, with chord
symbols.

FERGUSON, MACK.
A dream (that won't come true);
music by Mack Ferguson, words
by Mack Ferguson and Bert
Bartlett. © Midwest Music
Publishers, Kansas City, Kan.;
15Jun45; EP13383.

FERNÁNDEZ, IVÁN.
Dice mi gallo ... letra y música
de Iván Fernández, [arr. by
Pérez Prado] © Peer International Corp., New York;
19Dec46; EF3422.

FERNÁNDEZ PORTA, MARIO.
Canción por tu regreso ... letra
y música de Mario Fernández
Porta. © Peer International
Corp., New York; 30Dec46;
EF5558.

Pasión tropical ... letra y
música de Mario Fernández
Porta. © Peer International
Corp., New York; 30Dec46;
EF5557.

Que me importa ... letra y
música de Mario Fernández Porta.
N[ew] Y[ork] Southern Music
Pub. Co., representantes para
Cuba: Excelsior Music Co.,
Habana. © Peer International
Corp., New York; 11Dec46;
EF5580.

Vuelvo a querer ... letra y
música por Mario Fernández
Porta. © Peer International
Corp., New York; 30Dec46;
EF5559.

FERNANDO, DENNIS D
I'm sad again, I'm blue again tonight;
words and music by Dennis D. Fernando ... arrangement ... by C. Maurice
King. © The Popular Song Club, N.C.
Davis, exclusive owner, Hollywood,
Calif.; 19Oct46; EP6357. For voice
and piano, with guitar diagrams
and chord symbols.

FERRARI, LOUIS.
Blotti sur ton épaule; paroles de
Jacques Plante, musique de
Louis Ferrari. © Ste. ame. fse.
Chappell, Paris; 17Feb47;
EF5258.

FERRETÉ, LÉON M   1890-
Mariguana ... paroles
françaises de Joan Cis,
paroles mexicaines de E.
Enderiz, musique de L. M.
Ferreté. © Éditions Salabert,
Paris; 25Jan47; EF3809.

Mariguana ... paroles méxicaines
de E. Enderiz, paroles
françaises de Jean Cis [pseud.],
musique de L. M. Ferreté, arrt.
de Francis Salabert ... Y a un
accordéon ... paroles de
Louis Poterat, musique de
Marguerite Monnot, arrt. de
Francis Salabert. © Éditions
Salabert, Paris; on arrangement; 15Feb47; EF3555. Piano-
conductor score (orchestra,
with words), and parts.

FERRY, CHARLES T   1884-
I'm pleading for the wings;
(spiritual) solo and chorus,
words by Harriet Lyon Leonard,
music by Charles T. Ferry. ©
Wesley Webster, San Francisco;
23Apr47; EP13817.

The Lord hath done great things
for thee ... words by Frances
Ridley Havergal, music by
Charles T. Ferry. © Wesley
Webster, San Francisco; 5Jun47;
EP14912.

Songs; by Charles T. Ferry and
[words by] Harriet Lyon Leonard.
© Wesley Webster, San Francisco;
on 6 songs; 24Dec46. Contents.-
[v.1] A Welsh ballad (© EP10776)-
[v.2] Hushed are the stars
(© EP10777)- [v.3] I shall not
lack for music (© EP10778)-
[v.4] Nordic lullaby (© EP10779)-
[v.5] The day is over (© EP10780)-
[v.6] Whispering pines (© EP10781)

FEWELL, C   MARVIN.
Did Jesus stay with grief and
sorrow? ... The text and
music by C. Marvin Fewell.
© The H. W. Gray Co., inc.,
New York; 14Mar47; EP12849.
Score: chorus (SATB) and
piano reduction.

FIBICH, ZDENĚK, 1850-1900.
Poem; [by] Zdeněk Fibich, accordeon
(piano-concert) arr. [by] J.
Kálach. [Words by Karel Balling]
© Fr. A. Urbánek & Synové,
Praha, Czechoslovakia; on arrange-
ment; 50ct42; EF5084. Czech and
German words.

Poème; by Zdenko Fibich ... transcribed by Howard M. Peterson. ©
Mills Music, inc., New York; on
arrangement; 25Feb47; EP6647.
Score (marimba or xylophone and
piano) and part.

FICHTHORN, CLAUDE L
Behold, the angel of the Lord;
Easter anthem ... text from the
Scriptures, [music by] Claude L.
Fichthorn. © The Oliver Ditson
Co., Philadelphia; 10Jan47;
EP11397. Score: SATB and organ.

FIEHN, ERIK, 1907-
Hvem er det, der banker? ...
Musik: Erik Fiehn & Max Hansen,
tekst: Viggo Barfoed. ©
Wilhelm Hansen, Musik-Forlag,
Copenhagen; 21Mar41; EF5045.
Piano-conductor score
(orchestra, with words) and
parts.

FIELD, JOHN.
Rondo in E ... [by] John Field,
rev. and ed. by Alec Rowley. ©
Edwin Ashdown, ltd., London; on
arrangement; 20Jan47; EF3115.
For piano solo.

FIELDS, FRANK GASKIN.
"An Oklahoma scene" ... by Frank
Gaskin Fields. © Regent Music
Corp., New York; 10Jan47;
EP11844. Score: orchestra.

FIELDS, IRVING.
The goofy gal of Tegucigalpa
... Lyric by Albert Gamse,
music by Irving Fields. ©
Jewel Music Publishing Co.,
inc., New York; 9Jun47;
EP14625.

Miami beach rumba ... Lyric by
Albert Ganse, Spanish lyric by
Johnnie Camacho, music by
Irving Fields. © Edward B. Marks
Music Corp., New York; 26Dec46;
EP10767. For voice and piano,
with chord symbols.

Miami Beach rumba; lyric by Albert
Gamse, Spanish lyric by Johnnie
Camacho. Music by Irving Fields,
arr. by George Snowhill. ©
Edward B. Marks Music Corp., New
York; on arrangement; 30Dec46;
EP10977. Piano-conductor score
(orchestra, with words) and parts.

FIGUEROA, OTILIA.
Es de noche en el mar ... de
Otilia Figueroa. © Promotora
Hispano Americana de Música,
s.a., Mexico, D. F.; 27Dec46;
EF4864. Piano-conductor score
(orchestra), condensed score
and parts.

[FILLASTRE, GEORGETTE DE] 1914-
Comme autrefois; paroles de Cine
Money [pseud.], musique de G.
Viala [pseud.] © Éditions
Musicales Nuances, Paris,
15Feb47; EF3495.

FINA, JACK, 1913-
Dream sonata; by Jack Fina, and
[words by] Harold Spina. ©
Martin Music, Hollywood, Calif.;
1Apr47; EP13829. For piano solo,
with words.

FINCH, HAROLD N
Roadways; for chorus of mixed
voices S.A.T.B. a cappella,
poem by John Masefield, music
by Harold N. Finch, ed. by
Walter Aschenbrenner. © Carl
Fischer, inc., New York; 17May47;
EP15194.

FINLAYSON, WALTER.
Storm king ... [by] Walter Finlayson.
© Boosey & Hawkes, inc., New
York; 31Dec46; EP10999. Condensed
score (band) and parts.

[FINOCCHIOLI, AMEDEO]
Mamma non piangere! Vorsi e musica
by Er Sor Capanna-Mariarosa
[pseud.] © Amedeo Finocchioli,
Brooklyn; 1Nov46; EP11584.
Melody and words.

FIORITO, TED.
Charley, my boy ... by Gus Kahn
and Ted Fiorito, arr. by Jimmy
Dale. © Bourne, inc., New York;
on arrangement; 21Apr47;
EP13824. Piano-conductor score
(orchestra) and parts.

FISCHER, CARL, 1912-
Promise; words by Bill Carey ...
music by Carl Fischer. © Royal
Music Publisher, Hollywood,
Calif.; 21Nov46; EP6365.

FISCHER, CHARLES.
Lonely one; words by Mike Zimnocha,
music by Charles Fischer.
© Nordyke Publishing Co., Los
Angeles; 18Jul46; EP14777.

She's the picture of my mother;
words by Shirley Tough, music
by Charles Fischer. © Nordyke
Publishing Co., Los Angeles;
5Mar47; EP13271.

[FISCHER, IRWIN L   ] 1903-
Waltz reverie, by Edwin Marshal,
[pseud.] © Clayton F. Summy
Co., Chicago; 29May47; EP14832.
For piano solo.

FISHER, ARTHUR P   1899-
Jesus is a friend of mine; [by]
Arthur P. Fisher, arr. by W.
M. Thorne. (In Church of the
Nazarene. Michigan District.
Nazarene Young Peoples Society.
Choruses of the N. Y. P. S.
p.17) © Michigan District,
Nazarene Young Peoples Society,
Flint, Mich.; 25Jul46; EP13043.
Close score: SATB.

FISHER, DORIS.
(The corpse came C.O.D.) Warm
kiss (and a cold heart) ...
[from the picture] The corpse
came C.O.D. by Allan Roberts
and Doris Fisher. © Mood
Music Co., inc., New York;
29May47; EP14773. For voice and
piano, with chord symbols.

FISHER, DORIS. Cont'd.
(Down to earth) Let's stay young
forever. By Allan Roberts and
Doris Fisher ... [from] "Down to
earth." © Mood Music Co., inc.,
New York; 16Jun47; EP15219.
For voice and piano, with chord
symbols.

(Down to earth) They can't
convince me ... from the ...
picture "Down to earth" ...
by Allan Roberts and Doris
Fisher, arr. by Johnny
Warrington. © Mood Music Co.,
inc., New York; on arrangement; 21Apr47; EP13807.
Piano-conductor score
(orchestra, with words) and
parts.

They can't convince me. See her
Down to earth.
Warm kiss (and a cold heart) See
her The corpse came C.O.D.

When Johnny brings Lelahani home;
words and music by Allan Roberts
and Doris Fisher. © Sun Music
Co., inc., New York; 2Jan47;
EP11026.

FISHER, FRED.
Peg o' my heart; words by Alfred
Bryan, music by Fred Fisher.
[Revised version] New York,
Robbins Music Corp. © Leo
Feist, inc., New York; on new
words; 12May47; EP15131.

FISHER, GLADYS W
Wake, my heart; (S.A.B.) [words]
from "Hark, my soul" by John
Austin. © J. Fischer & Bro.,
New York; 3Jun46; EP4706.

FISHER, MARVIN, 1916-
Money, money, money, money, money!
The miser's serenade ... words and
music by Fred Patrick, Claude Reese
[and] Marvin Fisher. © Sunset Music
Publishers, New York; 10Feb47;
EP12067.

You don't learn that in school;
words by Roy Alfred, music by
Marvin Fisher. © Vanguard
Songs, Hollywood, Calif.;
8Apr47; EP13732.

FITCH, THEODORE F 1900-
Thine is the glory; anthem for
four-part chorus of mixed
voices with organ acc., text
from Matthew VI:13, music by
Theodore F. Fitch. © The
Boston Music Co., Boston;
27Feb47; EP12382.

FLACK, DUKE KEN, 1923-
Kiss my tears away; [melody by]
Duke Flack, [words by Helen
Palmer] © Helen Florine Palmer
[and] Duke Ken Flack, Ottumwa,
Iowa; 1Mar47; EP14669.

FLAGLER, ROBERT S
Easter dawn; SAB accompanied,
with solo voices, text taken
from St. Matthew, music by
Robert S. Flagler, arr. by
Wallingford Riegger. © Harold
Flammer, inc., New York; on
arrangement; 14Mar47; EP13463.

Easter dawn; SSA accompanied, with
solo voices, text taken from St.
Matthew, music by Robert S.
Flagler, arr. by Wallingford
Riegger. © Harold Flammer, inc.,
New York; on arrangement;
12Mar47; EP13464.

FLANDERS, JANE A
Ah, Revere! Ah, Revere! Words
and music by Jane A. Flanders.
[c1946] © Bruce Humphries,
inc., Boston; 3Feb47; EP11768.

FLANDORF, WALTER.
The Lord's prayer; [by] Walter
Flandorf. © Walter Flandorf,
Chicago; 30Dec46; EP11078.
Close score: SSATB.

FLAVIA, CH., pseud. See
Beauregard, Abel.

FLEENER, WOODDIE O
Would you like for me to love
you? Words and music by Wooddie
O. Fleener. © Nordyke Publishing Co., Hollywood, Calif.;
17Dec46; EP10791.

FLEGL, JOSEF, 1881-
Dětská suita; [music by] Josef
Flegl. [Op. 17] © Karel Barvitius, Praha, Czechoslovakia;
20Mar46; EP5371. For piano solo.

Malá taneční suita; na motivy
československých lidových písní,
Op.23. [By] Josef Flegl.
© Urbánek, Fr. A. & Synové,
Praha, Czechoslovakia; 1Jun46;
EP4964. For piano solo.

Union-marche; [music by] Josef
Flegl [Op. 3] © Mojmír Urbánek,
Praha, Czechoslovakia; 12Aug39;
EP5375. Piano-conductor score
(orchestra) and parts.

FLEISCHER, MONIA.
Dream of you; words and music by
Monia Fleisher. © Nordyke
Publishing Co., Los Angeles;
7May47; EP14792.

FLEMING, CHRISTOPHER LE. See
Le Fleming, Christopher.

FLEMING, LEN.
Ev'ry day ... words by Jacob H.
Kieselmann, music by Len Fleming.
© Jacob H. Kieselmann, St. Louis;
26Dec46; EP10726.

FLETCHER, JOHN.
The quilting party; words by
Frances Kyle, music by John
Fletcher. [Easy piano arrange-
ment with keyboard charts by
Victor Lakos Martin] © Songs
You Remember Publishing Co. (V.
L. Martin, proprietor) Atlanta;
on arrangement and playing in-
structions; 20Dec46; EP11336.

FLETCHER, LEILA.
Leila Fletcher's Music lessons have
begun; for the piano. © The
Boston Music Co., Boston;
10Mar47; AA50926.

On the merry-go-round; [by]
Lenore Montgomery [pseud.]
© Century Music Publishing
Co., New York; 12May47;
EP14268. For piano solo.

FLICKINGER, GRACE SPEER.
Maytime in the Ozarks; words and
music by Grace Speer Flickinger.
© Grace Speer Flickinger, Little
Rock, Ark.; 18Jun47; EP6969.

[PLODIN, SVEN]
Ensam vid mitt fönster ... text
och musik: Sven Goon [pseud.],
arr.: Karl-Henrik Norin. ©
Skandinaviska Odeon, a.b.,
Stockholm; 1Jan44; EP3751.
Piano-conductor score
(orchestra), and parts.

FLOOD, DORA FLICK.
O small feas'd flower; for two
voices and piano, S.A. [Words by
William Barnes, music by] Dora
Flick Flood. © G. Ricordi & Co.,
New York; 28Jan47; EP6617.

FLOR DE LIMON. (Lemon blossom) ...
Folk song of Janitzio Isle, Lake
Patzcuaro, Mexico, [English words
adapted by Albert Gamse] [in
André, Julio, ed. Songs from south
of the border. p.28-29) © Edward
B. Marks Music Corp., New York; on
English adaptation; 28Dec46;
EP10871.

FLORENTINE, sister.
Two offertories in honor of St.
Joseph: 1. Lauda Jerusalem. 2.
Veritas mea ... [music by] Sr. M.
Florentine ... [for 2 equal voices)
© McLaughlin & Reilly Co., Boston;
12Nov46; EP11183.

FLORES, NICK.
Horas negras ... Música y letra
de Nick Flores, [arr. by Jose A.
Gallardo] Corpus Christi, Tex.,
Gallardo Music Co. © Nick
Flores, Corpus Christi, Tex.;
3Feb47; EP11910.

[FLOWERS, PAUL D   ] 1924-
Free again; song ... by Rendell Lee
Manning [pseud.] © Rendell Lee
Manning, Los Angeles; 24Dec46;
EP10897.

FLUITER, HENRY DE. See
De Fluiter, Henry.

[FLUSS, STELLA D   ] 1892-
Shadow hills; words and music by
Starr von Fluss, [pseud., arr.
by Dan J. Michaud] Hollywood,
Calif., W. von Fluss. © Starr
von Fluss, Hollywood, Calif.;
27Mar47; EP13331.

FLYNN, CLEMENT.
Within Thy sight; sacred song, words
and music by Clement Flynn. ©
The Boston Music Co., Boston;
9Jul46; EP11886.

FOCH, DIRK.
Valse nostalgique. Op.43, no. 1,
by Dirk Foch. © Carl Fischer,
inc., New York; 17May47; EP14719.
For piano solo.

FÖDERL, KARL, 1885-
Spatzen-Polka. Alle Spatzen von
Wien pfeifen Straussmelodien
... Musik: Karl Föderl, Worte:
Hans Hauenstein. © Ludwig
Doblinger (Bernhard Herzmansky)
K. G., music publisher, Vienna;
9Dec44; EP3318.

FOERSTER, JOSEF BOHUSLAV, 1859-
Dva impromptus; [by] Jos. B.
Foerster ... rev. [by] prof.
Viktor Nopp. © Hudební Matice
Umělecké Besedy, Praha, Czecho-
slovakia; 11Jun42; EP4951. Score
(violin and piano) and part.

(Trio, piano & strings, no. 2)
Zweites klavier-trio, B dur, von
Jos. B. Foerster. Op. 38. Wien,
Universal-Edition. © Associated
Music Publishers, inc., New
York; 1Jan19; EP4825. Score
(violin, violoncello and piano)
and parts.

FOGARTY, ALEX.
Broodle-oo, broodle-oo (said the
pigeon); words by Pete Smith,
music by Alex Fogarty. © Chappell & Co., inc., New York;
10Jun47; EP15286.

[FOLDES, ANDOR] 1913-
I can not be gay; words by Alice
Nadine Morrison, music by Ted
Bromley [pseud.] © Morrison
Music Co., Seattle; 1Jan47;
EP10907. For voice and piano,
with chord symbols.
Two pieces for piano: Introvert
[and] Extrovert [by] Andor
Foldes. New York, Marks Ed. ©
Edward B. Marks Music Corp., New
York; 30Apr47; EP14134.

FOLGER, BILLY, 1915-
If I'd only been true to you;
words and music by Andy Walsh
and Billy Folger. © Adams, Vee
& Abbott, inc., Chicago; 24Oct46;
EP13346.

FOLPRECHT, ZDENĚK, 1900-
Dvanást' l'udových piesní slovenských;
[by] Zdenek Folprecht. Op. 9.
© Hudební Matice Umělecké Besedy,
Praha, Czechoslovakia; 28Oct40;
EF4946. For voice and piano.

Suita; [by] Zdeněk Folprecht.
Op. 2. © Hudební Matice
Umělecké Besedy, Praha,
Czechoslovakia; 6April;
EF4948. For piano solo.

FONTANALS, FRANCISCO.
Cuba y Méjico ... letra y
música de Francisco Fontanals,
arreglo de Pérez Prado. ©
Peer International Corp., New
York; EF5435. Parts:
orchestra.

FONTENOY, MARC, pseud. See
Schwab, Alexandre.

FORBES, ROGER, arr.
Melodies from masterworks ... arr.
for piano solo by Roger Forbes.
© New World Publishers, ltd.,
London; on selection & arrange-
ment in v. 3, 21Jan47; on
arrangement in v. 5, 28Mar47;
EF4991, 5568.

FORBES, MEL.
The devil's train; words and
music by Cliff Carlisle and
Mel Force. © Acuff-Rose
Publications, Nashville;
14May47; EP14351.

Journey's end; by Claude Casey
and Mel Foree. [c1946]
© Bourne, inc., New York;
14May47; EP12745. For voice
and piano, with chord symbols.

FORESYTHE, REGINALD.
Molloy, my boy ... by Reginald
Foresythe. © Arcadia Music
Publishing Co., ltd., London;
17Sep46; EF3776. For voice
and piano.

FORET, FELICIEN HENRI, 1891-
Eglogue; [by] Félicien Foret.
Paris, L. de Lacour, Editions
Costallat. © Lucien de Lacour,
Paris; 15Oct46; EF3290. Score
(oboe and piano) and part.

La rose du jardin ... pour chant
et piano, [by] Félicien Foret,
poésie de Jean Moréas [pseud.]
Paris, L. de Lacour, Editions
Lucien de Lacour, Paris; 15Oct46;
EF5237.

(Sonata, oboe & piano) Sonate
en sol majeur ... [by]
Félicien Foret. Paris, L. de
Lacour, Editions Costallat.
© Lucien de Lacour, Paris;
30Nov46; EF3642. Score and
part.

FORTIS, JOHNNY, 1913-
Gotta go to St. Joe, Mo.; [words]
by Max Spickol [and] Alan
Fielding, [music by] Johnny
Fortis. © Farrow Music, inc.,
New York; 5May47; EP14808.

FORTNER, RED.
Take my word the way you took my
heart; lyric by Tommy Coley,
music by Red Fortner. © Unique
Music Publishers, Detroit;
1Dec46; EP12028.

[FOSTER, ALBERT H   ] 1888-   comp.
Anthems choir and congregation enjoy;
[comp. by Albert H. Foster] © Clayton F. Summy Co., Chicago; 10Mar47;
EP12546. Score: SATB, in part with
organ.

For me and my piano ... progressive
piano pieces, [comp. by Albert
H. Foster] © Clayton F. Summy
Co., Chicago; bk.1, 3, 10Feb47;
bk.2, 14Feb47; EP12060, 12890,
12059.

Singing keys; graded piano pieces
[comp. by Albert H. Foster]
© Clayton F. Summy Co., Chicago;
bk.4. 2May47; EP14185.

Twelve twin tunes; standard composi-
tions for two pianos, [comp. by
Albert H. Foster, jr.] © Clayton
F. Summy Co., Chicago; 2Jan47;
EP11221. Score: piano 1-2.

FOSTER, CHARLES.
Roll it over; by Charles Foster.
© Preview Music Co., Chicago;
13Jul46; EP12077. For voice and
piano, with chord symbols.

FOSTER, CHUCK.
Busybody; music and lyrics by Hal
Pruden, Lyle Moraine [and]
Chuck Foster. © Advanced Music
Corp., New York; 18Jun47;
EP15279.

FOSTER, DOROTHY FAY, 1915-
Dingdong, dingdong; [by] Dorothy
Fay Foster. (In Poulton, D.
F., comp. Songs for preschool
children. p. 8) © Dorothy
Fay Foster, Cincinnati;
1Sep46; EP13168.

What can I give Him? [Words by]
Christina G. Rossetti, [music
by] Dorothy Fay Foster. (In
Poulton, D. F., comp. Songs
for preschool children. p. 49)
© Dorothy Fay Foster, Cincinnati;
1Sep46; EP13177.

FOSTER, DOROTHY GUTEKUNST.
God's love hush and other songs;
[by Dorothy Gutekunst Foster.
© Atwood Foster, Salem, Or.;
16May47; EP14637.

FOSTER, IVOR R
Three songs with pianoforte
accompaniment; [by] Ivor R.
Foster. Op. 36. Poems by
Thomas Hardy. © Alfred
Lengnick & Co., ltd., London;
2Apr47; EF3197.

FOSTER, MYLES B
O! For a closer walk with God;
for ... S.S.A. (incidental
solo: soprano) opt. [By] Myles
B. Foster, arr. by Roy Lathrop
[pseud. Words by] William
Cowper. © Pro Art Publications,
New York; on arrangement; '
21Apr47; EP13602.

FOSTER, STEPHEN COLLINS, 1826-1864.
Camptown races; by Stephen Foster,
arr. by Dorothy Gaynor Blake.
© Clayton F. Summy Co., Chicago;
on arrangement; 1May47; EP14183.
Two scores for piano 1-2.

FOUKES, MARY SELISH.
Reminiscing with you; words and music
by J. P. Foukes and M. S. Foukes.
[c1946] © J. P. Foukes [and] M.
S. Foukes, San Diego, Calif.;
7Jan47; EP11555.

FOUTS, MURIEL.
Children's easy piano pieces;
signs of spring series, by
Muriel Fouts. © Edward Schuberth
& Co., inc., New York; 14Mar47.
Contents.- [v. 1] Playing marbles (© EP12610)- [v. 2] Roller
skating (© EP12611)- [v. 3]
Bicycle riding (© EP12612)-
[v. 4] Balloons (© EP12613)-
[v. 5] Sling shots. Tricycle
ride (© EP12614)- [v. 6] Bubble
gum. Easy hopscotch (© EP12615)-
[v. 7] Walking on stilts
(© EP12616)- [v. 8] Hop scotch
(© EP12617)- [v. 9] Floating
balloons (© EP12618)- [v. 10]

Play with me. A day in spring
(© EP12619)- [v. 11] Waltz in A
minor (© EP12620)- [v. 12] Waltz
in F major (© EP12621)- [v. 13]
Prelude in G major (© EP12605)-
[v. 14] Riding horseback
(© EP12606)- [v. 15] Indian baby
(© EP12607)- [v. 16] A flower
sings (© EP12608)- [v. 17] Two
ways (© EP12609)- [v. 18] The
hammer song (© EP12604)- [v. 19]
I will see you. Baby kitty
(with words) (© EP12603)- [v. 20]
The snoopy rabbit (© EP12601)-

[v. 21] Going to town (with words)
(© EP12600)- [v. 22] Jumping on
the bed. I know something (with
words) (© EP12602)- [v. 23] Cowboy song. Nap time (with words)
(© EP12599)

Fun on the keys; forty-seven easy
piano pieces, (some with words),
[by] Muriel Fouts. Illus. by
Jeanne Tallec. © G. Schirmer,
inc., New York; 2May46; EP11611.

FOWLER, GEORGE, 1863-
Just abide in Jesus; [and My
pilot; by] George Fowler.
[c1946] (In his Two stories)
© George Fowler, Philadelphia;
3Feb47; EP15054-15055. Close
score: SATB.

[FOWLER, JOHN WALLACE] 1917-   comp.
Lowell Blanchard's Folio of Mid-day
Merry-go-round favorites; [comp.
by Wally Fowler. Words and music
by Wally Fowler, Curly Kinsey,
Johnny New and others. c1945] ©
Wallace Fowler Publications, Nash-
ville; bk. 1, 4Nov46; EP12927.
Melody and chord symbols, with
words.

Smilin' Bill Waters Home folk
songs; [words and music by
Smilin' Bill Waters and others]
© Wallace Fowler Publications,
Nashville; 25Feb47; EP13028.

FOWLER, WALLY. See
Fowler, John Wallace.

FOX, FRANK, 1902-
Amerika hat Rhythmus und Wien
hat Melodie ... Worte: Erich
Meder, Musik: Frank Fox.
© Ludwig Doblinger (Bernhard
Herzmansky) K. G., music
publisher, Vienna; 12Nov45;
EF3315.

Kaugummi (Ich muss den Jonny
küssen) ... English words by
Ezra Lapides, Worte: Erich
Meder, Musik: Frank Fox.
© Ludwig Doblinger (Bernhard
Herzmansky) K. G., music
publisher, Vienna; 12Nov45;
EF3314.

"Oh-yes!" ... Worte: Erich
Meder, (English words by
Franklyn W. Everts] Musik:
Frank Fox. © Ludwig Doblinger
(Bernhard Herzmansky), K. G.,
Vienna; 15Mar46; EF3403.

Und das war verboten! Potpourri
von Frank Fox. [c1945] ©
Ludwig Doblinger (Bernhard
Herzmansky), K. G., Vienna;
12Jun46; EF3402. For piano
solo, with words.

FOX, LEO, 1914-
Down in old New Jersey; words and
music by Leo Fox, arr. by Dan
J. Michaud. © Leo Fox, Hollywood, Calif.; 24Apr47; EP13918.

FOX, RED.
Nothin' but you; words and music by
"Red" Fox. © Hill and Range
Songs, inc., Hollywood, Calif.;
8Mar47; EP12586.

47

FOX, RED. Cont'd.
Stop now; words and music by "Red" Fox. © Hill and Range Songs, inc., Hollywood, Calif.; 8Mar47; EP12585.

FRANCA, IDA.
We pray to Thee ... carol, music and poem by Ida Franca. © Ida Franca, New York; 22Dec46; EP11023. Close score: SSAA.

FRANCE, WILLIAM EDWARD, 1912-
A child's prayer to the shepherd; anthem for junior choir, two part; words by Rev. T. B. Pollock ... Music by William E. France. © The Frederick Harris Music Co., ltd., Oakville, Ont., Can.; 8Mar47; EF5291.

FRANCESCHI, PASQUALE, 1890-
Napoli sorride; parole di E. A. Bellitti, musica del Mo. Pasquale Franceschi. New York, The Music Lyre. © Eugenio Angelo Bellitti, New York; 6Jan47; EP11260.

FRANCK, CÉSAR AUGUSTE, 1822-1890.
Father most merciful. Panis angelicus. For four-part chorus of mixed voices with piano acc. [by] César Franck, arr. by Kenneth Downing, [pseud.] © G. Schirmer, inc., New York; EP13189.

The Lord's prayer. (Panis angelicus) TTB accompanied, with optional violin obligato; words adapted by Alfred Marlhom, [music by] César Franck, arr. by Wallingford Riegger. © Harold Flammer, inc., New York; on arrangement; 14Mar47; EP15475.

The Lord's prayer. (Panis angelicus) TTBB accompanied, with optional violin obligato; words adapted by Alfred Marlhom, [music by] César Franck, arr. by Wallingford Riegger. © Harold Flammer, inc., New York; on arrangement; 14Mar47; EP15476.

FRANCO LUGO, GABRIEL.
Dile que venga otra vez ... [words and music by] Gabriel Franco Lugo, arreglo de Juan Bruno Farraza. © Editorial Mexicana de Música Internacional, s. a., Mexico; 30Dec46; EF5807. Condensed score (orchestra), piano-conductor score and parts.

FRANGEUL, FERNAND.
M'ap resodou. (To think I thought so much of you) ... [By] Fernand Frangeul, [English words adapted by Albert Gamse] (In André, Julie, ed. Songs from south of the border. p.30-31) © Edward B. Marks Music Corp., New York; on English adaptation; 28Dec46; EP10872.

FRANGKISER, CARL, 1894-
The Argonaut ... [by] Carl Frangkiser. © Belwin, inc., New York; 3Mar47; EP12756. Condensed score (band) and parts.

Buffalo Bill; by Carl Frangkiser. © Pro Art Publications, New York; 3Feb47; EP11754. Condensed score (band) and parts.

The high vision ... [by] Edward Rayner [pseud.] © Belwin, inc., New York; 24Dec46; EP10702. Score (band), condensed score and parts.

Rapture of spring; choral finale (optional), by Carl Frangkiser. © Pro Art Publications, New York; 7Apr47; EP12981. Condensed score (chorus: SATB and band) and parts for band.

The rapture of spring; words and music by Carl Frangkiser. © Pro Art Publications, New York; 19May47; EP14448. Score: chorus (SSA) and piano.

Rendezvous with destiny ... by Carl Frangkiser. © Carl Fischer, inc., New York; 19Dec46; EP11215. Condensed score (band) and parts.

Scene from a campanile ... [by] Carl Frangkiser. © Belwin, inc., New York; 24Dec46; EP10701. Score (band), condensed score and parts.

Under the big top; (a figment of the imagination) © Pro Art Publications, New York; 30Sep46; EP8255. Condensed score (band) and parts.

FRANK, J L
Singing as I go; words and music by Pee Wee King and J. L. Frank. © Acuff-Rose Publications, Nashville; 12Mar47; EP12628.

FRANKE, G H
Darling mother of mine; words and music by G. H. Franke, arr. by E. H. Brey. © G. H. Franke, Manitowoc, Wis.; 16May47; EP14641.

FRANKEL, BENJAMIN.
(Quartet, strings, no. 2) Quartet no. 2. Op. 15. For two violins, viola & violon-cello. [By] Benjamin Frankel. © Augener ltd. (British), London; 9Apr47; EF3323. Miniature score.

FRANKLIN, DAN.
(Gotta get to) Oklahoma City; by Don Reed [and] Dan Franklin. © Hometown Music Co., inc., New York; 24Mar47; EP13568. For voice and piano, with chord symbols.

FRANKLIN, DAVE.
Deep down in your heart; lyric and music by Cliff Friend and Dave Franklin. © Triangle Music Corp., New York; 28Apr47; EP14100.

Dreamer's holiday; lyric and music by Cliff Friend and Dave Franklin. © Bregman, Vocco and Conn, inc., New York; 28Apr47; EP14106.

FRANZ, ROBERT.
Lord, as we part ... for mixed voices, [by] Robert Franz, arr. by C. D. Glauque. © Oliver Ditson Co., Philadelphia; on arrangement; 8Apr47; EP13484.

FRAZER, DONALD.
A carol in captivity; for S.A.T.B. Words by Maurice Wilson ... music by Donald Frazer, arr. Elizabeth Poston. London, J. Curwen & Sons. © Donald Frazer, Aldershot, Eng.; 9Dec46; EF14765.

FREDERICK, SCHIEFELBEIN ALBERT, pseud. See Schiefelbein, Frederick Albert.

FREEBURG, DONALD S
Beaver flight song; [official centennial song, College of the City of New York] ... Words and music by Philip R. Benjamin and Donald S. Freeberg. © Shapiro, Bernstein & Co., inc., New York; 7May47; EP14336.

FREED, FRED, pseud. See Goldbaum, Friedrich.

FREED, ISADORE.
Crossing the plains; song with piano acc., [words by Joaquin Miller] music by Isadore Freed. © Carl Fischer, inc., inc., New York; 8May47; EP15019.

Prayers of Israel; for conservative, reform & orthodox services ... by Isadore Freed. © Hatikvah Music Publishing Co., (Mrs. Janot S. Roskin, sole owner) Indianapolis; on 5 pieces; 10Mar47. Score: 2-4 mixed voices and organ. Contents.- I. Friday evening service music. [v. 1.] V'shomeru. © EP6674)- [v. 2.] Yismechu I. © EP6670)- [v. 3.] Yismechu II. © EP6671)- [v. 4.] A prayer for peace. May the words. (© EP6673) II. Sabbath morning service music. [v. 5] Etz chayim. © EP6672)

FREED, JACK N 1908-
The glorious resurrection; words by Jessie W. Menzies, music by Jack N. Freed. © Jack N. Freed [and] Jessie W. Menzies, Inglewood, Calif.; 16Jun47; EP15093.

FREEMAN, BUD.
Atomic era ... [by] Bud Freeman [and Ray McKinley] © Robbins Music Corp., New York; 6Dec46; EP11010. Score (saxophone and piano) and parts for saxophone and drums. Edition for E flat alto saxophone.
----Edition for B flat tenor saxophone. © Robbins Music Corp., New York; 6Dec46; EP11011.

A study in augmented intervals [by] Bud Freeman. B♭ tenor saxophone solo, with piano accompaniment. © Robbins Music Corp., New York; 29Nov46; EP11005. Score (saxophone and piano) and part.

A study in augmented intervals; E♭ alto saxophone ... [by] Bud Freeman. © Robbins Music Corp., New York; 14Nov46; EP11012. Corrected by EP12318. Score (saxophone and piano) and part.

FREY, ERIK, 1904-
Recompense ... music by Erik Frey, arr. for mixed voices by Walter J. Goodell. © Erik Frey, Chicago; 1Jan47; EP15113.

FREY, HUGO, 1874- arr.
A greeting to you; folk melody ... [words by Elsie-Jean, pseud.] arr. by Hugo Frey. © Hamilton S. Gordon, inc., New York; on arrangement and words; 11Jun47; EP15059. For piano solo, with words.

FREY, HUGO, 1874- ed. and arr.
Music for millions; a collection of world famous piano pieces, ed. by Hugo Frey. © J. J. Robbins & Sons, inc., New York; on arrangements; v. 1, 23Apr47; EP15291.

FREY, HUGO, 1874-
When Gran'ma danced the polka; music by Hugo Frey, vocal arrangement by the composer, words by Harry R. Wilson. © J. J. Robbins and Sons, inc., New York; 2Jun47; EP14857. Score: SATB and piano.

48

FRIBOULET, GEORGES EDMOND, 1910-
Quarante leçons d'harmonie;
faciles, moyenne difficulté,
difficiles; 3 basses et chants
alternés, 17 basses données,
20 chants donnés. Par
Georges Friboulet, préface
d'Henri Busser. © Henry
Lemoine & Cie., Paris; v. 1-
2, 22Jul46. Contents.- 1.
Textes seuls. (© EF5539)-
2. Textes réalisés. (© EF3538)

FRIEBER, LOUIS. See also
Raymond, Louis, pseud.

Parade of the marionettes; by
De Romney, [pseud.] & Sidney
Crooke. © Schauer & May,
London; 1Nov46; EF5160. For
piano solo.

FRIEDELL, HAROLD.
Jesus, so lowly; anthem for
mixed voices, [words by] Edith
Williams, [music by] Harold
Friedell. © The H. W. Gray
Co., inc., New York; 30Apr47;
EP14071.

FRIEZIERER, BENJAMIN, 1922-
Melody bars. Melody bars in 4/4
time; [for] piano accordion, by
Benjamin Friezierer. © Melody
Music Co., New York; 28Oct46;
EP11187.

FRIML, RUDOLF, 1881-
L'amour, toujours l'amour. (Love
everlasting; music by Rudolf
Friml, arr. by Jimmy Dale. ©
Harms, inc., New York; on arrangement; 29May47; EP15002. Piano-
conductor score (orchestra) and
parts.

(The firefly) Sympathy ... from
the comedy-opera "The firefly";
for two-part chorus of women's
voices with piano accompaniment.
Words by Otto Harbach, [music
by] Rudolf Friml, arranged by
Chas. Dews [pseud.] © G.
Schirmer, inc., New York; on
arrangement; 30Dec46; EP11603.

Indian love call ... Transcribed
by F. Campbell-Watson. © Harms,
inc., New York; on arrangement;
20Mar46; EP2564. Piano-conductor score (orchestra) and parts.

Love is the time. See his
Northwest outpost.

(Northwest outpost) Love is the
time, from the ... picture,
"Northwest outpost," lyric by
Edward Heyman, music by Rudolf
Friml. © Edwin H. Morris & Co.,
inc., New York; 23May47;
EP14759.

(Northwest outpost) Raindrops
on a drum, from the ... picture,
"Northwest outpost," lyric by
Edward Heyman, music by Rudolf
Friml. © Edwin H. Morris & Co.
inc., New York; 23May47; EP14760.

(Northwest outpost) Tell me with
your eyes; from the ... picture,
"Northwest outpost," lyric by
Edward Heyman, music by Rudolf
Friml. © Edwin H. Morris &
Co., inc., New York; 23May47;
EP14758.

Raindrops on a drum. See his
Northwest outpost.

(Rose Marie) The mounties; from
"Rose Marie" ... S.A. or T.B.,
lyric by Otto Harbach and Oscar
Hammerstein ... music by Rudolf
Friml and Herbert Stothart, arr.
by Douglas MacLean, [pseud.]
© Harms, inc., New York; on ar-
rangement; 30Jan47; EP12022.

Sympathy. See his The Firefly.

Tell me with your eyes. See his
Northwest outpost.

FRISCH, AL.
A chocolate sundae on a Saturday
night; by Fred 'Jise, Hal David
[and] Al Frisch. © Barton
Music Corp., New York; 23Jun47;
EP15206. For voice and piano,
with chord symbols.

Pancho Maximilian Hernandeez (the
best president we ever had) ...
by Bob Hilliard and Al Frisch.
© United Music Corp., New York;
1May47; EP14108. For voice and
piano, with chord symbols.

[FRISIA, ATTILIO]
Il piccolo Friol ... un metodo che
insegna ... la fisarmonica, dalla
piccola a 12 bassi all' completa. © Carisch, s.a., Milano;
30Sep43; EF4529. For accordion.

FROMM, HELEN ELIZABETH, 1900-
Jesus' name, how sweet to me ...
Life! Life! Life! ... [by]
Helen E. Fromm. © Helen
Elizabeth Fromm, Philadelphia;
22Dec46; EP11762. Hymns, with
music.

FROSINI, PIETRO, 1885-
Chile beans ... by P. Frosini.
© Accordion Music Publishing
Co., New York; 23Dec46; EP11272.
For accordion solo.

Sicilian scronade ... by P. Frosini.
© Accordion Music Publishing
Co., New York; 23Dec46; EP11271.
For accordion solo.

FRYBERG, MART.
Will you? By Eddie Seiler, Sol
Marcus [and] Mart Fryberg, arr.
by Allan Small. © Leeds Music
Corp., New York; 16Jun47;
EP15092. Piano-conductor score
(orchestra) and parts.

FRYDAN, CAMILLA, 1890-
America united; words by Jay
Rohman, music by Camilla
Frydan. New York, National
March Music Co. © Camilla
Frydan & Jay Rohman, New York;
26May47; EP14675.

[FRYKMAN, ERIK]
En dörr på glänt ... text och
musik [by] Fritz-Gustaf [pseud.
and] Fryman [pseud.] ©
Skandinaviska Odeon, a.b.,
Stockholm; 1Jan46; EF3756.

Jag ligger ut igen ... av
Fryman [pseud. and] Fritz-
Gustaf [pseud.], arr: Julius
Jacobsen. © Skandinaviska
Odeon, a.b., Stockholm;
1Jan46; EF3754. Piano-con-
ductor score (orchestra), and
parts.

FRYMAN, pseud. See
Frykman, Erik.

FRYXELL, REGINA HOLMEN, 1899-
The Lord's prayer ... [by]
Regina Holmen Fryxell. ©
Regina Holmen Fryxell, Rock
Island, Ill.; 12Dec46;
EP10895. Close score: mixed
chorus.

To the hills I lift mine eyes;
[by] Regina Holmen Fryxell,
[words] from the Psalms,
metrical version by Rollin
Pease. © Regina Holmen Fryxell,
Rock Island, Ill.; 12Dec46;
EP10894. Close score: SATB.

FUCHS, ARNO.
El a b c de la música; juegos
para niños, con notas, figuras
y canciones infantiles. (México, Editorial de México)
© Arno Fuchs, Tacubaya, D. F.,
México; 22Apr47; EF3370.

La hora de cantar; segunda parte
de le serie de coros a 3 voces
para escuelas, [by] Arno Fuchs.
[México, Editorial de México]
© Dr. Arno Fuchs, Tacubaya,
D. F., México; 21Apr47; EF3371.

FUCILLI, PASQUALE.
Cerco la mia piccola casetta ...
testo di C. Deani, musica di
Pasquale Fucilli. (In Un
sorriso e 20 canzoni. p. 12-13)
© Edizioni Leonardi, s.a.r.l.,
Milano; 70ct45; EF4915. For
voice and piano.

Rose per una santa ... testo e
musica di P. Fucilli. (In Un
sorriso e 20 canzoni. p. 10-
11) © Edizioni Leonardi, s.a.r.l.,
Milano; 11Nov45; EF4914. For
voice and piano.

FUENTES, RICARDO.
Rumbeame. (When you dance with
me) ... English words by Joe
Davis, Spanish words by Jaime
Yamin, music by Ricardo Fuentes.
© Caribbean Music, inc., New
York; 12May47; EP14215.

FULEIHAN, ANIS.
(Rhapsody, violoncello & string
orchestra) Rhapsody, for cello
and string orchestra; by Anis
Fuleihan. Cello and piano version.
© Carl Fischer, inc., New York;
10Apr47; EP13482.

FULKERSON, MAUDE.
I'll bless your darlin' heart; by
Maude Fulkerson. © Cine-Mart
Music Publishing Co., Hollywood,
Calif.; 1Nov46; EP11722. For
voice and piano, with chord
symbols.

FULLER, H   J
Bring back my Bonnie; words and
music by H. J. Fuller. [Easy
piano arrangement with keyboard
charts by Victor Lakos Martin]
© Songs You Remember Publishing
Co. (V. L. Martin, proprietor),
Atlanta; on arrangement and
playing instructions; 20Dec46;
EP11334.

FULLER, PAUL, pseud. See
Howorth, Wayne.

FULTON, JACK.
My baby didn't even say goodbye;
by Jimmy Hilliard and Jack
Fulton, arr. by Johnny Warrington. © Pic Music Corp., Chicago;
on arrangement; 1Apr47; EP13591.
Piano-conductor score (orchestra,
with words) and parts.

My baby didn't even say goodbye; by
Jimmy Hilliard and Jack Fulton.
© Pic Music Corp., Chicago; 4Jan47;
EP12142. For voice and piano, with
chord symbols.

FULTON, NORMAN.
Serenade for strings, by Norman
Fulton. © Oxford Univ. Press,
London; 12Dec46; EF4733.

FUMERO, J. CLARO. See
Claro Fumero, J.

FURBY, ARTHUR.
My inspiration. See his She
wanted a cream front door.

49

FURBY, ARTHUR. Cont'd.
(She wanted a cream front door)
My inspiration ... (from) "She
wanted a cream front door" ...
words by Mai Bacon, music by
Arthur Furby & Reg Sellick,
[piano arrangement by Chris
Langdon] © Chappell & Co.,
ltd., London; 21Mar47; EF5481.

FURNEY, ALBERT J   1887-
Climbing hills ... words and
music ... by Al Furney, arr.
Harry Powell. © Al J. Furney,
San Francisco; 12Jun47;
EP15113.

If I flew blind (to paradise) ...
words and music ... by Al Furney,
arr. [by] Harry Powell. © Albert
J. Furney, San Francisco; 31Dec46;
EP13349.

Let's get launched ... words and
music ... by Al Furney [arr. by
Harry Powell. c1946] © Albert
J. Furney, San Francisco;
22Apr47; EP14120.

On de Embarcadero ... words and
music ... by Al Furney, arr.
Harry Powell. © Al Furney,
San Francisco; 12Jun47; EP15114.

They (we) never met again ...
words and music ... by Al Furney,
arrangement [by] Harry Powell.
© Albert J. Furney, San Francisco;
31Dec46; EP11352.

Wolf whistle bait; words and music...
by Al Furney ... arrangement [by]
Harry Powell. © Albert J. Furney,
San Francisco; 31Dec46; EP11350.

Would if I could ... words and music...
by Al Furney, arrangement [by] Harry
Powell. © Albert J. Furney, San
Francisco; 31Dec46; EP11351.

FYLER, GEORGE WILLIAM, 1906-
Lilac time in Lombard; lyrics
and music [by] George W.
Fyler, arr. by Marjorie
Street. © George William
Fyler, Lombard, Ill.; 21May47;
EP14631.

G

[GABRIEL, CHARLES H   ] 1856-
1932.
An evening prayer (A prayer
anthem) [words by C. M.
Battersby, music by Gabriel-
Shelly] arr. by Griffith J.
Jones. Winona Lake, Ind.,
Rodeheaver Hall-Mack Co.
© The Rodeheaver Co., Winona
Lake, Ind.; 10Feb47; EP12153.
Score: soprano, SATB and piano.

GADDIS, RACHEL M
Abraham, the pilgrim; [words by
T. H. Gaddis] The soldier's
triumph; [words by Peter Fagins]
... Jesus, the dearest Friend
[and] Oh, so happy; [words by
R. M. G.] Music by Rachel M.
Gaddis. Winona Lake, Ind.,
Gaddis Moser Evangelistic Party.
© Rachel M. Gaddis, Winona Lake,
Ind.; 10Apr47; EP13598. Close
score: SATB.

GADE, JACOB.
Jalousie. (Jealousy) ... lyric by
Vera Bloom, Spanish text by Belen
Ortega, music by Jacob Gade, a
Johnny Sterling arrangement.
© Harms, inc., New York; on ar-
rangement; 8Apr47; EP13690.
Piano-conductor score(orchestra,
with words) and parts.

The last Viking. © Sprague-Cole-
man, New York; 10Apr40; EP4467.
Piano-conductor score (orchestra)
and parts.

GADSBY, HENRY.
He is risen ... for combined junior
(S.A.) and senior (S.A.T.B.)
choirs with piano or organ acc.,
[by] Henry Gadsby, arr. by Carl
F. Mueller. Words adapted from
the Bible. © Carl Fischer, inc.,
New York; on arrangement; 27Jan47;
EP12428.

GAGE, A   F
Call me not hence, O Lord; (The
workman's prayer) Words by
Anna P. Slattery, music by A.
F. Gage, sr. © A. F. Gage, sr.
& T. E. Conerly, Chicago;
5May47; EP14602. Close score:
SATB.

GAGE, HORACE ANDREW, 1906-
All my love to you; lyric by
Florence C. Gage, music by
Horace A. Gage. © Horace
Andrew Gage & Florence Com-
stock Gage, Detroit; 28May47;
EP14886.

GAGE, WILLIS J   1907-
Marchiesta; by Willis Gage.
Dallas, Stamps-Baxter Music
& Printing Co., inc. ©
Willis Gage, Dallas; 15Jun46;
EP14320. For piano solo.

GAGNIER, JEAN J   1885-
Trois esquisses musicales; pour
piano. Three musical sketches;
for the piano [by] J. J. Gagnier.
© Editions A. Passio, Lachute,
Que., Canada; 1Apr47;
EP5327-5329. Contents.- Prélude.
- Reflets.- Têtes d'enfants.

GAINES, SAMUEL RICHARDS,   d. 1945
Gwendolyn waltzes; for full
chorus of women's voices with
piano acc., words and music by
Samuel Richards Gaines. © G.
Schirmer, inc., New York;
3Apr47; EP14058.

GALAVERNI, ITALO, 1879-
La famiglia Brambilla alla
fiera del Milano; sei pezzi
facili per pianoforte, [by]
Italo Galaverni. © Carisch,
s.a., Milan; 16May47; EP3787.

I piccoli concertisti; [by]
Italo Galaverni. 4 pezzi di
media difficoltà. © Carisch,
società anonima, Milan; 20Sep39;
EP5244. For piano 4 hands.

Scherzi per pianoforte; [by]
Italo Galaverni. © Carisch,
s.a., Milan; on 3 pieces;
28Feb42. Contents.- [1] No. 1.
© EP3846.- [2] No. 5.
© EP3847.- [3] No. 6.
© EP3848.

GALINDO, BLAS.
Springtime. La primavera ...
Music and Spanish text by Blas
Galindo, English text by Olga
Paul. © Leeds Music Corp.,
New York; 31Dec46; EP14692.
Score: SATB and piano.

GALINDO, PEDRO.
(Easy to wed) Viva México! (Viva
América!) English lyric by Al
Stewart ... Spanish lyric by P.
Galindo. © Peer International
Corp., New York; on English
lyric; 31Dec45; EP4973. For
voice and piano, with chord sym-
bols.

Viva México! See his Easy to
wed.

GALLA-RINI, ANTHONY, 1904-   arr.
Galla-Rini's collection of
hymns for accordion; [arr.
by Galla-Rini] © Chart Music
Publishing House, inc., Chicago;
on arrangement; 15Apr47;
EP6835.

GALLIARD, JOHANN ERNST.
(Sonatas, bassoon & harpsichord)
Six sonatas ... [by] Johann
Ernst Galliard; figured bass
set by Edith Weiss-Mann,
foreword by Josef Marx. New
York, McGinnis & Marx.
(Music for wind instruments
by 18th century masters ...
no.II) © Josef Marx, New
York; on setting of figured
bass & foreword; 4Dec46;
EP12623. Score (bassoon or
cello and piano) and parts.

GALLIPOLI, ALFREDO A
La conga de los novios ... letra
y música de Julio Nistal y
Alfredo A. Gallipoli. ©
Editorial Argentina de Música
Internacional, s. de r., ltda.,
Buenos Aires; 30Dec46; EP5217.

GALLO, pseud. See
Gorni, Francesco.

GALLOIS MONTBRUN, RAYMOND, 1918-
Les rêves de Janceline; douze pièces
faciles ... [by] Raymond Gallois
Montbrun. © Alphonse Leduc et
Cie., Paris; on 12 pieces; 2Jan47.
Contents.- 1. Quadrille des soldats
de plomb (© EP3543) - 2. Complainte du petit bossu (© EP3544)
- 3. Confidences d'une vieille
horloge (© EP3545) - 4. Sourire
à Morphée (© EP3546) - 5. Le
manège des sept nains (© EP3547)
- 6. Chagrin près d'une fontaine
(© EP3548) - 7. Polka du
rossignol (© EP3551) - 8. Siciliette, reine des Siciles (© EP3550)
- 9. Minuetti, prince de la
danse (© EP3549) - 10. Le jardin
des ombres (© EP3542) - 11.
Remords de Carabouse (© EP3541)
- 12. La ronde des grillons
(© EP3540)

Pages de sonatine ... [by] Raymond Gallois Montbrun. ©
Alphonse Leduc et Cie., Paris;
on 5 pieces. Score (violin
and piano) and part. Con-
tents.- 1. page. Prélude.
(© 21Oct46; EP5206)- 2. page.
Courante (© 21Oct46; EP5205)-
3. page. Andante (© 9Oct46;
EP5204)- 4. page. Pastorale
(© 21Oct46; EP5203)- 5. page.
Saltarelle (© 21Oct46; EP5202)

GALLOP, SAMMY.
I'd do the impossible for you;
words and music by Sammy Gallop.
© Edwin H. Morris & Co., inc.,
New York; on changes in words
and music; 27Dec46; EP13583.

GALLOS, ANNA GEROTHEOU, 1920-   arr.
The divine liturgy of Saint John
Chrysostom; from the Byzantino,
comp., arr. and harmonized by
Anna Gerotheou Gallos. © Anna
Gerotheou Gallos, New Haven,
Conn.; 31Dec46; EP10900. Cover-
title: A liturgy for the Greek
Orthodox church. Score: chorus
(SSA) and organ or chorus (SATB);
Greek words.

GALOVA, TRUDIE, 1886-
Arizona baby; written & composed by
Trudie Galova. Southend-on-
Sea (Eng.) Arthur's Music Co.
© Trudi Galova Duffton, Glasgow;
16Apr47; EF6061. For voice
and piano.

GALVÁN, ARGENTINO L.
Cafetín ... letra de Homero A.
Expósito, música de Argentino
L. Galván. © Editorial Argentina de Música Internacional,
s. de r., ltda. Buenos Aires;
30Dec46; EP5602.

50

GALVEZ, MANUEL.
Probably; American adaptation of
"Mascarada" ... English lyric by
Albert Gamse, music and Portuguese
lyric by Manuel Galvez. © Edward
B. Marks Music Corp., New York;
4Dec46; EP11971.

GANNAWAY, AL, 1920-
Movie to-night; by Walt Farrar
and Al Gannaway. © Shapiro,
Bernstein & Co., inc., New York;
28Apr47; EP14097. For voice and
piano, with chord symbols.
Uptown Saturday night; words and
music by Walt Farrar and Al
Gannaway. © Martin Music,
Hollywood, Calif.; 17Jan47;
EP11521.

GANNON, RUTH ELLEN, 1894-
I'll stand by our grand old
U. S. ship; lyrics and music
by Ruth Ellen Gannon. San
Francisco, Gannon Pub. House.
[c1944] © Ruth Ellen Gannon,
San Francisco; 7Mar47;
EP12472.
A red, red rose; poem by Robert
Burns, music by Ruth E. Gannon.
© Ruth Ellen Gannon, San Fran-
cisco; 13Mar47; EP12743.
The right partner; lyrics and
music by Ruth Ellen Gannon.
San Francisco, Gannon Pub.
House. © Ruth Ellen Gannon,
San Francisco; 7Mar47;
EP12471.

GANZ, RUDOLPH.
Dialogue; for piano, [by]
Rudolph Ganz. © McKinley
Publishers, inc., Chicago;
28Feb47; EP12406.
Four short pieces; [by] Rudolph
Ganz. © McKinley Publishers,
inc., Chicago; 28Feb47;
EP12405. For piano solo.
The snow is falling; [by]
Rudolph Ganz. For piano.
© McKinley Publishers, inc.,
Chicago; 28Feb47; EP12407.

GARCIA, FERNANDO.
Mi vaca lechera ... Letra de
Jacobo Morcillo, música de
Fernando Garcia, arreglo de
Manuel Salina. Buenos Aires,
Editorial Argentina de Música
International. © Southern
Music Publishing Co., inc.,
New York; 23Dec46; EF3336.

GARCIA, JOSÉ
Esta noche de luna ... letra de
Héctor Marcó, música de José
García y Graciano M. L. Gomez,
arr. de D. Savino. © Robbins
Music Corp., New York; on arrangement; 2Jan47; EP11817. Piano-
conductor score (orchestra, with
words) and parts.

GARCIA CURIEL, NICOLÁS.
Espuelas de oro; letra y música
de N. García Curiel. © Promotora Hispano Americana de
Música, s.a., México; 28Aug46;
EF5593.
Mi Chinita ... letra y música
de Nicolás García Curiel. ©
Promotora Hispano Americana
de Música, s.a., Mexico;
28Aug46; EF5597.

GARDNER, ANN.
Stars and sunshine; words & music
by Ann Gardner. © Nordyke Publishing Co., Los Angeles; 27Sep46;
EP13546.

GARDNER, DONALD YETTER, 1913-
All I want for Christmas (is my
two front teeth) ... words and
music by Don Gardner. [c1946]
© M. Witmark & Sons, New York;
3Jun47; EP15127.

GARDNER, SAMUEL.
The very first violin book; by
Samuel Gardner. © The Boston
Music Co., Boston; 1May47;
AA51440.

GARETT, GARY.
Is there somebody else? ... Words
and music by Tom Fowler and
Gary Garett. © Peer International Corp., New York.
10Apr47; EP13701.

GARNER, ERROLL, 1920-
Five piano solos ... by Erroll
Garner, transcribed and ed. by
Olin B. Adams. c1946. © Bell-
tone Music Publishers, inc.,
New York; 21Apr47; EP14138.
Cover-title: Compositions for
piano.

GASKILL, CLARENCE.
Close the door, Dora! By Clarence
Gaskill. © Pauli-Pioneer Music
Corp., New York; 18Apr47;
EP13882. For voice and piano.
Hail Mary; (Prayer), musical setting
by Clarence Gaskill. © Robbins
Music Corp., New York; 4Dec46;
EP11004. For voice and piano.

GASSMANN, REMI, 1908-
Serenade; [words by] Kenton
Kilmer, [music by] Remi
Gassmann. (Contemporary
American songs for medium voice
and piano, 3d ser.) © Asso-
ciated Music Publishers, inc.,
New York; 15Apr47; EP14477.

GASTE, LOUIS.
Album des six derniers succès de
Louis Gasté. © Éditions Micro,
Paris; 28Feb45; EF601. For
voice and piano.
Deuxieme album des derniers
succès de Louis Gasté. © Éditions Micro, Paris; 28Feb45;
EF602. For voice and piano.
Vagabond; music by Louis Gasté,
lyric by Bob Musel & John
Turner. © Imperia Music Co.
ltd., London; 28Nov46; EF4818.
For voice and piano, with chord
symbols; melody also in tonic
sol-fa notation.
Vagabond; music by Louis Gaste,
words by Bob Musel & John Turner,
arr. by Stan Bowsher [and three
beautiful words of love, words &
music by Billy Reid, arr. by Bert
Read] © on Vagabond, Imperia Music
Co., ltd., London; © on Three
beautiful words of love, Peter
Maurice Music Co., ltd , New York;
on arrangement; 6Dec46; EF4901-
4902. Piano conductor score
(orchestra, with words), and
parts.

GASTON, E   THAYER.
The way to music on the trombone;
by E. Thayer Gaston. © McKinley
Publishers, inc., Chicago; 10Feb47;
EP12049.

GATES, GEORGE M
You're grand ... music by George
M. Gates, arr. by Lee Hudson.
© George M. Gates Music Publi-
cations, New York; 24Jul47;
EP14498. Piano-conductor
score (orchestra) and parts.

GATES, JOHN.
There's a new white cross in
Normandy tonight; words and
music by John Gates, arr.
by Horace A. Cronk. © Nordyke Publishing Co., Los
Angeles; 16Sep46; EP13687.

GAUL, HARVEY BARTLETT, 1881-1945.
Juniata bound; an American work
song ... S.A.T.B., with tenor
solo. From old Pennsylvania
canal fragments, pieced together by Harvey Gaul. © M.
Witmark & Sons, New York; on
arrangement & adaptation;
17Dec46; EP11557.
Oh, I drive oxen; an American work
song ... S.A.T.B., with baritone
solo. Pennsylvania lumber camp
song, arr. by Harvey Gaul. ©
M. Witmark & Sons, New York; on
arrangement & adaptation; 17Dec46;
EP11556.
Ohio River farewell song; an American
work song ... S.A.T.B., with
baritone solo ... Freely pieced
together by Harvey Gaul. © M.
Witmark & Sons, New York; on
arrangement & adaptation; 17Dec46;
EP11558.
Song of the halutzim; based on
Palestinian folk motifs, by Harvey
Gaul ... S.A.T.B. with soprano
solo. © M. Witmark & Sons, New York;
31Dec46; EP11138.

GAUL, HARVEY BARTLETT, 1881-1945, arr.
Ohio River bound; an American work
song, four part mixed voices,
S.A.T.B., with baritone solo ...
An old Ohio River chanty freely
arranged by Harvey Gaul. © M.
Witmark & Sons, New York; 16Jan47;
EP11400.
Timber cutter's chant; an American
work song, four part mixed voices,
S.A.T.B., with baritone solo.
Allegheny mountain lumber camp
tune, arr. by Harvey Gaul. © M.
Witmark & Sons, New York; 16Jan47;
EP11399.

GAY, NOEL.
I'll always love you. See his
Sweetheart mine.
My little pet lamb sings tra-la-la;
words & music by Ralph Butler,
Hugh Charles & Noel Gay.
London, Clover Music Co. © Noel
Gay, inc., New York; 17May46;
EP5648.
(Sweetheart mine) I'll always
love you, from Sweetheart mine;
by Frank Eyton and Noel Gay.
London, Clover Music Co., sole
selling agents, N. Gay Music Co.
© Noel Gay, inc., New York;
15Aug46; EP5646. For voice and
piano, with chord symbols;
melody also in tonic sol-fa
notation.

GEARHART, LIVINGSTON.
Dry bones; a rhythmic spiritual,
arr. by Livingston Gearhart [for]
T.T.B.B. [with string bass (ad
lib.) and percussion. c1946]
© Words and Music, inc., New York;
on arrangement; 28Jan47; EP11900.

GEE, LAURA REBECCAH, 1908-
Lord have mercy on me; words and
music by Laura Gee. Chicago,
Martin's Studio of Music.
© Laura Rebeccah Gee, Salem,
N. J.; 4Feb47; EP13316.

GEEHL, HENRY ERNEST, 1881-
The easiest way; a very simple and
modern method of learning to
play the violin, by Henry Geehl.
© J. H. Larway (Proprietors:
Edwin Ashdown, ltd.), London;
27Dec46; EF4981.

GENTEMEN, M. ELAINE, sister. See
Elaine, sister.

GENTEMEN, MARY ELAINE. See
Elaine, sister.

GEOFFRION, ORAETTA. See
Schaeffer, Oraetta.

GEORGE, CHARLES.
Sleepy head; a juvenile operetta in
one act (for unchanged voices),
book, lyrics and music by
Charles George. © T. S. Denison
& Co., Minneapolis; 20Jan47;
DP1194.

Streamlined Cinderella; an operetta
in one act (for unchanged voices),
libretto, lyrics and music by
Charles George. © T. S. Denison
& Co., Minneapolis; 27Feb47;
DP1173.

GEORGE, DON R
It was at an old Hawaiian luau;
lyric by Paul Page, music by
Don R. George. © Southern
Music Publishing Co., inc.,
New York; 10Apr47; EP13700.

It's all wicky wacky in Hawaii; words
by Paul Page, music by Don R.
George ... Piano arrangement by
Larry Stanton. © Southern Music
Publishing Co., inc., New York;
13Dec46; EP11171. For voice and
piano, with chord symbols.

GEŌRGIADĒS, ALEKOS GIANNĒS, 1906-
E zōgraphia sou ... etichoi
Chr. Chairopoulou, mousikē
Al. Geōrgiadou. Athēnai,
Ekdoseis Gaïtanou. © Michael
Gaetanos, Athens; 10Mar47;
EP5542. For voice and piano.

GÉRARD, M. PHILIPPE- pseud. See
Bloch, Philippe Gérard.

GERLAY, PAUL.
Du ciel bleu, du soleil ...
paroles de Albert Sarrou,
musique de Paul Gerlay. ©
Ste. ame. fse. Chappell,
Paris; 29Apr47; EF3783.

GERMAN, EDWARD.
(Merrie England) The yeomen of
England, from "Merrie England";
arranged as a quartet for T.T.B.B.
Words by Basil Hood, music by
Edward German, arr. by Clarence
Lucas. © Chappell & Co., ltd.,
London; on arrangement; 7Jan47;
EF4842.

O peaceful England; music by
Edward German, words by Basil
Hood, arr. for mixed voices
(S.A.T.B.) by Clarence Lucas.
© Chappell & Co., ltd., London;
on arrangement; 18Mar47;
EF5479.

The yeomen of England. See his
Merrie England.

GERSHWIN, ARTHUR.
What's come over you? Lyric by
Jack Ellis, music by Arthur
Gershwin. © Fred Fisher Music
Co., inc., New York; 21May47;
EP14538.

GERSHWIN, GEORGE, 1898-1937.
Embraceable you; [by] George
Gershwin, arr. by Johnny Sterling. © New World Music Corp.,
New York; on arrangement;
1May47; EP14413. Score
(trumpet or cornet and piano)
and parts.

Gershwin made easy for the piano;
by Ada Richter. © New World
Music Corp., New York; on
arrangement; v.1, 20Dec46;
v.2, 25Apr47; EP11066, 14285.

(Girl crazy) I got rhythm, from
"Girl Crazy" ... S.A.T.B.,
words by Ira Gershwin, music
by George Gershwin, choral arrangement by Clay Warnick.
(New York, Harms) © New World
Music Corp., New York; on arrangement; 7May47; EP14408.

I got rhythm. See his Girl Crazy.

(Lady be good) The man I love,
[from "Lady be good"] music
by George Gershwin, arr. for
organ by Charles R. Cronham.
© Harms, inc., New York; on
arrangement; 11Jun47; EP15200.
Includes registration for Hammond organ.

The man I love. See his Lady be
good.

Oh, lady be good; [by] George
Gershwin, arr. by J. Louis
Merkur, piano duet. © Harms,
inc., New York; on arrangement;
9May47; EP14409.

GHESTEM, GEORGES, 1903-
Console-moi ... paroles de Maurice
Ygor [pseud.], musique de Georges
Ghestem. © Éditions Musicales
Nuances, Paris; 15Dec46; EF3494.

GIAKOBLEPH, N. See
Iakobleph, Nikolaos Petros.

GIANNEO, LUIS, 1897-
Villancico; para piano, [by]
Luis Gianneo. © Editorial
Argentina De Música (E.A.M.),
Buenos Aires; 21Apr47;
EF5673.

GIANNETTO, pseud. See
Culotta, Illuminato.

GIANNIDĒS, KOSTA, pseud. See
Konstantinidēs, Giannēs Geōrgios.

GIANNINI, VITTORIO.
Variations on a cantus firmus;
for pianoforte, [by] Vittorio
Giannini. © Elkan-Vogel Co.,
inc., Philadelphia; on 4
volumes; 28Feb47; EP13104-
13107. Contents.- [v.1]
Moderato, var.1-10.- [v.2]
Aria, var. 11-12.- [v.3]
Toccata, var.13-22.- [v.4]
Interlude, var.23-24.

GIBBANY, ETTA MAY HOLMES, 1883-
Moon over Missouri; words and
music by Etta May Holmes
Gibbany. St. Louis, Distribu-
tors, Shattinger Piano & Music
Co. © Etta May Holmes Gibbany,
Jefferson City, Mo.; 20May47;
EP14495.

GIBSON, ARBIE.
The darling song; by Arbie Gibson.
© Preview Music Co., Chicago;
11Mar46; EP12078. For voice and
piano, with chord symbols.

Don't turn your back on me; by Rex
Allen and Arbie Gibson. © Preview
Music Co., Chicago; 11Mar46; EP12136.
For voice and piano, with chord
symbols.

The wages of sin; by Arbie Gibson.
© Preview Music Co., Chicago;
11Mar46; EP12135. For voice and
piano, with chord symbols.

GIDEON, MIRIAM.
Canzona; for piano solo, [by]
Miriam Gideon. (New music, a
quarterly publishing modern
compositions; v. 20, no. 2)
© New Music, New York; 3Feb47;
EP12488.

GIERLACH, CHESTER.
Village festival dances ... by
Chester Gierlach. © Mills Music,
inc., New York; 12Mar47; EP6693.
Score (string orchestra) and
parts.

GIERSDORF, HAROLD WESLEY, 1904-
I'm talkin' to you; words and
music by Roy George, Hal Hor-
ton and Rip Giersdorf.
© Metro Music, Dallas; 16Apr47;
EP14442.

GIERSDORF, RIP. See
Giersdorf, Harold Wesley.

GIL, ALFREDO.
No trates de mentir. (Don't ever
lie to me) ... English words by
Joe Davis, Spanish words and
music by Alfredo Gil. ©
Caribbean Music, inc., New York;
12May47; EP14218.

Olvídate de mí. (Forgot about me,
dear) Spanish words by José
Jesus "Chucho" Navarro, music
by Alfredo Gil, English words by
Joe Davis. © Caribbean Music,
inc., New York; 17Mar47; EP12641.

Solo para tí. (Suddenly in love)
... Spanish words by José Jesus
"Chucho" Navarro, music by
Alfredo Gil, English words by
Leo Paris. © Caribbean Music,
inc., New York; 17Mar47; EP12638.

GIL, CARLOS MARTINEZ. See
Martinez Gil, Carlos.

GIL, CHARRO. See
Gil, Felipe.

GIL, FELIPE.
Tilín tilón ... de Felipe Gil
(Charro Gil) © Promotora
Hispano Americana de Música,
s.a., Mexico; 24Apr47; EF3209.
For voice and piano.

GILARDINI, RENZO.
Triste sera ... [testo di C. Deani,
pseud.], musica di Renzo Gilardini. Bella Ciquita ... [testo
e] musica di Giuseppe Ald. ©
Edizioni Leonardi, s.a.r.l.,
Milano; 20May46; EP5061. Piano-
conductor score (orchestra, with
words) and parts.

GILBERT, CARL J.
The spirit of youth ... [by] Carl
J. Gilbert, arr. [by] Harold
Moss. c1945. © Bosworth & Co.,
ltd., London; on arrangement;
16Jul46; EF5163. Parts: band.

GILBERT, HAZEL M   1891-
Ceremonial march; by Hazel Gilbert.
© Gilbert Publishing Co., Detroit;
1Dec46; EP11857. For piano solo.

God's rainbow shines for you; by
Hazel Gilbert, [author of words
unknown] © Gilbert Publishing Co.,
Detroit; 1Dec46; EP11856.

GILBERT, JEAN.
Novoletto; by J. Gilbert. New
York, Harmonia Edition. ©
Harmonia Edition Publishing
Co., New York; 30Dec46; EP6462.
For piano solo.

GILLAR, MAC, pseud. See
Panzuti, Virgilio.

GILLESPIE, "DIZZY." See
Gillespie, John.

GILLESPIE, JOHN.
Night in Tunisia; by Frank
Paparelli [and] John "Dizzy"
Gillespie, arr. by Red Bone.
© Leeds Music orp., New York;
on arrangement 14Apr47;
EP13717. Condensed score
(orchestra) and parts.

GILLETTE, JAMES ROBERT, 1886-
Fable ... by James R. Gillette.
© Neil A. Kjos Music Co.,
Chicago; 28Jan47; EP13549.
Condensed score (band) and
parts.

52

GILLIAM, LLOYD A
Black mood; words & music by
Lloyd A. Gilliam. © Nordyke
Publishing Co., Los Angeles;
27Sep46; EP14783.

GILLIS, CURTIS EUGENE, 1907-
How can I forgot you? By Curtis
Eugene Gillis. © Curtis
Eugene Gillis, Oakland, Calif.;
1Feb47; EP11766. For voice and
piano, with chord symbols.

Thy sweetness is my life; by
Curtis Eugene Gillis. ©
Curtis Eugene Gillis, Oak-
land, Calif.; 23Apr47;
EP13218. For voice and
piano, with chord symbols.

GILLOCK, BILL, 1917-
My sweetheart ... Lyrics by
Philip A. Montroy, music by
Bill Gillock. © Philip A.
Montroy, Jennings, La. &
Bill Gillock, Larussell,
Mo.; 26May47; EP14805.

GILMORE, CHESTER.
Carry you through ... words & music
by Chester Gilmore, arr. by
Goldie P. Rhodes. © Chester Gil-
more, Chicago; 7Apr47; EP13659.
Close score: SATB.

GILMORE, THOMAS S   1944-
Four new songs: The peek-a-boo
lullaby, Caressed by a
memory, Candlelight mood
[and] Cellophane heart,
arrangements by Schaefer,
music and lyrics by Gilmore.
© Thomas S. Gilmore, Boston;
12Apr47; EP13793.

GINDER, RICHARD.
Missa Martialis; [for] T.T.B.B.
alternating with unison.
© J. Fischer & Bro., New York;
3Jun46; EP8709.

GINDHART, TOM.
Blue rangor; music by Tom Gind-
hart, words by Jack Howard.
(In Cousin Lee book of original
songs, p.10-11) © Jack
Howard Publications, inc.,
Philadelphia; on changes in
lyrics; 30Dec46; EP11731.

Git along, git along cowboy; words
and music by Tom Gindhart. (In
Cousin Lee book of original
songs, p.5-7) © Jack Howard
Publications, inc., Philadelphia;
30Dec46; EP11729.

GIRNATIS, WALTER, 1894-
Festliche Hausmusik; für 3 Violinen und Violoncello (auch 2
Violinen und Klavier) oder an-
dere Melodieinstrumente. © Henry Litolff's Verlag, Leipzig;
3Nov41; EP2595. Score and parts.

GIRÓN, ADOLFO.
Violins and violets; by ...
Adolfo Girón, arr. by Allan
Small. © Leeds Music Corp.,
New York; 16Jun47; EP15090.
Piano-conductor score (orches-
tra) and parts.

GIUSSANI, GEO.
Spacco tutto.... musica di Geo
Giussani, testo di Arassich.
Voglio cantare a te ... musica
di Carletto Concina, testo di
C. Deani [pseud.] © Edizioni
Casiroli, s.a.r.l., Milano;
2Jan47; EP5276. Piano-conduc-
tor score (orchestra, with
words), and parts.

Spacco tutto ... testo di Arassich,
musica di Geo Giussani. (In
Un sorriso e 20 canzoni. p.
40-41) © Edizioni Casiroli,
s.a.r.l., Milano; 12Jan47; EP4929.
For voice and piano.

GLANZBERG, NORBERT.
Tout le long des rues; paroles de
Jacques Larue [pseud.]
musique de Norbert Glansberg.
c1947. © Les Nouvelles
Editions Méridian, Paris;
30Dec46; EF3591.

GLARUM, LEONARD STANLEY, 1908-
The beatitudes; anthem for mixed
voices, a cappella (S.S.A.A.T.T.
B.B.) [by] L. Stanley Glarum.
[Words from] Matthew 5:3-12. ©
Hall & McCreary Co., Chicago;
12Apr47; EP13759.

GLAZER, FRANK.
Cassandra; [words by] Orlando
Weber jr., [music by] Frank
Glazer. © Broadcast Music,
inc., New York; 10Mar47;
EP14728.

July ... by Frank Glazer, [words
by Orlando F. Weber, jr.]
© Broadcast Music, inc., New
York; 25Mar47; EP13779.

A Maverick heart ... by Frank
Glazer, [words by Orlando
F. Weber, jr.] © Broadcast
Music, inc., New York;
10Mar47; EP13780.

My love ... by Frank Glazer,
[words anon.] © Broadcast
Music, inc., New York;
10Mar47; EP13781.

Reuben Jones ... by Frank Glazer,
[words by Orlando F. Weber, jr.]
© Broadcast Music, inc., New
York; 10Mar47; EP13778.

GLICKMAN, FRED.
Let me be the first (to say I'm sorry);
lyric by Johnny Lange, music by Fred
Glickman. © Milene Music, Nashville;
21Jan47; EP11440.

GLIÈRE, REINHOLD MORITSEVICH, 1875-
Cortège from "The red poppy";
[by] Reinhold Glière, orchestration by Arthur Cohn. © Elkan-
Vogel Co., inc., Philadelphia;
on orchestration; 24Dec46;
EP11460. Score, condensed
score and parts.

GLOSSON, LONNIE A
Rockin' chair money; by Bill
Carlisle and Lonnie A.
Glosson. © Hometown Music
Co., inc., New York; 19Feb47;
EP12376. For voice and
piano, with chord symbols.

GLOVER, JOE.
Angel; words by John Latouche,
music by Joe Glover. © Chappell & Co., inc., New York;
EP14514.

[GLYNN, BETTY] arr.
The barnyard polka ... arr. by
[Betty Glynn of] the Oahu staff.
(Oahu modern note method for
electric and Hawaiian guitars,
[lesson 35FN]) © Oahu Publishing Co., Cleveland; on arrangement; 7Jan47; EP6980. For
soprano and alto, with chord
symbols. Includes lesson on
seventh chord building and the
discussion: Hymns come to us.

Danube waves ... arr. by [Betty
Glynn of] the Oahu staff. (Oahu
modern note method for electric
and Hawaiian guitars, [lesson
34PN]) © Oahu Publishing Co.,
Cleveland; on arrangement;
7Mar47; EP6879. For guitar solo.
Includes lesson on minor chord
harmonizing and the discussion:
Festival music.

Danube waves; lyric by Jean Dietzel, [arr. by Betty Glynn of the
Oahu staff] (Oahu "rhythm style"
note course for plectrum guitar
(octave notation), [lesson 49PG])
© Oahu Publishing Co., Cleveland;
on arrangement & lyrics; 23Apr47;
EP6883. For voice and guitar.
Includes lesson on minor chords
and the discussion: Lullabies.

Honolulu stomp; [arr. by Betty
Glynn of the Oahu staff] (Oahu
E-Z method, [lesson 72EZ]) ©
Oahu Publishing Co., Cleveland;
on arrangement; 16Apr47; EP6875.
For guitar solo. Includes
discussion: Career ahead.

Jonny Lind polka; (plectrum guitar
duet), lyric by Joan Dietzel,
arr. by [Betty Glynn of] the
Oahu staff. (Oahu "rhythm style"
note course for plectrum guitar
(octave notation), [lesson 34PG])
© Oahu Publishing Co., Cleveland;
on arrangement & lyrics; 30Sep46;
EP6982. Includes lesson on
chords and the discussion:
Stephen Collins Foster.

Near the cross; arr. by [B. Glynn
of] the Oahu staff. (Oahu E-Z
method, [lesson 6EZ]) © Oahu
Publishing Co., Cleveland; on
arrangement; 24Jul46; EP6871.
For voice and piano. Includes
discussion: How do we "study"
music?

Opuu lani ... lyric by Jean Dietzel, arr. by [Betty Glynn of] the
Oahu staff. (Oahu E-Z method,
[lesson 41EZ]) © Oahu Publishing Co., Cleveland; on arrangement & lyrics; 15Jul46; EP6873.
For voice and guitar. Includes
lesson on the slur and care of
the strings and the discussion:
Greece gave us music.

GOATLEY, ALMA, 1889-
Summer evening at Bryanston ...
[by] Alma Goatley. London,
Boosey & Hawkes. © Hawkes &
Son (London), ltd., London;
8Apr47; EF5450. Score
(clarinet and piano) and
part.

GODARD, BENJAMIN LOUIS PAUL, 1849-1895.
A golden lullaby; music by Benjamin
Godard, words by Clarence Lucas,
arr. as a two-part song by Henry
Geehl. © Edwin Ashdown, ltd.,
London; on arrangement; 30Apr47;
EF5624.

(Jocelyn) Lullaby, from Jocelyn;
arr. for piano and ... instruments ... [by] Walter Rosemont,
lyrics by Jack Edwards] © Edwards Music Co., New York; on
arrangement & lyrics; 14Nov46;
EP10558.

Lullaby. See his Jocelyn.

GODINI, ANTIGONO, 1901-
Tanto, tanto ... Zitta, zitta ...
Parole di A. Natili, musica di
A. Godini. © Carisch, società
anonima, Milan; 20Dec46; EP5489.
Piano-conductor score (orches-
tra, with words), and parts.

GOEB, ROGER.
Suite in folk style ... [By]
Roger Goeb. © Broadcast Music,
inc., New York; 21May47; EP15235.
Score (4 clarinets) and parts.

GOEHR, RUDOLPH, 1906-
All of a sudden it's you; words by
John Latouche, music by Rudolph
Goehr. © Chappell & Co., inc.,
New York; 27Jan47; EP12011.

53

GOEHR, WALTER.
(Great expectations) Great
expectations waltz; composed
by Walter Goehr for the ...
film Great expectations, [arr.
by George Zalva] © Southern
Music Publishing Co., ltd.,
London; 18Apr47; EF5591. For
piano solo.

GOELL, KERMIT.
I wanna be a friend of yours;
P. D. children's song adapted
by Kermit Goell. © Hudson
Music Corp., New York; on new
words; 3Apr47; EP13967.

GÜLLNER, KONRAD, 1914-
Ein Weg zur Polyphonie; in 50
zweistimmigen Kanons, sowie
Präludium und Fuge, im Fünfton-
raum für Klavier. [By] Konrad
Güllner. Op. 23. © Ludwig
Doblinger (Bernhard Herzmansky),
K. G., Vienna; 5Apr45; EF3313.

GÖRLING, UNO.
Blue sorrow blues ... musik och
special arr.: Miff Görling.
© Edition Sylvain, a.b.,
Stockholm; 1Jan45; EF3764.
Piano-conductor score
(orchestra), and parts.

I like boogie woogie ... musik:
Miff Görling [and] Jonny
Bossman [pseud.], arrangemang:
Miff Görling, text: Jonny
Bossman. © Edition Sylvain,
a.b., Stockholm; 1Jan45;
EF3749. Piano-conductor
score (orchestra), and parts.

Det var en lek ... musik och
arr.: Miff Görling, text:
Rune Strand. © Edition
Sylvain, a.b., Stockholm;
1Jan45; EF3758. Piano-conductor score (orchestra),
and parts.

GOETSCHIUS, MARJORIE.
New moon in New Mexico; words and
music by Marjorie Goetschius.
© Emory Music, inc., New York;
2May47; EP14006.

[GOLDBAUM, FRIEDRICH] 1903-
Accordéon; paroles de Marcel
Paul [pseud.], musique de
Fred Freed [pseud.] [c1946]
© Éditions Salmer, Paris;
14Dec45; EF5184.

Elle et moi; paroles de Géo Koger
[pseud.], musique de Fred Freed
[pseud.] Paris, Salabert.
© Salabert, inc., New York;
31Jan47; EF3464.

Nuits du Brésil ... paroles de
Marcel Paul, musique de Fred
Freed [pseud.] et Jacques
R. Breux. © Éditions E. M. U.
L., Paris; 26Dec45; EF3618.

Valse obsédante; paroles de Géo
Koger [pseud.], musique de Fred
Freed [pseud.] Paris, Salabert.
© Salabert, inc., New York;
31Jan47; EF3531.

GOLDMAN, EDWIN FRANKO.
The bugler; by Edwin Franko Goldman
... arr. by Erik Leidzen. © Mills
Music, inc., New York; on arrangement; 23May47; EP6934. Condensed
score (solo cornet or trumpet and
band) and parts.

GOLDMAN, MAURICE.
The rich and the poor. ("A zemerle.")
Paraphrase on a humorous Jewish
folk song for solo, mixed voices
and piano, [by] Maurice Goldman.
© Transcontinental Music Corp.,
New York; 20Jan47; EP11340.
Yiddish words (transliterated)

GOLDMAN, RICHARD FRANKO.
The Lee rigg; by Richard Franko
Goldman; transcribed for piano
solo by Andor Foldes. © Mercury
Music Corp., New York; on ar-
rangement; 16Jun47; EP15250.

[GOLDSEN, MICHAEL H   ]
The King Cole Trio novelty song
parade; words and music [adapted
by Michael H. Goldsen] © Capitol
Songs, inc., New York; 24Feb47;
EP12157.

[GOLDSEN, MICHAEL H   ] arr.
The Pied Piper modern arrangements for 4 voices, with piano
accompaniment; [comp. and arr.
by Michael H. Goldsen] ©
Capitol Songs, inc., New
York; 1Apr47; EP13354.

[GOLDSEN, MICHAEL H   ] ed.
Tex Ritter all star song folio;
[comp. and ed. by Michael H.
Goldsen] © Tex Ritter Music
Publications, inc., New York; 17Jun47;
EP15007. For voice and piano, with
chord symbols.

GOLDSWORTHY, WILLIAM A
Mizpah ... S.A.T.B. Genesis
31: 49; [by] William A.
Goldsworthy. © Edwin H.
Morris & Co., inc., New
York; 22Jan47; EP11430.

O Lord, Thou hast searched me out;
for four-part chorus of mixed
voices (S.A.T.B.-a cappella);
text from Psalm 139, music by
W. A. Goldsworthy. © Carl
Fischer, inc., New York
19May47; EP14714.

Silver lamps; anthem for junior
and senior choirs combined,
or for mixed voices with two
solo voices ... [By] W. A.
Goldsworthy, [words by]
William C. Dix. © The H. W.
Gray Co., inc., New York;
9May47; EP14378.

GOLETTI, NELLY.
L'auberge du Goujon qui Rit;
paroles de L. D. Kerambrun,
musique de Nelly Goletti. ©
Editions Paris-Broadway, Paris;
31Dec46; EF3840.

Un quat, une robe, un chapeau;
paroles de André Ledur, musique de Nelly Goletti. ©
Editions Paris-Broadway, Paris;
31Dec46; EF3844.

Jeux; paroles de France Mortagne,
musique de Nelly Goletti. ©
Editions Paris-Broadway, Paris;
31Dec46; EF3820.

Mains câlines; paroles de André
Ledur; musique de Nelly
Goletti. © Editions Paris-
Broadway, Paris; 31Dec46;
EF3821.

GOMES, RUTH FARNUM.
The V-day waltz; words by Joe
Gomes, music by Ruth Farnum
Gomes. © Nordyke Publishing
Co., Los Angeles; 23Aug45;
EP15528.

GOMEZ, EDDIE.
Solos solitos ... Letra y música
de Eddie Gomez. © Peer International Corp., New York;
18Mar47; EP13978.

GOMEZ, GRACIANO.
Tu intimo secreto ... Letra de
Héctor Marcó, música de
Graciano Gómez, [piano
arrangement by Domenico
Savino] © Robbins Music
Corp., New York; on piano
arrangement; 21Feb47;
EP12390.

GONZALES, VINCENT.
I've waited for someone like you
to come along; words & music
by Vincent Gonzales. Los
Angeles, Leftwich Publishing Co.
© Vincent Gonzales, Los Angeles;
6Nov46; EP15178.

GONZALEZ, AARÓN.
Negrita no me dejes ... letra y
música de Aarón Gonzalez.
© Peer International Corp.,
New York; 13Dec46; EP13618.

GONZALEZ, LEOPOLDO.
Maldicion. (Conscience) ...
English words by Joe Davis,
Spanish words and music by
Leopoldo Gonzalez. © Cari-
bbean Music, inc., New York;
17Mar47; EP12637.

Mi cancion. (My song) ... English
words by Joe Davis, Spanish
words and music by Leopoldo
Gonzalez. © Caribbean Music,
inc., New York; 12May47; EP14219.

GONZALEZ, VIRGILIO.
Doggie. (Recuerdon la ola marina)
Blossner ... Spanish words and
music by Virgilio Gonzales. ©
Peer International Corp., New
York; on English words; 13Feb47;
EP12231.

No quiere cocinar ... letra y
música de Virgilio González,
arreglo de Tito. © Peer
International Corp., New
York; 30Dec46; EF5432.
Parts: orchestra.

GONZALEZ RUIZ, JUANA.
Es de mi sitio la caña ... Letra
y música de Juana González
Ruiz. Habana. © Peer International Corp., New York;
15May47; EF3340.

GOODCHILD, ARTHUR.
Chivalry; words by Jan Struther,
music by Arthur Goodchild.
© Novello & Co., ltd., London;
24Mar47; EF5322.

Twice three tongue-twisters; ...
Words collected and music composed by Arthur Goodchild.
© Novello & Co., ltd., London;
15May47; EF3328.

GOODHART, AL.
Heart breakin'; words and music by
Kay Twomey, Al Urbano and Al Good-
hart. © Woodward Music, inc.,
New York; 11Mar47; EP12544.

I'm living a lie; words and music by
Kay Twomey, Al Urbano and Al Good-
hart. © Woodward Music, inc., New
York; 11Mar47; EP12543.

GOODSELL, EVELYN MARIE, 1904-
comp.
Popular piano breaks [and Introduc-
tions and endings]; compiled by
Evelyn Goodsell. © The Good-
sell Style (of Popular Piano),
Fullerton, Calif.; 11Feb47;
EP12093.

Self teaching popular piano; comp.
by Evelyn Goodsell. © The Goodsell Style, Fullerton, Calif.;
bk. 1, 11Jun47; EP14954.

GOODWILL, PHIL, pseud. See
Phillips, John Howard.

GOODWIN, WALTER, 1885-
The house of O'Brien; [words] by
Walter and Alice Goodwin,
[music by Walter Goodwin] ©
Alice and Walter Goodwin,
Chicago; 22Mar47; EP13414.

GOON, SVEN, pseud. See
Flodin, Sven.

GORDON, HUGH, pseud. See
Nordon, Hugo.

GORE, RICHARD T
Today did Christ arise ... [for]
S.A.T.B. Dutch melody ... words
[and arrangement] by Richard
T. Gore. © J. Fischer & Bro.,
New York; on words & arrangement;
27May47; EP6957.

GORLING, MIFF. See
Görling, Uno.

GORMAN, PAT.
I'd like to be a cow in Switzerland; by Pat Gorman, [words by]
Nick Kenny and Charles Kenny,
by Billy Taylor. © Gold-
mine Music, inc., New York;
6May47; EP48833.

[GORNI, FRANCESCO] 1885-
I ballabili campagnoli; di Gallo
[pseud.] © Carisch, s.a.,
Milan; 1Mar47; EF5644. Piano-
conductor score (orchestra) and
parts.

I ballabili campagnoli di Gallo
[pseud.] © Carisch, s.a., Milan;
17Feb47; EF5493. Piano-conductor
score (orchestra) and parts.

GORNSTON, DAVID.
David Gornston's Trumpet velocity
... ed. by Harry Huffnagle.
© Edwin H. Morris & Co., inc.,
New York; 24Mar47; EP13369.

Fun with scales; for saxophone ...
by David Gornston and Ben Paisner.
© Leeds Music Corp., New York;
21Mar47; EP12862.

GORRESE, VICENTE.
Criolla linda ... letra de Luis
Rubistein, música de Vicente
Gorrese y Bernardo Germino.
[c1947] © Corporación Musical
Argentina-Comar-s.a., Buenos
Aires; 29Dec46; EF3156.

GOSPEL BELLS ... authors, Frank H.
Stamps, O. A. Parris, Robt. E.
Arnold [and others] © Stamps
Quartet Music Co., inc.,
Dallas; 25Jan47; EP12356.
Hymns, with music, shape-note
notation.

GOULD, C   WALLACE.
Of unsung heroes; overture [by]
C. Wallace Gould. © C. Wallace
Gould, Springfield, S. D.;
22Apr47; EP14253. Condensed
score (band) and parts.

GOULD, MORTON, 1913-
Ballad for band; [by] Morton
Gould. © G & C Music Corp.,
New York; 27May47; EP15028.
Condensed score and parts.

GOULD, R   E
There's a little white house;
words and music by R. E. Gould.
© Nordyke Publishing Co., Los
Angeles; 8Mar47; EP13554.

GOULDING, EDMUND.
J'aime ta pomme. See his The
razor's edge.
The lovely song my heart is
singing; for voice and piano,
words and music by Edmund
Goulding. New York, G. Schir-
mer, inc. © Edmund Goulding,
Beverly Hills, Calif.; 15Feb47;
EP12738.

Mam'selle. See his The razor's
edge.

(The razor's edge) J'aime ta
pomme, from the ... picture
"The razor's edge", lyric by
Jacques Surmagne, music by
Edmund Goulding. New York, L.
Feist. © Twentieth Century
Music Corp., New York; 30Apr47;
EP14140. French words.

(The razor's edge) Mam'selle, theme
from ... "The razor's edge;" lyric
by Mack Gordon, music by Edmund
Goulding. New York, L. Feist.
© Twentieth Century Music Corp.,
New York; 10Mar47; EP12798.

To rest in the glory; for voice
and piano, words and music by
Edmund Goulding. New York, G.
Schirmer, inc. © Edmund
Goulding, Beverly Hills, Calif.;
15Feb47; EP12739.

GOUNARÈS, NIKOLAOS KONSTANTINOS,
1915-
Poios se pêre kai mouphyges ...
etichoi K. Kophiniōtē, mousikē
N. Gounarē. 6. ekdosē. ©
"S.O.P.E." Copyright Protection
Society, Athens; 17Aug46;
EF3230. For voice and piano.

GOUNOD, CHARLES FRANÇOIS, 1818-1893.
Ave Maria; [by] Ch. Gounod, on a
prelude of J. S. Bach, arr. for
piano and organ by Allenson
Brown. © Parnasse Musical,
Lachute, Que., Can.; on
arrangement; 1May46; EF4853.

Ave Maria; de Gounod, arr. par
Johan Algra [for] piano.
© Edition Heuwekemeyer (Firm
A. J. Heuwekemeyer & B. F. van
Gaal), Amsterdam, The Nether-
lands; on arrangement; 25Apr46;
EF5136. With words.

Ave Maria. Father, to Thee we
pray; based on the first prelude from Bach's "Well-tempered
clavier". For three-part
chorus of women's voices with
piano or organ acc. [by] Charles
Gounod, arr. by Kenneth Downing, [pseud.] © G. Schirmer, inc.,
New York; on arrangement; 30Dec46;
EP14052.

O divine Redeemer; for three-
part chorus of women's voices
with organ or piano acc., [by]
Charles Gounod, arr. by Bryceson Treharne. © G. Schirmer,
inc., New York; on arrangement;
6Feb47; EP14059.

Praise be to Mary ... words:
Robert Wood ... music: Ch.
Gounod, arr. by G.J.E.S. Op. 2,
no. 1. © Gerard J E. Sullivan,
Dayton, Ohio; on arrangement;
12May47; EP14661. Close score:
SATB.

Praise ye the Father; SA accompanied,
[by] Charles Gounod, arr. by
Wallingford Riegger. © Harold
Flammer, inc., New York; on
arrangement; 7May47; EP14371.

Praise ye the Father; SSA accompanied,
[by] Charles Gounod, arr. by
Wallingford Riegger. © Harold
Flammer, inc., New York; 7May47;
EP14372.

Teach us purity; S.A.T.B. a
capella, [by] Gounod-Messiter,
arr. by Griffith J. Jones,
[words by Ninde-Plumpier] ©
Belwin, inc., New York; on
arrangement; 31Dec46; EP11225.

There is a green hill far away;
for three-part chorus of
women's voices with organ or
piano acc. [By] Charles
Gounod, arr. by Bryceson Treharne. © G. Schirmer, inc.,
New York; on arrangement;
6Feb47; EP12737.

(The razor's edge) J'aime ta
pomme, from the ... picture
"The razor's edge", lyric by
Jacques Surmagne, music by
Edmund Goulding. New York, L.
Feist. © Twentieth Century
Music Corp., New York; 30Apr47;
EP14140. French words.

GOURNAY, ROGER DE, 1898-
Caresse ... Musik von Roger de
Gournay, Arrangement von
Michael Braumüller. © Ludwig
Doblinger (Bernhard Herzman-
sky), k.g., Vienna; 19Sep46;
EF3794. For piano solo.

GRAENER, PAUL, 1872-1944.
Vier Lieder ... Von Paul Graener.
Op. 50. [Words by Christian
Morgenstern & Max Dauthenday]
Wien, Universal-Edition A. G.
© Associated Music Publishers,
inc., New York; 22Mar19; EF5306.

GRAFF, GEORGE.
Dear mother; words by Samuel H.
Harris, music by George Graff,
jr. © Lawrence Music Co.,
Los Angeles; 5Mar47; EP13270.

GRAFSTRÖM, GUSTAV.
En gammal historia; [by] Gustav
Grafström, arr. [by] William
Lind. © Nordiska Musikförlaget, a.b., Stockholm;
1Jan46; EF3755. Piano-conductor score (orchestra), and
parts.

GRAHAM, ANNE CRUMELL, 1913-
Prayer changes things ... words
and music by Anne C. Graham. ©
Anne Crumell Graham, sole owner of
Graham's Studios of Gospel Music,
New York; 10ct46; EP11094. Close
score: SATB.

GRANATA, SALVADOR.
Borron de niebla ... letra de
Gerónimo Yorio, música de
Salvador Granata y Orlando
Romanelli. © Editorial
Argentina de Música Inter-
nacional, s. de r., ltd.,
Buenos Aires; 30Dec46; EF5598.

GRANATO, LAWRENCE.
I'll have my love for you; words
and music by Larry Granato, jr.
© Nordyke Publishing Co., Los
Angeles; 23Dec45; EP10861. For
voice and piano.

It just shows to go ya; words and
music [by] Larry Granato, jr.
© Lawrence Granato & Son, Dayton, Ohio; 27Dec46; EP10980.
For voice and piano, with guitar
diagrams and chord symbols.

GRAND, ROBERT LE. See
Le Grand, Robert.

GRANIER, JULES.
Hosanna; for three-part chorus
of women's voices with organ
br piano acc. [By] Jules
Granier, arr. by Kenneth
Downing [pseud.] © G. Schirmer, inc., New York; on arrangement; 6Feb47; EP12734.

GRANT, ADA (BILLSON), 1910-
Goodwill unto man; secular chorus
for mixed voices, acc. ... By
Ada Billson. [Words] from "A
Christmas Carmen" [by] John
Greenleaf Whittier. © Hall &
McCreary Co., Chicago; 12Apr47;
EP13760.

GRANT, PHIL.
Chasing the beat ... ([for]
two snare drums, cymbals,
and bass drum] ... by Phil
Grant. © Mercury Music
Corp., New York; 11Apr47;
EP13353.

Double bubble; a snare drum
duet ... by Phil Grant. ©
Mercury Music Corp., New York;
11Apr47; EP13352.

GRASSO, FRANK T
Alicia's story; [by] Frank T.
Grasso, [for grade school orchestra] © George F. Briegel, inc.,
New York; 24Mar47; EP13400.
Piano-conductor score and parts.

GRaTIA, LOUIS E   1878-
L'harmonium pour tous; 23 pièces
pour harmonium sans difficultés,
pour tous les services religieux,
par L. E. Gratia. © Editions
Philippo, Paris; 29Nov46;
EF3288.

GRATTON, HECTOR.
La joie de vivre ... [by] Hector
Gratton. Op. 1, no. 1. (In Le
Passe-Temps. no. 890, p. 8-10)
© Les Editions du Passe-Temps, inc.,
Montreal; 20Sep45; EF3093.
For piano solo.

GRAVINA, F
La joselito ... paroles de F.
Maenza, musique de F. Gravina.
© Julio Garzon, Paris; 15Jul46;
EF5005. Piano-conductor score
(orchestra) and parts.

GRAY, ALLAN.
(A matter of life and death)
Stairway to heaven; by Allan
Gray. The prelude from the
film "A matter of life and
death." © Peter Maurice
Music Co., ltd., London;
13May47; EF3781. For piano
solo.

Stairway to heaven. See his A matter of life and death.

GRAY, RUBY A
Fellowship with Jesus; [by]
Ruby Gray, arr. by W. M. T.
(In Church of the Nazarene.
Michigan District. Nazarene
Young Peoples Society.
Choruses of the N. Y. P. S.
p.54) © Michigan District,
Nazarene Young Peoples Society,
Flint, Mich.; 25Jul46;
EP13074. Close score: SATB.

GREAN, CHARLES.
Jenny kissed me; lyric adapted
from a poem by Leigh Hunt.
Words and music by Jordan
Smith and Charles Grean. ©
Mutual Music Society, inc.,
New York; 27Mar47; EP13008.

GREAT GRAND DAD; [arr.] by Lawrence
Wilson [pseud.] © Bob Miller, inc.,
New York; 30Dec46; on arrangement;
EP10744. For voice and piano,
with chord symbols.

GRECHANINOV, ALEKSANDR TIKHONOVICH,
1864-
Deuxieme sonate; pour pianoforte
[by] Alexandre Gretchaninoff.
Op.174. © Axelrod Publications,
inc., Providence; 5May47;
EF14133.

Petite suite; by Alexandre
Gretchaninoff. Op. 176. ©
Century Music Publishing Co.,
New York; v.1-2, 15Apr47; v.3-5,
12May47. For piano solo. Contents.- [1] Etude (© EP13227)-
[2] Romance (© EP13226) - [3]
Polka (© EP14270) - [4] Wistful
mazurka (© EP14271) - [5]
Russian dance (© EP14272)

GRECO, V
Rodriguez Peña ... paroles espagnoles
[by J. M. Velich] et musique de
V. Greco [and Amoureux; (alejandro);
musique de Manuel Pizarro] ©
Julio Garzon, Paris; 15Jul46;
EF2630. Piano-conductor score
(orchestra, with words), and parts.

GREEN, ANNE.
Eight new sacred choruses; words
and music by Mrs. Anne Green,
arr. by K. Y. Plank. © Fred
Green, Alliance, Ohio; on 8
songs; 15Apr47. Contents.-
Keep your little cup
(© EP14245).- He died for you
(© EP14246).- Walking and
talking with Jesus (© EP14244).
- Pray, pray, pray (© EP13889).
- Down deep in my heart
(© EP13888).- When the early
morn is breaking (© EP13887).-
Listening (© EP13886).- Lord,
help me (© EP13885)

Keep me 'neath the shadow of Thy
cross, and Are you here tonight without Jesus? Words
and music by Mrs. Anne Green,
arr. by K. Y. Plank. © Fred
Green, Alliance, Ohio; 5May47;
EP14603-14604. Close score:
SATB.

GREEN, JOHNNY.
I love a mystery. See his Something
in the wind.

I'm happy-go-lucky and free. See
his Something in the wind.

It's only love. See his Something in the wind.

(Something in the wind) I love a
mystery, [from the Universal-International picture "Something in
the wind"]; lyric by Leo Robin,
music by Johnny Green. New York;
Robbins Music Corp. © Universal
Music Corp., New York; 29May47;
EP14961.

(Something in the wind) I'm happygo-lucky and free, [from the Universal-International picture "Something in the
wind"]; lyric by Leo Robin, music by
Johnny Green, New York, Robbins Music
Corp. © Universal Music Corp., New
York; 29May47; EP14962.

(Something in the wind) It's only
love, [from the Universal-International picture "Something
in the wind"]; lyric by Leo Robin,
music by Johnny Green, New York,
Robbins Music Corp. © Universal
Music Corp., New York; 29May47;
EP14963.

(Something in the wind) You
wanna keep your baby lookin'
right, [from the Universal-International picture "Something in the wind"]; lyric by
Leo Robin, music by Johnny
Green. New York, Robbins
Music Corp. © Universal Music
Corp., New York; 29May47;
EP14964.

You wanna keep your baby lookin'
right. See his Something in
the wind.

GREEN, PHIL.
Scottish patrol ... composed &
arr. by Phil Green. c1946.
© Noel Gay Music Co., ltd.,
London; 28Apr47; EF3659.
Piano-conductor score
(orchestra), condensed score
and parts.

GREEN, RAY.
Dance theme and variations; a
piano solo by Ray Green.
© Mercury Music Corp., New York;
16Jun47; EP15251.

GREENBURG, RALPH GILBERT.
Impression; by Ralph G. Greenburg.
© Ralph G. Greenburg, Indianapolis; 10Jun47; EP15148. For
piano solo.

GREENE, JOE.
Across the alley from the Alamo;
by Joe Greene. © Leslie Music
Corp., New York; 1Apr47;
EP13356. For voice and piano,
with chord symbols.

Across the alley from the Alamo;
by Joe Greene, arr. by Van
Alexander. New York, Capitol
Songs, inc. © Leslie Music
Corp., New York; on arrangement; 17May47; EP14382. Pianoconductor score (orchestra,
with words) and parts.

Don't let the landlord gyp you;
words and music by Joe Greene.
© Northern Music Corp., New
York; 25Mar47; EP13203.

I'm mindin' my business (and
Baby, my business is you);
words and music by Joe Greene.
© Northern Music Corp., New
York; 17Mar47; EP12795.

GREENE, SAMMY NEWELL, 1907-   comp.
"Sacred songs and hymns" ... comp.
by S. N. Greene. Oklahoma City,
S. N. Greene. Shape-note notation.

GREENHILL, HAROLD W
Three pieces for organ; by H. W.
Greenhill. © Novello & Co.,
ltd., London; on 3 pieces;
6May47; EF3329-3331. Contents.
-Allegretto.- Offertoire.
Folk song.

GREGG, HUBERT.
(Between ourselves) I always
know the way to Piccadilly,
[from the] revue Between
ourselves; words and music by
Hubert Gregg. © Peter Maurice
Music Co., ltd., New York;
19Mar47; EF5524.

I always know the way to Piccadilly.
See his Between ourselves.

GREGORY, BOBBY, 1900-
Bobby Gregory and his Ramblin'
Hobo's Album of hobo songs.
© American Music Publishing
Co., New York; no. 12,
2Jan47; EP11091.

GREIR, ARNOLD. See
Greir, Robert Arnold.

GREIR, ROBERT ARNOLD.
The souls of the righteous ...
composed by Arnold Greir ... by
Robert Arnold Greir, London;
30Oct46; EF3100. Score: solo
voices (TB), chorus (SATB)
and organ.

GRENET, ELISEO.
El guajiro alegre ... letra y
música de Eliseo Grenet. Buenos
Aires, Editorial Argentina de
Música Internacional. © Southern
Music Publishing Co., inc., New
York; 28Dec45; EF5615.

Te ves de mi ... música por:
Eliseo Grenet, letra por:
Ruddy Lagury. Habana, Peer
International Corp. © Peer
International Corp., New York;
13Aug46; EF4783. For voice
and piano.

GRENET, ERNESTO.
Sueño guajiro ... música y letra
de Ernesto Grenet. © Hnos.
Márquez, s. de r. l., México;
1Dec45; EF3905.

GRETCHANINOFF, ALEXANDRE. See
Grechaninov, Aleksandr Tikhonovich.

GRÉTRY, ANDRÉ ERNEST MODESTE,
1741-1813.
Suite rococo ... [by] Grétry-
Bazelaire. © Schott Frères,
Brussels; on arrangement;
31Jul42; EF3573. Score:
violoncello and string orchestra.

Suite rococo; pour violoncelle
& orchestre, [by] Grétry-
Bazelaire. © Schott Frères,
Brussels; on arrangement;
31Jul42; EF3574. Score
(violin and piano) and part.

GREY, LANNY.
Pete; by Lanny Grey. New York,
Capitol Songs, inc.. © Criterion Music Corp., New York;
30Apr47; EP14061. For voice
and piano, with chord symbols.

GRIDER, FRANCIS J
All is over (but the shouting); words
and music by Francis J. Grider.
© Cine-Mart Music Publishing Co.,
Hollywood, Calif.; 1Dec46; EP12111.

Waltz melody; words and music by
Francis J. Grider. [c1946]
© Whitehouse Publishing Co.,
Hollywood, Calif.; 13Jan47;
EP11988.

GRIEG, EDVARD HAGERUP, 1843-1907.
(Concerto, piano) Grieg's concerto
march; adapted from themes from the
"Piano concerto in A minor. Opus
16" ... arr. by Dick Jacobs. ©
Bregman, Vocco and Conn, inc.,
New York; 7Feb47; EP11898. Con-
densed score (band) and parts.

(Concerto, piano) Themes from
Grieg's piano concerto. [Op.
16. Arr. by Hugo Frey]
© Hamilton S. Gordon, inc.,
New York; on arrangement;
27Jan47; EP13517. For piano
solo.

Grieg for the young; selected,
arr. and ed. for piano solo by
Leopold W. Rovenger. © Rubank, inc.; Chicago;;
15Apr47; EP13222.

Grieg's concerto march. See his
Concerto, piano.

I love thee; chorus for treble
voices, acc. (S.S.A.) [by]
Edward Grieg, arr. by Donald
E. Sellew. [Words by] Hans
Christian Andersen. English
version by D. E. S. © Hall
& McCreary Co., Chicago; on
English words & arrangement;
28Apr47; EP11279.

Norwegian dance no.2; [by] Grieg,
arr. for easy piano solo by
Mark Ashley [pseud.] © Century
Music Publishing Co., New York;
on arrangement; 31May47; EP14735.

Themes from Grieg's piano concerto.
See his Concerto, piano.

GRIER, JIMMIE.
The object of my affection ... by
Pinky Tomlin, Coy Poe and Jimmie
Grier, arr. by Van Alexander.
© Bourne, inc., New York; on
new arrangement; 25Jun47;
EP15290. Piano-conductor score
(orchestra, with words) and
parts.

GRIFFIN, REX.
How can I be sure; words and music
by Ernest Tubb and Rex Griffin.
© Ernest Tubb Music, inc., Hollywood, Calif.; 22Apr47; EP13966.

GRIFFIS, ELLIOT, 1893-
Yellow rose ... for piano, by
Elliot Griffis. © Dorothea
Louise Schroeder, Flushing,
N. Y.; 9Jun47; EP14906.

GRIFFIS, J   W
Arab temple ... [by] J. W.
Griffis. © Arab Temple,
Topeka, Kan.; 27Dec46;
EP11756. Parts: band.

GRIMM, CHRISTIAN A   1875-
Life's winding road; words by
Alma Timian, music by Christian
A. Grimm. © General Music
Sales, Chicago; 3Mar47; EP12310.

Peek-a-boo ... words and music by
Virginia Hale [pseud.] and
Christian A. Grimm. © General
Music Sales, Chicago; 12Oct47;
EP9338.

GRINDY, ROY M   1899-
Behold the Lamb of God; words
from St. John 1:35-37, 40-42,
[music by] R. M. Grindy,
[and St. Andrew hymn; by
R. M. Grindy] Arr. by Stanley
P. Stevens. © Roy M.
Grindy, Marblehead, Mass.;
21Mar47; EP12866.

Prayer hymn; words and music by
R. M. Grindy, arr. by S. P.
Stevens. © Roy M. Grindy,
Marblehead, Mass.; 18Apr47;
EP13917.

GROFÉ, FERDE, 1892-
Deep nocturne; by Ferde Grofé ...
[piano arrangement by D. Savino]
© Robbins Music Corp., New York;
23May47; EP14938.

GROOCOCK, JOSEPH.
Five nursery rhymes; for
unaccompanied choir, S.A.T.B.,
by Joseph Groocock. ©
Chappell & Co., ltd., London;
1Feb47; EF5165.

GROSS, CHARLES.
Rain drops fall; words and music
by Norris Jones and Charles
Gross. © Nordyke Publishing
Co., Los Angeles; 8Mar47;
EP13236.

GROSS, WALTER.
Bubble gum ... piano solo, by Walter
Gross. © Robbins Music Corp.,
New York; 12Dec46; EP11013.

Tenderly; lyric by Jack Lawrence,
music by Walter Gross. ©
Edwin H. Morris & Co., inc.,
New York; 13Mar47; EP12665.

Winter moon ... piano solo, by
Walter Gross. © Robbins Music
Corp., New York; 12Dec46; EP11014.

GROUYA, TED, 1910-
Whom am I gonna kiss you good
morning? Lyric by Eddie de
Lange ... music by Ted Grouya.
© Martin Music, Hollywood,
Calif., 17Jan47; EP11520.

GROSVENOR, RALPH L
What good does a long face do?
S.A. accompanied, words and
music by Ralph L. Grosvenor.
© Harold Flammer, inc., New
York; 7May47; EP14375.

GRUBER, FRANZ.
Silent night; Hawaiian guitar solo,
by Franz Gruber, arr. by Hibbard
A. Perry. © Perry Music Studio,
(Hibbard A. Perry, owner)
Providence; on arrangement;
6Dec46; EP11548.

Silent night, holy night; for
piano, by F. Gruber, arr. [by]
Arthur S. Loam. © Allan & Co.,
pty. ltd., Melbourne, Australia;
29Dec46; EF3752.

Silent night; words by Joseph
Mohr, music by Franz Gruber.
[Easy piano arrangement with
keyboard charts by Victor
Lakes Martin] © Songs You
Remember Publishing Co. (V.
L. Martin, proprietor),
Atlanta; on arrangement and
playing instructions; 20Dec47;
EP11337.

GRUN, BERNARD.
Magic interlude. See his White
Cradle Inn.

(White Cradle Inn) Magic inter-
lude, from the film "White
Cradle Inn"; music by Bernard
Grun. © Keith, Prowse & Co.,
ltd., London; 23May47; EF3344.
For piano solo.

GUADALUPE ALVAREZ, JOSÉ.
Última noche ... letra y música de
J. Guadalupe Alvarez. © Pro-
motora Hispano Americana de
Música, s.a., México; 23Dec46;
EF5074.

GUARINO, JOHN B
Vieux Carré sérénade. (Old
square); words and music by
John B. Guarino. © John B.
Guarino, New Orleans; on ar-
rangement; 3Feb47; EP12320.

GUARNIERI, CAMARGO, 1907-
"Chôro" torturado; for piano
solo [by] Camargo Guarnieri.
© Associated Music Publishers,
inc., New York; 19May47;
EP15128.

Toccata; for piano solo, [by]
Camargo Guarnieri. © Associated
Music Publishers, inc., New
York; 6Jun47; EP15244.

GUERRA, JESÚS.
El cuá cuá ... letra y música de
Jesús Guerra, arreglo de Pérez
Prado. © Peer International
Corp., New York; 28Dec45;
EF5612. Parts: orchestra.

GUEVARA, LUIS.
Mirándote; letra y música de Luis
Guevara. © Editorial Mexicana
de Música Internacional, s.a.,
México; 30Dec46; EF5550.

GUGLIELMI, LOUIS, 1916-
C'est un soir. See his Le destin
s'amuse.

Dans la vie faut du cran. See his
Ploum ploum tra la la.

(Le destin s'amuse) C'est un soir,
chanson du film "Le destin
s'amuse"; paroles de L. et J.
Poterat, André Tabet et J.
Companeez, musique de Louiguy
[pseud.] © Editions Regis,
Paris; 1Mar47; EF3882.

(Le destin s'amuse) Pâquerette,
chanson du film "Le destin
s'amuse"; paroles de L. et J.
Poterat, André Tabet et J.
Companeez, musique de Louiguy
[pseud.] © Editions Regia,
Paris; 1Mar47; EF3883.

Le hasard fait bien les choses;
paroles de Jacques Plante,
musique de Louiguy [pseud.]
© Editions Joubert, Paris;
31Dec46; EF3620.

Le hasard fait bien les choses;
paroles de Jacques Plante,
musique de Louiguy [pseud.]
© Editions Joubert, Paris;
31Dec46; EF3852. Piano-
conductor score (orchestra,
with words), and parts.

Je suis un pauvre gars. See his
Ploum ploum tra la la.

57

GUGLIELMI, LOUIS, 1916-   Cont'd.
Mademoiselle Hortensia; paroles de
Jacques Plante, musique de
Louiguy [pseud.] © Éditions
Musicales Hortensia, Paris;
15Sep46; EF5212.
Pâquerette. See his Le destin
s'amuse.

(Ploum ploum tra la la) Dans
la vie faut du cran ... dans
le film: "Ploum ploum tra la
la"; paroles de Paul Fékété,
musique de Louiguy [pseud.]
© Société d'Éditions Musicales
Internationales (S.E.M.I.),
Paris; 20Mar47; EF3889.

(Ploum ploum tra la la) Je suis
un pauvre gars ... dans le film:
"Ploum ploum tra la la"; paroles
de Paul Fékété, musique de
Louiguy [pseud.] © Société
d'Éditions Musicales Internationales (S.E.M.I.), Paris;
20Mar47; EF3843.

GUIDA, PEDRO, 1902-
"Irenita" ... paroles de Bertal
[pseud. and] Maubon, musique de
Pedro Ouida. © Éditions EIMEP-
OPERA, Paris; 1Mar47; EF3454.
Parts: orchestra. French and
Spanish words.

Rumba viva ... paroles de Bertal
[pseud. and] Maubon, musique
de Pedro Ouida. © Éditions
EIMEP-OPERA, Paris; 1Mar47;
EF3455. Parts: orchestra.
French and Spanish words.

GUILLIAT, VERONICA ARLENE, 1921-
Why not choose life; [by] Arlene
Guilliat. © Veronica Arlene
Guilliat, Cass City, Mich.;
20Feb47; EP12773. Close score:
SATB.

GUION, DAVID W
God's golden West; song with piano
acc., words and music by David
W. Guion ... medium voice.
© Carl Fischer, inc., New York;
12Jun47; EP15220.

Roll along little dogies; song
with piano acc., words and
music by David W. Guion.
Medium voice. © Carl Fischer,
inc., New York; 9Jun47; EP15221.

GULIZIA, MARIO
Bella donna ... testo e musica di
Mario Gulizia. (In Un sorriso
e 20 canzoni. p. 28-29) ©
Edizioni Leonardi, s.a.r.l.,
Milano; 7Jun45; EF4923. For
voice and piano.

Bella donna ... [words by P. Sacchi],
musica di M. Gulizia. Cerco la mia
casetta ... [words by C. Deani],
musica di P. Fucilli. Arrangiamenti
di A. Giacomazzi. © Edizioni
Leonardi, s.a.r.l.; Milan; 4Mar46;
EF4802. Piano-conductor score
(orchestra, with words) and parts.

GULLMAR, KAI, pseud. See
Bergström, Gulli.

GUTIÉRREZ, JULIO.
Compendio ... letra y música de
Julio Gutiérrez. © Peer Interna-
tional Corp., New York; 17Dec42;
EF5613.

GUY, HELEN. See
Rhodes, Helen (Guy).

GUZMAN, RAFAEL.
Si, señorita, sí ... by Rafael
Guzman. © Grimes Music Publish-
ers, Philadelphia; 28Jan47;
EP12328. For voice and piano,
with chord symbols.

GYLDMARK, SVEN, 1904-
(Bedstemor gaar amok) Nu gaar Bed-
stemor amok; Tekst: Victor
Skaarup. © Wilhelm Hansen, Mu-
sik-Forlag, København; 3Oct44;
EF732. For voice and piano.

Chanson d'amour. See his Elly
Petersen.
Den er go' med Marianne. See his
Elly Petersen.

(Elly Petersen) Chanson d'amour.
(Kaerlighedens Sang) ... Den er
go' med Marianne ... Dansk og
fransk Tekst: Mogens Dam. ©
Wilhelm Hansen, Musik-Forlag,
København; 28Jul44; EF733. For
voice and piano.

En lille Krog i Kaerlighedens Land.
See his Jeg elsker en anden.

Et godt Humør, et flot Humør. See
his Panik i Familien.

(Frøken Vildkat) Kom, naar Lykken
kalder! ... Der skal Kaerlighed
til alt. Theobald. Tekst: Poul
M. Jørgensen. © Wilhelm Hansen, Musik-Forlag, København;
28Aug42; EF730. For voice and
piano.

(Hans Onsdags-Veninde) Kaerlighed
og du og jeg; Tekst: Poul M.
Jørgensen. © Wilhelm Hansen,
Musik-Forlag, København; 28Apr43;
EF731. For voice and piano.

(Jeg elsker en anden) En lille
Krog i Kaerlighedens Land, [from
Jeg elsker en anden] Tekst:
Mogens Dam, Musik: Sven Gyldmark.
© Wilhelm Hansen, Musik-Forlag,
Copenhagen; 24Sep46; EF4822. For
voice and piano.

Kaerlighed og du og jeg. See his
Hans Onsdags-Veninde.

Kom, naar Lykken kalder! See his
Frøken Vildkat.

Nu gaar bedstemor amok. See his
Bedstemor gaar amok.

(Panik i Familien) Et godt Humør,
et flot Humør ... Tekst: Victor
Skaarup. © Wilhelm Hansen,
Musik-Forlag, København; 6Aug45;
EF735. For voice and piano.

Der skal Kaerlighed til alt, Theobald. See his Frøken Vildkat.

Ta' Briller paa! ... Tekster: Poul
Sørensen. © Wilhelm Hansen, Mu-
sik-Forlag, København; 10Jun42;
EF729. For voice and piano.

Teatertosset ... Tekster: Mogens
Dam. © Wilhelm Hansen, Musik
-Forlag, København; 28Feb44;
EF734. For voice and piano.

[GYLLENHAMMAR, ULLA MARGARETA]
Brevet du skrev om kärlek;
musik: Evelyn Naylor [pseud.],
text: Naylor [and] Fritz
Gustaf [pseud.] © Nordiska
Musikförlaget, a.b., Stockholm; 1Jan46; EF3762.

H

H., ROGELIO DIHIGO. See
Dihigo H., Rogelio.

HAAG, GÖSTA.
Yes, of course ... musik och
special arr.: Gösta Haag. ©
Edition Sylvain, a.b.,
Stockholm; 1Jan45; EF3728.
Piano-conductor score
(orchestra), and parts.

HAAG, SVEN GÖSTA. See

HAAS, GEORGE DE. See
De Haas, George.

HAASE, KARL.
Six wedding processionals or
recessionals; for the organ, by
Karl Haase. © Karl Haase, Lincoln,
Neb.; 23Apr47; AA51816.

HABER, RHEA, 1918-
I found the one I want; words and
music by Dan Silverstein and
Rhea Haber. Philadelphia,
Maurie Swerdlow Music. © Dan
Silverstein, Camden, N. J. &
Rhea Haber, Philadelphia;
16May47; EP14488.

HACKNEY, JUNE MARIE.
Every time I dream, I think about
you; words by June Marie Hackney,
music arranged by Al Landon
Music Co. Newark, Ohio, Ohio
Pub. Co. © John Seylor Burris,
Newark, Ohio; 20Dec46; EP11747.

HADDAD, SONYA SADE', 1916-
Ev'ryday is mother's day (in
this heart of mine); lyric
by Stephen Boswell, music by
Sonya Haddad, arr. by Jack
Hunter. © Stephen Francis
Boswell and Sonya Sade'
Haddad, sole owners of B & H
Music Publishing Co., Akron,
Ohio; 30Mar47; EP13573.

HANDEL, GEORG FRIEDRICH, 1685-
1759.
Air varié; by George Fredrick
Handel, arr. and ed. for
organ by Robert Leech Bedell.
© Edward Schuberth & Co.,
inc., New York; 25Mar47;
EP12875.

(Concerto, oboe, no. 1) Concerto no. 1 in B major, for
oboe and strings [by] G. F.
Handel ... arr. by Arthur
Willner. London, Boosey &
Son (London) ltd., London on
arrangement; 13May47; EF3287.
Score (oboe and piano) and
part.

(Concerto, oboe, no. 2) Concerto
no. 2 in B major ... [by] G.
F. Handel; arr. by Arthur
Willner. London, Boosey &
Hawkes. © Hawkes & Son (London) ltd., London; on arrangement; 14May47; EF3283. Score
(oboe and piano) and part.

(Concerto, oboe, no. 3) Concerto
no. 3 in G minor ... [by] G. F.
Handel, arr. by Arthur Willner.
© Hawkes & Son (London) ltd.,
London; on arrangement; 14May47;
EF3282. Score (oboe and piano)
and part.

Dear Lord and Father; sacred song
for medium voice, the music by
G. F. Händel, the music and
text adapted by Katherine H.
Davis. © R. D. Row Music Co.,
Boston; on words and changes
in music; 8May47; EP14201.

Fugue in F major; by G. F. Handel,
transcribed ... by Russell
Harvey. © Elkan-Vogel Co., inc.,
Philadelphia; on transcription;
26Nov46; EP11457. Condensed
score (band) and parts.

The gods go a-begging. Ballet suite
[from operas of Handel] arr. by
Sir Thomas Beecham. [Arr. for
military band by W. J. Duthoit,
rev. for American band by Erik
Leidzen] New York, Chappell &
Co., inc. © Chappell & Co., ltd.,
London; on arrangement & revision
for American band; 17Jun47;
EF15201. Condensed score (band)
and parts.

HÄNDEL, GEORG FRIEDRICH, 1685-1759.
Cont'd.
Guardian angels; (from "The tri-
umph of time and truth") ... tr.
from the Italian ... [and] arr.
with descant by Hugh Ross. (In
Ross, Hugh, arr. Sacred cho-
ruses for women's or girls'
voices. p. 37-42) © G. Schir-
mer, inc., New York; on arrange-
ment; 30Sep46; EP9783.
Hallelujah chorus, from "The
Messiah"; for ... S.S.A., [by]
George Frederic Handel, arr. by
Paul Fuller [pseud.] © Pro Art
Publications, New York; on ar-
rangement; 21Apr47; EP13612.
Largo. (Ombra mai fù) From
"Xerxes," by G. F. Handel, arr.
for voice with piano or organ
acc., and with secular text:
Oh thou cooling shade, and
sacred text: When I prayed to
God, by Nelson Eddy. © Carl
Fischer, inc., New York; on
arrangement and English words;
5Jun47; EP15023.
Largo. See his Xerxes.
Lord, God divine; by G. F. Händel,
arr. by Charles H. Maskell,
[words by C. H. M.] © Theodore
Presser Co., Philadelphia; on
arrangement & text; 14Dec28;
EP12163. Score: tenor, SATB
and piano.
(The Messiah) O thou that tellest
good tidings; from the "Messiah"
for three choirs, [words] Isaiah
xl:9. ••• [by] George Friederich
Händel, arr. by Kenneth E. Runkel.
© Harold Flammer, inc., New York;
on arrangement; 14Mar47; EP13477.
Minuet from Berenice. See his
Berenice.
O thou that tellest good tidings.
See his Messiah.
Ombra mai fù. See his Xerxes.
Pastorale: The faithful shepherd;
[by] G. F. Handel, arr. by E.
Power Biggs. © The H. W. Gray
Co., inc., New York; on arrange-
ment; 14Mar47; EP12926. For organ
solo.
A summer carol; (for mixed voices)
[by] Händel, choral version by
Margretho Hokanson, adapted
from text by Bess Berry Carr.
© Clayton F. Summy Co., Chicago;
on arrangement; 29May47;
EP14826.
Thanks be to Thee, O Lord,
(Arioso from Cantata con
stromenti) ... [by] Georg
Friedrich Händel ... arr. by
Gwynn S. Bement, English version
by Louis Victor Saar. © E. C.
Schirmer Music Co., Boston;
23Apr47; EP14471. Score: alto,
chorus (SSAA) and piano.
Where'er you walk; for four-
part chorus of boys' voices
with piano acc. [by] George
F. Handel, arr. by Robert
W. Gibb. © The Boston
Music Co., Boston; on arrange-
ment; 19May47; EP14814.
Where'er you walk ... From
Händel's "Semele", adapted &
arr. by J. Henry Francis.
© Sam Fox Publishing Co., New
York; on arrangement; 10Mar47;
EP12733. Score: solo voice
(S or A), chorus (SATB) and
piano.

HAESELER, WILLIAM, 1901-
Camp Pioneer; words and music
by William Haeseler, jr.
© William Haeseler, jr.,
North Tonawanda, N. Y.;
19Mar47; EP12834.

HAGEMAN, RICHARD.
A lady comes to an inn; [words by]
Elizabeth Coatsworth, [music by]
Richard Hageman. © Galaxy Music
Corporation, New York; 23May47;
EP6914.

HAGEN, JACK. See
Hagen, John Elmer.

HAGEN, JOHN ELMER, 1928-
You mean so much to me; music &
words by Jack Hagen. © John
Elmer Hagen, Des Plaines, Ill.;
8May47; EP14321.

HAINES, W   D
St. Omar commandory march; [by]
W. D. Haines. © Paul A. Giles,
Fort Oglethorpe, Ga.; 3Feb47;
EP11917. Parts: band.

HALAMA, FRANK JEROME, 1903-
At the range on the other
side; words by Jeanne Lane,
music by Frank J. Halama.
© Frank J. Halama Publica-
tions, Chicago; 7Apr47;
EP13219.
If I ever got you in my arms (I'll
never let you get away); words
by Tommy Hand, music by Frank
J. Halama. © Frank J. Halama
Publications, Chicago; 28Apr47;
EP13953.

HALBEE, S   WALTER.
Keys to happiness; the A-B-C
way for you to learn how to
play piano ... conceived and
written by S. Walter Halbee,
illus. by Helen Walter. ©
Paull-Pioneer Music Corp.,
New York; 7Jan47; EP11099.

HALL, ALVIN R
The boy that is not coming back;
words and music by Alvin R.
Hall. © Nordyke Publishing Co.,
Los Angeles; 18Sep45; EP6452.

HALL, C   G
I chased horses (in the middle of
the stream); words and music by
C. C. Hall. © Dixie Music Pub-
lishing Co., New York; 30Jun44;
EP14132.

HALL, JOHN HUBERT, ed.
Favorite melodies ... (shaped
notes) © Hall Music Co., Mary-
ville, Tenn.; 1Sep46; EP6308.
Hymns.

HALL, LYLE WEAVER.
Love sleeps in a rose ... for
medium voice with piano acc., by
Lyle Weaver Hall. © Broadcast
Music, inc., New York; 23Dec46;
EP13845.

HALL, R   E
On our honeymoon in the air; lyric
by Wm. R. Meyers, music by R. E.
Hall. New York, Jack Mills, inc.
© Mills Music, inc. (Successors
in interest to: Jack Mills, inc.),
New York; 22Jul19; EP6456.

HALLER, MICHAEL.
Sacred Heart hymns; by Michael
Haller. For low mass, holy
hours, [and] first Fridays
(unison or solo voice) © Mc-
Laughlin & Reilly Co., Boston;
27Dec46; EP12301.

HALMY, LOU.
Western skies ... [for] concert
band. © Carl Fischer, inc., New
York; 27Jun46; EP5023.

HAMILTON, DONALD ARTHUR, 1921-
Jesus satisfies; [by] Don Hamilton. © Donald A. Hamilton, Los
Angeles; 8Apr47; EP15581. Close
score: SATB.

HAMILTON, JIMMY
Blues for clarinet ... [by] Jimmy
Hamilton. © Robbins Music Corp.,
New York; 25Feb47; EP12439.
Score (clarinet and piano) and
part.
Blues in my music room ... [by]
Jimmy Hamilton. © Robbins Music
Corp., New York; 25Feb47; EP12438.
Score (clarinet and piano) and
part.
Slapstick ... [by] Jimmy Hamilton.
© Robbins Music Corp., New
York; 25Feb47; EP12440. Score
(clarinet and piano) and part.

HAMPTON, DONNAH, 1916-
V-i-c-t-o-r-y; [by] Donnah
Hampton, arr. by W. M. Thorne.
(In Church of the Nazarene.
Michigan District. Nazarene
Young Peoples Society.
Choruses of the N. Y. P. S.
p.18) © Michigan District,
Nazarene Young Peoples Society,
Flint, Mich.; 25Jul46;
EP13044. Close score: SATB.

HAMPTON, LIONEL, 1915-
The lamplighter; composed by
Lionel Hampton [and] Milton
Buckner, scored by Charlie
Shirley. [c1946] © Swing &
Tempo Music Publishing co.,
inc., New York; 16Jun47;
EP14820. Parts: orchestra.
The pencil broke; composed by
Lionel Hampton, Gladys Neal
[and] Curley Hammer, scored by
Elton Hill. [c1946] © Swing
& Tempo Music Publishing Co.,
inc., New York; 16Jun47;
EP14819. Piano-conductor
score (orchestra) and parts.
Overtime ... Composed by Lionel
Hampton and Milton Buckner.
[c1946] © Swing & Tempo
Music Publishing Co., inc.,
New York; 16Jun47; EP14814.
Punching Judy; composed by Lionel
Hampton [and] Joe Morris. [c1946] © Swing
& Tempo Music Publishing Co.,
inc., New York; 16Jun47;
EP14817. Piano-conductor score
(orchestra) and parts.
Robbins in your hair; composed
by Lionel Hampton, scored by
Joe James. © Swing & Tempo
Music Publishing Co., inc.,
New York; 16Jun47; EP14815.
Piano-conductor score (orches-
tra) and parts.
Tempo's birthday; composed by
Lionel Hampton [and] Joe Morris,
scored by Joe Morris. ©
Swing & Tempo Music Publishing
Co., inc., New York; 16Jun47;
EP14816. Piano-conductor
score (orchestra) and parts.
Tempo's boogie; composed by
Lionel Hampton, scored by
Edgar Battles. [c1946]
© Swing & Tempo Music Publish-
ing Co., inc., New York;
16Jun47; EP14818. Piano-con-
ductor score (orchestra) and
parts.

[HANBY, BENJAMIN R   ]
Darling Nellie Grey; [by Benjamin R. Hanby], arr. by Jeff
Muston. © Irwin Dash Music
Co., ltd., London; on arrangement; 18Mar47; EP3301. Piano-
conductor score (orchestra),
and parts.

[HAND, JOHN RAYMOND] 1886-
Hoosier harmonies ... by The
Hoosier Schoolmaster, [pseud.,
words by Mona Atkinson, Mary

[HAND, JOHN RAYMOND] 1886-   Cont'd.
Miller, and others] Crawfordsville, Ind., The Trawler, [c1946] © John Raymond Hand, Crawfordsville, Ind.; no.1, 12Jan47; EP13117. Principally close score: SATB.

HANDEL, GEORGE FREDERIC. See Händel, Georg Friedrich..

HANDMAN, DOREL, 1906-
Sept mélodies pour chant et piano; [by] Dorel Handman. [c1947] © Durand & Cie., Paris; 31Dec46; EP3500.

HANDY, WILLIAM C   1873-   arr.
Go down, Moses (let my people go); Negro spiritual, arr. by W. C. Handy. © William C. Handy, New York; on arrangement; 2Jan30; EP12055. Cornet conductor score (band) and parts.

HANKWITZ, ANITA MATILDA.
M.S.T.C., words ... by A. M. Hankwitz. © Anita Matilda Hankwitz, Shorewood, Wis.; 1Nov45; EP2737. For voice and piano.

[HANLEY, JAMES F   ]
Rose of Washington Square; [by Ballard MacDonald and James F. Hanley] arranged by Jimmy Dale. © Shapiro, Bernstein & Co., inc., New York; 27Dec46; EP10753. Score (orchestra) and parts.

HANLON, BERT.
Round on the end and high in the middle, O-hi-o; [by] Alfred Bryan and Bert Hanlon, arr. by William C. Schoenfeld. New York, Music Publishers Holding Corp. © Remick Music Corp., New York; on arrangement; 19Mar47; EP13211. Parts: band.

HANNA, PHIL.
Lynne; by Phil Hanna. © Shapiro, Bernstein & Co., inc., New York; 3Feb47; EP11686. For voice and piano, with chord symbols.

HANSON, HOWARD, 1896-
Symphony no.1 in E minor, "Nordic"; [by] Howard Hanson. [Op.21. Rome] American Academy in Rome; [American agents: C. C. Birchard & Co., Boston] [Publications of the Department of Music of the American Academy in Rome, vol.I] © Howard Hanson, Rochester, N. Y.; 1Jan29; EF5330.

HANSSON, STIG. See also Sylvain, Jules, pseud.
Mud en enkel tulipan ... Musik: Jules Sylvain [pseud.], text: Paddock [pseud.] © Edition Sylvain 6/6, Stockholm; 1Jan38; EF5032.

HARBRIDGE, AL J. See Harbridge, Albert James.

HARBRIDGE, ALBERT JAMES, 1876-
She's got ev'rything; words and music by Al. J. Harbridge. © Albert James Harbridge, Trinidad, Colo.; 10Mar47; EP12626.

HARDELOT, GUY D', pseud. See Rhodes, Helen (Guy)

[HARDEN, JOHN]
Maralee waltz; for the piano, by G. A. Brown [pseud.] © Harold Flammer, inc., New York; 4Nov46; EP10750.

HARDING, BUSTER, 1916-
Bedford drive; by Buster Harding, arr. by Artie Shaw. London, Bosworth & Co. [c1945] © Winfield Music, inc., New York; on arrangement; 17Dec46; EP4732. Piano-conductor score (orchestra), condensed score and parts.

What'll I have? Words and music by Jack Palmer and Buster Harding. © Little Jazz Music Publications, inc., New York; 21Feb47; EP12864.

HARDING, CHUCK. See Harding, Gladyn Edward.

HARDING, GLADYN EDWARD, 1910-
Swingbilly revue folio; complete with words and music [by Chuck Harding, Pete Pyle and Cousin Joe Maphis], arr. for piano, accordion, guitar. © Country Music Publishers, owner: Russ Hull, Chicago; bk. no.2, 20Mar47; EP12870.

HARDY, ALFA B
Yosemite; words and music by Alfa B. Hardy. Whittier, Calif., V. Warner Publications. © Alfa B. Hardy, Whittier, Calif.; 12Jun47; EP15047. For voice and piano; version of chorus for TTBB at end.

HARGROVE, ELIZABETH D
I wonder when we'll meet again; words and music by Elizabeth D. Hargrove. © Cine-mart Music Publishing Co., Hollywood, Calif.; 30Dec46; EP11953.

[HARING, ROBERT C   ] 1896-
The old lamp-lighter; by Charles Tobias and Nat Simon, [piano paraphrase by Robert C. Haring] © Shapiro, Bernstein & Co., inc., New York; on piano paraphrase; 3Mar47; EP12378.

HARLAM, LOUIS G   1893-
Oraia kai glykeia mou; words and music by Louis G. Harlam. North Hollywood, Calif., © Louis G. Harlam, North Hollywood, Calif.; 28Mar47; EP14262. Greek words.

While you are in my arms; words and music by Louis G. Harlam. North Hollywood, Calif., Elite Publishing Co. © Louis G. Harlam, North Hollywood, Calif.; 28Mar47; EP13220.

HARLEY, FRANCES, arr.
Croatian serenade; for chorus of mixed voices, S.A.T.B. a cappella, arr. by Frances Harley in collaboration with Walter Aschenbrenner. Translation by F. H. © Carl Fischer, inc., New York; on arrangement; 17May47; EP14722.

[HARLEY, HOWARD McTYERE]
The grasshopper hop; [lyric by Tim Creighton, music by Howard Harley and Bill Murray] © Kayton Co., inc., Charleston, S. C.; 19Apr47; EP13847.

HARLINE, LEIGH.
(Honeymoon) I love geraniums, from the ... picture Honeymoon; lyric by Mort Greene, music by Leigh Harline. © Edwin H. Morris & Co., inc., New York; 19Mar47; EP12792.

(Honeymoon) Ven aqui; lyrics by Mort Greene, music by Leigh Harline ... [from] Honeymoon. © Edwin H. Morris & Co., inc., New York; 10Apr47; EP13654. English words.

I love geraniums. See his Honeymoon.

(Nocturne) Nocturne; music by Leigh Harline, lyrics by Mort Greene. From the RKO picture, Nocturne. © Edwin H. Morris & Co., inc., New York; 3Jan47; EP11126. For voice and piano, with chord symbols.

Ven aqui. See his Honeymoon.

HARPER, JAMES, 1910-
Johnny Bach; (based on a Welsh traditional air "Sospan Fach"), words and music by Hal Evans, Jack Lowry and Jimmy Harper. © Evans and Lowry, ltd., London; 17Jan47; EF5310.

HARPER, ROBERT H
Ney, but you who do not love her; [words by] Robert Browning, [music by] Robert H. Harper. © Clayton F. Summy Co., Chicago; 17Feb47; EP12495. Sqoro: chorus (SATB) and piano reduction.

HARRINGTON, TIMOTHY, 1902-
Down the road; words and music by Timothy Harrington. © Shelby Music Publishing Co., Detroit; 7Apr47; EP14324. .

HARRIS, BILL. See Harris, Willard P.

HARRIS, EDWARD.
Agatha Morley; song with piano accompaniment, words by Sydney King Russell, music by Edward Harris. © Carl Fischer, inc., New York; 19Dec46; EP11129.

HARRIS, ERNEST E   1914-
Young America at the violin ... [by] Ernest E. Harris ... Raymond Burrows ... [and] Ella Mason Ahearn. © C. C. Birchard & Co., Boston; bk. 2, 17Jan47; EP13938.

HARRIS, GEORGE EMANUEL, 1884-
Back to dear old Oklahoma; [words and music by George E. Harris] © George Emanuel Harris, Oklahoma City; 6Jan47; EP13578.

Old Oklahoma moon; words and music by George E. Harris. [c1947] © George Emanuel Harris, Oklahoma City; 10Dec46; EP13577.

Old Wyoming waltz ... Words and music by George E. Harris. © George Emanuel Harris, Oklahoma City; 16Dec46; EP13576.

When I lost her tiny footprints in the snow ... Words and music by George E. Harris. © George Emanuel Harris, Oklahoma City; 16Dec46; EP13575.

HARRIS, LEO ALBERT, 1890-
We will be valiant; a song for mixed voices by Leo A. Harris. © Leo Albert Harris, Ogden, Utah; 10Mar47; EP13384.

HARRIS, RALPH A   1895-
O be joyful in the Lord ... the 100th Psalm, [by] Ralph A. Harris. SATB accompanied. © Harold Flammer, inc., New York; 31Dec46; EP11424.

HARRIS, WILLARD P
"Everywhere"; music by Bill Harris, arr. by Joe Bishop. © Charling Music Corp., New York; 11Apr47; EP13644. Piano-conductor score (orchestra) and parts.

HARRIS, WILLIAM HENRY, 1883-
Thou hast made me; motet for double choir, words by John Donne (from the Holy sonnets), music by William H. Harris. © Novello & Co., ltd., London; 29May47; EF3779.

HARRIS, WILLIAM HENRY, 1883-   Cont'd.
Collect for St. George ... music by
William H. Harris. © a. & C.
Black, ltd., London; 23Apr47;
EP5262. Versions for mixed
chorus (close score: SATB) and
men's chorus (close score: TTBB)
Voice parts also in tonic sol-
fa notation.

HARRISON, ANNIE F
In the gloaming; words by Meta
Orrod, music by Annie F.
Harrison. [Easy piano arrange-
ment with keyboard charts by
Victor Lakes Martin] © Songs
You Remember Publishing Co.
(V. L. Martin, proprietor),
Atlanta; on arrangement and
playing instructions; 20Dec46;
EP11335.

HARRISON, JULIUS, 1885-
The dark forest; part-song for
S. A. T. B.; poem by Edward
Thomas, music by Julius
Harrison. © Boosey & Co., ltd.,
London; 28Mar47; EP5318.

Troubadour suite; by Julius Harrison,
for strings and harp (or piano)
London, Boosey & Hawkes. © Hawkes
& Son (London), ltd.; 31Dec46;
EP4773.

HARROP, FAYE.
In slumberland I dream of you;
words and music by Faye Harrop.
© Cine-Mart Music Publishing
Co., Hollywood, Calif.; 1Dec46;
EP12102.

HARSCH, HAROLD.
Benediction; [by] Harold Harsch.
© Clayton F. Summy Co., Chicago;
6Feb47; EP11957. For organ solo.

HART, DANNY, pseud. See
Choisser, Joseph Daniel.

HART, FLORENCE WIMER.
Our glorius old U. S. A.; words
and music by Florence Hart,
arrangement by Harold Potter.
© Florence Wimer Hart, Washington, D. C.; 20Jul44;
EP11446.

HARTEVELD, WILHELM, d. 1927, arr.
Karl XII:s marsch. See his Marcia
Carolus XII, svecorum rex.

Marcia Carolus XII, svecorum rex;
[originally arr. by] Wilh.
Harteveld ... [arr. for orchestra by] Sven Sköld. © Nordiska
Musikförlaget, a.b., Stockholm;
on arrangement; 1Jan41; EP3253.
Parts.

(Marcia Carolus XII, svecorum rex)
Karl XII:s marsch. (Marcia
Carolus XII, svecorum rex)
Lifgardet 1707. Restaurerad
[and arr.] av prof. Wilhelm
Harteveld. © Nordiska Musik-
förlaget, a.b.; Stockholm; on
arrangement; 1Jul20; EP3254.
For piano solo.

HARTS, HARRY L
Our country; a patriotic chorus
for four part men's voices and
orgnn, optional Christmas text:
Today be joy in every heart.
[Patriotic] words by ... John
Reynell Wreford ... and one
stanza by John Greenleaf Whit-
tier ... [Christmas words by]
Frederic Lucian Hosmer ...
Music by Harry L. Harts.
© McLaughlin & Reilly Co.,
Boston; 10Apr47; EP13631.

[HARTUSCH, MIREILLE]
Pourquoi; paroles et musique de
Mireille [pseud.] © Societe
d'Éditions Musicales Inter-
nationale (S.E.M.I.), Paris;
7Mar47; EP3841.

Vive la tour Eiffel. (Ça, vous
voyez, mademoiselle) Paroles
de Jean Nohain [pseud.],
musique de Mireille [pseud.]
© Éditions Vianelly, Paris;
3May47; EP3245.

HARWOOD, C   EDWIN, 1913-
Evening prayer; [by] C. Edwin
Harwood, arr. by W. M.
Thorne. (In Church of the
Nazarene. Michigan District.
Nazarene Young Peoples Society.
Choruses of the N. Y. P. S. p.
15) © Michigan District,
Nazarene Young Peoples Society,
Flint, Mich.; 25Jul46; EP13041.
For 3 treble voices and piano.

HARWOOD, R   ERNESTINE, 1914-
In the morning He is with me;
[by] Ernestine Harwood, arr.
by W. M. T. (In Church of the
Nazarene. Michigan District.
Nazarene Young Peoples Society.
Choruses of the N. Y. P. S.
p.35) © Michigan District,
Nazarene Young Peoples Society,
Flint, Mich.; 25Jul46; EP13061.
Close score: SATB.

HASENAUER, EMIL E
There's no gal like mine; words
and music by Emil E. Hasenauer.
© Nordyke Publishing Co., Los
Angeles; 8Mar47; EP13258.

HASKINS, WILL R
Me and Captain Kidd ... [From]
"Me and Captain Kidd," words by
Will A. Heelan, music by Will R.
Haskins. New York, Will R.
Haskins Co. © Denton & Haskins
Corp., as assignee, New York;
27Oct19; EP13411.

HASLER, KAREL, 1879-1941.
Vspominky; na Karla Haslera.
[Words and music] by Karel Has-
ler. © Mojmir Urbánek, Praha,
Czechoslovakia; 12Jun46;
EP5411.

HASTINGS, THOMAS, 1784-1872.
Rock of ages; words by Augustus
M. Toplady, music by Thomas
Hastings. [Easy piano arrange-
ment with keyboard charts by
Victor Lakes Martin] © Songs
You Remember Publishing Co. (V.
L. Martin, proprietor), Atlanta;
on arrangement and playing in-
structions; 20Dec46; EP11335.

HATCH, EDITH.
Essential rudiments; a concise
and melodious introduction to
the art of pianoforte playing,
by Edith Hatch. [Rev. ed.]
© The Arthur P. Schmidt Co.,
Boston; on changes in text &
music of bk.3; 11Jul47;
EP15650.

HATCHER, CLARENCE E
Come, let us walk together in the
Lord ... Arr. by Kenneth Woods,
jr., words & music by Clarence
E. Hatcher. © Clarence E.
Hatcher, Brooklyn; 15Feb45;
EP6745.

I have resolved to keep the faith
... Words and music by Clarence
E. Hatcher. [arr. by Virginia
Davis] Brooklyn, Hatcher Music
House. © Clarence E. Hatcher,
Brooklyn; 12Jun44; EP6747.

Toll the bells in Zion; words and
music by Clarence E. Hatcher, [arr.
by Kenneth Woods, jr.] Brooklyn,
Hatcher Music House. © Clarence
E. Hatcher, Brooklyn; 10Mar45;
EP6746.

HAUFRECHT, HERBERT, arr.
More than one hundred songs and
games every child should know
... comp. and arr. by Herbert
Haufrecht, ed. by Alex Kramer.
© Capitol Songs, Inc., New
York; 3Mar47; EP12349.

HAUSDÖRFER, FRED, 1916-
Trompet-capriciolon; [by] Fred
Hausdörfer. © Edition
Houwekemeyer (Firm A. J.
Houwekemeyer & B. F. van Gaal),
Amsterdam; 8Apr45; EP5137. Score
(trumpet 1, trumpet 2 ad lib.
and piano) and part.

HAWKE, H   WILLIAM, ed.
Elkun-Vogel organ series, [cd. and
comp. by] H. William Hawke.
© Elkan-Vogel Co., inc., Phila-
delphia; v.1, 3-4. 25Mar47; v.2,
11Mar47. Contents.- v.1. Early
Italian (© EP14874)- v.2. Early
English (© EP14875)-v.3. Early
German (© EP14876)- v.4. Dietrich
Buxtehude (© EP14877)

HAWKINS, COLEMAN.
Disorder at the border; [by] Coleman Hawkins, [arr. by Murray
Feldman] © Robbins Music Corp.,
New York; on arrangement;
12Nov46; EP11506. Score (saxophone and piano) and part.

Feeling zero [by] Coleman Hawkins,
[arr. by Murray Feldman] ©
Robbins Music Corp., New York;
on arrangement; 5Dec46; EP11815.
Score (saxophone and piano) and
part.

HAWKINS, ERSKINE, 1914-
I had a good cry; lyric by Sid
Prosen, music by Erskine
Hawkins and Carol Lang. ©
Burke & Van Heusen, inc.,
New York; 13Jan47; EP14282.

HAWKINS, HERMAN CHARLES.
Down the aisle of life; by Herman Charles Hawkins [arr. by
Lindsay McPhail] © Victor
Publishing Co., Dallas;
15Dec46; EP14500. For voice
and piano, with chord symbols.

Down the aisle of life; by Herman
Charles Hawkins. [arr. by Lindsay McPhail] © Victor Publishing Co., Dallas; 17Apr47;
EP13819. Piano-conductor score
(orchestra, with words) and
parts.

HAWKINS, JAMES.
Merciful Lord. (In Ross, Hugh,
arr. Sacred choruses for women's
or girls' voices. p. 98-100)
© G. Schirmer, inc., New York;
on arrangement; 30Sep46; EP9789.

HAWKINSON, FRANCES IRENE, 1890-
Serenity; lyrics by Ada S. Sher-
wood, music by Frances Hawkin-
son. [c1946] © Frances
Hawkinson, Los Angeles; 15Jan47;
EP12460.

HAYDEN, ROGER THAYER, 1915-   comp.
One hundred hymns for men ... pre-
pared by Roger T. Hayden and
Arthur S. Hayden. Melrose, Mass.,
The Hayden Publishing Co. ©
Roger Thayer Hayden. Arthur
Stuart Hayden, d.b.a. The Hayden
Publishing Co., Melrose, Mass.;
27Dec46; EP10844.

[HAYDN, J   MICHAEL]
O worship the king ... [words by
Robert Grant, music by J.
M. Haydn], arranged for piano
... by Mildred Ortlip. M.
Ortlip. © Mildred Ortlip Keel,
Flushing, L. I., N. Y.; on
arrangement; 31Dec46; EP11462.

HAYDN, JOSEPH, 1732-1809.
(Concerto, violoncello) Concerto
for clarinet, B♭ major, freely
transcribed from the D major
cello concerto. [By] Haydn,
[arr. by] De Caprio. © Gamble
Hinged Music Co., Chicago; on
arrangement; 10Jan47; EP11090.
Score (clarinet and piano) and
part.

Gipsy rondo; [by] Joseph Haydn,
special arrangement for accordion by Charles Magnante.
© Chart Music Publishing House,
inc., Chicago; on arrangement;
9May47; EP14563.

Haydn-Schaum for piano ...
biographical continuity by
Nora Schaum, musical adaptation by John W. Schaum.
© Belwin, inc., New York; bk.1,
9May47; EP14466.

The heavens are telling. ([from]
The creation) For ... S.S.A.,
[by] Josef Haydn, arr. by
Russell Watson [pseud.] © Pro
Art Publications, New York; on
arrangement; 21Apr47; EP13606.

Lo, my Shepherd is divine. (from
Mass in G, no.7) [by] Franz
Joseph Haydn, freely arranged by
Kenneth E. Runkel. For junior choir
(SA) and senior choir (SATB) ©
Harold Flammer, inc., New York; on
arrangement; 31Dec46; Er11419.

Menuetto and finale from Symphony
no. 1 in E♭. See his Symphony,
no. 1.

Some of the happy melodies from
Haydn's chamber music; arr. for
pianoforte by J. Michael
Diack. © Paterson's Publications, ltd., London; on arrangement; 14Apr47; EF3307.

(Symphony, no. 1) Menuetto and
Finale from Symphony no. 1 in
E♭, [by] Joseph Haydn, arr. ...
by W. J. Duthoit. (The Army
journal for full military band,
no. 730) © Chappell & Co.,
ltd., London; on arrangement;
31Dec46; EF5098.

HAYDN, M
So dim with tears. Caligaverunt
oculi mei ... From a motet by
M. Haydn, ed. and arr. by Noble
Cain. English version by Noble
Cain. © Choral Art Publications,
New York; on arrangement; 20Jun47;
EP15246. Score: SATB and piano
reduction.

HAYES, BILLY, 1906-
I feel better since I got your
letter; by Billy Hayes.
© Dawn Music, inc., New York;
21Jan47; EP13995. For voice
and piano, with chord symbols.

HAYES, CHARLES.
A little too fer; by Charles
Hayes. (c1946) © Capitol
Songs, inc., New York;
30Apr47; EP14242. For voice
and piano, with chord symbols.

HAYES, EARL.
United victory march; music by Earl
Hayes. © Cine-Mart Music Publish-
ing Co., Hollywood, Calif.; 1Nov46;
EP15949. For piano solo.

HAYES, HARRY
Blue charm; by Harry Hayes.
c1947. © Edward Kassner Music
Co., ltd., London; 15Oct46;
EF4894. Piano-conductor score
(orchestra), and parts.

HAYES, OPAL LOUISE.
The Swiss clock; piano solo
(with optional second piano
part) by Opal Louise Hayes
[arr. by N. Louise Wright]
© The Boston Music Co., Boston;
30Apr47; EP14070.

The wooly black lamb; piano solo
by Opal Louise Hayes. © The
Willis Music Co., Cincinnati;
3Apr47; EP13359.

HAYWOOD, ERNEST.
Country gardens, and Staines morris;
arr. by Ernest Haywood. © Keith
Prowse & Co., ltd., London; on
arrangement; 24Jan47; EF4835.
For piano solo.

The decent Irish boy; (Hollo,
Patsy Fagan) song, arr. by
Ernest Haywood. © Keith,
Prowse & Co., ltd., London;
on arrangement;16Apr47;
EF5468.

HAZELLE, EARL, 1906-
The active accordionist; by Earl
Hazelle, containing supplementary
solos and recital pieces in conjunc-
tion with the Belwin (or any other)
accordion course. © Belwin, inc.,
New York; on bk. 1-2; 11Mar47;
EP12569, 12570.

HECKMAN, GEORGE J
Poème; [by] George J. Heckman.
© Theodore Presser Co., Phila-
delphia; 17May47; EP14610.
Score (violin and piano) and
part.

HEFFER, FRANK.
Fantasie pastorale; (Through
darkness to light); for organ or
Hammond organ, by Frank Heffer.
© Edward Schuberth & Co., inc.,
New York; on revision and Hammond
organ registration; 9Dec46;
EP11929.

HEFFNER, EDWARD C
Oriole's march; words and music
by Edward C. Heffner. © The
Orioles, Reading, Pa.; 10Mar47;
EP13925. For piano solo, with
words.

[HEIFETZ, JASCHA] 1901-
Hora swing-eato ... words ... by
Marjorie Goetschius and music
[by] Jim Hoyl [pseud.] © Carl
Fischer, inc., New York; on
arrangement and new words; 5Dec46;
EP11299.

HEIMANN, MOGENS, 1915-
Modern violin-studies; [by] Mogens
Heimann. © Wilhelm Hansen, Musik-
Forlag, Copenhagen; 9Nov46;
EF4826.

HELBLING, DeVON WILLIS.
Ambassadors for Christ; [words by
D. W. Helbling] and Have faith
in God ... [words and music by]
Fred G. Walker [arr. by] D. W.
Helbling. © on Ambassadors for
Christ, DeVon Willis Helbling,
Pineland, Tex.; © on Have faith
in God, Fred Gerald Walker,
Pineland, Tex.; 16Nov46; EP6249,
6248. For voice and piano.

HELENE, sister. See
Mary Helene, sister.

HELLARD, ROBERT A
Knickknacks; a novelty for piano
by Robert A. Hellard. ©
Theodore Presser Co., Philadelphia; 26May47; EP14699.

On dress parade; march for piano
[by] Robert A. Hellard. ©
Theodore Presser Co., Philadelphia;
26May47; EP14700.

HELLEBRANTH, ELENA DE. See
De Hellebranth, Elena.

HELLER, RUTH, 1920-   arr.
O come, all ye faithful. Adeste
fideles. Christmas chorus for
senior and junior choirs, acc.
... Arranged by Ruth Heller; Latin
hymn tr. by Frederick O. Keley.
© Hall & McCreary Co., Chicago;
on arrangement; 12Apr47; EP13754.

HELLSTRÖM, DAVID.
Bohuslänska valsen; ord av
Göran Svenning, musik [by]
David Hellström. ©
Skandinaviska Odeon, a.b.,
Stockholm; 1Jan46; EF3763.

[HELMLE, LOUISE BAKER] 1902-
arr.
Polka zu dreien. (Polka for
three) German dance, [arr.
by Louise Baker Helmle,
directions for the dance by
Eugene Tso] © Louise Baker
Helmle & Eugene Tso, New York;
on arrangement; 1Nov46;
EP11764. For piano solo
Road to the Isles; [Scotch
song arr. by Louise Baker
Helmle, directions for the
dance by Eugene Tso] ©
Louise Baker Helmle & Eugene
Tso, New York; on changes
in music; 1Nov46; EP11763.
Melody only.

HELY-HUTCHINSON, VICTOR, 1901-
More ruthless rhymes for heartless
homes; music by Victor Hely-
Hutchinson, words by Harry
Graham, illustrations by Ridge-
well. London, E. Arnold [c1946]
© Victor Hely-Hutchinson,
London; 30Jan47; EF5105.

HEMEL, OSCAR LOUIS VAN, 1892-
(Sonata, viola & piano) Sonate ...
[by] Oscar van Hemel. ©
Edition Heuwekemeijer (Firm
Heuwekemeijer & van Gaal),
Amsterdam; 21Feb47; EF3584.
Score (viola and piano) and
part.

HENDERSON, RAY.
Birth of the blues; music by Ray
Henderson, arr. by Jimmy Dale.
© Harms, inc., New York; on
arrangement; 29May47; EP15001.
Piano-conductor score (orchestra)
and parts.

Just a memory ... words by B. G.
DeSylva and Lew Brown, music
by Ray Henderson, a Ken Macomber arrangement. © Harms,
inc., New York; on arrangement;
1Apr47; EP13707. Piano-conductor
score (orchestra, with words)
and parts.

HENDRICKS, CHARLES F
Prelude and fugue; by Charles F.
Hendricks, jr. Op.9. Arr. by
Robert Leech Bedell ... [for]
organ solo. © Mills Music, inc.,
New York; on arrangement;
23May47; EP6937.

HENDRIX, BYRON. See
Hendrix, Edward Byron.

HENDRIX, EDWARD BYRON, 1911-
Search me, I don't know; words
and music by Margaret Hendrix
& Byron Hendrix. © Edward
Byron Hendrix [&] Margaret
Sims Hendrix, Monroeville, Ala.;
6Jun47; EP14901.

Shag-a-tag rag; words and music by
Margaret Hendrix [and] Byron
Hendrix. © Margaret Sims
Hendrix [&] Edward Byron Hendrix,
Monroeville, Ala.; 6Jun47;
EP14902.

HENEY, JOHN J
The carnival of Venice ... By John
J. Heney. Cincinnati, Fillmore
Music House. © Fillmore Bros.
Co., Cincinnati; 22Mar47; EP6738.
Score (xylophone and piano) and
part.

HENMAN, GEOFFREY.
Un jour sans toi; paroles de Jean
Solar [pseud.], musique de Geoffrey
Henman. © Ste. ame. fse. Chappell,
Paris; 18Dec46; EF4843. For voice
and piano.

HENNEFIELD, NORMAN, 1902-   ed.
Masterpieces of organ music ...
Norman Hennefield, editor. ©
Liturgical Music Press, inc.,
New York; on arrangement;
no. 53, 25Jun47; EP15073.

Masterpieces of organ music ...
Norman Hennefield, editor. ©
Liturgical Music Press, inc.,
New York; on arrangement; no.38,
8May46; no.41, 5Jul46; no.47,
15Dec46; no.48, 24Jan47; no.49
& 50, 7Mar47; no.51, 29Apr47;
no.52, 24May47; no.54, 29Jul47;
no.55, 29Jul47; EP10951, 10950,
10772, 12086, 12632, 13937,
14677, 15924, 15923.
Special issues: no.1, ed.
by Norman Hennefield and
George Mead. © Liturgical
Music Press, New York;
on arrangement; 15Mar47;
EP13231.

HENRY, CHARLES.
Noël swing. © Durand et Cie,
Paris; 15Jun46; EF2790. For
piano solo.

HENRY, MAC, pseud. See
McHenry, Elmer W.

HENSLEY, HAROLD.
I hear you knockin'; words and
music by Harold Hensley.
© Hill and Range Songs, inc.,
Hollywood, Calif.; 17May47;
EP14580.

I'll be satisfied; by Claude
Casey, Mel Foree [and] Harold
Hensley. © Bourne, inc., New
York; 5Mar47; EP12454. For
voice and piano, with chord
symbols.

HENSON, JOHN MELVIN, comp.
Gleams of glory; a choice collection
of gospel songs ... by J. M.
Henson, [Alfred Barratt and
others] Atlanta, J. M. Henson
Co. © John Melvin Henson,
Atlanta; 1Jul46; EP11188. Shape-
note notation.

Star of promise ... by J. M. Henson, [Alfred Barratt and others]
Atlanta, J. M. Henson Music Co.
© John Melvin Henson, Atlanta;
1Jan46; EP11189. Hymns, with
music; shape-note notation.

HERBERT, VICTOR, 1859-1924.
The birds and the bees ... [By]
Victor Herbert, paraphrased by
Domenico Savino. © J. J.
Robbins & Sons, inc., New York;
on arrangement; 2Jun47; EP14864.
For piano solo.

Canzonetta; [by] Victor Herbert,
paraphrased by Domenico Savino.
© J. J. Robbins & Sons, inc.,
New York; on arrangement;
21Apr47; EP14460. For piano
solo.

Eventide; [by] Victor Herbert,
paraphrased by Domenico Savino.
© J. J. Robbins & Sons, inc.,
New York; on arrangement;
2Jun47; EP14868.

(The fortune teller) Gypsy love
song (from The fortune teller),
music by Victor Herbert, arr.
for organ by Charles R. Cronham.
© M. Witmark & Sons, New York; on
arrangement; 6Jun47; EP15170.
For organ solo; includes registration for Hammond organ.

(Gypsy lady) Keepsakes ... from
the operetta, "Gypsy lady,"
lyric by Robert Wright and
George Forrest, music by
Victor Herbert. © M. Witmark
& Sons, New York; 15May47;
EP14585.

(Gypsy lady) My treasure, from
the operetta "Gypsy lady,"
lyric by Robert Wright and
George Forrest, music by
Victor Herbert. © M. Witmark
& Sons, New York; 15May47;
EP14586.

(Gypsy lady) Springtide ... from
the operetta "Gypsy lady,"
lyric by Robert Wright and
George Forrest, music by Victor
Herbert. © M. Witmark & Sons,
New York; 2May47; EP14401.

Happy harlequin; [by] Victor
Herbert, paraphrased by
Domenico Savino. © J. J.
Robbins & Sons, inc., New
York; on arrangement; 21Apr47;
EP14457. For piano solo.

Heart song; [by] Victor Herbert,
paraphrased by Domenico
Savino. © J. J. Robbins &
Sons, inc., New York; on ar-
rangement; 21Apr47; EP14455.
For piano solo.

In a Viennese garden; [by] Vic-
tor Herbert, paraphrased by
Domenico Savino. © J. J.
Robbins & Sons, inc., New York;
on arrangement; 21Apr47;
EP14459. For piano solo.

Italian street song; [by] Victor
Herbert, arr. by J. Louis Merkur, piano duet. © M. Witmark
& Sons, New York; on arrangement; 1May47; EP14412.

Keepsakes. See his Gypsy lady.

A kiss in the dark. See his
Orange blossoms.

Love's lament; [by] Victor Herbert,
paraphrased by Domenico Savino.
© J. J. Robbins & Sons, inc.,
New York; on arrangement; 2Jun47;
EP14867. For piano solo.

My treasure. See his Gypsy lady.

On parade. See his Sweethearts.

Por tu amor. See his Orange
blossoms.

(Orange blossoms) A kiss in the
dark. "Por tu amor." From
the operetta, "Orange blossoms";
Spanish text by Johnnie Camacho,
English text by B. G. De Sylva,
music by Victor Herbert. ©
M. Witmark & Sons, New York;
on Spanish words; 29May47;
EP14997.

Puppet's holiday ... [By] Victor
Herbert, paraphrased by
Domenico Savino. © J. J.
Robbins & Sons, inc., New
York; on arrangement; 21Apr47;
EP14454. For piano solo.

The red mill; selection, [by]
Victor Herbert. Bless the bride;
selection, [by] Vivian Ellis.
[Arr. by W. J. Duthoit] (The
army journal for full military
band, no.733) © The red mill;
M. Witmark & sons, New York;
Bless the bride; Chappell & Co.,
ltd., London; on arrangement;

27Jun47; EF5782-5783. Condensed
score and parts.

Romance in F; [by] Victor Her-
bert, paraphrased by Domenico
Savino. © J. J. Robbins &
Sons, inc., New York; on ar-
rangement; 21Apr47; EP14456.
For piano solo.

Serenade; [by] Victor Herbert,
paraphrased by Domenico
Savino. © J. J. Robbins &
Sons, inc., New York; on ar-
rangement; 21Apr47; EP14458.
For piano solo.

Song without words; [by] Victor
Herbert, paraphrased by Domenico
Savino. © J. J. Robbins & Sons,
inc., New York; on arrangement;
2Jun47; EP14866. For piano
solo.

Spring morn; [by] Victor Herbert,
paraphrased by Domenico Savino.
© J. J. Robbins & Sons, inc.,
New York; on arrangement;
2Jun47; EP14865. For piano
solo.

Springtime. See his Gypsy lady.

Sweethearts, from the comic opera
"Sweethearts"; for two-part
chorus of women's voices with
piano acc., [words by] Robert
B. Smith, [music by] Victor
Herbert, arr. by Jeffrey Marlowe,
[pseud.] © G. Schirmer, inc.,
New York; on arrangement;
30Dec46; EP11633.

(Sweethearts) On parade, from
"Sweethearts"; for two-part
chorus of women's voices with
piano acc. [Words by] Bob
Wright and Chet Forrest, [music
by] Victor Herbert, arr. by
Jeffrey Marlowe, [pseud.] ©
G. Schirmer, inc., New York;
on arrangement; 30Dec46; EP11634.

HERBRUCK, JOHN P 1903-
Rudiments of music; by John P.
Herbruck. © John P. Herbruck,
Rockford, Ill.; 4Apr47;
AA51090.

HERING, SIGMUND.
24 advanced etudes for the trumpet
or cornet; by Sigmund Hering.
© Carl Fischer, inc., New York;
31Mar47; EP13493.

HERNANDEZ, PEDRO. See
Hernandez Sanchez, Pedro.

HERNANDEZ, RAFAEL.
Canta, canta; letra y música de
Rafael Hernandez. Mexico,
Editorial Mexicana de Música
Internacional. © Peer Inter-
national Corp., New York;
30Dec46; EP11647.

Diez años ... letra y música de
Rafael Hernández. © Peer
International Corp., New York;
28Dec45; EP13646.

HERNANDEZ SANCHEZ, PEDRO.
Rumba en el patio ... Autores
Alfredo Boloña y Pedro
Hernandez Sanchez. Habana.
© Peer International Corp.,
New York; 15May47; EF3337.
Parts: orchestra (with words)

HERPIN.
En écoutant mon coeur chanter.
(All of a sudden my heart sings)
Paroles de Jamblan [pseud.] et
[English words by] Harold Rome;
musique de Herpin. La nouv.
version française du ... succès
"Ma mie." © Raoul Breton,
Paris; on new French words;
9Dec45; EF3711.

HERRMANN, BERNARD, 1911-
For the fallen; [by] Bernard
Herrmann. © American Music
Center, Inc., New York;
8Oct46; EP13101. Score:
orchestra.

HERRON, JOEL.
Paging Mr. Husing; (theme song
of the Ted Husing Bandstand);
words and music by Joel
Herron. © Burke & Van Heusen,
inc., New York; 4Mar47;
EP14340.

HERSCHER, LOUIS, 1894-
The best years in our lives,
(keep them forever in bloom);
[words] by Ruth Herscher and
Louis Herscher ... [arr.] by
Louis Herscher] based on a
theme by Rosas. © Bell Song
Publishing Co., Hollywood,
Calif.; on lyrics and arrange-
ment; 18Mar47; EP12629.
Can't get myself together; by
Phil Cohen [and] Louis Herscher
... arr. by Lou Halmy. ©
Bell Song Publishing Co., Holly-
wood, Calif.; 8Jan47; EP10929.
For voice and piano, with chord
symbols.
O chuca-chuca ... Words and
music by Joseph Frengel and
Louis Herscher, Portugese
lyric by Jose Telles, arr. by
Lou Halmy. © Bell Song Pub-
lishing Co., Hollywood, Calif.;
27Feb47; EP12197.

HERZON, HAL.
Nocturnal episode; piano solo by
Hal Herzon. © American Academy
of Music, inc., New York;
31Dec46; EU64461.

HESELTINE, PHILIP, 1894-1930.
Andantino tranquillo. See his
Capriol suite.
(Capriol suite) Andantino tran-
quillo; (Pieds-en-l'air) ...
from the "Capriol suite" by
Peter Warlock [pseud.], arr.
for organ solo by Stanley Roper.
© J. Curwen & Sons, ltd., London;
on arrangement; 24Jan47; EF5067.

HESS, JOHNNY, 1915-
Passing by; music by John Hess and
Paul Misraki, French lyric by
Charles Trenet, American version
by Jack Lawrence. © Chappell &
Co., inc., New York; on English
words; 19Apr47; EF5626. English
words.
Soyez bref; paroles de Jacques
Larue [pseud.], musique de
Johnny Hess. © Editions
Salabert, Paris; 15Jun46;
EF3561.

HETHERINGTON, ELA JONES.
My heart's in stitches; words and
music by Ela Jones Hetherington.
© Cine-Mart Music Publishing
Co., Hollywood, Calif.; 1Nov46;
EP11718.

HEUSEN, JAMES VAN. See
Van Heusen, James.

HEYWOOD, DONALD.
Stokey Bailey; words by Henry
Creamer, music by Donald
Heywood and Bob Schafer.
New York, J. Mills. © Mills
Music, inc. (successors in
interest to Jack Mills, inc.)
New York; 18Sep23; EP6859.

HEYWOOD, EDDIE.
Coquette; [by Gus Kahn, Carmen
Lombardo and John W. Green]
... transcription for piano
[by] Eddie Heywood. © Leo
Feist, inc., New York; on
arrangement; 27Nov46; EP11821.

Heywood blues ... for piano. ©
Robbins Music Corp., New York;
12Dec46; EP11016.
Loch Lomond ... transcription for
piano. © Robbins Music Corp.,
New York; on arrangement;
12Dec46; EP11017.

HIBBELER, RAYMOND OSCAR, 1892-
Behind my masquerade; words by
Helen E. Jones, music by Ray
Hibbeler. © Helen Evalyn
Jones, Corpus Christi, Tex.;
5Feb47; EP13313.
Do you ever dream of me? Words
& music by Frantz Clark and Ray
Hibbeler. © Frantz Hampton
Clark, Wilmington, Del.;
19Jun47; EP15255.
Drifting down the stream of love;
words by Sylvia Gae Utermarck,
music by Ray Hibbeler. ©
Sylvia Gae Utermarck, Milwaukee;
28Mar47; EP13150.
I bless you in ev'ry prayer;
words by Mildred Sloan, music
by Ray Hibbeler. © Mildred
Maude Sloan, Peoria, Ill.;
7Apr47; EP13459.
I'd like to have a cottage all our
own; words & music by Ruth
Trietsch Gaudlitz and Ray
Hibbeler. © Ruth Trietsch
Gaudlitz, Springfield, Ill.;
10Apr47; EP13834.
In the land of golden dreams;
words by Hazel C. Capp, music
by Ray Hibbeler. © Hazel
Caroline Capp, Perry, Iowa;
6Jun47; EP15029.
Let's tell the world we're in love;
words by Lu Rafferty, music by
Ray Hibbeler. © Lu Elinor Rafferty,
Delavan, Wis.; 25Feb47; EP12290.
Lovely, lovely; words by Walter M.
Hemmerly, music by Ray Hibbeler.
© Walter Merritt Hemmerly,
Philadelphia; 15May47; EP14678.
Mine alone; words & music by
Esther Mugan Bush and Ray
Hibbeler. © Esther Mugan
Bush, San Diego, Calif.;
10Jun47; EP11239.
My dreams of you; words by Helen
E. Jones, music by Ray Hibbeler.
© Helen Evalyn Jones, Corpus
Christi, Tex.; 5Feb47; EP13314.
My heart once sang all day;
words by Annie De Witt,
music by Ray Hibbeler. ©
Annie Martha De Witt, San
Jose, Calif.; 19Mar47;
EP13090.
There's a bright moon shining
tonight; words by Columbia
Gallant, music by Ray
Hibbeler. © Columbia Rita
Gallant, Boston; 6Mar47;
EP13025.
This is my own sweet melody;
words & music by Ruth Trietsch
Gaudlitz and Ray Hibbeler. ©
Ruth Trietsch Gaudlitz, Spring-
field, Ill.; 10Apr47; EP13833.
You are a part of my heart; words
and music by Eleanor Karnes
and Ray Hibbeler. © Eleanora
Lona Karnes, Hot Springs, Ark.;
on changes in words & music;
30Jan47; EP12198.

HIBBS, CLEO ALLEN, 1907-
The pledge to the flag ... by
Cleo Allen Hibbs. © Wesley
Webster, San Francisco; 5Jun47;
EP14910. Score: SATB and
piano reduction.

HICKEY, BILLY, 1890-
When the shamrock meets the
palm; [words by] Ginni Moran
[and] Murray Tannen, [music
by] Billy Hickey, [arr. by
Lindsay McPhail] © Jo
Golden, Music Publisher,
Brooklyn; 15Apr47; EP14332.

HILE, RUTH, 1902-
Sweet dreams, goodbye; [words by
G. G. Russell, [music by] Ruth
Hile. © Superior Melodies Pub-
lishing Co., Chicago; 15Jul46;
EP14920.

HILL, ALFRED.
(Quartet, strings, no. 11) String
quartet in D minor, [by] Alfred
Hill. © Chappell & Co., ltd.,
Sydney & Allan & Co., pty. ltd.,
Melbourne, Australia; 15Nov46;
EF4788.
String quartet in D minor. See his
Quartet, strings, no. 11.

HILL, BILLY.
The last round-up; fox trot [by
Billy Hill] arranged by Jimmy
Dale. © Shapiro, Bernstein &
Co., inc., New York; on arrange-
ment; 31Dec46; EP11071. Piano-
conductor score (orchestra) and
parts.

HILL, EMMA.
The east bound Harlem train;
words and music by Emma Hill.
© Nordyke Publishing Co., Los
Angeles; 22Oct45; EP13556.

HILL, EUGENE, 1909-
(Chorale preludes, organ) Four
choral preludes ... by Eugene
Hill. © Waterloo Music Co.,
Waterloo, Ont., Can.; on
arrangement; 1Feb47; EF4978.
Four chorale preludes for organ.
See his Chorale preludes, organ.

HILL, HARRY, 1893- ed.
The singing period book of carols
... ed. and comp. by Harry Hill.
© Waterloo Music Co., Waterloo,
Ont., Can.; 2Dec46; EF4937.
Close score: SATB.

HILL, HERMAN, 1928-
I got ya' covered, Mister Buzzard;
by Herman Hill. © Popular Music
Co., New York; 13Jun47; EP15044.
For voice and piano, with chord
symbols.

HILL, LEWIS EUGENE. See
Hill, Eugene.

HILL, MAYME BERRY, 1915-
Life forever; words by Anna Goode
Berry, music by Mayme Berry Hill,
arr. by Loretta Cessor Manggrum.
© Anna Goode Berry, Cincinnati;
8May47; EP14898.

HILL, TOLBERT JUNIOR, 1910-
The wind rolls the clouds; a
little song for little tots,
written and composed by
Tolbert Junior Hill. ©
Tolbert J. Hill, individually,
and Tolbert J. Hill, as
trustee for Saralind Ann Hill
jointly, Champaign, Ill.;
3Feb47; EP13026.

HILL AND COUNTRY RADIO SONGS. [A
compilation] © John Bava, Davis,
W. Va.; 9Jun47; EP15203.

HILLEBRAND, FRED.
I worry 'bout you; words and
music by Fred Hillebrand.
© Fred Hillebrand, sole owner
of Fred Hillebrand Publications, Bayside, N. Y.;
12May47; EP14804.

64

HILLIAM, BENTLEY COLLINGWOOD, 1890-
Ladies of Leamington ... [by]
B. C. Hilliam, orchestrated by
George Linstead. © Ascherberg,
Hopwood, & Crew, ltd., London; on
arrangement; 10Mar47; EF5077.
Piano-conductor score (orchestra)
and parts.

HILLMAN, ROC.
I met her in a revolving door; words
and music by Roc Hillman. © Leo
Feist, inc., New York; 14Feb47;
EP12089.

[HINDERER, EVERETT R]
In the note that I wrote you last
night; words by Ted A. Brince-
field, music by Shorty Cook,
[pseud.] © Adams, Vee & Abbott,
inc., Chicago; 16Dec46; EP11347.

HINES, CLAUDE V 1886-
Let's sing it! Gospel songs and
choruses ... comp. by Claude V.
Hines. © Claude V. Hines,
Peoria Heights, Ill.; 16Sep46;
EP10892. Principally by Claude
V. Hines.

[HINSHAW, FRANK M]
Good news melodious; [words and
music by Frank M. Hinshaw and
V. W. Hinshaw] © Frank M.
Hinshaw, Hayward, Calif.;
10Jan47; EP6477.

HIRSCH, JOSEPH E
Texas and Pacific; words and
music by Jack Wolf Fine and
Joseph E. Hirsch; words by
Johnny Warrington. © Pic Music
Corp., Chicago; on arrangement;
1Mar47; EP13351. Piano-conductor score (orchestra, with
words) and parts.

HIRSCH, LOUIS ACHILLE, 1881-1924.
(Mary) The love nest, from the
musical comedy "Mary;" words
by Otto Harbach, music by Louis
A. Hirsch, [arranged by Ken
Macomber] © Harms, inc., New
York; on arrangement; 20Dec46;
EP11063. Piano-conductor
score (orchestra) and parts.

HITCHCOCK, ARLENE RUTH, 1916-
The wild rose of Ioway; words by ...
Myrle Thomas, music by Arlene
Hitchcock.[arr. by Gertrude L.
Brannan] [c1945] © Myrle Madge
Thomas & Arlene Ruth Hitchcock,
Muscatine, Iowa; 25Jun46; EP11550.

HIVELY, WELLS.
Habana suite ... composed and
arr. by Wells Hively. ©
Broadcast Music, inc., New
York; no.1, 27Dec46; no.2,
12Mar47; no.3, 9Apr47; no.4,
12May47. Piano-conductor
score (orchestra) and parts.
Contents.- no.1. San Cristó-
bal de la Habana (© EP11842)-
no.2. Plaza de armas
(© EP13776) - no.3. La cabaña
(© EP15238) -no.4. Paseo
(© EP15237)

HLOBIL, EMIL, 1901-
Druhý kvartet. See his Quartet,
strings, no. 2.

(Quartet, strings, no. 2) Druhý
kvartet; pro dvoje housle, violu
a violoncello. [By] Emil Hlobil.
Op. 15. © Hudební Matice Umělecké
Besedy, Praha, Czechoslovakia;
14Jun45; EF4958.

(Quintet, strings) Kvintet; pro
dvoje housle, dvě violy a
violoncello, [by] Emil Hlobil.
Op. 1. © Hudební Matice Umělecké Besedy, Praha, Czechoslovakia; 22Apr43; EF4962.

Tri piano; [by] Emil Hlobil. Op.
8. [Words by Josef Chaloupka
and S. K. Neumann] © Hudební
Matice Umělecké Besedy, Praha,
Czechoslovakia; 31Mar42; EF4950.
For voice and piano.

HOBBS, PEGGY.
The love I threw away; words and
music by Johnny Rion and Peggy
Hobbs. © Peer International
Corp., New York; 18Mar47;
EP13975.

HODGE, A J
Have you counted the cost? [Words
by] A.J.H. (In Dunlop, Merrill,
arr. Choral selections, #3.
p. 9) © Homer A. Rodeheaver,
d.b.a. The Rodeheaver Co.,
Winona Lake, Ind.; on arrangement; 15Nov46; EP10332.

HODGES, JIMMIE.
I'll see you again; words and
music by Bob Miller and Jimmie
Hodges. © Bob Miller, inc.,
New York; 2May47; EP14175.

Sweetheart of yesterday; words and
music by Jimmie Hodges. © Bob
Miller, inc., New York; 2May47;
EP14176.

HOEPLE, CARL.
The bubble gum song; words by
Del Porter ... music by Carl
Hoefle. © Tune Towne Tunes,
Hollywood, Calif.; 8Apr47;
EP13725.

Topeka polka; by Spade Cooley,
Del Porter [and] Carl Hoefle.
© Tune Towne Tunes, Hollywood,
Calif.; 8Apr47; EP13731. For
voice and piano, with chord
symbols.

HOFFMAN, AL.
Heartaches; [music by Al Hoffman,
arr. by Joseph P. Elsnic] Chicago,
Vitak-Elsnic Co. © Leeds Music
Corp., New York; on arrangement;
26May47; EP14693. For concertina.

Heartaches ... music by Al Hoffman,
arr. by William Teague. © Leeds
Music Corp., New York; on arrangement; 15May47; EP14418.
Condensed score (band) and
parts.

HOFFMAN, CHARLOTTE FEAST. See
Feast, Charlotte.

HOFFMAN, MAL.
Terang boelan. Malayan moon.
Words by Frank Harling Parker,
music by Mal Hoffman. © Allan
& Co., pty. ltd., Melbourne,
Australia; 5Sep46; EF3090. For
voice and piano, with guitar
diagrams and chord symbols.

HOFFMANN, HORST.
Stars ... by H. Hoffmann. New
York, Harmonia Edition. ©
Harmonia Edition Publishing Co.,
New York; 30Dec46; EP6464. For
piano or organ solo.

HOFLAND, SIGVART A 1889-
At sundown; (S.A.T.B. div.) music
by Sigvart A. Hofland, words by
David T. Nelson. © Neil A.
Kjos Music Co., Chicago; .
12Mar47; EP14004.

HOFNER, ADOLPH.
Sweetheart, this is goodbye;
words and music by Adolph
Hofner ... piano arrangement by
Dick Kent. [and I can't keep
the tears out of my eyes; by
Charlie Wilkins and Curt
Barrett] © Peer International
Corp., New York; 15May47;
EP14575-14576. For voice and
piano, with chord symbols.

HOFSTAD, MILDRED.
Bombardier's return ... for piano,
by Mildred Hofstad. © The
Boston Music Co., Boston;
4Apr47; EP13358.

HOGAN, GORDON ALBION, 1923-
I could believe in dreams; by
Gordon Hogan. © Gordon Albion
Hogan, Corona, Calif.; 30May47;
EP15211. For voice and piano.

HOHMANN, WALTER HUGO, 1892-
Christ walks into the hills; sacred
chorus for mixed voices, optional
a cappella (S.A.T.B.-divided)
[By] Walter H. Hohmann, [words by]
W. H. H. © Hall & McCreary Co.,
Chicago; 12Apr47; EP13761.

Po' good Jesus ... for mixed voices
with soprano solo, optional
a cappella (S.A.T.B., div.) [By]
Walter H. Hohmann, [words by]
Waring Cuney. © Hall & McCreary
Co., Chicago; 14Apr47; EP13762.

HOKANSON, MARGRETHE.
Song of the pilgrim; for mixed
voices. Italian church melody
... arr. by Margrethe Hokanson,
text by Bernhard Ingemann, tr.
by Baring-Gould. © Clayton F.
Summy Co., Chicago; 12May47;
EP14799.

HOLBROOKE, JOSEF.
Night by the sea. From the
Grande suite moderne (no. 2)
(Op. 18 B, no. 3) by Josef
Holbrooke, arr. for organ by
Purcell J. Mansfield. ©
Ascherberg, Hopwood & Crew,
ltd., London; on arrangement;
24Mar47; EF5340.

[HOLDRIDGE, IONE]
Let's get married; words and music by
Art Kassel [and Ione Holdridge]
© Loop Music Co., Chicago; 23Dec46;
EP6495.

HOLLAENDER, VICTOR.
Ballet ... by Victor Hollaender,
New York, Harmonia Edition. ©
Harmonia Edition Publishing co.,
New York; 30Dec46; EP6465. or
piano or organ solo.

HOLLIS, CHARLES, pseud.
The church's one foundation ...
Ed. and arr. for junior choir,
by Charles Hollis, [words by
Samuel J. Stone] © Choral Press,
Evanston, Ill.; 10ct46; EP11704.

[HOLMBERG-AASTRUP, PER]
Lolita ... [words and] musik!
Arne Nielson [pseud.], arr:
Thore Ehrling. © Edition
Sylvain, a.b., Stockholm;
1Jan45; EF3722. Piano-con-
ductor score (orchestra, with
words), and parts.

HOLMES, G E
Vanity fair ... By G. E. Holmes.
© Mills Music, inc., New York;
30Apr47; EP6870. Condensed
score (band) and parts.

Woodland serenade; by G. E. Holmes.
© Mills Music, inc., New York;
30Apr47; EP6869. Condensed score
(band) and parts.

HOLMES, LESLIE.
The wedding of the brush and
comb; words and music by Leslie
Sarony and Leslie Holmes.
© Peter Maurice Music Co., ltd.,
New York; 31Dec46; EF5064.

HOLROYD, CAROLYN I M
I love a married Jew; words by
Mary Marcella Janda, music by
Carolyn I. M. Holroyd and Gladys
Anderson Bros. Wilber, Neb.,
Marcella Janda. © Gary Marc
Bros., Wilber, Neb., 26Dec46;
EP10730.

HOLST, AGNES M
We believe, we all believe (Old
Danish hymn - 1524); credo for
mixed voices harmonized and arr.
by Agnes M. Holst. [Translation
by A. M. H.] © Broadcast Music,
inc., New York; on arrangement
& translation; 1May47; EP15227.

HOLST, MARIE SEUEL.
Three woodland scenes ... by
Marie Seuel Holst. [Op. 42]
© Clayton F. Summy Co., Chicago; on 3 pieces. For piano
solo, with words. Contents.-
[1] Pines on the hillside
(© 25Apr47; EP13970) - [2]
Dogwood in April (© 29May47;
EP14831) - [3] The runaway
brooklet (© 22May47; EP14835)

HOLT, HILDA.
Carl Fischer note-spellor; a music-
writing book progressively
arranged for beginning piano
students, by Hilda Holt. © Carl
Fischer, inc., New York; 12Mar47;
AA50452.

HOLT, JOHN MAX, 1900-
There'll be no invasion in heaven;
lyrics and music by J. Max
Holt. © J. Max Holt, Denver;
10Jun47; EP15094.

HOLTON, FRED B., pseud. See
Wilson, Ira Bishop.

HOLZMANN, ABE.
Blaze of glory ... [by] Abe Holzmann, arr. by Don Bowdon. ©
Hawkes & Son (London), ltd.; on
arrangement; 31Dec46; EF4769.
Piano-conductor score (orchestra)
and parts.

HOLZWORTH, ALFRED, 1882-
The Spirit of light; [words by
Christopher Wordsworth,
[music by] Alfred Holzworth.
(In Moody Bible institute of
Chicago. The voice of thanks-
giving, no.5. Hymn no.130)
© The Moody Bible Institute
of Chicago, Chicago; 23Sep46;
EP10885. Close score: SATB.

Thou art my hiding place; [words
by] Thomas Raffles, [music
by] Alfred Holzworth. (In
Moody Bible institute of
Chicago. The voice of thanksgiving, no.5. Hymn no.203)
© The Moody Bible Institute
of Chicago, Chicago; 23Sep46;
EP10886. Close score: SATB.

HOMER, BENJAMIN.
Ridin' on the gravy train;
words by Sunny Skylar, [pseud.]
and Steve Graham, music by
Ben Homer. New York, Capitol
Songs, inc. © Criterion
Music Corp., New York;
14Dec45; EP14281.

HOMER, SIDNEY.
Sheep and lambs; for two-part
chorus of women's voices, with
piano acc., [words by] Katharine
Tynan Hinkson, [music by] Sidney
Homer. Op.31, arr. by Carl
Deis. © G. Schirmer, inc., New
York; on arrangement; 24Mar47;
EP13426.

HONEGGER, ARTHUR, 1892-
O salutaris; pour soprano ... avec
accompagnement d'orgue et piano
(ou harpe) ad libitum. © Heugel,
Au Ménestrel, Paris; 31Dec43;
EF52.

Symphonic liturgique; [by] Arthur
Honegger. Partition d'orchestre.
Paris, Salabert. © Salabert,
inc., New York; 15Nov46;
EF3294.

HOORNSTRA, PAUL Z   1920-
If you would give Christ to the
nations; [words by] P. Z. H.
and C. E. H., [music by] Paul
Z. Hoornstra, arr. by W. M. T.
(In Church of the Nazarene.
Michigan District. Nazarene
Young Peoples Society. Choruses
of the N. Y. P. S. p.42-43) ©
Michigan District, Nazarene
Young Peoples Society, Flint,
Mich.; 25Jul46; EP13065. Close
score: SATB.

THE HOOSIER SCHOOLMASTER, pseud.
See Hand, John Raymond.

HOPKINS, ANTONY, 1921-
The just vengeance; a festival
passion play, words by Dorothy
Sayers, music by Antony Hopkins.
Chorus part. (London, J. & W.
Chester) © Antony Hopkins, Lon-
don; 1Jul46; EP4885.

(Sonata, piano) Sonata in D
minor for pianoforte; by Antony
Hopkins. © J. & W. Chester,
ltd., London; 27May47; EF3897.

HOPKINS, HARRY P
Clothes-pin soldiers ... by H.
P. Hopkins. © McKinley Publishers,
inc., Chicago; 31Dec46; EP11677.
For piano solo.

Happy and gay; [by] H. P. Hopkins.
© Century Music Publishing Co.,
New York; 15Apr47; EP13224.
For piano solo.

Hawaiian breezes ... by H. P.
Hopkins. © McKinley Publishers,
inc., Chicago; 31Dec46; EP11678.
For piano solo.

The ice cream man; [by] H. P.
Hopkins. © Century Music
Publishing Co., New York;
15Apr47; EP13800. For piano
solo, with words.

Lady bird's waltz ... By H. P.
Hopkins. © McKinley Publish-
ers, inc., Chicago; 31Dec46;
EP12184. For piano solo.

A mystery story; [by] H. P.
Hopkins. [Ed. by Walter
Rolfe] © Century Music
Publishing Co., New York;
12May47; EP14265. For piano
solo.

Playful kitty ... By H. P.
Hopkins. © McKinley Publishers,
inc., Chicago; 31Dec46;
EP12185. For piano solo.

A song for Annie Lou; [by] H. P.
Hopkins. © Century Music
Publishing Co., New York;
15Apr47; EP13223. For piano
solo, with words.

HOPKINS, HARRY P   arr.
The marine's hymn; arr. by H. P.
Hopkins. © McKinley Publishers, inc., Chicago; on arrangement; 31Dec46; EP12188. For
piano solo.

Polly wolly doodlo; arrW by H. P.
Hopkins. © McKinley Publishers,
inc., Chicago; on arrangement;
31Dec46; EP12189. For piano
solo.

HOPKINS, JOHN HENRY.
We three kings of Orient are ...
[words by] J. H. Hopkins, jr.
... with descants by Hugh
Ross. (In Ross, Hugh, arr.
Sacred choruses for women's or
girls' voices. p. 155-160) ©
G. Schirmer, inc., New York; on
arrangement; 30Sep46; EP9797.

HOPKINS, JOSEPH M
Dusk dreams; for piano [by]
Joseph M. Hopkins. © Theodore
Presser Co., Philadelphia;
26May47; EP14698.

HOPKINS, MAUDE D
Desert starlight; words and music
by Maude D. Hopkins. © Cine-
Mart Music Publishing Co., Hollywood, Calif.; 15Dec46; EP11951.

Golden dream of love; words and music
by Maude Hopkins. © Cine-Mart Music
Publishing Co., Hollywood, Calif.;
1Nov46; EP12123.

HORE, CHARMION, 1898-
En las playas uruguayas. (On the
Uruguayan beaches) ... Words and
music [by] Charmion Hore, piano
accompaniment [by] Harry Walker.
[Buenos Aires, Lottermoser]
© Charmion Hore & Harry Walker,
Buenos Aires; 1Nov46; EP5252.

Eventido ... Piano acc. [by]
Harry Walker, words and music
[by] Charmion Hore. Buenos
Aires, Casa Lottermoser.
© Charmion Hore and Harry Walker,
Buenos Aires; 1Nov46; EP5357.

Interlude; song, words and music
[by] Charmion Hore, piano
accompaniment [by] Harry
Walker. [Buenos Aires,
Lottermoser] © Charmion Hore
& Harry Walker, Buenos Aires;
1Nov46; EP5251.

My lady; words and music [by]
Charmion Hore, piano
accompaniment [by] Harry Walker.
[Buenos Aires, Lottermoser] ©
Charmion Hore & Harry Walker,
Buenos Aires; 1Nov46; EP5253.

HORGAN, MARY STANISLAUS, sister, 1887-
Ave Maria; by Sister Mary
Stanislaus. © Sisters of
Mercy, Omaha; 13May46; EP10763.
For 2 treble voices and piano.

O salutaris. Tantum ergo; by
Sister Mary Stanislaus. ©
Sisters of Mercy, Omaha; 20May46;
EP10764. For 2 treble voices
and piano.

HORN, CHARLES VAN. See
Van Horn, Charles.

HORN, EDIE M. VAN. See
Van Horn, Edie M.

HORST, ADAM GOOD, 1880-
The joy of His Presence. King
and Teacher evermore. Dwell in
my heart. "For God so loved"
... By A. G. Horst. [c1946]
© Adam Good Horst, Portland,
Or.; 14Mar47; EP12774-12777.
Close score: SATB.

HORTON, LEWIS HENRY.
Ancient of days; for five-part
chorus of mixed voices (S.S.A.T.
B. a cappella) Hymn by William
C. Doane, music by Lewis Henry
Horton. © Carl Fischer, inc.,
New York; 17May47; EP14720.

HORTON, VAUGHN, 1911-
Deep delta blues; words and music
by Denver Darling and Vaughn
Horton. © Northern Music Corp.,
New York; 2Jun47; EP14967.

Dixie cannon ball; by Gene Autry,
"Rod" Foley and Vaughn Horton.
© Western Music Publishing Co.,
Hollywood, Calif.; 17Dec46;
EP10792.

Juke joint mama; words and music
by Denver Darling and Vaughn
Horton. © Northern Music
Corp., New York; 12May47;
EP14381.

HOSKIN, R   W   S
Michigan; words and music by R.
W. S. Hoskin. Menominee, Mich.,
Sheridan Publishing Co. © R.
W. S. Hoskin, Menominee, Mich.;
15Apr47; EP14243.

HOUDINI, WILMOTH.
Arima to-night, Sangre Grande
to-morrow night; words and
music by Wilmoth Houdini. ©
Northern Music Corp., New
York; 27Nov46; EP12387.

Black but sweet; words and music by
Wilmoth Houdini. © Northern
Music Corp., 27Nov46; EP12344.

HOUSE, CHARLIE EDWARD.
The light in your eyes (lit a
flame in my heart); words and
music by Charlie Edward House.
© Nordyke Publishing Co., Los
Angeles; 11Oct46; EP13543.

HOUSER, JOHN GARNETT.
The Lord's prayer; [by] J. Garnett
Houser. © John Garnett Houser,
jr., Chicago; on arrangement;
27May47; EP14674. Score:
mixed voices and piano.

HOVELMANN, CHRISTINA.
The clown; by Christina Hovemann, for
the piano. © Harold Flammer,
inc., New York; 4Nov46; EP10751.

It's snowing! Piano solo with words
by Christina Hovemann. © Harold
Flammer, inc., New York; 31Dec46;
EP11426.

Twilight shadows; piano solo for
left hand alone, by Christina
Hovemann. © Harold Flammer, inc.,
New York; 4Nov46; EP10752.

HOVEN, GEORGE, 1913-
Hi ball polka; by George Hoven.
Solo for piano accordion.
New York, O. Di Bella Music
Co. © Onofrio Di Bella, New
York; 15Apr47; EP14305.

Pittsburgh polka; by George
Hoven. Solo for piano
accordion. New York, O. Di
Bella Music Co. © Onofrio
Di Bella, New York; 15Apr47;
EP14304.

HOVEY, VAHAN, 1918-
I'm bewildered; [by] George
Fragos and Vahan Hovey. ©
Westchester Music Co., New
York; 15Mar47; EP13095. For
voice and piano, with chord
symbols.

HOWARD, EDDY.
Lynn; words and music by Eddy
Howard. © Lake Shore Publishing
Co., Chicago; 31Dec46; EP11079.

My last goodbye ... music by Eddy
Howard, arr. by Jimmy Dale. ©
Bourne, inc., New York on arrangement; 21Mar47; EP12925. Piano-
conductor score (orchestra) and
parts.

HOWARD, JOHN TASKER.
I will lift up mine eyes; S.A.T.B.
[Words from] Psalm 121, [music
by] John Tasker Howard. ©
Edwin H. Morris & Co., inc.,
New York; 26May47; EP14949.

In the valley at home; for three-
part chorus of women's voices
with piano acc. Words by
Josephine Hemsley, music by
John Tasker Howard, arr. by
Bryceson Treharne. © The Boston
Music Co., Boston; on arrange-
ment; 2May47; EP14467.

O did you hear the meadow lark?
For chorus of women's voices,
three-part, [by] John Tasker
Howard ... [words by] Lorraine
Noel Finley. © Galaxy Music
Corp., New York; 12May47;
EP6895.

HOWARD, JOSEPH EDGAR, 1880-
Goodbye, my lady love; by Joseph E.
Howard, arr. by Paul Weirick. ©
Mills Music, inc., New York; on
arrangement; 23May47; EP6930.
Piano-conductor score (orchestra,
with words) and parts.

I wonder who's kissing her now;
lyrics by Will M. Hough and
Frank R. Adams, music by Joseph
E. Howard, [arr. by Claude
Garreau] for four part male
voices T.T.B.B. © Edward B.
Marks Music Corp., New York;
on arrangement; 23Jun47;
EP15207.

I wonder who's kissing her now;
lyrics by Will M. Hough and Frank
R. Adams, music by Joseph E.
Howard [from] "I wonder who's
kissing her now." [Arr. by Paul
Weirick] © Edward B. Marks Music
Corp., New York; on fox-trot arrangement & waltz arrangement;
23Apr47; EP13861-13862. Piano-
conductor score (orchestra, with
words) and parts. Score and
parts of waltz version on verso
of score and parts of fox-trot
version.

What's the use of dreaming? By
Joseph E. Howard, arr. by Paul
Weirick. © Mills Music, inc.,
New York; on arrangement; 23May47;
EP6932. Piano-conductor score
(orchestra, with words) and
parts.

HOWARD, RICHARD.
You've laughed at me for the last
time; words and music by
Richard Howard. © Sun Music
Co., inc., New York; 21Mar45;
EP13376.

HOWE, MARY.
When I died in Berners Street;
for voice and piano, words by
Elinor Wylie, music by Mary
Howe. © G. Schirmer, inc.,
New York; 24Mar47; EP13134.

HOWELL, INEZ, 1885-
Lullaby; piano solo, by Inez
Howell. © Belwin, inc., New
York; 31Dec46; EP11226.

[HOWORTH, WAYNE] 1895-
Cielito lindo. (Beautiful heaven)
For ... S.S.A. Mexican folk song
arr. by Paul Fuller [pseud.]
© Pro Art Publications, New York;
on arrangement; 21Apr47;
EP13613. English words.

Dry bones; for women's voices
S.S.A., harmonized and arr.
by Russell Watson, [pseud.]
© Belwin, inc., New York; on
arrangement; 14May47;
EP14628.

Hallelujah! For ... S.S.A. and
solo; spiritual [arr. by] Wayne
Howorth. © Pro Art Publications,
New York; 21Apr47; EP13607.

Hold on! For ... S.S.A. (incidental solo for soprano)
Spiritual, [arr. by] Wayne
Howorth. © Pro Art Publications, New York; on arrangement; 21Apr47; EP13603.

Little David play on yo' harp;
for ... S.S.A. (incidental solo:
soprano) Spiritual, arr. by
Russell Watson [pseud.] © Pro
Art Publications, New York; on
arrangement; 21Apr47; EP13604.

Were you there? [Spiritual] S.A.T.B.
(with solo for low voice) harmonized
and arr. by Wayne Howorth. © Belwin,
inc., New York; on arrangement;
13Feb47; EP12074.

HOWORTH, WAYNE, 1895-
Go down Moses; for mixed voices,
S.A.T.B. with solo for medium
voice, a cappella; spiritual
arranged by Wayne Howorth. ©
Belwin, inc., New York; on
arrangement; 21Jan47; EP12200.

HOYL, JIM, pseud. See
Heifetz, Jascha.

HUBBELL, FRANK ALLEN, 1907-
"Grumpy Shark"; record, music,
story [and] comic book, written
... by Bob Bollem, music ... by
Frank Hubbell. Told by Marvin
Miller, funnies by Mel Millar.
© Belda Record and Publishing
Co., Pasadena, Calif.; on The
smile song; 23Jan47; EP11728.
Includes The smile song: p. [2-
3] of cover of album.

HUBEAU, JEAN, 1917-
Concerto héroïque; 1. concerto
en si majeur, en deux hymnes,
[for] piano et orchestre, [by]
Jean Hubeau. © Editions
Durand & Cie., Paris; 31Oct46;
EP5238. Two scores for piano
1-2.

HUBER, BOB.
Mon rêve; paroles de Louis Poterat,
musique de Bob Huber. © SIDEM,
Société Intercontinentale
d'Editions Musicales, Vaduz,
Ginevra; 18Oct46; EF4935. For
voice and piano.

HUDGINS, EUGENE.
I know you didn't mean to say
goodbye ... Words and music by
Eugene Hudgins. © Peer International Corp., New York;
24Mar47; EP13428.

Only a friend ... Words and music
by Eugene Hudgins. © Peer
International Corp., New York;
24Mar47; EP13430.

HUDSON, J V
My boot training; words and music
by J. V. Hudson. © Nordyke
Publishing Co., Los Angeles;
12Dec46; EP14784.

HUERGO, MARUJA PACHECO. See
Pacheco Huergo, Maruja.

HUESTON, BILLY.
Why should I tell you? (Macy's
don't tell Gimbel's) Words and
music by Clarence Maher and Billy
Hueston. © Mills Music, inc.,
New York; 23May47; EP6929.

HUFFNAGLE, HARRY, 1899-
16 smart studies; by Harry
Huffnagle, ed. by David
Gornston. © Gate Music Co.,
New York; 9Apr47; EP13795.
For trumpet solo.

HUGG, GEORGE C
No, not one! [Words by] Johnson
Oatman, [music by] Geo. C.
Hugg. (In Eddy Arnold's radio ...
favorites song book. no. A-1,
p.45.) © Adams, Vee & Abbott,
inc., Chicago; on arrangement;
17Jun46; EP11229. Close score:
SATB, with guitar diagrams and
chord symbols.

HUGHES, HAROLD KENNETH, 1911-
My gift ... Poem by Jay Rumney ...
music by Harold K. Hughes.
[c1947] © Harold Kenneth Hughes,
Hudson Heights, N. J.; 30Dec46;
EP13413.

[HUGUET Y TAGELL, ROGELIO JOSE]
1882-
Hurra pour l'Espagne! ... Léa,
Lili, Lole, Loulou ... paroles
de Fremique [pseud.], musique de
Dorcine [pseud.] © Editions
Salabert, Paris; 8Jul47; EF6408.
Piano-conductor score (orchestra,
with words) and parts.

HULEN, L   E
True blue and gold; words and music
by LeHulen. © L. E. Hulen, Fort
Worth, Tex.; 26Jun47; EP15218.

[HULL, RUSSELL EUGENE] 1911-   comp.
Famous family album of radio
favorites; [by Famous Tim Lashua,
Russell Eugene Hull and others]
© Country Music Publishers,
(Russ Hull, owner), Chicago; bk.
no.1, 2Jun47; EP15103. For
voice and piano, with guitar
diagrams and chord symbols.

Lonnie Glosson and his talking
harmonica ... favorite home and
sacred songs, [words and music by
Lonnie Glosson, Russell Eugene
Hull, Fred G. Henry, and others]
© Country Music Publishers (owner,
Russ Hull) Chicago; 30Apr47;
EP14123.

HUMMEL, FERDINAND.
Hosanna; anthem for mixed voices
with bass or alto solo ...
[words by] Heinrich Rupprecht,
English text by Helen A. Dickin-
son [music by] Ferdinand Hummel,
arranged by Clarence Dickinson.
© The H. W. Gray Co., inc., New
York; on arrangement; 3Jan47;
EP11054. English words.

HUMPERDINCK, ENGELBERT, 1854-1921.
Come, sing and dance; from ...
Hansel and Gretel; [by] E.
Humperdinck, arr. [and English
translation] by the Krones,
Beatrice and Max. Chicago,
Neil A. Kjos Music Co. © Max
& Beatrice Krone, Los Angeles;
on arrangement and English words;
26Apr47; EP14925. Score: cho-
rus (SA or SSA) and piano.

The dance in the cottage, from
Hansel and Gretel, [by] E.
Humperdinck, arr. [and English
translation by the Krones, Bea-
trice and Max. Chicago, N. A.
Kjos Music Co. © Max & Beatrice
Krone, Los Angeles; on arrange-
ment and English words; 26Apr47;
EP14926. Score: chorus (SSA)
and piano.

Song of the dew fairy, from
Hansel and Gretel; [by] E.
Humperdinck, arr. [and English
text] by the Krones, Beatrice
and Max. Chicago, N. A. Kjos
Music Co. © Max & Beatrice
Krone, Los Angeles; on arrange-
ment and English text; 2May47;
EP14923. Score: chorus (SA or
SSA) and piano.

Susie, little Susie, from Hansel
and Gretel; [by] E. Humperdinck,
arr. [and English translation]
by the Krones, Beatrice and Max.
Chicago, N. A. Kjos Music Co.
© Max & Beatrice Krone, Los
Angeles; on arrangement and
English words; 2May47; EP14924.
Score: chorus (SA or SSA) and piano.

HUNTER, BASIL, 1918-
Cosmic serenade; for piano.
© Western Music Co.,
ltd., Vancouver, B. C.; 13Dec46;
EP4936.

HUNTER, SAM, pseud.   See
Smith, Robert E.

HURNIK, ILJA, 1922-
Dívčí písně. [Op. 7. By] Ilja
Hurnik. © František Chadim,
Praha, Czechoslovakia;
10Dec46; EP3363. For voice
and piano.

HURRAN, DICK.
Betty Lou; arr. by Will Hudson,
words and music [by] Dick
Hurran. New York, American
Academy of Music, inc. ©
Francis, Day & Hunter, ltd.,
London; on arrangement; 23Dec46;
EP6631. Piano-conductor score
(orchestra, with words) and
parts.

HUTCHINS, DARWIN FRANK.
I wonder, I wonder, I wonder;
words and music by Daryl
Hutchins. Oakland, Calif.,
Trilon Publishers. © Daryl
Hutchins, Oakland, Calif.;
2Jan47; EP13657.

I wonder, I wonder, I wonder;
words and music by Daryl
Hutchins. © Robbins Music
Corp., New York; on changes
in melody and lyrics and
piano arrangement; 7Mar47;
EP12684.

HUTCHINS, DARYL.   See
Hutchins, Darwin Frank.

HUTCHINSON, THERESA, 1904-
There's peace in the valley for
me; by Theresa Hutchinson, ar-
rangement by Virginia Davis.
Chicago, The Martin Studio of
Gospel Music. © Theresa Hutch-
inson, New York; 20Dec45;
EP14922. For voice and piano.

HUTCHINSON, VICTOR HELY-   See
Hely-Hutchinson, Victor.

HYMES, MARY E
The enchanted song; words and music
by Mary E. Hymes. © Cine-Mart
Music Publishing Co., Hollywood,
Calif.; 11Nov46; EP11415.

I

IAKOBIDES, Z.
Agapoula, agapoula; etichoi M.
Margaritē [pseud.], mousikē Z.
Iakōbidē. Athēnai, Ekdoseis
Gaitanou. © Michael Gaetanos,
Athens; 10Nov46; EF3130. For
voice and piano.

Gyrna kai pali; etichoi M.
Margaritē [pseud.], mousikē
Z. Iakōbidē - N. Iakōbleph.
Athēnai, Ekdoseis Gaitanou.
© Michael Etienne Gaetanos,
Athens; 14Jan47; EF5344.
For voice and piano.

Kardies'pou smixane ... etichoi:
M. Margaritē [pseud.],
mousikē Z. Iakōbidē. Athēnai,
Ekdoseis Gaitanou. © Michael
Gaetanos, Athens; 17Feb47;
EF5545. For voice and piano.

M'ena phili erōs den zei ...
etichoi M. Margarito
[pseud.], mousikē Z.
Iakōbidē [and] N. Iakōbleph.
Athēnai, Ekdoseis Gaitanou.
© Michael Etienne Gaetanos,
Athens; 14Jan47; EF5341. For
voice and piano.

Na to parōs to koritsi ...
etichoi: K. Nikolaidē, mousikē
Z. Iakōbidē. 3. ekdosis.
Athēnai, Ekdoseis A.
Charikiopoulos, "Melody". ©
S O P E Copyright Protection
Society, Athens; 2Mar47;
EF3769. For voice and piano.

Sphixe me, sphixe me ... etichoi:
M. Margaritē [pseud.], mousike:
Z. Iakōbidē. [Athens]
Gaitanos. © Michael Gaetanos,
Athens; 19Feb47; EF5544. For
voice and piano.

Tha meinō gia panta konta sou
... etichoi: K. Nikolaidē,
mousikē: Z. Iakōbidē.
Athēnai, Ekdoseis A.
Charikiopoulos, "Melody".
© SOPE Copyright Protection
Society, Athens; 2Mar47;
EF3770. For voice and piano.

IAKOBLEPH, NIKOLAOS PETROS, 1909-
Koimēsou mes tēn ankalia mou;
[music by] Nikolaou
Giakobleph, [words by] Kōsta
Kophiniōtē. Athēnai,
Ekdoseis Gaitanou. © Michael
Etienne Gaetanos, Athens;
4Jun45; EF5349. For voice and
piano.

ICE, WILLARD.
Handle with care; words and music
by Willard Ice. © Cine-Mart
Music Publishing Co., Hollywood, Calif.; 1Nov46; EP11481.

IDEN, RAYMOND JOHN, 1890-
Hail to Thee, oh Jesus; [by] Raymond
J. Iden, [words by] C. F. Davidson.
© Cyrenius Franklin Davidson,
Midway, Pa.; 3Jan47; EP11565.
Close score: SATB.

I must walk the way with Jesus;
[by] Raymond J. Iden. Mt. Vernon,
Ohio, Christian Music Pub. Co.
© Raymond John Iden, Mt. Vernon,
Ohio; 5Feb47; EP11920. Close
score: SATB.

In the perfect tomorrow; [words by]
Milda McCroskey, [music by] Ray-
mond J. Iden. [c1946] © Armilda
Margaret (Allgood) McCroskey,
Fairgrove, Mo.; 2Feb47; EP12267.
Close score: SATB.

My mother ... [words by] Alta M.
Brooks, [music by] Raymond J.
Iden. © Alta M. Brooks, Freeland-
ville, Ind.; 24Jan47; EP11673.
Close score: SATB.

ILDA, LEWIS.
May I call you sweetheart? Words
and music by Muriel Watson, Jack
Denby & Lewis Ilda. © Irwin
Dash Music Co., ltd., London;
1Jan47; EF5133. For voice and
piano, with chord symbols; melody
also in tonic sol-fa notation.

INGRAHAM, ROY.
Cuttin' capers on the campus; words
and music by Dave Oppenheim and
Roy Ingraham ... piano arr. by
Dick Kent. © Southern Music
Publishing Co., inc., New York;
20Nov46; EP13770.

IREY, FRANCIS, 1909-
Hallelujah, praise the Lord,
amen! [by] Francis Irey.
(In Church of the Nazarene.
Michigan District. Nazarene
Young Peoples Society.
Choruses of the N.Y.P.S. p.
16) © Michigan District,
Nazarene Young Peoples Society,
Flint, Mich.; 25Jul46; EP13042.
Close score: SATB.

IRONS, EARL D
The elder statesman ... By Earl
D. Irons. © Carl Fischer,
inc., New York; 27Feb47;
EP12430. Condensed score
(band) and parts.

ISAAC, MERLE J
Orchestral exercises ... by
Merle J. Isaac. © Boosey &
Hawkes, inc., New York;
pt.2, 14Mar47; EP12662.
Piano-conductor score and
parts.

ISEL, WILL, 1901-
There I stood (smoking a ciga-
rette; words by Tommy Carey,
music by Will Isel. © Thomas
J. Carey, Bradley Beach, N.
J. (Will Isel, Washington,
D. C.; 20May47; EP14429.

68

[ISRAEL, MARCEL] 1881-
A Bagatelle; paroles de Hubert
Ithier [pseud.], musique de
Learsi [pseud.] © Edition
Selector, Gentilly, France;
15Dec46; EF3515.

A Venise, le soir ... paroles de
Telly [pseud.], musique de Learsi
[pseud.] © Editions Selector,
Gentilly, France; 1Mar47; EF3516.

Un buisson ... un oiseau; paroles
de Vline [pseud.] et Buggy
[pseud.], musique de Learsi
[pseud.] © Edition Selector,
Gentilly, France; 1Mar47;
EF3514.

La fille du Nord; paroles de Hubert
Ithier [pseud.], musique de
Learsi [pseud.] © Edition
Selector, Gentilly, France;
15Dec46; EF3512.

Tout cela n'est rien sans vous;
paroles de Vincent Telly
[pseud.], musique de Learsi
[pseud.] © Salabert, inc.,
New York; 31Jan47; EF3811.

Viens, petite amie ... paroles de
Vline [pseud.] et Buggy [pseud.]
musique de Learsi [pseud.]
© Edition Selector, Gentilly,
France; 15Dec46; EF3475.

IVANOVICI, J
Der chasene waltz. (The wedding
waltz) ... music by Ivanovici,
arr. for voice and piano by
Henry Lefkowitch. New York;
Metro Music. © Henry Lefkowitch,
New York; on arrangement and
words; 28Feb47; EP14187.
Yiddish words (transliterated)

Danube waves; by Jan Ivanovici ...
[words by Elsie-Jean, pseud.]
arr. by Hugo Frey. © Hamilton
S. Gordon, inc., New York; on
arrangement and words; 6Jun47;
EP15065. For piano solo, with
words.

Mother and dad's favorite
wedding songs: Waves of the
Danube [by J. Ivanovici] ...
The golden wedding [by Gabriel-
Marie. Lyrics by Jack Edwards,
arr. by Walter L. Rosemont]
© Edward Music Co., New York;
on new lyrics and arrangements;
4Mar47; EP13308.

Waves of the Danube; by Ivanovici,
piano solo arrangement by John
W. Schaum. © Belwin, inc.,
New York; on arrangement; 29Apr47;
EP14048.

Waves of the Danube; [by] Ivanovici
... simplified arrangement by
Mark Nevin. © Schroeder &
Gunther, inc., Rhinebeck, N. Y.;
on arrangement; 16Jun47; EP6966.

Waves of the Danube; by J.
Ivanovici. For piano solo,
simplified, [arr. by Chester
Wallis, pseud.] © The Boston
Music Co., Boston; on arrange-
ment; 12Mar47; EP12758.

Waves of the Danube; [by] J.
Ivanovici, easy arrangement for
piano ... and all C melody instru-
ments ... by V. P. Frangipane.
© Edward Schuberth & Co., inc.,
New York; 14Apr47; EP13495.

Waves of the Danube ... by I.
Ivanovici, piano accordion
solo ... transcribed by
Michael Edwards. © Mills
Music, inc., New York; on
transcription; 21Apr47;
EP6849.

Waves of the Danube; by J.
Ivanovici, piano solo ed. and
arr. by Leopold W. Rovenger.
© Bourne, inc., New York; on
arrangement; 25Apr47; EP14810.

Waves of the Danube; by Joseph
Ivanovici. Simplified piano
arrangement by Bruce Carleton.
© Theodore Presser Co., Philadelphia; on arrangement;
21May47; EP14694.

Waves of the Danube ... by J.
Ivanovici ... transcribed by
Michael Edwards. © Mills
Music, inc., New York; on
transcription; 21Apr47;
EP6848. Score (clarinet and
piano) and part.

Waves of the Danube ... by J.
Ivanovici ... transcribed by
Michael Edwards. © Mills
Music, inc., New York; on
transcription; 21Apr47;
EP6850. Score (trumpet and
piano) and part.

Waves of the Danube ... by J.
Ivanovici ... transcribed by
Michael Edwards. © Mills
Music, inc., New York; on
transcription; 21Apr47;
EP6851. Score (violin and
piano) and part.

Waves of the Danube ... by J.
Ivanovici ... transcribed by
Michael Edwards. © Mills
Music, inc., New York; on
transcription; 21Apr47;
EP6852. Score (saxophone and
piano) and part.

Waves of the Danube ... by J. Ivan-
ovici ... transcribed by Philip
J. Lang. © Mills Music, inc.,
New York; on arrangement; 3Mar47;
EP6706. Condensed score (band)
and parts.

Waves of the Danube; paraphrase
for piano solo arr. and ed. by
Cromweed, original theme by
Ivanovici. © Axelrod
Publications, inc., Providence;
on arrangement; 20May47;
EP13348.

IVES, DAVID LIVINGSTONE, 1921-
comp.

Singecstasy; gospel songs and choruses,
comp. by David Livingstone Ives.
Archbold, Ohio, The Ives Music
Press.

Specials; gospel solos & duets,
[by Richard E. Gerig, Thomas
O. Chisholm, Harry Dixon Loes
and others], comp. by David
Livingstone Ives and R. Win-
grove Ives. Archbold, Ohio,
Ives Music Press. © David L.
Ives, Archbold, Ohio; 10May47;
EP14350.

J

JACKSON, BULL MOOSE.
I know who threw the whiskey (in
the well); by Bull Moose Jackson.
© Pic Music Corp., Chicago;
12Aug46; EP12040. For voice and
piano, with chord symbols.

JACKSON, CHUBBY. See also
Jackson, Grieg.

Beachcomber; [by] Chubby Jackson.
© Robbins Music Corp., New York;
5Feb47; EP11870. Score: guitar,
bass, drums and piano.

Four men on a horse; music by
Chubby Jackson, arr. by Joe
Bishop. © Charling Music Corp.,
New York; 14Apr47; EP13643.
Piano-conductor score (orchestra)
and parts.

Mino; [by] Chubby Jackson. ©
Robbins Music Corp., New York;
5Feb47; EP11868. Score: guitar,
bass, drums and piano.

Oh! how I love off-beats; [by]
Chubby Jackson. © Robbins Music
Corp., New York; 5Feb47; EP11869.
Score: guitar, bass, drums and
piano.

Scratch sheet; [by] Chubby Jackson.
© Robbins Music Corp., New York;
5Feb47; EP11867. Score: guitar,
bass, drums and piano.

JACKSON, GRIEG. See also
Jackson, Chubby.

[JACKSON, JAMES ALBERT] 1903-
Guide me Lord I pray; [words and
music by A. Jackson, re-arr. by
Jesse Barron] Birmingham, Ala.,
Jackson Music Co. © Albert
Jackson, Birmingham, Ala.;
4May47; EP15070. Close score:
SATB.

JACKSON, LAURETTA MAY, 1906-
By faith; [by] L. M. Jackson.
© Lauretta May Jackson,
Detroit; 22Jan47; EP11503.
For 3 treble voices.

For Jesus spoke peace to my
soul; [by] L. M. Jackson. ©
Lauretta May Jackson (Mrs.
Stirling P.), Detroit;
10May47; EP14329. For 3
treble voices.

He is all the world to me; [by]
L. M. Jackson. © Lauretta
May Jackson, Detroit; 22Jan47;
EP11502. For 3 treble voices.

Take heart, weary soul, take
heart; [by] L. M. Jackson.
© Lauretta May Jackson,
Detroit; 22Jan47; EP11504.
For 3 treble voices.

JACKSON, MYRTLE ETHEL, 1911-
I promised I'd serve Him (going
to keep my word); by Myrtle
Jackson. A Martin arrange-
ment. © Myrtle Jackson,
Chicago; 6May47; EP13021.
For voice and piano.

I'm living by faith and grace ...
words and music by Myrtle Jack-
son, arr. by Jeanette Tall.
Chicago, M. Jackson Studio of
Gospel Music. © Myrtle Jackson,
Chicago; 8Sep46; EP13686.

Oh, yes, I want to make a
soldier ... words and music
by Myrtle Jackson, arr. by
Jeanette Toll. © Myrtle Jackson, Chicago; 25Jul46;
EP14803.

JACKSON, MRS. STIRLING P. See
Jackson, Lauretta May.

JACKSON, T   K
For you; words and music by T. K.
Jackson. © Nordyke Publishing
Co., Los Angeles; 5Mar47;
EP13566.

JACOBI, VICTOR, d. 1921.
(Apple blossoms) You are free;
from "Apple blossoms," by Victor
Jacobi, transcribed by F.
Campbell-Watson. © Harms, inc.,
New York; on arrangement;
30Jan47; EP12024. Piano-
conductor score (orchestra) and
parts.

JACOBS, DICK.
Schumann's concerto march; adapted
from themes from the Concerto in
A minor. Op. 54 ... arr. by
Dick Jacobs. © Bregman, Vocco
and Conn, inc., New York;
29May47; EP14846. Condensed
score (band) and parts.

Waves of the Danube; adapted from
Ivanovici's Waves of the Danube
... arr. by Dick Jacobs.
© Bregman, Vocco and Conn, inc.,
New York; 29May47; EP14845.
Condensed score (band) and parts.

[JACOBS, MILTON]
On the open road; [by] Milton
James [pseud.] © Century Music
Publishing Co., New York;
15Apr47; EP13228. For piano
solo.

[JACOBS, MILTON] arr.
Boogie woogie step-by-step; by
Albert H. Stanley, [pseud.]
© Century Music Publishing Co.,
New York; on arrangement of 6
pieces; 12May47. For piano solo.
Contents.- pt.1. The old gray
mare and Little brown jug
(© EP14267) - pt.2. Auld lang
syne and Good night ladies
(© EP14263)-pt.3. Dark eyes and
Comin' through the rye
(© EP14276) - pt.4. Hand me down
my walkin' cane and She'll be
comin' round the mountain
(© EP14274) -pt.5 Old MacDonald
had a farm (© EP14273) pt.6
Jingle bells.   (© EP14264)

JACOBSON, MAURICE.
Carousal; for pianoforte, [by]
Maurice Jacobson. © Alfred
Lengnick & Co., London;
26Nov46; EF3096.

Suite of four pieces; [by] Maurice
Jacobson. © Augener, ltd.,
London; 26Sep46; EF3103. Score
(violin or flute, violoncello
and piano) and parts for flute
and violoncello.

JACOBUS, DALE ASHER.
Technic teasers; for the piano,
by Dale Asher Jacobus. © G.
Schirmer, inc., New York;
30Dec46; EP11601.

JADASSOHN, S
Scherzo; [by] S. Jadassohn, arr.
by Allanson G. Y. Brown.
© Parnasse Musical, Lachute,
Que., Cnn.; on arrangement;
1May46; EF4852. For organ solo;
includes Hammond organ
registration.

Scherzo in canon form; [by] S.
Jadassohn, [arr. by Vittorio
Giannini] © Harmonia Edition
Publishing Co., New York; on
arrangement; 27Jan47; EP6551.
Score: (string orchestra) and
parts.

JÄRNEFELT, ARMAS.
Berceuse. Cradle song; for chorus
of mixed voices with soprano
solo and piano acc., S.A.T.B.
[By] Armas Järnefelt. Arr. by
Frances Harley in collaboration
with Walter Aschenbrenner.
Text by F. H. © Carl Fischer,
inc., New York; on arrangement;
17May47; EP14723.

JAFFE, CHARLES.
Tea for two; [by] Vincent Youmans,
paraphrased by Charles Jaffe.
© Harms, inc., New York; on
arrangement; 25Mar47; EP13207.
Score (violin and piano) and
part.

JAMES, LANGFORD FRANCIS, 1912-
When elephants roost in bamboo
trees; [words and music by
Langford Francis James, arr. by
Martin Delman] Detroit, Martin
Delman. © L. Francis James &
Martin Delman, Detroit; 30Jun45;
EP13230.

JAMES, MILTON, pseud.   See
Jacobs, Milton.

JAMES, PHILIP.
E. F. G. overture; composed ...
by Philip James. © Leeds Music
Corp., New York; 21Mar47;
EP12858. Condensed score (band)
and parts.

Novellette; (La maison grise) By
Philip James. © H. W. Gray Co.,
inc., New York; 13Jun47; EP15157.
For organ solo.

Our town; suite for piano solo,
by Philip James. © Elkan-
Vogel Co., inc., Philadelphia;
6Feb47; EP13108.

Song of the miners; for chorus of
men's voices, [by] Philip James,
[words by] Brychan B. Powell.
© The H.W. Gray Co., inc., New
York; 11Apr47; EP13627.

JAMES, PHOEBE L   1898-
Accompaniments for rhythmic
expressions; children's music
for children, primary and upper
grades, by Phoebe James. ©
Phoebe James, Pacific Palisades,
Calif.; 1Nov46; EP10762.

JAMES, WILLIS LAURENCE.
Cabin boy call; song for voice
and piano, by Willis Laurence
James. © G. Schirmer, inc.,
New York; 30Dec42; EP13188.

JAMESSON EDITH HATCH. See
Hatch, Edith.

JANÁČEK, LEOŠ, 1854-1928.
Po zarostlém chodníčku; drobné
skladby ... [by] Leoš Janáček,
rev. prof. Frant. Schäfer.
© Hudební Matice Umělecké
Besedy, Praha; rada 2, 11Mar47;
EF4944. For piano solo.

Výlety Páně Brouškovy; opera ...
složil Leoš Janáček, libretto
podle Svatopluka Čecha, první
část napsal V. Dyk, druhou Fr.
S. Procházka; klavírní výtah
pořídil Roman Veselý. Vídeň,
Universální Edici. © Associated
Music Publishers, inc., New
York; 14Oct19; EF3194. Piano-
vocal score.

JANÁČEK, KAREL, 1903-
Duo; [by] Karel Janáček. Op. 19.
© Hudební Matice Umělecké Besedy,
Praha, Czechoslovakia; 8Feb39;
EF4943. Score: violin and viola.

Introdukce a fuga; [by] Karel
Janáček. Op. 22. © Hudební
Matice Umělecké Besedy, Praha,
Czechoslovakia; 31Mar42; EF4945.
For piano solo.

[JANSSENS, HUBERT] 1897-
The Canadian battle march;
accordeon solo, [by] J. Huss-
berg [pseud.] © Prop, Gustave-
Marie-Louis-Norbert, sole
owner of Edition Metropolis,
Antwerp; 6Sep45; EF5571.
Piano-conductor score (orchestra), and parts.

JAPHET, CLIFF.
(I'm gonna) dust off my saddle;
words and music by Cliff Japhet.
© Peer International Corp., New
York; 18Mar47; EP13979.

JARRATT, LOWELL E
Lonesome for you; lyric and music
by Lowell E. Jarratt. © Lowell
E. Jarratt, Music Publisher,
Denver; 19May47; EP14686.

JÁUREGUI, FERNANDO LOYOLA. See
Loyola Jáuregui, Fernando.

JEANES, DOMINIQUE, 1907-
Mon bonheur; paroles de René Hardy,
musique de Dominique Jeanès.
© Smyth, Paris; 12Feb47; EF3518.
For voice and piano, and voice
part.

JEFFERIES, STANTON.
My love for you; song, words by
Jane Renn [pseud.], music by
Stanton Jefferies. © Keith,
Prowse & Co., ltd., London;
29May47; EF3624.

JEFFERSON, ROBERT ALBERT, 1907-
Love goes on through the fall;·
words and music by R. A.
Jefferson. © Robert Albert
Jefferson, Clayton, Mo.;
1Mar47; EP12309.

JEFFRIES, HERB.
All the world is new; words and
music by Charlie Beal and Herb
Jeffries. © Northern Music
Corp., New York; 25Mar47;
EP13202.

JELESNIK, EUGENE.
The Mormon trail; words by Kay
Smith, music by Eugene Jelesnik.
© George F. Briegel, inc., New
York; 21Apr47; EP13993.

JENKINS, JIMMY.
Let's roll out the barrel once
again ... words and music by Jack
Robel and Jimmy Jenkins, arr. by
Jimmy Jenkins. © James E.
J. Robel, © James E. Jenkins,
Pottsville, Pa.; 2Nov46; EP12527.
Piano-conductor score (orchestra)
and parts.

JENSEN, ADOLF.
Murmuring zephyr ... (S.A.T.B.
divided) [words] adapted from
the Spanish, [music by] Adolf
Jensen. Op. 21, no. 4.
Transcribed by William J.
Reddick. © Oliver Ditson Co.,
Philadelphia; on adaptation
and transcription; 16Apr47;
EP14361.

Murmuring zephyrs; [by] Adolf Jensen,
transcribed for piano by Julie
Rive-King, [rev. by Chester Nordman, Rev. ed.] © Shattinger Piano
& Music Co., St. Louis; on revision;
31Dec46; EP11257.

JENSEN, GERTHA.
Longing for you; words and music
by Gertha Jensen. © Nordyke
Publishing Co., Los Angeles;
8Mar47; EP13257.

JEPPERSON, SAM.
Autumn rain; (Indian rain song)
[for] three part women's voices
S.S.A., words by Marguerite
Jepperson and Tom Jepperson,
music by Sam Jepperson. © M.
Witmark & Sons, New York;
23Apr47; EP13947.

JEPPESEN, KNUD, 1892-
Te Deum danicum. Æt dansk Te Deum.
[By] Knud Jeppesen. © Wilhelm
Hansen, Musik-Forlag, Copenhagen;
4Mar46; EF4838. Piano-vocal
score.

JEROME, M   K   1894-
(Love and learn) Would you believe me? From the Warner
Bros. pict. "Love and learn"
lyric by Charles Tobias, music
by M. K. Jerome and Ray Hein-
dorf. © Remick Music Corp.,
New York; 4Mar47; EP12415.

(Nora Prentiss) Who cares what people
say? Music by M. K. Jerome, words
by Jack Scholl. From the picture
"Nora Prentiss." © Harms, inc., New
York; 5Feb47; EP13846.
Who cares what people say? See his
Nora Prentiss.

Would you believe me? See his
Love and learn.

70

JESSE, MARY RUTH, 1895-
Play-easies; by Mary Ruth Jesse.
© Shattinger Piano & Music Co.,
St. Louis; 6May47; EP14230.
For piano solo.

[JESSEL, LEON]
Parade of the wooden soldiers;
[by Leon Jessel] ... Arr. by
Louis Sugarman. © Edward B.
Marks Music Corp., New York;
on arrangement; 17Feb47;
EP12240. For piano solo.

JESUS MORALES, JOSE DE.
Ahora y siempre: Letra y música
de J. de Jesús Morales. © Pro-
motora Hispano Americana de
Música, s.a., México; 22Mar46;
EF5619.

El huérfano. See his Cuando lloran
los valientes.

Lo ves mujer ...letra y música
de José de Jesús Morales. ©
Promotora Hispano Americana
de Música, s.a., México;
30Dec46; EF5454.

No te quiero ver ... [words and
music] de José de J. Morales.
© Promotora Hispano Americana
de Música, s.a., Mexico;
8oct46; EF5535. Piano-conductor score (orchestra), and
parts.

Ya lo ves ... letra, música y
arreglo de José de Jesús Morales.
© Promotora Hispano Americano
de Música, s.a., Mexico, D. F.;
30Dec46; EF4904. Piano-
conductor score (orchestra),
condensed score and parts.

JEVONS, REGINALD, 1901-
School piano class method ... by
Reginald Jevons. Student's book.
© Joseph Williams, ltd., London;
12Feb47; EF4990.

JIMENEZ LOPEZ, RICARDO.
"Las cinco novias" ... letra y
música de Ricardo Jiménez
López, arreglo de Ruben Calzado.
© Peer International Corp.,
New York; 18Dec46; EF5585.
Piano-conductor score (orches-
tra), and parts.

JIRAK, KAREL BOLESLAV, 1901-
(Quartet, strings, no. 5) III.
smyčcový kvartet, [by] K. B.
Jirák. Op. 41, © Hudební
Matice Umelecké Besedy, Praha,
Czechoslovakia; 30Jun42; EF4957.

JIRAK, KAREL BOLESLAV, 1891-
Rok; cyklus 12 písní [by] K. B.
Jirák. Op. 42. Na básně Jaroslava
Seiferta, dvanácti kresbami
doprovází Karel Svolinský. ©
Hudební Matice Umelecké Besedy,
Praha, Czechoslovakia; 11May44;
EF4942. For voice and piano.

Tretti smyčcový kvartet. See his
Quartet, strings, no. 3.

JOHNNY, OLLE.
Anders bilgaspel ... [music] av
Olle Johnny, arr.: Sigurd
Agren. [With words] ©
Skandinaviska Odeon, a.b.,
Stockholm; 1Jan44; EF3767.
Piano-conductor score
(orchestra), and parts.

JOHNS, VARNER JAY, 1890-
Just a few more shadows; [by]
Varner J. Johns. © Varner J.
Johns, Arlington, Calif.;
14Jun47; EP15213. Close score:
SATB.

JOHNSON, ALFRED H
Battle array; (S.A.T.B.) [by]
Alfred H. Johnson, [words by]
Vachel Lindsay. © J. Fischer
& Bro., New York; 27Mar47;
EP6807.

[JOHNSON, CHARLES LESLIE] 1876-
arr.
S. A. R. sonance; song of the Sons
of the American revolution...
words by Edgar Ponder Elzey,
music traditional [German melody,
arr. by Charles L. Johnson]
© Edgar Ponder Elzey, Parkersburg,
W. Va.; on changes in words;
23Sep46; EP13963.

JOHNSON, CLAIR W
Artemis and Orion ... [by] Clair
W. Johnson. © Rubank, inc.,
Chicago; 24May47; EP14776.
Condensed score (band) and
parts.

JOHNSON, CLAIR W   arr.
Eastertide; selection, [arr.
by] Clair W. Johnson. ©
Rubank, inc., Chicago;
15Apr47; EP13221. Condensed
score (band) and parts.

JOHNSON, EDWARD J
The song of you; words and music
by Edward J. Johnson. © Nordyke Publishing Co., Los
Angeles; 28Jan47; EP12719.

JOHNSON, GEORGE A
Modern etudes; for teaching popular music. © Modern Music Studios, Omaha; v. 1, 1Mar46;
EP1814.

JOHNSON, GORDON H
The twin ballots; words by H. S.
Taylor, music by Gordon H.
Johnson, [arr. by B. D. Ackley]
Winona Lake, Ind., Rodeheaver
Hall-Mack Co. © The Rodeheaver
Co., Winona Lake, Ind.; on
arrangement; 7Apr47; EP13884.

JOHNSON, Mrs. H   S   1914-
Worship the Lord; [by] Mrs. H.
S. Johnson, arr by W. M.
Thorne. (In Church of the
Nazarene. Michigan District.
Nazarene Young Peoples Society.
Choruses of the N. Y. P. S.
p.12) © Michigan District,
Nazarene Young Peoples Society,
Flint, Mich.; 25Jul46; EP13038.
Close score: SATB.

JOHNSON, HALL.
I've been 'buked; for four-part
chorus of mixed voices, a cappella.
Negro spiritual, arranged by Hall
Johnson. © G. Schirmer, inc., New
York; 30Dec46; EP11615.

Lord, I want to be a Christian; for
seven-part chorus of mixed
voices with incidental solo
soprano, a cappella. Negro
spiritual, arranged by Hall Johnson. © G. Schirmer, inc., New
York; 30Dec46; EP11619.

Oh Lord, have mercy on me; for nine-
part chorus of mixed voices with
soprano solo, a cappella. Negro
spiritual, arranged by Hall Johnson.
© G. Schirmer, inc., New York;
30Dec46; EP11617.

River chant; for chorus of mixed
voices (divided) with baritone
solo, a cappella; words and
music by Hall Johnson. © Carl
Fischer, inc., New York;
3Mar47; EP12596.

When I was sinkin' down; for four-
part chorus of mixed voices, a
cappella. Old American hymn,
arranged by Hall Johnson. © G.
Schirmer, inc., New York; 30Dec46;
EP11616.

on the dusty road. EP12424.

JOHNSON, J   C   1896-
I wasn't meant for love (love
wasn't meant for me); by J.
C. Johnson. © Jaybille Music
Publishing Co., inc., New
York; 23May47; EP14630. For
voice and piano, with chord
symbols.

JOHNSON, J   ROSAMOND.
Give me a rod, a reel (a boat and a
creel); words by Ernie Ford,
music by J. Rosamond Johnson.
© Oliver Ditson Co., Philadelphia;
6Mar47; EP12592.

Lift ev'ry voice and sing; lyric
by James Weldon Johnson, music
[and arr.] by J. Rosamond
Johnson. © Edward B. Marks
Music Corp., New York; on
arrangement; 15Apr40; EP14490.

JOHNSON, MERRITT.
Technic book, for piano; by Merritt
Johnson. Aberdeen, S. D., College
Book Store. © Merritt Johnson,
Aberdeen, S. D.; 26Dec46; EP10735.

JOHNSON, ODELL.
Echo in the valley; by Odell Johnson. North Hollywood, Calif.,
Husseo Music. © Odell Johnson,
North Hollywood, Calif.;
31Dec46; EP11325. For voice
and piano.

JOHNSON, REGINALD NOEL- See
Noel-Johnson, Reginald.

JOHNSON, THOMAS ARNOLD.
Scherzo for two pianos; by Thomas
Arnold Johnson. © Chappell &
Co., ltd., London; 13Jan47;
EF4992.

JOHNSON, VERDA, 1926-
Jesus keeps me singing; [by]
Verda Johnson, arr. [by] W. M.
Thorne. (In Church of the
Nazarene. Michigan District.
Nazarene Young Peoples Society.
Choruses of the N. Y. P. S.
p.9) © Michigan District,
Nazarene Young Peoples Society,
Flint, Mich.; 25Jul46; EP13035.
Close score: SATB.

JOHNSON, VIRGINIA G   arr.
Carolettes ... traditional Christmas
melodies ... to sing or play,
adapted by Virginia G. Johnson and
Eric Belmont [pseud.] Rev. ed. ©
Shattinger Piano & Music Co., St.
Louis; on additional music;
31Dec46; EP11259.

JOHNSON, WILLIAM, 1912-
Don't you think I ought to know?
Words by Mel Wettergreen, music
by William Johnson. © Fowler
Music Co., New York; 7May47;
EP14208.

JOHNSTON, EDDIE.
My heart-beat put to music (and ev'ry
heart-beat says I love you); words
and music by Ethel M. Herman and
Eddie Johnston. [c1946] © Nordyke
Publishing Co., Los Angeles; 30Jan47;
EP12088.

JOHNSTON, LUCILE MOORE.
That's what the Daughters do;
Daughters of the American
Revolution, words and music
by Lucile Moore Johnston.
© Lucile Moore Johnston,
Thomaston, Ga.; 17Apr47;
EP13669.

JOIO, NORMAN DELLO. See
Dello Joio, Norman.

JOLIVET, ANDRE.
Etude sur des modes antiques;
pour piano, [by] André
Jolivet. Nouv. notation
simplifiée Nicolas Obouhow.
© Durand & Cie., Paris;
15Mar47; EF3654.

JOLSON, AL, 1886-
(The egg and I)" The egg and I ...
From the Universal-International
picture "The egg and I" ... words
and music by Harry Akst, Herman
Ruby, Bert Kalmar [and] Al Jolson.
© Miller Music Corp., New York;
2Jan47; EP11025.
(The Jolson story) Anniversary song
... [from] "The Jolson story" ...
By Al Jolson and Saul Chaplin,
based on a theme by Ivanovici.
[Simplified piano edition arr. by
Lucy-Ann Bryant [pseud.] © Mood
Music Co., inc., New York; on arrange-
ment; 31Mar47; EP13592. For voice and
piano, with chord symbols.

JONES, ALBERT A
Bursting bubbles; (The bubble
queen) [by Albert Jones] ©
Albert A. Jones, Lima, Ohio;
17Apr47; EP13620. For voice and
piano.

JONES, BERTHA VIOLA, 1896-
The fragrant rose; words and
music by Bertha V. Jones.
© Bertha Viola Jones, Santa
Clara, Calif.; 2Feb47;
EP14627.

The fragrant rose; words and
music by Bertha V. Jones. ©
Bertha V. Jones, Santa Clara,
Calif.; 22Apr47; EP6824.

JONES, CHARLES.
(Sonatina, violin & piano)
Sonatina for violin and piano,
by Charles Jones. New York,
Published for the Society for the
Publication of American Music.
26th season, 1944-45) © Charles
Jones, New York; 16Nov46;
EP11614.

JONES, GRANDPA.
Don't sweet talk me; words and
music by "Grandpa" Jones.
© Hill and Range Songs, inc.,
Hollywood, Calif.; 17May47;
EP14579.

Eight more miles to Louisville;
words and music by "Grandpa"
Jones. © Hill and Range
Songs, inc., Hollywood, Calif.;
17May47; EP14583.

Get things ready for me, Ma;
words and music by "Grandpa"
Jones. © Hill and Range Songs,
inc., Hollywood, Calif.;
17May47; EP14689.

JONES, GRIFFITH JOHN, 1875-
Life more abundant; [words by D.
Stratford Scadeng] O Jesus
Christ I come; [words by Mari-
anne Farningham] Duets, by
Griffith J. Jones. Winona Lake,
Ind., Rodeheaver Hall-Mack Co.
© The Rodeheaver Co., Winona
Lake, Ind., 20Jan47; EP11659,
11660.

JONES, HEYWOOD S
Brass on parade ... [By] Heywood
S. Jones. © George F. Briegel,
inc., New York; 24Feb47;
EP12433. Condensed score
(band) and parts.

JONES, ISHAM.
It had to be you; music by Isham
Jones, arr. by Jimmy Dale. ©
Remick Music Corp., New York;
on arrangement; 9May47;
EP14403. Piano-conductor
score (orchestra) and parts.

JONES, J   GRAYSON.
I don't want to remember that night;
words and music by J. Grayson
Jones, [arr. by F. Henri Klickmann]
© J. Grayson Jones Music Co.,
Freeland, Pa.; 15May47; EP6946.

JONES, S   TURNER.
Suite moderne ... by S. Turner
Jones. © Volkwein Bros., inc.,
Pittsburgh; 8Mar47; EP12450.
Score (4 clarinets) and parts.

JONES, SPIKE, 1911-
All hail, Coinegie Tech ... words
and music by Spike Jones, Mickey
Katz [and] Howard Gibeling.
© Novel-Airs, Beverly Hills,
Calif.; 28Jan47; EP11896.

JONES, SPIKE, 1911-   arr.
The Jones laughing record; intro-
ducing the flight of the bumble
bee. Special arrangement by Spike
Jones. © Arenas Stars, inc.,
Beverly Hills, Calif.; 15Jan47;
EP11569.

JONES, W   BRADWEN.
Be present, O merciful God ...
Words from "An order for compline,"
music by W. Bradwen Jones.
© Novello & Co., ltd., London;
15Apr47; EF5525. Score: chorus
(SATB) and piano reduction.

JONES, WILLIE D
Don't let Satan keep you away; by
Willie D. Jones, arrangement by
Livingston's Studio. © Living-
ston's Studio, Baltimore;
26Dec46; EP10727.

JONSSON, JOSEF, 1887-
Tre visor; [by] Josef Jonsson.
Op. 16 ... Till dikter av Emil
Kléen. © Nordiska Musikförlaget,
a/b, Stockholm; on 3 songs;
1Jan20. Contents.- Jungfru
Margits värvisa (© EF3707)- En
visa (© EF3708)- Berceuse
(© EF3709)

JORDAN, ROY.
Svenska flicka. (Swedish girl);
words and music by Roy Jordan.
New York, Capitol Songs, inc.
© Criterion Music Corp., New
York; 15Jun47; EP14985. English
words.

JOY, JEANNE ALDEN.
The river of the water of life;
sacred song, the music by
Jeanne Alden Joy, the words
from the Bible (Rev.22) © R.
D. Row Music Co., Boston;
8May47; EP14812.

JUDE, WILLIAM H   1851-1895.
Jesus calls us ... hymn-anthem for
choir and congregation (S.A.T.B.)
... arr. by W. B. Olds. [Words
by] Cecil F. Alexander. © Hall
& McCreary Co., Chicago; on arrangement; 3Jun46; EP4701.

JUDELL, MAXSON FOXHALL, 1894-
The challenge of U. C. L. A.; words
and music by Maxson F. Judell.
© Maxson F. Judell, Hollywood,
Calif.; 14Dec46; EP10820.

JURGENS, DICK.
Careless ... by Lew Quadling,
Eddy Howard [and] Dick Jurgens;
arr. by Jimmy Dale. © Bourne,
inc., New York; on arrangement;
24Jan47; EP11499. Piano-conductor score (orchestra) and
parts.

K

KAAI, BERNIE KEOKI.
Au-we ... words and music by
Bernie Kaai. Oakland, Calif.,
Golden Gate Publications. ©
Ray Meany, Golden Gate Publica-
tions, Oakland, Calif.; 22Apr47;
EP14121. For voice and 2 guitars;
also diagrams and chord symbols
for ukelele.

KABALEVSKIĬ, DMITRIĬ BORISÓVICH,
1904-
(Preludes, piano) 24 preludes;
for piano [by] Dmitri Kabalevsky. Op.38. [Ed. with special
annotations by Leo Smit]
© Leeds Music Corp., New York;
on foreword and editing;
15May47; EP14417.

24 preludes. See his Preludes,
piano.

Variations; for piano, [Op.40,
by] Dmitri Kabalevsky, [edited
with special annotations by
Joseph Wolman] © Leeds Music
Corp., New York; on editing
and foreword; 14Feb47; EP12179.

KACPRZAK, MATTHEW.
Tears follow my dreams; words and
music by Matthew Kacprzak ...
piano arr. by Dick Kent.
© Peer International Corp.,
New York; 13Dec46; EP13619.

KADISON, PHILIP.
A trout, no doubt; words by
Thomas B. Howell, music by
Philip Kadison. © Mutual
Music Society, inc., New York;
3Apr47; EP13455.

KADOSA, PAUL.
Small pieces for small people ...
Tízenkét kis gyermekdarab; [by]
Paul Kadosa. Op. 35/b. ©
Edition Cserépfalvi, Budapest,
Hungary; 4Feb46; EF3159. For
piano solo.

KAHLER, WILLIAM THADDEUS, 1868-
Let me dream sweet dreams of you;
music by Wm. T. Kahler, lyrics
by Ruby Jane Thomas. Vinita,
Okla., R. J. Thomas. © William
Thaddeus Kahler, Olive View,
Calif.; 28Dec46; EP11758.

Queen of the Osage Hills; lyrics
by Ruby Jane Thomas, music by
W. T. Kahler. Bartlesville,
Okla., R. J. Thomas. © William
Thaddeus Kahler, Olive View,
Calif.; 28Dec46; EP11757.

KAHN, MARVIN.
Modern styles and harmonic construction
for popular piano playing; by Marvin
Kahn. © Mills Music, inc., New
York; 12Mar47; EP6692.

KAISER, JEAN.
Santa drives again; a Christmas
"radio" play with music for
middle and upper grades by Lyla
Waterbury Haynes and Jean Kaiser.
© Row, Peterson & Co., Evanston,
Ill.; 11Nov46; DP1221.

Thanksgiving in the cupboard; a
play with music for middle and
upper grades by Lyla Waterbury
Haynes and Jean Kaiser. © Row,
Peterson & Co., Evanston, Ill.;
11Nov46; DP1222.

KALLSTENIUS, EDVIN, 1881-
Fyra sånger. (Vier Lieder) Av
Edvin Kallstenius. Op. 9.
Översättningar av tonsättaren.
© Nordiska Musikförlaget, a/b,
Stockholm; on 4 songs; 1Jan21;
EF5402-5405. Contents.- No. 1.
Minnas. Gedenken; words by Hed-
vig Lan.- No. 2. Hösbörgningen.
Heuernte; words by Karl Erik
Forsslund.- No. 3. Luise Hensels
barneftonbön. Milde bin ich,
geh zur Ruh; words by Luise
Hensel.- No. 4. Välkommen äter,
snälla sol. Willkommen, liebe
Sonne, Du! Words by August
Strindberg.

KALMAN, EMMERICH. See
Kálmán, Imre.

KÁLMÁN, IMRE, 1882-
(Countess Maritza) Play gypsies,
dance gypsies; from "Countess
Maritza" ... words by Harry B.
Smith, music by Emmerich Kálmán,
a Ken Macomber arrangement.
© Harms, inc., New York; on ar-
rangement; 3Apr47; EP13709.
Piano-conductor score (orchestra,
with words) and parts.
Play gypsies, dance gypsies. See
his Countess Maritza.

KANE, KILROY. See
Kane, Murray.

KANE, MURRAY, 1915-
Kilroy really was here; words and
music by Murray "Kilroy" Kane. ©
Nero Music, inc., New York; 1Feb47;
EP11669.

KAPPELMANN, E   G
Kilbourn centennial greeting ...
Words by Henry Schwab, music by
E. G. Kappelmann, [and Kilbourn
centennial hymn ... Words by
Henry Schwab, arr. by E. G.
Kappelmann] © Kilbourn Lodge
No.3, F. & A. M., Milwaukee;
17Feb44; EP6751-6752. Close
score: SATB.

KARG-ELERT, SIGFRID.
Three musical portrait miniatures
from the romantic school ... by
Sigfrid Karg-Elert, arr. by
Robert Leech Bedell ... [for]
organ solo. © Mills Music, inc.,
New York; on arrangement;
23May47; EP6935.

KARLIN, AARON, 1903-
Gypsy hearts; (based on Karlinsky's
concerto in E minor), arr. the
harmonic way by Aaron Karlin,
[words by Mac Slovis] © Harmonic
Studio of Piano Playing, Brooklyn;
19Feb47; EP12213.

While dancing the dream waltz with
you ... by Aaron Karlin, [words
by Mac Slovis] © Harmonic
Studio of Piano Playing,
Brooklyn; 15Apr47; EP13794.
Contains a version for voice
and piano, preparatory studies
and 2 arrangements for piano
solo.

KARLIN, AARON, 1903-   arr.
Auld lang syne; (arr. three separate
times) Arr. the harmonic way by
Aaron Karlin. © Harmonic Studio
of Piano Playing, Brooklyn; 19Feb47;
EP12214.

KASSCHAU, HOWARD.
Gypsy whirl; piano solo, by Howard
Kasschau. © Schroeder & Gunther,
inc., Rhinebeck, N. Y.; 16Jun47;
EP6965.

KASSEL, ART.
The echo said "no"; words and
music by Art Kassel. ©
Lombardo Music, inc., New York;
28Apr47; EP14099.

KASTRIOTĒS, GIANNĒS MITSOS, 1905-
San to palĕo baiseki; etichoi
Or. Laskou, mousikē Giannē
Kastriotĕ. [Athens] Gaftanos.
© Michael Etienne Gaetanos,
Athens; 26Feb47; EF53546.
For voice and piano.

KATCHKO, ADOLPH.
Five musical settings of Hashkivenu
... for cantor (either tenor or
baritone), mixed choir, with and
without organ accompaniment, by
Rev. Adolph Katchko. New York,
Bloch Publishing Co. © Adolph
Katchko, New York; 17Jan47;
EP6549. Hebrew words (transliter-
ated)

KATRIBANOS, DĒMĒTRIOS KONSTANTINOS,
1904-
Perimenō gramma sou; etichoi-
mousikē M. Katribanou. 2.
ekdosis. Athēnai, Ekdoseis A.
Charikiopoulou, "Melody". ©
"S.O.P.E." Copyright Protection
Society, Athens; 18Nov45;
EF3235. For voice and piano.

KATZ, ERICH, arr.
Recorder consort ... [arr. by]
Erich Katz for a trio of
recorders. © E. C. Schirmer
Music Co., Boston; bk.1, on
arrangement; 3Apr47;
EP13333.

[KATZMAN, HENRY]
The traffic light song; words and
music by Ervin Drake, Jimmy
Shirl [pseud.] and Henry Manners
[pseud.] © Broadcast Music, inc.,
New York; 26Nov46; LP11841.

KAUFMAN, ALVIN S   1910-
Ask anyone who knows; words
and music by Eddie Seiler,
Sol Marcus and Al Kaufman.
© M. Witmark & Sons, New
York; 25Mar47; EP13010.

You can't hide your heart behind a
kiss; by Eddie Seiler, Sol Marcus
[and] Al Kaufman. © George
Simon, inc., New York; 12Mar47;
EP12552. For voice and piano,
with chord symbols.

KAUFMAN, IRVING J.
You fell out of a star; lyric by
Andrew J. Tartaglione, music by
Dr. Irving J. Kaufman [and]
Charles Del Monte. © Leeds
Music Corp., New York; 14Apr47;
EP13741.

KAVANAUGH, RAY MATTHEWS, 1896-
Lynn, Massachusetts, U. S. A.;
lyrics by Lorraine Todd, music
by Ray Kavanaugh. © Ray Kavanaugh, Sunnyside, L. I., N. Y.;
22Mar47; EP12919.

KAY, JULIAN.
The dum dot song (Dye dut da
denny in da dum dot) (I put
a penny in the gum slot); by
Julian Kay. © Sinatra
Songs, inc., New York;
24Feb47; EP12374. For voice
and piano, with chord symbols.

KEARNEY, JAMES, III.
What's needed in love; lyric by
Alexander Lee [pseud.] Music by
James Kearney III. © Broadcast
Music, inc., New York; 9Apr47;
EP15237.

KEATH, ROBERT.
In love; lyrics by Buddy Ebsen,
music by Robert Keath & Griff
Williams. © Buddy Ebsen and
Robert Keath, Chicago; 14Jun46;
EP15139.

KEATING, LAWRENCE.
Travail and triumph; an Easter
cantata for the volunteer choir,
the words written and selected by
C. W. Waggoner, the music by
Lawrence Keating. © Theodore
Presser Co., Philadelphia; 3Jan47;
EP11134.

KEITH, GEORGE D
Scherzo and continuo ... [by]
George D. Keith. © Gamble
Hinged Music Co., Chicago;
28Dec46; EP12312. Score
(flute 1-3) and parts.

KELLAR, BERTHA, 1907-
Jesus has saved me from sin;
[by] Bertha Kellar, arr. by
R. A. Cosselman. (In Church

---

of the Nazarene. Michigan
District. Nazarene Young
Peoples Society. Choruses
of the N. Y. P. S. p.28-29) ©
Michigan District, Nazarene
Young Peoples Society, Flint,
Mich.;25Jul46; EP13055. Close
score: SATB.

KELLER, LUE ALICE.
Hear us, O Father; a prayer, for
four-part chorus of women's
voices with piano or organ
acc., arr. from J. S. Bach's
Prelude no.8 by Lue Alice
Keller, words by Lue Alice
Keller. © The Boston Music
Co., Boston; on arrangement;
27Feb47; EP12383.

KELLETTE, JOHN WILLIAM.
I'm forever blowing bubbles ...
Arranged by Ken Macomber ...
lyric and music by Jaan Kenbrovin
[pseud.] and John William
Kellette. © Remick Music Corp.,
New York; on arrangement;
30Jan47; EP12021. Piano-conductor
score (orchestra, with words)
and parts.

KELLEY, BIRTIE M
Don't steal my kisses and then
skidoo; words & music by Birtie
M. Kelley, arr. by Harold Potter.
© Birtie M. Kelley, Atlanta;
2Jun47; EP15138.

KELLY, CARLOS.
We never mention Aunt Clara;
adapted by Carlos Kelly. ©
Carlos Kelly, c/o Clayton F.
Summy Co., Chicago; on
adaptation; 9Apr47; EP13788.

KELLY, FRANCES.
Can it be true? Words and music
by Frances Kelly. © Master
Melodies Music Publishers, inc.,
Baltimore; 9Apr47; EP13674.

KELLY, NORMAN, 1920-
Day in, day out; lyric by Marie
Blair Collura, music by
Norman Kelly, piano arr. by
Pietro Vargas. © Kelly Music
Publications, Franklin, Pa.;
31Dec46; EP13296.

Golden memories of by-gone
days. [On wings of love I
send a kiss to thee. Welcome
home, soldier] Words by
Hubert S. Covert, music by
Norman Kelly [and Go all the
way with me; words by Oma
Anderson, music by Norman
Kelly] © Kelly Music Publications, Franklin, Pa.; 31Dec46;
EP13300-13303.

Kiss me goodnight, love. [Will
the moon carry the message
of my love for you? The
waltz of the snowflake. Tell
me again (that you love me)]
Words by Hubert S. Covert,
music by Norman Kelly. ©
Kelly Music Publications,
Franklin, Pa.; 31Dec46;
EP13299, 13304-13306.

KEMENY, EGON.
Hókusz-pókusz ... Szenes Iván,
verse, Komény Egon, zenéje
[c1946] © Edition Cscrépfalvi,
Budapest, Hungary; 20Dec45;
EF3158. For voice and piano.

KEMPINSKI, LEO A
Gracious Lord who givest blessing;
(S.A.T.B.) text by Margaret
Bristol, music by Leo A. Kempinski.
© Leeds Music Corp., New York; on
arrangement; 24Jan47; EP11809.

KEMPINSKI, LEO A   Cont'd.
Gracious Lord who givest blessing ... by Leo A. Kempinski, text by Margaret Bristol. © Leeds Music Corp., New York; 31Dec46; EP10843. Piano-conductor score (chorus: SATB and band) and parts for band.

KENBROVIN, JAAN, pseud.
I'm forever blowing bubbles; music by Jaan Kenbrovin [pseud.] and John William Kellette, arr. by Jimmy Dale. © Remick Music Corp., New York; on arrangement; 14May47; EP14713. Piano-conductor score (orchestra) and parts.

KENDIS, JAMES. See Kenbrovin, Jaan, pseud.

KENNAN, KENT.
Night soliloquy ... By Kent Kennan, [arr. by the composer] © Eastman School of Music, Rochester, N. Y.; on arrangement; 17May47; EP14718. Score (flute and piano) and part.

KENNEDY, AL, 1911-
Darling, what shall I do? Words by Sam Mumford, music by Al Kennedy. © Al Kennedy, Barre, Vt.; 1Apr47; EP13092.

I've got stuff. There's a spook in that juke box; music ... by Al Kennedy, [words by] John Kelly and Tracy Hall. © Al Kennedy, Barre, Vt.; 15Apr47; EP14043-14044.

New songs ... Words [by Al Kennedy and Stan Williams] ... music by Al Kennedy. © Al Kennedy, Barre, Vt.; 1Mar47; EP12769-12771. Contents.- Since I've been in love with you.- Femininity (Masculinity)- Ain't got nothin' now.

Quarter of a watermelon; music by Al Kennedy, words ... [by] John Kelly [and] Tracy Hall. © Al Kennedy (Kennedy Music Co.), Barre, Vt.; 24Jun47; EP15215.

KENNEDY, AMANDA.
Star of the sea; [by] Amanda Kennedy ... for piano, arr. and ed. by Maxwell Eckstein. © Carl Fischer, inc., New York; 8May47; EP15021.

KENNEDY, MARGARET.
Good news! [Words and music by] Margaret Kennedy. c1945. (In Beginner teacher. v.17, no.2, p.[3] of cover) © Broadman Press, Nashville; 6Apr47; B5-123.

KENNEY, JACK.
T-E-X-A-S; words and music by Jack Kenney. © Lone Star Music Co., Hollywood, Calif.; 1Jan47; EP6521.

KENNY, JACK.
I'm buildin' a stairway in to Heaven; by Jack Kenny. © Capitol Songs, inc., New York; 8Feb47; EP11964. For voice and piano, with chord symbols.

KENNY, NICK.
Do you love me just as much as ever? Words and music by Nick and Charles Kenny. © Goldmine Music, inc., New York; 9Jan47; EP11137. For voice and piano, with chord symbols.

KENNY, SEAN W   1907-
Killarney and you ... Written and composed by Sean W. Kenny. [c1946] © The D'Olier Music Co., Dublin, Eire; 29Jan47; EP5409. For voice and piano,

KENT, ARTHUR, pseud. See also Kronenberger, Arthur Lawrence.

Upper Fifth Avenue; by Arthur Kent, for piano. © J. J. Robbins & Sons, inc., New York; 16Jun47; EP15214.

KENT, ERWIN.
Cling a little closer; words by Mitchell Parish, music by Erwin Kent, [piano score by Michael Edwards] © Mills Music, inc., New York; 16Apr47; EP6830.

Cling a little closer; words by Mitchell Parish, music by Erwin Kent, arr. by Johnny Warrington. © Mills Music, inc., New York; on arrangement; 23May47; EP6931. Piano-conductor score (orchestra, with words) and parts.

KENT, WALTER.
(Down Missouri way) Just can't get that guy, [from the P.R.C. picture "Down Missouri way"]; lyric by Kim Gannon, music by Walter Kent. © Southern Music Publishing Co., inc., New York; 28Aug46; EP13989.

I'm drownin' in your deep blue eyes; words and music by Ray Gilbert and Walter Kent. © George Simon, inc., New York; 10Apr47; EP13460.

KENTON, STAN.
Artistry in boogie; arr. by Pete Rugolo, composed by Stan Kenton & Pete Rugolo. © Leslie Music Corp., New York; 25Jan47; EP11381. Piano-conductor score (orchestra) and parts.

Fantasy; composed and arr. by Stan Kenton, ed. by Van Alexander. © Leslie Music Corp., New York; 10Feb47; EP11871. Piano-conductor score (orchestra) and parts.

KERLIN, ADELE S
She makes a fuss over me; words and music by Adele S. Kerlin. © Cine-Mart Music Publishing Co., Hollywood, Calif.; 31Dec46; EP14018.

KERN, CARL WILHELM, d. 1945.
Easter triumph. Op. 688. [By] C. W. Kern. © Theodore Presser Co., Philadelphia; 3Jan47; EP11032. For organ solo; includes registration for Hammond organ.

Valse piquante; for the piano [by] Carl Wilhelm Kern. [Op. 725] © Oliver Ditson Co., Philadelphia; 24Feb47; EP12279.

KERN, JEROME, 1885-1945.
Make believe. See his Show boat.

(Show boat) Make believe; [from the musical play "Show boat,"] music by Jerome Kern, words by Oscar Hammerstein 2nd, simplified teaching ed. for piano [arr. by Albert Sirmay]. © T. B. Harms Co., New York; on arrangement; 7Mar47; EP12680.

KERR, HARRISON, 1899-
Four preludes for piano. See his Preludes, piano.

(Preludes, piano) Four preludes ... by Harrison Kerr. © Arrow Music Press, inc., New York; 24Mar47; EP13783.

Symphony no. 1, in one movement; [by] Harrison Kerr. © Arrow Music Press, inc., New York; 15Sep46; EP12223. Score.

KERR, PHILLIP STANLEY, 1906-
There is a way; [and The day is coming; by] Phil Kerr, [words by] Esther V. Peterson. © Esther V. Peterson, Los Angeles; 15Jan47; EP12016-12017. Close score: SATB.

KERR, ROBERT NOLAN.
Tunes for little players; a piano book ... by Robert Nolan Kerr. © Theodore Presser Co., Philadelphia; 3Feb47; EP11685.

KESNAR, MAURITS.
Seven pieces ... [by] Maurits Kesnar. © Gamble Hinged Music Co., Chicago; 5May47; EP14128. Score (violin and piano) and part. Contents.- [v.1] Americana (© EP14126)- [v.2] Evening campfire (© EP14127)- [v.3] Festival frolic (© EP14128)- [v.4] In memoriam (© EP14129)- [v.5] Minuet antique (© EP14130)- [v.6] Puppet dance (© EP14131)- [v.7] Shadow picture (© EP14125)

KESSLER, CLAUDE S   1900-   ed. and comp.
Bassoon passages; ed. and comp. by Claude S. Kessler. © Belwin, inc., New York; on bk. 1-2; 13Mar47; EP12562, 12563.

KESTER, CLARA M
Spring; words and music by Clara M. Kester. © Clara M. Kester, Loto, Mont.; 26Dec46; EP10720.

KETTERER, ELLA.
Let's play; A piano book for young beginners; by Ella Ketterer. © Theodore Presser Co., Philadelphia; 17Mar47; EP12842.

KHATAB-SALIM. See Salim, Khatab.

KILBOURNE, TOMMY.
Don't say goodbye; words by Gordon E. Willey, music by Tommy Kilbourne. © Nordyke Publishing Co., Los Angeles; 18Sep45; EP6508.

KIMBALL, KENNETH VANHOUGHTEN, 1897-
Wanta-wanta; words by Den M. Franklin, music by Ken Kimball. © Benjamin M. Franklin, Boston; 12Feb47; EP12082.

KING, CHARLES E
Aloha serenade; by Chas. E. King. Honolulu; C. E. King. © Charles E. King, Elmhurst, L. I., N. Y.; 9Apr47; EP6901. For voice and piano, with chord symbols; English and Hawaiian words.

Flowers of Hawaii. [Pua carnation] A song ... by Chas. E. King. Honolulu, C. E. King. © Charles E. King, Elmhurst, L. I., N. Y.; 9Apr47; EP6902. English and Hawaiian words.

KING, ERWIN.
I traced her little footprints in the snow ... [words] by Bradley Kincaid and [music by] Erwin King. © Edwards Music Co., New York; on new lyrics & arrangement; 17Mar47; EP13398.

KING, FELIX.
Paddling in the stream; words and music by Howard Barnes & Felix King, [piano score by Kenneth Essex] © Bradbury Wood, ltd., London; 23May47; EP3797.

KING, FRANK. See also King, Pee Wee.

Covered wagon lullaby; words and music by J. L. Frank and Pee Wee King. © Acuff-Rose Publications, Nashville; 4Mar47; EP12325.

KING, FRANK. Cont'd.
I just don't care anymore; words
and music by J. L. Frank and
Pee Wee King. © Acuff-Rose
Publications, Nashville;
4Mar47; EP12423.
Let's both say we're sorry; words
and music by J. L. Frank and
Pee Wee King. ©-Acuff-Rose
Publications, Nashville; 4Mar47;
EP12324.

KING, HOWARD, 1913-
Guaracha; letra de Tony
Martinez, música de Howard
King. © Howard King,
North Hollywood, Calif.;
20Jan47; EP12891.

KING, IRVING, pseud. See
Campbell, James.

KING, JAN, pseud. See
Grenfell, Joyce.

KING, LAWRENCE, 1889-
Girl with the advertising smile;
words by Jeners S. Johnson and
Ben Neff, music by Lawrence
King, arr. by Will Livernash.
© Jeners S. Johnson, Los Angeles;
27Mar47; EP13330.
Race track blues; [words] by Jeners
Johnson, [music by Lawrence King]
© Jeners S. Johnson, Los Angeles;
14Dec46; EP12061.
When I dream I'm in your arms;
words by Macie Verity Ballard,
music by Lawrence King. ©
Art Music Co., New York;
1Apr47; EP13148.

KING, LOTUS RAY.
Astrea dear; words and music by
Lotus Ray King, arr. by
Frederick Landwehr. © Saint
Germain Press, inc., Chicago;
2Apr47; EP13596.

KING, MARJORIE KELLY, comp.
Music tablet ... rudiments of music
and transposition, comp. by Mar-
jorie Kelly King. © Marjorie
Kelly King, Wichita, Kan.; 30Dec46;
EP11075.

KING, PEE WEE. See also
King, Frank.
Southland polka; by Redd Steward
and Pee Wee King. © Acuff-Rose
Publications, Nashville; 19May47;
EP14537. For voice and piano,
with guitar diagrams and chord
symbols.

KING, SIDNEY.
Jolie blonde. (Pretty blonde);
by Sammy Gallop [and] Sid King.
© Leeds Music Corp., New York;
14Feb47; EP12181. For voice
and piano, with chord symbols;
English words.

KING, STANFORD.
Junior Miss plays the piano; pieces
a modern girl will like, by Stanford
King. © Mills Music, inc., New
York; 20Jan47; EP6498.
Junior Mister plays the piano;
pieces a modern boy will like, by
Stanford King. © Mills Music,
inc., New York; 20Jan47; EP6499.
Put your little foot. La varsov-
iana. Piano solo by Stanford
King. © Mills Music, inc.,
New York; on arrangement;
16Apr47; EP6834.
Spring holiday; by Stanford King,
piano solo. © Theodore Presser
Co., Philadelphia; 16Apr47;
EP13893.

KINGSBURY, EDDIE W
When love comes stealing; words
and music by Eddie W. Kings-
bury. © Eddie W. Kingsbury,
Auburn, Wash.; 1May47;
EP14513.

KINKADE, ARLIE.
Visions of mother; words by Babe
Proctor, music by Arlie
Kinkade, arr. by Carl Heide-
mann. © Arlie Kinkade, Can-
ton, Ohio; 1Jun47; EP6864.

KISTLER, DEWEY E   1897-
Day dream; words, music and arrange-
ment by Dewey E. Kistler. © Dewey
E. Kistler, Gary, Ind.; 23Jan47;
EP11674. Close score: TTBB.

[KLAVARSKRIBO INSTITUTE, KINGSTON,
MASS.]
Music book [for] correspondence
course for piano. © Klavarskribo
Slikkerveer, Holland; v.1,
2Jun47; 1c 28Feb47; AI-757.
Vol.1, by Cornelis Pot.

KLEIN, JOHN, 1915-
Breath of heather; for piano,
[by] John Klein. © Oliver
Ditson Co., Philadelphia;
12Mar47; EP12844.
The maxims of Solomon; for four-
part chorus of mixed voices a
cappella, words from Pro-
verbs chap.25, music by John
Klein. © The Boston Music
Company, Boston; 27Feb47;
EP12384.
Sonnet to the sea; [by] John
Klein, [words by] Joanne
Hislop. (Contemporary
American songs for medium
voice and organ, 3d ser.)
© Associated Music Publishers,
inc., New York; 3Mar47;
EP12840.
To evening; [by] John Klein,
[words by] Joanne Hislop.
(Contemporary American songs
for medium voice and organ,
3d ser.) © Associated Music
Publishers, inc., New York;
3Mar47; EP12841.

KLEINSINGER, GEORGE.
Pee-Wee, the piccolo; for narrator
and piano. Words by Paul Tripp,
music by George Kleinsinger.
New York, Sole selling agents;
G. Schirmer, inc. © George Kleinsinger and Paul Tripp, New York;
15Jan47; EP11618.

KLEMANS, TED ADAM, 1905-
I'm waiting for April; words and
music by Ted Klemans, [arr. by
Dave Kaplan] © Ted Klemans,
Clifton, N. J.; 1May47; EP14540.
Sweet, sweet Daisy; words and
music by Ted Klemans. ©
Ted Klemans, Clifton, N. J.;
5Jan47; EP11744.

KLENAU, PAUL VON, 1883-1946.
Paolo and Francesca; aus Dante;
Divina comedia. Inferno. V.
Gesang. Symphonische Dichtung
für grosses Orchester von Paul
v. Klenau. Wien, Universal-
Edition. © Associated Music
Publishers, inc., New York;
1Jan19; EP4798.

KLERK, ALBERT DE. See also
Klerk, Josef Albert de.
Klerk, Albert Jozef de.
Sarabande en Sicilienne; voor
fluit en hobo, [by] Albert de
Klerk. © Edition Heuwekemeyer
(Firm A. J. Heuwekemeyer & B.
F. van Gaal), Amsterdam, the
Netherlands; 31May46; EF5152.

KLERK, ALBERT JOZEF DE.   See also
Klerk, Albert de.
Klerk, Josef Albert de.

KLERK, ALBERT JOZEF DE, 1917-
Tien orgelwerken; [by] Albert de
Klerk. [c1946] © Edition
Heuwekemeijer (Firm Heuwekemeijor
& van Gaal), Amsterdam; deel 1,
26Mar47; EF3343. Contents.-
deel 1. No. 1-5.

KLERK, JOSEF ALBERT DE, 1917-
Élegie ... [by] Albert de Klerk.
© Edition Heuwekemeyer (Firm
A. J. Heuwekemeyer & B. F. van
Gaal), Amsterdam, The Nether-
lands; 24Jul43; EF5106. Score
(violin and piano) and part.

KLERK, JOZEF ALBERT DE. See
Klerk, Albert de.

KLERK, JOSEF ALBERT DE. See also
Klerk, Albert Jozef de.
Klerk, Albert de.

[KLICKMANN, F   HENRI] ed.
E Z favorite (Bb tenor) saxophone
solos; with piano acc. © Wm. J.
Smith Music Co., inc., New York;
2May46; EP3507. Score and part.
E Z favorite (Eb alto) saxophone
solos; with piano acc. © Wm. J.
Smith Music Co., inc., New York;
2May46; EP3508. Score and part.
E Z favorite trumpet solos; with
piano acc. © Wm. J. Smith Music Co., inc., New York; 2May46;
EP3506. Score and part.

[KLINGSTEDT, PAUL THEODORE] 1890-
Alma mater hymn; Oklahoma A. and M.
college [by Paul T. Klingstedt]
© Paul T. Klingstedt, Stillwater,
Okla.; 15Oct46; EP12748.

KLOSE, FRIEDRICH, 1862-1942.
Fünf Gesänge ... Von Friedrich
Klose. Gedichte von Giordano
Bruno. Wien, Universal-Edition
A.-G. © Associated Music Pub-
lishers, inc., New York; 1Apr19;
EF5307. For voice and piano.

KLOSE, H
Celebrated method for the clarinet;
[by] H. Klosé, rev. and enl.
by Simeon Bellison. c1946.
© Carl Fischer, inc., New
York; on additional material
in v.1-2, 2Jan47, 26Dec46;
EP11661, 1128.

KLUMPKEY, JULIA, 1877-
"Among the things"; song ... by
Julia Klumpkey. © Wesley
Webster, San Francisco; 5Jun47;
EP14913.
I sent my love; words by Constance
Grovenor Alexander, music by
Julia Klumpkey. © Wesley Webster,
San Francisco; 24Dec46; EP10784.
Prayer ... words by Margaret
Herrick, music by Julia Klump-
key. © Wesley Webster, San
Francisco; 5Jun47; EP14911.
Two songs by Julia Klumpkey;
words by Henry Wadsworth Long-
fellow. 1. Ships that pass in
the night. 2. The tide rises,
the tide falls. © Wesley
Webster, San Francisco; 5Jun47;
Ep14914.

KLUSE, FRANCES LOVINA, 1889-
Popular piano; introductions,
breaks, endings; written ...
by Frances Lovina Kluse.
© Frances Lovina Kluse, Alta-
dena, Calif.; 23Dec46; EP10855.

KNECHT, JUSTIN H   1752-1817.
O Jesus, Thou art standing ...
hymn-anthem for choir and congregation (S.A.T.B.) ... arr.
by W. B. Olds. [Words by] William Walsham How. © Hall &
McCreary Co., Chicago; on
arrangement; 4Jun46; EP4703.

KNIGHT, GEORGE H   1905-
Carmen Ludi Qualicani; song of
Qualicum Beach School, Van-
couver Island, B.C., Canada.
Words and music by Geo. H.
Knight. © George H. Knight,
Qualicum Beach, V.I., B.C.,
Can.; 18Feb47; EF5246.

KNIGHT, JIMMY DE. See
DeKnight, Jimmy.

KNUTSON, TRACY.
I'm goin' home where I belong;
by Tracy Knutson. © Tracy
Knutson, Roseland, Neb.; 26Dec46;
EP10725. For voice and piano.

I'm not the reason why girls leave
home; by Tracy Knutson. ©
Tracy Knutson, Roseland, Neb.;
26Dec46; EP10729. For voice
and piano.

KOCH, FREDA POSTLE, 1915-
Making habits' fun; a story with
songs to help parents teach
little tots ... words and music
by Freda Postle Koch, acc. by
Rodger Borror. © Freda Postle
Koch, Worthington, Ohio; on
changes in 5 songs; 5Jun47;
EP14899.

KOCH, SIGURD VON, 1879-1919.
Morgenländische Liebeslieder; [by]
Sigurd v. Koch, (words by] Hans
Bethge, nach chinesischen Dich-
tern) Österländska kärleks-
sanger [tr. by Ragnar von Koch]
© Nordiska Musikförlaget, a/b,
Stockholm; on 4 songs; 1Jan20.
Contents.- Auf dem Flusse. På
floden. (Thu-Fu) © EF3703) Am
Teefeld. På tefältet. (Schei-
Min) © EF3704) Das Blatt der
Frühlingsweide. Videbladet om
våren. (Tschan-Tiu-Lin) (©
EF3705) Liebeslied. Kärleks-
visa. (Schei-Min) (© EF3706)

Die wilden Schwäne; [by] Sigurd v.
Koch, [German words by Hans
Bethge, Swedish translation by
Ragnar von Koch] © Nordiska
Musikförlaget, a/b, Stockholm;
on 3 songs; 1Jul19. Contents.-
Der Frühlingsregen. Varnatts-
regnet. (Thu-Fu) (© EF3686)
Das Los des Menschen. Mänskans
lott. (Khong-Fu-Tse) (© EF3687)
Die wilden Schwäne. De vilda
svanarna. (Ly-y-Han) (© EF3688)

KODÁLY, ZOLTÁN, 1882-
Gyermektáncok. Children's dances.
Piano solo, [by] Zoltán Kodály.
London, Boosey & Hawkes. ©
Hawkes & Son (London), ltd.,
London; 29May47; EF3418.

... Missa brevis; [for] mixed
chorus and organ [by] Zoltán
Kodály. © Boosey & Hawkes,
inc., New York; 14Mar47;
EP12663.

KOEHLER, C   FRANZ.
The goldfish pool; piano solo,
by C. Franz Koehler. ©
The Willis Music Co.,
Cincinnati; 11Mar47; EP12837.

KOEPKE, PAUL.
Vignette ... [by] Paul Koepke.
© Theodore Presser Company,
Philadelphia; 17May47; EP14609.
For organ solo; includes regis-
tration for Hammond organ.

KOKI, SAM.
Ka nalu. (The waves) Lyric by
Ted Matheson, music by Sam Koki,
arr. by [Betty Glynn of] the
Oahu staff. (Oahu advanced harmony note course for Hawaiian
and electric guitar, [lesson
44PT]) © Oahu Publishing Co.,
Cleveland; on arrangement;
4Mar47; EP6879. For voice and
guitar. Includes lesson on
sixth chords.

KOMST, MARINUS JOHANNES, 1908-
Dix études brillantes; pour
trompette, cornet à pistons ou
bugle, [by] Marinus Komst. ©
Edition Heuwekemeyer (Firm A.
J. Heuwekemeyer & B. F. van
Gaal), Amsterdam, The Nether-
lands; 1Dec45; EF5151.

Flying notes ... [by] Marinus
Komst. © Edition Heuwekemeyer
(Firm A. J. Heuwekemeyer & B. F.
van Gaal), Amsterdam, The
Netherlands; 1Mar41; EF5150.
Score (trumpet or cornet and
piano) and part.

Hurry, hurry ... [by] Marinus
Komst. © Edition Heuwekemeyer
(Firm A. J. Heuwekemeyer & B. F.
van Gaal), Amsterdam, The Netherlands; 1Mar41; EF5149. Score
(trumpet or cornet and piano)
and part.

[KONSTANTINIDES, GIANNES GEORGIOS]
1900-
Etsi ein' ē zoē ... etichoi: D.
Euangelidē, mousikē Kosta
Giannidē [pseud.] athēnai,
Ekdoseis G. Konstantinidē. ©
"S.O.P.E." Copyright Protection
Society, Athens; 4Mar43; EF3232.
For voice and piano.

KOPPEL, HERMAN D
(Ditte Menneskebarn) Spindevise,
fra ... Ditte Menneskebarn.
[Words by Martin Andersen Nexø,
music by] Herman D. Koppel.
[c1947] © Wilhelm Hansen,
Musik-Forlag, Copenhagen;
22Dec46; EF3438.

Spindevise. See his Ditte
Menneskebarn.

KOPYLOV, ALEXANDER.
God is a Spirit; for four-part
chorus of men's voices (a
cappella) [by] Alexander
Kopylov ... [words from] St.
John, 4:24, adapted by V.o.O.T.,
arr. by Gwynn S. Bement. © M.
C. Schirmer Music Co.; Boston;
on arrangement; 22Apr47;
EP15853.

KORB, ARTHUR, 1909-
It takes time; by Arthur Korb.
© London Music Corp., New York;
5Feb47; EP11675. For voice and
piano, with chord symbols.

KORNAUTH, EGON, 1891-
Klarinettenquintett. See his
Quintet, clarinet & strings.

(Quintet, clarinet & strings)
Klarinettenquintett; [by] Egon
Kornauth. Op. 33. © Ludwig
Doblinger (Bernhard Herz-
mansky), K. G., Vienna;
26Mar41; EF3319. Miniature
score.

(Quintet, clarinet & strings)
Klarinettenquintett, für Klari-
nette, 2 Violinen, Bratsche
und Cello, [by] Egon Kornauth
... Op. 33. © Ludwig Doblin-
ger (Bernhard Herzmansky), K.
G., Vienna; 26Mar41; EF3320.
Parts.

KOSLOF, ABRAHAM TED. See
Koslof, Ted.

KOSLOF, TED, 1914-
Chew chaw chaw; by Phil Cohen,
Robert Hyman [and] Ted Koslof
... arr. by Lou Halmy. ©
Boll Song Publishing Co., Holly-
wood, Calif.; 8Jan47; EP10930.
For voice and piano, with chord
symbols.

KOSMA, JOSEPH, 1905-
Chanson des enfants; paroles de
Jacques Prévort, musique de
Joseph Kosma. © Salabert,
inc., New York;
31Jul46; EF4849. For voice and
piano.

Les feuilles mortes; paroles de
Jacques Prévort, musique de
Joseph Kosma. © Enoch & Cie.,
Paris; 3Feb47; EF4891. For
voice and piano.

Les portes de la nuit; [music by]
Joseph Kosma. © Enoch & Cie.,
Paris; 28Mar47; EF5319. For
piano solo.

KOŠŤÁL, ERNO, 1889-
Pohádka o popolce ... Opus 242.
Slova: V. V. Paleček, grafická
výzdoba: Věra Korecká, [music
by] Erno Košťál. © Karel
Barvitius, Praha, Czechoslovakia; 23Apr42; EF5366. For piano
solo, with words.

Zoologická zahrádka; [music by]
Erno Košťál ... Opus 237.
Slova a grafická výzdoba: F. V.
Voborský. © Karel Barvitius,
Praha, Czechoslovakia; 30May42;
EF5367. For piano solo, with
words.

KOUNTZ, RICHARD.
The Lord is great in Zion; anthem
for chorus of mixed voices, with
tenor solo and soprano and alto
duet] [Words from] psalms 97,
v19 [and] 99; verses 2,3,5, [music
by] Richard Kountz. © Galaxy
Music Corporation, New York;
19May47; EP6911.

KOUTZEN, BORIS, 1901-
Concert piece (for 'cello solo
and string orchestra) [by]
Boris Koutzen. © Elkan-Vogel
Co., inc., Philadelphia;
3Dec46; EP11448.

Concert piece for 'cello solo
and string orchestra; [by]
Boris Koutzen, [piano
accompaniment arr. by Boris
Koutzen] © Elkan-Vogel Co.,
inc., Philadelphia; on piano
accompaniment; 24Dec46;
EP12192. Score (violoncello
and piano) and part.

Valley Forge; [by] Boris Koutzen.
© American Music Center, inc.,
New York; 8Oct46; EP13100.
Score: orchestra.

KOVAŘOVIC, KAREL, 1862-1920.
Havířská polka; slova: Fr. Kudrna,
[music by] Karel Kovařovic.
© Mojmir Urbánek, Praha,
Czechoslovakia; 8Jul42;
EF3365. For voice and piano.

KRAFT, ALVAR.
För gamla Sveriges väl. See his
Kalle på Spången.

Från "Blyge Anton" till "En sjöman
till häst" ... musik: Alvar
Kraft. © Sylvain Edition a/b,
Stockholm; on 5 songs, 1Jan41.
Contents.- Vid brasan, from
Blyge Anton (Ch. Henry, pseud.)
(© EF3426)- Av sitt värdegrenhet,
from Blyge Anton (Alvar Kraft]
(© EF3427)- När jag ser dig så
ser jag våren; words and music
by Alvar Kraft and Sven Goon,
pseud.; from Blyge Anton
(© EF3428)-

KRAFT, ALVAR. Cont'd.

Alla m' vi sjöman på livets
stora hav, from En sjöman till
hämt (Ch. Henry) (© EF5429)-
Hembygd du rika, from En sjöman
till hämt (A. Richter) (© EF5430)
Det går ett tåg mot drömmens land.
See his Stinsen på Lyckås.

Den glada skräddaren ... Musik:
Alvar Kraft, text: Ch. Henry
[pseud.] (© Edition Sylvain
a/b, Stockholm; on 4 songs;
1Jan45. Contents.- [v.1]
Vända och sy om (© EF5029)-
Du kan drömma om allt (© EF5030)-
[v.2] Lite hit, lite dit
(© EF5027)- När som jägarn går
på jakt (© EF5028)

Jag har bott vid en landsväg i
hela mitt liv. See his Kalle
på spången.

(Kalle pa Spången) För gamla
Sveriges väl ... ur Edvard Persson-
filmen "Kalle pa Spången"; ord av
Ch. Henry [pseud.], musik av Alvar
Kraft. © Carl Uchrmans Musikförlag,
a/b, Stockholm; 1Jan39; EF4829.
For voice and piano.

Klockorna i Gamla stan ... I vårens
första natt ... Musik: Alvar
Kraft, text: Nils Hellström.
© Edition Sylvain a/b, Stockholm;
1Jan46; EF5037.

Klockorna i Gamla stan ... Klockorna
i Gamla stan; musik: Alvar Kraft,
text: Ch. Henry [pseud.]
© Edition Sylvain a/b, Stockholm;
1Jan46; EF5036.

Klockorna i Gamla stan ... När
livet var ungt; musik: Alvar
Kraft, text: K. G. Ossiannilsson.
© Edition Sylvain a/b, Stockholm; 1Jan46; EF5035.

Livet på landet; musik: Alvar
Kraft, sångtexter: Gabriel
Jönsson. © Edition Sylvain
a/b, Stockholm; on 4 songs;
1Jan43; EF5038-5041. Contents.-
Välkomstvisa.- Det gamla
trädet.- Julvisa.- Dryckesvisa.

När seklet var ungt ... musik:
Alvar Kraft. © Edition Sylvain
a/b, Stockholm; 1Jan44; EF5024-
5026. For voice and piano,
with chord symbols. Contents.-
Kvarnen; text: K. G. Ossiannilsson.- När seklet var ungt; text:
K. G. Ossiannilsson.- Ett hem;
text: Berco [pseud.]

När livet var ungt. See his
Klockorna i Gamla stan.

(Stinsen på Lyckås) Det går ett
tåg mot drömmens land ... text:
Nils-Georg [pseud.], musik:
Alvar Kraft, arr.: Miff Görling.
[From the film, Stinsen på
Lyckås] © Nils-Georgs Musik-
förlag, a/b, Stockholm; on
arrangement; 1Jan43; EF5423.
Piano-conductor score (orchestra,
with words) and parts.

(Stinsen på Lyckås) Det går ett
tåg mot drömmens land ... ur
filmen "Stinsen på Lyckås"; text:
Nils-Georg [pseud.], musik: Alvar
Kraft. © Nils-Georgs Musikförlag,
a/b, Stockholm; 1Jan42; EF4828.

(Stinsen på Lyckås) Stinsvisan,
ur "Stinsen på Lyckås"; text:
Sven Gustafson, musik: Alvar
Kraft. © Nils-Georgs Musikför-
lag, a/b, Stockholm; 1Jan42;
EF5425.

Stinsvisan. See his Stinsen på
Lyckås.

Tre sma ord ... Text: S. S.
Wilson [pseud.], musik: Alvar
Kraft. © Edition Sylvain a/b,
Stockholm; 1Jan42; EF5034.
Vid brasan. See his Blyge Anton.

KRAMER, ALEX C 1914-
Ain't nobody here but us chickens;
words and music by Joan Whitney
[pseud., band] Alex Kramer. ©
Sun Music Co., inc., New York;
2Jan47; EP11027.

Ain't nobody here but us chickens;
words and music by Joan Whitney
and Alex Kramer, arr. by Johnny
Warrington. Chicago, Pic
Music Corp. © Sun Music Co.,
New York; on arrangement;
1Apr47; EP14807. Piano-conductor score (orchestra, with
words) and parts.

My dearest Uncle Sam ... By
Joan Whitney [and] Alex C.
Kramer, New York, Leeds
Music Corp. © Sun Music
Co., inc., New York; 21Mar47;
EP12863. For voice and
piano, with chord symbols.

Two weeks with pay; by Joan Whitney and Alex Kramer. © Beaux-
Arts Music, inc., New York;
7April7; EP13434. For voice and
piano, with chord symbols.

KRAMER, SID, 1911-
Funny what love can do; words &
music by Lee Crane & Sid Kramer.
© Crane Music, inc., New York;
4Sep46; EP12266.

KRAMER, WILLIAM CHARLES, 1898-
I know I can't forget you; words
and music by William C. Kramer.
[c1946] © William Charles
Kramer, Philadelphia; 16Jan47;
EP12191.

[KRANCHER, WILLY CARL] 1900-
Schenk mir dein Herz ... Worte:
John Ernie [pseud.], Musik:
Peter Fitt [pseud.] © Albert
Lüthold, Musikverlag "Arpeggio,"
Zürich, Switzerland; 6Mar46;
EF5338. For voice and piano;
part for accordion (or violin)
laid in.

KRANZ, JULIUS.
Valse piquante; [by] Julius
Kranz. © Theodore Presser
Co., Philadelphia; 17May47;
EP14606. Score (violin and
piano) and part.

KRAWITZ, ELFRED HARRIS.
Twilight memories; lyrics by John
Sutor and Loah Kale, music by E.
Harris Krawitz. [c1946] ©
Superior Melodies Pub. Co.,
Chicago; 10Jan47; EP11670.

KREAGER, JAMES S
Jitterbug jazz; words and
music by James Kreager.
© Nordyke Publishing Co.,
Los Angeles; 5Mar47; EP13284.

KREGAL, MAURICE.
I'll never fall in love anymore;
words and music by Ray Langham
and Maurice Kregal ... Piano arr.
by Dick Kent. © Peer International Corp., New York; 20Nov46;
EP11172. For voice and piano, with
chord symbols.

KREJČÍ, MIROSLAV, 1891-
Kvintet, B dur. See his Quintet,
strings.

(Quintet, strings) Kvintet, B dur
... pro dvoje housle, dve violy
a violoncello. [by] Miroslav
Krejčí. Op. 15. © Hudební
Matice Umělecké Besedy, Praha,
Czechoslovakia; 8Dec44; EF4961.

(Sonata, viola & piano)
Sonata, cis moll, [by]
Miroslav Krejčí. Op. 57.
© Hudební Matice Umělecké
Besedy, Praha, Czechoslovakia;
18Sep44; EF4970. Score and
part.

KRENZ, WILLIAM.
I bow my head in silent prayer;
words and music by Don McNeill,
Samuel Gallop [and] William
Krenz. [Arranged by Robbins
Music Corp. Rev. ed.] ©
Robbins Music Corp., New York;
on arrangement; 5Dec46; EP11168.
For voice and piano.

KRESA, HELMY.
Be the good Lord willing; lyric by
Bissell Palmer, music by Helmy
Kresa. © Bregman, Vocco & Conn,
inc., New York; 23Jan47; EP11658.

KRESS, CARL.
There's a train out for dreamland;
words by Fred Heider, music by
Carl Kress. © Regent Music
Corp., New York; 8Apr47;
EP13454.

KREUTZ, ARTHUR, 1906-
Symphonic blues ... [By] Arthur
Kreutz; arr. by the composer.
© Broadcast Music, inc., New
York; 15May47; EP15236. Piano-
conductor score (orchestra)
and parts.

KŘIČKA, JAROSLAV, 1882-
Druhý smyčcový kvartet. See his
Quartet, strings, no. 2.

(Quartet, strings, no. 2) II.
smyčcový kvartet, e-moll;
[by] Jaroslav Křička. Op. 70.
© Hudební Matice Umělecké
Besedy, Praha, Czechoslovakia;
13Nov42; EF4960.

(Sonata, violin & piano) Sonata,
E moll ... [by] Jaroslav Křička.
Op.40. Revidoval Stan. Novák
a Karel Solc. © Hudební Matice
Umělecké Besedy, Praha, Czechoslovakia; 1Jun42; EF4973. Score
and part.

KRIETEMEYER, EDWARD WILLIAM, 1913-
Aloha lani; Hawaiian song, arr. and
composed by Eddie Krietemeyer. ©
Eddie Krietemeyer Publications,
Evansville, Ind.; 2Dec46;
EP10761. Score: 3 Hawaiian
guitars.

Rudiments of music; [for] Hawaiian
steel guitar. © Eddie Krietemeyer
Publications, Evansville, Ind.;
on 3 pieces; 12Dec46. Contents.-
[v.1] Lessons 1 and 2 (© EP11282)-
[v.2] Lesson 3 (© EP11281)-
[v.3] Lesson 4 and 5 (© EP11280)

KROEPFL, WALTER JOHN, 1914-
Concert waltz ... [by] Walter J.
Kroepfl. © Walter J. Kroepfl,
St. Paul; 1Jan47; EP11152. For
piano solo.

KROEPSCH, FRITZ.
416 progressive daily studies for
the clarinet; [by] F. Kroepsch,
rev. by Simeon Bellison.
© Carl Fischer, inc., New York;
on revision & phrasing in bk.
1-2; 27Dec46; EP11132, 11131.

KROLL, BOBBY.
Joseph in his brudders; by Barbara Belle, Louis Armstrong
[and] Bobby Kroll. © International Music, inc., New
York; 15Mar47; EP12661. For
voice and piano, with chord
symbols.

KROMNOW, AXEL.
En kväll i april; text:
Cepcan [pseud.], musik: Sam
Croner [pseud.] © Nordiska
Musikförlaget, a.b., Stock-
holm; 1Jan46; EF3754.

KRONE, BEATRICE PERHAM, 1901-
The happy peasant girl; [for] S.S.A.
Roumanian folk song, arranged by
the Krones, Beatrice and Max, [tr.
by B. P. K.] © Belwin, inc., New
York; on arrangement; 13Feb47;
EP12073.

The happy peasant girl; S.A.B.,
Roumanian folk song, arr. by
the Krones, Beatrice and Max.
© Belwin, inc., New York; on
arrangement; 3Apr47; EP13197.

My true love. La hilacha nueva
and La alegria. S.A.B., Roumanian folk songs, text and arr.
by the Krones, Beatrice and Max.
Chicago, N. A. Kjos Music Co.
© Max & Beatrice Krone, Los
Angeles; on arrangement & text;
19Jun47; EP15191. English
words.

KRONE, BEATRICE PERHAM, 1901-   arr.
My love is o'er the sea; S. A. T. B.
Scottish folk song, arr. by the
Krones, Beatrice and Max. © Belwin,
inc., New York; on arrangement;
21Jan47; EP11358.

My love is o'er the sea; S. S. A.
Scottish folk song, arr. by the
Krones, Beatrice and Max.
© Belwin, inc., New York; on ar-
rangement; 21Jan47; EP11359.

A world in tune; [arr. by
Beatrice and Max Krone]
Chicago, N. A. Kjos Music Co.
© Max & Beatrice Krone, Los
Angeles; on arrangement,
English texts & translations
of explanations in bk.5;
25Feb47. For 2-3 voices and
piano. Contents.- book V.
Folksongs of Brazil; arr. by
José Vieira Brandão, with
English texts and translations
of explanations by Max and
Beatrice Krone (© EP13803)

KRONENBERGER, ARTHUR LAWRENCE. See also
Kent, Arthur, pseud.
You never miss the water till
the well runs dry; music by
Arthur Kent, [pseud.] words
by Paul Secon. © United
Music Corp., New York;
22Mar47; EP12872.

KRTIČKA, STANISLAV, 1887-
Velká cvoudílná škola pro normální a francouzský klarinet.
(S hmatovými tabelami) V
přílaze; Soubor solových míst
z děl českých a slovanských
skladatelů. Napsal Stanislav
Krtička. © Ladislav Hnyk,
Hradec Králové, Czechoslovakia;
10Oct39; EF3368.

KRYGER, BRUNON, 1898-
Brunon Kryger, "king of the polkas,"
dance album; [by Brunon Kryger and
Leander Castellani] Wilkes-Barre,
Pa., Brunon Kryger Music Co. ©
Brunon Kryger, Wilkes-Barre, Pa.;
no. 1, 15Oct46; EP11748. For piano
accordion.

KUAANA, DANNY KUAI, 1902-
E kuu lei my darling; words and
music by Danny K. Kuaana,
piano arrangement by Dick Kent.
© Peer International Corp.,
New York; 31Dec45; EP14062.

KUHN, DICK. See
Kuhn, Richard S.

KUHN, RICHARD S   1907-
The Black Hills of South Dakota;
by Eddie White and Dick Kuhn.
© Dick Kuhn Music Corp., New
York; 20Jan47; EP11297. For
voice and piano, with chord
symbols.

KUKOL, CARL T
Jungle rhyme; words and music by
Carl T. Kukol, arr. by Fedy S.
Aquino. © Nordyke Publishing
Co., Los Angeles; 16Dec46;
EP14787.

Too hasty was I; words and music
by Carl Kukol, arr. by Mary
York. © Nordyke Publishing
Co., Los Angeles; 15Feb47;
EP14786.

KULVYANSKIA, W   A
Nothing; by W. A. Kulvyanskia.
© Cine-Mart Music Publishing
Co., Hollywood, Calif.;
1Nov46; EP11482. For voice
and piano, with chord symbols.

KUMMER, GASPARD.
(Quintet, 2 flutes, strings &
guitar) Quintet for two flutes,
viola, cello and guitar; by
Gaspard Kummer, ed. by Harry
Volpe. © Volpe Music Co.,
Jackson Heights, L. I., N. Y.;
on arrangement & editing; 4Jan47;
EP6481.

KVAPIL, JAROSLAV, 1892-
Intimní obrázky ... [by] Jaroslav
Kvapil, rev. [by] prof. Viktor
Nopp. © Hudební Matice Umelecké
Besedy, Praha, Czechoslovakia; v. 1-2,
30Jun43; EF4959. Score
(violin and piano) and part.

(Quartet, strings, no. 4) IV.
smyčcový kvartet; [by] Jaroslav
Kvapil. © Hudební Matice
Umělecké Besedy, Praha, Czechoslovakia; 8Dec43; EF4959.

Sivrty smyčcový kvartet. See his
Quartet, strings, no. 4.

L

LA MONICA PÉREZ. (Monica Perez)
[English words adapted by Albert
Gamse] (In André, Julie, ed.
Songs from south of the border.
p.42-43) © Edward B. Marks Music
Corp., New York; on English
adaptation; 28Dec46; EF10877.

LABEDZ, VIC.
My Indiana home; words and music
by Hubert McIlvaine and Vic
Labedz, arr. by Gabe Wellner,
Phil Warner and Larry Oliver.
Chicago, H. A. McIlvaine Music
Pub. Co. © Hubert A. McIlvaine,
Geneva, Ill.; 22Apr47; EP14254.

LACEY, WILLIAM, 1889-
With all of your faults; words
and music by Will Lacey, [piano
arrangement by Phil Runzo]
Baltimore, Willacy Publishing
Co. © William Lacey, Baltimore; 27Dec46; EP13193.

LAFARGE, GUY PIERRE MARIE, 1904-
Aqui Radio-Andorra ... paroles de
François Llenas & Jean Hebey
[pseud.], musique de Guy Lafarge.
© Editions Musicales Nuances,
Paris; 15Feb47; EF3497.

Douceur; paroles de Lull
Micaelli, musique de Guy La-
farge. © Editions Joubert &
Royalty, Paris; 25Nov46; EF5234.
Piano-conductor score (orches-
tra), and parts.

Mon bien aimé; paroles de F.
Llenas & Guy Lafarge, musique
de Guy Lafarge. © Editions
Royalty, Paris; 31Mar47; EF3891.

Le monsieur du troisième; paroles
de Jean Valmy, musique de Guy
Lafarge. © Editions Joubert,
Paris; 31Mar47; EF3813.

Paris; paroles de Lull Micaelli,
musique de Guy Lafarge. ©
Editions Joubert, Paris;
25Nov46; EF5230.

Le petit cousin; paroles de
Henri Kubnick, musique de Guy
Lafarge. © Editions Royalty,
Paris; 25Nov46; EF5185.

Le p'tit cousin; paroles de Henri
Kubnick, musique de Guy Lafarge,
arr. [by] Raymond Legrand.
© Editions Royalty, Paris;
31Dec46; EF3874. Piano-conductor
score (orchestra), and parts.

LaFORGE, EARL LeROY, 1898-
Beautiful California (I've fallen
in love with you) ... Words and
music by Earl LaForge. © Earl
LeRoy LaForge, Portland, Or.;
16Jun47; EP15184.

LAFOSSE, ANDRE, 1890-
Méthode complète de trombone à
coulisse; [by] André Lafosse
... Nouv. ed., entièrement
rev. par l'auteur et considér-
ablement augm. d'exercices et
d'études. Complete method of
slide-trombone. © Alphonse
Leduc et cie, Paris; v. 1-2,
18Oct46; EF5240, 5198.

LAGERHEIM-ROMARE, MARGIT.
Möte i gründen ... av Margit
Lagerheim-Romare. 4. tusendet.
© Carl Gehrmans Musikförlag,
Stockholm; 1Jan46; EF4892.
For voice and piano, with
chord symbols.

Möte i gründen ... text och
musik: Margit Lagerheim-
Romare, arrangemang Andrew
Walter. © Carl Gehrmans
Musikförlag a/b; 1Jan46;
EF4875. Piano-conductor score
(orchestra), and parts for
violin 1-2 and accordion.

LA GUIRLANDE; chansonnier
polyphonique de la jeunesse.
[c1945] © Henry Lemoine et
Cie., Paris; 1. cahier,
20Jul46; EF3528. Vol. 1-
arr. by César Geoffray and
William Lemit. Contents. -
1. Trente chansons popu-
laires françaises, harmonisées
à trois voix égales.-

LAHMER, REUEL ELI, 1912-
Hear, Lord; S.S.A.T.B., adapted
from Psalms 4,27, 102 [by] Reuel
Lahmer. © Neil A. Kjos Music
Co., Chicago; 19Jun47; EP15138.

LAKE, GENEVIEVE.
The goose boy; by Genevieve Lake.
Piano solo. © Harold Flammer,
inc., New York; 31Dec46; EP14429.

The jump ng mouse; piano solo,
by Genevieve Lake. © The
Boston Music Co., Boston;
11Mar47; EP12846.

Little singer; piano solo by
Genevieve Lake. © The Willis
Music Co., Cincinnati; 23May47;
EP14690.

There's a rainbow; piano solo by
Genevieve Lake. © Harold Flammer,
inc., New York; 31Dec46; EP11428.

Trick riders; triplet studyette
for piano, by Genevieve
Lake. © The Boston Music
Co., Boston; 11Mar47;
EP12845.

78

LAKE, HAROLD C.
Sweet, come again! madrigal for
five voices, words by Thomas
Campian, music by Harold C.
Lake. © Novello & Co., ltd.,
London; 30Dec46; EF4790.

LAKE, MAYHEW.
In the land of Shangri-la; grand
opera a la carte. © George F.
Briegel, inc., New York;
27May46; EP3892. Condensed
score (narrator and band) and
parts.

LALANDE, MICHEL RICHARD DE.
Sinfonie du Te Deum, [from]
Sinfonies pour les soupers du
roi. [1st suite, by] Lalande,
réalisation de Roger Désormière.
Paris, L'Oiseau-Lyre, D. B.
M. Dyer. © Louise B. M. Dyer,
Paris; on realization;
30Dec46; EF3830. Parts:
orchestra.

LALO, EDOUARD.
Andante. See his Symphonie espagnole.

Scherzando. See his Symphonie espagnole.

(Symphonie espagnole) Andante,
from Symphonie espagnole. Op.
21. [by] Edouard Lalo, arr. by
Gustave Langenus. © The Ensemble
Music Press, East Northport, N.Y.;
on arrangement; 29Nov46; EP6361.
Score (clarinet and piano) and
part.

(Symphonie espagnole) Scherzando
from Symphonie espagnole. Op.
21. [by] Edouard Lalo, arr. by
Gustave Langenus. © The Ensemble
Music Press, East Northport, N.Y.;
on arrangement; 29Nov46; EP6350.
Score (clarinet and piano) and
part.

LAMA, GAETANO.
M'aggio sunnato Napule; versi di
Vincenzo Capillo, musica di
Gaetano Lama. [Napoli] "La
Canzonetta." © Italian Book
Co., New York; 3Feb47; EF5641.
Melody and chord symbols, with
words.

LAMA, JERRY.
Have you forgotten? Words by
Al Newton, music by Jerry
Lama, arr. by Dave Kaplan.
[c1946] © Al Newton,
Mobile, Ala.; 20May47;
EP6899.

LAMARR, RICARDO.
Rancho serenade ... by Ricardo
Lamarr. © Southern Music
Publishing Co., ltd., London;
14Mar46; EF5578. For voice and
piano, with chord symbols;
melody also in tonic sol-fa
notation.

LAMARTER, ERIC DE. See
De Lamarter, Eric.

LAMB, LOUIS.
Have I been mean to you? Words and
music by Al Dexter and Louis
Lamb. Hollywood, Calif., Hill and
Range Songs. © Hill and Range
Songs, inc. & Al Dexter Music
Publishing Co., Hollywood, Calif.;
22Jan47; EP11665.

[LAMBERT, RENÉ] 1896-
Je pense a vous ... You did not
love me ... Paroles de René
Lambert, musique et arrangements
de Eler [pseud.] Paris, Les
Tangos de Eler. © Eler, Paris;
26Dec46; EF3506. Piano-conductor
score (orchestra,
with French words) and parts.

No tengo gana; musique de Eler
[pseud.] Je t'en prie ...
paroles françaises de René
Lambert, musique de Eler et
Roger de Molière. Paris, Les
Tangos de Eler. © Eler, Paris;
26Dec46; EF3507. Piano-conductor
score (orchestra, with words)
and parts.

Que no vas ... paroles françaises
de René Lambert, musique de Eler
[pseud.] Noche encantada!
Paroles françaises de R. Lambert,
musique de Eler et Roger de
Molière. Paris, Les Tangos de
Eler. © Eler, Paris; 26Dec46;
EF3508. Piano-conductor score
(orchestra, with words) and parts.

LAMBILLOTTE, LOUIS.
On this day, O Beautiful Mother;
music by Louis Lambillotte,
[arr. by Victor Hamello] © Jos.
L. Armstrong, Philadelphia; on
arrangement; 8May47; EP11895.
For 1-2 voices and piano.

LAMKOFF, PAUL.
Dream time; words by Nell Freeman,
music by Paul Lamkoff. © Cine-
mart Music Publishing Co., Hollywood, Calif.; 30Dec46; EP11954.

Dreams do often come true; words
by Marie R. Whitehouse, music
by Paul Lamkoff. © Cine-Mart
Music Publishing Co., Hollywood, Calif.; 1Dec46; EP11485.

My heart and I; words by Betty
Heflin, music by Paul Lamkoff.
© Nordyke Publishing Co., Los
Angeles; 25Jul46; EP13544.

There's a cabin in the pines in
Wisconsin; words by Harry
McDonald, music by Paul Lamkoff.
© Cine-mart Music Publishing
Co., Hollywood, Calif.; 1Aug46;
EP10960. For voice and piano,
with chord symbols.

You're the bad apple in the basket;
words by Wilbur M. Weakley, music
by Paul Lamkoff. © Cine-Mart
Music Publishing Co., Hollywood,
Calif.; 1Dec46; EP12119.

LANCE, ADDIE EMILY.
Eternally yours; by Addie Emily
Lance, [arr. by Jimmie Crane]
© Addie E. Lance, West Ashe-
ville, N. C.; 20Dec46; EP10981.
For voice and piano.

LANE, BOYD.
Footprints in the snow ... words
and music by Boyd Lane. © Peer
International Corp., New York;
10Apr47; EP13699.

LANE, BURTON, 1912-
Feudin' and fightin'; words by
Al Dubin and Burton Lane, music
by Burton Lane. New York,
Chappell & co., inc. © Mara-
Lane Music Corp., New York;
23May47; EP14952.

(Finian's rainbow) Excerpts
from Finian's rainbow; new
musical comedy. Lyrics by
E. Y. Harburg, music by Burton
Lane, for orchestra by Russell
Bennett. New York, Crawford
Music Corp. © The Players
Music Corp., New York; on
arrangement; 12May47; EP14386.
Piano-conductor score
(orchestra) and parts.

(Finian's rainbow) How are things
in Glocca Morra? From the
musical play "Finian's rainbow,"
male voices (T.T.B.B.) arr. by
William Stickles, words by E.
Y. Harburg, music by Burton
Lane. [New York, Crawford Music
Corp.] © The Players Music
Corp., New York; on arrangement;
31Dec46; EP12675.

(Finian's rainbow) How are things
in Glocca Morra? From the
musical play "Finian's rainbow,"
mixed voices (S.A.T.B.) arr. by
William Stickles, words by E.
Y. Harburg, music by Burton Lane.
[New York, Crawford Music Corp.]
© The Players Music Corp., New
York; on arrangement; 31Dec46;
EP12676.

(Finian's rainbow) How are things
in Glocca Morra? From "Finian's
rainbow," words by E. Y. Harburg,
music by Burton Lane, arr. for
band by Erik Leidzen. New York;
on arrangement; 28Apr47; EP14159.
Condensed score (band with words)
and parts.

(Finian's rainbow) How are
things in Glocca Morra? From
the musical play "Finian's
rainbow," female voices (S.S.A.)
arr. by William Stickles, words
by E. Y. Harburg, music by
Burton Lane. [New York, Crawford Music Corp.] © The
Players Music Corp., New York;
on arrangement; 31Dec46;
EP12677.

(Finian's rainbow) If this isn't
love, from the musical play "Finian's
rainbow" ... [(for) S.A.T.B.] arr.
by William Stickles; words by E. Y.
Harburg, music by Burton Lane.
[New York, Crawford Music Corp.] ©
The Players Music Corp., New York;
on arrangement; 31Dec46; EP12916.

(Finian's rainbow) If this isn't love,
from the musical play "Finian's
rainbow" ... [(for) S.S.A.] arr.
by William Stickles; words by E. Y.
Harburg, music by Burton Lane.
[New York, Crawford Music Corp.]
© The Players Music Corp., New York;
on arrangement; 31Dec46; EP12915.

(Finian's rainbow) Look to the
rainbow [from "Finian's rainbow"] Words by E. Y. Harburg,
music by Burton Lane. ©
The Players Music Corp., New
York; 10Feb47; EP12090.

(Finian's rainbow) Old devil
moon, from the musical play
"Finian's rainbow" ... [(for)
S.A.T.B.] arr. by William
Stickles. Words by E. Y. Har-
burg, music by Burton Lane.
New York, Crawford Music Corp.
© The Players Music Corp., New
York; on arrangement; 31Dec46;
EP13343.

(Finian's rainbow) Old devil
moon, from the musical play
"Finian's rainbow" ... [(for)
T.T.B.B.] arr. by William
Stickles. Words by E. Y. Har-
burg, music by Burton Lane.
New York, Crawford Music Corp.
© The Players Music Corp., New
York; on arrangement; 31Dec46;
EP13342.

(Finian's rainbow) Something
sort of grandish; [from] Finian's
rainbow. Words by E. Y. Harburg,
music by Burton Lane. [New
York, Chappell & co., inc.] ©
The Players Music Corp., New
York; 20May47; EP14878.

(Finian's rainbow) When I'm not
near the girl I love; [from]
"Finian's rainbow," words by
E. Y. Harburg, music by Burton
Lane. [New York, Chappell &
Co.] © The Players Music
Corp., New York; 19Dec46;
EP10612. Corrected by EP12317.

LANE, BURTON, 1912-   Cont'd.
(Finian's rainbow) When I'm
not near the girl I love,"
[from] "Finian's rainbow,"
words by E. Y. Harburg, music
by Burton Lane. © The Players
Music Corp., New York; 23Dec46;
EP12317. Correcting EP10612.

How are things in Glocca Morra?
See his Finian's rainbow.

If this isn't love. See his
Finian's rainbow.

Look to the rainbow. See his
Finian's rainbow.

Old devil moon. See his Finian's rainbow.

When I'm not near the girl I love.
See his Finian's rainbow.

LANG, C   S
Love is a babel; part song for
S.A.T.B., words from Robert
Jones' Second book of airs
(1601), music by C. S. Lang.
Op. 46. © Novello & Co., ltd.,
London; 16Jun47; EF3801.

LANG, CARL, 1903-
Let's not waste the moonlight;
by Carl Lang. © Shelby Music
Publishing Co., Detroit;
28Dec46; EP11120. For voice
and piano, with guitar diagrams
and chord symbols.

LANG, EDITH, 1885-
The Psalm of David; for four-part
chorus of mixed voices, with
piano acc. Old Testament text,
music by E. Lang. © The Boston
Music Co., Boston; 7Jan47; EP13051.

The twenty-fourth Psalm; for four-
part chorus of mixed voices with
organ or piano accompaniment.
Music by E. Lang, Psalm XXIV:
1-6. © The Boston Music Co.,
Boston; 9Apr47; EP13639.

LANG, HANS, 1908-
Wann der Steffel wieder wird,
so wie er war ... Worte:
Erich Meder, Musik: Hans Lang.
© Ludwig Doblinger (Bernhard
Herzmansky), k.g., Vienna;
20Aug46; EF3790.

LANG, PHILIP J
School days fantasy; by Will D.
Cobb and Gus Edwards ... trans-
cribed for band by Philip J.
Lang. © Mills Music, inc., New
York; on arrangement; 9Dec46;
EP6523. Condensed score (band)
and parts.

LANGE, IRENE.
Somebody's heaven; words & music
by Irene Lange. © Nordyko
Publishing Co., Los Angeles;
9Nov46; EP11532.

LANGE-MUELLER, P   E
Lead on, O King Eternal! [Words
by] Ernest W. Shurtleff ...
[music by] P. E. Lange-Mueller
... arr. and chorus by Harry
Dixon Loes. (In Moody Bible
institute of Chicago. The voice
of thanksgiving, no.5. Hymn
no.372) © Hope Publishing Co.,
Chicago; on arrangement & chorus,
1Jul46; EP13682. Close score:
SATB.

LANGER, DOLFI, 1906-
Zamilované klarinety ... Clarinets in love, solo for 2 clarinets ... [by] Dolfi Langer.
© František Kudelík, Praha,
Czechoslovakia; 12Mar46;
EF3367. Piano-conductor score
(2 clarinets and orchestra),
and parts.

LANGEY, OTTO.
Langey-Carl Fischer tutors: for
violoncello. New rev. ed; ©
Carl Fischer, inc., New York;
on new instructive material &
exercises; 31Dec46; EP11101.

LANGEY-CARL FISCHER TUTORS; for guitar ... New rev. ed. © Carl Fischer, inc., New York; on new instructive material & exercises;
15Nov46; EP9720.

LANGHAM, RAY.
A pair of baby shoes; words and
music by Maurice Kregal and Ray
Langham ... piano arr. by Dick
Kent. © Peer International
Corp., New York; 29Oct46;
EP13622.

LANGLAIS, JEAN.
(Symphony, organ, no. 1) Première
symphonie. © H. Hérelle & Cie,
Paris; 20May45; EF626.

LANGSTROTH, IVAN, 1887-
Fantasie and fugue; for organ by
Ivan Langstroth. © The H. W.
Gray Co., inc., New York; 23May47;
EP14762.

Toccata and fugue; for the
organ by Ivan Langstroth.
© M. Witmark & Sons, New
York; 30Apr47; EP14292.

LANJEAN, MARC.
Quand il pleut sur la maison;
paroles et musique de Marc
Lanjean. © Éditions Paris-
Broadway, Paris; 31Mar45;
EF3076.

LANTIER, PIERRE LOUIS, 1910-
Andante et scherzetto; [by]
Pierre Lantier. © Pierre
Noël, Paris; 15Sep42;
EF5536. Parts: 4 saxophones.

LAO SCHOR, ALBERTO, 1882-
Visione ... elaborazione di A.
Lao Schor e Amleto Fiorini
dalla Ballata n. 1 [by] Chopin.
© Carisch, s.a., Milan;
28Mar47; EF3845. For voice
and piano.

LAPARCERIE, MIARKA, 1912-
Mon coeur est un violon; d'après
un poème de Jean Richepin,
paroles et musique de Miarka
Laparcerie. © Éditions Salabert, Paris; 15Nov46; EF5197.

LAPO, CECIL ELWYN, 1910-
When wilt Thou save the people?
Anthem for mixed voices, music
by Cecil E. Lapo, based on tune:
Commonwealth, by Josiah Booth.
Words by Ebenezer Elliott. ©
C. Albert Scholin, Brentwood,
Mo.; 16Jan47; EP11767.

LARA, AGUSTIN.
Album ... de canciones del músico
poeta Agustín Lara. © Promotora
Hispano Americana de Música,
s.a., Mexico; no.7, 30Dec46;
EP5534. For voice and piano.

María bonita.... letra y música
de Agustín Lara, arreglo de
Evaristo Fafoya. © Promotora
Hispano Americana de Música,
s.a., México; 28Mar47;
EF5494. Piano-conductor score
(orchestra), and parts.

LARKIN, MILTON, 1910-
Larkin's blues; by Milton Larkin.
© Popular Music Co., New York;
20Jun47; EP15210. For voice
and piano, with chord symbols.

LA ROSA, ORLANDO DE. See
Rosa, Orlando de la.

LARSSON, LARS-ERIK.
Liten marsch; av Lars-Erik
Larsson, arr. [by] William
Lind. © Nordiska Musik-
förlaget, a.b., Stockholm;
1Jan46; EF3721. Piano-conductor score (orchestra), and
parts.

LASSERE, GENEVIEVE LAKE. See
Lake, Genevieve.

LAST, JOAN.
First of all; an album of 15
piano pieces by Joan Last. ©
Chappell & Co., ltd., London;
2May47; EF3631.

LASZLO, SANDOR, 1895-
"Das ist das Glück!" zwölf Lieder
nach Gedichten von Else Luz ...
von Sándor László. Op. 7.
Berlin, N. Simrock. © Associated
Music Publishers, inc., New
York; v.1-2, 1Mar20; EF4850-4851.
For voice and piano.

LATHROP, JACK.
I like to have you like to have me
love you; words and music by Jack
Lathrop. © Robbins Music Corp.,
inc., New York; 24Jan47; EP11657.

LA TORRE, HECTOR DE. See
Torre, Hector de la.

LAUBENSTEIN, PAUL F   1892-
They that go down to the sea in
ships ... Psalm CVII: 23-31,
music by Paul F. Laubenstein.
© M. Witmark & Sons, New York;
30Apr47; EP14291. Score:
solo voices (TB) and organ or
piano.

LAVINE, LAWRENCE PAUL, 1908-
A tribute to mother; words and
music by Lawrence Lavino. ©
Lawrence Paul Lavino, Des
Moines; 23Apr47; EP14366.

LAVISTA, RAÚL.
(Cuando lloran los valientes)
Tal vez me puedan matar ... de
la película, "Cuando lloran los
valientes"; música de Raúl
Lavista, letra de Ernesto M.
Cortázar; y Traición ingrata;
letra y música de Ernesto
Alarcón Leal. © Promotora
Hispano Americana de Música,
s.a., México; 29Oct46; EF5496,
5495.

Tal vez me puedan matar. See his
Cuando lloran los valientes.

LAWRANCE, ALF   J
Hello Spring! This is love ...
words and music by Robyn
Teakle and Alf. J. Lawrance. ©.
Chappell & Co., ltd., Sydney;
24Mar47; EF3269.

LAWRENCE, ELLIOT, pseud. See
Broza, Elliot Lawrence.

LAWRENCE, JACK.
Please don't play that old song;
by Jack Lawrence. © Whale
Music Corp., New York; 14Apr47;
EP13492. For voice and piano.

LAWRENCE, WILLIAM, arr.
They led my Lord away; arranged
by William Lawrence. © Mc-
Laughlin & Reilly Co., Boston;
on arrangement; 10Mar47;
EP12778.

LAWSON, JIMMIE.
I just can't forgive you anymore;
by Jimmie Lawson. © Acuff-Rose
Publications, Nashville; 21Jan47;
EP14439. For voice and piano, with
guitar diagrams and chord symbols.

LAZARUS, DANIEL, 1898-
Épitaphe; [by] Daniel Lazarus,
poème de Charles Oulmont,
pour voix de contralto,
chant et piano. © Durand &
Cie, Paris; 25May47; EF5939.

Rythmes de guerre ... Piano à deux
mains. © Durand & Cie, Paris;
5Jun45; EF632. Cover-title:
Carnaval héroïque.

LEACOCK, LEONARD H
God bless our Canada ... words by
Frank Baker, music by Leonard H.
Leacock. Toronto, Whaley, Royce
& Co. © Frank Baker, Creston,
B. C., Can.; 28Oct46; EF4767.
For voice and piano.

LEAL, EDUARDO ALARCÓN. See
Alarcón Leal, Eduardo.

[LEAMAN, GEORGE]
The girl with the gold in her
hair; adapted from the duet
from Don Giovanni by Mozart,
lyric by Sammy Gallop, [music
arr. by Geo. Leaman]
© Sinatra Songs, inc., New
York; 15May47; EP14524.

LEAP, GLENN CECIL, 1889-
There's a stairway to heaven; ...
[words by] Velma C. Fine,
[music by] Glenn C. Leap.
Indianapolis, Glenn C. Leap.
© Velma C. Fine, Indianapolis;
20May47; EP14532. Close score:
SATB.

Won't you come to Jesus today?
[Words by] Velma C. Fine, [music
by] Glenn C. Leap. Indianapolis,
Glenn C. Leap. © Velma C. Fine,
Indianapolis; 20May47; EP14531.
Close score: SATB.

LEARSI, pseud. See
Israel, Marcel.

LEAS, LYLE.
Indiana blues; words and music
by Lyle Leas. © Nordyke
Publishing Co., Los Angeles;
7Mar47; EP13245.

LEBECK, PAULINE.
You are the one I love; words and
music by Pauline Lebeck. [c1946]
© Whitehouse Publishing Co.,
Hollywood, Calif.; 2Jan47;
EP11986.

LECA, HENRY, 1914-
Bikini; paroles de Michel de Bry
[and] Ralph Derby [pseud.],
musique de Henry Leca. ©
Éditions du Lido, Paris; 15Nov46;
EF3450. Piano-conductor score
(orchestra, with words), and
parts.

Bikini; paroles de Michel de
Bry & Ralph Derby [pseud.],
musique de Henry Leca. ©
Éditions du Lido, Paris;
25Nov46; EF5183. Melody and
chord symbols, with words.

Voilà, voilà, Paris; paroles de
Ralph Derby [pseud.], musique
de Henry Leca. © Éditions du
Lido, Paris; 25Nov46; EF5214.
Score (voice and piano) and
voice part.

LECOCQ, CHARLES.
Les cent vierges ... Version nou-
velle de André Mouëzy-Éon et Albert Willemetz. © Éditions Joubert, Paris; v. 1-2, 31Dec42;
EF375-374. For voice and piano.

LECUONA Y CASADO, ERNESTO, 1895-
(Carnival in Costa Rica) Maracas
... [from] Carnival in Costa
Rica ... Spanish lyric and
music by Ernesto Lecuona,
[English] lyric by Harry Ruby.
© Edward B. Marks Music Corp.,
New York; 4Dec46; EP11969.

La comparsa. (Cuban processional)
... [By] Ernesto Lecuona, [English
words adapted by Albert Gumsol
(In André, Julio, ed. Songs from
south of the border. p.5-9) ©
Edward B. Marks Music Corp., New
York; on English adaptation;
28Dec46; EP10864.

La comparsa. See his Danzas afro-
cubanas.

(Danzas afro-cubanas) La
comparsa. Carnival pro-
cession; from "Danzas afro-
cubanas" suite by Ernesto
Lecuona, arr. ... by Paul
Yoder. © Edward B. Marks
Music Corp., New York; on
arrangement; 21May47; EP14544.
Condensed score (band) and
parts.

Gitanerías, from Andalucia
suite espagnolo; [by] Ernesto
Lecuona, arr. ... by Paul
Yoder. © Edward B. Marks
Music Corp., New York; on
arrangement; 17Jun47; EP15111.
Condensed score (band) and
parts.

Malaguena; [by] Ernesto [Lecuona]
... Arr. by Louis Sugarman.
© Edward B. Marks Music Corp.,
New York; on arrangement;
17Feb47; EP12247. For piano
solo.

Maracas. See his Carnival in Costa
Rica.

LEE, ALFRED.
The man on the flying trapeze;
for ... S.S.A. (solo for medium
voice) [by] Alfred Lee, arr. by
Russell Watson [pseud. Words
by] George Leybourne. © Pro
Art Publications, New York; on
arrangement; 21Apr47; EP13609.

LEE, ARIVERS.
Do you remember, sweetheart
(because I do); words & music
by Arivers Lee. © Nordyke
Publishing Co., Los Angeles;
9Aug46; EP10858. For voice
and piano, with chord symbols.

LEE, BERNIE.
Como on and kiss me; words and music
by Dave Ringle ... Low Tobin and
Bernie Lee. © Dave Ringle, inc.,
New York; 6Jan47; EP11045.

LEE, DAI-KEONG.
Forgetfulness; (S.A.T.B.) Text
by Hart Crane, music by Dai-
keong Lee. © Leeds Music
Corp., New York; 21Mar47;
EP12853.

Joyous interlude ... by Dai-Keong
Lee. © Mills Music, inc., New
York; 17Feb47; EP6605. Con-
densed score (band) and parts.

October, November; (S.A.T.B.)
Text by Hart Crane, music by
Dai-keong Lee. © Leeds
Music Corp., New York;
21Mar47; EP12854.

LEE, JOHNNIE ROBERT, 1909-
Where do I come in? Words and
music by Johnnie Lee. © Metropolitan Music Co., Houston,
Tex.; 12Jun47; EP14958.

LEE, JULIA.
Gotta gimme whatcha got; by Julia
Lee. © Capitol Songs, inc.,
New York; 12Jan47; EP11127. For
voice and piano, with chord symbols.

Since I've been with you; words
and music by Julia Lee.
© Capitol Songs, inc., New York;
17Jun47; EP15121.

LEE, LESTER.
Inflation; words and music by Zeke
Manners and Lester Lee. © Bob
Miller, inc., New York; 30Dec46;
EP10742.

Naughty Angelino; words and music
© George Simon, inc., New York;
4Jun47; EP14853.

LEEDS, MILTON, pseud. See
Liberman, Milton.

LEFEBVRE, CHANNING, arr.
Fourteen folk tunes for young men ...
arr. for 3 part male chorus
(T.B.B.) by Channing Lefebvre.
© Galaxy Music Corp., New York;
on arrangement; 7Mar47; EP6664.

Somebody's knockin' at your door;
for chorus of men's voices;
negro spiritual arr. by Channing
Lefebvre. © Galaxy Music Corp.,
New York; on arrangement; 14Jan47;
EP6479.

LEFEVRE, AUGUSTE.
Sleepytime lullaby; by Auguste
Lefevre. © Dix, ltd., London;
1Apr47; EF3342. For piano
solo.

LEFKOWITCH, HENRY, 1891- arr.
Ani ma-amin ... Arr. for voice
and piano by Henry Lefkowitch
as notated and sung by Moshe
Nathanson. New York, Metro
Music. © Henry Lefkowitch,
New York; 28Feb47; EP14188.
Hebrew words (transliterated)

LE FLEMING, CHRISTOPHER, 1908-
Five psalms; for soprano solo,
chorus and orchestra, music by
Christopher Le Fleming. Vocal
score. © J. & W. Chester,
ltd., London; 22Apr47; EF3299.

[LEGGETT, LEWIS ERNEST] 1893-1943.
My twilight tango. (A la
puesta del sol) English lyric
by Derek Elphinstone, music
by José Muriello [pseud. and
Goodnight, beloved; lyric by
Benny Lamarr, pseud., music
by Billy Mack, pseud. & Ray
Barry pseud., arr. by Den
Berry] © Cosmo Music Co.,
(London) ltd., London; on My
twilight tango, 27Dec46;
EF3658; on Goodnight, beloved,
12Aug46; EF3639. Piano-
conductor score (orchestra,
with words) and parts.

LEGNINI, AMERICO.
Ave Maria; [music] by Americo
Legnini. © Americo Legnini,
Havertown, Pa.; 12Dec46;
EP11467. For voice and
piano.

LE GRAND, ROBERT, 1894-
Amaryllis; choeur à 4 voix
mixtes, poème attribué à
Louis XIII, musique de Robert
Le Grand. Op. 34, no. 1.
Paris, Rouart, Lerolle et
Cie., vente exclusive, Éditions
Salabert, inc., New York; 31Dec46; EF3556.

Le boiteux mary de Vénus; choeur
à 4 voix mixtes, poème de
Ronsard, musique de Robert Le
Grand. Op. 34, no. 3. Paris,
Rouart, Lerolle et Cie, vente
exclusive, Éditions Salabert.
© Salabert, inc., New York;
31Dec46; EF3595.

Cinq chansons de Bilitis; [by]
Robert Le Grand, d'après les
poèmes de Pierre Louÿs. [Op.
43] © Rouart, Lerolle et
Cie., Paris; 31May46; EF3564.
For voice and piano.

LE GRAND, ROBERT, 1894-   Cont'd.
Légende slave; pour violoncelle
et orchestre ou piano, [by]
Robert Le Grand. Op. 8. ©
Durand & Cie., Paris; 3Jan47;
EF3499. Score (violoncello and
piano) and part.

Le premier jour du mois de mai;
choeur à 4 voix mixtes,
poésie de Ranchin ... musique
de Robert Le Grand. Op. 34,
no. 2. Paris, Rouart, Lerolle
et Cie., vente exclusive,
Editions Salabert, inc., New York; 31Dec46;
EF3552.

LEGUERNEY, JACQUES, 1906-
Deux mélodies sur des poèmes d'
Apollinaire; [by] Jacques
Leguerney. © Durand & Cie.,
Paris; 3Jan47; EF3504.

LEHÁR, FERENC, 1870-
Dream girl ... By Franz Lehár.
© Peter Maurice Music Co., ltd.,
New York; 6Mar47; EF5359. For
piano solo.

Frasquita serenade; (My little
nest of heavenly blue); by
Franz Lehár ... Arr. by Louis
Sugarman. © Edward B. Marks
Music Corp., New York; on
arrangement; 17Feb47; EP12245.
For piano solo.

Schillornder Falter; Koloraturlied,
Musik van Franz Lehár, Worte von
M. C. Krüger. © Ludwig Doblinger
(Bernhard Herzmansky), K. G.,
Vienna; 25Aug42; EF3399. Score
(soprano, soprano ad lib.,
unison chorus ad lib. and piano)
and part for voices.

Song of the Volga, from the operetta
"The Czarevitch", by Bella Jen-
bach and Heinz Reichert; English
lyric by Harry S. Pepper, music
by Franz Lehár. ©1927-1935. ©
Glocken Verlag, ltd., London;
on English translation; 17Mar47;
EF3195.

Sunday in the park ... by Franz
Lehár. © The Peter Maurice
Music Co., ltd., New York;
6Mar47; EF5360. For piano
solo.

LEHMAN, EVANGELINE.
Lamb of God. Agnus Dei. Sacred
song, adapted to the "Little
Prelude in C minor," by J. S.
Bach, [melody by] Evangeline
Lohman. © Oliver Ditson Co.,
Philadelphia; 26May47; EP14703.

LEHULEN. See
Hulen, L. E.

LEICEA, CALIXTO.
"Rumbambaramba" ... letra y
música de Calixto Leicea,
arreglo del autor. © Peer
International Corp., New
York; 30Dec46; EF5445.
Parts: orchestra.

LEIDZÉN, ERIK W   G   1894-
Doxology. S.A.T.B. [by] Leidzén.
© Leeds Music Corp., New York;
24Jan47; EP11810.

Hymn of thanksgiving ... (S.A.T.B.)
Netherlands hymn, [music by]
Erik Leidzen. © Leeds Music
Corp., New York; 2Jun47; EP14969.

LEIGHTON, HERB.
The things you left in my heart;
by Buddy Kaye, Hugo Talani and
Herb Leighton. © Lewis Music
Publishing Co., inc., New York;
on words & arrangement; 14Jan47;
EP11240.

LEINBACH, E   W
Hosanna ... [By] E. W. Leinbach,
ed. and arr. by James Christian
Pfohl. [Charlotte, N. C., Sole
selling agent: Brodt Music Co.]
© Moravian Church. Southern
Province, Winston-Salem, N. C.;
13Dec43; EP6753. Score: chorus
(SATB, SATB) and piano reduction.

LEJAY, ANDRÉ, 1903-
Bora Bora ... paroles de Marcel
Gayd, musique de André Lejay.
© Édition "La Fauvette,"
Paris; 20Nov46; EF5211.

LEKBERG, SVEN, 1899-
And a very great multitude ...
Sacred song, [words from] Matthew
XXI:8,9. Music by Sven Lekberg.
© M. Witmark & Sons, New York;
23May47; EP14704.

How long wilt Thou forget me, O
Lord? ... Sacred Song, [words
from] psalm XIII from the St.
Dunstan Psalter. Music by
Sven Lokberg. © M. Witmark &
Sons, New York; 23May47; EP14706.

I will lift up mine eyes ...
Sacred song, [words from] Psalm
CXXI, from the St. Dunstan
Psalter. Music by Sven Lokberg.
© M. Witmark & Sons, New York;
23May47; EP14705.

LEMAIRE, CHARLES.
Chanson à manger. In praise of
food ... Transcribed by J. B.
Weckerlin; English version by
Lorraine Noel Finley. (In
[Hodges, Lester] comp. John
Charles Thomas album of favorite
songs and arias. p. 9-11) ©
G. Schirmer, inc., New York;
21Jun46; EP10218.

LENNERTS, WILLIAM JOSEPH, 1914-
Merry Christmas; words and music
by Bill Lennerts, [arr. by
Ewing Reid] Detroit, Lennerts
Music Publishers. © William J.
Lennerts, d.b.a. Lennerts Music
Publications, Detroit; 18Dec46;
EP10854. For voice and piano,
with chord symbols.

LENOIR, JEAN, pseud. See also
Neuburger, Jean Bernard.
Je sais une chanson; paroles &
musique de Jean Lenoir. ©
Continental Leeds Music Co.,
Paris; 27Dec46; EF3658.

La madone aux yeux de ciel;
paroles de Pierre Jacob,
musique de Jean Lenoir. ©
Continental Leeds Music Co.,
Paris; 27Dec46; EF3657.

LEONARD, ANITA, 1922-
I'm gonna hop on a cloud; words
by Morton Parnes, music by
Anita Leonard. © Fowler Music
Co., New York; 25Apr47;
EP14040.

LEONARD, CONRAD, 1898-
I'm in love with a song ... words
by Carroll Levis, music by
Conrad Leonard. © Lawrence
Wright Music Co., ltd., Lon-
don; 7May47; EF3258.

LEONARDI, ROBERTO.
Ritmo senza amore ... di Roberto
Leonardi, [words by P. Sacchi]
© Edizioni Leonardi, s.a.r.l.,
Milano; 11Feb46; EF4906.
Piano-conductor score (orches-
tra, with words), and parts.

LEONCAVALLO, RUGGIERO, 1858-1919.
(I pagliacci) I am the prologue,
from R. Leoncavallo's opera
"I Pagliacci" in a modern

English version, by Dmitri
Dobkin, Fred G. Moritt [and]
Irwin M. Cassel, [arr. by I. M.
Cassel] © Congress Music
Publications, Miami, Fla.; on
arrangement & English words;
9Dec46; EP10889. For voice and
piano; Italian and English words.

LEONE, FRANCESCO DE. See
De Leone, Francesco.

LEOPOLD, J   WALTER.
Old chuck wagon ... lyric by
Monte Howard, music by J.
Walter Leopold. © Columbia
Music Carpold Co., Hollywood,
Calif.; 16Jan47; EP6483.

LEPITRE, ANDRÉ CHARLES, 1884-
Le concours d'Annick; pièce
facile pour piano, [by]
André Lepitre. © Henry Lemoine
& Cie., Paris; 30Nov46;
EF3583.

LERNER, AL, 1919-
Hinkty man; [words] by Buddy
Feyne, [music by] Al Lerner
[and] Irving Miller. ©
Fowler Music Co., New York;
18Apr47; EP13808.

LESLIE, EDGAR.
Love will keep us young; (based on
Johannes Brahms' waltz in A♭.
Op. 39), adaptation and lyric
by Edgar Leslie. © Lombardo
Music, inc., New York; 12Jun47;
EP15053.

LE STRANGE, RAY, 1895-
Don't spoil those pretty eyes (with
tears dear); words and music
by Marty Ingram and Ray Le
Strange. © Nordyke Publishing
Co., Hollywood, Calif.; 17Jan47;
EP11524.

LESUR, DANIEL JEAN, 1908-
Chansons cambodgiennes ... textes
recueillis et traduits par
Albert Tricon, musique de
Daniel-Lesur. © Durand &
Cie., Paris; 15Mar47; EF3645.

Deux chansons de L'étoile de
Séville; [by] Daniel-Lesur,
[words by Claude Roy] Paris,
L. de Lacour, Editions Cos-
tallat. © Lucien de Lacour,
Paris; 31Oct46; EF3622.

Deux noëls; [for] piano, [by]
Daniel-Lesur. Grenoble, 1945.
© Amphion, Paris; 31Dec46;
EF3529.

LETELLIER, DÉSIRÉ.
Amalia; paroles de François
Llenas, musique de Désiré
Letellier. © Ste. ame. fse.
Chappell, Paris; 24May47;
EF3910.

[LEVEILLER, CHARLES P   J
1889-
I'm glad I'm Sioux City Sue; words
and music by Jean Avril [pseud.]
© Chas. P. J. Leveiller, LeMars,
Iowa; 15Jan47; EP13410.

LEVENGER, GEORGIA, 1912-
Kiddies' polka; medley of nursery
rhymes, words and music by
Harold Potter, Eddie Dorr [and]
Georgia Levenger. © Royal
Crown Music Co., New York;
24Feb47; EP12215.

LEVERTON, BUCK.
I'll come back; words and music
by Dave Denney and Buck Leverton.
© Vogue Music Corp., New York;
6Feb47; EP13372.

LEWIS, CARROLL, 1910-
The miners' song; arr. for ...
(T.T.B.B.) with piano acc., words
and music by Carroll Lewis, [arr.
by Clarence Lucas] © Chappell &
Co., ltd., London; on arrangement; 15Apr47; EF5642.

The miners' song; by Carroll
Lewis. © Chappell & Co.,
ltd., London; 3Mar47;
EF5418.

The miners' song; [by] Carroll
Lewis, arr. [by] W. J. Duthoit.
© Chappell & Co., ltd., London;
on arrangement for brass band;
23Apr47; EF3274. Cornet-conductor score (band) and parts.

The miners' song; [by] Carroll
Lewis, arr. [by] W. J. Duthoit.
© Chappell & Co., ltd., London;
on arrangement for military
band; 23Apr47; EF3273. Cornet-
conductor score (band), and
parts.

Nobody loves my baby like me ...
Words and music by Carroll
Lewis. © Lawrence Wright Music
Co., ltd., London; 17Feb47;
EF5023.

[LEVY, MICHEL MAURICE] 1883-
D'Artagnan; opérette héroïque.
Couplets de L. Marion [pseud.],
musique de Bétovo [pseud.]
© Editions Royalty, Paris;
1. recueil, 31Dec45; EF5186.

Strasbourg; hymne à l'Alsace, a
voix mixtes; paroles de Joë
Bridge [pseud.], musique de
Bétove [pseud.] © Rouart
Lerolle et Cie., Paris;
15Nov46; EF5191.

LEWANDOWSKI, LOUIS, 1823-1894.
Psalm 150; Halleluja, praise ye the
Lord ... (S.A.T.B.) [By] Louis
Lewandowski, ed. by Harry Robert
Wilson, [words] adapted from Psalm
150 by H. R. W. © Hall & McCreary
Co., Chicago; on adaptation of text;
13Jan47; EP14434.

LEWIS, ARTHUR, 1907-
The greatest Pilot; words and music
by Arthur Lewis, [arr. by William
Walker Combs] © Arthur Lewis,
Effingham, Ill.; 21Mar47; EP13667.

LEWIS, JIM.
I'm tellin' you; words and music
by Billy Hughes and Texas Jim
Lewis. © Hill and Range Songs,
inc., Hollywood, Calif.;
7Jan47; EP11205.

LEWIS, SANFORD IRWIN, 1925-
As lovely as a rose; words & music
by Sanford Lewis. c1946. ©
Sanford Irwin Lewis, Wilmette,
Ill.; 19Feb47; EP13587.

Serenade to Helen; words & music by
Sanford Lewis, Wilmette, Ill.,
19Feb47; EP13389.

When I met you for the first time;
words and music by Sanford Lewis.
c1946. © Sanford Irwin Lewis,
Wilmette, Ill.; 19Feb47; EP13388.

LEWIS, TEXAS JIM. See
Lewis, Jim.

LEZZA, CARLO.
Ritmo di felicità ... Testo di
C. Denni, musica di Carlo
Lezza. [©1946] © Edizioni
Leonardi, s. a. r. l., Milano;
1Jan47; EP5302. Piano-conduct-
or score (orchestra, with words)
and parts.

LIADOV, ANATOLII KONSTANTINOVICH,
1855-1914.
Lullaby; for four-part chorus of
women's voices and soprano
solo, a cappella; words by I.
B., [music by] Anatol Liadov,
transcribed and ed. by Igor
Buketoff. © G. Schirmer, inc.,
New York; 11Apr47; EP14077.

LIBBY, RUTH.
Sweet story; for the piano [by] Ruth
Libby. © The Oliver Ditson Co.,
Philadelphia; 16Dec46; EP11559.

[LIBERMAN, MILTON]
Castanets and lace; words and
music by Bob Hilliard, Dave
Mann and Milton Leeds, [pseud.]
© Republic Music Corp., New
York; 19May47; EP14383.

Met a Texas gal; words and music
by Billy Hayes, Denver Darling
[and] Milton Leeds, [pseud.]
© Southern Music Publishing
Co., inc., New York; 10Apr47;
EP13694.

Who else? Words and music by
Billy Hayes [and] Milton Leeds,
[pseud.] © Robbins Music Corp.,
New York; 21Apr47; EP14771.

LIEFELD, JO.
Famous themes in the modern
manner; styled for piano
solo, by Jo Liefeld. ©
Rubank, inc., Chicago; on
arrangement; 2Jun47;
EP14740.

LIEMOHN, EDWIN.
O Christ, Thou Lamb of God ...
For mixed voices S.A.T.B.
(divided) a cappella ad lib.
[By] Edwin Liemohn. © Gamble
Hinged Music Co., Chicago;
9May47; EP14277.

[LIETA, THELMA] 1929-
Sweet darling; [words] by Yodelin'
Bob [pseud.] and [words by]
Thelma [pseud.] and All thru the
years, the melody of love, The
song I saved for you [and] Lullaby
to the evening star; [words] by
Hubert S. Covert and [music by]
Norman Kelly. © Kelly Music
Publications, Franklin, Pa.;
31Dec46; EP11020.

LIGGINS, JOE.
T.W.A.; [by] Joe Liggins. ©
Recordo Music Publishers, Holly-
wood, Calif.; 20May47; EP14534.
For voice and piano, with chord
symbols.

LIGHT, FRANCES M
Bears in the woods; piano solo, by
Frances M. Light. © Theodore
Presser Co., Philadelphia; 21Feb47;
EP12291.

LIGHTFRITZ, EDITH
Missing in action; words by Henry
Nelson Waterfield, music by
Edith Lightfritz. © Nordyke
Publishing Co., Los Angeles;
28Nov45; EP11551.

LIGTELIJN, JOHANNES LAMBERTUS, 1902-
Bagatelle; pour piano, [by] Johan
Ligtelijn. © Edition Heuweke-
meyer (Firm A. J. Heuwekemeyer
& B. F. van Gaal), Amsterdam,
The Netherlands; 27Jan46;
EF5130.

Historiette; [by] Johan Ligtelijn,
pour piano. © Edition Heuweke-
meyer (Firm A. J. Heuwekemeyer
& B. F. van Gaal), Amsterdam,
The Netherlands; 27Jan46;
EF5131.

Papillonne; [by] Johan Ligtelijn,
pour piano. © Edition Heuweke-
meyer (Firm A. J. Heuwekemeyer
& B. F. van Gaal), Amsterdam,
The Netherlands; 27Jan46;
EF5155.

LILLENAS, HALDOR, 1885-
Face the music; by Haldor Lillenas.
© Haldor Lillenas, Tuscumbia, Mo.;
1Mar47; EP6669.

A living Saviour; music by Haldor
Lillenas, words by Raymond
Stoffer. © Raymond Stoffer,
North Georgetown, Ohio; 20Feb47;
EP12489. Close score: SATB.

There is no better Friend than
Jesus; music by Haldor Lille-
nas, words by Raymond Stoffer.
© Raymond Stoffer, North
Georgetown, Ohio; 17May47;
EP14496. Close score: SATB.

We're looking for a city. Jesus
ransomed me; words by Cecil W.
Brown, music by Haldor Lillenas.
© Cecil W. Brown, Nashville,
Ind.; 24Jun47; EP9972.

LILLIS, THOMAS JOSEPH, 1872-
Old Jersey City, N. J.; words
and music by Thomas J. Lillis.
© Thomas J. Lillis, Jersey
City; 24Apr47; EP14042.

LIMA, ALBERTO DE.
Malas carnes ... Lotra y música
de Alberto de Lima. © Peer
International Corp., New York;
30Dec46; EP11873.

Velo y corona ... Letra y música
de Alberto de Lima. © Peer
International Corp., New York;
30Dec46; EP11175. For voice and
piano, with chord symbols.

[LINCKE, PAUL]
Glow-worm; [by] Paul Lincke] ...
Arr. by Louis Sugarman. © Edward B. Marks Music Corp.,
New York; on arrangement;
17Feb47; EP12246. For piano
solo.

LINCOLN, JOHN.
Sincerely; words & music by John
Lincoln. © Nordyke Publishing
Co., Los Angeles; 15Nov46;
EP14785.

LINDBERG, OSKAR, 1887-
En längtans vals; [av] Oscar
Lindberg. © Nordiska Musikförlaget, a/b, Stockholm;
1Jul19; EF5398. For piano solo.

Två sånger; för en röst med piano
av Oskar Lindberg. - Nordiska
Musikförlaget, a/b, Stockholm;
on 2 songs; 1Jan20. For voice
and piano. Contents.- [v.1]
Alskade, sjung; dikt av Axel
Krook. (© EF5400).- [v.2] Sov;
dikt av Olof Thurman (© EF5399)

Vår; för piano, [by] Oskar
Lindberg. © Nordiska Musikförlaget, a/b, Stockholm;
1Jan20; EF5401.

LIPPMAN, SIDNEY, 1914-
After graduation day. See his
Barefoot boy with cheek.

(Barefoot boy with cheek) After
graduation day, [from] "Barefoot boy with cheek." Words
by Sylvia Dee, [pseud] music
by Sidney Lippman. © Chappell
& Co., inc., New York; 24Feb47;
EP12304.

(Barefoot boy with cheek) I
knew I'd know, [from] "Barefoot
boy with cheek"; words by Sylvia
Dee [pseud.], music by Sidney
Lippman. © Chappell & Co., inc.,
New York; 14Mar47; EP12723.

LIPPMAN, SIDNEY, 1914-   Cont'd.
(Barefoot boy with cheek) It's
too nice a day to go to school.
[from] Barefoot boy with
cheek; words by Sylvia Dee
[pseud.], music by Sidney
Lippman. © Chappell & Co.,
inc., New York; 8Mar47;
EP12678.

(Barefoot boy with cheek) The
story of Carrot; [from "Barefoot boy with cheek"] words by
Sylvia Dee, [pseud.], music
by Sidney Lippman. ©
Chappell & Co., inc., New
York; 5May47; EP14344.

(Barefoot boy with cheek) When
you're eighteen, [from] "Barefoot
boy with cheek"; words by Sylvia Dee,
[pseud.] music by Sidney Lippman.
© Chappell & Co., inc., New York;
11Mar47; EP12785.

I knew I'd know. See his Barefoot boy with cheek.

It's too nice a day to go to school.
See his Barefoot boy with cheek.

The story of Carrot. See his
Barefoot boy with cheek.

When you're eighteen. See his
Barefoot boy with cheek.

LISBONA, EDDIE, 1905-
I don't wanna dream again;
written and composed by Joe
Lubin and Eddie Lisbona. ©
Lawrence Wright Music Co.,
ltd., London; 13Jun47;
EF3716.

LISTER, BILL. See
Lister, Weldon Edwin.

LISTER, WELDON EDWIN, 1923-
This time, sweetheart, we're really
through; words & music by Bill
Lister. © Uhl & Ware, San
Antonio; 7Feb47; EP12289.

LISZT, FRANZ, 1811-1886.
Ave Maria; [by] Arcadelt-Liszt,
transcribed ... by Russell
Harvey. © Elkan-Vogel Co.,
inc., Philadelphia; on transcription; 26Nov46; EP11449.
Condensed score (band) and
parts.

Dream of love. (Liebestraum, no.
3) For chorus of soprano I &
II, and alto, [by] Franz Liszt,
arr. by Robert W. Gibb. [Words
by] Mary B. Austin. © The B. F.
Wood Music Co., Boston; on words
& arrangement; 21Apr47; EP13814.

Dream of love. (Liebestraum, no.
3) Two-part chorus, [by] Franz
Liszt, arr. by Robert W. Gibb.
[Words by] Mary B. Austin.
© The B. F. Wood Music Co.,
Boston; on words & arrangement;
21Apr47; EP13813.

Liebestraum. Dream of love; by
Franz Liszt, [arr. by Hugo
Frey] © Hamilton S. Gordon,
inc., New York; on arrangement;
14Apr47; EP13738. For piano
solo.

LISZTOFF, GREGORY.
In a little candy store; music
and lyrics by Gregory Lisztoff.
© Popular Melody Publisher,
Loyalhanna, Pa.; 20Mar47;
EP13142.

LITOLF, ANTON, 1890-
How could I know? .Words by Percy
Edgar, music by Anton Litolf.
© B. Feldman & Co., ltd.,
London; 18Feb47; EF5079.

LITTLE, JACK, 1900-
In a shanty in old Shanty
Town ... Lyric by Joe Young,
music by Little Jack Little
and John Siras [pseud.] A
Johnny Sterling arrangement.
© M. Witmark & Sons, New
York; on arrangement; 25Apr47;
EP14404. Piano-conductor
score (orchestra, with words)
and parts.

You broke the only heart that
ever loved you ... (S.A.T.B.)
arr. by William Stickles.
Words and music by Freddy
James and Little Jack Little.
© Chappell & Co., inc., New
York; on arrangement; 31Dec46;
EP11432.

You broke the only heart that
ever loved you ... (T.T.B.B.)
arr. by William Stickles.
Words and music by Freddy
James and Little Jack Little.
© Chappell & Co., inc., New
York; on arrangement; 31Dec46;
EP11433.

LITTLE, LITTLE JACK. See
Little, Jack.

LIVINGSTON, JAY HAROLD, 1915-
A coach and four. See his
Monsieur Beaucaire.

(Monsieur Beaucaire) A coach and
four; words and music by J.
Livingston and Ray Evans. ©
Famous Music Corp., New York;
6Jun46; EP7031.

LIVINGSTON, JERRY, 1909-
Chi-baba, chi-baba (my bambino
go to sleep); words and music
by Mack David, Al Hoffman [and]
Jerry Livingston. © Oxford
Music Corp., New York; 21Apr47;
EP13831.

Give me something to dream about;
by Mack David, Al Hoffman and
Jerry Livingston, arranged by Van
Alexander. [c1946] © Capitol Songs,
inc., New York; on arrangement;
28Jan47; EP11393. Piano-conductor
score (orchestra, with words) and
parts.

Give me something to dream about;
by Mack David, Al Hoffman [and]
Jerry Livingston. © Capitol
Songs, inc., New York; 22Jan47;
EP11308. For voice and piano,
with chord symbols.

A heart full of love; lyric by
Al Hoffman, music by Jerry Living-
ston. © Bob Stephens, inc.,
New York; 6Feb47; EP11878.

I had too much to dream last night ...
by Al Hoffman, Jack Segal [and]
Jerry Livingston, arr. by Johnny
Warrington. [c1946] © ABC Music
Corp., New York; on arrangement;
21Mar47; EP12924. Piano-conductor
score (orchestra, with words) and
parts.

Polly Pigtails; words and music
by Mack David, Al Hoffman &
Jerry Livingston. © World
Music, inc., New York; 9Jun47;
EP14943.

Rose of Santa Rosa; words and music
by Al Hoffman, Allan Roberts and
Jerry Livingston. © Sun Music
Co., inc., New York; 15Apr47;
EP13772.

LIZÉE, GILLES M
Sweetheart; words and music by
Gilles M. Lizée. © Cine-Mart
Music Publishing Co., Hollywood,
Calif.; 30Dec46; EP14015.

LJUNGGREN, AXEL.
Storsktern-valsen; text o[ch]
musik: Axel Ljunggren.
© Edition Sylvain a/b, Stockholm; 1Jan43; EF5033.

LA LLORONA. (Cry baby) ... Folk song
of Oaxaca, Mexico, [English words
adapted by Albert Gamse] (In
André, Julio, ed. Songs from south
of the border. p.18-21) © Edward B. Marks Music Corp., New
York; on English adaptation;
28Dec46; EP10868.

LOBOS, HEITOR VILLA. See
Villa-Lobos, Heitor.

LOEB, JOHN JACOB.
If my heart had a window; words
by Lou Holzer, music by John
Jacob Loeb, [piano arr. by
Helmy Kresa] © Mutual Music
Society, inc., New York; on
new words and arrangement;
27Mar47; EP13734.

The maharajah of Magador; words
and music by Lewis Harris [and]
John Jacob Loeb. © Mutual
Music Society, inc., New York;
1May47; EP14443.

You'll know when it happens ... by
Carmen Lombardo and John Jacob
Loeb, arr. by Johnny Warrington.
[c1946] © Bourne, inc., New
York; on arrangement; 20Mar47;
EP12821. Piano-conductor score
(orchestra, with words) and parts.

LÜHR, HERMANN.
Chorus, gentlemen! Words by Mark
Ambient, music by Hermann Lühr,
arr. for ... T. T. B. B. by
Clarence Lucas. © Chappell &
Co., ltd., London; on arrange-
ment; 1May47; EF5415.

LOEILLET, JEAN BAPTISTE.
Sonata in C major ... [by] J. B.
Loeillet, figured bass realised
by A. Gibilaro, ed. and arr.
by Evelyn Rothwell. © J. &
W. Chester, ltd., London; on
arrangement; 1Jun47; EF5896.
Score (oboe and piano) and
part.

LOES, HARRY DIXON.
Look unto the Saviour; [by] Harry
Dixon Loes, [words by] John J.
Keating, sr. © John J. Keating,
sr., Omaha, Neb.; 15Mar47;
EP15142. Close score; SATB.

The Saviour lives; [words by]
Oswald J. Smith, [music by]
Harry Dixon Loes. (In Moody
Bible institute of Chicago.
The voice of thanksgiving, no.
5. Hymn no.109) © Hope
Publishing Co., Chicago;
1Jul46; EP13680. Close score;
SATB.

LOESSER, FRANK, 1910-
(The perils of Pauline) I wish I
didn't love you so; by Frank
Loesser. [From the Paramount
picture "The perils of Pauline",
piano arr. by Jerry Phillips]
© Famous Music Corp., New York;
10Apr47; EP13496. For voice and
piano, with chord symbols.

(The perils of Pauline) Poppa, don't
preach to me, as sung in the ...
picture "The perils of Pauline";
by Frank Loesser. © Famous Music
Corp., New York; 12Mar47; EP12757.
For voice and piano, with chord
symbols.

LOESSER, FRANK, 1910-   Cont'd.
(The perils of Pauline) Rumble,
rumble, rumble, as sung in
the ... picture "The perils
of Pauline"; by Frank Loesser.
© Famous Music Corp., New
York; 14Mar47; EP12639. For
voice and piano, with chord
symbols.

(The perils of Pauline) The sewing
machine; by Frank Loesser. [From
the Paramount picture "The perils
of Pauline", piano arr. by Jerry
Phillips] © Famous Music Corp.,
New York; 10Apr47; EP13497. For
voice and piano, with chord symbols.

Poppa don't preach to me. See his
The perils of Pauline.

Rumble, rumble, rumble. See his
The perils of Pauline.

Tallahassee. See his Variety
girl.

(Variety girl) Tallahassee, as
featured in the ... picture
"Variety girl"; by Frank Loesser.
© Famous Music Corp., New York;
15Apr47; EP13652. For 1-2 voices and piano, with chord
symbols.

LOEWE, FREDERICK.
Almost like being in love. See his
Brigadoon.

(Brigadoon) Almost like being in
love ... [from] Brigadoon ...
lyrics by Alan Jay Lerner,
music by Frederick Loewe.
Cleveland, S. Fox Pub. Co.
© Alan Jay Lerner & Frederick
Loewe, New York; 13Mar47;
EP12727.

(Brigadoon) Almost like being in
love ... from the ... musical,
Brigadoon, lyrics by Alan Jay
Lerner, music by Frederick
Loewe, dance arrangement by
Paul Weirick. New York, S. Fox
Publishing Co. © Alan Jay
Lerner [and] Frederick Loewe,
New York; on arrangement;
11Apr47; EP13692. Piano-con-
ductor score (orchestra, with
words) and parts.

(Brigadoon) Almost like being in
love, [from the new musical
"Brigadoon"]; lyrics by Alan
Jay Lerner ... music by
Frederick Loewe, arr. by Victor
Lamont, [pseud.] © Frederick
Loewe and Alan Jay Lerner,
New York; on arrangement;
2Jun47; EP15027. Piano-con-
ductor score (orchestra, with
words) and parts.

(Brigadoon) Brigadoon ... [from]
Brigadoon ... lyrics by Alan
Jay Lerner, music by Frederick
Loewe, Cleveland, S. Fox Pub.
Co. © Alan Jay Lerner &
Frederick Loewe, New York;
13Mar47; EP12730.

(Brigadoon) Come to me, bend to
me ... [from] Brigadoon ...
lyrics by Alan Jay Lerner,
music by Frederick Loewe. Cleveland, S. Fox Pub. Co. © Alan
Jay Lerner & Frederick Loewe,
New York; 13Mar47; EP12725.

(Brigadoon) Come to me, bend to
me; waltz from the ... musical
"Brigadoon." Lyrics by Alan
Jay Lerner, music by Frederick
Loewe, dance arrangement by
Paul Weirick. New York, Sam
Fox Publishing Co. © Alan Jay
Lerner & Frederick Loewe, New
York; on arrangement; 17Apr47;
EP13866. Piano-conductor score
(orchestra) and parts.

(Brigadoon) Come to me, bend to
me, [from the new musical
"Brigadoon"]; lyrics by Alan Jay
Lerner ... music by Frederick
Loewe, arr. by Victor Lamont,
[pseud.] © Frederick Loewe and
Alan Jay Lerner, New York; on ar-
rangement; 2Jun47; EP15026.
Piano-conductor score (orchestra,
with words) and parts.

(Brigadoon) Down on MacConnachy
Square ... [from] Brigadoon ...
lyrics by Alan Jay Lerner,
music by Frederick Loewe.
Cleveland, S. Fox Pub. Co.
© Alan Jay Lerner & Frederick
Loewe, New York; 13Mar47;
EP12731.

(Brigadoon) From this day on ...
[from the] musical, Brigadoon ...
lyrics by Alan Jay Lerner, music
by Frederick Loewe. New York, S.
Fox Pub. Co. © Frederick Loewe
[and] Alan Jay Lerner, New York;
7May47; EP14397.

(Brigadoon) The heather on the
hill ... [from] Brigadoon ...
lyrics by Alan Jay Lerner,
music by Frederick Loewe.
Cleveland, S. Fox Pub. Co.
© Alan Jay Lerner & Frederick
Loewe, New York; 13Mar47;
EP12729.

(Brigadoon) The heather on the
hill ... from the ... musical,
Brigadoon, lyrics by Alan Jay
Lerner, music by Frederick
Loewe, dance arr. by Paul
Weirick. New York, S. Fox
Publishing Co. © Alan Jay
Lerner [and] Frederick Loewe,
New York; on arrangement;
10Apr47; EP13691. Piano-con-
ductor score (orchestra, with
words) and parts.

(Brigadoon) The heather on the
hill, [from the new musical
"Brigadoon"]; lyrics by Alan Jay
Lerner ... music by Frederick
Loewe, arr. by Victor Lamont,
[pseud.] © Frederick Loewe and
Alan Jay Lerner, New York; on ar-
rangement; 2Jun47; EP15024.
Piano-conductor score (orchestra,
with words) and parts.

(Brigadoon) I'll go home with
bonnie Jean ... [from] Briga-
doon ... lyrics by Alan Jay
Lerner, music by Frederick
Loewe. Cleveland, S. Fox
Pub. Co. © Alan Jay Lerner
& Frederick Loewe, New York;
15Mar47; EP12697.

(Brigadoon) There but for you go
I ... [from] Brigadoon ... lyrics
by Alan Jay Lerner, music by
Frederick Loewe. Cleveland, S.
Fox Pub. Co. © Alan Jay Lerner
& Frederick Loewe, New York;
13Mar47; EP12726.

(Brigadoon) Waitin' for my dearie
... [from] Brigadoon ... lyrics
by Alan Jay Lerner, music by
Frederick Loewe. Cleveland,
S. Fox Pub. Co. © Alan Jay
Lerner & Frederick Loewe, New
York; 13Mar47; EP12728.

Come to me, bend to me. See his
Brigadoon.

Down on MacConnachy Square. See
his Brigadoon.

From this day on. See his
Brigadoon.

The heather on the hill. See his
Brigadoon.

I'll go home with bonnie Jean.
See his Brigadoon.

There but for you go I. See his
Brigadoon.

Waitin' for my dearie. See his
Brigadoon.

LOMBARDO, CARMEN.
You'll know when it happens; by
Carmen Lombardo [and] John
Jacob Loeb. [c1946] © Bourne,
inc., New York; 8Apr47; EP13911.
Condensed score (orchestra)
and parts.

LONERGAN, MOYA.
Just like Darby and Joan; words
and music by Moya Lonergan.
© Allan & Co., pty. ltd.,
Melbourne, Australia; 5Feb47;
EF3355.

LONG, GRAYCE E
Tiny tunes. New York, J. Day Co.
© Grayce E. Long, Hartford,
Conn.; 29Apr46; EP4666.

LONG, LOUISE.
Road closed, bridge out, detour;
words and music by Louise
Long. © Harry Warren Music,
inc., New York; 20May47;
EP14558.

LONG, NEWELL H   1905-
Chestnuts ... [by] Newell H. Long.
© Rubank, inc., Chicago; 1Mar47;
EP12272. Piano-conductor score
(narrator and band) and parts.

LONG, SHORTY.
Just say so long (and not goodbye)
... music by Shorty Long, [words
by] Jack Day. (In Cousin Lee
book of original songs. p.14-
15) © Jack Howard Publications,
inc., Philadelphia; 30Dec46;
EP11733.

LONGING; traditional Russian folk
song ... [English lyric by
Wladimir Lakond] © Edward
B. Marks Music Corp., New York;
on English lyric; 18Dec46;
EP12031. Score: TB and oboe.

LOOSLI, EUGENE, 1884-
Little two by four; words and
music by Eugene Loosli.
© Eugene Loosli, Elmira, N. Y.;
on new words; 18Aug38;
EP14453.

LOPEZ, FRANCIS, 1916-
(La belle de Cadix) Pour toi,
Pepita ... de l'opérette: "La
belle de Cadix" ... Lyrics de
Maurice Vandair [pseud.],
musique de Francis Lopez ...
La belle histoire ... du film:
"Adventure sur la côte"; paroles de Pierre Farny, musique
de Henri Martinet, arr. de
Francis Salabert. © Salabert,
inc., New York; 30Nov46;
EF3869. Piano conductor score
(orchestra, with words), and
parts.

(Le cavalier noir) La plus belle;
paroles de Marcel Bertou. ©
Éditions Paul Beuscher, Paris;
30Jun44; EF524. For voice and
piano.

Jungle serenade. (Refrain sauvage)
French lyric by Francois Llenas
& Pierre Hiegel, English lyric
by Renaldo C. Lyonel, music by
Francis Lopez. [c1946] © Camp-
bell, Connelly & co., ltd.,
London; 1Feb47; EF5288.

La plus belle. See his Le cavalier noir.

LOPEZ, FRANCIS, 1916-   Cont'd.
Pour toi, Pepita. See his La belle
de Cadix.
Rendez-vous sous la lune; de
l'opérette "La belle de Cadix"
... Lyrics de Maurice Vandair
[pseud.] musique de Francis
López. © Salabert, inc., New
York; 31Oct46; EP5193.

LOPEZ, MANO.
Mi corazón ... Letra y música de
Maño Lopez. © Peer Internation-
al Corp., New York; 18Apr47;
EP13974.

LOPEZ, RICARDO JIMENEZ. See
Jiménez López, Ricardo.

LÓPEZ MENA, DOMÍNGO.
Adios corazon ... de D. López Mena.
Echenle agua no hagan polvo ...
de Felipe Bermejo. © Pro-
motora Hispano Americana de
Música, s.a., Mexico; 24Apr47;
EF3202-3203. For voice and
piano.

LOPEZ VIDAL, FRANCISCO. See
Vidal, Francisco Lopez.

LORA, ANTONIO.
Improvisation and burlesque ... by
Antonio Lora. © Broadcast Music,
inc., New York; 10Mar47; EP13777.
Score (flute and piano) and part.

LORD, RACHEL.
Lord, let me learn of Thee; [words
by] R. L. (In Gospel choruses.
no. 3, p. 2] © Rachel Lord, Pasadena, Calif.; 4Jun46; EP4312.
Close score: SATB.

Since Jesus' love I've found; words
by S. S. Plank and Doris Woodard,
music by Rachel Lord. (In Four
gospel songs, no.4. p.[2])
© Rachel Lord, Doris Woodard & S.
S. Plank, Baldwin Park, Calif.;
10Sep46; EP12034.

LORENZ, ELLEN JANE, 1907-
God is here; four-part chorus of
mixed voices ... a cappella,
words by Gerhard Tersteegen,
music by Ellen Jane Lorenz. ©
Carl Fischer, inc., New York;
16Apr47; EP13899.
Memories of Easter morn; an S.S.
A. Easter choir cantata ... text
arr. and music, based on familiar
Easter hymns, composed by Ellen
Jane Lorenz. © Lorenz Publishing Co., Dayton, Ohio; on arrangement; 2Jan47; EP14129.

LORENZ, ELLEN JANE, 1907-   comp.
Get-together hymns ... comp. by
Ellen Jane Lorenz. © Lorenz
Publishing Co., Dayton, Ohio;
14Dec46; EP12127. With music.

Lorenz's organ and piano duets;
[comp. by Ellen Jane Lorenz]
© Lorenz Publishing Co., Dayton, Ohio; no.2, 12May47;
EP15257.

Lorenz's organ chimes folio; comp.
by Ellen Jane Lorenz. © Lorenz
Publishing Co., Dayton, Ohio;
13Jun47; EP15258.

LORENZ'S ORGAN ALBUM; [comp. by
Ellen Jane Lorenz] © Lorenz
Publishing Co., Dayton,
Ohio; no.4, 21Jan47; no.5,
2Jul47; EP12673, 16552.

LOTH, L   LESLIE.
Little elfin piper ... [words by]
Maude Hall Lyman, [music by]
L. Leslie Loth. © Oliver
Ditson Co., Philadelphia,
7May47; EP14484.

LOU, TANTE, pseud. See
Cursan, Marie Louise.

LOUIGUY, pseud. See also
Guglelmi, Louis.

LOUIS, DEL ST. See
St. Louis, Del.

LOURIÉ, ARTHUR.
The crucifix by the sea. A Cristo
crucificado ante el mar. Song
for baritone (or mezzo-soprano)
and piano, by Arthur Lourié,
[Spanish words by José Bergamin,
English version by Erminie Huntress]
© G. Schirmer, inc., New York;
8Apr46; EP11610.

LOVEDAY, CARROLL, 1895-
The hills of Dannemora; words and
music by Carroll Lovoday. ©
Gate Music Co., New York;
2Jan47; EP11019.

LOVEJOY, HELEN.
Autumn barcarolle; by Helen
Lovejoy. © Axelrod Publications, inc., Providence;
1Apr47; EP12833. For
piano solo.

LOVELACE, AUSTIN C
Easter paean; anthem for mixed
voices, the text and music by
Austin C. Lovelace. © The H.
W. Gray Co., inc., New York;
3Jan47; EP11060.

LOWE, RALPH.
I sing to the sea ... the words
and music by Ralph Lowe. © R.
D. Row Music Co., Boston;
8May47; EP14811.

LOWRY, ROBERT, 1826-1899.
I need Thee every hour; [by]
Lowry, transcribed by H. F. Hopkins. © Century Music Publishing Co., New York; on arrangement;
31May47; EP14737. For piano solo.

Who'll be the next? ... By M.
Lowry, arr. for violin by John
Chestnut, [© John Chestnut,
Jr., Philadelphia; on arrange-
ment; 31Mar47; EP14871. Score
(violin and piano) and part.

LOYOLA, FERNANDO. See
Loyola Jáuregui, Fernando.

LOYOLA JAUREGUI, FERNANDO, 1874-
Obras para piano y canto; [by]
Fernando Loyola. © Fernando
Loyola Jáuregui, Querétaro,
Qro., México; album no.1-2,
15Nov46; EP4873-4874.

LUBIN, JOE.
Don't fall in love; words and
music by Eddie Lisbona and Joe
Lubin, [piano score by Kenneth
Essex] © Bradbury Wood, ltd.,
London; 30Jan47; EF5099.

I get up ev'ry morning. (What do
I do, what do I do, what do I
do?) By Eddie Lisbona and Joe
Lubin, piano score by Kenneth
Essex. © Bradbury Wood, ltd.,
London; 22Apr47; EF5263. For
voice and piano; melody also in
tonic sol-fa notation.

Ignorance is bliss; words and
music by Eddie Lisbona and
Joe Lubin, [piano score by
Kenneth Essex] The signature
tune from the ... B.B.C.
feature. © Bradbury Wood,
ltd., London; 3May47;
EF3782.

LUCAS, HARVEY W
Your final decision ... words by
Charles A. Reinert, music by
Harvey W. Lucas. © Harvey W.
Lucas, Philadelphia; 3Feb47;
EP11915.

LUCCHESI, ROGER.
Douce biguine. In my dreams.
Paroles et musique de Roger
Lucchesi, English version by Don
Titman. Lachute, Qué., Can.,
Parnasse Musical. © Editions A.
Fassio, Lachute, Qué., Can.,
1Feb47; EF5054.

LUCKE, KATHARINE ELEANOR, 1875-
Practical drill in keyboard
harmony ... by Katharine E.
Lucke. [4th ed.] Baltimore,
G. F. Krans Music Co. ©
Katharine E. Lucke, Baltimore; bk.1, on new set of
modulations & harmonization
of figured & unfigured basses;
24Mar47; EP13347.

LULLY, VICTOR.
Passacaille; [by] Lully,
réalisation et annotations de
Paul Bazelaire. © Alphonse
Leduc et Cie., Paris; on
arrangement; 5Dec46; EF5201.
Score (violoncello and piano)
and part.

LUNDKVIST, PER. See
Lundquist, Per.

LUNDQUIST, MATTHEW.
Go forth, my heart, and seek delight ... for four part male
chorus (unaccompanied) Old
French folk-melody arr. and ed.
by Matthew Lundquist; text a-
nonymous. © McLaughlin &
Reilly Co., Boston; on arrangement; 10Apr47; EP13629.

LUNDQUIST, PER.
Med folket för fosterlandet;
([words by] Ragnhild Lundquist) ... Av Per Lundquist.
© Nordiska Musikförlaget,
a.b., Stockholm; 1Jan45;
EF3723. For voice and piano.

LUPI, ROBERTO, 1908-
(Partita, harp] Partita per
arpa; (da intavolature per liuto
della metà del secolo XVII],
[by] Roberto Lupi. © Carisch,
società anonima, Milan;
20Feb42; EF5216.

LUPO, PINO, 1905-
Lo studio dei bassi ... metodo
di perfezionamento per la
mano sinistra, [by] Pino Lupo.
© Carisch, s.a., Milan;
11Nov40; EF3718. Studies and
exercises for accordion.

LUPTON, BELLE GEORGE.
Memories of Idaho; words by Her-
bert Lupton, music by Belle
George Lupton. © Belle George
Lupton, Ashton, Idaho; 26Dec46;
EP10716.

LUTÈCE, JEAN, pseud. See also
Chardon, Julien.

Reviens vers moi; paroles de
Jacques Larue [pseud.], musique
de Jean Lutece. © Sté Ame Pac
Chappell, Paris; 8May47; EF3414.

LUTHER, MARTIN, 1483-1546.
A mighty fortress is our God;
melody by Luther, arr. ... by
Lucien Cailliet. © Boosey &
Hawkes, inc., New York; on
arrangement; 27Dec46; EP13382.
Piano-conductor score (orchestra)
and parts.

A mighty fortress is our God;
melody by Luther, arr. by
Lucien Cailliet. S.A.T.B. ©
Boosey & Hawkes, inc., New
York; on arrangement; 31Dec46;
EP10998.

LUTHER, MARTIN, 1483-1546. Cont'd.
A mighty fortress is our God;
melody by Luther, arr. by
Lucien Cailliet. S.S.A. ©
Boosey & Hawkes, inc., New
York; on arrangement; 31Dec46;
EP10997.

A mighty fortress is our God; music
by Luther, arr. by Lucien
Cailliet ... T.T.B.B. ©
Boosey & Hawkes, inc., New
York; on arrangement; 27Dec46;
EP10995.

LUTHOLD, NIKOLAUS ALBERT, 1893-
Liebe vergeht; Worte: Theo A.
Körner, Musik: Albert Lüthold.
© Albert Lüthold, Musikverlag
"Arpeggio," Zürich, Switzerland;
6Mar46; EF5339. For voice and
piano, parts for orchestra
laid in.

LUTYENS, ELISABETH.
Five intermezzi; [by] Elisabeth
Lutyens. Op. 9. [For] piano
solo. © Alfred Lengnick &
Co., ltd., London; 2Apr47;
EF3198.

(Quartet, strings, no. 2) String
quartet no. 2. Op. 5, no. 5.
[By] Elisabeth Lutyens. ©
Alfred Lengnick & Co., ltd.,
London; 2Apr47; EF3199. Parts.

LUVAAS, MORTEN J   1896-
As the snowflakes gently fall;
French carol, S.A.T.B. [Words
by] Jane Lewis McKnight, [arr.
by] Morten J. Luvaas. © Neil
A. Kjos Music Co., Chicago;
on arrangement & words; 1Jul46;
EP10989.

The pines of home; for four-part
chorus of mixed voices a cappella.
Poem by Virginia Grant Collins,
music by Morten J. Luvaas.
© Carl Fischer, inc., New York;
10Feb47; EP12161.

Ye bells of Bethlehem; melody from
Freylinghausen's Gesangbuch ...
S.S.A., with acc. [Words by]
Valerio Simpson, [alternate text
... by Woissel, tr. Catherine Wink-
worth, arr., by] Morten J. Luvaas.
© Neil A. Kjos Music Co., Chicago;
on arrangement & words; 1Jul46;
EP10988.

[LUVAAS, MORTEN J   ], 1896-
arr.
Light of light; choral melody by
J. S. Bach, [words by] Benjamin
Schmolck ... [arr. by] Peter
Norman, [pseud.] © Neil A. Kjos
Music Co., Chicago; on arrange-
ment; 19Jun47; EP15187. Score:
soprano or children's choir,
chorus (SATB) and piano or organ.

LUYPAERTS, GUY.
Une enseigne au vent. The
ancient sign. Paroles de
Rachèle Thoreau, musique de
Guy Luypaerts, English
version by Don Titman. ©
Éditions A. Fassio, Lachute,
Qué., Can.; 20Jun47; EF3934.

LYNCH, STEVE.
Let's pretend; words and music by
Steve Lynch, arrangement by Harold
Potter. © Stephen J. Lynch,
Utica, N. Y.; 3Feb47; EP11907.

LYNTON, EVERETT, 1888-
Pretty little dirty face; by
Algy More and Everett Lynton.
© Lawrence Wright Music Co.,
ltd., London; 24Jan47; EF4066.
For voice and piano, with chord
symbols; melody also in tonic
sol-fa notation.
Rose coloured world; written and
composed by Charlie Chester, Ken
Morris and Everett Lynton. ©
Lawrence Wright Music Co., ltd.,
London; 24Apr47; EF5625. For
voice and piano, with chord sym-
bols; melody also in tonic sol-fa
notation.
Sweetheart (you're like my favour-
ite song); by Charlie Chester,
Ken Morris & Everett Lynton.
© Lawrence Wright Music Co.,
ltd., London; 27Mar47; EF5473.

M

MAAS, GEORGE H
Hokey pokey man; words by Julia R. Maas, music by George H. Maas. © George R. Maas, Milwaukee; 12May47; EP14595.

McBRIDE, DICKIE.
Nobody's waiting for me; words and music by Floyd Tillman and Dickie McBride. © Northern Music Corp., New York; 12Feb47; EP12172.

McBRIDE, ROBERT.
Lonely landscape; composed ... by Robert McBride. © Leeds Music Corp., New York; 21Mar47; EP12857. Condensed score (band) and parts.

McCARGAR, DOROTHY.
The scarecrow's friend; an operetta for the upper grades in one act, libretto by Millis Cavorly, music by Dorothy McCargar. © Row, Peterson & Co., Evanston, Ill.; 18Dec46; DP1223.

McCARTHY, PAT.
I'm afraid to love you ('fraid I might like it); by Harry Stride, Bert Douglas and Pat McCarthy; arr. by Paul Weirick. © Bob Stephens, inc., New York; on arrangement; 31Dec46; EP11312. Piano-conductor score (orchestra, with words) and parts.

McCAUGHERTY, IRENE ELEANOR, 1914-
Come to me, lonesome baby; words and music by Irene McCaugherty, [music arrangement by W. Brad] © Irene Eleanor McCaugherty, N. Vancouver, B. C.; 1May47; EP31443.

McCLELLAN, CLARK, 1917-
I'll never grieve (oh no! oh no!) Words by Fred Perrazzano, music by Clark McClellan. © McClennan Music Co., New York; 18Apr47; EP13724.

McCOMAS, THOMAS JEFFERSON, 1909-
So much for so little, (who am I to ask for more)? Words and music by T. J. McComas. © Thomas Jefferson McComas, Englewood, Colo.; 1Sep46; EP11742.

MACOMBER, KEN.
(Humoresque) Humoresque (humor it!); with apologies to Anton Dvorak, featured in the Warner Bros. picture "Humoresque". A Ken Macomber ... arrangement. © Remick Music Corp., New York; on arrangement; 18Feb47; EP12255. Piano-conductor score (orchestra) and parts.

McCONNELL, MAMIE.
Big Chief Wahoo; for piano, [by] Mamie McConnell. © Theodore Presser Co., Philadelphia; 17Feb47; EP12392.

McCUTCHEON, VEDA MARIE.
Dark river; words and music by Veda Marie McCutcheon. © Nordyke Publishing Co., Los Angeles; 20ct45; EP13531.

McDERMOTT, ALFRED.
Chiming bells; words and music by Alfred McDermott. © Alfred McDermott, Pound, Wis.; 27Feb47; EP13414.

McDIARMID, DONALD P   1898-
Aloha nui loa, dear ... words and music by Don McDiarmid. © Donald P. (Don) McDiarmid, Honolulu; 14May47; EP14431.

MacDOWELL, EDWARD ALEXANDER, 1861-1908.
Deserted; [by] Edward MacDowell. Op.9, no.1. Arr. by Hugo Norden. (In MacDowell, E. A. 6 transcriptions ... for violin and pianoforte. p.12-13) © The Arthur P. Schmidt Co., Boston; on arrangement; 31Dec46; EP11857. Score (violin and piano) and part.

MACELL, JERRY.
Midnight lady; words & music by Jerry Macell. © Nordyke Pub. Co., Los Angeles; 9Aug46; EP11921.

I'm just an old man; words and music by Alfred McDermott. © Alfred McDermott, Pound, Wis.; 27Feb47; EP13418.

Just another headache; words and music by Alfred McDermott. © Alfred McDermott, Pound, Wis.; 27Feb47; EP13417.

McENERY, ALBERTA.
I'm a married man; words and music by Alberta McEnery. © Hill and Range Songs, inc., Hollywood, Calif.; 10Jun47; EP15084.

McENERY, DAVID L
I don't want to lose you now; words and music by "Red River" Dave McEnery. © Stasny Music Corp., New York; 31May47; EP6942.

Tired and weary old cowboy; words by Peggy Ann Munson, music by Dave McEnery (Red River Dave) (In Cousin Lee book of original songs. p.28-29) © Jack Howard Publications, inc., Philadelphia; 30Dec46; EP11739.

McENERY, RED RIVER DAVE. See McEnery, David L.

MACFAYDEN, JOHN H
(Clear the track) More like an angel; lyric by Marc Lawrence ... music by John H. MacFayden ... [from the] Princeton University Triangle Club ... production ... Clear the track. © Broadcast Music, inc., New York; 12Dec46; EP11838.

More like an angel. See his Clear the track.

McGHEE, BERRY M
I am Alpha and Omega; words & music by Berry M. McGhee [arr. by Harry P. Guy] © Berry M. McGhee, Detroit; 3Feb47; EP11911. Close score: SATB.

McGLOOK, SPOOK. See Dahle, Alexander A.

McGRANE, PAUL.
To bed early; by Jimmy Eaton & Paul McGrane. London, Clover Music Co. © Noel Gay, inc., New York; 17May46; EP5647. For voice and piano, with chord symbols; melody also in tonic sol-fa notation.

MacGREGOR, CHUMMY, 1903-
Why don't we say we're no sorry? Lyric by Harry Harris, music by Chummy MacGregor. [arr. by Jerry Phillips] © Crystal Music Publishers, inc., Hollywood, Calif.; 15Jan47; EP12832.

McGUFFIN, KATHLEEN W. FACE, 1891-
Sorghum; [by] Mrs. Kathleen W. Face McGuffin. © Kathleen W. Face McGuffin, Jackson Heights, N. Y.; 14Apr47; EP13916. For piano solo.

McGURK, WILLIAM ROBERT JAMES, 1884-
Sunset and evening ... words and music by Bill McGurk, [tr. by Theo. Weinrich and Mrs. Paul Vogeler, arr. by Ed. Donovan] [c1946] © William H. J. McGurk, Holyoke, Mass.; on arrangement; 11Jun47; EP14420. German and English words.

McHENRY, ELMER W
To you, from me, all my love; words & music by Mac Henry, [pseud.] © Elmer W. McHenry, Decatur, Ga.; 21Jun47; EP6974.

MACHESNEY, ART.
My dream about you; words and music by Art Machesney. © Master Melodies Music Publishers, inc., Baltimore; 9Apr47; EP13675.

MACHO, GUSTAV, 1882-
Wiener serenade; [by] Gustav Macho. © Ludwig Doblinger (Bernhard Herzmansky), K. G., Vienna; 15Nov44; EF3398. Score (violin and piano) and part.

McHUGH, JAMES FRANCIS, 1894-
(Calendar girl) Calendar girl; words by Harold Adamson, music by James McHugh ... [from the] picture "Calendar girl." © Mayfair Music Corp., New York; 24Mar47; EP13371.

(Calendar girl) I'm telling you now; words by Harold Adamson, music by James McHugh ... [From] Calendar girl. © Mayfair Music Corp., New York; 25Feb47; EP12524.

(Calendar girl) Lovely night to go dancing; words by Harold Adamson, music by James McHugh ... [From] Calendar girl. © Mayfair Music Corp., New York; 25Feb47; EP12523.

(Hit parade of 1947) Is there anyone here from Texas? From the ... picture "Hit parade of 1947;" lyric by Harold Adamson, music by Jimmy McHugh. © Melrose Music Corp., New York; 19Mar47; EP12790.

I guess I'll have that dream right now. See his Hit parade of 1947.

I'm telling you now. See his Calendar girl.

Is there anyone here from Texas? See his Hit parade of 1947.

Lovely night to go dancing. See his Calendar girl.

On the sunny side of the street; by Dorothy Fields and Jimmy McHugh, [arr. by Charlie Ventura] © Shapiro, Bernstein & Co., inc., New York; on arrangement; 10Jun47; EP14979. Score (B♭ tenor saxophone and piano) and part.

MACIAS FEMAT, MIGUEL.
Zopilote ... de M. Macias Femat, [words by Amado Vicario] © Promotora Hispano Americana de Música, s.a., México; 23Dec46; EF5072.

McILWRAITH, ISA.
Christ our Passover; chant setting in unison ... by Isa McIlwraith. © The H. W. Gray Co., inc., New York; 3Jan47; EP11055.

MacINNIS, MURDOCK DONALD.
(Clear the track) Princeton victory march; words by Asa S. Bushnell, III ... music by M. Donald MacInnis ... [from the] Princeton University Triangle Club ... production ... Clear the track. © Broadcast Music, inc., New York; 12Dec46; EP11840.

Princeton victory march. See his Clear the track.

MACISTE, MANUEL ALVAREZ.
Toreros y flores ... [words and music] de Manuel A. Maciste. © Hnos. Márquez, s. de r. l., México; 3Jun46; EF5907. Piano-conductor score (orchestra), and parts.

MACISTE, MANUEL ALVAREZ. See also Alvarez Maciste, Manuel.

88

McKAY, FRANCIS R
The captive; chorus for mixed
voices, S.A.T.B., a cappella,
text by Harold Vinal, music by
Francis McKay. © Clayton F.
Summy Co., Chicago; 9May47;
EP14589.
Nocturne ... S.A.T.B., a cap-
pella, text by Harold Vinal,
music by Francis McKay.
© Clayton F. Summy Co.,
Chicago; 13May47; EP14798.

McKAY, GEORGE FREDERICK, 1899-
American panorama; seven
pieces in the American folk
idiom ... quartet for ...
violins ... horns ... saxophones ... trumpets ... [or]
clarinets ... by George
Frederick McKay. © Carl
Fischer, inc., New York;
23May47; EP14715. Score
and parts.
Port Royal, 1861; folksong suite
... (based on old Negro songs
collected in the Port Royal
Islands, S. C. in 1861) ...
[by] George Frederick McKay.
(Op. 48) © C. C. Birchard &
Co., Boston; 11Feb47; EP12263.
Score (string orchestra) and
parts.

McKINLEY, RAY.
Hoodle addle; lyric and music by
Ray McKinley. © Triangle Music
Corp., New York; 16Jan47; EP11313.
Howdy friends; words and music
by Ray McKinley. © Edray
Music Publishing Co., New
York; 25May47; EP14287.

McKITTRICK, ANNE VERSTEEG.
We love the place, O God ... for
mixed voices, [words by]
William Bullock ... [music by]
Anne Vorsteeg McKittrick. ©
The H. W. Gray Co., inc., New
York; 21Feb47; EP12252.

MACKLIN, YVETTE.
Put Your spirit over me ...
words & music by Yvette
Macklin, arr. by V. Bates.
[c1946] © Yvette Macklin,
Chicago; 24Apr47; EP6862.
Teach me how to serve Thee,
Father; words and music
by Yvette Macklin, arr.
by V. Bates. [c1946] ©
Yvette Macklin, Chicago;
24Apr47; EP6861.
Work for the Master today ...
words and music by Yvette
Macklin, arr. by V. Bates.
[c1946] © Yvette Macklin,
Chicago; 24Apr47; EP6863.

McLEAN, DAVID W   1884-
San Marino greeting song; [by]
Dave McLean. © San Marino
Kiwanis Club, San Marino, Calif.;
28Jan47; EP14835. Close score;
SATB.
San Marino welcome song; [by] Dave
McLean. © San Marino Kiwanis
Club, San Marino, Calif.; 28Jan47;
EP14834. Close score; SATB.

McMILLEN, HARRY.
The bridge by Yosemite Falls; words
and music by Clara E. Porter and
Harry McMillen, piano score by
Harry A. Powell. © Harry L. Mc-
Millen, Marguerite Porter Mc-
Millen and Clara E. Porter, Mill-
brae, Calif.; 16Dec46; EP10771.
For voice and piano, with chord
symbols.

MACMURROUGH, DERMOT, pseud. See
White, Harold Robert.

McNEIL, JAMES CHARLES, 1902-
Butterflies; words by Marion
Greeley, music by J. Chas.
McNeil. © Cine-Mart Music
Publishing Co., Hollywood,
Calif.; 31Mar47; EP14653.
Just have to know; words by E. L.
Lawson, music by J. Chas. McNeil.
© Nordyke Publishing Co., Los
Angeles; 5Mar47; EP13273.
My Sally gal; words by William H.
Sheppard, music by J. Chas.
McNeil. © Nordyke Publishing
Co., Los Angeles; 5Mar47;
EP13260.
My Virginia rose; words by
Jack Alfred Carter, music by J.
Chas. McNeil. © Nordyke
Publishing Co., Los Angeles;
8Mar47; EP13288.
One of my three; words by Edward
C. Heinz, music by J. Chas.
McNeil. © Nordyke Publishing
Co., Los Angeles; 1Jul47;
EP10863. For voice and piano,
with chord symbols.
Take care of my heart; words by
Albert Joseph Perez, music by
J. Chas. McNeil. [c1943] ©
Nordyke Publishing Co., Los
Angeles; 15Feb44; EP10862. For
voice and piano.
What can it mean? Words by Rudy
Burkhart, music by J. Chas.
McNeil. © Nordyke Publishing
Co., Los Angeles; 23Aug45;
EP6504.
You're my heart; words by Alma
Horne, music by J. Chas. McNeil.
© Cine-mart Music Publishing Co.,
Hollywood, Calif.; 1Aug46; EP10953.
For voice and piano, with chord
symbols.
You're on my mind; words by Al
Douglas, music by J. Chas
McNeil. © Nordyke Publishing
Co., Hollywood, Calif.; 25Jul46;
EP11530.

McPHAIL, LINDSAY.
I've found the rainbow's end;
lyrics by Margaret Billings,
music by Lindsay McPhail.
© Victor Publishing Co.,
Dallas; 8May47; EP14508.
The Texas polka; [lyrics] by
Charles A. Francis, [music by
Lindsay McPhail] © Victor
Publishing Co., inc., Dallas;
10Jan47; EP11355.

McRAE, BOBB, 1913-
Not bad, Bascomb; by Bobb McRae.
© Fowler Music Co., New York;
16Apr47; EP13796. For piano
solo.

McVEA, JACK.
Open the door, Richard! Words by
"Dusty" Fletcher [and] John Mason,
music by Jack McVea [and] Dan
Howell. © Duchess Music Corp.,
New York; 14Feb47; EP12175.
Open the door, Richard; words by
"Dusty" Fletcher [and] John
Mason, music by Jack McVea
[and] Dan Howell, [arranged by
Vic Schoen] © Duchess Music
Corp., New York; on arrange-
ment; 14Feb47; EP12177.
Piano-conductor score (orches-
tra, with words) and parts.

MADER, CARL.
Salute to the twin cities, (Sterling-
Rock Falls, Illinois); by
Carl Mader. © Ziegler Band
Music Publ. Co., Sterling, Ill.;
3Feb47; EP11916. Condensed
score (band) and parts.

I. Title.

MADERNA, OSMAR HECTOR.
Lirio ... letra de José María
Contursi, música de Osmar
Héctor Maderna. Buenos Aires,
Editorial Argentina de Música
Internacional. © Peer Inter-
national Corp., New York;
28Aug46; EF5551.

MAEKELBERGHE, AUGUST.
The office of the holy communion;
set to music ... by August
Maekelberghe. Op. 15. © The
H. W. Gray Co., inc., New
York; 30Apr47; EP14072. Score:
chorus (SATB) and organ.

MAESTRON, CARMAN.
Drums away; composed by Carman
Maestron, arr. by Ray McKinley.
© Peter Maurice Music Co., ltd.,
New York; 13Dec46; EF5053.
Piano-conductor score (orchestra),
condensed score and parts.

MAGIC MELODIES of the gay nineties;
a collection of the songs of
yesterday ... © Remick Music
Corp., New York; on compilation
and arrangement; 12Mar46;
EP11065.

MAGNANI, A.
Méthode complète de clarinette;
[by] Magnani. Ed. con tradu-
ione in lingua italiana. ©
Alphonse Leduc & Cie.; Paris;
v. 1-2, 15Dec46; EF3597-3598.

MAGNER, MARY ALINE.
America, my country; words and
music by Mary Aline Magner.
© Grimes Music Publishers,
Philadelphia; 10Mar47; EP12330.

MAGNUSON, ARVID.
Twenty-five compositions for
piano; by Arvid Magnuson.
© Arvid Magnuson, Highland
Park, Ill.; 11Mar47;
EP13111.

MAGRAM, ROY A
My lovely little Dresden doll;
words and music by Roy A.
Magram. © Broadcast Music,
inc., New York; 19Mar47;
EP13782.

MAHER, MIKE. See
Maher, Rosamond E.

MAHER, ROSAMOND E
You sold my love for a lie; words
and music by Mike Maher. © Cine-Mart
Music Publishing Co., Hollywood,
Calif.; 1Dec46; EP12099.

MARIEUX, EDMOND, 1886-
L'amour est roi; paroles de
Nelly-Andrée [pseud.], musique
de Edmond Mahieux. Paris, Salabert. © Salabert, inc., New
York; 31Jan47; EP3471.
Sur la Place de la Bastille ...;
paroles de J. Rodor [pseud.],
musique de Edmond Mahieux, arrt.
de Francis Salabert ... L'amour
est roi ... paroles de Nelly
André [pseud.], musique de Edmond
Mahieux, arrt. de Francis Salabert. Paris, Éditions Salabert.
© Salabert, inc., New York; on
arrangement; 15Dec46; EF3460.
Piano-conductor score (orchestra,
with words) and parts.
Sur la Place de la Bastille;
paroles de Jean Rodor [pseud.],
musique de Edmond Mahieux.
Paris, Salabert. © Salabert,
inc., New York; 31Jan47;
EF3585.

MAHNGOTAYSEE, SCAN.
Red bloomed a rose; words and
music by Scan Mahngotaysee.
Chicago, Lone Tree Music Studios.
© Scan Mahngotaysee, Chicago;
7Apr47; EP13662.

MAHON, GEORGE.
The royal minuet; written &
composed by George Mahon, arr.
by Stan Bowsher [and Whisper
"I love you"; by Ross Parker,
Michael Carr & Gerald Plato,
arr. by Stan Bowsher] © Peter
Maurice Music Co., ltd., New
York; on arrangement; 28May47;
EF3664-3665. Piano-conductor
score (orchestra, with words)
and parts.
The royal minuet; written and com-
posed by George Mahon. London,
Macmelodies. © Peter Maurice
Music Co., ltd., New York;
23Apr47; EF3260.

MAINGUENEAU, LOUIS.
Suite brève; pour basson et
orchestre, [by] Louis
Maingueneau. © Durand &
Cie., Paris; 15Mar47; EF3860.
Score (bassoon and piano) and
part.

MAJO, RODRIGO A. DE SANTIAGO. See
Santiago Majo, Rodrigo A. de.

MAJOR, ERVIN, comp.
Ut a szonatához; The way leading
to the sonata ... [comp. by]
Major Ervin [and] Szelényi István
... A collection of piano pieces.
© Edition Cserépfalvi, Budapest,
Hungary; v. 1, 15Dec45; EF3157.

MALÁT, JAN, 1843-1915.
Což neřekl Ti zrak můj tisíckrát
... (Mám Tě rádi) [By] J.
Malát ... [words by J. Rokyta]
© František Chadím, Praha,
Czechoslovakia; 10Oct39;
EF5421. For voice and piano.

MALEC, ANNA.
Ciemnym borem nad wieczorem ...
In the evening through the dark
forest waltz ... for piano and
piano accordion ... words and
music by Anna Malec, arr. by F.
Przybylski. [c1946] © Władysław
H. Sajowski, Chicago; 11Feb47;
EF6660. Polish words.
Czy pamiętasz moja miła ... (Do you
remember, my darling?) ... for
piano and piano accordion ...
words and music by Anna Malec,
arr. by F. Przybylski. [c1946]
© Władysław H. Sajowski, Chicago;
11Feb47; EF6657. Polish words.
Iskiereczka ognia ... (Sparks of
fire krakowiak) ... for piano and
piano accordion ... words and
music by Anna Malec, arr. by F.
Przybylski. [c1946] © Władysław
H. Sajowski, Chicago; 11Feb47;
EF6661. Polish words.
Kochałam się, Jasiu ... (I loved you
Johnny) ... for piano and piano
accordion ... words and music by
Anna Malec, arr. by F. Przybylski.
[c1946] © Władysław H. Sajowski,
Chicago; 11Feb47; EF6656. Polish
words.
Ludzie mi to za złe mają ...
(People say I am naughty oberek)
... for piano and piano accordion
... words and music by Anna Malec,
arr. by F. Przybylski. [c1946] ©
Władysław H. Sajowski, Chicago;
11Feb47; EF6655. Polish words.
Świeci miesiączek na niebie ...
(The moon in the sky waltz) ...
for piano and piano accordion
... words and music by Anna Malec,
arr. by F. Przybylski. [c1946] ©
Władysław H. Sajowski, Chicago;
11Feb47; EF6654. Polish words.
U mego tatusia ... (In my father's
garden polka) ... for piano and
piano accordion ... words and
music by Anna Malec, arr. by
F. Przybylski. [c1946] ©
Władysław H. Sajowski, Chicago;
11Feb47; EF6659. Polish words.

W prost do mego okieneczka ... (The
apple tree at my window polka)
... for piano and piano accordion
... words and music by Anna Malec,
arr. by F. Przybylski. [c1946]
© Władysław H. Sajowski, Chicago;
11Feb47; EF6658. Polish words.

MALLIDÈS, GIORGOS NIKOLAOS, 1910-
Enas charoumenos alētēs ...
etichoi-mousikē Giorgou Mallidē.
Athēnai, Ekdoseis Gaïtanou. ©
Michael Etienne Gaetanos,
Athens; 28Aug46; EF5350. For
voice and piano.

MALNECK, MATT.
Those New York City kind of
blues; by Tom Adair, Milton
Delugg and Matty Malneck.
[c1946] © Saunders Publications, inc., New York; 25Jan47;
EP11854. For voice and piano,
with chord symbols.

MALOOF, ALEXANDER.
In the style of Hanon; 28 original
progressive studies for piano,
by Alexander Maloof. © Carl
Fischer, inc., New York;
30Dec46; EP11376.

MALOTTE, ALBERT HAY.
Life eternal; for voice and piano,
by Albert Hay Malotte. © G.
Schirmer, inc., New York;
13May47; EP14553.
The Lord's prayer; by Albert Hay
Malotte ... vocal duet [for]
soprano and alto [arr. by
Carl Deis] © G. Schirmer, inc.,
New York; on arrangement;
30Dec46; EP11510.
© G. Schirmer, inc., New York; on
arrangement; 30Dec46; EP11512.
The twenty-third Psalm; for four-
part chorus of men's voices, with
piano acc., [by] Albert Hay
Malotte, arr. by Kenneth Downing,
[pseud.] © G. Schirmer, inc.,
New York; on arrangement;
24Mar47; EP13125.
Wee Hughie; for voice and piano;
by Albert Hay Malotte. [words
by Elizabeth Shane] © G.
Schirmer, inc., New York;
16Nov46; EP131390.

MALTZEFF, ALEXIS.
Lord, now lettest Thou Thy servant ... anthem for mixed
voices with tenor solo, a
cappella, [by] Alexis Maltzeff,
text adapted by Theresa Maltzeff. © Oliver Ditson Co.,
Philadelphia; 17May47;
EP14605.
Spring is nigh; chorus for
mixed voices, a cappella [by]
Alexis Maltzeff. [Words]
from the Russian of Feodor
Tutchev, tr. unknown. ©
Oliver Ditson Co., Phila-
delphia; on arrangement;
23Apr47; EP14241.

MALVIN, ARTIE.
Blues of the record man; by Harold
Dickinson, Bill Conway and Artie
Malvin. © Edwin H. Morris &
Co., inc., New York; 11Apr47;
EP15746. For voice and piano,
with chord symbols.

MANA-ZUCCA, pseud.
Ten etudettes; in thirds and
sixths, for piano, by Mana-
Zucca, [pseud.] Op. 172-173.
© Theodore Presser Co.,
Philadelphia; 20May47;
EP14626.

MANCINI, ALBERT, 1899-
Trumpet studies with modernistic
rhythms; by Albert Mancini.
Hollywood, Calif., A.G.M.
Music Publishers. © Albert
Mancini, Hollywood, Calif.;
3Feb47; EP12486.

MANGIAGALLI, RICCARDO PICK. See
Pick Mangiagalli, Riccardo.

MANN, FRED C
Dancing to the beat of my heart;
lyric by Beatrice A. Smith, music
by Fred C. Mann and Jacob
Musnitsky. [c1946] © Beatrice
A. Smith, Wilmington, Del.;
3Feb47; EP12319.

MANNERS, HENRY, pseud. See
Katzman, Henry.

MANNERS, ZEKE.
Fat man blues; words by Bill Cane,
music by Zeke Manners. © Bob
Miller, inc., New York; 2May47;
EP14169.

MANNING, RENDELL LEE, pseud. See
Flowers, Paul D.

MANNO, VINCENZO.
Una notte a Vienna ... musica di
Vincenzo Manno. © Edizioni
Musicali Cora, Milano; 26Jul43;
EP5051. Piano-conductor score;
orchestra.

MANRING, ERNEST.
Mills elementary method for clari-
net. © Mills Music, inc., New
York; 26Dec45; EP46.

MANUS, JACK 1909-
Midnight masquerade; by Bernard
Bierman, Arthur Berman and Jack
Manus. © Shapiro, Bernstein &
Co., inc., New York; 31Dec46;
EP11392. For voice and piano,
with chord symbols.
Midnight masquerade ... by Ber-
nard Bierman, Arthur Berman and
Jack Manus ... arr. by Paul
Weirick. © Shapiro, Bernstein
& Co., inc., New York; on
arrangement; 10Mar47; EP12652.
Piano-conductor score (orches-
tra, with words) and parts.
Unless it can happen with you; [words
and music] by Bernard Bierman,
Arthur Berman [and] Jack Manus. ©
Stevens Music Corp., New York;
14Jan47; EP11182. For voice and
piano, with chord symbols.

MARAIS, STEPHANUS LeROUX, 1896-
My eerste musiek boek; deur S.
le R. Marais. © R. Mülier,
pty. ltd., Cape Town, South
Africa; 27Dec46; EF3636.
Studies and exercises for
piano, in part with words.

MARCEDO, DON.
Panama; composed and arr. by
Don Marcedo. © Noel Gay
Music Co., ltd., London;
28Apr47; EF3660. Piano-conductor score (orchestra), and
parts.
El samba; composed and arr. by
Don Marcedo. © Noel Gay
Music Co., ltd., London;
28Apr47; EF3661. Piano-conductor score (orchestra), and
parts.

MARCELL, RAY, 1896-
Lady of old Shanty Town ...
music by Ray Marcell and
"Pappy" Howard, [words by Ray
Marcell] © Ray Marcell,
Cleveland & "Pappy" Howard,
Southington, Conn.; 13Feb47;
EP12149.

MARCELLI, RICO.
Wear your American smile; by
Audrey Call & Rico Marcelli.
Chicago, CallMar Publishers.
© Audrey Call, Chicago;
7Apr47; EP13665. For voice and
piano, with guitar diagrams and
chord symbols.

MARCHESE, VINCE.
By the shores of Monterey; words
and music by Vince Marchese.
© L. J. Tuck, Pacific Grove,
Calif.; 12Jun47; EP15115.

MARCHESE, VINCE. Cont'd.
Roses in June; words and music by
Vince Marchese. © L. J. Tuck,
Pacific Grove, Calif.; 12Jun47;
EP15116.

MARCHISIO, CARLOS.
Somos ... letra de Jose M.
Suñe, música de Carlos Marchisio.
© Editorial Argentina de Música
Internacional, s. de r., ltd.,
Buenos Aires; 30Dec46; EP5216.

MARDEN, ROBERT, 1908-   ed.
Everybody's favorite standard
overtures; arr. for piano duet.
Selected and ed. by Robert
Marden. © Amsco Music Publishing Co., New York; on compiling
& editing; 15Apr47; EP13658.

MARESCOTTI, ANDRÉ FRANÇOIS, 1902-
Vergers; [by] A. F. Marescotti
... sur des poèmes de R. M.
Rilke. © Jean Jobert, Editeur,
Paris; 15May47; EF6424.

MARGETSON, EDWARD.
Preserve me, O God; for four-part
chorus of mixed voices, a
cappella. Psalm XVI: 1, 2, 3, 8,
11. © G. Schirmer, inc., New
York; 13Feb46; EP2399.
Strong Son of God, Immortal Love;
for four-part chorus of mixed
voices with soprano solo and organ accompaniment. [Words by]
Lord Alfred Tennyson. © Boston
Music Co., Boston; 22Mar46;
EP2660.

MARIDÈS, LÉO.
Valse nordique; paroles et musique
de Léo Maridès. © Société
Éditions Musicales Paris-Monde,
Paris; 31Dec46; EF3881.

[MARIE NOELIE] sister.
Rosette ... [by] Frances T.
Martin [pseud.] © Frederick
Harris Music Co., ltd., Oak-
ville, Ont., Can.; 3Jun47;
EF3570. For piano solo.

MARIER, THEODORE N   1912-
A hymn of thanks to the blessed
Virgin Mary; poem by Edward
C. Currie, music by Theodore
Marier. © McLaughlin &
Reilly Co., Boston; 24Mar47;
EP13012.
Standard Gregorian chants;
[comp. by Theodore N. Marier]
© McLaughlin & Reilly Co.,
Boston; 2Dec46; EP12442.

MARINIER, PAUL, 1866-
Barcarolle romantique; paroles et
musique de Paul Marinier.
© Éditions Salabert, Paris;
15Feb47; EF3465.
La chanson du vent sous la
porte; paroles et musique de
Paul Marinier. Paris, Salabert.
© Salabert, inc., New York;
31Dec46; EF5593.
Le chemin d'autrefois; paroles et
musique de Paul Marinier. ©
Éditions Salabert, Paris;
15Feb47; EF3596.
Minuit sonne à tous les clochers;
paroles et musique de Paul
Marinier. © Éditions Salabert,
Paris; 15Feb47; EF3462.
Si le bonheur était à vendre;
paroles et musique de Paul
Marinier. © Éditions Sala-
bert, Paris; 15Feb47; EF3562.

MARION, RUSTY.
I beg your humble pardon, little
girl; words and music by Dixie
Boy Jordan, Sterling F. O'Bittle
and Rusty Marion ... piano arr.
by Dick Kent. © Peer International Corp., New York; 28Aug46;
EP13990.

MARKLAND, LAWRENCE, 1882-
In the morning ... words ... by
Mary Dixon Thayer ... music
[by] Lawrence Markland.
© Lawrence Markland, Baltimore;
28Feb47; EP13310.

MARKS, GERALD.
All of me; [words and music] by
Seymour Simons and Gerald Marks
... arrangement ... by Joe
Leahy. © Bourne, inc., New York
on arrangement; 23Jun47; EP15205.
Condensed score (orchestra) and
parts.
You can wait beneath that apple tree;
words and music by Gerald Marks.
© Bob Miller, inc., New York;
30Dec46; EP10740.

MARKS, GODFREY.
Sailing; words and music by
Godfrey Marks. [Easy piano
arrangement with keyboard
charts by Victor Lakes Martin]
© Songs You Remember Publishing Co. (V. L. Martin, proprietor), Atlanta; on arrange-
and playing instructions;
20Dec46; EP11538.

MARKS, MANLEY.
That wonderful something; words
and music by Manley Marks.
© Peer International Corp.,
New York; 18Mar47; EP13980.

MARLOW, JUDY KAY, 1935-
Heaven on the islands; words
and music by Leo Winters and
Judy Marlow. [c1946] ©
Hawaii Conservatory Publishing Co., Los Angeles
14Jan47; EP13027.

MARLY, ANNA.
Une chanson à trois temps;
paroles et musique de Anna
Marly. © Éditions Raoul
Breton, Paris; 18Mar47; EF5334.
For voice and piano, with chord
symbols.
Pour un foulard; paroles et
musique de Anna Marly. ©
Raoul Breton, Paris; 18Dec46;
EF3713.
Reminiscence ... For the piano
[by] Ralph E. Marryott. ©
Oliver Ditson Co., Philadelphia;
21Apr47; EP13943.
Sur un pont; paroles et musique
de Anna Marly. © Éditions
Vianelly, Paris; 18Dec46;
EF3712.
Wake from your slumbers; Easter anthem
for mixed voices, a cappella, by Ralph
E. Marryott, [words by] Thomas Tiplady
© The Oliver Ditson Co., Philadelphia;
10Jan47; EP11398

MAROUDAS, TONE.
Tha phygoume me mia barkoula;
etichoi K. Kophiniotē,
moustikē Tonē Marouda. ©
Ekdoseis Gattanou. © Michael
Gaetanos, Athens; 20Nov46;
EF3127. For voice and piano.

MARRACO, J   SANCHO.
O come, Jesus, my salvation ...
tr. and ed. by Hugh Ross. (In
Ross, Hugh, arr.   Sacred choruses for women's or girls'
voices. p. 111-116) © G. Schirmer, inc., New York; on arrangement; 30Sep46; EP9790.

MARRODÁN, FRANCISCO.
Arruza ... letra de Gerardo
Gonzalez, música de Francisco
Marrodán, y Enrique Geravilla.
New York, Sole selling agent,
Peer International Corp.
© Promotora Hispano Americana
de Música, s.a., Mexico;
16Dec46; EF5052.

MARRYOTT, RALPH E
Hosanna!   Blessed is He; [by] Ralph
E. Marryott ... for men's voices,
a cappella. © The Oliver Ditson
Co., Philadelphia; 3Jun47; EP11030.
I worship Him ... for unison
chorus [by] Ralph E. Marryott,
[words by] Thomas Tiplady. ©
Oliver Ditson Co., Philadelphia;
16Apr47; EP13892.
Légende triste; [by] C. H. Marsh.
© Edward Schuberth & Co., inc.,
New York; 14Apr47; EP13733.
For organ solo; includes regis-
tration for Hammond organ.
My only sweetheart; by Charles
Henry Marsh. © Charles Henry
Marsh, New Haven; 19May47;
EP6908. For voice and piano,
with chord symbols.

MARSH, CHARLES HENRY.
A cradle song; for piano, [by]
Charles H. Marsh. © McKinley
Publishers, inc., Chicago;
26Dec46; EP10850.
Eternal Father, strong to save
... [by] C. H. Marsh, [words by
W. Whiting] © Edward Schuberth
& Co., inc., New York; 13Jun47;
EP11102.   Score: SATB and piano.
Indian legend; for piano, [by]
Charles H. Marsh. © McKinley
Publishers, inc., Chicago;
26Dec46; EP10849.

MARSH, CHARLES HOWARD, 1885-
Arm of the Lord, awake!   For
S.A.T.B., [by] Charles H.
Marsh, [words by] W. Shrubsole.
© Dorothea Louise Schroeder,
Flushing, N. Y.; 31Mar47;
EP13396.
The strife is o'er; Easter chorus
for mixed voices, acc. [By]
Charles H. Marsh, [words from
the Latin, tr. by Francis Pott.
© Hall & McCreary Co., Chicago;
7Apr47; EP13757.

MARSH, SIMEON B   1798-1875.
Jesus, lover of my soul; words
by Charles Wesley, music by
Simeon B. Marsh. [Easy piano
arrangement with keyboard
charts by Victor Lakes Martin]
© Songs You Remember Publishing Co. (V. L. Martin,
proprietor), Atlanta; on
arrangement and playing
instructions; 20Dec46;
EP11339.

MARSHAL, EDWIN, pseud.   See
Fischer, Irwin L.

[MARSHALL, RENDA] 1917-   RENDER
The spider and the fly; [by] Myra
Taylor [pseud. c1946] © Blasco
Music, inc., Kansas City, Mo.;
16Jan47; EP11891. For voice and
piano, with chord symbols.

MARSHALL, W   S
Blessed quietness; [words by]
Manie Payne Ferguson, [music by]
W. S. Marshall. (In Eddy Arnold's
radio favorites song book. No.
A-1, p.44.) © Adams, Vee &
Abbott, inc., Chicago; on arrange-
ment; 17Jun46; EP11228. Close
score: SATB, with guitar diagrams
and chord symbols.

MARTELL, CHARLES.
What time is it in heaven? Words
by Furniss Peterson, music by
Charles Martell. © Bob Miller,
inc., New York; 2May47; EP14172.

91

MARTELLI, HENRI ERNEST, 1899-
Deuxième petite suite, pour piano;
[by] Henri Martelli. [Op.38,
no.2] Paris, L. de Lacour,
Éditions Costallat. © Lucien de
Lacour, Paris; 15Oct46; EF3289.

MARTH, HELEN JUN, 1903-
Jesus in the garden; (mixed voices)
[Words and music by] Helen Jun
Marth. St. Louis, Distributors,
Hunleth Music Co. © C. Albert
Scholin, St. Louis; 9Jan47;
EP10925.

The Lord reigneth; [for] S.A.T.B.,
by Helen Jun Marth, [with
Scriptural text] © Belwin,
inc., New York; 13Feb47;
EP12749.

Praise ye servants of the Lord;
S.A.T.B. [Psalm 113,] music by
Helen Jun Marth. © Belwin,
inc., New York; 31Dec46;
EP11224.

Serve the Lord with gladness;
for two choirs, choir I
S.A.T.B., choir II S.A.B.
[Psalm 95] by Helen Jun
Marth. © Belwin, inc.,
New York; on arrangement;
3Apr47; EP13196.

Sleep, little Jesus; (jr. and sr.
choirs) [Words and music by]
Helen Jun Marth. St. Louis,
Distributors, Hunleth Music Co.
© C. Albert Scholin, St. Louis;
9Jan47; EP10926.

MARTIN, ENOCH NATHANIEL, 1921-
I want some bread, I said; words
by Buddy Payne, music by Enoch
Martin. © Fowler Music Co.,
New York; 19May47; EP14529.

I'm henpecked; by Enoch Martin.
© Fowler Music Co., New York;
7May47; EP14207. For voice and
piano, with chord symbols.

MARTIN, FRANCES T., pseud. See
Marie Noelie, sister.

MARTIN, ISAIAH GUYMAN, 1862-
The G. I. battle hymn; [by] I. G.
Martin. © Isaiah Guyman Martin,
Pasadena, Calif.; 22Apr47;
EP14666. Close score: SATB.

MARTIN, JAMES.
You know you can't say no; words
and music by James Martin. ©
Nordyke Publishing Co., Los
Angeles; 7Mar47; EP13246.

MARTIN, KENNETH, pseud. See
Weinschenk, Bertlies.

MARTIN, SAM.
You're not my darlin' anymore; by
Fred Rose ... Rosalie Allen
and Sam Martin. © Western Music
Publishing Co., Hollywood, Calif.;
20Dec46; EP11098. For voice and
piano, with chord symbols.

[MARTIN, VICTOR LAKES] 1903-   arr.
Juanita; [words by Caroline Norton,
an old Spanish melody arr. by
Victor Lakes Martin] Easy piano
arrangement with keyboard charts.
© Songs You Remember Publishing
Co., (V. L. Martin, Proprietor),
Atlanta; on arrangement; 5Apr47;
EP14753.

MARTINET, HENRI.
La belle histoire ... paroles de
Pierre Farny, musique de
Henri Martinet. © Salabert,
inc., New York; 25Jan47;
EF3828.

La belle histoire. See his Aventure sur la côte.

Un petit nuage ... paroles de
Pierre Farny, musique de Henri
Martinet. © Salabert, inc.,
New York; 25Jan47; EF3879.

MARTINEZ GIL, CARLOS.
Falsaria; (La canción audaz) ...
arr. por los hnos. Martínez
Gil. © Promotora Hispano
Americana de Música, s.a.,
México; on arrangement;
28Aug46; EF5595. For voice and
piano.

Que voy a hacer ... letra y
música de los hnos. Martínez
Gil. © Promotora Hispano
Americana de Música, s.a.;
Mexico; 28Aug46; EF5609.

MARTINI, G   B
Gavotte antique; by Padre G. B.
Martini, arr. by Harvey B.
Gaul. © Volkwein Bros., inc.,
Pittsburgh; on arrangement;
9May47; EP14309. Score
(violin 1-2, viola, violoncello and double-bass) and
parts.

[MARTINO, RODOLFO DE]
L' hanno ritrovata ... ma chi? ...
Zazà ... musica di Paisaniello
[pseud.], testo di Arrigo. È
una pagina d'amore ... testo e
musica di Enrico Frati. ©
Edizioni Casiroli, s.a.r.l.,
Milano; 2Jan47; EF5272. Piano-
conductor score (orchestra,
with words), and parts.

MARTINON, JEAN FRANCISQUE ÉTIENNE,
1910-
Concerto giocoso; pour violon et
orchestre ou piano, [by] Jean-
Martinon. Op. 18. Paris, L.
de Lacour, Éditions Costallat.
© Lucien de Lacour, Paris;
51Oct46; EF3291. Score (violin
and piano) and part.

Suite nocturne ... [by] Jean-Martinon. Paris, L. de Lacour, Éditions Costallat. © Lucien de Lacour, Paris; 31Oct46; EF3292.
Score (violin and piano) and
part.

MARTINSON, BERTHOLD.
Midsommarnattsvals; musik:
Berthold Martinsson, arr.:
Sixten Liedbeck, text: Rune
Strand. © Edition Sylvain,
a.b., Stockholm; 1Jan5;
EF372u. Piano-conductor score
(orchestra, with words), and
parts.

MARTINSSON, BERTHOLD. See
Martinson, Berthold.

MARTINU, BOHUSLAV, 1890-
Double concerto ... [by] Bohuslav
Martinu. London, Sole selling
agents, Boosey & Hawkes. © Hawkes
& Son (London), ltd.; 7Dec46;
EF4775. Parts: two string orchestras,
piano and kettle-drums.

Lidice; [by] Bohuslav Martinů.
© Melantrich, ltd., Praha,
Czechoslovakia; 6Jun46;
EF5295. Score: orchestra.

MARVIN, CARRIE B
The American step; by Carrie B.
Marvin. © Carrie B. Marvin,
Hannibal, Mo.; 3Feb47; EP11904.
For piano solo.

MARX, JOSEPH, 1882-
(Quartet, strings) Quartetto in
modo antico; [by] Joseph Marx.
© Ludwig Doblinger (Bernhard
Herzmansky), K. G., Wien;
21Nov45; EF3397. Miniature
score.

(Quartet, strings) Streich-
Quartett in modo antico; [by]
Joseph Marx. © Ludwig Dob-
linger (Bernhard Herzmansky),
K. G., Vienna; 21Nov45;
EF3400. Parts.

(Quartet, strings) Streich-Quar-
tett in modo classico; [by]
Joseph Marx. © Ludwig Doblinger
(Bernhard Herzmansky), K. G.,
Vienna; 19Feb45; EF3316. Mini-
ature score.

(Quartet, strings) Streich-
Quartett in modo classico;
[by] Joseph Marx. © Ludwig
Doblinger (Bernhard Herzman-
sky), K. G., Vienna; 19Feb45;
EF3317. Parts.

Streich-Quartett in modo antico.
See his Quartet, strings.

MARY FLORENTINE, sister. See
Florentine, sister.

MARY HELENE, sister.
Jeanne Mance song; words by
Alfreda Gardiner Ricketts,
music by Sister Mary Helene.
© Sister Mary Helene, C.S.M.,
Antigonish, N. S.; 1May47;
EP14881.

MARY RACHEL, sister. See
Rachel, sister.

MARY STANISLAUS, sister. See
Horgan, Mary Stanislaus, sister.

MASON, LOWELL.
When I survey the wondrous cross
... hymn-anthem for choir and
congregation (S.A.T.B.) ... arr.
by W. B. Olds. [Words by] Isaac
Watts. © Hall & McCreary Co.,
Chicago; on arrangement; 3Jun46;
EP4702.

MASON, MARY BACON, comp. and arr.
Classics in Key-Kolor; for the piano.
Standard notation adapted for easy
reading in the hard keys ... comp.
and arr. by Mary Bacon Mason. ©
Oliver Ditson Co., Philadelphia;
25Mar47; EP12994.

MASONIER, CLEM.
Maybe you think you're foolin'
me; words and music by Clem
Masonier. © Nordyke Publish-
ing Co., Los Angeles; 25Jul46;
EP13542.

MASSENET, JULES ÉMILE FRÉDÉRIC,
1842-1912.
(Hérodiade) Salomé! English version by Marcia Short. [In
[Hodges, Lester] comp. John
Charles Thomas album of favorite
songs and arias. p. 55-61)
© G. Schirmer, inc., New York;
21Jun46; EP10277.

MASSIS, A
Poème; [arr. by A. Massis] © Lucien de Lacour, Paris; 25Jul45;
EF639. Score (viola and piano)
and part.

MATHIEU, ANDRE, 1929-
Fantaisie brésilienne ... by
André Mathieu. Lachute, Que.,
Parnasse Musical. © Editions
A. Passio, Lachute, Que., Can.;
15Dec46; EF4856. Score
(violin and piano) and part.

MATOS, MANUEL G
(Gay señorita) Llanero es, from the
... picture "Gay señorita" ... letra
y música de Manuel G. Matos. © Peer
International Corp., New York; 13Dec46;
EP13621.

(Gay señorita) Te quiero besar,
from the ... picture "Gay
señorita"; letra y música de
Manuel G. Matos. © Peer International Corp., New York;
13Dec46; EP13620.

Llanero es. See his Gay señorita.

Te quiero besar. See his Gay
señorita.

MATOS RODRIGUEZ, G. H. See
Rodriguez, G. H.

MATTES, WILHELM.
"The prince of Kandapora" ...
Music by Willy Mattes, lyric by
Einar Moberg, English version by
William Cameron. © Reuter &
Reuter Förlags, a/b, Stockholm;
1Jul46; EFL834. Piano-vocal
score. English words.

MATTES, WILLY. See
Mattes, Wilhelm.

MATTESON, MAURICE J   1893-
Joy and pain; words by Nell
Mellichamp, music by Maurice
Matteson. © Shattinger Piano &
Music Co., St. Louis; 31Dec46;
EP11250.
A silver pool; words by Nell
Mellichamp, music by Maurice
Matteson. © Shattinger Piano
& Music Co., St. Louis; 31Dec46;
EP11249.
Sweet soldier boy [North Carolina
folk-song, recorded and arr. by
Maurice Matteson] © G. Schirmer,
inc., New York; 30Dec46; EP11517.
Score: chorus (SATB) and piano.

MATTHIAS, JACK.
Leave some; music by Jack
Matthias, words by Eddie
Cherkose. © Stevens Music
Corp., New York; on words;
10Apr47; EP13791. Piano-
conductor score (orchestra,
with words) and parts.

MATTLIN, MATT, 1904-
I want a man; words and music by
Matt Mattlin. [c1947] © Matt
Mattlin, Spring Lake, N. J.;
2Dec46; EP12334.

MATTSSON, CARL OTTO.
Tommy min pojke ... text och
musik [by] Carl Otto Mattsson.
© Skandinaviska Odeon, a.b.,
Stockholm; 1Jan46; EF3737.

MAUR, LOUIS.
I love you; words & music by Louis
Maur. © Grimes Music Publishers,
Philadelphia; 10Mar47; EP12533.
My marinerette ... words & music
by Louis Maur. © Grimes Music
Publishers, Philadelphia;
10Mar47; EP12534.
Pennsylvania hills; words &
music by Louis Maur. © Grimes
Music Publishers, Philadelphia;
10Mar47; EP12535.

MAXWELL, RICHARD, 1897-
The chapel in my heart; by ...
Richard Maxwell. © Will
Rossiter, Chicago; 10May47;
EP14322. For voice and piano,
with chord symbols.

MAXWELL, RICHARD, comp.
Songs of cheer and comfort;
selected by Richard Maxwell.
Chicago, Rodeheaver Hall-Mack
Co. © Richard Maxwell, New York;
15Sep38; EP13684. Hymns, with
music.

MAY, HANS.
Break of day; arr. as a duet for
soprano and tenor. Words by
Alan Stranks, music by Hans
May. © Keith, Prowse & Co.,
ltd., London; on arrangement;
20May47; EF3349.
Here's to music. See his Spring
song.
Laugh is life; arr. as a duet
for soprano and tenor. Words
by Alan Stranks, music by Hans
May. [c1946] © Keith, Prowse
& Co., ltd., London; 16May47;
EF3346.

775306 O - 48 - 7

(Spring song) Here's to music,
from the ... film "Spring song";
[by] Hans May, arr. [by] W. J.
Duthoit. London, Chappell &
Co. © Victoria Music Publishing Co., ltd., London; on arrangement for brass band;
23Apr47; EF3272. Cornet-conductor score (band), and parts.
(Spring song) Here's to music,
from the ... film "Spring song";
[by] Hans May, arr. [by] W. J.
Duthoit. London, Chappell &
Co. © Victoria Music Publishing Co., ltd., London; on arrangement for military band;
23Apr47; EF3271. Cornet-
conductor score (band) and parts.
Spring song; selection, arr. for
orchestra by Geo. L. Zalva.
[By] Hans May. © Victoria
Music Publishing Co., ltd.,
London; on selection for
orchestra; 24Dec46; EF4867.
Piano-conductor score
(orchestra), and parts.
Spring song; selection, [by] Hans
May. Centennial summer; se-
lection, [by] Jerome Kern.
[Arr. by W. J. Duthoit] (The
army journal for full military
band, no.732) © Spring song:
Victoria Music Publishing Co.,
ltd., London; Centennial
summer: T. B. Harms Co., New
York; on arrangement; 23Apr47;
EF3964-3965. The selection from
Centennial summer includes All
through the day © Williamson
Music, inc., New York; 23Apr47;
EF3966) Condensed score and
parts.
This is the happiest day of my
life. (Heut' ist der schönste)
ukulele arr. by R. S. Stoddon
... English words by Tommie
Connor, music by Hans May. ©
B. Feldman & Co., ltd., London;
on arrangement for ukulele &
English words; 12May47;
EF3281.

MAYER, .C   ISABEL.
Don't cry, little darling ...
words by Theo Lorene Jordan,
music by C. Isabel Mayer.
Portland, Or., C. I. Mayer
Music Publishing. [c1946]
© Theo Lorene Jordan, Jennings,
Okla.; 10Feb47; EP12455.
Pasadena Rose; words by Ora Paul
Hollingsworth, music by C.
Isabel Mayer. Portland, Or.,
C. Isabel Mayer Music Pub. ©
Ora Paul Hollingsworth, Canoga
Park, Calif.; 2Dec46; EP11021.

MAYER, CLARENCE.
My prayer; [by] Clarence Mayer.
Lansdowne, Pa., Reyam Music
House. © Elsie and Clarence
Mayer, Lansdowne, Pa.; 8May47;
EP14742. For orchestra (parts
for French horn, trombone,
violin, violoncello or bassoon)

MAYER, ROBERT M   1910-   comp.
Oboe passages; extracted by Robert
M. Mayer from the works of ...
world famous composers. ©
Belwin, inc., New York; on bk.
1-2; 11Mar47; EP12575, 12574.

MAYERL, BILLY.
In my garden (springtime) ... for
piano, by Billy Mayerl. ©
Keith, Prowse & Co., ltd.,
London; 10Jun47; EF3903.
In my garden (summertime) ... for
piano, by Billy Mayerl. ©
Keith, Prowse & Co., ltd.,
London; 10Jun47; EF3902.

MAYLOR, EVELYN, pseud. See
Gyllenhammar, Ulla Margareta.

MAZELLIER, JULES.
Complainte pour Noël; variations
pastorales pour piano, [by]
Jules Mazellier. Paris, L.
de Lacour, Éditions Costellat.
© Lucien de Lacour, Paris;
30Nov46; EF3652.

MEACHAM, F   W
American patrol; [by] Meacham,
arr. for easy piano solo by
Mark Ashley [pseud.] © Century
Music Publishing Co., New York;
on arrangement; 31May47; EP14739.

MEANS, CLAUDE.
Blessed are they, O Lord ...
[by] Claude Means, (canticle
for mixed voices) © Oliver
Ditson Co., Philadelphia;
29Jan47; EP11882.
We will carol joyfully; Easter
carol for mixed voices with
soprano solo or children's
choir ad lib. Anonymous [words,
music by] Claude Means. ©
The H. W. Gray Co., inc., New
York; 3Jan47; EP11058.

MEEK, P   CLESS.
That old cow path; words & music
by P. Cless Meek. © Nordyke
Publishing Co., Los Angeles;
11Oct46; EP12716.

MEEKS, VIRGINIA FERN, 1925-
Rise up ye sons of Frankfort;
[by] Virginia F. Meeks, [words
by] Dean G. Felker. © Frankfort
Pilgrim College, Frankfort, Ind.;
14May47; EP14489. Close score:
SATB.

MÉHUL, ÉTIENNE-NICOLAS.
O brother mine; scene from the
opera "Joseph and his brethren."
For four-part chorus of mixed
voices with piano acc., S.A.T.B.
... Music by Étienne-Nicolas
Méhul, arr. by W. A. Goldsworthy.
© Carl Fischer, inc., New York;
on arrangement; 17May47; EP14721.

MEIJLINK, COR. See
Meijlink, Cornelis Johannes.

MEIJLINK, CORNELIS JOHANNES, 1894-
Capriccioso ... [by] Cor Meijlink.
© Edition Heuwekemeyer (Firm
A. J. Heuwekemeyer & B. F. van
Gaal), Amsterdam, The Nether-
lands; 24Jul43; EF5113. Score
(flute and piano) and part.
Valse élégante; pour saxophone-
alto et piano, [by] Cor Meijlink.
© Edition Heuwekemeyer. (Firm
A. J. Heuwekemeyer & B. F. van
Gaal), Amsterdam; 14May47;
EF3387. Score (saxophone and
piano) and part.

MEISSNER, JOSEPH JAMES.
Leavin' town; by Lee Jarvis and
Joseph James Meissner ... arr. by
"Zep" Meissner. © American Academy
of Music, inc., New York; on arrange-
ment; 23May47; EP6940. Piano-con-
ductor score (orchestra, with words)
and parts.
Leavin' town; words by Lee Jarvis,
music by Joseph James Meissner.
© American Academy of Music,
inc., New York; 31Dec46; EP6460.
Louella; words by Elizabeth La
Voie and Irving Mills, music by
Joseph James Meissner. © Am-
erican Academy of Music, inc., New
York; 31Dec46; EF6459.

MEISSNER, ZEP.
Dixie down beat; by Zep Meissner
and Irving Mills ... arr. by
"Zep" Meissner. © American
Academy of Music, inc., New
York; 30Apr47; EP6865. Piano-
conductor score (orchestra)
and parts.

93

MEL, LEW, pseud. See
Mulé, Louis.

MELACHRINO, GEORGE MILTIADES,
1909-
Portrait of a lady; [by] George
Melachrino. © Arcadia Music
Publishing Co., ltd., London;
11Mar47; EF3774. Score
(violin and piano) and part.
Together and apart; [by] George
Melachrino, [words by Edwin
Radford] © Arcadia Music
Publishing Co., ltd., London;
28Nov46; EF3775.
Vision d'amour. See his Woman to
woman.
Winter sunshine; [by] George Mela-
chrino, [adapted from the origi-
nal score by Geo. L. Zalva.
c1946] © Arcadia Music Publish-
ing Co., ltd., London; 27Jan47;
EF5003. Piano-conductor score
(orchestra) and parts.
(Woman to woman) Vision d'amour.
(Vision of love) by George
Melachrino. Theme from the
British national film "Woman
to woman". © Arcadia Music
Publishing Co., ltd., London;
3Feb47; EF5163.

MELECCI, ADELMO, 1900-
Clock strikes at midnight; [by]
A. Melecci. © Frederick
Harris Music Co., ltd., Oak-
ville, Ont., Can.; 2Apr47;
EF5566. For piano solo.
Composing with the composers;
by A. Melecci. A series of
lessons. © Frederick Harris
Music Co., ltd., Oakville,
Ont., Can.; 3Jun47; EF3571.
Jenny Lind waltz; [by] A.
Melecci. © Frederick Harris
Music Co., ltd., Oakville,
Ont., Can.; 2Apr47; EF5567.
For piano solo.
Toys on parade; [by] A. Melecci.
© Frederick Harris Music Co.,
ltd., Oakville, Ont., Can.,
2Apr47; EF5565. For piano solo.

MELICHAR, ALOIS, 1896-
(Triumph der Liebe) Schaukel-
lied, aus dem ... Film "Triumph
der Liebe" ... Text: Kurt
Heuser [and] Hans Werner, Musik;
Alois Melichar, [arr. by Viktor
Hruby] © Josef Weinberger, ltd.,
London; 1May47; EF3575.

MELKA, HARRIET.
Grandma's turned over again; words
and music by H. Melka. © Acuff-
Rose Publications, Nashville;
31Dec46; EP10899.

MELLER, LLOYD P
Give ear to my words O Lord ...
Ps. 5:1-3, 12, [by] Lloyd P.
Moller. © Lloyd P. Meller,
Chattanooga; 18Sep46; EP13908.
Close score: SATB.
Jesus is waiting for me. When
Jesus comes; by Lloyd P.
Meller. © Lloyd P. Meller,
Chattanooga; 18Sep46; EP13909.
Hymn, with music.
Jesus saved me ... [by] Lloyd P.
Meller. © Lloyd P. Meller,
Chattanooga; 29Nov46; EP13907.
Close score: SATB.

MELLIER, MARIO.
Lo dicono le stelle ... [words by
Franco Molinari], musica di Mario
Mellier. Rose per una santa ...
[words and] musica di P. Fucilli.
© Edizioni Leonardi, s.a.r.l.,
Milan; 4Mar46; EF4812 & EF4811
(on arrangement) Piano-conductor
score (orchestra, with words) and
parts.

MELSHER, IRVING.
Always keep your promise; words
by Remus Harris, music by
Irving Melsher. © Bob Miller,
inc., New York; 2May47; EP14471.
Too tired to care; words by Cy
Coben, music by Irving Melsher.
© Bob Miller, inc., 30Dec46;
EP10745.

MENA, DOMÍNGO LÓPEZ. See
López Mena, Domingo.

MENASCE, JACQUES DE.
Hebrew melodies ... by Jacques
de Menasce. © G. Schirmer,
inc., New York; on 3 pieces;
15Feb47. Score (violin and
piano) and parts. Contents.-
[v.1] Dance (© EP12740) -
[v.2] Lullaby (© EP12741) -
[v.3] Rhapsody (© EP12742)

MENDELIN, WILLIAM.
Fourteen melodies; by William
Mendelin. Chicago, Mendelin
Publications. © William Men-
delin, Chicago; 7Apr47;
EP12247. For voice and piano.

MENDELSSOHN, JACK.
You're breaking in a new heart
(while you're breaking mine);
words and music by Ervin Drake
and Jimmy Shirl, [pseud.]
© Record Songs, inc., New York;
6Jun47; EP15285.

MENDELSSOHN-BARTHOLDY, FELIX, 1809-1847.
Andante and rondo capriccioso;
by Mendelssohn. [Op. 14.
Arr. by Victor Ambroise]
© Lawrence Wright Music Co., ltd.,
London; on arrangement; 9Apr47;
EF5474. For piano solo.
Fingal's cave ... by F. Mendelssohn,
arr. by J. S. Seredy. © Carl
Fischer, inc., New York; on arrange-
ment; 19Dec46; EP12317. Piano-
conductor score (band) and parts.
How lovely are the messengers, from
"St. Paul." Romans X: 15, 18.
[Music by] Mendelssohn, arranged by
Wallingford Riegger. SA accompanied.
© Harold Flammer, inc., New York; on
arrangement; 4Nov46; EP11164.
How lovely are the messengers, from
"St. Paul." Romans X: 15, 18. [Music
by] Mendelssohn, arranged by Walling-
ford Riegger. SSA accompanied, solo
voices optional. © Harold Flammer,
inc., New York; on arrangement; 4Nov46;
EP11163.
How sweet I roam'd ... [Words] by
William Blake, [music by] F.
Mendelssohn, op. 30, no. 1, arr.
for three part chorus of women's
voices by Lute Cummins Drum.
© Elkan-Vogel Co., inc., Phila-
delphia; on arrangement; 7Apr47;
EP13933.
If with all your hearts ...
From Mendelssohn's "Elijah",
arr. by J. Henry Francis.
© Sam Fox Publishing Co., New
York; on arrangement; 10Mar47;
EP12732. Score: soprano or
junior choir, chorus (SATB)
and piano.
A selection of famous Mendelssohn
melodies; arr. for the piano-
forte in a simplified manner by
Howard Ward. © Peter Maurice
Music Co., ltd., New York; on
arrangement; 31Dec46; EF3261.
Spring song; [by] Felix Mendelssohn.
Op. 62, no. 6. Arr. by William
Teague. © Broadcast Music, inc.,
New York; on arrangement; 16Dec46;
EP11837. Piano-conductor score
(orchestra) and parts.
Spring song, by Mendelssohn;
and Melody in F, by Rubinstein.
[Arr. by Victor Ambroise] ©
Lawrence Wright Music Co.,
ltd., London; on arrangement;
7May47; EF3256. For piano solo.

Symphony no.4 (third movement);
[by] Felix Mendelssohn-Bartholdy.
Op.90. Arr. by Harold Sanford.
© Broadcast Music, inc., New
York; on arrangement; 15May47;
EP15243. Piano-conductor score
(orchestra) and parts)
Tears, idle tears ... [Words] from
The princess by Alfred Tennyson,
[music] by F. Mendelssohn, op.
30, no. 3, arr. for three part
women's voices by Lute Cummins
Drum. © Elkan-Vogel Co., inc.
Philadelphia; on arrangement;
7Apr47; EP13932.
Too tired to care; words by Cy
Coben, music by Irving Melsher.
© Bob Miller, inc., 30Dec46;
EP10745.

MENDEZ, BILLY.
Dentro de mí ... Letra y música
de Billy Mendez. © Peer Inter-
national Corp., New York; 29Jan47;
EP11875.
Qué lío, tío! ... Letra de Alberto
Salinas, música de Billy Mendez.
© Peer International Corp., New
York; 29Jan47; EP11877.

MENDOZA, ROBERTO.
Se que te vas. (Think of me some-
time) ... English words by
Joe Davis, Spanish words and
music by Roberto "Tito"
Mendoza. © Caribbean Music,
inc., New York; 17Mar47;
EP12639.

MENDOZA, TITO. See
Mendoza, Roberto.

MENÉNDEZ, J. CARBO. See
Carbo Menendez, J.

MENÉNDEZ, NILO.
Lavandera ... Music by Nilo
Menendez and Felix De Cola.
English lyric by Nilo De Cola,
Spanish lyric by Nilo Menéndez.
© Peer International Corp., New
York; 18Mar47; EP13982.

MENZEL, ALFREDO.
Cajita de música ... para piano,
original de Alfredo Menzel.
[Op. 24] © Editorial de
México, México; 7Apr47; EF5250.

MERCADO, FRANCISCO.
Tu mirar. (Your eyes) ... English
words by Joe Davis, Spanish
words and music by Francisco
Mercado. © Caribbean Music,
inc., New York; 12May47; EP14222.

MERCER, JOHNNY. •
Dream; words and music by Johnny
Mercer, simplified piano solo
with words. [arr. by Alex
Kramer] © Capitol Songs, inc.,
New York; on arrangement;
4Feb47; EP11965.

MERCERON, MARIANO.
O. K. Jones ... [by] Mariano
Mercerón. © Editorial
Mexicana de Música Inter-
nacional, México; 30Dec46;
EF3312. Piano-conductor
score (orchestra), and parts.

MEREDITH, I H
The empty tomb; an Easter
pageant, book by Edwin E.
Jacques, lyrics by Philip
Jordan, incidental music
by I. H. Meredith. © Tul-
lar-Meredith Co., New York;
13Jan47; EP12671.
Gifts most precious; [by] I. H.
Meredith. © I. H. Meredith, New
York; 23Nov46; EP12130. Close
score: SATB.

MEREDITH, I   H   comp.
Golden hours; a service for
Children's Day, comp. by
I. H. Meredith. © Tullar-
Meredith Co., New York;
5Apr47; EP14485.

94

MERETTA, LEONARD V
Aurora ... by Leonard V. Meretta.
© Mills Music, inc., New York;
12Mar47; EP6690. Score (cornet
1-3 and piano) and parts.

MERS, EDDY, pseud. See
Mersson, Boris.

[MERSSON, BORIS]
Inséparables; paroles de Ruy Blag
[pseud.], musique de Eddy Mers
[pseud.] (sur un thème de Schu-
bert) © Imuta, F. Heiber,
International Music, Theatre
Edition and Agency, Basle,
Switzerland; 15Dec46; EF4999.

MESSINI, JIMMY.
Don Patrick Alphonso O'Toole;
words and music by Desmond
O'Connor & Jimmy Messini. ©
Noel Gay Music Co., ltd., Lon-
don; 3Mar47; EF5460.

MĒTSAKES, GEORGIOS STEPHANOS,
1921-
Pasle brochoula epiase ... To
Mētsakē. Etichoi-mousikē G.
Mētsakē. Athēnai, Ekdoseis
Gaïtanou. © Michel Gaetanos,
Athens; 20Nov46; EF5126. For
voice and piano.

MEYER, JOSEPH.
The bachelor and the bobby-soxer;
[words] by Don Meyer [and]
Howard Phillips, [music by]
Joseph Meyer. © Paull-Pioneer
Music Corp., New York; 3Jun47;
EP15134.
If you knew Susie (like I know
Susie); by B. G. DeSylva and
Joseph Meyer. © Shapiro, Bern-
stein & Co., inc., New York;
18Mar25; EP14915. Correcting
Eb10519. For voice and piano,
with guitar diagrams and chord
symbols.

MEYER, LUIS CARLOS.
Micaela ... De Luis Carlos Meyer.
© Promotora Hispano Americana de
Musica, s. a., Mexico; 30Dec46;
EF5815. For voice and piano.

MEYER, MARY VINCENT, sister.
For Christ Our King through Mary;
words and music by Sister Mary
Vincent Meyer ... (school song)
[for] Our Lady of Mercy school,
Detroit, Michigan. © Sister
Mary Vincent Meyer, R.S.M.,
Grand Rapids; 1Jul46; EP6486.

MEYER, RALPH LOUIS, 1907-
Affectionately (I send
greetings to you); [words
and] music by Lou Meyer,
arr. by Larry Royal. ©
Personal Songs, New York;
27Mar47; EP13091. For
voice and piano. On cover:
Affectionately to (Mary).

MEYER, VINCENT, sister. See
Meyer, Mary Vincent, sister.

MEYERS, CHARLES J
Holding you in my arms; words &
music by Charles J. Meyers. ©
Nordyke Publishing Co., Los
Angeles; 9Nov46; EP12711.
Someone like you; words and music by
Charles J. Meyers. © Nordyke
Publishing Co., Los Angeles;
18Jul46; EP12715.

MICHAEL, PATRICK.
Terang boulan. (Malayan song of
love) Words and music by Robert
Nestor, Ernest Wilson & Patrick
Michael. © Campbell Connelly &
Co., ltd., London; 3Jan47;
EF4977. English words.

MICHALSON, ABRAHAM SEVERIN, 1887-
Too-ra-loo; [by A. S. Michalson]
© Abraham S. Michalson,
Minneapolis; 14Dec46; EP11668.
For voice and piano.

MIEIR, AUDREY MAE.
Three little pigs; [by Audrey Mae
Mieir, words by A. M. M.] ©
Songs by Audrey, Alhambra, Calif.;
23Dec46; EP11855.

MIER, PEDRO.
La mosca [words by Pedro Mier];
Camino a Mexico; y, Muchachas
de quince años; tres polkas de
Pedro Mier. © Promotora His-
pano Americana de Música, s. a.,
Mexico; 30Dec46; EF5530, 5532,
5531. For piano solo.
"Saludamos a Texas" y "Asi son las
mujeres"; [words by Jorge Radare
... Music] de Pedro Mier.
© Promotora Hispano Americana de
Música, s.a., México; 23Dec46;
EF5068-5069. "Saludamos a Texas"
is for piano solo.

MIKITA, ANDREW.
The very first band and orchestra
book; rev. by Andrew Mikita.
© Andrew Mikita, Macomb, Ill.;
on new instrument parts;
28Dec45; EP13138. Part for
cornet 1-2.

MILENA, LUCIO.
Mamma, dammi venti lire ... (Mam,
give me 20 lire) Parole e
musica di Lucio Milena, arr. by
Lionel Alan. Tramonto sul
fiume ... (Twilight on the
river) Parole e musica di Gilberto Forti, arr. by Lionel
Alan. © Edizioni Musicali
Millen, Modena, Italy; 24Sep46;
EF5059. Piano-conductor score
(orchestra) and parts.

MILES, C   AUSTIN, d. 1946.
In the garden ... by C. Austin
Miles, arranged by Griffith J.
Jones. Winona Lake, Ind., The
Hall-Mack Co. © The Rodeheaver
company, Winona Lake, Ind.;
15Jan47; EP11851. For 2 treble
voices and piano.

MILES, DICK.
Banana boat; by Bob Hilliard and
Dick Miles. © Pic Music Corp.,
Chicago; 28Dec45; EP12041. For
voice and piano.
Sunny weather; by Bob Hilliard and
Dick Miles. © Pic Music Corp.,
Chicago; 22May46; EP12038. For
voice and piano, with chord
symbols.

MILES, RUSSELL HANCOCK.
Love's redeeming work is done;
[by] Russell Hancock Miles,
[words by] Archer T. Gurney ...
[and] Charles Wesley. © The
Arthur P. Schmidt Co., Boston;
14Jan47; EP11207. Score:
SSATB and piano.

MILFORD, ROBIN.
(Sonata, flute & piano) Sonata in
C [by] Robin Milford. ©
Augener, ltd., (British), London;
3Jan47; EF3161. Score (flute and
piano) and part.

MILHAUD, DARIUS, 1892-
(Concerto, violoncello, no.2)
Concerto no. 2, pour violon-
celle et orchestre [by] Darius
Milhaud. © Associated Music
Publishers, inc., New York;
16May47; EP15050. Minia-
ture score.
(Concerto, violoncello, no. 2)
Concerto no. 2, pour violon-
celle et orchestre, réduction de
l'orchestre au piano de l'auteur.
© Associated Music Publishers,
inc., New York; 9May47; EP15051.
Score (violoncello and piano)
and part.

Elegie ... [by] Darius Milhaud.
© Boosey & Hawkes, inc., New
York; 9Jul46; EP12321. Score
(violoncello and piano) and
part.
(Sonata, violin & harpsichord)
Sonata for clavecin (or piano)
and violin; [by] Darius Mil-
haud. © Elkan-Vogel Co., inc.,
Philadelphia; 20Dec46; EP11461.
Suite francaise; composed ... by
Darius Milhaud. © Leeds Music
Corp., New York; on arrange-
ment; 21Mar47; EP12859. Con-
densed score (band) and parts.
Une journee. (One day), by Darius
Milhaud, piano solo. © Mercury
Music Corp., New York; 12May47;
EP14082.

MILLER, BOB.
The longest train I ever saw; by
Bob Miller. [©1946] © Bob
Miller, inc., New York; 2May47;
EP14170. For voice and piano,
with chord symbols.
Seven women in one; words by Billy
Moll, music by Bob Miller. ©
Bob Miller, inc., New York;
30Dec46; EP10758.

MILLER, EDDIE.
(Love's got me in a) lazy mood;
words [by] Johnny Mercer, music
[by] Eddie Miller. © Capitol
Songs, inc., New York; 26Jun47;
EP15259.

MILLER, ERVIN G   1902-
Meditation; [by] Ervin G. Miller,
arr. by W. M. Thorne. (In
Church of the Nazarene.
Michigan District. Nazarene
Young Peoples Society.
Choruses of the N. Y. P. S.
p.3) © Michigan District,
Nazarene Young Peoples Society,
Flint, Mich.; 25Jul46;
EP13029. Close score: SATB.

MILLER, ETHEL H
Child's prayer; words by Irene
Kane Latta, music by Ethel H.
Miller, based on a melody by
Beethoven. © Emhall Music Co.,
Ethel Hall Miller, sole owner,
Rochester, N. Y.; 5Feb47;
EP11930.

MILLER, MRS. HOWARD.
Mrs. Howard Miller's chord and note
or ear piano method; for students of
any age. © Mrs. Howard Miller, New
Philadelphia, Ohio; on bk. 1; 18Mar47;
EP12968.

MILLER, IRVING.
Ugga ugga boo; Ugga boo boo ugga,
by Eddie Cherkose, Mel Blanc,
Mac Benoff and Irving Miller.
© Tune Towne Tunes, Hollywood,
Calif.; 8Apr47; EP13726. For
voice and piano, with chord
symbols.

MILLER, LESLIE ALTON.
My own; words and music by Leslie
Miller, arr. by Pee Wee Weber.
© Leslie Alton Miller, Lincoln,
Mont.; 3Feb47; EP11913.
Western lullaby; words and music
by Leslie Miller, arr. by Pee
Wee Weber. © Leslie Alton
Miller, Lincoln, Mont.; 3Feb47;
EP11912.

MILLER, MARION CATHERINE, 1903-
Be still and know; words by Thomas
Brindley, music by Marion C.
Miller. [c1946] © Marion C.
Miller, Lynn, Mass.; 19Jan47;
EP12199.

MILLER, NELSON S
My mother's lullaby; words and
music by Nelson S. Miller. ©
Nelson S. Miller, Defiance,
Ohio; 23Sep46; EP11194.

MILLINDER, LUCKY.
More, more, more; words and music
by Henri Woode, Joe Purnell and
Lucky Millinder. © Northern
Music Corp., New York; 12Feb47;
EP12170.

MILLS, ANNETTE.
Hopscotch! ... by Annette Mills.
© Peter Maurice Music Co., ltd.,
New York; 17Jan47; EF4897. For
voice and piano, with chord
symbols; melody also in tonic
sol-fa notation.
London in the spring; words and
music by Annette Mills. © Irwin
Dash Music Co., ltd., London;
1Jan47; EF3134. For voice and
piano, with chord symbols; melody
also in tonic sol-fa notation.

MILLS, GEORGE WARREN, 1881-
I will lead you safely through;
[by] Geo. W. Mills, [arr. by
Haldor Lillenas] © George
Warren Mills, Osceola, Ind.;
11Nov44; EP12466. For voice
and piano.

MILLS, IRVING.
Blue Lou; by Edgar Sampson and
Irving Mills, inc., New York; on
arrangement 21Apr47; EP6844;
Piano-conductor score (orchestra)
and parts.

MILLS, KATHERINE MAE, 1891-
Made whole; [by] Mae Mills, [words
by] M. M. [c1939] © Katherine
Mae Mills, Osceola, Ind.;
8Feb46; EP11858. Close score;
SATB.

MILNE, ANITA.
Drifting (you know the reason
why); words & music by Anita
Milne. © Grimes Music
Publishers, Philadelphia;
10Mar47; EP12332.

MILTON, JAY, 1910-
Aunt Hetty; by Jay Milton. ©
Bel-Air Music, Hollywood,
Calif.; on additional lyrics
& changes in music; 15May47;
EP14345. For voice and piano,
with chord symbols.
You can't take Texas out of me;
by Jay Milton. © Bel-Air
Music, Hollywood, Calif.;
7Mar47; EP12452. For voice
and piano, with chord symbols.

MINCHELLA, ERNEST
Minchella complete modern method
for piano accordion, bass clef.
Detroit, Minchella Music Pub-
lisher. © Ernest Minchella,
Detroit; 23May47; EP14825.

MINCHELLA, ERNEST, comp.
Minchella's accordion favorites.
Detroit, Minchella Music Publish-
er. © Ernest Minchella, Detroit;
bk.1,3, 9Apr47. Contents.- bk.1.
Party and banquet songs
© EP13678) - bk.3. Cowboy songs
© EP13679)

MINEO, ENRICO, 1876-
Le forosette danzano ... per
pianoforte, [by] Enrico Mineo.
© Carisch, società anonima,
Milan; 27Dec46; EP5487.
La gavottina delle bambole; per
pianoforte, [by] Enrico Mineo.
© Carisch, società anonima,
Milan; 27Dec46; EP5486.
Plenilunio ... per pianoforte, di
Enrico Mineo. © Carisch,
società anonima, Milan;
27Dec46; EP5488.

MINNELLA, LENA.
Connie; lyrics and music by Lena
Minnella. © Cine-Mart Music
Publishing Co., Hollywood, Calif.;
1Nov46; EP11721.

MIRAL, LUCIANO.
Déjame en paz ... letra y música
de Luciano Miral. © Editorial
Mexicana de Música International.
s.a., México; 23Dec46; EF5075.

MIREILLE, pseud. See
Hartusch, Mireille.

MIRO, FAUSTINO.
Aunque te vayas ... letra y música
de Faustino Miró. N[ew] Y[ork],
Southern Music Pub. Co., repre-
sentantes para Cuba, Excelsior
Music Co., Habana. © Peer
International Corp., New York;
28Dec45; EP5617.
"Oye un coco" ... letra y
música por Faustino Miró. ©
Peer International Corp., New
York; 18Dec46; EP5589. Piano-
conductor score (orchestra), and
parts.
Pero ... que mulata! ... letra y
música por Faustino Miró.
Habana. © Peer International
Corporation, New York; 30Dec46;
EF5311. Parts: orchestra.

MIROVITCH, ALFRED, ed.
The student pianist ... Ed. by Alfred
Mirovitch. © Leeds Music Corp., New
York; v.1, 2Jun47; v.2, 16Jun47; v.3
(on foreword & editing), 3Jul47;
EP14975, 15346, 15433. Contents.-v.
1-2. Alfred Mirovitch, comp. 55 piano
pieces.- v.3. Anton Arensky. Six
recital pieces for piano duet. Op.34.

MITCHELL, HORACE E
Call of freedom ... by Horace E.
Mitchell, arr. ... by Cliff Barnes.
© Horace E. Mitchell, Cleveland;
7Mar47; EP12804. Condensed score
(band) and parts.

MITCHELL, JOSEPH BLAINE, 1886-
If I could dream forever; words
and music by Joseph Blaine
Mitchell, [arranged by David
Gussin] © Joseph Blaine
Mitchell, Hollywood, Calif.;
16Jan47; EP11324.
It's girls like you; words and
music by Joseph Blaine Mitchell,
[arranged by David Gussin] ©
Joseph Blaine Mitchell, Holly-
wood, Calif.; 16Jan47; EP11323.
Rough ridin' Willie; words and
music by Joseph Blaine Mitchell,
[arranged by David Gussin]
© Joseph Blaine Mitchell,
Hollywood, Calif.; 16Jan47;
EP11322.

MITSAKI, G   1897-
Kompologaki; words & music: G.
Mitsaki. © Colonial Music Publish-
ing Co. inc., New York; 24Feb47;
EP12277. Greek words.
O loulas; words & music: G. Mitsaki.
© Colonial Music Publishing Co.,
inc., New York; 24Feb47; EP12276.
Greek words.

MITTLER, FRANZ, 1893-
Kleine walzer ... von Frans Mittler.
Op.4. Wien, Universal-Edition.
© Associated Music Publishers,
inc., New York; 1Feb19; EF4824.
For piano solo.

MIZZY, VIC.
Mama, do I gotta? Lyric by Mann
Curtis, music by Vic Mizzy. ©
Miller Music Corp., New York;
4Jan47; EP11863.
What did you put in that kiss? Words
by Mann Curtis, [pseud.] music by
Vic Mizzy. © Chappell & Co.,
inc., New York; 25Jan47; EP11651.
You grew up to be some baby;
lyric by Mann Curtis, [pseud.]
music by Vic Mizzy. © Miller
Music Corp., New York;
25Apr47; EP14065.

MOE, CHRISTOPHER CHARLES.
The litany or general supplication;
(as used by the Holy Catholic
Church of Illumination) Music
and text by ... C. C. Moe. ©
Christopher Charles Moe, New
York; 19Jun46; EP11111.

MÖLLER-HOLST, AGNES.
Three portraits of old Denmark;
[by] A. Möller-Horst. © Volkwein
Bros., inc., Pittsburgh; on
arrangement; 9May47; EF14310.
Score (violin 1-2, viola,
violoncello and double-bass)
and parts.

MOERAN, E   J
Sinfonietta; by E. J. Moeran.
Full score. © Novello & Co.,
ltd., London; 24Feb47; EF5220.

MOFFITT, DE LOYCE W
Rocking in a plastic chair ; ...
by De Loyce W. Moffitt. ©
Charling Music Corp., New
York; 25Feb47; EP13367.
Condensed score (band) and
parts.

MOHRING, MILDRED MARIE.
Glad tidings, Youth for Christ;
[by] Mildred Mohring, [words by]
M. M. c1946. © Mildred Marie
Mohring, Chicago; 25Jan47;
EP6652. Close score: SATB.

MOIETTA, BEPPE.
La Pepina ... [words by Tettoni]
musica di Beppe Moietta.
Fulvia ... [words by B.
Bacarelli] musica di Mario
Chesi. © Edizioni Leonardi,
Milano; 18Jun46; EF4907.
Piano-conductor score
(orchestra), and parts.
Schüler und Rythmus. "Ritmo in
conservatorio." Von Beppe
Moietta. Mailand, Leonardi-
Piero Musikverlag. © Edizioni
Leonardi, s.a.r.l., Milano;
8May44; EF5058. Piano-conductor
score (orchestra) and parts.
T' amo ... testo di F. Tettoni,
musica di Beppe Moietta. (In
Un sorriso e 20 canzoni, p.
4-5) © Edizioni Leonardi,
s.a.r.l., Milano; 25May45;
EF4911. For voice and piano.
Tenerezze; testo di C. Deani,
musica di Beppe Moietta. ©
Edizioni Leonardi, s.a.r.l.,
Milan; 5Jan46; EF4815. For
voice and piano.

MOINEAU, GEORGES.
Noël nouvelet; (XVe siècle),
choeur à 4 voix mixtes,
harmonisé par Georges Moineau.
Paris, Rouart, Lerolle et Cie.,
vente exclusive, Éditions
Salabert. © Salabert, inc.,
New York; on harmonization;
31Dec46; EF3854.
On entend partout carillon ...
choeur à 4 voix mixtes,
harmonisé par Georges Moineau.
Paris, Rouart, Lerolle et
Cie., vente exclusive, Éditions
Salabert. © Salabert, inc.,
New York; on harmonization;
31Dec46; EF3855.

MOISSE, SEVERIN, 1898-
Variations sur un thème de
Paganini; pour piano, par
Séverin Moisse. © Parnasse
Musical, Lachute, Que., Can.;
1May46; EF4854.

MOLEN, ALBERT VAN DER. See
Van der Molen, Albert.

MOLIÈRE, ROGER DE.
Bonsoir, mon amour; paroles de Jean
Jouenne et J. Pacaud, musique de
Roger de Molière et Eler. ©
Éditions Colibri, Paris; 15Oct46;
EF3147.

MOLIERE, ROGER DE. Cont'd.
Chérie, c'est a toi que je rêve;
paroles de Jean Jouenne & Géo
Remy. musique de Roger de
Molière & Éler. © Éditions
Colibri, Paris; 15May46; EF3145.

MOLINARE, NICANOR.
Chiu, chiu; [by] Nicanor Molinare,
arr. by Harry Breuer. c1946.
© Chart Music Publishing House,
inc., Chicago; on arrangement;
17Mar47; EP13164. Score
(marimba or xylophone and piano)
and part.
Chiu, chiu; [by] Nicanor Molinare,
... arrangement for accordion by
Charles Magnante. © Chart Music
Publishing House, inc., Chicago;
on arrangement; 2Jun47; EP14936.
Chiu, chiu; English lyrics by
Alan Surgal, Spanish lyrics
and music by Nicanor Molinare.
For voice and piano with piano
acc.; playable also as duet
for Spanish and Hawaiian guitars (or two Spanish guitars)
Arr. by George M. Smith.
© Chart Music Publishing House,
inc., Chicago; on arrangement
for Spanish guitar & piano
acc.; 9May47; EP14565.
Valparaíso ... [by] Nicanor
Molinare. [n.p.] Southern
Music International. © Peer
International Corp., New York;
30Dec46; EF5560. For voice
and piano.

MOLTÓ, ANDRÉS.
Madrid 1800 ... letra, música y
arreglo de Andrés Moltó. ©
Andrés Moltó, Madrid; 1Jan47;
EF4903. Piano-conductor score
(orchestra, with words), and
parts.

MONAHAN, JOSEPH BERNARD, 1894-
Down the lane to home sweet home;
words & music by Joseph B. Monahan.
© Monahan Music Publications,
New York; 2Jan47; EP12125.

I'm lost without you; words &
music by Joseph B. Monahan.
© Monahan Music Publications,
New York; 9Apr47; EP13594.

MONDRAGÓN, SAMUEL.
Sarape oaxaqueño. (Song of a Mexican
sarape) ... Music by Samuel
Mondragón ... Spanish lyric by
Juan O. Vasconcelos, [English
words adapted by Albert Gamse]
(In André, Julie, ed. Songs from
south of the border. p.50-53)
© Edward B. Marks Music Corp.,
New York; on English adaptation;
28Dec46; EP10881.

MONGE, CHUCHO. See
Monge, Jesús.

MONGE, JESÚS.
Este dolor ... Letra y música de
Chucho Monge (Jesús Monge)
, © Promotora Hispano Americana de
Música, s. a., Mexico; 30Dec46;
EF5528.

Fiesta ... letra y música de Chucho
Monge (Jesús Monge) © Promotora
Hispano Americana de Música, s.a.,
México; 28Aug46; EF5611.
La Genoveva ... letra y música
de Chucho Monge (Jesús Monge)
© Promotora Hispano Americana
de Música, s.a., México;
30Dec46; EF5458.
Mi guitarra y yo ... Letra y música
de Chucho Monge (Jesús Monge)
© Promotora Hispano Americana de
Música, s. a., Mexico; 29Oct46;
EF5501.
La mujer que quiere a dos ...
Letra y música de Chucho Monge
(Jesús Monge). © Promotora
Hispano Americana de Música,
s. a., Mexico; 30Dec46; EF5285.

Sus ojitos .. ... Letra y música
de Jesús Monge (Chucho Monge)
© Promotora Hispano Americana
de Música, s.a., Mexico; 7May47;
EF3335.

[MONK, WILLIAM H   ]
Abide with me; [words by Henry F.
Lyte, music by William H. Monk,
arr. by Victor Lakes Martin]
Easy piano arrangement with
keyboard charts. © Songs You
Remember Publishing Co., (V. L.
Martin, Proprietor), Atlanta; on
arrangement; 5Apr47; EP14748.

MONNOT, MARGUERITE.
Un coin tout bleu. See her
Montmartre sur Seine.
(Montmartre sur Seine) Un coin
tout bleu. © Éditions Paul
Beuscher, Paris; 30Nov11; EF490.
For voice and piano, and voice
part.

MONROE, BILL. See
Monroe, William Smith.
MONROE, WILLIAM SMITH.
Mother's only sleeping; words and
music by Bill Monroe. © Peer
International Corp., New York;
18Apr47; EP13983.

MONSON, ISADORA, 1869-
When you strike it rich! Words and
music by Isadora Monson. ©
Isadora Monson, Denver; 11Feb47;
EP14425.

MONTBRUN, RAYMOND GALLOIS- See
Gallois-Montbrun, Raymond.

MONTE, COR, pseud. See
Berg, Cornelis Jacobus van den.

MONTEFALCO, ALBERT.
Where can you be? Words and
music by Albert Montefalco.
© Nordyke Publishing Co.,
Los Angeles; 22Apr47; EP14790.

MONTGOMERY, BRUCE.
On the resurrection of Christ;
words by William Dunbar, music
by Bruce Montgomery. © Novello
& Co., ltd., London; 15Apr47;
EF5526. Score: chorus
(SSAATTBB) and piano.

MONTGOMERY, LEE S   1906-
Casey at the bat; [words by] Ernest
L. Thayer, [music by] Lee S.
Montgomery. © Ruval Music Co.,
Hollywood, Calif.; 3Feb47;
EP12485.

MONTGOMERY, LENORE, pseud. See
Fletcher, Leila.

MONTGOMERY, MARVIN.
Bear Creek hop ... words and music
by Marvin Montgomery. © Peer
International Corp., New York;
10Apr47; EP13697.

MONTGOMERY, ROMAYNE.
Lonesome for love; words by
Morris Montgomery, music by
Romayne Montgomery. ©
Nordyke Publishing Co., Los
Angeles; 8Mar47; EP13287.

MONTGOMERY, VIRGINIA.
The music fun book; a work book
for young piano beginners, by
Virginia Montgomery. ©
Theodore Presser Co., Phila-
delphia; 3Jun47; EP15126.

MOODY, JAMES, 1907-
Parakeet in paradise; by James
Moody. © Evans and Lowry, ltd.,
London; 18Jan47; EF5309. For
piano solo.

MOORE, DONALD LEE.
Midnight ... words by Adelaide
Van Wey, music by Donald Lee
Moore. © Theodore Presser Co.,
Philadelphia; 19Feb47;
EP12164.

MOORE, DOUGLAS.
Not this alone; for voice and
piano, [words by Pierson Underwood, music] by Douglas Moore.
© G. Schirmer, inc., New York;
3Apr47; EP14053.

MOORE, DOUGLAS S
Good night, Harvard (Yale football
song); march, by Douglas S. Moore,
arranged by Paul Yoder. © Shapiro,
Bernstein & Co., inc., New York;
on arrangement; 31Dec46; EP13632.
Condensed score (band) and parts.

MOORE, E   C   1887-
Classroom method for the fife;
by E. C. Moore. © Trophy
Products Co., Cleveland;
30Dec46; EP12069. Cover title:
The Moore classroom fife
method.

MOORE, FLEECIE.
Ain't that just like a woman? By
Claude Demetrius and Fleecie Moore.
© Preview Music Co., Chicago;
13Apr46; EP12079. For voice and
piano, with chord symbols.
Beware, brother, beware; words and
music by Morry Lasco, Dick Adams
[and] Fleecie Moore, arr. by
Johnny Warrington. © Preview
Music Co., Chicago; on arrange-
ment; 1Feb47; EP12563. Piano-
conductor score (orchestra, with
words) and parts.
Caldonia (What makes your big head
so hard?) By Fleecie Moore, arr.
by Johnny Warrington. © Preview
Music Co., Chicago; on arrangement; 1Feb47; EP12364. Piano-
conductor score (orchestra, with
words) and parts.
Caldonia. See also his No leave,
no love.
Let the good times roll; by Sam
Theard and F. Moore. © Preview
Music Co., Chicago; 8Oct46; EP12134.
For voice and piano, with chord symbols.
(No leave, no love) Caldonia
(what makes your big head so
hard) Featured in the ...
picture "No leave, no love", by
Fleecie Moore. [c1945] © Preview Music Co., Chicago; on new
title page by Robert Holley;
21Aug46; EP13114.

MOORE, FLOYD C
Lord, let me live today; by
Floyd C. Moore, arr. by
Danforth Simonton, [words by
W. Wyttenbach] © Theodore
Presser Co., Philadelphia;
on arrangement; 20Mar47;
EP12884. Score: chorus
(SaTB) and organ.

MOORE, GEORGE D
The haven of rest; [words by] H.
L. Gilmore, [music by] Geo. D.
Moore. (In Eddy Arnold's radio
favorites song book. no. A-1,
p.46) © Adams, Vee & Abbott,
inc., Chicago; on arrangement;
17Jun46; EP11230. Close score:
SATB, with guitar diagrams and
chord symbols.

MOORE, MARY CARR, 1873-
Intuition. [Op.103, no.1] and
Dance. [Op.98, no.5] Two short
songs; [words] by Mary Carr Moore.
© Wesley Webster, San Francisco;
24Dec46; EP10782.
Message; by Mary Carr Moore.
Op. 98, no.6. © Wesley
Webster, San Francisco;
15Apr47; EP13589. For voice
and piano.

MOORE, MILTONA.
Island fantasy ... by Miltona Moore.
© McKinley Publishers, inc.,
Chicago; 10Feb47; EP12044. For
piano solo.

MOORE, MILTONA. Cont'd.
Nocturne; for [piano], left hand
alone, [by] Miltona Moore. ©
McKinley Publishers, inc.,
Chicago; 26Dec46; EP10853.
Street carnival; for piano [by]
Miltona Moore. © McKinley
Publishers, inc., Chicago;
28Feb47; EP12404.
Young Mister Playboy; [by]
Miltona Moore, for piano.
© McKinley Publishers, inc.,
Chicago; 7May47; EP14316.

MOORE, NADINE, 1888-
I heard a bird at break of day ...
[words by] William Alexander
Percy, [music by] Nadine Moore.
SSA accompanied. © Harold Flammor,
inc., New York; 31Dec46; EP14423.

MOORE, OSCAR.
Oscar Moore's Guitaristics ...
original guitar solos with
piano and 2nd guitar acc.
© Leeds Music Corp., New York;
21Mar47; EP12861.

MOORE, WILTON.
(Carnegie Hall) The pleasure's
all mine; by Frank Ryerson [and]
Wilton Moore, featured ... in
the ... picture "Carnegie Hall."
© Leeds Music Corp., New York;
31Dec46; EP13719. For voice and
piano, with chord symbols.
The pleasure's all mine. See his
Carnegie Hall.

MOPPER, IRVING, 1914-
The frog; for four-part chorus of
men's voices, a cappella, [by]
Irving Mopper. Text anonymous.
© The Boston Music Co., Boston;
10Jun47; EP14992.

MOQUIN, AL, 1891-
I hate to spend another lonely day;
by Dick Reynolds and Al Moquin.
© Stevens Music Co., San Antonio;
3Feb47; EP11914. For voice and
piano, with chord symbols.

MORAINE, LYLE.
Christmas Island; words and
music by Lyle Moraine, [arr.
by Vic Schoen] New York, The
Peter Maurice Music Co., ltd.
© Northern Music Corp., New
York; on arrangement;
31Dec46; EP14280. Piano-
conductor score (orchestra,
with words) and parts.
Christmas Island; words and music
by Lyle Moraine. New York, The
Peter Maurice Music Co., Ltd.
© Northern Music Corp., New York;
31Dec46; EP14166.

MORALES, JOSÉ DE JESÚS. See
Jesús Morales, José de.

MORALES, NORO, 1912-
Wha' happeen, baby? (I got to
know); lyric by Al Stillman,
music by Noro Morales.
© Robbins Music Corp., New York;
27May47; EP14347.
You better mind your mama; words
and music by Leo Corday, Leon
Carr and Noro Morales.
Robbins Music Corp., New York;
19Dec46; EP11002.

MORAN, EDGAR.
Adiosita; words and music by
Edgar Moran. © Broadcast
Music, inc., New York; 31Dec46;
EP12768. English words.

MOREAU, CELIA MARY, 1904-
Piano chords; by Celia Moreau.
Self-instruction in playing
popular music. New York,
Sole selling agent, Edward
Schuberth & Co. © Celia
Mary Moreau, Providence; bk. 2,
18Feb47; EP12174.

MORENA, MORENA ... Brazilian song,
[English words adapted by Albert
Gamse] (In André, Julie, ed.)
Songs from south of the border.
p.38-39) © Edward B. Marks Music
Corp., New York; on English
adaptation; 28Dec46; EP10875.

MORES, MARIANITO.
Sin palabras ... letra de Enrique
Santos Discépolo, música de
Marianito Mores. © Editorial
Argentina de Música Inter-
nacional, s. de r., ltd.,
Buenos Aires; 30Dec46; EF5218.

MORETTI, RAOUL.
Pense à moi; paroles et musique
de Raoul Moretti. ©
Ste. ame. fse. Chappell,
Paris; 29May47; EF3911.

MORGAN, HAYDN.
God is the Light of the world;
for ... SSATBB [by] Haydn
Morgan. [Words] from the
Scriptures. © The B. F. Wood
Music Co., Boston; 21Apr47;
EP13810.
Hide not Thy face; four-part chorus
for mixed voices ... a cappella,
words adapted from the Psalms,
music by Haydn Morgan. © Carl
Fischer, inc., New York; 16Apr47;
EP13900.

MORGAN, LOUMELL, 1917-
Riffin' Rufus; by Loumell Morgan.
© Popular Music Co., New York;
13Jun47; EP15034. For voice and
piano, with chord symbols.

MORGAN, R   DUKE.
'Tain't no fun what you've done;
lyric by Blanche Calloway,
music by R. Duke Morgan. ©
Kay & Kay, inc., New York;
18Feb47; EP6612.

MORGAN, RHYS.
Love that never fails; sacred song.
Words by James Cowden Wallace,
music by Rhys Morgan. © Delmar
Publications (Gwladys K. Long-
more, sole owner), New York;
30Apr45; EP6735.

MORRIS, KENNETH, 1917-
Christ is all; words and music
by Kenneth Morris. Chicago,
Martin and Morris Music
Studio. © Kenneth Morris,
Chicago; 31Oct46; EP12464.
He will give me rest ... words
and music by Kenneth Morris.
Chicago, Martin & Morris Music
Studio. © Kenneth Morris,
Chicago; 10Aug46; EP12463.
Just like Jesus; words and music
by Kenneth Morris. Chicago,
Martin and Morris Music Studio.
© Kenneth Morris, Chicago;
13Dec46; EP12461.
When I reach that city over
there; words and music by
Kenneth Morris. Chicago,
Martin & Morris Music Studio.
© Kenneth Morris, Chicago;
13Dec46; EP12462.
Yes, I want to rest; original
words by James Sands, rev.
lyrics and music by Kenneth
Morris. © Kenneth Morris &
James Sands, Chicago; on
arrangement; 15Sep45; EP13801.

KORRISON, JOHN, 1910-
Afterglow; tone poem for the
piano by John Morrison. ©
Shattinger Piano & Music Co.,
St. Louis; 6May47; EP14235.

MORRISSEY, JOHN J
Interlude ... by John J.
Morrissey. © Remick Music
Corp., New York; 14May47;
EP14548. Condensed score
(clarinet and band) and parts.

MORROS, BORIS, arr.
(Carnegie Hall) Souvenir album
of piano music, from the motion
picture "Carnegie Hall"; tran-
scribed [and arr.] ... by Boris
Morros and Gregory Stone.
© Omega Music Edition, New
York; on arrangement; 24Apr47;
EP13961.

MORTARI, VIRGILIO, 1902-
Due laude; [by] Virgilio Mortari,
da un antico codice della
Confraternità de' Disciplinati
di Santa Croce in Urbino. ©
Carisch, società anonima,
Milan; 30Dec46; EF5484. Score
(voice, flute, violoncello
and piano) and parts.
Trittico; [by] Virgilio Mortari,
per soprano, mezzo soprano,
coretto femminile e orchestra.
Riduzione per canto e pianoforte.
© Carisch, società anonima,
Milan; 30Dec46; EF5485.

MOSBERGER, STEVE G
Now it's my turn to turn you
down; words and music by
Steve G. Mosberger. [A Jean
Walz arrangement] © Hartmann
& Van Horn Music Publishing
Co., La Grange, Ill.;
22Apr47; EP14462.

MOSER, FRANZ, 1880-1939.
Aus meinem Leben; zwölf
Klavierstücke von Franz Moser.
Op. 12. Wien, Universal-
Edition A. G. © Associated
Music Publishers, inc., New
York; 15Dec19; EF5321.
For piano solo.

MOSES, ABRAM.
Sabbath morning synagogue service;
for four-part chorus of mixed voices
and organ, with baritone solo. ©
G. Schirmer, inc., New York; 30Dec46;
EP13513.

MOSLEY, SNUB, 1906-
Blues at high noon; by Snub Mosley.
© Popular Music Co., New York;
13Jun47; EP15037. For voice and
piano, with chord symbols.
Snub's boogie; by Snub Mosley
[and] Herman Flintall. ©
Popular Music Co., New York;
5May47; EP12403. For piano
solo.
Squash head; words by Buddy
Feyne, music by Snub Mosley
[and] Herman Flintall. © Popular Music Co., New York;
4Jun47; EP14889.
You and the Devil; by Snub Mosley.
© Fowler Music Co., New York;
19May47; EP14530. For voice and
piano, with chord symbols.

MOSSMAN, TED, 1914-
Don't you worry, don't you care
(love will come to you); words
and music by Ted Mossman, based on
the Roumanian rhapsody, no. 1, by
Georges Enesco. © Edwin H.
Morris & Co., inc., New York;
10Jun47; EP11180. For voice
and piano, with chord symbols.
I love to love you in my dreams;
words and music by Ted Mossman.
© Gaumont Music Publishers, New
York; 1Apr47; EP6739.
A thousand and one nights ... by
Ted Mossman ... [words by] Jack
Segal. © Barton Music Corp.,
New York; 22Jan47; EP11387.

MOSSMAN, TED, 1914-   arr.
The Arkansaw fiddler; piano solo,
words and arrangement by Ted
Mossman. © Belwin, inc., New
York; on words and arrangement;
24Dec46; EP11260.

98

MOSSMAN, TED. Cont'd.
Blow the man down; (a song of the sea) piano solo, words and arrangement by Ted Mossman. © Belwin, inc., New York; on words & arrangement; 18Dec46; EP11966.

Deep river; (a spiritual) piano solo, words and arrangement by Ted Mossman. © Belwin, inc., New York; on words and arrangement; 24Dec46; EP11263.

The Erie Canal; piano solo; words and arrangement by Ted Mossman. © Belwin, inc., New York; on words and arrangement; 24Dec46; EP11264.

Mohoo; piano solo; words and arrangement by Ted Mossman. © Belwin, inc., New York; on words and arrangement; 24Dec46; EP11265.

Polly wolly doodle; (American folk song) Piano solo, words and arrangement by Ted Mossman. © Belwin, inc., New York; on words and arrangement; 24Dec46; EP11266.

That big rock candy mountain; piano solo, words and arrangement by Ted Mossman. © Belwin, inc., New York; on words and arrangement; 24Dec46; EP11261.

MOSZKOWSKI, MORITZ.
Etude caprice; by Moszkowski-Waln. © Belwin, inc., New York; on arrangement; 31Dec46; EP11765. Piano-conductor score (clarinet and band) and parts.

MOURIN, NEVILLE.
Our Lady of Fatima; chorus for two-part treble voices, by Cleophas Nevillo [pseud.] © Harold Flammer, inc., New York; 4Nov46; EP10827.

MOYSE, LOUIS JOSEPH, 1912-
Sept caprices pour flûte; par Louis Moyse. © Louis Moyse, Rueil-Malmaison, Seine & Oise, France; v.2, 22Dec46; v.3, 1Mar47. Vol.2 has piano accompaniment. Contents.- 2. Scherzo (© EF5530) - 3. Pastorale (© EF5812)

MOYZES, ALEXANDER, 1906-
Divertimento, piano à 2 ms. Op.11. [By] Alexander Moyzes. © Hudební Matice Umělecké Besedy, Praha, Czechoslovakia; 28Oct39; EF5012.

MOZART, JOHANN CHRYSOSTOM WOLFGANG AMADEUS, 1756-1791.
(Concerto, bassoon) Concerto for bassoon and orchestra; [by] W. A. Mozart. K. V. 191 ... Arr. by John S. Weissmann. The bassoon part rev. and the cadenzas added by Archie Camden. © Boosey & Hawkes, ltd., London; on arrangement; 29May47; EF5419. Score (bassoon and piano) and part.

(Concerto, clarinet, K.622) Concerto for clarinet and orchestra; [by] W.A. Mozart. K. V. 622 ... Arranged by Ernest Roth, the clarinet part revised by Frederick Thurston. © Boosey & Hawkes, ltd., London; on arrangement; 31Dec46; EF4771. Score (clarinet and piano) and part.

(Concerto, horn) Horn concerto in E flat; by [by] W. A. Mozart. K. V. 447 ... Arr. by W. Salomon. © Boosey & Hawkes, ltd., London; on arrangement; 29May47; EF5421. Score (horn and piano) and part.

Divertimento in C major; [by] W. A. Mozart, transcribed by Gregor Piatigorsky. © Elkan-Vogel Co., inc., Philadelphia; on transcription; 28Feb47; EP13110. Score (violoncello and piano) and part.

Divertimento in C major; [by] W. A. Mozart, transcribed by Gregor Piatigorsky, [viola part ed. by Henri Elkan] © Elkan-Vogel Co., inc., Philadelphia; on transcription ; 28Feb47; EP13109. Score (violoncello and piano) and part for viola.

Don Giovanni; opera in two acts by Wolfgang Amadeus Mozart; words by Lorenzo da Ponte, English version by Edward J. Dent, vocal score by Ernest Roth, London, Boosey & Hawkes. © Boosey & Co., ltd., London; on new vocal score; 4Feb47; EF4888.

18th century theme from sonata in C major. See his Sonata, piano.

Gloria in excelsis, from Mozart's 12th mass; arr. for 3 choirs by C. Albert Scholin. [St. Louis, Distributors, Hunleth Music Co.] © C. Albert Scholin, St. Louis; on arrangement; 8Jan47; EP10928.

Great melodies from Mozart's operas; [arr.] by Eric Steiner for the young pianist. © Elkan-Vogel Co., inc., Philadelphia; on arrangement & revision; 20Dec46; EP11455.

Horn concerto in E flat. See his Concerto, horn.

Jesus, I my cross have taken ... hymn-anthem for choir and congregation with soprano solo (S.A.T.B.) ... arr. by W. B. Olds. [Words by] Henry F. Lyte. © Hall & McCreary Co., Chicago; on arrangement; 4Jun46; EP4699.

(Eine kleine Nachtmusik) Serenade; [by] W. A. Mozart, [arr. for] piano, deux mains [by] Johan Ligtelijn. © Edition Heuwekemeyer (Firm A. J. Heuwekemeyer & B. F. van Gaal), Amsterdam, The Netherlands; on arrangement; 7Feb46; EF5114.

(Eine kleine Nachtmusik) Sérénade; Petite musique de nuit. Small night music. Eine kleine Nachtmusik. (Köchel no. 525) Réduction pour piano par Jean Martinon. Paris, L. de Lacour, Éditions Costallat. © Lucien de Lacour, Paris; on arrangement; 30Nov46; EF5648.

The marriage of Figaro. See his Le nozze di Figaro.

Menuetto; [by] W. A. Mozart, arr. and ed. by Andrea Del Vecchio. © Carl Fischer, inc., New York; on arrangement; 9Jun47; EP15222. Score (solo instrument and piano) and part for flute.

Mozart-Schaum for piano ... biographical continuity by Nora Schaum, musical adaptation by John W. Schaum. © Belwin, inc., New York; on adaptation and compilation; bk. 1; 29Apr47; EP14665.

(Le nozze di Figaro) The marriage of Figaro; opera in four acts by Wolfgang Amadeus Mozart, words by Lorenzo da Ponte, English version by Edward J. Dent, vocal score by Ernest Roth. New York, Boosey & Hawkes. © Boosey & Co., ltd., London; on vocal score; 29Apr47; EF5627. Italian and English words.

Sérénade. See his Eine kleine Nachtmusik.

Sleep and rest; S A accompanied, [by] Mozart, arr. and adapted by Frances Williams. © Harold Flammer, inc., New York; on arrangement; 7May47; EP14374.

Some of the happy melodies from Mozart's chamber music; arr. for pianoforte by J. Michael Diack. © Paterson's Publications, ltd., London; 14Apr47; EF5309.

(Sonata, piano) 18th century theme from sonata in C major; [by] W. A. Mozart, arr. by Art Jolliff. © Rubank, inc., Chicago; on arrangement; 1May47; EP14083. Score (marimba or xylophone and piano) and part.

(Sonata, piano) Sonata in C; [by] Mozart. [Köchel no. 545. Arr. by Victor Ambroise] © Lawrence Wright Music Co., ltd., London; on arrangement; 9Apr47; EF5475.

Two pieces (I. Canon; II. Minuetto) [by] Wolfgang A. Mozart. For two alto recorders and one tenor recorder. Arr. by George Hunter. (Earls Court repertory for recorder) © E. C. Schirmer Music Co., Boston; 25Jan47; EP11885.

MRACZEK, JOSEPH GUSTAV, 1878-
Ikdar; Oper in drei Aufzügen; Dichtung von Guido Glück, Musik von Joseph Gustav Mraczek, Klavierauszug mit Text von Josef Rosenstock. Vienna, Universal-Edition, a..8,. © Associated Music Publishers, inc., New York; 1Mar19; EF5157.

MUCHACHA BONITA. (The maid with the mole on her cheek) [English words adapted by Albert Gamse] (In André, Julie, ed. Songs from south of the border. p.36-37) © Edward B. Marks Music Corp., New York; on English adaptation; 28Dec46; EP10874.

MUELLER, CARL F
O blessed day of motherhood ... S A B, with optional solos, [words by] Ernest F. McGregor, [music by] Carl F. Mueller. © Harold Flammer, inc., New York; on arrangement; 14mar47; EP13478.

O blessed day of motherhood ... SSA accompanied, [by] Carl F. Mueller, [words by] Ernest F. McGregor. © Harold Flammer, inc., New York; on arrangement; 7May47; EP14367.

O for a thousand tongues ... for four-part (divided) chorus of mixed voices with baritone (or contralto) solo (S.A.T.B.) a cappella) Music by Carl F. Mueller ... words by Rev. Charles Wesley. © Carl Fischer, inc., New York; 27Jan47; EP12429.

O God, our Help in ages past; SAB accompanied, [by] Carl F. Mueller, [words by] Isaac Watts. © Harold Flammer, inc., New York; on arrangement; 7May47; EP14377.

Prayer of St. Francis; for ... chorus of mixed voices with tenor (or soprano) solo, S.A.T.B. a cappella. Music by Carl F. Mueller ... text by St. Francis of Assisi. © Carl Fischer, inc., New York; 10Apr47; EP13764.

Whither shall I go from Thy spirit? For four-part chorus of mixed voices, with piano or organ acc. ... Psalm CXXXIX; 7-12 [by] Carl F. Mueller. © Carl Fischer, inc., New York; 16Apr47; EP13898.

MUELLER, CARL F arr.
Two-part anthem book; for junior or women's choirs ... arr. with organ or piano acc. [by] Carl F. Mueller. © Carl Fischer, inc., New York; on arrangement; 11Mar47; EP12836.

99

MUELLER, P. E. LANGE- See
Lange-Mueller, P. E.

MUFFAT, GEORG.
Passacaglia; [by] George Muffat,
for string orchestra, transcribed by R. Temple Savage.
Full score. © J. & W. Chester,
ltd., London; on transcription;
27May47; EP3898.

MULCAHY, MARGARET AGNES, 1898-
Yankee soldiers' march; words by
Ellen M. Mulcahy, music by
Margaret A. Mulcahy. New York,
Waterford Music Publishers.
© Margaret A. Mulcahy, New
Milford, Conn.; 20Oct42;
EP13996.

MULDER, HAROLD J   1903-
It's Easter time once more;
words by Harold Charter,
music by Harold Mulder. ©
Mulder & Charter, Muskegon,
Mich.; 27Mar47; EP13093.

[MULÉ, LOUIS]
Just one dream after another;
words and music by Lou Clair
and Lew Mel [pseud.] © Nordyke Publishing Co., Los
Angeles; 26Oct45; EP13535.

A rose, a smile, a prayer; music
by Lew Mel [pseud.] and Win
Roland, words by Jesse Rogers
and Jack Howard. (In Cousin
Lee book of original songs.
p.24-25) © Jack Howard
Publications, inc., Philadelphia;
30Dec46; EP11737.

MULLICAN, MOON.
New pretty blonde; (New Jole
Blon) By Sydney Nathan and
Moon Mullican. © Hill and
Range Songs, inc., Hollywood,
Calif.; 17May47; EP14582.
For voice and piano, with
guitar diagrams and chord
symbols.

MUNDAHL, ROGER OBED, 1926-
Why did it happen to me? Words
and music by Roger Mundahl,
[arr. by Harold Burton Edstrom,
simplified arrangement by Gilmore Frederick Mason] © Roger
Mundahl, Peterson, Minn., on
simplified arrangement; 29May47;
EP14947.

[MUNDLIN, LOIS]
Big town gal; lyrics and music by
Spook McGlook [pseud.], Arizona
Mulligan [pseud. and] Marion
Aldrich [pseud.] © Hillcrest
Music Publications, Omaha;
8Apr47; EP14441.

MUNOZ, RAFAEL.
Baile del tambah. (The tambah)
... English words by Joe Davis,
Spanish words and music by
Rafael Munoz. © Caribbean
Music, inc., New York; 17Mar47;
EP12646.

MUNRO, RONNIE.
Musical typist ... by Ronnie Munro,
arr. by Philip J. Lang. New York,
Mills Music, inc. © Noel Gay
Music Co., ltd., London; on arrangement; 23May47; EP6939. Score
(solo piano, xylophone or accordion
and band) and parts.

MUNTE, MANUEL DEL, pseud. See
Cassard, Emmanuel.

MURAY, PAULE.
Ay ay ay, mama! ... paroles de
Noël Barcy [pseud.], musique de
Paule Muray. © Publications
Francis Day, Paris; 31Oct46;
EF3577. Melody and words.

MURIELLO, JOSÉ, pseud. See
Leggett, Lewis Ernest.

MURILLO, EMILIO.
Pajarillo. (Pretty pa-ha-reel-yo)
... [By] Emilio Murillo, [English
words adapted by Albert Gamse]
(In André, Julio, ed. Songs from
south of the border. p.26-27) ©
Edward B. Marks Music Corp., New
York; on English adaptation;
28Dec46; EP10870.

MURPHEY, HULET. See
Murphey, James Hulet.

MURPHEY, JAMES HULET.
Our prayer; words and music by:
Hulet Murphey. © James H.
Murphey, Evansville, Ind.;
25Mar47; EP6748. Close score:
SATB.

MURPHY, JOSEPH A   1880-
Te Deum laudamus; Gregorian chant
and three equal voices (S.S.A. -
or T.T.B.) a cappella with
popolo part, ad lib., by Joseph
A. Murphy. [c1946] © The St.
Gregory Guild, inc., Philadelphia;
10Jan47; EP12015.

MURPHY, LYLE SPUD, 1908-
Modern dance band harmony and
system of progressions; by
Lyle Spud Murphy. © Lyle
Spud Murphy, Hollywood,
Calif.; 1May47; EP14147.

MURRAY, ALAN.
Too tired to sleep; song, words
by Carlene Graham [pseud.],
music by Alan Murray. ©
Keith, Prowse & Co., ltd.,
London; 30May47; EF3625.

MURRAY, DAVID DANIEL, 1911-
Are you just pretending, dear?
Words and music by Dave Murray.
© David Daniel Murray, Arling-
ton, Va.; on revision of words
and music; 10Mar47; EP12453.

MURRAY, LYN.
Comin' thro' the rye; version by
Lyn Murray, arr. by Jeff
Alexander ... S.A.T.B. ©
Boosey & Hawkes, inc., New
York; on arrangement; 27Dec46;
EP10992.

The farmer in the dell; version by
Lyn Murray ... S.A.T.B. ©
Boosey & Hawkes, inc., New York;
on arrangement; 27Dec46; EP10994.

Twinkle, twinkle little star;
version by Lyn Murray, arr. by
Jeff Alexander ... S.A.T.B.
© Boosey & Hawkes, inc. New
York; on arrangement; 27Dec46;
EP10993.

MURRY, TED, 1900-
My young and foolish heart; words
and music by Charles Tobias,
Al Lewis [and] Ted Murry. ©
Edwin H. Morris & Co., inc.,
New York; 24Feb47; EP12375.

Pineapples; words by Charles
Tobias; music by Ted Murry.
© Edwin H. Morris & Co.,
inc., New York; 24Feb47;
EP12373.

MUSCAT, ANDRÉ.
Harmonie ... paroles de René Dez,
musique de André Muscat. ©
Éditions Musicales Nuances,
Paris; 28Nov46; EF3151.

MUSEL, BOB.
Saturday night at the palais; [by]
Bob Musel & Eddie Lisbona, arr.
by Dave Rose. [c1946] © Peter
Maurice Music Co., ltd., New
York; 19Mar47; EF5523. Piano-
conductor score (orchestra) and
parts.

THE MUSICAL SALVATIONIST. © Salvationist Publishing & Supplies,
ltd., London. Vol.50, pt.6,
v.51, pt.1-2, comp. by Dram-
well Coles. v. 50, pt. 6;
25Nov46; © EF3117.   v. 51,
pt. 1; 10Feb47; © EF3180.
v. 51, pt. 2; 24Apr47; © EF3670.

MUSTELIER, ALEJANDRO.
El cocinero ... de Alejandro
Mustelier. © Peer International
Corp., New York; 17Dec42; EF5618.
For voice and piano.

El testamento del Congo ... letra
y música de Alejandro
Mustelier, arreglo de R. Calzado.
© Peer International Corp.,
New York; 30Dec46; EF5440.
Piano-conductor score
(orchestra) and parts.

MY FIRST CHRISTMAS SONGS. © Art
Publication Society, Clayton, Mo.;
on design & arrangements in
study no.159-162, 22Nov46. For
piano solo, with words. Vol.
159-162 arr. by Lillie-Mayes
Dodd. · Contents.- study no.159.
Three kings of Orient and I
heard the bells on Christmas
day (© EP10913) - study no.160.
A carol from Poland and Silent
night. (© EP10914) - study no.161.
O come, all ye faithful and The
first noel (© EP10915) - study
no.162. Hark! the herald angels
sing and It came upon the midnight
clear (© EP10916)

[MYDDLETON, WILLIAM]
Down South; [by William Myddleton]
... Arr. by Louis Sugarman.
© Edward B. Marks Music Corp.,
New York; on arrangement;
17Feb47; EP12244. For piano
solo

MYNATT, ALBERTA.
Chimes of Zion; words and music
by Alberta Mynatt, ed. by Artie
Matthews. Cincinnati, Cos-
mopolitan School of Music Press.
© Alberta Mynatt and C. S. of M.,
Lockland, Ohio; 17Apr47; EP14672.
For voice and piano.

MYROGIANNES, GEORGIOS CHRISTOS,
1911-
Na ti pē Ellada; version by
K. Kiouse, mousikē: G. Myrogi-
annēs. 3. ekdosis. Athenai
Ekdoseis O. Konstantinidē. ©
"S.O.F.E." Copyright Protection
Society, Athens; 16Feb45;
EF3234. For voice and piano.

MYROW, JOSEF, 1910-
Autumn nocturne; music by Josef
Myrow. © Advanced Music Corp.,
New York; on arrangement;
7Jun47; EP15168. For organ
solo; includes registration for
Hammond organ.
(If I'm lucky) Jam session in Brazil
... lyric by Edgar Do Lange, music
by Josef Myrow. Featured in the
... picture "If I'm lucky."
Mills Music, inc., New York;
31Dec46; EP6431. For voice and
piano, with chord symbols.
Jam session in Brazil. See his
If I'm lucky.

Moon of jade; [by] Josef Myrow.
© Triangle Music Corp., New
York; 14Apr47; EP13711. For
piano solo.

MYSELS, SAMMY.
His feet too big for de bed; by
Dick Sanford, Bernardez Brana
and Sammy Mysels. © Capitol
Songs, inc., New York; 24Feb47;
EP12158. For voice and piano,
with chord symbols.
His feet too big for de bed; by
Hernandez Brana, Dick Sanford
and Sammy Mysels, arr. by Van
Alexander. © Capitol Songs,
inc., New York; on arrangement;
1Apr47; EP13355. Piano-
conductor score (orchestra,
with words) and parts.
Red silk stockings and green
perfume; by Dick Sanford,
Bob Hilliard [and] Sammy
Mysels. © Edwin H. Morris
& Co., inc., New York;
13Mar47; EP12664. For voice
and piano, with chord symbols.

MYSELS, SAMMY. Cont'd.
A strawberry moon (in a blueberry
sky); [words] by Bob Hilliard
... [music by] Sammy Mysels.
[arr. by Bob Kahn] © Jefferson
Music Co., inc., New York;
21Feb47; EP6575.

N

NADYVAL.
Images; paroles de Guy
Fayereau, musique de Nadyval.
© Éditions E.M.U.L., Paris;
31Jul46; EF3616.

[NAGELI, HANS G   ]
Blest be the tie that binds;
[words by John Fawcett, music
by Hans G. Nageli, arr. by Vic-
tor Lakes Martin] Easy piano ar-
rangement with keyboard charts.
© Songs You Remember Publishing
Co., (V. L. Martin, Proprietor),
Atlanta; on arrangement; 5Apr47;
EP14750.

NAGLE, ROY B
Friendship; words by Florence H.
Staniels, music by Roy B.
Nagle. Reading, Pa., Nagle
Studio of Music. © Florence
H. Staniels, Passaic, N. J. &
Roy B. Nagle, Reading, Pa.;
15May47; EP6900.

NAGLE, WILLIAM S
Benedictus, es Domine; set to
music in the key of C for mixed
voices by William S. Nagle.
© The H. W. Gray Co., inc.,
New York; 3Jan47; EP11056.

NAGLE, WILLIAM S   arr.
Shepherds song; French folk tune,
transcribed by William S. Nagle.
© Elkan-Vogel Co., inc., Philadelphia; on transcription;
24Dec46; EP11459. For organ
solo.

NAGLER, FRANCISCUS.
A song in praise of the Lord;
four part anthem for mixed
voices ... [by] Franciscus
Nagler, arr. by Clarence
Dickinson, English text
by Helen A. Dickinson. ©
The H. W. Gray Co., inc.,
New York; on arrangement; 3Jan47;
EP12395.

NATHAN, LLOYD.
Why did it have to be you? Words
and music by Lloyd Nathan. ©
Bell Song Publishing Co.,
Hollywood, Calif.; 31Jan47;
EP11519.
You can't save me for a rainy day;
words and music by Lloyd Nathan.
© Bell Song Pub. Co., Hollywood,
Calif.; 11Feb47; EP11927.

NATHAN, SYDNEY.
Steppin' out kind; words and
music by Sid Nathan. © Hill
and Range Songs, inc., Hollywood, Calif.; 17May47;
EP14557.

NAVARRO, AURORA.
Asi te queria ... [words and
music by] Aurora Navarro,
arreglo de Antonio Núñez M.
© Editorial Mexicana de Música
Internacional, s. a., Mexico;
14Jul47; EP5808. Condensed score
(orchestra), piano-conductor
score and parts.

NAVARRO, CHUCHO. See
Navarro, José Jesus.

NAVARRO, JOSÉ JESUS.
Perdida. (I'm lost) ... English
words by Joe Davis, Spanish words
and music by José Jesus "Chucho"
Navarro. © Caribbean Music,
inc., New York; 12May47; EP14221.

NECKES, Father.
Pascha nostrum; Easter communion
for two equal or four mixed
voices, [by] Fr. Neckes, arr.
by T. N. M. © McLaughlin &
Reilly Co., Boston; on arrangement; 10Mar47; EP12782.

NEDD, J   B
Our Father; words and music by J.
B. Nedd, arr. by Virginia Davis.
[c1946] © Rev. J. B. Nedd,
Cleveland; 1Jan47; EP6975.
Hymn.

NEIDLINGER, WILLIAM.
Lord, with glowing heart;
anthem for mixed voices with
tenor or soprano solo, [by]
William Neidlinger, [words
by] Francis Scott Key. ©
The H. W. Gray Co., inc.,
New York; 28Feb47; EP12398.

NEILSON, JAMES.
The music road ... [by] James
Neilson ... [and] Ruth M. Shafer
... Drawings and cover [by]
Wilhelmina M. Blanchard. ©
Harlow Publishing Corp., Oklahoma
City; bk.1, 25Mar47; AA48317.
A workbook for elementary grades.

NELSON, EDWARD G   1886-
Downright lonely, downright blue;
words and music by Steve Nelson,
Milton Leeds, [pseud.] and Ed.
Nelson. © Bob Miller, inc.,
New York; 2May47; EP14177.

NELSON, FREDA N
The musical man from San Berdoo;
lyrics and music by Freda B.
Nelson. © Freda B. Nelson,
Muroc, Calif.; 15Mar47; EP6817.

NELSON, HERBERT, 1910-
In your arms; words and music by
Herbert Nelson, [arrangement:
Martin Roman] © Imuta, P.
Heiber, International Music,
Theatre Edition and Agency,
Basle, Switzerland; 15Dec46;
EP4985.
Love, l'amour, amore; words and
music by Herbert Nelson,
[arrangement: Martin Roman]
© Imuta, P. Heiber, Inter-
national Music, Theatre Edition
and Agency, Basle, Switzerland;
15Dec46; EP4989.
Never more; words and music by
Herbert Nelson, [arrangement:
Martin Roman] © Imuta, P.
Heiber, International Music,
Theatre Edition and Agency,
Basle, Switzerland; 15Dec46;
EP4988.
Romeo and Juliet; words and music
by Herbert Nelson, [arrangement:
Martin Roman] © Imuta, P.
Heiber, International Music,
Theatre Edition and Agency,
Basle, Switzerland; 15Dec46;
EP4986.
Stop the world; words and music by
Herbert Nelson, [arrangement:
Martin Roman] © Imuta, P.
Heiber, International Music,
Theatre Edition and Agency,
Basle, Switzerland; 15Dec46;
EP4987.
"Your heart and my heart"; words
and music [by] Herbert Nelson,
[arrangement: Martin Roman]
© Imuta, P. Heiber, International
Music, Theatre Edition and
Agency, Basle, Switzerland;
15Dec46; EP4984.

NELSON, KENNETH F   1911-
(There's) a blue heart (to-night
in the mountains); words
by Billy Fairmann, music by
Ken Nelson. © Adams, Vee
& Abbott, inc., Chicago;
16Dec46; EP13345.

NELSON, MILTON.
You must be blind; words and music
by Lorenzo Pack and Milton
Nelson. © Northern Music Corp.,
New York; 6Jul45; EP13375.

NEMO, HENRY.
Baby, come out of the clouds;
lyric by Lee Pearl, music by
Henry Nemo. © Leeds Music
Corp., New York; 2Jun47;
EP14971.

NENE, pseud. See
Enriso, Rafael.

NERO, PAUL.
Frantic fantasy; for four fiddles,
by Paul Nero. © Carl Fischer,
inc., New York; 29May47; EP15016.
Score (4 violins) and parts.

NEŠIĆ, MARKO.
Sedi, Boso, dei (Sit beside me,
Boso!) Song ... Tamisvár polka;
by M. Nešić, arr. by Rud
Cernkovich. © Rudolph
Cernkovich, Bradley, Mich.; on
arrangement; 5Feb47; EP12650.
Parts: string orchestra; Sedi,
Boso, dei has Croatian words.

NETHERCOTT, DICK.
I light a cigarette; melody and
lyrics by Dick Nethercott.
© Murray Hill Publishing Co.,
Detroit; 12May47; EP14596.

NETTLES, WILLIAM EDWARD, 1895-
My aggravatin' wife; words and
music by Bill Nettles. ©
Lynn Music Corp., New York;
15May47; EP14330.
Too many blues; by Bill Nettles.
© Bourne, inc., New York; 12Feb47;
EP12075. For voice and piano, with
chord symbols.
Trouble's all I've ever known;
words and music by Bill
Nettles. © Peer Inter-
national Corp., New York;
24Apr47; EP14239.

NEUBERGER, JEAN BERNARD, 1891-
Un coeur m'attend; paroles de
Pierre Andrieu, musique de
Jean Lenoir [pseud.] © Publica-
tions Francis Day, Paris;
31Oct46; EF5467.
Vous savez bien ... paroles et
musique de Jean Lenoir [pseud.]
© Publications Francis Day,
Paris; 31Oct46; EF3466.

NEUBERGER, JEAN BERNARD, 1891- See also
Lenoir, Jean, pseud.

NEVELOFF, AL, 1906-
If you roll out the barrel once too
often, the barrel will roll
over you; words and music by
Harry Vogel and Al Neveloff.
Brooklyn, Stanow Publications,
[c1946] © Harry Vogel & Al
Neveloff, d.b.a. Stanow Publications, Brooklyn; 28Jan47; EP11880.

NEVILLE, CLEOPHAS, pseud. See
Mourin, Neville.

NEVILLE, DEREK, 1911-
Neville let it be said; by Derek
Neville. London, Cavendish
Music Co., sole selling agents,
Boosey & Hawkes. © Boosey &
Co., ltd., London; 31Dec46;
EF4771. Score (saxophone and
piano) and parts.

NEVIN, ETHELBERT WOODBRIDGE, 1862-
1901.
Barchetta; [by] Ethelbert Nevin.
Op. 21, no. 3, transcribed by
Lloyd Marvin. © Chart Music
Publishing House, inc., Chicago;
on arrangement; 2Jun47; EP14935.

NEVIN, ETHELBERT WOODBRIDGE, Cont'd.
Narcissus; by Ethelbert Nevin ...
arr. by Hugo Frey, [words by
Elsie-Jean, pseud.] © Hamilton
S. Gordon, inc., New York; on
arrangement and words; 23Jun47;
EP15288. For piano solo, with
words.
Narcissus; [by] Ethelbert Nevin.
Op. 13, no. 4, transcribed by
Lloyd Marvin. © Chart Music
Publishing House, inc., Chicago;
on arrangement; 2Jun47; EP14934.
For piano solo.
Narcissus, by Nevin; and Minuet,
by Boccherini. [Arr. by Vic-
tor Ambroise] © Lawrence
Wright Music Co., ltd., London;
on arrangement; 16May47;
EP3322. For piano solo.

NEVINS, MORTY.
Beatrice (your lovely name); lyric
by Sammy Gallop, music by Morty
Nevins, Artie Dunn [and] Al
Nevins. © Alba Music, inc.,
New York; 22Apr47; EP13826.

NEWMAN, BOB.
Baby doll; words and music by Bob
Newman. © Tim Spencer Music,
inc., Hollywood, Calif.; 21Feb47;
EP12210.
The leaf of love; by "Tex" Williams
and Bob Newman. © Golden West
Melodies, inc., Hollywood, Calif.;
17Dec46; EP10793. For voice and
piano, with chord symbols.

NEWMAN, ROY.
Sicilian lullaby; for two-part
chorus of women's voices with
piano acc., [by] Roy Newman,
arr. by Richard Harding [pseud.]
Folksong tr. by Sophie Jewett.
© The Willis Music Co., Cincinnati; on arrangement; 2May47;
EP14164.
There be none of Beauty's daughters;
song. the poem by Lord Byron,
the music by Roy Newman. © The
John Church Co., Philadelphia;
23Dec46; EP11068.

NICHOLLS, HORATIO, 1888-
Among my souvenirs. See his
The best years of our lives.
(The best years of our lives)
Among my souvenirs, from "The
best years of our lives". Lyric
by Edgar Leslie, music by Horatio
Nicholls, vocal orch. by Oscar
Catsiff. © Crawford Music Corp.,
New York; on vocal orchestration;
31Dec46; EP11431.

NICHOLS, PEE WEE. See
Nichols, W. H.

NICHOLS, W   H
Girls don't worry my mind ... words
and music by Rupert McClendon and
W. H. "Pee Wee" Nichols. © Peer
International Corp., New York;
10Apr47; EP13698.
I found you last night in my
dreams; words and music by
Rupert McClendon [and] W. H.
(Pee Wee) Nichols. © Peer
International Corp., New York;
27Nov46; EP13985.

NICKY BLAIR'S CARNIVAL SOUVENIR SONG
FOLIO; additional lyrics by Ted
Fetter, [new arrangements by
Domenico Savino] © J. J. Robbins
& Sons, inc., New York; on new
lyrics & new arrangements;
27Nov46; EP11218.

NICOLO, MARIO.
Il mandolinista popolare; [words
and music] di Mario Nicolo.
Napoli, Edizione "Mia."
© Edward Rossi, New York;
2Feb47; EF5337.

NIELAND, HERMAN. See
Nieland, Hermanus Jacobus Josephus.
NIELAND, HERMANUS JACOBUS JOSEPHUS,
1910-
Het kinder paradijs. Children's
paradise ... [By] Herman
Nieland; 7 stukjes voor piano.
© Edition Heuwekemeyer (Firm
A. J. Heuwekemeyer & B. F. van
Gaal), Amsterdam, The Nether-
lands; 24Oct46; EF5109.
Op school ... acht voortrachtstuk-
jes voor piano. [by] Herman
Nieland. [Jc1946] © Edition
Heuwekemeijer & van Gaal),
Amsterdam; 24Mar47; EF3382.

NIELAND, JAN. See
Nieland, Johannes Harmannus
Ignatius Maria.
NIELAND, JOHANNES HARMANNUS IGNATIUS
MARIA, 1903-
Arabesque; [by] Jan Nieland, pour
le piano. © Edition Heuweke-
meyer (Firm A. J. Heuwekemeyer
& B. F. van Gaal), Amsterdam,
The Netherlands; 3Jun44; EF5110.
Bij den boer; een ser. lichte
stukjes voor piano, [by] Jan
Nieland. © Edition Heuweke-
meyer (Firm A. J. Heuwekemeyer
& B. F. van Gaal), Amsterdam,
The Netherlands; 15Dec45;
EF5108.
Ciaconna e fuga; per organo; [by]
Jan Nieland. © Edition Heuweke-
meyer (Firm A. J. Heuwekemeyer &
B. F. van Gaal), Amsterdam, The
Netherlands; 12Oct45; EF5121.
Le coucou ... pour piano, [by]
Paul Roland [pseud.] © Edition
Heuwekemeyer (Firm A. J. Heuweke-
meyer & B. F. van Gaal), Amster-
dam, The Netherlands; 18Jul46;
EF5132.
Een dagje buiten; zes stukjes ...
[by] Jan Nieland. © Edition
Heuwekemeyer (Firm A. J. Heu-
wekemeyer & B. F. van Gaal),
Amsterdam, The Netherlands;
29Dec45; EF5126. For piano 4
hands.
Etudes melodiques; pour piano,
[by] Jan Nieland. © Edition
Heuwekemeyer (Firm A.J.
Heuwekemeyer & B.F. van Gaal),
12Oct45; EF5129.
Fantasia e fuga sopra B.A.C.H.;
per organo, [by] Jan Nieland.
© Edition Heuwekemeyer (Firm
A. J. Heuwekemeyer & B. F. van
Gaal), Amsterdam, The Nether-
lands; 28May46; EF5123.
(Fantasia, organ) Fantasie ...
[by] Jan Nieland. © Edition
Heuwekemeyer (Firm A. J. Heu-
wekemeyer & B. F. van Gaal),
Amsterdam, The Netherlands;
28May46; EF5122.
Feestmarschje; [by] Paul Roland
[pseud.] © Edition Heuwekemeyer
(Firm A. J. Heuwekemeyer & B. F.
van Gaal), Amsterdam, The Nether-
lands; 15Jul46; EF5127. For
piano solo.
Gavotte; [by] Jan Nieland.
© Edition Heuwekemeyer (Firm
A. J. Heuwekemeyer & B. F. van
Gaal), Amsterdam, The Nether-
lands; 3Apr44; EF5128. Score
(violin and piano) and part.
Lentebloemen ... een ser. stukjes
voor piano; [by] Jan Nieland.
© Edition Heuwekemeyer (Firm
A. J. Heuwekemeyer & B. F. van
Gaal), Amsterdam, The Nether-
lands; 28Jan46; EF5111.
Lyrische stukken; voor piano, [by]
Jan Nieland. [c1946] © Edition
Heuwekemeijer (Firm Heuwekemeijer
& van Gaal), Amsterdam; bk. 1,
3Jun44; bk. 2-3, 22Sep45;
EF3388-3390.

Marche triomphale; pour grand
orgue, [by] Jan Nieland.
© Edition Heuwekemeyer (Firm
A. J. Heuwekemeyer & B. F. van
Gaal), Amsterdam, The Nether-
lando; 12Nov43; EF5120.
Melodia; pieces pour harmonium ou
orgue, [by] Jan Nieland. ©
Edition Heuwekemeijer (Firm
Heuwekemeijer & van Gaal),
Amsterdam; livre 1, 22Oct46;
livre 2, 31Dec46; EF3394-3395.
Nocturne naar een thema van E. H.
Hens-Boendermaker, [for] piano,
[by] Jan Nieland. © Edition
Heuwekemeyer (Firm A. J. Heuwe-
meyer & B. F. van Gaal), Amster-
dam, The Netherlands; 22Dec41;
EF5148.
Pastorale; [by] Jan Nieland.
© Edition Heuwekemeyer (Firm
A. J. Heuwekemeyer & B. F. van
Gaal), Amsterdam, The Nether-
lands; 3Apr44; EF5146. Score
(violin and piano) and part.
Petite suite; [by] Jan Nieland.
© Edition Heuwekemeyer (Firm
A. J. Heuwekemeyer & B. F. van
Gaal), Amsterdam, The Netherlands;
10Dec43; EF5117. For piano 4
hands.
Prélude, choral et variations;
pour grand orgue, [by] Jan
Nieland. © Edition Heuweke-
meyer (Firm A. J. Heuwekemeyer
& B. F. van Gaal), Amsterdam,
The Netherlands; 12Nov43;
EF5125.
Serenata; [by] Jan Nieland.
© Edition Heuwekemeyer (Firm
A. J. Heuwekemeyer & B. F. van
Gaal), Amsterdam, The Nether-
lands; 3Apr44; EF5147. Score
(violin and piano) and part.
6 sketches ... [by] Jan Nieland.
© Edition Heuwekemeyer (Firm
A. J. Heuwekemeyer & B. F. van
Gaal), Amsterdam, The Nether-
lands; 31Oct43; EF5149. For
piano 4 hands.
Stap voor stap; etudes en stuk-
jes voor piano, [by] Jan Nie-
land. © Edition Heuwekemeijer
(Firm Heuwekemeijer & van
Gaal), Amsterdam; bk.1-3,
18Sep45; EF3391-3393.
Suite française; pour le piano,
[by] Jan Nieland. © Edition
Heuwekemeyer (Firm A. J.
Heuwekemeyer & B. F. van Gaal),
Amsterdam, The Netherlands;
7May46; EF5133.
Valse; [by] Jan Nieland. © Edition
Heuwekemeyer (Firm A. J. Heu-
wekemeyer & B. F. van Gaal),
Amsterdam, The Netherlands;
3Apr44; EF5145. Score (violin
and piano) and part.
Valse triste; pour piano, [by]
Jan Nieland. © Edition Heuweke-
meyer (Firm A. J. Heuwekemeyer
& B. F. van Gaal), Amsterdam,
The Netherlands; 12Oct45; EF5144.
Zestig kleine etudes [for] piano,
[by] Jan Nieland. © Edition
Heuwekemeyer (Firm A. J.
Heuwekemeyer & B. F. van Gaal),
Amsterdam, The Netherlands;
19Apr46; EF5134.

NIELSON, ARNE, pseud. See
Holmberg-Aastrup, Per.

NIETZER, CHARLES, 1890-
My best for Jesus; by C.
Nietzer. © Charles Nietzer,
Brooklyn; 15May47; EP14621.
For voice and piano.
My hands ... By C. Nietzer. ©
Charles Nietzer, Brooklyn;
15May47; EP14622. For voice
and piano.

NIGRIS, NETTIE DE. See
De Nigris, Nettie.

102

NILES, JOHN JACOB.
Green beds; folk-song, adapted
and arr. by John Jacob Niles.
© G. Schirmer, inc., New York;
11Apr47; EP14081. Two scores
for piano 1-2.

I wonder as I wander; Appalachian
carol, adapted and arr. by John
Jacob Niles. © G. Schirmer,
inc., New York; on adaptation
and arrangement; 28Apr47;
EP15195. For piano, 4 hands.

Jesus, Jesus, rest Your head;
Appalachian carol, adapted and
arr. by John Jacob Niles.
© G. Schirmer, inc., New York;
on adaptation and arrangement;
28Apr47; EP15196. For piano,
4 hands.

Jesus the Christ is born;
Appalachian carol collected
and arr. by John Jacob Niles.
© G. Schirmer, inc., New York;
on arrangement; 28Apr47;
EP15197. For piano, 4 hands.

The story of the bee; folk-song,
"Do take care of the bee boys,"
adapted and arr. by John Jacob
Niles. © G. Schirmer, inc.,
New York; 11Apr47; EP14080.
Two scores for piano 1-2.

Sweet little boy Jesus; for four-
part chorus of mixed voices, a
cappella. Words and music by John
Jacob Niles, arranged by Arrand
Parsons. © G. Schirmer, inc., New
York; on arrangement; 16Nov46;
EP11608.

Sweet little boy Jesus; for three-
part chorus of women's voices, a
cappella. Words and music by John
Jacob Niles, arranged by Arrand
Parsons. © G. Schirmer, inc., New
York; on arrangement; 16Nov46;
EP11607.

NILES, JOHN JACOB, arr.
I wonder as I wander ... piano
acc. as played by Lester Hodges.
(In Swarthout, Gladys, comp.
Gladys Swarthout album of con-
cert songs and arias. p. 66-68)
© G. Schirmer, inc., New York;
on piano accompaniment; 21Feb47;
EP2418.

NILES, JOHN JACOB, ed. and arr.
The singing campus; a song book for
girls' schools, ed. and arr. by
John Jacob Niles. © G. Schirmer,
inc., New York; 16Nov46;
EP13645. (Contents (each also ©
separately; new matter (except
EP12912); optional alto part)-
My little Mohee (EP12900) - I had
a sister Susan (EP12901)- Whistle,
daughter, whistle (EP12902)- One
morning in May (EP12903) - Down
in that valley (EP12904) - I
wonder as I wander (EP12905) -
Little willie (EP12906) - The
carrion crow; or, The tailor and
the crow (EP12907) - The farmer's
curst wife (EP12908) - Barbary
Ellen (EP12909) - Fairest Lord
Jesus (EP12910) - The church's
one foundation (EP12911) - Grace
before meals: Show pity, Lord;
As little children; and For God
so loved the world; words and
music by J. J. Niles (EP12912)

NILSSON, NILS KNUT SIGVARD.
Tonett-polka; [by] Nils Nilsson.
© Nordiska Musikförlaget,
a.b., Stockholm; 1Jan43;
EF3728. For piano solo, with
chord symbols.

[NILSSON, STIG]
Portvakten ... text: Nils Bie-
Persson [pseud.], musik:
Torsten Stignel [pseud.]
© Nordiska Musikförlaget,
a.b., Stockholm; 1Jan46;
EF3730.

NOBAR, BOB.
Freight train boogie; words and
music by Jim Scott and Bob
Nobar. © Hill and Range Songs,
inc., Hollywood, Calif.; 13Mar47;
EP12683.

NOBLE, EMILIE DUNN.
The flag salute of America; music
by Emilie Dunn Noble. © Miller
Music Corp., New York; 20Jan47;
EP11416. For voice and piano.

NOBLE, THOMAS TERTIUS, 1867-
Drop, drop, slow tears; three
part chorus for women's
voices, [by] T. Tertius
Noble, the text by Phineas
Fletcher. © The H. W.
Gray Co., inc., New York;
28Feb47; EP12400.

Morning hymn; four part chorus
for women's voices, [by]
T. Tertius Noble, text by
Paul Gerhardt, trans. by J.
Brownlio. © The H. W.
Gray Co., inc., New York;
28Feb47; EP12594.

NOD, DE, pseud. See
Doneddu, A.

NOEL, LEE.
Underneath the Texas moon; words &
music by Lee Noel. © M. M. Cole
Publishing Co., Chicago; 23Apr47;
EP13920.

NOEL-JOHNSON, REGINALD.
Three far-away trees; song ...
words by Kathleen Egan, music
by Reginald Noel-Johnson.
© Chappell & Co., ltd.,
London; 16Jan47; EF4899.

NOELIE, sister. See
Marie Noelie, sister.

NOLAN, TOMMY.
Death by the roadside; by Dorsey
Dixon and Tommy Nolan. New
York, Sole selling agent,
Burke and Van Heusen. ©
Hometown Music Company, inc.,
New York; 2May47; EP14339.
For voice and piano, with
chord symbols.

[NOLASCO, FELIX A] arr.
Latin-American dance album;
[arr. by Felix A. Nolasco]
© Onofrio Di Bella, New
York; on arrangement of
bk.7; 16Dec46; EP12955.
Parts: orchestra.

NOLI, JUAN F
[Que lucha! ... música de Juan F.
Noli. c1946] © Editorial
Argentina de Música Internacional,
s. de r. ltd., Buenos Aires;
24Apr47; EF3208. For piano solo,
with chord symbols.

NOLL, ALBERT W
Ambrosia, a feast for the gods;
words and music by Albert W.
Noll. © W. Harold Howatt,
Springfield, Mass.; 28Mar47;
EP6736.

NOLL, LAURA A
Garden of gold; words and music
by Laura Noll, arr. by Bélle
Schrag. Aberdeen, Wash.,
Lindstrom's Music Publishing
Co. © Laura A. Noll, Aberdeen,
Wash.; 12Jun47; EP15117.

Laura Noll's prediction song;
words and music by Laura Noll,
[arr. by Belle Schrag] Aberdeen,
Wash. © Lindstrom's Publishing
Co. © Laura A. Noll, Aberdeen,
Wash.; 12Jun47; EP15112.

NOLTE, ROY E
The risen Savior; an Easter choir
cantata for mixed voices, text
by Elsie Duncan Yale, music by
Roy E. Nolte. © Lorenz Publishing Co., Dayton, Ohio; 3Jan47;
EP12131.

[NORDEN, HUGO] 1909-
Hark! The voice of love and
mercy; [by] Hugh Gordon
[pseud.], on a theme by S.
Stanley, [words by] Jonathan
Evans. © The Arthur P. Schmidt
Co., Boston; on adaptation &
arrangement; 14Jan47; EP11209.
Score: SATB and piano.

NORDEN, N LINDSAY.
Lift up your heads; from Psalm
XXIV. Anthem for mixed voices
by N. Lindsay Norden. © Broadcast Music, inc., New York;
15May47; EP15232.

Music; song for high voice, music
by N. Lindsay Norden, words by
F. Cresson Schell. © N. Lindsay
Norden, Philadelphia; 15Dec46;
EP6482.

NORDMAN, CHESTER, 1895-
Behold what manner of love ... for
four-part chorus of mixed voices,
with soprano solo and piano or
organ acc., words from the
Scriptures, music by Chester
Nordman. © The Willis Music Co.,
Cincinnati; 20Jan47; EP11562.

Mother; words by Mary E. Linton,
music by Anton Rubinstein.
Song adaptation by Chester
Nordman. © Shattinger Piano
& Music Co., St. Louis; on
adaptation; 6May47; EP14232.

NORDQVIST, GUSTAF.
Bisp Thomas' frihetssang;
tonsatt för solo eller unison
kör med piano av Gustaf
Nordqvist. © Nordiska
Musikförlaget, a.b., Stockholm; 1Jan44; EF3766.

NORDRAAK, RIKARD.
Rikard Nordraak, forfäret i norsk
musikk; arrangement av sangene
ved Arne Dørumsagaard. © Musikk-
Huset, a/s, Oslo, Norway; on
compilation & arrangement;
25Jan46; EF5089. Partly for
piano solo, partly for voice
and piano.

NORDSTROM, DAGMAR.
Remembering you ... Music by Dagmar
Nordstrom, arr. by Freddy A.
Miller. © Leeds Music Corp., New
York; on arrangement; 14Apr47;
EP13745. Condensed score (orches-
tra) and parts.

NORLIN, LLOYD B 1918-
(Break the news) A day like this,
from Break the news; words and
music by Lloyd B. Norlin. ©
Northwestern University Waa-Mu
Show, Evanston, Ill.; 22Feb47;
EP6610.

(Break the news) Every time we say
good night, from Break the news;
words and music by Lloyd B. Norlin.
© Northwestern University Waa-Mu
Show, Evanston, Ill.; 22Feb47;
EP6609.

"Break the News!"; musical se-
lections, music and lyrics by
Lloyd B. Norlin, Bill Stone,
Leonard Norman, and others]
© Northwestern University
Waa-Mu Show, Evanston, Ill.;
6May47; EP14849.

A day like this. See his Break
the news.

Every time we say good night.
See his Break the news.

NORRIS, GERTRUDE, 1879-
Just an old fashioned girl in a new
fashioned bonnet; by Gertrude Norris.
© Shelby Music Publishing Co.,
Detroit; 31Dec46; EP12141. For
voice and piano, with guitar diagrams
and chord symbols.

NORRIS, GERTRUDE. Cont'd.
You're beautiful; by Gertrude
Norris. © Shelby Music Publishing Co., Detroit; 6Dec46;
EP11121. For voice and piano,
with guitar diagrams and chord
symbols.

NORT, ISABEL VAN. See
Van Nort, Isabel.

NORTH, JAMES D., pseud.
Praise the Lord, ye heavens adore;
[old Welsh tune, anonymous words]
... ed. and arr. for mixed chorus,
SATB, by James D. North. © Choral
Press, Evanston, Ill.; on arrangement; 10ct46; EP11701.
Spirit of God, descend ... Ed. and
arr. for junior choir, by James D.
North, [words by George Croly,
altered and adapted by J. D. N.]
© Choral Press, Evanston, Ill.;
10ct46; EP11703.

NORTH, MICHAEL.
London calling! song, lyric by
Harry Dawson, music by Michael
North. © Ascherberg, Hopwood &
Crew, ltd., London; 8Jan47; EF4819.

NORTIMA, FRANK D
Sentimental love song ... Words by
Frank Di Martino, music by Frank D.
Nortima. © Frank Di Martino, Jersey
City; 11Feb47; EP22081.

NOVÁČEK, SLÁVA EMANUEL, 1911-
Až uvidíte "J1" ... [Všechno ti
feknu mlčením] Hudba: S. E.
Nováček, slova: Vilda Dubský.
© Mojmír Urbánek, Praha, Czech-
oslovakia; 10Oct46; EF5372.
Piano-conductor score (orchestra,
with words) and parts.

NOVÁK, VÍTĚZSLAV, 1870-
De profundis; [by] Vítězslav
Novák. Op. 67. © Hudební
Matice Umělecké Besedy, Praha,
Czechoslovakia; 5Mar45;
EF4940. Score: orchestra.
Lady Godiva; Ouvertüre für
grosses Orchester, overture for
great orchestra ... by ...
Vítězslav Novák. Op. 41.
Score. Wien, Universal-
Edition. © Associated Music
Publishers, inc., New York;
1Apr19; EF5247.
Svatováclavský triptych; (toccata,
ciacona, fuga) ... k tisku
revidoval a rejstříkováním
opatřil B. A. Wiedermann. [By]
Vítězslav Novák. Op. 70. ©
Hudební Matice Umělecké Besedy,
Praha, Czechoslovakia; 3Nov43;
EF5087. For organ solo.

NÚÑEZ DE BORBÓN, ALFREDO.
Abismo ... de Alfredo Núñez de
Borbón. © Promotora Hispano
Americana de Música, s.a., México;
15Dec42; EF5616. For voice and
piano.
La vida dirá ... De: Alfredo
Núñez de Borbón. © Promotora
Hispano Americana de Música,
s. a., México; 30Dec46; EF5280.
Piano-conductor score (orchestra,
with words) and parts.

NUTTER, CARL HALL, 1893-
I just gotta talk about you; words
and music by Carroll Lucas,
Bobby Lane [pseud.] and Carl
Nutter. © Radio-Recording Songs,
inc., New York; 27Nov46; EP10758.
I know it's love; words and music
by Frank Carbon [pseud.] and
Carl Nutter. © Radio-Recording
Songs, inc., New York; 27Nov46;
EP10757.

NUTTING, HARLIE.
Thanks for a wonderful evening;
words and music by Harlie
Nutting. © Nordyke Publish-
ing Co., Los Angeles; 8Mar47;
EP13552.

NYSTROM, GOSTA, 1890-
Hjärtat; dikt av Bo Bergman,
tonsatt av Gösta Nyström. Op.
15, nr. 1. © Nordiska
Musikförlaget, a/b, Stockholm;
1Jan21; EF5396. For voice and
piano.
Natt vid sättern; dikt av
Christian Günther, för sång med
piano av Gösta Nyström. ©
Nordiska Musikförlaget, a/b,
Stockholm; 1Jul19; EF5397.
For voice and piano.

O

O, HOW MUCH WE OWE, JESUS; (Tune,
"What a Friend we have in Jesus");
words by Rev. Pearl Townsend. ©
Pearl Townsend, Grand Rapids,
Mich.; on new words; 11Jan47;
EP13451. Close score: SATB.

OAHU PUBLISHING CO., arr.
The heel and toe polka ... lyric
by Thelma Ottoson, arr. by the
Oahu staff. (Oahu modern note
method for electric and Hawaiian
guitars, [Lesson 45FN]) © Oahu
Publishing Co., Cleveland; on
lyrics; 22Jul46; EP6581. For
voice and 2 guitars. Includes
lesson on dexterity and speed
and the discussion: The rhythm
section takes over.

OAKLAND, BEN.
(Song of the thin man) You're not
so easy to forget ... [from] the
... picture "Song of the thin
man," lyric by Herb Magidson,
music by Ben Oakland. © Leo
Feist, inc., New York; 25Apr47;
EP14064.
You're not so easy to forget. See
his Song of the thin man.

OBENCHAIN, VIRGINIA PAULI.
The circus horse; for the piano,
by Virginia Obenchain. © G.
Schirmer, inc., New York; 16Nov46;
EP11606.

OBERG, O   SCHELDRUP.
Drifting thoughts; meditation for
piano [by] O. Scheldrup Oberg.
© Theodore Presser Co., Phila-
delphia; 16Jun47; EP15224.
Faded memories; piano solo by O.
Scheldrup Oberg. © Theodore
Presser Co., Philadelphia;
26Apr47; EP14098.
A frolic in May; piano solo, by
O. Scheldrup Oberg. ©
Theodore Presser Co.,
Philadelphia; 7May47; EP14482.
Old spinning wheel; [by] O.
Scheldrup Oberg. © Theodore
Presser Co., Philadelphia;
7Feb47; EP11902. For piano
solo.

OBRADORS, FERNANDO J
Canciones clásicas; [by] F. J.
Obradors. © Unión Musical
Española, Madrid; v.2-3,
30Dec41; EF5569. For
voice and piano.
Canciones clásicas españolas;
[by] Fernando J. Obradors. ©
Unión Musical Española,
Madrid; v.1, 30Dec21; v.2,
30Dec30; EF5566, 3568. For
voice and piano. Partial
contents.- 2. Las gracïosas
La fracasada; letra y música de
Doroteo Ochoa; y, Orgullo ranch-
ero; letra y música de Pedro M.
Colmenero. © Promotora Hispano
Americana de Música, s.a.,
México; 30Dec46; EF5516, 5515.
Lagos de Moreno ... letra y
música de Doroteo Ochoa. ©
Promotora Hispano Americana
de Música, s.a., México;
30Dec46; EF5455.

O'CONNELL, WILLIAM HENRY, cardinal,
1859-1944.
Hymns for low mass; (for 3 equal
voices), by William Cardinal
O'Connell, arr. by Edward Grey
[pseud.] © McLaughlin &
Reilly Co., Boston; on arrange-
ment; 2Dec46; EP12446.
Hymns for low mass; for unison
or S.A.T.B. voices, by William
Cardinal O'Connell, arr. by
Edward Grey [pseud.] © Mc-
Laughlin & Reilly Co., Boston;
on arrangement; 2Dec46; EP12447.

O'CONNOR, D   G
O lumen; hymn to St. Dominic ...
for unison or two-part singing.
[Liturgical words] English
words by Rev. J. J. McLarney,
music by Rev. D. G. O'Connor.
[c1946] © McLaughlin & Reilly
Co., Boston; 10Mar47; EP12780.

O'DELL, EDWARD OSCAR.
Jim and Jon, the cowboys;
words & music by Ed O'Dell.
© Edward Oscar O'Dell,
Lubbock, Tex.; 16May47;
EP14640.

ODEN, MARGARET MUSE, 1916-
Job's God is true; [words by] ...
S. N. Greene, [music by] Mar-
garet Muse Oden. (In Greene,
S. N., comp. Sacred songs and
hymns. No. 1) © Sammy Newell
Greene, Oklahoma City; 1Mar45;
EP11672. Shape-note notation.

O'DONNELL, WALTER.
Carnival echoes; for piano,
[by] Walter O'Donnell. ©
Theodore Presser Co., Philadelphia; 17Feb47; EP12293.

ÖSTLING, HERBERT STEEN- See
Steen-Östling, Herbert.

OFFENBACH, JACQUES, 1819-1880.
Offenbach (simplified); fourteen
favorite compositions arr. for
piano solo by Richard Harding
[pseud.] © The Willis Music
Co., Cincinnati; on arrangement; 29Jan47; EP11794.
Prima-ballerina; ballettpantomime
in 3 bildern, musik von J.
Offenbach, zusammengestellt
und bearbeitet von Einar
Nilson. © Universal-Edition,
a. g., Wien; on compilation &
arrangement; 2Dec19; EF3242.
For piano solo.

O'FLYNN, CHARLES.
Something for nothing; words and
music by Willard Robison and
Charles O'Flynn. © Harms,
inc., New York; 23Apr47;
EP13945.

O'HAGAN, JACK.
One little kiss in the moonlight;
words and music by Jack O'Hagan.
© Allan & Co., pty. ltd., Melbourne, Australia; 18Sep46;
EP3087. For voice and piano,
with guitar diagrams and chord
symbols.

O'HARA, GEOFFREY, 1882-
Bright is the ring of words ...
music by Geoffrey O'Hura ...
poem by Robert Louis Stevenson.
© R. D. Row Music Co., Boston;
on arrangement; 8May47; EP14203.
Bright is the ring of words ...
music by Robert Louis Stevenson,
music by Geoffrey O'Hara. © R.
D. Row Music Co., Boston;
31Mar47; EP13325. Score: TTBB
and piano.
I walked today where Jesus
walked ... [By] Geoffrey
O'Hara, arr. by Kenneth
Downing [pseud.], [words by]
Daniel S. Twohig. © G. Schirmer, inc., New York; on arrangement; 13Feb47; EP12735.
Score: chorus (SABar) and
piano.

O'HARA, GEOFFREY. Cont'd.
Let us walk in the light of the
Lord; [by] Harry R. Wilson and
Geoffrey O'Hara. For mixed
voices and piano. © G. Ricordi
& Co., New York; 21Apr47;
EP14141.
O little hills of Nazareth;
Christmas anthem, two part S.A.
or T.B. Words by Herbert J.
Brandon, music by Geoffrey
O'Hara, arr. by Douglas MacLean
[pseud.] © M. Witmark & Sons,
New York; on arrangement;
29May47; EP15000.
This is the story of Jesus;
sacred song, words by Daniel
S. Twohig, music by Geoffrey
O'Hara. © The Boston Music
Co., Boston; 28Feb47; EP12380.
White birches; by Geoffrey
O'Hara. © Bregman, Vocco
and Conn, inc., New York; on
arrangement; 9May47; EP14337.
Score (violin, violoncello
and piano) and parts.

O'HARA, MARY.
Green grass of Wyoming ... words and
music by Mary O'Hara ... arr. by
Paul Weirick. © Sam Fox Publishing Co., New York; on arrangement;
17Feb47; EP12345. Piano-conductor
score (orchestra, with words) and
parts.

O'HARE, ELIZABETH.
I think of you, my son; words and
music by Elizabeth O'Hare. ©
Nordyke Publishing Co., Los
Angeles; 23Jan46; EP6509.

THE OLD-TIME RELIGION. (In Eddy
Arnold's radio favorites song book.
no. A-2, p.47) © Adams, Vee
& Abbott, inc., Chicago; on
arrangement; 17Jun46; EP11231.
Close score: SATB, with guitar
diagrams, and chord symbols.

[OLDEN, CHARLIE]
Every Saturday night; written
and composed by Ted May
[pseud.] © B. Feldman & Co.,
ltd., London; 9Apr47; EF5561.

OLDRATI ROSSI, RENZO, 1903-
Armonie! ... Testo di G. C.
Testoni, musica di R. Oldrati
Rossi. © Odeon, società
anonima, Milan; 21Dec46;
EF5482.
Strada delle mimose ... Come una
rondine ... musica di Renzo
Oldrati Rossi, parole di L. L.
Martelli. © Odeon, società
anonima, Milan; 15Jan47; EF5483.
Piano-conductor score (orches-
tra, with words), and parts.

OLDS, WILLIAM BENJAMIN, 1874-
Hee-haw! Chorus for male voices,
a cappella (T.T.B.B.) [by] W.
B. Olds, [words by] Esther M.
Hoisington. © Hall & McCreary
Co., Chicago; 12Apr47; EP13756.
Let us praise God; a canticle for
treble voices with speech choir
or reader (S.S.A.) [by] W.B.
Olds, [words by] Percy Dearmer.
© Hall & McCreary Co., Chicago;
12Apr47; EP13753.

OLIVADOTI, JOSEPH.
South of the Rio; selection of
Latin American melodies [by]
J. Olivadoti. © Rubank, inc.,
Chicago; on arrangement;
16Jun47; EP15104. Condensed
score (band, with words) and
parts.

OLIVEIRA, MILTON DE.
Não tenho lagrimas ... (No tengo
lágrimas) (Let's speak of love)
Portuguese lyric and music by
Max Bulhões and Milton de Olivèira,
Spanish lyric by Myrta Silva,
English lyric by Benjamin Blossmer.
© Peer International Corp., New
York; on Spanish & English lyrics;
20Nov46; EP13768.

OLIVER, GEORGE.
Original themes for piano; [by]
George Oliver. © Mike-Tunes,
Chicago; on 2 pieces; 12May47;
Contents.- [v.1] Glacier
(© EP14592)- [v.2] Sylvanesque
(© EP14593)

OLIVER, HERBERT, 1883-
Coming home ... [by] Herbert Oliver.
London, Sole selling agents,
Boosey & Hawkes. © Hawkes &
Son (London), ltd.; 27Dec46;
EF4768. Parts: band.
Gentleman Jim; song. Words by
Harry A. Parr, music by Her-
bert Oliver. © Keith Prowse &
Co., ltd., London; 14May47;
EF3345.
Laughing patrol; by Herbert Oliver,
for piano. © Keith Prowse & Co.,
ltd., London; 20Feb47; EF5102.
Remembrance ... [by] Herbert
Oliver. London, Boosey &
Hawkes. © Hawkes & Son
(London), ltd., London;
8Apr47; EF5451. Score
(violin and piano) and part.

OLIVER, SY.
Deep river ... arr. by Sy Oliver
... ed. by Dick Jacobs. ©
Embassy Music Corp., New York;
on arrangement; 13Dec46;
EP11197. Piano-conductor score
(orchestra) and parts.

OLIVIERI, DI CEGLIE- See
Ceglie-Olivieri, di.

OLIVIERI, DINO.
Dedy ... testo e musica di Dino
Olivieri. (In Un sorriso e 20
canzoni. p. 58-59) © Edizioni
Casiroli, s.a.r.l., Milano,
3Jan46; EF4928. For voice and
piano.
Good bye, Milanesina ... testo di
E. Prati, musica di Dino Olivieri.
(In Un sorriso e 20 canzoni.
p.22-23) © Edizioni Leonardi,
s.a.r.l., Milano; 15Jun45;
EF4920. For voice and piano;
Italian and English words.
Ritornei ... musica di Dino
Olivieri, parole di Nino Rastelli.
© Edizioni Leonardi, s.a.r.l.,
Milan; 6Nov45; EF4814. For
voice and piano.
Tutto il mondo canta Tornerai;
raccolta di 15 canzoni del Mo.
Dino Olivieri. © Edizioni
Leonardi, s.a.r.l., Milan; on
15 songs. Contents.- Tornerai
(N. Rastelli) - Eternamente tu
(Niaa [pseud.]) (© 20Dec45;
EF3918) - Vorrei sognar (N.
Rastelli) (© 20Dec45; EF3919) -
Suonando una romanza di Puccini
(R. Micheli) (© 28Jan46; EF3920)
- Il valzer delle rose zago
(C. Deani [pseud.]) (© 28Jan46;
EF3921) - Girotondo (C. Deani)
(© 28Jan46; EF3922) - Un giorno
(E. Frati) (© 28Jan46; EF3923) -
Il cuore è stanco di sognare
(R. Micheli) (© 28Jan46;
EF3924) - Canto della soli-
tudine (E. Frati) (© 28Jan46;
EF3925) - Facciamo ancora un
po' di strada insieme (R.
Micheli) (© 28Jan47; EF3926) -
Malinconia (C. Deani) (©
28Jan46; EF3927) - Pucci, Pucci
(D. Olivieri) (© 28Jan46;
EF3928) - So che ti chiami Lucia
(C. Deani) (© 28Jan46; EF3929) -
Incantesimo (C. Deani) (©
28Jan46; EF3930) - Il giardino
dei ricordi (P. Sacchi) (©
28Jan46; EF3931) - O bella
bionda (© 27Mar47; EF3932)

OLSON, CARL W
Sing for me, the night is falling;
words and music by Carl W. Olson.
© Renascent Music Publishing Co.,
Minneapolis; 26Mar47; EP6915.
Solitude; words and music by Carl
W. Olson. © Renascent Music
Publishing Co., Minneapolis.
26Mar47; EP6741.
White star lily ... Words and music
by Carl W. Olson. © Renascent
Music Publishing Co., Minneapolis;
26Mar47; EP6742.

OLSON, ROBERT G
Who did? For four-part chorus of
men's voices with piano acc.
Old college tune, freely arr.
for male voices [by] Robert G.
Olson. © The Boston Music Co.,
Boston; on arrangement; 4Jun47;
EP14988.

OLVIRADES, JOSE.
Lolita Lopez; [The belle of El
Salvador], lyric by Albert
Gamse, music by Jose Olvirades.
© Encore Music Publications,
inc., New York; 14Apr47;
EP14801.

ONDŘÍČEK, FRANTIŠEK, 1857-1922.
(Quartet, strings) Smyčcový
kvartet, as-dur; [by] František
Ondříček. Op. 22. © Hudební
Matice Umělecké Besedy, Praha,
Czechoslovakia; 7Oct44; EF4956.
Smyccovy kvartet, as-dur. See his
Quartet, strings.

O'NEILL, CHARLES, 1882-
Majesty ... by Charles O'Neill.
© Remick Music Corp., New York;
18Feb47; EP12167. Condensed score
(band) and parts.

OPPECKER, FRANZ BERTHOLD, 1895-
(Romance Viennese) Sweethearts try
to explain, from "Romance Viennese";
words and music by Franz B.
Oppecker. Camden, N. J., Oppecker
& Sons [c1941] © Frenz Berthold
Oppecker, Camden, N. J.; 8Oct46;
EP11786. For soprano, tenor and
piano.
Sweethearts try to explain. See
his Romance Viennese.

ORCUTT, J   BRUCE.
Your number, please; by J. Bruce
Orcutt, [arr. by Jean Walz] ©
J. Bruce Orcutt, Miles City,
Mont.; 26Dec46; EP10717. For
voice and piano, with chord
symbols.

ORENT, MILTON.
Whistle blues; words and music
by Mary Lou Williams and
Milton Orent. © Harman
Music, inc., New York;
21Mar47; EP12850.

ORLOB, HAROLD.
(Citizen saint) Saint Frances Cabrini;
words & music by Harold Orlob,
from ... [the] motion picture
Citizen saint. New York, Milton
Music Co. © Harold Orlob, New
York; 24Dec46; EP11605. For
voice and piano.
Saint Frances Cabrini. See his
Citizen saint.

ORTIZ, C   A
Flores negras. (Black flowers) ...
[By] C. A. Ortiz, [English words
adapted by Albert Gamse] (In
André, Julio, ed. Songs from
south of the border. p.15-17)
© Edward B. Marks Music Corp.,
New York; on English adaptation;
28Dec46; EP10867.

ORTIZ, RAFAEL.
"Rapindey" ... letra y música de
Rafael Ortiz, arreglo de Pedro
Ouida. © Peer International
Corp., New York; 30Dec46;
EF5446. Parts: orchestra.

ORTLIP, MILDRED, arr.
My country, 'tis of thee ... arr.
... by Mildred Ortlip, [tune
"America" by Henry Carey, words
by Samuel F. Smith] Flushing,
N. Y., Miro Publishing Co. ©
Mildred Ortlip Keel, Flushing,
N. Y.; on arrangement; 7Apr47;
EP13928. For piano solo, with
words.

OSBORN, IRENE CAIN, 1882-
(Christ our Redeemer) He will
judge between the nations,
[from the oratorio "Christ our
Redeemer"] ... for mixed voices,
[by] Irene Cain Osborn.
© (Irene Cain Osborn d.b.a.)
"The Irene Cain Osborn Haven of
Melody," Washington, D. C.;
20May47; EP14821.
He will judge between the nations.
See her Christ our Redeemer.

OSBORNE, WILL.
Dry bones; T.T.B.B., [words and
music] by Dick Rogers and Will
Osborne, arranged by William
Stickles. © Leeds Music Corp.,
New York; on arrangement;
14Feb47; EP12178.

O'SHAUGHNESSY, MILDRED WARD.
You are my destiny; words and
music by Mildred Ward
O'Shaughnessy, arr. by Dave
Kaplan. © Monahan Music
Publications, New York;
9Apr47; EP13593.

OSTLING, ACTON E   1906-
America in rhythm ... by Acton
Ostling. © Belwin, inc., New
York; 22Jan47; EP11360. Score
(drum 1-2) and part.
Drummer's patrol; drum quartet by
Acton Ostling. © Belwin, inc.,
New York; 30Jan47; EP12750.
Score.
Drumming in triplicate; drum trio
by Acton Ostling. © Belwin,
inc., New York; 30Jan47;
EP12126.
A pair of diddlers ... by Acton
Ostling. © Belwin, inc., New
York; 22Jan47; EP11361. Score
(drum 1-2) and part.
Three R's for snare drum: reading,
rhythms, rudiments; by Acton
E. Ostling. [v. 2: c1946] ©
Belwin, inc., New York; on bk.
1-2; 11Mar47; EP12577-12578.

OSTROW, ABE, pseud. See
Ostrowsky, Abraham M.

[OSTROWSKY, ABRAHAM M   ]
Desire; lyric by George Howe,
music by Abe Ostrow, [pseud.]
© Arthur Steven Publications,
Venice, Calif.; 2May47;
EP6881.
The toy-town masquerade; lyric by
Bernie Hubon [pseud.] and Tommy
Kahn, music by Abe Ostrow [pseud.]
© Arthur Steven Music Publications,
Venice, Calif.; 3Feb47; EP6650.

OTEO, ALFONSO ESPARZA. See
Esparza Oteo, Alfonso.

[OTERO, JOSEPH]
When you're near; words and music
by Joseph Terry, [pseud.], arr.
by Lindsay McPhail. © Nordyke
Publishing Co., Los Angeles;
7Mar47; EP13248.

O'TOOLE, WILLIAM.
Pony rido; by William O'Toole.
New York, Creative Music
Publishers, [c1946] ©
William O'Toole, New York;
12May47; EP6893. For piano
solo, with words.

OUTLEY, MOZELLE TE, 1886-
Were you there? A new arrangement of an old spiritual,
arranged by Mozelle Te Outley.
© Mozelle Te Outley, Los
Angeles; on arrangement;
15Feb47; EP12194. Score:
mixed voices and piano or
organ.

OVERHOLT, CHARLES E
Moonflowers; a piano solo, by
Charles E. Overholt. © Theodore
Presser Co., Philadelphia;
16Apr47; EP13894.

OVIEDO, IGNACIO DIAZ Y. See
Diaz y Oviedo, Ignacio.

OWENS, HARRY ROBERT, 1902-
Lazy Joe; words and music by
Harry Owens. © Royal Music
Publisher, Hollywood, Calif.;
20May47; EP14487.

OWENS, HILDA.
Home; words and music by Hilda
Owens, arr. by H. Robinson.
© Nordyke Publishing Co., Los
Angeles; 8Mar47; EP13256.

OWENS, LAURA M
Melody valley; words and music by
Laura M. Owens. © Studio Staff
Productions, Hollywood, Calif.;
21Sep46; EP13688.

OWENS, TEX.
Love me now; by Tex Owens. © Tex
Ritter Music Publications, inc.,
New York; 29Dec46; EP11080. For
voice and piano, with chord
symbols.

P

PACE, CHARLES H
He keeps the fire burning down in
my soul; words & music by Chas.
H. Pace. Pittsburgh, The Old Ship
of Zion [c1947] © Chas. H. Pace,
Pittsburgh; 19Dec46; EP6457.
Score: chorus (SATB) and piano.
Roll, memories, roll; a bass solo,
by Chas. H. Pace, Pittsburgh,
The Old Ship of Zion. © Chas.
H. Pace, Pittsburgh; 21Apr47;
EP6815.

PACHECO HUERGO, MARUJA.
Qué será, doctor? ... letra y
música original de Maruja Pacheco
Huergo. Buenos Aires, Editorial
Argentina de Música Internacional.
© Peer International Corp., New
York; 14Jun46; EF5620.

PACHMANN, LIONEL DE, 1887-
Les muses en fuite; (sur un vieux
refrain) Musique de Lionel
de Pachmann. Poésie de Edmond
Roche. © Societe Anonyme des
Editions Ricordi, Paris;
27Feb47; EF3305.

PADILLA, JOSÉ, 1899-
Mon habanera; paroles de Henri
Varna et Marc-Cab [pseud.]
musique de José Padilla. ©
Salabert, inc., New York;
31Aug46; EF3810.
Papa Noël ... paroles espagnoles
de Emilio Vanner [pseud.] ...
musique de José Padilla.
© Julio Garzon, Paris; 2Jan47;
EF3479. Spanish words.
Valencia; [by] José Padilla, arr.
by J. Louis Merkur, piano
duet. © Harms, inc., New York;
on arrangement; 1May47;
EP14447.
Le vent du souvenir; paroles de
Henri Varna et Marc-Cab [pseud.],
musique de José Padilla. ©
Salabert, inc., New York;
31Aug46; EF3808.

Who'll buy my violets; fox trot,
words by E. Ray Goetz, music by
José Padilla, [arranged by
Johnny Sterling] © Harms, inc.,
New York; on arrangement; 20Dec46;
EP11064. Piano-conductor score
(orchestra) and parts.

PADULA, JOSÉ L   1878-
Nueve de julio ... de José L.
Padula, arrt. de Francis
Salabert ... El choclo ... de
A. G. Villoldo, arrt. de
Francis Salabert. © Éditions
Salabert, Paris; on arrange-
ment; 31Jan47; EF3554. Piano-
conductor score (orchestra),
and parts.

PAEZ, MANUEL.
Revivir. (Love came back) ...
English words by Joe Davis,
Spanish words and music by
Manuel Paez. © Caribbean
Music, inc., New York; 12May47;
EP14216.

PAFUMY, JOSÉ.
Cuando estoy junto a tí ... Música de José Pafumy, letra de
Alberto Salinas. © Peer International Corp., New York;
18Mar47; EF13981.

PAGANINI, NICOLO, 1782-1840.
Niccolo Paganini for guitar solo;
special arrangement by Harry
Volpe. © Volpe Studios,
Jackson Heights, L. I., N. Y.;
bk.1, 8Jan47; EP6480.

PAGANUCCI, ANTHONY.
Alla luna; song, [words by F. Villa,
music by] Anthony Paganucci. ©
G. Ricordi & Co., New York;
27Dec46; EP6616. Italian words.

PAGOT, JEAN.
L'amour de moy; chanson du XVe.
siècle, 4 voix mixtes et ténor
solo, harmonisée par Jean
Pagot. Paris, Rouart Lerolle
& Cie., vente exclusive,
Éditions Salabert. © Salabert,
inc., New York; on arrangement;
26Oct46; EF3651.

PAINE, J   WELDON.
Sailing home ... words and music
by J. Weldon Paine, arr. by
[Betty Glynn or] the Oahu staff.
(Oahu E-Z method, [lesson 32EZ])
© Oahu Publishing Co., Cleveland;
on arrangement; 27Aug46; EP6972.
For voice and 2 Guitars. Includes lesson on reverse steel
position and the discussion: The
land of the dragon fly.

PAISANIELLO, pseud. See
Martino, Rodolfo de.

PAISLEY, WILLIAM M
Do ya s'pose? Song by William
M. Paisley. © The John
Church Co., Philadelphia;
26Feb47; EP12372.

PAISNER, BEN, 1913-
19 swing etudes; for trombone, by
Ben Paisner. © David Gornston,
New York; on arrangement; 14Mar47;
EP12813.

PALACIOS, CHUCHO. See
Palacios, Jesús.

PALACIOS, JESÚS.
Miguel Alemán ... de Chucho
Palacios (Jesús Palacios) ©
Promotora Hispano Americana de
Música, s.a.; México; 30Dec46;
EF5536. For voice and piano.

PALAU, RAFAEL.
¡Ese pollo! ... letra de Eduardo
Saborit, música y arreg. [by]
Rafael Palau. © Peer International Corp., New York;
18Dec46; EF5584. Parts: orchestra.

PALESTRINA, GIOVANNI PIERLUIGI DA,
1525?-1594.
Gloria Patri ... English translation
by Jacqueline Sneed, music by
Palestrina, arr. for 2 choirs by
C. Albert Scholin. © Bolwin, inc.,
New York; on arrangement; 19Feb47;
EP12270. Latin and English words.

PALMER, JACK.
Oh! My achin' heart; by Freddy
James [pseud.], Little Jack
Little and Jack Palmer.
© Mood Music Co., inc., New
York; 5Jun47; EP14884. For
voice and piano, with chord
symbols.

PALMGREN, SELIM.
The dragonfly; by Selim Palmgren,
arr. for 'cello and piano by
Mary Dann. © Carl Fischer,
inc., New York; on arrangement;
29Apr47; EP14089. Score and
part.

PANKRATZ, ARTHUR JOHN, 1899-
"Joy complete"; [by] Arthur
J. Pankratz. © Arthur J.
Pankratz, Elmwood Park,
Ill.; 15Apr47; aP13805.

"Ye shall receive power"; [by]
Arthur J. Pankratz. © Arthur
J. Pankratz, Elmwood Park,
Ill.; 15Apr47; EP13806.

PANTA, LEO, pseud. See
Broeck, Leo van den.

PANZUTI, VIRGILIO.
Basta un po' di swing ... [testo di
Danpa], musica di Virgilio Panzuti. L'usignolo è triste ...
[versi di F. Tettoni], musica di
Umberto Chiccohio. © Edizioni
Leonardi, s.a.r.l., Milano;
22May46; EP5062. Piano-conductor
score (orchestra, with words)
and parts.

Buona notte, angelo mio ... testo
italiano di Danpa-Pallesi,
musica di Mac Gillar [pseud.]
(In Un sorriso e 20 canzoni.
p. 16-17) © Edizioni Leonardi,
s.a.r.l., Milano; 4Dec45;
EP4917. For voice and piano.

Insieme ... testo di Pallesi,
musica di Virgilio Panzuti.
(In Un sorriso e 20 canzoni.
p. 24-25) © Edizioni Leonardi,
s.a.r.l., Milano; 10Jan46;
EP4921. For voice and piano.

Lacrime di pioggia ... testo di
Danpa, musica di Virgilio
Panzuti. (In Un sorriso e 20
canzoni. p. 20-21) © Edizioni
Leonardi, s.a.r.l., Milano;
6Jan46; EP4919. For voice and
piano.

Niuba (Luna algerina) ... di
Virgilio Panzuti, [words by
C. Deani] © Edizioni Leonardi,
s.a.r.l., Milano; 25Mar46;
EP4910. Piano-conductor score
(orchestra, with words),
and parts.

Oggi no! ... testo di Danpa, musica
di V. Panzuti. (In Un sorriso
e 20 canzoni. p. 26-27) ©
Edizioni Leonardi, s.a.r.l.,
Milano; 5Dec45; EP4922. For
voice and piano.

Pino solitario ... testo di Danpa,
musica di V. Panzuti. (In Un
sorriso e 20 canzoni. p. 30-31)
© Edizioni Leonardi, s.a.r.l.,
Milano; 8May45; EP4924. For
voice and piano.

La scuola del ritmo ... musica di
Panzuti, [words by Danpa] Non
mi vuoi dir chi sei ... [made
by] F. Dongilli, [words by E.
Frati] © Edizioni Casiroli,
s.a.r.l., Milano; 31Dec46;
EP5266. Piano-conductor score
(orchestra, with words), and
parts.

Scuola del ritmo ... testo di
Danpa, musica di Virgilio
Panzuti. (In Un sorriso e 20
canzoni. p. 42-43) © Edizioni
Casiroli, s.a.r.l., Milano;
15Jan46; EP4930. For voice
and piano.

Svogliati e canta ... testo di
Danpa, musica di V. Panzuti. ©
Edizioni Leonardi, s.a.r.l.,
Milano; 4Mar46; EP4804. Piano-
conductor score (orchestra, with
words) and parts.

Vecchietto arzillo ... testo di
Pallesi, musica di Virgilio
Panzuti. (In Un sorriso e 20
canzoni. p. 18-19) © Edizioni
Casiroli, s.a.r.l., Milano;
12Sep45; EP4918. For voice and
piano.

PAPADOPOULOS, THEODOROS GIANNES,
1905-
Pōs me methas ... etichoi S.
Makē [pseud.] mousikē Th.
Papadopoulou. Athēnai,
Ekdoseis Gaētanou [c1946]
© Michael Etienne Gaetanos,
Athens; 18Jan47; EF5347.
For voice and piano.

PAPAÏŌANNOS, GIANNĒS PETROS, 1912-
Treis megales laïkes epitychies
tou dēmophilous synthetou
laïkōn tragoudiōn, I.
Papaïōannou. Athēnai,
Ekdoseis Gaētanou. ©
Michael Gaetanos, Athens;
12Mar47; EF5543. For voice
and piano.

PAPAJOHN, GREGORY J   1906-
O apomachos. The veteran ...
By Gregory Papajohn. [c1946]
© Gregory J. Papajohn, New
York; 15May47; EF14331. For
voice and piano; Greek words.

PAPARELLI, FRANK.
Kind treatment (will make me love
you); by Alberta Hunter [and]
Frank Paparelli. © Leeds Music
Corp., New York; 24Jan47; EP11807.
For voice and piano, with chord
symbols.

Lights and shadows; by Frank
Paparelli [and] John "Dizzy"
Gillespie, arr. by Red Bone.
© Leeds Music Corp., New York;
14Apr47; EP13743. Condensed
score (orchestra) and parts.

Newton's boogie woogie; by Frank
Paparelli, arr. by Red Bone.
© Leeds Music Corp., New York;
on arrangement; 14Apr47; EP13742.
Condensed score (orchestra) and
parts.

PARCE , RALPH R   1899-
Seeking his sheep; [by] Ralph
R. Parce. © Ralph R. Parce,
Chicago; 15Feb47; EP13723.
Close score; SATB.

PARES, GABRIEL.
Saint Hubert overture ... Arr. by
L. W. Chidester. © Neil A. Kjos
Music Co., Chicago; on arrange-
ment; 21Dec46; EP10655. Con-
densed score (band) and parts.

PARIS, JAMES BYRON.
Faithfully yours; words by Frankie
Sabas, music by James B. Paris.
© Midget Music, inc., Jackson-
ville, Tex.; 27May47; EP14919.

PARK, PHIL.
Mamula moon; words by Phil Park,
music adapted by Phil Park. ©
Sterling Music Publishing Co.,
ltd., London; on adaptation;
31Dec46; EP4841. For voice and
piano.

PARK, STEPHEN, 1911-
Pastorale ... by Stephen Park.
© The Composers Press, inc.,
New York; 5Apr47; EP13334.
Score (flute, violin 1,
violin 2, or viola, and
violoncello) and parts.

PARKE, DOROTHY, 1910-
The house and the road; song,
words by Josephine Peabody,
music by Dorothy Parke.
[London] Boosey & Hawkes. ©
Boosey & Co., ltd., London;
24Jun47; EF3849.

PARKER, ANDY.
Here today and gone tomorrow; by
Fred Strykor [and] Andy Parker.
© Fairway Music Co., Hollywood,
Calif.; 17Jan47; EP11525.
For voice and piano, with chord
symbols.

PARKER, BEULAH, 1906-
Shadow and sun; by Beulah Parker.
© Wesley Webster, San Francisco;
24Dec46; EP10775. For piano solo.

PARKER, EMMA ESTHER, 1893-
Have faith in God; [words by]
E.E.P. (In Gospel choruses.
no. 3, p. 4) © Emma Esther
Parker, Pasadena, Calif.; 4Jun46;
EP4316. Close score; SATB.

I am rejoicing; [words by] E.E.P.
(In Gospel choruses. no. 3,
p. 4) © Emma Esther Parker,
Pasadena, Calif.; 4Jun46; EP4317.

Oh, publish the story; [words by]
E.E.P. (In Gospel choruses.
no. 3, p. 3) © Emma Esther Parker, Pasadena, Calif.; 4Jun46
EP4314. For voice and piano.

Oh, why don't you let Him come in?
Words by Emma Esther Parker [and]
James F. Parker, [music by] Emma
Esther Parker. (In Four gospel
songs, no.4, p.[1]) © Emma
Esther Parker, Pasadena, Calif.;
10Sep46; EP12033.

Take the world, but give me Jesus;
[words by] E.E.P. (In Gospel
choruses. no. 3, p. 3) © Emma
Esther Parker, Pasadena, Calif.;
4Jun46; EP4315.

'Tis so sweet to trust in Jesus;
words by Mary E. Johnson, music
by Emma Esther Parker. (In Four
gospel songs, no.4, p.[4])
© Emma Esther Parker, Pasadena,
Calif.; 10Sep46; EP12034.

PARKER, HENRY.
Jerusalem; [for] three choirs; SA,
SAB, SATB, [by] Henry Parker,
arr. by Kenneth E. Runkel. ©
Harold Flammer, inc., New York;
on arrangement; 31Dec46; EP11425.

PARKER, RAYMOND C   1920-
My truest friend; [words by]
R. C. P. (In Gospel choruses.
no. 3, p. [1]) © Raymond C.
Parker, Pasadena, Calif.;
4Jun46; EP4311. For voice and
piano.

Yes, He is mine; verse lyrics by
Ruth E. Thompson, chorus lyrics by
Emma Esther Parker, music by Ray-
mond C. Parker. (In Four gospel
songs, no.4, p.[5]) © Raymond C.
Parker & Ruth E. Thompson, Pasadena,
Calif.; 10Sep46; EP12035.

PARKS, HOLLIS.
There's a home for us in glory;
[words by] H. P. and G. E. H.
[music by] Hollis Parks, arr.
by W. M. T. (In Church of the
Nazarene. Michigan District.
Nazarene Young Peoples Society.
Choruses of the N. Y. P. S.
p.50-51) © Michigan District,
Nazarene Young Peoples Society,
Flint, Mich.; 25Jul46; EP13071.
For voice and piano.

PARR, PATSY, 1937-
The Brownies' welcome; words by
Margaret Murray, music by
Brownie Patsy Parr. ©
Boosey & Hawkes (Canada), ltd.,
Toronto; 12May47; EF32l6.

PARRA, ALFREDO.
Amigablemente ... [words and mus-
ic by] Alfredo Parra, [arr. de
M. Ruiz Armengol] © Editorial
Mexicana de Música Internacion-
al, s. a., Mexico; 14Jul47;
Condensed score (orchestra),
piano-conductor score and parts.

PARRA, EMILIO.
My rancho (in California); words
and music by Emilio Parra. ©
George Simon, inc., New York;
18Apr47; EP15809. English and
Spanish words.

PARRA, GILBERTO.
Amor de los dos ... musica y
letra de Gilberto Parra. ©
Hnos. Márquez, s. de r. l.,
México; 15Aug46; EF3908.

PARRISH, CARL.
Chorale prelude on the Welsh hymn
tune "Jabes" for the organ, by
Carl Parrish, [ed. by Catharine
Crozier] © M. Witmark & Sons,
New York; 11Apr47; EP13704.
Chorale prelude on the Welsh
hymn tune "Llansanan" for the
organ, by Carl Parrish, [ed.
by Catharine Crozier] © M.
Witmark & Sons, New York;
11Apr47; EP13703.
Chorale prelude on the Welsh
hymn tune "St. Denio" for the
organ, by Carl Parrish, [ed.
by Catharine Crozier] © M.
Witmark & Sons, New York;
11Apr47; EP13705.
Mary's baby; a Christmas anthem,
three part women's voices,
S.S.A.; poem by Shaemas O'Sheal,
music by Carl Parrish. © M.
Witmark & Sons, New York; on
arrangement; 17Jun47; EP15272.

PARROTT, IAN.
Theme and six variants; for pianoforte,
[by] Ian Parrott. © Alfred
Lengnick & Co., ltd., London;
7Feb47; EF3155.

PARRY, C   HUBERT H
Jerusalem ... stanzas from William
Blake's Prophetic books, set to
music by C. Hubert H. Parry; ed.
with organ accompaniment arr. by
G. T. Thalben-Ball. London, J.
Curwen & Sons, New York, G.
Schirmer, sole agents. © Lady
Dorothea Ponsonby (executrix of
the late Sir Hubert Parry), Has-
lemere, Surrey, Eng.; on arrangement; 24Jun47; EF5065. For
unison chorus and organ.

PARTAIN, DOROTHY.
Our Lady's Martinites; words by
seventh and eighth grades [of
St. Martin Hall] San Antonio,
Mother's Club of St. Martin
Hall, Demonstration School, Our
Lady of the Lake College. ©
Our Lady of the Lake College,
San Antonio; 4Apr46; EP2848.
For voice and piano.

PARTICHELA, F   A
Mexican hat dance ... [by] F. A.
Partichela, arr. by Charles
Nunzio [for] piano accordion.
© Edward B. Marks Music Corp.,
New York; on arrangement;
15Jan47; EP11570.

PARYS, GEORGES VAN, 1902-
(Circonstances attenuantes) One
more kiss for the road ...
from the film "Circonstances
attenuantes" ... English words
by Stanley Taylor [pseud.],
music by Georges van Parys.
© Ascherberg, Hopwood & Crew,
ltd., London; on English
words; 17Dec46; EF5227.

J'suis Parigote ... paroles de
Jean Manse, musique de G. van
Parys. © Éditions Royalty,
Paris; 31Dec46; EF3887.
Ne t'en fais pas, mon vieux! ...
Paroles de Jean Manse, musique
de G. van Parys. © Éditions
Royalty, Paris; 31Dec46;
EF3892.
One more kiss for the road. See
his Circonstances attenuantes.
Pour les amants. See his Le
silence est d'or.
(Le silence est d'or) Pour les
amants (c'est tous les jours
dimanche), du film "Le silence
est d'or"; paroles de René Clair
[pseud.] musique de Georges van
Parys. © Éditions Philippe Pares,
Paris; 31Jan47; EF3480.
La valse qui chante ... paroles
de Jean Manse, musique de G.
van Parys. © Éditions Royalty,
Paris; 31Dec46; EF3895.

PASCARELLA, ENZO.
Lullaby; song. [words by James J.
Wills, music by] Enzo Pascarolla.
© G. Ricordi & Co., New York;
28Jan47; EP6618.

PASERO, PIERO.
Ho licenziato la cameriera ...
musica di Piero Pasero, testo
di Chiosso. Un bacio ... musica
di Beppe Moietta, testo di P.
Tettoni. © Edizioni Leonardi,
s.a.r.l., Milano; 9Jan47;
EP5268. Piano-conductor score
(orchestra, with words), and
parts.

PASSANI, ÉMILE BARTHÉLÉMI, 1905-
Saltarelle; pour piano, [by]
Émile Passani. © Heugel & Co.,
Paris; 11Oct46; EF6436.

PASSER, ROLF.
Darling, let's go to Sonoma;
words and music by Rolf Passer.
San Francisco, Spotlite Music.
© Rolf Passer, San Francisco;
2Jan47; EP11348.

PASZTOR, GEORGE ALBERT, 1910-
Gone are you; words and music by
George Pasztor. © George A.
Pasztor, White Plains, N. Y.;
15Apr47; EP13892.

PATITUCCI, ELVIRA.
All the time; words and music by
Elvira Patitucci. © Grimes
Music Publishers, Philadelphia;
28Jan47; EP12329.

PATTI, SANTO T
The beautiful Bay of Milwaukee ...
by Santo T. Patti. © Patti
Bros. Music House, Milwaukee;
26Dec46; EP10710. For accordion
solo.
Gay life of Milwaukee ... by Santo
T. Patti. © Patti Bros. Music
House, Milwaukee; 26Dec46;
EP10709. For accordion solo.
The young musician's progress ...
by Santo T. Patti. © Patti
Bros. Music Co., Milwaukee;
26Dec46; EP10714. For accordion
solo.

PAULOS, N   E   1886-
Inspiración ... musique de N.
Poulos, arrangement de Francis
Salabert. Eternamente ...
musique de Julio F. Falcon,
arrangement de Francis Salabert.
© Éditions Salabert, Paris; on
arrangement; 15Feb47; EF3527.
Piano-conductor score (orchestra)
and parts.

PAULSEN, RALPH E
Between ourselves; words and music
by Ralph E. Paulsen. © Cine-
mart Music Publishing Co.,
Hollywood, Calif.; 1Aug46;
EP10954. For voice and piano,
with chord symbols.

PAULSON, JOSEPH.
High ridin'; by Joseph Paulson.
© George F. Briegel, inc.,
New York; on arrangement;
25Feb47; EP12434. Condensed
score (band) and parts.

PAULY, FRANCIS.
In my dreams; words and music by John
Dayfotis and Francis Pauly. © Art
Music Co., New York; 22Jan47;
EP11442.

PAVARD, ALBERT CHARLES AUGUSTE,
1895-
Voilà l'hiver ... paroles de A.
Pierre Pani [pseud.], musique
de Albert Pavard. © Albert
Pavard, Rouen (S.I.) France;
5Dec46; EF5194.

PAVESIO, PIERO.
Non ci comprendiamo più ... testo
di F. Tettoni, musica di Piero
Pavesio. © Edizioni Leonardi,
s.a.r.l., Milano; 9Jan47;
EP5275. Piano-conductor score
(orchestra, with words), and
parts.

PAZ, RAFAEL DE.
Con el alma en los labios ...
letra, música y arreglo de
Rafael de Paz. © Editorial
Mexicana de Música Inter-
national, s.a., Mexico, D. F.;
27Dec46; EF4863. Piano-conductor score (orchestra), condensed score and parts.

PAZANDAK, AL.
On the trail to home, sweet home;
words by Al Pinkard, music by
Al Pazandak. © Nordyke Publish-
ing Co., Los Angeles; 14Sep46;
EP11278.
On the trail to home sweet home;
words by Al Pinkard, music by
Al Pazandak. © Nordyke Publish-
ing Co., Los Angeles; 2Dec46;
EP10859. For voice and piano,
with chord symbols.

PEARSALL, ROBERT LUCAS, 1795-1856.
Praise Jehovah ... Psalm 146,
[music by] Robert Lucas Pear-
sall ... ed. [and arr.] by
Matthew Lundquist. © Sam
Fox Publishing Co., New York;
on arrangement; 2Jun47;
EP15025. Score; chorus
(SATB) and piano reduction.

PEARSON, DOROTHY.
Let Jesus lead you all the way;
words by William E. Hudson,
music by Dorothy Pearson. ©
William E. Hudson, Philadelphia;
12May47; EP14548. Close score;
SATB.

PEARSON, G   ALBERT, 1907-
Be Thou my vision; [words by
Eleanor Hull, music] by G.
Albert Pearson. © Choral Press,
Evanston, Ill.; 15Apr47; EP14192.
Score; solo voices (soprano or
junior choir and baritone),
chorus (SATB) and piano re-
duction.

PEDROLLO, ARRIGO.
La regina di Cirta. Die Königin
von Cirta. Tragedia lirica in tre atti di
Antonio Lega. (Für die deutsche
Opernbühne übersetzt von Karl
Ernst) Riduzione per canto e
pianoforte dell' autore. ©
Casa Musicale Giuliana, Trieste,
Italia; 30Sep41; EF3214. Piano-
vocal score.

PEETERS, FLOR, 1903-
Aria; voor orgel, [by] Flor
Peeters. © Edition Heuwekemeyer
(Firm A. J. Heuwekemeyer & B. F.
van Gaal), Amsterdam, The Neth-
erlands; 28Feb46; EF5124.

108

PEETERS, FLOR. Cont'd.
Mère. (Moeder) Six mélodies
pour voix grave et piano ...
[by] Flor Peeters. Op. 41.
Poésie de Maurice Carême,
nederlandsch van Alba [pseud.]
© Edition Heuwekemeyer (Firm
A. J. Heuwekemeyer & B .F.
van Gaal), Amsterdam, The
Netherlands; 24Sep46; EP5154.
Steenhof; tien landelijke schetsen
voor piano ... door Flor Peeters.
Op. 53. © Edition Heuwekemeijer
(Firm A. J. Heuwekemeijer & B.
F. van Gaal), Amsterdam; 30Nov46;
EP3380.
Te Deum. Lord God, we praise
Thee... by Flor Peeters.
Op. 57. English text by
Edward C. Currie. © McLaugh-
lin & Reilly Co., Boston; on ar-
rangement; 24May47; EP15009.
Score; TTB and organ.
Te Deum. Lord God we praise
Thee. For four mixed voices
and organ, by Flor Peeters.
Op.57. English text by Edward
C. Currie. © McLaughlin &
Reilly Co., Boston; 10Mar47;
EP12781.
Variations and finale on an old
Flemish song; [by] Flor Peeters
... for organ. Op.20. © Elkan-
Vogel Co., inc., Philadelphia;
31Dec46; EP11463.
Variations on an original theme;
[for] organ, [by] Flor Peeters.
Op. 58. © Elkan-Vogel Co., inc.,
Philadelphia; 11Mar47; EP13936.
PEETERS, FRANS FLORENTIUS. See
Peeters, Flor.
PELLEGRINI, GIAN MARCO, 1905-
Metodo per saxofono; [by] G.
M. Pellegrini. © Carisch,
s.a., Milan; 16May47;
EP3784.
PELOQUIN, CHARLES ALEXANDER, 1918-
The Christmas Child. Quand
Dieu naquit à Noël. (A French
noel) ... S.A.T.B., a cappella.
English version by C. A.
setting by C. Alexander Pelo-
quin. © M. Witmark & Sons,
New York; on English words &
arrangement; 14May47; EP14613.
PELOSI, DON.
The world belongs to you, little
man; by Leo Towers & Don Pelosi.
© Strauss Miller Music Co., ltd.,
London; 20Jan47; EF3149. For
voice and piano, with chord symbols.
Melody also in tonic sol-fa
notation.
PELT, MERRILL B. VAN. See
Van Pelt, Merrill B.
PENDLETON, EMMET.
April wisdom; words by Grace Mar-
garet Robinson, music by Emmet
Pendleton, inc., Boston; 10Apr47; EP13915.
Blue moon; words by Elton Williams,
music by Emmet Pendleton.
© Bruce Humphries, inc., Boston;
10Apr47; EP13336.
The catkins; words by Zuella
Sterling, music by Emmet
Pendleton. © Bruce Humphries,
inc., Boston; 10Apr47; EP13337.
From moon-filled sky; a
collection of six songs, words
by Harry William Nelson,
music by Emmet Pendleton. ©
Bruce Humphries, inc., Boston;
1May47; EP13784.
Leaf smoke; words by Roberta
Rinear, music by Emmet Pendle-
ton. © Bruce Humphries, inc.,
Boston; 10Apr47; EP13339.
Love on a hill; words by Jessie
Goddard Broman, music by
Emmet Pendleton. © Bruce
Humphries, inc., Boston
10Apr47; EP13338.

Quiet paths; two songs: 1. These
woods of light and shadow. 2.
Intricate is the weaving. Words
by Stanton Coblentz, music by
Emmet Pendleton. [c1946] ©
Bruce Humphries, inc., Boston;
17Feb47; EP11895.
This is my plea; words by Grace
Andrews, music by Emmet Pendleton.
[c1946] © Bruce Humphries, inc.,
Boston; 10Feb47; EP11893.
Winter night; words by Harriett
Lightfoot, music by Emmet Pendle-
ton. © Bruce Humphries, inc.,
Boston; 10Apr47; EP13912.
PENNY, LEE.
A lot of elbow room; words and
music by Lee Penny. © Hill
and Range Songs, inc., Holly-
wood, Calif.; 24Mar47;
EP13204.
My prairie serenade; words and
music by Ken Curtis and Lee
Penny. © Hill and Range
Songs, inc., Hollywood, Calif.;
24Mar47; EP13205.
PENTUFF, ODOREDO.
I'd never give you up ... Words
and music written by Odoredo
Pentuff. (In Tampa morning
tribune. v.53, no.80, p.9)
© Odoredo Pentuff, Tampa, Fla.;
29Mar47; EF6799. Melody and
words.
Mauna Loa ... words and melody by
Miss Odoredo Pentuff. (In
Tampa Morning Tribune. v. 53,
no. 130, p. 20) © Odoredo
Pentuff, Tampa, Fla.; 10May47;
B5-5.
PEPPER, BUDDY.
Don't tell me. See his The huck-
sters.
(The hucksters) Don't tell me,
[from] the ... picture, "The
hucksters," words and music by
Buddy Pepper. © Robbins Music
Corp., New York; 14May47;
EP14765.
PEREZ, JUANITA, pseud. See
Dubarbie, Jeanne.
PERGAMENT, MOSES.
I natt skall jag dö. [Tonight I
must die. Words by] Harriet
Löwenhjelm, [music by] Moses
© Nordiska Musikförlaget, a.b.,
Stockholm; 1Jan43; EF3747.
Score (voice and piano) and
voice part.
Vem spelar i natten ... [Who
plays in the night-time ...
words by] Pär Lagerkvist, [tr.
by Noel Wirén, music by] Moses
Pergament. © Nordiska
Musikförlaget, a.b., Stockholm; 1Jan43; EF3741. Score
(voice, flute ad lib. and
piano) and part for voice and
flute.
PERGOLESI, GIOVANNI BATTISTA, 1710-1736.
Glory to God in the highest! (The
angel's song); SAB accompanied.
[by] Giovanni Battista Pergolesi
... arr. by Wellingford Riegger,
acc. by Vincent Novello, [words:]
St. Luke, 2:14. © Harold Flammer,
inc., New York; on arrangement;
4Nov46; EP10853.
Glory to God in the highest! (The
angel's song); SATB accompanied,
[by] Giovanni Battista Pergolesi
... arr. by Wellingford Riegger,
acc. by Vincent Novello, [words:]
St. Luke, 2:14. © Harold Flammer,
inc., New York; on arrangement;
4Nov46; EP10858.

PERNE, NILS.
Tänker du på mej? ... Av Nils
Perne och Sven Paddock [pseud.]
© Carl Gehrmans Musikförlag,
a/b, Stockholm; 1Jan45; EP5001.
For voice and piano, with chord
symbols.
Tänker du på mej?... Musik och text!
Perne-Paddock [pseud.], arrangemang:
G. Lundén-Welden. © Carl Gehrmans
Musikförlag, a/b, Stockholm, on
arrangement; 1Jan45; EP5000.
Piano-conductor score (orchestra)
and parts.
PERPER, BOB.
The time, the place and you;
music by Bob Perper, lyrics by
Bebe Starr. © Kaiser Music Co.,
New York; 1Apr47; EP13415.
PERSICHETTI, VINCENT.
Poems for piano; [by] Vincent
Persichetti. © Elkan-Vogel
Co., inc., Philadelphia; v.
1, 25Mar47, v. 2, 11Mar47;
EP13921, 13103.
[PERSSON, HARRY ARNOLD]
Lazy lagoon blues; musik och
arr.: Harry Arnold [pseud.]
© Edition Sylvain, a.b.,
Stockholm; 1Jan46; EP3720.
Piano-conductor score (orchestra),
and parts.
PESCARA, AURELIO PATERAS.
Tibet. © Associated Music Pub-
lishers, inc., New York;
24Dec45; EP468. Miniature
score: orchestra.
[PESSL, YELLA] ed. and comp.
The art of the suite; eight
suites of dances by Jacques
Champion de Chambonnières,
Johann Jacob Froberger, Henry
Purcell [and others, ed. and
comp. by Yella Pessl] © Ed-
ward B. Marks Music Corp., New
York; on compilation; 14May47;
EP14358. For harpsichord (or
piano) solo.
PETERSON, J   EMIL.
Tho blue Hawaiian moon; words &
music by J. E. Peterson. Wash-
ington, D. C., Peterson Pro-
ductions. © J. Emil Peterson,
Washington, D. C.; 22Jan47;
EP12490.
PETERSON, JOHN CHARLES.
I'm jealous of your dream; words &
music by John Charles Peterson.
© Jack Wallner Publishing Co.,
Duluth; 7Apr47; EP13664.
PETERSON, JOHN WILLARD, 1921-
[Gospel songs] words and music
by John W. Peterson. Wichita,
Kan., Norse Gospel Trio.
© John Willard Peterson,
Wichita, Kan.; on 3 songs;
6Apr47. Contents.- When I
took it to Jesus in prayer
© EP14916) Glad tidings!
© EP14918)- I must tell
others © EP14917)
[PETERSON, KARL-ERIK]
Du är välkommen hem ... [music]
av Carle [pseud. and Malm,
[words by] Moberg; arr.: Kurt
Blomquist. © Skandinaviska
Odeon, a.b., Stockholm;
1Jan44; EP3757. Piano-con-
ductor score (orchestra), and
parts.
När det skymmer ... av Eric
Carle [pseud.], arr.: Ch.
Byrd [pseud. Words by Fritz
Gustaf] © Skandinaviska Odeon,
a.b., Stockholm; 1Jan44;
EP3729. Piano-conductor score
(orchestra), and parts.
PETERSON, ROBERT A
I'll never be sorry I care; words
and music by Robert A. Peterson.
[c1945] © Nordyke Publishing Co.,
Los Angeles; 14Jun46; EP11996.

109

775306 O - 48 - 8

PETIVAN, ART.
Does your conscience ever hurt you?
By Art Petivan. © Sunset Music
Publications, New Orleans; 28Dec45;
EP1547. For voice and piano,
with guitar diagrams and chord
symbols.

PETRIE, HENRY W
I don't want to play in your yard;
by Henry W. Petrie ... [words
by Philip Wingate] arr. by Hugo
Frey. © Hamilton S. Gordon,
inc., New York; on arrangement;
11Jun47; EP15066. For piano
solo, with words.

PETRŽELKA, VILÉM, 1889-
Čtyři impromptus ... Op. 36.
[By] Vilém Petrželka. ©
Hudební Matice Umělecké
Besedy, Praha, Czechoslovakia;
1Sep44; EF4966. Score
(violin and piano) and part.
Písně milostné; na slova perského
básníka Bábá Tahira, [by]
Vilém Petrželka. Op. 35. ©
Hudební Matice Umělecké Besedy,
Praha, Czechoslovakia; 8Dec43;
EF4966. For voice and piano.
Sonata, violoncello solo. Op.
23. [By] Vilém Petrželka,
revidoval V. Černý. ©
Hudební Matice Umělecké
Besedy, Praha, Czechoslovakia;
13Nov42; EF4972.

PETYREK, FELIX, 1892-
Zwei Lieder aus dem "Buch der Seele"
von Richard Schaukal; vertont
von Felix Petyrek. Wien,
Universal-Edition. © associated
Music Publishers, inc., New York;
1Jan19. Vol.1, score (voice,
violin and piano) and part for
violin. Contents.- 1. Spät
(© EF4823)

PEYRONNIN, JEAN HUBERT, 1901-
Emile et Ferdinand; paroles de
Rene Nazelles [pseud.], musique
de Joan Peyronnin et René
Nazelles. Paris, Salabert. ©
Salabert, inc., New York; 31Aug47;
EF4848. For voice and piano.

PHILIPP, ISIDOR.
Coordinated piano method ... written
in collaboration with Louis Sugar-
man; illustrations by Richard and
Elsie Erdoes, lyrics by Alfred Gamse.
© Edward B. Marks Music Corp., New
York; bk.2, 23Apr47; EP13860.
Coordinated piano method, eye, ear,
hand ... written in collaboration
with Louis Sugarman. © Edward
B. Marks Music Corp., New York;
bk. 1, 20Nov46; EP9533.
Phalenes. (Moths) Piano solo,
[by] Isidor Philipp. (Con-
temporary composers ser.)
© Edward B. Marks Music Corp.,
New York; 30Apr47; EP14806.
Progressive piano exercises;
[by] Isidor Philipp, preface
by Rudolph Ganz. © McKinley
Publishers, inc., Chicago;
10Feb47; EP12411.

PHILIPPE-GÉRARD, M., pseud. See
Bloch, Philippe-Gérard.

PHILLIPS, DONALD, 1913-
Concerto in jazz; pianoforte solo
by Donald Phillips. © Lawrence
Wright Music Co., ltd., London;
28Feb47; EF5166.

PHILLIPS, "FLIP." See
Phillips, Joe.

PHILLIPS, JOE.
Lost weekend; arr. by Joe Bishop,
music by Joe "Flip" Phillips.
© Charling Music Corp., New
York; 25Apr47; EP14065. Piano-
conductor score (orchestra)
and parts.

With someone new; by Joe "Flip"
Phillips, arr. by Joe Bishop.
© Charling Music Corp., New
York; 15Apr47; EP13865. Piano-
conductor score (orchestra) and
parts.

[PHILLIPS, JOHN HOWARD] 1878-
Through as dreamer, through as
opposer; words ... [and] music
by Phil Goodwill, [pseud., arr.
by George H. Wade] © John
Howard Phillips, Richmond;
28May47; EP14772.

PHILLIPS, PETER.
Sing, gondolier ... words by
Martyn Mayne [pseud.], music
by Peter Phillips. © Schauer
& May, London; 1Nov46; EF5161.

PÍCHA, FRANTIŠEK, 1893-
Trio quasi una fantasia ... [by]
František Pícha. Op.21.
© Hudební Matice Umělecké
Besedy, Praha, Czechoslovakia;
3Nov43; EF5008. Score (violin,
viola and piano) and parts.

PICK MANGIAGALLI, RICCARDO, 1882-
Angelus ... [by] R. Pick Mangiagalli. © Carisch, s.a.,
Milan; 28Apr47; EF5900. Score
(mixed chorus and piano) and
parts for women's voices and
men's voices.

PIERNÉ, GABRIEL.
En barque. Boat song. [Words by]
E. Guinand, English version by
Lorraine May Finley. (In
[Hodges, Lester] comp. John
Charles Thomas album of songs
and arias. p. 73-80) © G. Schir-
mer, inc., New York; 21Jun46;
EP10220.

PIERRON, JOSEPH JAMES, 1875-
22 hymns in honor of the Sacred
Heart, B. V. Mary and St. Joseph;
for S.A.T.B., by ... Jos. J.
Pierron. Sheboygan, Wis.,
Zohlen Music Studio. © Joseph
James Pierron, Campbellsport,
Wis.; 18Mar47; EP12942.

PIKE, MORRIS DONALD, 1928-
Youth, O youth; [by] Morris D.
Pike, [words by] Doris C. Kinsley.
[c1946] © Doris C. Kinsley,
Montpelier, Vt. & Morris D.
Pike, Stowo, Vt.; 15Jan47; EP12269.

PIKE, RUSS.
I won't hang around you anymore;
words and music by Russ Pike.
© Peer International Corp.,
New York; 29Oct46; EP15615.

PIMSLEUR, SOLOMON, 1900-
(Suite of transformations) Fugal
fantasie and Ode to intensity,
from Suite of transformations,
op. 10, [no. 4-5] for piano
solo. © Solomon Pimsleur, New
York, 20c146; EP11746.

[PINKARD, EDNA BELLE ALEXANDER] 1899-
I'll always remember; [music by
Alex Belledna, pseud., words]
by Morris Filowitz and Alex
Belledna [pseud.] © Pinkard
Publications, inc., New York;
30Dec46; EP12014.

PINKARD MACEO, 1897-
Don't cry, little girl, don't
cry; by Maceo Pinkard, [arr.
by Robert C. Haring] ©
Shapiro, Bernstein & Co., inc.,
New York; on arrangement and
changes in words; 16May47;
EP14616. For voice and
piano, with chord symbols.
That fascinatin', procrastinatin'
gal o'mine ... by Maceo Pinkard.
© Pinkard Publications, inc.,
New York; 30Dec46; EP11671. For
voice and piano, with chord symbols.

PINKHAM, DANIEL R 1923-
Motet I[-III; by] Daniel Pinkham,
[words from the Psalms] © Daniel
Pinkham, Lynn, Mass.; 14Feb47;
EP12140. Score: chorus (SSA) and
unfigured bass; Latin words.

PINTERALLY, AL. See
Pinterally, Alfred.

PINTERALLY, ALFRED, 1919-
Always be with me, God; music and
lyrics by Al Pinterally.
© Alfred Pinterally, Chicago;
7Jun47; EP14903.
Christmas love; music and lyrics
by Al Pinterally. © Alfred
Pinterally, Chicago; 7Jun47;
EP14905.

PIRES VERMELHO, ALCYR.
Rio ... music and Portuguese
lyric by Oswaldo Santiago and
Alcyr Pires Vermelho, lyric by
Mack David ... arr. by Gaó,
[pseud.] © Remick Music Corp.,
New York; on arrangement;
11Mar47; EP13708. Piano-conductor score (orchestra, with
words) and parts.

PISANO, GIGI, comp.
Piedigrotta Pisano-Cioffi, 1941-
42, XIX. [Comp. by Gigi Pisano,
words by G. Pisano, Nisa and
others, music by Giuseppe Cioffi,
Nino Casiroli and others] ©
Casa Musicale La Canzone, Naples;
6Oct41; EF3431.

PISTON, WALTER, 1894-
Divertimento, for nine instruments;
by Walter Piston. Score and parts.
© Broadcast Music, inc., New York;
16Dec46; EP13843.

PISTON, WALTER, 1894-
(Quintet, flute & strings)
Quintet, for flute and string
quartet; [by] Walter Piston. ©
Arrow Music Press, inc., New
York; 13Jul46; EP12220. Mini-
ature score.

PITMAN, HENRY M 1879-
If you want it, Dixie has it;
words and music by Henry M.
Pitman. © Uhl & Ware, San
Antonio; 1Jan47; EP10898.

PITT, PETER, pseud. See
Krancher, Willy Carl.

PITTS, JOE F
The new liberty bell; by Joe F.
Pitts, sr., arr. by John N.
Klohr. © Joe F. Pitts, sr.,
Sharon, Tenn.; 24Sep46;
EP12532. Parts: band.

PIZZOGLIO, WILLIAM.
Missa in honorem "Sanctae
Franciscae Xaveriae Cabrini";
for S.A.T.B. voices with organ
acc. ... by ... William Pizzoglio. Boston, McLaughlin &
Reilly Co. © William Pizzoglio, Utica, N. Y.; 27Dec46;
EP12391.

PLATO, G
(You are my sweetheart) Melodia;
words by H. P. D., music by G.
Plato, [piano arrangement by
Chris Langdon] © Chappell & Co.,
ltd., London; 25Mar47; EF5471.

PLATO, GERALD.
Whisper I love you; words and
music by Ross Parker, Michael
Carr and Gerald Plato. © The
Peter Maurice Music Co., ltd.,
London; 15Apr47; EF5630.

POGGÉS, ANDREAS ERMÉS, 1908-
Klapse phtôchô kardia mou;
etichoi K. Manesă, mousikê
Andrea Poggé, athênai,
Ekdoseis Gaïtanou. ©
Michael Etienne Gaetanos,
Athens; 8May46; EF5348.
For voice and piano.

POLL, LEO, pseud. See
Polnareff, Leib.

POLLA, WILLIAM C   d.1939.
Dancing tambourine; [by] W. C.
Polla, arr. by Juan Gossette,
[pseud.] © Harms, inc., New
York; on arrangement; 24May47;
EP14709. Score (B♭ trumpet or
cornet and piano) and part.
Dancing tambourine ... [By] W. C.
Polla ... arr. by Walter Beeler.
© Harms, inc., New York; on
arrangement; 29May47; EP14995.
Score (B♭ baritone (or euphonium)
and piano) and part.

POLLACK, ROBERT, 1900-
I'm just a Yankee too; words by
Olga Duboy, music by Robert
Pollack. © Cine-Mart Music
Publishing Co., Hollywood,
Calif.; 1Nov46; EP11940.
There's an angel waiting for
you; words by W. P. Sloan,
music by Robert Pollack.
© Nordyke Publishing Co.,
Los Angeles; 7Mar47;
EP15567.

POLLET, BARBARA.
More straw for the scarecrow; a
three-act play for children with
music and dances, by Betty
Kelley ... music by Barbara
Pollet. © Row, Peterson & Co.,
Evanston, Ill.; 19Nov46; DP1220.

POLLINO, NICHOLAS.
Your love is everything to me;
words and music by Nicholas
Pollino. © Nicholas Pollino,
Wilmington, Del.; 23Sep46;
EP11191.

[POLNAREFF, LEIB] 1899-
Tant pis ... tant mieux ... paroles
de Maurice Druon & Jean Kessel;
musique & arrangement de Léo
Poll [pseud.] © Éditions Musicales Nuances, Paris; 15Feb47;
EF34686.

POLOVINA, MICHAEL JOSEPH, 1911-
I'll be coming back your way;
lyrics by Joseph S. Klebosits
and [music by] Michael J.
Polovina. South Bend, Ind.,
Essex Music Publishers. ©
Joseph S. Klebosits and Michael
J. Polovina, South Bend, Ind.;
on changes in words & music;
2Jun47; EP14852.
These things I know will happen
(then how happy I'll be);
words by Joseph S. Klebosits,
music by Michael J. Polovina,
South Bend, Ind., Mid-west
Music Publishers. © Michael
Joseph Polovina & Joseph Steven
Klebosits, South Bend, Ind.;
on changes in music; 7Apr47;
EP11117.

POMARES, GUILLERMO.
Mentiras. (Foolish lies) ...
English words by Joe Davis,
Spanish words and music by
Guillermo Pomares. ©
Caribbean Music, inc., New
York; 17Mar47; EP12633.
Sin rencor. (No hard feelings)
... English words by Joe
Davis, Spanish words and music
by Guillermo Pomares. ©
Caribbean Music, inc., New
York; 17Mar47; EP12633.

PONCE, MANUEL.
Little star. (Estrellita) For...
S.S.A. and soprano solo, [by]
Manuel Ponce, arr. by Russell
Watson [pseud.] © Pro Art
Publications, New York; on ar-
rangement; 21Apr47; EP13610.

POND, FRANK G   1866-
Whisper that you love me. When
it's apple blossom time again
... words and music by Frank
Pond. © Frank G. Pond,
Mountain View, N. Y.; 28Oct46;
EP13350.

PORDARSON, SIGURDUR.
(I álbgum) Tíu sönglög. Textar
eftir Dagfinn Sveinbjörnsson.
© Gunnar R. Paulsson, Baldwin,
N.Y.; 11Dec45; EP1337. For
voice and piano.
Tíu sönglög. See his I álbgum.

PORTA, MARIO FERNÁNDEZ. See
Fernández Porta, Mario.

PORTER, CLARA E
Everything comes first; words and
music by Clara E. Porter. ©
Harry L. McMillen, Marguerite
Porter McMillen and Clara E.
Porter, Millbrae, Calif.; 1Apr47;
EP13443.

PORTER, COLE, 1892-
(Anything goes) Anything goes ...
Music by Cole Porter, piano
adaptation by Henry Levine.
© Harms, inc., New York; on
arrangement; 3Feb47; EP12005.
(Anything goes) You're the top...
Music by Cole Porter, piano adap-
tation by Henry Levine. © Harms,
inc., New York; on arrangement;
3Feb47; EP12002.
(Gay divorcee) Night and day; for
xylophone or marimba with piano
accompaniment, by Cole Porter,
arranged by F. Henri Klickmann.
© Harms, inc., New York; on ar-
rangement; 5Feb47; EP12003.
(Gay divorcee) Night and day.
(Noche y día) From "Gay
divorcee," Spanish text by
Johnnie Camacho, lyric and
music by Cole Porter. ©
Harms, inc., New York; on
Spanish text; 14May47; EP14711.
I get a kick out of you ... music
by Cole Porter, piano adaptation
by Henry Levine. © Harms, inc.,
New York; on adaptation; 2Jan47;
EP11212.
In the still of the night; by
Cole Porter, symphonic arrange-
ment ... by Hans Spialek. ©
Chappell & Co., inc., New York;
on arrangement; 16Dec46; EP11751.
Piano-conductor score (orchestra)
and parts.
(Jubilee) Begin the beguine ...
From the musical production
"Jubilee." Words and music by
Cole Porter, Spanish version by
Maria Grever. [Arr. by William
Stickles] © Harms, inc., New
York; on arrangement; 19May47;
EP14712. Score: solo voices
(SA or SBA) and piano.
(Jubilee) Just one of those things
... Music by Cole Porter, piano
adaptation by Henry Levine.
© Harms, inc., New York; on ar-
rangement; 3Feb47; EP12001.
Let's do it ... music by Cole
Porter, piano adaptation by
Henry Levine. © Harms, inc.,
New York; on arrangement; 3Feb47;
EP11999.
Night and day. See his Gay
divorcee.
(Wake up and dream) What is this
thing called love? From "Wake up
and dream;" by Cole Porter.
Transcribed for band by John J.
Morrissey. © Harms, inc., New
York; on arrangement; 11Jun47;
EP15198. Condensed score (band)
and parts.

What is this thing called love?
... music by Cole Porter, piano
adaptation by Henry Levine.
© Harms, inc., New York; on
adaptation; 2Jan47; EP11214.

PORTER, DEL, 1902-
My pretty girl; words and music by
Ray Johnson [and] Del Porter.
© Tune Towne Tunes, North Holly-
wood, Calif.; 17Dec46; EP10785.

PORTER, FRANK ADDISON, 1859-1941.
Seven and twenty easy pieces; composed
and adapted by F. Addison Porter.
Rev. ed. by Laura Huxtable Porter.
Boston, C. W. Homeyer and Co. [c1946]
© Laura Huxtable Porter, Belmont,
Mass.; on additional music; 25Jan47;
EP12949. For piano solo.

PORTER, LEW.
A pillow of sighs and tears; by
Lew Porter. © Northern Music
Corp., New York; 10Mar47;
EP12759. For voice and piano,
with chord symbols.

POSAMANICK, BEATRICE.
Praise; (S.A.T.B. with contralto
(or baritone) solo) [by]
Beatrice Posamanick. [words
by Gerard Manley Hopkins]
© Galaxy Music Corp., New
York; 29Apr47; EP6860.

POSEY, EDWIN, 1893-
I'm sometimes weeping; words and
music by ... Edwin Posey, sr.,
arr. by Odessa Steward. ©
Edwin Posey, sr., Chicago; 10Oct46;
EP12257.

POST, THEODORE HAROLD, 1892-
The sweet promised land of
Nevada; words: Walter Van
Tilberg Clark, music: Theodore
H. Post. © Theodore Harold
Post, Reno, Nev.; 3Mar47;
EP12316.

POST, WILLIAM HARVEY, 1919-
There's a rainbow in the rain; words
and music by Bill H. Post, [arr. by
Don Robertson] © Post and Postel
Publishing Co., Los Angeles; on
arrangement & changes in melody &
words; 11Feb47; EP12084.

POTERAT, LOUIS, 1901-
Valse des regrets ... paroles
[and music] de Louis Poterat,
sur les motifs de la célèbre
Valse en la de Johannes Brahms,
Op. 39, no. 15. © Éditions
Salabert, Paris; 31Oct46;
EF5195.

[POTHIER, RICHARD]
Jack, you're dead! Lyric by
Walter Bishop, music by Dick
Miles, [pseud.] © Pic Music
Corp., Chicago; 1Apr47;
EP13584.

POTTER, ALMA LEONARD.
No place for June; words and music
by Alma Leonard Potter. © Alma
Leonard Potter, Lisbon, N. D.;
26Dec46; EP10734.

POTTER, HAROLD, 1906-
In my garden of memory; words
and music by Florence Erisman
and Harold Potter. © Rich-
mond Melodies, Staten Island,
N. Y.; 17Mar47; EP12630.
Rosie Marie and me; lyric by W.
Frank Brown, music by Harold
Potter. Keokuk, Iowa, Dr.
Billie Song Shoppe. © W.
Frank Brown, Keokuk, Iowa;
23Sep46; EP11193.

POTTLE, LOUISE KNAPP.
Mary's manger song; SSAA with option-
al violin obligato, [by] Louise
Knapp Pottle, [words by] William
Channing Gannett. © Harold
Flammer, inc., New York; 4Nov46;
EP10829.

111

POULTON, DOROTHY F   1904-
The flowers in their pretty hats;
[by] Dorothy F. Poulton. (In
Poulton, D. F., comp. Songs
for preschool children. p. 62)
© Dorothy F. Poulton, Columbus,
Ind.; 1Sep46; EP13182.
God, make me know; [words by]
John A. Martin, [music by]
Dorothy F. Poulton. (In Poul-
ton, D. F., comp. Songs for
preschool children. p.52)
© Dorothy F. Poulton, Columbus,
Ind.; 1Sep46; EP13178.
God sends the snow like wool;
[by] Dorothy F. Poulton. (In
Poulton, D. F., comp. Songs
for preschool children. p. 74)
© Dorothy F. Poulton, Columbus,
Ind.; 1Sep46; EP13184.
Heav'nly Father, be Thou near me;
[words by] Dorothy Errett,
[music by] Dorothy F. Poulton.
(In Poulton, D. F., comp.
Songs for preschool children.
p. 16) © Dorothy F. Poulton,
Columbus, Ind. [&] The Standard
Publ. Co., Cincinnati; 1Sep46;
EP13171.
The Heav'nly Father loves the
birds; 1st verse by Lillie A.
Faris, 2nd verse by Cecil
Frances Alexander, [music by]
Dorothy F. Poulton. (In Poul-
ton, D. F., comp. Songs for
preschool children. p 37)
© Dorothy F. Poulton, Columbus,
Ind. [&] The Standard Publ. Co.,
Cincinnati; 1Sep46; EP13173.
Here is the church; [by] Dorothy F
Poulton. (In Poulton, D. F.,
comp. Songs for preschool
children. p. 8) © Dorothy F.
Poulton, Columbus, Ind.;
1Sep46; EP13167.
I have a small family here; [by]
Dorothy F. Poulton, [words by]
Frances Weld Danielson. (In
Poulton, D. F., comp. Songs
for preschool children. p. 74)
© Dorothy F. Poulton, Columbus,
Ind.; 1Sep46; EP13185.
I want to send a whisper song;
[words by] Mrs. O. W. Scott,
[music by] Dorothy F. Poulton.
(In Poulton, D. F., comp.
Songs for preschool children.
p. 57) © Dorothy F. Poulton,
Columbus, Ind.; 1Sep46;
EP13181.
I'll help my mother; [by] Dorothy
F. Poulton. (In Poulton, D. F.,
comp. Songs for preschool
children. p 31) © Dorothy
F. Poulton, Columbus, Ind.;
1Sep46; EP13174.
Jesus loves the little children;
by Dorothy F. Poulton. (In
Poulton, D. F., comp. Songs
for preschool children. p 57)
© Dorothy F. Poulton, Columbus,
Ind.; 1Sep46; EP13180.
Let the little ones come unto
Me; [by] Dorothy F. Poulton.
(In Poulton, D. F., comp.
Songs for preschool children.
p. 28) © Dorothy F. Poulton,
Columbus, Ind.; 1Sep46;
EP13173.
Let us sing unto the Lord; [by]
Dorothy F. Poulton. (In Poul-
ton, D. F., comp. Songs for
preschool children. p. 12)
© Dorothy F. Poulton, Columbus,
Ind.; 1Sep46; EP13170.
The Lord is my Shepherd; [oy]
Dorothy F. Poulton. (In Poul-
ton, D. F., comp. Songs for
preschool children. p. 21)
© Dorothy F. Poulton, Columbus,
Ind.; 1Sep46; EP13172.

Oh, little children, do you
know? [Words by] Louise M.
Oglevee, [music by] Dorothy F.
Poulton. (In Poulton, D. F.,
comp. Songs for preschool
children. p. 53) © Dorothy
F. Poulton, Columbus, Ind.;
1Sep46; EP13179.
Open, shut them; [by] Dorothy F.
Poulton. (In Poulton, D. F.,
comp. Songs for preschool
children. p. 67) © Dorothy
F. Poulton, Columbus, Ind.;
1Sep46; EP13183.
Red, white and blue; by Dorothy
F. Poulton. (In Poulton, D.
F., comp. Songs for preschool
children. p 76) © Dorothy F.
Poulton, Columbus, Ind.;
1Sep46; EP13186.
Thank You for the world so sweet;
[by] Dorothy F. Poulton. (In
Poulton, D. F., comp. Songs
for preschool children. p. 38)
© Dorothy F. Poulton, Columbus,
Ind.; 1Sep46; EP13176.
This is the day that God has
made; [by] Dorothy F. Poulton.
(In Poulton, D. F., comp.
Songs for preschool children.
p. 11) © Dorothy F. Poulton,
Columbus, Ind.; 1Sep46; EP13169.
POUPARD, HENRI, 1901-   See also
Sauguet, Henri, pseud.
Petite messe pastorale; à 2
voix égales avec accompagne-
ment d'orgue, [by] Henri
Sauguet [pseud.] © Rouart,
Lerolle et Cie., Paris;
31Dec46; EF3559.
POWELL, EDNA.
Baby, that's what I can do; words
by Gloria Powell, music by Edna
Powell. © Cine-Mart Music
Publishing Co., Hollywood, Calif.;
30Dec46; EP11952.
POWELL, TEDDY.
Flea on a spree; by Teddy Powell
and Ben Homer, arr. by Ben Homer.
© Bregman, Vocco and Conn, inc.,
New York; 28Apr47; EP14104.
Piano-conductor score (orchestra)
and parts.
Ridin' the subways; composed by
Teddy Powell and Ray Conniff,
arr. by Ray Coniff. © Bregman,
Vocco and Conn, inc., New York;
28Apr47; EP14105. Piano-conductor
score (orchestra) and parts.
Some day; composed by Teddy Powell
and Ben Homer, arr. by Ben Homer.
© Bregman, Vocco and Conn, inc.,
New York; 28Apr47; EP14100.
Piano-conductor score (orchestra)
and parts.
The sphinx; by Teddy Powell and
Ben Homer, arr. by Ben Homer.
© Bregman, Vocco and Conn, inc.,
New York; 28Apr47; EP14102.
Piano-conductor score (orchestra)
and parts.
POWERS, MARY, 1895-
June, June; by Mary Powers. ©
Shelby Music Publishing Co.,
Detroit; 4Dec46; EP11122.
For voice and piano, with
guitar diagrams and chord
symbols.
POWERS, MAXWELL M   1911-
Boogie woogie nocturne; [by]
Maxwell Powers. New York,
Marks Ed. © Edward B. Marks
Music Corp., New York; 30Apr47;
EP11137.
The bugler and the drummer; [by]
Maxwell Powers. © Belwin,
inc., New York; 31Dec46;
EP10935. For piano solo.
Outdoor song; for piano, by Max-
well Powers. © The Boston Music
Co., Boston; 24Apr47; EP13941.

POYNTER, ARTHUR ROBERT, 1913-
My heart shall truly love you;
words by Joshua Sylvester, music
by Arthur Robert Poynter. ©
Frederick Harris Music Co., ltd.,
Oakville, Ont., Can.; 29Dec46;
EF4782. For voice and piano.
PRATER, EMERY.
The black and the gold; words
and music by Dick Lillard and
Emery Prater, arrangement by
Loren R. Williams. © The Stu-
dent Council, Neosho High
School, Neosho, Mo.; 20Mar47;
EP13141.
PRAY, ADA JORDAN.
Songs of love; music by Ada Jordan
Pray [words by Ina Coolbrith,
Alan Abbey, Grace Porterfield
Polk and others] San Francisco,
Jordan Publishing Co. © Ada
Jordan Pray, Durham, Calif.;
18May47; EP14535.
PRESTON, ELLA PURVIS.
Is this you, world, that used to be?
Words and music by Ella Purvis
Preston. © Nordyke Publishing
Co., Los Angeles; 31Aug45;
EP6571.
PRETINHO, PRINCIPE, 1882-
A vitoria é nossa ... de Principe
Pretinho, arrangement de Francis
Salabert. Direito de amar ...
de Arthur Costa et Delé, arrange-
ment de Francis Salabert. ©
Éditions Salabert, Paris; on
arrangement; 15Jan47; EF2526.
Piano-conductor score (orchestra)
and parts.
PRICE, FLORENCE B
Witch of the meadow; (S.S.A.)
[by] Florence B. Price, [words
by Mary Rolofson Gamble]
© Gamble Hinged Music Co.,
Chicago; 20Jul47; EP15049.
PRIMA, LOUIS.
Baciagaloop makes love on da stoop;
by Sid Tepper, Roy Brodsky and
Louis Prima. © Mills Music,
inc., New York; 16Apr47; EP6829.
For voice and piano, with chord
symbols.
PRINTZ, WARD FERNLEY, 1896-
Goodnight! God bless you ... [By]
Ward F. Printz. (In Ives, D. L.,
comp. Singcostasy. No. 109) ©
Ward F. Printz, Reading, Pa.;
20Sep46; EP11095.
I am the place where God shines
thru ... [by] Ward F. Printz,
[words] anon. (In Ives, D. L.,
comp. Singcestasy. No. 91) ©
Ward F. Printz, Reading, Pa.;
20Sep46; EP11096. Close score;
SATB.
Jesus! How wonderful Thou art to
me; by Ward F. Printz. (In Ives,
David Livingstone, comp. Specials.
[no.] 41) © Ward F. Printz, Read-
ing, Pa.; 10May47; EP14633.
Hymn.
PROKOF'EV, SERGEI SERGEEVICH, 1891-
(Concerto, violin, no.2) Concerto
no. 2 ... [by] Serge Prokofieff.
Op.63. [Ed. with special annotations by Louis Persinger]
© Leeds Music Corp., New York; on
foreword and editing; 15May47;
EP14415. Score (violin and piano)
and part.
Gavotte; (3rd movement from
"Classical symphony"); [by]
Serge Prokofieff. Op.25. As
arr. and played by Galla-Rini.
© Chart Music Publishing House,
inc., Chicago; on arrangement;
9May47; EP14566. For accordi-
on solo.

PROKOF'EV, SERGEI SERGEEVICH. Cont'd.

Marche, from "The love for three oranges." [By] Serge Prokofieff. Op.33. Arranged by Clair W. Johnson. © Rubank, inc., Chicago; on arrangement; 15Apr47; EP13499. Condensed score (band) and parts.

Peter and the wolf; by Serge' Prokofieff.... [words by Elsie-Jean, pseud.] arr. by Hugo Frey. © Hamilton-S. Gordon, inc., New York; on arrangement and words; 6Jun47; EP15062. For piano solo, with words.

Peter and the wolf, themes; by Sergei Prokofieff, [arr. by Hugo Frey] © Hamilton S. Gordon, inc., New York; on arrangement; 14Apr47; EP13737. For piano solo.

(Sonata, piano, no. 1) Sonata no. 1 (in F minor) for piano, [by] Serge Prokofieff. Op.1. [Ed. with special annotations by Harry Cumpson] © Leeds Music Corp., New York; on foreword and editing; 15May47; EP14419.

Ten pieces, from the ballet "Cinderella" [by] Serge Prokofieff. Op.70. For piano, ed. with special annotations by Ernõ Balogh. © Leeds Music Corp., New York; on foreword, editing; 15May47; EP14416.

Three pieces ... [by] Serge Prokofieff. Op. 96. Ed. with [foreword and] special annotations by Harry Cumpson. © Leeds Music Corp., New York; on foreword & editing; 14Apr47; EP13718. For piano solo.

PROSSER, IORWERTH W
Serenade; [words by] Henry W. Longfellow, [music by] Iorwerth W. Prosser. © Clayton F. Summy Co., Chicago; 3Apr47; EP13216. Score: TTBB.

PROVO, HARRY OTTO, 1913-
Waiting for you; lyrics by Milton C. Pfeiffer, music by Harry Provo, [arr. by Malcolm Lee] © Shelby Music Publishing Co., Detroit; on arrangement; 19Oct46; EP12032.

PUCCINI, GIACOMO, 1858-1924.
(La Bohème) Musetta's waltz-song, [from] La Bohème, by G. Puccini, arr. ... by Sidney Crooke. [c1946] © G. Ricordi & Co. (London) ltd., London; on arrangement; 27Feb47; EF5691. Score (violin and piano) and part.

Musetta's waltz-song. See his La Bohème.

PULLEN, OLIVE DUNGAN.
Tropical tunes ... music [by] Clive Dungan, lyrics [by] Gertrude Gore [pseud.], illustrations [by] H. Lawson. © The Boston Music Co., Boston; 15Jan47; EP13306. For piano solo, with words.

PURCELL, HENRY, 1658 or 9-1695.

The blessed Virgin's expostulation; [by] Henry Purcell ... the figured basses realized by Benjamin Britten, the vocal parts ed. by Peter Pears. London, Boosey & Co., ltd., London; on realisation of figured bass; 15Apr47; EF5546. For voice and piano.

Fantasia (no. 3) [by] Henry Purcell, for soprano, alto and tenor recorders, adapted by George Hunter. © E. C. Schirmer Music Co., Boston; 17Mar47; EP13403.

Glory and worship are before Him; [by] Henry Purcell ... for four-part chorus of women's voices, Psalm; 96:6,10, arr. by Gwynn S. Bement. © E. C. Schirmer Music Co., Boston; on arrangement; 22Apr47; EP13852.

Orpheus britannicus; [by] Henry Purcell, the figured basses realised by Benjamin Britten, the vocal parts ed. by Peter Pears. Seven songs. London, Boosey & Hawkes. © Boosey & Co., ltd., London; on realization of the figured bass & arrangement; 24Jan47; EF4868.

PURVIS, RICHARD.
Communion service; (Mass of Saint Nicholas), by Richard Purvis. © Coleman-Ross Co., inc., New York; 23Jan47; EP11681. Score: solo voice, chorus (SSAATTBB) and organ.

The road's end ... [Words by] Theodosia Garrison, [music by] Richard Purvis. © Elkan-Vogel Co., inc., Philadelphia; 25Mar47; EP13934. Score: soprano, chorus (SSA) and piano.

Spiritual; (from Four carol preludes) by Richard Purvis. © Leeds Music Corp., New York; 15May47; EP14421. For organ solo.

Winter passes over ... (S.S.A.), by Richard Purvis. © Leeds Music Corp., New York; on arrangement; 21Mar47; EP12852.

PUSA-TERI, COSMO ROOSEVELT.
Asperges me ... Vidi aquam. © J. Fischer & Bro., New York; 15Aug46; EP5749. For unison voices and piano or organ.

PUSCHECK, ADRIA BROWN, 1913-
Lost in love; lyric by Gordon Vanderburg, music by Adria Brown. © Graham Publishing Co., Hollywood, Calif.; 17Apr47; EP14194.

PUTNAM, GEORGE.
Rain on my heart; words by Claude Reese, music by George Putnam. © Chappell & Co., inc., New York; 1Feb47; EP12012.

PYLE, IVY MARIE, 1918-
Ambassadors for Jesus ... [By] Ivy M. Pyle. © Ivy M. Pyle, New Park, Pa.; 21Mar47; EP12835. Close score: SATB.

Q

QUATRE CANONS; [French words by B. Forest] © Rouart, Lerolle & Cie, Paris; on adaptation & French words; 1Mar41; EF1634. Score: 3-6 treble voices.

[QUEVIDO, RAYMOND]
Ann Sheridan; comp. by George Muttoo, lyrics and music by Radio, [pseud.] and Atilla, [pseud.] © Remick Music Corp., New York; 2May47; EP14286.

QUIROGA, MANUEL L
One miss for good measure; American adaptation of "Te lo juro yo", English lyric by Albert Gamse, Spanish lyric by Rafael De Leon, music by Manuel L. Quiroga. © Edward B. Marks Music Corp., New York; 14Dec46; EP11968.

QUISENBERRY, PHYLLIS W   1921-
B. T. C.; [by] Phyllis Quisenberry, [words by] Phyllis and Charles Quisenberry. © Charles M. and Phyllis W. Quisenberry, Pasadena, Calif.; 16Sep46; EP11567.

Heaven; duet ... arr. by Phyllis Quisenberry. © Phyllis W. and Charles M. Quisenberry, Pasadena, Calif.; 16Sep46; EP11568.

"Pressing toward perfection" ... [by Phyllis Quisenberry, words] by Charles and Phyllis Quisenberry. © Phyllis W. and Charles M. Quisenberry, Pasadena, Calif.; 16Sep46; EP13118.

R

RAAFF, ADRIANUS CORNELIS DE, 1911-
Papillon; [by] André de Raaff. Solo pour saxophone-alto & piano. © Edition Heuwekemeijer (Fa. A. J. Heuwekemeijer & B. F. van Gaal), Amsterdam; 28Dec46; EF5377. Score (saxophone and piano) and part.

RAAFE, ANDRE DE. See Raaff, Adrianus Cornelis de.

[RABE, ROBERT]
Rhythmic variety in piano music; [comp. by Robert Rabe]. © Theodore Presser Co., Philadelphia; on compilation; 10Apr47; EP13949.

RACHEL, sister, arr.
Polskie koledy. Polish Christmas carols; in ... easy arrangements with chords for piano accordion, by Sister Mary Rachel. Chicago, Felician Sisters Convent. © Felician Sisters, O.S.F., Chicago; 30Dec44; EP6756. For piano solo; Polish words.

RACHMANINOFF, SERGEI, 1873-1943.
(Concerto, piano, no. 1) Concerto no. 1. Op. 1. For piano and orchestra. New York, Charles Foley music pub. © Charles Foley, New York; on changes in music; 10Nov19; EP11354.

(Concerto, piano, no. 2) Melody from second piano concerto; [by] Sergei Rachmaninoff, arr. by Ada Richter. © Theodore Presser Co., Philadelphia; on arrangement; 28Dec46; EP10887. For piano solo.

(Concerto, piano, no. 2) Rachmaninoff's concerto march; adapted from themes from the "Concerto no. 2 in C minor. Opus 18" ... arr. by Dick Jacobs. © Bregman, Vocco and Conn, inc., New York 7Feb47; EP11897. Condensed score (band) and parts.

(Concerto, piano, no.2) Second concerto. Op. 18. First movement, by Sergei Rachmaninoff, abridged concert transcription by Walter Stockhoff. © Shattinger Piano & Music Co., St. Louis; on transcription; 21Mar47; EP11256. For piano solo.

(Concerto, piano, no. 2) Second concerto, opus 18, third movement; by Sergei Rachmaninoff. Abridged concert transcription by Walter Stockhoff. © Shattinger Piano & Music Co., St. Louis; on arrangement; 20May47; EP14844.

(Concerto, piano, no.2) Themes from Rachmaninoff's second concerto. [Op. 18. Transcription by Hugo Frey] © Hamilton S. Gordon, inc., New York; on arrangement; 27Jan47; EP13318. Caption title: Two themes from Rachmaninoff concerto no. 2. For piano solo.

(Concerto, piano, no.2) Themes from second concerto, by S. Rachmaninoff. Op.18. Arr ... by David Bennett. © Carl Fischer, inc., New York; on arrangement; 18Mar47; EP13160. Condensed score (band) and parts.

RACHMANINOFF, SERGEI. Cont'd.
Northern dream; English translation
by Wladimir Lakond, English adaptation by Olga Paul, music by
S. Rachmaninoff. © Edward B.
Marks Music Corp., New York;
on English translation & adaptation; 18Dec46; EP12029. Score:
SAA and piano.
Prelude; (Bells of Moscow) ...
[by] Sergei Rachmaninoff. Op.3,
no.2. Arr. by Ada Richter. ©
Theodore Presser Co., Philadelphia;
on arrangement; 28Dec46; EP10902.
For piano solo.
Rachmaninoff memory album; ed. and
arr. by Loopold W. Rovenger. ©
Bourne, inc., New York; on
arrangement; 12Jun46; EP6445. For
piano solo.
Rachmaninoff's concerto march. See
his Concerto, piano, no. 2.

Themes from Rachmaninoff's second
concerto. See his Concerto,
piano, no. 2.

RACK, RUDOLPH R   1912-
Moses; song, [words] by Lou Segal &
[music by] Rudy Rack. © Musicmakers, inc., Philadelphia;
28Feb47; EP12365.

RADICH, JOSEPH.
Orao polka, (The eagle); by
Joseph Radich, arr. by Rud.
Cornkovich. © Rudolph
Cornkovich, Bradley, Mich.;
on arrangement; 10Feb47;
EP12648. Parts: string
orchestra.

RAEZER, CORA MAE.
Dance lightly; for the piano, by
Cora Mae Raezer. © G. Schirmer,
inc., New York; 11Apr47; EP14079.
Pop-corn ... By Cora Mae Raezer.
© G. Schirmer, inc., New York;
13May47; EP14554. For piano
solo, with interlinear words.

RAINS, GRAY.
Easy pickin's; by Gray Rains, a
special arrangement by Frankie
Carle [pseud.] for piano. ©
Bregman, Vocco and Conn, inc., .
New York; on arrangement;
3Apr47; EP13362.

RALTON, HARRY. See
Raymond, Louis, pseud.

RAM, BUCK, 1908-
How big can you get? Words and
music by Dana Slawson and Buck
Ram. © Chappell & Co., inc.,
New York; 3Mar47; EP12784.

RAMEAU, JEAN PHILLIPE, 1683-1764.
(Hippolyte et Aricie) Hymn to
hight; (from the opera, "Hippo-
lyte et Aricie") ... with trans-
lation by Hugh Ross. (In Ross,
Hugh, arr. Sacred choruses for
women's or girls' voices.
p. 66-69) © G. Schirmer, inc.,
New York; on arrangement;
30Sep46; EP9786.
Les paladins; 1. suite, [by]
J.-Ph. Rameau, réalisation de
Roger Désormière. Paris,
L'Oiseau-Lyre, L. B. M. Dyer.
© Louise B. M. Dyer, Paris;
on realization; 30Dec46;
EF3829. Miniature score:
orchestra.

Hymn to night. See his Hippolyte
et Aricie.

RAMEY, VELMA.
A garden of Eden; words and music
by Velma Ramey. © Nordyke
Publishing Co., Los Angeles;
8Mar47; EP13524.

RAMIREZ, RAFAEL.
Esta noche, (To-night) ...
English words by Joe Davis,
Spanish words and music by
Rafael Ramirez. © Caribbean
Music, inc., New York;
23Jun47; EP15145.
Nuestro amor. (Our wonderful
love) ... English words by
Joe Davis, Spanish words and
music by Rafael Ramirez. ©
Caribbean Music, inc., New
York; 17Mar47; EP12645.
¿Por qué insistes? Bolero, letra
y música de Rafael Ramirez.
© Peer International Corp.,
New York; 27Feb47; EP12762.
Yo quisiera ... letra y musica de
Rafael Ramirez. © Peer Inter-
national Corp., New York;
29Oct46; EP13616.

RAMIREZ, ROGER.
(Boy, what a girl) I just refuse to
sing the blues; [music] by Roger
"Ram" Ramirez and [words by]
Walter Bishop. Featured ... in the
Herald picture "Boy, what a girl".
© Walter Bishop, New York;
17Mar47; EP6666.
I just refuse to sing the blues.
See his Boy, what a girl.

RAMIREZ, SANTOS.
Que celosal ... Letra y música
de Santos Ramirez (Niño),
arreglo de H. Bello. Habana.
© Peer International Corp.,
New York; 15May47; EP3338.
Piano-conductor score (orches-
tra, with words) and parts.

RAMPONI, GIACOMO, 1911-
La fisarmonica in orchestra;
breve metodo di perfezionamento,
[by] Giacomo Ramponi. ©
Carisch, s.a., Milan; 16May47;
EF3786.

RANDEGGER, ALBERT, 1832-1911.
Save me, O God ... [by] Albert
Randegger, choral arrangement
by H. Lindsay Nordan. © Clayton F. Summy Co., Chicago; on
arrangement; 3Feb47; EP12249.
Score: chorus (SATTBB) and
organ.

RANGSTROM, TURE, 1884-
Ur Kung Eriks visor; av Gustaf
Fröding, för en röst med piano
av Ture Rangström. © Nordiska
Musikförlaget, a/b, Stockholm;
on 5 songs; 1Jul19; EF5390-5394.
For voice and piano. Contents.-
I. En visa om när jag var lustig
med Welam Welamsson.- II. En
visa om mig och herren Herkules.-
III. En visa till Karin när
V. Kung Eriks sista visa.

RAPLEY, FELTON, 1907-
Breton berceuse; for organ, by
Felton Rapley. © Ascherberg,
Hopwood & Crew; ltd., London;
30Apr47; EF5270.

RAPP, RAYMOND E   1895-
Round Table song; words by Horace L.
Stevenson, music by Raymond E. Rapp.
© Round Table International, Denver;
27Mar47; EP12960. Close score: SATB.

RASCHIG, ANITA.
London Bridge; for the piano, by
Anita Raschig. © G. Schirmer,
inc., New York; 13May47;
EP14555.

RASLEY, JOHN M
Alleluia carol; by John M. Rasley.
© Theodore Presser Co., Phila-
delphia; 3Jan47; EP11028.
Score: chorus (SATB) and piano.

RATCLIFFE, DESMOND.
In Salutation; carol for S.A.T.B.,
(unacc.), words by May Sarson,
music by Desmond Ratcliffe. ©
Novello & Co., ltd., London;
15Nov47; EF3459.

RATH, HELEN.
Lullaby land; by Helen Rath, for the
piano. © Herold Flammer, inc.,
New York; 31Dec46; EP11427.

RATHAUS, KAROL, 1895-
The boatman and the maiden.
Wodnik i dziewczyna, Polish
folk song; four part mixed
voices, S.A.T.B., English version by F. C. W., choral setting by Karol Rathaus. © M.
Witmark & Sons, New York; on
arrangement & English words;
18Jun47; EP15279.
The boatman and the maiden.
Wodnik i dziewczyna; Polish
folk song, three part women's
voices, S.S.A. English version
by F.C.W., choral setting by
Karol Rathaus. © M. Witmark &
Sons, New York; on arrangement
and English words; 18Jun47;
EP15276.
Oh, yody, yody. Kaj się działy one
lata. Polish folk song, four
part mixed voices ... English
version by F. C. W., choral
setting by Karol Rathaus. ©
M. Witmark & Sons, New York; on
English version and choral setting;
6Jun47; EP15003.
Oh, Yody, Yody. Kaj się działy one
luta. Polish folk song, three
part women's voices: S.S.A.
English version by F. C. W.,
choral setting by Karol Rathaus.
© M. Witmark & Sons, New York;
on English version and choral
setting; 6Jun47; EP15006.
There will I don my cloak. Wezme
ja kontusz. Polish folk song ...
English version by F. C. W.,
choral setting by Karol Rathaus.
© M. Witmark & Sons, New York;
on English version and choral
setting; 6Jun47; EP15004. Score:
SSSA and piano.
There will I don my cloak. Wezma
ja kontusz. Polish folk song,
four part mixed voices ... English
version by F. C. W., choral setting
by Karol Rathaus. © M. Witmark &
Sons, New York; on English version
and choral setting; 6Jun47; EP15005.
Three English songs, for high or
medium voice and piano; [music by]
Karol Rathaus. © Associated
Music Publishers, inc., New York;
on 3 songs. Contents.- [v.1] As
I ride, As I ride (through the
Metidja to Abd-El-Kadr); words by
Robert Browning © 16Dec46;
EP11142) - [v.2, The oblation;
words by Algernon Charles Swinburne
(© 20Dec46; EP11143) - [v.3] Sweet
music; words by William Shakespeare
(© 16Dec46; EP11144)

RAVANELLO, ORESTE.
Mass in honor of St. Albert; for
unison or two-part with organ
acc., by Oreste Ravanello.
Op. 24, Arr. and ed. by Cyr
de Brant [pseud.] © J. Fischer
& Bro., New York; on arrangement; 27Mar47; EP6811.

RAVASINI, NINO, 1900-
Serenatella a mamma ... musica di
N. Ravasini. © Casa Editrice
Musicale "Sonorfilm," Milano;
9Sep46; EF3227. Piano-conductor
score: orchestra.

RAVASINI, NINO. Cont'd.
Sola ... (in una notte di
tormento) ... [by] D. Vasin
[pseud.], parole di P.
Rost e Malatesta. © Carisch,
s. a., Milan; 3Mar40; EF3717.
Piano-conductor score
(orchestra, with words), and
parts.
Il tamburo della banda d'Affori
... di Rastelli, Panzeri [and]
Ravasini. Milano, Edizioni
Musicali Irradio di N.
Casiroli. © Casa Editrice
"Nazionale" Musicale, Milano;
4Nov46; EF3225. For voice and
piano, with chord symbols.
Triste serenata ... musique de
Nino Ravasini, parolee de G.
C. Testoni. © SIDEM, Société
Intercontinentale d'Éditions
Musicales, Vaduz - Geneva,
Switzerland; 31Dec46; EF5159.
Italian words.

RAVEL, MAURICE, 1875-1937.
Jeux d'eau; [by] Ravel [arr. by
Castelnuovo Tedesco, a tran-
scription for violin and piano,
violin part ed. by Joseph
Szigeti. © Carl Fischer, inc.,
New York; on transcription;
16Apr47; EP13902. Score and
part.
Pavane for a dead princess; [by]
Ravel, arr. for easy piano solo
by Mark Ashley [pseud.] ©
Century Music Publishing Co.,
New York; on arrangement; 31May47;
EP14734.

RAVIZE, ANGÈLE, 1887-
Trente-deux leçons de solfège sans
altérations; préparatoires aux
concours interscolaires, par
Angèle Ravize. © Durand & Cie.,
Paris; 10Jan47; EF34446.

RAWICZ, MARYAN.
Snow-flakes ... by Maryan
Rawicz. © Arcadia Music
Publishing Co., ltd., London;
11Mar47; EF3772. For piano
solo.
Spinning-wheel ... by Maryan
Rawicz. © Arcadia Music
Publishing Co., ltd., London;
on alterations & one new
movement; 11Mar47; EF3773.
For piano solo.

RAWSON, DOERING HECTOR ADOLPHE
FRANÇOIS, 1904-
Traité d'harmonisation pratique
... ouvrage complet sur la do-
cumentation technique de l'accor-
deon [by H. Rawson and M. Camia]
© M. Camia, Paris; 31Jul46;
EF4605.

RAWSON, H. See
Rawson, Doering Hector Adolphe
Francois.

RAY, TED, pseud. See
Olden, Charlie.

RAYBURN, RHETHA, 1896-
Tune up time for love; words and
music by Rhetha Rayburn. ©
Rhetha Rayburn, Los Angeles;
15Feb47; EP12095.
When you were mine; words and music
by Rhetha Rayburn. © Rhetha
Rayburn, Los Angeles; 15Feb47;
EP12096.

RAYE, DON.
Bounce me brother with a solid four;
by Don Raye [and] Hughie Prince,
arr. by Fud Livingston. © Leeds
Music Corp., New York; on arrangement; 14Apr47; EP13744. Condensed score (orchestra) and parts.

RAYMOND, LOUIS, pseud. See also
Frieber, Louis.

Waltz of my dreams ... Music by
Louis Raymond, orch. by Geo. L.
Zalva. © Arcadia Music Pub.
Co., London; 26Jul46; EF3097.
Piano-conductor score:
orchestra.

RAYNA, JEAN.
Rien qu' avec toi; paroles de Jean
Rayna, musique de Jean Rayna &
Maurizi. © Éditions Paris-Broad-
way, Paris; 31Dec46; EF3877.

RAYNER, EDWARD, pseud. See
Frangkiser, Carl.

READ, GARDNER, 1913-
Six intimate moods; for violin
and piano. Op.35 ... By Gardner
Read. © Carl Fischer, inc.,
New York; 10Apr47; EP13483.

[READ, GEORGE]
Dancing on the moon. (Bailando en
la luna) Words and music by Jorge
Chileno [pseud.] © Croxton
Publishing Co., Los Angeles;
3Feb47; EP12085.

READE, CHARLES.
Stockin' full of blues; by Dick
Charles, [pseud.] Phil Perry,
[pseud.] [and] Charles Reade.
© Leeds Music Corp., New York;
24Jan47; EP11805. For voice and
piano, with chord symbols.

REBE, LOUISE CHRISTINE.
In a Hungarian market place;
piano solo by Louise
Christine Rebe. © Clayton
F. Summy Co., Chicago;
14Apr47; EP13790.

RED RIVER DAVE, pseud. See
McEnery, David.

REDEEMING LOVE; a book of gospel songs
... Authors: Nolin Jeffress ... T.
S. Williams [and others] ©
Jeffress Music Co., Crossett,
Ark.; 15Nov46; EP11034.

REED, HENRY.
You are my world; song, words
by Eric Maschwitz, music by
Henry Reed. © Keith, Prowse
& Co., ltd, London; 28May47;
EF3626.

REEDER, JUNE WEYBRIGHT. See
Weybright, June.

REES-DAVIES, IEUAN.
Close thine eyes. (Cyn cau
llygaid) For chorus (or quartet) of female voices, (S.S.A.A)
(unaccompanied) Words attributed to King Charles I, translation by Wil Ifan, music by
Ieuan Rees-Davies. London, J.
Curwen, New York, G. Schirmer,
sole agents. © Ieuan Rees-
Davies, London; 20Mar47;
EF5466.

REESE, CLAUDE.
I'm always dreaming about you; words
and music by Claude Reese. ©
Cine-Mart Music Publishing Co.,
Hollywood, Calif.; 1Dec46; EP12104.

REEVES, WALTER LEE, 1902-
Be ready judgement day; words and
music by Walter L. Reeves. ©
Walter Lee Reeves, sr., Brooklyn;
22Apr47; EP13951. Hymn.

REID, BILLY.
Three beautiful words of love;
words and music by Billy Reid
[London], World Wide Music Co.
© Peter Maurice Music Co., ltd.,
New York; 28Nov46; EF4787.
When China boy meets China girl;
words and music by Billy Reid.
London, Macmelodies. © Peter
Maurice Music Co., ltd., New
York; 1May47; EF5358. For voice
and piano, with chord symbols.
Melody also in tonic sol-fa
notation.

REID, DON.
Dit-dot-dit (in twenty-five words
or less); words and music by
Don Reid. © Chappell & Co.,
inc., New York; 12May47;
EP14515.
The old square dance is back again.
See his People are funny.
(People are funny) The old square
dance is back again; [words and
music]by D. Reid and Henry To-
bias. © Leeds Music Corp., New
York; on additional lyrics;
5Apr46; EP4670.

REILLY, JAMES A   1854-1940.
Easter choral repertoire; for
four mixed voices and organ,
comp. by James A. Reilly. ©
McLaughlin & Reilly Co.,
Boston; on compilation of
v.3; 24Mar47; EP13011.

REILLY, JAMES A   1854-1940,
comp.
Easter choral repertoire; for
four mixed voices and organ,
comp. by James A. Reilly.
© McLaughlin & Reilly Co.,
Boston; v.1; 19Feb47; v.2;
10Mar47; EP12302, 12779.
Part of the words in Latin,
part in English.
Liturgical motets; for four part
men's voices, comp. by James
A. Reilly. © McLaughlin &
Reilly Co., Boston; 19Feb47;
EP12300.

REINHARDT, DONALD S
Trumpet mechanisms; a streamlined
school of technique ... by D. S.
Reinhardt and David Gornston.
© Leeds Music Corp., New York;
on new exercises & additions;
20Jun46; EP4870.

REISFELD, BERT.
Fiesta de las flores; by Bert
Reisfeld, for piano. © Breg-
man, Vocco and Conn, inc.,
New York; 14Mar47; EP13502.

REISFELD, BERT, arr.
Deep river; arr. by Bert Reisfeld.
© Century Music Publishing Co.,
New York; on arrangement;
31May47; EP14738. For piano
solo, with interlinear words.
Standin' in the need of prayer;
arr. by Bert Reisfeld. ©
Century Music Publishing Co.,
New York; on arrangement;
31May47; EP14732. For piano
solo, with interlinear words.

REISTRUP, JAMES, 1892-
The brook; for piano, [by]
James Reistrup. © McKinley
Publishers, inc., Chicago;
28Feb47; EP12412.
Sunday morning; for piano, by
James Reistrup. © The Com-
posers Press, inc., New York;
EP14908.

RENAULT, ANDRÉ, 1906-
Danse no.1; piano à deux mains,
[by] André Renault. © Durand &
Cie., Paris; 3Jan47; EF3502.
Danse no. 2; piano à deux mains,
[by] André Renault. © Durand
& Cie., Paris; 3Jan47; EF3503.
Divertissement; pour piano, [by]
André Renault. © Durand & Cie.,
Paris; 3Jan47; EF3520.
Sérénade de fantasio; pour piano,
[by] André Renault. © Durand
& Cie., Paris; 3Jan47; EF3519.

RENSTROM, MOISELLE.
You haunt me; words & music by
Moiselle Renstrom. © Nordyke
Pub. Co., Los Angeles; 15Nov46;
EP11924.

115

REUTER, ADELADE MAY, 1897-
Consecration; by Adelade M.
Reuter. [c1946] © Adelade May
Reutor, Foxboro, Mass.; 2Jan47;
EP11558. For voice and piano.

REVEL, HARRY, 1905-
(Earl Carroll's vanities)
Rolling along, from Earl
Carroll's vanities; lyrics
by Earl Carroll, music by
Harry Revel. © Harry Von
Tilzer Music Pub. Co., New
York; 12Jun47; EP15031.
(Earl Carroll's vanities) You,
wonderful you, from Earl
Carroll's vanities; lyrics by
Earl Carroll, music by Harry
Revel. © Harry Von Tilzer
Music Pub. Co., New York;
12Jun47; EP15030.
(It happened on Fifth Avenue) It's
a wonderful, wonderful feeling;
words and music by Harry Revel.
Featured in "It happened on Fifth
Avenue." © Chappell & Co., inc.,
New York; 21Jan47; EP11652.
(It happened on Fifth Avenue) Speak,
my heart! Words and music by Harry
Revel. Featured in "It happened on
Fifth Avenue." © Chappell & Co.,
inc., New York; 21Jan47; EP11653.
(It happened on Fifth Avenue) You're
everywhere; words by Paul Francis
Webster, music by Harry Revel.
Featured in "It happened on Fifth
Avenue". © Chappell & Co., inc.,
New York; 21Jan47; EP11650.
It's a wonderful, wonderful feel-
ing. See his It happened on
Fifth Avenue.
Rolling along. See his Earl
Carroll's vanities.
Speak, my heart! See his It hap-
pened on Fifth Avenue.
Stay as sweet as you are; four
part male chorus ... arr. by
William Stickles. Lyric and
music by Mack Gordon and Harry
Revel. © Crawford Music Corp.,
New York; on arrangement;
13Jun47; EP15152.
Stay as sweet as you are; four
part mixed chorus ... arr. by
William Stickles, lyric and
music by Mack Gordon and Harry
Revel. © Crawford Music Corp.,
New York; on arrangement;
13Jun47; EP15150.
Stay as sweet as you are; three
part female chorus (S.S.A.)
arr. by William Stickles, lyric
and music by Mack Gordon and
Harry Revel. © Crawford Music
Corp., New York; on arrange-
ment; 10Jun47; EP15122.
You, wonderful you. See his Earl
Carroll's vanities.
You're everywhere. See his It
happened on Fifth Avenue.

RHEA, RAYMOND.
The everlasting mercies of our
Lord; by Raymond Rhea, arr.
and ed. for mixed chorus,
S.S.A.A.T.T.B.B., by Noble
Cain. [Words by Ralph E.
Storey] © Choral Art
Publications, New York; on
arrangement; 8May47; EP14392.
Ferns; by Raymond Rhea, arr. and
ed. for women's chorus, S.S.A.A.,
by Noble Cain. © Choral Art
Publications, New York; on
arrangement; 8May47; EP14394.

[RHODES, HELEN (GUY)]
Because; music by Guy d'Hardelot
[pseud.], transcribed for piano
by Albert Sirmay. N[ew] Y[ork],
Chappell & Co. © Chappell & Co.,
ltd., London; on transcription;
21Jan47; EP4844.

RHODES, MRS. W. I. See
Rhodes, Helen (Guy)

RHYNES, MYLES ANDREW J . 1885-
I'm so glad God knows my heart;
by ... M.A.J. Rhynes. © Myles
Andrew J, Rhynes, Fayetteville,
N. C.; 1Sep46; EP11093. Close
score: SATB.
When will that day of rest come?
By ... M.A.J. Rhynes. © Myles
Andrew J. Rhynes, Fayetteville,
N. C.; 1Sep46; EP11092. Close
score: SATB.

RICCA, LOU.
Horizontal; words by Hal David,
music by Lou Ricca. © Leeds
Music Corp., New York; 24Jan47;
EP11806.

RICCIARDI, V
Suspiro 'e chitarra ... versi di
L. Cacciapuoti, musica di V.
Ricciardi. Napoli, Gesa. ©
Italian Book Co., New York;
5Dec46; EP5577.

RICE, ROBERT R
I'll step aside; words by Della E.
Rice, music by Robert R. Rice.
© Cine-Mart Music Publishing Co.,
Hollywood, Calif.; 1Dec46; EP12109.

RICE, MRS. WILLIAM HENRY.
Don't go away without Jesus ... [words
by] Wm. H. Rice, arr. by Mrs. W. H.
R. © William Henry Rice, Wheaton,
Ill.; 23Nov46; EP12251. Close score:
SATB.

RICH, MAX.
I'm looking for a word; words and
music by Rose Cardinal and Max
Rich. © Bob Miller, inc., New
York; 30Dec46; EP11378.
Love lost it's way; words and music
by Manuel M. Warner and Max Rich.
© Bob Miller, inc., New York;
30Dec46; EP11377.

RICHARD, LEO, 1883-
An aunt; words by Josephine A.
Zakrzewski, music by Leo &
Hector Richard. © Nordyke
Publishing Co., Los Angeles;
5Mar47; EP13242.
Escape; words by Anna T. Braye.
© Anna T. Braye, Hollywood, Calif.;
7Aug46; EP11544.
I am now in your arms; words
by Alexander C. Andrzejczak,
music by Leo and Hector
Richard. © Alexander C.
Andrzejczak, Erie, Pa.;
21Feb47; EP15022.
Indiana Jim; words by Naomi
Thilking, music by Leo and
Hector Richard. © Nordyke
Publishing Co., Los Angeles;
5Mar47; EP13259.
Last night; words by Lucy Byrd, music
by Leo and Hector Richard. ©
Lucy Byrd, Montclair, N. J.; 10Aug46;
EP11689.
Mother; words by Ethel Pierce,
music by Leo and Hector Rich-
ard. © Ethel Pierce, Waterloo,
Iowa; 12May47; EP14594.
Our allies were convoying; words
by Lenard W. Monroe, music by
Leo & Hector Richard. [c1946]
© Nordyke Publishing Co., Los
Angeles; 5Mar47; EP13565.
Our most precious boys, they move no
more; words by Alexander C. Andrzej-
czak, music by Leo and Hector Richard.
[c1946] © Alexander C. Andrzejczak,
Erie, Pa.; 24Jan47; EP12065.
Salute to victory; words by Anna
T. Braye, music by Leo and
Hector Richard. © Anna T.
Braye, Hollywood, Calif.;
25Jan46; EP12458.

RICHARD BROS.
Darling mother; words by J. D.
Scholes, music by Richard Bros.
© Nordyke Publishing Co., Los
Angeles; 8Mar47; EP13522.

[RICHARDS, DON]
How your trulove to know; song
with piano acc., words by
Elizabeth Madox Roberts, music
by Martin Diller, [pseud.] ©
Carl Fischer, inc., New
York; 20Mar47; EP15201.

RICHARDS, JOHN HERBERT, 1900-
Why did you? ... Words by Dorothy
M. Cornell, music by Johnny
Richards. © John (Johnny) H.
Richards, Philadelphia; 14Jun47;
EP15076.
You were not true; by Johnny
Richards. © John H. Richards,
Philadelphia; 21Apr47; EP14204.
For voice and piano, with chord
symbols.
You were not true ... words &
music by Johnny Richards. ©
John H. Richards, Philadelphia;
on arrangement; 2May47; EP14205.
For guitar solo.

RICHARDS, MARION ROE, 1905-
Breathe on me, breath of God ...
music by Marion Richards.
[words from Episcopal hymn book]
Toledo, A. V. Higgins. © Marion
Roe Richards, Toledo; 7Apr47;
EP13671.
Life eternal ... by Marion Roe
Richards, Toledo, A. V. Higgins.
© Marion Roe Richards, Toledo;
4Apr47; EP13802. For voice and
organ.
Pal of my memories ... music by
Marion Richards ... [lyrics by
James La Roque] Toledo, A. V.
Higgins. © Marion R. Richards
& James La-Roque, Toledo;
7Apr47; EP13670.

RICHARDSON, CLIVE.
Romantic interlude; piano solo by
Clive Richardson. © Chappell
& co., ltd., London; 19Mar47;
EP5503.

RICHEPIN, TIARKO FRANCOIS DENIS, 1884-
L'auberge qui chante; [words by]
Georges Hirsch & André de Badet,
musique de T. Richepin, airs
additionnels de A. de Badet ...
& Trémolo. © C. Joubert & Cie,
Paris; 10ct41; EP382.
Le forgeron de Gretna-Green ...
paroles de Louis Bergen-
Leplay, musique de Tiarko
Richepin. © Henry Lemoine &
Cie., Paris; 25Dec46; EP3582.

RICHTER, ADA.
You can play the piano! A book
for the older beginner by Ada
Richter. © Theodore Presser
Co., Philadelphia; on new
music and arrangements; pt. 1,
13Jun47; EP15088.

RICHTER, WILLIAM BENSON, 1901-
Eenee, meenee, mynee, moe;
words and music by William
Benson Richter. © William
Benson Richter, Philadelphia;
31Mar47; EP13152.

RIDGWAY, JOHN.
Jack's boogie ... By John Ridgway
and Joseph Goldberg. © Grimus
Music Publishers, Philadelphia;
6May47; EP14184. For piano solo.

RIEGGER, WALLINGFORD, 1885-
Children of the heavenly Father;
S.S.A. with soprano solo ...
Swedish folk song, arr. by
Wallingford Riegger. © Harold
Flammer, inc., New York; on
arrangement; 7May47; EP14368.
New and old; twelve pieces for
piano, complete with an analy-
sis and explanation of modern
terms by Wallingford Riegger.
© Boosey & Hawkes, inc., New
York; 24Apr47; EP13869.

116

RIEGGER, WALLINGFORD. Cont'd.
(Quartet, strings, no.1) String
quartet no. 1. Opus 30. [By]
Wallingford Riegger. © Arrow
Music Press, inc., New York;
31Dec46; EP12221. Miniature
score.
Skip to my Lou; mountain dance tune
arr. by Wallingford Riegger for
chorus of mixed voices. © Harold
Flammer, inc., New York; on arrangement; 31Dec46; EP11422.

RIETI, VITTORIO, 1898-
Sinfonia tripartita; (symphony
no. 4) [by] Vittorio Rieti.
© Associated Music Publishers, inc.,
New York; 18Apr47; EP14069.
Miniature score.

RIFENBERG, IDA O   1873-
Somebody here needs the Savior ...
by ... Ida O. Rifenberg. © Ida
O. Rifenberg, Hot Springs, Ark.;
8May47; EP15056. Close score:
SATB; shape-note notation.

RIFKIN, IRVING, 1918-
Whistle-stop town; words and
music by Vic Lourie and Irving
Rifkin. © Top Music Publishers,
inc., New York; 14Apr47;
EP13583.

RIGGS, SYLVIA K
It gets me; words and music by
Sylvia K. Riggs. © Nordyke
Publishing Co., Los Angeles;
5Mar47; EP13563.

RIGHTER, CHARLES B
Taps; arr. by C. B. Righter, for
solo cornet, echo cornet, brass
harmony, and tympani or muffled
snare drum. © Gamble Hinged
Music Co., Chicago; on arrangement; 19May47; EP14494. Condensed score and parts.

RIIS, AMDI, 1911-
Byt, byt, byt. See his Naar Katten
er ude.
(Naar Katten or ude) Byt, byt,
byt. Tror du paa Eventyr.
[From] Asa-Filmen "Naar Katten
er ude"; Tekst: Arvid Müller,
Musik; Amdi Riis. © Wilhelm
Hansen, Musik-Forlag, Copenhagen;
17Feb47; EF3437, 3436.
(Tivoli-Revyen 1946) Naar Skovon er
grøn, [from Tivoli-Revyen 1946];
tekst: Epe [pseud.] musik: Amdi
Riis. © Wilhelm Hansen, Musik-Forlag,
Copenhagen; 6Jul46; EF4837. For
voice and piano.
Tror du paa Eventyr. See his Naar
Katten er ude.

RIISAGER, KNUDÅGE, 1897-
(Pilatus) Drømme ømme, tyssende,
stille; Julius Sang af Kaj
Munk's Skuespil "Pilatus," [by]
Knudåge Riisager. © Wilhelm
Hansen, Musik-Forlag, Copenhagen;
3Feb47; EF5441.

RILEY, LOWELL.
The eternal search; words by ...
Roy A. Burkhart, music by
Lowell Riley, [for] S.A.T.B.
© Boosey & Hawkes, inc., New
York; 24Apr47; EP13848.

[RIMSKIĬ-KORSAKOV, NIKOLAĬ ANDREEVICH]
1844-1908.
The flight of the bumble bee; [by]
N. Rimsky-Korsakoff, transcribed by
Walter L. Rosemont] Bumble bee
boogie; [adaptation by Jack Edwards
and Walter L. Rosemont] © Edwards
Music Co., New York; on adaptation;
17Feb47; EP13386. For piano solo.
Lost love; [based on] (Song of India)
music by Rimsky-Korsakoff, words
by Lou Segal, [arr. by R. R. Rack]
© Musicmakers, inc., Philadelphia;
on words; 15Mar47; EP12366.

(Scheherezade) The young prince
and the young princess from
'Scheherezade' ... [by N.
Rimsky-Korsakoff, words by
Elsie-Jean, pseud.] arr. by
Hugo Frey. © Hamilton S.
Gordon, inc., New York; on
arrangement and words; 6Jun47;
EP15064. For piano solo, with
words.
the young princess. See his
Scheherezade.

RINGLE, DAVE, 1894-
I should have used my head and
not my heart; words and music
by Rudy Russo and Dave Ringlo.
© Dave Ringlo, Jersey City;
18Jun47; EP15179.
This red, red rose is so like you;
lyric and melody by Edward Dillen
and Dave Ringlo. © Dave Ringlo,
New York; 15Dec46; EP11554.

RINGWALD, ROY.
The song of Christmas; the story of
the Nativity as told in Christmas
songs, carols, and Biblical verses,
by Roy Ringwald. For soloists,
narrators, and mixed chorus, with
four-hand piano or organ acc. ...
[c1946] © Words and Music, inc.,
New York; 28Jan47; EP11899.

RINI, ANTHONY GALLA- See
Galla-Rini, Anthony.

RIO, PEPE DEL. See
Del Rio, Pepe.

RITSIARDĒS, IOSEPH MICHAEL, 1900-
Dyo mayra matia me gelasane. See
his Prosphygē stēn O. E. E.
(Eythymes peripeteies) Tha
brō kainourgia agapē ...
etichoi: G. Iōannidē, mousikē:
I. Ritsiardē. Apo tēn
epitheōresi Eythymes peripeteies,
2. ekdosis. Athēnai, Ekdoseis
Gaftanou. © Michael Etienne
Gaetanos. Athens; 5Jan47;
EP5345. For voice and piano.
Pane tosa chronia. See his
Prosphygē stēn O. E. E.
(Prosphygē stēn O.E.E.) Dyo
mayra matia me gelasane ...
apo tēn ... theatrikē
epityehia "Prosphygē stēn
O.E.E." ... Etichoi: K.
Maniatakē, mousikē: I.
Ritsiardē. Athēnai, Ekdoseis
Gaftanou. © Michael Etienne
Gaetanos, Athens; 22Feb47;
EP5343. For voice and piano.
(Prosphygē stēn O.E.E.) Pane
tosa chronia ... apo tēn ...
theatrikē epityehia Prosphygē
stēn O.E.E. ... Etichoi
Kōsta Maniatakē, mousikē I.
Ritsiardē. © Michael Etienne
Gaetanos, Athens; 22Feb47;
EP5342. For voice and piano.
Tha brō kainourgia agapē. See his
Eythymes peripeteies.

RITTER, TEX.
Rye whiskey; Tex Ritter's version.
© Tex Ritter Music Publications,
inc., New York; 15Feb47; EP12010.
For voice and piano, with chord
symbols.

RITTER, WALTER SCHNELL, 1894-
Saint Nicholas; [by Walter S.
Ritter, words by Walter S.
Ritter and Gertrude E. Ritter]
© Walter S. Ritter & Gertrude
E. Ritter, Detroit; 15Feb47;
EP10896.

RIVERA,   C   arr.
Philippine folk songs, re-arr.
by J. C. Rivera. San Francisco, Agcaoili Music Co. ©
J. C. Rivera, San Francisco;
31Dec46; EP15149.

RIVERA, PETE.
No me haces falta. (I do not
love you) ... English words by
Joe Davis, Spanish words and
music by Pete Rivera. ©
Caribbean Music, inc., New York;
28Apr47; EP13955.
Por primera vez. (You're the
answer to my dreams) ... English
words by Joe Davis, Spanish
words and music by Pete Rivera.
© Caribbean Music, inc., New
York; 28Apr47; EP13957.
Que vida. (What a life) ... Eng-
lish words by Joe Davis, Spanish
words and music by Pete Rivera.
[c1946] © Caribbean Music,
inc., New York; 28Apr47;
EP13956.
Te esperare. (I'm waiting for you)
... English words by Joe Davis,
Spanish words and music by Pete
Rivera. © Caribbean Music, inc.,
New York; 28Apr47; EP13954.

RIVERO, FACUNDO.
Learning Latin (from Latin songs)
(Yo estoy aprendiendo inglés)...
Music and Spanish lyric by Fa-
cundo Rivero, English lyric by
Benjamin Blossner. © Peer Inter-
national Corp., New York; on
English lyric; 13Dec46; EP13625.

[RIVERS, JACK]
Texas tornado; by Jimmy Wakely
[and Jack Rivers] © Fairway
Music Co., Hollywood, Calif.;
31Dec46; EP11326. For voice
and piano, with chord symbols.

RIVIER, JEAN FERNAND ALEXIS FÉLIX,
1896-
(Concerto, piano, no. 1) Con-
certo no. 1, en ut; pour piano
et orchestre, [by] Jean Rivier.
Paris, L. de Lacour, Éditions
Costallat. © Lucien de Lacour,
Paris; 31Oct46; EP3293.
Score: piano 1-2.

RIZZO, ANDY, comp. and arr.
The Andy Rizzo program album;
for piano-accordion, a collection
of marches, polkas and waltzes,
selected and arr. by Andy
Rizzo. © Carl Fischer, inc.,
New York; on arrangements and
selection; 6Mar47; EP12654.

RIZZO, Joe.
Never like this. Así eres tu.
English lyrics by Bill Ficarnoy,
Spanish lyrics by Eddie Gomez,
music by Joe Rizzo. © Peer
International Corp., New York;
18Apr47; EP13984.

ROBB, J   D   1892-
Pictures of New Mexico; [by J. D.
Robb ... For piano solo. ©
Associated Music Publishers, inc.,
New York; 2May47. Contents.-
[v.1] The bells of the mission.
Horseback over the sagebrush
plain (© EP15164)- [v.2] In the
Indian village. Siesta time
(© EP15165)- [v.3] In the
cottonwood (© EP15163)

ROBBIANI, IGINO, 1884-
Guido del popolo. © Carisch,
s.a., Milano; on arrangement of
selections; 30Jun45; EF2815.
Miniature score: orchestra.
Introduzione, Danza delle 9 muse,
Orchesis di Apollo. See his
Roma dei Cesari.
(Roma dei Cesari) Introduzione,
Danza delle 9 muse, Orchesis
di Apollo, (dall' atto I.
dell' opera Roma dei Cesari);
trascrizione da concerto per
pianoforte solo di G. E.
Moroni. © Garisch Società
Anonima, Milan; 16Dec46;
EF3243.

ROBBINS MUSIC CORP., comp.
Bill Hardey's Songs of the good
old days. © Robbins Music Corp,
New York; 8Aug46; EP7775.

ROBERDAY, FRANÇOIS.
Caprice in F; for brass quartet
... transcribed and ed. by
Roger Smith ... Score. ©
Mercury Music Corp., New
York; on arrangement; 21Mar47;
EP12598.

ROBERT, CAMILLE.
Le chant des F.F.I. [Marche offi-
cielle de la résistance] ...
paroles de Valentin Tarault,
orchestré par Félicien Foret.
© Editions Salabert, Paris; on
arrangement; 30Jan45; EF2482.
Piano-conductor score (band,
with words) and parts.

ROBERTON, HUGH STEVENSON, 1874-
Blake's cradle song; for choir (or
trio) of equal voices, S. S. C.,
unaccompanied. Words by William
Blake, music by Hugh S. Roberton.
London, J. Curwen & Sons. ©
Hugh S. Roberton, Glasgow; 9Dec46;
EF4764.

For to-night a King is born in
Bethlehem; for chorus (or
quintet) ... S.S.C.T.B.
(unaccompanied) Words by Mary
Sim, music by Hugh S. Roberton.
London, J. Curwen & Sons. ©
Hugh S. Roberton, Glasgow;
18Apr47; EF3278.

I got a robe; traditional Negro
spiritual, arr. for choir (or
trio) ... S.S.C. (unaccompanied)
by Hugh S. Roberton. London,
J. Curwen & Sons. © Hugh S.
Roberton, Glasgow; on arrangement; 18Apr47; EF3279.

My luve is like a red, red rose;
traditional Scottish air, arr.
for choir (or quartet) ...
(T.T.B.B.) (unaccompanied) by
Hugh S. Roberton, words
adapted from an old English
folk song by Burns. London,
J. Curwen & Sons. © Hugh S.
Roberton, Glasgow; on arrangement; 18Apr47; EF3277.

Nativity cradle song; for choir
(or quartet) ... (TTBB)
(unaccompanied) [Words by]
Narayan Vaman Tilak, tr. from
the Marathi by Nicol Macnicol,
music by Hugh S. Roberton.
London, J. Curwen & Sons. ©
Hugh S. Roberton, Glasgow; on
arrangement; 24Mar47; EF5066.

Nobody know de trouble I've seen;
traditional Negro spiritual arr.
for choir (or trio) of women's
(or children's) voices, S.S.C.
by Hugh S. Roberton. London, J.
Curwen & Sons, New York, G.
Schirmer, sole agents. © Hugh
Stevenson Roberton, Glasgow; on
arrangement; 24Mar47; EF5066.

O western wind; for choir (or
quartet) of men's voices,
(T.T.B.B.) (unaccompanied) ...
Words anon., 16th cent., music
by Hugh S. Roberton. London,
J. Curwen, New York, G.
Schirmer, sole agents. ©
Hugh S. Roberton, Glasgow;
20Mar47; EF5463.

When de stars begin to full
traditional Negro spiritual,
arr. for chorus (or trio) ...
(S.S.C.) (unaccompanied) by
Hugh S. Roberton. London,
J. Curwen & Sons. © Hugh S.
Roberton, Glasgow; on arrange-
ment; 18Apr47; EF3280.

ROBERTS, ALLAN.
(Cigarette girl) It's all in the
mind; by Allan Roberts and Doris
Fisher. [From] Cigarette girl.
© Mood Music Co., inc., New York;
31Mar47; EP13393.

(Singin' in the corn) I'm a gal of
property; by Allan Roberts and
Doris Fisher ... [From] Singin'
in the corn. © Mood Music Co.,
inc., New York; 31Mar47; EP13390.
For voice and piano, with chord
symbols.

(Singin' in the corn) An old love
is a true love; by Allan Roberts
and Doris Fisher ... [From] Singin'
in the corn. © Mood Music Co., inc.,
New York; 31Mar47; EP13391. For
voice and piano, with chord symbols.

ROBERTS, LEE S
Ave Maria; sacred song (with
violin or 'cello obbligato,
ad lib) by Lee S. Roberts.
© The Boston Music Co., Boston;
22Apr47; EP13880. Latin and
English words.

ROBERTS, MERVYN.
(Chorales, 2 pianos) Two chorales
... by Mervyn Roberts. ©
Novello & Co., ltd., London;
21Apr47; EP5658-5659. Score.

Pilgrim song; unison or two-part
song, words by John Bunyan,
music by Mervyn Roberts. ©
Novello & Co., ltd., London;
2May47; EP5251.

Two chorales for two pianos. See
his Chorales, 2 pianos.

ROBERTS, MYRON S
Carillon; by Myron J. Roberts.
© The H. W. Gray Co., inc., New
York; 23May47; EP14763.

ROBERTSON, LEROY, 1896-
Novelette; for the piano, by
LeRoy Robertson. © Morrison
Music Co., Seattle; 27Feb47;
EP12470.

ROBIN, SID.
If it's love you want baby, that's
me; by Sid Robin. © Pic Music
Corp., Chicago; 3Jul46; EP12039.
For voice and piano, with chord
symbols.

That's the way it goes; by Alec
Wilder and Sid Robin. © Regent
Music Corp., New York; 26Jun47;
EP15261. For voice and piano,
with chord symbols.

ROBINSON, ANNE.
Chattering monkeys ... by Anne
Robinson. © McKinley Publishers,
inc., Chicago; 10Feb47; EP12048.
For piano solo.

Here comes the band ... by Anne
Robinson. © McKinley Publishers,
inc., Chicago; 10Feb47; EP12047.
For piano solo.

Little comrade march ... by
Anne Robinson. © McKinley
Publishers, inc., Chicago;
10Feb47; EP12046. For
piano solo.

Spooks ... by Anne Robinson.
© McKinley Publishers, inc.,
Chicago; 10Feb47; EP12045. For
piano solo.

Three very easy piano pieces; by
Anne Robinson. © Clayton F.
Summy Co., Chicago; on 3 pieces.
Contents.- [1] My hobby horse
(© 22May47; EP14636) - [2] Swing-
ing (© 16May47; EP14437) - [3]
Bow-wow and meow (© 16May47;
EP14438)

ROBINSON, EARL.
(California) California, from the
Paramount picture "California";
words by E. Y. Harburg, music
by Earl Robinson. [c1946] ©
Paramount Music Corp., New York;
3Feb47; EP11824.

(California) California or bust, from
the Paramount picture "California";
words by E. Y. Harburg, music by
Earl Robinson. [c1946] © Paramount
Music Corp., New York; 3Feb47;
EP11825.

California or bust. See his
California.

Far from my darling. See his The
Missouri story.

I come from Missouri. See his The
Missouri story.

(The Missouri story) Far from my
darling, [from] the ... picture,
"The Missouri story," lyric by
Lewis Allan, music by Earl Robin-
son. © Robbins Music Corp., New
York; 21Apr47; EF14768.

(The Missouri story) I come from
Missouri, [from] the ... picture,
"The Missouri story," lyric by
Lewis Allan, music by Earl Robin-
son. © Robbins Music Corp., New
York; 21Apr47; EF14769.

Said I to my heart, said I. See
his California.

ROBINSON, ELSA.
Just blame it on fate; words and
music by Bill Nettles and Elsa
Robinson. © Peer International
Corp., New York; 29Oct46;
EP13623.

ROBINSON, J   RUSSEL.
Meet me at no special place (and
I'll be there at no particular
time); lyric by Arthur Terker
and Harry Pyle, music by J.
Russel Robinson. © Leeds Music
Corp., New York; 2Jun47;
EP14973.

ROBINSON, RUSSELL D   1927-
Short course song; words and
music by Russ Robinson. ©
Russell D. Robinson, Mauston,
Wis.; 8Mar47; EP13307.

ROBINSON, WILLIE CHURCHILL.
It will all be over by and by;
words and music by Willie C.
Robinson, arr. by Mamie Dan-
dridge. Baltimore, National
Gospel Workers Aid Society. ©
Mamie Louise Dandridge, Balti-
more; 20Mar47; EP6723.

ROBISON, WILLARD.
Give us peace; by Willard
Robison. © Bob Miller, inc.,
New York; 2May47; EP14573.
For voice and piano.

ROCHE, PIERRE LUCIEN ANDRÉ JOSEPH.
Bal du faubourg ... paroles de
Charles Aznavour [pseud.],
musique de Pierre Roche.
© Editions Paris-Broadway,
Paris; 31Dec45; EF3839.

C'est pas tous les jours dimanche
... paroles de Charles
Aznavour [pseud.], musique de
Pierre Roche. © Publications
Francis Day, Paris; 31Oct46;
EF3581. Score (voice and
piano) and voice part.

Voyez, c'est le printemps ...
paroles de Charles Aznavour
[pseud.], musique de Pierre
Roche. © Editions Paris-
Broadway, Paris; 31Dec46;
EF3817.

ROCKWELL, HARRY J   1911-
Tonight, sweetheart, tonight;
words and music by Harry J.
Rockwell, [arranged by Gene
Engle. c1945] © Gene
Engle Music, Indianapolis;
15Mar46; Eri3024.

RODGERS, IRENE.
A third piano book for little
Jacks and Jills; by Irene
Rodgers, illustrations by
Joanne Wood. © G. Schirmer,
inc., New York; 30Dec46;
EP11515.

RODGERS, RICHARD, 1902-
(The boys from Syracuse) Falling in
love with love, from the musical
comedy, "The boys from Syracuse".
Scored ... by Hans Spialek, music by
Richard Rodgers. © Chappell & Co.,
inc., New York; on arrangement;
18Feb47; EP12091. Piano-conductor
score (orchestra) and parts.
(A Connecticut Yankee) My heart
stood still; from "A Connecticut
Yankee"; four part male voices,
T.T.B.B., words by Lorenz Hart,
music by Richard Rodgers, arr.
by William Stickles. © Harms,
inc., New York; EP15275.
A(Connecticut Yankee) My heart stood
still, from the musical comedy "A
Connecticut Yankee"; words by Lorenz
Hart, music by Richard Rodgers, [arr.
by William Stickles] © Harms, inc.,
New York; on arrangement; 29May47;
EP15994. Score: solo voices (SA or
SBar and piano.
Falling in love with love. See
his The boys from Syracuse.

(The girl friend) The blue room;
from "The girl friend" ...
T.T.B.B., words by Lorenz Hart,
music by Richard Rodgers,
arr. by Douglas MacLean, pseud.
© Harms, inc., New York; on ar-
rangement; 30Jan47; EP12023.
My heart stood still. See his
A Connecticut yankee.
My romance; four part male chorus
... arr. by William Stickles.
Words by Lorenz Hart, music by
Richard Rodgers, New York, T.
B. Harms. © T. B. Harms Co. &
Max Dreyfus, New York; on ar-
rangement; 13Jun47; EP15154.
My romance; four part mixed chorus
... arr. by William Stickles.
Words by Lorenz Hart, music by
Richard Rodgers, New York, T. B.
Harms. © T. B. Harms Co. & Max
Dreyfus, New York; on arrangement;
13Jun47; EP15156.
My romance; three part female
chorus (S. S. A.), arr. by
William Stickles. Words by
Lorenz Hart, music by Richard
Rodgers, New York, T. B. Harms.
© T. B. Harms Co. & Max Dreyfus,
New York; on arrangement;
13Jun47; EP15155.
My romance; three part mixed chorus
(S. A. B.), arr. by William
Stickles. Words by Lorenz Hart,
music by Richard Rodgers. New
York, T. B. Harms. © T. B.
Harms Co. & Max Dreyfus, New
York; on arrangement; 13Jun47;
EP15153.
Oh, what a beautiful mornin'. See
his Oklahoma.
Oklahoma; from the musical play
"Oklahoma!" Three-part mixed
chorus (S.A.B.) arr. by William
Stickles. Words by Oscar
Hammerstein II, music by
Richard Rodgers. New York,
Crawford Music Corp. © William-
son Music, inc., New York; on
arrangement; 14Apr47; EP13867.
(Oklahoma) Many a new day; from
the musical play "Oklahoma!"
Three part female voices (S.S.A.)
arr. by William Stickles.
Words by Oscar Hammerstein II,
music by Richard Rodgers. New
York, Crawford Music Corp.
© Williamson Music, inc., New
York; on arrangement; 16May47;
EP14754.
(Oklahoma) Many a new day; from the
musical play "Oklahoma!" Three
part mixed chorus (S.A.B.) arr.
by William Stickles. Words by
Oscar Hammerstein II, music by
Richard Rodgers. New York,
Crawford Music Corp. © William-
son Music, inc., New York; on
arrangement; 16May47; EP14755.

(Oklahoma) Many a new day; from
the musical play "Oklahoma!"
Two part chorus arr. by
William Stickles. Words by
Oscar Hammerstein II, music
by Richard Rodgers. [New
York, Crawford Music Corp.]
© Williamson Music, inc., New
York; on arrangement; 13May47;
EP14598.
(Oklahoma) Oh, what a beautiful
mornin'; [from the musical play
"Oklahoma!"] Music by Richard
Rodgers, lyric by Oscar Hammer-
stein, arr. by Albert
Sirmay] © Williamson Music,
inc., New York; on arrangement;
7Mar47; EP12682.
(Oklahoma) Oh, what a beautiful
mornin'; from the musical
play "Oklahoma!" Three part
mixed chorus (S.A.B.) arr. by
William Stickles. Words by
Oscar Hammerstein II, music
by Richard Rodgers. [New York,
Crawford Music Corporation] ©
Williamson Music, inc., New
York; on arrangement; 13May47;
EP14399.
(Oklahoma) Oh, what a beautiful
mornin'; from the musical play
"Oklahoma!" Two part chorus
arr. by William Stickles. Words
by Oscar Hammerstein II, music
by Richard Rodgers. New York,
Crawford Music, inc., New York; on
arrangement; 14Apr47; EP13868.
(Oklahoma!) Out of my dreams,
from the musical play "Okla-
homa!" ... ([For] S.S.A.) arr.
by William Stickles. Words by
Oscar Hammerstein II, music by
Richard Rodgers. New York,
Crawford Music Corp. ©
Williamson Music, inc., New
York; on arrangement; 1Apr47;
EP13345.
(Oklahoma!) Out of my dreams,
from the musical play "Okla-
homa!" [For] two part chorus,
arr. by William Stickles.
Words by Oscar Hammerstein II,
music by Richard Rodgers. New
York, Crawford Music Corp. ©
Williamson Music, inc., New York;
on arrangement; 1Apr47; EP13344.
(Oklahoma!) People will say we're
in love, from the musical play
"Oklahoma!" ... ([For] S.A.B.)
arr. by William Stickles, music by
Richard Rodgers, words by Oscar
Hammerstein, II. © Williamson
Music, inc., New York; on arrange-
ment; 14Apr47; EP13765.
(Oklahoma!) People will say we're
in love, from the musical play
"Oklahoma!" Two part chorus,
arr. by William Stickles, music
by Richard Rodgers, words by
Oscar Hammerstein, II. © William-
son Music, inc., New York; on
arrangement; 14Apr47; EP13764.
Oklahoma; selection, [by] Richard
Rodgers ... arr. ... by W. J.
Duthoit. (The army journal for
full military band, no.734)
© Williamson Music, inc., New
York; on arrangement; 17Jul47;
EP6177. Condensed score and
parts.
(Oklahoma) The surrey with the
fringe on top; [from the musical
play "Oklahoma!"] Music by
Richard Rodgers, words by Oscar
Hammerstein 2nd, simplified
teaching ed. for piano [arr. by
Albert Sirmay]. © Williamson
Music, inc., New York; on arrange-
ment; 7Mar47; EP12681.

(Oklahoma) The surrey with the
fringe on top; from the musical
play "Oklahoma!" Three part
mixed chorus (S.A.B.) arr. by
William Stickles. Words by Oscar
Hammerstein, II, music by Richard
Rodgers. © Williamson Music
Corp. © Williamson Music, inc.,
New York; on arrangement; 16May47;
EP14756.
(Oklahoma!) The surrey with the
fringe on top, from the musical
play "Oklahoma!" Two part chorus
arr. by William Stickles; words
by Oscar Hammerstein II, music
by Richard Rodgers. [New York,
Crawford Music Corp.] © Williamson
Music, inc., New York; on arrange-
ment; 19Mar47; EP12914.
Out of my dreams. See his
Oklahoma.
People will say we're in love.
See his Oklahoma.
The surrey with the fringe on top.
See his Oklahoma.
Where or when; by Richard
Rodgers, piano solo arr. by
Trude Rittman. © Chappell &
Co., inc., New York; on ar-
rangement; 14May47; EP14520.
Where or When ... ([for] T.T.B.B.)
arr. by William Stickles, music
by Richard Rodgers, words by
Lorenz Hart. © Chappell & Co.,
inc., New York; 7Aug47; on
arrangement; EP16274.
With a song in my heart; [by]
Richard Rodgers, arr. by J.
Louis Merkur [for] piano duet.
© Harms, inc., New York; on
arrangement; 5Jun47; EP15172.
With a song in my heart. See also his
Spring is here.

RODRIGUEZ, G   H
La Cumparsita. (The masked one)
... [By] G. H. Rodriguez, arr.
by Rudolph Goehr. © Edward B.
Marks Music Corp., New York;
on arrangement; 21May47;
EP14541. Score (solo instrument
and piano) and part for Bb
clarinet.
La Cumparsita. (The masked one)
... [By] G. H. Rodriguez, arr.
by Rudolph Goehr. © Edward B.
Marks Music Corp., New York; on
arrangement; 21May47; EP14542.
Score (solo instrument and
piano) and part for Bb cornet.
La Cumparsita. (The masked one)
... [By] G. H. Rodriguez, arr.
by Rudolph Goehr. © Edward B.
Marks Music Corp., New York;
on arrangement; 21May47; EP14543.
Score (solo instrument and piano)
and part for violin.

RODRIGUEZ, JOHNNY.
Fichas negras. (Gambling with
love) ... English words by
Joe Davis, Spanish words and
music by Johnny Rodriguez. ©
Caribbean Music, inc., New
York; 17Mar47; EP12654.

ROE, MARION. See
Richards, Marion Roe.

ROEMMELD, HEINZ, 1902-
Heaven only knows; from Nero
production "Heaven only knows"
... Lyrics by Bill Carey, music
by Heinz Roemheld. © Martin
Music, Hollywood, Calif.; 31Mar47;
EP13452.

RÖNTGEN, JOHAINES, 1898-
Hot lied van de jeugd. The song
of youth. Woorden van Tom Bouws,
English transl. [by] Harold C.
King; [music by] Johannes
Röntgen. © Edition Heuwekemeijer
(Fa. A. J. Heuwekemeijer & B.
F. van Gaal), Amsterdam; 21Dec46;
EP3381.

ROFF, HARVEY.
Sign on the dotted line; words
and music by Harvey Roff.
© Hill and Range Songs, inc..
Hollywood, Calif.; 13May47;
EP14425.

ROGER, KURT GEORGE, 1895-
Nacht. (Night); song for medium
voice and piano by Kurt George
Roger. [Op.21, no.3. Poem by
Christian Morgenstern, English
translation by Grace Yerbury]
© Kurt George Roger, New York;
15Dec46; EP10765.

ROGERS, BENJAMIN, 1614-1698.
Give thanks and praise; chorale
for mixed voices (a cappella),
[by] Benjamin Rogers ... edited
by Matthew Lundquist; [words from]
Psalm 118. © Sam Fox Pub. Co.,
New York; on arrangement; 23Sep46;
EP11750.

ROGERS, BERNARD.
Characters from Hans Christian
Andersen; [four drawings for
small orchestra] [by] Bernard
Rogers. © Elkan-Vogel Co.,
inc., Philadelphia; 20Dec46;
EP11446.

ROGERS, CHAUNCEY EPHRIAM, 1908-
The best wishes to you; music
and lyric by Chauncey Rogers.
© Chauncey Ephriam Rogers,
Philadelphia; 10Mar47;
EP13579.

ROGERS, EDDY.
Hand in hand; words by Leonard
Whitcup, music by Eddy Rogers.
© Shapiro, Bernstein & Co., inc.,
New York; 28Apr47; EP14095.

ROGERS, JIMMY.
Could it be I love you; words by
Thelma Lawyer, music by Jimmy
Rogers. © Nordyke Publishing
Co., Los Angeles; 7Mar47;
EP13570.
My cottage of dreams; words by
Irene Zellers, music by Jimmy
Rogers. © Nordyke Publishing
Co., Los Angeles; 2Dec46;
EP11048.

ROGERS, MILTON.
Igor ... music by Milton "Shorty"
Rogers and Red Norvo, arr. by
Joe Bishop. © Charling Music
Corp., New York; 15May47;
EP15525. Piano-conductor score
(orchestra) and parts.
Nero's conception; music by Milton
"Shorty" Rogers and Red Norvo,
arr. by Joe Bishop. © Charling
Music Corp., New York; 15Apr47;
EP13864. Piano-conductor score
(orchestra) and parts.
Steps; music by Milton "Shorty"
Rogers and Red Norvo, arr. by
Joe Bishop. © Charling Music
Corp., New York; 14Apr47;
EP13642. Piano-conductor
score (orchestra) and parts.

ROGERS, SHORTY. See
Rogers, Milton.

ROGERS, WARREN A
I will mind God; by Warren A.
Rogers [harmonized by Ruth
A. Boy] © Warren A. Rogers,
Detroit; 20Mar47; EP13144.

ROGET, HENRIETTE, 1910-
Deux prières; pour grand orgue,
[by] H. Roget. © Henry
Lemoine & Cie., Paris;
15Dec46; EF3586.

ROHLER, ROBERT G
Carry on; words and music by Bob
Rohler. © Cine-Mart Music
Publishing Co., Hollywood, Calif.,
1Nov46; EP11941.

[ROHRBOUGH, LYNN] 1900- comp.
Twenty festival songs; [choice folk
melodies from 12 European countries,
comp. by Lynn Rohrbough] Delaware,
Ohio, Handy Songs. © Cooperative
Recreation Service, Delaware, Ohio;
20Dec46; EP11542.

ROIG, GONZALO.
Loving you (as I do); American
adaptation of "Yo te ame" ...
English lyric by Albert Gamse,
Spanish lyric by Agustín Rodrigues,
music by Gonzalo Roig. © Edward
B. Marks Music Corp., New York;
4Dec46; EP11970.

ROJO, GUADALUPE.
Mujota caprichosa. (Fickle you)
... English words by Joe Davis,
Spanish words by Jaime Yamir,
music by Guadalupe Rojo. ©
Caribbean Music, inc., New
York; 17Mar47; EP12642.
Secretos del corazon. (My secrets
of love) ... English words by
Joe Davis, Spanish words by
Jaime Yamir, music by Guadalupe
Rojo. © Caribbean Music, inc.,
New York; 12Mar47; EP14217.

ROLAND, PAUL, pseud. See
Nieland, Johannes Harmannus
Ignatius Maria.

ROLLAND, CLARENCE R
Irma; words and music by Clarence
R. Rolland. © Nordyke Publish-
ing Co., Los Angeles; 16Sep46;
EP12717.

ROMANELLI, FRANK.
Where ever you are; words by
Melvin Spohrholtz, music by
Frank Romanelli. © Nordyke
Publishing Co., Los Angeles;
10May47; EP14794.

ROMARE, MARGIT LAGERHEIM- See
Lagerheim-Romare, Margit.

ROMBERG, SIGMUND, 1887-
Deep in my heart, dear. See his
The student prince.
Lover come back to me. See his
The new moon.
(Maytime) Will you remember?
(Sweetheart) from "Maytime".
(Lyrics by Rida Johnson Young,
music by Sigmund Romberg, arr.
by Chas. Dews, pseud.] © G.
Schirmer, inc., New York; on
arrangement; 30Dec46; EP11516.
Score; chorus (SAB) and piano.
(The new moon) Lover, come back
to me. "Quando vuelvas a mi."
From the operetta "The new moon";
Spanish text by Johnnie Camacho,
English text by Oscar Hammer-
stein, II, music by Sigmund
Romberg. © Harms, inc., New
York; on Spanish words; 29May47;
EP14996.
(The new moon) Wanting you, [from
"the new moon"], music by
Sigmund Romberg, arr. for organ
by Charles R. Cronham. © Harms,
inc., New York; on arrangement;
11Jun47; EP15199. Includes
registration for Hammond organ.
(The night is young) When I grow
too old to dream; from the
M-G-M picture "The night is
young"] ... lyric by Oscar
Hammerstein II, music by Sigmund
Romberg, scored by Johnny
Warrington. © Robbins Music
Corp., New York; on arrange-
ment; 14Jan47; EP11507. Piano-
conductor score (orchestra,
with words) and parts.
Quando vuelvas a mi. See his
The new moon.
Romberg made easy for the piano;
by Ada Richter. © Harms, inc.,
New York; on arrangement in
v. 2, 25Apr47; EP14284.

Serenade. See his The student
prince.
Serenade. See his Der studentenprinz.
"Softly, as in a morning sunrise"
... by Sigmund Romberg, transcribed by F. Campbell-Watson.
© Harms, inc., New York; on
arrangement; 18Feb47; EP12254.
Piano-conductor score (orchestra)
and parts.
(The student prince) Deep in my
heart, dear, from "The student
prince"; by Sigmund Romberg ...
arr. ... by Charles R. Cronham.
© Harms, inc., New York; on
arrangement; 17Jun47; EP15281.
For organ solo; includes registration for Hammond organ.
(The student prince) Golden
days; from "The student
prince;" four part mixed
voices ... Words by Dorothy
Donnelly, music by Sigmund
Romberg, choral arrangement
by Clay Warnick. © Harms,
inc., New York; on arrangement;
7May47; EP14400.
(The student prince) Serenade,
from "The student prince" ...
[by] Sigmund Romberg, arr. by
Jean Gossette [pseud.] © Harms,
inc., New York; 13Jun47;
EP15271. Score (trumpet or
cornet and piano) and part.
(Der Studentenprinz) Serenade;
arr. and orchestrated by F.
Campbell-Watson. © Harms, inc.,
New York; on arrangement;
6Aug46; EP8234. Piano-conductor
score and parts.
Wanting you. See his The new
moon.
When I grow too old to dream. See
his The night is young.
Will you remember? See his
Maytime.

ROME, HAROLD JACOB, 1908-
(Call me Mister) Going home train;
from "Call me Mister," [for] T.T.
B.B., words and music by Harold
Rome, arr. by Joseph Wood. © M.
Witmark & Sons, New York; on ar-
rangement; 3Feb47; EP12020.

ROMERO, GARET, pseud. See
Catsos, Nicholas A.

ROMITA, ELENA, 1920-
Piccolo zoo; pezzettini facili
per pianoforte a 2 e a 4 mani,
[by] Elena Romita. ©
Carisch, S.a.., Milan; 16May47;
EF3785.

ROMNEY, DE, pseud. See
Frieber, Louis.

ROMNEY, GERALD.
Save a little sunbeam for a rainy
day; words by Stanley Lloyd,
music by Gerald Romney.
Southend-on-Sea, Essex, Arthur's
Music Co., in conjunction with
the Watson Music Co. © Stanley
Lloyd, Ottawa; 19Feb46; EF5002.

ROMNEY, LUCILE TURLEY, 1926-
My prayer; by Lucile Turley
Romney, words by ... Melville
L. Trimble. © Lucile T.
Romney, El Paso, Tex.;
26Apr47; EP14836. For 3
treble voices and piano.

ROSA, ORLANDO DE LA.
La mazucamba; letra y música de
Orlando de la Rosa. © Peer
International Corp., New York;
30Dec46; EP11174. For voice
and piano, with chord symbols.

ROSAS, JUVENTINO.
Over the waves; by Juventino
Rosas, for piano solo, simplified
[by Peter Randall, pseud.] ©
The Boston Music Co., Boston;
on arrangement; 24Apr47; EP13940.

120

ROSATO, ANTHONY.
Rosina ... piano solo, by Anthony
Rosato. © Mutual Music Society,
inc., New York; 24Jan47; EP11656.

ROSE, CLARKSON.
They christened the baby; words &
music by Clarkson Rose. © Peter
Maurice Music Co., ltd., 31Dec46;
EF4839. For voice and piano,
with chord symbols; melody also
in tonic sol-fa notation.

ROSE, DAVID.
David Rose trio album. © Breg-
man, Vocco and Conn, inc.,
New York; on 6 arrangements;
17Mar47; EP12667. Score
(violin, violoncello and
piano) and parts.
The happy ice cube ... for piano,
by David Rose. © Bregman, Vocco
and Conn, inc., New York;
11Apr47; EP13633.
No rest for the weary; lyric by
Bob Russell, music by David
Rose. © Bregman, Vocco and
Conn, inc., New York; 16May47;
EP14568.
Vienna sings again; composed and
arr. ... by David Rose. ©
Bregman, Vocco and Conn, inc.,
New York; 7Mar47; EP12584.
Condensed score (string orches-
tra) and parts.
Waukegan concerto; [by] David Rose.
Arr by David Rose for orchestra.
© Bregman, Vocco and Conn, inc.,
New York; on arrangement;
11Apr47; EP13634. Condensed
score (orchestra) and parts.
Waukegan concerto ... for piano,
by David Rose. © Bregman, Vocco
& Conn, inc., New York; 20Jan47;
EP11371.

ROSE, FRED, 1897-
Lazy morning; by Fred Rose.
© Milene Music, Nashville; 28Apr47;
EP14039. For voice and piano;
with guitar diagrams and chord
symbols.
Lovebug, Tennessee; by Fred Rose.
© Milene Music, Nashville;
14May47; EP14355. For voice
and piano, with guitar diagrams
and chord symbols.
Oklahoma City; words and music by
Fred Rose. © Milene Music,
Nashville; 31Dec46; EP10911.
For voice and piano, with guitar
diagrams and chord symbols.
Rose of ol' Pawnee; words and
music by Fred Rose. © Milene
Music, Nashville; 14Jun47;
EP15046.
Some folks call it Texas; by Fred
Rose. © Milene Music, Nashville;
14May47; EP14356. For voice and
piano, with guitar diagrams and
chord symbols.
Somebody else's trouble; words and
music by Fred Rose. © Milene
Music, Nashville; 26Dec46; EP10774.
Texas Toni Lee; by Fred Rose.
© Milene Music, Nashville;
3Apr47; EP13217. For voice
and piano, with guitar
diagrams and chord symbols.
There's a big rock in the road;
by Fred Rose. © Milene Music,
Nashville; 31Dec46; EP10910.
For voice and piano, with chord
symbols.
This crazy obsession of mine;
words and music by Fred Rose.
© Leeds Music Corp., New York;
14Feb47; EP12183.

ROSE, PETER DE. See
De Rose, Peter.

ROSEMONT, WALTER L   arr.
Two guitars; [and] Dark eyes;
in one ed., [lyric by Jack
Edwards] ... arr. by Walter
L. Rosemont. © Edwards Music
Co., New York; on arrangement;
11Jan47; EP11342. For voice
and piano, with chord symbols;
parts for 2 instruments, or small
orchestra.

ROSENBERG, KAI, 1898-
(Det gaeldor din Frihed) Det
gaeldor din Frihed, fra Filmen af
samme Titel; musik: Kai Rosenberg,
tekst: Karl Roos. © Wilhelm
Hansen, Musik-Forlag, Copenhagen;
12April6; EF4836.

ROSENTHAL, MANUEL.
Saint François d'Assise. © Jean
Jobert, Paris; 25Feb45; EF449.
Score: mixed voices, without the
accompaniment.

ROSETTER, BERTHA.
Safety on the farm; words by
Bertha Rosetter, music arr.
by Bertha Rosetter, Agnes
Peterson & Amanda Haughland.
© Bertha Rosetter, Granite
Falls, Minn.; on arrangement;
3Mar47; EP13137. Score:
SSA and piano.

ROSS, HUGH, 1898-
The Coventry carol ... English
melody, 1591 ... [words by]
Robert Croo. (In Ross, Hugh,
arr. Sacred choruses for women's or girls' voices. p. 28-
31) © G. Schirmer, inc., New
York; on arrangement; 30Sep46;
EP9781.

ROSS, HUGH, 1898-   arr.
A pastoral; (from an anonymous
"Messiah") ... Durham Cathedral
ms. (In Ross, Hugh, arr. Sacred chofuses for women's or
girls' voices. p. 141-145) ©
G. Schirmer, inc., New York; on
arrangement; 30Sep46; EP9794.
Sacred choruses for women's or
girls' voices. New York, G.
Schirmer.

ROSSI, RENZO OLDRATI, 1903-
Questo à swing ... [by] R.
Oldrati Rossi, parole di L.
L. Martelli ... Programma B. B.
C. ... [by] Giaco Ricci,
parole di G. Maicochi. ©
Odeon, s. a., Milan; 11Mar47;
EF3627. Piano-conductor score
(orchestra, with words), and
parts.

ROSSINI, CARLO, ed.
The ecclesiastical organist; preludes, interludes, postludes,
in the contrapuntal style ...
for pipe or reed organ, comp.
and ed. by Carlo Rossini. ©
J. Fischer & Bro., New York;
on compilation & arrangement
of v.2, 2Jun47; EP6961.

ROSSINI, CARLO, ed. and arr.
The Gregorian organist; contrapuntal
preludes and postludes in the modal
and semi-modal Gregorian style for
pipe or reed organ, arr., comp. and
ed. by Carlo Rossini. © J.
Fischer & Bro., New York; on
arrangement and compilation;
27May47; EP6960.

ROSSINI, GIOACCHINO ANTONIO,
1792-1868.
O Thou, whose power; from "Moses
in Egypt" ... words adapted from
George S. Parker's translation
by Hugh Ross. (In Ross, Hugh,
arr. Sacred choruses for women's or girls' voices. p. 129-
135) © G. Schirmer, inc., New
York; on arrangement; 30Sep46;
EP9792.

HOTGERS, RALPH.
Rumba swing ... lotra de Johnnie
Camacho, música dc Ralph
Rotgers. © Robbins Music Corp.,
New York; 23Dec46; EP11008.

ROTH, ELTON MENNO, 1891-
Elton Menno Roth's Hymns, solos and
choir selections. © Elton Menno
Roth, Los Angeles; 10Jan46;
EP11148.

ROTH, HOWARD HAINES, 1907-
How could I ever forget? By
Howard Roth. © Howard H. Roth
& Co., inc., Clearwater, Fla.;
22Jan47; EP11390. For voice
and piano, with chord symbols.
I'm keepin' tabs on you; by
Howard Roth. © Howard H. Roth
& Co., inc., Clearwater, Fla.;
22Jan47; EP11391. For voice and
piano, with chord symbols.
ROUNDUP OF SONG HITS for radio
and recording; [by Emory
Stroup, Red Belcher, Clarke
Van Ness, pseud., and others]
© Dixie Music Pub. Co., New
York; bk. no. 13, 15Mar46;
bk. no. 14, 30Sep46; EP12986-
12987.

ROUSE, ERVIN T
Bum bum blues; words and music by
Ervin T. Rouse. © Bob Miller,
inc., New York; 2May47; EP14179.
Craven county blues; words and
music by Ervin T. Rouse.
© Bob Miller, inc., New York;
2May47; EP14178.
The Orange Blossom Special; [by]
Ervin T. Rouse. © Bob Miller,
inc., New York; 2May47; EP14180.
For voice and piano.
The Silver Meteor; by Ervin T.
Rouse. © Bob Miller, inc.,
New York; 2May47; EP14181. For
voice and piano.

ROUX, M
Messe "Haec dies"; à deux voix
égales ... [by] Chanoine M.
Roux. © Georges Delrieu & Cie.,
Nice, France; 25Nov46; EF5208.

ROVENGER, LEOPOLD W   arr.
Celestial echoes ... transcriptions for piano, arr. by Leopold W. Rovenger. © Chart
Music Publishing House, inc.,
Chicago; on arrangements;
17Mar47; EP13163.

[ROW, RICHARD D   ] 1899-
Solitude; (T.T.B.B.) words and
music by Andre Dotevsky, [pseud.]
© R. D. Row Music Co., Boston;
31Mar47; EP13527.

ROWLEY, ALEC, 1892-
Can't you dance the polka?
Sea-shanty, arr. for male voices
by Alec Rowley. © Boosey &
Co., ltd., London; on arrange-
ment; 11Feb47; EF4995.
Fire down below ... arr. for male
voices by Alec Rowley. ©
Boosey & Co., ltd., London; on
arrangement; 4Feb47; EF4890.
Five nocturnes ... for piano solo,
[London] Boosey & Hawkes.
© Boosey & Co., ltd., London;
v. 3-5, 8Apr47; Contents.-
no.3. in G © EF5448) - no.4.
In E © EF5449) - no.5. In F
(© EF5447)
Hullabaloo balay; sea-shanty, arr.
for male voices by Alec Rowley.
© Boosey & Co., ltd., London;
on arrangement; 11Feb47; EF4996.
Jesus Christ is risen today;
Easter anthem for mixed voices
by Alec Rowley. © The H. W.
Gray Co., inc., New York;
3Jan47; EP11059.

121

ROWLEY, ALEC. Cont'd.
The little wave; unison song, music
by Alec Rowley; words by Edward
Shenton. © Edward Arnold & Co.,
London; 12Dec46; EF4748.
Milking song; unison song, words by
May Sarson, music by Alec Rowley.
© Novello & Co., ltd., London;
7May47; EF5239.
Parisian scenes; [by] Alec Rowley,
orchestrated by Henry Geehl.
© Joseph Williams, ltd.,
London; 7May47; EF5649.
Piano-conductor score (orchestra)
and parts.
Pipe and tabor, and The hare and the
tortoise ... by Alec Rowley.
London; J. Curwen & Sons. © Alec
Rowley, Kew Gardens, Surrey,
Eng.; 9Dec46; EF4766. For piano,
4 hands.
Rio Grande; sea-shanty, arr. for
male voices by Alec Rowley.
© Boosey & Co., ltd., London; on
arrangement; 11Feb47; EF4997.
Shenandoah ... arr. for male
voices by Alec Rowley. ©
Boosey & Co., ltd., London; on
arrangement; 4Feb47; EF4889.
Suite; pour piano, par Alec
Rowley. © Editions Durand &
Cie., Paris; 31Oct46; EF5176.
Trumpet march; composed by Alec
Rowley. © Joseph Williams, ltd.,
London; 30Dec46; EF4776. Score;
orchestra.
Wee Jesu and Saint Johnnikin; words
from the Flemish, 17th century,
[tr. by Adrian Porter] © Joseph
Williams, ltd., London; 29Mar46;
EF867. Score: chorus (SATB) and
piano.

ROY, MARY CAMPBELL, 1900-
Sittin' on a hilltop; words and
music by Mary Roy. © Mary Roy,
Palo Alto, Calif.; 14Jan47;
EP11238.

RUBBRA, EDMUND.
Lyric movement [by] Edmund Rubbra.
Op. 24. © Alfred Lengnick &
Co., ltd., London; 2Apr47;
EF3238. Score (violin 1, violin
2, viola, violoncello and piano)
and parts.
The morning watch; motet for chorus
and orchestra [by] Edmund
Rubbra. Op. 55. Words by Henry
Vaughan ... Vocal score. ©
Alfred Lengnick & Co., ltd.,
London; 2Apr47; EF3237.

RUBÍN, ISAURO CADENA. See
Cadena Rubín, Isauro.

RUBINSTEIN, ANTON, 1829-1894.
Melody in F. (Op.3, no.1) [By]
A. Rubinstein, arr. by Calla-
Mini. © Chart Music Publishing
House, inc., Chicago; on ar-
rangement; 9May47; EP14562.
For accordion solo.
Mother; words by Anton Rubinstein,
music by Mary E. Linton, arr.
by Chester Nordman. © Shat-
tinger Piano & Music Co.,
St. Louis; on arrangement;
6May47; EP14225. Score: SATB
and piano.
Mother; words by Mary E. Linton,
music by Anton Rubinstein, arr.
by Chester Nordman. © Shattinger
Piano & Music Co., St. Louis;
on arrangement; 6May47; EP14226.
Score: SSA and piano.

[RUCKSTUHL, JOHNNIE]
Little French pal; words and music
by John W. Briggs [pseud.;
arrangement: Martin Roman]
© Imuta, P. Heiber, International
Music, Theatre Edition and
Agency, Basle Switzerland;
15Dec46; EF4983.

RUDOLPH, FRANK.
Who's tellin'? Words and music
by Frank Rudolph, arr. by
Harry and Mildred Bell. ©
Frank Rudolph, Phoenix, Ariz.;
28Dec45; EP13156.

RUEDA, JAVIER RUÍZ. See
Ruíz Rueda, Javier.

RÚNO, SVEN.
Annu i mång-tusende år. See his
Sol över Klara.
De' hurra vi får. See his Sol
över Klara.
De' skall vara en mållare till de'.
See his Sol över Klara.
Sol över Klara; Edvard Perssons
Europafilm-succés. [Words by
Nils-Georg, pseud., & Charles Henry
pseud., music by Sven Runo & Alvar
Kraft] © Nils-Georgs Musikförlag,
a/b, Stockholm; on 4 songs; 1Jan42.
Contents.- [v.1] Sol över Klara;
words by Nils-Georg, music by Sven
Rúno (© EF4832)- [v.2] Annu i
mång-tusende år; words by Nils-
Georg, music by Sven Rúno (© EF4830)-
[v.3] De' hurra vi får; words by
Charles Henry, music by alvar Kraft
(© EF4833)- [v.4] De' skall vara
en mållare till de'; words by Nils
Georg, music by Sven Rúno.
(© EF4831)

RUFTY, HILTON.
Hobby-on-the-green; [by] Hilton
Rufty, arr. ... by Elizabeth
Gest. © G. Schirmer, inc.,
New York; on arrangement;
13Mar47; EP14551. Two scores
for piano 1-2.

RUGOLO, PETE.
Artistry in bolero ... by Pete
Rugolo, ed. by Van Alexander.
© Leslie Music Corp., New York;
8Feb47; EP11822. Piano-conductor
score (orchestra) and parts.
Artistry in percussion; composed and
arr. by Pete Rugolo, ed. by Van
Alexander. © Leslie Music Corp.,
New York; 27Jan47; EP11417.
Piano-conductor score (orchestra)
and parts.
Como back to Sorrento; adapted and arr.
by Pete Rugolo, ed. by Van Alexander.
© Leslie Music Corp., New York; on
adaptation & arrangement; 27Jan47;
EP12132. Piano-conductor score
(orchestra) and parts.
Machito; composed and arr. by
Pete Rugolo, ed. by Van Alexander.
© Leslie Music Corp., New York;
15Jun47; EP14986. Piano-conductor
score (orchestra) and parts.
Rhythm, inc.; parts 1 & 2, ed. by
Van Alexander, composed and arr.
by Pete Rugolo. © Leslie Music
Corp., New York; 7Jun47;
EP14966. Piano-conductor score
(orchestra) and parts.
Safranski ... by Pete Rugolo,
ed. by Van Alexander. ©
Leslie Music Corp., New York;
4Feb47; EP11823. Piano-
conductor score (orchestra)
and parts.

RUHF, DORIS P   1921-
Australia for Jesus; [by] D. P.
Ruhf, arr. [by] R. A. Cossel-
mon. (In Church of the
Nazarene. Michigan District.
Nazarene Young Peoples Society.
Choruses of the N. Y. P. S.
p.60) © Michigan District,
Nazarene Young Peoples Society,
Flint, Mich.; 25Jul46; EP13080.
Close score: SATB.
Ever with me; [words by] Faythe
M. Eastman, [music by] Doris
P. Ruhf, arr. by W. M. Thorne.
(In Church of the Nazarene.
Michigan District. Nazarene
Young Peoples Society.

Choruses of the N. Y. P. S. p.
11) © Michigan District,
Nazarene Young Peoples Society,
Flint, Mich.; 25Jul46; EP13037.
Close score: SATB.

RUIZ, GABRIEL.
Que cosa es el amor? ... letra y
música de Gabriel Ruíz. New
York, Peer International Corp.
© Promotora Hispano Americana
de Música, s. a., México;
10Apr47; EF13693.
Velaré tu sueño ... palabras de
Ricardo López Méndez, música
de Gabriel Ruíz. © Promotora
Hispano Americana de Música,
s.a., México, D. F.; 27Dec46;
EF4861. Piano-conductor score
(orchestra), condensed score
and parts.

RUÍZ, JUANA GONZÁLEZ. See
González Ruíz, Juana.

RUÍZ RUEDA, JAVIER.
Alarde ... de Javier Ruíz Rueda,
letra de: Alfredo Rode. © Pro-
motora Hispano Americana de
Música, s.a., México; 23Dec46;
EF5076. Piano-conductor score
(orchestra) and parts.
Qué pasa, mi cuate ... letra de
José Antonio Zorrilla, música
de Javier Ruíz Rueda. © Pro-
motora Hispano Americana de
Música, s.a., México; 30Dec46;
EF5537.

RUNYAN, WILLIAM M
The beauty of Jesus; [words by]
Albert Orsbon, [music by]
William M. Runyan. (In Moody
Bible institute of Chicago.
The voice of thanksgiving, no.
5. Hymn no.386) © Hope Publish-
ing Co., Chicago; 1Jul46;
EP13683. Close score: SATB.

RUNYEON, GEORGE ELLIS, 1886-
Forgiving love; by George Ellis
Runyeon. © Sholby Music
Publishing Co., Detroit;
3Dec46; EP11769. For voice
and piano, with guitar diagrams
and chord symbols.

RUSCONI, ERNESTO.
Invocazione ... parole di L.
Ferruccio, musica di E. Rusconi.
[c1947] © Edizioni Diesis, Milano;
31Dec46; EF4931.
Nostalgia di Napoli ... testo di M.
Panseri. Canzone a Maria ...
testo di C. Deani [pseud.]
Musiche di E. Rusconi. [c1945]
© Edizioni Leonardi, s.a.r.l.,
Milano; 7Aug44; EF5060. Piano-
conductor score (orchestra, with
words) and parts.
Una notte a Venezia; versi di R.
Friggieri, musica di E. Rusconi.
Milano, Edi. NUFA, conces. R.
Friggieri. © Italian Book Co.,
New York; 10Dec46; EF3599.

RUSCONI, OTTO.
Liliana ... testo di C. Bruno,
musica di O. Rusconi. c1947.
© Edizioni Diesis, Milano;
31Dec46; EF4932.

RUSSELL, BENE.
Anthem of the United Nations ...
(S.A.T.B.) [by] Bené Russell,
arr. by Harry R. Wilson. ©
Bourne, inc., New York; 24Jan47;
EP11500.
Anthem of the United Nations;
song by Bene Russell, arr. by
Harry Robert Wilson. © Bourne,
inc., New York; 31Jan47;
EP11852.

RUSSELL, VELMA A
Look down from Heaven, O God ...
for four-part chorus of mixed
voices, with piano or organ acc.
[Words from] Deuteronomy: 26,
[music by] Velma A. Russell. ©
The Willis Music Co., Cincinnati;
17Jan47; EP11561.

RUSSIN, JACK.
My love; words by Don Russin,
music by Jack Russin. ©
Northern Music Corp., New York;
24Sep46; EP13373.

RUSSO, F   MARIO, comp.
Album musicale "F. Mario Russo" ...
[words by Amedeo Greco, F. M.
Russo and others, music by G.
Tavernier, Oreste Mantovani,
and others] Napoli, F. M.
Russo. © Italian Book Co.,
New York; 7Jan47; EF5574.

[RUSSO, S   ] comp.
I successi della CESA, 1944-45.
CESA's latest song hits of
1944-45. [Words by V. Dura
and others, music by E. A.
Mario, M. Festa, and others,
comp. by S. Russo] © Italian
Book Co., New York; 7Sep45;
EF3396. Italian words.

RUSTIN, EDDIE.
Arizona; words and music by Eddie
Rustin. © Royal Music Publisher,
Hollywood, Calif.; 11Apr47;
EP14900.

RUTSKY, LESTER.
You're gonna be sorry; by Maceo
Pinkard & Lester Rutsky.
© Pinkard Publications, inc.,
New York; 30Dec46; EP12013.
For voice and piano with chord
symbols.

RYAN, CHARLES.
How do you measure love? ...
Words and music by Dagmar Van
Haur, Bernie Weisman and
Charles Ryan, piano arr. by
Dick Kent. © Peer Inter-
national Corp., New York;
10Apr47; EP37702.

RYDBERG, SAM.
Kungl. Norra skanska
infanteriregementets marsch;
musik [by] Sam Rydberg. ©
Nordiska Musikförlaget, a.b.,
Stockholm; on arrangement;
1Jan46; EF3743. Piano-conductor score (orchestra), and
parts.
Kungl. Norra skånska infanteriregementets marsch; musik
[by] Sam Rydberg. ©Nordiska
Musikförlaget, a.b., Stockholm;
1Jan46; EF3744. For piano
solo, with chord symbols.

RYDER, NOAH FRANCIS, 1914-
Noah F. Ryder's Five sketches
for piano. © Handy Brothers
Music Co., inc., New York;
26May47; EP14664.

RYNNING, ETHEL FROLICH.
Polk-a-dots; words by Margueritte
Frolich, music by Ethel Frolich Rynning. © Nordyke Publishing Co., Los Angeles;
8Mar47; EP13239.

S

SABORIT,
El caballo y la montura ...
Letra de Clavelito, música de
Saborit, arreglo de Pérez
Prado. Habana. © Peer Inter-
national Corp., New York;
15May47; EP3339. Parts;
orchestra (with words)

SABORIT, EDUARDO.
Ponme la mano caridad ... letra
y música de Eduardo Saborit,
arreglo de; Pedro Guida. ©
Peer International Corp.,
New York; 30Dec46; EF5430.
Piano-conductor score
(orchestra) and parts.

SÁCASAS, ANSELMO.
Te seguiré queriendo ... música de
Anselmo Sacasas, letra de Carlos
De La Cima. © Peer International
Corp., New York; 28Aug46; EP13771.

SACCARDO, ERNIE.
Without you; words & music by Ernie
Saccardo. © Nordyke Publishing
Co., Los Angeles; 24Sep45; EP6505.

SACCO, JOHN C
Brother Will, Brother John; for
voice and piano, by John
Sacco, [words by Elizabeth
Charles Welborn] © G. Schirmer,
inc., New York; 24Mar47;
EP13135.
An echo; song for voice and piano
by John Sacco. [Words by Grace
Hyde Trine] © The Boston Music
Co., Boston; 29Apr47; EP14145.
Railroad reverie; for four-part
chorus of mixed voices and
piano, with tenor solo; [words
by] E. R. Young, [music by]
John Sacco. © G. Schirmer,
inc., New York; 11Apr47;
EP14078.
Sky-rider ... poem by Katherine
Beasely, music by John Sacco.
© Carl Fischer, inc., New York;
16Apr47; EP13963.

[SACHS, BENNO]
Strutting; [by] Edward Stanton
[pseud.] © Century Music Publishing Co., New York; 15Apr47;
EP13229. For piano solo.

SACHS, HENRY E
The little worm ... An encore
song by Henry Sachs. © Harold
Flammer, inc., New York;
14Mar47; EP15471.
The little worm; SSA accompanied;
words and music by Henry E.
Sachs, arr. by Wallingford
Riegger. © Harold Flammer, inc.,
New York; on arrangement;
14Mar47; EP13472.

SACK, AL.
Midnight reverie ... For piano,
by Al Sack. © Triangle Music
Corp., New York; 14Apr47;
EP13712.

SAENZ CRUZ, ALEJANDRO.
Dueña de mi alma ... Letra y
música de A. Saenz Cruz. © Pro-
motora Hispano Americana de
Música, s. a., Mexico; 30Dec46;
EF5281. For voice and piano.

SAEVERUD, HARALD, 1897-
(Siljustøl) Slåtter og stev fra
Siljustøl for klaver ... [by]
Harald Saeverud. Op.22.
© Musikk-Huset, a/s, Oslo; on 5
pieces in hefte 2; 16May46.
Contents.- hefte 2. Revebjølle
(© EF3137) Kvernaslått (© EF3138)
Den siste bålnlat (© EF3139) På
kingelvevstrenger (© EF3140)
Kjempevise-slåtten (© EF3141)
Sinfonia dolorosa; per orchestra,
opus 19, [by Harald Saeverud]
Partitura. [c1945] © Musikk-
Huset a/s, Oslo, Norway;
7Nov46; EF5021.

SAGUE, JACK.
Tu me vas a llorar ... letra y
música de Jack Sagué. © Peer
International Corp., New York;
30Dec46; EF5548.

ST. LOUIS, DEL.
I wish that my dreams were true; words
and music by Del St. Louis. © Cine-
Mart Music Publishing Co., Hollywood,
Calif.; 1Dec46; EP12113.

SAINT-YVES, JEAN.
Nous aurions pu passer ...
paroles de Jean Saint-Yves,
musique de Jean Saint-Yves et
André Popp. © Éditions Paris-
Broadway, Paris; 31Mar46;
EF3823.

Premier madrigal; paroles de
Jean Saint-Yves, musique de J.
Saint-Yves et André Popp. ©
Éditions Paris-Broadway,
Paris; 30Jun46; EF3858.

SAKELLARIOU, ANTONIOS.
Oriental rapsody; for piano solo
... by Antonios Sakellariou. New
York, Hermes Music Publishing Co.
© Antonios Sakellariou, New York;
13May47; EP6945.
To xoupó heftaixa ... words and
music by Antonios Sakellariou.
New York, Hermes Music Publish-
ing Co. © Antonios Sakellariou,
New York; 13May47; EP6897.
Greek words.

SALAMI, A
Dark eyes. [Music by A. Salami]
Arr. by Will Hudson ... 3 way
dance orchestration. © Lewis
Music Publishing Co., inc., New
York; on arrangement; 2Jun47;
EP14851. Piano-conductor score
(orchestra) and parts.

[SALERNO, NICOLA]
La luna e sei soldi ... Dal film
omonimo; testo di T. Gramantieri,
musica di A. Selyrn [pseud.]
© Edizioni Leonardi s. a. r. l.,
Milano; 15Jan47; EF5301. Piano-
conductor score (orchestra, with
words) and parts.

SALIM, KHATAB.
Hey daddy-o; words and music by
Khatab-Salim. © Embassy Music
Corp., New York; 26Apr47;
EP13919.

SALTA, MENOTTI, 1894-
Nocturne; for orchestra, [by]
Menotti Salta. © G. Ricordi
and Co., New York; on arrangement; 18Feb47; EP12386.
Piano-conductor score
(orchestra) and parts.

SALTZMAN, MAX MATTHEW, 1914-
Find the woman; lyrics and music
by Max Matthew Saltzman. Los
Angeles, Manuscript Music Pub.
Co. © Max Matthew Saltzman,
Los Angeles; 10Mar47; EP14402.

THE SALVATION ARMY BRASS BAND JOURNAL.
© Salvationist Publishing & Supplies,
ltd., London. Score and parts,
nos. 1269-1272, 1273-1276, comp.
by Bramwell Coles. Sep46, nos.
1269-1272; 18Nov46; © EF3096.
Dec46, nos. 1273-1276; 31Jan47;
© EF3182.
Festival series. © Salvationist
Publishing & Supplies, ltd.,
London. Score and parts.
Jul46, nos. 137-140, 1Nov46;
© EF3095. Jan47, nos. 141-144,
25Apr47; © EF3671.
[2d ser.] © Salvationist Publish-
ing & Supplies, ltd., London.
Score and parts. Nos. 393-396,
397-400, comp. by Bramwell Coles.
Jul-Oct46, nos. 393-396; 3Feb47;
© EF3181. Jan47, nos. 397-400;
11Apr47; © EF3671.

SAMPSON, GODFREY.
The bells; [words] by Edgar Allan
Poe ... For double chorus and
orchestra. © Novello and Co.,
ltd., London; 29Jan46; EP248.
With piano accompaniment.

SAMSON, SAM.
Miss Peggy ... musik och arr.:
Sam Samson. © Edition
Sylvain, a.b., Stockholm;
1Jan45; EF3726. Piano-conductor score (orchestra), and
parts.

SAMUELS, JOSEPH WILSON.
When the rainbow of love appears;
words by Lewis & Young, music
by Joseph Wilson Samuels.
New York, Waterson-Berlin &
Snyder Co. (Successors in interest
to Waterson, Berlin & Snyder
Co.) New York; 12Jul19;
EP5892.

SAMUELS, WALTER.
I'm dreaming of you; lyric by Edna
Lauwaert ... music by Walter Sam-
uels. Friend, Neb., S.T.A. Music
Pub. Co. © Leta S. Bendor, Friend
Neb.; 28Oct46; EP6633.
One night to love; lyric by Edward
J. Lauwaert, music by Walter Sam-
uels. Friend, Neb., S.T.A. Music
Pub. Co. © Edward J. Lauwaert,
Elmhurst. Ill.: 27Feb47; EP6634.

SANBORN, EDGAR RUSSELL, 1879-
The Lord's prayer; musical setting
by E. Russell Sanborn. Concord,
N. H., Mondamin Press. © Edgar
Russell Sanborn, Concord, N. H.;
21Mar47; EP14139. For voice and
piano.

SANCAN, PIERRE, 1916-
Mouvement; pour piano, [by] Pierre
Sancan. © Durand & Cie., Paris;
30Nov46; EF3501.

SANCHEZ, PEDRO HERNANDEZ. See
He_nan_e, Sanches, Pedro.

SÁNCHEZ VÁZQUEZ, PABLO.
Pero vuelve ... letra y música de
Pablo Sánchez Vázquez. © Pro-
motora Hispano Americana de
Música, s.a., México; 23Dec46;
EP5071.
Súplica del alma ... de Pablo
Sánchez Vázquez. © Promotora
Hispano Americana de Música,
s.a., Mexico; 24Apr47; EP5210.
For voice and piano.
Tristezas del alma ... letra y
música de Pablo Sánchez
Vazquez. © Promotora Hispano
Americana de Música, s.a.,
México; 31Dec46; EP5538.

SANDERS, ALMA.
The cuckoo-cheena. See her
Louisiana lady.
Dream-away Lane. See her Ire-
land today.
Flying home. See her Ireland
today.
I remember when. See her Ire-
land today.
(Ireland today) Dream-away Lane;
lyrics ... by Monte Carlo and
music [by] Alma Sanders from ...
"Ireland today." © Bob Miller,
inc., New York; 18Jun47; EP15266.
(Ireland today) I remember when;
lyrics ... by Monte Carlo and
music [by] Alma Sanders, from
... "Ireland today." © Bob
Miller, inc., New York; 18Jun47;
EP15268.
(Ireland today) A lovely day; lyrics
... by Monte Carlo and music [by]
Alma Sanders from ... "Ireland
today." © Bob Miller, inc., New
York; 18Jun47; EP15267.
(Ireland today) Mike O'Day;
lyrics ... by Monte Carlo and
music [by] Alma Sanders, from ...
"Ireland today." © Bob Miller,
inc., New York; 18Jun47; EP15269.
(Ireland today) My Ireland, lyrics
... by Monte Carlo and music [by]
Alma Sanders from ... "Ireland
today." © Bob Miller, inc.,
New York; 18Jun47; EP15264.
(Louisiana lady) The cuckoo-
cheena, [from] "Louisiana lady";
words by Monte Carlo, music by
Alma Sanders. New York, Chappell
& Co. © Alma Sanders and Monte
Carlo, New York; 12May47;
EP14519.

(Louisiana lady) The night was
all to blame, [from] "Louisiana
lady"; words by Monte Carlo,
music by Alma Sanders. New York,
Chappell & Co. © Alma Sanders
and Monte Carlo, New York;
12May47; EP14516.
(Louisiana lady) That's why I
want to go home, [from] "Louisiana lady"; words by Monte Carlo,
music by Alma Sanders. New York,
Chappell & Co. © Alma Sanders
and Monte Carlo, New York;
12May47; EP14517.
(Louisiana lady) When you are
close to me, [from] "Louisiana
lady"; words by Monte Carlo,
music by Alma Sanders. New
York, Chappell & Co. © Alma
Sanders and Monte Carlo, New
York; 12May47; EP14518.
A lovely day. See her Ireland
today.
Mike O'Day. See her Ireland
today.
My Ireland. See her Ireland
today.
The night was all to blame. See
her Louisiana lady.
That's why I want to go home. See
her Louisiana lady.
When you are close to me. See her
Louisiana lady.

[SANDERS, GEORGE H   ]
Scheherazada suite; three songs
adapted from themes by Rimsky-
Korsakoff ... lyrical setting by
Phil Martin [pseud.] and [musical
adaptation by] Glen Dexter [pseud.]
© Cavalcade Music Co., New York;
on lyrics & adaptation of 3 songs;
v.1, 9April47, v.2-3, 28Feb47;
Contents.- 1. Scheherazada, from
ballet motifs (© EP13592) - 2.
Río samba, from "Caprice espagnol"
(© EP12327)- Desert serenade,
from "Hymn to the sun" (©
EP12326)

SANDERS, J
Adiós, muchachos. (Farewell, com-
panions) ... Music by J. Sanders
... Spanish lyric by C. F. Vedani,
[English words adapted by Albert
Gamse] [In andré, Julie, ed.
Songs from south of the border.
p.58-60) © Edward B. Marks Music
Corp., New York; on English
adaptation; 28Dec46; EP10883.

SANDERS, LENNY.
Ridin' thru Cool Canyon; words
and music by Roy West and Lenny
Sanders. © Edward Schuberth &
Co., inc., New York; 27Jan47;
EP11413. For voice and piano,
with guitar diagrams and chord
symbols.

[SANDERS, OLCUTT] 1915-   comp.
Amigos cantandos; [comp. and tr. by
Olcutt Sanders] Delaware, Ohio,
Handy Songs. © Cooperative Recreation Service, Delaware, Ohio;
30Dec46; EP11541. Melody and
words.

SANDOVAL, MIGUEL.
Christ, the Redeemer; for mixed
voices and piano, S.A.T.B.
[Words by Carmela Ponselle]
© G. Ricordi & Co., New York;
on arrangement; 7Jun46; EP4715.

SANG, B
Pizzicato polka; by B. Sang. New
York, Harmonia Edition. © Har-
monia Edition Publishing Co.,
New York; 30Dec46; EP6467. For
piano or organ solo.

SANJUAN, PEDRO.
Ritual ... English text by Olga
Paul, music and Spanish text by
Pedro Sanjuan. © Leeds Music
Corp., New York; 12Apr47; EP14970.
Score: chorus (SSATTBarB) and
piano reduction.

SANTA, ELMA, 1921-
Ohio Valley polka; by Elma Santa,
arr. by Joe Biviano [for]
accordion solo. © Viccas Music
Co., New York; 12May47; EP15099.

SANTIAGO MAJO, RODRIGO A   DE.
Estampés vascas; [by] Rodrigo A.
de Santiago. Madrid. (Harmonia:
revista musical, 1. sección,
no.289) © Rodrigo A. de
Santiago, Madrid; 30Dec43;
EP3600. Condensed score: band.

SANTOS, PEARL.
Christmas chimos; by Pearl Santos.
© Bob Millor, inc., New York;
30Dec46; EP10739. For voice
and piano, with chord symbols.

SARGENT, FRED WALTER, 1878-
The Ballards; words and music by
Fred Sargent, arr. by Fred and
Lydia Sargent. © Fred and
Walter Sargent & Lydia Lillethun
Sargent, Chicago; on words &
revised arrangement; 14Feb47;
EP13409.

SARGENT, LESTER LYMAN, 1882-
Christmas angels; song by Lester
L. Sargent with violin obligato
[arr. by L. L. Sargent and A.
Papalardo] Washington, D. C.,
Festival Music Co. © Lester L.
Sargent, Washington, D. C.; on
arrangement; 13Oct46; EP14897.
Score: chorus (SATB) and violin.
Holiday moods; by Lester L. Sargent.
Washington, D. C., Festival Music
Co. © Lester L. Sargent, Wash-
ington, D. C.; 18Sep46; EP14869.
Score (violin and piano) and
part.

SARRAT, ANDRE JOSEPH ISIDORE, 1908-
Ils ont tout vu! ... Paroles et
musique de André Sarrat. ©
Éditions André Sarrat, Montpellier,
France; 2Nov46; EF3296. Melody
and words.
Mon saucisson ... paroles et
musique de André Sarrat. ©
Éditions André Sarrat, Mont-
pellier, France; 2Nov46;
EF5297. Melody and words.

SAS, ANDRES, 1900-
(Ollantay) Kashwa; (from choral
triptych "Ollantay") (S.A.T.B.)
English text by Olga Paul,
music and Spanish text by
Andrés Sás. © Leeds Music
Corp., New York; 21Mar47;
EP12855.
(Ollantay) Melopeya; (from choral
triptych "Ollantay") (S.A.T.B.
English text by Olga Paul,
music and Spanish text by
Andrés Sás. © Leeds Music
Corp., New York; 21Mar47;
EP12856.

SATTERFIELD, TOM.
Sunday in Now York; by Tom Satterfield, for piano. © J. J.
Robbins & Sons, inc., New York;
3Apr47; EP13830.

SAUGUET, HENRI, pseud. See also
Poupard, Henri.
Les forains; ballet, réduction
pour piano. © Rouart, Lerolle
& Cie, Paris; 28Feb46; EF1981.

SAULNIER, MAURICE, 1908-
Le retour du printemps ... paroles
& musique de Maurice Saulnier.
© Éditions Musicales Nuances,
Paris; 15Dec46; EF3488.

SAUNDERS, GEORGE EDWARD, 1901-
He is bidding for you; congrega-
tional, words and music by Lila
G. Gfell [and] Geo. E. Saunders.
© The Silhouetted Lyre; George
E. Saunders & Lila G. Gfell,
Detroit; 6Mar47; EP14003.

124

SAUNDERS, GEORGE EDWARD. Cont'd.

He is bidding for you; vocal,
words and music by Lila G.
Gfell [and] Geo. E. Saunders.
© The Silhouetted Lyre; George
E. Saunders & Lila G. Gfell,
Detroit; 6Mar47; EP14002.

SAUTER, EDDIE.
Hangover Square ... By Eddie
Sauter. © Regent Music
Corp., New York; 21Mar47;
EP12887. Piano-conductor
score (orchestra) and
parts.

Sandstorm ... By Eddie Sauter.
© Regent Music Corp., New
York; 21Mar47; EP12888.
Piano-conductor score
(orchestra) and parts.

This believing world ... Composed by Eddie Sauter. ©
Regent Music Corp., New York;
17May47; EP14567. Score
(trumpet and piano) and part.

SAUTEREAU, CÉSAR 1913-
(Concerto, string orchestra)
Concert pour orchestre à
cordes; [by] C. Sautereau.
© Pierre Noël, Paris; 9Sep47;
EF3537.

SAVINO, DOMENICO, 1882-
Cuban concerto; for piano, with
orchestra guide for second piano.
© J. J. Robbins & Sons, inc.,
New York; 27Dec46; EP12119.
Score: piano 1-2.

Dream fantasy; for piano, by Dom-
onico Savino. © Robbins Music
Corp., New York; 29Nov46;
EP11007.

Dream lullaby; music by Domenico
Savino, vocal arrangement by
the composer. Words by Harry R.
Wilson. © J. J. Robbins & Sons,
inc., New York; 26Feb47; EP13399.
Score: soprano, chorus (SSA) and
piano.

The emperor waltz; song based on
the Johann Strauss waltz; words
by Ted Fetter, music by Domenico
Savino. © Hamilton S. Gordon,
inc., New York; on words & arrangement of music; 9Apr47;
EP11450.

Faith, hope and charity; music by
Domenico Savino, vocal arrange-
ment by the composer, words by
Harry R. Wilson. © J. J. Robbins
& Sons, inc., New York; 2Jun47;
EP14862. Score: SSATB and piano.

The little band; music by Domenico
Savino, vocal arrangement by the
composer, words by Harry R.
Wilson. © J. J. Robbins & Sons,
inc., New York; 2Jun47; EP14861.
Score: SSAATB and piano.

A merry Christmas; music by
Domenico Savino, vocal arrange-
ment by the composer, words by
Harry R. Wilson. © J. J. Robbins
& Sons, inc., New York; 2Jun47;
EP14860. Score: SSATB and
piano.

Neapolitan serenade; music by
Domenico Savino, vocal arrange-
ment by the composer, words by
Harry R. Wilson. © J. J. Robbins
& Sons, inc., New York; 2Jun47;
EP14859. Score: SATS and piano.

The prince and the maiden; music
by Domenico Savino ... words by
Harry R. Wilson. © J. J. Robbins
& Sons, inc., New York; 30Jan47;
EP11932. Score: SSAATTBB and
piano.

A symphony of flowers; music by
Domenico Savino, vocal arrange-
ment by the composer, words by
Harry R. Wilson. © J. J. Robbins
& Sons, inc., New York; 2Jun47;
EP14858. Score: SSA and piano.

To America; music by Domenico
Savino, vocal arrangement by the
composer, words by Harry R.
Wilson. © J. J. Robbins & Sons,
inc., New York; 2Jun47; EP14863.
Score: soprano, chorus (SATB)
and piano.

The wedding of a marionette; music
by Domenico Savino ... words by
Harry R. Wilson. © J. J. Robbins
& Sons, inc., New York; 30Jan47;
EP11931. Score: SSAATTBB and
piano.

SAWAYA, JESS.
You've done it again; composed and
arr. ... by Jess Sawaya. ©
Sawaya Publications, inc.,
Trinidad, Colo.; 21Jun46;
EP12668. Piano-conductor score
(orchestra) and parts.

SAXON, DAVID, 1919-
Ain't no hurry, baby; words by
Stan Rhodes, music by David
Saxon. © Stuart Music, inc.,
New York; 12Mar47; EP14731.

The sweetest words in the world;
lyric by Robert S. Marvin, music
by David Saxon. © Stevens Music
Corp., New York; 14Jan47; EP11181.
For voice and piano with chord symbols

SAXTON, STANLEY E
The noble nature; for chorus of
women's voices, [by] Stanley E.
Saxton, [words by] Ben Johnson.
© The H. W. Gray Co., inc.,
New York; 11Apr47; EP13626.

SCALA, TANI, 1915-
C'est le dernier rendez-vous ...
Paroles de Bertal [pseud. and]
Maubon; musique de Tani Scala &
Fayrac [pseud.] © Éditions
EIMEP-OPERA, Paris; 10Jan47;
EF3452. Parts: orchestra.

Constellation ... [by] Tani Scala.
© Éditions EIMEP-OPERA, Paris;
10Jan47; EF3453. Piano-conductor
score (orchestra), and parts.

Dansons encore; paroles de
Roger Varnay, musique de Tani
Scala. © Éditions E.M.U.L.,
Paris; 4Jun46; EF3615.

Si vous n'étiez pas si jolie ...
paroles de Bertal [pseud. and]
Maubon, musique de Tani Scala.
© Édition EIMEP-OPERA, Paris;
10Jan47; EF3456. Piano-conductor
score (orchestra, with words),
and parts.

SCARLATTI, DOMENICO, 1685-1757.
Capriccio; [by] Scarlatti-Tausig,
ed. by Ernest Haywood. Piano
solo. © Keith, Prowse & Co.,
ltd., London; on arrangement;
8Aug46; EF5263.

(Sonata, harpsichord) Sonata no.
4 in E minor; (Bibl. marc. bk.
XIV, no. 46) [by] Domenico
Scarlatti, arr. by Lionel Salter.
© Augener, ltd., (British), Lon-
don; on arrangement; 10Dec46;
EF3114. Score (violin and
harpsichord) and part.

35 sonatas for piano; by Domenico
Scarlatti, after the ed. of
Alessandro Longo, [comp. by
Clara Silvers] © Carl Fischer,
inc., New York; on compilation,
new thematic index and text;
v. 1-2; 29Apr47; EP14093-14094.

SCARMOLIN, A   LOUIS.
My creed; words by Elias
Lieberman, music by A.
Louis Scarmolin, for mixed
voices (S.A.T.B.) a cappella.
© Mills Music, inc., New
York; 30Apr47; EP6868.

Nostalgia; for four-part chorus of
mixed voices with piano acc. ...
text by Marion J. Daly, music by
A. Louis Scarmolin. © Carl
Fischer, inc., New York; 29Apr47;
EP14092.

Twilight's rosary; for four-part
chorus of mixed voices with
piano acc. ... text by Marion
J. Daly, music by A. Louis
Scarmolin. © Carl Fischer,
inc., New York; 29Apr47;
EP14091.

SCHADE, C   FRED, 1876-
Oh, mother, little mother mine...
by C. Fred Schade. © C. Fred
Schade, Portland, Or.; 1May47;
EP14907. For voice and piano.

SCHAFER, FRANTIŠEK, 1905-
Furiant. [Op.11. By] František
Schäfer; rev. prof. Vilém Kurz.
(Klavírní repertoir, 22) ©
Hudebni Matice Umělecké Besedy,
Praha, Czechoslovakia; 13Nov42;
EF5081. For piano solo.

(Sonatinas, piano) 3 sonatiny;
pro dospívající mládez, [by]
František Schäfer. Op.6/II ...
(Pratoklady opatrila V. Schä-
ferová-Zelená) © Hudební
Matice Umělecké Besedy, Praha,
Czechoslovakia; 6Apr44; EF5083.
For piano solo.

(Sonatinas, piano) 3 sonatiny;
pro mládez, [by] František
Schäfer. Op. 6/I ...
(prstoklady opatrila V.
Schäferová-Zelená) © Hudební
Matice Umělecké Besedy,
Praha, Czechoslovakia; 6Apr44;
EF5082. For piano solo.

SCHAEFER, JACOB, 1888-1936.
"Moshiach Ben Yosef" ... for soprano solo, chorus and piano
acc., by Jacob Schaeffer [text
by Beinush Shteinman] New York,
Jewish Music Alliance. © Laye
Schaefer, New York; 1Sep45;
EP14476. Yiddish words (transliterated)

SCHAEFER, THEODOR, 1904-
Klavírní etudy. Op. 8. [By]
Theodor Schaefer; rev. prof. R.
Kurzová. © Hudební Matice
Umělecké Besedy, Praha,
Czechoslovakia; 10Oct39;
EF5080.

Romantické skladby; [by] Theodor
Schaefer ... Op.7. Rev. dr. L.
Kundera. © Hudební Matice
Umělecké Besedy, Praha, Czecho-
slovakia; 31Mar42; EF5086. For
piano solo.

SCHAEFFER, ORAETTA.
Let's pretend; words and music
by Oraetta Geoffrion. © Nordyke Publishing Co., Los Angeles;
13Nov45; EP13541.

SCHALIT, HEINRICH, 1886-
The 98th Psalm. (Sing unto the
Lord a new song) For tenor
solo, mixed voices and organ
(S.A.T.B.) © Heinrich Schalit,
Providence; 16May47; EP14491.
Words in Hebrew (transliter-
ated) and English.

SCHAUM, JOHN W   1905-
Johnny jumped the ocean; piano solo
... words and music [by] John W.
Schaum. © Belwin, inc., New
York; 24Dec46; EP10696.

Turkey in the straw; [arr. by]
John W. Schaum. © Belwin, inc.,
New York; on arrangement;
29Apr47; EP14049. For 2
pianos, 8 hands.

SCHAUM, JOHN WESLEY, 1933-
Fiesta in Costa Rica; piano solo
... by John Wesley Schaum, jr.,
[ed. and fingered by John W.
Schaum] © Belwin, inc., New
York; 9May47; EP14465.

SCHAUM, JOHN W   1905-   arr.
Mexican "clap hands" dance ...
[arr. by] John W. Schaum. ©
Belwin, inc., New York; on
arrangement; 29Apr47; EP14051.
For 2 pianos, 8 hands.

SCHEER, LEO.
Scheer violin method ... by
Leo Scheer. © Belwin, inc.,
New York; bk.3, 3Apr47;
EP13200.

SCHER, WILLIAM.
By the wigwam; [by] William Scher.
© Theodore Presser Co.
Philadelphia; 26May47; EP14702.
For piano solo.

La coquette; piano solo, by
William Scher. © Theodore
Presser Co., Philadelphia;
7May47; EP14481.

Dreaming of old Vienna; piano
solo, by William Scher. ©
Mills Music, inc., New York;
16Apr47; EP6827.

Old English; piano solo, by
William Scher. © Mills Music,
inc., New York; 16Apr47;
EP6828.

[SCHIEFELBEIN, FREDERICK ALBERT] 1887-
At the tulip festival; by S. A.
Frederick [pseud.] © Volkwein
Brothers,inc., Pittsburgh;
17Jan47; EP11288. For piano
solo.

Fleeting fancies; by Fred A.
Schiefelbein. © Volkwein Brothers,
inc., Pittsburgh; 17Jan47;
EP11295. For piano solo.

Lazy river; by Fred A. Schiefelbein. © Volkwein Brothers,
inc., Pittsburgh; 17Jan47;
EP11289. For piano solo.

Off to camp ... by S. A.
Frederick [pseud.] © Volkwein
Brothers, inc., Pittsburgh;
17Jan47; EP11294. For piano
solo.

On green meadows; [by] S. A.
Frederick [pseud.] © Volkwein
Brothers, inc., Pittsburgh; 17Jan47;
EP11292. For piano solo.

Russian peasant dance; by Fred
A. Schiefelbein. © Volkwein
Brothers, inc., Pittsburgh;
17Jan47; EP11291. For piano solo.

Sunset hour ... by S. A. Frederick
[pseud.] © Volkwein Brothers,
inc., Pittsburgh; 17Jan47;
EP11293. For piano solo.

Village bells; pedal study, by
Fred A. Schiefelbein. © Volkwein Brothers, inc., Pittsburgh;
17Jan47; EP11296. For piano
solo.

A weird tale; by Fred A. Schiefelbein. © Volkwein Brothers,
inc., Pittsburgh; 17Jan47;
EP11290. For piano solo.

SCHIMMERLING, HANNS ALDO.
Koupím já si koně vraný. The
thorn in the rose, for full chorus
of mixed voices a cappella. The
English text by Edwin McKinley,
music (based on a Czech folk tune)
by H. A. Schimmerling. © Broadcast Music, inc., New York; on
arrangement & English words;
19Mar47; EP14724.

SCHIMMERLING, HANNS ALDO, arr.
Ja som baća velmi starý. The old
shepherd. Chorus for mixed voices
a cappella arr. by H. A.
Schimmerling. English text by
Edwin McKinley. © Broadcast
Music, inc. New York; on arrange-
ment & English text; 12Mar47;
EP14726.

Sadlu muška. The bee (Slovak
folk tune) Chorus for mixed voices
a cappella, arr. by H. A. Schimmerling. English text by Edwin
McKinley. © Broadcast Music,
inc., New York; on arrangement
& English text; 12Mar47; EP14725.

SCHLOSSER, PAUL.
Huit pièces très faciles pour
piano; sur cinq notes, sans
changement de position.
Pentacordes d'ut et de sol
... Par Paul Schlosser, paroles
de Alice Paul Schlosser. ©
Durand & Cie., Paris;
15Mar47; EP3653.

SCHMIDT, MARGUERITE COOK.
Wedding march; by Marguerite Cook
Schmidt. © Marguerite C,
Schmidt, Aurora, Ill.; 26Dec46;
EP10733. For piano solo.

SCHMITT, ALOYS.
Exercices préparatoires. Pre-
paratory exercises ... [By]
Schmitt. Op. 16, [with
supplement by] Jan Nieland. ©
Edition Heuwekemeyer (Firm
A. J. Heuwekemeyer & B. F.
van Gaal), Amsterdam, The
Netherlands; 28Aug45; EP5135.

SCHMITT, FLORENT, 1870-
(Trio, strings) Trio à cordes;
[by] Florent Schmitt. Op. 105.
© Durand & Cie., Paris; 31Dec46;
EP3498.

(Trio, strings) Trio à cordes;
[by] Florent Schmitt. Op. 105.
© Durand & Cie., Paris; 31Dec46;
EP3457. Miniature score.

SCHOECK, OTHMAR, 1886-
Don Ranudo; komische Oper in vier
Aufzügen, nach einer Komödie von
Holberg von Armin Rüeger. Musik
von Othmar Schoeck, Klavierauszug
mit Text von Otto Singer. Leip-
zig, Breitkopf & Härtel. ©
Breitkopf Publications, inc.,
New York; 1Feb19; EP4797. Piano-
vocal score.

SCHOENBERG, ARNOLD, 1874-
Variations on a recitative;
[by] Arnold Schoenberg. [Op.
40. Ed. by Carl Weinrich]
© The H. W. Gray Co., inc.,
New York; 9May47; EP14379.
For organ solo.

SCHOLIN, CARL ALBERT, 1896-
Czecho-Slovakian dance song;
for two choirs ... S.S.A.
[and] ... S.A.T.B., arr. by
C. Albert Scholin. [Words
by Ruth B. Scholin] © Belwin,
inc., New York; on arrangement;
3Mar47; EP12754.

Dear Land and Father of mankind ...
for mixed voices with soprano or
tenor solo; music by C. Albert
Scholin, words by John G.
Whittier. [St. Louis, Distributors, Hunleth Music Co.]
© C. Albert Scholin, St. Louis;
26Apr47; EP14006.

Let our gladness know no end;
for senior and intermediate
choirs, [Bohemian carol] arr.
by C. Albert Scholin. ©
Belwin, inc., New York; on
arrangement; 3Apr47; EP13195.

Were you there? [For] mixed
voices, Negro spiritual arr.
by C. Albert Scholin.
[St. Louis, Distributors,
Hunleth Music Co.] © C.
Albert Scholin, St. Louis;
on arrangement; 26Apr47;
EP14007.

SCHONBRUN, BERNARD.
Sin tu amor. (Without your love)
... English words by Bernard
Schonbrun, Spanish words by
Tony Carrillo, music by Ber-
nard Schonbrun. © Caribbean
Music, inc., New York; 17Mar47;
EP12655.

SCHOR, ALBERTO LAO. See
Lao Schor, Alberto.

SCHOSTAKOVICH, D. See
Shostakovich, Dmitrii Dmitrievich.

SCHOTT, JIM, 1917-
Vous ... paroles de René Gonot,
musique de Jim Schott.
© Éditions Musicales Nuances,
Paris; 15Feb47; EF5481.

SCHRAD, ED
Rondino; by Ed. Schrad. New York,
Harmonia Edition. © Harmonia
Edition Publishing Co., New York;
30Dec46; EP6466. For piano or
organ solo.

SCHRADER, MOGENS, d.1934.
I de lyse naetter ... Af M.
Schrader, tekst: D. Schrader.
© Wilhelm Hansen, Musik-Forlag,
Copenhagen; 3Jul30; EF5046.

SCHREIER-BOTTERO.
Tango of roses. (Tango delle rose)
By Schreier-Bottero, arr. for piano
solo by F. Gonzales. © Edward B.
Marks Music Corp., New York; on
arrangement; 30Dec46; EP11571.

SCHROEDER, JOHN H
Old Antico waltzes; by John H.
Schroeder. © J. H. Schroeder,
Wausau, Wis.; 31Dec46; EP6476.
For piano solo.

SCHRØDER, WALTHER ANTON, 1895-
Rebild Bakker; Dansk Rhapsodi.
Rebild National Park;
Danish rhapsody ... for
Orkester, [by] Walther
Schrøder. Op. 15. ©
Skandinavisk Musikforlag
Aktieselskab, København;
28Mar47; EF3601.

SCHUBERT, FRANZ PETER, 1797-1828.
Ave Maria; [by] Schubert, adapted
by A. Siegel. © McKinley
Publishers, inc., Chicago; on
arrangement; 26Dec46; EP10817.
For piano solo, with words.

Ave Maria. God of our Father ...
For junior and senior choirs,
music by Franz Schubert, arr. by
C. Albert Scholin. English version by Ruth B. Scholin. © Belwin, inc., New York; on English
words & arrangement; 3Apr47;
EP14009.

Ave Maria. God of our Father ...
For mixed voices with tenor
solo, S.A.T.B. Music by Franz
Schubert, arr. by C. Albert
Scholin. English version by
Ruth B. Scholin. © Belwin, inc.,
New York; on English words &
arrangement; 3Apr47; EP14011.

Ave Maria. God of our Father ...
For ... S.S.A., music by Franz
Schubert, arr. by C. Albert
Scholin. English version by
Ruth B. Scholin. © Belwin, inc.,
New York; on English words & ar-
rangement; 3Apr47; EP14010.

The cross of faith; (from "Das
Gebet des Herrn") ... words
adapted from Henry Francis Lyte
by Hugh Ross. (In Ross, Hugh,
arr. Sacred choruses for women's
or girls' voices. p. 32-36) ©
G. Schirmer, inc., New York; on
arrangement; 30Sep46; EP9782.

Ecossaise in D, [by] F. Schubert.
Minuet in Bb [by] G. F. Handel.
For drums, tambourines, triangles
and cymbals, arr. by Rowena
Cohen. [London] Boosey & Hawkes.
© Boosey & Co., ltd., London; on
arrangement; 29May47; EF3420.

Gott im Frühling. God in springtime. [Words by] J. P. Uz, English version by Lorraine Noel
Finley. (In Swarthout, Gladys,
comp. Gladys Swarthout album of
concert songs and arias. p. 14-
17) © G. Schirmer, inc., New
York; on English version;
21Feb46; EP2414.

SCHUBERT, FRANZ PETER. Cont'd.

Jesus, to Thy table led ... for mixed voices, [by] Franz Schubert, arr. by Frederick E. Starke, [words by] Robert H. Baynes. © Oliver Ditson Co., Philadelphia; on arrangement; 16Apr47; EP13890.

Marche militaire; [by] Franz Schubert. Op.51, no.1. Piano arrangement in concert-style by Carl Tausig ... rev. and ed. by Maxwell Eckstein. © Carl Fischer, inc., New York; on revision; 14Dec46; EP11133.

La mer. By the sea. (Am Meer) ... [By] F. Schubert, arr. by A. Passio. © Éditions A. Passio, Lachute, Que.; on arrangement; 26May47; EF3522. Score (trombone or baritone and piano) and part.

SCHUBERT, FRANZ PETER, 1797-1828.
Minuet, from Symphony no. 5 in B major. See his Symphony no. 5 in B major.

Minuet (in F); [by] Franz Schubert, [arr. by] Reuven Kosakoff, [ed. by Stella Nahum and Lillian Reznikoff Wolfe] © Clayton F. Summy Co., Chicago; 26Jun46; EP11109. Score: piano 1-2.

Moment musical; [by] Schubert, arr. by Jeff Muston. © Irwin Dash Music Co., ltd., London; on arrangement; 18Mar47; EF3300. Piano-conductor score (orchestra), and parts.

The omnipotence; SAB accompanied, [by] Schubert, arr. by Wallingford Riegger. © Harold Flammer, inc., New York; on arrangement; 14Mar47; EP13468.

Schubert (a bouquet of music); [arr. by Victor Ambroise. c1946] © Lawrence Wright Music Co., ltd London; 2May47; EF3257. For piano solo.

Schubert's serenade [and] Drigo's serenade; in one ed. .... arr. by Walter L. Rosemont. © Edwards Music Co., New York; on arrangement; 11Jan47; EP11341. Parts for piano and 2 instruments, or small orchestra.

Song of the brook. Wohin. By F. Schubert; arr. and ed. for women's chorus, S.S.A., by Noble Cain. [Words by Wilhelm Mueller, free translation by Noble Cain] © Choral Art Publications, New York; on arrangement; 8May47; EP14390. English text.

Souvenirs from the great masters, Schubert; selected and arr. by G. H. Clutsam. © Keith Prowse & Co., ltd., London; on arrangement; 30Dec46; EF4796. For piano solo.

(Symphony no. 5) Minuet, from Symphony no. 5 in Bᵇ major; [by] Franz Schubert, arr. by Eric Steiner. © G. Schirmer, inc., New York; 11Apr47; EP14076. Two scores for piano 1-2.

Ter sanctus; (from the German mass) ... tr. by Hugh Ross. (In Ross, Hugh, arr. Sacred choruses for women's or girls' voices. p. 146-150) © G. Schirmer, inc., New York; on arrangement; 30Sep46; EP9795.

Unfinished symphony; by Franz Schubert ... [words by Elsie-Jean, pseud.] arr. by Hugo Frey. © Hamilton S. Gordon, inc., New York; on arrangement and words; 11Jun47; EP15061. For piano solo, with words.

SCHUETKY, FR JOS
Send forth Thy Spirit. Emitte Spiritum Tuum. For ... S.S.A., [by] Fr. Jos. Schuetky, arr. by Frederic Fay Swift. © Pro Art Publications, New York; on arrangement; 25Mar47; EP13402.

SCHÜTZ, HEINRICH, 1585-1672.
Lord, be pleased to deliver me; (no. 2 of "Five small sacred concerts") ... tr. by Hugh Ross. (In Ross, Hugh, arr. Sacred choruses for women's or girls' voices. p. 88-97) © G. Schirmer, inc., New York; on arrangement; 30Sep46; EP9788.

SCHUTZ, ALFRED.
Papaveri di Montecassino. (Czerwone maki na Monte Cassino) Testo di Felix Conarschi-Rofren, versione italiana di Marino, musica di Alfred Schütz. © Edizioni Musicali Sciacca, Roma; 1Jun46; EF3223. Italian words.

SCHULMAN, ROSE MARIE, 1914-
I've got April in my heart; words and music by Rose Marie Schulman, [arr. by Ewing Reid] Vandalia, Ill., J. J. Shulman. © Rose Marie Schulman, Vandalia, Ill., 7Apr47; EP13786.

Not a minute too soon; words and music by Martha Nelle Welch [and] Rose Marie Schulman. Vandalia, Ill., J. J. Shulman. © Rose Marie Schulman & Martha Nelle Welch, Vandalia, Ill.; 7Apr47; EP13785.

Will you care? Words and music by Rose Marie Schulman, [arr. by Ewing Reid] Vandalia, Ill., J. J. Shulman. © Rose Marie Schulman, Vandalia, Ill.; 7Apr47; EP13787.

SCHUMAN, WILLIAM H
Holiday song ... [by] William Schuman, [words by Genevieve Taggard, arr. by the composer] © G. Schirmer, inc., New York; on arrangement; 30Dec46; EP11514.

Undertow; choreographic episodes ... for orchestra, [by] William Schuman. © G. Schirmer, inc., New York; 30Dec46; EP11688.

SCHUMANN, ROBERT ALEXANDER, 1810-1856.
Album for the young; [by] Robert Schumann. Op.68. For the piano, ed. by Harold Bauer. © G. Schirmer, inc., New York; on instructions & directions; 13Aug46; EP10937.

Fantasia; [by] Robert Schumann. Op.17. For the piano, ed. by Harold Bauer. © G. Schirmer, inc., New York; on instructions & directions; 13Aug46; EP10938.

Faschingsschwank aus Wien ... [by] Robert Schumann. Op.26. For the piano, ed. by Harold Bauer. © G. Schirmer, inc., New York; on instructions & directions; 5Sep46; EP10936.

Happy farmer; by Robert Schumann ... with words [by Elsie-Jean, pseud.] ... arr. by Hugo Frey. © Hamilton S. Gordon, inc., New York; on arrangement and words; 23Jun47; EP15287.

Papillons. Op. 2. [Ed. de travail par] Alfred Cortot. © Éditions Salabert, Paris; on study edition; 2Dec45; EF2230. For piano solo.

Robert Schumann. [A collection of selected compositions] ... Comp. by Alex M. Kramer, ed. by Ben Kendall. © Bregman, Vocco and Conn, inc., New York; 28Mar47; EP13457. For piano solo.

Scenes from childhood; for the piano, [by] Robert Schumann. Op. 15. Edited by Harold Bauer. © G. Schirmer, inc., New York; on instructions & directions; 23Mar47; EP6146.

Schumann, excerpts from his greatest works; [arr. by Victor Ambroise] © Lawrence Wright Music Co. ltd., London; 20Jun47; EF3934. For piano solo.

(Symphony, no. 4) Symphony no. four (in D minor); [by] Robert Schumann, for piano two hands. Ed. and annotated by Percy Goetschius. (Analytic symphony series, no. 35) © Oliver Ditson Co., Philadelphia; on biography, critical note, preface & editorial annotations; 9Feb40; EP11997.

SCHUSTER, IRA, d.1946.
Dance of the paper dolls; two part, S.A., words and music by Johnny Tucker, Joe Schuster and John Siras, [pseud.], arr. by Douglas MacLean, [pseud.] © M. Witmark & Sons, New York; on arrangement; 5Jun47; EP15167.

[SCHWAB, ALEXANDRE] 1910-
Carillon du clocher; paroles et musique de Marc Fontenoy [pseud.] © Éditions Salmer, Paris; 6Feb47; EF3505.

SCHWARTZ, ARTHUR, 1900-
Dancing in the dark; by Arthur Schwarts, transcribed by F. Campbell-Watson. © Harms, inc., New York; on arrangement; 10Feb47; EP12004. Piano-conductor score (orchestra) and parts.

SCIONTI, SILVIO, 1900-
Road to piano artistry; a collection of classic and romantic compositions comp., graded and ed. ... with interpretative and technical comment by Silvio Scionti. © Carl Fischer, inc., New York; on compiling, editing & grading; v.6. 24Feb47; v.7, 8May47; v.8, 5Aug47; EP12432, 15022, 16267.

SCIVER, ESTHER VAN. See Van Sciver, Esther.

SCOTT, CHARLES WESLEY.
Tulips for you; words and music by Charles Wesley Scott. © Cine-Mart Music Publishing Co., Hollywood, Calif.; 1Nov46; EP11720.

SCOTT, JIM.
The midnite special; words and music by Jim Scott. © Peer International Corp., New York; 30Dec46; EP11636.

Remember I feel someone, too; words and music by Jim Scott, piano arrangement by Larry Stanton. © Peer International Corp., New York; 27Dec46; EP11635.

SCOTT, LANNIE, 1908-
Jim jam boogie; by Lannie Scott. © Popular Music Co., New York; 4Jun47; EP14887. For piano solo, with chord symbols.

SCOTT, RAYMOND.
In an eighteenth century drawing room ... By Raymond Scott, arr. by F. Henri Klickmann. © Advanced Music Corp., New York; on arrangement; 15May47; EP14708. Score (xylophone or marimba and piano) and part.

127

SCOTT, TOM.
Down the wind; choral fantasia with orchestral acc. Music composed and arr. by Tom Scott, lyrics written and adapted by Joy Scott. [For] mixed chorus. [c1946] © Words and Music, inc., New York; 28Jan47; EP11901.

SCOTTO, VINCENT BAPTISTE, 1874-
L'aventure est au coin de la rue; paroles de Daniel Norman & Jean Rodor [pseud.] © Éditions réunies Ver Luisant-Codini-Julsam, Paris; 15Jun44; EF2033. For voice and piano.

La chanson du soleil; paroles de Géo Koger [pseud.] & Vincent Scotto, musique de Vincent Scotto. © Éditions Royalty, Paris; 25Nov46; EF5190.

Les Cosaques du Don; paroles de Jean Rodor [pseud.], musique de Vincent Scotto. © Éditions Royalty, Paris; 15Dec46; EF5187.

SCULL, HAROLD T
Sing ivy; unison song, music by Harold T. Scull, words traditional. © Edward Arnold & Co., London; 12Dec46; EF4754.

SEAMAN, FLOYD MONROE.
One great love ... lyrics, music, and text arr. ... by Floyd Monroe Seaman. © Monroe Music Co., Uniontown, Pa.; 28Feb47; EP5214. Score: solo voices, mixed chorus and piano.

SECORD, GEORGIA KING.
Everything is lovely when the sun shines; words and music by Georgia King Secord. [c1946] © Georgia King Secord, Trumansburg, N.Y.; 22Apr47; EP14251.

SEDLON, JOSEF HARRY.
Introducing the accordion, 12 to 120 bass; by J. H. Sedlon. © Sam Fox Publishing Co., New York; 28Apr47; EP14240.

SEDLON, JOSEPH HARRY, 1907-
The Sedlon method for the modern pianist; [composed and arr. by Joseph Harry Sedlon, comp. and ed. by Constance K. Sedlon] © Sedlon Music Co., Joseph H. and Constance Sedlon, sole owners, Cleveland; bk.3, 18Oct46; EP10906.

SEEGR, JOSEPH, 1716-1782.
Acht Toccaten und Fugen für die Orgel; von Joseph Seegr ... mit einer Vorrede von Daniel Gottlob Türk. [New pref. and revision by Piet Visser] © Edition Heuwekemeyer (Firm A. J. Heuwekemeyer & B. F. van Gaal), Amsterdam; on revision; 23Feb46; EF3385.

SEGOND, PIERRE, 1913-
Trois mélodies; pour chant et piano, [by] Pierre Segond ... [words by] Francis Carco ... [and] Tristan Derème ... © Durand & Cie., Paris; 10Jan47; EF3478.

SEIBER, MATYAS, 1905-
Yugoslav folk-songs; for mixed voices (unaccompanied) English words by A. L. Lloyd and Fred Harry, [music arr. by] Mátyás Seiber. © Boosey & Co., ltd., London; on arrangement & English words; 13May47; EF3286.

SEITZ, HARRY.
A Lenten song; for S.S.A.T.T.B., music by Harry Seitz, words by Delphine Schmitt. © McLaughlin & Reilly Co., Boston; 1May47; EP14882.

SELYRN, A., pseud. See
Salerno, Nicola.

SENAILLE, JEAN BAPTISTE.
Introduction and Allegro spiritoso; euphonium solo, [by] J. B. Senaillé ... arr. [by] Denis Wright. © William Paxton & Co., ltd., London; on arrangement; 25Nov46; EF9432. Cornet-conductor score (band) and parts.

SENDREY, AL.
I'll write myself a letter; words by Iona Howell, music by Al Sendrey. © Cine-mart Music Publishing Co., Hollywood, Calif.; 1Aug46; EP10962. For voice and piano, with chord symbols.

SENÉE, HENRI.
Tircis ... by Henri Senée, arr. by L. W. Chidester. © Southern Music Co., San Antonio; on arrangement; 14May47; EP15045. Condensed score (band) and parts.

SENTIS, JOSÉ, 1888-
Blanca Rosa ... de José Sentis, arrt. de Francis Salabert. Volveras ... paroles espagnoles de R. Medina et J. Teruel [pseud.], musique de José Sentis, arrt. de Francis Salabert. Paris, Salabert. © Salabert, inc., New York; on arrangement; 15Jan47; EF3594. Piano conductor score (orchestra, with words), and parts.

Bulorias; chants andalous, paroles de Medina et Teruel [pseud.], musique de José Sentis. © Éditions Salabert, Paris; 31Jan41; EF3878.

Coqueta ... musique de José Sentis, arrangement de Francis Salabert ... Cielito mio ... musique de Osvaldo N. Fresedo, arrangement de Francis Salabert. © Éditions Salabert, Paris; 10Feb47; EF3805. Piano-conductor score (orchestra), and parts.

[SESSIONS, JAMES BYRL] 1911-   ed.
For your tunejoyment; songs, old & new, [compiled and edited by Evang. and Mrs. J. B. Sessions] © The Family Worship Hour, Fairmont, W. Va.; 1Aug46; EP12053.

SESSLER, JAMES RUSSELL, 1924-
For the Master's use; [by] Russell Sessler, jr. © Russell Sessler, jr., Uniontown, Pa.; 31Mar47; EP13212. Close score: SATB.

SESSLER, RUSSELL. See
Sessler, James Russell.

SEUEL-HOLST, MARIE.
June morning ... For piano, by Marie Seuel-Holst. [c1946] © The Willis Music Co., Cincinnati; 18Apr47; EP13879.

[SEVIER, LORRAINE]
Whistling Jerry; [by Lorraine Sevier] © Lorraine Magney, Cora, Mo.; 10Jan47; EP11354. For voice and piano.

SEVIER, MERTIE MAE.
Spanish noodle waltz; by Mertie Mae Sevier, Cora, Mo.; 26Dec46; EP10732. For voice and piano.

SEYMER, WILLIAM, 1890-
Sånger av William Seymer. © Nordiska Musikförlaget, a/b, Stockholm; on 3 songs; 1Aug19; EF5387-5389. For voice and piano. Contents.- [1] Med röde roser; words by Knut Hamsun.- [2] Stiller gang; words by Dehmel, tr. by Vilh. Ekelund.- [3] Dryaden; words by A. Österling.

Skogsnymfen dansar; av William Seymer, arr. [by] Sven Sköld. © Nordiska Musikförlaget, a.b., Stockholm; 1Jan44; EF3733. Piano-conductor score (orchestra), and parts.

Strofer i sol och skugga .... Strophes in sun and shadow. För piano, av William Seymer. Op.6. © Nordiska Musikförlaget, a/b, Stockholm; on 14 pieces; 1Sep19. Contents.- häfte 1. Sommarmorgon. Summer morning (© EF3689) Stilla manskensnatt. Quiet moonshiny night (© EF3690) En vårvals. A spring walts (© EF3691) Vid en skogstjärn. At a woodland tarn (© EF3692) Mott kväll. Song at eve (© EF3693) Heden blommar. The heath in bloom (© EF3694) Gra oktoberdag. Grey October day (© EF3695) Stjärnnatt. Starry night (© EF3696) Ett gammalt minne. An old memory (© EF3697) - häfte 2. Gryning pa havet. Dawn on the sea (© EF3698) Varstycke. A piece of spring (© EF3699) Nattlig dyning. Swelling waves in the night (© EF3700) Det var en gang. Once upon a time (© EF3701) Högsommar. In the height of summer (© EF3702)

SEYMOUR, JOHN LAURENCE.
Elegiac tone poem no. 2, in F minor; [by] John Laurence Seymour. Op.9, no.2. San Francisco, Banner Play Bureau, inc. © John Laurence Seymour, San Francisco; 8Jun46; EP12145. Score (viola and piano) and part.

The Lord victorious; anthem for mixed choir (SATB) with organ accompaniment, by John Laurence Seymour. Op. 52. [Text: I Chronicles 29:1 11-13] San Francisco, Banner Play Bureau. © John Laurence Seymour, San Francisco; 20Dec46; EP10978.

Six melodic pieces; [by] John Laurence Seymour. Op.8. San Francisco, Banner Play Bureau. © John Laurence Seymour, Sacramento, Calif.; no.5, 23Sep46; EP11195. Score (violin and piano) and part. Contents.- no.5. By the sundial.

SGAMBELLONE, GUIDO.
No longer blue; words by J. H. Goodman, music by Guido Sgambellone. © Nordyke Publishing Co., Los Angeles; 5Mar47; EP13549.

SHADWELL, CHARLES, 1898-
Down with the curtain ... [by] Charles Shadwell, arr. by Ronald Hanmer. © Ascherberg, Hopwood & Crew, ltd., London; on arrangement; 10Apr47; EF5629. Piano-conductor score (orchestra) and

[SHAFTEL, ART]
There's that lonely feeling again; words and music by Bobb Arthur [pseud.]. © Mellin Music, inc., New York; 28Apr47; EP14346.

SHAND, TERRY.
Dream street; lyric by "By" Dunham, music by Terry Shand. © George Simon, inc., New York; 2Jan47; EP11087.

Possum song; (Six, tall, slim, slick, sycamore saplin'); lyric by "By" Dunham, music by Terry Shand. © Harry Warren Music, inc., New York; 14Feb47; EP12150.

Where does it get you in the end? Lyric by "By" Dunham, music by Terry Shand. © George Simon, inc., New York; 6Jan47; EP11088.

SHANNON, GRACE.
Yes, yes, honey (you've got me
eatin' right out of your hand);
words by Wiley Patterson, music
by Grace Shannon. © Chelsea
Music Corp., New York; 15Jan47;
EP11518.

SHAPIRO, GEORGE H
Seventeen to sing; lyrics by
Gladys L. Adshead, music by
George H. Shapiro, pictures by
Decie Merwin. © Oxford Uni-
versity Press, New York, inc.,
New York; 23Dec46; EP12322.

SHAPIRO, TED.
Far-away island; by Benny Davis
and Ted Shapiro, [arranged by
Vic Schoen] © Leeds Music Corp.,
New York; on arrangement;
31Dec46; EP12007. Piano-conductor score (orchestra, with
words) and parts.
Far-away island; by Benny Davis
and Ted Shapiro, special vocal background arr. by Bob Morse. C orig.
© Leeds Music Corp., New York;
31Dec46; EP10842. Piano-conductor
score (orchestra, with words) and
parts.
Far-away island; by Benny Davis
[and] Ted Shapiro, special
vocal background arr. by Bob
Morse. [Key of] G. © Leeds
Music Corp., New York; 31Dec46;
EP10841. Piano-conductor
score (orchestra, with words)
and parts.
Far-away island; by Benny Davis
[and] Ted Shapiro, © [c1947]
© Leeds Music Corp., New York;
31Dec46; EP12009. For voice
and piano, with chord symbols.

SHARP, VERNON LATHOM.
Serenade to happiness. ("Some-
times life is all of roses")
Song, words and music by
Vernon Lathrom Sharp. ©
Lawrence Wright Music Co., ltd.,
London; 31Dec46; EF4730.

SHARPLES, ROBERT, arr.
Scottish Paul Jones; a selection
of Scottish melodies specially
arr. in the modern manner for a
Paul Jones by Robert Sharples.
© Bradbury Wood, ltd., London;
on arrangement; 9Dec46; EF4784.
Piano-conductor score (orchestra, with words) and parts.

SHAW, GEOFFREY, 1879-1944.
Laugh and be merry; arr. for chorus
of mixed voices (S.C.T.B.) by
Martin Shaw. Words by John Masefield ... music by Geoffrey Shaw.
© J. Curwen & Sons, ltd., London;
on arrangement; 9Dec46; EF4762.

SHAW, MARTIN.
The bubble song; words by Mabel
Dearmer, music by Martin Shaw,
arr. for ... S. S. A. by Clarence
Lucas. © Chappell & Co., ltd.,
London; on arrangement; 1May47;
EF3416.

SHAW, OLIVER.
For the gentlemen; [by] Oliver
Shaw, for woodwind quartet
(flute, oboe or clarinet in
B♭, and bassoon) Rev. and ed.
by Roger Smith. © Mercury
Music Corp., New York; on
arrangement; 21Mar47; EP12597.

SHAY, VIRGINIUS H
His kisses made a Mrs. out of me;
words and music by V. H. Shay.
© Puritan Publishing Co., inc.,
Chicago; 10Sep46; EP11235.

SHEFFIELD, CORA.
Come to Utah ... Words and music
by Cora and Ralph Sheffield.
© Sheffield Enterprises, Salt
Lake City; 1Apr47; EP13442.

SHELLABARGER, CARL ELWOOD, 1905-
Rural community ... By Carl E.
Shellabarger. [Op. 199]
© Fireside Publications,
(owned by Carl Elwood & Mary
Lovina Shuelabarger), Syracuse,
N. Y.; 18Apr47; EP14475. For
piano solo.

SHELLEY, H   R
Christian, the morn breaks sweetly
o'er thee; for ... S.S.A. (incidental soli: soprano-contralto)
opt. [By] R. R. Shelley, arr.
by Russell Watson [pseud.]
© Pro Art Publications, New York;
on arrangement; 21Apr47;
EP13601.

SHELLY, LOU.
Be yourself (and you'll be you);
words and music by Joe Schuster,
Johnny Tucker and Lou Shelly.
© Mills Music, inc., New York;
23May47; EP6927.

SHELTON, BERTHA.
Let's be sweethearts always; by
Bertha Shelton, [words by]
Norman Kelly [and I'll never
be sweetheart again; words
and music by Al Stewart and
Ellen Steen] © Kelly Music
Publications, Franklin, Pa.;
31Dec46; EP13297-13298.

SHENK, LOUIS, 1881-
Two heroic hymns of praise ...
By Louis Shenk. Philadelphia,
The Philadelphia Music Press.
© Louis Shenk, Philadelphia;
on new music & changes in
words; 7Apr47; EP13927. Con-
tents.- Jesus, Thy boundless
love to me (Paul Gerhardt)-
Jesus, our mighty Lord (James
Miller)

SHEPARD, RILEY.
Handle with care; by Billy Hayes
and Riley Shepard. © Robbins
Music Corp., New York; 19Dec46;
EP11003. For voice and piano,
with chord symbols.
Twenty years of sorrow; by Billy
Hayes, Milton Leeds [pseud. and]
Riley Shepard. © Edwin H. Morris
& Co., inc., New York; 8Jan47;
EP11125. For voice and piano,
with chord symbols.
Who's your baby, Hoosier baby?
Words and music by Erwin King
and Riley Shepard. © Peer
International Corp., New York;
15May47; EP14577.

SHERMAN, ALICE E
Eastern Star of light and glory;
by Alice E. Sherman. Plattsburg, N. Y., Sherman Publications.
© Alice E. Sherman, Plattsburg,
N. Y.; 26Dec46; EP10731. For
piano solo.

SHIELD, LEROY.
Cuban carnival ... for piano, by
Leroy Shield, [arr. by D. Savino]
© Robbins Music Corp., New York;
on arrangement; 27Nov46; EP11812.

SHIELD, ROY.
The golden spike. See his Union
Pacific suite.
(Union Pacific suite) The golden
spike; from the Union Pacific
suite, composed and arr. by Roy
Shield. © Bregman, Vocco and
Conn, inc., New York; on arrange-
ment; 28Apr47; EP14101. Con-
densed score (band) and parts.

SHIRL, JIMMY, pseud. See
Mendelsohn, Jack.

SHOFFNER, MAGGIE FOGLEMAN.
There's a garden where Jesus was
praying; words and music by
Maggie Fogleman Shoffner. [c1941]
© Maggie Fogleman Shoffner,
Burlington, N. C.; 4Mar47; EP6494.
Close score: SATB.

SHORT, LEON.
Dissatisfied; by Jimmie and Leon
Short. © Acuff-Rose Publications,
Nashville; 21Jan47; EP11437. For
voice and piano, with guitar diagrams
and chord symbols.

SHOSTAKOVICH, DMITRII DMITRIEVICH,
1906-
Dance from "Golden age;" by
D. Shostakovich, arranged
for violoncello and piano by
Joseph Schuster. © Edward
B. Marks Music Corp., New
York; on arrangement; 28Mar47;
EP13096.
Nine pieces for piano; [by]
Shostakovich. (Contemporary
masterpieces, album no.19) ©
Edward B. Marks Music Corp., New
York; on 3 pieces; 9Apr47;
EP13437-13439. Partial contents
(Selections from Lady Macbeth of
Mtsensk, arr. by Frederick Block) -
Dance prelude.- Interlude.-
Grotesque scene.
(Quartet, strings, no. 2) Quartet no.
2; [by] Dmitri Shostakovich. [Op.
69] [Ed. with special annotations
and foreword by Harold Sheldon]
© Leeds Music Corp., New York; on
editing and foreword; 2Jun47;
EP14976. Parts: 2 violins, viola
and violoncello.
(Sonata, violoncello and piano)
Sonata for violoncello and piano,
[op. 40, by] Dmitri Shostakovich,
ed. with special annotations [and
foreword] by Gregor Piatigorsky.
© Leeds Music Corp., New York; on
foreword and editing; 2Jun47;
EP14974. Score and part.
(Trio, piano, violin & violoncello) Trio for piano,violin
and violoncello; [by] Dmitri
Shostakovich. [Op. 67] Ed.
with special annotations [and
foreword] by Harold Sheldon.
© Leeds Music Corp., New York;
on editing and foreword;
2Jun47; EP14977. Score and
parts.
Two pieces; for string octet.
[Op. 11. Ed. with special annotations by Harold Sheldon] ©
Leeds Music Corp., New York; on
foreword; 26Apr47; EP4231.

SHOUCAIR, CARL G
When it's Easter lily time; words
and music by Carl G. Shoucair.
© Carl G. Shoucair, New York;
1Apr47; EP13992.

SHRADER, JOHN L
No atheists in foxholes; words
by Lora K. Mayes, music by
John L. Shrader. © Lora K.
Mayes, Ft. Payne, Ala.;
9Apr47; EP13676. Score: SATB
and piano, with guitar diagrams
and chord symbols.

SHUART, BILLY.
Poor Maggie Brown; words and
music by Gene Roland, Vido
Musso [and] Billy Shuart.
© Regent Music Corp., New
York; 19Feb47; EP12468.

SHURE, RALPH DEANE, 1885-
The carpenter's Son; ten choral
anthems for treble voices
(S.A.), by R. Deane Shure.
© Mills Music, inc., New
York; 30Apr47; EP6667.
God of the wind and wave; S.A.T.B.
... by R. Deane Shure. ©
Bolwin, inc., New York; 31Dec46;
EP10932.
God of the wind and wave; S.S.A.
... by R. Deane Shure. ©
Bolwin, inc., New York; 31Dec46;
EP10933.

129

SHURE, RALPH DEANE. Cont'd.
He walketh upon the wings of the wind; S.S.A., a capella, [music] by R. Deane Shure. [Scriptural text] © Belwin, inc., New York; 31Dec46; EP10934.

An old spring madrigal; [by] R. Deane Shure, [words by Thomas Weelkes] (For mixed voices, a cappella) © Oliver Ditson Co., Philadelphia; 5Feb47; EP11880.

On Jordan's stormy banks; S.A.T.B., white spiritual. [Words by Samuel Stennett, music] by R. Deane Shure. © Belwin, inc., New York; 31Dec46; EP10931.

Prayer abiding ... Words by Samuel Ellsworth Kiser, music by R. Deane Shure. St. Louis, Hunleth Music Co. © C. Albert Scholin, St. Louis; on arrangement; 20Feb47; EP12080.

Thou purple morn rejoice; (mixed voices) [Music by] R. Deane Shure, [words from St. Francis of Assisi] St. Louis, Distributors, Hunleth Music Co. © C. Albert Scholin, St. Louis; 8Jan47; EP10927.

SIBELIUS, JEAN, 1865-
The Lord's prayer; Our Heavenly Father, the music by Jean Sibelius [Finlandia], arr. by Richard D. Row. © R. D. Row Music Co., Boston; on adaptation; 31Mar47; EP13329. For voice and piano.

SICKLE, ROBERT VAN. See Van Sickle, Robert.

THE "SIDE BY SIDE SERIES" OF PIANO DUETS. © Edwin Ashdown, ltd., London; bk. 9, 8Feb47; EF3119. Bk. 9, by Alec Rowley.

SIECZYNSKI, RUDOLF.
Vienna dreams; four part male voices T.T.B.B., words by Irving Caesar, music by Rudolf Sieczynski, arr. by William Stickles. © Harms, inc., New York; on arrangement; 17Jun47; EP15273.

SIEGEL, ARSENE FREDERIC.
Dance of the puppets; [by] Arsene Siegel, for piano. [c1946] © McKinley Publishers, inc., Chicago; 7May47; EP14317.

Little Boy Blue boogie; by Frederic Darsen, [pseud.] © McKinley Publishers, inc., Chicago; 26Dec46; EP10846. For piano solo.

Little Boy Blue boogie; by Frederic Darsen [pseud.] © McKinley Publishers, inc., Chicago; 31Dec46; EP12187. For piano solo.

Mr. Boogie Woogie, junior; by Frederic Darsen, [pseud.] © McKinley Publishers, inc., Chicago; 26Dec46; EP10845. For piano solo.

Mr. Boogie Woogie Junior; by Frederic Darsen [pseud.] © McKinley Publishers, inc., Chicago; 31Dec46; EP12186. For piano solo.

Toy train; for piano, [by] Arsene Siegel. © McKinley Publishers, inc., Chicago; 31Dec46; EP12410.

Wild West boogie; by Frederic Darsen [pseud.] © McKinley Publishers, inc., Chicago; 10Feb47; EP12043. For piano solo.

SIEGEL, IRVING URBAN ANTON.
"Good-bye, old Mexico moon"; [music] by Irving Siegel & [words by] Hazel Jarvis. © Irving Urban Anton Siegel, Marshfield, Wis.; 15Sep46; EP6478. Melody and words.

SIEGEL, PAUL, 1914-
A cigarette in Europe; music and words; Paul Siegel ... deutsche Worte: Erich Meder, 2. Chorusstrophe: Dr. Pauli Kuchelbacher. © Ludwig Doblinger (Bernhard Herzmansky), k.g., Vienna; 18Jun46; EP3791.

In Vienna so far away; music and words [by] Paul Siegel, (German words by Erich Meder) © Ludwig Doblinger (Bernhard Herzmansky), k.g., Vienna; 26Jun46; EF3789.

SIEGEL, RALPH MARIA.
Rondinella pellegrina ... testo di C. Deani, musica di R. M. Siegel. (In Un sorriso e 20 canzoni. p. 8-9) © Edizioni Leonardi, s.a.r.l., Milano; 7Nov45; EF4913. For voice and piano.

SIEGL, OTTO, 1896-
(Sonata, violin & piano, no.2) Zweite sonate, (c-moll) ... von Otto Siegl ... Op. 117. © Ludwig Doblinger (Bernhard Herzmansky), K. G., Vienna; 16Apr41; EF3404. Score and part.

Zweite sonate. See his Sonata, violin & piano, no. 2.

SIEGMEISTER, ELIE, 1909-
American legends; six songs for voice and piano composed by Elie Siegmeister. © Edward B. Marks Music Corp., New York; on 4 songs, 19Mar47. EP13407 has new matter: English lyric & arrangement. Contents.- Paul Bunyan; words by Leo Paris (© EP13404) - Nancy Hanks; words by Rosemary Benet (© EP13405)- John Reed; words by Lewis Allan (© EP13406) - Johnny Appleseed; words by Rosemary Benet. Lazy afternoon, from "Ozark set"; words by Leo Paris (© EP13407) - The Lincoln penny; words by Alfred Kreymborg.

The devil and the farmer's wife; for mixed voices S.A.T.B., arr. by Elie Siegmeister. © Edward B. Marks Music Corp., New York; on arrangement; 23Jun47; EP15208.

SIEGMEISTER, ELIE, 1909-   arr.
Singing down the road; songs ... chosen and arr. for male voices by Elie Siegmeister ... and Rufus A. Wheeler. © Ginn and Co., Boston; 28Mar47; A13127.

SIEM, KARE, 1914-
Skorgelaten; [by] Kare Siem. [Oslo] Musikk-Huset. © Kare Siem, Oslo, Norway; 17Nov45; EF5088. Score (violin and piano) and part.

SIEMONN, GEORGE.
Ulysses; for voice and piano, [words by Berton Braley, music] by George Siemonn. © G. Schirmer, inc., New York; 11Apr47; EP14075.

SIENKIEWICZ, ALFRED J
Love is a dream .. words and music by Alfred J. Sienkiewicz, [arrangement by Zygmond Rondomanski] Norwich, Conn., Mellow Music Co. © Alfred J. Sienkiewicz, Norwich, Conn.; 30Apr47; EP14511.

SIGMA ALPHA MU.
Girl of Sigma Alpha Mu ... national sweetheart song, [by] Sigma Alpha Mu Fraternity, scored by Don Freeberg. © Sigma Alpha Mu Fraternity, inc., New York; 1Mar47; EP13192.

SIGMA PHI GAMMA.
Sigma Phi Gamma International Sorority song book. © Sigma Phi Gamma International Sorority, Cincinnati; 31May47; EP15044.

SIGMAN, CARL.
Ballerina; lyric by Bob Russell, music by Carl Sigman. © Jefferson Music Co., inc., New York; 23May47; EP6910.

Come in out of the rain; lyrics by Bob Russell, music by Carl Sigman, [arr. by Bob Kahn] © Jefferson Music Co., inc., New York; 23May47; EP6838.

SIGNORELLI, FRANK.
Yo tengo amor. (I have love) ... English words by Dorothy Dolen, Spanish words by Jaime Yamin, music by Frank Signorelli and Charlie Bourne. © Caribbean Music, inc., New York; 23Jun47; EP15146.

SILCHER, FRIEDRICH.
The Loreley. Ich weiss nicht, was soll es bedeuten. For ... S.S.A. (incidental solo for soprano) [by] Friedrich Silcher, arr. by Wayne Howorth. (Words by] Heinrich Heine, English text by Wayne Howorth. © Pro Art Publications, New York; on arrangement; 21Apr47; EP13600. English words.

SILVA, OWEN DA. See Da Silva, Owen.

SILVERS, LOUIS.
April showers. See his Bombo.

(Bombo) April showers; (from "Bombo") music by Louis Silvers, arr. by Jimmy Dale. © Harms, inc., New York; on arrangement; 1May47; EP14362. Piano-conductor score (orchestra) and parts.

SILVI, JOHNNY.
Where are you now? Words and music by Johnny Silvi. © Puritan Publishing Co., Chicago; 3Apr46; EP11233.

SIMINGTON, GRACE ELINOR, 1905-
When I tell my heart; by Grace E. Simington, [arr. by Edwin Le Roy McKenzie] © Morrison Music Co., Seattle; 1Jan47; EP10908. For voice and piano, with chord symbols.

SIMMONDS, HARRY.
Alpha eleven; words and music by Harry Simmonds. © Nordyke Publishing Co., Los Angeles; 28Jan47; EP12720.

[SIMON, BILL] 1920-
Time and again. (Nunca sabrás)... [By Bill Simon] English lyric by Marty Konwood and Matt Kingsley, Spanish lyric by Johnnie Camacho. © Edward B. Marks Music Corp., New York; 11Jun47; EP14959.

SIMON, FRANK, 1889-
March of the majorettes; [by] Frank Simon. © Neil A. Kjos Music Co., Chicago; 27Mar47; EP14005. Condensed score (band) and parts.

SIMON, GEORGE.
The singing Pakapika; words and music by George Simon, [arr. by Betty Glynn of the Oahu staff] (Oahu advanced harmony note course for Hawaiian and electric guitar, [lesson 40PT]) © Oahu Publishing Co., Cleveland; on arrangement; 17Feb47; EP6676. For voice and guitar. Includes a musical quiz.

SIMON, LOUISE MARIE, 1903-
Arrieu, Claude, pseud.
See also SINGER, ABRAHAM.

Chanson de marin ... musique de
Claude Arrieu [pseud.], paroles
de Roudanez. © Henry Lemoine &
Cie., Paris; 31Dec39; EF3534.
Melody and words.

SIMON, NAT.
An apple blossom wedding; by Jimmy
Kennedy and Nat Simon. ©
Shapiro, Bernstein & Co., inc.,
New York; 22Apr47; EP13906. For
voice and piano, with chord
symbols.

My eight o'clock date; lyric by
Charles Tobias, music by Nat
Simon. © Leo Feist, inc., New
York; 11Apr47; EP13747.

The old lamp-lighter; by ... Nat
Simon ... arr. by George F. Briegel.
© Shapiro, Bernstein & Co., inc.,
New York; on arrangement; 27Jan47;
EP11828. Piano-conductor score
(band) and parts.

The old lamp-lighter; words by
Charles Tobias, music by Nat Simon,
arr. for male voices (T.T.B.B.,
with piano acc. by Robert C.
Haring. © Shapiro, Bernstein &
Co., inc., New York; on arrangement; 31Jan47; EP11829.

The old lamp-lighter; words by
Charles Tobias, music by Nat
Simon, simplified piano solo
(with words) ... arranged by
Lucy-Ann Bryant [pseud.] ©
Shapiro, Bernstein & Co., inc.,
New York; on arrangement;
31Dec46; EP11072.

SIMON, WALTER C   arr.
Go down, Moses (let my people go);
Negro spiritual, arr. by W. C.
Handy, [with] pipe organ adaptation
by Walter C. Simon. [c1950] ©
William C. Handy, New York; on
adaptation; 6Mar51; EP12054.

SIMONS, MOÏSES.
Chibo que rompe tambó. (The goat
who ate the drum) ... [By] Moïses
Simons, [English words adapted by
Albert Gamse] (In André, Julio,
ed. Songs from south of the border,
p.54-57) © Edward B. Marks Music
Corp., New York; on English adaptation; 28Dec46; EP10882.

ŠÍN, OTAKAR, 1881-1943.
(Quartet, strings, no.2) Smyčcový
kvartet, č.2, [by] Otakar Šín.
[Op.10] © Hudební Matice
Umělecké Besedy, Praha, Czecho-
slovakia; 11Mar42; EF4976.
Parts.

Smyčcový kvartet, č. 2. See his
Quartet, strings, no. 2.

(Sonata, violoncello & piano)
Sonata ... [by] Otakar Šín.
Op.11. © Hudební Matice
Umělecké Besedy, Praha, Czecho-
slovakia; 7Oct41; EF5011.
Score.

SINES, EDWARD.
Lotus City love; words and music by
Edward Sines. © Edward Sines,
Toledo; 16Jun47; EP11892.

SINGENBERGER, JOHN B   1848-
1924.
Ave Maria ... [By] John B. Singenberger ... rev. & arr. by J.
Alfred Schehl. © McLaughlin &
Reilly Co., Boston; on arrangement; 2Jun47; EP15011. Score:
soprano or tenor, chorus (SATB)
and organ.

Jubilate Deo. Veni Creator
Spiritus. O salutaris. Pange
lingua; Tantum ergo ... [By] John
B. Singenberger. © McLaughlin &
Reilly Co., Boston; 2Jun47;
EP15012. Score: TTBB and organ.

Shabos Kodesh. (Holy Sabbath) ...
words and music by Abraham
Singer, arr. by Harry Ellstein.
New York, Metro Music Co. ©
Abraham Singer, Brooklyn; ˇ
10Jun47; EP6722. Yiddish words
(transliterated)

SINGER, LOU, 1912-
Atom and evil; (The atom bomb
song) ... lyric by Hy Zaret,
music by Lou Singer.
© Argosy Music Corp., New York;
10Apr47; EP13792.

Listen to the green grass growing;
lyric by Hy Zaret, music by Lou
Singer. © Argosy Music Corp.,
New York; 28Jan47; EP11684.

SINGING WORDS; by the boys and girls
of Prospect Hill School, Pelham,
New York. © Prospect Hill School,
Pelham Manor, N. Y.; 25Apr47;
AA51565.

SINGLETON, WHITELEY.
To the cuckoo; two-part song, music
by Whiteley Singleton, words by
John Logan. © Edward Arnold &
Co., London; 12Dec46; EF4758.

SINIAVINE, ALEC. See
Siniavine, Alexandre.

SINIAVINE, ALEXANDRE, 1906-
J'attends dans un rêve ... paroles
de Gine Money [pseud.], musique
de Alec Siniavine. © Editions
Colibri, Paris; 22Jun46; EF3476.

SINZIG, PETRUS, father, 1876-
Missa "Rosa mystica"; for S.A.T.B.
voices with organ accompaniment
... Op. 71b. © McLaughlin &
Reilly Co., Boston; 30Jul46;
EP7729.

SIQUEIRA, JOSE.
Reminiscência; for medium voice and
piano [by] José Siqueira, [words
by Raul Machado, English version
by Harvey Officer] © Associated
Music Publishers, inc., New York;
28Mar47; EP13763.

SIRAS, JOHN, pseud.   See
Schuster, Ira.

SISK, THEODORE ROOSEVELT, 1907-   ed.
Divine praise; our 1947 song book
... Theodore Sisk, music editor.
© The Sisk Music Co., Toccoa, Ga.;
on new songs; 9Jun47; AA55172.

SISSON, C   T
May fancies; for the piano by C.
T. Sisson, introduction [by
Chester Nordman. Rev. ed.] ©
Shattinger Piano & Music Co.,
St. Louis; on introduction;
31Dec46; EP11244.

SIZEMORE, ASHER.
I'll be fightin' old Satan 'til
I die; words and music by Gordon
Sizemore and Asher Sizemore.
© Kelly Music Publications,
Franklin, Pa.; 15Jun47; EP15077.

SKILTON, EMMA.
Phantom shadows; [by] Emma Skilton
... For piano. © Theodore
Presser Co., Philadelphia;
16Jun47; EP15225.

SKOLD, SVEN J
Svensk allmogemarsch; [music and]
arr.: Sven Sköld. © Nordiska
Musikförlaget, a.b., Stockholm;
14Jan44; EF3734. Piano-conductor score (orchestra), and
parts.

SLACK, FREDDIE.
Behind the eight beat; by Freddie
Slack, scored by Will Hudson.
© Robbins Music Corp., New York;
on arrangement; 9Dec46; EP11818.
Piano-conductor score (orchestra)
and parts.

SLEOR, LYNE.
My love; paroles de Jean Berger,
musique de Lyne Sleor et
Marceau Crocq. © Editions
Paris-Broadway, Paris;
31Dec45; EF3837. For voice
and piano. French words.

Si vous écoutez ma chanson;
paroles de Jean Berger,
musique de Lyne Sleor et
Marceau Crocq. © Editions
Paris-Broadway, Paris;
31Mar45; EF3826.

SLONIMSKY, NICOLAS, 1894-
Thesaurus of scales and melodic
patterns; [by] Nicolas Slonimsky. © Coleman-Ross Co., inc.,
New York; 5Apr47; EP14153.

SMALE, LOLA GWIN, 1875-
A prayer; words by Emma Dickin-
son Avery, music by Lola Gwin
Smale. © Emma Dickinson Avery
and Lola Gwin Smale, Hollywood,
Calif.; 15Apr47; EP15588.

Star of gold; words ... by Francesca
Falk Miller and music [by] Lola
Gwin Smale. © Francesca Falk
Miller, Chicago & Lola Gwin
Smale, Hollywood, Calif.;
16Dec46; EP11972.

SMALL, ALLAN.
Lullaby medley ... arr. by Allan
Small. © Leeds Music Corp.,
New York; on arrangement;
16Jun47; EP15089. Piano-conductor score (orchestra) and
parts.

SMALL, GEORGE.
Have a heart, have a sweetheart;
words by Lionel M. Taylor,
music by George Small, jr.
© Nordyke Publishing Co., Los
Angeles; 7Mar47; EP13261.

SMAREGLIA, ANTONIO.
(I pittori fiamminghi) Serenata
di primavera. (Spring-serenade)
... (dai Pittori fiamminghi di
A. Smareglia) © Casa Musicale
Giuliana, Trieste, Italia;
18Sep46; EF3224. Score (violin
and piano) and part.

Serenata di primavera. See his
I pittori fiamminghi.

SMETANA, BEDŘICH, 1824-1884.
Braniboři v Čechách; [music by]
Bedřich Smetana, smès ...
upravil: Karol Barvitius, ml.
© Karel Barvitius, Praha,
Czechoslovakia; on arrangement;
1Mar45; EF5368. For piano solo.

Čertova stěna; [music by] Bedřich
Smetana, smès ... upravil:
Karel Barvitius, ml. © Karel
Barvitius, Praha, Czecho-
slavakia; on arrangement;
18Mar45; EF5369. For piano solo.

Libuše; [music by] Bedřich
Smetana, smès ... upravil:
Karel Barvitius, ml. © Karel
Barvitius, Praha, Czechoslo-
vakia; on arrangement; 5Feb49;
EF5370. For piano solo.

Večerní písně; [by] Bedřich
Smetana. Slova: Vítězslav Hálek,
pro klavír ... upravil [by]
Ladislav Lásko. © Karel
Barvitius, Praha, Czechoslovak-
ia; on arrangement; 15May46;
EF5376. For piano solo, with
words.

SMITH, Mrs. CARMA, 1912-
I'll take Jesus with me; [by]
Mrs. Carma Smith, arr. by
W. M. T. (In Church of the
Nazarene. Michigan District.
Nazarene Young Peoples Society.
Choruses of the N. Y. P. S. p.
48) © Michigan District,
Nazarene Young Peoples Society,
Flint, Mich.; 25Jul46;
EP13069. Close score: SATB.

131

SMITH, Mrs. CARMA. Cont'd.
Look ever to Jesus; [words by]
Mrs. C. S. and Lois Blanchard,
[music by] Mrs. Carma Smith,
arr. by W. M. Thorne. (In
Church of the Nazarene. Michi-
gan District. Nazarene Young
Peoples Society. Choruses of
the N. Y. P. S. p. 61) ©
Michigan District, Nazarene
Young Peoples Society, Flint,
Mich.; 25Jul46; EP13081. Close
score: SATB.
Wonderful what Jesus did for me;
[by] Mrs. Carma Smith, arr.
by W. M. T. (In Church of the
Nazarene. Michigan District.
Nazarene Young Peoples Society.
Choruses of the N. Y. P. S. p.
56) © Michigan District,
Nazarene Young Peoples Society,
Flint, Mich.; 25Jul46; EP13076.
For voice and piano.

SMITH, ERIC.
As now the sun's declining
rays ... words by C. Coffin,
(tr. [by] J. Chandler], music by
Eric Smith. © Novello & Co.,
ltd., London; 15Jan47; EF4900.
Score: chorus (SATB) and organ.

SMITH, GEORGE M   1912-
George M. Smith collection of solos
for the plectrum guitar. ©
Guitarists' Publications, Los
Angeles; on v.1-2; 17Dec46;
EP10789-10790.

SMITH, HARMIE.
Tomorrow begins another year; by
Webb Pierce [and] Harmie Smith.
© Leeds Music Corp., New York;
24Jan47; EP11803. For voice and
piano, with guitar diagrams and
chord symbols.

SMITH, HAROLD M
The instant-modulator; [by
Harold M. Smith] New Bruns-
wick, N. J., The Marvin Music
Ed. © Harold M. Smith, New
Brunswick, N. J.; 31Dec46;
EP11471.

SMITH, HARRISON GODWIN, 1895-
Lena; song by Harrison Smith,
arr. by Robert Cloud. ©
Harrison Godwin Smith,
Brooklyn; 2Aug47; on new
lyrics; EP16036.

SMITH, JACK, ed.
Jack Smith's Radio favorites;
song folio ... with guitar
diagrams and chords. ©
Shapiro, Bernstein & Co.,
inc., New York; 4Feb47;
EP13187.

SMITH, LORAINE McINNIS.
Mother's hands ... Words and
music by Loraine McInnis Smith.
© Loraine McInnis Smith,
Hattiesburg, Miss.; 2May47;
EP14156.

SMITH, ORMOND G
Lonely rider; words and music by
Ormond G. Smith. © Peer International Corp., New York;
18Mar47; EP13976.

SMITH, OUIDA S
Good morning; words and music
by Ouida M. Smith. © Nordyke
Publishing Co., Los Angeles;
5Mar47; EP13243.

[SMITH, ROBERT E   ] 1915-
Where is Sam? Words and music by
Edward Kean, Robert Unger [and]
Sam Hunter [pseud.] © Record
Songs, inc. (successor to Record
Songs Co.), New York; 20May47;
EP14843.

SMITH, ROY LAMONT, d. 1916.
Mice in the cupboard of old Mother
Hubbard; for the piano, by Roy
Lamont Smith. © G. Schirmer, inc.,
New York; 30Dec46; EP11622.

SMITH, VERNON GEECHIE.
(The frog song) Him ain't got no
tail; by Nat Leslie and Vernon
Geechie Smith. © Capitol Songs,
inc., New York; 18May47; EP14363.
For voice and piano, with chord
symbols.

SMITH, VORA MAUD.
Keep our country free; a song ...
words and music by Vora Maud
Smith ... Including arrangement
for mixed voices. © M. Baron
Co., New York; 5Dec46; EP10856.

SMITH, WALTER, 1887-
Barfly; [words] by Dominic J.
Palmisano and [music by]
Walter Smith. © Dominic
J. Palmisano, d.b.a. Radio
Electric Service, San
Francisco; 15Aug46;
EP13115.
They tell me I'm just a dreamer;
[words] by Thersa Erickson [and]
Eric A. Erickson ... [music by]
Walter Smith. Corning, Calif.,
E. A. Erickson. © Thersa
Erickson & Eric A. Erickson,
Corning, Calif.; 1Apr47;
EP13424.

SMITH, WILLIE.
Conversation on Park Avenue; by
Willie (The Lion) Smith,
[transcribed for piano by Robert
C. Haring] © Shapiro, Bernstein
& Co., inc., New York; 27Dec46;
EP10890.

SMITH, WILLIE MAE FORD.
Just keep still; words and music
by Mrs. Willie Mae Ford
Smith. © Willie Mae Ford
Smith, St. Louis; 10Sep38;
EP6836.

SMOLEN, JOHNNY CHARLES, 1901-
Oh, Mother Cabrini; music and
lyrics by Johnny Smolen, [arr.
by Jean Walz] © Johnny Charles
Smolen, Chicago; 12Dec47;
EP12467.

SNEED, ED ALEXANDER..
Oh come get in my automobile;
words and music by E. Alexander
Sneed. © Ed Alexander Sneed,
Los Angeles; 27Sep46; EP11958.

SNOW, FRANCIS W
O praise the Lord; for chorus of
mixed voices, Psalm 135:1,3,
[by] Francis W. Snow. © The
B. F. Wood Music Co., Boston;
21Apr47; EP13816.

SNYDER, HOWARD.
Songs of abounding love; [words
by Luetta Snyder, music by
Howard Snyder, comp. by Howard
Snyder and Luetta Snyder] ©
Luetta Pearl Snyder, Mauch
Chunk, Pa.; 26Dec46; EP14837.

SNYDER, TED.
Who's sorry now? By Bert Kalmar,
Harry Ruby and Ted Snyder ...
arr. by "Zep" Meissner. ©
Mills Music, inc., New York;
on arrangement; 21Apr47; ©
Piano-conductor score (orchestra)
and parts.

SNYDER, VIRGINIA.
Let not your heart be troubled;
for voice and piano, by Virginia
Snyder, [words from John XIV]
© Elkan-Vogel Co., inc.,
Philadelphia; 16Apr47; EP13924.

SÖDERLUNDH, BROR AXEL.
Den stora kometen; text: Nils
Ferlin, musik: Lille Bror
Söderlundh. © Nordiska
Musikförlaget, a.b., Stock-
holm; 1Jan44; EF3760.

SÖDERLUNDH, LILLE BROR. See
Söderlundh, Bror Axel.

SOLER, RAUL, d. 1946.
(This time for keeps) Un poquito
de amor, [from] the M-G-M picture
"This time for keeps"; lyric by
Ralph Freed, music by Raul Soler
[and] Xavier Cugat, Spanish lyric
by Raul Soler. © Robbins Music
Corp., New York; 4Dec46; EP11001.
English and Spanish words.

SOLLO, HARRY A
Dream ships; words by Celeste H.
Sollo, music by Harry A. Sollo.
© C. & H. Music Publishing Co.,
Colorado Springs; 26Dec46;
EP10711.

SOLOMON, NOAH, 1901-
(All those in favor) 10 hit
songs, from "All those in favor";
lyrics by Hy Teich and Frances
Solomon, music by Noah Solomon.
© Solomon & Teich, Boston;
7May47; EP14259.
Black or brown or slightly tan;
and "Willie Earle"; words by
H. M. Teich, music by Noah
Solomon. © Publications, inc.,
Boston; 14Jun47; EP15074-15075.

SOLOMON, SAMUEL, 1894-
Main land eretz-Israel. Palestino
is mine! Lyrics by Oscar Ostroff,
music by Samuel Solomon. ©
Oscar Ostroff & Samuel Solomon,
Chicago; 28Nov46; EP11318.
Yiddish words, transliterated.

SOMALVICO, GIACOMO.
Topo, topo, topolino ... testo di
N. Rastelli, musica di Giacomo
Somalvico. (In Un sorriso e
20 canzoni. p. 14-15) © Edizioni
Casiroli, s.a.r.l., Milano;
4May45; EF4916. For voice and
piano.

SOMMERS, HENRY J
I love somebody who doesn't love me;
[by] Henry J. Sommers. © Henry J.
Sommers, Washington, D. C.;
17Jan47; EP13595. For voice and
piano, with chord symbols.

SOOTER, RUDY.
It's dark outside (and I'm
skeered); words and music by
Spade Cooley and Rudy Sooter.
© Hill and Range Songs, inc.,
Hollywood, Calif.; 13May47;
EP14428.

SOROA, MANOLO.
Vida mia. (You're my life) ...
English words by Joe Davis,
Spanish words and music by
Manolo Soroa. © Caribbean
Music, inc., New York; 17Mar47;
EP12656.

SORRELLS, ROBERT DAVID, 1905-
Let us never walk alone; anthem
for mixed voices, [by] R. D.
Sorrells. [St. Louis, Distributors, Hunleth Music Co.]
© C. Albert Scholin, St. Louis;
26Apr47; EP14008.

UN SORRISO E 20 CANZONI; album ...
dei piu grandi successi radiofonici.
Milano, Edizioni Leonardi. For
voice and piano.

SOUGIOUL, M.
Kane mou lige sintrophia ...
etichoi K. Maniataké, mousiké
M. Sougioul. Athénai, Ekdoseis
Gaitanou [c1947] © Michael
Gaetanos, Athens; 20Nov46;
EF3128. For voice and piano.

THE SOUL MUST BEAR THE CROSS; an
ancient spiritual dialogue from
the Corner collection 1631.
Anthem for mixed voices with
youth choir or solo ... arr.
by Heinrich Reimann and Clarence
Dickinson, the English text by
Helen A. Dickinson. © The H.
W. Gray Co., inc., New York; on
arrangement; 3Jan47; EP11928.

SOUSA, JOHN PHILIP, 1854-1932.
The high school cadets; by John Philip Sousa, arranged by David Bennett. © Bregman, Vocco and Conn, inc., New York; 11Apr47; EP13635. Condensed score (band) and parts.

Our flirtation; by John Philip Sousa, arranged by David Bennett. © Bregman, Vocco and Conn, inc., New York; 11Apr47; EP13657. Condensed score (band) and parts.

The Picadore march; by John Philip Sousa, arranged by David Bennett. © Bregman, Vocco and Conn, inc., New York; 11Apr47; EP13636. Condensed score (band) and parts.

Semper fidelis ... By John Philip Sousa, arr. by Lloyd Marvin. © Chart Music Publishing House, inc., Chicago; on arrangement; 2Jun47; EP14932. Score (4 accordions) and parts.

Semper fidelis; by John Philip Sousa, arr. for piano solo by Maxwell Eckstein. © Carl Fischer, inc., New York; on arrangement; 12May47; EP15018.

Sound off; by John Philip Sousa, arranged by David Bennett. © Bregman, Vocco and Conn, inc., New York; 11Apr47; EP13638. Condensed score (band) and parts.

The thunderer ... by John Philip Sousa, arr. by Paul Yoder. © Carl Fischer, inc., New York; on arrangement; 18Mar47; EP13162. Piano-conductor (band) and parts.

Washington Post; march [by] John Philip Sousa, arr. by C. Paul Herfurth. © Carl Fischer, inc., New York; 29May47; EP15014. Piano-conductor score (orchestra) and parts.

The Washington Post march ... By John Philip Sousa, arr. by Lloyd Marvin. © Chart Music Publishing House, inc., Chicago; on arrangement; 2Jun47; EP14933. Score (4 accordions) and parts.

SOUTHWICK, GLADYS HEATHCOCK.
The young king; an operetta in three acts for junior high schools, adapted from Oscar Wilde's story of the same title. Dialogue and lyrics by Nellie McCaslin, music written and arr. by Gladys Heathcock Southwick, dance instructions by Ruth Ferguson. © Row, Peterson & Co., Evanston, Ill.; 29Oct46; DP1224.

SOWERBY, LEO.
Poem; for viola (or violin) and organ, by Leo Sowerby. © The R. W. Gray Co., inc., New York; 13Jun47; EP15159. Score and parts.

Sonatina; for organ by Leo Sowerby. © The H. W. Gray Co. inc., New York; 13Jun47; EP15158.

SPAETH, SIGMUND.
Telling time; [words by John Kendrick Bangs] and The snow; [words by Alice Van Leer Carrick] Composed and arr. by Sigmund Spaeth [for] S.S.A. © Pro Art Publications, New York; 21Apr47; EP13599.

SPALDING, ALBERT.
Four piano pieces; by Albert Spalding. Op. 6. New York, Composers' Music Corp. © Carl Fischer, inc., New York; v.1, 18Nov20. Contents.-
1. Prelude (© EP13145)

SPARKLER, BOB.
I ain't mad at you; by Bob Sparkler. New York, Capitol Songs. © Criterion Music Corp., New York; 6Mar47; EP12305. For voice and piano, with chord symbols.

SPARTAKOS, GIANNES, 1910-
Tha se parō na phygoume; stichoi: ... Sakellariou, mousikē: Glannē Spartakou. 8. ekdosis. Athēnai, Ekdoseis G. Konstantinide. © "S.O.P.E." Copyright Protection Society, Athens; 22Nov44; EF3236. For voice and piano.

SPECIAL SONGS for young people's anniversaries and festal occasions. New ser. © Salvationist Publishing & Supplies, ltd., London; no.9, 25Mar47; EF3669. No.9 comp. by Bramwell Coles.

SPELLMAN, GEORGE F
When we're back together again; words and music by George F. Spellman. © Nordyke Publishing Co., Los Angeles; 5Sep45; EP12713.

SPELMAN, TIMOTHY M
Jamboree; a rustic carnival. © Broadcast Music, inc., New York; 31Jan46; EP2577. Piano-conductor score (orchestra) and parts.

SPENCE, A   L   arr.
The chase; based on the old English air "Green sleeves", lyrics by A. L. Spence. London, Cinephonic Music Co. [1945] © Classical Music Co., Ltd., London; on lyrics and arrangement; 31Jan46; EP1378. For voice and piano; melody also in tonic sol-fa notation.

SPENCE, HARRIET SWAN.
Nebraska's glad refrain; words and music by Harriet Swan Spence. © Harriet Swan Spence, Crab Orchard, Neb.; 7Apr47; EF15663.

SPENCER, HERBERT.
Underneath the stars ... music by Herbert Spencer, piano adaptation by Henry Levine. © Remick Music Corp., New York; on adaptation; 2Jan47; EP11213.

SPENCER, LUCILLE DENTHRIFF, 1905-
I'm going there and see; words and music by Lucille Spencer, [arr. by D. Norman Tillman. c1946] © Lucille Denthriff Spencer, Cleveland; 22Jan47; EP11787.

SPENCER, TIM.
Cigareetes, whusky and wild, wild women; words and music by Tim Spencer. © Tim Spencer Music, inc., Hollywood, Calif.; 10Jun47; EP15033.

The everlasting hills of Oklahoma; words and music by Tim Spencer. © Tim Spencer Music, inc., Hollywood, Calif.; 10Jun47; EP15032.

SPIALEK, HANS, 1894-
The Danube (from a plane); based on Johann Strauss' "The blue Danube," by Hans Spialek. © Chappell & Co., inc., New York; 31Dec46; EP11179. Piano-conductor score (orchestra) and parts.

SPICER, HAZEL, 1902-
At the end of a dream; words and music by Wm. D. Steving ... [and] Hazel Spicer. © William Doty Steving, Berry Creek, Calif. and Hazel Spicer, Chico, Calif.; 14Aug46; EP13590.

SPIER, LARRY.
Memory lane; two part, S.A. or T.B., words by B. G. De Sylva, music by Larry Spier and Con Conrad, arr. by Douglas MacLean, [pseud.] © Harms, inc., New York; on arrangement; 17Jun47; EP15274.

SPIVAK, SAMUEL, 1888-
Children's very first piano pieces; with lyrics, arr. and ed. by Samuel Spivak. © Edward Schuberth & Co., inc., New York; 1Apr47; EP12989.

SPIVAK, SAMUEL, 1888-   arr.
48 tuneful technical studies; comp. and arr. by Samuel Spivak. © Edward Schuberth & Co., inc., New York; bk. 2, 21Jan47; EP11415.

SPOHR, LOUIS, 1784-1859.
Children, pray this love to cherish; (from the cantata "God, Thou art great") ... English adaptation by Morley Chubb. (In Ross, Hugh, arr. Sacred choruses for women's or girls' voices. p. 18-27) © G. Schirmer, inc., New York; on arrangement; 30Sep46; EP9780.

Thy love is every morning new; (from "The Christian's prayer") ... [Words by] Edward Taylor, after the German of A. Mahlmann. (In Ross, Hugh, arr. Sacred choruses for women's or girls' voices. p. 151-154) © G. Schirmer, inc., New York; on arrangement; 30Sep46; EP9796.

SPROSS, CHARLES GILBERT.
In a little Irish village; song, words by Gerald Fitzgerald, music by Charles Gilbert Spross. © The John Church Co., Philadelphia; 5Feb47; EP11881.

SQUIRES, HARRY D
I let spring go to my head; by Harry D. Squires. © Irving Arthur Music Publications, Brooklyn; 14Apr47; EP6816. For voice and piano, with chord symbols.

STAAB, HAROLD B   1891-
Colleen, my own ... words and music by Hal B. Staab, arr. by Charles M. Merrill. [c1946] © Harold B. Staab, Northampton, Mass.; 10Jan47; EP11926. Close score; TTBB.

[STADBURY]
Little Red Riding Hood; [by Don Pelosi and Stadbury] © Bradbury Wood, ltd., London; 19Dec46; EP4789. For piano solo, with words.

STAIRS, LOUISE E
Christ the Lord is risen today; by Louise E. Stairs [words by Charles Wesley] © Theodore Presser Co., Philadelphia; 3Jan47; EP11029. Score: chorus (SATB) and piano.

STALEY, KARL ARTHUR, 1900-
Ohio; [by] Karl Staley, [arr. by] Cæs Rowe. © Karl A. Staley, Madison, Ohio; 16May47; EP14891. Close score: SATB.

STANDEFER, JOHNNY.
I'm smiling to hide an aching heart; words & music by Cliff Japhet & Johnny Standefer, arr. by Belle Schragg. © Joe McDaniel Music Co., New York; 10Apr47; EP6890.

STANISLAUS, sister. See Horgan, Mary Stanislaus, sister.

STANLEY, ALBERT H., pseud. See Jacobs, Milton.

STANLEY, BOB.
Dziadwuka polka. (Beggars' polka); music by Bob Stanley, arr. by Joe Biviano [for] accordion solo. © Viccas Music Co., New York; 12May47; EP15100.

Polka na lewo. (Polka to the left); music by Bob Stanley, arr by Joe Biviano [for] accordion solo. © Viccas Music Co., New York; 12May47; EP15102.

STANPHILL, IRA FOREST, 1914-
Hymntime harmonies ... by Ira
and Zelma Stanphill. © Ira
Forest Stanphill, Springfield,
Mo.: 19Sep46; EP11790.

STANTON, EDWARD, pseud. See
Sachs, Benno.

STANTON, FRANCIS HAYWARD, 1913-
Foldin' money; words and music
by Happy Felton, Vi Bradley &
Frank Stanton. © Nationwide
Songs, inc., New York;
28Apr47; EP14347.

STANTON, FRANK. See
Stanton, Francis Hayward.

STAPP, H   RUSSELL.
"Rotary bell"; by H. Russell
Stapp. © H. Russell Stapp &
The Rotary Club of South Bend,
South Bend, Ind.; 21May47;
EP6950. For voice and piano.

THE STAR SPANGLED BANNER; an arrangement ... by John C. Zeran. © John
Courtney Zeran, Los Angeles; on
arrangement; 5Feb47; EP11934.
Score (bugle and drum corps)
and parts.

STARR, KATHLEEN GERELDA CURTIS, 1922-
Christ the way; [by] Kathleen G.
Starr, [words by] Claude H.
Curtis. © Claude Hamilton
Curtis, San Francisco; 1Nov46;
EP11105. Close score: SATB.

I know; [by] Kathleen G. Curtis,
© Claude Hamilton Curtis, San
Francisco; 1Nov46; EP11104.
Close score: SATB.

My God is able ... [by] Kathleen
G. Starr, har. [by] Herbert G.
Tovey, [words by] K.G.S. ©
Claude Hamilton Curtis, San
Francisco; 1Nov46; EP11107.

Trust Him; [by] Kathleen G.
Curtis. © Claude Hamilton
Curtis, San Francisco; 1Nov46;
EP11106. Close score: SATB.

STAUB, DIANA.
Manèges; paroles et musique de
Diana Staub. © Editions
Paris-Broadway, Paris;
31Dec46; EP3836.

Mon coin de banlieue; paroles
et musique de Diana Staub. ©
Éditions Paris-Broadway, Paris;
31Dec46; EP3822.

Ritournelle; paroles et musique de Diana Staub. ©
Éditions Paris-Broadway, Paris;
31Dec46; EP3825.

STEBBINS, GEORGE C   b. 1846.
Thy will, O Lord; [words by] John
D. Bacon, [music by] George C.
Stebbins. © John D. Bacon,
Dallas; 23Dec46; EP10946. Close
score: SATB, in shape-note
notation.

STEELE, J   A
Leaves from an Austral garden; for
piano, by J. A. Steele. © Allan
& Co., pty. ltd., Melbourne, Australia; 30ct46; EF3122.

STEELE, TED.
Smoke dreams ... by Lloyd Shaffer,
John Klenner [and] Ted Steele.
© Stopt, inc., New York;
15May47; EP14364. For voice
and piano, with chord symbols.

STEEN, HERBERT. See
Stéen-Ostling, Herbert.

STÉEN-ÖSTLING, HERBERT.
Vill du tänka på mej? ... Musik:
Herbert Stéen, arr: Kewe
Wickman, text: Harry Iseborg.
© Edition Sylvain, a.b.,
Stockholm; 1Jan45; EF3727.
Piano-conductor score
(orchestra, with words), and
parts.

STEIN, GLADYS M
Soldiers on parade; piano solo by
Gladys M. Stein. © Mills Music,
inc., New York; 31Dec46; EP6444.

[STEIN, SIEGFRIED] 1903-
There is no breeze (to cool the
flame of love) [De tout mon
coeur] lyric by Alstone, [pseud.]
... lyric by Dorothy Dick, French
lyric by Andre Tabet and roger
Bernstein. New York, Robbins
Music Corp. © Editions Salabert,
Paris; on English lyric; 13Sep46;
EP3312. Correcting EP6444.

STEINBACH, BARBARA, 1922-
Modern miniatures; for the piano,
by Barbara Steinbach. © G.
Schirmer, inc., New York; on 7
pieces; 30Dec46. Contents.-
[v.1] The lark and At Church
(© EP11623)- [v.2] The rooster
and The alarm clock (© EP11624)-
[v.3] The little dance and
Rain (© EP11621)- [v.4] The
hurdy gurdy (© EP11625)- [v.5]
March (© EP11626)- [v.6] Playing
hop scotch (© EP11627)- [v.7]
Hunting song (© EP11628)

[STEINER, ERIC]
On tiptoes; [by] Edgar L.
Stone [pseud.] © Century
Music Publishing Co., New
York; 12May47; EP14269. For
piano solo.

Sword dance; [by] Edgar L.
Stone [pseud.] © Century
Music Publishing Co., New
York; 12May47; EP14275.
For piano solo.

STEINER, HOWARD.
Funny how you got along without
me; lyric by Sammy Gallop,
music by Howard Steiner. ©
Sun Music Co., inc., New York;
9Dec46; EP13377.

STEINER, MAX.
Deep Valley, from the ... pict.
"Deep Valley"; lyric by Charles
Tobias, music by Max Steiner.
© Remick Music Corp., New York;
18Jun47; EP15278.

Symphonic moderne; on a theme by
Max Rabinowitsch, composed by
Max Steiner, transcribed for
band after the original score
by Frank Marsales. © Remick
Music Corp., New York; on
arrangement; 16Jan47; EP11401.
Condensed score (band) and
parts.

STELIBSKY, JOSEF, 1909-
Hledám stín. See his Pro kamaráda.

Ostrov milováni; opereta ...
hudba: Jos. Stelibský; J.
Mottl [and] K. Melisek ...
klavírní úprava [by] B. Niko-
dem. © Mojmír Urbánek, Praha,
Czechoslovakia; 15Aug40;
EF3358. For voice and piano.

(Pro kamaráda) Hledám stín ... z
filmu: "Pro kamaráda" ... slova:
J. Mottl, hudba: Jos. Stelibský.
(In Co Praha tancí a spívá. v.10,
p.2-3) © Mojmír Urbánek, Praha,
Czechoslovakia; 3Feb41; EF5377.
For voice and piano.

STENHAMMAR, WILHELM, 1871-1927.
Fyra dikter; av Verner von
Heidenstam, för en röst med
piano av Wilh. Stenhammar.
Op. 37. © Nordiska Musik-
förlaget, a/b, Stockholm; on 4
songs, 10ct19; EF5379-5382.
For voice and piano. Contents.-
Jutta kommer till Folkungarna.-
I lönnens skymning.- Mänljuset.-
Vore jag ett litet barn.

Fyra Stockholmsdikter; av Bo
Bergman, ... [music] av Wilhelm
Stenhammar. Op. 38. © Nordiska
Musikförlaget, a/b, Stockholm;
on 4 songs, 10ct19; EF5383-
5386. For voice and piano.
Contents.- no. 1. Kväll i Klara.-
ne. 2 I en skogsbacke.- no. 3
Mellan broarna.- no. 4. En
positivvisa

STEPT, SAM H
I'll always be in love with you;
by Bud Green, Herman Ruby and
Sam H. Stept, [arr. by Charlie
Ventura] © Shapiro, Bernstein
& Co., inc., New York; on
arrangement; 10Jun47; EP14983.
Score (Bb tenor saxophone and
piano) and part.

STERN, EMIL, 1913-
Have you change for a dream?
(Ou-es tu, mon amour?) Lyric
by Henry Lemarchand, English
version by Stanley Adams,
music by Emil Stern. ©
Edwin H. Morris & Co., New
York; 13Mar47; EP12666.
English words.

Mon amour me tient chaud; [words
by] Henry Lemarchand, [music by]
Emil Stern. © H. Lemarchand &
E. Stern, Paris; 16Jul46; EF3532.

STEVENS, MABEL BUCHANAN. See
Buchanan, Mabel.

STEVENS, THAD.
Lazy blues; by Thad Stevens. ©
Parker Music Publications,
Indianapolis; 22Apr47;
EP14252. For voice and piano,
with chord symbols.

Our town; lyrics by Maye Shake
Brooks, music by Thad Stevens.
© Parker Publications, Indian-
apolis; 23Apr47; EP14157.

STEVENSON, SIR JOHN.
Hark, the vesper hymn is stealing;
for ... S.A.T.B., from Sir John
Stevenson's original setting of
a Russian air, arr. by Wayne
Howorth. Words by Thomas Moore.
© Pro Art Publications, New
York; on arrangement; 21Apr47;
EP13608.

STEWART, ALBERT CHESTON, 1880-
Unblamable and unreprovable ...
[by] Albert C. Stewart ...
[arr. by] Walter Manley.
[c1946] © Albert Cheston
Stewart, Tucson, Ariz.; 5Feb47;
EP11919. Close score: SATB.

[STEWART, ARTHUR SHARPE] 1911-
At the gin mill; [by Arthur Sharpe
Stewart] arr. by Doris Simpson
Stewart] © Arthur Sharpe Stewart,
Pittsburgh; 12Feb47; EP12083. For
voice and piano.

STICKLES, WILLIAM, 1883-   arr.
Bing Crosby's favorite hymns;
arr. by William Stickles. ©
Burke and Van Heusen, inc.,
New York; on arrangement;
8Apr47; EP13656.

Bing Crosby's selection of sacred
songs and hymns; arr. by
William Stickles. © Burke and
Van Heusen, inc., New York;
on arrangement; 8Apr47;
EP13655.

College songs; for male quartet
or chorus, arr. by William
Stickles. [c1946] © Melrose
Music Corp., New York;
13Jun47; EP15120.

STIGNIEL, TORSTEN, pseud. See
Nilsson, Stig.

STOCK, LARRY.
The man who paints the rainbow; words
and music by Cy Coben, Irving
Melsher [and] Larry Stock.
© Mutual Music Society, inc., New
York; 2Jan47; EP11124. For voice
and piano, with chord symbols.

STOCKS, H   C   L
Grant, we beseech Thee; anthem for
S. A. T. B. (unacc.) by H. C.
L. Stocks. © Novello & Co.,
ltd., London; 15Mar47; EF5293.

STOCKTON, J   H
Glory to His name; [words by] E. A.
Hoffman, [music by] J. H. Stockton. (In Eddy Arnold's radio
favorites song book. no. A-1,
p. 48) © Adams, Vee & Abbott,
inc., Chicago; on arrangement;
17Jun46; EP11232. Close score:
SATB, with guitar diagrams and
chord symbols.

STOKES, HAROLD.
This evening; words and music by
Mary Hartline and Harold Stokes,
piano arrangement by Dick Kent.
© Peer International Corp., New
York; 30Dec46; EP11637.

STOLTZE, ROBERT, 1910-
Green earth; for piano by Robert
Stoltze. © The Composers Press,
inc., New York; 15May47; EP14359.

Miniatures; for piano ... by
Robert Stoltze. © The Composers
Press, inc., New York; 1Apr47;
EP13426.

Traffic dance; for piano, by
Robert Stoltze. © The Composers
Press, inc., New York; 5Apr47;
EP13335.

STOLZ, ROBERT.
Uber die Au (Spazieren Fritz und
Frieda) Von Robert Stolz.
Op.760. Text [von] Robert
Gilbert. © Edition Turicaphon,
a.g., Zurich, Switzerland;
20Jun47; EF5824.

STONE, EDGAR L., pseud. See
Steiner, Eric.

STONE, GREGORY, 1900-
Boogie-woogie etude; [by] Gregory
Stone. © Chappell & Co., inc.,
New York; 22Jan47; EP14449. Two
scores for piano 1-2.

Boogie-woogie etude; [by] Gregory
Stone. [For] piano solo. [Piano
solo ed.] © Chappell & Co., inc.,
New York; on arrangement; 5Feb47;
EP11903.

El boogie-woogie Mexicano; [by] Gregory
Stone, [for] piano solo. © Chappell
& Co., inc., New York; 17Feb47;
EP12092.

(Carnegie Hall) Sometime we will
meet again; words and music
by William Le Baron, Boris
Morros and Gregory Stone,
featured ... in ... "Carnegie
Hall." © Leo Feist, inc., New
York; 17Jan47; EP11366.

Dancing in the dark; [by] Arthur
Schwartz, paraphrased by
Gregory Stone. © Harms, inc.,
New York; on arrangement;
25Mar47; EP13209. Score
(violin and piano) and part.

El iorito enamorado ... letra y
musica de Gregory Stone.
© Editora Interludio, New York;
10Aug44; EP11977.

One kiss; [by] Sigmund Romberg,
paraphrased by Gregory Stone.
© Harms, inc., New York; on
arrangement; 25Mar47; EP13208.
Score (violin and piano) and
part.

Sometime we will meet again. See
his Carnegie Hall.

You are free; [by] Victor Jacobi
paraphrased by Gregory Stone.
© Harms, inc., New York; on
paraphrase; 3Apr47; EP13706.
Score (violin and piano) and
part.

STONE, JUSTIN.
Saddle serenade; words and music
by Larry Markes and Justin Stone.
© Bob Miller, inc., New York;
2May47; EP14182.

STORER, H   J
"Miss Lou Rose;" words by Harriet
Lyon Leonard, music by H. J.
Storer. © Wesley Webster, San
Francisco; 23Apr47; EP13818.

STORIE, BENJAMIN ENOCH, 1892-
Hen-pecked papa; words and music
by Ben Storie. © Ben E. Storie,
Brownfield, Tex.; 13Nov46;
EP12238.

Rocky mountain moon; words by
Louise Murphy, music by Ben E.
Storie. Holbrook, Ariz., L.
Murphy. © Louise Murphy and Ben
E. Storie, Brownfield, Tex.;
30Apr47; EP14547.

Sweet home blues; words and music
by Ben E. Storie. © Ben E. Storie,
Brownfield, Tex.; 2Jan47; EP11353.

Sweet home blues; words and music
by Ben E. Storie. © Ben E.
Storie, Brownfield, Tex.; 1Jan47;
EP12239.

STORM, BARRY.
Wherever you are; words and
music by Barry Storm. ©
Nordyke Publishing Co., Los
Angeles; 29Apr47; EP14634.

STORONI, J   1872-
Amapa ... de J. Storoni, arrt. de
Francis Salabert ... Dengoso
... de Ernesto Nazareth, arrt.
de Francis Salabert. ©
Editions Salabert, Paris; on
arrangement; 15Feb47; EF3555.
Piano-conductor score
(orchestra), and parts.

STORY, HELEN APRIL, 1902-
The magic carpet; by H. Story.
© H. Story, East Los Angeles,
Calif.; 1Apr47; EP13421. For
piano solo.

STORY, JAMES, 1902-
James Story band book; [by J.
Story, arrangements by James
Story, Ralph Barber, James E.
Son, Lou Halmy] © Jim Tom
Music Publishing Co., Long
Beach, Calif.; 3Apr46;
EP12193. Parts: band.

STOUT, CLARENCE A
Fooling me; words and music by
Clarence A. Stout. © Mills
Music, inc., New York; 28Feb40;
EP6531.

STOUT, OAKLEY.
Señorita chiquita; (Little miss),
words and music by Oakley
Stout. © Nordyke Publishing
Co., Los Angeles; 7Mar47;
EP13268.

STOWE, L   HUDSON.
The war is won and I am going
home; words and music by
L. Hudson Stowe. © S. J.
Melody Music Publisher,
Sewell, N. J.; 24Dec46;
EP11458.

STRAUSS, ART.
Stay out of my dreams ... music
by Art Strauss & [words by]
Sonny Miller. © Strauss Miller
Music Co., ltd., London; 28Jan47;
EF3148.

STRAUSS, JOHANN, 1825-1899.
The blue Danube; a choral
arrangement for mixed voices
to be sung to the acc. of the
two piano adaptation by Abram
Chasins ... text and arrangement ... by Harvey Enders. ©
J. Fischer & Bro., New York;
on text & arrangement; 17Apr47;
EP6904.

The blue Danube ... [by] Johann
Strauss, arr. by Eddie
Griffiths. [London, Sole
selling agents, Bossey &
Hawkes] © Hawkes & Son
(London) ltd., on arrangement;
24Jan47; EF4869. Piano-
conductor score (orchestra),
and parts.

Emperor waltz; [by] J. Strauss,
easy arrangement ... by Victor
P. Frangipane. © Edward Schuberth & Co., inc., New York;
10Jun47; EP15133. For piano
solo.

Emperor waltz ... [by] Johann
Strauss. Op.437. Abridged and
transcribed by Kathleen Armour
[pseud.] © Century Music Publishing Co., New York; on arrangement;
15May46; EP10987. For piano solo.

The emperor waltz, from the Para-
mount picture "The emperor waltz";
lyric by Johnny Burke, music by
Johann Strauss. © Burke and Van
Heusen, inc., New York; 15Apr47;
EP15863.

(Die Fledermaus) The bat. Die
Fledermaus; selection [by] Johann
Strauss, arr. by L. P. Laurendeau,
rev. and arr. by Julius S. Seredy,
arr. for modern bands with new
parts by H. R. Kent [pseud.] ©
Carl Fischer, inc., New York; on
arrangement with new parts;
19Dec46; EP11216. Piano-conductor
score (band) and parts.

Die Fledermaus; selection, music by
Johann Strauss, arr. by Arthur
Wood. © William Paxton & Co.,
ltd., London; on arrangement;
23Dec46; EF3563. Piano-conductor
score (orchestra), and parts.

Love wherever I roam; ("They say
love makes the world go round")
from The gipsy baron, by
Johann Strauss. English lyric
by Bruce Sievier. © Josef
Weinberger ltd. & Cranz & Co.,
ltd., London; on English lyric;
1Apr47; EF3409.

1001 nights ... [by] Johann
Strauss, arr. by Cecil Woods.
[London, Boosey & Hawkes]
© Hawkes & Son (London) ltd.,
London; on arrangement; 11Feb47;
EF4994. Piano-conductor score
(orchestra) and parts.

Souvenirs from the great
masters, Johann Strauss;
selected & arr. by G. H.
Clutsam. © Keith Prowse &
Co., ltd., London; on arrangement; 30Dec46; EF4795. For
piano solo.

Tales of the Vienna woods [lyric by
Jack Edwards, and] The beautiful
blue Danube ... Arranged by Walter L. Rosemont. © Edwards Music
Co., New York; on arrangement;
24Jan47; EP11860. Parts for piano
and 2 instruments, or small orchestra.

Viennese waltz medley ... [Melodies
by Johann Strauss] Arr. by Will
Hudson ... 3 way dance orchestration. © Lewis Music Publishing
Co., inc., New York; on arrangement; 2Jun47; EP14850. Piano-
conductor score (orchestra) and
parts.

STRAUSS, JOHANN, 1825-1899. Cont'd.
Viennese waltzes; [by] Strauss and
Waldteufel ... selected and ed.
by Robert Marden. © Amsco Music
Publishing Co., New York; on
compiling, arranging & editing;
31Dec46; EP111141. Score (violin
and piano) and part.

Voices of spring. Voci di
primavera. By Johann Strauss.
Transcription for voice with
piano acc., cadenza and flute
obbligato by Frank La Forge.
[English translation from
original German lyrics by Frank
La Forge, Italian text by Italo
Celesti] © Carl Fischer, inc.,
New York; on arrangement &
English words; 23May47; EP14716.

STRAUSS, RICHARD, 1864-
All Souls' day, [by] Richard Strauss,
arranged by Harvey Gaul. © G.
Schirmer, inc., New York; on arrangement; 22Mar46; EP11612. For organ
solo; includes registration for
Hammond organ.

STRAVINSKII, IGOR' FEDOROVICH,
1882-
Dance of the princesses, from
"The fire-bird"; [arr. by
Quinto Maganini, viola part
transcribed by Rudolph Forst]
© Edition Musicus - New York,
inc., New York; on arrangement
of viola part; 23Oct46;
EP13721. Score (viola and
piano) and part.

Ebony concerto; by Igor Stravinsky. Miniature score. ©
Charling Music Corp., New York;
31Dec46; EP11136.

Ode; elegiacal chant in three
parts, [by] Igor Stravinsky.
London, Schott and Co., ltd.,
© Associated Music Publishers,
inc., New York; 10Feb47
EP12203. Miniature score.

STRICKLAND, BEN.
There's a time; words and music
by Ben Strickland. © Nordyke
Publishing Co., Los Angeles;
7Mar47; EP13262.

STRICKLAND, LILY.
Fog in the harbour; for mixed
chorus and piano, words and
music by Lily Strickland. ©
Elkan-Vogel Co., inc., Philadelphia; 7Apr47; EP13930.

Peace shall prevail ... Words by
Irwin Rowan ... music by Lily
Strickland. © Elkan-Vogel Co.,
Philadelphia; 7Apr47; EP13929.
Score; chorus (SATB) and piano.

STRICKLER, DAVID, arr.
MacDonald's farm; for full chorus
of mixed voices, a cappella,
arr. by David Strickler, traditional [words] © O. Shire,
inc., New York; 3Apr47c m r
EP14057.

STRIDE, HARRY.
Lulu had a sweetheart; [words] by
Pat McCarthy [and] Micky Stoner,
[music by] Harry Stride. © Bob
Stephens, inc., New York;
10Feb47; EP12018.

STRIMER, JOSEPH.
Le petit farfadet; [by] Joseph
Strimer. [In Le Passe-Temps.
no. 891, p. 8] © Les Éditions
du Passe-Temps, inc., Montreal;
20Oct45; EF3136. For piano
solo.

STRÖMBERG-ANDERSSON, FRITHIOF.
En liten bld förgät mig ej ...
text och musik [by] Frithiof
Strömberg-Andersson. ©
Skandinaviska Odeon, a.b.,
Stockholm; 1Jan46; EF3752.

STUART, EVEN P
Branded with love; words and music
by Even P. Stuart. © Robert
B. Montfort, Hot Springs, Ark.;
28Dec45; EP13158.

Time changes things; words and
music by Even P. Stuart. ©
R. B. Montfort, Hot Springs,
Ark.; 28Dec45; EP13159.

STURK, BURTON FINNIS, 1900-
Songs that last; [words and music
principally] by Rev. and Mrs.
B. F. Sturk. Ashley, Mich.,
B. F. Sturk. Flint, Mich.; 15Aug46;
EP10755. Close score; SATB.

STUTSCHEWSKY, JOACHIM, arr.
Sammlung moderner und klassisher
Einzelstücke ... bearbeitet und
genau bezeichnet von J. Stutschewsky. Mains, B. Schott's
Söhne. © Associated Music
Publishers, inc., New York; on
arrangement in heft 1-4; 1Mar19;
EF5057, 5248, 5249, 5257. Two
scores for violin and violoncello. Vol.3 has title: Sammlung ausgewählter Einzelstücke.

STYNE, JULE.
The Brooklyn bridge. See his It
happened in Brooklyn.

I believe. See his It happened
in Brooklyn.

I'm still sitting under the apple
tree; lyric by Sammy Cahn, music
by Jule Styne. © Melrose
Music Corp., New York; 23Jun47;
EP15247.

(It happened in Brooklyn) The Brooklyn
bridge, from the ... picture It
happened in Brooklyn; lyric by
Sammy Cahn, music by Jule Styne.
© Sinatra Songs, inc., New York;
19Mar47; EP12788.

(It happened in Brooklyn) It's
the same old dream, from the
... picture "It happened in
Brooklyn"; lyric by Sammy
Cahn, music by Jule Styne.
© Sinatra Songs, inc., New
York; 10Mar47; EP12581.

(It happened in Brooklyn)
The song's gotta come from
the heart; lyrics by Sammy
Cahn, music by Jule Styne ...
[from] "It happened in
Brooklyn." © Sinatra Songs,
inc., New York; 24Mar47;
EP13370.

(It happened in Brooklyn) Time
after time, from the ...
picture "It happened in Brooklyn"; lyric by Sammy Cahn,
music by Jule Styne. © Sinatra
Songs, inc., New York; 10Mar47;
EP12583.

(It happened in Brooklyn) Whose baby
are you? From the ... picture "It
happened in Brooklyn;" lyric by
Sammy Cahn, music by Jule Styne.
© Sinatra Songs, inc., New York;
19Mar47; EP12794.

It's all up to you (to make North
Carolina no. 1 in good health) ...
[words] by Sammy Cahn, [music by]
Jule Styne. © Edwin H. Morris &
Co., inc., New York; 31Dec46;
EP11135. For voice and piano,
with chord symbols.

It's the same old dream. See his
It happened in Brooklyn.

(Ladies' man) I gotta gal I love
(in North and South Dakota) ...
[from the Paramount picture
"Ladies' man"]; words by Sammy
Cahn, music by Jule Styne.
[c1946] © Famous Music Corp.,
New York; 3Jan47; EP11053.

(Ladies' man) What am I gonna do
about you? [From the Paramount
picture "Ladies' man"]; words
by Sammy Cahn, music by Jule
Styne. [c1946] © Paramount
Music Corp., New York; 3Jan47;
EP11074.

The song's gotta come from the
heart. See his It happened in
Brooklyn.

Time after time. See his It
happened in Brooklyn.

We knew it all the time; words by
George R. Brown, music by Jule
Styne. © Melrose Music Corp.,
New York; 11Mar47; EP12851.

Whose baby are you? See his It
happened in Brooklyn.

SUÁREZ, HUMBERTO.
Que le voy a hacer ... letra y
música de Humberto Suárez.
© Peer International Corp., New
York; 17Dec42; EF5622.

Siguiéndote... (I'll follow
you); lyric by Mack David,
music and Spanish lyric by
Humberto Suárez. ©
Remick Music Corp., New
York; 13Mar47; EP12851.

SUAREZ, SENEN.
Bagels in Mexico. (Mi bumba né)
... Spanish lyrics and music by
Senen Suarez, English lyrics
by Benjamin Blossner. © Peer
International Corp., New York;
on English lyric; 20Nov46;
EP13769.

SUGGS, CHARLEY.
Rumpelstiltskin; by Kacy and
Charley Suggs, arrangement by
Dorothy Ritter. Chicago,
Dramatic Publishing Co. ©
Kacy Suggs and Charley Suggs,
New Haven; 27Dec46; EP14671.
Piano-vocal score.

SUK, JOSEF, 1874-1935.
Epilog; symfonická skladba ...
[By] Josef Suk. Op.37.
© Hudební Matice Umělecké Besedy,
Praha, Czechoslovakia; 11Apr39;
EF5017. Score; solo voices
(SBarB), mixed chorus and
orchestra.

Pod jabloní; dramatická legenda
o šesti obrazech, [by] Josef
Suk. Op. 20. Na slova Julia
Zeyera. Klavírní výtah s
textem upravil Karel Šolc. ©
Hudební Matice Umělecké Besedy,
Praha, Czechoslovakia;
14Jun45; EF4963. Piano-vocal
score.

Praga ... Složil Jos. Suk. Op. 26.
Klavírní výtah na 4 ruce od
skladatele ... Rev. by R.
Tanner. © Mojmír Urbánek,
Prague, Czechoslovakia; on
arrangement; 14Jul39; EF5365.
For piano 4 hands.

3 klavírní skladby; [by] Josef
Suk ... revidoval prof. Vilém
Kurz. © Hudební Matice Umělecké
Besedy, Praha, Czechoslovakia;
3Nov43; EF5014. For piano solo.

SULLIVAN, SIR ARTHUR SEYMOUR, 1842-
1900.
The lost chord; by Sir Arthur
Sullivan, arranged by Alfred
d'Auberge. © Accordion Music
Publishing Co., New York; on
arrangement; 30Dec46; EP10769.
For accordion solo.

The lost chord; for combined choral
groups, a cappella ... Poem by
Adelaide Proctor, [music by] Sir
Arthur Sullivan, choral setting
by Arthur F. A. Witte. © M.
Witmark & Sons, New York; on
arrangement; 14Mar47; EP13950.

*(It happened in Brooklyn) I
believe. EP12582. See 1950 CCE*

SULLIVAN, SIR ARTHUR SEYMOUR. Cont'd.
The lost chord; S.A.T.B. (with
baritone solo) by Sir Arthur
Sullivan, arr. by Wayne
Howorth, [words by Adelaide A.
Proctor] © Belwin, inc., New
York; on arrangement; 3Apr47;
EP13198.
The lost chord; S.S.A. (with solo
for medium voice) by Sir
Arthur Sullivan, arr. by Wayne
Howorth, [words by Adelaide
A. Proctor] © Belwin, inc.,
New York; on arrangement;
3Apr47; EP13199.
Oh Lord, Redeemer; S.A.T.B. ...
arr. by George F. Strickling;
text from the Psalms. © Broad-
cast Music, inc., New York; on
arrangement; 30Apr46; EP4716.
Onward, Christian soldiers ... [by]
Sullivan, arr. by Maxine Tannehill.
© J. Merrill Tannehill, St. Paul;
on arrangement; 1Nov46; EP11553.
Parts: marimba and piano.

SULLIVAN, GENE.
Kansas City blues; words and music
by Wiley Walker and Gene
Sullivan, [piano arr. by Dick
Kent, and (I love you) Mary Lou;
words and music by Jimmy Heavner
and Slim Haynes] © Peer International Corp., New York;
24Mar47; EP13431, 13433.
Take away those blues around my
heart ... Words and music by
Alex Morrison, Wiley Walker &
Gene Sullivan. © Peer International Corp., New York;
19Mar47; EP13429.

SULLIVAN, GERARD JOSEPH E
Brother, 1911—
Ave Maria; (in Bb) [by] G.J.E.S.
Op. 1, no. 2. © Gerard J. E.
Sullivan, Dayton, Ohio; 12Mar47;
EP14659. Close score: SATB.

---- ---- Ed. in E flat. © Gerard
J. E. Sullivan, Dayton, Ohio;
11Feb47; EP14660.

SUMERLIN, MACON D
Mother, I'm coming home ... [words
by] John O. Harrell, [music
by] Macon D. Sumerlin. © John
Oscar Harrell, sr., Abilene,
Tex ; 10May46; EP11330.

SUNI, GRIKOR MIRZOEFF, 1876-
1939.
Armenian song bouquet; original
compositions and others comp.
by Grikor M. Suni. © Lucy
E. Gulezian, executor of the
estate of Grikor M. Suni,
Philadelphia; v.3-4, 16Apr47;
EP14872-14873.

SUPPE, FRANZ VON, 1819-1895.
Overture, Franz Schubert ... [by]
Suppé, arr. [by] Denis Wright,
© William Paxton & Co., ltd.,
London; on arrangement; 23Dec46;
EF5433. Piano-conductor score
(band) and parts.

SURDAM, THEO JANET.
Bridges; [by] T. Janet Surdam.
© T. Janet Surdam, Henrietta,
N.Y.; 5Dec46; EP11082.
Close score: SATB.

SURER, VERNA MEADE, 1912-
Mother's Day; words and music by
Verna Meade Surer. Philadelphia,
Epler & Geist. © Verna Meade
Surer, Bala-Cynwyd, Pa.; 28Mar47;
EP13926.

SUSPIROS DEL CHANCHAMAYO. By the Rio
Chanchamayo. [English words adapted
by Albert Gamse] (In André, Julie,
ed. Songs from south of the border.
p.40-41) © Edward B. Marks
Music Corp., New York; on English
adaptation; 28Dec46; EP10876.

SUTTON, VIVIAN.
I'm traveling the King's high-
way; [words by] Elsie Hobaugh,
[music by] Vivian Sutton,
arr. by R. A. Cosselmon. (In
Church of the Nazarene.
Michigan District. Nazarene
Young Peoples Society.
Choruses of the N. Y. P. S. p.
4-5) © Michigan District,
Nazarene Young Peoples Society,
Flint, Mich.; 25Jul46; EP13031.
Close score: SATB.

SVECENSKI, BERTHA.
My train; for the piano, by
Bertha Svecenski. © G.
Schirmer, inc., New York;
16Nov46; EP12879.

SVOJIK, FRANTIŠEK, 1909-
Růžová krinolína; hudba: Fr.
Svojík, slova: Vl. E. Port.
© Mojmír Urbánek, Praha,
Czechoslovakia; 24Apr39;
EF336U. For voice and piano.

SWEATMAN, JUANITA M
I won't cry over you. words and
music by Juanita M. Sweatman.
© Nordyke Publishing Co., Los
Angeles; 5Mar47; EP13547.

SWEATMAN, WILBUR C
Down home rag; fox trot [by Wilbur
C. Sweatman], arranged by Jimmy
Dale. © Shapiro, Bernstein &
Co., inc., New York; on arrange-
ment; 31Dec46; EP11070. Piano-
conductor score (orchestra) and
parts.

SWEET, MILO.
Indiana Varsity; by Milo Sweet,
arr. by Chas. N. Fielder.
© Thornton W. Allen Co., New
York; on arrangement; 19Nov46;
EP12865. Parts: band.
Men of Duke ... words and music by
Milo Sweet. © Melrose Music Corp.,
New York; 14Jan47; EP11837.
Stand up and fight for Tennessee;
words and music by Milo Sweet.
© Melrose Music Corp., New York;
16Dec43; EP10704.

SWIFT, FREDERIC FAY, 1907-
Evening reverie; for ... S.S.A.A.,
words and music by Frederic Fay
Swift. © Pro Art Publications,
New York; 21Apr47; EP13611.
Every time I feel the Spirit;
S.A.T.B. arr. by Frederic
Fay Swift. © Belwin, inc.,
New York; on arrangement;
31Dec46; EP11222.
In Jesus' name; words and music by
Frederic Fay Swift, [for] S.S.A.
© Pro Art Publications, New York;
25Mar47; EP13401.
Lullaby; words and music by
Frederic Fay Swift. © Robbins
Music Corp., New York; 12Dec46;
EP11015.
Lullaby; words and music by
Frederic Fay Swift, [four part
S.A.T.B. arranged by the com-
poser] © Robbins Music Corp.,
New York; on arrangement;
5Mar47; EP12766.
Lullaby; words and music by
Frederic Fay Swift, [three
part S.S.A. arranged by the
composer] © Robbins Music
Corp., New York; on arrange-
ment; 5Mar47; EP12767.
Nobody knows de trouble I've
seen; [for] S.A. Negro spirit-
ual, arr. by Frederic Fay
Swift. © Belwin, inc., New
York; on arrangement; 5Mar47;
EP12751.
Thunder; words and music by
Frederic Fay Swift. © Pro
Art Publications, New York;
19May47; EF14449. Score:
chorus (SATB) and piano.

SWIFT, FREDERIC FAY, 1907-   arr.
Three blind mice ... special arrangement by Frederic Fay Swift [for]
girl's trio and girl's chorus (S.A.)
© Belwin, inc., New York; on arrangement; 13Feb47; EP12070.

SWIFT, FREDERIC FAY, 1907-
comp. and arr.
String class method; by Frederic
Fay Swift. © Belwin, inc.,
New York; on arrangement and
compilation; 12Jun47; EP15141.
Extra violin part, 11Apr47;
EP13458. Score(violin, viola,
violoncello, bass and piano)
and parts.

SWINEFORD, LAURA PROPHET.
In old Missouri; words and music by
Laura Prophet Swineford. © Paul
Swineford, Springfield, Mo.;
8May47; EP14502.

SWING, ROBERT, pseud. See
Bosmans, Robert.

SWINSTEAD, FELIX.
Russian rhapsody; for pianoforte, by
Felix Swinstead. © Alfred
Lengnick & Co., ltd., London;
7Feb47; EF5354.

SYLVAIN, JULES, pseud. See also
Hansson, Stig.

Rumba Zorina; [by] Jules
Sylvain, piano arr. [by]
Jerry Högstedt, text:
Schütz [and] Baudisch, [tr. by]
Hyltén-Cavallius [and] S. S.
Wilson [pseud.] Stockholm,
Nordiska Musikförlaget. ©
Teaterförlag Arvid Englind,
a.b., Stockholm; 1Jan43;
EF3768. For voice and piano,
with chord symbols. Swedish
words.

SYLVIANO, RENE, pseud. See
Caffot, Sylvère Victor Joseph.

SZENDREI, ALADAR, 1884-
Der türkisenblaue Garten; ein
Spiel von Liebe und Tod in
einem Akt von Rose Silberer,
Musik von Aladàr Szendrei,
Wien, Universal-Edition. ©
Associated Music Publishers,
inc., New York; 1Mar19; EF5103.
Piano-vocal score.

SZERVANSZKY, ENDRE.
Sonatine pour le piano, [by] Endre
Szervánszky. © Edition Cserépfalvi,
Budapest, Hungary; 15May46;
EF3160.

T

TABET, GEORGES.
Boogie-woogie partout; paroles
& musique de Georges Tabet.
© Continental Leeds Music Co.,
Paris; 27Mar47; EF5423.

TAFF, GEORGE, pseud. See
Zahoratos, George Taff.

TAGLIAFERRI, ERNESTO.
Raccolta delle celebri canzoni di
Ernesto Tagliaferri ... versi
di Ernesto Murolo ... [and]
Tullio Gentili. [Comp. by
Valentina Bideri] © Casa
Editrice Ferdinando Bideri,
Napoli; ser. 1, 31Aug46;
EF3220.

TAJČEVIC, M
Macedonian courting dance; by M.
Tajčević ... arr. for violin and
piano by Jascha Herzog. © Carl
Fischer, inc., New York; on
arrangement; 19Dec46; EP11130.

TAKENS, MAXINE L   1923-
Draw me closer to Calvary; [by]
Maxine Takens, arr. by W. M.
Thorne. (In Church of the
Nazarene. Michigan District.
Nazarene Young Peoples Society.
Choruses of the N. Y. P. S.
p.8) © Michigan District,
Nazarene Young Peoples Society,
Flint, Mich.; 25Jul46; EP13034.
For voice and piano.

Heaven's in my heart today;
[by] Maxine Takens, arr. by
W. M. T. (In Church of the
Nazarene. Michigan District.
Nazarene Young Peoples Society.
Choruses of the N. Y. P. S.
p.27) © Michigan District,
Nazarene Young Peoples Society,
Flint, Mich.; 25Jul46; EP13053.
For 2 treble voices and piano.

Jesus never fails; [by] Maxine
Takens, arr. by W. M. T.
(In Church of the Nazarene.
Michigan District. Nazarene
Young Peoples Society.
Choruses of the N. Y. P. S.
p.25) © Michigan District,
Nazarene Young Peoples Society,
Flint, Mich.; 25Jul46;
EP13049. For voice and piano.

TALBOT, ALICE. See
Yoder, Alice Talbot.

TALLIS, THOMAS.
Magnificat and Nunc dimittis; [or-
gan part by Ernest White] © Music Press, New York; on preface
& realization of figured bass;
7Feb46; EP11280.

TALMA, LOUISE.
Alleluia, in form of toccata; for
piano, by Louise Talma. © Carl
Fischer, inc., New York; 28Jan47;
EP11687.

TALMADGE, ARTHUR S
See Jesus the Saviour; for four-
part chorus of women's voices, a
cappella. Folk carol, recorded in
Morgan County, Kentucky, 1913, by
John Jacob Niles; arranged by
Arthur S. Talmadge. © G. Schirmer,
inc., New York; on arrangement;
16Nov46; EP11609.

TAM, FRANKIE, 1915-
Flamenco chant ... by Frankie
Tam and Arthur Gardner.
Washington, D. C., Maureen
Music Co. © Frankie Tam,
Washington, D. C.; 19May47;
EP14432. For voice and piano;
arbitrary syllables as text.

TANNEHILL, MAXINE BROWNLEE, 1909-
Christmas medley; arr. ... by
Maxine Tannehill. St. Paul,
Tannehill Music Publishers.
© J. Merrill Tannehill, St.
Paul; on arrangement 25Nov46;
EP11452. Parts: marimba and
piano.

"Wonderful words of life" ... [By
P. P. Bliss], arr. by Maxine
Tannehill. St. Paul, Tannehill
Music Publishers. © J. Merrill
Tannehill, St. Paul; on arrange-
ment; 15May47; EP14536. Score
(marimba and piano) and part.

TANNEHILL, MAXINE BROWNLEE, 1909-
arr.
Very easy sacred solos ... [by
Redner, Franz Gruber, Converse
and others] comp. and arr. by
Maxine Tannehill. St. Paul,
Tannehill Music Publishers. ©
J. Merrill Tannehill, St. Paul;
on arrangement 20Dec46; EP11083.
Parts: cornet and piano.

TANTE LOU, pseud. See
Cursan, Marie Louise.

TATUM, ART, arr.
Art Tatum improvisations ... ed.
by Murray Feldman. © Robbins
Music Corp., New York; no. 2,
on arrangement; 14Mar46;
EP9394.

TAVARES, HEKEL.
Favela ... Letra en español de
Pedro Berriós, lutra en portugués
de Jornoy Camargo, [piano arrange-
ment by Domenico Savino] ©
Robbins Music Corp., New York; on
Spanish words and piano arrange-
ment; 21Feb47; EP12388.

TAYLOR, BEN E
Perpetual spring; [by] B. E.
Taylor. © Ben E. Taylor,
Seattle; 3Mar47; EP12533.
Parts: band.

TAYLOR, BOB ALFRED, 1905-
The stars and you; words and music
by Bob A. Taylor. © Bob Alfred
Taylor, Romoland, Calif.;
23Nov46; EP15202.

TAYLOR, COLIN.
Aconite; unison song, music by
Colin Taylor, words by Jan
Struther [pseud.] © Edward
Arnold & Co., London; 12Dec46;
EP14736.

Alexander the Great ... two-part
song, music by Colin Taylor,
words by Eleanor and Herbert
Farjeon. © Edward Arnold & Co.,
London; 12Dec46; EP14737.

Boadicea ... unison song, music by
Colin Taylor, words by Eleanor and
Herbert Farjeon. © Edward Arnold
& Co., London; 12Dec46; EP14739.

The Duke of Marlborough ... two-
part song, music by Colin
Taylor, words by Eleanor and
Herbert Farjeon. © Edward
Arnold & Co., London; 12Dec46;
EP14742.

Frosty night; unison song, music
by Colin Taylor, words by Wilfrid Thorley. © Edward Arnold
& Co., London; 12Dec46; EP14743.

George Washington ... unison song,
music by Colin Taylor, words by
Eleanor and Herbert Farjeon. ©
Edward Arnold & Co., London;
12Dec46; EP14744.

He and she; unison song, music by
Colin Taylor, words anonymous.
© Edward Arnold & Co., London;
12Dec46; EP14745.

It is not the tear; three-part song,
traditional air arr. by Colin
Taylor, words by Thomas Moore.
© Edward Arnold & Co., London;
12Dec46; EP14747.

Timour the Tartar ... two-part
song, music by Colin Taylor, words
by Eleanor and Herbert Farjeon.
© Edward Arnold & Co., London;
12Dec46; EP14757.

TAYLOR, EDNA.
Valse mignonne; piano solo by
Edna Taylor. © Carl Fischer,
inc., New York; 8May47; EP14549.

TAYLOR, FRED ALLSOBROOKE, 1883-
One hundred years ago; by Fred
Taylor. © Fred Allsobrooke
Taylor, Salt Lake City;
7Apr47; EP14084. For voice
and piano.

TAYLOR, IRVING.
You can take my word for it, baby;
by Tickor Freeman [and] Irving Taylor. © Sinatra Songs,
inc., New York; 15Jan47; EP11830.
For voice and piano; with chord
symbols.

TAYLOR, MAURICE D
Intermediate steps to the band; by
Maurice D. Taylor. © Mills Music,
inc., New York; on 13 pts.
Parts: basses (© 23May47; AA34515),
bassoon (© 29May47; AA34591), Bb
cornet or trumpet (© 16Apr47;
AA34039), Bb tenor saxophone
(© 29May47; AA34587), C flute
(© 23May47; AA34511), Db piccolo
(© 23May47; AA34514), drums
(© 29May47; AA34586), Eb alto horn
or mellophone (© 29May47; AA34588),
F horn (© 23May47; AA34512), oboe
or C saxophone (© 23May47; AA34510),
piano accompaniment (© 29May47;
AA34589), trombone & baritone
(bass clef) (© 23May47; AA34513),
trombone & baritone (truble clef)
(© 29May47; AA34590)

TAYLOR, MYRA, pseud. See
Marshall, Renda.

TAYLOR, PETE.
I round-up the stars (every evening);
words ... by Jack Howard, [music by]
Pete Taylor and Jimmy DeKnight.
© Jack Howard Publications, inc.,
Philadelphia; 30Dec46; EP10974.
For voice and piano, with chord
symbols.

TAYLOR, ROUMEL WILLIAM, 1921-
This same Jesus cares for you and
me; words and music by Roumel
Wm. Taylor, arr. by Ernest
Haywood. © Roumel William
Taylor, Philadelphia; 24Jun46;
EP10920. For voice and piano.

TCHAIKOVSKY, PETER ILYITCH. See
Chaikovskii, Petr Il'ich.

TCHEREPNINE, ALEXANDRE. See
Cherepnin, Aleksandr Nikolaevich.

TEAL, JOHN.
Calling; words and music by John
Teal. © Nordyke Publishing Co.,
Los Angeles; 5Mar47; EP14921.

EL TECOLOTE. (Lament of the owl) ...
Folk song of Michoacan, Mexico,
[English words adapted by Albert
Gamse] [In André, Julie, ed.
Songs from south of the border.
p.12-14] © Edward B. Marks Music
Corp., New York; on English
adaptation; 28Dec46; EP10866.

TEDESCO, MARIO CASTELNUOVO- See
Castelnuovo-Tedesco, Mario.

[TENINTY, ORBA HOY]
Money makes the world go 'round;
[by O. H. (Tim) Teninty] © Orba
Hoy Teninty, Idaho Falls, Idaho;
15Aug46; EP11365.

TENINTY, TIM. See
Teninty, Orba Hoy.

TERI, COSMA ROOSEVELT PUSA- See
Pusa-Teri, Cosma Roosevelt.

TERII, JAMES, 1902-
Underneath the cherry tree; by
James Terii, [arr. by Ed Le Roy
McKenzie] © James Terii, Seattle;
1Feb47; EP11955. For voice and
piano, with chord symbols.

TERRY, FRANCES.
Chanson d'amour; for the piano,
by Frances Terry. © G.
Schirmer, inc., New York;
30Dec46; EP11604.

TERRY, JOSEPH, pseud. See
Otero, Joseph.

TERRY, RICHARD RUNCIMAN, 1865-1938.
Richard de Castre's prayer to
Jesus; carol, A.D. 1430. [By]
R. R. Terry, arr. [by] Maurice
Jacobson. London, J. Curwen &
Sons. © Harold Robinson & Mrs.
Marion Lee Squire, (executors of
the estate of Sir Richard Terry)
& Maurice Jacobson, London; on
arrangement; 16Nov46; EP14887.
For unison voices and piano;
melody also in tonic sol-fa
notation.

TERSMEDEN, GERARD A   H
Solitaire; by Gerard Tersmeden.
Piano solo arr. by Albert
Sirmay. © Chappell & Co.,
inc., New York; on arrangement;
5May47; EP14333.

En sommarllNkt ... text: inga
Roos, musik: G. Tersmeden.
© Gerard Tersmeden, formerly
called Edition Cnnto, Stockholm;
1Jan46; EF4879. For voice and
piano.

Vals nr. 5; [by] Gerard Tersmeden.
© Gerard Tersmeden, Stockholm;
1Jan47; EF4800. Score: orchestra.

TERUEL, J., pseud. See
Sentis. José.

TEXIDOR DALMAU, JAIME.
Fiesta en La Caleta ... letra
y música de Texidor. Bilbao,
España, Ediciones Texidor. ©
Jaime Texidor Dalmau, Bilbao,
Spain; 1Dec46; EF5256. Piano-
conductor score (orchestra),
and parts.

THELMA, pseud. See
Lista, Thelma.

TRIMAN, ERIC HARDING, 1900-
Departure ... words by William
Browne ... music by Eric H.
Thiman. © Novello & Co., ltd.,
London; 7May47; EF5240. Score:
chorus (SSA) and piano.

Preludes and voluntaries ... for
the organ, by Eric H. Thiman.
London, J. Curwen & Sons. ©
Eric H. Thiman, London; bk.3,
20Mar47; EF5467.

A tune for the tuba; by Eric H.
Thiman. © Novello & Co., ltd.,
London; 16Jun47; EF3803. For
organ solo.

THOMAS, ANDRE, 1910-
Le Tombeau de Mex Jacob; prélude
et toccata pour piano [by]
André Thomas. © Lucien de
Lacour, Editeur, Paris; 1Jul47;
EF4545.

THOMAS, CHRISTOPHER.
Then sing; for four-part chorus of
mixed voices, a cappella, [by]
Christopher Thomas, [words by]
Wordsworth. © The Willis Music
Co., Cincinnati; 23Jan47; EP11664.

THOMAS, DICK.
I've gah a gal in Laramie; words
and music by Max C. Freed-
man ... [and] Dick Thomas.
© National Music Publishing
Corp., New York; 31Dec46;
EP12867.

A lonely cowboy's dream; words and
music by Max C. Freedman and
Dick Thomas. © Shapiro, Bernstein & Co., inc., New York;
25Jun47; EP15282.

THOMAS, HAROLD.
On the isle of my dreams; lyrics
by Frank Viggiani, music by
Harold Thomas. © Frank Viggiani,
sole owner of Big Boy Music
Publishers, New York; 1Jan47;
EP11975.

THOMAS, HARVEY VERN, 1920-
Try and forget a little harder;
by Harvey V. Thomas. © Harvey
Vern Thomas, Seattle; 27Feb47;
EP12451. For voice and piano,
with chord symbols.

THOMAS, J   J
Here we go [By] J. J. Thomas
... for piano. © Theodore
Presser Co., Philadelphia;
7May47; EF14483.

Sleepy bird; piano solo by J. J.
Thomas. © Theodore Presser Co.,
Philadelphia; 26May47; EP15058.

Swing up, swing down; Piano solo,
by J. J. Thomas. © Theodore
Presser Co., Philadelphia;
16Apr47; EP13095.

THOMAS, KARL M
Time to tell; words and music by
Karl M. Thomas, arr. by Anson C.
Jacobs. © Nordyke Publishing
Company, Los Angeles; 5Mar47;
EP14461.

THOMAS, MILLARD GALWESTON, 1894-
My prayer; by Millard Thomas.
© Thomas & Son, Music Pub-
lishers, Newark, N. J.; 15Apr47;
EP13952. For voice and piano,
with chord symbols.

THOMAS, RAY, 1878-
Tho church by tho side of tho road;
[by] Ray Thomas. © Ray Thomas,
Indianapolis; 1Dec46; EP11279.
Close score: SATB.

THOMPSON, CHARLOTTE P
Hail! Hail! Ohio; words and music by
Charlotte P. Thompson. © Charlotte
P. Thompson, Jewett, Ohio; 27Mar47
EP12967.

THOMPSON, GERALD.
My Valparaiso; words and music by
Gerald Thompson. © Lawrence
Wright Music Co., ltd., London;
30Dec46; EF4785.

THOMPSON, HARRY C
From Hand to Hand ... by Harry C.
Thompson. © Ziegler Band
Music Publ. Co., Sterling,
Ill.; 3Feb47; EP11918. Con-
donsed score (band) and parts.

THOMPSON, HENRY WILLIAM, 1925-
"Whoa! Sailor," [and A lonely
heart knows] by Hank Thompson.
© Metro Music, Dallas;
16Apr47; EP14443-14444. For
voice and piano, with chord
symbols.

THOMPSON, IOLA.
Sunset dreams; by Iola Thompson,
[arr. by R. W. Gieradorf. © Victor Publishing Co., inc., Dallas;
10Jan47; EP11356.

Whistles ... by Iola Thompson.
© Victor Publishing Co.,
Dallas; 2May47; EP14501.
For voice and piano, with
chord symbols.

THOMPSON, RICHARD W   1928-
Mood impetuous ... [By] Richard
W. Thompson. © Wesley Webster,
San Francisco; 15Apr47;
EP13587. For piano solo.

THOMPSON, RUTH E
He is there; [words by] R.E.T. ...
arr. [by] Emma Esther Parker.
(In Gospel choruses. no. 3, p.
27 © Ruth E. Thompson & Emma
Esther Parker, Pasadena, Calif.;
4Jun46; EP4313. For voice and
SATB.

THOMPSON, WILLIAM H
Did anyone over tell you you're a
pretty girl? Words by Harriet
W. Schab, music by William H.
Thompson. © Nordyke Publishing
Co., Los Angeles; 2Dec46;
EP11047.

THORDARSON, SIGURDUR. See
Pórdarson. Sigurdur.

THORNE, WAYNE M   1913-
All things work for good; [words
by] C. E. H., [music by]
W. M. T. (In Church of the
Nazarene. Michigan District.
Nazarene Young Peoples Society.
Choruses of the N. Y. P. S. p.
49) © Michigan District.
Nazarene Young Peoples Society,
Flint, Mich.; 25Jul46; EP13070.
Close score: SATB.

Built upon the Rock; [words by]
W. M. T. [and] C. E. H.,
[music by] Wayne M. Thorne.
(In Church of the Nazarene.
Michigan District. Nazarene
Young Peoples Society. Choruses
of the N. Y. P. S. p. 26-27) ©
Michigan District, Nazarene
Young Peoples Society, Flint,
Mich.; 25Jul46; EP13052. For
voice and piano.

Come, Holy Spirit; [words by]
Marvin S. Cooper, [music by]
Wayne M. Thorne. (In Church
of the Nazarene. Michigan
District. Nazarene Young
Peoples Society. Choruses of
the N. Y. P. S. p.21) ©
Michigan District, Nazarene
Young Peoples Society, Flint,
Mich.; 25Jul46; EP13047.
Close score: SATB.

His grace is sufficient ...
[words by] Lois Blanchard,
[music by] W. M. T. (In
Church of the Nazarene.
Michigan District. Nazarene
Young Peoples Society.
Choruses of the N. Y. P. S.
p.19) © Michigan District,
Nazarene Young Peoples Society,
Flint, Mich.; 25Jul46;
EP13045. Close score: SATB.

I'll hide in Jesus; [words by] E.
M. Murrill, [music by] Wayne M.
Thorne. (In Church of the Nazarene.
Michigan District. Nazarene Young
Peoples Society. Choruses of the
N. Y. P. S. p.70-71) © Michigan
District, Nazarene Young Peoples
Society, Flint, Mich.; 25Jul46;
EP13089. For voice and piano.

Jesus has died that we might
live; [words by] Mary Cole
and Lois Blanchard, [music
by] Wayne M. Thorne. (In
Michigan District. Nazarene
Young Peoples Society.
Choruses of the N. Y. P. S.
p.33) © Michigan District,
Nazarene Young Peoples Society,
Flint, Mich.; 25Jul46; EP13059.
Close score: SATB.

Jesus is my friend and brother;
[words by] Mrs. Arloa L. Vincent,
[music by] W. M. T. (In Church
of the Nazarene. Michigan Dis-
trict. Nazarene Young Peoples
Society. Choruses of the N. Y.
P. S. p.67) © Michigan District,
Nazarene Young Peoples Society,
Flint, Mich.; 25Jul46; EP13086.
Close score: SATB.

Let me shine; [words by] Russell
Spray and C. E. H., [music by]
W. M. T. (In Church of the
Nazarene. Michigan District.
Nazarene Young Peoples Society.
Choruses of the N. Y. P. S.
p.34) © Michigan District,
Nazarene Young Peoples Society,
Flint, Mich.; 25Jul46; EP13060.
Close score: SATB.

N. Y. P. S. rally song; [words by]
Madge Bugbee, [music by] Wayne
M. Thorne. (In Church of the Naz-
arene. Michigan District. Naz-
arene Young Peoples Society.
Choruses of the N. Y. P. S. p.
62-63) © Michigan District,
Nazarene Young Peoples Society,
Flint, Mich.; 25Jul46; EP13082.
For voice and piano.

None but Christ can satisfy; old
hymn, [music by] Wayne M.
Thorne. (In Church of the
Nazarene. Michigan District.
Nazarene Young Peoples Society.
Choruses of the N. Y. P. S.
p.4) © Michigan District,
Nazarene Young Peoples Society,
Flint, Mich.; 25Jul46
EP13050. For 2 treble voices
and piano.

There is a name more precious;
[words by] Matilda Walker Hunter,
[music by] Wayne M. Thorne. (In
Church of the Nazarene. Michigan
District. Nazarene Young Peoples
Society. Choruses of the N. Y.
P. S. p.66) © Michigan District,
Nazarene Young Peoples Society,
Flint, Mich.; 25Jul46; EP13085.
For voice and piano.

139

THORNE, WAYNE M. Cont'd.
To Theo, O Christ, I give my
love; [words by] C. E. H.,
[music by] W. M. T. (In
Church of the Nazarene.
Michigan District. Nazarene
Young Peoples Society.
Choruses of the N. Y. P. S.,
p.38-39) © Michigan District,
Nazarene Young Peoples Society,
Flint, Mich.; 25Jul46; EP13063.
For voice and piano.
Whatever betide us, He will be
near; [words by] Wayne M.
Haynes, [music by] Wayne M.
Thorne. (In Church of the
Nazarene. Michigan District.
Nazarene Young Peoples Society.
Choruses of the N. Y. P. S.
p.51) © Michigan District,
Nazarene Young Peoples Society,
Flint, Mich.; 25Jul46; EP13057.
Close score: SATB.
Why do I love Jesus? ... [Words by]
C. Edwin Harwood, [music by]
Wayne M. Thorne. (In Church of
the Nazarene. Michigan District.
Nazarene Young Peoples Society,
Choruses of the N. Y. P. S. p.64-65)
© Michigan District, Nazarene Young
Peoples Society, Flint, Mich.;
25Jul46; EP13083. Close score:
SATB.

THORNTON, A. DE MOSS. See
Thornton, Armenta Fadora (De Moss)
THORNTON, ARMENTA FADORA (DE MOSS)
1913-
Jesus requires of you to be true;
music by Mrs. A. De Moss Thorn-
ton, words by Rev. Edward K.
Wilson. © Edward Knox Wilson
and Armenta De Moss Thornton,
Los Angeles; 14Jun47; EP15173.
For voice and piano.
THUILLIER, EUGENE, 1945-
Methode; [par] Eug. Thuillier;
1ère année, piano. Pièces
récréatives du S..Raynaud
Zurfluh. Paris, Editions
Aug. Zurfluh. © Zurfluh,
Paris; 2Jan47; EF5168.
THURSTON, FREDERICK, 1901-
Passage studies; for the Bb clari-
net, [by] Frederick Thurston.
London, Boosey & Hawkes.
© on v.1-2, Hawkes & Son (London)
ltd., London; © on v.3, Boosey &
Hawkes, ltd., London; on arrange-
ment; 28Mar47. Contents.- 1.
Easy studies © EF5314) - 2.
Moderately difficult studies
(© EF5315) - 3. Difficult studies
(© EF5608)
TIERSOT, JULIEN.
L'amour de moi. Love of my heart.
Fifteenth century song ... Eng-
lish version by Lorraine Noel
Finley. (In [Hodges, Lester]
comp. John Charles Thomas album
of favorite songs and arias.
p. 6-8) © G. Schirmer, inc.,
New York; on English version;
21Jun46; EP10217.
TIGERSTROM, STEN GUNNAR
Min lilla ocearina ... Text och
musik: Gunnar Tigerström.
© Edition Sylvain a/b,
Stockholm; 10et45; EF5313.
TILLMAN, FLOYD.
Come back to my lonely heart; by
Floyd Tillman. © Northern Music
Corp., New York; 12Feb47;
EP12173. For voice and piano,
with chord symbols.
Go out and find somebody new;
words and music by Floyd Till-
man, [and I wish we'd never
met; words and music by Ekko
Whelan and Bill Boyd] © Peer
International Corp., New York;
1May47; EP14571-14572.

TILZER, HARRY VON. See
Von Tilzer, Harry.
TIMBERG, HERMAN.
What's with your heart? By Dude
Dorman and Herman Timberg. ©
Mills Music, inc., New York;
16Apr47; EP6832. For voice
and piano, with chord symbols.
TIMBERG, SAMMY.
Help yourself to my heart; lyric
by Buddy Kaye, music by Sammy
Timberg. © Sinatra Songs, inc.,
New York; 12Jun47; EP15192.
TINTURIN, PETER.
The funny thing called love; words
and music by Peter Tinturin.
© Robbins Music Corp., New
York; 7Mar47; EP12653.
On an evening in Paris; words
and music by Peter Tinturin.
© Robbins Music Corp., New York;
21Apr47; EP14770.
TIOMKIN, DIMITRI.
Duel in the sun. The Orizaba
dance; fantasia for piano by
Dimitri Tiomkin, from the David
O. Selznick production, Duel in
the sun. © Edwin H. Morris & Co.,
inc., New York; 18Feb47;
EP12152.
TIPPETT, MICHAEL KEMP, 1905-
(Quartet, strings, no. 1) String
quartet no. 1; [by] Michael
Tippett. © Schott & Co., ltd.,
London; 11Dec46; EF14817.
Close score: SATB.
TIPPITT, WARNIE T 1921-
Like the Saviour; [words by]
W. T. and C. E. H., [music
by] Warnie T. Tippitt, arr. by
W. M. T. (In Church of the
Nazarene. Michigan District.
Nazarene Young Peoples Society.
Choruses of the N. Y. P. S.,
p.55) © Michigan District,
Nazarene Young Peoples Society,
Flint, Mich.; 25Jul46; EP13075.
Close score: SATB.
TOBIAS, HENRY H
Give a broken heart a break;
words and music by Don Reid
and Henry Tobias. © Northern
Music Corp., New York;
12Sep46; EP12724.
Who pushed the button? ...Words and
music by Charlie Tobias, Jack
Ellis and Henry Tobias.
© Mutual Music Society, inc.,
New York; 1May47; EP14144.
TOBIN, LOUIS, 1904-
The banner song; words by Augusta
Netzell, music by Lew Tobin.
© Cine-Mart Music Publishing
Co., Hollywood, Calif.; 31Mar47;
EP14654.
Beloved star; words by Dorothy Rose
Keller, music by Lew Tobin. ©
Nordyke Publishing Co., Los
Angeles; 23Aug45; EP6506.
Bloom in my garden of memories;
words by Eugene J. Mullane,
music by Lew Tobin. ©
Nordyke Publishing Co., Los
Angeles; 7Mar47; EP13293.
Darling little girl; words by
Doris Manuel, music by Lew
Tobin. © Cine-mart Music
Publishing Co., Hollywood, Calif.;
1Aug46; EP10952. For voice
and piano, with chord symbols.
Caption title: Dear little girl.
Darling Nell; words by M. O.
Fiorillo, music by Lew Tobin.
© Cine-mart Music Publishing
Co., Hollywood, Calif.; 1Aug46;
EP10956. For voice and piano,
with chord symbols.
Digging with jive; words by
Myrtle L. Spargo, music by Lew
Tobin. [c1946] © Whitehouse
Publishing Co., Hollywood,
Calif.; 2Jan47; EP11979.

Goodnight sailor; words by
Marie O'Shea, music by Lew
Tobin. © Cine-Mart Music
Publishing Co., Hollywood,
Calif.; 31Mar47; EP14644.
The humming bird; words by Charles J.
LeBlanc, music by Lew Tobin.
© Cine-Mart Music Publishing Co.,
Hollywood, Calif.; 1Dec46; EP12112.
I just hate to take you home
tonight; words by Ferdind
Kunkel, music by Lew Tobin.
© Nordyke Publishing Co.,
Los Angeles; 5Mar47; EP13283.
I'm picking up the pieces of my
heart; words by Jean S. Watson,
music by Lew Tobin. [c1946]
© Nordyke Publishing Co., Los
Angeles; 29Jan47; EP14789.
Kiss your boy goodbye; words by
Josephine A. Zakzevski, music by
Lew Tobin. © Cine-Mart Music
Publishing Co., Hollywood, Calif.;
1Dec46; EP12120.
Let's follow the clouds; words by
Dorothy Lind, [pseud.], music
by Lew Tobin. © Dorothy Lind-
strom, St. Paul; 20Mar47;
EP13965.
The long-waited letter; words by
Gilbert Domingue, music by Lew
Tobin. © Cine-Mart Music Pub-
lishing Co., Hollywood, Calif.;
1Nov46; EP14118.
Main Street; words by Charles H.
Dunlavy, music by Lew Tobin.
© Cine-Kart Music Publishing
Co., Hollywood, Calif.; 30Dec46;
EP14034.
My kisses are limited; words by
Virgil L. Cotton, music by Lew
Tobin. © Nordyke Publishing
Co., Los Angeles; 13Jul46;
EP14782.
My little yeller buckskin; words
by Vande Ward, music by Lew
Tobin. © Vande Ward, Kalamazoo,
Mich.; 12May47; EP14600.
A poet's place; words by Nenio
Bekay [pseud.], music by Lew
Tobin. © Cine-mart Music
Publishing Co., Hollywood,
Calif.; 1Aug46; EP10955. For
voice and piano, with chord symbols.
Somebody's kissing her now;
words by Fred D. Johnson,
music by Lew Tobin. © Nordyke
Publishing Co., Los Angeles;
8Mar47; EP13235.
This day; words by Joseph Gardi,
music by Lew Tobin. © Nordyke
Publishing Co., Los Angeles;
27Sep46; EP12714.
To you it was just a fling;
words by Lela Coffield, music
by Lew Tobin. © Nordyke
Publishing Co., Los Angeles;
31Oct45; EP13530.
Waiting for a call from you;
words by Emma Marie Saccone,
music by Lew Tobin. © Nor-
dyke Publishing Co., Los
Angeles; 30Apr46; EP13534.
When you call me up (please don't
call me down); words by Artie
Stevens, music by Lew Tobin.
© Dave Ringle, inc., New York;
18Jun47; EP15180.
You can't stop my dreams; words
by Helen O. Aymami, music by
Lew Tobin. © Nordyke Publish-
ing Co., Los Angeles; 7Mar47;
EP15253.
TOCH, ERNST.
Quintet. Op. 64. [By] Ernst
Toch. © Delkas Music Publishing
Co., Los Angeles; 26Feb47;
EP6665. Score (violin 1-2, viola,
violoncello and piano) and parts.

TOCZEK, FRANK.
My Tex; words and music by Frank
Toczek. © Nordyke Publishing
Co., Los Angeles; 7Mar47;
EP13264.

TODD, TOM T
Tom foolery ... ed. by Van Alexander, composed by Tom T. Todd.
© Embassy Music Corp., New York;
14Apr47; EP13500. Piano-conductor score (orchestra) and
parts.

TOELLE, FRANCES B
Easter alleluya; (S.S.A.) [by]
Frances B. Toelle, [words by]
Isaac Watts. © J. Fischer
& Bro., New York; 27Mar47;
EP6808.
—— Ed. for SATB. © J. Fischer
& Bro., New York; 27Mar47; EP6809.

TOLLEFSEN, AUGUSTA, 1885-
Gay little pieces; by Augusta
Tollefsen, for piano. © The
Composers Press, inc. New
York; on 3 pieces; 25Feb47.
Contents.- [v.1] Norwegian
dance (© EP12241)-[v.2] Water-
sprite (© EP12240) - [v.3]
Gaiety (© EP12242)

TOMELLE, FERDINAND DE LA, 1854-1928.
Savior of my heart; motet for two-
part chorus, S.A. or T.B. [words
and music by] Ferdinand de la
Tombelle, arr. [and tr.] by
Robert Leech Bedell. © Clayton
F. Summy Co., Chicago; on arrange-
ment and translation; 30Dec46;
EP10985.

TOMBLINGS, PHILIP.
Osme's song. See his Sylvia.
(Sylvia) Osme's song, (from
"Sylvia"; or, The May queen);
words by George Darley, music by
Philip Tomblings. © Elkin
& Co., ltd., London; 1May47;
EP3196. Score: chorus (SATB)
and piano reduction. Voice
parts also in tonic sol-fa
notation.

TOME, JOSE.
Manolete" ... letra y música de
José Tomé, arr. de A. Varona
C. © Peer International Corp.,
New York; 18Dec46; EP5586.

TOMKINS, THOMAS, 1545-1626.
Oh, pray for the peace of
Jerusalem; by Thomas Tomkins,
arr. and ed. for mixed chorus
... by Wm. Cosman. [Psalm
122:6, rev. by W.C.] © Choral
Art Publications, New York;
on arrangement; 8May47;
EP14389.

TOMSHA, WILLIAM.
Just a flower; words and music by
William Tomsha. © Nordyke
Publishing Co., Los Angeles;
12Sep45; EP6450.

TORANZO, UNDELINO.
Jueves; (Dia de moda) ... de
Udelino Toranzo y Rafael Rossi.
Editorial Argen-
tina de Música Internacional.
© Peer International Corp.,
New York; 28Aug46; EP5600.
Piano-conductor score: orches-
tra.

TORCH, SIDNEY.
All strings and fancy free;
piano solo, by Sidney Torch.
© Chappell & Co., ltd., London;
5May47; EP3629.

Samba sud; piano solo, by
Sidney Torch. © Chappell &
Co., ltd., London; 5May47;
EP3628.

TORJUSSEN, TRYGVE, 1885-
30 pedal studies; in progressive order
for pianoforte, with harmonic analysis, composed by Trygve Torjussen.
Op. 70. © The Arthur P. Schmidt Co.,
Boston; on harmonic analysis; 23Jan47
EP13246.

TORMÉ, MELVIN HOWARD.
Born to be blue; words and music by
Robert Wells [and] Mel Tormé.
© Stevens Music Corp., New York;
11Feb47; EP12066.

TORRE, HECTOR DE LA.
Dios lo quiere ... letra y
música de Hector de la Torre.
© Editorial Mexicana de Música
Internacional, s.a., Mexico,
D. F.; 27Dec46; EP4865. For
voice and piano.

TOSTI, F   PAOLO.
The serenade. La serenata. For four-
part chorus of mixed voices with
piano acc., words by G. A. Cesareo,
English version by Nathan Haskell
Dole. [Music by] F. Paolo Tosti,
arranged by Josef Furgiuele. ©
G. Schirmer, inc., New York; on
arrangement; 22Mar46; EP11613.

TOUGH, DAVE.
Dave Tough's Advanced paradiddle
exercises; ed. by Bill West.
© Mutual Music Society, inc.,
New York; 27Mar47; EP13009.

TOURNEMIRE, CHARLES.
Pièce symphonique; by Charles Tourne-
mire. [Op.16] Arr. by Robert
Leech Bedell ... [for] organ solo.
© Mills Music, inc., New York; on
arrangement; 23May47; EP6936.

TOURTE, ROBERT, 1895-
Méthode du tambour et caisse
claire d'orchestre; par Robert
Tourte. © Éditions Salabert,
Paris; 1Oct46; EP5196.

TOUTJEAN, VARTAN, 1897-
I am in love; lyrics by E. Miles
Thayer, music by Vartan
Toutjean. Oakland, Calif.,
Toutjean Studios. © Vartan
Toutjean, jr., Oakland, Calif.
& Eleanor Miles Thayer,
Berkeley, Calif.; on revision
of words & music; 15Mar47;
EP13799.

TOVEY, EVA MARGARET.
I cannot fathom Calvary; [by]
Eva Margaret Tovey, [words by]
Herbert G. Tovey. © Herbert G.
Tovey, Los Angeles; 6Aug43;
EP13516. Close score: SATB.

The way everlasting ... for soli,
choir, and organ, the one hundred
and thirty ninth Psalm, music by
Eva Margaret Tovey. Los Angeles,
The Sacred Music Foundation.
© Herbert G. Tovey, Los Angeles;
6Mar45; EP13512.

TOVEY, HERBERT GEORGE, 1888-
Alone with Jesus; [words by]
Margaret Donovan Moore, [music
by] Herbert G. Tovey. © Herbert
G. Tovey, Los Angeles; 6Jan42;
EP13501.

Always for Jesus; [by] Herbert G.
Tovey, [words by] Elizabeth
Nord. © Herbert G. Tovey, Los
Angeles; 6Jun40; EP13520.
Close score: soprano and chorus
of 4 treble voices.

Break with the tie; [by] Herbert
G. Tovey, [words by] H. G. T.
© Herbert G. Tovey, Los Angeles;
10Sep44; EP13514. Close score:
SATB.

Ceaseless prayer; [by] Herbert
G. Tovey, [words by] Eva Margaret
Tovey. © Herbert G. Tovey, Los
Angeles; 10Jan43; EP13513. Close
score: SATB.

Eternity somewhere; [by] Herbert
G. Tovey, [words by] H. G. T.
© Herbert G. Tovey, Los Angeles;
10Sep45; EP13517. Close score:
SATB.

Grateful hearts; ladies trio
[by] Herbert G. Tovey, [words
by] Marion Tovey. © Herbert
G. Tovey, Los Angeles;
6Aug40; EP13518.

Heaven is real; [by] Herbert G.
Tovey, [words by] H. G. T. ©
Herbert G. Tovey, Los Angeles;
20Jul41; EP13519. Close score:
SATB.

In the regions beyond; [by]
Herbert G. Tovey. © Herbert
G. Tovey, Los Angeles;
10Jan45; EP13510. Close score:
SATB.

Into my heart I've taken my Lord;
[by] Herbert G. Tovey. © Herbert
G. Tovey, Los Angeles; 10Oct44;
EP13507. Partly for voice and
piano, partly close score:
SATB.

Love for others; [by] Herbert
G. Tovey, [words by] Mrs. J. M.
Dick. © Herbert G. Tovey, Los
Angeles; 24Feb47; EP13506.

On the sands of time ... [by]
Herbert G. Tovey. © Herbert G.
Tovey, Los Angeles; 6Jul45;
EP13508. For voice and piano.

The Saviour calls, prepare! ...
[by] Herbert G. Tovey. © Herbert
G. Tovey, Los Angeles; 20Feb47;
EP13511. Close score: SATB.

Tarry near the cross; words by
Mabel Long, music by Herbert G.
Tovey ... solo or duet for low
voices with a male quartet or
male chorus acc. © Herbert G.
Tovey, Los Angeles; 6Feb39;
EP13505.

That dream will come true ...
[by] Herbert G. Tovey.
© Herbert G. Tovey, Los Angeles;
20Feb40; EP13504. Close score:
SATB.

The touch of God; [by] Herbert
G. Tovey, [words by] H. G. T.
© Herbert G. Tovey, Los Angeles;
10Sep44; EP13515. Close score:
SATB.

The unseen hand ... [by] Herbert
G. Tovey. © Herbert G. Tovey,
Los Angeles; 25May44; EP13503.
Close score: SATB.

When the gold star came ... In
three settings ... Words and
music by Herbert G. Tovey.
Los Angeles, The Sacred Music
Foundation. © Herbert G. Tovey,
Los Angeles; 10Jan45; EP13521.
Close score: SATB, TTBB or SSA.

A yielded life; [by] Herbert G.
Tovey, [words by] Eva Margaret
Tovey. © Herbert G. Tovey,
Los Angeles; 6Jan43; EP13502.

You may preach! ... [by] Herbert
G. Tovey, [words by] Eva Margaret
Tovey. © Herbert G. Tovey, Los
Angeles; 6Sep43; EP13509.

TOWERS, LEO, pseud. See also
Blitz, Leonard.

The little old mill (went round and
round); words and music by Don
Pelosi, Lewis Ilda & Leo Towers.
© Irwin Dash Music Co., ltd.,
London; 1Jan47; EP3152. For voice
and piano, with chord symbols;
melody also in tonic sol-fa
notation.

TOWNSEND, PEARL DEA ETTA, 1886-
I am coming to the Cross ... Lead
me gently home; words and music
by Rev. Pearl Townsend, arr. by
Bernice H. Washington. © Pearl
Townsend, Grand Rapids, Mich. &
Bernice H. Washington, Darby,
Pa.; on 2 hymns, 11Jan47;
EP13449, 13448. Close score:
SATB.

I'm glad His blood reaches me;
words and music by ... Pearl
Townsend, arr. by Bernice H.
Washington. © Pearl Townsend,
Grand Rapids & Bernice H.
Washington, Darby, Pa.; 15Jul46;
EP11035. Close score: SATB.

TOWNSEND, PEARL DEA ETTA. Cont'd.

Jesus gives me victory; words and
music by ... Pearl Townsend, arr.
by Bernice H. Washington. ©
Pearl Townsend, Grand Rapids &
Bernice H. Washington, Darby,
Pa.; 15Jul46; EP11039.

Jesus is my friend; words and
music by ... Pearl Townsend,
arr. by Bernice H. Washington.
© Pearl Townsend, Grand Rapids
& Bernice H. Washington, Darby,
Pa.; 15Jul46; EP11037. Close
score: SATB.

Jesus loves me; words and music
by Rev. Pearl Townsend, arr. by
Bernice H. Washington. © Pearl
Townsend, Grand Rapids, Mich.
& Bernice H. Washington, Darby,
Pa.; 11Jan47; EP13447. Close
score: SATB.

No room in the inn; words and music
by ... Pearl Townsend, arr. by
Bernice H. Washington. © Pearl
Townsend, Grand Rapids & Bernice
H. Washington, Darby, Pa.;
15Jul46; EP11038. Close score:
SATB.

Roll away Jordan; words and music
by ... Pearl Townsend, arr. by
Bernice H. Washington. ©
Pearl Townsend, Grand Rapids &
Bernice Washington, Darby, Pa.;
30Apr46; EP11040. Score: chorus
(SATB) and piano.

Weighed in the balance; words and
music by Rev. Pearl Townsend,
arr. by Bernice H. Washington.
© Pearl Townsend, Grand Rapids,
Mich. & Bernice H. Washington,
Darby, Pa.; 11Jan47; EP13450.
Close score: SATB.

When I take leave for heaven; words
and music by ... Pearl Townsend,
arr. by Bernice H. Washington.
© Pearl Townsend, Grand Rapids &
Bernice H. Washington, Darby, Pa.;
15Jul46; EP11036. Close score:
SATB.

TRACE, AL.

Duluth, M-I-double-N ... Words &
music by Al Trace. © Franklin
Music Co., New York; 26May47;
EP6953.

Pork 'n beans; words and music by
Ferney De Persia and Al Trace.
© Melomusic Publications, New
York; 16Jan47; EP6489.

TRAFICANTE, EDWARD.

The Traficante certified system;
for piano accordion [by Edward
Traficante] © Edward Traficante,
Minneapolis; 30Dec46; EP10986.

TRAMS, CHARLES H

That bloom in May; by Drewey King
and C. H. Trams. © Chords
Music Publishers, New York;
5May47; EP15103. For voice and
piano, with chord symbols.

TRAVIS, BOBBS.

Dance of the paper dolls; for
the piano, [by] Bobbs Travis.
© Oliver Ditson Co., Philadelphia; 7May47; EP14480.

Jack-in-the-box ... for the piano,
[by] Bobbs Travis. © Oliver
Ditson Co., Philadelphia; 16Apr47;
EP13896.

TRAVIS, M

Heart stealin' mama; words and
music by "Grandpa" Jones and
M. Travis. © Hill and Range
Songs, inc., Hollywood, Calif.;
17May47; EP14581.

[TRAVNICEK, ANDRE 1898-
Belle Andalousie ... La estocada
... Paroles de Georges Thibault,
musique de A. T. Cekow [pseud.]
© Éditions Musicales A. T. Cekow,
Paris; 3Jul46; EP5233. Parts:
orchestra.

Je suis a toi ... paroles de Jack
Jym, musique de A. T. Cekow
[pseud. and A la Fazenda; musique
de A. T. Cekow] © Éditions
Musicales A. T. Cekow, Paris;
30Jan47; EP5447. Piano-conductor
score (orchestra) and parts.

Josélito; [and Canari, By] ... A.
T. Cekow [pseud.] © Éditions
Musicales A. T. Cekow, Paris;
30Jan47; EP5446. Piano-conductor
score (orchestra), and parts.

Swing huit ... & Bravo toro ...
[by] A. T. Cekow [pseud.]
© Éditions Musicales A. T.
Cekow, Paris; 11Nov46; EP5232.
Parts: orchestra.

TRAXLER, JIŘÍ, 1912-
6x Jiří Traxler; [words and music
by Jiří Traxler] © Mojmír
Urbánek, Praha, Czechoslovakia;
12Jun46; EP5413.

TREAT, JASPER WILLIE, 1907- ed.
Cantos espirituales; para usarse
en todos los servicios de la
Iglesia de Cristo, arr. por J.
W. Treat. [n.p.] Impr. a su
orden, Harding College Press,
H. Howk. © Jasper Willie
Treat, Abilene, Tex.; 27Apr47;
EP14422. Hymns with music.

TREHARNE, BRYCESON, 1879-
Again in unison we stand; for four-
part chorus of mixed voices with
... piano acc.; poem by A. G.
Prys-Jones. © Boston Music Co.,
Boston; 22Jan46; EP14043.

[TREHARNE, BRYCESON] 1879- arr.
Music lovers' book of grand
opera ... comp. and arr. by
Chester Wallis [pseud.] © The
Boston Music Co., Boston; on
compilation and arrangement;
23Jun47; EP15260. For piano
solo.

TREMBLAY, EDWARD, 1902-
As long as you are near ... Words
and music by Edward Tremblay. ©
Edward Tremblay, Ancon, C. Z.;
on changes in words; 9May47;
EP14870.

TRENET, CHARLES, 1913-
Ding! Dong! Paroles et musique
de Charles Trenet. © Éditions
Salabert, Paris; 31Mar45; EP3588.

Une noix; musique de Charles
Trenet et Albert Lasry.
© France-Music Co., New York;
3Jun47; EP3710. For piano solo.

N'y pensez pas trop; paroles de
Charles Trenet, musique de
Charles Trenet & Albert Lasry.
© Éditions Vianolly, Paris;
3Apr47; EP5422.

Quand un facteur s'envole ...
paroles et musique de
Charles Trenet. © Éditions
Salabert, Paris; 10Feb43;
EP3916.

Quartier latin; paroles et
musique de Charles Trenet. ©
Éditions Salabert, Paris; 31Mar45;
EP3563.

Retour à Paris; paroles de
Charles Trenet, musique de
Charles Trenet & Albert Lasry.
© Raoul Breton, Paris; 21Mar47;
EP5332. For voice and piano
with chord symbols.

Le soleil a des rayons de
pluie; paroles et musique de
Charles Trenet. © Éditions
Salabert, Paris; 10Feb43;
EF3915.

Le violon du diable; musique de
Charles Trenet et Albert
Lasry. © France-Music Co.,
New York; 3Jun47; EP3715.
For piano solo, with chord
symbols.

TREVIÑO, PACO.

Lluvia de estrellas ... [words and
music] de Paco Treviño, arreglo
de Luis Márquez. © Promotora
Hispano Americana de Música, s.a.,
México; 28Aug46; EF5604. Piano-
conductor score (orchestra),
and parts.

Por que te quieres ir? ... Música
y letra de Paco Treviño. ©
Hnos. Márquez, s. de r. l.,
México; 5Jul46; EF3906.

TREW, CHARLES A

Cornish carnival; the Helston
floral dance, by Charles A.
Trew. Piano solo. © Keith,
Prowse & Co., ltd., London;
26Feb47; EF5261.

Cornish carnival; the Helston
floral dance, by Charles A.
Trew. Piano solo (simplified)
© Keith, Prowse & Co., ltd.,
London; 26Feb47; EF5262.

TREWHELA, RALPH HENRY, 1911-
The Princess Elizabeth waltz;
words & music by Ralph Trewhela.
Johannesburg, Gallo (Africa)
ltd. © Ralph Henry Trewhela,
Johannesburg, S. Africa;
3Mar47; EF5531.

TRIETSCH, KEN.

The first thing I do every morning;
words and music by Lee Penny and
Ken Trietsch. © Hill and Range
Songs, inc., Hollywood, Calif.;
22Jan47; EP11667.

TRINE, VERNA.

Studios in port de bras for beginners; music by Verna Trine,
choreography by Edna Lucile Baum.
© Edna Lucile Baum, Chicago;
5Aug46; EP10921. For piano solo.

TRISTAN, YVON, 1908-
Un oeillet fané ... paroles de Guy
Favoreau, musique de Yvon Tristan,
arr. by Henry Leca. © Éditions
du Lido, Paris; on arrangement;
15Dec46; EF5449. Piano-conductor
score (orchestra, with words),
and parts.

Venez danser, baby ... paroles
de Sergelys, musique de Yvon
Tristan & Armand Fort. ©
Éditions E.M.U.L., Paris;
15Oct45; EF3844.

TROILO, ANIBAL.

Tango triste ... letra de José
Maria Contursi, música de
Anibal Troilo. © Editorial
Argentina de Música Inter-
nacional, s. de r., ltd.,
Buenos Aires; 24Mar47; EF5599.

TROTTER, DORIS, 1928-
Smile, smile, smile; [by] Doris
Trotter, arr. by W. M.
Thorne. (In Church of the
Nazarene. Michigan District.
Nazarene Young Peoples Society.
Choruses of the N. Y. P. S.
p.13) © Michigan District,
Nazarene Young Peoples Society,
Flint, Mich.; 25Jul46;
EP13039. Close score: SATB.

TROUP, BOBBY. See also
Troup, Robert William.

Swingin' in thirds; words and
music by Bobby Troup. © Harman
Music, inc., New York; 21May47;
EP14521.

[TROUP, JOHN B]
Valley of the moon; [by John
B. Troup] © John Daniel,
Nashville; 23Sep46; EP6818.
Close score: SATB; shape-
note notation.

TROUP, ROBERT WILLIAM. See also
Troup, Bobby.

The three bears; by Bobby Troup.
© Mayfair Music Corp., New
York; 19Mar47; EP12791. For
voice and piano, with chord
symbols.

TROWBRIDGE, LUTHER, 1892-
Chorale ... by Luther Trowbridge.
© The Composers Press, inc.,
New York; 23Dec46; EP10687.
Score (trumpet, cornet or flugel-
horn 1-4) and parts.
In meadow and forest ... for piano,
by Luther Trowbridge. [c1946]
© The Composers Press, inc., New
York; on 4 pieces; 13Jan47.
Contents.- [v.1] Crocodile
(© EP11153) - [v.2] Hootie the
owl (© EP11154) - [v.3] Peter
Rabbit (© EP11155) - [v.4] Daddy
Longlegs (© EP11156)
Nature tone-poems; for piano, by
Luther Trowbridge. © The
Composers Press, inc., New
York; on 3 pieces; 28Feb47;
Contents.- [v. 1] Will o'th
wisp (© EP12313) - [v. 2] Robin
Redbreast (© EP12314) - [v. 3]
Firefly (© EP12315)
Pensively ... by Luther Trowbridge.
© The Composers Press, inc., New
York; 21Mar47; EP12812. Score
(clarinet, violin, viola and
violoncello) and parts.
Tranquillo ... by Luther Trow-
bridge. © The Composers Press,
inc., New York; 23Dec46; EP10688.
Score (trumpet, cornet or flugel-
horn 1-3) and parts.

TRUED, S   CLARENCE, 1895-
Thy Word is like a garden, Lord...
[for] mixed voices; words by
T. H. Gill, music by S. Clarence
Trued. © Dorothea Louise
Schroeder, Flushing, N. Y.;
31Mar47; EP13395.
Thy Word is like a garden, Lord
... Words by T. H. Gill, music
by S. Clarence Trued. ©
Dorothea Louise Schroeder,
Flushing, N. Y.; 31Mar47;
EP13394. Score: chorus (SA)
and piano.

TSCHAIKOWSKY, PETER. See
Chaĭkovskiĭ, Petr Il'ich.

TUBB, ERNEST.
Don't look now (but your broken
heart is showin'); words and
music by Ernest Tubb. © Ernest
Tubb Music, inc., Hollywood,
Calif.; 2May47; EP14195.

TUCCI, TERIG.
La bamba de Vera Cruz; English
lyric by Ted Mossman, Spanish
lyric by Chuco Navarro, music
by Terig Tucci. © Kelton, inc.,
New York; 22Mar47; EP13883.

TUKES, SUSIE.
I'm going home to see my Saviour;
words and music by Susie Tukes,
arr. by Virginia Davis.
Chicago, L. King's Studio of
Music. © Susie Tukes, Chicago;
23Sep46; EP12459.

TURINA, JOAQUIN.
Sinfonia sevillana; para orquesta,
[by] Joaquin Turina. © Union
Musical Española, Madrid;
20Dec25; EF3186.

TURNER, CAROLYN AYERS.
Peace; words by Cleta Clemmer,
music by Carolyn Turner.
© Cleta Alice Clemmer, Indianapolis; 30Dec46; EP11761.

TURNER, GODFREY BIRKETT, 1913-
Fanfare, chorale & finale; [by]
Godfrey Turner. © Arrow
Music Press, inc., New York;
11Sep46; EP12222. Score:
brass instruments.
(Sonata, piano, no. 1) Pianoforte
sonata no. 1 [by] Godfrey Turner.
© American Music Center, inc.,
New York; 13Nov46; EP13099.

TURNER, LEIGE. See
Turner, Monroe.

TURNER, MONROE, 1913-
Lonesome little darling; words ...
by Red ... Turner. (In Old Favorites music book of the Sohio
hayride gang. p. [11]) © Monroe
Turner & Ulys Turner, Cincinnati;
7Nov46; EP9715.

TURNER, ROY J
The old flying "L"; words and
music by Roy J. Turner, [piano
arr. by Larry Stanton] © Peer
International Corp., New York;
18Mar47; EP13977.
Saddle 'n' ride; words and music
by Roy J. Turner. © Peer International Corp., New York;
1May47; EP14573.

TURNER, ZEB.
It's a sin; by Fred Rose and Zeb
Turner. © Milene Music,
Nashville; 14May47; EP14354.
For voice and piano, with guitar
diagrams and chord symbols.

TWINN, SYDNEY.
I will lift up mine eyes; sacred
song with piano or organ acc.,
text from Psalm 121, music by
Sydney Twinn. © Carl Fischer,
inc., New York; 12May47;
EP15020.

TYLE, RODNEY VAN. See
Van Tyle, Rodney.

TYLER, GERALD.
Magnificat; (E minor) [by] Gerald
Tyler, [arr. by Chester Nord-
man] Rev. ed. © Shattinger
Piano & Music Co., St. Louis;
on arrangement; 31Dec46; EP11246.
Score: chorus (SATB) and piano
or organ.

TYLER, JOHNNY.
Oakie boogie; words and music by
Johnny Tyler. © Hill and Range
Songs, inc., Hollywood, Calif.;
21Feb47; EP12211.
This troubled mind o' mine; words
and music by Billy Hughes and
Johnny Tyler. © Hill and Range
Songs, inc., Hollywood, Calif.;
22Jan47; EP11666.

TYLER, LLOYD J
Land next to heaven; by Lloyd J.
Tyler. © Cine-Mart Music Publishing Co., Hollywood, Calif.;
1Dec46; EP11412. For voice and
piano, with chord symbols.

TYRWHITT-WILSON, GERALD HUGH. See
Berners, Gerald Hugh Tyrwhitt-
Wilson, baron.

U

UDALL, FRED, 1915-
The girl in the polka dot dress;
words and music by Fred Udall.
© Lyric Music Publishers, inc.,
New York; 30Dec46; EP13420.

UHER, BRUNO.
Wenn der Jasmin blüht ... Text und
Musik von Bruno Uher. © SIDEM,
Société Intercontinentale
d'Editions Musicales, Vaduz,
Ginevra; 18Oct46; EF4934. For
voice and piano.

UNDERWOOD, JESSE L
I hope you won't be sorry (because you left me all alone);
by Jesse L. Underwood. ©
Cine-Mart Music Publishing
Co., Hollywood, Calif.;
1Nov46; EP11495. For voice
and piano.

UNRUH, DAVID P
I shall come again ... Anthem for
mixed voices, S.S.A.T.B.B.;
words from scriptures, music by
David P. Unruh. Oakland, Calif.,
Unruh Music Studios. © David
P. Unruh, Oakland, Calif.;
30Apr47; EP14545.

UPTEGROVE, WILLIAM ELLIOTT, 1907-
Let us sing praises to our God;
words and music by W. E.
Uptegrove. © William Elliott
Uptegrove, Georgetown, S. C.;
12Mar47; EP13855. Close score:
SATB.

UPTON, ANNE, 1892-
The Lord's prayer; by Anne Upton.
© Phoenix, Los Angeles; 3Feb47;
EP12064. For voice and piano.
My mother; by Anne Upton. © Phoenix,
Los Angeles; 24Dec46; EP12062.
For voice and piano.
Never to part again; by Anne Upton.
© Phoenix, Los Angeles; 3Feb47;
EP12063. For voice and piano,
with chord symbols.

URYGA, PETER.
Modern city polka; words by S.
L. Drobac, music by P. Uryga.
© Grand Central Music Co.,
Chicago; 21Jun46; EP12669.

USÁK, JAROSLAV, 1892-
Škola pro smičcový či tahový
pozoun ... napsal Jaroslav
Usák. © Ladislav Hnyk, Hradec
Králové, Czechoslovakia;
10Oct39; EF3359.

USERA, MONCHO. See
Usera, Raymond.

USERA, RAYMOND.
A la vuelta. ('Round the corner)
... English words by Joe Davis,
Spanish words and music by Raymond "Moncho" Usera. © Caribbean Music, inc., New York;
30Dec46; EP10676.

UYTTENBOOGAARD, FRITS, 1895-
Victimae Paschali ... [by] Frits
Uyttenboogaard. Op. 32.
[c1946] © Edition Heuwoke-
meijer (Fa. A.J. Heuwekemeijer
& B. F. van Gaal), Amsterdam;
18Jan47; EF3374. Close score:
SSAA.

V

VAČKÁŘ, DALIBOR C   1906-
Extempore; piano solo. Op.24.
[By] Dalibor C. Vačkář.
© Hudební Matice Umělecké
Besedy, Praha, Czechoslovakia;
11Mar43; EF4975.

VAČKÁŘ, VACLAV, 1881-
Sérénade, Vzpomínka na Zbiroh ...
[By] Václav Vačkář. Opus 180.
[Slova: Adolf Wenig] © Karel
Barvitius, jun., Praha,
Czechoslovakia; 16Jun46; EP5410.
Violin-conductor score (orches-
tra, with words) and parts.
Sérenáda; Vzpomínka na Zbiroh.
Op. 180. [By] Václav Vačkář.
[c1944] © Karel Barvitius,
jun., Praha, Czechoslovakia;
8Jul45; EF3362. Score (violin
and piano) and part.

VACKÁR, VACLAV. Cont'd.
Šohaj ... hudbu složil Vaclav
Vackar. Mužně vpřed ... hudbu
složil Josef Hanžl. © Jaroslav Stožický, Brno Czechoslovakia; 9Jun46; EF3366. Condensed score (band), and parts.

VAILLANT, H
Tenues rythmiques pour l'indépendance des doigts;
(moyenne force) Rythmical
sustained notes for the independence of the fingers;
(medium degree) ... [By]
H. Vaillant. © Georges
Delrieu & Cie., Nice, France;
31Mar47; EF3862. For piano.

VAL, JACK, 1897-
All dressed up with a broken
heart; words and music by Fred
Patrick, Claude Reese [and]
Jack Val, [piano arr. by Marvin
Fisher] © Sunset Music Pub-
lishers, New York; 21Feb47;
EP12236.

VALDERRAMA, CARLOS.
Chola andina ... Música de
Cárlos Valderrama, letra de
Haydée Hoyle de Valderrama.
© Peer International Corp.,
New York; 27Feb47; EP12764.

VALDES, GILBERTO.
Drumi ogguere ... letra y música
de Gilberto Valdés. © Robbins
Music Corp., New York; 9Jun47;
EP15130.

Flor do mi amar ... letra de
Johnnie Camacho, música de
Gilberto Valdés. © Robbins
Music Corp., New York; 9Jun47;
EP15129.

VALDON, JEAN.
Ma chanson d'Espagne ... paroles de
Gine Money, musique de Jean
Valdon. © Éditions Colibri,
Paris; 15May46; EF3146.

VALENCIA, CASTRO.
Sin título... [by] Pepe Del Rio,
Ruben Berrios [and] Castro
Valencia. © Peer International
Corp., New York; 15May47;
EP14578. For piano solo.

VALENTE, NICOLA.
Addio, mia bella Napoli; testo
di Tito Manlio, musica di
Nicola Valente, dal film
omonimo. © Edizioni Leonardi,
s.a.r.l.; 27Mar47; EF3408.

Sirmo 'e Napule ... paisà ...;
versi di Puppino Fiorelli,
musica di Nicola Valente. ©
Italian Book Co., New York;
30Dec46; EP14679.

VALLADARES, MIGUEL ANGEL.
Frio en el alma ... letra y
música de Miguel Angel
Valladares. © Promotora
Hispano Americana de Música,
s.a., México; 14Apr47;
EP5594.

VAN BUREN, BURRELL.
I see Jesus everywhere; lyrics
by W. Frank Brown, music by
Burrell Van Buren. © W. Frank
Brown, Keokuk, Iowa; 23Sep46;
EP11192.

VAN DEN BERG, CORNELIS JACOBUS. See
Berg, Cornelis Jacobus van den.

VANDENBERG, DON G 1912-
Entreat me not to leave thee; by
Don Vandenberg, [words, Ruth 1:16],
ed. and arr. for mixed chorus,
SATB, by Noble Cain. © Choral
Press, Evanston, Ill; 15Jun46;
EP11694.

Responses for general use; by Don
Vandenberg, ed. and arr. for
mixed chorus, SATB. © Choral
Press, Evanston, Ill.; 15Jun46;
EP11694.

Thanksgiving ... Ed. and arr. for
women's chorus, SSA, by Don Vandenberg, [words by Isabel Vendenberg]
© Choral Press, Evanston, Ill.;
10ct46; EP11706.

VAN DEN BROECK, LEO. See
Broeck, Leo van den.

VANDERBURG, GORDON JAMES, 1913-
Never leave me; lyric by Eva Adams,
music by Gordon Vanderburg. ©
Graham Publishing Co., Hollywood,
Calif.; 28Apr47; EP14193.

You are my story; lyric by William
Macy Gray, music by Gordon Van-
derburg. © Graham Publishing
Co., Hollywood, Calif.; 19May47;
EP14931.

You are the only one in the
world; lyric by Helen
Schueler, music by
Gordon Vanderburg. ©
Graham Publishing Co.,
Hollywood; 19May47; EP14632.

VANDERCOOK, H A
On the wing ... [by] VanderCook.
© Rubank, inc., Chicago;
1May47; EP12820. Piano-conductor score (band) and parts.

Salute to youth ... [by] VanderCook.
© Rubank, inc., Chicago; 1May47;
EP12819. Piano-conductor score
(band) and parts.

VAN DER MOLEN, ALBERT, 1882-   comp.
Latin American airs ... comp. by
Albert Van der Molen. © Alpha
Music, New York; 1Mar47; EP12874.
Partly for piano solo, partly
for voice and piano. Spanish
words.

VAN DUUREN, HENDRIK JOHANNES. See
Duuren, Hendrik Johannes van.

VAN HEUSEN, JAMES, 1913-
As long as I'm dreaming. See his
Welcome stranger.

Bing Crosby's Songs for young
hearts (from 6 to 60); words
by Johnny Burke, music by
Jimmy Van Heusen. © Burke and
Van Heusen, inc., New York;
10Apr47; EP13655.

Country style. See his Welcome
stranger.

(Cross my heart) It hasn't been
chilly in Chile, [from] "Cross
my heart", a Paramount picture;
words by Johnny Burke, music by
Jimmy Van Heusen. © Paramount
Music Corp., New York; 29Dec46;
EP10703.
It hasn't been chilly in Chile.
See his Cross my heart.

My heart is a hobo. See his
Welcome stranger.
Smile right back at the sun. See
his Welcome stranger.

(Variety girl) Harmony ... [From]
the Paramount picture "Variety
girl." Lyric by Johnny Burke, music
by James Van Heusen. © Burke
& Van Heusen, inc., New York;
12Jun47; EP15193.

(Welcome stranger) As long as I'm
dreaming, from the Paramount picture
"Welcome stranger"; lyric by Johnny
Burke, music by James Van Heusen.
© Burke & Van Heusen, inc., New York;
30Jan47; EP11834.

(Welcome stranger) Country style,
from the Paramount picture "Welcome
stranger"; lyric by Johnny Burke,
music by James Van Heusen. © Burke
& Van Heusen, inc., New York;
30Jan47; EP11833.

(Welcome stranger) My heart is a
hobo, from the Paramount picture
"Welcome stranger"; lyric by Johnny
Burke, music by James Van Heusen.
© Burke & Van Heusen, inc., New York;
30Jan47; EP11832.

(Welcome stranger) Smile right back
at the sun, from the Paramount pic-
ture "Welcome stranger"; lyric by
Johnny Burke, music by James Van
Heusen. © Burke & Van Heusen, inc.,
New York; 30Jan47; EP11835.

VAN HORN, CHARLES. See also Von Horn,
Charles.
I hear my Saviour call; [by]
Charles Van Horn, arr. by W.
M. T. (In Church of the
Nazarene. Michigan District.
Nazarene Young Peoples Society.
Choruses of the N. Y. P. S.
p.28) © Michigan District,
Nazarene Young Peoples Society,
Flint, Mich.; 25Jul46; EP13054.
For voice and piano.

VAN HORN, EDIE M 1920-
Some day I'll forget you; words
by Charles L. Clair, music by
Edie Van Horn. © Hartmann &
Van Horn Music Publishing Co.,
La Grange, Ill.; 22Apr47; EP14465.

VAN HULSE, CAMIL, 1897-
Elegy ... By Camil Van Hulse.
Opus 38. © The Composers Press, inc.,
New York; 9Jun47; EP14909. Score
(violin, violoncello and piano)

VAN NESS CLARKE, pseud. See
Clark, C. Van Ness.

VAN NORT, ISABEL.
Gay butterflies in springtime; piano
solo, by Isabel Van Nort. ©
Mills Music, inc., New York;
23May47; EP6928.

VAN PARYS, GEORGES. See
Parys, Georges van.

VAN PELT, MERRILL B
How to play the flutophone; a
simplified, comprehensive classroom method, by Merrill B. Van
Pelt [and] J. Leon Ruddick. ©
Trophy Products Co., Cleveland;
1May47; EP6920.

VAN SCIVER, ESTHER.
Ida-Idaho; words by Dave Denney &
Steve Nelson. © Bob Miller,
inc., New York; 13Dec46; EP10364.
For voice and piano, with chord
symbols.

VAN SICKLE, ROBERT, 1891-
Ida from Idaho; words by Luther
Denick, music by Robert Van
Sickle. © Luther Denick, Sedan,
Kan.; 3Feb47; EP11909.

Just as my heart; words by
Elsie Bell Becker, music by
Robert Van Sickle. © Nordyke
Publishing Co., Los Angeles;
5Mar47; EP13280.

VAN TYLE, RODNEY.
Lovers' lane; words by J. A. Adams,
music by Rodney Van Tyle. ©
Nordyke Publishing Co., Los
Angeles; 23Aug45; EP6449.

Mists of memories; words by James A.
Shelburn, music by Rodney Van
Tyle. © Nordyke Publishing Co.,
Los Angeles; 12Oct45; EP6507.

VAN ZANDT, JAMES.
I'm always sleepin' (at the
wrong time); words by Millicent
Victoria Steen, music by James
Van Zandt, arr. by Harold
Potter. © Van Vada Music,
Indianapolis; 30Apr47;
EP14510.

VAN ZANDT, JAMES. Cont'd.
Peace (with love); words and
music by James Van Zandt, arr.
by Harold Potter. © Van Vada
Music, Indianapolis; 30Apr47;
EP14509.

VARELA, HECTOR.
Te espero en Rodríguez Peña ...
letra de Carlos Waiss, música
de Hector Varela. Buenos
Aires, Editorial Argentina de
Música Internacional. © Peer
International Corp., New York;
30Dec46; EF5552.

VARNER, RED.
Quirk of a dirk ... Composed and
arr. by (Red) Varner. © Milton
G. Wolf Publications, Chicago;
23Dec43; EP6759. Score (guitar
and piano) and part.

VARONA, LOUIS.
Por tu amor; lotra de Luis Del
Campo, música de Louis Varona,
arr. de D. Savino. © J. J.
Robbins & Sons, inc., New York;
27Dec46; EP11119.
Por tu amor ... Letra de Luis
Del Campo, música de Louis
Varona, arreglo de D. Savino.
[Rev. ed.] © J. J. Robbins &
Sons, inc., New York; on new
words; 31Mar47; EP13960.
Sabrosura; letra de Luis Del
Campo, música de Louis Varona,
arreglo de D. Savino. © J. J.
Robbins & Sons, inc., New York;
31Mar47; EP13959.

VAŠATA. RUDOLF LEO, 1888-
Poslední pření... The last will.
[By] Rudolf Leo Vašata. © Edition Continental (B. Leopold
kom. spol.), Praha, Czechoslovakia; 5Dec44; EF3359.
Piano-conductor score (orchestra), and parts.

VASIN, D., pseud. See
Ravasini, Nino.

VAZQUEZ, ERNESTO.
Bongo ... letra y música de Ernesto
Vazques. © Peer International
Corp., New York; 30Dec46;
EP13649.
Invocando a cambg; letra y música
de Ernesto Vazquez. © Peer
International Corp., New York;
30Dec46; EP11173. For voice
and piano, with chord symbols.

VAZQUEZ, PABLO SÁNCHEZ. See
Sánchez Vázquez, Pablo.

VEGA, CELSO.
Celos ... letra y música de Celso
Vega. © Peer International
Corp., New York; 10Apr47;
EP13695.
Un clavo saca otro clavo ...
Letra y música de Celso Vega.
© Peer International Corp.,
New York; 31Mar47; EP13432.

VELÁSQUEZ, CONSUELO.
Aunque tengas razón ... letra y
música de Consuelo Velásquez.
© Promotora Hispano Americana
de Música, s.a., México;
14Apr47; EF5590.
"Será por eso" ... de Consuelo
Velázquez. [c1946] © Pro-
motora Hispano Americana de
Música, s.a., México; 14Apr47;
EF5592. For voice and piano.

VELAZQUEZ, VICTORINO.
Quién te ha traído! ... versos y
música de Francisco Fiorentino,
Astor Piazzola y Victorino
Velázquez. Buenos Aires,
Editorial Argentina de Música
Internacional. © Peer Inter-
national Corp., New York;
11Jun46; EF5621.

VENÉ, RUGGERO, 1897-
Billy and me; for two part and
piano [by] Ruggero Vené, [words
by James Hogg] © G. Ricordi &
Co., New York; 21Apr47; EP13904.
Peggy; for two part and piano
[by] Ruggero Vené, [words by
Allan Ramsay] © G. Ricordi &
Co., New York;.21Apr47; EP13905.

VERMELHO, ALCYR PIRES. See
Pires Vermelho, Alcyr.

VEROLI, DONATO DI, 1921-1943.
Tema con variazioni; [by] Donato
di Veroli. © Carisch, società
anonimå, Milan; 30Dec46; EF5492.
Score: orchestra.

VERRES, LEON, 1893-
I do not ask, O Lord; anthem for
mixed chorus with organ, by
Leon Verres ... text by Adelaide
Proctor. © The Composers
Press, inc., New York; 30Apr47;
EP14038.

VESELY, STANLEY.
Foundation to cornet playing ...
by Stanley Vesely. Cedar
Rapids, Iowa, Sole selling
agents, Hiltbrunner Music Co.
© Stanley Vesely, Cedar Rapids,
Iowa; 28Dec45; EP13157.

VÉTHEUIL, PAULETTE.
Mon coeur a retrouvé l'espoir;
paroles de Léo Mariâts, musi-
que de Paulette Vétheuil. ©
Société Éditions Musicales
Paris-Monde, Paris; 31Dec46;
EF3814.

VIALA, GEORGETTE, pseud. See
Fillastre, Georgette de.

[VICHERY, LEONA] 1897-
Walking in the sunshine; words
& music by Pat Dillma [pseud.)
© Shelby Music Publishing Co.,
Detroit; 11Apr47; EP14325.

VIDAL, FRANCISCO LOPEZ.
Lagrimas del corazoh. (Tears in
my heart ... English words by
Joe Davis, Spanish words and
music by Francisco Lopez Vidal.
© Caribbean Music, inc., New
York; 7Apr47; EP15340.

VIDALITA. (Little song of life)
[English words adapted by Albert
Gamse] (In André, Julie, ed.
Songs from south of the border.
p.48-49) © Edward B. Marks
Music Corp., New York; on
English adaptation; 28Dec46;
EP10880.

VILLA-LOBOS, HEITOR.
Bachianas brasileiras no. 5;
for soprano and orchestra of
violoncelli, [by] Heitor
Villa-Lobos, [text by Ruth V.
Corrêa, English version by
Harvey Officer] © Associated
Music Publishers, inc., New
York; 6May47; EP14588. Minia-
ture score.

[VILLATTE, JEAN LÉON] 1897-
comp.
Collection de chants choisis;
pour le brevet élémentaire,
[comp. by J. L. Villatte] ©
Henry Lemoine & Cie., Paris;
1. cahier, 31May46; EF3535.
Contents.- 1. 10 chants.-

VILLOLDO, A   G
Arrimate, vida mia. (Draw closer,
my love) ... [By] A. G. Villoldo,
[English words adapted by Albert
Gamse] (In André, Julie, ed.
Songs from south of the border.
p.46-47) © Edward B. Marks Music
Corp., New York; on English
adaptation; 28Dec46; EP10879.

VINAVER, CHEMJO, 1895-
Yom hashviy. The seventh day; a
Friday evening service for cantor
and choir, by Chemjo Vinaver.
[n.p.] Rabbinical Assembly of
America and the United Synagogue
of America, 1946. © Chemjo
Vinaver, New York; 20Jan47;
EP11319. Score: tenor, chorus
(SATB) and organ; Hebrew words
(transliterated)

VINCENT, BESSIE L   1901-
Take Him with you; [by] Bessie
L. Vincent, arr. by W. M. T.
(In Church of the Nazarene.
Michigan District. Nazarene
Young Peoples Society.
Choruses of the N. Y. P. S.
p.40-41) © Michigan District,
Nazarene Young Peoples Society,
Flint, Mich.; 25Jul46; EP13064.
For voice and piano.

VINCENT, CHARLES.
As it began to dawn ... S.A.B. accompanied, [by] Charles Vincent,
arr. by Wallingford Riegger. ©
Harold Flammer, inc., New York; on
arrangement; 4Nov46; EP10834.

VINCENT, LARRY.
The freckle song; by Larry Vincent.
© Leeds Music Corp., New York;
24Jan47; EP11804. For voice and
piano, with chord symbols.

VINCENT, NATHANIEL M.   See also
Kenbrovin, Jaan, pseud.
That's where the West begins;
words by Edward F. Gill,
music by Nat Vincent. ©
Nordyke Publishing Co., Los
Angeles; 8Mar47; EP13289.

VIOLA, AL.
Gee, but it's good to be; words
and music by Bobby Troup and
Al Viola. © Regent Music
Corp., New York; 22May47   ;
EP14587.

VISTA, FIDEL ARMANDO.
Corrido veracruzano; letra y
música de Fidel A. Vista. ©
Promotora Hispano Americana de
Música, s.a., México; 28Aug46;
EF5596.
Ya perdí la esperanza ... letra
y música de Fidel A. Vista. ©
Promotora Hispano Americana de
Música, s.a., México; 31Dec46;
EF5539.

VIVALDI, ANTONIO, 1680 (ca.)-1741.
Concerto, G minore, [by] Antonio
Vivaldi, [arr. for] organo [by]
Paul Eraly. Op.12. © Edition
Heuwekemeyer (Firm A. J. Heu-
wekemeyer & B. F. van Gaal),
Amsterdam, The Netherlands; on
arrangement; 13Aug46; EP5119.
(Concerto, orchestra) Concerto
... in do maggiore; [by]
Antonio Vivaldi, elaborazione
di Alfredo Casella. Partitura.
© Carisch, s.a., Milan;
13Nov43; on elaboration;
EF6224.

VLAG, HARREND, 1913-
Ballade; [by] Harrend Vlag.
© Edition Heuwekemeyer (Firm
A. J. Heuwekemeyer & B. F. van
Gaal) Amsterdam, The Nether-
lands; 24Oct46; EF5107. Score
(clarinet and piano) and part.

VOGEL, HARRY, 1893-
North America, take it away! Words
and music by Al Neveloff and
Harry Vogel. Brooklyn, Stanow
Publications, [c1946] © Al
Neveloff & Harry Vogel, d.b.a.
Stanow Publications, Brooklyn;
28Jan47; EP11679.

VOL, FRANK DE. See
DeVol, Frank.

VOLPE, HARRY, 1906-
Childhood scenes; suite for plectrum guitar in four movements, by Harry Volpe. © Volpe Music Co., Jackson Heights, N. Y.; 5May47; EP14214.

Harry Volpe's Concert pieces for guitar. © Volpe Music Co., Jackson Heights, L. I., N. Y.; bk.2, 14Jun47; EP15304.

Harry Volpe's Concert pieces for guitar. © Volpe Music Co., Jackson Heights, N. Y.; on arrangements in bk.1, 5May47; EP14215.

Harry Volpe's masterpieces for plectrum guitar; [by Harry Volpe] © Volpe Music Co., Jackson Heights, L. I., N. Y.; on original compostions and arrangements; bk. 1-4, 7Apr47; bk. 5, 14Apr47; EP6819-6823.

Manhattan soliloquy; modern suite for plectrum guitar in three movements, by Harry Volpe. © Volpe Music Co., Jackson Heights, L.I., N.Y.; 1May47; EP14357.

Suite miniature; for plectrum guitar in three movements, by Harry Volpe. © Volpe Music Co., Jackson Heights, N. Y.; 28Apr47; EP14452.

Twelve swing choruses for guitar; [arr. by Harry] Volpe. © Volpe Music Co., Jackson Heights, L.I., N. Y.; on arrangement; 1Feb47; EP6529.

Volpe's Guitar journal. © Volpe Music Co., Jackson Heights, L. I., N. Y.; on editing & arrangement in no.1, 1Feb47; EP6530. Contains original compositions and works by various composers arranged by Harry Volpe.

VOMAČKA, BOLESLAV, 1887-
Dvě balady a píseň; na slova J. W. Goetheho, pro nižší hlas s orchestrem. Op. 26. [By] Boleslav Vomáčka. © Hudební Matice Umělecké Besedy, Praha, Czechoslovakia; 20May43; EF4967. For voice and piano.

Noční nálady; sedm drobných skladeb ... (revidoval prof. V. Kurz] Op.36. [By] Boleslav Vomáčka. © Hudební Matice Umělecké Besedy, Praha, Czechoslovakia; 20May43; EF5013. For piano solo.

Písně letní noci; cyklus písní ... Op. 34. [By] Boleslav Vomáčka, [words by Jaroslav Kvapil] © Hudební Matice Umělecké Besedy, Praha, Czechoslovakia; 19Oct42; EF4971. For voice and piano.

Quartettino. Op.31/a. [By] Boleslav Vomáčka. © Hudební Matice Umělecké Besedy, Praha, Czechoslovakia; 11Jun42; EF4969. Parts: violin 1, violin.2, viola and violoncello.

Sluncem a stínem; pět písní ... Op. 35. [By] Boleslav Vomáčka, [words by Jaroslav Vrchlický, Adolf Heyduk and others] © Hudební Matice Umělecké Besedy, Praha, Czechoslovakia; 5Apr45; EF5006. For voice and piano.

[VON BERGE, HERMAN] 1871- comp.
Lorenz's Select anthems; a collection of easy anthems, quartets, sentences and responses [comp. by H. Von Berge and Paul Jordon Monroe] © Lorenz Publishing Co., Dayton, Ohio; 10Jun46; EF7830.

VON BERGEN, RALPH J
That's right, you're wrong; by Ralph J. Von Bergen. © Cine-Mart Music Publishing Co., Hollywood, Calif.; 30Dec46; EP12122. For voice and piano, with chord symbols.

VONEL, RÉSY.
Par lui; paroles et musique de Résy Vonel. © Éditions Paris-Broadway, Paris; 31Dec45; EF3824.

VON PLUSS, STARR, pseud. See Fluss, Stella D.

VON HORN, CHARLES. See also Van Horn, Charles.
Wonderful love of Calvary; [by] Chas. Von Horn, arr. by W. M. Thorne. (In Church of the Nazarene. Michigan District. Nazarene Young Peoples Society. Choruses of the N. Y. P. S. p.10) © Michigan District, Nazarene Young Peoples Society, Flint, Mich.; 25Jul46; EP13056. For 2 treble voices and piano.

VON KLENAU, PAUL. See Klenau, Paul von.

VON KOCH, SIGURD. See Koch, Sigurd von.

VON TILZER, HARRY, 1872-1946.
Bagpipes on parade. See his Earl Carroll's Vanities.
(Earl Carroll's Vanities) Bagpipes on parade, from Earl Carroll's Vanities; lyrics by Earl Carroll, music by Harry Von Tilzer [adapted from "When Highland Mary did the Highland fling," lyrics by Jack Mahoney. c1946] © Harry Von Tilzer Music Pub. Co., New York; on modified lyrics; 24Feb47; EP12234.

VORE, GLADYS DE. See De Vore, Gladys.

VOXMAN, HIMIE, arr.
Ensemble classics for brass quartet [arr.] by H. Voxman. © Rubank, inc., Chicago; bk.1-2, 1May47; EP13461-13462.

VRÁNA, FRANTIŠEK, 1914-
(Sonata, piano) Sonata ... [by] František Vrána. Op.11. © Hudební Matice Umělecké Besedy, Praha, Czechoslovakia; 30Jan42; EF5016.

VUILLERMOZ, EMILE.
Bourrée de Chapdes Beaufort ... musique de Emile Vuillermonz, transcription pour choeur à 3 voix égales par René Berthelot. © Rouart, Lerolle et Cie., Paris; on transcription; 10Jan47; EF3605.

Jardin d'amour; chanson populaire canadienne, musique de Emile Vuillermoz, transcription ... par René Berthelot. © Rouart, Lerolle et Cie., Paris; on transcription; 10Jan47; EF3856. Score: soprano and women's chorus, without the piano accompaniment.

Les trois princesses; chanson populaire canadienne, musique de Emile Vuillermoz, transcription ... par René Berthelot. © Rouart, Lerolle et Cie., Paris; on transcription; 10Jan47; EF3853. Score: soprano and women's chorus, without the piano accompaniment.

VYČPÁLEK, LADISLAV, 1882-
České requiem; (Smrt a spasení); na náboženské texty pro sbory, sóla a orchestr ... složil Ladislav Vyčpálek. Op.24. © Hudební Matice Umělecké Besedy, Praha, Czechoslovakia; 13Nov42; EF5015. Piano-vocal score.

W

WADELY, F   W
The Saints of God; full anthem,
words by Archbishop Maclagan,
music by F. W. Wadely. ©
Novello & Co., ltd., London;
16Sep47; EF6546. Score: SATB
and organ.

WAGNER, CHARLES.
You look good in them pants;
song, words by Abe Samya,
music by Charles Wagner.
Memphis, Music-Mart Publishers.
© Samya and Wagner, Memphis;
28Dec45; EP13155.

WAGNER, J   F
Jolly lumberjack ... Tiroler
Holzhacker Buab'n. [By] J. F.
Wagner, [for] concertina, arr. by
Joseph P. Elsnic. © Vitak-Elsnic
Co., Chicago; on arrangement;
17May46; EP11563.

WAGNER, JOSEPH.
Eulogy; composed ... by Joseph
Wagner. © Leeds Music Corp.,
New York; 21Mar47; EP12860.
Condensed score (band) and
parts.

WAGNER, JOSEPH FREDERICK, 1900-
From the Monadnock region; suite
for piano. © Edition Musicus-
New York, inc., New York;
20Sep46; EP8811.

WAGNER, LARRY.
The men of Iwo Jima ... Words and
music by Edward L. Bertz and
Larry Wagner, [optional setting
for TTBB arr. by Larry Wagner]
© Carl Fischer, inc., New York;
28May47; EP15017. Condensed
score (band, with words) and
parts.

WAGNER, RICHARD, 1813-1883.
Eucharist. See his Parsifal.

O du, mein holder Abendstern. See
his Tannhäuser.

(Parsifal) Eucharist; music
from Parsifal, by Richard
Wagner, arr. for mixed chorus,
tenor or baritone solos, and
organ by Charlotte Garden,
sacred text by John J. Momont.
© J. Fischer & Bro., New York;
on arrangement & text; 27Mar47;
EP6813.

(Tannhäuser) O du, mein holder
Abendstern. To the evening star.
English version by Dorothy
Kaehler Thomas. (In (Hodges,
Lester) comp. John Charles Thomas album of favorite songs and
arias. p. 36-40) © G. Schirmer,
inc., New York; on English version; 21Jun46; EP10219.

[WAHLBERG, HERBERT]
Till henne dMrhemma ... musik: Hr.
Bert [pseud.], text: Ch. Henry
[pseud.] © Sylvain Edition, a/
b, Stockholm; 1Jan41; EF3424.

WAITE, MILDRED GRACE, 1924-
Oh, to know Christ ... [words
by] M. K. Kasler, [music
by] M. G. Waite. © Mary
Kathryn Kasler & Mildred
Grace Waite, Johnson City,
N. Y.; 21Mar47; EP12869.
Close score: SATB.

WAKELY, JIMMY, 1914-
Follow thru; by Jimmy Wakely.
© Fairway Music Co., Hollywood,
Calif.; 17Jan47; EP11526. For
voice and piano, with chord
symbols.

WAKEMAN, FRANK MERWIN, 1870-
Psalm 146 ... [by] F. M. Wakeman.
© Frank Merwin Wakeman, Pawling,
N. Y.; 4May47; EP14352. Score:
SATB and piano.

WAL-BERG.
Le destin s'amuso ... dans le
film "Le destin s'amuso";
paroles de L. et J. Poterat,
André Tabet et J. Companeoz,
musique de Wal-Berg. ©
Editions Regia, Paris; 1Mar47;
EF3884.
(Le destin s'amuse) Ritournelle
de Paris ... dans le film
"Le destin s'amuse"; paroles
de L. et J. Poterat, André
Tabet et J. Companeoz, musique
de Wal-Berg. © Editions
Regia, Paris; 1Mar47; EF3861.

Ritournelle de Paris. See his
Le destin s'amuse.

WALBERG, BETTY JEAN, 1921-
Accompaniments for the modern dance;
[by] Betty Walberg. © Betty
Walberg, New York; 15Mar47;
EP12921. For piano solo.

WALDEN, F
Los gracieux ... [by] F. Walden.
[New York, Harmonia Edition]
© Harmonia Edition Publishing
Co., New York; 30Dec46; EP6463.
For piano solo.

WALDTEUFEL, ÉMILE.
The children's Waldteufel ...
easy arrangements for piano
duet by Ernest Haywood. ©
Ascherberg, Hopwood & Crew,
ltd., London; on arrangement;
28Feb47; EF5259.

WALKER, CINDY.
Here's to the ladies; by Gene Autry
and Cindy Walker. © Golden
West Melodies, inc., Hollywood,
Calif.; 17Dec46; EP10794. For
voice and piano, with chord symbols.

Kokomo Island; words and music
by Al Dexter and Cindy Walker.
© Hill and Range Songs, inc.
and Al Dexter Music Publishing Co., Hollywood, Calif.;
20Feb47; EP12195.

New broom boogie; words and music
by Al Dexter and Cindy Walker.
Hollywood, Calif., Hill and
Range Songs. © Hill and Range
Songs, inc. and Al Dexter
Music Publishing Co., Holly-
wood, Calif., 13May47; EP14427.

WALKER, LARRY, 1899-
Carolina calling; words and music
by Larry Walker. © Lynn Music
Corp., New York; 20Jan47; EP11199.

WALKER, LEOLA MAE, 1919-
Here under the sun; lyric by
Samuel Walker, music by Leola
Walker. © Walker Music Pub.
Co., owned by Samuel R. Walker,
jr. & Leola M. Walker, Houston,
Tex.; 15Jan47; EP11788.

WALLACE, MAUDE ORITA.
The turkey and the pumpkin; words and
music by Maude Orita Wallace. ©
Eldridge Entertainment House, inc.,
Franklin, Ohio; 1Sep46; EP6492.

WALLACE, WILLIAM V   1814-1865.
Immortal love, forever full ...
hymn-anthem for choirs and con-
gregation (S.A.T.B.) ... arr. by
W. B. Olds. [Words by] John
Greenleaf Whittier. © Hall &
McCreary Co., Chicago; on
arrangement; 3Jun46; EP4700.

WALLBRIDGE, RICHARD LLEWELLYN
ANTHONY.
I walk with Love; sacred song,
the music by Richard L. A.
Wallbridge, the words by Minnie
M. H. Ayers. © R. D. Row Music
Co., Boston; 8May47; EP11200.

WALLEN, HAROLD HENRY, 1900-
Where you're concerned; by Harold
Wallen. © Metropolis Publications,
Sheridan, Mont.; 5Mar44; EP12051.
For voice and piano, with chord
symbols.

WALLER, "FATS", 1904-1943.
"Fats" Waller's famous London
suite; for the piano. © The
Peter Maurice Music Co., ltd.,
New York; 7Feb47; EF5170.

WALLER, MAURICE.
I will be there; words and music
by Oscar Porter and Maurice
Waller. © Arberne Music Co.,
New York; 23May47; EP10474.

WALLER, THOMAS W.   See
Waller, "Fats."

WALSH, MARY E
Black hawk waltz; [by] Mary E.
Walsh ... for piano, arr. and
ed. by Maxwell Eckstein. ©
Carl Fischer, New York; on
arrangement; 5May47; EP14550.

WALSH, NICOLAS E
Miserere illi; [by] Nicolas E.
Walsh. Mullan, Idaho, Saint
Michael's Guild. © Nicolas E.
Walsh, Mullan, Idaho; 6Aug46;
EP11785. Close score: SATB;
Latin words.

WALTER, CY.
The Astaire ... Lyric by Andrew
Rosenthal, music by Cy Walter.
© Leo Feist, inc., New York;
7Mar47; EP12796.

WALTER, FORREST G
The magic carpet; a fantasy-
pageant for Children's Day,
book and lyrics by Lucile
Crites and Philip Jordan, music
by Forrest G. Walter. ©
Tullar-Meredith Co., New York;
5Apr47; EP14486.

WALTER, SERGE.
Darling I love you ... lyric by
Robert MacGimsey, music by Serge
Walter. © Carl Fischer, inc.,
New York; 16Apr47; EP13901.

Gimme a good horse (when I'm a-
straddle of my saddle again); music
by Serge Walter ... lyric by Doris
Mayer, arr. by Lindsay McPhail.
© Stasny Music Corp., New York;
31May47; EP6941.

WALTERS, HAROLD L   1918-
Bobby sox suite ... by Harold L.
Walters. © Ludwig Music Pub.
Co., Cleveland; 14Mar47; EP12979.
Condensed score (band) and parts.

Rocket-rhythm; [by] Harold L.
Walters. © Gamble Hinged
Music Co., Chicago; 5May47;
EP14124. Condensed score
(band) and parts.

WALTERS, OSCAR W
Sanctus ... words and music by
Oscar W. Walters. © D. Davis
& Co., pty. ltd., Sydney;
13Mar47; EF3252.

Shine on, O star ... words and
music by Oscar W. Walters.
[c1945] © D. Davis & Co., pty.
ltd., Sydney; 15Nov46; EF4647.
For voice and piano.

WALTERS, OSCAR W. Cont'd.
This, and every day; words and music by Oscar W. Walters. © D. Davis & Co. Pty., ltd., Sydney; 17Feb47; EP5292.

WALTHUIS, FRED, 1887-
La hacienda California. California is my home; words and music by Fred Walthuis [arr. by Harold Zweifel] © Fred Walthuis, Los Angeles; on changes in words and music; 25Apr47; EP13856. English words.

WALTON, JAMES G
Lord! Give us faith! Based on "Faith of our fathers," for ... S.S.A. [By] James G. Walton, arr. by Frederic Fay Swift. Words by Frederick Faber. © Pro Art Publications, New York; on arrangement; 17Mar47; EP12932.

WANSBOROUGH, HAROLD.
Cherry blossoms; by Harold Wansborough ... for piano. © Theodore Presser Co., Philadelphia; 16Apr47; EP13897.

The cuckoo and the bull frog ... by H. Wansborough. © McKinley Publishers, inc., Chicago; 10Feb47; EP12042. For piano solo.

Waltz of the wooden shoes ... By H. Wansborough. © McKinley Publishers, inc., Chicago; 7May47; EP14315. For piano solo.

WARD, ARTHUR E   arr.
Classic songs; arr. for soprano and alto (duet or chorus) by Arthur E. Ward. © Harold Flammer, inc., New York; on arrangement & English versions; 31Dec46; EP11418.

WARD, C   B
The band played on; [for] S.A. By C. B. Ward, arr. by Frederic Fay Swift. © Belwin, inc., New York; on arrangement; 3Mar47; EP12752.

WARD, HERBERT RALPH.
Let nothing trouble thee; sacred song, the music by Herbert Ralph Ward, [anonymous words] © R. D. Row Music Co., Boston; 8May47; EP14202.

WARD, SAMUEL A   1847-1903.
America, the beautiful ... (S.A.T.B. and descant) [By] Samuel A. Ward, arr. by Harry Robert Wilson, [words by] Katharine Lee Bates. © Hall & McCreary Co., Chicago; on arrangement; 10Jan47; EP14435.

America, the beautiful; words by Katherine Lee Bates, music by Samuel A. Ward. [Easy piano arrangement with keyboard charts by Victor Lakes Martin] © Songs You Remember Publishing Co. (V. L. Martin, proprietor), Atlanta; on arrangement and playing instructions; 20Dec46; EP13332.

WARE, GILBERT, 1910-
You are mine because you want to be; words by Maude Linn [pseud.], music by Gilbert L. Ware. © Uhl & Wars, San Antonio; 5Apr47; EP13445.

WARLOCK, PETER, pseud. See Heseltine, Philip.

WARMACK, JOHN, 1874-
The glory of creation; [by] John Warmack. © John Warmack, Fort Smith, Ark.; 19Jun47; EP15293. Close score: SATB.

[WARNER, EUGENE A   ]
Moyer's charted harmony chords for the guitar; [now text by Eugene A. Warner] © Chart Music Publishing House, inc., Chicago; on new text; 2Jan47; EP6448.

[WARNER, EUGENE A   ] comp.
Five star collection of cowboy songs; [comp. by Eugene A. Warner] © Chart Music Publishing House, inc., 9May47; EP14564.

WARNER, KEN.
To an Irish lake; by Ken Warner. London, Peter Maurice Music Co. © Peter Maurice, inc., New York; 31Dec46; EP14896. Piano-conductor score (orchestra), and parts.

WARNER, M
Darling, you and only you; words by Calvin Jerry, music by M. M. Warner. © Cine-mart Music Publishing Co., Hollywood, Calif., 14Aug46; EP10963. For voice and piano, with chord symbols.

WARNICK, BOB, 1926-
Concert of love; words ... by Dick Deutsch, [music by] Bob Warnick. © Bob Warnick & Richard Price Deutsch, New York; 29Apr47; EP14440.

WARREN, ELINOR REMICK.
The heart of night; S.S.A. accompanied, [by] Elinor Remick Warren, [words by] Bliss Carman. © Harold Flammer, inc., New York; 7May47; EP14369.

Light the lamps up; for voice and piano, [words by Eleanor Farjeon, music] by Elinor Remick Warren. © G. Schirmer, inc., New York; 11Apr47; EP14074.

WARREN, HARRY, 1893-
Afraid to fall in love. See his Summer holiday.

Carnival. (Carnaval) Lyric by Bob Russell, Spanish lyric by Clotilde Arias, music by Harry Warren. © Triangle Music Corp., New York; on arrangement & Spanish words; 23Jan47; EP11663.

Dan-Dan-Dannville High. See his Summer holiday.

Every so often; lyric by Johnny Mercer, music by Harry Warren. © Harry Warren Music, inc., New York; 12Jun47; EP15132.

Independence Day. See his Summer holiday.

Spring isn't everything. See his Summer holiday.

The Stanley steamer. See his Summer holiday.

(Summer holiday) Dan-Dan-Dannville High, [from] the ... picture, "Summer holiday," lyric by Ralph Blane, music by Harry Warren. © Harry Warren Music, inc., New York; 14May47; EP14559.

(Summer holiday) Independence Day, from the ... picture, "Summer holiday," lyric by Ralph Blane, music by Harry Warren. © Harry Warren Music, inc., New York; 14May47; EP14560.

(Summer holiday) Spring isn't everything; [from] the M-G-M picture "Summer holiday," Lyric by Ralph Blane, music by Harry Warren. © Harry Warren Music, inc., New York; 17Jan47; EP11384.

(Summer holiday) The Stanley steamer [from Summer holiday]; lyric by Ralph Blane, music by Harry Warren. © Harry Warren Music, inc., New York; 7Mar47; EP12498.

(Summer holiday) The weary blues, [from the M-G-M picture "Summer holiday"]; lyric by Ralph Blane, music by Harry Warner. © Harry Warren Music, inc., New York; 27May47; EP14944.

WARREN, PAUL D
I loved you when I met you; words and music by Paul D. Warren. © Cine-Mart Music Publishing Co., Hollywood Calif.; 1Dec46; EP12110.

WARRINGTON, JOHNNY.
(Carnegie Hall) Carnegie Hall dance medley; containing classic themes from the picture "Carnegie Hall" ... Scored by Johnny Warrington. © Robbins Music Corp., New York; on arrangement; 7May47; EP15223. Piano-conductor score (orchestra) and parts.

WATERS, MEL.
Let's go 'round again; words and music by Michael Ravell, Murray Gans [and] Mel Waters. © Regent Music Corp., New York; 27Feb47; EP12253.

WATKINS, MILDRED CECILIA, 1913-
I've changed my mind (about you); by Mildred Watkins. © La Mar Music Publishers, inc., Canton, Ohio; 10May47; EP14353. For voice and piano.

WATSON, ANNA EDWARDS.
Pioneer baby; (A pioneer lullaby), words by Hallie Gardner Grigg and Anna Edwards Watson, music by Anna Edwards Watson. © Anna Edwards Watson, St. Anthony, Idaho; 24Jun47; EP6973.

WATSON, DEEK.
Long legg'd Lizzie; words and music by Deek Watson and Herman Fairbanks. © RYTVOC, inc., New York; 30Dec46; EP6589. For voice and piano, with chord symbols.

WATSON, O   M
Charlene ... words and music by Raymond C. McCollister, Tony Ferragamo [and] O. M. Watson. New York, Television-Radio Music Publications. © Raymond C. McCollister, Wichita, Kan.; 30Dec46; EP11077.

WATSON, RUSSELL, pseud. See Howorth, Wayne.

WATT, JANE CHURCHILL, 1894-
American names; chorus for male voices, a cappella (T.T.B.B.) [by] Jane C. Watt, [words by] Stephen Vincent Benét. © Hall & McCreary Co., Chicago; 12Apr47; EP13755.

WAVERLY, JACK, 1896-
A cowboy's last goodbye; words and music by Jack Waverly. © Jack Waverly, Bellmore, N. Y.; 1Jul45; EP14199.

I was doin' all right; words and music by Jack Waverly. © Jack Waverly, Bellmore, N. Y.; 10Mar47; EP12551.

My gal is your gal now; words and music by Jack Waverly. © Jack Waverly, Bellmore, N. Y.; 12Jan47; EP14198.

Song of the farmer; by Jack Waverly. © Jack Waverly, Bellmore, N. Y.; 10Mar47; EP12550. For voice and piano, with chord symbols.

Uncle Jeremiah's gen'ral store; words and music by Jack Waverly. © Jack Waverly, Bellmore, N. Y.; 27Mar47; EP13097.

WAYNE, BERNIE.
(Calcutta) This is madness
[from] "Calcutta"; words by
Ben Raleigh, music by Bernie
Wayne, French words by Ted
Grouya. © Famous Music Corp.,
New York; 3Jun47; EF15124.

This is madness. See his
Calcutta.

Walkin' with my shadow; lyric by
Ben Raleigh, music by Bernie
Wayne. © Vanguard Songs, Holly-
wood, Calif.; 17Dec46; EP10795.

WEBB, ALLIENE BRANDON.
The endless song; by Alliene Brandon
Webb, for ... S.S.A. with piano
acc. © Mills Music, inc., New
York; 23May47; EP6921.

WEBBER, RUSSELL, 1900-
Fiddle fun for the young soloist
... by Russell Webber. ©
Belwin, inc., New York; 21Jan47;
EP11362. Score (violin and
piano) and part.

WEBER, FRED, 1912-
Belwin intermediate band method;
by Fred Weber. © Belwin,
inc., New York; on arrangement & compilation; 13Jun47;
EP15504. Extra cornet part,
11Mar47; EP12571. Condensed
score and parts.

WEBSTER, CARTER.
Why am I alone? Words by Marion
E. Hockenhull, music by Carter
Webster. © Hockenhull's Music
Publications, Chicago; 26Dec46;
EP10712.

WEED, BUDDY.
Whoopsie doodle; words and music
by Danny Loroy, Joe Leroy and
Buddy Weed. c1946. © Beverly
Music Corp., New York; 1May47;
EP14109.

WEELKES, THOMAS, d. 1623.
Let Thy merciful ears, O Lord;
by Thomas Weelkes, arr. and
ed. for mixed chorus ... by
Wm. Cosman. (Text rev. by
Wm. Cosman) © Choral Art
Publications, New York; on
arrangement; 8May47; EP14396.

WEHNER, CHARLES FLORIAN, 1895-
arr.
Swinging the scales ... arranged
by C. F. Wehner. © Charles F.
Wehner, Roxbury, Mass.; on 15
additional lessons; 15Jan47;
EP11320.

WEIGL, VALLY.
Shepherdess Moon; for treble choir,
[by] Vally Weigl. © Broadcast
Music, inc., New York; 19Mar47;
EP13774.

This is the day of light; anthem
for mixed voices by Vally Weigl.
[Words by John Ellerton] ©
Broadcast Music, inc., New York;
28Apr47; EP15228.

WEIGLE, CHARLES FREDERIC, 1871-   ed.
Sing a new song ... gospel songs
... ed. and comp. by Charles F.
Weigle and Gladys B. Muller.
Chicago, Van Kampen Press. ©
True Life Library, Holland,
Mich.; 30Dec46; EP11103.
Partial contents © 15Dec46)- words
by C. F. Weigle, music by G. B.
Muller, unless stated.- We'll
sing a new song © EP10796)- No
longer lost © 10797)- How can I
forget? Words and music by C. F.
Weigle © EP10798)- After the
darkness comes dawn © EP10799)-
Life is now so wonderful to me
© EP10800)- I will not doubt,
words and music by C. F. Weigle

© EP10801)- I'm so glad I let
Jesus come in © EP10802)- I saw
the cross of Jesus, words by F.
Whitfields, music by G. B. Muller
© EP10803)- I know I love Jesus
© EP10804)- I'd rather walk
with Jesus © EP10805)- Jesus
abides with me, words and music
by C. F. Weigle © EP10806)-
In Gethsemane © EP10807)- I'm
walking with Jesus © EP10808)-
When Jesus smiles on me © EP10809)-
He was found worthy, arr. by C.
F. Weigle © EP10810)- I have
made my reservation, words and
music by C. F. Weigle © EP10811)-
Lead me home, words and music by
C. F. Weigle © EP10812)- Some
one is calling you © EP10813)-
Jesus, my Lord © EP10814)- I
need my Saviour near me © EP10815)-
Christ is more to me than ever
© EP10816)- We are waiting for
the coming of the Lord © EP10817)-
Ransomed © EP10818)- I love to
sing of home © EP10819)

WEILL, KURT, 1900-
A boy like you. See his Street
scene.

Lonely house. See his Street
scene.

Moon-faced, starry eyed. See his
Street scene.

(Street scene) A boy like you, [from]
"Street scene;" words by Langston
Hughes, music by Kurt Weill. New
York, Chappell & Co., inc.. © Kurt
Weill & Langston Hughes, New York;
3Mar47; EP12786.

(Street scene) Lonely house [from]
"Street scene"; words by Lang-
ston Hughes, music by Kurt Weill.
[New York] Chappell. © Kurt
Weill and Langston Hughes, New
York; 31Dec46; EP11178. For
voice and piano.

(Street scene) Moon-faced, starry-
eyed [from] "Street scene"; words
by Langston Hughes, music by Kurt
Weill. New York, Chappell & Co.
© Kurt Weill & Langston Hughes,
New York; 17Jan47; EP11654.

(Street scene) We'll go away together [from] "Street scene";
words by Langston Hughes, music
by Kurt Weill. [New York]
Chappell. © Kurt Weill & Langston Hughes, New York; 7Jan47;
EP11176. For voice and piano,
with chord symbols.

(Street scene) What good would the
moon be? [From] "Street scene";
words by Langston Hughes, music
by Kurt Weill. [New York]
Chappell. © Kurt Weill and Langston Hughes, New York; 31Dec46;
EP11177. For voice and piano, with
chord symbols.

We'll go away together. See his
Street scene.

What good would the moon be? See
his Street scene.

WEINBERG, JACOB.
Haganah. Song of liberation;
English words by Abraham Bur-
stein, Hebrew and Yiddish
translations by Michael
Atzmoni, music by Jacob Wein-
berg. [For] mixed voices (S.A.T.B)
© Transcontinental Music Corp.,
New York; 1Mar47; EP13323. The
Hebrew and Yiddish words are
trans-   literated.

WEINBERGER, JAROMIR, 1896-
Une cantilène jalouse ... par
Jaromir Weinberger. Wien,
Universal-Edition. © Asso-
ciated Music Publishers, inc.,
New York; 17Feb20; EP5563.
Score (violin and piano) and
part.

Colloque sentimental; prélude
d'après le poème de Paul
Verlaine ... par Jaromir
Weinberger. Wien, Universal-
Edition. © Associated Music
Publishers, inc., New York;
10Feb20; EP5562. Score
(violin and piano) and part.

Three Bohemian pieces ... concert
version by the composer, ed. by
Felix Guenther. © Associated
Music Publishers, inc., New
York; on concert version for
v.1, 31Mar47. Score: orchestra.
Contents.- 1. Bohemian song,
from "Shvanda, the bagpiper"
© EP13640)

WEINGARTEN, ANN.
Repeat performance; words and
music by Patrece Snydur and Ann
Weingarten. [From] "Repeat
Performance." © Beverly Music
Corp., New York; 2Jun47; EP14839.

WEINGARTNER, FELIX, 1863-1942.
Meister Andres; komische Oper mit
Dialog in zwei Akten nach E.
Geibels gleichnamigem Lustspiel,
von Felix Weingartner. Op.66.
Wien, Universal-Edition.
© Associated Music Publishers,
inc., New York; 1Apr19; EP5056.
Piano-vocal score.

Musik zu Shakespeare's "Der Sturm";
von Felix Weingartner. Op.65.
Klavierauszug mit Text von Alois
Hába. Wien, Universal-Edition.
© Associated Music Publishers,
inc., New York; 1Mar19; EP5055.
Piano-vocal score.

[WEINSCHENK, BERTLIES]
Sleep, darling, sleep; for chorus
of women's voices, three-part,
[by] Kenneth Martin, [pseud.,
words by] Adele M. Freund.
© Galaxy Music Corp., New
York; 12May47; EP5447.

WEIRICK, JOHN.
It has no ending; by John Weirick.
© Cine-Mart Music Publishing Co.,
Hollywood, Calif.; 1Nov46;
EP11488. For voice and piano,
with chord symbols.

WEIS, JYTTE, 1919-
Emigrantens Sang; Musik: Jytte Weis,
Tekst: Victor Skaarup. © Wilhelm
Hansen, Musik-Forlag, Copenhagen;
25Nov46; EP4821. For voice and
piano.

WEISMAN, BEN. See also
Weisman, Bernie.
Don't (keep our two hearts cryin');
by Ben Weisman. © Ben Weisman,
Los Angeles; 1May47; EP14674.
For voice and piano.

WEISMAN, BERNIE. See also
Weisman, Ben.
You are my love; lyric by Jack
Lathrop and Charlie Ryan, music
by Ben Weisman. © Broadcast
Music, inc., New York; 31Mar47;
EP15226.

WEISMANN, WILHELM.
Mein schwäbisches Liederbuch. ©
Henry Litolff's Verlag, Leipzig;
1Dec43; EF2592.

WEISS, GEORGE, 1921-
I can't get up the nerve to kiss
you; words and music by Bennie
Benjamin and George Weiss. ©
Santly-Joy, inc., New York;
8Apr47; EP13435.

I want to thank your folks; words
and music by Bennie Benjamin and
George Weiss. © Oxford Music Corp.,
New York; 21Jan47; EP11543.

Speaking of angels; words and music by
Bennie Benjamin and George Weiss.
© Santly-Joy, inc., New York;
18Feb47; EP12098.

WEISS, GEORGE. Cont'd.
When tonight is just a memory;
words and music by Bennie
Benjamin and George Weiss.
© Oxford Music Corp., New York;
9Jun47; EP14930.

WEISS, STEPHAN.
Alone with you; words by Howard
Dietz, music by Stephan Weiss.
© Beverly Music Corp., New
York; 3Jan47; EP10923. For
voice and piano, with chord
symbols.

WEISSBUCH, ANTONIA SCHATZBERG.
These loving hearts; wedding
song ... by Antonia S.
Weissbuch. Campgaw, N. J.;
21May47; EP14619.

[WEISSHAUS, EDMEE ANNE LEONIE
(LOUIN)]1913-
Travaillons en chantant; avec
Edmée Arma [pseud.] et Villemot.
© Éditions Ouvrières, Paris;
4Nov46; EP5181.

[WEISSHAUS, IMRE] 1904-
A la jeunesse; pour chant et
piano, [by] Paul Arma [pseud.],
... couverture dessinée par Pablo
Picasso. © Henry Lemoine & Cie.,
Paris; 28Feb45; EF3533.
Chansons pour Miroka; imaginées
par Edmée Arma [pseud.],
paroles par Jean-Lançois
[pseud.], mises en images par
Maurice Tranchant sur des
musiques de Paul Arma [pseud.]
© Éditions Ouvrières, Paris;
18Nov46; EP5180.
Flûtes qui chantent; 17 morceaux
pour 2 flûtes égales (ou pour
tous autres instruments
mélodiques), sur des airs
populaires de divers peuples,
[by] Paul Arma [pseud.];
couverture dessinée par Guy
Georget. © Henry Lemoine &
Cie., Paris; on arrangement;
31Mar44; EF3576.

[WEISSHAUS, IMRE] 1905- arr.
Neuf choeurs; à 4, 5 et 6 voix
mixtes sur les noëls tradi-
tionnels de divers peuples
(harm. par Paul Arma, pseud.,
adaptation française de Jean
Lançois, pseud.) © Éditions
Ouvrières, Paris; on harmonization & French words; 16Dec46;
EP5179.

WEITZEL, G J 1884-
Ein herrlicher Heiland! [An
excellent Saviour! By] G. J.
Weitzel. © G. J. Weitzel,
Portland, Or.; 25Feb47;
EP12308. Close score; SATB.

WELDON, FRANK.
Strictly as advertised; words by
Alan Kent, music by Frank Weldon.
© Shapiro, Bernstein & Co., inc.,
New York; 25Jun47; EP15283.

WELDY, GEORGE W
Behold the dawn; by George W. Weldy,
Jr. © Theodore Presser Co.,
Philadelphia; 13Jan47;
EP11298. Score; SATB and organ.

WELLER, BEN, 1890-
Weller school of popular piano
playing; ten primary lessons [by
Ben Weller] © Ben Weller, Kansas City, Mo.; 10Nov46; EP11113.

WELLS, CHANNING, pseud.
Down by the banks of Jordan; by
Channing Wells [pseud.], ed. and
arr. for women's chorus, SSA.
© Choral Press, Evanston, Ill.;
1Sep46; EP11700.

WELLS, CREVELYN DYER, 1902-
I love you best; words and
music by Crevelyn D. Wells.
© Crevelyn Dyer Wells, New
York; 15Mar47; EP13295.

WELTY, JOSEPHINE TOTT, 1904-
Friendship march; by Josephine T.
Welty. © Gilbert Publishing Co.,
inc., Cleveland; 1Dec46; EP12522.
For piano solo.
A poppy for remembrance; words
and music by Josephine Tott
Welty. © Josephine T. Welty,
Spirit Lake, Iowa; 12May47;
EP14599.

WENRICH, PERCY.
Moonlight bay; music by Percy
Wenrich, arr. by Jimmy Dale.
© Remick Music Corp., New York;
on arrangement; 10Jun47;
EP15245. Piano-conductor score
(orchestra) and parts.

WERRENRATH, REINALD.
One man stuff; T.T.B.B. [words
by] Albert Stillman, [music by]
Reinald Werrenrath. © R. D. Row
Music Co., Boston; 31Mar47;
EP13328.

WESTERLUND, GÖSTA.
Lolita hambomazurka; musik [by]
Gösta Westerlund [and] Martin
Livén. © Nordiska
Musikförlaget, a.b., Stockholm;
1Jan46; EF3725. For piano
solo, with chord symbols.

WESTMORELAND, PAUL.
Oklahoma bound; words and music
by Paul Westmoreland. © Hill
and Range Songs, inc., Hollywood, Calif.; 4Feb47; EP11956.

WESTON, PAUL.
Ain'tcha ever comin' back? By
Irving Taylor, Axel Stordahl
and Paul Weston. © Sinatra
Songs, inc., New York; 25Apr47;
EP15057. For voice and piano,
with chord symbols.

WESTPHAL, FRANK.
When you come to the end of the day;
for four-part chorus of mixed
voices, S.A.T.B., words by Gus
Kahn, music by Frank Westphal,
arr. by Harry R. Wilson.
© Bourne, inc., New York; on arrangement; 14Apr47; EP13332.
When you come to the end of the day
... music by Frank Westphal, arr.
by Jimmy Dale. © 1946; © Bourne
,inc., New York; on arrangement;
22Jan47; EP11436. Piano-conductor
score (orchestra) and parts.

WETZEL, RAY.
Intermission riff; ed. by Van
Alexander, composer and arr.
by Ray Wetzel. © Capitol
Songs, inc., New York; 25Jan47;
EP11380. Piano-conductor score
(orchestra) and parts.

WEYBRIGHT, JUNE.
Oft heard tunes; arr. by June
Weybright, [comp. by Albert H.
Foster, Jr.] © Clayton F.
Summy Co., Chicago; 19Feb47;
EP12148. For piano solo.
Technic for pianists of junior
grade; by June Weybright. ©
Mills Music, inc., New York;
bk.1-2, 18Mar47; EP6717, 6716.

WHEATON, HOMER DAMIAN, 1905-
Hush! my dear, lie still and
slumber; words by Isaac Watts,
music by Homer D. Wheaton. ©
Homer Damian Wheaton, Millbrook,
N. Y.; 2Jan47; EP13453.

WHEELER, ALFRED.
May joy be yours; song, words and
music by Alfred Wheeler. ©
Chappell & Co., ltd., Sydney;
1Nov46; EF4781.

WHISTLER, HARVEY S 1907-
Modern Arban-St. Jacome comprehensive course for trombone or
baritone, by Harvey S. Whistler;
a compilation of two famous
methods, entirely rev., re-ed.
and re-styled. © Rubank, inc.,
Chicago; on compilation; 1Aug46;
EP7593.

WHISTLER, HARVEY S 1907- ed.
Modern Hohmann-Wohlfahrt beginning
method for violin ... a compilation of two famous methods, entirely rev., re-ed. and re-
styled ... by Harvey S. Whistler.
© Rubank, inc., Chicago; v.2,
2Jan47; EP11046.

WHITCOMB, ELSIE.
Progressive exercises for basic
ballet turns; choreographed by
Edna Lucile Baum, music by Elsie
Whitcomb. © Clayton F. Summy Co.,
Chicago; 2May47; EP14186.

WHITE, ANNA B
Heaven; words and music by Anna B.
White, [arr. by Virginia Davis
& Theodore R. Frye] © Theodore
R. Frye Publishers, Chicago;
30Mar46; EP5637.

WHITE, CARL.
Forever in my heart; words by
Harvey E. Havor, music by Carl
White. © Cine-Mart Music Pub-
lishing Co., Hollywood, Calif.;
31Mar47; EP14649.

WHITE, DANIEL J
J'suis un p'tit môme de
Levallois; paroles de Roger
Normand, musique de Daniel
J. White. © Éditions Paris-
Broadway, Paris; 31Mar46;
EF3853.

WHITE, DORIS.
I know my God is able to deliver
me; words and music by Doris
White. © Doris White, Lansing,
Mich.; 24Mar47; EP6800. Close
score; SATB.

WHITE, GRACE.
Major, minor; for the piano (with
words) by Grace White. ©
Shattinger Piano & Music Co.,
St. Louis; 31Dec46; EP11252.
Steps forward; for the piano (with
words) by Grace White. ©
Shattinger Piano & Music Co.,
St. Louis; 31Dec46; EP11251.

[WHITE, HAROLD ROBERT] 1872-1943.
Cheerio! Two-part song... [words
by] P. J. O'Reilly, [music by]
Dermot Macmurrough [pseud.]
© William Paxton & Co., ltd.,
London; 27Dec46; EF3637.

WHITE, HELEN LEE, 1927-
He is mine! [By] Helen Lee White,
arr. by Wayne M. Thorne. [In
Church of the Nazarene. Michigan
District. Nazarene Young Peoples
Society. Choruses of the N. Y.
P. S. p.65) © Michigan District,
Nazarene Young Peoples Society,
Flint, Mich.; 25Jul46; EP13081.
For voice and piano.

WHITE, LIZZIE O BORGESON.
A pioneer mother's lullaby; words
and music by Lizzie O. Borgeson
White. © Lizzie O. Borgeson
White, Salt Lake City; 29May47;
EP6954.

WHITE, MARY.
We're on our way to heaven;
[words by] M. W. and C. E. H.,
[music by] Mary White, arr. by
W. M. T. (In Church of the
Nazarene. Michigan District.
Nazarene Young Peoples Society.
Choruses of the N. Y. P. S.
p.44) © Michigan District,
Nazarene Young Peoples Society,
Flint, Mich.; 25Jul46; EP13066.
Close score; SATB.

WHITE, MATHEW.
I was born in Hoboken; words and
music by Mathew White. © Nordyke
Publishing Co., Los Angeles;
31Oct45; EP6701.

WHITE, MAUDE VALÉRIE.
So we'll go no more a roving; arr.
for ... S.A.T.B. by Clarence
Lucas, words by Lord Byron,
music by Maude Valérie White.
© Chappell & Co., ltd., London;
on arrangement; 15Apr47; EF5643.

WHITE, PAUL.
Idyl ... [by] Paul White. ©
Elkan-Vogel Co., inc., Phila-
delphia; 24Dec46; EP13321.
Score (orchestra), condensed
score and parts.

WHITEFIELD, BERNARD, 1910-
Modern miniatures ... [By]
Bernard Whitefield. Piano
solo. © Mercury Music Corp.,
New York; 13May47; EP14158.
Three sonnet sonatas; for the
piano, [by] Bernard White-
field. © Paragon Music
Publishers, New York; 3Apr47;
EP13213.

WHITFORD, JAMES KEITH. See
Whitford, Keith.

WHITFORD, KEITH, 1917-
He gave Himself for me; [by] Keith
Whitford, [words by] K. W.
© J. Keith Whitford, Dayton, Or.;
27Dec46; EP10823.
He's the lover of my soul; [by]
Keith Whitford, [words by]
K. W. © J. Keith Whitford,
Dayton, Or.; 27Dec46; EP10824.
No sunset in God's tomorrow; [by]
Keith Whitford, [words by]
K. W. © J. Keith Whitford,
Dayton, Or.; 27Dec46; EP10821.
Close score: SATB.
What undying love; [by] Keith Whit-
ford, [words by] K. W. © J.
Keith Whitford, Dayton, Or.;
27Dec46; EP10822.

WHITFORD, ROBERT H
Break sheets for piano; [by]
Robert Whitford. © Robert
H. Whitford, Erie, Pa.,
no.25-26, 28Feb47; no.29-30,
12Aug47; EP6626-6627, 16705-
16706.
Morning mood; [by] Robert Whitford.
Erie, Pa., Robert Whitford
Publications. © Robert H.
Whitford, Erie, Pa.; 28Feb47;
EP6628. For piano solo.
Our serenade; [by] Robert Whit-
ford. Erie, Pa., Robert Whit-
ford Publications. © Robert H.
Whitford, Erie, Pa.; 28Feb47;
EP6624. For piano solo.
Rhapsody in rhythm; [by] Robert
Whitford. Erie, Pa., Robert
Whitford Publications. © Robert
H. Whitford, Erie, Pa.; 10Dec46;
EP6487. For piano solo.
Rhythm lullaby; [by] Robert Whitford.
Erie, Pa., Robert Whitford
Publications. © Robert H. Whit-
ford, Erie, Pa.; 28Feb47; EP6623.
For piano solo.
Robert Whitford break sheets for
piano. Erie, Pa., R. Whitford
Publications. © Robert H. Whit-
ford, Erie, Pa.; no. 13-20,
31Dec45; no. 23-24, 10Dec46;
EP501-508, 6296-6297.

WHITNEY, MAURICE C
A song of faith; S.A.T.B. with
baritone solo, words and music
by Maurice C. Whitney. © J.
Fischer & Bro., New York;
27Mar47; EP6802.
Soon; [by George Gershwin,
paraphrased for piano by
Maurice C. Whitney. © New
World Music Corp., New
York; on paraphrase; 24Mar47;
EP13210.

WHITNEY, RAYMOND KEITH.
Minnesota lowland; words and
music by Raymond Keith Whitney,
piano arrangement by James S.
Allen. © Raymond Keith Whitney, Minneapolis; 2Nov46;
EP12525.

WHITTAKER, NOLA.
Utah, home of mine; lyrics and
music by Esther Wiltshire
and Nola Whittaker [arr. by
Robert E. Miller] © Nola
Whittaker and Esther Wiltshire,
Circleville, Utah; 22Apr47;
EP6825.

WHITTREDGE, EDWARD B
The Pilot; chorus for men's
voices [by] Edward B.
Whittredge, [words by]
Carleton F. Shaw. © The B.
F. Wood Music Co., Boston;
21Apr47; EP13812.

WIANT, BLISS, 1899- arr.
The pagoda; thirteen songs from China
arr. for group singing [and tr.
by Bliss Wiant] © Cooperative
Recreation Service, Delaware, Ohio;
5Dec46; EP11540.

WICKENS, CLITUS M
I'll see you again little darlin';
words and music by Clitus M.
Wickens. © Universal Music
Sales, Chicago; 26Apr47;
EP6854.
In the Dells of old Wisconsin;
words and music by Clitus M.
Wickens. © Universal Music
Sales, Chicago; 26Apr47;
EP6855.
The merry maker's polka; [and
I'm not just a whistling
Dixie] words and music
by Clitus M. Wickens. ©
Universal Music Sales,
Chicago; 26Apr47; EP6856,
6857.

WICKSMAN, HELEN.
The typist's serenade; words by
Martha L. Spain, music by Helen
Wicksman. © Nordyke Publishing
Co., Los Angeles; 12Dec45;
EP15526.

WIDÉEN, IVAR.
Tre Pär Lagerkvist-dikter;
tonsatta av Ivar Widéen. ©
Nordiska Musikförlaget a.b.,
Stockholm; v.2-3, 1Jan43.
Contents.-2. Landet (© EF3719)-
3. Hembygden (© EP3750) For
voice and piano, and voice part.

WIDQVIST, VIKTOR.
Under blagul fana ... av Viktor
Widqvist arr. ... av
komponisten. © Nordiska
Musikförlaget, a.b., Stockholm; 1Jan42; EF3740. Piano-
conductor score (orchestra),
and parts.

WIENER, JEAN, 1896-
Nous continuons la France; paroles
de Pierre Migennes [pseud.],
musique de Jean Wiener. © Le
Chant du Monde, Paris; 10Feb47;
EF3458.

WILBUR, EDNA.
Snowdrifts and gardenias ...
arrangement by Frank Furlott
... words and music by Edna
Wilbur. © Puritan Publishing
Co., inc., Chicago; 7Jan47;
EP11321. Piano-conductor
score (orchestra) and parts.
Snowdrifts and gardenias; words
and music by Edna Wilbur.
[c1946] © Puritan Publishing
Co., inc., Chicago; 8Jan47;
EP11237.

WILCOXON, CHARLEY.
The drummer on parade; by Charley
Wilcoxon. 50 rudimental-swing
street beats. Cleveland [Wil-
coxon's Drum Shop] © Chas. S.
Wilcoxon, Cleveland; 23Apr47;
EP14154.

WILDER, ALEC.
Did you ever cross over to
Snedon's? ... By Alec Wilder.
© Edwin H. Morris & Co., inc.,
New York; 2May47; EP14341.
For voice and piano.
What will you bring me? For
voice and piano, by Alec
Wilder, [words by William
Engvick] © G. Schirmer,
inc., New York; 30Sep46;
EP12877.

WILHITE, MONTE.
Ce soir cherie; words by Mack
David, music by Monte Wilhite.
© Famous Music Corp., New York;
15May47; EP14478. English
words.

WILHOUSKY, EMIL.
Our song of love; words by Muriel
Burton, music by Emil Wilhousky.
© Lincoln Music Corp., New York;
2May47; EP14150.

WILKINS, CHARLIE.
Foolish pride (can break your
heart); words and music by
Curt Barrett and Charlie
Wilkins. © Peer International
Corp., New York; 1May47;
EP14570.

WILKINSON, CHARLES ANGELO RICHARD,
1885-
Jesu, Word of God Incarnate. Ave
Verum. Motet, music by Charles
A. R. Wilkinson, four-part, S.A.T.B. Oakville,
Ont., Can., F. Harris Music Co.,
ltd. [c1946] © Charles A.
Wilkinson, Simcoe, Ont., Can.;
24Jan47; EF4979.

WILLIAMS, CHARLES LOBER, 1923-
Wild desires; words and music
by Charles L. Williams.
[Philadelphia] Prediction
Music, inc. © Charles Lober
Williams, Philadelphia;
12May47; EP14328.

WILLIAMS, CLARENCE.
Ugly chile (you're some pretty doll);
by Clarence Williams. © Shapiro,
Bernstein & Co., inc., New York;
100ct46; EP11372. For voice and
piano, with chord symbols.

WILLIAMS, DAVID W
I would see Jesus in glory ...
[by] David W. Williams,
[words by] Frank E. Roush.
© Frank E. Roush, Lynchburg,
Ohio; 3May47; EP6866. Close
score: SATB.
Saved because I love Him ... [words
by] Frank E. Williams, [music by]
David W. Williams. © Frank
Edgar Roush, Lynchburg, Ohio;
22May47; EP6912. Close score:
SATB.

WILLIAMS, DOOTSIE. See
Williams, Walter Dootsie.

WILLIAMS, EDDIE, 1912-
Drifting blues; by Johnny Moore,
Charles Brown [and] Eddie
Williams. © Aladdin Music
Publications, Hollywood, Calif.;
14Jan47; EP6684. For voice and
piano, with chord symbols.
Drifting blues; by Johnny Moore,
Charles Brown [and] Eddie
Williams. © Aladdin Music
Publications, Hollywood, Calif.;
17Jan47; EP11527. For voice
and piano, with chord symbols.

151

WILLIAMS, EDDIE. Cont'd.
What's mine is mine; music by Enoch
"Sonny" Williams, words by Buddy
Fayne. © Fowler Music Co., New
York; on words; 7Jan47; EP11150.
For voice and piano, with chord
symbols.

WILLIAMS, ENOCH. See also
Williams, Sonny.

WILLIAMS, ERNEST S
Little classics for cornet or
trumpet ... by Ernest S.
Williams. Saugerties, N. Y.,
Ernest Williams School of
Music. © Ernest S. Williams,
Saugerties, N. Y.; on 12
pieces; 28Dec46. Score (cornet
or trumpet and piano) and part.
Contents.- [v.] 1. Concertone
(© EP11782) - [v.] 2. Sarabande
and Bourrie (© EP11777) - [v.]
3. Osseo fantazia (© EP11778)-
[v.] 4. Wyalusing polka
(© EP11779) - [v.] 5. Winema
waltz (© EP11780) - [v.] 6.
Mitena gavotte (© EP11781) -
[v.] 7. Wanatuska march
(© EP11776) - [v.] 8. Chemung
rondino (© EP11775) - [v.] 9.
Chenango schottisch (© EP11774)-
[v.] 10. Temecula waltz
(© EP11773) - [v.] 11. The
Adirondacks polka (© EP11771) -
[v.] 12. The Catskills polka
(© EP11772)

WILLIAMS, FRANCES.
In Bethlehem's lowly manger; SA
accompanied (optional descent)
Words by Theodore H. Kenworth,
music by Frances Williams. ©
Harold Flammer, inc., New York;
on arrangement; 4Nov46; EP10830.
In Bethlehem's lowly manger; SAB
accompanied (optional descent)
Words by Theodore H. Kenworth,
music by Frances Williams. ©
Harold Flammer, inc., New York;
on arrangement; 4Nov46; EP10831.
In Bethlehem's lowly manger; SSA
accompanied (optional descent)
Words by Theodore H. Kenworth,
music by Frances Williams. ©
Harold Flammer, inc., New York;
on arrangement; 4Nov46; EP10832.
A King is born today; SATB with solo
voice, [by] Frances Williams and
Rhoda Newton. © Harold
Flammer, inc., New York; 4Nov46;
EP10748.
Silent are the meadows ... SATB
accompanied; [by] Frances Williams,
words by Theodore H. Kenworth.
© Harold Flammer, inc., New
York; 4Nov46; EP10746.

WILLIAMS, GLENNA J   1929-
I want to live for Jesus; words
by] G. J. W. and Lois Blanchard,
[music by] Glenna J. Williams.
(In Church of the Nazarene.
Michigan District. Nazarene
Young Peoples Society.
Choruses in the N. Y. P. S.
p.46-47) © Michigan District,
Nazarene Young Peoples Society,
Flint, Mich.; 25Jul46; EP13068.
Close score: SATB.

WILLIAMS, HENRY AUGUSTUS, 1895-
Happy birthday ... words & music by
Henry A. Williams. © Charles
Wynn Publications, New York;
on changes in words and music;
23Nov46; EP10942. For voice
and piano, with chord symbols.

WILLIAMS, LATHAN LEWIS, 1921-
I will never forget; words and
music by Lathan L. Williams.
© Lathan Lewis Williams, Los
Angeles; 20Mar47; EP15080.

My heart is taking a beating;
words and music by Lathan
L. Williams. © Lathan
Lewis Williams, Los Angeles;
2Mar47; EP15215.
There's a mood for everything;
words and music by Lathan L.
Williams. © Lathan Lewis
Williams, Los Angeles; 20Mar47;
EP15079.
The three little monkeys; words
and music by Lathan L.
Williams. © Lathan Lewis
Williams, Los Angeles;
2Mar47; EP15214.

WILLIAMS, RALPH EDWIN, 1916-
Give ear unto my voice ... [By]
Ralph E. Williams, text ...
from Psalm CXLI. © Neil A.
Kjos Music Co., Chicago;
6May47; EP14928. Score: chorus
(SSAATTBB) and piano reduction.
Praise our God, all ye His servants ... [by] Ralph E.
Williams, [words from] Rev.,
ch. 19, v. 5-6. © Neil A.
Kjos Music Co., Chicago;
6May47; EP14927. Score:
chorus (SSAATTBB) and piano
reduction.

WILLIAMS, SONNY. See also
Williams, Enoch.
That ain't right (to boogie on
Sunday); words by Charles
Davenport [and] Peggy Daven-
port, music by Sonny Williams.
© Popular Music Co., New York;
23Jan47; EP11533.

WILLIAMS, SPENCER.
Dish me a dish; by Jack Simpson
& Spencer Williams. [c1946]
© Cameo Music Publishing Co.,
London; 14Jan47; EF5576. For
voice and piano, with chord
symbols; melody also in tonic
sol-fa notation.
Only a dream away; by Jean Cavall
& Spencer Williams. [c1946] ©
Cameo Music Publishing Co.,
London; 14Jan47; EF5575. For
voice and piano, with chord
symbols; melody also in tonic
sol-fa notation.

WILLIAMS, WALTER DOOTSIE.
Bobby sox blues; words and music
by Dootsie Williams. © Hill
and Range Songs, inc., Hollywood, Calif.; 13May47;
EP14424.

WILLIAMS-BIGGERS, LELA MACK.
Troubles and trials; words and
melody by Lela M. Williams
... Harmonized by A. DeMoss
Thornton. Los Angeles,
Biggers Business College. ©
Lela M. Williams-Biggers, Los
Angeles; 15Mar47; EP14434.

WILLIAMSON, GEORGE.
I'll be true to you, my darling,
(love you till the end of time);
words and music by Ted Daffan
and George Williamson. ©
Northern Music Corp., New York;
15Nov46; EP13374.

WILLING, FOY.
Vout cowboy; by Sid Robin [and]
Foy Willing. © Leeds Music
Corp., New York; 24Jan47;
EP11801. For voice and piano,
with guitar diagrams and chord
symbols.

WILLINGSBY, GEORGE E. pseud.
Dear Lord and Father; by George
E. Willingsby, [pseud., from Op.
67, no. 5 by F. Mendelssohn,
words by John G. Whittier.] Ed.
and arr. for junior choir by
George E. Willingsby, [pseud.]
© Choral Press, Evanston, Ill.; on
arrangement & adaptation; 10ct46;
EP11692.

Dear Lord and Father; [from Op. 67,
no. 5, by F. Mendelssohn] ... Ed.
and arr. for mixed chorus, SATB,
by George E. Willingsby. [Words
by John G. Whittier, adapted and
revised by G. E. W.] © Choral
Press, Evanston, Ill.; on arrangement and adaptation of words;
10ct46; EP11702.

WILLIS, S   P
The aspen train; by Hayden Simp-
son and S. P. (Slim) Willis.
© Richardson Songs, Beverly
Hills, Calif.; 8Apr47;
EP13730. For voice and piano,
with chord symbols.

WILLIS, SLIM. See
Willis, S. P.

WILSON, DON.
Beggar's opera fantasy ... (S.S.A.)
Music adapted and arr. by Don
Wilson, [words by] John Gay ...
rev. by Edward Bradley. © Bourne,
inc., New York; on arrangement &
revision of lyrics; 28Oct46;
EP10922.

WILSON, FAITH CHAMBERS.
In time for Easter ... [Words by]
Kathryn Blackburn Peck, [music
by] Faith Chambers Wilson. (In
Primary Bible lesson leaflets.
v.9, no.3, p.[4]) © Nazarene
Publishing House, Kansas City,
Mo.; 1Mar47; EP6729.

WILSON, GERALD HUGH TYRWHITT- See
Berners, Gerald Hugh Tyrwhitt-
Wilson, baron.

WILSON, HARRY ROBERT, 1901-
Opportunity; text by John W.
Bratton, music by Harry Robert
Wilson and Geoffrey O'Hara,
S.A.T.B., arr. by Harry Robert,
Wilson. © Robbins Music Corp.,
New York; 17Apr47; EP14767.
The song of the swamps; lyric by
Florence Tarr, music by Harry
Robert Wilson. © Robbins Music
Corp., New York; 20May47;
EP14760.

WILSON, HARRY ROBERT, 1901- arr.
Skip to my Lou; chorus for mixed
voices, original a cappella ...
American dance tune arr. by
Harry Robert Wilson. [Words]
traditional. © Hall & Mc-
Creary Co., Chicago; on arrange-
ment; 12Apr47; EP13758.

[WILSON, IRA BISROP] 1880-
Children of the King; lyrics and
exercises by Paul Monroe, music
by Ruth Dale [pseud.] © Lorenz
Publishing Co., Dayton, Ohio;
28Feb47; EP13488.
The cross triumphant; an Easter
choir cantata for mixed voices,
music by Herman Von Berge, music
by Ira B. Wilson. © Lorenz
Publishing Co., Dayton, Ohio;
3Jan47; EP12128.
Easter is here; an Easter service,
[text by E. S. Tillotson, music
by Fred B. Holton, pseud.] ©
Lorenz Publishing Co., Dayton,
Ohio; 11Jan47; EP12672.
Lorenz song specials for choir
use; a collection of songs and
special numbers ... Compiled and
arranged by Ira B. Wilson. ©
Lorenz Publishing Co., Dayton,
Ohio; 21Dec46; EP13490.

WILSON, ROGER C   1912-
Beauty for ashes; [words by]
Herman von Berge, [music by]
Roger C. Wilson. © Lorenz
Publishing Co., Dayton, Ohio;
17Mar47; EP13489. Close
score: SATB.

152

WILSON, ROGER C. Cont'd.

Song of the holy night; a Christmas choir cantata for mixed voices, based on the familiar carol "Silent night, holy night." Text written and comp. by Edith Sanford Tillotson, music composed by Roger C. Wilson. © Lorenz Publishing Co., Dayton, Ohio; 13Jun47; EP15256.

WILSON, S   H
It's nothing but love; words and music by S. H. Wilson. © Nordyke Publishing Co., Los Angeles; 8Mar47; EP13238.

WILSON, STANLEY R
The rooster's serenade; words & music ... by Stanley R. Wilson. © Stanley R. Wilson, Williamsport, Pa.; 5Jun47; EP6952.

WINDSOR, A   D
The national anthem of Israel; Answer to the wailing wall, lyric by J. David Guelph de Windsor, music by A. B. Windsor. © Emma H. Munson, Los Angeles; 6Jun47; EP15177.

WINKLER, GERHARD.
Fishermen of Capri; music [by] Gerhard Winkler. © Peter Maurice Music Co., ltd., New York; 21Mar47; EF5438.

[WINNER, SEPTIMUS] 1827-1902.
Listen to the mocking bird; [by Septimus Winner] version by Lyn Murray ....S.A.T.B. © Boosey & Hawkes, inc., New York; on arrangement; 27Dec46; EP10996.

WINSETT, R   E
Revival message; ed. by R. E. Winsett. © R. E. Winsett, song book publisher, Dayton, Tenn.; 15Jul47; AA35150. Hymns, with music.

WINSETT, R   ed.
Abiding faith; edited and compiled by R. E. Winsett. © R. E. Winsett, music publisher, Dayton, Tenn.; 28Mar47; AA35933. Hymns, with music in shape-note notation.

WINSTEAD, KENNETH COLLINS.
Ida reed; an American folk song. Four part male voices, with tenor solo ... a cappella, arr. by Kenneth Winstead. © M. Witmark & Sons, New York; on arrangement; 1Apr47; EP13710.

WINSTON, ELWYN.
One room kitchenette; words ... by David Ellis, and music [by] Elwyn Winston, arr. by Frank Furlett. © Puritan Publishing Co., inc., Chicago; 10Nov46; EP11234.

WINSTONE, ERIC HENRY, 1913-
Saratoga; [by] Eric Winstone. © Cosmo Music Co. (London), ltd., London; 23Dec46; EF34434. Piano-conductor score (orchestra), and parts.

WIRGES, WILLIAM FRANCIS, 1900-
Ages ago in Galilee; [words by] Richard Maxwell ... [music by] William Wirges. © Maxwell-Wirges Publications, inc., New York; 15Jan47; EP11963. Close score: SATB.

Smile songs; by Richard Maxwell and William Wirges. © Maxwell-Wirges Publications, inc., New York; 15Sep46; EP11211.

Smile songs; by Richard Maxwell and William Wirges. © Maxwell-Wirges Publications, inc., New York; 15Sep46; EP11210. Cover-title: Rainbow smile songs.

WISE, AL, employer for hire. See Bennett, Elsie M.
Marden, Robert.

WISE, CHUBBY.
Shenandoah waltz; words by Clyde Moody, music by Chubby Wise. © Acuff-Rose Publications, Nashville; 9Jun47; EP14929.

WISE, FRED.
Gone, gone, gone (but not forgotten); by Billy Hayes, Milton Leeds [pseud.] and Fred Wise. © Milene Music, Nashville; 31Dec46; EP10909. For voice and piano, with guitar diagrams and chord symbols.

WISEMAN, SCOTTY. See Wiseman, Skyland.

WISEMAN, SKYLAND.
Why in the dickens don't you milk that cow? Words and music by Chester Rice, Geer Parkinson and Skyland "Scotty" Wiseman. © Peer International Corp., New York; 24Apr47; EP14238.

WITTE, ALFRED DE. See De Witte, Alfred.

WOLF, ALOIS, 1914-
Mistral; [by] Alois Wolf [and Jupiter; by] Alois Wolf, arr. by Alois Wolf and Zdeněk Krotil] © R. A. Dvorský, Praha, Czechoslovakia; 12Aug46; EF5427. Piano-conductor score (orchestra) and parts.

WOLF, AUDREY HAY.
Are you a "numbers" fan? Words and music by Audrey May Wolf. © Grimes Music Publishers Philadelphia; 10Mar47; EP12331.

WOLF, DANIEL.
Open your window; for three-part chorus of women's voices with piano acc. (S.S.A.) Lyric by Mabel Livingstone, music by Daniel Wolf. © Carl Fischer, inc., New York; 14Mar47; EP12883.

The pretzel man ... Lyric by Mabel Livingstone, music by Daniel Wolf. © Leeds Music Corp., New York; 14Apr47; EP13720.

WOLF, JACK.
From rocking horse to rocking chair; words and music by Irving Melshur, Remus Harris and Jack Wolf. © Mutual Music Society, inc., New York; 31Dec46; EP11307.

WOLF, OLGA.
Sure short cut for learning to play the accordion; by Olga Wolf. © The Boston Music Co., Boston; bk. 1, 27Mar47; AA50927.

WOLFE, JACQUES.
The shoemaker of the stars and his tunes; 11 piano pieces with words. Poems by S. A. De Witt, music by Jacques Wolfe. © Carl Fischer, inc., New York; 15Apr47; EP11682.

WOLFF, S. DRUMMOND-   See also Drummond-Wolff, S.

O praise God in His holiness; [words from Psalm 150] © Gordon V. Thompson, ltd., Toronto; 12Dec46; EF3077. Score: SATB and organ.

WOLFSON, LOUIS HAIMAN, 1875-
Starlight waltz; by Louis H. Wolfson. © Louis Haiman Wolfson, Tuscaloosa, Ala.; 23Jan47; EP11472. For piano solo.

WOLKEN, LEWIS ALBERT, 1897-
"Love one another" (as I have loved you"); words by Melville Pendleton, music by Lewis Wolken. Erie, Pa., Advance Printing & Litho Co. © Cecil Melville Pendleton, Erie, Pa.; 5Apr47; EP13597.

WOOD, GUY.
Sweet nothings; words by James Cavanaugh ... music by Guy Wood. © Woodward Music, inc., New York; 11Mar47; EP12545.

WOOD, HAYDN, 1882-
The horse guards, Whitehall ... arr. for piano solo by the composer, Haydn Wood. © Chappell & co., ltd., London; 26Feb47; EF5536.

I bended unto me a bough of May; [music by] Haydn Wood, words by T. E. Brown. © Ascherberg, Hopwood & Crew, ltd., London; 26Feb47; EF5241.

London cameos. No. 1. The city; miniature overture by Haydn Wood. © Ascherberg, Hopwood & Crew, ltd., London; 31Mar47; EF5527. Piano-conductor score (orchestra) and parts.

WOOD, IONE.
I knew my Shepherd's voice; [by] Ione Wood, arr. by William Wirges. © Maxwell-Wirges Publications, inc., New York; 15Jan47; EP11962. Close score: SATB.

WOODBRIDGE, CHARLOTTE LOUISE, 1888-
See also Woodbridge, Louise.
Sing unto the Lord; [by] Louise Woodbridge. © Charlotte Louise Woodbridge, Pasadena, Calif.; 20Apr47; EP14323. Close score: SATB.

WOODBRIDGE, LOUISE. See also Woodbridge, Charlotte Louise.
Dance of the gnomes; [by] Louise Woodbridge. © Theodore Presser Co., Philadelphia; 17May47; EP14607. Score (violin and piano) and part.

[WOODBURY, I   B   ]
Stars of the summer night; [words by Longfellow, music by I. B. Woodbury, arr. by Victor Lakes Martin] Easy piano arrangement with keyboard charts. © Songs You Remember Publishing Co., (V. L. Martin, Proprietor), Atlanta; on arrangement; 5Apr47; EP14747.

WOODE, HENRI.
How big can you get, little man? Words by Al J. Neiburg, music by Henri Woode [and] Lucky Millinden © Northern Music Corp., New York; 11Feb47; EP12171.

My Evelyn; words and music by Henri Woode. © Mutual Music Society, inc., New York; 17Apr47; EP13740.

[WOODFORD, GORDON ROBERT] 1917-
A dance for two; words by Victor A. Torsello, music by James Welland [pseud.] © Cine-mart Music Publishing Co., Hollywood, Calif.; 1Aug46; EP10966. For voice and piano, with chord symbols.

Moonshine Valley mamma; words by Harry Herker, music by R. Woodie [pseud.] © Cine-Mart Music Publishing Co., Hollywood, Calif.; 1Nov47; EP11713.

WOODGATE, HUBERT LESLIE, 1902-
Simon Peter; an oratorio, words from the Bible and other sources, music by Leslie Woodgate. © Hubert Leslie Woodgate, Wembley Park, Middlesex, Eng.; 28Feb47; EF5260. Piano-vocal score.

WOODGATE, HUBERT LESLIE, 1902-arr.
Lil brack sheep; negro spiritual. Melody by J. H. Maunder, freely arr. for mixed voices by Leslie Woodgate. © Ascherberg, Hopwood & Crew, ltd., London; on arrangement; 10Mar47; EF5308.

WOODGATE, LESLIE. See
Woodgate, Hubert Leslie.

WOODMAN, R   HUNTINGTON.
The gate of the year; for
four-part chorus of mixed
voices and piano or organ,
with incidental soprano
or tenor solo. [Words by]
M. Louise Haskins, [music by]
R. Huntington Woodman, arr.
by Kenneth Downing [pseud.]
© G. Schirmer, inc., New
York; on arrangement; 24Mar47;
EP13124.

WOODS, HARRY.
I happen to love you; by Harry
Woods. © Sinatra Songs, inc.,
New York; 13Jan47; EP11505.
For voice and piano, with
chord symbols.

WOODS, J   SHERMAN, 1888-
Crown for cross ... Words by
Will H. Ruebush, music by J.
Sherman Woods, [and Out of the
shadows; words by Harry Dixon
Loes, music by J. Sherman
Woods] © J. Sherman Woods,
Auburn, Calif.; 30Apr47;
EP14301.

He won my heart on Calvary;
quartet for mixed voices ...
(organ or piano acc.)   Words by
T. O. Chisholm ... music by J.
Sherman Woods. © J. Sherman
Woods, Auburn, Calif.;
30Apr47; EP14296.

The homeland; song for medium
voice, words by Will H. Ruebush,
music by J. Sherman Woods. ©
J. Sherman Woods, Auburn,
Calif.; 30Apr47; EP14294.

How much I owe; hymn for
quartet (S.A.T.B.) and choir,
(piano or organ acc.)   Words
by Dr. Oswald J. Smith, music
by J. Sherman Woods, [and
Be a blessing today; words by
C. Austin Miles, music by J.
Sherman Woods] © J. Sherman
Woods, Auburn, Calif.; 30Apr47;
EP14299.

I heard the Lord; sacred song
for medium or low voice, words
by Mary Stoner Wine ... Music
by J. Sherman Woods. © J.
Sherman Woods, Auburn, Calif.;
30Apr47; EP14295.

I know; trio for women's voices
(S.S.A.) Words by Dr. Oswald
J. Smith ... music by J.
Sherman Woods. © J. Sherman
Woods, Auburn, Calif.;
30Apr47; EP14297.

Mother, listen for me; song for
medium voice ... Words by
Mary Stoner Wine, music by J.
Sherman Woods. © J. Sherman
Woods, Auburn, Calif.;
30Apr47; EP14298.

The straying sheep; hymn for
mixed choir. Words by Harry
Dixon Loes, music by J.
Sherman Woods, Auburn, Calif.;
30Apr47; EP14300.

WOODSIDE, JAMES, 1895-1945.
Hope thou in God ... Text adapted
from Psalms XLII and CIII,
music by James Woodside.
© The Boston Music Co.,
Boston; 4Mar47; EP12873.
Score: chorus (SATB) and
piano reduction.

I like the lad with the golden
hair; for three-part chorus
of women's voices with piano
acc., English version by
James Woodside. Spanish
folk-song arr. by James Woodside. © The Boston Music
Co., Boston; 27Feb47; EP12381.

WOODWARD, H   H
The radiant morn hath passed
away; by H. H. Woodward, arr.
and ed. for mixed chorus ...
by Albert Ayers. [Words by
Godfrey Thring] © Choral
Art Publications, New York;
on arrangement; 8May47;
EP14391.

WOODWARD, LYNN, pseud.
I will lift up mine eyes; [Psalm
121] by Lynn Woodward, [pseud.]
Ed. and arr. for mixed chorus,
SATB. © Choral Press, Evanston,
Ill.; 15Jun46; EP11696.

I will lift up mine eyes; [Psalm
121] by Lynn Woodward, [pseud.]
Ed. and arr. for women's chorus,
SSA. © Choral Press, Evanston,
Ill.; 15Jun46; EP11695.

WORDSWORTH, WILLIAM.
Three songs with pianoforte
accompaniment, [by] William Wordsworth. © Alfred Lengnick & Co.,
ltd., London; 30Dec46; EP31214.

WORK, HENRY CLAY.
Crossing the Rhineland; words
[and arrangement] By E. J.
Samuelson, music by Henry C.
Work. © E. J. Samuelson,
Chicago; on words and arrange-
ment; 15Jun45; EP13382.

The day of jubilo; piano solo; [by
Henry Clay Work], words and
arrangement by Ted Mossman. ©
Belwin, inc., New York; on words
and arrangement; 24Dec46; EP11262.

Grandfather's clock; by Henry C.
Work ... [arr. by] John W.
Schaum. © Belwin, inc., New
York; on arrangement; 29Apr47;
EP11050. For 2 pianos, 8 hands.

WORTH, BOBBY.
"Truer words were never spoken;"
lyrics and music by Bobby Worth,
arr. by Lou Halmy. © Martin
Music, Hollywood, Calif.;
26May47; EP14663.

WRIGHT, CHARLES C
Wait a little while; words and
music by Charles C. Wright.
© Nordyke Publishing Co., Los
Angeles; 23Feb46; EP13527.

WRIGHT, ELLIOT.
Franklin D. Roosevelt; words by
Louis L. Lawman, music by
Elliot Wright. © Louis Lester
Lawman, Estherville, Iowa; 26Dec46;
EP10715.

WRIGHT, HELEN SNYDER, 1915-
Salute to Glenville; words by H.
Laban White, music by Helen Wright.
© Alumni Association of Glenville
State College, Glenville, W. Va.;
9May47; EP14890.

WRIGHT, JAMES, 1887-
"Got away from that door;" words &
music by James Wright. © James
Wright, Paterson, N. J.; 18Feb47;
EP12496. Melody and words.

WRIGHT, N   LOUISE.
The banjo picker; for N. Louise
Wright, arr. for piano duet by
Emanuel Lowenstein. © The
Willis Music Co., Cincinnati;
on arrangement; 22Apr47;
EP13878.

A gigue ... By N. Louise Wright.
© McKinley Publishers, inc.,
Chicago; 7May47; EP14313. For
piano solo.

A May day picnic; for piano, [by]
N. Louise Wright. © McKinley
Publishers, inc., Chicago;
26Dec46; EP10852.

Stepping stones ... By N. Louise
Wright. © McKinley Publishers,
inc., Chicago; 7May47;
EP14314. For piano solo.

White caps; for the piano, [by]
N. Louise Wright. © McKinley
Publishers, inc., Chicago;
26Dec46; EP10851.

WRIGHT, NORMAN SÖRENG.
One hundred twenty-first Psalm;
[by] Norman Söreng Wright.
© Delkas Music Publishing
Co., Los Angeles; 22Apr47;
EP6841. Score: chorus (SSA)
and organ.

WRUBEL, ALLIE, 1905-
I do, do, do like you; words and
music by Allie Wrubel. © Harms,
inc., New York; 2Apr47; EP13361.

The lady from 29 palms; music
and lyrics by Allie Wrubel
... arr. by Lou Halmy. ©
Martin Music, Hollywood,
Calif.; 11May47; EP14278.

"When the white roses bloom"
("down in Red River valley");
music by Allie Wrubel, lyrics
by Paul Herrick, arr. by Lou
Halmy. © Martin Music, Hollywood, Calif.; 19May47; EP14662.

WULFFAERT, HESTER.
I light a cigarette and dream;
words and music [by] Hester
Wulffaert. © Hester Wulffaert,
Cambridge, Mass.; 9Apr47;
EP13673.

WYLIE, DONNA ARLEEN, 1927-
I am crucified with Christ ... [By]
Donna A. Wylie. © Donna Wylie,
Johnson City, N. Y.; 2May47;
EP14197. Close score: SATB.

Y

YAKOVLEFF, NICOLAS PETROS. See
Iakobleph, Nikolaos Petros.

YAMIN, JAIME, 1913-
Aquel recuerdo ... letra de Mario
Fuentes, música de Jaime Yamin.
N[ew] Y[ork], Sole selling agent,
Southern Music Pub. Co. © Peer
International Corp., New York,
27Dec46; EP11641.

Desconfianza de tu amor. (I've
lost all confidence in you)
... Spanish words and music
by Jaime Yamin, English words
by Joe Davis. © Caribbean
Music, inc., New York; 17Mar47;
EP12643.

Despierta ... letra de Mario
Fuentes, música de Jaime Yamin.
N[ew] Y[ork], Sole selling
agent, Southern Music Pub. Co.
© Peer International Corp., New
York; 27Dec46; EP11643.

Hoy te vas. (If I only knew) ...
English words by Joe Davis,
Spanish words and music by
Jaime Yamin. © Caribbean
Music, inc., New York; 30Dec46;
EP10674.

Mi amada ... letra de Mario Fuentes,
música de Jaime Yamin. N[ow] Y[ork],
Sole selling agent, Southern
Music Pub. Co. © Peer Inter-
national Corp., New York; 27Dec46;
EP11643.

Mujer ajena ... letra y música
de Jaime Yamin. N[ew] Y[ork],
Sole selling agent, Southern
Music Pub. Co. © Peer International Corp., New York;
27Dec46; EP11646.

Por que tu lloras? (Why are you
crying?) ... English words by
Joe Davis, Spanish words and
music by Jaime Yamin. © Caribbean Music, inc., New York;
23Jun47; EP15144.

154

YAMIN, JAIME. Cont'd.
Si tu me adoraras ... letra y
música de Jaime Yamin. N[ew]
Y[ork], Sole selling agent,
Southern Music Pub. Co. ©
Peer International Corp., New
York; 27Dec46; EP11644.
Sufro su ausencia ... letra y
música de Jaime Yamin. N[ew]
Y[ork], Sole selling agent,
Southern Music Pub. Co. ©
Peer International Corp.,
New York; 27Dec46; EP11645.

YANCEY, ELISE.
Mother's voice; words and music by
Elise Yancey, a Robert Anderson's
arrangement. Gary, Ind., Robert
Anderson's Good Shepherd Music
House. © Robert Anderson & Elise
Yancey, Gary, Ind.; 21May46;
EP11276. Close score: SATB.

YAW, RALPH.
Balboa bash; composed by Ralph
Yaw, arranged by Stan Kenton,
edited by Jiggs Noble.
© Capitol songs, inc., New
York; 16Feb47; EP12006.
Piano-conductor score (orches-
tra) and parts.
Down in Unihuahua ... by Johnny
Richards and Ralph Yaw. ©
Leslie Music Corp., New York;
28Dec46; EP11509. For voice
and piano, with chord symbols.

YAYSNOFF, I   1919-
Revelation; text and music by
J. [and] I. Yaysnoff. © G.
Winthrop & Co., New York; 31Dec46;
EP10901. For voice and piano.

YEAZEL, CHESTER.
[Gospel songs; words by] Violet Mc-
Pherson. © Violet McPherson,
Flint, Mich.; on 4 songs; 20Feb47.
Contents.- Homesick for heaven,
by Chester Yeazel [© EP12491]-
Jesus knows and understands, by
Chester Yeazel, arr. by Violet Mc-
Pherson [© EP12492]- Jesus will
care for His own, by Violet Mc-
Pherson [© EP12493]- Consecrate
me, Lord, by Violet McPherson
[© EP12494]

YODER, ALICE TALBOT, 1914-
Jesus is the lover of my soul; [by]
Alice Talbot, arr. by W. M. T.
(In Church of the Nazarene.
Michigan District. Nazarene Young
Peoples Society. Choruses of the
N. Y. P. S. p.69) © Michigan
District, Nazarene Young Peoples
Society, Flint, Mich.; 25Jul46;
EP13088. Close score: SATB.

YODER, PAUL, arr.
Rambling wreck from Georgia
Tech.; arr. by Paul Yoder.
© Melrose Music Corp., New
York; 21May47; EP15119.
Piano-conductor score (band)
and parts.

YORK, RAYMOND, 1893-
The popping the question waltz
... and Perth on the Swan
... words by C. M. Huggins,
music by Raymond York.
© Messrs Cecil Murray Huggins
and Raymond York, West Perth,
West Australia; 18Dec45;
EF3936, EF3935.

YOST, GAYLORD, 1888-
Five pieces for violin and piano
in the first position; by
Gaylord Yost. © Volkwein
Brothers, inc., Pittsburgh; on
5 pieces; 11Mar47. Score
(violin and piano) and part.
Contents.- [v.1] The dawn greets
the rose (© EP12476)- [v.2] The
funny clown (© EP12477)- [v.3.] The
leaves are falling (© EP12478)-
[v.4] The merry elves (© EP12474)
[v.5] The sleeping princess (©
EP12475)

Yost violin method. © Volkwein
Bros., inc., Pittsburgh;
v. 2, 15Mar47; EP12710.

YOUMANS, VINCENT, d. 1946.
(No, no Nanette) Tea for two;
from the musical comedy "No,
no Nanette," words by Otto
Harbach and Irving Caesar ...
Music by Vincent Youmans, [arr.
by Johnny Sterling] © Harms,
inc., New York; on arrangement;
29May47; EP14998. Piano-conductor score (orchestra, with
words) and parts.

YOUNG, BARNEY, 1911-
Truman flew to Mexico; words and
music by Gloria Parker, William
Forest Crouch and Barney Young.
© Winfield Music, inc., New York;
9Apr47; EP13582.

YOUNG, HATTIE.
Swanee River boogie; by H.
Young [based on song by
Stephen Foster] ... Piano solo.
© Preview Music Co., Chicago;
on arrangement; 15Apr47;
EP13385.

YOUNG, JAMES.
Life is fine; by James "Trummie"
Young, arr. by Roger Segure.
© Leeds Music Corp., New York;
14Apr47; EP13713. Condensed
score (orchestra) and parts.

YOUNG, "TRUMMIE." See
Young, James.

YOUNG, VICTOR, 1900-
Edison march ... by Victor Young,
orchestration by Adolf Schmid.
© The John Church Co., Philadel-
phia; on orchestration; 13Jan47;
EP13574. Piano-conductor score
(orchestra, with words) and parts.
Edison march; ... by Victor Young,
scored for band by Erik Leidzén.
© The John Church Co., Philadelphia;
on arrangement; 24Jan47; EP11655.
Condensed score (band, with words)
and parts.
Little patch o' land; words by
Bissell Palmer, music by Victor
Young. © Theodore Presser Co.,
Philadelphia; on arrangement;
28Jan47; EP11884. Score:
S.A.T.B. and piano.
Pearls on velvet; by Victor Young.
[Arrangement for two pianos by
Mario Braggiotti] © Robbins
Music Corp., New York; on arrange-
ment; 12Nov46; EP11816. Two scores
for piano 1-2.
Stella by starlight ... words by
Ned Washington, music by Victor
Young. © Famous Music Corp.,
New York; 30Dec46; EP10919. For
voice and piano, with chord symbols.
Sweet Sue - just you; by Will J.
Harris and Victor Young, [arr.
by Charlie Ventura] © Shapiro,
Bernstein & Co., inc., New York;
on arrangement; 10Jun47; EP14982.
Score (B♭ tenor saxophone and
piano) and part.

YOUNG, WILLIAM M   Jr.
Amber eyes; lyric by Van Cunning-
ham, music by William M. Young,
Jr. © Broadcast Music, inc.,
New York; 9Apr47; EP15240.

YRADIER, SEB
La paloma waltz. (The dove.
Golubica) By Seb. Yradier, arr.
& Croatian version by ... R.
Cernkovich. © Rudolph Cernko-
vich, Bradley, Mich.; on arrange-
ment; 20Feb47; EP13315. Parts;
string orchestra; Croatian words.

YUILL, M   1898-
Finger frolics; sixteen recrea-
tional studies for the piano,
by M. Yuill. © Shattinger
Piano & Music Co., St. Louis;
6May47; EP14229.

YVAIN, MAURICE, 1891-
Chanson gitane; opérette ...
Couplets de L. Poterat, musique
de Maurice Yvain. © Editions
Royalty, Paris; 1.-2.recueil,
3Jan47; EF5189, 5188.

YVES, JEAN SAINT- See
Saint-Yves, Jean.

Z

ZADRA, REMY.
Hymn to Saint Frances Xavier
Cabrini; words by Rev. Norman
Herman, music by Rev. Remy
Zadra. © McLaughlin & Reilly
Co., Boston; 10Mar47; EP12783.
For unison chorus and organ.

[ZAHOROTOS, GEORGE TAFF.]
Darling, my heart is calling you;
words and music by George Taff
[pseud.] New York, G. Taff.
© George Zahoratos, New York;
9Jun47; EF6956.
I'm riding alone; words and music
by George Taff [pseud.] New York,
G. Taff. © George Zahoratos,
New York; 9Jun47; EF6955.

ZAJC, FRANK.
Jolly rhythm polka; by Ernie
Benedict [and] Frank Zajc.
© Peer International Corp.,
New York; 28Aug46; EP13987.
For piano solo, with chord
symbols.

ZANDT, JAMES VAN. See
Van Zandt, James.

ZANELLA, AMILCARE.
L'isola dei sogni. The island of
dreams ... Azione coreografica
di Otello Pagliai, con musiche
sinfoniche di Amilcare Zanella.
Riduzione per pianoforte dell'
autore. © Casa Musicale Giuliana,
Trieste, Italia; 5Feb47; EF3215.

ZARET, HY.
A home of my own; words and music
by Harry Woods and Hy Zaret. ©
Bob Miller, inc., New York;
30Dec46; EP10741.

ZEE, ALLAN.
Make the stars shine bright for
the women in white ... Words
and music by Allan Zee. © Leo
Feist, inc., New York; 7Mar47
EP12797.

ZELIBOR, GUSTAV, 1903-
Unverhofft; ein Spiel in 3
Akten, frei nach Johann
Nestroy, von Bruno Hardt-
Warden, Musik: Gustav Zelibor.
© Ludwig Doblinger (Bernhard
Herzmansky), k.g., Vienna;
24Jul46; EF3795. For voice
and piano.

ŽEMAITAITIS, JONAS PETRAS, 1890-
Kaip berneli aš vilojau ...
muzika parašė Jonas P.
Zemaitaitis, [words by Žod.
Rožytes] 1946. © Jonas
Petras Zemaitaitis, Brooklyn;
15May47; EP14885.

ZEPP, ARTHUR.
Row, row, row your boat ...
[with an acc. figure borrowed
from Tschaikowsky] by Arthur
Zepp. © Clayton F. Summy Co.,
Chicago; on arrangement;
27Feb47; EP12288. For piano
solo.
Spice on the ice; piano solo by
Arthur Zepp. © Clayton F.
Summy Co., Chicago; 28Apr47;
EP14645.

155

ZERAN, JOHN COURTNEY, 1899-
Arranging for drum and bugle corps;
using G and D bugles employing
free-valve, by John C. Zeran. ©
John Courtney Zeran, Los Angeles;
31Jan47; EP11690.

ZICH, JAROSLAV, 1912-
Letmý host; cyklus písní pro
střední hlas s orchestr, na slova
Viktora Dyka. [By] Jaroslav
Zich. Op.2. Klavírní úprava
skladatelova. © Hudební Matice
Umělecké Besedy, Praha, Czechoslovakia; 19Oct42; EF5009. For
voice and piano.

ZICH, OTAKAR, 1879-1934.
(Trio, violin, violoncello &
piano) Trio, E moll ... [by]
Otakar Zich. © Hudební Matice
Umělecké Besedy, Praha, Czecho-
slovakia; 8Jan45; EF5010.
Score and parts.

ZIEGLER, ELMER.
The service star; by Elmer
Ziegler. © Ziegler Band
Music Publishing Co., Sterl-
ing, Ill.; 2Nov46; EP12526.
Condensed score (band) and
parts.

ZIEHLER, JACK.
There was a little pig; words and
music by Jack Ziehler. © Mills
Music, inc., New York; 20Jan47;
EP6496.

ZINSSER, WILLIAM K
(Clear the track) You've gotta
have me; words and music by
Mark Lawrence ... and Bill
Zinsser ... [from the]
Princeton University Triangle
Club ... production ... Clear
the track. © Broadcast Music,
inc., New York; 12Dec46; EP11839.

You've gotta have me. See his
Clear the track.

ZIRPOLI, PATRICK ANTHONY, 1923-
Someday you'll learn to love me;
words and music by Pat Zirpoli,
[arranged by Frank V. Turner]
© Charles Wynn Publications, New
York; 20Jan47; EP11859.

ZOELLER, CHARLES H
"Glory! Hamilton High!" ... Words
and music by Charles H. Zoeller.
© Charles H. Zoeller, Hamilton,
Ohio; 11Mar47; EP12554.

ZOELLNER, PETE.
Steel guitar blues ... music by
Pete Zoellner, lyric [and ar-
rangement] by Betty Glynn.
(Oahu advanced harmony note
course for Hawaiian and electric
guitar, [lesson 41PT]) © Oahu
Publishing Co., Cleveland; on
arrangement & lyrics; 4Mar47;
EP6877. For voice and guitar.
Includes lesson on C#minor
tuning and harmonic intervals.

ZORLIG, KURT.
Personal message ... [by] Kurt
Zorlig. [Now York, Harmonia
Edition] © Harmonia Edition
Publishing Co., New York; 30Dec46;
EP6468. For piano or organ solo.

ZOUBEK, KAREL.
A sheaf of first position pieces for
violin ... by Karel Zoubek. ©
Allan & Co., pty. ltd., Melbourne, Australia; 14Oct46;
EF3121. Score (violin and
piano) and part.

ZUCCHERI, LUCIANO.
Non so come si chiami ... testo
di S. Corti, musica di Luciano
Zuccheri. Ti chiamo amore ...
testo di C. Deani [pseud.],
musica di Virgilio Panzuti.
© Edizioni Leonardi, s.a.r.l.,
Milano; 15Jan47; EF5274. Piano-
conductor score (orchestra, with
words), and parts.
Oggi ancor ... musica di L.
Zucchori, (arrang. dell' autore)
Nube Rosa ... musica di Piero
Vidale, (arrang. dell' autore)
© Edizioni Leonardi, s.a.r.l.,
Milano; 21Dec46; EF5269. Piano-
conductor score (orchestra,
with words), and parts.

ZYGMAN, EDMUND.
Mazurka-phantasy; for piano solo,
[by] Edmund Zygman. © Elkan-
Vogel Co., inc., Philadelphia;
24Dec46; EP11466.

All dressed up with a broken heart.
  Val, J.
All dressed up with no place to go.
  Rinker, A.
All for you.
  Beaton, J.
All glory, laud, and honor.
  Bach, J. S.
All hail, Coinegie Tech.
  Jones, S.
All Hollow's Eve.
  Bedell, R. L.
All I have is love.
  Chappelear, L. I've learned my
    lesson.
All I want for Christmas (is my two
    front teeth).
  Gardner, D. Y.
All is over (but the shouting).
  Grider, F. J.
All my love to you.
  Gage, H. A.
All of a sudden it's you.
  Goehr, R.
All of a sudden my heart sings.
  Herpin. En écoutant mon coeur
    chanter.
All of me.
  Marks, G.
All on account of you.
  Watchorn, A. B. Big teardrops are
    falling, all on account of you.
All people that on earth.
  Farnes, E., pseud.
All Souls' day.
  Strauss, R.
All star song folio.
  Goldsen, M. H., ed. Tex Ritter all
    star song folio.
All strings and fancy free.
  Torch, S.
All suit! No man.
  Coots, J. F.
All that I know is.
  Furney, A.
All the time.
  Patitucci, E.
All the world is new.
  Jeffries, H.
All the world to me.
  Buchanan, M.
All things work for good.
  Thorne, W. M.
All those in favor.
  Solomon, N.
All through the day.
  May, H. Spring song.
All thru the years.
  Lieta, T. Sweet darling.
All-time popular songs.
  Carmichael, H.
Alla å vi sjöman på livets stora hav.
  Kraft, A. Fran "Blyge Anton" till
    "En sjöman till håst."
Alla luna.
  Paganucci, A.
Alla marcia.
  Trowbridge, L.
Alle fontane.
  Casalini, V.
Allegretto.
  Greenhill, H. W. Three pieces for
    organ.
Allegretto [from] Symphony no. 3.
  Brahms, J. Symphony, no. 3.
Alleluia.
  Elaine, sister.
Alleluia carol.
  Rasley, J. M.
Alleluia! Christ is risen.
  Edmundson, M.
Alleluia, in form of toccata.
  Talma, L.
All's well that ends well.
  Buys, P.
Alma mater hymn.
  . Klingstedt, P. T.

Almost like being in love.
  Loewe, F. Brigadoon.
Aloha lani.
  Krietemeyer, E. W.
Aloha nui loa, dear.
  McDiarmid, D. P.
Aloha serenade.
  King, C. E.
Alone.
  Bunker, L.
  Dellon, H.
Alone with Jesus.
  Tovey, H. G.
Alone with you.
  Weiss, S.
Along the pineapple trail.
  Faber, B.
Along this way.
  Donald, J. S.
Alpha eleven.
  Simmonds, H.
Altalena della bambola.
  Catalano, A.
Although another separates us.
  Arthur, W.
Although you've broken my heart.
  Day, L.
Always.
  Berlin, I.
  Berlin, I. Accordion transcriptions.
Always alone with me.
  Pinterally, A.
Always be with me, God.
  Tovey, H. G.
Always keep your promise.
  Melsher, I.
Am meer.
  Schubert, F. P. La mer.
Am teefeld.
  Koch, S. v. Morgenländische liebes-
    lieder.
Amalia.
  Letellier, D.
Amapa.
  Storoni, J.
Amaryllis.
  Le Grand, R.
Amateur organist. See title entry
  in composer list.
Ambassadors for Christ.
  Helbling, D. W.
Ambassadors for Jesus.
  Pyle, I. M.
Amber eyes.
  Young, W. M., jr.
Ambrosia, a feast for the gods.
  Noll, A. W.
America. See title entry in composer
  list.
America in rhythm.
  Ostling, A.
America, my country.
  Magner, M. A.
America, the beautiful.
  Ward, S. A.
America united.
  Frydan, C.
American folk music.
  Bryan, C. F., arr.
American legends.
  Siegmeister, E.
American names.
  Watt, J. C.
American panorama.
  McKay, G. F.
American patrol.
  Meacham, F. W.
American step.
  Marvin, C. B.
American youth.
  Bannon, R. E.
Americana.
  Kesnar, M. Seven pieces.
America's best guitar note and diagram
  song folio.
  Martell, J., arr.

America's best piano accordion folio.
  Deiro, P., arr.
Amerika hat rhythmus und Wien hat
  melodie.
  Fox, F.
Amigablemente.
  Parra, A.
Amigos cantandos.
  Sanders, O., comp.
Amolador.
  Echevarria, E.
Among my souvenirs.
  Nicholls, H. The best years of our
    lives.
Among the daffodils.
  Dittenhaver, S. L. Four piano com-
    positions.
Among the things.
  Klumpkey, J.
Amor de los dos.
  Parra, G.
Amor llamó.
  Ahlert, F. E.
Amor, non mi lar ciar.
  Carenzio, R.
Amour de moi.
  Tiersot, J.
Amour de moy.
  Pagot, J.
Amour est roi.
  Mahieux, E.
  Mahieux, E. Sur la Place de la
    Bastille.
Amour! ... L'amour.
  Durand, P.
Amour, toujours l'amour.
  Friml, R.
Amoureux.
  Greco, V. Rodriguez Pena.
Analytic symphony series, no. 35.
  Schumann, R. A. Symphony, no. 4.
Ancient of days.
  Horton, L. H.
Ancient sign.
  Luypaerts, G.
And a very great multitude.
  Lekberg, S.
And Jesus said.
  Antes, J.
Andante.
  Gallois Montbrun, R. Pages de
    sonatine.
Andante et scherzetto.
  Lantier, P. L.
Andante from Symphonie espagnole.
  Lalo, E. Symphonie espagnole.
Anders bälgaspel.
  Johnny, O.
Andy Rizzo program album.
  Rizzo, A., comp. & arr.
Angel.
  Glover, J.
Angel of my dreams.
  Pericola, V.
Angels are singing for mother.
  Ellsworth, A. B.
Angelus.
  Pick Mangiagalli, R.
Ani ma-amin.
  Lefkowitch, H., arr.
Anima Christi.
  Auer, J.
  Briggs, E. F.
Ann Sheridan.
  Quevido, R.
Annie get your gun.
  Berlin, I.
Annie Laurie.
  Scott, J. D., lady.
Anniversary song.
  Chaplin, S.
Annu I mang-tusende år.
  Runo, S. Sol över Klara.
Anoche platicamos.
  Baena, F.
Another echo song.
  Hruby, F. M.

Anthem of the United Nations.
  Russell, B.
Anthems choir and congregation enjoy.
  Foster, A. H., <u>comp.</u>
Anyone can dream.
  Lilley, J. J.
Anything goes.
  Porter, C.
Apologies to Farmer MacDonald.
  Dorr, A. I.
Apotheosis.
  Berlioz, H. Symphony.
Appassionata sonata.
  Beethoven, L. van. Sonata, piano.
Apple blossom wedding.
  Simon, N.
Apple blossoms.
  Jacobi, V.
Apple tree at my window polka.
  Malec, A. W prost do mego okienec-
  zka.
April is in my mistress' face.
  Morley, T.
April showers.
  Silvers, L. Bombo.
April song.
  Duro, J.
April wisdom.
  Pendleton, E.
April's a lovely lady.
  Dunhill, T. F.
Aquel recuerdo.
  Yamin, J.
Aquí Radio-Andorra.
  LaFarge, G.
Arab temple.
  Griffis, J. W.
Arabesque.
  Nieland, J. H. I. M.
  Schumann, R. A.
Archipel.
  Humel, C.
Are he gone? Have he went.
  Webb, A. B.
Are you a numbers fan.
  Wolf, A. M.
Are you facing the world all alone.
  Rogers, J.
Are you here tonight without Jesus.
  Green, A. Keep me 'neath the shadow
  of Thy cross.
Are you just pretending, dear.
  Murray, D. D.
Argentinita.
  Salerno, F.
Argonaut.
  Frangkiser, C.
Aria.
  Peeters, F.
Ariel.
  Bacher, E.
Arima to-night, Sangre Grande to-morrow
  night.
  Houdini, W.
Arise, all nations.
  Deis, C.
Arise, Lord.
  Bortniansky, D. S.
Aristocrat.
  Spier, H. R.
Arizona.
  Rustin, E.
Arizona baby.
  Galova, T.
Arkansaw fiddler.
  Mossman, T., <u>arr.</u>
Arlette.
  Yost, G.
Arm of the Lord, awake.
  Marsh, C. H.
Armenian song bouquet.
  Suni, G. M.
Armonie.
  Oldrati, Rossi.
Army catering corps.
  Dean, J. F., <u>arr.</u>
Army journal for full military band.

Belton, J. Time marches on.
Herbert, V. The red mill.
Army made a man out of Joe.
  Carleton, R. L.
Arnljot Gelline.
  Beck, T.
Arranging for drum and bugle corps.
  Zeran, J. C.
Arrimate, vida mia.
  Villoldo, A.
Arrullos de hamaca.
  Brenes Candanedo, G.
Arruza.
  Marrodán, F.
Art of fugue.
  Bach, J. S.
Art of the suite.
  Pessl, Y., <u>ed.</u> & <u>comp.</u>
Art Tatum improvisations.
  Tatum, A., <u>arr.</u>
Artemis and Orion.
  Johnson, C. W.
Artistry in bolero.
  Rugolo, P.
Artistry in boogie.
  Kenton, S.
Artistry in percussion.
  Rugolo, P.
Artist's life.
  Strauss, J.
As I ride, as I ride (through the Metidja
  to Abd-El-Kadr).
  Rathaus, K. Three English songs.
As it began to dawn.
  Vincent, C.
As long as I have you.
  Bailes, L.
As long as I'm dreaming.
  Van Heusen, J. Welcome stranger.
As long as you are near.
  Tremblay, E.
As lovely as a rose.
  Lewis, S. I.
As now the sun's declining rays.
  Smith, C.
As on the night.
  Carr, A.
As the days go by.
  Fullenwider, P.
As the snowflakes gently fall.
  Luvaas, M. J.
As torrents in summer.
  Elgar, Sir E. W.
  Elgar, E. King Olaf.
  Brahms, J. Four serious songs.
As ye sow shall ye reap.
  Boland, C. A. Chris crosses.
As years go by.
  De Rose, P. Song of love.
Así eres tú.
  Rizzo, J. Never like this.
Así son las mujeres.
  Mier, P. Saludamos a Texas.
Así te quería.
  Navarro, A.
Ask anyone who knows.
  Kaufman, A. S.
Aspen train.
  Willis, S. P.
Asperges me.
  Pusa-Teri, C. R.
Astaire.
  Walter, C.
Astrea dear.
  King, L. R.
At a woodland tarn.
  Seymer, W. Strofer i sol och skugga.
At church.
  Steinbach, B. Modern miniatures.
(At last I've found) the kind of girl I've
  dreamed of.
  Tepper, S.
At sundown.
  Donaldson, W.
  Hofland, S. A.
At the ballet.
  Beck, M.

At the end of a dream.
  Spicer, H.
At the feet of Jesus.
  Harper, T.
At the gin mill.
  Stewart, A. S.
At the range on the other side.
  Halama, F. J.
At the tulip festival.
  Schiefelbein, F. A.
Atom and evil.
  Singer, L.
Atomic era.
  Freeman, B.
Au Tyrol.
  Close, H.
Auberge du Goujon qui rit.
  Goletti, N.
Auberge qui chante.
  Richepin, T.
Auf dem flusse.
  Koch, S. v. Morgenländische liebes-
  lieder.
Auld lang syne.
  Jacobs, M., <u>arr.</u> Boogie woogie step-
  by-step.
  Karlin, A., <u>arr.</u>
Aunque lo quieran o no.
  Esperón, M.
Aunque te vayas.
  Miró, F.
Aunque tengas razon.
  Velásquez, C.
Aunt.
  Richard, L.
Aunt Hetty.
  Milton, J.
Aurora.
  Meretta, L. V.
Aus der Tiefe rufe ich.
  Bach, J. S. Forty days and forty
  nights.
Aus meinem leben.
  Moser, F.
Australia for Jesus.
  Ruhf, D. P.
Autumn barcarolle.
  Lovejoy, H.
Autumn nocturne.
  Myrow, J.
Autumn rain.
  Jepperson, S.
Au-we.
  Kaai, B. K.
Av ren välgörenhet,
  Kraft, A. Fran "Blyge Anton" till
  "En sjöman till hast".
Ave Maria.
  Aubanel, G.
  Brahms, J.
  Drumm, G.
  Gounod, C. F.
  Horgan, M. S., <u>sister.</u>
  Legnini, A.
  Liszt, F.
  Roberts, L. S.
  Schubert, F. P.
  Singenberger, J. B.
  Sullivan, G. J. E., <u>brother,</u>
  Zalewski, B. J.
Ave maris stella.
  Bingham, S.
Ave Regina.
  Charpentier, M. A. Hail Thee.
Ave verum.
  Aubanel, G.
  Wilkinson, C. A. R. Jesu, Word of
  God incarnate.
Aventure est au coin de la rue.
  Scotto, V.
Aventure sur la côte.
  Lopez, F. (La belle de Cadix) Pour
  toi, Pepita.
Aventures de Casanova.
  Caffot, S. V. J.
Awake, my soul.
  Diggle, R.

Awake 'tis spring.
Elliott, M.
Axel Christensen's break studies.
Christensen, A. W.
Ay, ay, ay, ay! My serenade.
Guizar, T.
Ay ay ay, mama.
Muray, P.
Ay corazón.
Alarcón Leal, E.
Az ti bude smutno.
Cuma, A. Hvezda a její stín.
Az uvidíte 'ji'.
Novácek, S. E.
B. T. C
Quisenberry, P. W.
Babe is born in Bethlehem.
Bach, J. S.
Baby.
Brigada, A.
Baby boogie.
Broza, E. L.
Baby, come out of the clouds.
Nemo, H.
Baby doll.
Newman, B.
Baby kitty.
Fouts, M. Children's easy piano pieces.
Baby, that's what I can do.
Powell, E.
Baby, the joke's on me.
Carleton, R. L.
Baby, you can't get me down.
Daffan, T.
Bachelor and the bobby-soxer.
Meyer, J.
Bachianas brasileiras no. 5.
Villa-Lobos, H.
Baciagaloop makes love on da stoop.
Prima, L.
Bacio.
Pasero, P. Ho licenziato la camer-
iera.
Back in the good old days.
Canary, M. T.
Back to dear old Oklahoma.
Harris, G. E.
Bagatelle.
Ligtelijn, J. L.
Bagatells.
Bartos, J. Z. Malickosti.
Bagel and lox.
Brodsky, R.
Bagels in Mexico.
Suárez, S.
Bag-pipes on parade.
Von Tilzer, H. Earl Carroll's Vani-
ties.
Bailadores.
Bekes, R.
Bailando en la luna.
Read, G. Dancing on the moon.
Baile del tambah.
Munoz, R.
Baja California.
Bustillos, F.
Bal des mariniers.
Capronnier, M.
Bal du faubourg.
Roche, P.
Balboa bash.
Yaw, R.
Balinese dance.
Nevin, M.
Balla il boogie woogie.
Chiocchio, U.
Ballabili campagnoli.
Gorni, F.
Ballad for band.
Gould, M.
Ballade.
Vlag, H.
Ballards.
Sargent, F. W.
Ballerina.
Sigman, C.

Ballet.
Hollaender, V.
Balloons.
Fouts, M. Children's easy piano pieces.
Bamba de Vera Cruz.
Tucci, T.
Banana boat.
Miles, D.
Band played on.
Ward, C. B.
Bang, bang.
Davis, J. I'm gonna write myself a
lette.
Banjo picker.
Wright, N. L.
Banner song.
Tobin, L.
Banners of victory.
Barsotti, R.
Banzi, you-all.
Carleton, R. L.
Barbara Ann.
Moon, L. W.
Barbara Ann is skating.
Gray, T.
Barbary Ellen.
Niles, J. J., ed. & arr. The singing
campus.
Barcarolle.
Schwartz, H.
Trowbridge, L.
Barcarolle romantique.
Marinier, P.
Barchetta.
Nevin, E. W.
Barefoot boy with cheek.
Lippman, S.
Barfly.
Smith, W.
Barn dance.
Elliott, M.
Barnyard polka.
Glynn, B., arr.
Barnyard reel.
Daly, J.
Bartender's ball.
Baumgart, G. P.
Bassoon passages.
Kessler, C. S., ed. & comp.
Basta un po' di swing.
Panzuti, V.
Bat.
Strauss, J. Die fledermaus.
Battle array.
Johnson, A. H.
Be a blessing today.
Woods, J. S. How much I owe.
Be present, O merciful God.
Jones, W. B.
Be ready judgement day.
Reeves, W. L.
Be still and know.
Miller, M. C.
Be still, and know that I am God.
Bitgood, R.
Be strong and faithful.
Breydert, F. M. Estote fortes.
Be the good Lord willing.
Kresa, R.
Be Thou exalted, O God.
Demarest, C.
Be Thou my vision.
Pearson, G. A.
Be yourself.
Shelly, L.
Beachcomber.
Jackson, C.
Bear Creek hop.
Montgomery, M.
Bears in the woods.
Light, F. M.
Beatitudes.
Bush, J. M.
Glarum, L. S.
Beatrice (your lovely name).
Nevins, M.

Beau soir.
Debussy, C.
Beautiful Bay of Milwaukee.
Patti, S. T.
Beautiful Beckley.
Cole, L. P.
Beautiful blue Danube.
Strauss, J. Tales of the Vienna
woods.
Beautiful blue Hudson.
Broekman, D.
Beautiful California.
LaForge, E. L.
Beautiful girl.
De Rose, P. Earl Carroll Vanities.
Beautiful heaven.
Howorth, W. Cielito lindo.
Beautiful Killarney.
Canary, M. T. K.
Beauty for ashes.
Wilson, R. C.
Beauty of Jesus.
Runyan, W. M.
Beaver fight song.
Freeburg, D. S.
Because.
Rhodes, H. G.
Because He died on Calvary.
Evangel special sacred songs, no. 1.
Because I love you so.
Barnes, O. C.
Because I'm already in love.
Carleton, R. L.
Bedford drive.
Harding, B.
Bedstemor gaar amok.
Gyldmark, S.
Bee.
Schimmerling, H. A., arr. Sadla
muska.
Bee and the buttercup.
Eckhardt, F. G.
Beethoven.
Beethoven, L. van.
Beethoven overtures.
Beethoven, L. van.
Beethoven (simplified).
Beethoven, L. van.
Beggar's holiday.
Ellington, D.
Beggar's opera fantasy.
Wilson, D.
Beggars' polka.
Stanley, B. Dziaduwka polka.
Begin the beguine.
Porter, C. Jubilee.
Begräbnisgesang.
Brahms, J.
Behind my masquerade.
Hibbeler, R. O.
Behind the eight beat.
Slack, F.
Behold! I stand at the door.
Cain, N.
Behold the angel of the Lord.
Fichthorn, C. L.
Behold the dawn.
Weldy, G. W.
Behold the Lamb of God.
Grindy, R. M.
Behold what manner of love.
Nordman, C.
Belenciano soy.
Diaz y Oviedo, I.
Bell-man.
Belchamber, E. Two songs from
Herrick.
Bell witch.
Bryan, C. F.
Bella Ciquita.
Gilardini, R. Triste sera.
Bella donna.
Gulizia, M.
Belle Andalousie.
Travnicek, A.
Belle de Cadix.
Lopez, F.

Belle histoire.
 Martinet, H.
Belles of the Rio Grande.
 Bunn, A.
Bells.
 Sampson, G.
Bells across the meadows.
 Ketelby, A. W.
Bells of the mission.
 Robb, J. D. Pictures of New Mexico.
Beloved star.
 Tobin, L.
Belwin intermediate band method.
 Weber, F.
Benediction.
 Harsch, H.
Benediction manual.
 Tappert, H.
Benedictus es, Domine.
 Nagle, W. S.
Benjie's bubble.
 Goodman, B.
Berceuse.
 Järnefelt, A.
 Jonsson, J. Tre vis or.
Berenice.
 Händel, G. F.
Beside still waters.
 Marsh, C. H.
Beside the railroad.
 Connelly, R.
Beside you.
 Evans, R. My favorite brunette.
Best wishes to you.
 Rogers, C. E.
Best years in our lives.
 Herscher, L.
Best years of our lives.
 Barlow, H.
 Hart, P.
 Nicholls, H.
Betty Lou.
 Hurran, D.
Between ourselves.
 Gregg, H.
 Paulsen, R. E.
Beware, brother, beware.
 Moore, F.
Bicycle built for two.
 Dacre, H.
Bicycle riding.
 Fouts, M. Children's easy piano
 pieces.
Bicycle song.
 Blane, R.
Big Chief Wahoo.
 McConnell, M
Big moon.
 Warfel, M.
Big rock in the road.
 Rose, F. There's a big rock in the
 road.
Big teardrops are falling, all on account
 of you.
 Watchorn, A. B.
Big town gal.
 Mundlin, L.
Biguine à Bikini.
 Beauregard, A. La rumba à Doudou.
Bij den boer.
 Nieland, J. H. I. M.
Bikini.
 Leca, H.
Bill Hardey's Songs of the good old days.
 Robbins music corp., comp.
Billy.
 Castellani, L. Olemka.
Billy and me.
 Vene, H.
Bimkom haerez.
 Roskin, J, S., arr.
Bing Crosby's favorite hymns.
 Stickles, W., arr.
Bing Crosby's selection of sacred songs
 and hymns.
 Stickles, W., arr.
Bing Crosby's songs for young hearts.
 Van Heusen, J.

Birdies' petite nocturne.
 Day, R. E.
Birds and the bees.
 Herbert, V.
Birds will sing no more.
 Broekman, D.
Birth of the blues.
 Henderson, R.
Bisp Thomas' frihetssang.
 Nordqvist, G.
Bist du bei mir.
 Bach, J. S.
Bitter sweet.
 Coward, N.
Black and the gold.
 Prater, E.
Black but sweet.
 Houdini, W.
Black flowers.
 Ortiz, C. A. Flores negras.
Black hawk waltz.
 Walsh, M. E.
Black Hills of South Dakota.
 Kuhn, R, S.
Black man's return.
 Dickinson, D.
Black mood.
 Gilliam, L. A.
Black or brown or slightly tan.
 Solomon, N.
Blake's cradle song.
 Roberton, H. S.
Blanca luz.
 Domínguez, E.
Blanca Rosa.
 Sentis, J.
Blatt der Frühlingsweide.
 Koch, S. v. Morgenländische
 liebeslieder.
Blaze of glory.
 Holzmann, A.
Blaze of noon.
 Deutsch, A.
Bless the bride.
 Ellis, V.
 Herbert, V. The red mill.
Bless you for being an angel.
 Baker, D.
Bless your little heart.
 Starcher, B.
Blessed art Thou, O Lord.
 Means, C.
Blessed quietness.
 Marshall, W, S.
Blessed Virgin's expostulation.
 Purcell, H.
Blest be the tie that binds.
 Nageli, H. G.
Bloeiende ranken.
 Duuren, H. J. van.
Blomsterflickan.
 Pergament, M. Tre små sånger.
Bloom in my garden of memories.
 Tobin, L.
Blotti sur ton épaule.
 Ferrari, L.
Blow the man down.
 Mossman, T., arr.
Blue as the night.
 Brobst, H.
Blue, blue eyes.
 Daniels, W.
Blue charm.
 Hayes, H.
Blue Danube.
 Strauss, J.
Blue Hawaiian moon.
 Peterson, J. E.
Blue Lou.
 Mills, I.
Blue Monday.
 Arthur, W.
Blue moon.
 Pendleton, E.
Blue Mountain ballads.
 Bowles, P.
Blue ranger.
 Gindhart, T.

Blue room.
 Rodgers, R. The girl friend.
Blue skies.
 Berlin, I.
 Berlin, I. Accordion transcriptions.
Blue sorrow blues.
 Görling, U.
Bluebonnets.
 Bailey, A. S.
Blueprint for two.
 Casey, T.
Blues at high noon.
 Mosley, S.
Blues for clarinet.
 Hamilton, J.
Blues in my music room.
 Hamilton, J.
Blues of the record man.
 Malvin, A.
Blumenstück.
 Schumann, R. A. Arabesque.
Boadicea.
 Taylor, C.
Boat song.
 Pierne, G. En barque.
Boatman and the maiden.
 Rathaus, K.
Bobby Gregory and his Ramblin' Hobo's
 Album of hobo songs.
 Gregory, B.
Bobby sox blues.
 Cotton, D. W.
 Williams, W. D.
Bobby sox suite.
 Walters, H. L,
Boga rodzica najświetsza panno.
 Cieszykowski, L. A.
Bohème.
 Puccini, G.
Bohemian song.
 Weinberger, J. Three Bohemian pieces.
Bohuslänska valsen.
 Hellström, D.
Boiteux mary de Vénus.
 Le Grand, R.
Bombardier's return.
 Hofstad, M.
Bombo.
 Silvers, L.
Bongo.
 Vazquez, E.
Bonnie lassie.
 Joyce, J. A wee braw lassie.
Bonsoir, mon amour.
 Molière, R. de.
Boogie beat Pete.
 Brobst, H.
Boogie blues.
 Biondi, R.
Boogie woogie.
 Ceglie-Olivieri, Di.
Boogie-woogie etude.
 Stone, G.
Boogie-woogie mexicano.
 Stone, G.
Boogie-woogie na Favela.
 Brean, D. The bumble boogie samba.
Boogie woogie nocturne.
 Powers, M.
Boogie-woogie partout.
 Tabet, G.
Boogie woogie step-by-step.
 Jacobs, M., arr.
Book of bells.
 Bentley, B. B.
Bora Bora.
 Lejay, A.
Born to be blue.
 Torme, M. H.
Borron de niebla.
 Granata, S.
Bortoli's accordion method.
 Bortoli, F.
Bosco and his doghouse.
 Stegmeyer, W.
Boulevard.
 Bloch, P. G.
Bounce me brother with a solid four.
 Raye, D.

Bouquet of Croatian folk songs.
 Cernkovich, R.
Bouquet of music.
 Schubert, F. P. Schubert.
Bourrée de Chapdes Beaufort.
 Vuillermoz, E.
Bow low, elder.
 Decker, H. A., arr.
Bow Tie Jim.
 Morgan, R.
Bow-wow and meow.
 Robinson, A. Three very easy piano
 pieces.
Boy like you.
 Weill, K. Street scene.
Boy that is not coming back.
 Hall, A. R.
Boy, what a girl.
 Ramirez, R.
Boys from Syracuse.
 Rodgers, R.
Boys will be home for Xmas.
 Halloway, D.
Bozzetti montani.
 Culotta, I.
Brahms at the piano.
 Brahms, J.
Brahms' Lullaby.
 Brahms, J.
Brahms' Third symphony.
 Brahms, J. Symphony, no. 3, F major.
Branded with love.
 Stuart, E. P.
Braniboři v Cechách.
 Smetana, B.
Brass bass method (tuba-sousaphone).
 Eidson, A. B.
Brass on parade.
 Jones, H. S.
Bravo toro.
 Travnicek, A. Swing huit.
Brazilian bolero.
 Coots, J. F.
Bread of God.
 Cain, N.
Break, break, break.
 Ashe, J. H.
Break, new-born year.
 De Lamarter, E.
Break of day.
 May, H.
Break sheets for piano.
 Whitford, R. H.
Break studies for piano.
 Christensen, A. W.
Break the news.
 Norlin, L. B.
Break with the tie.
 Tovey, H. G.
Breath of heather.
 Klein, J.
Breathe on me, breath of God.
 Richards, M. R.
Breton berceuse.
 Rapley, F.
Brevet du skrev om kärlek.
 Gyllenhammar, U. M.
Bridal song.
 Cieszykowski, L. A. Boga rodzica
 najświetsza panno.
Bridge by Yosemite Falls.
 McMillen, H.
Bridges.
 Surdam, T. J.
Brigadoon.
 Loewe, F.
Bright is the ring of words.
 O'Hara, G.
Bright tomorrow.
 Satterfield, T.
Bright was the day.
 Coward, N. Pacific 1860.
Bring back my Bonnie.
 Fuller, H. J.
Bring me nearer heaven.
 Williams, D. W.
Bring the money in.
 Bruce, R.

Broken hearted one you left alone.
 Creasy, J. M.
Broken promise means a broken heart.
 Bohn, D.
Broken vow will mean a broken heart.
 Carson, J.
Broken vows.
 Daffan, T.
Broodle-oo, broodle-oo.
 Fogarty, A.
Brook.
 Reistrup, J.
Brooklyn breeze.
 Clayton, B.
Brooklyn bridge.
 Styne, J. It happened in Brooklyn.
Brother Will, Brother John.
 Sacco, J. C.
Brouillard.
 Durand, P.
Brown Danube.
 Borne, H. Carnegie Hall.
Brownies' welcome.
 Parr, P.
Brumes.
 Chardon, J.
Brunilde.
 Ciliberti, A.
Brunon Kryger, king of the polkas, dance
 album.
 Kryger, B.
Brurleik fra Lesja.
 Beck, T. L. Dansar fra Gudbrands-
 dal.
Bubble gum.
 Fouts, M. Children's easy piano
 pieces.
 Gross, W.
Bubble gum song.
 Hoefle, C.
Bubble song.
 Shaw, M.
Buenos Aires.
 Bermudez, L. E.
Buffalo Bill.
 Frangkiser, C.
Bugler.
 Goldman, E. F.
Bugler and the drummer.
 Powers, M.
Built upon the Rock.
 Thorne, W. M.
Buisson ... un oiseau.
 Israel, M.
Bulerias.
 Sentis, J.
Bum bum blues.
 Rouse, E. T.
Bumble bee boogie.
 Rimskii-Korsakov, N. A. The
 flight of the bumble bee.
Bumble boogie samba.
 Brean, D.
Bunte Blätter.
 Schumann, R. A.
Buona notte, angelo mio.
 Panzuti, V.
Burgmüller-Schaum for piano.
 Burgmüller.
Burning love.
 Manzano, W. Fervor.
Bursting bubbles.
 Jones, A. A.
Busybody.
 Foster, C.
But no nickel.
 Carr, L.
Butterflies.
 McNeil, J. C.
Butterfly.
 Dunhill, T. F. Tommy Perkins.
Butterfly study.
 Chopin, F. F. Etude in E major.
Buying a home.
 Slater, W. W.
By faith.
 Jackson, L. M.

By grace, thru faith, plus nothing.
 Webb, W. A.
By his stripes ye are healed.
 Carlson, F. H.
By the Kea-la Ke-kua Bay.
 Colonna, D. R.
By the light of the silvery moon.
 Edwards, G.
By the Rio Chanchamayo.
 Suspiros del Chanchamayo.
By the river.
 Dunhill, T. F.
By the sea.
 Schubert, F. P. Lamer.
By the shores of Monterey.
 Marchese, V.
By the singin' river.
 Siegel, I. U. A.
By the sundial.
 Seymour, J. L. Six melodic pieces.
By the waters of Babylon.
 Dvořák, A.
By the wigwam.
 Scher, W.
Byt, byt, byt.
 Riis, A. Naar Katten er ude.
C. A. R. sonance.
 Johnson, C. L. arr.
Ca' vous voyez, mademoiselle.
 Hartusch, M. Vive la tour Eiffel.
Caballo y la montura.
 Saborit.
Cabaña.
 Hively, W. Habana suite.
Cabin.
 Bowles, P. Blue Mountain ballads.
Cabin boy call.
 James, W. L.
Cadence.
 Beethoven, L. van.
Cadenza.
 Carpi, G.
Cafetín.
 Galvan, A. L.
Cailliet clarinet studies.
 Cailliet, L.
Cajita de música.
 Menzel, A.
Calandria.
 Castillo, N. El chichihua.
Calcutta.
 Wayne, B.
Caldonia.
 Moore, F.
 Moore, F. No leave, no love.
Calendar girl.
 McHugh, J. F.
Calgary blues.
 Kenney, J.
California.
 A'Dair, J. A hymn to California.
 Robinson, E.
California is my home.
 Walthuis, F. La hacienda California.
California or bust.
 Robinson, E. California.
California sings.
 Van Dyke, G. M. Van Dyke's
 songfolio.
Caligaverunt oculi mei.
 Haydn, M. So dim with tears.
Calinda.
 Delius, F. Koanga.
Call me Mister.
 Rome, H. J.
Call me not hence, O Lord.
 Gage, A. F.
Call of freedom.
 Mitchell, H. E.
Calling.
 Teal, J.
Camino a Mexico.
 Mier, P. La mosca.
Camp Pioneer.
 Haeseler, W.
Campaign specials.
 Davis, J. C., comp.
Camping out.
 Baumer, C.

Camptown races.
  Foster, S. C.
Campus chimes.
  Cailliet, L.
Can I ever forget.
  Van Tyle, R.
Can it be true.
  Kelly, F.
Can you hear the call of the Saviour.
  Elliot, J. An evangel in song.
Can you look me in the eyes.
  McMichael, J.
Canaan. see title entry in composer list.
Canadian battle march.
  Janssens, H.
Canari.
  Trąvnicek, A. Josélito.
Canción del viento.
  Esparza Oteo, A.
Canción por tu regreso.
  Fernández Porta, M.
Canciones clasicas.
  Obradors, F. J.
Canciones clasicas españolas.
  Obradors, F. J.
Candide.
  Castelnuovo-Tedesco.
Candlelight mood.
  Gilmore, T. S. Four new songs.
Candy man.
  Segal, L.
Canon.
  Mozart, J. C. W. A. Two pieces.
Can't you dance the polka.
  Rowley, A.
Canta, canta.
  Hernandes, R.
Cantilena.
  Arnaud, W.
Cantilène jalouse.
  Weinberger, J.
Canto al amor.
  Elizondo, R.
Canto della solitudine.
  Olivieri, Dino. Tutto il mondo canta
    Tornerai.
Canto triste.
  Piubeni, V. Mi place improvvisar.
Cantos espirituales.
  Treat, J. W., ed.
Canzona.
  Gideon, M.
Canzone a Maria.
  Rusconi, E. Nostalgia di Napoli.
Canzonetta.
  Herbert, V.
Capriccioso.
  Meijlink, C. J.
Caprice espagnol.
  Sanders, G. H. Scheherazada suite.
Capriol suite.
  Heseltine, P.
Captive.
  McKay, F. H.
Caravan of songs.
  Casey, C., comp.
Careless.
  Jurgens, D.
Caresse.
  Gournay, R. de.
Caressed by a memory.
  Gilmore, T. S. Four new songs.
Caribbean serenade.
  Josefovits, T.
Carillon.
  Roberts, M. J.
Carillon du soir.
  Schwab, A.
Carl Fischer note-speller.
  Holt, H.
Carmen.
  Bizet, G.
Carmen Ludi Qualicani.
  Knight, G. H.
Carnaval.
  Warren, H. Carnival.

Carnaval héroique.
  Lazarus, D. Rythmes de guerre.
Carnegie Hall.
  Borne, H.
  D'Artega, A.
  Moore, W.
  Morros, B., arr.
  Stone, G.
  Warrington, J.
Carnegie Hall dance medley.
  Warrington, J. Carnegie Hall.
Carnival.
  Raezer, C. M.
  Warren, H.
Carnival capers.
  Botsford, T.
Carnival echoes.
  O'Donnell, W.
Carnival in Costa Rica.
  Lecuona Y Casado, E.
Carnival of Venice.
  Heney, J. J.
Carnival procession.
  Lecuona Y Casado, E. Danzas
    afro-cubanas.
Carol from Poland.
  My First Christmas songs.
Carol in captivity.
  Fraser, D.
Carol of the annunciation.
  Burgess, E.
Carolettes.
  Johnson, V. G., arr.
Carolina calling.
  Walker, L.
Carolina Caroline.
  Royall, C. T.
Carousal.
  Jacobson, M.
Carpenter's Son.
  Shure, R. D.
Carretera de Estepona.
  Bowles, P.
Carrion crow.
  Niles, J. J., ed. & arr. The
    singing campus.
Carry me back to old Virginny.
  Bland, J. A.
Carry on.
  Rohler, R. G.
Carry you through.
  Gilmore, C.
Casey at the bat.
  Lenz, J. N.
  Montgomery, L. S.
Casinorevyn, 1943.
  Byhmar, S.
Cassandra.
  Glaser, F.
Cast your burden on the Lord.
  Elliot, J. An evangel in song.
Castanets and lace.
  Liberman, M.
Catkins.
  Pendleton, E.
Catskills polka.
  Williams, E. S. Little classics for
    cornet or trumpet.
Caught in the wind.
  Klemm, G.
Cavalier noir.
  Lopez, F.
Cavalleria rusticana.
  Mascagni, P.
Ce soir cherie.
  Wilhite, M.
Ceaseless prayer.
  Tovey, H. G.
Celebrity hop.
  Clayton, B.
Celestial echoes.
  Rovenger, L. W., arr.
Cellophane heart.
  Gilmore, T. S. Four new songs.
Celos.
  Vega, C.

Cent vierges.
  Lecocq, C.
Centennial summer.
  May, H. Spring song.
Cerco la mia casetta.
  Gulizia, M. Bella donna.
Cerco la min piccola casetta.
  Fucilli, P.
Ceremonial march.
  Gilbert, H. M.
Certova stena.
  Smetana, B.
Ceskych tancu c. 7.
  Sevcik, O.
C'est le dernier rendez-vous.
  Scala, T.
C'est le peuple de Paris.
  Pavard, A.
C'est pas tous les jours dimanche.
  Roche, P. L. A. J.
C'est toi le pays de mes rêves.
  Dumas, R.
C'est un soir.
  Guglielmi, L. Le destin s' amuse.
Chagrin près d'une fontaine.
  Gallois-Montbrun, R. Les rêves
    de Janceline.
Challenge of U. C. L. A.
  Judell, M. F.
Champu de cariño.
  Delgado, P.
Chanson à manger.
  Lemaire, C.
Chanson à trois temps.
Chanson d'amour.
  Gyldmark, S. Elly Petersen.
  Terry, F.
Chanson de marin.
  Simon, L. M.
Chanson de Venise.
  Caffot, S. V. J. Les aventures de
    Casanova.
Chanson des enfants.
  Kosma, J.
Chanson du soleil.
  Scotto, V. B.
Chanson du vent sous la porte.
  Marinier, P.
Chanson gitane.
  Yvain, M.
Chansons cambodgiennes.
  Lesur, D.
Chansons pour Miroka.
  Weisshaus, I.
Chant des F.F.I.
  Robert, C.
Chant des jeunes mineurs de France.
  Champagne, P.
Chant of the Amazon.
  Broekman, D.
Chant of the Brahmans.
  Delibes, L. Lakme.
Chante, chante, mon coeur.
  Caffot, S. V. J.
Chanteur inconnu.
  Marcuse, A.
Chaparrita cuerpo de uva.
  Esperon, M. No basta ser charro.
Chapel in my heart.
  Maxwell, R.
Characters from Hans Christian
    Andersen.
  Rogers, B.
Charlene.
  Watson, O. M.
Charley, my boy.
  Fiorito, T.
Charlot's revue.
  Braham, P.
Charmingly.
  Carleton, R. L.
Charoumenos Aletes.
  Mallides, G. N.
Chase.
  Spence, A. L., arr.
Chasene waltz.
  Ivanovici, J.
Chasing the beat.
  Grant, P.

163

Chatita querida.
  Pérez Leyva, N.
Chattering monkeys.
  Robinson, A.
Cheeriette.
  Ahlstrand, D.
Cheerio.
  White, H. R.
Chemin d'autrefois.
  Marinier, P.
Chemung rondino.
  Williams, E. S. Little classics
    for cornet or trumpet.
Chenango schottisch.
  Williams, E. S. Little classics for
    cornet or trumpet.
Cheri.
  Bensenberg, N.
Chérie, c'est à toi que ja rêve.
  Molière, R. de.
Cherry blossoms.
  Wansborough, H.
Cherubim song.
  Bordeau, C.
  Bortniansky, D. S.
Chester.
  Billings, W. Compositions.
Chestnuts.
  Long, N. H.
Chew chaw chaw.
  Koslof, T.
Chi-baba, chi-baba.
  Livingston, J.
Chiapanecas.
  Campo, M. V. de.
Chibo que rompe tambo.
  Simons, M.
Chicago Tribune march.
  Chambers, W. P.
Chichihua.
  Castillo, N.
Childhood scenes.
  Volpe, H.
Children of the Heavenly Father.
  Riegger, W.
Children of the King.
  Wilson, I. B.
Children, pray this love to cherish.
  Spohr, L.
Children's dances.
  Kodály, Z. Gyermektancok.
Children's day helper. See title entry
  in composer list.
Children's paradise.
  Nieland, H. J. J. Het kinder paradijs.
Children's very first piano pieces.
  Spivak, S.
Children's Waldteufel.
  Waldteufel, É.
Child's prayer.
  Miller, E. H.
Child's prayer to the shepherd.
  France, W. E.
Chile beans.
  Frosini, P.
Chimes of Zion.
  Mynatt, A.
Chiming bells.
  McDermott, A.
China clipper.
  Schaum, J. W.
Chinese carillon.
  Rózsa, M. Kaleidoscope.
Chiomadoro.
  Cioffi, G.
Chiu, chiu.
  Molinare, N.
Chivalry.
  Goodchild, A.
Chocio.
  Padula, J. L. Nueve de Julio.
  Villoldo, A. G.
Chocolate sundae on a Saturday night.
  Frisch, A.
Chola andina.
  Valderrama, V.
Choo choo ch'boogie.
  Gabler, M.
Chopin-Schaum.
  Chopin, F. F.

Chopin's polonaise.
  Chopin, F. F. Polonaise.
Choral prelude on Dundee.
  Curry, W. L.
Chorale.
  Trowbridge, L.
Chorale prelude.
  Parrish, C.
Chorale prelude on the Welsh hymn
  tune Llansanan.
  Parrish, C.
Chôro torturado.
  Guarnieri, C.
Chorus, gentlemen.
  Lohr, H.
Chris crosses.
  Boland, C. A.
Christ born in Bethlehem.
  Woods, J. S.
Christ is all.
  Morris, K.
Christ is more to me than ever.
  Weigle, C. F. Sing a new song.
Christ is real.
  Crockett, A. B. Crockett's
    spirituals.
Christ is risen to-day.
  Davis, K. K.
Christ our Passover.
  McIlwraith, I.
Christ our Redeemer.
  Osborn, I. C.
Christ the Lord is risen today.
  Drummond-Wolff, S.
  Stairs, L. E.
Christ, the Redeemer.
  Sandoval, M.
Christ the way.
  Starr, K. G. C.
Christ walks into the hills.
  Hohmann, W. H.
Christ, whose glory fills the skies.
  Cain, N.
Christ will be your friend.
  Evangel special sacred songs, no. 1.
Christian, in a world below.
  Elliot, J. An evangel in songs.
Christian soldiers.
  Cumming, J. W. W.
Christian, the morn breaks sweetly
  o'er thee.
  Shelley, H. R.
Christmas.
  Goers, M. J.
Christmas angels.
  Sargent, L. L.
Christmas bells their anthems ringing.
  Boss, B. D.
Christmas Child.
  Peloquin, C. A.
Christmas chimes.
  Bernard, P. J.
  Santos, P.
Christmas eve.
  Dunhill, T. F.
  Jacobsen, S.
Christmas island.
  Moraine, L.
Christmas love.
  Pinterally, A.
Christmas medley.
  Tannehill, M, B.
Christmas time's the time for love.
  Evis, F.
Chromatico.
  Trowbridge, L.
Chubasco.
  Rodriguez, J.
Church by the side of the road.
  Thomas, R.
Church's one foundation.
  Hollis, C., pseud.

Niles, J. J., ed. & arr. The singing
  campus.
Ciacona in E minor.
  Buxtehude, D.
Ciaconna e fuga.
  Nieland, J. H. I. M.
Cielito lindo.
  Howorth, W.
Cielito mio.
  Sentis, J. Coqueta.
Ciemnym borem nad wieczorem.
  Malec, A.
Cigareetes, whusky and wild, wild women.
  Spencer, T.
Cigarette girl.
  Roberts, A.
Cigarette in Europe.
  Siegel, P.
Cinco novias.
  Jiménez López, R.
Cinderella.
  Prokof'ev, S. S. Ten pieces.
Cinq chansons de Bilitis.
  Le Grand, R.
Cinq divertissements.
  Damais, É.
Cinquante-nuit canons.
  Chailley, J., ed.
Cinque liriche romantiche.
  Davico, V.
Circonstances attenuantes.
  Parys, G. van.
Circus horse.
  Obenchain, V. P.
Ciribiribin.
  Ferraro, J., arr.
Citizen saint.
  Orlob, H.
City.
  Wood, H. London cameos.
Claddagh ring.
  Colahan, A.
Clarinets in love.
  Langer, D. Zamilované klarinety.
Classic songs.
  Ward, A. E., arr.
Classics in Key-Kolor.
  Mason, M. B., comp. & arr.
Classroom method for the fife.
  Moore, E. C.
Clavo saca otro clavo.
  Vega, C.
Clear the track.
  MacFayden, J. H.
  MacInnis, M. D.
  Zinsser, W. K.
Climbing hills.
  Furney, A. J.
Climbing up our apple tree.
  Dittenhaver, S. L. Four piano
    compositions.
Cling a little closer.
  Kent, E.
Cloches des bois.
  Nedbal, O.
Clock strikes at midnight.
  Melecci, A.
Close dem pretty eyes.
  Ashe, J.
Close the door, Dora!
  Gaskill, C.
Close thine eyes.
  Rees-Davies, L.
Closer walk with Jesus.
  Elliot, J. An evangel in song.
Clothes-pin soldiers.
  Hopkins, H. P.
Clouds.
  Demuth, N.
Clouds rained trouble down.
  Cargill, I.
Clown.
  Hovemann, C.
Clownerie.
  Berg, C. J. van den.
Coach and four.
  Livingston, J. H. Monsieur Beaucaire.

164

Cocinero.
  Mustelier, A.
Cockney capers.
  Crantock, P.
Coeur est un oiseau qui chante.
  Lejay, A.
Coeur m'attend.
  Neuburger, J. B.
Cogiendo agua.
  Díaz, J.
Coin tout bleu.
  Monnot, M. Montmartre sur Seine.
Collect for St. George.
  Harris, W. H.
Collection de chants choisis.
  Villatte, J. L., comp.
Collection of California Polytechnic
  College school songs.
  Davidson, H. P.
Collection of Polish dances.
  Przybylski, F., arr.
Colleen, my own.
  Staab, H. B.
College songs.
  Stickles, W., arr.
Colloque sentimental.
  Weinberger, J.
Colorado's calling.
  Cooper, W. B.
Come back to my lonely heart.
  Tillman, F.
Come back to Sorrento.
  Curtis, E. de.
  Rugolo, P.
Come, Holy Spirit.
  Thorne, W. M.
Come in, Mister Santa.
  Carleton, R. L.
Come in out of the rain.
  Sigman, C.
Come, let us walk together in the Lord.
  Hatcher, C. E.
Come now, ye shepherds.
  Elmore, R.
Come on and kiss me.
  Lee, B.
Come on, boys, it's everywhere now.
  Lodree, E. J.
Come, sing and dance.
  Humperdinck, E.
Come to me, bend to me.
  Loewe, F. Brigadoon.
Come to me, lonesome baby.
  McCaugherty, I. E.
Come to Utah.
  Sheffield, C.
Come, ye that weep.
  Fauré, J., B. O salutaris hostia.
Comin' thro' the Rye.
  Murray, L.
  Jacobs, M., arr. Boogie woogie step-
    by-step.
Coming home.
  Oliver, H.
Comme autrefois.
  Fillastre, G. de.
Commit thy way unto the Lord.
  Elliot, J. An evangel in song.
Commit thy ways to Jesus.
  Bach, J. S.
Communion service.
  Purvis, R.
Como visten las mujeres.
  Casamor, E.
Comparsa.
  Lecuona y Casado, E.
  Lecuona y Casado, E. Danzas afro-
    cubanas.
Compasión.
  Angel, M.
Compendio.
  Gutiérrez, J.
Complainte du petit bossu.
  Gallois-Montbrun, R. Les rêves de
    Janceline.
Complainte pour Noël.
  Mazellier, J.

Complete method of slide-trombone.
  Lafosse, A. Méthode complete de
    trombone à coulisse.
Composing with the composers.
  Melecci, A.
Compositions.
  Billings, W.
Compréndeme.
  Alma, M.
Con el alma en los labios.
  Paz, R. de.
Con la bella in calessino.
  Concina, C. Don Pasquà.
Con todo mi corazon.
  Condercuri, A.
Concert miniatures for orchestra.
  Delamater, E., arr.
Concert of love.
  Warnick, B.
Concert piece.
  Koutzen, B.
Concert piece on Forest green.
  Diggle, R.
Concert pieces for guitar.
  Volpe, H. Harry Volpe's Concert
    pieces for guitar.
Concert pour orchestre à cordes.
  Sautereau, C. Concerto, string
    orchestra.
Concert rondo.
  Dallin, L.
Concert waltz.
  Kreopfl, W. J.
Concerto en ut majeur.
  Djabadary, H. Concerto, violoncello, no. 1.
Concerto for bassoon and orchestra.
  Mozart, J. C. W. A. Concerto, bassoon.
Concerto for clarinet and orchestra.
  Mozart, J. C. W. A. Concerto, clarinet,
    K. 622.
Concerto for clarinet, Bb major.
  Haydn, J.
Concerto, violoncello.
Concerto for harp and orchestra.
  Berezowsky, N. T. Concerto, harp.
Concerto, G minore.
  Vivaldi, A.
Concerto giocoso.
  Martinon, J., F. E.
Concerto heroïque.
  Hubeau, J.
Concerto in D major.
  Bach, J. C. Concerto, piano.
Concerto in do maggiore.
  Vivaldi, A. Concerto, orchestra.
Concerto in jazz.
  Phillips, D.
Concerto-jazz.
  Deltour, E.
Concerto miniature.
  Klauss, N.
Concerto no. 1, en ut.
  Rivier, J. F. A. F. Concerto, piano,
    no. 1.
Concerto no. 1 in Bb major.
  Händel, G. F. Concerto, oboe, no. 1.
Concerto no. 2.
  Prokof'ev, S. S. Concerto, violin, no. 2.
Concerto no. 2 in Bb major.
  Händel, G. F. Concerto, oboe, no. 2.
Concerto no. 2, pour violoncelle et
  orchestre.
  Milhaud, D. Concerto, violoncello,
    no. 2.
Concerto no. 3 in G minor.
  Händel, G. F. Concerto, oboe, no. 3.
Concertone.
  Williams, E. S. Little classics for
    cornet or trumpet.
Conchitina.
  D'Angelo, L.
Concours d'Annick.
  Lepitre, A., C.
Confidences d'amour.
  Chauvet, R.
Confidences d'une vieille horloge.
  Gallois-Montbrun, R. Les rêves de

Janceline.
Confused.
  Davis, J.
Conga de los novios.
  Gallipoli, A. A.
Connecticut Yankee.
  Rodgers, R.
Connie.
  Minnella, L.
Conscience.
  Gonzalez, L. Maldición.
Consecrate me Lord.
  Yeazel, C. Gospel songs.
Consecration.
  Reuter, A. M.
Console-moi.
  Ghestem, G.
Constellation.
  Scala, T.
Contrition.
  Yost, G.
Conversation on Park Avenue.
  Smith, W.
Cooks in Trinidad.
  Houdini, W.
Coordinated piano method.
  Philipp, I.
Copacabana.
  Coslow, S.
Coqueta.
  Sentis, J.
Coquette.
  Heywood, E.
  Scher, W.
Coraline.
  Caffot, S. V. J. Les aventures de
    Casanova.
Corazón mexicano!
  Los Cuates Castilla (Musicians)
Corbleur, eh, Marion!
  Charette, V., arr.
Corn-tassel dance.
Cornet method.
  Eidson, A. B.
Cornish carnival.
  Trew, C. A.
Coronado.
  Arthur, W.
Corpse came C.O.D.
  Fisher, D.
Corrido veracruzano.
  Vista, F. A.
Cosa ai milioni.
  Consiglio, M. Gran premio.
Cortège.
  Glière, R. M.
Cosaques du Don.
  Spotto, V. B.,
Cose, cose, cose.
  Castro, A.
Cose da nulla.
  Chiocchio, U. Balla il boogie woogie.
Cosmic serenade.
  Hunter, B.
Cossack's song.
  Chaikovskiĭ, P. I.
Cottage for rent.
  Leonard, G.
Cotton eyed Joe.
  Duncan, T.
  McEnery, D.
Coucou.
  Nieland, J. H. I. M.
Could it be I love you.
  Rogers, J.
Couli-couri.
  Dubarbie, J.
Countess Maritza.
  Kálmán, I.
Counting sheep.
  Davies, H. P. The Shephard show.
Country gardens.
  Haywood, E.
Country style.
  Van Heusen, J. Welcome stranger.

Courante.
Gallois Montbrun, R. Pages de
sonatine.
Courtly scene.
Boykin, H.
Coventry carol.
Ross, H.
Covered wagon lullaby.
King, F.
Cowboy dad.
DeKnight, J.
Cowboy song.
Fouts, M. Children's easy piano
pieces.
Cowboy songs.
Minchella, E., comp. Minchella's
accordion favorites.
Cowboy's last goodbye.
Waverly, J.
Což neřekl Ti zrak muj tisíckrát.
Malát, J.
Cradle song.
Duffy, J. J.
Marsh, C. H.
Roberton, H. S.
Craven county blues.
Rouse, E. T.
Crazy 'cause I love you.
Cooley, D. C.
Crazy, lazy and in love.
Carleton, R. L.
Cream-cake-Charlie.
Dahlquist, L. E.
Creation.
Haydn, J. The heavens are telling.
Crepuscule.
Beydts, L.
Engelen, F.
Criolla linda.
Gorrese, V.
Croatian serenade.
Harley, F., arr.
Crockett's spirituals.
Crockett, A. B.
Crocodile.
Trowbridge, L. In meadow and forest.
Cronies.
Bown, P. B.
Cross my heart.
Van Heusen, J.
Cross of faith.
Schubert, F. P.
Cross triumphant.
Wilson, I. B.
Crossing the plains.
Freed, I.
Crossing the Rhineland.
Work, H. C.
Crown for cross.
Woods, J. S.
Crucifix by the sea.
Lourie, A.
Cry baby.
La Llorona.
Crying.
Chernis, J.
Čtortý smyčcový kvartet.
Kvapil, J. Quartet, strings, no. 4.
Čtyři impromptus.
Petrželka, V.
Cua cua.
Guerra, J.
Cuando estoy junto a tí.
Pafumy, J.
Cuando lloran los valientes.
Jesús Morales, J. de.
Lavista, R.
Cuba, Havannah, Hawaii, Tahiti och
Florida.
Dahlquist, L. E.
Cuba y Méjico.
Fontanals, F.
Cuban carnival.
Shield, L.
Cuban concerto.
Savino, D.

Cuban processional.
Lecuona y Casado, E. La comparsa.
Cuckoo and the bull frog.
Wansborough, H.
Cuckoo-cheena.
Sanders, A. Louisiana lady.
Cuento oriental.
Dalmar, Alvaro.
Cuerudo.
Castillo, N.
Cumparsita.
Rodríguez, G. H.
Cuore é stanco di sognare.
Olivieri, D. Tutto il mondo canta
Tornerai.
Cuore viaggiatore.
Simi, G.
Cupid is love.
Carleton, R. L.
Cupid on a shelf.
Clyde, T.
Curtains of sorrow.
Allen, R.
Cute little dimples.
Carleton, R. L.
Cuttin' capers on the campus.
Ingraham, R.
Cymbal Simon.
Franks, A.
Cyn cau llygaid.
Rees-Davies, I. Close thine eyes.
Czardas II.
Erhardt, S.
Czecho-Slovakian dance song.
Scholin, C. A.
Czerny-Schaum.
Czerny, C.
Czerwone maki na Monte Cassino.
Schütz, A. Papaveri di Montecassino.
Czy pamiętasz moja miła.
Malec, A.
D'ombre red et soleil.
Beydts, Louis.
Dacent Irish boy.
Haywood, E.
Daddy Longlegs.
Trowbridge, L. In meadow and
forest.
Daddy's little pin-up girl.
Denby, J.
Dag kjem aldri at eg deg glóymer.
Egge, K.
Dagje buiten.
Nieland, J. H. I. M.
Dainty buttercup.
Thomas, J. J.
Dainty toes.
Besthoff, M.
Dame à la licorne.
Baudrier, Y. M.
Dan-Dan-Dannville High.
Warren, H. Summer holiday.
Dan, the old grinder man.
Echevarria, E. El amolador.
Dan, the piccolo man.
Munn, W. O.
Dance.
Menasce, J. de. Hebrew melodies.
Dance for two.
Woodford, G. R.
Dance from Golden age.
Shostakovich, D. C.
Dance in the cottage.
Humperdinck, E.
Dance lightly.
Raezer, C. M.
Dance of the gnomes.
Woodbridge, J.
Dance of the paper dolls.
Schuster, I.
Travis, B.
Dance of the princesses.
Stravinski, I. F.
Dance of the puppets.
Siegel, A. F.
Dance theme and variations.
Green, R.
Dances from Gudbrandsdal.
Beck, T. L. Dansar fra Gudbrandsdal.

Dancing and dreaming.
Bartlett, F.
Dancing Dolores.
Besthoff, M.
Dancing elf.
Thomas, J. J.
Dancing in the dark.
Schwartz, A.
Stone, G.
Dancing on the moon.
Read, G.
Dancing tambourine.
Polla, W. C.
Dancing to the beat of my heart.
Mann, F. C.
Dang! That gal o' mine.
Joyce, J.
Daniël.
Miller, J.
Danmark.
Börding, A. H.
Dans la vie faut du cran.
Guglielmi, L. Ploum ploum tra la la.
Dans le ciel de tes yeux.
Darrys, R.
Dansar fra Gudbrandsdal.
Beck, T. L.
Danse no. 1.
Renault, A.
Danse no. 2.
Renault, A.
Danses de Jacarémirim.
Milhaud, D.
Dansk Te Deum.
Jeppesen, K.
Dansons encore.
Scala, T.
Danube (from a plane).
Spialek, H.
Danube waves.
Glynn, B., arr.
Ivanovici, J.
Danzas afro-cubanas.
Lecuona y Casado, E. Danzas afro-
cubanas.
Dare to let you know.
Bowman, W. L.
Daring.
Atkinson, A. B.
Dark eyes.
Jacobs, M., arr. Boogie woogie
step-by-step.
Rosemont, W. L., arr. Two guitars.
Salami, A.
Dark forest.
Harrison, J.
Dark river.
McCutcheon, V. M.
Darlin', now I know the reason why.
Davis, S.
Darling I love you.
Browne, L. B.
Walter, S.
Darling, let's go to Sonoma.
Passer, R.
Darling little girl.
Tobin, L.
Darling little Irishman.
Carleton, R. L.
Darling mother.
Richard Bros.
Darling mother of mine.
Franke, G. H.
Darling, my heart is calling you.
Zahoratos, G. T.
Darling Nell.
Tobin, L.
Darling Nellie Grey.
Hanby, B. R.
Darling song.
Gibson, A.
Darling, what shall I do?
Kennedy, A.
Darling, you and only you.
Warner, M. M.
D'Artagnan.
Levy, M. M.

166

David Rose trio album.
Rose, D.
David's lamentation.
Billings, W. Compositions.
Dawn greets the rose.
Yost, G. Five pieces for violin and piano.
Dawn on the sea.
Seymer, W. Strofer i sol och skugga.
Day after day.
Engle, G.
Day dream.
Kistler, D. E.
Day in, day out.
Kelly, N.
Day in spring.
Fouts, M. Children's easy piano pieces.
Day in the mountains.
Hibbs, C. A.
Day is coming.
Kerr, P. S. There is a way.
Day is over.
Ferry, C. T. Songs.
Day like this.
Norlin, L. B. Break the news.
Day of jubilo.
Work, H. C.
Day you came along.
Dorsett, L. E.
Daybreak.
Binge, R. Madrugado.
Days are long, nights are lonely.
Foree, M.
De' hurrà vi för.
Runo, S. Sol över Klara.
De profundis.
Nova, V.
De' skall vara en malâre till de'.
Runo, S. Sol över Klara.
De tout mon coeur.
Stein, S. There is no breeze (to cool the flame of love).
Deaf old woman.
Davis, K. K. Three American folksongs.
Dear little girl.
Tobin, L. Darling little girl.
Dear Lord and Father.
Händel, G. F.
Willingsby, G. E., pseud.
Dear Lord and Father of mankind.
Scholin, C. A.
Dear Lord, take my life.
Wolverton, M. H.
Dear mother.
Graff, G.
Dear mother of mine.
Dacon, C. M.
Dear one.
Brooks, M.
Van Tyle, R.
Dear Ruth.
Dolan, R. E.
Death by the roadside.
Nolan, T.
Declamation and toccata.
Cohn, A.
Dedy.
Olivieri, D.
Deep delta blues.
Horton, V.
Deep down in the heart of a rose.
Crane, J.
Deep down in your heart.
Franklin, D.
Deep in my heart, dear.
Romberg, S. The student prince.
Deep nocturne.
Grofé, F.
Deep river.
Mossman, T.
Oliver, S.
Reisfeld, B., arr.
Deep Valley.
Steiner, M.

Déjame en paz.
Miral, I.
Délivrance.
Corroyez, G.
Demain.
Combe, R. F.
Den er go'med Mar-lanne.
Gyldmark, S. Elly Petersen, Chanson d'amour.
Den petrazei.
Chairopoulos, C. K.
Dengozo.
Storoni, J. Amapa.
Denn es gehet dem menschen.
Brahms, J. Four serious songs.
Dentro de mi.
Mendez, B.
Departure.
Thiman, E. H.
Desconfianza de tu amor.
Yamin, J.
Desert serenade.
Sanders, G. H.
Desert starlight.
Hopkins, M. D.
Deserted.
MacDowell, E. A.
Desire.
Ostrowsky, A. M.
Despierta.
Yamin, J.
Destin s'amuse.
Guglielmi, L.
Wal-Berg.
Det går ett tåg mot drömmens land.
Kraft, A. Stinsen på Lyckås.
Det gaelder din Frihed.
Rosenberg, K.
Detska suita.
Fiegl, J.
Deux chansons de L'étoile de Séville.
Lesur, D.
Deux mélodies sur des poèmes d'Apollinaire.
Leguerney, J.
Deux noëls.
Lesur, D. J.
Deux prières.
Roget, H.
Deux tambours.
Daneau, S.
Deuxième album des derniers succès de Louis Gasté.
Gasté, L.
Deuxième petite suite.
Martelli, H. E.
Deuxième sonate.
Grechaninov, A. T.
Devi ricordare.
Casiroli, N. Le sorprese del vagone letto.
Devil and the farmer's wife.
Siegmeister, E.
Devil's train.
Foree, M.
Dialogue.
Ganz, R.
Dialogue for lovers.
Broekman, D.
Dice mi gallo.
Fernández, I.
Did anyone ever tell you you're a pretty girl?
Thompson, W. H.
Did Jesus stay with grief and sorrow?
Fewell, C. M.
Did the moon tap on your window last night?
De Rose, P.
Did you ever cross over to Snedon's?
Wilder, A.
Didn't my Lord deliver Daniel?
Miller, J. D.
Diez años.
Hernández, R.
Digging with jive.
Tobin, L.

Dile que venga otra vez.
Franco Lugo.
Ding! Dong!
Trenet, C.
Dingdong, dingdong.
Foster, D. F.
Dios lo quiere.
Torre, H. de la.
Direito de amar.
Pretinho, P. A vitoria é nossa.
Dish me a dish.
Williams, S.
Disorder at the border.
Hawkins, C.
Dissatisfied.
Short, L.
Dit-dot-dit (in twenty-five words or less).
Reid, D.
Ditte Menneskebarn.
Koppel, H. D.
Divčí pisně.
Hurník, I.
Divertimento.
Moyzes, A.
Divertimento.
Piston, W.
Divertimento in B flat for orchestra.
Berkeley, L.
Divertimento in C major.
Mozart, J. C. W. A.
Divertissement.
Renault, A.
Divine liturgy of Saint John Chrysostom.
Gallos, A. G., arr.
Divine praise.
Sisk, T. R., ed.
Divinus Infans.
Plante, A. T.
Dix études brillantes.
Komst, M. J.
Dix pièces de J. S. Bach.
Bach, J. S.
Dix-huit ans, de l'opérette L'ingénue de Londres.
Blareau, R. L'ingénue de Londres.
Dixie.
Emmett, D.
Dixie cannon ball.
Horton, V.
Dixie down beat.
Meissner, Z.
Dixieland detour.
Dorsey, J.
Do a little bus'ness on the side.
Allen, B.
Do ya s'pose?
Paisley, W. M.
Do you ever dream of me?
Hibbeler, R. O.
Do you have rivers?
Benner, H., arr.
Do you love me just as much as ever?
Kenny, N.
Do you remember?
Arthur, W.
Do you remember, my darling?
Malec, A. Czy pamiętasz moja miła.
Do you remember, sweetheart.
Lee, A.
Dörr på glänt.
Frykman, E.
Does aloha mean goodbye?
Shockey, L.
Does your conscience ever hurt you?
Petivan, A.
Doggie.
Gonzalez, V.
Dogwood in April.
Holst, M. S. Three woodland scenes.
Doin' what comes natur'lly.
Berlin, I. Annie get your gun.
Don Giovanni.
Mozart, J. C. W. A.
Don Pasqua.
Concina, C.
Don Patrick Alphonso O'Toole.
Messini, J.

Don Ranudo.
  Schoeck, O.
Donde me la pinten brinco!
  Bermejo, F.
Don't ask me to give up Jesus.
  Neale, S.
Don't be afraid to dream.
  Capano, F.
Don't blame it all on me.
  King, F.
Don't change sweethearts.
  Evans, R. B.
Don't cry, little darling.
  Mayer, C. I.
Don't cry, little girl, don't cry.
  Pinkard, M.
Don't ever doubt my love for you.
  Ancheta, L. L.
Don't ever lie to me.
  Gil, A. No trates de mentir.
Don't fall in love.
  Lubin, J.
Don't forget that you live in the pres-
  ence of the King.
  Coleman, H.
Don't go away without Jesus.
  Rice, Mrs. W. H.
Don't house me up.
  Carleton, R. L.
Don't keep her waiting.
  Carleton, R. L.
Don't (keep our two hearts cryin').
  Weisman, B.
Don't let Satan keep you away.
  Jones, W. D.
Don't let the landlord gyp you.
  Greene, J.
Don't let the light burn low.
  Dickson, A.
Don't let the moon get you.
  Carleton, R. L.
Don't look now.
  Tubb, E.
Don't say goodbye.
  Kilbourne, T.
Don't spoil those pretty eyes.
  Le Strange, R.
Don't steal my kisses and then skidoo.
  Kelley, B. M.
Don't sweet talk me.
  Jones, G.
Don't tell me.
  Pepper, B. The hucksters.
Don't throw me over for somebody else.
  Costa, J. S. da.
Don't turn your back on me.
  Gibson, A.
Don't worry 'bout that mule.
  Groner, D.
Don't you do that, what you want to do,
  to do that to me.
  Davis, N. C.
Don't you make me high.
  Barker, D.
Don't you think I ought to know?
  Johnson, W.
Don't you worry, don't you care.
  Mossman, T.
Dort wo die Zeder.
  Roskin, J. S., arr. Bimkom haerez.
Dos almas.
  Fabian, D.
Dos grillitos.
  Baltor, H. Two little crickets.
Dos luceros.
  Bermejo, F.
Double bubble.
  Grant, P.
Double concerto.
  Martinu, B.
Double trouble on my mind.
  King, F.
Douce biguine.
  Lucchesi, R.
Douceur.
  Lafarge, G. P. M.
Douze fables de La Fontaine.
  Crémieux, O.

Dove.
  Yradier, S. La paloma waltz.
Dóve sta Zazá?
  Cioffi, G.
Dove sta Zazá?
  Cioffi, G. Has anyone seen my
    beautiful Rosa?
Down by the banks of Jordan.
  Wells, C., pseud.
Down by the old Bayou.
  Bennett, D.
Down by the Sally gardens.
  Donovan, R.
Down deep in my heart.
  Green, A. Eight new sacred choruses.
Down from the hills.
  Diggle, R.
Down home rag.
  Sweatman, W. C.
Down in Chihuahua.
  Yaw, R.
Down in old New Jersey.
  Fox, L.
Down in that valley.
  Niles, J. J., ed. & arr. The singing
    campus.
Down Missouri way.
  Kent, W.
Down on Claiborne Avenue.
  De Vore, Q.
Down on MacConnachy Square.
  Loewe, F. Brigadoon.
Down South.
  Myddleton, W.
Down that old moonlit trail.
  Bell, M.
Down the aisle of life.
  Hawkins, H. C.
Down the lane to home sweet home.
  Monahan, J. B.
Down the road.
  Harrington, T.
Down the wind.
  Scott, T.
Down through the river of dreams.
  Williamson, D. D.
Down to earth.
  Fisher, D.
Down with the curtain.
  Shadwell, C.
Downright lonely, downright blue.
  Nelson, E. G.
Doxology.
  Leidzen, F. W. D.
Dragonfly.
  Palmgren, S.
Draw closer, my love.
  Villoldo, A. G. Arrímate, vida mía.
Draw me closer to Calvary.
  Takens, M. L.
Dream.
  Mercer, J.
Dream again.
  Kulma. (If I wasn't in your dream
    last night), dream again.
Dream-away Lane.
  Sanders, A. Ireland today.
Dream concerto.
  D'Artega.
Dream fantasy.
  Savino, D.
Dream girl.
  Lehár, F.
Dream lullaby.
  Savino, D.
Dream of love.
  Liszt, F.
  Liszt, F. Liebestraum.
Dream of reality.
  Allee, E. E.
Dream of you.
  Fleisher, M.
Dream ships.
  Sollo, H. A.
Dream sonata.
  Fina, J.
Dream street.
  Shand, T.

Dream (that won't come true).
  Ferguson, M.
Dream time.
  Lamkoff, P.
Dreamboat.
  Evans, R. B.
Dreamboats.
  Arthur, W.
Dreamer's holiday.
  Franklin, D.
Dreaming dreams.
  Chanslor H.
Dreaming of old Vienna.
  Scher, W.
Dreaming of the past at twilight.
  Dean, C. W.
Dreamland baby.
  Edgar, L.
Dreams are a dime a dozen.
  Mysels, S.
Dreams do often come true.
  Lamkoff, P.
Dreamy Cocoanut Island.
  Kaai, B. K.
Drifting.
  Milne, A.
Drifting along.
  Hibbs, C. A.
Drifting away from the day into the night.
  Arthur, W.
Drifting blues.
  Williams, E.
Drifting down the stream of love.
  Hibbeler, R. O.
Drifting thoughts.
  Oberg, O. S.
Drömme ömme, tyssende, stille.
  Riisager, K. Pilatus.
Drop, drop, slow tears.
  Candlyn, T. F. H.
  Noble, T. T.
Druhy kvartet.
  Hlobil, E. Quartet, strings, no. 2.
Druhy smyccový kvartet, e-moll.
  Kricka, J. Quartet, strings, no. 2.
Drumi ogguere.
  Valdes, G.
Drummer on parade.
  Wilcoxon, C.
Drummer's patrol.
  Ostling, A. E.
Drumming in triplicate.
  Ostling, A. E.
Drums away.
  Maestren, C.
Dry bones.
  Gearhart, L.
  Howorth, W.
  Osborne, W.
Dryaden.
  Seymer, W. Sånger.
Dryckesvisa.
  Kraft, A. Livet på landet.
Du är välkommen hem.
  Peterson, K.-E.
Du ciel bleu, du soleil.
  Gerlay, P.
Du kan drömma om allt.
  Kraft, A. Den glada skräddaren.
Du skrev om kärlek.
  Gyllenhammar, U. M. Brevet.
Du sover bak sex små fönster.
  Pergament, M. Tre små sånger.
Ducky.
  Ellis, V. Bless the bride.
Due laude.
  Mortari, V.
Duel in the sun.
  Tiomkin, D.
Dueña de mi alma.
  Saenz Cruz, A.
Duke of Marlborough.
  Taylor, C.
Duluth, M-I-double-N.
  Trace, A.
Dum dot song.
  Kay, J.

Dundee.
  Curry, W. L.
Duo.
  Janeček, K.
Dusk dreams.
  Hopkins, J. M.
Dust of snow.
  Carter, E.
Dust off my saddle.
  Japhet, C. I'm gonna dust off my
    saddle.
Dust on the trail.
  De Knight, J.
Dvanást ľudových piesní sloven-
  ských.
  Folprecht, Z.
Dvě balady a píseň.
  Vomáčka, B.
Dve impromptus.
  Foerster, J. B.
Dve klavírní skladby.
  Borkovec, P.
Dvouhlasé invence.
  Bartoš, J. Z.
Dwell in my heart.
  Horst, A. G. The joy of His Presence.
Dye dut da denny in da dum dot.
  Kay, J. The dum dot song.
Dyo mayra matia me gelasane.
  Ritsiardēs, I. M. Prosphygē stēn
    O.E.E.
Dziaduwka polka.
  Stanley, B.
E, F, G. overture.
  James, P.
E kuu lei my darling.
  Kuaana, D. K.
È una pagina d'amore.
  Martino, R. de. L'hanno ritrovata ...
    ma chi?
E Z favorite (Bᵇ tenor) saxophone solos.
  Klickmann, F, H., ed.
E Z favorite (Eᵇ alto) saxophone solos.
  Klickmann, F. H., ed.
E Z favorite trumpet solos.
  Klickmann, F. H., ed.
Eagle.
  Radich, J. Orao polka.
Earl Carroll vanities.
  De Rose, P.
Earl Carroll's vanities.
  Revel, H.
  Von Tilzer, H.
Easiest way.
  Geehl, H. E.
East bound Harlem train.
  Hill, E.
Easter.
  Schimmerling, H. A.
Easter alleluya.
  Toelle, F. B.
Easter choral repertoire.
  Reilly, J. A.
Easter dawn.
  Flagler, R. S.
Easter helper, no. 47.
  Ackley, B. D., comp.
Easter is here.
  Wilson, I. B.
Easter joy.
  Otis, E. C.
Easter morn.
  Miller, M. C.
Easter paean.
  Lovelace, A. C.
Easter parade.
  Berlin, I. Accordion transcriptions.
Easter tidings.
  Diestelhorst, H. J., arr.
Easter triumph.
  Kern, C. W.
Eastern star of Indiana.
  Himelick, V. B.
Eastern Star of light and glory.
  Sherman, A. E.
Eastertide.
  Johnson, C. W., arr.

Easy come, easy go.
  Evans, R.
Easy pickin's.
  Rains, C.
Easy solos for accordion.
  Bennett, E. M., ed. & arr. Everybody's
    favorite Easy solos for accordion.
Easy to wed.
  Galindo, F.
Ebony concerto.
  Stravinskii, I. F.
Ecce panis.
  Dubois, T.
Ecclesiastical organist.
  Rossini, C., ed.
Echenle agua no hagan polvo.
  Lopez Mena, D. Adios corazon.
Echo.
  Sacco, J.
Echo de la forêt.
  Lanzone, R.
Echo in the valley.
  Johnson, O.
Echo polka.
  Azzaro, A.
Echo said no.
  Kassel, A.
Echoes in the night.
  Baron, V.
Echoes of love.
  Leonard, L.
Echoes of the past.
  Dennée, C.
Ecossaise in D.
  Schubert, F. P.
Ecstasy.
  Boykin, H.
Eddie Alkire's Hawaiian hula songs.
  Alkire, E. H.
Eddie Alkire's Hawaiian waltz songs.
  Alkire, E. H.
Edison march.
  Young, V.
Eenee, meenee, mynee, moe.
  Richter, W. B.
Eeny meeny Dixie deeny.
  Bryant, H.
Efter alla dessa ar.
  Aspelin, S. En sjöman till hast.
Egg and I.
  Jolson, A.
Eglogue.
  Foret, F. H.
Eight more miles to Louisville.
  Jones, G.
Eight new sacred choruses.
  Green, A.
18th century theme from sonata in C
  major.
  Mozart, J. C. W. A. Sonata, piano.
Eileen, my colleen.
  Barrett, P. D.
Elder statesman.
  Irons, E. D.
Elegiac tone poem no. 2.
  Seymour, J. L.
Élegie.
  Klerk, J. A. de.
  Milhaud, D.
Elegy.
  Van Hulse, C.
Elenden sollen essen.
  Bach, J. S.
Elfins' frolic.
  Conklin, M. H.
Elijah.
  Mendelssohn-Bartholdy, F. If with all
    your hearts.
Elizabeth waltz.
  Evans, W. W. J.
Elkan-Vogel organ series.
  Hawke, H. W., ed.
Elle et moi.
  Goldbaum, F.
Elly Petersen.
  Gyldmark, S.

Elton Menno Roth's Hymns, solos and
  choir selections.
  Roth, E. M.
Emanuel.
  Billings, W. Compositions.
Embraceable you.
  Gershwin, G.
Embrasse-moi.
  Barelli, A.
Emigrantens Sang.
  Weis, J.
Emile et Ferdinand.
  Peyronnin, J. H.
Emitte Spiritum Tuum.
  Schuetky, F. J. Send forth Thy Spirit.
Emperor Norton.
  Campbell, W. W.
Emperor waltz.
  Savino, D.
  Strauss, J.
Empty arms.
  Arthur, W.
Empty chair and memories.
  Denby, J.
Empty tomb.
  Meredith, I. H.
En barque.
  Pigrne, G.
En écoutant mon coeur chanter.
  Herpin.
En las playas uruguayas.
  Hore, C.
En tu ausencia.
  Carbo Menendez, J. J'attends ton
    retour.
Enchanted song.
  Hynes, M. E.
Endless sleep.
  Webb, A. B.
Enredadora.
  Bermejo, G.
Ensam vid mitt fönster.
  Flodin, S.
Enseigne au vent.
  Luypaerts, G.
Ensemble classics for brass quartet.
  Voxman, H., arr.
Entreat me not to leave thee.
  Vandenberg, D.
L'Épi rouge.
  Charette, W., arr. Corbleur, eh,
    Marion!
Epilog.
  Suk, J.
Épitaphe.
  Lazarus, D.
Erie Canal.
  Mossman, T., arr.
Ernest.
  Lopez, F.
Es de mi sitio la caña.
  Gonzalez Ruiz, J.
Es de noche en el mar.
  Figueroa, O.
Esbyse enas megalos erōtas.
  Bellas, G. G.
Escape.
  Richard, L.
Escargot sans coquille.
  Delettre, J.
Escena clásica.
  Boladeres, G. de.
Escena oriental.
  Boladeres, G. de.
Escena romántica.
  Boladeres, G. de. Escena clásica.
Ese pollo!
  Palau, R.
España.
  Chabrier, E.
Espejismo.
  Elena, J.
Espuelas de oro.
  García Curiel, N.
Essential rudiments.
  Hatch, E.
Esta noche.
  Ramírez, R.

169

Esta noche de luna.
  Garcia, J.
Estamos en paz.
  Alcantara, R.
Estampas vascas.
  Santiago Majo, R. A. de.
Esto dolor.
  Monge, J.
La estocada.
  Travnicek, A. Belle Andalousie.
Estote fortes.
  Breydert, F. M.
Estrellita.
  Ponce, M. Little star.
Estudio sobre la sonata De la aurora de
  Beethoven.
  Boladeres, G. de.
Estudio sobre la sonata Patética de
  Beethoven.
  Boladeres. G. de.
Eternal Father, strong to save.
  Marsh, C. H.
Eternal search.
  Riley, L.
Eternally yours.
  Lance, A. E.
Eternamente.
  Paulos, N. E. Inspiración.
Eternamente tu.
  Olivieri, D. Tutto il mondo canta
    Tornerai.
Eternity somewhere.
  Tovey, H. G.
Etsi ein' e zoe.
  Konstantinidēs, G. G.
Etude.
  Grechaninov, A. T. Petite suite.
Etude caprice.
  Moszkowski, M.
Etude de concert.
  Czerny, C.
Etude for violins and love.
  Broekman, D.
Etude in E major.
  Chopin, F. F.
Étude sur des modes antiques.
  Jolivet, A.
Etudes melodiques.
  Nieland, J. H. I. M.
Etz chayim.
  Freed, I. Prayers of Israel.
Eucharist.
  Wagner, R. Parsifal.
Eulogy.
  Wagner, R.
Evangel in song.
  Elliot, J.
Evangel special sacred songs, no. 1.
  See title entry in composer list.
Even me, even me.
  Bradbury, W. B.
Evening campfire.
  Kesnar, M. Seven pieces.
Evening prayer.
  Gabriel, C. H.
  Harwood, C. E.
Evening reverie.
  Swift, F. F.
Eventide.
  Herbert, V.
  Hore, C.
Ever after on.
  Handy, W. C.
Ever with me.
  Ruhf, D. P.
Everlasting hills of Oklahoma.
  Spencer, T.
Everlasting love.
  Arthur, W.
Everlasting mercies of our Lord.
  Rhea, R.
Every day.
  Ford, H. J.
Every Saturday night.
  Olden, C.
Every so often.
  Warren, H.

Every time I dream, I think about you.
  Hackney, J. M.
Every time I feel the Spirit.
  Swift, F. F.
Every time we say good night.
  Everybody's favorite Chopin album.
  Chopin, F. F.
Everybody's favorite Easy solos for
  accordion.
  Norlin, L. B. Break the news.
Everybody's favorite standard over-
  tures.
  Bennett, E. M., ed. & arr.
Everyone knew it but me.
  Dodd, B.
Everything comes first.
  Porter, C. E.
Everything is lovely when the sun shines.
  Secord, G. K.
Everything's movin' too fast.
  Barbour, D.
Everywhere.
  Harris, W. P.
Evocacion Incaica.
  Barragan, R.
Ev'ry day.
  Fleming, L.
Ev'ry day blues.
  Djal, H.
Ev'ryday is mother's day.
  Haddad, S. S.
Ev'ryone like to rhumba.
  Davis, J.
Evviva l'allegria.
  Concina, C.
Excellent Saviour.
  Weitzel, G. J. Ein herrlicher Heiland!
Excerpts from concertos.
  Ambroise, V. arr.
Excerpts from Finian's rainbow.
  Lane, B. Finian's rainbow.
Exercises preparatoires.
  Schmitt, A.
Extempore.
  Vackar, D. C.
Extrovert.
  Foldes, A. Two pieces for piano.
Eythymes peripeteies.
  Ritsiardes, I. M.
Fable.
  Dello Joio, N.
  Gillette, J. R.
Facciamo ancora un po' di strada insieme.
  Olivieri, D. Tutto il mondo canta Tor-
    neral.
Face the music.
  Lilienas, H.
Faded memories.
  Oberg, O. S.
Fairest Lord Jesus.
  Niles, J. J., ed. & arr. The singing
    campus.
Fairest of the fair.
  Clyde, T.
Fairy news.
  Brook, H.
Faith, hope and charity.
  Savino, D.
Faith that keeps us.
  Elliot, J. An evangel in song.
Faithful heart.
  Belton, J. Time marches on.
Faithful shepherd.
  Handel, G. F. Pastorale.
Faithfully yours.
  Paris, J. B.
Falling in love with love.
  Rodgers, R. The boys from Syracuse.
Falsarja.
  Martinez Gil, C.
Falto de cariño.
  Cruz Artigas, H.
Famigiia Brambilla alla fiera di Milano.
  Galaverni, I.
Famous family album of radio favorites.
  Hull, R. E., comp.

Famous sounds from the operas.
  Cernkovich, R., arr.
Famous themes in the modern manner.
  Liefeld, J.
Fanfare, chorale & finale.
  Turner, G. B.
Fantaisie brésilienne.
  Mathieu, A.
Fantasi i Halling.
  Egge, K.
Fantasia.
  Purcell, H.
  Schumann, R. A.
Fantasia e fuga sopra B.A.C.H.
  Nieland, J. H. I. M.
Fantasie.
  Kapr, J.
  Nieland, J. H. I. M. (Fantasia, organ)
Fantasie and fugue.
  Langstroth, I.
Fantasie pastorale.
  Heffer, F.
Fantasy.
  Kenton, S.
  Samuels, W.
Fantasy overture.
  Chaikovskii, P. I.
Far-away island.
  Shapiro, T.
Far from my darling.
  Robinson, E. The Missouri story.
Farandoles.
  Dehette, M.
Fare you well, my friends.
  Billings, W. Compositions.
Farewell, companions.
  Sanders, J. Adiós, muchachos.
Farmer in the dell.
  Murray, L.
Farmer's curst wife.
  Niles, J. J., ed. & arr. The singing
    campus.
Farr-away blues.
  Farr, H.
Faschingsschwank aus Wien.
  Schumann, R. A.
Fascinating polka.
  Cirelli, L.
Fat man blues.
  Manners, Z.
Father most merciful.
  Franck, C. A.
Father, to Thee we pray.
  Gounod, C. F. Ave Maria.
Fats Waller's famous London suite.
  Waller, F.
Fault is all your own.
  Carleton, R. L.
Faut pas bouder Bouddha.
  Dumas, R.
Favela.
  Tavares, H.
Favorite melodies.
  Hall, J. H., ed.
Favorite songs.
  Cole (M.M.) Publishing co., comp.
Federal shield song.
  Beatty, R. J.
Feeling zero.
  Hawkins, C.
Féerie laotienne.
  Tomasi, H.
Feestmarschje.
  Nieland, J. H. I. M.
Fellowship with Jesus.
  Gray, R. A.
Femininity (Masculinity)
  Kennedy, A. New songs.
Femme s'en va.
  Datin, J.
Ferns.
  Rhea, R.
Fervor.
  Manzano, W.
Festa di Vendemmia in Sicilia.
  Culotta, I.

Festival frolic.
 Kesnar, M. Seven pieces.
Festliche Hausmusik.
 Girnatis, W.
Feudin' and fightin'.
 Lane, B.
Feuilles mortes.
 Kosma, J.
Fichas negras.
 Rodriguez, J.
Fickle you.
 Rojo, G. Mulata caprichesa.
Fiddle fun for the young soloist.
 Webber, R.
Fiddler's folly.
 Engleman, J.
Fidelio overture.
 Beethoven, L. v.
Fiesta.
 Monge, J.
Fiesta de las flores.
 Reisfeld, B.
Fiesta en La Caleta.
 Texidor Dalmau, J.
Fiesta in Costa Rica.
 Schaum, J. W.
Fiesta time.
 Eckstein, M.
Fifth Avenue jive.
 Ferguson, D.
55 piano pieces.
 Mirovitch, A., ed. The student pianist.
Figaro.
 Collin, J.
Figaro 46.
 Rossini, G. A.
Fight on ye Bruins.
 Crossman, A. G.
Filipino baby.
 Clark, C. V.
Fille du Nord.
 Israel, M.
Find the woman.
 Saltzman, M. M.
Fine thing.
 Dolan, R. E. Dear Ruth.
Fingal's cave.
 Mendelssohn-Bartholdy, F.
Finger frolics.
 Yuill, M.
Finger talk.
 Templeton, V.
Finian's rainbow.
 Lane, B.
Fiori.
 Davico, V. Cinque liriche romantiche.
Fire-bird.
 Stravinskii, I. F.
Fire down below.
 Rowley, A.
Firefly.
 Friml, R.
 Trowbridge, L. Nature tone-poems.
First angel.
 Goldsworthy, W. A.
First arrangement.
 Alexander, V.
First edition.
 Hayes, H.
First jump.
 Baker, K.
First Noel.
 Balogh, L. L.
 Childe, R. S., arr.
First of all.
 Last, J.
First thing I do every morning.
 Trietsch, K.
First-year violin method.
 Cohen, E.
Fisarmonica in orchestra.
 Ramponi, G.
Fish seller.
 Dungan, O.
Fishermen of Capri.
 Winkler, G.

Five fantasies on Polish Christmas
 carols.
 Bax, A.
Five intermezzi.
 Lutyens, E.
Five keys to heaven.
 Ayer, N. D.
Five musical settings of Hashkivenu.
 Katchko, A.
Five nocturnes.
 Rowley, A.
Five nursery rhymes.
 Groocock, J.
Five piano solos.
 Garner, E.
Five psalms.
 Le Fleming, C.
Five responses.
 Diggle, R.
Five star collection of cowboy songs.
 Warner, E. A., comp.
Flag salute of America.
 Noble, E. D.
Flamenco chant.
 Tam, F.
Flauta e pandeiro.
 Lacerda, O.
Flea on a spree.
 Powell, T.
Fledermaus.
 Strauss, J.
Fleeting fancies.
 Schiefelbein, F. A.
Fleurs de mousse.
 Cockenpot, F.
Fleurs d'or.
 Cockenpot, F.
Flickorna fran gamla sta'n.
 Bauman, E.
Flight of the bumble bee.
 Rimskii-Korsakov, N. A.
Flitting butterflies.
 Brown, L.
Floating balloons.
 Fouts, M. Children's easy piano
  pieces.
Flor de mi amor.
 Valdes, G.
Floral message.
 Cosgray, O. Once a star shone bright.
Flores negras.
 Ortiz, C. A.
Flower girl.
 Pergament, M. Tre små sånger.
Flower sings.
 Fouts, M. Children's easy piano
  pieces.
Flowering shoots.
 Duuren, H. J. v. Bloeiende ranken.
Flowers in their pretty hats.
 Poulton, D. F.
Flowers of Hawaii.
 King, C. E.
Flutes qui chantent.
 Weisshaus, I.
Flying home.
 Sanders, A. Ireland today.
Flying notes.
 Komst, M. J.
For gamla Sveriges väl,
 Kraft, A. Kalle på Spången.
Fog in the harbour.
 Strickland, L.
Fold me in your arms.
 De Rienzo, S.
Foldin' money.
 Stanton, F. H.
Folio of mid-day merry-go-round
 favorites.
 Fowler, J. W., comp. Lowell Blanch-
  ard's Folio.
Folk song.
 Greenhill, H. W. Three pieces for organ.
Folk-song arrangements.
 Britten, B., arr.
Folk song of Oaxaca, Mexico.
 La Llorona. Cry baby.

Folksongs of Brazil.
 Krone, B. P., arr. A world in tune.
Follow thru.
 Wakely, J.
Fooling me.
 Stout, C. A.
Foolish lies.
 Pomares, G. Mentiras.
Foolish pride.
 Wilkins, C.
Footprints in the snow.
 King, E. I traced her little footprints
  in the snow.
 Lane, B.
For Christ Our King through Mary.
 Meyer, M. V., sister.
For God so loved.
 Horst, A. G. The joy of His Presence.
For him.
 Dasher, J. L.
For Jesus spoke peace to my soul.
 Jackson, L. M.
For me and my piano.
 Foster, A. H., comp.
For sentimental reasons.
 Best, W. I love you.
For the fallen.
 Herrmann, B.
For the gentlemen.
 Shaw, O.
For the Master's use.
 Sessler, J. R.
For to-night a King is born in Bethle-
 hem.
 Roberton, H. S.
For you.
 Jackson, T. K.
For you and me.
 Decker, A. A.
For your tunejoyment.
 Sessions, J. B., ed.
Forains.
 Sauguet, H.
Forest chimes.
 Bragdon, S. C.
Forest dreams.
 Ettema, T. A.
Forest scenes.
 Schumann, R. A.
Forever and after that.
 Carleton, R. L.
Forever in my heart.
 White, C.
Forgeons.
 Delfau, R.
Forgeron de Gretna-Green.
 Richepin, T. F. D.
Forget about me, dear.
 Gil, A. Olvidate de mi.
Forgetfulness.
 Lee, D.
Forgiving love.
 Runyeon, G. E.
Formosa.
 Doneddu, A.
Forosette danzano.
 Mineo, E.
Fortune teller.
 Herbert, V.
Forty days and forty nights.
 Bach, J. S.
48 tuneful technical studies.
 Spivak, S., arr.
Forward together with Christ.
 Brown, W. N.
Foundation to cornet playing.
 Vesely, S.
Four American variations on a theme
 by Paganini.
 Perl, L.
Four and twenty elders.
 Dorsey, J. E., arr. Two negro spirit-
  uals.
Four choral preludes.
 Hill, E. Chorale preludes, organ.

171

Four dance episodes from Rodeo.
Copland, A. Rodeo.
Four eclogues.
De Lamarter, E.
Four gospel songs. See title entry
in composer list.
416 progressive daily studies for the
clarinet.
Kroepsch, F.
Four keys.
Baumer, C.
Four men on a horse.
Jackson, G.
Four new songs.
Gilmore, T. S.
Four piano compositions.
Dittenhaver, S. L.
Four piano pieces.
Spalding, A.
Four preludes.
Kerr, H. Preludes, piano.
Four sacred sonnets.
Wordsworth, W.
Four serious songs.
Brahms, J.
Four short pieces.
Ganz, R.
Fourteen folk tunes for young men.
Lefebvre, C., arr.
Fourteen melodies.
Mendelin, W.
Fox and the hare.
Kjerulf, H.
Från Blyge Anton till En s jöman
till häst.
Kraft, A.
Fragrant rose.
Jones, B. V.
Frank Luther's holiday music folio
of popular children's songs.
Engel, L. K.
Franklin D. Roosevelt.
Wright, E.
Frantic fantasy.
Nero, P.
Frantic rhapsody.
Stegmeyer, W.
Franz Schubert.
Suppe, F. v. Overture.
Frasquita serenade.
Lehár, F.
Freckle song.
Vincent, L.
Free again.
Flowers, P. D.
Free eats.
Basie, V.
Free fantasia.
Ball, E.
Freight train boogie.
Nobar, B.
French horn method.
Edison, A. B.
Friendship.
Nagle, M. S.
Friendship march.
Welty, J. T.
Frio en el alma.
Valladares, M. A.
Fröken Vildkat.
Gyldmark, S.
Frog.
Mopper, I.
Frog song.
Smith, V. G.
Frolic in May.
Oberg, O. S.
From an old legend.
Harvey, N. W.
From cross to glory.
Unruh, D. P.
From Hand to Hand.
Thompson, H. C.
From Khaki to civies.
Brune, A.
From moon-filled sky.
Pendleton, E.
From now on.
Clark, C.
From out of Heaven.
Bonnell, W. C.

From rocking horse to rocking chair.
Wolf, J.
From the far-off hills.
Seymour, J. L.
From the Monadnock region.
Wagner, J. F.
From this day on.
Loewe, F. Brigadoon.
Frosty night.
Taylor, C.
Frühlingsregen.
Koch, S. v. Die wilden Schwäne.
F 'taint one thing it's another.
Ba efel, E.
Fünf, Gesänge.
Klose, F.
Fugal fantasia.
Pimsleur, S. Suite of transformations.
Fugue in F major.
Händel, G. F.
Fulvia.
Moietta, B. La Pepina.
Fun on the keys.
Fouts, M.
Fun with scales.
Gornston, D.
Fun with violin technic.
Cremin, A. T.
Funeral song.
Brahms, J. Begräbnisgesang.
Funiculi funicula.
Denza, L.
Funny clown.
Yost, G. Five pieces.
Funny how you get along without me.
Steiner, H.
Funny thing called love.
Tinturin, P.
Funny what love can do.
Kramer, S.
Furiant.
Schäfer, F.
Fyra dikter.
Stenhammar, W.
Fyra sånger.
Kallstenius, E.
Fyra Stockholmsdikter.
Stenhammar, W.
Fyrtjet.
Christiansen, E.
G. I. battle hymn.
Martin, I. G.
G minor spin.
Barnes, G.
Gaiety.
Tollefsen, A.
Galla-Rini's collection of hymns for
accordion.
Galla-Rini, A., arr.
Gambling with love.
Rodriguez, J. Fichas negras.
Gamla sta'n.
Baumann, E. Flickorna fran gamla
sta'n.
Gamla trädet.
Kraft, A. Livet på landet.
Gammal historia.
Grafström, G.
Gammalt minne.
Seymer, W. Strofer i sol och skugga.
Gant, une robe, un chapeau.
Le.
Garden is a lovesome thing.
Mopper, I.
Garden of Eden.
Ramey, V.
Garden of gold.
Noll, L. A.
Gate of the year.
Woodman, R. H.
Gavotte.
Nieland, J. H. I. M.
Prokof'ev, S. S.
Gavotte antique.
Martini, G. B.
Gavottina delle bambole.
Mineo, E.

Gay butterflies in springtime.
Van Nort, I.
Gay divorcee.
Porter, C.
Gay life of Milwaukee.
Patti, S. T.
Gay little pieces.
Tollefsen, A..
Gay señorita.
Matos, M. G.
Gdy sie Chrystus rodzi.
Bement, G. S. When the Saviour Christ
is born.
Gebet des Herrn.
Schubert, F. P. The cross of faith.
Gedenken.
Kallstenius, E. Fyra sånger.
Gee, but it's good to be.
Viola, A.
Gene Autry's popular music folio of
Western songs.
Engel, L. K., comp.
Genevieve.
Bryant, D. B.
Genie on the spot.
Hogan, G. A. Overture.
Genoveva.
Monge, J.
Gentleman Jim.
Oliver, H.
George M. Smith collection of solos for
the plectrum guitar.
Smith, G. M.
George Washington.
Taylor, C.
Gershwin made easy for the piano.
Gershwin, G.
Gesa, nuovi successi.
Fiore, F., comp.
Get away from that door.
Wright, J.
Get things ready for me, Ma.
Jones, G.
Get-together hymns.
Lorenz, E. J., comp.
Get up those stairs, mademoiselle.
Brent, R.
Giardino dei ricordi.
Olivieri, D. Tutto il mondo canta
Tornerai.
Gifts most precious.
Meredith, I. H.
Gigue.
Wright, N. L.
Gimme a good horse.
Walter, S.
Gingham dog and the calico cat.
Binney, A. S.
Giorno.
Olivieri, D. Tutto il mondo canta
Tornerai.
Gipsy baron.
Strauss, J. Love wherever I roam.
Gipsy rondo.
Haydn, J.
Girl crazy.
Gershwin, G.
Girl friend.
Rodgers, R.
Girl in the polka dot dress.
Udall, F.
Girl like you.
Clark, R.
Girl of my dreams.
Clapp, S.
Girl of Sigma Alpha Mu.
Sigma Alpha Mu.
Girl that I marry.
Berlin, I. Annie get your gun.
Girl with the advertising smile.
King, L.
Girl with the gold in her hair.
Leaman, G.
Girl with the Spanish drawl.
Camacho, J.
Girls don't worry my mind.
Nichols, W. H.

Girotondo.
    Olivieri, D. Tutto il mondo canta
        Tornerai.
Giselle.
    Adam, A.
Git along, git along cowboy.
    Gindhart, T.
Gitanerias.
    Lecuona y Casado, E.
Giv mig dit Hjerte, Maria.
    Deneke, E. V. M.
Give a broken heart a break.
    Tobias, H. H.
Give Christ to all the world.
    Fero, G. L.
Give ear to my words O Lord.
    Meller, L. P.
Give ear unto my voice.
    Williams, R. E.
Give me a faith.
    Bitgood, R.
Give me a rod, a reel.
    Johnson, J. R.
Give me something to dream about.
    Livingston, J.
Give me the country!
    Schneider, J. L.
Give me the night so enchanting.
    Crosley, E. J.
Give me tomorrow.
    De Hellebranth, E.
Give me twenty nickels for a dollar.
    Brandt, A.
Give thanks and praise.
    Rogers, B.
Give us peace.
    Robison, W.
Glacier.
    Oliver, G. Original themes for
        piano.
Glad tidings!
    Peterson, J. W. Gospel songs.
Glad tidings, Youth for Christ.
    Mohring, M. M.
Glada skräddaren.
    Kraft, A.
Gleams of glory.
    Henson, J. M., comp.
Gloria in excelsis.
    Mozart, J. C. W. A.
Gloria Patri.
    Palestrina, G. P. da.
Glorieux Canada.
    Donnell, R. This Canada of ours.
Glorious resurrection.
    Freed, J. N.
Glory and triumph.
    Berlioz, H.
Glory and worship are before Him.
    Purcell, H.
Glory! Hamilton High!
    Zoeller, C. H.
Glory of creation.
    Warmack, J.
Glory to God in the highest.
    Erb, J. L.
    Pergolesi, G. B.
Glory to His name.
    Stockton, J. H.
Glow-worm.
    Lincke, P.
Glueck in Jesu.
    Weitzel, G. J. Liebe Seele'
        steh' im Glauben.
Go all the way with me.
    Kelly, N. Golden memories of by-gone
        days.
Go down, Moses.
    Chiaffarelli, A., arr.
    Handy, W. C., arr.
    Howorth, W., arr.
    Simon, W. C., arr.
Go forth, my heart, and seek delight.
    Lundquist, M.
Go gather in the grain.
    Bostwick, F. J. I am satisfied with
        Jesus.

Go out and find somebody new.
    Tillman, F.
Go to sleepy, little baby.
    Canova, J.
Go West, young man, go West.
    Garfield, L.
Goat who ate the drum.
    Simons, M. Chibo que rompe tambó.
God be in my head.
    Ashfield, R. Two introits.
    Clokey, Joseph W.
God bless our Canada.
    Leacock, L. H.
God in springtime.
    Schubert, F. P. Gott im Frühling.
God is a Spirit.
    Bennett, W. S.
    Kopylov, A.
God is here.
    Lorenz, E. J.
God is the Light of the world.
    Morgan, H.
God is very close.
    Truss, I. T.
God, make me know.
    Poulton, D. F.
God of our Father.
    Schubert, F. P. Ave Maria.
God of the wind and wave.
    Shure, R. D.
God, save America!
    Butler, W. G.
God sends the snow like wool.
    Poulton, D. F.
Gods go a-begging.
    Händel, G. F.
God's golden West.
    Guion, D. W.
God's love hush and other songs.
    Foster, D. G.
God's mountains.
    Swift, F. F.
God's rainbow shines for you.
    Gilbert, H. M.
Godt Humør, et flot Humør.
    Gyldmark, S. Panik i Familien.
Going home train.
    Rome, H. J. Call me Mister.
Going to town.
    Fouts, M. Children's easy piano
        pieces.
Golden age.
    Shostakovich, D. D. Dance.
Golden day is dying.
    Bement, G. S., arr.
Golden days.
    Romberg, S. The student prince.
Golden dream of love.
    Hopkins, M.
Golden hours.
    Meredith, I. H., comp.
Golden lullaby.
    Godard, B. L. P.
Golden memories of by-gone days.
    Kelly, N.
Golden Rule.
    Carleton, R. L.
Golden spike.
    Shield, R. Union Pacific suite.
Golden star.
    Tobin, L.
Golden sunset.
    West, M.
Golden wedding.
    Ivanovici, J. Mother and dad's favorite
        wedding songs.
Goldfish pool.
    Koehler, C. F.
Golondrinas.
    Alarcón Leal, E.
Golubica.
    Yradier, S. La paloma waltz.
Gone are you.
    Pasztor, G. A.
Gone, gone, gone.
    Wise, F.

Gonna give you back to the Indians.
    Carson, J. L.
Good ale.
    Donovan, R.
Good bye, Milanesina.
    Olivieri, D.
Good evening to you.
    Dolan, J.
Good morning.
    Smith, O. M.
Good news!
    Kennedy, M.
Good news melodious.
    Hinshaw, F. M.
Good night, Harvard.
    Moore, D. S.
Good night ladies.
    Jacobs, M., arr. Boogie woogie step-
        by-step.
Goodbye, my lady love.
    Howard, J. E.
Goodbye, old Mexico moon.
    Siegel, I. U. A.
Goodnight, beloved.
    Leggett, L. E. My twilight tango.
Goodnight! God bless you!
    Printz, W. F.
Goodnight sailor.
    Tobin, L.
Goodwill unto man.
    Grant, A. B.
Goofy gal of Tegucigalpa.
    Fields, I.
Googie-woogie.
    Brodsky, R.
Goose boy.
    Lake, G.
Gospel songs.
    Peterson, J. W.
    Yeazel, C.
Got a ring around Rosie's finger.
    Carver, Z.
Got the mother-in-law blues.
    McNeil, J. J.
Gott im Frühling.
    Schubert, F. P.
Gotta get to Oklahoma City.
    Franklin, D.
Gotta gimme whatcha got.
    Lee, J.
Gotta go to St. Joe, Mo.
    Fortis, J.
Gotta make love.
    Carleton, R. L.
Gra oktoberdag.
    Seymer, W. Strofer i sol och
        skugga.
Grace before meals.
    Niles, J. J., ed. & arr. The singing
        campus.
Gracieux.
    Walden, F.
Graciosas.
    Obradors, F. J. Canciones clásicas
        español's.
Gracious Lord who givest blessing.
    Kempinski, L. A.
Gran premio.
    Consiglio, M.
Grand symphony for band.
    Berlioz, H. Symphony.
Grandfather's clock.
    Work, H. C.
Grandma's turned over again.
    Melka, H.
Grant, we beseech Thee.
    Stocks, H. C. L.
Grasshopper hop.
    Harley, H. M.
Grateful hearts.
    Tovey, H. G.
Great expectations.
    Goehr, W.
Great expectations waltz.
    Goehr, W. Great expectations.
Great grand dad. See title entry in
    composer list.

775306 O - 48 - 12

Great melodies from Mozart's operas.
　Mozart, J. C. W. A.
Greatest Pilot.
　Lewis, A.
Green beds.
　Niles, J. J.
Green earth.
　Stoltze, R.
Green grass of Wyoming.
　O'Hara, M.
Greeting to you.
　Frey, H., arr.
Greetings to Milwaukee.
　Patti, S. T.
Gregorian organist.
　Rossini, C., ed. & arr.
Grey October day.
　Seymer, W. Strofer i sol och skugga.
Grieg for the young.
　Grieg, E. H.
Grieg's concerto march.
　Grieg, E. H. Concerto, piano.
Grieving my heart over you.
　Carleton, R. L.
Grumpy Shark.
　Hubbell, F. A.
Gryning pa hafvet.
　Seymer, W. Strofer i sol och skugga.
Guajirita mia.
　Escarpenter, J.
Guajiro alegre.
　Grenet, E.
Guaracha.
　King, H.
Guardian angels.
　Händel, G. F.
Guide me Lord I pray.
　Jackson, J. A.
Guido del popolo.
　Robbiani, I.
Guitar journal.
　Volpe, H. Volpe's Guitar journal.
Guitaristics.
　Moore, O. Oscar Moore's Guitaristics.
Gun-totin' mama.
　Copas, C.
Gwendolyn waltzes.
　Gaines, S. R.
Gyermekdancok.
　Kodaly, Z.
Gypsy and her donkey.
　Chaves, A.
Gypsy camp fire.
　Slater, L.
Gypsy hearts.
　Karlin, A.
Gypsy lady.
　Herbert, V.
Gypsy love song.
　Herbert, V. The fortune teller.
Gypsy whirl.
　Kasschau, H.
Gyrna kai pali.
　Iakôbides, Z.
Habana suite.
　Hively, W.
Habanera.
　Bizet, G. Carmen.
Hacienda California.
　Walthuis, F.
Haganah.
　Weinberg, J.
Hail, Breath of Life.
　Clokey, J. W.
Hail! Hail! Ohio.
　Thompson, C. P.
Hail Mary.
　Bickel, W. J.
　Gaskill, C.
Hail Thee.
　Charpentier, M. A.
Hail to Thee, oh Jesus.
　Iden, R. J.
Hallelujah.
　Howorth, W.
　Woods, J. S.
Hallelujah chorus.
　Händel, G. F.

Hallelujah, Christ arose.
　Brown, L. F.
Hallelujah, praise the Lord.
　Irey, F.
Halleluja, praise ye the Lord.
　Lewandowski, L. Psalm 150.
Halling fra Lom.
　Beck, T. L. Dansar fra Gudbrandsdal.
Hammer song.
　Fouts, M. Children's easy piano
　　pieces.
Hand in hand.
　Rogers, E.
Hand me down my walkin' cane.
　Jacobs, M., arr. Boogie woogie
　　step-by-step.
Handle with care.
　Ice, W.
　Shepard, R.
Hands around the globe.
　Davol, R.
Hangover Square.
　Sauter, E.
Hanno ritrovata.
　Martino, R. de.
Hans Onsdags-Veninde.
　Gyldmark, S.
Hansel and Gretel.
　Humperdinck, E. Susie, little Susie.
Happiness.
　Rodde, V.
Happy again.
　Bunner, G. G.
Happy and gay.
　Hopkins, H. P.
Happy birthday.
　Williams, H. A.
Happy farmer.
　Schumann, R. A.
Happy, happy Easter!
　Benner, H. C.
Happy harlequin.
　Herbert, V.
Happy ice cube.
　Rose, D.
Happy melodies from Beethoven's
　chamber music.
　Beethoven, L. v. Some of the happy
　　melodies from Beethoven's chamber
　　music.
Happy melodies from Haydn's chamber
　music.
　Haydn, J. Some of the happy melodies
　　from Haydn's chamber music.
Happy melodies from Mozart's chamber
　music.
　Mozart, J. C. W. A. Some of the happy
　　melodies from Mozart's chamber
　　music.
Happy peasant girl.
　Krone, B.
Happy Utah.
　Ballif, S. C.
Hare and the tortoise.
　Rowley, A. Pipe and tabor.
Hark! The herald angels sing.
　My First Christmas Songs.
Hark! The voice of love and mercy.
　Norden, N.
Hark, the vesper hymn is stealing.
　Stevenson, Sir J.
Harke, how the minstrils gin to shrill
　aloud.
　Cole, W.
Harmonie.
　Muscat, A.
Harmonium pour tous.
　Gratia, L. E.
Harmony.
　Van Heusen, J. Variety girl.
Harmony gems.
　Baxter, J. R., comp.
Harry Volpe's Concert pieces for guitar.
　Volpe, H.
Harry Volpe's masterpieces for plectrum
　guitar.
　Volpe, H.

Has anyone seen my beautiful Rosa?
　Cioffi, G.
Hasard fait bien les choses.
　Guglielmi, L.
Hashkivenu.
　Katchko, A. Five musical settings
　　of Hashkivenu.
Hasta que perdió Jalisco.
　Esperón, M.
Hatikvah.
　Roskin, J. S., arr.
Havana holiday.
　Dickson, R.
Have a heart, have a sweetheart.
　Small, G.
Have faith in God.
　Helbing, D. W. Ambassadors for
　　Christ.
　Parker, E. E.
Have I been mean to you?
　Lamb, L.
Have you change for a dream?
　Stern, M.
Have you counted the cost?
　Hodge, A. J.
Have you forgotten?
　Lama, J.
Haven of rest.
　Moore, G. D.
Havírská polka.
　Kovaľcovic, K.
Hawaiian breezes.
　Hopkins, H. P.
Hawaiian hula songs.
　Alkire, E. H. Eddie Alkire's
　　Hawaiian hula songs.
Hawaiian waltz songs.
　Alkire, E. H. Eddie Alkire's
　　Hawaiian waltz songs.
Haydn-Schaum for piano.
　Haydn, J.
He and She.
　Taylor, C.
He can do abundantly.
　Blanchard, J.
He answereth prayer.
　Betz, M. H.
He died for you.
　Green, A. Eight new sacred choruses.
He gave Himself for me.
　Whitford, K.
He has come home to stay.
　Carleton, R. L.
He is Able.
　Ford, H. J.
He is all the world to me.
　Jackson, J. A.
He is bidding for you.
　Saunders, G. E.
He is coming back for me.
　Johnson, J. L.
He is mine!
　White, H. L.
He is risen.
　Gadsby, H.
He is there.
　Thompson, R. E.
He is with me.
　Bugbee, M.
He keeps the fire burning down in my
　soul.
　Pace, C. H.
Evangel special sacred songs.
He lives again for aye.
　Slote, J. W.
He that believes in Jesus.
　Bacon, J. D.
He that doeth truth.
　Cain, N.
He took my sins away.
　Cryor, W. M.
He understands.
　Burt, J. G.
He walketh upon the wings of the wind.
　Shure, R. D.
He was a pal of mine.
　Carleton, R. L.

174

He was found worthy.
  Weigle, C. F., ed. Sing a new song.
He who would valiant be.
  Elmore, R.
He will give me rest.
  Morris, K.
He will judge between the nations.
  Osborn, I. C. Christ our Redeemer.
He won my heart on Calvary.
  Woods, J. S.
Healing leaves.
  Eley, L. C.
Hear, Lord.
  Lahmer, R. E.
Hear my crying.
  Dvořák, A.
Hear my prayer, O Lord.
  Dvořák, A.
Hear us, O Father.
  Keller, L. A.
Heart breakin'.
  Goodhart, A.
Heart full of love.
  Livingston, J.
Heart of night.
  Warren, E. R.
Heart song.
  Herbert, V.
Heart stealin' mama.
  Travis, M.
Heart that is breaking for you.
  King, F.
Heartaches.
  Hoffman, A.
Heart's desire.
  Grey, F.
Heat wave.
  Berlin, I. Blue skies.
Heath in bloom.
  Seymer, W. Strofer i sol och skugga.
Heather on the hill.
  Loewe, F. Brigadoon.
Heaven.
  Quisenberry, P. W., arr.
  White, A. B.
Heaven above.
  Coleman, E.
Heaven is real.
  Tovey, H. G.
Heaven on the islands.
  Marlow, J. K.
Heaven only knows.
  Roemheld, H.
Heavenly grass.
  Bowles, P. Blue mountain ballads.
Heavens are telling.
  Haydn, J.
Heaven's in my heart today.
  Takens, M. L.
Heav'nly Father, be Thou near me.
  Poulton, D. F.
Heav'nly Father loves the birds.
  Poulton, D. F.
Hebraic study.
  Cohn, A.
Hebrew chants.
  Braslavsky, S. G., arr.
Hebrew melodies.
  Menasce, J. de.
Heden blommar.
  Seymer, W. Strofer i sol och
    skugga.
Hee-haw!
  Olds, W. B.
Heed now the voice.
  Clayton, N. J.
Heel and toe polka.
  Oahu publishing co., arr.
Heimisher bulgar.
  Ellstein, A.
Hello Daddy.
  Crawford, R. L.
Hello Montana.
  Dahle, A. A.
Hello, Patsy Fagan.
  Haywood, E. The dacent Irish boy.
Hello Spring!
  Lawrance, A. J.

Help me to help my neighbor.
  Berlin, I.
Hem.
  Kraft, A. När seklet var ungt.
Hembygd du rika.
  Kraft, A. Fran "Blyge Anton"
    till "En sjöman till häst."
Hembygden.
  Widéen, I. Tre Pår Lagerkvist-
    dikter.
Hen-pecked papa.
  Storie, B. E.
Hep step.
  Carleton, R. L.
Here comes the band.
  Robinson, A.
Here I go.
  Wilson, E. M.
Here is the church.
  Poulton, D. F.
Here today and gone tomorrow.
  Parker, A.
Here under the sun.
  Walker, L. M.
Here we go!
  Thomas, J. J.
Here's to music.
  May, R. Spring song.
Here's to the ladies.
  Walker, C.
Héritage infernal.
  Trenet, C.
Hérodiade.
  Massenet, J. E. F.
Heroic poem.
  Britain, R.
Herr Dandolo.
  Siegel, R.
Herr Jesu Christ, Dich zu uns wend'.
  Bach, J. S.
Herrlicher Heiland!
  Weitzel, G. J.
He's all right.
  Pace, C. H. He's everything to me,
    He's all right.
He's everything to me, He's all right.
  Pace, C. H.
He's goin' away.
  Davis, K. K. Three American folksongs.
  (He's my darlin') precious little sonny
    boy.
  Denney, D.
He's the lover of my soul.
  Whitford, K.
Heuernte.
  Kallstenius, E. Fyra sånger.
Heut' ist der schönste.
  May, H. This is the happiest day of my
    life.
Hey daddy-o.
  Salim, K.
Hey! Mama, he's tryin' to kiss me.
  Coblin, K.
Heywood blues.
  Heywood, E.
Hi ball polka.
  Hoven, G.
Hide not Thy face.
  Morgan, H.
High heaven.
  Bailey, R. M.
High meadow.
  Dyson, G.
High ridin'.
  Paulson, J.
High school cadets.
  Sousa, J. P.
High vision.
  Kallstenius, E. Fyra sånger.
Highest praise.
  Baxter, J. R., comp.
Highland scenes.
  Thiman, E.
Highway to Estepona.
  Bowles, P. Carretera de Estepona.
Highway to heartache.
  Hunnicutt, W.

Hilacha nueva.
  Krone, B. P. My true love.
Hills of Dannemora.
  Loveday, C.
Him ain't got no tail.
  Smith, V. G. The frog song.
Hinkty man.
  Lerner, A.
Hippolyte et Aricie.
  Rameau, J. P.
His feet too big for de bed.
  Mysels, S.
His grace is sufficient.
  Thorne, W. M.
His kisses made a Mrs. out of me.
  Shay, V. H.
His love for me.
  Carveth, W.
His love, like a sunbeam.
  Clayton, N. J.
Histoire de fou.
  Datin, J.
Historiette.
  Ligtelijn, J. L.
Hit parade of 1947.
  McHugh, J. F.
Hjärtat.
  Nystrom, G.
Hjerternes Vals.
  Christiansen, E. Fyrtøjet.
Hledam stín.
  Stelibsky, J. Pro kamaráda.
Ho il cuor cosi greve di pianto.
  Davico, V. Cinque liriche roman-
    tiche.
Ho licenziato la cameriera.
  Pasero, P.
Hobby-on-the-green.
  Rufty, H.
Hodie Christus natus est.
  Pollak, W. T. Today is Christ born.
Höbärgningen.
  Kallstenius, E. Fyra sånger.
Högsommar.
  Seymer, W. Strofer i sol och skugga.
Hofnung.
  Roskin, J. S., arr. Hatikvah.
Hokey pokey man.
  Maas, G. H.
Hókusz-pókusz.
  Kemeny, E.
Hold on!
  Howorth, W.
Holding you in my arms.
  Meyers, C. J.
Holiday moods.
  Sargent, L. L.
Holiday overture.
  Carter, E. C.
Holiday song.
  Schuman, W. H.
Holly and the ivy.
  Boughton, R., arr.
Hollywood stars.
  Arthur, W.
Holy City.
  Adams, S.
Holy Name of Jesus.
  Tegtmeyer, W. C.
Holy Sabbath.
  Singer, A. Shabos Kodesh.
Holy Spirit, Truth Divine.
  Brown, L. F.
Homage to Chopin.
  Trowbridge, L.
Home.
  Owens, H.
Home folk songs.
  Fowler, J. W., comp. Smilin' Bill
    Waters Home folk songs.
Home, give me a home.
  Chanslor, H.
Home in Idaho.
  Clyde, T.
Home of my own.
  Zaret, H.
Home on the range.
  Bland, J. A. Carry me back to old
    Virginny.

Homesick for Heaven.
  Yeazel, C. Gospel songs.
Homeland.
  Woods, J. S.
Homing.
  Del Riego.
Honest injun.
  Carson, J. L.
Honey doll.
  Carleton, R. L.
Honey, I'm bound to go.
  Houdini, W.
Honey, it's you.
  Carleton, R. L.
Honeymoon.
  Cocciardi, F.
Honeymoon.
  Harline, L.
Honolulu march.
  Cernkovich, R., arr.
Honolulu stomp.
  Glynn, B., arr.
Hoodie addie.
  McKinley, R.
Hoosier harmonies.
  Hand, J. R.
Hoosier hop.
  Edwards, B., comp.
Hootie the owl.
  Trowbridge, L. In meadow and
    forest.
Hope thou in God.
  Woodside, J.
Hop-o'-my-thumb.
  Burton, E.
Hopscotch.
  Fouts, M. Children's easy piano
    pieces.
  Mills, A.
Hora de cantar.
  Fuchs, A.
Hora staccato.
  Dinicu.
Hora swing-cato.
  Heifetz, J.
Horas negras.
  Flores, A.
Horizontal.
  Ricca, L.
Horn concerto in E flat.
  Mozart, J. C. W. A. Concerto horn.
Hornicky koník.
  Beneš, B.
Horse guards, Whitehall, arr.
  Wood, H.
Horseback over the sagebrush plain.
  Robb, J. D. Pictures of New Mexico.
Hosanna.
  Granier, J
  Hummel, F.
  Leinbach, E. W.
  Marryott, A.
Hosanna to the Son of David.
  Carr, A.
House and the road.
  Parke, D.
House of funny mirrors.
  Schaum, J. W.
House of O'Brien.
  Goodwin, W.
How are things in Glocca Morra?
  Lane, B. Finian's rainbow.
How big can you get?
  Ram, D.
How big can you get, little man?
  Woode, H.
How can I be sure?
  Griffin, R.
How can I forget?
  Weigle, C. F., ed. Sing a new song.
How can I forget you?
  Gillis, C. E.
How can I make you care?
  Carleton, R. L.
How can I say I love you.
  Coben, C.
How could I ever forget?
  Roth, H. H.

How could I know?
  Litolf, A.
How do you measure love?
  Ryan, C.
How long wilt Thou forget me, O Lord?
  Lekberg, S.
How lovely are the messengers.
  Mendelssohn-Bartholdy, F.
How lucky you are.
  Cassen, E.
How much I owe.
  Woods, J. S.
How sweet I roam'd.
  Mendelssohn-Bartholdy, F.
How to play Hawaiian guitar by note in
    different keys.
  Chaney, W. C., arr.
How to play the flutophone.
  Van Pelt, M. B.
How your trulove to know.
  Richards, D.
Howdy friends.
  McKinley, R.
Howdy! Have a coke!
  Bushkin, J.
Hoy te vas.
  Yamin, J.
Huckleberry Finn.
  Blake, D. G.
Hucksters.
  Pepper, B.
Huérfano.
  Jesús Morales, J. de. Cuando
    lloran los valientes.
Huit pieces très faciles pour piano.
  Schlosser, P.
Hullabaloo balay.
  Rowley, A.
Humming bird.
  Tobin, L.
Humoreske.
  Schumann, R. A.
Humoresque.
  Chalkovskií, P. I.
  Dvořák, A.
  Macomber, K.
  Powers, M.
Hunting song.
  Steinbach, B. Modern miniatures.
Hurdy gurdy.
  Steinbach, B.
Hurra pour l'Espagne!
  Huguet y Tagell, R, J.
Hurricane on de islan'.
  Dungan, O.
Hurry, hurry.
  Komst, M.
Hush! my dear, lie still and slumber.
  Wheaton, H. D.
Hushed are the stars.
  Ferry, C. T. Songs.
Hvem er det, der banker?
  Hall, C.
Hvězda a její stín.
  Cuma, A.
Hymn of thanks to the blessed Virgin
    Mary.
  Marier, T. N.
Hymn of thanksgiving.
  Leidzén, E. W. G.
Hymn of the angels.
  Daley, P. A. Hymnus angelorum.
Hymn of the immortals.
  Williams, D. M.
Hymn to America.
  Bergen, A. H.
(Hymn to)California.
  A'Dair, J.
Hymn to night.
  Rameau, J. P. Hippolyte et Aricie.
Hymn to Saint Frances Xavier Cabrini.
  Zadra, R.
Hymn to the Holy Name.
  O'Connell, W., cardinal.
Hymn to the night.
  Donovan, R.
Hymn to the sun.
  Sanders, G. H. Scheherazada suite.

Hymns for low mass.
  O'Connell, W. H., cardinal.
Hymntime harmonies.
  Stanphill, I. F.
Hymnus angelorum.
  Daley, P. A.
I álogum.
  Pórdarson, S.
I ain't mad at you.
  Sparkler, B.
I always know the way to Piccadilly.
  Gregg, H. Between ourselves.
I am Alpha and Omega.
  McGhee, B. M.
I am coming to the Cross.
  Townsend, P. D. E.
I am crucified with Christ.
  Wylie, D. A.
I am digging at the end of the rainbow.
  Brown, J. W.
I am in love.
  Toutjean, V.
I am now in your arms.
  Richard, L.
I am rejoicing.
  Parker, E. E.
I am satisfied with Jesus.
  Bostwick, F. J.
I am so happy.
  Crosby, V. M.
I am the place where God shines thru.
  Printz, W. F.
I am the prologue.
  Leoncavallo, R. I pagliacci.
I beg your humble pardon, little girl.
  Marion, R.
I believe.
  Styne, J. It happened in Brooklyn.
I bended unto me a bough of May.
  Wood, H.
I bless you in ev'ry prayer.
  Hibbeler, R. O.
I bow my head in silent prayer.
  Krenz, W.
I can not be gay.
  Foldes, A.
I cannot fathom Calvary.
  Tovey, E. M.
I cannot go beyond nor do less.
  Bacon, J. D.
I can't believe it was all make-believe.
  Coots, J. F.
I can't forget the day we met.
  Dossey, W. G.
I can't forget your smile.
  De Witte, A.
I can't get up the nerve to kiss you.
  Weiss, G.
I can't keep the tears out of my eyes.
  Hofner, A. Sweetheart, this is good-
    bye.
I changed horses.
  Hall, C. G.
I come from Missouri.
  Robinson, E. The Missouri story.
I could believe in dreams.
  Hogan, G. A.
I could not live without Jesus.
  De Fluiter, H.
I couldn't forget you.
  Arthur, W.
I cried my last cry last night.
  Arthur, W.
I de lyse naetter.
  Schrader, M.
I do, do, do like you.
  Wrubel, A.
I do not ask, O Lord.
  Verres, L.
I do not love you.
  Rivera, P. No me haces falta.
I don't dread this journey.
  Farmer, W. L.
I don't mind being all alone.
  Mills, I.
I don't wanna dream again.
  Lisbona, E.

176

I don't want to lose you now.
McEnery, D. L.
I don't want to play in your yard.
Petrie, H. W.
I don't want to remember that night.
Jones, J. G.
I dream of Jeanie.
Foster, S. C.
I dreamt I was back in Paris.
Ellis, V.
I en skogsbacke.
Stenhammar, W. Fyra Stockholmsdikter.
I feel better since I got your letter.
Hayes, B.
I feel with my heart.
Carleton, R. L.
I fell for you.
Briggs, F.
I fell in love.
Docking, L.
I found the one I want.
Haber, R.
I found you last night in my dreams.
Nichols, W. H.
I get a kick out of you.
Porter, C.
I get up ev'ry morning.
Lubin, J.
I got a robe.
Roberton, H. S.
I got lost in his arms.
Berlin, I. Annie get your gun.
I got rhythm.
Gershwin, G. Girl crazy.
I got the sun in the morning.
Berlin, I. Annie get your gun.
I got ya' covered, Mister Buzzard.
Hill, H.
I gotta gal I love.
Styne, J. Ladies' man.
I gotta get an awful lot of lovin' baby.
Muller, L.
I greet Thee, my Redeemer.
Bourgeois, L.
I guess I'll have that dream right now.
McHugh, J. F. Hit parade of 1947.
I had a good cry.
Hawkins, E.
I had a sister Susan.
Niles, J. J., ed. & arr. The singing
campus.
I had too much to dream last night.
Livingston, J.
I happen to love you.
Wood, H.
I hate to spend another lonely day.
Moquin, A.
I have a small family here.
Poulton, D. F.
I have love.
Signorelli, F. Yo tengo amor.
I have made a promise and I can't turn
around.
Farmer, Miss W. L.
I have made my reservation.
Weigle, C. F., ed. Sing a new song.
I have resolved to keep the faith.
Hatcher, C. E.
I have waited too long.
Ellstein, A.
I hear my Saviour call.
Van Horn, C.
I hear the sighing winds.
Warren, E. R.
I hear you knockin'.
Hensley, H.
I heard a bird at break of day.
Moore, N.
I heard a great voice.
Billings, W. Compositions.
I heard the bells on Christmas day.
My first christmas songs.
I heard the Lord.
Woods, J. S.
I Held a candle.
Brennan, J. R.

I hope you won't be sorry.
Underwood, J. L.
I just can't forgive you anymore.
Lawson, J.
I just don't care anymore.
King, F.
I just gotta talk about you.
Nutter, C. H.
I just hate to take you home tonight.
Tobin, L.
I just refuse to sing the blues.
Ramirez, R. Boy, what a girl.
I knelt at Jesus' feet.
Ditmar, W.
I knew I'd know.
Lippman, S. Barefoot boy with
cheek.
I knew my Shepherd's voice.
Wood, I.
I knew what I wanted.
Ballard, R.
I know.
Starr, K. G. C.
Woods, J.
I know Christ Jesus understands.
Evangel special sacred songs, no. 1.
I know I can't forget you.
Kramer, W. C.
I know I love Jesus.
Weigle, C. F., ed. Sing a new song.
I know it's love.
Nutter, C. H.
I know my God is able to deliver me.
White, D.
I know something.
Fouts, M. Children's easy piano
pieces.
I know what you're puttin' down.
Allen, B.
I know who threw the whiskey.
Jackson, B. M.
I know you didn't mean to say goodbye.
Rudgins, E.
I learned about love from you.
Dexter, A.
I left my boots and saddle home.
Docking, L.
I let spring go to my head.
Squires, H. D.
I light a cigarette.
Nethercott, D.
I light a cigarette and dream.
Wulffaert, H.
I like boogie woogie.
Görling, U.
I like the Bible book.
Benner, H. C.
I like the lad with the golden hair.
Woodside, J.
I like to have you like to have me love
you.
Lathrop, J.
I like what you say.
Arthur, W.
I lönnens skymning.
Stenhammar, W. Fyra dikter.
I love a married Jew.
Holroyd, C. I. M.
I love a mystery.
Green, J. Something in the wind.
I love geraniums.
Harline, L. Honeymoon.
I love her more.
Bolick, E.
I love my love.
Darwin, L.
I love somebody who doesn't love me.
Heintz, H. J.
I love thee.
Grieg, E. H.
I love to love you in my dreams.
Mossman, T.
I love to sing of home.
Weigle, C. F., ed. Sing a new song.
I love you.
Maur, L.

I love you best.
Wells, C. D.
(I love you) for sentimental reasons.
Best, W.
I love you Mary Lou.
Sullivan, G. Kansas City blues.
I love you so sincerely.
Ferguson, F. M.
I love you still to-day.
Carleton, R. L.
I loved you Johnny.
Malec, A. Kochalam sie, Jasiu.
I loved you when I met you.
Warren, P. D.
I met her in a revolving door.
Hillman, R.
I miss you, dear.
Tobin, L.
I must tell others.
Peterson, J. W. Gospel songs.
I must walk the way with Jesus.
Iden, R. J.
I natt skall jag dö.
Pergament, M.
I need a man.
Houdini, W.
I need my Saviour near me.
Weigle, C. F., ed. Sing a new song.
I need Thee every hour.
Lowry, R.
I never had a chance.
Rose, F.
I never knew what it meant to be lonesome.
Evans, W.
I promised I'd serve Him.
Jackson, M. E.
I put a penny in the gum slot.
Kay, I.
I remember when.
Sanders, A. Ireland today.
I round-up the stars.
Taylor, P.
I saw heaven in disguise.
D'Angelo, L.
I saw no shadow.
Coward, N. Pacific 1860.
I saw the cross of Jesus.
Weigle, C. F., ed. Sing a new song.
I see Jesus everywhere.
Van Buren, B.
I send you my love.
Nurnberg, V.
I sent my love.
Klumpkey, J.
I shall be near to you.
Bush, G.
I shall come again.
Unruh, D. P.
I shall not lack for music.
Ferry, C. T. Songs.
I shall not walk alone.
Edwards, J. B.
I should have used my head and not
my heart.
Ringle, D.
I sing to the sea.
Löwe, R.
I sing unto the Lord.
Bach, J. S. Lobt Ihn mit Herz und
Munde.
I sure got it from you.
Blankenhorn, E.
I think I'll shed a tear.
Arthur, W.
I think of you, my son.
O'Hare, E.
I took a day to search for God.
Dawson, A. E.
I traced her little footprints in the
snow.
King, E.
I varens första natt.
Kraft, A. Klockorna i Gamla stan.
I walk with Love.
Wallbridge, R. L. A.
I walk with my Master each day.
Carleton, R. L.
I walked today where Jesus walked.
O'Hara, G.

I wanna be a friend of yours.
Goell, K.
I want a man.
Mattlin, M.
I want some bread, I said.
Martin, E. N.
I want some love, baby.
Carleton, R. L.
I want to be loved.
Churchill, S.
I want to concentrate on you.
Baird, W. G.
I want to live for Jesus.
Williams, G. J.
I want to send a whisper song.
Poulton, D. E.
I want to sing for Jesus.
Cartwright, F.
I want to thank your folks.
Weiss, G.
I was born a hundred years too late.
Dahle, A.
I was born in Hoboken.
White, M.
I was doin' all right.
Waverly, J.
I was never kissed before.
Ellis, V. Bless the bride.
I wasn't meant for love.
Johnson, J. C.
I wasn't wanting to fall in love.
Edgar, L.
I will be there.
Waller, M.
I will extol Thee.
Diggle, R.
I will lead you safely through.
Mills, G. W.
I will lift up mine eyes.
Bampton, R.
Howard, J. T.
Lekberg, S.
Twinn, S.
Woodward, L., pseud.
I will mind God.
Rogers, W. A.
I will move on up a little higher.
Davis, V.
I will never forget.
Williams, L. L.
I will not doubt.
Weigle, C. F., ed. Sing a new song.
I will see you.
Fouts, M. Children's easy piano
pieces.
I will sing new songs of gladness.
Dvořák, A.
I wish I didn't love you so.
Loesser, F. The perils of Pauline.
I wish I had a pal.
Carnes, J. R.
I wish that my dreams were true.
St. Louis, D.
I wish we'd never met.
Tillman, F. Go out and find somebody
new.
I wish you could love me.
Carver, Z.
I wonder as I wander.
Niles, J. J., arr.
I wonder, I wonder, I wonder.
Hutchins, D. F.
I wonder when we'll meet again.
Hargrove, E. D.
I wonder who's kissing her now.
Howard, J. E.
I wonder why I do not hear from you.
Carleton, R. L.
I won't be home any more when you call.
Fairman, B.
I won't cry over you.
Sweatman, J. M.
I won't hang around you anymore.
Pike, R.
I worry 'bout you.
Hillebrand, F.
I worship Him.
Marryott, R. E.

I would see Jesus in glory.
Williams, D. W.
Ice cream man.
Hopkins, H. P.
Ich freue mich im Herrn.
Bach, J. S. Lobt Ihn mit Herz und
Munde. I sing unto the Lord.
Fox, F. Kaugummi.
Ich wandte mich und sahe an.
Brahms, J. Four serious songs.
Ich weiss nicht, was soll es bedeuten.
Silcher, F. The Loreley.
I'd do the impossible for you.
Gallop, S.
I'd give a lot.
Edgar, L.
I'd like to be a cow in Switzerland.
Gorman, P.
I'd like to have a cottage all our own.
Hibbeler, R. O.
I'd never give you up.
Pentuff, O.
I'd rather have a poor man than a
rich man.
Carleton, R. L.
I'd rather walk with Jesus.
Weigle, C. F., ed. Sing a new song.
I'd trade all of my tomorrows.
Carson, J. L.
Ida from Idaho.
Van Sickle, R.
Ida-Idaho.
Van Sciver, E.
Ida red.
Winstead, K. C.
Idol of my heart.
Wolfson, L. H.
Idyl.
White, P.
Idyll.
A'Dair, J.
If God forgot.
O'Hara, G.
If I could dream forever.
Mitchell, J. B.
If I could steal you.
Grimes, D. A.
If I ever get you in my arms.
Halama, F. J.
If I ever make you cry.
King, F.
If I fall in love again.
Felton, G.
If I flew blind.
Furney, A. J.
If I only knew.
Yamin, J. Hoy te vas.
If I wasn't in your dream last night,
dream again.
Kulma.
If I'd only be true to you.
Folger, B.
If I'm lucky.
Myrow, J.
If it's love you want baby, that's me.
Robin, S.
If it's love you'll know it.
Browne, L. B.
If it's Thy will.
Ellis, S. L.
If love stays away from my door.
Kieselmann, J. H.
If my heart had a window.
Loeb, J. J.
If this isn't love.
Lane, B. Finian's rainbow.
If with all your hearts.
Mendelssohn-Bartholdy, F.
If you are near.
Bach, J. S. Bist du bei mir.
If you can't be the bell cow, fall in
behind.
Cooke, L.
If you knew Susie.
Meyer, J.
If you roll out the barrel once too often,
the barrel will roll over you.
Neveloff, A.

If you talk just right to me.
Davis, N. C.
If you want it, Dixie has it.
Pitman, H. M.
If you were the only girl in the world.
Ayer, N. D.
If you would give Christ to the nations.
Boornstra, P. Z.
If your love goes away the birds will
sing no more.
Broekman, D.
Ignorance is bliss.
Lubin, J.
Igor.
Rogers, M.
Ikdar.
Mraczek, J. G.
Il a le regard francais.
Delettre, J.
Il était une fois.
Chantrier, A.
I'll always be in love with you.
Stept, S. H.
I'll always love you.
Gay, N. Sweetheart mine.
I'll always remember.
Pinkard, E. B. A.
I'll be at rest.
Ford, H. J.
I'll be coming back your way.
Polovina, M. J.
I'll be fightin' old Satan 'til I die.
Sizemore, A.
I'll be satisfied.
Hensley, H.
I'll be there.
Stept, S. H.
I'll be true to you, my darling.
Williamson, G.
I'll bless your darlin' heart.
Fulkerson, M.
I'll come back.
Leverton, B.
I'll follow you.
Suarez, H. Siguiéndote.
I'll forget if you'll forgive.
Darling, D.
I'll get along somehow.
Posey, E.
I'll get under her umbrella.
Hibbeler, R. O.
I'll go all the way with Jesus.
Webb, W. A.
I'll go home with bonnie Jean.
Loewe, F. Brigadoon.
I'll help my mother.
Poulton, D. F.
I'll hide in Jesus.
Thorne, W. M.
I'll never be sorry I care.
Peterson, R. A.
I'll never be sweetheart again.
Shelton, B. Let's be sweethearts
always.
I'll never fall in love anymore.
Kregal, M.
I'll never grieve.
McClellan, C.
I'll remember that in the moonlight.
Carleton, R. L.
I'll save my love for you.
Granato, L.
I'll say I do.
Buller, B.
I'll see you again.
Hodges, J.
I'll see you again little darlin'.
Wickens, C. M.
I'll sing and be happy.
Van Tyle, R.
I'll smile again.
Gray, H.
I'll stand by our grand old U. S. ship.
Gannon, R. E.
I'll step aside.
Rice, H.
I'll take Jesus with me.
Smith, Mrs. C.

178

I'll tell my lonely heart.
  Czajkowski, F. T.
I'll tell the world I love you.
  Carleton, R. L.
I'll write myself a letter.
  Sendrey, A.
Illusion.
  Cugat, X.
Ils ont tout vu!
  Sarrat, A. J. I.
I'm a cowboy.
  Navarro, J. J. Soy ranchero.
I'm a gal of property.
  Roberts, A. Singin' in the corn.
I'm a married man.
  McEnery, A.
I'm a millionaire.
  Baird, W. G.
I'm afraid to love you.
  McCarthy, P.
I'm all down in the dumps.
  Carleton, R. L.
I'm always dreaming about you.
  Reese, C.
I'm always sleepin'.
  Van Zandt, J.
I'm always thinking of you.
  Cassady, E. E.
I'm an eagle.
  Berendsohn, B.
I'm bewildered.
  Hovey, V.
I'm bringing a rose from old Ireland.
  Cantwell, N.
I'm buildin' a stairway in to Heaven.
  Kenny, J.
I'm comin' home.
  Becker, W.
I'm crazy over the moon.
  Wickens, C. M.
I'm dreaming of you.
  Arthur, W.
  Samuels, W.
I'm drownin' in your deep blue eyes.
  Kent, W.
I'm falling in love with you.
  Chittenden, E.
I'm forever blowing bubbles.
  Kellette, J. W.
  Kenbrovin, J., pseud.
I'm glad His blood reaches me.
  Townsend, P. D. E.
I'm glad I'm Sioux City Sue.
  Leveiller, C. P. J.
I'm glad that I met my sunshine.
  Karr, J. J.
I'm goin' home where I belong.
  Knutson, T.
I'm going home to see my Saviour.
  Tukes, S.
I'm going there and see.
  Spencer, L. D.
I'm going to make it in.
  Posey, E.
I'm gonna be boss.
  Ashlock, J.
I'm gonna dust off my saddle.
  Japhet, C.
I'm gonna hop on a cloud.
  Leonard, A.
I'm gonna write myself a letter.
  Davis, J.
I'm happier unhappy with you.
  Arthur, W.
I'm happy-go-lucky and free.
  Green, J. Something in the wind.
I'm henpecked.
  Martin, E.
I'm in love with a song.
  Leonard, C.
I'm in love with you.
  Brewer, J.
I'm jealous of your dream.
  Peterson, J. C.
I'm just a bachelor, I.
  Carleton, R. L.
I'm just a Yankee too.
  Pollack, R.

I'm just an old man.
  McDermott, A.
I'm keepin' tabs on you.
  Roth, H. H.
I'm like a raindrop.
  Carleton, R. L.
I'm living a lie.
  Goodhart, A.
I'm living by faith and grace.
  Jackson, M. E.
I'm living for God.
  Edwards, J. M.
I'm longing for love 'cause it's spring-
    time.
  Carleton, R. L.
I'm looking for a Jack of all trades.
  Carr, M.
I'm looking for a word.
  Rich, M.
I'm lost.
  Navarro, J. J. Perdida.
I'm lost without you.
  Monahan, J. B.
I'm mindin' my business.
  Greene, J.
I'm not just a whistling Dixie.
  Wickens, C. M. The merry maker's
    polka.
I'm not the reason why girls leave home.
  Knutson, T.
I'm on my way to heaven.
  Bennett, D. E.
I'm picking up the pieces of my heart.
  Tobin, L.
I'm pleading for the wings.
  Perry, C. T.
I'm riding alone.
  Zahoratos, G. T.
I'm sad again, I'm blue again tonight.
  Fernando, D. D.
I'm saving my kisses for you.
  Brooks, G. C.
I'm seeking for a city.
  Ford, H. J.
I'm singing this song to you.
  Cernkovich, R. Pjesmu ti pjevam.
I'm smiling to hide an aching heart.
  Standefer, J.
I'm so glad God knows my heart.
  Rhynes, M. A. J.
I'm so glad I let Jesus come in.
  Weigle, C. F., ed. Sing a new song.
I'm somebody's something today.
  Carleton, R. L.
I'm sometimes weeping.
  Posey, E.
I'm sorry to see Sunday go by.
  Bergere, R.
I'm still sitting under the apple tree.
  Styne, J.
I'm talkin' to you.
  Giersdorf, H. W.
I'm telling you.
  Lewis, J.
I'm telling you now.
  McHugh, J. F. Calendar girl.
I'm the romancing king.
  Arthur, W.
I'm through with other lovers.
  Rodrigues, J.
I'm traveling the King's highway.
  Sutton, V.
I'm under a cloud, dear.
  Carleton, R. L.
I'm waiting for April.
  Klemans, T. A.
I'm waiting for you.
  Rivera, P. Te esperare.
I'm walking with Jesus.
  Weigle, C. F., ed. Sing a new song.
Images.
  Nadyval.
Immortal love, forever full.
  Wallace, W. V.
Imp.
  Alford, H.
Impresario.
  Cimarosa, D.

Impression.
  Greenburg, R. G.
Improvisation.
  Achron, I.
Pick, R. S.
Improvisation and burlesque.
  Lora, A.
In a glass of water before retiring.
  Bergsma, W.
In a Hungarian market place.
  Rebe, L. C.
In a little bungalow just built for two.
  Arthur, W.
In a little candy store.
  Lisztoff, G.
In a little Irish village.
  Spross, C. G.
In a shanty in old Shanty Town.
  Little, J.
In a summer garden.
  Bentley, B. B.
In a Viennese garden.
  Herbert, V.
In an autumn garden.
  Evans, L.
In an eighteenth century drawing
    room.
  Scott, R.
In Bethlehem's lowly manger.
  Williams, F.
In David's town.
  Elmore, R.
In days of old.
  Woods, J. S.
In deepest need.
  Dieterich, M.
In endless song.
  Booth, G.
In Gethsemane.
  Weigle, C. F., ed. Sing a new song.
In God's book.
  Truss, I. T.
In heavenly love abiding.
  Bixby, A. K.
In Jesus' name.
  Swift, F. F.
In love.
  Keath, R.
In love with my wonderful Lord.
  Webb, W. A.
In meadow and forest.
  Trowbridge, L.
In memoriam.
  Kesnar, M. Seven pieces.
In my dreams.
  Lucchesi, R. Douce biguine.
  Pauly, F.
In my father's garden polka.
  Malec, A. U mego tatusia.
In my garden of memory.
  Potter, H.
In my garden (springtime).
  Mayerl, B.
In my garden (summertime).
  Mayerl, B.
In my heart.
  Arthur, W.
In my home over there.
  Ford, H. J.
In my moonlit garden.
  Carleton, R. L.
In old Missouri.
  Swineford, L. P.
In praise of food.
  Lemaire, C. hanson a manger.
In primeval forest.
  Hokanson, M.
In quiet pastures.
  Coleman, B.
In retrospect.
  Trowbridge, L.
In salutation.
  Ratcliffe, D.
In slumberland I dream of you.
  Harrop, F.
In the beginning.
  Gipson, T. L.

In the cottonwood.
  Robb, J. D. Pictures of New Mexico.
In the Dells of old Wisconsin.
  Wickens, C. M.
In the depths of my heart.
  Carleton, R. L.
In the desert.
  Anson, G.
In the evening by the moonlight.
  Bland, J. A.
In the evening through the dark forest
    waltz.
  Malec, A. Ciemnym borem nad
    wieczorem.
In the garden.
  Miles, C. A.
In the gloaming.
  Harrison, A. F.
In the height of summer.
  Seymer, W. Strofer i sol och skugga.
In the Indian village.
  Robb, J. D. Pictures of New Mexico.
In the land of golden dreams.
  Hibbeler, R. O.
In the land of Shangri-la.
  Lake, M.
In the little red school house.
  Brennan, J. A.
In the morning.
  Markland, L.
In the morning He is with me.
  Harwood, R. E.
In the note that I wrote you last night.
  Hinderer, E. R.
In the perfect tomorrow.
  Iden, R. J.
In the regions beyond.
  Tovey, H. G.
In the still of the night.
  Porter, C.
In the style of Hanon.
  Maloof, A.
In the vale of Tempe.
  Cronham, C. R.
In the valley at home.
  Howard, J. T.
In time for Easter.
  Wilson, F. C.
In Vienna so far away.
  Siegel, P.
In your arms.
  Nelson, H.
Incantesimo.
  Olivieri, D. Tutto il mondo canta
    Tornerai.
Incognito.
  Clayton, B.
Independence Day.
  Warren, H. Summer holiday.
Indian baby.
  Fouts, M. Children's easy piano
    pieces.
Indian legend.
  Marsh, C. H.
Indian love call.
  Friml, R.
Indiana blues.
  Leas, L.
Indiana Jim.
  Richard, L.
Indiana Varsity.
  Sweet, M.
Inflation.
  Lee, L.
Ingénue de Londres.
  Blareau, R.
  Blareau, R. Souviens-toi.
  Blareau, R. Le sport.
  Blareau, R. Valse des coeurs.
  Blareau, R. La vie de printemps.
Ingénue de mon coeur.
  Blareau, R. L'ingenue de Londres.
Inseparables.
  Mersson, B.
Insieme.
  Panzuti, V.
Inspiracion.
  Paulos, N. E.

Instant-modulator.
  Smith, H. M.
Interlude.
  Boland, C. A. Chris crosses.
  Hore, C.
  Morrissey, J. J.
Intermediate steps to the band.
  Taylor, M. D.
Intermezzo for a day in May.
  Broekman, D.
Intermission riff.
  Wetzel, R.
Intimní obrázky.
  Kvapil, J.
Into my heart I've taken my Lord.
  Tovey, H. G.
Intrata quasi springar.
  Beck, T. L. Dansar fra Gudbrandsdal.
Intricate is the weaving.
  Pendleton, E. Quiet paths.
Introducing the accordion, 12 to 120 bass.
  Bedlon, J. H.
Introduction and Allegro spiritoso.
  Senaillé, J. B.
Introduction to Hanon.
  Bezdek, J.
Introductions and endings.
  Goodsell, E. M., comp. Popular
    piano breaks.
Introdukce a fuga.
  Janecek, K.
Introduzione, Danza delle 9 musè,
    Orchesis di Apollo.
  Robbiani, I. Roma dei Cesari.
Introvert.
  Földes, A. Two pieces for piano.
Intuition.
  Moore, M. C.
Invocando a changé.
  Vazquez, E.
Invocation.
  Addinsell, R.
Invocazione.
  Rusconi, E.
Ireland today.
  Sanders, A.
Irenita.
  Guida, P.
Irma.
  Rolland, C. R.
Irwin Dash selection of serenades.
  Cleve, J. H., arr.
Is there anyone here from Texas?
  McHugh, J. F. Hit parade of 1947.
Is there somebody else?
  Garett, G.
Is this you, world, that used to be?
  Preston, E. P.
Iskiereczka ognia.
  Malec, A.
Island fantasy.
  Moore, M.
Island of dreams.
  Zanella, A. L'isola dei sogni.
Island paradise.
  Dunagan, E.
Isola dei sogni.
  Zanella, A.
Israel.
  Durrant, F.
Israel's keeper.
  Binder, A. W. Shomer Yisroel.
  Das ist das Glück!
    Laszlo, S.
It came upon the midnight clear.
  My first Christmas songs.
It gets me.
  Riggs, S. K.
It had to be you.
  Jones, I.
It happened in Brooklyn.
  Styne, J.
It happened on Fifth Avenue.
  Revel, H.
It has no ending.
  Weirick, J.
It hasn't been chilly in Chile.
  Van Heusen, J. Cross my heart.

It is not the tear.
  Taylor, C.
It is sweet to walk with Jesus.
  Jenkins, E. M.
It just ain't right.
  Stevenson, H. P.
It just shows to go ya.
  Granato, L.
It might have been a different story.
  Addy, M. J.
It seems I can't forget.
  Ellsworth, A. B.
It takes time.
  Korb, A.
It was at an old Hawaiian luau.
  George, D. R.
It wasn't the rum.
  Joyce, J.
It will all be over by and by.
  Robinson, W. C.
It won't be long.
  D'Angelo, L.
Italian street song.
  Herbert, V.
It's a good day.
  Barbour, D.
It's a moonlight night.
  Deane, B.
It's a sin.
  Turner, Z.
It's a wonderful, wonderful feeling.
  Revel, H. It happened on Fifth Avenue.
It's all in the mind.
  Roberts, A. Cigarette girl.
It's all up to you.
  Styne, J.
It's all wicky wacky in Hawaii.
  George, D. R.
It's as simple as that.
  Arden, N.
It's dark outside.
  Sooter, R.
It's Easter time once more.
  Mulder, H. J.
It's girls like you.
  Mitchell, J. B.
It's nothing but love.
  Wilson, S. H.
It's only love.
  Green, J. Something in the wind.
It's snowing.
  Hovemann, C.
It's so important.
  Jackson, M. E.
It's the color of my eyes.
  Cotton, V. L.
It's the same old dream.
  Styne, J. It happened in Brooklyn.
It's the same old moon.
  Carr, F. L.
It's the same the whole world over.
  Boland, C. A. Chris crosses.
It's the twink, twink, twinkle in your
    eye.
  Campbell, T.
It's too nice a day to go to school.
  Lippman, S. Barefoot boy with cheek.
I've been buked.
  Johnson, H.
I've changed my mind.
  Watkins, M. C.
I've fallen in love with an angel.
  Ellison, J. M.
I've found the rainbow's end.
  McPhail, L.
I've got a gal in Laramie.
  Thomas, D.
I've got April in my heart.
  Schulman, R. M.
I've got stuff.
  Kennedy, A.
I've got you.
  Carlisle, J.
I've learned my lesson.
  Chappelear, L.
I've lost all confidence in you.
  Yamin, J. Desconfianza de tu amor.

I've waited for someone like you to
come along.
  Gonzales, V.
Ivy.
  Carmichael, H.
J'ai laissé mon coeur à Paris.
  Delettre, J.
J'ai tout donné.
  Blareau, R. L'ingénue de Londres.
J'ai un beau chapeau.
  Dumas, R.
J'aime ta pomme.
  Goulding, E. The razor's edge.
J'attends dans un rêve.
  Siniavine, A.
J'attends ton retour.
  Carbo Menendez, J.
J'en ai un p'tit bout.
  Blareau, R. L'ingénue de Londres.
J'entends mon amour.
  Durand, P. J.
J'suis Parigote.
  Parys, G. v.
J'suis un p'tit môme de Levallois.
  White, D. J.
Ja som bača velmi starý.
  Schimmerling, H. A., arr.
Jack-in-the-box.
  Travis, B.
Jack, you're dead!
  Pothier, R.
Jackanapes.
  Evans, H. P.
Jack's boogie.
  Ridgway, J.
Jack's ideas.
  Dieval, J.
Jag blott tango dansa vill.
  Ahl, H.
Jag lägger ut igen.
  Frykman, E.
Jaliscienses.
  Bermejo, F.
Jalousie.
  Gade, J.
Jam session in Brazil.
  Myrow, J. If I'm lucky.
Jamboree.
  Spelman, T. M.
James Story band book.
  Story, J.
Jan.
  Benjamin, A.
Jap and it.
  Walker, F. A. E.
Jardin d'amour.
  Vuillermoz, É.
Jardin des ombres.
  Gallois-Montbrun, R. Les rêves de
    Janceline.
Java du champagne.
  Blareau, R. L'ingénue de Londres.
Je cueille un bouquet.
  Droniou, R.
Je n'ai rien oublié.
  Emer, M.
Je ne sais plus qi tu m'aimes.
  Perrari, L.
Je t'peux pas m'expliquer.
  Dumas, R.
Je pars!
  Chairopoulos, C. K.
Je pense a vous.
  Lambert, R.
Je sais une chanson.
  Lenoir, J.
Je suis a toi.
  Travnicek, A.
Je suis un pauvre gars.
  Guglielmi, L. Ploum ploum tra la la.
Je t'en prie.
  Lambert, R. No tengo gana.
Je vous aime.
  Coslow, S. Copacabana.

Jealousy.
  Gade, J. Jalousie.
Jeanne Mance song.
  Mary Helene, sister.
Jeg elsker en anden.
  Gyldmark, S.
Jennie was a lady.
  Blane, R.
Jenny kissed me.
  Grean, C.
Jenny Lind polka.
  Glynn, B., arr.
Jenny Lind waltz.
  Melecci, A.
Jephtha.
  Carissimi, G. Plorate filii Israel.
Jericho road.
  McCrossan, D. S.
Jerusalem.
  Parker, H.
  Parry, C. H. H.
Jesu, joy of man's desiring.
  Bach, J. S.
  Bach, J. S. Herz und Mund and That
    und Leben.
Jesu Leiden Pein und Tod.
  Bach, J. S. Jesus suffered pain and
    death.
Jesu, Word of God Incarnate.
  Wilkinson, C. A. R.
Jesus abides with me.
  Weigle, C. F., ed. Sing a new song.
Jesus calls us.
  Jude, W. H.
Jesus Christ is risen today.
  Rowley, A.
Jesus Christ our Lord.
  Cadwallader, J. R.
Jesus Christ, our Saviour.
  Bach, J. S. Jesus Christus, unser
    Heiland.
Jesus Christus, unser Heiland.
  Bach, J. S.
Jesus, dear and precious Saviour.
  Christman, T. L.
Jesus, fount of joy and peace.
  Bach, J. S.
Jesus gives me victory.
  Townsend, P. D. E.
Jesus has died that we might live.
  Thorne, W. M.
Jesus has saved me from sin.
  Kellar, B.
Jesus! How wonderful Thou art to me.
  Prints, W. F.
Jesus, I my cross have taken.
  Mozart, J. C. W. A.
Jesus in the garden.
  Marth, H. J.
Jesus is a friend of mine.
  Fisher, A. P.
Jesus is calling.
  Slater, W. W.
Jesus is my friend.
  Townsend, P. D. E.
Jesus is my friend and brother.
  Thorne, W. M.
Jesus is the lover of my soul.
  Yoder, A. T.
Jesus is waiting for me.
  Meller, L. P.
Jesus is waiting to save you.
  Elliot, J. An evangel in song.
Jesus is with me.
  Wolverton, M. H.
Jesus, Jesus, rest Your head.
  Niles, J. J.
Jesus keeps me singing.
  Johnson, V.
Jesus knows.
  Cosselmon, R. A.
Jesus knows and understands.
  Yeazel, C. Gospel songs.
Jesus knows it's hard for me to bear.
  McDuffy, M. L.
Jesus, lover of my soul.
  Marsh, S. B.

Jesus loves me.
  Townsend, P. D. E.
Jesus loves the little children.
  Poulton, D. F.
Jesus, my Lord.
  Weigle, C. F., ed. Sing a new song.
Jesus' name, how sweet to me.
  Fromm, H. E.
Jesus never fails.
  Takens, M. L.
Jesus, only Saviour.
  Evangel special sacred songs, no. 1.
Jesus, our mighty Lord.
  Shenk, L. Two heroic hymns of praise.
Jesus put a song in my soul.
  Ford, H. J.
Jesus ransomed me.
  Lillenas, H. We're looking for a city.
Jesus requires of you to be true.
  Thornton, A. F. D.
Jesus satisfies.
  Hamilton, D. A.
Jesus saved me.
  Meller, L. P.
Jesus, so lowly.
  Friedell, H.
Jesus suffered pain and death.
  Bach, J. S.
Jesus the Christ is born.
  Niles, J. J.
Jesus, the dearest Friend.
  Gaddis, R. M. Abraham, the pilgrim.
Jesus, the very thought of Thee.
  Dykes, J. B.
Jesus, Thou my heart's delight.
  Bach, J. S.
Jesus, Thy boundless love to me.
  Shenk, L. Two heroic hymns of
    praise.
Jesus, to Thy table led.
  Schubert, F. P.
Jesus will care for His own.
  Yeazel, C. Gospel songs.
Jeux.
  Goletti, N.
Jeux d'eau.
  Ravel, M.
Jim and Jon, the cowboys.
  O'Dell, E. O.
Jim jam boogie.
  Scott, L.
Jimmy de Harlem.
  Delettre, J.
  Jacobs, M., arr. Boogie woogie
    step-by-step.
Jingles all the way.
  Cable, H. R.
Jitterbug jazz.
  Kreager, J. S.
Job's God is true.
  Oden, M. M.
Jocelyn.
  Godard, B. L. P.
Jock of Hazeldean.
  Castelnuovo-Tedesco, M.
Joe Palooka.
  Mossman, T.
John Reed.
  Siegmeister, E. American legends.
John Shirley's prayer.
  Monk, H.
Johnny Appleseed.
  Alexander, J. Three American
    episodes.
Johnny Bach.
  Harper, J.
Johnny jumped the ocean.
  Schaum, J. W.
La joie de vivre.
  Gratton, H.
Jole Blon.
  Acuff, R., arr. Our own Jole Blon.
Jolie blonde.
  Earlee, P.
  King, S.
Jolly Bob från Aberdeen.
  Dahlquist, L. E.

Jolly lumberjack.
  Wagner, J. F.
Jolly rhythm polka.
  Zajc, F.
Jolson story.
  Berlin, I.
  Chaplin, S.
  Jolson, A.
Jones laughing record.
  Jones, S., arr.
Jorden är blott du och jag och mull.
  Eriksson, J. Två dikter.
Josélito.
  Gravina, F.
  Travnicek, A.
Joseph and his brethren.
  Méhul, É.-N. O brother mine.
Joseph 'n his brudders.
  Kroll, B.
Jour sans toi.
  Hepman, G.
Journée.
  Milhaud, D.
Journey's end.
  Foree, M.
Joy and pain.
  Matteson, M.
Joy complete.
  Pankratz, A. J.
Joy of His Presence.
  Horst, A. G.
Joyous interlude.
  Lée, D.-K.
Juanita.
  Martin, V. L., arr.
Jubilate Deo.
  Blake, L.
  Elaine, sister.
  Singenberger, J. B.
Jubilee.
  Porter, C.
Jubilee cantata.
  Burk, A. E.
Jueves.
  Toranzo, U.
Juggling clown.
  Carter, B.
Juke box blues.
  Copas, C.
Juke joint mama.
  Horton, V.
Julian porteño.
  Donato, E.
Julvisa.
  Kraft, A. Livet pa landet.
July.
  Glazer, F.
Jumping beans.
  Templeton, V.
Jumping mouse.
  Lake, G.
Jumping on the bed.
  Fouts, M. Children's easy piano
    pieces.
Jumping rope rhyme.
  Coupland, L. H.
June in our hearts.
  Carleton, R. L.
June, June.
  Powers, M.
June morning.
  Sequel-Holst, M.
Jungfru Margits vårvisa.
  Jonsson, J. Tre visor.
Jungle rhyme.
  Kukol, C. T.
Jungle serenade.
  Lopez, F.
Juniata bound.
  Gaul, H.
Junior Miss plays the piano.
  King, S.
Junior Mister plays the piano.
  King, S.
Just a cabin in the mountains.
  Carleton, R. L.

Just a few more shadows.
  Johns, V. J.
Just a flower.
  Tomsha, W.
Just a little blue.
  Mead, J. F.
Just a little tugboat.
  Carleton, R. L.
Just a memory.
  Henderson, R.
Just a sigh of love.
  Clyde, T.
Just abide in Jesus.
  Fowler, G.
Just an old fashioned girl in a new
    fashioned bonnet.
  Norris, G.
Just an old forgotten letter.
  Carlisle, C. R.
Just an old love of mine.
  Barbour, D.
Just another headache.
  McDermott, A.
Just as you are.
  Van Sickle, R.
Just as you are.
  Van Tyle, R.
Just beyond my dreams.
  Dasher, J. D.
Just blame it on fate.
  Robinson, E.
Just blue delphinium and you.
  Erisman, F.
Just call me your love, love.
  Arthur, W.
Just hangin' on.
  Call, I.
Just have to know.
  McNeil, J. C.
Just keep still.
  Smith, W. M. F.
Just lazin' around.
  Carleton, R. L.
Just leave it all with Jesus.
  Ackley, A. H.
Just like Darby and Joan.
  Lonergan, M.
Just like Jesus.
  Morris, K.
Just one dream after another.
  Mulé, L.
Just one of those things.
  Porter, C. Jubilee.
Just plain love.
  Cowan, J.
Just say so long.
  Long, S.
Just suppose.
  Arthur, W.
Just to be with you tonight.
  Chanslor, H.
Just vengeance.
  Hopkins, A.
Just want to be loved by Bill.
  Clarke, I. V.
Jutta kommer till Folkungarna.
  Stenhammar, W. Fyra dikter.
Ka nalu.
  Koki, S.
Kärleksvisa.
  Koch, S. v. Morgenländische
    Liebeslieder.
Kaerlighed og du og jeg.
  Gyldmark, S. Hans Onsdags-Veninde.
Kaerlighedens Sang.
  Gyldmark, S. (Elly Petersen)Chanson
    d'amour.
Kain berneli as viliojau.
  Zemaitaitis, J. P.
Kaj się dzialy one lata.
  Rathaus, K. Oh, Yody, Yody.
Kaleidoscope.
  Cyl, C. Orientale.
  Rózsa, M.
Kalinka.
  Krone, B.
Kalle på Spången.
  Kraft, A.

Kane mou ligē sintrophia.
  Sougioul, M.
Kansas City blues.
  Sullivan, G.
Kardies pou smixane.
  Iakōbidēs, Z.
Karl XII:s marsch.
  Harteveld, W., arr. Marcia
    Carolus XII, svecorum rex.
Kashwa.
  Sas, A. Ollantay.
Kate, have I come too early, too late?
  Berlin, I.
Katjesspel.
  Berg, C. J. van den.
Kaugummi.
  Fox, F.
Keep America singing.
  Thorne, F. H.
Keep me humble, Lord.
  Pace, C. H.
Keep me 'neath the shadow of Thy
    cross.
Keep our country free.
  Smith, V. M.
Keep pushing along.
  Simpson, W. G.
Keep smiling.
  Ellsworth, A. B.
Keep the faith.
  Carrier, V.
Keep your lamps trimmed.
  Cain, N.
Keep your little cup.
  Green, A. Eight new sacred
    choruses.
Keep your mind on what you're doin'.
  Chittenden, E.
Keepsakes.
  Herbert, V. Gypsy lady.
Kenvreuriez ar Viniouerin..
  Arnoux, G., comp.
Keys to happiness.
  Halbee, S. W.
Kiddies' polka.
  Levenger, G.
Kilbourn centennial greeting.
  Kappelmann, E. G.
Kilbourn centennial hymn.
  Kappelmann, E. G.
Killarney and you.
  Kenny, S. W.
Killyburn braes.
  Dawn, M.
Kilroy boy.
  Ahlstrand, D.
Kilroy really was here.
  ˙ Kane, M.
Kilroy was here.
  Edwards, J.
Kilroy's no kill-joy.
  Arthur, W.
Kind of girl I've dreamed of.
  Tepper, S. (At last I've found)the kind of
    girl I've dreamed of.
Kind treatment.
  Paparelli, F.
Kinder paradi js.
  Nieland, H. J. J.
King.
  Basie, C.
King and Teacher evermore.
  Horst, A. G. The joy of His Presence.
King Christian stood by the lofty mast.
  Darcy, T. F., arr. National anthem
    of Denmark.
King Cole Trio novelty song parade.
  Goldsen, M. H.
King is born today.
  Williams, F.
King of love my Shepherd is.
  Cain, N.
King Olaf.
  Elgar, E.
King Winter.
  Dunhill, T. F.
Kiss in the dark.
  Herbert, V. Orange blossoms.

Kiss me goodnight, love.
  Kelly, N.
Kiss my tears away.
  Flack, D. K.
Kiss your boy goodbye.
  Tobin, L.
Kjempevise-slåtten.
  Saeverud, H. Siljustøl.
Klapse phtōchē kardia mou.
  Poggès, A. E.
Klarinettenquintett.
  Kornauth, E. Quintet, clarinet &
    strings.
Klavervaerker.
  Buxtehude, D.
Klavírní etudy.
  Schaefer, T.
Klavírní repertoir.
  Petrželka, V. Suita pro klavír.
  Schäfer. Furiant.
Klavírní variace na vlastní thema.
  Blažek, Z.
Kleine kontrapunktische Stücke.
  Brockt, J. Piccoli pezzi kontrapuntistici.
Kleine Nachtmusik.
  Mozart, J. C. W. A.
Kleine walzer.
  Mittler, F.
Klockorna i Gamla stan.
  Kraft, A.
Knickknacks.
  Hellard, R. A.
Koanga.
  Delius, F.
Kochajam się, Jasiu.
  Malec, A.
Königin von Cirta.
  Pedrollo, A. La regina di Cirta.
Koimēsou mes tēn ankalia mou.
  Iakobleph, N. P.
Kokomo Island.
  Walker, C.
Kom, naar Lykken kalder!
  Gyldmark, S. Fröken Vildkat.
Kompologaki!
  Mitsaki, G.
Koupim ja si koně vraný.
  Schimmerling, H. A.
Kreisleriana.
  Schumann, R. A.
Krysař.
  Bořkovec, P.
Kung Eriks sista visa.
  Rangstrom, T. Ur Kung Eriks
    visor.
Kungl.
  Rydberg, S.
En kväll i april.
  Kromhow, A.
Kväll i Klara.
  Stenhammar, W. Fyra Stockholms-
    dikter.
En kväll på Henriksberg.
  Dahlquist, L. E.
Kvarnen.
  Kraft, A. När seklet var ungt.
  Pergament, M. Tre små sånger.
Kvernslått.
  Saeverud, H. Siljustøl.
Kvintet.
  Hlobil, E. Quintet, strings.
  Krejčí, M. Quintet, strings.
Kytice písní českých.
  Axman, E.
Labor.
  Devonshire, T.
Lacrime di pioggia.
  Panzuti, V.
Ladies' man.
  Styne, J.
Ladies of Leamington.
  Hilliam, B. C.
Lady be good.
  Gershwin, G.
Lady bird's waltz.
  Hopkins, H. P.
Lady comes to an inn.
  Hageman, R.

Lady from 29 palms.
  Wrubel, A.
Lady Godiva.
  Novák, V.
Lady of old Shanty Town.
  Marcell, R.
Laendler no. 11.
  Elsnic, J. F.
Längtans vals.
  Lindberg, O.
Lagos de Moreno.
  Ochoa, D.
Lágrimas de sangre.
  Coen, A.
Lágrimas del corazon.
  Vidal, F. L.
Laissons dormir nos souvenirs.
  Alongi, F.
Lakmé.
  Delibes, L.
Lalo estuvo aquí.
  Del Río, P.
Lamb of God.
  Lehman, E.
Lambda Chi welcome song.
  Davis, A.
Lament of Pan.
  Battate, A. E.
Lament of the owl.
  El tecolote.
Lamentation for a day of mourning.
  Breydert, F. M. Vox in Rama.
Lamento.
  Tizol, F.
The lamplighter.
  Hampton, L.
Land next to heaven.
  Tyler, L. J.
Land of the Midnight Sun.
  Carleton, R. L.
Landel.
  Wideen, I. Tre Pär Lagerkvist-
    dikter.
Langey-Carl Fischer tutors.
  Langey, O.
  See also title entry in composer list.
Largo.
  Händel, G. F.
Lark.
  Emery, W.
  Steinbach, B. Modern miniatures.
Larkin's blues.
  Larkin, M.
Last man I'll ever lose.
  Campbell, B.
Last night.
  Richard, L.
Last round-up.
  Hill, B.
Last Viking.
  Gade, J.
Last will.
  Vašata, R. L. Poslední přání.
Latin American airs.
  Van Der Molen, A., comp.
Latin-American dance album.
  Nolasco, F. A., arr.
Laugh and be merry.
  Shaw, G.
Laugh at life.
  May, H.
Laughing patrol.
  Oliver, H.
Laura Noll's prediction song.
  Noll, L. A.
Lavandera.
  Menendez, N.
Lay down your soul.
  Ande, G.
Lay your habits down.
  Bernhardt, C.
Lay your hand upon my shoulder.
  Baggett, N.
Lazy afternoon.
  Siegmeister, E. American legends.
Lazy blues.
  Stevens, T.

Lazy buckaroo.
  Deane, B.
Lazy Joe.
  Owens, H. R.
Lazy lagoon blues.
  Persson, H. A.
Lazy mood.
  Miller, E. (Love's got me in a) lazy
    mood.
Lazy morning.
  Rose, F.
Lazy river.
  Schiefelbein, F. A.
Lea, Lili, Lola, Loulou.
  Huguet y Tagell, R. J. Hurra pour
    l'Espagne!
Lead, kindly light.
  Dykes, J. B.
Lead me gently home.
  Townsend, P. D. E. I am coming
    to the Cross.
Lead me home.
  Weigle, C. F., ed. Sing a new song.
Lead on, O King Eternal!
  Lange-Mueller, P. E.
Leaf of love.
  Newman, B.
Leaf smoke.
  Pendleton, E.
Learning Latin.
  Rivero, F.
Leave some.
  Matthias, J.
Leaves are falling.
  Yost, G. Five pieces for violin
    and piano in the first position.
Leaves from an Austral garden.
  Steele, J. A.
Leavin' town.
  Meissner, J. J.
Lee rigg.
  Goldman, R. F.
Legend.
  Chaĭkovskiĭ, P. I.
Légende slave.
  Le Grand, R.
Légende triste.
  Marsh, C. H.
Lemon blossom.
  Flor De Limon.
Lena.
  Smith, H. G.
Lentebloemen.
  Nieland, J. H. I. M.
Lenten song.
  Seitz, H.
Les bounce.
  Harding, B.
Lesser power.
  Bond, J.
Let Jesus fix it for you.
  Crockett, A. B. Crockett's spirituals.
Let Jesus help you, He understands.
  Banks, E. V.
Let Jesus lead you all the way.
  Pearson, D.
Let me be the first.
  Glickman, F.
Let me dream sweet dreams of you.
  Kahler, W. T.
Let me shine.
  Thorne, W. M.
Let me sing and I'm happy.
  Berlin, I. The Jolson story.
Let me take a taste of your sweet lips.
  Chanslor, H.
Let not your heart be troubled.
  Snyder, V.
Let nothing trouble thee.
  Ward, H. R.
Let our gladness know no end.
  Scholin, C. A.
Let the good times roll.
  Moore, F.
Let the little ones come unto Me.
  Poulton, D. F.
Let those Christmas bells ring.
  Bailey, R. M.

Let Thy merciful ears, O Lord.
  Weelkes, T.
Let us dream.
  Pace, F.
Let us never walk alone.
  Sorrells, R. D.
Let us praise God.
  Olds, W. B.
Let us sing praises to our God.
  Uptegrove, W. E.
Let us sing unto the Lord.
  Poulton, D. F.
Let us wait upon the Lord.
  Anderson, R.
Let us walk in the light of the Lord.
  O'Hara, G.
Letmy host.
  Zich, J.
Let's be sweethearts always.
  Shelton, B.
Let's both say we're sorry.
  King, F.
Let's dance.
  Howorth, W.
Let's do it.
  Porter, C.
Let's do it up right.
  Muncaster, C. K.
Let's follow the clouds.
  Tobin, L.
Let's get launched.
  Furney, A. J.
Let's get married.
  Holdridge, I.
Let's go 'round again.
  Waters, M.
Let's go walking.
  Templeton, V.
Let's not waste the moonlight.
  Lang, C.
Let's play.
  Ketterer, E.
Let's play duets.
  Dittenhaver, S. L.
Let's pretend.
  Lynch, S.
  Schaeffer, O.
Let's pretend we're in love.
  Ellison, J. M.
Let's roll out the barrel once again.
  Jenkins, J.
Let's share romance together.
  Engelhard, E.
Let's sing a love song.
  Day, S.
Let's sing it!
  Hines, C. V.
Let's speak of love.
  Oliveira, M. de. Não tenho lagrimas.
Let's stay young forever.
  Fisher, D. Down to earth.
Let's take it easy.
  Brennan, J. A.
Let's tell the world we're in love.
  Hibbeler, R. O.
Let's try it again.
  Carleton, R. L.
Letter from Stresa.
  Bruni, M.
Letter marked unclaimed.
  Nolan, B.
Letter to Freddy.
  Bowles, P.
Levee lullaby.
  Keegan, F.
Libuše.
  Smetana, B.
Lidice.
  Martinů, B.
Liebe Seele, steh' im Glauben
  Weitzel, G. J.
Liebe vergeht.
  Luthold, N. A.
Liebeslied.
  Koch, S. v. Morgenländische Liebes-
    lieder.

Liebestraum.
  Liszt, F.
  Liszt, F. Dream of love.
Lied.
  Djabadary, H. Nocturne.
Lied van de jeugd.
  Röntgen, J.
Life eternal.
  Malotte, A. H.
Life eternal.
  Richards, M. R.
Life forever.
  Hill, M. B.
Life has loveliness to sell.
  Ceiga, G. E.
Life is fine.
  Young, J.
Life is now so wonderful to me.
  Weigle, C. F., ed. Sing a new song.
Life! Life! Life!
  Fromm, H. E. Jesus' name, how sweet
    to me.
Life more abundant.
  Jones, G. J.
Life of Tchaikovsky.
  Chaĭkovskiĭ, P. I.
Life was meant to be a sweet romance.
  Behrens, E.
Life's rainbow.
  Kantner, T. R.
Life's winding road.
  Grimm, C. A.
Lift ev'ry voice and sing.
  Johnson, J. R.
Lift up your heads.
  Norden, N. L.
Light in your eyes.
  House, C. E.
Light of light.
  Luvaas, M. J., arr.
Light of love.
  Carleton, R. L.
Light the lamps up.
  Warren, E. R.
Lights and shadows.
  Paparelli, F.
Lights of home.
  Bacon, J. P.
Like as the Father.
  Cherubini, L.
Like as the hart.
  Koepke, P.
Like the Saviour.
  Tippitt, W. T.
Lil brack sheep.
  Woodgate, H. L., arr.
Lilac-scented night.
  Fisher, E. M.
Lilac time in Lombard.
  Fyler, G. W.
Liliana.
  Rusconi, O.
Lille Klumpedump.
  Dahlquist, L. E.
Lille Krog i Kaerlighedens Land.
  Gyldmark, S. Jeg elsker en anden.
Lily Christine.
  Aspelin, S. En sjöman till häst.
Lily lay.
  Johnson, A. H.
Limehouse blues.
  Braham, P.
  Braham, P. Charlot's revue.
Lincoln.
  Elwell, H.
Lincoln penny.
  Siegmeister, E. American
    legends.
Linda rumba.
  Di Bella, O.
Line on the highway.
  Dyer, D.
Lingering.
  Danberger, W. D.
Linked together.
  De Haas, G.
Lirio.
  Maderna, O. H.

Listen to the green grass growing.
  Singer, L.
Listen to the mocking bird.
  Winner, S.
Listening.
  Green, A. Eight new sacred
    chrouses.
Litany of general supplication.
  Moe, C. C.
Lite hit, lite dit.
  Kraft, A. Den glada skräddaren.
Liten blå förgät mig ej.
  Strömberg-Andersson, F.
Liten marsch.
  Larsson, L.-E.
Little band.
  Savino, D.
Little bit more besides.
  Charles, H.
Little bit of heaven.
  Ball, E. R.
Little bit of love.
  Johnson, J. R.
Little Boy Blue boogie.
  Siegel, A. F.
Little brown jug.
  Jacobs, M., arr. Boogie woogie
    step-by-step.
Little classics for cornet or trumpet.
  Williams, E. S.
Little comrade march.
  Robinson, A.
Little dance.
  Steinbach, B. Modern miniatures.
Little David play on yo' harp.
  Howaorth, W.
Little elfin piper.
  Loth, L. L.
Little French pal.
  Ruckstuhl, J.
Little green elf.
  Dunhill, T. F. Summer, the piper.
Little houses.
  Worth, A.
Little Jim.
  Fain, S. Little Mister Jim.
Little Lordeen.
  Baldwin, R. L.
Little madonna.
  Edgar, L.
Little miss.
  Stout, O. Senorita chiquita.
Little Miss Muffet.
  Burnam, E. M.
Little Mister Jim.
  Fain, S.
Little old mill.
  Towers, L.
Little pansies in my garden.
  Hibbeler, R. O.
Little patch o' land.
  Young, V.
Little red hen.
  Bampton, R.
Little Red Riding Hood.
  Stadbury.
Little singer.
  Lake, G.
Little sonata.
  Fenner, B. Two little piano
    sonatas.
Little song of life.
  Vidalita.
Little star.
  Ponce, M.
Little too far.
  Hayes, C.
Little two by four.
  Loosli, E.
Little wave.
  Rowley, A.
Little Willie.
  Niles, J. J., ed. & arr. The singing
    campus.
Little worm.
  Sachs, H. E.
Little you cared.
  Burns, H.

Liturgical motets.
  Reilly, J. A., comp.
Liturgy for the Greek Orthodox church.
  Gallos, A. G., arr. The divine liturgy
    of Saint John Chrysostom.
Livet på landet.
  Kraft, A.
Living Saviour.
  Lillenas, H.
Livre d'orgue.
  Chaumont, L.
Llanero es.
  Matos, M. G. Gay señorita.
Lluvia de estrellas.
  Treviño, F.
Lo dicono le stelle.
  Mellier, M.
Lo, my Shepherd is divine.
  Haydn, J.
Lo nitka od.
  De Haas, G. Linked together.
Lo que siente el alma.
  Elizondo, R. Un canto al amor.
Lo, the full, final sacrifice.
  Finzi, G.
Lo ves mujer.
  Jesus Morales, J. de.
Lobt Ihn mit Herz und Munde.
  Bach, J. S.
Loch Lomond.
  Deis, C. .
  Heywood, E.
Loi de l'amour.
  Caffot, S. V. J. Les aventures de
    Casanova.
Lolita.
  Holmberg-Aastrup, P.
Lolita hambomazurka.
  Westerlund, G.
Lolita Lopez.
  Olvirades, J.
London Bridge.
  Raschig, A.
London calling!
  North, M.
London cameos.
  Wood, H.
London in the spring.
  Mills, A.
London suite.
  Waller, F. Fats Waller's famous
    London suite.
London waltz.
  Enticknap, C. G.
Londonderry air.
  Lovejoy, H., arr.
Lonely.
  Crane, J.
  Kranz, J. A.-A.
Lonely cowboy's dream.
  Thomas, D.
Lonely heart knows.
  Thompson, H. W. Whoa! Sailor.
Lonely house.
  Weill, K. Street scene.
Lonely is the word.
  Matt, J. J.
Lonely landscape.
  McBride, R.
Lonely moments.
  Williams, M. L.
Lonely night.
  Carleton, R. L.
Lonely one.
  Fischer, C.
Lonely rider.
  Smith, O. G.
Lonesome for love.
  Montgomery, R.
Lonesome for you.
  Jarratt, L. E.
Lonesome heart.
  Lamkoff, P.
Lonesome little darling.
  Turner, M.
Lonesome man.
  Bowles, P. Blue Mountain ballads.

Lonesome shepherd.
  Powers, M.
Long ago.
  Buck, C. C.
Long ago at candle-light.
  Dunhill, T. F.
Long gone, baby.
  Atcher, B.
Long legg'd Lizzie.
  Watson, D.
Long, lonely way.
  Samuels, W.
Long, long ago.
  Bayly, T. H.
Long-waited letter.
  Tobin, L.
Longest train I ever saw.
  Miller, B.
Longing.
  Arnaud, W.
  Arthur, W.
  Bull, O. B.
Longing for you.
  Jensen, G.
Lonnie Glosson and his talking har-
    monica.
  Hull, R. E., comp.
Look down from Heaven, O God.
  Russell, V. A. Look down from
    Heaven, O God.
Look ever to Jesus.
  Smith, Mrs. C.
Look in the looking glass.
  Casey, C.
Look to the rainbow.
  Lane, B. Finnian's rainbow.
Look unto the Saviour.
  Loes, H. D.
Lord, as we part.
  Franz, R.
Lord, be pleased to deliver me.
  Schütz, H.
Lord Christ, reveal Thy holy face.
  Bach, J. S. Herr Jesu Christ, Dich
    zu uns wend'.
Lord! Give us faith!
  Walton, J. G.
Lord God Almighty.
  Dreier, M.
Lord, God divine.
  Händel, G. F.
Lord God, we praise Thee.
  Peeters, F. Te Deum.
Lord, grant us everlasting peace.
  Bach, J. S.
Lord hath done great things for thee.
  Ferry, C. T.
Lord have mercy on me.
  Gee, L. R.
Lord, help me.
  Green, A. Eight new sacred chor-
    uses.
Lord, I adore Thee.
  Carnes, J. R.
Lord, I want to be a Christian.
  Johnson, H.
Lord if I try.
  Posey, E.
Lord is great in Zion.
  Kountz, R.
Lord is my Shepherd.
  Cain, N.
  Poulton, D. F.
  Cain, N.
Lord, let me learn of Thee.
  Lord, R.
Lord, let me live today.
  Moore, F. C.
Lord, let me shine!
  Bugbee, M.
Lord, now lettest Thou Thy servant.
  Maltzeff, A.
Lord of Hosts.
  Durham, G. H.
Lord reigneth.
  Marth, H. J.
Lord victorious.
  Seymour, J. L.

Lord, with glowing heart.
  Neidlinger, W.
Lord's prayer.
  Beethoven, L. v.
  Flandorf, W.
  Franck, C. A.
  Fryxell, R. H.
  Houser, J. G.
  Malotte, A. H.
  Sanborn, E. R.
  Sibelius, J.
  Upton, A.
Lord's table.
  Maness, I. W.
Loreley.
  Silcher, F.
Lorenz's organ album. See title entry
    in composer list.
Lorenz's organ and piano duets.
  Lorenz, E. J., comp.
Lorenz's organ chimes folio.
  Lorenz, E. J., comp.
Lorenz's Select anthems.
  Von Berge, H., comp.
Lorenz's song specials for choir use.
  Wilson, I. B.
Lorito enamorado.
  Stone, G.
Das Los des Menschen.
  Koch, S. v. Die wilden Schwäne.
Lost chord.
  Sullivan, Sir A. S.
Lost in love.
  Carleton, R. L.
  Puscheck, A. B.
Lost love.
  Rimskii-Korsakov, N. A.
Lost weekend.
  Phillips, J.
Lot of elbow room.
  Penny, L.
Lotus City love.
  Sines, E.
Lotus flower.
  Duncan, C.
Louella.
  Meissner, J. J.
Louisiana hayride.
  Colicchio, M. R.
Louisiana lady.
  Sanders, A.
Love and learn.
  Jerome, M. K.
Love and the weather.
  Berlin, I.
Love came back.
  Paez, M. Revivir.
Love, could I only tell thee.
  Capel, J. M.
Love everlasting.
  Friml, R. L'amour, toujours l'amour.
Love for others.
  Tovey, H. G.
Love for three oranges.
  Prokof'ev, S. S. Marche.
Love goes on through the fall.
  Jefferson, R. A.
Love I threw away.
  Hobbs, P.
Love is a babel.
  Lang, C. S.
Love is a dream.
  Sienkiewicz, A. J.
Love is the time.
  Friml, R. Northwest outpost.
Love, l'amour, amore.
  Nelson, H.
Love lost it's way.
  Rich, M.
Love me as I love you.
  Amame mucho.
Love me now.
  Owens, T.
Love nest.
  Hirsch, L. A. Mary.
Love of my heart.
  Tiersot, J. L'amour de moi.

185

Love on a hill.
  Pendleton, E.
Love one another.
  Wolken, L. A.
Love sets me free.
  Cosselmon, R. A.
Love sick.
  Erby, J.
Love sleeps in a rose.
  Hall, L. W.
Love song.
  Suk, J. Píseň lásky.
Love star.
  Carleton, R. L.
Love that never fails.
  Morgan, R.
Love wherever I roam.
  Strauss, J.
Love will keep us young.
  Leslie, E.
Love will rule our hearts.
  Hibbeler, R. O.
Lovebug, Tennessee.
  Rose, F.
Loveliest night.
  Brace, B.
Lovely California moon.
  Fears, W. A.
Lovely day.
  Sanders, A. Ireland today.
Lovely lady of lover's lane.
  Bjornson, F.

Lovely, lovely.
  Hibbeler, R. O.
Lovely night to go dancing.
  McHugh, J. F. Calendar girl.
Lovely song my heart is singing.
  Goulding, E.
Lovely sweetheart of mine.
  Carleton, R. L.
Lover, come back to me.
  Romberg, S. The new moon.
Lovers' lane.
  Van Tyle, R.
(Love's got me in a) lazy mood..
  Miller, E.
Love's lament.
  Herbert, V.
  Tizol, F. Lamento.
Love's redeeming work is done.
  Miles, R. H.
Loving you.
  Roig, G.
Low voice melodies.
  Clayton, N. J., comp.
Lowell Blanchard's Folio of Mid-day
  Merry-go-round favorites.
  Fowler, J. W.
Ludzie mi to za zle maja.
  Malec, A.
Luise Hensels barnaftonbön.
  Kallstenius, E. Fyra sånger.
Lullaby.
  Brahms, J.

  Davis, D.
  Godard, B. L. P. Jocelyn.
  Howell, I.
  Liadov, A. K.
  Menasce, J. de. Hebrew melodies.
  Pascarella, E.
  Swift, F. F.
Lullaby land.
  Rath, H.
Lullaby medley.
  Small, A.
Lullaby moon.
  Brown, B.
Lullaby of the trail.
  Bonner, R.
Lullaby to the evening star.
  Lieta, T. Sweet darling.
Lulu had a sweetheart.
  Stride, H.
Luma e sei soldi.
  Salerno, N.
Lynn.
  Howard, E.
Lynn, Massachusetts, U. S. A.
  Kavanaugh, R. M.
Lynne.
  Hanna, P.
Lyric movement.
  Rubbra, E.
Lyrische stukken.
  Nieland, J. H. I. M.

M.S.T.C.
  Hankwitz, A. M.
Ma belle Marguerite.
  Ellis, V. Bless the bride.
Ma chanson d'Espagne.
  Valdon, J.
Ma mère l'oye.
  Nieland, J. H. I. M.
Mänljuset.
  Stenhammar, W. Fyra Dikter.
Mabel, I'll tell the world.
  Carleton, R. L.
MacDonald's farm.
  Strickler, D., arr.
Macedonian courting dance.
  Tajčević, M.
Machito.
  Rugolo, P.
Machuquillo con puerco.
  Claro Fumero, J.
Madame de Sévigné.
  Chardon, J.
Made whole.
  Mills, K. M.
Mademoiselle Hortensia.
  Guglielmi, L.
Madone aux yeux de ciel.
  Lenoir, J.
Madrid 1800.
  Moltó, A.
Madrigal.
  Dello Joio, N.
Madrugado.
  Binge, R.
Människans lott.
  Koch, S. v.
M'aggio sunnato Napule.
  Lama, G.
Magic carpet.
  Story, H. A.
  Walter, F. G.
Magic city of the angels.
  Canning, J. J.
Magic interlude.
  Grun, B. White Cradle Inn.
Magnificat.
  Tallis, T.
  Tyler, G.
Maharajah of Magador.
  Loeb, J. J.
Mahzel.
  Beekman, J.
Maid with the mole on her cheek.
  Muchacha Bonita.
Main Street.
  Tobin, L.
Mains Câlines.
  Goletti, N.
Maizales.
  Briseño, S.
Majesty.
  O'Neill, C.
Major, minor.
  White, G.
Make believe.
  Kern, J. Show boat.
Make the stars shine bright for the
  women in white.
  Zee, A.
Making habits fun.
  Koch, F. P.
Mala racha.
  Alarcón Leal, E.
Malá tanečni suita.
  Flegl, J.
Malaguena.
  Lecuona, E.
Malas carnes.
  Lima, A. de.
Malayan moon.
  Hoffman, M. Terang boelan.
Malayan song of love.
  Michael, P. Terang boulan.
Maldición.
  Gonzalez, L.
Maličkosti.
  Bartoš, J. Z.

Malinconia.
  Olivieri, D. Tutto il mondo canta
    Tornerai.
Malvinas.
  Bordino, F.
Mam, give me 20 lire.
  Milena, L. Mamma, dammi venti lire.
Mama, do I gotta?
  Mizzy, V.
Mamma, dammi venti lire.
  Milena, L.
Mamma non piangere!
  Finocchioli, A.
Mamma santa.
  Ancillotti, G.
Mam'selle.
  Goulding, E. The razor's edge.
Mamula moon.
  Park, P.
Man I love.
  Gershwin, G. Lady be good.
Man of sorrows.
  Evangel special sacred songs, no. 1.
Man on the flying trapeze.
  Lee, A.
Man that I've got.
  Allen, C. F.
Man who paints the rainbow.
  Stock, L.
Manana.
  Colonna, D. R.
Mande, lipa mande!
  Cernkovich, R., arr. Oj, jesenske
    duge noči!
Mandolin.
  Dupont, G. Mandoline.
Mandoline.
  Dupont, G.
Il mandolinista popolare.
  Nicolo, M.
Mandy.
  Berlin, I.
Manège des sept nains.
  Gallois-Montbrun, R. Les rêves de
    Danceline.
Manèges.
  Staub, D.
Manhattan samba.
  Dalmau, J.
Manhattan soliloquy.
  Volpe, H.
Manolete.
  Tomé, J.
Many-a-mile away.
  Cobb, H.
Many a new day.
  Rodgers, R. Oklahoma.
M'ap resodou.
  Frangeul, F.
Maracas.
  Lecuona y Casado, E. Carnival in
    Costa Rica.
Maralee waltz.
  Harden, J.
March.
  Beethoven, L. van
  Steinbach, B. Modern miniatures.
March chromatic.
  Brose, E. O.
March modernistic.
  Edwards, M.
March of the majorettes.
  Simon, F.
March of the Twirling corps.
  Dorr, A. I.
March time.
  Templeton, V.
Marche.
  Prokof'ev, S. S.
Marche militaire.
  Schubert, F. P.
Marche solennelle.
  Bourdon, E.
Marche triomphale.
  Nieland, J. H. I. M.
Marchiesta.
  Gage, W. J.

Marcia Carolus XII, svecorum rex.
  Harteveld, W., arr.
María bonita.
  Lara, A.
Marianna mia.
  Lambert, H.
Marie.
  Berlin, I.
Marie Marie.
  Chauliac, L.
Mariguana.
  Ferreté, L. M.
Marimba capers.
  Caneva, E. O.
Marina.
  Caymmi, D.
Marine's hymn.
  Hopkins, H. P., arr.
Marriage of Figaro.
  Mozart, J. C. W. A. Le nozze di Figaro.
Mary.
  Hirsch, L. A.
Mary and-a Martha.
  Cronham, C. R.
Mary Ann.
  Castro, A.
Mary Lou.
  Sullivan, G. Kansas City blues.
Mary Magdalene.
  Eichhorn, H. W.
Mary's baby.
  Parrish, C.
Mary's lullaby.
  Sejts, H.
Mary's manger song.
  Pottle, L. K.
Mascarada.
  Galvez, M. Probably.
Masked one.
  Rodriguez, G. H. La Cumparsita.
Mass in honor of Our Lady.
  Da Silva, O.
Mass in honor of Padre Junipero Serra.
  Bienbar, A. M.
Mass in honor of St. Albert.
  Ravanello, O.
Mass in honor of St. Anthony of Padua.
  Becker, R. L.
Mass in honor of St. Frances X.
  Cabrini, Mother Cabrini.
  Bonk, W.
Masterpieces of organ music.
  Hennefield, N., ed.
Matrimony in disguise.
  Ahlstrand, D.
Matter of life and death.
  Gray, A.
Mauna Loa.
  Pentuff, O.
Maverick heart.
  Glazer, F.
Maxims of Solomon.
  Klein, J.
May day picnic.
  Wright, N. L.
May fancies.
  Sisson, C. T.
May I call you sweetheart?
  Iida, L.
May joy be yours.
  Wheeler, A.
May the words.
  Freed, I. Prayers of Israel.
Maybe you think you're foolin' me.
  Masonier, C.
Maybe you'll be there.
  Bloom, R.
Maytime.
  Romberg, S.
Maytime in the Ozarks.
  Flickinger, G. S.
Mazucamba.
  Rosa, O. de la.
Mazurka - phantasy.
  Zygman, E.
Me and Captain Kidd.
  Haskins, W.

Me go where you go, amigo.
  Christy, B.
Me voy pá Sibanicú.
  Delgado, P.
Mean mama don't worry me.
  Carlisle, C. R.
The measuring-worm.
  Blake; D. G.
Med en enkel tullipan.
  Hansson, S.
Med folket för fosterlandet.
  Lundquist, P.
Med røde roser.
  Seymer, W. Sånger av William
  Seymer.
Meditation.
  Miller, E. G.
Meet me at no special place.
  Robinson, J. R.
Meet me by the ice house, Lizzie.
  Harty, R. E.
Mein land eretz-Isroel.
  Solomon, S.
Mein Mädel hat einen Rosenmund.
  Brahms, J.
Mein schwäbisches Liederbuch.
  Weismann, W.
Meister Andrea.
  Weingartner, F.
Mellan broarna.
  Stenhammar, W. Fyra Stockholmsdik-
  ter.
Melodia.
  Nteland, J. H. I. M.
  Piato, G. You are my sweetheart.
Melodie on a theme by S. Rachmaninoff.
  Rachmaninoff, S.
Melodies from masterworks.
  Forbes, R., arr.
Melodies of life.
  Clayton, N. J., comp.
Melody.
  Beletzky, V.
Melody bars.
  Friezierer, B.
Melody from Polonaise.
  Chopin, F. F. Polonaise, piano, op. 53.
Melody from second piano concerto.
  Rachmaninoff, S. Concerto, piano.
  no. 2.
Melody in E flat.
  Duke, J.
Melody in F.
  Mendelssohn-Bartholdy, F. Spring
  song.
  Rubinstein, A.
Melody of love.
  Engelmann, H.
  Lieta, T. Sweet darling.
Melody swing.
  Bisio, N.
Melody valley.
  Owens, L. M.
Mélopée du serpent.
  Djabadary, H.
Melopeya.
  Sás, A. Ollantay.
Memorial concert.
  Bliss, A.
Memories.
  Van Alstyne, E.
Memories of Easter morn.
  Lorenz, E. J.
Memories of Idaho.
  Lupton, B. G.
Memories of spring.
  Alford, E.
Memories of you.
  Blake, E.
Memories of you dear.
  Colonna, D. R.
Memory lane.
  Spier, L.
Memory of youth.
  Bunner, G. G.

Men of Duke.
  Sweet, M.
Men of Iwo Jima.
  Wagner, L.
Men of the fenlands.
  Durieux, G.
M'ena phili erōs den zei.
  Iakōbidēs, Z.
Mene mlada oženiše.
  Cernkovich, R., ed. & arr.
Mentiras.
  Pomares, G.
Menuetto.
  Mozart, J, C. W.A.
Menuetto and Finale.
  Haydn, J. Symphony, no. 1.
Mer.
  Schubert, F. P.
Merciful Lord.
  Hawkins, J.
Mère.
  Peeters, F.
Merrie England.
  German, E.
Merry autumn days.
  Dunhill, T. F.
Merry Christmas.
  Lennerts, W. J.
  Savino, D.
Merry elves.
  Yost, G. Five pieces for violin and
  piano in the first position.
Merry maker's polka.
  Wickens, C.
Message.
  Moore, M.
Message of the bells.
  Day, R. E.
Messe "Haec dies."
  Roux, M.
Messenger star.
  Bryans, J. F.
Messiah.
  Händel, G. F.
  Händel, G. F. Hallelujah chorus.
Met a Texas gal.
  Liberman, M.
Methode.
  Thuillier, E.
Méthode complète de clarinette.
  Magnani, A.
Méthode complète de trombone à
  coulisse.
  Lafosse, A.
Méthode de tambour et caisse claire
  d'orchestre.
  Tourte, R.
Metodo per saxofono.
  Pellegrini, G. M.
Mexican "clap hands" dance.
  Schaum, J. W., arr.
Mexican hand-clapping song.
  Campo, M. V. de. Chiapanecas.
Mexican hat dance.
  Partichela, F.,A.
Mi amada.
  Yamin, J.
Mi baile es asi.
  Enrico, R.
Mi bumba né.
  Suárez, S. Bagels in Mexico.
Mi canción.
  Gonzales, L.
Mi Chinita.
  García Curiel, N.
Mi corazón.
  Lopez, M.
Mi décima canción.
  Márquez Rojo, R.
Mi guitara y yo.
  Monge, J.
Mi "lea" no baila.
  Cairo, P.
Mi Panama querido.
  Efrón, T.
Mi place improvvisar.
  Piubeni, V.

Mi triste corazón.
  Gioe, J.
Mi vaca lechera.
  Garcia, F.
Miami Beach rumba.
  Fields, I.
Miami sunshine and you.
  Heck, M. J.
Micaela.
  Meyer, L. C.
Mice in the cupboard of old Mother Hub-
  bard.
  Smith, R. L.
Michael Aaron piano primer.
  Aaron, M.
Michigan.
  Hoskin, R. W. S.
Midnight.
  Moore, D. L.
Midnight blues.
  Williams, L. L.
Midnight lady.
  Macell, J.
Midnight masquerade.
  Manus, J.
Midnight reverie.
  Sack, A.
The midnite special.
  Scott, J.
Midsommarnattsvals.
  Martinson, B.
Mighty fortress is our God.
  Luther, M.
Miguel Alemán.
  Palacios, J.
Mijn derde oefenboek.
  Duuren, H. J. van.
Mijn eerste oefenboek.
  Duuren, H. J. van.
Mijn tweede oefenboek.
  Duuren, H. J. van.
Mike O'Day.
  Sanders, A. Ireland today.
Mikrokosmos.
  Bartók, B.
Milking song.
  Rowley, A.
Mill.
  Pergament, M. Tre små sånger.
Mills elementary method for clarinet.
  Manring, F.
Milwaukee second century.
  Patti, S. T.
Min lilla occarina.
  Tigerström, S. G.
Mina de oro.
  Esperón, M. Albur de amor.
Minchella complete modern method for
  piano accordion, bass clef.
  Minchella, E.
Mind if I tell you I love you.
  Willson, M.
The mind of God.
  Wolfe, J. F.
Mine alone.
  Hibbeler, R. O.
The miners' song.
  Levis, C.
Miniatures.
  Stoltze, R.
Miniver Cheevy.
  Bornschein, F. C.
Minnas.
  Kallstenius, E. Fyra sanger.
Minnesota loveland.
  Whitney, R. K.
Mino.
  Jackson, C.
Minuet.
  Händel, G. F. Berenice.
  Nevin, E. W. Narcissus.
  Schubert, F. P.
  Schubert, F. P. Symphony no. 5.
Minuet antique.
  Kesnar, M. Seven pieces.
Minuet in swing.
  Cooley, D. C.

Minuet in the candlelight.
 Frank, L.
Minuetti, prince de la danse.
 Gallois-Montbrun, R. Les rêves de
 Janceline.
Minuetto.
 Mozart, J. C. W. A. Two pieces.
Minuit sonne à tous les clochers.
 Marinier, P.
Mirándote.
 Guevara, L.
Miserere illi.
 Walsh, N. E.
Miss Lou Rose.
 Storer, H. J.
Miss Peggy.
 Samson, S.
Missa "Adeste fideles."
 Rossini, C.
Missa brevis.
 Kodály, Z.
Missa in honorem Reginae Pacis.
 Bragers, A. P.
Missa in honorem Sanctae Franciscae
 Xaveriae Cabrini.
 Pizzoglio, W.
Missa Marialis.
 Ginder, R.
Missa regina angelorum.
 Capocci, F.
Missa "Rosa mystica."
 Sinzig, P., father.
Missing in action.
 Lightfritz, E.
Missing one.
 Wallace, V. M.
Missouri story.
 Robinson, E.
Mr. Boogie Woogie, junior.
 Siegel, A. F.
Mistral.
 Wolf, A.
Mrs. Howard Miller's chord and note or
 ear piano method.
 Miller, Mrs. H.
Mists of memories.
 Van Tyle, R.
Mitena gavotte.
 Williams, E. S. Little classics for
 cornet or trumpet.
Mixup.
 Alpert, H.
Mizpah.
 Goldsworthy, W. A.
Modern Arban-St. Jacome comprehensive
 course for trombone or baritone.
 Whistler, H. S.
Modern city polka.
 Uryga, P.
Modern dance band harmony and system
 of progressions.
 Murphy, L. S.
Modern etudes.
 Johnson, G. A.
Modern miniatures.
 Steinbach, B.
 Whitefield, B.
Modern styles and harmonic construction
 for popular piano playing.
 Kahn, M.
Modern tunes for young violinists.
 Cooper, I.
Modern violin-studies.
 Heimann, M.
Modrý zvonek.
 Nedbal, O. Les cloches des bois.
Moeder.
 Peeters, F. Mère.
Möte i gründen.
 Lagerheim-Romare, M.
Mohee.
 Mossman, T., arr.
Molloy, my boy.
 Foresythe, R.
Moment musical.
 Schubert, F. P.
Moments from the passion.
 Becker, J. J.

Moments vécus.
 Djabadary, H.
Mon amour me tient chaud.
 Stern, E.
Mon bien aimé.
 Lafarge, G.
Mon bonheur.
 Jeanès, D.
Mon coeur a retrouvé l'espoir.
 Vétheuil, P.
Mon coeur attend.
 Broeck, L. van den. My heart is
 yours.
Mon coeur est un violon.
 Laparcerie, M.
Mon coin de banlieue.
 Staub, D.
Mon habanera.
 Padilla, J.
Mon p'tit copain du cinéma.
 Durand, P.
Mon rêve.
 Huber, B.
Mon saucisson.
 Sarrat, A. J. I.
Mon triste coeur.
 Bouillon, J.
Money makes the world go 'round.
 Teninty, O. H.
Money, money, money, money, money!
 Fisher, M.
Monica Pérez. See title entry in
 composer list.
Monsieur Beaucaire.
 Livingston, J. H.
Monsieur du troisième.
 Lafarge, G.
Montana.
 Howard, J. E.
Montana bound.
 Clyde, T.
Montmartre sur Seine.
 Monnot, M.
Mood Hollywood.
 Dorsey, J.
Mood impetuous.
 Thompson, R. W.
Moon complaining.
 Bury, W.
Moon-faced, starry-eyed.
 Weill, K. Street scene.
Moon in my window waltz.
 Malec, A. Zaświć miesiaczku w okno
 moje.
Moon in the sky.
 Malec, A. Świeci miesiaczek na
 niebie.
Moon of jade.
 Myrow, J.
Moon over Easterland.
 Crouse, V. V.
Moon over Missouri.
 Gibbany, E. M. H.
Moon river.
 David, L.
Moon was yellow.
 Ahlert, F. E.
Moonbeams in your hair.
 Carleton, R. L.
Moonflowers.
 Overholt, C. E.
Moonlight.
 Beethoven, L. van.
Moonlight bay.
 Wenrich, P.
Moonlight dreams.
 Chanslor, H.
Moonlight over Manhattan.
 Dye, W. K.
Moonlight sonata.
 Beethoven, L. van. Sonata, piano,
 no. 14.
Moonshine Valley mamma.
 Woodford, G. R.
Moore classroom fife method.
 Moore, E. C. Classroom method for
 the fife.

More choral gems from the masters.
 Grant, L., comp.
More like an angel.
 MacFayden, J. H.
More, more, more.
 Millinder, L.
More precious to me.
 Arthur, W.
More ruthless rhymes for heartless
 homes.
 Hely-Hutchinson, V.
More straw for the scarecrow.
 Pollet, B.
More than one hundred songs and
 games every child should know.
 Haufrecht, H., arr.
Morgenländische Liebeslieder.
 Koch, S. von.
Mormon trail.
 Jelesnik, E.
Morning hymn.
 Noble, T. T.
Morning mood.
 Whitford, R. H.
Morning song.
 Bax, A.
 Powers, M.
Morning watch.
 Rubbra, E.
Morning wind.
 Dieterich, M.
Mosca.
 Mier, P.
Moses.
 Rack, R. R.
Moses in Egypt.
 Rossini, G. A. O Thou, whose power.
Moshiach Ben Yosef.
 Schaefer, J.
Motet.
 Pinkham, D. R.
Mother.
 Nordman, C.
 Richard, L.
 Rubinstein, A.
Mother and dad's favorite wedding songs.
 Ivanovici, J.
Mother beloved.
 Dunlap, E. E.
Mother Duck.
 Dunhill, T. F.
Mother, I'm coming home.
 Sumerlin, M. D.
Mother, listen for me.
 Woods, J. S.
Mother's Day.
 Surer, V. M.
Mother's Day hymn.
 Barnes, E. S.
Mother's Day prayer.
 Jones, T. M.
Mother's fallen tears.
 Carleton, R. L.
Mother's hands.
 Smith, L. M.
Mother's only sleeping.
 Monroe, W. S.
Mother's voice.
 Yancey, E.
Moths.
 Philipp, I. Phalènes.
Mott kväll.
 Seymer, W. Strofer i sol och skugga.
Mounties.
 Friml, R. Rose Marie.
Mouvement.
 Sancan, P.
Mouvement perpétuel.
 Cherepnin, A. N.
 Demuth, Norman.
Movie to-night.
 Gannaway, A.
Moyer's charted harmony chords for the
 guitar.
 Warner, E. A.
Mozart-Schaum for piano.
 Mozart, J. C. W. A.

Muchacha Bonita. See title entry in
  composer list.
Müde bin ich, geh zur Ruh.
  Kallstenius, E. Fyra sånger.
Mujer ajena.
  Yamin, J.
Mujer que quiere a dos.
  Monge, J.
Mujer vanidosa.
  Sánchez Vázquez, P.
Mulata caprichosa.
  Rojo, G.
Murmuring zephyr.
  Jensen, A.
Murmuring zephyrs.
  Jensen, A.
Muses en fuite.
  Pachmann, L. de.
Musetta's waltz-song.
  Puccini, G. La Bohême.
Music.
  Norden, N. L.
Music book [for] correspondence
  course for piano.
  Klavarskribo Institute, Kingston,
  Mass.
Music for millions.
  Frey, H., ed. & arr.
Music fun book.
  Montgomery, V.
Music lessons have begun.
  Fletcher, L.
Music lovers' book of grand opera.
  Treharne, B., arr.
Music lovers' book of symphonies.
  Treharne, B., arr.
Music of life.
  Cain, N.
Music on a quiet theme.
  Bergsma, W. L.
Music road.
  Neilson, J.
Music tablet.
  King, M. K., comp.
Music you remember.
  Chaĭkovskiĭ, P. I. Tschaikowsky's.
Musical box.
  Duuren, H. J. van. De speeldoos.
Musical man from San Berdoo.
  Nelson, F. B.
Musical quiz.
  Essex, K., arr.
Musical typist.
  Munro, R.
Musik zu Shakespeare's Der Sturm.
  Weingartner, F.
Musique pour Mitzi.
  Bulterman, J.
Must Jesus bear the cross?
  Allan, G. N.
Mutton leg.
  Basie, C.
Mužné vpřed.
  Vačkář, V. Sohaj.
My aggravatin' wife.
  Nettles, W. E.
My baby didn't even say goodbye.
  Fulton, J.
My beautiful Rosa.
  Cioffi, G. Has anyone seen my
  beautiful Rosa?
My beauty is you, Marilou!
  Carleton, R. L.
My best for Jesus.
  Nietzer, C.
My boot training.
  Hudson, J. V.
My broadside gal.
  Camarata, M.
My bungalow dream girl.
  Brodersen, M.
My cottage of dreams.
  Rogers, J.
My country, 'tis of thee.
  Ortlip, M., arr.
My creed.
  Scarmolin, A. L.

My dainty little maid.
  Bell, A.
My darling Blue eyes.
  Crane, J.
My darling Clementine.
  Montrose, P.
My darling little Peggy.
  David, W. R.
My darling's lips are a petaled rose.
  Brahms, J. Mein Mädel hat einen
  Rosenmund.
My dear, don't tell me no.
  Canoro, L.
My dear one.
  Bennett, E.
My dearest Uncle Sam.
  Kramer, A. C.
My dream about you.
  Machesney, A.
My dream came true.
  Arden, N.
My dream girl.
  Bonnell, W. C.
My dreamland sweetheart.
  Carleton, R. L.
My dreams of you.
  Hibbeler, R. O.
My eerste musiek boek.
  Marais, S. L.
My eight o'clock date.
  Simon, N.
My Evelyn.
  Woode, H.
My fair Hawaii.
  Dunagan, E.
My fairy queen.
  Carleton, R. L.
My favorite brunette.
  Evans, R. B.
My favorite tune.
  Cobb, H.
My first Christmas songs. See title
  entry in composer list.
My first love affair.
  Beddig, H.
My Florida.
  Alewine, H. N.
My gal is your gal now.
  Waverly, J.
My gal, my plane and I.
  Crawford, R. M.
My gift.
  Hughes, H. K.
My God is able.
  Starr, K. G. C.
My guajirita.
  Escarpenter, J. Guajirita mia.
My hands.
  Nietzer, C.
My heart and I.
  Lamkoff, P.
My heart belongs to you.
  Dencher, S.
My heart is a hobo.
  Van Heusen, J. Welcome stranger.
My heart is taking a beating.
  Williams, L. L.
My heart is yours.
  Broeck, L. van den.
My heart once sang all day.
  Hibbeler, R. O.
My heart remembers.
  Bartlett, F.
My heart shall truly love you.
  Poynter, S. R.
My heart stood still.
  Rodgers, R. A Connecticut Yankee.
My heart was crying.
  Condon, L.
My heart was doing a bolero.
  Coslow, S. Copacabana.
My heart-beat put to music.
  Johnston, E.
My heart's in stitches.
  Hetherington, E. J.
My heaven is where I find you.
  Brix, A. E.
My hobby horse.
  Robinson, A. Three very easy piano
  pieces.

My Indiana home.
  Labedz, V.
My inspiration.
  Furby, A. She wanted a cream front
  door.
My Ireland.
  Sanders, A. Ireland today.
My Jerusalem.
  Fairman, G.
My kisses are limited.
  Tobin, L.
My lady.
  Hore, C.
My lady of the roses.
  Fabian, D. Dos almas.
My last goodbye.
  Howard, E.
My lesson learned.
  Chanslor, H.
My little dog got kittens.
  Bernhardt, C.
My little dude ranch gal.
My little Mohee.
  Niles, J. J., ed. & arr. The singing
  campus.
My little nest of heavenly blue.
  Lehár, F. Frasquita serenade.
My little pat of butter.
  Copell, P.
My little pet lamb sings tra-la-la.
  Gay, N.
My little spot of sunlight.
  Crane, J.
My little white boat.
  Dunhill, T. F.
My little wooden cradle.
  Bartlett, F.
My little yeller buckskin.
  Tobin, L.
My love.
  Glazer, F.
  Russin, J.
  Sleor, L.
My love, dear, is all for you.
  Van Sickle, R.
My love for you.
  Jefferies, S.
My love goes with you.
  Dexter, A.
My love is o'er the sea.
  Krone, B., arr.
My lovely little Dresden doll.
  Magram, R. A.
My luve is like a red, red rose.
  Roberton, H. S.
My marinerette.
  Maur, L.
My Master's own trail.
  Stoughton, R. S.
My mom.
  Donaldson, W.
My mother.
  Iden, R. J.
  Upton, A.
My mother's lullaby.
  Miller, N. S.
My name is Kelly.
  Nelson, E. G.
My old fashioned rose.
  Carleton, R. L.
My old fashioned sweetheart.
  Crawford, J. D.
My only sweetheart.
  Marsh, C. H.
My own.
  Miller, L. A.
My Ozark mountain home.
  King, C. M.
My pet squirrel.
  Dittenhaver, S. L. Four piano
  compositions.
My picture of you.
  Carleton, R. L.
My pilot.
  Fowler, G. Just abide in Jesus.
My prairie serenade.
  Penny, L.

My prayer.
　Mayer, C.
　Romney, L. T.
　Thomas, M. G.
My prayer for home.
　Benner, H. C.
My pretty blonde.
　Davis, L.
　King, S.
My pretty girl.
　Porter, D.
My queen.
　Malani, C.
My rancho.
　Parra, E.
My red wagon.
　Dittenhaver, S. L. Four piano compositions.
My romance.
　Rodgers, R.
My sailor husband.
　Carleton, R. L.
My Sally gal.
　McNeil, J. C.
My secrets of love.
　Rojo, G. Secretos del corazon.
My song.
　Gonzalez, L. Mi cancion.
　Lewis, F. G.
My song is a threnody.
　Dickinson, D.
My song of love.
　Blitz, L. Mia canzone d'amore.
My sweetheart.
　Crane, J.
　Gillock, B.
My Tex.
　Toczek, F.
My theme of love.
　Beittel, R. H.
My thoughts seem to wander to you.
　Arthur, W.
My tones will tell.
　Blekhman, J.
My train.
　Svecenski, B.
My treasure.
　Herbert, V. Gypsy lady.
My true love.
　Krone, B. P.
My truest friend.
　Parker, R. C.
My turn.
　Faglier, J.
My twilight rose.
　Carleton, R. L.
My twilight tango.
　Leggett, L. E.
My Valparaiso.
　Thompson, J.
My Virginia rose.
　McNeil, J. C.
My young and foolish heart.
　Murry, T.
Mystère de Lyon et de Notre Dame.
　Chatillon, E.
Mystery story.
　Hopkins, H. P.
N. Y. P. S. rally song.
　Thorne, W. M.
N' ora 'e felicita.
　Cioffi, G. One happy hour with you.
N'y pensez pas trop.
　Trenet, C.
Na ti tha pē Ellada.
　Myrogiannēs, G. C.
Na to parēs to koritsi.
　Iakōbidēs, Z.
Naar katten er ude.
　Riis, A.
Naar Skoven er grøn.
　Riis, A. Tivoli-Revyen 1946.
Nacht.
　Roger, K. G.
Når det skymmer.
　Peterson, K. E.

När jag ser dig så ser jag varen.
　Kraft, A. Från "Blyge Anton" till "En sjöman till häst.
När livet var ungt.
　Kraft, A. Klockorna i Gamla stan.
När seklet var ungt.
　Kraft, A.
När som jägarn går på jakt.
　Kraft, A. Den glada skräddaren.
Namboro.
　Barreto, J.
Nancy Hanks.
　Siegmeister, E. American legends.
Não tenho lagrimas.
　Oliveira, M. de.
Nap time.
　Fouts, M. Children's easy piano pieces.
Napoli sorride.
　Franceschi, P.
Narcissus.
　Nevin, E. W.
National anthem of Afghanistan.
　Darcy, T. F., arr.
National anthem of Argentine.
　Darcy, T. F., arr.
National anthem of Denmark.
　Darcy, T. F., arr.
National anthem of Israel.
　Windsor, A. B.
National anthem of Saudi Arabia.
　Darcy, T. F., arr.
National anthem of Siam.
　Darcy, T. F., arr.
National anthem of Sweden.
　Darcy, T. F., arr.
Nation's prayer.
　Alberti, S.
Nativity cradle song.
　Roberton, H. S.
Natt vid sätern.
　Nyström, G.
Nattlig dyning.
　Seymer, W. Strofer i sol och skugga.
Nature tone-poems.
　Trowbridge, L.
Naughty Angeline.
　Lee, L.
Naval patrol.
　Essex, K., arr.
Nay, but you who do not love her.
　Harper, R. H.
Ne t'en fais pas, mon vieux!
　Parys, G. van.
Neapolitan serenade.
　Savino, D.
Near the cross.
　Glynn, B., arr.
Nebraska's glad refrain.
　Spence, H. S.
Necesito de ti.
　Delgado, N.
Negrita no me dejes.
　Gonzalez, A.
Negro spirituals.
　Alexander, J. Three American episodes.
Nero's conception.
　Rogers, M.
Netherlands roundelay.
　Bruinsma, H. A.
Neuf choeurs.
　Weisshaus, I., arr.
Never leave me.
　Vanderburg, G. J.
Never like this.
　Rizzo, J.
Never more.
　Bartlett, F.
　Nelson, H.
Never to part again.
　Upton, A.
Neville let it be said.
　Neville, D.
New and old.
　Riegger, W.
New broom boogie.
　Walker, C.
New century march.
　Steele, H.
New liberty bell.
　Pitts, J. F.

New moon.
　Romberg, S.
New moon in New Mexico.
　Goetschius, M.
New moon is changing to gold.
　Broughton, H.
New pretty blonde.
　Mullican, M.
New songs.
　Kennedy, A.
New songs of a Christian.
　Dunlop, M.
New Year song.
　Viebrock, W. H.
Newton's boogie woogie.
　Paparelli, F.
Nicholas Nickleby.
　Berners, G. H. Tyrwhitt-Wilson, baron.
Nicky Blair's carnival souvenir song folio. See title entry in composer list.
Night.
　Roger, K. G. Nacht.
Night and day.
　Porter, C. Gay divorcee.
Night by the sea.
　Holbrooke, J.
Night has a thousand eyes.
　Ashe, J. H.
Night in Tunisia.
　Gillespie, J.
Night is young.
　Romberg, S.
Night piece.
　Belchamber, E. Two songs from Herrick.
Night soliloquy.
　Kennan, K.
Night was all to blame.
　Sanders, A. Louisiana lady.
Night we fell in love.
　McNeil, J. C.
Nimrod.
　Elgar, Sir E. W.
Niña.
　Doneddu, A. Formosa.
　Smith, H.
Nine bass boogie.
　Carrozza, C. A.
Nine pieces for piano.
　Shostakovich, D. D.
19 swing etudes.
　Paisner, B.
98th Psalm.
　Schalit, H.
Ninety-nine years is a long time.
　Howard, P. M.
Nita corazon.
　Beauregard, A.
Niuba.
　Panzuti, V.
No atheists in foxholes.
　Shrader, J. L.
No basta ser charro.
　Esperon, M.
No children allowed.
　Parker, D.
No hard feelings.
　Pomares, G. Sin rencor.
No leave, no love.
　Moore, F.
No longer blue.
　Scambellone, G.
No longer lost.
　Weigle, C. F., ed. Sing a new song.
No me haces falta.
　Rivera, P.
No me jures.
　Castillo, J. P.
No mo' bench and board.
　Houdini, W.
No more goodnight sweetheart.
　Evans, T.
No more roamin'.
　King, F.
No, no Nanette.
　Youmans, V.

No, not one!
  Hugg, G. C.
No one knows our secret but the moon.
  Colgin, G. L.
No place for Jesus.
  Potter, A. L.
No quiere cocinar.
  González, V.
No room in the inn.
  Townsend, P. D. E.
No se por qué.
  Esperon, M. El ahijado de la muerte.
No sunset in God's tomorrow.
  Whitford, K.
No te quiero ver.
  Jesus Morales, J. de.
No tengo gana.
  Lambert, R.
No tengo lágrimas.
  Oliveira, M. de. Não, tenho lágrimas.
No tengo más amores.
  Rodriguez, J.
No trates de mentir.
  Gil, A.
Noah F. Ryder's Five sketches for piano.
  Ryder, N. F.
Noble nature.
  Saxton, S. E.
Nobody but you.
  Clark, N.
Nobody know de trouble I've seen.
  Roberton, H. S.
Nobody knows de trouble I've seen.
  Swift, F. F.
Nobody loves my baby like me.
  Levis, C.
Nobody's waiting for me.
  McBride, D.
Noche encantada!
  Lambert, R. Que no vas.
Noche está serena.
  Elaine, sister, arr.
Noche y día.
  Porter, C. (Gay divorcee) Night and day.
Noche y Marfil.
  Federico, D. S.
Nočni nálady.
  Vomáčka, B.
Nocturnal episode.
  Herzon, H.
Nocturne.
  Bratten, I. F.
  Chopin, F. F.
  Dahl, V.
  Djabadary, H.
  Dukelsky, V.
  Harline, L.
  McKay, F. H.
  Moore, M.
  Nieland, J. H. I. M.
  Salta, M.
Noël nouvelet.
  Moineau, G.
Noël pastoral.
  Bowman, C. B.
Noël swing.
  Henry, C.
Noix.
  Trenet, C.
Nokturna.
  Chlubna, O.
Nola.
  Arndt, F.
Nomás porque sí.
  Alarcon Leal, E. Mala racha.
Non ci comprendiamo più.
  Pavesio, P.
Non mi vuoi dir chi sei.
  Panzuti, V. La scuola del ritmo.
Non so come si chiami.
  Zuccheri, B.
None but Christ can satisfy.
  Thorne, W. M.
Nora Prentiss.
  Jerome, M. K.
Nordic lullaby.
  Ferry, C. T. Songs.

North America, take it away!
  Vogel, H.
Northern dream.
  Rachmaninoff, S.
Northwest outpost.
  Friml, R.
Norwegian dance.
  Grieg, E. H.
  Tollefsen, A. Gay little pieces.
Nostalgia.
  Comstock, F.
  Scarmolin, A. L.
Nostalgia di Napoli.
  Rusconi, E.
Not a minute too soon.
  Schulman, R. M.
Not bad, Bascomb.
  McRae, B.
Not this alone.
  Moore, D.
Note speller.
  Holt, H. Carl Fischer note-speller.
Nothin' but you.
  Fox, R.
Nothing.
  Kulvyanskia, W. A.
Nothing but a dream?
  A'Dair, J.
Notte a Venezia.
  Rusconi, E.
Notte a Vienna.
  Manno, V.
Nous aurions pu passer.
  Saint-Yves, J.
Nous continuons la France.
  Wiener, J.
Novelette.
  Gilbert, J.
  Robertson, L.
Novellette.
  James, P.
Novelty song parade.
  Goldsen, M. H. The King Cole Trio.
Now I lay me down to sleep.
  Edwards, J.
Now it's my turn to turn you down.
  Mosberger, S. G.
Noyé.
  Datin, J.
Nozze di Figaro.
  Mozart, J. C. W. A.
Nu gaar Bedstemor amok.
  Gyldmark, S. Bedstemor gaar amok.
Nube Rosa.
  Zuccheri, L. Oggi ancor.
Nuestro amor.
  Ramirez, R.
Nueve de julio.
  Padula, J. L.
Nuit.
  Datin, J.
Nuits du Brésil.
  Goldbaum, F.
Nun me dicite No.
  Canoro, L.
Nunc dimittis.
  Erb, J. L.
  Tallis, T. Magnificat.
Nunca.
  Cardenas, G. Your love or no love.
Nunca sabrás.
  Simon, B. Time and again.
Nuovi successi.
  Cioffi, G.
Nut cracker suite.
  Chaikovskii, P. I. Cossack's song.
O. K. Jones.
  Mercerón, M.
O.N.U.!
  Chobillon, C.
O apomachos.
  Papajohn, G. J.
O be joyful in the Lord.
  Diggle, R.
  Harris, R. A.
O bella bionda.
  Olivieri, Dino. Tutto il mondo canta Tornerai.

O blessed day of motherhood.
  Mueller, C. F.
O, blessed is he.
  Bortniansky, D. S.
O blessed Jesu.
  Palestrina, G. P. da.
O bone Jesu.
  Palestrina, G. P. da.
O brother mine.
  Méhul, E. N.
O Christ, Thou Lamb of God.
  Liemohn, E.
O chuca-chuca.
  Herscher, L.
O come, all ye faithful.
  Heller, R., arr.
  My first christmas songs.
O come and mourn.
  Means, C.
O come, Jesus, my salvation.
  Marraco, J. S.
O dame, get up and bake your pies.
  Bax, A.
O death.
  Brahms, J. Four serious songs.
O did you hear the meadow lark?
  Howard, J. T.
O divine Redeemer.
  Gounod, C.
O du, mein holder Abendstern.
  Wagner, R. Tannhäuser.
O, ever I'll follow.
  Elliot, J. An evangel in song.
O everlasting God.
  Bullock, E.
O! For a closer walk with God.
  Foster, M. B.
O for a thousand tongues.
  Mueller, C. F.
O give thanks.
  Constantini, A.
O God of love, O King of peace.
  Baker, H. W.
O God, our Help in ages past.
  Mueller, C. F.
O holy night.
  Adam, A.
O, how much we owe Jesus. See title entry in composer list.
O Jesus Christ I come.
  Jones, G. J. Life more abundant.
O Jesus, Lord of heavenly grace.
  Baker, H. W.
O Jesus, Thou art standing.
  Knecht, J. H.
O light divine.
  Arkhangel'skii, A. A.
O little hills of Nazareth.
  O'Hara, G.
O Lord, support us all the day long.
  Chapman, M. C.
O Lord, Thou hast searched me out.
  Goldsworthy, W. A.
O loulas.
  Metsakēs, G. S. To kompologaki.
  Mitsaki, G.
O love divine.
  Brace, B.
O lumen.
  O'Connor, D. G.
O peaceful England.
  German, E.
O popelce.
  Koštál, E. Pohádka.
O praise God in His holiness.
  Wolff, S. D.
O praise the Lord.
  Erb, J. L.
  Snow, Francis W.
O risen Lord.
  Lovelace, A. C.
O Sacred Head surrounded.
  Bedell, R. L.
O salutaris.
  Aubanel, G.
  Honegger, A.
  Horgan, M. S., sister.

O'Connell, W., cardinal. Hymn to
the Holy Name.
Singenberger, J. B. Jubilate Deo.
O salutaris hostia.
Fauré, J. B.
O saving victim.
Callaway, P.
O small feac'd flower.
Flood, D. F.
'O sole mio!
Bideri, Valentina, comp.
O soul, why in darkness?
Baker, L. M.
O swallow, swallow.
Diggle, R.
O, tell me of Jesus, my Saviour.
Elliot, J. An evangel in song.
O thou that tellest good tidings.
Händel, G. F. The Messiah.
O Thou who camest.
Bach, J. S.
O Thou, whose power.
Rossini, G. A.
O tod, wie bitter bist du.
Brahms, J. Four serious songs.
O western wind.
Roberton, H. S.
Oahu advanced harmony note course for
Hawaiian and electric guitar. See
title entry in composer list.
Oahu, dreamy island.
Faber, Billy.
Iona, Andy.
Oahu E-Z method. See title entry in
composer list.
Oahu modern note method for electric
and Hawaiian guitars. See title
entry in composer list.
Oahu "rhythm style" note course for
plectrum guitar (octave notation)
See title entry in composer list.
Oakie boogie.
Tyler, J.
Object of my affection.
Grier, J.
Oblation.
Rathaus, K. Three English songs.
Oblio.
Bisio, N. Melody swing.
Oboe passages.
Mayer, R. M., comp.
Obras para piano y canto.
Loyola Jáuregui, F.
Occasional overture.
Handel, G. F.
October, November.
Lee, D. K.
Od Našega rastanka.
Cernkovich, R., arr.
Ode.
Stravinskiĭ, I. F.
Ode to intensity.
Pimsleur, S. Suite of transforma-
tions.
Oeillet fané.
Tristan, Y.
Österländska kärlekssanger.
Koch, S. von.
Of passion blue.
Pentuff, O.
Of unsung heroes.
Gould, C. W.
Off to camp.
Schiefelbein, F. A.
Offenbach (simplified).
Offenbach, J.
Offertoire.
Greenhill, H. W. Three pieces for
organ.
Office of the holy communion.
Maekelberghe, A.
Oft heard tunes.
Weybright, J.
Oggi ancor.
Zuccheri, L.
Oggi no!
Panzuti, V.

Oh boy, oh boy, oh boy.
Dahlquist, L. E.
Oh, clap your hands.
Edwards, C., pseud.
Oh come get in my automobile.
Sneed, E. A.
Oh hear these, our words.
Morgan, H.
Oh, how can you do it?
Arthur, W.
Oh! how I love off-beats.
Jackson, C.
Oh how I loved you then.
Carleton, R. L.
Oh, I drive oxen.
Gaul, H.
Oh, Jesus, help me when I pray.
Street, E.
Oh, lady be good.
Gershwin, G.
Oh, little children, do you know?
Poulton, D. F.
Oh Lord, have mercy on me.
Johnson, H.
Oh Lord, Redeemer.
Sullivan, Sir A. S.
Oh, Mother Cabrini.
Smolen, J. C.
Oh, mother, little mother mine.
Schade, C. F.
Oh! My achin' heart.
Palmer, J.
Oh Ninna and Anninia.
Diggle, R.
Oh, pray for the peace of Jerusalem.
Tomkins, T.
Oh promise me.
De Koven, R.
Oh, publish the story.
Parker, E. E.
Oh, so happy.
Gaddis, R. M. Abraham, the pilgrim.
Oh, to know Christ.
Waite, M. G.
Oh, what a beautiful mornin'.
Rodgers, R. Oklahoma.
Oh, why don't you let Him come in?
Parker, E. E.
Oh, worship the King.
Cain, N.
Oh—yes!
Fox, F.
Oh, yes, I want to make a soldier.
Jackson, M. E.
Oh, Yody, Yody.
Rathaus, K.
O-hi-o.
Hanlon, B. Round on the end and high
in the middle, O-hi-o.
Ohio.
Staley, K. A.
Ohio River bound.
Gaul, H. B., arr.
Ohio River farewell song.
Gaul, H.
Ohio Valley polka.
Santa, E.
Oi Mari.
Ceglie, C. di.
Oiseau fidèle.
Caffot, S. V. J.
Oj, jesenske duge noči!
Cernkovich, R., arr.
Oklahoma!
Rodgers, R.
Oklahoma bound.
Westmoreland, P.
Oklahoma City.
Franklin, D. (Gotta get to) Oklahoma
City.
Rose, F.
Oklahoma scene.
Fields, F. G.
Oklahoma stomp.
Cooley, D. C.
Old Abram Brown.
Britten, B.

Old Antigo waltzes.
Schroeder, J. H.
Old chuck wagon.
Leopold, J. W.
Old devil moon.
Lane, B.
Old English.
Scher, W.
Old fashion love.
Clyde, T.
The old flying. "L."
Turner, R. J.
Old folks at home.
Foster, S. C.
An old friend is the best friend.
Wilder, A.
Old gray mare.
Jacobs, M., arr. Boogie woogie
step-by-step.
Old Jersey City, N. J.
Lillis, T. J.
Old lamp-lighter.
Haring, R. C.
Simon, N.
Old love is a true love.
Roberts, A. Singin' in the corn.
Old MacDonald had a farm.
Jacobs, M., arr. Boogie woogie
step-by-step.
Old memory.
Seymer, W. Strofer i sol och
skugga.
Old musician and his guitar.
Charnoph, C.
Old Oklahoma moon.
Harris, G. E.
Old shepherd.
Schimmerling, H. A., arr. Ja som
bača velmi starý.
Old Spanish trail.
Fears, W. A.
Old spinning wheel.
Oberg, O. S.
Old spring madrigal.
Smure, R. D.
Old square.
Guarino, J. B. Vieux Carré sérénade.
Old square dance is back again.
Reid, D.
Old-time religion. See title entry in
composer list.
Old white goose.
Austin, G. L.
Old Wyoming waltz.
Harris, G. E.
Olé Maléna!
Delvoie, J. C.
Olemka.
Castellani, L.
Olivia.
Stearns, W. L.
Ollantay.
Sas, A.
Olvídate de mí.
Gil, A.
Ombre di sogno.
Concina, S.
Ombra mai fù.
Händel, G. F. Largo.
Omnipotence.
Schubert, F. P.
On a ferriswheel.
Dallam, H.
On a heavenly isle in Tahiti.
Faber, B.
On an evening in Paris.
Tinturin, P.
On de Embarcadero.
Furney, A. J.
On dress parade.
Hellard, R. A.
On entend partout carillon.
Moineau, G.
On green meadows.
Schiefelbein, F. A.
On Jordan's stormy banks.
Shure, R. D.

On our honeymoon in the air.
Hall, R. E.
On parade.
Herbert, V. Sweethearts.
On the dusty road.
Johnson, H.
On the isle of my dreams.
Thomas, H.
On the lone prairee.
Blake, D. G.
On the merry-go-round.
Fletcher, L.
On the mountain.
Arcos, E. Por la sierra.
On the open road.
Jacobs, M.
On the resurrection of Christ.
Montgomery, B.
On the sands of time.
Tovey, H. G.
On the sunny side of the street.
McHugh, J. F.
On the trail to home, sweet home.
Pazandak, A.
On the Uruguayan beaches.
Hore, C. En las playas uruguayas.
On the wing.
Vandercook, H. A.
On the wrong side of the railroad track.
Ellington, D. Beggar's holiday.
On this day, O Beautiful Mother.
Lambillotte, L.
On tiptoes.
Steiner, E.
On wings of love I send a kiss to thee.
Kelly, N. Golden memories of
by-gone days.
On wings of melody.
Dean, E. B.
On wings to romance.
Nurnberg, V.
Once a lady was here.
Bowles, P.
Once a star shone bright.
Cosgray, O.
Once more, beloved.
Dittenhaver, S. L.
Once on a time Christ came to us here.
Cornelius, P.
Once upon a moonlight night.
Bibo, I.
Once upon a time.
Dodd, D.
Powers, M.
Seymer, W. Strofer i sol och skugga.
One day.
Milhaud, D. Une journée.
One day on Calvary.
Woods, J. S.
One evening.
Clyde, T.
One evening at the circus-theatre.
Culotta, I. Una serata al circo.
One great love.
Seaman, F. M.
One happy hour with you.
Cioffi, G.
One hundred hymns for men.
Hayden, R. T., comp.
One hundred twenty-first Psalm.
Wright, N. S.
One hundred years ago.
Taylor, F. A.
One kiss.
Stone, G.
One kiss for good measure.
Quiroga, M. L.
One little kiss in the moonlight.
O'Hagan, J.
One man stuff.
Werrenrath, R.
One more kiss for the road.
Parys, G. van. Circonstances
attenuantes.
One morning in May.
Carmichael, H.
Niles, J. J., ed. & arr.

One night.
Woode, H.
One night to love.
Samuels, W.
One of my three.
McNeil, J. C.
One room kitchenette.
Winston, E.
1001 nights.
Strauss, J.
One, two, three.
Coward, N. Pacific 1860.
Only a dream away.
Williams, S.
Only a friend.
Hudgins, E.
Only in dreams.
Bergman, M.
Only you.
Arnold, A. A.
Onward, Christian soldiers.
Sullivan, Sir A. S.
Op en top.
Berg, C. J. van den.
Op school.
Nieland, H. J. J.
Open, shut them.
Poulton, D. F.
Open the door, Richard!
McVea, J.
Open the gates of promise.
Hanna, E.
Open your window.
Wolf, D.
Opou ki an pas.
Chairopoulos, C. K.
Opportunity.
Wilson, H. R.
Opuu lani.
Glynn, B., arr.
Oraia kai glykeia mou.
Harlan, L. G.
Orange Blossom Bay.
Carleton, R. L.
Orange Blossom Special.
Rouse, E. T.
Orange blossoms.
Herbert, V.
Orao polka.
Radich, J.
Orchard.
Brook, H.
Orchestral exercises.
Isaac, M. J.
Organ chimes folio.
Lorenz, E. J., comp.
Organito de la tarde.
Castillo, C.
Organum metamorphosis.
Trowbridge, L.
Oriental rapsody.
Sakellarious, A.
Oriental tale.
Dalmer, A. Cuento oriental.
Orientale.
Cui, C.
Origin of valentines.
Enders, H.
Original piano solos.
Chittison, H.
Original themes for piano.
Oliver, G.
Oriole's march.
Heffner, E. C.
Orizaba dance.
Tiomkin, D. Duel in the sun.
Orpheus britannicus.
Purcell, H.
Oscar Moore's Guitaristics.
Moore, O.
Oshkosh, Wis.
Brodsky, R.
Osme's song.
Tomblings, P. Sylvia.
Osseo fantasia.
Williams, S. Little classics for
cornet or trumpet.

Ostrov milováni.
Stelibský, J.
Ou-es tu, mon amour?
Stern, E. Have you change for a
dream?
Our allies were convoying.
Richard, L.
Our country.
Harts, H. L.
Our Father.
Nedd, J. B.
Our flirtation.
Sousa, J. P.
Our glorious old U. S. A.
Hart, F. W.
Our Lady of Fatima.
Mourin, N.
Our Lady's Martinites.
Partain, D.
Our most precious boys, they move no
more.
Richard, L.
Our own Jole Blon.
Acuff, R., arr.
Our prairie padre.
Ash, T. J.
Our prayer.
Murphey, J. H.
Our serenade.
Whitford, R. H.
Our town.
James, P.
Stevens, Thad.
Our resurrected Lord.
Uptegrove, W. E.
Our song of love.
Wilhousky, E.
Our strength, O church of God, thou art.
Bach, J. S.
Our wonderful love.
Ramirez, R. Nuestro amor.
Out in Nevada.
Erskine, H. E. R.
Out of my dreams.
Rodgers, R. Oklahoma!
Out of the shadows.
Woods, J. S. Crown for cross.
Out on the range where dreams come
true.
Carleton, R. L.
Outdoor song.
Powers, M. M.
Over the waves.
Rosas, J.
Overlander's song.
Dawson, H.
Overtime.
Hampton, L.
Overture.
De Lamarter, E.
Overture, Franz Schubert.
Suppé, F. von.
Oye.
Delgado, P.
Oye un coco.
Miró, F.
Pa floden.
Koch, S. von. Morgenländische
Liebeslieder.
Pa tófället.
Koch, S. von. Morgenländische
Liebeslieder.
Pa kingelvevstrenger.
Saeverud, H. Siljustöl.
Paa min Faerden gennem Verden.
Christiansen, E. Fyrtøjet.
Pacific 1860.
Coward, N.
Paddling in the stream.
King, F.
Pages de sonatine.
Gallois Montbrun, R.
Paging Mr. Husing.
Herron, J.
Pagliacci.
Leoncavallo, R.
Pagoda.
Wiant, B., arr.

Pair of baby shoes.
  Langham, R.
Pair of diddlers.
  Ostling, A.
Pajarillo.
  Murillo, E.
Pal of my memories.
  Richards, M. R.
Paladins.
  Rameau, J. P.
Pale blue slippers.
  Dungan, O.
Palestine is mine!
  Solomon, S. Mein land evetz-Israel.
Palm Sunday and Easter organ book.
  Ashmall, W. E., arr.
Palms.
  Faure, J. B.
Paloma waltz.
  Yradier, S.
Panama.
  Marcedo, D.
Pancho Maximilian Hernandeez.
  Frisch, A.
Pane tosa chronia.
  Ritsiardes, I. M. Prosphyge sten O.E.E.
Pange lingua.
  Singenberger, J. B.
Panik i Familien.
  Gyldmark, S.
Panis angelicus.
  Charpentier, M. A.
  Franck, C. A. Father most merciful.
Paolo und Francesca.
  Klenau, P. von.
Papa Noël.
  Padilla, J.
Papaveri di Montecassino.
  Schütz, A.
Papillon.
  Raaff, A. C. de.
Papillonne.
  Ligtelijn, J. L.
Papillons.
  Schumann, R. A.
Papylon.
  Castro, A.
Pâquerette.
  Guglielmi, L. Le destin s'amuse.
Par lui.
  Vonel, R.
Par ona storia.
  Clerici, A.
Parade of the marionettes.
  Frieber, L.
Parade of the wooden soldiers.
  Jessel, L.
Parakeet in paradise.
  Moody, J.
Paraphrase on "Jesus Christ is risen today."
  Campbell, E.
Paris.
  Lafarge, G. P. M.
Parisian scenes.
  Rowley, A.
Partita.
  Bentzon, N. V. Partita, piano.
Partita per arpa.
  Lupi, R. Partita, harp.
Partizanen.
  Pokrass.
Party and banquet songs.
  Minchella, E., comp. Minchella's accordion favorites.
Pasadena Rose.
  Mayer, C. I.
Pascha nostrum.
  Neckes, father.
Paseo.
  Hively, W. Habana suite.
Pasión tropical.
  Fernández Porta, M.
Pass to the North.
  Bollman, W. H.
Passacaglia.
  Muffat, G.
  Wolpe, S.

Passacaille.
  Lully, V.
Passage studies.
  Thurston, F.
Passé.
  Meyer, J.
Passing by.
  Hess, J.
Passion of Jesus.
  Miles, C. A.
Pastoral.
  Ross, H., arr.
Pastorale.
  Gallois Montbrun, R. Pages de sonatine.
  Händel, G. F.
  Nieland, J. H. I. M.
  Park, S.
Pastorale at dawn.
  Balogh, E.
Pathways in music.
  Cole, A. L.
Pathways to the proms.
  Barrington, J.
Paul Bunyan.
  Siegmeister, E. American legends.
Paul Bunyan suite.
  Bergsma, W.
Pavane for a dead princess.
  Ravel, M.
Peace.
  Turner, C. A.
Peace shall prevail.
  Strickland, L.
Peace (with love)
  Van Zandt, J.
Pearls on velvet.
  Young, V.
Pedal tunes for the Hammond student.
  Ceiga, G. E., arr.
Pedlar.
  Dunhill, T. F. Mother Duck.
Pee-Wee, the piccolo.
  Kleinsinger, G.
Peek-a-boo.
  Grimm, C. A.
Peek-a-boo lullaby.
  Gilmore, T. S. Four new songs.
Peg o' my heart.
  Fisher, F.
Peggy.
  Vené, R.
Pena gris.
  Canaro, M.
Pennsylvania hills.
  Maur, L.
A penny for your thoughts.
  Carson, J. L.
Peñón de las ánimas!
  Esperón, M.
Pense à moi.
  Moretti, R.
Pensively.
  Trowbridge, L.
People are funny.
  Reid, D.
People say I am naughty oberek.
  Malec, A. Ludzie mi to za zle maja.
People will say we're in love.
  Rodgers, R. Oklahoma!
Pepina.
  Moletta, B.
Pepito Santa Cruz.
  Choisser, J. D.
Perdida.
  Navarro, J. J.
Perfect friend.
  Wolverton, M. H.
Perhaps, perhaps, perhaps.
  Farrés, O. Quizas, quizas, quizas.
Perils of Pauline.
  Loesser, F.
Perimenó gramma sou.
  Katribanos, D. K.
Periwigs and ruffles.
  Nordman, C.
¡Pero ... que mulata!
  Miró, F.

Pero vuelve.
  Sánchez Vázquez, P.
Perpetual spring.
  Taylor, B. E.
Personal message.
  Zorlig, K.
Perth on the Swan.
  York, R. The popping the question waltz.
Pete.
  Grey, L.
Peter and the wolf.
  Prokof'ev, S. S.
Peter Rabbit.
  Trowbridge, L. In meadow and forest.
Petit cousin.
  Lafarge, G. P. M.
Petit Farfadet.
  Strimer, J.
Petit nuage.
  Martinet, H.
Petit poucet noir.
  Emer, M.
Petite messe pastorale.
  Poupard, H.
Petite musique de nuit.
  Mozart, J. C. W. A. Eine kleine Nachtmusik.
Petite suite.
  Chaikovskii, P. I.
  Grechaninov, A. T.
  Nieland, J. H. I. M.
Petite valse de concert.
  Belton, J. Time marches on.
Phalenes.
  Philipp, I.
Phantasy in Halling.
  Egge, K. Fantasi i Halling.
Phantom shadows.
  Skilton, E.
Philippine folk songs.
  Rivera, J. C., arr.
Piano accordion album.
  Cowlin, R., ed. & arr.
Piano chords.
  Moreau, C. M.
Piano duet book of gospel hymns.
  Dorsey, T. A.
Piano pieces for the youth.
  Boscovich, A. U.
Piano portrait.
  Fina, J.
Pianoforte sonata no. 1.
  Turner, G. B. Sonata, piano. no. 1.
Picadore march.
  Sousa, J. P.
Piccoli concertisti.
  Galaverni, I.
Piccoli pezzi kontrapuntistici.
  Brockt, J.
Piccolo Friel.
  Frisia, A.
Piccolo sentiero.
  Culotta, I.
Piccolo zoo.
  Romita, E.
Pickaninny in the dark.
  Bown, P. B. The cronies.
Picture parade.
  Beaver, J.
Pictures in melody.
  Ketèlbey, A. W.
Pictures of New Mexico.
  Robb, J. D.
Piece of spring.
  Seymer, W. Strofer i sol och skugga.
Pièce symphonique.
  Tournemire, C.
The Pied Piper.
  Goldsen, M. H., arr.
Piedigrotta Bideri 1946.
  Bideri, V., comp.
Piedigrotta Pisano-Cioffi, 1941-42, XIX.
  Pisano, G., comp.
Pieds-en-l'air.
  Heseltine, P. Capriol suite.

195

Pig foot Pete.
  DePaul, G.
Pilatus.
  Riisager, K.
Pilgrim song.
  Roberts, M.
Pillow of sighs and tears.
  Porter, L.
Pilot.
  Whittredge, E. B.
Pine Ridge mountain rendezvous.
  Davidson, L. D.
Pineapples.
  Murry, T.
Pines.
  A'Dair, J.
Pines of home.
  Luvaas, M. J.
Pines on the hillside.
  Holst, M. S. Three woodland scenes.
Pino solitario.
  Panzuti, V.
Pinto Ben.
  DeVol, F.
Pioggia d'ottobre.
  Davico, V. Cinque liriche romantiche.
Pioneer.
  Chenette, E.
Pioneer baby.
  Watson, A. E.
Pioneer mother's lullaby.
  White, L. O. B.
Pioneer sweetheart.
  Merrill, C.
Pipe and Tabor.
  Rowley, A.
Pipe dreams.
  Carleton, R. L.
Piquante.
  Bacher, E.
Píseň lásky.
  Suk, J.
Písně letní noci.
  Vomáčka, B.
Písně milostné.
  Petržela, V.
Pittori fiamminghi.
  Smareglia, A.
Pittsburgh polka.
  Hoven, G.
Pizzicato caprice.
  Engleman, J.
Pizzicato polka.
  Sang, B.
Pjesmu ti pjevam.
  Cernkovich, R.
Plain Mary.
  Feldman, W.
Play gypsies, dance gypsies.
  Kálmán, I. Countess Maritza.
Play with me.
  Fouts, M. Children's easy piano
    pieces.
Play-easies.
  Jesse, M. R.
Playful kitty.
  Hopkins, H. P.
Playful pixies.
  Aulbach, F. E.
Playing at love.
  Chanslor, H.
Playing hop scotch.
  Steinbach, B. Modern miniatures.
Playing marbles.
  Fouts, M. Children's easy piano
    pieces.
Plaza de Armas.
  Hively, W. Habana suite.
Please don't play that old song.
  Lawrence, J.
Please, Mama.
  Elman, Z.
Please play a dreamy waltz.
  Carty, D.
Please tell me a lie.
  Trommer, J.
Pleasure's all mine.
  Moore, W. Carnegie Hall

Pledge to the flag.
  Elaine, sister.
  Hibbs, C. A.
Plenilunio.
  Davico, V. Cinque liriche roman-
    tiche.
  Mineo, E.
Plorate filii Israel.
  Carissimi, G.
Ploum ploum tra la la.
  G. glie. mi, L.
Po' good Jesus.
  Hohmann, W. H.
Po zarostlém chodníčku.
  Janáček, L.
Pod jabloní.
  Suk, J.
Pod tým naším okieneškom.
  Schimmerling, H. A. Yarmila.
Poem.
  Fibich, Z.
  Sowerby, L.
Poème.
  Fibich, Z.
  Heckman, G. J.
  Massis, A.
Poems for piano.
  Persichetti, V.
Poet's place.
  Tobin, L.
Pohádka o popelce.
  Koštál, E.
Poios se pere kai mouphyges.
  Gounares, N. K.
Polish Christmas carols.
  Rachel, sister, arr. Polskie koledy.
Polka.
  Grechaninov, A. T. Petite suite.
Polka du rossignol.
  Gallois-Montbrun, R. Les rêves de
    Janceline.
Polka for three.
  Helmle, L. B., arr. Polka zu dreien.
Polka na lewo.
  Stanley, B.
Polka to the left.
  Stanley, B. Polka na lewo.
Polka zu dreien.
  Helmle, L. B., arr.
Polk-a-dots.
  Rynning, E. F.
Polkatrinka.
  Ettore, E.
Polly Pigtails.
  Livingston, J.
Polly wolly doodle.
  Hopkins, H. P., arr.
  Mossman, T., arr.
Polonaise.
  Chopin, F. F.
Polonaise in A flat.
  Chopin, F. F.
Polskie koledy.
  Rachel, sister, arr.
Polynesian swing.
  Dominici, H.
Ponme la mano caridad.
  Saborit, E.
Pony ride.
  O'Toole, W.
Poor Maggie Brown.
  Shuart, B.
Pop-corn.
  Raezer, C. M.
Poppa, don't preach to me.
  Loesser, F. The perils of Pauline.
Popping the question waltz.
  York, R.
Poppy for remembrance.
  Welty, J. T.
Popular piano.
  Kluse, F. L.
Popular piano breaks.
  Goodsell, E. M., comp.
Poquito de amor.
  Soler, R. This time for keeps.
Por confiado.
  Cadena Rubín.

Por la sierra.
  Arcos, E.
Por primera vez.
  Rivera, P.
¿Por qué insistes?
  Ramírez, R.
Por que te quieres ir?
  Treviño, P.
Por que tu lloras?
  Yamin, J.
Por tu amor.
  Herbert, V. Orange blossoms. A
    kiss in the dark.
  Varona, L.
Pork 'n beans.
  Trace, A.
Port Royal, 1861.
  McKay, G. F.
Portes de la nuit.
  Kosma, J.
Portrait of a lady.
  Melachrino, G. M.
Portvakten.
  Nilsson, S.
Pōs me methas.
  Papadopoulos, T. G.
Positive[ly]
  Lambertz, A.
Positivvisa.
  Stenhammar, W. Fyra Stockholmsdik-
    ter.
Poslední pīsñí.
  Vašata, R. L.
Possum song.
  Shand, T.
Pour les amants.
  Parys, G. van. Le silence est d'or.
Pour lui.
  Barelli, A.
Pour toi, Pepita.
  Lopez, F. La belle de Cadix.
Pour un foulard.
  Marly, A.
Pour vous, madame.
  Dehette, M. Farandoles.
Practical drill in keyboard harmony.
  Lucke, K. E.
Praga.
  Suk, J.
The prairie trail.
  Ellsworth, A. B.
Praise.
  Posamaniek, B.
Praise be to Mary.
  Gounod, C. F.
Praise His holy name.
  Everhart, L.
Praise Jehovah.
  Pearsall, R. L.
Praise, my soul, the King.
  Farnes, E., pseud.
Praise, my soul, the King of Heaven.
  Duncan, C.
Praise our God, all ye His servants.
  Williams, R. E.
Praise the Lord, ye heavens adore.
  North, J. D., pseud.
Praise ye servants of the Lord.
  Marsh, H. J.
Praise ye the Father.
  Gounod, C. F.
Praise ye the Lord.
  Bostwick, F. J.
  Campbell, L. E.
Praise ye the name of the Lord.
  Cherepnin, N. N.
Pray, pray, pray.
  Green, A. Eight new sacred choruses.
Prayer.
  Hore, C.
  Klumpkey, J.
  Smale, L. G.
Prayer abiding.
  Shure, R. D.
Prayer changes things.
  Graham, A. C.
Prayer for peace.
  Freed, I. Prayers of Israel.

196

Prayer hymn.
  Grindy, R. M.
Prayer of St. Francis.
  Mueller, C. F.
Prayer of trust.
  Schumann, R. A.
Prayers of Israel.
  Freed, I.
Precious.
  Koehler, R. H.
Precious little sonny boy.
  Denney, D. (He's my darlin')
    precious little sonny boy.
Preferible es llorar.
  Domínguez, A.
Pregonera.
  Angelis, A. de.
Prélude.
  Gallois Montbrun, R. Pages de
    sonatine.
Prelude and fugue.
  Hendricks, C. F.
Prelude, C minor.
  Gardner, M. A.
Prélude, choral et variations.
  Nieland, J. H. I. M.
Prelude in A minor, no. 2.
  Beyer, E. Prelude, piano, no. 2.
Prelude in G major.
  Fouts, M. Children's easy piano
    pieces.
Prelude moderne.
  Signorelli, F.
Prélude pastoral.
  Chabrier, E.
Preludes and voluntaries.
  Thiman, E. H.
Premier jour du mois de mai.
  Le Grand, R.
Premier madrigal.
  Saint-Yves, J.
Première symphonie.
  Langlais, J. Symphony, organ, no. 1.
Preparatory exercises.
  Schmitt, A. Exercices préparatoires.
Près de la petite source.
  Charney, L.
Présent.
  Beydts, L.
Preserve me, O God.
  Margetson, E.
Pressing toward perfection.
  Quisenberry, P. W.
Pretending.
  Sherman, A.
Pretty blonde.
  King, S. Jolie blonde.
Pretty butterfly.
  Castro, A. El papylon.
Pretty girl is like a melody.
  Berlin, I. Accordion transcriptions
    of Irving Berlin melodies.
Pretty little dirty face.
  Lynton, E.
Pretty pa-ha-reel-yo.
  Murillo, E. Pajarillo.
Pretty, pretty.
  Navarro, J. J. Que bonito.
Pretzel man.
  Wolf, D.
Prières pour le pain.
  Cockenpot, F.
Prima-ballerina.
  Offenbach, J.
Primavera.
  Galindo, B. Springtime.
Prince and the maiden.
  Savino, D.
Prince of Kandapora.
  Mattes, W.
Princely courtiers.
  Downey, S. E.
Princess and the flute player.
  Ber₂man, V. M.
Princess Elizabeth waltz.
  Trewhela, R. H.
Princeton victory march.
  MacInnis, M. D. Clear the track.

Principles of extensions in violin
  fingering.
  Babitz, S.
Prinsessans strumpeband.
  Björklund, N.
Printemps.
  Durand, P. J.
Prisoner's last letter.
  Anderson, G, A.
Prisonnier de l'amour.
  Chobillon, C.
  Chobillon, C. O. N. U.
Pro kamaráda.
  Stelibský, J.
Probably.
  Galvez, M.
Programma B. B. C.
  Rossi, R. O. Questo è swing.
Progressive exercises for basic ballet
  turns.
  Whitcomb, R.
Progressive piano exercises.
  Philipp, I.
Promenade.
  Anderson, L₁roy EP 6718 Dec. 18, 1947
Promise.
  Fischer, C.
Promised land.
  Eisen, N. Dos versprochene land.
Prosphyge stēn O.Ế.E.
  Ritsiardēs, I. M.
Psalm of David.
  Lang, E.
Psalm 150.
  Lewandowski, L.
Psalm 146.
  Wakeman, F. M.
Psalm 25.
  Bruinsma, H. A.
Psilē brochoula epiase.
  Metsakēs, G. S.
P'tit cousin.
  Lafarge, G.
Pua carnation.
  King, C. E. Flowers of Hawaii.
Pucci, Pucci.
  Olivieri, D. Tutto il mondo canta
    Tornerai.
Punching Judy.
  Hampton, L.
Puppet dance.
  Kosnar, M. Seven pieces.
Puppet's holiday.
  Herbert, V.
Puppets on parade.
  Chenoweth, W.
Put, put, put, went the Evinrude.
  Bergen, A. H.
Put your little foot.
  King, S.
Put Your spirit over me.
  Macklin, Y.
Quadrille des soldats de plomb.
  Gallois-Montbrun, R. Les rêves de
    Janceline.
Quand Dieu naquit à Noël.
  Peloquin, C. A. The Christmas Child.
Quand il pleut sur la maison.
  Lanjean, M.
Quand un facteur s'envole.
  Trenet, C.
Quand verrai-je les îles?
  Arrieu, C.
Quando vuelvas a mi.
  Romberg, S. The new moon. Lover,
    come back to me.
Quarante lecons d'harmonie.
  Friboulet, G. E.
Quarter of a watermelon.
  Kennedy, A.
Quartet in C major.
  Berger, A. V. Quartet, wind.
Quartet no. 2.
  Frankel, B. Quartet, strings, no. 2.
  Shostakovich, D. D. Quartet, strings,
    no. 2.

Quartettino.
  Vomáčka, B.
Quartetto in modo antico.
  Marx, J. Quartet, strings.
Quartier latin.
  Trenet, C.
Quattro successi.
  Barile, E.
Quatuor à cordes (no. 2)
  Bloch, E. Quartet, strings, no. 2.
Que bonito.
  Navarro, J. J.
Que celosa!
  Ramirez, S.
Que, cosa es el amor?
  Ruiz, G.
Que le voy a hacer.
  Suárez, H.
Que lindo es mi amor.
  Elena, J.
Qué lío, lío!
  Mendez, B.
¡Que lucha!
  Noli, J. F.
Que me importa.
  Fernández Porta, M.
Que no, que no!
  Curbelo, J.
Que no vas.
  Lambert, R.
Qué pasa, mi cuate.
  Ruiz Rueda, J.
Qué será, doctor?
  Pacheco Huergo, M.
Que vida.
  Rivera, P.
Que voy a hacer.
  Martínez Gil, C.
Queen.
  Ramirez, J. La reina.
Queen of the Osage Hills.
  Kahler, W. T.
Quel tuo rosso.
  Carenzio, R.
Questo è swing.
  Rossi, R. O.
¿ Quién sabe?
  Cunliffe, D.
Quién te ha traído!
  Velázquez, V.
Quiet, don't cry, my heart.
  Calla, no llores.
Quiet moonshiny night.
  Seymer, W. Strofer i sol och skugga.
Quiet paths.
  Pendleton, E.
Quietude.
  Trowbridge, L. R.
Qu'il fait bon chanter!
  Bloch, P. G.
Quilting party.
  Fletcher, J. S.
Quintet.
  Toch, E.
Quintet, for flute and string quartet.
  Piston, W. Quintet, flute & strings.
Quirk of a dirk.
  Varner, R.
Quittez, pasteurs.
  Moineau, G.
Quizas, quizas, quizas.
  Farrés, O.
Rabbit jumps.
  Coupland, L. H.
Raccolta delle celebri canzoni.
  Tagliaferri, E.
Raccolta di successi.
  Crescenzo, V. de, comp.
Race track blues.
  King, L.
Rachmaninoff memory album.
  Rachmaninoff, S.
Rachmaninoff's concerto march.
  Rachmaninoff, S. Concerto, piano,
    no. 2.
Radiant morn hath passed away.
  Blake, G.
  Woodward, W. H.

197

Radiant star of ocean.
  Bingham, S. Ave maris stella.
Radio favorites.
  Smith, J., ed. Jack Smith's Radio
  favorites.
Railroad reverie.
  Sacco, J.
Rain.
  Steinbach, B. Modern miniatures.
Rain drops fall.
  Gross, C.
Rain on my heart.
  Putnam, G.
Rainbow River.
  Bruns, G.
Rainbow smile songs.
  Wirges, W. F. Smile songs.
Rainbows and roses.
  Cooper, L. A.
Raindrop.
  Chopin, F. F.
Raindrops on a drum.
  Friml, R. Northwest outpost.
Raising of Lazarus.
  Davis, K. K.
Ralph Barfell method for playing
  Hawaiian Guitar.
  Barfell, R. A.
Ralph Federer's piano solo album.
  Federer, R., comp.
Rambling rose.
  Burke, J.
Rambling wreck from Georgia Tech.
  Yoder, P., arr.
Ramiro.
  Codevilla, P. Tango habanera.
Ramuntcho.
  Scotto, V. B.
Rancho de mis recuerdos.
  Rufz, F.
Rancho serenade.
  Lamarr, R.
Ransomed forever.
  Elliot, J. An evangel in song.
Rapindey.
  Ortiz, R.
Rapture of spring.
  Frangkiser, C.
Rask Soldat.
  Christiansen, E. Fyrtøjet.
Rattenfänger.
  Bořkovec, P. Krysař.
Razor's edge.
  Goulding, E.
Re quin tin pla.
  Amat, R.
Rebild Bakker.
  Schrøder, W. A.
Rebild National Park.
  Schrøder, W. A. Rebild Bakker.
Recitative and prayer.
  Berlioz, H.
Recompense.
  Frey, E.
Reconversion blues.
  Moore, F.
Recorder consort.
  Katz, E., arr.
Recuerden la ola marina.
  Gonzales, V. Doggie.
Red ball line.
  Battle, E.
Red bird sang in a green, green tree.
  Cadman, C. W.
Red bloomed a rose.
  Mahngotaysee, S.
Red candles.
  Farr, H. B.
Red mill.
  Herbert, V.
Red poppy.
  Glière, R. M. Cortège.
Red, red rose.
  Gannon, R. E.
Red silk stockings and green perfume.
  Mysels, S.

Red, White and Blue.
  Dunagan, I. D., arr.
  Poulton, D. F.
Redeeming love. See title entry in
  composer list.
Redfeather.
  Stein, G. M.
Reflets.
  Gagnier, J. J. Trois esquisses
  musicales.
Refrain sauvage.
  Lopez, F. Jungle serenade.
Regina di Cirta.
  Pedrollo, A.
Regrets.
  Djabadary, H.
Reina.
  Ramirez, J.
Rejoice in Zion.
  Chajes, J.
Religion is a fortune.
  Cain, N.
Remember I feel lonesome, too.
  Scott, J.
Remember when.
  Barnes, O. C.
Remembering you.
  Nordstrom, D.
Remembrance.
  Oliver, H.
Reminiscence.
  Marryott, R. E.
Reminiscência.
  Siqueira, J.
Reminiscing.
  Arthur, W.
Reminiscing with you.
  Foukes, M. S.
Remords de Carabosse.
  Gallois-Montbrun, R. Les rêves de
  Janceline.
Rendez-vous sous la lune.
  Lopez, F.
Rendezvous with destiny.
  Frangkiser, C.
Rendezvous with memory.
  Dale, J.
Reno town.
  Butler, T. S.
Repeat performance.
  Weingarten, A.
Requiem.
  Brahms, J.
Responses for general use.
  Vandenberg, D.
Responses for special occasions.
  Riley, L.
Responses for the church service.
  Barnes, E. S.
Rest well, Beloved, sweetly sleeping.
  Bach, J. S.
Reste encore.
  Luypaerts, G. G.
Resurrection hymn.
  McCarty, E. R.
Retour à Paris.
  Trenet, C. L.
Retour des saisons.
  Trenet, C. L.
Retour du printemps.
  Saulnier, M.
Reuben and Cynth'a.
  Dillon, W. A.
Reuben Jones.
  Glazer, F.
Revebjølle.
  Saeverud, H. Siljustøl.
Revelation.
  Yaysnoff, I.
Reverie.
  Debussy, C.
  Fastofsky, S.
Rêves de Janceline.
  Gallois-Montbrun, R.
Reviens vers moi.
  Lutece, J.
Revival message.
  Winsett, R. E.

Revivir.
  Paez, M.
Revoltillo.
  Ulloa, M.
Rhapsodie géorgienne.
  Djabadary, H.
Rhapsody.
  Fuleihan, A. Rhapsody, violoncello
  & string orchestra.
  Menasce, J. de. Hebrew melodies.
Rhapsody in rhythm.
  Whitford, R. H.
Rhapsody in scales.
  Nevin, M.
Rhubarb song.
  Coffin, J. E.
Rhythm.
  Duchâc, M.
Rhythm, inc.
  Rugolo, P.
Rhythm lullaby.
  Whitford, R. H.
Rhythmic variety in piano music.
  Rabe, R.
Rich and the poor.
  Goldman, M.
Richard de Castre's prayer to Jesus.
  Terry, R. R.
Ricreazioni.
  Bossi, R.
Ricreazioni di antiche musiche.
  Bossi, R., arr.
Ridin' on the gravy train.
  Homer, B.
Ridin' the subways.
  Powell, T.
Ridin' thr' Cool Canyon.
  Sanders, L.
Riding along.
  Templeton, V.
Riding horseback.
  Fouts, M. Children's easy piano
  pieces.
Riding on a rainbow.
  Battle, E.
Ri en qu' avec toi.
  Rayna, J.
Riffin' Rufus.
  Morgan, L.
Right off the ice.
  Barefield, E.
Right out of a dream.
  Duane, H.
Right partner.
  Gannon, R. E.
Rikard Nordraak, foråret i norsk musikk.
  Nordraak, R.
Ring, ring de banjo.
  Foster, S. C.
Rio.
  Pires Vermelho, A.
Rio Grande.
  Rowley, A.
Rio samba.
  Sanders, G. H. Scheherazada suite.
Rise up ye sons of Frankfort.
  Meeks, V. F.
Risen Savior.
  Nolte, R. V.
Ri tmo di felicità.
  Lezza, C.
Ritmo in conservatorio.
  Moietta, B. Schüler und Rythmus.
Ritmo senza amore.
  Leonardi, R.
Rittornoi.
  Olivieri, D.
Ritournelle.
  Staub, D.
Ritournelle de Paris.
  Wal-Berg. Le destin s'amuse.
Ritual.
  Sanjuan, P.
River.
  A'Dair, J.
River chant.
  Johnson, H.

River of the water of life.
Joy, J. A.
Road closed, bridge out, detour.
Long, L.
Road to piano artistry.
Scionti, S., ed.
Road to the Isles.
Helmle, L. B., arr.
Road's end.
Purvis, R.
Roadways.
Finch, H. N.
Robbins in your hair
Hampton, L.
Robe of righteousness.
Coryell, M.
Robert Schumann.
Schumann, R. A.
Robert Whitford break sheets for piano.
Whitford, R. H.
Robin Redbreast.
Trowbridge, L. Nature tone-poems.
Rock of ages.
Hastings, T.
Rock pool.
Dunhill, T. F.
Rocket-rhythm.
Walters, H. L.
Rockin' chair money.
Glosson, L. A.
Rocking in a plastic chair.
Moffitt, D. W.
Rocky mountain moon.
Storie, B. E.
Rodeo.
Copland, A.
Rodriguez Peña.
Greco, V.
Roger, righto, Rogers.
Donahue, I.
Rok.
Arak, K. B.
Roll along little dogies.
Guion, D. W.
Roll away Jordan.
Townsend, P. D. E.
Roll it over.
Foster, C.
Roll, memories, roll.
Pace, C. H.
Roller skating.
Fouts, M. Children's easy piano
pieces.
Rolling along.
Revel, H. Earl Carroll's vanities.
Roma dei Cesari.
Robbiani, I.
Romance.
Chaïkovski, P. I.
Grechaninov, A. T. Petite suite.
Romance arabesque.
Eckstein, M.
Romance au moulin.
Duclaye, E.
Romance in Carnegie Hall.
D'Artega, A. Carnegie Hall.
Romance in F.
Herbert, V.
Romance Viennese.
Oppecker, F. B.
Romances.
Schumann, R. A. Arabesque.
Romantic interlude.
Richardson, C.
Romantické skladby.
Schaefer, T.
Romberg made easy for the piano.
Romberg, S.
Romeo and Juliet.
Chaïkovski, P. I. Fantasy overture.
Nelson, H.
Rondas de niños.
Brenes Candanedo, G.
Ronde des grillons.
Gallois-Montbrun, R. Les rêves de
Janceline.
Rondine di maggio.
Concina, C.

Rondinella pellegrina.
Siegel, R. M.
Rondini.
Davico, V. Cinque liriche roman-
tiche.
Rondino.
Schrad, E.
Rondo in E.
Field, J.
Rondondons.
Betti, H.
Rondos.
Chopin, F. F.
Rooster.
Steinbach, B. Modern miniatures.
Rooster's serenade.
Wilson, S. R.
Rosa, Nina, Stella.
Caffot, S. V. J.
Rosario.
Alongi, F.
Rose.
Bell, A.
Rose, a smile, a prayer.
Mulé, L.
Rose-bud.
Cole, W.
Rose coloured world.
Lynton, E.
Rose du jardin.
Foret, F. H.
Rose family.
Carter, E.
Rose Marie.
Friml, R.
Rose of ol' Pawnee.
Rose, F.
Rose of Santa Rosa.
Livingston, J.
Rose of the Alamo.
Hughes, B.
Rose of Washington Square.
Hanley, J. F.
Rose per una santa.
Fucilli, P.
Mellier, Mario. Lo dicono le stelle.
Rose still grows beyond the wall.
Verner, H. C.
Roses in june.
Marchese, V.
Roses in the rain.
Carlone, F. N.
Rosette.
Marie Noelle, sister.
Rosie Marie and me.
Potter, H.
Rosina.
Rosato, A.
Rossini on Ilkla Moor.
Fenby, E.
Rotary bell.
Stapp, H. R.
Rough ridin' Willie.
Mitchell, J. B.
Round on the end and high in the middle,
O-hi-o.
Hanlon, B. J.
Round Table song.
Rapp, R. E.
'Round the corner.
Usera, R. A la vuelta.
Round-up lullaby.
Barnes, C. W.
Roving.
Rowley, A.
Row, row, row your boat.
Zepp, A.
Royal minuet.
Mahon, G.
Ruby.
Creasy, J. M.
Rudiments of music.
Herbruck, J. P.
Krietemeyer, E. W.
Ruffy and Tuffy.
Schaum, J. W.
Ruins of Athens.
Beethoven, L. v. March.

Rule Britannia!
Arne, T. A. Alfred.
Rumania, Rumania.
Lebedeff, A.
Rumba.
Dungan, O.
Rumba a Doudou.
Beauregard, A.
Rumba en el patio.
Hernandez Sanchez, P.
Rumba swing.
Rotgers, R.
Rumba viva.
Guida, P.
Rumba Zorina.
Sylvain, J.
Rumbambaramba.
Leicea, C.
Rumbeame.
Fuentes, R.
Rumble, rumble, rumble.
Loesser, F. The perils of Pauline.
Rumpelstiltskin.
Suggs, C.
Run and help us tell.
Davis, V.
Runaway brooklet.
Holst, M. S. Three woodland scenes.
Rural community.
Shellabarger, C. E.
Russian dance.
Grechaninov, A. T. Petite suite.
Russian lullaby.
Berlin, I. Accordion transcriptions.
Russian peasant dance.
Schiefelbein, F. A.
Russian picnic.
Enders, H.
Russian rhapsody.
Swinstead, F.
Ruth's entreaty.
Cronham, C. R.
Ružová krinolina.
Svojík, F.
Rye is growing green.
Malec, A. Wszystkie się żytko
zazieleniło.
Rye whiskey.
Ritter, T.
Rythmes de guerre.
Lazarus, D.
Rythmical sustained notes for the inde-
pendence of the fingers.
Vaillant, H. Tenues rythmiques.
S. A. R. sonance.
Johnson, C. L., arr.
Sa får som en flicka kan bli.
Ågren, S.
Sång till Hälsingland.
Eriksson, J.
Sabbath morning synagogue service.
Moses, A.
Sabrosura.
Varona, L.
Sacred choruses for women's or girls'
voices.
Ross, H., arr.
Sacred Heart hymns.
Haller, M.
Sacred songs and hymns.
Greene, S. N., comp.
Sacred songs for home and choir.
Bruinsma, H. A., ed.
Saddest gal in town.
D'Angelo, L.
Saddle call.
Kruslak, D.
Saddle 'n' ride.
Turner, R. J.
Saddle serenade.
Stone, J.
Sadla muska.
Schimmerling, H. A., arr.
Bull, O. B. Longing.
Safety on the farm.
Rosetter, B.

Safranski.
  Rugolo, P.
Sage brush shuffle.
  Clark, J.
Sailing.
  Marks, G.
Sailing home.
  Paine, J. W.
St. Andrew hymn.
  Grindy, R. M. Behold the Lamb of
    God.
Saint Frances Cabrini.
  Orlob, H. Citizen saint.
Saint François d'Assise.
  Rosenthal, M.
Saint Hubert overture.
  Pares, G.
Saint Nicholas.
  Ritter, W. S.
St. Omer commandery march.
  Haines, W. D.
St. Paul.
  Mendelssohn-Bartholdy, F. How
    lovely are the messengers.
St. Petersburg.
  Damm, P. F.
Saints of God.
  Wadely, F. W.
Salomé!
  Massenet, J. E. F. Hérodiade.
Salt Pork, West Virginia.
  Tennyson, W.
Saltarelle.
  Gallois Montbrun, R. Pages de
    sonatine.
  Passani, E. B.
Saludamos a Texas.
  Mier, P.
Salute to Glenville.
  Wright, H. S.
Salute to the twin cities.
  Mader, C.
Salute to victory.
  Richard, L.
Salute to youth.
  Vandercook, H. A.
Salvation Army Brass Band Journal.
  See title entry in composer list.
Sam, the paper man.
  Sullivan, W. A.
Samba.
  Marcedo, D.
Samba of the orchids.
  Broekman, D.
Samba sud.
  Torch, S.
Same old blues.
  Bloom, R.
Same old Mary.
  James, B.
Sammlung ausgewählter Einzelstücke.
  Stutschewsky, J., arr. Sammlung
    moderner und klassisher Einzel-
    stücke.
Sammlung moderner und klassisher
    Einzelstücke.
  Stutschewsky, J., arr.
San Cristóbal de la Habana.
  Hively, W. Habana suite.
San Joaquin Valley blues.
  Carleton, R. L.
San Marino greeting song.
  McLean, D. W.
San Marino welcome song.
  McLean, D. W.
San to paleo balsaki.
  Kastriotès, G. M.
Sanctus.
  Breydert, F. M.
  Walters, O. W.
Sand in your shoes.
  Stedman, J. H.
Sandstorm.
  Sauter, E.
Sandy.
  Carleton, R. L.
Sangue blu.
  Barberis, A. Tutto è leggero.

Santa Ana.
  Fábrega, R.
Santa, dear Santa.
  Diestelhorst, H. J.
Santa drives again.
  Kaiser, J.
Santa's favorite carols.
  Ango, J., arr.
  Boothman, E., arr.
Sanzasoen Barami.
  Darcy, T. F., arr. National anthem
    of Siam.
Sarabande and Bourrie.
  Williams, E. S. Little classics for
    cornet or trumpet.
Sarabande en Sicilienne.
  Klerk, A. de.
Sarape oaxaqueño.
  Mondragon, S.
Saratoga.
  Cummings, R.
  Winstone, E. H.
Saturday night at the palais.
  Musel, B.
Saudi Arabia.
  Darcy, T. F., arr. National anthem.
Save a little sunbeam for a rainy day.
  Romney, G.
Save me, O God.
  Randegger, A.
Save your nickels, save your dimes!
  Crosby, A. D.
Saved because I love Him.
  Williams, D. W.
Savior of my heart.
  Tombelle, F. de la.
Saviour calls, prepare!
  Tovey, H. G.
Saviour, help me bear my cross.
  Evangel special sacred songs.
Saviour is calling.
  Cottingham, F.
Saviour lives.
  Evangel special sacred songs.
  Loes, H. D.
Savoir ce que l'on veut.
  Dumas, R.
Say bye-bye.
  Carleton, R. L.
Say bye-bye but never good-night.
  Carleton, R. L.
Say it and play it.
  Crane, H. A. G.
Say no more.
  Akst, H.
Scarecrow's friend.
  McCargar, D.
Scars upon my heart.
  Carlisle, C. R.
Scene from a campanile.
  Frangkiser, C.
Scenes from childhood.
  Schumann, R. A.
  Bach, J. S. Sheep may safely graze.
Schaukel-Lied.
  Melichar, A. Triumph der Liebe.
Scheer violin method.
  Scheer, L.
Scheherazada.
  Sanders, G. H. Scheherazada suite.
Scheherazada suite.
  Sanders, G. H.
Scheherezade.
  Rimskii-Korsakov, N. A.
Schenk mir dein Herz.
  Krancher, W. C.
Scherzando from Symphonie espagnole.
  Lalo, E. Symphonie espagnole.
Scherzi per pianoforte.
  Galaverni, I.
Scherzo.
  Jadassohn, S.
Scherzo and continuo.
  Keith, G. D.
Scherzo and fugue.
  Diggle, R.

Scherzo for two pianos.
  Johnson, T. A.
Scherzo in canon form.
  Jadassohn, S.
Scherzo polyphonic.
  Mueller, O.
Schillernder Falter.
  Lehár, F.
School days fantasy.
  Lang, P. J.
School piano class method.
  Jevons, R.
Schoolmates.
  Cobb, H.
Schubert (a bouquet of music).
  Schubert, F. P.
Schüler und Rythmus.
  Moietta, B.
Schumann, excerpts from his greatest
    works.
  Schumann, R. A.
Schumann's concerto march.
  Jacobs, D.
Scottish patrol.
  Green, P.
Scottish Paul Jones.
  Sharples, R., arr.
Scratch sheet.
  Jackson, C.
Scufflin'.
  Donahue, S.
Scuola del ritmo.
  Panzuti, V.
Scuola dello jazz.
  Elio, V.
Se equivoca compay gato.
  Salazar, R.
Se il grano potesse parlar.
  Cioffi, G.
Se que te vas.
  Mendoza, R.
Sea woman.
  Goldsworthy, W. A.
Seafoam.
  Boykin, H.
Search me, I don't know.
  Hendrix, E. B.
Second concerto.
  Rachmaninoff, S. Concerto, piano,
    no. 2.
Second joyful mystery.
  Chanler, T.
Second piano parts to First solo book
    pieces.
  Diller, A.
Second Timothy 2:15.
  Carrier, V.
Secret dreams.
  Brunelle, G.
Secretos del corazon.
  Rojo, G.
Sedi, Boso, de!
  Nešić, M.
Sedlon method for the modern pianist.
  Sedlon, J. H.
See Jesus the Saviour.
  Talmadge, A. S.
Seeking his sheep.
  Parce, R. R.
Selection of Brahms Hungarian dances.
  Brahms, J.
Selection of famous Mendelssohn melo-
    dies.
  Mendelssohn-Bartholdy, F.
Self teaching popular piano.
  Goodsell, E. M., comp.
Semper fidelis.
  Sousa, J. P.
Send forth Thy Spirit.
  Schuetky, F. J.
Señorita chiquita.
  Stout, O.
Sentimental love song.
  Nortima, F. D.
Sentimental me.
  Bosmans, R.
Senza pate, e' nnammurata!
  Donadio, L.

Sept caprices pour flûte.
　Moyse, L. J.
Sept complaintes pour les coeurs
　serrés.
　Bourgeois, H.
Sept mélodies pour chant et piano.
　Handman, D.
Será por eso.
　Velázquez, C.
Serata al circo.
　Culotta, I.
Serbian girl kolo.
　Bajić, I. Srpkinja kolo.
Sérenáda.
　Vačkář, V.
Serenade.
　Borodin, A. P.
　Herbert, V.
　Mozart, J. C. W. Eine kleine Nacht-
　　musik.
　Prosser, I. W.
　Romberg, S. The student prince.
　Romberg, S. Der Studentenprinz.
　Tosti, F. P.
　Vačkář, V.
Sérénade de fantasio.
　Renault, A.
Serenade for strings.
　Fulton, N.
Serenade to an old-fashioned girl.
　Berlin, I. Blue skies.
Serenade to happiness.
　Sharp, V. L.
Serenade to Helen.
　Lewis, S. I.
Serenade to no-one in particular.
　Connor, T.
Serenata.
　Annunziata, M. R.
　Nieland, J. H. I. M.
　Tosti, F. P. The serenade.
Serenata ad un angelo.
　Castroli, N.
Serenata di primavera.
　Smareglia, A. I pittori fiamminghi.
Serenata preferita.
　Cristalli, O.
Serenata serena.
　Falcocchio, E.
Serenata tapatía.
　Esperón, M. El peñón de las ánimas!
Serenatella a mamma.
　Ravasini, N.
Serene night.
　Elaine, sister, arr. La noche esta
　　serena.
Serenity.
　Hawkinson, F. I.
Serve the Lord with gladness.
　Marth, H. J.
Service star.
　Ziegler, E.
6x Jiří Traxler.
　Traxler, J.
Seven and twenty easy pieces.
　Porter, F. A.
Seven golden buttons.
　Eisenstein, J. K.
Seven pieces.
　Bartók, B. Mikrokosmos.
　Kesnar, M.
Seventeen to sing.
　Shapiro, G. H.
Seventh day.
　Vinaver, C. Yom hashviy.
Seventh veil.
　Bernard, B.
Seventh veil waltz.
　Bernard, B. The seventh veil.
Sewing machine.
　Loesser, F. The perils of Pauline.
Shabos Kodesh.
　Singer, A.
Shadow and sun.
　Parker, B.
Shadow hills.
　Fluss, S. D.

Shadow picture.
　Kesnar, M. Seven pieces.
Shady lane.
　Carleton, R. L.
Shag-a-lag rag.
　Hendrix, E. B.
She makes a fuss over me.
　Kerlin, A. S.
She wanted a cream front door.
　Furby, A.
Sheaf of first position pieces for violin.
　Zoubek, K.
Sheep and lambs.
　Homer, S.
Sheep may safely graze.
　Bach, J. S.
She'll be comin' round the mountain.
　Jacobs, M., arr. Boogie woogie
　　step-by-step.
Shelter of His wings.
　Eisele, F. W.
Shenandoah.
　Rowley, A.
Shenandoah waltz.
　Wise, C.
Shephard show.
　Davies, H. P.
Shepherd, show me how to go.
　Roberts, L. S.
Shepherdess Moon.
　Weigl, V.
Shepherds.
　Cornelius, P.
Shepherds, by night, were watching.
　Huston, F. C. Two songs.
Shepherd's hymn.
　Duncan, C.
Shepherds song.
　Nagle, W. S., arr.
She's got everything.
　Harbridge, A. J.
She's just a wee tot.
　Cooper, W. B.
She's the picture of my mother.
　Fischer, C.
S-H-I-N-E.
　Dabney, F.
Shine on my silvery moon.
　Andersen, D.
Shine on, O star.
　Walters, O. W.
Shine, shine.
　Mynatt, A.
Ships ahoy!
　MacLachlan, T. R.
Ships that pass in the night.
　Klumpkey, J. Two songs.
Shivisi adonoy.
　Lewandowski, L.
Shoemaker of the stars and his tunes.
　Wolfe, J.
Shomer Yisroel.
　Binder, A. W.
Short Course song.
　Robinson, R. D.
Short Te Deum.
　Diggle, R.
Show boat.
　Kern, J.
Show me the way to go home.
　Campbell, J.
Shure they call it Ireland.
　Ball, E. R. A little bit of heaven.
Shvanda, the bagpiper.
　Weinberger, J. Three Bohemian pieces.
Si le bonheur était à vendre.
　Marinier, P.
Si, señorita, si.
　Guzman, R.
Si tu me adoraras.
　Yamin, J.
Si tu me quisieras.
　Canaro, F.
Si vous écoutez ma chanson.
　Sieor, L.
Si vous n'étiez pas si jolie.
　Scala, T.

Si vous vouliez, madame.
　Delettre, J.
Sicilian lullaby.
　Newman, R.
Sicilian serenade.
　Frosini, P.
Sicilienne.
　Klerk, A. de. Sarabande en
　　Sicilienne.
Siciliette, reine des Siciles.
　Gallois-Montbrun, R. Les rêves de
　　Janceline.
Side by side series of piano duets. See
　title entry in composer list.
Siesta time.
　Robb, J. D. Pictures of New Mexico.
Sigan tomando, muchachos!
　Bonavena, A.
Sight-reading made easy.
　Bradley, D.
Sigma Phi Gamma International Sorority
　song book.
　Sigma Phi Gamma.
Sign on the dotted line.
　Roff, H.
Signs of spring series.
　Fouts, M. Children's easy piano
　　pieces.
Siguéndote.
　Suarez, H.
Silence est d'or.
　Parys, G. van.
Silent are the meadows.
　Williams, F.
Silent night.
　Gruber, F.
　My First Christmas Songs.
Siljustøl.
　Saeverud, H.
Silkeborg.
　Andersen, K. N.
Silver.
　Begley, M.
Silver dream ship.
　Austin, G. L.
Silver lamps.
　Goldsworthy, W. A.
Silver Meteor.
　Rouse, E. T.
Silver pool.
　Matteson, M.
Sim'chu b'tzion.
　Chajes, J. Rejoice in Zion.
Simmo' e Napule.
　Valente, N.
Simon Peter.
　Woodgate, H. L.
Simple faith.
　Bacon, J. D., arr.
Simple rengaine.
　Bruno, D.
Sin palabras.
　Mores, M.
Sin rencor.
　Pomares, G.
Sin título.
　Valencia, C.
Sin tu amor.
　Schonbrun, B.
Since at the Father's throne.
　Blanchard, L. F.
Since He took my sins away.
　Cottingham, F. The Saviour is calling.
Since I have a sweetheart like you.
　Arthur, W.
Since I've been in love with you.
　Kennedy, A. New songs.
Since I've been with you.
　Lee, J.
Since Jesus' love I've found.
　Lord, R.
Since Jesus touched me.
　Ford, H. J.
Since we parted.
　Cernkovich, R., arr. Od Našega
　　rastanka.
Sincerely.
　Lincoln, J.

Sinfonia dolorosa.
  Saeverud, H.
Sinfonia from Cantata 75.
  Bach, J. S. Die Elenden sollen essen.
Sinfonia sevillana.
  Turina, J.
Sinfonia tripartita.
  Rieti, V.
Sinfonie du Te Deum.
  Lalande, M. R. de.
Sinfonies pour les soupers du roi.
  Lalande, M. R. de. Sinfonie du Te
  Deum.
Sinfonietta.
  Moeran, E. J.
Sing.
  Cioffi, G. Has anyone seen my beauti-
  ful Rosa?
Sing a happy song and smile.
  Clyde, T.
Sing a new song.
  Weigle, C. F., ed.
Sing a song of America.
  Clyde, T.
Sing-a-while leaflet.
  Buck, C. C.
Sing alleluia forth.
  Buck, D.
Sing for me, the night is falling.
  Olson, C. W.
Sing glory.
  Etoll, G. W.
Sing, gondolier.
  Phillips, P.
Sing ivy.
  Scull, H. T.
Sing of Calvary.
  Ellis, V. B., ed.
Sing the mass.
  De Nigris, N., ed.
Sing to the Son of David.
  Rawls, K. H.
Sing unto the Lord.
  Emery, D. R.
  Woodbridge, C. L.
Sing unto the Lord a new song.
  Schalit, H. The 98th Psalm.
Singecstasy.
  Ives, D. L., comp.
Singin' in the corn.
  Roberts, A.
Singing a song of love.
  Crookham, D. D.
Singing as I go.
  Frank, J. L.
Singing brook.
  Earle, E.
Singing campus.
  Niles, J. J., ed. & arr.
Singing choruses.
  Davies, A.
Singing down the road.
  Siegmeister, E., arr.
Singing keys.
  Foster, A. H., comp.
Singing Pakapika.
  Simon, G.
Singing period book of carols.
  Hill, H., ed.
Singing strings.
  Dominici, H.
Singing the boogie.
  Davis, N. C.
Singing words. See title entry in
  composer list.
Sippin' cider with my Ida.
  Cocts, J. F.
Sir Roger de Coverley.
  Krein, M.
Siste bå'nlat.
  Saeverud, H. Siljustøl.
Sit beside me, Boso!
  Nešic, M. Sedi, Boso, del
Sittin' on a hilltop.
  Roy, M. C.
Six Christmas hymns.
  Tonner, P.

Six intimate moods.
  Read, G.
Six recital pieces for piano duet.
  Mirovitch, A., ed. The student
  pianist.
6 sketches.
  Nieland, J. H. I. M.
Six sonatas.
  Galliard, J. E. Sonatas, bassoon &
  harpsichord.
Six wedding processionals or reces-
  sionals.
  Haase, K.
16 smart studies.
  Huffnagle, H.
Sjöman till häst.
  Aspelin, S.
Ska' man inte va' gla'.
  Ahde, S.
Skies of the west.
  Carleton, R. L.
Skip to my Lou.
  Riegger, W.
  Wilson, H. R., arr.
Skogsnymfen dansar.
  Seymer, W.
Skola pro normální a francouzský klarinet.
  Krtička, S. Velká dvoudílná škola.
Škola pro snižcový ti tahový pozoun.
  Ušák, J.
Skomagerdrengen.
  Christiansen, E. Fyrtøjet.
Skorgelaten.
  Siem, K.
Sky-rider.
  Sacco, J.
Slåtter- og stev fra Siljustøl.
  Saeverud, H.
Slab in the lab.
  Kelly, N.
Slapstick.
  Hamilton, J.
Sleep and rest.
  Mozart, J. C. W. A.
Sleep, darling, sleep.
  Weinschenk, B.
Sleep, little Jesus.
  Marth, H. J.
Sleeping beauty.
  Chalkovskii, P. I.
Sleepy bird.
  Thomas, J. J.
Sleeping princess.
  Yost, G. Five pieces.
Sleepy bugler polka.
  Fryberg, M.
Sleepy head.
  George, C.
Sleepy lagoon.
  Coates, E.
Sleepytime lullaby.
  Lefevre, A.
Slightly fantastic.
  Fields, I.
Sling shots.
  Fouts, M.
Slow movement.
  Brahms, J. Sonata, clarinet & piano,
  no. 1.
Slumber song.
  Consentino, A. B. Songs.
Sluncem a stínem.
  Vomáčka, B.
Small night music.
  Mozart, J. C. W. A. Eine kleine
  Nachtmusik.
Small pieces for small people.
  Kadosa, P.
Smile right back at the sun.
  Van Heusen, J. Welcome stranger.
Smile, smile, smile.
  Trotter, D.
Smile song.
  Hubbell, F. A. Grumpy Shark.
Smile songs.
  Wirges, W. F.
Smilin' Bill Waters Home folk songs.
  Fowler, J. W., comp.

Smoke dreams.
  Steele, T.
Smoke gets in your eyes.
  Kern, J.
Smoky Hollow tune.
  Bornschein, F.
Smoochin'.
  Cook, W.
Smyčcový kvartet.
  Sín, O. Quartet, strings, no. 2.
Snoopy rabbit.
  Fouts, M. Children's easy piano
  pieces.
Snow.
  Spaeth, S. Telling time.
Snow drop tree.
  Krone, B. Kalinka.
Snow-flakes.
  Rawicz, M.
Snow is falling.
  Ganz, R.
Snowdrifts and gardenias.
  Wilbur, E.
Snub's boogie.
  Mosley, S.
So che ti chiami Lucia.
  Olivieri, D. Tutto il mondo canta
  Torne_ai.
So dim with tears.
  Haydn, J.
So I returned.
  Brahms, J. Four serious songs.
So jealous of you.
  Carleton, R. L.
So much for so little.
  McComas, T. J.
So see I, sez I, the moon.
  Chanslor, H.
So weary.
  Bergere, R.
So we'll go no more a roving.
  White, M. V.
Soaring falcons.
  Altbayer, B.
Social drag.
  Campbell, B.
Sørgemarch.
  Andersen, K. N. Silkeborg.
Softly, as in a morning sunrise.
  Romberg, S.
Sohaj.
  Vačkař, V.
Sol över Klara.
  Runo, S.
Sola.
  Ravasini, N.
Soldier.
  Davis, K. K. Three American
  folksongs.
Soldiers on parade.
  Stein, G. M.
The soldier's triumph.
  Gaddis, R. M. Abraham, the pilgrim.
Soleil à des rayons de pluie.
  Trenet, C.
Solfège élémentaire.
  Favre, G.
Solitaire.
  Tersmeden, G.
Solitude.
  Ellington, D.
  Olson, C. W.
  Row, R. D.
Sollozo.
  Curiel, G.
Solo para tí.
  Gil, A.
Solo una lacrima.
  Boffa, I.
Solos solitos.
  Gomes, E.
Som Fuglen i Buret.
  Christiansen, E. Fyrtøjet.
Some clay without a sculptor.
  Confrey, E. E.
Some day.
  Powell, T.

Some day I'll forget you.
  Van Horn, E. M.
Some day when it's spring.
  Deal, J. H.
Some folks call it Texas.
  Rose, F.
Some of the happy melodies from Beethoven's chamber music.
  Beethoven, L. v.
Some of the happy melodies from Haydn's chamber music.
  Haydn, J.
Some of the happy melodies from Mozart's chamber music.
  Mozart, J. C. W. A.
Some one is calling you.
  Weigle, C. F., ed. Sing a new song.
Some sweet tomorrow.
  Dexter, N.
Some time.
  English, B.
Somebody else's trouble.
  Rose, F.
Somebody here needs the Savior.
  Rifenberg, I. O.
Somebody stole my moustache cup.
  Cochrane, N.
Somebody's boy.
  Bratton, J. W.
Somebody's heaven.
  Lange, I.
Somebody's knockin' at your door.
  Lefebvre, C., arr.
Somebody's Rose.
  Weber, B.
Someday I'll find you.
  Coward, N.
Someday you'll learn to love me.
  Zirpoli, P. A.
Someone like you.
  Carr, F. L.
  Meyers, C. J.
Something for nothing.
  O'Flynn, C.
Something in the wind.
  Green, J.
Something sort of grandish.
  Lane, B. Finian's rainbow.
Something to remember.
  Bartlett, F.
Sometime we will meet again.
  Stone, G. Carnegie Hall.
Somewhere in Utah.
  Baker, N.
Sommarmorgon.
  Seymer, W. Strofer i sol och skugga.
Somos.
  Marchisio, C.
Sonar.
  Los Cuates castilla (Musicians)
Sonata.
  Benjamin, A. Sonata, viola & piano.
  Berkeley, L. Sonata, piano.
  Broennemuller, E.
  Delachi, P. Sonata, violin & piano.
  Fastofsky, S. Sonata, piano.
  Hopkins, A. Sonata, piano.
  Krejčí, M. Sonata, viola & piano.
  Klička, J. Sonata, violin & piano.
  Loeillet, J. B.
  Milford, R. Sonata, flute & piano.
  Milhaud, D. Sonata, violin & harpsichord.
  Mozart, J. C. W. A. Quartet, oboe & strings.
  Petrželka, V.
  Prokof'ev, S. S. Sonata, piano, no. 1.
  Scarlatti, D. Sonata, harpsichord.
  Shostakovich, D. D. Sonata, violoncello and piano.
  Šín, O. Sonata, violoncello & piano.
  Vrána, F. Sonata, piano.
Sonate.
  Hemel, O. L. v. Sonata, viola & piano.
Sonate en sol majeur.
  Foret, F. Sonata, oboe & piano.

Sonate en ut dièze.
  Decruck, F.
Sonate pour violon seul.
  Damais, E.
Sonatina.
  Borkovec, P. Sonatina, violin & piano.
  Bowles, P.
  Jones, C. Sonatina, violin & piano.
  Sowerby, L.
Sonatine.
  Arrieu, C. Sonatina, flute & piano.
Sonatine pour le piano.
  Szervánszky, E.
Song at eve.
  Seymer, W. Strofer i sol och skugga.
Song for Annie Lou.
  Hopkins, H. P.
Song I saved for you.
  Lieta, T.
Song in praise of the Lord.
  Nagler, F.
Song may bring two hearts together.
  Martino, P.
Song of a Mexican sarape.
  Mondragon, S. Sarape oaxaqueño.
Song of Christmas.
  Ringwald, R.
Song of destiny.
  Brahms, J.
Song of faith.
  Whitney, M. C.
Song of freedom.
  Ricketts, C.
Song of home.
  Cameron, J.
Song of liberation.
  Weinberg, J. Haganah.
Song of love.
  De Rose, P.
Song of palms.
  Howe, M.
Song of spring.
  Norden, N. L.
Song of the Armored division.
  Chadwick, N.
Song of the brook.
  Schubert, F. P.
Song of the dew fairy.
  Humperdinck, E.
Song of the farmer.
  Waverly, J.
Song of the gauche.
  Berry, P. L.
Song of the halutzim.
  Gaul, H.
Song of the holy night.
  Wilson, R. C.
Song of the miners.
  James, P.
Song of the pilgrim.
  Hokanson, M.
Song of the Sierras.
  Wakely, J.
Song of the swamps.
  Wilson, H. R.
Song of the thin man.
  Oakland, B.
Song of the Volga.
  Lehár, F.
Song of the Volga boatmen.
  Lovejoy, H., arr.
Song of the West.
  Petrillo, C.
Song of you.
  Johnson, E. J.
Song of youth.
  Röntgen, J. Het lied van de jeugd.
Song on May morning.
  Emery, W.
Song on the road.
  Seymour, J. L.
Song specials for choir use.
  Wilson, I. B. Lorenz's song specials for choir use.
Song to Hawaii.
  Pryce, B., arr.
Song to the forest.
  Chaikovskii, P. I.

Song without words.
  Herbert, V.
  Cascio, C.
Songs.
  Consentino, A. B.
Songs and choruses.
  Coletta, L. B. S.
Songs and games every child should know.
  Haufrecht, H., arr. More than one hundred songs and games.
Songs for the hour.
  Bowlby, G. W., comp.
Songs for worship.
  Brown, A. G. Y., arr.
Songs for young hearts.
  Van Heusen, J. Bing Crosby's Songs for young hearts.
Songs from south of the border.
  Andre, J., ed.
Songs from the heart.
  Buck, W.
Song's gotta come from the heart.
  Styne, J. It happened in Brooklyn.
Songs of abounding love.
  Snyder, H.
Songs of cheer and comfort.
  Maxwell, R., comp.
Songs of love.
  Pray, A. J.
Songs of my youth.
  Alkire, E. H.
Songs of the dawn.
  Schumann, R. A.
Songs of the gay '90's.
  Edwards, B., comp.
Songs of the good old days.
  Robbins Music Corp., comp. Bill Hardey's Songs of the good old days.
Songs of the hills and plains.
  Bava, J., comp.
Songs that last.
  Sturk, B. F.
Sonnet, no. 2.
  Achron, J.
Sonnet to the sea.
  Klein, J.
Soon.
  Whitney, M. C.
Soothe me.
  Greene, J.
Sorghum.
  McGuffin, K. W. F.
Sorprese del vagone letto.
  Casiroli, N.
Soul must bear the cross. See title entry in composer list.
Souls of the righteous.
  Greir, R. A.
Sound off.
  Sousa, J. P.
Sourire a Morphée.
  Gallois-Montbrun, R. Les rêves de Janceline.
Sous le beau ciel du Canada.
  Lejay, A.
South American serenade.
  Clark, P.
South in my soul.
  Farr, H.
South of the Rio.
  Olivadoti, J.
Southland polka.
  King, P. W.
Souvenir.
  Charney, L.
Souvenir album.
  Morros, B., arr. Carnegie Hall.
Souvenir d'un jour.
  Caffot, S. V. J.
Souvenir de Hongrie.
  Djabadary, H. Concerto, violoncello, no. 1.
Souvenirs from the great masters.
  Brahms, J.

Delibes, L.
  Schubert, F. P.
  Strauss, J.
Souviens-toi.
  Blareau, R.
Soy bahiano.
  Caymmi, D.
Soy ranchero.
  Navarro, J. J.
Soyez bref.
  Hess, J.
Spacco tutto.
  Giussani, G.
Spacious firmament.
  Diggle, R.
Spanish Main.
  Baynon, A.
Spanish needle waltz.
  Sevier, M. M.
Sparkling burgundy.
  Josefovits, T.
Sparks of fire krakowiak.
  Malec, A. Iskiereczka ognia.
Spatzen-Polka.
  Föderl, K.
Split.
  Petyrek, F. Zwei Lieder.
Speak, my heart!
  Revel, H. It happened on Fifth
    Avenue.
Speaking of angels.
  Weiss, G.
Special songs for young people's anni-
  versaries and festal occasions.
  See title entry in composer list.
Specials.
  Ives, D. L., comp.
Speeldoos.
  Duuren, H. J. v.
Sphinx.
  Powell, T.
Sphixe me, sphixe me.
  Iakobides, Z.
Spice on the ice.
  Zepp, A.
Spider and the fly.
  Marshall, R.
Spindevise, fra.
  Koppel, H. D. Ditte Menneskebarn.
Spinning-wheel.
  Rawicz, M.
Spirit of God, descend.
  North, J. D., pseud.
Spirit of light.
  Holsworth, A.
Spirit of youth.
  Gilbert, C. J.
Spiritual.
  Purvis, R.
Spooks.
  Bacher, E.
  Robinson, A.
Sport.
  Blareau, R.
Spring.
  Kester, C. M.
Spring again.
  Van Tyle, R.
Spring holiday.
  King, S.
Spring in Donegal.
  De Leone, F.
Spring is coming.
  Bragdon, S. C.
Spring is here.
  Benner, H. C.
Spring is nigh.
  Maltzeff, A.
Spring isn't everything.
  Warren, H. Summer holiday.
Spring morn.
  Herbert, V.
Spring of the year.
  Dunhill, T. F.
Spring-serenade.
  Smareglia, A. I pittori fiamminghi.
Spring song.
  May, H.
  Mendelssohn-Bartholdy, F.

Spring waltz.
  Seymer, W. Strofer i sol och
    skugga.
Springtide.
  Herbert, V. Gypsy lady.
Springtime.
  Galindo, B.
Springtime in Nevada.
  Birdsley, A. E.
Square dances with calls, polkas, jigs
  and reels.
  Potter, R., arr.
Squash, head.
  Mosley, S.
Srpkinja kolo.
  Bajic, I.
Staccato waltz.
  Allender, N. D.
Staines morris.
  Haywood, E. Country gardens.
Stairway to heaven.
  Gray, A. A matter of life and death.
Stand up and fight for Tennessee.
  Sweet, M.
Standard Gregorian chants.
  Marier, T. N., comp.
Standard overtures.
  Marden, R., ed. Everybody's favorite
    standard overtures.
Standin' in the need of prayer.
  Reisfeld, B., arr.
Stanley steamer.
  Warren, H. Summer holiday.
Stap voor stap.
  Nteland, J. H. I. M.
Star of gold.
  Smale, L. G.
Star of promise.
  Henson, J. M., comp.
Star of the sea.
  Kennedy, A.
Starkle, starkle, little twink.
  Brandon, A.
Starlight love.
  Forke, G.
Starlight waltz.
  Wolfson, L. H.
Starry night.
  Seymer, W. Strofer i sol och skugga.
Stars.
  Hoffmann, H.
Stars and sunshine.
  Gardner, A.
Stars and you.
  Taylor, B. A.
Stars are kisses.
  Arthur, W.
Stars hide their faces.
  Sandefur, H.
Stars of the summer night.
  Woodbury, I. B.
Stay a little longer.
  Duncan, T. E.
Stay as sweet as you are.
  Revel, H.
Stay out of my dreams.
  Strauss, A.
Steel guitar blues.
  Zoellner, P.
Steel guitar rag.
  McAuliffe, L.
Steenhof.
  Peeters, F.
Stella by starlight.
  Young, V.
Steppin' out kind.
  Nathan, S.
Steppin' out tonight.
  Byrne, W. L.
Stepping out.
  Cobb, H.
Stepping stones.
  Wright, N. L.
Steps.
  Rogers, M.
Steps forward.
  White, G.
Stick to your pony.
  Clark, P.

Sticky fingers.
  Carleton, R. L.
Stilla manskensnatt.
  Seymer, W. Strofer i sol och skugga.
Stiller gang.
  Seymer, W. Sånger av William
    Seymer.
Stinsen på Lyckås.
  Kraft, A.
Stinsvisan.
  Kraft, A. Stinsen på Lyckås.
Stjärnnatt.
  Seymer, W. Strofer i sol och skugga.
Stockin' full of blues.
  Reade, C.
Stokey Bailey.
  Heywood, D.
Stomping room only.
  Marks, H.
Stop breaking my heart.
  Buffington, F.
Stop coming and come.
  Houdini, W.
Stop now.
  Fox, R.
Stop the world.
  Nelson, H.
Stopping the hiccoughs.
  Burnam, E. M.
Stora kometen.
  Söderlundh, B. A.
Storm king.
  Finlayson, W.
Storsätern-valsen.
  Ljunggren, A.
Story of Carrot.
  Lippman, S. Barefoot boy with cheek.
Story of the bee.
  Niles, J. J.
Strada delle mimose.
  Oldrati Rossi, R.
Stranger things have happened.
  Coslow, S. Copacabana.
Strasbourg.
  Levy, M. M.
Strawberry moon.
  Mysels, S.
Straying sheep.
  Woods, J. S.
Streamlined Cinderella.
  George, C.
Street carnival.
  Moore, M.
Street scene.
  Weill, K.
Streich-Quartett in modo classico.
  Marx, J. Quartet, strings.
Strictly as advertised.
  Weldon, F.
Strife is o'er.
  Marsh, C. H.
String bass passages.
  Fahsbender, R., ed. & comp.
String class method.
  Swift, F. F., comp. & arr.
String quartet.
  Hill, A. Quartet, strings, no. 11.
  Lutyens, E. Quartet, strings, no. 2.
  Riegger, W. Quartet, strings, no. 1.
  Tippett, M. K. Quartet, strings, no. 1.
Strofer i sol och skugga.
  Seymer, W.
Strong Son of God, Immortal Love.
  Margetson, E.
Strophes in sun and shadow.
  Seymer, W. Strofer i sol och skugga.
Stručak hrvatskih pučkih pjesama.
  Cernkovich, R. Bouquet of Croatian
    folk songs.
Strutting.
  Sachs, B.
Student pianist.
  Mirovitch, A., ed.
Student prince.
  Romberg, S.
Studentenprinz.
  Romberg, S.

Studies in port de bras for beginners.
  Trine, V.
Studies in waltz time.
  Lanner, J.
Studio dei bassi.
  Lupo, P.
Studio 24.
  Engelen, F.
Study in augmented intervals.
  Freeman, B.
Stumbling home.
  Bellovich, T. J.
Stuvarevalsen.
  Dahlquist, L. E.
Su con la vita.
  Ceglie, C. di.
Subway squeeze.
  Clayton, B.
Successi della CESA.
  Russo, S., comp.
Such is life.
  Usera, R.
Suddenly in love.
  Gil, A. Solo para ti.
Suegras.
  Dominguez, P.
Sueño fue.
  Gomez Barrera, C.
Sueño guajiro.
  Grenet, E.
Sufro su ausencia.
  Yamin, J.
Sugar and spice.
  Dean, J. F., arr. Army Catering
    Corps.
Sugar in the cane.
  Bowles, P. Blue Mountain ballads.
Suita.
  Folprecht, Z.
Suita pro klavír.
  Petrželka, V.
Suite.
  Rowley, A.
Suite baroque.
  Telemann, G. P.
Suite brève.
  Maingueneau, L.
Suite brève en trio.
  Bozza, E.
Suite française.
  Milhaud, D.
  Nieland, J. H. I. M.
Suite in folk style.
  Goeb, R.
Suite miniature.
  Volpe, H.
Suite moderne.
  Jones, S. T.
Suite nocturne.
  Martinon, J. F. É.
Suite of four pieces.
  Jacobson, M.
Suite of transformations.
  Pimsleur, S.
Suite rococo.
  Grétry, A. E. M.
Suite Swanee.
  Nevin, M.
Suite symphonique.
  Bloch, E.
Summer carol.
  Händel, G. F.
Summer evening at Bryanston.
  Goatley, A.
Summer holiday.
  Warren, H.
Summer morning.
  Light, F. M.
Summer morning.
  Seymer, W. Strofer i sol och skugga.
Summer night.
  Eitzen, L.
Summer, the piper.
  Dunhill, T. F.
Sunday in New York.
  Satterfield, T.
Sunday in the park.
  Lehár, F.

Sunday morning.
  Reistrup, J.
Sundown and sorrow.
  King, F.
Sunlit way.
  Baxter, J. R., comp.
Sunny weather.
  Miles, D.
Sunny youth.
  Duuren, B. J. v. Zonnige jeugd.
Sunrise is coming.
  Del Riego, T.
Sunset and evening.
  McGurk, W. R. J.
Sunset Carson mountain ballads [and]
    cowboy songs.
  Carson, S., comp.
Sunset dreams.
  Thompson, I.
Sunset hour.
  Schiefelbein, F. A.
Sunshine Mission melodies.
  Dillon, W. A., comp.
Suonando una romanza di Puccini.
  Olivieri, D. Tutto il mondo 'canta
    Tornerai.
Súplica del alma.
  Sánchez Vázquez, P.
Supplement to Beginner's band book.
  Broughton, W. F.
Supplication.
  Dunlap, E. E.
Sur la Place de la Bastille.
  Mahieux, E.
Sur la tombe de Barczy Marguit.
  Djabadary, H. Moments vécus.
Sur un pont.
  Marly, A.
Sure short cut for learning to play the
    accordion.
  Wolf, O.
Surely, I'm sure of Shirley.
  Choisser, J. D.
Surrey with the fringe on top.
  Rodgers, R. Oklahoma!
Sus ojitos.
  Monge, J.
Susie, little Susie.
  Humperdinck, E.
Suspiro 'e chitarra.
  Ricciardi, V.
Svatováclavský triptych.
  Novák, V.
Svegliati e canta.
  Panzuti, V.
Svensk allmogemarsch.
  Sköld, S. J.
Svenska flicka.
  Jordan, M.
Sveriges hemvärn.
  Björklund, N.
Swallow-birds.
  Dunhill, T. F. By the river.
Swan.
  Saint-Saens, C.
Swanee.
  Colicchio, M.
Swanee River boogie.
  Young, H.
Sweet and low.
  Barnby, J.
Sweet bells.
  Sawaya, J.
Sweet, come again!
  Lake, H. C.
Sweet darling.
  Lieta, T.
Sweet dreams, goodbye.
  Hile, R.
Sweet home blues.
  Storie, B. E.
Sweet is the air.
  Mascagni, P. Cavalleria rusticana.
Sweet little boy Jesus.
  Niles, J. J.
Sweet memories of you.
  Carleton, R. L.
Sweet music.
  Rathaus, K. Three English songs.

Sweet nothing.
  Wood, G.
Sweet Papa Willie.
  Houdini, W.
Sweet promised land of Nevada.
  Post, T. H.
Sweet rain
  Johnson, J. R.
Sweet sleep.
  Bentley, B. B.
Sweet soldier boy.
  Matteson, M. J.
Sweet story.
  Libby, R.
Sweet Sue - just you.
  Young, V.
Sweet, sweet Daisy.
  Klemans, T. A.
Sweetest words in the world.
  Saxon, D.
Sweetheart.
  Lizée, G. M.
  Lynton, E.
Sweetheart mine.
  Gay, N.
Sweetheart of yesterday.
  Hodges, J.
Sweetheart, this is goodbye.
  Hofner, A.
Sweethearts.
  Herbert, V.
Sweethearts of Aggieland.
  Turner, W. M.
Sweethearts try to explain.
  Oppecker, F. B. Romance Viennese.
Swelling waves in the night.
  Seymer, W. Strofer i sol och skugga.
Swieci miesiaczek na niebie.
  Malec, A.
Swing huit.
  Travnicek, J.
Swing up, swing down.
  Thomas, J. J.
Swingbilly revue folio.
  Harding, G. E.
Swingin' in Sweden.
  Bonfils, K.
Swingin' in thirds.
  Troup, B.
Swingin' up and down.
  Stegmeyer, W.
Swinging.
  Robinson, A. Three very easy piano
    pieces.
Swinging on your gate.
  Carleton, R. L.
Swinging the scales.
  Wehner, C. F., arr.
Swiss clock.
  Hayes, O. L.
Swoon of a goon.
  Barnes, G. G minor spin.
Sword dance.
  Steiner, E.
Sylvanesque.
  Oliver, G. Original themes for piano.
Sylvia.
  Tomblings, P.
Sympathy.
  Friml, R. The firefly.
Symphonic blues.
  Kreutz, A.
Symphonic toccata.
  Coke-Jephcott, N.
Symphonie espagnole.
  Lalo, E.
Symphonie liturgique.
  Honegger, A.
Symphonie moderne.
  Steiner, M.
Symphony no. 1.
  Hanson, H.
  Kerr, H.
Symphony no. 4.
  Mendelssohn-Bartholdy, F.
  Schumann, R. A.
Symphony of flowers.
  Savino, D.

T.W.A.
    Liggins, J.
T' amo.
    Moietta, B.
Ta' Briller paa!
    Gyldmark, S.
Tänker du på mej?
    Perne, N.
'Tain't no fun what you've done.
    Morgan, R. D.
Take a little off the top.
    Carr, L.
Take away those blues around my heart.
    Sullivan, G.
Take care of my heart.
    McNeil, J. C.
Take heart, weary soul, take heart.
    Jackson, L. M.
Take Him with you.
    Vincent, B. L.
Take love easy.
    Ellington, D. Beggar's holiday.
Take me back to Arizona.
    De Armond, E. N.
Take me, take me!
    Castro, A.
Take my word the way you took my
    heart.
    Fortner, R.
Take our love song into your heart.
    Arthur, W.
Take the world, but give me Jesus.
    Parker, E. E.
Take Thou my hand.
    Bradford, M.
Tal como fuiste.
    Los Cuates Castilla (Musicians)
Tal es la vida.
    Usera, R.
Tal vez me puedan matar.
    Lavista, R. Cuando lloran los
    valientes.
Tale of the high seas.
    Woods, J. S. One day on Calvary.
Tales of the Vienna woods.
    Strauss, J.
Tallahassee.
    Loesser, F. Variety girl.
Tambah.
    Munoz, R. Baile del tambah.
Tamburo della banda d'Affori.
    Ravasini, N.
Tango de notre amour.
    Marcuse, A. Le chanteur inconnu.
Tango delle rose.
    Schreier-Bottero. Tango of roses.
Tango habanera.
    Codevilla, P.
Tango of roses.
    Schreier-Bottero.
Tango triste.
    Troilo, A.
Tannhäuser.
    Wagner, R.
Tant pis ... tant mieux.
    Polnareff, L.
Tanto, tanto.
    Godini, A.
Tantum ergo.
    Aubanel, G.
    Horgan, M. S., sister. O salutaris.
    O'Connell, W., cardinal. Hymn to the
    Holy Name.
Tap dancer's nightmare.
    Dorsey, T.
Taps.
    Righter, C. B.
Tarry near the cross.
    Tovey, H. G.
Te Deum.
    Peeters, F.
Te Deum danicum.
    Jeppesen, K.
Te Deum laudamus.
    Murphy, J. A.
Te esperare.
    Rivera, P.

Te espero en Rodríguez Peña.
    Varela, H.
Te has de acordar de mi.
    Colmenero, P. M.
"Te lo juro yo."
    Quiroga, M. L. One kiss for a good
    measure.
Te quiero besar.
    Matos, M. G. Gay señorita.
Te quiero que.
    Alea, M. M.
Te seguire queriendo.
    Sacasas, A.
Te' vas de mi.
    Grenet, E.
Tea for two.
    Jaffe, C.
    Youmans, V. No, no Nanette.
Teach me how to serve Thee, Father.
    Macklin, Y.
Teach us purity.
    Gounod, C. F.
Tears follow my dreams.
    Kacprzak, M.
Tears from my heart.
    Coen, A. Lagrimas de sangre.
Tears, idle tears.
    Mendelssohn-Bartholdy, F.
Tears in my heart.
    Deceico, I.
    Vidal, F. L. Lagrimas del corazon.
Teatertosset.
    Gyldmark, S.
Technic book, for piano.
    Johnson, M.
Technic for pianists of junior grade.
    Weybright, J.
Technic teasers.
    Jacobus, D. A.
Tecolote. See title entry in composer
    list.
Tell me again (that you love me)
    Kelly, N. Kiss me goodnight, love.
Tell me, what is love?
    Carleton, R. L.
Tell me with your eyes.
    Friml, R. Northwest outpost.
Telling time.
    Spaeth, S.
Tema con variazioni.
    Veroli, D. di.
Temecula waltz.
    Williams, E. S. Little classics for
    cornet or trumpet.
Temisvar polka.
    Nejć, M. Sedi, Boso, de!
Tempo's birthday.
    Hampton, L.
Tempo's boogie.
    Hampton, L.
Temps des cerises.
    Renard, A.
Tempus fugit.
    Sandoval, M.
Ten enudettes.
    Mana-Zucca, pseud.
10 hit songs.
    Solomon, N. All those in favor.
Ten pieces, from the ballet "Cinderella."
    Prokof'ev, S. S.
Tenderly.
    Gross, W.
Tenerezze.
    Moietta, B.
Tenues rythmiques pour l'indépendance
    des doigts.
    Vaillant, H.
Ter sanctus.
    Schubert, F. P.
Terang boelan.
    Hoffman, M.
Terang boulan.
    Michael, P.
Teresini Teresini Teresini
    Cioffi, G.
Testamento del Congo.
    Musteljer, A.
Têtes d'enfants.
    Gagnier, J. J. Trois esquisses musi-
    cales.

Tex Ritter all star song folio.
    Goldsen, M. H., ed.
T-E-X-A-S.
    Kenney, J.
Texas and Pacific.
    Hirsch, J. E.
Texas polka.
    McPhail, L.
Texas Toni Lee.
    Rose, F.
Texas tornado.
    Rivers, J.
Tha brö kainoūrgia agapē.
    Ritsiardēs, I. M. Eythymes peri-
    peteies.
Tha meinō gia panta konta sou.
    Iakōbidēs, Z.
Tha phygōi
    Chairopoulos, C. K. Je pars!
Tha phygoume me mia barkoula.
    Maroudas, T.
Tha se parō na phygoume.
    Spartakos, G.
Tha se philēsō ki'as mēn to theleis.
    Bellas, G. G.
Thank God.
    Ballantine, E.
Thank you.
    Crawford, J.
Thank You for the world so sweet.
    Poulton, D. F.
Thanking you.
    Enticknap, C. G.
Thanks be to Thee, O Lord.
    Händel, G. F.
Thanks for a wonderful evening.
    Nutting, H.
Thanks, soldier boy.
    Carleton, R. L.
Thanksgiving.
    Vandenberg, D. G.
Thanksgiving in the cupboard.
    Kaiser, J.
That ain't right (to boogie on Sunday)
    Williams, S.
That big rock candy mountain.
    Mossman, T.
That bloom in May.
    Trams, C. H.
That cheap look in your eye.
    King, F,
That chick's too young to fry.
    Hilliard, J.
That cute little girl down at the roadside
    inn.
    Dexter, A.
That dream will come true.
    Tovey, H. G.
That fascinatin', procrastinatin' gal
    o' mine.
    Pinkard, M.
That fascinating smile.
    Buck, R.
That feeling of falling in love.
    Deering, J.
That Holy City will be my home.
    Jenkins, E. M.
That Holy Thing.
    Bristol, L. H.
That is why I love my Saviour.
    Evangel Special Sacred Songs, no. 1.
That old cow path.
    Meek, P. C.
That rhythmy rhythm.
    Bender, A.
That wonderful something.
    Marks, M.
That'll be the day.
    Denny, D.
That's between the desert and me.
    Krakeur, J.
That's my desire.
    Kresa, H.
That's my love.
    Lee, J.
That's right, you're wrong.
    Von Bergen, R. J.

That's the way it goes.
  Robin, S.
That's what the Daughters do.
  Johnston, L. M.
That's when I knew I loved you.
  Bailes, L.
That's when my dreams all fade out.
  Angeloni, J.
That's where I came in.
  De Rose, P.
That's where the West begins.
  Vincent, N.
That's why I want to go home.
  Sanders, A. Louisiana lady.
That's why I'm in love with you.
  Beuckmann, H.
Theme and cadenza.
  Bliss, A. Memorial concert.
Theme and six variants.
  Parrott, I.
Theme from Brahms' third symphony
  (third movement)
  Brahms, J. Symphony, no. 3.
Theme [from] "Dream concerto."
  D-Artega. Dream concerto.
Theme from Tschaikowsky's concerto
  no. 1.
  Chaikovskii, P. I. Concerto, piano,
  no. 1.
Themes from Grieg's piano concerto.
  Grieg, E. H. Concerto, piano.
Themes from Rachmaninoff's second
  concerto.
  Rachmaninoff, S. Concerto, piano,
  no. 2.
Themes from second concerto.
  Rachmaninoff, S. Concerto, piano,
  no. 2.
Themes from the 9th symphony.
  Beethoven, L. van. Symphony, no. 9.
Themes from Tschaikowsky's Fifth.
  Chaikovskii, P. I. Symphony, no. 5.
Then I met you.
  Barris, H.
Then sing.
  Thomas, C.
There be none of Beauty's daughters.
  Newman, N.
There but for you go I.
  Loewe, F. Brigadoon.
There I stood.
  Isel, W.
There is a green hill far away.
  Gounod, C. F.
There is a name more precious.
  Thorne, W. M.
There is a way.
  Kerr, P. S.
There is no better Friend than Jesus.
  Lillenas, H.
There is no breeze.
  Stein, S.
There is no end.
  Burrows, R.
There is someone new in town.
  Arthur, W.
There really ain't enough to go around.
  Levine, L.
There was a little pig.
  Ziehler, J.
There will always be.
  Arthur, W.
There will I don my cloak.
  Rathaus, K.
There'll be a happy time in heaven one
  of these days.
  Banks, E. V. McK.
There'll be no invasion in heaven.
  Holt, J. M.
There's a big rock in the road.
  Rose, F.
(There's) a blue heart.
  Nelson, K. F.
There's a bright light shining in my soul.
  Pace, C. H.
There's a bright moon shining tonight.
  Hibbeler, R. O.

There's a cabin in the pines in Wisconsin.
  Lamkoff, P.
There's a garden where Jesus was pray-
  ing.
  Shoffner, M. F.
There's a home for us in glory.
  Parks, H.
There's a little white house.
  Gould, R. E.
There's a look in your eye.
  Egger, T. W.
There's a mood for everything.
  Williams, L. L.
There's a new white cross in Normandy
  tonight.
  Gates, J.
There's a rainbow.
  Lake, G.
There's a rainbow in the rain.
  Post, W. H.
There's a spook in that juke box.
  Kennedy, A.
There's a stairway to heaven.
  Leap, G. C.
There's a star and a flag in my window
  for a lad.
  Kimberlin, E. W.
There's a story.
  Evangel Special Sacred Songs, no. 1.
There's a time.
  Strickland, B.
There's a train out for dreamland.
  Kress, C.
There's an angel waiting for you.
  Pollack, R.
There's fun out on the farm.
  Carleton, R. L.
There's no gal like mine.
  Hasenauer, E. E.
There's peace in the valley for me.
  Hutchinson, T.
There's that lonely feeling again.
  Shaftel, A.
Thesaurus of scales and melodic pat-
  terns.
  Slonimsky, N.
These loving hearts.
  Weissbuch, A. S.
These things I know will happen.
  Polovina, M. J.
These woods of light and shadow.
  Pendleton, E. Quiet paths.
They all ask for you.
  Robles, A. Todo me habla de ti.
They can't convince me.
  Fisher, D. Down to earth.
They christened the baby.
  Rose, C.
They led my Lord away.
  Dorsey, J. E., arr. Two negro
  spirituals.
  Lawrence, W., arr.
They married me young.
  Cernkovich, R., ed. & arr. "Mene
  mlada oženise."
They never met again.
  Furney, A. J.
They say it's wonderful.
  Berlin, I. Annie get your gun.
They tell me I'm just a dreamer.
  Smith, W.
They that go down to the sea in ships.
  Laubenstein, P. F.
They'll fight you anyway.
  Riggs, M. L.
Thine is the glory.
  Fitch, T. F.
Things I like about you.
  Carleton, R. L.
Things you do to me.
  Carleton, R. L.
Things you left in my heart.
  Leighton, H.
Think of me sometime.
  Mendoza, R. Se que te vas.
Third piano book for little Jacks and Jills.
  Rodgers, I.

3rd piano concerto.
  Bartók, B. Concerto, piano, no. 3.
Third string quartet in F.
  Bax, A. Quartet, strings, no. 3.
35 sonatas for piano.
  Scarlatti, D.
30 pedal studies.
  Torjussen, T.
This, and every day.
  Walters, O. W.
This believing world.
  Sauter, E.
This Canada of Ours.
  Donnell, R.
This crazy obsession of mine.
  Rose, F.
This day.
  Tobin, L.
This evening.
  Stokes, H.
This is a changing world.
  Coward, N. Pacific 1860.
This is it!
  Carleton, R. L.
This is madness.
  Wayne, B. Calcutta.
This is my dream.
  Carleton, R. L.
This is my lovely day.
  Ellis, V. Bless the bride.
This is my own sweet melody.
  Hibbeler, R. O.
This is my plea.
  Pendleton, E.
This is the day of light.
  Weigl, V.
This is the day that God has made.
  Poulton, D. F.
This is the happiest day of my life.
  May, H.
This is the inside story.
  Bierman, B.
This is the story of Jesus.
  O'Hara, G.
This red, red rose is so like you.
  Ringle, D.
This same Jesus cares for you and me.
  Taylor, R. W.
This time for keeps.
  Soler, R.
This time, sweetheart, we're really
  through.
  Lister, W. E.
This troubled mind o' mine.
  Tyler, J.
Thorn in the rose.
  Schimmerling, H. A. Koupim já si
  koně vraný.
Those New York City kind of blues.
  Malneck, M.
Thou art my hiding place.
  Holzworth, A.
Thou hast made me.
  Harris, W. H.
Thou leadest me.
  Bugbee, M.
Thou purple morn rejoice.
  Shure, R. D.
Though I speak with the tongues of men.
  Brahms, J. Four serious songs.
Thousand and one nights.
  Mossman, T.
Three American episodes.
  Alexander, J.
Three American folksongs.
  Davis, K. K.
Three bears.
  Troup, R. W.
Three beautiful words of love.
  Gaste, L.
  Reid, B.
Three blind mice.
  Swift, F. F., arr.
Three Bohemian pieces.
  Weinberger, J.
Three brothers.
  Feasel, D.

Three childhood impressions.
Arnell, R.
Three fantasies.
Bergsma, W.

Three far-away trees.
Noel-Johnson, R.
Three humorous pieces.
Lora, A.
Three kings of Orient.
My First Christmas Songs.
The three little monkeys.
Williams, L. L.
Three little pigs.
Mieir, A. M.
Three musical portrait miniatures from
the romantic school.
Karg-Elert, S.
Three musical sketches.
Gagnier, J. J. Trois esquisses musi-
cales.
Three octave scales and chords for
saxophone.
Allard, J. A.
Three pieces.
Choveaux, N.
Prokof'ev, S. S.
Three pieces for organ.
Greenhill, H. W.
Three pieces from "Album for children."
Chaĭkovskiĭ, P. I.
Three portraits of old Denmark.
Möller-Holst, A.
Three R's for snare drum.
Ostling, A. E.
Three songs with pianoforte accompani-
ment.
Foster, I. R.
Wordsworth, W.
Three sonnet sonatas.
Whitefield, S.
Three very easy piano pieces.
Robinson, A.
Three woodland scenes.
Holst, M. S.
Through as dreamer, through as opposer.
Phillips, J. H.
Through darkness to light.
Heffer, F. Fantasie pastorale.
Thunder.
Swift, F. F.
Thunderer.
Sousa, J. P.
Thy grace is sufficient for me.
Elliot, J. An evangel in song.
Thy love is every morning new.
Spohr, L.
Thy name is great.
Bruinsma, H. A.
Thy sweetness is my life.
Gillis, C. E.
Thy will, O Lord.
Stebbins, G. C.
Thy Word is like a garden, Lord.
Trued, S. C.
Ti chiamo amore.
Zuccheri, L. Non so come si chiami.
Ti manderò una cartolina da Milano.
Clerici, A. La par ona storia.
Tibet.
Pescara, A. P.
Tick-tack polka.
Cernkovich, R.
The tide rises, the tide falls.
Klumpkey, J. Two songs.
Tien orgelwerken.
Klerk, A. J. de.
Tiin tiión.
Gil, F.
Till He come.
Cumming, J. W. W.
Till henne därhemma.
Wahlberg, H.
'Till my Saviour comes again.
Bay, A. L. Upon the mountain side.
Till you came along.
Arthur, W.
Timber cutter's chant.
Gaul, H. B., arr.

Time after time.
Styne, J. It happened in Brooklyn.
Time and again.
Simon, B.
Time cannot change a faithful heart.
Belton, J. Time marches on.
Time changes things.
Stuart, E. P.
Time is drawing near.
Famous Blue Jay Singers, arr.
Time marches on.
Belton, J.
Time-out for my heart and you.
Critelli, L.
Time, the place and you.
Perper, B.
Time to tell.
Thomas, K. M.
Timour the Tartar.
Taylor, C.
Tiny tunes.
Long, G. E.
Tircis.
Senee, H.
Tired and weary old cowboy.
McEnery, D.
Tired hikers.
Belchoff, M.
Tired Tim.
Belchamber, E. Two songs from
De La Mare.
Tiroler Holzhacker Buab'n.
Wagner, J. F. Jolly lumberjack.
Tiruliru.
Bocheros, L.
'Tis a privilege to live in Colorado.
Courtney, A.
'Tis safe to follow Him.
Cummings, M. H.
'Tis so sweet to trust in Jesus.
Parker, E. E.
Tṛú sḥṅglög.
Pórdarson, S. I ḷlögum.
Tivoli-Revyen 1946.
Riis, A.
Tizenkét kis gyermekdarab.
Kadosa, P. Small pieces for small
people.
To a waterfowl.
Crist, B.
To America.
Cowell, H.
Savino, D.
To an Irish lake.
Warner, K.
To bed early.
McGrane, P.
To Calvary.
Bogert, L. E.
To evening.
Klein, J.
To God all praise shall be.
Elliot, J. An evangel in song.
To kompologaki.
Mētsakēs, G. S.
To love you forever.
Barile, M.
To Mētsakē.
Mētsakēs, G. S. Psilē brochoula
epiase.
To music, to becalm his fever.
Adrian, W.
To my brother, Bob.
Van Tyle, R.
To rest in the glory.
Goulding, E.
To the cuckoo.
Singleton, W.
To the evening star.
Wagner, R. Tannhäuser.
To the hills I lift mine eyes.
Fryxell, R. H.
To Thee, O Christ, I give my love.
Thorne, W. H.
To think I thought so much of you.
Frangeul, F. M'ap resodou.
To this temple, where we call Thee.
Ashfield, R. Two introits.

To xeupō neftaixa.
Sakellariou, A.
To you, from me, all my love.
McHenry, E. W.
To you it was just a fling.
Tobin, L.
To you, sweetheart.
Byers, F.
Toccata.
Guarnieri, C.
Toccata and fugue.
Langstroth, I.
Today and always I will serve the Lord.
Ford, H. J.
Today be joy in every heart.
Harts, H. L. Our country.
Today did Christ arise.
Gore, R. T.
Today is Christ born.
Pollak, W. T.
Todo me habla de ti.
Robles, A.
Todos gustan bailarlo.
Davis, J. Ev'ryone like to rhumba.
Together and apart.
Melachrino, G. M.
Toledo polka.
Dawson, S. B.
Toll the bells in Zion.
Hatcher, C. E.
Tom foolery.
Todd, T. T.
Tombeau de Max Jacob.
Thomas, A.
Tommy min pojke.
Mattsson, C. O.
Tommy Perkins.
Dunhill, T. F.
To-morrow.
Colonna, D. R. Manana.
Tomorrow begins another year.
Smith, H.
Tomorrow Mountain.
Ellington, D. Beggar's holiday.
Ton coeur est la forteresse.
Fassio, A.
"Tonadas del trópico niño."
Brenes Candanedo, G. Rondas de
niños.
Tonett-polka.
Nilsson, N. K. S.
To-night.
Ramirez, R. Esta noche.
Tonight I must die.
Pergament, M. I natt skall jag dö.
Tonight, sweetheart, tonight.
Rockwell, H. J.
Tonight there's no heaven (where there
is no you)
Weisman, B. Tonight there's no heaven.
Too hasty was I.
Kukol, C. T.
Too many blues.
Nettles, W. E.
Too tired to care.
Melsher, I.
Too tired to sleep.
Murray, A.
Too-ra- loo.
Michalson, A. S.
Topeka polka.
Hoefle, C.
Topo, topo, topolino.
Somalvico, G.
Toreros y flores.
Maciste, M. A.
Tornerai.
Olivieri, D. Tutto il mondo canta
Tornerai.
Tortillas.
Alshin, H. A.
Tota pulchra es Maria.
Bruckner, A.
Touch of God.
Tovey, H. G.
Tout cela n'est rien sans vous.
Israel, M.

Tout le long des rues.
　Glanzberg, N.
Tower bells.
　Aulbach, F. E.
Toy band parade.
　Besthoff, M.
Toy-town masquerade.
　Ostrowsky, A. M.
Toy train.
　Siegel, A. F.
Toys in my room.
　Consentino, A. B. Songs.
Toys on parade.
　Melecci, A.
Traditional Hebrew chants.
　Braslavsky, S. G., arr.
Traffic dance.
　Stoltze, R.
Traffic light song.
　Katzman, H.
Traficante certified system.
　Traficante, E.
Tragic march.
　Beckhelm, P. B.
Traición ingrata.
　Lavista, R. Cuando lloran los
　valientes.
Traité d'harmonisation pratique.
　Rawson, D. H. A. F.
Tramonto sul fiume.
　Milena, L. Mamma, dammi venti
　lire.
Tranquillo.
　Trowbridge, L.
Travail and triumph.
　Keating, L.
Travaillons en chantant.
　Weisshaus, E. A. L. L.
Tre gator.
　Byhmar, G. Casinorevyn, 1943.
Tre Pär Lagerkvist-dikter.
　Widéen, I.
Tre sma ord.
　Kraft, A.
Tre sma sånger.
　Pergament, M.
Tre visor.
　Jonsson, J.
Trees in the rain.
　Cadman, C. W.
Treis megales laikes epitychies.
　Papaïoannos, G. P.
Trente- deux lecons de solfège sans
　altérations.
　Ravizé, A.
Tretí smyčcový kvartet.
　Jirak, K. B. Quartet, strings, no. 3.
Tri klavírní skladby.
　Suk, J.
Tři písne.
　Hlobil, E.
3 sonatiny.
　Schäfer, F. Sonatinas, piano.
Tri Toccaty.
　Dobias, V.
Tribute to Chopin.
　Eckstein, M.
Tribute to mother.
　Lavine, L. P.
Trick riders.
　Lake, G.
Tricycle ride.
　Fouts, M. Children's easy piano
　pieces.
Triflin' woman blues.
　Bernhardt, C.
Trio à cordes.
　Schmitt, F. Trio, strings.
Trio, E moll.
　Zich, O. Trio, violin, violoncello &
　piano.
Trio for piano, violin and violoncello.
　Shostakovich, D. D. Trio, piano,
　violin & violoncello.
Trio in B flat.
　Bax, A. Trio, piano & strings.
Trio quasi una fantasia.
　Pícha, F.

Trip to Hollywood.
　Choisser, J. D.
Triste sera.
　Gilardini, R.
Triste serenata.
　Ravasini, N.
Tristezas del alma.
　Sánchez Vázquez, P.
Trittico.
　Mortari, V.
Triumph der Liebe.
　Melichar, A.
Triumphant praises.
　Wolverton, M. H.
Trois esquisses musicales.
　Gagnier, J. J.
Trois mélodies.
　Segond, P.
Trois noëls niçois.
　Delrieu, G.
Trois poëmes.
　Devriès, D. M.
Trois princesses.
　Vuillermoz, É.
Trombone method.
　Eidson, A. B.
Trompet- capriolen.
　Hausdörfer, F.
Trop tard.
　Delettre, J.
Tropical tunes.
　Pullen, O. D.
Tror du paa Eventyr.
　Riis, A. Naar Katten er ude.
Troubadour suite.
　Harrison, J.
Trouble's all I've ever known.
　Nettles, W. E.
Troubles and trials.
　Williams-Biggers, L. M.
Trout, no doubt.
　Kadison, P.
Truck driving fever.
　Carleton, R. L.
True blue and gold.
　Hulen, L. E.
True to the Navy.
　LaMarche, A.
"Truer words were never spoken."
　Worth, B.
Truman flew to Mexico.
　Young, B.
Trumpet march.
　Rowley, A.
Trumpet mechanisms.
　Reinhardt, D. S.
Trumpet studies with modernistic
　rhythms.
　Mancini, A.
Trumpet velocity.
　Johnson, G. H.
Trust God for everything.
　Berry, Mrs. W.
Trust Him.
　Starr, K. G. C.
Try and forget a little harder.
　Thomas, B. V.
Tschajkowsky's music you remember.
　Chaikovskiĭ, P. I.
Tu dis, demain.
　Chekler, E.
Tu íntimo secreto.
　Gómez, G.
Tu me vas a llorar.
　Sagué, J.
Tu mirar.
　Mercado, F.
Tucuman.
　Codevilla, P. Uraguayana.
Türkisenblaue Garten.
　Szendrei, A.
Tulip time.
　Schubert, F. P.
Tulips for you.
　Scott, C. W.
Tune for the tuba.
　Thiman, E. H.

Tune my heart.
　Bacon, J. D.
Tune up time for love.
　Rayburn, R.
Tuneful graded studies.
　Bradley, D., arr.
Tunes for little players.
　Kerr, R. N.
Turkey and the pumpkin.
　Wallace, M. O.
Turkey in the straw.
　Schaum, J. W., arr.
Turkish patrol.
　Michaelis, T.
Tutto è leggero.
　Barberis, A.
Tutto il mondo canta Tornerai.
　Olivieri, D.
Tuya es mi serenata.
　Barcelata, L.
Tvä dikter.
　Eriksson, J.
Tvä sånger.
　Lindberg, O.
Twelve swing choruses for guitar.
　Volpe, H.
Twelve twin tunes.
　Foster, A. H., comp.
Twenty festival songs.
　Rohrbough, L., comp.
Twenty-five compositions for piano.
　Magnuson, A.
Twenty-five selected songs.
　Fauré, G. U.
24 advanced etudes.
　Hering, S.
24 preludes.
　Kabalevskiĭ, D. B. Preludes, piano.
Twenty-fourth Psalm.
　Lang, E.
21 special.
　Ducháč, M. Rhythm.
Twenty-third psalm.
　Acheson, M. W.
　Malotte, A. H.
22 hymns.
　Pierron, J. J.
Twenty years of sorrow.
　Shepard, R.
Twice three tongue-twisters.
　Goodchild, A.
Twilight memories.
　Krawitz, E. H.
Twilight on the river.
　Milena, L. Mamma, dammi venti lire.
Twilight shadows.
　Hovemann, C.
Twilight's rosary.
　Scarmolin, A. L.
Twin ballots.
　Johnson, G. H.
Twinkle, twinkle little star.
　Murray, L.
Twintig melodische etuden.
　Duuren, H. J. van.
Two bits in my pocket.
　Broughton, H. The new moon is
　changing to gold.
Two choral preludes.
　Bach, J. S. Chorale preludes, organ.
Two chorales.
　Roberts, M. Chorales, 2 pianos.
Two fatal words.
　Davis, T.
Two folk-songs from the planet Mars.
　Bosmans, A.
Two guitars.
　Rosemont, W. L., arr.
Two heroic hymns of praise.
　Shenk, J.
Two introits.
　Ashfield, S.
Two little crickets.
　Baltor, H.
Two little piano sonatas.
　Fenner, B.
Two miniatures.
　Foldes, A.

Two negro spirituals.
Dorsey, J. E., arr.
Two offertories in honor of St. Joseph.
Florentine, sister.
Two-part anthem book.
Mueller, C. F.
Two pieces.
Mozart, J. C. W. A.
Two pieces for piano.
Foldes, A.
Two pieces for string octet.
Shostakovich, D. D.
Two playtime pieces.
Bragdon, S. C.
Two seventeenth century clavier arias.
Brydson, J. C., arr.
Two songs.
Klumpkey, J.
Two songs from De La Mare.
Belchamber, E.
Two songs from Herrick.
Belchamber, E.
Two sweethearts.
Clyde, T.
Two take away one.
Wilson, E. M.
Two themes from Rachmaninoff concerto no. 2.
Rachmaninoff, S. Concerto, piano, no. 2.
Two tickets to Loveland.
Carleton, R. L.
Two ways.
Fouts, M. Children's easy piano pieces.
Two weeks with pay.
Kramer, A. C.
Tympani passages.
Cross, R. A., arr.
Typist's serenade.
Wicksman, H.
Tyve-fem lette klaverstykker i urtekstutgave.
Bach, J. S.
Tzu lang hob ich gevärt oif dir.
Ellstein, A. I have waited too long.''
U mego tatusia.
Malec, A.
Uber die Au.
Stolz, R.
Ugga ugga boo.
Miller, I.
Ugly chile.
Williams, C.
Uh-Huh.
Christiansen, E. Fyrtøjet.
Uit Leopold Mozart's notenboek.
Duuren, H. J. van, arr.
Ultima noche.
Collazo, B.
Guadalupe Alvarez, J.
Ultima palabra.
Barcelata, L.
Ulysses.
Siemonn, G.
Un | deux | trois |
Dumas, R.
Unblamable and unreprovable.
Stewart, A. Ç.
Uncle Jeremiah's gen'ral store.
Waverly, J.
Und das war verboten!
Fox, F.
Under blågul fana.
Widqvist, V.
Under the big top.
Frangkiser, C.
Under the southern sky.
Albéniz, I. M. F.
Under the Texas moon.
Bellin, B.
Undercurrent.
Brahms, J.
Underneath the cherry tree.
Terii, J.
Underneath the stars.
Spencer, H.
Underneath the Texas moon.
Noel, L.

Underneath the tropic moon.
Arthur, W.
Undertow.
Schuman, W.
Unfinished symphony.
Schubert, F. P.
Union-marche.
Flegl, J.
Union Pacific suite.
Shield, R.
United victory march.
Hayes, E.
Unless it can happen with you.
Manus, J.
The unseen hand.
Tovey, H. G.
Until you come home.
Carleton, R. L.
Unverhofft.
Zelibor, G.
Up and down the scale.
Amstell, B.
Up in my window.
Choisser, J. D. Pepito Santa Cruz.
Upon the mountain side.
Bay, A. L.
Upper Fifth Avenue.
Kent, A.
Uptown Saturday night.
Gannaway, A.
Ur Kung Eriks visor.
Rangstrom, A.
Uruguayana.
Codevilla, P.
Usignolo é triste.
Panzuti, V. Basta un po' di swing.
Usta moi molchat.
Blekhman, J. My tones will tell.
Ût a szonátához.
Major, E., comp.
Utah, home of mine.
Whittaker, N.
Utrillo.
Chardon, J.
The V-day waltz.
Gomes, R. F.
Vår.
Lindberg, O.
Vårstycke.
Seymer, William. Strofer i sol och skugga.
En varvals.
Seymer, W. Strofer i sol och skugga.
Välkommen åter, snälla sol.
Kallstenius, E. Fyra sånger.
Vålkomstvisa.
Kraft, A. Livet på landet.
Vända och sy om.
Kraft, A. Den glada skräddaren.
Vagabond.
Brose, E. O.
Gaste, L.
Vagabond heaven.
Ansell, E. N.
Valencia.
Padilla, J.
Valley Forge.
Koutzen, B.
Valley of the moon.
Troup, J. B.
Valparaíso.
Molinare, N.
Vals.
Tersmeden, G. A. H.
Vals-romanza.
Boladeres, G. de. Escena oriental.
Valse.
Nieland, J. H. I. M.
Valse de Walma.
Dominici, H., arr.
Valse des coeurs.
Blareau, R.
Valse des regrets.
Poterat, L.
Valse élégante.
Meijlink, C. J.
Valse éternelle.
Bouillon, J.

Valse from Symphony, no. 5.
Chalkovski, P. I. Symphony, no. 5.
Valse lente.
Drigo, R.
Valse mignonne.
Taylor, E.
Valse nordique.
Maridés, L.
Valse nostalgique.
Foch, D.
Valse obsédante.
Goldbaum, F.
Valse piquante.
Kern, C. W.
Kranz, J.
Valse qui chante.
Parys, G. van.
Valse simplice.
Böke, J. P. F.
Valse triste.
Nieland, J. H. I. M.
Valse viennoise.
Tillery, H.
Valsette.
Borowski, F.
Valser dello zigo zago.
Olivieri, D. Tutto il mondo canta Torneral.
Van Dyke's song folio.
Van Dyke, G. M.
Vanity fair.
Holmes, G. E.
Vaquero Johnny.
A'Dair, J.
Var en gang.
Seymer, W. Strofer i sol och skugga.
Var en lek.
Görling, U.
Var lilla komedi.
Dahlquist, L. E.
Variations.
Kabalevski, D. B.
Variations and finale on an old Flemish song.
Peeters, F.
Variations and fugue on a theme of Purcell.
Britten, B. The young person's guide to the orchestra.
Variations on a cantus firmus.
Giannini, V.
Variations on a recitative.
Schoenberg, A.
Variations on an original theme.
Peeters, F.
Variations on the name ''Abegg.''
Schumann, R. A.
Variations sur un chant hongrois.
Djabadary, H.
Variations sur un thème de Paganini.
Moisse, S.
Variety girl.
Van Heusen, J.
Varnattsregnet.
Koch, S. v. Die wilden Schwäne.
Varsoviana.
King, S. Put your little foot.
Veċhietto arzillo.
Panzuti, V.
Veċernf písně.
Smetana, B.
Veeda.
Alden, J.
Velaré tu sueño.
Rufa, G.
Velká dvoudílná škola pro normální a francouzský klarinet.
Krtiċka, S.
Velo y corona.
Lima, A. de.
Velvet shoes.
Evans, L.
Vem spelar i natten.
Pergament, M.
Ven aquí.
Harline, L. Honeymoon.
Venez danser, baby.
Tristan, Y.

210

Veni Creator Spiritus.
  Singenberger, J. B. Jubilate Deo.
Vent dans arbres.
  Elaine, sister.
Vent du ciel.
  Cassard, E.
Vent du souvenir.
  Padilla, J.
Vergers.
  Marescotti, A. F.
Verrò.
  Cioffi, G. Teresin!
Versprochene Land.
  Eisen, N.
Very easy sacred solos.
  Tannehill, M. B., arr.
Very first band and orchestra book.
  Mikita, A.
Very first violin book.
  Gardner, S.
Very last time.
  Lilley, J. J.
Very, very welcome hem, Mister Swans-
   son.
  Dahlquist, L. E. Very welcome home,
   Mr. Swanson.
Very welcome home, Mr. Swanson.
  Dahlquist, L. E.
Veteran.
  Papajohn, G. J. O apomachos.
Veteran's friend.
  Boyt, E.
Vi drikker, vi drikker.
  Christiansen, E. Fyrtøjet.
Vi har gungat uppå havet.
  Aspelin, S. En sjöman till häst."
Victimae Paschali.
  Uyttenboogaard, F.
V-i-c-t-o-r-y.
  Hampton, D.
Victory is our eternal song.
  Downing, L. J.
Vid brasan.
  Kraft, A. Från "Blyge Anton"
   till "En sjöman till häst."
Vid en skogstjärn.
  Seymer, W. Strofer i sol och skugga.
Vida castiga.
  Alvarez Maciste, M.
Vida мía.
  Nuñez De Borbón, A.
Vida mia.
  Soroa, M.
Videbladet om varen.
  Koch, S. v. Morgenländische
   Liebeslieder.
Vidi aquam.
  Pusa-Teri, C. R. Asperges me.
Vie, de printemps.
  Blareau, R.
Vieille valse.
  Blanc, J. R.
Vienna dreams.
  Sieczynski, R.
Vienna sings again.
  Rose, D.
Viennese waltz medley.
  Strauss, J.
Viennese waltzes.
  Strauss, J.
Viens, petite amie.
  Israël, M.
Vier ernste Gesänge.
  Brahms, J. Four serious songs.
Vier Lieder.
  Graener, P.
  Kallstenius, E. Fyra sånger.
Vieux Carré serenade.
  Guarino, J. B.
Vignette.
  K.,ep,e, P.
Vijften melodische etudes.
  Böke, J. P. F.
Vilda svanarna.
  Koch, S. v. Die wilden Schwäne.
Vill du tänka på mej?
  Steen-Östling, H.

Village bells.
  Schiefelbein, F. A.
Village festival dances.
  Gierlach, C.
Villancico.
  Gianneo, L.
Vimalei.
  Lefkowitch, H., arr.
Vin corse.
  Agostini, F. U vinu corsu.
Vine à verte.
  Bucino, M.
Vinu corsu.
  Agostini, F.
Violetta rumba.
  Nolasco, F. A.
Violins and violets.
  Giron, A.
Violon du diable.
  Trenet, C. L.
Visa.
  Jonsson, J. Tre visor.
Visa om mig och narren Herkules.
  Rangstrom, T. Ur Kung Eriks
   visor.
Visa om när jag var lustig med Welam
  Welamsson.
  Rangstrom, T. Ur Kung Eriks visor.
Visa till Karin när hon hade dansat.
  Rangstrom, T. Ur Kung Eriks visor.
Visa till Karin ur fängelset.
  Rangstrom, T. Ur Kung Eriks visor.
Vision.
  Dungan, O.
Vision d'amour.
  Melachrino, G. M. Woman to woman.
Visione.
  Lao Schor, A.
Visions of mother.
  Kinkade, A.
Vita è ritmo.
  Simi, G. Cuore viaggiatore.
Viva México! (Viva America!)
  Galindo, P. Easy to wed.
¡Viva mi suerte!
  Alarcón Leal, E.
Vive la tour Eiffel.
  Hartusch, M.
Voce del violino.
  Arassich.
Voci di primavera.
  Strauss, J. Voices of spring.
Voglio cantare a te.
  Giussani, G. Spacco tutto.
Voices of spring.
  Strauss, J.
Voilà l'hiver.
  Pavard, A. C. A.
Voilà, voilà, Paris.
  Leca, M.
Volveras.
  Sentis, J. Blanca Rosa.
Vore jag ett litet barn.
  Stenhammar, W. Fyra dikter.
Vorrei sognar.
  Olivieri, D. Tutto il mondo canta
   Tornerai.
Vous.
  Schott, J.
Vous et moi.
  Bosmans, R.
Vous saves bien.
  Neuburger, J. B.
Vous trouv'rez tout ca chez moi!
  Delettre, J.
Vout cowboy.
  Willing, F.
Vox in Rama.
  Breydert, F. M.
Voyes, c'est le printemps.
  Roche, P.
Všechno ti řeknu mlčením.
  Nováček, S. E. Až uvidíte "Ji."
V'shomeru.
  Freed, I. Prayers of Israel.
V'shom'ru no. 2.
  Nowakowski, D.

Vuelvo a querer.
  Fernández Porta, M.
Výlety Pané Broučkovy.
  Janáček, L.
Vzpominka na Zbirch.
  Vačkář, V. Sérénade.
Vzpominky.
  Hasler, K.
W prost do mego okieneczka.
  Malec, A.
Wages of sin.
  Gibson, A.
Wait a little while.
  Wright, C. C.
Waitin' for my dearie.
  Loewe, F. Brigadoon.
Waiting for a call from you.
  Tobin, L.
Waiting for you.
  Ajax, I.
  Provo, H. O.
Wake, my heart.
  Fisher, G. W.
Wake up and dream.
  Porter, C.
Walkin' on air.
  Arthur, W.
Walkin' with my shadow.
  Wayne, B.
Walking and talking with Jesus.
  Green, A. Eight new sacred choruses.
Walking in the light.
  Benson, C. G.
Walking in the sunshine.
  Vichery, L.
Walking on stilts.
  Fouts, M. Children's easy piano
   pieces.
Waltz in A minor.
  Fouts, M. Children's easy piano
   pieces.
Waltz in F major.
  Fouts, M. Children's easy piano
   pieces.
Waltz melody.
  Grider, F. J.
Waltz-mosaic.
  Worden, W.
Waltz of my dreams.
  Raymond, L., pseud.
Waltz of the flowers.
  Chaikovskii, P. I.
Waltz of the ladybugs.
  Bright, A.
Waltz of the snowflake.
  Kelly, N. Kiss me goodnight, love.
Waltz of the willows.
  Bugbee, L. A.
Waltz of the wooden shoes.
  Wansborough, H.
Waltz reverie.
  Fischer, I. L.
Waltzing thru' Erin.
  Cassen, E., arr.
Wanatuska march.
  Williams, E. S. Little classics for
   cornet or trumpet.
Wanderlust.
  Oberg, O. S.
Wandering miller.
  Schubert, F. P.
Wann der Steffel wieder wird, so wie er
   war.
  Lang, H.
Wanta-wanta.
  Kimball, K. V.
Wanted: a place to live!
  Bauer, E. T.
Wanting you.
  Romberg, S. The new moon.
War is over.
  Carleton, R. L.
War is won and I am going home.
  Stowe, L. H.
Warm kiss.
  Fisher, D. The corpse came C.O.D.
Warm weather baby.
  Rack, R. R.

Warsaw concerto.
  Addinsell, R.
Warsaw polka.
  Stanley, B. Warsawska polka.
Warsawska polka.
  Stanley, B.
Washboard blues.
  Mills, I.
Washington Post march.
  Sousa, J. P.
Wasn't it a pity how they did my Lord?
  Farmer, W. L.
Watching for Him.
  Woods, J. S.
Water colors.
  Nevin, M.
Watersprite.
  Tollefsen, A. Gay little pieces.
Waukegan concerto.
  Rose, D.
Waves.
  Koki, S. Ka nalu.
Waves of the Danube.
  Ivanovici, J.
  Ivanovici, J. Mother and dad's favorite
    wedding songs.
Way everlasting.
  Tovey, E. M.
Way leading to the sonata.
  Major, E., comp. Ut a szonátánoz.
Way of holiness.
  Cosselmon, R. A.
'Way over in Egypt land.
  Work, J. W.
Way to music on the trombone.
  Gaston, E. T.
Way to the stars.
  Belton, J. Time marches on.
We are waiting for the coming of the Lord.
  Weigle, C. F., ed. Sing a new song.
We believe, we all believe.
  Holst, A. M.
We can be more than friends.
  La Ro, K.
We come to worship Thee, O Lord.
  Evans, D. M.
We knew it all the time.
  Styne, J.
We love the place, O God.
  McKittrick, A. V.
We never mention Aunt Clara.
  Kelly, C.
We never met again.
  Furney, A. J.
We praise Thee.
  Buketoff, I.
We pray to Thee.
  Franca, I.
We thank Thee.
  Christie, C. A.
We three kings of Orient are.
  Hopkins, J. H.
We two in a lean-to.
  Feast, C.
We will be valiant.
  Harris, L. A.
We will carol joyfully.
  Means, C.
We wish we had it but we ain't.
  Dixon, G.
We won't be strangers long.
  Carleton, R. L.
Wear your American smile.
  Marcelli, R.
Weary blues.
  Warren, H. Summer holiday.
Wedding march.
  Schmidt, M. C.
Wedding of a marionette.
  Savino, D.
Wedding of the brush and comb.
  Pleis, J.
Wedding prayer.
  Dunlap, F. G.
Wedding waltz.
  Faber, B.
  Ivanovici, J. Der chasene
    waltz.

Wee braw lassie.
  Joyce, J.
Wee Hughie.
  Malotte, A. H.
Wee Jesu and Saint Johnnikin.
  Rowley, A.
Weep little Mary.
  Fenner, B.
Weeping willow.
  Bergman, M.
Weg zur Polyphonie.
  Göllner, K.
Weighed in the balance.
  Townsend, P. D. E.
Weinendes Herz.
  Bordino, F. Las Malvinas.
Weird tale.
  Schiefelbein, F. A.
Weiser?
  Birlew, E. C.
Welcome home, soldier.
  Kelly, N. Golden memories of by-
    gone days.
Welcome stranger.
  Van Heusen, J.
Welcome that star.
  Cain, N.
We'll be shadows in the moonlight.
  Fellowes, L.
We'll go away together.
  Weill, K. Street scene.
We'll sing a new song.
  Weigle, C. F., ed. Sing a new song.
Weller school of popular piano playing.
  Weller, B.
Welsh ballad.
  Ferry, C. T. Songs.
Wenn der Jasmin blüht.
  Uher, B.
Wenn ich mit Menschenund mit Engels-
    zungen.
  Brahms, J. Four serious songs.
We're going to Tokio.
  Barbee, E. C.
We're gonna catch up on romancing.
  Carleton, R. L.
We're looking for a city.
  Lillenas, H.
We're on our way to heaven.
  White, M.
Were you there?
  Howorth, M.
  Outley, M. T.
  Scholin, C. A.
Western lullaby.
  Miller, L. A.
Western skies.
  Halmy, L.
Western wagons.
  Alexander, J. Three American episodes.
We've been partners on the prairie.
  Capano, F.
We've found our Sioux City Sue.
  Crookham, D. D.
Wezme ja kontusz.
  Rathaus, K. There will I don my
    cloak.
Wha' happen, baby?
  Morales, N.
Whack-fol-de-diddle-ol.
  Carolan, E. T.
What a life.
  Rivera, P. Que vida.
What am I gonna do about you?
  Styne, J. Ladies man.
What can I give Him?
  Foster, D. F.
What can it mean?
  McNeil, J. C.
What-cha got in mind?
  Pleis, J.
What did you put in that kiss?
  Mizzy, V.
What good does a long face do?
  Grosvenor, R. L.

What good would the moon be?
  Weill, K. Street scene.
What is this thing called love?
  Porter, C.
What is this thing called love?
  Porter, C. Wake up and dream.
What kinder shoes?
  Johnson, H.
What makes your big head so hard.
  Moore, F. No leave, no love.
What might have been.
  Caldwell, H.
What time is it in heaven?
  Martell, C.
What undying love.
  Whitford, K.
What was her name?
  Dowle, F.
What will you bring me?
  Wilder, A.
Whatever betide us, He will be near.
  Thorne, W. M.
What'll I have?
  Harding, B.
What's come over you?
  Gershwin, A.
What's mine is mine.
  Williams, E.
What's needed in love.
  Kearney, J., III.
What's the use of dreaming?
  Howard, J. E.
What's with your heart?
  Timberg, H.
When am I gonna kiss you good morning?
  Grouya, T.
When China boy meets China girl.
  Reid, B.
When de stars begin to fall.
  Roberton, H. S.
When dreaming is through.
  Carleton, R. L.
When elephants roost in bamboo trees.
  James, L. F.
When G. I. Joe comes marching home.
  McCredie, W. L.
When good children sleep.
  Barnes, O. C.
When Gran'ma danced the polka.
  Frey, H.
When I died in Berners Street.
  Howe, M.
When I dream I'm in your arms.
  King, L.
When I grow too old to dream.
  Romberg, S. The night is young.
When I live with Jesus.
  Williams, R. N.
When I look in your eyes.
  Embil, J. R.
When I lost her tiny footprints in the
    snow.
  Harris, G. E.
When I met you for the first time.
  Lewis, S. I.
When I reach that city over there.
  Morris, U.
When I send white orchids.
  Banbury, G. E.
When I speak your name.
  Campbell, E. L.
When I survey the wondrous cross.
  Mason, L.
  Noble, T. T.
When I take leave for heaven.
  Townsend, P. D. E.
When I tell my heart.
  Simington, G. E.
When I took it to Jesus in prayer.
  Peterson, J. W. Gospel songs.
When I walk with you.
  Ellington, D. Beggar's holiday.
When I was sinkin' down.
  Johnson, H.
When I write my song.
  Anson, B.

When I'm not near the girl I love.
Lane, B. Finian's rainbow.
When Irish eyes are smiling.
Ball, E. R.
When it's apple blossom time again.
Pond, F. G. Whisper that you love
me.
When it's cherry pickin' time at the North
Pole.
Scholz, P.
When it's Easter in April.
Rader, D.
When it's Easter lily time.
Shoucair, C. G.
When it's peach bloom time.
Alongi, M.
When Jesus comes.
Meiler, L. P. Jesus is waiting for
me.
When Jesus smiles on me.
Weigle, C. F., ed. Sing a new song.
When Johnny brings Lelahani home.
Fisher, D.
When love comes stealing.
Kingsbury, E. W.
When Pa put the baby to bed.
Ellsworth, A. B.
When Silvia sings.
Berwald, W.
When the early morn is breaking.
Green, A. Eight new sacred choruses.
When the gold star came.
Tovey, H. G.
When the moonbeams come out tonight.
Barnum, K. R.
When the rainbow of love appears.
Samuels, J. W.
When the robins come again.
Carleton, R. L.
When the Saviour Christ is born.
Bement, G. S.
When the shamrock meets the palm.
Hickey, D.
When the snow-birds cross the Rockies.
Autry, G.
When the swallows homeward fly.
Munk, V.
When the 13th comes on Friday.
Alexander, R. R.
When the white roses bloom.
Wrubel, A.
When the Yanks come home again.
Heck, M. J.
When tonight is just a memory.
Weiss, G.
When we lift our eyes to pray.
Dieterich, M.
When we're back together again.
Spellman, G. F.
When will that day of rest come?
Rhynes, M. A. J.
When wilt Thou save the people?
Lapo, C. E.
When you and I were young, Maggie.
Butterfield, J. A.
When you are close to me.
Sanders, A. Louisiana lady.
When you call me up.
Tobin, L.
When you come to the end of the day.
Westphal, F.
When you dance with me.
Fuentes, R. Rumbeame.
When you get back home to visit Mother.
Conner, M. B.
When you left me.
Sharples, W.
When you said goodbye.
Alkire, E. H.
When you strike it rich!
Monson, I.
When you were mine.
Rayburn, H.
When you're around.
McCarter, B.
When you're eighteen.
Lippman, S. Barefoot boy with cheek.
When you're near.
Otero, J.

Where are you now?
Silvi, J.
Where can you be?
Where do I come in?
Lee, J. R.
Where does it get you in the end?
Shand, T.
Where ever you are.
Romanelli, F.
Where is Sam?
Smith, R. E.
Where or when.
Rodgers, R.
Where the moonbeams kiss the river
Rio Grande.
Drake, G.
Where willows bend.
Elliott, M.
Where you're concerned.
Wallen, H. H.
Where'er you walk.
Handel, G. F.
Where's my sweetie?
Butler, M. J.
Wherever you are.
Storm, B.
While dancing the dream waltz with
you.
Karlin, A.
While the sun shines.
Brodsky, N.
While the tears drop.
Sowulewski, E.
While you are in my arms.
Harlam, L. G.
Whirling the firestick.
Carter, B., arr.
Whisper I love you.
Mahon, G. The royal minuet.
Plato, G.
Whisper that you love me.
Pond, F. G.
Whispering pines.
Ferry, C. T. Songs.
Whistle blues.
Orent, M.
Whistle, daughter, whistle.
Niles, J. J., ed. & arr. The singing
campus.
Whistle-stop town.
Rifkin, I.
Whistles.
Thompson, I.
Whistling Jerry.
Sevier, L.
White birches.
O'Hara, G.
White caps.
Wright, N. L.
White Christmas.
Berlin, I. Accordion transcriptions.
White Cradle Inn.
Grun, B.
White orchids.
Banbury, G. E. When I send white
orchids.
White star lily.
Olson, C. W.
Whither shall I go from Thy spirit?
Mueller, C. F.
Who cares what people say?
Jerome, M. K. Nora Prentiss.
Who did?
Olson, R. G.
Who do you love, I hope.
Berlin, I. Annie get your gun.
Who else?
Koch, S. von
Who knows?
Cunliffe, D. ¿Quién sabe?
Who plays in the night-time.
Pergament, M. Vem spelar i
natten.
Who pushed the button?
Tobias, H. H.

Who was old Zip Coon?
Davies, O., pseud.
Whoa! Sailor.
Thompson, H. W.
Who'll be the next?
Lowry, R.
Who'll buy my violets.
Padilla, J.
Whoopsie doodle.
Weed, B.
Who's goin' stay with me tonight?
Bryan, C. F.
Who's sorry now?
Snyder, T.
Who's tellin'?
Rudolph, F.
Who's your baby, Hoosier baby?
Shephard, R.
Whose baby are you?
Styne, J. It happened in Brooklyn.
Why?
Arthur, W.
Why am I alone?
Webster, C.
Why are you crying?
Yamin, J. Por que tu lloras?
Why did I teach my girl to drive?
Cohen, C.
Why did it happen to me?
Mundahl, R. O.
Why did it have to be?
Carlisle, C.
Why did it have to be you?
Nathan, L.
Why did we have to part, dear?
Dunlap, M.
Why did you?
Richards, J. H.
Why do I feel the way that I do about
you?
Capano, F.
Why do I love Jesus?
Thorne, W. M.
Why do you say to Him nay?
Cottingham, F. The Saviour is
calling.
Why don't we say we're sorry?
MacGregor, C.
Why don't you smile?
Barth, J. F.
Why dream dreams of you.
Carleton, R. L.
Why in the dickens don't you milk
that cow?
Wiseman, S.
Why is the sky so blue?
Brooks, H. O.
Why not choose life.
Guilliat, V. A.
Why should I tell you?
Hueston, B.
Why should I worry?
Carleton, R. L.
Why should I worry now.
Carrier, J. A.
Why should I worry over you?
Ellsworth, A. B.
Wiener serenade.
Macho, G.
Wiggie, woogie, wiggie.
Pane, G. A.
Wild desires.
Williams, C. L.
Wild rose of Ioway.
Hitchcock, A. R.
Wild West boogie.
Siegel, A. F.
Wilden Schwäne.
Koch, S. von
Will o'th wisp.
Trowbridge, L. Nature tone-poems.
Will the moon carry the message of
my love for you?
Kelly, N. Kiss me goodnight, love.
Will you?
Fryberg, M.

Will you care?
　　Schulman, R. M.
Will you remember?
　　Romberg, S. Maytime.
Willie Earle.
　　Solomon, N. Black or brown
　　　or slightly tan.
Willkommen, liebe Sonne, Du!
　　Kallstenius, E. Fyra sånger.
Wind and girl.
　　Eakin, V.
Wind in the trees.
　　Elaine, sister. Le vent dans arbres.
Wind rolls the clouds.
　　Hill, T. J.
Window.
　　Belchamber, E. Two songs from De
　　　La Mare.
Window to the sea.
　　Stockton, R.
Winema waltz.
　　Williams, E. S. Little classics for
　　　cornet or trumpet.
Wings of a dove.
　　English, G.
Winter Alaska.
　　Lademann, L. L.
Winter moon.
　　Gross, W.
Winter night.
　　Pendleton, E.
Winter passes over.
　　Purvis, R.
Winter sunshine.
　　Melachrino, G. M.
Winter wonderland.
　　Bernard, F.
Wishes.
　　Martin, A. K. E.
Wistful.
　　Courtney, A. G.
Wistful mazurka.
　　Grechaninov, A. T. Petite suite.
Witch of the meadow.
　　Price, F. B.
With a song in my heart.
　　Rodgers, R.
With all of your faults.
　　Lacey, W.
With someone new.
　　Phillips, J.
Within Thy sight.
　　Flynn, C.
Without you.
　　DuFour, B.
　　Evans, D.
　　Saccardo, E.
Without your love.
　　Schonbrun, B. Sin tu amor.
Witness for my Lord.
　　Huston, F. C. Two songs.
Wodnik i dziewczyna.
　　Rathaus, K. The boatman and the
　　　maiden.
Wohin.
　　Schubert, F. P. Song of the brook.
Wolf whistle bait.
　　Furney, A. J.
Woman, if she loves you (will sleep
　　on a board)
　　Rox, J.
Woman is a worthy thing.
　　Chavez, C.
Woman to woman.
　　Melachrino, G. M.
Wonderful love of Calvary,
　　Von Horn, C.
Wonderful what Jesus did for me.
　　Smith, Mrs, C.
Wonderful words of life.
　　Tannehill, M. B.
Won't you come back to me.
　　Brennan, J. A.
Won't you come to Jesus today?
　　Leap, G. C.

Wood of the cross.
　　Byles, B. D.
Woodland serenade.
　　Hokmes, G. E.
Wooly black lamb.
　　Hayes, O. L.
Work for the Master today.
　　Macklin, Y.
Working together with Him.
　　Helsing, R. C.
World belongs to you, little man.
　　Pelosi, D.
World has lost all its attraction.
　　Evangel Special Sacred Songs.
World in tune.
　　Krone, B. P., arr.
Worship the Lord.
　　Johnson, Mrs. H. S.
Worthy is the Lamb who died to set us free.
　　Brazier, E. L.
Would if I could.
　　Furney, A. J.
Would you believe me?
　　Jerome, M. K. Love and learn.
Would you blame me?
　　Arthur, W.
Would you do me a favor?
　　Bernhardt, C.
Would you like for me to love you?
　　Fleener, W. O.
Wrap your troubles in dreams.
　　Barris, H.
Wszystk-ie sie żytko zazielenifo.
　　Malec, A.
Wyalusing polka.
　　Williams, E. S. Little classics for
　　　cornet or trumpet.
Y a un accordéon.
　　Ferreté, L. M. Mariguana.
Y dicen por ahi.
　　Esperón, M.
Ya lo ves.
　　Jesus Morales, J. de.
Ya lo viste mujer.
　　Palacios, J.
Ya perdí la esperanza.
　　Vista, F. A.
Yankee soldiers' march.
　　Mulcahy, M. A.
Yard dog.
　　Eldridge, R.
Yarmila.
　　Schimmerling, H. A.
Ye bells of Bethlehem.
　　Luvaas, M. J.
Ye shall receive power.
　　Pankratz, A. J.
Yellow rose.
　　Griffis, E.
Yeomen of England.
　　German, E. Merrie England.
Yes, He is mine.
　　Parker, R. C.
Yes, I want to rest.
　　Morris, K.
Yes, it's true what they say about
　　Dixie.
　　Clarkson, F.
Yes, of course.
　　Haag, G.
Yes or no.
　　Chapman, J.
Yes, yes, honey.
　　Shannon, G.
Yielded life.
　　Tovey, H. G.
Yismechu.
　　Freed, I. Prayers of Israel.
Yo.
　　Close, N.
Yo estoy aprendiendo inglés.
　　Rivero, F. Learning Latin.
Yo quisiera.
　　Ramirez, R.

Yo te ame.
　　Roig, G. Loving you.
Yo tengo amor.
　　Signorelli, F.
Yom hashviy,.
　　Vinaver, C.
Yosemite.
　　Hardy, A. B.
Yosemite suite.
　　Cope, F.
Yost violin method.
　　Yost, G.
You and the Devil.
　　Mosley, S.
You are a part of my heart.
　　Hibbeler, R. O.
You are everything in my life.
　　Arthur, W.
You are free.
　　Jacobi, V. Apple blossoms.
　　Stone, G.
You are mine because you want to
　　be..
　　Ware, G.
You are my destiny.
　　O'Shaughnessy, M. W.
You are my love.
　　Weisman, B.
You are my story.
　　Vanderburg, G.
You are my sweetheart.
　　Plato, G.
You are my world.
　　Reed, H.
You are the one I love.
　　Lebeck, P.
You are the only one in the world.
　　Vanderburg, G.
You are there.
　　Carlone, F. N.
You better change your ways.
　　Daffan, T.
You better get down on your knees and
　　pray.
　　Horton, V.
You better mind your mama.
　　Morales, N.
You broke the only heart that ever loved
　　you.
　　Little, J.
You can bet your boots on me, little
　　darlin'.
　　Fortner, R.
You can count on me.
　　Cosselmon, R. A.
You can play the piano!
　　Richter, A.
You can take my word for it, baby.
　　Taylor, I.
You can wait beneath that apple tree.
　　Marks, G.
You can't break a heart.
　　Adams, C. P.
You can't hide your heart behind a kiss.
　　Kaufman, A.
You can't save me for a rainy day.
　　Nathan, L.
You can't stop my dreams.
　　Tobin, L.
You can't take Texas out of me.
　　Milton, J.
You did not love me.
　　Lambert, R. Je pense a vous.
You don't fall into love.
　　Arthur, W.
You don't learn that in school.
　　Fisher, M.
You fell out of a star.
　　Kaufman, I. J.
You got the river of Jordan to cross.
　　Windom, A. B.
You grew up to be some baby.
　　Mizzy, V.
You had your say.
　　Catsos, N. A.
You haunt me.
　　Renstrom, M.

You keep coming back like a song.
  Berlin, I. Blue skies.
You keep going your way.
  Ellsworth, A. B.
You know you can't say no.
  Martin, J.
You left me in September.
  Bonnell, W. C.
You live in a world all your own.
  Copas, C.
You look good in them pants.
  Wagner, C.
You may preach!
  Tovey, H. G.
You mean so much to me.
  Hagen, J. E.
You must always remember.
  Kramer, O.
You must be blind.
  Nelson, M.
You my friend me.
  Davol, R.
You never miss the water till the
  well runs dry.
  Kronenberger, A. L.
You oughta be ashamed.
  King, J. T.
You said it!
  Carleton, R. L.
You smile at me.
  Brodsky, R.
You sold my love for a lie.
  Maher, R. E.
You wanna keep your baby lookin' right.
  Green, J. Something in the wind.
You went too far and stayed too long.
  Campbell, B.
You were not true.
  Richards, J. H.
You were the cause of it all.
  King, F.
You, wonderful you.
  Revel, H. Earl Carroll's vanities.
You'll know when it happens.
  Loeb, J. J.
  Lombardo, C.
You'll see the day.
  King, F.
Young America at the piano.
  Burrows, R. M.
Young America at the violin.
  Harris, E. E.
Young and old.
  Ashe, J. H.
Young king.
  Southwick, G. H.
Young Mister Playboy.
  Moore, M.
Young musician's progress.
  Patti, S. T.
Young person's guide to the orchestra.
  Britten, B.
Young piano prodigy.
  Besthoff, M.
Young prince and the young princess.

Rimskii-Korsakov, N. A. Scheherezade.
Your eyes.
  Mercado, F. Tu mirar.
Your eyes have told me so.
  Blaufus, W.
Your final decision.
  Lucas, H. W.
Your heart and my heart.
  Nelson, H.
Your love is everything.
  Pollino, N.
Your love or no love.
  Cardenas, G.
Your love will linger.
  Bell, E. W.
Your number, please.
  Orcutt, J. B.
You're beautiful.
  Norris, G.
You're breaking in a new heart.
  Mendelssohn, J.
You're breaking my hear..!
  Blew, E. M.
You're crying for the moon.
  Castle, J.
You're everywhere.
  Revel, H. It happened on Fifth
  Avenue.
You're gonna be sorry.
  Rutsky, L.
You're gonna miss your daddy.
  Carleton, R. L.
You're grand.
  Gates, G. M.
You're heaven sent.
  Essex, L.
You're laughing up your sleeve.
  Carson, J. L.
You're living a lie.
  Copas, C.
You're my heart.
  McNeil, J. C.
You're my heart's desire.
  Boatner, E.
You're my life.
  Soroa, M. Vida mia.
You're my ray of sunshine.
  Rodriguez, J. Chubasco.
You're not my darlin' anymore.
  Martin, S.
You're not so easy to forget.
  Oakland, B. Song of the thin man.
You're on my mind.
  McNeil, J. C.
You're really doin' something to me.
  Dawn, M.
You're some pretty doll.
  Williams, C. Ugly chile.
You're tempting.
  Piehl, H. W.
You're the answer to my dreams.
  Rivera, P. Por primera vez.
You're the bad apple in the basket.
  Lamkoff, P.

You're the only pebble on the beach.
  Baker, D.
You're the top.
  Porter, C. Anything goes.
You're what's the matter with me.
  Elly, J.
Youth, O youth.
  Pike, M. D.
Youth triumphant.
  Belton, J. Time marches on.
You've done it again.
  Sawaya, J.
You've got the River of Jordan to
  cross.
  Windom, A. B.
You've gotta have me.
  Zinsser, W. K. Clear the track.
You've gotta quit makin' me blue.
  Carson, J. L.
You've had your way, now I'm having
  mine.
  Carson, J.
You've laughed at me for the last time.
  Howard, R.
Yugoslav folk-songs.
  Seiber, M.
Zafa.
  Barcelata, L.
Zamilované klarinety.
  Langer, D.
Zaswic miesiaczku w okno moje.
  Malec, A.
Zbiór tancow polskich.
  Przybylski, F., arr. Collection of
  Polish dances.
Zdrowas Mario.
  Zalewski, B. J. Ave Maria.
Zebra twins.
  Lake, G.
Zemerle.
  Goldman, M. The rich and the poor.
Zestig kleine etudes.
  Nieland, J. H. I. M.
Zigeuner.
  Coward, N.
  Coward, N. Bitter sweet.
Zitta, zitta.
  Godini, A. Tanto, tanto.
Zōgraphia sou.
  Geōrgiadēs, A. G.
Zonnige jeugd.
  Duuren, R. J. van.
Zoologická zahrádka.
  Koštal, E.
Zopilote.
  Marcias Femat, M.
Zwei Lieder aus dem Buch der Seele.
  Petyrek, F.
Zweite sonate.
  Siegl, O. Sonata, violin & piano,
  no. 2.
Zweites klavier-trio.
  Foerster, J. B. Trio, piano
  & strings, no. 2.

U. S. GOVERNMENT PRINTING OFFICE : O—1948

.

CATALOG OF COPYRIGHT ENTRIES

Third Series

VOLUME I, PART 5 A, NUMBER 2

Published Music

JULY–DECEMBER

1947

COPYRIGHT OFFICE

THE LIBRARY OF CONGRESS

WASHINGTON 25, D. C.

PUBLISHED MUSIC

CONTENTS

PREFACE

THE Catalog of Copyright Entries for the year 1947 is issued in a new series and an enlarged format, a change designed to increase and extend the usefulness of the compilation. Inquiries, suggestions and comments on all details of the Catalog are solicited, and should be addressed to the Chief of the Cataloging Division, Copyright Office, Library of Congress, Washington 25, D. C.

CONTENTS. This part of the Catalog of Copyright Entries contains a list of published music registered in the Copyright Office from July 1, 1947, through December 31, 1947, in Class E, together with selected musical works registered in other classes. Renewal registrations of music made in this period are listed in Part 14B of the Catalog.

ARRANGEMENT. The first section of this catalog consists of complete entries under main headings (composer, editor, arranger, or, in some cases, title). It is followed by an index by title for all registrations listed.

ENTRY. Under the main heading each entry includes the title, followed by the names of all authors. Name of publisher and place of publication are given when they differ from the name and address of the claimant. Filing titles are supplied in some entries to bring together all excerpts from one work, or to file works with non-distinctive titles under the name of the musical form. Filing titles are placed in curves in front of the title as taken from the work, for example:

(Spring Is Here) With a Song in my Heart,
   from "Spring Is Here."

(Sonata, viola & piano, no. 2) 2ème
   Sonate ...

COPYRIGHT DATA. The statement giving the copyright facts is preceded by the copyright symbol ©. This is followed by the name and address of the claimant, the date of publication as defined in the Copyright Act, and the registration number. The registration number is preceded by one of the following symbols: EP (musical compositions published in the United States, registered in class E); EF (musical compositions published abroad, registered in class E); A (books proper, registered in class A); AA (selected pamphlets, registered in class A); B5 (contributions to periodicals, registered in class B); DP (published dramatic compositions, registered in class D). If the claim is based on new matter, a brief description of the new matter is given between the date and registration number.

DEPOSIT OF COPIES. In the case of every copyright entry listed in the catalog, the deposit of copies (or copy) as required by Title 17, U.S.C., Secs. 12, 13 has been made.

AUTHORITY. The Catalog of Copyright Entries is published pursuant to the authority given in the provisions of Title 17, U.S.C., Secs. 210 and 211. Section 210 provides that the Catalog "shall be admitted in any court as prima facie evidence of the facts stated therein as regards any copyright registration."

ORGANIZATION OF THE CATALOG. This issue of the Catalog is part of Volume I of the new Third Series. The parts are numbered according to the alphabetical sequence of classes as listed in Title 17, U.S.C., Sec. 5. Letters are used to designate subdivisions. The following is the plan of publication for 1947:

Part 1A - Books and Selected Pamphlets.
Part 1B - Pamphlets, Serials and Contributions to
    Periodical Literature.
Part 2 - Periodicals.
Parts 3 & 4 - Dramas and Works Prepared for Oral Delivery.
Part 5A - Published Music.
Part 5B - Unpublished Music.
Part 6 - Maps.
Parts 7-11A - Works of Art, Reproductions of Works of
    Art, Scientific and Technical Drawings,
    Photographic Works, Prints and Pictorial
    Illustrations.
Part 11B.-Commercial Prints and Labels.
Parts 12 & 13 - Motion Pictures.
Part 14A -Renewal Registrations - Literature, Art, Film.
Part 14B -Renewal Registrations - Music.

SUBSCRIPTION. The annual subscription price for the complete yearly Catalog of Copyright Entries is $10.00, payable in advance to the Superintendent of Documents, Government Printing Office, Washington 25, D. C., to whom inquiries and orders concerning the complete Catalog or any of its parts should be addressed.

COPYRIGHT REGISTRATIONS OF PUBLISHED MUSIC - CALENDAR
  YEAR 1947

EP	Musical compositions published in the United States	10,484
EF	Musical compositions published abroad	3,555
	Total	14,039

The above figures show the registrations for published music for the calendar year 1947, but do not represent the exact number of entries in this part of the catalog. A few registrations made prior to 1947 are included and a few made in 1947 are omitted and held for inclusion in a later issue of this part of the catalog.

A

ABELENDA, ANA MARIA.
Mi Ruego‼ ... Letra y música de
Ana María Abelenda. © Corpor-
acion Musical Argentine - Comar,
s.s., Buenos Aires; 15Jul47;
EF6797.

ABERNATHY, LEE ROY, 1913-
Everybody's Gonna Have a Wonderful
Time Up There; (Gospel boogie)
by Lee Roy Abernathy. © Lee Roy
Abernathy, Canton, Ga.; 15Nov47;
EP19025. For voice and piano;
shape-note notation.

Lord, I'm Feeling Mighty Fine Today; by Lee Roy Abernathy.
[Canton, Ga., Abernathy Publishing Co.] © Lee Roy Abernathy,
Canton, Ga.; 14Sep47; EP18095.
Close score: SATB; shape-note
notation.

Lord I'm Ready Now to Go; by Lee
Roy Abernathy. © Lee Roy
Abernathy, Canton, Ga.;
24Feb46; EP17777. Close score:
SATB; shape-note notation.

My Home ... by Lee Roy Abernathy.
© Lee Roy Abernathy, Canton, Ga.;
24Feb46; EP17776. Close score:
SATB; shape-note notation.

You Can't Believe Everything You
Hear; by Lee Roy Abernathy. ©
Lee Roy Abernathy, Canton, Ga.;
15Nov47; EP19026. For voice and
piano; shape note notation.

[ABRAHAM, IRVIN] 1909-
Every Day's My Birthday ... by
Irvin Graham [pseud.] © Edward
B. Marks Music Corp., New York;
5Dec47; EP19182. For voice and
piano, with chord symbols.

I Know It ... by Irvin Graham
[pseud.] © Edward B. Marks
Music Corp., New York; 3Dec47;
EP19183. For voice and piano,
with chord symbols.

ACHRON, JOSEPH, 1886-
Sicilienne (in the old style) ...
[by] J. Achron. [Op.21,no.3]
Transcribed by Edmund Kurtz.
© Boosey & Hawkes, inc., New
York; 19Jun46; on arrangement;
EP18542. Score (violoncello
and piano) and part.

[ACKLEY, BENTLEY D   ]
Our Living Lord; [words by B. C.
Getsinger] Out to Win; [words
by Margaret A. Fassitt. Music
by B. D. Ackley] Winona Lake,
Ind., The Rodeheaver Hall-Mack
Co., © The Rodeheaver Co., Winona Lake, Ind.; 10Oct47; on 2
hymns; EP18421-18422.

ACUFF, ROY.
I'm Dying a Sinner's Death; words
and music by Roy Acuff. © Acuff-
Rose Publications, Nashville;
18Oct47; EP18149.

Searching for a Soldier's Grave;
words and music by Roy Acuff.
© Acuff-Rose Publications,
Nashville; 30Oct47; EP17673.

Short-changed in Love; words and
music by Roy Acuff. © Acuff-
Rose Publications, Nashville;
9Sep47; EP16711.

This World Can't Stand Long;
words and music by Roy Acuff.
© Acuff-Rose Publications,
Nashville; 24Oct47; EP18236.

ACUÑA, MANUEL S
Confesión ... (words and music by)
Manuel S. Acuña. Mexico, Editorial Mexicana de Música Internacional, s. a. © Peer International Corp., New York; 30Dec46;
EP5810. Condensed score
(orchestra), piano-conductor
score and parts.

ADAMS, ERNEST HARRY, 1886-
The Toy Doll; by Ernest Harry
Adams. © The Arthur P. Schmidt
Co., Boston; 1Jul47; on arrange-
ment; EP15393. Score: piano 1-2.

Two Little Etudes for piano-
forte ... by Ernest Harry
Adams. © The Arthur P.
Schmidt Co., Boston; 7Aug47.
Contents.- [v.1] The Bouncing
Ball (© EP16106)-[v.2] Leap
Frog (© EP16105)

ADAMS, FRANKIE.
My Little Red-Head; by Max C.
Freedman and Frankie Adams.
© Shapiro, Bernstein & Co., inc.,
New York; 12Aug47; EP16296.
For voice and piano, with
chord symbols.

ADAMS, PERCY H
Dizzy Joe; words and music by Percy H. Adams. © Nordyke Publishing Co., Los Angeles; 15Jun46;
EP15905.

ADAMS, ROBERT LOVE, 1910-
I Will Gladly Tell the Story; by
Robert L. Adams. © Robert Love
Adams, Winchester, Va.; 14Jun47;
EP18266. Close score: SATB.

ADAMS, STEPHEN.
The Holy City; sacred song, words
by F. E. Weatherly, music by
Stephen Adams [arr. by Charles
R. Cronham] © Boston Music Co.,
Boston; 14Nov47; on arrangement;
EP18916. For organ solo; in-
cludes registration for Hammond
organ.

The Holy City; two keys in one ed.:
low [and] high. Music by
Stephen Adams, words by F. E.
Weatherly, [arr. by Walter L.
Rosemont] © Edwards Music Co.,
New York; 3Sep47; on arrangement;
EP16661. For voice and organ.

ADAMS, WALLACE D   1902-
I'm Working for My Savior; words
and music by Wallace D. Adams,
arr. by Margarite Brown. Chicago, Martin & Morris Studio.
© Wallace D. Adams, Chicago;
1Dec47; EP19267.

There Is Room in Heaven for You;
words and music by Wallace D.
Adams, [arr. by Margarite Brown]
Chicago, Martin and Morris Music
Studios. © Wallace D. Adams,
Chicago; 19Jun47; EP15388.

Tired of Wandering; words and
music by Wallace D. Adams.
Chicago, Martin and Morris Music
Studios. © Wallace D. Adams,
Chicago; 10Nov47; EP18689.

ADAMS, WALTER D
When the Lights Go On in My Life
Again; words and music by Walter
D. Adams, transcription by Anita
Adams. © Nordyke Publishing Co.,
Los Angeles; 21Aug47; EP16601.

ADAMS, WELLINGTON, 1879-
Drifting ... Words and music by
Wellington Adams. © Wellington
Adams, Brooklyn; 26Sep47;
EP17848.

ADAMS, WELLINGTON, 1879-   arr.
What a Friend We Have in Jesus;
quartet or chorus with obbligato and female trio, an arrangement by Wellington Adams.
© Wellington Adams, Brooklyn;
15Aug47; on arrangement;
EP17959.

ADDINSELL, RICHARD.
Festival. See his Trespass.

Harmony for False Lovers. See his
Trespass.

I Like Life. See his Tuppence Coloured.

I'm Going to See You Today; [words]
by Joyce Grenfell; [music by]
Richard Addinsell, arr. by Allan
Small. New York, Leeds Music
Corp. © Keith, Prowse & Co., ltd.,
London; 16Jun47; on arrangement;
EP15348. Piano-conductor score
(orchestra) and parts.

A Jabberwocky Song. See his Tuppence
Coloured.

Sing, Child, Sing. See his Tuppence
Coloured.

Sing, Sweet Nightingale. See his
Tuppence Coloured.

(Trespass) Festival; from Emlyn
Williams' play "Trespass," by
Richard Addinsell; [arr. by H.
Boynton-Power] © Keith Prowse
& Co., ltd., London; 18Jul47;
on arrangement; EF6687.

(Trespass) Harmony for False Lovers,
from Emlyn Williams' play, "Trespass"; by Richard Addinsell. ©
Keith, Prowse & Co., ltd., London;
18Jul47; EF6241. For piano solo.

(Tuppence Coloured) I Like Life;
words by Joyce Grenfell, music
by Richard Addinsell, sung... in
Tuppence Coloured. © Keith,
Prowse & Co., ltd., London; 4Dec47;
EF7174.

(Tuppence Coloured) A Jabberwocky
Song; lyrics by Leonard Gershe,
music by Richard Addinsell ...
[from the revue] Tuppence Coloured.
© Keith, Prowse & Co., ltd.,
London; 25Sep47; EF6601.

ADDINSELL, RICHARD. Cont'd.
(Tuppence Coloured) Sing, Child,
Sing; lyrics by Leonard Gershe,
music by Richard Addinsell ...
[from the revue] Tuppence
Coloured. © Keith, Prowse & Co.,
ltd., London; 20Nov47; EF7208.
(Tuppence Coloured) Sing, Sweet
Nightingale; lyrics by Joyce
Grenfell, music by Richard
Addinsell ... [from the revue]
Tuppence Coloured. © Keith,
Prowse & Co., ltd., London;
25Sep47; EF6600.

A'DENE, DON, pseud. See
Numsen, Adena.

ADLER, HUGO CH
Elijah, the Prophet. Eliyahu
Hanavi. Transcribed for mixed
voices (S.A.T.B.) by Hugo Ch.
Adler. © Transcontinental
Music Corp., New York; 19Dec47;
on arrangement; EP20150. Heb-
rew words (transliterated)

ADLER, MYRA
Lambs in the Meadow; for the piano
[by] Myra Adler. © Oliver
Ditson Co., Philadelphia; 31Jul47;
EP16344.
Little Piggies; piano solo with
words, by Myra Adler. ©
Oliver Ditson Co., Philadelphia;
5Sep47; EP16380.

ADLER, SAMUEL HANS, 1928-
Concert Piece; [by] Samuel H. Adler
North Easton, Mass., Music for
Brass. © Samuel Hans Adler,
Worcester, Mass.; 15Aug47;
EP16660. Score: brass instru-
ments and kettle drums.
Praeludium; [by] Samuel H. Adler,
North Easton, Mass., Music for
Brass. © Samuel Hans Adler,
Worcester, Mass.; 30May47; EP16667,
Score: brass instruments and
kettle drums.

ADRIAN, WALTER.
Give Me a Song; for voice and
piano by Walter Adrian.
© Oliver Ditson Co., Philadelphia; 26Jun47; EP15376.

ADRIANCE, BONNIE E
My Flower; words by Leo N.
Williams, music by Bonnie
E. Adriance. © Nordyke
Publishing Co., Los Angeles;
16Jul47; EP17487.

AGAY, DENES.
Gypsy Polka; by Denes Agay ...
for piano. © Bregman, Vocco
and Conn, inc., New York;
12Sep47; EP17125.

AGOSTI, GUIDO, 1901-
Due Liriche; [by] Guido Agosti.
Op. 3. © Carisch, s.a., Milan;
1Jul47; EP6209. For voice and
piano; French words. Contents.-
Appel (Ly-Y-hano) La Robe de
Soie (Chio Ko-fou)
Scherzo ed Epigramma; [by] Guido
Agosti. © Carisch, s.a., Milan;
1Jul47; EP6211. For voice and
piano; French words. Contents.-
Qui Prétend que l'Amour Est Bon?
Le Mépris du Mépris (Tristan L'
Hermite)
Tre Liriche; [by] Guido Agosti.
Op. 2. © Carisch, s.a., Milan;
1Jul47; EP6210. For voice and
piano. Contents.- Danse (Simonide)
Il Mio Diletto EPartito. Preghiera
(Francesco d' Albizzo)

AGUARIGUAY, pseud. See
hafaelli, Mario.

AHDE, SVERKER.
En 3Jönsnsvisa; musik; Sverker
Ahde. En Gammal Bateman; musik:
Sven Goon [pseud.] Tva visor av
Prins Wilhelm. © Reuter & Reu-
ter förlags, a.-b., Stockholm;
1Jan43; on 2 songs; EF6954-6955.

AHLEFELD, FRED WILLIAM, 1900-
My Heart Depends on You; [words]
by Stephen Hudak, [music by]
Fred Wm. Ahlefeld, 3rd [and]
Ruth Hile. © Superior Melodies
Publishing Co., Chicago; 15Jul47;
EP20416. Melody and chord sym-
bols, with words.

AHLERT, FRED.
Caravan of Dreams; lyric by
Edgar Leslie, music by Fred
Ahlert. © Bregman, Vocco and
Conn, inc., New York; 8Aug47;
EP16279.

AHLSTRAND, DAVID.
Oklahoma Pioneers; words by Mrs.
B. W. Ealey, music by David
Ahlstrand. © Nordyko Publish-
ing Co., Los Angeles; 1Jan47;
EP16835.
On, On, Old Glory; music by
David Ahlstrand, words by
Francis Robert Davis. ©
Francis Robert Davis, Oswego,
N. Y.; 10Aug47; EP16580.

AHRENS, CORA BELLE, 1891-
Ear Training ... by Cora B. Ahrens.
© Boosey & Hawkes (Canada) ltd.,
Toronto; grade 1, 11Nov47;
EP7179.

AJAYE, HALLIE Q
The Savior Soon' Is Coming Back to
Earth ... words by Rev. John L.
Bell, music by Hallie Q. Ajaye.
© John L. Bell, Belle Glade, Fla.;
14Nov47; EP18830. Close score;
SATB.

AKEY, CLEVE NICHOLAS, 1884-
Bands Away; [by] Cleve N. Akey,
[arr. by Howard Weeks] ©
Cleve N. Akey, Wisconsin Rapids,
Wis.; 10Jul47; EP16072. Parts:
band.

AKST, HARRY.
All My Love; words and music by Al
Jolson, Saul Chaplin and Harry
Akst. [Based on a theme by
Emile Waldteufel] © Remick
Music Corp., New York; 25Jun47;
EP15361.
Intrigue, from the ... picture
"Intrigue" ... words and music
by Sam Lerner and Harry Akst.
© Triangle Music Corp., New
York; 26Sep47; EP17697.

ALARCÓN LEAL, EDUARDO.
"Porque Te Quiero" y "Fiesta Brava"
... letra y música de Eduardo
Alarcón Leal. © Promotora His-
pano Americana de Música, s.a.,
México; 27Aug47; EP6704, 6703.

ALBANESE, LUIGI, d.1945.
Andante Religioso; [by] L. Alba-
nese. © Ricordi Americana,
S.A.E.C., Buenos Aires; 17May46;
EP6965. Score (violin and piano
or harp) and part.

ALBENIZ, ISAAC.
Granada; [by] I. Albeniz,
[arr. by] Andres Segovia.
© Celesta Publishing Co.,
New York; 1Aug47; on arrange-
ment; EP16240. For guitar
solo.
Granada ... plectrum guitar solo,
[by] I. Albéniz, arr. as played by
Harry Volpe. c1939. © Albert
Rocky Co., New York; 10Jan40; on
arrangement; EP20187.

ALBERTA SLIM, pseud. See
Edwards, Eric.

ALCANIZ FARRE, ARMANDO.
Cuando Llora el Corazón. (Tears
Fill My Heart) ... Spanish words
and music by Armando Alcaniz
Farre, English words by Joe Davis.
© Caribbean Music, inc., New York;
29Aug47; EP17077.

ALEXANDER, PERRY, 1895-
Ev'rybody's Buying My Love Song
(just to get a picture of you);
[words] by Jack Rollins [and]
Lou Shelly, and [music by] Perry
Alexander. © Dubonnet Music
Publishing, New York; 26Jun47;
EP15299.

ALEXANDER, W
Hep Step and Jump; by W. Alexander,
arr. by N. Paramor & N. Gold.
© Cinephonic Music Co., ltd.,
London; 21Mar47; EP6053. Piano-
conductor score (orchestra)
and parts.

ALFRED, J., pseud. See
Peltier, Alfred James.

ALKIRE, EDDIE. See
Alkire, Elbern H.

ALKIRE, ELBERN H   1907-
All about doggies ... All about
stars [and All about jugs.
Easton, Pa., E. Alkire Publica-
tions] [Spanish guitar lesson,
no. 8] © Elbern H. Alkire,
Easton, Pa.; on studies &
arrangement; 15Apr48; EP3557.
Down in Salinas; [by] Eddie Alkire.
Easton, Pa., E. Alkire Publica-
tions. © Elbern H. "Eddie" Al-
kire, Easton, Pa.; 16Dec47;
EP20431. For voice and 2 guitars.
Eavesdropping; [by] Eddie Alkire.
Easton, Pa., E. Alkire Publica-
tions. © Elbern H. "Eddie" Alkire,
Easton, Pa.; 16Dec47; EP20433.
For voice and 2 guitars.
Eddie Alkire's A Love Story ...
music for ... Spanish guitar,
[with words] Easton, Pa., E.
Alkire Publications, © Elbern
H. "Eddie" Alkire, Easton, Pa.;
10Sep47; on arrangement &
studies; EP18696.
Eddie Alkire's Be My Beau. Easton,
Pa., E. Alkire Publications. ©
Elbern H. "Eddie" Alkire, Easton,
Pa.; 16Dec47; EP20429. For voice
and 2 guitars.
Eddie Alkire's Darling, Keep on
Dreaming ... music for ...
Spanish guitar. Easton, Pa., E.
Alkire Publications. © Elbern
H. "Eddie" Alkire, Easton, Pa.;
10Sep47; on arrangement &
studies; EP18696.
Eddie Alkire's Dreams of Hawaii
... music for Spanish guitar,
[with words] Easton, Pa., E.
Alkire Publications © Elbern
H. "Eddie" Alkire, Easton,
Pa.; 25Aug47; on arrangement &
study; EP18700.
Eddie Alkire's In Old Virginia ...
music for ... Spanish guitar.
Easton, Pa., E. Alkire Publica-
tions. © Elbern H. "Eddie"
Alkire, Easton, Pa.; 10Sep47;
on arrangement & studies;
EP18697.
Eddie Alkire's When Dreams Come
True ... music for Spanish
guitar, [with words] Easton, Pa.,
Alkire Publications. © Elbern H.
"Eddie" Alkire, Easton, Pa.;
10Sep47; on arrangement &
studies; EP18707.
Eddie Alkire's You're My Only
Sweetheart ... music for ...
Spanish guitar [with words]
Easton, Pa., E. Alkire Publica-
tions. © Elbern H. "Eddie"
Alkire, Easton, Pa.; 10Sep47; on
arrangement & studies; EP18695.
Flower Lois ... By Eddie Alkire.
[Easton, Pa., Eddie Alkire
Publications] © Elbern H.
"Eddie" Alkire, Easton, Pa.;
24Jul47; on arrangement & pre-
paratory studies; EP17091.
For Hawaiian guitar solo or duet.

218

ALKIRE, ELBERN H. Cont'd.

I'm a Well Adjusted Cowboy; by Eddie Alkire. Easton, Pa., E. Alkire Publications. © Elbern H. "Eddie" Alkire, Easton, Pa.; 19Jul47; on changes in words and music; EP15984. For voice and piano, with chord symbols.

I'm Lonely for You ... [by] Eddie Alkire. Easton, Pa., E. Alkire Publications. © Elbern H. "Eddie" Alkire, Easton, Pa.; 16Dec47; on words, arrangement & counter melody; EP20435. For voice and 2 guitars.

It's Been So Long; [for] Spanish guitar ... [by] Eddie Alkire, [with words] Easton, Pa., E. Alkire Publications. © Elbern H. "Eddie" Alkire, Easton, Pa., 10Sep47; on arrangement; & studios; EP18699.

It's Been So Long Since You Said "So Long"; by Eddie Alkire. [Easton, Pa., E. Alkire Publications] © Elbern H. "Eddie" Alkire, Easton, Pa.; 19Jul47; EP15986. For voice and piano, with chord symbols.

Johnnie's Blue; [by] Eddie Alkire. Easton, Pa., E. Alkire Publications. © Elbern H. "Eddie" Alkire, Easton, Pa.; 16Dec47; EP20430. For voice and 2 guitars.

Kahdewatah ... [by] Eddie Alkire. Easton, Pa., E. Alkire Publications. © Elbern H. "Eddie" Alkire, Easton, Pa.; 16Dec47; EP20432. For voice and 2 guitars.

Lazy Little Latin; by Eddie Alkire, (melody from a Mexican folk song) [Easton, Pa., E. Alkire Publications] © Elbern H. "Eddie" Alkire, Easton, Pa.; 40ct47; on lyrics & arrangement; EP18705. For 2 treble voices with chord symbols.

A Love Story; by "Eddie" Alkire. Easton, Pa., E. Alkire Publications. © Elbern H. "Eddie" Alkire, Easton, Pa.; 19Jul47; on changes in music & new words; EP15985. For voice and piano, with chord symbols.

Riding on the Prairie; [by] Eddie Alkire. Easton, Pa., E. Alkire Publications. © Elbern H. "Eddie" Alkire, Easton, Pa.; 16Dec47; EP20427. For voice and 2 guitars.

Silent Night; [arr. by] Eddie Alkire. Easton, Pa., E. Alkire Publications. © Elbern H. "Eddie" Alkire, Easton, Pa.; 20Nov47; on arrangement; EP20436. For voice and 2 guitars.

Symptoms of Love; by Eddie Alkire. © Elbern H. "Eddie" Alkire, Easton, Pa.; 30Sep47; on changes in words & music; EP17694. For voice and piano, with chord symbols.

Two Hearts Will Know; [by] Eddie Alkire. Easton, Pa., E. Alkire Publications. © Elbern H. "Eddie" Alkire, Easton, Pa.; 16Dec47; on words, arrangement & counter melody; EP20434. For voice and 2 guitars.

Waiting for You; by Eddie Alkire, (melody from Chopin prelude no. 7) [Easton, Pa., E. Alkire Publications] © Elbern H. "Eddie" Alkire, Easton, Pa.; 40ct47; on lyrics and arrangement; EP18706. Includes versions for voice and piano and for 2 treble voices, with chord symbols.

When Dreams Come True; by Eddie Alkire. [Easton, Pa., E. Alkire Publications] © Elbern H. "Eddie" Alkire, Easton, Pa.; 19Jul47; EP15987. For voice and piano, with chord symbols.

You and I; [by] Eddie Alkire. Easton, Pa., E. Alkire Publications. © Elbern H. "Eddie" Alkire, Easton, Pa.; 16Dec47; on arrangement & counter melody; EP20428. For voice and 2 guitars.

You Tell Me Your Dream, (I'll toll you mino); rev. lyrics and arr. by Eddie Alkire. [Easton, Pa., E. Alkire Publications] © Elbern H. "Eddie" Alkire, Easton, Pa.; 24Jul47; on new lyrics and arrangement; EP17090. For Hawaiian guitar solo or duet.

You're Mine; by Eddie Alkire, (melody from an old Polynesian theme) [Easton, Pa., E. Alkire Publications] © Elbern H. "Eddie" Alkire, Easton, Pa.; 40ct47; on music and lyric adaptation; EP18704. For 2 treble voices with chord symbols.

You're My Only Sweetheart; by Eddie Alkire. Easton, Pa., E. Alkire Publications. © Elbern H. "Eddie" Alkire, Easton, Pa.; 30Sep47; on arrangement & changes in words & music; EP17692. For voice and piano, with chord symbols.

ALLAIRE, BLANCHE LUPTON.
Roll Does Eyes Around, Honey; words and music by Blanche Lupton Allaire. [a1946] © Blanche Lupton Allaire, Hackensack, N. J.; 12Sep47; EP17076.

[ALLEGRA, ARMAND T]
I'm Afraid; [by Armand T. Allegra] © Armand T. Allegra, Hartford; 21Nov47; EP20272. Melody and words.

ALLEN, BARCLAY.
Beginner's Boogie; by Barclay Allen [and] Bob Ballard. © Martin Music, Hollywood, Calif.; 18Aug47; EP16219. For piano solo.

ALLEN, GIL.
I'm Out to Forget Tonight; by Gil Allen. © Algonquin Music, inc., New York; 25Sep47; EP17337. For voice and piano, with chord symbols.

ALLEN, ROY.
Spring Is the Time for Love; words by E. P. Domen, music by Roy Allen. © Nordyke Publishing Co., Los Angeles; 23Sep47; EP20032.

ALLEN, RUE KELLOGG, 1885-
On My Pinto Pony; by Rue Kellogg Allen. Piano solo. © Harold Flammer, inc., New York; 28Jul47; EP16260.

On the Tester; piano solo by Rue Kellogg Allen. © Harold Flammer, inc., New York; 28Jul47; EP16258.

ALLENDER, N   D
Go to Sleep Our Baby Boy; words and music by N. D. Allender. © Bob Wills Music, inc., Hollywood, Calif.; 14Nov47; EP18773.

ALLEVA, JOHN J
Have a Little Patience;... Music and lyrics by John J. Alleva, [arr. by Robert Girlamo] Philadelphia, E. B. Swisher. © John J. Alleva, Norristown, Pa.; 1Dec47; EP19555.

ALLUE, JORGE GONZÁLEZ. See Gonzalez Allue, Jorge.

ALLYN, GLADYS FERN.
June Time and You; words and music by Gladys Fern Allyn. © Nordyke Publishing Co., Los Angeles; 10May47; EP16827.

ALMANGANO, SERGIO, 1914-
Tarántola; musica di Sergio Almangano. © Carisch, s.a., Milan; 18Jan47; EF7159. Piano-conductor score (orchestra) and parts.

ALOMA, HAL.
The Night You Said Aloha to Me; words and music by Hal Aloma and John Leal, [arr. by Betty B. Glynn] (Oahu E-Z method, [lesson] 70EZ) © Oahu Publishing Co., Cleveland; 14Oct47; on arrangement; EP19606. For voice and guitar. Includes lesson on technical exercises in C# minor tuning and the discussion Music of Today.

ALPERT, S   L
The Broadcaster, march [by] S. L. Alpert, arr. by Antonio Zordan. © Chart Music Publishing House, inc., Chicago; 13Nov47; on arrangement; EP19127. For accordion solo.

ALPHENAAR, GERARD, ed. and comp.
Chapel Voluntaries; for organ, harmonium or piano (with Hammond organ registration) ed. and comp. by Gerard Alphenaar. © Edward B. Marks Music Corp., New York; bk. 1, 24Jul47; EP17242.

ALTAMIRANO, LUIS DÍAZ. See Díaz Altamirano, Luis.

ALTER, LOUIS.
(Living in a Big Way) Fido and Me; lyric by Edward Heyman, music by Louis Alter ... [From the M-G-M picture] "Living in a Big Way." © Leo Feist, inc., New York; 5Jun47; EP16227.

ALVAREZ RIOS, MARIO.
Shadows of the Past ... Words and music by Don Mario (Don Mario Alvarez Rios) © Antobal Music Co., New York; 15Jul47; EP16962.

ALWYN, WILLIAM, 1905-
Suite of Scottish Dances; arr. for small orchestra by William Alwyn. © Oxford Univ. Press, London; 20Oct47; on arrangement; EF6916.

AMBROISE, VICTOR, 1888-   arr.
Excerpts from Concertos; arr. for piano solos by Victor Ambroise. © Lawrence Wright Music Co., ltd., London; 24Oct47; on arrangement; EF7005.

AMBROSE, PAUL, 1868-1941.
Tomorrow Comes the Song; [by] Paul Ambrose. Op.42. Arr. by Hugh Gordon [pseud., arr. by] Maltbie D. Babcock. © The Arthur P. Schmidt Co., Boston; 1Jul47; on arrangement; EP15392. Score: TTBB and piano.

AMBROSIO, AMEDEO D', 1909-
Por Voi, Signora ... composto da A. d'Ambrosio. © Carisch, s.a., Milan; 10Aug47; EF6249. For accordion solo.

AMES, J. J. pseud. See Thompson, John.

AMFITHEATROF, DANIELE.
Lost Moment; lyrics by Jack Brooks, music by Daniele Amfitheatrof. From ... "The Lost Moment." © Robert Music Corp., New York; 20Nov47; EP19065.

AMSTELL, BILLY.
Don't Fuss ... composed and arr. by Billy Amstell. © Peter Maurice Music Co., ltd., New York; 1Dec47; EF7355. Piano-conductor score (orchestra) and parts.

AMSTERDAM, MOREY.
I Cain't Get offa My Horse; words
and music by Morey Amsterdam.
© Leo Feist, inc., New York;
30Apr47; EP16228.

ANCLIFFE, CHARLES.
You with the Mona Lisa Eyes;
written and composed by C. S.
Diamond and Charles Ancliffe. ©
Diamond Music Publishing Co.,
London; 14Aug47; EF6259. For
voice and piano; melody also in
tonic sol-fa notation.

ANDERS, T., pseud. See
Reuterskiöld, Lennart.

ANDERSEN, ARTHUR OLAF, 1880-   arr.
Sing, Girls Sing! Three-part
treble choruses arr. by Arthur
Olaf Andersen. © Hall &
McCreary Co., Chicago; 9Oct47;
on arrangements & original
compositions; EP17989.

ANDERSEN, C   WESLEY, 1907-
Lullaby for Mary's Son; (S.S.A.)
words by Leith Shackel, music by
C. Wesley Andersen. © Paul A.
Schmitt Music Co., Minneapolis;
27Oct47; EP18925.

ANDERSEN, KAI NORMANN, 1900-
Dagmar Revyen, 1947; [by] Kai
Normann Andersen, [words by]
Mogens Dam [and] Poeten [pseud.]
© Wilhelm Hansen, Musik-Forlag,
Copenhagen; 8May47; on 7 songs.
Contents.- Det Er Jo Ogsaa No'et,
Der Gør (Mogens Dam) (© EP6347)
Naar Man Elsker Hinanden Maa
Himlen Vente (Mogens Dam) (©
EP6341) Købt og Betalt (Mogens
Dam) (© EP6342) Natten Er Til
Bare for Os (Poeten) (© EF6343)
Kan Man Nu Forstaa Det? (Mogens
Dam) (© EF6345) Se Op og Smil--
Vaer Optimist (Poeten) (©
EP6345) Her Kommer Jeg med det
Lille, Jeg Har (Poeten) (©
EP6346)

Det Er Jo Ogsaa No'et, Der Gør. See his
Dagmar Revyen, 1947.

Her Kommer Jeg med det Lille, Jeg Har.
See his Dagmar Revyen, 1947.

Kan Man Nu Forstaa Det? See his
Dagmar Revyen, 1947.

Købt og Betalt. See his Dagmar Revyen,
1947.

Naar Man Elsker Hinanden Maa Himlen Vente.
See his Dagmar Revyen, 1947.

Natten Er Til Bare for Os. See his
Dagmar Revyen, 1947.

Se Op og Smil-- Vaer Optimist. See his
Dagmar Revyen, 1947.

ANDERSON, DUKE.
Just by Chance; words by Artie
Clark, music by Duke Anderson.
© Nordyke Publishing Co., Los
Angeles; 16Jul47; EP17598.

ANDERSON, IRMA KLEINFELD.
I Bowed in the Shadow of the Cross;
by Irma Kleinfeld Anderson. ©
Irma Kleinfeld Anderson, Providence; 35ep47; EP18926. Close
score; SATB.

ANDERSON, JOSEPH.
The Open Sky Home; words and music
by Joseph Anderson. © Nordyke
Publishing Co., Los Angeles;
25Jun47; EP17411.

ANDERSON, LEROY.
Fiddle-Faddle ... by Leroy Anderson. © Mills Music, inc., New
York; 29Aug47; EP17939. Score
(string orchestra), piano-
conductor score and parts.

ANDERSON, MARION.
Carolare; ten carols for movement,
arr. by Marion Anderson. ©
The Oxford University Press,
London; 19Dec46; on arrangement;
EF6101. For piano solo.

ANDERSON, ROBERT.
Technicolored Garden; words and
music by Robert Anderson. ©
Robert Anderson, Hector, Minn.;
28Jul47; EP16016.

ANDERSON, ROBERT E   1903-
Introspection; and Retrospection;
two miniatures for piano, by
Robert E. Anderson. San Francisco, W. Webster. © Robert E.
Anderson, San Francisco;
20Oct47; EP18229.

ANDERSON, WILLIAM H   1882-
As I walked in Bethlehem ... S.A.T.B.
Words by Audrey Alexander Brown,
music by W. H. Anderson. © West-
ern Music Co., ltd., Vancouver,
B. C., Can.; 26Nov47; EF7181.

As Mary Sings ... for ladies' voices
(S.S.A.) words by Jean Paul Tal-
bot, music by W. H. Anderson. ©
Western Music Co., ltd., Vancouver,
B. C., Can.; 26Nov47; EF7185.

Bread of the World; communion
motet for S.A.T.B., [words by]
Bishop H. Hober, [music by]
Hugh Garland [pseud.] ©
Western Music Co., ltd.,
Vancouver, B. C., Can.; 3Nov47;
EF6926.

Five Introits and Vespers ...
[by] W. H. Anderson. ©
Western Music Co., ltd.,
Vancouver, B. C., Can.; 1Nov47;
EF6925. Close score; SATB.

I Know a Bank; for ladies' voices
(S.S.A.) a capella, [words by]
W. Shakespeare, [music by] Hugh
Garland [pseud.] © Western Music
Co., ltd., Vancouver, B. C.,
Can.; 20Sep47; EF6599.

Liberty; part song for mixed
voices (S.A.T.B.) [words by]
Kathleen Blanchard, [music by]
W. H. Anderson. © Western Music
Co., ltd., Vancouver, B. C.,
Can.; 20Sep47; EF6598.

Music, When Soft Voices Die;
S.S.A., words by P. B. Shelley,
music by Hugh Garland [pseud.]
© Western Music Co., ltd., Van-
couver, B. C., Can.; 22Sep47;
EF6597.

Popping Corn; unison song, words by
R. H. Grenville, music by W. H.
Anderson. © Western Music Co.,
ltd., Vancouver, B. C., Can.;
26Nov47; EF7184.

ANDERSON, WILLIAM HENRY, 1882-
The Holy Child; carol anthem for
S.A.T.B., words by Constance
Barbour, music by W. H. Anderson.
© C. C. Birchard & Co., Boston;
20Nov47; EP19032.

ANDREW, JOHN FRED, 1892-
The Gift Divine; [by] J. Fred
Andrew. © John Fred Andrew,
Fort Wayne; 22Oct47; EP19043.
Close score; SATB.

ANDREW, PAUL.
The Winding Road; arr. for male
voices by T. J. Hewitt, words by
David Arale, music by Paul Andrew.
© Keith, Prowse & Co., ltd.,
London; 26Sep47; on arrangement;
EF6776.

ANDREWS, H   K
Rest; the words by Christina
Rosetti, set to music by H. K.
Andrews. © The Oxford
University Press, London;
3Jul47; EF7185.

ANDREWS, JAMES FINLEY, 1907-
Afraid of the Rain; words and music
by J. F. Andrews ... [arr. by]
E. Cox Todd ... [and] Gene
Worth. © James Finley Andrews,
Portland, Or.; 10ct47; EP18109.

THE ANDREWS BROTHERS.
Go to Sleep, My Darling Curly Head;
words and music by the Andrews
brothers. (c1946) © D. Davis &
Co., pty. ltd., Sydney; 15Oct47;
EF7168.

ANÈPETA, G
Cchiù Zitto ... di Anèpeta,
[words by] Fiorelli. Rome,
Vesuvio. © Edward Rossi, New
York; 16Jul47; EF6306. Melody
and chord symbols, with words.

ANGEL, JAMES.
Villagers All, this Frosty Tide;
words from "The Wind in the
Willows" by Kenneth Grahame,
music by James Angel. Arr. as
a two part song by the composer.
© Novello & Co., ltd., London;
30Aug47; EF6554.

ANGELO, LANI D'   See
D'Angelo, Lani.

ANGELONI, JOHN.
In France They Say - Tout Jour
l'Amour Tout Jour; words and
music by John Angeloni, arr. by
Dan J. Michaud. © John Angeloni,
Los Angeles; 25Aug47; EP16971.

Lo, It's a Meadow Lark! Words &
music by John Angeloni, arr. by
Dan J. Michaud. © John
Angeloni, Los Angeles;
9Jul47; EP16236.

Remomber? words and music by John
Angeloni, arr. by Dan J. Michaud.
© John Angeloni, Los Angeles;
25Aug47; EP16970.

ANGELSON, CHRISTY ANDREW.
Zeramba; words and music by
Christy Andrew Angelson. © Nordyke Publishing Co., Los Angeles; 25May46; EP19552.

ANGULO RODRÍGUEZ, PEDRO, 1923-
Mujer, No Puedo Perdonarte ...
letra y música de Pedro Angulo
Rodríguez. © Pedro Angulo Rodríguez, Habana; 1Aug47; EF7169.

ANIK, H   E
Pensée Élégiaque; [by] H. E. Anik.
(In Alphonaar, Gerard, ed. and
comp. Chapul Voluntaries. bk.1,
p.4-5) © Edward B. Marks Music
Corp., New York; 23Jul47;
EP16496. For organ solo or
harmonium or piano; includes
registration for Hammond organ.

ANSON, BILL.
Some Things Will Never Change;
based on Tschaikowsky's "Waltz
of the flowers," by Ted Mossman and Bill Anson. © Santly-
Joy, inc., New York; 23Oct47;
EP18296. For voice and piano,
with chord symbols.

ANSON, GEORGE.
The Old Witch; [by] George
Anson. © Oliver Ditson Co.,
Philadelphia; 11Aug47; EP16300.
For piano solo.

ANTHEIL, GEORGE.
Fourth Symphony, "1942." See his
Symphony, no. 4.

(Symphony, no.4) Fourth Symphony,
"1942," [by] George Antheil.
Full score. © Boosey & Hawkes,
inc., New York; 28Mar47; EP16065.

ANTOINE, BROTHER, 1900-
Apple Blossoms; piano solo for
young players, by Frère Antoine. © Bach Music Co. (Henry
Dellafield, sole owner), Boston;
10Oct47; EP18098.

The Drum Major; piano solo for
young players, by Frère Antoine. © Bach Music Co. (Henry
Dellafield, sole owner), Boston;
10Oct47; EP18100.

ANTOINE, BROTHER. Cont'd.
Sunrise; piano solo for young
players, by Frère Antoine.
© Bach Music Co. (Henry Dellafield, sole owner), Boston;
10ct47; EP18099.

The Young Hero; piano solo for
young players, by Frère Antoine. © Bach Music Co. (Henry
Dellafield, sole owner), Boston;
10ct47; EP18101.

ANZI, GIOVANNI D'.
(È Bello Qualche Volta Andare a
Piedi) Mattinata Fiorentina
... dalla rivista "È Bello
Qualche Volta Andare a Piedi."
Parole di M. Galdieri, musica
di G. d'Anzi. © Edizioni
Curci, s.a., Milan; 26Sep41;
EP6558.

Maria Mia.... (Marie-Laurence)
Lyric by Carl Sigman, music by
G. d'Anzi, French lyric by
Jacques Plante, Italian lyric
by M. Galdieri, [arr. by Rob-
bins Music Corp.) © Robbins
Music Corp., New York; 27May47;
on English lyric and arrange-
ment; EP17735. French and Eng-
lish words.
Mattinata Fiorentina. See his È Bella
Qualche Volta Andare a Piedi.

AQUINO, ANTONIO G
Your Money and You; words and
music by ... A. G. Aquino.
[c1945] © Nordyke Publishing
Co., Los Angeles; 27Oct47;
EP16306.

ARANT, BURTON.
Dolly's Lullaby; [by] Burton
Arant. © Theodore Presser Co.,
Philadelphia; 26Jun47; EP15374.
For piano, 4 hands.

ARBELAEZ, HANNIBAL.
Happy Hitchy Hiker; words & music
by Hannibal Arbelaez. © Nordyke Publishing Co., Los Angeles; 15Aug46; EP19933.

AROE, JESÚS GUZMÁN.
Murio como un "Heroe" ... por
Jesús Guzmán Aroe. © Jesús
Guzmán Aroe, Houston, Tex.;
1Jul47; EP15806. For voice
and piano.

ARFINE, LEWIS IRVING, 1902-
Comprehensive Chordal Etudes ...
by Lewis Arfine, for saxophone
or clarinet. © Lewis Arfine,
New York; 23Jun47; EP15302.

ARLYS, FRED, 1908-
Avez-vous vu Louise? Paroles de
André Tabet & Bruno Coquatrix,
musique de Fred Arlys & Bruno
Coquatrix. © Editions Roger
Bernstein, Paris; 31Jan47;
EP5887.

ARMA, PAUL, pseud. See
Weisshaus, Imre.

ARMENGOL, MARIO RUIZ. See
Ruiz Armengol, Mario.

ARMSTRONG, LOUIS.
Louis Satchmo Armstrong's Immortal
Trumpet Solos; [comp. by Lee
Castle] © Leeds Music Corp.,
New York; v.1, 27Jun47; EP15366.
Score (trumpet and piano) and
part. Principally by Louis
Armstrong.

ARNE, THOMAS.
[The Tempest] Where the Bee Sucks
(from 'The Tempest'), air by
Thomas Arne, arr. for mixed
voices (S.C.T.B.) [by] Norman
Stone, [words by] Shakespeare.
© The Oxford University Press,
London; 3Jul47; on arrangement;
EP6126.
Where the Bee Sucks. See his The Tempest

ARNEY, JACQUES.
Barcarolle d'Automne; [by] Jacques
Arney. © L. Maillochon, Éditeur
de musique, Paris; 18Jun23;
EP6803. Score (violin and
piano) and part.

Fragment Lyrique ... [by] Jacques
Arney. © L. Maillochon, Paris;
18Jun24; EP6804. Score (violin
and piano) and part.

ARNOLD, J   H
Oxford Liturgical Settings of the
Holy Communion; ed. by J. H.
Arnold. © Oxford Univ. Press,
London; no.6, 29May47; no.7,
18Sep47; EP6123, 6914. By Mar-
tin Shaw; no.6 for S.A.B. unacc.;
no.7 for S.S.A. or T.T.B. unacc.
Simple Three-Part Evening
Canticles; (eight tones & faux-
bourdons) S.A.A. or T.T.B.,
without organ, [by] J. H.
Arnold. © The Oxford Univ.
Press, London; 18Sep47; EP6915.

ARNOLD, MALCOLM.
(Concerto, horn) 2nd Movement
from Concerto for horn & orchestra; [by] Malcolm Arnold, arr.
by the composer. © Alfred
Lengnick & Co., ltd., London;
12Sep47; EP6743. Score (horn
and piano) and part.
2nd Movement from Concerto for horn & or
chestra. See his Concerto, horn.

ARNOLD, TONY.
Our Baby; words and music by
Tony Arnold. © Clover Music
Co., ltd., London; 19Jun47;
EP6353.

ARRIEU, CLAUDE, pseud. See also
Simon, Louise Marie.
Prélude, forlane et gigue; pour
piano, [by] Claude Arrieu. ©
Enoch & Cie., Paris; 28Mar47;
EP5320.

ARTER, WALTER J
The High Cost of Living; words
and music by Walter J. Arter.
© Nordyke Publishing Co., Los
Angeles; 15Feb47; EP19934.

ARTHUR, WILLIAM.
Absolutely Impossible; words by
Claude W. Vaughn, music by
William Arthur. © Nordyke
Publishing Co., Los Angeles;
25Jun47; EP17568.
All Over Again; words by Christina
Cheever, music by William Arthur.
© Nordyke Publishing Co., Los
Angeles; 27Jul47; EP19467.
America, My Native Land; words by
Grover S. Slayter, music by
William Arthur. © Nordyke Pub-
lishing Co., Los Angeles;
9Apr47; EP18214.
American Girl; words by Louis
Sarcinella, music by William
Arthur. [c1946] © Nordyke Pub-
lishing Co., Los Angeles; 28Jan47;
EP19786.
As Fancy Free (as a melody);
words by Richard Wm. Chesley,
music by William Arthur. ©
Nordyke Publishing Co., Los
Angeles; 11Jul47; EP17570.
As Long As We Live; words by Lee
Goodpasture, music by William
Arthur. © Nordyke Publishing
Co., Los Angeles; 19Jun47;
EP17424.
As Time Goes By; words by Zoltan
Domik, music by William Arthur
© Nordyke Publishing Co., Los
Angeles; 11Jul47; EP17571.
Beautiful, Beautiful Ohio; words
by Ruth Phelps, music by William
Arthur. © Nordyke Publishing
Co., Los Angeles; 22Jul47;
EP19726.

The Beautiful Thing That Is You;
words by Adele Steede, music by
William Arthur. [c1946] © Nor-
dyke Publishing Co., Los Angeles;
29Jan47; EP19495.
Because of You; words by Margaret
Iarussi, music by William Arthur.
© Nordyke Publishing Co., Los
Angeles; 28Jar47; EP16749.
Believe Me, Dear; words by Wilfrid
Dusseault, music by William
Arthur. © Nordyke Publishing
Co., Los Angeles; 27Mar47;
EP16720.
Bugs Bunny; words by Eleanor
V. Williams, music by William
Arthur. © Nordyke Publishing
Co., Los Angeles; 16Jul47;
EP17564.
Can't You See It My Way for a
Change; words by Winnie Daniel,
music by William Arthur. ©
Nordyke Publishing Co., Los
Angeles; 28Mar47; EP16785.
Chicks Come Home To Roost; words
by Irene Brewster Owen, music
by William Arthur. © Nordyke
Publishing Co., Los Angeles;
5Jun47; EP16866.
Combination to My Heart; words by
Charley Middlestetter, music by
William Arthur. © Nordyke
Publishing Co., Los Angeles;
1Jun47; EP16953.
Counting the Falling Stars; words
by Dona Rae [pseud.), music by
William Arthur. © Nordyke Pub-
lishing Co., Los Angeles; 29Apr47;
EP16847.
Dancing on the Stars; words by
Howard O. Long, music by William
Arthur. © Nordyke Publishing
Co., Los Angeles; 31Jul47;
EP19730.
Darling, I Love You I Do; words by
Ricky Milt Wood, music by William
Arthur. © Nordyke Publishing Co.,
Los Angeles; 10Jun47; EP16864.
Darling, I Mean Them Still; words
by Lois Manchester, music by
William Arthur. © Nordyke Pub-
lishing Co., Los Angeles; 1Jun47;
EP16849.
A Dear Little Someone That
Makes Me Think of You; words by
Dorothy Olds George, music by
William Arthur. © Nordyke
Publishing Co., Los Angeles;
29Jul47; EP17587.
Dear One; words by Juanie Fatzinger,
music by William Arthur. ©
Nordyke Publishing Co., Los
Angeles; 17May47; EP16848.
Dirty Moon; words by Glen Smith,
music by William Arthur. ©
Nordyke Publishing Co., Los
Angeles; 24Jul47; EP17586.
The Doghouse Cafe; words by Er-
nest Watson, music by William
Arthur. © Nordyke Publishing
Co., Los Angeles; 5Aug47;
EP17594.
Don't Deny It; words by Del Carter,
music by William Arthur.
© Nordyke Publishing Co., Los
Angeles; 1Jun47; EP16940.
Dream Girl; words by Nellie
Schumacher, music by William
Arthur. © Nordyke Publishing
Co., Los Angeles; 25Jun47;
EP17632.
Dreaming Is Believing; words by
Shirley Hammond, music by
William Arthur. © Nordyke
Publishing Co., Los Angeles;
29Jan47; EP19437.
Dreams of You; words by Julia Pal-
mer, music by William Arthur.
© Nordyke Publishing Co., Los
Angeles; 24Jul47; EP19731.

221

ARTHUR, WILLIAM. Cont'd.

Empty Arms; words by Irma V. Dee, music by William Arthur. © Nordyke Publishing Co., Los Angeles; 25Jun47; EP17630.

The End of a Wonderful Dream; words by Zoltan Domik, music by William Arthur. © Nordyke Publishing Co., Los Angeles; 28Mar47; EP16768.

Fond Memories; words by Ella Redfearn, music by William Arthur. © Nordyke Publishing Co., Los Angeles; 12Apr47; EP16800.

The Girls of Idaho; words by Hattie E. Morgan, music by William Arthur. © Nordyke Publishing Co., Los Angeles; 29Aug47; EP20347.

Got a Kiss on My Mind; words by Sonny O'Day [pseud.], music by William Arthur. © Nordyke Publishing Co., Los Angeles; 29Jul47; EP17624.

Green Pastures; words by Esther M. Mostert, music by William Arthur. © Nordyke Publishing Co., Los Angeles; 10Jun47; EP16950.

Happy; words by Mildred Coleman, music by William Arthur. © Nordyke Publishing Co., Los Angeles; 28Jul47; EP19938.

Has Someone Taken My Place? Words by Virginia Lee Somers, music by William Arthur. © Nordyke Publishing Co., Los Angeles; 15May47; EP17527.

Has Someone Taken My Place? Words by Virginia Lee Somers, music by William Arthur. © Nordyke Publishing Co., Los Angeles; 17May47; EP16930.

Haunting Melody; words by Katharine M. Patty, music by William Arthur. © Nordyke Publishing Co., Los Angeles; 29May47; EP16922.

Have You Found Somebody New? Words by Tony Rogers, music by William Arthur. © Nordyke Publishing Co., Los Angeles; 10May47; EP16858.

Heading for the End of the Rainbow; words by John H. Stone, music by William Arthur. © Nordyke Publishing Co., Los Angeles; 27Mar47; EP16727.

Hello, Little Darling, Hello! Words by E. Arthur Johnson, music by William Arthur. © Nordyke Publishing Co., Los Angeles; 16Jul47; EP17622.

Home to My Heart; words by Eleanor McDonough, music by William Arthur. © Nordyke Publishing Co., Los Angeles; 16Dec46; EP16721.

How Can I Tell You? Words by Billie Hemrick, music by William Arthur. [c1946] © Nordyke Publishing Co., Los Angeles; EP19939.

How Could You Do This to Ke? Words by Thelma Anne Dean, music by William Arthur. © Nordyke Publishing Co., Los Angeles; 14Mar47; EP16760.

How Far Is Heaven? Words by Charlie Orem, music by William Arthur. © Nordyke Publishing Co., Los Angeles; 11Jul47; EP17529.

How Your Love Came to Me; words by J. Stuart Oates, music by William Arthur. © Nordyke Publishing Co., Los Angeles; 22Jul47; EP19513.

I Asked the Birds to Sing; words by Agnes E. Harris, music by William Arthur. © Nordyke Publishing Co., Los Angeles; 22Jul47; EP19517.

I Caught a Rainbow; words by Grace L. Davis, music by William Arthur. © Nordyke Publishing Co., Los Angeles; 24May47; EP16879.

I Don't Want To Be Adored; words by Charlotte Turman, music by William Arthur. © Nordyke Publishing Co., Los Angeles; 22Apr47; EP16900.

I Had a Lovely Dream; words by Mrs. Harry Clevenson, music by William Arthur. © Nordyke Publishing Co., Los Angeles; 16Jul47; EP17615.

I Have That Certain Feeling; words by Helen Beall, music by William Arthur. © Nordyke Publishing Co., Los Angeles; 12Apr47; EP16804.

I Haven't a Heart; words by June Silva, music by William Arthur. © Nordyke Publishing Co., Los Angeles; 27Mar47; EP16805.

I Knew What Heaven Could Be; words by Elma Hughes, music by William Arthur. © Nordyke Publishing Co., Los Angeles; 22Jul47; EP19523.

I Need You; music by William Arthur, words by Albert K. Ysabel. © Nordyke Publishing Co., Los Angeles; 29Apr47; EP16874.

I Still Love You; words by Marie Tarkelson, music by William Arthur. © Nordyke Publishing Co., Los Angeles; 21Feb47; EP19516.

I Was Never in Love Before; words by Frank Casciottolo, music by William Arthur. © Nordyke Publishing Co., Los Angeles; 16Jul47; EP17614.

I Will Write You a Love Song; words by Elvia R. Lacarra, music by William Arthur. © Nordyke Publishing Co., Los Angeles; 19Jun47; EP17532.

I Wouldn't Know; words by Eva Bailey Reed, music by William Arthur. © Nordyke Publishing Co., Los Angeles; 28Mar47; EP16754.

I'll Wait for You; words by Ethel Cormier, music by William Arthur. © Nordyke Publishing Co., Los Angeles; 10May47; EP16882.

I'm Burning a Torch for You; words by L. B. (Bill) Bryant, jr., music by William Arthur. © Nordyke Publishing Co., Los Angeles; 5Jun47; EP17574.

I'm Going to Get a Patent; words by Vennette White Sherman, music by William Arthur. © Nordyke Publishing Co., Los Angeles; 28Mar47; EP16786.

I'm Going to Marry Marion; words by Joe Dervin, music by William Arthur. © Nordyke Publishing Co., Los Angeles; 5Aug47; EP19799.

I'm in Heaven with You; words by Andrew A. Preader, music by William Arthur. © Nordyke Publishing Co., Los Angeles; 11Jun47; EP17580.

I'm in Love with You; words by Adele Steeds, music by William Arthur. © Nordyke Publishing Co., Los Angeles; 27Mar47; EP16808.

I'm Recording a Memory of You in My Heart; words by Roberta Summer, music by William Arthur. © Nordyke Publishing Co., Los Angeles; 9Nov46; EP19792.

It Happened in Spring; words by Betty J. Carter, music by William Arthur. © Nordyke Publishing Co., Los Angeles; 25Jun47; EP17604.

It's About Time; words by Milton H. Pairbank, music by William Arthur. © Nordyke Publishing Co., Los Angeles; 27Mar47; EP16881.

I've Been Dreaming Too Long; words by William Solly, music by William Arthur. © Nordyke Publishing Co., Los Angeles; 29Mar47; EP16733.

I've Chased My Blues (to the blue horizon); words by William J. Cramer, music by Nordyke Publishing Co., Los Angeles; [c1946] © Nordyke Publishing Co., Los Angeles; 12Apr47; EP16772.

I've Closed the Door on You; words by Emily D. Stowell, music by William Arthur. © Nordyke Publishing Co., Los Angeles; 14Nov47; EP19697.

I've Cried My Last Time over You; words by Lois G. Holden, music by William Arthur. © Nordyke Publishing Co., Los Angeles; 31Jul47; EP19496.

I've Discovered Heaven; words by Edythe Stryker, music by William Arthur. © Nordyke Publishing Co., Los Angeles; 10Jun47; EP16898.

I've Never Tried to Forget You; words by Louise Wright Howard, music by William Arthur. © Nordyke Publishing Co., Los Angeles; 12Apr47; EP16773.

Just Another Number in Your Book; words by Harold Harris, music by William Arthur. © Nordyke Publishing Co., Los Angeles; 25Jun47; EP17596.

Just for Two; words by Myrtie Blood, music by William Arthur. © Nordyke Publishing Co., Los Angeles; 5Jun47; EP16779.

Last Night I Dreamed a Dream of You; words by Nell Johnson, music by William Arthur. © Nordyke Publishing Co., Los Angeles; 15Feb47; EP17545.

Let's Fall in Love; words by Elvon Kinney, music by William Arthur. © Nordyke Publishing Co., Los Angeles; 3Sep47; EP19969.

Life Is a Dream; words by Mary Alice Duncan, music by William Arthur. © Nordyke Publishing Co., Los Angeles; 3Sep47; EP19344.

A Lifetime with You; words by Bob Wright, music by William Arthur. © Nordyke Publishing Co., Los Angeles; 29Jul47; EP17595.

The Lights Above; words by Les Marino, music by William Arthur. © Nordyke Publishing Co., Los Angeles; 29Apr47; EP16814.

The Little White House; words by Bessie Wright, music by William Arthur. © Nordyke Publishing Co., Los Angeles; 16Dec46; EP19479.

Living in the Land of Make Believe; words by Mrs. Ora Marshall, music by William Arthur. © Nordyke Publishing Co., Los Angeles; 30Jan47; EP19963.

Love Hasn't Changed; words by Carl E. King, music by William Arthur. © Nordyke Publishing Co., Los Angeles; 19Jun47; EP17534.

Love Is Best; words by Darwinia Wood Love, music by William Arthur. © Nordyke Publishing Co., Los Angeles; 3Sep47; EP19346.

ARTHUR, WILLIAM. Cont'd.

Love Never Dies; words by Art Prager, music by William Arthur. © Nordyke Publishing Co., Los Angeles; 17May47; EP16818.

Love Triangle; words by Grace V. Leach, music by William Arthur. © Nordyke Publishing Co., Los Angeles; 24Jul47; EP17507.

Magic Moon; words by Etta Gant, music by William Arthur. © Nordyke Publishing Co., Los Angeles; 13Nov46; EP19688.

Me, Baby, Me; words by Richard Cecil Rogers, music by William Arthur. © Nordyke Publishing Co., Los Angeles; 27Mar47; EP16809.

Memories of Kentucky; words by Leta Creekmore, music by William Arthur. © Nordyke Publishing Co., Los Angeles; 21Feb47; EP19438.

A Million Dreams; words by Oscar H. Minton, music by William Arthur. © Nordyke Publishing Co., Los Angeles; 14Jun47; EP17432.

The Moon Winks His Eye; words by Girdia Romine, music by William Arthur. © Nordyke Publishing Co., Los Angeles; 24Jul47; EP17495.

Mother Dear; words by Helen Cedile, music by William Arthur. [c1946] © Nordyke Publishing Co., Los Angeles; 14Jan47; EP19454.

My Angel; words by Harry C. Fox, music by William Arthur. © Nordyke Publishing Co., Los Angeles; 16Jul47; EP17557.

My Heart Is Aching over You; words by Junior Dager, music by William Arthur. © Nordyke Publishing Co., Los Angeles; 10May47; Ep16854.

My Heart Will Tag Along; words by Eleanor Saso, music by William Arthur. © Nordyke Publishing Co., Los Angeles; 27Mar47; EP16810.

My Kansas Pawnee, Wanda Rose; words by Franklin M. Owen, music by William Arthur. © Nordyke Publishing Co., Los Angeles; 31Jul47; EP17492.

My Love for You; words by Eddie Bleck, Jr., music by William Arthur. © Nordyke Publishing Co., Los Angeles; 16Dec46; EP19456.

My Love for You; words by Flaurence Stewart, music by William Arthur. [c1946] © Nordyke Publishing Co., Los Angeles; 7Feb47; EP19705.

My Love for You; words by Jack Burda, music by William Arthur. © Nordyke Publishing Co., Los Angeles; 29Apr47; EP16859.

My Love for You; words by Mareta Arent, music by William Arthur. © Nordyke Publishing Co., Los Angeles; 14Jun47; EP17430.

My Love Will Always Be the Same; words by Carrie Fisher, music by William Arthur. © Nordyke Publishing Co., Los Angeles; 21Aug47; EP19353.

My Lucky Day; words by William H. Jones, music by William Arthur. © Nordyke Publishing Co., Los Angeles; 29Mar47; EP16750.

My Peachy Packing Pal; words by Harry Craft, music by William Arthur. © Nordyke Publishing Co., Los Angeles; 9Nov46; EP19442.

My Rose under the Lilac Tree; words by Earl Thompson, music by William Arthur. © Nordyke Publishing Co., 21Feb47; EP19710.

My Sweet Has Turned Sour on Me; words by Winifred B. Jones, music by William Arthur. © Nordyke Publishing Co., Los Angeles; 29May47; EP16878.

My Sweetheart; words by Doris Imogene Brothers, music by William Arthur. © Nordyke Publishing Co., Los Angeles; 27Mar47; EP16954.

My Sweetheart; words by Jay Sell, music by William Arthur. [c1946] © Nordyke Publishing Co., Los Angeles; 20Jan47; EP19738.

My Tahiti Rose; words by George R. Howarth, music by William Arthur. © Nordyke Publishing Co., Los Angeles; 22Aug47; EP20092.

My Treasure; words by Cleo C. Owings, music by William Arthur. © Nordyke Publishing Co., Los Angeles; 16Jun47; EP17552.

My Window Pane; words by Richard Wm. Chesley, music by William Arthur. © Nordyke Publishing Co., Los Angeles; 5Aug47; EP19676.

My Yesterdays; words by Joe Hunt, music by William Arthur. © Nordyke Publishing Co., Los Angeles; 11Jul47; EP17531.

Nebraska; words by Bud Nelson, music by William Arthur. [c1946] © Nordyke Publishing Co., Los Angeles; 30Jan47; EP20331.

Never; words by Emil L. Vigeant, music by William Arthur. [c1946] © Nordyke Publishing Co., Los Angeles; 29Jan47; EP19643.

Never Give Up Your Dreams; words by Mary Garrison, music by William Arthur. © Nordyke Publishing Co., Los Angeles; 27Mar47; EP16780.

Night and Morning; words by J. C. Griggs, music by William Arthur. © Nordyke Publishing Co., Los Angeles; 25Jul47; EP17425.

Nobody Loves Me Anymore; words by Clifton F. Smith, music by William Arthur. © Nordyke Publishing Co., Los Angeles; 29Mar47; EP16771.

Number One Hit Parader; words by Wm. H. Walden, music by William Arthur. © Nordyke Publishing Co., Los Angeles; 12Jul47; EP17426.

Oh, What a Lovely Evening; words by Carl W. Carlson, music by William Arthur. [c1946] © Nordyke Publishing Co., Los Angeles; 30Jan47; EP19402.

Old Memories; words by Dess A. Hartford, music by William Arthur. © Nordyke Publishing Co., Los Angeles; 22Jul47; EP19532.

On Again, Off Again, Gone Again; words by B. Boyd, music by William Arthur. © Nordyke Publishing Co., Los Angeles; 19Nov46; EP19407.

On the Beaches of the Salt Lake Shore; words by Lyda Anderson, music by William Arthur. © Nordyke Publishing Co., Los Angeles; 22Jul47; EP19331.

One More October; words by Milton Harris, music by William Arthur. © Nordyke Publishing Co., Los Angeles; 10May47; EP16855.

Only a Dreamer; words by Charles F. Gross, Jr., music by William Arthur. © Nordyke Publishing Co., Los Angeles; 25Jun47; EP17410.

Pennsylvania Moon; words by Winifred Virginia Mitnick, music by William Arthur. © Nordyke Publishing Co., Los Angeles; 3Jul47; EP17417.

Pick a Peach in the Garden of Love; words by Mary G. Frishmuth, music by William Arthur. © Nordyke Publishing Co., Los Angeles; 3Jul47; EP17415.

Please Say It's Not Good-bye; words by Bruce Leon Stratton, music by William Arthur. © Nordyke Publishing Co., Los Angeles; 29Mar47; EP16729.

Pretending; words by Virg Brown, music by William Arthur. © Nordyke Publishing Co., Los Angeles; 15Aug47; EP20488.

The Rhythm of the Raindrops; words by Frank (Johnny) Philips, music by William Arthur. © Nordyke Publishing Co., Los Angeles; 12Aug47; EP17468.

The Same, Same Old Story; words by Jack Dillon, music by William Arthur. © Nordyke Publishing Co., Los Angeles; 29May47; EP16910.

San Clemente Moon; words by Philip Gordon, music by William Arthur. © Nordyke Publishing Co., Los Angeles; 14Nov46; EP19529.

School Days; words by Robert C. Dyste, music by William Arthur. © Nordyke Publishing Co., Los Angeles; 16Jul47; EP17396.

Shattered Dreams; words by Mrs. George Schuler, music by William Arthur. [c1946] © Nordyke Publishing Co., Los Angeles; 30Jan47; EP19646.

She's a Rose in Old Virginia; words by Samuel B. Richardson, music by William Arthur. © Nordyke Publishing Co., Los Angeles; 29Apr47; EP16901.

So Lonely and Blue; words by Tandy W. Henry, music by William Arthur. © Nordyke Publishing Co., Los Angeles; 14Jun47; EP17393.

Softly; words by Pauline Collins, music by William Arthur. © Nordyke Publishing Co., Los Angeles; 30Oct47; EP19627.

Some Little Something; words by Mabel Katherine Hanna, music by William Arthur. © Nordyke Publishing Co., Los Angeles; 29Mar47; EP16752.

Someday I'll Find My Love; words by Verna Leigh Merritt, music by William Arthur. [c1946] © Nordyke Publishing Co., Los Angeles; 2Jan47; EP20327.

Something in Your Eyes; words by R. Ruth Wolfe, music by William Arthur. © Nordyke Publishing Co., Los Angeles; 14Jun47; EP17549.

The Song of Love; words by Don Jackson, music by William Arthur. © Nordyke Publishing Co., Los Angeles; 10May47; EP16891.

Stop Your Fooling Me; words by Henry Larson, music by William Arthur. © Nordyke Publishing Co., Los Angeles; 14Jun47; EP17544.

The Sweetest Smile I Know; words by Roxie Bane, music by William Arthur. © Nordyke Publishing Co., Los Angeles; 10May47; EP17539.

ARTHUR, WILLIAM. Cont'd.

Take a Little Trip Down South;
words by Sarah Sellers McDougald,
music by William Arthur. ©
Nordyke Publishing Co., Los
Angeles; 22Jul47; EP19372.

That Night; words by Jean
Gallatin, music by William
Arthur. © Nordyke Publishing
Co., Los Angeles; 3Sep47;
EP20044.

That's All There Is (there is no
more) words by Joseph A.
Ferrara, music by William
Arthur. © Nordyke Publishing
Co., Los Angeles; 3Sep47;
EP19328.

That's What You Did Do; words by
Glen Devine, music by William
Arthur. © Nordyke Publishing
Co., Los Angeles; 10Jun47;
EP16861.

There Was a Time; words by Flor-
ence Ray, music by William
Arthur. © Nordyke Publishing
Co., Los Angeles; 9Nov46;
EP20039.

There's Fish in the Ocean,
There's Fish in the Sea; words
by Jessie Sposeto, music by
William Arthur. © Nordyke
Publishing Co., Los Angeles;
3Sep47; EP20478.

Think It Over; words by Raymond
Nelson, music by William
Arthur. © Nordyke Publishing
Co., Los Angeles; 24Jul47;
EP17466.

Thinking of You; words by
Annette Schoch, music by
William Arthur. [c1949]
© Nordyke Publishing Co.,
Los Angeles; 28Jan47; EP19659.

This Is It; words by Blanche
Lewis, music by William Arthur.
© Nordyke Publishing Co., Los
Angeles; 22Jul47; EP19537.

Through a Lighted Window Pane;
words by W. E. Perry, music by
William Arthur. © Nordyke
Publishing Co., Los Angeles;
28Jun47; EP20336.

Tonight Is the Night for Love; words
by Florence B. Ball, music by
William Arthur. © Nordyke Publishing
Co., Los Angeles; 3Jul47; EP17389.

Tread Lightly for You're Treading
on My Dreams; words by Grace
Thompson, music by William
Arthur. © Nordyke Publishing
Co., Los Angeles; 14Jun47;
EP17481.

Two Days Ago; words by Kenneth
Dippol, music by William
Arthur. © Nordyke Publishing
Co., Los Angeles; 29Aug47;
EP19298.

Underneath the Stars; words by
E. Francis Rivers, music by
William Arthur. © Nordyke
Publishing Co., Los Angeles;
29Aug47; EP19300.

Until You Came Along; words by
Anthony Nieder, music by William
Arthur. © Nordyke Publishing
Co., Los Angeles; 2Sep47;
EP19301.

Waiting Up; words by Mary Ainsle
McMichael, music by William
Arthur. © Nordyke Publishing
Co., Los Angeles; 3Dec46;
EP19391.

Wanna Be Loved (as only you can
love) words by Laura Mitchell,
music by William Arthur.
© Nordyke Publishing Co.,
Los Angeles; 7Feb47; EP19396.

What Did I Ever Do? Words by
Louise Feuerstein, music by
William Arthur. © Nordyke
Publishing Co., Los Angeles;
23May47; EP16911.

What My Heart Can't Say; words by
Lodemia Hurley, music by William
Arthur. © Nordyke Publishing
Co., Los Angeles; 27Mar47;
EP16916.

What's the Use? Words by Lois G.
Holden, music by William
Arthur. © Nordyke Publishing
Co., Los Angeles; 22Jul47;
EP14446.

When I Hear Your Name; words by
Shep Paxton, jr., music by
William Arthur. © Nordyke
Publishing Co., Los Angeles;
5Aug47; EP17477.

When I Hold Your Hand in Mine;
words by Mary Scott Saint-Amand,
music by William Arthur.
© Nordyke Publishing Co., Los
Angeles; 27Mar47; EP16917.

When I'm Alone with You; words by
Tracy P. Hall, music by William
Arthur. © Nordyke Publishing
Co., Los Angeles; 25Jun47;
EP17449.

When It's Moonlight on the Lake;
words by William C. Darden,
music by William Arthur. ©
Nordyke Publishing Co., Los
Angeles; 22Jul47; EP19449.

Wherever You Are; words by
Roxie Bane, music by William
Arthur. © Nordyke Publishing
Co., Los Angeles; 8Mar47; EP16795.

Why Do I? Words by Leota B. Hod-
son, music by William Arthur.
© Nordyke Publishing Co., Los
Angeles; 22Aug47; EP20066.

Why Don't You Get Yourself
Together? Words by Manvel Rod,
music by William Arthur. ©
Nordyke Publishing Co., Los
Angeles; 13Aug47; EP19318.

Why Don't You Try to Remember the
Things I Try So Hard to Forget?
Words by Joe Rinebolt, music by
William Arthur. © Nordyke
Publishing Co., Los Angeles;
22Jul47; EP17475.

Why Must I Keep on Loving You?
Words by Rachelle D. Le Fevre,
music by William Arthur. ©
Nordyke Publishing Co., Los
Angeles; 11Aug47; EP17474.

Will There Be a Sunset Tomorrow?
Words by Leota B. Hodson, music
by William Arthur. © Nordyke
Publishing Co., Los Angeles;
3Sep47; EP19309.

The Wind That Blows in My Hair;
words by L. Randolph Whitehead,
music by William Arthur.
© Nordyke Publishing Co., Los
Angeles; 20Aug47; EP19315.

With Your Head upon My Heart; words
by Onella Sawyer, music by William
Arthur. © Nordyke Publishing
Co., Los Angeles; 27Mar47;
EP16744.

Within My Reach; words by
Catherine Maria, music by
William Arthur. © Nordyke
Publishing Co., Los Angeles;
28Mar47; EP16782.

Wonderful Beautiful You; words by
Laura Oedekoven, music by
William Arthur. © Nordyke
Publishing Co., Los Angeles;
29Aug47; EP19319.

Yaller Gal; words by Elton
(pseud.), music by William Arthur. © Nordyke Publishing
Co., Los Angeles; 16Jul47;
EP17454.

You; words by Marie Nordblad,
music by William Arthur. ©
Nordyke Publishing Co., Los
Angeles; 22Aug47; EP19283.

You Are My Temptation; words by
H. N. (Casey) Jones, music by
William Arthur. © Nordyke
Publishing Co., Los Angeles;
5Aug47; EP17470.

You Can't Get Along without Love;
words by Ann Pettigrew, music
by William Arthur. © Nordyke
Publishing Co., Los Angeles;
12Jul47; EP17465.

You Know I Still Care; words by
Lillian G. Pierce, music by
William Arthur. © Nordyke Publishing Co., Los Angeles;
11Oct46; EP20057.

You're in My Arms Again; words by
Mabel Witwer Goodwin, music by
William Arthur. © Nordyke
Publishing Co., Los Angeles;
29Nov46; EP19387.

You're Playing a Quiz Game with
My Heart; words by Augie M.
Graf, music by William Arthur.
© Nordyke Publishing Co., Los
Angeles; 16Jul47; EP17457.

You're Still the Sunshine of My
Heart; words by Grace Hudson,
music by William Arthur. © Nordyke Publishing Co., Los Angeles;
22Jul47; EP20373.

You're the Spice of My Life; words
by Myrtle Graham, music by William Arthur. [c1946] © Nordyke
Publishing Co., Los Angeles;
15Feb47; EP19745.

You're the Tick Tick Tock in My
Heart; words by Rachelle D.
LeFevre, music by William Ar-
thur. © Nordyke Publishing
Co., Los Angeles; 5Aug47;
EP20485.

You've Caused Me Lots of Trouble;
words by Docimao Scruggs, music
by William Arthur. © Nordyke
Publishing Co., Los Angeles;
3Sep47; EP20375.

You've Turned the Tables on Me;
words by Writha G. Hudson,
music by William Arthur. ©
Nordyke Publishing Co., Los
Angeles; 11Oct46; EP19527.

ARTHUR TALLMAN MUSIC FEATURES - YOU;
trumpet, tenor sax [or] clarinet.
© Arthur Tallman, New York;
12Nov47; EP20228. Part.

ASH, GERTRUDE.
Listen To Me; words and music by
Gertrude Ash. © Gertrude F.
Ash, Toledo; 18Aug47; EP16528.

We're Going on a Vacation; words
and music by Gertrude Ash.
© Nordyke Publishing Co., Los
Angeles; 2Jul46; EP20072.

ASHE, JOHN HAROLD.
Love's Philosophy; words by Shel-
ley, music by John Ashe.
© John Harold Ashe, Townsville,
Queensland, Australia; 2Sep47;
EF6857.

O World! O Life! O Time! ...
[Words] by Shelley, music by
John Ashe. © John Harold Ashe,
Townsville, Queensland, Austra-
lia; 2Sep47; EF6859.

A Widow Bird Sate Mourning; words
by Shelley, music by John Ashe.
© John Harold Ashe, Townsville,
Queensland, Australia; 2Sep47;
EF6858.

ASHNALL, WILLIAM E   arr.
Processionals and Postludes for
Organ Solo; selected from "The
Organists' Journal," arr. by
William E. Ashnall. © McLoughlin
& Reilly Co., Boston; 2Jun47; on
arrangement & compilation;
EP16390.

ASHMALL, WILLIAM EDWIN, 1860-1927.
Missa Pro Pace; (Mass in C major)
for quartett and chorus with organ
acc., composed by Wm. Edwin Ashmall. Op.205. Arlington, N. J.,
W. E. Ashmall. © Florence M. Ashmall (in notice: Wm E. Ashmall)
Downer's Grove, Ill.; 31Dec19;
EP20152.

ATKINSON, GEORGE HECTOR, 1889-
Music for Ballet Exercises ...
music by T. E. Atkinson, from
directions by Espinosa. ©
William Paxton & Co., ltd.,
London; v. 1-2, 23Dec46;
EF5708, 5710. For piano.
Contents.- [1] Grades I, II
and III. [2] Grades IV and V.

ATKINSON, T   E   See
Atkinson, George Hector.

ATSELL, BERT.
Would You Mind? Words and music by
Bert Atsell. © Nordyke Publishing
Co., Los Angeles; 10Jun47;
EP169144.

ATTERBERG, KURT..
De Favitska Jungfrurna; rapsodi på
svenska folkmotiv. The Wise and
the Foolish Virgins; rhapsody on
old Swedish folksongs, [by] Kurt
Atterberg. Op.17. Stockholm, Ed.
Suecia. © A. B. Nordiska Musikförlaget, Stockholm; 1Jan21;
EF7091. Score: orchestra.

ATTERBURY, LYNN L   1876-
Dunking the Doughnut; words and
music by Lynn L. Atterbury. ©
Lynn L. Atterbary, Waukegan,
Ill.; 15Nov47; EP19037.
Star Light; words and music by
Lynn L. Atterbury. © Lynn L.
Atterbury, Waukegan, Ill.;
15Jul47; EP16139.

ATTERBURY, GEORGE ALVIN, 1892-
Beautiful Oregon, I Love You. See his
Oregon Melody.

(Oregon Melody) Beautiful Oregon,
I love you; orchestration ...
featured in ... movie short
"Oregon Melody," [words and
music by George Atterbury, arr.
by Whetmore]. © Portland, Or.,
Atterbury Music Enterprises.
© George A. Atterbury, Portland,
Or.; 12Mar47; on arrangement;
EP17938. Parts: orchestra.

ATWOOD, HARRY GARDENIER, 1901-
Baby, You're Mine for Keeps;
words by Louis Herscher ...
music by Harry Atwood. © Bell
Song Publishing Co., Hollywood,
Calif.; 100ct47; EP17921.
Lonely Souls at Sea; lyric by
Louis Herscher ... music by
Harry Atwood. © Bell Song Pub-
lishing Co., Hollywood, Calif.;
30Oct47; EP18170.
You'll Never Break My Heart Again;
words by Louis Herscher ...
music by Harry Atwood. © Bell
Song Publishing Co., Hollywood,
Calif.; 10Oct47; EP17922.

AUBANEL, GEORGES PIERRE PHILIPPE,
1896-
Ah! Quand Reviendra-t-il le Temps
...; [Quouro Tournara lou Tèms
...] Choeur à 4 voix mixtes;
noël de N. Saboly ... tr. et
harmonisé par Georges Aubanel.
© Heugel & Cie, Paris; 29Nov46;
on translation & harmonization;
EF6518.

C'est le Bon Lever, Doux Pastour-
eau ... Noël populaire de
Provence, tr. et harmonisé par
Georges Aubanel. © Heugel &
Cie, Paris; 29Nov46; on trans-
lation & harmonization; EF6497.
Score: soprano, baritone, chorus
(SATB) and piano reduction;
Provençal and French words.

Nuit de Félicité; choeur à 4
voix mixtes. Noël populaire
languedocien traduit et
harmonisé par Georges Aubanel.
© Heugel & Cie, Paris;
29Nov46; on arrangement &
translation; EF6555.
Sont Trois Hommes Fort Sages (Soun
Tres Ome Fort Sage) Choeur à
4 voix mixtes, noël de N. Saboly
... tr. et harmonisé par
Georges Aubanel. © Heugel &
Cie, Paris; 29Nov46; on translation & arrangement; EF6430.

AUBUCHON, CLIFFORD.
The National Guard March; words
and music by Clifford Aubuchon.
© Dreyer Music Corp., New York;
3Dec47; EP19197.

AUDINOT, RAFAEL.
Rumba Rhapsody; [by] Rafael Audinot & Alberto de Bru, transcribed by Gregory Stone [for]
piano duet. © Remick Music
Corp., New York; 10Nov47; on
arrangement; EP18873.

AUFDEMBERGE, EDGAR HERBERT, 1922-
Blessed Are the Sons of God; SSA
a cappella, with optional solo
voices. Words by Joseph Humphreys, [music] based on hymn
tunes ... arr. by Edgar H.
Aufdemberge. © Harold Flammer,
inc., New York; 14Nov47; on
arrangement; EP19157.

Comfort Ye, My People; SSA a
cappella, with optional solo
voices. [Words by] Johann
Olearius, tr. by Catherine Winkworth; (music from) "Freu dich
sehr" [by] Bach, [arr. by]
Aufdemberge. ? Harold Flammer,
inc., New York; 14Nov47; on
arrangement; EP19154.

AULBACH, FRANCIS K
Silver Shadows; piano solo by
Francis E. Aulbach. © Clayton
F. Summy Co., Chicago; 26Sep47;
EP17352.

AULD, WILDA JACKSON.
Sacred Transcriptions; for the
piano, for four hands by Wilda
Jackson Auld. Kansas City, Mo.,
Lillenas Publishing Co. ©
Haldor Lillenas, Kansas City,
Mo.; 1Jul47; EP15746.

AURIC, GEORGES, 1899-
Trois Impromptus; pour piano, [by]
Georges Auric. © Éditions Max
Eschig, Paris; 30Jun46; EP7225.

AVILAR, RAMON, pseud. See
Vanner, Emilio.

AWAI, KEOKI E   arr.
The Superior Collection of Steel
Guitar Solos ... [arr.] by Keoki
E. Awai, [comp. by Miller Music
Corp.] San Francisco, Sherman,
Clay. © Miller Music Corp., New
York; v.2, 29Dec19; EP20410.

AXELSSON, STEN.
Duga-Duga ... [by] Sten Axelsson,
arr. [by] Ch. Redland. Stockholm, Musikaliska knuten. ©
Novelty Music Edition, Spånga,
Sweden; 1Jan46; EF7090. Piano-
conductor score (orchestra) and
parts.

B

BACCARI, ANGELO, 1894-
United Nations; lyrics by James A.
McGrano, music by Angelo Baccari.
© The McGrano Music Co., James
A. McGrano, sole owner, Ossining,
N. Y.; 10Sep47; EP17828.

BACH, JOHANN CHRISTIAN.
(Concerto, violin & piano) Concerto en ut mineur, de J. Chr.
Bach, réalisé, harmonisé et
orchestré par Henri Casadesus
[pseud.] © Salabert, inc., New
York; 2Jun47; EF5923. Score
(viola and piano) and part.

BACH, JOHANN SEBASTIAN, 1685-1750.
(Ach Herr, Mich Armen Sünder) O
Lord, This Grieving Spirit. Ach
Herr, Mich Armen Sünder. Sacred
cantata no. 135 ... by Johann Sebastian Bach. ed. and acc. arr. by
Ifor Jones, original text by Cy-
riacus Schneegass, English version
by J. M. Stein and Ifor Jones. ©
G. Schirmer, inc., New York;
28Apr47; on editing, translation
& piano reduction; EP20287.

All Nature Is Smiling. See his
Weichet Nur.

Alleluja! See his Uns Ist ein Kind Geboren.

Aria, "Forget Me Not"; [by] J. S.
Bach, arr. by Edwin Arthur Kraft.
© Edward Schuberth & Co., inc.,
New York; 22Dec47; on arrangement;
EP20274. For organ solo; includes
registration for Hammond organ.

Bach for the Clarinet; transcribed by Eric Simon... © G.
Schirmer, inc., New York;
29Jul47; on 3 forewords & 3
vols. of transcriptions. Score
and parts. Contents. - pt. 1.
Clarinet and piano (© EP17747)-
pt. 2. Clarinet solo./ Clarinet
duet (© EP17748) - pt. 3.
Clarinet trio. Clarinet quartet
(© EP17749)

Beside Thy Cradle Here I Stand.
Ich Steh an Deiner Krippen Hier.
Choral from the "Christmas
Oratorio," [by] Johann Sebastian
Bach ... [Words by] Paul Gerhardt
... English version by Rev. John
Troutbeck... arr. by B. Warren.
© E. C. Schirmer Music Co.,
Boston; 28Jul47; on arrangement;
EP15975. Score: SA and piano.

Capriccio on the Departure of a
Beloved Brother; for piano, [by]
Johann Sebastian Bach, ed. by
James Friskin, with new preface.
© J. Fischer & Bro., New York;
3Sep47; on editing and preface;
EP17386.

Christmas Symphony; (And there
were shepherds abiding in the
field) [by] J. S. Bach, arr.
... by W. A. Goldsworthy.
© J. Fischer & Bro., New York;
27Aug47; on arrangement;
EP17773. Score: organ and
piano.

Come, Kindly Death. See his Komm Süsser
Tod.

Complete Organ Works; [by] Johann
Sebastian Bach, [prepared by Alexander Lipsky, preface tr. by Theodore Front] © Edwin F. Kalmus,
New York; v.1, 3, 15Dec47; on
translation; A19725-19726.

Complete Organ Works; [by] Johann
Sebastian Bach, [prepared by Theodore Front, preface tr. by Alexander Lipsky] © Edwin F. Kalmus,
New York; v.2, 4, 10Oct47; v.5,
22Sep47; v.8, 10Oct47; A17718,
17721, 17720, 17719.

Dear Christians, Let Us Now Rejoice; [by] J. S. Bach, arr. by
E. A. Kraft. © Edward Schuberth & Co., inc., New York;
24Nov47; on arrangement;
EP18906. For organ solo; includes registration for Hammond
organ.

BACH, JOHANN SEBASTIAN. Cont'd.
(Du Wahrer Gott und Davids Sohn)
Thou Very God and David's Son.
Du wahrer Gott und Davids Sohn.
Sacred cantata no. 23, by Johann
Sebastian Bach, ed. and acc. arr.
by Ifor Jones, English version by
J. M. Stein and Ifor Jones. © G.
Schirmer, inc., New York; 28Apr47;
on editing, translation & piano
reduction; EP20285. English and
German words.

First Sinfonia from Cantata 35, by
J. S. Bach, arr. ... by Walter
Emery. © Novello & Co., ltd.,
London; 8Aug47; on arrangement;
EF6178. Score: piano 1-2.

For As the Rain and Snow from Heaven
Fall. See his Gleich Wie der Regen
und Schnee vom Himmel Fällt.

Fugue in C minor; from the Well
Tempered Clavichord [by] J. S.
Bach, transcribed by Marc Tar-
low. © Elkan-Vogel Co., inc.,
Philadelphia; 17Jul47; on
arrangement; EP15801. Score
(flute, clarinet and bassoon)
and parts.

(Gleich Wie der Regen und Schnee
vom Himmel Fällt) For As the
Rain and Snow from Heaven Fall.
Gleich Wie der Regen und Schnee
vom Himmel Fällt. Sacred cantata
no. 18 ... by Johann Sebastian
Bach, ed. and acc. arr. by Ifor
Jones, original text by Erdmann
Neumeister, English version by J.
M. Stein and Ifor Jones. © G.
Schirmer, inc., New York; 11Apr47;
on editing, translation & piano
reduction; EP20286.

God's Loving Kindness, [by] Johann
Sebastian Bach. Four-part chorus
for boy's glee club arr. by
Robert W. Gibb, [words by] Paul
Gerhardt, English version by
Christine T. Curtis. © Boston
Music Co., Boston; 15Dec47; on
arrangement & English text;
EP20402.

If Now You Truly Love Me. See his
Willst Du Dein Herz Mir Schenken.

Jesus suffered pain and death.
(Jesu Leiden, Pein und Tod)
[By] Bach, arr. by Harvey Gaul.
© Volkwein Bros., inc., Pittsburgh; on arrangement; 9May47;
on arrangement; EP14311. Score (flute, violin
1-2, viola, violoncello and
double-bass) and parts.

(Komm Süsser Tod) Come, Kindly
Death, by J. S. Bach, ed., with
English translation, by Emily
Daymond. [c1946] © The Oxford
University Press, London;
9Jan47; on arrangement and
translation; EF6091. For voice
and piano; English words.

Lord of Life, and King All Glorious
... from cantata no. 8, [by] J.
Johann Sebastian Bach, arr. by
Edwin Arthur Kraft. © Harold
Flammer, inc., New York; 14Nov47;
on arrangement; EP19160. Score:
SSA and organ or piano.

My Heart Ever Faithful; (aria)
[by] J. S. Bach, arr. by Ernest
Haywood [for] piano solo.
[c1946] © Keith, Prowse & Co.,
ltd., London; 25Jul47; on arrangement; EP6243.

My Heart Ever Trusting; [by] J. S.
Bach, arr. by Norman Richardson.
London, Sole selling agents, Boosey
& Hawkes. © Hawkes & Son (London)
ltd., London; 26Nov47; on arrangement; EF7191. Condensed score
(band) and parts.

O Ever Faithful God; (melody,
anonymous, 1679) [by] J. S. Bach,
arr. by Edwin Arthur Kraft. ©
Edward Schuberth & Co., inc.;
14Oct47; EP19258. For organ solo;
includes registration for Hammond
organ.

(O Jesu Christ, Mein's Lebens Licht)
O Jesu Christ, My Life and Light.
O Jesu Christ, Mein's Lebens
Licht. Scored cantata no. 118 by
Johann Sebastian Bach, ed. and
acc. arr. by Ifor Jones, original
text by Martin Behm, English ver-
sion by J. M. Stein and Ifor
Jones. © G. Schirmer, inc., New
York; 28Apr47; on editing, trans-
lation and piano reduction;
EP20285.

O Jesus Christ, My Life and Light.
See his O Jesu Christ, Mein's Lebens
Licht.

O Lord, This Grieving Spirit. See his
Ach Herr, Mich Armen Sünder.

Oh God, Thou Faithful God; from
cantata no. 129. [By] Johann
Sebastian Bach, arr. by Edwin
Arthur Kraft. © Harold Flammer,
inc., New York; 14Nov47; on
arrangement; EP19161. Score:
SA and organ.

Oh Haste Thee, My Soul, aria from
cantata no. 124, [by] Johann
Sebastian Bach, arr. by Edwin
Arthur Kraft. © Harold Flammer,
inc., New York; 14Nov47; on
arrangement; EP19158. Score:
SA and organ.

Organ Toccata. See his Toccata, organ.

Organ Toccata and Fugue. See his
Toccata & Fugue, organ.

Sarabande; (French Suite in D
Minor) [by] J. S. Bach; arr.
... by Gordon Phillips. © The
Oxford Univ. Press, London;
90ct47; on arrangement; EF6997.
Score (violin and piano) and
part.

Second Bach Book; for pianoforte,
adapted, arr. and ed. by Arthur
Foote. A sequel to "First Year
Bach." © Arthur P. Schmidt Co.,
Boston; 23Sep47; on adaptation,
arrangement & compilation;
EP18220.

(Selig, Wer am Jesum Denkt)
Bless'd Are They Who in Jesus
Live. (Selig, Wer am Jesum
Denkt) For four-part chorus of
women's voices (a cappella) [by]
Johann Sebastian Bach ... arr.
by Arthur S. Talmadge, [words
by] A.G.B., English version by
A.S.T. © R.C. Schirmer Music
Co., Boston; 20ct47; on arrange-
ment; EP18151. English words.

Sheep May Safely Graze. See his Was Mir
Behagt.

Short Pieces for the Organ, from
the Anna Magdalena Book, by J. S.
Bach, ed. [with extra parts added]
by Henry Coleman. © The Oxford
Univ. Press, London; 23Oct47; on
arrangement and extra parts;
EF7176.

(Sonata, violoncello, no.1)
Three Pieces; (from 1st Sonata
for 'cello solo) arr. ... by
Maurice Johnstone. [c1946]
© Alfred Lengnick & Co., ltd.,
London; 30May47; on arrange-
ment; EF6685. Score (viola
and piano) and part.

Thou Very God and David's Son. See his
Du Wahrer Gott und Davids Sohn.

Three Pieces. See his Sonata, violoncello, no. 1.

To My Jesus Do I Cling, from cantata no. 124, [by] Johann Sebastian Bach, arr. by Edwin Arthur
Kraft. © Harold Flammer, inc.,
New York; 14Nov47; on arrangement; EP19159. Score: SSA and
organ.

Toccata and Fugue; in D minor,
[by] Johann Sebastian Bach,
transcribed ... by York Bowen.
© Elkin & Co., ltd., London;
2Dec47; on arrangement; EF7567.
Two scores for piano 1-2.

(Toccata & Fugue, organ) The
Organ Toccata & Fugue in D minor;
arr. ... by C. H. Stuart Duncan.
© Alfred Lengnick & Co., ltd.,
London; 10Jul47; on arrangement;
EF6350. Score: piano 1-2.

(Toccata & Fugue, organ) Organ
Toccata and Fugue; in D minor
[by] J. S. Bach, transcribed
for piano solo by Eric Lewis.
© Forsyth Brothers, ltd.,
London; 13Jun47; on transcription;
EF6062.

(Toccata, organ) Organ Toccata in
F, [by] J. S. Bach, arr. by
Vivian Langrish. © The Oxford
University Press, London;
3Jul47; on arrangement;
EF6127. Two scores for piano
1-2.

(Uns Ist ein Kind Geboren)
Alleluja! Choral from the
cantata: 'Uns Ist ein Kind
Geboren' ('Unto Us a Child
Is Born') For three-part
chorus of mixed voices. Melody
attributed to Kaspar Füger,
the younger, harmonized by
Johann Sebastian Bach ... arr.
by Victoria Glaser, [words]
from the Christmas hymn: 'Wir
Christenleut,' by Kaspar
Füger ... English version by
Charles Sanford Terry, ed. by
H. Clough Leighter. © E. C.
Schirmer Music Co., Boston;
18Aug47; on arrangement;
EP16510. German and English
words.

Victoria Merrylees, arr. III.
Terry, Charles Sanford, tr.
IV. Clough-Leiter, H., ed. V.
Title. VI. Title: Uns Ist ein
Kind Geboren.

(Was Frag' Ich nach der Welt?)
Who Cares Alone for This Blind
World, by J. S. Bach, arr.
Hubert Somervell. © The
Oxford University Press, London;
29May47; on arrangement;
EF6148. Two scores for piano
1-2.

(Was Mir Behagt) Sheep May
Safely Graze ... aria [from
Cantata no. 208] by Bach, arr.
for piano solo by King Palmer.
© W. Paxton & Co., ltd.,
London; 12Aug46; on arrange-
ment; EF5698.

(Was Mir Behagt) 'Sheep May Safely
Graze,' aria from secular cantata
no. 208, by J. S. Bach, arr.
... by Watson Forbes. © The
Oxford University Press, London;
12Dec46; on arrangement; EF6067.
Score (violin and piano) and
part, and alternative parts for
viola and violoncello.

(Was Mir Behagt) Sheep May Safely
Graze; by J. S. Bach, arr. for
two solo violins and strings by
Reginald Jacques. Score. ©
The Oxford University Press,
London; 24Jul47; on arrangement;
EF6257.

(Was Mir Behagt) Sheep May Safely
Graze. (Schafe Können Sicher
Weiden) From the secular
cantata, no. 208, "Was Mir Behagt." [By] J. S. Bach, English words
by Albert Howe. © W. Paxton &
Co., ltd., London; 25Oct46; on
arrangement; EF5750. For voice
and piano.

(Weichet Nur) All Nature Is Smiling; words by May Sarson, music
by J. S. Bach (from the secular
cantata, 'Weichet Nur') © Novello & Co., ltd., London;
17Dec47; on new text; EF7357.
For voice and piano.

Who Cares Alone for This Blind World?
See his Was Frag' Ich nach der Welt?

BACH, JOHANN SEBASTIAN. Cont'd.
.(Willst Du Dein Herz Mir Schenken)
If Now You Truly Love Me, by J.
S. Bach, ed., with English trans-
lation, by Emily Daymond.
[c1946] © The Oxford University
Press, London; 9Jan47; on ar-
rangement and translation;
EF6090. For voice and piano;
English words.

BACH, WILHELM FRIEDEMANN, 1710-1784.
Sonata in C Minor; for viola and
harpsichord (or pianoforte), by
W. F. Bach, ed. © The Oxford Univer-
Yella Pessl. © The Oxford University Press, London; 13Nov47; on
arrangement; EF7266.

BACHMAN, AL. See
Bachman, Alvin.

BACHMAN, ALVIN, 1920-
Sleeping in the Hay; words and
music by Dan Marcotte and Al
Bachman. © Wise Music Pub-
lications, New York; 5Aug47;
EP16068.

BACON, ERNST.
From Emily's Diary; secular cantata for four-part chorus of
women's voices and small orchestra with incidental soprano
and contralto soli by Ernst
Bacon, poems by Emily Dickinson.
© G. Schirmer, inc., New York;
27Aug47; EP18727. Piano-vocal
score.

BAER, CATHERINE EVELYN, 1914-
He Abideth Faithful ... [by]
Evelyn Baer. © Catherine Eve-
lyn Baer, Altoona, Pa.;
2Nov47; EP20218. Close score;
SATB.

BAER, EVELYN. See
Baer, Catherine Evelyn.

BAGGERS, MARIUS.
Dans le Temple d'Isis ... [by]
Marius Baggers. © L. Maillo-
chon, éditeur, Paris; 9Dec22;
EF6802. Score (violin and
piano) and part.

BAIL, GRACE S   1906-
Little Fingers; a collection of
fifteen short piano pieces for
study and amusement, by Grace
Bail. © Wesley Webster, San
Francisco; 10Dec47; EP19580.

BAILES, FRANKIE.
Oh, So Many Years; words and
music by Frankie Bailes.
© Acuff-Rose Publications,
Nashville; 16Oct47; EP18150.

BAILES, WALTER.
Don't Cry over Me (when I'm gone)
words and music by the Bailes
brothers (Johnnie & Walter)
© Acuff-Rose Publications,
Nashville; 24Oct47; EP18238.

The Drunkard's Grave; words
and music by the Bailes
brothers (Johnnie & Walter)
© Acuff-Rose Publications,
Nashville; 30Oct47; EP17672.

I Can't Help Wondering; words and
music by the Bailes Brothers
(Johnnie & Walter) © Acuff-
Rose Publications, Nashville;
13Oct47; EP17988.

I Want to Be Loved; words and
music by Bailes Brothers (Johnny & Walter) © Acuff-Rose
Publications, Nashville;
26Sep47; EP17344.

I'd Like to Be a Man like Daniel;
words and music by the Bailes
brothers (Johnnie & Walter)
© Acuff-Rose Publications,
Nashville; 30Oct47; EP17671.

Just Leave Me Here Behind; words
and music by the Bailes Brothers
(Johnnie & Walter) © Acuff-Rose
Publications, Nashville; 18Oct47;
EP18151.

When the Eastern Skies Shall
Open; words and music by the
Bailes brothers (Johnnie &
Walter) © Acuff-Rose Publica-
tions, Nashville; 30Oct47;
EP17670.

Whiskey Is the Devil (in liquid
form); words and music by the
Bailes brothers (Johnnie &
Walter) © Acuff-Rose Publica-
tions, Nashville; 30Oct47;
EP17669.

Why Did You Say Goodbye? Words
and music by The Bailes Brothers
(Johnnie & Walter) © Acuff-Rose
Publications, Nashville;
18Oct47; EP18152.

Why Pretend? Words and music by
the Bailes Brothers (Johnnie &
Walter) © Acuff-Rose Publications, Nashville; 18Oct47;
EP18153.

You'll Always Be the Only One;
words and music by the Bailes
Brothers (Johnnie & Walter)
© Acuff-Rose Publications,
Nashville; 13Oct47; EP17987.

BAILEY, FARRELL J
My Darling's Lullaby; words and
music by Farrell J. Bailey.
© Nordyke Publishing Co., Los
Angeles; 29Aug47; EP19366.

BAILEY, MILDRED VIRGINIA, 1911-
I Wonder if You Remember; by
Mildred Bailey, [arr. by Thomas
Alexander Phillips] © La Mar
Music Publishers, inc., Canton,
Ohio; 8Dec47; EP20112. For
voice and piano.

BAINES, WILLIAM.
Christmastide ... for mixed
voices, [by] William Baines.
© Theodore Presser Co., Philadelphia; 8Sep47; EP17286.

Dancing Dewdrops; by William
Baines. © Theodore Presser Co.,
Philadelphia; 31Jul47; EP16337.
For piano solo.

Purple Asters; piano solo by
William Baines. © Theodore
Presser Co., Philadelphia;
21Oct47; EP18418.

BAIRSTOW, SIR EDWARD C   1874-
1947.
While Shepherds Watched Their
Flocks by Night; Christmas
hymn [by Edward C. Bairstow,
[words by] Nahum Tate. © Oxford University Press, London; 11Sep47; EF6659. For mixed
chorus and organ.

BAKER, EVELYN.
Please Don't Pretend; words &
music by Evelyn Baker. © Nordyke Publishing Co., Los Angeles;
11Nov46; EP20329.

BAKER, HAZEL FRANCES, 1902-
Tune-Tech Class Method; featuring
tunes and techniques for the vio-
lin ... written by Hazel F. Baker,
Homer LaGassey [and] Bernard I.
Silverstein. © Neil A. Kjos Music
Co., Chicago; bk.2, 23Oct47;
EP19206.

BAKER, PAUL.
Followed by Your Prayer; words by
Albin Fleming, music by Paul Baker.
© Albin Fleming, Ft. Worth, Tex.;
1Jan47; EP14957.

BAKER, PHIL.
A Lovely Dream; words and music
by Phil Baker. © Richardson
Songs, Beverly Hills, Calif.;
25Sep47; EP17826.

BAKER, TOM.
Somewhere under the Stars; words
by Waneita Hughes, music by
Tom Baker. © Nordyke Publish-
ing Co., Los Angeles; 11Jun46;
EP19417.

BAKER, WARD.
Behold the Lamb of God; for mixed
chorus, words and music by Ward
Baker, Delano, Calif., W.
Baker Music Publishing Co. ©
Ward Baker, Delano, Calif.;
5Nov47; EP18679.

Calling you; words and music by
Ward Baker. © Ward Baker,
Delano, Calif.; 5Nov47; EP18680.
For 3 treble voices and piano.

Desert Flower; words and music by
Ward Baker, Delano, Calif., W.
Baker Publishing Co. © Ward
Baker, Delano, Calif.; 5Nov47;
EP18681. Score: SSA and piano.

BALÁZS, ÁRPÁD.
Össze Tudnék Csokolgatni. (Since
the Time I Saw My Darling) English lyric by Olga Paul, music by
BaláZs Árpád. (In Pasti, Barbara,
comp. Memories of Hungary. p.
10-11) © Edward B. Marks Music
Corp., New York; 19Nov47; on English lyric; EP18992.

Valakinek Muzsikálnek. (Music
Played for Someone Sweetly)
English lyric by Olga Paul, music
by BaláZs Árpád. (In Pasti, Bar-
bara, comp. Memories of Hungary.
p. 8-9) © Edward B. Marks Music
Corp., New York; 19Nov47; on
English lyric; EP18991.

Valamikor Szerettelek. (Once I
Used to Love You Dearly) English
lyric by Olga Paul, music by Balázs Árpád. (In Pasti, Barbara,
comp. Memories of Hungary.
p. 6-7) © Edward B. Marks Music
Corp., New York; 19Nov47; on
English lyric; EP18990.

BALDWIN, FERNE STARR, 1882-
So Deep in My Heart; words and
music by Ferne Starr Baldwin,
[arr. by Gene Engle] © Ferne
Starr Baldwin, Indianapolis;
23Aug47; EP16978.

BALES, GERALD ALBERT, 1919-
Toccata; piano solo by Gerald Bales.
© BMI Canada, ltd., Toronto;
28Sep47; EF6595.

BALL, ERIC.
Conchita ... [By] Eric Ball. London, Sole selling agent: Boosey
& Hawkes. © Hawkes & Son (London) ltd., London; 15Aug47;
EF6895. Condensed score (solo
cornet and band) and parts.

Four Preludes; [by] Eric Ball.
London, Boosey & Hawkes. ©
Hawkes & Son (London) ltd., London; 6Nov47; EF7010. Score:
band.

BALLANTINE, EDWARD.
Early in the Morning; and other
pieces for pianoforte, by
Edward Ballantine. © The
Arthur P. Schmidt Co., Boston;
11Jul47; EP15651.

BALLARD, FRANCIS DRAKE.
Inktaminika Honika Zunk; by Pat
Ballard. © Francis Drake
Ballard, Tuckahoe, N. Y.;
3Sep47; EP16621. For voice
and piano.

BALLATORE, PIETRO.
Little Goldfish; for the piano,
by Pietro Ballatore. [Op. 98]
© G. Schirmer, inc., New York;
27Aug47; EP18032.

BALLATORE, PIETRO, 1888- arr.
Battle Hymn of the Republic; arr.
by P. Ballatore. (In Ballatore,
Pietro comp. So Easy. p.10-11)
© Edward B. Marks Music Corp.,
New York; 9Dec47; on arrangement;
EP19507. For piano solo.

Believe Me If All Those Endearing
Young Charms; Irish folksong, arr.
by P. Ballatore. (In Ballatore,
Pietro comp. So Easy. p.9) ©
Edward B. Marks Music Corp., New
York; 9Dec47; on arrangement;
EP19586. For piano solo.

Green Sleeves ... arr. by P. Ballatore. (In Ballatore, Pietro, comp.
So Easy, p.12) © Edward B. Marks
Music Corp., New York; 9Dec47; on
arrangement; EP19588. For piano
solo.

Home on the Range; American folk-
song arr. by P. Ballatore. (In
Ballatore, Pietro, comp. So Easy,
p.6-7) © Edward B. Marks Music
Corp., New York; 9Dec47; on arrangement; EP19584. For piano solo.

Santa Lucia; Italian folksong, arr.
by P. Ballatore. (In Ballatore,
Pietro, comp. So Easy, p.20-21)
© Edward B. Marks Music Corp.,
New York; 9Dec47; on arrangement;
EP19594. For piano solo.

Wearing of the Green; Irish folk-
song, arr. by P. Ballatore. (In
Ballatore, Pietro, comp. So Easy.
p.22) © Edward B. Marks Music
Corp., New York; 9Dec47; on arrangement; EP19595. For piano
solo.

BALLATORE, PIETRO, 1888- comp.
So Easy; 15 piano pieces for young
folks, comp. and arr. by P. Ballatore. New York, E. B. Marks
Music Corp.

BALLIETT, GEORGE.
I Believe in Santa Claus; words
and music by George Balliett,
[arr. by Harold Potter] ©
George Balliett, Boise, Idaho;
20Nov47; EP19049.

I Found a Gold Mine (when I found
you); words and music by George
Balliett. © Nordyke Publishing
Co., Los Angeles; 27Mar47;
EP16718.

Thumbing My Way (to the top of the
world); words and music by George
Balliett. © Nordyke Publishing
Co., Los Angeles; 10May47;
EP16170.

BALTEL, JEAN RAYMOND, 1914-
Voulez-Vous Danser, Grand'mère?
Paroles de Jean Lenoir [pseud.],
musique de J. R. Baltel et Alex.
Padou [pseud.] © Éditions Magali,
Marseille, France; 26Jun47;
EF7318.

BAMPTON, RUTH.
Pioneers; for mixed voices [by]
Ruth Bampton, [words by] Walt
Whitman. © Abbey Music Co.,
Hollywood, Calif.; 16Apr47;
EP16170.

BANBURY, GEORGE E
New Jersey ... words and music by
George E. Banbury. © George F.
Briegel, inc., New York; 27Oct47;
EP18961.

BANCHIERI, ADRIANO.
Two Fantasias in Four Parts; for
brass quartet ... transcribed and
ed. by Sydney Beck. © Mercury
Music Corp., New York; 30Sep47;
on arrangement; EP17722. Score
(trumpet 1-2 and trombone 1-2
(or horn and baritone) and parts.

BANDINI, AL.
Deep Blue Waters; words and music
by Tedd Lawrence and Al Bandini.
© Standard Music Publishers,
ltd., New York; 14Aug47;
EP18243.

BANKS, HARRY.
Hark! Hear the Merry Bells;
Christmas carol for mixed voic-
es, words and music by Harry
Banks. © The John Church Co.,
Philadelphia; 16Sep47; EP17288.

BANTOCK, SIR GRANVILLE, 1868-1946,
ed.
Songs of Scotland; selected and
ed. by Granville Bantock. © W.
Paxton & Co., ltd., London;
bk.2, 22Jul46; on compilation;
EF5747.

Songs of Wales; selected and ed.
by Granville Bantock. Welsh
and English words. © William
Paxton & Co., ltd., London;
bk.2, 17Dec46; on compilation;
EF5709.

BANTOCK, GRANVILLE RANSOME, 1868-
1946.
Three Songs of Sister Miriam;
words by Sister Miriam, music
by Granville Bantock. ©
Goodwin & Tabb, ltd., London;
21Jun46; EF5697.

BARAN, LOUIS.
For All That I Want; words and
music by Marion Aldrich, Al
Dahle [and] Louis Baran. ©
Mardi Gras Music Co., Buffalo;
29Aug47; EP18265.

BARBIC, FRANK STANLEY.
Jitterbug; words and music by
Frank Stanley Barbic. [c1945]
© Nordyke Publishing Co., Los
Angeles; 12Jun46; EP20321.

BARBIROLLI, JOHN, 1899-
(Concerto, oboe & string
orchestra) Concerto ... on
themes of Arcangelo Corelli, by
John Barbirolli. London,
Boosey & Hawkes. © Hawkes &
Son (London) ltd., London;
24Sep47; on arrangement; EF6649.

BARKER, DANNY.
Save the Bones for Henry Jones
('cause he don't eat no meat)
music by Danny Barker, words by
Vernon Lee. New York, Capitol
Songs. © Criterion Music Corp.,
New York; 27Oct47; EP18528.

BARKLA, NEIL.
Miniature Suite ... [by] Neil Barkla.
© The Oxford Univ. Press, London;
30Oct47; EF7176. Two scores for
2 pianos.

BARLOW, WAYNE.
Lyrical Piece ... By Wayne
Barlow, [transcribed by the
composer from the original
score for clarinet and string
orchestra] © Carl Fischer,
inc., New York; 25Jun47;
EP15368. Score (clarinet and
piano) and part.

BARNBY, JOSEPH, 1838-1896.
When Morning Guilds the Skies ...
for choirs and congregation
with soprano and alto solos (S.
A.T.B.) [by] Joseph Barnby ...
arr. by W. B. Olds, [words from
the] Katholisches Gesang buch ...
tr. by Edward Caswall. © Hall
and McCreary Co., Chicago;
22Aug47; on arrangement; EP17026.

BARNES, EDWARD SHIPPEN.
Bethlehem; Christmastide anthem,
S. A. T. B. [Words by]
Howard Patrick McConnell,
[music by] Edward Shippen
Barnes. © J. Fischer & Bro.,
New York; 3Sep47; EP17385.

If Love Should Come ... for three-
part chorus of women's voices
with piano acc. [by] Edward
Shippen Barnes, [words by]
Edward Fuller. © The Boston
Music Co., Boston; 2Sep47;
EP17299.

Peace ... [words by] Wm. L.
Stidger, music by Edward Shippen
Barnes. © The Arthur P. Schmidt
Co., Boston; 23Sep47; EP17322.

BARNES, JEWEL E
Billy Boy; lullaby, words and
music by Jewel E. Barnes.
© Jewel E. Barnes, Modesto,
Calif.; 30Jun47; EP15692.

BARNETT, JACK.
The Secretary Song ... words and
music by Sammy Fain and Jack Barnett. © Leo Feist, inc., New
York; 4Dec47; EP20408.

BARON, MAURICE.
Ode to Democracy; a musical
setting of Lincoln's Gettysburg
address, for baritone solo, with
or without mixed chorus, and
orchestra or piano, by Maurice
Baron ... Vocal score. © M.
Baron Co., New York; 10Oct47;
EP18003.

BARR, L   STEWART.
In Mother's Arms; song, lyric and
music by L. Stewart Barr. ©
L. Stewart Barr, New York;
19Sep47; EP17245.

BARRAINE, ELSA, 1910-
Improvisation; pour saxophone alto
et piano [by] Elsa Barraine.
© Lucien de Lacour, Éditeur,
Paris; 1Jul47; EF6573. Score
and part.

Marche du Printemps sans amours;
[by] Elsa Barraine. © Éditions
Musicales "Le Chant du Monde,"
Paris; 4Jun47; EF5920.

BARRAUD, HENRY.
(Concerto, piano) Concerto ...
[by] Henry Barraud, réduction
... por l'auteur. © Lucien de
Lacour, Éditeur, Paris; 1Jul47;
EF6575. Score; piano 1-2.

BARRAUD, HENRY HIPPOLYTE, 1900-
Le Testament Villon; cantate de
chambre pour ténor, piano et
choeur à capella; poème de
François Villon, [music by]
Henry Barraud. © Durand & Cie,
Paris; 25May47; EF5852.

BARRERA, CARLOS GÓMEZ.   See
Gómez Barrera, Carlos.

BARRET, GEORGE FRANCIS.
You Made Me Crazy 'Bout You; words
and music by George Francis
Barret. © Nordyke Publishing
Co., Los Angeles; 16Sep46;
EP20312.

BARRETO, JUSTI.
Llegaste Tarde! ... Letra y
música de Justi Barreto, arreglo de Pérez Prado. © Peer
International Corp., New York;
6Jun47; EF5736. Parts:
orchestra.

BARRETT, LYDIA.
You're the One in My Heart; words
and music by Lydia Barrett. ©
Nordyke Publishing Co., Los
Angeles; 27Sep46; EP20355.

BARRIS, ELIZABETH PULITZER.
Glorious Old Glory; words and
music by Elizabeth Pulitzer
Barris. © Nordyke Publishing
Co., Los Angeles; 13Aug47;
EP19482.

BARRIS, HARRY.
Torchy; lyrics by John Seeley and
Harry Jans, music by Harry
Barris, [arr. by Lou Halmy]
© Mills Music, inc., New York;
29Aug47; EP17944.

BARRIS, HARRY. Cont'd.
Wrap Your Troubles in Dreams (and
dream your troubles away) words
by Ted Koehler and Billy Moll,
music by Harry Barris, [arr. by
Robert C. Haring] © Shapiro,
Bernstein & Co., inc., New York;
17Nov47; on arrangement; EP19248.

[BARRITEAU, CARL ALDRIC STANLEY]
1914-
I'm Tired but I Don't want to
Sleep; [by] Spencer Williams
and Martin Granger [pseud.]
© Box and Cox (Publications),
London; 10Jun47; EF5790. For
voice and piano; melody also
in tonic sol-fa notation.

BARRO, JOÃO DE.
Copacabana; lyric by Al Stillman,
music by João de Barro and Al-
berto Ribeiro. © Robbins Music
Corporation, New York; 24Oct47;
EP19122.

BARRON, BARRY, 1910-
Cuddle Me in the Clover. © The
Irwin Dash Music Co., ltd.,
London; 13Jun47; EF5857. For
voice and piano, with chord
symbols. Melody also in tonic
sol-fa notation.

BARROS, JOSÉ.
El Gallo Tuerto ... de: José
Barros. Arreglo de: Rafael de
Paz. © Promotora Hispano Americana de Música, s.a., México;
30Dec46; EF6713. Piano-conductor score (orchestra) condensed score and parta.

[BARTH, HAROLD]
Traum, Kleines Baby ... Musik:
Mac Paxton Bill [pseud.],
deutscher Text von Karl Ferber,
paroles françaises de C. Casali,
parole italiane di C. Casali.
© Édition Turicaphon ltd.,
Zürich, Switzerland; 28Apr47;
EF5873.

BARTHELSON, JOYCE, 1900-
Christmas Prayer; for two-part
chorus of women's voices with
piano acc., words by Marc
Edmund Jones, music by Joyce
Barthelson. © The Boston Music
Co., Boston; 20Oct47; EP17796.

Hail to the Bells; for four-part
chorus of mixed voices with
piano accompaniment. Words by
Marc Edmund Jones, music by
Joyce Barthelson. © Boston
Music Co., Boston; 17Sep47;
EP17359.

Ring Now, Ring Wide; for four-
part chorus of mixed voices
with piano accompaniment.
Words by Marc Edmund Jones,
music by Joyce Barthelson.
© Boston Music Co., Boston;
17Sep47; EP17358.

Savannah ... by Joyce Barthelson.
© Carl Fischer, inc., New York;
20Nov47; EP19167. Piano-conductor score (orchestra) and parts.

BARTHOLDY, CARL.
Someday I Knew I'd See You; words
and music by Carl Bartholdy.
[c1945] © Nordyke Publishing
Co., Los Angeles; 21Jun46;
EP19459.

BARTHOLOMEW, MARSHALL.
Along the Street I Hear; for chorus
of male voices unacc. Burgundian
carol arr. by Marshall Bartholomew
... [words by] Bernard de la
Monnoye, English version by
Alfred R. Bellinger. © Galaxy
Music Corp., New York; 13Aug47;
on arrangement and English text;
EP17022.

BARTHOLOMEW, MARSHALL, arr.
Eight Burgundian Carols; arr. by
Marshall Bartholomew, [words by
Bernard de la Monnoye, tr. by
Alfred R. Bellinger] (Publica-
tions of the Carol Society,
vol.XIX) © Galaxy Music Corp.,
New York; 21Aug47; on arrange-
ment & English text; EP17017.

Sister Mary Wore Three Lengths of
Chain; Negro spiritual for men's
chorus with tenor or baritone
solo, from "Six Spirituals" collected by Jean Taylor, arr. by
Marshall Bartholomew. © H. W.
Gray Co., inc., New York; 12Dec47;
on arrangement; EP20278.

BARTLETT, ETHEL.
Elizabethan Suite; arr. by Ethel
Bartlett. © The Oxford
University Press, London;
22May47; on arrangement;
EF6121. Two scores for piano
1-2.

BARTLETT, FLOYD.
Along the Blue Muskingum; words
by Sylvia G. Morrison, music by
Floyd Bartlett. © Nordyke
Publishing Co., Los Angeles;
13Jul46; EP19427.

Always Keep Busy; words by Elmer
Muter, music by Floyd Bartlett.
© Nordyke Publishing co., Los
Angeles; 15Aug46; EP20351.

Bent on Love; words by Verna G.
Durbin, music by Floyd Bartlett.
© Nordyke Publishing co., Los
Angeles; 18Jul46; EP19759.

Bottoms Up; words by Roy Schmaltz,
music by Floyd Bartlett. ©
Nordyke Publishing co., Los
Angeles; 11Oct46; EP19788.

The Chapel of Broken Dreams;
words by Joseph L. McCrea,
music by Floyd Bartlett. [c1945]
© Nordyke Publishing Co., Los
Angeles; 21Jun46; EP19953.

Come On Out and Be with Me; words
by Monroe Jones, music by Floyd
Bartlett. © Nordyke Publishing
Co., Los Angeles; 2Jul46;
EP19955.

Come What May; words by Lill B.
Ernst, music by Floyd Bartlett.
© Nordyke Publishing Co., Los
Angeles; 1Jul46; EP19948.

Dancing in the Blue; words by
Pauline Bailey, music by Floyd
Bartlett. © Nordyke Publishing
Co., Los Angeles; 16Sep46;
EP19462.

Darling, Why Did You Leave Me?
Words by Mary E. Shank, music by
Floyd Bartlett. © Nordyke
Publishing Co., Los Angeles;
11Oct46; EP19702.

Ev'ry time I See a Rose; words by
Pat Judge, music by Floyd Bart-
lett. © Nordyke Publishing Co.,
Los Angeles; 11Jun46; EP19727.

The Fonder You Are to My Heart;
words by William Weeks, music
© Nordyke Publishing co., Los
Angeles; 13Jul46; EP20362.

Foolish Pride; words by Ruth Yancey, music by Floyd Bartlett.
[c1945] © Nordyke Publishing
Co., Los Angeles; 21Jun46;
EP19735.

For Your Heart Will Break, Not
Mine; words by Donna Mark, music by Floyd Bartlett. © Nordyke Publishing co., Los Angeles;
16Sep46; EP20360.

Headin' Back to West Virginia;
words by Willis J. Burrows,
music by Floyd Bartlett. ©
Nordyke Publishing Co., Los
Angeles; 10Jan46; EP16823.

Just Dreaming; words by Mary C.
Cookingham, music by Floyd
Bartlett. © Nordyke Publish-
ing Co., Los Angeles; 11Jun46;
EP19940.

Just Plain Lazy; words by Lill B.
Ernst, music by Floyd Bartlett.
© Nordyke Publishing Co., Los
Angeles; 1Jul46; EP19760.

Kid Stuff; words by Joseph Mayzik
and Leslie Sabo, jr., music by
Floyd Bartlett. © Nordyke
Publishing Co., Los Angeles;
9Aug46; EP19335.

Loneliness in View; words by Mary
Jane Parrish, music by Floyd
Bartlett. © Nordyke Publishing
Co., Los Angeles; 8Aug46;
EP20339.

Lost Love; words by Mrs. E. M.
Jones, music by Floyd Bartlett.
[c1945] © Nordyke Publishing
Co., Los Angeles; 27Sep46;
EP19970.

Love Is a Wonderful Feeling;
words by Conard F. Gray,
music by Floyd Bartlett.
© Nordyke Publishing Co.,
Los Angeles; 26Oct45;
EP17502.

Love Jumped over a Pin Ball
Machine; words by Musa Millard
Gross, music by Floyd Bartlett.
© Nordyke Publishing Co., Los
Angeles; 25May46; EP19965.

Memories of Old New York; words by
Tom Moran, music by Floyd Bart-
lett. © Nordyke Publishing Co.,
Los Angeles; 7Aug46; EP20305.

Moon Lullaby; words by Marcine
Yarbrough, music by Floyd
Bartlett. © Nordyke Publish-
ing Co., Los Angeles; 16Sep46;
EP19475.

The More I See of You; words by
Marie R. Whitehouse, music by
Floyd Bartlett. © Nordyke
Publishing Co., Los Angeles;
27Sep46; EP20084.

My Alabama Rose; words by Bobbie
L. Nichols, music by Floyd
Bartlett. © Nordyke Publishing
Co., Los Angeles; 27Sep46;
EP16735.

My Dove; words by Ethel Roberta
Lewis, music by Floyd Bartlett.
© Nordyke Publishing Co., Los
Angeles; 25Jul46; EP20087.

My Prairie Home; words by Howard
Boyer; music by Floyd Bartlett.
© Nordyke Publishing Co., Los
Angeles; 8Aug46; EP16793.

My Queen of Hearts; words by
Margaret Shannon, music by
Floyd Bartlett. © Nordyke
Publishing Co., Los Angeles;
16Sep46; EP19721.

My Senorita; words by Bernice
Crutchfield, music by Floyd
Bartlett. © Nordyke Publishing
Co., Los Angeles; 12Jun46;
EP19351.

Night for Loving; words by Marie
S. Lagarde, music by Floyd
Bartlett. © Nordyke
Publishing Co., Los Angeles;
9Aug46; EP19662.

Our Dreams; words by Geraldine
McConahay, music by Floyd
Bartlett. [c1945] ©
Nordyke Publishing Co., Los
Angeles; 24Jun46; EP19404.

Radar Beams; words by Trudie P.
Wilkins, music by Floyd Bart-
lett. © Nordyke Publishing
Co., Los Angeles; 2Jul46;
EP19657.

Rhythm; words by Eppie Sydnor,
music by Floyd Bartlett.
© Nordyke Publishing
Co., Los Angeles; 31May46;
EP19650.

229

BARTLETT, FLOYD. Cont'd.
Road to Your Heart; words by
Alice G. Sehrt, music by
Floyd Bartlett. © Nordyke
Publishing Co., Los Angeles;
16Sep46; EP19656.

Sentimental; words by Martin C.
Graham, music by Floyd Bartlett.
[c1946] © Nordyke Publishing
Co., Los Angeles; 26Jan47; EP17394.

She's Like Pink Roses; words by
Annie Batson, music by Floyd
Bartlett. © Nordyke Publish-
ing Co., Los Angeles; 31May46;
EP19460.

Sight of Happiness; words by Barney
Lukaschuk, music by Floyd Bart-
lett. © Nordyke Publishing Co.,
Los Angeles; 11Oct46; EP20494.

Staking a Claim on the Moon;
words by W. Paul Hanson, music
by Floyd Bartlett. © Nordyke
Publishing Co., Los Angeles;
27Sep46; EP19414.

The Stars Will Shine Tonight;
words by Roy Harrell, music by
Floyd Bartlett. © Nordyke
Publishing Co., Los Angeles;
11Jun46; EP19416.

Stranger; words by Nettie Rogers,
music by Floyd Bartlett. ©
Nordyke Publishing Co., Los
Angeles;16Sep46; EP20031.

Texas Star; words by Virginia
Dantzler, music by Floyd Bart-
lett. © Nordyke Publishing Co.,
Los Angeles; 15Aug46; EP19753.

There's a Rainbow in Your Tears;
words by Cora Mason, music by
Floyd Bartlett. [c1945] ©
Nordyke Publishing Co., Los
Angeles; 14Jun46; EP20477.

There's Something I Want; words
by Beatrice O'Brien, music by
Floyd Bartlett. [c1945] © Nordyke
Publishing Co., Los Angeles;
14Jun46; EP20338.

Tomorrow May Be Too Late; words
by Ella Spence, music by Floyd
Bartlett. [c1945] © Nordyke
Publishing Co., Los Angeles;
8Aug46; EP19535.

Too Tired; words by Agnes D. Maze,
music by Floyd Bartlett. ©
Nordyke Publishing Co., Los
Angeles; 11Jun46; EP20476.

Waiting with Tears in My Heart;
words by Blanche M. Smith, music
by Floyd Bartlett. [c1946] ©
Nordyke Publishing Co., Los
Angeles; 21Aug47; EP16609.

We've Been Strangers Too Long;
words by Virgil E. Sprague,
music by Floyd Bartlett. [c1945]
© Nordyke Publishing
Co., Los Angeles; 12Jun46;
EP19709.

What'll I Do? Words by Joseph R.
Phillips, music by Floyd Bart-
lett. © Nordyke Publishing
Co., Los Angeles; 16Sep46;
EP20054.

Won't You Remember; words by Cecil
Edwards, music by Floyd Bartlett.
© Nordyke Publishing Co., Los
Angeles; 11Nov46; EP19751.

Would It Make Any Difference?
Words by Effie Sanders, music
by Floyd Bartlett. © Nordyke
Publishing Co., Los Angeles;
14Jun46; EP19770.

Wouldn't It Be Grand, My Dear;
words by Leta Selby, music by
Floyd Bartlett. [c1946] © Nordyke Publishing Co., Los Angeles;
30Oct47; EP19633.

You Are Never Off My Mind; words
by Isaac Whitworth, music by
Floyd Bartlett. © Nordyke
Publishing Co., Los Angeles;
6Oct45; EP17452.

You Are So Beautiful; words by
Oscar Wright, music by Floyd
Bartlett. © Nordyke Publishing
Co., Los Angeles; 11Oct46;
EP19476.

You Came into My Heart; words by
Jimmy Corra, music by Floyd
Bartlett. © Nordyke Publishing
Co., Los Angeles; 30May46;
EP20587.

You Can't Remember (and I can't
forget); words by Rosemary Smiley,
music by Floyd Bartlett. © Nordyke Publishing Co., Los Angeles;
27Sep46; EP19739.

You Kissed Me in My Dreams; words
by A. M. Lunson, music by Floyd
Bartlett. © Nordyke Publishing
Co., Los Angeles; 27Sep46;
EP20583.

You Locked My Heart; words by
H. H. Harris, music by Floyd
Bartlett. © Nordyke Publishing
Co., Los Angeles; 18Jul46;
EP19384.

You, My Beautiful You; words by
Francis W. Earsley, music by
Floyd Bartlett. © Nordyke
Publishing Co., Los Angeles;
9Aug46; EP19749.

Your Little Kiss; words by C. H.
Taylor, music by Floyd Bartlett.
© Nordyke Publishing Co., Los
Angeles; 16Sep46; EP20316.

You're a Revelation to Me; words
by Mildred Thatcher, music by
Floyd Bartlett. © Nordyke
Publishing Co., Los Angeles;
18Jul46; EP19485.

You're My Precious Darling; words
by Charlotte Roberts Wodin, music by Floyd Bartlett. © Nordyke Publishing Co., Los Angeles;
25May46; EP20374.

You're the Castle of My Dreams;
words by Lillie Murph, music
by Floyd Bartlett. © Nordyke
Publishing Co., Los Angeles;
28Jun46; EP20586.

You're the Love of My Heart;
words by Marcella Roberts,
music by Floyd Bartlett.
© Nordyke Publishing Co., Los
Angeles; 30May46; EP20059.

BARTÓK, BÉLA, 1881-1945.
(Concerto, Piano, No. 3) 3rd
Piano Concerto; [by] Béla
Bartók, reduction for two
pianos, four-hands by Mátyás
Seiber. © Hawkes & Son,
(London), ltd., London;
18Jul47; on arrangement;
EP5800. Score: piano 1-2.

BARTON, GLEN, pseud. See
Klemm, Gustav.

BASHAM, LENARD.
American Dance; [by] L. Basham.
© Carl Fischer, inc., New York;
23Sep47; EP18065. Score
(clarinet and piano) and part.

BASIE, COUNT, 1906-
Brand New Wagon; by Jimmy Rushing
and Count Basie ... arr. by Will
Hudson. © Bregman, Vocco and
Conn, inc., New York; 17Nov47;
EP18775. Piano-conductor score
(orchestra, with words) and
parts.

House Rent Boogie; by Count Basie,
Buster Harding and Milton Ebbins
... arr. by Buster Harding. ©
Bregman, Vocco and Conn, inc.,
New York; 17Nov47; EP18776.
Piano-conductor score (orchestra)
and parts.

One O'clock Boogie; by Count Basie,
Jimmy Mundy and Milton Ebbins.
© Bregman, Vocco and Conn, inc.,
New York; 24Jul47; EP15831.
Piano-conductor score (orchestra)
and parts.

BASTIDA, RAMON G
Farolito de Madrid ... música del
Mtro. Ramon G. Bastida, letra
de Salvador Valverde, [arr. by
Laito Castro] © Peer Interna-
tional Corp., New York; 6Jun47;
EP6174. Piano-conductor score
(orchestra) and parts.

BASTIEN, ANDRÉ, 1908-
Eldorado ... [by] A. Bastien. La
Barranca ... [by] Mario Melfi
[and] Félix Antonini. © Éditions espagnoles Julio Garzon,
Paris; 14Oct47; EF7331. Piano-
conductor score (orchestra) and
parts.

BATES, AUBREY ELIAS, 1924-
Through the Eyes of Jesus [and]
Show Me the Way to Go Home;
[words by] A. E. Bates, [music by]
Aubrey E. Bates. © Aubrey
Elias Bates, North Charleston,
S. C.; 20Jul47; EP15740-15741.

BATH, HUBERT.
Cornish Rhapsody; by Hubert Bath,
[lyrics by Al Stillman, arr.
by Victor Lamont. Standard
od.] © Sam Fox Publishing
Co., New York; 12Aug47; on
arrangement & lyrics; EP16414.

Cornish Rhapsody; lyric by Al
Stillman, music by Hubert Bath,
[arr. by Victor Lamont] Popular
vocal ed. © Sam Fox Publishing
Co., New York; 12Aug47; on
arrangement & lyrics; EP16415.

BATISTICH, JOSEPH, 1894-
Room for Two; words by Robert
Clairmont, music by Joseph
Batistich. © Handy Brothers
Music Co., inc., New York;
15Jul47; EP15387.

BATTISTE, LAWRENCE LeBARON.
Blue Eyed Mary Lou; words and
music by Lawrence LeBaron
Battiste. © Nordyke Publishing
Co., Los Angeles; 29Jan47;
EP19453.

BATTLE, BERNARD GARY, 1916-
I'm Going to Sing Hallelujah Bye
and Bye; words and music by Ber-
nard G. Battle, arr. by Mary E.
Lacy Moore. © Washington, D.C.,
Battle & Odom. © Bernard Gary
Battle, Washington, D.C.;
16Jun47; EP19282. Close score:
SATB.

BATTLE, EDGAR.
Serenade in Rhythm ... by Edgar
Battle. © Rudine Music, inc.,
New York; 17Jun47; EP15457.
Piano-conductor score (orchestra)
and parts.

BAUER, BILLY.
Pam ... music by Billy Bauer, arr.
by Joe Bishop. © Charling Music
Corp., New York; 26May47;
EP15510. Piano-conductor score
(orchestra) and parts.

BAUER, MARION.
The Harp ... by Marion Bauer,
[words by Edna Castleman Bailey]
© Broadcast Music, inc., New
York; 25Jul47; EP18208.

Swan ... By Marion Bauer, [words by
Edna Castleman Bailey, pseud.]
© Broadcast Music, inc., New York;
25Jul47; EP18047.

230

BAUM, GEORGETTE, 1917-
It's Better That Way; lyric by
Jerry Hochberg, music by Geor-
gette Baum. © Alan Courtney
Music Co., New York; 24Nov47;
EP19860.
It's Gonna Rain; lyric by Jerry
Hochberg, music by Georgette
Baum. © Alan Courtney Music Co.,
New York; 24Nov47; EP19859.
The Lovers' Waltz; lyric by Carol
Lynne [and] Jerry Hochberg,
music by Georgette Baum. © Alan
Courtney Music Co., New York;
17Nov47; EP19090.
There's Only Lonely Me; lyric by
Jerry Hochberg, music by Geor-
gette Baum. © Alan Courtney
Music Co., New York; 17Nov47;
EP19091.

BAUMGARTNER, MARGUERITE.
Paradise Waltz; words and music
by Marguerite Baumgartner.
© Nordyke Publishing Co., Los
Angeles; 12Sep47; EP20484.

BAWCOMB, JOHN.
Pearls; song, words by Joseph
Murrells, music by John
Bawcomb. © Chappell & Co.,
ltd., London; 12Jun47;
EP5721.

BAWCOMB, JOHN WILLIAM, 1904-
Green Fingers ... lyric by
Joseph Murrells, music by John
Bawcomb. [c1946] © Dix, ltd.,
London; 13Jun47; EP6377.

BAX, ARNOLD, 1883-
Epithalamium (for S.A.T.B. in uni-
son and organ) [by] Arnold Bax.
[words from Edmund Spenser] ©
Chappell & Co., ltd., London;
7Nov47; EF7205.
Five Greek Folk Songs; English
translation from the Greek and
readjustment of text by M. D.
Calvocoressi, arr. for S.A.T.B.
by Arnold Bax. © Chappell &
Co., ltd., London; 14Jul47;
EF6232.
Four Pieces; for flute & piano,
by Arnold Bax. © Chappell &
Co., ltd., London; 24Sep47;
EF6830. Score and part.

BAXTER, JESSE R   1887-   comp.
Garden of Melody ... [comp. by] J. R.
Baxter, jr., [music ed. by] V. O.
Fossett ... [words ed. by] B. B.
Edmiaston. © Stamps-Baxter Music
and Printing Co., Dallas; 15Oct47;
EP19881. Shape-note notation.

BAXTER, LILLY.
Waltzing thru' My Dreams; words and
music by Lilly Baxter. © Nordyke Publishing Co., Los Angeles;
25Jul46; EP20308.

[BAY, MELBOURNE E   ]
The Mel-Bay Chord System; for the
modern orchestral guitar, [by
Mel Bay] © Joseph Lemantraut,
jr., d.b.s. Louis Retter Music
Co., St. Louis; 25Jul47; EP16707.

BAYHA, CHARLES ANTHONY, 1893-
I'd Rather Be in Miami; by Charles
A. Bayha. [arr. by Howard Ross]
© Charles Anthony Bayha, New
York; 12Aug47; EP16153. For
voice and piano.
On Biscayne Bay, Down Miami Way
... By Charles A. Bayha, [arr.
by Frank Turner] © Charles
Anthony Bayha, New York;
12Aug47; EP16152. For voice
and piano, with chord symbols.

BAYNON, ARTHUR.
Diversions; for piano ... By
Arthur Baynon. © Keith
Prowse & Co., ltd., London;
8Jul47; EP5754.

BEACH, FLOYD O   1898-
Sleep Weary Soldier; by Floyd O.
Beach. © Floyd O. Beach, East
Orange, N. J.; 14Aug47;
EP16500. For voice and piano.

BEACH, FOSTER.
Takin' My Time (you'll surely be
mine) words and music by Foster
Beach. © Lake Music Publishing
Co., New York; 18Oct47; EP18168.

BEACH, HELEN.
He Came Back to Me Just Like He
Used to Be; words and music by
Helen Beach. [c1946] © Nor-
dyke Publishing Co., Los Angeles;
14Jan47; EP19498.

BEADLE, WILBUR.
It's the Waltz You Must Dance;
words and music by Wilbur Beadle. [c1946] © Nordyke Publishing Co., Los Angeles;
16Sep47; EP17913.
One More Goodbye; words and music
by Wilbur Beadle. [c1946]
© Nordyke Publishing Co., Los
Angeles; 16Sep47; EP17915.

BEANE, RAYMOND A   1911-
Siena Victory March; words and
music by Raymond A. Beane. ©
St. Bernadine of Siena College,
Loudonville, N. Y., 6Oct47;
EP18281.

BEAR, NOEL.
You've Got Something There; words
by Charles Fink, music by
Noel Bear. © Nordyke Publish-
ing Co., Los Angeles; 4Sep47;
EP19321.

BEARD, CLARENCE M
We Have to Wear Galoshes; words
and music by Clarence M. Beard.
© Nordyke Publishing Co., Los
Angeles; 22Jul47; EP19540.

BEAVER, GUBE.
The Great Judgment Day; by Cliff
Carlisle, Sid Prosen and Pappy
Gube Beaver. © Hometown Music
Co., inc., New York; 13Aug47;
EP16427. For voice and piano,
with chord symbols.

BEAVER, WILMA.
Prairie Du Chein; words and music
by Billie Beaver. © Nordyke
Publishing Co., Los Angeles;
10Jun47; EP16946.

BECHLER, MARJORIE FRANKLIN.
I'll Go Along; words and music by
Marjorie Franklin Bechler.
© Nordyke Publishing Co., Los
Angeles; 16Jun47; EP17620.

BECK, CONRAD, 1901-
(Trio, strings, no. 2)   Trio II
... [by] Conrad Beck.   Score.
© Schott & Co., ltd., London;
5Jun47; EP5791. Score; violin,
viola and violoncello.

BECKER, HELEN.
Oh, What Am I Gonna Do with You?
words and music by Helen Becker.
© Nordyke Publishing Co., Los
Angeles; 12Jun46; EP19500.

BECKHARD, ROBERT L   1917-
Four Epitaphs; for full chorus of
mixed voices a cappella, [by]
Robert L. Beckhard, [words by]
Sylvia Townsend Warner. © The
Boston Music Co., Boston;
10Nov47; EP20161.

BECKWITH, LILAH L
Rogue River Valley; words and
music by Lilah L. Beckwith.
[c1946] © Nordyke Publishing
Co., Los Angeles; 20Jan47;
EP19961.

BEDELL, ROBERT LEECH, 1909-   ed.
Baroque Suite; for organ, ed. by
Robert Leech Bedell. © Edition
Musicus-New York, inc., New
York; 23May47; on harmonic &
rhythmic changes, organ registra-
tion & preface; EP16162.
Contents.-Prelude, by G. P.
Palestrina.- Fugue, by H. L.
Hassler.- Toccata, by Girolamo
Frescobaldi.
Messe Basse; (suite brève
religieuse) For organ, by
Robert Leech Bedell. © The H.
W. Gray Co., inc., New York;
23Oct47; EP18485.
Prelude-offertoire (pour messe
basse); organ solo by Robert
Leech Bedell. © Mills Music,
inc., New York; 8Dec47; EP19906.

BEDOUIN, PAUL, 1897-
Fantaisie ... [by] P. Bedouin.
© Alphonse Leduc & Co., Paris;
30Apr47; EF6421. Score
(trumpet and piano) and part.

BEER, ALEX.
You Ought To Know I Miss You;
words by Anita Gerson, music by
Alex Beer. © Nordyke Publishing
Co., Los Angeles; 27Mar47;
EP16955.

BEETHOVEN, LUDWIG VAN, 1770-1827.
Bagatelle; in G minor, by
Beethoven. Op. 119. Arr. by
Arthur Baynon. © Oxford University Press, London; 28Aug47;
on arrangement; EF6657. Two
scores for piano 1-2.
For Elise; [by] Beethoven, ed. by
Ernest Haywood. Piano solo.
© Keith, Prowse & Co., ltd.,
London; 25Jun47; on editing &
arrangement; EF6246.
Hymn to Courage; four-part chorus
for boys' glee club, [by] Ludwig van Beethoven, arr. by
Robert W. Gibb, English version
by Christine P. Curtis. © Boston Music Co., Boston; 28Nov47;
on arrangement; EP19808.
Minuet in G ... Arr. by Hugo Frey,
[words by Elsie-Jean, pseud.]
© Hamilton S. Gordon, inc., New
York; 16Jun47; on words and arrangement; EP15743. For piano
solo, with words.
Moon of Dawn; (Moonlight sonata)
lyric by Joseph McCarthy, Jr.,
music by Ludwig van Beethoven,
arr. by Hugo Frey ... [for] two
part ... treble voices. © The
John Franklin Co., inc., New
York; 7Oct47; on arrangement;
EP18127.
Moon of Dawn; (Moonlight sonata)
lyric by Joseph McCarthy, Jr.,
music by Ludwig van Beethoven,
arr. by Hugo Frey ... S.A.B.
© The John Franklin Co., inc.,
New York; 7Oct47; on arrangement; EP18126.
Moon of Dawn; (Moonlight sonata)
lyric by Joseph McCarthy, Jr.,
music by Ludwig van Beethoven,
arr. by Hugo Frey ... S.A.T.B.
© The John Franklin Co., inc.,
New York; 7Oct47; on arrangement; EP18128.
Moon of Dawn; (Moonlight sonata)
lyric by Joseph McCarthy, Jr.,
music by Ludwig van Beethoven,
arr. by Hugo Frey ... S.S.A.
© The John Franklin Co., inc.,
New York; 7Oct47; on arrangement; EP18125.
Moonlight Sonata. See his Sonata, piano

BEETHOVEN, LUDWIG VAN. (Cont'd.)
Prayer; for four-part chorus of boys'
voices with piano accompaniment,
[words oy] Walker W. Daly, [music
by] Ludwig van Beethoven, arr. by
Robert ... Gibb. © Boston Music
Co., Boston; 15Dec47; on arrangement; EP20396.

(Sonata, piano) Moonlight Sonata;
guitar solo, [by] L. van Beethoven,
arr. by Harry Volpe. c1939. ©
Albert Rocky Co., New York;
10Jan40; on arrangement; EP20199.

(Sonata, piano) Theme and Two
Variations from Beethoven's
Appassionata Sonata (second
movement) for piano solo, sim-
plified by Chester Wallis
[pseud.] © The Boston Music Co.,
Boston; 30Jul47; on arrangement;
EP19038.

(Sonata, violoncello) Sonata in
G minor, Op. 5, no. 2. [By]
Beethoven, [ed. by Donald F. To-
vey] Arr. for viola & piano by
Lionel Tertis. © Augener, ltd.,
London; 7Nov47; on arrangement;
EF7361. Score (violoncello and
piano) and part for viola.

Theme and Two Variations from Beethoven'
Appassionata Sonata. See his Sonata,
piano.

Three Equale; for four trombones,
[by] Beethoven, adapted for trumpet and 3 trombones by Emil Kahn.
© Edward B. Marks Music Corp., New
York; 19Nov47; on adaptation & arrangement; EP18988. Score and
parts.

Variations on a Theme by Diabelli;
[by] Ludwig van Beethoven. Op.
120. [For] piano solo, ed. and
annotated by Artur Schnabel.
© Carl Fischer, inc., New York;
15Aug47; on Spanish text; EP16619.
English, French and Spanish annotations; those in Spanish tr. by
Maria Paz Gainsborg.

BELL, BEATRICE.
The Rainbow Trail; words and music
by Beatrice Bell. © Nordyke
Publishing Co., Los Angeles;
12Apr47; EP16801.

BELL, HARRY, 1885-
Madelene, I Had a Dream; words
by William E. Monroe, music by
Harry & Mildred Bell. ©
Nordyke Publishing Co., Los
Angeles; 27Sep46; EP19445.

My Heart Goes Out to a Soldier;
words by Pauline E. Ausenbaugh,
music by Harry & Mildred Bell.
© Nordyke Publishing Co., Los
Angeles; 27Jul46; EP19675.

BELL, HUGO J
Sleepy Moon; words and music by
Hugo J. Bell. © Nordyke Publishing Co., Los Angeles;
29Mar47; EP16744.

BELL, MAUD E   1918-
Lord, I'm Trying, Is My Way All
Right? Words and music by
Maud E. Bell. © Maud E. Bell,
Buffalo; 8Aug47; EP16115.

BELLA, ONOFRIO DI. See
Di Bella, Onofrio.

BELLAS, GIANNES GEORGIOS, 1910-
Aphese Me na Phileso ... Etichoi;
K. Kophiniote, mousiké Gianné
Bella. Athénai, Ekdoseis
Gaitanou. © Michael Gaetanos,
Athens; 15May47; EF5768. For
voice and piano.

Ena Mpoukéto Menexedes ... stichoi;
G. Photide, mousiké Gianné Bella.
Athénai, Ekdoseis Gaitanou. ©
Michael Gaetanos, Athens; 2May47;
EF5769. For voice and piano.

BELLE, BARBARA.
Early Autumn; words and music by
Stan Rhodes and Barbara Belle.
© Enterprise Music Corp., New
York; 28Aug47; EP17931.

BELLIN, LEWIS.
Let's Pick Up Where We Left Off;
by Jay Milton and Lewis Bellin.
© Bel-Air Music Corp., Hollywood, Calif.; 26Sep47; EP17580.
For voice and piano, with chord
symbols.

BELLINI, G   B
If You Loved. (Se Amassi)
Italian words by E. Colisciani,
English translation and vocal
setting by Exa Blount Lucchesi,
music by G. B. Bellini. ©
Mrs. Exa Blount Lucchesi,
Nashville; 13Aug47; on trans-
lation & vocal setting;
EP16309.

BELTRAN RUIZ, PABLO.
Injusticia ... Letra y música de
Pablo Beltrán Ruiz. © Editorial
Mexicana de Música Internacion-
al, s.a., Mexico; 14Jul47;
EF5804.

BEMENT, GWYNN SMITH, 1895-   arr.
Early One Morning; English folk-
song arr. by Gwynn S. Bement
for four-part chorus of men's
voices (a cappella) © E. C.
Schirmer Music Co., Boston;
30Apr47; EP15475.

Early One Morning; for three-part
chorus of women's voices (a
cappella), English folk-song
arr. by Gwynn S. Bement,
traditional English text. ©
E. C. Schirmer Music Co., Boston; 29Sep47; on arrangement;
EP18142.

Let All Things Now Living; three-
part chorus, with descant, for
women's voices, [words by]
John Cowley, traditional Welsh
melody, arr. by Gwynn S. Bement.
© E. C. Schirmer Music Co.,
Boston; 29Jul47; on arrangement; EP16486.

BENATZKY, RALPH, 1887-
Am End! Macht "Er" Alles Allright
... Text und Musik von Ralph
Benatzky. © Edition Turicaphon
a.g., Zürich, Switzerland;
15Sep47; EF6814.

Brief Maria Theresias an Fried-
rich den Grossen; Text und
Musik von Ralph Benatzky.
© Edition Turicaphon a.g., Zur-
ich, Switzerland; 11Jul47;
EF6798.

Drei Tage aus dem Leben Frédéric
Chopin's; Text und Musik von
Ralph Benatzky. © Edition Turicaphon AG., Zurich, Switzerland;
10Aug47; EF7037.

Kleinstadt Zauber; ein musikalisches
lustspiel, die charaktere sind
teilweise basiert auf Nikolaus
Gogol's lustspiel "Der Revisor."
Buch, verse und musik von Ralph
Benatzky. © Edition Turicaphon
ag., Zürich, Switzerland; 1Jul47;
D pub 11076. Libretto.

Kleinstadt Zauber; ein musikalisches
lustspiel, die charaktere sind
teilweise basiert auf Nikolaus
Gogol's lustspiel "Der Revisor."
Buch, verse und musik von Ralph
Benatzky. © Edition Turicaphon
ag., Zürich, Switzerland; 1Jul47;
D pub 11076. Piano-vocal score.

Die Neuberin; Text und Musik v.
Ralph Benatzky. © Edition Turicaphon a.g., Zürich, Switzerland; 11Jul47; EF6799.

Xanthippe; Text und Musik von
Ralph Benatzky. © Edition Turicaphon, AG., Zurich, Switzerland;
10Aug47; EF7038.

BENDER, ALENE.
Unforgettable You; words and
music by Alene Bender. ©
Nordyke Publishing Co., Los
Angeles; 21Feb47; EP19468.

BENDER, LETA S   1894-
Tied to My Heart; by Leta S. Ben-
der, [words by] Claribel L.
Thomas, Raymond A. Sterling
[and Leta S. Bender] Friend,
Neb., S.T.A. Music Pub. Co.
© Leta S. Bender, Friend, Neb.;
8Sep47; EP18181.

You Think I Don't Care; words by
Lillian Turtur, melody by Leta
S. Bender. © Lillian Turtur,
Elizabeth, N. J.; 24Oct47;
EP18428.

BENEDICT, EDWARD.
Here Am I, Send Me; missionary
hymn, [by] E. E. Greenwood [and]
Edw. Benedict. © E. E.
Greenwood, Chicago; 11Aug47;
EP16290.

BENEDICTION HYMNS FOR FOUR MEN'S
VOICES.
© McLaughlin & Reilly Co., Boston;
18Jul47; on arrangement of 2
hymns; EP15873. Partial
contents (arr. by J. A. Reilly)-
Ave Verum Corpus (W. A. Mozart)-
Panis Angelicus (Baini, attr. to
C. C. Casciolini)

BENES, JARA.
Barbara ... Deutscher Text von
Stephanie Kurzer, parole italiane di Carlo Deani, paroles
françaises de Ruy Blag, Musik
von Jara Benes. © Edition
Turicaphon a.g., Zürich, Switzerland; 22Mar47; EF5866.

BENJAMIN, ARTHUR, 1893-
The Fire of Your Love; words by
Frank Eyton, music by Arthur
Benjamin. [London] Boosey &
Hawkes. © Boosey & Co., ltd.,
London; 20Aug47; EF6262.

Linstead Market; a Jamaican folk-
song, set to music by Arthur
Benjamin. London, Boosey &
Hawkes. © Boosey & Co., ltd.,
London; 18Aug47; on new setting;
EF6313.

The Red River Jig; [by] Arthur Benjamin. © Hawkes & Son (London)
ltd., London; 6Nov47; EF7013.
Score: orchestra.

BENNETT, ROBERT RUSSELL.
Vu. (Seen in Paris) 20 études
en miniature pour piano ...
[by] Robert Russell Bennett.
© Publications Raoul Breton &
Co., Paris; 18Sep34; EF5773.

BENSON, JOHN, pseud. See
Pimperal, John Mathew.

BENSON, ROYAL E
Every Night When It Is Twilight;
words and music by Royal E.
Benson. [c1946] © Nordyke
Publishing Co., Los Angeles;
27Oct47; EP18400.

BENTLEY, BERENICE BENSON.
Long, Long Ago; [by] Berenice
Benson Bentley, words anon-
ymous. © Clayton F. Summy Co.,
Chicago; 26Sep47; EP17351. For
piano solo, with words.

Two Piano Solos; by Berenice
Benson Bentley. © Clayton F.
Summy Co., Chicago; v.1, 26Sep47;
v.2, 2Sep47. Contents,- [1] The
Skaters (© EF17350) - [2] Ship
Ahoy (© EP17326)

BENTLY, GUS.
If It's True; words and music by
Don Redman, Jule Penrose and
Gus Bently, arr. by Johnny Warrington. © American Academy
of Music, inc., New York;
18Sep47; on arrangement;
EP18246. Piano-conductor
score (orchestra, with words)
and parts.

BENTZON, NIELS VIGGO, 1919-
Koncertetude ... [by] Niels Viggo
Bentzon. Op. 40. © Wilhelm
Hansen, Musik-Forlag, Copen-
hagen; 30May47; EF6296. For
piano solo.

Toccata ... [by] Niels Viggo
Bentzon. Op. 10. © Wilhelm
Hansen, Musik-Forlag, Copenhagen;
1Apr47; EF6290. For piano solo.

BENZ, VIOLA E
The Tale of Peter Rabbit; an operetta for primary grades by Thelma M. Parker, music by Viola E.
Benz. © Row, Peterson & Co.,
Evanston, Ill.; 20Oct47; D pub
11134.

BEOBIDE, JOSÉ MARIA, 1882-
Tantum Ergo. God Our Father, Lord
of Heaven; for three-part chorus
of mixed voices (a cappella)
[Words by] St. Thomas Aquinas ...
English text by John Cowley,
[music by] José Maria Beobide ...
Arr. by Victoria Glaser. © E. C.
Schirmer Music Co., Boston;
25Jul47; on arrangement; EP16051.

BERALDI, MARINO, 1901-   comp.
Breve Metodo per l'Allievo
Pianista; basato sulle opere
di Beyer, Burgmüller, Duvernoy
... e di altri autori, con
l'aggiunta di un riassunto
teorico e note tecniche sul
pianoforte. © Carisch, s.a.,
Milan; v. 1, 26May47; v.2,
31May47; EF3978, 3979.

BERG, GÖSTA, pseud. See
Jensen, Harry.

BERG, NATANAEL.
(Engelbrekt) Det Sitter en Duva
på Liljekvist, ur op. Engelbrekt, [by] Natanael Berg. ©
Föreningen svenska tonsättare,
Stockholm; 1Jan46; EF7122. For
voice and piano.

Engelbrekt; förspel [by] Natanael
Berg. Stockholm, Ed. Suecia.
© Föreningen svenska tonsättare,
Edition Suecia, Stockholm;
1Jan45; EF7076. Score: orches-
tra.

Det Sitter en Duva på Liljekvist. See
his Engelbrekt.

BERGDAHL, EDITH.
That's What I Like about the West;
words and music by Robert Mac
Gimsey and Edith Bergdahl. ©
Tex Ritter Music Publications,
inc., New York; 27Oct47; EP18509.

BERGEIM, JOSEPH.
Chimes of Victory; march by Joseph
Bergeim. New York, Boosey &
Hawkes. © Hawkes & Son (London)
ltd., London; 22Aug47; EP17144.
Condensed score (band) and parts.

The Skywriter; march by Joseph
Bergeim. New York, Boosey &
Hawkes. © Hawkes & Son (London)
ltd., London; 22Aug47;
EP17143. Condensed score (band)
and parts.

BERGH, ARTHUR, 1898-
Music, When Soft Voices Die; song
for medium voice, poem by Shelley,
music by Arthur Bergh. [Op.37,
no.1] © Wesley Webster, San
Francisco; 2Jul47; EP15444.

The Night Has a Thousand Eyes;
song for high voice, poem by
Francis William Bourdillon,
music by Arthur Bergh. [Op.37,
no.2] © Wesley Webster, San
Francisco; 2Jul47; EP15443.

BERGMAN, DEWEY, 1900-
If I Can't Believe in You; lyric
by Jack Segal, music by Dewey
Bergman. © Paull-Pioneer Music
Corp., New York; 24Oct47;
EP18451

Melancholy; words and music by
Jack Segal and Dewey Bergman.
© Bregman, Vocco and Conn,
inc., New York; 16Oct47;
EP18297.

BERGSMA, WILLIAM.
Six Songs; to poems by E. E. Cummings
for voice and piano, music by
William Bergsma. © Carl Fischer,
inc., New York; 22Sep47; EP18068.

BERK, MORTY, 1898-
My "Jo" in Idaho; by Monty Berk
... [words by] Chas. Dumont.
© Chas. Dumont & Son, Philadelphia; 4Aug47; EP18623.

BERLE, MILTON, 1908-
I'll Never Make the Same Mistake
Again; by Herb Magidson, Ben
Oakland [and] Milton Berle.
© Mayfair Music Corp., New
York; 30Jun47; EP15787. For
voice and piano, with chord
symbols.

BERLIN, BORIS, 1907-
Two Pieces; for pianoforte, [by]
Boris Berlin. © The Frederick
Harris Music Co., ltd., Oak-
ville, Ont., Can.; 25Oct47; on
2 pieces. Contents: - [1]
Squirrels at Play (© EF6853) -
[2] Yanina (© EF6854)

BERLIN, IRVING, 1888-
(Annie Get Your Gun) Irving Berlin's
I Got Lost in His Arms; from ...
Annie Get Your Gun ... arr. by
Jimmy Dale. New York, I. Berlin
Music Corp. © Irving Berlin, New
York; 8Aug46; on arrangement;
EP11302. Piano-conductor score
(orchestra, with words) and parts.

The Freedom Train ... music by
Irving Berlin ... arr. by Eric
Leidzén. New York, I. Berlin
Music Corp. © The American
Heritage Foundation, Washington,
D. C.; 12Nov47; on arrangement;
EP18783. Condensed score (band)
and parts.

The Freedom Train ... Words and
music by Irving Berlin, arr. by
Erik Leidzén. New York, I.
Berlin Music Corp. © The
American Heritage Foundation,
Washington, D.C.; 30Oct47; on
arrangement; EP18780. Score;
TTBB and piano.

The Freedom Train ... Words and
music by Irving Berlin, arr. by
Erik Leidzén. New York, I.
Berlin Music Corp. © The
American Heritage Foundation,
Washington, D.C.; 30Oct47; on
arrangement; EP18781. Score;
SSA and piano.

The Freedom Train ... Words and
music by Irving Berlin, arr. by
Erik Leidzén. New York, I.
Berlin Music Corp. © The
American Heritage Founda-
tion, Washington, D. C.;
30Oct47; on arrangement;
EP18782. Score; SATB and piano.

The Freedom Train; words and music
by Irving Berlin. A Larry
Wagner arrangement. New York,
I. Berlin Music Corp. © The
American Heritage Foundation,
Washington, D.C.; 38ep47; on
arrangement; EP18784. Piano-
conductor score (orchestra, with
words) and parts.

The Freedom Train; words and music
by Irving Berlin. [New York] I.
Berlin Music Corp. © The American Heritage Foundation, New
York; 8Jul47; EP15511.

Help Me to Help My Neighbor ...
music by Irving Berlin, arr. by
Erik Leidzén. New York, I. Berlin Music Corp. © Irving Berlin,
New York; 17Jun47; on arrangement; EP18778. Condensed score
(band) and parts.

I Got Lost in His Arms. See his Annie
Get Your Gun.

Irving Berlin Waltzes ... for
voice and piano [comp. by Irving
Berlin] New York, I. Berlin
Music Corp. © Irving Berlin,
New York; no. 2, 8Apr47; on
compilation; EP18785.

Kate (have 1 come to early, too
late); words and music by
Irving Berlin. A Johnny Warrington arrangement. New York, I.
Berlin Music Corp. © Irving
Berlin, New York; 27Jun47; on
arrangement; EP18779. Parts;
orchestra.

Love and the Weather; words and
music by Irving Berlin, a Johnny Warrington arrangement. New
York, I. Berlin Music Corp.
© Irving Berlin, New York;
17Jun47; on arrangement;
EP18891. Piano-conductor score
(orchestra, with words) and
parts.

BERMEJO, GUILLERMO.
El Abrojo ... letra y música de
Guillermo Bermejo. © Promotora
Hispano Americana de Música,
s.a., México; 27Aug47; EF6712.

BERMONT, GEORGES, 1901-
Waltzing Marionettes ... [by]
Georges Bermont. (In Hirsch-
berg, David, ed. and comp.
Pieces Are Fun. bk. 1, p. 30-
31) © Musicord Publications,
New York; 2Jul47; EP15939.
For piano solo.

BERNARD, BEN.
Bow Bells. See his Dancing with Crime.

(Dancing with Crime) Bow Bells;
words by Harold Purcell, music
by Ben Bernard ... [From the
film] "Dancing with Crime." ©
Edward Kassner Music Co., ltd.,
London; 9Jul47; EF6871.

I'm Not in Love. See his Night Beat.

(Night Beat) I'm Not in Love;
words by Harold Purcell, music
by Ben Bernard ... [From the
film] "Night Beat." © Edward
Kassner Music Co., ltd.,
London; 30Jul47; EF6869.

(Night Beat) When You Smile; words
by Harold Purcell, music by Ben
Bernard ... [From the film]
"Night Beat." © Edward Kassner
Music Co., ltd., London; 13Oct47;
EF6870.

When You Smile. See his Night Beat.

BERNARD, FELIX.
Winter Wonderland; words by Dick
Smith, music by Felix Bernard,
[arr. by Sophie Bostelmann]
Children's ed. © Bregman,
Vocco and Conn, inc., New York;
31Oct47; on children's edition;
EP18464.

BERNARD, GUY, pseud. See
Delapierre, Guy Bernard.

BERNARD, PAUL, arr.
Douze Pièces Mélodiques; études et
exercices pour tuba et saxhorn
basse [transcribed by] Paul Bernard. Extraites de la collection
de vocalises-études pub. sous la
direction de Al. Hettich. ©
Alphonse Leduc, Éditions
musicales, Paris; 1. recueil,
30Apr47; on transcription;
EF6420.

BERNART DE VENTADORN, 12th cent.
Music of the Troubadours; six
songs in Provençal by Bernart
de Ventadorn ... transcribed
and arr. by Egon Wellesz.
[French versions by César
Sfeir] © Oxford University
Press, London; 6Feb47; on
arrangement; EP6144. For voice,
with violin, viola or recorder
accompaniment.

BERNSTEIN, MARTIN, ed.
Score Reading; a series of graded
excerpts, comp. and ed. by Martin
Bernstein. Rev. ed. © M. Witmark
& Sons, New York; 5Dec47; EP19997.

BERR, FRÉDÉRIC.
Méthode Complète de Clarinette ...
[by] Berr. Nouv. éd. entièrement
rev., annotée et augm. par P.
Lefevre ... d'après l'éd. de P.
Mimart. © Alphonse Leduc & Co.,
Éditions musicales, Paris; v. 1,
28Mar47; on revision, annotation
& augmentation; EP6414.

[BERRY, DENNIS ALFRED] 1921-
Something for the Boys; by Jack
Sharp, [pseud.] © Cosmo Music
Co., [London] ltd., London;
26Aug46; EP5704. Piano-
conductor score (orchestra)
and parts.

BERRY, EDDIE, 1914-
El Po Ka Pu (el po ka pi-ya);
English lyric by Ken Hecht,
Spanish lyric by Manuel Palma,
music by Eddie Berry. © Eagle
Music Publishing Corp., New York;
14Aug47; EP16067. English and
Spanish words.

BERRY, THOMAS DAVIS, 1891-
Have You Got a Bad Hangover?
Words and music by Thomas Davis
Berry. Gulfport, Miss., Berry
Song Service Productions.
© Thomas Davis Berry, Gulfport,
Miss.; 10Jul47; EP15657.

BERTAIL, INEZ, arr.
Lullabies from Every Land; arrange-
ments by Inez Bertail, illustra-
tions by Steffie E. Lerch. Garden
City, N. Y., Garden City Pub. Co.
© Duenewald Printing Corp., New
York; 60ct47; A17713. For voice
and piano.

BERTAIL, INEZ, ed. and arr.
Complete Nursery Song Book; ed. and
arr. by Inez Bertail, illus. by
Walt Kelly. © Lothrop, Lee &
Shepard Co., inc., New York;
23Oct47; A16888.

BESKIN, GERALD S   1903-
"Legion Air;" words and music by
... G. S. Beskin. © Independ-
ent Music Publishers, New
York; 27Aug47; EP18247.

BEST, WILLIAM.
(I love you) for sentimental
reasons; lyric by Deek Watson,
music by William Best, arr. for
Hawaiian, electric & plectrum
guitar (note and diagram) [by
the Onhu staff) © Duchess Music
Corp., New York; on arrangement;
24Jan47; EP11808.

BÉTOUS, LOUISE.
Lenoc; (Always) words and music
by Louise Bétous. © Nordyke
Publishing Co., Los Angeles;
10May47; EP17540.

BÉTOVE, pseud. See
Levy, Michel Maurice.

BETTARINI, LUCIANO, 1914-
Canzone del Mare. See his Ombra della
Valle.

Canzone della Valle. See his Ombra dell
Valle.

(Ombra della Valle) Canzone del
Mare ... dal film "Ombra della
Valle"; [by] Luciano Bettarini.
© Carisch, s.a., Milan;
31May47; EP5776. For voice
and piano.

(Ombra della Valle) Canzone
della Valle, dal film "Ombra
della Valle"; [by] Luciano
Bettarini. © Carisch, s.a.,
Milan; 31May47; EP5812. For
voice and piano.

BETTI, ANGE EUGÈNE. See also
Betti, Henri, 1917-

Chanson Populaire; paroles de
Maurice Vandair [pseud.] &
Maurice Chevalier, musique de
Henri Betti. © Éditions Paul
Beuscher, Paris; 20Jul45;
EP6459.

Mandarinade ... Une chanson de
Maurice Chevalier & Pierre
Gilbert ... [music] de Henri
Betti. © Éditions Paul Beusch-
er, Paris; 20Jul45; EP6572.

Monotone ... paroles de Maurice
Vandair [pseud.], musique de
Henri Betti. © Éditions Paul
Beuscher, Paris; 15Jun45;
EP6610. For voice and piano,
and voice part.

BETTI, HENRI. See also
Betti, Ange Eugène.

Une Aiguille dans un Tas de Foin.
See his Mam'selle Printemps.

L'Amour de Ninette. See his Mam'zelle
Printemps.

Le Baccalauréat. See his Mam'zelle
Printemps.

Le Bandonéon. See his Mam'zelle Printemps.

Le Berlingot. See his Mam'zelle
Printemps.

Farandole en Provence. See his Mam'zelle
Printemps.

Mam'zelle Printemps, de l'opérette
"Mam'zelle Printemps" ... paroles
de Maurice Vandair [pseud.],
musique de Henri Betti. Paris,
Paris-Monde, c1946. © Maurice
Vandair & Henri Betti, Paris;
15Feb47; EP5954.

(Mam'zelle Printemps) Une Aiguille
dans un Tas de Foin, de l'opérette
"Mam'zelle Printemps" ...
paroles de Maurice Vandair [pseud.]
musique de Henri Betti. Paris,
Paris-Monde, c1946. © Maurice
Vandair & Henri Betti, Paris;
15Feb47; EP5910.

(Mam'zelle Printemps) L'Amour de
Ninette, de l'opérette "Mam'zelle
Printemps" ... paroles de Maurice
Vandair [pseud.] musique de Henri
Betti. Paris, Paris-Monde,
c1946. © Maurice Vandair & Henri
Betti, Paris; 15Feb47; EP5911.

(Mam'zelle Printemps) Le
Baccalauréat, de l'opérette
"Mam'zelle Printemps" ...paroles
de Maurice Vandair [pseud.]
musique de Henri Betti. Paris,
Paris-Monde, c1946. © Maurice
Vandair & Henri Betti, Paris;
15Feb47; EP5912.

(Mam'zelle Printemps) Le Bandonéon,
de l'opérette "Mam'zelle Printemps"
... paroles de Maurice Vandair
[pseud.] musique de Henri Betti.
Paris, Paris-Monde, c1946. ©
Maurice Vandair & Henri Betti,
Paris; 15Feb47; EP5913.

(Mam'zelle Printemps) Le Berlingot,
de l'opérette "Mam'zelle Prin-
temps" ... paroles de Maurice
Vandair, [pseud.] musique de
Henri Betti. Paris, Paris-Monde,
c1946. © Maurice Vandair &
Henri Betti, Paris; 15Feb47;
EP5914.

(Mam'zelle Printemps) Farandole en
Provence, de l'opérette "Mam'zelle
Printemps" ... paroles de Maurice
Vandair [pseud.] musique de Henri
Betti. Paris, Paris-Monde, c1946.
© Maurice Vandair & Henri Betti,
Paris; 15Feb47; EP5915.

(Mam'zelle Printemps) Octave, de
l'opérette "Mam'zelle Printemps"
... paroles de Maurice Vandair
[pseud.], musique de Henri Betti. ©
Maurice Vandair & Henri Betti,
Paris; 15Feb47; EP5971.

(Mam'zelle Printemps) Si Tu Voulais,
de l'opérette "Mam'zelle Printemps"
... paroles de Maurice Vandair
[pseud.], musique de Henri Betti.
Paris, Paris-Monde, c1946. ©
Maurice Vandair & Henri Betti,
Paris; 15Feb47; EP5973.

(Mam'zelle Printemps) Son Amour,
de l'opérette "Mam'zelle Printemps"
... paroles de Maurice Vandair
[pseud.], musique de Henri Betti.
Paris, Paris-Monde, c1946. ©
Maurice Vandair & Henri Betti,
Paris; 15Feb47; EP5974.

(Mam'zelle Printemps) Toujours d'
Accord, de l'opérette "Mam'zelle
Printemps" ... paroles de Maurice
Vandair [pseud.], musique de
Henri Betti. Paris, Paris-Monde,
c1946. © Maurice Vandair &
Henri Betti, Paris; 15Feb47;
EP5975.

(Mam'zelle Printemps) Valse Joyeuse,
de l'opérette "Mam'zelle Printemps"
... paroles de Maurice Vandair
[pseud.], musique de Henri Betti.
Paris, Paris-Monde, c1946. ©
Maurice Vandair & Henri Betti,
Paris; 15Feb47; EP5976.

Octave. See his Mam'zelle Printemps.

Le Régiment des Mandolines ...
paroles: Maurice Vandair [pseud.],
musique: Henri Betti. Paris,
Paris-Monde. © Maurice Vandair
& Henri Betti, Paris; 8Oct46;
EP5972.

Si Tu Voulais. See his Mam'zelle
Printemps.

Son Amour. See his Mam'zelle Printemps.

Toujours d'Accord. See his Mam'zelle
Printemps.

Valse Joyeuse. See his Mam'zelle Printemps.

BEVERLY, JAMES W
If the Shoe Fits; words by Otis B.
Scott, music by James W. Beverly,
arr. by Belle Schrag. [c1946]
© Nordyke Publishing Co., Los
Angeles; 20Jan47; EP19699.

BEYDTS, LOUIS, 1895-
En Arles.... [by] Louis Beydts,
poème de P. J. Toulet. ©
Durand & Cie, Paris; 19Mar47;
EP6317. Score (voice, flute
ad. lib. and piano) and part
for flute.

BEYER, EMIL.
Ocean Echoes; for voice and piano,
medium or high. Poem by Phyllis
Ernst, music by Emil Beyer.
Cincinnati, Beyer Music Studios.
© Emil Beyer, Cincinnati;
12Nov47; EP19202.

BEYER, FERDINAND.
Preliminary School for the Pianoforte; [by] Beyer, with
additional compositions by
Victor Herbert, Domenico Savino,
and Hugo Frey, [ed. by J. Frank
Level] © Hamilton S. Gordon,
inc., New York; 14Aug47; on
compilation and new pieces;
EP16054.

234

BIBO, IRVING.
Am I Wasting My Time on You? ....
Words and music by Howard Johnson ... and Irving Bibo ... new
arr. by Lindsay McPhail. ©
Stasny Music Corp., New York;
1Sep47; on arrangement; EP18380.

Beeg Palloons; words by Sidney
Clare, music by Irving Bibo.
© Mills Music, inc., New York;
29Aug47; EP17943.

BIERMAN, BERNARD.
Can It Ever Be the Same; by Jack
Manus, Arthur Berman and Bernard
Bierman. © Johnstone Music, inc.,
New York; 24Nov47; EP18774. For
voice and piano, with chord sym-
bols.

I Wouldn't Be Surprised; words and
music by Jack Manus and Bernard
Bierman. © Republic Music Corp.,
New York; 10ct47; EP17717.

BIGARD, ALBANY.
Mood Indigo; words and music [and
arrangement] by Duke Ellington,
Irving Mills and Albany Bigard.
© Gotham Music Service, inc.,
New York; 21Feb31; on lyric &
arrangement; EP17918.

BIGGERS, LELA MACK WILLIAMS.
See Williams-Biggers, Lela Mack.

BIGLER, JEAN E.
Through the Lonely Pines; words and
music by Jean E. Bigler. © Jean E.
Bigler, Morgantown, W. Va.;
2Aug47; EP17089.

BILL, MAC PAXTON, pseud. See
Barth, Harold.

BILLINGS, WILLIAM, 1746-1800.
Compositions ... ed. by Oliver
Daniel. Ser. II. © C. C.
Birchard and Co., Boston;
v. 1-3, on arrangement, notes
& foreword, 5Aug46; v. 4-5,
29Nov46; EP8749, 8747, 8748,
10309, 9559. For mixed chorus,
with piano reduction. Contents.-
[1] David's lamentation.- [2]
I heard a great voice.- [3]
Fare you well, my friends.-
[4] Emanuel.- [5] Chester.

BINDER, RAY.
Mélodie Calme et Triste; [by] Ray
Binder. © Ste. Ame. Fse. Chappell,
Paris; 1Aug47; EF6365. Piano-
conductor score (orchestra) and
parts.

BING CROSBY'S FAVORITE HYMNS ...
arr. by William Stickles. [Rev.
ed.] © Burke & Van Heusen, inc.,
New York; 3Nov47; on additional
music; EP18924.

BINGE, RONALD, 1910-
Madrugada. (Daybreak) [By] Ronald
Binge. © Ascherberg, Hopwood
& Crew, ltd., London; 22Sep47;
on arrangement; EF6633. Piano-
conductor score (orchestra)
and parts.

BINKLEY, FLORENCE FENDER.
Tone Tune Technic; for beginners
in piano ... by Florence Fender
Binkley, the drawings are by
Lucile Strector. © Mills Music,
inc., New York; bk. 1-2, 29Aug47;
EP17956, 17955.

BIRCSAK, THUSNELDA, 1897-
Lullaby of the Christ Child; for
two-part chorus of treble voices,
[words by] T. B., music by Thusnelda Bircsak. © Raymond A.
Hoffman Co., Chicago; 21Oct47;
EP19081.

BIRD, MILLIE WINIFRED, 1898-
"The Lord's Prayer"; written and
composed by M. W. Bird.
Adelaide, South Australia,
Australian Songwriters' and
Music Publishers' Agency. ©
Millie Winifred Bird, Royston
Park, South Australia; 31May46;
EF7049. For voice and piano.

BIRMINGHAM BLUE JAY SINGERS. See
Famous Blue Jay Singers.

BISHOP, DICK.
This Night Is Mine; words and
music by Dick Bishop. ©
Nordyke Publishing Co., Los
Angeles; 21Aug47; EP20483.

BISHOP, HENRY ROWLEY.
Deep in My Heart; song, by Henry
Rowley Bishop, arr. and ed. by
Alec Rowley. [London] Boosey
& Hawkes. © Boosey & Co., ltd.,
London; 12Aug47; on arrangement
and editing of text; EF6061.

BISHOP, JOE.
Indian Boogie Woogie; by Joe
Bishop [and] Woody Herman, arr.
by Joe Bishop. © Leeds Music
Corp., New York; 18Aug47; on
arrangement; EP16402. Piano-
conductor score (orchestra) and
parts.

BITSCH, MARCEL, 1921-
Marvellous Dreams; twelve easy
pieces for the piano. Les Songes
Merveilleux ... [by] Marcel
Bitsch. © Alphonse Leduc & Cie,
Paris; 28Feb47; EF5970.

BIVENS, BURKE.
My Heart Jumped over the Moon;
words by Alfred Ludwig, music
by Burke Bivens. © Nordyke
Publishing Co., Los Angeles;
9Nov46; EP19669.

BIXIO, C'   A
(La Canzone dell'Amore) Song of
Love. La Canzone dell'Amore ...
del film omonimo ... English
lyric by Olga Paul, Italian
music by B. Cherubini, music by
C. A. Bixio. (In Memories of
Italy. p.40-43) © Edward B.
Marks Music Corp., New York;
16Jul47; on English lyric;
EP15825.

BIZET, GEORGES, 1838-1875.
(L'Arlésienne) Le Carillon,
([from] Suite L'Arlésienne), by
Georges Bizet, arr. from the
orchestral score for organ by
M. P. Ingle. © The H. W.
Gray Co., inc., New York;
23Oct47; on arrangement;
EP18489.

Carmen Fantasia; [by] Georges
Bizet, arr. by Theo. M. Tobani,
arr. for modern bands with new
parts by H. R. Kent, [pseud.]
© Carl Fischer, inc., New
York; 25Jul47; on modern band
arrangement; EP15910. Piano
conductor score (band) and
parts.

(Carmen) March from Carmen [by]
Georges Bizet ... [Arr.] for
piano accordion [by Lloyd Marvin]
© Chart Music Publishing House,
inc., Chicago; 13Nov47; on arrangement; EP19126.

BLACK, JOHN STEWART.
Dardanella; by Fred Fisher, Felix
Bernard and Johnny S. Black,
[arr. by Marvin Fisher] © Fred
Fisher Music Co., inc., New
York; 10Oct47; on arrangement;
EP17898. For piano solo, with
chord symbols.

BLACK, MARION R
Stepping Stones; piano solo, [by]
Marion R. Black. © Theodore
Presser Co., Philadelphia;
2Dec47; EP19254.

BLACKBURN, HUBERT.
Garden of Mem'ries; words and music by Hubert Blackburn. © Nordyke Publishing co., Los Angeles;
12Sep47; EP20363.

BLAHA, VACLAV.
I Waited for You ... by Václav
Bláha, [arr. by Joseph Cerny]
© Vitak-Elsnic Co., Chicago;
on arrangement; 25Apr47;
EP15757. Piano-conductor
score (orchestra) and parts.

BLAHNÍK, ROMAN, 1897-
Maskovaná milenka; opereta, hudba:
Roman Blahník, slova: Pavel
Skála. © František Chadím,
Praha, Czechoslovakia; 15Dec46;
EF5363. Excerpts, for voice and
piano.

BLAIN, KENNETH.
Songs and Monologues; written and
composed by Kenneth Blain. ©
Reynolds & Co. (Music Publish-
ers) ltd., London; 1Jul47;
EF6013.

Songs and Monologues; written and
composed by Kenneth Blain.
© Reynolds & Co. (Music Publishers) ltd., London; 2Sep47;
EF6693.

BLAINE, JEAN.
Gosh Darn It, I'm Crazy 'bout
You; words and music by Jean
Blaine. © Kanes Music Publish-
ers, New York; 30Jul47;
EP16174.

BLAIR, HAL.
Let's Go Sparkin'; words and music
by Eddie Dean and Hal Blair,
piano arrangement by Dick Kent.
© Peer International Corp., New
York; 31Oct47; EP18571.

Spring Has Come to Old Missouri;
words and music by Eddie Dean
and Hal Blair. © Peer
International Corp., New York;
31Oct47; EP18578.

Stars over Texas; words and music
by Eddie Dean and Hal Blair.
(In Bourne, inc., comp. Eddie
Dean [song folio] p.4-6) ©
Bourne, inc., New York; 22Jul47;
EP15861.

Why Can't We Be Sweethearts Again?
Words and music by Eddie Dean
and Hal Blair. (In Bourne, inc.,
comp. Eddie Dean [song folio]
p.33-35) © Bourne, inc., New
York; 22Jul47; EP15864.

BLAIR, HUGH.
Angels Are Singing. See his The New
Born King.

(The New Born King) Angels are
Singing, from the cantata
"The New Born King," [by] Hugh
Blair, arr. by Hugh Gordon
[pseud.] © The Arthur P.
Schmidt Co., Boston; 23Sep47;
on arrangement; EP17319. Score:
SA and piano.

BLAKE, C   D
Clayton's Grand March; [by] C. L.
Blake ... for piano, arr. and
ed. by Maxwell Eckstein. ©
Carl Fischer, inc., New York;
5Sep47; on arrangement &
editing; EP18078.

BLAKE, DOROTHY GAYNOR, 1893-
The Brook; piano solo by Dorothy
Gaynor Blake. © The Willis
Music Co., Cincinnati; 9Dec47;
EP20008.

With a "Yo Heave Ho!" Piano solo
[with words] by Dorothy Gaynor
Blake. © The Willis Music Co.,
Cincinnati; 16Oct47; EP18514.

BLAKESLEE, S   EARLE.
I Adore Thee, Blessed Savior; anthem for mixed voices, S.A.T.B.
... words by William W. Bray,
music by S. Earle Blakeslee, arr.
by the composer. © Pallma Music
Products Corp., Chicago; 15Oct47;
EP18927.

BLANC, JANE EUPHEMIE, 1915-
How Ireland Got Its Music; words by
James J. O'Brien ... music by
Jane Euphemie Blanc. © Loyola
University, New Orleans; 26Jun47;
EP15487.

BLANC, MANNY.
Dixieland Traveller ... arrangement
of the Arkansas traveller, by
Manny Blanc. © David Gornston,
New York; 21Oct47; on arrangement;
EP20241. Condensed score (band)
and parts.

BLANCHARD, DONALD.
Goin' to the Old Barn Dance; words
& music by Donald (Red)
Blanchard. © M. M. Cole
Publishing Co., Chicago; 14Nov47;
EP18692.

Sally's Gone to Sante Fe; words &
music by Donald (Red) Blanchard.
© M. M. Cole Publishing Co.,
Chicago; 14Nov47; EP18693.

BLANCHARD, RED. See
Blanchard, Donald.

BLANCHARD, WILLIAM GODWIN, 1905-
Envoy; for full chorus and orches-
tra, music by William G.
Blanchard, text by ... Theodore
C. Agins ... orchestral score
arr. for two pianos. © William
Godwin Blanchard, Claremont,
Calif.; 1Jul47; EP15907.
Score: chorus (SATB) and piano
"-?

BLANCO, JULIO.
Batamú ... Lyric by Marion Sun-
shine, music and Spanish words
by Marcelino Guerra and Julio
Blanco. © Antobal Music Co.,
New York; 15Jul47; EP16961.

BLANCO LEONARD, JULIO.
Encadenado. (Enchained) ... English lyric by Marjorie Harper
... music & Spanish words by
Julio Blanco Leonard. © Antobal Music Co., New York;
15Oct47; EP18564.

BLAND, JAMES A   1854-1911.
Carry Me Back to Old Virginny; [by]
James Bland, arr. by P. Ballatore.
(In Ballatore, Pietro, comp. So
Easy. p. 14-15) © Edward B.
Marks Music Corp., inc., New York;
9Dec47; on arrangement; EP19590.
For piano solo.

BLANE, RALPH, 1914-
(Good News) Pass that Peace Pipe,
from the ... picture "Good
News"; by Roger Edens, Hugh
Martin and Ralph Blane. [New
York, Chappell & Co.] ©
Robbins Music Corp., New York;
14Oct47; EP18280. For voice
and piano, with chord symbols.

Pass that Peace Pipe. See his Good News.

BLANK, WILLIAM D
Somewey, Somehow; words and music
by William D. Blank. [c1946]
© Nordyke Publishing Co., Los
Angeles; 29Jan47; EP19458.

BLASIO, GENNARO.
"Nu Vaso a 'Na Cerasa" ... [music
by] Gennaro Blasio e [words by]
Filippo Surio. Napoli, Edizioni
E.M.C.D. © Italian Book Co.,
New York; 1Sep47; EP6619.

BLAUFUSS, WALTER.
My Isle of Golden Dreams ... words
by Gus Kahn, music by Walter
Blaufuss, arr. by Jerry Sears.
© Remick Music Corp., New York;
30Oct47; on arrangement;
EP18474. Piano-conductor score
(orchestra, with words) and
parts.

BLISS, ARTHUR, 1891-
March, "The Phoenix"; by Arthur
Bliss. © Novello & Co., ltd.,
London; 10Oct47; on pts. for
1st violin, 2d violin, viola,
violoncello & contra bass;
EP6885-6889.

BLISS, PHILIP PAUL, 1838-1876.
The Light of the World Is Jesus;
[by] P. P. Bliss, arr. by L. R.
S. © Lawrence R. Schoenhals,
Seattle; 13Dec47; on arrange-
ment; EP20108. Close score;
SATB.

The Stars Will Remember (so will I)
... music and lyric by Don Pelosi
and Leo Towers' [pseud.], scored
by Jerry Sears. © E. Feldman &
Co., ltd., London; 25Sep47;
on vocal orchestration; EP17732.
Piano-conductor score (orchestra,
with words) and parts.

[BLITZ, LEONARD]
The Stars Will Remember, (So Will
I) ... words and music by Don
Pelosi and Leo Towers [pseud.]
A Johnny Warrington arrangement.
New York, Harms. © B. Feldman &
Co., ltd., London; 25Aug47; on
dance orchestration; EP17154.
Piano-conductor score and parts.

The Stars Will Remember, (so will
I); words and music by Don
Pelosi and Leo Towers [pseud.]
© B. Feldman & Co., ltd., London;
15Aug47; on arrangement; EP6440.

BLOCH, ERNEST, 1880-
Nigun; (improvisation) from "Baal
Shem" [by] Ernest Bloch, [arr.]
by Joseph Schuster. © Carl
Fischer, inc., New York; 4Nov47;
on arrangement; EP18872. Score
(violoncello and piano) and
part.

BLONDIS, MARTE.
You Never Went Away; words by
Ralph Wolf, music by Marte
Blondis. © Nordyke Publishing
Co., Los Angeles; 23Dec46;
EP19477.

BLOW, JOHN, d. 1708.
The "Whitehall" Suite; by John
Blow, arr. and ed. by H. Watkins
Shaw. © The Oxford Univ. Press,
London; 9Oct47; on arrangement;
EP6996. Score: string orches-
tra and piano reduction.

BLOWER, MARY AGNES, 1898-
Virginia City Moon; words and music
by Mary A. Blower. © B. & M.
Music Publications, Alhambra,
Calif.; 18Aug47; EP16446.

Sing, O Heavens; anthem, S.A.T.B.,
[words from] Isaiah XLIX, vs.
13-16, music by Maurice Blower.
London, J. Curwen, New York, G.
Schirmer, sole agents. ©
Maurice Blower, Rake, near Liss,
Hampshire, Eng.; 23Oct47;
EP6942.

BLUE JAY SINGERS. See
Famous Blue Jay Singers.

BLYTHE, BILL.
Yerra Go On; Words & music by
Bill Blythe. © William John
Blythe t/a William John & Co.,
Dublin, Eire; 14Jun47; EP6554.

BOATMAN, HENRY.
Lazy John; words and music by
Johnnie Lee Wills and Henry
Boatman. © Bob Wills Music,
inc., Hollywood, Calif.;
30Jul47; EP16040.

BOB NOLAN'S SONS OF THE PIONEERS;
cowboy songs. Hollywood, Calif.,
T. Spencer Music.

BODDIFORD, EVIE LEE.
Bashful and Shy; words and music
by Evie Lee Boddiford. [c1946]
© Nordyke Publishing Co., Los
Angeles; 30Jan47; EP19452.

BODE, ARNOLD G   H
O That Men Would Praise the Lord;
anthem for mixed voices, words
from Psalm 107 and Isaac Watts,
[music by] Arnold G. H. Bode.
© Clayton F. Summy Co., Chicago;
11Sep47; EP6996.

BODGE, PETER.
I Just Said Good-Evening; words by
Irving Superior, music by Peter
Bodge. © Broadcast Music, inc.,
New York; 1Jul47; EP18205.

BODROGI, ZSIGMOND.
Szép, Tavaszi Álmok. (Lovely
Dreams of Springtime) English
lyric by Olga Paul, words by
Bodrogi Zsigmond. (In Festi,
Barbers, comp. Memories of Hun-
gary. p. 31) © Edward B. Marks
Music Corp., New York; 19Nov47;
on English lyric; EP19002.

BOGDAN, MAE.
I'm Waiting for the Sunshine in
the Rain; words and music by
Mae Bogdan. © Nordyke Publishing Co., Los Angeles;
23May47; EP17606.

I'm Waiting for the Sunshine in
the Rain; words and music by
Mae Bogdan. © Nordyke Publishing Co., Los Angeles; 23May47;
EP16876.

BOGGS, NOEL.
Boggs Boogie; by Noel Boggs, and
Jimmy Wyble & Spade Cooley.
© Hill and Range Songs, inc.,
Hollywood, Calif.; 23Jul47;
EP14435. For piano solo.

BOILES, E   CELESTE.
Sweetheart, I'll Be True; words
and music by E. Celeste Boiles.
[c1945] © Nordyke Publishing
Co., Los Angeles; 24Jun46;
EP19461.

BOLAND, CLAY ALOYSIUS.
(Chris Crosses) Holiday, from the
Univ. of Pennsylvania 59th annual
Mask and wig show "Chris Crosses."
Words by Fred Waring and Moe Jaffe,
music by Clay Boland. © Words &
Music, inc., New York; 4Dec47;
EP19619.

Happy Go Lucky. See his Juleo and
Romiet.

Holiday. See his Chris Crosses.

I'm Feeling Happy Go Lucky. See his
Juleo and Romiet.

(Juleo and Romiet) I'm Feeling
Happy Go Lucky; music by Clay
Boland, lyrics by Moe Jaffe.
[From] the Mask and Wig Club
[production] ... "Juleo and Ro-
miet." © Words and Music, inc.,
New York; 3Dec47; EP19196.

BOLICK, BILL.
Como to the Saviour ... music
by Bill and Earl Bolick, and
[words by] Thomas Daniel Lynn.
© Acuff-Rose Publications,
Nashville; 29Sep47; EP17381.

There's Been a Change ... music
by Bill and Earl Bolick, and
[words by] Calvin Van Pelt.
© Acuff-Rose Publications,
Nashville; 29Sep47; EP17382.

BONADE, DANIEL, 1896-   comp.
Orchestra Studies for clarinet;
comp. and rev. by Daniel Bonade.
© Daniel Bonade, New Hope, Pa.;
10Sep47; EP18340.

BONCOMPAGNI, SOLAS, 1925-
Ho un Segreto sul Cuor ... Canzone
d'Autunno ... Parole e musica di
S. Boncompagni. © Carisch, s.a.,
Milan; 30ct47; EF7165. Piano-
conductor score (orchestra, with
words) and parts.

BOND, ARTHUR JOEL, 1869-
America; [words by] Rev. Samuel
Francis Smith, melody by Arthur
Joel Bond, harmonized by W. Jud-
son Kibby. © Arthur Joel Bond,
Chicago; 10ct47; EP19210. Close
score; SATB.

BOND, JASPER.
War Is Hell! By Jasper Bond.
© Jasper Bond, San Fernando,
Calif.; 25Sep47; EP17821. For
voice and piano.

BOND, JOHNNY.
Rock My Cradle (once again); words
and music by Billy Folger and
Johnny Bond ... piano arrange-
ment by Dick Kent. © Peer
International Corp., New York;
14Jul47; EP15869.
Too Many Years Too Late; words and
music by Johnny Bond. © Peer
International Corp., New York;
11Jun47; EP15620.
You Can't Tell the Depth of the
Well (by the Length of the Handle
on the Pump); words and music by
Johnny Bond. © Mellin Music,
inc., New York; 20Aug47; EP16558.

BONI, MARGARET BRADFORD, 1893-   ed.
Fireside Book of Folk Songs;
selected and ed. by Margaret
Bradford Boni, arr. for the
piano by Norman Lloyd, illus. by
Alice and Martin Provensen. ©
Simon & Schuster, inc. & Artists
& Writers Guild, inc., New York;
10Oct47; A19681.

BONK, ANGELA.
The Toy Shop; a musical playlet for
Christmastide, for kindergarten
and first grade. Libretto by Lu-
cille Landon and Leona Van
Nostrand, music by Angela Bonk.
© Row, Peterson & Co., Evanston,
Ill.; 13Oct47; D pub 11133.

LA BONNE CHANSON. Accompagnements
de la Série des jeunes, par
Conrad Latendre. © Charles-
Emile Gadbois, St. Hyacinthe,
Que., Can.; 15May45; on
accompaniments; EF6851. For
voice and piano.

LA BONNE CHANSON; [by Charles-
Emile Gadbois, Gabriel Cusson,
Conrad Latendre, and others,
words by Georges Boileau, and
others] © Charles Emile Gadbois,
Séminaire de St- Hyacinthe,
Que., Can.; 3. année, 30Apr39;
4. année, 8Sep39; 5. année,
15Oct39; 6. année, 20Dec39; 7.
album, 1Dec46; on illustrations
and new words and music;
EF6076, 6075, 6074, 6073, 6072.
For 1-3 treble voices.

--- --- Accompagnements. © Charles
Emile Gadbois, Séminaire de St-
Hyacinthe, Que., Can.; 1.
année, 19Jun39; 2. année,
7Nov39; 3. album, 15Oct46;
on new music and arrangement;
EF6078, 6077, 6669. For 1-3
treble voices and piano.

LA BONNE CHANSON À l'ÉCOLE; [by]
Joseph Beaulieu, and others, words
by A. B. Routhier, and others,
arr. by Charles-Emile Gadbois]
© Charles-Emile Gadbois, Séminaire de St-Hyacinthe, Que.,
Can.; 1-2. année, 4-8. année,
15Sep43; EF6071, 6070, 6069,
6068, 6067, 6066, 6066. EF6066
6068-6070 have new matter; new
words and music, 6067, new
words; 6065, new music. For 1-
3 treble voices.

BONNER, JAN.
I'm So In Love with Love; words and
music by Jan Bonner. © Nordyke
Publishing Co., Los Angeles;
5Jun47; EF16812.

BONNIVAR, FLORENCE, 1894-
This Old Time Religion. Oh! How I
Love Him Today; [by] Florence
Bonnivar, [harmonized by Mar-
jorie P. McColloch] © Florence
Bonnivar, Havana, Ill.; 31Jul47;
EP17655, 17656. Close score;
SATB.

BONPORTI, FRANCESCO ANTONIO.
Concerto ... realizzazione del
basso continuo e revisione
istrumentale di Alceo Toni. ©
Carisch, s. a., Milan; 15Jul42;
on realization of figured bass
and revision; EF6228. Score:
violin, string orchestra and
organ.
Concerto in fa maggiore ... [by]
F. A. Bonporti. Op.XI, n.5.
Trascrizione di Guglielmo Barblan.
© Carisch, s.a., Milan; 26Feb44;
on transcription; EF6279.
Score: violin, string orchestra
and harpsichord.

BOONE, CLAUDE.
Wedding Bells; by Claude Boone.
© Hometown Music Co., inc., New
York; 21Nov47; EP19796. For
voice and piano, with chord
symbols.

BOOTE, HERBERT, arr.
El Campo Junior; plectrum guitar
solos, arr. by Herbert Boote. ©
Don Santos Pub. Co., Rochester,
N. Y.; 20Dec47; EP2025L.

BOOTH, F   CARLTON, comp.
Living Above Songs and Choruses;
comp. by F. Carlton Booth.
[c1947]

BORG, M   L
We'll Just Be Friends; words &
music by M. L. Borg. ©
Nordyke Publishing Co., Los
Angeles; 11Oct46; EP19393.

[BORGAZZI, FABIO]
Le Dodici Ragazze ... Fra le
Stelle ... parole di Pinchi,
musica di G. Fabor [pseud.]
© Edizioni Italcarisch, Milano;
on Le Dodici Ragazze, 29May46;
on Fra le Stelle, 1Mar46;
EF6764, 6765. Piano-conductor
score (orchestra, with words)
and part for violins.
Rosangela ... di Fabor-Natili
[pseud.] © Edizioni Ritmi
& Canzoni, Milano; 10Apr47;
EF6767. Melody and chord
symbols, with words.

BORGUNO, AGUSTIN.
Down by the Glenside; (Old Irish
song) ... musical setting by
Agustin Borguno. © Oliver
Ditson Co., Philadelphia;
22Sep47; on musical setting;
EP17557.

BORNSCHEIN, FRANZ.
Our Worship, Lo! (S.A.T.B.) [by]
Franz Bornschein ... Latin text
by St. Anatolius ... tr. by J.
Brownlie. © R. D. Row Music
Co., Boston; 8Nov47; EP18429.
English words.
Thy Temple, Lord; anthem for mixed
voices, optional a cappella
(S.A.T.B.) Adapted from Psalm
48: 9-14, [music by] Franz Born-
schein. © Hall & McCreary Co.,
Chicago; 10Nov47; EP18908.

BORNSCHEIN, FRANZ C
Day; for women's voices (SSA) with
piano acc.; incidental solos for
soprano and contralto. The music
by Franz Bornschein, the words by
Sigbjörn Obstfelder. © R. D. Row
Music Co., Boston; 24Dec47;
EP20294.

BORNSCHEIN, FRANZ CARL, 1879-
Peace; S.A.T.B., [by] Franz Born-
schein, [words by] Frederic
Manley. © C. C. Birchard & Co.,
Boston; 30Oct47; EP18386.

BORTKIEWICZ, SERGEI, 1877-
Vier Klavierstücke; [by] Sergei
Bortkiewicz. Op. 65. © Ludwig
Doblinger (Bernhard Herzmansky),
K.G., Music Publisher, Vienna;
11Jun47; EF6235. For piano solo.

BORTOLI, FRANK, 1911-
Connie Polka. © Frank Bortoli,
Chicago; 25Jul47; EP16136. For
accordion solo.
Dancing on the Keyboard;
accordion solo ... by Frank
Bortoli. © Frank Bortoli,
Chicago; 19Jul47; EP16037.

BOSSI, LUIS M
Acordes ... letra de Alfredo Roldán,
música de Luis M. Bossi. ©
Editorial Argentina de Música
Internacional, s. de r. ltd.,
Buenos Aires; 1Dec47; EF4382.
For voice and piano.

BOSSI, MARCO ENRICO.
Crepuscolo; for organ [by] M. En-
rico Bossi. © Edward B. Marks
Music Corp., New York; 24Sep47;
EP18093.
Preludio e Fuga for organ, [by] M.
Enrico Bossi. © Edward B. Marks
Music Corp., New York; 24Sep47;
EP18092.

BOSSI, RENZO, arr.
Ricreazioni di antiche musiche.
© Carisch, s.a., Milano; 3. ser.,
21May45; EF4503. Score: string
orchestra.

BOSTWICK, FRANCES JOHNSON.
At the Mercy Seat ... [by] Frances
Johnson Bostwick. © Frances
Johnson Bostwick, Venice,
Calif.; 1Jul47; EP15810. Close
score: SATB.
Send Forth the Gospel; From Glory
to Glory; and others, by Frances
Johnson Bostwick. © Frances
Johnson Bostwick, Venice, Calif.;
1Jun47; on 2 hymns. Partial
contents.- From Glory to Glory
(© EP15484) - Send Forth the
Gospel (© EP15485)

BOTTI, CARDENIO, 1891-
Composizioni per tromba o pianoforte; [by] Cardenio Botti. ©
Carisch, s. a., Milan; 1Jul47;
on 3 pieces. Score (trumpet
and piano) and part. Contents.-
[v.1] Scherzo (© EP6189)- [v.2]
Romanza (© EF6188)- [v.3]
Allegro da Concerto (© EF6187)

BOURNE, PATRISHA RONALD, 1899-
My Heart for You ... words and
music by Patrisha Ronald Bourne.
[London] Boosey & Hawkes.
© Boosey & Co., ltd., London;
16Oct47; EF6817.

BOURNE, inc., comp.
Eddie Dean [song folio] © Bourne,
inc., New York; 22Jul47; EP15451.
Jolson Songs. © Bourne, inc.,
New York; 2Jun47; EP15553.

Whitey and Hogan's Mountain
Memories; [comp. by Bourne, inc.]
© Bourne, inc., New York; 6Jul47;
EP15463. For voice and piano,
with chord symbols.

237

BOURQUIN, JULES STARBUCK, 1906-
The March Way to Drumming; by Jules
and Ruth Bourquin. © Jules S.
Bourquin & Ruth L. Bourquin,
Bartlesville, Okla.; 8Sep47;
AA69788.

BOURTAYRE, HENRI, 1915-
Baisse un Peu l'Abat-jour ...
Paroles de Marcel Delmas, musi-
que de Henri Bourtayre. ©
Éditions Paul Beuscher, Paris;
20Jul45; EP6454.

(Le Chanteur Inconnu) Tout Bleu
... du film "Le Chanteur Inconnu";
paroles de André Hornez, musique
de Henri Bourtayre. © Éditions
Paul Beuscher, Paris; 30Nov46;
EP6583.

La Dactylo ... paroles de Henri
Kubnick, musique de Henri
Bourtayre. © Arpège Éditions
Musicales, Paris; 2Jan47;
EP6604. For voice and piano
and voice part.

Feu Follet ... Paroles de Henri
Kubnick, musique de Henri Bour-
tayre. © Éditions Paul Beuscher,
Paris; 20Jul45; EP6469.

Une Fleur sur l'Oreille ...
Paroles de Henri Kubnick,
musique de Henri Bourtayre.
© Arpège Éditions Musicales,
Paris; 31Dec46; EP6611. For
voice and piano, and voice part.

Imaginez ... Didn't you know? ...
Paroles françaises de Jacques
Poterat, paroles anglaises de
Bobby Astor [pseud.], musique de
James H. Midway [pseud.] ©
Éditions Paul Beuscher, Paris;
20Jul45; EP6467.

Le Pas du Hareng. Feet of Fish
... Paroles de Maurice Vandair
[pseud.] & Syam [pseud.], musique de Henri Bourtayre et Émile
Prud'Homme. © Éditions Paul Beuscher, Paris; 2Jan46; EP6584.

Pastourelle à Nina; paroles de
Maurice Vandair [pseud.],
musique de Henri Bourtayre.
[cl946] © Éditions Paul Beuscher, Paris; 10Dec45; EP6495.

Quand On A, Comme Vous ... Paroles
de André Hornez & Syam [pseud.]
musique de Henri Bourtayre. ©
Arpège Éditions Musicales,
Paris; 13Mar47; EP6447.

Simple Histoire ... Paroles de
André Hornez, musique de Henri
Bourtayre. © Éditions Paul
Beuscher, Paris; 30Nov46;
EP6585.

Le Swing à l'École ... Paroles de
Syam [pseud.] & Georgius
[pseud.], musique de Henri Bourtayre. [cl946] © Éditions Paul
Beuscher, Paris; 10Dec45;
EP6582. Score (voice and
accordion or piano) and voice
part.

Tout Bleu. See his Le Chanteur Inconnu.

BOVE, ALEXANDER L
You're Playing Hookey from Heaven;
words and music by Alexander L.
Bove. © Nordyke Publishing Co.,
Los Angeles; 10May47; EP16938.

BOVÉ, J   HENRY, 1897-
An Indian Epic in Song; words and
music by J. Henry Bové. New York,
Hill-Coleman. © J. Henry Bové,
New York; 15Jun36; EP16979.

BOWEN, YORK.
Arabesque ... [by] York Bowen.
(Op.119) © Oxford Univ. Press,
London; 16Oct47; EP6994. Two
scores for 2 pianos.

BOWER, SHIRLEY, 1926-
Open Mine Eyes ... [by] Shirley
Bower, [words by] Nancy Lee
Thompson. © Kappa Phi, National
Club of Methodist College Wo-
men, Cambridge, Mass.; 6Sep47;
EP18143.

BOWERS, FREDERICK V
Because; lyric by Charles Horwitz,
music [and new verse] by Freder-
ick V. Bowers, [arr. by Robert
C. Haring] © Shapiro, Bernstein
& Co., inc., New York; 17Nov47;
on new verse and arrangement;
EP17974.

BOWLES, PAUL, 1911-
Folk Preludes; for piano solo [by]
Paul Bowles. © Mercury Music Corp.,
New York; 15Dec47; EP19981.

BOWMAN, EUDAY L
12th Street Rag; by Euday L. Bowman ... [arr.] by Charles Magnante. © Shapiro, Bernstein &
Co., inc., New York; 14Oct47;
on arrangement; EP18020. For
accordion solo.

BOWMAN, H   H
Once; words and music by H. H.
Bowman. © Nordyke Publishing
Co., Los Angeles; 24Jul47;
EP19499.

BOWN, PEARL BOYCE.
A Bayou Tale; piano composition
with words by Pearl Boyce Bown.
© Mills Music, inc., New York;
8Dec47; EP19892.

Dusting the Piano; piano solo by
Pearl Boyce Bown. © Mills Music,
inc., New York; 8Dec47; EP19893.

The Reluctant Camel; piano solo
by Pearl Boyce Bown. © Mills
Music, inc., New York; 8Dec47;
EP19891.

BOX, HAROLD ELTON, pseud. See
Cox, Harold Elton.

BOYCE, WILLIAM.
Rail No More, Ye Learned Asses;
by William Boyce, for bass
voice and pianoforte, arr. by
Archibald Jacob. © Oxford
University Press, London;
11Sep47; on arrangement;
EF6655.

BOYD, JEANNE.
Descants on Eight Hymns; by
Jeanne Boyd. © H. T. Fitz-
Simons Co., Chicago; 29Sep47;
EP18119.

BOYKINS, CONNIE.
The Zig-Zag Boogie; words and music by Connie Boykins. © Nordyke Publishing Co., Los Angeles;
27Jul46; EP20353.

BOYLES, RAY.
Baby, Can't You See That's Class;
words & music by Ray Boyles.
© Nordyke Publishing Co., Los
Angeles; 29Nov46; EP19494.

BOZI, HAROLD, 1887-
Esclave d'Amour ... paroles de Delph
et Julsam [pseud.], musique de
Harold de Bozi, arr. de Dorcine
[pseud.] ... Valse Obsédante ...
paroles de Géo Koger [pseud.],
musique de Fred Freed [pseud.] arrt.
de Francis Salabert. © Éditions
Salabert, Paris; 22Jul47; EP7257.
Piano-conductor score (orchestra,
with words) and parts.

BOZI, HAROLD DE, 1887-   arr.
Accordéonia; 24 pièces célèbres
pour accordéon ... [arr. by]
Harold de Bozi. © Alphonse Leduc
& Cie, Paris; v. 1-2, 31May47;
on arrangement; EF7299, 7297.

BOZZA, EUGÈNE, 1905-
Jeux de Plage; [by] Eugène Bozza,
ballet en un acte, argument de
José Bruyr. [Op. 62] © Alphonse
Leduc & Cie, Éditions musicales,
Paris; 30May47; EF6418.

Tableau Instrumental; [by] E.
Bozza. Indiquant l'étendue, la
notation écrite et les sons
réels de tous les instruments
principaux des orchestres
symphoniques et militaires,
complétés par un tableau annexe
concernant les instruments
divers, ainsi que les claviers
et les instruments à percussion.
© Alphonse Leduc & Co., Éditions
musicales, Paris; 30May47; EF6416.

BOYD, BILL.
New Fort Worth Rag; by Bill Boyd.
© Hill and Range Songs, inc.,
Hollywood, Calif.; 28Nov47;
EP19140. For piano solo.

Tellin' Lies; words and music by
Bill Boyd. © Peer International
Corp., New York; 25Nov47;
EP19847.

[BRAD, WILLIAM RALPH] 1891-
Maple Leaf ... [by Willaim Ralph
Brad, words by] W.L. Webber.
© William Lester Webber, Van-
couver, B.C., Can.; 15Aug47;
EF6790.

No Regrets ... [by Willaim Ralph
Brad, words by] W. L. Webber.
© William Lester Webber, Van-
couver, B.C., Can.; 15Aug47;
EF6789.

BRADEN, EDWIN.
Forever in My Heart; words by
Edwin Braden, music by Alan
Reeve-Jones. © The Individual
Music Co., ltd., London; 19Jul47;
EF5802.

Red Sky; words by Alan Reeve-Jones,
music by Edwin Braden. © Individual Music Co., ltd., London;
13Aug47; EF6374.

BRADFORD, THOMAS, 1913-
We Need a Little Touch from Jesus;
words and music by Thomas Bradford. © Beacon Publishing Co.,
Toronto; 14Nov47; EF7026. Close
score; SATB.

BRADLEY, DOROTHY.
Sight-Reading Made Easy; a complete
graded course for the pianoforte
[by] Dorothy Bradley & J. Raymond
Tobin. © Joseph Williams, ltd.,
London; bk.4-5, 29Oct47. -Contents.
- bk.4 Lower (© EF6636) - bk.5.
Higher (© EF6637.

BRADLEY, JOSÉ.
Remember Me; by José Bradley,
[piano arrangement by Geo. H.
Record] © Cinephonic Music Co.,
ltd., London; 5Oct45; EF6043.
For voice and piano, with chord
symbols; melody also in tonic
sol-fa notation.

[BRADLEY, KARL] comp.
Bing Crosby's Hits of the Day;
popular song folio [compiled by Karl
Bradley] © Edwin H. Morris &
Co., inc., New York; 1Aug47;
EP16330.

BRAGDON, SARAH COLEMAN.
Lord, in Adoration Kneeling;
words by Lorraine F. Rude,
music by Sarah Coleman Bragdon. © Theodore Presser Co.,
Philadelphia; 10Oct47;
EP17991.

BRAGERS, ACHILLE PIERRE, 1887-   arr.
Proprium de Tempore. The Proper of
the Time. Le Propre du Temps.
Gregorian chant acc. by Achille P.
Bragers. © McLaughlin & Reilly
Co., Boston; v.2, 25Jul47; on har-
monization; EP16392. Contents.-
v.2, From Easter to Advent.

BRAHAM, PHILIP.
(Charlot's Revue) Limehouse
Blues;(from "Charlot's Revue"),
music by Philip Braham, arr.
by Jimmy Dale. © Harms, inc.,
New York; 25Aug47; on arrangement; EP17156. Piano-conductor
score (orchestra, with words)
and parts.
Limehouse Blues; [by] Philip
Braham, arr. by J. Louis Merkur.
© Harms, inc., New York; 17Dec47;
on arrangement; EP20280. Two
scores for piano 1-2.

BRAHE, MAY H
Matthew, Mark, Luke and John; song,
lyric adapted by Walter de la
Mare, music by May H. Brahe,
[London] Boosey & Hawkes. ©
Boosey & Co., ltd., London;
20Aug47; EP6260.

BRAHMS, JOHANNES, 1833-1897.
(Anchors Aweigh) Cradle Song.
(Wiegenlied) By Brahms, arr.
to English words by King
Palmer; sung ... in the ...
picture "Anchors Aweigh." ©
W. Paxton & Co., ltd., London;
11Jul46; on arrangement &
English words; EP5748.

Brahms' Cradle Song ... arr. by
Harry Huffnagle. © David Gorn-
ston, New York; 27Oct47; on
arrangement; EP20240. Score
(3 trumpets, 2 trombones and
tuba, ad lib.) and parts.
Brahms; (excerpts from his great-
est works) [arr. by Victor
Ambroise] © Lawrence Wright
Music Co., ltd., London;
19Sep47; on arrangement; EP6638.
For piano solo.
Brahms' Lullaby; piano solo, an
arrangement by Genevieve Lake.
© Pallma Music Products, Chica-
go; 27May47; on arrangement;
EP15665.
Brahms' Songs of Love; his most
popular melodies [arr. by
Walter L. Rosemont, words by
Jack Edwards] © Edwards Music
Co., New York; 6Nov47; on
simplified arrangement & words;
EP18670. For piano solo,
partly with words.
Brahms' string quintet in F Minor
... reconstructed by Sebastian H.
Brown. © Stainer & Bell, ltd.,
London; 23Oct47; on arrangement;
EP6085. Parts: 2 violins, viola
and 2 violoncellos.
Brahms' Waltz. (Op. 39, no. 15)
... arr. by Harry Huffnagle.
© David Gornston, New York;
27Oct47; on arrangement;
EP20239. Score (3 trumpets,
2 trombones and tuba, ad lib.)
and parts.
Cadenza for the violin concerto. Op. 77
See his Concerto, violin.

(Concerto, violin) Cadenza for the
violin concerto [by] Joh. Brahms.
Op. 77. [By] Jascha Heifetz. ©
Carl Fischer, inc., New York;
20Nov47; EP19170.

Cradle Song; [by] Johannes Brahms,
arr. by P. Ballatore. (In Ballatore, Pietro, comp. So easy.
p.16) © Edward B. Marks Music
Corp., New York; 9Dec47; on arrangement; EP19591. For piano
solo.

Cradle Song. See his Anchors Aweigh.

Es Ist ein' Ros' Entsprungen.
(A Rose Breaks into Blossom)
Choral prelude no. 8 for organ,
by Johannes Brahms, ed. by
Stanley Roper. © The Oxford
University Press, London;
10Jul47; on arrangement;
EP6165.

Ever Lighter Grow My Slumbers; for
four-part women's voices, by
Johannes Brahms, arr. by Walter
Goodell, [words by Hermann Ling,
tr. by Claire Goodell] © H. T.
FitzSimons Co., Chicago;
29Sep47; on arrangement;
EP18121.

The Lord Is Our Fortress. See his
Symphony, no.1.

A Night in June; [by] Johannes
Brahms, S.S.A. arr. by Frederick
Wick. © Frederick Wick, Minneapolis; 28Aug47; on words &
arrangement; EP17934.

(Symphony, no.1) The Lord Is
Our Fortress; from the Finale
of Symphony no.1 [by] Johannes
Brahms, text by Gena Branscombe,
arr. for women's voices S.S.A.A.
by Gena Branscombe. © J.
Fischer & Bro., New York;
30Sep47; on words and arrangement; EP17702.

Symphony no.3; (Third movement)
[by] Johannes Brahms, arr. by
Mark White. © Broadcast Music,
inc., New York; 8Aug47; on
arrangement; EP18043. Piano-
conductor score (orchestra)
and parts.

BRAKEBUSH, HAL.
Until Now; words by Hal Brakebush. ©
Nordyke Publishing Co., Los
Angeles; 28Mar47; EP16788.

[BRAND, ALTON L   ]
Simplex Fingering Slide Rule; for
French horns in F, Eb or Bb, also
double horns in F and Bb, [by
Alton L. Brand] © Mills Music,
inc., New York; 16Dec47; AA70402.

BRANDÃO, JOSÉ VIEIRA. See
Vieira Brandão, José.

BRANDT, ALAN.
Now He Tells Me; words and music
by Don Wolf and Alan Brandt. ©
King Cole Music, inc., New York;
27Nov47; EP19215.
You Can't Get a Tahicab in Mehico;
by Don Wolf and Alan Brandt.
© Republic Music Corp., New
York; 23Sep47; EP17642. For
voice and piano, with chord
symbols.

[BRANNAN, WALTER LEW] 1884-
Out on the Chisholm Trail; [by
Walter Brannan, arr. by Karl
Johnson. Wichita, Kan., Van
Tine Printing Co.] © Walter
Lew Brannan, Wichita, Kan.;
1Sep47; EP18619. For voice and
piano.

BRANSON, DAVID.
Spanish Jazz; for pianoforte [by]
David Branson. [c1946] © The
Oxford University Press, London;
9Jan47; EP6096.

BRANT, ADA, 1891-
Arpeggietto; (The balance wand)
piano solo by Ada Brant. ©
Boston Music Co., Boston;
29Oct47; EP18654.

BRATTON, OSCAR.
The Sun Comes over the Mountain;
words and music by Oscar Bratton.
© Nordyke Publishing Co., Los
Angeles; 29Mar47; EP16743.

BREACH, MICHAEL, 1902-
I Can't Fall in Love All Over
Again; words by Walter Howe,
music by Michael Breach. ©
B. Feldman & Co., ltd., London;
5Aug47; EP6251.

BRECK, EDWARD S   arr.
Christmas in Song and Carol;
sixteen familiar Christmas
selections for three-part chorus
(or trio) of treble voices, or
one- two- or three-part junior
choir with piano or organ acc.,
arr. by Edward S. Breck. ©
Carl Fischer, inc., New York;
21Aug47; on arrangement;
EP17305.

BRENES CANDANEDO, GONZALO, 1907-
Las Voces Matinales; del libro
"Tonadas del Trópico Niño,"
música de Gonzalo Brenes.
Mexico, Editorial de Mexico.
© Gonzalo Brenes Candanedo, San
José, Costa Rica; 16Apr46;
EP5825.

BRENNAN, JAMES A
The Dream I Dreamed of You; words
by Alice Young, music by James
A. Brennan, arr. by Phil J.
Schaefer. © Nordyke Publishing
Co., Los Angeles; 24Oct47;
EP18395.
That Country Place Where I Was
Born; lyrics by Henry J. Sweeney,
music by James A. Brennan [arr.
by Phil Schaefer] © Henry J.
Sweeney, Lowell, Mass.; 7Jul47;
EP15874.

BRENT, ROYAL.
Get up Those Stairs, Mademoiselle;
by Clifford Jackson [and] Royal
Brent ... arr. by Fred Weissman-
tel. © Duchess Music Corp., New
York; 27Jun47; on arrangement;
EP15364. Piano-conductor score
(orchestra, with words) and parts.

BRERO, CÉSAR JULIO, 1908-
Toccata; [by] C. Brero, para piano.
© Ricordi Americana, S.A.E.C.,
Buenos Aires; 21Apr47; EP6969.

BREWSTER, MEL.
Hawaiian Memories; words and music
by Mel Brewster and Fred Asmus,
[arr. by Betty B. Glynn] (Oahu
E-Z method, [lesson] 64E2) ©
Oahu Publishing Co., Cleveland;
22Sep47; on arrangement; EP19608.
For 2 guitars, with words.

BREWSTER, THEODORE.
Searching for Love; words and
music by Ted. Brewster.
© Broadcast Music, inc., New
York; 24Sep47; EP17902.

BREZINA, WILLIAM, 1926-
Winter Time; music by W. Brezina,
words by Martha Young. ©
Martha Young, Glendale, N. Y.
& William Brezina, New York;
29Aug47; on introduction,
arrangement & changes in
music; EP16583.

BRIDGES, RONALD.
As Irish as Dublin Town; by Ronald
Bridges. © Box & Cox Publications,
ltd., London; 25Nov47; EF7273.
For voice and piano, with chord
symbols.
The Lord Is My Shepherd; (Psalm 23)
music by Ronald Bridges. ©
Asherberg, Hopwood & Crew, ltd.,
London; 30Jun47; EF5704. For
voice and piano.

BRIGGS, EVERETT FRANCIS, 1908-
Panis Angelicus; music and English
translation by ... E. F. Briggs.
© Everett F. Briggs, Lakewood,
N. J.; 30Jul47; EP15992. Close
score: SATB; Latin and English
words.

BRINK, BO, pseud. See
Ullvén, Uno H.J.

BRIOSO, RAFAEL INCIARTE. See
Inciarte Brioso, Rafael.

BRISBEN, NED. See
Brisben, William Edward.

BRISBEN, WILLIAM EDWARD, 1915-
Keep Away from Me! Lyrics [by]
Tom Johnstone, music [by] Ned
Brisben. © William Edward
(Ned) Brisben, d.b.a. Fairfax
Music Co., Alexandria, Va.;
19Sep47; EP17232.

BRISTON, M   RUTH.
Because You Went Away; words and
music by M. Ruth Briston. ©
Nordyke Publishing Co., Los Angeles; 25Jul46; EP19489.

BRITO, ALFREDO.
You and Your Love. (Ansias de
Amar) Music and Spanish
lyric by Alfredo Brito, lyric
by Al Stillman. © Remick
Music Corp., New York;
18Aug47; EP16433.

BRITO, JULIO.
Mira Que Eres Linda ... Letra y
música de Julio Brito. ©
Peer International Corp., New
York; 6Jun47; EF5741.

BRITTEN, BENJAMIN, 1913-
Fish in the Unruffled Lakes; song
with piano [by] Benjamin Britten,
words by W. H. Auden. [London]
Boosey & Hawkes. © Boosey &
Co., ltd., London; 6Nov47;
EF7012.
(Peter Grimes) Old Joe Has Gone
Fishing, round from the opera
"Peter Grimes"; [by] Benjamin
Britten. New York, Boosey &
Hawkes. © Boosey & Hawkes, ltd.,
London; 5Sep47; on arrangement;
EP17147. Score: SATB and piano.
(Peter Grimes) Song of the Fisher-
men ... from the opera "Peter
Grimes"; [by] Benjamin Britten.
© Boosey & Hawkes, ltd., London;
5Sep47; on arrangement; EP17146.
Score: SATB and piano.
The Rape of Lucretia. Der Raub
der Lukrezia. [Op. 37] An
opera in two acts, libretto
after André Obey's play "Le
viol de Lucrèce" by Ronald
Duncan, German translation by
Elisabeth Mayer, vocal score by
Henry Boys, [composed and rev.
by] Benjamin Britten. Rev. ed.
© Boosey & Hawkes, ltd., London;
24Sep47; on revision & German
translation; EP18507.

BROADHEAD, G   F
Changing Seas; [by] G. F. Broadhead.
© Oliver Ditson Co., Philadelphia;
6Dec47; EP20448. For piano solo.
Joie de Vivre. (Joy of Life) ...
For the piano by G. F. Broad-
head. © Oliver Ditson Co.,
Philadelphia; 11Aug47;
EP16301.

BROBST, HAROLD.
Dreaming of Hawaii; words and
music by Harold Brobst, arr.
by composer [and Waltz of the
Strings; words and music by Ray
Meany, arr. by Harold Brobst]
© Ray Meany, Golden Gate Publi-
cations, Oakland, Calif.; 3Dec47;
EP19864. For voice and guitar.
Sing Your Blues Away; words and
music by Harold Brobst. [Arr.
by composer] © Ray Meany,
Golden Gate Publications,
Oakland, Calif.; 2Sep47;
EP17214. For voice and 2
guitars; also diagrams and
chord symbols for ukulele.

That's the Hawaiian Swing; words
and music by Harold Brobst, arr.
by Bernie Kaai. © Ray Meany,
Golden Gate Publications,
Oakland, Calif.; 4Aug47; EP16117.
For voice and 2 guitars; also
diagrams and chord symbols for
ukulele.

BROCKMAN, JOSEPH.
My Western Home; words and music
by Joseph Brockman, sr. ©
Nordyke Publishing Co., Los
Angeles; 11Jun46; EP19457.

BRODSKY, NICHOLAS, 1905-
Canzone della Terra. See his A Man about
the House.
(A Man about the House) Canzone
della Terra. (Song of the
Earth) From [the film] "A Man
about the House." [By] Nicholas
Brodsky. © Chappell & Co.,
ltd., London; 17Oct47; EF6904.
For piano solo.

BRODSKY, ROY.
Dance with me; words and music by
Sid Tepper and Roy Brodsky,
[based on a theme by Waldteufel,
piano score by Michael Edwards]
© Mills Music, inc., New York;
4Aug47; on new words, adapta-
tion of music & arrangement;
EP19258.
Five Kisses Till Midnight; words
and music by Sid Tepper and Roy
Brodsky. © Mills Music, inc.,
New York; 4Aug47; EP18257.
Money, Money, Money; words and
music by Sid Tepper and Roy
Brodsky. © Mills Music, inc.,
New York; 29Aug47; EP17942.
Summer Serenade; by Sid Tepper and
Roy Brodsky. © Mills Music, inc.,
New York; 4Aug47; EP18262. For
voice and piano, with chord
symbols.
Water Faucet; Drip, drip drip,
words and music by Sid Tepper
and Roy Brodsky, [piano score
by Michael Edwards] © Mills
Music, inc., New York; 29Aug47;
EP17949.

BRODSZKY, NICHOLAS. See
Brodsky, Nicholas.

BRONSON, MARGARET.
Life - Keep a Song in My Heart;
for four-part chorus of men's
voices with piano acc. Poem
and music by Margaret Bronson.
© R. L. Huntzinger, inc.,
New York; 8Sep47; EP17209.

BROOK, HARRY, 1893-
Christmas Lullaby; unison song,
with optional descant for voices
or descant recorders and piano-
forte acc. Poem by Leonard
Clark ... music by Harry Brook.
London, J. Curwen, New York, G.
Schirmer, sole agents. ©
Harry Brook, Woodbridge,
Suffolk, Eng.; 23Oct47; EF6939.

BROOKING, ROSIE L
You Had My Heart; words & music
by Rosie L. Brooking. © Nordyke
Publishing Co., Los Angeles;
11Nov46; EP20513.

BROOKS, HARRY JOHN, 1893-
Majorette, on Parade; by Marie
Carr and Harry J. Brooks.
Fairmont, W. Va., H. J. Brooks.
© Mario Carr, Pawtucket, R. I.
& Harry John Brooks, Fairmont,
W. Va.; 18Oct46; EP15508. For
voice and piano, with chord
symbols.

BROOKS, JACK.
Saturday Date; by Jack Brooks.
© Burke and Van Heusen, inc.,
New York; 24Oct47; EP18458.
For voice and piano, with chord
symbols.

BROOKS, WELKER BERNARD.
Watching the Moonbeams Fade;
words and music by Welker Bernard Brooks. © Nordyke Publishing Co., Los Angeles; 15Aug47;
EP20074.

BROWN, ALLANSON G   Y
O Lamb of God; [by] Allanson G. Y.
Brown. © The Arthur P. Schmidt
Co., Boston; 18Aug47; EP16378.
Score: chorus (SSAATB) and piano.
Three Religious Pieces; for organ,
by Allanson G. Y. Brown. ©
McLaughlin & Reilly Co., Boston;
1Aug47; EP16384.

BROWN, ARTHUR L
Ballet on Skates; piano solo, by
Arthur L. Brown. Op. 126.
© The B. F. Wood Music Co.,
Boston; 14Jul47; EP15539.
Lonesome Doll; piano solo, by
Arthur L. Brown. Op. 125.
© The B. F. Wood Music Co.,
Boston; 14Jul47; EP15540.
Stars over Normandy; for piano by
Arthur L. Brown. [Op.127]
© Theodore Presser Co., Phila-
delphia; 31Oct47; EP18847.
Swinging down the Road; a piano solo
by Arthur L. Brown. Op.128.
© The B. F. Wood Music Co.,
Boston; 8Sep47; EP16658.

BROWN, BEN F
Twilight Shadows Bring Sweet
Dreams of You; words and music
by Ben F. Brown. © Nordyke
Publishing Co., Los Angeles;
29Aug47; EP19296.

BROWN, CARTHELL C
I Will Follow the Lord ... words
and music by Carthell C. Brown.
© Carthell C. Brown, Dayton,
Ohio; 4Dec47; EP19201. Score:
SATB.

BROWN, CHAD.
Sunbeams March; by Chad Brown. ©
Chad Brown, Madison, Wis.;
12Nov47; EP19200. For piano
solo.

BROWN, HAZEL SHEARER.
My Shack (out in the West) words
and music by Hazel Shearer
Brown. © Nordyke Publishing
Co., Los Angeles; 25May46;
EP19678.

BROWN, LEWIS.
Chain of Daisies; piano solo by
Lewis Brown. © Theodore Presser
Co., Philadelphia; 16Jun47;
EP15351.
Desert night; by Lewis Brown, for
piano. © J. Fischer & Bro.,
New York; 19Sep47; EP17797.
A Sleepy Song; [by] Lewis Brown.
© J. Fischer & Bro., New York;
9Sep47; EP17708. For piano
solo.

BROWN, NACIO PORTER, 1921-
Who Put That Dream in Your Eyes?
Lyric by Al Stewart, music by
Nacio Porter Brown. © Stuart
Music, inc., New York; 28Nov47;
EP19089.

BROWN, PEARL BOYCE. See
Bown, Pearl Boyce.

BROWN, RANDALL.
Sarabande and Gavotte ... by Randall
Brown. © Elkin & Co., ltd., London; 2Dec47; EF7368. Two scores
for piano 1-2.

BROWN, RAYMOND H
Vermont Infantry March; [by]
Raymond H. Brown. © George F.
Briegel, inc., New York;
EP17920. Condensed score (band)
and parts.

240

BROWN, REGINALD PORTER- See
Porter-Brown, Reginald.

BROWN, RUSSELL J   1891-
How Long Wilt Thou Forget Me?
[Words from] Psalm 13. Sacred
duet for high and low voices
by Russell J. Brown. © The
Boston Music Co., Boston;
31Oct47; EP18467.

BROWN, SAMUEL S
Song of the Angels; words and
music by Samuel S. Brown.
[c1945] © Nordyke Publishing
Co., Los Angeles; 13Jul46;
EP19527.

BROWN, WARD RILEY, 1888-
Lonely Heart of Mine; by Ward
Riley Brown. © Shelby Music
Publishing Co., Detroit; 3Jun47;
EP15384. For voice and piano,
with guitar diagrams and chord
symbols.

BROWNE, BRADFORD.
Two Eyes Two Lips but No Heart;
words and music by Alex Sullivan,
Doyle O'Dell and Bradford Browne.
(In Bob Nolan's Sons of the
Pioneers. p. 32-33) © Tim
Spencer Music, inc., Hollywood,
Calif.; 30Jul47; EP16031.

BROWNE, LEE B   See
Browne, Leland B

BROWNE, LELAND B
Little I Care; words by Decimae
Scruggs, music by Lee B. Browne.
© Nordyke Publishing Co., Los
Angeles; 10May47; EP16830.

Patty McGee; words by Robert R.
MacGregor, music by Lee B.
Browne.[c1945] © Nordyke Publishing Co., Los Angeles;
12Jun46; EP20486.

Song in My Heart; words by
Dorothy Guinn, music by Lee B.
Browne. © Nordyke Publishing
Co., Los Angeles; 11Oct46;
EP19665.

Your Parade of Broken Hearts; words
by Mabel Hubbard, music by Lee B.
Browne. © Nordyke Publishing Co.,
Los Angeles; 29Apr47; EP16841.

BROWNELL, WILLIAM, 1920-
The Ice Cream Song; words and
music by Richard Klaus & Bill
Brownell. © Musicmakers, inc.,
Philadelphia; 1Sep47;
EP17255.

BRUGGEN, JOHN VER. See
Ver Bruggen, John.

BRUMBELOW, INEZ.
Where Have You Been Hiding?
Words & music by Inez Brumbelow.
© Nordyke Publishing Co., Los
Angeles; 27Sep46; EP19401.

BRUNDLE, JOHN.
Canada, My Home; words and music
by John Brundle. © John Brundle,
Roche's Point, Ont., Can.;
30Jul47; EP6392. Version for
voice and piano and for mixed
chorus and piano.

Yes, 'Tis Thon I'll Boot You There;
words and music by John Brundle.
Ont., Can.; 30Jul47; EP6393.

BRUNNER, VIDA GRACE, 1897-
A Severn Serenade; words and
music by Vi Brunner. © Vida G.
Brunner, Crownsville, Md.;
9Dec47; EP19918.

BRYAN, CHARLES FAULKNER, 1911-
Jesus Born in Bethlehem; S.A.T.B.
with soprano solo, [by] Charles
F. Bryan. ©C. C. Birchard &
Co., Boston; 13Nov47; EP18664.

BRYDSON, JOHN.
Peter Pan; an easy suite for piano,
by John Brydson. © Alfred
Lengnick & Co., ltd., London;
10Jul47; EF6351.

BUCHANAN, ANNABEL MORRIS.
Mary Through a Thornwood's Gone
... [by] Annabel Morris Buchanan, traditional German carol,
English translation by Richard
Chase and A.M.B. © J. Fischer
& Bro., New York; 27Aug47; on
arrangement & English translation; EP17271. Score: soprano,
chorus (SATB) and piano reduction.

BUCHANAN, LESTER.
Dreamy Eyes; words and music by
Chester Buchanan, Elsie Buchan-
an and Lester Buchanan. © Main
Street Songs, inc., New York;
14Oct47; EP17996.

BUCHTEL, FORREST LAWRENCE, 1899-
arr.
Fair Are the Meadows; (S.A.T.B.)
Czech melody, words ... [and]
arr. by Forrest L. Buchtel.
© Neil A. Kjos Music Co.,
Chicago; 8Jul47; on arrange-
ment; EP16134.

Scale-Time Band Book; by Forrest
L. Buchtel. © Neil A. Kjos Music
Co., Chicago; 12Aug47; EP17121.
Piano-conductor score (band)
and parts.

BUCK, RONALD, 1907-
Give Me a Dolly; words by Emil C.
Hasenauer, music by Ronald Buck.
[c1946] © Nordyke Publishing
Co., Los Angeles; 30Jan47;
EP20348.

Gone But Not Forgotten; words by
Irene Zemkus, music by Ronald
Buck. © Nordyke Publishing Co.,
Los Angeles; 2Sep47; EP20349.

The Hobo without a Frown; lyrics
by Jasper Bond, music by Ronald
Buck. © Jasper Bond, San Fernando, Calif.; 25Sep47; EP17825.

It Was June in December; words
by Andy Bryan, music by Ronald
Buck. © Nordyke Publishing
Co., Los Angeles; 11Jul47;
EP17618.

Joy Ride; words by Emil C. Hase-
nauer, music by Ronald Buck.
© Nordyke Publishing Co., Los
Angeles; 17Jun47; EP17441.

Lonely Cowboy; words by Harold S.
Oneyear, music by Ronald Buck.
© Nordyke Publishing Co., Los
Angeles; 15Aug47; EP19350.

My Charming Dream; words by George
Steinbeck, music by Ronald Buck.
© Nordyke Publishing Co., Los
Angeles; 12Apr47; EP16790.

My Shawnee Miss; words by Ollie
Cooper, music by Ronald Buck.
© Nordyke Publishing Co., Los
Angeles; 4Feb47; EP19441.

My Star of Love; words by John A.
Ryser, music by Ronald Buck. ©
Nordyke Publishing Co., Los
Angeles; 12Sep47; EP19355.

Rocky Mountain Melody; words by
Mary Ann Sievers, music by Ron-
ald Buck. © Nordyke Publishing
Co., Los Angeles; 21Aug47;
EP20015.

Your Heart Spoke to My Heart;
words by Frank Kolenc, music by
Ronald Buck. © Nordyke Publishing
Co., Los Angeles; 19Jun47; EP17437.

BUCKLEY, WILLIAM H
That Glorious Song of Old; [by]
William H. Buckley ... (for
mixed voices, junior choir ad
libitum, with piano, and organ
ad lib.) [words by E. H. Sears]
© Oliver Ditson Co., Philadelphia; 28Sep47; EP17285.

BUCKNER, HARRIET EDDINGS.
My Bonnie Lass; piano solo [by]
Harriet Eddings Buckner. © Carl
Fischer, New York; 1Dec47;
EP20289.

BUEROSSE, GEORGE J
Strolling under Magic Moon ...
Music: George Buerosse ... words:
George Buerosse & Milton Groose,
arr. by Milton Groose. Beaver
Dam, Wis., G. J. Buerosse
Publishing Co. © George J.
Buerosse, Beaver Dam, Wis.,
18Sep47; EP17810.

BUGATCH, SAMUEL.
A Zemer ... words by Aron Zeitlin,
music by Samuel Bugatch, song
for voice and piano. New York,
Metro Music Co. © Henry
Lefkowitch, New York; 13Nov47;
EP18686. Words in both
Yiddish and Yiddish
transliterated.

BULLOCK, ERNEST, 1890-
Close Now Thine Eyes; the words
by Francis Quarles, set to
music by Ernest Bullock.
[c1946] © The Oxford University Press, London; 9Jan47;
EF6095.

O For a Closer Walk with God ...
for choir (S.A.T.B.) and organ,
[by] Ernest Bullock, [words by]
William Cowper. © The Oxford
University Press, London;
3Jul47; EF6124.

Three Songs from "Twelfth Night"
... words by William Shakespeare, set for tenor and
pianoforte by Ernest Bullock.
[c1946] © The Oxford University Press, London; 9Jan47.
Contents.- No. 1. O Mistress
Mine (© EF6094)- No. 2, Come
Away, Death (© EF6093)- No. 3.
When That I Was and a Little
Tiny Boy (© EF6092)

I. Shakespeare, William, 1564-1616,
lyricist. II. Title. III. Each
contents title.

BUNN, FLOYD S
Starlight Honeymoon; words and
music by Floyd S. Bunn.
© Nordyke Publishing Co., Los
Angeles; 25May46; EP19421.

BUNTE, OTTO VANDER. See
Vander Bunte, Otto.

BUREN, BURRELL VAN. See
Van Buren, Burrell.

BUREN, NEWTON JAMES, 1892-
Lullaby; by Newton J. Buren.
Tacoma, Lakewood Music Publish-
ing Co. © Newton J. Buren,
Tacoma; 21Oct47; EP18639. For
piano solo.

BURKHARD, SAMUEL T
Fairest Lord Jesus; (Crusaders'
hymn) for three-part chorus of
mixed voices (a cappella) Sil-
esian folk-tune, arr. by S. T.
Burkhard, [words] of unknown
authorship. © E.C. Schirmer
Music Co., Boston; 29Sep47; on
arrangement; EP18139.

BURLI, ANGELO.
Bncancita ... musica de A. Burli.
© Publications Raoul Breton &
Cie, Paris; 12Mar31; EF5993.
Piano-conductor score: orchestra.

Corazoncito ... [for] piano, [by]
Angelo Burli. © Publications
Raoul Breton & Co., Paris;
9Nov29; EF5995.

Mala-Pata ... de Angelo Burli.
© Publications Raoul Breton &
Co., Paris; 9Nov29; EF5998.
Piano-conductor score: orches-
tra.

241

BURLI, ANGELO. Cont'd.
Me Voy Compañeros ... de Angelo
Burli. © Publications Raoul
Breton & Cie, Paris; 27Mar30;
EF5999. Piano-conductor score:
orchestra.

Muñequita de Paris ...de Angelo
Burli. © Publications Raoul
Breton & Co., Paris; 9Nov29;
EF6000. Piano-conductor score:
orchestra.

Primer Amor ... musique de Angelo
Burli, paroles de Alfonso de
Silva. © Publications Raoul
Breton et Co., Paris; 6Jun29;
EF6001. Spanish words.

Solitario ... musique de Angelo
Burli. © Publications Raoul
Breton & Cie, Paris; 18Sep31;
EF5992. Piano-conductor score:
orchestra.

BURNET, WILLIAM PORTER.
Dearest Beloved; words and music
by William Porter Burnet. ©
Nordyke Publishing Co., Los
Angeles; 3Dec46; EP20299.

BURNETT, ERNIE, 1884-
Christmas Comes But Once a Year;
words by Harry Edelheit, music
by Ernie Burnett. © Burnett,
ltd., Saranac Lake, N. Y.;
15Dec47; EP20211.

BURNS, DON.
Yankee Land (and you) words by
Lee Holdridge, music by Don
Burns. [c1945] © Nordyke
Publishing Co., Los Angeles;
14Jun46; EP19385.

BURNS, JOE.
Let's Have Some Fun; words and
music by Joe Burns. © Nordyke
Publishing Co., Los Angeles;
5Aug47; EP19341.

BURROWS, ABE.
The Girl with the 3 Blue Eyes; by
Abe Burrows. © Edwin H. Morris
& Co., inc., New York; 13Nov47;
EP19111. For voice and piano,
with chord symbols.

BURROWS, REX, 1903-
My Heart Is Yours; song, words by
Kathleen Egan [pseud.], music by
Rex Burrows. © Ascherberg,
Hopwood & Crew, ltd., London;
20Aug47; EF6360.

BURTON, LARRY.
Sweet California Moon; words by
Hazel Burton, music by Larry
Burton. © Nordyke Publishing Co.,
Los Angeles; 13Jul46; EP20322.

BUSBY, BOB.
Happy Days. See his Holiday Camp.

(Holiday Camp) Happy Days; by
Louis Levy & Bob Busby ...
[from] Holiday Camp. ©
Chappell & Co., ltd., London;
16Sep47; EF6637. For voice
and piano; melody also in
tonic sol-fa notation.

BUSCH, WILLIAM, d. 1945.
Suite ... [by] William Busch,
[violoncello part ed. by Florence
Hooton, c1946] © The Oxford
University Press, London;
23Jun47. Score (violoncello
and piano) and part. Contents.-1
Prelude (© EF6109)- 2. Capriccio
(© EF6111)- 3. Nocturne (©
EF6110)- 4. Tarantella (© EF6108)

BUSH, GRACE, 1900-
Two Christmas Songs; Far Away in
Bethlehem [rnd] Hail, Holy Child;
text by Patricia O'Neill, music
by Grace Bush. © Wesley Webster,
San Francisco; 10Dec47; EP19577.

BUSHKIN, JOE, 1916-
Boogie Woogie Blue Plate; words
by John De Vries, music by
Joe Bushkin. © Northern Music
Corp., New York; 24Sep47;
EP17698.

BUSI, DOROTHY DE. See
De Busi, Dorothy.

BUSSER, HENRI, 1872-
Trois Antiennes à la Sainte Vierge
Marie; [by] Henri Busser. Op.
115 ... Pour quatre voix égales
(a capella) © Durand & Cie,
Paris; 30Jun47; EF6527. Latin
words.

BUTERA, JOSIE.
Sweetheart America; words & music
by Josie Butera. © Nordyke
Publishing Co., Los Angeles;
8Aug46; EP19690.

BUTLER, PRISCILLA, 1916-
A Little Suite; by Priscilla
Butler. © Forsyth Brothers,
ltd., London; 14Oct47; EF6860.
For piano solo.

BUXTEHUDE, DIETRICH, 1637-1707.
Six Organ Preludes on Chorales ...
by D. Buxtehude, ed. by Henry G.
Ley. © The Oxford University
Press, London; 15May47; on
editing; EF6114.

BYRNE, W   L   1885-
Let's Put the Moon to Bed; by
W. L. Byrne. © W. L. Byrne, Los
Angeles; 9Sep47; EP17000. For
voice and piano.

C

CABALLERO, REGINO GARNICA. See
Garnica Caballero, Regino.

CABLE, E   L
The Night Is Fine; words and
music by E. L. Cable. © Nordyke
Publishing Co., Los
Angeles; 12Sep47; EP19291.

CABRERA, ANA S   DE, 1903-
Canciones y Danzas Argentinas;
para canto y piano [by] Ana S.
Cabrera. © Ricordi Americana,
s.a.e.c., Buenos Aires; cuaderno 3, 18May42; EF7157. Cuaderno 1 has title: Cantos Nati-
vos y Danzas del Norte Argentino; cuaderno 2, Danza y Canciones Argentinas.

CABY, ROBERT JOSEPH AUGUSTE, 1905-
Chanson de la Servante ... poésie
de Henri Weitzmann, musique de
Robert Caby. © Enoch & Cie,
Editeurs, Paris; 10Jun47; EF5962.

Lo Pusillé; poème de Jacques
Prévert, musique de Robert Caby.
© Enoch & Cie, Editeurs, Paris;
10Jun47; EF5883.

Poèmes de Guillaume Apollinaire,
musique de Robert Caby. ©
Enoch & Cie, Editeurs, Paris;
30Apr47; EF5884.

CADMAN, CHARLES WAKEFIELD, 1881-1946.
The Road I Have Chosen ... words
by Aaron Kramer, music by
Charles Wakefield Cadman. ©
Leeds Music Corp., New York;
31Oct47; EP18646.

Song of Forest Lawn; music by
Charles Wakefield Cadman, lyrics
by Edward Lynn. © Forest Lawn
Memorial-Park Assn., inc., Glendale, Calif.; 10Nov47; EP16665.

CADOU, ANDRÉ PIERRE, 1885-
Alles Lui Dire que Je L'Aime ...
paroles de Louis Sauvat [pseud.]
musique de André Cadou. ©
Editions Masspacher, Paris;
15Jan47; EF6960.

[CAFFOT, SYLVÈRE] 1903-
Je Crois en Mon Étoile ... Paroles
de René Rousseud & Maurice Van-
dair [pseud.], musique de René
Sylviano [pseud.] © Editions
Choudens, Paris; 22Jul47;
EF6570.

CAIN, ANN E
Prospectin' Papa; words and
music by Ann E. Cain. ©
Nordyke Publishing Co., Los
Angeles; 24Jul47; EP20492.

CAIN, NOBLE, 1896-
The Arrow and the Song; [words
by] Longfellow. [c1933] © The
Raymond A. Hoffman Co., Chicago;
28Feb34; EP15589. Score: mixed
chorus and piano reduction.

Chillun' Come on Home; for a cappella chorus of male voices,
[arr.] by Noble Cain. © The
Raymond A. Hoffman Co., Chicago;
22Dec32; EP15581.

Come, Ye Faithful, Raise the
Strain; words by John of Damascus
... [tr. by John H. Neale] Music
by Noble Cain. © Boosey & Hawkes,
inc., New York; 30Jun47; EP16063.
Score: SSAATTBB and piano reduction.

A Day in June; [words by] Lowell.
[c1933] © The Raymond A. Hoffman Co., Chicago; 12Apr34;
EP15593. Score: mixed chorus
and piano.

Dey're a Ghost 'Roun' de Corner.
[c1933] © The Raymond A. Hoffman Co., Chicago; 23Feb34;
EP15595. Score: mixed chorus
and piano reduction.

The Eagle; [words by] Tennyson.
[c1933] © The Raymond A. Hoffman Co., Chicago; 28Feb38;
EP15588. Score: mixed chorus
and piano.

Hymn to the Night; [words by]
Longfellow. © The Raymond A.
Hoffman Co., Chicago; 25Jul33;
EP15597. Score: mixed chorus
and piano reduction.

I Got Shoes (Heaven, Heaven);
[for] TB or TTBB accompanied.
Negro spiritual arr. by
Noble Cain. © Harold Flammer,
inc., New York; 28Jul47; on
arrangement; EP16249.

I Got Shoes (heaven, heaven) Negro
spiritual, arr. by Noble Cain
... S.A.T.B. © Harold Flammer,
inc., New York; 14Nov47; on arrangement; EP19147.

I Got Shoes (heaven, heaven) Negro
spiritual, arr. by Noble Cain ...
S.S.A. © Harold Flammer, inc.,
New York; 14Nov47; on arrangement;
EP19146.

I Will Pour Out My Spirit ...
[words] from an early King James
version of Joel 2 and Isaiah 32,
[music by] Noble Cain. © Harold
Flammer, inc., New York; 14Nov47;
EP19152. Score: SSATTBB and
piano reduction.

My Lord's Goin' to Rain Down Fire.
[c1933] © The Raymond A. Hoffman
Co., Chicago; 23Feb34; EP15594.
Score: mixed chorus and piano
reduction.

Three Limericks; [by] unknown
poet. [c1933] © The Raymond
A. Hoffman Co., Chicago; 12Apr34;
EP15592. Score: chorus (SATB)
and piano.

When All Thy Mercies, Oh, My God
... [words by] Joseph Addison.
[c1933] © The Raymond A. Hoffman Co., Chicago; 17Jun34;
EP15596. Score: mixed chorus
and piano.

CAINES, GRACIA.
Happy Songs for Children; words
and music by Gracia Caines. ©
The Willis Music Co., Cincinnati;
16Oct47; EP18515.

CAIRNS, CLIFFORD IRVING, 1880-
My Lord Is in the Mountains; words
and music by Clifford Cairns.
Winona Lake, Ind., Rodeheaver
Hall-Mack Co. © The Rodeheaver
Co., Winona Lake, Ind.; 20Nov47;
EP19163.

Now I Lay Me Down to Sleep; words
and music by Clifford Cairns.
Winona Lake, Ind., Rodeheaver
Hall-Mack Co. © The Rodeheaver
Co., Winona Lake, Ind.; 20Nov47;
EP19164.

CAIRO, PABLO.
El Chismecito de Moda ... Letra
y música de Pablo Cairo, arreglo
de Juan E. Lazaga. © Peer
International Corp., New York;
16Dec46; EP5732. Parts:
orchestra.

Como Me Da la Gana Soy Yo ...
Letra y música de Pablo Cairo,
arreglo de Juan E. Lazaga.
© Peer International Corp.,
New York; 6Jun47; EP5742.
Parts: orchestra.

CAIX D'HERVELOIS, LOUIS DE, ca.
1670-ca. 1760.
La Gracieuse; [by] Caix d'Hervelois ... transcribed by Rudolf
Forst. © Edition Musicus New
York, inc., New York; 30Sep47;
on arrangement; EP20244. Score
(flute and piano) and parts for
2 flutes.

CALDER, GEORGE.
Mother, Dear to Me; words by
Bob Lavall & George Calder,
music by George Calder. ©
M. M. Cole Publishing Co.,
Chicago; 6Aug47; EP16084.

CALDWELL, HOWARD C
When It's Love; words and music
by Howard C. Caldwell. © Art
Music Co., New York; 26Nov47;
EP19057.

CALLAERTS, JOSEPH.
Toccata; by Joseph Callaerts,
arr. by Robert Leech Bedell ...
[for] organ solo. © Mills
Music, inc., New York; 28Jul47;
on arrangement; EP16194.

CALLENDER, CHARLES ROYAL, 1911-
Cornered; lyric by Niski Callender, music by Chuck Callender
[and] Redd Harper. © Laura-
Lea Music, Hollywood, Calif.;
15Oct47; EP18228.

CALLENDER, CHUCK. See
Callender, Charles Royal.

CALZA, EDVIGE.
Metodo per lo Studio Elementare
del Pianoforte; [by] Edvige
Calza, brani musicali di Enzo
Masetti, riduzioni di antiche
musiche italiane di F. Balilla
Pratella. Milano, Carisch.
© Edvige Calza, Milano; v. 2,
20Sep39; EF7162.

CAMACHO, JOHNIE, 1916-
When You Cross Your Heart. (Cuando
Aprenderás?) ... words and music
by Henry Stano, José Curbelo
[and] Johnnie Camacho. © Edward
B. Marks Music Corp., New York;
16Jul47; EP15815.

CAMERON, PEARL ANNA.
Old Pals; words and music by
Pearl Anna Cameron. © Nordyke
Publishing Co., Los Angeles;
11Jul47; EP17418.

CAMPBELL, BILL, 1904-
Don't Bring Me No News; by Bill
Campbell. © Popular Music Co.,
New York; 15Sep47; EP17228.
For voice and piano, with
chord symbols.

Like He's Never Loved Before;
by Bill Campbell. © Popular
Music Co., New York; 15Sep47;
EP17229. For voice and piano,
with chord symbols.

CAMPBELL, CECIL.
Hawaiian Moon; words and music by
Cecil Campbell. © Hill and
Range Songs, inc., Hollywood,
Calif.; 14Nov47; EP18769.

Little Hula Shack in Hawaii; words
and music by Cecil Campbell. ©
Hill and Range Songs, inc.,
Hollywood, Calif.; 21Aug47;
EP16514.

'Neath Hawaiian Palms; by Cecil
Campbell. © Hill and Range
Songs, inc., Hollywood, Calif.;
14Nov47; EP18766. For piano
solo; chords in guitar diagrams
and symbols.

She's Got the Cutest Eyes; words
& music by Bamer Shelton [and]
Cecil Campbell. © Bourne, inc.,
New York; 22Aug47; EP16559.

Steel Guitar Hop; by Cecil Campbell. © Hill and Range Songs,
inc., Hollywood, Calif.;
15Dec47; EP20133. For piano
solo, with guitar diagrams and
chord symbols.

CAMPBELL, WISHART NEIL MUNRO, 1906-
Two Anthems for Chorus; texts by
Wallace McAlpine, music by
Wishart Campbell. © BMI Canada,
ltd., Toronto; 28Sep47; on 2
anthems; EF6591-6592. Contents.
- Lead Us, O God. - Grant Us Thy
Care.

CAMPOS, OLIVER.
I'd Jump at the Chance; words and
music by Oliver Campos. © Nordyke
Publishing Co., Los Angeles;
28Mar47; EP16742.

CANDANEDO, GONZALO BRENES. See
Brenes Candanedo, Gonzalo.

CANDELLA, ALEX.
No Matter Where You Go; words and
music by Alex Candella. © Nordyke Publishing Co., Los Angeles; 3Sep47; EP19290.

CANDLYN, T   FREDERICK H
Music, When Soft Voices Die; [com-
posed and arr. by] T. Frederick
H. Candlyn, [words by] P. B.
Shelley. © The Arthur P. Schmidt
Co., Boston; 23Sep47; on arrange-
ment; EP17520. Score: TTBB and
piano reduction.

CANFIELD, RAY.
My Sweetheart; words and music by
Ray Canfield, arr. by [Betty B.
Glynn of] the Oahu Staff. (Oahu
advanced harmony note course for
Hawaiian and electric guitar,
lesson] 61FT) © Oahu Publishing
Co., Cleveland; 30Oct47; on arrangement; EP20242. For voice and
2 guitars. Includes swing arrangement for 2 guitars.

CANORA, L   1888-
Night of Love ... solo for piano
accordion [by L. Canora], arr.
by J. Peppino. New York, O.
Di Bella Music Co. © Onofrio
Di Bella, New York; 3Nov47;
EP19916.

CANTELOUBE, JOSEPH, 1879-
O Houp! Chant populaire du Langue-
doc, recueilli, noté et harmonisé pour 4 voix mixtes par
Joseph Canteloube ... adaptation
française de G. Daumas et J.
Chailley. © Rouart Lerolle &
Cie, Paris; 17Aug47; on adaptation and harmonization; EF7339.

CANTELOUBE, MARIE JOSEPH. See
Canteloube, Joseph.

LE CANZONI DEL 1940-1947; [by Gino
Camposo, F. Langella and others,
words by Salv. di Costanzo, M.
Galdieri, and others] Napoli,
Epifani. © Italian Book Co.,
New York; 15Oct46; EP6008.

CAPANO, FRANK, 1899-
As Long As There Is Love (We'll
Be Happy thru the Years); words
and music by Mary Cianfrani and
Frank Capano. © Tin Pan Alley,
Philadelphia; 21Aug47; EP17054.

Counting the Stars; words and
music by Rose Montgomery, Duke
Morgan and Frank Capano. © Tin
Pan Alley, Philadelphia;
21Aug47; EP17057.

I Was Wrong; words and music by
Jack Ziehler, Samuel Slater and
Frank Capano. [c1946] © Tin
Pan Alley, Philadelphia;
21Aug47; EP17056.

Va-zap-pa; ... Words and music by
Tony Starr and Frank Capano.
© Mills Music, inc., New York;
29Aug47; EP17951.

CAPES, DENIS.
Mary, Mary, Quite Contrary ...
[by] Denis Capes. © Oxford Univ.
Press, London; 28Aug47; EF6665.
Two scores for piano 1-2.

CAPOZZOLO, ISIDORO.
When I Was a Young Boy; words and
music by Isidoro Capozzolo.
© Nordyke Publishing Co., Los
Angeles; 16Dec46; EF20306.

CAPRI, ANGELO, pseud. See
Capriotti, Angelo.

[CAPRIOTTI, ANGELO]
A Toast to Our Love; words and music
by Angelo Capri [pseud.] ©
Nordyke Publishing Co., Los
Angeles; 29Apr47; EP16842.

CARBAJO, ROQUE.
Recompensa ... letra y música de
Roque Carbajo. [© Robbins
Music Corp.] © Robbins Music
Corp., New York; 29Aug47; on
arrangement; EP17734.

Recompensa ... música ; letra de
Roque Carbajo, arreglo de
Pancho Montes. © Hnos. Márquez,
s. de r. l., editores, México;
12Apr46; EF6382. Piano-conductor
score (orchestra) and parts.

CARBUTT, ANN.
The Willow Song; words by William
Shakespeare, music by Ann Car-
butt. © Peter Maurice Music
Co., ltd., New York; 28Nov47;
EF7356.

CARDEW, PHIL.
Alto Reverie; by Phil Cardew.
© The Edward Kassner Music Co.,
ltd., London; 14Oct47; EF6876.
Score (saxophone and piano)
and part.

CARDONE, F
Nun Turnà; versi e musica di F.
Cardone. Napoli, Edizioni
E.M.C.D. © Italian Book Co.,
New York; 4Aug47; EF6618.

CAREY, HENRY, d. 1743.
My Country 'Tis of Thee; [by] H.
Carey, arr. by P. Ballatore. (In
Ballatore, Pietro, comp. So easy.
p.13) © Edward B. Marks Music
Corp., New York; 9Dec47; on ar-
rangement; EP19589. For piano
solo.

CARIBOU, JOHN.
Bird Symphony ... By John Caribou,
arr. by B. F. Stuber. © The
Raymond A. Hoffman Co., Chicago;
14Mar33; EP15571. Condensed
score (orchestra) and parts.

CARLE, FRANKIE, pseud. See
Carlone, Francis N.

CARLETON, ROBERT L   1888-
Back Home with You; words by Lloyd
J. Tyler, music by Bob Carleton.
© Nordyke Publishing Co., Los
Angeles; 15Aug46; EP19493.

Deep in My Heart; words by Emmaline
Flick, music by Bob Carleton. ©
Nordyke Publishing Co., Los An-
geles; 31Jul47; EP19729.

Dreamy Eyes; words by Gertrude
Splitt, music by Bob Carle-
ton. © Nordyke Publishing
Co., Los Angeles; 25Jun47;
EP17633.

Every Time I See You; words by
Neal Hemer, music by Bob
Carleton. © Nordyke Publishing
Co., Los Angeles; 2May47;
EP16959.

Fool Am I; words by Barbara
Allen, music by Bob Carleton.
[c1945] © Nordyke Publishing
Co., Los Angeles; 12Feb46;
EP17626.

Going Home Today; words by Tillie
Thayer, music by Bob Carleton.
© Nordyke Publishing Co., Los
Angeles; 18Jul46; EP19484.

Gosh Oh Friday (I wish I was free)
words by Harry Craft, music by
Bob Carleton. © Nordyke
Publishing Co., Los Angeles;
9Nov46; EP19484.

Have I a Chance? Words by
Gertrude Splitt, music by Bob
Carleton. © Nordyke Publishing
Co., Los Angeles; 29Apr47;
EP16824.

I Am Living in a Dream; words by
Evelyn B. Taylor, music by
Bob Carleton. [c1946] © Nor-
dyke Publishing Co., Los
Angeles; 28Jun47; EP19661.

It Is Sleepy Time Now; words by
Areta E. Powers, music by Bob
Carleton. © Nordyke Publishing
Co., Los Angeles; 11Aug47;
EP19695.

It's to Laugh; words by Ellen
Petersen, music by Bob Carleton.
© Nordyke Publishing Co., Los
Angeles; 29Mar47; EP16753.

June's Got Me! Words by Joseph
Gardi, music by Bob Carleton.
© Nordyke Publishing Co., Los
Angeles; 16Jul47; EP17599.

Like a Lovely Melody; words by
Charlotte Hadley Saxon, music
by Bob Carleton. © Nordyke
Publishing Co., Los Angeles;
8Aug46; EP19772.

Little Did I Know; words by Calvin
Jorry, music by Bob Carleton.
© Nordyke Publishing Co., Los
Angeles; 27Mar47; EP16802.

Marvelous Mysteries Sublime;
words by Bea Kaylor, music by
Bob Carleton. © Nordyke
Publishing Co., Los Angeles;
11Oct46; EP19560.

Music of the Jungle; words by
Louise Maxwell, music by Bob
Carleton. [c1945] © Nordyke
Publishing Co., Los Angeles;
21Aug47; EP16603.

My Dream Girl; words by James V.
Shears, music by Bob Carleton.
© Nordyke Publishing Co., Los
Angeles; 9Aug46; EP19714.

One Sweet Day; words by I. O. C.
Wood, music by I. O. C.
Wood. © Nordyke Publishing Co., Los
Angeles; 29Mar47; EP16770.

Peace and Freedom; words by Eli
J. Klingensmith, music by Bob
Carleton. © Nordyke Publishing
Co., Los Angeles; 18Jul46;
EP19957.

Racing for the Moon; words by
Mary Seaman, music by Bob
Carleton. [c1945] © Nordyke
Publishing Co., Los Angeles;
21Jun46; EP19651.

Reach for the Stars; words by
Clara Victoria Sherman, music
by Bob Carleton. © Nordyke
Publishing Co., Los Angeles;
8Aug46; EP19652.

Tell Me That You Love Me; words by
Mabel Galatos Arn, music by Bob
Carleton. © Nordyke Publishing
Co., Los Angeles; 10Jul47;
EP16945.

That Matters Much to Me; words
by Linda Jayne [pseud.] music
by Bob Carleton. © Nordyke
Publishing Co., Los Angeles;
15Aug47; EP20431.

Waterfall; words by Joe McClinton,
music by Bob Carleton. © Nordyke Publishing Co., Los Angeles;
23Jul46; EP19642.

Wedding Ring in the spring; words
by Florence Wells Jones, music
by Robert L. Carleton. ©
Nordyke Publishing Co., Los
Angeles; 10Oct47; EP19305.

What Good Is the Moon? Words by
Vincent Pantano, music by Bob
Carleton. © Mills Music, inc.,
New York; 29Aug47; EP17940.

Whoa, Texas! Words by Bill Alden
[pseud.], music by Bob Carleton. © Nordyke Publishing Co.,
Los Angeles; 15Aug47; EP20075.

[CARLONE, FRANCIS N   ]
I Don't Want to Meet Any More People;
lyric by Stanley Adams, music by
Frankie Carle. [pseud.] © Dreyer
Music Corp., New York; 21Jul47;
EP15895.

CARLSON, ALEX PHYLANDER, 1898-
Alex Carlson Violin School, Elemen-
tary Course. © Alex Carlson,
Portland, Or.; bk.3, 21Sep47;
EP17805.

CARLSON, MILLIE E
The Time I Think of You; words
and music by Millie E. Carlson.
© Nordyke Publishing Co., Los
Angeles; 5Aug47; EP19536.

CARMICHAEL, CLARA JANET.
I Thank My Lucky Star; words
and music by Clara Janet
Carmichael. © Nordyke
Publishing Co., Los Angeles;
28Mar47; EP16765.

CARMICHAEL, HOAGY.
Casanova Cricket; by Hoagy
Carmichael, Larry Markes [and]
Dick Charles. © Burke and
Van Heusen, inc., New York;
12Aug47; EP16407. For voice
and piano, with chord symbols.

Star Dust; by Mitchell Parish and
Hoagy Carmichael. Organ solo
with annotations for Hammond
organ [arr. and] ed. by Robert
Leech Bedell. © Mills Music,
inc., New York; 28Jul47; on
arrangement; EP16197.

CARNES, JOSEF R
Remember Me (at close of day) ...
song, by Josef R. Carnes. ©
Josef A. Carnes, Hillsboro, Ind.;
28Jul47; EP16014.

CARON, ALLAN.
If You're the Girl; Rendezvous ...
lyrics and music by Allan Caron.
© The Mello Music Pub. Co.,
Winnipeg, Manitoba, Can.;
20Oct47; EP18323.

Slumber Song; lyrics and music by
Allan Caron. © Mello-Music
Pub. Co., Winnipeg, Man., Can.;
18Aug47; EP16529.

Think! Brother; Cosmopolitan
International song, [words and
music] ... by Allan Caron. ©
Allan Caron, Winnipeg, Manitoba,
Can.; 30Jun47; EP5885.

You're the Answer to My Dreams;
lyrics and music by Allan Caron.
© The Mello Music Pub. Co.,
Winnipeg, Manitoba, Can.;
20Oct47; EP18322.

CARPENTER, IMOGEN.
If Winter Comes; theme from the
... picture, "If Winter Comes."
Lyric by Kim Gannon, music by
Imogen Carpenter. New York,
Robbins Music Corp.; 24Nov47; EP19123.

CARPENTIER, JEAN M
The Chimes Love Waltz; words &
music by Jean M. Carpentier.
© Nordyke Publishing Co. Los
Angeles; 11Oct46; EP19411.

CARR, ARTHUR, arr.
As on the Night; for three-part
chorus of women's voices with
piano acc., adapted from George
wither's "Hymns and Songs of the
Church." 1623 [by] Arthur Carr.
© G. Schirmer, inc., New York;
27Aug47; on arrangement; EP18728.

CARR, KEITH.
Lullaby of the Raindrops; music
by Keith Carr, words by Ray
Meany, arr. by Melo Dominici.
© Ray Meany, Golden Gate Publications, Oakland, Calif.;
11Aug47; EP16315. For voice
and 2 guitars; also tablature
and chord symbols for ukulele.

Lullaby of the Raindrops; words
by Ray Meany ... music by Keith
Carr ... piano arrangement by
Dick Kent. © Peer International
Corp., New York; 26Sep47;
EP17854.

CARR, LEON, 1910-
A Man Could Be a Wonderful Thing;
words ... by Leo Corday, [music
by] Leon Carr, [piano arr. by
George Sumner] © Ritchie Music
Co., inc., New York; 18Jul47;
EP15971.

CARR, MICHAEL.
The Things I Do for Love; words by
Michael Carr & Sid Colin, music
by Michael Carr. © Noel Gay
Music Co., ltd., London; 3Sep47;
EP6692.

(When Moonbeams Kiss) the Little
Homes of Ireland ... lyric by
Richard W. Pascoe, music by
Michael Carr. © Leeds Music
Corp., New York; 31Oct47;
EP18643.

CARRIER, COTTON.
Careless Love Boogie; words and
music by Cotton Carrier.
© Carson-Carrier Publications,
Atlanta; 30Jun47; EP15548.

CARRINGTON, OTIS M
The Shepherd's Christmas; Christmas operetta in three scenes ...
words and music by Otis M. Carrington. © Otis M. Carrington,
Redwood City, Calif.; 22Aug47;
D pub 1550.

CARROLL, BERT.
Love Is Love; words by Lois G.
Johnson, music by Bert Carroll.
© Nordyke Publishing Co., Los
Angeles; 29Mar47; EP16732.

Lover's Plea; words by E. M. J.
Keller, music by Bert Carroll.
© Nordyke Publishing Co., Los
Angeles; 9Nov46; EP19971.

CARROLL, JIMMY.
Helen-Polka; by Walt Dana,
Albert Gamse [and] Jimmy
Carroll. © Bregman, Vocco and
Conn, inc., New York; 12Dec47;
EP20467. For voice and piano,
with chord symbols.
In Santiago, Chile ('tain't chilly
at all); lyric by Albert Gamse,
music by Jimmy Carroll. c1948.
© Encore Music Publications,
inc., New York; 18Dec47; EP20237.
Melody and chord symbols, with
words.

CARSON, JENNY LOU.
Behind the Eight Ball; words and
music by Jenny Lou Carson.
© Hill and Range Songs, inc.,
Hollywood, Calif.; 30Oct47;
EP18345.
Never Trust a Woman; words and
music by Jenny Lou Carson.
© Home Folks Music, inc., Hol-
lywood, Calif.; 30Oct47;
EP18341.
Out in the Rain Again; words and
music by Jenny Lou Carson.
© Tim Spencer Music, inc.,
Hollywood, Calif.; 15Dec47;
EP20109.
Songs; by Jenny Lou Carson. Album
no.1. © Hill and Range Songs,
inc., Hollywood, Calif.; on 6
songs, 15Dec47. Partial contents.-
Too Good to Be True (© EP20113)-
Purgatory (© EP20114)- Foolish
Tears (© EP20115)- Somebody No-
body Loves (© EP20116)- Lassie
Come Home (© EP20117)- The Burning
of the Winecoff (© EP20118)
You'll Live to Regret It (wait and
see); words and music by Jenny
Lou Carson. © Hill and Range
Songs, inc., Hollywood, Calif.;
30Jul47; EP16048.

CARSON, RUBY BARRETT.
Allegro Brillante; for piano solo
by Ruby Barrett Carson. © The
Boston Music Co., Boston;
15Oct47; EP18636.

CARTER, JOHN, 1917-
Angel (I've fallen for you);
written and composed by Armand
Mora, Fred Sutton, John A. Carl-
sen [and] John Carter. © Lawrence
Wright Music Co., ltd., London;
5Dec47; EF7369. For voice and
piano, with chord symbols; melody also in tonic sol-fa notation.
I. Mora, Armand, joint composer. II. Sutton,
Fred, 1919-   joint composer. III. Carl-
sen, John A., 1915-   joint composer.
IV. Title.

CARTURAN, CARLO.
Two Christmas Offertories; by Carlo
Carturan ... For three equal
voices. © McLaughlin & Reilly
Co., Boston; 18Jul47; EP15879.

CARULLI, F
Nocturne no.1-[3; by].F. Carulli.
Op.128. (Arr. by) Victor & Volpe.
c1939. © Albert Rocky Co., New
York; 10Jan40; on 3 arrangements;
EP20205-20207. Parts: 4 guitars.

CARVER, ZEB.
Did You Mean That Last Goodbye?
By Sam Martin and Zeb Carver.
© Golden West Melodies, inc.,
Hollywood, Calif.; 28Apr47;
EP16149. For voice and piano,
with chord symbols.

[CASADESUS, FRANCIS] 1870-
Canta per Me. Chante Encore
pour Moi ... sur les motifs
d'Albert Petit, paroles françaises et italiennes de
Custy [pseud.] et Dutnil,
musique de F. C. Sénéchal
[pseud.] © A. Jullien-Grenval,
Paris; 15Apr47; EF5984.

Deux Pièces pour Alto; a. Romance
Provençale. b. Danse. [By]
Francis Casadesus, doigtés et
coups d'archets de Maurice Vieux.
Paris, H. Lemoine. © Francis
Casadesus, Paris; 26Aug47; EF7221.
Score (viole and piano) and part.
(Hurricane-Express) Noël Américain;
choeur à 4 voix mixtes, chanté
dans le film "Hurricane-Express."
Paroles de J. Ercé [pseud.], musique
de Francis Casadesus. Paris,
H. Lemoine. © Francis Casadesus,
Paris; 26Aug47; EF7222.

Noël Américain. See his Hurricane-Express.

Romance Provençale et Danse; deux
pièces pour saxophone alto en mi
b, [by] Francis Casadesus, tran-
scrites par Marcel Mule. Paris,
H. Lemoine. © Francis Casadesus,
Paris; 26Aug47; EF7223. Score
(saxophone and piano) and part.

CASADESUS, ROBERT, 1899-
(Sonata, piano, no. 1) Première
Sonate; [by] Robert Casadesus,
Op.14. © Salabert, inc., New
York; 15Sep47; EF7247.

CASADO, ERNESTO LECUONA Y. See
Lecuona y Casado, Ernesto.

CASAMOR, EUTIMIO.
"Eloísa la China" ... Letra de
José Casamor, música de Eutimio
Casamor, arreglo de Juan B.
Lazaga. © Peer International
Corp., New York; 3Jul47;
EP5727. Parts: orchestra.
Oye! Destapa la Botella ... letra
y música de Eutimio Casamor,
arreglo de Juan E. Lazaga.
© Peer International Corp., New
York; 30Sep47; EP6825. Piano-
conductor score (orchestra) and
parts.

CASAMOR, JOSE.
Caridá No Tá Viní ... Letra y
música de José Casamor,
arreglo de Juan E. Lazaga.
© Peer International Corp.,
New York; 3Jul47; EP5728.

CASELLA, ENRIQUE M   1891-
Estudio en fa; [by] Enrique M.
Casella, para piano. © Ricordi
Americana, S.A.E.C., Buenos
Aires; 9Oct46; EP6970.

CASEY, J   D
My Girl of Yesteryear; words and
music by J. D. Casey. © Nordyke
Publishing Co., Los Angeles; 10May47;
EP16936.

CASEY, TONY, 1908-
Just a Faded Picture (in a dusty
frame); words and music by Ross
Leonard, Ernie Towle & Tony Casey.
© Top Music Publishers, inc., New
York; 25Aug47; EP16373.

CASILAO, ALFREDO.
Underneath the Tropical Moonlight; words and music by Alfredo Casilao. © Nordyke Publishing Co., Los Angeles;
25Jun47; EP17448.

CASLAR, DAN.
(E Bello Qualche Volta Andare a
Piedi) Sorrentina (Ricciolina)
dalla rivista "E Bello Qualche
Volta Andare a Piedi," parole di
M. Galdieri, musica di D. Caslar.
© Edizioni Curci, s. a., Milan;
31Dec41; EF6330. Melody and
chord symbols, with words.
Sorrentina. See his E Bello Qualche
Volta Andare a Piedi.

CASLER, CHARLES HENRY, 1908-
Mother Read Those Stories; words
and music by Charles Casler.
Philadelphia, F. Steiger.
© Charles Henry Casler, Phila-
delphia; 19Aug47; EP17984.

[CASSEL, TORSTEN MAGNUS]
Love in Spring. Kärleks-Vår ...
Musik: Guy Lessac [pseud.],
arr.: Gösta Theselius. © Svala
och Söderlund, kungl. hovmusik-
handel, Stockholm; 1Jan44;
EF7057. Piano-conductor score
(orchestra) and parts.

CASSONE, MICHAEL.
Rainbow Serenade; words and music
by Michael Cassone. © Mills
Music, inc., New York; 4Aug47;
EP18263.

CASTAGNETTA, GRACE, 1912-   arr.
Song of Robin Hood; selected & ed.
by Anne Malcolmson, music arr.
by Grace Castagnetta, designed &
illus. by Virginia Lee Burton.
[Boston] Houghton Mifflin Co. ©
Anne Burnett Malcolmson, Alexandria, Va. & Virginia Lee Demetrios, Gloucester, Mass.;
15Oct57; A17994.

CASTELBERG, MARTHA VON, 1892-
Sieben Geistliche Lieder ... [by]
Martha von Castelberg. © Hug
& Co., Music-Publishers, Zurich,
Switzerland; 15Sep47; EF6844.
For voice and piano; part of the
words in Latin, part in German.

CASTELLANI, LEANDER.
Pittston Polka. Nanticoke Polka.
... By Leander Castellani. ©
Leander Costellani, Wyoming,
Pa.; 10Jul47; EP15733-15734.
For accordion solo.
Scranton Polka; modern accordion
solo by Leander Castellani.
© Leander Castellani, Wyoming,
Pa.; 10Jul47; EP15735.

CASTELLANOS, AL.
Are You Kidding? Ta Jugando? By
Al L. Castellanos. © Peer In-
ternational Corp., New York;
25Nov47; EP19857. For voice and
piano; Spanish words.
Mish-Mash ... letra y música de
Al Castellanos. © Peer Inter-
national Corp., New York;
25Nov47; EP19858.
Talk to Me. "Háblame." Letra y
música de Al Castellanos.
© Peer International Corp., New
York; 27Aug47; EP17862.

CASTILLO, NICANDRO.
El Engreído! ... Letra y música de
Nicandro Castillo. © Promotora
Hispano Americana de Música,
s.a., México; 27Aug47; EP6711.
Sueño ... y El Cantador; letra
y música de Nicandro Castillo.
© Promotora Hispano Americana
de Música, s. a., Mexico;
29Jul47; EF3986. 3985.

CASTRO, ARMANDO.
Jinguili Jonjolo ... English words
by Joe Davis, Spanish words by
Romulo Contreras, music by Ar-
mando Castro. © Caribbean Music
Co., New York; 4Dec47; EP20233.

CASTRO, JOSÉ MARÍA, 1892-
Pequeña Marcha; para piano.
[c1946] © Editorial
Argentina de Música (E.A.M.)
Buenos Aires; 9Jan47; EF3991.
Tres Estudios. © Editorial
Argentina de Música (E.A.M.),
Buenos Aires; 28Sep46;
EF3992. Score (violoncello
and piano) and part.
Vals Miniatura; para piano. ©
Editorial Argentina de Música
(E.A.M.), Buenos Aires;
22Jan47; EF3992.

CASTRO, JUAN JOSÉ, 1895-
"Casi Polka"; para piano. ©
Editorial Argentina de Música
(E.A.M.), Buenos Aires;
22Jan47; EF3993.

245

CASTRO, JUAN JOSÉ. Cont'd.
Intrata y Danza Rustica ...
[by] Juan José Castro.
[c1946] © Editorial Argentina De Música (E.A.M.),
Buenos Aires; 9Jan47; EF5652.
Score (violin and piano) and
part.

CASTRO, WASHINGTON, 1909-
Cuatro Piezas sobre Temas In-
fantiles; para piano [by]
Washington Castro. © Editorial
Argentina De Música (E.A.M.),
Buenos Aires; 6Jul45. Contents.-
1. Juegos (© EF5664)- 2.
Haciendo Nonito (© EF5663)-
3. Era un Pajarito (© EF5662)-
4. Ronda (© EF5661)

CATALÁN, MANUEL ANTONIO.
Vuela, Vuela Pajarito! ... Letra
y música de Manuel A. Catalán.
© Promotora Hispano Americana
de Música, s.a., México; 30Dec46;
EF6060.

CATE, HAROLD WEBSTER.
Our Homeland; Voice of Lawrence
... words and music by Harold
Webster Cate. Boston, N. N.
Homeyer & Co. © Harold Webster
Cate, Lawrence, Mass.; 15May47;
EP6985.

CATES, MATTIE D
The Land of Golden Sunsets; words
and music by Mattie D. Cates.
© Nordyke Publishing Co., Los
Angeles; 22Apr47; EP16937.

CATLETT, SID.
Humoresque Boogie; arr. by Sid
Catlett, piano solo. © Duchess
Music Corp., New York; 18Aug47;
on arrangement; EP16397.

CAVALLINI, E
Douze Études; pour clarinette,
[by] Cavallini. Nouv. éd.
entièrement rev., corr. et
annotée par François Étienne.
© Alphonse Leduc & Co., Éditions
musicales, Paris; 30Jun47;
on revision, correction &
annotation; EF6419.

CAVANAUGH, DANIEL PATRICK, 1892-
Just Because We've Got no Sense;
words and music by Danny
Cavanaugh. Boston, N. N.
Homeyer & Co., distributors.
© Danny Cavanaugh, Boston;
25Sep47; EP17249.

CAVI, FRED
Why Should I Have a Heart for
You? Words and music by Fred
Cavi. © Standard Music Pub-
lishers, ltd., New York;
15Aug47; EP18241.

CAYMMI, DORIVAL.
Karina [words and music by]
Dorival Caymmi. Q. E. S.
Mangione, editor, São Paulo,
Brazil; 12Mar47; EF6778. Piano-
conductor score (orchestra) and
parts.

CAZA, ILEEN, 1920-
That's Why I Love Only You; by
Ileen Caza. © Shelby Music Publishing Co., Detroit; 3Dec47;
EP19884. For voice and piano,
with guitar diagrams and chord
symbols.

CAZES, MARIUS, 1890-
Prière d'Amour ... paroles de Pierre
Decourt [pseud.], musique de Mario
Cazes. © Éditions Salabert, Paris;
4Aug47; EF7246.

CECILIA, sister.
Swaying Blossoms; piano solo by
Sister Cecilia. © The Boston
Music Co., Boston; 21Oct47;
EP18411.

CEELEY, LYN.
Gardenia Lady ... [from] a new
musical, Gardenia Lady; music
... & lyrics by Lyn Ceeley. ©
Chappell & Co., ltd., London;
6Oct47; EF7007.

(Gardenia Lady) My Heart Is
Yours ... [from] a new musical,
Gardenia Lady; music ... &
lyrics by Lyn Ceeley. © Chap-
pell & Co., ltd., London;
7Oct47; EF7004.
My Heart Is Yours. See his Gardenia
Lady.

CEKOW, A. T., pseud. See
Travnicek, André.

CERNKOVICH, RUDOLPH, 1889-
Nebo Je Čisto, Jasno. (The Sky
Is Clear and Bright) Original
matter and arrangement by Rud.
Cernkovich. © Rudolph Cernkovich, Bradley, Mich.; 28Oct47;
on Croatian words, interlude &
arrangement; EP18434. Parts:
string orchestra; Croatian
words.
Nine O'Clock Polka ... original
matter and arrangement by Rud.
Cernkovich. © Rudolph
Cernkovich, Bradley, Mich.;
18Aug47; on original introduction, 2d part & arrangement;
EP16668. Parts: string
orchestra.
Pod mojim Okancem. (Under My
Window) Original matter and
arrangement by Rud. Cernkovich.
© Rudolph Cernkovich, Bradley,
Mich.; 20Aug47; on original
introduction, trio & 1st verse,
Croatian translation of 2d, 3d
& 4th verses & arrangement;
EP16669. Parts: string
orchestra, with Croatian words.
Sjedaš Li Se Onog Sata? (Do You
Remember?) ... Po Gradini Mjesečina Sija Meka. (Moonlight
over the Fields) Ed. & arr. by
R. Cernkovich. © Rudolph Cernkovich, Bradley, Mich.; 30Oct47;
on arrangement; EP18433. Parts;
string orchestra; Croatian
words.

CERNY, RALPH J
Did You Mean It? Words and music
by Ralph J. Cerny. © Nordyke
Publishing Co., Los Angeles;
11Aug47; EP17588.

CHADWICK, CECIL, 1896-
To Jane ... words by Shelley,
music by Cecil Chadwick. ©
Boosey & Co., ltd., London;
12Aug47; EF6082.

CHADWICK, GEORGE WHITEFIELD, 1854-
1931.
Allah; [music by] G. W. Chadwick,
arr. by Hugh Gordon [pseud.]
words by] H. W. Longfellow. ©
The Arthur P. Schmidt Co., Boston; 4Sep47; on arrangement;
EP16638. Score: chorus (SSA) and
piano.

CHADWICK, LOLA K
Baby's Lullaby; words and music
by Lola K. Chadwick. © Wire
Co., Publishers, Salt Lake
City; 18Oct47; EP18435.

CHAĬKOVSKIĬ, PETR IL'ICH, 1840-1893.
Arab Dance; [based on a theme from
Tschaikowsky's "Nutcracker Suite")
Arr. by Claude Thornhill.
© Mutual Music Society, inc.,
New York; 11Jun47; on arrangement; EP15352. Piano-conductor
score (orchestra) and parts.
The Best Known Music of Tschaikowsky; [with arrangements and transcriptions by Hugo Frey] © Hamilton S. Gordon, inc., New York;
2Dec47; on arrangements & transcriptions; EP19268. For piano
solo.

(Concerto, piano, no. 1) Piano
concerto no. 1; by Peter I.
Tchaikovsky, abridged version
for piano solo by Albert Harland. © Chappell & Co., ltd.,
London; 1Aug47; on arrangement;
EP6623.

(Concerto, piano, no. 1) Tschaikowsky's Concerto no. 1, arr.
by A. J. Condaris. © Scholastic
Music Co.; New York; 14ov47;
14ov47; on arrangement for
school orchestra; EP19604.
Piano-conductor score and parts.

Dance of the Sugar Plum Fairy;
[from "The Nutcracker Suite" by
Peter Tschaikowsky] ... Arr. by
Hugo Frey. (Words by Leda
Joyce] © Hamilton S. Gordon,
New York; 28Oct47; on
words and arrangement; EP18748.
For piano solo, with words.

Danse des Mirlitons; [from]
(Nutcracker Suite) [by] Peter
Ilyitch Tschaikowsky, arr. by
William Teague. © Broadcast
Music, inc., New York; 25Jul47;
on arrangement; EP18042. Piano-
conductor score (orchestra) and
parts.

Lady on a Fan; [by] P. I. Tschai-
kowski, an arrangement of the
Chinese dance from the Nutcracker suite, with flute obbligato ad lib., [words by
Edith Sanford Tillotson, arr.
by Ira B. Wilson] © Lorenz
Publishing Co., Dayton, Ohio;
24Sep47; on vocal arrangement;
EP17892. Score: flute, chorus
(SSA) and piano.

March, from the Nutcracker Suite;
[by] Tschaikowsky, arr. for easy
piano solo by Walter Rolfe.
© Century Music Publishing Co.,
New York; 10Jul47; on arrangement; EP15488.

None but the Lonely Heart; by
Peter Tschaikowsky. [Arr. by
Hugo Frey] © Hamilton S. Gordon,
inc., New York; 9Jul47; on arrangement; EP15610. For voice
and piano.

Overture Miniature; (Nutcracker
suite) [by] Peter Ilyitch
Tschaikowsky, arr. by William
Teague. © Broadcast Music, inc.,
New York; 5Jun47; on arrangement; EP18213. Piano-conductor
score (orchestra) and parts.

Romeo and Juliet; [by]
(Tschaikowsky), piano solo,
theme from the fantasy-
overture, arr. by King
Palmer. © William Paxton
& Co., ltd., London; 18Sep46;
on arrangement; EP5714.

Selected Dances; [by] Tchaikovsky
... arr. for piano solo by Roger
Forbes. © New World Publishers,
ltd., London; 23Jul47; on
arrangement; EP6622.

(Serenade, string orchestra)
Waltz, from Serenade for
strings; by P. I. Tschaikowsky,
piano solo, a John W. Schaum
arrangement. © Belvin, inc.,
New York; 20Nov47; on arrangement; EP18802.

(Serenade, string orchestra) Waltz,
from Serenade. Op.48, by P.
Tchaikovsky, arr. ... by
Pevel, [pseud.] © Carl Fischer,
inc., New York; 14Jul47; on
arrangement; EP15701. Condensed
score (band) and parts.

Waltz, from Serenade. Op. 48. See
Serenade, string orchestra.

CHAIKOVSKII, PETR IL'ICH. Cont'd.
Waltz, from "Serenade for Strings."
Op. 48. [By] Tschaikowsky, arr.
by Roy Douglas. London, Sole
selling agents, Boosey & Hawkes,
ltd. © Hawkes & Son (London)
ltd., London; 12Aug47; on arrange-
ment; DP6083. Piano-conductor
score (orchestra) and parts.
Waltz of the Flowers, from."The
Nutcracker Suite" by P. Tschai-
kowsky; S.A., arr. by C. Albert
Scholin, [words by Ruth B.
Scholin] © Belwin, inc., New
York; 18Dec47; on arrangement;
EP19928.

CHAILLEY, JACQUES, 1910-   comp.
Les Chansons du Jamboree; réunies
par Jacques Chailley, William
Lemit [and] César Geoffray. ©
Rouart Lerolle & Cie, éditeurs,
Paris; 4Jul47; on compilation;
EF7342. For 1-4 voices.
J'ay Vu la Beauté Ma Mie; chanson
du XVe siècle, choeur à 4 voix
mixtes, harmonisée par Jacques
Chailley. © Rouart, Lerolle &
Cie, Paris; 20Mar47; on harmoni-
zation; EF5977.
Le Menuisier du Roi; mélodie
pour chant et piano, paroles
de Maurice Fombeure, [music by]
Jacques Chailley. © Lucien De
Lacour, Paris; 31Mar47;
EF5908.

CHAJES, JULIUS THEODORE, 1910-
Evening Song; from "Out of the
Desert" by Julius Chajes, lyric
by Michael Atzmoni [pseud.]
New York, Bloch Pub. Co.
© Julius Chajes & Michael
Atzmoni Keen, Detroit; 10Jun47;
EP15518. Score (voice and
piano; English words) and voice
part (Hebrew words with trans-
literation)
Song of the Camel Driver; [Gamal,
G'malli], from the opera "Out
of the Desert" by Julius
Chajes, lyric by Michael
Atzmoni [pseud.] New York,
Bloch Pub. Co. © Julius
Chajes & Michael Atzmoni Keen,
Detroit; 28Jul47; EP17241.
Words in Hebrew (transliterat-
ed) and English.
Song of the Jewish Partisans; text
by Hirsh Glick, setting for ...
S.A.T.B. by Julius Chajes. ©
Transcontinental Music Corp.,
New York; 18Nov47; on arrange-
ment; EP18826. Score; SAATBB and
piano reduction; words in both Yiddish
and Yiddish transliterated.

CHALFANT, BLANCHE PAGE.
Please Show Me the Way to the
Cross; [words by Granville E.
Davis] © The La Casa Del Rio
Music Publishing Co., inc.,
Toledo; 14Dec45; EP15605.
Close score; SATB.

CHAMINADE, C
The Silver Ring. (L'anneau
d'argent) For three-part chorus of women's voices ... arr.
by Wayne Howarth, [words by]
Rosamondo Gerard, English version [by] W. H. © The Raymond
A. Hoffman Co., Chicago;
11Sep40; EP15575. English
words.

CHAMINADE, CECILE.
Pas des Echarpes. (Scarf Dance)
[By] C. Chaminade ... rev. and
ed. by Maxwell Eckstein. © Carl
Fischer, inc., New York; 10Dec43;
EP17141. For piano solo.

CHAMPION, S
Crazy Summer; words and music by
S. Champion. © Nordyke Publish-
ing Co., Los Angeles; 21Feb47;
EP19409.

CHANDLER, GUS.
Canadian Capers; [by] Henry Cohen
Bert White and Gus Chandler,
transcribed by Gregory Stone.
© Remick Music Corp., New York;
21Nov47; on arrangement; EP19174.
Score (violin and piano) and
part.

CHANEY, WILBUR CLIFFORD.
Chaney's Rapid-Note-Reader ...
comp. and arr. by W. Clifford
Chaney. © The Norman Music
Publishing Co., (Wilbur Clifford
Chaney, sole owner) Detroit;
pt.1, 1Aug47; MP16069.

CHANLER, THEODORE.
The Doves; [music by] Theodore
Chanler, [words by Leonard
Feeney] © Hargail Music Press,
New York; 1Jul46; EP17119.

CHANSLOR, HAL, 1903-
April and Tulip Time; words by
Winnifred Brown Daniel, music by
Hal Chanslor. © Nordyke Pub-
lishing Co., Los Angeles;
12Aug47; EP19717.
Choo Choo Baby; words by Clovo
Hilsman, music by Hal Chanslor.
© Nordyke Publishing Co., Los
Angeles; 29Jan47; EP19949.
The Fighting Marines; words by
Edward J. Poirier, music by Hal
Chanslor. © Nordyke Publishing
Co., Los Angeles; 1May46; EP16763.
I Don't Want To Live without you;
words by Mamie Teague, music by
Hal Chanslor. © Nordyke
Publishing Co., Los Angeles;
10Jun47; EP16885.
Just Show Me You Do; words by Eda
Belle Love Canady, music by Hal
Chanslor. © Nordyke Publishing
Co., Los Angeles; 13Aug47;
EP19943.
Like Millions Have Done; words by
Joseph Wyant, music by Hal
Chanslor. © Nordyke Publishing
Co., Los Angeles; 15Jul46;
EP19966.
Live in My Memory; words by Ray-
mond Kiecker, music by Hal
Chanslor. © Nordyke Publishing
Co., Los Angeles; 9Nov46;
EP19972.
Lonesome and Blue; words by Vir-
ginia Sproof, music by Hal Chan-
slor. © Nordyke Publishing Co.,
Los Angeles; 11Jun46; EP19507.
Lover's Serenade; words by Edna
Ivey, music by Hal Chanslor.
© Nordyke Publishing Co.,
Los Angeles; 29Jul47; EP17508.
Meet Me Tonight in the Moonlight;
words by Albert Weder, music by
Hal Chanslor. © Nordyke Pub-
lishing Co., Los Angeles;
11Jun46; EP19685.
Mr. Moon; words by Stanley
Erickson, music by Hal Chanslor.
© Nordyke Publishing Co., Los
Angeles; 20Aug45; EP16715.
Moon Magic; words by Beverly
Page [pseud.], music by Hal
Chanslor. © Nordyke Publishing
Co., Los Angeles; 5Jul47; EP17490.
Night Shift Blues; words by Ruth
Smith, music by Hal Chanslor.
[c1946] © Nordyke Publishing
Co., Los Angeles; 21Feb47;
EP20298.
Riding the Rainbow; words by
Mary Rose Jones, music by Hal
Chanslor. © Nordyke Publishing
Co., Los Angeles; 13Aug47;
EP19962.
Rolling Waves; words by Norman L.
White, music by Hal Chanslor.
© Nordyke Publishing Co., Los
Angeles; 12Apr47; EP16759.

Singing to the Rhythm of the
Saddle; words by Bessie Mc-
Clain, music by Hal Chanslor.
© Nordyke Publishing Co., Los
Angeles; 14Jun47; EP17535.
Until You Came Along; words by
Norman Hoffman, music by Hal
Chanslor. © Nordyke Publishing
Co., Los Angeles; 29Jul47;
EP19531.
Waiting and Yearning; words by
Elizabeth Barrett, music by Hal
Chanslor. © Nordyke Publishing
Co., Los Angeles; 10May47;
EP16851.
When Peace Has Come; words by
Edward J. Poirier, music by Hal
Chanslor. © Nordyke Publishing
Co., Los Angeles; 6Oct45;
EP16748.
Why, oh why, oh why? Words by
Clifford A. Myers, music by Hal
Chanslor. © Nordyke Publishing
Co., Los Angeles; 18Jul46;
EP20309.
Will Your Eyes Look into Mine?
Words by Gerald M. Morris,
music by Hal Chanslor. [c1946]
© Nordyke Publishing Co., Los
Angeles; 29Jan47; EP19398.
You; words by Don Paull, music by
Hal Chanslor. [c1946] ©
Nordyke Publishing Co., Los
Angeles; 29Jan47; EP19382.
You Are My World; words by Zola
Barnes, music by Hal Chanslor.
© Nordyke Publishing Co., Los
Angeles; 27Sep46; EP20314.
(The Jolson Story) Anniversary
Song; by Al Jolson and Saul
Chaplin, [arr. by Robert C.
Haring] Based on the theme by
Ivanovici. From the ... picture,
"The Jolson Story." © Mood
Music Co., inc., New York;
18Nov47; on arrangement; EP19219.
La Canzone dell' Anniversario. See his
The Jolson Story.

CHAPLIN, SAUL.
Anniversary Song. See his The Jolson
Story.
(The Jolson Story) La Canzone dell'
Anniversario. (Anniversary Song)
...[from The Jolson Story... by
Al Jolson and Saul Chaplin,
based on a theme by Ivanovici,
Italian lyric by Nicola Paone.
© Mood Music Co., inc., New
York; on Italian lyric; 14Jul47;
EP15730. For voice and piano,
with chord symbols; Italian words.

CHAPMAN, EDWARD THOMAS, 1902-
It Was a Lover and His Lass; canon
for equal soprano voices, words
by William Shakespeare, music by
Edward T. Chapman. © A. & C.
Black, ltd., London; 18Jun47;
EF5990.

CHAPPOTIN, FELIX.
Que Se Vaya ... Letra y música de
Felix Chappotin. © Peer International Corp., New York;
3Jul47; EP5726. Parts: orchestra.

CHARDON, FÉLIX, 1911-
Y Avait Une Fois Deux Amoureux;
paroles de Raymond Asso,
musique de Félix Chardon &
Albert Lasry. © Éditions
Salabert, Paris; 14Apr47;
EF5934.

[CHARDON, JULIEN] 1909-
L'Enfant au Coeur d'Or; choeur à
4 voix d'hommes, paroles de
Jacques Larue [pseud.], musique
de Juan Lutèce [pseud.] ©
Rouart, Lerolle & Cie, Paris;
20Mar47; EF5879.
Entre dans le Danse; paroles de
Louis Hennevé, musique de Juan
Lutèce [pseud.] © Sté Ame Fse
Chappell, Paris; 10Nov47; EF7200.
Melody and chord symbols, with
words.

247

CHARLES, DICK, pseud. See
Krieg, Richard Charles.

CHARLES, ERNEST.
O Lovely Words; for voice and piano
by Ernest Charles. [Words by
Velma Hitchcock] © G. Schirmer,
inc., New York; 17Jul47; EP17042.

Save Me, O God; for voice and piano
by Ernest Charles. [Words
adapted from Psalm 69] © G.
Schirmer, inc., New York;
17Jul47; EP17041.

CHASE, NEWELL.
Tanglewood Pool ... (music and
arrangement) by Newell Chase,
ed. by Arthur Fiedler. © Mills
Music, inc., New York; 24Apr45;
on arrangement and editing;
EP16144. Piano-conductor score
(orchestra) and parts.

CHATTERTON, TOMMY.
Sweetheart Darlin'; words and mu-
sic by Tommy Chatterton. ©
Peer International Corp., New
York; 25Nov47; EP19841.

CHAUMONT, LAMBERT.
Livre d'orgue (1695) ... présenté
en notation moderne avec notices
explicatives par Charles Hens
... et Roger Bragard. Liège,
Belgique, Éditions Dynamo, P.
Aelberts. (Monumenta leodien-
sium musicorum. sér. A, v. 1)
© Pierre Aelberts, Liège, Belgique; on modern notations with
explanatory notes; 30Dec39;
EF2261.

CHAUVIGNY, ROBERT, 1916-
Un Refrain Courait dans la Rue;
paroles de Edith Piaf [pseud.]
musique de Robert Chauvigny. ©
Arpège Éditions Musicales, Paris;
5Mar47; EF6448. For voice and
piano, and voice part.

CHAVIS, LEE.
I'm Cryin' All over Again; words
and music by Lee Chavis. ©
Rujanart Music Publications,
Encino, Calif.; 8Apr47;
EP16167.

CHEATHAM, EUGENE CALVIN, 1895-
You Must Live Like the Bible Say;
words and music [by] ... E. C.
Cheatham, arr. by Earl A. Hess.
© Eugene Calvin Cheatham, Cin-
cinnati; 28Jun47; EP15480.

CREERS, JACK, 1908-
Rhythm Solitude; words by William
R. Westfield, music by Jack
Cheers. © William R. Westfield,
Princeton, Wis.; 1Nov47;
EP19059.

CHEKLER, EDWARD EUGÈNE, 1917-
Il Fait des ... ; paroles de
Edith Piaf [pseud.], musique de
Edward Chekler. © Éditions
Paul Beuscher, Paris; 10Jul47;
EF6466.

CHENETTE, ED. 1898-
Oh You Basketball ... by Ed
Chenette. © Southern Music Co.,
San Antonio; 17Nov47; EP18834.
Piano-conductor score (band,
with words) and parts.

Texas Tech on Parade ... by Ed
Chenette. © Southern Music Co.,
San Antonio; 17Nov47; EP18835.
Piano-conductor score (band)
and parts.

CHEREPNIN, N
The Standard Bearers; by N.
Tcherepnin ...(a cappella) S.A.
T.B. [English translation by
Wladimir Lakond, English adap-
tation by Olga Paul] © Edward
B. Marks Music Corp., New York;
14Oct47; on English adaptation;
EP18366.

CHESNOKOV, P
May Thy Blessed Spirit; for four-
part male chorus, by P. Tschesnokoff, arr. by Frank B. Cookson. © H. T. FitzSimons Co.,
Chicago; 29Sep47; on arrangement; EP18120.

Nunc Dimittis; for chorus of mixed
voices, [by] Tschesnokoff.' From
the Greek liturgy, tr., ed. and
arr. by Noble Cain, [and Gloria,
composed by Noble Cain after
Tschesnokoff] © The Raymond A.
Hoffman Co., Chicago; 19Dec31;
EP15598.

CHETTICK, HAPPY JACK. See
Chettick, Jonathan Marr.

CHETTICK, JONATHAN MARR.
Back on the Range in My Sunny
Texas Home ... words & music by
Happy Jack Chettick. © Jonathan
Marr Chettick, Houston, Tex.;
31Oct47; EP18939.

There Is Two Loving Arms Wanting
You ... words and music by
Happy Jack Chettick. © Jonathan
Marr Chettick, Houston, Tex.;
31Oct47; EP18938.

Where the Rio Colorado Wends Its
Way ... words and music by
Happy Jack Chettick. © Jonathan
Marr Chettick, Houston, Tex.;
31Oct47; EP18937.

CREVALS, MAURICE, d. 1943.
Solfège scolaire; [by] Maurice
Chevals. Nouv. éd. ... con-
forme aux instructions
ministérielles, considérable-
ment augm. d'exercices et de
chants à une et à deux voix
et orientant vers le chant
choral. 745 morceaux variés.
c1946. © Alphonse Leduc et
Cie., Paris; on new edition;
v. 1, 14Nov46; v. 2, 1Jan47;
EF5200, 6315.

CHEYETTE, IRVING, arr.
Loads o' Fun Band Book; by Irving
Cheyette. © Bregman, Vocco &
Conn, inc., New York; v. 1-2,
12Sep47; EP17126-17127. Contents.- [1] Part for flutophones,
song flutes, sweet winds and
tonettes.- [2] Part for drums
and bell lyra.

Loads o' Fun Band Book; [comp. and
arr.] by Irving Cheyette. ©
Bregman, Vocco and Conn, inc.,
New York; v. 3, 7Nov47; EP19850.
Contents.- [3] Piano-conductor.

CHILDE, MANTLE.
Lazy Sheep; a pianoforte solo
based on an old French melody,
[by] Mantle Childe. © The
Oxford Univ. Press, London;
16Oct47; on arrangement;
EF6995.

CHILDE, ROBERT S   1899-
Dark Eyes; Russian folk song,
S.A.T.B. arr. by Robert Childe.
© Neil A. Kjos Music Co., Chica-
go; 10Oct47; on arrangement;
EP18820.

Workin' on de Railroad; arr. by
Robert Childe. © Neil A. Kjos
Music Co., Chicago; 26Jun47;
on arrangement; EP16059. Score:
SSATB and piano.

CHITTY, ADA WINIFRED IVY, 1901-
Rhythmic Games and Dances for
Juniors; by A. W. I. Chitty.
© William Paxton & Co., ltd.,
London; 2Dec46; EF5705.

CHOBILLON, CHARLES, 1891-
A Mélodie le Dimanche ...
Paroles de Lucien Rimels
[pseud.], musique de Charles
Chobillon. © Éditions Salabert,
Paris; 19Jun47; EF5900.

CHODOROV, DAVID.
Yours till the End; words by Beth
Renard, music by David Chodorov.
© Nordyke Publishing co., Los An-
geles; 31Jul47; EP20354.

[CHOISSER, JOSEPH DANIEL] 1925-
In the Mexican Cafe; by Danny
Hart [pseud.] arr. by Univ.
Music Co.] © Univ. Music Co.,
Hollywood, Calif.; 7May47;
EP14468. For voice and piano,
with chord symbols.

CHOPIN, FRYDERYK FRANCISZEK, 1810-
1849.
Fantaisie Impromptu; by Chopin,
[arr. by Victor Ambroise] ©
Lawrence Wright Music Co.,
ltd., London; 23Sep47; on
simplification; EF6634. For
piano solo.

Minute Waltz; music by Fr. Chopin,
[arr. by Jerry Sears] © Broadcast
Music, inc., New York; 2Sep47;
on arrangement; EP18055. Piano-
conductor score (orchestra)
and parts.

(Nocturne, piano) Romance Lointaine;
sur les motifs du "Nocturne. Op.
9, no.2" de Frédéric Chopin,
paroles de Louis Poterat et Jack
Jym [pseud.], arrangement de
André Lodge [pseud.] © Salabert,
inc., New York; 19Jun47; on
arrangement; EF5953.

Preludio; [by] Chopin. Plectrum
guitar solo, arr. as played by
Harry Volpe. c1939. © Albert
Rocky Co., New York; 10Jan40;
on arrangement; EP20202.

Romance Lointaine. See his
Nocturne, piano.

Sleep, Little Child of Mine; by
Chopin, [text by R. L. P.]
© Theodore Presser Co., Phila-
delphia; 28Sep47; on arrangement;
EP17283. Score: SATB and piano.

CHRISTENSEN, ALBERT OLAI.
Proper of the Service; for the
church year, set to Gregorian
psalm-tones with organ acc., by
Albert Olai Christensen and Harold
Edward Schuneman. © H. W. Gray
Co., inc., New York; 58ep47;
A17130.

CHRISTENSEN, AXEL WALLEMAR, 1881-
Axel Christensen's Break Studies ...
Anita Sampson, associate and arranger. © Axel Waldemar Christensen, Los Angeles; no.73, 15May47;
no.74, 12Jul47; no.75, 16Sep47;
no.76, 22Oct47; no.77, 3Dec47;
EP20177, 20176; 20175; 20174;
20173. For piano solo.

CHRISTIANSEN, PAUL J
From Afar; Christmas song for mixed
voices [by] Paul J. Christianson.
© Paul A. Schmitt Music Co.,
Minneapolis; 4Sep47; EP16654.

CHRISTY, VAN AMBROSE, 1900-
Sleep of the Infant Jesus; carol
for ... (S.S.A.), French noel
arr. by Van A. Christy. English
text by V. A. C. © Hall &
McCreary Co., Chicago;
18Aug47; on text & arrangement; EP16548.

Sleep of the Infant Jesus;
Christmas carol for mixed
voices, optional a cappella
(S.S.A.T.B.B.) French carol,
arr. by Van A. Christy, English
text by V.A.C. © Hall &
McCreary Co., Chicago; 22Aug47;
on English text and arrangement;
EP17028.

CHRYSOSTOM, sister. See
Koppes, Mary Chrysostom, sister.

CIMAGLIA, LIA, 1908-
Recuerdos de Mi Tierra; suite
para piano, [by] Lia Cimaglia.
© Ricordi Americana, s.a.e.c.,
Buenos Aires; 25Mar42; EF6982.

CIMAROSA, DOMENICO.
Penelope; sinfonia dell'opera,
[by] D. Cimarosa, rev. di N.
Negrotti. © Carisch, s. a.,
Milan; 12Jun44; on revision;
EF6275. Score: orchestra.

CIOFFI, GIUSEPPE.
Raccolta di Successi Cioffi, 1947-48;
[music by] Giuseppe Cioffi, [words
by Nello De Lutio, Gigi Pisano,
Enzo Bonagura and others] © Ital-
ian Book Co., New York; 1Nov47;
EF7190.
Though You Are Pretty. Guance
rosate. English lyric by Olga
Paul, Italian lyric by F.
- Caccavale, music by G. Cioffi.
(In Memories of Italy. p.48-51)
© Edward B. Marks Music Corp.,
New York; 16Jul47; on English
lyric; EP15827.

CLARK, AARON ALFRED.
Where the Old Missouri Winds Its
Way; words by Oscar W. Smith,
music by Aaron A. Clark. © Oscar
W. Smith, Strasburg, Mo.; 17Nov47;
EP19036.

CLARK, AARON AUGUSTIN, 1907-
My Mother, an Angel in Disguise;
words by Edna Locklar Norman,
music by Aaron A. Clark. ©
Edna Locklar Norman, Knob Noster,
Mo.; 29Oct47; EP18326.

CLARK, ARTHUR.
Jackie Robinson; words and music
by Artie Clark. © Nordyke
Publishing Co., Los Angeles;
11Aug47; EP17597.

CLARK, ARTIE.
Blue Darling; words and music by
Artie Clark. © Nordyke Publish-
ing Co., Los Angeles; 31Jul47;
EP19724.

[CLARK, C   VAN NESS] 1894-
All on Account of You; (song) by
Pat McCarthy and Clarke Van Ness
[pseud.] © Rialto Music Pub.
Corp., New York; 20Aug47;
EP18981.
The Plight of the Bumble Bee;
(The bumble bee can't fly, but
he does) by Clarke Van Ness
[pseud.] © Dixie Music Pub. Co.,
New York; 25Aug47; EP18979.
For voice and piano, with guitar
diagrams and chord symbols.

CLARK, EDDIE, 1909-
Vitamin You; music by Eddie Clark,
words by Vick Knight. © Hollywood Melodies, Music Publishers,
Los Angeles; 1Jul47; EP16666.

CLARK, FRANCES OMAN.
ABC Papers; the interval approach
to reading, a work and play book,
by Frances Oman Clark. © Clayton
F. Summy Co., Chicago; 31Jul47;
EP16022.

CLARK, HAROLD.
Two Songs; for tenor or soprano,
[by] Harold Clark. © Elkin &
Co., ltd., London; v. 1-2,
25Jul47; EF6379-6380. Contents.-
Como, Sloop (Beaumont and
Fletcher) - Flowers for Heliodora
(From the Greek Anthology)

CLARK, MRS. K   R
Bahama Nights; words and music by
Mrs. K. R. Clark. © Nordyke
Publishing Co., Los Angeles;
11Aug47; EP17566.

CLARK, LUTHER A
Pennsylvania Roof Garden; music by
Luther A. Clark, words by Chester
W. Cramer. © Chester Cramer,
Somerset, Pa.; 25Aug47; EP16614.

When the Leaves Were Young and
Green; words by Elma G. Hughes,
music by Luther A. Clark. ©
Nordyke Publishing Co., Los
Angeles; 31Jul47; EP19447.

CLARK, PALMER J   1893-
Song of Courage; unison chorus,
anonymous words] © The Raymond
A. Hoffman Co., Chicago; 12Oct35;
EP15568.

CLARKE, ARTHUR W
Two Choral Preludes; A Greek air
and Leoni, for organ by Arthur
W. Clarke. © Alfred Lengnick &
Co., ltd., London; 26Sep47;
EF7133.

[CLARKE, C   VAN NESS] 1894-
Regular Guy; (song) by Pat
McCarthy, Harold Hillock and
Clarke Van Ness [pseud.] ©
Rialto Music Pub. Corp., New
York; 20Aug47; EP18985.

CLARKE, HARRY DUDLEY, 1888-
Open the Door [and] We Want Every-
body to Be Happy; [words by]
H. D. C. [music by] Harry D.
Clarke. © Harry D. Clarke,
Gerards Port, Pa.; 25Jul47;
EP15904-15905. Close score;
SATB.

CLARO FUMERO, JOSE.
"Doña Bonifacia" ... Letra y
música de José Claro Fumero,
arreglo de Generoso Jiménez. ©
Peer International Corp.,
New York; 6Jun47; EF5731.
Parts: orchestra.

CLAVELLI, MARIO. See
Clavell, Miguel Mario.

CLAVELL, MIGUEL MARIO.
Porque Tú Lo Quieres ... letra y
música de M. Mario Clavell.
© Editorial Julio Korn, Buenos
Aires; 27Jul45; EF6806.

CLAYTON, NORMAN JOHN, 1903-
Praise Him Forevermore; [words by]
N. J. C. [music by] Norman J.
Clayton. © Norman John Clayton,
Malverne, N. Y., 15Nov47;
EP19060.

CLEMENTS, BERNIE.
This Can Never Happen Again; words
and music by Dale Koch and Bernie
Clements. © Nordyke Publishing
Co., Los Angeles; 29Jul47; EP17392.

CLEMENTS, JOHN.
Steal Away; spiritual, S. A. T. B.
(unaccompanied), arr. by John
Clements. © Keith, Prowse &
Co., ltd., London; 16Jul47;
on arrangement; EF6369.
Were You There? Spiritual, S. A.
T. B. (unaccompanied), arr. by
John Clements. © Keith, Prowse
& Co., ltd., London; 16Jul47;
on arrangement; EF6368.

CLEVE, FRIEDA.
Love's Hope; words and music by
Frieda Cleve. © Nordyke Publishing
Co., Los Angeles; 19Jun47; EP17499.

CLINE, J   DeFOREST
Hush Ye, 'Tis Mary; for chorus of
mixed voices, a cappella, words
by Vivian Yeiser Laramore,
music by J. DeForest Cline. ©
Paul A. Schmitt Music Co.,
Minneapolis; 7Jul47; EP16061.
Score: SATB and piano reduction.

CLITHEROE, FRED, 1882-
Ave Maria; music by Fred Clitheroe.
© Fred Clitheroe, Kenosha, Wis.;
15Sep47; EP17060. For voice and organ.
Fifty-seventh Session March; by
Fred Clitheroe. © Fred Clitheroe,
Kenosha, Wis.; 15Sep47; EP17061.
For piano solo.

CLOÉREC, RENÉ, 1911-
L'Amour N'est Qu'une Comédie. See his
Monsieur Alibi.

(Monsieur Alibi) L'Amour N'est
Qu'une Comédie, du film:
Monsieur Alibi ... paroles de
Henri Jeanson, musique de René
Cloérec. © Éditions Musicales
Robert Salvet, Paris; 28Feb47;
EF5933.

CLOKEY, JOSEPH W
Pretense; T.T.B.d. [by] Joseph W.
Clokey, [words by] George
Elliston. © J. Fischer & Bro.,
New York; 27Aug47; EP17272.
Six Sacred Pieces; for men's voices,
by Joseph W. Clokey. © C. C.
Birchard & Co., Boston; 30Oct47;
EP20213.
Two Dwellings; [by] Joseph W.
Clokey, [words by] Thomas
Washbourne. © J. Fischer &
Bro., New York; 17Jul47;
EP20358. Score: SA and piano.

CLOSE, GENE, 1893-
Grey Symphony; lyric by Ada Frances [pseud.], music by Gene
Close. [c1948] © Close Harmony
Publications, Hollywood, Calif.;
10Dec47; EP20106.
Visions in the Night; lyric by Hal
West, music by Gene Close.
[c1948] © Close Harmony Publications, Hollywood, Calif.;
10Dec47; EP20107.

[CLYDE, MERLING D   ] 1885-
Covered Wagon Home; [by Merling D.
Clyde, arr. by Clarice Gowers]
© Merling D. Clyde, Provo, Utah
& Clarice Gowers, Nephi, Utah;
22Jul47; EP17073. For voice and
piano.

CLYDE, TED.
Ain't It a Pity; words by Bob
L. Bowers, music by Ted Clyde.
© Nordyke Publishing Co., Los
Angeles; 14Nov46; EP19426.
All of My Life; words by Agnes E.
Sandbeck, music by Ted Clyde.
© Nordyke Publishing Co., Los
Angeles; 28Jun47; EP19060.
At the Foot of the Hill; words by
Vera Mae Dale, music by Ted
Clyde. © Nordyke Publishing
Co., Los Angeles; 27Jul46;
EP19433.
Beloved California; words by Per-
cival Phillips, music by Ted
Clyde. © Nordyke Publishing Co.,
Los Angeles; 11Oct46; EP19725.
Boogie Boogie Feet; words by
Susan Rose Moriel, music by Ted
Clyde. © Nordyke Publishing
Co., Los Angeles; 25Jul46;
EP19755.
Broadway Shuffle; words by Martin
C. Graham, music by Ted Clyde.
[c1946] © Nordyke Publishing Co.,
Los Angeles; 13Jul47; EP17561.
Christmas on the Ranch; words by
Cora Mason, music by Ted Clyde.
© Nordyke Publishing Co., Los
Angeles; 27Sep46; EP19931.
Every Day Is a Rainy Day for Me;
words by Worthy Scott, music
by Ted Clyde. © Nordyke Pub-
lishing Co., Los Angeles;
21Feb47; EP19446.
The Farm Is the Place for Me;
words by Charles A. Jones, mu-
sic by Ted Clyde. [o 1945]
© Nordyke Publishing Co., Los
Angeles; 12Jun46; EP20358.
Grieving; words by Lou Caro, [pseud.],
music by Ted Clyde. © Nordyke
Publishing Co., Los Angeles;
1Jun47; EP16863.
Hi There, Hello! Words by John
L. Adams, music by Ted Clyde.
© Nordyke Publishing Co., Los
Angeles; 11Oct46; EP17526.

CLYDE, TED. Cont'd.

How You All? Words by Leah Wright Dugat, music by Ted Clyde. © Nordyke Publishing Co., Los Angeles; 9Nov46; EP19435.

I Am Coming Back to You; words by Sadie Bigsby, music by Ted Clyde. © Nordyke Publishing Co., Los Angeles; 27Mar47; EP16736.

I'll Never Forget; words by Frank E. Stevens, music by Ted Clyde. © Nordyke Publishing Co., Los Angeles; 17May47; EP16889.

I'll Settle for You; words by Ann Wyatt, music by Ted Clyde. © Nordyke Publishing Co., Los Angeles; 27Mar47; EP16784.

Is Cupid Ever Stupid; words by Newt Jones, music by Ted Clyde. © Nordyke Publishing Co., Los Angeles; 10Jun47; EP16884.

Juke Box Heck; words by Ray Will, music by Ted Clyde. [c1946] © Nordyke Publishing Co., Los Angeles; 27Oct47; EP18402.

Kassie; words by Ragna O. Malom, music by Ted Clyde. [c1946] © Nordyke Publishing Co., Los Angeles; 14Jan47; EP19334.

Lilacs; words by Margaret P. Reed, music by Ted Clyde. © Nordyke Publishing Co., Los Angeles; 21Feb47; EP19974.

Love Is Like a Checkerboard; words by Joseph Wyant, music by Ted Clyde. © Nordyke Publishing Co., Los Angeles; 25May46; EP19509.

Lover's Evening; words by Joe Eberts, music by Ted Clyde. © Nordyke Publishing Co., Los Angeles; 10May47; EP16813.

Love's Lullaby; words by Stella Teller, music by Ted Clyde. © Nordyke Publishing Co., Los Angeles; 29Apr47; EP16951.

Moonlight and You, Sweetheart; words by Viola Johnson, music by Ted Clyde. © Nordyke Publishing Co., Los Angeles; 29Apr47; EP16840.

Mother; words by John S. Edwards, music by Ted Clyde. © Nordyke Publishing Co., Los Angeles; 5Jul47; EP17576.

My Dearest Dreams of You; words by Trudie F. Wilkins, music by Ted Clyde. © Nordyke Publishing Co., Los Angeles; 13Jul46; EP19471.

My Fondest Hope; words by Lila Sturte [pseud.], music by Ted Clyde. © Nordyke Publishing Co., Los Angeles; 22Apr47; EP17444.

My Grandboy; words by Dencie W. Corliss, music by Ted Clyde. © Nordyke Publishing Co., Los Angeles; 22Apr47; EP16825.

My Miami Gal; words by Lee McKeta, music by Ted Clyde. © Nordyke Publishing Co., Los Angeles; 27Jul46; EP19671.

My Mountain Sweetheart; words by Caleb Fitzgerald, music by Ted Clyde. [c1946] © Nordyke Publishing Co., Los Angeles; 15Aug47; EP16995.

My Pal; words by Gabriel Giovanni, music by Ted Clyde. © Nordyke Publishing Co., Los Angeles; 22Apr47; EP17583.

My Whole Life Long; words by Lois Manchester, music by Ted Clyde. © Nordyke Publishing Co., Los Angeles; 10May47; EP16941.

Our Ivory Tower; words by Emile E. Thornton, music by Ted Clyde. © Nordyke Publishing Co., Los Angeles; 8Aug46; EP19736.

Singin' to the Dogies on the Range; words by Carl B. Craig, music by Ted Clyde. © Nordyke Publishing Co., Los Angeles; 29May47; EP16907.

The Sky Is Grey in Loveland; words by William Robbinette, music by Ted Clyde. © Nordyke Publishing Co., Los Angeles; 12Jun46; EP20063.

Strolling in the Moonlight; words by Stella Teller, music by Ted Clyde. © Nordyke Publishing Co., Los Angeles; 12Jul47; EP17398.

Sunny Curls; words by James A. Burchett, music by Ted Clyde. © Nordyke Publishing Co., Los Angeles; 13Jul46; EP19431.

That's How I Stay Happy; words by Adele Linn [pseud.] music by Ted Clyde. © Nordyke Publishing Co., Los Angeles; 22Apr47; EP16822.

Trailin' My Herd; words by Jos. Brockman, arr., music by Ted Clyde. © Nordyke Publishing Co., Los Angeles; 1Jul47; EP16956.

True Love; words by Eleanor Dewsnap, music by Ted Clyde. © Nordyke Publishing Co., Los Angeles; 29Apr47; EP16836.

Unlock the Door to My Heart; words by Theodosia Walker, music by Ted Clyde. © Nordyke Publishing Co., Los Angeles; 17May47; EP16920.

Violet; words by Foy T. Quan, music by Ted Clyde. © Nordyke Publishing Co., Los Angeles; 16Dec46; EP19351.

Wandering Around; words by Ada Warren, music by Ted Clyde. © Nordyke Publishing Co., Los Angeles; 23May47; EP16856.

The Way You Speak; words by Frances Dollie, music by Ted Clyde. [c1946] © Nordyke Publishing Co., Los Angeles; 30Jan47; EP19589.

When the Mountains Start Calling Me Home; words by Eli Parker, music by Ted Clyde. © Nordyke Publishing Co., Los Angeles; 23Feb46; EP17451.

The White Hills of St. John; words by Lucille Klaus, music by Ted Clyde. © Nordyke Publishing Co., Los Angeles; 15Aug46; EP20053.

You Owe Me a Kiss; words by Emily E. Semler, music by Ted Clyde. © Nordyke Publishing Co., Los Angeles; 16Dec46; EP19741.

You Smiled and Said I Love You; words by Marguerite Gallacher, music by Ted Clyde. © Nordyke Publishing Co., Los Angeles; 1Jul46; EP19746.

You're the Girl That I Love; words by Ernest Clark, music by Ted Clyde. [c1945] © Nordyke Publishing Co., Los Angeles; 24Jun46; EP20053.

COBB, HAZEL.
Getting Acquainted with the Keyboard; practice patterns by Hazel Cobb. © Mills Music, inc., New York; 8Dec47; EP19895.

That Promised Land ... piano solo by Hazel Cobb. © Mills Music, inc., New York; 8Dec47; EP19894.

To the Duck Pond; piano solo, by Hazel Cobb. © Mills Music, inc., New York; 3Jul47; EP6995.

COBB, HAZEL, arr.
Sweet Sabbath; [The oldtime religion] a piano solo [arr.] by Hazel Cobb. © Clayton F. Summy Co., Chicago; 20Oct47; on arrangement; EP16182.

COBEN, CY.
This Is a Fine Time (to wanna leave me); words and music by Lewis Harris and Cy Coben. © Mutual Music Society, inc., New York; 19Nov47; EP18808.

When You See Those Flying Saucers; words and music by Charles Grean and Cy Coben. © Bob Miller, inc., New York; 27Oct47; EP18604.

COCHRAN, LESLIE TUDOR, 1903-
Facility; [by] Leslie T. Cochran, words by Robert W. Service. © G. Ricordi & Co. (London) ltd., London; 28Aug47; EF6612.

COCHRANE, PEGGY.
Irish Blarney; suite for pianoforte by Peggy Cochrane. © Campbell, Connelly & Co., ltd., London; no.2-3, 22Aug47; EF6961.

COCKSHOTT, GERALD.
All in the Morning; traditional carol, arr. for S.S.C., (unacc.) by Gerald Cockshott. © Novello & Co., ltd., London; 3Dec47; on arrangement; EF7291.

The Cobbler; unison song, words traditional, music by Gerald Cockshott. c1944. © A. & C. Black, ltd. (in notice: H. F. W. Deane & Sons, The Year Book Press, ltd.) London; 20Feb47; EF5756.

Sans Day Carol; traditional carol, arr. for S.S.C. (unacc.) by Gerald Cockshott. © Novello & Co., ltd., London; 5Dec47; on arrangement; EF7292.

CODY, WAYNE.
"Dear Cowboy Santa Claus;" words ... by Eddie Malle ... [and] Frank Stein, music [by] Wayne Cody. © Jack Howard Publications, inc., Philadelphia; 5Dec47; EP19546.

COFFEY, EDWIN J.
The Vale of the Hudson; words and music by Edwin J. Coffey. © Nordyke Publishing Co., Los Angeles; 10Jun47; EP16947.

COGHLAN, A V
Rose Time; words and music by A. V. Coghlan. © Nordyke Publishing Co., Los Angeles; 14Jun46; EP19525.

COGHLAN, ARTHUR V
There's a Great Time Coming; words and music by Arthur V. Coghlan. © Nordyke Publishing Co., Los Angeles; 25May46; EP20303.

COLBORN, ARTHUR GEORGE.
In Bethlehem; (Christmas carol) [by] Arthur G. Colborn, arr. by Hugo Nordun, [words by] J. M. Neale, last stanza by A.G.C. © The Arthur F. Schmidt Co., Boston; 18Aug47; on arrangement; EP16979. Score: SATB and piano.

COLDREY, ALBERT GEORGE JEFFERY, 1903-
(Bandit prince) Let us romance together, excerpt from "Bandit prince" operetta; words & music by Jeff Coldrey. © Albert George Jeffery Coldrey, sole owner of South Pacific Star Music Publishing Co., Melbourne, Australia; 14Oct46; EF5378.

COLE, ADAM, pseud. See Wilson, Roger C.

COLE, JOHNNY, pseud. See Kowalski, John Leo.

COLE, WILLIAM.
The Evening Hour; part-song for
S. A. T. B., words by Byron,
music by William Colo. ©
Novello & Co., ltd., London;
4Sep47; EF6307.

Love in Thy Youth, Fair Maid;
part-song for S.A.T.B., words by
W. Porter ... music by William
Colo. © Novello & Co., ltd.,
London; 4Sep47; EF6386.

COLIN, CHARLES, 1913-
Advanced Dance Studies; [for] trombone, [by] Charles Colin. ©
Charles Colin, New York; 5Dec47;
on arrangement; EP19552.

Melodious Fundamentals; [by]
Charles Colin [for] trumpet. ©
Charles Colin, New York; 18Nov47;
on compilation; EP18742.

COLL, RAMON.
Manola ... musique de Ramón Coll.
© L. Maillochon, Paris;
27Sep20; EF6805. For piano
solo.

COLLINS, ANTHONY VINCETT BENEDICTUS,
1893-
Dreams; S.S.A.A. [By] Anthony Collins, [words by Byron] © Keith,
Prowse & Co., ltd., London;
2Dec47; EF7173.

COLLINS, JANE.
Sleepless Nights, My Love; words
and music by Walter and Jane
Collins. © Nordyke Publish-
ing Co., Los Angeles; 24Jul47;
EP19526.

COLLINS, WALTER, 1891-
Forward ... composed by Walter
Collins. © Swan & Co. (Music
Publishers) ltd., London;
20Jun47; EF5686. For piano
solo.

COLLINSON, FRANCIS MONTGOMERY,
1898- arr.
Songs from the Countryside; as
featured in "Country Magazine,"
[music] selected & [arr.] by
Francis M. Collinson and [words
ed. by] Francis Dillon. ©
William Paxton & Co., ltd.,
London; bk.1, 10Oct46; on
selecting & editing; EF3972.
For voice and piano.

COLOMBO, JOSEPH, 1900-
Bambola ... de Joseph Colombo.
Thérésy ... de Joseph Colombo
et Igino Papiri. © (Editions
Espagnoles) Julio Garzon,
Paris; 25Jul47; EF6484. Parts:
orchestra.

Vals Chinoise; [by] Joseph
Colombo et Georges Ghestam.
© Les Editions Metropolitaines,
Paris; 5Feb47; EF6501.

COLVILLE, ALAN, pseud. See
Wilcoxen, Frank Samuel.

COMBS, W   W
God Lives Today ... [by] W. W.
Combs, [words by] Loella Hob-
son. © Loella M. Hobson, Fort
Wayne; 20Oct47; EP18354. Score:
SATB.

COMO, OSCEOLA.
Living God; words and music by
Osceola Como. © Osceola Como,
Grand Rapids; 28Jul47; EP16008.
Close score: mixed voices.

COMPAGNO, GRACE MARIE.
Berceuse for Bethlehem; for mixed
voices S.A.T.B. and soprano
solo by Grace Marie Compagno,
[words by Charles J. Quirk] ©
Groene Music Publishing Co.,
San Francisco; 1Oct47; EP17815.

COMPTON, HAROLD.
Just Pretending; words and music
by Harold Compton. © Nordyke
Publishing Co., Los Angeles;
5Jun47; EP16867.

CONCONE, GIUSÉPPE, 1810-1861.
Twenty-five Easy and Progressive
Melodic Studies for Piano. [By]
J. Concone. Op.24. Rev. and
ed. by Maxwell Eckstein. ©
Carl Fischer, inc., New York;
8Dec47; on revision and editing;
EP17137.

CONCONE, J. See
Concone, Giuseppe.

CONDARIS, ALCO JAMES, 1919-   arr.
Chiapanecas. (Mexican Clapping
Song) Arr. by A. J. Condaris.
© Scholastic Music Co., Port
Chester, N. Y.; 1Nov47; on ar-
rangement for school orchestra;
EP19600. Piano-conductor score
and parts.

Dark Eyes; arr. by A. J. Condaris.
© Scholastic Music Co., Port
Chester, N. Y.; 1Nov47; on ar-
rangement for school orchestra;
EP19596. Piano-conductor score
and parts.

Ole Ark's A-Moverin'; arr. by A.
J. Condaris. © Scholastic
Music Co., Port Chester, N. Y.;
1Nov47; on arrangement for
school orchestra; EP19599.
Piano-conductor score and parts.

Short'nin Bread; arr. by A. J.
Condaris. © Scholastic Music
Co., Port Chester, N. Y.; 1Nov47;
on arrangement for school orchestra; EP19602. Piano-conductor score and parts.

Turkey in Swing; arr. by A. J.
Condaris. © Scholastic Music
Co., Port Chester, N. Y.; 1Nov47;
on arrangement for school
orchestra; EP19598. Piano-conductor score and parts.

CONN, CHESTER.
Why Should I Cry over You?
Words and music by Ned Miller
and Chester Conn, [arr. by
Helmy Kresa] © Leo Feist,
inc., New York; 15Jul47; on
arrangement; EP16231.

CONN, FRANCES VIVIAN, 1910-
Put Yourself in a Frame for Love
... Words and music by Frances
V. Conn. © Frances V.
Conn, New York; 10Jul47; EP15731.

CONN, MERVIN AARON, 1920-
You'd Better Be Good While I'm
Gone; lyric by Raymond Leveen
... music by Mervin Conn.
© Mervin A. Conn, Washington,
D. C.; 15Jun47; EP15305.

CONN, PETER.
It's Jack the Bell Boy Time; by
Dardnnelle [pseud.] and Peter
Conn. © Burke & Van Heusen, inc.,
New York; 25Aug47; EP16679. For
voice and piano, with chord
symbols.

CONNELL, GRANT.
Nymphs and Goblins; piano solo by
Grant Connell. © Schroeder &
Gunther, inc., Rhinebeck, N. Y.;
5Sep47; EP16649.

CONNIFF, RAY, 1916-
Familiar Moe; [by] Ray Conniff,
[arr. by] Artie Shaw. London.
Bosworth. © Winfield
Music, inc., New York; 13Jun47;
on arrangement; EF7156. Piano-
conductor score (orchestra) and
parts.

CONNOR, TOMMIE, 1904-
Down in the Glen; song, words
and music by Harry Gordon and
Tommie Connor. © Lawrence
Wright Music Co., ltd., London;
26Sep47; EF6635.

I'm Mashuga for My Sugar; words
and music by Tommie Connor.
© Noel Gay Music Co., ltd.,
London; 16Jun47; EF5862.

CONRARDY, HATTIE C
In the Shade of Our New Apple
Tree; words and music by
Hattie C. Conrardy. © Nordyke
Publishing Co., Los Angeles;
22Apr47; EP16896.

CONRAY, AL.
Why Did You Say You Loved Me?
Words and music by Max & Harry
Nesbitt and Al Conray. ©
Irwin Dash Music Co., ltd.,
London; 21Apr47; EF3941.

CONROY, MARCIE.
Cutie, You Are a Beauty; words &
music by Margie Conroy. ©
Nordyke Publishing Co., Los
Angeles; 11Oct47; EP19410.

CONSERVATORY OF MUSIC OF TORONTO. See
Toronto. Conservatory of Music.

CONSTANTINE, FRED.
Crying 'Cause I'm Happy; words
and music by Fred Constantine.
© Nordyke Publishing Co., Los
Angeles; 16Jul47; EP17568.

CONWAY, OLIVE F
Little Things, My Lord; for voice
and piano, words by Marian Fos-
ter Smith, music by Olive F.
Conway. © Volkwein Bros., inc.,
Pittsburgh; 24Oct47; EP18287.

COOK, H   MAX.
My Dreams; words and music by H.
Max Cook. [c1945] © Nordyke
Publishing Co., Los Angeles;
21Jun46; EP20332.

COOK, JOE.
Everyone Has Their Dreams; words
and music by Albert Millis and
Joe Cook. © Nordyke Publishing
Co., Los Angeles; 25Jun47;
EP17629.

COOK, LAWRENCE HARLEY, 1922-
It Won't Be Long; [music by]
Lawrence Cook, [words by] Daniel
Keller. © Daniel Keller, Dallas
Center, Iowa; 3Sep47; EP17066.

Make Your Honeymoon To Last; [music
by] Lawrence Cook, [words by]
Daniel Keller. © Daniel Keller,
Dallas Center, Iowa; 3Sep47;
EP17067. Close score: SATB.

COOK, LESTER.
Happy As a Schoolboy; lyric and
music by G. Everett Allen and
Lester Cook. © Allen and Klink
Music Publishers, Bowling Green,
Ky.; 30Jun47; EP15512.

I Found the Key; words and music
by Ray Brooks and Lester Cook.
© Nordyke Publishing Co., Los
Angeles; 11Jun47; EP17577.

COOK, MAE, pseud. See
Koch, Clara Mae

COOK, MYRTLE ELIZABETH.
Sweetie Pie; words by Catherine A.
Weedin, music by Myrtle Eliza-
beth Cook. © Nordyke Publish-
ing Co., Los Angeles; 27Jul46;
EP19693.

Why, Oh Why! Words by Catherine A.
Weedin, music by Myrtle Elizabeth Cook. © Nordyke Publishing Co., Los Angeles; 9Aug46;
EP20067.

COOKE, JAMES FRANCIS.
Song of the North; Norwegian
barcarolle for piano. © Theodore
Presser Co., Philadelphia; 28Jul47;
EP15960.

COOKSON, FRANK B   1897-
Joshua Fit de Battle ob Jericho;
for two-part chorus of male
voices. Negro spiritual, arr.
by Frank B. Cookson. [c1941]
© The Raymond A. Hoffman Co.,
Chicago; 28Nov42; EP18521.

That's More to My Mind! ... For
three-part chorus of women's
voices, folk song arr. by Frank
B. Cookson. © H. T. Fitzsimons
Co., Chicago; 29Sep47; on arrangement; EP18122.

COOLEY, D   C
Cowbell Polka; by Spade Cooley, Larry (Pedro) De Paul and Andrew Soldi. © Hill and Range Songs, inc., Hollywood, Calif.; 15Dec47; EP20121. For piano solo, with guitar diagrams and chord symbols.

Spadella; by Spade Cooley. © Hill and Range Songs, inc., Hollywood, Calif.; 15Sep47; EP17223. For piano solo, with guitar diagrams and chord symbols.

Yodeling Polka; by Spade Cooley, Larry (Pedro) De Paul and Andrew Soldi. © Hill and Range Songs, inc., Hollywood, Calif.; 15Dec47; EP20119. For piano solo, with guitar diagrams and chord symbols.

COOLIDGE, Mrs. ELIZABETH PENN (SPRAGUE) 1864-
(Sonata, oboe and piano) Sonata ... by E. S. Coolidge. © Carl Fischer, inc., New York; 24Nov47; EP20459. Score (oboe and piano) and part.

COOMBS, GLORIA, 1911-
Ain't the Right One; by Gloria Coombs. © Clock Publishing Co., inc., Santa Monica, Calif.; 20Nov47; EP20424. Melody and chord symbols, with words.

A Heart May Break; by Gloria Coombs. © Clock Publishing Co., inc., Santa Monica, Calif.; 20Nov47; EP20425. Melody and chord symbols, with words.

Love Turned Out a Bitter Brew; lyric and music by Gloria Coombs. © Clock Publishing Co., inc., Santa Monica, Calif.; 20Nov47; EP20423. Melody and chord symbols, with words.

COOPER, BILL, 1914-
The Thrill of Love; [based on Grieg's concerto in A minor] lyric by Morton Parnes, adapted by Bill Cooper and Pat Lixon. © Gaynote Music Co., New York; 16Oct47; on words & changes in music; EP18090.

COOPER, ESTHER.
Lord, Hold Out Your Hand to Me; from "Negro sketches," music by Esther Cooper, words by Helen Williams. © Volkwein Bros., inc., Pittsburgh; 24Oct47; EP18284.

Preachin'; from "Negro sketches," music by Esther Cooper, poem by Helen Williams. Low [voice] © Volkwein Bros., inc., Pittsburgh; 24Oct47; EP18286.

Silver Horn; from "Negro sketches," music by Esther Cooper, poem by Helen Williams. © Volkwein Bros., inc., Pittsburgh; 24Oct47; EP18285.

COOPER, FRANCES .
Who-who-oo; words by Marie Rasberry, music by Frances Cooper. [c1945] © Nordyke Publishing Co., Los Angeles; 24Jun46; EP20052.

COOPER, HARRISON.
Have You Ever Been Told? Words and music by Benny Goodman [and] Harrison Cooper. © Regent Music Corp., New York; 25Jul47; EP15836.

COOPER, JOE.
Julie; music by Joe Cooper, words by George Jessel [and] Eddie De Lange. © George Simon, inc., New York; 21Aug47; EP16448.

COOPERSMITH, HARRY.
By the Waters of Babylon. Al Naharot Bavel. [Words from] Psalm 137. [music by] Harry Coopersmith. © Transcontinental Music Corp., New York; 25Jul47; EP15897. Score: SATB and piano; English and Hebrew words (transliterated)

COOPERSMITH, SYLVIA, 1915-
Sha! Shtill! Words by Lou Segal, music by Sylvia Coopersmith & Rudy Rock. © Musicmakers, inc., Philadelphia; 15Sep47; EP17253.

You Charm the Night; lyrics by Joe Coopersmith, music by Sylvia Coopersmith. © Musicmakers, inc., Philadelphia, 15Sep47; EP17256.

COOTS, J   FRED.
Encore, Cherie; lyric by Alice D. Simms, music by J. Fred Coots. © Miller Music Corp., New York; 24Oct47; EP18510. English words.

Nora; words by Edward Eager, music by J. Fred Coots. © Mills Music, inc., New York; 4Aug47; EP18260.

COPE, CECIL.
I See His Blood upon the Rose; [by] Cecil Cope, [words by] Joseph Mary Plunket. © The Oxford University Press, London; 19Jun47; EP6153. Score: chorus (SATB) and piano.

COPE, DICK.
Lonely; words and music by Dick Cope. © Nordyke Publishing Co., Los Angeles; 9Jul47; EP17505.

COPELAND, H   H
Onward, Kermit High School; by H. H. Copeland. © Victor Publishing Co., Dallas; 7Nov47; EP18832. Includes versions for voice and piano, and for mixed chorus.

COPLAND, AARON, 1900-
Fantasia Mexicana. See his Fiesta.

(Fiesta) Pantasia Mexicana. (Mexican Fantasy); from Aaron Copland's El Salon Mexico, adapted by Johnny Green, a piano solo. [from] Fiesta. © Boosey & Hawkes, inc., Lynbrook, N. Y.; 27Jun47; on adaptation; EP15427.

In the Beginning; [by] Aaron Copland, [text from Genesis, Chap. 1:1-II:7] For mixed chorus a cappella with mezzo-soprano solo. © Boosey & Hawkes, inc., New York; 11Nov47; EP19233.

Statements; [by] Aaron Copland. Full orchestral score. [New York] Boosey & Hawkes. © Hawkes & Son (London) ltd., London; 11Nov47; EP19232.

(Symphony, no.3) Third Symphony; [by] Aaron Copland. © Boosey & Hawkes, ltd., London; 8Aug47; EP16286. Miniature score.

COQUATRIX, BRUNO.
Le Rythme de Paris; paroles et musique de Bruno Coquatrix. © Editions Salabert, Paris; 14Jun42; EP6271. Score (voice and piano) and voice part.

CORDOUAN, GERHARD.
Peace on Earth; words by Margarete Stephenson, music by Gerhard Cordouan. © Mrs. Margarete Elder Stephenson, Chicago; 15Jul47; EP15712.

CORELLI, ARCANGELO, 1653-1713.
Concerto Grosso for string orchestra, from the violin sonatas of Arcangelo Corelli, ed. and arr. by John Barbirolli. © The Oxford University Press, London; 24Jul47; on arrangement; EP6256. Score.

Serenata; by A. Corelli, for brass quintet. © Mills Music, inc., New York; 28Dec45; on arrangement; EP718. Score (2 cornets, horn, baritone and tuba) and parts.

Serenata ... for brass quintet ... © Mills Music, inc., New York; 28Dec45; on arrangement; EP718.

Seven Transcriptions for organ [by] Arcangelo Corelli, [arr.] by R. S. Stoughton. © The Arthur P. Schmidt Co., Boston; 11Jul47; on arrangement; EP15649.

COREY, WESLEY B
What Would You Do? Words and music by Wesley B. Corey. [c1946] © Nordyke Publishing Co., Los Angeles; 30Jan47; EP19545.

CORLET, TOM.
Oh, Professor, How Could You! Words by Virgil L. Cotton, music by Tom Corlet. © Virgil L. Cotton, Flint, Mich.; 28Jul47; EP16015.

CORMIER, BILL.
44 Original Canadian Jigs and Reels for Square Dances. © Harry E. Jarman, Toronto; 7Jul47; EF3990. For violin solo.

[CORNETT, ALICE]
The Miners' Song; (Down, down, down), [words by] Bob Richards [pseud., music by] Erasie Palmer [pseud.] and Dick Milton [pseud.] ... arrangement by Irwin King. © Quality Music Co., inc., New York; 28Jul47; EP15970.

CORNILLE, GEORGES, 1918-
La Chèvre de Monsieur Seguin; paroles de Georges Bérard & Pierre Calmon, musique de Georges Cornille & Cd Bouillon. © Editions Musicales Nuances, Paris; 30Jul47; EF6502.

CORTÉS, QUIRINO F. MENDOZA Y. See Mendoza y Cortés, Quirino F.

CORTESE, LUIGI, 1889-
Preludio e Fuga; per orchestra, [by] Luigi Cortese. Op. 16. Partitura. © Carisch, s.a., Milan; 1Jul47; EF6208.

CORY, GEORGE.
"Deep Song;" words by Douglass Cross, music by George Cory. © Northern Music Corp., New York; 31Oct47; EP20159.

COSBY, ESCHOL. See Cosby, Robert Eschol.

COSBY, ROBERT ESCHOL, 1910-
Just Inside the Door; [and Come to Jesus] by Eschol Cosby. © Robert Eschol Cosby, Los Angeles; 20Aug47; EP18543. Close score: SATB.

COSENTINO, MARIO, comp.
Piedigrotta 1947-48; compilatore. Mario Consentino, [words by Dom. Furnò, G. Savarese and others, music by Attilio Staffelli and others] Napoli, Casa Musicale Napoletana. © Italian Book Co., New York; 15Sep47; EF6620.

COSLOW, SAM, 1902-
Sleep My Love, from the picture "Sleep My Love"; words and music by Sam Coslow. © Chappell & Co., inc., New York; 24Nov47; EP19804.

COSTA, ENRICO DA. See Da Costa, Enrico.

COSTA, PEDRO VALENTI. See Valenti Costa, Pedro.

COSTE, Marius, 1908-
C'est un Village; paroles de
Georges Berard & Jacques Severac
[pseud.], musique de Marius
Coste & Raymond Legrand. ©
Royalty, Paris; 31Dec43;
EF5903.

COTTON, VIRGIL L
That Cute Little Usheretto; words
and music by Doris W. Cotton,
Margaret Gerrow and Virgil L.
Cotton. © Virgil L. Cotton,
Flint, Mich.; 17Nov47; EP19216.

COUËT, JEANNE D   1917-
L'Amour a le Boogie Woogie; [by]
Fernand Robidoux [and] J. D.
Couët. © Adanac Music Co.,
Toronto; 20Feb47; EF6331.
Melody and chord symbols, with
words.

Plus Rien; [by] Fernand Robidoux
[and] J. D. Couët, [Spanish
lyrics by Manolita Del Veyo] ©
Adanac Music Co., Toronto;
20Feb47; EF6332. Melody and
chord symbols, with words.

COUPERIN, FRANÇOIS.
Soeur Monique ... [by] François
Couperin ... rev. and annotated
by Arthur Foote. © The Arthur
P. Schmidt Co.; Boston; 11Jul47;
on arrangement; EP15648. For
piano solo.

COURAUD, MARCEL, 1912-
Cahiers de Polyphonie Vocale; (en-
traînement au chant choral) [by]
Marcel Couraud. © Rouart Lerolle
& Co., éditeurs, Paris; sér. A: 1.
cahier, 10ct47; EF7343. Contents.-
sér. A (âge moyen 12 ans) 1. cahier.
Chants de Noel.

COVINGTON, TOMMY.
I Didn't Have Time; words and music
by Tommy Nolan and Tommy Covington. © Hometown Music Co,,
inc., New York; 21Nov47; EP19795.

COWAN, JESSE, 1900-
Jesse Cowan's Musical Time Method;
for all instruments and voices.
© Jesse Cowan, Chicago; 4Dec47;
on changes in description & an
illustrated cross reference added;
AA70023.

COWARD, NOËL PIERCE, 1899-
(Bitter Sweet) I'll See You Again,
from the musical comedy "Bitter
Sweet" ... words and music by
Noël Coward. A Ken Macomber
arrangement. © Harms, inc.,
New York; 22Oct47; on arrangement; EP18480. Piano-conductor
score (orchestra, with words)
and parts.

(Bitter Sweet) I'll See You Again.
Sé Que Te Veré. From the musical
comedy "Bitter Sweet." Spanish
text by Johnnie Camacho, words and
music by Noel Coward. © Harms,
inc., New York; 2Dec47; on Spanish
words; EP19820.

"Bitter Sweet" Overture; by Noël
Coward, transcribed for band by
David Bennett. © Harms, inc.,
New York; 22Oct47; on arrange-
ment; EP18471. Condensed score
and parts.

(Bitter Sweet) Zigeuner. "Ziga-
na." From the musical comedy,
"Bitter Sweet." Spanish text by
Johnnie Camacho, words and music
by Noel Coward. © Harms, inc.,
New York; 17Nov47; on Spanish
words; EP19241.

I'll Follow My Secret Heart;
four part male chorus
(T.T.B.B.) arr. by William
Stickles. Words and music by
Noël Coward. New York,
Chappell. © Chappell & Co.,
ltd., London; 14Jul47; on
arrangement; EP15781.

I'll Follow My Secret Heart;
four part male chorus
(T.T.B.B.) arr. by William
Stickles. Words and music by
Noël Coward. New York,
Chappell. © Chappell & Co.,
ltd., London; 17Jul47; on
arrangement; EP15778.

I'll Follow My Secret Heart;
four part mixed chorus
(S.A.T.B.) arr. by William
Stickles. Words and music by
Noël Coward. New York,
Chappell. © Chappell & Co.,
ltd., London; 14Jul47; on
arrangement; EP15780.

I'll Follow My Secret Heart ...
(S.S.A.) arr. by William
Stickles. © Chappell & Co.,
ltd., London; 17Jul47; on
arrangement; EP15776.

I'll Follow My Secret Heart;
two part mixed chorus (S.A.) arr.
by William Stickles. Words
and music by Noël Coward.
New York, Chappell. ©
Chappell & Co., ltd., London;
17Jul47; on arrangement;
EP15777.

I'll See You Again. See his Bitter
Sweet.

Pacific 1860; a musical romance
in three acts by Noel Coward.
Vocal score. © Chappell & Co.,
ltd., London; 15Jul47; EF6231.

Sé Que Te Veré. See his Bitter Sweet.

Someday I'll Find You; four part
mixed chorus (S.A.T.B.) arr. by
William Stickles, words and
music by Noël Coward. © Chappell
& Co., ltd., London; 10Jul47;
on arrangement; EP15461.

Someday I'll Find You; four part
male chorus (T.T.B.B.) arr. by
William Stickles, words and
music by Noël Coward. © Chappell
& Co., ltd., London; 10Jul47; on
arrangement; EP15462.

Zigeuner; [by] Noel Coward, transcribed by J. Louis Merkur. ©
Harms, inc., New York; 17Dec47;
on arrangement; EP20281. Two
scores for piano 1-2.

Zigeuner. See his Bitter Sweet.

COWELL, HENRY, 1892-
(Sonata, violin & piano) Sonata.
New York; 20Jun47; EP15372.
Score and part.

COWELL, HENRY, 1897-
Tom Binkley's Tune. New York,
Sole selling agent, Mercury
Music Corp. © Merrymount Music
Press, New York; 22Dec47;
EP20418. Score (Bb baritone
and piano) and parts for Bb bari-
tone and euphonium.

[COWEN, WESLEY]
Test your A.Q.; arranging quotient,
with arrange-a-grams; problems
and solutions in arranging [by
Wesley Cowen] © King Brand
Publications, New York; v.1,
series 4, 8Mar47; AA50374.

COWLES, CECIL.
Bonnie Lassie; song, words by
Robert Burns, music by Cecil
Cowles. © Theodore Presser Co.,
Philadelphia; 15Jul47; EP15676.

COX, DESMOND. See also
Elton, Louis, pseud.

COX, HAROLD ELTON. See also
Elton, Louis, pseud.

COX, HERBERT C
Dreams; words and music by
Herbert C. Cox. © Nordyke
Publishing Co., Los Angeles;
10Jun47; EP16942.

COX, JOHN J   1880-
The Lone Wayward One; music by
J. W. Cox, [arrangement and]
words by Chas. W. Slifer.
[c1946] © Chas. W. Slifer,
Wichita, Kan.; 1Jun47; EP16208.

CRABBE, GUY SNIDER.
Your Mother Always Has a Smile
for You; words and music by
Guy Snider Crabbe. © Guy
Snider Crabbe, Galesburg, Ill.;
18Aug47; EP16533.

CRAIG, DAVIS.
My Heart Remembers; words and
music by Davis Craig. [c1945]
© Nordyke Publishing Co., Los
Angeles; 19Aug47; EP16597.

CRAIG, FRANCIS.
Near You; lyric by Kermit Goell,
music by Francis Craig. ©
Supreme Music Corp., New York;
25Jul47; EP15888.

CRAMER, HANK. See
Cramer, Henry Gearhead.

CRAMER, HENRY GEARHEARD.
Why? Words by Russ Jones, music
by Hank Cramer. © Nordyke Publishing Co., Los Angeles;
19Jun47; EP17439.

CRANDALL, CARRIE M
Come My Love, Take a Ride With
Me; words and music by Carrie
M. Crandall. © Nordyke Publish-
ing Co., Los Angeles; 12Aug47;
EP19781.

CRANE, HARRY.
Chidabee, Chidabee, Chidabee (yah!
yah! yah!) by Jimmy Durante,
Harry Harris, and Harry Crane,
[arr. by Jerry Phillips] ©
Jimmy Durante Music Publishing
Co., inc., Hollywood, Calif.;
20Nov47; EP19052. For voice
and piano, with chord symbols.

CRANE, J
Jolly Hay Ride; words by Alfred &
Helen Semperisi, music by J.
Crane. [c1945] © Nordyke Pub-
lishing Co., Los Angeles;
14Jun47; EP19743.

My Homestead Is Waiting; words
by C. A. Eley, music by J.
Crane. © Nordyke Publishing
Co., Los Angeles; 9Nov46;
EP19666.

My Only Love; words by Grace Good-
man, music by J. Crane. [c1946]
© Nordyke Publishing Co., Los
Angeles; 14Jan47; EP19762.

Shall We Still Remember Yet; words
by Hank Withrow, music by J. Crane.
© Nordyke Publishing Co., Los
Angeles; 12Apr47; EP16811.

CRANE, JAMES.
Her Kisses; words by Victor
Berger, music by J. Crane.
© Nordyke Publishing Co., Los
Angeles; 11Oct46; EP19463.

Our U. S. Army Boys; words by
Clara Jewell Durkin, music by
J. Crane. © Nordyke Publish-
ing Co., Los Angeles; 27Jul46;
EP19429.

Tomorrow Is the Day; words by
Roy Jacobson, music by J. Crane.
© Nordyke Publishing Co., Los
Angeles; 3Sep47; EP19373.

CRANE, JIMMIE, 1910-
Christ Is the Light of the World;
words by Milda McCroskey,
music by J. Crane, arr. by
H. H. H. © Armilda Margaret
(Allgood) McCroskey, Fairgrove,
Mo.; 31Aug47; EP16713.

Home and Eternal Bliss; words by
Milda McCroskey, music by J.
Crane, arr. by H. H. H. ©
Armilda Margaret (Allgood)
McCroskey, Fairgrove, Mo.;
31Aug47; EP16712.

CRANE, JIMMIE. Cont'd.
My Bad Habit Is You; words by
Ethel Wiley Edwards, music by
J. Crane. © Nordyke Publishing Co., Los Angeles;
18Sep45; EP167644.
Your Smile Is Like a Red Rose in
Bloom; words by Susan McCollum,
music by Jimmie Crane. © Nordyke Publishing Co., Los Angeles; 3Sep47; EP19288.

RAWFORD, JOHN D
Sophia's Sofa; words and music by
John Crawford. © John D. Craw-
ford, Canton, Ohio; 19Jun47;
EP155398.
You and I Together; words and music
by John Crawford. © John D.
Crawford, Canton, Ohio; 19Jun47;
EP155395.

CRAWFORD, JOHN DANIEL, 1901-
I Like the Way You Say Goodnight;
by John Crawford. © La Mar
Music Publishers, inc., Canton,
Ohio; 8Nov47; EP18792. For
voice and piano.

CRERIE, E   EDWING.
Gaily Tripping;[by] E. Edwing
Orerie, arr. by Antonio Zordan.
© Chart Music Publishing House,
inc., Chicago; 13Nov47; on ar-
rangement; EP19129.

CRIPPS, HENRY.
Rondinello; [by] Henry Cripps.
© Boosey & Hawkes (Australia)
pty. ltd., Sydney; 6Nov47;
EF7009. Score (saxophone and
piano) and part.

CRISCUOLO, JENNIE D'ALESSIO, 1886-
I Am Waiting; original song by
Jennie Criscuolo. New York,
M. G. Cefola [c1946] © Jennie
D'Alessio Criscuolo, New York;
29Aug47; EP17831.
Nina Nana ... By Jennie Criscuolo.
New York, M. G. Cefola [c1946]
© Jennie Criscuolo, New York;
29Aug47; EP17832. For voice
and piano.

CROASDALE, ROWLAND.
Steal a Kiss (then run for your
life); words & music by Rowland
Croasdale. [c1947] © Nordyke
Publishing Co., Los Angeles;
21Aug47; EP16602.

CROFT, CARL W
The Language of Your Eyes; words
and music by Carl W. Croft. ©
Nordyke Publishing Co., Los
Angeles; 23May47; EP16829.

CRONHAM, CHARLES RAYMOND, 1896-
Choral Benediction and Amen;
S.A.T.B., words by John Newton
... music by Charles R. Cronham. © Edwin H. Morris & Co.,
inc., New York; 24Apr47;
EP17327.

The Kings of the Orient ...
based on "We three kings of Orient are," [arr.] by Charles
Raymond Cronham ... [for]
piano, four-hands. © The Boston Music Co., Boston; 25Apr47;
on arrangement; EP17742.

Nativity Scenes; suite for organ by
Charles Raymond Cronham. © Boston
Music Co., Boston; v. 1-3, 25Nov47;
EP19131-19133. Includes registra-
tion for Hammond organ. Contents.-
1. The Journey to Bethlehem.- 2.
Dialogue between the Innkeeper and
Joseph.- 3. The Shepherds and the
Heavenly Host.

On a Winter's Night ... for
chorus of mixed voices with
alto solo and organ or piano
accompaniment, [by] Charles R.
Cronham, based on a French
carol. © The Boston Music Co.,
Boston; 30Sep47; on arrangement & words; EP17746.

CROSBY, MARIE.
The Funny Old Clown; [by]
Marie Crosby. © Century
Music Publishing Co., New
York; 6Aug47; EP16125. For
piano solo.

CROSS, SYLVESTER L
I've Fallen for the Man in the
Moon; words by Edith Cole, music
by Sylvester L. Cross. © Nordyke
Publishing Co., Los Angeles;
12Aug47; EP17500.
When Johnny Strolls with Me;
words by Laura K. Cook, music
by Sylvester L. Cross. © Nordyke Publishing Co., Los Angeles; 12Aug47; EP17551.

CROSSMAN, ARTHUR GORDON, 1920-
Tulsa University Alma Mater; words,
music [and] arrangement by
Arthur G. Crossman. c1946. ©
Arthur Gordon Crossman, West
Los Angeles, Calif.; 10ct47;
on changes in words; EP17818.
Close score: SATB.

CRÜGER, JOHANN.
Now Thank We All Our God; [by]
Johann Crüger, arr. ... by
Lucien Cailliet. © Boosey &
Hawkes, inc., New York; 25Jul47;
on arrangement; EP15886. Score
and piano-conductor score
(chorus (SATB) and orchestra)
and parts for orchestra.
Now Thank We all Our God; [by]
Johann Crüger ... arr. by Lucien
Cailliet. S.A.T.B. © Boosey
& Hawkes, inc., New York; 25Jul47;
on arrangement; EP15835.
Now Thank We All Our God; [by]
Johann Crüger ... arr. by Lucien
Cailliet. S.S.A. © Boosey &
Hawkes, inc., New York; 25Jul47;
on arrangement; EP15833.
Now Thank We All Our God; [by]
Johann Crüger, arr. for band by
Lucien Cailliet. © Boosey &
Hawkes, inc., New York; 25Jul47;
on arrangement; EP15834. Full
score, condensed score (band,
with words) and parts.

CRYOR, JESSE, 1906-
Chop-Chop Tim-m-m-m-berl. By Jesse
Cryor. © Songwriters' Publishing Corp., Hollywood, Calif.;
12Nov47; EP18643. For voice
and piano, with chord symbols.

LOS CUATES CASTILLA. (Musicians)
"El Amor de Mi Vida" ... do los
Cuatos Castilla. © Promotora
Hispano Americana de Música, s.
a., México; 30Dec46; EP6194.
Piano-conductor score (orchestra)
and parts; with words.

CUGAT, XAVIER, 1904-
Rhumba Fantasy; [adapted from Rimsky-Korsakoff's "Capriccio Español"], musical adaptation and
arrangement by Xavier Cugat and
Jose Morand [pseud.] © Pemora
Music Co., inc., New York;
24Oct47; on adaptation & arrangement; EP18321. For piano solo.
The Story of Sorrento; lyric by
Bob Russell and S. T. Gallagher,
[pseud.], musical adaptation by
Xavier Cugat. © Pemora Music
Co., inc., New York; 16Jul47;
on English lyric and musical
adaptation; EP15972.

CULBERSON, CHARLIE.
Little Hoop of Gold; words and
music by Charlie Culberson.
© Peer International Corp.,
New York; 25Nov47; EP19843.

CUNNINGHAM, BILL.
Honey Mine; words and music by
Bill Cunningham. [c1946]
© Nordyke Publishing Co., Los
Angeles; 30Jan47; EP19436.

CUNNINGHAM, VAN.
After Dark; words and music by Van
Cunningham. © Broadcast Music,
inc., New York; 25Jul47; EP18051.

CUNNINGHAM, WILLIAM FRANCIS, 1899-
You're the One and Only; lyric
and music by W. F. Cunningham.
© William (Bill) Francis Cunning-
ham, Washington, D. C.; 16Dec47;
EP20252.

CURIEL, GONZALO.
(Angel o Demonio) "La Capitana"
... (words and music) de:
Gonzalo Curiel. Instrumentación
de: Sergio Guerrero. De la
película: "Angel o Demonio."
© Promotora Hispano Americana
de Música, s.a., México;
31Oct47; EP6937. Piano-conductor score (orchestra) and
parts.
La Capitana. See his Angel o Demonio.

CURRAN, WILLIAM JOSEPH, 1880-
The Meeting in the Air; words by
W. J. Galvin, music by W. J.
Curran. © William J. Galvin,
Staten Island, N. Y.; 10ct47;
EP18961.

CURRY, JESSIE GUNN, 1896-
[Embellishments on Standard Tune
"Tallahassee"; by Jessie Gunn
Curry] © Jessie Gunn Curry
Studio (Jessie Gunn Curry, sole
owner), Lynn, Mass.; 15Sep47;
EP18544. For piano solo.
Improve Your Piano Playing with
Jessie Gunn Curry Figures. ©
Jessie Gunn Curry, sole owner of
Jessie Gunn Curry Studio, Lynn,
Mass.; 15Sep47; EP17778.

CURTIS, DICK.
My Irish Colleen; words and music
by Dick Curtis. © Tim Spencer
Music, inc., Hollywood, Calif.;
14Nov47; EP18763.

CURTIS, DORIS.
Like Reaching for the Sky; words
by Sid Curtis, music by Doris
Curtis. © Nordyke Publishing
Co., Los Angeles; 5Jun47;
EP18215.
Mister Moon; words and music by
Sid and Doris Curtis. © Nor-
dyke Publishing Co., Los An-
geles; 16Jun47; EP17556.

CURTIS, ERNESTO DE
Come Back to Sorrento; by Ernesto
de Curtis, lyric by Joseph
McCarthy, Jr. (arr. by D.
Savino] © Hamilton S. Gordon,
New York; 12Nov47; on new
lyrics & arrangement; EP18675.
Come Back to Sorrento. Torna a
Surriento. Music by Ernesto de
Curtis, English text by Claire
Stafford [pseud.], Italian text
by G. B. de Curtis, [ed. by G.
A. Sears] © Remick Music Corp.,
New York; 2Dec47; on English
version, arrangement & editing;
EP19821.
Come Back to Sorrento. (Torna a
Surriento) Song with English
and Italian text [by] Ernesto
de Curtis, arr. by Sandy King.
© Edward Schuberth & Co., inc.,
New York; 12Nov47; EP18902.
Ed. for low voice.

--- --- Ed. for medium voice. © Edward Schuberth & Co., inc., New
York; 17Nov47; EP18903.

CURTIS. ERNESTO DE. Cont'd.

--- --- Ed. for high voice. © Edward Schuberth & Co.., inc., New York; 17Nov47; EP1o9O4.

Come Back to Sorrento. Torna a Surriento. Song with piano acc., Italian text by C. B. DeCurtis, English words by Alice Mattullath, music by Ernesto De Curtis ... medium voice. © Carl Fischer, inc., New York; 4Nov47; on English words; EP18871.

Torno a Surriento. (Come Back to Sorrento) Plectrum guitar solo, [by] E. de Curtis, arr. as played by Harry Volpe. c1939. © Albert Rocky Co., New York; 10Jan40; on arrangement; EP20203.

CURTIS, FULTON EVERETT.
The Wedding Bells Are Sweetly Chiming; words and music by Fulton Everett Curtis. © Nordyke Publishing Co., Los Angeles; 10ct47; EP19306.

CURTIS, NELLIE GORDON, 1889-
He's Engraving His Name on My Heart; words and music by Rev. Nellie Gordon Curtis. © Nellie Gordon Curtis, Newport, Or.; 26Nov47; EP19621.

CURZON, FREDERIC.
Bonaventure ... by Frederic Curzon, [arr. by Norman Richardson] London, Sole selling agents, Boosey & Hawkes. © Hawkes & Son (London) ltd., London; 24Sep47; on arrangement; EF6641. Condensed score (band) and parts.

D

DA COSTA, ENRICO.
Each Little Hour; by John Moran & Enrico Da Costa, [piano arrangement by Geo..H. Record] © Cinephonic Music Co., ltd., London; 4Dec46; EF6023. For voice and piano, with chord symbols; melody also in tonic sol-fa notation.

DACRE, HENRY.
Daisy ... words and music by Henry Dacre, arr. by Phil Embury. © Society for the Preservation and Encouragement of Barber Shop Quartet Singing in America, inc., Detroit; 2Sep47; on arrangement; EP17237. Close score: TTBB.

DAFFAN, TED.
Are You Satisfied Now? Words and music by Ted Daffan. © Hill and Range Songs, inc., Hollywood, Calif.; 29Aug47; EP16588.

"Careless Sweetheart," words and music by Ted Daffan. © Northern Music Corp., New York; 31Oct47; EP20160.

Go On, Go On; words and music by Ted Daffan. © Peer International Corp., New York; 25Nov47; EP19831.

My Fallen Star; words and music by Ted Daffan. © Hill and Range Songs, inc., Hollywood, Calif.; 29Aug47; EP16587.

DAILEY, PAULINE, 1910-
I'm Building a Mansion ... [by] Pauline Dailey. © Pauline Dailey, Anderson, Ind.; 14Jun47; EP16083. Close score: SATB.

DALE, JAMES.
Who Do You Think You're Foolin' Baby? Words and music by Lil Mortlock, Murray Semos [and] Jimmy Dale, [piano arr. by Marvin Fisher] © Sunset Music Publishers, New York; 1Dec47; EP19560.

DALE, JOHNNY.
Dear Old Mother of Mine; words by Oscar A. Pice, music by Johnny Dale. © Nordyke Publishing Co., Los Angeles; 28Mar47; EP16725.

Knowing You Care; words by Lou Dare, music by Johnny Dale. © Nordyke Publishing Co., Los Angeles; 24Jul47; EP19338.

My Atomic Gal; words by William Lyke, music by Johnny Dale. © Nordyke Publishing Co., Los Angeles; 16Sep46; EP19664.

DALEY, F.
Hymnus Angelorum. (Hymn of the Angels) ... for S.S.A. chorus, words by Sister M. J., translation by Sister E. L., music [and arrangement] by F. A. Daley. © McLaughlin & Reilly Co., Boston; 26Sep47; on arrangement; EP17878.

DALLAPICCOLA, LUIGI, 1904-
(Marsia) Frammenti Sinfonici dal Balletto "Marsia" ... Partitura. © Carisch, s.A., Milan; 31May47; EF3977.

DALTRY, JOSEPH SAMUEL, 1899-
Les Anges dans Nos Campagnes. Old French carol arr. by Joseph S. Daltry. © Joseph Samuel Daltry, Middletown, Conn.; 21Oct47; on arrangement & English words; EP18167. Close score: SATB; French and English words.

DAMASE, JEAN MICHEL, 1928-
(Trio, flute, harp & violoncello) Trio ... musique de Jean-Michel Damase. © Henry Lemoine & Cie, Paris; 24Jun47; EF7350. Score and parts.

D'AMBROSIO, AMEDEO. *See* Ambrosio, Amedeo d'.

DANDELOT, GEORGES, 1895-
Vingt Leçons d'Harmonie; de moyenne difficulté, (basses-chants-alternés) [by] Georges Dandelot ... Ed.A. Textes donnés. © Lucien de Lacour, Paris; 31Dec46; EF5495.

Vingt Leçons d'Harmonie; de moyenne difficulté (basses-chants-alternés) [by] Georges Dandelot. Ed. B. Réalisation de l'auteur. © Lucien de Lacour, Paris; 31Dec46; EF6240.

D'ANGELO, LANI, 1915-
The Death of Mamie Brown; words and music by Lani D'Angelo. © Lani D'Angelo, Brooklyn; 12Nov47; EP18762.

Festival of Love; words and music by Lani D'Angelo. © Lani D'Angelo, Brooklyn; 26Nov47; EP19181.

I Gave You the Best of My Life; words and music by Lani D'Angelo. © Lani D'Angelo, Brooklyn; 12Nov47; EP18761.

Merry Christmas; words and music by Lani D'Angelo. © Lani D'Angelo, Brooklyn; 2Nov47; EP18443.

DANICAN, FRANÇOIS ANDRÉ. *See* Philidor, François André Danican, *known as.*

DANIEL, KATHRYN, 1878-
Drowsy June; piano solo by Kathryn Daniel. © The Willis Music Co., Cincinnati; 8Dec47; EP20006.

DANIELS, AMY JULIE.
Mater Admirabilis; by Amy Julie Daniels. [Elkhart, Ind., Daniels Co.] © Amy J. Daniels, North Wilbraham, Mass.; 30Sep47; EP17668. For voice and piano; Latin words.

[DANIELS, CHARLES NEIL] 1878-1943.
Love Came Smiling Through; words by Harry Tobias, music by Neil Moret [pseud.] New York Sole selling agent, Chappell & Co., inc. © Charles N. Daniels, inc., New York; 8Sep47; EP17204.

DANIELS, WANDA.
I'm Gonna Marry Mary; by Jimmy Wakely and Wanda Daniels. © Mono-Music, North Hollywood, Calif.; 28Apr47; EP16148. For voice and piano with chord symbols.

DANKS, HART PEASE, 1834-1903.
Silver Threads Among the Gold; words by Eben E. Rexford, music by Hart P. Danks [arr. by D. Savino] © Hamilton S, Gordon, inc., New York; 12Nov47; on arrangement; EP18674.

Silver Threads among the Gold; words by Eben E. Rexford, music by Hart P. Danks, arr. by Hugo Frey ... S.S.A. © The John Franklin Co., inc., New York; 7Oct47; on arrangement; EP18124.

DANTE, ADRIAN.
La Venusmmia Overture. (Vintage Time) ... Composed by Adrian Dante. © Modern Accordion Publications, ltd., London; 20Nov47; EF7270. For accordion solo.

D'ANZI, GIOVANNI. *See* Anzi, Giovanni d'.

DARBY, KENNETH LORIN, 1909-
Slow Down; lyric by Winston Hibler, music by Ken Darby. © Dreamhouse Publications, inc., Hollywood, Calif.; 4Aug47; EP16116.

Your Dream House; lyric by Winston Hibler, music by Ken Darby. © Dreamhouse Publications, inc., Hollywood, Calif.; 4Aug47; EP16113.

DARCIEUX, FRANCISQUE. *See* Darcieux, François.

DARCIEUX, FRANÇOIS, 1880-
Les Cygnes; [by] Francisque Darcieux, poème de Emile Dousset. Chant et piano. © Durand & Cie, Paris; 30Apr47; EF5940.

Les Libellules; [by] Francisque Darcieux, poème de Emile Dousset. Chant et piano. © Durand & Cie, Paris; 25May47; EF5936.

DARLING, AUDRE'MAE.
Moondust; words and music by Audre'mae Darling. © Nordyke Publishing Co., Los Angeles; 2Sep47; EP20091.

DARLING, GRACE.
Singin' Blues; words and music by Grace Darling. © Nordyke Publishing Co., Los Angeles; 10Jun47; EP16909.

DARLING, ROY.
Smiley ... song, words and music by Roy Darling. © Boosey & Hawkes (Australia) pty. ltd , Sidney; 17Dec47; EF7290.

DARNELL, BILL.
I'm in Love; [by] Grace Shannon and Bill Darnell. © Robert Lee Music Publishers, New York; 1946 [in notice] EP7904. For voice and piano, with chord symbols.

DARNTON, CHRISTIAN.
Cantilena; for string orchestra, by Christian Darnton. © Alfred Lengnick & Co., ltd., London; 10Jul47; EF6348.

DARRELL, LEON, 1907-
The Echo; [by] Leon Darrell,
accordion duet arrangement.
© John Krachtus Co., Chicago;
3Sep47; EP16656.

D'ARTEGA, ALFONSO.
Valley of Dreams-come-true; words
and music by Jack Lawrence, Paul
Reif and D'Artega. © Bob
Miller, inc., New York; 27Oct47;
EP18600.

[DASH, IRWIN] 1892-
Turn over a New Leaf; words and
music by Jos. Geo. Gilbert &
Lewis Ilda [pseud.] © The
Irwin Dash Music Co., ltd.,
London; 13Jun47; EF5860.

D'AUBURGE, ALFRED, 1901-
Bolerito ... Solo for the accordion
by Alfred d'Auberge. ©
Accordion Music Publishing Co.,
New York; 18Jul47; EP15739.

DAVID, HAL.
Down the Milky Way; words and mu-
sic by Joe Bollon, Billy Ward
[and] Hal David. © Kansa Music
Publishers, New York; 18Nov47;
EP20251.

DAVID, LEE.
Moody Monday; by James Cavanaugh,
John Redmond & Lee David. ©
Mills Music, inc., New York;
4Aug47; EP18261. For voice and
piano, with chord symbols.
You Can't Go Wrong Doing Right;
words and music by John Redmond,
Gene West and Lee David. ©
Bob Miller, inc., New York;
27Oct47; EP18627.

DAVID, MACK, 1912-
At the Candlelight Café. See his Tisa.
Blue and Sentimental; by Count
Basie, Jerry Livingston and
Mack David. © Bregman, Vocco
and Conn, inc., New York;
30Oct47; on verse; EP18657. For
voice and piano, with chord
symbols.
(Tisa) At the Candlelight Café,
from the ... picture "Tisa." By
Mack David. © M. Witmark &
Sons, New York; 5Dec47; EP18874. For
voice and piano, with chord symbols.

DAVIDENKO, ALEXANDER.
My Mother; words by J. Utkin,
English adaptation by Olga
Paul, [music by] Alexander
Davidenko. (In Haywood, Charles,
ed. Art Songs of Soviet Russia,
p.4-8) © Edward B. Marks Music
Corp., New York; 16Sep47; EP17174.
English and Russian words.

DAVIDSON, DALE.
My Pinto; words and music by Dale
Davidson. © Nordyke Publishing
Co., Los Angeles; 15Aug47;
EP20089.

DAVIDSON, ERNIE.
Kiss-Kiss-Kissin' in the Corn;
words by Ken Taylor, music by
Ernie Davidson. © D. Davis &
Co., pty. ltd., Sydney;
15Apr47; EF5680.

DAVIES, HARRY PARR.
(The Lisbon Story) Pedro, the Fisherman, from "The Lisbon Story";
words by Harold Purcell, music
by Harry Parr Davies, arr. as
a part-song for T.T.B.B. by
John A. Derbyshire. © Chappell
& Co., ltd., London; 20ct47; on
arrangement; EF6771.

Pedro, the Fisherman. See his The Lisbon Story.

DAVIES, HUBERT, 1893-
Variations on The Grey Cuckoo;
(Y Gog Lwydlas) Welsh melody ...
By Hubert Davies. © Hubert
Davies, Aberystwyth, Cardigan-
shire, Wales; 17Jul47; on
arrangement; EF5785. Score
(viola and piano) and part.

DAVIS, BENNY.
Margie ... by Con Conrad, J.
Russel Robinson and Benny
Davis, transcribed by Eddy
Rogers. © Mills Music, inc.,
New York; 28Jul47; on arrange-
ment; EP16198. Score (violin
and piano) and part.

DAVIS, CYRIL E
What Did You Do Last Night? Words
and music by Cyril E. Davis.
© Nordyke Publishing Co., Los
Angeles; 5Aug47; EP19543.

DAVIS, DALLAS MERIAN.
The Unfinished Dance; an adaptation
of the "Margarita waltz" from
Gounod's "Faust"; lyric by Tom
Adair, music adaptation by D. M.
Davis. © FDS Music Publishers,
Hollywood, Calif.; 12Aug47;
EP18934.

[DAVIS, DELLA S]
Tell Me, Whose Darling Are You?
Words and music by Kathleen
Shannon [pseud.] © Nordyke
Publishing Co., Los Angeles;
16Jul47; EP17485.

DAVIS, J M
That Arizona Moon and You; words
and music by J. M. Davis. ©
Nordyke Publishing Co., Los
Angeles; 7Feb47; EP19752.

DAVIS, JOE, 1896-
I Drove You into Someone Else's
Arms ... words and music by Joe
Davis. © Joe Davis Music Co.,
inc., New York; 24Nov47; EP18760.
Joe! Joe! Joe! (Yo, Yo, Yo) ...
English words and music by Joe
Davis, Spanish words by Romulo
Contreras. © Caribbean Music,
inc., New York; 29Aug47; EP16562.

DAVIS, KATHERINE K
Be Ye Kind, One to Another; for
chorus of mixed voices, with alto
(or baritone) solo, [by] Katherine
K. Davis, [words from] Ephesians
4:32,31. © Galaxy Music Corp.,
New York; 30Sep47; EP17715.

DAVIS, KATHERINE K   arr.
Summer Evening; song for low voice.
Finnish folk song, arr. by Ka-
therine K. Davis, [English ver-
sion of text by Jane & Deems
Taylor and Kurt Schindler] ©
The H. W. Gray Co., inc., New
York; 17Oct47; on arrangement;
EP18487.

DAVIS, LILLIAN B
Afraid of Love; words and music
by Lillian B. Davis. [c1946]
© Nordyke Publishing Co., Los
Angeles; 15Feb47; EP19432.

DAVIS, LINK.
Love Lanes of Yesterday; words
and music by Al Dexter and
Link Davis. Hollywood, Calif.,
Hill and Range Songs. © Hill
and Range Songs, inc., and
Al Dexter Music Publishing Co.,
Hollywood, Calif.; 15Sep47;
EP17226.

DAVIS, MIKE.
Imagine (if you loved me too);
words by Barbara Beck, music by
Mike Davis. © Sherwood Music
Co., Los Angeles; 8Oct47;
EP17816.

DAVIS, RALPH W
Forget and Forgive Me; words and
music by Ralph W. Davis. © Main
Street Songs, inc., New York;
14Oct47; EP17994.

DAVIS, RUTH ALLEN
A Day Is Dawning This Side of Heaven;
words and music by Ruth Allen Da-
vis. Burbank, Calif., Wideworld
Publications. © Ruth Allen Davis,
Burbank, Calif.; 18Dec47; EP20143.

DAVIS, STU.
Lips That Lie; words and music by
Stu Davis. © Peer Internation-
al Corp., New York; 25Nov47;
EP19844.
My San Fer-nan-do Rose; words and
music by Stu Davis. © Peer
International Corp., New York;
25Nov47; EP19842.

DAVIS, TONY.
Now You're Alone and I'm Alone;
words and music by Tony Davis.
© Nordyke Publishing Co., Los
Angeles; 12Jul47; EP17427.

DAVIS, VIRGINIA.
Have You Tried My Blessed
Saviour, He's Alright;[music
and arrangement by Virginia
Davis, words by Hattie Turner]
© The Famous Blue Jay Singers,
Chicago; 1Feb47; EP15794.
My God's Going to Get Tired After
While; [words by Hattie Turner,
music and arrangement by Vir-
ginia Davis] © The Famous Blue
Jay Singers, Chicago; 1Feb47;
EP15792.

DAWES, EDWARD, 1911-
"One Minute Musical Announcement";
words and music by Edward Dawes.
© International Resistance Co.,
Philadelphia; 23Apr47; EP16004.
Melody and words.

DAWN, MARILOU.
When It's Spring (And You're in
Love); lyric and music by Carrie
Hoffman and Marilou Dawn.
[c1946] © Unique Music Pub-
lishers, inc., Detroit; 15Jun47;
EP15688.

DAWN, MURIEL.
The Maid of Mourne Shore; County
Derry, collected and arr. by
Muriel & Douglas Dawn. ©
Novello & Co., ltd., London;
30Aug47; on collecting &
arrangement; EF6552. For uni-
son chorus and piano.

DAWSON, BART.
The Daughter of Jole Blon; by
Bart Dawson. © Milene Music,
Nashville; 16Jul47; EP15656.
For voice and piano, with
guitar diagrams and chord
symbols.

DAY, GEORGE HENRY.
Blessed Art Thou, O Lord ...
For unison voices [by] George
Henry Day. [Text from the
Scriptures] © Theodore
Presser Co., Philadelphia;
9Sep47; EP17166.

DAY, RUTH E   1901-
Birdies' First Flight; piano solo
with words, by Ruth E. Day.
© Willis Music Co., Cincinnati;
12Dec47; EP20394.
Nature Spirits; a tone impression
for piano, by Ruth E. Day. ©
Willis Music Co., Cincinnati;
12Dec47; EP20395. With words.

DEA, DAVID YOUNG.
The Lost Heart; words and music
by David Young Dea. © Nordyke
Publishing Co., Los Angeles;
3Jul47; EP17506.

DEAL, J   S
Old Moon Say "Hello"; words
and music by J. S. Deal.
[c1945] © Nordyke Publishing
Co., Los Angeles; 12Jun46;
EP19430.

256

DEAN, EDDIE.
Don't Believe a Thing They Say;
by Eddie Dean. (In Bourne, inc.,
comp. Eddie Dean [song folio]
p.30-32) © Bourne, inc., New
York; 22Jul47; EP15865. For
voice and piano, with chord
symbols.
Don't Keep Me Waitin' Too Long;
words and music by Eddie Dean.
(In Bourne, inc., comp. Eddie
Dean [song folio] p.42-43) ©
Bourne, inc., New York; 22Jul47;
EP15862.
My Mistake Cost Me You; words and
music by Eddie Dean. (In Bourne,
inc., comp. Eddie Dean [song folio]
p.19-21) © Bourne, inc., New
York; 22Jul47; EP15866.

DEAN, JIMMIE.
Suzanne; words and music by Jimmie
Dean. © Nordyke Publishing Co.,
Los Angeles; 11Aug47; EP17401.

DEAREST, pseud.
I'm Laughing with a Tear in My Eye;
words and music by Eddie Dean and
Dearest. (In Bourne, inc., comp.
Eddie Dean [song folio] p.40-41)
© Bourne, inc., New York; 22Jul47;
EP15863.

DEB DYER AND HIS GOSPEL SINGIN' BEE;
original and favorite songs [by
Deb Dyer, Ted West, Nellie
Brown and others] © M. M. Cole
Publishing Co., Chicago; 9Jul47;
EP15517.

DE BARRO, JOÃO. See
Barro, João de.

DE BOZI, HAROLD. See
Bozi, Harold de.

DE BUSI, DOROTHY.
It's Love, To Be Loved by You;
words and music by Dorothy De
Busi. © Nordyke Publishing
Co., Los Angeles; 5Jun47;
EP16899.

DEBUSSY, CLAUDE, 1862-1918.
La Chevelure ... [by] Debussy,
[transcribed by] Jascha Heifetz.
© Carl Fischer, inc., New York;
8Sep47; on transcription; EP18075.
Score (violin and piano) and part.
Clair de Lune. See his Suite
Bergamasque.
Nocturne (in D flat); [by] Claude
Debussy, rev. and ed. by Eugene
Valber [pseud.] © Carl Fischer,
inc., New York; 8Jul38; on
revision & edition; EP17134.
For piano solo.
(Suite Bergamasque) Clair de Lune,
de la Suite Bergamasque, [by]
Claude Debussy, [transcription
pour 2 pianos par Henri Datilleux]
© Jean Jobert, Éditeur, Paris;
15May47; on transcription;
EP5991. Two scores for piano
1-2.
(Suite Bergamasque) Clair de
Lune, de la Suite Bergamasque;
pour piano, [by] Claude Debussy
(Simplified ed., by Émile
Nerini) © Jean Jobert, Éditeur,
Paris; 30Jun47; on arrangement;
EP6425.

DECRUCK, FERNANDE.
(Sonata, saxophone & piano) Sonate
en ut dièze. © Lucien de Lacour,
Paris; 15Jun45; EP648. Score
(alto saxophone and piano) and
part.

DE CURTIS, ERNESTO. See
Curtis, Ernesto de.

DE FALLA, MANUEL. See
Falla, Manuel de.

DE FRUMERIE, GUNNAR.
Fyra Sånger; [by] Gunnar de Frumerie.
© Föreningen svenska tonsättare,
Stockholm; on 4 songs, 1Jan45.
Contents. - 1. En Gång Blir All-
ting Stilla (Pär Lagerkvist)
(© EF7107) -2. Livsbåten (Pär
Lagerkvist) (© EF7108) - 3. Regnet
(Harry Blomberg) (© EF7109) - 4.
Ute i Skären (Ebbe Lindqvist)
(© EF7110)
Tre Sånger; till text av Pär Lager-
kvist, [by] Gunnar de Frumerie.
© Föreningen svenska tonsättare,
Stockholm; 1Jan46; EF7106.

DEHETTE, MAURICE.
Pour Vous, Madame! ... Paroles
de Edouard Rombeau & René
Bernoville, musique de Maurice
Dehette & Pierre Drucbert. ©
Sté. ame. fse. Chappell, Paris;
26Sep47; on arrangement;
EF6899.

DEIS, CARL.
Arise, All Nations! For chorus of
mixed voices. [Words by] Albert
C. Lisson, [music by] Carl
Deis. © Galaxy Music Corp.,
New York; 14Aug47; EP16353.
Come Up, Come In with Streamers;
for chorus of mixed voices with
piano acc., [by] Carl Deis.
[words by] Alfred Noyes.
© Galaxy Music Corp., New York;
1Dec47; EP20003.
Come Up, Come In with Streamers;
(T.T.B.B.) [by] Carl Deis,
[words by] Alfred Noyes] ©
Galaxy Music Corp., New York;
3Sep47; EP17307.
I'd Like to Live Forever! ... for
voice and piano, words and music
by Carl Deis ... High [voice]
© The Boston Music Co., Boston;
20Nov47; EP19162.
--- --- Ed. for medium or low voice.
My Mother's Eyes; a song for
voice and piano by Carl Deis
to a poem by Margaret Bristol.
© G. Schirmer, inc., New York;
27Aug47; EP18740.

DE KOVEN, REGINALD.
Oh, Promise Me; by ... Reginald
De Koven, [words by] Clement
Scott, choral version for mixed
voices by Noble Cain. © Broad-
cast Music, inc., New York;
30May47; on arrangement;
EP18195.

De LAMARTER, ERIC, 1880-
The Bread of Life; four part mixed
voices, S.A.T.B. with alto solo
[by] Eric De Lamarter, text
adapted from Scripture. © M.
Witmark & Sons, New York;
21Nov47; EP20168.
Forever, [by] Jehovah, Thy Word;
four part mixed voices S.A.T.B.
a cappella [by] Eric De Lamarter, [text from the Scriptures]
© M. Witmark & Sons, New York;
21Nov47; EP20169.
God Came, the Holy One; four part
mixed voices S.A.T.B. with soprano solo [by] Eric De Lamarter,
text from Habakkuk III. © M.
Witmark & Sons, New York;
21Nov47; EP20170.
Lord, Our Dwelling Place; four
part mixed voices S.A.T.B. a
cappella with soprano solo, [by]
Eric De Lamarter, text from
Psalm 90. © M. Witmark & Sons,
New York; 11Jul47; EP15841.

DELANNOY, MARCEL, 1898-
Nanou Filhadoué ... paroles de
Henri Jacques [pseud.], musique
de Marcel Delannoy. © Éditions
Mondia, s.a., Paris; 10Mar47;
EP5228.

[DELAPIERRE, GUY BERNARD] 1907-
En avant les Copains ... Paroles
et musique de Guy Bernard
[pseud.] © Éditions Musicales
"Le Chant du Monde," Paris;
30Apr47; EF5921.
Le Minervois; pertition musicale
du film, musique de Guy Bernard
[pseud.] © "Le Chant du Monde,"
Éditions Musicales, Paris;
15Jul47; EF6579.

DELETTRE, JEAN, 1902-
Dors, Mon Amour ... paroles de
Max François, musique de Jean
Delettre. © Arpège Édition
Musicale, Paris; 25Jul47;
EF6605.
Le Petit Bal du Sam'di Soir ...
paroles de J. Drejac [pseud.]
& Jean Delettre, musique de
Jean Delettre & Borel Clerc.
[c1946] © Éditions Paul Beuscher,
Paris; 20Dec45; EF6494. For
voice and accordion or piano,
and voice part.

DELFAU, RENÉ, 1902-
Forgeron! ... A quatre voix mixtes
ou à deux voix égales; paroles de
Émile Ohlmann, musique de René
Delfau. © Rouart, Lerolle et Cie,
Paris; 30Sep46; EF3469.
Rossignolet du Bois; 4 chansons
à 2, 3 et 4 voix égales ou
mixtes, [arr. by] René Delfau.
© Rouart, Lerolle et Cie, Paris;
10Apr47; on harmonization;
EF5093.

DELPOLIE, VALÉRY.
Trésor des Plus Belles Mélodies de
Tous les Temps et de Tous les Pays;
avec notices historiques, commen-
taires littéraires et esthétiques
[by] V. Delfolie. Nouv. éd. rev.
et augm. Chambéry (Savoie) Éditions Edsco. © Éditions Scolaires,
Chambéry, Savoie; 30Jun47; AF4777.

DEL GROSSO, PETER.
The Val Taro Musette; popular
dance hits for piano accordion,
[music by Peter Del Grosso, arr.
by Louis Canoro] © Joseph
Cerabino, New York; v.1, 1Oct47;
EP18313.

DEL HOYO, FAUSTINO. See
Hoyo, Faustino Del.

DELIBES, LÉO, 1836-1891.
(Lakmé) Bell Song. Où va la
jeune indoue; from "Lakme."
Lyric by Walter Hirsch, music
by Leo Delibes. [Piano arrange-
ment by Hugo Frey] New York,
Leo Feist, inc. © Loew's, inc.,
New York; 12Jun47; on piano
arrangement; EP16230.
Passepied. See his Le Roi S'Amuse.
Pizzicato Polka. See his Sylvia.
(Le Roi S'Amuse) Passepied; (from
Le Roi S'Amuse), music by Leo
Delibes [arr. by Jerry Sears]
© Broadcast Music, inc., New
York; 25Jul47; on arrangement;
EP18053. Piano-conductor score
(orchestra) and parts.
(Sylvia) Pizzicato Polka (from
the ballet "Sylvia") [by] Léo
Delibes, arr. by Leo Kempinski.
© Broadcast Music, inc., New
York; 10Oct47; on arrangement;
EP18456. Piano-conductor score
(orchestra) and parts.

DELL, CARMEN, pseud. See
Del Sesto, Salvatore.

DELLAFIELD, HENRY, 1870-
Hidden Violets ... piano solo, by
Henry Dellafield. [Op. 610]
© Bach Music Co. (Henry Della-
field, sole owner), Boston;
1Oct47; EP18107.

DELLAFIELD, HENRY. Cont'd.
Under the Stars ... piano solo by
Henry Dellafield. [Op. 609]
© Bach Music Co. (Henry Della-
field, sole owner), Boston;
10ct47; EP18105.

DELLO, CARMEN.
My Lovely Angel; words and music
by Carmen Dello. © Peer International Corp., New York;
27Aug47; EP17864.

DELLO JOIO, CASIMIRO.
Notturno Napolentuno. © Edward
Schuberth & Co., inc., New York;
28Jul47; EP15890. For organ
solo; includes registration for
Hammond organ.

DELLO JOIO, NORMAN.
A Jubilant Song; for full chorus of
women's voices with piano, [by]
Norman Dello Joio. [Words]
adapted from Walt Whitman.
© G. Schirmer, inc., New York;
17Ju47; on arrangement;
EP17040.

DELMORE, HARRY ANDREW, 1896-
Steal away; [for] mixed voices arr.
by Harry Delmore. New York,
Gilroth Publishing Co. ©
Mary Delmore, New York; 1Jul47;
on arrangement; EP15969.

DeLOACH, A   L   1904-
She's out of This World; words
and music by A. L. "Buddy"
DeLoach, jr. © A. L. "Buddy"
DeLoach, jr., Monroe, La.;
1Jul47; EP16041.

DeLOACH, BUDDY.   See
DeLoach, A   L

DEL PELO, A   See
Pelo, A   del.

[DEL SESTO, SALVATORE]
Haven't Seen the Likes of You;
words by John Welch, music by
Carmen Dell [pseud.] © Kenmore
Music Co., Boston; 12Nov47;
EP18817.

DEL VECCHIO, TONY.
My Little Dream Girl; words and
music by Nick Doom and Tony
Del Vecchio. [c1945] © Nordyke
Publishing Co., Los Angeles;
12Jun46; EP19439.

DE MARCO, JAY.   See
De Marco, Josephine Rita.

DE MARCO, JOSEPHINE RITA, 1912-
In a Dream; lyric by Gladys
Burns, music by Jay De Marco.
© Wise Music Publications, New
York; 10ct47; EP17638.

DE MARCO, MICHAEL, 1922-
One Cloudy Night; music by Mike
De Marco, lyrics by Joey Lane.
© Candell Music Publishers, inc.,
Oakland, Calif.; 5Sep47;
EP17116.

DEMAREST, VICTORIA BOOTH, 1890-
You Were a Workingman, My Lord;
sacred song by Victoria Booth
Demarest. High. © Boston
Music Co., Boston; 3Nov47;
EP18653.

--- --- Ed. for medium or low voice.

DeMAY, AL.
So Many Dreams; words and music by
Al DeMay. © Nordyke Publishing
Co., Los Angeles; 300ct47;
EP19628.

You Told Me You Loved Me; words
and music by Al DeMay. [c1946]
© Nordyke Publishing Co., Los
Angeles; 300ct47; EP20388.

DE MICHELLE, BILL.
Sometimes Dreams Come True; words
and music by Bill de Michelle.
© Nordyke Publishing Co., Los
Angeles; 13Aug47; EP19773.

DE MONFRED, AVENIR.   See
Monfred, Avenir de.

DE MORAES, NINO.
Bela Cumbancha. (I Love To Watch
the Dancers) ... Spanish words
and music by Nino De Moraes,
English words by Joe Davis.
© Caribbean Music, inc.,
New York; 25Aug47; EP16521.

DE MOYA, ROBERTO.   See
Moya, Roberto de

DENE, DON A', pseud.   See
Nunsen, Adene.

DENEGRI, GILBERTO.
De quién es tu corazón ... Letra y
música de G. Denegri, arreglo de
Rafael de Paz. © Editorial
Mexicana de Música Internacional,
s. a., Mexico; 14Jul47; EP5806.
Condensed score (orchestra),
piano-conductor score and parts.

DENMAN, JOE T
My Best Gal Has Gone; words and
music by Joe T. Denman. ©
Nordyke Publishing Co., Los
Angeles; 14Jun47; EP17479.

Will You Meet Me in the Moonlight
Tonight? Words and music by Joe
T. Denman. © Nordyke Publishing
Co., Los Angeles; 12Jul47;
EP17463.

DENNE, CARLE.
Moonlight and music; lyrics and
music by Carle Denné. © The
Mello-Music Pub. Co., Winnipeg,
Man., Can.; 130ct47; EP18038.

DENNI, LUCIEN, d. 1946.
Alfalfa Rose; lyric by Roger
Lewis, music by Lucien Denni.
© Leeds Music Corp., New York;
8Dec47; EP20472.

DENNIS, MATT, 1914-
Natchi Lyric by Cooper Paul,
music by Matt Dennis. ©
Crystal Music Publishers, inc.,
Hollywood, Calif.; 20Jul47;
EP16156.

DENNY, WILLIAM D
Lux Fulgebit Hodie; [Quem Vidis-
tis, Pastores? and Hodie Christ-
tus Natus Est; by] William Denny. © William D. Denny, Berkeley, Calif.; 19Nov47; EP20217.
Score; chorus (SSATBB)

DENTON, EUNITA.
Was it You and I? Words and
music by Eunita Denton. ©
Nordyke Publishing Co., Los
Angeles; 29Apr47; EP16839.

DENZA, LUIGI, 1846-1922.
Funiculi-Funicula. (A Merry
Heart) [For] S.A. with
soprano solo [by] Luigi Denza,
arr. by Wallingford Riegger.
[Words by] Edward Oxenford.
© Harold Flammer, inc., New
York; 28Jul47; EP16251.

Funiculi-funicula; music by Luigi
Denza, [arr. by] Jerry Sears.
© Broadcast Music, inc., New
York; 4Sep47; on arrangement;
EP18050. Piano-conductor score
(orchestra) and parts.

DE OLIVEIRA, MILTON.   See
Oliveira, Milton de.

DE ORUE, JUAN.   See
Orue, Juan de.

DE PACE, BERNARDO, 1881-
Dream Valse; [by] Bernardo De
Pace. © Bernardo De Pace,
Brooklyn; 25Jul46; RP17218.
For mandolin solo.

Triste. [By] Bernardo De
Pace. © Bernardo De Pace,
Brooklyn; 25Jul46; RP17219.
For mandolin solo.

DePAUL, GENE.
Have I Ever Told You? Words ...
by Don Raye and [music by] Gene
DePaul. © Edwin H. Morris &
Co., inc., New York; 1Aug47;
EP16558.

Your Red Wagon, from the ... picture "Your Red Wagon." Words ...
by Don Raye, music [by] Gene de
Paul [and] Richard M. Jones,
arr. by Fred Weismantel. ©
Leeds Music Corp., New York;
8Dec47; on arrangement; EP19995.
Piano-conductor score (orchestra,
with words) and parts.

Your Red Wagon; words by Don Raye,
music by Gene de Paul [and]
Richard M. Jones, female ...
vocal background arr. by Bob
Morse. © Leeds Music Corp.,
New York; 8Dec47; on arrangement;
EP19993. Piano-conductor score
(orchestra, with words) and
parts.

Your Red Wagon; words by Don Raye,
music by Gene de Paul [and]
Richard M. Jones, male ... vocal
background arr. by Bob Morse.
© Leeds Music Corp., New York;
8Dec47; on arrangement; EP19994.
Piano-conductor score (orchestra,
with words) and parts.

DE PAUL, LARRY.
Banjo Polka; by Larry (Pedro)
De Paul and Andrew Soldi. ©
Hill and Range Music, inc.,
Hollywood, Calif.; 15Dec47;
EP20123. For piano solo, with
words, guitar diagrams and
chord symbols.

DER, MARK, pseud.   See
Kwong, Mark Der K.

DeREEDER, PIERRE, 1887-
Dreams Do Come True; [music] by
Pierre DeReeder [and] John
Shubert, [words by John Shubert]
and Charles Abbott. © Century
Library, inc., New York;
4Jul47; EP18656.

DERMYER, D   D
That's Why I Go to the Nazarene
Sunday School; [by] D. D. Der-
myer. © D. D. Dermyer, Reed
City, Mich.; 3Jul47; EP15394.
For voice and piano.

DE ROSE, PETER.
Babe ... words by Charles Tobias,
music by Peter De Rose. ©
Tobias and Lewis, New York;
11Aug47; EP16555.

Twenty-five Chickens, Thirty-five
cows ... lyric by Al Stillman,
music by Peter De Rose. © Robbins Music Corp., New York;
28Nov47; EP19824.

DESCHÊNES, JEANNINE, 1921-
Christmas Together; words & music
by Jeannine Deschênes. [c1946]
© François Marcel Deschênes,
Shawinigan Falls, Que., Can.;
28Jul47; EF6003.

I Wish You a Happy Birthday;
words & music by Jeannine
Deschênes. © François Marcel
Deschênes, Shawinigan Falls,
Que., Can.; 28Jul47; EF6002.

DESMOND, PEGGY.
Night in Rio; piano solo, by
Peggy Desmond. © Chronophonic
Music Co., ltd., London;
18Jul46; EF6014.

DESORT, FRANK.
My, My, Oh Why! Words and
music by Frank Desort. ©
Nordyke Publishing Co., Los
Angeles; 3Jul47; EP17489.

DESPORTES, YVONNE BERTHE MÉLINA,
1907-
Vingt-cinq Leçons de Solfège Très
Difficiles; en clés de sol 2.
et fa 4. avec acc. de piano,
par Yvonne Desportes. ©
Heugel & Cie, Paris; 12Nov46;
EF6427.

D'ESPOSITO, ARNALDO. See
Esposito, Arnaldo d'

DE TORRE, EMILIO, 1900-
Rumba Royal; (a Recipe for Romance),
English lyric by Marty Kenwood
and Matt Kingeley, Spanish lyric
and music by Emilio de Torre.
© Vander Music Co., New York;
25Jun47; EP15696.

DEUTSCH, EMERY.
Play Fiddle Play; [by] Emery
Deutsch [and] Arthur Altman,
arr. by L. Sugarman. © Edward B.
Marks Music Corp., New York;
3Sep47; on arrangement; EP16629.
For piano solo.

DE VELDE, ERNEST VAN. See
Velde, Ernest van de.

DE VENTADORN, BERNART. See
Bernart de Ventadorn.

DEVEY, GENE.
I've Tried to Forget You; song,
by Gene Devey. © Gene Levey,
Ogden, Utah; 2Dec47; EP20265.

My Girl; song by Gene Devey. ©
Gene Devey, Ogden, Utah; 2Dec47;
EP20264.

DEVINE, DOC. See
Devine, William M

DEVINE, WILLIAM M
In Flanders' Field; words by ...
John McRae, music by Doc. De-
vine. © Nordyke Publishing
Co., Los Angeles; 14Jun47;
EP17607.

DE VOL, FRANK, 1911-
Too Many Sweethearts; by Frank
De Vol, [arr. by Lou Halmy]
© Vanguard Songs, Hollywood,
Calif.; 4Jun47; EP16212. For
voice and piano, with chord
symbols.

DEXTER, AL.
Can This Love Be Real? Words and
and music by Al Dexter. Holly-
wood, Calif., Hill and Range
Songs. © Hill and Range Songs,
inc., and Al Dexter Music
Publishing Co., Hollywood,
Calif.; 15Dec47; EP20126.

I Told My Heart; words and music
by Al Dexter. Hollywood, Calif.,
Hill and Range Songs. © Hill
and Range Songs, inc., and Al
Dexter Music Publishing Co.,
Hollywood, Calif.; 15Dec47;
EP20127.

I Waited Too Long; words and
music by Al Dexter. Hollywood,
Calif., Hill and Range Songs.
© Hill and Range Songs, inc.,
and Al Dexter Music Publishing
Co., Hollywood, Calif.; 15Dec47;
EP20128.

Who's Gonna Love You When I'm Gone?
Words and music by Al Dexter.
Hollywood, Calif., Hill and
Range Songs. © Hill and Range
Songs, inc. and Al Dexter Music
Publishing Co., Hollywood, Calif.;
30Jul47; EP16050.

D'HERVELOIS, CAIX. See
Caix d'Hervelois. Louis de.

DIAMOND, C   S
Come for a Dance in the Moonlight;
written and composed by C. S.
Diamond. © Diamond Music Publishing Co., London; 8Aug47;
EF6260. For voice and piano;
melody also in tonic sol-fa
notation.

Johnny Moore; written and composed by C. S. Diamond. © The
Diamond Music Publishing Co.,
London; 21Jul47; EF5987. For
voice and piano; melody also
in tonic sol-fa notation.

DIAMOND, DAVID. LEO, 1915-
5 Songs; by David Diamond. © Elkan-Vogel Co., inc., Philadelphia; v. 1-5, 17Oct47; EP18970-
18971, 18968, 18967, 18965.
Contents.- (1) This World Is Not
My Home (anonymous) - [2] A
Portrait (Herman Melville) -
[3] Monody (Herman Melville) -
[4] Somewhere (Logan Pearsall
Smith) - [5] The Epitaph (Logan
Pearsall Smith)

2 Pieces; [by] David Diamond. ©
Elkan-Vogel Co., inc., Philadelphia; v. 1-2, 17Oct47;
EP18972, 18966. Score (violin
and piano) and part. Contents.-
[1] Canticle.- [2] Perpetual
Motion.

DIAZ, JESUS.
Las Cosas del Encargado ...
By Jesús.Díaz, arreglo [by]
Eulogio Casteleiro (Yoyo)
© Peer International Corp.,
New York; 6Jun47; EP5735.
Parts: orchestra.

DIAZ ALTAMIRANO, LUIS.
Un Destino y un Amor. (It's forever) ... English words by Joe
Davis, Spanish words and music
by Luis Díaz Altamirano. ©
Caribbean Music Co., New York;
5Dec47; EP19615.

DIBDIN, CHARLES, 1745-1814.
Tom Bowling; arr. as part-song
for men's voices [by] S. E.
Lovatt, words and melody by
Charles Dibdin. © The Oxford
University Press, London;
17Jul47; on arrangement;
EF6132.

DI BELLA, ONOFRIO, 1885-
Flora ... piano accordion solo
by O. Di Bella [and J. Peppino]
New York, O. Di Bella Music Co.
© Onofrio Di Bella, New York;
3Nov47; EP19917.

O. Di Bella Italian Dance Albums for
orchestra. New York, O. Di Bella
Music Co. © Onofrio Di Bella, New
York; bk.8, 15Nov47; on arrangement; EP19913. Parts.

DICKASON, GEORGENA MAY.
The Birds Will Be Singing
Brightly; music by Georgena
May Dickason, words by E. H.
Purdy. Hope Bay, B.C.,
Canada, G.M. Dickason & E.
Purdy. © Georgena May Dickason,
Hope Bay, B.C., Can.;
1Aug47; EF16493.

DICKENSON, HAL.
The Jingle Bell Polka; words and
music by Hal Dickenson. © Peter
Maurice Music Co., ltd., New
York;31Oct47; EP20407.

DICKERHOFF, DWITE WILLIAM, 1905-
Don't Ask Me Why; by Dwite Dickerhoff. © La Mar Music Publishers,
inc., Canton, Ohio; 14Jul47;
EP15600. For voice and piano,
with chord symbols.

DICKINSON, CLARENCE.
A Christmas Carol from Lapland;
for chorus of women's voices.
English text by Helen A.
Dickinson, traditional [music],
arr. by Clarence Dickinson.
© H. W. Gray Co., inc., New
York; 12Sep47; on arrangement;
EP17571.

DICKS, ERNEST A
Glory! Praise and Power; [words
by] Clorinda Roberts, [music
by] Ernest A. Dicks. [Arr. by
The Arthur P. Schmidt Co.] Rev.
ed. © The Arthur P. Schmidt
Co., Boston; 25Jul47; on arrangement; EP15900. Score: SATB and
organ.

DICKSON, ART.
The Night Herder; words and music
by Art Dickson. © Peer International Corp., New York;
11Jul47; EP15616.

DIEHM, DICK.
So in Love; words and music by
Jack Chiarelli and Dick Diehm.
© Nordyke Publishing Co., Los
Angeles; 17May47; EP16893.

DIEKEMA, WILLIS A   1891-
Keep America Singing ... words and
music by Willis A. Diekema, arr.
for men's chorus by the composer.
© Willis A. Diekema, Holland,
Mich.: 15Aug47; EP20413.

DIETERICH, MILTON, 1900-
Nocturne; for four-part men's
voices [by] Milton Dieterich ...
[words by] Amelia Josephine Burr.
© Clayton F. Summy Co., Chicago;
22Sep47; EP17845.

DIGGLE, ROLAND, 1887-
(Alice in Wonderland Suite) Alice
Sings a Song, from "Alice in
Wonderland Suite," by Roland
Diggle. © McKinley Publishers,
inc., Chicago; 8Jul47; EP15522.
For piano solo.

(Alice in Wonderland Suite) The
Cheshire Cat Goes to Sleep. The
Duchess Takes a Bow [and] The
White Rabbit Is Tired; from
"Alice in Wonderland Suite," by
Roland Diggle. © McKinley
Publishers, inc., Chicago;
8Jul47; EP15521. For piano solo.

(Alice in Wonderland Suite) The
King and Queen Were Talking;
from "Alice in Wonderland Suite,"
by Roland Diggle. © McKinley
Publishers, inc., Chicago;
8Jul47; EP15519. For piano solo.

(Alice in Wonderland Suite) The
Mock Turtle Marches On, from
"Alice in Wonderland Suite," by
Roland Diggle ... for piano. .
© McKinley Publishers, inc.,
Chicago; 8Jul47; EP15520.

Alice Sings a Song. See his Alice in
Wonderland Suite.

Birds in the Garden ... by Roland
Diggle. © McKinley Publishers,
inc., Chicago; 8Jul47; EP15524.
For piano solo.

The Cheshire Cat Goes to Sleep. See his
Alice in Wonderland Suite.

Chiaroscuro; piano solo [by]
Roland Diggle. © Delkas Music
Publishing Co., Los Angeles;
1Jul47; EP15466.

Christmas Rhapsody; [by] Roland
Diggle. © Edward Schuberth &
Co., inc., New York; 5Nov47;
EP18466. For organ solo; in-
cludes registration for Ham-
mond organ.

Christ's Loving Children ... [by]
Roland Diggle. © Edward Schuberth & Co., inc., New York;
18Nov47; EP18901. Score: SATB
and piano.

The Duchess Takes a Bow. See his Alice
in Wonderland Suite.

The Grasshopper. See his Summer
Sketches.

The King and Queen Were Talking. See
his Alice in Wonderland Suite.

The Little Shepherd ... by Roland
Diggle. © McKinley Publishers,
inc., Chicago; 8Jul47; EP15523.
For piano solo.

Little White Lily. See his Summer
Sketches.

Lord, Speak to Me; [for] three
part mixed voices S.A.B. Text
by Frances R. Havergal, music
by Roland Diggle. © M. Witmark
& Sons, New York; 2Dec47;
EP19816.

259

DIGGLE, ROLAND, Cont'd.
May Morning. See his Summer Sketches.

The Mock Turtle Marches on. See his
Alice in Wonderland Suite.

Solemn Epilogue; on Canticum re-
fectionis, by Roland Diggle.
© Leeds Music Corp., New York;
20Oct47; EP18895. For organ
solo; includes registration for
Hammond organ

Summer Evening. See his Summer Sketches

(Summer Sketches) The Grasshopper;
and Little White Lily, from
"Summer Sketches" by Roland
Diggle. © McKinley Publishers,
inc., Chicago; 10Nov47;
EP18714. For piano solo.

(Summer Sketches) May Morning;
and Summer Evening, from
"Summer Sketches", by Roland
Diggle. © McKinley Publishers,
inc., Chicago; 10Nov47; EP18715.
For piano solo.

The White Rabbit is Tired. See his
Alice in Wonderland Suite.

DILBECK, THOMAS CHRISTOPHER, 1905-
I'll Hold You in My Heart ('till
I can hold you in my arms);
words and music by Eddy Arnold,
Hal Horton and Tommy Dilbeck.
© Adams, Vee & Abbott, inc.,
Chicago; 15May47; EP16027.

DIMOCK, CLOYD, 1898-
Indonesia ... by Cloyd Dimock,
[arr. by Grattan Guerin] ©
C. D. Smith, Rivera, Calif.;
18Sep47; EP17244. Score
(violin and piano) and part.

DINICU.
Hora Staccato; by Dinicu-Heifetz,
arr. by David Bennett. © Carl
Fischer, inc., New York; 17Jul47;
on arrangement; EP15751. Condensed score (band) and parts.

DION, YVONNE.
Moonlight Stroll; words by Lionel
S. Cadorette, music by Yvonne
Dion. © Nordyke Publishing
Co., Los Angeles; 1May46;
EP18096.

DISNEY (WALT) PRODUCTIONS, LTD.
Beanero. See its Fun and Fancy Free.

Fee-fi-fo-fum. See its Fun and Fancy
Free.

(Fun and Fancy Free) Beanero;
music [by] Oliver Wallace ...
[from the] motion picture "Fun
and Fancy Free." © Santly-Joy,
inc., New York; 2Jul47; EP15452.
For piano solo.

(Fun and Fancy Free) Fee-fi-fo-
fum; words [by] Arthur Quenzer,
music [by] Paul J. Smith ...
[from the] motion picture "Fun
and Fancy Free." © Santly-Joy,
inc., New York; 2Jul47; EP15451.

(Fun and Fancy Free) Lazy
Countryside; words and music
[by] Bobby Worth ... [from the]
motion picture "Fun and Fancy
Free." © Santly-Joy, inc.,
New York; 2Jul47; EP15449.

(Fun and Fancy Free) My favorite
Dream; words [by] William Walsh,
music [by] Ray Noble ... [from
the] motion picture "Fun and
Fancy Free." © Santly-Joy, inc.,
New York; 2Jul47; EP15450.

(Fun and Fancy Free) Say It with a
Slap; words and music [by] Eliot
Daniel ... [from the] motion
picture "Fun and Fancy Free."
© Santly-Joy, inc., New York;
2Jul47; EP15447.

(Fun and Fancy Free) Too Good to
Be True; words [by] Buddy
Kaye, music [by] Eliot Daniel
... [from the] motion picture
"Fun and Fancy Free." ©
Santly-Joy, inc., New York;
2Jul47; EP15446.

Fun and Fancy Free; words and
music [by] Bennie Benjamin and
George Weiss ... [from the]
motion picture "Fun and Fancy
Free." © Santly-Joy, inc.,
New York; 2Jul47; EP15448.

Lazy Countryside. See its Fun and Fancy
Free.

My Favorite Dream. See its Fun and
Fancy Free.

Say It with a Slap. See its Fun and
Fancy Free.

Too Good to Be True. See its Fun and
Fancy Free.

DITTENHAVER, SARAH LOUISE. ©
Mardi Gras; for piano, by Sarah L.
Dittenhaver. © J. Fischer & Bro.,
New York; 9Sep47; EP17714.

DIXON, ESTHER.
Iowa Poppy Song; words and music
by Esther Dixon. Lenox, Iowa,
Dixon Music Co. © Esther Dixon,
Lenox, Iowa; 14Jun47; EP15471.

DIXON, WILLIE.
The Jungle King; (You ain't a dog-
gone thing) by Willie Dixon,
arr. by Joe Bishop. © Leeds
Music Corp., New York; 18Aug47;
on arrangement; EP16403.
Piano-conductor score (orchestra,
with words) and parts.

The Jungle King; (You ain't a
dog-gone thing) by Willie Dixon.
© Leeds Music Corp., New York;
18Aug47; EP16400. For voice and
piano, with chord symbols.

Lonely and Roamin'; words and
music by Willie Dixon. © Leeds
Music Corp., New York; 8Dec47;
EP20471.

DOCZY, JÓZSEF.
A Kanyargó Tisza Partján Ott Szület-
tem. (Born There ... where the
winding Tisza ...) English lyric
by Olga Paul, music by Dóczy
József. (In Pasti, Barbara, comp.
Memories of Hungary, p. 12-13)
© Edward B. Marks Music Corp.,
New York; 19Nov47; on English
lyric; EP18993.

Szeretöd Keresek. (I Must Have a
Sweetheart) English lyric by
Olga Paul, music by Dóczy József.
(In Pasti, Barbara, comp. Memories
of Hungary. p. 16-17) © Edward
B. Marks Music Corp., New York;
19Nov47; on English lyric;
EP18995.

Vett a Rózsám Piros Selyem Viganót.
(I Received a Dress) English
lyric by Olga Paul, music by
Dóczy József. (In Pasti, Barbara,
comp. Memories of Hungary. p.
14-15) © Edward B. Marks Music
Corp., New York; 19Nov47; on
English lyric; EP18994.

DOHNÁNYI, ERNŐ, 1877-
Six Piano Pieces. Op.41. [By]
Dohnányi. © Alfred Lengnick &
Co., ltd., London; 30Oct47;
EP17134.

DOLAN, ANN.
I'm Gonna Buzz-Buzz-Buzz; words
and music by Ann Dolan. © Nordyke Publishing Co., Los Angeles;
27Mar47; EP16717.

DOMINGUEZ, ARMANDO.
Aventura ... letra y música de
Armando Domínguez, [arr. by
Robbins Music Corp.] © Robbins
Music Corp., New York; 6Oct47;
EP17900.

DOMÍNGUEZ B , ALBERTO.
Fermín Rivera ... letra, música y
arreglo de: Alberto Domínguez B.
© Promotora Hispano Americana de
Música, s.a., México; 30Dec46;
EF6709. Piano-conductor score
(orchestra) and parts

Vivir para Soñar ... [words and
music] de: Alberto Domínguez B.
© Promotora Hispano Americana de
Música, s.a., México; 30Dec46;
EF6708. Piano-conductor score
(orchestra) and parts.

DONATI, PINO, 1907-
Notte, Divina Notte; per voce di
soprano o orchestra da camera,
su testo di Ada Negri ... [by]
Pino Donati, trascrizione per
canto e pianoforte di Antonio
Brainovich. © Carisch, s.a.,
Milan; 10Jul44; on transcription;
EF6240.

DONNARUMMA, G
If You Would Know. Villaggio.
English lyric by Olga Paul,
Italian lyric by A. Trusiano,
music by G. Donnarumma and A.
Cavaliero. (In homerics of
Italy. p.20-23) © Edwin B.
Marks Music Corp., New York;
16Jul47; on English lyric;
EP15820.

DORCINE, R., pseud. See also
Huguet y Tagell, Rogelio José.

DORTA, ARMANDO.
You'll Always Care; words by Frank
Summa, music by Armando Dorta,
jr. © Nordyke Publishing Co.,
Los Angeles; 10Oct47; EP19281.

DOUGLAS, FRED M
When the Moon Shines upon Sweet
Roses; words and music by Fred
M. Douglas. © Nordyke Publish-
ing Co., Los Angeles; 22Jul47;
EP19312.

DOUGLAS, MARY, pseud. See
Nunes, John.

DOUGLAS, WINIFRED, d. 1944.
Two Hymn Preludes; by Winfred
Douglas. © H. W. Gray Co.,
inc., New York; 12Sep47;
EP17376. For organ solo

Two Responses; for mixed voices,
by Winfred Douglas. ©
R. W. Gray Co., inc., New York;
12Sep47; EP17372.

DOUNIS, DEMETRIUS CONSTANTINE, 1887-
The Development of Flexibility ...
for violin ... by D. C. Dounis.
© Mills Music, inc., New York;
bk.2. 8Dec47; EP19890. Contents.-
bk.2. Change of Position Studies.

Essential Scale Studies; on scienti-
fic basis for violin ... by D. C.
Dounis. Op.37. © Mills Music,
inc., New York; 8Dec47; EP19889.

DOUTY, NICHOLAS.
The Sea at Dusk; (Twilight) [for]
low voice, words and music by
Nicholas Douty. © Oliver Dit-
son Co., Philadelphia; 20Nov47;
EP20166.

DRAKE, OLIVER.
Moon over Montana; from the Mono-
gram picture "Moon over Montana,"
by Jimmie Wakely and Oliver
Drake. © Mono-Music, North
Hollywood, Calif.; 28Apr47;
EP16145. For voice and piano,
with chord symbols.

DREW, NELLIE LEE.
Give Me an Atom of Love; words
and music by Nellie Lee Drew.
© Nordyke Publishing Co., Los
Angeles; 20Aug47; EP19371.

DREYER, FRANZ, 1877-
Zwei und Zwanzig Etuden für Posaune;
[by] Franz Dreyer. © Ludwig
Doblinger (Bernhard Herzmansky)
k. G., Music Publisher, Vienna;
3Aug46; EF6237.

260

DRIGO, RICHARD.
Valse Bluette; guitar duet, [by]
R. Drigo, arr. as played by Harry
Volpe. c1939. © Albert Rocky
Co., New York; 10Jan40; on ar-
rangement; EP20198.

DRIVER, ANN.
New Songs for Old; words by
Trevor Blakemore, music arr. by
Ann Driver. © The Oxford
University Press, London;
10Apr47; on arrangements,
v. 1-4. Contents.- 1. The High
Street. The Green Field. The
Cool Sea. The Quiet Lane
(© EP6163)- 2. The Blackbird
(© EP6164-). King.Cups. Fruit
Song (© EP6162)- 4. Three Blind
Mice (© EP6161).

DRUMMOND-WOLFF, S
Let Us With a Gladsome Mind; hymn-
anthem ... words from John Milton
... music by S. Drummond Wolff.
© Gordon V. Thompson, ltd.,
Toronto; 23Sep47; EP6686.

DUDGEON, FRANK.
"Be Careful with My Heart"; words
... by Mary Jean Shurtz [and]
Chaw Mank ... [music by] Frank
Dudgeon. © Chaw Mank Blue Ribbon Music Co., Staunton, Ill.;
1Sep47; EP19616.

DUGAT, LEAH W
Palomino, Pal of Mine; words &
music by Leah W. Dugat. ©
Nordyke Publishing Co., Los
Angeles; 27Sep46; EP19958.

DUKAS, PAUL.
The Sorcerer's Apprentice [by]
Dukas, (condensed version by
Milton James, [pseud.]) ©
Century Music Publishing Co.,
New York; 6Aug47; on arrange-
ment; EP16128. For piano
solo.

DUKE, VERNON, pseud. See
Dukelsky, Vladimir.

[DUKELSKY, VLADIMIR] 1903-
Le Bal des Blanchisseuses. (The
Washerwomen's Ball); ballet in
one act by Boris Kochno, music
by Vernon Duke, [pseud.] Piano
score. © Carl Fischer, inc.,
New York; 14Jul47; EP15700.

Ogden Nash's Musical Zoo; tunes by
Vernon Duke [pseud.] Boston,
Little, Brown. © Ogden Nash,
Baltimore & Vernon Duke, New York;
5Nov47; A18530. For voice and
piano.

(Walk-a Little Faster) April in
Paris. "Avril à Paris," from the
musical revue "Walk a Little
Faster"; French version by
Emelia Renaud, words by E. Y.
Harburg, music by Vernon Duke
[pseud.] © Harms, inc., New York;
1Aug47; on French version;
EP16287.

DULMAGE, WILL.
It Was Christmas in London; words
by Richard W. Pascoe, music by
Will Dulmage & H. O'Reilly Clint.
© Mills Music, inc., New York;
8Dec47; EP19898.

DUMAS, ROGER, 1897-
J'ai un Beau Chapeau; paroles de
Jean Manse, musique de Roger
Dumas. c1946. © Éditions
Royalty, Paris; 2Jun47;
EP5927. Piano-conductor
score (orchestra) and parts.

DUMLER, MARTIN G   1882-
(Quartet, strings) String Quartet,
for two violins, viola [and] violoncello, by Martin G. Dumler.
Score. © The Composers Press,
inc., New York; 17Dec47; EP19919.

String Quartet. See his Quartet,
strings.

DUNBAR, EDITH.
A Lover's Dream; words & music by
Edith Dunbar. © Nordyke Publish-
ing Co., Los Angeles; 15Aug46;
EP19757.

DUNCAN, CARLYLE, 1893-
My Lady Walks in Loveliness; for
four-part chorus of men's voices,
a cappella, words by Mona Modini
Wood, music by Carlyle Duncan.
© Boston Music Co., Boston;
13Nov47; EP18917.

The Night Has a Thousand Eyes; for
four-part chorus of men's voices,
a cappella, [words by] F. W.
Bourdillon, [music by] Carlyle
Duncan. © Boston Music Co.,
Boston; 13Nov47; EP18918.

Still, Still with Thee; for four-
part chorus of men's voices a
cappella, music by Harriet B.
Stowe, music by Carlyle Duncan.
© The Boston Music Co., Boston;
28Sep47; EP17297.

Were You There When They Crucified
My Lord? For four-part chorus
of mixed voices, a cappella ad
lib. Negro spiritual, arr. by
Carlyle Duncan. © Boston Music
Co., Boston; 13Nov47; on arrangement; EP18919.

DUNCAN, TOMMY.
Brain Cloudy Blues; words and
music by Bob Wills and Tommy
Duncan. © Bob Wills Music,
inc., Hollywood, Calif.; 26Jun47;
EP15307.

THE DUNCAN SISTERS.
It's Somebody's Birthday Today;
words and music by the Duncan
Sisters. © Duncan Sisters
and Merrill Music Publishing
Co., San Francisco; 4Aug47;
EP16119.

Welcome Stranger; lyric by
Blanche Merrill, music by
the Duncan Sisters. ©
Duncan Sisters and Merrill
Music Publishing Co., San
Francisco; 4Aug47; EP16120.

DUNFORD, JESSIE WARNER.
Ring Out, Christmas Bells! Mixed
voices, words and music by Jessie Warner Dunford. © California
Publishing Co., Los Angeles;
8Dec47; EP20255.

DUNGAN, OLIVE.
Down South; piano solo by Olive
Dungan. © The Boston Music Co.,
Boston; 7Aug47; EP16285.

DUNHILL, THOMAS FREDERICK, 1877-1946.
The Frog; (unison song for treble
voices) [by] Thomas F. Dunhill,
[words by] Margaret Rose. ©
Banks & Son, York, Eng.; 22Oct47;
EP7153.

Pastime & Good Company; suite of
pieces for orchestra, by
Thomas F. Dunhill. Op.70.
Full score. © The Oxford
University Press, London;
17Apr47; EP6102.

The Wheel of Progress; melodious
pianoforte studies ... by Thos.
Dunhill. © Associated Board
of the Royal Schools of Music,
London; bk.4-5, 10Sep47. Contents.
- bk.4. Higher to Intermediate
(© EP6796) - bk.5. Intermediate
to advanced (© 6795)

DUNN, MICHAEL.
Dearest Santa; words and music by
Bonnie Boyd and Michael Dunn.
© Beverly Music Corp., New York;
6Nov47; EP18442.

DUNN, REBECCA WELTY.
Vitamins and Villains; an operetta
for children ... libretto by
Edna Becker, music by Rebecca
Welty Dunn. © Row, Peterson &
Co., Evanston, Ill.; 3Nov47;
D pub 11441.

DUPRÉ, MARCEL.
Sinfonia; for piano and organ, by
Marcel Dupré. Op. 42. © The H.
W. Gray Co., inc., New York;
7Nov47; EP19265.

DURAND, PAUL, 1907-
Cheveux au Vent ... paroles de
Raymond Vincy [pseud.], musique
de Paul Durand. © Arpège Éditions
Musicales, Paris; 3Mar47; EP6603.
For voice and piano, and voice
part.

Éternellement ... paroles de
François Llenas, musique de
Paul Durand. © Arpège Éditions
Musicales, Paris; 31Dec46;
EP6606.

DURANT, CHRISTINE.
O Worship tho King; anthem for
mixed voices based on the tune
"Lyons" adapted from J. M.
Haydn. [Words by] Robert Grant,
[music by] Christine Durant.
© Theodore Presser Co., Philadelphia; 15Jul47; on arrangement; EP15672.

We Thank Thee, Lord; words by
Una Morse Gibson, music by
Christine Durant. © Theodore
Presser Co., Philadelphia;
11Aug47; EP16299.

DURANTE, JIMMY.
You're One in a Million; lyric by
Harry Harris, music by Jimmy
Durante, [arr. by Jerry Phillips]
© Jimmy Durante Music Publish-
ing Co., Hollywood, Calif.;
20Nov47; EP19053.

DUREY, LOUIS, 1888-
Les Constructeurs; paroles de
Pierre Seghers, musique de Louis
Durey. © Éditions Musicales
"Le Chant du Monde," Paris;
30Apr47; EP5853.

DURHAM, GEORGE H
Happy Christmas Morning; for full
chorus of mixed voices a
cappella, [by] George H.
Durham. © The Boston Music
Co.; 18Aug47; EP16440.

Other Christmas Voices; for full
chorus of mixed voices, [music
by] George H. Durham, [words
by] Frances Ridley Havergal.
© The Boston Music Co., Boston;
13Aug47; EP16439.

The Sweet Refrain; for four part
chorus of men's voices with
piano accompaniment, [by]
George H. Durham. © The Boston
Music Co.; 13Aug47;
EP16438.

Ye Heavens Adore Him; for full
chorus of mixed voices, a
cappella, [by] George H.
Durham, [words] anon. © The
Boston Music Co., Boston;
29Aug47; EP17015.

DURLAK, JOSEPH P
Czyja To Dziewczyna ... (Whose Girl
Are You) ... Words and music by
Joseph P. Durlak, arr. by F.
Przybylski. © Wladyslaw H.
Sajewski, Chicago; 1Aug47;
EP17037. For voice and piano
(or accordion); Polish words.

Do Berna Chłopcy Do Berna ...
(Bern-Waltz) ... Words and music
by Joseph P. Durlak, arr. by
F. Przybylski. © Wladyslaw H.
Sajewski, Chicago; 1Aug47;
EP17038. For voice and piano
(or accordion); Polish words.

Kuku-Kuku; (Kokoszka) ... words
and music by Joseph P. Durlak,
arr. by F. Przybylski. ©
Wladyslaw H. Sajewski, Chicago;
1Aug47; EP17039. For voice and
piano (or accordion)

DURUFLÉ, MAURICE GUSTAVE, 1902-
Scherzo ... [by] Maurice
Duruflé. Op.8. © Durand &
Cie, Paris; 30Apr47; EF5968.
Score: orchestra.

DUSHKIN, DAVID, 1899-
Music Magic; a book of musical
games, devised and progressively arr. by David Dushkin. [Chi-
cago, Musicgames] © David
Dushkin, Winnetka, Ill., 4Oct47;
EP17760

DUTAILLIS, JACQUES PETIT. See
Petit Dutaillis, Jacques.

DUTAILLY, JACQUES, pseud. See
Petit Dutaillis, Jacques.

DUTILLEUX, HENRI, 1916-
(Sonata, oboe & piano) Sonate;
pour hautbois et piano [by] Henri
Dutilleux. © Lucien de Lacour,
Éditeur, Paris; 1Jul47; EF6563.
Score and part.

DUTTON, GENE.
Forgive Me; words and music by
Gene Dutton. © Nordyke Publishing co., Los Angeles;
20Aug47; EP20357.

DUUREN, HENDRIK JOHANNES VAN, 1895-
Mijn eerste-(derde) oefenboek ...
etuden voor piano ... [By] H. J.
v. Duuren. © Edition Heuwekemeijer (Firm A. J. Heuwekemeyer
& B. F. van Gaal), Amsterdam,
The Netherlands; v. 1-2, 14Jan46;
v. 3, 30Nov46; EF5138-5139, 3378.

DVOŘÁK, ANTONÍN, 1841-1904.
Humoresque; by Anton Dvorak, arr.
by Will Hudson. © Lewis Music
Publishing Co., inc., New York;
10Jul47; EP15410. Piano-conductor score
(orchestra) and parts.
Songs My Mother Taught Me; by
Anton Dvořák. [Arr. by Hugo
Frey] © Hamilton S. Gordon,
inc., New York; 9Jul47; on
arrangement; EP15611. For
voice and piano.
Songs My Mother Taught Me; by Antonín Dvořák ... transcribed by
Howard M. Peterson. © Mills
Music, inc., New York; 12Sep47;
on arrangement; EP18350. Score
(marimba or xylophone and piano)
and part.
(Symphony, no.5) From the New
World. Symphony No. 5, 1st
movement; by Anton Dvořák.
[Op.95] Transcribed for band by
Erik Leidzén. © Mills Music,
inc., New York; 28Jul47; on
arrangement; EP16205. Condensed
score (band) and parts.

DVORAK, RAYMOND F
Valse Renene; duet. [c1941] ©
Chart Music Publishing House,
inc., Chicago; 23Jul47; EP15966.
Score (clarinets and piano)
and part.

DYKES, JOHN B
Holy, Holy, Holy, Lord God Almighty; hymn anthem ... [words
by] Reginald Heber ... [music
by] John B. Dykes ... arr. by R.
Deane Shure. © Edwin H. Morris
& Co., inc., New York; 17Nov47;
on arrangement; EP19112. Score;
mixed chorus and piano reduction.
Sleep, Holy Babe! S.A.T.B. (divided) [with] contralto solo ...
harmonized and arr. by Wayne
Howorth, [words by] E. Caswall.
© The Raymond A. Hoffman Co.,
Chicago; 22Nov39; EP15582.

E

EARLE, RAYMOND EDWARD, pseud. See
Garman, William McKinley.

EASTER, TEDDY.
I Want to Be Home on Christmas
Morning; words and music by
Teddy Easter. [c1945] © Nor-
dyke Publishing Co., Los
Angeles; 27Oct47; EP18398.

EASTERLING, GENE.
Stars over the Prairie; words and
music by Gene Easterling. ©
Nordyke Publishing Co., Los
Angeles; 12Aug47; EP17404.

EASTERLING, MARION WESLEY, 1910-
America's Favorite Radio Songs ...
[comp. by] Marion W. Easterling.
© Marion Wesley Easterling,
Clanton, Ala.; 2Dec47; AA70925.
Hymns, with music.

EBBINS, MILTON.
I Ain't Had at You; by Count Basie;
Freddy Green and Milton Ebbins ...
arr. by Will Hudson. © Bregman,
Vocco and Conn, inc., New York;
22Aug47; EP16550. Piano-conduct-
or score (orchestra, with words)
and parts.

EBERHLE,
Glory to Christ the King;
·[by] Eberhle, arr. for three
equal voices by J. A. Murphy.
© McLaughlin & Reilly Co.,
Boston; 1Nov47; on arrangement;
EP18465.

EBLINGER, JEAN.
Ploum, Ploum, Ploum ... paroles de
P. Briquet, musique de J. Eblinger.
© Éditions Maillochon, Raoul
Breton et Cie., Paris; 30ct28;
EF6204. Score (voice and piano)
and voice part.

ECHAVARRÍA FERRER, ANGEL, 1907-
Llanto del Alma ... Para piano por
Angel Echavarría Ferrer. ©
Angel Echavarría Ferrer, Santur-
ce, P. R.; 10ct47; EP18315.

ECKHARDT, FANNY G
From the Russian Steppes; [by]
Fanny G. Eckhardt. © Century
Music Publishing Co., New York;
10Jul47; EP15490. For piano
solo.
The Grasshoppers' Holiday; [by]
Fanny G. Eckhardt. © Century
Music Publishing Co., New York;
10Jul47; EP15491. For piano
solo.
Pillow Fight; [by] Fanny G.
Eckhardt. © Century Music
Publishing Co., New York;
6Aug47; EP16126. For piano
solo.

ECKHARDT, FANNY G   arr.
Heav'n, Heav'n; arr. by Fanny G.
Eckhardt. © Century Music
Publishing Co., New York;
10Jul47; on arrangement; EP15492.
For piano solo, with words.
Songs of America; arr. by Fanny G.
Eckhardt. © Century Music
Publishing Co., New York;
10Jul47; on arrangement;
EP15493. For piano solo, with
words.
Songs of France; arr. by Fanny G.
Eckhardt. © Century Music
Publishing Co., New York;
10Jul47; on arrangement, trans-
lation & adaptation of text;
EP15494. For piano solo, with
French and English words.
Songs of Italy; arr. by Fanny G.
Eckhardt. © Century Music
Publishing Co., New York;
10Jul47; on arrangement, transla-
tion & adaptation of texts of
Ciribiribin & Carnival of Venice;
EP15495. For piano solo, with
words.

Songs of Scotland; arr. by Fanny
G. Eckhardt. © Century Music
Publishing Co., New York;
10Jul47; on arrangement;
EP15496. For piano solo, with
words.

ECKSTEIN, MAXWELL, arr.
Let Us Have Music for Christmas;
39 famous songs for piano with
words, ten of which are also arr.
as piano duets. Comp. and arr.
by Maxwell Eckstein. © Carl
Fischer, inc., New York; 15Sep47;
on compilation & arrangement;
EP18060.

ECKSTEIN, MAXWELL, ed. and arr.
Let Us Have Music for Singing;
seventy-seven famous songs for
voice and piano, arr. and ed.
by Maxwell Eckstein. © Carl
Fischer, inc., New York; 20Nov47;
on arranging & editing; EP19266.
Picture Pointers for Piano Tech
nic; 44 melodious and progressive studies in the early grades
by the master etude writers,
adapted, arr. and annotated by
Maxwell Eckstein. © Carl Fischer, inc., New York; 20Nov47; on
adaptation, arrangement & annotation; EP19169.

EDEN, ANITA.
Santo Dominican Way; words and
music by Anita Eden. © Melrose
Music Corp., New York; 1Aug47;
EP16328.

EDLIN, I   A
I'm a Lone Cowboy; words and music
by I. A. (Ted) Edlin. © Uhl &
Ware, San Antonio; 18Nov47;
EP19103.
No Rose in San Antone; words and
music by I.A. (Ted) Edlin.
© Uhl & Ware, San Antonio;
17Oct47; EP18180.

EDLIN, TED. See
Edlin, I. A.

EDMUNDS, CHRISTOPHER.
The Windmill; for viola & piano,
[by] Christopher Edmunds. ©
Alfred Lengnick & Co., ltd.,
London; 14Jul47; EF6292.

EDMUNDSON, GARTH.
Prelude on a Benedictine Plainsong "Adoro Devote," for organ
by Garth Edmundson. © J.
Fischer & Bro., New York;
27Aug47; EP17274.

[EDUCATIONAL METHODS, INC.]   arr. and
comp.
Visual Method Class Piano. Adult
course. © Educational Methods,
inc., Wilmington, Del; 16Jul47;
on arrangements and compilation
with instructions for students;
EP16160.

EDVARD PERSSONS 5 BÄSTA. © Nils-
Georg Musikförlag, A/B, Stockholm
(EF5304) © Sonora Musikförlags
A/B, Stockholm; on 5 songs.
Contents.-Litet grann från ovan,
ur Edvard Persson-filmen "Kalle
på spången," text och musik:
Lasse Dahlquist (© 1Jan39;
EF5296)- Kalle på spången, ur
filmen "Kalle på spången," text
och musik: Lasse Dahlquist (©
1Jan39; EF5297)- Jag har bott
vid en landsväg i hela mitt liv,
ur filmen "Kalle på spången,"
text och musik: Alvar Kraft &
Charles Henry [pseud.] (© 1Jan40;
EF5304)- En liten vid kanin,
text och musik: Sven Gustafson
(© 1 Jan43; EF5298)- Vi klarar
oss nog ändå, text & musik:
Lasse Dahlquist (© 1 Jan39;
EF5299)

EDWARDS, AUSTYN R   1891-
Valse Brilliant ... by Austyn R.
Edwards. © Paul A. Schmitt
Music Co., Minneapolis; 26Sep47;
EP17348. Score (cornet and
piano) and part.

[EDWARDS, ERIC]
Alberta Slim's Western Songs.
© Gordon V. Thompson, ltd.,
Toronto; no. 1, 16Jul47;
EF5840.

EDWARDS, HAL.
Lazy Day; words and music by
Hal Edwards. © Nordyke
Publishing Co., Los Angeles;
12Jul47; EP17503.

EDWARDS, SHERMAN, 1919-
Let's Sit the Next One Out ...
By Don Meyer, Elise Bretton
[and] Sherman Edwards. ©
Edward B. Marks Music Corp.,
New York; 17Sep47; EP17192.
For voice and piano, with
chord symbols.

[EGNER, PHILIP]
The Official West Point March ...
[by Philip Egner] arr. by Paul
Yoder. © Shapiro, Bernstein &
Co., inc., New York; 28Oct47; on
arrangement; EP18586. Condensed
score (band) and parts.

EICHHORN, FLORA.
Danzetta; [by] Flora Eichhorn. ©
Oliver Ditson Co., Philadelphia;
6Dec47; EP20449. For piano solo.

EICHHORN, HERMENE WARLICK.
Cockle Shells; old English song,
arr. for S.S.A. with mezzo-
soprano solo ... [by] Hermene
Warlick Eichhorn. © J. Fischer
& Bro., New York; 12Aug47; on
arrangement; EP17661.

EILENBERG, RICHARD, d. 1925.
Le Moulin de la Forêt Noire.
[The Mill in the Black Forest,
by] Richard Eilenberg. Op. 52.
[Rev. L. Wilmet] [c1947] ©
Albert William Oranz, Bruxelles;
8Nov46; EF5671. For piano
solo.

EISEMANN, MIHALY.
Szeret-e Még? (Do You Love Me?)
English lyric by Olga Paul, music
by Eisemann Mihály, (In Pesti)
Barbora, comp. Memories of Hun-
gary. p. 40-41) © Edward B.
Marks Music Corp., New York;
19Nov47; on English lyric;
EP19007.

EISENSTEIN, ALFRED.
Life Was Beautiful (only for you)
words by Alfred Eisenstein and
Charles J. White, music by
Alfred Eisenstein. © Chappell
& Co., inc., New York; 13Aug47;
EP17005.
Life Was Beautiful (only for
you) words by Alfred
Eisenstein and Charles J.
White, music by Alfred
Eisenstein. © Chappell &
Co., inc., New York; 13Aug47;
EP17165.

ELAM, CLAUDE M   1881-
Bub-bub-bubble; words by Alvah
Duke, music by Claude Elam.
© Pre-View Publications, Rich-
mond; 15Oct47; EP17681.

(Harlem) Talking to the Wind,
from the ... musical "Harlem,"
words by Alvah Duke, music by
Claude Elam. © Pre-View
Publications, Richmond; 15Jul47;
EP15503.

Talking to the Wind. See his Harlem.

ELGAR, SIR EDWARD WILLIAM, 1857-1934.
Salute d'Amour; plectrum guitar
solo, [by] E. Elgar. Op. 12.
Arr. as played by F. Victor.
c1939. © Albert Rocky Co., New
York; 10Jan40; on arrangement;
EP20200.

ELLINGTON, DUKE, 1899-
(Beggar's Holiday) A Collection of
Songs, from Beggar's Holiday;
music by Duke Ellington ... lyrics
by John Latouche. © Chappell &
Co., inc., New York; 20Nov47;
EP20155.
A Collection of Songs. See his Beggar's
Holiday.

It's Kind of Lonesome out Tonight;
words by Don George ... music by
Duke Ellington. © Jewel Music
Publishing Co., inc., New York;
2Jul47; EP15370.

ELLIOTT, LESLIE.
That Little Old Lady I Love; words
& music by Leslie Elliott. ©
Chappell & Co., ltd., London;
6Oct47; EF7006.

ELLIOTT, LEWIS E   1921-
One Time - So Long Ago; words by
Bobbie Berry, music by Lewis
Elliott. © Lewis E. Elliott,
Jr., Martin, Tenn.; 17Sep47;
EP17233.

ELLIOTT, MARJORIE, 1890-
Christmas Bells ... (S.A.B.) ...
arr. by Don Wilson. © The Raymond A. Hoffman Co., Chicago;
13Nov44; EP15570.

March on, America; words by
Charles H. Elliott. © The
Raymond A. Hoffman Co.,
Chicago; 15Jun44; EP15599.
For voice and piano, with
guitar diagrams and chord
symbols.

On a Lovely Summer Evening;
American country scene, for
chorus of mixed voices. © The
Raymond A. Hoffman Co., Chicago;
15Jun44; EP15580.

The Storm King; for mixed voices
S.A.B. [by] Marjorie Elliott.
© Gamble Hinged Music Co.,
Chicago; 1Jul47; EP15297.

ELLIS, A   A
Scottish Emblem ... by A. A.
Ellis. Piano solo. © Chappell
& Co., ltd., London; 22Sep47;
EF6640.

ELLIS, FRANK ALFRED, 1905-
A Life for God; book, lyrics and
music by Frank A. Ellis.
© Frank Alfred Ellis, Rockford,
Ill.; 24Oct47; EP18294. Prin-
cipally close score: SATB.

ELLIS, HERB.
I Told Ya I Love Ya, Now Get Out!
Words and music by John Frigo,
Lou Carter [and] Herb Ellis.
New York, Capitol Songs. © Cri-
terion Music Corp., New York
18Dec47; EP20470.

ELLIS, SEGER.
I Left Myself Wide Open; words
and music by Seger Ellis. ©
Famous Music Corp., New York;
11Sep47; EP17160.

Little Jack Frost Get Lost; words
and music by Al Stillman and
Seger Ellis. © Dreyer Music
Corp., New York; 19Jun47;
EP15458.

"What You Don't Know Won't Hurt
You;" words and music by Russ
Morgan and Seger Ellis. ©
Supreme Music Corp., New York;
6Nov47; EP19214.

ELLIS, VIVIAN.
Bless the Bride; selection. [By]
Vivian Ellis, arr. by W. G.
Lemon. (Chappell's Brass and
reed band journal, no. 162) ©
Chappell & Co., ltd., London;
5Nov47; on arrangement; EF7276.
Condensed score and parts.

ELLMENREICH, ALBERT.
Spinning Song; by Albert Ellmenreich, piano solo, a John W.
Schaum arrangement. © Belwin,
inc., New York; 20Nov47; on arrangement; EP18803.

ELLSTEIN, ABE.
The Bulgar Song. Shpiel Klesmer
Shpiel ... Words by I. Lillian
and J. Jacobs, music by Abe Ell-
stein. © J. & J. Kammen Music
Co., New York; 26May47; EP6936.
Yiddish words, transliterated.

ELLSTEIN, ABRAHAM.
(Just My Luck) Shtarker Fun
Liebe ... (Stronger than Love);
from the operetta "Just My Luck"
... words by Isidor Lillian and
Jacob Jacobs, music by Abraham
Ellstein. New York, Metro Music
Co. © Henry Lefkowitch, New
York; 13Nov47; EP18687. Words
in both Yiddish and Yiddish
transliterated.
(Just My Luck) Such a Year on Me
... (Aza Yur Oif Mir) From the
operetta "Just My Luck" ...
words by Isidor Lillian and
Jacob Jacobs, music by Abraham
Ellstein. New York, Metro Music
Co. © Henry Lefkowitch, New
York; 13Nov47; EP18685. Words
in both Yiddish and Yiddish
transliterated.

ELMER, KAY.
For Better, for Worse; words and
music by Kay Elmer. © Nordyke
Publishing Co., Los Angeles;
29May47; EP16877.

ELMORE, ROBERT.
I Will Bless the Lord; for chorus
of women's voices with mezzo
soprano solo ... [Words] from
the thirty-fourth Psalm, [music
by] Robert Elmore. © Galaxy
Music Corp., New York; 4Aug47;
EP16352.
The Manger at Bethlehem; Christmas
anthem for chorus of mixed
voices, with alto (or baritone)
solo. [Words by] Robert B.
Reed, [music by] Robert Elmore.
© Galaxy Music Corp., New York;
4Aug47; EP16354.

ELSNIC, JOSEPH PAUL, 1895-
Chicago Waltz; [for] concertina.
© Vitak-Elsnic Co., Chicago;
25Oct46; on arrangement;
EP15760.

ELSNIC, JOSEPH PAUL, 1895-   arr.
Finger Polka [and Domino Polka.
(Koketka) For] piano accordion.
© Vitak-Elsnic Co., Chicago;
18Apr47; on arrangement;
EP15766.
Silver Lake. © Vitak-Elsnic Co.,
Chicago; 23Nov46; on arrange-
ment; EP15767. For piano solo.

ELTON, LOUIS, pseud.
Teddy O'Neil; additional words by
Jimmy Dolan, additonal music by
Louis Elton. © Box and Cox
(Publications) London; 6Aug47;
on additional words & music;
EF6626.

ELWELL, H   B
God's Afterward ... [by] H. B.
Elwell. © H. B. Elwell, Pitts-
burgh; 1Jul47; EP15805. For
voice and piano.
Only Believe; [words by] H. B. E.,
[music by] H. B. Elwell. © H.
B. Elwell, Pittsburgh; 1Jul47;
EP15802. Close score: SATB.

ELWELL, H. B. Cont'd.
The Rainbow of His Love ... [by]
H. B. Elwell. © H. B. Elwell,
Pittsburgh; 1Jul47; EP15804.
For voice and piano.

Walk Beside Me, O My Saviour ...
[by] H. B. Elwell. © H. B.
Elwell, Pittsburgh; 1Jul47;
EP15803. Close score: SATB.

EMER, MICHEL.
On Ne Sait Pas Qui On Est; paroles
de Jean Delettre & Jean Deyrmon,
musique de Michel Emer & Jean
Delottre. c1930. © Éditions
Paris-Broadway, Paris; 31Dec46;
EF0303.

Solitaire; paroles & musique de
Michel Emer. © Éditions
Wishely, Paris; 17Mar37; EF6307.

EMERY, DOROTHY RADDE.
Christ Is Risen; (for S.A.B.)
text, Luke 24:1-6, music by Dor-
othy Radde Emery. © J. Fischer
& Bro., New York; 20Oct47;
EP18307.

EMERY, WALTER.
The Spring; words by Thomas
Carew ... music by Walter Emery.
© Novello & Co., ltd., London;
15Jul47; EP5779. Score: SATB
and piano reduction.

EMMEL, JOHN CLIFTON, 1907-
The New Look; words and music by
Arthur Hugét [and] John Emmel.
© Arthur John Hugét & John
Clifton Emmel, Portland, Or.;
10Oct47; EP18173.

ENDERS, HARVEY.
Russian Picnic ... by Harvey
Enders. © G. Schirmer, inc.,
New York; 27Aug47; on arrange-
ment; EP18739. Two scores for 2
pianos.

[ENGEL, LYLE K.], 1915-   comp.
Latest Popular Music Folio (with words
and music) also arranged for piano,
uke, guitar [and] banjo. © 20Feb46;
Movie Songs, inc., New York.; EP3433.

Popular Music Folio of Hit Songs (with
words and music) also arranged for
piano, uke, guitar [and] banjo. ©
19Apr46; Movie Songs, inc., New York;
EP3433.

ENTICKNAP, CLIFFORD G
The Day I Fell in Love with You;
words by Harold Crook, composed
... by Clifford G. Enticknap.
London, Selling agents, Walsh,
Holmes. © London Music Pub-
lishing Co., High Wycombe, Bucks,
Eng.; 22Mar47; EF6723.

ERHARDT, JOSEPH, 1912-
I Can Hear Church Bells Ringing;
[by Joseph Erhardt] © Joseph
Erhardt, Minneapolis; 7Aug47;
EP16171. For voice and piano.

ERWIN, LEE.
Can't Get the Cork out of Grand-
pappy's Jug; lyric by Mal
West, music by Lee Erwin. ©
Southern Music Publishing Co.,
inc., New York; 27Aug47; EP17858.

Mary Jane; words by Mal Howard,
music by Lee Erwin. © Peer
International Corp., New York;
27Aug47; EP17863.

Old Fashioned Cowboy; lyric by
Mal Howard, music by Lee Erwin.
© Peer International Corp.,
New York; 27Aug47; EP17865.

ERWIN, RALPH.
I Kiss Your Hand, Madame. "Jo
Rêve de Vos Youx, Madame."
[Original text by Fritz Rotter],
French version by Emelia Renaud,
American version by Sam Lewis
and Joe Young, music by Ralph
Erwin ... Vocal solo ...
(English and French text) ©
Harms, inc., New York; 15Aug47;
on French version; EP16394.

ESPERÓN, MANUEL.
Maldita Sea Me Suerte. See his Los Tres
García.

(No basta ser charro) Fiesta
mexicana ... de la película "No
basta ser charro"; letra de Ernesto M. Cortázar, musica de
Manuel Esperón. © Promotora
Hispano Americana de Música,
s.a., México; 29Oct46; EF5453.
Qué Gusto Da. See his Soy Charro de
Rancho Grande.

(Soy Charro de Rancho Grande) La
Motivosa ... y Me Voy por "Ai"
[from the film, Soy Charro de
Rancho Grande] ... letra de Ernesto M. Cortázar, música de
Manuel Esperón. © Promotora
Hispano Americana de Música,
s.a., México; 27Aug47; on 2
songs; EF6707, 6706.

(Soy Charro de Rancho Grande)
"Qué Gusto Da" [from the film,
Soy Charro de Rancho Grande] ...
letra de Ernesto M. Cortázar,
música de Manuel Esperón. ©
Promotora Hispano Americana de
Música, s.a., México; 27Aug47;
EF6705.

(Los Tres García) Maldita Sea Mi
Suerte ... [from "Los 3 García"]
letra de Pedro Urdimalas, musica
de Manuel Esperón. © Promotora
Hispano Americana de Música,
s.a., México; 29Jul47; EF5817.

(Los Tres García) Mi Cariñito
... de la película "Los 3
García" ... Letra de Pedro
Urdimalas, música de Manuel
Esperón. © Promotora Hispano
Americana de Música, s.a.,
México; 29Jul47; EF6206.

(Los Tres García) Mi Consentida
... de la película "Los 3
García" ... música de Manuel
Esperón. © Promotora Hispano
Americana de Música, s.a.,
México; 29Jul47; EF6204.

ESPINOL, ROLANDO LLUIS. See
Lluis Espinol, Rolando.

ESPOSITO, ARNALDO D', 1907-1945.
Preludio y Fuga; para piano [by]
Arnaldo d'Esposito, revisión
de R. Locatelli. © Ricordi
Americana, s.a.e.c., Buenos
Aires; 1Apr44; EF6990.

Tres Piezas; para canto y piano.
[by] A. d'Esposito, [words by
Hector Iglesias Villoud, and
others] © Ricordi Americana,
s.a.e.c., Buenos Aires; 17Dec43;
EF6992.

ESSENBURG, EDITH, 1882-
Beautiful City; [words and music
by] Edith Essenburg. © Edith
Essenburg, Oakville, Wash.;
29Nov47; EP19867.

Christ Is Coming Again; [words and
music by] Edith Essenburg. ©
Edith Essenburg, Oakville, Wash.;
29Nov47; EP19865.

Help Somebody as You Go Along;
[words and music by] Edith Essenburg. © Edith Essenburg, Oakville, Wash.; 29Nov47; EP19866.

In the Summer Land up Yonder; [and
When We Meet with Christ Our
King. Words and music by] Edith
Essenburg. © Edith Essenburg,
Oakville, Wash.; 29Nov47;
EP19868-19869.

Oh, To Be like the Master; [and
Awakening Song. Words and music
by] Edith Essenburg. © Edith
Essenburg, Oakville, Wash.;
29Nov47; EP19870-19871.

ESTERS, HELEN V   1894-
I Will Follow Jesus; arr. by Ter-
esa Sanders, words and music by
Helen V. Esters. © Helen V.
Esters, Indianapolis; 7Oct47;
EP18303. Close score: SATB.

Oh, for a Heart to Serve Jesus;
arr. by Teresa Sanders, words
and music by Helen V. Esters.
© Helen V. Esters, Indianapolis;
7Oct47; EP18302.

Won't You Pray ... words and
music by Helen V. Esters, arr.
by Teresa Sanders. © Helen V.
Esters, Indianapolis; 7Oct47;
EP18301. Close score: SATB.

ESTRELLA, JOSEPH C
Because I'm in Love with You;
words and music by Joseph C.
Estrella. © Nordyke Publishing
Co., Los Angeles; 28Mar47;
EP16769.

ETLER, ALVIN DERALD, 1913-
(Sonata, winds & viola) Sonata
... [by] Alvin Etler. South
Hadley, Mass., Valley Music
Press. © Alvin Derald Etler,
Urbana, Ill.; 18Aug47; EP18547.
Score (viola, clarinet and viola)
and parts.

ETOLL, GEORGE W
Never Wander, Never Stray; parts
prima of twin tunes (one melody -
two thoughts) [By] Geo. W. Etoll.
© George W. Etoll, Bryan, Ohio;
27Jul47; EP16964.

ETTORE, EUGENE, 1921-
Chansonette ... By Eugene Ettore,
arr. by Joe Biviano. © Viccas
Music Co., New York; 25Aug47;
EP17834. For accordion solo.

EUGENIA, VICTORIA.
Mi Changuita ... Letra y música
de Victoria Eugenia. New York,
Peer International Corp. ©
Promotora Hispano Americana de
Música, s. a., México; 29Jul47;
EF5730.

EULALIA, SISTER, 1889-
Ave Maria; chorus for women's
voices, S.S.A., with piano acc.,
by Sister M. Eulalia. © The
Composers Press, inc., New York;
2Dec47; EP19088. Latin words.

EULLER, CARLTON RUSSELL, 1924-
Your Someone New; lyric and music
by Carl Euller. © Carlton R.
Euller, East Aurora, N. Y.;
23Aug47; EP16560.

EVANS, CLAY, 1925-
Bye and Bye ... Words and music
by Clay Evans, arr. by Jeanette Tall. © Clay Evans, jr.,
Chicago; 5Jul47; EP16574.

EVANS, GARDNER.
Psalm 100. (Jubilate Deo). [By]
Gardner Evans. © The B. F.
Wood Music Co., Boston; 14Jul47;
EP15538. Score: chorus (SATB)
and piano; English words.

EVANS, HAL.
My Honey's Back Home ... lyric
by Alec Howard, music by Hal
Evans, orchestrated by Hal
Evans & Don Berry. © Cosmo
Music Co., (London) ltd.,
London; 2May46; EF5696.
Piano-conductor score (orches-
tra. with words) and parts.

EVANS, TONI.
There Are Those Times; words and
music by Toni Evans. © Nordyke
Publishing Co., Los Angeles;
13Jul46; EP19554.

EWANS, KAI, 1906-
Det Er Saa Lidt Der Skal Til;
Tekst: Knud Pheiffer, Musik: Kai
Ewans. (In his Tiffer Revuen
1947. Strliber pau Stregbe's.
p.[6]-[7]) © Jac. Boesens Musik-
forlag, a/s, Copenhagen; 16May47;
EF7000.

EWANS, KAI. Cont'd.
Tiffer Revuen 1947. Striber paa
Strøget; Lusik: Kai Ewans og
Hans Schreiber [and others].
Tekst: Knud Pheiffer. Køben-
havn, J. Boesens Musikforlag.

EWEN, DAVID. 1907-   ed.
Songs of America ... ed. with
commentaries by David Ewen,
arrangements by Mischa and
Wesley Portnoff. © Ziff-Davis
Publishing Co., Chicago;
30ct47; A18403.

EYBEL, ALMA S   1893-
Belwin Method for Song Bells ...
by Alma S. Eybel. © Belwin,
inc., New York; bk. 1-3, 90ct47;
on compilation, arrangement &
new compositions; EP18618, 18617,
18616. For 1-2 toy xylophones
and piano.

F

FABOR, G., pseud. See
Borgazzi, Fabio.

FABOR-NATILI, G., pseud. See
Borgazzi, Fabio.

FADANELLI, GIUSEPPE.
Grido d'Amore; versi o musica di
Giuseppe Fadanelli. Napoli, Edi-
zioni E.L.C.D. © Italian Book
Co., New York; 4Sep47; EF6615.

FAIN, SAMMY.
(The Birds and the Bees) The
Dickey-Bird Song, in the M-G-M
picture "The Birds and the Bees";
lyric by Howard Dietz, music by
Sammy Fain. © Robbins Music Corp.,
New York; 19Aug47; EP16545.

Church Bells on Sunday Morning;
lyric by Jack Yellen, music by
Sammy Fain. © Leo Feist, inc.,
New York; 29Apr47; EP16229.

The Dickey-Bird Song. See his The Birds
and the Bees.

Don't Kill the Goose (that lays
the golden egg) lyric by Herb
Magidson, music by Sammy Fain.
© Mayfair Music Corp., New York;
160ct47; EP18526.

I Thank You Weenk! ... Lyric by
George Marion, jr., music by
Sammy Fain. © Edwin H. Morris
& Co., inc., New York; 26Sep47;
EP17696.

Never Make Eyes (at the gals with
the guys who are bigger than
you) words by Jack Yellen,
music by Sammy Fain. © Jack
Yellen and Sammy Fain, New York;
24Oct47; EP18532.

The Wildest Gal in Town; words
by Jack Yellen, music by
Sammy Fain. © Yellen & Fain,
New York; 14Aug47; EP16436.

FAIR, HAROLD.
On the Sea of Sleep; by Harold
Fair. © Broadcast Music, inc.,
New York; 19May47; EP18210.
For voice and piano.

FAITH, PERCY, 1908-
Noche Caribe. (Caribbean Night);
by Percy Faith. © Harms, inc.,
New York; 30ct47; EP17801. For
piano solo.

FALCOCCHIO, EDUARDO.
Serenata Serena; versi di Enzo
Bonagura, musica di E.
Falcocchio. © Edizioni
Musicali E. Falcocchio, Napoli;
3May47; EF6481.

FALLA, MANUEL DE, 1876-1946.
Nocturno; para piano, [by] M.
de Falla. © Unión Musical
Española, Madrid; 30Dec40;
EF6005.

FAMA, RUSSELL, 1910-
Brilliant Star ... by Russell
Fama. © Accordion Music Pub-
lishing Co., New York; 2Jul47;
EP16567. For accordion solo.

Seguidille; for voice and piano
by Manuel de Falla, English
lyric by Olga Paul, French
lyric by Théophile Gautier.
© Edward B. Marks Music Corp.,
New York; 27Feb42; on English
lyric; EP18337.

Serenata Andaluza; para piano,
[by] M. de Falla. © Unión
Musical Española, Madrid;
30Dec40; EF6006.

Tus Ojillos Negros ... poesía de
Cristóbal de Castro, música de
Manuel de Falla. © Unión
Musical Española, Madrid;
30Dec40; EF6007.

Vals-Capricho; para piano [by]
M. de Falla. © Unión Musical
Española, Madrid; 30Dec40;
EF6004.

FAMOUS BLUE JAY SINGERS.
Jesus' Love Just Flowing Over in
My Soul; [by] the Famous Blue
Jay Singers, [arr. by V.
Bates] © Birmingham Blue Jay
Singers, Chicago; 1Feb47;
EP16502. Close score: SATB.

There'll Be No More Crying ...
words and music by] the
Famous Blue Jay Singers,
[arr. by V. Bates] © Bir-
mingham Blue Jay Singers,
Chicago; 1Feb47; EP16501.

FAMOUS FOLIO OF SONGS TO REMEMBER;
[words and music by Budge and Fudge
Mayse, George York and others]
© Dixie Music Pub. Co., New York;
bk. 2, 150ct47; EP18984.

FANSLER, PAULINE.
You've Been Two-timin' Me; words
and music by Pauline Fansler.
© Nordyke Publishing Co., Los
Angeles; 10ct47; EP15285.

FARKAS, IMRE.
Megállok a Keresztútnál. (In the
Summer at These Crossroads)
English lyric by Olga Paul, music
by Farkas Imre. (In Pasti, Barbara, comp. Memories of Hungary.
p. 60-61) © Edward B. Marks Music Corp., New York; 19Nov47; on
English lyric; EP19016.

FARMER, WILLIE LUE, 1914-
Flag of Stars for Victory; [by]·
... Willie Lou Farmer ... arr.
by Margarite Brown. © Rev.
Miss Willie Lou Farmer, Chicago;
15Sep47; EP17770. For voice
and piano.

I Must Join That Heavenly Choir;
words and music by Rev. Miss
Willie Farmer. [Arr. by Odessa
Steward] © Rev. Miss W. L.
Farmer, Chicago; 2Jul47;
EP15358.

FARMERS EDUCATIONAL AND COOPERATIVE
UNION OF AMERICA.
Singing Farmers; a songbook of the
Farmers Educational and Coopera-
tive Union of America, arrange-
ments by Harry Robert Wilson.
© National Farmers Union, Denver;
10Oct47; on arrangement;
EP18118.

FARR, CARL.
Farr Brothers' Stomp; by Carl and
Hugh Farr. © Tim Spencer Music,
inc., Hollywood, Calif.; 2Jul47;
EP15413. For piano solo, with
guitar diagrams and chord
symbols.

Texas Skiparoo; by Carl and Hugh
Farr. © Tim Spencer Music, inc.,
Hollywood, Calif.; 2Jul47;
EP15412. For piano solo, with
guitar diagrams and chord
symbols.

FARROW, JOHNNY.
I Have But One Heart. ['O Marena-
riello] Words by Marty Symes,
music by Johnny Farrow [Italian
words by Marty Symes and Johnny
Farrow, c1945] © Barton Music
Corp., New York; 30Jul47; on
Italian words: EP18615.

FASSONE, V
A Cup of Coffee. 'A Tazza 'e
Caffè English lyric by Olga
Paul, Italian lyric by G.
Capaldo, music by V. Fassone.
(In Memories of Italy. p.62-64.)
© Edward B. Marks Music Corp.,
New York; 16Jul47; on English
lyric; EP15830.

FAURÉ, JEAN BAPTISTE, BAPTISTE, 1830-1914.
The Palms; [by] Jean Batiste
Fauré, choir I, S.A.T.B.,
II, S.A.T.B., arr. by C. Albert
Scholin. © Belwin, inc., New
York; 18Dec47; oh arrangement;
EP19929.

The Palms; [by] Jean Batiste
Faure, [tr. from the French by
T. T. Barker] Junior, intermediate and senior choirs, arr.
by Guy Chambers Filkins. © Belwin, inc., New York; 20Nov47;
on arrangement; EP18759.

FAVRE, GEORGES, 1905- Paris. Ecoles
Solfèges de Concours; à 1 et 2
voix (1947) par Georges Favre,
Robert Planel, Raymond Weber,
Madeleine Larose [and] Michel
Boulnois. © Durand & Cie, Paris;
15Jul47; EF6526.

FEDERER, RALPH.
The Devil's Night Out; piano solo
by Ralph Federer. © Mills Music,
inc., New York; 8Dec47; EP19896.

Fantasy in F-sharp minor ... by
Ralph Federer. © Theodore
Presser Co., Philadelphia;
25Jul47; EP15909. Two scores
for piano 1-2.

Forgotten Melody; piano solo.
© Theodore Presser Co. Philadelphia; 18Jul47; EP15753.

The Girl in the Picture Hat; piano
solo by Ralph Federer. © Mills
Music, inc., New York; 8Dec47;
EP19897.

Lonely Dancer; for piano by Ralph
Federer. © Theodore Presser
Co., Philadelphia; 26Jun47;
on arrangement; EP15373.
For piano, 4 hands.

Night in Vienna; by Ralph Federer.
© Theodore Presser Co.,
Philadelphia; 27Oct47; on
arrangement; EP18651. For piano
4 hands.

Sophisticated Sophie ... piano
solo by Ralph Federer. ©
Oliver Ditson Co., Philadelphia; 15Aug47; EP16444.

When Twilight Falls ... Arr. for
organ by R. S. Stoughton.
© Theodore Presser Co., Philadelphia; 18Jul47; on arrangement; EP15754. Includes registration for Hammond organ.

FEIN, SUSIE BELLE.
Am I Worthy of You? Words and
music by Susie Belle Fein,
[arr. by Burrell Van Buren]
© Nordyke Publishing Co., Los
Angeles; 16Jul47; EP17569.

The Whippoorwill Will Soon Be
Singing; words and music by
Susie Belle Fein. © Nordyke
Publishing Co., Los Angeles;
5Aug47; EP19450.

FELL, FRANK PRESLY, 1927-
Why Don't You Come Around Any
More? by Frank Fell. © La Mar
Music Publishers, inc., Canton,
Ohio; 14Jul47; EP15659. For
voice and piano.

265

FELLER, SHERMAN.
I'm Cooked, Boiled 'n' Toasted
(I'm in love); by Sherman Feller.
© Broadcast Music, inc., New
York; 12Aug47; EP18044. For
voice and piano, with chord
symbols.

FENDER, INA MAE.
There's a Moon Tonight; words
and music by Ina Mae Fender,
arr. by Lindsay McPhail.
© Nordyke Publishing Co., Los
Angeles; 22Apr47; EP17445.

FENERTY, MARTIN E.
I Paid for the Kiss I Stole;
words and music by Martin E.
Fenerty. © Nordyke Publishing
Co., Los Angeles; 11Jul47;
EP17612.

[FENSTERSTOCK, BELLE]
Be an Angel; words by Frederick
N. Polangin, music by Belle
Fenstock [pseud., piano score
by Michael Edwards] © Mills
Music, inc., New York; 29Aug47;
EP17941.

FENSTOCK, BELLE, pseud. See
Fensterstock, Belle.

FERGO, TONY.
Gavilán! Suelta los pollos ...
letra y música: Tony Fergo. ©
Ediciones Atlas, s.a., México;
31Dec46; EP6773.

La Televisión; letra y música
de J. Carbó Menéndez y Tony
Fergo. © Regent Music Corp.,
New York; 22Jul47; EP16420.

FERNSTROM, JOHN.
Chaconne; [by] Fernström. [Op. 31]
... G moll. Stockholm, Ed.
Suecia. © Föreningen svenska
tonsättare, Edition Suecia, Stockholm; 1Jan40; EF7060. Score
(violoncello and piano) and part.

I Stolta Städer; till text av Nils
Ferlin, [by] John Fernström.
[Op.50a] © Föreningen svenska
tonsättare, Stockholm; 1Jan46;
EF7123.

Intima Miniatyrer ... Op.2. [By]
John Fernström. Stockholm, Ed.
Suecia. © Föreningen svenska
tonsättare, Edition Suecia,
Stockholm; 1Jan45; EF7073.
Score: string orchestra.

Sex Sånger; [by] John Fernström.
Stockholm; 1Jan45; on 6 songs.
Contents.- Rollige Bror (Nils
Ferlin) © EF7067)-En Vandrande
Pierrot (Py Sörman) (© EF7068)-
Flickan och Göken (Gabriel Jönsson)
(© EF7072)-Nymäne (Dagmar Sten-
berg) (© EF7071)-Rokoko (Dagmar
Stenberg) (©EF7070)-Strandvialen
(Elof Akesson) (© EF7069)

FERRARI, ERMANNO WOLF- See
Wolf-Ferrari, Ermanno.

FERRARI, GIACOMO GOTIFREDO, 1759-1842.
Introduzione all'opera La Villanella
Rapita. See his La Villanella Rapita.

(La Villanella Rapita) Introduzione
all'opera La Villanella Rapita
di F. Bianchi ... [by] J. G.
Ferrari, elaborazione di F.
Quaranta. © Carisch, S. A.,
Milan; 30Apr46; on elaboration;
EF6280. Score: orchestra.

FERRARI, JACOPO GOTTIFREDO. See
Ferrari, Giacomo Gotifredo.

FERRARI, LOUIS, 1910-
Joue contre Joue ... Paroles de
Jacques Plante, musique de Louis
Ferrari. © Editions Paul
Beuscher, Paris; 20Jul46; EF6468.

Tout Doux ... paroles de Jacques
Larue [pseud.], musique de Louis
Ferrari. © Editions E.M.U.L.,
Paris; 30Dec44; EF6492.

Volo, Mon Coeur, Volo; paroles de
Jacques Plante, musique do Louis
Ferrari. © Sté. Ame. Fse.
Chappell, Paris; 26Jun47; EF6233.

FERRARO, ATTILIO.
Turmiento; versi di Amleto Brus-
sati, musica di Attilio Ferraro.
Napoli, Ed. E.M.C.D. © Italian
Book Co., New York; 5Sep47;
EF6855.

FERRÉ, LÉO, 1916-
Paris; paroles et musique de
Léo Ferré. © Editions Musi-
cales "Le Chant du Monde,"
Paris; 2May47; EF5919.

FERRER, ANGEL ECHAVARRIA. See
Echavarría Ferrer, Angel.

FERRERA, JOHN BATTISTA, 1913-
Musical Chart; showing absolute
pitch and range of the voice,
band and chief orchestral instruments in relation to the
piano, designed and comp. by
John B. Ferrera. © John
Battista Ferrera, Hialeah, Fla.;
24Oct47; EP18622.

FERRETE, LEON M   1890-
Rumba de Amores ... [by] L. M.
Ferreté. © [Editions Espagnoles]
Julio Garzon, Paris; 23Jun47;
EF6511. Piano-conductor score
(orchestra) and parts.

[FERRIER, LUCIEN] 1897-
Judo; film documentaire ...
musique de L. Ferrier Jourdain
[pseud.] © Les Editions du
Coquelicot, Paris; 21Jul47; .
EF6490. For piano solo.

FERRIER JOURDAIN, L., pseud. See
Ferrier, Lucien.

FERRY, CHARLES T   1884-
Benedictus; song for low voice,
words by Harriet Lyon Leonard,
music by Charles T. Ferry. ©
Wesley Webster, San Francisco;
24Jul47; EP15918.

Breezes from the Hilltop; words
by Harriet Lyon Leonard, music
by Charles T. Ferry. © Wesley
Webster, San Francisco; 10Dec47;
EP15578.

Constancy; lyric by Harriet Lyon
Leonard, music by Charles T.
Ferry. © 2Oct47; EP18331.

Desire; song for high voice, music
by Charles T. Ferry, [words
anonymous] © Wesley Webster,
San Francisco; 2Jul47; EP15445.

Sonnet; song for medium voice,
lyric by Harriet Lyon Leonard,
music by Charles T. Ferry.
© Wesley Webster, San Francisco;
2Oct47; EP18332.

PERRY, FRANCES.
It's Me for You; lyric by Pat Ballard and Johnny Winters, music
by ... Frances Ferry. © F. D.
Ballard & Roger Bower, Bronx-
ville, N. Y.; 28Jun47; EP17757.

FICHER, JACOBO, 1896-
Azúcar, Malvones, Menta ...
(Zucchero, Gerani, Menta) [by]
Jacobo Ficher. Op. 45, [no.]
5. De las Siete Canciones de
Amado Villar, textos: español
e italiano, version italiana
de: Honorio Siccardi. ©
Editorial Argentina De Música
(E.A.M.), Buenos Aires;
30Apr45; EF5657.

Déjame Dormir, Amor. (Lasciami
Dormire, Amore) [by] Jacobo
Ficher. Op. 45, [no.] 6. De
las Siete Canciones de Amado
Villar, textos: español e
italiano, version italiana de:
Honorio Siccardi. © Editorial
Argentina De Música (E.A.M.),
Buenos Aires; 30Apr45; EF5656.

El Desfile; [de las "5 Piezas
Infantiles". Op. 39, no. 5]
para piano, [by] Jacobo Ficher.
© Editorial Argentina De
Música (E.A.M.), Buenos
Aires; 20Mar47; EF5674.

Me Dice Palabras Tiernas. (Mi
Esprime Verbi d'Amore) [by]
Jacobo Ficher. Op. 45, [no.]
4. De las Siete Canciones de
Amado Villar, textos: español
e italiano, version italiana
de: Honorio Siccardi. ©
Editorial Argentina De Música
(E.A.M.), Buenos Aires;
30Apr45; EF5658.

Polvo, Caldén, Espinillo ...
(Rena, Caldón e Spiniglipo)
[by] Jacobo Ficher. Op. 45,
[no.] 3. De las Siete
Canciones de Amado Villar,
textos: español e italiano,
version italiana de: Honorio
Siccardi. © Editorial
Argentina De Música (E.A.M.),
Buenos Aires; 30Apr45; EF5659.

Tres Danzas en Estilo Popular
Argentino; para piano, [by]
Jacobo Ficher. Op. 43. ©
Editorial Argentina De Música
(E.A.M.), Buenos Aires;
30Sep46; EF3995.

FICHTHORN, CLAUDE L.
Behold, What Manner of Love;
sacred song, text from the
Scriptures, [music] by Claude
L. Fichthorn. © The John
Church Co., Philadelphia;
15Jul47; EP15679.

FIDANZINI, VIERI.
See If I Care. (Eso Eres Tu)
Music and Spanish lyric by Mario
Clavell and Vieri Fidanzini,
English lyric by Mack David.
© Remick Music Corp., New York;
29Oct47; EP18478.

FIEDEL, SAMUEL SOLOMON.
Elf on a Sleigh Ride; piano solo
by Sam S. Fiedel. © Bob Miller,
inc., New York; 27Oct47; EP18628.

Who Cares (for I love you); words
and music by Sam Fiedel. ©
Bob Miller, inc., New York;
27Oct47; EP18632.

Who Cares (for I love you); words
and music by Sam S. Fiedel ...
arrangement by Sam S. Fiedel.
[n.p.] Dorian Music Publishers.
© Bob Miller, inc., New York;
27Oct47; on arrangment; EP18910.
Piano-conductor score (orchestra)
and parts.

FIELDS, IRVING.
Hugo and Igo (in Mexico); by
David Gale and Irving Fields.
© Mayfair Music Corp., New York;
11Aug47; EP16325. For voice and
piano, with chord symbols.

Moroccan Market ... by Irving
Fields. © Remick Music Corp.,
New York; 11Jul47; EP15840.
For piano solo.

Pigeon-toed Penguin; a piano
novelty in the modern idiom. by
Irving Fields. © Remick Music
Corp., New York; 18Aug47;
EP16435.

FILAS, THOMAS, 1908-
America for Me ... by Edward
Ballantine [and] Thomas Filas,
[words by Edward Ballantine,
Thomas Filas and] W. R.
Williams [pseud.] © Will
Rossiter, Chicago; 10Oct47;
EP17792.

FILAS, THOMAS J   1908-
"Hut-2-3-4," ... by Thomas J. Filas.
© Will Rossiter, Chicago; 11Dec47;
EP19562. Principally for piano
solo; in part for voice and piano.

FILKINS, GUY CHAMBERS, 1892-
The Ageless Miracle; an Easter
anthem for chorus and high soli
voices ... [words by] Mary
Hallet ... [music by] Guy
Chambers Filkins. © Guy
Chambers Filkins, Detroit;
20Dec46; EP17378.

Paean ... for mixed chorus, antiphonal choirs I and II and organ [by] Guy Chambers Filkins,
words adapted from Scriptures.
© Guy Chambers Filkins, North-
ville, Mich.; 28Dec40; EP18240.

Prayer Response; [by] Guy Chambers
Filkins. © Guy Chambers Filkins,
Ann Arbor, Mich.; 1Oct47;
EP17765. Close score; SATB.

Te Deum; in G (chorus & soli) [by]
Filkins. © Guy Chambers Fil-
kins, Ann Arbor, Mich.; 3Sep47;
EP17962. English words.

FILLGROVE, EDNA.
Hot Tamale Rose; words and music
by Edna Fillgrove, arr. by L.
McPhail. © Nordyke Publishing
Co., Los Angeles; 2Dec46;
EP20341.

FILLMORE, FRED A   1850-1926/
All My Hope on Earth Is Jesus ...
[by] Fred A. Fillmore, [words
by] Frank E. Roush. © Frank E.
Roush, Lynchburg, Ohio; 1Oct47;
EP17636. Close score; SATB.

Wonderful Story of Grace ... [by]
Fred A. Fillmore, [words by]
Frank E. Roush. © Frank E.
Roush, Lynchburg, Ohio; 8Oct47;
EP18372. Close score; SATB.

FINCH, HARRY ELLSWORTH, 1915-
Ouija ... words & music by Harry
E. Finch. © Harry E. Finch,
Torrance, Calif.; 22Oct47;
EP18291.

FINK, FREDERICK A
City Guardians ... by Fred Fink.
© Volkwein Brothers, inc.,
Pittsburgh; 9Sep47; EP16696.
Piano-conductor score (band)
and parts.

FINKE, JOHN.
Cynthia; for piano, [by] John
Finke, jr. © Theodore Presser
Co., Philadelphia; 26Jun47;
EP15375.

FINKLEHOFFE, FRED F
Albuquerque; words and music by
Sid Silvers ... [and] Fred F.
Finklehoffe ... [arr.] 24Feb47;
Co., Hollywood, Calif.; 24Feb47;
EP15456.

FINN, THOMAS.
'Though You're in Love with Somebody Else; by Thomas Finn. ©
Cinephonic Music Co., ltd.,
London; 9Apr46; EP6648. For
voice and piano, with chord
symbols; melody also in tonic
sol-fa notation.

FINNEY, THEODORE M
One Elect of Stars; S.A.T.B.,
[by] Theodore M. Finney,
[words by Doris Jack] ©
Volkwein Brothers, inc.,
Pittsburgh; 9Sep47; EP16695.

FINZI, GERALD, 1901-
An Ode for St. Cecilia's Day; for
tenor solo, chorus and orchestra, words by Edmund Blunden,
music by Gerald Finzi. [London,
Sole selling agents, Boosey &
Hawkes] © Boosey & Co., ltd.,
London; 29Oct47; EP6898. Part
for chorus.

FIORILLO, DANTE, 1908-
Chorale March; for band, by Dante
Fiorillo ... Conductor's con-
densed score. © Educational
Publishing Institute Corp.,
New York; 23Oct47; EP18957.

Crescendo for Band; by Dante
Fiorillo ... Conductor's con-
densed score. © Educational
Publishing Institute Corp., New
York; 23Oct47; EP18958.

South American Holiday; for band
by Dante Fiorillo ... Conductor's
condensed score. © Educational
Publishing Institute Corp., New
York; 23Oct47; EP18959.

[FIRON, GUY] 1919-
Rêve d'un Soir ... Paroles de
Henry Lemarchand, musique de Joë
Bellingham [pseud.] © Editions
Europa, Paris; 15Jan47;
EF5886.

[FISCHER, IRWIN L   ]
Mists of the Morning; by Edwin
Marshal [pseud.] © Clayton F.
Summy Co., Chicago; 2Sep47;
EP17325. For piano solo.

Northern Lights; by Edwin Marshal
[pseud.] © Clayton F. Summy Co.,
Chicago; 30Jun47; EP15453. For
piano solo.

A Woodland Stream; by Edwin Marshal,
[pseud.] © Clayton F. Summy Co.,
Chicago; 19Jun47; EP15331. For
piano solo.

FISCHER, WILLIAM G
I Love to Tell the Story; [by]
Fischer, transcribed by H. P.
Hopkins. © Century Music
Publishing Co., New York;
10Jul47; on arrangement;
EP15501. For piano solo.

FISHER, DORIS.
Now You Tell Me; words and music
by Allan Roberts and Doris
Fisher. © Sun Music Co., inc.,
New York; 25Jul47; EP17421.

(The Strawberry Roan) Texas Sandman; by Allan Roberts and Doris
Fisher ... [from] The Strawberry Roan. © Mood Music Co.,
inc., New York; 14Nov47;
EP18983. For voice and piano,
with chord symbols.

Texas Sandman. See her The Strawberry
Roan.

FISHER, DOUGLAS R   arr.
Song-a-log; specially comp. and
arr. for mixed choirs by Douglas
R. Fisher. © Van Kampen Press,
Chicago; 23Sep47; EP18352.

FISHER, MARVIN.
For Once in Your Life; lyric by
Jack Segal, music by Marvin
Fisher. © Dreyer Music Corp.,
New York; 13Jun47; EP15459.

FISHER, MITCHELL.
You Are My Dream Girl; words and
music by Mitchell Fisher. ©
Nordyke Publishing Co., Los
Angeles; 31May46; EP19750.

FISHER, SHUG, arr.
"The Crawdad Song;" arrg; Shug
Fisher. © Century Songs, inc.,
Chicago; 14Nov47; on arrangement
& words; EP18771. Melody and
chord symbols, with words.

FISK, DANNY FRED, 1929-
This Romance; words and music by
Danny F. Fisk. © Danny Fred
Fisk, Tulsa, Okla.; 4Sep47;
EP17122.

Tropical Ecstasy; words and music
by Danny F. Fisk. © Danny Fred
Fisk, Tulsa, Okla.; 12Aug47;
EP17098.

FLEMING, ALICE.
If I Could Sing; words and music
by Alice Fleming. © Nordyke
Publishing Co., Los Angeles;
12Jul47; EP17516.

FLEMING, CHRISTOPHER LE. See
Le Fleming, Christopher.

FLEMING, LEN.
In the Spring; words by Carl G.
Johnson, music by Len Fleming.
© Nordyke Publishing Co., Los
Angeles; 16Jul47; EP17627.

I've Fallen in Love with You;
words by Troy A. Thompson,
music by Len Fleming. © Nordyke
Publishing Co., Los Angeles;
10May47; EP16894.

[FLETCHER, LEILA]
Cello Song; [by] Lenore
Montgomery, [pseud.] ©
Century Music Publishing
Co., New York; 8Aug47;
EP16124. For piano solo.

FLEURY, ANDRÉ, pseud. See also
Orakton, E. Marie.

Allegro Symphonique; pour orgue,
[by] André Fleury. © Editions
Musicales Herelle & Cie, Paris;
10Jun47; EF5964.

FLOOD, DORA FLICK, 1885-
Twinkle, Twinkle, Little Star;
S.A. [by] Dora Flick Flood,
lyric by Jane Taylor. © Dorothea Louise Schroeder, Flushing, N.Y.; 18Dec47; EP19923.

FLORY, SYLVIO.
Carioca Album of Brazilian Songs
... music by Sylvio Flory,
Portuguese lyrics by Ceiṕão
Barreto, English lyrics by
Carol R. Wood & Albert Gamse.
© Edward B. Marks Music Corp.,
New York; 20Aug47; on English
lyrics; EP16464. Contents.-
Saudade do Brazil. (Salute to
Brazil) (© EP16453)- Rio de
Janeiro (© EP16454)- Pão de
Assucar, (Sugar Loaf Mountain)
(© EP16455)- Ipanema
(© EP16456)- Flamengo (©
EP16457)- Urca (© EP16458)-
Tijuca (© EP16459)- Leme (©
EP16460)- Corcovado, -
Copacabana (© EP16461)- Gávea
(© EP16462)- Leblon (© EP16463)

FLOTSAM, pseud. See
Hilliam, Bentley Collingwood.

FLOYD, ALAN. See
Floyd, H. Alan.

FLOYD, H   ALAN.
Hosea; anthem for mixed voices
(with tenor and baritone solos),
text adapted from the book of
Hosea by Bernard C. Clausen ...
music by Allan Floyd. ©
Broadcast Music, inc., New York;
25Aug47; EP18057.

FOGARTY, DANIEL F
You Were Just Seventeen; words
and music by Daniel F. Fogarty,
arr. by Edward F. Geoghegan.
© Nordyke Publishing Co., Los
Angeles; 11Jul47; EP17455.

FONTANALS, FRANCISCO.
Fuego en Panamá ... Letra y
musica de Francisco Fontanals,
arreglo de Pérez Prado. © Peer
International Corp., New York;
3Jul47; EF5725. Parts: orchestra.

FONTENOY, MARC, pseud. See
Schwab, Alexandre.

FORBES, ROGER, arr.
First Collection of Waltz Classics
... selected and arr. for piano
solo by Roger Forbes. © New World
Publishers, ltd., London; 19Jul47;
on arrangement; EF6621.

FORD, FRANK.
Old Glory; words by Jack Smith,
music by Frank Ford. © Nordyke
Publishing Co., Los Angeles;
16Jul47; EP17413.

FORD, THOMAS.
Since First I Saw Your Face;
melody by Ford ... words
anonymous. [From the Arnold
Book of Old Songs, arr. by
Roger Quilter] London, Boosey
& Hawkes. © Boosey & Co., ltd.,
London; 24Sep47; on arrange-
ment; EF6646.

FOREST, B   pseud. See
Souriac, Blanche.

FORMELL M   FRANCISCO.
Quiero Oir Tu Voz; letra y música
de Francisco Formell M. © Peer
International Corp., New York;
30Dec46; EF6827. Parts: orchestra.

FORREST, SIDNEY.
Flowers for Mother; by Sidney
Forrest. © Theodore Presser Co.,
Philadelphia; 11Aug47; EP16298.
For piano solo, with words.

FORT, ELEANOR H
Pic-a-nic-in' (in the park);
words and music by Hank Fort.
© Champagne Music Corp.,
Chicago; 15Jul47; EP16709.

FORT, HANK. See
Fort, Eleanor H

[FOSTER, ALBERT H   ] 1888-
comp.
Marching Away; eight ... marches
for assembly and school use,
[comp. by Albert H. Foster, jr.]
© Clayton F. Summy Co.,
Chicago; 27Jun47; EP15303.

Piano Pieces Boys Like to Play;
[comp. by Albert H. Foster]
© Clayton F. Summy Co., Chicago;
4Jun47; EP16071.

Piano Pieces Girls Like to play.
© Clayton F. Summy Co., Chicago;
7Aug47; EP16130.

FOSTER, ARNOLD.
Red Top-knots. (Tappagyn Jiargey)
Manx folk song, air from Moore's
"Manx Ballads," English version
of the Manx traditional words
by Mona Douglas, arr. as a two
part song with pianoforte acc.
by Arnold Foster. © Stainer &
Bell, ltd., London; 22Oct47; on
arrangement; EF6861. Score:
2 sopranos and piano.

FOSTER, FAY
Margaret O'Brien ... Favorite
Songs and Stories; stories and
lyrics by Florence Tarr, music
by Fay Foster, drawings by
Seymour Jaffe. © Robbins Music
Corp., New York; 14Oct47;
EP18425.

FOSTER, IVOR R
101 Unfigured Melodies & Basses
for Harmonization; primary
triads to dominant seventh &
simple modulation, by Ivor R.
Foster. © Alfred Lengnick &
Co., ltd., London; 20Aug47;
EF6689.

FOSTER, STEPHEN COLLINS, 1826-1864.
Barndoorshemmet i Kentucky. (My
Old Kentucky Home, Good Night)
[By] S. C. Foster, arr. av
Josef Jonsson. © Nordiska
musikförlaget, a.b., Stockholm;
on arrangement; EF7088.
Close score: TTBB.

Beautiful Dreamer; by Stephen C.
Foster, [arr. by Hugo Frey]
© Hamilton S. Gordon, New York;
12Nov47; on arrangement;
EP18675. For voice and piano.

Beautiful Dreamer; pianoforte solo, [arr.
by King Palmer] © William
Paxton & Co., ltd., London;
24Dec46; on arrangement;
EF5707.

Beautiful Dreamer. See also his Duel in
the Sun.
(Duel in the Sun) · Beautiful
Dreamer, words and music by
Stephen C. Foster ... from the
... production Duel in the Sun,
[arr. by Chris Langdon] ©
Chappell & Co., ltd., London;
10Jul47; on arrangement; EF6229.

I Dream of Jeanie; for two-part
chorus of male voices ... arr.
by Frank B. Crokson. © The Raymond A. Hoffman Co., Chicago;
22Sep38; EP15585.

Oh, Susanna; TTBB accompanied.
[By] Stephen Foster, arr. by
Noble Cain. © Harold Flammer,
inc., New York; 14Nov47; on
arrangement; EP19156.

Old Folks at Home; [by] Stephen C.
Foster, arr. by F. Bellstore.
(In Bellstore, Pietro, comp. So
Easy. p.5) © Edward B. Marks
Music Corp., New York; 9Dec47;
on arrangement; EP19503. For
piano solo.

Swanee River; [by Stephen Collins
Foster, arr. by Edward Robert
Pripps and] Zep Meissner. ©
Joseph James (Zep) Meissner,
North Hollywood, Calif.; 23May47;
on arrangement; EP19076. Parts:
orchestra.

FOUNTAIN, FORREST ROLAND, 1922-
Cougars Fight; [words by] Marion
Ford, jr. [music by Marion Ford,
jr., and] Forrest Fountain. ©
Marion Edwin Ford, jr., Pasa-
dena, Tex. & Forrest Roland
Fountain, Houston, Tex.;
18Oct47; EP18932.

FOUSER, CHARLES ELLIOTT, d. 1946.
Te Deum; for full chorus of mixed
voices, alto solo, organ acc.
and timpani, [by] Charles Elliott Fouser. © The Willis
Music Co., Cincinnati; 17Nov47;
EP19222. English words.

FOWLER, JOHN WALLACE.
City of Memphis; words and music
by Beasley Smith ... and Wally
Fowler. © F & M Publishing
Co., inc., New York; 1Aug47;
EP16327.

FOWLER, WALLACE, 1917-
Texas Red; by Louie Buck, Curley
Kinsey [and] Wally Fowler. ©
F & M Publishing Co. inc.,
New York; 30Jun47; EP15786.
For voice and piano, with
chord symbols.

FOX, CURLY.
Even Tho' I'll Shed a Million
Tears; words and music by Texas
Ruby and Curly Fox. © Peer
International Corp., New York;
25Nov47; EP19834.

FOX, HARRY CLAY, 1884-
I Dreamed; words & music by
Harry C. Fox. © Harry C. Fox,
Detroit; 8Oct47; EP17015.

I'll Give All My Dreams to You;
words & music by Harry C. Fox.
© Harry Clay Fox, Detroit;
17Oct47; EP18154.

FRAGNA, ARMANDO.
Guitarrita; English lyric by Olga
Paul, Italian lyric by B.
Cherubini, music by Armando
Fragna. (In Memories of Italy.
p.28-33) © Edward B. Marks
Music Corp., New York; 16Jul47;
on English lyric; EP15822.

FRANCE, WILLIAM.
It Was a Lover and His Lass; [by]
Shakespeare ... from "As You
Like It," set to music by
William France, for chorus of
women's voices, three-part, un-
acc. © Galaxy Music Corp., New
York; 21Aug47; EP17018.

268

FRANCE, WILLIAM EDWARD, 1912-
Lord of All Power and Might;
anthem for mixed voices, music
by William E. France. © The
Frederick Harris Music Co.,
ltd., Oakville, Ont., Can.;
14Jul47; EF5751.

FRANCIS, HERBERT.
The Lord Is Our Comfort; three
part S.S.A., [by] Herbert
Francis, arr. by Dora Flick
Flood, text by Daniel Twohig.
© Dorothea Louise Schroeder,
Flushing, N. Y.; 5Sep47; on
arrangement; EP17775.

FRANCIS, J   HENRY.
Sleep! Dear Christ-Child; [by] J.
Henry Francis. © The Arthur P.
Schmidt Co., Boston; 4Sep47;
EP16639. Score: chorus (SATB)
and piano.

FRANCK, CÉSAR AUGUSTE, 1822-1890.
Extract from first movement, violin
sonata. See his Sonata, violin.

(Hulda) Lutte de l'Hiver et du
Printemps; ballet allégorique
extrait de "Hulda," légende
scandinave, [by] César Franck ...
transcription pour piano à deux
mains par Gustave Samazeuilh.
© Choudens, Éditeurs, Paris;
22Jul47; on transcription;
EF6549.

Larghetto. See his Quartet, strings.

Lutte de l'Hiver et du Printemps. See
his Hulda.

Prelude, Fugue and Variation;
transcribed for piano solo by
Anis Fuleihan. [By] César
Franck. © Heritage Music Publications, inc., New York;
1Nov47; on arrangement;
EP18367.

(Quartet, strings) Larghetto,
from the string quartet by
César Franck, arr. for organ by
... Gregory Murray. © The Oxford
University Press, London; 10Jul47;
on arrangement; EF6169.

(Sonata, violin) Extract from
first movement, violin sonata,
[by] César Franck, arr. for
organ by C. H. Stuart Duncan.
© Edwin Ashdown, ltd., London;
7Jun47; on arrangement; EF6746.

FRANKLIN, DAVE.
Lone Star Moon; words and music
by Cliff Friend and Dave Franklin. © Advanced Music Corp.,
New York; 26Nov47; EP19118.

FRANKLIN, RUBY MILDRED, 1907-
He's Mine, This Christ, the Naz-
arene; [by] Mrs. W. M. Frank-
lin. © Mrs. W. M. Franklin,
Fargo, N. D.; 20Oct47; EP18148.
Close score: SATB.

FRANKO, NAHAN.
Unity March; by Nahan Franko ...
arr. by Erik Leidzén. © Mills
Music, inc., New York; 1Aug47;
EP18254. Condensed score
(band) and parts.

FRAMS, ALFIE.
Boogie Mood; by Alfie Franks.
© Cinephonic Music Co., ltd.,
London; 8Jun45; EF6027. For
piano solo.

FRÁTER, LORÁND.
Elmegyek Ablakod Elött. (When I
Pass before Your Window) English
lyric by Olga Paul, music by
Fráter Loránd. (In Pasti, Barbara,
comp. Memories of Hungary. p.
20-21) © Edward B. Marks Music
Corp., New York; 19Nov47; on
English lyric; EP18997.

FRATER, LORAND, Cont'd.
Száz Száz Gyertyát, Száz Itce Bort.
(Hundred Candles, Hundred Bottles)
English lyric by Olga Paul, music
by Fráter Lóránd. (In Pasti, Barbara, comp. Memories of Hungary.
p.18-19) © Edward B. Marks Music
Corp., New York; 19Nov47; on English lyric; EP18996.

FRAZEE, GERALD F
From the Realms of Glory; a Christ-
mas choir cantata for mixed
voices, text by Elsie Duncan
Yale, music by Gerald F. Frazee.
© Lorenz Publishing Co., Dayton,
Ohio; 28Jul47; EP16611.

FRED, HERBERT W
Fantasy on an American Air ... for
band by Herbert W. Fred. © H.
T. FitzSimons Co., inc., Chicago;
25Nov47; on arrangement; EP19055.
Condensed score (band) and parts.

FREDERICKS, CHARLES R
Hawaiian Paradise; words & music
by Charles R. Fredericks. © Nordyke Publishing Co., Los Angeles;
25Jul46; EP19744.

FREED, FRED.
On the Avenue; Ab ... lyric by
Harold Rome, music by Fred Freed,
arr. by Bob Horse. © Leeds
Music Corp., New York; 30Jul47;
on arrangement; EP15999. Piano-
conductor score (orchestra, with
words) and parts.

On the Avenue; C orig. ... lyric
by Harold Rome, music by Fred
Freed, arr. by Bob Horse. ©
Leeds Music Corp., New York;
30Jul47; on arrangement;
EP16001. Piano-conductor score
(orchestra, with words) and
parts.

On the Avenue; lyric by Harold
Rome, music by Fred Freed. ©
Leeds Music Corp., New York;
30Jul47; EP16002.

On the Avenue; lyric by Harold
Rome, music by Fred Freed, arr.
by Fred Weismantel. © Leeds
Music Corp., New York; 30Jul47;
on arrangement; EP16000. Piano-
conductor score (orchestra, with
words) and parts.

FREED, FRED, pseud. See also
Goldbaum, Friedrich.

FREEMAN, TICKER
(I Don't Gare) That's All I Want
to Know; words and music by
Sunny Skylar [pseud.] and
Ticker Freeman. © Beverly Mus-
ic Corp., New York; 12Aug47;
EP16154.

Ready, Set, Go! Lyric by Sunny
Skylar [pseud.], music by Ticker
Freeman. © Robbins Music Corp.,
New York; 210ct47; EP18424.

FRELEIGH, DARRELL. See
Freleigh, Richard Darrell.

FRELEIGH, RICHARD DARRELL, 1909-
Before the Harvest Days Are Over;
[by] Darrell Freleigh. © R. D.
Freleigh, Merriam, Kan.;
24Oct47; EP18176. Close score;
SATB.

FRENCH, MOLLIE PERCY.
Little Bridget Flynn; song, words
by Percy French, traditional
air arr. by Mollie Percy French.
© Keith, Prowse & Co., ltd.,
London; 16Oct47; on words &
arrangement; EP6909.

FRENCH, PERCY.
Phil, the Fluter's Ball; by Percy
French, arr. by Norman Impey.
© Keith, Prowse & Co., ltd.,
London; 31Oct47; on arrangement;
EP7287. Piano-conductor score
(orchestra) and parts.

FRESCO, JOAN.
Violinade; for violin and piano,
by Joan Fresco. [Op. 40] © Keith,
Prowse & Co., ltd., London;
28Nov47; EP7171. Score and part.

FREY, HUGO, arr.
Jumbo Note Folk Songs; arr. by
Hugo Frey. © Chas. H. Hansen
Music Co., New York; 1Jul47;
EP16103. For piano solo, with
words.

Lawrence Welk's Favorite Polkas;
a collection for the clarinet,
solos, duets, trios with piano
acc [and piano-accordion chord
symbols arr. by Hugo Frey] ©
J. J. Robbins & Sons, inc., New
York; 27Oct47; on arrangements;
EP18498. Piano-conductor score
and part.

Lawrence Welk's Favorite Polkas;
a collection for the Eb saxophone, solos, duets, trios with
piano acc. [arr. by Hugo Frey]
© J. J. Robbins & Sons, inc.,
New York; 27Oct47; on arrangements; EP18497. Piano-conductor
score and part.

Lawrence Welk's Favorite Polkas;
a collection for the trumpet,
solos, duets, trios with piano
acc. [and piano-accordion chord
symbols arr. by Hugo Frey] ©
J. J. Robbins & Sons, inc., New
York; 27Oct47; on arrangements;
EP18498. Piano-conductor score
and part.

[FREY, HUGO] 1874-   comp. and arr.
Sammy's Bowery Follies; songs of
yesterday, [comp. and arr. by
Hugo Frey] © J. J. Robbins
& Sons, inc., New York;
28Jul47; on compilation and
arrangement; EP15955.

FREY, HUGO, 1874-   ed. and arr.
Music for Millions; a collection of
world famous songs, ed. by Hugo
Frey. © J. J. Robbins & Sons,
inc., New York; v.2, 29Oct47; on
arrangement & new words; EP19269.
Contains special arrangements by
Domenico Savino, with new lyrics
by Joseph McCarthy, Jr., Ted
Fetter, Jeanne Burns and Marjorie
Harper.

FRIEDMAN, LEO.
Let Me Call You Sweetheart ...
music by Leo Friedman ... [arr.]
by Charles Magnante. New York,
Shapiro, Bernstein & Co. © Sha-
piro, Bernstein & Co., inc. and
Paull-Pioneer Music Corp., New
York; 14Oct47; on arrangement;
EP18024. For accordion solo.
Includes "Straight version" and
"A Charles Magnante interpreta-
tion."

FRIEL, J   J
Dixie Lee; words and music by J. J.
Friel. © Nordyke Publishing Co.,
Los Angeles; 21Aug47; EP19635.

FRIEND, CLIFF.
I Love to Sing a Duet; by Cliff
Friend. © Leeds Music Corp.,
New York; 31Dec46; EP17257.
For voice and piano, with
chord symbols.

FRIML, RUDOLF, 1881-
Giannina Mia, from "The Firefly"
by Rudolf Friml; arr. for the
piano by James Palmeri. © G.
Schirmer, inc., New York;
17Jul47; on arrangement;
EP17043.
Nearer and Dearer. See his Northwest
Outpost.

(Northwest Outpost) Nearer and
Dearer ... from ... Northwest
Outpost; music by Rudolf Friml,
lyrics by Edward Heyman. ©
Edwin H. Morris & Co., inc.,
New York; 5Jun47; EP15342.

Sympathy Waltz, from "The Firefly"
by Rudolf Friml; arr. for the
piano by James Palmeri. © G.
Schirmer, inc., New York;
17Jul47; on arrangement;
EP17044.

FRISCH, AL.
A-N-G-E-L Spells Mary; words and
music by Fred Wise, Steve Nelson
and Al Frisch. © United Music
Corp., New York; 15Sep47;
EP17112.

FRISQUE, BOB.
My Dream of Tomorrow Is You; music
by Bob Frisque, lyrics by Teddy
Hurd. © Nordyke Publishing Co.,
Los Angeles; 12Sep47; EP19356.

FROST, BERNICE.
The Bell at the Fountain; piano
solo by Bernice Frost. © The
Boston Music Co., Boston; .
1Aug47; EP16342.

Bernice Frost's Companion Series;
for the piano ... classics,
folk tunes [and] original compositions. © The Boston Music Co.,
Boston; bk. 1, 2Sep47; EP17298.

A Gay Promenade; piano solo by
Bernice Frost. © The Boston
Music Co., Boston; 1Aug47;
EP16344.

March of the Wild Geese; piano
solo by Bernice Frost. © The
Boston Music Co., Boston; 1Aug47;
EP16343.

FROST, BERNICE, ed.
Six Sonatas; for piano, by
Beethoven ... [and others],
collected, rev. and ed. by
Bernice Frost. © J. Fischer &
Bro., New York; 30Sep47; on
collecting, revising, editing
& preface; EP17703.

FRUMERIE, GUNNAR DE. See
De Frumerie, Gunnar.

FRYDAN, CAMILLA, 1890-
(Ladies Know How) Muchachita ...
English lyric by Albert Gamse,
Spanish lyric by Clotilde Arias,
music by Camilla Frydan. From
the musical revue "Ladies Know
How." © Empress Music Publish-
ers, New York; 9Jul47; EP16977.
Piano-conductor score (orchestra,
with words) and parts.

(Ladies Know How) Muchachita,
from the musical revue Ladies
Know How ... lyrics by Albert
Gamso, music by Camilla Frydan.
[Spanish lyric by Clotilde
Arias] © Empress Music
Publishers, New York; 9Jul47;
EP16965.

Muchachita. See her Ladies Know How.

FRYE (THEODORE R) PUBLISHERS, ed.
Clarence H. Cobbs Songs of Zion;
comp. and ed. by the Theodore
R. Frye Publishers, Georgiana
M. Rose and Myrtle Jackson. ©
Theodore R. Frye, d. b. a. The
[Theodore R.] Frye Publishers,
Chicago; 8Jan47; EP17196.

Lucie E. Campbell Superior Song
Book; for use in all Christian
religious services, [ed. and
comp. by Theodore R. Frye
Publishers] © Theodore R.
Frye, Chicago; 17May46;
EP17198.

President Jemison Special Song
Book no.2; an all purpose book
of gospel songs adaptable for
all departments of the church.
Ed. ... by the Theodore R.
Frye Publishers © Theodore
R. Frye, d. b. a. The [Theodore
R.] Frye Publishers, Chicago;
17May46; EP17199.

FRYE, THEODORE ROOSEVELT, 1901–
God Answers Prayer; words and
music by Virginia Davis and
Theodore R. Frye, [arr. by
Virginia Davis] Chicago, T.
R. Frye. © Virginia Davis and
Theodore R. Frye, Chicago;
30Apr46; EP17197.

FRYKLÖF, HARALD, d. 1919.
Sonata alla Leggenda ... [by] Harald
Fryklöf, rev. av Charles Barkel.
© A.-b. Nordiska musikförlaget,
Stockholm; 15Dec19; on revision;
EF7187. Score (violin and piano)
and part.

FUCHS, LILLIAN.
Jota; [by] Lillian Fuchs. © M.
Witmark & Sons, New York; 18Dec47;
EP20279. Score (violin and piano)
and part.

FULEIHAN, ANIS.
The Bailiff's Daughter; English
ballad [transcribed for] piano
solo [by] Anis Fuleihan. © Carl
Fischer, inc., New York; 8Sep47;
on transcription; EP18076.

The Bailiff's Daughter, [transcribed for] two
pianos [by] Anis Fuleihan. ©
Carl Fischer, inc., New York;
23Sep47; EP18066. Two scores
for 2 pianos.

The Blighted Swain; old English
melody transcribed by Anis
Fuleihan. © Carl Fischer, inc.,
New York; 23Sep47; on transcription; EP18064. For piano solo.

Fugue; [by] Anis Fuleihan ... for
piano. © Carl Fischer, inc.,
New York; 8Sep47; EP18077.

Set of Five; piano solo [by]
Anis Fuleihan. © Mercury Music
Corp., New York; 18Dec47;
EP19980.

The Slighted Swain. See his The
Blighted Swain.

FULLER, FRANK R
Into Our Garden of Love; lyric by
Ralph T. Taylor, music by Frank
R. Fuller. San Francisco, R.T.
Taylor. © Ralph T. Taylor and
Frank R. Fuller, San Francisco;
18Oct47; EP18436.

FUMERO, JOSÉ CLARO. See
Claro Fumero, José.

FURLOW, BROWN, 1927–
Love's a Lovely Thing; words and
music by Brown Furlow. © Dial
Music Corp., Great Neck, L. I.,
N. Y.; 27Jan47; EP15954.

FURNEY, ALBERT J 1887–
Blue Jacket Blues; words and
music ... by Al Furney, arr.
[by] Harry Powell. © Albert
J. Furney, San Francisco;
11Aug47; EP16312.

"Right Wheel, Left Wheel,"
(storm clouds ahead); words and
music ... by Al Furney, arr.
[by] ... Harry Powell. ©
Albert J. Furney, San Francisco;
11Aug47; EP16316.

G

GABRIEL, CHALVAR AXEL, 1892–
Singing Along the Way ... [music by]
Chalvar A. Gabriel, Duluth; v.1, 18Nov47;
Gabriel. © Chalvar A.
A. Maker and others.
Gabriel; v.1, 18Nov47; Vol. 1 has words by J.

GABRIEL, CHARLES H 1856–1932.
An Evening Prayer ... solo for
soprano voice ... words by C. M.
Battersby, music by Chas. H.
Gabriel, special arrangement by
B. D. Ackley. Winona Lake, Ind.,
The Rodeheaver Hall-Mack Co.
© The Rodeheaver Co., Winona
Lake, Ind.; 23Oct47; on arrange-
ment; EP18508.

O That Will Be Glory; [for] male
voices [by] Chas. H. Gabriel,
arr. by Griffith J. Jones.
[Words by] Chas. H. Gabriel [and]
G. W. Davis. [Winona Lake, Ind.,
Rodeheaver Hall-Mack Co.] © The
Rodeheaver Co., Winona Lake, Ind.;
5Sep47; on arrangement; EP17128.
Includes There Is Glory in My Soul.

GABRIEL-MARIE, JEAN, 1907–
Do Si, La Sol, Fa Mi, Ré Do;
berceuse enfantine ... [by] Jean
Gabriel-Marie, rev. et doigtée
par Zino Francescatti. © Durand
& Co., Paris; 31May47; EF7220.
Score (violin and piano) and
part.

Do Si, La Sol, Fa Mi, Ré Do;
berceuse enfantine pour piano,
[by] Jean Gabriel-Marie. ©
Durand & Cie, Paris; 25May47;
EF5938.

GABRIELIDES, MICHAEL GEORGIOS, 1908–
01? agapē "As Millésoume Pali" ...
etichoi: G. Giannakopoulou,
mousikē, Mich. Gabrielidē. 2.
ekdosis. Athēnai, Ekdoseis
Gaitanou. © Michael Gaetanos,
Athens; 18May47; EF6809. For
voice and piano.

GADDIS, RACHEL M.
Repentance. Heaven, Our Home.
[Music by Rachel M. Gaddis, words
by T. H. Gaddis] ... Jesus Is
Calling; [words and] music by
Rachel M. Gaddis. Winona Lake,
Ind., Gaddis Moser Evangelistic
Party. © Rachel M. Gaddis, Winona
Lake, Ind.; 30Aug47; EP16660.
Close score; SATB.

GADE, JACOB.
Jalousie (Jealousy) [By] Jacob
Gade, arr. by Jerry Sears. ©
Harms, inc., New York; 28Oct47;
on arrangement; EP18724. Score
(trombone and piano) and part.

Jalousie. (Jealousy) ... [For]
S.A.B., music by Jacob Gade,
arr. by Douglas MacLean [pseud.]
Words by Vera Bloom, Spanish
text by Belen Ortega. © Harms,
inc., New York; 21Jul47; on
arrangement; EP16541.

Jalousie. (Jealousy) ... [For]
T.T.B.B., music by Jacob Gade,
choral setting by Clay Warnick.
Words by Vera Bloom, Spanish
text by Belen Ortega. ©
Harms, inc., New York;
28Jul47; on arrangement;
EP16542.

Jalousie. (Jealousy) Music by
Jacob Gade, arr. by Jerry Sears.
© Harms, inc., New York;
20Jun47; on arrangement; EP15362.
Piano-conductor score (orchestra)
and parts.

GAEVERT, E   A   See
Gevaert, François Auguste.

GAGE, AGNES PETERSON, 1869–
Medley of Christmas Carols; by
Agnes Peterson Gage. Chicago,
Senga Music Publishers. © Agnes
Peterson Gage, Chicago; 1Dec46;
on arrangement; EP20268. For
harp solo.

GAGE, HORACE ANDREW, 1906–
All My Dreams Come True; lyric
by Florence Gage, music by
Horace Andrew Gage. © Horace Andrew
Gage – Florence Comstock Gage,
Detroit; 15Aug47; EP16495.

Dancing, Dear, with You in My
Arms; lyric by Florence C. Gage.
© Horace Andrew Gage & Florence
Comstock Gage, Detroit; 9Jul47;
EP15564. For voice and piano,
with chord symbols.

Merry Christmas to You; lyric by
Florence Gage, music by Horace
Gage. © Horace Andrew Gage &
Florence Comstock Gage, Detroit;
19Nov47; EP19027.

Shootin' Just in Fun; lyric by
Florence Gage, music by Horace
Gage. © Horace Andrew Gage &
Florence Comstock Gage, Detroit;
5Nov47; EP18560.

That Night of Nights; lyric by
Florence Gage, music by Horace
Gage. © Horace Andrew Gage &
Florence Comstock Gage, Detroit;
19Sep47; EP18110.

GAGLIO, JOSEPH, 1925–
Just Me, Without You; words by Kay
Randazzo, music by Joe Gaglio.
© Shelby Music Publishing Co.,
New York; 10Jun47; EP15386.

GAGNEBIN, HENRI DAVID, 1886–
Vingt-trois Pièces Récréatives et
Progressives; pour servir à
l'etude de la flûte, [by] H.
Gagnebin. © Alphonse Leduc &
Co., Paris; 31May47; EF6417.

GAGNON, SELMA JULIETTE.
Turn to Jesus; [by] Selma J.
Gagnon. (In Hymn Writers'
Magazine. v.1, no.2, p.27)
© Selma J. Gagnon, Los Angeles;
28Aug47; B5-2512. Close score;
SATB.

GAILING, BENJAMIN, 1898–
Bet a Yid Rosh Hashono; words
and music by Ben Gailing, arr.
by George J. Siegel. © Benjamin Gailing, Mattapan, Mass.;
18Sep47; EP17246. Words in
Yiddish (transliterated)

GALLANT, MICHAEL, pseud. See
Golletz, Michael, 1896–

GALLA-RINI, ANTHONY, 1904–
Paragon March; [by] Galla-Rini.
© Chart Music Publishing House,
inc., Chicago; 17Oct47;
EP18483. For accordion solo.

Paragon March; for accordion band,
by Galla-Rini. © Chart Music
Publishing House, inc., Chicago;
17Oct47; EP18482. Score and
parts.

GALLO, pseud. See
Gorni, Francesco.

GALLOIS MONTBRUN, RAYMOND, 1918–
Douze Études-Caprices de Concert;
pour violon, [by] R. Gallois
Montbrun. © Alphonse Leduc &
Cie, Paris; 28Feb47; EF5905.

GAMAUF, LADISLAUS C 1890–
Betrothal Prayer; wedding song,
words by Jane E. Tower, music
by Ladislaus C. Gamauf. ©
Ladislaus C. Gamauf, Hollywood,
Calif.; 19Nov47; EP19004.

[GAMBARDELLA, S]
Comme Facette Mammeta? [Words by
G. Capaldo, music by S.
Gambardella] © Italian Book
Co., New York; 24Jul47;
EP15913. Melody and words.

GARABRANT, MAURICE.
Benedictus Es, Domine; for S. A.
or S. S. in the key of A major,
by Maurice Garabrant. © H. W.
Gray Co., inc., New York;
12Sep47; EP17375. English
words.

GARCERÁN, RAFAEL QUINTERO. See
Quintero Garcerán, Rafael

GARCIA MORILLO, ROBERTO, 1911–
Marlborough's Return. (La Vuelta
de Mambrú) de los Cuentos
para Niños Traviesos, [by]
Roberto García Morillo. ©
Editorial Argentina De Música
(E.A.M.), Buenos Aires;
6Jul45; EF5660. For piano
solo.

GARCIA MORILLO, ROBERTO. Cont'd.
Variaciones 1942. (op. 10) Para
piano [by] Roberto Garcia
Morillo. ℗ Ricordi Americana,
s.a.e.c., Buenos Aires; 3Apr44;
EF6981.

GARDEL, CARLOS.
Melodía de Arrabal; de la película
del mismo nombre ... letra de
Alfredo le Pera y Mario
Battistella, música de Carlos
Gardel. ℗ Editorial Julio
Korn, Buenos Aires; 5Dec38;
EF6791.

GARDNER, ANN E
My Baby's Waiting for a Kiss;
words-and music by Ann E. Gardner. © Nordyke Publishing Co.,
Los Angeles; 16Dec46; EP19683.

GARDNER, EDDIE.
No, Baby, No! Words and music by
Fletcher Henderson, Bobby Troup,
Frank Lewis and Eddie Gardner.
© Regent Music Corp., New York;
18Oct47; EP18298.

GARLAND, HUGH, pseud. See
Anderson, William H.

GARLAND, JOSEPH COPELAND.
In the Mood ... music by Joe Garland ... [arr.] by Charles Magnante. © Shapiro, Bernstein
& Co., inc., New York; 14Oct47;
on arrangement; EP18022. For
accordion solo.

GARMAN, WILLIAM McKINLEY, 1899-
Bondage; composition for piano
[by] William McKinley Garman.
[Op. 397] Los Angeles, Garman
Music Publications. © William
McKinley Garman, Los Angeles;
20Nov47; EP19101.

Concerto Petite; piano solo by
Raymond Edward Earle [pseud.]
Los Angeles, Garman Music Publi-
cations. © William McKinley
Garman, Los Angeles; 20Nov47;
EP19100.

Gambol of the Gnomes; composition
for piano [by] William McKinley
Garman. [Op. 282] Los Angeles,
Garman Music Publications. ©
William McKinley Garman, Los
Angeles; 20Nov47; EP19099.

Jingle Jungle; piano solo by
William Garman. Los Angeles,
Garman Music Publications. ©
William McKinley Garman, Los
Angeles; 20Nov47; EP19098.

Kitty-Cat; piano solo with words,
by Marita Roberts [pseud.] Los
Angeles, Garman Music Publications. © William McKinley Garman, Los Angeles; 20Nov47;
EP19097.

Little Concert Master; piano solo
by William Garman. Los Angeles,
Garman Music Publications. ©
William McKinley Garman, Los
Angeles; 20Nov47; EP19096.

Tango Español; piano solo by William McKinley Garman. Los Angeles, Garman Music Publications.
© William McKinley Garman, Los
Angeles; 20Nov47; EP19095.

Toy-Town Band; by Frederick Joyce
[pseud.] Los Angeles, Garman
Music Publications. © William
McKinley Garman, Los Angeles;
20Nov47; EP19094. For piano solo.

Waltz Melody; piano solo by Allan
Printz [pseud.] Los Angeles,
Garman Music Publications. ©
William McKinley Garman, Los An-
geles; 20Nov47; EP19093.

GARNICA CABALLERO, REGINO.
Que Aparezca la Piña ... Letra
y música de Regino Garnica
Caballero. © Peer Internation-
al Corp., New York; 6Jun47;
EF5738. Parts: orchestra.

GARTLAN, GEORGE H
Dublin and Belfast United; words
by Daniel J. Hickey, music by
George H. Gartlan. © Robbins
Music Corp., New York; 31Oct47;
EP18462.

JARVIN, MARY.
Lovely Lady; words and music by
Mary Garvin. © Nordyke Publishing
Co., Los Angeles; 18Jun47;
EP17501.

GARY, HOLLAND MERRICK, 1911-
Muskingum Moon; words and music
by Holland M. Gary. © Holland
M. Gary, Zanesville, Ohio;
15Sep47; EP18111.

GASTÉ, LOUIS, 1908-
C'Etait un Grand Garçon; paroles de
Mireille Brocey [pseud.], musique
de Louis Gasté. © Éditions Micro,
Paris; 20Nov46; EF7303.

Ce N'Etait Pas Original ... paroles de Françoise Giroud
[pseud.], musique de Louis
Gasté. © Éditions Micro,
Paris; 31Dec43; EF3983.

Le Complet Gris; paroles et musique de Louis Gasté. © Éditions Micro, Paris; 10Dec45;
EF7324.

Il N'Etait Pas Sentimental; pa-
roles de A. Hornez, musique de
Louis Gasté. © Éditions Micro,
Paris; 20Nov46; EF7323.

(L'Ile d'Amour) Tendre Sérénade ...
dans le film "L'Ile d'Amour."
Paroles de Claude Marcy [pseud.],
S. Pizella & R. Lucchesi, musique
de Louis Gasté, arr. par Al Kiwi
[pseud.] © Éditions Max Eschig,
Paris; 5Mar47; on arrangement;
EF7229. Piano-conductor score
(orchestra) and parts.

Jamais Deux sans Trois; paroles de
Françoise Giroud [pseud.] & de
Marguenat, musique de Louis Gasté.
© Éditions Micro, Paris; 14Mar46;
EF6768.

Nous Deux; paroles de H. Kubnick,
musique de Louis Gasté. ©
Éditions Micro, Paris; 20Nov46;
EF7322.

Le Porte-Bonheur; paroles de Henri
Kubnick, musique de Louis Gasté.
c1945. © Éditions Micro, Paris;
15Jul46; EF6769.

Si J'Avais la Chance; paroles de
H. Kubnick, musique de L. Gasté.
© Éditions Micro, Paris; 25Mar47;
EF7321.

Tendre Sérénade. See his L'Ile.d'Amour.

GAUL, HARVEY BARTLETT, 1881-1945.
George Washington's Prayer; for
soprano solo and chorus of mixed
voices, [by] Harvey Gaul, [words
by] George Washington. © The H.
W. Gray Co., inc., New York;
7Nov47; EP19260.

Moravian Evening Hymn; based on a
Moravian hymn-tune ... "Old 29th"
[by] Harvey Gaul. © The H. W.
Gray Co., inc., New York;
23Oct47; EP18488. For organ
solo.

Prayer for an American Sailor;
for the organ, by Harvey Gaul.
© G. Schirmer, New York;
16Jun47; EP16689.

A Prelude for Pentecost; for the
organ, by Harvey Gaul. ©
G. Schirmer, inc., New York;
16Jun47; EP16688.

Tennessee Twilight Tune; for the
organ, by Harvey Gaul. ©
G. Schirmer, inc., New York;
16Jun47; EP16690.

GAVAERT, E   A   See
Gevaert, François Auguste.

GAWTHROP, ADALINE H
My Heart's on My Sleeve; words
and music by Adaline H. Gawthrop.
© Nordyke Publishing Co., Los
Angeles; 12Jul47; EP17486.

GAY, NOEL.
There's a Lovely Little Lady; words
and music by Noel Gay. © Noel
Gay Music Co., ltd., London;
3Sep47; EP6691.

GEEHL, HENRY, 1881-
In Tudor Days; [by] Henry Geehl,
for brass band. © Besson & Co.,
ltd., London; 16Oct47; EF6823.

GEIST, ELECTA ALMA (GROOVER) 1905-
Love Me Dear; words & music by
Electa Alma Groover. © Electa
Alma (Groover) Geist, Indian-
apolis; 24Nov46; EP18144.

GELABERT, JOSÉ.
Macatalina ... letra y música de
José Gelabert, arreg. [by] Pérez
Prado. © Peer International
Corp., New York; 23Sep47; EF6717.
Parts: orchestra.

GELLER, HAROLD.
El Toreador; by ... Harold Geller
[words by] Bob Howard. ©
Cinephonic Music Co., ltd.,
London; 13May47; EF6631. For
voice and piano, with chord
symbols; melody also in tonic
sol-fa notation.

GENDRON, JULIETTE C
Bird Sketches; for piano, by
Juliette C. Gendron. © The
Boston Music Co., Boston;
12Sep47; on 3 pieces. Contents.
- 1. Flock of Sparrows (© EP
17300) - 2. Bob White (© EP
17301) - 3. Humming Bird
(© EP17303)

GEORGE, CHARLES
A Christmas Story; an operetta in
one act, based on Charles Dickens' "Christmas Carol," book,
lyrics and music by Charles
George. © T. S. Denison & Co.,
Minneapolis; 20Oct47; D pub 11196.

My Old Rag Doll; [words and music
by Charles George] © T. S.
Denison & Co., Minneapolis;
1Aug47; EP16963.

Sister Susie Started Swingin';
lyric and music by Charles
George. © T. S. Denison & Co.,
Minneapolis; 26Aug47; EP19070.

Wild Rose; a musical comedy in two
acts, book, lyrics, and music by
Charles George. © T. S. Denison
& Co., Minneapolis; 25Sep47; D
pub 11015.

GEORGE, DON.
I Want You to Be a Part of Me;
words by Anna Boyer, music by
Don George. © Nordyke Publishing Co., Los Angeles;
12Aug47; EP17600.

Nina Nana ... lyric by Don
George, music by Don George
[and] Carmen Passin. © Encore
Music Publications, inc., New
York; 27Oct47; EP18245.

Sentimental Souvenirs; words and
music by Lionel Newman, Harry
James and Don George. © Jewel
Music Publications, inc., New
York; 23Sep47; EP19136.

The Story of the Two Stars; words
by Kenneth L. Herron, music by
Don George. © Nordyke Publishing
Co., Los Angeles; 23Sep47;
EP20495.

Where in the World Is Heaven; by
Lionel Newman, Wilton Moore
[and] Don George. © Grand Music
Corp., New York; 3Jul47; EF6979.
For voice and piano, with chord
symbols.

GEORGE, EARLE, pseud. See
Metcalfe, George E.

GEORGE, GRAHAM.
O Worship the King; anthem for
mixed voices, based on the old
104th Ravenscroft's Psalter,
1621. [By] Graham George, [words
by] Robert Grant. © The H. W.
Gray Co., inc., New York; 7Nov47;
EP19261.

GERMAINE, ADELAIDE ST., pseud. See
Long, Norman Russell.

GERMAN, Sir EDWARD, 1862-1936.
Long Live Elizabeth. See his Merrie
England.
(Merrie England) Long Live Eliza-
beth, from "Merrie England";
words by Basil Hood, music by
Edward German. © Chappell & Co.,
ltd., London; 8Sep47; EP6602.
Score: chorus (SATB) and piano.

GEROUX, LUDGER.
I Will Say; words and music by
Ludger Geroux. © Nordyke
Publishing Co., Los Angeles;
16Jul47; EP17494.

GERSHWIN, GEORGE, 1898-1937.
Andante and Finale. See his Rhapsody in
Blue.
George Gershwin Selection; tran-
scribed ... by David Bennett. ©
New World Music Corp., New York;
20Nov47; on arrangement; EP19177.
Condensed score (band) and parts.

George Gershwin's Second Prelude
(Andante con moto) For trumpet
and piano, transcribed by Gregory Stone. © New World Music
Corp., New York; 13Nov47; on
arrangement; EP18890. Score
and parts.

George Gershwin's Second Prelude.
(Andante con moto) For violin,
'cello and piano, transcribed
by Gregory Stone. © New World
Music Corp., New York; 13Nov47;
on arrangement; EP18889. Score
and parts.

The Man I Love; [by] George
Gershwin, arr. by Jean Gossette
[pseud.] © Harms, inc., New
York; 8Sep47; on arrangement;
EP17276. Score (trombone and
piano) and part.

Of Thee I Sing, from the musical
comedy "Of Thee I Sing"; music
by George Gershwin, lyric by
Ira Gershwin, [arr. by Jerry
Sears] © New World Music Corp.,
New York; 30Jul47; on arrangement; EP16539. Piano-
conductor score (orchestra,
with words) and parts.

(Oh, Key) Someone To Watch over Me,
from the musical comedy "Oh, Key";
music by George Gershwin, words
by Ira Gershwin ... scored by Ken
Macomber. © Harms, inc., New York;
25Aug47; on vocal orchestration;
EP17150. Piano-conductor score
(orchestra, with words) and parts.

(Oh, Key) Clap Yo' Hands; from the
musical production "Oh, Key!"
Three part women's voices, S.S.A.,
words by Ira Gershwin, music by
George Gershwin, choral setting
by Clay Warnick. © Harms, inc.,
New York; 29Jul47; on arrangement;
EP16369.

Oh, Lady Be Good; solo for E flat
alto saxophone with piano acc.,
[by] George Gershwin, arr. by
Jerry Sears. © Harms, inc., New
York; 6Nov47; on arrangement;
EP18074. Score and part.

--- --- Ed. for B flat tenor saxophone. © Harms, inc., New York;
6Nov47; on arrangement; EP18075.

(Rhapsody in Blue) Andante and
Finale, from George Gershwin's
Rhapsody in Blue; for accordion
solo (bass clef) arr. by Roberto
Carreno. © Harms, inc., New
York; 19Aug47; on arrangement;
EP17094.

(Rhapsody in Blue) Andante and
Finale, from George Gershwin's
Rhapsody in Blue ... transcribed
by David Grunes. © Harms, inc.,
New York; 19Aug47; on arrangement;
EP17096. Score (violoncello and
piano) and part.

GEVAERT, FRANÇOIS AUGUSTE, 1828-1908.
Two Christmas Carols; S.A.T.B. I.
The Sleep of the Baby Jesus [by]
F. A. Gevaert, [words and arr.
by Frederic Fay Swift] II. O
Little Town of Bethlehem; words
by Phillips Brooks ... music by
Frederic Fay Swift. © Belwin,
inc., New York; 7Nov47; on ar-
rangement; EP18539.

GIACOME, ANTONIO.
Luna Bugiarda ... parole di Pinchi,
musica di A. Giacone (arr. di F.
Rizza) A-ulf-ulé ... musica e
arr. di G. Fabor [pseud.]
Parole di Lodo e Gomez. © [c1947]
© Edizioni Italcarisch, Milano;
on Luna Bugiarda, 29Nov46; on
A-ulf-ulé, 24Aug46; EP6762,
6761. Piano-conductor score;
orchestra, with words.

GIANELLA, P.
Gee, I Love You; words and music
by P. Gianella. © Nordyke Publishing Co., Los Angeles;
14Jun47; EP17548.

GIANNEO, LUIS, 1897-
Alba con Lanas; canto y piano,
[by] Luis Gianneo, letra de
Alfredo R. Bufano. © Editorial
Argentina De Música (E.A.M.),
Buenos Aires; 9Nov46; EP5651.

Caminito de Belén; para piano,
[by] Luis Gianneo. ©
Editorial Argentina De Música
(E.A.M.), Buenos Aires;
21Apr47; EP5672.

La Danza de las Liebres; [for]
canto y piano, [by] Luis
Gianneo; versos de Conrado
Nalé Roxlo. © Editorial
Argentina De Música (E.a.M.),
Buenos Aires; 9Nov46; EP3998.

Lied; canto y piano, [by] Luis
Gianneo, versos de Alfredo R.
Bufano. © Editorial Argentina
De Música, Buenos Aires;
9Nov46; EP5650. Spanish words.

GIBBONS, ORLANDO.
Fantasie (in three parts); [by]
Orlando Gibbons; for soprano,
alto and tenor recorders.
Adapted by George Hunter. ©
E. C. Schirmer Music Co.,
Boston; 12Aug47; on adaptation;
EP16557.

GIBSON, EVELYN LOUISE, 1925-
Christ, the Answer; [by] Evelyn
Louise Gibson. © Evelyn Louise
Gibson, Akron, Ohio; 13Dec47;
EP19852. Close score; SATB.

[GIBSON, HERBERT MURDOCH] 1897-
Serenade to a Beautiful Day; words
by Hubert Sands [pseud.], music by
Peter Revell [pseud.] © Edwin
Ashdown, ltd., London; 14Dec47;
on additional score; EP7271.

GIBSON, HUGH.
Honeymoon Trip to the Moon; words
and music by Hugh Gibson. ©
Nordyke Publishing Co., Los
Angeles; 22Apr47; EP16828.

So, Now We're Through; words and
music by Hugh Gibson. © Nordyke
Publishing Co., Los Angeles;
29Apr47; EP16905.

GIBSON, KENNETH.
Do You Remember? Words and music
by Kenneth Gibson. © Nordyke
Publishing Co., Los Angeles;
10Jun47; EP16957.

GIL, CARLOS MARTINEZ. See
Martinez Gil, Carlos.

GILARDI, GILARDO, 1889-
Canción de Cuna India; para canto
y piano, [by] Gilardo Gilardi,
letra de Ana Serrano Redonnet.
© Ricordi Americana, s.a.e.c.,
Buenos Aires; 25Nov42; EP6977.

La Pesarosa; [by] Gilardo Gilardi
para coro a 4 voces mixtas con
acompañamiento de piano; letra
de Ana Serrano de Redonnet.
© Ricordi Americana, S.A.E.C.,
Buenos Aires; 14Sep42; EP6964.

GILBERT, FRANK.
Don't Leave Me Alone; words and
music by Frank Gilbert, [arr. by
Lou Halmy] © Starlight Pub.
Co., Los Angeles; 24Feb47;
EP15455.

There'll Never Be Another Sister
McPherson; words by Frank
Gilbert and James Boersma and
music [by Frank Gilbert] ©
X-L Music Publications, Los
Angeles; 25Sep47; EP17824.

GILBERT, HARRY.
Fantasie on Swedish Folk Songs;
for chorus of men's voices
with English text and music by
Harry Gilbert. © H. W. Gray
Co., inc., New York; 12Sep47;
EP17369.

GILBERT, LEE, pseud. See
Parmelee, Gilbert.

GILBERT, NORMAN.
Let All the World; [by] Norman
Gilbert, [words by] George
Herbert. © The Oxford University Press, London; 5Jun47;
on arrangement; EP6116. For 3
treble voices and piano.

GILBERT, ROBERT.
Der Holunderbusch blunt. [Down
the Green Hudson Valley] ...
Musik und Worte von Robert
Gilbert. [c1946] © Edition
Turicaphon, ltd., music publish-
ers (in notice: Edition Suizo-
Beltic a.g.) Zurich, Switzer-
land; 1Apr47; EP5830.

Puzzle ... [by] R. Guilbert.
© Alphonse Leduc & Cie., Paris;
30May47; EP6415. Score (horn
and piano) and part.

GILBERTSON, HALTON.
My Melody; [music by] Hal Gilbertson,
[words by] La Verne B. Christianson.
© La Verne Bosworth Christianson,
Chicago; 27Jun47; EP17095. Close
score: SATB.

GILL, HARRY.
About My Father's Farm; the
words by Edward Wright, set to
music by Harry Gill. © The
Oxford University Press,
London; 19Jun47; EP6151.

GILLETTE, JAMES ROBERT, 1886-   arr.
Short Classics for Band; 17th cen-
tury compositions arr. by James R.
Gillette. © Carl Fischer, inc.,
New York; 3Nov47; on arrangement;
EP19165. Condensed score and
parts.

GILLIS, DON.
Portrait of a Frontier Town; [by]
Don Gillis. London, Hawkes. ©
Boosey & Hawkes, inc., New York;
17Dec47; EP-02275. Score: orches-
tra.

GILLUM, RUTH HELEN, 1907-
Roll Jordan Roll ... Arr. by R. H.
Gillum. © Ruth Helen Gillum,
Durham, N. C.; 5Jul47; on arran-
gement; EP16137. Score: mixed
voices.

GINASTERA, ALBERTO E   1916-
Malambo; para piano [by] Albert.
E. Ginastera. © Ricordi
Americana, s.a.e.c., Buenos
Aires; 16Jul42; EF6978.

GINDHART, THOMAS J   1908-
Ev'rybody Knows I Love You; by
Jack Ziehler, Bert Kripaitis,
and Tom Gindhart. Philadelphia, Sole selling agent, Tin
Pan Alley. © Thomas J. Gindhart, Philadelphia; 1Aug47;
EP19926. For voice and piano,
with chord symbols.

[GIOE, JOSEPH] 1885-
Randy ... piano accordion solo
[by] J. Joy, pseud.], arr. by J.
Peppino. New York, O. Di Bella
Music Co. © Onofrio Di Bella,
New York; 3Nov47; EP19914.

GISELA, MARY, sister, comp.
Mount Mary Motet Book; for equal
voices, comp. by Sister Mary
Gisela ... Acc. ed. © McLaughlin
& Reilly Co., Boston; 20Jun47;
on compilation; EP15883.

GIULIANI, AMERICO.
Capinera; English lyric by Olga
Paul, music and Italian lyric
by Americo Giuliani. (In
Memories of Italy, p.44-47) ©
Edward B. Marks Music Corp.,
New York; 16Jul47; on English
lyric; EP15826.

GIULIANI, VITTORIO.
Ti Porterò ... (nel Paraguay) ...
parole di Pinchi, musica di V.
Giuliani [arr. di F. Bergamini]
Rimani ... musica e arr. di L.
Rosentini. [c1947] © Edizioni
Italcanarisch, Milano; on Ti
Porterò, 29Nov46; on Rimani,
28Mar47; EF6766, 6765. Piano-
conductor score (orchestra, with
words) and part for saxophone 3.

GIUSSANI, GEO.
Pochi Soldi ... Tanto Amore ...
testo di Gianipa [pseud.],
musica di Giussani [and]
Arcsrich, [c1945] © Edizioni
Leonardi, s.a.r.l., Milano;
22Jan46; EF6239. Piano-conductor
score (orchestra) and parts

GLANZBERG, NORBERT, 1910-
Moi J'M'En Fous; paroles de André
Hornez, musique de Norbert
Glanzberg. c1946. © Editions
Roger Bernstein, Paris;
31Jan47; EF5888.

GLARUM, LEONARD STANLEY, 1908-
The Chimes of the Sabbath;
Norwegian folk tune arr. by
L. Stanley Glarum [words by]
Oscar R. Overby. © Neil A.
Kjos Music Co., Chicago;
8Jul47; on arrangement; EP16133.
Score SSAATTBB and piano re-
duction.

GLAZER, FRANK.
Stopping by Woods on a Snowy Eve-
ning ... by Frank Glazer, [words
by Robert Frost] © Broadcast
Music, inc., New York; 19May47;
EP18209.

GLIÈRE, REINHOLD MORITSEVICH, 1875-
Intermezzo; [by] Reinhold Glière.
Op.35,no.11. [ed. with special
annotations by Harold Sheldon]
© Leeds Music Corp., New York;
20Oct47; on foreword, editing &
special annotations; EP18892.
Score (horn and piano) and part.

GLASER, VICTORIA MERRYLEES.
Fireflies; for three-part chorus
of mixed voices (a cappella).
Russian [folksong] arr. by
Victoria Glaser, English version
by Nathan Haskell Dole. © E.
C. Schirmer Music Co., Boston;
28Jul47; on arrangement;
EP15976.

The Three Holy Kings; [for] SATB
and soprano solo [by] R. M.
Glière, arr. by N. Lindsay
Norden. [Words by] Heinrich
Heine, tr. by N. L. N. ©
Harold Flammer, inc., New York;
28Jul47; on arrangement &
translation; EP16256.

GLOGAU, JACK.
Lucky Day ... by Jack Glogau ...
ed. and arr. by Thomas J. Filas.
© Will Rossiter, Chicago;
17Dec47; EP20101.

Single File ... by Jack Glogau,
ed. and arr. by Thomas J.
Filas. © Will Rossiter, Chicago; 11Oct47; EP17909. For
piano solo.

[GLYNN, BETTY B   ] 1914-
The Arkansas Traveler; (plectrum
guitar duet) ... by [Betty B.
Glynn of] the Oahu staff. (Oahu
"rhythm style" note course for
plectrum guitar (octave notation),
[lesson] 31FG) © Oahu Publishing
Co., Cleveland; 26May47; on arrangement; EP19607. Includes
lesson on chord acc. and the discussion "Oh, Susannah."

GNECCO, FRANCESCO, 1769-1810.
Sinfonia all' Italiana; per
orchestra da camera, [by] F.
Gnecco ... trascrizione di A.
F. Lavagnino. Partitura. ©
Carisch, s.a., Milan; 10Apr41;
on transcription; EF6217.

GOBLE, DORIS.
When I See Cy Press Cider; words
and music by Doris Goble.
© Nordyke Publishing Co., Los
Angeles; 16Jul47; EP17453.

GODARD, BENJAMIN LOUIS PAUL, 1849-
1895.
O Love Divine; hymn-anthem for
women's voices (S.S.A.) Text
adapted from hymns by Anna
Steele and Oliver Wendell
Holmes, [music by] Benjamin
Godard, arr. by William C.
Steere. © Theodore Presser
Co., Philadelphia; 9Sep47;
on arrangement; EP17169.

GODINI, ANTIGONO, 1901-
Crodimi ... [by] A. Godini, testi
di A. Natili. © Odeon, s. a.,
Milan; 30Sep42; EF6193. Piano-
conductor score (orchestra,
with words) and parts.

GODY, LOUIS.
Eho ... Compagnero! ... Paroles
de Jacques Plante, musique de
Louis Gody. © Arpège Edition
Musicale, Paris; 31Dec46;
EF6606. French words.

GOEDICKE, ALEXANDER F
Twelve Dances and Sketches; composed by Alexander F. Goedicke,
piano solos arr. and ed. by
Elizabeth Quaile. © Carl
Fischer, inc., New York; pt.1-2,
17Oct47; on arrangement & editing; EP18404-18405.

GOGNIAT, JOSEPH, 1881-
Hymne Patriotique à Nicolas de
Flue. Bruder-Klausen-Marsch.
Paroles de M. Strub, texte
allemand de A. Rohrbesser,
musique de Joseph Gogniat. ©
The Refousse Music Publishing
Co., New York; 17Oct47; EP18087.

GOLD, ERNEST, 1921-
Sleepy Hollow Heaven; lyrics by
Don McCray and Narda Stokes,
music by Ernest Gold. © Crys-
tal Music Publishers, inc.,
Hollywood, Calif.; 8Oct47;
EP17911.

GOLD, HAL.
It's the Little Things; words and
music by Art Waner, Ed. Weiner
and Hal Gold. © Leo Feist,
inc., New York; 15Jul47;
EP16252.

GOLD, HENRY. See
Gold, Henryk.

GOLD-ZAHAVI, HENRY, pseud. See
Gold, Henryk.

GOLDBAUM, FRIEDRICH, 1903-
See also   Freed, Fred.
On the Avenue; lyric by Harold
Rome, music by Fred Freed
[pseud.], arr. for Hawaiian,
electric & plectrum guitar [by
the Oahu staff] © Leeds Music
Corp., New York; 10ct47; on
arrangement; EP17751.

On the Avenue ... music by Fred
Freed [pseud.], arr. by Harold
L. Walters. © Leeds Music Corp.,
New York; 20Oct47; on arrange-
ment; EP18894. Condensed score
(band) and parts.

GOLDEN, ERNIE.
Toymaker's Dream; [by] Ernie
Golden, arr. by L. Sugarman.
© Edward B. Marks Music Corp.,
New York; 29Aug47; on arrange-
ment; EP16578. For piano solo.

GOLDEN STEPS ... [by] Frank H.
Stamps, O. A. Parris, Robt. E.
Arnold [and others] © Stamps
Quartet Music Co., Dallas;
1Jun47; EP19212. Hymns, with
music; shape-note notation.

GOLDSPINK, HECTOR.
I Sink in Deep Mire; from the
Psalms of King David, music
by Hector Goldspink. ©
Joseph Carlton, New York;
1Aug47; EP16484.

GOLDSWORTHY, WILLIAM A
Of the Father's Love Begotten ...
based on a 12th century plain
song, [for] SATB accompanied,
[music by] W. A. Goldsworthy.
Words by Aurelius Clemens
Prudentius, tr. by Neale and
Baker. © Harold Flammer, inc.,
New York; 28Jul47; EP16253.

GOLLATZ, MICHAEL, 1896-
Night After Night Dreaming of You;
words and music by Gay Claridge
& Michael Gallant [pseud.] ©
Gollatz Music Publishers, Chi-
cago; 15Oct47; EP19209.

GOLLEDGE, ED
I'm a Lucky Boy; words by Ethel S.
Stowell, music by Ed Golledge and
Osie Butler. © Nordyke Publish-
ing Co., Los Angeles; 15Jul46;
EP19791.

GOLLWELL, JOHN.
Stovka Není Nic, Láska To Je Víc
... hudba, J. Gollwell, slova,
Gero [and Gollwell] © Zdeněk
Vlk, Praha, Czechoslovakia;
4Feb44; EF6794. Part for 2
treble voices.

GOLZ, WALTER, 1881-
Etude for piano, by Walter Golz.
© The Composers Press, inc.,
New York; 28Jul47; EP15915.

Romanza ... by Walter Golz. ©
The Composers Press, inc., New
York; 28Jul47; EP15914. Score
(violoncello or bassoon and
piano) and parts.

GOMEZ, EDDIE.
Tabo Tabo ... Letra y música de
Eddie Gomez. © Peer International Corp., New York;
1Jul47; EP15622.

GOMEZ, VICENTE.
The Princess; Peruvian Inca dance
[by] Vicente Gomez. © Mills
Music, inc., New York; 8Dec47;
EP19908. For Spanish guitar
solo.

Valse Lento; [by] Vicente Gomez.
© Mills Music, inc., New York;
8Dec47; EP19907. For Spanish
guitar solo.

273

GÓMEZ BARRERA, CARLOS.
Sólo con Mi Dolor ... música y
letra de Carlos Gómez Barrera.
© Hnos. Marquez, S. de R. L.
Editores, Mexico; 13Jan45;
EF6180.

GONZALEZ, AARON, 1908-
Two Shadows in the Moonlight;
music by Aaron Gonzales, lyric
by Fred Stryker, Spanish version by Aaron Gonzalez. ©
Royal Music Publisher, Hollywood, Calif.; 10Jul47; EP18314.

GONZALEZ, LEOPOLDO.
Evocación ... letra y música de
Leopoldo Gonzalez. © Peer
International Corp., New York;
11Sep47; EP17266.

Hembra Malai (Wicked Woman) ...
English words by Joe Davis,
Spanish words and music by
Leopoldo Gonzalez. © Carib-
bean Music Co., New York;
20Oct47; EP18609.

GONZALEZ ALLUE, JORGE.
Por Eso Tengo Miedo ... Letra y
música de Jorge Gonzalez Allue.
© Peer International Corp.,
New York; 6Jun47; EP5740.

GOODHART, AL.
Those Things Money Can't Buy;
lyric by Ruth Poll, music by
Al Goodhart. © Robbins Music
Corp., New York; 19Aug47;
EP18546.

Who Were You Kissing (when you
kissed me last night?) ...
Words and music by Kay Twomey
and Al Goodhart, arr. by Johnny
Warrington. © Bourne, inc.,
New York; 27Oct47; on arrangement; EP18300. Piano-conductor
score (orchestra, with words)
and parts.

Who Were You Kissing (when you
kissed me last night)? Words
and music by Kay Twomey and Al
Goodhart. © Bourne, inc., New
York; 3Nov47; EP18390.

GOODMAN, BENNY.
Tattletale; by Benny Goodman and
Tommy Todd ... piano solo.
© Regent Music Corp., New York;
9Aug47; EP17016.

GORDON, CARL.
How to Play the Violin; the visual
method, by Carl Gordon. © N.
Stalker, Burbank, Calif.; bk.1,
28Jun47; EP15991.

GORDON, HAMILTON S., INC., comp.
Ten of the Best World Famous Piano
Solos; [comp. by Hamilton S. Gor-
don, inc., principally arr. by
Hugo Frey] © Hamilton S. Gordon,
inc., New York; 18Dec47; EP20178.

Ten of the Best World Famous Songs;
[comp. by Hamilton S. Gordon, inc.]
© Hamilton S. Gordon, inc., New
York; 18Dec47; EP20179.

GORDON, HUGH, pseud. See
Norden, Hugo.

GORDON, JAY.
Could It Be? Words and music by
Jay Gordon. © Nordyke Publish-
ing Co., Los Angeles; 29Jul47;
EP17559.

GORDON, JAY H
I Hung a Star in My Window; words
and music by Jay H. Gordon.
[c1945] © Nordyke Publishing
Co., Los Angeles; 16Sep47;
EP17914.

GORNEY, JAY.
Mailu. See his Ziegfeld Follies of 1931

[Ziegfeld Follies of 1931]
Mailu; words by E. Y. Harburg,
music by Jay Gorney and Hugo
Riesenfeld, [from] Ziegfeld
Follies. © Miller Music Corp.,
(formerly Miller Music, inc.),
New York; 6Jul31; EP19908.

[GORNI, FRANCESCO] 1885-
I Ballabili Campagnoli; di Gallo
[pseud.] © Carisch, s. a., Milan;
6Jul47; EF6191. Piano-conductor
score (orchestra) and parts.

GORNSTON, DAVID.
David Gornston's Clarinet Velocity;
a modern school of speed studies,
ed. by Harry Huffnagle. ©
Edwin H. Morris & Co., inc.,
New York; 12Aug47; EP16408.

David Gornston's Saxophone
Velocity; a modern school of
speed studies, ed. by Harry
Huffnagle. © Edwin H. Morris
& Co., inc., New York; 26Sep47;
EP17695.

GOSLOWSKY, GEORGE.
A Date to Be with You; words and
music by George Goslowsky. ©
Nordyke Publishing Co., Los
Angeles; 11Jun47; EP15857.

GOSS, HOWARD ARCHIBALD, 1883-   comp.
Pentecostal Praises; a complete
church hymnal, comp. by ... H. A.
Goss [and] ... V. H. Kidson.
Shape notes only. Houston, Tex.,
Herald Pub. House. © V. E.
Kidson, Houston, Tex.; 24Jul47;
EP17665.

GOSZ, ROMAN.
Dakota Waltz; piano solo, arr. by
Joseph P. Elsnic. [c1946]
© Vitak-Elsnic Co., Chicago;
28Feb47; on arrangement;
EP15762.

Grandfather's Joy ... [For] concertina, arr. by Joseph P. Elsnic.
© Vitak-Elsnic Co., Chicago;
24Apr47; on arrangement; EP15764.

Lover's Waltz; [by] Romy Gosz,
[arr. by Joseph Paul Elsnic,
for] piano accordion. © Vitak-
Elsnic Co., Chicago; 30Apr47;
on arrangement; EP15763.

Lover's Waltz; by Romy Gosz ...
arrangement by Red McLeod.
© Vitak-Elsnic Co., Chicago;
6Jan47; on arrangement; EP15770.
Piano-conductor score (orchestra) and parts.

Musical Clock Polka; by Romy
Gosz ... arrangement by Red
McLeod. © Vitak-Elsnic Co.,
Chicago; 17Dec46; on arrange-
ment; EP15769. Piano-conduc-
tor score (orchestra) and parts.

GOSZ, ROMY. See
Gosz, Roman.

GOTTLER, ARCHIE.
I Hate to Lose You (I'm so used to
you now); lyric by Grant Clarke,
music by Archie Gottler, [arr. by
Marvin Fisher] © Fred Fisher
Music Co., inc., New York; 10Dec47;
on arrangement and change in
words; EP20461.

GOTTSCHALK, LOUIS MOREAU.
Pasquinade; by Louis Moreau
Gottschalk ... arr. ... by Erik
Leidzén. © Carl Fischer, inc.,
New York; 21Jul47; on arrange-
ment; EP15889. Condensed score
(band) and parts.

GOTTUSO, TONY.
I Wonder If You Care; words by
Lee Gould, music by Tony Gottuso.
© Bob Miller, inc., New York;
27Oct47; EP18631.

GOUDEY, MAURICE RUSSEL. See
Goudey, Russel.

GOUDEY, RUSSEL, 1907-
Christmas Comes Once a Year.
[Navidad] Words ... by John
Paris ... music [by] Russel
Goudey, Spanish lyric by Augusto
Coén. © Rich Music Publications,
New York; 24Dec47; EP20502.

GOULD, DANNY, 1921-
Running Arpeggios; a new approach in
developing the left hand style and
technique of the pianist, by Danny
Gould. © Danny Gould, Brooklyn;
15Dec47; EP20102.

GOULD, MORTON.
American Salute; based on "When
Johnny Comes Marching Home," by
Morton Gould. Full orchestral
score. © Mills Music, inc.,
New York; 18Sep47; on full
orchestral score; EP18911.
Miniature score.

(American Symphonette no.2)
Pavanne, from American Symphonette no.2, by Morton Gould, ed.
and arr. by Laurence Taylor.
© Mills Music, inc., New York;
28Jul47; on arrangement;
EP16196. Score (flute, oboe,
clarinet, horn and bassoon) and
parts.

(Americana) Hillbilly, from
Americana; by Morton Gould, arr.
... by David Bennett. © Carl
Fischer, inc., New York;
2Jul47; on arrangement; EP15422.
Condensed score (band) and
parts.

(Americana) Indian Nocturne, from
Americana; mood sketches [com-
posed and arr.] for symphonic
orchestra by Morton Gould. ©
Carl Fischer, inc., New York;
23Oct47; on arrangement;
EP18589. Piano-conductor score
and parts.

Deep River; spiritual, a Morton
Gould string choir arrangement.
© Mills Music, inc., New York;
12Sep47; on arrangement;
EP18249. Score (celeste, harp
and string orchestra) and parts.

Londonderry Air; a Morton Gould
string choir arrangement. ©
Mills Music, inc., New York;
12Sep47; on arrangement;
EP18250. Score (celeste, harp
and string orchestra) and parts.

Pavanne. See his American Symphonette
no. 2.

Revival; a fantasy on six spirituals ... by Morton Gould. ©
Mills Music, inc., New York;
12Sep47; on adaptation & arrangement; EP18251. Condensed score
(orchestra) and parts.

Rumbolero; by Morton Gould. ©
Carl Fischer, inc., New York;
29Oct47; EP18469. Condensed
score (band) and parts.

GOULDING, EDMUND.
So That You May Know; lyric by
George Jessel, music by Edmund
Goulding. © Robbins Music
Corp., New York; 5Dec47;
EP20010.

GOUNOD, CHARLES FRANÇOIS, 1818-1893.
Ave Maria; meditation on the 1st
prelude of J. S. Bach, [by]
Charles Gounod, arr. by Eric
Hauser. [c1928] © Carl Fischer,
inc., New York; 26Jul37; on arrangement; EP18305. Score (horn
and piano) and part.

Father in heaven. Ave Maria.
English text by Lorraine Noel
Finlay, [music by] Bach-Gounod,
arranged by Wallingford Riegger.
SATB accompani. © Harold
Flammer, inc., New York; on
arrangement; 4Nov46; EP11165.

(Faust) Valentine's Farewell,
from "Faust," by Charles Gounod.
Four-part chorus for boy's glee
club arr. by Robert W. Gibb,
English version by Mary B. Austin.
© Boston Music Co., Boston;
15Dec47; on arrangement & English
text; EP20401.

GOUNOD, CHARLES FRANCOIS. Cont'd.
Holy Morn; for four-part chorus of
mixed voices with piano acc.
Based on the Bach-Gounod "Ave
Maria", text and arrangement by
Margaret Bronson. © R. L. Hunt-
zinger, inc., Cincinnati;
17Nov47; on text & arrangement;
EP19220.

Judex [and Hosanna in Excelsis] ..
from "Mors et Vita" [by] Gounod,
arr. by Frank Wright. London,
Boosey & Hawkes. (Boosey &
Hawkes brass
band journal, no.832) © Hawkes &
Son (London) ltd., London; 18Jul47;
on arrangement; EF5799. Piano-conductor score (band) and parts.

Sanctus; from "Messe Solennelle"
(St. Cecilia) ... by Charles
Gounod, arr. for 3 choirs by
C. Albert Scholin. [St. Louis,
Hunleth Music Co.] © G. Albert
Scholin, St. Louis; 15Jul47; on
arrangement; EP15686.

Valentine's farewell. See his Faust.

GOW, DAVID GODFREY, 1924-
Country Pictures; seven easy pieces
for piano, by David Gow. ©
Augener, ltd., London; 24Nov47;
EF7213.

GOWER, WILLIAM.
Rubank Advanced Method for French
Horn ... by Wm. Gower ... and
H. Voxman. © Rubank, inc.,
Chicago; 9Jul47; EP15516.

GRADSTEIN, ALFRED, 1904-
Hommage à Chopin; douze études
pour piano (nos. 2 à 13), [by]
Alfred Gradstein. Paris, Rouart,
Lerolle & Cie. © Salabert, inc.,
New York; 31Mar47; EF5981.

GRAFF, MEL.
Wilda; words and music by Mel
Graff. © Edwin H. Morris & Co.,
inc., New York; 21Nov47;
EP19797.

GRAHAM, BILLY.
In Dear Old Glasgow Toon; (Hearts
of Glasgow) Words by John F.
Stevenson, music by Billy
Graham. © Chappell & Co., ltd.,
London; 20Aug47; EF6383.

GRAHAM, IRVIN, pseud. See
Abraham, Irvin.

GRAHAM, JOHNNY.
After What You Said Last Night;
words and music by Johnny
Graham. © Kanes Music Publish-
ers, New York; 30Jul47;
EP16175.

GRAHAM, MARTIN C
Piano Queen (from Port of Spain);
words and music by Martin C.
Graham. © Nordyke Publishing
Co., Los Angeles; 3Jan46; EP17412.

GRANADOS, ENRIQUE. See
Granados y Campina, Enrique.

GRANADOS Y CAMPINA, ENRIQUE, 1867-
1916.
Danza Española No. 6; guitar solo,
[by] E. Granados, arr. as played
by Harry Volpe. c1939. © Albert
Rocky Co., New York; 10Jan40; on
arrangement; EP20189.

Playera ... [by] Enrique Granados,
arr. by Amedeo De Filippi. ©
Broadcast Music, inc., New York;
23Sep47; on arrangement; EP18052.
Piano-conductor score (orchestra
and parts.

GRANATO, LAWRENCE.
When I Get Back to Dayton (Will
You Be Waitin')? Words and music
by Lawry Granato, jr. © Lawrence
Granato & Son, Dayton, Ohio;
20Aug47; EP17087.

GRAND, ROBERT LOUIS LE. See
Le Grand, Robert Louis.

GRANDJANY, MARCEL.
Harp Album; [by] Marcel Grandjany.
(Op.27] © M. Baron Co., New
York; 21Nov47; EP19040.

Two Duets; for harps, [by] Marcel
Grandjany. Op. 26. © M. Baron
Co., New York; v. 1-2, 14Nov47;
EP20259-20260. Contents.- 1.
Sally and Dinny Duet.- 2. Elea-
nor and Marcia Duet.

GRANGER, MARTIN, pseud. See
Barriteau, Carl Aldric Stanley.

GRANT, FREDDY.
Comin' In on the C. P. R.; words and
music by Freddy Grant. © Gordon
V. Thompson, ltd., Toronto;
11Dec47; EP7275.

GRANT, JOAQUIN, 1880-
Calle de Alcalá ... letra de F.
Maenza [and] L. Grajales,
música de Joaquín Grant.
© (Ediciones Espagnoles) Julio
Garzon, Paris; 17Apr47; EF6486.

Sérénade à Ma Belle. See his Visions
Iberiques.

Tirolliro ... paroles de Chamfleury
[pseud.] et Liogar [pseud.],
musique et arrangement de Joaquin Grant. © (Editions Espagnoles) Julio Garzon, Paris;
17Apr47; on arrangement; EP6515.
French and Portuguese words.

(Visions Iberiques) Sérénade à Ma
Belle, du film: "Visions Iberiques";
paroles françaises de Chamfleury
[pseud.] & Liogar [pseud.], musique
de J. Grant. © Éditions espagnoles
Julio Garzon, Paris; 100ct47;
EF7336.

GRANT, JOAQUIN, arr.
L'Hirondelle. (La Golondrine)
Paroles de R. Chamfleury [pseud.
and] Liogar [pseud.], arrangement de J. Grant. © (Editions
Espagnoles) Julio Garzon, Paris;
17Apr47; on arrangement; EF6487.

GRANT, LEONARD G LE. See
LeGrant, Leonard G

GRANT, LORD INVADER. See
Grant, Rupert.

GRANT, RUPERT.
Found Your Plantain in a Mortar
... Words and music by Rupert
Grant (Lord Invader) © Peer
International Corp., New York;
23Sep47; EP7851.

GRANT-SCHAEFER, G A
Good Morning! Unison chorus,
poem by Theodosia Paynter.
© The Raymond A. Hoffman Co.,
Chicago; 12Oct35; EP15576.

Officer Buzz Advises; unison cho-
rus, poem by Theodosia Paynter.
© The Raymond A. Hoffman Co.,
Chicago; 12Oct35; EP15569.

Paganini Suite ... By G. A. Grant-
Schaefer, arr. by B. F. Stuber.
[c1941] © The Raymond A. Hoffman Co., Chicago; 25Jun44;
EP15572. Parts: orchestra.

GRANVILLE, NORMAN.
Aubade ... by Norman Granville.
© Volkwein Brothers, inc.,
Pittsburgh; 9Sep47; EP16699.
Score (violin and piano) and
part.

GRASSI, ANDRÉ, 1911-
La Marie; paroles et musique de
André Grassi. © Société
d'Éditions Musicales Internationales (S.E.M.I.), Paris;
11Apr47; EF5943.

GRASSI, ANDRE JOSEPH, 1911-
Nuit sans Amour; paroles de Louis
Poterat, musique de André
Grassi. © Les Editions Metro-
politaines, Paris; 30Sep46;
EF5856.

GRAVES, RICHARD.
Pamela Mary's Piano Album; ten
little pieces for young pianists,
by Richard Graves. © Alfred
Lengnick & Co., ltd., London;
3Jun47; EF5676.

GRAY, CLEDA. See
Underwood, Cleda Gray.

GRAY, THOMAS JAMES, 1893-
How Long Has It Been? Words and
music by Thomas J. Gray, sr.,
[arr. by Howard Bernard Weeks]
© Thomas J. Gray, sr., Milwaukee;
21Nov47; EP19068.

It's Love; words and music by
Thomas J. Gray, Sr. [arr. by
Howard Bernard Weeks] © Thomas
J. Gray, Sr., Milwaukee; 21Nov47;
EP19045.

GRAYSON, BOB.
I Fell in Love Last Night; words
and music by Bob Grayson.
© Nordyke Publishing Co., Los
Angeles; 12Aug47; EP19512.

GREAVES, RALPH.
A Psalm of Thanksgiving; "Whoso
dwelleth"; set for unaccompanied
mixed choir by Ralph Greaves.
[Words from Psalm XCI] ©
Oxford University Press, London;
14Aug47; EF6663.

GRECHANINOV, ALEKSANDR TIKHONOVICH,
1864-
Chanson Militaire. (Military
Song) For piano, by A. Gretchan-
inoff. © J. Fischer & Bro.,
New York; 17Jun47; EP6482.

Credo. For chorus of mixed voices
and solo voice (alto or baritone) [by] A. Gretchaninoff,
arrangement and Latin adaptation by Valmond H. Cyr. © The
Boston Music Co., Boston;
20Oct47; on arrangement & Latin
adaptation; EP18533. Latin and
English words.

Hail, O Virgin; T.T.B.B. a cappella [by] A. Gretchaninoff,
[arr. by A. Gretchaninoff]
© C. C. Birchard & Co., Boston;
7Oct47; on arrangement;
EP18363.

GREEN, CALVIN EDW.
Boogie Man; [words by] Mattie Lou
Anderson, [music by] Calvin Edw.
Green [and] George A. Gibbs, jr.
© Kelly Music Publications,
Franklin, Pa.; 15Oct47; EP17690.

GREEN, HAROLD, 1915-
I've Waited for Years (for this
moment); words and music by
Harold Green. © Peerless Music
Co., New York; 5Sep47; EP16628.

GREEN, JOHNNY.
Body and Soul; featured in ...
"Body and Soul" ... words by
Edward Heyman, Robert Sour and
Frank Eyton, music by Johnny
Green, a Jerry Sears arrange-
ment. © Harms, inc., New York;
10Oct47; on orchestration;
EP17752. Piano-conductor score
(orchestra, with words) and parts.

Body and Soul; for xylophone or
marimba with piano acc. by
Johnny Green, arr. by F. Henri
Klickmann. © Harms, inc.,
New York; 11Aug47; on arrange-
ment; EP17205. Score and part.

Body and Soul. See his Three's a Crowd.

(Cynthia) Melody of Spring; lyric
by Ralph Freed, music by Josef
Strauss, adapted by Johnny
Green ... [from] Cynthia. ©
Robbins Music Corp., New York;
16Sep47; EP17737.

Melody of Spring. See his Cynthia.

GREEN, JOHNNY. Cont'd.
'Round, an' 'Round, an' 'Round. See his
Something in the Wind.
Something in the Wind. [from] the
... picture "Something in the
Wind". lyric by Leo Robin, music
by Johnny Green. New York,
Miller Music Corp., © Universal
Music Corp., New York; 23May47;
EP15044.
(Something in the Wind) The Turn-
table Song; ('Round, an' 'Round,
an' 'Round) [from] the ...
picture "Something in the Wind,"
lyric by Leo Robin, music by
Johnny Green. Music Corp. © Universal Music
Corp. © Universal Music
Corp., New York; 23May47;
EP15043.
(Three's a Crowd) Body and Soul.
"Todo Me Ser." From the musical
comedy "Three's a Crowd".
Spanish text by Johnnie Camacho,
English text by Edward Heyman,
Robert Sour and Frank Eyton,
music by Johnny Green. © Harms,
inc., New York; 22Oct47; on
Spanish text; EP18481.
The Turntable Song. See his Something
in the Wind.
GREEN, PHIL, 1911-
Sleepy San Benito; words and
music by Phil Green. ©
Lawrence Wright Music Co., ltd.,
London; 28Aug47; EF6321.
GREEN, SANFORD.
Saddle in the Sky; words by Harry
Ross, music by Sanford Green. ©
Mutual Music Society, inc.,
New York; 30Oct47; EP18659.
GREENE, JOE.
"Bluejay"; words and music by
Rex Stewart, Joya Sherrill
[and] Joe Greene, [piano arr.
by Adrien Harris] © Republic
Music Corp., New York; 28Jul47;
EP16523.
GREENE, WALTER.
(Jack and Joy in Yonderland)
Songs for Young America, from
Jack and Joy in Yonderland ...
songs by Walter Greene, [words
by] Dave Fleischer and [Henry
Williams] New York, Sole sell-
ing agents: Broadcast Music. ©
Music for Young America Co.,
New York; 30May47; EP18212.
Songs for Young America. See his Jack
and Joy in Yonderland.
GREENFIELD, ALFRED M
Here, O My Lord; for S.A.T.B. - a
cappella. [Words adapted from]
Horatius Bonar, [music by] Al-
fred M. Greenfield. © Carl
Fischer, inc., New York; 17Jul47;
EP15871.
GREENHALGH, MADELINE
Homeland; words and music by Made-
line Greenhalgh. © Nordyke Pub-
lishing Co., Los Angeles; 9Aug47;
EP19789.
GREENWOOD, NORMAN.
What a Mess We've Made; words and
music by Norman Greenwood. ©
Nordyke Publishing Co., Los
Angeles; 24Jul47; EP17469.
GREER, JAMES B   1922-
Everybody's Baby; words and music
by James B. Greer. © Clock
Publishing Co., inc., Santa
Monica, Calif.; 22Nov47;
EP20421. Melody and chord symbols,
with words.
Save It for Me; lyric and music by
James B. Greer. © Clock Publish-
ing Co., inc., Santa Monica,
Calif.; 22Nov47; EP20422. Melody
and chord symbols, with words.
Why Couldn't I Have You? By James
B. Greer. © Clock Publishing
Co., inc., Santa Monica, Calif.;
22Nov47; EP20420. Melody and
chord symbols, with words.

GREGORY, BOBBY, 1900-
Tonight (when I say goodbye); .
words and music by Thomas
Colangelo [and] Bobby Gregory.
© American Music Publishing Co.,
New York; 16Jun47; EP15502.
GREGORY, VANCE.
Since You've Gone; words and music
by Vance Gregory. © Nordyke
Publishing Co., Los Angeles;
2Dec47; EP17395.
GRENET, ELISEO. See
Grenet Sánchez, Eliseo.
GRENET SÁNCHEZ, ELISEO, 1893-
Librito ... letra y música por
Eliseo Grenet. Havana, Grenet
Music Corp. © Eliseo Grenet
Sánchez, Habana; 8May47; EF6394.
GRETCHANINOFF, A. See
Grechaninov, Aleksandr Tikhonovich.
GREW, GERRY.
You're So Dear; words and music
by Gerry Grew. © Nordyke Pub-
lishing co., Los Angeles;
15Aug47; EP20372.
GRIBBS, CURLY, 1920-
I Just Fell out of Love with You;
words & music by Denver Darling,
Rosalie Allen [and] Curly Gribbs.
© N. F. D. Music Pub. Co., inc.,
New York; 24Jun47; EP17065.
GRIEG, EDVARD HAGERUP, 1843-1907.
Anitra's Dance ... [by] Grieg,
arr. as played by Harry Volpe.
c1939. © Albert Rocky Co.,
New York; 10Jun40; on arrangement;
EP20195. For 2 guitars.
Anitra's Dance. See his Peer Gynt.
The Best Known Music of Grieg;
[arr. by Hugo Frey] © Hamilton
S. Gordon, inc., New York;
12Nov47; on arrangement; EP18676.
For piano solo.
(Concerto, piano) Concerto in A
minor, Op.16. Themes from 1st
movement; [by] Edvard Grieg,
arr. by Alfred d'Auberge. ©
Accordion Music Publishing Co.,
New York; 11Aug47; on arrange-
ment; EP16973. For accordion
solo.
(Peer Gynt) Anitra's Dance, from
"Peer Gynt" suite [by] Edvard
Grieg, piano solo, a John W.
Schaum arrangement. © Belwin,
inc., New York; 20Nov47; on ar-
rangement; EP18801.
Peer Gynt Suite ... [By] Edvard
Grieg. Op.46. Arr. by Mayhew L.
Lake, arr. for modern bands with
new parts by H. R. Kent [pseud.]
© Carl Fischer, inc., New York;
21Aug47; on arrangement; EP16618.
Condensed score (band) and parts.
GRIFFO, GIOVANNI.
"Nun Si' Cchiù Chella"; versi di
Eduardo Nicolardi, musica di
Giovanni Griffo. Napoli,
Edizioni E.N. C.D. © Italian
Book Co., New York; 7Sep47;
EF6616.
GRIGGS, FRANK.
Toccatina; [by] Frank Griggs. ©
Joseph Williams, ltd., London;
10Oct47; EF6742. For piano solo.
GRILL, ANDREW.
Chatterbox Polka. © Vitak-Elsnic
Co., Chicago; 20Mar47; EP15768.
Piano-conductor score (orches-
tra) and parts.
Rainbow Polka; [for] concertina,
arr. by Joseph F. Elsnic. ©
Vitak-Elsnic Co., Chicago;
6Dec46; on arrangement;
EP15759.
[GRILL, KARL RUDOLF N   ] 1896-
Go! Wausau High; words by Sheldon
Disrud, music by X [pseud.]
© Senior High School, Wausau,
Wis.; 7Oct47; EP17788.

The School Pledge; words by Sharon
and Shirley Onstad, music by
K. R. N. Grill. © Senior High
School, Wausau, Wis.; 7Oct47;
EP17787.
GRIMSTVEDT, DORIS M
Here in My Heart; words and music
by Doris M. Grimstvedt. © Nor-
dyke Publishing Co., Los Angeles;
11Jun46; EP19624.
GRISWOLD, GEORGE LUTHER, 1904-
My Mansion in Glory; [by] G. L.
Griswold. © Geo. Luther Gris-
wold, White Plains, N. Y.;
19Aug47; on changes in harmony;
EP16319. Close score: SATB.
GROOVER, ELECTA ALMA. See
Geist, Electa Alma (Groover)
GROTHE, FRANZ.
Abendlied ... Musik: Franz Grothe,
Arrangement von Helmut Gardens
... Ein Tango-Märchen; Musik und
Arrangement von Josef Rixner.
© Edition Turicaphon, AG., Zü-
rich, Switzerland; 11Aug47; on
2 pieces; EF7035-7036. Piano-
conductor score (orchestra) and
parts.
GROVER, RALPH S
Crucifixus; [for] SATB accompa-
nied, [music by] Ralph S.
Grover. © Harold Flammer, inc.,
New York; 28Jul47; EP16246.
GRUBB, LEWIS W
A Prayer to Saint Catherine of
Sienna; (patroness of unmarried
women) chorus for women's
voices (S.S.A.A.) by Lewis W.
Grubb, [words anonymous] ©
Broadcast Music, inc., New
York; 22Sep47; EP17903.
GRUBBS, JAMES HERSCHEL, 1884-
Railway Mail; words & music by
James H. Grubbs. © James H.
Grubbs, Washington, D. C.;
18Aug47; EP16317.
[GRUBER, FRANZ X   ]
Silent Night; [by Franz Gruber]
arr. by Den Berry [and The
First Nowell; arr. by Sid
Wright] © Cosmo Music Co.,
(London) ltd., London; 21Oct46;
on arrangement; EF5745, 5700.
Piano-conductor score (orches-
tra, with words) and parts.
Silent Night, Holy Night; [by] F.
X. Gruber, arr. by P. Ballestore.
(In Ballestore, Pietro, comp. So.
Ecsy. p.8) © Edward B. Marks
Music Corp., New York; 9Dec47;
on arrangement; EP19585. For
piano solo.
GRUMMONS, RUTH NORINE, 1906-
He's Coming; and The Lord Is My
Shepherd; composed by ... Nor-
ine Grummons, [words by Emma
Lindeman] © Ruth Norine Grum-
mons, Fort Wayne; 15Oct47;
EP18117.
I'm So Glad That Jesus Found Me;
[words by Norine Grummons] and
God's Time; [words by Loella
Hobson], composed by ... Norine
Grummons, Fort Wayne; 15Oct47;
EP18115. Close score: SATB.
Jesus, Come and Be My Lord; [by]
Norine Grummons, [words by]
Emma Lindeman. © Ruth Norine
Grummons, Fort Wayne; 15Oct47;
EP18116. Close score: SATB.
O Be Ready ... [by] Norine Grum-
mons, [words by] Loella Hobson.
© Loella M. Hobson, Fort Wayne;
20Oct47; EP18355. Close score:
SATB.
GRUNDMAN, CLARE E
Two Moods ... [by] Clare E. Grund-
man. New York; Boosey & Hawkes.
© Hawkes & Son (London) ltd.,
London; 24Oct47; EP18505. Score
(band) and parts.

GUARINO, GIAN MARIO, 1908-
Intimità ... parole di G. C.
Testoni, musica e arr. di G.
M. Guarino ... Strada del
Mio Quartiere ... parole di
L. L. Martelli, musica e
arr. di G. M. Guarino. ©
Odeon, s.a., Milan; 20May47;
EF3973. Piano-conductor
score (orchestra, with words),
and parts.

GUASTAVINO, CARLOS, 1912-
Proposito; [by] C. Guastavino.
© Ricordi Americana, s.a.e.c.,
Buenos Aires; 28Jul44; EF6979.
For voice and piano.

Pueblito, Mi Pueblo ... [by]
Carlos Guastavino, [words by
Francisco Silva] © Ricordi
Americana, s.a.e.c., Buenos
Aires; 5May42; EF6976. For 1
or 2 treble voices and piano.

Tierra Linda; [by] C. Guastavino,
. para piano. © Ricordi
Americana, s.a.e.c., Buenos
Aires; 30Jul42; EF6980.

GUBITOSI, EMILIA, 1887-
Notturno; [by] E. Gubitosi.
© G. Ricordi & Co., Milan;
10ott4; EF6079. Score: orchestra.

GUENTHER, FELIX, arr.
Kol Nidre; traditional melody arr.
for voice and piano or organ by
Felix Guenther. English adapt-
ation by Olga Paul. © Edward
B. Marks Music Corp., New York;
23Jul47; on English adaptation
and arrangement; EF15791.
Transliterated Hebrew and
English words.

GUENTHER, FELIX, 1886-   ed.
Dances by Great Masters; album for
piano, ed. and comp. by Felix
Guenther. © Edward B. Marks
Music Corp., New York; 10Jul47;
on arrangement of 3 pieces.
Partial contents.- Gavotte,
from "Iphigenie in Aulis," by
Chr. W. Gluck (© EF16983) -
Dance of the Blessed Spirits,
from "Orpheus and Eurydice,"
by Chr. W. Gluck (© EF16984) -
Congratulation Minuet, by L. van
Beethoven (© EF16985)

GUENTZEL, GUS.
Bas-Bleu ... [by] Gus Guentzel.
© C. L. Barnhouse Co., Oska-
loosa, Iowa; 17Sep47; EP18556.
Score (flute, oboe, clarinet,
horn and bassoon) and parts.

Festival Days; brass quartet (four
cornets or two cornets and two
trombones) [by] Gus Guentzel.
© C. L. Barnhouse Co., Oskaloosa, Iowa; 17Sep47; EP18557.
Score and parts.

Impromptu ...[by] Gus Guentzel.
© C. L. Barnhouse Co., Oskaloosa,
Iowa; 17Sep47; EP18558. Score
(2 cornets, horn and baritone)
and parts.

In the Meadow ... [by] Gus Guentzel. © C. L. Barnhouse Co.,
Oskaloosa, Iowa; 17Sep47;
EP18555. Score (flute, oboe,
clarinet, horn and bassoon)
and parts.

GUERIN, GRATTAN.
From This Day On. See his Gloria.

(Gloria) From This Day On, from
the musical show Gloria; by
Grattan Guerin. © Gay Rin Pub,
Co., Whittier, Calif.; 14Aug47;
EP18917. For voice and piano,
with chord symbols.

[GUGLIELMI, LOUIS] 1916-
Aye! Mama ... Paroles de Jacques
Plante, musique de Louiguy [pseud.]
© Éditions musicales Hortensia,
Paris; 14Dec46; EF7320.

Comme une Etoile. See his Trente et
Quarante.

La Danseuse Est Créole; paroles de
Jacques Plante, musique de Louiguy
[pseud.] © Éditions musicales
Hortensia, Paris; 31Dec46; EF7319.

(Trente et Quarante) Comme une
Étoile ... du film, Trente et
Quarante; paroles de J. Larue
[pseud.], musique de Louiguy
[pseud.] © Éditions Paul
Beuscher, Paris; 30Nov45; EF6461.

(Trente et Quarante) La Garme et
l'Amour; une chanson du film ...
Trente et Quarante ... Paroles de
J. Larue [pseud.], musique de
Louiguy [pseud.] © Éditions Paul
Beuscher, Paris; 30Nov45; EF6464.

La Vie en Rose ... Paroles de
Edith Piaf [pseud.], musique de
Louiguy [pseud.] c1946. ©
Arpège Édition Musicale, Paris;
2Jan47; EF6451. For voice and
piano, and voice part.

GUIDA, PEDRO.
"Rica Samba" ... paroles de Bertal
[pseud., and] Maubon, musique de
Pedro Guida & Raimundo Palau,
[and] "El Tamalero" ... paroles
de Chamfleury [pseud.], musique
de José Riestra, arr. de Pedro
Guida. © Éditions Eimef-Opera,
Paris; 14crl47; EF6318. Parts:
orchestra.

GUILDHALL SCHOOL OF MUSIC AND DRAMA,
LONDON.
Pianoforte Examinations. London,
J. Williams. © The Corporation
of the City of London, London;
v. 1, 23Jul47. Contents.- [1]
Introductory examination,
composed by R. Barclay Wilson
(© EF5778)-

GUILLON, JEAN, 1898-
A la Porte du Square; paroles de
Berjos [pseud.], musique de
Jean Guillon. © Éditions
Musicales Claribela, Orléans
(Loiret) France; 31Mar47;
EF5957. Piano-conductor score
(orchestra, with words) and
parts on p. [4]

La Valse Est une Câline; paroles
de Burjos [pseud.], musique de
Jean Guillon. © Éditions
Musicales Claribela, Orléans
(Loiret), France; 31Mar47;
EF5958. Piano-conductor score
(orchestra, with words) and
parts on p. [4]

GUILLORY, ELLIS J
That's Why I'm Dreaming of You;
words and music by Ellis J.
Guillory. © Nordyke Publishing
Co., Los Angeles; 14Jun47;
EP17482.

GUINOPOULOS, MICHEL, 1920-
Cinq Épilogues ... et Deux Danses
alla Grecque ... Pour piano [by]
Michel Guinopoulos. © Choudens,
Editeur, Paris; 22Jul47; EF6567.

GUION, DAVID W
Pastoral; for the piano by David
Guion. © G. Schirmer, inc.,
New York; 20Aug47; EP18031.

GUIZAR, TITO.
Fiesta in Santa Fé. (Fiesta de
Santa Fé) Words and music by
Marjorie Harper [and] Tito
Guizar. © Rytvoc, inc., New York;
10Jul47; EP15600.

GUNSALLUS, JULIA.
It's Leant to Be; words and music
by Julia Gunsallus. © Nordyke
Publishing Co., Los Angeles;
12Apr47; EP16757.

GUPTILL, ARTHUR LEIGHTON, 1920-
Three Be-Bop Solos for piano; by
Leighton Guptill. © Arthur
Leighton Guptill, Jr., New York;
24Jul47; EP16074.

GUPTILL, LEIGHTON. See
Guptill, Arthur Leighton.

GUTHRIE, CLARENCE ARLINGTON.
It's Wonderful to Live This Day;
by Clarence Arlington Guthrie.
© Clarence Arlington Guthrie,
New Kensington, Pa.; 27Oct47;
EP18493. For voice and piano.

Swimming in the Briny Deep; words
and music by Clarence Arlington
Guthrie. © Clarence Arlington
Guthrie, New Kensington, Pa.;
30Oct47; EP18230.

GUTHRIE, JACK.
Oklahoma's Calling; words and
music by Jack Guthrie. © Hill
and Range Songs, inc., Hollywood, Calif.; 15Dec47; EP20130.

Please, Oh Please; words and music
by Jack Guthrie. © Hill and
Range Songs, inc., Hollywood,
Calif.; 28Nov47; EP19139.

GUTIERREZ, BIENVENIDO J
"Hasta que Se Rompa el Coco" ...
Letra y música de Bienvenido J.
Gutierrez. © Peer Internation-
al Corp., New York; 6Jun47;
EF5734. Parts: orchestra.

GUZMÁN ARCE, JESÚS. See
Arce, Jesús Guzmán.

GYLDMARK, HUGO GODTFRED SKOVGAARD,
1899-
(Ave Maria) Praeludium af Kay
Rostgaard-Frøhne's Højrespil, Ave
Maria; Musik; Hugo Gyldmark. ©
Nyt Dansk Musikforlag, Copenhagen; 7Jul40; EF6589. Piano-
conductor score (string orchestra)
and parts; with words.

(Ave Maria) Praeludium af Kai
Rostgaard-Frøhnes Højrespil, Ave
Maria; Musik: Hugo Gyldmark. ©
Nyt Dansk Musikforlag, Copen-
hagen; 7Jul40; EF6590. For
voice and piano.

H

HABER, RHEA, 1916-
Sing, Little Gypsy, of Love; words
and music by Rhea Haber. Phila-
delphia, M. Swerdlow. © Rhea
Haber, Philadelphia; 5Oct47;
EP18940.

HABING, FLOYD F
All the Good Things Come from
Missouri; words by Ben E. Woody,
Jr., music by Floyd F. Habing.
© Dix-E-Ana Music Publishers,
Kingston, Tenn.; 18Aug47;
EP16530.

HACKFORTH, NORMAN.
Don't Give It Another Thought;
song, words and music by Norman
Hackforth. © Chappell & Co.,
ltd., London; 5Aug47; EF17007.

HADDEN, HAZEL HUNT, 1895-
Rest at Evening. He Is Waiting
There for Me. God Is, He Knows
and Cares. Words and music by
Hazel Hunt Hadden. © Hazel Hunt
Hadden, Oakland, Calif.; 15Feb47;
EP16974, 16976, 16975. Close
score: SATB.

HADDOX, CHET.
So Blue; words and music by Chet
Haddox. © Nordyke Publishing
Co., Los Angeles; 31Jul47;
EP19528.

HANDEL, GEORG FRIEDRICH, 1685-1759.
Airs de Ballet; [by] G. F. Händel
... [arr. by] Hermann Müller.
© Hug & Co., Music Publishers,
Zürich, Switzerland; 18Jul47;
on arrangement; EF6839. Score
(violin and piano) and part.

(Alcina) Overture to "Alcina";
for string orchestra by G. F.
Handel, arr. by Reginald
Jacques. © Oxford University
Press, London; 10Jul47; on
arrangement; EF6166.

HANDEL, GEORG FRIEDRICH. Cont'd.
(Almira) Rigaudon, from "Almira,"
[by] G. F. Handel, arr. by
Leopold J. Beer. © Theodore
Presser Co., Philadelphia;
5Sep47; on arrangement; EP17281.
For piano solo.
Aria (from the opera "Ptolemy") See his
Ptolemy.

Ask If Yon Damask Rose Be Sweet. See
his Susannah.

Concerto in A major for pianoforte
and orchestra [by] Handel-
Beecham, (the orchestra arr. for
a second piano) [by Beecham]
© Mills Music, inc., New York;
14Aug47; on arrangement; EP18349.
Score: 2 pianos.
Courante. See his Suite, harpsichord.

Glory to God. See his The Messiah.

Händel Simplified; ten favorite
compositions, arr. for piano
solo by Peter Randall,
[pseud.] © The Willis
Music Co., Cincinnati;
30Jul47; on arrangement;
EP16095.

The Hallelujah Chorus. See his The
Messiah.

Haste Thee, Nymph, from
"L'Allegro"; for eight-part
double chorus of mixed voices
with piano accompaniment ad lib
... [By] G. F. Handel, arr. by
Carlton Martin, ed. by John
Finley Williamson; text by John
Milton. © Carl Fischer, inc.,
New York; 15Aug47; on arrange-
ment; EP16409.

In Thee, O Lord, Have I Put My
Trust. (In Te Domine) For three-
part chorus of mixed voices [by]
Georg Friedrich Händel ... arr.
by Victoria Glaser, [words from]
Psalm 71:1,2. © E.C. Schirmer
Music Co., Boston; 29Sep47; on
arrangement; EP18138. English
words.

(Judas Maccabeus) See, the Conqu'ring Hero Comes ... from
Handel's "Judas Maccabeus";
freely arr. for unison or massed
singing by E. Markham Lee. ©
Banks & Son, York, Eng.; 22Oct47;
on arrangement; EP7152.

Marches; for five wind instruments
[arr. and ed. by Sydney Beck.
© Mercury Music Corp., New York;
80ct47; on arrangement and realization of basso continuo; EP17721.
Score (clarinet 1-2 (or oboe 1-2),
trumpet 1-2 and bassoon, (or bass
clarinet or baritone)) and parts.

Messiah; an oratorio [by] G. F.
Handel, ed. from the original
sources by J. M. Coopersmith. ©
Carl Fischer, inc., New York;
3Jul47; on prefatory material,
editing and compilation of alternative versions; LP15750. Piano-
vocal score.

(The Messiah) Glory to God, from
"The Messiah" (S.A.T.B., with
piano or organ acc.) [by] G. F.
Handel, arr. by Edward S. Breck.
© Carl Fischer, inc., New York;
24Sep47; on arrangement; EP18073.

(The Messiah) The Hallelujah
Chorus from Handel's The Messiah
simplified, [arr. by Walter L.
Rosemont, for] voice [and] organ
[or] piano. © Edwards Music
Co., New York; 6Nov47; on
simplified arrangement for piano
& organ; EP18671.

(The Messiah) Overture to "The
Messiah"; arr. for piano duet
by Cecil Arburn. © Augener, ltd.,
London; 3Nov47; on arrangement;
EF7212.

Minuet in G minor [by] G. F. Handel,
arr. by Keith Phillips [pseud.]
© J. Fischer & Bro., New York;
9Sep47; on arrangement; EP17713.
For piano solo.

The Musick for the Royal Fireworks; by George Frederic
Handel, arr. for pianoforte
by Granville Bantock. ©
William Paxton & Co., ltd.,
London; 2Dec46; on arrangement; EF5712.

Prelude and Fugue in F minor. See his
Suite, harpsichord, no.8.

(Ptolemy) Aria (from the opera
"Ptolemy") [by] George F. Handel,
arr. by Edwin Arthur Kraft. ©
Edward Schuberth & Co., inc.,
New York; 4Dec47; EP19257. For
organ solo; includes registration for Hammond organ.

Rigaudon. See his Almira.

See, the Conqu'ring Hero Comes. See his
Judas Maccabeus.

(Suite, harpsichord) Courante;
(Harpsichord Suite in D minor)
[by] G. F. Händel, arr. by
Gordon Phillips. © The Oxford
Univ. Press, London; 9Oct47;
on arrangement; EF6991. Score
(violin and piano) and part.

(Suite, harpsichord, no.8) Prelude
and Fugue in F minor, from the
eighth Suite for Harpsichord, by
George Frederick Handel, arr. by
Don Malin. © Carl Fischer, inc.,
New York; 12Dec47; on arrangement;
EP19991. Condensed score (band)
and parts.

(Susannah) Ask If Yon Damask Rose
Be Sweet; (from Susannah); for
four-part chorus of mixed
voices, [by] Georg Frederick
Händel ... arr. by B. Warren,
[words] of unknown authorship.
© E. C. Schirmer Music Co.,
Boston; 29Sep47; on arrangement;
EP18141.

Thanks Be to Thee; [by] Handel,
[arr. by] O.C.C., (English version by O.C.C.) © Neil A. Kjos
Music Co., Chicago; 30Jul47;
on arrangement & English words;
EF 17976. Score: unison chorus
and piano or organ.

The Water Musick; of George
Frederick Handel, arr. for
pianoforte by Granville
Bantock. © William Paxton &
Co., ltd., London; 2Dec46;
on arrangement; EF5711.

HAESELER, WILLIAM, 1901-
Be Strong and of a Good Courage ...
by William Haeseler, jr. ©
William Haeseler, jr., North Ton-
awanda, N. Y.; 15Oct47; EP16626.
Close score: S.ATB.

HAHN, REYNALDO, 1874-1947.
O Holy Saviour ... words by Elsie
Duncan Yale, music by Reynaldo
Hahn. © The John Church Co.,
Philadelphia; 2Dec47; on words;
EP19253.

(Quartet, piano & strings, no. 3)
Troisième quatuor en sol majeur
... [by] Reynaldo Hahn. ©
Heugel & Cie., Paris; 22Oct46;
EF6438. Score and parts.

HAIGHT, JEANNE.
My Day Dreams; words and music by
Jeanne Haight. © Nordyke Publishing Co., Los Angeles;
25Jul46; EP19680.

HAJOS, JOE, 1907-
A Part Vous ... Paroles de Jean
Boyer, musique de Joë Hajos.
© Éditions Roger Bernstein,
Paris; 15Dec46; EF5896.

Eperdument. See his L'Éventail.

(L'Eventail) Eperdument ... du
film."L'Eventail"; paroles de
Jacques Larue [pseud.], musique
de Joe Hajos. © Arpège Éditions
Musicales, Paris; 13Mar47;
EF6609. For voice and piano,
and voice part.

HALAMA, FRANK JEROME, 1903-
May-be Next Year; words and music
by Frank J. Halama. © Frank J.
Halama Publications, Chicago;
23Jul47; EP15689.

HALBARDIER, BARBARA HENSLEY, 1923-
Pull You Down a Moonbeam; by
Barbara Hensley Halbardier. ©
Uhl & Ware, San Antonio; 10Jul47;
EP15719. For voice and piano,
with chord symbols.

HALDEMAN, OAKLEY, 1909-
Here Comes Santa Claus (right
down Santa Claus Lane) words
and music by Oakley Haldeman.
© Gene Autry Music Publishing,
inc., Hollywood, Calif.;
20Nov47; EP19051.

Pretty Mary (that sure is a
pretty dress you're a-wearin')
[by] Jim MacDonald, Bob Mitchell, Gene Autry [and] Oakley
Haldeman. © Gene Autry Music
Publishing, inc., Hollywood,
Calif.; 12Nov47; EP18044. For
voice and piano, with chord
symbols.

[HALDEMAN, OAKLEY] 1911-   comp.
Tex Williams and His Western
Caravan Song Folio, [by Tex
Williams and others] © Golden
West Melodies, inc., Hollywood,
Calif.; 28Apr47; EP16150. For
voice and piano with chord
symbols.

HALINÄS, HILDING.
Två Sånger; till text av Gunnar
Ekelöf, [by] Hilding Halinäs.
© Föreningen svenska tonsättare,
Stockholm; 1Jan45; EF7116.

HALL, CHARLOTTE GOOLD.
The First Love Song; words and
music by Charlotte Goold Hall.
© Nordyke Publishing Co., Los
Angeles; 14Jun47; EP17546.

HALL, CLARENCE L.
Gloria; mixed chorus ... by Robert
Hall. © Broadcast Music, inc.,
New York; 1Jul47; EP18200.

HALL, DAVID.
All My Dreams; words by Audrey
Sylvester, music by David Hall.
© Nordyke Publishing Co., Los
Angeles; 31Jul47; EP17919.

And, Now I'm Lonely; words by
Ardith Fischer, music by David
Hall. © Nordyke Publishing Co.,
Los Angeles; 13Jul47; EP17918.

Call Me What You Will; words by
T. Harrison, music by David
Hall. © Nordyke Publishing
Co., Los Angeles; 12Aug47;
EP17592.

Changeable as the Weather; words
by Daisy Major Pearman, music by
David Hall. © Nordyke Publishing
Co., Los Angeles; 31Jul47;
EP19723.

A Christmas Souvenir; words by Al-
fred Perez, music by David Hall.
© Nordyke Publishing Co., Los
Angeles; 31Jul47; EP19722.

Don't You Care; words by Helen La
Raviere, music by David Hall.
© Nordyke Publishing Co., Los
Angeles; 31Jul47; EP19732.

Dreaming of You; words by William
V. Justice, music by David Hall.
© Nordyke Publishing Co., Los
Angeles; 12Aug47; EP17589.

HALL, DAVID. Cont'd.
The First Robin of Spring; words
by Helen McCutcheon, music by
David Hall. © Nordyke Publish-
ing Co., Los Angeles; 31Jul47;
EP19506.

Freckles; words by Johnnie Lansin
[pseud.], music by David Hall.
© Nordyke Publishing co., Los
Angeles; 21Aug47; EP20361.

Goodbye to Love; words by Peggy
Matthews, music by David Hall.
© Nordyke Publishing Co., Los
Angeles; 31Jul47; EP19511.

Goodnight, My Dream, Goodnight;
words by Louis Mazzei, music by
David Hall. © Nordyke Publishing co., Los Angeles; 21Aug47;
EP20368.

A Harvest of Love; words by Harry
J. Brooks, music by David Hall.
© Nordyke Publishing Co., Los
Angeles; 11Aug47; EP19486.

Hello; words by Alfred Perez,
music by David Hall. © Nordyke Publishing Co., Los Angeles; 12Aug47; EP17522.

How Long? Words by Richard Shaw,
music by David Hall. © Nordyke Publishing Co., Los Angeles; 12Aug47; EP17523.

I Promised the Moon; words by
Harry C. Fox, music by David
Hall. © Nordyke Publishing
Co., Los Angeles; 31Jul47;
EP19522.

I'm Alone; words by E. L. Bula,
music by David Hall. © Nordyke
Publishing Co., Los Angeles;
31Jul47; EP19694.

I've Gathered All Your Tears;
words by Ershal G. Foster, music
by David Hall. © Nordyke Publishing Co., Los Angeles;
31Jul47; EP19497.

Keep a Little Place in Your Heart
for Dreams; words by Tressa M.
Buckles, music by David Hall.
© Nordyke Publishing Co., Los
Angeles; 22Jul47; EP19557.

Last Night; words by E. J. Kinzig,
music by David Hall. © Nordyke
Publishing Co., Los Angeles;
29Aug47; EP19542.

Lazy May; words by Cora Taylor,
music by David Hall. © Nordyke
Publishing Co., Los Angeles;
4Sep47; EP19543.

Lonesome Blues; words by Jennie
Liles, music by David Hall. ©
Nordyke Publishing Co., Los
Angeles; 3Sep47; EP19545.

Love Is Like a Theme Song; words
by Josiah C. Sharp, music by
David Hall. © Nordyke Publishing Co., Los Angeles; 21Aug47;
EP19549.

Love Mood; words by Savannah
Downie, music by David Hall.
© Nordyke Publishing Co., Los
Angeles; 12Sep47; EP19339.

Magic of October; words by Made-
leine Pezda, music by David Hall.
© Nordyke Publishing Co., Los
Angeles; 31Jul47; EP19734.

La Margareta; words by Martha
Padon Parrish, music by David
Hall. © Nordyke Publishing
Co., Los Angeles; 2Sep47;
EP19540.

Maybe I'm Only Dreaming; words
by Jarvis Marvin, music by
David Hall. © Nordyke Publishing Co., Los Angeles; 31Jul47;
EP17478.

Memories of You; words by Julia
Schultz, music by David Hall.
© Nordyke Publishing Co., Los
Angeles; 12Sep47; EP19359.

Moon Madness; words by Sharon Mc-
Coy [pseud.], music by David
Hall. © Nordyke Publishing Co.,
Los Angeles; 11Aug47; EP19703.

My Danny; words by Tommy Thomp-
son, music by David Hall.
© Nordyke Publishing Co., Los
Angeles; 22Aug47; EP19682.

My Darling, I Miss You Tonight;
words by Ruby H. McMillan,
music by David Hall. © Nordyke
Publishing Co., Los Angeles;
2Sep47; EP19667.

My Dream of Dreams; words by Bill
Kelley, music by David Hall.
© Nordyke Publishing Co., Los
Angeles; 2Sep47; EP19677.

My Heart's on a Strike; words by
Helen Bishop, music by David
Hall. © Nordyke Publishing
Co., Los Angeles; 4Sep47;
EP19364.

My Love; words by Ernest Jenkins,
music by David Hall. © Nordyke
Publishing Co., Los Angeles;
12Aug47; EP19674.

My Love for You; words by Daisy
Coleman, music by David Hall.
© Nordyke Publishing Co., Los
Angeles; 11Aug47; EP17498.

My Luck Has Changed; words by
Ann Freehling, music by David
Hall. © Nordyke Publishing Co.,
Los Angeles; 4Sep47; EP19365.

My Old Sweet Story; words by
Mary M. Parker, music by
David Hall. © Nordyke Publish-
ing Co., Los Angeles; 2Sep47;
EP19363.

Never Before; words by Frances R.
Ward, music by David Hall. ©
Nordyke Publishing Co., Los
Angeles; 12Aug47; EP19429.

No Romance for Him; words by
Andy Anderson, music by David
Hall. © Nordyke Publishing
Co., Los Angeles; 2Sep47;
EP19293.

O! Now You Tell Me; words by
Pearl Johnson, music by David
Hall. © Nordyke Publishing Co.,
Los Angeles; 14Aug47; EP19408.

One Alone; words by John Koprosky,
music by David Hall. © Nordyke
Publishing Co., Los Angeles;
12Aug47; EP19713.

Our Remember Melody; words by
Jimmie McGreevy, music by David
Hall. © Nordyke Publishing Co.,
Los Angeles; 3Sep47; EP19330.

Out of the Mist; words by Arnold
Hensley, music by David Hall.
© Nordyke Publishing Co., Los
Angeles; 12Aug47; EP17422.

Please Tell Me; words by Harold
Soul-Thorpe, music by David Hall.
© Nordyke Publishing Co., Los
Angeles; 12Aug47; EP17421.

Roses I Remember; words by Erik O.
Brattstrom, music by David Hall.
© Nordyke Publishing Co., Los
Angeles; 12Aug47; EP19503.

Selfish Me; words by Jon Trepasso,
music by David Hall. © Nordyke
Publishing Co., Los Angeles;
31Jul47; EP19419.

Smoke Stacks of Home; words by
Gladys Gengo, music by David
Hall. © Nordyke Publishing
Co., Los Angeles; 12Aug47;
EP17402.

Some Day, Yes, Some Day; words by
J. O. Kessler, music by David
Hall. © Nordyke Publishing Co.,
Los Angeles; 11Aug47; EP17405.

Something Never For Sale; words
by C. K. Leang, music by David
Hall. © Nordyke Publishing
Co., Los Angeles; 10ct47;
EP20024.

Somethin's Wrong with My Heart;
words by Ann Wonders, music by
David Hall. © Nordyke Publishing Co., Los Angeles; 10ct47;
EP20022.

Sometime, Someplace, and Somewhere;
words by Edna Mae Watson, music
by David Hall. © Nordyke
Publishing Co., Los Angeles;
2Sep47; EP20496.

The Song Eternal; words by Grover
C. Evans, music by David Hall.
© Nordyke Publishing Co., Los
Angeles; 21Aug47; EP19629.

The Song in the Trees; words by
Frances Brancato, music by
David Hall. © Nordyke Publish-
ing Co., Los Angeles; 12Sep47;
EP20021.

Starlight and Moonbeams; words by
George W. Corn, music by David
Hall. © Nordyke Publishing
Co., Los Angeles; 21Aug47;
EP20523.

Summer Romance; words by Ray F.
Parks, music by David Hall.
© Nordyke Publishing Co., Los
Angeles; 10ct47; EP20023.

Talking to Myself about You; words by
Eddie Markie, music by David Hall.
© Nordyke Publishing Co., Los Angeles;
12Aug47; EP17591.

Tell Me; words by Frank Matchett,
music by David Hall. © Nordyke
Publishing Co., Los Angeles;
10ct47; EP20038.

There's No Prescription for Love;
words by Della Stephenson,
music by David Hall. © Nordyke
Publishing Co., Los Angeles;
22Jul47; EP19295.

Thunder in My Aching Heart; words
by Billy Mann, music by David
Hall. © Nordyke Publishing Co.,
Los Angeles; 10ct47; EP20010.

Tickle My Heart; words by Lois
Manchester, music by David
Hall. © Nordyke Publishing
Co., Los Angeles; 10ct47;
EP20045.

What You Do to Me; words by Millie
Jenkins, music by David Hall.
© Nordyke Publishing Co., Los
Angeles; 31Jul47; EP19544.

Whatcha' Doin' About Love? Words
by George Reinke, music by
David Hall. © Nordyke Publishing Co., Los Angeles; 2Sep47;
EU19317.

When I Hear Your Lovely Voice;
words by P. Gianella, music by
David Hall. © Nordyke Publishing Co., Los Angeles; 20Aug47;
EP20096.

When Lovers Meet; words by
Lynn C. Flake, music by
David Hall. © Nordyke
Publishing Co., Los Angeles;
11Aug47; EP17473.

When the Roses Bloom Again; words
by Nancy Hayes [pseud.], music
by David Hall. © Nordyke
Publishing Co., Los Angeles;
10ct47; EP19302.

Where the Mississippi Begins;
words by Arthur M. Lystad, music
by David Hall. © Nordyke
Publishing Co., Los Angeles;
2Sep47; EP20098.

Why; words by Theresa Gallagher,
music by David Hall. © Nordyke
Publishing Co., Los Angeles;
270ct47; EP18399.

Within Your Eyes; words by
Elizabeth Jane Leonard, music
by David Hall. © Nordyke
Publishing Co., Los Angeles;
10ct47; EP19307.

Without You; words by Cora E.
Lane, music by David Hall. ©
Nordyke Publishing Co., Los
Angeles; 22Aug47; EP20093.

279

HALL, DAVID. Cont'd.
Won't You Waltz with Me? Words
by Esther Lee, music by David
Hall. © Nordyke Publishing Co.,
Los Angeles; 21Aug47; EP20094.
You Broke a Precious Vow; words by
Mrs. Rufus Easters, music by Da-
vid Hall. © Nordyke Publishing
co., Los Angeles; 31Jul47;
EP20352.
You Haven't Got a Chance; words by
Fred Johnson, music by David
Hall. © Nordyke Publishing Co.,
Los Angeles; 21Aug47; EP19578.
You Thrilled My Eyes; words by
George E. Wilson, music by
David Hall. © Nordyke Publish-
ing Co., Los Angeles; 29Aug47;
EP19323.
Your Letter; words by Judy A.
Ferndell, music by David Hall.
© Nordyke Publishing Co., Los
Angeles; 21Aug47; EP19326.
You're Home to Stay; words by
Esther Runge, music by David
Hall. © Nordyke Publishing Co,
Los Angeles; 11Aug47; EP19747.
You're Still on My Mind; words by
Jean Cox, music by David Hall.
© Nordyke Publishing Co. Los
Angeles; 11Aug47; aP17434.

HALL, J   E
When I Saw You; words and music by
J. E. Hall. © Chappell & Co.,
ltd., London; 21Nov47; EF7268.

HALL, JIMMY.
Tulsa, Straight Ahead; words and
music by Jimmy Hall. © Cherio
Music Publishers, inc., New York;
7Nov47; EP18394.

HALL, JOHANN BAPTIST VAN. See
Wanhal, Johann Baptist.

HALL, JOHN T
Wedding of the Winds ... by John T.
Hall, arr. for modern bands with
new parts by H. R. Kent [pseud.]
© Carl Fischer, inc., New York;
20Oct47; on arrangement; EP18588.
Condensed score and parts.

HALL, MARGARET.
There's a Bluebird in the Weeping
Willow Tree; words and music
by Margaret Hall. © Nordyke
Publishing Co., Los Angeles;
12Sep47; EP20041.

HALL, ROBERT. See
Hall, Clarence L

HALL,WINONA LAUGHING-EYES, 1909-
Garden City, We Love You; words
and music by Winona L. Hall,
arr. by Chick Moore. ©
Winona L. Hall, Garden City,
Mich.; 28Jun47; EP15389.

HALLE, FRED.
(I've had enough of your two-
timin') You've Had Enough of My
Bankroll; words and music by
Claire Smith [and] Fred Halle.
© Century Songs, inc., Chicago;
18De c47; EP20504. Melody and
chord symbols, with words.

HALLE, FRED JAMES, 1912-
Cream of Kentucky [words by]
Claire Smith. © Century Songs,
inc., Chicago; 30Jun47;
EP15558. Melody and chord
symbols, with words.
Pretty Mama Boogie; [words by]
Claire Smith. © Century Songs
inc., Chicago; 30Jun47;
EP15565. Melody and chord
symbols, with words.

HALLETT, JOHN CHESTER, 1917-
33 Solos and Duets; written and
selected by Johnnie Hallett.
[Ridgewood, N. J., Radio Gospel
Publishers] © John Chester Hallett,
Ridgewood, N. J.; 11Nov46; on 4
songs. Partial contents.- Father
in Heaven, words by Avis B. Christiansen (© EP15725)- It Was the
Cross, words by Victor Hatfield
(© EP15726)- When Jesus Calls,
words by Avis B. Christiansen (©
EP15727)- Walking with Him, words
by Harriet Gates. c1943
(© EP15728)

HALLETT, JOHN CHESTER, 1917-   comp.
Singing Along; a collection of
gospel songs and choruses comp.
... by Johnnie Hallett. Ridge-
wood, N. J., Radio Gospel
Publishers] © John Chester
Hallett, Ridgewood, N. J.;
22Mar47; on 5 songs. Partial
contents (words and music by
J. C. Hallett unless stated)-
Through the Day; words by Char-
lotte Arnold. c1946 (© EP15720)-
Stand up, Shout out! (© EP15721)-
I Know He Loves Me words by
Ruth O. Hallett. c1946 (© EP15722)-
Are You Listening in? c1946
(© 15723)- "Goodbye". c1946
(© EP15724)

HALLETZ, ERWIN.
Ein Kleiner Bär mit Grossen Ohren.
© Edition Turicaphon, ltd.,
Zurich, Switzerland; 14Apr47;
EF5831. For voice and piano.

HALLNÄS, HILDING.
Hymn; (motiv ur Vedasangerna) till
text av Dan Andersson, [by]
Hilding Hallnäs. © Föreningen
svenska tonsättare, Stockholm;
1Jan45; EF7111.
Tre Sänger; till text av Nils Perlin,
[by] Hilding Hallnäs. © Föreningen
svenska tonsättare, Stockholm;
1Jan45; EF7115.

HALPIN, JOE F
A Lonely Prayer; words by Ray F.
Spitz, music by Joe F. Halpin.
[c1946] © Nordyke Publishing
Co., Los Angeles; 28Jan47;
EP19508.

HLUEL, GEORGES LOUIS FRANÇOIS, d.
1917.
Perles de Cristal ... de Georges
Hluel, arrangement et transcrip-
tion pour accordéon, par M.
Camin. © "A L'Intermédiaire"
Germain Louis, Paris; 30Apr47;
on arrangement; EF5960.

HAMER, GEORGE F   1862-1945.
Flight of the Fairies; for
pianoforte, by George F.
Hamer. © The Arthur P.
Schmidt Co., Boston; 7Aug47;
EP16109.

HAMILTON, ARTHUR, 1926-
Along El Camino Real;lyric & music
by Neely Plumb & Arthur Hamil-
ton. © Neely Plumb Publishing
Co., North Hollywood, Calif.;
28Nov47; EP19198.
"Everything But You", words ...
by Peter Potter and Arthur Ham-
ilton, [music by Arthur Hamilton]
© Neely Plumb Publishing Co.,
North Hollywood, Calif.; 1Nov47;
EP19179.
Is It Real? Lyrics ... by Don
Otis and Arthur Hamilton, [music
by Arthur Hamilton] © Neely
Plumb Publishing Co., North
Hollywood, Calif.; 1Nov47;
EP19180.

HAMILTON, JIMMIE.
Independent Superintendant; (song)
by Pat McCarthy and Jimmie
Hamilton. © Rialto Music Pub.
Corp., New York; 20Aug47;
EP18980.

HAMILTON, MARIE.
You're Haunting My Life; words
and music by Marie Hamilton.
[c1946] © Nordyke Publishing
Co., Los Angeles; 14Jan47;
EP19588.

HAMILTON, ORD.
I'll Keep My Faith ... by Ord
Hamilton. © Cinephonic Music
Co., ltd., London; 21Mar47;
EF6029. For voice and piano.
(Rhythm of the Dawn) Theme from
Rhythm of the Dawn, by Ord
Hamilton. [Op.57] © Cinephonic
Music Co., ltd., London;
18Jul46; EF6015. For piano
solo.
Theme from Rhythm of the Dawn. See his
Rhythm of the Dawn.

HAMMANN, FRED B   1881-
Put Me off at Baltimore; words and
music by Fred B. Hammann. ©
Dubonnet Music Publishing, New
York; 26Jun47; EP15300.

HAMMITT, ORLIN.
Goin' Steady with the Moon; words
and music by Andy D. Patterson
[and] Orlin Hammitt. © Broadcast Music, inc., New York;
3Nov47; EP19144.

HAMMOND, HARRY DONALD, 1914-
Stay Out Of the North (this year)
... words and music by Harry D.
Hammond. © Harry D. Hammond,
Tampa, Fla.; 14Oct47; EP20227.

HAMMONDS, EARL. See
Hammonds, Richard.

HAMMONDS, RICHARD.
I Married the Girl of My Dreams;
words and music by Richard "Earl"
Hammonds. © Nordyke Publishing
Co., Los Angeles; 30Jan47;
EP16740.

HAMPTON, LIONEL, 1915-
Beulah's Boogie ... By Lionel
Hampton, [scored by Gil Fuller.
c1946] © Swing & Tempo Music
Publishing Co., inc., New York;
16Jun47; EP16321. Piano-
conductor score (orchestra)
and parts.
Jivin' with Jarvis; by Lionel
Hampton. c1941. © Regent Music
Corp., New York; 5Jul47;
EP15431. Melody only.
No Good Woman Blues; words and
music by Vaughn Horton [and]
Lionel Hampton. © Rytvoc, inc.,
New York; 10Jul47; EP6997.

HANDAL, LYDIA.
El Bananero. (The Banana Vendor)
... English words by Joe Davis,
Spanish words and music by
Lydia Handal. © Caribbean
Music Co., New York; 10Nov47;
EP19177.

HANDL, J
Adoramus Te, Jesu Christe; double
chorus ... [by] J. Handl, ed. &
arr. by Noble Cain. © Boosey &
Hawkes, inc., New York; 20Oct47;
on arrangement; EP19875.

HANDLON, JAMES B
Business in B♭. © Fillmore Bros.
Co., Cincinnati; 15Jul47;
EP15813. Condensed score (band)
and parts.

HANDLON, JAMES ELWIN, 1901-
Jungle Jump. © Neil A. Kjos
Music Co., Chicago; 23Jul47;
EP16135. Condensed score (band)
and parts.

HANISH, OTOMAN ZAR-ADUSHT, d. 1936.
Avesta in Song; by Dr. Otoman
Zar-Adusht Hanish. [Rev. ed.]
© Mazdaznan Press, Los Angeles;
24Dec46; on new songs & changes
in old songs; A14795.

HANKIN, WALLY.
I'll Be Near; words and music by
Sol Parker and Wally Hankin,
[adapted from the Adagio
Pathétique by Benjamin Godard.
c1946] © Famous Music Corp.,
New York; 3Jul47; on words and
arrangement; EP17430.

HAULEY, JAMES F
Indiana; (Back Home Again in
Indiana); by Ballard MacDonald
and James F. Hanley ... arr.
especially by Johnny Warrington.
© Shapiro, Bernstein & Co.,
inc., New York; on
arrangement; EP16242. Piano-
conductor score (orchestra) and
parts.

HANNAH, PHOEBE JOHN.
Mom's Baked Beans; words & music
by Phoebe John Hannah. © Nordyke Publishing Co., Los Angeles; 11Oct46; EP19765.

HANNON, BETTY.
The Old Timers; words by Charles
R. Taylor, music by Billy Hannon.
© Nordyke Publishing Co., Los
Angeles; 1Jul47; EP16870.

[HANSEN, BILL]
Samba-Samba; (Bota Fogo, Nao-nao)
[By Carol and Dale Wood, pseud.
arr. by Joseph Wood. © Chas.
H. Hanson Music Co., New York;
20Jun47; EP15566. Piano-
conductor score (orchestra,
with words) and parts.

HANSON, BOB.
Mellow Moon; words and music by
Bob Hanson. © Nordyke Publish-
ing Co., Los Angeles; 14Jun47;
EP17542.

HANSON, HOWARD.
(Concerto, organ) Concerto for
organ, strings, and harp; by
Howard Hanson. Opus 22 no.3. ©
Carl Fischer, inc., New York;
15Aug47; EP16620. Score: organ
and piano.

HANTAKAS, GEORGE.
I Miss Your Arms; words and music
by George Hantakas. © Nordyke
Publishing Co., Los Angeles;
13Aug47; EP19655.

HAQUINIUS, ALGOT.
Tre Sånger; [by] Algot Haquinius,
[words by Pär Lagerkvist, Sara
Bohlin and Erik Blomberg] ©
Föreningen svenska tonsättare,
Stockholm; 1Jan46; EF7124.
Väverskan; till text av E. A.
Karlfeldt, [by] Algot Haquinius.
© Föreningen svenska tonsättare,
Stockholm; 1Jan45; EF7105.

HARDMAN, CARLOTA DAWNEY, 1906-
Lullaby; words and music by C.
Dawney Hardman. [Buenos Aires,
Casa Lottermoser] © Carlota
Dawney Hardman, FCCA, Argentina;
28Dec46; EF6832.

HARDY, AL FABRIZIO, 1894-
Sweet Susabella Come under My
Umbrella; lyric and music by
Al Hardy; [arr. by Lou Halmy]
© Van Brunt Music Pub. Co.,
Hollywood, Calif.; 19Sep47;
EP17234.

HARDY, ALFA B
A Little Bit of Heaven (A-shinin'
in Your Eyes); lyric and music
by Alfa B. Hardy. Whittier,
Calif., Vicki Warner Publica-
tions. © Alfa B. Hardy,
Whittier, Calif.; 27Jun47;
EP15336.
Sweetheart; lyric and music by
Alfa B. Hardy. Whittier, Calif.,
V. Warner Publications. © Alfa
B. Hardy, Whittier, Calif.;
24Jun47; EP15416.

HARE, MARY.
You Must Be in Love; words and music
by Mary Hare. © Nordyke Publishing
Co., Los Angeles; 28Mar47; EP16724.

HARKNESS, ROBERT, 1877-
But Thanks Be to God ... [Words
from] I Cor.15:57, [music by]
Robert Harkness. (In A Doc
Bundle of Songs, p.1) © W.
Clyde Haslett, El Monte, Calif.;
12Jul47; EP17100. Close score:
SATB.

HARLEY, FRANCES.
The Erie; for chorus of men's
voices with piano acc. ...
Folk-song of old New York arr.
by Frances Harley, ed. by
Walter Aschenbrenner. © Carl
Fischer, inc., New York;
11Jul47; on arrangement;
EP15697.
Hangtown Gals; for chorus of men's
voices with piano acc. ... Folk-
song of Old California arr. by
Frances Harley in collaboration
with Walter Aschenbrenner.
© Carl Fischer, inc., New York;
11Jul47; on arrangement;
EP15699.

HARM, MARJORIE LEA.
All Aboard! ... [By] Marjorie Lea
Harm. © Marjorie Lea Harm,
Shaker Heights, Ohio; 14Oct46;
EP17829. For voice and piano.
Lullaby ... [By] Marjorie Lea
Harm. © Marjorie Lea Harm,
Shaker Heights, Ohio; 14Oct46;
EP17830. For voice and piano.

HARMAN, GEORGE FRANKLIN, 1923-
Fall in Love; words and music by
George Harman. © George F. Har-
man, Jr., Sharon Hill, Pa.;
22Dec47; EP20506.
Wouin's the Doin'; words and
music by George Harman. ©
George Franklin Harman, Jr.,
Sharon Hill, Pa.; 8Dec47;
EP19547.

HARMON, FRANK.
I'm Gonna Miss You; words and music
by Frank Harmon, sr. © Tin Pan
Alley, inc., New York; 19Aug46;
EP7992.

HARPER, ETHELYN GLENORE, 1916-
The C.M.A. Is Marching Onward;
[by] Ethelyn Harper, [arr. by]
Frank Lee Collier. © Frank Lee
Collier & Ethelyn Harper, Erie,
Pa.; 28Jul47; EP20262.

HARPER, MARJORIE.
La Flor de Valencia. [The Flower
of Valencia]; [by] Marjorie
Harper. © Oliver Ditson Co.,
Philadelphia; 15Jul47; EP15677.

HARPER, NIC.
Wishing for Hawaii; words and
music by Roy Kaiser and Nic
Harper ... piano arrangement
by Dick Kent. © Peer International Corp., New York;
27Aug47; EP17866.

HARPER, REDD, 1903-
Mail Order Mama; by Frances Kane
[and] Redd Harper. © Fairway
Music Co., Hollywood, Calif.;
23Jul47; EP15997. For voice
and piano, with chord symbols.

HARR, BILL.
Ev'ry Little Bug; music by Bill
Harr, lyric by Will Eisner.
© Robbins Music Corp., New
York; 15Aug47; EP16437.

HARRELL, TOMMY.
When the Fire Comes Down; by
Wally Fowler, Milten Estes,
Curly Kinsey [and] Tommy Harrell. New York, Sole selling
agent, E. H. Morris. © F & M
Publishing Co., inc., New York;
18Sep47; EP17647. For voice
and piano, with chord symbols.

HARRIS, CUTHBERT, 1870-1932.
Five Postludes for Organ; (on two
staves) by Cuthbert Harris. ©
Arthur P. Schmidt Co., Boston;
7Nov47; EP19104.

Ponder My Words, O Lord; [by]
Cuthbert Harris, [words from]
Psalm V, v: 1,2. © The Arthur
P. Schmidt Co., Boston; 1Jul47;
on arrangement; EP15391. Score:
SATB and organ.
Sailors' Dance; [by] Cuthbert
Harris, [arr. by the Arthur
P. Schmidt Co.] © The Arthur
P. Schmidt Co., Boston; 4Sep47;
on arrangement; EP16645. For
piano solo.

HARRIS, DORA, 1880-
Little Brown Bear; words and music
by Dora Harris. © Dora Harris,
Philadelphia; 21Aug47; EP17058.

HARRIS, GRACE E
The Little Red Cottage; words and
music by Grace E. Harris, arr.
by Lew Tobin. © Nordyke Publishing Co., Los Angeles; 28Mar47;
EP16738.

HARRIS, HOMER.
Sing, Tom Kitty; by Bill Carlisle
and Homer Harris. © Hometown
Music Co., inc., New York;
13Aug47; EP16426. For voice
and piano, with chord symbols.

HARRIS, O   W
Reminiscing; words & music by O.
W. Harris. © Nordyke Publish-
ing Co., Los Angeles; 27Sep46;
EP20014.

HARRIS, PHYLLIS BLANDFORD.
uniforms; unison song, words by
N. G. ... music by Phyllis
Blandford Harris. © J. Curwen
& Sons, ltd., London; 23Oct47;
EF6943.

HARRIS, ROY, 1898-
American Ballads; for piano ...
by Roy Harris. © Carl Fischer,
inc., New York; Set 1, 4Nov47;
EP18870.
Blow the Man Down; a free improvisation of the sailor's ballad,
for four-part chorus of mixed
voices with contralto and
baritone solos and symphonic
orchestra, by Roy Harris. Vocal
score. © Carl Fischer, inc.,
New York; 17Aug47; EP18406.
Melody; by Roy Harris. © Carl
Fischer, inc., New York; 12Nov47;
EP18942. Piano-conductor score
(orchestra) and parts.
Radio piece; by Roy Harris. ©
Carl Fischer, inc., New York;
12Nov47; EP18941. Piano-conductor score (orchestra) and
parts.

HARRIS, WILLIAM HENRY, 1883-
I Heard a Voice from Heaven;
(anthem for full choir) [by]
William H. Harris. © Oxford
University Press, London;
19Jun47; EF6152.
Magnificat and Nunc Dimittis ...
music by William H. Harris.
© A. & C. Black, ltd., London;
18Jun47; EF6682. Score: SATB
and organ; English words.

HARRISON, TED.
Pixie; composed and orchestrated
by Ted Harrison. [c1947] ©
Cinephonic Music Co., ltd.,
London; 28Oct46; EF6033. Piano-
conductor score (orchestra) and
parts.

HARROLD, SARA.
The Rest of the Way; words and mu-
sic by Sara Harrold, arr. by
Karl Heler. © Nordyke Publish-
ing Co., Los Angeles; 16Dec46;
EP20382.

HARSANYI, TIBOR, 1898-
(Concerto, violin) Concerto pour
violon et orchestre; [by] Tibor
Harsanyi. Réduction. ©
Editions Salabert, Paris;
1Sep47; EF6770. Score (violin
and piano) and part.
Divertimento no. 1; (Concertino)
pour deux violons et orchestre de
chambre, [by] Tibor Harsanyi.
Réduction. © Editions Salabert,
Paris; 15Sep47; EF7264. Score
(2 violins and piano) and parts.

HARSCH, HAROLD L
Prelude; (Chanson des Pivoines)
[by] Harold Harsch. © Clayton
F. Summy Co., Chicago; 31Oct47;
EP18339. For organ solo.

HART, DANNY, pseud. See
Choisser, Joseph Daniel.

HARTER, ALLEN.
This Can't Be Me; words by Rosa
Harter, music by Allen Harter.
© Nordyke Publishing Co., Los
Angeles; 10Jun47; EP16927.

HARTLEY, FRED.
The Flowers o' Edinburgh ...
freely arr. by Fred Hartley.
© The Peter Maurice Music Co.,
ltd., New York; 29Sep47;
EF6814. Piano-conductor score
(orchestra) and parts.

HARTLEY, RENE.
You Cut a Fancy Figure in My
Heart ... Music by Rene Hartley,
words [by] Leo Gilbert [pseud.]
© Melotone Music Publishers,
Chicago; 5Oct47; EP17683.

HARTMAIER, FRANCES BENZIGER.
Our Church Bells; words and
music by Frances Benziger
Hartmaier. © Frances
Benziger Hartmaier, Rosendale,
N. Y.; 7Aug47; EP16090.

HARTMAN, C P
Warner's Collection of Clarinet
Ensembles; suitable for ren-
dition as solo, duet, trio,
quartet or for four Bb clarinets by
C. P. Hartman, ed. by T. L.
Mesang. © Chart Music Publishing House, inc., Chicago;
3Sep47; on arrangement; EP17202.

HARTMAN, S
San Francisco by the Golden Gate;
lyric by S. Costa, music by S.
Hartman. San Francisco, S and S
Music Publications.
Hartman, San Francisco; 18Oct47;
EP18438.
Silly Little Quarrels; lyric by
S. Costa, music by S. Hartman.
San Francisco, S and S Music
Publications. © S. Hartman,
San Francisco; 18Oct47;
EP18437.

HARTMANN, MAURIE MERL.
The Old Accordion; words by Milt
Gabler, music by Maurie Hart-
mann. © Rytvoc, inc., New York;
24Oct47; EP18188.
Smiling Shadows; words by Billy
Faber, music by Maurie Hartmann.
© Rytvoc, inc., New York;
7Nov47; EP18393.
What's It to You; words by Billy
Faber, music by Maurie Hartmann.
© Rytvoc, inc., New York;
7Nov47; EP18392.

HARTSHORN, WILLIAM C
The Offering of the Grateful Heart;
an offertory response [by]
William C. Hartshorn, text para-
phrased from John G. Whittier.
© C. C. Birchard & Co., Boston;
11Dec47; on arrangement;
EP19911. Score: SSAATTBB.

[HARTUSCH, MIREILLE]
Quand un vicomte ... paroles de
Jean Nohain [pseud.] musique de
Mireille [pseud.] © Editions
Raoul Breton, Paris; 17Sep35; EF6059.
Le Vieux Chateau ... paroles de
Jean Nohain [pseud.] musique de
Mireille [pseud.] © Publications
Raoul Breton & Co., Paris;
9Jun33; EF6057.

HARVEY, LENA, 1900-
I Know He Will Remember Me; words
and music by Lena Harvey.
© Lena Harvey, St. Louis;
21Jun47; EP17960.
I'm Going On with Jesus; words
and music by Lena Harvey.
© Lena Harvey, St. Louis;
21Jun47; EP17961.

HARVEY, SHEENA, 1922-
My Dear, Remember; ('Until we
part for aye'); song, words
and music by Sheena Harvey. ©
Lawrence Wright Music Co.,
ltd., London; 23Sep47; EF6636.

HARVEY, VIVIEN.
Summer; chorus for mixed voices,
poem by George Peele ... music
by Vivien Harvey. © Broadcast
Music, inc., New York; 11Jul47;
EP18206.

HASKINS, VERNON C 1909-
In the Moonlight; song, words
adapted from Sappho, music by
Vernon C. Haskins. [c1942]
© Wesley Webster, San Francis-
co; 10Dec47; EP19576.
Preludes Miniatures. © Wesley
Webster, San Francisco; 12Aug47;
EP16159. For piano solo.

HAŠLER, KAREL, 1879-1941.
Česka písníčka. See his Písníčkář.
(Písníčkář) Česká písníčka, z
filmu "Písníčkář"; [by] Karel
Hašler. © Mojmír Urbánek, Praha,
Czechoslovakia; 10Oct46; EF5362.
For voice and piano.

HASLETT, RUTH, 1893-
The Blessed Hope; [words by] W.
Clyde Haslett, [music by] Mrs.
W. Clyde Haslett, [arr. by
Robert Harkness] (In A Wee
Bundle of Songs, p.11) © Dr.
and Mrs. W. Clyde Haslett, El
Monte, Calif.; 12Jul47; EP17102.
Close score: SATB.
Jesus, I Love Thee; [words by] W.
Clyde Haslett, [music by] Ruth
Haslett, arr. [by] G. E. H.
(In A Wee Bundle of Songs, p.2-
3) © Dr. and Mrs. W. Clyde
Haslett, El Monte, Calif.; 12Jul47;
EP17101. Close score: SATB.
Waitings; [words by] W. Clyde
Haslett, [music by] Mrs. W.
Clyde Haslett, [arr. by Robert
Harkness] (In A Wee Bundle of
Songs, p.18-19) © Dr. and Mrs.
W. Clyde Haslett, El Monte,
Calif.; 12Jul47; EP17099. Close
score: SATB.

HASLETT, MRS. W. CLYDE. See
Haslett, Ruth.

HASSEL, MILDRED.
Pitchin' a Little Woo; Words and
music by Herb Hassel and Mildred
Hassel. © Nordyke Publishing
Co., Los Angeles; 24Jul47;
EP20491.

HASSLER, HANS LEO, 1564-1612.
O Sing unto the Lord; for three-
part chorus of mixed voices (a
cappella) [by] Hans Leo Hassler
... arr. by Victoria Glaser,
[words from] Psalm 96:1,2,3;
adapted by V.G.G.T. © E. C.
Schirmer Music Co., Boston;
29Sep47; on arrangement;
EP18137.

HATLEM, CECELIA.
High Sierra Home; words and music
by Maxine Schlapp and Cecelia
Hatlem. © Nordyke Publishing
Co., Los Angeles; 12Jun46;
EP19653.

HAUCK, MARSETTE L
New Moon in the Sky; words by
Marsette L. Hauck. © Nordyke
Publishing Co., Los Angeles;
14Jun46; EP19425.

HAUSER, WILLIAM, 1891-
De Sun Done Rose; words and music
by William Hauser, arr. by Georgia Lee Thorn, Cleveland;
15Oct47; EP18338.

HAWKINS, JESSIE MAE, 1913-
What More Can Jesus Do? ...
Words and melody by Sis. J.
Hawkins, arr. by A. B. Windom.
St. Louis, A. B. Windom Studio.
© Jessie Mae Hawkins, St. Louis;
24Jul47; EP16164.

[HAWTHORNE, MARCY]
Say It with a Flower; words and
music by Roy Lynn [pseud.]
and Margy Lynn [pseud.]
Oakland, Calif., Golden Gate
Publications. © M. L.
Hawthorne, Seattle; 28Sep47;
EP17215.

HAYDN, JOSEPH, 1732-1809.
God's Word; [music by] Jos. Haydn,
[words by] Margarete E. Frit-
schel] (In The words of Jesus,
Oct. issue, p. [2]) © Margarete
E. Fritschel, Clinton, Iowa;
27Sep47; on words; EP18361.
Gypsy Rondo. See his Trio, piano &
strings, no.5.
Little Symphony. See his Trio.
for orchestra by Anthony Collins.
Full score. © Keith, Prowse &
Co., ltd., London; 24Sep47; on
arrangement; EF6836. "This work
may be played by strings alone."
Presto in C major. See his Quartet,
Strings.
(Quartet, strings) Presto in C
major; from the String Quartet.
Op. 1, no. 6, [by] Joseph
Haydn, arr. ... by Eric Steiner.
© Elkan-Vogel Co., inc., Phila-
delphia; 26Jun47; on arrangement;
EP15846. Two scores for piano 1-2.
(Quartet, strings) Serenade;
by Joseph Haydn [from String
Quartet in F] Theme melody in
the B.B.C. feature, "Music in
Miniature." [Arr. by Victor
Ambrose.] © Lawrence Wright
Music Co., ltd., London;
16Sep47; on arrangement;
EF7353. For piano solo.
Serenade. See his Quartet, strings.
(Trio, piano & strings, no.5)
Gypsy Rondo. Ungarisches Rondo.
From Trio no.5 in G by Franz
Joseph Haydn, arr. by Joe
Biviano. © Vicoas Music Co.,
New York; 25Aug47; on arrange-
ment; EP17835.
Twelve Grey Dwarfs; [from] Haydn-
Symphony in G ... by Franz
Joseph Haydn] arr. by Hugo Frey.
[Words by Martha Ostense]
Hamilton S. Gordon, inc., New
York; 22Oct47; on lyrics and
arrangement; EP18743. For piano
solo, with words.
Ungarisches Rondo. See his Trio, piano
& strings, no.5.

HAYES, BILLY S
A Smile Will Chase Away a Tear;
words and music by Milton Leeds
[pseud.] and Billy Hayes. ©
Northern Music Corp., New York;
24Nov47; EP19250.

HAYES, BILLY S. Cont'd.
You Laughed and I Cried; by Ray Whitley, Milton Leeds [pseud., and] Billy Hayes. © Western Music Publishing Co., Hollywood, Calif.; 12Nov47; EP18848. For voice and piano, with chord symbols.

HAYES, CLANCY. See Hayes, Clarence.

HAYES, CLARENCE.
George Washington, Abraham Lincoln, Ulysses S., Robert E. Lee; [music] by Clancy Hayes and [words by] Kermit Goell. © Hudson Music Corp., New York; 19Aug47; EP18336.

HAYES, OPAL LOUISE.
4 Easy Etudes; for the development of technic for piano solo, [by] Opal Louise Hayes. © Elkan-Vogel Co., inc., Philadelphia; on 4 pieces, 24Sep47. Contents.- no. 1, G major © EP17970) - no. 2. A minor © EP17971) - no. 3. Ab major © EP17972) - no. 4. G major © EP17969)

Sea Idyl; for the piano [by] Opal Louise Hayes. © Oliver Ditson Co., Philadelphia; 6Dec47; EP20451.

Three Easy Piano Pieces; by Opal Louise Hayes. © Elkan-Vogel Co., inc., Philadelphia; on 3 pieces; 24Sep47. Contents. - [1] A Summer Evening (© EP17966) - [2] Little Tattler (© EP17967) - [3] The Jester (© EP17968)

Twenty Teachable Tunes; for piano, by Opal Louise Hayes. © Theodore Presser Co., Philadelphia; 10ct47; EP17754.

HAYWOOD, CHARLES, ed.
Art Songs of Soviet Russia ... Comp. and ed. by Charles Haywood, with the original text. Literal text translation by Charles Haywood, English adaptations by Olga Paul. © Edward B. Marks Music Corp., New York; 16Sep47; EP17173. English and Russian words.

HAYWOOD, ERNEST.
Practice Makes Perfect; seven graded pieces with preparatory studies by Ernest Haywood. © Keith, Prowse & Co., ltd., London; 10ct47; on arrangements & editing of the solos; EF6777.

HAZELLE, EARL, 1906-
The Active Accordionist; by Earl Hazelle, containing supplementary solos and recital pieces. © Belwin, inc., New York; bk.3, 24Sep47; on arranging & compiling; EP18224.

Belwin ... Accordion Course ... by Earl Hazelle. © Belwin, inc., New York. EP18216-18218 have new matter; compilation & arrangement. Contents.- For young beginners: bk.3. Grade 2 1/2 (© Mar47; EP12934) - For adult beginners: bk.1 (© 27Mar47; EP12977) bk.2. Grade 1 1/2 (© 27Mar47; EP12977) bk.3, Grade 2 1/2 (© 14May47; EP14629) - bk.4. Grade 3 (© 23Sep47; EP18216) - bk.5. Grade 4 (© 23Sep47; EP18218) - bk.6.
Grade 5 (© 23Sep47; EP18217)

HEAD, MICHAEL, 1900-
The Little Road to Bethlehem; words by Margaret Rose, music by Michael Head, arr. by Noble Cain. © Boosey & Hawkes, inc., New York; 30Jun47; on arrangement; EP16062. Score: SATB and piano.

The Little Road to Bethlehem; words by Margaret Rose, music by Michael Head, arr. by Noble Cain. © Boosey & Hawkes, inc., New York; 30Jun47; on arrangement; EP16064. Score: SATB and piano.

HEAPS, RAYMOND.
When We Meet; words by Ken Ferguson, music by Raymond Heaps. © Nordyke Publishing Co., Los Angeles; 10Jun47; EP16928.

HEATON, SYD.
Good Night, Machree; words and music by Joe Wall and Syd Heaton. © Jerry Vogel Music Co., inc., New York; 31Jul47; EP16284.

[HECIMOVICH, JOHN]
A Girl Has a Right To Change Her Mind; words and music by Johnny Louis [pseud.] © Nordyke Publishing Co., Los Angeles; 22Apr47; EP16932.

HEDGREN, VIKTOR, 1905-
The Christmas Story; a cantata by Viktor Hedgren, for soloists, choir and organ or piano, with a narrative by ... L. A. Reed. © Universal Publishing Co., Chicago; 10ct47; EP18333. Piano-vocal score and part for narrator.

[HEIFETZ, JASCHA]
Hora Swing-cato; adapted from "Hora Staccato" by Dinicu-Heifetz. Words and music by Jim Hoyl [pseud.] and Marjorie Goetschius ... Johnny Worrington dance orchestration. © Carl Fischer, inc., New York; 15Sep47; on arrangement; EP18062. Piano-conductor score (orchestra, with words) and parts.

HEILNER, IRWIN.
Every Day Is Friday to a Seal ... words by Claire Berger, music by Irwin Heilner and Gerald Marks. © Bob Miller, inc., New York; 270ct47; EP18633.

HEINZ, ALICE STURDEVANT, 1896-
I Am Ready ... [by] Alice S. Heinz. © Albert H. Heins, Columbus, Ohio; 20Aug47; EP19558. Close score: SATB.

HELFER, WALTER.
To the Chief Musician ... [words from Psalm 23] for three-part chorus of treble voices, acc. for percussion, bass viols (celli) by Walter Helfer. © Clayton F. Summy Co., Chicago; 7Jul47; EP15465.

HELFMAN, MAX, arr.
Kol Nidre; for cantor (tenor) and mixed choir with or without organ accompaniment, setting by Max Helfman. © Transcontinental Music Corp., New York; 19Aug47; on arrangement; EP16049.

HELLARD, ROBERT A
Winding Wistaria; piano solo by Robert A. Hellard. © Theodore Presser Co., Philadelphia; 210ct47; EP18417.

HELLER, FRANÇOIS, 1905-
Le Petit Horloger; paroles de Ruy Blag, musique de François Heller. © SIDEM Société Intercontinentale d'Éditions Musicales, Vaduz, Liechtenstein; 19Nov47; EF7189.

HELLSTRÖM, DAVID.
Bröllopsvalsen; musik: David Hellström, text: Göran Svenning. © Reuter & Reuter förlags, a.-b., Stockholm; 1Jan44; EF6952.

HELM, ERNEST.
It Might's Been Vitamin "B"; words by Tom Johnstone, music by Ernest Helm. © Nordyke Publishing Co., Los Angeles; 11Aug47; EP17520.

HELM, EVERETT.
Sonata Brevis; [by] Everett Helm. © Hargail Music Press, New York; 15Jul47; EP16625. For piano solo.

HELPENSTELL, MAX H
It's the Natural Thing To Do; words and music by Max H. Helpenstell. © Nordyke Publishing Co., Los Angeles; 22Apr47; EP16471.

My Dream for Tonight; words and music by Max H. Helpenstell. © Nordyke Publishing Co., Los Angeles; 29Apr47; EP16833.

Someone I Knew; words and music by Max H. Helpenstell. © Nordyke Publishing Co., Los Angeles; 12Sep47; EP20020.

HEMMERLE, JOSEPH, 1882-
Adoro To. O Salutaris; [by] Joseph Hemmerle. © Les Éditions Ouvrières, Paris; 20May47; EF5898. For voice and organ or harmonium.

Chansons du Blé Qui Lève; [comp. by] Joseph Hemmerle ... illustrées par Jean-Paul Raxnvet, préface de Henri Colas. © Les Éditions Ouvrières, Paris; 5May47; EF5492. For 1-3 treble voices.

REMY, HENRY F
Faith of Our Fathers ... for choir (S.A.T.B.) and congregation [by] Henry F. Remy ... arr. by W. B. Olds, [words by] Frederick W. Faber. © Hall & McCreary Co., Chicago; 28Nov47; on arrangement; EP19801.

HENDERSON, MAX.
Why Can't You Wait? Words and music by Max Henderson. [c1945] © Nordyke Publishing Co., Los Angeles; 28Jun46; EP20069.

HENDERSON, RAY, 1896-
The Best Things in Life Are Free. See his Good News.

(Good News) The Best Things in Life Are Free ... from the ... picture "Good News"; words and music by B. G. De Sylva, Lew Brown and Ray Henderson, dance orchestration by Paul Weirick. © Crawford Music Corp., New York; 210ct47; on arrangement; EP18531. Piano-conductor score (orchestra, with words) and parts.

An Old Sombrero (und an old Spanish shawl) by Lew Brown and Ray Henderson. © Shapiro, Bernstein & Co., inc., New York; 18Nov47; EP19247. For voice and piano, with chord symbols.

HENDL, WALTER, 1917-
(Dark of the Moon) Prelude to "Dark of the Moon"; by Walter Hendl. Piano solo. © Hargail Music Press, New York; 14Aug46; EP16576.

HENMAN, GEOFFREY.
The Charm Waltz ... melody for strings and woodwind, music by Geoffrey Henman, arr. for orchestra by Sidney Torch. © Chappell & Co., ltd., London; 5Nov47; on arrangement; EP16576. Piano-conductor score (orchestra) and parts.

The Songs of Love; song ... words by Christopher Hassall, music by Geoffrey Henman. © Chappell & Co., ltd., London; 12Jun47; EF5722.

HEN..EBERG, ALBERT.
(Serenade, string orchestra)
Serenad för stråkorkester ...
[by] Albert Henneberg. Op.20.
Partitur. Stockholm, Ed. Suecia.
© Föreningen svenska tonsättare,
Edition Suecia, Stockholm;
1Jan45; EF7074.

Tva Kärlekssänger; [by] Albert
Henneberg, till text av Erik
Axel Karlfeldt. © Föreningen
svenska tonsättare, Stockholm;
1Jan46; EF7100.

Två Sånger; till text av Richard
Vullner, [by] Albert Henneberg.
[Op.9] © Föreningen svenska
tonsättare, Stockholm; 1Jan45;
EF7117.

HENNEFIELD, NORMAN, 1902- ed.
Masterpieces of Organ Music ...
Norman Hennefield, editor.
Liturgical Music Press, inc.,
New York; no.56, 29Aug47; no.57,
22Oct47; no.58, 20Nov47; on
arrangement; EF16982, 17343,
18787.

Masterpieces of Organ Music ... Norman Hennefield, editor. © Liturgical Music Press, inc., New York;
folio 59-60, 20Dec47; on arrangement; EP20415, 20414.

HENNESSY, HERBERT, 1918-
"At Last"; written and composed
by Herbert Hennessy. Adelaide,
South Australia, Australian
Songwriters' and Music Publish-
ers' Agency. © Herbert
Hennessy, Goodwood, South
Australia; 30May47; EF6671.
For voice and piano.

HENNESSY, NELLIE, 1917-
Carpet of Gold; written and
composed by Nellie Hennessy.
Adelaide, South Australia,
Australian Songwriters' and
Music Publishers' Agency. ©
Nellie Hennessy, Goodwood,
South Australia; 30May47;
EF6670. For voice and piano.

HENNINGER, GEORGE, 1895-
Sunset Lullabye; lyric by W. R.
Williams [pseud.], music by
George Henninger. © Will
Rossiter, Chicago; 17Nov47;
EP18690.

HENRI, PAUL.
Too Long; words and music by Paul
Henri. © Broadcast Music, inc.,
New York; 19May47; EP18046.

HENRICSON, RAOUL.
Underbara Ogon ... musik; Raoul
Henricson, text; Holge Stråby,
arrangemang; ... B. Stålhandske.
© Edition Raoul Henricson,
Orebro, Sweden; 1Jan46; on arrangement; EF7084. Piano-
conductor score (orchestra) and
parts.

Underbara Ogon; musik; Raoul
Henricson, text, Holge Stråby.
© Edition Raoul Henricson,
Orebro, Sweden; 1Jan46; EF7083.

HENRIKSEN, EDYTHE GERTRUDE) 1914-
I Love To Be Surprised; words and
music by Faith Palmer [pseud.]
© Palmer Music, inc., Faith
Palmer & Edythe Henriksen, sole
owners, New York; 14Aug47;
EP16678.

This Time the Torch Is on Me;
words and music by Faith Palmer
[pseud.] © Palmer Music, inc.,
Edythe G. Henrikson & Faith
Palmer, sole owners, New York;
14Aug47; EP16677.

HENRY VIII, king of England, 1491-
1547.
Trenchmore; (one of King Henry's
mirth or freemen's songs) arr.
for mixed voices (S.C.T.B.)
... [by] Norman Stone. © Oxford University Press, London;
14Sep47; on arrangement;
EF6664.

HENRY, CHARLES, 1909-
Trois plus Trois; six petites
pièces faciles ... musique de
Charles-Henry. © Henry Lemoine
& Cie, Paris; 8May47; EF7332.
For piano 4 hands.

HENSCHEL, GEORGE, 1850-1934.
The Lamb; [by] George Henschel,
arr. by Hugh Gordon [pseud.],
words by] William Blake. ©
The Arthur P. Schmidt Co.,
Boston; 23Sep47; on arrangement; EF17321. Score: SSA and
piano.

HERBERT, BLANCHE.
My Heart Begins to Cry; words and
music by Blanche Herbert. ©
Nordyke Publishing Co., Los
Angeles; 12Jul47; ©P17491.

HERBERT, IVY.
The Linnet; the words by Robert
Bridges, set to music by Ivy
Herbert. © The Oxford Univer-
sity Press, London; 19Jun47;
EF6155.

Two Songs; (1) Jenny Kiss'd Me,
words by Leigh Hunt. (2) A
Widow Bird Sat Mourning, words
by Percy Bysshe Shelley, set to
music by Ivy Herbert. © The
Oxford University Press, London;
19Jun47; EF6154.

HERBERT, VICTOR, 1859-1924.
(The Fortune Teller) Gypsy Love
Song; by Victor Herbert, tran-
scribed by F. Campbell-Watson.
© M. Witmark & Sons, New York;
30Oct47; on arrangement;
EP18477. Piano-conductor
score (orchestra) and parts.

(The Fortune Teller) Gypsy Love
Song, from "The Fortune Teller,"
music by Victor Herbert.
Concert ed. © M. Witmark &
Sons, New York; 6Aug47; on
arrangement; EP17004. Piano-
conductor score (orchestra)
and parts.

Gypsy Love Song ... by Victor
Herbert, arr. by F. Henri
Klickmann. © M. Witmark & Sons,
New York; 3Sep47; on arrange-
ment; EP17277. Score (xylophone
or marimba and piano) and part.

Gypsy Love Song. See his The Fortune
Teller.

A Kiss in the Dark. See his Orange
Blossoms.

(Orange Blossoms) "A Kiss in the
Dark"; by Victor Herbert,
transcribed by F. Campbell-
Watson. © M. Witmark & Sons,
New York; 25Aug47; on arrangement; EP17053. Condensed score
(orchestra) and parts.

Star Light, Star Bright ... [for]
S.S.A., music by Victor Herbert,
arr. by Otto Wick. Words by
Harry B. Smith. © Edward
Schuberth & Co., inc., New York;
28Aug47; EP16674.

Thine Alone; by Victor Herbert,
transcribed by F. Campbell-Watson. © M. Witmark & Sons, New
York; 15Oct47; on arrangement;
EP18410. Piano-conductor score
(orchestra) and parts.

Victor Herbert Made Easy for the
piano, [arr.] by Ada Richter. ©
M. Witmark & Sons, New York; v.1,
20Nov47; on arrangement; EP19176.

Victor Herbert Made Easy for the
Piano; by Ada Richter. © M. Witmark & Sons, New York; v.2,
15Dec47; on arrangement; EP20542.

Victor Herbert String Americana;
a collection of solos for cello
and piano, arr. by F. Campbell-
Watson. © M. Witmark & Sons,
New York; bk. 1, 24Oct47; bk.2,
28Oct47; on arrangement;
EP18473, EP18726. Score and
part.

Victor Herbert String Americana;
a collection of solos for viola
and piano, arr. by F. Campbell-
Watson. © M. Witmark & Sons,
New York; bk.1, 24Oct47; bk.2,
28Oct47; on arrangement;
EP18472, EP18725. Score and
part.

Victor Herbert String Americana;
a collection of solos for
violin and piano, arr. by F.
Campbell-Watson. © M. Witmark
& Sons, New York; bk.1, 30Oct47;
on arrangement; EP18475. Score
and part.

Victor Herbert String Americana; a
collection of solos for violin
and piano, arr. by F. Campbell-
Watson. © M. Witmark & Sons,
New York; bk. 1, 30Oct47; bk. 2,
20Nov47; on arrangement;
EP18475, 19239. Score and part.

Victor Herbert String Americana;
a ser. of string ensembles in
varied combinations with piano
acc., arr. by F. Campbell-Watson.
© M. Witmark & Sons, New York;
on arrangement of 20 pts. Contents.- bk. 1: Piano acc. (©
20Nov47; EP19237) Violin A (©
13Nov47; EP18888) Violin B (©
12Nov47; EP18879) Violin C (©
20Nov47; EP19236) Violin D (©
31Oct47; EP18661) Violin E (©
31Oct47; EP18660) Viola (©

12Nov47; EP18883) 'Cello A (©
5Nov47; EP18499) 'Cello B (©
5Nov47; EP18500) String bass
(© 13Nov47; EP18885) - bk. 2.
Piano acc. (© 20Nov47; EP19240)
Violin A (© 12Nov47; EP18886)
Violin B (© 13Nov47; EP18886)
Violin C (© 5Nov47; EP18504)
Violin D (© 12Nov47; EP18880)
Violin E (© 12Nov47; EP18881)
Viola (© 12Nov47; EP18882)
'Cello A (© 13Nov47; EP18887)
'Cello B (© 20Nov47; EP19238)
String bass (© 12Nov47;
EP18884)

Victor Herbert Waltz Medley;
[words by Henry Blossom and
George Gard DeSylva] A Jerry
Sears arrangement. © M. Witmark & Sons, New York; 15Oct47;
on arrangement; EP18409. Piano-
conductor score (orchestra, with
words) and parts.

HERFORD, JULIUS G 1901-
ed.
Humor in Vocal Music; six canons
and a quodlibet in 7 parts.
Music of Kuhlau, Mozart,
Beethoven ... Ed. by Julius
G. Herford. (Music Education
Series, v. 2) © Hargail Music
Press, New York; 10Oct46; on
words, arrangement, and compila-
tion, and composition of "Not
so easy"; EP16623.

Preparing for the Music of Bach
and Mozart; 23 short and easy
piano pieces ... by Türk, Mozart,
Mattei and others ... Ed. by
Julius G. Herford. (Music
Education Series, v.1) © Hargail
Music Press, New York; 3Sep45;
EP16577.

HERMAN, THE HERMIT, pseud.
Big Sue; words and music by
Herman, the Hermit. © Hill
and Range Songs, inc.,
Hollywood, Calif.; 30Jul47;
EP16046.

HERMANN, RODOLPHE. See
Hermann, Rudolph Adolf Joseph.

HERMANN, RUDOLPH ADOLF JOSEPH, 1875-
Six Petites Pièces Faciles; pour
piano [by] Rodolphe Hermann.
© Lucien de Lacour, Éditeur,
Paris; 17Jul47; EF6562.

Six Pièces Brèves; pour le piano
[by] Rodolphe Hermann. Paris,
Rouart Lerolle; vente exclusive:
Éditions Salabert. © Salabert,
inc., New York; 17Aug47; EF7243.

HERNANDEZ, PABLO VALDES. See
Valdés Hernández, Pablo.

HERNANDEZ, VICTOR MARIN. See
Marin Hernandez, Victor.

HERNRIED, ROBERT.
Chinese Dance; [by] R. Hernried.
© Carl Fischer, inc., New York;
17Oct47; EP18407. Score (solo
instrument and piano) and part
for clarinet.

HERSENHOREN, SAMUEL, 1908-
(Bush Pilot) True Love; musical
theme of the motion picture
"Bush Pilot," by Gordon Fleming, Harold Moon, and Samuel
Hersenhoren. © North
American Music, ltd., Toronto;
8Jan47; EF6376. For voice
and piano, with chord symbols.

True Love. See his Bush Pilot.

HERVELOIS, CAIX D'. See
Caix d' Hervelois, Louis de.

[HESELTINE, PHILIP]
Capriol ... a suite based on dance
tunes from Arbeau's Orchéso-
graphie (1588) by Peter Warlock
[pseud.] arr. ... by Maurice
Jacobson. London, J. Curwen,
New York, G. Schirmer, sole
agents. © Maurice Jacobson,
London; 22Aug47; on arrangement;
EF6741. Two scores for piano
1-2.

HESS, JOHN.
Maman Ne Vends Pas la Maison ...
paroles de Charles Trenet, musique
de John Hess. Je M'y Crois
Plus; paroles de Louis Sauvat
[pseud.], musique de Alek
Siniavine. © Éditions Raoul
Breton, Paris; 3Sep35; EF6058.

Passing By; four part male chorus
(T.T.B.B.) (a cappella ad lib.)
arr. by William Stickles, American version by Jack Lawrence,
music by John Hess and Paul
Misraki. © Chappell & Co., inc.
New York; 28Aug47; on arrangement; EF17012.

Passing By; four part mixed
chorus (S...T.B.) arr. by
William Stickles, American
version by Jack Lawrence, music
by John Hess and Paul Misraki.
© Chappell & Co., inc., New
York; 28Aug47; on arrangement;
EF17013.

Passing By; three part female
chorus (S.S.A.) arr. by
William Stickles, American ver-
sion by Jack Lawrence, music by
John Hess and Paul Misraki. ©
Chappell & Co., inc., New York;
28Aug47; on arrangement;
EF17011.

HESS, JOHNNY.
Le Duel; paroles de Charles Trenet,
musique de John Hess. ©
Éditions Raoul Breton et Co.,
Paris; 17May34; EF6206.

HETTICH, A   L
Répertoire Moderne de Vocalises-
Études; pub. sous la direction
de A. L. Hettich.

HEUZEROER, R
(The Emperor Waltz) The Kiss in
Your Eyes, (from) the Paramount
picture, "The Emperor Waltz",
music by R. Heuberger, lyric by
Johnny Burke. © Bosworth & Co.,
inc., New York; 12Jun47; on
lyrics; EF16349.

The Kiss in Your Eyes. See his The
Emperor Waltz.

HEUSEN, JAMES VAN. See
Van Heusen, James.

HEYS, JOHN ALEXANDER, 1910-
The Lord's Prayer; [music by]
Rev. John A. Heys. © John
Alexander Heys, Grand Rapids;
5Sep47; EP17230. Close score;
SATB.

Our Father Which in Heaven
Art; [music by] Rev. John A.
Heys. © John Alexander Heys,
Grand Rapids; 5Sep47; EP17231.
Close score; SATB.

HEYWARD, SAMMY, 1906-
(Checkin' on the) Freedom Train;
by ... Sammy Heyward, [words by]
Langston Hughes. © Handy Brothers Music Co.,inc., New York;
6Oct47; EP17650.

HIBBARD, HELEN, 1903-
The House Shortage Blues; words and
music by Helen Hibbard. © Helen
Hibbard, Chester, Pa.; 21Aug47;
EP17055.

HIBBELER, RAYMOND OSCAR, 1892-
Four-pointed Kiss; words by Cor-
nelius G. Van Schelven, music
by Ray Hibbeler. © Cornelius
Gerard Van Schelven, Arlington,
Va.; 18Sep47; EP20049.

How Can I Forget? Words by Jack
Haines, music by Ray Hibbeler.
© Nordyke Publishing Co., Los
Angeles; 11Jul47; EP17528.

I Can't Forget My Sorrow; words
by Joseph A. Klima, music by
Ray Hibbeler. © Joseph
Anthony Klima, Baltimore;
3Jul47; EP16448.

I Lost My Heart to You; words &
music by Elsie Spehar and Ray
Hibbeler. © Elsie Antonia Spehar,
Lake Orion, Mich.; 29Aug47;
EP17079.

I Truly Love You, Darling; words
by Edna Mae Fryer, music by
Ray Hibbeler. © Edna Mae Fryer,
Harrison, Ohio; 12Nov47;
EP18755.

I Wonder if She'd Answer Me (if I
would say 'hello'); words by
Henry J. Willems, music by Ray
Hibbeler. © Henry Joseph
Willems, Kenosha, Wis.; 23Jul47;
EP15899.

If I Could Write a Song about
You; words & music by Leslie L.
Burbick & Ray Hibbeler. ©
Leslie Lea Burbick, Rogers,
Ohio; 29Oct47; EP17916.

I'm Flying without Wings; words &
music by Mabel Petersen and Ray
Hibbeler. © Mabel Rosoland
Petersen, Rock Falls, Ill.;
21Aug47; EP16561.

I've Forgotten How to Smile; words
and music by Henry E. Stiles and
Ray Hibbeler. © Nordyke Publishing Co., Los Angeles; 10Jun47;
EP16862.

Just an Old Tin-type Picture of
You; words by Nettie Johnson,
music by Ray Hibbeler. © Nordyke Publishing Co., Los Angeles;
12Apr47; EP16756.

Log Cabin Lady; words by Angeline
Warburton, music by Ray Hibbeler. © Angeline Juliet Warburton, St. Paul; 23Sep47; EP17338.

Moonlight through My Window;
words by Sue Taylor, music by
Ray Hibbeler. © Nordyke
Publishing Co., Los Angeles;
27Mar47; EP16918.

My Heart Beats in Hawaii; words
& music by Virginia Hurlock &
Ray Hibbeler. © Virginia Hurlock, Newark, Del.; 23Sep47;
EP18155.

My Sweetheart Jane of Tennessee;
words by Clara Jewell Durkin,
music by Ray Hibbeler. ©
Nordyke Publishing Co., Los
Angeles; 18Jul46; EP19440.

Song of the Bluebird; words by
Finette Kennedy, music by Ray
Hibbeler. © Finette Elizabeth
Kennedy, Shiocton, Wis.;
16Sep47; EP17315.

There's Music in Your Voice; words
by Charlotte C. Meyher, music by
Ray Hibbeler. © Charlotte
Caroline Meyher, Detroit; 4Sep47;
EP16998.

Tippin' Tug-boats; words by John
Pontician, music by Ray Hibbeler. © John Pontician, Pottsville, Pa.; 3Jul47; EP15789.

Way out West; words by Julia Barker,
music by Ray Hibbeler. © Julia
Halstad Barker, Inavale, Neb.;
10Sep47; EP17172.

We Need a Girl and a Boy; words &
music by Lorraine I. Kralovetz
& Ray Hibbeler. © Lorraine
Inez Kralovetz, Found, Wis.;
23Sep47; EP17649.

Where Did You Get Those Charms?
Words and music by Melanie Field
Hampton and Ray Hibbeler. ©
Nordyke Publishing Co., Los Angeles;
11Jun47; EP17579.

HIBBS, CLEO ALLEN.
Mist; for piano [by] Cleo Allen
Hibbs. © J. Fischer & Bro.,
New York; 19Sep47; EP17798.

Waltz Moderne; by Cleo Allen
Hibbs. © Volkwein Brothers,
inc., Pittsburgh; 9Sep47;
EP16698. For piano solo.

White Mice; by Cleo Allen Hibbs.
© Volkwein Brothers, inc.,
Pittsburgh; 9Sep47; EP16697.
For piano solo.

HICKMAN, ROGER M
Break Forth into Joy; anthem for
four-part chorus of mixed voices
with soprano and alto duet and
piano or organ accompaniment,
[words from] Isaiah 52:9, [music
by] Roger M. Hickman. © Boston
Music Co., Boston; 15Dec47;
EP20398.

[HICKS, TOM]
I'm Going to Get a Puppet; [by
Tom Hicks, c1945] © Nordyke
Publishing Co., Los Angeles;
16Sep47; EP17916. For voice
and piano.

HIGGINBOTHAM, IRENE.
It's Mad, Mad, Mad Lyric by Syd
Shaw, music by Irene Higgin-
botham. © Sinatra Songs, inc.,
New York; 13Nov47; EP18810.

HIGGINBOTHAM, LUTHER.
I Don't Know Where to Go but I'm
Goin'; words and music by Luther
Higginbotham. © Forster Music
Publisher, inc., Chicago;
26Aug47; EP17113.

HIGGINS, RAY.
My Album of Dreams; words and
music by Ray Higgins. © Nordyke Publishing Co., Los
Angeles; 14Dec46; EP19764.

285

HIGGINS, RUTH BELL.
Glad Tidings Hymnal; [by] Ruth Bell Higgins. © Ruth Bell Higgins, Rushville, Neb.; 3Nov47; A10593.

[HIGGINSON, J VINCENT] arr.
Melodies of Christendom; (S.A.B.) (Christmas) [arr. by] Cyr de Brant [pseud.] (First series) © The Arthur P. Schmidt Co., Boston; 9Oct47; on arrangement; EP18637.

HILE, RUTH, 1902-
The Jitta Rumba; by Ruth Hile, [words by] Charles C. Legler [and] Betty Mae Harris. © Superior Melodies Publishing Co., Chicago; 1Nov47; on changes in words and music; EP20417.

HILL, ALFRED.
Come Again, Summer; piano solo by Alfred Hill. © Chappell & Co., ltd., Sydney; 4Aug47; EP6542.

Highland Air. Och As Ochan Mo Chàradh. (Uses He for Charlie) Air collected by Captain S. Fraser ... arr. for the pianoforte by Alfred Hill. [c1946] © Chappell & Co., ltd., Sydney; 24Jun47; on arrangement; EP6621.

HILL, BILLY.
The Last Round-up; by Billy Hill. Arr. for ... S.A.B. (with piano acc.) by William Stickles. © Shapiro, Bernstein & Co., inc., New York; 30Jun47; on arrangement; EP15359.

HILL, CHARLES LEE.
Little Joe, the Wrangler. © Carl Fischer, inc., New York; 3Jul47; EP15749. Condensed score (band) and parts.

Swinging on the Range; by Charles Lee Hill. © Southern Music Co., San Antonio; 17Nov47; EP18836. Condensed score (band) and parts.

HILL, MIRRIE.
In Spite of All; song, music by Mirrie Hill, words by Gloria Rawlinson. © Chappell & Co., ltd., Sidney; 24Oct47; EP7277.

HILL, NORMAN E
After the Dawn Tomorrow; words & music by Norman E. Hill. © Nordyke Publishing Co., Los Angeles; 9Nov46; EP19428.

HILL, TOLBERT JUNIOR, 1910- arr.
Old Hundred ... (A chorale setting for three voices) with new words. Written and arr. by Tolbert Junior Hill [with the assistance of Thelma Willott] © Tolbert J. Hill, Champaign, Ill.; 28Jun47; on arrangement & new words; EP15556.

HILLIAM, BENTLEY COLLINGWOOD, 1890-
(Flotsam's Follies) Selection with words from Flotsam's Follies; by B. C. Hilliam. © Ascherberg, Hopwood & Crew, ltd., London; 1Dec47; EP7362. For piano solo.

Ladies of Lemington; words and music by B. C. Hilliam, arr. as part-song for mixed voices, S.A.T.B., by Clarence Lucas. © Ascherberg, Hopwood & Crew, ltd., London; 20Oct47; on arrangement; EP6959.

HINKLE, LILLIAN.
The Flustered Flea; piano solo, by Lillian Hinkle. © The Boston Music Co., Boston; 30Jul47; EP16094.

The Quilting Bee; piano solo, by Lillian Hinkle. © The Boston Music Co., Boston; 31Jul47; EP16003.

HINMAN, RALPH EMMERSON.
Hangin' Round a Country Store; words and music by Ralph Emmerson Hinman. © Tin Pan Alley, inc., New York; 19Aug46; EP7995.

HINSON, WILKS.
Baby, Don't You "No, no" Me; words and music by Wilks Hinson. © Nordyke Publishing Co., Los Angeles; 10May47; EP16934.

HIRSCHBERG, DAVID, 1899-
Little Dutch Dance ... [by] David Hirschberg. (In Hirschberg, David, ed. and comp. Pieces Are Fun. bk. 1, p. 8-9) © Musicord Publications, New York; 2Jul47; EP15929. For piano solo.

Peasant Dance ... [by] David Hirschberg. (In Hirschberg, David, ed. and comp. Pieces Are Fun. bk. 1, p. 32-33) © Musicord Publications, New York; 2Jul47; EP15940. For piano solo.

Sunny Rays ... [by] David Hirschberg. (In Hirschberg, David, ed. and comp. Pieces Are Fun. bk. 1, p. 16-17) © Musicord Publications, New York; 2Jul47; EP15932. For piano solo.

HIRSCHBERG, DAVID, 1899- ed. and comp.
Classics Are Fun ... selected classics comp., ed. and annotated by David Hirschberg ... illus. by Richmond E. Lawlor. © Musicord Publications, New York; 2Jun47; EP15402. For piano solo.

Pieces Are Fun ... selected pieces, comp., ed. and annotated by David Hirschberg. © Musicord Publications, New York; bk. 1, 2Jul47; EP16239. For piano solo.

HIRST, RICHARD.
Interlude in Waltz Time; by Richard Hirst, [for] piano. © Ascherberg, Hopwood & Crew, ltd., London; 24Jul47; EP6247.

HISCOCKS, HARRY.
Smile, Chum, Smile; words by Henry P. Bateman, music by Harry Hiscocks. © Nordyke Publishing Co., Los Angeles; 10Jun47; EP17195.

HITCHCOCK, MOTT.
Carmel Valley; words and music by Mott Hitchcock. [c1946] © Nordyke Publishing Co., Los Angeles; 30Oct47; EP19954.

HODEIGE, OCTAVE JEAN.
Ne Rame Pas; paroles de Pierre Jarjailles & Louis Charco, musique de O. Jean Hodeige. © Éditions Raoul Breton, Paris; 18Nov35; EP6310.

La Petite Boutique; paroles de Roméo Carlès, musique de Octave Hodeige. © Éditions Vianelly, Paris; 3Sep57; EP6308.

HODGES, EDWARD LEWIS, 1867-
Evening Prayer; words and music by Edward Lewis Hodges. © Christian Fellowship Organization, San Mateo, Calif.; 2Dec47; EP20212. Close score; SATB.

HOFFMAN, JUANITA.
Won't You Believe Me? Words and music by Juanita Hoffman. [c1946] © Nordyke Publishing Co., Los Angeles; 27Oct47;

HOFSTAD, MILDRED, 1905-
Roller Coaster; piano solo by Mildred Hofstad. © The Willis Music Co., Cincinnati; 22Oct47; EP18412.

HOISHOLT, MARY SPENCER, 1878-
Communion Anthem; [for] SA with soprano solo, music by Mary Spencer Hoisholt, words from hymn "Shepherd of souls." © Harold Flammer, inc. New York; 28Jul47; EP16247.

HOKANSON, MARGRETHE.
Adventus; (Juletid) [arr. by] Margrethe Hokanson. © J. Fischer & Bro., New York; 30Sep47; on arrangement; EP18306. For organ solo.

Infant Jesu; S.A.T.B. ... (a cappella or with accompaniment) [by] Margrethe Hokanson, [words by] Agnes P. Olsen. © J. Fischer & Bro., New York; 30Sep47; EP17706.

A Song at Evening. Aften Sang. [By] Margrethe Hokanson, versification of Norwegian translation by Mlodzik and Benfield. © Clayton F. Summy Co., Chicago; 2Jul47; EP15380. Score; SSAATBB.

HOLDATE, E LINFORD. See Holgate, Elsie Dorothy.

HOLGATE, ELSIE DOROTHY, 1888-
Music for Rhythmic Movement; for nursery school or kindergarten, by E. Linford Holgate. © William Paxton & Co., ltd., London; 21Oct46; EP5716. For piano.

Play Songs for the Nursery School; by E. Linford Holgate. © William Paxton & Co., ltd., London; bk. 1-2, 21Oct46; EP5715, 5763.

HOLLER, JOHN.
The Little Jesus; a Christmas folk song. Unison sacred song [by] John Holler, [words by] Lizette W. Reese. © The H. W. Gray Co., inc., New York; 31Oct47; EP18486.

HOLLINGSWORTH, CRYSTAL B 1891-
On a Holy Night; by Crystal B. Hollingsworth. © Crystal B. Hollingsworth, Connersville, Ind.; 28Sep47; EP16593. For voice and piano.

HOLLIS, L P 1923-
Don't Be That Way to Me; [by] L. P. Hollis, Jr. © L. P. Hollis jr., Greenville, S. C.; 30Nov47; EP20292. Melody and words.

I'm Helpless; [by] L. P. Hollis, jr. © L. P. Hollis, jr., Greenville, S. C.; 30Nov47; EP20291. Melody and words.

HOLLIS, PETE. See Hollis, L. P.

HOLLIS, RUBY SHAW, 1920- arr.
Carol of the New Year; S.S.A.A. (a cappella), 14th century English carol adapted and arr. by Ruby Shaw. Traditional [words] © C. C. Birchard & Co., Boston; 21Nov47; on arrangement; EP19022.

HOLLY, ANDY.
It Must Have Been an Ill Wind; words and music by Andy Holly. © Nordyke Publishing Co., Los Angeles; 12Jul47; EP17517.

HOLMES, MINOR, 1915-
Let Jesus Fix It for You ... words & music by Minor Holmes, arr. by Virginia Davis. © Minor Holmes, Chicago; 26Jun47; EP15296.

HOLST, EDUARD, 1843-1899.
The June Bug's Dance ... for the piano by Eduard Holst [ed. by Peter Randall, pseud.] © Boston Music Co., Boston; 28Nov47; on editing; EP19809.

HOLST, GUSTAV, 1874-1934.
Scherzo; by Gustav Holst. Full
score. © Hawkes & Son (London)
ltd., London; 16Oct47; EF6819.
For orchestra.

HOLST, IMOGEN.
In Heaven It Is Always Autumn; set
for unacc. female voices (S.S.S.A.
A.) [by] Imogen Holst, the words
by John Donne. © The Oxford
University Press, London; 3Jul47;
EF6172.

HOLST, IMOGEN, arr.
Folk Songs of the British Isles.
Chansons Populaires des Iles
Britanniques. Canciones Populares
de las Islas Británicas.
Selected and set for piano by
Imogen Holst. Traductions
françaises par M. du Chastain.
Traducciones españolas para C.
Alonso. © Hawkes & Son (London)
ltd., London; 20Aug47; on arrange-
ment; EF6261. For piano solo,
with English, French and Spanish
words.
Six Traditional Carols; arr. for
S.S.A. unaccompanied by Imogen
Holst. © Oxford Univ. Press,
London; 21Aug47; on arrangement;
EF6661.

HOLSTEIN, BEULAH D   1907-
Witnessing for Christ; [by] Beulah
Holstein, har. Esther Scott.
© Beulah D. Holstein, Wilmington,
Calif.; 17May47; EP15295. Close
score: SATB.

HOLSTROM, EYELA JANETTE.
Darling, I Love You; words and
music by Eyela Janette Hol-
strom. © Nordyke Publishing
Co., Los Angeles; 12Jul47;
EP17634.

HOLTON, BEN.
Ain't I Losing You? Words and
music by Ben Holton. © Lois
Publishing Co., Hollywood,
Calif.; 15Sep47; EP17224.

HOLTON, FRED B., pseud. See
Wilson, Ira Bishop.

HOLUB, JAMES.
Sleepy-Time; words and music by
James Holub. © Nordyke Publish-
ing Co., Los Angeles; 3Sep47;
EP20018.

HOLT, ALFRED, 1866-
Dreizig Kurze Harfensätze zum
Gebrauch beim Unterricht; musik:
Alfred Holt. Op.35. © Ludwig
Doblinger (Bernhard Herzmansky)
k.g., Vienna; 23Jul46; EF6236.

HOLY NAME SOCIETY.
The Official Holy Name Hymnal;
comp. by J. J. McLarney. ©
National Headquarters of Holy
Name Societies, New York; 10Oct47;
EP17879.

HOLZMANN, RUDOLPH, 1910-
Tres Madrigales; (Pablo Neruda)
para canto y piano ... [by]
Rudolph Holzmann. © Editorial
Argentina de Música (E.A.M.),
Buenos Aires; 7Nov46; EF5996.

HONEGGER, ARTHUR, 1892-
Intrada ... [by] Arthur Honegger.
© Éditions Salabert, Paris;
25Jul47; EF6409. Score
(trumpet and piano) and part.

Mimaamaquim; (Psaume CXXX) [by]
Arthur Honegger. © Éditions
Salabert, Paris; 25Jul47;
EF6406. For voice and piano.

Petit Cours de Morale; extrait de
"Suzanne et le Pacifique" de Jean
Giraudoux. © Éditions Salabert,
Paris; 18Aug47; EF7251. For voice
and piano.

Quatre Chansons; pour voix grave,
[by] Arthur Honegger. (Words by
Archag Tchobanian, William Aguet,
Paul Verlaine and Pierre de Ronsard) © Éditions Salabert, Paris;
5Aug47; EF7244.

Sérénade à Angélique; [by] Arthur
Honegger, pour petit orchestre.
© Éditions Salabert, Paris;
25Jul47; EF6402.

Souvenir de'Chopin; pour piano
[by] A. Honegger. © Choudens,
éditeur, Paris; 22Jul47; EF6577.

(Symphony, no. 4) Symphonie no
IV (Delicias basilienses) [by]
Arthur Honegger. © Éditions
Salabert, Paris; 25Jul47; EF6403.

HOPFIELD, HERBERT FERDINAND, 1894-
Then I Knew You Were Mine; words
& music by Herb Hopfield. [c1946]
© Herbert Ferdinand Hopfield,
Baltimore; 16Apr47; EP16224.

HOPKINS, EDWIN.
Crosstown Stroll; an operetta in
three movements for soprano and
contralto; words and music by
Edwin Hopkins. © Edwin Hopkins,
New York; 8Sep47; EP18271.

HOPKINS, H   P   1900-
Camping Out ... [by] H. P. Hopkins. (In Hirschberg, David,
ed. and comp.   Pieces Are Fun.
bk. 1, p. 2-3) © Musicord
Publications, New York; 2Jul47;
EP15926. For piano solo.

Circus Parade ... [by] H. P.
Hopkins. (In Hirschberg, David,
ed. and comp.   Pieces Are Fun.
bk. 1, p. 18-19) © Musicord
Publications, New York;
2Jul47; EP15933. For piano solo.

Pretty Rainbow ... [by] H. P.
Hopkins. (In Hirschberg, David,
ed. and comp.   Pieces Are Fun.
bk. 1, p. 6-7) © Musicord
Publications, New York; 2Jul47;
EP15928. For piano solo.

HOPKINS, HARRY P
The Big Bass Drum; by H. P.
Hopkins. Piano solo. ©
Harold Flammer, inc., New York;
28Jul47; EP16259.

HOPKINS, HARRY P. TERSON, 1890-
Night Magic; chorus for treble
voices, accompanied (S.S.A.)
[by] H. P. Hopkins, text adapted
from the French by H. P. H.
© Hall & McCreary Co., Chicago;
20Oct47; on music & adaptation of
text; EP18039.

HOPKINS, HARRY PATTERSON.
Hippity-Hop; [by] H. P. Hopkins,
[ed. by Walter Rolfe] ©
Century Music Publishing Co.,
New York; 6Aug47; EP16123.
For piano solo.

Indian Flute; (invocation) [by]
H. P. Hopkins. © Edward Schubert & Co., inc., New York;
24Nov47; EP18905. For organ
solo; includes registration
for Hammond organ.

Snow Girl; [by] H . P. Hopkins
based on a Canadian lyric. ©
The Arthur P. Schmidt Co.,
Boston; 4Sep47; EP16104.
Score: SSA and piano.

Summer Nocturne; [by] Harry
Patterson Hopkins. © The
Arthur P. Schmidt Co., Boston;
4Sep47; EP16266. For piano
solo.

HOPKINS, JOSEPH M
April Nosegay; for piano [by]
Joseph M. Hopkins. © Theodore
Presser Co., Philadelphia;
21Oct47; EP18416.

I Waited for the Lord; [by] Joseph
M. Hopkins, text: Psalm 40 from
the Psalter hymnal. © Volkwein
Bros., inc., Pittsburgh;
24Oct47; EP18288. Score: SATB
and piano.

Let Not Your Heart Be Troubled;
sacred vocal solo by Joseph M.
Hopkins, [words from John 14: 1-
3. c1946] © Volkwein Bros.,
inc., Pittsburgh; 24Oct47;
EP18621.

HOPPER, HAL.
The Riddle Song; words and music
by Hal Hopper. New York,
Capitol Songs, inc. © Criterion
Music Corp., New York; 30Aug47;
EP17038.

HORACEK, LEO.
The Way to Music on the Guitar;
by Leo Horacek. © McKinley
Publishers, inc., Chicago;
23Sep47; EP17819.

HORNETT, SPIKE.
Alto Mood at Midnite; composed
and arr. by Spike Hornett. ©
Cinephonic Music Co., ltd.,
London; 21Oct46; EF6042. Piano-
conductor score (orchestra)
and parts.

HORST, ADAM G
The Prince of Peace; [a Christmas
cantata] by Adam G. Horst. ©
Adam G. Horst, Portland, Or.;
12Oct46; EP15995.

HORST, MYRON.
You Rate High with Me; words and
music by Myron Horst. © Nordyke Publishing Co., Los Angeles; 13Aug47; EP19768.

HORTON, VAUGHN, 1911-
Ball and Chain Boogie; words and
music by Vaughn Horton. © Rytvoc, inc., New York; 10Jul47;
EP6996.

Sold Down the River; words and
music by Vaughn Horton. © Rytvoc, inc., New York; 10Jul47;
EP6999.

Sweet Corrina Blues; words and
music by Vaughn Horton. © Rytvoc, inc., New York; 10Jul47;
EP6998.

Teardrops in My Heart; words and
music by Vaughn Horton. ©
Southern Music Publishing Co.,
inc., New York; 27Aug47;
EP17859.

You Should Live So Long; words
and music by Vaughn Horton.
© Rytvoc, inc., New York;
24Oct47; EP18167.

HOUCK, CLARK, 1916-
This Time the Joke's on Me; music
and lyrics by Clark Houck. ©
Hollywood Melodies, Hollywood,
Calif.; 14Aug47; EP15983.

HOUGH, BASSETT W
Benedictus Es, Domine; set to
music in the key of G by
Bassett W. Hough. © H. W. Gray
Co., inc., New York; 12Sep47;
EP17374. Score: SATB and
organ; English words.

HOUSE, CHARLIE, 1914-
New Mexico Sunset; words by
Daisy Dean [pseud.], music by
Charlie House. © Kelly Music
Publications, Franklin, Pa.;
15Oct47; EP17691.

HOUSE, L   MARGUERITTE.
Professor Owl; or, Adventures in
Storyland; an operetta for the
elementary schools in one act,
by L. Margueritte House. © Row,
Peterson & Co., Evanston, Ill.;
4Nov47; D pub 11440.

HOVEN, GEORGE, 1913-
Hot Stuff Polka; accordion solo,
music by George Hoven, arr. by
Ray F. Maus. [c1946] ©
George Hoven, Chester, Pa.;
30Oct47; EP17678.

HOVEN, GEORGE. Cont'd.
Ocean City Polka; accordion solo,
music by George Hoven, arr. by
Philip Dubas. [c1946] ©
George Hoven, Chester, Pa.;
30ct47; EP17677.

Streamline Polka; accordion solo,
music by George Hoven, arr. by
Michael Ostrowski. [c1946] ©
George Hoven, Chester, Pa.;
30ct47; EP17676.

The Ward Grille Polka ... Accordion solo, music [and words] by
George Hoven, arr. by Ben Matu-
sek. © George Hoven, Chester,
Pa.; 30ct47; EP17675.

Woogie-boogie polka; accordion
solo, music by George Hoven,
arr. by Henri B. Butler. [c1946]
© George Hoven, Chester, Pa.;
30ct47; EP17674.

HOVEY, SERGE.
Lullaby for a Union Man; music by
Serge Hovey, words by Les Pine
and Harold Bernardi. © Music
Publications inc., Elkins Park,
Pa.; 16Dec47; EP19927.

[HOWARD, JACK] comp.
101 Ranch Boys; [music by Andy
Reynolds, Clifford L. Brown and
others, words by George Long
and others, comp. by Jack
Howard] © Jack Howard Publications, inc., Philadelphia;
1Jul47; EP16986.

HOWARD, JOHN TASKER. —
It Is Christmas in This House;
[S.A.T.B. divided, a cappella]
[by] John Tasker Howard, [poem
by Abigail Cresson] © Carl Fischer,
inc., New York; 24Sep47; EP18070.

HOWARD, JOSEPH EDGAR, 1880-
Be Sweet to Me Kid. See also his I
Wonder Who's Kissing Her Now.

Honeymoon. See also his I Wonder Who's
Kissing Her Now.

"Honeymoon" Medley. See his I Wonder
Who's Kissing Her Now.

I Wonder Who's Kissing Her Now
... by Joseph E. Howard, a Hal
Leonard arrangement. © Edward
B. Marks Music Corp., New York;
12Nov47; on arrangement; EP13666.
Condensed score (band) and parts.

(I Wonder Who's Kissing Her Now)
"Honeymoon" Medley, introducing
"Be Sweet to Me, Kid," both from
"I Wonder Who's Kissing Her Now"
... lyrics by Will M. Hough &
Frank R. Adams, music by Joseph
E. Howard, arr. by George Snow-
hill. © Edward B. Marks Music
Corp., New York; 27Jun47; on
arrangement; EP15482. Piano-
conductor score (orchestra, with
words) and parts.

(I Wonder Who's Kissing Her Now)
Honeymoon; [The waning honey-
moon], lyrics by Will M. Hough
and Frank R. Adams, music by
Joseph E. Howard. [French lyric
by Mario-Anne. From] "I Wonder
Who's Kissing Her Now." ©
Edward B. Marks Music Corp.,
New York; 12Sep47; on French lyric;
EP17117. French and English words.

I Wonder Who's Kissing Her Now;
music by Joseph E. Howard, arr.
for piano accordion by Charles
Nunzio. © Edward B. Marks Music
Corp., New York; 5Sep47; on
arrangement; EP16673.

I Wonder Who's Kissing Her Now,
music by Joseph E. Howard,
lyrics by Will M. Hough and
Frank R. Adams, arr. for
Hawaiian, electric & plectrum
guitar (note & diagram) [by]
Oahu Pub. Co. © Edward B.
Marks Music Corp., New York;
on arrangement; 17Jul47;
EP15656.

(I Wonder Who's Kissing Her Now)
What's the Use of Dreaming? From
"I Wonder Who's Kissing Her Now"
... words and music by Joseph E.
Howard, arr. by George Snowhill.
© Edward B. Marks Music Corp.,
New York; 27Jun47; on arrange-
ment; EP15483. Piano-conductor
score (orchestra, with words)
and parts.

What's the Use of Dreaming? See also
his I Wonder Who's Kissing Her Now.

HOWELL, INEZ, 1885-
A Bobolink in May; a piano solo
by Inez Howell. © Belwin,
inc., New York; 130ct47;
EP18013.

Easter Lily; piano solo by Inez
Howell. © Belwin, inc., New
York; 130ct47; EP18017.

Golliwogg's Dance; for piano solo
by Inez Howell. Ⓓ The Willis
Music Co., Cincinnati; 24Oct47;
EP18450.

Lilac Time; piano solo by Inez
Howell. © Belwin, inc., New
York; 130ct47; EP18016.

Sleigh Bells in the Snow ; a piano
solo by Inez Howell. © Belwin,
inc., New York; 130ct47; EP18012

HOWELL, MARVIN.
In the Fair Twilight Hour; words
by Stan Tucker; music by Marvin Howell. © Nordyke Publishing Co., Los Angeles; 19Jun47;
EP17440.

HOWELLS, HERBERT.
Magnificat and Nunc Dimittis ...
by Herbert Howells. © Novello
& Co. ltd., London; 31Jul47;
EP5946. In part for chorus
(SSATB) and organ; in part for
tenor, chorus (SATBB) and organ.
English words.

Magnificat and Nunc Dimittis ...
by Herbert Howells. © Novello
& Co. ltd., London; 13Aug47;
EP6276. Score; mixed chorus
and organ; English words.

HOWORTH, WAYNE, 1895-
As Lately We Watched; S.A.T.B.
(divided) [with] tenor solo.
Austrian, arr. by Wayne Howorth.
© The Raymond A. Hoffman Co.,
Chicago; 30Nov39; EP15585.

Deep River; [spiritual] S.A.T.B.
with solo for medium voice, harmonized and arr. by Wayne Howorth. © Belwin, inc., New York;
5Dec47; on arrangement; EP19273.

Deep River; [spiritual] S.S.A.
with contralto solo harmonized
and arr. by Wayne Howorth. ©
Belwin, inc., New York; 5Dec47;
on arrangement; EP19272.

The First Noel; S.A.T.B. (divided),
[with] solo. Traditional,
arr. by Wayne Howorth. © The
Raymond A. Hoffman Co., Chicago;
22Nov39; EP15574.

Let Our Gladness Know No End;
S.S.A. (a capella ad. lib.) Old
Bohemian Christmas carol, arr.
by Ole Ryg [pseud.] © Belwin,
inc., New York; 18Dec47; on arrangement; EP19930.

Let Our Gladness Know No End; S.S.
A. (a capella ad lib.), Old Bo-
hemian Christmas carol, arr. by
Ole Ryg [pseud.], traditional
© Belwin, inc., New
York; 6Nov47; on arrangement;
EP18540.

HOYL, JIM, pseud. See
Heifetz, Jascha.

HOYO, FAUSTINO DEL, 1909-
Preludio y Doble Fuga; [by]
Faustino Del Hoyo, piano solo.
© Edward B. Marks Music Corp.,
New York; 7Jul47; EP15442.

HUBAY, JENO.
Minek Turbékoltok. (Tell Me Why
You're Always Cooing) English
lyric by Olga Paul, music by Hubay Jeno. (In Festi, Barbara,
comp. Memories of Hungary. p.
56-57) © Edward B. Marks Music
Corp., New York; 19Nov47; on
English lyric; EP19014.

HUBBARD, HAL.
I'm So Helpless in Your Arms;
lyrics by Earl Carroll, music
by Hal Hubbard. ♩ Piantadosi
Music Publications, Encino,
Calif.; 8Apr47; EP16168.

HUBBARD, THOMAS H 1913-
He Is My Song; [by] Thomas H.
Hubbard. Ⓓ Thomas H. Hubbard,
Columbus, Ohio; 15Jun47;
EP16085. For voice and piano.

HUBBELL, FRANK ALLEN, 1907-
Chirpy Cricket; record, music,
story & comic book. Story by
Frank Bonham ... Drawings by
Mel Millar, music ... by Frank
Hubbell. Told by Daws Butler and
"Tip" Corning. © Belda Record
and Publishing Co., Pasadena,
Calif.; 20Apr47; on Dance of
the Crickets; EP16165. Includes
Dance of the Crickets, p.[2-3]
of cover of album.

HUBBELL, RAYMOND.
(The Big Show) Poor Butterfly,
from the musical production,
"The Big Show" ... words by John
L. Golden, music by Raymond
Hubbell. A Jerry Sears arrangement. Ⓓ Harms, inc., New York;
20Nov47; on arrangement;
EP19173. Piano-conductor score
(orchestra, with words) and
parts.

Poor Butterfly. See his The Big Show.

HUBER, HARRY SOLAND, 1892-
Three Little Kittens; words and
music by Harry Huber. © Harry
Huber, Hackensack, N. J.;
10Jun47; EP15454.

HUBER, WERNER, 1894-
Der Köbu u der Chrigu u der
Sepp; Jodel-Lied von Werner
Huber. © Edition Helbling,
Zürich, Switzerland; 10Feb37;
EF3953.

HUCKLENUTT, INKY, pseud. See
Miller, Bob.

HUDSON, JEAN T
Because I Love You So; words and
music by Jean T. Hudson. ©
Nordyke Publishing Co., Los
Angeles; 18Jul46; EP19395.

HUERTER, CHARLES.
A Little Dutch Dance; for the
piano, by Charles Huerter. ©
Sam Fox Publishing Co., New
York; 15Sep47; EP17295.

HUESTON, BILLY, 1893-
Ev'ry Thing'll Be All Right; words
and music by Bonnie Martini,
Clarence Maher and Billy Hueston,
[piano arr. by Dick Jacobs] ©
Bee-C-Bee Music Corp., New York;
18Aug47; EP16993.

I'm Having a Lot of Fun Growing
Old; words and music by Bonnie
Martini, Clarence Maher and
Billy Hueston, [piano arr. by
Dick Jacobs] © Bee-C-Bee Music
Corp., New York; 18Aug47;
EP16992.

When I Say I Love You, It's Really
My Heart That Speaks; words and
music by Bonnie Martini, Clarence
Maher and Billy Hueston, [piano
arr. by Dick Jacobs] © Bee-C-Bee
Music Corp., New York; 18Aug47;
EP16991.

HUFFMAN, CARL H
Autumn's Waning ... clarinet
quartet [for] two E♭, alto and
bass clarinets or four B♭ clarinets, [by] Carl H. Huffman. ©
C. L. Barnhouse Co., Oskaloosa,
Iowa; 17Sep47; EP18549. Score
and parts.

HUFFNAGLE, HARRY.
Black Velvet; by Harry Huffnagle,
trumpet solo with dance
orchestra. [c1946] © David
Gornston, New York; 25Sep47;
EP17243. Piano-conductor score
(orchestra) and parts.

HUGET, ARTHUR JOHN, 1918-
Here I Am, Lord; music and lyrics
by Arthur Huget. © Arthur John
Huget, Portland, Or.; 10Oct47;
EP18172.

HUGHES, BILLY.
Ain't That Too Bad; words and
music by Billy Hughes. © Hill
and Range Songs, inc., Hollywood,
Calif.; 14Nov47; EP18768.
Nobody's Fool; words and music by
Billy Hughes. © Hill and Range
Songs, inc., Hollywood, Calif.;
26Jun47; EP15316.

HUGHES, JOHN.
Love Divine, from Jesus Flowing;
S.S.A. with descant ... arr. by
Griffith J. Jones. Words by
General Booth. [Winona Lake, Ind.,
The Rodeheaver Hall-Mack Co.] ©
The Rodeheaver Co., Winona Lake,
Ind.; 28Mar46; on arrangement;
EP2718.

HUMPHREYS, DONALD EDWIN.
I Will Lift Up Mine Eyes unto the
Hills; (Psalm 121) ... by Don
Humphreys. High. © The Boston
Music Co., Boston; 29Apr47;
EP17331.

--- --- Ed. for low voice.
The Lord Is My Light; (Psalm
XXVII,) sacred song by Edwin
McDonald [pseud.] Low [voice]
© The Boston Music Co., Boston;
15Aug47; EP16422.

— — Edition for high voice.
© The Boston Music Co., Boston;
15Aug47; EP16423.

[HUGUET Y TAGELL, ROGELIO JOSÉ]
1882-
Les Deux Manières ... Je Te
Pardonne ... paroles de Frami-
que [pseud.], musique de R.
Dorcine [pseud.] © Éditions
Salabert, Paris; 8Jul47; EP6407.
Piano-conductor score (orches-
tra, with words) and parts.

Les Deux Manières ... Paroles de
Framique [pseud.], musique de
R. Dorcine [pseud.] © Éditions
Salabert, Paris; 10Apr47;
EP5922.

Hurra pour l'Espagne! ... Paroles
de Framique [pseud.], musique
de R. Dorcine [pseud.] ©
Éditions Salabert, Paris,
10Apr47; EP5880.

Je Te Pardonne ... Paroles de
Framique [pseud.], musique de
R. Dorcine [pseud.] © Éditions
Salabert, Paris; 10Apr47;
EP5882.

Léa Lili, Lola, Loulou! ... Paroles
de Framique [pseud.], musique de
R. Dorcine [pseud.] © Éditions
Salabert, Paris; 10Apr47; EP5959.

HULIN, DAMARIS, 1897-
Gypsy Trails and Rainbow Trails; two
songs for medium voice, words by
Agnes Davenport Bond, music by
Damaris Hulin. © Wesley Webster,
San Francisco; 12Aug47; EP16158.

HULIN, DONALD NEWTON, 1919-
Absolute Surrender ... [by]
Donald N. Hulin, [harmonized by
Earle Freeman Hulin] c1946.
(In Booth, F. Carlton, comp.
Living Above Songs and Choruses.
no.51) © Earle Freeman Hulin,
Cranston, R. I.; 4Apr47;
EP18951. Close score: SATB.

Jesus Is the Same ... [by] Donald
N. Hulin, [harmonized by Earle
Freeman Hulin] c1946. (In
Booth, F. Carlton, comp. Living
Above Songs and Choruses. no.
65) © Earle Freeman Hulin,
Cranston, R. I.; 4Apr47;
EP18955. Close score: SATB.

The Path of the Just ... [by]
Donald N. Hulin, [harmonized by
Earle Freeman Hulin] c1946.
(In Booth, F. Carlton, comp.
Living Above Songs and Choruses.
no.9) © Earle Freeman Hulin,
Cranston, R. I.; 4Apr47;
EP18945. Close score: SATB.

That My Lord May Live ... [by]
Donald N. Hulin, [harmonized by
Earle Freeman Hulin] c1946.
(In Booth, F. Carlton, comp.
Living Above Songs and Choruses.
no.18) © Earle Freeman Hulin,
Cranston, R. I.; 4Apr47;
EP18947.

HULIN, EARLE FREEMAN, 1916-
Give Me a Burden ... [by] Earle F.
Hulin. c1946. (In Booth F.
Carlton, comp. Living Above
Songs and Choruses. no.59) ©
Earle Freeman Hulin, Cranston,
R. I.; 4Apr47; EP18952. Close
score: SATB.

I Need Thee, Lord ... [by] Earle
F. Hulin. c1946. (In Booth,
F. Carlton, comp. Living Above
Songs and Choruses. no.55)
© Earle Freeman Hulin, Cranston,
R. I.; 4Apr47; EP18949.

I Want My Life to Count for Jesus
... [by] Earle F. Hulin. c1946.
(In Booth, F. Carlton, comp.
Living Above Songs and Choruses.
no. 11) © Earle Freeman Hulin,
Cranston, R. I.; 4Apr47;
EP18946. Close score: SATB.

I Want to Rise Above the World ...
[by] Earle F. Hulin. c1946.
(In Booth, F. Carlton, comp.
Living Above Songs and Choruses.
no. 1) © Earle Freeman Hulin,
Cranston, R. I.; 4Apr47;
EP18944.

I Would Like to Have Seen Jesus ...
[by] Earle F. Hulin. c1946.
(In Booth, F. Carlton, comp.
Living Above Songs and Choruses.
no.26) © Earle Freeman Hulin,
Cranston, R. I., 4Apr47; EP18948.

Just to Know Him ... [by] Earle F.
Hulin. c1946. (In Booth, F.
Carlton, comp. Living Above
Songs and Choruses. no.46) ©
Earle Freeman Hulin, Cranston,
R. I.; 4Apr47; EP18950.

HULL, DOROTHY, 1916-
Color Blind; words by James Car-
hartt and Nicholas Winter,
music by Dorothy Hull. ©
Edward B. Marks Music Corp.,
New York; 25Nov47; EP19042.

[HULL, RUSSELL EUGENE] 1911- comp.
Sheriff Tom Owen's Cowboys; a
collection of favorite songs,
[by R. E. Hull, John Thomas
Yaklevich, and others, words
by Elmer Wickham, R. E. Hull,
and others, comp. by R. E. Hull]
© Country Music Publishers
(owner, Russ Hull), Chicago;
bk.1, 22Aug47; EP18221.

HUMEL, CHARLES, pseud. See
Melone, Michel Hubert.

HUMMER, DICK, 1914-
Ridin' on Two Flats; by Dick Hummer, [arr. by] Frankie Carle
[pseud.] © Bel-Air Music Corp.,
Hollywood, Calif., 26Sep47; on
arrangement; EP18222. For
piano solo.

HUMPERDINCK, ENGELBERT, 1854-1921.
Evening Prayer and Dream Pantomine;
from the opera "Hansel and
Gretel," for four-part chorus
of mixed voices with piano acc.
[By] E. Humperdinck, arr. by
Peter J. Wilhousky. English
text by Lorraine Noel Finley.
© Carl Fischer, inc., New York;
17Jul47; on arrangement and
English text; EP15070.

Prayer; from the opera "Hansel and
Gretel," for two equal voices,
[by] Engelbert Humperdinck, arr.
by E. C. Currie. Stanza 1 tr.,
stanza 2 composed by Edw. C.
Currie. © McLaughlin & Reilly
Co., Boston; 20Jun47; on arrangement and new text; EP15876.

HUNE, BILL.
Yes, I Do; words and music by Bill
Hune. © Nordyke Publishing Co.,
Los Angeles; 19Jun47; EP17435.

HUNT, BILLIE.
Make With the Music (bang it
around) words & music by
Billie Hunt. © Nordyke Publish-
ing Co., Los Angeles; 27Sep46;
EP19444.

HUNT, EARLE RADMORE.
Sing, Christian, Sing; [by] Earle
R. Hunt ... harmony by N. L.
Ridderhof. (In Hymn writers'
Magazine. v.I, no.1, p.14)
© Earle Radmore Hunt, Santa
Monica, Calif.; 1Jul47; B5-1050.
Close score: SATB.

HUNT, FLOYD.
Fool That I Am; lyric and music
by Floyd Hunt, [arr. by Floyd
Hunt] © St. Louis Music Corp.,
Hollywood, Calif.; 30Oct47; on
arrangement; EP18543.

Fool That I Am; lyric and music
by Floyd Hunt. © Melo Song
Publishers, New York; 8Jun46;
EP16710.

HUNT, OLIVER DAVID.
In a Honeymoon Teepee ... lyric
and music by Oliver David Hunt.
© Art Music Co., New York;
22Nov47; EP19020.

HUNT, REGINALD, 1891-
Meditation; [by] Reginald Hunt.
(London) Boosey & Hawkes. ©
Hawkes & Son (London) ltd., Lon-
don; 6Nov47; EP7011. Score
(clarinet and piano) and part.

HUNT, RICHARD G
I Done Did It; words and music
by Richard G. Hunt. ©
Nordyke Publishing Co., Los
Angeles; 28Mar47; EP16427.

HUNT, SCOTTY.
That Big Physique from Martinique;
words & music by Stephen McNeil
& Scotty Hunt. © Sherwood
Music Co., Los Angeles; 8Oct47;
EP17817.

HUNTLEY, ELIZABETH MADDOX.
The Ten Commandments ... by Elizabeth
Maddox Huntley. St. Louis,
Distributors, Hunluth Music Co.
© Elizabeth Maddox Huntley,
St. Louis; 10Jun47; EP15925.
For voice and piano.

HURST, GEORGE, 1926-
Music, When Soft Voices Die; poem
by Percy B. Shelley, music by
George Hurst. © BMI Canada, ltd.,
Toronto; 2Sep47; EF6594.

289

HURSTON, ZORA NEALE, comp.
Caribbean Melodies; for chorus of
mixed voices and soloists,
dancers ad libitum, with acc.
for piano and percussion instruments. Collected and annotated
by Zora Neale Hurston, arr. by
William Grant Still. D Oliver
Ditson Co., Philadelphia;
15Oct47; on collection, annotation & arrangement; EP18192.

HURTGEN, LEW.
A Star over Texas; words and
music by Lew Hurtgen. ©
Nordyke Publishing Co., Los
Angeles; 12Jun46; EP19415.

HUSTON, FRANK CLAUDE, 1871-
Hello, Ev'rybody! Let Us Get
Acquainted; [by] Frank C.
Huston. © Frank C. Huston,
Jacksonville, Fla.; 10Oct47;
EP17804. Close score: SATB.

Three New Songs ... by Frank C.
Huston. © Frank C. Huston,
Jacksonville, Fla.; 16Jul47;
Contents. - There's a Glad New
Joy (© EP17316) - Since I Stop-
ped and Listened to Jesus (©
17317) - Walking with Jesus
(© 17318)

HUTCHENS, FRANK.
Christmas Bells; by Frank Hutchens.
© Chappell & Co., ltd., London;
1Jul47; EP6230. Score: piano 1-2.

HUTCHINSON, VICTOR HELY, d. 1947.
Overture to a Pantomime; [by] Victor
Hely Hutchinson. © Keith, Prowse
& Co., ltd., London; 25Nov47;
EP7289. Score: orchestra.

HUTCHISON, CHARLES B.
She Is the One for Me; words and
music by Charles B. Hutchison.
© Nordyke Publishing Co., Los
Angeles; 10Oct47; EP20016.

HYDE, ALEXANDER.
American Wings Band Book; by Alex-
ander Hyde ... bandstrated from
composer's original scores by
Lou Halmy & Chas. Stevens. ©
Southern Music Publishing Co.,
inc., New York; 30Dec44; EP19249.
Piano-conductor score.

HYDE, MIRIAM.
Under the Milky Way; ten elementary piano pieces which may also be used as songs for children ... words and music by
Miriam Hyde. [c1946] ©
Chappell & Co., ltd., Sydney;
28Jan47; EP6324.

HYDEN, A   FRANKLIN.
My Golden Opportunity; words
and music by A. Franklin
Hyden. © Nordyke Publishing
Co., Los Angeles; 3Jul47;
EP17488.

HYDEN, WALFORD.
(Caravan) Oriana's Romance; by
Walford Hyden, from the ...
picture 'Caravan' © Cinephonic
Music Co., ltd., London;
18Jul46; EP6010. For piano
solo.

Oriana's Romance. See his Caravan.

HYDEN, WALFORD, comp.
Pavlova; an album of music with
illus. from Pavlova's famous
ballets, comp. by Walford Hyden.
© Chappell & Co., ltd., London;
20Oct47; EP6892. For piano solo.

HYNES, GERARD.
Dreaming Sweet Dreams; words and
music by Gerard Hynes. ©
Nordyke Publishing Co., Los
Angeles; 1Jun47; EP16952.

IAKOBIDES, Z
Apopse Th'artho na Se Klepso ...
etichoi; K. Nikolaide, mousikē
Z. Iakobidē. Athēnai, Ekdoseis
Gaitanou. © Michael Gaetanos,
Athens; 15May47; EP5770. For
voice and piano.

IBERT, JACQUES, 1890-
Les Amours de Jupiter; ballet en
cinq tableaux sur un scenario
de Boris Kochn., musique de
Jacques Ibert, transcription
pour piano par Irène Aitoff.
© Salabert, inc., New York;
21May47; on arrangement; EP5917.

(Barbe Bleue) Deux Chansons de
Melpomène; pour soprano avec
accompagnement de piano ...
Extraits de l'opéra-bouffe radio-
phonique "Barbe Bleue" ...
Paroles de William Aguet, musique
de Jacques Ibert. © Heugel & Cie,
Paris; 17Mar47; EP6504.

(Barbe Bleue) Quintette de la
Peur; avec acc. de piano ... de
l'opéra-bouffe radiophonique,
"Barbe Bleue" ... paroles de
William Aguet, musique de
Jacques Ibert. © Heugel & Cie,
Paris; 17Mar47; EP6437.

Deux Chansons de Melpomène. See his
Barbe Bleue.

IDEN, RAYMOND JOHN, 1890-
His Servants Never More than Ho;
[words by] Dorothy Ehernnan,
[music by] Raymond J. Iden. ©
Dorothy Ehernnan, Columbus
Grove, Ohio; 25Jul47; EP15903.
Close score: SATB.

Is Everybody Happy? [By] Raymond
J. Iden, [words by] Alfred Fedora. © Alfred Otto Fedora, Indianapolis; 2Aug47; EP18534.
Close score: SATB.

My Jesus Knows, and I Am Satisfied
... [words by] Alfred Fedora,
[music by] Raymond J. Iden. ©
Alfred Otto Fedora, Indianapolis;
2Aug47; EP18977. Close score:
SATB.

IDRISS, RAMEY.
(If You Know Susie) My Brooklyn Love
Song; words and music by George
Tibbles and Ramey Idriss, from the
... picture "If You Knew Susie."
© Triangle Music Corp., New York;
21Nov47; EP20164.

My Brooklyn Love Song. See his If You
Knew Susie.

Quintette de la Peur. See his Barbe
Bleue.

IGLESIAS VILLOUD, HECTOR, 1913-
La Chola Apasionada; [by] H. Iglesias Villoud, para piano.
[c1941] © Ricordi Americana,
s.a.e.c., Buenos Aires; 25Mar42;
EP6975.

ILDA, LEWIS, pseud. See also
Dash, Irwin.

A Shanty in Ypsilanti; words and
music by Box [pseud.], Cox and
Lewis Ilda. © Irwin Dash Music
Co., ltd., London; 21Apr47;
EF3940.

ILGENFRITZ, McNAIR.
As We Part; three-part chorus for
female voices, S.S.A. Words by
Fredrick Peterson, music by
McNair Ilgenfritz, arr. by Otto
Wick. © Edward Schuberth & Co.,
inc., New York; 14Aug47; on
arrangement; EP16357.

At the Opera; song by McNair Ilgenfritz. © Edward Schuberth & Co.,
inc., New York; 24Nov47;
EP18907.

Blow, Blow, Thou Winter Wind ...
Three-part chorus for female
voices, S.S.A. Lyric from "As
You Like It" [by] Shakespeare,
music by McNair Ilgenfritz, arr.
by Otto Wick. © Edward Schuberth
& Co., inc., New York; 14Aug47;
on arrangement; EP16356.

INCH, HERBERT.
The Return to Zion; (S.S.A. with
piano or organ acc.) [by] Herbert
Inch [words from Isaiah XXXV] ©
Carl Fischer, inc., New York;
24Sep47; EP18071.

INCIARTE BRIOSO, RAFAEL.
"El Baile Tijera" ... [By] Luis
Morleta Ruiz y Rafael Inciarte
Brioso. © Peer International
Corp., New York; 6Jun47;
EF5733. Parts: orchestra.

INGALL, OLIVE.
Idyll (Then comes the dawn) ...
words and music by Olive
Ingall. © Chappell & Co.,
ltd., Sydney; 17May47;
EF5694.

INGRAHAM, GRACE, 1906-
A Bird Sings in May; by Grace Ingraham, song for medium voice.
© Wesley Webster, San Francisco; 10Dec47; EP19575.

IPPOLITOV-IVANOV, MIKHAIL MIKHAILOVICH,
1859-1935.
Caucasian Sketches; suite in four
parts by M. Ippolitov-Ivanov.
Op.10. Arr. by F. Safranck,
arr. for modern bands with new
parts by H. R. Kent [pseud.]
© Carl Fischer, inc., New York;
3Jul47; on arrangement with new
parts; EP15752. Condensed score
(band) and parts.

O Praise the Lord, My Soul; for
three-part chorus of mixed voices
(a capella) [by] Mikail M.
Ippolitov-Ivanov ... arr. by
Victoria Glaser, Psalm 103: 1-4,
English text adapted by L. Harold
Geer. © E. C. Schirmer Music
Co., Boston; 14Aug47; on arrange-
ment; EP16372.

White Russian Legend; English
adaptation by Olga Paul,
[music by] M. Ippolitov-Ivanov.
Op.66. (In Haywood, Charles,
ed. Art Songs of Soviet Russia,
p.48-52) © Edward B. Marks
Music Corp., New York; 16Sep47;
on English adaptation; EP17187.
English and Russian words.

ISAACSON, HARRY.
Love Never Comes My Way; words and
music by Harry Isaacson. ©
Nordyke Publishing Co., Los
Angeles; 20Aug47; EP19540.

ISBELL, EUGENE, 1922-
Let Us Pray; lyrics & music by
Eugene Isbell, arr. by
Margarite Brown. Chicago,
Martin & Morris Music Studio.
© Eugene Isbell, Chicago;
6Aug47; EP16179.

Lord Have Pity; lyrics & music
by Eugene Isbell, arr. by
Margarite Brown. Chicago,
Martin & Morris Music Studio.
© Eugene Isbell, Chicago;
6Aug47; EP16180.

[ISRAEL, MARCEL] 1881-
Ton Amour Est Si Beau; paroles
de Battaille-Henri [pseud.],
musique de Marcel [pseud.].
© Editions Selection, Gentilly
(Seine) France; 30May47;
EF5946.

ISRAEL, MARILYN LENORE.
Pickin' Petals; words and music by
Max Dickman and Marilyn Israel.
© Broadcast Music, inc., New
York; 1Jul47; EP18197.

IVANOV, M. IPPOLITOV- See
Ippolitov-Ivanov, Mikhail Mikhailovich.

IVANOVICI, JAN.
Danube Waves; [by] J. Ivanovici
... for piano, arr. and ed.
by Maxwell Eckstein. ©
Carl Fischer, Inc., New York;
21Jul47; on arrangement and
editing; EP16101.
Danube Waves ... (Donauwellen) [by]
J. Ivanovici, arr. by William
Teague. © Broadcast Music, inc.,
EP18041. Piano-conductor score
(orchestra) and parts.
Donauwellen ... [by] J. Ivanovici,
arr. [by] Arthur Wood. © W.
Paxton & Co., ltd., London;
16Jul46; on arrangement;
EP5701. Piano-conductor score
(orchestra) and parts.
Little Red Shoes; [by] J. Ivano-
vici, S.A. arr. by Ira B. Wil-
son, [words by] Marion Wake-
man. © Lorenz Publishing Co.,
Dayton, Ohio; 24Sep47; on
vocal arrangement; EP17887.
Memory Waltz ... [arr. for] guitar
... [by] Eddie Alkire. Easton,
Pa., E. Alkire Publications.
Elbern H. "Eddie" Alkire, Easton,
Pa.; 25Aug47; on arrangement,
charts & minor studies; EP17693.
Waves of the Danube ... [by] J.
Ivenovici, arr. by F. Ballatore.
(In Ballatore, Pietro, comp. So
Easy. p. 18-19) © Edward B. Marks
Music Corp., New York; 9Dec47;
on arrangement; EP15593. For
piano solo.
Waves of the Danube ... by J. Ivano-
vici, arr. for accordion by
Charles Nunzio. © Alfred Music
Co., inc., New York; 10Oct47; on
arrangement; EP19087.
The Wedding Waltz; (Danube Waves),
words by Ted Fetter, music by
Jan Ivanovici, arr. by Hugo Frey.
© The John Franklin Co., inc.,
New York; 25Nov47; on arrange-
ment; EP19053. Score: SATB and
piano.
The Wedding Waltz; (Danube Waves),
words by Ted Fetter, music by
Jan Ivanovici, arr. by Hugo
Frey. © The John Franklin Co.,
inc., New York; 25Nov47; on
arrangement; EP19034. Score:
SSA and piano.
The Wedding Waltz; (Danube Waves),
words by Ted Fetter, music by
Jan Ivanovici, arr. by Hugo Frey.
© The John Franklin Co., inc.,
New York; 25Nov47; on arrange-
ment; EP19055. Score: SA and
piano.

IVES, CHARLES E
22; [and] Three Protests; [by]
Charles E. Ives, Two Woofs [by]
Henry Cowell [and] Air, by John Kirk-
patrick; [20th anniversary ed.]
(New Music; a quarterly pub.
modern compositions, v.21, no.1)
© New Music, New York; 10Dec47;
EP19912. Cover-title: Piano Works.

IVES, CHARLES EDWARD, 1874-
(Symphony, no.3) Third Symphony;
[by] Charles Ives. © Arrow
Music Press, inc., New York;
27Mar47; EP16520. Score.

IVES, DAVID LIVINGSTONE, 1921- comp.
Male Quartet; comp. by David
Livingstone Ives, music editor:
Richard E. Gerig, [words by]
Thomas O. Chisholm, Harry Dixon
Loes and others, music by D. L.
Ives, R. E. Gerig, H. D. Loes
and others] Archbold, Ohio,
Ives Music Press. © David
Livingstone Ives, Archbold,
Ohio; 10Oct47; EP18786.

J

JACEK, VALENTINE J
How Can I Forgive You? Words and
music by Valentine J. Jacek.
© Nordyke Publishing Co., Los
Angeles; 3Jul47; EP17530.

JACK, STORMY. See
Stormy Jack.

JACKS, HAZEL LILLIAN, 1909-
De Train Am Comin' Round de Bend;
Negro spiritual, words by Pearl
Jacks Gotschall, music by Hazel
Jacks. © Pearl Elizabeth Jacks
Gotschall & Hazel Lillian Jacks,
Marion, Ind.; 2Dec47; EP19622.

JACKSON, A   F
Hasta la Vista; words and music
by A. F. (Jack) Jackson. ©
Bob Miller, inc., New York;
27Oct47; EP18606. For voice
and piano, with chord symbols,
and voice part. English and
Spanish words.

JACKSON, CHARLES Q
You Belong to Me; words and music
by Charles Q. Jackson. ©
Nordyke Publishing Co., Los
Angeles; 17May47; EP16843.

JACKSON, CROFT.
Hrossey; diversions on a theme, for
pianoforte, by Croft Jackson.
© The Oxford University Press,
London; 29May47; EP6122.

JACKSON, JACK. See
Jackson, A. F.

JACKSON, KATHERINE CECELIA, 1913-
I've Got a Saviour ... words and
music by Katherine Cecelia
Jackson. Cleveland, Coleman's
Studio of Gospel Music. ©
Katherine Cecelia Jackson,
Cleveland; 5Nov47; EP18694.

JACKSON, LAURETTA MAY, 1906-
He Is the One; [by] L. M. Jackson.
© Lauretta May Jackson (Mrs.
Stirling P.), Detroit; 10Aug47;
EP16220. Close score; SSA.
Now Is the Time; [by] L. M. Jackson,
Detroit; 7Sep47;
EP17251. For voice and piano.
O Sinner, Give Heed; [by] L. M.
Jackson © Lauretta May Jack-
son, Detroit; 25May47; EP16221.
Safe Now Forever in Him; [by]
L. M. Jackson. © Lauretta May
Jackson, Detroit; 7Sep47;
EP17252. For voice and piano.

JACKSON, T   K
Follow Your Rainbow; words and
music by T. K. Jackson. © Nordyke Publishing Co., Los Angeles; 12Aug47; EP17628.
Sing Me a Song Tonight; words and
music by T. K. Jackson. ©
Nordyke Publishing Co., Los
Angeles; 15Feb47; EP20025.

JACOBI, FREDERICK.
Introduction and Toccata; for
piano [by] Frederick Jacobi.
© Axelrod Publications, inc.,
Providence; 12Nov47; EP18536.

JACOBS, ANSON C
Bright Star of Heaven; words by
O. Burton & Ernest O'Hara,
music by Anson C. Jacobs. ©
O. B. Hawkins, Franklin, Pa.;
28Jul47; EP16017.

JACOBS, DICK.
50 Questions 50 Answers; a
necessary reference guide to the
problems of advanced arranging.
© Bregman, Vocco and Conn, inc.,
New York; 8Aug47; EP16280.

JACOBSON, JAN. See also
Jacobson, William Jan.

JACOBSON, JAN, 1910-
You Can't Play Fair; words and music
by Dorlene Welch [and] Jan Jacobson. © Paragon Music Publications,
Hollywood, Calif.; 8Dec47; EP20430.

JACOBSON, MAURICE.
The Song of Songs; for low or
medium voice, [by] Maurice
Jacobson, [words from Solomon's
"Song of songs"] © Alfred
Lengnick & Co., ltd., London;
10Jun47; EP5684. For voice and
piano, ad lib.

JACOBSON, WILLIAM JAN, 1910-
Summer Song; words by Larry
Sullivan, music by Jan Jacobson.
© Paragon Music Publications,
Hollywood, Calif.; 16Jul47;
EP15714.

JACOBY, TED, 1919-
The Pig Latin Way; words & music
by Paul Kalet, Hernan Brana
[and] Ted Jacoby. © "Pops"
Music Co., New York; 19Aug47;
EP17772.

JACQUES, HENRI, pseud. See
Henri, Jacques, 1886-

JAFFE, MOE, 1901-
I'm My Own Grandpaw; by Dwight
Latham and Moe Jaffe. Boston,
Sole selling agents, Boston
Music Co. © General Music Pub-
lishing Co., inc., New York;
15Dec47; EP20210. For voice
and piano, with chord symbols.

[JAFFREY, JESSE CARL] 1909-
Eno Sunshine; words and music [by
John Henry Part and Jesse Carl
Jaffrey, words rev. by Arthur
Aloysius Starin] © J. C. Eno,
inc., Bloomfield, N. J.; 28Jan47;
EP15464.

JAMACK, PETER JOSEPH, 1907-
Music World; [by Peter Jamack, arr.
by Lee Hudson] © Peter J.
Jamack (World Music), Phila-
delphia; 20May47; EP15509. For
piano solo.
Snow-bound; lyrics and music by
Peter J. Jamack. © Peter J.
Jamack, Philadelphia; 16Jul47;
EP15635.

JAMES, A   W
At the Break of Day; words and music
by A. W. James. © Nordyke Pub-
lishing Co., Los Angeles; 28Apr47;
EP16755.
I'm Just a Dreamer of Dreams;
words and music by A. W. James.
© Nordyke Publishing Co., Los
Angeles; 29Apr47; EP16873.

JAMES, HUGH, pseud. See
Lally, James.

JAMES, INEZ.
That's the Way He Does It; words
and music by Buddy Pepper and
Ines James. © Robbins Music
Corp., New York; 16Dec47; EP20406.

JAMES, PHILIP, 1890-
Festal March; (Perstare et Praestare)
by Philip James. © Chappell &
Co., inc., New York; 19Nov47;
EP19115. Condensed score (band)
and parts.
Festal March "Perstare et
Praestare" [composed and arr.]
by Philip James. © The H. W.
Gray Co., inc., New York;
2Jul47; on arrangement; EP15705.
For organ solo.

JANDREAU, LLE, pseud. See
Jondrow, Leonore.

JANOWSKI, MAX.
Avodath Hakodosh Shel Kehilath
Anshe Maariv; musical Sabbath
service for mixed voices and
organ (ad lib.) by Max Janowski.
© Transcontinental Music Corp.,
New York; 13Sep47; EP17078.
Hebrew words (transliterated)

JANSEN, DAN.
If a Rose Could Speak; words & music by Dan Jansen. © Nordyke Publishing Co., Los Angeles; 22Apr47; EP16897.

When a 'Eighty One' Plays a run on the Piano; words & music by Dan Jansen. © Nordyke Publishing Co., Los Angeles; 11Oct46; EP20049.

[JANSEN, LEON DeBIERE] 1908-
Why Do You Make Promises? [By Rick O'Shay, pseud. Piano arr. by Jerry Bresler] © Le Jan Music Co., Maspeth, L. I., N. Y. 15Nov47; EP18691. For voice and piano, with chord symbols.

JAPHET, CLIFF.
Lonely Renfro Valley Rose; words ... by Chaw Mank, music by Cliff Japhet. [c1945] © Chaw Mank's Blue Ribbon Music Co., Staunton, Ill.; 1Dec47; EP20104.

JASON, WILL.
Out of the Blue; lyric by Henry Nemo, music by Will Jason ... [from] "Out of the Blue." New York; Leeds Music Corp. © Eagle-Lion Studios, inc., Hollywood, Calif.; 20Oct47; EP18897.

Sincerely Yours; lyric by Sid Robin, music by Will Jason, arr. by Carl Ladra. © Leeds Music Corp., New York; 31Oct47; on arrangement; EP18647. Piano-conductor score (orchestra, with words) and parts.

Sincerely Yours; lyric by Sid Robin, music by Will Jason. Female vocal, key of F ... special vocal background arr. by Bob Morse. © Leeds Music Corp., New York; 31Oct47; on arrangement; EP18648. Piano-conductor score (orchestra, with words) and parts.

Sincerely Yours; lyric by Sid Robin, music by Will Jason. © Leeds Music Corp., New York; 18Aug47; EP16396.

Sincerely Yours; lyric by Sid Robin, music by Will Jason. Male vocal, B♭ orig. ... special vocal background arr. by Bob Morse. © Leeds Music Corp., New York; 31Oct47; on arrangement; EP18649. Piano-conductor score (orchestra, with words) and parts.

JAY, FRED.
You Can't Put Out a Fire (by fanning the flame); words and music by Eddie Seiler, Sol Marcus and Fred Jay. © Northern Music Corp., New York; 1Aug47; EP16360.

JAY, JOHNNY, pseud. See
Steila, Johnny J.

JEANJEAN, PAUL, 1900-
Etudes Modernes; pour flûte, [by] Paul Jeanjean. © Alphonse Leduc & Co., Paris; 15Jun47; EP7311.

JEFFERIES, STANTON.
Two Hearts in Summertime ... words by Jane Renn [pseud.], music by Stanton Jefferies. © Ascherberg, Hopwood & Crew, ltd ., London; 25Sep47; EF6831.

JEMSAY, KAZIMIR.
The Magic Gypsy Eyes ... Lyric by Nicolai Batorin, music by Kazimir Jemsay. © Nickolai Batorin - Jemsay, Los Angeles; 8 Apr47; EP16169.

JENKINS, CORA W. 1870-
Blowing Bubbles ... [by] Cora W. Jenkins. (In Hirschberg, David, ed. and comp. Pieces Are Fun. bk. 1, p. 24-25) © Musicord Publications, New York; 2Jul47; EP15936. For piano solo.

Two Little Chipmunks ... [by] Cora W. Jenkins. (In Hirschberg, David, ed. and comp. Pieces Are Fun. bk. 1, p. 20-21) © Musicord Publications, New York; 2Jul47; EP15934. For piano solo.

JENKINS, GORDON.
Tomorrow; words and music by Gordon Jenkins. © Edwin H. Morris & Co., inc., New York; 25Apr47; EP17329.

JENKINS, JOEL LEON, 1909-
I Pray You'll Remember; words and music by Leon Jenkins. [Piano acc. by Bernie Clements] © Metropolitan Music Co., Houston, Tex.; 12Jul47; EP15609.

JENKINS, LEON. See
Jenkins, Joel Leon.

JENKINS, MERVIN HENRY, 1909-
Inspired Hymns of the Hour ... by Mervin Henry Jenkins. © Mervin Henry Jenkins, Portland, Or.; on 6 hymns in pt. 1, 23Dec47. Principally close score: SATB. Contents.- Wonderful Jesus (© EP20507) - Put Your Arm Around the Sinner (© EP20508) - Let's Tell the World about Jesus (© EP20509) - The Latter Rain (© EP20510) - A Cup of Cold Water (© EP20511) - Over and Over Again (© EP20512)

JENSEN, A.
The Kill; arr. as a two part song for treble voices by Alec Rowley, words by Doris Rowley, music by A. Jensen. © Keith, Prowse & Co., ltd., London; 30Sep47; on arrangement & words; EP6774.

[JENSEN, HARRY] 1911-
Bedre Sent end Aldrig; Tekst og Musik: Ogsta Berg [pseud.] © Jac. Boesens Musikforlag A/S, Copenhagen; 6Mar47; EF6999.

JEROME, M   K
Hush-A-Bye Wee Rose of Killarney. See his My Wild Irish Rose.

(My Wild Irish Rose) Hush-A-Bye Wee Rose of Killarney, from the ... picture "My Wild Irish Rose," lyric by Ted Koehler, music by M. K. Jerome. © M. Witmark & Sons, New York; 21Nov47; EP20167.

JESSEL, LEON.
Parade of the Wooden Soldiers; [by] Leon Jessel, arr. by Charles Nunzio. © Edward B. Marks Music Corp., New York; 21Nov47; on arrangement; EP20232. For accordion solo.

JESSYE, EVA SHEPHERD.
Simon the Fisherman; (a Negro story song) for chorus of mixed voices with narrators, arr. by Eva Jessye, [traditional words] © C. C. Birchard & Co., Boston; 10ct47; on arrangement; EP18123.

JOHANSSON, NISSE.
Fröken Johanssons Sjömansvals; text och musik: Nemo Ciacelli och Nisse Johansson. © Reuter & Reuter förlags, a.-b., Stockholm; 1Jan46; EF6951.

[JOHNDROW, LEONORE]
Goin' Home to Arizona; words by Edith M. Briggs, music by Lee Jandreau [pseud.] © Nordyke Publishing Co., Los Angeles; 22Apr47; EP16933.

JOHNSON, ALFRED H
The Agincourt Song; for chorus of mixed voices (unison) and junior choir. English song (15th century) freely arr. by Alfred H. Johnson. © Galaxy Music Corp., New York; 4Aug47; on arrangement; EP16555.

JOHNSON, CECIL.
Golden-Gate Boogie; by Cecil Johnson and Ray Meany, arr. by Bernie Kaai. © Ray Meany, Golden Gate Publications, Oakland, Calif.; 4Aug47; EP16118. For 2 guitars; also diagrams and chord symbols for ukulele.

JOHNSON, CLAIR W   1902-
Golden Glow ... [by] Clair W. Johnson. © Boosey & Hawkes, inc., New York; 29Sep47; EP17755. Score (band), condensed score and parts.

Prairie Skies ... [by] Clair W. Johnson. © Belwin, inc., New York; 18Sep47; EP17659. Condensed score (band) and parts.

Romantic Rhapsody; [by] Clair W. Johnson. Chicago; 1Nov47; EP18376. Condensed score (band) and parts.

JOHNSON, E   ARTHUR
Nobody Will Do But You; words and music by E. Arthur Johnson. [c1946] © Nordyke Publishing Co., Los Angeles; 7Feb47; EP19367.

JOHNSON, GEORGE. See
Johnson, Joseph George.

JOHNSON, HAL, pseud. See
Nelson, Kenneth Francis

JOHNSON, HERBERT W.
Dismas, the dying thief upon the cross; words & music by Herbert W. Johnson, arr. by Dorothy H. Johnson. Hutchinson, Kan., The H. W. Johnsons. © Herbert W. Johnson, Hutchinson, Kan.; 27Oct47; EP18494.

JOHNSON, IDA MAI.
World of Tomorrow; words and music by Ida Mai Johnson. © Nordyke Publishing Co., Los Angeles; 22Jul47; EP19314.

JOHNSON, J   C   1896-
Empty Bed Blues; words and music by J. C. Johnson. New York, Record Music Publishing Co. © J. C. Johnson, New York; 17Oct47; EP17687.

[JOHNSON, J   ROSAMOND]
Lift Ev'ry Voice and Sing; [by J. Rosamond Johnson], arr. by Robert Cray. © Edward B. Marks Music Corp., New York; 27Aug47; on arrangement; EP16701. Condensed score (band) and parts.

JOHNSON, JAMES P
Concerto Jazz-a-mine; [second movement], piano solo by James P. Johnson. © Mills Music, inc., New York; 4Aug47; EP18256.

JOHNSON, JOHN OSCAR, 1888-
Oh, Minnesota Moon; words and melody by John Oscar Johnson, piano acc. by Carol Glockzin. [c1942] © John Oscar Johnson, Long Prairie, Minn.; 10Jul47; EP16210.

JOHNSON, JOHNNY.
She Said She Loved Me; words & music by Johnny Johnson, arr. by Floyd Bartlett. © Nordyke Publishing Co., Los Angeles; 11Oct47; EP20027.

JOHNSON, JOSEPH GEORGE, 1913-
You Make My Life All Sunshine in My Dreams; lyric by N. R. Kuehner, music by George Johnson. © N. R. Kuehner, Laurel Springs, N. J.; 30Jul47; EP16082.

JOHNSON, JUNE CATHERINE.
Querida; words and music by June Catherine Johnson. © Nordyke Publishing Co., Los Angeles; 11Jun47; EP16958.

JOHNSON, KATHRYN KURTZ.
Within the Stable; Christmas carol
for four-part chorus of women's
voices a cappella, lyric and
music by Kathryn Kurtz Johnson.
© Boston Music Co., Boston;
17Sep47; EP17361.

JOHNSON, NETTIE.
Goodnight, Little Sweetheart;
words and music by Nettie Johnson. © Nordyke Publishing Co.,
Los Angeles; 13Jul46; EP19976.

JOHNSON, QUENTIN P
Lady Pepperell Waltz; by Quentin P.
Johnson. (In The Pepperell
Sheet. Oct. 1947, p.10-11) ©
Quentin P. Johnson, Biddeford,
Me.; 10ct47; B5-2361. For piano
solo.

JOHNSTON, LUCILE MOORE.
Dreamy Sleepy Town ... words and
music by Lucile Moore Johnston.
© Lucile Moore Johnston,
Thomaston, Ga.; 19Jun47; EP15397.

JOHNSTONE, MAURICE.
Dover Beach; for baritone or contralto solo & orchestra, words
by Matthew Arnold, arrangement
for voice and pianoforte [by]
Maurice Johnstone. © Alfred
Lengnick & Co., ltd., London;
14Jul47; EF6928.

So Are You to My Thoughts; music by
Maurice Johnstone, words by Shakespeare. © Alfred Lengnick & Co.,
ltd., London; 15Aug47; EF6690.

JOIO, CASIMIRO DELLO. See
Dello Joio, Casimiro.

JOIO, NORMAN DELLO. See
Dello Joio, Norman.

JOLER, GEORGE A.
·Think of Me; words and music by
George A. Joler. © Nordyke
Publishing Co., Los Angeles;
15Jun46; EP19376.

JOLIVET, ANDRE, 1905-
Le Chant de l'Avenir; paroles de
Pierre Migenne [pseud.],
musique de André Jolivet. ©
Editions Musicales "Le Chant du
Monde", Paris; 30Apr47; EF5854.

Cinq Danses Rituelles; pour piano,
[by] Andre Jolivet; © Durand &
Cie, Paris; 19Jun47; EF6522.

JOLSON, AL, 1886-
All My Love; based on a theme by
Emil Waldteufel. By Al Jolson,
Saul Chaplin and Harry Akst,
arr. by William C. Schoenfeld.
© Harms, inc., New York; Music Publishers
Holding Corp. © Harms, inc.,
New York; 25Aug47; on arrange-
ment; EP17150. Cornet-con-
ductor score (band) and parts.

JONAS, ARTHUR HERBERT, 1930-
She Walks in Beauty; poem by Lord
Byron, music by Arthur Jonas.
© Arthur Herbert Jonas, New
York; 26Oct47; EP18235.
Score: SA and piano.

JONASSON, J   EMANUEL.
GOk-Hambo ... musik och arr.; J. E.
Jonasson. © R. Westlings musik-
förlag, Stockholm; 1Jan45;
EF7066. Parts; orchestra.

JONES, ALICE F
That'll Do Me; words and music
by Alice F. Jones. © Nordyke
Publishing Co., Los Angeles;
21Aug47; EP20482.

JONES, CORLISS W
When the Lights Are Low; words
and music by Corliss W. Jones.
© Nordyke Publishing Co., Los
Angeles; 31Jul47; EP19448.

782058 O—48—6

JONES, GRANDPA.
It's Raining Here This Morning;
words and music by "Grandpa"
Jones. © Hill and Range Songs,
inc., Hollywood, Calif.;
26Jun47; EP15320.

JONES, GRIFFITH, 1875-   arr.
Three Sixteenth Century Melodies;
S.S.A. (a capella) arr. by
Griffith Jones. © Belwin, inc.,
New York; 28Nov47; on arrange-
ment; EP19064.

JONES, GRIFFITH J   1875-
Christ Understands. Have Faith
in God. Words by H. M. S.
Richards, music by Griffith J.
Jones. Winona Lake, Ind.,
Rodeheaver Hall-Mack Co. ©
Rodeheaver Co., Winona Lake,
Ind.; 18Jul47; EP17367.

Jesus, the Name I Love To Hear.
Plant Ydym Eto Dan ein Hoed ...
traditional melody arr. by
Griffith J. Jones. [Winona Lake,
Ind., Rodeheaver Hall-Mack Co.]
© The Rodeheaver Co., Winona
Lake, Ind.; 58ep47; on arrange-
ment; EP17129. Score: SATB and
piano.

Praise and Worship His Name;
arr. by Griffith J. Jones,
[words by Wransky] Winona Lake,
Ind., The Rodeheaver Hall-Mack
Co. © The Rodeheaver Co.,
Winona Lake, Ind.; 7Nov47; on
arrangement of words & music;
EP19251. Score: soprano, SATB
and piano.

JONES, LESTER.
Loving You; words and music by
Lester Jones. © Nordyke Publishing Co., Los Angeles;
16Jun47; EP17443.

JONES, NOLA LAVON
Just Be Sure What You Say Is All
True; words and music by Nola
Lavon Jones. © Nordyke Pub-
lishing Co., Los Angeles;
15Feb47; EP19941.

JONES, RICHARD M
Your Red Wagon ... [from] "Your Red
Wagon", [by] Richard M. Jones
[new words and changes in music]
by Don Raye ... [and] Gene De Paul.
© Leeds Music Corp., New York;
8Dec47; on new words & changes in
music; EP20473.

JONGEN, JOSEPH.
Pastorale for organ, by Joseph
Jongen, arr. by Robert Leech
Bedell. © Mills Music, inc.,
New York; 28Jul47; on arrange-
ment; EP16193.

JONSSON, JOSEF.
En Grav; till text av Oscar
Stjerne, [by] Josef Jonsson. ©
Föreningen svenska tonsättare,
Stockholm; 1Jan46; EF7112.

JORDAN, JACK.
Have a Go, Joe; by Jack Jordan.
© Cinephonic Music Co., ltd.,
London; 16Dec46; EF6030. For
voice and piano, with chord
symbols; melody also in tonic
sol-fa notation.

JORGENSEN, EDYTHE.
Not for Me; words and music by
Edythe Jorgenson. © Nordyke
Publishing Co., Los Angeles;
29Mar47; EP16754.

JOSEFOVITS, TERI.
Au Revoir Again; lyric by Nikki
Wasson, music by Teri Josefovits.
© Ben Bloom Music Corp., New
York; 1Dec47; EP19186.

JOSPE, ERWIN.
I Believe. Ani Mamin. Text from
"The 13 Principles of Faith" by
Maimonides, melody from the
Warsaw ghetto, setting for ...
S.A.T.B. by Erwin Jospe. ©
Transcontinental Music Corp.,
New York; 18Nov47; on arrange-
ment; EP18827. Score; soprano,
chorus (SATB) and piano.

Joyful Torah Song. V'natan Lanu
Torat Emet. Folk melody, freely
arr. for mixed voices (S.A.T.B.)
by Erwin Jospe. © Transcontinental Music Corp., New York;
19Dec47; on arrangement;
EP20147. Hebrew words (transliterated)

The Palestine Brigade. Shir Brigadah. English text adaptation
by Ben Aronin, setting for mixed
voices (S.A.T.B.) by Erwin
Jospe. © Transcontinental Music
Corp., New York; 19Dec47; on arrangement & English text;
EP20148. Words in English and
Hebrew (transliterated)

Sing Unto the Lord. Ashira Ladonai. Based on an Oriental melody
[arr.] for mixed voices (S.A.
T.B.) by Erwin Jospe; text from
"Miriam's song of triumph" (Ex-
odus XV) English text adaptation by Ben Aronin. © Transcontinental Music Corp., New
York; 19Dec47; on arrangement &
English text; EP20149. Words in
Hebrew (transliterated) and English.

JOURDAIN, L. FERRIER, pseud. See
Ferrier, Lucien.

JOY, J., pseud. See
Gloe, Joseph.

JOYCE, FREDERICK, pseud. See
Garman, William McKinley.

JURAFSKY, ABRAHAM, 1906-
Coplas; [by] A. Jurafsky, [words
by Luis L. Franco] © Ricordi
Americana, S.A.B.C., Buenos
Aires; 12Aug42; EF6974. For
voice and piano.

Tres Canciones; para canto y
piano, [by] A. Jurafsky [words
by Luis L. Franco] © Ricordi
Americana, s.a.o.c., Buenos
Aires; 12Aug42; EF6993.

[JURKOVICH, CATHERINE]
Strange; words and music by Kathryn King [pseud.] © Nordyke
Publishing Co., Los Angeles;
24Jul47; EP19625.

K

KABALEVSKY, D
Spudd Words by S. Kirsanoff,
English adaptation by Olga Paul,
[music by] D. Kabalevsky. [In
Haywood, Charles, ed. Art Songs
of Soviet Russia, p.12-15) ©
Edward B. Marks Music Corp.,
New York; 16Sep47; on English
adaptation; EP17176. English
and Russian words.

KABELL, LOUIS.
She's Changed; words and music by
L. Kabell. © Nordyke Publish-
ing Co., Los Angeles; 22Aug47;
EP20026.

KADAS, GYORGY.
Hogyha Olykor Éjféltájban. (If at
Night a Bend of Cypress) English
lyric by Olga Paul, music by Kádas
György. (In Pusti, Barbara, comp.
Memories of Hungary. p. 26-27)
© Edward B. Marks Music Corp.,
New York; 19Nov47; on English ly-
ric; EP19000.

KADISON, PHILIP, 1919-
Just for You; words by Thomas B.
Howell. © Chappell & Co., inc.,
New York; 27Jun47; EP15551.
For voice and piano, with
chord symbols.

293

KADISON, PHILIP. Cont'd.
Totem, Teepee and Tom-Tom; music by Philip Kadison, words by Thomas B. Howell. © Mutual Music Society, inc., New York; 12Sep47; EF17133.

KAHN, MARVIN.
Engagement Waltz; by Gladys Shelley and Marvin Kahn. [Based on the Waltz in A flat by Brahms] © Chappell & Co., inc., New York; 21Jun47; EP15367. For voice and piano, with chord symbols.

KAHN, PERCY B 1880-
The Bells of Heaven ... poem by Ralph Hodgson, music by Percy B. Kahn. © Lawrence Wright Music Co., ltd., London; 9Jul47; EF5693.

Summer Morning; piano solo, [by] Percy B. Kahn. © Lawrence Wright Music Co., ltd., London; 3Jul47; EF5692.

KAISER, GRACE C
Little Primrose ... for piano [by] Grace C. Kaiser. © Theodore Presser Co., Philadelphia; 30Oct47; EP18446.

KAISER, JEAN.
The Christmas Spelling Bee; or, Christmas at Snowbank Corners; a Christmas operetta for elementary schools. Libretto by Lila Waterbury Haynes, music by Jean Kaiser. © Row, Peterson & Co., Evanston, Ill.; 3Nov47; D pub 11442.

KAISER, MINNIE M
Alone in the Valley of Dreams; words and music by Minnie M. Kaiser. © Nordyke Publishing Co., Los Angeles; 25Jun47; EP17567.

KAISER, RALPH L
God Gave Me You; words and music by Ralph L. Kaiser, duet [for] high and low voices [arr. by Victor Lamont] © Sam Fox Publishing Co., New York; 20Oct47; on arrangement; EP18000.

KALES, NICK.
Your Beautiful Eyes; words and music by Nick Kales. © Nordyke Publishing Co., Los Angeles; 10Jun47; EP16923.

KALINNIKOFF.
Let All Creatures of God His Praises Sing; by Kalinnikoff, ed., and arr. by Noble Cain, English version by Noble Cain. © Boosey & Hawkes, inc., New York; 2Dec47; on arrangement & English words (SSAATTBB) and piano reduction.

KALINNIKOFF, V
Dawn; by V. Kalinnikoff ... (a cappella) S.S.A.A.T.T.B.B. [English translation by Wladimir Lekond, English adaptation by Olga Paul] © Edward B. Marks Music Corp., New York; 14Oct47; on English adaptation; EP18369.

KALINNIKOFF, BASILE.
Chanson Triste; [by] Basile Kalinnikow, [arr. by Quinto Maganini] © Edition Musicus New York, inc., New York; 30Sep47; on arrangement; EP20245. Score (flute and piano) and parts for flute and viola.

Chanson Triste; [by] Basile Kalinnikow, [arr. by Quinto Maganini] © Edition Musicus New York, inc., New York; 30Sep47; on arrangement; EP20246. Score (violin and piano) and parts for violin and violoncello.

Chanson Triste; [by] Basile Kalinnikow, [arr. by Quinto Maganini] © Edition Musicus New York, inc., New York; 30Sep47; on arrangement; EP20247. Score (flute and piano) and parts for flute and clarinet.

KALLSTENIUS, EDVIN.
För Vilsna Fötter Sjunger Gräset; [by] Edvin Kallstenius, till text av Hjalmar Gullberg. © Föreningen svenska tonsättare, Stockholm; 1Jan46; EF7098.

(Quartet, strings) Stråkkvartett (C moll) Op.8. [By] Edvin Kallstenius. Stockholm, Ed. Suecia. © Föreningen svenska tonsättare, Edition Suecia, Stockholm; 1Jan45; EF7075. Parts.

Vaggsång för Humpe; till text av Helge Åkerhielm, [by] Edvin Kallstenius. © Föreningen svenska tonsättare, Stockholm; 1Jan46; EF7114.

KALMAN, EMMERICH.
Play Gypsies, Dance Gypsies; [by] Emmerich Kálmán, transcribed by Gregory Stone. © Harms, inc., New York; 18Aug47; on transcription; EP17035. Score (violin, violoncello and piano) and parts.

KALMAN, IMRE, 1882-
Love's Own Sweet Song ... [by] Emmerich Kalman, arr. by L. Sugarman. © Edward B. Marks Music Corp., New York; 5Sep47; on arrangement; EP16671. For piano solo.

KAMP, PETER VAN DE. See
Van De Kamp, Peter.

KANITZ, ERNEST, 1894-
A Counterpoint Workbook ... by Ernest Kanitz. © Ernest Kanitz, Los Angeles; 6Dec47; AA70035.

KAPER, BRONISLAW.
(Green Dolphin Street) On Green Dolphin Street; theme of the ... picture "Green Dolphin Street"; lyric by Ned Washington, music by Bronislau Kapor. © Loew's, inc., New York; 24Sep47; EP17699.

KAPLIN, BILL.
The Lady's in Love; words and music by Danny and Joseph Leroy and Bill Kaplin. © Peer International Corp., New York; 14Jul47; EP15868.

KAPP, DAVID, 1904-
Home Is Where the Heart Is ... a Johnny Warrington arrangement; lyric by Charles Tobias, music by David Kapp. © Advanced Music Corp., New York; 25Aug47; on dance orchestration; EP17152. Piano-conductor score and parts.

Home Is Where the Heart Is; music by Dave Kapp, lyric by Charles Tobias. © Advanced Music Corp., New York; 20Aug47; on new arrangement for piano; EP16526.

Home Is Where the Heart Is; music by Dave Kapp, lyric by Charles Tobias ... scored by Jerry Sears. © Advanced Music Corp., New York; 25Aug47; on vocal orchestration; EP17153. Piano-conductor score and parts.

(The Last Round-up) A Hundred and Sixty Acres; words and music by David Kapp ... [from] The Last Round-up. © Leeds Music Corp., New York; 20Oct47; EP18893.

KAPPHAHN, THEODORE AUGUST, 1906-
Men of Boys Town; and Boys Town Victory March; by T. A. Kapphahn, arr. by Forrest L. Buchtel. © Neil A. Kjos Music Co., Chicago; 14Nov47; EP19551. Piano-conductor score (band) and parts.

KARLIN, AARON, 1903-
Rhumba-Loma; arr. the harmonic way by Aaron Karlin, [with rhythmic pattern aids], ed. and fingered by Harold M. Browner. ℗ Harmonic Studio of Piano Playing, Brooklyn; 10Nov47; EP18612. For piano solo.

KARLSSON, BROR, pseud. See
Sørensen, Wilhelm Gustav.

KAROLEVITZ, BOB.
Does No Lean No? Words and music by Bob Karolevitz. © Hargail Publishing Co., Los Angeles; 29Mar47; EP16731.

KARP, OTTO.
Burning Trails; words and music by Freddie Van, Alan Foster, Harold Potter [and] Otto Karp. © Catchy Songs Music Co., New York; 22Jul47; EP15716.

KARTZEV, A
The Partisan; words by J. Utkin, English adaptation by Olga Paul, [music by] A. Kartzov. (In Haywood, Charles, ed. Art Songs of Soviet Russia, p.61-64) © Edward B. Marks Music Corp., New York; 16Sep47; on English Adaptation; EF17190. English and Russian words.

KASSEL, ART.
Oh! What I Know About You; lyric by Sammy Gallop, music by Art Kassel. © Lombardo Music, inc., New York; 7Nov47; EP19213.

KASTALSKY, ALEXANDER DMITRIEVITCH, 1856-1926.
Hail, Holy Light! For four-part chorus of women's voices (a cappella) [Words by] John Milton ... adapted by Henry Wilder Foote, [music by] Alexander Dimitrievitch Kastalsky ... Arr. by Gwynn S. Bement. © E. C. Schirmer Music Co., Boston; 25Jul47; on arrangement; EP16052.

KATAN, BLANCH, 1913-
My Lips Will Be Calling; by H. Enners and B. Katan. © Dorothea Louise Schroeder, Flushing, N. Y.; 1Dec47; EP19058. For voice and piano.

KATCHER, ROBERT.
When Day Is Done ... words by B. G. DeSylva, music by Robert Katcher; a Jerry Sears arrangement. © Harms, inc., New York; 16Dec47; on arrangement; EP20344. Piano-conductor score (orchestra, with words) and parts.

KATZ, ERICH, 1900-
Sonatina, for two alto recorders or flutes or recorder and oboe, by Erich Katz. © Hargail Music Press, New York; 14Jul47; EP17120.

[KATZMAN, HENRY]
Gilly Gilly Wish Wash ... words and music by Henry Manners [pseud.] © Edward B. Marks Music Corp., New York; 12Nov47; EP18667.

We Could Make Such Beautiful Music; by ... Henry Manners [pseud.], concert transcription for band by William Teague. © Broadcast Music, inc., New York; 5Jun47; on arrangement; EP18194. Condensed score and parts.

KAUFMAN, AL. See
Kaufman, Alvin S

KAUFMAN, ALVIN S   1910-
How Many Kisses (does it take to
make you fall in love with me?
Words and music by Eddie Seiler,
Sol Marcus and Al Kaufman.
© Dreyer Music Corp., New York;
30Jun47; EP15381.

KAUS, OLGA.
You Are Mine, All Mine; by Olga
Kaus. © Olga Kaus, Dunkirk,
N. Y.; 30Jun47; EP15693. For
voice and piano.

KAVANAGH, PATRICK, 1907-
O'Grady's Tinwhistle Band; Irish
comedy song, words and music by
Patrick Kavanagh. © D'Oller Mu-
sic Co., Dublin, Eire; 5Dec47;
EF7371.

KAY, PAT.
I've Got a Boogie Woogie Baby!
By Pat Kay. © Cinephonic Music
Co., ltd., London; 30May47;
EF6026. For voice and piano,
with chord symbols; melody also
in tonic sol-fa notation.

KAY, SYDNEY JOHN.
Commedia Español; by Sydney
John Kay, adapted for the
piano by Paul Schramm. ©
Chappell & Co., ltd., London;
12Jun47; EF5723.
Lament; by Sydney John Kay,
adapted for the piano by Paul
Schramm. © Chappell & Co.,
ltd., London; 12Jun47; EF5724.

KAYE, SAMMY.
The Flow'r of Theta Chi; by Sammy
Kaye and Sunny Skylar [pseud.]
© World Music, inc., New York;
21Jun46; EP4880. Close score:
SATB.

KAYNE, BARBARA.
I Remember You; words and music
by Barbara Kayne. © Piantadosi
Music Publications, Encino,
Calif.; 20Nov47; EP19050.

KAZEL, TOM.
I Was Just Window Shopping; words
and music by Tom Kazel. © Nordyke Publishing Co., Los Angeles; 31Jul47; EP19518.

KEATH, ROBERT.
Who Do You Think You're Foolin'?
Lyric by Edna Rothbart, music
by Robert Keath. © Leo Feist,
inc., New York; 31Oct47;
EP18465.

KECK, PEARL.
Over the Snow; piano solo by
Pearl Keck. © Pallma Music
Products, Chicago; 27May47;
EP15661.

KEEFER, ARRETT MARWOOD.
Blue Rose of the Rio; words ...
by Ruth Keefer, music [by] Rusty
Keefer. © Myers Music, Philadelphia; 1Dec47; EP20144.
"Jukebox Cannonball;" words and
music by Rusty Keefer, [words
by] Jesse Rogers and Wayne
Barrie. © Jack Howard Publications, inc., Philadelphia;
5Jan47; EP17340. Melody and
words.

KEEFER, RUSTY.   See
Keefer, Arrett Marwood.

KEENE, WILLIAM HERBERT, 1916-
Jesus, Rose of Sharon; words and
music by Bill (W. H.) Keene.
© W. H. Keene, Seattle; 26Sep47;
EP17680.
The Land of Milk and Honey; words
and music by Bill W. H. Keene.
[Piano arr. by Wm. B. Coburn]
© William Herbert Keene, Seattle;
18Nov47; EP19021.

KEENER, ORRIN L   1893-
Love All Things Can Do; [by]
Orrin L. Keener. © Orrin L.
Keener, Berea, Ky.; 26Nov47;
EP19056. Close score: SATB.

KEITH, SID.
Bermuda; words and music by Al
Bandini and Sid Keith. © Stan-
dard Music Publishers, ltd.,
New York; 17Aug47; EP18242.

KELLER, ARMIN.
Satisfied; words by Andy
Christensen, music by Armin
Keller. © Andy Christensen &
Armin Keller, Chicago; 3Nov47;
EP18583.

KELLER, DEZSO.
Szegős Mályva, Gyöngyvirág. (Fragrant Malva, Pretty Flow'r) English lyric by Olga Paul, music by
Kellér Dezső. (In Pasti, Barbara,
comp. Memories of Hungary. p.
32-33) © Edward B. Marks Music
Corp., New York; 19Nov47; on
English lyric: EP19003.

KELLER, DON.   See
Keller, Edward McD.

KELLER, EDWARD McD.
Keller's Berkeley Band Book; a
collection of sixteen original
marches, [composed and arr. by
Don Keller] Piano-conductor.
© Edward McD. Keller, Berkeley,
Calif.; 2Sep47; EP17213.

KELLER, FAY, 1898-
Golden Years; words by Mona Weber,
music by Fay Keller. © Mona
Weber & Fay Keller, South Pasadena, Calif.; 24Jun47; EP15415.

KELLER, RICHARD.
Schade, Gestern Warst Du Süss
wie Schokolade ... Von Heino
Gaze und Richard Keller. ©
Edition Turicaphon a. g.,
Bühnen- und Musikverlag,
Zürich, Switzerland; 1Apr47;
EF5872. For voice and piano.

KELLEY, DEAN MAURICE, 1926-
Hymn of Affirmation ... [by] Dean
M. Kelley. © Dean M. Kelley,
Denver; 10Dec47; EP20146.
Close score: SATB.
Hymn of Thanksgiving ... [by] Dean
M. Kelley. © Dean M. Kelley,
Denver; 10Dec47; EP20145. Close
score: SATB.
Hymn of Triumph ... [by] Dean M.
Kelley. © Dean M. Kelley,
Denver; 3Jun47; EP17001. For
voice and piano.

KELSO, HAZEL, 1901-
The Orange Diamond Jubilee;
words and music by ... Hazel
Kelso [n.p.] Kansas State
Grange. © Hazel Kelso, Havana,
Kan.; 9Jul47; EP16177.

KEMMER, GEORGE W
The Infant Saviour; Christmas
anthem for mixed voices. [Words
by] Canon L. B. Ridgely,
[Music by] George W. Kemmer.
© H. W. Gray Co., inc., New
York; 12Sep47; EP17370.

KEMPINSKI, LEO A
Teach Us Thy Ways ... text by
David Ormont, music by Leo A.
Kempinski. © Leeds Music Corp.,
New York; 31Oct47; EP18644.

THE KEN CURTIS SONG CORRAL; [by Paul
Earlee, Lee Penny, Ken Curtis,
and others] © Preview Music Co.,
Chicago; 14Jul47; EP16708.

KENDALL, W   M
Glorious Victory ... [by] W. M.
Kendall. © Hawkes & Son (Lon-
don), ltd., London; 18Jul47;
EF5798.

KENDRICK, PAUL M
Snooze Your Blues Away; words and
music by Paul M. Kendrick. ©
Nordyke Publishing Co., Los
Angeles; 29Jul47; EP17400.

KENNARD, ALICE.
A Little Love Song; for voice and
piano by Alice Kennard. © G.
Schirmer, inc., New York;
17Jul47; EP17045.

KENNE, EVEREST ROMAN, 1924-
The Million Dollar Polka; words
[and piano acc.] by Bernie
Clements, music by Everest
Kenne. © Metropolitan Music
Co., Houston, Tex.; 12Jul47;
EP15608.

KENNEDY, AL, 1911-
Love Lives on Little Things; words
by John Kelly, music by Al
Kennedy. © Kennedy Music Co.,
Barre, Vt.; 15Jul47; EP15977.

KENNEDY, AMANDA.
Star of the East; words by George
Cooper, music by Amanda Kennedy,
[arr. by John Bach] © Calumet
Music Co., Chicago; 4Nov47; on
arrangement; EP19208.
Star of the East; words by George
Cooper, music by Amanda Kennedy,
arr. by [Betty B. Glynn of] the
Oahu staff. (Oahu advanced har-
mony note course for Hawaiian and
electric guitar, [lesson] 3pt) ©
Oahu Publishing Co., Cleveland;
22Sep47; on arrangement; EP20243.
For voice and 2 guitars. Includes
lesson on principal chords.

KENNEDY, JAMES, 1902-
On the Old Spanish Trail; by Kenneth
Leslie Smith and Jimmy Kennedy,
arr. by Bob Morse. © The Peter
Maurice Music Co., ltd., New York;
30Jul47; on vocal arrangement in
key of B♭; EP15980. Piano-conductor
score (orchestra, with words) and
parts.
On the Old Spanish Trail; by
Kenneth Leslie Smith and Jimmy
Kennedy, arr. by Bob Morse. ©
The Peter Maurice Music Co., ltd.,
New York; 30Jul47; on vocal
arrangement in key of D♭; EP15981.
Piano-conductor score (orchestra,
with words) and parts.
On the Old Spanish Trail; by
Kenneth Leslie Smith [and]
Jimmy Kennedy, arr. by Fred
Weismantel. © The Peter
Maurice Music Co., ltd., New
York; 30Jul47; on arrangement;
EP15979. Piano-conductor score
(orchestra, with words) and
parts.
"On the Old Spanish Trail," by
Kenneth Leslie Smith [and] Jimmy
Kennedy, [from] "On the Old
Spanish Trail." © Peter Maurice
Music Co., ltd., New York;
30Jul47; EP15978. For voice and
piano, with guitar diagrams and
chord symbols.

[KENNEDY, JIMMY]
Brussels Express; [by] Joe Le May,
[pseud.] arr. [by] A. Picon [and
Southern Solitude; by Joe Le May,
arr. by Arthur Young] © Hit Music
Co., Brussels; 15Apr46; EF7285-
7286. Piano-conductor score (or-
chestra) and parts.
Sleepy Trumpeter; [and Straight Cut
Stomp. By] Joe Le May [pseud.]
arr. [by] Arthur Young. © Hit
Music Co., Brussels; 15Apr46;
EF7283-7284. Piano-conductor
score (orchestra) and parts.

KENNEDY, MARGARET LeMASTER.
When I Think of My Friend, Called
Jesus; words, music and arrange-
ment by Margaret LeMaster
Kennedy. © Margaret LeMaster
Kennedy, Dallas; 14Jun47;
EP15467.

When I Think of My Friend, Called
Jesus; words, music and arrange-
ment by Margaret LeMaster Kennedy.
© Margaret LeMaster Kennedy,
Dallas; 5Sep47; EP17081. Score:
SABarB and piano.

KENNETH, GEORGE.
Putting Peas in Podzies; words and
music by George Kenneth. © Chappell & Co., ltd., London; 24Nov47;
EF7269.

KENNY, BILL.
Do You Feel That Way Too? By Paul
Flynn and Bill Kenny. © Barton
Music Corp., New York; 30ct47;
EP17758. For voice and piano,
with chord symbols.

KENNY, CHARLES.
The Old Ferris Wheel; words and
music by Nick and Charles Kenny.
© Goldmine Music, inc., New
York; 25Jul47; EP15964.

KENT, ARTHUR.
Upper Fifth Avenue; [by] Arthur
Kent. Rev. ed. © J.J. Robbins
& Sons, inc., New York; 10Oct47;
on additional material; EP18234.
For piano solo.

KENT, BOB.
I Lost My Heartaches; words and
music by Paul Sapp [and] Bob Kent.
© Century Songs, inc., Chicago;
17Nov47; EP20270. Melody and
chord symbols, with words.
"In the Shambles of My Heart;"
words ... by Billy Fairmann,
music [by] Bob Kent. © Century
Songs, inc., Chicago; 17Nov47;
EP18753. Melody and chord
symbols, with words.
"Sad and Blue;" words and music by
Bob Kent. © Century Songs,
inc., Chicago; 17Nov47; EP18752.
Melody and chord symbols, with
words.

KENT, BUDDY, pseud. See
Sarkissian, Barouyr.

KENT, WALTER.
Have You Seen My Colleen This
Mornin'? By Kim Gannon and
Walter Kent. © Edwin H. Morris
& Co., inc., New York; 16Oct47;
EP18525. For voice and piano,
with chord symbols.
That's What Your Heart Is For;
lyric by Bob Wells, music by
Walter Kent. © Robert Music
Corp., New York; 17Nov47;
EP18794.

KENTON, STAN.
Artistry in Boogie; composed by
Stan Kenton and Pete Rugolo,
scored by Pete Rugolo. © Leslie
Music Corp., New York; 27Nov47;
on condensed concert score;
EP19226. For orchestra.
Collaboration; composed and arr.
by Stan Kenton & Pete Rugolo,
ed. by Van Alexander. © Leslie
Music Corp., New York; 29Jun47;
EP19543. Piano-conductor score
(orchestra) and parts.
Fantasy; composed and scored by
Stan Kenton. © Leslie Music
Corp., New York; 27Nov47;
EP19227. Score: orchestra.

KENTWELL, WILBUR D
Conflict Concerto. See his The Intimat
Stranger.

(Roberta) Lovely to Look At; from
the musical play "Roberta" ...
S.A.B. arr. by William Stickles.
Words by Dorothy Fields and Jimmy
McHugh, music by Jerome Kern. ©
T. B. Harms Co., New York; 4Dec47;
on arrangement; EP20454.

(The Intimate Stranger) Conflict
Concerto; a modified piano
solo arrangement of selected
themes from the orchestral
score by Wilbur Kentwell,
featured in the ... film "The
Intimate Stranger." © W. H.
Paling & Co., ltd., Sydney;
4Jun47; EF5670.

KERN, JEROME, 1885-1945.
Can't Help Lovin' Dat Man; three
part female chorus (S.S.A.),
words by Oscar Hammerstein 2nd,
music by Jerome Kern, arr. by
William Stickles. © T. B. Harms
Co., New York; 28Oct47; on ar-
rangement; EP19873.
The Night Was Made for Love ... S.A.
B. arr. by William Stickles. Words
by Otto Harbach, music by Jerome
Kern. © T. B. Harms Co., New York;
9Dec47; on arrangement; EP20452.
The Night Was Made for Love; two
part chorus arr. by William
Stickles. Words by Otto Harbach,
music by Jerome Kern. © T. B.
Harms Co., New York; 9Dec47; on
arrangement; EP20453.
Ol' Man River. See his Show boat.
Selection of Jerome Kern Songs;
symphonic arrangement by Erik
Leidzen. © T. B. Harms Co.,
New York; 29Jul47; on arrangement;
EP16362. Condensed score (band)
and parts.
(Show boat) Ol' Man River, [from
the musical play "Show boat"];
music by Jerome Kern, words by
Oscar Hammerstein 2nd, simpli-
fied teaching ed. for piano
[arr. by Albert Sirmay] © T. B.
Harms Co., New York; on arrange-
ment; 15May47; EP14523.
They Didn't Believe Me ... S.A.B.
arr. by William Stickles. Lyric
by Herbert Reynolds, music by
Jerome Kern. © T. B. Harms Co.,
New York; 4Dec47; on arrangement;
EP20454.
They Didn't Believe Me; two part
chorus arr. by William Stickles.
Lyric by Herbert Reynolds, music
by Jerome Kern. © T. B. Harms
Co., New York; 4Dec47; on arrange-
ment; EP20455.
Why Was I Born? Words by Oscar
Hammerstein 2nd, music by Jerome
Kern ... S.A.B. arr. by William
Stickles. © T. B. Harms Co.,
New York; 70ct47; on arrange-
ment; EP18279.
Why Was I Born? Words by Oscar
Hammerstein 2nd, music by Jerome
Kern, two part chorus arr. by
William Stickles. © T. B.
Harms Co., New York; 70ct47;
on arrangement; EP18278.
You Are Love ... S.S.A. arr. by
William Stickles. Words by Oscar
Hammerstein 2nd, music by Jerome
Kern. © T. B. Harms Co., New York;
4Dec47; on arrangement; EP20456.
You Are Love; three part mixed
chorus (S. A. B.), words by
Oscar Hammerstein 2nd, music by
Jerome Kern, arr. by William
Stickles. © T. B. Harms Co.,
New York; 9Dec47; on arrange-
ment; EP19872.

KERR, HARRISON, 1899-
(Sonata, piano, no. 2) Piano
Sonata no. 2, [by] Harrison
Kerr. © Arrow Music Press,
inc., New York; 27Mar47;
EP16519.

KERR, JACK.
My Only Love; words and music by
Jack Kerr. © Nordyke Publish-
ing Co., Los Angeles; 12Aug47;
EP19524.

[KERR, PHILLIP STANLEY] 1906-
Christian Songs. [words by Esther
V. Peterson. Music by Phil Kerr]
© Esther V. Peterson, Los Angeles;
no.6, 10Oct47; AA66863.

KERSHAW, THEODORE R   1910-
Jump with Rhythm; words and music
by Theodore R. Kershaw.
© Theodore R. Kershaw, Philadelphia;
21Aug47; EP17059.

KESSLER, MADGE TUTTLE.
Blue River Waltz; words and music
by Madge Tuttle Kessler. ©
Nordyke Publishing Co., Los
Angeles; 5Jun47; EP16666.

KETELBEY, ALBERT W
Bells across the meadows; by Albert
W. Ketelbey. Trio arrangement ...
by Henry Bopkin. New York, Mills
Music, inc. © Keith, Prowse &
Co., ltd., London; on arrangement; 24Jan47; EP6648. Score
(violin, violoncello and piano)
and parts.

KETTERER, ELLA.
Ella Ketterer's Book of Piano
Pieces. © Theodore Presser Co.,
Philadelphia; 29Jul47; on
compilation; EP15961.

KHACHATURIAN, A
I'm Consumed by a Flame; Armenian
folk text tr. into Russian by
D. Ussov, English adaptation by
Olga Paul, [music by] A. Khachaturian. (In Heywood, Charles,
ed. Art Songs of Soviet Russia,
p.42-44) © Edward B. Marks
Music Corp., New York; 16Sep47;
on English adaptation; EP17185.
English and Russian words.

KHACHATURĪAN, ARAM IL'ICH, 1904-
(Concerto, piano) Concerto for
piano and orchestra; [by] Aram
Khachaturian. [Editing, foreword and special annotations
by Harold Sheldon] © Leeds
Music Corp., New York; 17Sep47;
on editing, foreword &
annotations; EP17264. Miniature
score.
Poem; [by] Aram Khachaturian,
[ed. with special annotations
by Gyorgy Sandor] © Leeds Music
Corp., New York; 8Dec47; EP20474.
For piano solo.
Sabre Dance, from "Gayne Ballet"
[by] Aram Khachaturian, for
piano, 4 hands, [ed. with special
annotations by Gyorgy Sandor]
© Leeds Music Corp., New York;
3Jul47; on foreword and editing;
EP15432.
Three Dances (Sabre Dance, Lullaby,
Dance of the Rose Maidens) from
"Gayne Ballet"; by Aram Khacha-
turian, scored ... by Erik Leidzén.
© Leeds Music Corp., New York;
8Dec47; on arrangement; EP20475.
Condensed score (band) and parts.

KIALLMARK, E
The Old Oaken Bucket; [by] E. Kiallmark, arr. by P. Bellatore. (In
Bellatore, Pietro, comp. So Easy.
p.4) © Edward B. Marks Music
Corp., New York; 9Dec47; on arrangement; EP19562. For piano
solo.

KICKLER, DeWITT CLINTON, 1875-
The Blood So Cleansing to Me;
[by] D. C. Kickler. © DeWitt
Clinton Kickler, Roanoke, Va.;
19May47; EP15652. Close score:
SATB, with chord symbols.
I Want to Make Sure of Heaven;
[by] D. C. Kickler. © DeWitt
Clinton Kickler, Roanoke, Va.;
19May47; EP15653. Close score:
SATB, with chord symbols.

KIECKER, LEONARD.
Pals of Long Ago; words and music
by Leonard Kiecker. © Nordyke
Publishing Co., Los Angeles;
18Jul46; EP19956.

KIERZSULIS, WALTER.
Album Polskich Tańców i Pieśni ...
Album [of] Polish Dances ... for
piano solo and piano accordion,
by W. Kierszulis. [Polish professional Music Pub., 1948] ©
Walter Kierszulis, Detroit; 1947
[in notice] EP12475. A few
pieces have words (in Polish)

[KIES, RALPH GEORGE] 1918-
Seek Ye the Lord; [by Ralph George
Kies] © Ralph George Kies,
Austin, Tex.; 13May47; EP15920.
Score: solo voices, mixed chorus
and piano.

KIESTER, EVERETT.
You're the Flower of My Heart (the
Only One Worth Living for);
words and music by Everett
Kiester. © Everett Kiester,
Fairmont, Minn.; 23Jun47;
EP15355.

KILPATRICK, J   F   1915-
Indian Choral Chants; by J. F.
Kilpatrick. © Boston Music Co.,
Boston; 16Dec47; EP20405. Score:
chorus (men's voices) and piano.

KINCAID, PAUL E
My Heart Knows Nothing Better;
words and music by Paul Kincaid.
© Kermore Music Co., Boston;
12Nov47; EP18818.

KINDER, RALPH.
Evening Prayer; (with chimes) [by]
Ralph Kinder. © Theodore Presser
Co., Philadelphia; 6Dec47; EP20441.
For organ solo.

KING, ANDREW F
Yes or No; words and music by John
Mack [pseud.] and Drewey King.
© Chorda Music Pub., New York;
18Aug47; EP16653.

KING, ARTHUR C   1866-
Once to Every Heart; (based on
"Mignon" by Thomas) lyric by
Frank Stanton, adapted by
Arthur C. King. © Nationwide
Songs, inc., New York;
28Apr47; on adaptation;
EP16471.

KING, DREWEY.   See
King, Andrew F.

KING, FRANK.
My Main Trial Is Yet to Come;
words and music by J.L. Frank
and Pee Wee King. © Acuff-Rose
Publications, Nashville;
24Oct47; EP18237.

KING, HAROLD, 1909-
Hail U. B. C.; words and music by
Harold King. © Alma Mater Society
of the Univ. of British Columbia,
inc., Vancouver, B. C., Can.;
10Nov47; EP17139.

KING, HENRY.
Boogie Express; by Henry King.
(c1945) © Cinephonic Music Co.,
ltd., London; 18Jul46; EF6017.
For piano solo.

KING, KATHRYN, pseud.   See
Jurkovich, Catherine.

KING, PEARL R
My Memories; words by Evelyn Todd,
music by Pearl R. King. ©
Pearl R. King, Anton, Colo.;
18Sep47; EP17808.

KING, PEE WEE.   See
King, Frank.

KING, REGINALD.
My Southern Rose ... words by
Harold Simpson, music by
Reginald King. © Peter
Maurice Music Co., ltd., New
York; 20Jun47; EF5688.
Where Water-Lilies Dream; [by]
Reginald King, arr. for orchestra
by Cecil Milner. © Peter Maurice
Music Co., ltd., New York;
1Aug47; EF4240. Piano-conductor
score (orchestra) and parts.

KING, STANFORD.
In Fond Remembrance ... for piano
by Stanford King. © Theodore
Presser Co., Philadelphia; 6Dec47;
EP20442.
In Lavender Silk; piano solo by
Stanford King. © Theodore
Presser Co., Philadelphia;
26Jun47; EP15377.

KING, WAYNE.
Lullaby for Latins; for the piano,
a modern suite in two parts by
Wayne King and Fabian Andre. ©
Brugman, Vocco and Conn, inc.,
New York; 28Aug47; EP16685.

KINGSLEY, MATT.
Tira-Lira-Li; song ... [by] Ray
Trotta, Marty Kenwood [and]
Matt Kingsley. © Sinatra
Songs, inc., New York; 1Aug47;
EP16524.

KINSEY, CURLY.
I Miss a Little Miss (in Mississip-
pi); words and music by Wally
Fowler and Curly Kinsey. © F &
M Publishing Co. inc., New York;
24Oct47; EP18457.

KIPPEL, MICKEY.
The Girl in the Cream Colored
Coat; words by Roy M. Schuldt
and Mickey Kippel, music by
Mickey Kippel. © Nordyke
Publishing Co., Los Angeles;
22Apr47; EP16820.

KIRBY, FRED.
Somewhere a Heart Is Breaking;
words and music by Fred Kirby.
© Main Street Songs, inc., New
York; 14Oct47; EP17999.

KIRCHGASSNER, PHOEBE H
These Times Will Be Old Times Sometime;
words and music by Phoebe H. Kirchgassner. © Nordyke Publishing Co.,
Los Angeles; 12Jul47; EP17390.

KIRK, EDDIE.
So Round, So Firm, So Fully
Packed; by Merle Travis,
Cliffie Stone [and] Eddie Kirk.
© American Music, inc., Holly-
wood, Calif.; 8Jan47; EP17334.
For voice and piano, with chord
symbols.

KIRSHNER, CARL.
I'm Restless; words and music by
Harlan Jensen and Carl Kirshner.
© Tim Spencer Music, inc., Holly-
wood, Calif.; 22Jul47; EP16980.

KLAMI, UUNO KALERVO, 1901-
Neljä suomalaista kansanlaulua;
sov. Uuno Klami. Op. 12.
© A/B Fazers Musikhandel, Helsingfors, Finland; on arrangement; 10Aug44; EF5415. Score:
piano and string orchestra.

KLAMP, PAUL, 1900-
Atoms; words and music by P. Klamp.
© Shelby Music Publishing Co.,
Detroit; 25Nov47; EP19885.

KLAUS, HOWARD M
There's No One Can Keep Out of Love;
words and music by Howard M. Klaus.
© Nordyke Publishing Co., Los Angeles; 18Jul47; EP17388.

KLEIN, JOHN.
Four Children's Pieces; [by] John
Klein. © Elkan-Vogel Co., inc.,
Philadelphia; 17Oct47; EP18969.
For piano solo.

KLEIN, MILDRED.
Goodnight, Baby Mine; words and
music by Mildred Klein. © Nordyke Publishing Co., Los Angeles; 31Jul47; EP19512.

KLEINSINGER, GEORGE.
Pan, the Piper ... music by George
Kleinsinger, story by Paul Wing.
(RCA Victor record story) ©
Radio Corp. of America, RCA
Victor Division, Camden, N. J.;
15Apr47; on prefatory matter;
A13236. Paul Wing, narrator,
with Russ Case and his orchestra.
Includes "The orchestra," by
Victor Millonzi (6 p.)
Young Pan America Sings; twelve
good neighbor songs, music by
George Kleinsinger, lyrics by
Beatrice Goldsmith Jacobson.
© Mercury Music Corp., New York;
1Aug47; EP15784.

KLEMM, EDWARD G   1910-
Desert Dance; for piano, by Edward
G. Klemm, Jr. © Composers
Press, inc., New York; 10Nov47;
EP18563.

KLEMM, GUSTAV.
The Magic Hour; [for] medium
voice [by] Gustav Klemm ...
[words by] Daniel S. Twohig.
© Oliver Ditson Co., Philadel-
phia; 10Oct47; EP17992.
March of the Smugglers, by Glen
Barton [pseud.], for piano.
© J. Fischer & Bro., New York;
9Sep47; EP17709.
My Dream of Vienna; song, words by
Hugh Kenyon, music by Gustav
Klemm. © Theodore Presser Co.,
Philadelphia; 27Oct47; EP18650.
My Friend, Bob White; [for] SA
accompanied, [music by] Gustav
Klemm. [words by] Glen Barton
[pseud.] © Harold Flammer, inc.,
New York; 28Jul47; EP16252.

KLENNER, JOHN.
Moonlight on the Purple Sage ...
by John Klenner, orchestrated by
Ronald Binge. [London] Sole
agents, Ascherberg, Hopwood & Crew.
© Skidmore Music Co., inc., New
York; 13Jul47; on arrangement;
EP7204. Piano-conductor score
(orchestra, with words) and parts.

[KLICKMANN, F   HENRI] arr.
Ed Durlacher's Country Dances; [pre-
pared by Ed Durlacher, medleys arr.
by F. Henri Klickmann] © Bob
Miller, inc., New York; bk.1,
10Sep47; AA70308.
Giant-Note Hymns; for the elementary
accordionist ... arr. by Bruno
Comini [pseud.] © Chas. H. Hansen
Music Co., New York; 9Aug47; on
arrangement; EP17105.

[KLICKMANN, F   HENRI] ed.
E favorite clarinet solos; with
piano acc. © Wm. J. Smith Music
Co., inc., New York; 2May46;
EP3505. Score and part.

KLOSTER, CHARLES.
I Met My Dream Boy in Person;
words by Shirley Murphy, music
by Charles Kloster. © Nordyke
Publishing Co., Los Angeles;
23Jun47; EP17433.

KLUMPKEY, JULIA, 1879-
"I Have Been Here Before"; words
by Dante Gabriel Rossette, music
by Julia Klumpkey; for medium
voice. © Wesley Webster, San
Francisco; 1Nov47; EP19579.

[KNIPPER, LEV KONSTANTINOVICH]
1898-
Cavalry Patrol; the popular
Russian song "Song of the
Steppes," arr. for piano
solo by King Palmer. © W.
Paxton & Co., ltd., London;
11Aug46; on arrangement;
EF5699.

KNOWLTON, LORRAINE E
Circle 'round the Moon; words
and music by Lorraine E. Knowlton. © Croxton Publishing Co.,
Los Angeles; 80ct47; EP18018.

[KOCH, CLARA MAE] 1887-
One Kiss, Just This; music by
Mae Cook [pseud.], words [by]
Lee Gilbert [pseud.] © Melotone
Music Publishers, Chicago;
5Oct47; EP17682.

KOCH, ERLAND VON.
Nordiskt Capriccio ... Op.26.
[By] Erland von Koch. Stock-
holm, Ed. Suecia. © Föreningen
svenska tonsättare, edition
Suecia, Stockholm; 1Jan45;
EF7065. Score: orchestra.

KOCH, ERLAND VON. cont'd.
Solstorm. (Sonnensturm) Till
text av Sigfrid Siwertz, [by]
Erland von Koch. © Föreningen
svenska tonsättare, Stockholm;
1Jan45; EF7113.

Två Sånger; till next av Erik Axel
Karlfeldt, [by] Erland von Koch.
© Föreningen svenska tonsättare,
Stockholm; 1Jan46; EF7125.

KOCH, MARTIN, d. 1940.
Lyckan; [by] Martin Koch, [arr.
by Gösta Hädell] © Nordiska
musikförlaget, a/b, Stockholm;
1Jan36; on arrangement; EF6950.
For voice and piano, guitar or
lute.

KOCH, SIGURD VON, 1879-1919.
Gammalsvenska wijsor; [by] Sigurd
v. Koch, (words by Lucidor and
Wivallius) © Nordiska
Musikförlaget, a/b, Stockholm;
on 13 songs; 1Jan21. Contents.-
1. Hvarföre skal iagh mig medh
sorger quälia' (Lucidor)
(© EF3673) Wivalli wijsa.
(© EF3674) Wivalli wijsa.
(© EF3675) Lasse Lucidors
dryckes-wijsa. (© EF3676) Wäll
then som vidt af höga klippor.
(Wivallius) (© EF3677) Du
hiärtans tröst och lilia.
(Wivallius) (© EF3678) Een
skiön wijsa. (Wivallius)
(© EF3679)- 2. Skulle iagh
sörja, då wore iagh tokot.
(Lucidor) (© EF3680) Jagh
stoorlig bekymbrat är.
(Wivallius) (© EF3681) Härmedh
faar väl, skiön damma!
(Wivallius) (© EF3682)
Svijklige världens oundvijklige
äd-dädligheets sorgrätstande
lijksäng. (Lucidor) (© EF3683)
Önske-wijsa. (Wivallius)
(© EF3684) Som een sißman
uthistoor fhaar. (Wivallius)
(© EF3685)

KOEHLER, CURTIS ALBERT, 1898-
I've Got a Feeling; by Curtis
Koehler. © La Mar Music Publishers, inc., Canton, Ohio;
16Jun47; EP15989. For voice and
piano, with chord symbols.

KOGEN, HARRY, 1895-
Bob White Polka; by Harry Kogen,
[for] piano accordion. ©
Southern Music Publishing Co.,
inc., New York; 26Sep47;
EP17855.

Happy Days Polka; by Harry Kogen,
[for] piano accordion. ©
Southern Music Publishing Co.,
inc., New York; 26Sep47;
EP17856.

If You Only Knew; words and music
by Vaughn Horton, Whitey Ber-
quist [and] Harry Kogen.
© Rytvoc, inc., New York;
24Oct47; EP18189.

March of the Drum Majorettes; by
Harry Kogen, arr. for piano sol
by Samuel Spivak. Lewis
Music Publishing Co., inc.,
New York; 30Oct47; EP18385.

"Uncle Will" March; by Harry Ko-
gen ... ed. and arr. by Thomas
J. Filas. © Will Rossiter,
Chicago; 17Dec47; EP20100.
For piano solo.

KOLETKA, ELIZABETH.
The Reflections of a Teacher; by
Elizabeth Koletka and Charles
Nupper. Washington, D. C.,
Dept. of Classroom Teachers,
National Education Assn. of the
United States, 1947.

KOMPANEETZ, ZINOVI.
Soviet Seamen; words by S. Bolotin,
English adaptation by Olga Paul,
[music by] Zinovi Kompaneetz.
(In Haywood, Charles, ed. Art
Songs of Soviet Russia, p.24-28)
© Edward B. Marks Music Corp.,
New York; 16Sep47; on English
adaptation; EP17180. English
and Russian words.

KOONTS, JONES CALVIN.
I'm Living in a Dream; words and
music by J. Calvin Koonts. ©
Jones Calvin Koonts, Lexington,
N.C.; 1Aug47; EP16494.

KOPPEL, HERMAN DAVID, 1908-
(Sextet, piano & winds) Sekstet,
for piano, flauto, oboe,
clarinetto in A, corno in F
og fagotto, [by] Herm. D.
Koppel. Op. 36. © Skandinavisk
Musikforlag Aktieselskab,
Copenhagen; 11Jun47; EF5687.
Miniature score.

KOPPES, CHRYSOSTOM, sister. See
Koppes, Mary Chrysostom, sister.

KOPPES, MARY CHRYSOSTOM, Sister,
1910-
Dedication ... words and music by
Chrysostom Koppes. © Mont St.
Scholastica, Atchison, Kan.;
24Nov47; EP19279. Score: SA and
piano; Latin words.

Down Bethlehem Way; for three-
part chorus of women's voices a
cappella. Words by Agnes Haga-
ney & Lillian Muell, music by
Chrysostom Koppes. © Willis
Music Co., Cincinnati; 28Nov47;
EP19803.

KOPYLOV, ALEXANDER.
God Is a Spirit; [by] Alexander
Kopylov ... arr. by K.K.D.
[words from] St. John, 9:24
[adapted] © E.C. Schirmer Music
Co., Boston; 29Sep47; on arrangement; EP18140. Score:
chorus (SA) and piano or organ.

KORCHMARYOV, KLIMENT.
Lullaby; words by N. P. Liubimov,
English adaptation by Olga Paul,
[music by] Kliment Korchmaryov.
(In Haywood, Charles, ed. Art
Songs of Soviet Russia, p.32-34)
© Edward B. Marks Music Corp.,
New York; 16Sep47; on English
adaptation; EP17182. English
and Russian words.

Matrena and the Deacon; words by
A. Lyubovsky, English adaptation
by Olga Paul, [music by] Kliment
Korchmaryov. (In Haywood,
Charles, ed. Art Songs of
Soviet Russia, p. 38-41.) ©
Edward B. Marks Music Corp., New
York; 16Sep47; on English adap-
tation; EP17184. English and
Russian words.

KORMAN, JAMES A
Mass in Honor of the Blessed
Sacrament; for 2 or 4 voices
[by] J. A. Korman. © McLaughlin
& Reilly Co., Boston; 25Jul47;
on arrangement; EP16389.

KORNGOLD, ERIC WOLFGANG.
(Escape Me Never) Love for Love,
from the ... pict. "Escape Me
Never"; lyric by Ted Koehler,
music by Eric Wolfgang Korngold.
© M. Witmark & Sons, New York;
20Aug47; EP16527.

(Escape Me Never) O Nené; Italian
lyric by Aldo Frenchetti, lyric
by Ted koehler, music by Erich
Wolfgang Korngold, from the ...
picture "Escape Me Never." ©
M. Witmark & Sons New York;
30Oct47; EP17800.

Love for Love. See his Escape Me Never.

O Nené. See his Escape Me Never.

KORSAKOFF, N. RIMSKY. See
Rimskii-Korsakov, Nikolai Andreevich.

KOSMA, JOSEPH, 1905-
Baptiste; pantomime en 6 tableaux,
de Jacques Prévert, d'après le
film ... "Les Enfants de Paradis,"
musique de Joseph Kosma. © Enoch
& Cie, Paris; 31Mar47; EF5967.
For piano solo; includes
directions for pantomime.

D'Autres Chansons ... [words by]
Jacques Prévert et [music by]
Joseph Kosma. © Enoch et Cie,
Paris; v.2, 10Nov47; EF7206.

Rhapsodie; variations a vocalisea
pour soprano léger [by] Joseph
Kosma. © Enoch & Cie, Paris;
11Nov47; EF7207. For voice and
piano; without words.

Suite Languedocienne; pour piano,
[by] Joseph Kosma. © Enoch &
Cie, Éditeurs, Paris; 30Apr47;
EF5885.

KOSS, JOSEPH.
Miami Moon; words and music by
Joseph Koss. © Art Music Co.,
New York; 4Aug47; EP16066.

KOTEL, MARTIN.
Rollin' Along; by Rose Cooper and
Martin Kotel. © Western Music
Publishing Co., Hollywood, Calif.;
28Jun47; EP15990. For voice and
piano, with chord symbols.

KOUNTZ, RICHARD.
Rise Up Early; Christmas carol for
chorus of women's voices, three-
part, [by] Richard Kountz ...
based on a Slovak Christmas
carol. © Galaxy Music Corp.,
New York; 13Aug47; EP7020.

Rise Up. Early; (S.A.T.B.) [by].
Richard Kountz. © Galaxy Music
Corp., New York; 13Aug47; EP
17021.

KOVAL, MARIAN.
Red Rico; original poem in
Hungarian by Antal Mádas, tr.
into Russian by M. Room, English
adaptation by Olga Paul, [music
by] Marian Koval. (In Haywood,
Charles, ed. Art Songs of
Soviet Russia, p.53-57) © Edward
B. Marks Music Corp., New York;
16Sep47; on English adaptation;
EP17188. English and Russian
words.

Times Have Changed; words by H.
Asseev, English adaptation by
Olga Paul, [music by] M. Koval.
(In Haywood, Charles, ed. Art
Songs of Soviet Russia, p.20-21)
© Edward B. Marks Music Corp.,
New York; 16Sep47; on English
adaptation; EP17178. English
and Russian words.

KOWALSKI, JOHN [LEO] 1913-
I Had a Lot of Friends; music ...
by Johnny Cole [pseud.], lyrics
[by] Buddy Kaye. © Mrs. Joan M.
Garvey, Jackson Heights, N. Y.;
18Sep47; EP18320.

KRAFT, ALVAR, 1902-
En Hälsning från det Gamla Landet.
Tre Flaggor; musik: Alvar Kraft,
text: Nils Hellström. © Scan-
dinavian Music House, inc., New
York; 28Aug46; EF18292.

KRAMER, A WALTER, 1890-
Music, When Soft Voices Die; S.A.
T.B. [by] A. Walter Kramer,
[words by] Percy Bysshe Shelley.
© C. C. Birchard & Co., Boston;
30Oct47; on arrangement;
EP20214.

You Saw Your Soul in Mine! [Words]
by Mary E. Coleridge, [music by]
A. Walter Kramer. © Galaxy
Music Corp., New York; 22Oct47;
EP18414.

KRAMER, ALEX CHARLES.
His Fraternity Pin; words and
music by Joan Whitney and Alex
Kramer. © Beaux Arts Music,
inc., New York; 30Jul47;
EP15973.

298

KRAMER, ALEX CHARLES. Cont'd.
What Would It Take? Words and
music by Joan Whitney [pseud.]
and Alex Kramer. © Sun Music Co.,
inc., New York; 31Oct47; EP20412.

KRASEV, M
Song of the Tartar Maiden; words by
M. Klokov, English adaptation by
Olga Paul, [music by] M. Krasov.
(In Haywood, Charles, ed. Art
Songs of Soviet Russia, p.45-47)
© Edward B. Marks Music Corp.,
New York; 16Sep47; on English
adaptation; EP17186. English
and Russian words.

KRECKEL, PHILIP GEORGE, 1886-
The Parish Organ Book; composed
and arr. by Philip G. Kreckel.
© J. Fischer & Bro., New York;
pt.2, 30Sep47; EP17705. Contents.- pt.2. Interludes,
Offertories and Communions.

KREISLER, FRITZ, 1875-
Liebesleid; [by] Fritz Kreisler,
arr. for one piano, four hands
by Hermene W. Eichhorn. ©
Charles Foley, New York;
13May47; on arrangement;
EP15537.
Schön Rosmarin; [by] Fritz
Kreisler, arr. for one piano,
four hands by Hermene W. Eichhorn. © Charles Foley, New York;
13May47; on arrangement;
EP15536.

KREITNER, FRANZ.
We'll Meet Again. (Wenn Wir Uns
Wiedersehn) Music [by] Franz
Kreitner, lyrics [by] Helen
Opsata, adapted from Viennese
text of Alois Eckhardt and Eng-
lish translation of Victor S.
Scharbau. © Washington Music
Bazaar, R. H. Greenwell, sole
owner, New York; 3Jun47; on
arrangement and English words;
EP15687. English words.

KREMSER, EDUARD.
Prayer of Thanksgiving; old Dutch
folk-tune ... arr. from Eduard
Kremser, by Roger C. Wilson.
© The Raymond A. Hoffman Co.,
Chicago; 17Jun36; EP15584.
Score: chorus (men's voices)
and piano.
Prayer of Thanksgiving; (old
Dutch folk tune) arr. from
Eduard Kremser by Roger C.
Wilson. © The Raymond A.
Hoffman Co., Chicago; 24Nov34;
EP15587. Score: mixed chorus
and piano.

KRENZ, BILL, 1899-
Early Riser ... by Bill Krenz ...
ed. and arr. by Thomas J. Filas.
© Will Rossiter, Chicago;
24Nov47; EP18824. For piano
solo.

KREPS, WILLIAM H
At the Tavern Ball; words and
music by William H. Kreps. ©
William H. Kreps, Lincoln, Neb.;
17Nov47; EP19217.

KRESA, HELMY.
That's My Desire; by Carroll
Loveday and Helmy Kresa, transcribed by Stanford King.
© Mills Music, inc., New York;
28Jul47; on simplified arrangement; EP16199. For piano solo.

KREUDER, PETER.
Abschied ... Worte von H. F.
Beckmann und Erich Meder, Musik
von Peter Kreuder. © Edition
Turicaphon, ltd., music publish-
ers, Zurich, Switzerland;
1Apr47; EP5831.
Alles Vurstoh'n Hoisst Alles
Vorzeih'n; Musik: Peter
Kreuder, Worte: H. F. Beckmann.
© Edition Turicaphon a. g.,
Bühnen- und Musikverlag, Zurich,
Switzerland; 22Mar47; EP5870.

Das Blaue Halstuch ... text von
Kurt Meuser, musik von Peter
Kreuder [and] Ich Nenne Alle
Frauen Baby ... text von
Fritz Böttger, musik von Benny
De Weille. © Edition Turi-
caphon A G, Zurich, Switzer-
land; 1Jun47; EP5678-5679.
Parts: voice and orchestra.

Enten Blues; Worte von Josef
Petrak, [music by] Peter Kreud-
er. Zurich, Edition-Suizo-
Baltic a.g., [c1946] © Edition
Turicaphon a.g. (in notice;
Edition Suizo-Baltic a.g.) /
Zurich, Switzerland; 1Apr47;
EP5829.

Herzen Träumen in der Dämmerung
... Musik: Peter Kreuder, Text:
Josef Petrak. © Edition Turicaphon s.g., Zurich, Switzerland; 11Jul47; EP6800. Parts:
voice and orchestra.

(Das Singunden Haus) Lass Uns von
der Liebe Redon ... aus dem
Kollektivfilm ... "Das Singende
Haus" ... Text: Bruno Hardt und
Aldo v. Pinelli, Musik: Peter
Kreuder. © Edition Turicaphon
ng., Bühnen- und Musikverlag,
Zürich, Switzerland; 22Mar47;
EP5668.

Die Türe Müsste Aufgehn! Worte:
H. F. Beckmann, Musik: Peter
Lippen Küsse ... © Edition Turicaphon
a. g., Bühnen- und Musikverlag,
Zürich, Switzerland; 22Mar47;
EP5871.

Wege der Liebe; 6 Chansons von
Peter Kreuder, Texte von H. F.
Beckmann. [c1946] © Edition
Turicaphon a. g., Bühnen- und
Musikverlag, Zürich, Switzer-
land; 1Apr47; on 5 songs. Con-
tents.- Abschied.- Ich Kann bei
Gewitter Nicht Allein Sein!
(© EF5874)- Wenn Ich Deine
Lippen Küsse ... (© EF5875)-
Mit einer Träne in der Stimme
(© EF5876)- Konversation!
(© EF5877)- Lasst Mir Doch
Meine Träume! (© EF5878)

[KRIEG, RICHARD CHARLES]
I Ain't A-Gonna Leave My Love No
More; words and music by Larry
Markes, Eddie Waldman and Dick
Charles [pseud.] © Bob Miller,
inc., New York; 27Oct47; EP18629.
It Takes a Long Long Train with a
Red Caboose (to carry my blues
away); words and music by Larry
Markes and Dick Charles [pseud.]
© Bob Miller, inc., New York;
27Oct47; EP18607.
It Takes a Long Long Train with a
Red Caboose (to carry my blues
away); words and music by Larry
Markes and Dick Charles [pseud.],
arrangement by Johnny Warrington.
© Bob Miller, inc., New York;
5Dec47; EP19828. Piano-conductor
score (orchestra, with words)
and parts.
You Did Your Best to Break My Heart;
lyric by Sid Prosen, music by
Dick Charles [pseud.] © Empire
Music Co., inc., New York; 1946
(in notice) EP7903.

KRISZ, SPEED.
The Georgia Waltz; words and music
by Speed Krise. © Nordyke
Publishing Co., Los Angeles;
2Jul46; EP19977.

KRISH, EDWARD, 1902-
A Song for You ... words by Peter
Carroll, music by Edward Krish.
[London] Boosey & Hawkes.
© Boosey & Co., ltd., London;
16Oct47; EF6816.

KRISSEL, WALTER D
Things Are No Different Now;
music by Walter D. Krissel,
lyric by Stanley Adams. ©
Edwin H. Morris & Co., inc.,
New York; 1Aug47; EP16329.

KRÖNE, BEATRICE PERHAM, 1901-
El Capotin. (The Raincoat Song)
(S.A.B.) Mexican folk tune,
text and arr. by the Krones,
Beatrice and Max. Chicago,
N.A. Kjos Music Co. © Max &
Beatrice Krone, Los Angeles;
6Nov47; on arrangement & text;
EP19548. English words.
Christ the Lord Is Risen Today
... S.S.A., from the Krones,
Beatrice and Max, [words by]
Charles S. Wesley. Chicago,
N. A. Kjos Music Co. © Max &
Beatrice Krone, Los Angeles;
8Sep47; on arrangement;
EP17977.
Christmas Is Coming; Old English
Christmas songs arr. by the
Krones, Beatrice and Max, des-
cant by Constance Pearson.
Chicago, N. A. Kjos Music Co.
© Max & Beatrice Krone, Los
Angeles; 29Oct47; on arrange-
ment & descant; EP18821. Score:
/chorus (SA) and piano.
On Christmas Day; traditional
English carol, S.S.A. arr. by
the Krones, Beatrice and Max,
Chicago, N. A. Kjos Music Co.
© Max & Beatrice Krone, Los
Angeles; 17Oct47; on arrange-
ment; EP18822.

KROPP, GEORGE W   1907-
I'll Always Love You; words by
Bernice Kouba Horney, music by
George W. Kropp. © Shelby Music
Publishing Co., Detroit; 29May47;
EP15583.

KROUSE, MORTON.
Baby, I Don't Cry over You;
by Morton Krouse. © Northern
Music Corp., New York; 1Aug47;
EP16413. For voice and piano,
with chord symbols.

KRUPA, GENE.
Disc Jockey Jump; by Gene Krupa
and Gerry Mulligan ... arr.
by Will Hudson. © Robbins
Music Corp., New York; 1Aug47;
EP16544. Piano-conductor score
(orchestra) and parts.

KUAANA, DANNY KUAI, 1902-
Auana (the song of the wanderer);
lyric by Bernie Kaai, melody by
Danny K. Kuaana. © Ray Meany,
Golden Gate Publications, Oakland, Calif.; 5Jul47; EP15642.
For voice and two guitars; also
diagrams and chord symbols for
ukulele.
Tahiti, My Tahiti; words and
music by Danny K. Kuaana, arr.
by Bernie Kaai. © Ray Meany,
Golden Gate Publications, Oakland, Calif.; 5Jul47; EP15641.
For voice and two guitars;
also diagrams and chord symbols
for ukulele.

KUHLA, GEORGE J   T
I Know What Love Can Do; words and
music by George J. T. Kuhla.
© Nordyke Publishing Co. Los
Angeles; 10Jun47; EP16888.

KUKUK, WAYNE.
Julie; words & music by Wayne
Kukuk. © Nordyke Publishing
Co., Los Angeles; 16Sep46;
EP19942.

KULMA, LOUISE, 1912-
My Own Darby and Joan; [by]
Box [pseud.] Cox and Kulma.
© Box and Cox (Publications),
London; 8Apr47; EF5755. For
voice and piano, with chord
symbols; melody also in tonic
sol-fa notation.

299

KUNC, PIERRE, 1877-1941.
Rapsodie; [by] Pierre Kunc. © Editions Max Eschig, Paris; 22May46;
EF7340. Score (viola and piano)
and part.

KUNTZ, P EMIL.
1. O Gloriosa Virginum. 2.
Veni Sponsa Christi. By P.
Emil Kuntz, for three equal
voices. © McLaughlin & Reilly
Co., Boston; 2Jun47; EP16683.

KURTH, BURTON, 1890-
A Cookie for Snip and The Tired
Moon; unison songs, words by
Margaret Hutchison, music by
Burton Kurth. © Western Music
Co., ltd., Vancouver, B.C., Can.;
6Oct47; EP6683.

Daffodil and White Dreams; unison
songs, words by Margaret
Hutchison, music by Burton Kurth.
© Western Music Co., ltd.,
Vancouver, B.C., Can.; 2Oct47;
EP6684.

Kitty's Tongue; and Candle Talk; unison songs, words by Margaret Hutchison, music by Burton Kurth. ©
Western Music Co., ltd., Vancouver,
B. C., Can.; 5Dec47; EP7209.

KURUCZ, JANOS.
Bukony Erdon Sir a Gerle. (There's
a Dove within the Forest) English lyric by Olga Paul, music
by Kurucz János. (In Pesti, Barbara, comp. Memories of Hungary.
p. 36-37) © Edward B. Marks
Music Corp., New York; 19Nov47;
on English lyric; EP19005.

Ha Eldbr Hozzád. (If, when You Hear
My Song) English lyric by Olga
Paul, music by Kurucz János. (In
Pesti, Barbara, comp. Memories
of Hungary. p. 34-35) © Edward
B. Marks Music Corp., New York;
19Nov47; on English lyric;
EP19004.

Valahol. (Somewhere) English lyric
by Olga Paul, music by Kurucz
János. (In Pesti, Barbara, comp.
Memories of Hungary. p. 62. ©
Edward B. Marks Music Corp., New
York; 19Nov47; on English lyric;
EP19017.

KURZEN, PEARL CAROLYN.
Sweetheart, You're a Heartache;
words and music by Pearl
Carolyn Kurzen. © Nordyke
Publishing Co., Los Angeles;
15Aug47; EP20035.

[KWONG, MARK DER K] 1886-
Christmas Day ... song by Mark Der,
[pseud.] © Mark Der (i.e., Mark
Der K, Kwong) Malden, Mass.;
15Sep47; on revised words;
EP19054.

L

LABASTILLE, IRMA.
The World's Your Home ... by Irma
Labastille. © Pan American Airways, inc., New York; 10Sep47;
EP18304. Melody and chord symbols, with words.

LABBE, ALBERT.
Bangkok. See his Un Vent de Folie.

(Un Vent de Folie) "Bangkok,"
[from the] revue ... "Un Vent
de Folie"; music by W. Sterling
[pseud.] and J. Betty [pseud.]
© Éditions L. Maillochon, Paris;
12Mar26; EF6285. For piano solo.

LACALLE, JOSEPH M
Amapola; [by] Jos. M. Lacalle, arr.
by L. Sugarman. © Edward B.
Marks Music Corp., New York;
5Sep47; on arrangement; EP16670.
For piano solo.

LaFARGE, GUY, 1904-
Black! Paroles de François
Llenas, musique de Guy LaFarge.
© Éditions Royalty, Paris;
2Jun47; EF5904. French words.

Bonne-femme; paroles et musique de
Guy Lafarge. © Éditions Joubert,
Paris; 10Oct47; EF7258.

Les Jeunes Filles de Bonne Famille;
paroles de Henri Kubnick, musique
de Guy Lafarge. © Éditions Joubert, Paris; 10Oct47; EF7259.

Mars! Avril! Mai Juin!
Paroles de Jamblan [pseud.]
musique de Guy LaFarge.
Éditions Joubert, Paris;
31Mar47; EF6866.

Le Milliardaire Américain;
paroles de Andrée Demetz,
musique de Guy Lafarge. c1946. ©
Éditions Roger Bernstein, Paris;
31Jun47; EF5955.

Petit Noël; paroles de François
Llenas & Guy Lafarge, musique
de Guy Lafarge. © Éditions
Joubert et Royalty, Paris;
2Jun47; EF5962.

Valse! Paroles de François Llenas
& Roger Lanzac, musique de Guy
Lafarge. © Éditions Joubert et
Royalty, Paris; 31Mar47; EF5983.

LAFFERTY, WILLIAM HENRY, 1891-
Sixteen; [by] W. H. Lafferty.
[Arr. by William Henry Lafferty
and Marguerite May Henricks] ©
William Henry Lafferty, Toledo;
22Jul47; EP18994. Melody and
chord symbols, with words.

The Years We Left Behind; [by]
W. H. Lafferty, [arr. by W. H.
Lafferty and Marguerite May
Henricks] © William Henry
Lafferty, Toledo; 22Jul47;
EP18702. Melody and chord
symbols, with words.

LAGERKRANS, KARL OLOF.
Förråk Inte mod Mej, Fröken ...
ur filmen mod samma namn, musik;
Kocko Lagerkrans, text: Åke
Söderblom, arr.: Sam Samson. ©
Edition Sylvain, a.b., Stockholm; 1Jan45; on arrangement;
EP7086. Piano-conductor score
(orchestra, with words) and
parts.

Förråk Inte mod Mej, Fröken ...
ur Kungs-filmen mod samma namn;
musik: Kocko Lagerkrans, text:
Åke Söderblom. © Edition
Sylvain, a.b., Stockholm;
1Jan45; EP7085.

LAGERKRANS, KOCKO. See
Lagerkrans, Karl Olof.

LAINE, FRANKIE.
Put Yourself in My Place, Baby;
by Hoagy Carmichael and Frankie
Laine. © Burke & Van Heusen,
inc., New York; 12Sep47;
EF17292. For voice and piano,
with chord symbols.

LAIR, JOHN.
Keep Them Cold Icy Fingers off
Me; words and music by John
Lair. © Hill and Range Songs,
inc., Hollywood, Calif.;
7May47; EP15318.

LAJTAI, LAJOS.
Én Nem Szeretek Mást csak Téged.
(I Love Nobody Else but You,
Dear) English lyric by Olga Paul,
music by Lajtai Lajos. (In Pesti,
Barbara, comp. Memories of Hungary. p. 44-46) © Edward B.
Marks Music Corp., New York;
19Nov47; on English lyric;
EP19009.

LAKE, GENEVIEVE, 1892-
Ballerina; piano solo by Genevieve Lake. © The Willis Music
Co., Cincinnati; 9Dec47;
EP20007.

Candy Town Tunes; six pieces for
piano solo by Genevieve Lake.
© Willis Music Co., Cincinnati;
v.3, 6, 8Aug47. Contents.-
3. Candy Parade (© EP16282)-
6. The Candy Clock (© EP16283)

Dancing on a Rainbow; piano solo
by Genevieve Lake. © Pallma
Music Products, Chicago; 27May47;
EP15668.

Gliders; piano solo by Genevieve
Lake. © Pallma Music Products,
Chicago; 27May47; EP15667.

If Wishes Were Fishes; piano solo
by Genevieve Lake. © Pallma
Music Products, Chicago;
27May47; EP15666.

Snaps and Snails ... Piano solo by
Genevieve Lake. © Clayton F.
Summy Co., Chicago; 11Sep47;
EP16997.

Sugar and Spice ... piano solo by
Genevieve Lake. © Clayton F.
Summy Co., Chicago; 2Aug47;
EP16331.

There She Goes; piano solo by
Genevieve Lake. © The Boston
Music Co., Boston; 8Dec47;
EP20000.

The Watchdog; piano solo by
Genevieve Lake. © Pallma
Music Products, Chicago;
27May47; EP15665.

Woodpeckers at Work; piano solo
by Genevieve Lake. © Pallma
Music Products, Chicago;
27May47; EP15662.

LAKS, SIMON, 1901-
Passacaille; [by] Simon Laks. Paris
Rouart, Lerolle; vente exclusive:
Éditions Salabert, inc., New York; 30Jun47; on arrangement; EF7250. Score (violoncello and piano) and part.

[LALLY, JAMES]
Remember Me? 'Cause I Remember
You! Words by Bill Eladon,
music by Hugh James [pseud.]
© Ideal Music Publishers,
London; 30Jun47; EF3980.

LAMA, GAETANO.
I Hear You Sweetly Singing.
Vieneme 'nzuonno. English lyric
by Olga Paul, Italian lyric by
F. Fiore, music by Gaetano Lama.
(In Memories of Italy. p.52-55)
© Edward B. Marks Music Corp.,
New York; 16Jul47; on English
lyric; EP15828.

Like April's Roses. Come le rose.
English lyric by Olga Paul,
Italian lyric by A. Gonise,
music by Gaetano Lama. (In
Memories of Italy. p.24-27)
© Edward B. Marks Music Corp.,
New York; 16Jul47; on English
lyric; EP15821.

My Dearest Darling. Cara Piccina;
English lyric by Olga Paul, music
by Gaetano Lama. (In Memories
of Italy. p.34-35) © Edward B.
Marks Music Corp., New York;
16Jul47; on English lyric;
EP15823.

Tik-a-tee, Tik-a-tay. Tic-ti
Tic-tà. English lyric by Olga
Paul, Italian lyric by Uff. F.
Peola, music by Gaetano Lama.
(In Memories of Italy. p.56-59)
© Edwin B. Marks Music Corp.,
New York; 16Jul47; on English
lyric; EP15829.

LAMA, JERRY.
I'll Never Fall in Love Again ...
Words and music by Jerry Lama.
[c1945] © The La Casa del Rio
Music Publishing Co., inc.,
Toledo; 4Jan46; EP15607.

LA MAR, CHARLIE, pseud. See
Shean, Charles La Mar.

LaMAR, ESTELLE HILL.
The Cat Song; words and music by
Estelle Hill LaMar. © Estelle
Hill LaMar, Houston, Tex;
6Oct47; EP17095.

LaMAR, ESTELLE HILL. Cont'd.
Down Texas Way; words and music
by Estelle Hill LaMar. ©
Estelle Hill LaMar, Houston,
Tex.; 22Sep47; EP17364.
It's You, Dear; words and music
by Estelle Hill LaMar. ©
Estelle Hill LaMar, Houston,
Tex.; 22Sep47; EP17365.
LA MARGE, JIMMIE, 1910-
Blessed Event Song; (Have a cigar)
... words and music by Jimmie
Franklin ... Abe Farbman and Jimmie
La Marge. © Peerless Music Co.,
New York; 5Sep47; EP16627.
LAMARRE, RENNY.
The Day I Left Alsace Lorraine; by
Jack Harris, Russ Donahoe [and]
Renny LaMarre. New York, Trilon
Publishing Co. © Trilon Record
Mfg. Co., d.b.a. Trilon Publish-
ing Co., Oakland, Calif.;
10ct47; EP17812. For voice and
piano, with chord symbols.
LAMARTER, ERIC DE. See
De Lamarter, Eric.
LAMB, FRED W
Nancy Sue; words & music by
Fred W. Lamb. © Nordyke
Publishing Co., Los Angeles;
27Sep46; EP19388.
LAMBERT, CECILY.
The Cuban Spell ... by Cecily
Lambert. © The Boston Music
Co., Boston; 11Aug47; EP16294.
Score (violin and piano) and
part.
Two Piano Duets; by Cecily Lambert.
© The Boston Music Co., Boston;
25Sep47. Contents. - 1. A Droll
Tale (© EP17723) - 2. Larch with
Bells (© EP17724)
LAMBERTSON, MILAN WARD, 1923-
This Is the Victory ... for voice
and piano, words taken from the
Bible, music by M. Lambertson.
© Milan Ward Lambertson, Cam-
denton, Mo.; 1Nov47; EP18366.
LANBERTUCCI, ROBERTO, 1915-
Mi Dolor ... de Don Filinto
[pseud.], Aguariguay [pseud.] y
Lambertucci. © Editorial
Musical "El Cometa," Buenos
Aires; 31May47; EF6672. For
voice and piano.
LAMKOFF, PAUL.
Because of You; words by Thelma
Buchanan, music by Paul Lamkoff.
© Nordyke Publishing Co., Los
Angeles; 3Jul47; EP17565.
Belle of Bali; words by Jean
Ogden, music by Paul Lamkoff.
© Nordyke Publishing Co., Los
Angeles; 29Apr47; EP16819.
Don't Ache, My Heart; words by
Ella Frances Whaley, music by
Paul Lamkoff. © Nordyke Pub-
lishing Co., Los Angeles;
15Aug47; EP19636.
F. D. Roosevelt; words by Ann Steffy,
music by Paul Lamkoff. © Nordyke
Publishing Co., Los Angeles;
31May46; EP19649.
Going Fishing; words by Esther S.
Coup, music by Paul Lamkoff.
© Nordyke Publishing Co., Los
Angeles; 23May47; EP16948.
Grandpa, I Want to Be a Soldier;
words by Edward Fisher, music by
Paul Lamkoff. © Nordyke Publish-
ing Co., Los Angeles; 16Sep46;
EP19975.
Saddle My Horse; words by
Katherine Elizabeth McDonald,
music by Paul Lamkoff. © Nordyke
Publishing Co., Los
Angeles; 10May47; EP16892.
A Song in My Heart; words by Her-
bert C. Hilton, music by Paul
Lamkoff. © Nordyke Publishing
Co., Los Angeles; 16Sep46;
EP19691.

The V. J. Song; words by Robert
O. Wheeler, music by Paul Lam-
koff. © Nordyke Publishing
Co., Los Angeles; 1Jul46;
EP20064.
You Bore Me; words by Mary F. El-
saesser, music by Paul Lamkoff.
[c1945] © Nordyke Publishing
Co., Los Angeles; 14Jun46;
EP19748.
LANCASTER, RICHARD, 1887-
San Francisco, You're the Town for
Me; words and music by Richard
Lancaster, [piano arr. by Frank
R. Fuller] San Francisco, Ryland
Music Pub. Co. © Richard
Lancaster, San Francisco; 5Jul47;
EP15644.
LANDL, ERNST.
Babdadu ... Text von Max Schinke
und Peter Wehle, Musik von
Ernst Landl. © Edition Turi-
caphon, ltd., music publishers,
Zurich, Switzerland; 1Apr47;
EF5832.
Fräulein Rosmarie ... Text von
Aldo von Pinelli, Musik von
Ernst Landl. © Edition Turi-
caphon, e. g. Zurich, Switzerland;
31May47; EF5828. Piano-conduct-
or score (orchestra, with words)
and parts.
LANDOWSKI, MARCEL, 1915-
Edina; poème symphonique [by]
Marcel Landowski. Op. 37.
Partition d'orchestre. ©
Éditions Choudens, Paris;
15Jul47; EF6568.
Poème; [by] Marcel Landowski. ©
Choudens, Éditeur de Musique,
Paris; 22Jul47; EF5571. Condensed
score; piano and orchestra.
LANDRY, NORMAN F
To-morrow; words & music by Norman
P. Landry. © Norman P. Landry,
New Orleans; 27Nov47; EP20226.
LANE, BILL.
I'm Ready for Love; words and
music by Bill Lane. © Nordyke
Publishing Co., Los Angeles;
29Apr47; EP16890.
LANE, VERNON.
Caribbean Moonlight; for piano [by]
Vernon Lane. © Theodore Presser
Co., Philadelphia; 6Dec47; EP20447.
Shores of Waikiki; piano solo
[by] Vernon Lane. © Theodore
Presser Co., Philadelphia;
17Oct47; EP18518.
LANG, EDITH, 1885-
Lord, Teach Us How to Pray; hymn-
anthem for mixed voices [or]
optional unison or soprano solo,
words from "Amore Dei", 1825,
music by Edith Lang, based on a
theme by Spohr. © Boston Music
Co., Boston; 15Dec47; on ar-
rangement; EP20399.
Surely God Is in This Place; [by]
Edith Lang, [words by
Bible] © The Arthur P. Schmidt
Co., Boston; 90ct47; EP18007.
Score: solo voices, chorus
(SATB) and organ.
LANG, HANS.
Miramare ... Worte von Erich
Meder, Musik von Hans Lang.
© Edition Turicaphon, ltd.,
music publishers, Zurich, Switz-
erland; 14pr47; EF5833.
LANG, MARGARET RUTHVEN.
Ghosts; [by] Margaret Ruthven
Lang, arr. by Hugh Gordon, [pseud.],
words by Munkittrick. © The
Arthur P. Schmidt Co., Boston;
18Aug47; on arrangement; EP16377.
Score: SSA and piano.

[LANGDON, CHRIS], arr.
I'll Marry a Maid; (Turkeyloney)
[arr. by Chris Langdon] ©
Chappell & Co., ltd., London;
13Oct47; on arrangement; EF7002.
For voice and piano; melody
also in tonic sol-fa notation.
LANGEY, OTTO, 1851-1922.
Langey-Carl Fischer tutors for
baritone, bass clef, 3 valves.
New rev. ed. [by Julius S.
Seredy] © Carl Fischer, inc.,
New York; 31Dec46; on new
instructive material, exercises
& solos; EP17052.
Langey-Carl Fischer tutors for
slide trombone, bass clef.
New rev. ed. [by Julius S.
Seredy] © Carl Fischer, inc.,
New York; 31Dec46; on new
instructive material, exercises
& solos; EP17051.
LANGLAIS, JEAN, 1907-
Suite Brève; pour orgue, [by] Jean
Langlais. © S. Bornemann, éditeur,
Paris; 20Aug47; EF7329.
LANGSTROTH, IVAN.
Four Chorale Preludes. © The H. W.
Gray Co., inc., New York;
2Jul47; on 2 pieces. For organ
solo. Partial contents.- Come
Thou Saviour of Mankind (© EP-
15702) - Now Dawns a Glorious
Day (© EP15703)
LANJEAN, MARC, pseud. See
Marcland, Jean.
LANTIER, PIERRE.
Le Roman Breton; paroles de René
Rousseau, musique de Pierre Lan-
tier. © Sté Ame Fse Chappell,
Paris; 10Nov47; EF7199.
LAPARCERIE, MIARKA, 1912-
Contredanse à la Sous-Préfecture;
paroles et musique de Miarka
Laparcerie. © Éditions Salabert,
Paris; 4Aug47; EF7263.
LAPELL, DOROTHY, 1897-
"You're the Doctor"; by Dorothy
Lapell. c1947; © Dorothy
Lapell, Hollywood, Calif.;
28Dec46; EP16573. For voice
and piano, with chord symbols.
LAPO, CECIL E 1910-
Love Came Down at Christmas; for
combined junior and senior
choirs or solo and S.A.T.B.,
from "Poetical Works" by
Christina Rossetti ... music by
Cecil E. Lapo. © Edwin H.
Morris & Co., inc., New York;
12Aug47; EP16404.
A Prayer for Youth; S.S.A.A.T.T.
B.B. Words by Dorothy Clarke
Wilson, music by Cecil E. Lapo.
© Belwin, inc., New York;
6Nov47; EP18538.
The Shepherds Had an Angel; for
combined junior and senior
choirs, or solo and S.A.T.B. a
cappella. Music by Cecil E.
Lapo, [words] from "Poetical
works" by Christina Rossetti.
© Edwin H. Morris & Co., inc.,
New York; 12Aug47; EP18405.
LARA, AGUSTÍN.
Pecadora ... letra y música de
Agustín Lara. © Promotora His-
pano Americana de Música, s.a.,
México; 31Jul47; EF6195.
LARCHET, JOHN F
The Cormorant; poem by Emily Law-
less, music by John F. Larchet.
© Stainer & Bell, ltd., London;
9Dec47; EF7366.
LAROE, DON.
(Fair Follics of '47) A Moonlight
Fantasy, words by Mary K. Sarlow,
music by Don Laroe ... [from]
Fair Follics of '47. © Mary K.
Sarlow, Ionia, Mich.; 4Aug47;
EP16025.

A Moonlight Fantasy. See his Fair Follies of '47.

LARRIEU, PIERRE.
Le Portrait ... musique de Pierre Larrieu, paroles de Robert Voleire [pseud.] © Editions L. Maillochon, Raoul Breton & Cie, Paris; 27Feb27; EF6311.

LARSON, EARL ROLAND, 1897-
Carrousel ... words adapted by John Stuart Wengenstein, Swedish folk song arr. by Earl Roland Larson. © Paul A. Schmitt Music Co., Minneapolis; 1Nov47; arrangement & words, new & adapted; EP19613. Score: chorus (SATB) and piano reduction.
Harbor in Moonlight; piano solo by Earl Roland Larson. © Clayton F. Summy Co., Chicago; 20Oct47; EP18185.
Hurdy-gurdy; [words by] Frances Frost, [music by] Earl Roland Larson. © Paul A. Schmitt Music Co., Minneapolis; 7Jul47; EP16060. Score: SATB and piano reduction.
Journeying; [words by] Edith Tatum, traditional melody, [Shenandoah], arr. by Earl Roland Larson. © Paul A. Schmitt Music Co., Minneapolis; 1Nov47; on words & arrangement; EP19612. For mixed chorus with piano reduction.
Wonder ... [for] S.S.A., [music by] Earl Roland Larson, arr. by Margrethe Hokanson. [Words by] Lucia Trent. © Clayton F. Summy Co., Chicago; 4Aug47; on arrangement; EP16676.

LARSON, EARL ROLAND, arr.
Organ Album ... with registration for pipe organ and Hammond organ, comp. and arr. by Earl Roland Larson. © Belwin, inc., New York; v.1, 29Oct47; on new compositions, compilation & arrangement; EP18330.

LARSON, WALTER VALENTINE, 1907-
Palm Springs Californiay; words and music by Walter Valentine Larson. © Walter Valentine Larson, Palm Springs, Calif.; 14Nov47; on new words & changes in words & music; EP18683.

LASH, EDDIE.
Power House Polka; by Eddie Lash. Concertina arr. by Rudy Patek. © Patek Music Co. (Rudy Patek, sole owner), Chicago; 28Sep47; EP17842.

LASRY, ALBERT.
Piano d Vendre; paroles de André Grassi, musique de Albert Lasry. Paris, R. Breton. © France Music Co., New York; 3Nov47; EF7027.

LASSERE, GENEVIEVE LAKE. See Lake, Genevieve.

LASSO, ORLANDO DI. See Lassus, Orland de.

LASSUS, ORLAND DE, d.1594.
Valley, Deep Valley. Valle Profonda. For two antiphonal five-part choruses of mixed voices (each S.S.A.T.B.-a cappella) English words by Lorraine Noel Finley, music by Orlando di Lasso, ed. by John Finley Williamson. © Carl Fischer, inc., New York; 11Aug47; on editing and piano reduction; EP17211.

LATERRA, JOHN L.
Why Dream? Words and music by John L. Laterra. © Nordyke Publishing Co., Los Angeles; 19Jun47; EP17446.

LAURA, ANNIE.
Dreaming; words and music by Annie Laura. © Nordyke Publishing Co., Los Angeles; 3Jul47; EP17635.

LAURENCE, RAY, 1903-
Guatemala; music by Ray Laurence, lyric by Albert Gamse. © Magnet Music, inc., New York; 5Sep47; EP16694.

LAVAGNINO, A F
Canto Bretone ... [by] Lavagnino, [violoncello part transcribed by] Cassadó. © Carisch, s.a., Milan; 31May47; on transcription; EF3974. Score (violin or violoncello and piano) and part for violoncello.

LAVERTY, LAWSON S 1891-
"Our Martha" in Blossom Time; [words] by Henry J. Zinn, [music by Lawson S. Laverty] © Henry J. Zinn, Dunmore, Pa.; 22Sep47; EP18445.

LAVISTA, RAUL.
El Caballo Blanco. See his Cuando Lloran los Valientes.

(Cuando Lloran los Valientes)
El Caballo Blanco ... de la película "Cuando Lloran los Valientes" ... música de Raul Lavista, letra de Ernesto M. Cortázar. © Promotora Hispano Americana de Música, s.a., México; 29Jul47; EF3984.

(Cuando Lloran los Valientes) Mi Lindo Monterrey ... [from "Cuando Lloran los Valientes"] letra de Ernesto M. Cortázar, música de Raul Lavista. © Promotora Hispano Americana de Música, s.a., Mexico; 22Jul47; EF5816.

(Cuando Lloran los Valientes)
Ramito de Azahar ... [from "Cuando Lloran los Valientes"] letra de Ernesto M. Cortázar, música de Raul Lavista. © Promotora Hispano Americana de Música, s.a., México; 22Jul47; EF5819.

Mi Lindo Monterrey. See his Cuando Lloran los Valientes.

Ramito de Azahar. See his Cuando Llorar los Valientes.

LAVOTTA, RUDOLF.
Honnan Jő a Fény. (Whence Comes All Our Light?) English lyric by Olga Paul, music by Lavotta Rudolf. (In Pesti, Barbara, comp. Memories of Hungary. p. 38-39) © Edward B. Marks Music Corp., New York; 19Nov47; on English lyric; EP19006.

Mezei Bokréta. (I Have Made a Fine Bouquet) English lyric by Olga Paul, music by Lavotta Rudolf. (In Pesti, Barbara, comp. Memories of Hungary. p. 22-23) © Edward B. Marks Music Corp., New York; 19Nov47; on English lyric; EP18998.

LAVRY, MARC, 1903-
Emek; poème symphonique, [by] Marc Lavry. © Editions Salabert, Paris; 21May47; EF5969. Score: orchestra.

Kukijah; variations sur un thème populaire palestinien, pour orchestre de chambre. © Editions Salabert, Paris; 2May47; EF5849. Score.

LAWRANCE, ALFRED JOHN, 1886-
Riding Home ... Words and music by Alfred J. Lawrance. © Allan & Co., pty. ltd., Melbourne, Australia; 25Oct46; EF5777.

LAWRENCE, JACK, 1912-
Hand in Hand; by Jack Lawrence. © Mayfair Music Corp., New York; 12Sep47; EP17293. For voice and piano, with chord symbols.

I'll Hate Myself in the Morning; words and music by Jack Lawrence. © Chappell & Co., inc., New York; 3Sep47; EP17294.

LAWRENCE, SIDNEY.
Three Early Grade Pieces; for piano solo by Sidney Lawrence. © The Boston Music Co., Boston; 15Aug47; Vol.2-3; have words' by Lawrence Braun. Contents.-1. The Cuckoo and the Cockatoo (© EP16421) - 2. The Home Run King (© EP17032) - 3. Echo Is a Copycat; (© EP17031)

LAWRENCE, WILLIAM.
Let Us Break Bread Together ... for S.A.T.B. voices, Negro spiritual, arr. by William Lawrence. © McLaughlin & Reilly Co., Boston; 7Jul47; on arrangement; EP16382.
Roll Jordan Roll; for four part mixed chorus. Negro spiritual arr. by William Lawrence. © McLaughlin & Reilly Co., Boston; 7Jul47; on arrangement; EP15872.

LAWSON, JORDANELLE.
I Found a Rose in Sicily; words and music by Jordanbelle Lawson. © Nordyke Publishing Co., Los Angeles; 10Jun47; EP16887.
Why Shouldn't You Remember Me; words and music by Jordanbelle Lawson. © Nordyke Publishing Co., Los Angeles; 31Mar47; EP16806.

LAWTON, DAVID, comp.
Selected Second Grade Studios; for piano, comp. by David Lawton. © Theodore Presser Co., Philadelphia; 2Sep47; EP17284.

LAZARUS, DANIEL, 1898-
Mouettes; [by] Daniel Lazarus, poème de Charles Oulmont, pour voix de contralto, chant et piano. © Durand & Cie, Paris; 25May47; EF5935.
Sonnet XVII; poème de Jean Cassou, [music by] Daniel Lazarus; pour voix de contralto, chant et piano. © Durand & Cie, Paris; 25May47; EF5848.
Sonnet XXII; poème de Jean Cassou, [music by] Daniel Lazarus; pour voix de contralto, chant et piano. © Durand & Cie, Paris; 25May47; EF5847.

LEACH, JIMMY.
When tho Thrill Has Gone, Will You Still Love Me? By J. Leach. © Cinephonic Music Co., Ltd., London; 9Apr46; EF6046. For voice and piano, with chord symbols; molody also in tonic sol-fa notation.

LEAL, EDUARDO ALARCON. See Alarcón Leal, Eduardo.

LEARSI, pseud. See Israel, Marcel.

LEAS, LYLE S
Goodnight, But Not Goodbye; words and music by Lyle S. Leas. © Nordyke Publishing Co., os Angeles; 28Jun46; EP1997.

LECUONA Y CASADO, ERNESTO.
Andalucia; [by] Ernesto Lecuona, arr. by L. Sugarman. © Edward B. Marks Music Corp., New York; 5Sep47; on arrangement; EP16669. For piano solo.
La Comparsa. (Carnival Procession) From album no. 3, Afro-Cuban dances; [by] Ernesto Lecuona, transcription by Louis Sugarman. © Edward B. Marks Music Corp., New York; 11Dec47; on arrangement; EP19857. For piano solo.
Gitanerias, from "Andalucia Suite"; [by] Ernesto Lecuona, transcription by Louis Sugarman. c1942. © Edward B. Marks Music Corp., New York; 11Dec47; on arrangement; EP19856. For piano solo.
Malaguena; [by] Ernesto Lecuona, arr. by Charles Nunzio. © Edward B. Marks Music Corp., New York; 21Nov47; on arrangement; EP20229. For accordion solo.

LECUONA Y CASADO, ERNESTO. Cont'd.
Malagueña; from Andalucía [by] Ernesto Lecuona, arr. for the Hammond organ (with additional pipe organ registration) by Don Baker. © Edward B. Marks Music Corp., New York; 22Oct47; on arrangement; EP18318.

LEDRU, JACK. See Ledru, Jacques.

LEDRU, JACQUES, 1922-
C'est la Chanson des Accordéons ... Paroles de Gine Money [pseud.], musique de Jack Ledru. © Editions Paul Beuscher, Paris; 31Dec44; EF6457.

LEDRUT, JEAN CLAUDE EMILE, 1902-
Boléro; melodie (sur les motifs du Boléro pour piano), paroles de Bataille-Henri, musique de Jean-Claude Ledrut. © Editions Paul Beuscher, Paris; 30Dec46; EF6456. For voice and piano, and voice part.

Rumba d'Amour ... Paroles de Jean Loysel [pseud.], musique de Jean-Claude Ledrut. © Arpège Editions Musicales, Paris; 25Feb47; EF6449.

LEE, E   MARKHAM.
Pianoforte Sight Playing Exercises; in eight grades, by E. Markham Lee. © Chappell & Co., ltd., London; bk. 1-2, 10ct47; EF6902; 6905. Contents.- bk. 1. (Grades I-IV) - bk. 2. (Grades V-VIII)

[LEE, ESTHER] comp.
Bill Monroc's Grand Ole Opry; WSM song folio, [comp. by E. Lee] © Peer International Corp., New York; no.1, 29Jul47; EP16363.

Hillbilly Hit Parade; [comp. by Esther Lee] © Peer International Corp., New York; 1946 issue, 11Jun47; 1947 issue, 11Jun47; EP15618-15619. For voice and piano, principally with chord symbols.

LEE, FRED.
The Union Pacific "Streamliner"; words by Charles Hathaway [and] Bud Averill, music by Fred Lee, Naomi Meyor, [and] Hayden Simpson. © Richardson Songs, Beverly Hills, Calif.; 4Jun47; EP15951.

LEE, HOWARD.
The End of a Journey; lyrics by John Moran, music by Howard Lee. © Cinephonic Music Co., ltd., London; 18Jul46; EF6051.

LEE, LESTER.
Christmas Dreaming; (A little early this year), by Irving Gordon and Lester Lee, arr. by Bob Morse. © Leeds Music Corp., New York; 17Sep47; on arrangement in C, EP17261; on arrangement in A flat, EP17262; on arrangement in E flat, EP17263. Piano-conductor score (orchestra, with words) and parts.

Christmas Dreaming; (A little early this year), by Lester Lee [and] Irving Gordon. © Leeds Music Corp., New York; 17Sep47; EP17258. For voice and piano, with chord symbols.

I'm Sorry I Didn't Say I'm Sorry. See his When a Girl's Beautiful.

(When a Girl's Beautiful) I'm Sorry I Didn't Say I'm Sorry; by Allen Roberts and Lester Lee, from the ... picture, "when a Girl's Beautiful." © Mood Music Co., inc., New York; 6Oct47; EP17802. For voice and piano, with chord symbols.

(When a Girl's Beautiful) I'm Sorry I Didn't Say I'm Sorry ... from the ... picture, "when a Girl's Beautiful"; by Allan Roberts and Lester Lee, arr. by Johnny Warrington. © Mood Music Co., inc., New York; 3Nov47; on arrangement; EP18652. Piano-conductor score (orchestra, with words) and parts.

LEE, RICHARD EVERETT, 1918-
Springtime; words and music by Dick Lee. © Richard Everett Lee, Beltsville, Md.; 18Aug47; EP16308.

LEE, SALLY.
Choo Choo Blues; words and music by LeRoy Redman and Sally Lee. © Dave Ringle, New York; 10Dec47; EP19854.

The Houndin' Blues; words and music by LeRoy Redman and Sally Lee. © Dave Ringle, New York; 15Nov47; EP18757.

LEE, SUNGSIK. See Sungsik, Lee.

LEE, WATERS J
Orncie; words and music by Waters J. Lee. © Nordyke Publishing Co., Los Angeles; 5Jun47; EP16865.

LEEKER, ABE, 1899-
When Will the Sun Shine Once More for Me? By Abe Leeker. © Clock Publishing Co., inc., Santa Monica, Calif.; 20Nov47; EP20426. Melody and chord symbols, with words.

LE FLEMING, CHRISTOPHER.
O Mortal Folk, You Hay Behold and See; (an epitaph) Two-part song with pianoforte accompaniment, words by Stephen Hawes, music by Christopher Le Fleming. Op. 16, no. 1. © J. Curwen & Sons, ltd., London; 5Jun47; EF6282.

LE GRAND, ROBERT LOUIS, 1894-
Tombe, Tombe, Pluie Légère ... de Robert Le Grand. [c1946] © Heugel & Cie., Paris; 7Jan47; EF6428. For voice and piano.

Le GRANT, LEONARD G
We'll Be Happy Day By Day; words and music by Leonard G. LeGrant, arr. by Sylvester L. Cross. © Nordyke Publishing Co., Los Angeles; 18Aug47; EP19320.

LEHAR, FERENC, 1870-
Frasquita Serenade; [by] Franz Lehar, arr. by Charles Nunzio. © Edward B. Marks Music Corp., New York; 21Nov47; on arrangement; EP20231. For accordion solo.

Lehárianna; Potpourri nach Motiven der beliebtesten Operetten von Franz Lehár, von Viktor Hruby ... Ausg. für Blasmusik, [arr. by Hermann Wermecke] © Ludwig Doblinger (Bernhard Herzmansky), K. G., Wien; 26Mar42; on arrangement; EF5786. Condensed score (band) and parts.

Vilia, from "The Merry Widow," S.A.T.B. [By] Franz Lehar, arr. by Robert Childe. © Neil A. Kjos Music Co., Chicago; 2Dec47; on arrangement; EP19549.

LEHAR, FRANZ. See Lehár, Ferenc.

LEHMANN, LYOLF.
Drömmen om Hawaii; Saa drömmer jeg nig bare til Hawaii; Tekst [by] Aase G. Krogh, Musik [by] E. Lehmann. © Wilhelm Hansen, Musik-Forlag, Copenhagen; 16May47; EF6294.

LEIDZEN, ERIK W   arr.
1894-
Crawford Quick-step Band Book; arrangements by Erik Leidzen. © Crawford Music Corp., New York; 28Apr47; on arrangement; EP15832. Condensed score (band) and parts.
--- --- Extra parts for clarinet and cornet. © Crawford Music Corp., New York; 28Apr47; on arrangement; EP14161, 14160.

Jolene ... by Erik Leidzen. © Mills Music, inc., New York; 29Aug47; EP17957. Score (cornet and piano) and part.

LEISHOUT, EDWARD MCKINLEY VAN. See Van Leishout, Edward McKinley.

LEISRING, VOLKMAR.
Ye Sons and Daughters of the King. (O Fil111 Filiae) Antiphonal for double-chorus of mixed voices (a cappella), [by] Volkmar Leisring ... (chorus II arr. for mixed voices [by H. Clough-Leighter]), words by V.G.G.T., ed. by H. Clough-Leighter. © E. C. Schirmer Music Co., Boston; 10Oct47; on arrangement; EP19277. English words.

LEITER, BELLE.
I'll Be with You; words and melody by Belle Leiter, harmony by N. L. Ridderhof. (In Hymn Writers' Magazine. v.1, no.1, p.19) © Grace May Ramont (Mrs. W. Paul Ramont), Inglewood, Calif.; 1Jul47; B5-1053. Close score; SATB.

Trial Testing Time in the Valley; words and music by Belle Leiter ... harmony by N. L. Ridderhof. (In Hymn Writers' Magazine. v.1, no.2, p.26) © Grace May Ramont, Inglewood, Calif.; 28Aug47; B5-1850. Close score; SATB.

LELIWA, ROGER. See Leliwa-Tyszkiewicz, Roger.

LELIWA-TYSZKIEWICZ, ROGER, 1920-
Symphony in Blue ... words and music [by] Roger Leliwa, arrangement [by] Frank Engelen. © Editions Ch. Bens, Brussels; 1Jun47; EF7042. Piano-conductor score (orchestra, with words) and parts.

LEMARE, EDWIN HENRY, 1865-1934.
Lemare's Andantino; arr. by A. J. Condaris. © Scholastic Music Co., Port Chester, N. Y.; 1Nov47; on arrangement for school orchestra; EP19603. Piano-conductor score and parts.

LE MAY, JOE, pseud. See Kennedy, Jimmy.

LEMIT, WILLIAM, 1908-
Ensemble; un chansonnier pour les colonies de vacances et les groupes d'enfants et de jeunes gens ... chansons nouvelles ... par william ... chansons populaires ... [arr.] par William Lemit ... rondes et jeux chantés avec les évolutions. © Rouart Lerolle & Cie, Paris; 4Jul47; EF7344. For 1-2 voices.

Il Faudrait Faire une Chanson; choeur à 4 voix mixtes, paroles et musique de William Lemit. © Rouart, Lerolle & Cie, Paris; 20Mar47; EF5978.

LEMON, SAMUEL DAVID.
Meet Me in Galilee; words and music by S. D. Lemon, arr. by Harry Rush. © Samuel David Lemon, Philadelphia; 5Apr47; EP6990.

LEMONS, SAMUEL HARVEY, 1916-
"Prepare Your Soul!" a sacred song by Samuel H. Lemons. St. Louis, Distributed by Shattinger. © Samuel Harvey Lemons, Du Quoin, Ill.; 8Nov47; EP18678.

LEMONT, CEDRIC W   1879-
By Starlight ....[by] Cedric W.
Lemont. (In Hirschberg, David,
ed. and comp. Pieces Are Fun.
bk. 1, p. 26-29) © Musicord
Publications, New York; 2Jul47;
EP159358. For piano solo.
The Drum Major ... [by] Cedric
W. Lemont. (In Hirschberg,
David, ed. and comp. Pieces
Are Fun. bk. 1, p. 42-43)
© Musicord Publications, New
York; 2Jul47; EP159945. For
piano solo.
The Lonesome Pine ... [by] Cedric
W. Lemont. (In Hirschberg,
David, ed. and comp. Pieces Are
Fun. bk. 1, p. 38-39) ©
Musicord Publications, New
York; 2Jul47; EP159943. For
piano solo.
On to Glory ... [by] Cedric W.
Lemont. (In Hirschberg, David,
ed. and comp. Pieces Are Fun.
bk. 1, p. 44-45) © Musicord
Publications, New York;
2Jul47; EP159946. For piano
solo
Poppies Are Blooming ... [by]
Cedric W. Lemont. (In Hirsch-
berg, David, ed. and comp.
Pieces Are Fun. bk. 1, p. 36-
37) © Musicord Publications,
New York; 2Jul47; EP159942.
For piano solo.
LENNERTS, WILLIAM JOSEPH, 1914-
A Blonde in Blue; words and
music by Bill Lennerts, piano
arr. by Ewing Reid. © Wil-
liam J. Lennerts, d.b.a.
Lennerts Music Publications,
Detroit; 10Sep47; EP17191.
LENOIR, JEAN, pseud. See
Neuberger, Jean Bernard Daniel.
LEONARD, DUKE ROBERT.
Mary Ann O'Toole; words and music
by Henry Tobias and Duke Leo-
nard, [piano score by Michael
Edwards] © Mills Music, inc.,
New York; 29Aug47; EP179947.
My Town; by Charlie McCord, Ed
Nelson, jr., [and] Robert Leo-
nard. © Shermack Music
Co., New York; 1Apr42; EP18815.
For voice and piano.
Saint Paul "Min" and Kansas City
"Moe"; by Marty Bloom and Duke
Leonard. © Chas. H. Hansen
Music Co., New York; 7Jul47;
EP15438. For voice and piano,
with chord symbols.
LEONARD, JULIO BLANCO. See
Blanco Leonard, Julio.
LEONCAVALLO, RUGGIERO.
Mattinata; [by] Ruggiero Leonca-
vallo, arr. by Leo Kempinski.
© Broadcast Music, inc.. New
York; 10Oct47; on arrangement;
EP184455. Piano-conductor score
(orchestra) and parts.
LEPONTE, FABIUS, pseud. See
Loponte, Fabius.
LEPPONEN, ERIC.
As Blue As I Am; words by Hans
Lepponen, music by Eric Lepponen.
© Nordyke Publishing Co., Los
Angeles; 20Aug47; EP19632.
LERNER, MARY.
You Are an Angel from the Sky;
words & music by Mary Lerner.
© Nordyke Publishing Co., Los
Angeles; 29Nov46; EP19377.
LESLIE-SMITH, KENNETH.
Sweet Yesterday; a musical romance,
book by Philip Leaver, music by
Kenneth Leslie-Smith, lyrics by
James Dyrenforth and Max Kester.
© Keith, Prowse & Co., ltd.,
London; 4Apr47; EP5437. Piano-
vocal score.
LESSAC, GUY, pseud. See
Cassel, Torsten Magnus.

LESTER, FLOYD.
Santa Fe Blues; words and music by
Floyd Lester. © Nordyke Publish-
ing Co., Los Angeles; 16Dec46;
EP20030.
LESUR, DANIEL JEAN YVES, 1908-
(Lieder, voice, flute, strings &
harp) Quatre Lieder; avec
accompagnement instrumental.
[Words by Cécile Sauvage and
Henri Heine] © Durand & Co.,
Paris; 30Jul47; EP6585. Score.

--- --- Parts. © Durand & Co., Paris;
30Jul47; EP6524.
Variations; [by] Daniel-Lesur.
© Lucien de Lacour, Éditeur,
Paris; 1Jul47; EP6520. Score
(piano and string orchestra)
and parts for strings.
Quatre Lieder. See his Lieder, voice,
flute, strings & harp.
LeVEILLE, CECILE, 1923-
"Hookey"; prelude no. 5, book 1.
Piano solo [by] Cecile LeVeille.
© Charles Standish Scribner,
Lawrence, Mass.; 2Dec47; EP19187.
Improvisation. Op. 22. Piano
solo [by] Cecile LeVeille. ©
Charles Standish Scribner, Law-
rence, Mass.; 2Dec47; EP19189.
Red Roses; prelude 5, book 3.
Piano solo [by] Cecile LeVeille.
© Charles Standish Scribner,
Lawrence, Mass.; 2Dec47; EP19188.
LEVENSON, BORIS.
The Lord Hath Done Great Things for
Us; anthem for junior choir (uni-
son) [by] Boris Levenson. Op. 92,
no. 2 ... Psalm 126, metrical
version by Rollin Pease. © Oli-
ver Ditson Co., Philadelphia;
27Oct47; EP19849.
LEVERTON, BUCK.
The Swiss Boy. (Schweizer Bub')
Words and music by Lawrence Du-
chow and Buck Leverton. © Peer
International Corp., New York;
13Dec47; EP12227.
LEVEY, HAROLD, 1900-
Ballad of the People; [words] by
Cameron Hawley, music composed
by Harold Levey. © Armstrong
Cork Co., Lancaster, Pa.; 12Dec47;
EP20439. Score: solo voices,
mixed chorus and piano.
LEVINE, HENRY.
More Themes from the Great Con-
certos; arr. for piano solo by
Henry Levine. © Theodore
Presser Co., Philadelphia;
19Sep47; on arrangement;
EP17359.
LEVY, LOUIS, arr.
(Carnegie Hall) Piano Selection,
arr. by Louis Levy ... from
"Carnegie Hall." © Chappell &
Co., ltd., London; 26Jul47;
on arrangement; EP5758.
[LEVY, MICHEL MAURICE] 1883-
Strasbourg; hymne à l'Alsace,
paroles de Joë Bridgo [pseud.],
musique de Bétove [pseud.]
© Rouart, Lerolle & Cie, Paris;
31Jul47; EP5905.
LeWINTER, DAVID.
You're the Prettiest Thing I've
Seen Tonight; words and music by
Margo Dean [and] David LeWinter.
© Duchess Music Corp., New York;
17Sep47; EP17259.
LEWIS, ELMER BULKLEY, 1879-
Our Colorado; by E. D. Lewis. ©
Elmer Bulkley Lewis, Brighton,
Colo.; 16Jun47; EP15893.
LEWIS, HUNTER MERIWETHER.
Dreamland Waltzes; by Hunter Meri-
wether Lewis. © Hunter Meriwether
Lewis, La Plata, Md.; 15Aug47;
EP16967.

LEWIS, JULIAN.
Late Evening Blues; words and
music by Johnnie Lee Wills,
Henry Boatman, [and] Julian
Lewis. © Bob Wills Music,
inc., Hollywood, Calif.;
30Jul47; EP16039.
LEWIS, LOUISE HILLS.
Marriage Blessing; words and
music by Louise Hills Lewis.
© Louise Hills Lewis, Indepen-
dence, Mo.; 13Oct47; EP18037.
Includes versions in close
score for SATB and SSA.
Prayer of Thanksgiving; [and
Thanksgiving] words and music
by Louise Hills Lewis. © Lou-
ise Hills Lewis, Independence,
Mo.; 13Oct47; EP18036. Close
score; SATB.
LEWIS, LUX. See
Lewis, Meade.
LEWIS, MEADE.
Honky Tonk Train ... by Meade
(Lux) Lewis ... [arr.] by
Charles Magnante. © Shapiro,
Bernstein & Co., inc., New
York; 14Oct47; on arrangement;
EP18027. For accordion solo.
LEWIS, URSULA
Children's Suite; 1 piano,
4 hands, by Ursula Lewis. ©
Elkan-Vogel Co., inc., Phila-
delphia; 12Aug47; EP16181.
LEWIS, VIC.
Etude to Eileen; [by] Vic Lewis.
[c1944] © Cinophonic Music Co.,
ltd., London; 9Apr46; EP6049.
Piano-conductor score (orchestra)
and parts.
LEWIS, WINNIE.
Give Me Romance; words and music
by Winnie Lewis. © Nordyke
Publishing Co., Los Angeles;
5Jun47; EP19649.
LEY, HENRY G
Anthem for a Harvest Festival;
[by] Henry G. Ley, words:
1928 Prayer Book (modified)
© The Oxford University Press,
London; 12Jun47; EP6159.
Score; chorus (SATB) and
organ.
LEYVA, NICOLAS PÉREZ. See
Pérez Leyva, Nicolas.
LEZZA, CARLO.
Amo Solo la Fiarmonica ... testo di
C. Deani, musica di Carlo Lezza
... Dove Andrai? ... Testo e Mu-
sica di Enrico Frati. © Edizioni
Casiroli, s.a.r.l., Milano;
15Jan47; EP5303. Piano-conductor
score (orchestra, with words) and
parts.
LICHNER, HEINRICH.
In the Meadow, [by] Heinrich
Lichner. Op.95, [no.2] Rev.
and ed. by Maxwell Eckstein.
© Carl Fischer, inc., New York;
10Dec43; on revision & edition;
EP17139. For piano solo.
LIDHOLM, INGVAR, 1908-
Fem Sånger; [by] Ingvar Lidholm.
© Föreningen svenska tonsättare,
Stockholm; on 6 songs, 1Jan46.
Contents. - För Vilana Fötter
Sjunger Gråset (Hjalmar Gullberg)
(© EF7092) - Vid Medelhavet (Hjal-
mar Gullberg) (© EF7093) - Den
Sista Människan (Hjalmar Gullberg)
(© EF7094) - Saga (Erik Höringe)
(© EF7095) - Jungfrulin (Erik
Höringe) (© EF7096) - Madonnans
Vaggvisa (Lope de Vega, tr. by K.
A. Hagberg) (© EF7097)
LIEMOHN, EDWIN.
Holy, Holy, Holy; (Sanctus) (no.3
from Concert mass in four move-
ments) ... [For] S.A.T.B.
(divided) a cappella ad lib.
[Music by] Edwin Liemohn.
© Gamble Hinged Music Co.,
Chicago; 9Sep47; EP16650.

LIEMOHN, EDWIN. Cont'd.
O God, Have Mercy upon Us; (Kyrie) by Edwin Liemohn [for] mixed voices. © Gamble Hinged Music Co., Chicago; 10Oct47; EP177O9.

LIEURANCE, THURLOW.
By the Waters of Minnetonka ... by Thurlow Lieurance, arr. ... by Bruno Reibold as a concert transcription or as an acc. for vocal solo. © Theodore Presser Co., Philadelphia; 22Oct47; on arrangement; EP18419. Piano-conductor score (orchestra, with words) and parts.

LIFERMAN, GEORGES, 1922-
Clic; (Danse du photographe) paroles de Jacques Mareuil [pseud.], musique de Georges Liferman, [arr. by Léo Poll, [pseud.] © Éditions Musicales Nuances, Paris; 30Jun47; on arrangement; EF6503. Piano-conductor score (orchestra, with Nous Deus ... Tant Mieux! Paroles de Henri Contet, musique de Georges Liferman. © Composers' Royalty, Paris; 14Aug47; EF7341.

LIFSON, HARRY, 1878-
"In Coney Island;" words and music by Harry Lifson. © Harry Lifson, New York; 15May47; EP18559.

LIGHT, FRANCES M
Joy Ride; piano solo [by] Frances M. Light. © Theodore Presser Co., Philadelphia; 6Dec47; EP20444.
The Rooster's Serenade; [by] Frances M. Light ... for piano. © Theodore Presser Co., Philadelphia; 9Dec47; EP19999.

LILJEFORS, INGEMAR.
Två Sånger; till text av Olof Thunman, [by] Ingemar Liljefors. © Föreningen svenska tonsättare, Stockholm; on 2 songs, 1Jan45. Contents. - 1. I Skymningen (© EF7103) - 2. Höstsang (© EF7104)

LILLEY, JOSEPH J
(The Emperor Waltz) Friendly Mountains, [from] ... the ... picture "The Emperor Waltz," lyric by Johnny Burke, music arr. by Joseph J. Lilley, from traditional Swiss airs. © Burke and Van Heusen, inc., New York; 16Oct47; EP18527.
Friendly Mountains. See his The Emperor Waltz.

LILLY, ALFRED, 1881-
Within My Memory and Little Token; solos for violin, by Alfred Lilly. © Alfred Lilly, Banks, Or.; 30Oct47; Within My Memory, EP17685; Little Token: on changes in words and music, EP17686. Melody and words.

LILLYA, CLIFFORD.
Summer Evening Serenade; by Merle J. Isaac and Clifford Lillya. © Sam Fox Publishing Co., New York; 25Aug47; EP17149. Condensed score (band) and parts.

LINCKE, PAUL.
The Glow-worm; [by] Paul Lincke, arr. by Charles Nunzio. © Edward B. Marks Music Corp., New York; 21Nov47; on arrangement; EP20230. For accordion solo.

LINDBERG, OSKAR.
Pingst; [music by] Oskar Lindberg. © Nordiska musikförlaget, a.b., Stockholm; 1Jan46; EF7052. Score: SSAATTBB.

LINDSTROM, VICTOR.
When the Maple Leaves Change Color in the Fall; by Victor Lindstrom, sr., arrangement by Belle Schrag. Aberdeen, Wash., The Lindstrom's Publishing Co. © Victor Lindstrom, sr., Aberdeen, Wash.; 10Oct47; EP17814. For voice and piano, with chord symbols.

LINDVALL, OTTO DAVID, 1876-1943.
Konvaljens Avsked; [by] Otto Lindwall ... för piano 2 händer (med text) © Nordiska musik-förlaget, a/b, Stockholm; 1Jan31; EF6949.
LINDVALL, OTTO DAVID. See Lindvall, Otto David.

LINTON, WALTER T
Why Did It Have to Be Me? Words and music by Walter T. Linton. © Nordyke Publishing Co., Los Angeles; 2Sep47; EP20008.

LIPPMAN, SIDNEY, 1914-
After Graduation Day ... ([for] S.A.) arr. by William Stickles, music by Sidney Lippman, words by Sylvia Dee [pseud.] New York, T. B. Harms Co. © Chappell & Co., inc., New York; 5Aug47; on arrangement; EP16269.
After Graduation Day ... ([for] S.A.B.) arr. by William Stickles, music by Sidney Lippman, words by Sylvia Dee [pseud.] New York, T. B. Harms Co. © Chappell & Co., inc., New York; 5Aug47; on arrangement; EP16270.
After Graduation Day ... ([for] S.A.T.B.) arr. by William Stickles, music by Sidney Lippman, words by Sylvia Dee [pseud.] New York, T. B. Harms Co. © Chappell & Co., inc., New York; 5Aug47; on arrangement; EP16276.
After Graduation Day ... ([for] S.S.A.) arr. by William Stickles, music by Sidney Lippman, words by Sylvia Dee [pseud.] New York, T. B. Harms Co. © Chappell & Co., inc., New York; 7 Aug47; on arrangement; EP16277.
After Graduation Day ... ([for] T.T.B.B.) arr. by William Stickles, music by Sidney Lippman, words by Sylvia Dee [pseud.] New York, T. B. Harms Co. © Chappell & Co., inc., New York; 5Aug47; on arrangement; EP16275.
(Barefoot boy with check) After graduation day, [from] "Barefoot boy with check." Words by Sylvia Dee, [pseud.] music by Sidney Lippman. © Chappell & Co., inc., New York; 24Feb47; EP12304.

LISBONA, EDDIE.
There's a New Moon Over the Ocean; by Joe Lubin and Eddie Lisbona. © Cinephonic Music Co., ltd., London; 12Feb47; EF6021. For voice and piano, with chord symbols; melody also in tonic sol-fa notation.

LIST, GEORGE, 1911-
The Little Jesus; SATB a cappella. [Words by] Lizette Woodworth Reese, [music by] George List. © Harold Flammer, inc., New York; 11Nov47; EP19153.

LISZT, FRANZ, 1811-1886.
La Campenella; by N. Paganini, transcribed by Franz Liszt, rev. and ed. by Maxwell Eckstein. © Carl Fischer, inc., New York; 15Nov46; on revision & edition; EP17138. For piano solo.
Liebestraum; [by Franz Liszt], arr. by A. J. Condaris. © Scholastic Music Co., Port Chester, N. Y.; 1Nov47; on arrangement for school orchestra; EP19597. Piano-conductor score and parts.
Liebestraum no.3. (Dream of Love) (simplified) for piano solo [by] Liszt, arr. and ed. by Thomas J. Gerald. © Paragon Music Publishers, New York; 20Oct47; on simplified arrangement; EP18171.

Liszt; excerpts from his greatest works, [arr. by Victor Ambroise] © Lawrence Wright Music Co., ltd., London; 18Jul47; on arrangement; EF5701.
Rhapsodie Hongroise, no.2; piano solo by Franz Liszt, arr. by William Coburn. © Clayton F. Summy Co., Chicago; 22Sep47; on arrangement; EP17846.
Sonetto CIV del Petrarca; [by] Franz Liszt, freely rev. by Rudolph Ganz. © Composers' Music Corp., New York; 29Jan21; on free revision; EP19116. For piano solo.

LITOLF, ANTON.
The Gollywog Fantesy; by Anton Litolf. © Cinephonic Music Co., ltd., London; 6May47; EF6020. For piano solo.

LITTLE, GEORGE A
Heaven with You; words & music by Kenneth Hart, Joseph Denise and George A. Little. © Mills Music, inc., New York; 14Aug47; EP18259.

LIVERNASH, WILL.
Lost in a Dream (that comes from my heart) words by LeRoy Redman, music by Will Livernash. © Dave Ringle, New York; 15Nov47; EP18756.

LIVERNASH, WILL. arr.
Estul Lee's Arizona Wildcats; outstanding collection of Western and hillbilly songs ... comp. and arr. by Will Livernash. © Edward Schuberth & Co., inc., New York; 25Sep47; EP17044.

LIVINGSTON, JERRY, 1909-
Don't You Love Me Anymore? Words and music by Mack David, Al Hoffman and Jerry Livingston. © Oxford Music Corp., New York; 9Sep47; EP17080.
Ma-ha-loni Papa-doo (hoy hoy) words and music by Mack David, Al Hoffman [and] Jerry Livingston. © Santly-Joy, inc., New York; 14Oct47; EP18089.
None But the Lonely Heart; adapted from Tschaikowsky by Mack David, Al Hoffman [and] Jerry Livingston. © Santly-Joy, inc., New York; 14Oct47; EP18620. For voice and piano, with chord symbols.
Our Hour; (the puppy love song), words and music by Mack David, Al Hoffman and Jerry Livingston. © Santly-Joy, inc., New York; 22Jul47; EP15795.

LLOSSAS, JUAN.
Granada ... Musik: Juan Llossas, Arrangement von Hugo Rausch ... Ewige Sonne ... Musik: Juan Llossas, Arrangement des Komponisten. © Edition Turicaphon, AG., Zürich, Switzerland; 11Aug47; on 2 pieces; EF7040-7041. Piano-conductor score (orchestra) and parts.

LLUIS ESPINOL, ROLANDO.
Caña y Azúcar ... letra, música y arreglo de Rolando Lluis Espinol. © Peer International Corp., New York; 30Sep47; EF6828. Parts: orchestra.

LOCATELLI, PIETRO.
Sonata per il flauto traverso; [by] Pietro Locatelli, [herausgegeben und für den praktischen Gebrauch eingerichtet von Alexander Kowetschoff] c1947. © Hug & Co., Music Publishers, Zurich, Switzerland; 7Oct43; EF6843. Score (flute and piano) and part.

LOCEY, HARRIET.
National W.A.R.M.A. Loyalty Song;
words and music by Harriet
Locey. © Womens Auxiliary
Railway Mail Association,
Webster Groves, Mo.; 16Aug47;
EP16491.

LOCKE, HAROLD.
Joyous Autumn Days; [by] Harold
Locke. © Theodore Presser
Company, Philadelphia; 26Nov47;
EP19134. For piano solo.

LOCKETT, FLORA ELLEN.
A Rose for You; words and music
by Flora Ellen Lockett. ©
Nordyke Publishing Co., Los
Angeles; 3Sep47; EP20029.

Wanderlust Blues; words and music
by Flora Ellen Lockett. ©
Nordyke Publishing Co., Los
Angeles; 17May47; EP16858.

LOCKIN, HANK.
I Always Lose; by Zeke Clements
[and] Hank Lockin. © Bourne,
inc., New York; 5Dec47;
EP19563. For voice and piano,
with chord symbols.

LODGE, ANDRE, pseud. See
Norman, André.

LOEB, JOHN JACOB.
Boulevard of Memories; music by
John Jacob Loeb, lyric by
Edward Lane. © Mutual Music
Society, inc., New York;
13Aug47; EP16411.

LOEILLET, J   B
Minuet; [by] Loeillet, [arr. by
Quinto Maganini] © Edition Musicus New York, inc., New York;
30Sep47; on arrangement;
EP20248. Score (flute and piano) and parts for 2 flutes.

LOES, HARRY DIXON.
The Christmas Spirit in gospel
solos and duets; for mixed
voices, by Harry Dixon Loes [and]
George S. Schuler. © Van
Kampen Press, Chicago; 29Aug47;
EP16622.

In the Valleys Below; [words by]
John J. Keating, [music by]
Harry Dixon Loes. © John J.
Keating, sr., Chicago; 4Aug47;
EP17194. Close score; SATB.

Just behind the Cloud ... [by]
Loella Hobson. [words by]
Harry Dixon Loes. © Loella M.
Hobson, Fort Wayne; 20ct47;
EP18553. Close score; SATB.

LOESSER, FRANK.
Bloop, Bleep! By Frank Loesser,
[piano arr. by Jerry Phillips]
© Paramount Music Corp., New
York; 11Jun47; EP15353. For
voice and piano, with chord
symbols.

Frank Loesser's A Tune for Humming. © Paramount Music Corp.,
New York; 20Oct47; EP18529. For
voice and piano, with chord
symbols.

(Variety Girl) He Can Waltz; [from
the Paramount picture "Variety
Girl"], by Frank Loesser. ©
Famous Music Corp., New York;
16Jul47; EP15774. For voice and
piano.

(Variety Girl) Your Heart Calling
Mine; by Frank Loesser. [From]
"Variety Girl." © Famous Music
Corp., New York; 27Aug47; EP16691.
For voice and piano.

What Are You Doing New Year's Eve?
By Frank Loesser. © Famous
Music Corp., New York; 11Jul47;
EP15624. For voice and piano,
with chord symbols.

LOEWE, FREDERICK.
Almost Like Being in Love. See his
Brigadoon.

(Brigadoon) Almost Like Being in
Love ... [from] Brigadoon ...
lyrics by Alan Jay Lerner, music
by Frederick Loewe ... arr. for
Hawaiian and electric guitar
(note and diagram) [by the Oahu
staff] New York, S. Fox Pub.
Co; Cleveland, Oahu Publishing
Co., Sole distributor. © Alan
Jay Lerner & Frederick Loewe,
New York; 3Nov47; on arrange-
ment; EP20171.   xW293

(Brigadoon) Almost Like Being in
Love ... from the musical play,
Brigadoon ... music by Frederick
Loewe. A Harold E. walters arrangement. New York, S. Fox Pub.
Co. © Alan Jay Lerner & Frederick Loewe, New York; 20Nov47;
on arrangement; EP19242. Condensed score (band) and parts.

(Brigadoon) Choral Selection of
the Musical Play Brigadoon ...
lyrics by Alan Jay Lerner, music
by Frederick Loewe, arrangement
by Erik Leidzén. New York, S.
Fox Pub. Co. © Alan Jay Lerner
& Frederick Loewe, New York;
24Nov47; on arrangement; EP19244.
Score: SSAATTBB and piano.

(Brigadoon) There But for You
Go I ... from the ... musical
Brigadoon; lyrics by Alan Jay
Lerner, music by Frederick Loewe,
dance arrangement by Paul Weirick. New York, S. Fox Publishing Co. © Alan Jay Lerner &
Frederick Loewe, New York;
15Oct47; on arrangement; EP18273.
Piano-conductor score (orchestra,
with words) and parts.

Choral Selection of the Musical Play
Brigadoon. See his Brigadoon.

LOFTON, THEODORE McMURRAY.
He Is Mine Today; words and music
by Theodore Lofton. © Theodore
McMurray Lofton, Boston; 18Sep47;
EP19609.

LOMBARDO, CARMEN.
Oahu; words and music by Carmen
Lombardo. © Lombardo Music,
inc., New York; 23Oct47;
EP18642.

LOMUTO, VICTOR, 1895-
Pepita ... paroles de Jean Rodor
[pseud.], musique de Victor
Lomuto. © Éditions espagnoles
Julio Garzon, Paris; 10Oct47;
EF7337.

LONG, BILLY W
Could It Be You? Words by Dwight
Perkins, music by Billy W. Long
and Wally Akers. © Nordyke
Publishing Co., Los Angeles;
5Aug47; EP17560.

LONG, GEORGE.
"That Mother-in-law;" by George
Long. © Kelly Music Publica-
tions, Franklin, Pa.; 15Dec47;
EP19561. Melody and words.

LONG, KENNETH R
Evening Service in F; for boys'
voices, [by] Kenneth R. Long.
© The Oxford University Press,
London; 26Jun47; EF6156.

[LONG, NORMAN RUSSELL] 1895-
Mi-ne-ap-o-lus; music and lyric
by Adelaide St. Germaine,
[pseud.] arr. by Henry A.
Frisch. © Norman Russell Long,
Charleston, N. H.; 10May47;
on arrangement; EP16188.

LONG, W   FRANK.
You're All That I Need; words and
music by W. Frank Long, arr. by
Harold Pottor. © Nordyke Publishing co., Los Angeles;
16Dec46; EP20569.

LONGÁS, FEDERICO, 1895-
Canción; poesía de Gabriel de Lara,
música de F. Longás. © Ricordi
Americana, S.A.E.C., Buenos
Aires; 31May44; EF6973.

Duérmete ... [by] Federico Longás,
poesía de Carmen Moreno de Flores. © Ricordi Americana,
S.A.E.C., Buenos Aires; 9Apr42;
EF6972. For voice and piano.

Mírame Chiquilla! ... Música de
Federico Longás, poesía de Juan
García. © Ricordi Americana,
S.A.E.C., Buenos Aires; 9Apr42;
EF6971.

Tres Claveles Rojos; canción
española, [by] F. Longás,
letra de Maria Echeverria. ©
Ricordi Americana, s.a.e.c.,
Buenos Aires; 20Nov42; EF6987.

Vuelve; canción ... [by] F.
Longás, [words by Alejandro
Flores] © Ricordi Americana,
s.a.e.c., Buenos Aires; 10Dec43;
EF6986.

LOPEZ, FRANCIS. See
Lopez, Francisco.

Banco. See his Trente et Quarante.

Aux Quatre Coins de Paris. See his Les
Trois Cousines.

LOPEZ, FRANCISCO, 1916-
À Deux Pas de Mon Coeur. See his
Destins.

(Destins) À Deux Pas de Mon Coeur
... dans le film "Destins",
Paroles de Jacques Larue [pseud.],
musique de Francis Lopez, arr. par
Al. Kiwi [pseud.] © Éditions Max
Eschig, Paris; 22Feb47; on arrangement; EF7298. Piano-conductor
score (orchestra) and parts.

(Destins) À Deux Pas de Mon Coeur
... [From] le film "Destins";
paroles de Jacques Larue [pseud.],
musique de Francis Lopez.
Éditions Max Eschig, Paris;
22Dec46; EF6477.

En Voulez-Vous? See his Les Trois
Cousines.

Je Vous Veux. See his Les Trois
Cousines.

Macouba. See his Les Trois Cousines.

Madame la Chance; paroles de Jean
Solar [pseud.], musique de Francis
Lopez. © Éditions Joubert, Paris;
10Oct47; EF7296.

Magdalena. See his Trente et Quarante.

Mélopée Lointaine ... paroles de
Georges Bernié, musique de
Francis Lopez ... Créole
Sérénade ... paroles de Ch.
Flavia [pseud.], musique de
Pierre Buflet & Ch. Flavia.
Arrt de Francis Salabert. ©
Salabert, inc., New York;
10May47; on arrangement;
EF5951. Piano-conductor
score (orchestra, with words)
and parts.

Moi, Je N'Aim' Pas Ça. See his Les
Trois Cousines.

Oh! Que C'Est Haut, le Haut des
Marches. See his Les Trois Cousines

Le P'tit Louis ... Paroles de
Raymond Vincy [pseud.], musique
de Francis Lopez. © Arpège
Éditions Musicales, Paris;
26Feb47; EF6446.

(Trente et Quarante) Banco ... du
film, "Trente et Quarante,"
paroles de Jacques Larue [pseud.]
musique de Francis Lopez. ©
Éditions Paul Beuscher, Paris;
30Nov45; EF6445.

(Trente et Quarante) Magdalena;
une chanson du film ... Trente
et Quarante ... Paroles de J.
Larue [pseud.] musique de F.
Lopez. © Éditions Paul Beuscher,
Paris; 30Nov45; EF6471. For
voice and piano, and voice part.

(Les Trois Cousines) Aux Quatre
Coins de Paris ... du film "Les
Trois Cousines"; paroles de Jean
Boyer & André Hornez, musique de
Francis Lopez. © Arpège Éditions
Musicales, Paris; 7Feb47; EF6506.
For voice and piano, and voice
part.

LOPEZ, FRANCISCO. Cont'd.
(Les Trois Cousines) En Voulez-
Vous? ... Du Film "Les Trois
Cousines"; paroles de Jean Boyer
& André Hornez, musique de Francis
Lopez. © Arpège Editions Musicales,
Paris; 25Feb47; EF6607. For
voice and piano and voice part.
(Les Trois Cousines) Je Vous
Voux ... du film, Les 3 Cousines
... paroles de Jean Boyer &
André Hornez, musique de Francis
Lopez. © Arpège, Editions
musicales, Paris; 3Mar47;
EF6441.
(Les Trois Cousines) Macouba ...
du film, Les 3 Cousines ...
musique de Francis Lopez,
paroles de Jean Boyer & André
Hornez. © Arpège, Editiones
musicales, Paris; 5Feb47;
EF6442.
(Les Trois Cousines) Moi, Je
N'Aim' Pas Ca ... du film, "Les
Trois Cousines"; paroles de Jean
Boyer & André Hornez, musique de
Francis Lopez. © Arpège, Editions
musicales, Paris; 3Mar47; EF6443.
(Les Trois Cousines) Oh! Que
C'Est Haut, le Haut des
Montagnes ... du film, Les 3
Cousines ... paroles de Jean
Boyer [and] André Hornez,
musique de Francis Lopez. ©
Arpège, Editions musicales,
Paris; 2Jan47; EF6444.
(Les Trois Cousines) Prends en Un
... Prends en Deuxi Du film Les
3 Cousines ... Musique de Francis
Lopez, paroles de Jean Boyer &
André Hornez. © Arpège Editions
Musicales, Paris; 5Feb47; EF6470.
LÓPEZ, ISRAEL.
Basta Cuando! ... Letra y música
de Rafael Ortiz [and] I. López,
arreglo de Pérez Prado. © Peer
International Corp., New York;
23Sep47; EF6716. Parts: orches-
tra.
LOPEZ, TILY.
Recuerdo de un Cocktail. (At
Last My Dream Came True)
Letra y música de Tily Lopez
... arr. by A. Silva. © X-L
Music Publications, Los Angel-
es; 16Apr47; EF16171. Piano-
conductor score (orchestra,
with words) and parts; Spanish
and English words.
LOPEZ MARTIN, A
¡Como Goza! ... Letra y música
[by] A. López Martin, arreglo
de Pérez Prado. © Peer
International Corp., New York;
3Jul47; EF5729. Parts:
orchestra.
"Hay Que Inventar" ... letra y
música de A. López Martin,
arreglo de Juan E. Lazaga.
© Peer International Corp., New
York; 23Sep47; EF6715. Piano-
conductor score (orchestra) and
parts.
[LOPONTE, FABIUS] 1881-
Belle Genève, à Toi Nos Coeurs;
chanson, musique de Fabius
Leponte [pseud.], paroles de
Rosa-Marie de Luisi. © Fabius
Leponte, Genève; 30Dec46;
EF6412.
LORD, DANIEL ALOYSIUS, 1888-
Let's Get Together; a musical foot-
note to history in one act and
several scenes, book, lyrics and
music by Rev. Daniel A. Lord.
© McLaughlin & Reilly Co., Boston;
25Jul47; EP16387.
LORD, JAMES RUSSELL, 1893-
I'll Be Waiting at the Chapel in
the Valley; words and music by
Russ Lord. © Song-Hit Music
Publishing Co., New York;
23Oct47; EP18325.

LORD, RUSS. See
Lord, James Russel.
LORD INVADER, pseud. See
Grant, Rupert.
LORENZ, ELLEN JANE, 1907-
The Ballad of Pocahontas; S.A.
[by] Ellen Jane Lorenz, [words
by] Mildred Lewis Kerr. © Lor-
enz Publishing Co., Dayton,
Ohio; 24Sep47; EP17886.
Beauty Shop Quartet; a medley,
by Ellen Jane Lorenz, [words by
Edith Sanford Tillotson] ...
four-part treble (S.S.A.A.)
© Lorenz Publishing Co., Dayton,
Ohio; 24Sep47; EP17890.
Beauty Shop Quartet; a medley,
by Ellen Jane Lorenz, [words by
Edith Sanford Tillotson] ...
three-part treble (S.S.A.)
© Lorenz Publishing Co., Dayton,
Ohio; 24Sep47; EP17891.
The Big Rock Candy Mountains ...
arr. from the traditional hobo
song [and words adapted] by
Ellen Jane Lorenz ... four-
part mixed voices, (S.A.T.B.)
© Lorenz Publishing Co., Day-
ton, Ohio; 24Sep47; on choral
arrangement & adaptation of
words; EP17882.
Johnny Appleseed; an operetta for
the middle and upper grades (un-
changed voices) (with sugges-
tions for a supplementary Apple
Festival) Book and lyrics by
Mildred Lewis Kerr, music by
Ellen Jane Lorenz. © Lorenz
Publishing Co., Dayton, Ohio;
20Oct47; EP18911.
Lorenz's Hymn-tune Anthems ... for
... S.A.T.B., comp. by Ellen Jane
Lorenz. © Lorenz Publishing Co.,
Dayton, Ohio; 8Jul47; EP16555.
Lorenz's S.S.A. Concert Choruses;
[comp. by Ellen Jane Lorenz]
© Lorenz Publishing Co., Dayton,
Ohio; 14Jun47; EP16554.
Women's Gospel Trios ... arr. for
the use of women's trios (S.S.A.)
or women's quartets (S.S.A.A.)
or women's choruses ... [Comp.] by
Ellen Jane Lorenz. © Lorenz Pub-
lishing Co., Dayton, Ohio; no.2,
22Sep47; EP17809.
Yankee Doodle Fantasy; a part song
by Ellen Jane Lorenz ... three-
part mixed (S. A. B.) ©
Lorenz Publishing Co., Dayton,
Ohio; 24Sep47; on arrangement;
EP18680.
Yankee Doodle Fantasy; a part
song by Ellen Jane Lorenz ...
two-part treble (S. A.) ©
Lorenz Publishing Co., Dayton,
Ohio; 24Sep47; on arrangement;
EP18881.
LOTH, JOHN FERRIS, 1908-
Piano Play for Every Day; by John
Ferris Loth. © Waterloo Music
Co., Waterloo, Ont., Can.; bk.5,
7Sep47; EF6391.
LOTTI, ANTONIO.
Agnus Dei. (Lamb of God) (from
Mass VII) four-part chorus
of women's voices (a cappella)
[by] Antonio Lotti ... arr. by
Arthur S. Talmadge. © E. C.
Schirmer Music Co., Boston;
29Sep47; on arrangement;
EP18130.
Salve Regina; by A. Lotti, arr.,
ed., and new text adapted by
Noble Cain. © Boosey & Hawkes,
inc., New York; 2Dec47; on ar-
rangement & new text; EP19879.
Score: chorus (SATTBB) and
piano reduction.
LOUCHEUR, RAYMOND, 1899-
Hialmar; [by] Raymond Loucheur.
© Durand & Cie., Paris; 30Apr47;
EF5937. Score (trombone and
piano) and part.

LOUD, JOHN HERMANN.
Useful Organ Music for the Church
Service; by John Hermann Loud.
© William E. Ashmall Co., Boston;
2Jun47; EP16391.
LOUIGUY, pseud. See
Guglielmi, Louis.
LOUIS, JOHNNY, pseud. See
Hecimovich, John.
LOURIE, ARTHUR.
Lament; from Dante's Vita nuova,
composed for women's voices and
string orchestra [by] Arthur
Lourié, [English version by
Joseph Cottler] Ed. for ...
S.S.A.A. © Elkan-Vogel Co.,
inc., Philadelphia; 6Feb47;
EP15332. English and Italian
words.
LOUVEL, JEAN, 1909-
La Valse Grise ... paroles d'un
prisonnier mort pour la France,
revues et arr. par Jean Louvel,
musique de Jean Louvel. © Jean
Louvel, Paris; 17Jul47; EF7309.
LOVATT, S   E
The Bonny Earl of Moray; arr. for
men's voices [by] S. E. Lovatt,
Scottish folk song. © The
Oxford University Press, London;
17Jul47; on arrangement; EF6133.
The Three Ravens; arr. as part
song for mixed voices [by] S. E.
Lovatt. © The Oxford Univer-
sity Press, London; 17Jul47;
on arrangement; EF6134.
LOVEDAY, CARROLL.
A Prayer in Song; by Carroll Love-
day. © Gate Music Co., New
York; 19Nov47; EP19092. For
voice and piano.
LOVELESS, WENDELL P
Christmas in the Heart; [by]
Wendell P. Loveless, [words by]
William M. Runyan. (In
Loveless, Wendell P., comp.
Radio Songs and Choruses of the
Gospel. p. [28a]) © Hope
Publishing Co., Chicago; (in
notice: Loveless and Runyan)
15May34; EP16509.
He Came to Me One Day; [by]
Wendell P. Loveless, [words by]
William M. Runyan. (In
Loveless, Wendell P., comp.
Radio Songs and Choruses of the
Gospel. p.24-25) © Hope Pub-
lishing Co., Chicago; (in
notice: Loveless and Runyan)
15May34; EP16508.
He Loves, He Saves, He Keeps, He
Satisfies; [by] Wendell P.
Loveless, [words by] William M.
Runyan. (In Loveless, Wendell
P., comp. Radio Songs and
Choruses of the Gospel. p.14-
15) © Hope Publishing Co.,
Chicago; (in notice: Loveless
and Runyan) 15May34; EP16507.
Jesus, Oh, What a Name! [By]
Wendell P. Loveless, [words by]
William M. Runyan. (In
Loveless, Wendell P., comp.
Radio Songs and Choruses of the
Gospel. p.30-31) © Hope
Publishing Co., Chicago; (in
notice: Loveless and Runyan)
15May34; EP16467.
A Manger; [by] Wendell P. Loveless,
[words by] William M. Runyan.
(In Loveless, Wendell P., comp.
Radio Songs and Choruses of the
Gospel. p. [28b]) © Hope
Publishing Co., Chicago; (in
notice: Loveless and Runyan)
15May34; EP16466.
Oh, What Love! ... [By] Wendell
P. Loveless, [words by] William
M. Runyan. (In Loveless,
Wendell P., comp. Songs and
Choruses of the Gospel. p.9)
© Hope Publishing Co., Chicago;
(in notice, Loveless and Runyan)
15May34; EP16505.

LOVICK, TED.
Jersey City, N.J.; words & music
by Ted Lovick, [piano arrangement by Dick Kent] © Peer
International Corp., New York;
11Jun47; EP15617.

LOVICK, THEODORE L
You're Laughing at Me (while I'm
crying) words by Mary E. Hub-
bard, music by Ted Lovick. ©
Mary E. Hubbard, Seattle &
Theodore L. Lovick, Starford,
Pa.; 8Nov47; EP19039. Melody
and chord symbols, with words.

LOVINGGOOD, PENMAN, 1895-
I Am Sure My Love; (a song of happiness), words by Zella [pseud.]
music by Penman Lovinggood. Los
Angeles, Lovinggood Songs.
© Penman Lovinggood, Los Angeles; 1Nov47; EP18347.

LOWE, HELEN L
Fickle You; words by Helen L.
Lowe and June Jolly, music by
Helen L. Lowe. © Nordyke Pub-
lishing Co., Los Angeles;
19Jun47; EP17438.

LOWE, JERRY.
These Beautiful Things; words by
Ralph E. Paulsen, music by
Jerry Lowe. © Nordyke Publishing
Co., Los Angeles; 16Dec46;
EP20337.

LOWELL, CLYDE ROY.
They Cry on My Shoulder (over
someone else) words and music
by Clyde Roy Lowell. © Nordyke
Publishing Co., Los Angeles;
2Jul46; EP20500.

LOWRY, TONY.
Valse d'Amour; piano solo by
Tony Lowry. © Chappell & Co.,
ltd., London; 17Oct47; EF6903.

LOZANO, PEDRO.
The Young Trumpeter; or, The art
of perfect phrasing. © Pedro
Lozano Publishing Co., Syracuse,
N. Y.; 12Aug47; EP16182.

LUBIN, ERNEST.
O Friend Song ... [words by]
Bahá'u'lláh, [tr. by Shoghi
Effendi] music by Ernest
Lubin. © The Arthur P.
Schmidt Co., Boston; 7Aug47;
EP16108.

LUBIN, JOE, 1917-
When the One You Love, Loves You;
[by] Eddie Lisbona and Joe
Lubin. © B. Feldman & Co., ltd.
London; 11Sep47; EF6439. For
voice and piano, with ukulele
diagrams and chord symbols.
Melody also in tonic sol-fa
notation.

LUBOSHUTZ, PIERRE.
We Love and Dream ... music by
Pierre Luboshutz, text by
Marks Levine. High. © J.
Fischer & Bro., New York;
12Aug47; EP17662.

LUCAS, CLARENCE.
When Stars Are in the Quiet Skies
... for mixed voices S.A.T.B.,
words by Lord Lytton, composed
and arr. by Clarence Lucas.
© Chappell & Co., ltd., London;
1Aug47; EF6523.

LUCCHESI, ROGER ANTOINE, 1912-
Au Coin du Feu; paroles de Jean
Jacques Rouff, musique de Roger
Lucchesi. © Éditions Salabert,
Paris; 15Sep47; EF7260.

Ba-Da-Boum ... paroles de Roger
Lucchesi, musique de Roger Lucchesi et Bernard Hilda [pseud.]
© Éditions Salabert, Paris;
15Sep47; EF7261.

Complainte Corse. See his L'Ile d'Amou
Étrange Mélodie. See his Sérénade aux
Nuages.

Feux de Camp. See his Le Gardian.

(Le Gardian) Feux de Camp ... dans
le film "Le Gardian." Paroles et
musique de Roger Lucchesi, arr.
par Al. Kiwi [pseud.] © Éditions
Max Eschig, Paris; 16Jun47; on arrangement; EF7216. Piano-conductor score (orchestra) and parts.

Hello!!! See his Sept Jours au Paradis

(L'Ile d'Amour) Complainte Corse
... dans le film "L'Ile d'Amour."
Paroles de Carulu Giovoni et Roger
Lucchesi, musique de Roger Luc-
chesi. © Éditions Max
Eschig, Paris; 15Jan45; EF7315.
French and Italian words.

(Sept Jours au Paradis) Hello!!!
[From the film, "7 Jours au Paradis." Words by Maurice Chevalier,
par Al. Kiwi [pseud.] ©
Éditions Max Eschig, Paris;
15May46; on arrangement; EF7218.
Piano-conductor score (orchestra)
and parts.

(Sérénade aux Nuages) Etrange
Mélodie ... dans le film "Sérénade aux Nuages" ... Paroles et
musique de Roger Lucchesi, arr.
par Al. Kiwi [pseud.] © Éditions
Max Eschig, Paris; 15May46; on
arrangement; EF7219. Piano-conductor score (orchestra) and
parts.

(Sérénade aux Nuages) Tout Près
de Toi, Qu'il Fait Bon ... dans
le film "Sérénade aux Nuages."
Paroles de Roger Lucchesi et
Maurice Vandair [pseud.], musique
de Roger Lucchesi [arr. by Al.
Kiwi, pseud.] © Éditions Max
Eschig, Paris; 27Jul46; on arrangement; EF7227. Piano-conductor score (orchestra) and parts.

Tout Près de Toi, Qu'il Fait Bon. See
his Sérénade aux Nuages.

LUCE, JANICE.
So Long; words by Andy Razaf,
music by Janice Luce. © Sun
Music Co., inc., New York;
31Oct47; EP20411.

LUCKIE, E   G
You're Goin' to Need Somebody on
Your Bond ... Negro spiritual
by E. G. Luckie. [Arr. by E. G.
Luckie] © The La Casa del Rio
Music Publishing Co., inc.,
Toledo; 14Dec45; EP15606.

LUCKY, DON.
You Never Miss the Water Till
the Well Runs Dry; words and
music by Spade Cooley, Dick
and Don Lucky. © Hill and
Range Songs, inc., Hollywood,
Calif.; 15Sep47; EP17225.

LUCRAFT, HOWARD.
What Goes On (comes off!) Music
by Howard Lucraft, lyric by
Desmond O'Connor. © Cosmo
Music Co. (London) ltd., London;
21Oct46; EF5749.

LUDARTE, FRANK VON. See
Von Luehrte, Frank.

LUFCY, EVERETT.
I Don't Want to Leave; words and
music by Everett Lufcy. ©
Nordyke Publishing Co., Los
Angeles; 11Jul47; EP17511.

LUGO, GABRIEL FRANCO. See
Franco Lugo, Gabriel.

LUKAS, PETER.
(A Voice Is Born) With All My
Heart; [from the Columbia picture
"A Voice Is Born"] Lyric by
George Blake, music by Peter
Lukas. © Mutual Music Society,
inc., New York; 21Jul47; EP15837.

LUNDQUIST, MATTHEW NATHANAEL.
Cradle Here among the Kine;
S.A.T.B. (a cappella) with
soprano solo. Christmas Carol
... from "Songs of the Salzburg
Monks" arr. by Matthew N. Lund-
quist, English version by M. N.
L. © C. C. Birchard & Co.,
Boston; 20Nov47; on arrangement;
EP19030.

LUNDVIK, HILDOR.
Som ett Blommande Mandelträd;
([words by] Pär Lagerkvist)
(music by) Hildor Lundvik. ©
Nordiska musikförlaget, a.b.,
Stockholm; 1Jan46; EF7053.
Close score; mixed chorus.

LUNEAU, OMER J
Mother of God; words & music by
O. J. Luneau. © Omer J. Luneau,
Concord, N. H.; 25Jul47; EP16386.

LUPE, JOHNNIE.
When I Find the Sweetheart of My
Dreams; words and music by
Johnnie Lupe. [c1946] © Nor-
dyke Publishing Co., Los An-
geles; 28Jan47; EP19641.

LUPO, PINO.
Lacrime ... testo di Gianipa
[pseud.], musica de Pino Lupo.
Quando Tu Vorrai ... parole di
Pinchi, musica di G. Fabor
[pseud.] © Edizioni Italगarisch,
Milano; on Lacrime, 26Sep46; on
Quando Tu Vorrai, 4Apr46; EF6760,
6759. Piano-conductor score
(orchestra, with words) and
part for violins.

LUPTON, HAROLD J   1662-
The Bells Are Ringing; S.A.T.B.
(with descant) words by Kathleen
Blanchard, music by Harold J.
Lupton. © Western Music Co.,
ltd., Vancouver, B. C., Can.;
26Nov47; EF7182.

LUTCHER, NELLIE.
He's a Real Gone Guy; by Nellie
Lutcher. New York, Capitol
Songs, inc. © Criterion
Music Corp., New York;
10Sep47; EP17159. For voice
and piano, with chord symbols.

Hurry on Down; by Nellie Lutcher
New York, Capitol Songs.
© Criterion Music Corp., New
York; 15Jul47; EP15625. For
voice and piano, with chord
symbols.

You Better Watch Yourself, Bub;
by Nellie Lutcher. New York,
Capitol Songs, inc. © Criterion
Music Corp., New York; 30Aug47;
EP17039. For voice and piano,
with chord symbols.

LUTÈCE, JEAN, pseud. See
Chardon, Julien.

LUTHER, MARTIN, 1483-1546.
A Mighty Fortress Is Our God ...
Anthem for mixed voices,
[words by] Martin Luther,
tr. [by] Frederick H. Hedge,
[music by] Martin Luther,
arr. by Reginald Martin. ©
Theodore Presser Co.,
Philadelphia; 9Sep47; on arrangement; EP17167.

A Mighty Fortress Is Our God; for
women's voices S.S.A. and contralto solo, [by] Martin Luther
... arr. by Wayne Howorth. ©
Belwin, inc., New York; 5Dec47;
on arrangement; EP19271. Cover-
title: A Mighty Father Is Our
God.

LUTKIN, PETER CHRISTIAN.
The Lord Bless You and Keep You;
from the Farewell anthem with
sevenfold amen, by Peter Christian Lutkin. High voice [solo
arrangement by Milton Dieter-
ich] © Clayton F. Summy Co.,
Chicago; 20Oct47; on arrangement; EP18183.

LUTKIN, PETER CHRISTIAN. Cont'd.
The Lord Bless You and Keep You;
from the Farewell anthem with
sevenfold amen, by Peter Christian Lutkin. Low voice [solo arrangement by Milton Dieterich]
© Clayton F. Summy Co., Chicago; 20Oct47; on arrangement;
EP18184.

LUTYENS, ELISABETH.
(Quartet, strings, no. 2) String
Quartet no. 2; [by] Elisabeth
Lutyens. Op. 5, no. 5. Parts.
© Alfred Lengnick & Co., ltd.,
London; 10Jul47; EF6349.

LUTZ, BENJAMIN F
Plant the Stars; words by Paul Y.
Livingston... music by Benjamin
F. Lutz. © Nordyke Publishing
Co., Los Angeles; 25May46;
EP20489.

LUVAAS, MORTEN J .   1896-
A Christmas Wish; (S,S,A,) [by]
Morten J. Luvaas, [words by]
Valorie Simpson] © Neil A,
Kjos Music Co., Chicago;
2Dec47; EP19550.

Ecstasy; S.A.T.B. with baritone
solo, [by] Morten J. Luvaas,
[words by] Virginia Grant
Collins. © C. C. Birchard &
Co., Boston; 30Jul47; EP16489.

Merry Christmas Time; S.A,T,B,
adapted and arr. by Morten J,
Luvaas. © Neil A. Kjos Music
Co., Chicago; 19Nov47; on arrangement; EP19205.

LUZZATTO, LIVIO MOISE.
Geremia; opera Biblica. Zürich,
Europa Verlag, a. g. © Livio
Moise Luzzatto, Milano; 1Aug47;
EF6867. Piano-vocal score.

LYLE, TOMMY.
With You, I'm in Love; words and
music by Tommy Lyle. © Nordyke
Publishing Co., Los Angeles;
29Apr47; EP16921.

LYNCH, PAT.
Boogie Concerto; piano solo by
Pat Lynch. © D. Davis & Co.
Pty., ltd., Sydney; 15Sep47;
EF6813.

LYNN, GEORGE.
Steal Away; spiritual, paraphrase
by George Lynn, for mixed
voices S.A.T.B. a cappella. ©
Mills Music, inc., New York;
28Jul47; on arrangement and
adaptation; EP16189.

LYNN, MARGY, pseud.   See
Hawthorne, Margy.

LYNTON, EVERETT, 1888-
There'll Never Be a Girl Like
You; written and composed by
Charlie Chester, Ken Morris
and Everett Lynton. ©
Lawrence Wright Music Co., ltd.,
London; 23Sep47; EF6659. For
voice and piano, with chord
symbols; melody also in tonic
sol-fa notation.

The Wedding of the Royal Princess;
written and composed by Tommie
Connor and Everett Lynton. ©
Lawrence Wright Music Co., ltd.,
London; 3Sep47; EF6384. For
voice and piano, with chord
symbols. Melody also in tonic
sol-fa notation..

LYON, JAMES.
Baby Lions' Lullaby; (for solo
voice or unison singing) Poem
by Marjorie Lyon, music by James
Lyon. © Chappell & Co., ltd.,
London; 10ct47; EF6900.

Serenity; part-song for male
voices, T.T.B.B. Poem by
Marjorie Lyon, music by James
Lyon. Opus 107, no. 1. ©
Chappell & Co., ltd., London;
10ct47; EF6901.

M

McALLISTER, DARYL DeWAYNE, 1906-
Oklahoma Home; by Daryl McAllis-
ter. © Daryl McAllister,
Hollywood, Calif.; 31Jul47;
EP16157. For voice and piano.

McALLISTER, LOUISE.
Purple Twilight; piano solo by
Louise McAllister. © The Arthur
P. Schmidt Co., Boston; 4Sep47;
EP16643.

McBRIDE, ELSIE IRENE, 1907-
Heigh-ho! ... chorus for treble
voices, acc., (S.A.) [by] Elsie
McBride. © Hall & McCreary Co.,
Chicago; 22Aug47; EP17024.

McBRYDE, ED.
You Took My Heart; words and
music by Ed McBryde. ©
Nordyke Publishing Co., Los
Angeles; 20Aug47; EP19329.

McCLELLAN, CLARK.   See
McClellan, John Clark.

McCLELLAN, JOHN CLARK, 1917-
Flibber Flabber, Jibber Jabber;
by Clark McClellan. © McClellan
Music Co., New York; 4Sep47;
EP17779. For voice and piano,
with chord symbols.

McCLINTOCK, J. Lorene.   See
McClintock, Lorene.

McCLINTOCK, LORENE, 1912-
Teach Yourself to Play the Piano;
based on the "Interval method,"
[by] Lorene McClintock. New York,
T. Y. Crowell Co. © Lorene
McClintock, Slaton, Tex.; 5Dec47;
A19540.

McCOLLIN, FRANCES, 1892-
Christmas Bells; words by H. W.
Longfellow, music by Frances
McCollin ... S.S.A. with piano
acc. © Mills Music, inc., New
York; 8Dec47; EP19886.

McCORMICK, BOB.
Everything's the Same But You;
words and music by Bob McCor-
mick. © Nordyke Publishing
Co., Los Angeles; 29Jul47;
EP17631.

McCULLOCH, WILLIAM CAMPBELL.
In the Year That King Uzziah Died;
anthem in four parts for mixed
voices, [words from] VI Isaiah,
1-8, [music] by William C. Mc-
Culloch, jr. © William Campbell
McCulloch, jr., Portland, Ore;
12Nov47; EP19610.

McDERMOTT, STEVE.
My Heart Is Yours to Break;
words and music by Bill and
Steve McDermott. © Nordyke
Publishing Co., Los Angeles;
16Jul47; EP17558.

McDONALD, EDWIN, pseud.   See
Humphreys, Donald Edwin.

MacDONALD, PERCY WICKER.
Song of Autumn; [by] Percy Wicker
MacDonald. © Theodore Presser
Co., Philadelphia; 5Sep47;
EP17280. For organ solo;
includes registration for
Hammond organ.

MacDOWELL, EDWARD ALEXANDER, 1861-1908.
Transcriptions for the Organ from
the Works of Edward MacDowell;
[arr. by Roy S. Stoughton] ©
Arthur P. Schmidt Co., Boston;
3d ser., 4Sep47; on arrangement;
EP16647.

To a Wild Rose.   See his Woodland
Sketches.

To a Water-Lily; [by] Edward Mac-
Dowell. Op. 51, no. 6. Tran-
scribed ... by Gaylord Yost.
© The Arthur P. Schmidt Co.,
Boston; 4Sep47; on arrangement;
EP16644. Score (violin and
piano) and part.

(Woodland Sketches) To a Wild
Rose; [by] Edward MacDowell.
Op. 51, no. 1. Transcribed by
Edward G. Simon. © The Arthur
P. Schmidt Co., Boston; 18Aug47;
on simplified version; EP16380.
Score (violin, violoncello and
piano) and parts, and alterna-
tive part for viola.

(Woodland Sketches) To a Wild
Rose, (from "Woodland Sketches")
[by] Edward MacDowell. Op. 51,
no. 1. Transcribed by Hugo
Norden. © The Arthur P. Schmidt
Co., Boston; 18Aug47; on arrangement; EP16381. Score (violin,
violoncello or viola, and piano
or harp) and parts.

McDOWELL, LUCIEN L   comp.
Memory Melodies; a collection of
folk songs from middle Tennessee
[comp.] by Lucien L. McDowell and
Flora Lassiter McDowell. © Flora
Lassiter McDowell, Smithville,
Tenn.; 29Aug47; A17157. Melody
and words.

McDUFF, THOMAS, pseud.   See
Mesang, Theodore Lawrence.

McELDUFF, MARY PAT.
A Long, Long Year; words and music
by Mary Pat McElduff. © Nordyke
Publishing Co., Los Angeles;
14Dec46; EP19756.

McELLIOT, BOB, pseud.   See
Mills, Carley.

McEVOY, TERESA.
California Lullaby; words and
music by Teresa McEvoy. © Nordyke Publishing Co., Los Angeles; 3Jul47; EP17591.

McFEETERS, RAYMOND.
Gentle Mary; Catalan folk song,
arr. for voice and piano by
Raymond McFeeters, [words by]
Martha Daughn Locker] © G.
Schirmer, inc., New York;
20Aug47; on arrangement;
EP18033.

Gentle Mary; for four-part chorus
of mixed voices with piano acc.,
Catalan folk song arr. by Raymond McFeeters. [Words by]
Martha Daughn Locker. © G.
Schirmer, inc., New York;
27Aug47; on arrangement; EP18730.

Gentle Mary; for three-part chorus
of women's voices with piano
acc., Catalan folk song arr. by
Raymond McFeeters. [Words by]
Martha Daughn Locker. © G.
Schirmer, inc., New York;
27Aug47; on arrangement; EP18729.

McGEE, DON.
Champion Folio ... for drum and
bugle corps, by Don McGee and
Keith P. Lacey. © C. L. Barnhouse Co., Oskaloosa, Iowa;
no.1, 23Sep47; EP17927. Score
and parts.

McGEE, JOHN A
The Monon Centennial Show;
lyrics by John A. McGee,
music by John A. McGee and Owen
Haynes. © Chicago, Indiana-
polis and Louisville Railway
Co., Chicago,; [v. 1-6, 8]
28Jul47; [v.7] 18Aug47. Con-
tents.— [v.1] Up and down the
Monon (© EP16009)- [v.2]
Hoosier Time (© EP16010)-
[v.3] Sleepy Little Town in the
Brown County Hills (© EP16011)-
[v.4] The Belle of the Monon
(© EP16013)- [v.5] The Gentle-
man Who Paid My Fare
(© EP16018)- [v.6] Monticello
Moon (© EP16019)- [v.7] Last
Call for Dinner (© EP16531)-
[v.8] Indiana Is So Rich;
lyrics by John A. McGee and
Chester W. Cleveland
(© EP16005)

MacGIMSEY, ROBERT.
When You Got a Man on Your Mind;
words and music by Robert
MacGimsey. New York, Capitol
Songs, inc. © Criterion Music
Corp., New York; 30Aug47;
EP17037.

MacGREGOR, CHUMMY. See
MacGregor, John Chalmers.

MacGREGOR, JOHN CHALMERS, 1903-
(I'm Gonna Wait) a Little Bit
Longer (for that never-on-time
baby of mine); words and music
by Chummy MacGregor. © M.
Witmark & Sons, New York;
12Aug47; EP16442.

McGUILL, LAWRENCE, 1917-
Jesus, Only Jesus; [by] Larry
McGuill; [arr. by John C. Hal-
lett] (In Hallett, J. C. Introducing New Radio Songs.
p. [4]) [c1942] © Lawrence
McGuill, Ridgewood, N. J.;
20Sep43; EP17653. Close score:

McGUIRE, GAYWOOD.
The Absentee's Jive; words and
music by Gaywood McGuire.
[c1945] © Nordyke Publishing Co., Los
Angeles; 21Aug47; EP16605.

McHUGH, JAMES FRANCIS, 1894-
Exactly like You. See his International
Revue.
(If You Knew Susie) My, How the
Time Goes by, from the ...
picture "If You Knew Susie."
Words by Harold Adamson, music
by Jimmy McHugh. New York,
Chappell. © McHugh & Adamson
Music, inc., New York; 9Sep47;
EP17203.
(International Revue) Exactly Like
You [from Lew Leslie's Interna-
tional Revue] Lyric by Dorothy
Fields, music by Jimmy McHugh
... Arr. ... by Johnny Warring-
ton. © Shapiro, Bernstein & Co.,
inc., New York; 24Nov47; on ar-
rangement; EP19125. Piano-con-
ductor score (orchestra, with
words) and parts.
(International Revue) Exactly
like You; [from Lew Leslie's
"International Revue"] ...
music by Jimmy McHugh ... [arr]
by Charles Magnante. © Shap-
iro, Bernstein & Co., inc., New
York; 14Oct47; on arrangement; EP18021. In-
cludes "Straight version" and
"A Charles Magnante interpreta-
tion."
(International Revue) On the Sunny
Side of the Street [from Lew
Leslie's International Revue]
Lyric by Dorothy Fields, music
by Jimmy McHugh ... Arr. ... by
Johnny Warrington. © Shapiro,
Bernstein & Co., inc., New York;
24Nov47; on arrangement; EP19124.
Piano-conductor score (orchestra,
with words) and parts.
(International Revue) On the
Sunny Side of the Street; [from
Lew Leslie's "International
Revue"] ... music by Jimmy Mc-
Hugh ... [arr.] by Charles Mag-
nante. © Shapiro, Bernstein &
Co., inc., New York; 14Oct47;
on arrangement; EP18021. In-
cludes "Straight version" and
"A Charles Magnante interpreta-
tion." For accordion solo.
My, How the Time Goes by. See his
If You Knew Susie.
On the Sunny Side of the Street. See
his International Revue.

MACIEL, ENRIQUE.
El Aguatero Porteño; (Agua fresca)
letra de F. M. Carbonaro
(Tito Sobral) música de Enrique
Maciel. © Editorial Argentina de
Música Internacional, s. de r.
ltda., (EDAMI), Buenos Aires;
27Aug47; EF6699.

McINTOSH, FOREMAN BILL.
Rendezvous Bend; words and music
by Rusty Jorge and Foreman Bill
McIntosh. © Peer International
Corp., New York; 25Nov47;
EP19840.

MACK, E
General Grant's Grand March; [by]
E. Mack ... for piano, arr. and
ed. by Maxwell Eckstein. ©
Carl Fischer, inc., New York;
5Sep47; on arrangement &
editing; EP18079.

McKAY, FRANCIS H
Bainbridge Island Sketches ...
[by] F. H. McKay. © C. L.
Barnhouse Co., Oskaloosa, Iowa;
17Sep47; EP18551. Score (flute,
oboe, clarinet, horn and bassoon)
and parts.
Chromatic Caprice; clarinet
quartet [for] two Bb, alto and
bass clarinets or four Bb
clarinets [by] F. H. McKay. ©
C. L. Barnhouse Co., Oskaloosa,
Iowa; 17Sep47; EP18552. Score
and parts.
Festival Prelude ... [by] F. H.
McKay. © C. L. Barnhouse Co.,
Oskaloosa, Iowa; 17Sep47;
EP18554. Score (4 trombones)
and parts.
Sextet in A major ... [by] F. H.
McKay. © C. L. Barnhouse Co.,
Oskaloosa, Iowa; 17Sep47;
EP18550. Score (2 trumpets,
horn, trombone, baritone and
tuba) and parts.

McKAY, GEORGE F
Song of the Voyageurs; (Canadian
boat song) [for] mixed voices
[by] George F. McKay, [words
by] Thomas Moore. © J. Fischer
& Bro., New York; 12Aug47;
EP17660.

McKAY, GEORGE FREDERICK, 1899-
Christmas Morning ... by George
Frederick McKay. © Albert J.
Andraud, Wind Instrument Music
Library, Cincinnati; 21Aug47;
EP16966. Score (flute 1-4)
and parts.
On a Nankin Plate; S.S.A.A., music
by George Frederick McKay, poem
by Austin Dobson. © C. C.
Birchard & Co., Boston; 29Oct47;
EP18383.
A Remembered Happiness; for piano,
by George Frederick McKay.
© J. Fischer & Bro., New York;
17Jun47; EP6984.
The Robin and the Woodpecker; for
piano, by George Frederick
McKay. © J. Fischer & Bro.,
New York; 17Jun47; EP6983.

McKEE, JEANELLEN, 1920-
Brush Up; exercise sheet no. 1-[8,
by Jeanellen McKee] © Forjedor
Publishing Co., Detroit; on nos.
1-8, 1Dec47; EP19564-19571. For
piano.

McKINLEY, RAY.
A Man's Best Friend Is a Bed;
words & music by Ray McKinley.
© Edray Music Publishing Co.,
New York; 11Jul47; EP15839.
Melody and chord symbols, with
words.

McKINLEY, ROBERT CLIFFORD, 1911-
Health Notes; twelve songs of
health for children, words and
music by Robert C. McKinley,
arr. by Angelo Scottolino.
© Dairy Council, inc., Philadelphia; 10ct47; EP17839.

McKINNEY, BAYLUS BENJAMIN, ed.
Voice of Praise; a collection of
standard hymns and gospel songs
... B. B. McKinney, music editor.
Printed in round ... notes. ©
Broadman Press, Nashville; 9Oct47;
A18707.

McKINNEY, HOWARD D
To a Hill-top; for S.S.A. [by]
Howard D. McKinney, arr. by
Francis L. Zavaglia, [words by]
Mildred Seitz. © J. Fischer &
Bro., New York; 17Jun47; on
arrangement; E86980.

McKISSICK, ELEANOR.
Outside Lookin' In: words and
music by Eleanor McKissick.
© Nordyke Publishing Co., Los
Angeles; 18Jul46; EP19405.

MacLACHLAN, T ROBIN.
Graded Melody Studies; modern
foundation material for development of touch, technic and
expression, by T. Robin
MacLachlan. © Schroeder &
Gunther, inc., Rhinebeck, N. Y.;
15Sep47; EP17786. For piano
solo.

McMEANS, JEWEL M
Waltz Me 'round the Rainbow;
words and music by Jewel M.
McMeans. © Nordyke Publish-
ing Co., Los Angeles; 29Aug45;
EP17450.

MacMICHAEL, MAXWELL, d. 1947.
Noël ... [for] SATB with junior
choir, words and music by
Maxwell MacMichael. © Harold
Flammer, inc., New York;
28Jul47; EP18248.

MacMILLAN, ERNEST, 1893-
Ballads of B. C.; words by John
Murray Gibbon, musical arrange-
ments by Ernest MacMillan. ©
Gordon V. Thompson, ltd.,
Toronto; 27Jun47; on new words
and arrangement; EP5681.

McMILLEN, HARRY LEITCH, 1914-
I Like How You Look; words and
music by Clara E. Porter and
Harry L. McMillen. © Harry L.
McMillen, Marguerite Porter Mc-
Millen & Clara E. Porter, Mill-
brae, Calif.; 15Dec47; EP20137.
Melody and chord symbols, with
words.

McNEIL, JAMES CHARLES, 1902-
Between Heaven and a Heartbreak;
words by James C. Murphy, music
by J. Chas. McNeil. [c1946]
© Nordyke Publishing Co., Los
Angeles; 30Jan47; EP19754.
Carlos, the Gaucho; words by
Charles Lepo, music by J. Chas.
McNeil. © Nordyke Publishing Co.,
Los Angeles; 12Aug47; EP19780.
Cupid Stole My Heart; words by
Mary Louise Hart, music by J.
Chas. McNeil. [c1945] ©
Nordyke Publishing Co., Los
Angeles; 12Jun46; EP17639.
The Garden Talk of Flowers (is
what my heart would say)
words by Harry C. Eversole,
music by J. Chas. McNeil.
© Nordyke Publishing Co., Los
Angeles; 25Jun47; EP17623.
Gertie; words by Murrell D. Clift,
music by J. Chas. McNeil. ©
Nordyke Publishing co., Los
Angeles; 12Sep47; EP20365.
The Gloomy Rain Blues; words by
James V. Shears, music by J.
Chas. McNeil. © Nordyke Publish-
ing Co., Los Angeles; 13Jul46;
EP19510.
Gold Star Mother; words by Mary
Spellman, music by J. Chas.
McNeil. © Nordyke Publishing
Co., Los Angeles; 10May47;
EP16935.
Harbor of Dreams; words by Bertha
Mae Brown, music by J. Chas.
McNeil. © Nordyke Publishing
Co., Los Angeles; 2Jul46;
EP19464.

310

McNEIL, JAMES CHARLES. Cont'd.
Heaven's Near; words by Dovie A.
Williams, music by J. Chas.
McNeil. © Nordyke Publishing
Co., Los Angeles; 2Jul46;
EP19487.

Home by the Susquehanna; words by
Tony Gughiocello, music by
J. Chas. McNeil. © Nordyke
Publishing Co., Los Angeles;
28Mar47; EP16739.

I Knew It; words by Walter E. Young,
music by J. Chas. McNeil.
[c1946] © Nordyke Publishing
Co., Los Angeles; 15Aug47; EP16598.

It Was the Month of June; words
by Dorothy Jane Hardee, music
by J. Chas. McNeil. © Nordyke
Publishing Co., Los Angeles;
23May47; EP16875.

It's Spring Again; words by Mabel
Marie Eades, music by J. Chas.
McNeil. © Nordyke Publishing
Co., Los Angeles; 12Jul47;
EP17518.

Just Me; words by Gwen E. Horton,
music by J. Chas. McNeil. ©
Nordyke Publishing Co., Los Angeles; 31Jul47; EP19502.

Just the Other Day; words by James
C. Murphy, music by J. Chas.
McNeil. [c1945] © Nordyke
Publishing Co., Los Angeles;
24Jun46; EP20319.

Kris, Kris, Krisella; words by
John F. Bockno, music by J.
Chas. McNeil.[c1946] © Nordyke
Publishing Co., Los Angeles;
28Jan47; EP19946.

More Than the Stars (in heaven
above); words by Rachel C.
Hockensmith, music by J. Chas.
McNeil. © Nordyke Publishing
Co., Los Angeles; 10ct47;
EP19358.

My Guns Are of Silver, My
Bullets of Gold; words by
James R. Davidson, music by
J. Chas. McNeil. © Nordyke
Publishing Co., Los Angeles;
5Aug47; EP17496.

My Heart Is Bursting with Love;
words by Agnes C. Sylvia, music
by J. Chas. McNeil. © Nordyke
Publishing Co., Los Angeles;
17May47; EP16831.

My Mother; words by Purney Noblitt,
music by J. Chas. McNeil. ©
Nordyke Publishing Co., Los
Angeles; 27Sep46; EP20317.

My Only One; words by Leslie F.
Crosby, music by J. Chas. Mc-
Neil. © Nordyke Publishing
Co., Los Angeles; 25May46;
EP19681.

Oh, That Memory; words by Alphonso
R. Miller, music by J. Chas.
McNeil. © Nordyke Publishing
Co., Los Angeles; 7Feb47;
EP19403.

Pin up the Corners of Your Mouth,
My Sweet; words by Katherine D.
Miller, music by J. Chas.
McNeil. © Nordyke Publishing
Co., Los Angeles; 27Jul46;
EP19959.

A Sailor's Dream; words by Herman
Norris, music by J. Chas. McNeil.
© Nordyke Publishing Co., Los
Angeles; 12Feb46; EP16730.

Someday I'll Travel Home; words
by William H. Pharo, music by
J. Chas. McNeil. © Nordyke Publishing Co., Los Angeles;
9Nov46; EP20061.

Songs of Love ... for soprano,
text by Mary Carr Moore, music
by J. Chas. McNeil. © Wesley
Webster, San Francisco; 24Jul47;
EP15919.

Such a Little While; words by
Mary Williamson, music by J.
Chas. McNeil. © Nordyke Publishing Co., Los Angeles;
16Sep46; EP19774.

Sunshine Blues; words by Sam Beeks,
music by J. Chas. McNeil, ed. and
rev. by C. Isabel Mayer. Portland, Or., C. I. Mayer Music
Publishing. © C. Isabel Mayer,
Portland, Or.; 23May47; EP15401.

Thinking Only of You; words by
Estella Barney, music by J.
Chas. McNeil. © Nordyke Pub-
lishing Co., Los Angeles; 12Apr47;
EP16758.

This Must Be Love; words by
Florente Luke, music by J. Chas.
McNeil. © Nordyke Publishing
Co., Los Angeles; 2Dec46;
EP20501.

The Ukkaa Song; words by Joseph
Bonuccelli, music by J. Chas.
McNeil. © Nordyke Publishing
Co., Los Angeles; 5Aug47;
EP19530.

What Is Love? Words by Myra
Johannesen, music by J. Chas.
McNeil. © Nordyke Publishing
Co., Los Angeles; 16Dec46;
EP19508.

When Springtime Comes; words by
Goldie Lynch, music by J. Chas.
McNeil. © Nordyke Publishing
Co., Los Angeles; 27Jul46;
EP20048.

Where the Willow Tree Whispers
"Good-Night"; words by Coral
Noble Kable, music by J. Chas.
McNeil. © Nordyke Publishing
Co., Los Angeles; 27Sep46;
EP19316.

Why Do You Treat Me So? Words by
Evelyn Hardin, music by J. Chas.
McNeil. © Nordyke Publishing
Co., Los Angeles; 21Feb47;
EP19394.

You Are the Dawn; words by Xelna
Tolbort, music by J. Chas. Mc-
Neil. © Nordyke Publishing co.,
Los Angeles; 22Apr47; EP20370.

You're My Great Big Bunch of
Sugar; words by Ada Line Davis,
music by J. Chas. McNeil. ©
Nordyke Publishing Co., Los
Angeles; 12Apr47; EP16781.

You've Been so Hard with Me;
words by Andrew Earl Johnson,
music by J. Chas. McNeil.
© Nordyke Publishing Co., Los
Angeles; 15Aug46; EP19369.

McPETERS, TAYLOR.
Mississippi Gal; words and music
by Sam Nichols, Daniel Cypert
and Taylor McPeters. © Hill and
Range Songs, inc., Hollywood,
Calif.; 26Jun47; EP15317.

McPHAIL, LINDSAY.
It's the Sweet Things You Say;
words by William Kapitz, music
by Lindsay McPhail. © Nordyke
Publishing Co., Los Angeles;
16Jul47; EP17613.

Minnesota Moon; by Margaret
Myers Lawrence and Lindsay
McPhail. © Victor Publish-
ing Co., Dallas; 24Jul47;
EP16093. For voice and
piano.

You Will Be My Dream Come True;
words by Verna Leigh Morritt,
music by Lindsay McPhail.
© Nordyke Publishing Co., Los
Angeles; 25Jul46; EP19380.

McVEA, JACK.
Open the door, Richard! Words by
"Dusty" Fletcher [and] John
Mason, music by Jack McVea [and]
Dan Howell, arr. by Skippy
Martin. © Duchess Music Corp.,
New York; on arrangement; 14Apr47;
EP13715. Piano-conductor score
(orchestra, with words) and parts.

MADEIRA, E   E   1868-
Comes At Times a Stillness; words
by ... I. Gregory Smith, music
by E. E. Madeira. © Dorothea
Louise Schroeder, Flushing, N.,
Y.; 18Dec47; EP19925. Score:
SATB and organ.

MADETOJA, LEEVI ANTTI, 1887-
HuvinäytelmN-alkusoitto; suurelle
orkesterille ... [by] Leevi
Madetoja. Op. 53. © A/B Fazers
Musikhandel, Helsingfors;
7Nov44; EF5416. Score: orchestra.

(Symphony, no. 2) Sinfonia no. 2;
[by] Leevi Medetoja. Op. 35.
© A/B Fazers Musikhandel, Helsingfors; 29Apr39; EF5417.

MAGALDI, ELVIRA.
Zamba de Mis Recuerdos ... letra
de Horacio Sanguinetti, música
de Elvira Magaldi. © Editorial
Argentina de Música Internacional (E.D.A.M.I.), Buenos
Aires; 27Aug47; EF6695.

MAGIDSON, HERB.
Midnight in Paris; words and
music by Con Conrad and Herb
Magidson, [words rev. by Herb
Magidson. © Movietone Music
Corp., New York; 25Sep47; on
revised lyrics; EP18516.

MAGILL, HARRY AUGUSTUS, 1864-
My Heart Belongs to You; words
and music by Harry A. Magill,
sr., arr. by John Bach. ©
Harry Augustus Magill, sr.,
Chicago; 12Jul47; EP16075.

MAGNANTE, CHARLES.
Minutes with Magnante; (rhythmic
paraphrase of Chopin's Minute
waltz) by Charles Magnante.
© Shapiro, Bernstein & Co.,
inc., New York; 14Oct47; on
arrangement; EP18026. For accordion solo.

MAGNEY, RUTH TAYLOR.
Lullaby, Little Jesus; Christmas
anthem for two part chorus [by]
Ruth Taylor Magney, [words by]
R. T. M. © The H. W. Gray Co.,
inc., New York; 230ct47; EP18490.

MAIER, GUY, ed.
Etudes for Every Pianist and How to
Study Them; selected, rev. and ed.
by Guy Maier. © Theodore Presser
Co., Philadelphia; 14Sep47; on
selection, revision & editing;
EP17291.

MAIR, ESTHER LOUISE, 1911-
In Fairy Land; by Esther Mair.
© La Mar Music Publishers, inc.,
Canton, Ohio; 16Jun47; EP15988.
For voice and piano, with chord
symbols.

MAKER, FREDERICK C
Dear Lord and Father of Mankind
... [by] Frederick C. Maker ...
[words by] John Greenleaf Whittier ... arr. by W. B. Olds for
choir and congregation with
alto solo (S.A.T.B.) © Hall &
McCreary Co., Chicago; 20Nov47;
on arrangement; EP20157.

Dear Lord and Father of Mankind;
SATB a cappella. Words by John
Greenleaf Whittier, [music by]
F. C. Maker. Harold Flammer,
inc., New York; 14Nov47; on arrange-
ment; EP19148.

MALAVSKY, SAMUEL, 1894-
Hebrew Traditional Cantorial
Masterworks; by Samuel Malavsky.
© Samuel Malavsky, Brooklyn;
15Jul47; EP15565. For voice
and piano; Hebrew words (transliterated)

MALDEREN, E   V
Le Tango du Rêve; paroles de
Jean Carwald, musique de E.
V. Malderen. © Éditions L.
Maillochon, Paris; 9Nov19;
EF5787.

MALIN, DON F   1896-   arr.
Praise the Lord, Ye Heavens Adore
Him; anthem for mixed and treble
choirs, Verses 1-2, The Found-
ling Collection, Verse 3 [by]
Edward Osler, Welsh tune - Hy-
frydol. By R. H. Prichard, arr.
by Don Malin. © C. C. Birchard
& Co., Boston; 20Nov47; on arrangement; EP19031.

MALIN, DONALD F   1896-
Ivy and Holly; Irish folk song,
[words by] John Keegan ... S.A.
T.B. arr. by Don Malin. © C.
C. Birchard & Co., Boston;
30Oct47; on arrangement; EP18387.

Prayer; for men's voices, a
cappella, tr. by Edward
Grabinski, Polish melody
arr. by Don Malin. ©
Clayton F. Summy Co.,
Chicago; 7Aug47; EP16129.

MALLIDÈS, GEORGIOS NIKITAS, 1909-
Ellenopoulo; Eisai e Pio Omorphe
Tou Kosmou; [words by] Lykiardo-
poulou, [music by] Mallidè.
[Athens] Gaitanos. © Michael
Gaetanos, Athens; 24Apr47;
EF6811.

MALMQUIST, TOMMY.
When I Join My Mother up There;
words and music by Tommy Malmquist. [c1946] © Nordyke
Publishing Co., Los Angeles;
14Jan47; EP20099.

MALOTTE, ALBERT HAY.
The Lord's Prayer; for three-part
chorus of women's voices and
soprano solo with piano accompaniment, [by] Albert Hay
Malotte, arr. by Carl Deis.
© G. Schirmer, inc., New York;
17Jul47; on arrangement;
EP17046.

MALTIN, BERNARD.
Rita; by Bernard Maltin, for
piano. © J. J. Robbins & Sons,
inc., New York; 17Nov47; EP19024.

MALTZEFF, ALEXIS.
I Sought the Lord; anthem for mixed
voices [by] Alexis Maltzeff.
Adapted from Psalm 34: 4, 8, by
Theresa Maltzeff. © Oliver Dit-
son Co., Philadelphia; 27Oct47;
EP19848.

Two Sentences or Responses; for
mixed voices by Alexis O.
Maltzeff. © The H. W. Gray
Co., inc., New York; 27Jun47;
EP15369.

MANCE, FRANK.
You Alone; words by Edd Hurshell,
music by Frank Mance. © Nordyke Publishing Co., Los Angeles; 16Jul47; EP17458.

MANCINO, MICHAEL A
I've Got My Love for You; words
and music by Michael A. Mancino. © Nordyke Publishing Co.,
Los Angeles; 12Jul47; EP17515.

MANK, CHARLES.
"Don't Play around Me Anymore;"
words and music by Billy Starr
& Chaw Mank. © Chaw Mank's
Blue Ribbon Music Co., Staun-
ton, Ill.; 15Aug47; EP18112.

MANK, CHAW. See
Mank, Charles.

MANLEY, GERTRUDE T
So Many Things Have Happened; words
and music by Gertrude T. Manley.
© Nordyke Publishing Co., Los
Angeles; 15Aug47; EP19630.

MANLEY, PEGGY.
No More; words and music by Peggy
Manley. © Nordyke Publishing
Co., Los Angeles; 18Jul46;
EP15289.

MANN, DAVE.
I Went Down to Virginia; by Redd
Evans and Dave Mann. c1948. ©
Jefferson Music Co., inc., New
York; 29Nov47; EP19067. For
voice and piano, with chord
symbols.

I've Only Myself to Blame; by Redd
Evans and Dave Mann. c1948. ©
Jefferson Music Co., inc., New
York; 29Nov47; EP19066. For
voice and piano, with chord sym-
bols.

Smorgasbord at the Swedish Cafe;
words and music by Bob Hilliard
and Dave Mann. © Republic
Music Corp., New York; 18Sep47;
EP17265.

These Will Be the Best Years;
words and music by Bob Hilliard
and Dave Mann. © Robbins Music
Corp., New York; 28Nov47; EP19823.

MANN, DAVID.
Passing Fancy; by Bob Hilliard &
Dave Mann. © Broadcast Music,
inc., New York; 10Oct47;
EP18454. For voice and piano,
with chord symbols.

MANN, ENID.
My Man Turned Up (and turned me
down); by Enid Mann. © Kanes
Music Publishers, New York;
30Jul47; EP16176. For voice
and piano, with chord symbols.

MANN, ROSCOE CONKLING, 1882-
Lest We Forget; America's first;
patriotic cantata, words and
music by Roscoe C. Mann. Council
Bluffs, Ia., American Publishing
Co. © Roscoe Conkling Mann, Council Bluffs, Ia.; 1Jun47; EP20269.

MANNERS, HENRY, pseud. See
Katzman, Henry.

MANNERS, MAXINE.
Mary, Marry Me; by Maxine
Manners. © Bourne, inc., New
York; 27Aug47; EP16564. For
voice and piano, with chord
symbols.

MANNING, DICK.
Chickasaw Limited; lyrics by
Buddy Kaye ... music by Dick
Manning. © Chas. K. Harris
Music Pub. Co., inc., New York;
27Aug47; EP17872.

The Treasure of Sierra Madre;
music by Dick Manning, lyric by
Buddy Kaye. © Remick Music
Corp., New York; 2Dec47; EP19822.

MANNING, RICHARD.
Twilight Trail; for voice and
piano, high ... by Richrd Manning, [words by Maxine Manners]
© G. Schirmer, inc., New York;
20Aug47; EP18029.

What Is This Fragrance? Quelle
Est Cette Odeur? Old French
carol, harmonized and arr. by
Richard Manning, French and
English texts. (English version by Richard Manning) Low
voice. © Galaxy Music Corp.,
New York; 12Aug47; on arrangement; EP17023.

MANSFIELD, RICHARD.
Please Come Back; words and music
by Glenn Larson and Richard
Mansfield. © Nordyke Publish-
ing Co., Los Angeles; 10Jun47;
EP16929.

MANUS, JACK, 1909-
A Bed of Roses; by Bernard Bierman,
Arthur Berman and Jack Manus.
© Johnstone Music, inc., New
York; 30Oct47; EP19611. For
voice and piano with chord sym-
bols.

Forgiving You; words and music by
Bernard Bierman and Jack Manus.
© Mellin Music, inc., New York;
28Jul47; EP15953.

Got the West on My Mind (take me
back); by Bernard Bierman,
Arthur Berman and Jack Manus.
© Shapiro, Bernstein & Co., inc.,
New York; 10Nov47; EP18719. For
voice and piano, with chord
symbols.

Here Comes the Milkman; by Bernard
Bierman and Jack Manus. ©
Republic Music Corp., New York;
24Nov47; EP18807. For voice and
piano, with chord symbols.

Hills of Colorado; by Bernard
Bierman [and] Jack Manus.
© London Music Corp., New York;
11Aug47; EP16332. For voice
and piano, with chord symbols.

My Cousin Louella; by Bernard
Bierman and Jack Manus. ©
Shapiro, Bernstein & Co., inc.,
New York; 23Oct47; EP18453. For
voice and piano, with chord sym-
bols.

Mar, Estelle Hill la. See
La Mar, Estelle Hill.

MARCELLI, NINO.
Song of the Andes. (Canción de
los Andes) ... For ...
(S.S.A.T.B. a cappella). Spanish
poem by N. M., English version
by Holon Bagg. © Carl Fischer,
inc., New York; 11Aug47; on
arrangement; EP16430.

MARCHESE, VINCE.
Flora Boogie; words and music by
Vince Marchese. Pacific Grove,
Calif., L. J. Tuck. © L. J.
Tuck and Vince Marchese, Pacific
Grove, Calif.; 5Jun47; EP15670.

MARCHMAN, HORTENSE.
Paradise; words by Jack Sawyer,
music by Hortense Marchman. ©
Nordyke Publishing Co., Los
Angeles; 29Apr47; EP16837.

[MARCLAND, JEAN] 1903-
Le Mariage de Ramuntcho ... musique
de Marc Lanjean [pseud., Vincent
Scotto and Paul Rocca, words by
P. Farge, pseud., M. Lanjean,
Jean Rodor, pseud. and André
Dassery] © Éditions Royalty,
Paris; 14Aug47; EP7235. Condensed
score: orchestra.

Maritchu; paroles de Marc Lanjean
[pseud.] & Paul Farge [pseud.],
musique de Marc Lanjean.
© Éditions Royalty, Paris;
31Mar47; EF5901.

MARCO, JEAN, pseud. See
Marcopoulos, Jean, 1923-

MARCOPOULOS, JEAN, 1923-
Faubourg Saint Honoré; paroles de
Jean Marco [pseud.] et Jean de
Jean Marco [pseud.] et Jean
Solar [pseud.] © Éditions Mondia,
s.a., Paris; 25Feb47; EF3806.

MARES, PABLO, arr.
Santa Fe Tipica Orchestra Folio;
music in the South of the Border
manner, arrangements ... by Pablo Mares. © Carl Fischer, inc.,
New York; 28Nov47; on arrangement; EP20392. Score and parts.

MARESCOTTI, ANDRÉ FRANÇOIS, 1902-
La Lampe d'Argile; [by] A.-F.
Marescotti, drame en cinq
actes de René Morax. ©
Adolphe Henn (Editions Henn),
Geneva; 31May47; EF6293.
Piano-vocal score.

MARGAT, YVES, 1896-
Impromptu Valse; par Yves Margat.
© Durand & Co., Paris; 30Jul47;
EF6523. For piano solo.

MARGETSON, EDWARD THEODORE, 1897-
O Lord, Support Us ... for four-
part chorus of mixed voices, a
cappella, [by] Edward Margetson,
[words from] Book of common
prayer. © Boston Music Co.,
Boston; 15Dec47; EP20400.

MARGRIS.
Valse Bleu; plectrum guitar solo,
[by] Margris, arr. as played
by Harry Volpe. c1939. © Albert
Rocky Co., New York; 10Jan40; on
arrangement; EP19709.

[MARIE, GABRIEL] 1852-1928.
Golden Wedding. (La Cinquantaine)
[By Gabriel-Marie], arr. by A. J.
Condaris. © Scholastic Music Co.,
Port Chester, N. Y.; 1Nov47; on
arrangement for school orchestra;
EP19601. Piano-conductor score
and parts.

MARIE, JEAN GABRIEL- See
Gabriel-Marie, Jean.

MARIER, THEODORE N   1912-
Jesus, the Very Thought of Thee;
[by] Theodore N. Marier, tr.
[by] ... E. Caswall. © Mc-
Laughlin & Reilly Co., Boston;
12Sep47; EP17876.

O Jesus, Thou the Beauty Art;
[by] Theodore N. Marier, tr.
[by] ... E. Caswall. © Mc-
Laughlin & Reilly Co., Boston;
12Sep47; EP17875.

MARIN HERNANDEZ, VICTOR.
La Misa Muerta; ... Letra y
música de Víctor Marin Hernan-
dez, arreglo de Luis Martinez.
© Peer International Corp.,
New York; 3Jul47; EP5744.
Parts; orchestra.

MARINIER, PAUL, 1866-
Les Plus Jolies Mélodies; de Paul
Marinier, [words by Paul
Marinier, Emile Bessière, Lucien
Boyer and Ernest Gustin, music
by Paul Marinier and Jean
Buffières, pseud.] Paris,
Éditions Salabert. © Salabert,
inc., New York; 28Apr47; EF6864.

MARIO, DON. See
Alvarez Rios, Mario.

MARIO, E   A
Santa Lucia, Far Away. Santa Lucia
Lontana. English lyric by Olga
Paul, music and Italian lyric by
E. A. Mario. (In Memories of
Italy, p3-5) © Edward B. Marks
Music Corp., New York; 16Jul47;
on English lyric; EP15816.

[MARIO, E   A   ] comp.
Piedigrotta Mario, 1947.
(Anno XXXII, n. 32. 2. ed.
Comp. by E. A. Mario. Words
by E. A. Mario, S. di Giacomo,
E. de Filippo and others;
Music by E, Nardella, E. A.
Mario and others) © Italian
Book Co., New York; 6Sep47;
EF5388.

MARKLE, EDWARD KING.
Sweet Suwanee Moon ... words and
music by Edward (Sailor) Markle.
© Edward King Markle, Avon Park,
Fla.; 7Jul47; EP15922.

MARKLE, SAILOR. See
Markle, Edward King.

MARKS, C   A
God of Mercy, God of Grace; two-
part hymn for treble voices.
[Words by] Henry F. Lyte, [music
by] C. A. Marks, arr. by Harold
K. Marks. © Theodore Presser
Co., Philadelphia; 15Jul47; on
arrangement; EP15674.

MARQUEZ, PEPE, arr.
La Raspa ... letra de Clotilde
Arias, arr. de Pepe Marquez, arr.
rev. de D. Savino. © Robbins
Music Corp. New York; 24Jun47;
on new piano arrangement and
words; EP15420.

MARROQUIN, JOSE SABRE. See
Sabre Marroquín, José.

MARRYOTT, RALPH E
Go, Tell It on the Mountains;
Negro spiritual. Christmas
chorus arr. for mixed voices
with baritone solo by Ralph E.
Marryott. © The H. W. Gray Co.,
inc., New York; 2Jul47; on
arrangement; EP15709.

Midwinter Carol; Christmas anthem
for mixed voices with solo or
children's choir. [Words by]
Christina G. Rossetti, [music
by] Ralph E. Marryott. © The
H. W. Gray Co., inc., New York;
2Jul47; EP15706.

Over Bethlehem's Town ... for
mixed voices, [by] Ralph E.
Marryott, [words by] Thomas
Tiplady. © Oliver Ditson Co.,
Philadelphia; 2Sep47; EP17282.

MARSH, CHARLES H
Little Chinese Dancer; piano
solo by Charles H. Marsh.
© Clayton F. Summy Co., Chicago;
26Sep47; EP17353.

MARSH, CHARLES HOWARD, 1885-
I Heard the Voice of Jesus Say
... for mixed voices, accompanied [by] Charles H. Marsh,
[words by] Horatius Bonar.
© Hall & McCreary Co., Chicago;
8Dec47; EP19983.

Te Deum Laudamus. We Praise Thee,
O God ... for mixed voices,
accompanied [by] Charles H.
Marsh, [text from] Episcopal
liturgy. © Hall & McCreary Co.,
Chicago; 8Dec47; EP19982.
English words.

MARSH, WILLIAM JOHN, 1880-
Choral Mass in Honor of the Infant
Jesus; [by] W. J. Marsh ... for
TTBB voices. © McLaughlin &
Reilly Co., Boston; 25Jul47;
on arrangement; EP16388.

MARSHAL, EDWIN, pseud. See
Fischer, Irwin L.

MARSHALL, DAVID.
I'm Living in Christ, My Savior;
words by Daniel S. Twohig,
music by David Marshall.
© Theodore Presser Co., Philadelphia; 17Oct47; EP18517.

MARSHALL, LOIS.K   1889-
A Country Lane; for piano solo by
Lois Marshall. © The Composers
Press, inc., New York; 28Oct47;
EP18327.

In a Canoe; for piano solo by
Lois Marshall. © The Composers
Press, inc., New York; 28Oct47;
EP18328.

MARTELLI, HENRI, 1895-
Fantaisiestück. Op.67. [By]
Henri Martelli. © Lucien de
Lacour, Éditeur, Paris; 1Jul47;
EF6574. Score (flute and piano)
and part.

(Trio, winds) Trio ... [by] Henri
Martelli. Op. 45. © Lucien de
Lacour, Éditeur, Paris; 1Jul47;
EF6566. Score (oboe, clarinet
and bassoon) and parts.

MARTENS, IB, 1918-
Huit Petits Instructives
Morceaux; pour piano, [by]
Ib Martens. © Wilhelm
Hansen, Musik-Forlag, Copen-
hagen; 30May47; EF6297.

MARTH, HELEN JUN, 1903-
Lo! The Angel of the Lord;
Christmas carol ... Words by
Helen Jun Marth. Cicilian
melody arr. by Helen Jun Marth.
[St. Louis, Hunleth Music Co.]
© C. Albert Scholin, St. Louis;
7Aug47; on arrangement; EP16140.
Score: 3 choirs (SA, SAB,
SATB) and piano.

MARTIN, DEAC.   See
Martin, C — T.

MARTIN, A   LOPEZ. See
López Martín, A.

MARTIN, C — T   1889-
arr.
How Can I Leave Thee? Old German
folk song arr. by Deac Martin.
© Society for the Preservation
and Encouragement of Barber
Shop Quartet Singing in America,
inc., Detroit; 15Nov47; on arrangement; EP19618.

MARTIN, GEORGE W
Not What My Hands Have Done; SATB
a cappella. Words by Horatius
Bonar, hymn tune by George W.
Martin, arr. by Gustav Nelson.
© Harold Flammer, inc., New York;
14Nov47; on arrangement; EP19149.

MARTIN, HAZEL.
I Would Have a Little Garden;
words by Elizabeth Stalnaker,
music by Hazel Martin. © Nordyke Publishing Co., Los Angeles; 12Aug47; EP19519.

MARTIN, JAMES.
Last Night I Counted Sheep; words
and music by James Martin.
© Nordyke Publishing Co., Los
Angeles; 28Mar47; EP16745.

MARTIN, LEONCE MARIE JOSEPH DE SAINT.
See
Saint-Martin, Léonce Marie Joseph Du.

MARTIN, MICHEL CHARLES, 1877-
Après les Devoirs ... [By] Robert
Charles Martin. Paris; 25May47; EF5845. For
piano solo.

MARTIN, ROBERT CHARLES. See
Martin, Michel Charles.

MARTIN, ROSE TURNER.
Which Way the Pig's Tail
Curl? Words and music by Guy
Wesley Martin and Rose Turner
Martin. © Nordyke Publishing
Co., Los Angeles; 11Jul47;
EP17462.

MARTINET, HENRI ALEXANDRE LEON, 1909-
(Destins) Petit Papa Noël ...
[From] le film "Destins";
paroles de Raymond Vincy [pseud.]
musique de Henri Martinet.
© Éditions Max Eschig, Paris,
23Dec46; EF6479.
Petit Papa Noël. See his Destins.

MARTINEZ, LEONARDO.
Nunca Más Volvera. (Nevermore to
Return) ... English words by Joe
Davis, Spanish words and music
by Leonardo Martinez. © Caribbean Music Co., New York;
4Dec47; EP20234.

MARTINEZ, LUIS, 1892-
Mi Casita ... paroles françaises
de Lioger [pseud.] & Chamfleury
[pseud.], paroles espagnoles de
L. Martinez, musique de L.
Martinez & J. Grant. © Éd-
itions Espagnoles] Julio Garzon,
Paris; 24Jul47; EF6488.

KARTINEZ GIL, CARLOS.
Revancha ... Letra y música de
Vos Hnos. Martines Gil. ©
Promotora Hispano Americana de
Musica, s, a., Mexico; 22Jul47;
EF5818.

MARTINON, JEAN, 1910-
(Sonatina, winds, no. 4) Sonatine
no. 4 ... [by] Jean-Martinon.
[Op. 26, no. 1] © Lucien de
Lacour, Éditeur, Paris; 1Jul47;
EF6564. Score (oboe, clarinet
and bassoon) and parts.

313

MARTINON, JEAN. Cont'd.
(Trio, strings) Trio ... [by]
Jean-Martinon. Op.32, no.2.
© Lucien de Lacour, Éditeur,
Paris; 1Jul47; EF6519. Score
and parts.

MARTINS, MARIA H   RUAS.
Padre Nosso. "The Lord's Prayer"
... Music by M. H. Ruas Martins.
© Mathilde Polla Ruas, Washington, D. C.; 15Aug47; EP16320.
For 2 treble voices and piano.

MARTINU, BOHUSLAV, 1900-
Symphony No.1; full score. ©
Hawkes & Son (London), ltd.,
London; 27Jun47; EF5989.

MARVIN, FRANKIE.
Two Broken Hearts; words and
music by Al Dexter and Frankie
Marvin. Hollywood, Calif.,
Hill and Range Songs. © Hill
and Range Songs, inc. and Al
Dexter Music Publishing Co.,
Hollywood, Calif.; 15Dec47;
EP20120.

MARVIN, LLOYD.
Hurdy-gurdy Man. © Chart Music
Publishing House, inc., Chicago;
23Jul47; EP15967. For piano
accordion solo.

Kolmar Grand March; accordion duet,
by Lloyd Marvin. © Chart Music
Publishing House, inc., Chicago;
13Nov47; EP19130.

MARY CHRYSOSTOM, sister.   See
Koppes, Mary Chrysostom, sister.

MARY EULALIA, sister. See
Eulalia, sister.

MARZ, RUDOLF.
Loin de Toi ... paroles de A. Viaud,
musique de R. Marz [arr. by Al.
Kiwi, pseud.] © Éditions Max
Eschig, Paris; 3Jul46; on arrangement; EF7234. Piano-conductor
score (orchestra) and parts.

MASON, JOHN.
The Joe-Bie Hop; written and
composed by John Mason.
[c1945] © Cinephonic Music
Co., ltd., London; 9Apr46;
EF6047. Piano-conductor score,
condensed score (orchestra) and
parts.

MASON, LOWELL, 1792-1872.
My Faith Looks Up to Thee; [by]
Lowell Mason, arr. by W. B.
Olds [for] S.A.T.B., [words by
Ray Palmer] © Hall & McCreary
Co., Chicago; 6Oct47; on
arrangement; EP18040.

MACONIER, CLEM.
You Made the Sun Shine thru the
Rain; words and music by Clem
Masonier. © Nordyke Publishing
Co., Los Angeles; 12Apr47;
EP16805.

MASSON, CLARICE C
I'm Saving My Pennies; words and
music by Clarice C. Masson.
© Nordyke Publishing Co., Los
Angeles; 12Jul47; EP17617.

MASTERS, FRANKIE.
Twinkle-Toes; words and music by
Sammy Gallop, Chester Conn and
Frankie Masters. © Triangle
Music Corp., New York; 16Oct47;
EP18225.

MATERN, MRS. LOUIS.
What If There Had Never Been a
Calvary? Music and lyrics by
Mrs. Louis Matern. Chicago,
Mrs. L. Matern. © Mr. and Mrs.
Louis Matern, Chicago; 6Oct47;
EP17496.

MATESKY, RALPH.
Prayer for Peace; text by Franklin
D. Roosevelt, music by Ralph
Matesky., For ... S.A.T.B. with
piano or organ acc. © Mills
Music, inc., New York; 8Dec47;
EP19888.

MATTHESON, JOHANN.
Sarabande; by J. Mattheson ... ed.
[i.e. arr.] by Arcady Dubensky.
© G. Ricordi & Co., New York;
30Jul47; on arrangement; EF16346.
Score; string orchestra.

MATTHEWS, HARRY ALEXANDER, 1879-
Danish Carol: O'er Bethlehem's
Plains; harmonized and arr. by
H. Alexander Matthews. © Elkan-
Vogel Co., inc., Philadelphia;
24Sep47; EP17965. Score: soprano, chorus (SATB) and piano
or organ reduction.

O Lord, Support Us All the Day
Long ... for mixed voices [by]
H. Alexander Matthews, [words by]
John Henry Newman. © Oliver
Ditson Co., Philadelphia; 29Sep47;
EP17731.

MAUL, GEORGE.
Stupid; words and music by
Fern Luhm & George Maul.
© Nordyke Publishing Co., Los
Angeles; 31Jul47; EP19420.

MAURO, BENOIT.
A Hymn to St. Frances Xavier Cabrini,
[by] Benoit Mauro. [n.p.] ©
Benoit Mauro, Brooklyn; 10Sep46;
EP6187. For voice and piano.

MAWHINNEY, EDNA A
Sad and Blue; words and music by
Edna A. Mawhinney, arr. by Walter W. Nowcomer. © Nordyke Publishing Co., Los Angeles;
21Feb47; EP20381.

MAXWELL, EDDIE.
Let's Be Sweethearts Again; by
Jerry Marlowe and Eddie Maxwell.
© Campbell-Porgie, inc., New
York; 23Oct47; EP18293. For
voice and piano, with chord
symbols.

MAY, AL DE. See
DeMay, Al.

MAY, E   G   1908-
Kitty O'Leary; song waltz, words
and music by E. G. May. ©
D'Olier Music Co., Dublin;
6Feb47; EF7135.

MAY, JOE LE, pseud. See
Kennedy, Jimmy.

MAY, JOHN M
Is It True? Words and music by
John M. May. © Nordyke Publishing Co., Los Angeles;
12Oct45; EP17605.

MAYE, PAUL.
Le Chant des Alpes; paroles et
musique de Paul Maye. © Ste.
Ame. Fse. Chappell, Paris;
20Jun47; EF5762.

Paname; paroles et musique de
Paul Maye. © Ste. Ame. Fse.
Chappell, Paris; 20Jun47; EF5760.

Tiens Bon l'Guidon; paroles et
musique de Paul Maye. © Ste.
Ame. Fse. Chappell, Paris;
20Jun47; EF5759.

Tout autour du Tour; chanson du
Tour de France 1947 ...
Paroles de Pierre Still &
Pierre Nival, musique de Paul
Maye. © Ste. Ame. Fse.
Chappell, Paris; 20Jun47;
EF5761.

MAYER, C   ISABEL.
Twilight on the Rose; ... Words
by Michael Reno, music by C.
Isabel Mayer. Portland, Or., C.
I. Mayer Music Publishing.
© Michael Reno, Fresno, Calif.;
26May47; EP15400.

When I Found You; words by Ora
F. Hollingsworth, music by C.
Isabel Mayer. Portland, Or.,
C. I. Mayer Music Pub. [c1945]
© Ora Paul Hollingsworth,
Canoga Park, Calif.; 18Jul47;
EP16470.

Where the Water Lillies Grow;
words by Mary Alice Marguerite
Milner, music by C. Isabel
Mayer. Portland, Or., C. I.
Mayer Music Pub. [c1946]
© Mary Alice Marguerite Milner,
Grants Pass, Or.; 3Jun47;
EP16469.

MAYERL, BILLY.
Romanesque; piano solo by Billy
Mayerl. © Keith Prowse & Co.,
ltd., London; 18Jul47; EF5753.

MAYO, O   W
The Queen of San Joaquin; words
and music by O. W. Mayo. ©
Bob Wills Music, inc., Hollywood,
Calif.; 14Nov47; EP18772.

MAYS, CLARA BELLE, 1887-
Making My Bust Better ... [By]
C. B. Mays. © Clara Belle Mays,
Texarkana, Ark.; 29Jul47;
EP15894. For unison chorus and
piano.

MAZELLIER, JULES, 1879-
Bercelonnette; [by] Jules Mazellier. © Lucien De Lacour,
Paris; 31Dec46; EF5918. For
piano solo.

Bercelonnette; [by] Jules
Mazellier, Paris, 31Dec46; EF5909. Score
(violin and piano) and part.

Nocturne; pour piano [by] Jules
Mazellier. © Lucien De Lacour,
Paris; 31Dec46; EF5907.

MAZZUCCHI, ALFREDO, 1882-
Palomma 'E 'Stu Core; Versi di
John Sturco, musica di Alfredo
Mazzucchi. Napoli, Edizioni
Bideri. © John Sturco, Long
Island City, N. Y.; 14Jul47;
EP6046.

MEACHAM, F   W
American Patrol; [by] F. W. Meacham, arr. by Herman A. Hummel.
© Rubank, inc., Chicago; 1Nov47;
on arrangement; EP19212. Score
(cornet or trumpet and piano)
and part, with part for cornet
or trumpet 2 ad lib.

MEDINA, ARTURO, pseud. See
Ullvén, Uno A.

[MEISSNER, JOSEPH JAMES] 1915-
Bluesalamode; [by Zep Meissner] ©
Joseph James (Zep) Meissner,
North Hollywood, Calif.; 23May47;
EP19077. Parts: orchestra.

Early Morning Blues; [by] Zep
Meissner. © Joseph James (Zep)
Meissner, North Hollywood,
Calif.; 23May47; EP19073. Parts:
orchestra.

Lazy Mood Blues; [by Zep Meissner]
© Joseph James (Zep) Meissner,
North Hollywood, Calif.; 10Oct47;
EP19078. Parts: orchestra.

Louella; words by Elizabeth La
Voie and Irving Mills, music by
Joseph James Meissner ... arr.
by "Zep" Meissner. [c1946] ©
American Academy of Music, inc.,
New York; on arrangement; 21Apr47;
EP6643. Piano-conductor score
(orchestra, with words) and parts.

The New Orleans Two Beat Shuffle;
[by Zep Meissner] © Joseph James
(Zep) Meissner, North Hollywood,
Calif.; 9Oct47; EP19072. Parts:
orchestra.

Randolph St. Strut; [by Zep Meissner and Edward Robert Pripps]
© Joseph James (Zep) Meissner,
North Hollywood, Calif.; 7Jul47;
EP19071. Parts: orchestra.

Smokehouse Stomp; by Zep Meissner.
© Joseph James (Zep) Meissner,
North Hollywood, Calif.; 23May47;
EP19075. Parts: orchestra.

MEISSNER, ZEP. See
Meissner, Joseph James.

314

MELCHERS, HENRIK MELCHER
(Quartet, strings) Strākkvartett
(G-dur) fōr tva violiner, viola
och violoncell. [by] H. M. Melchers. Op.17. Partitur. Stockholm, Ed. Suecia. © Fōreninger
svenska tonsāttare, Edition
Suecia, Stockholm; 1Jan45;
EF7064.

MELICHAR, ALOIS, 1896-
Schaukel-Lied. See his Triumph der
Liebe.

MELLERS, WILFRID.
Four Carols; for boys' (or women's)
voices with optional celesta,
by Wilfrid Mellers. [Words anon.
(Medieval)] © Alfred Lengnick
and Co., ltd., London; 14Jul47;
EF6291.

MELLS, H   F
Burden'd Chile ... By H. F. Mells.
© Handy Brothers Music Co., inc.,
New York; 6Oct47; EP17840. For
voice and piano.

[MELONE, MICHEL HUBERT] 1903-
Gomez de Santa Fé ... paroles et
musique de Charles Humel [pseud.]
© Charles Humel, Paris; 1Jul47;
EF6426.

Simbad le Marin ... paroles de
Roger Minier, musique de
Charles Humel [pseud.] ©
Editions Max Eschig, Paris;
25Jun47; EF6481.

MELSHER, IRVING.
Believe Me, I'll Be Leaving You;
words by Cy Coben, music by
Irving Melsher. © Bob Miller,
inc., New York; 27Oct47;
EP18605.

Forget Me; words by Cy Coben,
music by Irving Melsher. © Mutual Music Society, inc., New
York; 30Sep47; EP17880.

Red Hot Rella; words and music by
Cy Coben ... Charles Grean and
Irving Melsher. © Alamo Music,
inc., Hollywood, Calif.;
11Nov47; EP18758.

MELVIN, BETHEL, 1907-
The Cable Car Song; words and
music by Bethel Melvin. ©
Wesley Webster, San Francisco;
24Jul47; EP15917.

MEMORIES OF ITALY; an album of its
best-loved songs. New York, E. B.
Marks Music Corp.

MENDELSSOHN-BARTHOLDY, FELIX, 1809-
1847.
Canzonetta; guitar solo, [by] Felix
Mendelssohn, arr. as played by
Harry Volpe. c1939. © Albert
Rocky Co., New York; 10Jan40;
on arrangement; EP20196.

(Elijah) Be Not Afraid; from
"Elijah," for mixed voices.
[By] Felix Mendelssohn, arr.
by Homer Whitford. © Theodore
Presser Co., Philadelphia;
9Sep47; on arrangement;
EP17168.

(Elijah) Oh, Come Everyone That
Thirsteth, from "Elijah" by F.
Mendelssohn; arr. by Noble Cain.
© Boosey & Hawkes, inc., New
York; 11Nov47; on arrangement;
EP19234. Score: SSATB and piano.

Mendelssohn: Excerpts from His
Greatest Works; [arr. by Victor
Ambrose] © Lawrence Wright
Music Co., ltd., London;
12Nov47; on arrangement; EF7008.
For piano solo.

Oh, Come Everyone That Thirsteth. See
his Elijah.

Praeludium; [by] F. Mendelssohn, rev.
and ed. by Maxwell Eckstein. c1943.
© Carl Fischer, inc., New York;
24Jul44; on revision & edition;
EP17136. For piano solo.

Second Organ Sonata. See his Sonata,
organ. No.2.

Six Sonatas, Three Preludes and
Fugues; for organ, by Felix
Mendelssohn, ed. and rev. by
Edwin Arthur Kraft. © Theodore
Presser Co., Philadelphia;
17Sep47; on editing & revision;
EP17355.

(Sonata, organ, no.2) Second
Organ Sonata; [by] Felix
Mendelssohn, arr. for brass
band by Frank Wright. © Besson
and Co., ltd., London; 16Oct47;
on arrangement; EF6822.

MENDIOLEA, RODOLFO.
Siento Que Te Quiero ... de:
Rodolfo Mendiolea, arr. de:
Sergio Guerrero. © Promotora
Hispano Americana de Música, s.
a., México; 27Dec40; EF6173.
Piano-conductor score (orchestra)
and parts; with words.

MENDOZA, OCTAVIO.
La Botella; letra y música de Octavio Mendoza. © Peer International Corp., New York; 25Nov47;
EP19839.

MENDOZA, QUIRINO. See
Mendoza y Cortés, Quirino F.

MENDOZA Y CORTÉS, QUIRINO F
San Ignacio de Loyola ... de Quirino Mendoza. © Promotora Hispano Americana de Música, s.a.,
México; 27Aug47; EF6710. For
voice and piano.

MENNIN, PETER, 1923-
Folk Overture; [by] Peter Mennin.
© Hargail Music Press, New York;
27Jun46; EP16591. Score:
orchestra.

MEREDITH, I   H
Within My Heart a Song ... [by]
I. H. Meredith, [words by]
Charles S. Given. © Tullar-
Meredith Co., New York;
30Sep47; EF17885. Close score:
SATB.

MEREDITH, I   H   ed.
Primary and Junior Songs ... ed.
by I. H. Meredith. © Tullar-
Meredith Co., New York; no.2,
12Sep47; EP17720. — Contents.—
no.2. For Christmas.

MERETTA, LEONARD V
Holiday Polka ... by Leonard V.
Meretta. © Mills Music, inc.,
New York; 28Jul47; on arrange-
ment; EP16195. Score (trom-
bone 1-3 and piano) and parts.

MERICKA, V   O   1895-
Love Song of Old Vienna; [modern
adaptation of Viennese folk
song by V. O. Mericka. c1946]
© Mer-Uhl Co., Pasadena, Calif.;
15Jan47; on English words and
arrangement; EP16073.

MERLIN, ALFRED.
Piccadilly Polka; by Alfred
Merlin, arr. by Ken Warner.
© Peter Maurice Music Co.,
ltd., New York; 5Sep47; EF6752.
Piano-conductor score
(orchestra) and parts.

MERRILL, BOB.
Don't Bother to Cry; by Bob Merrill.
© Fairway Music Co., Hollywood,
Calif.; 23Jul47; EP15998. For
voice and piano, with chord
symbols.

Why Does It Have to Rain on Sunday? By Vi Ott and Bob Merrill.
© Johnstone Music Co., New
York; 15Oct47; EP18190. For
voice and piano, with chord
symbols.

MERRILL, RAY.
Roundup Polka; words and music
by Hal Ritchie and Ray Merrill.
© Capitol Songs, inc., New
York; 20Aug47; EP16412.

MERRITT, BABS RYAN.
Tennessee; T-E double-N E double-S
double-E, by Babs Ryan Merritt.
© Stevens Music Corp., New York;
16Jul47; EP15775. For voice and
piano, with chord symbols.

MERRITT, CHARLES EDWIN.
Symphony of the Seasons; words and
music by Charles E. Merritt.
Columbia, Mo., Missouri Music
Publications. © Charles Edwin
Merritt, Columbia, Mo.; 2Sep47;
EP17936.

MERSON, BILLY, pseud. See
Thompson, William Henry.

MESANG, THEODORE LAWRENCE, 1902-
Men of Wisconsin; march. ©
Fillmore Bros. Co., Cincinnati;
15Jul47; EP15812. Piano-
conductor score (band) and parts.

Tip Top March Book ... by Ted
Mesang, Harold Rusch, Thomas
McDuff [pseud.] and James Wendel
[pseud.] © Neil A. Kjos Music
Co., Chicago; 14Aug47; EP18954.
Piano-conductor score (band,
partly with words) and parts.

MESSIAEN, OLIVIER, 1908-
Vingt Regards sur l'Enfant-Jésus;
pour piano [by] Olivier Messiaen.
© Durand & Cie, Paris; 30Jun47;
EF6529.

MESSLER, OSCAR, 1876-
Heaven Is My Home; duet for so-
prano and alto with piano, words
and music by Oscar Messler.
Worcester, Mass., Messler Piano
Co. © Oscar Messler, Worcester,
Mass.; 20Nov47; EP19623.

METCALF, LEON V
Pastorale ... [by] Leon V. Metcalf.
© Boosey & Hawkes, inc., New
York; 2Dec47; EP19876. Score
(clarinet and piano) and part.

[METCALFE, GEORGE E   ]
Harmony Lane; words and music by
Earle George [pseud.] © Nor-
dyke Publishing Co., Los
Angeles; 12Aug47; EP19654.

METZLER, ARTHUR.
Tango-Villerupt; piano accordion
solo ... by Arthur Metzler. ©
Patek Music Co., (Rudy Patek,
sole owner) Chicago; 2Sep47;
EP17841.

MEYER, DEDE CAPLAN, 1928-
Melancholy Rain; words and music
by Dede Meyer. © Dede Caplan
Meyer, Lincoln, Neb.; 2Sep47;
EP17217.

MEYER, GEORGE.
In a Little Book Shop; words and
music by Kay Twomey, Al Goodhart and George Meyer. © Triangle Music Corp., New York;
16Oct47; EP18226.

MEYER, JOSEPH.
The Bachelor and the Bobby-Soxer
... [from] an RKO picture ...
"The Bachelor and the Bobby-
Soxer"; words by Don Meyer
[and] Howard Phillips, music by
Joseph Meyer, arr. by Will
Hudson. © Paull-Pioneer Music
Corp., New York; 3Jun47; on
arrangement; EP16266. Piano-
conductor score (orchestra,
with words) and parts.

Blue Music; words and music by Al
Jacobs, Marvin Fisher and Joseph
Meyer. © Famous Music Corp.,
New York; 24Jul47; EP15807.

California, Here I Come; by Al
Jolson, Bud De Sylva and Joseph
Meyer ... S.S.A. arr. by Douglas
MacLean [pseud.] © M. Witmark &
Sons, New York; 1Dec47; on ar-
rangement; EP19817.

MEYER, JOSEPH. Cont'd.
California, Here I Come; words
and music by Al Jolson [pseud.],
Bud De Sylva and Joseph Meyer,
arr. by Ken Macomber. © M.
Witmark & Sons, New York;
15Aug47; on arrangement;
EP16524. Piano-conductor score
(orchestra, with words) and
parts.
If You Knew Susie; by B. G. De
Sylva and Joseph Meyer, arr.
.. by Johnny Warrington.
© Shapiro, Bernstein & Co.,
inc., New York; 9Dec47; on ar-
rangement; EI20002. Piano-
conductor score (orchestra,
with words) and parts.
My Honey's Lovin' Arms; words by
Herman Ruby, music by Joseph
Meyer, [arr. by Michael Edwards]
© Mills Music, inc., New York;
28Jul47; on arrangement;
EP16201.

MEYERS, HERMAN.
To Sin Is Human; words & music by
Herman Meyers. © M. M. Cole
Publishing Co., Chicago;
25Sep47; EP17342.

MIASKOVSKY, NIKOLAI.
The Red Star Is Riding; (Song of
the air force), words by I.
Frenkel, English adaptation by
Olga Paul, [music by] Nikolai
Miaskovsky. (In Haywood, Charles,
ed. Art Songs of Soviet Russia,
p.29-31) © Edward B. Marks
Music Corp., New York; 16Sep47;
on English adaptation; EP17181.
English and Russian words.

MICHAELOFF, MISCHA.
Katuscha; danse russe, piano solo
by Mischa Michaeloff. © Moon
Melodies, ltd., London; 14Oct44;
EP6868.
2 Russian Dances ... by Mischa
Michaeloff. © The Edward
Kassner Music Co., ltd., London;
16Nov42; EF6878. For piano
solo.
Valse Vagabond; piano solo, by ...
Mischa Michaeloff. © The
Edward Kassner Music Co., ltd.,
London; 11Jun43; EF6879.

MICHEL, ALBERT.
I Just Can't Find the Words;
words by Wilfred Michel, music
by Albert Michel. © Nordyke
Publishing Co., Los Angeles;
14Jun47; EP17545.

MICHEL, JOSÉ ANTONIO.
No Se Va a Poder ... letra y mú-
sica de José Antonio Michel.
© Promotora Hispano Americana de
Música, s.a., México; 27Aug47;
EF6701.

MICHELS, WALTER.
I Want a Song (for Christmas);
by Lenora Carpenter, Lindsay
McPhail and Walter Michels.
© Victor Publishing Co., Dallas;
7Nov47; EP18833. For voice and
piano, with chord symbols.

MICHELSEN, B   FRANK.
Turn Thy Face from My Sins; an-
them for mixed voices, [words]
from Psalm 51, [music by] B.
Frank Michelsen. © Boston Music
Co., Boston; 15Dec47; EP20397.

MIDWAY, JAMES H., pseud. See
Bourayre, Henri.

MIKESKA, MRS. E   F
Brand New Saddle and Silver Spurs;
words and music by Mrs. E. F.
Mikeska. © Nordyke Publishing
Co., Los Angeles; 11Jun46;
EP19492.

MILES, RUSSELL HANCOCK.
In Deepening Faith ... [by]
Russell Hancock Miles. © The
Arthur P. Schmidt Co., Boston;
11Jul47; EP15647. Score: SATB
and organ.

MILFORD, ROBIN.
Easter Meditation no. 3 [-4] for
organ by Robin Milford. [c1946]
© The Oxford University Press,
London; 23Jan47; EF6107, 6106.
Fantasia in B minor; for string
quartet by Robin Milford.
Score. [c1946] © The Oxford
University Press, London;
10Apr47; EF6137.
The 121st Psalm; set to music for
four soloists (or semi-chorus)
and chorus unacc. by Robin Mil-
ford. © Alfred Lengnick & Co.,
ltd., London; 8Aug47; EF6847.
Seven Descant Carols; arr. from
the Oxford Carol Book, by Robin
Milford. © The Oxford University
Press, London; 19Dec46; on
arrangement; EF6098.

MILHAUD, DARIUS, 1892-
Chants de Misère; [by] Darius
Milhaud, poèmes de Camille
Pollerd. © Heugel & Cie, Paris;
16Oct46; EF6498. For voice and
piano.
Six Sonnets; composés au secret
par Jean Cassou, choeurs mixtes
ou quatuor vocal, musique de
Darius Milhaud. [c1946]
© Heugel & Cie., Paris; 6Jan47;
EF6432.
(Sonata, viola & piano, no. 2)
2ème Sonate ... [by] Darius
Milhaud. [c1946] © Heugel
& Cie, Paris; 6Jan47; EF6505.
Score and part.
Suite for violin and piano, [by]
Darius Milhaud. London, Boosey
& Hawkes. ℗ Boosey & Hawkes,
inc., New York; 16Oct47; EF6820.
Score (violin and piano) and
part.
Two Marches: In Memoriam [and]
Gloria Victoribus; [by] Milhaud.
(Michigan University. Band Series,
pt.1, no.2) © G. Schirmer, inc.,
New York; 17Sep47; EP20282.
Score (band) and parts.
Two Marches: I. In Memoriam. II.
Gloria Victoribus. [by] Darius
Milhaud. © G. Schirmer, inc.,
New York; 27Aug47; EP18732.
Score: orchestra.

MILKEY, EDWARD T   1908-
Fount of Liberty; for four-part
chorus of women's voices with
piano acc. [by] Edward T. Milkey, [words by] Edwin F. Scho-
field. © The Boston Music Co.,
Boston; 10Nov47; EP20163.

MILLARD, MARY.
The Angel Song; [by] Gene Autry,
Curt Massey [and] Mary Millard.
© Golden West Melodies, inc.,
Hollywood, Calif.; 12Nov47;
EP18845. For voice and piano,
with chord symbols.

MILLER, BOB.
Bite Your Tongue and Say You're
Sorry; words by Esther Van
Sciver and Shelby Darnell
[pseud.], music by Bob Miller.
© Bob Miller, inc., New York;
27Oct47; EP18594.
Pal in Palo Alto; words by Larry
Markes, music by Bob Miller.
© Bob Miller, inc., New York;
27Oct47; EP18595.
Wake Up, You Drowsy Sleepers!
By Elton Britt and Shelby Dar-
nell [pseud.] © Bob Miller,
inc., New York; 27Oct47;
EP18608. For voice and piano,
with chord symbols.
Welcome Back to My Heart; words
by Milton Leeds [pseud.], music
by Bob Miller. © Bob Miller,
inc., New York; 27Oct47;
EP18601.

When a Woman Yells Loud Enough
(she usually gets what she
wants); words and music by Inky
Hucklenutt [pseud.] © Bob
Miller, inc., New York; 27Oct47;
EP18599.

MILLER, BOB, arr.
Birmingham Jail; arr. by Bob
Miller. © Bob Miller, inc.,
New York; 27Oct47; on arrange-
ment; EP18598. For voice and
piano, with chord symbols.
Red River Valley; arr. by Bob
Miller. © Bob Miller, inc.,
New York; 27Oct47; on arrange-
ment; EP18597. For voice and
piano, with chord symbols.

MILLER, EDDIE.
(Love's Got Me in a) Lazy Mood;
Johnny Mercer, words, Eddie
Miller, music, arr. by Van
Alexander. © Capitol Songs,
inc., New York; 15Jul47; on
arrangement; EP15623.

MILLER, FRED.
Down the Sunny San Joaquin; words
and music by Fred Miller. ©
Nordyke Publishing Co., Los
Angeles; 22Apr47; EP17582.

MILLER, FREDA D   1911-
[Pre-classic Suite; by] Freda D.
Miller. © Freda D. Miller, New
York; 1Jan47; EP18158. For
piano solo.
Sebago Syncopation; [by] Freda D.
Miller. © Freda D. Miller, New
York; 1Aug47; EP18160. For
piano solo.
Time out for a Dream ... [by]
Freda D. Miller. © Freda D.
Miller, New York; 1Jan47;
EP18159. For piano solo.

MILLER, IRVING, 1907-
The New Mixmaster Song; lyrics
by Paul Franklin, music by
Irving Miller. © Fowler Music
Co., New York; 26Sep47;
EP17341.

MILLER, JOHN A
Answer to Rainbow at Midnight; by
Lost John Miller. © Shapiro,
Bernstein & Co., inc., New York;
28Nov47; on new words; EP19245.
For voice and piano, with chord
symbols.

MILLER, JOHNNY.
Sentimental Me; words and music
by Johnny Miller. © Nordyke
Publishing Co., Los Angeles;
11Aug47; EP17403.

MILLER, KATIE M   1900-
Seeking for that City; words by
Thomas J. Horton, music by
Katie M. Miller. © Thomas J.
Horton, Los Angeles; 30Oct47;
EP20225. Close score: SATB.

MILLER, LARRY.
The First Day of Summer; words by
Michael Littman & Ralph Butler,
music by Larry Miller & Eddie
Cassen. © The Edward Kassner
Music Co., ltd., London; 6May47;
EF6874.

MILLER, LOST JOHN. See
Miller, John A

MILLER, MARION CATHERINE, 1903-
Because I Walk with Thee, Dear
Lord; words and music by Marion
C. Miller. © Marion Catherine
Miller, Lynn, Mass.; 12Nov47;
EP18403.
God's Star; words by Minnie L.
Dove, music by Marion C. Miller.
© Marion Catherine Miller, Lynn,
Mass.; 12Nov47; EP18402.
My Mother's Song; words arr.
by Eleanor Mel, music by
Marion C. Miller. © Marion
Catherine Miller, Lynn, Mass.
[and] Eleanor Mel, Boston;
11May47; EP16497.

MILLER, ROSS.
  Look into My Eyes; words and
  music by Ross Miller. © Nor-
  dyke Publishing Co., Los An-
  geles; 29Jul47; EP19514.
MILLER, WILLIAM, 1896-
  Trusting My All to His Care; [by]
  William Miller. © William
  Miller, Brooklyn; 16Jun47;
  EP16226. Close score: SATB.
MILLER, WILLIAM NICHOLAS.
  O Little Town of Bethlehem; sacred
  song with piano or organ acc.,
  hymn by Phillips Brooks, music
  by William Nicholas Miller.
  High voice. © Carl Fischer, inc.,
  New York; 23Oct47; EP18587.
  O Little Town of Bethlehem; (S.A.T.B.
  with piano or organ acc.) [by]
  W. N. Miller, [words by Phillips
  Brooks] © Carl Fischer, inc., New
  York; 24Sep47; EP18069.
  O Little Town of Bethlehem; (S.S.A.
  with piano or organ acc.) by W. N.
  Miller, [words by Phillips Brooks]
  © Carl Fischer, inc., New York;
  10ct47; EP18063.
MILLER, WINSTON ReVALLE, 1914-
  I'm Saved! Saved! Saved! By
  Winston R. Miller. ©
  Winston R. Miller, Cincinnati;
  24Jul47; EP16038. For voice
  and piano.
MILLI, MIMI.
  What's the Meaning of That Dream;
  words and music by Genee and
  Mimi Milli. © Nordyke Publish-
  Co., Los Angeles; 18Aug47;
  EP19525.
MILLIGAN, U   A
  What's the Meaning of That Dream;
  words and music by U. A. Milligan.
  [c1945] © Nordyke Publishing
  Co., Los Angeles; 13Sep46;
  EP15856.
[MILLS, CARLEY] 1907-
  The Letter I Forgot to Mail;
  words and music by Art Lambert
  and Bob McElliot [pseud.]
  © Happy Songs, inc., New York;
  5Aug47; EP16445.
MILLS, DON.
  After You; lyric by Buddy Kaye,
  music by Don Mills. © Barton
  Music Corp., New York; 30ct47;
  EP17759.
MILLS, GEORGE WARREN, 1881-
  Ever Present Jesus; [by] Geo. W.
  Mills. (In his The Gospel in
  Song. no.20) © George Warren
  Mills, Osceola, Ind.; 5Jul47;
  EP16477.
  The Gospel in Song; [by Geo. and
  Mae Mills], comp. by Geo. W.
  Mills. Osceola, Ind., G. and
  M. Mills. © George Warren
  Mills, Osceola, Ind.; 5Jul47;
  EP16483.
  I'm Climbing Jacob's Ladder; [by]
  Geo. W. Mills. (In his The
  Gospel in Song. no.19) ©
  George Warren Mills, Osceola,
  Ind.; 5Jul47; EP16476. Close
  score: SATB.
  Jesus Calls Us; [by] Geo. W.
  Mills, [words by] Mae Mills.
  (In his The Gospel in Song.
  no.23) © George Warren Mills,
  Osceola, Ind.; 5Jul47; EP16480.
  Close score: SATB.
  Lay Your Burdens on Me ... [by]
  Geo. W. Mills, arr. by Haldor
  Lillenas. (In his The Gospel
  in Song. no.16) © George
  Warren Mills, Osceola, Ind.;
  5Jul47; EP16475.
  My Blessed Friend; [by] Geo. W.
  Mills. (In his The Gospel in
  Song. no.5) © George Warren
  Mills, Osceola, Ind.; 5Jul47;
  EP16473. Close score: SATB.

Oh! Yes We Will; [by] Geo. W.
  Mills. (In his The Gospel in
  Song. no. 26) © George Warren
  Mills, Osceola, Ind.; 5Jul47;
  EP16482. Close Score: SATB
Shining Jewels; [by] Geo. W.
  Mills, [words by] John J. Kwist.
  (In his The Gospel in Song.
  no.21) © George Warren Mills,
  Osceola, Ind.; 5Jul47; EP16478.
  Close score: SATB
The Whispering Woo; [by] Geo. W.
  Mills. (In his The Gospel in
  Song. no.22) © George Warren
  Mills, Osceola, Ind.; 5Jul47;
  EP16479. Close score: SATB.
MILLS, IRVING.
  New Orleans Masquerade; by
  Irving Mills and Joseph James
  Meissner ... arr. by "Zep"
  Meissner. © American Academy
  of Music, inc., New York;
  4Aug47; EP16503. Piano-con-
  ductor score (orchestra) and
  parts.
MILLS, KATHERINE MAE, 1891-
  One Day; [by] Mae Mills, [words
  by] Mrs. Maurice E. Tipton.
  (In Mills, George Warren. The
  Gospel in Song. no.8) © Mae
  Mills, Osceola, Ind.; 5Jul47;
  EP16474. Close score: SATB.
  Won't You Come to the Savior; [by]
  Mae Mills. (In Mills, George
  Warren. The Gospel in Song.
  no.25) © Katherine Mae Mills,
  Osceola, Ind.; 5Jul47; EP16481.
  Close score: SATB.
MILLS, MAE.
  See Mills, Katherine Mae.
MILTON, JAY.
  Red Hair and Green Eyes; words and
  music by Spude Cooley and Jay
  Milton. © Hill and Range Songs,
  inc., Hollywood, Calif.; 30Jul47;
  EP16047.
MILYUTIN, Y
  My Trusty Gun; words by Uralsky,
  English adaptation by Olga Paul,
  [music by] Y. Milyutin. (In
  Haywood, Charles, ed. Art Songs
  of Soviet Russia, p. 22-23) ©
  Edward B. Marks Music Corp.,
  New York; 16Sep47; on English
  adaptation; EP17179. English
  and Russian words.
MINGS, ROCKWELL.
  The Girl in the Valley; words by
  Rockwell Mings and Joe Westray,
  music by Rockwell Mings. [c1946]
  © Nordyke Publishing Co., Los
  Angeles; 14Jan47; EP20346.
MIRAMONTES R., ARNULFO, 1882-
  Adagio Cantabile ... para piano
  [by] Miramontes. © Arnulfo Mira-
  montes, Mexico City; 30Dec46; EP6781.
  Alado y Breve Primor ... [words by]
  F. M. de Olaguibel, [music by]
  Arnulfo Miramontes. © Arnulfo
  Miramontes, Mexico City; 30Dec28;
  EP7147.
  (Anáhuac) Minuetto (de la opera
  "Anáhuac") para piano, [by]
  Miramontes. © Arnulfo Miramon-
  tes, Mexico City; 30Sep47;
  EP6783.
  (Anáhuac) "Respiro"; [words by F.
  A. de Icaza] "Fugas"; [with
  words] y "Serenata"; [words by
  J. L. Mariscal] (De la opera,
  "Anáhuac") [by] Miramontes ...
  para canto y piano. © Arnulfo
  Miramontes, Mexico City; 30Sep47;
  EP6785.
  Arrulladora; en modo hipodorico,
  no. 4. [Op. 70. By] Miramontes.
  © Arnulfo Miramontes, Mexico
  City; 30Dec46; EP7146.
  Arrulladora; en sol bemol no.3,
  para piano. [Op.82,no.3. By]
  Miramontes. © Arnulfo Miramon-
  tes, Mexico City; 30Dec42;
  EF6786.

Dos Miniaturas: Arrulladora. [Op.
  123, no. 2] Vals. [Op. 122, no.
  1. By] Miramontes. © Arnulfo
  Miramontes, Mexico City;
  30Dec38; EP6779. For piano
  solo.
Eco. [Op. 69] Inquietud. [Op.
  88] Para piano, [by] Miramontes.
  © Arnulfo Miramontes, Mexico
  City; 30Dec46; EP7144.
Fugas. See his Anáhuac.
Hoja de Album; [by] Arnulfo Mira-
  montes R. Op. 11. [México, A.
  Wagner y Levien Sucs.] © Ar-
  nulfo Miramontes, Mexico City;
  30Dec20; EP7030. For piano solo.
"Las Hojas Caen;" romanza para
  canto y piano. Op. 77. [By]
  Miramontes, letra de Alfonso
  Iberri. © Arnulfo Miramontes,
  Mexico City; 30Sep47; EP6784.
Intermezzo en la. Momento Musical,
  no. 2. Momento Musical, no. 3.
  [By] Miramontes, para piano.
  © Arnulfo Miramontes, Mexico
  City; 30Dec46; EP7033.
Mazurka-Estudio; para piano, por
  A. Miramontes. © Arnulfo Mira-
  montes, Mexico City; 30Dec28;
  EF7145.
Minueto en fa para piano, [by]
  Miramontes. © Arnulfo Mira-
  montes, Mexico City; 30Dec28;
  EF6782.
Minuetto. See also his Anáhuac.
Minuetto; para piano, por A. Mira-
  montes. © Arnulfo Miramontes,
  Mexico City; 30Dec28; EF7143.
Momento Musical, no. 1. "Para
  Elvirita." [By] Miramontes, para
  piano. © Arnulfo Miramontes, para
  piano. © Arnulfo Miramontes,
  Mexico City; 30Dec46; EP7032.
Ninfas; para piano, por A. Mira-
  montes. © Arnulfo Miramontes,
  Mexico City; 30Dec46; EP7140.
El Niño ... [by] Arnulfo Mira-
  montes R. Op. 24. [México,
  A. Wagner y Levien Sucs.] © Ar-
  nulfo Miramontes, Mexico City;
  30Dec20; EP7029. For piano solo.
  Pastores; para piano, por A. Mira-
  montes. © Arnulfo Miramontes,
  Mexico City; 30Dec28; EF7148.
Porqué? ... [by] Arnulfo Mira-
  montes R. Op. 19. [México, A.
  Wagner y Levien Sucs.] © Ar-
  nulfo Miramontes, Mexico City;
  30Dec20; EP7031. For piano solo.
Preludio, núm.1; para piano, por
  A. Miramontes. © Arnulfo Mira-
  montes, Mexico City; 30Dec28;
  EF7141.
Preludio, núm.2; para piano, por
  A. Miramontes. © Arnulfo Mira-
  montes, Mexico City; 30Dec28;
  EF7142.
Preludio num. 3 en la menor, [by]
  Miramontes. [Op.92, no.3]
  © Arnulfo Miramontes, Mexico
  City; 30Dec38; EP6780. For
  piano solo.
Respiro. See his Anáhuac.
Serenata. See his Anáhuac.
MIREILLE, pseud. See
  Hartusch, Mireille.
MIROUZE, MARCEL, 1906-
  Humoresque; [by] M. Mirouze. ©
  Alphonse Leduc & Co., Editions
  musicales, Paris; 28Mar47;
  EP6423. Score (clarinet and
  piano) and part.
  Prélude, Thème et Variations; [by]
  Marcel Mirouze. © Editions Max
  Eschig, Paris; 25May46; EP7230.
  Score (double-bass and piano) and
  part.
MITCHELL, B   M
  Pearl; words and music by B. M.
  Mitchell. © Nordyke Publish-
  ing Co., Los Angeles; 31Jul47;
  EP20487.

MITCHELL, ROS. See
Mitchell, Robert Bostwick.

MITCHELL, CYRIL J
Rilloby-Rill; [by] Cyril J.
Mitchell, [words by] Henry New-
bolt. © The Oxford University
Press, London; 17Jul47; EF6135.
Score; unison chorus and piano;
melody also in tonic sol-fa
notation.

MITCHELL, GERALDINE.
Was It September? Words and music
by Jerry Mitchell. © Nordyke
Publishing Co., Los Angeles;
24May47; EP16914.

MITCHELL, JERRY. See
Mitchell, Geraldine.

MITCHELL, JOSEPH BLAINE.
Loved Only by You; words and music
by Joseph Blaine Mitchell ...
arr. by David Gussin. © Joseph
Blaine Mitchell, Hollywood,
Calif.; 9Sep47; EP16999.

Sentimental Bee; words and music
by Joseph Blaine Mitchell,
[arr. by David Gussin] ©
Joseph Blaine Mitchell, Hollywood, Calif.; 24Sep47; EP17651.

MITCHELL, MAE GERTRUDE, 1915-
Oh! Willie! I'm Waitin'; words
and music by Fred G. Moritt
[and] Mae Mitchell. © Lyric
Music Publishers, inc., New
York; 11Aug47; EP16334.

MITCHELL, R   C
Winds of the Rolling Prairies;
words and music by R. C.
Mitchell. © Nordyke Publishing
Co., Los Angeles; 11Jun47;
EP16959.

MITCHELL, ROBERT BOSTWICK, 1912-
Call to Worship; (church call)
S.A.T.B., words and vocal arr.
by Bob Mitchell. © Neil A. Kjos
Music Co., Chicago; 10Oct47; on
words & arrangement; EP18819.

MITTLER, FRANZ, 1893-
The Echo of a Whisper ... lyric by
Albert Gamse, music by Franz
Mittler. © Edward B. Marks
Music Corp., New York; 12Nov47;
EP18668.

The Happy Family ... [by] Franz
Mittler. (In Hirschberg, David,
ed. and comp. Pieces Are Fun.
bk. 1, p. 46-47) © Musicord
Publications, New York;
21Jul47; EP15947. For piano
solo.

Junior American Piano Concerto;
for two pianos. © Musicord
Publications, New York; 22Jul47;
EP15859. Score: piano 1-2.

Manhattan Suite; by Franz Mittler.
Cover design by Robert W. Loutrel.
© Musicord Publications, New
York; 24Aug47; EP16574. For
piano solo.

Suite in 3/4 Time; by Franz Mittler.
Cover design by Robert W. Loutrel.
© Musicord Publications, New York;
24Aug47; EP16575. For piano solo.

MIZZY, VIC.
With a Hey and a Hi and a Ho Ho
Ho! ... Words by Mann Curtis
[pseud.], music by Vic Mizzy,
arr. by Vic Mizzy. © Bourne,
inc., New York; 21Oct47;
EP18165. Piano-conductor score
(orchestra, with words) and
parts.

With a Hey and a Hi and a Ho Ho
Ho! Words by Mann Curtis
[pseud.], music by Vic Mizzy.
© Bourne, inc., New York;
3Nov47; EP18391.

MOBIGLIA, TULLIO, arr.
Dieci arrangiamenti per
Complesso Hot; [by] Tullio
Mobiglia. © Edizioni Casiroli,
s.a.r.l., Milano; 15Jun46; on
eight pieces. Piano-conductor
score (orchestra), and parts.
Two compositions not in L. C.
copy. Contents.- L'Orchestra
Innamorata, by Mario Mellier
(© EF3954) - L'Orchestra
Pazza, by Virgilio Panzuti
(© EF3955) - Quante Stelle,
by Arrigo Pagnini (© EF3956)
- Por Te Bambina, by Tullio
Mobiglia (© EF3957) Pel dì
Carota, by Geo Dan (© EF3958)
- Mezza Bottiglia d'Aria, by
Tullio Mobiglia (© EF3959) -
Alì Babà, by Tullio Mobiglia
(© EF3960) - Ti Sogno Bambina,
by Tullio Mobiglia (© EF3961)

MOCCIOLA, JOSÉ.
Oigan Amigos ... letra de Juan M.
Pinto y Andrés Sanguinetti,
música de José Mocciola. © Editorial Argentina de Música Internacional, s. de r. ltda., (EDAMI)
Buenos Aires; 27Aug47; EF6698.

MODIN, STAN.
Cupid's Got Me Corralled; words
and music by Stan Modin.
© Nordyke Publishing Co., Los
Angeles; 24Jul47; EP16960.

MOERAN, E   J   1894-
Concerto for violoncello and orchestra, by E. J. Moeran. © Novello &
Co., ltd., London; on piano score
and part for violoncello solo,
8Dec47; EF7359, 7360. Score (violoncello and piano) and part.

Fantasy Quartet; [by] E. J.
Moeran. © J. & W. Chester, ltd.,
London; 28Aug47; EF6631.
Miniature score: oboe, violin,
viola and violoncello.

Rahoon; the words by James Joyce,
set to music by E. J. Moeran.
© The Oxford University Press,
London; 3Jul47; EF6128.

MOFFAT, ALFRED, 1866-   arr.
The Lake ... ancient melody arr.
by Alfred Moffat. © The Arthur
P. Schmidt Co., Boston; 1Jul47;
on arrangement; EP15390.
Score: SA and piano.

MOISE, WILF.
My Saddle, My Broncho and You;
lyric by Artie Williams, melody
by Wilf Moise, arr. by Joe Leacsak. © United Music, inc.,
Pittsburgh; 10Oct47; EP20261.

MOKREJS, JOHN.
Valčik; in E flat for piano by
John Mokrejs. © J. Fischer &
Bro., New York; 9Sep47; EP17711.

MOM, MARIA MATILDE.
Como Te Quiero! ... De María
Matilde Mom. [c1942] ©
Editorial Julio Korn, Buenos
Aires; 12Mar45; EF6921. For
voice and piano.

MONACO, JAMES V
What a Fool I Have Been; lyric by
Ned Washington, music by James
V. Monaco. © James V. Monaco,
inc., New York; 16Oct47;
EP18272.

MONFORT, JEROME.
My Heart Is Yours. (Lejos De Ti)
Words and music by Marjorie
Harper [and] Jerome Monfort.
© Hytvoc, inc., New York;
10Jul47; EP18270.

MONFRED, AVENIR DE, 1903-
In Paradisum; pièce pour orgue par
Avenir de Monfred. Paris,
Éditions Salabert. © Salabert,
inc., New York; 16Jul47; EF7252.
For organ solo.

Une Jeune Fille Française ... petite
suite pour piano par Avenir de
Monfred. © Salabert, inc., New
York; 16Jul47; EF7224.

Moments Mystiques; sept petites
pièces pour orgue, par Avenir
de Monfred. © Salabert, inc.,
New York; 17Jul47; EF7253.

A Recital for Children. (Un Récital
pour Enfants) Suite pour piano
par Avenir de Monfred. © Salabert,
inc., New York; 16Jul47; EF7254.

MONGE, CHUCHO. See
Monge, Jesús.

MONGE, JESÚS.
A Todo Mecate ... Letra y música
de Chucho Monge (Jesús Monge)
© Promotora Hispano Americana
de Música, s.a., México;
22Jul47; EF5821.

El Colmenar ... letra y música de
Chucho Monge (Jesús Monge)
© Promotora Hispano Americana
de Música, s.a., México; 29Jul47;
EF6198.

"Dos Amores" y "Desde Cuándo" ...
letra y música de: Chucho Monge
(Jesús Monge) © Promotora His-
pano Americana de Música, s.a.,
México; 27Aug47; on 2 songs;
EF6721-6722.

MONK, WILLIAM H
Abide with Me ... for choir (S.A.
T.B.) and congregation [by]
William H. Monk ... arr. by W.
B. Olds, [words by] Henry F.
Lyte. © Hall & McCreary Co.,
Chicago; 28Nov47; on arrangement;
EP19800.

MONNOT, MARGUERITE, 1903-
C'Est Merveilleux. See her Étoile sans
Lumière.

C'Était un Jour de Fête; paroles
d'Édith Piaf [pseud.], musique
de M. Monnot. © Éditions Micro,
Paris; 8Oct41; EF7325.

Le Chant du Pirate. See her Étoile sans
Lumière.

Elle A ... paroles de Édith
Piaf [pseud.], musique de
Marguerite Monnot. [c1946]
© Éditions Paul Beuscher, Paris;
10Jul45; EF6463.

(Étoile sans Lumière) Adieu Mon
Coeur ... du film "Étoile sans
Lumière"; paroles de Henri
Contet, musique de Marguerite
Monnot. © Éditions Paul Beuscher,
Paris; 2Jan46; EF6461.

(Étoile sans Lumière) C'Est Mer-
veilleux, du film, "Étoile sans
Lumière"; paroles [by] Henri
Contet, musique [by] Marguerite
Monnot. © Éditions Paul
Beuscher, Paris; 10Dec45; EF6458.

(Étoile sans Lumière) Le Chant du
Pirate, du film, "Étoile sans
Lumière"; paroles [by] Henri
Contet, musique [by] Marguerite
Monnot. © Éditions Paul
Beuscher, Paris; 2Jan46; EF6460.

(Étoile sans Lumière) Meringe, du
film "Étoile sans Lumière";
paroles de: Henri Contet, musique
de: Marguerite Monnot. ©
Éditions Paul Beuscher, Paris;
25Oct46; EF6586.

La Grande Cité; paroles de Édith
Piaf [pseud.], musique de Mar-
guerite Monnot. © Éditions
Paul Beuscher, Paris; 10Jul45;
EF6465.

Mariage. See her Étoile sans Lumière.

Le Petit Homme; paroles de Henri
Contet, musique de Marguerite
Monnot. © Arpège Édition
Musicale, Paris; 27Feb47;
EF6445.

MONREAL, GENARO, 1894-
Ah! Les Femmes! (Chinita Chula...)
... Paroles espagnoles de Land-
cira [pseud.], paroles fran-
çaises de Chamrleury [pseud.]
& Liogar [pseud.] Musique de
Monreal & Arsque. © (Editions
Espagnoles) Julio Garzon, Paris;
27Jun47; EF6483.
MONROE, BILL.
Good-bye, Old Pal; words and music
by Bill Monroe. © Peer Inter-
national Corp., New York;
25Nov47; EP19832.
MONTA, F   H
In the Valley of Daffodils;
music by F. H. Monta, words by
Nettie May Berga. © Nordyke
Publishing Co., Los Angeles;
14Jun47; EP17602.
MONTBRUN, RAYMOND GALLOIS- See
Gallois-Montbrun, Raymond.
MONTEVERDI, CLAUDIO, 1567-1643.
Le Combat de Tancrède et Clorinde.
... Poème de Torquatt. Tasso,
réduction pour chant et piano
du G. Francesco Malipiero,
adaptation française de Xavier
de Courville. © Heugel & Cie,
Paris; 14Mar47; on arrangement
& adaptation; EF6499. Piano-
vocal score; French and Italian
words.
MONTGOMERY, BRUCE.
As Joseph Was A-walking; carol
for treble solo, mixed voices
and organ, [by] Bruce Mont-
gomery, the words from Hone's
Ancient Mysteries Described.
© The Oxford University Press,
London; 5Jun47; EF6118.
Fair Helen; song, words anonymous,
music by Bruce Montgomery. ©
Novello & Co., ltd., London;
10Oct47; EF6883.
MONTGOMERY, CECIL R
Alone with the Moon; words and
music by Cecil R. Montgomery.
© Nordyke Publishing Co.,
Los Angeles; 22Apr47; EP17585.
MONTGOMERY, LENORE, pseud. See
Fletcher, Leila.
MONTI, VITTORIO.
Czardas; [by] Vittorio Monti,
special arrangement for accordion
by Charles Magnanto. © Chart
Music Publishing House, inc.,
Chicago; 23Jul47; on arrangement;
EP15968.
MOODY, CLYDE, 1917-
Clyde "Caroline" Moody's Song
Folio; [words and music by Clyde
Moody, [wallace Fowler, Zeb
Turner and others] © Wallace
Fowler Publications, Nashville;
21Jul47; EP15736.
Lonely Broken Heart; words and
music by Gabriel Tucker [and]
Clyde Moody. © Peer Interna-
tional Corp., New York; 23Sep47;
EP17852.
MOOR, SYLVIA DONALDSON.
Wonder If You Know; words and music
by Sylvia Donaldson Moor. ©
Nordyke Publishing Co., Los An-
geles; 15Aug47; EP19634.
MOORE, BILL.
The Navy Blues; words and music by
Bill Moore. © Nordyke Publishing
Co., Los Angeles; 12Apr47;
EP16792.
MOORE, DOUGLAS.
Symphony in A Major; [by] Douglas
Moore. © G. Schirmer, inc.,
New York; 17Jul47; EP17048.
Miniature score.
MOORE, ERNEST A.
Still, Still with Thee; anthem
for S.A.T.B., words by H.B.
Stowe, music by Ernest A.
Moore. © Gordon V. Thompson,
ltd., Toronto; 16Jun47;
EF3942.

MOORE, JOHN, pseud.   See
Verrall, John.
MOORE, JUANITA, 1917-
Lee and Juanita's Songs of Home
and the Hills; [by Juanita
Moore] [n.p.] L. and J. Moore,
[c1940] © Juanita Moore, Charles-
ton, W. Va.; 24Sep47; EP18156.
Melody and chord symbols, with
words.
MOORE, PHIL.
I Feel So Smoochie; words and
music by Phil Moore. © Bregman,
Vocco and Conn, inc., New York;
26Nov47; EP19231.
MOORE, RALPH EUGENE.
The One Girl; words and music by
Ralph Eugene Moore. [c1946]
© Nordyke Publishing Co., Los
Angeles; 21Aug47; EF16604.
MOORE, RAYMON.
Sweet Marie; words by Cy Warman,
music by Raymon Moore, arr.
[and lyrics adapted] by the
Andrews Sisters. © Blossom
Music Corp., New York; 18Aug47;
on arrangement and adaptation
of lyrics; EP16398.
MOORE, RAYMOND.
(Life with Father) Sweet Marie;
from ... [the film] "Life with
Father;" words by Cy. Warman,
music by Raymond Moore [arr. by
Chris Langdon] © Chappell & Co.,
ltd., London; 29Aug47; on arrange-
ment; EF6395.
Sweet Marie; words by Cy Warman,
music by Raymond Moore, [arr. by
John Bach] © Calumet Music Co.,
Chicago; 17Nov47; on guitar
chords & piano arrangement;
EP18976.
Sweet Marie.   See his Life with Father.
MOORE, THURSTON W   1926-
Santa's on His Way; [by] T. Moore.
© Thurston Moore, Covington, Ky.;
2Dec47; EP19199. For voice and
piano, with chord symbols.
MOORE, WILTON.
The Chocolate Choo-Choo; words
and music by Ted Varnick and
Wilton Moore. © Lombardo
Music, inc., New York; 16Oct47;
EP18227.
MOOSE, C   EDGAR.
The West Is in My Soul; words &
music by Dale W. Starry and C.
Edgar Moose. © Nordyke
Publishing Co., Los Angeles;
3Dec46; EP19397.
MOPPER, IRVING, 1914-
And in That Day; for three-part
chorus of women's voices with
soprano solo and piano accom-
paniment [by] Irving Mopper,
text from Isaiah, chap. XII,
verses 1, 2, 4 and 6. © The
Boston Music Co., Boston;
30Sep47; EP17744.
The Lemon-colored Dodo; song for
voice and piano. [Text anonymous,
music] by Irving Mopper. © The
Boston Music Co., Boston; 12Sep47;
EP16351.
Play Me a Duet; five duets for one
piano, four hands, by Irving
Mopper. © The Boston Music Co.,
Boston; 12Sep47; EP17304.
Play Me a Mode; eight easy
pieces for piano by Irving
Mopper. © The Boston Music
Co., Boston; 11Aug47; EP16295.
MOQUIN, AL, 1881-
Garden of Love; words by John
Alvis, music by Al Moquin.
© Nordyke Publishing co., Los
Angeles; 24Jul47; EP20350.
I Guess I'll Always Love You;
words ... by Marilou Dawn [and]
Don B. Owens, jr. © The La Casa
Del Rio Music Publishing Co.,
inc., Toledo; 15Nov45; EP15604.
For voice and piano, with chord
symbols.

MORAKES, DEMETRIOS NICHOLAOS, 1907-
Elo mazy Mou kai Den Tha Chaeïs
... [words by] Kosta Kophinioti,
[music by] Tokē Morokē. Athēnai,
Ekdoseis Gaïtanou. © Michael
Gaetanos. Athens; 8Mar47; EF6807.
Otan Se Blepo ... etichoi; K.
Kophinioti, G. Oikonomidē;
mousikē; T. Morokē. Athēnai,
Ekdoseis Gaïtanou. © Michael
Gaetanos, Athens; 4May47; EF6808.
MORALES, MARIA TERESA.
Olo-lo-lo. (Forsaken) ... Span-
ish words and music by Maria
Teresa Morales, arr. by Obdulio
Morales, [English] lyric by
Marion Sunshine. © Antobal
Music Co., New York; 1Jul47;
EF15744.
MORALES, OBDULIO.
Dia de Reyes. (Day of Freedom)
· English lyric by Marion Sunshine
... music and Spanish words by
Obdulio Morales. © Antobal
Music Co., New York; 15Nov47;
EP19079.
El Sopón. (Cuban Stew) ... Lyric
by Marion Sunshine ... music &
Spanish words by Obdulio Mora-
les. © Antobal Music Co., New
York; 1Oct47; EP18316.
MORAN, JOHN.
My Lovely World and You; by John
Moran & Henry George, (lyric by
John Moran. © Cinephonic
Music Co., ltd., London; 6May47;
EF6032.
MORATH, LELAH P; pseud. See
Wister, Lelah Isabel (Morath)
MOREL, D'AVIGNON.
The Lord's Prayer; by D'Avignon
Morel. © D'Aignon Morel, Detroit;
28Jul47; EP16007. For voice and
piano.
MORGAN, ALBERT.
My Broken Heart and I; words by
Sylvester Melatti, music by
Albert Morgan. © Nordyke
Publishing Co., Los Angeles;
22Aug47; EP20088.
MORGAN, HAYDN, 1887-
Oo Down, Moses; spiritual, arr.
by Haydn Morgan. [c1935]
© The Raymond A. Hoffman Co.,
Chicago; 1Jun36; EP15577.
Score; chorus (TTBB) and piano
reduction.
MORGAN, HAYDN, 1898-
Christmas Everywhere ... S.S.A.
[by] Haydn Morgan, [words by]
Phillips Brooks. © C. C.
Birchard & Co., Boston; 30Jul47;
EP16488.
MORGAN, OTIS.
When the Robins Come Again; words
and music by Otis Morgan. ©
Nordyke Publishing Co., Los
Angeles; 14Jul46; EP20310.
MORGENSTERN, SAM.
Toccata Guatemala; for piano by
Sam Morgenstern. © Carl Fischer,
inc., New York; 9Dec47; EP19987.
MORILLO, ROBERTO GARCIA.   See
Garcia Morillo, Roberto.
MORIN, DOC WHEELER, 1910-
Information Please! words and
music by Doc Wheeler Morin and
Bill Kenny. © Jaybilee Music
Publishing Co., inc., New York;
on new words; 17Oct47; EP17925.
MORITZ, THEODORE L
The White Cross; words & music by
Theodore L. Moritz, [arr. by
Gertrude E. Reid] © Theodore
L. Moritz, Pittsburgh; 11Oct47;
EP17806.
MORLOTE R   LUIS.
Y Nadie Sabe Nal ... [words and
music by] Rafael Inciarte B. y
Luis Morlote R., arreglo de In-
ciarte. © Peer International
Corp., New York; 23Sep47; EF6718.
Parts; orchestra.

MORRIS, GLADYS ROTH.
Back in Your Loving Arms; words
and music by Gladys Roth Morris.
© Nordyke Publishing Co., Los
Angeles; 10Jun47; EP17575.

MORRIS, KENNETH, 1917-
Come Home ... and I Come to Thee
... words and music by Kenneth
Morris. Chicago, Martin and
Morris Music Studios. © Kenneth
Morris, Chicago; 15Oct47;
EP18178.

Some Glad Happy Day; words and
music by Kenneth Morris.
Chicago, Martin and Morris Music
Studios. © Kenneth Morris,
Chicago; 15Sep47; EP18179.

MORRIS, KENNETH, 1917-   arr.
I'm Going to Move on Up a Little
Higher ... [spiritual] arr. by
Kenneth Morris. © Martin &
Morris Music Studio, Chicago;
11Aug47; on arrangement; EP18267.

MORRISON, ALEX.
Take Me Back to Oklahoma (where
it's North, South, East and West
all rolled together) ... words
and music by Gayle V. Grubb and
Alex Morrison. © Peer International
Corp., New York; 11Jun47; EP15021.

MORTARI, VIRGILIO, 1902-
Due Canti d'Amore; [by] Virgilio
Mortari, [words by Torquato
Tasso and Leonardo Giustinian]
© Carisch, s.a., Milan; 3Nov47;
EF7158. Score: voice and violon-
cello.

Lamenti; [by] Virgilio Mortari;
© Carisch, s.a.; Milan; 3Nov47;
EF7156. For voice and piano.
Contents.- La forte e nova mia
disavventura (Guido Cavalcanti)-
Si ti lascio, mio ben (Parole
popolari italiane)

Piccolo serenata; per violoncello
solo, [by] Virgilio Mortari. ©
Carisch, s.a., Milan; 3Nov47;
EF7157.

Serenate; [by] Virgilio Mortari.
© Carisch, s.a., Milan; 3Nov47;
EF7155. For voice and piano.

Stabat Mater; per soprano, baritono
e orchestra, riduzione per canto
e pianoforte [by] Virgilio Mortari.
© Carisch s.a., Milan; 23Sep47;
on reduction for voice and piano;
EF7166. Score: soprano, baritone
and piano.

MORTENSEN, W   F
Let's Just Say Au Revoir; words
and music by W. F. Mortensen.
© Nordyke Publishing Co., Los
Angeles; 11Aug47; EP17509.

MORTON, FERDINAND JOSEPH, 1885-1941.
(Frog-i-more Rag) The Famous
Frog-i-more Rag; by Ferdinand J.
Morton ... piano solo ... ed. by
J. Lawrence Cook. © R. J.
Carew, Washington, D. C.; 20Jun47;
on arrangement; EP15486.

MORTON, JELLY ROLL. See
Morton, Ferdinand Joseph.

MOSER, DOLORES.
Tears, That Tell Me You're in
Love; words and music by
Donna Kratky and Dolores Moser.
© Nordyke Publishing Co., Los
Angeles; 4Sep47; EP20047.

MOSER, FRANZ, 1880-1939.
(Sextet, strings) Streichsextett,
F dur; für 2 Violinen, 2 Brats-
chen und 2 Violoncelle, von
Franz Moser. Op. 23. Wien, Uni-
versal-Edition. © Associated
Music Publishers, inc., New York;
8Oct19; EF5361. Miniature score.

MOSLEY, SNUB, 1906-
Herman's Boogie; music by Snub
Mosley [and] Herman Flintall,
words by Bill Campbell. ©
Popular Music Co., New York;
13Sep47; EP17227.

MOSSMAN, TED, 1914-
Dedication ... words and music by
Ted Mossman, based on Schumann's
Dedication. © Robbins Music
Corp., New York; 2Jul47; EP15419.

A Love Story: lyric by Ted Mossman,
music by Ted Mossman and Jack
Fina, based on Schumann's piano
concerto in A minor. © Robbins
Music Corp., New York; 2Jul47;
EP15418.

MOSZKOWSKI, MAURICE.
Caprice Espagnol; [by] Maurice
Moszkowski. Op.37. Rev. and ed.
by Maxwell Eckstein. © Carl
Fischer, inc., New York; 12Nov46;
on revision & edition; EP17140.
For piano solo.

MOURANT, WALTER BYRON, 1910-
Swing Low, Sweet Clarinet; by
Walter Mourant. © Stuart Music,
inc., New York; 15Sep47; EP17118.
For voice and piano, with chord
symbols.

MOYA, ROBERTO DE.
Arrimate ... Letra y música de
Roberto de Moya. © Antobal
Music Co., New York; 10Oct47;
EP18317.

Desengaño. (Disappointed); English
lyric by Don Mario, music and
Spanish lyric by Roberto De
Moya. © Antobal Music Co.,
New York; 5Jun47; EP6987.

MOZART, JOHANN CHRYSOSTOM WOLFGANG
AMADEUS, 1756-1791.
Alleluia. See his Exsultate, Jubilate.

(Ave Verum Corpus) Mighty Spirit,
All Transcending. (Ave Verum
Corpus) For three-part chorus
of mixed voices [by] Wolfgang
Amadeus Mozart ... arr. by Vic-
toria Glaser, [words by] Henry
Wilder Foote. © E.C. Schirmer
Music Co., Boston; 20Oct47; on
arrangement; EP18135. English
words.

(Bastien und Bastienne) Intrada;
by Mozart, [from "Bastien" and
"Bastienne"; arr. and ed. by
Robert Ernst Miller] © McKinley
Publishers, inc., Chicago;
8Jul47; EP15529. For piano
solo.

Collection of Dance Airs; by W. A.
Mozart ... For flute, recorder
or oboe and piano, ed. by Reba
Paeff Mirsky. © Hargail Music
Press, New York; 15Aug47; EP16624.
Score and part.

Dance; by A. Mozart ... ed. (i.e.
arr.] by Arcady Dubensky. ©
G. Ricordi & Co., New York;
30Jul47; on arrangement; EP16348.
Score: string orchestra.

(Don Giovanni) Minuet (from the
opera Don Giovanni) [by] W. A.
Mozart, arr. by P. Ballatore.
(In Ballators, Pietro comp. So
Easy, p.17) © Edward B. Marks
Music Corp., New York; 9Dec47;
on arrangement; EP19592. For
piano solo.

(Exsultate, Jubilate) Alleluia;
by W. A. Mozart [from motette
for soprano "Exsultate, Jubilate"] Soprano solo with junior,
intermediate and senior choirs
arr. by Guy Chambers Filkins.
© Belwin, inc., New York;
20Nov47; on arrangement;
EP18797.

Fantasie in F minor; [by] Mozart,
arr. for orchestra by Anthony
Collins. Full score. © Keith
Prowse & Co., ltd., London;
24Sep47; on arrangement; EF6835.

Figaro's Air; [from] Marriage of
Figaro. Minuet; [from] Don
Giovanni, by Mozart; [arr. and
ed. by Robert Ernst Miller]
© McKinley Publishers, inc.,
Chicago; 8Jul47; EP15528. For
piano solo.

Intrada. See his Bastien und Bastienne.

Minuet from "Don Juan"; by Wolfgang Mozart ... arr. by Hugo
Frey. [Words by Elsie-Jean,
pseud.] © Hamilton S. Gordon,
inc., New York; 27Oct47; on
lyrics and arrangement; EP18745.
For piano solo, with words.

Mozart; introducing all Mozart's
greatest works. [Arr. by
Victor Ambroise] © Lawrence
Wright Music Co., ltd., London;
31Oct47; on arrangement; EF6891.
For piano solo.

Mozart's Divertimenti; (7 movements) arr. by Carl A. Rosenthal
for 3 or 4 trumpets or clarinets
with timpani ad lib ... Nos.1
to 6 comprise the complete
divertimento K.188. No.7 is
taken from K.187. © Edwin H.
Morris & Co., inc., New York;
6Oct47; EP18524. Score (3 or 4
trumpets or clarinets) and part
for kettle drums.

(Quartet, oboe & strings) Quintet
in F major; from the Quartet
for violin, viola, cello and
oboe [by] W. A. Mozart,
transcribed by Lucien Cailliet.
© Elkan-Vogel Co., inc.,
Philadelphia; 26Jun47; on arrangement; EP15843. Score
(flute, oboe, clarinet, horn
bassoon) and parts.

(Quartet, oboe & strings) Sonata
after the quartet for oboe and
strings, K.V.370 ... arr. by
W. Salomon, th. oboe part rev.
by Leon Goossens. © Boosey &
Hawkes, ltd., London; 11Jul47;
on arrangement; EF5718. Score
(oboe and piano) and part.

Quintet in F major. See his Quartet,
oboe & strings.

Sinfonia. See his Symphony.

Sonata after the quartet for oboe and
strings. See his Quartet, oboe &
strings.

Twelve Duos; for two French horns,
[by] Wolfgang Amadeus Mozart.
K. 487. With an introduction by
Josef Marx. New York, McGinnis
& Marx. (Music for wind instruments by 18th century masters,
ed. by Josef Marx, no. 4) © Josef Marx, New York; 4Dec47;
on introduction, transposition
& articulation marks; EP20257.

MUELLER, CARL F
Dear Nightingale, Awake; [words]
anon., [music from] Bamberg
Hymn Book (1670), arr. by Carl
F. Mueller. © Carl Fischer,
inc., New York; 28Nov47; on
arrangement; EP20391. Score:
chorus (SA) with piano or organ.

The God of Abraham Praise; for
two-part chorus of treble
voices with piano or organ acc.
(S.A.) Hebrew melody arr. by
Carl F. Mueller ... [words by]
Daniel Ben Judah. © Carl
Fischer, inc., New York;
13Nov47; on arrangement;
EP18867.

Good Christian Men Rejoice; for
two-part chorus of treble
voices with piano or organ acc.
(S.A.) XIV century German melody
arr. by Carl F. Mueller ...med-
ieval Latin carol, tr. by John
M. Neale. © Carl Fischer, inc.,
New York; 13Nov47; on arrangement; EP18866.

Great Is the Lord; for four-part
chorus of mixed voices and junior
choir, with piano or organ acc.
Text from Psalm CXLV, music by
Carl F. Mueller. © Carl Fischer,
inc., New York; 26Nov47; EP19989.

MUELLER, CARL F. Cont'd.
The Marches of Peace; [by] Carl F.
Mueller, (S.A.T.B. divided, a
cappella) [words by John Greenleaf
Whittier] © Carl Fischer, inc.,
New York; 8Sep47; EP18074.
O God, Our Help in Ages Past;
[for] SSA accompanied, [music
arr. by] Carl F. Mueller.
[Words by] Isaac Watts. ©
Harold Flammer, inc., New York;
28Jul47; on arrangement;
EP16254.
We All Believe in One True God;
for four-part chorus of mixed
voices with piano or organ acc.
[by] Carl F. Mueller, [words by]
Tobias Clausnitzer ... chorale
melody from Darmstadt Gesang-
buch, 1699. © Carl Fischer,
inc., New York; 27Oct47; EP18468.
The Wise May Bring Their Learn-
ing; for two-part chorus of
treble voices with piano or or-
gan acc. (S.A.) English tradi-
tional melody arr. by Carl F.
Mueller ... words anonymous.
© Carl Fischer, inc., New York;
13Nov47; on arrangement;
EP18669.
MULDER, HAROLD.
I to You (and you to me) words &
music by Harold Mulder. [c1946]
© Nordyke Publishing Co., Los
Angeles; 16Sep47; EP17912.
MULOT, ARMAND M 1910-
Soirs; trois sonnets d'Albert
Samain extraits du recueil "Au
Jardin de l'Infante", musique
d'Armand A. Mulot. Op. 17. ©
Durand & Cie, Paris; v.1-3,
30Sep47; EF7327, 7300-7301.
Contents.- 1. Calmes aux Quais
Déserts.- 2. Le Séraphin des Soirs.
- 3. Le Ciel Comme un Lac d'Or
Pâle.
MUNDY, JIMMY.
Futile Frustration; by Jimmy
Mundy and Count Basie. © Breg-
man, Vocco and Conn, inc., New
York; 5Dec47; EP19880. Piano-
conductor score (orchestra) and
parts.
MUNIZ PEREZ, JUAN, 1895-
El Golpe Majá ... letra y música
de Juan Muñiz Pérez, arreglo de
F. Formell. © Juan Muñiz-Pérez,
Oriente, Cuba; 12May47; EF7046.
Mi Bayamesa ... letra y música de
Juan Muñiz Pérez, arreglo de F.
Formell. © Juan Muñiz-Pérez,
Oriente, Cuba; 15Oct47; EF7047.
MUNOZ, RAFAEL.
Por Ti. (Someone) ... English
words by Joe Davis, Spanish
words and music by Rafael Muñoz.
© Caribbean Music Co., New York;
12Dec47; EP18956.
Si Pudiera Decirte. (If I could
tell you) ... Spanish words and
music by Rafael Munoz, English
words by Joe Davis. © Caribbean
Music, inc., New York; 22Sep47;
EP17107.
MURENA, TONI, 1915-
Passion ... musique de A. Murena
et J. Colombo. © Editions
Salabert, Paris; 20Jan47;
EF6319. Piano-conductor score
(orchestra) and parts.
MURRAY, ALAN, 1890-
The Constant Flame; words by
Carlene Graham, music by Alan
Murray. © Paterson's
Publications, ltd., London;
1Au 47; EF6908.
MURRAY, CHARLES, 1918-
Beloved, Be Mine; lyric by Marjorie
Markes, music by Charles Murray.
© Edward B. Marks Music Corp.,
New York; 7Jul47; EP15440.

Beloved Be Mine ... Lyric by
Marjorie Markes, music by
Charles Murray, arr. by Paul
Weirick. © Edward B. Marks
Music Corp., New York; 15Jul47;
on arrangement; EP15654. Piano-
conductor score (orchestra, with
words) and parts.
Peace of Mind; by Charles Murray
[and] Bobby Goldman, [words by
Charles Murray] and Henry
Lawrence [pseud.] © Dubonnet
Music Publishing, New York;
26Jun47; EP15298.
MURRAY, JACK, comp.
Songs of Truth for Youth; [by
Eleanor Stephens Murray, and
others] comp. by Jack and
Eleanor Murray. Malverne, N. Y.,
Gospel Songs. © Eleanor S.
Murray, West Collingwood, N. J.;
5Jun47; EP15514. Principally
close score: SATB.
MURRAY, JAMES ALEXANDER.
"Loving Is the Thing To Do"; music
& lyrics by Jimmy Murray.
© James A. Murray Music Corp.,
Boston; 21Jul47; EP17123.
MURRAY, MARK.
My Adorable One; words and music
by Mark Murray. © Kanes Music
Publishers, New York; 18Nov47;
EP20250.
MURRY, TED, 1900-
Betty Blue ... music Ted Murry and
[words by] Raymond Leveen. ©
Ben Bloom Music Corp., New York;
10Oct47; EP19185.
MURTHA, ROBERT WILLIAM, 1915-
Living with a Dream of You; words
and music by Phil Wright and Bob
Murtha. Detroit, Bob Murtha.
© Philip O. Wright & Robert Wm.
Murtha, Detroit; 10Jul47;
EP18253.
MUSALE, EDWARD.
A Secret to Reveal; words and
music by Edward Musale. © Nor-
dyke Publishing Co., Los An-
geles; 3Sep47; EP20019.
MUSET, JOSE, 1890-
(Litany for Organ) Fifteen Organ
Works from the Litany for Organ;
by Rev. Joseph Muset ...
Biographical, historical and
analytical notes by Theodore
Marier ... French translations
by Rev. Angu-M. Portelance. ©
McLaughlin & Reilly Co., Boston;
v.1, 20Jun47; EP15844.
MUSET, JOSEPH. See
Muset, José.
THE MUSICAL SALVATIONIST. © Salva-
tionist Publishing & Supplies, ltd.,
London. Vol. 51, pt. 3-4, comp.
by Bramwell Coles.
MUSORGSKII, MODEST PETROVICH, 1839-1881.
Hopak; [by] M. Moussorgsky ... rev.
and ed. by Maxwell Eckstein.
© Carl Fischer, inc., New York;
14Oct43; on revision & edition;
EP17135. For piano solo.
MUSSON, ESTELLE, 1869-
In June; words by Eva Dean, music
by Estelle Musson. © Estelle
Musson, Akron, Ohio; 20Oct47;
EP18638.
MYERS, HAL.
I Know Why Angels Cry; by Hal
Myers. © Nordyke Publishing
Co., Los Angeles; 3Dec46;
EP16776. For voice and piano,
with chord symbols.
May I Come In out of the Rain?
Words and music by Hal Myers.
© Nordyke Publishing Co., Los
Angeles; 16Dec46; EP16775.
MYERS, MAXINE.
You'll Have Your Dreams; words
and music by Maxine Myers.
© Nordyke Publishing Co., Los
Angeles; 16Jul47; EP17461.

MYROW, JOSEF.
Fare-thee-well, Dear Alma Mater. See
his Mother Wore Tights.
Kokomo, Indiana. See his Mother Wore
Tights.
(Mother Wore Tights) Fare-thee-well,
Dear Alma Mater, from the musical
"Mother Wore Tights," lyric by
Mack Gordon, music by Josef
Myrow. New York Bregman, Vocco
and Conn. © Twentieth Century
Music Corp., New York; 17Jul47;
EP15695.
(Mother Wore Tights) Kokomo,
Indiana, from the ... musical
"Mother Wore Tights," lyric by
Mack Gordon, music by Josef
Myrow. New York, Bregman,
Vocco and Conn. © Twentieth
Century Music Corp., New York;
7Jul47; EP15545.
(Mother Wore Tights) Rolling down
Bowling Green on a Little Two-
seat Tandem, from the ...
musical "Mother Wore Tights,"
lyric by Mack Gordon, music by
Josef Myrow. New York, Bregman,
Vocco and Conn. © Twentieth
Century Music Corp., New York;
14Jul47; EP15681.
(Mother Wore Tights) There's
Nothing like a Song, from the
... musical "Mother Wore Tights,"
lyric by Mack Gordon, music by
Josef Myrow. New York, Bregman,
Vocco and Conn. © Twentieth
Century Music Corp., New York;
14Jul47; EP15683.
(Mother Wore Tights) This Is My
Favorite City, from the ...
musical "Mother Wore Tights,"
lyric by Mack Gordon, music by
Josef Myrow. New York, Bregman,
Vocco and Conn. © Twentieth
Century Music Corp., New York;
14Jul47; EP15682.
(Mother Wore Tights) You Do, from
the ... musical "Mother Wore
Tights," lyric by Mack Gordon,
music by Josef Myrow. New York,
Bregman, Vocco and Conn.
© Twentieth Century Music Corp.,
New York; 7Jul47; EP15546.
On a Little Two-seat Tandem. See his
Mother Wore Tights.
Rolling down Bowling Green on a Little
Two-seat Tandem. See his Mother Wore
Tights.
There's Nothing like a Song. See his
Mother Wore Tights.
This Is My Favorite City. See his
Mother Wore Tights.
You Do. See his Mother Wore Tights.
MYSELS, SAMMY.
The Elephant's Waltz; words and
music by Mart Fryberg, Dick
Sanford and Sammy Mysels. © May-
fair Music Corp., New York;
12Sep47; EP17643.
"Mention My Name in Sheboygan";
[by] Bob Hilliard, Dick Sanford
[and] Sammy Mysels, [piano arr.
by Adrian Harris] © World
Music, inc., New York; 28Jul47;
EP16322. For voice and piano,
with chord symbols.

N

NAGEL, JACK.
I've Been a Good Girl; by Ray
Katz and Jack Nagel. © Encore
Music Publications, inc., New
York; 31Jul47; EP16184. For
voice and piano, with chord
symbols.
NAGLE, WILLIAM S
Hark to the News, Neighbour;
Christmas carol for mixed
voices a cappella, words and mus-
ic by William S. Nagle. © Oliv-
er Ditson Co., Philadelphia;
16Sep47; EP17289.

NAGY, JOHN FRANCIS.
Aladdin's Lamp; by John Nagy,
[words by] Dorothy Carter and
Bill Kenny. © Jaybillee Music
Publishing Co., inc., New York;
29Dec47; on words & music of
verse; EP20134.

NAPOLITANO, EMILIO A 1907-
(Apurimac) Danza de las Bailari-
nas Cortesanas, del poema sim-
fónico-coreográfico "Apurimac,"
sobre la leyenda homónima de H.
Iglesias Villoud. Reducción
para piano [by] Emilio A.
Napolitano. [Op. 5] © Ricordi
Americana, s.a.e.c., Buenos
Aires; 11May45; on arrangement;
EP6988.
(Apurimac) Yaraví, del poema
sinfónico-coreográfico "Apuri-
mac," sobre la leyenda homónima
de H. Iglesias Villoud. Reduc-
ción para piano [by] Emilio A.
Napolitano. [Op. 5] © Ricordi
Americana, s.a.e.c., Buenos
Aires; 27Jul44; on arrangement;
EP6989.
La Canción del Saldan; para canto
y orquesta de camara, reducción
para canto y piano. [Op. 2,
no. 2] (Del poema "Bamba" de
Ataliva Herrera) © Ricordi
Americana, s.a.e.c., Buenos
Aires; 16Jul46; on reduction for
voice and piano; EP6963.
Danza de las Bailarinas Cortesanas.
See his Apurimac.
La Mariposa; cancion para canto
y piano [by] Emilio A.
Napolitano [words by Gaston
Figueira] © Ricordi Americana,
s.a.e.c., Buenos Aires; 28Jun44;
©P6985.
Yaraví. See his Apurimac.

NAPPI, WILLIAM, 1892-
Alabama on Parade; music by Bill
Nappi ... words [by] Herman
Goldstein. © William Nappi
[and] Herman S. Goldstein,
Birmingham, Ala.; 24Jun47;
EP15671.

NARAMORE, ARCH P
The Jayhawk Song; by Arch P.
Naramore. Wichita, Kan., Mid-
west Music Publishers. © Arch
P. Naramore, Wichita, Kan.;
13Sep47; EP17084. For voice and
piano.

NARDI, N
On the Hills of Galilee. Alêv
Giva. Poem by A. Broides;
melody by N. Nardi, transcribed
for ... S.S.A. by Lazar Weiner.
© Transcontinental Music Corp.,
New York; 18Nov47; on arrange-
ment; EP18828.

NASCA, JOSEPH.
The War Polka; words and music
by Joseph Nasca. © Nordyke
Publishing Co., Los Angeles;
25May46; EP19390.

NATILI, G. FABOR, pseud. See
Borgazzi, Fabio.

NAYLOR, ELMER ATKINSON, 1896-
A Joyous Christian ... [by] Elmer
A. Naylor, words by Howard K.
Williams. © Elmer Atkinson Nay-
lor, Philadelphia; 15Dec47;
EP20103. Close score; SATB.
Never without Him ... [words by]
Howard K. Williams ... [music
by] Elmer A. Naylor, Philadelphia;
1Dec47; EP19853. Close score;
SATB.

NEANDER, JOACHIM.
Hark, Ten Thousand Harps and
Voices; SSA accompanied. [Words
by] Thomas Kelly, [music by]
Joachim Neander, arr. by Edgar H.
Aufdemberge. © Harold Flammer,
inc., New York; 14Nov47; on
arrangement; EP19155.

NEHA-NEHA. (Now and Then) English
lyric by Olga Prul, [music] traditional. (In Pasti, Barbara, comp.
Memories of Hungary. p. 52-55)
© Edward B. Marks Music Corp.,
New York; 19Nov47; on English
lyric; EP19013.

NEIDLINGER, WILLIAM H
The Birthday of a King; a Christmas song, by William H. Neidlinger, [arr. by Roger C. Wil-
son] © Lorenz Publishing Co.,
Dayton, Ohio; 10ct47; on arrangement; EP17883.
The Birthday of a King; S.S.A.
[by] W. H. Neidlinger, arr.
H. D. McKinney. © J. Fischer &
Bro., New York; 27Aug47; on
arrangement; EP17269.

NEILLY, THERESA A
Jeanie; words & music by
Theresa A. Neilly. © Nordyke
Publishing Co., Los Angeles;
11Oct46; EP19944.

NEILSON, LENORD C 1887-
Song of the Mourning Doves; [words
and music by Lenord C. Neilson.
c1946] © Lenord C. Neilson,
Salt Lake City; 1Feb47; EP14477.
Score: SSSAAA and piano.

NELSON, EDWARD G 1886-
Dangerous Ground; words and music
by Steve Nelson and Milton Leeds
[pseud.] & Ed Nelson, jr. © Hill
and Range Songs, inc., Hollywood,
Calif.; 26Jun47; EP15519.
I've Got a Feelin' (somebody's
steelin' my darlin') words and
music by Milton Leeds [pseud.],
Fred Wise, Steve and Ed Nelson.
© Hill and Range Songs, inc.,
Hollywood, Calif.; 15Oct47;
EP18088.
Pretty Kitty Kelly; by Harry Pease
and Ed. G. Nelson, with solovox
arrangement [by Walter C. Simon,
new arrangement by Lindsay
McPhail, Rev. ed.] © Steany
Music Corp., New York; 15Dec46;
on new words & music & arrangement; EP18381. For voice and
piano, with chord symbols.

NELSON, GUSTAV, 1905-
O Vermeland; SATB a cappella.
Text from the Swedish of A. Fryxell; Swedish folk song arr. by
Gustav Nelson. © Harold Flammer,
inc., New York; 14Nov47; on
arrangement; EP19150.

NELSON, KEN. See
Nelson, Kenneth Francis.

NELSON, KENNETH FRANCIS, 1911-
Bats in Your Belfry; words by Billy
Fairmann, music by Ken Nelson.
© Tex Ritter Music Publications,
inc., New York; 1Jul47; EP15343.
Feelin' My Heart; lyric [by]
Billy Fairmann, music [by] Ken
Nelson [and] Fred Halle.
© Century Songs, inc., Chicago;
10Jul47; EP15559. Melody and
chord symbols, with words.
"Howdy, Friends, Good Evenin'
Neighbors"; lyrics [by] Billy
Fairmann [and] Randy Lake
[pseud.], music [by] Ken Nelson.
© Century Songs, inc., Chicago;
10Jul47; EP15562. Melody and
chord symbols, with words.
If It Hadn't Been for You; words
by Billy Fairmann, music by Ken
Nelson. © Century Songs, inc.,
Chicago; 18Nov47; EP20503.
"If You Don't Love Me;" words by
Billy Fairmann, music by Hal
Johnson [pseud.]. © Century
Songs, inc., Chicago; 1Oct47;
EP17667. Melody and chord
symbols, with words.

"Lonely Trail" (of memory) words
by Billy Fairmann, music by
Ken Nelson. © Century Songs,
inc., Chicago; 1Oct47;
EP17666. Melody and chord
symbols, with words.
"This Suspense Is Killin' Me;"
words by Billy Fairmann, music
by Ken Nelson. © Century Songs,
inc., Chicago; 17Nov47; EP18754.
Melody and chord symbols, with
words.
Where the Moon Plays Peek-a-boo
(Back of the Hills); lyric by
Dave Davis [pseud.], music by
Ken Nelson. © Century Songs,
inc., Chicago; 7Jul47; EP15561.
You Cooked Your Goose; lyric [by]
Billy Fairmann. © Century
Songs, inc., Chicago; 10Jul47;
EP15560. Melody and chord
symbols, with words.

NELSON, LOIS ISABELLE, 1927-
Mighty Pelicans ... words and
music by Lois Nelson ... arr.
by John Epley. © The Latin Club,
Klamath Union High School,
Klamath Falls, Or.; 28May47;
EP15732.

NELSON, MARDELLE.
No Heart at All; words and music
by Mardelle Nelson. © Nordyke
Publishing Co., Los Angeles;
28Mar47; EP16747.

NELSON, ROBIN H
Love's Awakening; words by Robin
H. Nelson & John Reed, music by
Robin H. Nelson. © Nordyke
Publishing Co., Los Angeles;
2Sep47; EP19968.

NELSON, STANLEY.
Get Swing Going; by Stanley Nelson,
tutor for violin. © Cinephonic
Music Co., ltd., London; 14Oct46;
EP6045.

NELSON, STEVE.
How Come the Mortgage Got Paid?
Words and music by Bob Hilliard,
Dave Mann and Steve Nelson. ©
World Music, inc., New York;
18Jun47; EP15885.

NEPPER, CHARLES. See
Nepper, James Charles.

NEPPER, JAMES CHARLES, 1910-
Baby, Baby, to Love You; (The
"ology" song) words and music
by Charles Nepper. (In Koletka,
Elizabeth. The Reflections of
a Teacher. p.50-52) © James
Charles Nepper, Huntington,
W. Va.; 6Oct47; EP18812.
Mature Theme ... [by] Charles
Nepper. (In Koletka, Elizabeth.
The Reflections of a Teacher.
p.49) © James Charles Nepper,
Huntington, W. Va.; 6Oct47;
EP18811. For piano solo.

NESS, CLARKE VAN, pseud. See
Clarke, C. Van Ness.

NETTLES, WILLIAM EDWARD, 1895-
High Falutin' Mama; words and mu-
sic by Bill Nettles. © Peer
International Corp., New York;
25Nov47; EP19845;
Hungry; words and music by Bill
Nettles. © Peer International
Corp., New York; 25Nov47;
EP19830.

[NEUBERGER, JEAN BERNARD DANIEL]
1891-
Il Revait; paroles de Robert
Malleron, musique de Jean
Lenoir [pseud.] © Smyth,
Paris; 28Apr47; EF5945.
L'Oasis du Bonheur; paroles de
Maurice Aubret, musique de Jean
Lenoir [pseud.] © Publications
Raoul Breton & Co., Paris;
21Jan51; EF6309.

322

[NEUBERGER, JEAN BERNARD DANIEL] Cont'd.
Ta Viox N'était Plus la Même;
paroles de Léo Lelièvre,
fils, musique de Jean Lenoir
[pseud.] © Smyth, Paris;
28Apr47; EF5944.

[NEUMAN, ANDRÉ] 1906-
Dans la Fumée des Cigarettes ...
paroles de Louis Poterat,
musique de André Lodge [pseud.]
© Les Editions Metropolitaines,
Paris; 30Sep46; EF5925. Score
(voice and piano, with chord
symbols) and voice part.

NEVIN, ETHELBERT WOODBRIDGE, 1862-
1901.
Little Boy Blue; by Ethelbert
Nevin ... arr. by Hugo Frey.
[Words by Eugene Field] ©
Hamilton S. Gordon, inc., New
York; 22Oct47; on arrangement;
EP18744. For piano solo, with
words.

Narcissus; [by] Ethelbert Nevin,
arr. by Harold L. Walters. ©
Rubank, inc., Chicago; 10Oct47;
on arrangement; EP17679.
Condensed score (band) and
parts.

Narcissus; by Ethelbert Nevin, transcribed by Herman A. Hummel. ©
Rubank, inc., Chicago; 1Nov47;
on arrangement; EP19211. Score
(cornet or trumpet and piano) and
part, with part for cornet or
trumpet 2 ad lib.

Narcissus; by Ethelbert Nevin.
[Op.13, no.4. Arr. by Hugo Frey]
© Hamilton S. Gordon, inc., New
York; 14Nov47; on arrangement;
EP18741. For piano solo.

Narcissus; [by] Ethelbert Nevin. Op.
13, no. 4. Ed. by Samuel Spivak.
© Edward Schuberth & Co., inc.,
New York; 7Oct47; EP17728. For
piano solo.

Narcissus; by Ethelbert Nevin,
[Op.13, no. 4. Arr. by Walter L,
Rosemont, special lyric by Jack
Edwards] © Edwards Music Co.,
New York; 6Nov47; on simplified
arrangement & new lyrics]
EP18669. Includes version for
voice and piano and parts for
piano and 2 instruments or small
orchestra.

Narcissus; [by] Ethelbert Nevin.
Op.13, no. 4. Simplified by Samuel
Spivak. © Edward Schuberth & Co.,
inc., New York; 6Oct47; EP17729.
For piano solo.

Narcissus; [by] Ethelbert Nevin.
[Op. 13, no. 11] Piano solo
[arr. by] Carl Richter. © Bach
Music Co., owner, Boston; 15Sep47;
on simplified arrangement;
EP17742.

Narcissus; by Ethelbert Nevin,
piano solo, a John W. Schaum
arrangement. © Belwin, inc.,
New York; 20Nov47; on arrangement; EP18806.

NEVIN, MARK.
Piccolo Pete; piano solo by Mark
Nevin. © Schroeder & Gunther,
inc., Rhinebeck, N. Y.; 21Nov47;
EP18837. With words.

NEW SONGS FOR YOUNG PEOPLE. © Salva-
tionist Publishing & Supplies, ltd.,
London; May 1947 issue, 4Jul47;
EF6687. Comp. by Bramwell Coles.

NEWELL, ROBERT C
Golden Sails, Silver Sails; lyric
by Earle C. Anthony, music by
Robert C. Newell. © Broadcast
Music, inc., New York; 6Oct47;
EP17904.

NEWHARD, DANA.
Tell Me; words and music by
Dana Newhard. © Nordyke Publishing Co., Los Angeles;
24Jul47; EP19375.

NEWMAN, ALFRED.
(Captain from Castile) Catana;
theme from the ... picture "Cap-
tain from Castile" ... lyric by
Eddie De Lange, music by Alfred
Newman. New York, Robbins Music
Corp. © Twentieth Century Music
Corp., New York; 5Dec47; EP20011.
Catana. See his Captain from Castile.

NEWMAN, BOB.
Shut Up and Drink Your Beer; words
and music by Bob Newman. © Tim
Spencer Music, inc., Hollywood,
Calif.; 15Dec47; EP20110.

NEWMAN, LIONEL.
My Flame Went Out Last Night;
words by Don George, music by
Lionel Newman. © Jewel Music
Publishing Co., inc., New York;
2Sep47; EP18809.

NEWMAN, MARION A
Open Range A-callin'; words and
music by Bob Newman and Slim
Newman. (In Bob Nolan's Sons of
the Pioneers. p. 40-41) © Tim
Spencer Music, inc., Hollywood,
Calif.; 30Jul47; EP16032.

NEWMAN, RUTH.
I Feel Like Crying; words and
music by Ruth Newman. ©
Nordyke Publishing Co., Los
Angeles; 3Jul47; EP17510.

NEWMAN, SLIM. See
Newman, Marion A

NEWTON, JOHN, 1899-
Guilty of Being in Love; lyrics
and music by John Newton. ©
New Harmony Music Publishers,
New York; 29Sep47; EP18312.

NEWTON, JOHN W
"Fight for Jersey!" Words by T.
G. Clarke, music by John W. New-
ton. © Thomas George Clarke,
Charleston, W. Va.; 11Dec47;
EP19620.

NICHOLAS, MORGAN.
England; words by Hugh Lyon, music
by Morgan Nicholas. © Banks &
Son, York, Eng.; 22Oct47;
EF7151. For unison voices and
piano; melody also in tonic sol-
fa notation.

NICHOLS, BOB, pseud. See
Wilkins, Robert Nichols.

NICHOLS, JUNE HOPSON
Roundelay ... by June Hopson
Nichols. © G. Schirmer, inc.,
New York; 25Aug47; EP18449.
Two scores for 2 pianos.

NICHOLS, SAM.
That Wild and Wicked Look in
Your Eye; words and music by
Sam Nichols. © Hill and Range
Songs, inc., Hollywood, Calif.;
18Aug47; EP16543.

NICOLETTI, LEONARD.
Unloved; words by Ken Ferguson,
music by Leonard Nicoletti.
[c1946] © Nordyke Publishing
Co., Los Angeles; 30Jan47;
EP18778.

NICOLO, MARIO.
Le Canzoni di Napoli; (per mando-
lino ... versi e musiche di
Mario Nicolò. © Edward Rossi,
New York; 16Jul47; EF6314.

Le Nuove Canzoni di Mario Nicolò
... versi e musica per
mandolino, violino, fisarmonica
... ecc. Napoli, Edizioni
M.I.A., Musicale italo-
americana di M. Nicolò. ©
Edward Rossi, New York; 11Oct47;
EF6923.

NIEDER, ANTHONY.
Oh Baby, No Baby (can do that to
me) words and music by Anthony
Nieder. © Nordyke Publishing
Co., Los Angeles; 16Jun47;
EP17553.

NIELAND, JOHANNES HARMANNUS IGNATIUS
MARIA, 1903-
Ma Mère l'Oye ... [by] Jan Nieland.
© Edition Heuwekemeyer (Firm
A. J. Heuwekemeyer & B. F. van
Gaal), Amsterdam, The Nether-
lands; 22Aug46; EF5118. For
piano 4 hands.

NIELSEN, HAROLD.
Violin Method for Young People;
especially prepared for beginners in elementary, junior and
senior high schools, by Harold
Nielsen. © H. Nielsen, Trenton,
Mich.; 27Oct47; EP18495.

NIEUMERE, GUSTAVE.
My Rhapsody of Love; by Gustave
Nieumere. © Cinephonic Music
Co., ltd., London; 24Sep46;
EF6628. For voice and piano;
melody also in tonic sol-fa
notation.

NILES, JOHN JACOB, 1892-
Sweet Marie and Her Baby; for two-
part chorus of women's voices
with piano acc., words and
music by John Jacob Niles. ©
G. Schirmer, inc., New York;
27Aug47; on arrangement;
EP18735.

Sweet Marie and Her Baby; for
three-part chorus of women's
voices with piano acc., words
and music by John Jacob Niles.
© G. Schirmer, inc., New York;
27Aug47; on arrangement;
EP18733.

Sweet Marie and Her Baby; for
four-part chorus of mixed voices
with piano acc., words and
music by John Jacob Niles. ©
G. Schirmer, inc., New York;
27Aug47; on arrangement;
EP18734.

NISWANDER, DWIGHT L
Are You Hiding the Word of God?
... [by] Dwight L. Niswander,
[words by] Wesley Duewel.
Columbus, Ohio, Christian
Music Press. © Thomas H.
Hubbard, Columbus, Ohio;
15Jun47; EP16498.

NIVEN, LEWIS.
A Song for the Little Jesus,
Cantico al Nino Dios. [For]
S. S. A. A. Verses 2 and 3 by
Maria de la Luz Grovas ...
Mexican folk song adapted and
arr. for women's voices by
Lewis Niven. © J. Fischer &
Bro., New York; 3Sep47; on
verses 2 & 3, adaptation &
arrangement; EP17384.

NIVERD, LUCIEN, 1879-
Vocalise-Etude; pour voix élevées,
[by] Lucien Niverd. (Répertoire
moderne de vocalises-études;
pub. sous la direction de A. L.
Hettich ... 159) © Alphonse
Leduc & Co., Paris; 30Jun47;
EF6413. For voice and piano.

NOBLE, HAROLD.
Hannaker Mill; part song for male
voices T. T. B. B. (unaccompanied),
words by Hilaire Belloc, music
by Harold Noble. © Ascherberg,
Hopwood & Crew, ltd., London;
16Jul47; EF6371.

Henry before Agincourt; part-song
for male voices (unacc.) words by
John Lydgate ... music by Harold
Noble. © Ascherberg, Hopwood &
Crew, ltd., London; 1Dec47;
EF7365.

NOBLE, MELBA LaFORCE, 1909-
The Man in the Turban; lyric and
music by Melba Noble. © Handy
Brothers Music Co., inc., New
York; 15Sep47; EP17062.

The Noble Accordion Course; [by Melba Noble) © Melba LaForce Noble,
Chicago; 3Dec47; EP20136.

323

NOBLE, THOMAS TERTIUS, 1867- ed.
and arr.
Service Music; for organ, arr.,
ed. and comp. by T. Tertius
Noble. © J. Fischer & Bro.,
New York; 30Sep47; EP17707.

NOBLE, W   S
My Dream; words and music by W.
S. Noble. © Nordyke Publishing
Co., Los Angeles; 30May46;
EP20318.

NOEL, ART.
I Don't Know What It'd Do without
You; by Art Noel, [piano arrangement by Geo. H. Record] ©
Cinophonic Music Co., ltd., London; 6Mar46; EP6044. For voice
and piano, with chord symbols;
melody also in tonic sol-fa
notation.

When London Is Saying Goodnight;
by Art Noel. © Cinophonic
Music Co., ltd., London; 18Jul46;
EP6050. For voice and piano,
with chord symbols; melody also
in tonic sol-fa notation.

NOLAN, BOB.
Ne-Hah-Ned. (Clear Water)
Words and music by Bob Nolan.
© American Music, inc., Holly-
wood, Calif.; 8Aug42; EP16043.
English words.

Old Forgotten Trails; words
and music by Bob Nolan. ©
American Music, inc., Hollywood, Calif.; 8Feb45;
EP16042.

NOLAN, Mrs. E   L
Clear Your Lines Before You Call;
[words and music by Mrs. E. L.
Nolan, arr. by Virginia Davis]
© The Famous Blue Jay Singers,
Chicago; 1Feb47; EP15793.

NOLAN, MICHAEL.
Annie Rooney ... words and music
by Michael Nolan, arr. by Phil
Embury. © Society for the
Preservation and Encouragement
of Barber Shop Quartet Singing
in America, inc., Detroit;
28Sep47; on arrangement;
EP17236. Close score: TTBB.

NOLAN, TOM.
That Gospel Train Is Comin'; by
Sid Prosen and Tom Nolan. ©
Hometown Music Co., inc., New
York; 13Nov47; EP19110. For
voice and piano, with chord
symbols.

NOLDER, MURL.
Baby Ann, Lullaby; words by
Bernadine Minzler, music by
Murl Nolder. Lynchburg, Ohio,
B. Minzler. © Bernadine Minz-
ler & Murl Nolder, Lynchburg,
Ohio; 18Sep47; EP17807.

NOMD, JOHN STANLEY, 1890-
Fun in the Sun at Las Vegas; words
and music by John S. Nord, arr.
by Lou Halmy] © John Stanley
Nord, Las Vegas, Nev.; 15Aug47;
EP16218.

If I Can't Have You; words ... by
Betty [Nord], music [by] John
S. Nord, [arr. by Lou Halmy]
© John Stanley Nord [and] Betty
R. Nord, Las Vegas, Nev.;
28Sep47; EP17908.

[NORDEN, HUGO] 1909-
Allegro Vigoroso; [by] Harold
Parkman [pseud.] © The Arthur P.
Schmidt Co., Boston; 23Sep47;
EP17324. Score (violin and
piano) and part.

Ayre for Dancing; [by] Mary
Norden. © The Arthur P.
Schmidt Co., Boston; 7Aug47;
EP16107. Score (violin and
piano) and part.

Come Hither, Ye Faithful; old
Welsh melody arr. by Hugh
Gordon [pseud.] Words from an
anonymous Latin hymn. © The
Arthur P. Schmidt Co., Boston;
4Sep47; on arrangement; EP16640.
Score: chorus (SA) and piano.

A Merry Tune; [by] Harold
Parkman, [pseud.] © The
Arthur P. Schmidt Co.,
Boston; 7Aug47; EP16110.
Score (violin and piano)
and part.

Jesu, My Lord, My God, My All;
[by] Hugh Gordon, [pseud.]
(based on a French folk-song)
[words] from a 19th century
anonymous poem. © The Arthur
P. Schmidt Co., Boston; 11Jul47;
on arrangement; EP15646. Score:
chorus (SA) and piano.

The Lord Be With Us; [by] Hugh
Gordon, [pseud.] (based on a
Danish folk-song) [words by]
John Ellerton. © The Arthur
P. Schmidt Co., Boston; 11Jul47;
on arrangement; EP15645. Score:
chorus (SA) and piano.

NORDQVIST, GUSTAF.
Ack, Saliga, Saliga; [(words by]
Harriet Löwenhjelm) [music by]
Gustaf Nordqvist, arr. av Karl-
Erik Svedlund. © Nordiska
musikförlaget, a.b., Stockholm;
1Jan46; on arrangement; EP7054.
Close score: mixed chorus.

NORGREN, JERRY.
Rainbow Girl; words and music by
Jerry Norgren. © Nordyke
Publishing Co., Los Angeles;
3Sep47; EP20493.

NORMAN, PIERRE.
The Miracle of the Bells, theme
of the ... picture "The Miracle
of the Bells"; lyric by Russell
Janney, music by Pierre Norman.
© Leo Feist, inc., New York;
24Sep47; EP17700.

NORT, ISABEL VAN. See
Van Nort, Isabel.

NORTH, BILL.
I Shall Remember; words by Ruth
Glenn [pseud.], music by Bill
North. © Nordyke Publishing
Co., Los Angeles; 11Jul47;
EP17512.

NORTON, BOB.
My Baby Doll; lyrics & music by
Hal Clark and Bob Norton. ©
Hillcrest Music Publications,
Omaha; 9Oct47; EP18491.

NORWORTH, JACK.
Shine on, Harvest Moon; by Nora
Bayes and Jack Norworth, [words
by Jack Norworth], T.B.B. arr.
by Douglas MacLean [pseud.]
© Remick Music Corp., New York;
12Dec47; on arrangement;
EP19984.

NORTH, MICHAEL, 1902-
If You Are There ... words by
Henrik Ege, music by Michael
North. [London] Boosey &
Hawkes. © Boosey & Co., ltd.,
London; 12Jun47; EP6080.

NOVAK, GEORGE S
(I've Been Lonely) "Ever Since You
Went Away"; by George S. Novak.
© Century Songs, inc., Chicago;
17Nov47; EP18750. Melody and
chord symbols, with words.

I've Got a Heart (that's broken
in two); by George S. Novak. ©
Century Songs, inc., Chicago;
17Nov47; EP18749. Melody and
chord symbols, with words.

"Mary Had a Little Lamb" (his
love was pure as snow) by George
S. Novak. © Century Songs, inc.,
Chicago; 17Nov47; EP18751.
Melody and chord symbols, with
words.

NOVELLI, SYL. See
Novelli, Sylvester.

NOVELLI, SYLVESTER P
Alone in Spring; lyrics by Sylvia
Dee [pseud.], music by Syl Nov-
elli. © Broadcast Music, inc.,
New York; 1Jul47; EP18199.

I've Done a Lot of Dreaming in My
Day; lyric by Sylvia Dee [pseud.]
music by Syl Novelli. © Broadcast Music, inc., New York;
1Jul47; EP18198.

A Little While from Now; lyric by
Sylvia Dee [pseud.], music by
Syl Novelli. © Broadcast Music,
inc., New York; 1Jul47; EP18202.

No One; lyric by Sylvia Dee
[pseud.], music by Syl Novelli.
© Broadcast Music, inc., New
York; 1Jul47; EP18201.

NOVELLO, IVOR.
Perchance To Dream; selection [by]
Ivor Novello, arr. W. G. Lemon.
(Chappell's Brass and reed band
journal, no. 160) © Chappell &
Co., ltd., London; 14May47; on
arrangement; EP3963. Cornet-
conductor score and parts.

We'll Gather Lilacs, from "Perchance to Dream"; S.A.T.B.;
words and music by Ivor Novello,
arr. by John A. Derbyshire. ©
Chappell & Co., ltd., London;
6Oct47; on arrangement; EP7003.

[NUMSEN, ADENE]
Stay Away from My Man; words and
music by Don A'Dene [pseud.]
© Nordyke Publishing Co., Los
Angeles; 4Sep47; EP20036.

[NUNES, JOHN] 1906-
Remember Denver; [by Mary Douglas,
pseud., cover design by Edward
J. Foth] © John Nunes and
Edward J. Foth, Denver; 10ct47;
EF17827. For voice and piano.

NUÑEZ M   ANTONIO.
Si Volviera a Querer ... [words
and music by] Antonio Nuñez M.
© Editorial Mexicana de Música
Internacional, s. a., Mexico;
14Jul47; EP5805. Condensed
score (orchestra), piano-conductor score and parts.

NUOVE CANZONI, 1947-1948; musiche di:
Bollini ... Ricciardi [and others]
... su versi di ... de Filippis
... Rossetti [and others] Napoli,
Santojanni. © Italian Book Co.,
New York; 1Sep47; EFb617.

NURNBERG, VICTOR.
Dream after Dream; lyric by
Mary de Zevallos, music by
Victor Nurnberg. New York
Tele-Publications. © Mary
de Zevallos and Victor
Nurnberg, New York; 17Jul47;
EP16087.

Hasta la Vista, My Sweet; lyric
by Mary de Zevallos, music
by Victor Nurnberg. New York
Tele-Publications. © Mary
de Zevallos and Victor
Nurnberg, New York; 1Aug47;
EP16088.

Romance in the Rain; lyric by
Mary de Zevallos, music by
Victor Nurnberg. © Tele-
Publications, New York;
17Jul47; EP16086.

When Will You Be Madam? Lyric
by Mary de Zevallos, music
by Victor Nurnberg. New
York, Tele-Publications. ©
Mary de Zevallos and Victor
Nurnberg, New York; 1Aug47;
EP16089.

NUTILE, E
Mother Always Wants to Know.
Mamma Mia, Che Vo Sape? English
lyric by Olga Paul, Italian lyric
by Ferd Russo, music by E. Nutile.
(In Memories of Italy. p.36-39)
© Edward B. Marks Music Corp.,
New York; 16Jul47; on English
lyric; EP15824.

NYGREN, DAVID F
No Theme Can Be Greater; [by]
David F. Nygren, [words by] D.
F. N. Duet: baritone and con-
tralto. © John T. Benson, jr.,
Nashville; 1Aug47; EP18268.
O Wondrous Peace; [by] David F.
Nygren. © John T. Benson, jr.,
Nashville; 1Aug47; EP18269.
Close score: SATB.

NYSTROEM, GOSTA.
Tva Sånger; [by] Gösta Nystroem.
© Föreningen svenska tonsättare,
Stockholm; on 2 songs, 1Jan45.
Contents. - 1. Gubben och Gum-
man Skulle mota Vall (© EF7126)-
2. Nocturne (Anders Osterling)
(© EF7118)

O

OAKES, ROBERT D   1915-
Southwind ... by Robert D. Oakes.
[c1948] © Belwin, inc., New
York; 29Oct47; EP18329. Condensed score (band) and parts.

OAKLAND, BEN.
I'll Dance at Your Wedding; lyric
by Herb Magidson, music by Ben
Oakland. © George Simon, inc.,
New York; 30ct47; EP17665.

O'BRIEN, KATHARINE ELIZABETH, 1901-
When I Set Out for Lyonnesse ...
chorus for treble voices, acc.
(S.S.A.) [by] Katherine E.
O'Brien, [words by] Thomas
Hardy. © Hall & McCreary Co.,
Chicago; 22Aug47; EP17025.

OBRUCA, RUDOLF, 1874-1941.
Slovanský pochod; [by] R. Obruča.
© Jaroslav Stožický, Brno,
Czechoslovakia; 9Jun46; EF5425.
Parts: band.

OCHS, RUDOLPH G
I Dreamed of You (a thousand
years ago) words and music by
Rudolph G. Ochs. © Nordyke
Publishing Co., Los Angeles;
11Jul47; EP17610.
I'm Burning Up with Love for You;
words and music by Rudolph G.
Ochs. © Nordyke Publishing Co.,
Los Angeles; 16Jul47; EP17387.

O'CONNELL, THOMAS, 1897-
That's What Ireland Means to Me;
words and music by Tommy
O'Connell. © Shelby Music
Publishing Co., Detroit; 12Jun47;
EP15385.

O'DELL, ED. See
O'Dell, Edward Oscar.

O'DELL, EDWARD OSCAR.
Voice of the Wind; words by Mrs.
W. C. Henry, music by Ed O'Dell.
© Edward Oscar O'Dell, Lubbock,
Tex.; 14Jun47; EP15470.

O'DONNELL, WALTER.
Little Lamb Polka. © Theodore
Presser Co., Philadelphia;
15Jul47; EP15678. For piano solo.
Neapolitan Festival; piano solo by
Walter O'Donnell. © Theodore
Presser Co., Philadelphia;
31Jul47; EP16338.

OFFENBACH, JACQUES, 1819-1880.
Barcarolle; [by] J. Offenbach, arr.
as played by Victor & Volpe.
c1959. © Albert Rocky Co., New
York; 10Jan40; on arrangement;
EP20181. For 2 guitars.

782058 O-48----8

Barcarolle; [from "Tales of
Hoffmann"] by Jacques Offenbach
... Arr. by Hugo Frey, [words
by Elsie-Jean, pseud.] ©
Hamilton S. Gordon, inc., New
York; 16Jul47; on arrangement &
words; EP15742. For piano solo,
with words.

OFTEDAHL, MARTIN, 1902-
When I Went to See My Nina Gal;
words and music by Martin Ofte-
dahl. © Martin Oftedahl, Eagle
Bend, Minn.; 2Jul47; EP15439.
Melody and words.

OGLE, CAROLINE, 1885-
His Mother's Gone; words and music
by Caroline Ogle. [c1946]
© Caroline Ogle, Spokane;
8Feb47; EP18356. Melody and
chord symbols, with words.
My Boy; words and music by Caroline Ogle. [c1946] © Caroline
Ogle, Spokane; 8Feb47; EP18357.
Melody and chord symbols, with
words.

O'HAGAN, JACK.
Let Me Die with My Boots on;
words and music by Jack
O'Hagan. © D. Davis & Co.,
pty. ltd., Sydney; 15May47;
EF5367.
A Little Ounce of Sunshine (is
worth a ton of rain); words and
music by Jack O'Hagan. © D.
Davis & Co., pty. ltd., Sydney;
15Jun47; EF6305.

O'HARA, ERNIE, 1910-
Headin' for Heaven ... words and
music by Dicksy Ayers and Ernie
O'Hara. © Top Music Publishers,
inc., New York; 19Nov47;
EP18688.

O'HARA, GEOFFREY, 1882-
Lane County Bachelor; [by]
Artells Dickson and Geoffrey
O'Hara. © G. Ricordi & Co.,
New York; 5Sep47; EP17161.
Close score: solo voice
(tenor) and chorus (TTBB)
We Call to Thee (Oh Lord of
men) ... for women's voices
S.S.A., words by Albert F.
Woods, music by Geoffrey
O'Hara. © Volkwein Brothers,
inc., Pittsburgh; 9Sep47;
EP16694.

OLCOTT, CHAUNCEY, d. 1932.
My Wild Irish Rose ... words and
music by Chauncey Olcott. A
Jerry Sears arrangement. © M.
Witmark & Sons, New York;
21Nov47; on arrangement; EP19172.
Piano-conductor score (orches-
tra, with words) and parts.

OLDRATI ROSSI, RENZO, 1905-
Buongiorno, Amore Mio ... [by] R.
Oldrati Rossi, testo di R.
Friggieri. Per una Furtiva
Lagrima ... [by] A. Sala, testo
di A. Dolci. © Odeon, s. a.,
Milan; 8Jul47; EF6192. Piano-
conductor score (orchestra, with
words) and parts.

OLDROYD, GEORGE.
A Hymn to Beauty; a song for
female voices and piano or
small orchestra, [by] George
Oldroyd, [words by] Horne
Ormsby. © The Oxford University Press, London; 26Jun47;
EF6157. Score: SSA and piano.
Paean of Remembrance; 'Let us now
praise famous men' for mixed
voices and orchestra or pianoforte, [by] George Oldroyd.
Words from Ecclesiasticus 44.
© Oxford Univ. Press, London;
28Aug47; EF6660. With piano
accompaniment.

325

OLDS, WILLIAM BENJAMIN, 1874-
The First Christmas Candle;
(S.A.T.B. divided, with narrator,
a cappella) [by] W. B. Olds.
© Carl Fischer, inc., New York;
22Sep47; EP18067.
Let Us Praise God ... for mixed
voices with speech choir or
reader, acc. (S.A.T.B.) [by]
W. B. Olds, [words by] Percy
Dearmer. © Hall & McCreary Co.,
Chicago; 22Aug47; EP17027.
Sun of My Soul ... for choir (S.A.
T.B.) and congregation with so-
prano, alto and tenor solos.
Adapted from Katholisches Gesang-
buch, 1774, arr. by W. B. Olds,
[words by] John Keble. © Hall
& McCreary Co., Chicago;
28Nov47; on arrangement; EP19799.

OLINGER, ANTHONY MATTHIAS, 1885-
Panis Angelicus; for alto or baritone solo with piano or organ acc.,
by Anthony M. Olinger. Sheboygan,
Wis., Zohlen Music Studio [c1945]
© Anthony M. Olinger, Milwaukee;
8Dec47; EP20296.

OLINGHOUSE, MAUD.
Talking to My Baby; words & music
by Maud Olinghouse. © Nordyke
Publishing Co., Los Angeles;
3Dec46; EP20340.

OLIVADOTI, J
Carnival of Roses ... by J.
Olivadoti. © Mills Music, inc.,
New York; 29Aug47; EP17958.
Condensed score (band) and parts.

OLIVEIRA, MILTON DE
Como te the Mardi Gras. (Não
tenho lagrimas) Lyrics by
Ervin Drake and Jimmy Shirl,
[pseud.], music by Max Bulhões
and Milton de Oliveira. © Peer
International Corp., New York;
11Jun47; on English lyric;
EP15615. English words.
Não Tenho Lagrimas ... Letra e
musica de Max Bulhões e Milton
de Oliveira. © Irmaos Vitale,
Sao Paulo, Brazil; 28Dec47;
EF5743.

OLIVER, CHIC.
Shadows; words and music by Chic
Oliver. © Nordyke Publishing
Co., Los Angeles; 3Jul47; EP17397.

OLIVER, HERBERT, 1885-
Looking Down at Me; song, the lyric
by Harry Parr, the music by
Herbert Oliver. © Albert Victor
Broadhurst, London; 5Jul47;
EF6367.
The Song for Me ... words by W. D.
Mathieson, music by Herbert Oliver.
© Keith, Prowse & Co., ltd., Lon-
don; 1Dec47; EF7172.
Vesper Song [and Canadian Boat
Song] Words by Thomas Moore,
music by Herbert Oliver. ©
Keith, Prowse & Co., ltd.,
London; 21Oct47; on arrangement;
EF6911. Score: chorus (TTBB)
and piano; voice parts also in
tonic sol-fa notation.

OLSEN, OTTO NORMAN.
While the Desert Blossoms as a
Rose ... song by Otto Norman
Olsen. © Otto Norman Olsen,
Hollywood, Calif.; 12Nov47;
EP18847.

OLSON, DANIEL.
Så Låt Oss Öppna Snart; (sv. ps.
223: 4 och 5 vers) Advent.
[Music by] Daniel Olson. ©
Nordiska musikförlaget, a.b.,
Stockholm; 1Jan46; EF7055.
Close score: SABar.

OLSON, DAVE, 1910-
Wait'll I Get My Sunshine in the
Moonlight; by Harry Glick,
Jimmy Lambert and Dave Olson.
© Vanguard Songs, Hollywood,
Calif.; 4Jun47; EP16211. For
voice and piano, with chord
symbols.

OLSON, ESTELL CLARA, 1912-
Sweetheart Dream with Me; words
and music by Estell Olson.
[Music arrangement by W. Brad]
© Mrs. Estell Clara Olson,
Edmonton, Alta., Can.; 16Sep47;
EP18788.

OLSON, RAY J
I'm Hitch-hiking to Heaven;
words by Howard D. Hechtner,
music by Ray J. Olson. © Nor-
dyke Publishing Co., Los
Angeles; 14Jun47; EP17547.
A Little Picture Album; by Ray J.
Olson. © Nordyke Publishing
Co., Los Angeles; 5Aug47;
EP19519. For voice and piano,
with chord symbols.

OLSSON, WALTER.
Storgårdsvalsen; musik; Walter
Olsson, text; Helge Sträby,
arrangemang ...B. Ståhlhandske.
© Edition Raoul Henricson,
Örebro, Sweden; 1Jan46; EF7050.
Parts: orchestra.

O'NEAL, BIRDO.
This Is the American Way of Life;
words and music by Birdo O'Neal.
© Nordyke Publishing Co., Los
Angeles; 3Sep47; EP20042.

ORAKTON, E. MARIE See also
Fleury, André, pseud.

[ORAKTON, E   MARIE] 1903-
(Symphony, organ, no. 1) Première
Symphonie, [by] André Fleury
[pseud.] © Henry Lemoine & Cie,
Paris; 8Apr47; EF7237.

ORGANUM AD ASPERGES ME ET VIDI
AQUAM; praeludia, moduli organo
comitati ... Preludes and
modes of organ-accompaniment
[by P. Leopold Beul, Otto
Rippl and others] © Paulus-
Verlag, G.m.b.H., Lucerne,
Switzerland; 10ct45; EF3938.

ORLANDO, MIGUEL, 1899-
Le Vieux Port. Viejo Puerto. Paroles espagnoles de Ramos Freda,
paroles françaises de Chamfleury
[pseud.] & Lemarchand, musique
de Miguel Orlando. © Éditions
espagnoles Julio Garzon, Paris;
21Jul47; EF7333.

ORMOND, RON.
It's a Boy; words and music by
Eddie Dean, Millard Guy [and]
Ron Ormond [and Two Broken
Hearts; words and music by Henry
G. Warren] © Peer International
Corp., New York; 31Oct47;
EP18576, 18579.

ORR, ROBIN.
Three Chinese Songs; the translations by Arthur Waley, set to
music by Robin Orr. © The Oxford University Press, London;
10Jul47; EF6168.

ORTLIP, MILDRED.
Saviour, like a Shepherd Lead Us;
[by Wm. B. Bradbury, words by
Dorothy A. Thrupp] as arr. for
chorus by Mildred Ortlip.
Flushing, N. Y., Miro Pub. Co.
© Mildred Ortlip Keel, Flushing,
L. I., N. Y.; 1Jul47; on arrange-
ment; EP15807.

ORUE, JUAN DE, 1902-
Laverito ... English words by Joe
Davis, Spanish words and music
by Juan de Orue. © Caribbean
Music Co., New York; 20Oct47;
EP18008.

Tierra del Sol ... [by] Orue.
El Manton de Manila ... [by]
J. Grant. © [Editions Espag-
oles] Julio Garzon, Paris;
2Jun47; EF6514. Piano-conductor
score (orchestra) and parts.

ORYNSKI, ISABELLA WANDA, 1883-
Love Song; [words and music by
Wanda Orynski] © Wanda Orynski,
Salt Lake City; 18Nov47; EP19028.

ORYNSKI, WANDA. See
Orynski, Isabella Wanda.

OSAGE, TOM.
Indian in Brooklyn; by Tom Osage
& Cheyenne Joe. [c1946] ©
Cinephonic Music Co., ltd.,
London; 6May47; EF6059. Piano-
conductor score (orchestra) and
parts.

Mohawk Mood; by Tom Osage &
Cheyenne Joe. [c1946] © Cinophonic Music Co., ltd., London;
6May47; EF6040. Piano-conductor
score (orchestra) and parts.

Pawnee Trail; by Tom Osage &
Cheyenne Joe. [c1946] ©
Cinephonic Music Co., ltd.,
London; 6May47; EF6058. Piano-
conductor score (orchestra) and
parts.

Sioux Serenade; by Tom Osage &
Cheyenne Joe. [c1946] ©
Cinephonic Music Co., ltd.,
London; 6May47; EF6036. Piano-
conductor score (orchestra) and
parts.

OSBORNE, STANLEY LLEWELLYN, 1907-
ed.
Music for Worship; ed. by S. L.
Osborne. © The Frederick Har-
ris Music Co., ltd., Oakville,
Ont., Can.; 25Oct47; EF6852.
Principally for unison chorus
and piano.

O'SHAY, RICK, pseud. See
Jansen, Leon DeSire.

OSSER, ABE.
What Ev'ry Woman Knows; by Edna
Osser. © Broadcast Music, inc.,
New York; 25Jul47; EP18045. For
voice and piano, with chord
symbols.

OSSER, GLENN. See
Osser, Abe.

OSTACH, MARTHA G
This Song; words by John A. Ostach,
music by Martha G. Ostach. ©
Nordyke Publishing Co., Los Angeles;
23Nov47; EP16857.

OSTERMANN, JOSEPH DIONYSIUS, 1894-
Mass in D in Honor of Christ the
King; by Rev. Joseph D.
Ostermann. Nanuet, N. Y., St.
Anthony's Shrine. © Joseph D.
Ostermann, Nanuet, N. Y.;
1Sep47; EP16981. Score: SATB
and organ.

OSTLING, ACTON E   1906-
arr.
Trio Album; for trombones, arr.
by Acton E. Ostling. © Belwin,
inc., New York; 18Sep47; on
arrangement; EP17658. Score:
3 trombones.

OSTROW, ABE, pseud. See
Ostrowsky, Abraham M

OSTROWSKY, ABRAHAM M., 1912-
It's December Again; lyric by
George Howe, music by Abe
Ostrow [pseud.] © Arthur Steven
Music Publications, Hollywood,
Calif.; 22Sep47; EP17539.

There Must Be a Reason; lyric by
George Howe, music by Abe Ostrow.
© Arthur Steven Music Publications,
Hollywood, Calif.; 15Jul47;
EP15713.

OTIS, EDNA COGSWELL.
Whence Those Sounds Symphonious;
for four-part chorus of women's
voices [and] for four-part
chorus of mixed voices a
cappella, [by] Edna Cogswell
Otis. © The Boston Music Co.,
Boston; 18Aug47; EP16441.

OTTS, PAUL A   1897-
My Daily Prayer; [by] Paul A. Otts.
© Paul A. Otts, Milledgeville,—
Ga.; 10Aug47; EP16216. Close
score: SATB.

OUELLETTE, RUSS.
This Dream of You; words and
music by Russ Ouellette.
© Nordyke Publishing Co., Los
Angeles; 14Nov46; EP20480.

OUR GOLDEN LADY; [collection of
songs, words by Grace Johnson,
Pamela Maude Long and others;
music by John L. McDonald,
Pamela Maude Long and others]
© Elvetta Grohl, Knights Ferry,
Calif.; 25Sep47; EP17212.

OVERLAND, ELNOR O
I Long for the Wide Open Spaces;
music by Elnor O. Overland,
words by Marguerite Lyane.
© E. O. Overland, Big Timber,
Mont.; 18Aug47; EP16532.

OVERLAND, H   V
Leave Me Alone; words and music by
H. V. Overland. © Nordyke
Publishing Co., Los Angeles;
21Aug47; EP20097.

OVERSTREET, W   BENTON.
There'll Be Some Changes Made;
lyric by Billy Higgins [and
Herbert Edwards], music by W.
Benton Overstreet. © Edward
B. Marks Music Corp., New
York; 27Aug47; on lyric;
EP16700.

OWEN, MRS. HULEN.
I Heard an Old Refrain ... by Mrs.
Hulen Owen. Winona Lake, Ind.,
The Rodeheaver Hall-Mack Co. ©
The Rodeheaver Co., Winona Lake,
Ind.; 7Nov47; EP19250. For
voice and piano.

OWEN, WILLIAM, 1881-
Songs of the New Age; [comp. by Wm.
Owen and Lulu May Holmes] © William Owen & Lulu May Holmes, Portland, Or.; 4Dec47; AA69502. Hymns,
with music.

OWENS, HARRY ROBERT, 1902-
Hawaii Will Be Paradise Once
More; based on Reginald De
Koven's "O Promise Me," words
and music by Harry Owens.
© Royal Music Publisher,
Hollywood, Calif.; 28Jul47;
EP16570.

OWENS, MARSHALL M
Your Smiles Have Done Something to
Me; words and music by Marshall
M. Owens. © Nordyke Publishing
Co., Los Angeles; 2Jul46;
EP19383.

OWERS, J   M
Shufflin' Jive; words & music by
J. M. Owers, arr. by Bernie
Clements. © Nordyke Publish-
ing Co., Los Angeles; 11Oct46;
EP19413.

P

PACE, BERNARDO DE. See
De Pace, Bernardo.

PACE, CHARLES H
He is Sweeter as the Years Roll
By; words & music by Chas. H.
Pace. Pittsburgh, Old Ship of
Zion. © Chas. H. Pace, Pitts-
burgh; 5Nov47; EP20236.
He Will Say Well Done Some Day;
words & music by Chas. H.
Pace. Pittsburgh, Old Ship of
Zion. © Chas. H. Pace,
Pittsburgh; 20Oct47; EP18573.
I Must Tell Jesus All; words &
music by Chas. H. Pace. Pitts-
burgh, Old Ship of Zion. © Chas.
H. Pace, Pittsburgh; 27Oct47;
EP18935. Score: SATB and piano.

PACE, CHARLES H. Cont'd.
Not a Word; a spiritual medley by
Chas. H. Pace. Pittsburgh, Old
Ship of Zion. © Chas. H. Pace,
Pittsburgh; 5Nov47; EP20235.
For solo voices, mixed chorus
and piano.
When I Get Home; words & music by
Chas. H. Pace. Pittsburgh, Old
Ship of Zion. © Chas. H. Pace,
Pittsburgh; 27Oct47; EP18936.
Score: SATB and piano.

PACE, FRANK.
Where She Goes, I Go; words and
music by Frank Pace. © Nordyke Publishing Co., Los Angeles; 16Jun47; EP17442.

PACIFICO, ACHILLE.
Inno a S. Antonio; a due voci pari,
versi di S. Pagliaro, musica di
A. Pacifico. © Achille Pacifico,
Mondragone, Italia; 15Jun47;
EP6629.
Inno alla SS. Vergine; a due voci
pari, versi di S. Pagliaro,
musica di A. Pacifico. ©
Achille Pacifico, Mondragone,
Italia; 15Jun47; EP6628.
Metodo Pratico-Popolare per
Fisarmonica; del prof. Achille
Pacifico. Contiene 20 nuovi
ballabili. Napoli, Editoria
musicale fratelli De Marino.
© Achille Pacifico, Mondragone,
Italia; 15Jun47; EP6630. For
accordion.

PADILLA, JOSE, 1889-
Cala d'Or ... paroles françaises
de Chamfleury [pseud.] et
Liogar [pseud.] paroles espag-
noles de José A. de Prada,
musique de José Padilla. ©
(Editions Espagnoles) Julio
Garzon, Paris; 17Jul47; EP6485.
Ciel d'Espagne; paroles de Henri
Varna [pseud.] et Marc-Cab
[pseud.] musique de José Padilla.
© Salabert, inc., New York;
30Sep46; EP6304.
Mujer de España. (Femme Espagnole)
... Paroles de Fremique [pseud.]
musique de José Padilla, arrt.
de Francis Salabert ... Guitarra
Andaluza ... de José Padilla,
arrt. de Francis Salabert. ©
Éditions Salabert, Paris; 8Jul47;
EP6404. Piano-conductor score
(orchestra) and parts.
La Nazarena ... paroles espagnoles
de José Andrés de Prada,
musique de José Padilla. ©
(Editions Espagnoles) Julio
Garzon, Paris; 17Apr47; EP6508.
Spanish words.
Ombres ... paroles françaises de
Jean Rodor [pseud.] musique de
José Padilla. © (Editions
Espagnoles) Julio Garzon, Paris;
17Jul47; EP6509.
Pepe Carmona ... paroles espag-
noles de José Andrés de Prada,
paroles françaises de Jean Ro-
dor [pseud.] musique de José
Padilla. © Éditions espagnoles
Julio Garzon, Paris; 16Oct47;
EP7338.
Pim-Pum-Pai ... paroles françaises
de Jean Rodor [pseud.] musique
de José Padilla. © Éditions es-
pagnoles Julio Garzon, Paris;
10Oct47; EP7335.
Recuerdos de un Tango; paroles
françaises de Chamfleury [pseud]
à Liogar [pseud.] paroles
espagnoles de José Andrés de
Prada. Musique de José Padilla.
© (Éditions Espagnoles) Julio
Garzon, Paris; 17Apr47; EP6510.
Spanish words only.

Voluptuosa ... Paroles espagnoles
et musique de José Padilla, arrt.
de Francis Salabert. Milonguita
... De Enrique Delfino (Delfy),
arrt. de Francis Salabert. ©
Éditions Salabert, Paris; 10Jun47;
on arrangement; EP5894.

PADWA, VLADIMIR, 1900-
Gypsy Waltz ... [by] Vladimir
Padwa. (In Hirschberg, David,
ed. and comp. Pieces Are Fun.
bk. 1, p. 40-41) © Musicord
Publications, New York;
2Jul47; EP15944. For piano
solo.

PAEZ, MANUEL.
Eternidad. (Eternity) ... Spanish
words and music by Manuel Paez,
English words by Joe Davis.
© Caribbean Music, inc., New
York; 22Sep47; EP17109.
Maldad. (Heartless) ... English
words by Joe Davis, Spanish
words and music by Manuel Paez.
© Caribbean Music Co., New
York; 10Nov47; EP18430.

PAGANINI, NICOLO, 1782-1840.
Caprice no. XXIV ... by Niccolo Pa-
ganini. With additional variations
and piano acc. [by] Mischa Elman.
© Carl Fischer, inc., New York;
20Nov47; EP19166. Score (violin
and piano) and part.
(Concerto, violin, no. 2) Secondo
Concerto in si minore (op.7 II
postuma) [By] Niccolò Paganini,
completamente ricostruito da
Carlo Zino. © Carisch, s.a.,
Milan; 14May40; on reconstruction;
EP6274. Score (violin and piano)
and part.
Moto Perpetuo; [by] N. Paganini.
Elaborazione ... di A. F.
Lavagnino. © Carisch, s.a.,
Milan; 5Sep40; on elaboration;
EP6216. Score: string orches-
tra.
Perpetual Motion; [by] Niccolo
Paganini. Op.11. Transcribed by
Rosalyn Tureck. © Carl Fischer,
inc., New York; 9Dec47; on
transcription; EP19990. For
piano solo.
Secondo Concerto. See his Concerto,
violin, no. 2.

PAHISSA, JAIME, 1880-
Nocturno; [by] J. Pahissa. © Ri-
cordi Americana, S.A.E.C., Bue-
nos Aires; 30Oct46; EP6967.
Score (violoncello or violin and
piano) and parts.
Piezas Infantiles; [by] Jaime
Pahissa, para piano. © Ricordi
Americana, s.a.e.c., Buenos
Aires; 20Dec43; EP6984.
Seis Canciones; [by] Jaime Pahissa.
© Ricordi Americana, S.A.E.C.,
Buenos Aires; 30Oct46; EP6968.
For voice and piano; principally
with Catalan and Spanish words.
Seis Canciones Populares Españolas
... [by] Jaime Pahissa. ©
Ricordi Americana, s.a.e.c.,
Buenos Aires; 10Oct46. EP6966
Principally for chorus: SA

PAISIELLO, GIOVANNI.
Sinfonia Funebre per la Morte
del Pontefice, Pio VI; [by]
G. Paisiello, ricostruzione di
G. Piccioli. © Carisch, s.a.,
Milan; 20Apr40; on arrange-
ment; EP6219. Score: orches-
tra.

PAISNER, BEN, 1912-
Minuet in Swing; piano solo [by]
Ben Paisner. [c1946] © Gate
Music Co., New York; 27Oct47;
on arrangement; EP18973.

PALACIOS, CHUCHO. See
Palacios, Jesús.

PALACIOS, JESUS.
Tres Cariños ... letra y musica
de Chucho Palacios (Jesús
Palacios) © Promotora Hispano
Americana de Música, s.a., México;
29Jul47; EP6203.
Ya para Qué Letra y música de
Chucho Palacios (Jesús
Palacios) © Promotora Hispano
Americana de Música, s.a.,
Mexico; 30Dec46; EP5814.

PALESTRINA, GIOVANNI PIERLUIGI DA,
1525?-1594.
(Adoramus Te) Alleluia, Lord God.
(Adoramus Te) For three-part
chorus of mixed voices (a cap-
pella) [by] Giovanni Pierluigi
de Palestrina ... arr. by Vic-
toria Glaser, words adapted by
Henry Wilder Foote. © E. C.
Schirmer Music Co., Boston;
29Sep47; on arrangement;
EP18134. English words.
Adoramus Te Christe; [by] Gio-
vanni Palestrina, [arr. by]
O.C.C. © Neil A. Kjos Music
Co., Chicago; 30Jul47; on ar-
rangement; EP17974. Score:
SATB and piano reduction.

PALMER, CEDRIC KING. See
Palmer, King.

PALMER, EDWINA.
Twenty Tunes for Beginners ...
[by] Edwina Palmer and Agnes
Best. © The Oxford University
Press, London; 10Apr47; EF6103.
Parts: viola and violoncello.

PALMER, ERASIE, pseud. See
Cornett, Alice.

PALMER, FAITH, pseud. See
Henriksen, Edythe Gertrude.

PALMER, JACK.
Oh! My Achin' Heart ... by Freddy
James, Little Jack Little and
Jack Palmer, arr. by Paul Weirick.
© Mood Music Co., inc., New York;
30Jun47; on arrangement; EP15460.
Piano-conductor score (orchestra,
with words) and parts.

PALMER, KING, 1913- arr.
Waltzing through the Years ...
arr. by King Palmer. © William Paxton & Co., ltd.,
London; 28Dec46; on arrangement, EF5706. Piano-conductor
score (orchestra) and parts.

PANEL, LUDOVIC.
Cansona; pour orgue [by] Ludovic
Panel. © S. Bornemann, Paris;
17Jul47; EF6581.

PANETTI, CHARLES.
Four Aces Polka; by Charles Panetti. © Roma Music Co., Cleveland; 15Oct47; EP18161. For
accordion solo.

PANIZZA, HECTOR, 1875-
Aurora; opera en tres actos y un
intermedio, libreto de Hector
Quesada y Luis Illica, versión
española de Angel Petitta y Josué
Quesada, música de Hector Panizza.
Partitura completa para canto y
piano, texto español e italiano.
© Ricordi Americana, s.a.e.c.,
Buenos Aires; 5Jun45; EP6962.

PAONE, NICOLA.
Mr. Police, That's Is My Gel
(a-what's-a matter you); by
Nicola Paone. © Shapiro, Bernstein & Co., inc., New York;
2Jul47; EP15423. For voice and
piano, with chord symbols.

PARCELL, FRANK.
She's My Girl Friend; words and
music by Frank Parcell, arr. by
Walter W. Newcomer. © Nordyke
Publishing Co., Los Angeles;
8Aug46; EP20324.

PARHALO, BROWNIE.
This Kind of Love; words and music
by Brownie Parhalo. [c1946]
© Nordyke Publishing Co., Los
Angeles; 21Aug47; EP16606.

PARIS, JAMES B
Am I to Blame? Words and music by
Al Dexter and James B. Paris.
Hollywood, Calif., Hill and
Range Songs. © Hill and Range
Songs, inc. and Al Dexter
Music Publishing Co., Hollywood,
Calif.; 30Jul47; EP16049.
Why Did It Have to Be; words and
music by Al Dexter and James B.
Paris. Hollywood, Calif., Hill
and Range Songs. © Hill and
Range Songs, inc., and Al Dexter
Music Publishing Co., Hollywood,
Calif.; 15Dec47; EP20129.

PARISH, MITCHELL.
Riverboat Shuffle; by Hoagy Carmichael, Dick Voynow, Irving
Mills and Mitchell Parish ...
arr. by "Zep" Meissner. ©
Mills Music, inc., New York;
28Jul47; on arrangement;
EP16190. Piano-conductor
score (orchestra) and parts.

PARKE, DOROTHY, 1910-
Christmas Carols; a short fantasia,
arr. ... by Dorothy Parke. ©
Edwin Ashdown, ltd., London;
20Sep47; EF6748. Two scores for
piano 1-2.

PARKER, JENNIE, 1930-
You went away and left me; words
and music by Jennie Parker.
© Box and Cox (Publications),
London; 16Apr47; EF3663.

PARKER, ROSS.
Aunt Hotty Likes; (The Puzzle
Song) Music by Ross Parker and
Wynne Smith, lyric by Ross
Parker and Michael Hilos. ©
Peter Maurice Music Co., ltd.,
New York; 24Jul47; EF6359.
I'll Make Up for Ev'rything; [by]
Ross Parker, arr. by Jordon
Rees [and My Girl's an Irish
Girl; by Jack Popplewell, arr.
by Stan Bowsher] © Peter
Maurice Music Co., ltd., New
York; 11Sep47; EF6666-6667.
Piano-conductor score (orches-
tra, with words) and parts.
I'll Make Up for Ev'rything; words
and music by Ross Parker.
London, Macmelodies. © The
Peter Maurice Music Co., ltd.,
New York; 23Oct47; EF6873.

PARKMAN, HAROLD, pseud. See
Norden, Hugo.

PARKS, BETTY.
Now, Listen to Me, Honey; words
by Elva Allen, music by Betty
Parks. © Nordyke Publishing Co.,
Los Angeles; 12Aug47; EP17428.

PARKS, P   EDWARD.
I Just Want to Talk about You;
words and music by F. Edward
Parks. © Nordyke Publishing
Co., Los Angeles; 11Jul47;
EP17608.

[PARMELEE, GILBERT] 1892-
I Like You, Valentine; words and
music by Lee Gilbert [pseud.]
© Melotone Music Publishers,
Chicago; 50ct47; EP17684.
The Up-to-date "Happy Birthday
Song"; words and music by Lee
Gilbert [pseud.] © Melotone
Music Publishers, Chicago;
30Sep47; EP17637.

PAROLINI, ALFRED C   1886-
The Sons and Daughters of Liberty; words and music by ... Alfred C. Parolini. © Alfred C.
Parolini, Los Angeles;
24Sep47; EP17652.

PARRA, GILBERTO.
Mala Mujer ... letra y música de
Gilberto Parra. © Promotora
Hispano Americana de Música,
s.a., México; 29Jul47; EP6205.

Pos Que Voy a Hacer ... letra y
música de Gilberto Parra.
© Promotora Hispano Americana
de Música, s.a., México; 29Jul47;
EP6202.
Sublime Inspiración ... de Gilberto
Parra. © Promotora Hispano
Americana de Música, s.a., México;
29Jul47; EP6196. For voice and
piano.

PARRIS, HERMAN.
3 Preludes; for piano solo, [by]
Herman Parris. © Elkan-Vogel
Co., inc., Philadelphia; 17Jul47;
EP15808.

PARRISH, CARL.
Little Turtle Dove So Lovely.
Cette Aimable Tourterelle.
French-Canadian folk song, four
part mixed voices S.A.T.B. with
baritone solo, choral setting
by Carl Parrish, [words] from
"Folk songs of French Canada,"
English version by C. P. © M.
Witmark & Sons, New York;
13Nov47; on arrangement;
EP18877.

PARTOS, JENO
Az a Szép. (Fine and True) English
lyric by Olga Paul, music by
Pártos Jenő. (In Pasti, Barbara,
comp. Memories of Hungary. p.
24-25) © Edward B. Marks Music
Corp., New York; 19Nov47; on
English lyric; EP16999.

PARYS, GEORGES VAN, 1902-
Le Silence Est d'Or; partition
cinématographique, paroles et
musique de Georges van Parys.
© Georges van Parys, Paris;
31Mar47; EF5941. Principally
for piano solo.

PASCAL, CLAUDE RENE GEORGES, 1921-
(Octet, winds & brass) Octuor,
pour instruments à vent, [by]
Claude Pascal. © Durand & Cie,
Paris; 30Apr47; EF5846. Parts:
flute 1-2, oboe, clarinet, bassoon
1-2, horn and trumpet.
--- --- Score. © Durand & Cie, Paris;
31Mar47; EF5960.

PASCAL, L
Dans les Rues d'Paname; paroles de
Ch. L. Pothier et Robert Valaire
[pseud.], musique de L. Pascal.
© Editions L. Maillochon, Paris;
12Jun27; EF5996.

PASHEZOGLU, PERRY.
Gone; words by Marjorie Arnold,
music by Perry Pashezoglu.
© Nordyke Publishing Co., Los
Angeles; 8Apr47; EP15852.

PASQUET, JEAN.
Father Omnipotent; S.A.T.B., text
and music by Jean Pasquet. ©
Edwin H. Morris & Co., inc.,
New York; 25Apr47; EP17328.

PASSANI, EMILE BARTHELEMI, 1905-
Brand' Vin. (Grund zum Trinken)
Chanson populaire allemande,
traduction de Guillot de Seix
[pseud.], harmonisation pour
choeur à 4 voix mixtes par
Emile Passani. © Heugel & Cie,
Paris; 11Oct46; on harmonization; EF6436.
Cueillons le Fraise et la Framboise; chanson populaire
tchécoslovaque, traduction de
Guillot de Seix [pseud.], harmonisation pour choeur à 4 voix
mixtes par Emile Passani. ©
Heugel & Cie, Paris; 11Oct46;
on harmonization; EF6500.
Le Ranz des Vaches; chanson
populaire suisse. Paroles de
Guillot de Seix [pseud.] (d'après
la tradition populaire),
harmonisation pour choeur à 4
voix mixtes par Emile Passani.
© Heugel & Cie, Paris; 11Oct46;
on arrangement; EF6433.

Le Raton des Rêves ... chanson
populaire lettone. Traduction
de Guillot de Seix [pseud.],
harmonisation pour choeur à 4
voix mixtes par Emile Passani.
© Heugel & Cie, Paris; 11Oct46;
on arrangement; EF6434.
Records; musique de: Emile Passani. © Henry Lemoine & Cie,
Paris; 15May47; EP7351. For
piano solo.
Santa Lucia; chanson populaire
italienne. Harmonisation pour
choeur à 4 voix mixtes par
Emile Passani. © Heugel & Cie.,
Paris; 11Oct46; on arrangement;
EF6431.
Sur le Bord de la Rivière; chanson
populaire provençale. Harmonisation pour choeur à 4 voix mixtes
par Emile Passani. © Heugel &
Cie., Paris; 11Oct46; on
arrangement; EF6429.

PASTI, BARBARA, comp.
Memories of Hungary. (Magyarország
Legszebb Dalai) ... A collection
of its best-loved songs comp. by
Barbara Pasti, with original Hungarian words, and English lyrics
by Olga Paul. © Edward B. Marks
Music Corp., New York; 19Nov47;
on English lyrics; EP6429.

PATRICK, BURTON E
Victory for Liberty; words & music by Burton E. Patrick, arr.
by E. J. Rohm. © Nordyke Publishing Co., Los Angeles;
25Jul46; EP20376.

PATTI, SANTO T
The Spirit of Milwaukee; by Santo
T. Patti. © Patti Bros. Music
House, Milwaukee; 22Sep47;
EP17366. For accordion solo.

PATTISON, PAT.
Rocky Mountain Rhythm; by Big
Bill Campbell and Pat Pattison.
© Southern Music Publishing
Co., ltd., London; 15Jul47;
EF5843. For voice and piano,
with chord symbols, melody also
in tonic sol-fa notation.

[PAUL, ALAN]
Hope and Pray; arr. for mixed voices
by T. J. Hewitt. Words by Joseph
Murrells, music by Peter Young
[pseud.] © Keith, Prowse & Co.,
ltd., London; 3Dec47; on arrangement; EF7170.
The Villages of England; part-song
for mixed voices S. A. T. B.,
words by Philip Brown, music by
Michael Strong [pseud.], arr.
by Clarence Lucas. © Ascherberg,
Hopwood & Crew ltd., London;
30Jun47; on arrangement; EF6255.
The Villages of England; part-song
for male voices T. T. B. B.,
words by Philip Brown, music by
Michael Strong [pseud.], arr.
by Clarence Lucas. © Ascherberg,
Hopwood & Crew, ltd., London;
5Aug47; on arrangement; EF6254.

PAUL, LES.
The Guitar Magic of Les Paul; ten
original guitar solos with
piano [by Les Paul. Piano
transcriptions by Bob Kersey
and Carl Bosler] © Leeds Music
Corp., New York; 30Jul47;
EP16099. Score (guitar and
piano) and part.

PAUL, RITA, pseud. See
Yoxsimer, Helen.

PAULSON, GUSTAF.
Fem Sånger; [by] Gustaf Paulson,
[words by Mårten Edlund, Ruth Hag-
man, Uno Florén, and others] ©
Föreningen svenska tonsättare,
Stockholm; 1Jan45; EF7099.

PAVEY, SALLY.
Spare the Love and Spoil the
Dream; words and music by Ed
Waldman and Sally Pavey.
© Broadcast Music, inc., New
York; 1Jul47; EP18196.

PAYMER, ADA, 1897-
Wynken, Blynken and Nod ... [by]
Ada Paymer. (In Hirschberg,
David, ed. and comp. Pieces
Are Fun. bk. 1, p. 22-23) ©
Musicord Publications, New
York; 2Jul47; EP15935. For
piano solo.

PAZ, HERBERTO.
Humoresque; pour piano, [by] Her-
berto Paz. [Op. 15, no. 1] ©
L. Maillochon, Paris; 9Sep23;
EP7044.
Mazurka; pour piano, dans le style
de Borodine, [by] Herberto Paz.
[Op. 13] © L. Maillochon, édi-
teur, Paris; 9Mar23; EP7043.
Scherzo; pour piano, [by] Herberto
Paz. [Op. 12, no. 1] © L.
Maillochon, Paris; 12Dec23;
EP7045.

PAZ, SUSY.
Fugitivo ... letra de Horacio San-
guinetti, música de Susy Paz.
© Editorial Argentina de Música
Internacional (EDAMI), s. de r.
ltda., Buenos Aires; 27Jul47;
EP6697.

PEACOCK, JOHN F
Whispering Moon; words by George
Quinan and John F. Peacock,
music by John F. Peacock.
© Nordyke Publishing Co., Los
Angeles; 29Jul47; EP19451.

PEARSON, AVEN J
You Are My Inspiration; words &
music by Aven J. Pearson.
© Nordyke Publishing Co., Los
Angeles; 15Aug46; EP19381.

PEASE, SHARON.
Snatch and Grab It; words and music
by Sharon Pease. New York, Capi-
tol Songs. © Criterion Music
Corp., New York; 18Nov47;
EP18920.

PEASE, SHARON, ed.
Down Beat's Styles of Famous 88'ers;
ed. by Sharon Pease. © Leeds
Music Corp., New York; 18Aug47;
EP16399. For piano solo.

PECKHAM, RUTH LEONA, 1905-
The Wounded Christ ... words by
Cora Elizabeth Barker, music by
Ruth Leona Peckham. © Cora El-
izabeth Barker, Elmira Heights,
N. Y.; 23Oct47; EP18299.

PEDREIRA, JOSÉ ENRIQUE, 1904-
No Podras Olvidarme ... letra:
Ana Santisteban, música: José
Enrique Pedreira. © Edward B.
Marks Music Corp., New York;
17Dec47; EP19920.

PEDRETTE, EDWARD A
Peace, Perfect Peace; for four-
part chorus of mixed voices, a
cappella, [by] Edward A. Pedrette,
[words by] E. H. Bickersteth.
© Boston Music Co., Boston;
12Dec47; EP19978.

PEERY, ROB ROY.
Two Guitars; Russian gypsy melody
for the pianoforte transcribed
by Rob Roy Peery. © Theodore
Presser Co., Philadelphia;
26Jul47; on arrangement;
EP15379. For piano, 4 hands.

PEETERS, FLOR.
Gavotte Antique. [Op.59, no.4]
© The H. W. Gray Co., inc., New
York; 2Jul47; EP15704. For organ
solo.

Morning Hymn. [Op.59, no.1] ©
The H. W. Gray Co., inc., New
York; 2Jul47; EP15711. For
organ solo.
Nostalgie. [Op.59, no.3] © The
H. W. Gray Co. inc., New York;
2Jul47; EP15710. For organ solo.
Thirty-five Miniatures; for organ
... Op.55. © McLaughlin &
Reilly Co., Boston; 20Jun47;
EP15881.

PEIA, ERNEST.
You're Only Teasin' Me; words and
music by Ernest Peia. © Nordyke
Publishing Co., Los Angeles;
2Sep47; EP19287.

PELO, A   DEL.
Malagueña ... paroles de Didier
Gold, musique de A. del Pelo.
© Les Éditions Carlton, Paris;
18Sep26; EP5997.

PELOQUIN, CHARLES ALEXANDER, 1918-
My Friend John. V'la l'Bon Vent.
French folk song ... English
version by Lionel Landry, S.S.A.
choral setting by C. Alexander
Peloquin. © M. Witmark & Sons,
New York; 16Dec47; on arrange-
ment; EP20343.

[PELTIER, ALFRED JAMES] 1893-
My Dreams Are Now a Reality;
words by Ida P. Rothtrock,
music by J. Alfred [pseud.]
© Nordyke Publishing Co.,
Los Angeles; 27Sep46; EP19670.
Orchids for You (dear Mother of
mine); words by Edmund H. Hentges,
music by J. Alfred [pseud.]
© Nordyke Publishing Co., Los
Angeles; 11Aug47; EP17420.
You'll Always Have My Heart;
words by Dominick Knox, music
by J. Alfred [pseud.] ©
Nordyke Publishing Co., Los
Angeles; 11Nov46; EP19379.

PENAU, ROGER.
Polichinelle et Colombine; [by]
Roger Pénau. © Editions L.
Maillochon, Paris; 9May24;
EP6312. For piano solo.

PENDLETON, CECIL MELVILLE, 1882-
Love, the Climax of Life; words
and music by Melville Pendleton.
[c1946] © Cecil Melville
Pendleton, Erie, Pa.; 25Oct47;
EP18492.

PENDLETON, MELVILLE. See
Pendleton, Cecil Melville.

PENNIMAN, DALE G
You Made a Fool Out of Me; words
and music by Dale G. Penniman.
© Nordyke Publishing Co. Los
Angeles; 10May47; EP18853.

PENNY, LEE.
Where Are You Now? Words and
music by Lee Penny. © Hill
and Range Songs, inc., Hollywood, Calif.; 15Dec47; EP20125.
Without a Doubt; words and music
by Lee Penny. © Hill and Range
Songs, inc., Hollywood, Calif.;
15Dec47; EP20122.

PENNY, MARTIN.
Old Gaelic Rune; traditional
words, set to music by Martin
Penny. © The Oxford University
Press, London; 10Jul47; EP6171.
There Was One; the words by Dorothy
Parker, set to music by Martin
Penny. © The Oxford University
Press, London; 10Jul47; EP6167.

PENROSE, BILLY.
Harlem Boogie; by Billy Penrose.
[c1945] © Cinephonic Music Co.,
ltd., London; 14Oct46; EP6037.
For piano solo.

PENTUFF, ODOREDO.
I Love It When It Rains ... words
and melody written by Odoredo
Pentuff. (In Tampa Morning
Tribune. no.211, p.13)
© Odoredo Pentuff, Tampa, Fla.;
30Jul47; B5-1690.

PEPIN, TED.
Calling to You, Sweetheart; words
and music by Ted Pepin. ©
Nordyke Publishing Co., Los
Angeles; 10May47; EP16045.

PEPPING, ERNST.
Laud Him! English version [by]
O. C. Christiansen, [music by]
Ernst Pepping, arr. [by] O. C.
C. © Neil A. Kjos Music Co.,
Chicago; 25Jun47; on arrangement;
EP16058. Score: SATB and piano
reduction.

PÉREZ, JUAN MUÑIZ. See
Muñiz Pérez, Juan.

PÉREZ LEYVA, NICOLAS.
Aunque Estes Lejos ... letra y
música de Nicolas Pérez Leyva.
© Promotora Hispano Americana
de Música, s.a., México; 27Aug47;
EP6702. For 2 voices and piano.

PERGAMENT, MOSES, 1893-
Romans ... av Moses Pergament. ©
Nordiska Musikförlaget, A/B,
Stockholm; on arrangement;
1Jul19; EP5395. Score (violin
and piano) and part.

PERGOLESI, GIOVANNI BATTISTA, 1710-
1736.
Air; [by] G. B. Pergolesi ... arr.
by Ernest Haywood [for] piano
solo. [c1946] © Keith, Prowse
& Co., ltd., London; 24Jul47;
on arrangement; EP6244.
Glory to God in the Highest ...
Text from Scripture, [music by]
G. B. Pergolesi, arr. by C.
Albert Scholin ... assa by
Vincent Novello. [St. Louis,
Hunleth Music Co.] © C. Albert
Scholin, St. Louis; 15Jul47;
on arrangement; EP15684. Score:
junior choir (SA), chorus (SATB)
and organ or piano.

PÉRISSAS, MADELEINE GENEVIÈVE
RAYMONDE, 1906-   arr.
La Bergère des Aravis; (Savoie),
chanson populaire harmonisée
pour 3 voix égales [by] Made-
leine Périssas, Paris; 20May47; on
Ouvrières, Paris; 20May47; on
arrangement; EP5897.
La Danaé; chanson populaire,
harmonisée pour 3 voix égales.
© Les Éditions Ouvrières,
Paris; 20May47; on arrangement;
EP5881.

PERKINS, FRANK.
Stars Fell on Alabama ... by
Mitchell Parish and Frank
Perkins, transcribed by Eddy
Rogers. © Mills Music, inc.,
New York; 28Jul47; on arrange-
ment; EP16200. Score (violin
and piano) and part.

PERKINS, HARKER.
The Lady in Slacks; words by
Irene E. Virden, music by
Harker Perkins. © Nordyke
Publishing Co., Los Angeles;
17May47; EP16826.
Reena; words by Irene E. Virden,
music by Harker Perkins. © Nor-
dyke Publishing Co., Los Angeles;
29Mar47; EP16728.

PERKINS, MARDAN.
Permelia; words and music by
Mardan Perkins. © Nordyke
Publishing Co., Los Angeles;
24Jul47; EP20490.

PEROSI, DON LORENZO. See
Perosi, Laurentius.

PEROSI, LAURENTIUS, 1872-
Mass in Honor of Saint Charles;
for two equal voices, [by]
Laurentius Perosi. ©
McLaughlin & Reilly Co., Boston;
20Jun47; EP15882.

PEROSI, LORENZO. See
Perosi, Laurentius.

PERRON, HELEN.
When Two Lights Are Burning;
words and music by Helen
Perron. © Nordyke Publishing
Co., Los Angeles; 12Aug47;
EP17476.

PERRY, CHARLES.
Overnight I Made a Hit with My
Baby; words by William Tisko,
music by Charles Perry and
Harry Reynolds. A Charles
Perry arrangement. © Joe
McDaniel Music Co.,New York;
9May47; EP16143.

PERRY, HELENE.
A Dream or Two; words and music
by Helene Perry. © Nordyke
Publishing Co., Los Angeles;
29Jul47; EP17572.
To the Love in My Heart; words
and music by Helene Perry.
© Nordyke Publishing Co., Los
Angeles; 10ct47; EP20046.

PERRY, JOSEPHINE HOVEY.
Musical Alphabet and Figures; for
the kindergartner and pre-school
pianist, by Josephine Hovey
Perry, illustrations by Joanne
Gilker. © Oliver Ditson Co.,
Philadelphia; 12Aug47; LP16303.

PERRY, JULIA.
Carillon Heigh-Ho; ([for]
S.A.T.B., divided, a cappella)
[By] Julia Perry, ed. by John
Finley Williamson. © Carl
Fischer, inc., New York;
14Aug47; EP16431.

PERRY, TONY JOHN, 1924-
If I Whisper "I Love You!" Words
and music by Tony Perry, piano
arrangement by Madeline Scott.
© Tony John Perry, Omaha;
17Jan47; EP17964.

PESENTI, RENÉ, 1898-
J'Attends; paroles de Maurice
Vandair [pseud.], musique de
René Pesenti. © Éditions
Mondia, s.a., Paris; 31Dec47;
EP3807.

PETER, C.
The Jolly Coppersmith ... [By]
C. Peter, arr. by Lloyd
Marvin. © Chart Music
Publishing House, inc.,
Chicago; 3Sep47; on arrange-
ment; EP17200. For piano
accordion solo.

PETERSON, CARL FREDERICK.
Once in a Lifetime; words &
music by Carl Frederick Peterson. © Nordyke Publishing Co.,
Los Angeles; 11Oct46; EP19406.

PETIT, PIERRE YVES MARIE CAMILLE,
1922-
"Le Jeu de l'Amour et du Hasard";
scène lyrique en un acte
(d'après Marivaux) par Charles
Clerc, musique de Pierre Petit.
© Heugel & Cie, Paris; 28Feb47;
EP6556. Piano-vocal score.
Mélodies; pour chant et piano [by]
Pierre Petit. © Heugel et Cie,
Paris; v.1-5, 26Mar47; EP6557-
6561. Contents.- 1. Le Besti-
aire du Chien à Ne Pas Mettre
Dehors (Claude Roy) - 2. La
Caravelle (Jean des Brosses) -
3. La Robe (Georges Neveux)-
4. Le Sou (Georges Neveux) - 5.
La Vague (Georges Neveux)

Rome, l'Unique Objet ... suite pour
le piano. © Heugel & Cie, Paris;
v.2, 2Jun47; EP6435. Contents.-2.
Néréides.
Six Petites Pièces; à quatre
mains, pour les enfants [by]
Pierre Petit. © Lucien De
Lacour, Paris; 31Mar47; EP5906.

[PETIT DUTAILLIS, JACQUES] 1924-
Il Fait Froid dans Mon Coeur ...
Paroles de Jacques Dutailly
[pseud.], musique de J.
Dutailly & Léo Poll [pseud.]
© Éditions Musicales Nuances,
Paris; 30Jul47; EP6472.
La Lettre Inutile; paroles de
Marion Vandal [pseud.], musique
de Jacques Dutailly [pseud.]
© Éditions Nuances, Paris;
30Jul47; EP6473.
Ma Chanson N'Est Pas Commerciale ..
... Paroles de Jacques Dutailly
[pseud.], musique de J. Dutailly
& Léo Poll [pseud.] © Éditions
Musicales Nuances, Paris;
30Jul47; EP6474.

PETRALIA, TITO, 1896-
Vado verso il Mio Paese ...
Parole di L. L. Martelli,
musica di Tito Petralia. La
Canzone delle Sonagliere ...
Adatt. ritmico di R. Morbelli,
musica di G. Simi. © Carisch,
s.a., Milan; 2Jun47; EF5775.
Piano-conductor score (orches-
tra, with words) and parts.

PETRIE, JOE.
The One I Adore; words by Joe
Payne, music by Joe Petrie.
© Nordyke Publishing Co., Los
Angeles; 14Jun47; EP17409.

PETRONIO, ARTUR, 1898-
Leçons de Solfège; pour développer
la concentration visuelle, par
A. Petronio. © Alphonse Leduc
& Co., Paris; v.1, 30May47; v.2,
30Apr47; v.3, 30Jun47; EP6536,
6535, 6534.

PETTIS, JACK.
Bugle Call Rag; by Jack Pettis,
Billy Meyers [and] Elmer Schoe-
bel, [arr. by Philip J. Lang]
© Mills Music, inc., New York;
18Sep47; on arrangement;
EP18252. Condensed score (band)
and parts.

PETTIT, ALICIA.
Take a Trip to Luzianne; words
and music by Judy Morris and
Alicia Pettit. © Judy Morris
and Alicia Pettit, Sioux City,
Iowa; 4Dec47; EP19203.

PEYRONNIN, JEAN, 1901-
Du Soleil ... du Printemps ...
Paroles de René Nazelles,
[pseud.], musique de Jean
Peyronnin. © Éditions Salabert,
Paris, 10May47; EP5916.
On Se Plaît ... paroles de Léo Le-
lièvre, musique de Jean Peyronnin.
© Éditions Salabert, Paris;
4Aug47; EF7249.
On Se Plaît ... paroles de Léo
Lelièvre, musique de Jean
Peyronnin ... Y avait Une Fois
Deux amoureux; paroles de
Ramond asso, musique de
Félix Chardon et Albert Lasry.
Arrt. de Francis Salabert. ©
Salabert, inc., New York;
12May47; on arrangement;
EF5952. Parts: orchestra.

PFLUEGER, CARL.
How Long Wilt Thou Forget Me?
Anthem for mixed voices, [words]
adapted from Psalm XIII, [music
by] Carl Pflueger, arr. by Danforth Simonton. © The John
Church Co., Philadelphia;
15Jul47; on arrangement;
EP15675.

PHELPS, RICHARD L
Lullaby of the Christ-Child; for
four-part chorus of mixed
voices. German folk-song arr.
by Richard L. Phelps, words by
R. L. P. © E. C. Schirmer Music
Co., Boston; 25Jul47; on arrangement; EP16053.

PHELPS, WILLIAM W
Now Let Us Rejoice; hymn for
mixed voices, [by].Wm. W.
Phelps] arr. by J. Spencer
Cornwall. © Choir Publishing
Co., Salt Lake City; 13Oct47;
EP18034.

PHILIDOR, FRANÇOIS ANDRE DANICAN,
1726-1795.
(Les Femmes Vengées) Overture to
Les Femmes Vengées ... [by]
Philidor (Francois André
Danican) ... arr. [and ed.] by
Adam Carse. © Augener, ltd.,
London; 14Jul47; on arrangement
& editing; EF6625. Score:
orchestra.

PHILLIPS, BURRILL, 1907-
Scene; for small orchestra, [by]
Burrill Phillips ... Score. ©
Hargail Music Press, New York;
21Jul47; EP16590.

PHILLIPS, C   HENRY, ca.
1906-1947.
To God the Mighty Lord ...
[by] C. Henry Phillips, [words
by] Tate and Brady ... Ps. 136.
© The Oxford University Press,
London; 1May47; EF6112. Score:
SATB and organ.

PHILLIPS, CLARE, 1878-
Alaskan Love Call; words and
music by Clare Phillips, arr.
by Aaron A. Clark. © Mrs.
A. H. Phillips, Washington,
D. C.; 11Aug47; EP16318.

PHILLIPS, DONALD, 1913-
Shopping Tour; [by] Donald
Phillips, piano solo. ©
Lawrence Wright Music Co.,
ltd., London; 3Jul47; EF5691.
Skyscraper Fantasy; complete
pianoforte solo. © Lawrence
Wright Music Co., ltd.,
London; 30Jun47; EF3971.
Tap Dancer ... piano solo, [by]
Donald Phillips. © Lawrence
Wright Music Co., ltd., London;
30Oct47; EF6890.

PHILLIPS, FRANK.
That Would Be Heaven for Two;
words and music by Frank
(Johnny) Phillips. © Nordyke
Publishing Co., Los Angeles;
15Aug47; EP19374.

PHILLIPS, LLOYD.
Unfinished Melody; piano solo by
Lloyd Phillips, based on the
theme from Schubert's "Unfinished
symphony." © Gate Music Co.,
New York; 27Oct47; on arrangement; EP18975.

PHILLIPS, MONTAGUE F
Blue-Bells; two-part song, arr. by
the composer, words by Doris A.
Kendall, music by Montague F.
Phillips. [Op. 25, no. 6] ©
Chappell & Co., ltd., London;
5Nov47; on arrangement; EF7279.
Cheer Up! Two-part song, arr. by
the composer, words by Harold Simpson, music by Montague F. Phillips.
(Op. 69, no. 2) © Ascherberg, Hopwood & Crew, ltd., London; 28Nov47;
on arrangement; EF7211.
Sing, Joyous Bird; three-part song,
arr. by the composer, words by
Nora C. Usher, music by Montague
F. Phillips. © Chappell & Co.,
ltd., London; 5Nov47; on arrangement; EF7280.

PHILLIPS, MONTAGUE F. Cont'd.
Spring Is a Lovely Lady; two-part
song, arr. by the composer, words
by Winifred May, music by Montague
F. Phillips. (Op. 56, no. 4) ©
Ascherberg, Hopwood & Crew, ltd.,
London; 28Nov47; on arrangement;
EF7210.

PHILLIPS, PETER.
Which Way Does the Wind Blow?
Words by Peter Phillips & Martyn
Mayne, music by Peter Phillips.
© Arcadia Music Publishing Co.,
ltd., London; 5Nov47; EF7570.

PHILPOT, EVA, 1910-
Hold Them Up in Prayer; [by] Mrs.
Eva Philpot. © Eva Philpot,
Hamilton, Ohio; 28Aug47; EP16636.
Close score: SATB, in shape-note
notation.

PHOUSKAGIANNĒS, pseud. See
Phouskas, Giannēs Konstantinos.

PHOUSKAS, GIANNĒS KONSTANTINOS, 1910-
Glyko Mou Agori ... etichoi: N.
Phatsea, mousikē: Phouskagiannē
[pseud.] Athēnai, Ekdoseis
Gaïtanou. © Michael Gaetanos,
Athens; 4Jun46; EF5771. For
voice and piano.

PHRANTZESKAKĒS, DĒMĒTRIOS GEORGIOS,
1906-
As Ein Kals e Thelos ap' tēn
Amerikē ... etichoi: G. Ioannidē,
mousikē, D. Phrantzeskakē.
Athēnai, Ekdoseis Gaïtanou. ©
Michael Gaetanos, Athens; 15May47;
EF5767. For voice and piano.

PIAZZI, GIUSEPPE.
Suite Retica; [by] Giuseppe Piazzi.
© Casa Musicale Sonzogno di
Piero Ostali, Milano; 21Dec46;
EF6929. Score: orchestra.

PICHÉ, BERNARD.
Rhapsody on Four Noëls; for organ,
by Bernard Piché. © The H. W.
Gray Co., inc., New York;
7Nov47; EP19264.

PICHON, FERNAND, 1893-
La Ritournelle de Nos Amours;
paroles et musique de Fernand
Pichon, arr. par Robert Bernay.
© Fernand Pichon, Nice, France;
15Jul47; on arrangement; EF7310.
For voice and piano, and voice
part.

PICON, ANTON, pseud. See
Spurgin, Anthony Martin.

PIEDIGROTTA "F. Mario Russo" 1947-48;
[words by Angelica Laurini, Amedeo
Greco and others, music by Alfonso
Neri, Giov. Donnarumma and others]
Napoli, F. M. Russo. © Italian
Book Co., New York; 3Sep47; EF6856.

PIEDIGROTTA 1947; [by Enzo Barile,
E. Nardella, and others, words by
E. Bonagura, Aldo Bovio, and
others] Napoli, Edizioni Musica-
li N. Gennarelli. © Italian
Book Co., New York; 30Sep47;
EF6858.

PIEDIGROTTA 1947 DE "LA CANZONETTA."
[Words by Francesco Fiore,
Michele Galdieri and others;
music by Gaetano Lama, G.
Bonavolontà and others] ©
Italian Book Co., New York;
5Aug47; EF6389.

PIERNÉ, GABRIEL.
In the Cathedral; [by] Pierné,
transcribed by Irving Cheyette.
(Michigan University. Band Series,
pt. 2, no. 2) © G. Schirmer, inc.,
New York; 23Sep47; on transcription;
EP20284. Score (band) and parts.

PIERCE, DORA.
An Introduction to Sight Reading;
[by] Dora Pierce and Lilian
Leavey. © The Oxford University
Press, London; 15May47; EF6115.

PIERNÉ, PAUL, 1904-
Bucolique Variée; trio [by] Paul
Pierné. © Lucien de Lacour,
Éditeur, Paris; 1Jul47; EF6576.
Score (oboe, clarinet and bassoon)
and parts.

PIERPONT, JAMES S
Jingle Bells; [by] J. Pierpont,
arr. for junior, intermediate
and senior choirs ... by Guy
Chambers Filkins. © Guy
Chambers Filkins, Ann Arbor,
Mich.; 15Dec46; on arrangement;
EP17763.

Jingle, Bells; by J. Pierpont,
arr. for S.A.T.B.B. [and words
adapted] by Leonard A. Temme.
© Hall & McCreary Co., Chicago;
16Oct47; on adaptation of text
& arrangement; EP18658.

Jingle Bells; for mixed chorus
arr. by Ray Charles. © The
Staff Music Publishing Co.,
Great Neck, N. Y.; 25Oct47;
on arrangement; EP18427.

PILDEROT, ENRIQUE TORRIENTE. See
Torriente Pilderot, Enrique.

[PIMPERAL, JOHN MATHEW] 1919-
I'm Dreaming of You; words and
music by John Benson [pseud.]
c1946. © John Mathew Pimperal,
Albany; 8Jul47; on new lyrics;
EP17963.

PINGAULT, CLAUDE, 1902-
Le Mousse du Bonaventure;
paroles de Maurice Ygor
[pseud.] musique de Claude
Pingault. c1947. © Société
d'Editions Musicales Internationales (S.E.M.I.),
Paris; 27Dec46; EF5942.

PINKSTON, QUEENIE F
Lonesome Me; words and music by
Queenie F. Pinkston. © Nordyke
Publishing Co., Los Angeles;
28Jul46; EP19973.

PINTO, WALTER.
With My Heart's Contentment;
words and music by Walter
Pinto. © Nordyke Publishing
Co., Los Angeles; 16Dec46;
EP20050.

PIPER, ELMER DAVID, 1917-
Revival Choruses (Number Two);
by Evangelist Elmer D. Piper.
© Elmer David Piper, Green-
ville, S.C.; 24Jun47; on 5
choruses. Close score:SATB.
Contents.- Jesus Is a Friend of
Mine (© EF15796).- He's Won My
Heart Completely (© EF15797) -
I've Been Set Free (© EF15798).-
Tell Me His Name Again (© EP
15799).- If Christ Would Live
and Reign in Me (© EF15800)

PIPON, LUCIEN, 1902-
L'Amour S'Amuse; comédie musicale en
3 actes, livret de H. Couarraze,
lyrics de Ch. L. Pothier et C. de
Morihon, musique de Lucien Pipon.
© Éditions Salabert, Paris;
18Sep47; EF7352. Piano-vocal
score.

L'Aveugle de Ma Rue ... Paroles
de Paul Alain [pseud.], musique
de Lucien Pipon, arrt. de Fran-
cis Salabert ... Triolets
Dansants ... musique de O.
Mirendola, arrt. de Francis
Salabert. © Éditions Salabert
Paris; 14Apr47; on arrangement;
EF5855. Piano-conductor
score (orchestra) and parts.

PIRONE, HARRY.
I Went to Cry; lyric by Lille
Randall, music by Harry Pirone.
© Excelsior Music Publishing
Co., New York; 18Nov47;
EP20249.

PISANI, DOMENICO.
Fior di Campāka ... Notti
Andaluse ... musiche di
Domenico Pisani, testi di
Mafalda Baccaglioni. ©
Edizioni Musicali "Lillium",
Milano; 15Mar47; EF3962.
Piano- conductor score
(orchestra, with words), and
parts.

PITFIELD, THOMAS BARON.
Ballet in Education, Children's
Examinations; music written
and compiled by Thomas B.
Pitfield. © Royal Academy of
Dancing, London; 17Jul47;
EF6182. For piano.

The Bold Pedlar; Russian gipsy
song, words tr. by Alice M.
Pitfield, arr. & English verse
by Thomas B. Pitfield. © The
Oxford University Press, London;
5Jun47; on arrangement; EF6117.
Score: SATB and piano reduction;
voice parts also in tonic sol-fa
notation.

The Country Road; unison song.
Words by Muriel Hilton, music by
Thomas B. Pitfield. © Banks &
Son, York, Eng.; 22Oct47;
EF7150.

Memorials; unison song, words
and music by Thomas B. Pitfield,
© A.& C. Black, ltd., London;
18Jun47; EF5989.

Night Music; choral suite for four,
five and six part voices (piano
acc. for practice only) by Thomas
B. Pitfield. © Augener, ltd.,
London; 28Oct47; EF7130.

Rondo Lirico ... by Thomas B.
Pitfield. © The Oxford
University Press, London;
10Apr47; EF6100. Score (oboe
and piano) and part,

The Runaway Showman; unison song,
words by Florence Harrison,
music by Thomas B. Pitfield. ©
A. & C. Black, ltd., London;
18Jun47; EF5988.

PITRE, BENOIT.
Old Glory Waves On Forever; words
and music by Benoit Pitre. [c1945]
© Nordyke Publishing Co., Los
Angeles; 15Aug47; EP16596.

PIZARRO, MANUEL.
Descamisado ... letra de Vicente
Toribio del Barrio, música de
Manuel Pizarro, música de
Argentina de Música Interna-
cional, s. de r. ltda., (EDAMI),
Buenos Aires; 27Aug47; EF6696.

PIZZINI, CARLO ALBERTO.
Al Piemonte; trittico sinfonico
per orchestra ... Partitura.
Roma, Edizioni de Santis. ©
Carlo Alberto Pizzini, Roma;
14Jun41; EF3982.

PJURA, WILLIAM JOSEPH, 1915-
Piano Polka; by Wm. J. Pjura.
© William J. Pjura, d.b.a. P. J.
Williams Co., Stratford, Conn.;
19Jul47; EP16333.

PLACHANSKI, JAN.
Clarinetka Polka [and Oberek
Janów; by] J. Plachanski, arr. by
Walter Ossowski. © Jan Plachanski, Johnson City, N. Y.;
23Jun47; EP15556-15557. Piano-
conductor score (orchestra) and
parts.

PLANEL, JEAN, 1903-
Sept Vocalises; pour soprano ou
ténor, par Jean Planel. © A.
Planel & Fils, Paris; 15Oct47;
EF7308.

PLANK, KINNEY YODER.
Pray about It ... [music by] K. Y.
Plank, [words by] B. Elliott
Warren. (In The Gospel Trumpet.
v.67, no.39, p.25) © Kinney
Yoder Plank, Springfield, Ill.
& Barney Elliott Warren, Spring-
field, Ohio; 20Sep47; B5-1808.
Close score; SATB.

With Him in Heaven; [music by]
K. Y. Plank, [words by] B. E.
Warren. (In The Gospel Music
Review. v.1, no.4, p.[10])
© Kinney Yoder Plank, Springfield, Ill.
& Barney Elliott
Warren, Springfield, Ohio;
1Jun47; B5-1270. Close score;
SATB.

PLEIS, JACK.
They're Mine, They're Mine, They're
Mine; lyric by Sonny Kane, music
by Jack Pleis. © Edwin H. Morris
& Co., inc., New York; 5Jun47;
EP15341.

PLUMB, BENJAMIN NEELY. See
Plumb, Neely.

PLUMB, NEELY, 1912-
"Dare It." Words and music by Neely
Plumb. © Neely Plumb Publishing
Co., North Hollywood, Calif.;
1Jul47; EP15952.

The Drugstore Cowboy's Lament;
words by Lou Marcelle, music by
Neely Plumb [and] Al Burton. ©
Neely Plumb Publishing Co.,
N. Hollywood, Calif.; 15Oct47;
EP18614.

"I Had a Million Dreams Last
Night;" words and music by
Neely Plumb. [c1945] ©
Neely Plumb, North Holly-
wood, Calif.; 1Aug47;
EP16513.

PLUMMER, HOWARD ALBERT.
How I Could Love You; words and
music by Howard A. Plummer, jr.
© Wise Music Publications, New
York; 12Sep47; EP17111.

POIRIER, EDWARD JOSEPH, 1903-
My Flaming Heart; words and music
by Edward J. Poirier [arr. by
Burrell Van Buren] © Edward
Joseph Poirier, Bay City, Mich.;
7Nov47; EP19046.

POLATSCHEK, VICTOR.
12 Etudes for Clarinet; by Victor
Polatschek. © Edward B. Marks
Music Corp., New York; 22Dec47;
EP20290.

POLITE, CHARLES R
What Lovely Music; words and
music by Charles R. Polite.
© Nordyke Publishing Co., Los
Angeles; 10Oct47; EP19303.

POLLA, WILLIAM C   d.1939.
Dancing Tambourine; [by] W. C.
Polla, piano duet arr. by J.
Louis Merkur. © Harms, inc.,
New York; 3Nov47; on arrange-
ment; EP18503.

POLLACK, ROBERT, 1900-
Down in the Valley; words by Al
Sizemore, music by Robert
Pollack. © Nordyko Publishing
Co., Los Angeles; 28Jul47;
EP16751.

Just Wanting You; words ... by
George M. Oates ... and Don B.
Owens, jr. [c1944] © The La
Casa Del Rio Music Publishing
Co., Toledo; 25Nov45;
EP15603. For voice and piano,
with guitar diagrams and chord
symbols.

Little Texas Queen; words by
Mildred Bowhall, music by
Robert Pollack. © Nordyke
Publishing Co., Los Angeles;
2Jul46; EP19466.

POLLET.
The Three Musketeers ... [by]
Pollet ... ed. and arr. by
Alec Rowley. © Joseph Wil-
liams, ltd., London; 2Jul47;
on arrangement; EF3943.
Score; orchestra.

POLOVINKIN, L   A
We Thank Our Great Leader; words
by I. Dobrovolsky, English adap-
tation by Olga Paul, [music by]
L. A. Polovinkin. (In Haywood,
Charles, ed. Art Songs of Soviet
Russia, p.35-37) © Edward B.
Marks Music Corp., New York;
16Sep47; on English adaptation;
EP17183. English and Russian
words.

PONCE, MANUEL M   1886-
Estrellita. Little Star; by
Manuel M. Ponce, lyric by Fred-
erick H. Martens ... [arr.] by
Hugo Frey] © Hamilton S.
Gordon, inc., New York; 9Jul47;
on arrangement; EP15612. Eng-
lish words.

[POND, CLARENCE ANDREW]
Beautiful City of Gold, Heaven's
Radio, [and Prophetic Song, by
C. A. Pond] © Clarence S.
Pansler, Akron, Ohio; 1Aug47;
EP16511. Caption title for
first hymn: The City of Gold.
Hymns with music.

POND, DOUGLAS.
Sandstorm; composed by Douglas
Pond and Don Bowden, arr. by
Don Bowden. © Hawkes & Son
(London) ltd., London; 23Jul47;
on arrangement; EF5795. Piano-
conductor score (orchestra) and
parts.

Woodwind ... [by] Douglas Pond.
[London] Boosey & Hawkes. ©
Hawkes & Son (London) ltd.,
London; 11Jul47; EF5720.
Score (clarinet and piano) and
part.

POND, FRANK GEORGE, 1866-
That's How I Know You Love Me;
words and music by Frank Pond.
© Frank George Pond, Mountain
View, N. Y.; 21Jul47; EP17333.

PONTAROLLO, MARY F
Seriously Speaking; words and
music by Mary E. Pontarollo.
© Nordyke Publishing Co., Los
Angeles; 22Jul47; EP20033.

PONZETTI, PAUL.
Sadness in the Rain; words and
music by Paul Ponzetti. © Nordyke Publishing Co., Los Angeles; 18Jul46; EP20062.

POPPLEWELL, JACK.
My Girl's an Irish Girl ... words
and music by Jack Popplewell.
© The Peter Maurice Music Co.,
ltd., New York; 20Oct47;
EF6833.

PORTER, COLE, 1892-
Cole Porter Selection; transcribed
... by David Bennett. © Harms,
inc., New York; 13Aug47; on
arrangement; EP17645. Condensed
score (band) and parts.

(Wake Up and Dream) What Is This
Thing Called Love [from the musi-
cal comedy "Wake Up and Dream"]
Music by Cole Porter, arr. by
Jerry Sears. © Harms, inc., New
York; 9Dec47; on arrangement;
EP19998. Piano-conductor score
(orchestra) and parts.

What Is This Thing Called Love? See his
Wake Up and Dream.

PORTER, ISRAEL HOYT, 1882-
Mother's Eyes: words [by] T. C.
Hoyt, music [by] Israel H.
Porter. © Israel Hoyt Porter,
Basalt, Idaho; 19Jul47; EP17258.

PORTER, J   SPENCER.
The Girl from the Production Line;
words and music by J. Spencer
Porter. © Nordyke Publishing
Co., Los Angeles; 29Mar47;
EP16798.

PORTER-BROWN, REGINALD, 1910-
The Little Ballerina; for pianoforte
[by] Reginald Porter-Brown. ©
Edwin Ashdown, ltd., London;
12Dec47; EF7272.

PORTNOFF, MISCHA
(Carnegie Hall) All the World Is
Mine, theme from "57th St.
Rhapsody" in the motion picture
"Carnegie Hall"; lyric by Dorothy
Dick, music by Mischa and Wesley
Portnoff. © Leo Feist, inc.,
New York; 11Aug47; EP16293.

POSFORD, GEORGE.
"Balalaika;" a play with music, by
Eric Maschwitz, music by George
Posford & Bernard Grün ... vocal
score by George Posford. © Keith
Prowse & Co., ltd., London;
28Jul47; EF6245.

The World Is Mine (tonight) lyric
by Holt Marvell, music by George
Posford ... duet [for] high and
low voices [arr. by Victor Lam-
ont] © Sam Fox Publishing Co.,
New York; 6Oct47; on arrangement; EP17999.

POST, BILL H   1919-
Doagie-boogie; words & music by
Bill H. Post, [arr. by Ralph
Flanagan] c1946. © Post and
Postel Publishing Co., Los
Angeles; 7Jul47; on arrange-
ment; EP15506.

POTTAG, MAX P   ed.
Sixty French Horn Duets ... ed.
by Max P. Pottag. © Belwin,
inc., New York; bk. 1, 18Sep47;
on editing; EP18562.

Sixty French Horn Duets ... bk. 2, ed. by
Max P. Pottag. © Belwin, inc.,
New York; bk.2, 30Oct47; on editing
& compiling; EP17919.

POTTER, ALMA LEONARD.
Dad and Mother Are There [and
Lord, I Hear Thy Call]; words
and music by Alma Leonard
Potter. © Alma Leonard Potter,
Lisbon, N. D.; 11Aug47;
EP16292, 16291.

POTTER, HAROLD HOLMES, 1891-
I Met Her in the Movies; words and
music by Freddie Van, George
Temple jr., Alan Foster [and]
Harold Potter. © Catchy Songs
Music Co., New York; 22Jul47;
EP15717.

It Was the Good Old Parson! ...
Music by Harold Potter; words
by W. Frank Brown. Keokuk,
Iowa, Dr. Billie Song Shoppe.
© W. Frank Brown, Keokuk, Iowa;
19Jun47; EP15596. Partly for
voice and piano with chord symbols; partly close score; SATB.

It's Easy to Fool the One Who Loves
You; music by Harold Potter,
lyric by Max Wartell. © Royal
Crown Music Co., New York;
17Sep47; EP17114.

So Much in Love; words and music
by George Temple, Freddie Van,
Alan Foster [and] Harold Potter.
© Catchy Songs Music Co., New
York; 22Jul47; EP15715.

POULENC, FRANCIS, 1899-
Le Disparu; [by] Francis Poulenc,
poème de R. Desnos. © Rouart
Lerolle & Co., éditeurs, Paris;
15Sep47; EF7347. For voice and
piano.

Intermezzo en lab majeur; pour
piano, [by] Francis Poulenc. ©
Editions Max Eschig, Paris;
12Mar47; EF7233.

POULENC, FRANCIS. Cont'd.
Main Dominée par le Coeur ... [by]
Francis Poulenc, poème de Paul
Eluard, [pseud.] © Rouart Lerolle
& Cie, éditeurs, Paris; 15Sep47;
EF7348. For voice and piano.

Paul et Virginie; poème de Raymond
Radiguet, musique de Francis
Poulenc. © Éditions Max Eschig,
Paris; 10Jan47; EF7231.

Le Pont. Un Poème. Deux mélodies
sur des poèmes de Guillaume
Apollinaire, musique de Francis
Poulenc. © Éditions Max Eschig,
Paris; 10Jan47; EF7232.

(Sonate, violin & piano) Sonate;
[by] Francis Poulenc. [c1944]
© Éditions Max Eschig, Paris;
12Jan45; EF7328. Score and part.

POUR, FRANK.
Patty; words & music by Frank
Pour, jr. © Nordyke Publishing
Co., Los Angeles; 27Sep46;
EP20485.

POVEDA, ENRIQUE SCHUMANN. See
Schumann Poveda, Enrique.

POWELL, DAISY.
Dreaming of You; words and music
by Daisy Powell. © Nordyke
Publishing Co., Los Angeles;
28Mar47; EP16746.

POWELL, RALPH E
A Cross of White (in Picardy to-
night) words and music by
Ralph E. Powell. © Nordyke
Publishing Co., Los Angeles;
14Jun47; EP17554.

POZO, Chano. See
Pozo, Luciano.

POZO, LUCIANO.
Uam-pam-piro ... letra y música
de Luciano (Chano) Pozo.
© Robbins Music Corp., New York;
24Jun47; EP15421.

POZO, M A
El Guarapo y la Melcocha ... au-
tores: Eduardo Saborit y M.A.
Pozo. © Peer International
Corp., New York; 30Sep47;
EP6829. Parts: orchestra; with
words.

PRATHER, ROBERT LYNN, 1918-
I'm Gonna Serve My Lord; words
and music by Robert L. "Bob"
Prather. © Robert L. Prather,
Atlanta; 8Sep47; EP17171.
Close score; SATB. Shape-note
notation.

PREADER, ANDREW A
Without You; words and music by
Andrew A. Preader. © Nordyke
Publishing Co., Los Angeles;
24Jul47; EP17467.

PRENTICE, WYNN S 1925-1946.
"In the Beginning;" by Wynn S.
Prentice, sacred song for medium voice, [text, 1st chap. of
Genesis, Op. 1, no. 6] © Wesley Webster, San Francisco;
10Dec47; EP19573.

PREOBRAJENSKY, VERA N
Am I Wastin' My Time? Words &
music by Tania and Vera Preobrajensky. © Nordyke Publishing Co., Los Angeles; 16Sep46;
EP19720.

Remember, June, That Night? Words
and music by Vera N. Preobrajensky. © Nordyke Publishing
Co., Los Angeles; 13Jul46;
EP20380.

PRESSLEY, BOB.
Silver and Gold; words by Lois
Markwalter, music by Bob Press-
ley. © Northern Music Corp.,
New York; 24Nov47; EP19229.

PRESTER, ARTHUR.
Symptoms of Love; words and music
by Arthur Prester. © Nordyke
Publishing Co., Los Angeles;
11Jun47; EP16908.

PRESTON, M L 1879-
Cowboy on a Rocking Horse ...
[by] M. L. Preston. (In
Hirschberg, David, ed. and comp.
Pieces Are Fun. bk. 1, p. 14-
15) © Musicord Publications,
New York; 2Jul47; EP15931. For
piano solo, with words.

PREUSS, THEO arr.
Christmas in Song; a treasury of
traditional songs, favorite
hymns, and choice carols, from
all ages and from many lands
... comp. and arr. for mixed
voices (S.A.T.B.) or unisonal
singing, by Theo. Preuss. ©
Rubank, inc., Chicago; 20Nov47;
EP18850.

PREVIN, ANDRÉ.
Previn's Boogie; by André Previn.
New York, Sinatra Songs. ©
Sinatra Music Publishing Corp.,
New York; 24Oct47; EP18460.

PRICE, ERNEST LELAND.
Land of Lakes and Mountains;
words and music by Ernest
Leland Price. © Nordyke
Publishing Co., Los Angeles;
16Jul47; EP17504.

PRICE, FLORENCE B 1888-
Criss Cross ... Rock-a-bye; by
Florence Price. © McKinley
Publishers, inc., Chicago;
8Jul47; EP15525. For piano
solo.

Here and There ... by Florence
Price. © McKinley Publishers,
inc., Chicago; 8Jul47; EP15527.
For piano solo.

March of the Beetles ... Clover
Blossom ... by Florence Price.
© McKinley Publishers, inc.,
Chicago; 8Jul47; EP15526. For
piano solo.

PRICE, THOMAS.
Your Love Fills My Heart, Virginia; words and music by Thomas
Price. © Nordyke Pub-
lishing Co., Los Angeles;
12Jun46; EP20058.

PRICHARD, R H
Joy of Heaven. (Llawenydd Nef)
For four-part chorus of men's
voices with piano accompaniment
... [by] R. H. Prichard, setting by Bryceson Treharne,
[words by] Charles Wesley,
Welsh translation by E. Cynol-
wyn Pugh. © The Boston Music
Co., Boston; 30Sep47; on arrangement & Welsh translation;
EP17745.

PRICHARD, ROWLAND H
Not Alone for Mighty Empire ...
[for] S.A.T.B., [music by]
Rowland H. Prichard, setting by
Earl Roland Larson. [Words by]
William P. Merrill. © Clayton
F. Summy Co., Chicago; 44u647;
on arrangement; EP16675.

PRIGMORE, BETTIE WILSON.
Darling, That's My Heart; words
and music by Bettee Wilson
Prigmore. © Nordyke Publishing
Co., Los Angeles; 25Jun47;
EP15858.

PRIMA, LOUIS.
Baciagaloop (makes love on da
stoop) words and music by Sid
Tepper, Roy Brodsky and Louis
Prima, arr. by Johnny Warring-
ton. © Mills Music, inc., New
York; 28Jul47; on arrangement;
EP16192. Piano-conductor score
(orchestra, with words) and
parts.

A Sunday Kind of Love; by Barbara
Belle, Anita Leonard ... Stan
Rhodes [and] Louis Prima. [Arr.
by Johnny Warrington] © The
Peter Maurice Music Co., ltd.,
New York; 30Jun47; on arrangement; EP15785. Piano-conductor
score (orchestra, with words)
and parts.

PRINTZ, ALLAN, pseud. See
Garman, William McKinley

[PRIPPS, EDWARD ROBERT] 1915-
Blizzard Head Blues; [by Edward
Robert Pripps] © Joseph James
(Zep) Meissner, North Hollywood,
Calif.; 7Jul47; EP19074. Parts:
orchestra.

PRITCHARD, WALLY.
Why Do I Love You, Oh Why? Words
and Music by Smokey Rogers and
Wally Pritchard. © Hill and
Range Songs, inc., Hollywood,
Calif.; 14Nov47; EP18764.

PROCHÁZKA, SLAVOJ.
Za Prahou ... [by] Slavoj Procház-
ka, [words by] Karel Šmíd [and]
Ant. Fanta. © Zdeněk Vlk,
Praha, Czechoslovakia; 1Feb44;
EF6793. Part for 2 treble
voices with chord symbols.

PROKOP'EV, SERGEI SERGEEVICH, 1891-
Gavotta; from the "Classical
symphony" ... arr. by Joseph
Schuster. © Carl Fischer, inc.,
New York; 3Jul47; on arrangement; EP15747. Score (violoncello and piano) and part.

Peter and the Wolf; a musical tale
by Serge Prokofieff. Op. 67.
[Simplified arrangement by Walter L. Rosemont] © Edwards Music Co., New York; 8Dec47; on
arrangement; EP19851. For narrator and piano.

(Quartet, strings, no. 2) Quartet
no. 2 [by] Sergo Prokofieff.
Op.92. [Ed. with special
annotations by Harold Sheldon]
© Leeds Music Corp., New York;
16Jun47; on editing & foreword;
EP15350. Parts.

PROVOST, WILLIAM.
Cinderella ... lyrics by Lee Rogow,
music by William Provost;
adapted by Michael Martin, piano
arrangements by Dorothy Cadzow.
© Merrymount Music Press, New
York; 3Jul47; EP15476.

PRUD'HOMME, ÉMILE LUCIEN, 1913-
Ta Chanson ... Paroles de Jean
Rafa [pseud.] & Syam [pseud.],
musique de Émile Prud'homme.
© Arpège Éditions Musicales,
Paris; 25Feb47; EP6450. For
voice and piano, and voice part.

[PRYCE, BETTY] arr.
A song to Hawaii. (Oahu modern
note method (lesson 19FN]) ©
Oahu Publishing Co., Cleveland;
on arrangement; 22Oct45; EP3980.
For 2 guitars, with interlinear
words.

PULITINI, JOSEPH, 1900-
Ocean View Waltz; for piano accordion by Joseph Pulitini. © Joseph Pulitini, Chicago; 10Nov47;
EP20216.

PURCELL, EDWARD.
Be Present at Our Table, Lord ...
[music by] Edward Purcell, arr.
by Griffith J. Jones, [words by]
John Cennick. [Prayer for Youth;
traditional English melody arr. by
O. J. Jones, words by W. woolsey
Stryker. Lord, We Thank Thee;
traditional air arr. by O. J. Jones,
words by William L. Stidger] ©
The Rodeheaver Co., Winona Lake,
Ind.; 5Sep47; on arrangement;
EP17130-17132. Close score; SATB,

333

PURCELL, HENRY, 1658 or 9-1695.
Blessed Is He Whose Unrighteousness Is Forgiv'n; (anthem) ed.
from the Purcell Society edition
by H. S. Middleton. [London]
Pub. for the Purcell Society by
Novello and Co. © Gerald M.
Cooper, London; 4Feb44; on new
continuo parts; EP6882. Score;
solo voices, chorus (SSATTB)
and organ.

The Blessed Virgin's Expostulation; [By] Henry Purcell. [arr.
from the figured bass by
Michael Tippett and Walter
Bergmann] (Voice and keyboard;
original compositions for
voice and figured bass, no.
1) © Schott & Co., ltd.,
London; 16Jun47; on arrangement; EP3944.

Comus; suite from the ballet ...
[by] Purcell, arr. by Constant
Lambert. [London, Boosey &
Hawkes] © Hawkes & Son (London)
ltd., London; 12Aug47; on
arrangement; EP6048. Parts:
orchestra.

Fairest Isle; [by] Henry Purcell,
arr. for solo instruments and
piano acc. (with optional second
parts) by Harold Farkman.[pseud.]
© The Arthur P. Schmidt Co.,
Boston; 10Oct47; on arrangement[?].
EP18377. Score and part.

Fantasia (no.1); [by] Henry Purcell,
for soprano, alto and tenor
recorders. Adapted by George
Hunter. © R. C. Schirmer Music
Co., Boston; 12Aug47; on adaptation; EP16556.

How Blest Are Shepherds. See his King
Arthur.

(The Indian Queen) Trumpet
Overture, from 'The Indian Queen'
by Henry Purcell, for trumpet,
strings, and timpani (optional),
arr. by Lionel Salter. Score.
© The Oxford University Press,
London; 5Jun47; on arrangement;
EP6120.

(King Arthur) How Blest Are Shepherds ... (from the opera, "King
Arthur") words by John Dryden,
music by Henry Purcell, arr. for
mixed voices (S.C.T.B.) by Norman Stone. © Ascherberg, Hopwood & Crew, ltd., London;
20Oct47; on arrangement; EP6958.

Music for a While; by Henry
Purcell, [arr. from the figured
bass by Michael Tippett and
Walter Bergmann] (Voice and
keyboard; original compositions
for voice and figured bass. no
2) © Schott & Co., ltd.,
London; 17Feb47; on arrangement;
EP3945.

(Preludes, piano) Two Preludes,
for piano; [by] Purcell-Bartók.
© Delkas Music Publishing Co.,
Los Angeles; 1Jul47; on transcription. Contents.-- [1] Prelude in
G Major (© EP17096) - [2] Prelude
in C Major (© EP17097)

Save Me, O God, for Thy Name's
Saku; anthem for S.S.A.T.T.B.,
by Henry Purcell. Psalm LIV.
[Arr. by Gerald M. Cooper]
London, Pub. for the Purcell
Society by Novello & Co. ©
Gerald M. Cooper, London;
24May39; on new continuo parts;
EP6880.

Sonata in G minor [by] Henry
Purcell ... [transcribed] by
Watson Forbes and Alan Richard-
son. (c1946) © The Oxford
University Press, London;
23Jan47; on arrangement; EP6140.
Score (viola and piano) and
part.

Trumpet Overture. See his The Indian
Queen.

"Welcome to All the Pleasures";
an ode for St. Cecilia's Day,
ed. from the Purcell Society
edition by Gerald M. Cooper.
[London] Pub. for the Purcell
Society by Novello and Co. ©
Gerald M. Cooper, London;
21Oct42; on new continuo parts;
EP6881. Score; solo voices,
mixed chorus and piano.

PYPER, GEORGE ROBERT, 1883-
I Took a Chance; by George Robert
Pyper. © George Robert Pyper,
Salt Lake City; 4Nov47; EP18831
For voice and piano, with chord
symbols.

Q

QUARATINO, PASCUAL, 1904-
El Embrujo de Zamba; [by] P.
Quaratino, para piano. ©
Ricordi Americana, s.a.e.c.;
Buenos Aires; 15Mar44; EP6983.

Organito; para piano [by] P.
Quaratino. © Ricordi Americana,
s.a.e.c., Buenos Aires; 19Mar42;
EP6991.

[QUILTER, ROGER] 1877-
The Ash Grove; old Welsh melody
[from the Arnold Book of Old
Songs, arr. by Roger Quilter]
English words by Rodney Bennett.
London, Boosey & Hawkes. ©
Boosey & Co., ltd., London;
24Sep47; on arrangement;
EP6645.

Believe Me, If All Those Endearing
Young Charms; old Irish melody
[from the Arnold Book of Old
Songs, arr. by Roger Quilter]
Words by Thomas Moore. London,
Boosey & Hawkes. © Boosey &
Co., ltd., London; 24Sep47; on
arrangement; EP6648.

Ca' the Yowes to the Knowes;
words by Burns, old Scottish
melody [from the Arnold Book of
Old Songs arr. by Roger Quilter]
London, Boosey & Hawkes. ©
Boosey & Co., ltd., London;
20Aug47; on arrangement;
EP6267.

Charlie is My Darling; words
anonymous, Scottish Jacobite
marching tune [from the Arnold
Book of Old Songs, arr. by Roger
Quilter] London, Boosey & Hawkes.
© Boosey & Co., ltd., London;
20Aug47; on arrangement; EP6263.

A Children's Overture; [by] Roger
Quilter, arr. [by] Denis Wright.
(Chappell's Brass and reed band
journal, no.161) © Chappell &
Co., ltd., London; 31Jul47; on
arrangement; EP6322. Cornet-
conductor score (band) and parts.
The Man behind the Plough. Le
Pauvre Laboureur. Old French
melody [from the Arnold Book
of Old Songs, arr. by Roger
Quilter] English words by Rod-
ney Bennett. London, Boosey
& Hawkes. © Boosey & Co., ltd.,
London; 30Sep47; on arrange-
ment; EP6650.

My Lady Greensleeves; old English
melody [from the Arnold Book
of Old Songs, arr. by Roger
Quilter] Words by John Irvine.
London, Boosey & Hawkes. ©
Boosey & Co., ltd., London;
30Sep47; on arrangement;
EP6651.
My Lady's Garden. L'Amour de Moi.
English words by Rodney Bennett,
old French melody [from the
Arnold Book of Old Songs, arr.
by Roger Quilter] London, Boosey
& Hawkes. © Boosey & Co., ltd.,
London; 20Aug47; on arrangement;
EP6264.

Oh! 'Tis Sweet to Think; words by
Thomas Moore, old Irish melody
[from the Arnold Book of Old
Songs, arr. by Roger Quilter]
London, Boosey & Hawkes. ©
Boosey & Co., ltd., London;
20Aug47; on arrangement; EP6265.
One Word Is Too Often Profaned;
[words by] Shelley, [music by]
Roger Quilter. [London] Curwen
Ed. © Roger Quilter, London;
16Sep47; EP6740.
Pretty Month of May. Joli Moi de
Mai. Words anonymous, old
French melody [from the Arnold
Book of Old Songs, arr. by
Roger Quilter] London, Boosey &
Hawkes. © Boosey & Co., ltd.,
London; 20Aug47; on arrangement;
EP6266.
Tulips; [by] Roger Quilter, words
by Herrick. © Ascherberg, Hopwood
& Crew, ltd., London; 25Nov47;
on arrangement; EP7205.
Ye Banks and Braes; old Scottish
melody [from the Arnold Book of
Old Songs, arr. by Roger
Quilter] Words by Burns.
London, Boosey & Hawkes. ©
Boosey & Co., ltd., London;
24Sep47; on arrangement;
EP6647.
QUINTERO GARCERÁN, RAFAEL.
La Negra Martica ... Letra y
música de Rafael Quintero
Garcerán, arreglo de Juan E.
Lazaga. © Peer International
Corp., New York; 6Jun47;
EP5737. Parts: orchestra.
QUIROGA, MANUEL.
Canto Amoroso; [by] Manuel Quiro-
ga. Paris, Publications R.
Breton. © Éditions. L. Maillo-
chon, Raoul Breton et Cie,
Paris; 18Mar28; EP6812. Score
(violin and piano) and part.
(Concerto, violin, no. 1)
Premier Concerto, dans le style
antique ... [by] Manuel
Quiroga, [harmonisation et
réalisation par Roger Pénau]
© Éditions L. Maillochon,
Paris; 9Jun25; EP6288. Score
(violin and piano) and part.
Emigrantes Celtas. Terra ... A
Nosa! Pour violon seul, [by]
Manuel Quiroga. © Éditions L.
Maillochon, Paris; 9Jun25;
EP6287.
Neuf Variations ... sur un thème
de Nicolò Paganini, [by] Manuel
Quiroga. © Éditions L. Maillochon,
Raoul Breton et Cie, Paris;
18Mar28; EP6289. For violin
alone.
Zortzico; danse basque, [by]
Manuel Quiroga. © Éditions L.
Maillochon, Raoul Breton et Cie,
Paris; 18Mar28; EP6290. Score
(violin and piano) and part.

R

RABAUD, HENRI, 1873-
Martine; cinq tableaux de Jean-
Jacques Bernard, musique de Henri
Rabaud. Partition pour chant et
piano réduite par l'auteur. ©
Henry Lemoine & Cie, Paris;
12Apr47; EF7240.
RABEY, RENÉ.
Suite Savoyarde; pour piano à
deux mains [by] René Rabey. ©
Durand & Cie, Paris; 30Apr46;
on 4 pièces. Contents.- 1. Au
Petit Trot des Mules (© EP2283)-
2. Sur le Lac Enchanté (©
EP2285)- 3. Cortège nocturne
dans la neige (© EP2282)- 4. La
Retraite des Gardes (© EP2288)
RABY, WARREN.
Can It Be True? Words and music
by Warren Raby. © Nordyke
Publishing Co., Los Angeles;
29Mar47; EP16767.

UNA RACCOLTA DI CANZONI PER VOI!
[Music by M. Ruccione, N. Valente
and others; words by Enzo Bonagura, C. Esposito and others]
© Mario Gennarelli, Naples;
10Sep46; EF5312.

RACHMANINOFF, SERGEI, 1873-1943.
The Best Known Music of Rachmaninoff;
[comp. by Hamilton S. Gordon, inc,
Vocalise transcribed by Hugo Frey]
© Hamilton S. Gordon, inc., New
York; 2Dec47; on transcription of
Vocalise; EP19553. For piano solo.

(Concerto, piano, no. 2) Rachmaninoff's Concerto no. 2, arr.
by A. J. Condaris. © Scholastic
Music Co., Port Chester, N. Y.;
1Nov47; on arrangement for
school orchestra; EP19605.
Piano-conductor score and parts.

Daisies ... [by] S. Rachmaninoff,
[transcribed by] Jascha Heifetz.
© Carl Fischer, inc., New York;
9Dec47; on transcription;
EP19988. Score (violin and
piano) and part.

Étude-Tableau (no. 2) ... [by]
Rachmaninoff, [transcribed by]
Jascha Heifetz. © Carl Fischer,
inc., New York; 9Dec47; on
transcription; EP18002. Score
(violin and piano) and part.

(Prelude, piano, no.5) Prelude
(No.5) ... [by] Rachmaninoff,
[arr. by] Jascha Heifetz. © Carl
Fischer, inc., New York; 24Nov47;
on arrangement; EP20160. Score
(violin and piano) and part.

Vocalise. Op.34, no.14; [by]
Rachmaninoff. © Charles Foley,
New York; 1Nov49; on revision;
EP15335. Score: violins and
orchestra.

We Do Worship and Praise Thee;
[by] Rachmaninoff ... ed. and
adapted to English words by A.
M. Henderson. © Bayley and
Ferguson, Glasgow; 14Aug47;
EF6927. Score: mixed chorus;
voice parts also in tonic sol-
fa notation.

RAE, RALPH.
Because I'm So in Love; by Art
Withall & Ralph Rae. © Broadcast Music, inc., New York;
14Nov47; EP19142. For voice and
piano, with chord symbols.

RAEZER, CORA MAE.
Cut the Pigeon Wing; piano solo
by Cora Mae Raezer. © Mills
Music, inc., New York;
29Aug47; EP17953.

Fairy Enchantment; piano solo by
Cora Mae Raezer. © Mills Music,
inc., New York; 29Aug47;
EP17952.

Hobby Horses; piano solo by Cora
Mae Raezer. © Mills Music,
Inc., New York; 29Aug47;
EP17950.

Step and Sway; piano solo by
Cora Mae Raezer. © Mills
Music, inc., New York;
29Aug47; EP17954.

[RAPAELLI, MARIO] 1910-
Rosanna ... de Don Filinto
[pseud.] y Aguariguay [pseud.]
© Editorial Musical "El
Cometa," Buenos Aires; 31May47;
EF6673. For voice and piano.

RAIDER, CLARA MARIE, 1900-
"Memories"; words and music by Clara
Raider. © Clara M. Raider,
Lorain, Ohio; 7Jul47; EP20293.

RAINIER, PRIAULX, 1905-
(Quartet, strings) Quartet for
strings, [by] Priaulx Rainier.
© Schott & Co., ltd., London;
3Apr47; EF3950. Miniature
score and parts.

RAKSIN, DAVID, 1912-
Forever Amber ... from the ...
picture "Forever Amber," lyric
by Johnny Mercer, music by David
Raksin. New York, Robbins Music
Corp. © Twentieth Century Music
Corp., New York; 10Nov47;
EP18914.

RALFO, C
Notturno ... parole e musica di
C. Ralfo, arr. [by] M. Flora.
Ritorna ... parole di C. Ralfo,
musica di M. Flora. © Edizioni
Musicali "PO," Torino, Italy;
29Jan47; EF6238. Piano-conductor
score (orchestra, with words)
and parts.

RAMEAU, JEAN PHILIPPE.
Votre Amour, Be.ger. Your Love,
Shepherd. From Cantates
Françoises, for three-part
chorus of women's voices with
soprano solo, [by] Jean-Philippe
Rameau ... arr. by Victoria
Glaser, English version adapted
by Corinne da Campagna-Pinto.
© E. C. Schirmer Music Co.,
Boston; 29-ep47; on arrangement;
EP18136.

RAMIREZ, ARTHUR R   1914-
José ... words and music by Arthur
R. Ramirez. © Arthur R. Ramirez,
San Antonio; 4Dec47; on changes
in words & music; EP19281.

RAMONT, GRACE MAY.
I Love You, Dear Jesus; words and
music by Grace Ramont, harmony
by N. L. Ridderhof. (In Hymn
Writers' Magazine. v.1, no.3,
p.27) © Grace May Ramont,
Inglewood, Calif.; 15Nov47;
B5-2943. Close score: SATB.

My Prayer; words and music by
Grace Ramont, harmony by N. L.
Ridderhof. (In Hymn Writers'
Magazine. v.1, no.1, p.15)
© Grace May Ramont (Mrs. W. Paul
Ramont), Inglewood, Calif.;
1Jul47; B5-1051. Close score:
SATB.

My Song of Songs; words and music
by Grace Ramont, harmony by
N. L. Ridderhof. (In Hymn .
Writers' Magazine. v.1, no.2,
p.22-23) © Grace May Ramont,
Inglewood, Calif.; 28Aug47;
B5-1829. For voice and piano.

Storm Shelter ... words and music
by Grace Ramont, harmony by N. L.
Ridderhof. (In Hymn Writers'
Magazine. v.1, no.1, p.18)
© Grace May Ramont, Inglewood,
Calif.; 1Jul47; B5-1052. Close
score: SATB.

RAMOS, S   R
El Rancho Grande; music by S. R.
Ramos, arr. by L. Sugarman. ©
Edward B. Marks Music Corp.,
New York; 5Sep47; on arrangement;
EP16672. For piano solo.

RAMSEY, ASTRID.
Fingers, Be Nimble, Fingers, Be
Quick! An interesting variety
of piano techniques in solo form,
by Astrid Ramsey. © The Willis
Music Co., Cincinnati; 4Sep47;
EP17306.

RAMSEY, STELLA.
Sweetheart of Mine; words and music
by Stella Ramsey. © Nordyko Publishing Co., Los Angeles; 21Aug47;
EP16607.

RANGSTRÖM, TURE, 1884-1947.
Brinnande Ljus; [by] Ture Rangström,
text av Karin Boye. © Föreningen
svenska tonsättare, Stockholm;
1Jan45; EF7120.

En Ghasel; text av Frans G.
Bengtsson, [by] Ture Rangström.
© Föreningen svenska tonsättare,
Stockholm; 1Jan45; EF7119.

Nordiskt; tre sänger till dikter
av Gunnar Ekelöf, [by] Ture
Rangström, Stockholm; 1Jan45;
EF7102.

Romans; [by] Ture Rangström.
Stockholm, Ed. Suecia. ©
Föreningen svenska tonsättare,
Edition Suecia, Stockholm; 1Jan40;
EF7058. Score (violoncello or
violin and piano) and parts.

Trots Allt; fem dikter av Bo Bergman i musik av Ture Rangström,
[tr. into German by Edvin Kallstenius and Ture Rangström]
Stockholm, Ed. Suecia, C. Gehrmans musikförlag i distribution
© Edition Suecia, Föreningen
svenska tonsättare, Stockholm;
1Jan42; EF7059.

Två Stockholmsdikter; [by] Ture
Rangström, [words by Tor Hed-
berg and Hjalmar Söderberg] ©
Föreningen svenska tonsättare,
Stockholm; 1Jan45; EF7101.

RAPELJE, MARIE.
Valentine Dance; [by] Marie Rap-
elje. © Theodore Presser Co.,
Philadelphia; 100ct47;
EP17990. For piano, 4 hands.

RAPOPORT, EDA, 1900-
Three Etchings; for pianoforte ...
by Eda Rapoport. © Eda Rapoport,
New York; 15Aug47; EP16659.

RASLEY, JOHN M   1913-
Assurance; [words by] Ethel L.
Ronnison, [music by] John M.
Rasley. © Raymond A. Hoffman
Co., Chicago; 210ct47; EP19005.
Score: baritone or mezzo-so-
prano, chorus (SATB) and piano.

Blessed Are the Peacemakers; [by]
John M. Rasley. © Raymond A.
Hoffman Co., Chicago; 210ct47;
EP19064. Score: solo voices,
mixed chorus and piano.

I Heard the Voice of Jesus Say;
[words by] Horatius Bonar,
[music by] John M. Rasley. ©
Raymond A. Hoffman Co., Chicago;
210ct47; EP19063. Score: tenor,
chorus (SATB) and piano.

Let Us Walk in the Spirit ...
[words from] Gal. 5:25, 6:7-8,
[music by] John M. Rasley. ©
Raymond A. Hoffman Co., Chicago;
210ct47; EP19082. Score: solo
voices (SATB) chorus (SATB) and
piano reduction.

RASMUSSEN, CLYDE.
You're Only the One I Adore;
words by Sonny B. Tagaban,
music by Clyde Rasmussen. ©
Nordyke Publishing Co., Los
Angeles; 23Sep47; EP19324.

RATCLIFFE, DESMOND.
The Vision; part song for S.A.T.
B., words by Laurence Swinyard,
music by Desmond Ratcliffe.
© Novello & Co., ltd., London;
15Aug47; EF6549.

RAVANELLO, ORESTE.
Mass in Honor of Saint Irenaeus;
composed by Oreste Ravanello,
arr. by Cyr de Brant [pseud.]
For unison or two part singing.
© McLaughlin & Reilly Co.,
Boston; 14Aug47; on arrangement;
EP17354.

Two Motets for Dedication of a
Church: 1. Tu Es Petrus
(Ravanello), 2. Caelestis Urbs
Jerusalem (Thermignon) For
three equal voices. © McLaughlin
& Reilly Co., Boston; 18Jul47;
EP15870.

RAVASINI, NINO.
Bolero Triste. © Edition Turicephon, ltd., music publishers,
Zurich, Switzerland; 19Apr47;
EF5836. For piano solo.

RAVAZZA, CARL.
Pedro; words and music by Carl
Ravazza. New York, Capitol
Songs. © Criterion Music Corp.,
New York; 29Nov47; EP20153.

RAWSON, DOROTHY.
You Say the Sweetest Things; words
and music by Dorothy Rawson.
[c1946] © Nordyke Publishing
Co., Los Angeles; 21Aug47;
EP16608.

RAWSTHORNE, ALAN, 1905–
Cortèges; [fantasy overture] for
orchestra, [by] Alan Rawsthorne.
© Oxford University Press,
London; 6Feb47; EF6141.

(Quartet, strings) String quartet;
[by] Alan Rawsthorne. [c1946]
© The Oxford University Press,
London; 23Jan47; EF6105. Score.
String Quartet. See his Quartet,
strings.

Symphonic Studies; for orchestra,
[by] Alan Rawsthorne. ©
Oxford University Press, London; 31Oct46; EF6147.

RAYBURN, RANDY.
"The Tune on the Tip of My Heart";
lyric: Ervin Drake [and] Jimmy
Shirl [pseud.]; music: Randy
Rayburn. © Encore Music Publi-
cations, inc., New York; 2Dec47;
EP20265. Melody and chord sym-
bols, with words.

RAYL, EVELYN H
Open Your Eyes; words and music
by Evelyn H. Rayl. © Nordyke
Publishing Co., Los Angeles; 19Jun47;
EP17436.

RAYMOND, RALPH, pseud. See
Williams, Ralph.

RAYNOR, JOHN.
The Californy Song; the words by
Hilaire Belloc, set to music
by John Raynor. © Oxford
University Press, London;
19Jun47; EF6150.

READ, BOB.
What's the Use? Words by Milli-
cent DeVere, music by Bob Read.
© Nordyke Publishing Co., Los
Angeles; 10ct47; EP19304.

READ, GARDNER.
De Profundis. Op.71a. By Gardner
Read. © Leeds Music Corp., New
York; 20Oct47; EP18896. For
organ solo; includes registra-
tion for Hammond organ.

READE, CHARLES.
Te Amo; Spanish lyric by Fausto
Curbelo, English lyric by Sy
Taylor, music by Charles Reade.
© George Simon, inc., New York;
30Sep47; EP17379.

READER, WILLIAM HENRY RALPH, 1905–
I'll Keep Following the Rainbow;
written and composed by Ralph
Reader. [Ukulele arr. by R. S.
Stoddon] © B. Feldman & Co.
ltd., London; 24Jul47; EF5825.
For voice and piano, with
guitar diagrams and chord
symbols.

REBIKOFF, V.
Cradle Song; by V. Rebikoff ...
S.S.A. [English translation by
Wladimir Lakond, English adapta-
tion by Olga Paul. © Edward B.
Marks Music Corp., New York;
14Oct47; on English adaptation;
EP18370.

RECH, LEO.
The Organ Grinder; words and
music by Leo Rech. © Nordyke
Publishing Co., Los Angeles;
2Sep47; EP19294.

RECLI, GIULIA, 1890–
La Cancion de un Muchacho ... per
voce di soprano o tenore. Testo
popolare argentino, versione
italiana di G. Recli, musica di
Giulia Recli. © Carisch, s.a.,
Milan; 13Oct47; EF7164.

Piangono gli Occhi Miei ... per
voce di soprano o tenore.
Parole del popolo di Sicilia,
versione italiana di G. Recli,
musica di Giulia Recli. ©
Carisch, s.a., Milan; 13Oct47;
EF7165.

REDMAN, REGINALD ERNEST, 1892–
From the Chinese; eleven songs,
translations from the Chinese
poets, music by Reginald
Redman. © Goodwin & Tabb,
ltd.; London; 21Aug46; EF5713.

REED, RAY.
The Old Black Steer; words and
music rev. by Ray Reed. © Bob
Wills Music, inc., Hollywood,
Calif.; 28Sep47; on adaptation
of words and arrangement;
EP17780.

Powderhorn; words and music by
Ray Reed. © Bob Wills Music,
inc., Hollywood, Calif.;
21Aug47; EP16515.

REEDER, PIERRE DE. See
DeReeder, Pierre.

REHM, IRVIN E
Midsummer Night in June; words by
Herbert C. Hilton, music by
Irvin E. Rehm. © Nordyke
Publishing Co., Los Angeles;
21Aug47; EP20081.

REICH, MARGARITE E
Your Nearness to Me; words and
music by Margarite E. Reich.
[c1946] © Nordyke Publishing
Co., Los Angeles; 13Jan47;
EP20060.

REICHA, ANTON JOSEPH.
Introduction and Allegro. See his
Quintet, winds.

(Quintet, winds) Introduction
and Allegro; [from Quintet.
Op.88, no.4. In D minor by]
Reicha, [rev. and ed. by
Richard Franko Goldman] ©
Mercury Music Corp., New York;
27Oct47; on arrangement;
EP18513. Score (flute, oboe,
clarinet, horn, and bassoon)
and parts.

REICHERT, FRANK E
Can't You Dream for Tonight?
Words and music by Frank E.
Reichert. [c1945] © Nordyke
Publishing Co., Los Angeles;
14Jun46; EP19952.

REID, BILLY, 1902–
I'm Gonna Hold You in My Arms.
© The Irwin Dash Music Co.
ltd., London; 13Jun47; EF5858.
For voice and piano, with chord
symbols. Melody also in tonic
sol-fa notation.

My First Love, My Last Love for
Always. © The Irwin Dash Music
Co., ltd., London; 25Jun47;
EF5859. For voice and piano,
with chord symbols. Melody also
in tonic sol-fa notation.

REILLY, JOSEPH.
I'm Wearing Last Night's Smile
Tonight; words and music by Sid
Tepper, Roy Brodsky, Warren Ro-
pickl & Joseph Reilly. [piano
score by Michael Edwards] ©
Mills Music, inc., New York;
29Aug47; EP17948.

REISFELD, BERT, 1906–   arr.
Nobody Knows the Trouble I've
Seen; arr. by Bert Reisfeld.
© Century Music Publishing Co.,
New York; 10Jul47; on arrange-
ment; EP15497. For piano solo,
with words.

Roll, Jordan, Roll; arr. by Bert
Reisfeld. © Century Music
Publishing Co., New York;
10Jul47; on arrangement;
EP15498. For piano solo, with
words.

Somebody's Knocking at Your Door;
arr. by Bert Reisfeld. © Century
Music Publishing Co., New York;
10Jul47; on arrangement;
EP15499. For piano solo, with
words.

Sometimes I Feel Like a Motherless
Child; arr. by Bert Reisfeld.
© Century Music Publishing Co.,
New York; 10Jul47; on arrangement;
EP15500. For piano solo, with
words.

REITER, EUSTELLA, sister, 1899–
Mother of Mine; words and music
by ... Eustolla Reiter.
Chicago, Srs. of Resurrection.
© Sister Eustella Reiter,
Chicago; 7Aug47; EP16114.

REITZ, ALBERT SIMPSON.
In His Presence There Is Peace;
[by] Albert Simpson Reitz,
[words by] A. S. R. © Hope
Publishing Co., Chicago (in
notice: Albert Simpson Reitz);
8Nov44; EP18382. Close score;
SATB.

Two Motets for Profession of Vows.
1. O Gloriosa Virginum; ([by]
Ruvanello) 2. Jesu Corona
Virginum; ([by] Thermignon)
For three equal voices. ©
McLaughlin & Reilly Co., Boston;
2Jun47; EP16385.

REIZENSTEIN, FRANZ, 1912–
Partita. © Schott & Co., ltd.,
London; 16Jan47; EF3949.
Score (flute or recorder and
piano) and parts.

Three Concert Pieces; [by] Franz
Reizenstein. © Hawkes & Son
(London) ltd., London; 11Jul47;
EF5801. Score (oboe and piano)
and part.

REMSEN, ALICE.
An Irish Slumber Song; words
and music by Alice Remsen.
© Alice Remsen, New York;
12Sep47; EP16704.

Lovely is the Lee; poem by Allan
Flynn ... music by Alice
Remsen. © Alice Remsen, New
York; 12Sep47; EP16703.

RENDALL, HONOR.
"A-tish-ool" Three-part song for
female voices, (S.S.C.) (unaccompanied) words by Walter De La
Mare ... music by Honor Rendall.
© J. Curwen & Sons, ltd., London; 16Sep47; EF6736.

RENÉ, HENRI.
Concerto for Squeeze Box; by
Henri René. © Sam Fox
Publishing Co., New York;
12Aug47; EP16416.

RENÉ, OTIS.
What a Fool I Was; words and
music by Otis René, [arr. by
Lou Halmy] © Mills Music, inc.,
New York; 29Aug47; EP17945.

RENNER, EDITH.
You Are My Sweetheart; words and
music by Edith Renner. © Nordyke Publishing Co., Los Angeles; 16Jul47; EP17460.

RETH, WILLIAM DONALD.
Waiting for You; words by Robert
H. Jump, music by William Donald
Reth. © Nordyke Publishing Co.,
Los Angeles; 16Dec46; EP19313.

RETTENBERG, MILTON.
Fill Your Community Chest; lyrics
by Robert Sour, music by Milton
Rettenberg. New York, Sole
selling agent, Associated Music
Publishers. © Broadcast Music,
inc., New York; 14Nov47;
EP19143.

[REUTERSKIÖLD, LENNART]
Vid Granskogens Bryn; musik och
text; T. Anders [pseud.] ©
Reuter & Reuter [Briggs, a.-b.,
Stockholm; 1Jan44; EF6947.

REVEL, HARRY, 1905-
Birmingham Boogie; words and music
by Harry Revel; [piano arrangement by Bob Bornstein] © Royal
Music Publisher, Hollywood, Calif.;
17Jul47; EP16217.

Harry Revel's Music out of the
Moon; a collection of piano
music ... arr. ... by Leslie
Baxter. © Capitol Songs, inc.,
New York; 15Aug47; EP16234.

"I'd Rather Look at You"; music by
Harry Revel, words by Walter
Sambor. © Hollywood Melodies,
Music Publishers, Los Angeles;
1Jul47; EP16665.

Love Thy Neighbor; lyric by Mack
Gordon, music by Harry Revel ...
S.A.B. arr. by William Stickles.
© Crawford Music Corp., New York;
26Nov47; on arrangement;
EP19825.

Love Thy Neighbor; lyric by Mack
Gordon, music by Harry Revel ...
S.S.A. arr. by William Stickles.
© Crawford Music Corp., New York;
26Nov47; on arrangement; EP19826.

Love Thy Neighbor; two part chorus
arr. by William Stickles. Lyric
by Mack Gordon, music by Harry
Revel. © Crawford Music Corp.,
New York; 26Nov47; on arrangement; EP19827.

When There's a Breeze on Lake
Louise; by Harry Revel. Arr.
by Allan Small. © Leeds Music
Corp., New York; 16Jun47; on
arrangement; EP15347. Piano-
conductor score (orchestra) and
parts.

REVELL, PETER, pseud. See also
Gibson, Herbert Murdoch.

REVELL, PETER, 1897-
The Confession; song, words and
music by Peter Revell. © Edwin Ashdown, ltd., London;
28Aug47; EF6749.

REVIL, 1916-
Il Pleurait. See his Pieges.

(Pieges) Il Pleurait ... paroles:
Maurice Vandair [pseud.], musique:
Révil. © Ray Ventura & Co., Paris;
31Dec39; EF7295. For voice and
piano, and voice part.

RHEINSCHMIDT, ERMA DOROTHY. See
Schachel-Rheinschmidt, Erma Dorothy.

RHODES, DAVID.
My Guitar Is My Sweetheart; by Alfio
Bargnesi [and] David Rhodes. ©
Bourne, inc., New York; 17Dec47;
EP20295. For voice and piano,
with chord symbols.

RHODES, STAN. See
Rhodes, Stanley.

RHODES, STANLEY.
A Girl That I Remember; words and
music by Stan Rhodes. ©
Broadcast Music, inc., New York;
12Aug47; EP16049.

RIBAUPIERRE, MILON DE
Swiss Lullaby; [by] Milon de Ribaupierre, arr. by Henry Sopkin.
© Carl Fischer, inc., New York;
20ct47; on arrangement; EP18084.
Score (string orchestra) and
parts.

RICARDEL, JOE.
My Corny Country Cousin; by
Frank Warren and Joe Ricardel.
© Smith-Foley Music Publica-
tions, New York; 5Aug47;
EP16122. For voice and piano,
with chord symbols.

RICH, MURRAY, 1912-
In One Ear and Out the Other; by
Bob Hilliard, Dick Miles [and]
Murray Rich. © Music Workshop,
New York; 290ct47; EP18567.
For voice and piano, with chord
symbols.

RICHARD, LEO, 1883-
Arizona Moon; words by Gene Scud-
der, music by Leo & Hector Richard. © Nordyke Publishing Co.,
Los Angeles; 30Jan47; EP19785.

Does the Moon Shine over Atlanta?
Music by Leo & Hector Richard,
words by Ruby Marie Aradis. ©
Nordyke Publishing Co., Los
Angeles; 1Jun47; EP16869.

Hold Me Close to You; words by
Laura Burns, music by Leo and
Hector Richard. c1946. © Laura
Burns, Los Angeles; 20Feb47;
EP17771.

I'll Love You Till I Die; words
by Doris Lee Stiles, music by
Leo and Hector Richard. © Art
Music Co., New York; 22Nov47;
EP19019.

Jive Is Sometimes the Real McCoy;
words by Mildred Gipson, music
by Leo & Hector Richard. ©
Nordyke Publishing Co., Los Angeles; 15Aug46; EP19761.

Little Sweetheart; words by Verna
Mae Davidson, music by Leo &
Hector Richard. © Nordyke Publishing Co., Los Angeles;
17May47; EP16816.

Moving No More; words by William
Holzman, music by Leo & Hector
Richard. © Nordyke Publishing
Co., Los Angeles; 12Jun46;
EP19443.

My Dream World; words by Lula
Saunders, music by Leo & Hector
Richard. © Nordyke Publishing
Co., Los Angeles; 16Dec46;
EP19715.

To Have and Not to Have; words by
Warren S. Bachhofer, music by
Leo and Hector Richard. © Nordyke Publishing Co., Los Angeles;
24Jun46; EP20301.

A Song to Pueblo; words by Dona
Collis, music by Leo and Hector
Richard. © Dona Collis, Pueblo,
Colo.; 23Jul47; EP16012.

A Song of Peace; words by Ervin
Schultz, music by Leo and
Hector Richard. © Nordyke
Publishing Co., Los Angeles;
18Jul46; EP19418.

What Have I Done to You? Words
by Johnnie Moore, music by Leo
and Hector Richard. © Nordyke
Publishing Co., Los Angeles;
31Jul47; EP19542.

When the Brown Bomber Goes to Town;
words by Eddie Johnson, music
by Leo and Hector Richard. ©
Eddie Johnson, Jacksonville,
Fla.; 200ct47; EP18324.

When the Night Birds Are Calling
You and Me; words by Oliver F.
Miller, sr., music by Leo and
Hector Richard. [c1946] © Nordyke
Publishing Co., Los Angeles;
270ct47; EP18401.

When Time Counts; words by
William Stancil, music by Leo
& Hector Richard. © Nordyke
Publishing Co., Los Angeles;
25Jul46; EP19592.

Where the River Maple Flows; words
by Nelson A. Pier, music by Leo
and Hector Richard. © Nordyke
Publishing Co., Los Angeles;
29Mar47; EP16844.

World upon World; words by Oscar
A. Rotan, music by Leo & Hector
Richard. [c1946] © Nordyke
Publishing Co., Los Angeles;
7Feb47; EP20051.

You May Be Gone Forever; words by
Curtiss Carlyle Eastland, ...
[music] by Leo & Hector Richard.
© Nordyke Publishing Co., Los
Angeles; 15Aug47; EP20384.

Your Memory Will Always Be My
Guide; words by Bonnie Morrison,
music by Leo and Hector Richard.
© Nordyke Publishing Co., Los
Angeles; 10Jun47; EP16943.

RICHARDS, AL.
Two Guitars; Russian gipsy song,
arr. for the piano accordion by
Al Richards. © W. Paxton & Co.,
ltd., London; 18Feb46; on arrangement; EF5702.

RICHARDS, J   J
Rainbow Pier ... [by] J. J.
Richards. © C. L. Barnhouse Co.,
Oskaloosa, Iowa; 23Sep47;
EP17926. Parts; band.

RICHARDS, KATHLEEN.
The Horn; for two voices and
pianoforte [by] Kathleen
Richards. Op. 16, no. 2.
[Words by] Walter De La Mare.
© The Oxford University Press,
London; 17Jul47; EF6130.

The Window; for two voices and
pianoforte, [by] Kathleen
Richards. Op. 16, no. 1.
[Words by] Walter De La Mare.
© The Oxford University Press,
London; 17Jul47; EF6131.

RICHARDS, MARION ROE.
Evening Prayer ... lyrics [by]
Andrew Sodick, music [by] Marion
Roe Richards. Toledo, A. V.
Higgins. © A. J. Sodick &
Marion R. Richards, Toledo;
14Jun47; EP15472.

Her Little Green Parasol; lyrics
[by] Andrew Sodick, music [by]
Marion Roe Richards. Toledo;
A. V. Higgins. © A. Sodick and
Marion R. Richards, Toledo;
18Sep47; EP17809.

RICHARDS, MAY.
Silly You; words and music by May
Richards. © May Richards,
Chicago; 150ct47; EP19029.

RICHARDSON, ALAN.
(Rondo, piano) Rondo; for pianoforte solo, [by] Alan Richardson.
© The Oxford Univ. Press, London;
230ct47; EF7177.

RICHARDSON, ARTHUR.
Too Fat Polka ... by Ross MacLean
and Arthur Richardson. © Shapiro, Bernstein & Co., inc.,
New York; 25Aug47; EP16616.

RICHARDSON, ARTHUR E
Our Faithful Friend; words by Arthur
E. Richardson and Flora E. Richardson, music by Arthur E. Richardson. [c1946] © Nordyke Publishing Co., Los Angeles; 30Jan47;
EP19533.

RICHARDSON, CLIVE.
A-Hunting We Will Go; transcribed
by Clive Richardson. [c1943] ©
Keith Prowse & Co., ltd., London;
7Aug47; on transcription;
EF6184. Piano-conductor score
(orchestra) and parts.

RICHARDSON, CLIVE. Cont'd.
Baa! Baa! Black Sheep! Transcribed by Clive Richardson. © Keith, Prowse & Co., ltd., London; 17Oct47; on transcription & arrangement; EP6910. Piano-conductor score (orchestra) and parts.

Come Lasses and Lads; transcribed by Clive Richardson. [c1944] © Keith Prowse & Co., ltd., London; 7Aug47; on transcription; EP6185. Piano-conductor score (orchestra) and parts.

The Farmer's Boy; transcribed by Clive Richardson. [c1946] © Keith Prowse & Co., ltd., London; 7Aug47; on transcription; EP6186. Piano-conductor score (orchestra) and parts.

The Irish Washerwomen; arr. by Clive Richardson. © Keith, Prowse & Co., ltd., London; 22Oct47; on transcription; EP6912. Piano-conductor score (orchestra) and parts.

On Ilkla Moor Baht' At ... transcribed by Clive Richardson. [c1943] © Keith Prowse & Co., ltd., London; 7Aug47; on transcription; EP6185. Piano-conductor score (orchestra) and parts.

Prelude to a Dream; [by] Clive Richardson, piano solo, [arr. by Henry Geehl] © Lawrence Wright Music Co., ltd., London; 11Apr47; on arrangement; EP3951.

Romantic Interlude; [by] Clive Richardson, arr. by Ronald Hanmer. © Chappell & Co., ltd., London; 17Jul47; on arrangement; EP6176. Piano-conductor score (orchestra) and parts.

RICHARDSON, LE SOTO E
Romance of Chief Tecumseh ... words by Frances Wright, music by De Soto E. Richardson. © Frank S. Wilut, music publisher, Lancaster, Pa.; 6Sep47; EP20215.

RICHARDSON, MAURINE K
Gorgeous; words and music by Maurine K. Richardson. © Nordyke Publishing Co., Los Angeles; 12Apr47; EP16799.

RICHEPIN, TIARKO, 1884-
C'Est à Champ-Dominelle ... paroles et musique de Tiarko Richepin. © Editions Royalty, Paris; 14Aug47; EP7346.

Départ dans la Nuit; paroles et musique de Tiarko Richepin. © Ste. ame. fse. Chappell, Paris; 20Nov47; EP7354.

RICHTER, ADA.
Organ Grinder Man; piano solo with words, by Ada Richter. © Theodore Presser Co., Philadelphia; 16Sep47; EP17290.

Revelry; [by] Ada Richter. © Theodore Presser Company, Philadelphia; 26Nov47; EP19135. For piano solo.

You Can Play the Piano! A book for the older beginner, by Ada Richter. © Theodore Presser Co., Philadelphia; pt.2, 31Oct47; EP18448.

[RICHTER, CARL] 1870-
The Carnival Suite ... for young players of the pianoforte, [by Carl Richter] © Bach Music Co. (Henry Dellafield, sole owner), Boston; 15Sep47; EP18108.

RICHTER, CARL, 1870- arr.
La Spagnola ... piano solo [arr. by] Carl Richter. © Bach Music Co., Henry Dellafield, sole owner, Boston; 15Sep47; on simplified arrangement; EP17783.

RICHTER, CARL ARTHUR, 1883-
Achtzehn Leichte Vortragsstücke ... Eighteen Easy Pieces ... [by] C. Arthur Richter. Op.34. © Ring & Co., Music-Publishers, Zurich, Switzerland; v. 1-2, 14Pr47; EP6012. Score (violin and piano) and parts.

RICHTER, WILLIAM BENSON, 1901-
Do You Ever Dream; words and music by William Benson Richter. © William Benson Richter, Philadelphia; 23Oct47; EP18814.

Kitty O'Malley; words and music by William B. Richter. © Dr. William Benson Richter, Philadelphia; 31Oct47; EP18589.

RICKETTS, CYRIL.
Song of Freedom; (for chorus and orchestra) [by] Cyril Ricketts. © Cyril Ricketts, Barmouth, Wales; 2Jun47; EP5780. Vocal score, in tonic sol-fa notation.

[RICKETTS, R   R   ]
Alamein ... [by] Leo Stanley [pseud.] © Hawkes & Son (London), ltd., London; 24Jul47; EP5794. Parts: band.

RICKUS, MARIE E
Hoping to Be Remembered; words and music by Marie E. Rickus. © Nordyke Publishing Co., Los Angeles; 12Apr47; EP16799.

RIDDERHOF, NICHOLAS LAMBERT.
Glory to God in the Highest; music by N. L. Ridderhof, words from Luke 2. (In Hymn Writers' Magazine. v.1, no.3, p.20) © Grace May Ramont, Inglewood, Calif.; 15Nov47; B5-2942. Close score: SATB.

RIDENOUR, RUTH CAMERON.
When Spring Is Here; words and music by Ruth Cameron Ridenour. © Nordyke Publishing Co., Los Angeles; 3Sep47; EP20073.

RIDLEY, WALTER.
I'll Keep You in My Heart; music by Walter Ridley, lyric by Desmond O'Connor [and] Tommy Connor. © The Edward Kassner Music Co., ltd., London; 25Jun47; EP6872.

RIGACCI, BRUNO, 1921-
Sciofar; melopoesi drammatica in 3 tempi per voce recitante e pianoforte, versi de Angiolo Orvieto, musica di Bruno Rigacci. © Carisch, s.a., Milan; 1Jul47; EP6207.

RIGG, J   BURLINGTON.
We Want Peace; words and music by J. Burlington Rigg. © J. Burlington Rigg, Chicago; 11Aug47; EP16289. Close score: SATB.

RIGGS, LORAINE.
Satisfied; words & music by Loraine Riggs. [c1946] © Nordyke Publishing Co., Los Angeles; 30Oct47; EP19626.

RIGHT, JOHNNY.
No One Else; words and music by Johnny Right. © Nordyke Publishing Co., Los Angeles; 24Jul47; EP19292.

RIIS, ADI, 1911-
Der Var Li'som en Hæmning. See his Tivoli Revyen.

Det Maa Man Godt. See his Tivoli Revyen.

For Hun'Er Saa Ung. See his Tivoli Revyen.

Den Gamle Stol. See his Tivoli Revyen.

I det Lille Grønne Land. See his Tivoli Revyen.

Ikke Ham. See his Tivoli Revyen.

Sødeste Børn. See his Tivoli Revyen.

Tivoli Revyen; Musik: Amdi Riis, Tekster: P. H., Poeten [pseud, and] Arvid Müller. © Wilhelm Hansen, Musik-Forlag, Copenhagen; 14May47; on 7 songs. Contents.- For Hun Er Saa Ung (Arvid Müller) (© EP6334) Den Gamle Stol (P. H.) (© EP6335) I det Lille Grønne Land (P. H.) (© EP6336) Ikke Ham (Arvid Müller) (© EP6337) Sødeste Børn (P. H.) (© EP6338) Det Maa Man Godt (P. H.) (© EP6339) Der Var Li'som en Hæmning (Poeten) (© EP6340)

RILEY, H   B
Sincere; words by E. Riley, music by H. B. Riley. © Nordyke Publishing Co., Los Angeles; 10May47; EP16906.

RIMSKII-KORSAKOV, NIKOLAI ANDREEVICH, 1844-1908.
Bumble Basses. See his Tsar Saltan.

(Scheherazade) The Young Prince and the Young Princess; third movement from Scheherazade [by] Rimsky-Korsakoff. Op. 35. Arr. for band by M. L. Lake, arr. for modern bands with new parts by H. R. Kent [pseud.] © Carl Fischer, inc., New York; 20Nov47; on arrangement for modern band; EP20172. Condensed score (band) and parts.

(Scheherazade) The Young Prince and the Young Princess; from [the symphonic suite] "Scheherazade" by Rimsky Korsakoff, arr. for accordion by Charles Nunzio. © Alfred Music Co., inc., New York; 10Oct47; on arrangement; EP19086.

A Song of India; by N. Rimsky-Korsakoff ... arr. by Hugo Frey. [Words by Leda Joyce] © Hamilton S. Gordon, inc., New York; 27Oct47; on words and arrangement; EP18747. For piano solo, with words.

Song of India; plectrum guitar solo, [by] Rimsky-Korsakoff, arr. as played by Harry Volpe. c1939. © Albert Rocky Co., New York; 10Jan40; on arrangement; EP20204.

Song of Scheherazade ... Based on "Young Prince and Princess" by N. Rimsky-Korsakoff. Lyric by Ted Fetter, arr. by Domenico Savino. © The John Franklin Co., inc., New York; 8Jul47; on words and arrangement; EP15633.

(Tsar Saltan) Bumble Basses; a ... left hand arrangement of Flight of the Bumble Bee, [by] N. Rimsky-Korsakoff, arr. by Pietro Deiro. © Accordion Music Publishing Co., New York; 14Sep47; on arrangement; EP18219. For accordion solo.

The Young Prince and the Young Princess. See his Scheherazade.

RIMSKY-KORSAKOFF, N. See Rimskii-Korsakov, Nikolai Andreevich.

RINDER, REUBEN R   1892- arr.
Kol Nidre; with traditional and revised texts for cantor, organ and choir, by Reuben R. Rinder. New York, Bloch Publishing Co. © Reuben R. Rinder, San Francisco; 21Aug47; on arrangement & revision of text; EP17932. Hebrew words (transliterated)

RINEHART, J   ALAN.
All of the Time; words and music by Holly O'Neill and J. Alan Rinehart. © Southern Music Publishing Co., inc., New York; 27Aug47; EP17861.

338

RINGGENBERG, LETHA L
Dreamy, Dreamy Moon Keep Shining;
words and music by Letha L.
Ringgenberg. © Nordyke Publish-
ing Co., Los Angeles; 27Mar47;
EP16762.

RINGLE, DAVE.
There's a Little Church in Wal-
pack; lyric and music by Mar-
celline Geer, "Bud" Clippinger
and Dave Ringle. © Sleepy
Valley Music, New York; 25Nov47;
EP19041.
There's an Old Fashioned Swing in
the Garden; words and music by
Josephine Clements and Dave
Ringle. © Maytone Music Pub-
lishers, New York; 1Dec47;
EP19137.

RIOS, MARIO ALVAREZ. See
Alvares Rios, Mario.

RITSIARDES, IOSEPH MICHAEL, 1900-
(Naylon'tou Akropol) M'Agapa ...
Den M'Agapa, apo tēn epitheorēsē,
"Naylon'tou Akropol." Etichoi:
D. Giannoukakē, mousikē: I.
Ritsiardē. Athēnai, Ekdoscis
Gaftanou. © Michael Gaetanos,
Athens; 23Apr47; EP6810. For
voice and piano.

RITSIARDES, JOSEPH MICHAEL, 1900-
M'Agapa ... Den M'Agapa. See his
Naylon'tou Akropol.

RITTER, WALTER S   1894-
Beginning of the Christmas Time;
(by Walter S. Ritter, words by
Walter S. Ritter and Gertrude
E. Ritter] © Walter S. Ritter
& Gertrude E. Ritter, Pontiac,
Mich.; 15Dec47; EP20139.

RIUS, FELIPE SANTIAGO. See
Santiago Rius, Felipe.

RIVAS, WELLO.
"Mi Agonía"; [words and music] de
Wello Rivas, [orchestrated by
Fernando Z. Maldonado] ©
Promotora Hispano Americana de
Música, s.a., México; 31Oct47;
EP6935. Piano-conductor score
and parts.

RIVERA, HECTOR.
Sin Protestar.   (I Won't
Protest) ... Spanish words
and music by Hector Rivera,
English words by Joe Davis.
© Caribbean Music, inc.,
New York; 25Aug47; EP16523.

RIVERS, JOHN.
Miss Elizabeth Brown; by John
Moran, Les Durbin & John Rivers.
© Cinephonic Music Co., ltd.,
London; 21Mar47; EF6024. For
voice and piano, with chord
symbols; melody also in tonic
sol-fa notation.

RIVIER, JEAN, 1896-
Concertino; pour alto et orchestre,
[by] Jean Rivier. Réduction.
© Editions Salabert, Paris; 15Sep47;
EF7262. Score (viola and piano)
and part.

Quatrième Symphonie. See his Symphony,
string orchestra, no. 4.

(Symphony, string orchestra, no. 4)
Quatrième Symphonie ... [by]
Jean Rivier. © Salabert, inc.,
New York; 2May47; EF5956. Score.

RIXNER, JOSEF.
Hiberia ... De Joe Rixner,
arrangement par Joe Rixner.
© Edition Turicaphon a. g.,
Zürich, Switzerland; 20Jun47;
EF5863. Piano-conductor score
(orchestra) and parts.

Spitzbub' ... Ragamuffin ...[by]
Joe Rixner. © Cesar R. Bahar,
Edition "Baltic," Berlin;
29May37; EF3981. Piano-
conductor score (orchestra),
and parts.

RIZZUTO, JOSE M
El Ultimo Beso ... [by] José M.
Rizzuto, arr. by Sydney Green.
© Broadcast Music, inc., New
York; 8Aug47; on arrangement;
EP17905. Piano-conductor
score (orchestra) and parts.

ROBBINS (J. J.) & SONS, INC., comp.
Sound Off! A collection of
marches from Schubert to Sousa,
[comp. by] J. J. Robbins & Sons,
inc.] © J. J. Robbins & Sons,
inc., New York; 18Dec47;
EP20180. For piano solo.

ROBERSON, EMOGENE.
I Have Found a Friend in Jesus;
words and music by Emogene
Roberson. © Emogene Roberson,
Pittsburgh; 7Aug47; EP16092.
Close score: SATB.

ROBERTON, HUGH STEVENSON, 1874-
De Battle ob Jerico; traditional
Negro spiritual, arr. for choir
(or trio) of women's voices,
(S.S.C.) by Hugh S. Roberton.
London, J. Curwen, New York, G.
Schirmer, sole agents. © Hugh
S. Roberton, Glasgow; 16Sep47;
on arrangement; EF6735.

Dream Pedlary; for chorus (or quar-
tet) of men's voices, (T.T.B.B.)
(unaccompanied) Words by Thomas
Lovell Beddoes ... music by Hugh
S. Roberton. London, J. Curwen,
New York, G. Schirmer, sole
agents. © Hugh S. Roberton,
Glasgow; 16Sep47; on arrangement;
EF6729.

Give a Man a Horse He Can Ride;
for chorus (or quartet) of men's
voices (T.T.B.B.) (unaccompanied)
Words by James Thomson ... music
by Hugh S. Roberton. London, J.
Curwen, New York, G. Schirmer,
sole agents. © Hugh S. Roberton, Glasgow; 22Aug47; EF6739.

Good Morrow to You, Springtime;
unison song. Words by F. A.
Grant, music by Hugh S. Roberton.
© Banks & Son, York, Eng.;
22Oct47; EF7149.

Iona Boat Song; traditional High-
land air, arr. for choir (or
quartet) of mixed voices,
(S.C.T.B.) by Hugh S. Roberton
... Words by Hugh S. Roberton.
London, J. Curwen, New York, G.
Schirmer, sole agents. © Hugh
S. Roberton, Glasgow; 16Sep47;
on arrangement; EF6728.

Iona boat song; traditional Highland air, arr. for tenor solo,
and choir (or quartet) ... T.T.B.B.
by Hugh S. Roberton ... Words by
Hugh S. Roberton. London, J.
Curwen & Sons. © Hugh S.
Roberton, Glasgow; on arrangement; 18Apr47; EF3276.

Iona Boat Song; words by Hugh S.
Roberton, traditional island
air arr. by Hugh S. Roberton.
London, J. Curwen, New York, G.
Schirmer, sole agents. © Hugh
S. Roberton, Glasgow; 5Jun47;
on arrangement; EF6283.

The Lark Now Leaves His Wat'ry
Nest; unison song, words by Sir
William Davenant ... music by
Hugh S. Roberton. London, J.
Curwen, New York, G. Schirmer,
sole agents. © Hugh S. Rober-
ton, Glasgow; 16Sep47; EF6737.

Listen to the Lambs; traditional
Negro spiritual arr. for choir
(or quartet) of men's voices
(T.T.B.B.) by Hugh S. Roberton.
London, J. Curwen, New York, G.
Schirmer, sole agents. © Hugh
Stevenson Roberton, Glasgow;
23Oct47; on arrangement; EF6940.

Lit'le David, Play on Yo' Harp;
traditional Negro spiritual, arr
for choir (or trio) of equal
voices, S.S.C., by Hugh S. Roberton. London, J. Curwen, New York,
G. Schirmer, sole agents. ©
Hugh S. Roberton, Glasgow;
16Sep47; on arrangement; EF6735.

Oh, By an' By; traditional Negro
spiritual, arr. for choir (or
trio) of equal voices, S.S.C.
(unaccompanied) by Hugh S. Roberton. London, J. Curwen, New
York, G. Schirmer, sole agents.
© Hugh S. Roberton, Glasgow;
16Sep47; on arrangement; EF6734.

Steal Away to Jesus; traditional
Negro spiritual arr. for choir
(or trio) of equal voices,
S.S.C. (unacc.) by Hugh S.
Roberton. London, J. Curwen,
New York, G. Schirmer, sole
agents. © Hugh S. Roberton,
Glasgow; 23Oct47; on arrange-
ment; EF6941.

Swing Low, Sweet Chariot; tradi-
tional Negro spiritual, arr. for
choir (or trio) of equal voices,
(S.S.C.) (unaccompanied) by Hugh
S. Roberton. London, J. Curwen,
New York, G. Schirmer, sole
agents. © Hugh S. Roberton,
Glasgow; 16Sep47; on arrangement;
EF6732.

Welsh Cradle Song; traditional
air, words and arrangement by
Hugh S. Roberton. ©
Paterson's Publications, ltd.,
London; 6Oct47; on words &
arrangement; EF6906. Score:
chorus (SA) and piano; voice
parts also in tonic sol-fa
notation.

Welsh Cradle Song; traditional
air, words and arrangement by
Hugh S. Roberton. ©
Paterson's Publications, ltd.,
London; 6Oct47; on words &
arrangement; EF6907. For
unison chorus and piano; melody
also in tonic sol-fa notation.

When de Stars Begin to Fall; Negro
spiritual, arr. for choir (or
quartet) of men's voices,
(T.T.B.B.) by Hugh S. Roberton.
Words traditional. London, J.
Curwen, New York, G. Schirmer,
sole agents. © Hugh S. Roberton,
Glasgow; 16Sep47; on arrangement;
EF6730.

ROBERTS, ANN.
The Farmer Took a Holiday; by
Paul and Ann Roberts. (In
Roberts, Paul. Paul and Ann
Roberts Favorite Cowboy and
Hillbilly Songs. v.1, p.20-21)
© Bob Miller, inc., New York;
29Oct47; EP18863. For voice
and piano, with chord symbols.

New England Is the Only Place for
Me; by Paul and Ann Roberts.
(In Roberts, Paul. Paul and
Ann Roberts Favorite Cowboy and
Hillbilly Songs. v.1, p. 10-11)
© Bob Miller, inc., New York;
29Oct47; EP18859. For voice
and piano with chord symbols.

ROBERTS, MARITA, pseud. See
Garman, William McKinley.

ROBERTS, MERVYN.
Christmas Day ... words by Andrew
Young, music by Mervyn Roberts.
© Novello & Co., ltd., London;
28Nov47; EF7198.
Elsewhere ... words by G. O. Warren,
music by Mervyn Roberts. © No-
vello & Co., ltd., London; 28Nov47;
EF7194.
Put a Rosebud on Her Lips ... words
by Francis H. King, music by
Mervyn Roberts. © Novello & Co.,
ltd., London; 28Nov47; EF7195.

ROBERTS, MERVYN. Cont'd.
Saint Govan ... words by A. G. Prys-
Jones, music by Mervyn Roberts.
© Novello & Co., ltd., London;
28Nov47; EF7197.

The Sentry ... words by G. O. Warren,
music by Mervyn Roberts. © Novello & Co., ltd., London; 28Nov47;
EF7196.

ROBERTS, PAUL.
Down in Mexico; by Paul Roberts.
(In his Paul and Ann Roberts
Favorite Cowboy and Hillbilly
Songs. v.1, p. 12-13) © Bob
Miller, inc., New York; 29Oct47;
EP18860. For voice and piano,
with chord symbols.

I Like to Hear the Old Songs; by
Paul Roberts. (In his Paul and
Ann Roberts Favorite Cowboy and
Hillbilly Songs. v.1, p. 8-9)
© Bob Miller, inc., New York;
29Oct47; EP18858. For voice
and piano, with guitar diagrams
and chord symbols.

The Jolly Mailman; by Paul Roberts.
(In his Paul and Ann Roberts
Favorite Cowboy and Hillbilly
Songs. v.1, p. 18-19) © Bob
Miller, inc., New York; 29Oct47;
EP18862. For voice and piano,
with chord symbols.

The Major of St. Lo; by Paul
Roberts. (In his Paul and Ann
Roberts Favorite Cowboy and Hillbilly Songs. v.1, p. 14-15) ©
Bob Miller, inc., New York;
29Oct47; EP18861. For voice and
piano, with chord symbols.

Neighbor, Have You Seen My Wife?
By Ann and Paul Roberts. (In
his Paul and Ann Roberts
Favorite Cowboy and Hillbilly
Songs. v.1, p. 24-25) © Bob
Miller, inc., New York; 29Oct47;
EP18865. For voice and piano,
with chord symbols.

Paul and Ann Roberts Favorite Cowboy and Hillbilly Songs. Book
1 [ed., comp. and arr. by
Shelby Darnell, pseud.] New
York, B. Miller [c1947] Songs
principally by Paul Roberts.

Read the Bible, if You Want to
Meet the Lord; by Paul Roberts.
(In his Paul and Ann Roberts
Favorite Cowboy and Hillbilly
Songs. v.1, p. 26-27) © Bob
Miller, inc., New York; 29Oct47;
EP18866. For voice and piano,
with chord symbols.

You Say You Don't Love Me; by Paul
Roberts. (In his Paul and Ann
Roberts Favorite Cowboy and
Hillbilly Songs. v.1, p. 22-23)
© Bob Miller, inc., New York;
29Oct47; EP18864.

ROBERTS, VIRGIL.
I Want More than a Sample of
Love; words and music by Virgil Roberts. © Nordyke Publishing Co., Los Angeles;
22Jul47; EP19520.

[ROBERTSON, BRUCE GILBERT] 1905-
My Future Address; [by Bruce
Robertson, har. by Norine
Grummons] and Will You Listen?
[By Norine Grummons] © Bruce
Gilbert Robertson, Anderson,
Ind.; on My Future Address,
15Oct47; EP18113. © Ruth
Norine Grummons, Fort Wayne; on
Will You Listen; 15Oct47;
EP18114. Close score: SATB.

ROBERTSON, HAZEL YORK.
If I Owned the Moon; words and
music by Hazel York Robertson.
© Nordyke Publishing Co., Los
Angeles; 11Jul47; EP17609.

ROBERTSON, HENRY E
I'm Stickin' Around; words and
music by Henry E. Robertson,
piano arrangement by Frank R.
Fuller. © Henry E. Robertson,
San Francisco; 11Aug47;
EP16313.

ROBERTSON, JEAN.
I Woke Up Crying; words and music
by Jean Robertson. © Nordyke
Publishing Co., Los Angeles;
3Jul47; EP17513.

ROBIN, SID.
I Miss You So; by Jimmy Henderson,
Bertha Scott [and] Sid Robin,
arr. by Fred Weismantel. ©
Leeds Music Corp., New York;
17Sep47; on arrangement;
EP17260. Piano-conductor score
and parts.

I Miss You So; by Jimmy Henderson, Bertha Scott and Sid Robin, special vocal background
arr. by Bob Morse. E° [ed.]
© Leeds Music Corp., New York;
20Oct47; on arrangement;
EP18898. Piano-conductor score
(orchestra, with words) and
parts.

ROBINSON, AL.
The Lost Grave; [and Ain't You
Ashamed?] Words and music by
Al Robinson. © Peer Internation-
al Corp., New York; 11Sep47;
EP17267-17268.

ROBINSON, ANNE, 1922-
A Barn Dance Shuffle; a piano
solo. © Clayton F. Summy Co.,
Chicago; 4Aug47; EP16070.

The Two Flutes; piano solo by
Anne Robinson. © Harold
Flammer, inc., New York;
28Jul47; EP16257.

ROBINSON, EARL, 1910-
Free and Equal Blues; words by
E. Y. Harburg, music by Earl
Robinson. © Chappell & Co.,
inc., New York; 21Jul47;
EP15783.

ROBINSON, J RUSSEL.
Beale Street Mamma; by Roy Turk
and J. Russel Robinson ...
arr. by "Zep" Meissner. ©
Mills Music, inc., New York;
28Jul47; on arrangement;
EP16191. Piano-conductor
score (orchestra) and parts.

Meet Me at No Special Place (and
I'll Be Happy at No Particular
Time); lyric by Arthur Terker and
Harry Pyle, music by J. Russel
Robinson, arr. by Fred Weismantel.
© Leeds Music Corp., New York;
16Jul47; on arrangement; EP15544.
Piano-conductor score (orchestra,
with words) and parts.

ROBINSON, WEYMAN.
Girl with the Corn Colored Hair;
words and music by Weyman Rob-
inson. © Nordyke Publishing
Co., Los Angeles; 29Jul47;
EP17625.

ROBISON, CARSON J
It's Gonna Take a Long Long Time
to Forget You; words and music
by Carson J. Robison. © Bob
Miller, inc., New York; 27Oct47;
EP18596.

Take Me to My Home Out on the
Prairie; words and music by
Carson J. Robison. © Bob
Miller, inc., New York;
27Oct47; EP18593.

ROBISON, HARRIS B
Try It, It's a Lot of Fun; words
and music by Harris B. Robison.
[c1946] © Nordyke Publishing
Co., Los Angeles; 13Jan47;
EP20055.

ROBISON, WILLARD.
When Are You Coming Home, My Baby?
By Jean Perricone and Willard
Robison. © Bob Miller, inc.,
New York; 27Oct47; EP18630.
For voice and piano, with chord
symbols.

ROBISON, WILLIAM RICHARD, 1879-
Since tho' Smoke Has Cleared Away;
by W. R. Robison. © William
Richard Robison, Graham, Okla.;
1Jul47; EP16635. Close score:
S.TB.

ROCCA, Paul. See
Rocca-Serra, Paul.

ROCCA-SERRA, PAUL, 1898-
Ferme Tes Yeux ... paroles de Paul
Rocca et André Dassary [pseud.],
musique de Paul Rocca. © Edi-
tions Royalty, Paris; 14Aug47;
EF7345. Basque and French words.

ROCHE, ALBERT T
California; words and music by
Albert T. Roche. © Albert T.
Roche, San Francisco; 5Nov47;
EP20266.

ROCHE, PIERRE, 1919-
J'ai Bu; paroles de Charles
Aznavour, musique de Pierre
Roche. © Société d'Éditions
Musicales Paris-Mélodies,
Paris; 31Jul46; EF5931.

RODGERS, RICHARD, 1902-
(Allegro) A Fellow Needs a Girl,
[from] "Allegro"; music by
Richard Rodgers, words by Oscar
Hammerstein 2nd. [New York,
Chappell & Co.] © Richard
Rodgers & Oscar Hammerstein
2nd, New York; 110ct47;
EP17009.

(Allegro) Come Home, [from] "Allegro," words by Oscar Hammerstein
2nd, music by Richard Rodgers. ©
Richard Rodgers and Oscar Hammerstein 2nd, New York; 20Oct47;
EP20156.

(Allegro) The Gentleman Is a Dope
... [from] Allegro ... music by
Richard Rodgers ... lyrics by
Oscar Hammerstein 2nd. New York,
Williamson Music. © Richard
Rodgers and Oscar Hammerstein
2nd, New York; 18Aug47; EP17014.

(Allegro) Money Isn't Ev'rything,
[from] "Allegro"; words by Oscar
Hammerstein 2nd, music by
Richard Rodgers. New York,
Williamson Music. © Richard
Rodgers and Oscar Hammerstein
2nd, New York; 110ct47; EP18274.

(Allegro) So Far, [from]
"Allegro"; music by Richard
Rodgers, words by Oscar Hammer-
stein 2nd. [New York, Chappell
& Co.] © Richard Rodgers &
Oscar Hammerstein 2nd, New York;
12Aug47; EP17008.

(Allegro) You Are Never Away,
[from] "Allegro"; music by
Richard Rodgers, words by Oscar
Hammerstein 2nd. [New York,
Chappell & Co.] © Richard
Rodgers and Oscar Hammerstein 2nd,
New York; 19Aug47; EP17010.

(Babes in Arms) Where or When,
from the musical comedy "Babes
in Arms" ... music by Richard
Rodgers, paraphrased ... by
Erik Leidzén. © Chappell & Co.,
inc., New York; 28Oct47; on
arrangement; EP18662. Condensed
score (band) and parts.

(Carousel) "Carousel" Choral Selection [from the musical play
"Carousel"] Words by Oscar
Hammerstein II, music by Richard
Rodgers. Transcription for
mixed voices (S.A.T.B) by Clay
Warnick. © Williamson Music,
inc., New York; 14Nov47; on
arrangement; EP19145.

RODGERS, RICHARD. Cont'd.
(Carousel) June Is Bustin' Out All Over; from the musical play "Carousel," S.A.B. arr. by William Stickles. Words by Oscar Hammerstein, 2nd, music by Richard Rodgers. © Williamson Music, inc., New York; 4Dec47; on arrangement; EP20464.

(Carousel) June Is Bustin' Out All Over; from the musical play "Carousel," two part chorus arr. by William Stickles. Words by Oscar Hammerstein 2nd, music by Richard Rodgers. © Williamson Music, inc., New York; 4Dec47; on arrangement; EP20462.

(Carousel) You'll Never walk Alone; from the musical play "Carousel," arr. by William Stickles. Words by Oscar Hammerstein 2nd, music by Richard Rodgers. © Williamson Music, inc., New York; 4Dec47; on arrangement; EP20463.

(Carousel) You'll Never Walk Alone, from the musical play "Carousel," music by Richard Rodgers, words by Oscar Hammerstein 2nd, three part mixed chorus (S.A.B.) arr. by William Stickles. © Williamson Music, inc., New York; 4Dec47; on arrangement; EP19805.

Come Home. See his Allegro.

(A Connecticut Yankee) My Heart Stood Still ... [from A Connecticut Yankee; by] Richard Rodgers, paraphrased by Gregory Stone. © Harms, inc., New York; 21Nov47; on arrangement; EP19175. Score (violin and piano) and part.

A Fellow Needs a Girl. See his Allegro

The Gentleman Is a Dope. See his Allegro.

June Is Bustin' Out All Over. See his Carousel.

Money Isn't Ev'rything. See his Allegro.

My Heart Stood Still. See his A Connecticut Yankee.

My Romance; two part chorus, arr. by William Stickles. Words by Lorenz Hart, music by Richard Rodgers. New York, T. B. Harms. © T. B. Harms Co. & Max Dreyfus, New York; 14Jul47; on arrangement; EP15782.

So Far. See his Allegro.

(Spring Is Here) With a Song in My Heart, from "Spring Is Here"; music by Richard Rodgers, arr. by Jimmy Dale. © Harms, inc., New York; 20Jun47; on arrangement; EP15363. Piano-conductor score (orchestra) and parts.

(Spring Is Here) With a Song in My Heart, from the musical comedy "Spring Is Here"; music by Richard Rodgers, words by Lorenz Hart, [arr. by Jerry Sears] © Harms, inc., New York; 30Jun47; on arrangement; EP16538. Piano-conductor score (orchestra with words) and parts.

Where or When. See his Babes in Arms.

Where or When ... ([for] S.A.B.) arr. by William Stickles, music by Richard Rodgers, words by Lorenz Hart. © Chappell & Co., inc., New York; 5Aug47; on arrangement; EP16272.

Where or When ... ([for] S.A.T.B.) arr. by William Stickles, music by Richard Rodgers, words by Lorenz Hart. © Chappell & Co., inc., New York; 7Aug47; or arrangement; EP16273.

Where or When ... ([for] S.S.A.) arr. by William Stickles, music by Richard Rodgers, words by Lorenz Hart. © Chappell & Co., inc., New York; 5Aug47; on arrangement; EP16271.

Where or When ... ([for] T.T.B.B.) arr. by William Stickles, music by Richard Rodgers, words by Lorenz Hart. © Chappell & Co., inc., New York; 7Aug47; on arrangement; EP16274.

Where or When; [for] two part chorus arr. by William Stickles, music by Richard Rodgers, words by Lorenz Hart. © Chappell & Co., inc., New York; 5Aug47; on arrangement; EP16268.

With a Song in My Heart. See his Spring Is Here.

You Are Never Away. See his Allegro.

You'll Never Walk Alone. See his Carousel.

RODNEY, DON.
Funny Little Money Man; words by Hal David, music by Don Rodney. © Shapiro, Bernstein & Co., inc., New York; 26Nov47; EP19246.

That's What Every Young Girl Should Know; music by Don Rodney, words by Mack David. [c1946]. © Beverly Music Corp., New York; 5Sep47; EP16652.

RODRIGUEZ, ARSENIO.
En Tampa ... De Arsenio Rodriguez. © Peer International Corp., New York; 23Sep47; EP17850. For voice and piano.

Un Sueño ... De Arsenio Rodriguez. © Peer International Corp., New York; 23Sep47; EP17849. For voice and piano.

RODRIGUEZ, CHUCHO. See Rodriguez, Jesús.

RODRIGUEZ, G   H
La cumparsita ... [by] G. H. Matos Rodriguez, arr. by Harry Breuer. © Chart Music Publishing House, inc., Chicago; on arrangement; 17Mar47; EP13165. Score (marimba or xylophone and piano) and part.

La cumparsita. The masked one ... by G. H. Matos Rodriguez, piano solo arr. and ed. by Harold Potter. © J. & J. Kammen Music Co., New York; on arrangement; 6May47; EP6917.

RODRIGUEZ, JESÚS.
"Lo Mismo Me Dá" ... [words and music] de: Chucho Rodriguez. Orquestación de: Antonio Nuñez M. © Promotora Hispano Americana de Música, s.a., México; 31Oct47; EF6936. Piano-conductor score (orchestra) and parts.

RODRIGUEZ, JOHNNY.
Ya Te Pesara. (You'll Regret) ... Spanish words and music by Johnny Rodriguez, English words by Joe Davis. © Caribbean Music, inc., New York; 22Sep47; EP17108.

RODRIGUEZ, M
La Cumparsita ... guitar solo, [by] M. Rodriguez, arr. as played by F. Victor. c1939. © Albert Rocky Co., New York; 10Jan40; on arrangement; EP20345.

RODRIGUEZ, MOISES SIMON. See Simon Rodriguez, Moises.

RODRIGUEZ, PEDRO ANGULO. See Angulo Rodriguez, Pedro.

ROETTKER, DAISY.
Until You Came Last Night Sweetheart; words and music by Daisy Roettker. © Nordyke Publishing Co., Los Angeles; 1Jul46; EP19299.

ROGELIO, JOSE HUGUET. See Huguet Rogelio, José.

ROGERS, BERNARD.
Elegy. © Elkan-Vogel Co., inc., Philadelphia; 11Jun47; EP15842. Score: orchestra.

ROGERS, DICK.
Two Blocks Down ... Turn to the left (on the right hand side of the street) By Freddy James (pseud.) and Dick Rogers. © Mood Music Co., inc., New York; 17Nov47; EP19218. For voice and piano, with chord symbols.

ROGERS, JESSE.
Mary from Maryland; words and music by Alvin Williams, Sally Rogers and Jesse Rogers. New York, B. Miller. © Main Street Songs, inc., New York; 14Oct47; EP17997.

ROHLF, EARL.
Keep Me in Mind; words and music by Bradford Browne and Earl Rohlf ... piano arrangement by Dick Kent. © Peer International Corp., New York; 25Nov47; EP19846.

ROHRER, T   1907–
Instrumental Music Primer; for ... beginners on orchestral and band instruments, by T. Rohner ... [for] bass clef instruments. © The Raymond A. Hoffman Co., Chicago; 12Nov35; EP15547.

ROIG, GONZALO.
Be Sure. (No Quiero Que Me Quieras) Lyric by Mack David, music and Spanish lyric by Gonzalo Roig. © Remick Music Corp., New York; 9Jul47; EP5766.

ROJO, GUADALUPE.
Mi Oracion. (My Prayer for You) ... English words by Joe Davis, Spanish words by Guadalupe Rojo. © Caribbean Music Co., New York; 20Oct47; EP18010.

Si Pudiera. (If I Could) ... English words by Joe Davis, Spanish words by Romulo Contreras, music by Guadalupe Rojo. © Caribbean Music Co., New York; 10Nov47; EP18432.

ROLLINS, JACK.
The Champion; by Jack Robbins. © Main Street Songs, inc., New York; 14Oct47; EP17995. For voice and piano, with chord symbols.

ROMA, VALENTINO.
The Dancer. (La Ballerina) by Valentino Roma, arr. for accordion duet by Galla-Rini. © Roma Music Co., Cleveland; 15Oct47; on arrangement; EP18162.

 RONANHAUSER, STANLEY.
The Rainbow March ... [by] Stanley Ronanhauser. © Stanley Ronanhauser, Columbus, Ohio; 21Jul47; EP15911. Close score: SATB.

ROMBERG, SIGMUND, 1887–
Deep in My Heart, Dear; from the operetta "The Student Prince." Words by Dorothy Donnelly; music by Sigmund Romberg; a Jerry Sears arrangement. © Harms, inc., New York; 16Dec47; on arrangement; EP20345. Piano-conductor score (orchestra, with words) and parts.

Deep in My Heart. See his The Student Prince.

(The Desert Song) French Military Marching Song, from "The Desert Song" by Sigmund Romberg, transcribed ... by C. Alexander Poloquin. © Harms, inc., New York; 18Jul47; on transcription; EP16537. Condensed score (band) and parts.

ROMBERG, SIGMUND. Cont'd.

(The Desert Song) The Riff Song,
from the operetta "The Desert Song"
... words by Otto Harbach and
Oscar Hammerstein, II, music by
Sigmund Romberg ... scored by Ken
Macomber. © Harms, inc., New York;
5Nov47; on arrangement; EP19119.
Piano-conductor score (orchestra,
with words) and parts.
French military marching song. See
his The desert song.

Lover Come Back to Me. See his The
New Moon.

Maytime; selection, by Sigmund Romberg, arr. by Mayhew Lake. © G.
Schirmer, inc., New York; 29Jul47;
on arrangement; EP19141. Condensed score (band) and parts.

(The New Moon) Lover Come Back to
Me, from the musical romance
"The New Moon" ... words by
Oscar Hammerstein II, music by
Sigmund Romberg, a Jerry Sears
arrangement. © Harms, inc.,
New York; 10oct47; on orchestra-
tion; EP17755. Piano-conductor
score (orchestra, with words)
and parts.

(The New Moon) Softly as in a
Morning Sunrise. "Quedo." From
the operetta "The New Moon,"
Spanish text by Johnnie Camacho,
English text by Oscar
Hammerstein, 2nd, music by
Sigmund Romberg. © Harms, inc.,
New York; 9Jul47; on Spanish
text; EP15627.

No Sufras por Mi. See his The Student
Prince.

Quedo. See his The New Moon.

The Riff Song. See his The Desert Song

Serenade, from "The Student
Prince" ... [by] Sigmund Romberg, arr. by Jean Gossette
[pseud.] © Harms, inc., New
York; 12Dec47; on arrangement;
EP19985. Score (trombone and
piano) and part.

Softly as in a Morning Sunrise. See
his The New Moon.

(The Student Prince) Deep in My
Heart, Dear. "No Sufras por
Mi." From the musical comedy
"The Student Prince"; Spanish
text by Johnnie Camacho, words
by Dorothy Donnelly, music by
Sigmund Romberg. © Harms, inc.,
New York; 25Jun47; on Spanish
text; EP15360.

ROMBY, PAUL, 1900-
Lorette; [by] Paul Romby ... arr.
de Julien Porret. © Le Chante
du Monde, Editions Musicales,
Paris; 30Jun47; EP64493. Piano-
conductor score (orchestra) and
parts.

The Advertising Song; (I
Believe), words & music by
Harold Rome. © Gemini Music
Co., inc., New York;
9Aug47; EP16417.

(Sitting on Your) Status Quo;
words & music by Harold Rome.
© Gemini Music Publishing Co.,
inc., New York; 9Aug47;
EP16419.

Small World; words & music by Harold
Rome. © Gemini Music Publishing
Co., inc., New York; 9Aug47;
EP16418.

ROMERO, GARET, 1912-
There's a Mansion in Heaven for
Me; words ... by ... Ben
Thomas [pseud.] and music by
Garet Romero, [piano arrange-
ment by Dick Kent] © Quality
Music Co., inc., New York;
28Aug47; EP17654.

RONALD, LANDON.
June Rhapsody; arr. by Alec Rowley
for mixed voices (S.A.T.B.)
words by Edward Lockton, music
by Landon Ronald. c1946. © Keith,
Prowse & Co., ltd., London;
7Oct47; on arrangement; EF6775.

RONCHETTO, LOUIS.
The way to Music on the accordion;
by Louis Ronchetto. © McKinley
Publishers, inc., Chicago;
23Sep47; EP17820.

ROONEY, MICKEY.
Until the Next Time; words and
music by Mickey Rooney, [arr.
by Lou Halmy] © Mills Music,
inc., New York; 29Aug47;
EP17946.

ROPARTZ, JOSEPH GUY MARIE, 1864-
Au Pied de l'Autel; [by] J. Guy Ro-
partz. © Rouart, Lerolle & Cie.,
Paris; 2.sér., 17Aug47; EF7236.
For harmonium solo.

Cinquième Quatuor Quasi una Fantasia.
See his Quartet, strings, no. 5.

(Quartet, strings, no.5) Cinquième
Quatuor Quasi una Fantasia, en
ré majeur, [by] J. Guy Ropartz.
© Durand & Cie, Paris; 30Apr47;
EF5844. Parts.

--- --- Miniature score. © Durand
& Cie, Paris; 30Apr47; EF5889.

ROSALES, MARCO.
Click Click Song ... Spanish
lyrics by Marco Rosales, English
lyric and music by Sylvia
Rosales and Marco Rosales.
© Southern Music Publishing Co.,
inc., New York; 23Sep47;
EP17857.

ROSE, CHARLES.
No Second Spring; words and music
by Charles Rose. © Nordyke
Publishing Co., Los Angeles;
11Jun47; EP17431.

ROSE, DAVID.
Manhattan Square Dance ... for
piano by David Rose. © Bregman,
Vocco and Conn, inc., New York;
12Sep47; EP17124.

Nostalgia; lyric by Edward Maxwell,
music by David Rose. © Bregman,
Vocco and Conn, inc., New York;
22Aug47; on lyric; EP16549.

The Outstanding Compositions of
David Rose; in a series of simplified arrangements, by Louis
Sugarman. © Bregman, Vocco and
Conn, inc., New York; 4Sep47;
on simplified editions of 5
pieces. Contents - [v.1]
Holiday for Strings (© EP17312)
- [v.2] Our Waltz (© EP17309) -
[v.3] Dance of the Spanish
Onion (© EP17311) - [v.4]
Nursery without Rhyme (© EP
17308) -   Continued on
[v.5] Nostalgia (© EP17310)

ROSE, FRED.
After We Say Goodbye; words and
music by Fred Rose. © Milene
Music, Nashville; 8Nov47;
EP18565.

The Last Mile; [by] Gene Autry,
Oakley Haldeman [and] Fred
Rose. © Western Music Publishing Co., Hollywood, Calif.;
12Nov47; EP18846. For voice
and piano, with chord symbols.

A Long Road Ahead; words and
music by Fred Rose. © Chas. K.
Harris Music Publishing Co.,
inc., New York; 27Aug47;
EP17873.

Someday You'll Thank Me; words and
music by Fred Rose. © Milene
Music, Nashville; 15Oct47;
EP18086.

Waltz of the Wind; words and music
by Fred Rose. © Milene Music,
Nashville; 15Oct47; EP18085.

(You've Got) a Sweet Kind of Love;
by Fred Rose. © Milene Music,
Nashville, Tenn.; 22Dec47; EP20297.
For voice and piano, with guitar
diagrams and chord symbols.

ROSE, MICKE.
I Never Told You; words and music
by Micke Rose. © Nordyke Publishing Co., Los Angeles;
11Jul47; EP17611.

ROSE, PETER DE. See
De Rose, Peter.

ROSEN, ARTHUR OLAF, 1901-
Minnen från Hembygden; ord av
John H. Rosen, music av Arthur
O. Rosen. [Seattle, Morrison
Music Co.] © Arthur Olaf Rosen,
John H. Rosen, Seattle; 4Jul47;
EP17781.

ROSENBERG, HILDING CONSTANTIN, 1892-
Johannes Uppenbarelse; symfoni IV...
koraler och slutkör, [by] Hilding
Rosenberg, [words by Hjalmar Gull-
berg] © A. b. Nordiska musikförlaget, Stockholm; 1Jan45; EP7186.
Principally for chorus (SATB)
with parts.

Suite nr 1 ur balett-pantomimen
Ytterata Domen. See his Ytterata
Domen.

Symphonische Suite; aus der Oper:
Die Reise nach Amerika, [by] Hilding Rosenberg. Stockholm, Ed.
Suecia. © Föreningen svenska tonsättare, Edition Suecia, Stockholm;
1Jan39; EP7063. Score: orchestra.

(Ytterata Domen) Suite nr 1 ur
balett-pantomimen Ytterata Domen
[by] Hilding Rosenberg. Stockholm,
Ed. Suecia. © Edition Suecia,
Föreningen svenska tonsättare,
Stockholm; 1Jan35; EP7080. Score:
orchestra.

ROSENKRANS, GEORGE.
With Bands and Banners ... by
George Rosenkrans, arr. by the
composer. © Volkwein Bros.,
inc., Pittsburgh; 2Jul46; on
conductor score, new parts &
editing; EP16969. Piano-
conductor score (band) and
parts.

ROSENTHAL, CARL A   arr.
Clarinet Trios; from Corelli to
Beethoven. Also suitable for
saxophone trios and violin
trios. Arr. by Carl A. Rosenthal. © Edwin H. Morris & Co.,
inc., New York; 6Oct47; EP18523.

ROSENTHAL, MANUEL, 1904-
La Pietà d'Avignon; six prières
pour quatre voix mixtes et
orchestre de cordes avec trompette, par Manuel Rosenthal.
© J. Jobert, Paris; 15Mar47;
EF5924. Score: SATB and piano.

Les Soirées du Petit Juas; huit
pièces ... par Manuel Rosenthal.
© Juan Jobert, Paris; 15Apr47;
EF5050. Parts: violin 1-2,
viola and violoncello.

ROSETTI, JOSEPH G
Let's Do It Again; words and music
by Joe Rosetti. © Joe Rosetti,
Olean, N. Y.; 3Nov47; EP18584.

ROSNER, BERNICE, 1912-
Big Note Boogie ... [by] Bernice
Rosner. (In Hirschberg, David,
ed. and comp. Pieces Are Fun.
bk. 1, p. 34-35) © Musicord
Publications, New York;
2Jul47; EP15941. For piano
solo.

Tomahawk Dance ... [by] Bernice
Rosner. (In Hirschberg, David,
ed. and comp. Pieces Are Fun.
bk. 1, p. 26-27) © Musicord
Publications, New York; 2Jul47;
EP15937. For piano solo, with
words.

ROSS, BEN.
Poor Little Polliwog; (The tadpole song], words by Bob Wald, music by Ben Ross. © Paull-Pioneer Music Corp., New York; 3Nov47; EP18718.

ROSS, BETTY.
Honolulu Lou; words and music by Betty Ross. © Nordyke Publishing Co., Los Angeles; 29Mar47; EP16807.

ROSS, CLEO E
My Heart Is a Violin; words and music by Cleo E. Ross. © Nordyke Publishing Co., Los Angeles; 12Aug47; EP19672.

ROSS, FLORENCE.
We Met in the Little White Church; words and music by Florence Ross. © Nordyke Publishing Co., Los Angeles; 31Jul47; EP19539.

ROSS, HELEN B
I've Changed My Mind; words and music by Helen Ross. © Broadcast Music, inc., New York; 30May47; EP18211.

ROSS, HELEN KATHERINE, 1914-
I'd Rather Be a Tither ... [by] Mrs. Helen Ross. © Mrs. Helen K. Ross, Ashford, W. Va.; 18Jun47; EP16235. Close score: SATB.

ROSSI, NINO, 1895   ed.
I Clavicembalisti Italiani; 20 composizioni accuratamente rivedute e diteggiate, da Nino Rossi. © Carisch, s. a., Milan; 27Jun46; on revision; EP62721 For piano solo.

ROSSI, RENZO OLDRATI. See
Oldrati Rossi, Renzo.

ROSSINI, GIOACCHINO ANTONIO, 1792-1868.
La Danza ... by Rossini, [arr. by Norman Richardson] London, Sole selling agents, Boosey & Hawkes. © Hawkes & Son (London) ltd., London; 28Aug47; on arrangement; EP6642. Condensed score (band) and parts.

The Italian in Algiers; overture [by] G. Rossini, arr. by Theo. Moses-Tobani, arr. for modern bands with new parts by H. R. Kent [pseud.] New York; © Carl Fischer, inc., New York; 17Oct47; on arrangement for modern band; EP18408. Condensed score (band) and parts.

L'Italiana in Algeri; Sinfonia, [by] Gioacchino Rossini, revisione di Giuseppe Piccioli. © Carisch, s.a., Milan; 25Mar39; on revision; EP6218. Score: orchestra.

(Quartet, winds) Quartet in F, for flute (or oboe), clarinet, horn [and bassoon; by] Rossini, [rev. and ed. by Richard Franko Goldman] © Mercury Music Corp., New York; 16Dec46; on revision & editing; EP16350. Miniature score and parts.

Sonata ... per due violini, violoncello e contrabbasso, [by] G. Rossini, rev. di Alfredo Casella. © Carisch, s. a., Milan; 8Aug43; on revision; EP6226. Score.

William Tell; by G. Rossini ... arr. by Hugo Frey. [Words by Elsie-Jean, pseud.] © Hamilton S. Gordon, inc., New York; 22Oct47; on words and arrangement; EP18746. For piano solo, with words.

ROTH, HOWARD HAINES, 1907-
Headin' West; words and music by Howard H. Roth. © Howard H. Roth & Co., inc., Clearwater, Fla.; 14Aug47; EP16215.

Waukegan Cowboy; words and music by Howard H. Roth. © Howard H. Roth & Co., inc., Clearwater, Fla.; 15Sep47; EP17221.

Ya Know What? Words and music by Howard H. Roth. © Howard H. Roth & Co., inc., Clearwater, Fla.; 25Jun47; EP15308.

ROTH, S   E
Sing of Our Saviour's Love; [by] S. E. Roth. © S. E. Roth, Woodburn, Or.; 13Sep47; EP17082. Close score: SATB.

ROUBANIS, N
Misirlou; music by N. Roubanis ... arr. by Michael Edwards. New York, Mills Music, inc. © Colonial Music Publ. Co., inc., New York; 28Jul47; on arrangement; EP16202. Parts: trumpet or cornet and piano.

Misirlou; music by N. Roubanis ... arr. by Michael Edwards. New York, Mills Music, inc. © Colonial Music Publ. Co., inc., New York; 28Jul47; on arrangement; EP16203. Parts: saxophone and piano.

Misirlou; music by N. Roubanis ... arr. by Michael Edwards. New York, Mills Music, inc. © Colonial Music Publ. Co., inc., New York; 28Jul47; on arrangement; EP16204. Parts: clarinet and piano.

Misirlou; music by N. Roubanis ... arr. by Philip J. Lang. New York, Mills Music. © Colonial Music Pub. Co., inc., New York; 12Sep47; on arrangement; EP18157. Condensed score (band) and parts.

[ROUSSEAU, PIERRE] 1889-1939.
Une Aventure de Babar; [by] Pierre Vellones [pseud.] Suite. © Henry Lemoine et Cie, Paris; 8May47; EF7349. For piano 4 hands.

Pluies; poème de Théophile Briant, [music by] Pierre Vellones [pseud.] Op. 49. Chant et piano. © Durand & Cie, Paris; 30Sep47; EF7314.

Soir d'Idumée; [by] Pierre Vellones. Op. 62. Poème de Gabriel Boissy. Chant et piano. © Durand & Cie, Paris; 30Sep47; EF7326.

ROUSSEL, ALBERT, 1869-1937.
Elpénor; poème radiophonique de Joseph Weterings, musique de Albert Roussel. (Op. 59) Texte et musique. © Durant & Cie, Paris; 30Sep47; EF7293. Play with incidental music. Score: flute, 2 violins, viola and violoncello.

ROVENGER, LEOPOLD W
Katinka; a Polish dance for piano, [by] Leopold W. Rovenger. © Theodore Presser Co., Philadelphia; 26Jun47; EP15378.

ROVENGER, LEOPOLD W   ed. and arr.
Adult Program Album; for piano, comp., arr. and ed. for the advancing pianist by Leopold W. Rovenger. © Rubank, inc., Chicago; 1Nov47; EP18626.

March Kings' Album for Piano; selected, arr. and ed.... by Leopold W. Rovenger. © Rubank, inc., Chicago; 5Aug47; on arrangements; EP16081.

ROWBOTHOM, HERBERT.
Sylvan Sprites; for the piano, by Herbert Rowbottom. © Theodore Presser Co., Philadelphia; 15Dec47; EP20395.

ROWDEN, HAZEN.
Take a Little Chance with Me; words and music by Hazen Rowden. © Nordyke Publishing Co., Los Angeles; 11Aug47; EP19660.

ROWLANDS, JOHNNY.
Bring On the Drums; by Johnny Rowlands, arr. by Norrie Paramor & Harry Gold. © Cinephonic Music Co., ltd., London; 9Apr46; EF6018. Parts: orchestra.

ROWLEY, ALEC, 1892-
Barcarolle ... by Alec Rowley. London, J. Curwen, New York, G. Schirmer, sole agents. © Alec Rowley, Kew Gardens, Surrey, Eng.; 23Oct47; EF6944. For piano 4 hands.

Corinna; two-part song for women's voices, words by Lord Lansdowne ... music by Alec Rowley. © Ascherberg, Hopwood & Crew, ltd., London; 15Sep47; EF6757.

Counting Sheep; music by Alec Rowley, words by Doris Rowley. © Edwin Ashdown, ltd., London; 24Nov47; EF6747.

The Gardener; words by Edward Shenton, music by Alec Rowley. © Western Music Co., ltd., Vancouver, B. C., Can.; 1Nov47; EF6924.

The Homeward Road ... (T.T.B.B.) words by Frederick Allen, music by Alec Rowley. London, Sole selling agents, Boosey & Hawkes. © Boosey & Co., ltd., London; 11Jul47; EF5717.

Miniature Concerto for piano and orchestra; [by] Alec Rowley. © Hawkes & Son (London) ltd., London; 16Oct47; EF6821. Two scores for 2 pianos.

Miniature Concerto; for piano and orchestra, [by] Alec Rowley. © Hawkes & Son (London) ltd., London; 6Nov47; EF7014. Nautical Toccata ... by Alec Rowley. London, J. Curwen, New York, G. Schirmer, sole agents. © Alec Rowley, Kew Gardens, Surrey, Eng.; 23Oct47; EF6945. For piano 4 hands.

The Ploughman; music by Alec Rowley, words by Dorothea Butler [pseud.] © Edwin Ashdown, ltd., London; 26Jul47; EF6724.

Sweet Was the Song the Virgin Sung; three-part song for treble voices S.S.A. (unacc.) Words 17th century, music by Alec Rowley. © Novello & Co., ltd., London; 15Oct47; EF6884.

Three Songs of Innocence; for female voices (S.S.A.) words by William Blake, music by Alec Rowley. © Novello & Co., ltd., London; 30Oct47; on 3 songs. Contents.- Piping down the Valleys Wild (© EF6725) Little Lamb (© EF6726) Holy Thursday (© EF6727)

The Winds of May; two-part song for treble voices with pianoforte acc., words by Bernard Christian Durrant, music by Alec Rowley. London, J. Curwen, New York, G. Schirmer, sole agents. © Alec Rowley, Kew Gardens, Surrey, Eng.; 23Oct47; EF6938.

ROX, JOHN J   BARBER HERRING.
Rainbow Hill; words and music by John Rox. © Broadcast Music, inc., New York; 11Jul47; EP18204.

ROYAL, LARRY.
If Ev'ry Day Was Christmas (and ev'ry night was New Year's Eve); by Larry Royal. © Chappell & Co., inc., New York; 8Aug47; EP17006. For voice and piano, with chord symbols.

ROYAL CONSERVATORY OF MUSIC OF TORONTO.
See Toronto. Conservatory of Music.

RUBBRA, EDMUND.
(Quartet, strings) String Quartet
in F minor. Op.35. [By] Edmund Rubbra. Score. © Alfred
Lengnick & Co., ltd., London;
26Sep47; EF7152.

Soliloquy; for solo violoncello
and string orchestra, horns and
tympani [by] Edmund Rubbra.
Op.57. © Alfred Lengnick & Co.,
ltd., London; 8Aug47; EF6948.

(Sonata, violoncello & piano)
Sonata in G minor; [by] Edmund
Rubbra. Op. 60. © Alfred
Lengnick & Co., ltd., London;
12Sep47; EF6744. Score and part.

String Quartet in F minor. See his
Quartet, strings.

Three Psalms; for low voice with
pianoforte acc. [by] Edmund
Rubbra. Op. 61. © Alfred Lengnick & Co., ltd., London;
8Aug47; EF6849.

RUBINSTEIN, ANTON, 1829-1894.
Kammenoi-Ostrow ... [by] A. Rubinstein. [arr. by] Harry Volpe.
c1939. © Albert Rocky Co., New
York; 10Jan40; on arrangement;
EP20194. For 2 guitars.

Melody in F ... [by] A. Rubinstein,
[arr. by] Harry Volpe. c1939.
© Albert Rocky Co., New York;
10Jan40; on arrangement; EP20201.
Parts: 4 guitars.

Melody in F; [by] Anton Rubinstein, for brass band [arr. by
Eric Ball] © Besson and Co.,
ltd., London; 16Oct47; on
arrangement; EF6815. Condensed
score (band) and parts.

Romance d'Autrefois; d'après la
"mélodie de fa," de Rubinstein.
Paroles de André Grassi et Albert
Leary. © Éditions Salabert, Paris;
5Aug47; on words; EF7245. For
voice and piano.

Shino on, oh Star. Kamennoiostrow. Four-part chorus of
male voices ... arr. [with
lyric] by Raymond Allyn Smith.
© The Raymond A. Hoffman Co.,
Chicago; 9Jun33; EP15579. English words.

RUBY, HARRY.
(Copacabana) Go West, Young Man,
featured in ... "Copacabana";
lyric by Bert Kalmar, music by
Harry Ruby, arr. by Vic Schoen.
New York, Blossom Music Corp.
© Sun Music Co., inc., New York;
18Aug47; on arrangement; EP16401.
Piano-conductor score (orchestra,
with words) and parts.

(Copacabana) Go West, Young Man,
featured in ... "Copacabana";
lyric by Bert Kalmar, music by
Harry Ruby. New York, Blossom
Music Corp. © Sun Music Co.,
inc., New York; 27Jun47;
EP15365.

Go West, Young Man. See his Copacabana

RUDY, ROBERT LEE, 1924-
Say You'll Be Mine; words and
music by Robert Rudy. © Cine-
Mart Music Publishing Co.,
Hollywood, Calif.; 20Jun47;
EP16206.

Say You'll Be Mine; words and
music by Robert Rudy. © Cine-
Mart Music Publishing Co.,
Hollywood, Calif.; 15Jul47;
EP16579.

RUGOLO, PETE.
Artistry in Bolero; composed and
scored by Pete Rugolo. © Leslie
Music Corp., New York; 27Nov47;
EP19224. Score: orchestra.

Artistry in Percussion; [composed
and]-scored by Pete Rugolo. ©
Leslie Music Corp., New York;
27Nov47; EP19225. Score: orchestra.

Interlude; composed and arr. by
Pete Rugolo, ed. by Van Alexander. © Leslie Music Corp.,
New York; 29Jun47; EP15542.
Piano-conductor score (orchestra) and parts.

Minor Riff; composed and arr. by
Pete Rugolo, ed. by Van
Alexander. © Leslie Music Corp.,
New York; 29Jun47; EP15544.
Piano-conductor score (orchestra)
and parts.

Safranski; composed and scored by
Pete Rugolo. © Leslie Music
Corp., New York; 27Nov47;
EP19228. Score: orchestra.

RUIZ, GABRIEL.
Miedo ... letra y música de
Gabriel Ruiz. New York, Sole
Selling Agent, Peer International Corp. © Promotora Hispano
Americana de Música, s.a.,
México; 11Sep47; EF6543.

A Solas Contigo ... letra de José
Antonio Zorrilla. Música de
Gabriel Ruiz. © Promotora Hispano Americana de Música, s.a.,
México; 30Dec46; EF6694. Condensed score (orchestra) and
parts.

RUIZ, PABLO BELTRAN. See
Beltrán Ruiz, Pablo.

RUIZ ARMENGOL, MARIO.
Muchachita ... by Mario Ruiz Armengol ... [Spanish words by]
Fernando Fernandez, English lyrics by Gus Arnheim, [arr. by
Lou Halmy] © Monterrey Music,
Hollywood, Calif.; 10Dec47;
EP20135.

RUNKEL, KENNETH E   1882-
The Christmas Bells Are Ringing;
S.A.T.B.B., [by] Kenneth E.
Runkel. © C. C. Birchard &
Co., Boston; 30Jul47; EP16490.

RUNYAN, WILLIAM M
The Gospel Homestead; [by] William
M. Runyan. [arr. by] William
Wendell F., comp. Radio Songs
and Choruses of the Gospel.
p.13) © Hope Publishing Co.,
Chicago; (in notice: W. M.
Runyan) 9Jun33; EP15579. English words.

Jesus Is My Sunshine; [by] William
M. Runyan. (In Loveless,
Wendell F., comp. Radio Songs
and Choruses of the Gospel.
p.6) © Hope Publishing Co.,
Chicago; (in notice: W. M.
Runyan) 15May34; EP16506.

RUOCCO, RENATO.
Palomma Mia ... versi di Salvatore
Stanzione, musica di Renato
Ruocco. Napoli, Edizioni E.N.C.D.
© Italian Book Co., New York;
4Sep47; EF6641.

RUSCH, H   W
Bandjive. © Fillmore Bros. Co.,
Cincinnati; 15Jul47; EP15811.
Condensed score (band) and
parts.

RUSH, NED.
Stand Behind the Great New U. S. A.;
words and music by Peter F.
Mondlak & Ned Rush. © Nordyke
Publishing Co., Los Angeles;
29Jan47; EP20326.

RUSHAN, KING GEORGE.
I Must Keep Workin'; words and
music by King George Rushan.
© Nordyke Publishing Co.,
Los Angeles; 29Mar47; EP16872.

[RUSHING, R   B   ]
Hurrah for Dear Miami; [by R. B.
Rushing] © R. B. Rushing, Music
Publisher, Miami, Fla.; 30ct47;
EP18231. Close score: SATB.

RUSSELL, JOHN WILLIAM.
Canoeing with You; words and
music by John Wm. Russell.
© Nordyke Publishing Co., Los
Angeles; 15Jun46; EP19947.

RUSSELL, KENNEDY.
"The Nightingale"; music by Kennedy Russell, book and lyric by
Michael Martin-Harvey and Sax
Rohmer. London, Ascherberg,
Hopwood & Crew. © Chappell &
Co., ltd., London; 14Aug47;
EF6325-6328. Contents.-
[1] There Is a Song My Heart
Will Always Sing. - [2] Lavender
Dreams. - [3] Cherry Blossom
Time. - [4] Let's Be Twenty-one.

(The Nightingale) Piano Selection
... [from] "The Nightingale";
music by Kennedy Russell. London,
Ascherberg, Hopwood & Crew.
© Chappell & Co., ltd., London;
11Aug47; EF6366.

Saint Christopher ... arr. as a
two-part song by Henry Geehl,
lyric by Arthur Stanley, music
by Kennedy Russell. © Edwin
Ashdown, ltd., London; 28Jun47;
on arrangement; EF6745.

RUSSELL, RICHARD S   1918-
"Too Careful"; music by Richard S.
Russell and Frank K. Primack,
words by Edgar De Lange. ©
Hollywood Melodies, Music Publishers, Hollywood, Calif.;
1Jul47; EP15921.

RUSSELL, VELMA K
Shindig ... for the piano, by
Volma A. Russell. © Oliver
Ditson Co., Philadelphia;
27Aug47; EP16684.

RUSTHOI, ESTHER KERR, 1909-
Gospel Songs; composed by Esther
Kerr Rusthoi. © Esther Kerr
Rusthoi, Pasadena, Calif.;
22Apr47; on 10 songs. Partial
contents.- Something Tells Me
That It Won't Be Long (©
EP15321)- Early in the Morning
(© EP15322)- Perhaps Today or
Tomorrow (© EP15323)- Forgiven
(© EP15324)- In the Secret
Place of Prayer (© EP15325)-
Just to Think (© EP15326)-
Heaven Is My Goal (© EP15327)-
Tenderly (© EP15328)- Ecstasy!
(© EP15329)- Keep Surrendered!
(© EP15330)

RUTHERFORD, ALFIE A
For You a Rose (in Portland
grows); words by Art Kirkham
... music by Alfie Rutherford,
[arrangement by Eliot Wright]
© Alfie A. Rutherford, Portland,
Or.; 6Jun47; EP16472.

RYDER, NOAH F
This Ol' Hammer; for four-part
chorus of men's voices and tenor
solo, a cappella. Traditional
Negro convict song, arr. by
Noah F. Ryder. © G. Schirmer,
inc., New York; 28May47; on
arrangement; EP17385.

RYDMAN, RALPH B
You're My First Love; words and
music by Ralph B. Rydman.
© Nordyke Publishing co., Los
Angeles; 5Aug47; EP20356.

RYERSON, FRANK.
Baby, Be Good; by Jimmy Eaton,
Wilton Moore [pseud., and]
Frank Ryerson. © Burke and Van
Heusen, inc., New York; 24Oct47;
EP18459. For voice and piano,
with chord symbols.

RYO, Ole, pseud. See
Howorth, Wayne.

S

SABLON, ANDRÉ.
(Un Chien Qui Rapporte) Coeur de
Parisienne, leit motif du film
parlant "Un Chien Qui Rapporte"
... paroles de Jean Choux et
Seider, musique de André Sablon.
© Publications Raoul Breton &
Cie, Paris; 3Jul31; EF5994.
Coeur de Parisienne. See his Un Chien
Qui Rapporte.

SABRE MARROQUIN, JOSÉ.
Jugando con el Tema. De: José Sabre
Marroquín. Arreglo de: Jaime López. © Promotora Hispano Americana de Música, s.a., México;
30Dec46; EF6700. Piano-conductor
score (orchestra) and parts.

SACCO, JOHN.
Maple Candy; words by Harold Van
Kirk, music by John Sacco.
© Bregman, Vocco & Conn, inc.,
New York; 12Dec47; EP20468.

SACCO, TONY, 1908-
Someday We'll Meet Again in
Montecatini; words and music by
Tony Sacco. © Tony Sacco,
Waterbury, Conn.; 23Sep47;
EP17248.

SADOWSKI, JOSEPHINE.
Mine Forever; words and music by
Josephine Sadowski. © Nordyke
Publishing Co., Los Angeles;
20Aug47; EP19361.
Mine To Be; words and music by
Josephine Sadowski. © Nordyke
Publishing Co., Los Angeles;
4Sep47; EP20082.

SAFRANSKI, EDDIE.
Concerto for Bass ... by Eddie
Safranski, arr. by Eddie
Safranski. © Mutual Music
Society, inc., New York; 2Jul47;
on arrangement; EP15426.
Piano-conductor score (double-
bass and orchestra) and parts.

ST. GERMAINE, ADELAIDE, pseud. See
Long, Norman Russell.

SAINT-MARTIN, LÉONCE MARIE JOSEPH
de, 1886-
OEuvres d'orgue de Léonce de Saint-
Martin. © H. Herelle, Paris;
10Jun47; on 2 pieces. Contents. -
[v.1] Postlude de Fête "Te
Deum Laudamus" (© EF5965)
[v.2] Le Salut à la Vierge; Ave
Maria, Ave Maria Stella (©
EF5966)

SAINT-SAËNS, CAMILLE, 1835-1921.
Le Carnaval des Animaux. See his
The Swan.
(Le Carnaval des Animaux) The
Swan ... [by] Saint-Saëns,
[transcribed by] Jascha Hei-
fetz. © Carl Fischer, inc.,
New York; 28Nov47; on transcrip-
tion; EP20390. Score (violin
and piano) and part.
Danse Macabre; [by] C. Saint-Saëns.
(Abridged ed.) Arr. by Merle J.
Isaac. © Carl Fischer, inc.,
New York; 20Nov47; on arrange-
ment; EP19168. Piano-conductor
score (orchestra) and parts.

SAKELLARIOU, ANTONIOS CH
Messenia, Messenia; stichoi:
Georgiou Zania, mousike:
Antoniou Sakellariou. New York,
Hermes Music Pub. Co. ©
Antonios Ch. Sakellariou, New
York; 13Jun47; EP17070. For
voice and piano.
O Aetos tes Kretes ... kai E Tru-
gona ... arr. by Antonios Sa-
kellariou. New York, Hermes
Music Pub. Co. © Antonios Ch.
Sakellariou, New York; 13Jun47;
on arrangement, of 2 songs;
EP17071-17072. For voice and
piano.

Ta Tria Phtaiximata ... kai Manna
Mou Rimaiphthisikos, e Arrostsa
sta Xeniteia. Words and music
by Antonios Sakellariou. New
York, Hermes Music Pub. Co. ©
Antonios Ch. Sakellariou, New
York; 13Jun47; EP17069.

SALES, JOE A
Yesterday, My Thought Was Only
You; words and music by Prof.
Joe A. Sales. © Nordyke
Publishing Co., Los Angeles;
3Dec46; EP19769.

SALFI, FRANCESCO, 1889-   arr.
Antiche Intavolature; libera in-
terpretazione o riduzione, per
pianoforte [by] Francesco Salfi.
© Carisch, s.a., Milan; 4Jan40;
on free interpretation and reduction; EF6273.

SALIERI, ANTONIO.
Axur, Re d'Ormus; sinfonia, [by]
A. Salieri, rev. di Nino Negrotti,
partitura. © Carisch, s. a.,
Milan; 28Apr47; on revision;
EF6277.

SALLER, ANTON.
Waltz Bohemia; [for] piano accor-
dion, arr. by Joseph P. Elsnic.
[°1946] © Vitak-Elsnic Co.,
Chicago; 1Feb47; on arrangement;
EP15761.

SALOMON, SIEGFRIED, 1885-
Hjaelp Mig at Følge Dig; Moster
mod den tunge Tornekrone; Digt
af Emi Munk, Musik af Siegfried
Salomon. © Wilhelm Hansen,
Musik-Forlag, Copenhagen;
22Mar47; EF6300. For voice and
piano.

SALZA, MENOTTI.
Nostalgic Serenade ... by Menotti
Salza. © Mills Music, inc., New
York; 8Dec47; EP19903. Score
(violin and piano) and part.

SALTAMACH, JOE.
School of Love; words and music
by Joe Saltamach. © Nordyke
Publishing Co., Los Angeles;
16Dec46; EP19480.
'Tho I Know; words and music by
Joe Saltamach. © Nordyke Pub-
lishing Co., Los Angeles; 9Aug46;
EP19783.

SALTER, LIONEL.
Scottish Reel; [by] Lionel Salter.
© Alfred Lengnick & Co., ltd.,
London; 8Aug47; EF6850. Two
scores for 2 pianos.
The Shepherdess; the words by
Alice Meynell; set to music by
Lionel Salter. © The Oxford
University Press, London;
3Jul47; EF6125.

THE SALVATION ARMY BRASS BAND JOURNAL.
© Salvationist Publishing & Supplies, ltd., London. Comp. by
Bramwell Coles. Score and parts.
(2d ser.) © Salvationist Publishing
& Supplies, ltd., London. Comp.
by Bramwell Coles. Score and
parts.

SAMAZEUILH, GUSTAVE, 1877-
Évocation; par Gustave Samazeuilh.
© Durand & Cie, Paris; 30Aug47;
EF7312. Score (violin or violon-
cello and piano) and parts.
Évocation; par Gustave Samazeuilh.
© Durand & Cie, Paris; 30Aug47;
EF7313. For piano solo.

SAMUELIAN, HARUTIUN S   1900-
Original Compositions ... [Ro-
mances and Songs, by] Harutiun
Samuelian. New York, Delphic
Press. © Harutiun Samuelian,
New York; v.1; 30Sep47; EP17847.
Words in both Armenian and
Armenian transliterated.

SAMUELS, WALTER, 1909-
Fort Worth Blues; words by
Victor Shropshire, music by Wal-
ter Samuels. © Nordyke Publish-
ing Co., Los Angeles; 29Jul47;
EP19733.

I'll Call It a Day; words by Edward
Lyle, music by Walter Samuels.
© Nordyke Publishing Co., Los
Angeles; 29Mar47; EP17581.

I'll Find You; words by John Kin-
zie, music by Walter Samuels.
© Nordyke Publishing Co., Los
Angeles; 19Jun47; EP17601.

Live, Love and Laugh; words by
Harold Bell, music by Walter
Samuels. © Nordyke Publishing
Co., Los Angeles; 27Jul46;
EP19465.

My Date; words by Virginia Lea
Wilder, music by Walter Samuels.
© Nordyke Publishing Co., Los
Angeles; 11Oct46; EP19778.

My Golden Dreams; words by W. C.
Logue, music by Walter Samuels.
© Nordyke Publishing Co., Los
Angeles; 15Nov46; EP19484.

My Honey Is on the Choo-Choo;
words by Leonard Franke, music by
Walter Samuels. © Nordyke
Publishing Co., Los Angeles;
27Mar47; EP16737.

My Pretty Blue Eyes; words by
Alice M. Berger, music by
Walter Samuels. © Nordyke
Publishing Co., Los Angeles;
15Jun46; EP19455.

My Quaker Queen; words by Johnny
Tucker, music by Walter Samuels.
© Nordyke Publishing Co., Los
Angeles; 21Feb47; EP19675.

Please Believe Me, Dear; words by
Bennie S. Cianciarula, music by
Walter Samuels. [c1945] ©
Nordyke Publishing Co., Los
Angeles; 21Jun46; EP20330.

Rain Blues; words by A. H. John-
son, music by Walter Samuels.
© Nordyke Publishing Co., Los
Angeles; 13Jul46; EP20013.

There Is Only One Sky (to cover
us all) words by Leora B.
Weddle, music by Walter
Samuels. © Nordyke Publishing
Co., Los Angeles; 4Sep47;
EP20043.

There's a Heart-warming Richness;
words by Nicholas Luke, music
by Walter Samuels. © Nordyke
Publishing Co., Los Angeles;
14Jun47; EP17480.

Why, Oh Why? Music by Walter
Samuels, lyric by Edna June
Lauwaert, Friond, Nob., S. T.
A. Music Pub. Co. © Edna June
Lauwaert, Elmhurst, Ill.;
26Jul47; EP16657.

You're Just Like Heaven; words by
Margaret Lou Hight, music by
Walter Samuels. © Nordyke
Publishing Co., Los Angeles;
2Dec46; EP19386.

SANCHEZ, ELISEO GRENET. See
Grenet Sánchez, Eliseo.

SÁNCHEZ VÁZQUEZ, PABLO.
Espera y Verás ... letra y música
de Pablo Sánchez Vázquez. ©
Promotora Hispano Americana de
Música, s.a., México; 22Jul47;
EP6720.
Para Que Volver ... letra y música
de Pablo Sánchez Vázquez. ©
Promotora Hispano Americana de
Música, s.a., México; 22Jul47;
EP6201.
Son Mis Gallos ... letra y música
de Pablo Sánches Vázquez. ©
Promotora Hispano Americana de
Música, s. a., Mexico; 22Jul47;
EP5820.
Soy Vagabundo ... lotra y música
de Pablo Sánchez Vázquez. ©
Promotora Hispano Americana de
Música, s.a., México; 29Jul47;
EP6197.

SAUDERS, ALMA.
(Ireland Today) A Little Green
Bonnet, from ... "Ireland Today,"
lyrics by Monte Carlo and music
by Alma Sanders. © Bob Miller,
inc., New York; 18Jun47;
EP15655.
A Little Green Bonnet. See her Ireland
Today.
SANDERS, GEORGE HARRY.
The Clock Song; by George H. San-
ders. © Cavalcade Music Co.,
New York; 30ct47; EP17664. For
voice and piano, with chord
symbols.
SANDERS, LENNY.
Baby Sitter; words and music by
Roy West, Ernest Benedict [and]
Lenny Sanders. © Remington
Music Corp., New York; 3Jul47;
EP6989.
SANDERS, PANSY SUBER- See
Suber-Sanders, Pansy.
SANDGREN, CLYDE D 1910-
The Cougar Song; of Brigham Young
University; words and music by
Clyde D. Sandgren. © Clyde D.
Sandgren, Provo, Utah; 23Oct47;
EP18295.
SANDLER, SIMON, 1918-
The Purple Mountains of Colorado;
for women's voices (S.S.A.) [by]
Simon Sandler. © Alexa Music
Co., New York; 10ct47; EP18359.
Their Songs We Sing ... for mixed
voices (S.A.T.B.) (a cappella)
[by] Simon Sandler. © Alexa
Music Co., New York; 10ct47;
EP18360.
SANDOR, JENŐ.
Halvány Sárga Rózsát. (Delicately
Tinted Are the Yellow Roses)
English lyric by Olga Paul, music
by Sándor Jenő. (In Pasti, Bar-
bera, comp. Memories of Hungary.
p. 47) © Edward B. Marks Music
Corp., New York; 19Nov47; on
English lyric; EP19010.
SANDOVAL, MIGUEL, 1903-
The Slave Market, El Mercado de
las Esclavas; [by] Miguel
Sandoval. English version by
Enrique Portes. [For] voice
and piano. © Delkas Music
Publishing Co., Los Angeles;
13Aug47; EP16487. English and
Spanish words.
SANDS, JAMES.
Christ Bled and Died for You and
Me; words and music by James
Sands, arr. by V. Bates.
© James Sands, Chicago;
18Sep47; EP18246.
SANTA CRUZ, CARLOS.
"Se Lo Voy a Decir" ... letra y
música de Carlos Santa Cruz,
arreglo de Pérez Prado. © Peer
International Corp., New York;
23Sep47; EP6714. Parts; orches-
tra.
SANTIAGO RIUS, FELIPE.
Labios de Clavel. (A Thread of
Scarlet) ... English lyric by
Marjorie Harper ... music &
Spanish words by Teodoro Bene-
melis and Felipe Santiago Rius.
© Antobal Music Co., New York;
15Oct47; EP18365.
SANTOS, DON.
Eldorado; easy plectrum guitar solos
(or duets) ... by Don Santos. ©
Don Santos Pub. Co., Rochester,
N. Y.; 20Dec47; EP20253. Princi-
pally composed by Don Santos.
SAPP, PAUL.
It's a Dirty Shame. © Century
Songs, inc., Chicago; 10Jul47;
EP15557. Melody and chord
symbols, with words.
"What I Want for Christmas";
words and music by Paul Sapp.
© Century Songs, inc., Chicago;
25Sep47; EP17377. Melody and
chord symbols, with words.

SARACINI, JOSEPH ALOYSIUS, 1906-
Samaritan Songs ... [music by] J.
A. Saracini, [arr. by Horace
Holmes, words by Vivian Ordon
Reeves and others] © Samaritan
Sacred Song Publishers, St.
Louis; 14Jul47; EP16987.
SARASATE Y NAVASCUES, PABLO MARTIN
MELITÓN DE, 1844-1908.
Spanish Dance. (Romanza Andaluza)
By Pablo de Sarasate. Op.22.
Arr. by Joe Biviano. © Viccas
Music Co., New York; 25Aug47;
on arrangement; EP17833. For
accordion solo.
SARDINA, FERNANDO TINTORER. See
Tintorer Sardiña, Fernando.
SARGES, LYNN, 1903-
My Atom Bomb; words and music by
Lynn Sarges. Los Angeles,
Star Publications. © Lynn
(Poor) Sarges, Los Angeles;
28Jul47; EP16485.
SARK, EINAR TRAERUP, 1921-
Lette Klaverstykker; [by] Einar
Traerup Sark. Op. 5a, © Wilhelm
Hansen, Musik-Forlag, Copen-
hagen; 14Apr47; EF6301. For
piano solo.
Toccata ... [by] Einar Traerup
Sark. Op. 6. © Wilhelm Hansen,
Musik-Forlag, Copenhagen;
14Apr47; EF6299. For piano solo.
[SARKISSIAN, BAROUYR]
That Dream of Mine; Words and
music by Buddy Kent [pseud.
c1946] © Nordyke Publishing
Co., Los Angeles; 29Jan47;
EP20479.
SARONY, LESLIE.
Sunday ... by Leslie Sarony. ©
Peter Maurice Music Co., ltd.,
New York; 26Aug47; EF6545.
For voice and piano.
SAS, NACI.
Erdőszélén Nagy a Zsivaj. (At the
Forest's Edge, There's a Celebra-
tion) English lyric by Olga Paul,
music by Sas Náci. (In Pasti,
Barbara, comp. Memories of Hun-
gary. p. 58-59) © Edward B.
Marks Music Corp., New York;
19Nov47; on English lyric;
EP19015.
Hogyha Szeretnélek. (Never Have I
Said I Loved You) English lyric
by Olga Paul, music by Sas Náci.
(In Pasti, Barbara, comp. Memo-
ries of Hungary. p. 48-49) ©
Edward B. Marks Music Corp., New
York; 19Nov47; on English lyric;
EP19011.
SATEREN, LELAND BERNHARD, 1913-
Accept My Heart; [music by] Leland
B. Sateren, [words by] Matthew
Bridges. © Paul A. Schmitt
Music Co., Minneapolis; 4Sep47;
EP16655. Score: SATB and piano.
God Walks Beside Thee; [music by]
Leland B. Sateren, [words by]
Grace Jewel Jensen. © Paul A.
Schmitt Music Co., Minneapolis;
26Aug47; EP16565. Score: SATB
and piano reduction.
Grieve Not the Holy Spirit ...
[words from] Ephesians 4:30-32,
[music by] Leland B. Sateren. ©
B. F. Wood Music Co., Boston;
23Dec47; EP20437. Score:
SSAATBB and piano reduction.
Most Wondrous Kingdom; (based on
an old chorale) [by] Leland B.
Sateren, [words by] N. F. S.
Gruntvig, tr. J. C. Aaberg. ©
Neil A. Kjos Music Co., Chicago;
20Oct47; on arrangement; EP19204.
Score: baritone or alto, chorus
(SSAATBB) and piano.
SATRA, MATTHEW, 1900-
Matthew Satra's "I'll Not Forget
So Soon." © Matthew Satra,
Brooklyn; 24Oct47; EP18444.
For voice and piano.

SAUNDERS, EDDIE P
The Babe of Bethlehem; duet, sop.
or tenor and alto [by] Eddie P.
Saunders. © Eddie P. Saunders,
Walterboro, S. C.; 13Oct47;
EP18035.
SAVAGE, MARION.
It's the Rage; words and music by
Marion Savage. © Nordyke Pub-
lishing Co., Los Angeles;
12Aug47; EP19696.
SAVARD, HENRY J
One Sunny Day; words and music by
Henry J. Savard. © Nordyke
Publishing Co., Los Angeles;
24Jul47; EP17412.
SAVILLE, TOM.
South Paw Special; by Tom Saville.
[c1945] © Cinephonic Music Co.,
ltd., London; 25Sep46; EF6019.
For piano solo.
SAVINO, DOMENICO, 1882-
Freedom and Brotherly Love; music
by Domenico Savino, vocal arrange-
ment by the composer, words by
Harry R. Wilson. © J. J.
Robbins & Sons, inc., New York;
8Apr47; EP15339. Score: SATB
and piano.
Hail to Tomorrow; based on "Piano
concerto" by Edvard Grieg, lyric
by Ted Fetter, arr. by Domenico
Savino. © The John Franklin Co.,
inc., New York; 21Aug47; on words
& arrangement; EP16652.
Moon of Dawn; (Moonlight sonata),
based on "First movement op.27,
no.2" by L. van Beethoven, lyric
by Jos. McCarthy, jr., arr. by
Domenico Savino. © The John
Franklin Co., inc., New York;
21Aug47; on words & arrangement;
EP16633.
My Heart Is Yours; based on "Concerto no.1" by Peter Ilich
Tschaikowsky, lyric by Ted Fetter,
arr. by Domenico Savino. © The
John Franklin Co., inc., New York;
21Aug47; on words & arrangement;
EP16631.
A New World; music by Domenico
Savino, vocal arrangement by the
composer, words by Harry R.
Wilson. © J. J. Robbins & Sons,
inc., New York; 8Apr47; EP15338.
Score: SATB and piano.
Peace of Mind; music by Domenico
Savino, vocal arrangement by the
composer, words by Harry R.
Wilson. © J. J. Robbins & Sons,
inc., New York; 8Apr47; EP15337.
Score: SATB and piano.
Samba Exótica; for piano [by]
Domenico Savino. © J. J.
Robbins & Sons, inc., New York;
25Jun47; EP15340.
To My Beloved; based on "Elegie"
by Jules Massonet, lyric by
Joanne Burns, arr. by Domenico
Savino. © The John Franklin Co.,
inc., New York; 21Aug47; on words
& arrangement; EP16630.
Valse Excentrique; for piano [by]
Domenico Savino. © J. J.
Robbins & Sons, inc., New York;
3Nov47; EP18663.
SAWAYA, JESS JOE.
Because I Think of You ... lyrics
and music by Jess Sawaya.
c1946. © The Sawaya Publica-
tions, inc., Trinidad, Colo.;
1Jan47; EP15314.
In Spite of It All ... lyric by
Johnny (Babe) Cartelli, music by
Jess Sawaya. c1946. © The
Sawaya Publications, inc., Trini-
dad, Colo.; 1Jan47; EP15313.
Is This How You Treat Ev'ryone? ...
lyric by Johnny (Babe) Cartelli,
music by Jess Sawaya. c1946.
© The Sawaya Publications, inc.,
Trinidad, Colo.; 1Jan47; EP15312.

346

SAWAYA, JESS JOE. Cont'd.
Jess Sawaya's As Long As I Live ...
words and music by Jess Sawaya.
c1946. © The Sawaya Publications, inc., Trinidad, Colo.;
1Jan47; EP15315.

'Neath the Cloud Lit Skies;
lyrics by Johnny (Babe)
Cartelli. © Sawaya Publications, inc., Trinidad, Colo.;
20Jun47; EP15555. For voice
and piano, with chord symbols.

Sweet Bells ... lyric by Johnny
(Babe) Cartelli, music by Jess
Sawaya. c1946. © The Sawaya
Publications, inc., Trinidad,
Colo.; 1Jan47; EP15311.

This, I Know ... lyrics by Johnny
(Babe) Cartelli, music by Jess
Sawaya. c1946. © The Sawaya
Publications, inc., Trinidad,
Colo.; 1Jan47; EP15310.

You've Done It Again ... lyric by
Johnny (Babe) Cartelli, music by
Jess Sawaya. c1946. © The
Sawaya Publications, inc., Trini-
dad, Colo.; 1Jan47; EP15309.

SAWYER, ADELLA, 1886-
Song of the Chimes; words & music
by Adella Sawyer. ©
Arlington Music, Hollywood,
Calif.; 15Jul47; EP16581.

SAWYER, STREET, pseud. See
Spector, Abner B.

SAWYER, VIRGINIA.
Gotta Have a Place to Hang My
Hat; words by Faye Wyatt, music
by Virginia Sawyer. © Nordyke
Publishing co., Los Angeles;
21Aug47; EP20366.

Tie a String around Your Heart;
words & music by Virginia Sawyer.
© Nordyke Publishing Co., Los
Angeles; 9Nov46; EP19784.

SAXON, DAVID.
Free; lyric by Sammy Gallop,
music by David Saxon. © United
Music Corp., New York; 17Dec47;
EP19921.

SAXON, IRV. See
Saxon, Joseph.

SAXON, JOSEPH.
Ev'rybody and His Brother; words
and music by Joseph (Irv) Saxon.
© Broadcast Music, inc., New
York; 11Jul47; EP18203.

SAXTON, STANLEY E.
My Soul Doth Magnify the Lord;
sacred song by Stanley E. Saxton.
High voice. © Galaxy Music
Corp., New York; 13Aug47;
EP17019.

SAYERS, HENRY J
Ta-ra-ra Boom-der-é; words and
music by Henry J. Sayers, [arr.
by John Bach] © Calumet Music
Co., Chicago; 20Oct47; on arrangement; EP18186.

SAYLOR, TED.
Utah Centennial; words by Clara
Nielson, music by Ted Saylor.
© Wire Co., Publishers, Salt
Lake City; 5Jul47; EP15639.

SCALA, TANI, 1915-
Sortilèges ... [by] T. Scala. La
Nuit Etend Son Voile ...
musique de Mario Melfi. ©
(Editions Espagnoles) Julio
Garzon, Paris; 7Jul47; EF6513.
Piano-conductor score (orches-
tra) and parts.

SCARBOROUGH, DUNCAN, 1896-
Hand in Hand with Jesus ... words
by Leah Kirberger, music by Duncan Scarborough. © Duncan Scarborough, West Orange, N. J.;
10Oct47; EP17762.

SCARLATTI, ALESSANDRO, 1660-1725.
Aria, from Toccata no. 2. Minuetto,
from Toccata no. 4. [By] Alessandro Scarlatti, [transcribed by]
Rosalyn Tureck. © Carl Fischer,
inc., New York; 1Dec47; on transcription; EP20288. For piano
solo.

(Cantata Pastorale) Christmas
Cantata. "Cantata Pastorale
per la Natività di Nostro
Signore Gesù Cristo." [By]
Alessandro Scarlatti, [words
by Cardinal Antonio Ottoboni,
English version by Edward J.
Dent], ed. by Edward J. Dent
for soprano solo, string quartet
and harpsichord. [c1945] ©
Oxford University Press, Lon-
don, 10Jan46; on editing;
EF6372. For voice and piano.

Capriccio, by D. Scarlatti ... ed.
[i. e. arr.] by Arcady Dubensky.
© G. Ricordi & Co., New York;
30Jul47; EP16345. Score; string
orchestra.

Christmas Cantata. See his Cantata
Pastorale.

Siebzehn Leichte Stücke ... 17
Easy Pieces for piano, [by]
Domenico Scarlatti, [arr. by]
Kurt Herrmann. © Hug & Co.,
Music-Publishers, Zurich,
Switzerland; 15Apr47; EF6011.

Sonata Allegro; (in G minor) [by]
Domenico Scarlatti, arr. ... by
Elizabeth Gest. © Elkan-Vogel
Co., inc., Philadelphia; 1Dec47;
on arrangement EP19556. Two
scores for 2 pianos.

SCARMOLIN, A. LOUIS, 1890-
The Foolish Dog; S.S.A. [by] A.
Louis Scarmolin ... [words by]
Frederick H. Martens. © Doro-
thea Louise Schroeder, Flushing,
N. Y.; 18Dec47; EP19992.

Marco Polo ... by A. Louis
Scarmolin. [Op.201] © Ludwig
Music Pub. Co., Cleveland;
5Aug47; EP16972. Condensed
score (band) and parts.

Scotch Plaid; [by] A. Louis
Scarmolin, [ed. by Walter
Rolfe] © Century Music
Publishing Co., New York;
6Aug47; EP16127. For piano
solo.

SCHACHEL-RHEINSCHMIDT, ERMA DOROTHY,
1911-
A Real Friend; words and music by
Erma Schachel-Rheinschmidt.
© Erma Schachel-Rheinschmidt,
Burlington, Iowa; 4Dec47;
EP19922.

SCHAEFER, G. A. GRANT. See
Grant-Schaefer, G. A.

SCHATENSTEIN, JACK.
High Hat; words by Michael Oles,
music by Jack Schatenstein.
© Nordyke Publishing Co., Los
Angeles; 29Jul47; EP17521.

SCHAUM, JOHN WALTER, 1905-
At My Teacher's Studio; piano solo
with words, by John W. Schaum.
© Belwin, inc., New York;
9Oct47; EP18145.

SCHAUM, JOHN WALTER, 1905- arr.
John W. Schaum March Album ...
[comp., arr. and ed. by John W.
Schaum] © Belwin, inc., New
York; 7Nov47; on compilation,
arrangement & editing; EP18541.
For piano solo.

The Man on the Flying Trapeze;
piano solo. © John W. Schaum
arrangement. © Belwin, inc.,
New York; 20Nov47; on arrangement; EP18804.

Three Blind Mice ... a John W.
Schaum arrangement. © Belwin,
inc., New York; 20Nov47; on arrangement; EP18799. For piano
6 hands.

SCHAUM, JOHN WALTER, 1905- comp.
John W. Schaum Christmas Album;
transcribed for piano accordion
by Earl Hazelle. © Belwin, inc,
New York; 17Sep47; on transcription; EP17657.

SCHEIN, JULIUS, 1910-
Disappointed; words and music by
Mack Key and Julius Schein.
© Music Workshop, New York;
9Oct47; EP17986.

SCHER, WILLIAM.
Chinese Scene; piano solo [by]
William Scher. © Theodore
Presser Co., Philadelphia;
20Nov47; EP20165.

Scarecrows in the Night ... for
piano [by] William Scher.
© Theodore Presser Co.,
Philadelphia; 11Aug47; EP16297.

10 Characteristic Dances; for
piano solo by William Scher.
© Mills Music, inc., New York;
8Dec47; EP19910.

SCHERS,
Sei Sonate per il flauto traverso solo.
See his Sonatas, flute & bass.

(Sonatas, flute & bass) Sei
Sonate per il flauto traverso
solo, o violino, e basso
continuo, del Signor Schers.
Libro primo. [Herausgegeben
von Joseph Bopp, Continuo
aussgesetzt von Eduard Müller.
c1947] © Hug & Co., Music
Publishers, Zurich, Switzerland;
v. 1-2, 18Dec42; EF6840, 6844.
Score (flute and piano) and
part. Contents.-1. No. 1, E
minor.- 2. No.2 major.

SCHEUERELL, FRANCIS J
I've Got a Funny Feeling; words
and music by Francis J. Scheuerell. [c1946] © Nordyke Publishing Co., Los Angeles; 20Jan47;
EP19698.

SCHIFFERLI, EDWIN, 1884-
Missa in Honorem SS. Trinitatis
et Beatissimae Mariae Virginis;
pro vocibus aequalibus cum
organo, composuit Edwin
Schifferli. © Hug & Co., Music
Publishers, Zurich, Switzerland;
30Jun47; EF6845.

SCHLAGER, KATHE VOLKART- See
Volkart-Schlager, Käthe.

SCHLOSSBERG, MAX, 1875-1936.
Daily Drills and Technical Studios
for Trombone; by Max Schlossberg,
[ed. by C. K. Schlossberg] ©
M. Baron Co., New York; 26Jun47;
EP15505.

SCHLOTFELDT, ALDEINA.
Only You; words & music by Aldeina
Schlotfeldt. © Nordyke Publish-
ing Co., Los Angeles; 11Oct46;
EP19712.

SCHMAH, IDA.
It Can't Be Done; words & music by
Ida Schmah. © Nordyke Publishing
Co., Los Angeles; 9Nov46;
EP19758.

SCHMIDT, LUCKI.
I've Tried All I Can; words and
music by Lucki Schmidt. © Nordyke Publishing Co., Los Angeles;
28Mar47; EP16726.

SCHMITT, ALOYS.
Five-finger exercises. Exercices
pour les cinq doigts. [By]
Schmitt. Op. 16. Additional
exercises by Healey Willan, with
supplementary exercises, scales
and arpeggios in various forms.
[c1946] © Frederick Harris
Music Co., ltd., Oakville, Ont.,
Can.; on additional exercises;
26Mar47; EF5326.

SCHMITT, FLORENT, 1870-
Clavecin Obtempérant; suite en 4
parties [by] Florent Schmitt.
Op.107. © Durand & Cie, Paris;
30Sep47; EF7241. For piano solo.

SCHMITT, FLORENT. Cont'd.
(Trios, women's voices & orchestra)
Trois Trios; pour voix de femmes
et orchestre (ou piano), [words
de Jean Cocteau ... René
Chalupt ... [and] Tristan Derème.
© Durand & Co., Paris; 30Jul47;
EF6528. Piano-vocal score..

SCHNABEL, ARTHUR.
Piece in Seven Movements; piano
solo [by] Artur Schnabel. ©
Edward B. Marks Music Corp.,
New York; 29Jul47; EP15958.

SCHOENBERGER, ALVA.
Every Cloud Would Wear a Rainbow
(if I had you, dear, only you)
words and music by Alva Schoenberger. © Alva Schoenberger,
Kecoughton, Va.; 11Jul47;
EP16023.

SCHOENBERGER, LEONARD.
Wouldn't You? Words by Frank Vig-
giani, music by Leonard Schoen-
berger. © Big Boy Music Publ.,
(Frank Viggiani, sole owner),
New York; 16Oct47; EP18177.

SCHOLIN, CARL ALBERT, 1896-
The Babe in Bethlehem; Christmas
carol for junior and senior
choirs. [Words] traditional,
English carol arr. by C. Albert
Scholin. (St. Louis, Hunleth
Music Co.] © C. Albert Scholin,
St. Louis; 7Aug47; on arrange-
ment; EP16141.
The First Noel; Christmas carol
for three choirs ... French
carol arr. by C. Albert Scholin.
[St. Louis, Hunleth Music Co.]
© C. Albert Scholin, St. Louis;
7Aug47; on arrangement; EP16142.
Score: S, SAB, SATB and piano
reduction.
God Rest You Merry, Gentlemen;
English carol arr. for junior
and senior choirs by C. Albert
Scholin. © Belwin, inc., New
York; 6Nov47; on arrangement;
EP18537.
O Lord, Most Holy; T.T.B.B. by
C. Albert Scholin. © Mills
Music, inc., New York; 8Dec47;
EP19887.
Prayer of Thanksgiving ... [for]
mixed chorus with junior choir
or solo voice, founded on the
tune "Netherlands" by Kremser,
arr. by C. Albert Scholin.
Translation by Wallingford
Riegger. © Harold Flammer, inc.,
New York; 28Jul47; on arrange-
ment & translation; EP16245.

SCHOLIN, CARL ALBERT, 1896- arr.
Deep River; [Negro spiritual],
arr. by C. Albert Scholin.
St. Louis, Hunleth Music Co.
© C. Albert Scholin, St. Louis;
15Jul47; on arrangement;
EP15685. Score: solo voices
(AB), chorus (SSATTBB) and
piano reduction.

SCHOLL, BEN.
God Bless Us, Darling; words by
Louise Maxwell, music by Ben
Scholl. © Nordyke Publishing
co., Los Angeles; 9Aug46;
EP20564.
Somebody New; words by Jewel
Sutherland, music by Ben Scholl.
[c1946] © Nordyke Publishing
Co., Los Angeles; 28Jan47;
EP19422.

SCHOONER, MAX, 1916-
My Prayer; words by Mary Cunning-
ham, music by Max Schooner.
© Schooner Music Co., Dearborn,
Mich.; 18Oct47; EP18175.

SCHREIBER, FREDERICK C
While Shepherds Watched; Christmas
carol for women's voices. [Words
by] Mahum Tate, [music by]
Frederick C. Schreiber. © The
H. W. Gray Co., inc., New York;
2Jul47; EP15708. Score: SSA and
organ.

SCHRODER, FRIEDRICH.
Über die Dächer der Grossen Stadt ;
... Musik: Friedrich Schröder,
Text: Peter Holm. © Edition
Turicaphon a. g., Zürich,
Switzerland; 20Jun47; EF5864.

Schroeder, Aaron. See
Kingsley, Matt.

SCHROEDER, ROY STEINER, 1897-
Underneath the Stars (in Texas);
by Roy Schroeder. © Roy Steiner
Schroeder, University Park, Md.;
38ep47; EP16592. For voice and
piano.

SCHUBERT, FRANZ, 1808-1878.
The Bee; [by] F. Schubert, plec-
trum guitar solo arr. ... by
Harry Volpe. c1939. © Albert
Rocky Co., New York; 10Jan40; on
arrangement; EP20208.

SCHUBERT, FRANZ PETER, 1797-1828.
(Ave Maria) Babe in a Manger
Born; for four-part chorus of
mixed voices with piano acc.
Based on Schubert's "Ave
Maria," text and arrangement
by Margaret Bronson. © The
Willis Music Co., Cincinnati;
8Sep47; on arrangement;
EP17208.
Ave Maria; guitar duet, [by] F.
Schubert, arr. as played by
Harry Volpe. c1939. © Albert
Rocky Co., New York; 10Jan40;
on arrangement; EP20191.
(Ave Maria) Hear Our Humble
Prayer; author of the words:
Ellen Jane Lorenz, music arr.
from "Ave Maria" by Franz
Schubert. [c1940] © Lorenz
Publishing Co., Dayton, Ohio;
10Oct47; on words; EP18582. For
voice and piano.
Ave Maria. (Heavenly Father)
Music by Franz Schubert.
(Op. 52, no. 6) English text
by Lorraine Noel Finley.
© Harold Flammer, inc., New
York; 28Jul47; on English
words; EP16262. For voice and
piano; Latin and English
words.
(Destin) Quand Reviendra le
Jour ... [From] le film "Destins";
paroles de André Hornez, musique
de Franz Schubert. © Éditions
Max Eschig, Paris; 23Dec46;
EF6480.
Good Is It To Thank Jehovah.
Lieblich Ist's dem Ew'gen
Danken. For four-part chorus
of mixed voices with baritone
or tenor solo a cappella, music
by Franz Schubert, ed. by John
Finley Williamson. English
text by Lorraine Noel Finley,
German words by Moses Mendels-
sohn. © Carl Fischer, inc.,
New York; 15Aug47; on English
text; EP16410.
Hear Our Humble Prayer. See his Ave
Maria.
How Uplifted My Heart. (To the
Infinite) anthem for mixed
voices, [by] Franz Schubert,
arr. by Clarence Dickinson.
English text by Helen A. Dickin-
son. © The H. W. Gray Co., inc.,
New York; 7Nov47; on arrangement;
EP19263.
Impromptu in Ab. Op.90, no.4.
[By] Franz Schubert ... rev. and
ed. by Maxwell Eckstein. © Carl
Fischer, inc., New York; 5Sep47;
on arrangement & editing;
EP18080. For piano solo.
Marche Militaire; for two pianos,
[by] Franz Schubert. Op. 51,
no. 1. Simplified arrangement
by Harold Flammer, inc., New York;
28Jul47; on arrangement;
EP16261.

Quand Reviendra le Jour. See his
Destins.
The Rosamunde Air; [by] Franz
Schubert, ed. by Maxwell Eckstein.
© Carl Fischer, inc., New York;
15Sep47; on revision & edition;
EP18061. For piano solo.
Round Dance; by F. Schubert, ed.
[i.e. arr.] by Arcady Dubensky.
© G. Ricordi & Co., New York;
30Jul47; on arrangement; EP16347.
Score: string orchestra.
Schubert (Simplified); fourteen
favorite compositions arr. for
piano solo by Peter Randall
[pseud.] © Willis Music Co.,
Cincinnati; 5Sep47; on arrange-
ment; EP17207.
Up Melody Lane with Schubert;
[arr. & comp. by Harold S.
Packer] for the piano. ©
Waterloo Music Co., Waterloo,
Ont., Can.; 28Sep47; EF6390.

SCHUITEMA, ANNA K. 1904-
Hymns for the Piano Accordion;
12 bass and up ... arr. by
Anna K. Schuitema. Winona Lake,
Ind., The Rodeheaver Co.. ©
Rodeheaver Hall-Mack Co. Wi-
nona Lake, Ind.; v.1, 10Oct47;
on arrangement; EP18423.

SCHUITEMA, ANNA K arr.
Jesus, Lover of My Soul. I Gave
My Life for Thee. Jesus Is
Calling. Near the Cross.
Hymns for the piano accordion,
12 bass and up, arr. by Anna K.
Schuitema. Winona Lake, Ind.,
Rodeheaver Hall-Mack Co. ©
Rodeheaver Co., Winona Lake,
Ind.; 18Jul47; on arrangement;
EP17568.

SCHULTZ, SVEND S 1913-
Koncert-Suite; [by] Sv. S.
Schultz. © Wilhelm Hansen,
Musik-Forlag, Copenhagen;
2Jun47; EF6302. For piano
solo.

SCHUMAN, WALTER.
The Other Side of the Hill; lyric
by James Sayers, music by Walter
Schuman. © Ben Bloom Music Corp.,
New York; 1Dec47; EP19184.

SCHUMANN, ROBERT ALEXANDER, 1810-1856.
The Best Known Music of Schumann;
[comp. by Hamilton S. Gordon,
inc.] © Hamilton S. Gordon, inc.,
New York; 2Dec47; EP19554. For
piano solo.
Children's Ball; piano, four hands.
[By R. Schumann, Op.130. Ed.
by Zelda Heller] © Edition
Musicus-New York, inc., New
York; 2May47; on preface,
rhythmic & harmonic changes &
fingering; EP16161.
Schumann-Schaum for piano ....
[arr., comp. and ed. by] John
W. Schaum. [Biographical continuity by Nora Schaum] ©
Belwin, inc., New York; bk.1,
14Nov47; on arrangement, compilation & editing; EP18677.
Schumann's Songs of Love; his most
popular melodies [arr. by Walter
L. Rosemont], including "Dedication," [words tr. by W. L. Rose-
mont] © Edwards Music Co.,
New York; 6Nov47; on simplified
arrangement & translation;
EP19641. Partly for voice and
piano, partly for piano solo;
with chord symbols.
(Sonata, piano) Sonate en fa# mineur;
[by] Schumann. Op. 11. [Ed. de
travail par Alfred Cortot.
c1946] © Salabert, inc., New
York; 8Oct47; on arrangement;
EF7242.
Träumerei (Dreaming) and Slumber-
song; by Schumann. Arr. by
Victor Ambroise] © Lawrence
Wright Music Co., ltd., London;
20Nov47; on arrangement; EF7278.
For piano solo.

SCHUMANN, ROBERT ALEXANDER. Cont'd.
Why? Warum? [By] Robert Schumann.
Op.12, no.3. Ed. [and rev.] by
Maxwell Eckstein. © Carl Fischer,
inc., New York; 15Sep47; on
revision & editing; EP18059.

SCHUMANN POVEDA, ENRIQUE.
New Vienna ... by Enrique Schumann
Poveda. © Enrique Schumann Poveda,
Santiago de Cuba; 4Dec47; EF7185.
For piano solo.

SCHUNK, P M 1904-
Sheriden, Wyoming, U. S. A.; words
and music by P. M. Schunk. ©
P. M. Schunk, Sheridan, Wyo.;
27May47; EP15411.

SCHVEDOFF, C
Come, Let Us Sing to the Lord;
[by] C. Schvedoff, ed. & arr. by
Noble Cain, English version by
N. C. © Boosey & Hawkes, inc.,
New York; 2Dec47; on arrange-
ment & English words; EP19876.
Score: chorus (SSAATTBB) and
piano reduction.

[SCHWAB, ALEXANDRE] 1910-
Le Taxi Fou; paroles et musique de
Marc Fontenoy [pseud.], arr.
[by] Raymond Legrand. ©
Editions Royalty, Paris; 2Jun47;
on arrangement; EF6475.
Le Taxi Fou; paroles et musique
de Marc Fontenoy [pseud.].
© Editions Royalty, Paris;
2Jun47; EF6476.
Vingt Ans; paroles de Maurice Chevalier & Marc Fontenoy [pseud.],
musique de Marc Fontenoy [pseud.].
© Editions Musicales Transatlan-
tiques, Paris; 31Dec46; EF7316.
For voice and piano, and voice
part.

SCHWANDT, WILBUR.
Whispers of Love; words by Leah W.
Dugat, music by Wilbur Schwandt.
© Nordyke Publishing Co., Los
Angeles; 10Jun47; EP16926.
Wishing You'd Come Back; words by
J. G. Cedillo, music by Wilbur
Schwandt. © Nordyke Publishing
Co., Los Angeles; 28Jan47;
EP16400.

SCHWARTZ, ARTHUR, 1900-
Dancing in the Dark; [by] Arthur
Schwartz, arr. by Jerry Sears.
© Harms, inc., New York; 3Nov47;
on arrangement; EP18502. Score
(trumpet and piano) and part.
(Revenge with Music) If There Is
Someone Lovelier Than You; from
"Revenge with Music." Three part
women's voices, S.S.A., words by
Howard Dietz, music by Arthur
Schwartz, choral setting by Clay
Warnick. © Harms, inc., New
York; 29Jul47; on arrangement;
EP16368.

SCIAMANNA, ENZO.
O Esca Viatorum; soprano (or tenor
solo) with chorus for T. B.
[by] Enzo Sciamanna. © J. Fischer & Bro., New York; 27Aug47;
EP17270.

SCIONTI, SILVIO, 1882-   ed.
Road to Piano Artistry; a collection of classic and romantic
compositions, comp., graded and
ed. ... with interpretative and
technical comment by Silvio
Scionti. © Carl Fischer, inc.,
New York; on compiling, grading
& editing of v.9; 16Sep47;
EP18058.

SCOTLAND, J
Lightly Tread; [by] J. Scotland,
arr. for solo instruments and
piano acc. (with optional combo
pa ts) by Harold Parkman [pseud.]
© The Arthur P. Schmidt Co.,
Boston; 10ct47; on arrangement;
EP18378. Score and part.

SCOTT, BERTHA.
I Miss You So; by Jimmy Henderson
[and] Bertha Scott, [new lyric
by] Sid Robin. © Leeds Music
Corp., New York; 18Aug47; on
new lyric; EP16395. For voice
and piano, with chord symbols.

SCOTT, CYRIL.
Theme & Variations ... [by]
Cyril Scott. © Elkin & Co.,
ltd., London; 26Aug47;
EF6381. Score: piano 1-2.

SCOTT, JOHN DOUGLAS, Lady.
Annie Laurie; [by] J. D. Scott, arr.
by F. Ballatore, [In Ballatore,
Pietro, comp. So Easy. p.3] ©
Edward B. Marks Music Corp., New
York; 9Dec47; on arrangement;
EP19581. For piano solo.

SCOTT, L   A
The Reason I Love You; words and
music by L. A. Scott. © Nordyke Publishing Co., Los Angeles; 2Sep47; EP20012.

SCOTT, RAYMOND.
In an Eighteenth Century Drawing
Room; [by] Raymond Scott, tran-
scribed by Gregory Stone. ©
Advanced Music Corp., New York;
3Dec47; on arrangement; EP19819.
Score (violin and piano) and
part.

SCOTT, THOMAS WAYNE, 1893-
Cannon Ball Wail; by Thos. W.
Scott. © Thos. W. Scott, Martin,
Tenn.; 24Sep47; EP17688. For
voice and piano.

SCOTTO, VINCENT.
(Au Pays des Cigales) Dans Notre
Roulotte ... dans le film "Au
Pays des Cigales." Paroles de
Marc-Cab [pseud.], R. Vincy
[pseud.] & H. Alibert, musique de
Vincent Scotto, arr. par Al. Kiwi
[pseud.] © Editions Max Eschig,
Paris; 14Jun47; on arrangement;
EF7215. Piano-conductor score
(orchestra) and parts.
(Au Pays des Cigales) La Valse
Douce ... dans le film "Au Pays
des Cigales." Paroles de Marc-
Cab [pseud.], R. Vincy [pseud.]
et H. Alibert. Musique de Vincent
Scotto. [Arr. par Al Kiwi, pseud.]
© Editions Max Eschig, Paris;
27Jul46; on arrangement; EF7305.
Piano-conductor score (orchestra)
and parts.
La Chanson de l'Etudiant; paroles
et musique de Vincent Scotto. ©
Vincent Scotto, Paris, 31Mar47;
EF6940.
Dans la Nuit J'Entends une Chanson
... Paroles de Jean Rodor [pseud.]
et Renée Thoreau, musique de Vin-
cent Scotto, arr. par Al. Kiwi
[pseud.] © Editions Max Eschig,
Paris; 22Feb47; on arrangement;
EF7214. Piano-conductor score
(orchestra) and parts.
Dans Notre Roulotte. See his Au Pays
des Cigales.
(Destins) Y A d'l'Amour ... dans le
film "Destins." Paroles de Géo
Koger [pseud.], musique de Vincent
Scotto, arr. par Al. Kiwi [pseud.].
© Editions Max Eschig, Paris;
16Jan47; on arrangement; EF7306.
Piano-conductor score (orchestra)
and parts.
(Destins) Y A d'l'Amour ... [From]
le film: Destins; paroles de Géo.
Koger [pseud.], musique de Vin-
cent Scotto. © Editions Max Eschig,
Paris; 23Dec46; EF6482.
Moineau de Paris; paroles et
musique de Vincent Scotto. ©
Vincent Scotto, Paris;
15Jan46; EF5948. Score
(voice and piano) and voice
part.

Non Mon Amour; paroles de
Baillie Duchateau & Vincent
Scotto. © Vincent Scotto,
Paris; 31Mar47; EF5947.
Score (voice and piano) and
voice part.
Le Pousse-Pousse; paroles et musique
de Vincent Scotto, arr. par Al.
Kiwi [pseud.] © Editions Max
Eschig, Paris; 14Jan47; on arrange-
ment; EF7226.
(Sérénade aux Nuages) Tango d'un
Soir ... dans le film "Sérénade
aux Nuages." Paroles de Géo
Koger [pseud.] & Vincent Scotto,
musique de Vincent Scotto, arr.
par Al. Kiwi [pseud.] © Editions
Max Eschig, Paris; 3Jul46; on
arrangement; EF7228. Piano-con-
ductor score (orchestra) and parts.
Tango d'un Soir. See his Sérénade aux
Nuages.
Two Loves Have I. (J'Ai Deux
Amours) French lyrics by Geo.
Koger [pseud.] and H. Varna,
English version by J. P. Murray
and Barry Trivers, music by
Vincent Scotto, [arr. by Helmy
Kresa] © Miller Music Corp.,
New York; 15Oct47; on piano
arrangement; EP18511.
La Valse Douce. See his Au Pays des
Cigales.
Ya d'l'Amour. See his Destins.

SCOTTY, pseud. See
Wiseman, Scott.

SEARS, EDWARD.
Serenade to Eileen; piano solo by
Edward Sears. [c1946] © The
Kassner Music Co., ltd.,
London; 28Feb47; EF6875.

SEARS, JERRY.
Irish Waltz Medley ... music by
J. R. Shannon [and] ... Walter Donaldson ... [and] Ernest
R. Ball, [words by Monty C.
Brice and others] A Jerry
Sears arrangement. © M. Witmark & Sons, New York; 30Oct47;
on arrangement; EP18476. Piano-
conductor score (orchestra, with
words) and parts.

SEAVER, BLANCHE EBERT.
Just for To-day ... a prayer by
Sybil F. Partridge, set to music
by Blanche Ebert Seaver, duet
[for] high and low voices [arr.
by Victor Lamont] © Sam Fox
Publishing Co., New York;
20ct47; on arrangement; EP17998.

SEBASTIANI, PIA.
Cuatro Preludios para Piano. ©
Editorial Argentino de Música
(E.A.M.), Buenos Aires; no. 1,
30Sep46; EF3994.

SEDLACK, JOHN.
You Can't Stop Me from Loving
You; words and music by John
Sedlack. © Nordyke Publishing
Co., Los Angeles; 13Aug47;
EP19286.

SEELY, NELL.
Don't Wait for the Sunrise Tomor-
row; lyrics ... [by] Addison
Jackson and music by Nell Seely.
© Hillcrest Music Publications,
Omaha; 9Oct47; EP18001.

SEGAL, JACK.
Fantasy; words and music by Ted
Mossman and Jack Segal, based
on Schumann's Träumerei.
© Robbins Music Corp., New York;
2Jul47; EP15417.
Green Grow the Lilacs; words and
music by Dewey Bergman and Jack
Segal. © Northern Music Corp.,
New York; 28Aug47; EP17148.

349

SEIBER, MATYAS, 1905-
Mordvin Lullaby; by Matyas Seiber, based on a Mordvinian folk-song. Words by Mark Lubbock, arr. for mixed voices and pianoforte by John Clements. © Matyas Seiber & J. Curwon & Sons, ltd., London; 5Jun47; on arrangement & English words; EP6281.
Pastorale and Burlesque; [for] flute and string orchestra, [by] M. Seiber. Full score. © Schott & Co., ltd., London; 19Mar47; EP5797.

SEIFERT, LILLIAN M
Just Because I Care; words and music by Lillian M. Seifert. [c1946] © Nordyke Publishing Co., Los Angeles; 15Feb47; EP19742.

SEIJO, RAFAEL.
Tu Nada Mas. (You Alone) ... Spanish words and music by Rafael Seijo, English words by Joe Davis. © Caribbean Music, inc., New York; 25Aug47; EP16522.

SELINSKY, VLADIMIR.
My Little Boy; song, words by Lester O'Keefe, music by Vladimir Selinsky. © Chappell & Co., inc., New York; 7Jul47; EP15550.

SELLEW, DONALD EDGAR, 1906-
Ben Jonson's Carol ... [[for] S.A.T.B., div.] [Music by] Donald E. Sellew. [words by] Ben Jonson. © Hall & McCreary Co., Chicago; 5..ug47; EP16264.
Still the Night with Snow So Deep; [by] Donald Sellew (hymn carol for mixed voices, a cappella) [words by Beatrice Gibbs] © Oliver Ditson Co., Philadelphia; 16Sep47; EP17287.
This Little Pilgrim; Christmas carol for mixed voices with soprano solo, optional a cappella (S.A.T.B.) [by] Donald E. Sellew, [words by] Robert Southwell. © Hall & McCreary Co., Chicago; 22Aug47; EP17029.
When Christ Was Born of Mary Free ... [[for] S.A.T.B., div.] [Music by] Donald E. Sellew, traditional [words] © Hall & McCreary Co., Chicago; 5Aug47; EP16265.

SELMER, MILDRED, 1900-
Praktisk Klaverskole. Oslo, J. G. Tanum. 1946. © Mildred Selmer, Oslo; del 1, 1May43; del 2, 1Jan46; del 3, 10ct46; EF3968-3970. Contents.- del 1. Laesen en lek; compiled and composed by Mildred Selmer.- del 2. Fra lek til alvor; compiled by Mildred Selmer, arr. by Fartein Valen, music by Anne Marie Orbeck, Eivind Groven and others.- del 3. Tonene lever; compiled by Mildred Selmer, music by Sparre Olsen, Eivind Groven, Irgens Jensen, Harald Saeverud, A. M. Orbeck and others.

SELVIN, BEN, comp.
Songs for Little Folks; a folio of 15 songs with lyrics set to the music of famous composers, lyrics by Albert Gamse, musical adaptation [and compilation] by Ben Selvin, simplified arr. by Louis Sugarman. © Bregman, Vocco and Conn, inc., New York; 27Oct47; EP18777.

SENDREY, AL. See Sendrey, Albert.

SENDREY, ALBERT.
Blue Rain; words by Howard G. Buckles, music by Al Sendrey. © Nordyke Publishing Co., Los Angeles; 16Jul47; EP17562.

The Captain and the Soldier; words by Robert and Gladys Hollingsworth, music by Al Sendrey. © Nordyke Publishing Co., Los Angeles; 10May47; EP16846.
Cowboy Joe; words by A. Iacobitti, music by Al Sendrey. © Nordyke Publishing Co., Los Angeles; 11Aug47; EP17593.
I Love You, Sweetheart Mine; words by Arthur Curry, music by Al Sendrey. © Nordyke Publishing Co., Los Angeles; 1Jun47; EP16895.
(Sonata, viola & piano) Sonata for viola and piano [by] Albert Sendrey. © Elkan-Vogel Co., inc., Philadelphia; 1Dec47; EP19557. Score and part.
Time Goes On; words by Doris Charles, music by Al Sendrey. © Nordyke Publishing Co., Los Angeles; 25Jul46; EP20302.
Two Hearts in Love; words by Hiram P. Nauma, music by Al Sendrey. © Nordyke Publishing Co., Los Angeles; 25Jul46; EP20335.
When Your Someone Loves You; words by Marie Gray, music by Al Sendrey. © Nordyke Publishing Co., Los Angeles; 16Jul47; EP17456.
Your Little Gremlin; words by Phyllis Love, music by Al Sendrey. © Nordyke Publishing Co., Los Angeles; 29Nov46; EP20371.

SENECHAL, F   C   pseud. See Cassagnac, Francis.

SENOB, CARL.
A Dilemma ... SSATTBB accompanied; words and music by Carl Senob. © Harold Flammer, inc., New York; 14Nov47; EP19151.

SERAO, ELIO.
In the Valley of Roses. (Canto per Ti) Lyric by Mack David, music and Spanish lyric by Fausto Curbelo and Elio Serao. © Remick Music Corp., New York; 1Aug47; EP16370.

SERGEEV, A
The Red Army Soldier's Son; words by D. Samarsky, English adaptation by Olga Paul, [music by] A. Sergeev. (In Haywood, Charles, ed. Art Songs of Soviet Russia, p.9-11) © Edward B. Marks Music Corp., New York; 16Sep47; on English adaptation; EP17175. English and Russian words.

SERGEY, JOHN MICHAEL, 1917-
Be Strong; [words by] Oswald J. Smith, [music by] John M. Sergey. © John Michael Sergey, Chicago; 12Apr47; EP19193. Close score: SATB.
I Must Be Up and Doing; [words by] Oswald J. Smith, [music by] John M. Sergey. © John Michael Sergey, Chicago; 12Apr47; EP19195. Close score: SATB.
If Your Heart Aches; [words by] Oswald J. Smith, [music by] John M. Sergey. © John Michael Sergey, Chicago; 12Apr47; EP19194. Close score: SATB.
Some Day I'll See My Saviour; [words by] Oswald J. Smith, [music by] John M. Sergey. © John Michael Sergey, Chicago; 12Apr47; EP19191. Close score: SATB.
When the Prodigal Son Came Home; [words by] Oswald J. Smith, [music by] John M. Sergey. © John Michael Sergey, Chicago; 12Apr47; EP19190. Close score: SATB.
Will You Not Come? [Words by] Oswald J. Smith, [music by] John M. Sergey. © John Michael Sergey, Chicago; 12Apr47; EP19192. Close Score: SATB.

SERRA, PAUL RUCCA- See Rocca-Serra, Paul.

SESSIONS, ROGER, 1896-
(Duet, violin & piano) Duo for violin and piano; [by] Roger Sessions. (New music [a quarterly publishing modern compositions, v. 21, no. 4]) © Roger Sessions, Berkeley, Calif.; 25Sep47; EP17822.
Duo for violin and piano. See his Duet. violin & piano.
From My Diary; piano solo [by] Roger Sessions. © Edward B. Marks Music Corp., New York; 8Oct47; EP17761.

SESTO, SALVATORE DEL. See Del Sesto, Salvatore.

SEVIER, LORRAINE.
Grand Coulee Serenade; by Lorraine Sevier. © Lorraine Magney, Cora, Miss.; 1Aug47; EP16492. For voice and piano.

SEVIER, MERTIE MAE.
Sacred Hill; by Mertie Mae Sevier. © Mertie Mae Sevier, Cora, Mo.; 22Sep47; EP17363. For voice and piano.

SEYMOUR, STANLEY A
Hope Chest; words and music by Stanley A. Seymour, arr. © Nordyke Publishing Co., Los Angeles; 12Apr47; EP16797.

SGAMBELLONE, GUIDO.
Toll No, Toll No; words by J. H. Goodman, music by Guido Sgambellone. © Nordyke Publishing Co., Los Angeles; 29Mar47; EP16719.

SHACKLETT, AL.
What Will I Do? Words and music by Al Shacklett. © Nordyke Publishing Co., Los Angeles; 1Jun47; EP16821.

SHACKLEY, GEORGE.
My Song Is Still Tonight; lyric by Carroll Loveday, music by George Shackley, adapted from "Phedre Overture" by Massenet. © Gate Music Co., New York; 15Oct47; on adaptation; EP18974.

SHAFFER, HELEN LOUISE, 1897-
Dear Little Boy; song, words by Agnes Davenport Bond, music by Helen Louise Shaffer. © Wesley Webster, San Francisco; 12Apr47; EP19574.

[SHAFTEL, SELIG] 1913-
Baby, Come Home; by Sunny Skylar [pseud.] © Skylar Music Corp., New York; 15Jul47; EP16663. For voice and piano, with chord symbols.
Hooray, Hooray, I'm Goin' Away; by Sunny Skylar, [pseud.] © George Simon, inc., New York; 28Jul47; EP15916. For voice and piano, with chord symbols.
I'm A Rollin'; words and music by Jackie Miles and Sunny Skylar [pseud.] © World Music, inc., New York; 10Sep47; EP17296.
It All Came True; by Sunny Skylar [pseud.] © Sinatra Songs, inc., New York; 30Jun47; EP15425. For voice and piano, with chord symbols.
Song of New Orleans; by Sunny Skylar [pseud.] © George Simon, inc., New York; 23Sep47; EP17216. For voice and piano, with chord symbols.
Sunny Skylar's Sister Arabella. © Skylar Music Corp., New York; 15Oct47; EP17983. For voice and piano, with chord symbols.

SHAIN, ROSE WIES.
Only in Dreams; words and music by Rose Wies Shain. Boston, Echo Music Publishing Co. © Rose Wies Shain, Brookline, Mass.; 23Jun47; EP15479.

SHAND, TERRY.
I'm A-Whistlin'; by Jimmy Eaton
and Terry Shand. © Shapiro,
Bernstein & Co., inc., New York;
17Oct47; EP18519. For voice
and piano, with chord symbols.
(I've Been So Wrong, for So Long,
but) I'm So Right Tonight;
lyric by "By" Dunham, music by
Terry Shand, arr. by Vic Schoen.
© Leeds Music Corp., New York;
16Jun47; on arrangement;
EP15345. Piano-conductor score
(orchestra, with words) and
parts.
(I've Been So Wrong, for So Long,
but) I'm So Right Tonight; lyric
by "By" Dunham, music by Terry
Shand. © Leeds Music Corp.,
New York; 16Jun47; EP16371.
Slow Train thru Arkansaw; by
Jimmy Eaton and Terry Shand. ©
Shapiro, Bernstein & Co., inc.,
New York; 10Nov47; EP18720.
For voice and piano, with chord
symbols.
Two Voices; by Charles O'Flynn ...
John Klenner ... and Terry Shand.
© Charles O'Flynn Publications
inc., New York; 2Dec47; EP19278.
For voice and piano.
You Can't Make Money Dreamin' (or
I'd be a millionaire); lyric by
"By" Dunham, music by Terry
Shand. © Leo Feist, inc., New
York; 27Oct47; EP18722.

SHANK, LOU.
Far Away; by Basil Ziegler and
Lou Shank. © Edwin H. Morris
& Co., inc., New York; 30Jun47;
EP15788. For voice and piano,
with chord symbols.

SHANNON, IRENE.
Farewell, from "The Thrush" by
Irene Shannon. © McKinley
Publishers, inc., Chicago;
10Nov47; EP18713. For piano
solo.
Learning to Fly, from "The Thrush"
by Irene Shannon. © McKinley
Publishers, inc., Chicago;
10Nov47; EP18712. For piano
solo.
Nesting, from "The Thrush" by
Irene Shannon. © McKinley
Publishers, inc., Chicago;
10Nov47; EP18711. For piano
solo.

SHANNON, KATHLEEN, pseud. See
Davis, Della S.

SHARP, DAVID S.
The Fairy Tale Parade; words and music
by David S. Sharp. Roturua, N. Z., /New-
son & Stroud Publications. © Sawaya Pu
blications, inc., Trinidad, Colo.; 27Jun
EP5789.

SHARP, JACK, pseud. See
Berry, Dennis Alfred.

SHARPE, EVELYN.
March of the Scouts; [by] Evelyn
Sharpe, [arr. by Hugo Norden]
© The Arthur P. Schmidt Co.,
Boston; 4Sep47; on arrangement;
EP16641; For piano 4 hands.

SHAUGHNESSY, ALFRED.
You Are My Favorite Dream; words
and music by Alfred Shaughnessy.
© Peter Maurice Music Co., ltd.,
London; 5Jul47; EF5784.

SHAW, ARTIE, 1910-
Summit Ridge Drive; by Artie Shaw,
special arrangement by Will Hudson. © Winfield Music, inc.,
New York; 25Jul47; on arrangement; EP19276. Piano-conductor
score (orchestra) and parts.

SHAW, MARTIN.
Let All the People Praise Thee,
O God; ... for soprano, alto,
and tenor or bass, by Martin
Shaw. Ps. lxvii, lxv. © Novello
& Co., ltd., London; 28Jul47;
EF6179.

SHEA, BEVERLY. See
Shea, George Beverly.

[SHEA, GEORGE BEVERLY] comp.
"Singing I Go;" with Beverly Shea
and his radio favorites, [comp.
by G. B. Shea] © Van Kampen
Press, Chicago; 7Feb47; EP18351.
Partly for voice and piano,
partly close score: SATB.

[SHEAN, CHARLES LA MAR] 1900-
Mon Aimé (My Love) By Charlie La
Mar [pseud.] © La Mar Music
Publishers inc., Canton, Ohio;
12Nov47; EP18791. For voice
and piano; English words.

SHEDD, JULIA LAWRENCE.
Waltzing with You; words and
music by Julia Lawrence Shedd.
© Nordyke Publishing Co., Los
Angeles; 21Aug47; EP20065.

SHEINWOLD, ELIZABETH, 1914-
First Tunes; for tonette or soprano
recorder by Elizabeth Sheinwold.
© Studios of Music Education,
New York; 4Dec47; AA70027.

SHEPHERD, ARTHUR, 1880-
Drive On! S.A.T.B. with baritone
solo, [music by] Arthur Shepherd,
[words by] Gary Merit. © C. C.
Birchard & Co., Boston; 4Aug47;
EP16209.

SHEPHERD, LELIA.
Heart of America; lyric by
Riley W. Geary, music by Lelia
Shepherd. © Riley W. Geary,
Phoenix, Ariz.; 12Aug47;
EP16452.

SHEPHERD, RONALD.
Sunshine and Flowers; words and
music by Ronald Shepherd, arr.
by June Day. © Nordyke Publishing Co., Los Angeles;
12Sep47; EP20017.

SHEPPARD, BUDDY.
It Wouldn't Be Christmas without
You; words by Murray Semos,
music by Buddy Sheppard. ©
Tune-House Publications, New
York; 25Nov47; EP16995.

SIERFEDINOV, Y
The Kolhoz; words by Tahir Hussein,
English adaptation by Olga Paul,
[music by] Y. Sherfedinov. [In
Haywood, Charles, ed. Art Songs
of Soviet Russia, p.16-17) ©
Edward B. Marks Music Corp.,
New York; 16Sep47; on English
adaptation; EP17177. English
and Russian words.

SHERMAN, RICHARD MORTON.
The Bard College Song; words and
music by Richard Morton Sherman.
© Bregman, Vocco and Conn, inc.,
New York; 12Dec47; EP20469.

SHERWIN, MANNING, 1902-
Skies; words by Michael Carr
[pseud.], music by Manning
Sherwin. © B. Feldman & Co.,
ltd., London; 5Aug47; EF6250.

SHIMMIN, SYDNEY.
Past Three o'Clock; old English
carol, a descant arrangement,
introducing other carol tunes,
[by] Sydney Shimmin. c1947.
© Oxford University Press,
London; 11Sep46; on arrangement; EF6656. For unison
treble chorus and piano, with
descant. Voice parts also in
tonic sol-fa notation.

SHIPPEE, DOT.
I'm Gonna Make Faces (at the moon);
words by Dick Bishop, music by
Dot Shippee. © Nordyke Publishing Co., Los Angeles;
5Aug47; EP17519.

SHLIMOVITZ, H   M
Little Su; snare drum solo by H.
M. Shlimovitz. © Mills Music,
inc., New York; 8Dec47; EP19901.

Nancy; snare drum solo by H. M.
Shlimovitz. © Mills Music, inc.,
New York; 8Dec47; EP19902.

SHOSTAKOVICH, DMITRII DMITRIEVICH,
1906-
Polka. Op.22. From the ballet
"L'Age d'Or" [by] D. Shostakovich, [ed., rev. and corr. by
Maxwell Eckstein] Piano solo.
© Carl Fischer, inc., New York;
31Aug42; on edition, revision &
correction; EP17050.

Symphony no. 5 (finale, by]
Dimitri Shostakovich, arr. ...
by Charles B. Righter. ©
Roosey & Hawkes, inc., New York;
30Sep47; on arrangement;
EP17756. Score (band),
condensed score and parts.

Fantastic Dances. Op.1. [By]
D. Shostakovich, [ed., rev. and
corr. by Maxwell Eckstein] Piano
solo. © Carl Fischer, inc., New
York; 31Aug42; on edition,
revision & correction; EP17053.

SHTREICHER, LYUDOV.
Always Working; words by D.
Hofshtein, English adaptation by
Olga Paul, [music by] Lyubov
Shtreichor. (In Haywood, Charles,
ed. Art Songs of Soviet Russia,
p.58-60) © Edward B. Marks Music
Corp., New York; 16Sep47; on
English adaptation; EP17189.
English and Russian words.

SHUMAN, FRANK.
Penguin at the Waldorf; words and
music by Jimmy Eaton, Larry
Wagner and Frank Shuman. ©
Dreyer Music Corp., New York;
30Jun47; EP15382.

SHURE, RALPH DEANE, 1885-
The Glad Trumpet; (white spiritual
for mixed voices) [by] R. Deane
Shure. St. Louis, Distributors,
Hunleth Music Co. © C. Albert
Scholin, St. Louis; 18Dec47;
EP20105.

SIBELIUS, JEAN, 1865-
Alla Marcia, from the Karelia Suite;
[by] Jean Sibelius, arr. by Norman
Richardson ... Military band score.
© Hawkes & Son (London) ltd., Lon-
don; 26Nov47; on arrangement;
EF7193.

Finlandia. Op.26, no.7. [By]
Jean Sibelius, [ed., rev. and
corr. by Maxwell Eckstein]
Piano solo. © Carl Fischer,
inc., New York; 7Dec42; on
edition, revision & correction;
EP17049.

Glade of Tuoni; for four part
chorus of mixed voices a cappella, [by] Jean Sibelius,
[words by] A. Kivi, English
version by Lorraine Noel Finley. © G. Schirmer, inc., New
York; 20Aug47; on English version; EP18030.

Maan virsi ... Hymn to the Earth;
for mixed chorus and orchestra
... Choral score. [Finnish
words by Eino Leino, Swedish
translation by Raf. Lindqvist,
English translation by Paul
Sjöblom, German translation by
Elisabeth Kurkiala. Op.95] ©
Oy. R. E. Westerlund,Ab., Helsingfors, Finland; 10Nov45; on
choral score; EF6853.

Romance; (from op. 21) [by] Jean
Sibelius, freely rev. by Rudolph Gans. © Composers' Music
Corp., New York; 29Jan21; on
free revision; EP19117. For
piano solo.

351

SIBELIUS, JEAN. Cont'd.
The Shepherd Song; (Pastorale),
for full chorus of mixed voices
with piano accompaniment ad
lib. Text by Boss Berry Carr,
[music by] Jean Sibelius,
choral version by Margrethe
Hokanson. © Boston Music Co.,
Boston; 2Sep47; on arrangement;
EP17362.

SICKLE, ROBERT VAN. See
Van Sickle, Robert.

SIECZYNSKI, RUDOLF.
Vienna, My City of Dreams; by Rudolf Sieczynski, transcribed for
piano by Herman Wasserman. ©
Harms, inc., New York; 1Dec47;
on arrangement; EP19818.

SIEGEL, CHARLES, 1909-
Ev'rything Shall Pass, My Love,
but You; lyric by Walter Cooper,
music by Chas. Siegel. © Music
Workshop, New York; 29Oct47;
EP18566.

SIEGEL, PAUL.
Kiss Me and Then Go Away. Gib
Mir einen Abschiedskuss ...
Music and English lyric by Paul
Siegel ... Deutscher Text von
Aldo von Pinelli. © Edition
Turicaphon a. g., Bühnen-
und Musikvorlag, Zürich,
Switzerland; 22Mar47; EP5869.

Vienna, New York, Shanghai ...
Music and English lyric ...
[by] Paul Siegel ... deutscher
Text von Aldo von Pinelli. ©
Edition Turicaphon a. g.,
Zürich, Switzerland; 1Jun47;
EP5865.

Die Zeit mit Dir War Schön ...
Musik von Paul Siegel ... Eng-
lish lyric by Paul Siegel,
Deutscher Text von Aldo von
Pinelli, paroles françaises de
Ruy Blag, parole italiane di
Carlo Deani. © Edition Turi-
caphon, ltd., Zürich, Switzer-
land; 28Apr47; EP5826.

SIEGER, RAYMOND.
For I Love You Dear; words and
music by Raymond Sieger.
© Nordyke Publishing Co., Los
Angeles; 16Jul47; EP17627.

SIEGMEISTER, ELIE, 1909-
Sunday in Brooklyn, piano solo,
[by] Siegmeister. New York,
Marks Ed. © Edward B. Marks
Music Corp., New York;
29Jul47; EP15997.

Sunday in Brooklyn; study score
[by] Siegmeister. © Edward B.
Marks Music Corp., New York;
19Nov47; on study score; EP18986.
For orchestra.

Wanderin' (S.A.T.B.) arr, by Elie
Siegmeister. © Northern Music
Corp., New York; 30Jun47; on
arrangement; EP15429.

You Better Mind; (S.A.T.B.) arr.
by Elie Siegmeister. © Northern
Music Corp., New York; 30Jun47;
on arrangement; EP15428.

SIEGMEISTER, ELIE, 1909- arr.
Singing down the road; songs ...
chosen and arr. for male voices
by Elie Siegmeister. ... and
Rufus A. Wheeler. © Ginn and
Co., Boston; 28Mar47; A13127.

SIFLER, PAUL J
Gloria in Excelsis Deo; mixed chorus
with antiphonal choir of women's
voices, by Paul J. Sifler. ©
Broadcast Music, inc., New York;
12Sep47; EP18040.

SIGMAN, CARL.
(Angel in the wings) The Thousand
Islands Song, from "Angel in the
Wings"; by Bob Hilliard and Carl
Sigman. © Edwin H. Morris &
inc., New York; 3Dec47; EP19252.
For voice and piano, with chord
symbols.

Civilization; (Bongo, Bongo,
Bongo), by Bob Hilliard and
Carl Sigman. © Edwin H. Morris
& Co., inc., New York;
20Aug47; EP16547. For voice
and piano, with chord symbols.

The Cutest Little Red-Headed Doll;
by ... Carl Sigman, [words by]
Jack Wolf. © United Music Corp.,
New York; 5Dec47; EP19280.

The Thousand Islands Song. See his
Angel in the Wings.

SILMON, MABEL.
My Longing Heart; words and music
by Mabel Silmon. © Nordyke
Publishing Co., Los Angeles;
29Mar47; EP16761.

SILVER, ABNER.
Sipping Cider by the Zuyder Zee;
words [by Fred Vise and Al
Frisch] ... music by Abner
Silver. © Ben Bloom Music Corp.,
New York; 18Jul47; EP15892.

SILVER, FRANK, 1897-
They're Jealous; by Al Curtis, Lou
Levy [and] Frank Silver. © Frank
Silver, New York; 29Jul47;
EP17064. For voice and piano,
with chord symbols.

SILVER, MARK, 1891-
Habein Yakir li Ephrayim ... for
cantor (tenor) with alto solo
and mixed chorus, with or
without organ, by Mark Silver.
New York, Bloch Pub. Co. ©
Mark Silver, Newark, N. J.;
15Aug47; EP16516.

Uvchein Yiskadash ... for cantor
(tenor) with baritone solo
and mixed chorus, by Mark
Silver. New York, Bloch Pub.
Co. © Mark Silver, Newark,
N. J.; 15Aug47; EP16518.

Vayechulu ... for voice (medium)
with organ or piano, by Mark
Silver. New York, Bloch Pub.
Co. © Mark Silver, Newark,
N. J.; 15Aug47; EP16517.

SILVERS, LOUIS, 1889-
April Showers; [by] Louis Silvers,
[for] piano duet arr. by J.
Louis Merkur. © Harms, inc.,
New York; 3Nov47; on arrange-
ment; EP18501.

SIMEONE, HARRY.
Grandma's Thanksgiving; poem by
Lydia Maria Child (expanded by
Frank Cunkle), music [and ar-
rangement] by Harry Simeone. ©
Shawnee Press, inc., New York;
18Nov47; EP19798. Score; chorus
(SSAATTBB) and piano.

Song of the Volga Boatmen ... arrangement of an old folk song
for mixed chorus, by Harry Simeone. © Shawnee Press, inc.,
New York; 27May47; on arrangement; EP20004.

SIMMONS, HOMER.
Gigue. © Clayton F. Summy Co.,
Chicago; 25Jul47; EP15860. For
piano solo.

SIMMS, A MARTINA.
The Grand's Song and Fraternal
Greeting Song ... Words and
music by Dt. Martina Simms. ©
A. Martina Simms, Baltimore;
23Aug47; EP17937.

SIMMS, MARTINA. See
Simms, A Martina.

SIMON, HOWARD.
Gonna Get a Girl; lyric by Al
Lewis, music by Howard Simon,
[arr. by Helmy Kresa] New York,
Miller Music. © Villa Moret,
inc., San Francisco; 22Sep47;
on piano arrangement; EP17701.

Simon, Louise Marie See also
Arrieu, Claude, pseud.

[SIMON, LOUISE MARIE] 1903-
Un Fiacre; paroles de Pierre Devaux,
musique de Claude Arrieu [pseud.]
© Enoch & Cie, Editeurs, Paris;
10Jun47; EP5961.

Scherzo [by] Claude Arrieu [pseud.]
© Enoch et Cie, Paris; 10Nov47;
EP7208. Score (violin or flute
and piano) and part for flute.

SIMON, NAT.
And Mimi ... by Jimmy Kennedy
and Nat Simon ... arr. by Jack
Mason. © Shapiro, Bernstein &
Co., inc., New York; 23Oct47;
on arrangement; EP18452. Piano-
conductor score (orchestra,
with words) and parts.

And Mimi; by Jimmy Kennedy and
Nat Simon. © Shapiro,
Bernstein & Co., inc., New
York; 11Aug47; EP16241.
For voice and piano, with
chord symbols.

An Apple Blossom Wedding ... by
Jimmy Kennedy and Nat Simon ...
arr. by Paul Weirick. © Shapiro,
Bernstein & Co., inc., New York;
22Jul47; on arrangement; EP15424.
Piano-conductor score (orchestra,
with words) and parts.

The Old Lamp-Lighter; words by
Charles Tobias, music by Nat
Simon. Christmas version, [by
Charles Tobias] © Shapiro,
Bernstein & Co., inc., New York;
13Nov47; on Christmas version;
EP18921.

The Prairie Song; (Ly-dee-i-dee-o),
words by Charles Tobias, music
by Nat Simon. © Shapiro, Bernstein & Co., inc., New York;
10Nov47; EP18721.

SIMON, WILLIAM J
Esquisse d'une Poeme; piano solo
[by] William J. Simon. ©
Edward B. Marks Music Corp.,
New York; 7Jul47; EP15441.

[SIMON RODRIGUEZ, MOISES]
The Peanut Vendor. (El Manisero)
... lyric by Marion Sunshine &
L. Wolfe Gilbert, music by Moises
Simons, [pseud.] arr. by Lawrence
Kempton. © Edward B. Marks
Music Corp., New York; 5Jul52;
on English lyric; EP15993.
English and Spanish words.

SIMONDS, WILL DEXTER, 1885-
Dance Night in the Valley; words
and music by Will Simonds. ©
Will Dexter Simonds, Santa Monica,
Calif.; 4Aug47; EP16077.

Yukon Jake; words and music by
Will Simonds. © Will Dexter
Simonds, Santa Monica, Calif.;
4Aug47; EP16076.

SIMONS, KATHRYN DANIEL. See
Daniel, Kathryn.

SIMONS, MOISES, pseud. See
Simon Rodriguez, Moises.

SIMPSON, JACK.
Spooks ... by Jack Simpson, [arr.
by Ray Terry] © Cinephonic Music Co., ltd., London; 12Dec46;
EF6035. Piano-conductor score
(orchestra) and parts.

SIMS, ALMA.
South Carolina, That's Home Sweet
Home to Me; words and music by
Alma Sims. [c1946] © Nordyke
Publishing Co., Los Angeles;
30Jan47; EP19689.

SINGENBERGER, JOHN B 1848-1924.
Ave Maria; for high solo and two-
part chorus (or three equal
voices) [By] John B. Singun-
berger, rev. & arr. by J. Alfred
Schehl. © McLaughlin & Reilly
Co., Boston; 20Jun47; on arrangement; EP15875.

SINGER, GEORGE G
Oh, Oh, I Love It So; words and music by Paul F. Senzer and George G. Singer, Jr. [c1946] © Nordyke Publishing Co., Los Angeles; 30Jan47; EP19431.

SINGER, LOU, 1912-
Little Songs on Big Subjects; lyrics by Hy Zaret, music by Lou Singer. © Argosy Music Corp., New York; 23Sep47; EP17314.

SIRATT, DOROTHY. See Yarbrough, Mrs. C

SIZEMORE, AL.
Lonely Valley; words and music by Al Sizemore. © Nordyke Publishing Co., Los Angeles; 12Apr47; EP16791.

SKERTICH, NICHOLAS.
Night Rose Polka. (Nočna Ruža) By Nick Skertich, arr. by Rud. Cernkovich. © Nicholas (Nick) Skertich, Whiting, Ind.; 29Oct47; EP18334. Parts: orchestra.

SKIDMORE, MELVIN B
Little Blue Lies; words and music by Melvin B. Skidmore. © Nordyke Publishing Co., Los Angeles; 18Jul46; EP19967.

SKOLD, INGVE, 1899-
(Concerto, violin) Violinkonsert. Op.40. [by] Yngve Sköld. Stockholm, Ed. Suecia. © Föreningen svenska tonsättare, Edition Suecia, Stockholm; 1Jan45; EF7079. Score (violin and piano) and part.

Det Harda Villkoret; till text av Akke Kumlien, [by] Yngve Sköld. © Föreningen svenska tonsättare, Stockholm; 1Jan45; EF7121.

SKOMRA, FRED.
There's Always a First Time; words and music by Fred Skomra. © Nordyke Publishing Co., Los Angeles; 1Jul46; EP19533.

SKORNICKA, JOSEPH E
The Boosey & Hawkes Band Method ... by Joseph E. Skornicka and Joseph Bergeim ... Full conductor's score. © Boosey & Hawkes, inc., New York; 22Aug47; EP17145.

Instrumentalist; (On parade) ... [by] Joseph E. Skornicka. © Boosey & Hawkes, inc., New York; 17Dec47; EP20277. Condensed score (band) and parts.

SKYLAR, SUNNY, pseud. See Shaftel, Selig.

SLADEK, PAUL.
From an Old Sketch Book; elegy ... by Paul Sladek. © Volkwein Bros., inc., Pittsburgh; 24Oct47; EP18289. Score (violin and piano) and part for viola.

From an Old Sketch Book; elegy ... by Paul Sladek. © Volkwein Bros., inc., Pittsburgh; 24Oct47; EP18290. Score (violin and piano) and part.

SLATER, ALETA VERA ROBERTS, 1900-
Rally 'Round for Freedom ... words and music by Aleta Roberts Slater. © Aleta Roberts Slater, Oakland, Calif.; 18Oct47; EP18282.

SLIM, ALBERTA, pseud. See Edwards, Eric.

SLONIMSKY, NICOLAS.
A Very Great Musician; [by] Nicolas Slonimsky, words by T. Marziale. © Axelrod Publications, inc., Providence; 12Nov47; EP18535.

SMALL, ALLAN, comp. and arr.
Leeds Am-Rus Album of Soviet Popular Songs; comp. and arr. by Allen Small ... with English lyrics [by Annemarie Ewing and others], Russian lyrics [and] Russian transliteration [by Aron Pressman] © Leeds Music Corp., New York; 3Jul47; on compilation, arrangements, transliteration and English lyrics; EP15434.

SMART, HAROLD.
Piccadilly Panorama; piano solo, by Harold Smart. © The Edward Kassner Music Co., ltd., London; 14Oct47; EF6877.

SMETANA, BEDRICH, 1824-1884.
The Bartered Bride; comic opera, concert version ed. and arr. by Julius Harrison, libretto by Karl Sabina, English version (from the Czech) by Rosa Newmarch. London, Boosey & Hawkes. © Boosey & Co., ltd., London; 29Oct47; D pub 11492. Score (orchestra).

SMIT, LEO, 1921-
Five Pieces for Young People; [for] piano solo [by] Leo Smit. © Edward B. Marks Music Corp., New York; 5Nov47; EP18440.

SMITAL, JOŽKA.
Got a Little, Give a Little Polka. Málo mám málo dám. [Arr. by Joseph Cerny] © Vitak-Elsnic Co., Chicago; 13Nov46; on arrangement; EP15771. Piano-conductor score (orchestra) and parts.

SMITH, ALFRED BERNHARD, 1916- comp.
A Gospel Song Service; comp. ... [by] Alfred B. Smith [and] Horace Perkins, jr. © Alfred B. Smith, Wheaton, Ill. and Horace Perkins, jr., Philadelphia; 2May39; EP16187. Close score; SATB.

SMITH, ANNA DUNCAN.
It Doesn't Take the Moon; words and music by Anna Duncan Smith. © Nordyke Publishing Co., Los Angeles; 1Jun47; EP16886.

SMITH, ARTHUR.
Blue Beat Boogie; by Arthur Smith. Guitar solo with piano or guitar acc. arr. by Ralph Colicchio. © Shapiro, Bernstein & Co., inc., New York; 14Jul47; EP16367. Score and part.

Countin' Blues; by Arthur Smith. Guitar solo with piano or guitar acc. arr. by Ralph Colicchio. © Shapiro, Bernstein & Co., inc., New York; 14Jul47; EP16366. Score and part.

Fingers on Fire; by Arthur Smith. Guitar solo, with piano or guitar acc., arr. by Ralph Colicchio. © Shapiro, Bernstein & Co., inc., New York; 14Jul47; EP16365. Score and part.

Guitar Jump; by Arthur Smith. Guitar solo, with piano or guitar acc., arr. by Ralph Colicchio. © Shapiro, Bernstein & Co., inc., New York; 14Jul47; EP16364. Score and part.

SMITH, BEASLEY.
Beg Your Pardon; words and music by Francis Craig and Beasley Smith. © Robbins Music Corp., New York; 14Oct47; EP18275.

SMITH, BESSIE LEE, 1914-
Around the Throne Afterwhile ... by Bessie L. Smith. © Bessie Lee Smith, Birmingham, Ala.; 26Aug47; EP16651. For voice and piano.

SMITH, CHARLES AUGUST.
I Winked at You; words and music by Charles August Smith. © Nordyke Publishing Co., Los Angeles; 18Jul46; EP19658.

SMITH, CLIFF.
Boogie Woogie Yodel Song; words and music by Kenny Roberts and Cliff Smith. © Adams, Vee & Abbott, inc., Chicago; 15May47; EP16028.

SMITH, EARL F
When All My Dreams Come True; words & music by Earl F. Smith. © Nordyke Publishing Co., Los Angeles; 27Sep46; EP19708.

SMITH, H H 1890-
Honey Gal; words and music by H. H. "Jumbo" Smith. © The Society for the Preservation and Encouragement of Barber Shop Quartet Singing in America, inc., Detroit; 10ct47; EP18624.

SMITH, HAROLD MARVIN, 1891-
The Instant-Modulator; [by H. M. Smith] New Brunswick, N. J., Marvin Music Ed. © Harold Marvin Smith, New Brunswick, N. J.; 9Oct47; on slide & changes in music; EP18319.

SMITH, HERBERT LESLIE.
Evening Service in C; for unison voices, choir and organ [by] Herbert Leslie Smith. © Stainer & Bell, ltd., London; 22Oct47; EF6862.

SMITH, J CLARENCE.
Blue Reminiscent Blues; words & music by J. Clarence Smith. © Nordyke Publishing Co., Los Angeles; 27Sep46; EP19787.

SMITH, JOHNNY, 1913-
W. C. Handy's Saint Louis Blues; jazz fantasia ... arr. by Johnny Smith. New York, Handy Bros. Music Co. © W. C. Handy, New York; 20Sep47; EP17769. Score (clarinet and piano) and part.

SMITH, JULIA.
In a Swan Boat; for piano by Julia Smith. © Theodore Presser Co., Philadelphia; 6Dec47; EP20146.

SMITH, JUMBO. See Smith, H. H.

SMITH, KENNETH LESLIE.
Down the Old Spanish Trail; [by] Jimmy Kennedy & Kenneth Leslie Smith, arr. by Stan Bowsher. © Peter Maurice Music Co., ltd., New York; 20Jun47; on arrangement; EP5689. Piano-conductor score (orchestra, with words) and part.

Down the Old Spanish Trail; words & music by Jimmy Kennedy & Kenneth Leslie Smith. © Peter Maurice Music Co., ltd., New York; 13Jun47; EP5690.

SMITH, LARRY.
Memories' Gardenias; words & music by Larry Smith. © Nordyke Publishing Co., Los Angeles; 25Jul46; EP19764.

SMITH, LEONARD B
Ecstasy ... by Leonard B. Smith. © Carl Fischer, inc., New York; 12Dec47; on arrangement; EP19992. Condensed score (cornet or trumpet or baritone and band) and parts.

SMITH, NORMAN O 1914-
Blessed Lord ... [music by] Norman O. Smith. © Western Music Co., ltd., Vancouver, B. C., Can.; 4Nov47; EF7015. Score: soprano,.chorus (SATB) and organ.

SMITH, T STEWART.
Suite for four equal clarinets
with optional 4th part for alto
clarinet [by] T. Stewart Smith.
© C. L. Barnhouse Co., Oskaloosa, Iowa; 17Sep47; EP18553.
Score and parts.

SMITH, WALTER L   1915-   ed.
Smith Brothers' Book of Selected
Radio and Revival Songs; a choice
collection of new and old songs
... [music by Mrs. Alvin Smith,
Virginia Martin, and others] ed.
and comp. by ... Walter and Irvin
Smith, assisted by Albert E. Brum-
ley. © Smith Brothers' Evangelistic Party, Mann, Okla.; 1Feb47;
EP20271. Close score: SATB; shape-
note notation.

SMITH, WILLIAM.
Baby, You Are Special Made; words
and music by William Smith, jr.
© Nordyke Publishing Co., Los
Angeles; 27Mar47; EP16931.
Without Fear; words and music by
William Smith, jr. © Nordyke
Publishing Co., Los Angeles;
27Mar47; EP16722.

SMITH, WYNNE.
My Irish Home, Sweet Home; words and
music by Wynne Smith. © Peter
Maurice Music Co., ltd ., New York;
12Nov47; EF7282.

SNIDER, LOU, 1910-
Missing; by Jackie Rae and Lou
Snider. © BMI Canada, ltd.,
Toronto; 2Sep47; EF6596. For
voice and piano, with chord
symbols.

SNOW, CLIFFORD R
I Love Only You; words and music by
Glea and Cliff Snow. © Clifford
R. Snow & Co., Des Moines;
20Aug47; EP17088.
My Heart Is Yours Alone; words and
music by Glea and Cliff Snow.
© Clifford R₀ Snow & Co., Des
Moines; 20Aug47; EP17085.

SNOW, FRANCIS W
Benedictus Es, Domine and Jubilate
Deo; set to Gregorian tones with
faux-bourdon verses by Francis W.
Snow. © The H. W. Gray Co., inc.,
New York; 2Dec47; EP19259.
Score: solo voices, SATB and
organ. English words.

[SØRENSEN, WILHELM GUSTAV] 1900-
Sømanden of Stjernen ... Musik:
Bror Karlsson [pseud.], Tekst:
Jesper [pseud. c1945] © Jac.
Boesens Musikforlag A/S,
Copenhagen; 22Nov44; EF7001.

SOLAR, JEAN, pseud. See
Gagon, Jean Adrien Antoine, 1906-

SOLDI, ANDREW.
Big Bass Polka; by Larry (Pedro)
De Paul and Andrew Soldi. ©
Hill and Range Songs, inc.,
Hollywood, Calif.; 15Dec47;
EP20124. For voice and piano,
with guitar diagrams and chord
symbols.

SOLIS, BENJAMIN F
The Lights Are On; words and
music by Benjamin F. Solis.
© Nordyke Publishing Co., Los
Angeles; 13Dec46; EP19964.

SOLOMON, DOLLY MARION, 1899-
Kissing; music and words by Dolly
Marion Solomon. © Mrs. Dolly
M. Solomon, Passaic, N. J.;
16Jul47; EP15630.

SOLOMON, SIDNEY HAROLD.
Ya, Sure - You Betcha (ay ban
tank ay do); by Sandy Oliver,
Paul Herrick [and] Sid
Solomon. © Patmar Music Co.,
inc., Hollywood, Calif.;
15Oct47; EP18813. For voice
and piano, with chord symbols.

SOMERS, HARRY STUART, 1925-
Strangeness of Heart; (piano solo)
by Harry Somers. © BMI Canada,
ltd., Toronto; 2Sep47; EF6593.

SOMERVELL, ARTHUR.
Nurse's Song; (two-part song for
treble voices) arr. by Alec
Rowley, words by William Blake,
music by Arthur Somervell. ©
Aschenberg, Hopwood & Crew, ltd.,
London; 15Sep47; on arrangement;
EF6756.

SOMIS, GIOVANNI BATTISTA.
Adagio and Allegro. See his Sonata,
violin & bass.
(Sonata, violin & bass) Adagio
and allegro from the D minor
sonata for violin solo and
basso continuo ... [by]
Giovanni Battista Somis, arr.
by Robert Hernried. © Carl
Fischer, inc., New York;
3Jul47; on arrangement;
EP16102. Score (flute, oboe,
clarinet, horn, and bassoon)
and parts.

SOMMERFELT, MAURICE.
Midsummer Dance. Midsommar Dans.
S.B.A.A. [by] Maurice Sommer-
felt. [Minneapolis, Wick Music
Publishing Co.] © Frederick
Wick, Minneapolis; 28Aug47;
EP17933.

SOOTER, RUDY.
Wearing My Heart on My Sleeve;
words and music by Rudy Sooter.
© Peer International Corp., New
York; 27Aug47; EP17871.

SOOY, ANITA.
In Caliente ... music by Anita
Sooy, English words by Joe Davis
and Anita Sooy, Spanish words by
J. A. Carbajal. © Caribbean
Music, inc., New York; 22Sep47;
EP17106.

SORNA, JOEL.
Bernice; words and music by Joel
Sorna. © Nordyke Publishing
Co., Los Angeles; 16Jul47;
EP17563.

SORS, FERNANDO.
Paraphrase on Mozart's Theme;
plectrum guitar solo, [by] F.
Sor, arr. as played by Harry
Volpe. c1939. © Albert Rocky
Co., New York; 10Jun40; on ar-
rangement; EP20192.

SOSEBEE, TOMMY.
Cryin' in Vain; by Tommy Sosebee.
© Hometown Music Co., inc., New
York; 13Nov47; EP19109. For
voice and piano, with chord
symbols.

SOUERS, MILDRED THOMSON.
Isle of Jamaica; words and music
by Mildred Souers. © Broadcast
Music, inc., New York; 25Jul47;
EP18207.

[SOURIAC, BLANCHE] 1896-
Soixante Leçons de Solfège; à une
voix pour le baccalauréat, [by]
B. Forest [pseud.] © Rouart,
Lerolle & Cie, Paris; 30Apr47;
EF5979.
Le Solfège à Deux Voix; l'enseigne-
ment du chant choral à l'école,
[by] B. Forest [pseud.] Paris,
Rouart, Lerolle; vente exclusive,
Salabert. © Salabert, inc., New
York; livre 1, 17Aug47; EF7256.

SOUSA, JOHN PHILIP, 1854-1932.
El Capitan ... [by] John Philip
Sousa, piano solo. A John W.
Schaum arrangement. © Belwin,
inc., New York; 5Dec47; on
arrangement; EP19275.
Semper Fidelis; by John Philip
Sousa, [arr. and ed. by Robert
Ernst Miller] © McKinley Pub-
lishers, inc., Chicago; 8Jul47;
EP15530. For piano solo.

The Thunderer ... [by] John Philip
Sousa, piano solo. A John W.
Schaum arrangement. © Belwin,
inc., New York; 5Dec47; on
arrangement; EP19274.
The Washington Post ... by John
Philip Sousa ... piano solo
[arr. by] Carl Richter. © Bach
Music Co. (Henry Dellafield,
sole owner) Boston; 15Sep47; on
simplified arrangement; EP17784.
The Washington Post March; by
John Philip Sousa, [arr. and ed.
by Robert Ernst Miller] © Mc-
Kinley Publishers, inc.,
Chicago; 8Jul47; EP15531. For
piano solo.

SOUTHALL, MITCHELL BERNARD.
Elf Dance; for the piano by
Mitchell B. Southall. © G.
Schirmer, inc., New York;
27Aug47; EP18738.

SOWULEWSKI, ED.
Till Ole Santa Will Come ... by
Ed Sowulewski. © United Artists Pub. Co., Saginaw, Mich.;
6Oct47; EP17897. For voice and
piano, with chord symbols.

SPEAKER, MARGARET.
Never Say 'No' to Your Sugar Daddy;
words & music by Margaret Speaker, arr. by Harold Potter. ©
Nordyke Publishing Co., Los Angeles; 27Sep46; EP19639.

SPEARMAN, FANNY TURNER.
A Bedtime Prayer; [by] Fanny Turner
Spearman. (In The Story Hour.
v.55, no.33, p.4) © Fanny Turner
Spearman, Atlanta; 17Aug47;
B5-2035. For voice and piano.

In My Family; [by] Fanny Turner
Spearman. (In The Story Hour.
v.55, no.19, p.4) © Fanny Turner
Spearman, Atlanta; 11May47;
B5-2034. For voice and piano.

[SPECTOR, ABNER B   ] 1917-
While I'm in This Mood; words and
music by Street Sawyer [pseud.]
© Abner B. Spector, Chicago;
21Apr47; EP18960.

SPENCER, BERNARD.
Popular Piano Playing; an elementary course in popular music,
by Bernard Spencer. © Oliver
Ditson Co., Philadelphia;
15Oct47; on arrangements;
EP18193.

SPENCER, TIM, 1908-
From the Bottom of My Heart; words
and music by Tim Spencer. (In
Bob Nolan's Sons of the Pioneers,
p.46-47) © Tim Spencer Music,
inc., Hollywood, Calif.; 30Jul47;
EP16035.
Out in Pioneertown; words and
music by Tim Spencer. © Tim
Spencer Music, inc., Holly-
wood, Calif.; 30Jul47;
EP16029.
Save the Pieces for Me; words and
music by Tim Spencer. (In Bob
Nolan's Sons of the Pioneers,
p. 42-43) © Tim Spencer Music,
inc., Hollywood, Calif.; 30Jul47;
EP16033.
Where Are You? Words and music by
Tim Spencer. (In Bob Nolan's
Sons of the Pioneers, p. 44-45)
© Tim Spencer Music, inc.,
Hollywood, Calif.; 30Jul47;
EP16034.

SPENCER, VICTOR.
Why Are You Ever So Distant?
Words and music by Victor
Spencer. © Nordyke Publishing
Co., Los Angeles; 22Apr47;
EP17537.

SPIALEK, HANS, 1894-
Because; (paraphrase), music by
Guy d'Hardelot [pseud.] ...
symphonic arrangement for
orchestra by Hans Spialek.
New York, Chappell & Co. ©
Chappell & Co., ltd., London;
5Aug47; on arrangement;
EP16278.

SPIER, LARRY.
Memory Lane ... [for] S.S.A.,
music by Larry Spier and Con
Conrad, arr. by Douglas MacLean
[pseud.] Words by B. G. De
Sylva. © Harms, inc., New
York; 21Jul47; on arrangement;
EP16543.

SPILLMAN, LOIS.
Be a Good Homemaker; words by
Dora E. Bush, music by Lois
Spillman. [c1946] © Nordyke
Publishing Co., Los Angeles;
20Jan47; EP19490.

SPINA, HAROLD, 1906-
It's Way Past My Bedtime; words by
Edward Heyman, music by Harold
Spina. © Spina-Green Music
Corp., Hollywood, Calif.;
15Jul47; EP18309.

One Little Tear Is an Ocean;
words by Artie Wayne, [Harold
Spina] and Bob Merrill, music
by Harold Spina. © Spina-Green
Music Corp., Hollywood, Calif.;
15Jul47; EP18943.

Santa Catalina (island of romance);
words and music by Harold Spina.
© Spina-Green Music Corp.,
Hollywood, Calif.; 15Dec46;
EP18308.

With the Roses in Her Hair; words
and music by Harold Spina.
© Beverly Music Corp., New York;
6Nov47; EP18441.

You Were Somebody Else's Sweetheart; words and music by Harold
Spina. © Spina-Green Music
Corp., Hollywood, Calif.;
15Aug46; EP18310.

SPINA, HENRY J
A Telephone Kiss from You; words
and music by Henry J. Spina.
© Nordyke Publishing Co., Los
Angeles; 14Jul46; EP19538.

SPIVAK, SAMUEL, 1888-   arr.
Giant Note Hymns; arr. by Samuel
Spivak. © Edward Schuberth &
Co., inc., New York; 8Dec47;
on arrangement; EP19814.

Giant Note Home Songs; arr. by
Samuel Spivak. © Edward Schuberth & Co., inc., New York;
8Dec47; on arrangement; EP19813.

Giant Note Kiddie Songs; arr. by
Samuel Spivak. © Edward Schuberth
& Co., inc., New York; 8Dec47; on
arrangement; EP19811.

Giant Note Waltzes; arr. by Samuel
Spivak. © Edward Schuberth & Co.,
inc., New York; 8Dec47; on arrangement; EP19812.

SPOLIANSKY, MISCHA.
Have I Told You? See his One, Two,
Three!

(One, Two, Three!) Have I Told
You? ... [From] One, Two, Three!
[Words and] music by Mischa Spol-
iansky. © Chappell & Co., ltd.,
London; 8Oct47; EP6893.

One, Two, Three! (Waltz mad) ...
[From] One, Two, Three! ...
[Words and] music by Mischa
Spoliansky. © Chappell & Co.,
ltd., London; 8Oct47; EP6894.

SPRING, MARGARET CATHERINE, 1895-
A Merry Merry Christmas; words
and music by Margaret C. Spring.
© Margaret Cesana Spring (Mrs.
L. E.), Stockton, Calif.;
13Oct47; EP17907.

SPROUSE, PETER.
From Now until Forever; words and
music by Peter Sprouse.
© Nordyke Publishing Co., Los
Angeles; 3Jun47; EP16880.

[SPURGIN, ANTHONY MARTIN] 1910-
Diabolero ... [by] A. Picon
[pseud.] © William Paxton &
Co., ltd., London; 8Oct46;
EP5703. Piano-conductor score
(orchestra) and parts.

SQUIRES, HARRY D   1897-
I'll Keep on Dreaming; by Harry
D. Squires. © Irving Arthur
Music Publications, Brooklyn;
22Sep47; EP17240. For voice
and piano, with chord symbols.

My Love Song; by Harry D. Squires.
© Irving Arthur Music Publications, Brooklyn; 22Sep47;
EP17239. For voice and piano,
with chord symbols.

STAAB, HAROLD BURTON, 1891-
Lovely Are Your Deep Blue Eyes;
words and music by Hal Staab,
arr. by Charles Merrill. ©
Harold B. Staab, Northampton,
Mass.; 20Aug47; EP17195.

When the Man in the Moon Says
"Hello" ... Words and music by
Hal Staab, arr. by Charles M.
Merrill. © Harold B. Staab,
Northampton, Mass.; 20Aug47;
EP17235. Close score: SATB.

STAIRS, LOUISE E
At Thy Feet; anthem for mixed
voices, [words by] James D.
Burns, [music by] Louise E.
Stairs. © Theodore Prosser
Co., Philadelphia; 15Jul47;
EP15673.

I Think I'll Plant a Garden;
piano solo with words by
Louise E. Stairs. © Theodore
Presser Co., Philadelphia;
9Sep47; EP17170.

There Were Shepherds; Christmas
cantata for mixed voices, words
by Elsie Duncan Yale, music by
Louise E. Stairs ... Vocal score.
© Theodore Presser Co., Philadelphia; 4Oct47; EP17794.

STAMITZ, CHARLES. See
Stamitz, Karl.

STAMITZ, KARL, 1746-1801.
(Quartets, strings) Two Quartets;
for clarinet or flute or oboe,
violin, viola and cello or string
quartet, [by] Carl stamitz, [ed.,
with preface, by Josef Marx]
string parts ed. by Emanuel Zet-
lin. New York, McGinnis & Marx.
(Music for wind instruments by
18th century masters, ed. by Josef
Marx, no.3) © Josef Marx, New
York; 4Dec47; on preface & editing
EP20258. Parts.

Symphonie Concertante do majeur
... C major, [by] Charles
Stamitz ... pour 2 violons solo
et orchestre, éd. et cadence
par ... Fr. Kneusslin. © Hug &
Co., Music-Publishers, Zurich,
Switzerland; 15Apr47; EF6010.
Score.

Two Quartets. See his Quartets, strings

STANLEY, JOHN.
Trumpet Tune; by John Stanley,
arr. for trumpet and string
orchestra (from a suite for
organ) by Henry Coleman.
[c1946] © Oxford University
Press, London; 9Jan47; on
arrangement; EP6146.

STANLEY, LEO, pseud. See
Ricketts, R. R.

STANTON, WALTER KENDALL.
Hail to the Lord's Anointed!
Anthem ... [Words by] James
Montgomery, [music by] W. K.
Stanton. © Stainer & Bell, ltd.,
London; 22Oct47; EF6863. Score:
SATB and organ.

STARBECK, ELLA TWETER.
Aquatennial Parade; words and
music by Ella Tweter Starbeck.
© Ella Tweter Starbeck,
Montevideo, Minn.; 18Aug47;
EP16534.

STAROMINSKY, MORDERAI, 1916-
Choral Suite; [by] Mordehai
Starominsky. © Mayer Joseph
Neidet, Tel-Aviv, Palestine;
1May47; EF6355. For solo voices
and mixed chorus; added t.-p.
and text in Hebrew.

STEADMAN, AGNES.
Aboard the Windjammer; piano solo
by Agnes Steadman. © The Willis
Music Co., Cincinnati; 8Aug47;
EP16281.

Hocus Pocus; piano solo on black
keys only by Agnes Steadman.
© The Willis Music Co., Cincinnati; 4Aug47; EP16559.

Silver Slippers; piano solo by
Agnes Steadman. © The Willis
Music Co., Cincinnati;
15Aug47; EP16424.

STEDMAN, JAMES HERBERT, 1877-
Sand in Your Shoes; the song of
Florida, words and music by
James H. Stedman. [Sarasota,
Fla., Stedman House] © James H.
Stedman, Sarasota, Fla.;
26Sep47; EP18929.

STEELE, DOUGLAS.
On Gibbon's Angel's Song; chorale
prelude for organ by Douglas
Steele. © Novello & Co., ltd.,
London; 4Dec47; EF7364.

STEELE, MARY C
At Eventide; words by Mary M.
Steele, music by Mary C.
Steele. © Nordyke Publishing
Co., Los Angeles; 19May47;
EP16925.

STEER, CLARENCE E
The Love Waltz; words and music by
Clarence E. Steer. © Nordyke
Publishing Co., Los Angeles;
13Aug47; EP19347.

STEGER, IRENE, 1901-
The Christ of Galilee; composed by
Rev. Irene Steger. © Rev. Irene
Steger, Indianapolis; 28Jul47;
EP15901. Close score: SATB.

Family Reunion in Heaven; composed
by Rev. Irene Steger. © Rev.
Irene Steger, Indianapolis;
25Jul47; EP15790. Close score:
SATB.

Take Me to Calvary; composed by
Rev. Irene Steger. © Rev.
Irene Steger, Indianapolis;
28Jul47; EP15902. Close score:
SATB.

STEIBELT, DANIEL.
Rondo in E flat; piano solo, [by]
Steibelt. [New ed., rev. and
fingered by Alec Rowley]
© Edwin Ashdown, ltd., London;
28Feb47; on editing, abridging
& fingering; EF6750.

[STEILA, JOHNNY J   ]
Music Box; words and music by
Johnny Jay [pseud.] © Nordyke
Publishing Co., Los Angeles;
28Mar47; EP16789.

STEIN, GRETA M
Your Heart and Mine; words and
music by Greta M. Stein. ©
Nordyke Publishing Co., Los
Angeles; 21Mar46; EP16650.

STEIN, LILLIAN FUCHS. See
FUCHS, LILLIAN.

355

[STEIN, SIEGFRIED ALEX] 1903-
Au Revoir ... Paroles anglaises
de Erwin Drake [and] Jimmy
Shirl, paroles françaises de
Jacques Larue [pseud.], musique
de Alstone [pseud.] © Éditions
Salabert, Paris; 19Jun47;
EF5899.

Au Revoir; words by Erwin Drake &
Jimmy Shirl [pseud.], music by
Alstone [pseud.] From "Gracie's
Working Party." © Chappell &
Co., inc., New York; 20Aug47;
EF6588.

(Destins) Destin ... dans le film
"Destins." Paroles de Jacques
Larue [pseud.] & André Hornez,
musique d'Alstone [pseud.],
arr. par Al. Kiwi [pseud.] ©
Éditions Max Eschig, Paris;
5Mar47; on arrangement; EF7217.
Piano-conductor score (orchestra)
and parts.

(Destins) Destin ... [From] le
film "Destins; paroles de Jacques
Larue [pseud.] et André Hornez,
musique d'Alstone [pseud.] ©
Éditions Max Eschig, Paris;
23Dec46; EF6470.

Harmonise ... paroles de Jacques
Poterat, musique de Alstone
[pseud.], c1946. © Éditions
Paul Beuscher, Paris; 10Dec45;
EF6507.

Imaginez; paroles de Jean Boyer,
musique de Alstone [pseud.] ©
Éditions Salabert, Paris; 15Sep47;
EF7255.

Sonata; paroles anglaises de Ervin
Drake [and] Jimmy Shirl [pseud.]
paroles françaises de Jacques
Larue [pseud.], musique de
Alstone [pseud.] © Éditions
Salabert, Paris; 25Jun47; on
French words; EF6316.

Sonata ... words by Ervin Drake
et Jimmy Shirl [pseud.], musique
de Alstone [pseud.] © Éditions Salabert,
Paris; 20Jan47; on arrangement;
EF6320. Piano-conductor score
(orchestra, with words) and
parts.

There Is No Breeze (to cool the
flame of love); music by Alstone
[pseud.] ... Lyric by Dorothy
Dick. New York, Robbins Music
Corporation. © Éditions Salabert,
Paris; 13Sep46; on English lyric
to De Tout Mon Coeur; EF6444.
Corrected by LP13312.

STEINER, ERIC.
Capriccietto; piano solo by Eric
Steiner. © Schroeder & Gunther,
inc., Rhinebeck, N. Y.; 21Nov47;
EP18838.

Zigzag; piano solo by Eric
Steiner. © Schroeder & Gunther,
inc., Rhinebeck, N. Y.; 21Nov47;
EP18839.

STEINER, MAX.
Arab Chant ... by Max Steiner.
© Mills Music, inc., New York;
3Jul47; EP6992. Score (oboe and
piano) and part.

STEININGER, FRANZ.
The Balalaika Serenade. See his Music
in My Heart.

Love Song. See his Music in My Heart.

(Music in My Heart) The Balalaika
Serenade; from the musical play
"Music in My Heart." Based on
Tchaikovsky's "June Barcarolle"
and "Romance," music by Forman
Brown, music adapted by Franz
Steininger, [piano arrangement by
Robbins Music Corp., New York; 10Oct47;
on piano arrangement; EP20273.

(Music in My Heart) Love Song;
based on Tchaikovsky's "Song
without words," from the musical
play "Music in My Heart"; words
by Forman Brown, music adapted
by Franz Steininger, [arr. by
Robbins Music Corp.] © Robbins
Music Corp., New York; 20Oct47;
on arrangement & changes in
words; EP18634.

(Music in My Heart) Once upon a
Time; based on themes from
Tchaikovsky's "Sleeping beauty
suite" and from "Piano concerto
in Bb minor," from the musical
play "Music in My Heart"; words
by Forman Brown, music adapted
by Franz Steininger. © Robbins
Music Corp., New York; 25Oct47;
EP18661.

(Music in My Heart) Stolen Kisses;
based on themes from Tchaikovsky's "String quartet" and from
the "Swan Lake suite" from the
musical play "Music in My heart,"
words by Forman Brown, music
adapted by Franz Steininger,
[arr. by Robbins Music Corp.]
© Robbins Music Corp., New York;
20Oct47; on arrangement & changes
in lyric; EP18669.

(Music in My Heart) While There's
a Song to Sing; based on
Tchaikovsky's "Sweet reverie,"
words by Forman Brown, music by
Franz Steininger. From the
musical play "Music in My Heart."
© Robbins Music Corp., New York;
25Sep47; EP17738.

Once upon a Time. See his Music in My
Heart.

Stolen Kisses. See his Music in My
Heart.

While There's a Song to Sing. See his
Music in My Heart.

STELIBSKÝ, JOSEF, 1909-
(Byli jsme a budem) Rád mám svoji
krásnou zem; (píseň o vlasti) ...
z operety ... "Byli jsme a
budem," hudba; J. Stelibský,
slova: K. Melíšek. © Mojmír
Urbánek, Praha, Czechoslovakia;
24Jul39; EF5574.

STELLA, SAMUEL JOHN, 1907-
Circus Day with You; words and
music by Samuel Stella. © Samuel J. Stella, Boston; 17Jul47;
EP18223.

STEPHENSON, MARGARETE ELDER, 1897-
Thank Thee, O Lord; (A New Year's
prayer) words & melody by M.
Stephenson, harmony; Clara Scott.
© Margarete Elder Stephenson,
Chicago; 12Dec47; EP19883.

STEPT, SAM H 1897-
Azusa, Cucamonga and Anaheim;
words and music by Sam H. Stept.
© Leo Feist, inc., New York;
10Dec47; EP20409.

Boing-n-n-ng; words & music by Sam
H. Stept. © Stept, inc., New
York; 27Jun47; EP15301.

Say Something Nice about Me;
words and music by Sam H. Stept.
© Chappell & Co., inc., New
York; 17Nov47; EP20154.

STERLING, ELIZABETH, 1928-
Sleep Not, Little One; song,
words by Clara J. Holmes, music
by Elizabeth Sterling. © Wesley Webster, San Francisco;
10Dec47; EP19572.

STERLING, WILLIAM, pseud. See
Labbe, Albert.

STERN, JOSEPH EBENEZZER, 1896-
Kansas City, My Home Town; male
quartette arrangement [by]
Joseph E. Stern. © Joseph E.
Stern, Kansas City, Mo.; 23Jul47;
EP15891.

STEVENS, EVERETT.
Animal Parade; [by] Everett Stevens,
for piano. © J. Fischer & Bro.,
New York; 9Sep47; EP17712.

Good-bye, Mr. Czerny; [by] Everett Stevens, for piano. © J.
Fischer & Bro., New York;
9Sep47; EP17861.

A Shepherd Sleeps; for piano
[by] Everett Stevens. © J.
Fischer & Bro., New York;
9Sep47; EP17710.

Three Piano Solos; by Everett
Stevens. © Clayton F. Summy
Co., Chicago; v.3, 26Sep47; on 3 pieces.
Contents.- [1] The Haunted
House (© EP17844) - [2] Jumping
Jacks (© EP17843) - [3] Southern
Mountain Tune (© EP17849)

STEVENS, MILO.
Gypsy Carnival; for the piano [by]
Milo Stevens. © Oliver Ditson
Co., Philadelphia; 6Dec47; EP20450.

STEVENSON, ROBERT M
Texas Suite; for piano by Robert
M. Stevenson. © The Boston
Music Co., Boston; 9Sep47; on 3
pieces.- Contents. - 1. Bronco
Bustin' (© EP17164) - 2. An Old
Spanish Mission (© EP17163) - 3.
The Lonesome Prairie (© LP17162)

STEWART, CHARLES H
The Evening We Went Out to Dine;
words & music by Charles H. Stewart. © Nordyke Music Co.,
Los Angeles; 25Jul46; EP19728.

STEWART, DOROTHY.
Now Is the Hour; (Maori farewell
song), words and music by Maewa
Kaihan, Clement Scott [and]
Dorothy Stewart, arr. by Carl
Ladra. © Leeds Music Corp.,
New York; 8Dec47; on arrange-
ment; EP19996. Piano-conductor
score (orchestra, with words)
and parts.

STEWART, HENRY.
Two Wrongs Don't Make a Right;
words and music by Ernest Tubb
and Henry "Red" Stewart.
© Ernest Tubb Music, inc.,
Hollywood, Calif.; 29Aug47;
EP17926.

STEWART, RED. See
Stewart, Henry.

[STICKLES, WILLIAM] 1883- arr.
Jumbo Note Lullabies; arr. by
Kathleen Hall [pseud.] © Chas.
H. Hansen Music Co., New York;
1Jul47; on new words for "The
Little Sandman," music and rev.
words for "Now I Lay Me down to
Sleep," and arrangements; EP17063.
For voice and piano. Partial
contents.- Now I Lay Me down to
Sleep, by William Stickles.-
The Little Sandman, words by
Charles Hansen, music by
Johannes Brahma.

STILL, WILLIAM GRANT.
Pastorela; [by] William Grant
Still, [ed. by Louis Kaufman]
© M. Witmark & Sons, New York;
1Jul47; EP15629. Score (violin
and piano) and part.

STILLERMAN, IRWIN.
My Atomic Sensation; words by
Frances Marvel Gnass, music by
Irwin Stillerman, arr. by L.
Leslie Loth. © Frances Marvel
Gnass, Royal Oak, Mich. &
Irwin Stillerman, Brooklyn;
16Mar47; EP17250.

STIVER, MARGARET.
Remember Me to You; words by Beart
Bernard [pseud.], music by Mar-
garet Stiver. © Nordyke Publish-
ing Co., Los Angeles; 5Aug47;
EP19504.

STOCK, LARRY.
I'll Never Be without a Dream
(As Long As I Have You); by
Freddy James [pseud.] and
Larry Stock; © Sun Music Co.,
inc., New York; 7Jul47; EP16304.
For voice and piano, with chord
symbols.

The Umbrella Man ... [by] James
Cavanaugh, Vincent Rose and
Larry Stock, arr. by William
Teague. New York, Music
Publishers Holding Corp. ©
Harms, inc., New York; 27Feb39;
on arrangement; EP17002. Parts:
band.

STOCKDALE, CLYDE EDISON, 1921-
My Pretty Miss; lyrics by Tom
Phillips, music by Clyde Stock-
dale. © La Mar Music Publishers,
inc., Canton, Ohio; 8Dec47;
EP20111.

Schade drum ... Musik von Robert
Stolz, Worte von Robert Gilbert.
© Edition Turicaphon, a. g.,
Zurich, Switzerland; 26Jun47;
EF5837.

Schicksal mit Musik; Musikalische
Komödie, worte: Karl Farkas,
musik: Robert Stolz. [Op.790]
© Ludwig Doblinger (Bernhard
Herzmansky) k. g., Music
Publisher, Vienna; 18Dec46;
EF6234. For voice and piano.

So Le La ... Musik von Robert
Stolz, Text von Robert Gilbert.
© Edition Turicaphon, a.g.,
Zürich, Switzerland; 1Jun47;
EF5827.

Sympathie ... Musik: Robert Stolz.
Op. 752. Lyric: Robert
Gilbert. © Edition Turicaphon
a. g., Bühnen- und Musikverlag,
Zürich, Switzerland; 22Mar47;
EF5867.

STOLZ, ROBERT, 1880-
Auf der Piazzetta, wo Caruso Sang
... Worte von Robert Gilbert,
Musik von Robert Stolz. Op.777.
© Edition Turicaphon, ltd.,
music publishers, Zurich,
Switzerland; 19Apr47; EF5835.

STONE, AARON ALFRED.
Funny as It Seems; words and music by Al Stone. © Nordyke Publishing co., Los Angeles; 3Sep47;
EP20359.

You've Got Plenty of Something;
words and music by Al Stone.
© Nordyke Publishing Co., Los
Angeles; 4Sep47; EP19322.

STONE, AL. See
Stone, Aaron Alfred.

STONE, CLIFFIE.
Divorce Me C.O.D.; words and
music by Merle Travis and
Cliffie Stone. © American
Music, inc., Hollywood, Calif.;
26Aug46; EP17335.

STONE, GREGORY, 1900-
Body and Soul; [by] Johnny Green,
paraphrased by Gregory Stone.
© Harms, inc., New York; 20Nov47;
on arrangement; EP19235. Score
(violin and piano) and part.

STONE, NORMAN.
The Cuckoo; for unaccompanied mixed voices (S. C. T. B.), West
Country folk-song, arr. [by]
Norman Stone. © Oxford University Press, London; 31Jul47; on
arrangement; EF6362.

STONER, MICKEY, 1911-
A Dollar Ain't a Dollar Anymore;
words & music by Denver Darling,
Elton Britt [and] Mickey Stoner.
© R. F. D. Music Pub. Co.,
inc., New York; 24Jun47;
EP16307.

I Still Say Your Name in My
Prayer; words & music by
Denver Darling, Elton Britt
[and] Mickey Stoner. ©
R. F. D. Music Pub. Co., inc.,
New York; 24Jun47; EP16306.

I'm Gonna Leave This Old Town;
words & music by Denver Darling,
Elton Britt [and] Mickey Stoner.
© R. F. D. Music Pub. Co., inc.,
New York; 24Jun47; EP16305.

STORM, CHARLES W
Ohio Valley Express; lyric by
Hon. John Storm, music by Chas.
W. Storm. © John Storm, Sardis,
Ohio; 12Jul47; on changes in
words; EP16136.

STORM, JOHN, 1889-
The Liberty Bell Special; words &
music by Hon. John Storm,
arrangement by Harold Potter.
© John Storm, Sardis, Ohio;
15Sep47; EP17115.

Marietta; words and music by John
Storm, arrangement by Harold
Potter. © John Storm, Sardis,
Ohio; 2Aug47; EP16692.

Parlor of the Valley; words &
music by John Storm, arr. by
Clarke Tate. © John Storm,
Sardis, Ohio; 7Oct47; EP17811.

Waiting on Broadway; words and
music by John Storm, arrangement by Harold Potter. © John
Storm, Sardis, Ohio; 22Sep47;
EP17313.

STORMY JACK.
Maggie Heubeil; words & music by
Stormy Jack, arrangement by
Harold Potter. © Cahoot, inc.,
Benwood, W. Va.; 12Dec47;
EP19855.

STORSETH, LARS.
Oh, My Darling Rose Marie; words
& music by Lars Storseth.
© Nordyke Publishing Co.,
Los Angeles; 16Sep46; EP16310.

STORY, H
Spangle Dance; by H. Story. © H.
Story, San Francisco; 5Nov47;
EP20267. For piano solo.

STORY, JAMES, 1902-
Honey Bunny ... by James Story,
arr. by J. R. King. © Jim Tom
Music Publishing Co., Long Beach,
Calif.; 12Nov47; EP18842.
Score (3 trumpets and piano) and
parts.

STOTHART, HERBERT.
Det Finnes Alltid Rosor. See his
Mrs. Miniver.

(Mrs. Miniver) Det Finnes Alltid
Rosor, ... ur ... storfilm Mrs.
Miniver, musik: Herbert Stothart,
svensk text: Tommy, Stockholm,
Reuter & Reuter. © Leo Feist,
inc., New York; 15Mar43; EF6063.

STOUGHTON, R   S
I Know a Beautiful Theme; anthem
for mixed voices, [by] R. S.
Stoughton, [words by] Ina Duley
Ogdon. © Theodore Presser Co.,
Philadelphia; 2Dec47; on arrange-
ment; EP19256.

STOUT, BILL.
You Darling, You Angel! Words
and music by Bill Stout. ©
Nordyke Publishing Co., Los
Angeles; 11Aug47; EP17471.

STOUT, CLARENCE.
Get Hep to the Lawd; words and
music by Clarence Stout. ©
Mills Music, inc., New York;
14Aug47; EP18264.

STOYE, PAUL.
Waltz Rhapsody; on themes from
Johann Strauss' "Roses from the
South." Piano solo by Paul
Stoye. © Clayton F. Summy Co.,
Chicago; 5Jun47; EP15534.

STRANGE, GLENN.
Maulin' Marandy; words and music
by Eddie Dean and Glenn Strange.
(In Bourne, inc., comp. Eddie
Dean [song folio] p.16-18) ©
Bourne, inc., New York; 22Jul47;
EP15867.

STRANKS, ALAN.
Blue Mediterranean; words and
music by Hans May & Alan Stranks.
© Cinephonic Music Co., ltd.,
London; 18Jul46; EF6622.

STRAUSS, JOHANN, 1825-1899.
Annen Polka; by Johann Strauss,
[arr. by Norman Richardson]
London, Sole selling agents,
Boosey & Hawkes. © Hawkes &
Son (London) ltd., London;
24Sep47; on arrangement; EF6644.
Condensed score (band) and
parts.

Emperor Waltz; piano solo by Johann Strauss, ... John W. Schaum
arrangement. © Belwin, inc.,
New York; 20Nov47; on arrangement; EP18800.

The Emperor Waltz; words by Ted
Fetter, music by Johann Strauss,
arr. by Hugo Frey ... for mixed
voices, S.A.T.B. © The John
Franklin Co., inc., New York;
17Nov47; on arrangement;
EP18796.

The Emperor Waltz; words by Ted
Fetter, music by Johann Strauss,
arr. by Hugo Frey [for] two
part ... treble voices. © The
John Franklin Co., inc., New
York; 17Nov47; on arrangement;
EP18795.

Pizzicato Polka; by Johann Strauss,
arr. for the piano by James
Palmeri. © G. Schirmer, inc.,
New York; 27Aug47; on arrangement; EP18737.

Pizzicato Polka; by Johann &
Josef Strauss, [arr. by Norman
Richardson] London, Sole
selling agents, Boosey & Hawkes.
© Hawkes & Son (London) ltd.,
London; 24Sep47; on arrangement;
EF6643. Condensed score (band)
and parts.

Tales from the Vienna Woods; by
Johann Strauss, arr. for the
piano by James Palmeri. © G.
Schirmer inc., New York;
17Jul47; on arrangement; EP17047.

Tales of the Vienna woods [lyric
by Jack Edwards, and] The beautiful blue Danube ... Arranged by
Walter L. Rosemont. © Edwards
Music Co., New York; on arrangement; 24Jan47; EP11060. Parts
for piano and 2 instruments, or
small orchestra.

STRAUSS, RICHARD, 1864-
Der Rosenkavalier; erste Walzer-
folge, first sequence of waltzes
... (1946) [by] Richard Strauss.
[Op. 59] © Boosey & Hawkes,
ltd., London; on arrangement;
28Mar47; EF5323. Score: orchestra.

STRAVINSKY, IGOR' FEDOROVICH, 1882-
(Concerto, string orchestra)
Concerto en ré pour orchestra à
cordes (1946) [by] Igor Strawin-
sky. London, Hawkes & Co. ©
Boosey & Hawkes, inc., New York;
24Sep47; EP18506.

Firebird ballet suite; for regular
orchestra [by] Igor Stravinsky.
New version augm. and rev. by the
author. © Leeds Music Corp.,
New York; 30Jul47; EP16097.
Miniature score: orchestra.

Summer Moon ... lyric by John
Klenner, music by Igor Stravin-
sky. © Leeds Music Corp.,
New York; 31Oct47; EP18645.

STRICKLAND, LILY TERESA, 1887-
"And on Earth Peace"; a Christmas
cantata for solo voices, mixed
chorus and organ or piano,
text from the New Testament.
© Chappell & Co. inc., New York;
5Nov47; EP18723.

Dreamin' Time, Mah Honey ... song,
words by John W. Bratton, music
by Lily Strickland. © Bourne,
inc., New York; 28Apr47; EP17110.

Go, Little Song! Words and music
by Lily Strickland. © Theodore
Presser Co., Philadelphia;
15Jul47; EP15680.

Grandma Loved a Soldier; (S.S.A.)
[by] Lily Strickland. © Galaxy
Music Corp., New York; 23Sep47;
EP17716.

Song of the Whippoorwill; words
by Theodosia Paynter, music by
Lily Strickland. © Oliver
Ditson Co., Philadelphia; 31Jul47;
EP16340.

With My Heart I Follow You; song,
words by Theodosia Paynter,
music by Lily Strickland. ©
Oliver Ditson Co., Philadelphia;
31Jul47; EP16339.

STRICKLING, GEORGE FRANKLIN, 1896-
We All Have Colds ... for mixed
chorus (S.A.T.B.) words by Allie
B. Leslie, music by George F.
Strickling. © Broadcast Music,
inc., New York; 11Jul47;
EP17901.

STRIDE, HARRY,
I Wish I Could Say the Same; words
by Nat Burton, music by Harry
Stride. © Northern Music Corp.,
New York; 1Aug47; EP16361.

STROMBERG, JOHN, d. 1902.
Ma Blushin' Rosie, (Ma Posie
Sweet); music by John Stromberg, lyrics by Edgar Smith ...
scored by Jerry Sears. ©
M. Witmark & Sons, New York;
30Jul47; on arrangement;
EP16596. Piano-conductor
score (orchestra, with words)
and parts.

STROMER, BERTLE WILLIARD.
Mornin', Nite and Noon; words and
music by Bertle Williard Stromer.
© Nordyke Publishing Co., Los
Angeles; 15Jun46; EP20085.

STRONG, CLIFTON E.
My Darling Baby; words by Petra E.
Harthun, music by Clifton E.
Strong. [c1945] © Nordyke
Publishing Co., Los Angeles;
21Jun46; EP19763.

STRONG, MAY A
King Midas; cantate fantasque
for two-part treble voices,
words by Celia Thaxter, music
by May A. Strong. © Theodore
Presser Co., Philadelphia;
15Oct47; EP18191.

STRONG, MICHAEL, pseud. See
Paul, Alan.

STROUSE, PAUL.
A Donkey Ride; piano solo by Paul
Strouse. © The Boston Music Co.,
Boston; 24Sep47; EP17726.

STRUM, EVELYN.
Ping Pong; piano solo by Evelyn
Strum. © Mills Music, inc.,
New York; 8Dec47; EP19905.

Sleep, My Little Papoose; piano
solo by Evelyn Strum. © Mills
Music, inc., New York; 8Dec47;
EP19904.

STUART, DONALD G
Theone; words and music by Donald
G. Stuart. © Nordyke Publish-
ing Co., Los Angeles; 29Aug47;
EP19297.

STUART, FRANK.
Love's Just a Funny Guy; words by
Tom McKee, music by Frank
Stuart. © Mills Music, inc.,
New York; 4Aug47; EP18255.

STUBBS, EDUARDO, 1891-
Zambre Gitana ... [by] Eduardo
Stubbs. © Éditions espagnoles
Julio Garzon, Paris; 10Oct47;
EF7334. For piano solo.

STURGILL, CLARA LEE.
Shadows on My Window; words and
music by Clara Lee Sturgill.
[c1946] © Nordyke Publishing
Co., Los Angeles; 28Jan47;
EP19644.

STUTCHEWSKY, JOACHIM, 1890-
Hassidic Dances; adapted for
piano by J. Stutchewsky. ©
Mayer Joseph Naidat, Tel-Aviv,
Palestine; 19Jun47; on arrange-
ment; EP6557.

[Roni 11; by Joachim Stutchewsky,
tr. into Hebrew by Dov Shtok
and Shimshon Meltser] © Mayer
Joseph Naidat, Tel-Aviv, Palestine; 12May47; EF6356. For
voice and piano; t.-p. and text
in Hebrew.

STYNE, JULE.
Can't You Just See Yourself? See his
High Button Shoes.

Get Away for a Day. See his High Button
Shoes.

(High Button Shoes) Can't You
Just See Yourself? ... [From]
High Button Shoes; lyrics by
Sammy Cahn and music [by] Jule
Styne. © Edwin H. Morris & Co.,
inc., New York; 29Sep47; EP17981.

(High Button Shoes) Get Away for
a Day, [from] ... the musical
comedy High Button Shoes; lyrics
... by Sammy Cahn, music [by]
Jule Styne. © Edwin H. Morris
& Co., inc., New York; 6Oct47;
EP18520.

(High Button Shoes) I Still Get
Jealous ... [from] the musical
comedy High Button Shoes; lyrics
... by Sammy Cahn and [music by]
Jule Styne. © Edwin H. Morris
& Co., inc., New York; 18Sep47;
EP17645.

(High Button Shoes) On a Sunday
by the Sea, from "High Button
Shoes"; lyric by Sammy Cahn,
music by Jule Styne. © Edwin
H. Morris & Co., inc., New York;
13Nov47; EP19108.

(High Button Shoes) Papa, Won't
You Dance with Me? ... [From]
the musical comedy High Button
Shoes; lyrics ... by Sammy Cahn
and [music by] Jule Styno. ©
Edwin H. Morris & Co., inc.,
New York; 18Sep47; EP17646.

(High Button Shoes) There's
Nothing like a Model T, [from]
... the musical comedy High
Button shoes; lyrics ... by
Sammy Cahn, music [by] Jule
Styne. © Edwin H Morris & Co.,
inc., New York; 20Oct47;
EP18521.

(High Button Shoes) You're My
Girl ... [from] High Button
Shoes; lyrics by Sammy Cahn and
music [by] Jule Styne. © Edwin
H. Morris & Co., inc., New York;
29Sep47; EP17982.

I Still Get Jealous. See his High
Button Shoes.

On a Sunday by the Sea. See his High
Button Shoes.

Papa, Won't You Dance with Me? See his
High Button Shoes.

Pico and Sepulveda ... Music by
Jule Styne, lyric by Eddie
Cherkose. © Mayfair Music
Corp., New York; 3Sep47;
EP18526. For solo voice, uni-
son chorus and piano.

There's Nothing like a Model T. See his
High Button Shoes.

You're My Girl. See his High Button
Shoes.

SUÁREZ, SENÉN.
"Vengo Cepillando" ... letra y mú-
sica de Senén Suárez, arreglo de
Carlos Faxas. © Peer Interna-
tional Corp., New York; 23Sep47;
EF6719. Parts; orchestra.

SUBER-SANDERS, PANSY, 1914-
Some Day Let My Soul Ever Be at
Rest; words and music by Pansy
Suber-Sanders. [Poem revision
and music arr. by Wellington
Adams] © Pansy Suber-Sanders,
Jamaica, N. Y.; 16Sep47;
EP17220.

SUESSE, DANA.
Night Sky ... for piano, by Dana
Suesse. © Robbins Music Corp.,
New York; 16Sep47; EP17736.

SULLIVAN, SIR ARTHUR SEYMOUR, 1842-
1900.
(H. M. S. Pinafore) "To Sail the
Ocean Blue, from "H. M. S.
Pinafore"; for two-part chorus
of male voices ... arr. by
Frank B. Cookson, [words by]
Wm. S. Gilbert. © The Raymond
A. Hoffman Co., Chicago; 22Sep38;
EP15586.

The Lost Chord; [by] Sir Arthur
Sullivan, words by Adelaide
Proctor, arr. for junior, inter-
mediate and senior choirs ...
by Guy Chambers Filkins. © Guy
Chambers Filkins, Ann Arbor,
Mich., 1Dec46; on arrangement;
EP17784.

The Lost Chord; (S.A.T.B. with
piano or organ acc.) arr. by
Edward S. Breck. [Music by]
Arthur Sullivan, [words by
Adelaide A. Procter] © Carl
Fischer, inc., New York; 17Oct47;
on arrangement; EP18655.

The Mikado and Pinafore; [by]
Gilbert and Sullivan, [arr. by
Walter L. Rosemont] © Edwards
Music Co., New York; 9Sep47;
EP16693. For piano solo with
interlinear words.

We Sail the Ocean Blue. See his
H. M. S. Pinafore.

SULLIVAN, BRENDA.
The Merry-go-round; for three-
part chorus of women's voices
and soprano solo with piano
acc., words and music by Brenda Sullivan. © The Willis
Music Co., Cincinnati; 14Nov47;
EP18900.

SULLIVAN, EUGENE T
Don't that Moon Look Lonesome;
[and Love Ain't Worryin' Me]
words and music by Wiley Walker
and Gene Sullivan. © Peer International Corp., New York;
27Aug47; EP17869. 1870.

SULLIVAN, GENE. See also
Sullivan, Eugene T

Bring Back the Sunshine; words and
music by Wiley Walker and Gene
Sullivan. © Peer International
Corp., New York; 25Nov47;
EP19836.

SULLIVAN, GERARD JOSEPH E
1911-
March into the Sun; words [and]
music: G. J. E. S. © Gerard
J. E. Sullivan, Dayton, Ohio;
10Jul47; EP16186.

SULLIVAN, HENRY.
(Wallflower) I May Be Wrong (but,
I think you're wonderful), featured in the ... picture "Wallflower"; words by Harry Ruskin,
music by Henry Sullivan ...
scored by Jerry Sears. © Advanced Music Corp., New York;
22Oct47; on arrangement; EP18479.
Piano-conductor score (orchestra,
with words) and parts.

SULLIVAN, MARTIN.
Don't Lay the Blame on Me; words
& music by Marvin Sullivan.
[c1946] © Nordyke Publishing
Co., Los Angeles; 15Aug47;
EP16600.

SULLIVAN, OSCAR. See
Sullivan, Rollin.

SULLIVAN, ROLLIN OSCAR
Cornbread and 'Lasses (sassafrass
tea) words and music by Lloyd
(Lonzo) George & Rollin (Oscar)
Sullivan. © Ernest Tubb Music,
inc., Hollywood, Calif.;
14Nov47; EP18759.
Take Them Cold Feet Outa My Back;
words and music by Lloyd Lonzo
George and Rollin Oscar Sulli-
van. © Ernest Tubb Music, inc.,
Hollywood, Calif.; 6Aug47;
EP16155.
Take Them Cold Feet outa My
Back; words and music by Lloyd
Lonzo George and Rollin Oscar
Sullivan. © Ernest Tubb Music,
inc., Hollywood, Calif.;
29Aug47; EP16584.

SULLIVAN, WILLIAM AUGUSTUS, 1876-
Why Do You Want Me Now? Words &
music by Will Sullivan. ©
Englewood Music House, Chicago;
28Jul47; EP15994.

SUMSION, HERBERT, 1899-
A Mountain Tune; intermezzo for
string orchestra by Herbert
Sumsion. Score. [c1946] © The
Oxford University Press, London;
9Jan47; EP6097.

SUNGSIK, LEE, 1914-
[Students! Korean Folk Song] Words
by Jun Chang Ho, music by Lee
Sungsik. [n.p.] Song Hahn Lee.
© Lee Sungsik, San.Fernando,
Calif.; 16Jul47; EP15014.
Title and text in Korean.

SUNSHINE, MARION.
Cuban Countryside. (Campina.Cu-
bana) ... Spanish lyric by Don
Mario, words and music by Mari-
on Sunshine. © Antobal Music
Co., New York; 15Nov47; EP19080.
They All Look Alike to Pancho.
© Antobal Music Co., New York;
1Jul47; EP15745. For voice
and piano.

SUPERNAL PRAISES; a book of gospel
songs ... 1947. Authors: Nolin
Jeffress, Mrs. Nolin Jeffress
... Curtis Shell [and others]
© Jeffress Music Co., Crossett,
Ark.; 6Jun47; EP15212.

SUPPÉ, FRANZ VON, 1819-1895.
Poet & Peasant; plectrum guitar solo
or duet, [by] Franz von Suppé,
arr. as played by Harry Volpe.
c1939. © Albert Rocky Co., New
York; 10Jan40; on arrangement;
EP20182.

SUSCINIO, JEAN, pseud. See
Texier. Henri Gustave.

SUSSMAN, JOSEPH.
I Wasn't Born in Ireland (but I
love it just the same) © Cherio
Music Publishers, inc., New
York; 10Jul47; EP15602. For
voice and piano, with chord
symbols.

SUTHERLAND, FLOYD A
Tip-toe to Fairyland; words and
music by Floyd A. Sutherland.
[c1945] © Nordyke Publishing
Co., Los Angeles; 15Jun46;
EP20499.

SWAN, DON, 1904-
(This Time for Keeps) Hokey Joe;
lyric by Juan Ricardo, music
by Don Swan ... [from] the
M-G-M production "This Time for
Keeps." © Vanguard Songs,
Hollywood, Calif.; 16Apr47;
EP16172.

SWAN, MARY.
Just for You; words & music by
Mary Swan. © Nordyke Publishing
Co., Los Angeles; 11Oct46;
EP20320.

SWANSON, CARL J
The Valley of the Sun; words and
music by Carl J. Swanson. ©
Peer International Corp., New
York; 25Nov47; EP19835.

SWANSON, ROY W
Love Goes 'Round an' 'Round (in
this heart of mine) by Roy W.
Swanson. © Nosnaws Music Co.,
Minneapolis; 70ct47; EP17973.
For voice and piano, with chord
symbols.

SWAYNIE, ETHEL WIRT.
Darling Jeanie; words by Hersel
Eugene Gutke, music by Ethel Wirt
Swaynie. [c1946] © Nordyke Pub-
lishing Co., Los Angeles; 30Jan47;
EP20300.

SWEET, MILO.
Fight for Ol' Missou'; words and
music by Milo Sweet. Song of
University of Missouri. ©
Melrose Music Corp., New York;
25Aug47; EP16643.
Fly, Eagles, Fly; (Boston College)
words and music by Milo Sweet.
© Melrose Music Corp., New York;
25Apr47; EP17530.
Go, Mustangs, Go! Song of Southern
Methodist University; words and
music by Milo Sweet. © Melrose
Music Corp., New York; 25Aug47;
EP16681.
T. C. U. Victory Song; words and
music by Milo Sweet. Song of
Texas Christian University. ©
Melrose Music Corp., New York;
25Aug47; EP16682.

SWERDLOW, MAURIE, 1895-
Someday, You and I; by Maurie
Swerdlow. © Maurie Swerdlow,
Philadelphia; 10Nov47; EP18564.
For voice and piano, with chord
symbols.

SWIERKOS, EVELINE.
Don't Ever Leave Me; words & music
by Eveline Swierkos. © Nordyke
Publishing Co., Los Angeles;
27Sep46; EP19701.

SWIFT, FREDERIC FAY
Three Blind Mice; girls trio and
mixed chorus, S.A.B. Special
arrangement by Frederic Fay
Swift. © Belwin, inc., New York;
5Dec47; on arrangement; EP19270.
Three Humming Themes; S.A.T.B. by
Frederic Fay Swift. © Belwin,
inc., New York; 28Nov47; on
arrangement; EP19061.
Three Humming Themes; S.S.A. by
Frederic Fay Swift. © Belwin,
inc., New York; 28Nov47; on
arrangement; EP19062.

SYLVAIN, JULES.
I Kärlekens Ortagard ... musik;
Jules Sylvain, arr.; Sune
Waldimir [pseud.], text; Karl
Ewert [pseud.] © Edition Syl-
vain, a.b., Stockholm; 1Jan45;
on arrangement; EP7082. Piano-
conductor score (orchestra,
with words) and parts.
(Svarta Rosor) I Kärlekens Orta-
gärd ... ur filmen "Svarta
Rosor"; musik: Jules Sylvain,
text: Karl Ewert [pseud.] ©
Edition Sylvain, a.b., Stock-
holm; 1Jan45; EP7081.
I Kärlekens Örtagård. See his Svarta
Rosor.

SYLVIANO, RENE, pseud. See
Caffot, Sylvère Victor Joseph.

SYMONS, THOMAS.
A Song of Endurance; (unison
song for treble voices) [by]
Dom Thomas Symons. © The
Oxford University Press, London;
17Jul47; EP6136.

SZÁNTO, MIHÁLY.
Tizenhat Esztendős Barna Kis Lány.
(My Sixteen Year Old Brown-Eyed
Young Maid) English lyric by
Olga Paul, music by Szánto Mihály.
(In Pasti, Barbara, comp. Memo-
ries of Hungary. p. 20-30) ©
Edward B. Marks Music Corp., New
York; 19Nov47; on English lyric;
EP19001.

SZYMANOWSKI, KAROL, 1883-1937.
Hagith; [by] Karol Szymanowski.
Op. 25. Oper in einem Aufzug
von Felix Dörmann ... TXomaczenie
polskie Stanisxawa Baraǒca.
Wien, Universal-Edition. ©
Associated Music Publishers,
New York; 18Aug20; EP6175.
Piano-vocal score.

T

TABB, JOHN DANIEL.
My Old Mellow Moon; words and
music by John Daniel Tabb. ©
Nordyke Publishing Co., Los
Angeles; 16Sep46; EP19707.

TABET, GEORGES ZACHARIE, 1905-
Avril aux Champs-Élysées; paroles
de Georges Tabet et André Tabet,
musique de Georges Tabet, arr.
par Pierre Larrieu. © Star-
Music Co., Paris; 27Sep47;
EP6001.
De la Madeleine à l'Opéra;
paroles et musique de Georges
Tabet. © Éditions Paul Beuscher,
Paris; 15Jun45; EP6462.

TACCANI, SANDRO, 1915-
Eterna Canzone ... Perchè Mi
Sfuggi? ... [By] S. Taccani,
testo di G. Taccani. © Odeon,
s.a., Milan; 17Feb47; EP7161.
Piano-conductor score (orches-
tra, with words) and parts.
Incanto Brasiliano ... Rosetera
Cubana ... Parole di Nisa,
musica di S. Taccani. ©
Carisch, s.a., Milan; 23Jun47;
EP5774. Piano-conductor score
(orchestra, with words) and
parts.
Il Pianto del Bosco; parole di
Nisa ... musica di S. Taccani.
Ritmo Tentatore; parole do
Gianipa [pseud.] ... musica di
V. Chiosa. © Carisch, s. a.,
Milan; 8Jul47; EP6190. Piano-
conductor score (orchestra, with
words) and parts.

TAFARELLA, PETER.
Dream of Love; words by Sarina
Tafarella, music by Peter Tafarella. [c1946] © Nordyke Publishing Co., Los Angeles;
30Oct47; EP19638.

TAGELL, ROGELIO JOSÉ HUGUET Y. See
Huguet y Tagell, Rogelio José.

TAGLIAFERRI, E
The Fisher of Pusilleco. Piscatore
'e Pusilleco. English lyric by
Olga Paul, Italian lyric by E.
Murolo, music by E. Tagliaferri.
(In Memories of Italy. p.13-15)
© Edward B. Marks Music Corp,
New York; 16Jul47; on English
lyric; EP15819.
Naples and Sorrento. Napule o
Surriento. English lyric by
Olga Paul, Italian lyric by E.
Murolo, music by E. Tagliaferri.
(In Memories of Italy. p.10-12)
© Edward B. Marks Music Corp,
New York; 16Jul47; on English
lyric; EP15818.

TAGLIAFERRI, E. Cont'd.
A Serenade to Naples. Mandulinata
a Napulo. English lyric by Olga
Paul, Italian lyric by E. Murolo,
music by E. Tagliaferri. (In
Memories of Italy. p.6-9) ©
Edward B. Marks Music Corp.,
New York; 16Jul47; on English
lyric; EP15617.

TALBOTT, OVA.
We Will Sing of Glory in Victory;
words by Sophia LaFrenz and Ova
Talbott, music by Ova Talbott.
[c1945] © Nordyke Publishing
Co., Los Angeles; 15Aug47;
EP16599.

TALLMAN, ARTHUR.
My Old Log Cabin Home (down in Vir-
ginia); words and music by Arthur
Tallman. © Arthur Tallman, New
York; 10Nov47; EP19069.

TALMADGE, CHARLES L
Autumn Thoughts; four-part song
for men's voices, [music by]
Charles L. Talmadge, [words by]
Kay Clark. © Oliver Ditson Co.,
Philadelphia; 11Aug47;
EP16302.

[TANN, LEE] 1916-
Cheer, Cheer, Cheer for Michigan;
[by Lee Tann] © Lee Tann,
Chicago; 20Oct47; EP18164. For
voice and piano, with chord
symbols.

TAPPIN, HAROLD, 1879-1934.
The Owl Song; music by Harold
Tappin ... words by Frazier
Curtis ... arr. by F. M.
Rackemann. © The Owl Club,
Cambridge, Mass.; 27Oct47;
EP18816.

TARDIF, HILAIRE MARIE, FATHER, 1903-
Triptique [Harial; pour orgue.
Harian Triptych ... Par ... R.
P. Hilaire-Marie Tardif. ©
Éditions A. Passic, Lachute,
Que., Can.; 20Jul47; on 3 pieces.
Contents.- Salutation (© EP6054)-
Contemplation (© EP6055)-
Jubilation (© EP6056)

TARKOWSKI, EDDIE.
I Sing My Songs; words and music
by Eddie Tarkowski. © Nordyke
Publishing Co., Los Angeles;
19Jun47; EP17603.

TARP, SVEND ERIK, 1898-
Snap-Shots; lette Smaastykker ...
by] Svend Erik Tarp. Op. 45.
© Wilhelm Hansen, Musik-Forlag,
Copenhagen; 14Apr47; EP6295.
For piano solo.

TARRANT, RABON.
Hey, Hey, Baby; words and music
by Rabon Tarrant. © Hill and
Range Songs, inc., Hollywood,
Calif.; 29Aug47; EP16585.

TARREGA, F
Lagrima; guitar solo, [by] F. Tar-
rega, arr. as played by Harry
Volpe. c1939. © Albert Rocky
Co., New York; 10Jan40; on ar-
rangement; EP20184.

TATE, ARTHUR F
Somewhere a Voice Is Calling;
four part mixed voices S.A.T.B.,
[words by] Eileen Newton [music
by] Arthur F. Tate, arr. by
William Stickles. © Harms, inc.
New York; 3Nov39; on arrangement; EP20465.

Somewhere a Voice Is Calling;
words by Eileen Newton, music
by Arthur F. Tate, orchestrated
by Jerry Sears. Concert ed.
© Harms, inc., New York;
25Aug47; on arrangement;
EP17157. Piano-conductor
score (orchestra) and parts.

TATE, PHYLLIS.
Fifteen Fingers; new settings of
nursery rhymes for three-hand
duet, by Phyllis Tate; foreword
by Dorothy Bradley. © The Oxford
Univ. Press, London; 30Oct47; on
arrangement; EP7175. For piano
3 hands.

Little Piggy; (tune Chopsticks),
[arr. by] Phyllis Tate, [words
by] Thomas Hood. © The Oxford
University Press, London; 10Oct46;
on arrangement; EP6086. For unison
chorus and piano; melody also in
tonic sol-fa notation.

Soldier, Won't You Marry Me? [by]
Phyllis Tate, words anon. © The
Oxford University Press, London;
12Jun47; EP6160. Score: SSA;
in both staff and tonic sol-fa
notation.

TÁUBE, EVERT.
Calle Schewens Vals; av Evert
Taube, [English version by Ed-
ward Adams-Ray] © Elkan &
Schildknecht, Emil Carelius,
Stockholm; 1Jan58; EP6957. For
voice and piano.

Vals Ombord; av Evert Taube. ©
Elkan & Schildknecht, Emil Care-
lius, Stockholm; 1Jan22; EP6956.
For voice and piano.

TAUBE, OSCAR.
My Last Days on the Ranch; words
by A. W. McAllister, music by
Oscar Taube. © A. W. McAllister,
Apopka, Fla.; 17Dec47; EP20138.

TAULMAN, MILDRED B
My Garden of Love; words and music
by Mildred B. Taulman. © Nordyke
Publishing Co., Los Angeles;
15Aug47; EP19352.

[TAVERNIER, FRANÇOIS EDOUARD]
The Tavie Boogie-woogie; piano
solo [by F. E. T.] © François
Edouard Tavernier, New York;
25Jun47; EP15658.

TAYLOR, ALFRED.
Nativity Miniatures; a Christmas
suite for organ, by Alfred
Taylor. © J. Fischer & Bro.,
New York; 30Sep47; EP17704.

TAYLOR, CORWIN H
Twenty Melodic Studies; for
trombone, baritone or bassoon,
by Corwin H. Taylor. © Fillmore Bros. Co., Cincinnati;
20Aug47; EP17923.

TAYLOR, DOROTHY JOHNSON, 1912-
Now Is the Time for Christmas; for
full chorus of mixed voices a
cappella, [words] anonymous
[music by] Dorothy Johnson Taylor. © G. Schirmer, inc., New
York; 27Aug47; EP18731.

TAYLOR, EDNA.
Starlight Dance; for the piano by
Edna Taylor. © Oliver Ditson Co.,
Philadelphia; 6Dec47; EP20140.

TAYLOR, GEORGE.
Some Day; words and music by
George Taylor. © Nordyke Publish-
ing Co., Los Angeles; 17May47;
EP16905.

TAYLOR, HARTY.
Blondes, Brunettes and Redheads;
words and music by Karl Davis
and Harty Taylor. © Hill and
Range Songs, inc., Hollywood,
Calif.; 30Oct47; EP18344.

The Chapel in the Hills; words
and music by Karl Davis and
Harty Taylor. © Hill and
Range Songs, inc., Hollywood,
Calif.; 23Aug47; EP16586.

Cheatin' Women; words and music
by Karl Davis and Harty Taylor.
© Hill and Range Songs, inc.,
Hollywood, Calif.; 14Nov47;
EP18765.

That Pretty Little Face; words
and music by Karl Davis and
Harty Taylor. © Hill and
Range Songs, inc., Hollywood,
Calif.; 30Jul47; EP16045.

TAYLOR, HAYDEN.
Downbeat Boogie; by Hayden Taylor,
arr. by Geo. Evans. © Cinephonic
Music Co., ltd., London; 21Mar47;
EP6052. Parts: orchestra.

TAYLOR, MARVIN.
Oh, How I Miss You (since you
went away) words and music by
Pete Cassell and Marvin Taylor
[and The Letter That Broke My
Heart; words and music by Texas
Ruby and Curley Fox] © Peer
International Corp., New York;
27Aug47; EP17867, 17868.

TAYLOR, MARY LYON.
Life Is a Dream; author unknown,
music by Mary Lyon Taylor.
© Mary Lyon Taylor, Beverly
Hills, Calif.; 27Nov47;
EP20142.

Now, I'm Always Dreaming; words
and music by Mary Lyon Taylor.
© Mary Lyon Taylor, Beverly
Hills, Calif.; 27Nov47;
EP20143.

TAYLOR, ROUMEL WILLIAM, 1921-
Since I Gave My Heart to the Lord;
words and music by Roumel Wm.
Taylor, [arr.] by Oscar Lewis.
© Roumel Wm. Taylor, Philadelphia;
6Jul47; EP15982.

TCHAIKOVSKY, P   See
Chaikovskiĭ, Petr Il'ich.

TCHEGODAEVA, IRENA.
Gitana ... by Irena Tchegodaeva.
© The Boston Music Co., Boston;
8Aug47; EP16263. Score
(violin and piano) and part.

TCHEREPNIN, N   See
Cherepnin, N

TEAKLE, BILL.
Fight for Our Nevada ... words
and music by Bill Teakle. ©
Bill Teakle, Reno, Nev.; 80ct47;
EP17790.

TEGNÉR, ALICE CHARLOTTE (SANDSTRÖM)
1864-1943.
Dags Visor; av Jeanna Oterdahl,
tonsatta av Alice Tegnér.
2. uppl. © A. B. Nordiska
musikförlaget (in notice: Alice
Tegnér), Stockholm; 4Dec19;
EP7025. Children's songs, principally for voice and piano.

"Sjung med Oss, Mamma!" ... utg. av
A. T., med fförord av Lea. [Words
by Anna M. Roos, Ebba Westberg,
Ernest Beckman, Emmy Köhler, Karl-
Erik Forsslund, Paul Nilsson, Nat-
anael Beskow, Elsa Beskow, Åke
Easén, Fanny Alving, Lin Detjen-
berg, Mildred Thorburn-Busch, and
others] © A. B. Nordiska musik-
förlaget (in notice: Alice Tegnér),
Stockholm; häfte 1-8, 4Dec19;
EP7017-7024.

svensk Jul. Fyra sånger för unga
röster af Alice Tegnér ...
[words by] Edv. Evers ... G. L.
Silverstolpe ... [and] Z. Tope-
lius. © A. B. Nordiska musikförlaget (in notice: Alice Tegnér), Stockholm; 4Dec19; EP7016.

TELEMANN, GEORG PHILIPP, 1681-1767.
Concerto for 4 clarinets, transcribed from "Concerto for 4
violins" by Eric Simon. ©
Edward B. Marks Music Corp.,
New York; 29Sep47; on arrangement; EP17924. Clarinet I
conductor score and parts.

TEMPLE, NAT.
It's a Pleasure; by Nat Temple,
arr. by Dave Foster. [c1945]
© Cinephonic Music Co. ltd.,
London; 31Mar47; EP6041. Piano-
conductor score (orchestra, with
words) and parts.

TEMPLETON, ALEC ANDREW, 1910-
Hast Thou Not Known; S.A.T.B.
[by] Templeton. © Leeds
Music Corp., New York;
16Jun47; EP16096.

TENEBRIA, JOSEPH B
Sadness; words and music by Harriet
Milling, Robert Pollack and
Joseph B. Tenebria. © Nordyke
Publishing Co., Los Angeles;
29Apr47; EP16904.

You're Breaking My Heart That Way;
words and music by Seymour Shor-
ser and J. B. Tenebria. [c1946]
© Nordyke Publishing Co., Los
Angeles; 13Jan47; EP19740.

TEOT, DOROTHY DURETT.
Memory Rose; words and music by
Dorothy Durett Teot. © Nordyke
Publishing Co., Los Angeles;
17May47; EP16919.

TERRY, AL.
That Atomic Bomb (excuse please)
words by Jean E. Joberg, music
by Al Terry. © Nordyke Publishing Co., Los Angeles; 18Jul46;
EP20498.

TERRY, FRANCES.
Spring Mood; for the piano [by]
Frances Terry. © Oliver Ditson
Co., Philadelphia; 13Oct47;
EP18019.

TERRY URRUTIA, SANTIAGO.
Total "Pa" Qué? ... Letra y
música de Santiago Terry
Urrutia, arrg. de Pérez Prado.
© Peer International Corp.,
New York; 6Jun47; EP5739.
Parts: orchestra.

[TEXIER, HENRI GUSTAVE] 1884-   comp.
Chansons de la Mer et de la Voile;
[comp. by Jean Suscinio, pseud.;
words principally by Henry
Jacques] © Henry Lemoine & Cie,
Paris; 10Feb47; EF7294. For 1-4
voices.

THAL, JEANETTE, 1900-
Bells in the Night. Op. 10, no. 3
... [By] Jeanette Thal. © Bach
Music Co. (Henry Dellafield,
sole owner), Boston; 10Oct47;
EP18103. For piano solo, with
words.

Ding-a-ling ... [Op. 10, no. 4.By]
Jeanette Thal. © Bach Music Co.
(Henry Dellafield, sole owner),
Boston; 10Oct47; EP18104. For
piano solo, with words.

Little Goldfish. Op. 10, no. 2
... [by] Jeanette Thal. © Bach
Music Co. (Henry Dellafield,
sole owner). Boston; 10Oct47;
EP18106. For piano solo, with
words.

Prairie Flower; [by] Jeanette
Thal. © Bach Music Co. (Henry
Dellafield, sole owner), Boston;
10Oct47; EP18102. For piano
solo, with words.

Tick-tock Polka. Op. 10, no. 1.
Piano solo [by] Jeanette Thal.
© Bach Music Co. (Henry Dellafield, sole owner), Boston;
10Oct47; EP18097.

THANKSGIVING; folksong, [words by
Margarete E. Fritschel] (In Thank
the Lord for He Is Good, [p]2)
© Margarete E. Fritschel,
Clinton, Iowa; 29Oct47; EP20238.

THAYER, TILLIE.
Dreaming of a Heaven for Two;
words and music by Tillie Thayer
[c1945] © Nordyke Publishing
Co., Los Angeles; 21Jun46;
EP19767.

THÉBAULT, VALENTIN, 1901-1942.
Buscando ... Sonia ... [by] Valentin Thébault. © Éditions espagnoles Julio Garson, Paris;
14Oct47; EP7330. Piano-conductor score (orchestra) and parts.

El Vagabundo ... Olvido ... [by]
Valentin Thébault. © Éditions
espagnoles Julio Garson, Paris;
14Oct47; EF7304. Piano-conductor
score (orchestra) and parts.

THECKSTON, NORM.
A Tuneful Little Tune; words and
music by Norm Theckston. ©
Nordyke Publishing Co., Los
Angeles; 21Feb47; EP19700.

THEODORE R. FRYE PUBLISHERS. See
Frye (Theodore R) Publishers.

THIEL, OLOF.
(En Prästkrage i Min Hand) Our
Dream Chalet in the Hills; [by]
Olof Thiel, words by Harold
Philton [pseud.], English ver-
sion of the famous Swedish song
En Prästkrage i Min Hand. ©
Ascherberg, Hopwood & Crew, ltd.,
London; 5Aug47; on English words;
EF6352.

Our Dream Chalet in the Hills. See his
En Prästkrage i Min Hand.

THIMAN, ERIC H
Praise the Lord of Heaven; anthem
for mixed voices ... [Words by]
T. B. Browne, [music by] Eric H.
Thiman. © The H. W. Gray Co.,
inc., New York; 2Jul47; EP15707.
Score: SATB and organ.

THOMAS, CARL.
I've Got a Dream to Share with
You; words and music by Carl
Thomas. © Nordyke Publishing
Co., Los Angeles; 12Jul47;
EP17616.

THOMAS, DANNY.
(The Unfinished Dance) Minor
Melody; words and music by Ray
Jacobs and Danny Thomas ...
[From] "The Unfinished Dance."
© Robbins Music Corp., New York;
28Sep47; EP17142.

THOMAS, EDWARD, 1924-
Ultra-Modern Guitar Solos; by
Edward Thomas, [ed. by Harry
Volpe] © Volpe Music Co.,
Jackson Heights, L. I., N. Y.;
bk.1, 23Aug47; EP16563.

THOMAS, GEORGE ALEXANDER.
The Dominant Spirit; words and
music by George Alexander
Thomas. © Nordyke Publishing
Co., Los Angeles; 7Feb47;
EP19779.

THOMAS, HELEN.
Tippie and the Hurdy-gurdy ...
words and music by Helen Thomas. © The Boston Music Co.,
Boston; 8Dec47; EP20001.

Tippie's Love Song. © The Boston
Music Co., Boston; 18Jul47;
EP15772. For voice and piano;
arrangement for piano solo on
page at end.

THOMAS, J   J
Keep in Stride ... [by] J. J.
Thomas. © Theodore Presser
Co., Philadelphia; 31Jul47;
EP16336. For piano solo.

Waltz of Spring; piano solo by J.
J. Thomas. © Theodore Presser
Co., Philadelphia; 2Dec47;
EP19255.

Winter echoes; [by] J. J. Thomas.
© Theodore Presser Co.,
Philadelphia; 15Aug47;
EP16443. For piano solo.

THOMAS, LEWYS, 1887-
The Bells of Aberdovey; for three-
part chorus of women's voices,
Old Welsh folk song arr. by
Lewys Thomas. © The Raymond A.
Hoffman Co., Chicago; 13Dec40;
EP15578.

[THOMPSON, JOHN J   ]
Bed-time Story; piano solo by J.
J. Ames [pseud.] © The Willis
Music Co., Cincinnati; 9Dec47;
EP20005.

The Little Rocking Horse; piano
solo by J. J. Ames [pseud.]
© The Willis Music Co., Cincinnati; 25Nov47; EP19223.

Longing; piano solo by J. J. Ames
[pseud.] © The Willis Music
Co., Cincinnati; 8Dec47;
EP20009.

Maracas; piano solo by John
Thompson, jr. © The Willis
Music Co., Cincinnati; 15Aug47;
EP16425.

[THOMPSON, JOHN SYLVANUS] 1889-
The Coquette; valse for piano by
Maurice Dupin [pseud.] © Willis
Music Co., Cincinnati; 3Dec47;
EP19802.

THOMPSON, MONTE. See
Thompson, Orlando Montrose.

THOMPSON, ORLANDO MONTROSE, 1879-
I Love to See You Smile ... words
and music by Monte Thompson,
[arr. by Harold Potter] New
York, Period Publishing Co. ©
Orlando Montrose Thompson, New
York; 28Jul47; EP18562.

Yours Sincerely ... words and
music by Monte Thompson,
[arrangement by Harold Potter]
New York, Period Publishing Co.
© Orlando Montrose Thompson,
New York; 30Oct47; EP18561.

THOMPSON, VIRGIL FRANCIS, 1920-
My Pretty Little Eileen; by Virgil
Thompson. [Arr. by Thomas
Alexander Phillips] © La Mar
Music Publishers, inc., Canton,
Ohio; 8Nov47; EP17897. For
voice and piano.

[THOMPSON, WILLIAM HENRY] d. 1947.
The Spaniard That Blighted My
Life; words and music by Billy
Merson [pseud.], arr. by Jerry
Sears. © Harms, inc., New
York; 15Aug47; on arrangement;
EP16525. Piano-conductor
score (orchestra, with words)
and parts.

THOMS, SHIRLEY, 1925-
Album of Hill Billy Songs; [by]
Shirley Thoms. © D. Davis & Co.,
pty. ltd., Sydney; 15Aug47;
EF7201. Cover-title: Album of
Shirley Thoms ... Hill Billy Songs.

THOMSON, VIRGIL.
Capitals, Capitals; for four men
and a piano, [music by] Virgil
Thomson, [words by] Gertrude
Stein. (New music [a quarterly
publishing modern compositions,
v. 20, no. 3]) © Virgil Thomson, New York; 19May47; EP16166.

THORIMBERT, LAWRENCE.
I Couldn't Dream a Better Dream,
Could You? Words and music by
Lawrence Thorimbert. © Nordyke
Publishing Co., Los Angeles;
18Jul46; EP19771.

THORNE, DONALD.
Fleshlight; piano solo. [By] Donald Thorne. © Liber-Southern,
ltd., London; 15Jul47; EF5822.

THORNTON, ARMENTA FADORA DE MOSS,
1913-
Grace, Joy, Peace and Happiness;
music by Mrs. A. De Moss Thorn-
ton, words by ... Edward K.
Wilson. Los Angeles, E. K.
Wilson. © Armenta De Moss
Thornton & Edward Knox Wilson,
Los Angeles; 18Jun47; EP15474.
Close score: SATB.

THORNTON, JAMES.
When You Were Sweet Sixteen; words and music by James Thornton, arr. for male voices (T.T.B.B.) (with piano acc.) by Robert C. Haring. © Shapiro, Bernstein & Co., inc., New York; 13Nov47; on arrangement; EP18922.

TIBBLES, GEORGE.
The Old Chaperone; lyric and music by Ramez Idriss and George Tibbles. © Supreme Music Corp., New York; 10Jul47; EP15654.

TIETZE, SAMUEL.
Teardrops and a Sunbeam in Your Eyes; words and music by Samuel Tietze. © Nordyke Publishing Co., Los Angeles; 12Jun46; EP19782.

TILBORROUGH, GAIL VAN. See Van Tilborrough, Gail.

TILLERY, HUBERT.
Jolly Hollander; for piano [by] Hubert Tillery. © Theodore Presser Co., Philadelphia; 6Dec47; EP20445.

TILLIA, HENRY.
Swinging in the Same Old Swing; by Herbert Gray [and] Henry Tillia. © Lake Music Publishing Co., New York; 18Oct47; EP18169. For voice and piano, with chord symbols.

TILLMAN, FLOYD.
Gotta Have Somethin'; words and music by Floyd Tillman. © Peer International Corp., New York; 25Nov47; EP19833.

TINTORER, FERNANDO. See Tintorer Sardiña, Fernando.

TINTORER SARDIÑA, FERNANDO, 1923-
El Caballo con Tres Frenos ... arreglo de: Tito Pérez, letra y música de Fernando Tintorer. © Fernando Tintorer Sardiña, Perico, Cuba; 1Dec47; EF7280. Piano-conductor score: orchestra.

Dime ¿Por Que Tu Eres Así? ... letra y música de: Fernando Tintorer, Perico, Cuba; 10Dec47; EF7274.

TINTURIN, PETER.
Santa Claus for President; words and music by Peter Tinturin. © Edwin H. Morris & Co., inc., New York; 12Aug47; EP16406.

Your Wish Is My Command! Words and music by Peter Tinturin. © Martin Music, Hollywood, Calif.; 23Jun47; EP17074.

TIOMKIN, DIMITRI.
Duel in the Sun (A duel of two hearts); music by Dimitri Tiomkin, lyric by Stanley Adams [and] Maxson F. Judell, love theme from ... "Duel in the sun." © Bourne, inc., New York; 27Jun47; EP15294.

"The Long Night;" lyrics by Ned Washington, music by Dimitri Tiomkin (based on theme from the seventh symphony by L. van Beethoven) ... [from the picture] The Long Night. © Dreyer Music Corp., New York; 3Dec47; EP19559.

TIPPETT, MICHAEL KEMP, 1905-
Preludio al Vespro di Monteverdi. For organ [by] Michael Tippett. © Schott & Co., ltd., London; 30May47; EF5792.

TITCOMB, EVERETT.
Jesus! Name of Wondrous Love ... for mixed voices [by] Everett Titcomb, [words by] W. Walsham How. © B. F. Wood Music Co., Boston; 26Dec47; EP20505.

TOBIAS, CHARLES, 1897-
The Mistletoe Song; words and music by Jack Owens and Charles Tobias. © Triangle Music Corp., New York; 1Dec47; EP19829.

TOBIN, LEW. See Tobin, Louis.

TOBIN, LOU. See Tobin, Louis.

TOBIN, LOUIS, 1904-
Another Man's Wife; words by A. W. McAlister, music by Lew Tobin. © A. W. McAlister, Apopka, Fla.; 8Oct47; EP17985.

The Army's Little Jeep; words by E. B. Sawyer, music by Lew Tobin. © Nordyke Publishing Co., Los Angeles; 2Dec46; EP19631.

Beautiful Hawaiian Islands of Love; words by Michael B. Valyo, music by Lew Tobin. © Nordyke Publishing Co., Los Angeles; 14Jun47; EP17550.

A Corner of My Heart; words by Lucille Hansen, music by Lew Tobin. © Nordyke Publishing Co., Los Angeles; 16Dec46; EP19950.

Darn It, Oh Darn It! She Knows (Heavenly Rose); words by Ed. J. Albright, music by Lew Tobin. © Ed. J. Albright, Wilmington, Ohio; 18Jul47; EP15690.

Desire; words by Audrey M. Wolf, music by Lew Tobin. © Nordyke Publishing Co., Los Angeles; 29Jan47; EP19766.

How'd You Like a Honeymooning? Words by V. J. Leotta, music by Lew Tobin. © Nordyke Publishing Co., Los Angeles; 25May46; EP19936.

Hurray! It's All Over, Over There; words by Michael Grella, music by Lew Tobin. © Nordyke Publishing Co., Los Angeles; 14Nov46; EP19955.

I Am a Soldier of the U.S.A.; words by Thelma Crockett, music by Lew Tobin. © Nordyke Publishing Co., Los Angeles; 5Jun47; EP17544.

I Knew Some Day I'd Meet Someone Like You; words by William H. Wilford, music by Lew Tobin. © William H. Wilford, Brooklyn; 14Jun47; EP15473.

I Love No One But You; words by Walter S. Sims, music by Lew Tobin. © Nordyke Publishing Co., Los Angeles; 22Apr47; EP17536.

I Still Remember; words by Domenick E. Schiavo, music by Lew Tobin. Brooklyn, C. Coleman, New York, selling agent, T. J. Lace. © Domenick Edward Schiavo, Brooklyn; 25Sep47; EP17336.

I'm in Love with You, Darling; words by Edmund B. Barrow, music by Lew Tobin. © Nordyke Publishing Co., Los Angeles; 16Jul47; EP17619.

Just Memories; words by Mollie McMullen, music by Lew Tobin. © Nordyke Publishing Co., Los Angeles; 27Jul46; EP19945.

Keep a Cool Head and Wear a Warm Smile; words by James W. Jewell, music by Lew Tobin. © Nordyke Publishing Co., Los Angeles; 21Aug47; EP19336.

Love-Hungry Heart; words by Louise Kuykendall, music by Lew Tobin. © Nordyke Publishing Co., Los Angeles; 29Apr47; EP16817.

Moon Gazing; words by Ashod K. Mirigian, music by Lew Tobin. © Nordyke Publishing Co., Los Angeles; 15Nov46; EP20334.

My Darling Today; words by Carl G. Carlson, music by Lew Tobin. © Bruce Humphries, inc., Boston; 3Sep47; EP17092.

My Heart Beats Only for You, Dear; words by Bill Wolters, music by Lew Tobin. © Nordyke Publishing Co., Los Angeles; 23Jan46; EP17538.

My Home; music by Lew Tobin, words by Louise Jotsch. © Louise Jotsch, Chicago; 25Aug47; EP16615.

My Love for You; words by Nellda Clark, music by Lew Tobin. [c1945] © Nordyke Publishing Co., Los Angeles; 14Jun46; EP20333.

My! My! Words by George Shingleton, music by Lew Tobin. © Nordyke Publishing Co., Los Angeles; 11Oct46; EP19716.

My Prayer; words by Edna Skipper, music by Lew Tobin. © Nordyke Publishing Co., Los Angeles; 14Nov46; EP19711.

My Selfish Prayer; words by George W. Wyatt, music by Lew Tobin. © Nordyke Publishing Co., Los Angeles; 2Jul46; EP19470.

No Moonlight, No Song; words by Art Hubbard, music by Lew Tobin. © Nordyke Publishing Co., Los Angeles; 25May46; EP19423.

Only the Thought of Her (is left to me now); words by Georgetta Sim, music by Lew Tobin. © Nordyke Publishing Co., Los Angeles; 29Jan47; EP19737.

Rustic Maid; words by Paul Florio, music by Lew Tobin. © Bruce Humphries, inc., Boston; 15Sep47; EF17094.

Set Me Aside; words by Lonnie Stidham, music by Lew Tobin. © Nordyke Publishing Co., Los Angeles; 31May46; EP20328.

Sugar Bowl; words by Emmit O'Banion, music by Lew Tobin. © Nordyke Publishing Co., Los Angeles; 28Mar47; EP16787.

Sugar Puss; words by Nicholas Luke [pseud.], music by Lew Tobin. © Bruce Humphries, inc., Boston; 11Sep47; EP17093.

Sweet Eilean; words by Fern Pratt, music by Lew Tobin. © Nordyke Publishing Co., Los Angeles; 3Dec46; EP20028.

Swinging Back; words by Stanford A. Wilson, music by Lew Tobin. © Nordyke Publishing Co., Los Angeles; 1Jul46; EP19775.

That Light in Your Eyes; words by George C. Rochow, music by Lew Tobin. © Nordyke Publishing Co., Los Angeles; 9Nov46; EP20056.

There'll Be Another Christmas; words by Waldor Haggans, music by Lew Tobin. © Nordyke Publishing Co., Los Angeles; 10Jun47; EP16915.

To My Gal; words by Mrs. Willie Waters, music by Lew Tobin. [c1945] © Nordyke Publishing Co., Los Angeles; 14Jun46; EP20497.

Twilight Shadows; words by Janet L. Syme, music by Lew Tobin. © Nordyke Publishing Co., Los Angeles; 11Jun46; EP20304.

The Victory Waltz; words by Mrs. J. Majeska, music by Lew Tobin. © Nordyke Publishing Co., Los Angeles; 25May46; EP20377.

Was Still Another Thing; words by Gertie Banford, music by Lew Tobin. © Nordyke Publishing Co., Los Angeles; 22Aug47; EP20070.

TOBIN, LOUIS. Cont'd.
We Are Going to Build a Highway
to the Sky; words by David
Vaughn, music by Lew Tobin.
© Nordyke Publishing Co., Los
Angeles; 5Aug47; EP19541.

When You're Around; words by
Robert Griffin, music by Lew
Tobin. © Nordyke Publishing
Co., Los Angeles; 12Apr47;
EP16796.

Wild Rose; words by Christie A.
Collins, music by Lew Tobin.
[c1946] © Nordyke Publishing
Co., Los Angeles; 15Feb47;
EP19399.

You Waited Too Long; words by
Bert Cooper, music by Lew
Tobin. © Nordyke Publishing
Co., Los Angeles; 27Mar47;
EP16783.

TOCE, ANDY.
The Trail to the Rio Grande;
words by Howard Boyer, music by
Andy Toce. [c1946] © Nordyke
Publishing Co., Los Angeles;
30Jan47; EP16794.

TOCH, ERNST, 1887-
Ideas; piano solo, [by] Ernst
Toch. © Delkas Music Publishing
Co., Los Angeles; 14Jul47;
EP15996.

TODD, E   COX, 1895-
Sambo's Banjo; piano solo by E.
Cox Todd. © Belwin, inc., New
York; 13Oct47; EP18011.

Tulip Time; piano solo [by] E.
Cox Todd. © Belwin, inc., New
York; 13Oct47; EP18014.

The Weasel Goes Modern; piano
solo [by] E. Cox Todd. © Belwin, inc., New York; 13Oct47;
EP18015.

TODD, M   FLORA.
Out of the Depths; for three-part
chorus of women's voices with
alto solo and organ or piano
accompaniment, Psalm 150 [by]
M. Flora Todd. © The Willis
Music Co., Cincinnati; 30Sep47;
EP17741.

TOELLE, FRANCES B
The Forest of Two Blue Skies;
three-part chorus for women's
voices with piano acc. Words
by Don Blanding, music by
Frances B. Toelle. © R. L.
Huntzinger, inc., Cincinnati;
17Nov47; EP19221.

TOLLERTON, NELLIE.
The Green Hills of Ireland; by
Billy Beadell & Nellie Tollerton.
© Cinephonic Music Co., ltd.,
London; 29Apr47; EF6025. For
voice and piano, with chord
symbols; melody also in tonic
sol-fa notation.

TOMASI, HENRI FREDIEN, 1901-
Les Gars de la Provence ...
d'Henri Tomasi ... arr. pour
harmonie ou fanfare par E. Alf
Borda. © Alphonse Leduc & Co.,
Éditions musicales, Paris;
30Jun47; EF6422. Condensed
score (band) and parts.

TOMMY TRENT'S DIXIE FUN BARN; song
folio, by Tommy Trent, Wally
Fowler, Curly Kinsey, and
others] © Wallace Fowler Publications, Nashville; no.1,
22Sep47; EP18232.

TONNER, PAUL.
The Musical Powder Box; by Paul
Tonner. © McKinley Publishers,
inc., Chicago; 10Nov47; EP18708.
For piano solo.

Scout Patrol; by Paul Tonner.
© McKinley Publishers, inc.,
Chicago; 10Nov47; EP18716. For
piano solo.

Silhouette; by Paul Tonner. ©
McKinley Publishers, inc.,
Chicago; 10Nov47; EP18710. For
piano solo.

The Silver Fawn; by Paul Tonner.
© McKinley Publishers, inc.,
Chicago; 10Nov47; EP18709. For
piano solo.

Thumbs Up, Thumbs Down; by Paul
Tonner. © McKinley Publishers,
inc., New York; 10Nov47;
EP18717. For piano solo.

TOOGOOD, EDWARD.
I'm Happy Again, It Is Spring;
words and music by Edward Toogood. © Nordyke Publishing Co.,
Los Angeles; 11Aug47; EP19790.

TORCH, SIDNEY.
Samba Sud; composed and arr. by
Sidney Torch. © Chappell &
Co., ltd., London; 22Aug47; on
arrangement; EF6385. Piano-
conductor score (orchestra) and
parts.

TORJUSSEN, TRYGVE, 1885-
Carnival; suite for piano, four
hands, by Trygve Torjussen.
Op.68. © Arthur P. Schmidt Co.,
Boston; v.3-4, 7Aug47. Contents.- 3. Tango (© EP16112) -
4. Danse Grotesque (© EP16111)

A Summer Reverie, [by] Trygve
Torjussen. Op.7, no.4. Arr.
by Hugo Norden. © The Arthur
P. Schmidt Co., Boston; 4Sep47;
on arrangement; EP16642. Score
(violin and piano) and part.

TORONTO. CONSERVATORY OF MUSIC.
Pianoforte Examination; [comp. &
arr. by Mary MacKinnon Shore]
Oakville, Can., F. Harris Music Co.,
ltd. © Royal Conservatory of Music
of Toronto; grade 7, 20Nov47;
on arrangement & compilation;
EF7138.

Pianoforte Examination; [comp. and
ed. by Mary MacKinnon Shore] Oakville, Can., Frederick Harris Music
Co. © Royal Conservatory of Music
of Toronto; grade 4, 17Jul47; on
compilation & editing; EF7188.

Pianoforte Examination; [comp. by
F. C. Silvester, ed. and arr. by
Boris Berlin and others, final
editing by Ettore Mazzoleni] ©
Frederick Harris Music Co., ltd.,
Oakville, Ont., Can.; grade 1,
19Jun47; grade 2, 28Aug47; ©
Royal Conservatory of Music of
Toronto; grade 3, 28Aug47; grade
5, 21Aug47; grade 6, 28Oct47;
(on arrangement & compilation
by Mary M. Shore; EF6674, 6677,
6676, 6675, 6934.

[TORRE, JOSEPH] 1893-
La Pianola ... solo for piano
accordion [by] J. Torre, arr.
by J. Peppino. New York, O. Di
Bella. New York; 3Nov47; EP19915.

TORRIENTE PILDEROT, ENRIQUE.
Pensamiento Mío ... letra y
música de Enrique Torriente
Pilderot, arreglo de Ramón
Valdés (Bebo) © Peer International Corp., New York;
30Sep47; EF6826. Parts: orchestra.

TOSTI, F   PAOLO.
Good Bye; (paraphrase) [by] F.
Paolo Tosti ... piano solo [arr.
by] Carl Richter. © Bach
Music Co., Henry Dellafield,
sole owner, Boston; 15Sep47; on
simplified arrangement; EP17705.

TOUGH, SHIRLEY.
Pal of My Heart; words and music
by Shirley Tough. [c1946]
© Nordyke Publishing Co., Los
Angeles; 28Jan47; EP19960.

TOURNIER, MARCEL LUCIEN.
Fresque marine; pour la harpe, [by]
Marcel Tournier. © Henry Lemoine
& Cie, Paris; 31Dec46; EF3504.

TOUTJEAN, VARTAN, 1897-
Little Miss Jealousy; music by
Vartan Toutjean, lyrics by Lee
Anderson. Oakland, Calif.,
Toutjean Studios. © Lee
Anderson & Vartan Toutjean,
Oakland, Calif.; 11Aug47;
EP16314.

Modern Piano in the Modern Manner;
condensed harmony for instructor
and student by Vartan Toutjean Jr.,
in collaboration with Prof. Joseph
von Hoenigsmann. Oakland, Calif.,
Modern Music Publications. © Vartan Toutjean, jr. & Joseph von
Hoenigsmann, Oakland, Calif.;
7Nov47; AA35998.

TOVEY, CHARLES.
It's a Great Life (if you don't
weaken); words by Clarkson Rose,
music by Charles Tovey, ukulele
arr. by R. S. Stoduon. © B. Fel-
man & Co., ltd., London; 5Dec47;
EF7202.

TOVEY, HERBERT G
Coming Then for Me ... Words by
Lora Petty Horton, music by
Herbert G. Tovey. © Lora Petty
Horton, Fulton, Ky.; 16Jun47;
EP16057. Close score: SATB.

Peace, Be Still ... Words by Lora
Petty Horton, music by Herbert
G. Tovey. © Lora Petty Horton,
Fulton, Ky.; 16Jun47; EP16056.
Close score: SATB.

Yielding; [by] Herbert G. Tovey,
[words by] Albert C. Stewart.
© Albert Cheston Stewart,
Tucson, Ariz.; 19Sep47;
EP17332. Close score: SATB.

TOWERS, LEE, pseud. See
Blitz, Leonard.

TOWERS, LEO.
The Little Old Mill (went 'round
and 'round) ... By Don Pelosi,
Lewis Ilda and Leo Towers ...
arr. by Paul Weirick. New York,
Shapiro, Bernstein. © Irwin
Dash Music Co., ltd., London;
30ct47; on arrangement; EP17795.
Piano-conductor score (orchestra
with words) and parts.

TOWSLEY, FLORENCE A
Marchas for piano ... by Florence
A. Towsley. © Florence A. Towsley, Battle Creek, Mich.; v.2,
11Jul47; EF1602L. Vol.2 includes the song, A New Day, with
words by Nettie Hahn.

TOYAS, PETER.
The Night That I First Met You;
words and music by Peter Toyas.
© Nordyke Publishing Co., Los
Angeles; 19Jun47; EP17423.

TRABUCCO, ROSE M
It Can't Be True; words and music
by Rose M. Trabucco. © Nordyke
Publishing Co., Los Angeles;
21Feb47; EP16777.

TRAFICANTE, EDWARD, 1903-
The Traficante Certified System for
Piano Accordion. © Edward Trafi-
cante, Minneapolis; 15Nov47;
AA68951.

[TRAFICANTE, EDWARD] 1903-   comp.
and arr.
The Traficante Certified System;
sacred series of solos with
duet acc. for piano accordion,
[rev. and ed. by E. Traficante]
© Edward Traficante, Minneapolis;
1May47; EP15554.

TRAINA, TEDDY.
My Future Is You; words and music
by Teddy Traina. © Nordyke
Publishing Co., Los Angeles;
20Aug47; EP19679.

TRAMS, CHARLES H 1904-
Who's Laughing Now; words and music by Drewey King and C. H.
Trams. © Chords Music Publishers, New York; 4Oct47; EP20256.

TRANCHANT, JEAN HONORE, 1904-
L'Amour Est un Jeu; paroles de
Jean Tranchant, musique de Jean
H. Tranchant. © Éditions Paul
Beuscher, Paris; 15Jun45;
EF6453.

TRAVIS, BOBBS.
Parade of the Wooden Toys; for
the piano, by Bobbs Travis. ©
G. Schirmer, inc., New York;
16Jun47; EP16686.

Playing Tag; for the piano, by
Bobbs Travis. © G. Schirmer,
inc., New York; 16Jun47;
EP16687.

TRAVIS, STAN.
Yesterday; words and music by Stan
Travis. © R S Rose Pub. Co.,
Philadelphia; 17Nov47; EP19023.

[TRAVNICEK, ANDRÉ] 1898-
Barbara la Créole ... Paroles de
Georges Thibault, musique de A.
T. Cekow, [pseud. and Ovacion
... Musique de A. T. Cekow,
pseud.] © Éditions Musicales
A. T. Cekow, Paris; 2Apr47;
EF5891. Parts: orchestra.

Dans Tes Yeux ... [words by Noël
Tomi, pseud.] Étoile des Tropiques; [music by] A. T. Cekow
[pseud.] © Éditions Musicales A.
T. Cekow, Paris; 2Jul47; EF6580.
Piano-conductor score (orchestra,
with words) and parts.

La Entrada ... [and Flores Rojas]
musique de A. T. Cekow [pseud.]
© Éditions Musicales A. T.
Cekow, Paris; 2Jul47; EF6578.
Piano-conductor score (orches-
tra) and parts.

Toujours Fin Prêt ... Musique de
A. T. Cekow, [pseud.] © Éditions
Musicales A. T. Cekow, Paris;
2Apr47; EF5890. Parts: orchestra.

TRECATE, LUIGI FERRARI, 1884-
Dal Pollice al Mignolo ...
pezzetti facilissimi per
pianoforte sulle 5 note, con
poesiole popolari. © Carisch,
s.a., Milan; v. 1-2, 31May47;
EF3975-3976.

TREHARNE, BRYCESON, 1879-
The Garden of Jamshyd; for four-
part chorus of men's voices,
[by] Bryceson Treharne, [words
by] Leigh Henry. © The Boston
Music Co., Boston; 29Apr47;
Er17003.

[TREHARNE, BRYCESON] 1879- arr.
Music Lovers' Piano Duets ... comp.
and arr. by Chester Wallis [pseud]
© Boston Music Co., Boston; bk.2,
24Nov47; on arrangement & compilation; EP19807.

[TREHARNE, BRYCESON] 1879- comp.
Finger Tricks; technic at the
piano, comp., titled and fingered
by Peter Randall [pseud.]
© The Boston Music Co., Boston;
bk. 1, 18Sep47; on compilation
& fingering; EP17302.

TRENET, CHARLES.
Coeur de Palmier; chanson genre
1925, paroles de Charles
Tranet, musique de Charles
Trenet & Albert Lasry. Paris,
En vente aux Éditions R.
Breton. © Éditions Vianelly,
Paris; 18Jun47; EF3937.

Douce France ... paroles et
musique de Charles Trenet,
arrt de Francis Salabert ...
Tout Cela N'est Rien sans
Vous ... paroles de Vincent
Télly [pseud.], musique de
Learsi [pseud.], arrt de
Francis Salbert. © Éditions
Salabert, Paris; 2Jun47; EF5926.
Piano-conductor score (orchestra,
with words) and parts.

Gala Poté ... Paroles de Charles
Trenet, musique de Charles
Trenet & Aloert Losry. ©
Éditions Vianelly, Paris;
18Jul47; EF5839.

Le Minou, le Cancon, la Baye ...
Paroles [de Charles Trenet],
musique de Charles Trenet &
[Albert Lasry] © Éditions
Vianelly, Paris; 18Jul47;
EF5838.

Rêve Espagnol; paroles de
Charles Trenet, musique de
Charles Trenet & André Popp.
Paris, R. Breton. © France
Music, New York; 9Jul47;
EF5772.

Votre Visage; paroles de Charles
Trenet, musique de Charles Tre-
net et Louis Unia. Paris, R.
Breton. © France Music Co.,
New York; 3Nov47; EF7028.

TRENET, LOUIS CHARLES. See
Trenet, Charles.

TREVANE, GEORGE.
Love and Hate; song, words & music
by George Trevare. © Chappell
& Co., ltd., Sydney; 22Jul47;
EF6364.

They Said It Wouldn't Last; words
and music by George Trevare. ©
D. Davis & Co., pty. ltd., Sydney;
15Aug47; EF7167.

TREVIÑO, PACO.
Por Qué Te Quieres Ir ... letra y
música de Paco Treviño, [arr.
by Robbins Music Corp.] © Robbins Music Corp., New York;
29Aug47; on arrangement;
EP17735.

Por Que To Quieres Ir ... música
y letra de Paco Treviño, arr do
Ramon Marquez. © Hnos. Marquez
Editores, Mexico; 30Apr44;
EF6181. Piano-conductor score
(orchestra) and parts.

TRIBBETT, SYLVIA.
Lord, Build Me a Cabin; [by] S.
Tribbett, [arr. by Edward G.
Margetson] © Tribbett's Music
Studio (Sylvia Tribbett, sole
owner) New York; 16Oct47;
EP18379.

TRISTAN, YVON EMILE, 1908-
Ma Bella Rumba; paroles de Ser-
gelys [pseud.], musique de
Yvon Tristan et Armand Fort.
© Éditions E.M.U.L., Paris;
30Dec46; EF6491.

TROTTER, GWYNNETH.
The Young Fiddler; early exercises
by Gwynneth Trotter, pianoforte
accompaniments by Kathleen Richards. © Elkin & Co., ltd.,
London; bk.1-2, 5Nov47; EF7127-
7128. Score (violin and piano)
and part.

TROUP, BOBBY, 1918-
Hickory Dickory Dock; [by] Bobby
Troup. © P.D.S. Music Publish-
ers, Hollywood, Calif.; 10Oct47;
EP18166. For voice and piano,
with chord symbols.

TRUMAN, CHARLES.
Your Star is Next to Venus, Dear;
words and music by Charles Truman. © Nordyke Publishing Co.,
Los Angeles; 16Jul47; EP17459.

TRUSSELLE, STANLEY P
Lament; [by] Stanley P. Trusselle.
© Theodore Presser Co., Philadelphia; 5Sep47; EP17278. Score
(violin and piano) and part.

The Windowpane; words by
Elizabeth Charles Welborn,
music by Stanley P. Trusselle.
© The John Church Co.,
Philadelphia; 31Jul47; EP16335.

TRYNER, FRANK.
Dutchman's Waltz; [for] concertina,
arr. by Joseph P. Elsnic.
© Vitak-Elsnic Co., Chicago;
21Feb47; on arrangement;
EP15758.

TRYON, EVERETTE EDDIE, 1893-
Daytona; words by Pete Salter,
music by Everette Eddie Tryon.
© Musicmakers, inc., Philadelphia; 15Sep47; EP17254.

TSCHAIKOWSKY, PETER. See
Chaikovskii, Petr Il'ich.

TSCHESNOKOFF, EDWARD. See
Chesnokov

TUBIN, EDWARD, 1905-
(Sonatine, piano) Sonatine ...
par Edvard Tubin. © Körlings
förlag.a.-b., Stockholm; 1Jan47;
EF6685.

TUCCI, TERIG.
La Bamba de Vera Cruz ... music
by Terig Tucci, English lyric by
Ted Mossman, Spanish lyric by
Chuco Navarro. Arr. by Johnny
Warrington. © Kelton, inc.,
New York; 22Mar47; on arrange-
ment; EF16432. Piano-
conductor score (orchestra, with
words) and parts.

TUCKER, ADA FOUTZ, 1904-
Hello; words by Duane Foutz,
music by Ada Tucker. Ogden,
Utah, A. Tucker. © Charles
Duane Foutz & Ada Foutz
Tucker, Ogden, Utah; 31Jul47;
EP18006.

TUCKER, E MONROE.
Goody Goody for You; by Frank A.
Haywood and E. Monroe Tucker.
© Nordyke Publishing Co., Los
Angeles; 13Jun47; EP15855. For
voice and piano, with chord
symbols.

I Know a Lot of Things; by Frank
A. Haywood and E. Monroe Tucker.
© Nordyke Publishing Co., Los
Angeles; 13Jun47; EP15853. For
voice and piano, with chord
symbols.

Love Me or Let Me Go; by Frank A.
Haywood and E. Monroe Tucker.
© Nordyke Publishing Co., Los
Angeles; 13Jun47; EP15854. For
voice and piano, with chord
symbols.

TUCKER, JOHN ALOYSEUS.
When You Walked Out with Shoes
on (I knew you were gone for
good); words by Doyle Williams,
music by Johnny Tucker. © Bob
Miller, inc., New York; 27Oct47;
EP18605.

TUELL, MARY JO.
So Thrilling; words and music by
Mary Jo Tuell. © Nordyke
Publishing Co., Los Angeles;
24Jul47; EP17599.

TULLAR, GRANT COLFAX, 1869-
That's Why I Love Jesus So ...
[by] Grant Colfax Tullar.
Glendale, Calif., Gospel
Music. © Phil Kerr, Glendale,
Calif.; 15Jul47; EP16450.
Close score: SATB.

Thou Art My Light at Eventide;
[words by] Gertrude Tullar
Pratt ... [music by] Grant
Colfax Tullar. © Mrs. Constance Pratt Swetenburg, Anderson, S. C.; 10Nov47; EP18613.

364

TURINA, JOAQUIN.
Rincón Mágico; desfile en forma
de sonata, para piano, [by] J.
Turina. [Op. 97] © Union
Musical Española, Madrid;
30Dec46; EF5675.

TURNER, ELIZABETH WILHELMSEN.
Copenhagen Waltz; music by Eliza-
beth Wilhelmsen Turner, arr.
by Prof. Emilio O'Brien Motta.
© Elizabeth Wilhelmsen Turner,
McComb, Miss.; 30Jun47; EP15691.

TURNER, EVA MAE.
Heaven Is My Home ... words and
music by Eva Turner. © Eva
Turner, Indianapolis; 11Aug47;
EP16288. Close score; SATB.

Take Jesus for Your Friend ...
arr. ... words and music by Eva
Turner. © Eva Mae Turner,
Indianapolis; 3Nov47; EP18585.

TURNER, JOE.
I'm Walking through Heaven with
You; words and music by Joe
Turner. © New Era Music Corp.,
New York; 25Jul47; EP15963.

TURNER, LEE.
We'll Soon Reach That Heaven;
words by Estella M. Snyder,
music by Lee Turner. [c1945] ©
Nordyke Publishing Co., Los
Angeles; 24Jun46; EP20311.

TURNER, MILTON M
Don't Disturb My Day Dream; words
and music by Milton M. Turner.
© Nordyke Publishing Co., Los
Angeles; 29May47; EP16834.

TURNER, ZEB, 1918-
Old Chihuahua City; words and
music by Wally Fowler, Cecil C.
Wilson and Zeb Turner. © F & M
Publishing Co., inc., New York;
20Oct47; EP18522.

Songs by Zeb Turner and His Fire-
side Boys; [words and music by
Zeb Turner, Wally Fowler, Curly
Kinsey, and others] © Wallace
Fowler Publications, Nashville;
22Sep47; EP18233.

You Hit the Nail Right on the
Head; words and music by Ernest
Tubb and Zeb Turner. © Ernest
Tubb Music, inc., Hollywood,
Calif.; 29Aug47; EP17930.

TURNEY, NORMA DEARBORN, 1897-
Four Chorus Gems; by Norma Dear-
born Turney and Jennie Lind
Dearborn Turney. © Norma
Dearborn Turney, Waverly, N. Y.;
30Apr47; EP17646.

TWYEFFORT, BARBARA, 1918-
Theme and Six Variations for organ
on "The Hebrew Children," [by]
Barbara Twyeffort. © Barbara
Twyeffort, New Rochelle, N. Y.;
27Jul47; on arrangement;
EP15996.

TYLE, RODNEY VAN. See
Van Tyle, Rodney.

TYLER, JOHNNY.
Jealous Blues; words and music by
Johnnie Bias and Johnny Tyler.
© Hill and Range Songs, inc.,
Hollywood, Calif.; 15Dec47;
EP20131.

TYNAN, THERON TIVERTON, 1891-
Rodeo Time in Sheridan, Wyo.;
[words and music by T. T.
Tynan. c1946] © T. T. Tynan,
Sheridan, Wyo.; 18Jul47;
EP16694.

TYSZKIEWICZ, ROGER LELIWA- See
Leliwa-Tyszkiewicz, Roger.

U

[ULLVÉN, UNO HJ   ]
GSW-Polka; [by] Brink [pseud.,
and] Byrd [pseud.] Stockholm,
Musikaliska knuten. © Novelty
Music Edition, Spånga, Sweden;
1Jan46; EP7087. For accordion
or piano.

I Väntan på Juntan ... [by] Brink
[pseud., and] Byrd [pseud.],
text: Jerico [pseud.] Stockholm, Musikaliska knuten. ©
Novelty Music Edition, Spånga,
Sweden; 1Jan45; EP7089. Piano-
conductor score (orchestra) and
parts.

Tango Intime; [by] Arturo Medina
[pseud.] arr.: E. Schleich.
Stockholm, Musikaliska knuten.
© Novelty Music Edition, Spånga,
Sweden; 1Jan46; EP7051. Piano-
conductor score (orchestra) and
parts.

ULMER, GEORGES, 1919-
Goût de Miel; paroles de Georges
Ulmer & Géo Koger [pseud.]
musique de Georges Ulmer &
Jean Payrac. © Éditions
Robert Salvet, Paris; 28Jun46;
EF5932.

Hôtel des Artistes. See his On A Volé
une Étoile.

Un Monsieur Attendait; paroles
... [and] musique de Georges
Ulmer & Géo Koger [pseud.]
© Éditions Musicales Robert
Salvet, Paris; 31Jan47; EF5928.

Nuits de Paris. See his On A Volé une
Étoile.

(On A Volé une Étoile) Hôtel des
Artistes, de l'opérette "On a
Volé une Étoile." Livret de
Jean Valmy [pseud.] & Géo Koger
[pseud.] ... musique de Georges
Ulmer. © Éditions Robert
Salvet, Paris; 30Apr47; EF6865.
For voice and piano, with chord
symbols.

(On A Volé une Étoile) Nuits de
Paris, de l'opérette On A Volé
une Étoile, livret de Jean Valmy
& Géo Koger [pseud.], ... musique
de Georges Ulmer. © Éditions
Robert Salvet, Paris; 30Apr47;
EF5930.

Un Petit Bout de Femme ...
paroles de Georges Ulmer &
Géo Koger [pseud.], musique
de Guy Luypaerts. ©
Éditions Robert Salvet,
Paris; 31Jan46; on arrangement; EF5950.

Quelqu'un Pleure; paroles de:
Georges Ulmer, musique de:
Georges Ulmer & Marius Coste.
© Éditions Robert Salvet,
Paris; 30Jun46; EF5929.

UNDER THE STARLIGHT; a Christmas
Service. © Tullar-Meredith Co.,
New York; 15Sep47; EP17888.
Partly for voice and piano;
partly close score: SATB.

[UNDERWOOD, CLEDA GRAY] 1888-
Centennial Whiskers; [lyric by]
Vesta Crawford, music by Cleda
Gray] Salt Lake City, C. G.
Underwood. © Vesta Pierce
Crawford [and] Cleda Gray
Underwood, Salt Lake City;
21Jun47; EP15950.

URBAN, MAX.
(Los Misterios del Hampa) El
Último Tango, de la película,
Los Misterios del Hampa; letra:
Fernando Fernández, música: Max
Urban. © Ediciones Atlas, s.a.,
México; 29Nov46; EF7772.

El Último Tango. See his Los Misterios
del Hampa.

URBANO, AL.
It's Like a Trip to Tipperary; words
and music by Kay Twomey, Al Goodhart and Al Urbano. © Mutual
Music Society, inc., New York;
25Aug47; EP16613.

Serenade of the Bells; words and
music by Kay Twomey ... Al Goodhart ... and Al Urbano. © Woodward Music, inc., New York;
7Jul47; EP15437.

URDAHL, O   N
Because; music by O. N. Urdahl.
© O. N. Urdahl, Minneapolis;
30Jun47; EP15547. For piano
solo.

URRUTIA, SANTIAGO TERRY. See
Terry Urrutia, Santiago.

V

VAIRIN, LOUISE.
Songs for voice and piano; [by]
Louise Vairin, poems by Lily
Strickland. © Elkan-Vogel Co.,
inc., Philadelphia; 26Jun47; on
4 songs. Contents.- [v.1] Oh,
Sweet Be Your Slumber (© EP15844)
- [v.2] Roses Remind Me (© EP15845)
- [v.3] Here in the Garden, Beloved (© EP15847)- [v.4] Springtime (© EP15848).

VAL, JACK, 1897-
All Dressed Up with a Broken Heart
... By Fred Patrick, Claude
Reese and Jack Val, arr. by Paul
Weirick. © Edward B. Marks
Music Corp., New York; 19Nov47;
on arrangement; EP18987. Piano-
conductor score (orchestra, with
words) and parts.

I Can't Go on Like This; words and
music by Fred Patrick, Claude
Reese [and] Jack Val. © Sunset
Music Publishers, New York;
3Nov47; EP18426.

(La la la la la la la) Lena!
Words and music by Fred Patrick,
Claude Reese [and] Jack Val.
© Sunset Music Publishers, New
York; 7Jul47; EP15738.

VALDELAMAR, EMA ELENA.
Te Sequiré Amando ... Letra y
música de Ema Elena Valdelamar.
© Editorial Mexicana de Música
Internacional, s. a., México;
30Dec46; EF5803.

VALDÉS, GILBERTO.
Brisas del Mar Tropical ... letra
y música de Gilberto Valdés.
© Robbins Music Corp., New York;
6Oct47; EP17899.

VALDES, MIGUELITO.
Letargo. (Long Live the Future)
English lyric by Albert Gamse,
Spanish-lyric and music by Mi-
guelito Valdes, arr. by George
Snowhill. © Edward B. Marks
Music Corp., New York; 14Oct47;
on arrangement; EP18571. Piano-
conductor score (orchestra) and
parts.

Rumba Rumbero ... English lyric
by Albert Gamse, Spanish lyric
and music by Miguelito Valdes.
© Edward B. Marks Music Corp.,
New York; 30Oct47; on new
English words and arrangement
of music; EP18625.

Rumba Rumbero; lyric by Albert
Gamse, music by Miguelito
Valdes, arr. by George Snowhill.
© Edward B. Marks Music Corp.,
New York; 5Nov47; on arrange-
ment; EP18439. Piano-conductor
score (orchestra, with words)
and parts.

VALDÉS HERNÁNDEZ, PABLO.
Maldita Suerte ... Letra y música
de Pablo Valdés Hernández.
© Editorial Mexicana de Música
Internacional, s. a.; 30Dec46;
EF5796.

VALENTI COSTA, PEDRO, 1905-
Seis Movimientos Corales a la
hamera Popular Argentina para
coros mixtos a "capella";
[by] Pedros Valenti Costa,
versos tomados del popular.
© Editorial Argentina De
Música (E.A.M.), Buenos Aires;
v.1, 14Aug45; v.2-4, 6,
10Sep45; v.5, 30Oct45. Con-
tents- 1. El Escondido
(© EF3999)- 2. El Cuando
(© EF5669)- 3. La Huella
(© EF5668)- 4. La Firmeza
(© EF5667)- 5. Vidala (José
R. Luna) (© EF5666)- 6.
Chacarera (© EF5665)

VALLEJO, FRANCISCA.
In Málaga; song, words by Inglis
Fletcher, music by Francisca
Vallejo. © Oliver Ditson Co.,
Philadelphia; 20Oct47; EP18415.

VANBROCK, FLORENCE.
My Dream; words & music by
Florence Vanbrock. © Nordyke
Publishing Co., Los Angeles;
15Aug46; EP19706.

VAN BUREN, BURREL.
My Garden of Dreams; words by Cora
M. Brassor, music by Burrel Van
Buren. © Nordyke Publishing
Co., Los Angeles; 12Sep47;
EP19354.
A Place in My Heart for You; words
by Mable Jones, music by Burrell
Van Buren. © Nordyke Publishing
Co., Los Angeles; 3Jul47; EP17416.
So Like a Perfect Rose You Are;
words by Rita Werril [pseud.],
music by Burrell Van Buren.
© Nordyke Publishing Co., Los
Angeles; 22Apr47; EP16902.

VANDAIR, MAURICE, pseud. See
Vandcrhaeghen, Maurice, 1905-

VAN DE KAMP, PETER.
Mal du Pays. (Nostalgia) For
the piano [by] Peter Van De
Kamp. © Oliver Ditson Co.,
Philadelphia; 19Aug47; EP16465.

VANDER BUNTE, OTTO.
Until the Mississippi Runs Dry;
words and music by Otto Vander
Bunte. © Nordyke Publishing
Co., Los Angeles; 21Feb47;
EP19469.
Where the Butterflies Fly;
words and music by Otto Vander
Bunte. © Nordyke Publishing
Co., Los Angeles; 19Jun47;
EP17447.

VANDERBURG, GORDON JAMES, 1913
Always and a Day; lyric by "Doug"
Singletary, music by Gordon
James Vanderburg. © Princess
Publications, Hollywood, Calif.;
23Jul47; EP18569.
Arizona Serenade; lyric by
Rawhide Gray, music by Red
Vanderburg. © Princess
Publications, Hollywood, Calif.;
15Aug47; EP18574.
Busy Gettin' Dizzy; lyric by Eve
Adams, music by Gordon Vander-
burg. © Princess Publications,
Hollywood, Calif.; 15Aug47;
EP18573.
Hang Your Stocking (and reminisce
on Christmas Eve) lyric by Ernie
Cuba, music by Gordon Vander-
burg. © Princess Publications,
Hollywood, Calif.; 9Oct47;
EP18005.
I'll Belong to You; lyrics by Eve
Adams, music by Gordon Vanderburg.
© Nordyke Publishing Co., Los
Angeles; 21Aug47; EP16610.
The Moon's a Magic Lantern; lyric
by Ernie Cuba, music by Gordon
Vanderburg. © Princess Publica-
tions, Hollywood, Calif.;
15Aug47; EP18570.

My Kitten's Always Puttin' On the
Dog; lyric by Tiny Hayes, music
by Red Vanderburg. © Princess
Publications, Hollywood, Calif.;
11Aug47; EP18572.
Nursin' One Beer; by Red
Vanderburg. © Princess Publica-
tions, Hollywood, Calif.;
23Jul47; EP18571. For voice
and piano, with chord symbols.
On the Farm; lyric by Althea
Pfeiffer, music by Gordon Vander-
burg. © Princess Publications,
Hollywood, Calif.; 9Jun47;
EP18575.
So Sure; lyric by Eve Adams,
music by Gordon Vanderburg. ©
Princess Publications, Hollywood,
Calif.; 15Aug47; EP18568.

VANDERBURG, RED. See
Vanderburg, Gordon James.

VANDERCOOK, HALE A.
Aces of the Air; [by] VanderCook.
© Rubank, inc., Chicago;
2ONov47; EP18857. Score (3
cornets or trumpets and piano)
and parts.
Arm in Arm; [by] VanderCook. ©
Rubank, inc., Chicago; 2ONov47;
EP18855. Score (2 cornets or
trumpets and piano) and parts.
Bonita; [by] VanderCook. [c1943]
© Rubank, inc., Chicago;
2ONov47; EP18853. Score(cornet
or trumpet and piano) and part.
The Commander; [by] VanderCook.
© Rubank, inc., Chicago;
2ONov47; EP18852. Score (cornet or trumpet and piano) and
part.
Debonnaire; [by] VanderCook.
[c1943] © Rubank, inc., Chicago; 2ONov47; EP18851. Score
(cornet or trumpet and piano)
and part.
Punchinello; [by] VanderCook.
[c1943] © Rubank, inc., Chicago; 2ONov47; EP18854. Score
(cornet or trumpet and piano)
and part.
Trumpet Twosome; [by] VanderCook.
© Rubank, inc., Chicago;
2ONov47; EP18856. Score (2
cornets or trumpets and piano)
and parts.

VAN DE VELDE, ERNEST. See
Velde, Ernest van de.

VANDEVERE, J   LILIAN, 1885-
The Two Robins ... [by] J. Lilian
Vandevere. (In Hirschberg,
David, ed. and comp. Pieces
Are Fun. bk. 1, p. 4-5) ©
Musicord Publications, New
York; 2Jul47; EP15927. For
piano solo, with words.

VANDEWELDE, ERNEST. See
Velde, Ernest van de.

VAN HALL, JOHANN BAPTIST. See
Wanhal, Johann Baptist.

VAN HEUSEN, JAMES.
Apalachicola, Fla. See his The Road to
Rio.
But Beautiful. See his The Road to Rio.
Experience. See his The Road to Rio.
(The Road to Rio) Apalachicola,
Fla., [from] the ... picture
"The Road to Rio"; words by
Johnny Burke, music by James
Van Heusen. © Burke and Van
Heusen, inc., New York;
EP18655.
(The Road to Rio) But Beautiful,
[from] "The Road to Rio"; lyric
by Johnny Burke, music by James
Van Heusen. © Burke and Van
Heusen, inc., New York; 17Nov47;
EP19113.

(The Road to Rio) Experience,
[from] "The Road to Rio"; words
by Johnny Burke, music by James
Van Heusen. © Burke and Van
Heusen, inc., New York; 13Nov47;
EP19106.
(The Road to Rio) You Don't Have to
Know the Language, [from] "The
Road to Rio"; words by Johnny
Burke, music by James Van Heusen.
© Burke and Van Heusen, inc., New
York; 13Nov47; EP19105.
You Don't Have to Know the Language.
See his The Road to Rio.

VAN HULSE, CAMIL, 1897-
Elegy ... By Camil Van Hulse.
Opus 38. © The Composers
Press, inc., New York; 9Jun47;
EP14909. Score (violin, violon-
cello and piano) and parts.
(Mass, Op. 27) Missa "Exultet
Orbis" ... Op. 27. © McLaugh-
lin & Reilly Co., Boston;
20Jun47; EP15877. Score; SATB
and organ.

VAN LEISHOUT, EDWARD McKINLEY.
Centennial Songs ... words and
music by Edward McKinley Van
Leishout. (Traverse City,
Mich.) Centennial Publishers.
© Edward McKinley Van Leishout,
Traverse City, Mich.; 30Jul47;
EP15694.

[VANNER, EMILIO] 1891-
Muñequita ... paroles françaises
de Liogar [pseud.], paroles
espagnoles et musique de Ramón
Avilar [pseud.] © (Éditions
Espagnoles) Julio Garzon, Paris;
2Jun47; EF6489. For voice and
piano, with violin obbligato and
chord symbols.

VAN NESS CLARKE, pseud. See
Clark, C. Van Ness.

VAN NORT, ISABEL.
Jack Be Nimble; piano composition
with words by Isabel Van Nort.
© Mills Music, inc., New York;
8Dec47; EP19899.
Jolly Little Playmates; piano solo
by Isabel Van Nort. © Mills
Music, inc., New York; 3Jul47;
EP6994.
Little Boy Blue (come blow your
horn); piano composition with
words by Isabel Van Nort. ©
Mills Music, inc., New York;
8Dec47; EP19900.
Nodding Tulips; piano solo by
Isabel Van Nort. © Mills Music,
inc., New York; 3Jul47; EP6993.

VAN PARYS, GEORGES. See
Parys, Georges van.

VAN PEURSEM, JAMES EUGENE, 1900-
A Study Outline for Public School
Music ... by James E. Van Peursem.
St. Louis, Planographed by J. S.
Swift Co. © James Eugene Van
Peursem, Richmond, Ky.; 15Feb47;
on revisions; AA6537.

VAN SICKLE, ROBERT, 1891-
Without You, Dear, I'm All Alone
... words by J. A. MacGregor,
music by Robert Van Sickle.
Aberdeen, Wash., Lindstrom's
Music Pub. Co. © J. A. Mac-
Gregor, Aberdeen, Wash.;
5Jul47; EP15643.

VAN TILBORROUGH, GAIL.
You're Tops with Me; words by
Mary Kemper, music by Gail Van
Tilborrough. [c1945] © Nordyke
Publishing Co., Los Angeles;
28Jun46; EP19370.

VAN TYLE, RODNEY.
I Found a Star; words by Ethel
M. Wilson, music by Rodney Van
Tyle. © Nordyke Publishing
Co., Los Angeles; 25Jul46;
EP19776.

VAN TYLE, RODNEY. Cont'd.

Memories of Your Love; words by
Dessie & Otis Wilkins, music by
Rodney Van Tyle. [c1945] ©
Nordyke Publishing Co., Los An-
geles; 30Oct47; EP20085.

My Heart Is Fenced in for You;
words by Kathryn J. H. Dupes,
music by Rodney Van Tyle. ©
Nordyke Publishing Co., Los
Angeles; 27Jun45; EP17407.

What Good Is Dreaming; words by
Mike Cantor, music by Rodney Van
Tyle. © Nordyke Publishing Co.,
Los Angeles; 27Jun46; EP20307.

You Fenced in My Heart; words by
Otis & Dessie Wilkins, music by
Rodney Van Tyle. [c1945] © Nordyke Publishing Co., Los Angeles;
30Oct47; EP20379.

VÁRADY, ALADÁR.

Hajlik a Jegenye. (Green Are the
Poplar Leaves) English lyric by
Olga Paul, music by Várady Aladár.
(In Pasti, Barbara, comp. Memo-
ries of Hungary. p. 63) © Ed-
ward B. Marks Music Corp., New
York; 19Nov47; on English lyric;
EP19018.

VARDELL, CHARLES GILDERSLEEVE, 1893-
Song in the Wilderness; cantata
for chorus and orchestra, with
baritone solo, poem by Paul Green,
music by Charles Vardell, [fore-
word by Hardin Craig] © The
University of North Carolina Press,
Chapel Hill, N. C.; 10May47;
EP15729. Piano-vocal score.

VARNEY, RICHARD, pseud. See
Humphries, Frederick.

VAUGHAN WILLIAMS, RALPH, 1872-
(Concerto, oboe & string orchestra)
Concerto for oboe and strings,
by R. Vaughan Williams, pianoforte
arrangement by Michael Mullinar.
© The Oxford University Press,
London; 6Feb47; EFu139. Score
(oboe and piano) and part.

Fantasia on Greensleeves. See his
Sir John is Love.

Greensleeves; adapted from an
old air by R. Vaughan Williams,
arr. for organ by Stanley Roper. © The Oxford University
Press, London; 24Apr47; on
arrangement; EF6104.

Introduction and Fugue ... by R.
Vaughan Williams. © Oxford
University Press, London;
13Mar47; EF6145. Score: piano
1-2.

The Lake in the Mountains; pianoforte solo, by R. Vaughan
Williams. © The Oxford University Press, London; 26Jun47;
EF6158.

My Soul, Praise the Lord; hymn,
words from the old metrical
version (slightly adapted) music
by R. Vaughan Williams. ©
Oxford University Press, London;
31Jul47; EF6363. Score: chorus
(SATB) and organ.

(Quartet, strings) String Quartet
in A minor ... [by] R. Vaughan
Williams. © Oxford University
Press, London; 30Jan47; EF6142.

(Sir John in Love) Fantasia on
Greensleeves, adapted from the
opera 'Sir John in Love' [by]
R. Vaughan Williams, arr. ...
by Watson Forbes. © Oxford
University Press, London;
19Jun47; on arrangement; EF6149.
Score (piano and viola) and
part, and alternative part for
violoncello.

The Souls of the Righteous; motet
for treble, tenor and baritone
soli, with treble, alto, tenor
and bass chorus a capella, [by]
R. Vaughan Williams, the words
taken from The Wisdom of Solomon,
III, 1-5. © The Oxford University
Press, London; 10Jul47; EF6170.

The Voice Out of the Whirlwind;
motet for chorus (S. A. T. B.)
and organ. The words from the
Book of Job ... [music by] R.
Vaughan Williams, adapted from
"Galliard of the Sons of the
Morning" "Job" scene VIII. ©
Oxford University Press, London;
13Nov47; on arrangement; EF7265.

VAUGHN, WAYNE.

Summer's on a Holiday; words &
music by Alex Mega, Herb Jenkins and Wayne Vaughn. © Nordyke Publishing Co., Los Angeles; 16Sep46; EP19692.

VÁZQUEZ, PABLO SÁNCHEZ. See
Sánchez Vázquez, Pablo.

VEILLE, CECILE LE. See
LeVeille, Cecile.

VEJVODA, JAROMIR.
Beer Barrel Polka; by Lew Brown,
Wladimir A. Timm and Jaromir
Vejvoda ... [arr.] by Charles
Magnante. © Shapiro, Bernstein
& Co., inc., New York; 14Oct47;
on arrangement; EP18023. For
accordion solo.

VELA, EDWARD L · 1916-
Take a Tip from My Heart. (Habla
Mi Corazon) Spanish & English
words by Lawrence Gutierrez and
Edward L. Vela, music by Edward
L. Vela. © Uhl and ware, San
antonio; 15Dec46; EP17766.

VELDE, ERNEST VAN DE, 1862-
Classiques-Albums; pour violon et
piano (avec 2me violon, ad
libitum), 38 morceaux choisis,
gradués, doigtés avec principes
d'analyse et de style, par
Ernest van de Velde. © Éditions
Van de Velde, Tours, France;
v.1, 30Jun47; EF6400. Score
(violin and piano) and part for
violin 1-2.

Le Déliateur; cours gradué de mé-
canisme. Graduated course of
mechanism. Curso graduado de
mecanismo. Technique moderne,
conseils des maîtres. [by]
Ernest van de Velde. © Éditions
Van de Velde, Tours, France;
30Jun47; EF6401. For piano.

Duos Choisis; pour deux violons,
transcrits, gradués et doigtés,
avec principes élémentaires
d'analyse et de style, par
Ernest van de Velde. © Éditions
Van de Velde, Tours, France;
v. 1, 30Jun47; EF6399.

École Orphéonique; [by] Ernest van
de Velde. Méthodes individuelles
pour tous les instruments de
cuivre et cours d'ensemble pour
tous les instruments de fanfare
et d'harmonie. © Éditions Van
de Velde, Tours, France; cahier
1, 30Jun47; EF6398. Contents.-
cahier 1. Instruments en si♭.
Méthode Complète ou Essentiellement Graduée de Clarinette;
système nouveau par Ernest Van
de Velde ... avec la collaboration de M. V. Joutet. © Éditions
Van de Velde, Tours, France;
30Jun47; EF6537.

Méthode Rose; par Ernest Van de
Velde. © Éditions Van de Velde,
Tours, France; 18re - 2e année,
30Jun47; EF6530, 6533. Contents.- [1] Méthode Rose. La
Première Année. Nouv. éd. -
[2] Vers des Buts Nouveaux.
2e Année de Piano.

Méthode Rythmique; A B C du rythme
et du solfège [by] Ernest Van de
Velde. © Éditions Van de Velde,
Tours, France; v.1, 30Jun47;
EF6531. Contents.--v.1 Cours
Élémentaire.

"Le Petit Paganini"; traité
élémentaire du violon, par Ernest
van de Velde. © Éditions Van de
Velde, Tours, France; v.1-2,
30Jun47; EF6539, 6538.

Pipeaux; cours élémentaire et
gradué de pipeau ou flûte douce
[by] E. Van de Velde. ©
Éditions Van de Velde, Tours,
France; 30Jun47; EF6397.

Solfège Populaire; basé sur le
rythme, par Ernest van de Velde.
Éd. A ... en clé de sol. ©
Éditions Van de Velde, Tours,
France; 30Jun47; EF6396.

Sonatines Graduées; "Sonatines-
album" [by] Ernest Van de Velde
... avec texte français, anglais,
espagnol. © Éditions Van de
Velde, Tours, France; v.1-2,
30Jun47; EF6540, 6532.

VELLONES, PIERRE, pseud. See also
Rousseau, Pierre.

VELLONES, PIERRE, 1889-1939.
Rapsodie ... [by] Pierre Vellones.
Op. 92. (Accompagnement harpe et
celesta) Réduction pour saxophone
alto et piano per Marcel Mule. ©
Henry Lemoine & Cie, Paris;
2Mar47; on arrangement; EF7239.
Score (saxophone and piano) and
part.

VENIS, GEOFFREY.
Swing Session at a Seance; by
Geoffrey Venis, [arr. by Norrie
Paramor] © Cinephonic Music
Co., ltd., London; 12Dec46;
EF6034. Parts: orchestra.

VENTADORN, BERNART DE. See
Bernart de Ventadorn.

VENUTI, JOE.
Ain't Doin' Bad Doin' Nothin'; lyric by Lee Jarvis, music by Joe
Venuti. © Edwin H. Morris & Co.,
inc., New York; 13Nov47; EP19107.

VER BRUGGEN, JOHN.
I Must Have Been Dreaming of You;
words and music by John Ver
Bruggen. © John Ver Bruggen,
West De Pere, Wis.; 14Jun47;
EP15468.

You're the Girl from Dixie, I'm
from Caroline; words and music
by John Ver Bruggen. © John Ver
Bruggen, West De Pere, Wis.;
14Jun47; EP15469.

VERDI, GIUSEPPE, 1813-1901.
Great Melodies from Verdi's
Operas; for the young pianist,
by Eric Steiner. © Elkan-
Vogel Co., inc., Philadelphia;
16May47; on arrangement;
EP15333.

[VERRALL, JOHN]
I Know Where I'm Goin'; old song
from County Antrim arr. by John
Moore [pseud.] for four-part
chorus of mixed voices with piano
acc. © Boston Music Co., Boston;
15Dec47; on arrangement; EP20403.

I Know Where I'm Goin'; old song
from County Antrim, arr. by John
Moore [pseud.] for three-part
chorus of women's voices with
piano acc. © Boston Music Co.,
Boston; 16Dec47; on arrangement;
EP20404.

(La Traviata) Prelude to Traviata;
[by] Verdi, arr. by Frederick
Block. © Century Music Publishing Co., New York; 10Jul47; on
arrangement; EP15489. For piano
solo.

VERRALL, JOHN. Cont'd.
Spirit Immortal; for bass solo
and chorus of men's voices
with piano accompaniment, [by]
Giuseppe Verdi, arr. by Vincent
H. Percy. © The Boston Music
Co., Boston; 29Sep47; on ar-
rangement; EP17743.

VESTAL, GERTRUDE LA V
Listen, Sinners; words and
music by Gertrude La V.
Vestal. © Nordyke Publishing
Co., Los Angeles; 29Apr47;
EP16815.

VICTORIA, TOMAS LUIS DE, 1540- (ca.)-
1611.
Gaudent in Caelis; motet for four-
part chorus of women's voices
(a cappella) [by] Ludovico Tommaso da Vittoria, arr. by Arthur
S. Talmadge. Antiphon from the
liturgy of the Roman Catholic
Church. © E. C. Schirmer Music
Co., Boston; 29Sep47; on arrangement; EP18129.

VIEIRA BRANDAO, JOSE.
A Riddle. (Adivinhação) S.A.T.B.
unacc., [arr. by] J. Vieira
Brandão, [words by] Martina
Alvarez, English translation
by the Krones, Beatrice and
Max. Chicago, N. A. Kjos Music
Co. © Max T. Krone, Los Angel-
es; 19Jun47; on arrangement and
translation; EP16185.

VIERNE, LOUIS, 1897-1937.
Marche Triomphale du Centenaire
de Napoléon 1er, [by] Louis
Vierne. [Op. 46] Pour 3
trompettes, 3 trombones, 3
timbales et grand orgue.
Partition. © Éditions Salabert,
Paris; 25Jul47; EF6405.

VILLOLDA, G
El Chaclo ... plectrum guitar solo,
[by] A. G. Villolda, arr. as
played by Harry Volpe. c1939.
© Albert Rocky Co., New York;
10Jan40; on arrangement; EP20193.
Sentimental Gaucho; music by A. G.
Villolda, words by Bob Musel &
Eddie Lisbona. © Southern
Music Publishing Co., ltd.,
London; 18Sep47; EF6544.

VILLOUD, HECTOR IGLESIAS. See
Iglesias Villoud, Hector.

VINCENT, JOSEPH B
Maria; words and music by Joseph
B. Vincent. [c1945] © Nordyke
Publishing Co., Los Angeles;
30Oct47; EP20086.

VINCENT, NAT. See
Vincent, Nathaniel H

VINCENT, NATHANIEL H. See also
Kenbrovin, Jaan, pseud.

VINCENT, NATHANIEL H
Great Soldier and Great Sailor;
words by Edward Poirier, music
by Nat Vincent. © Nordyke
Publishing Co., Los Angeles;
11Sep45; EP16721.
New world; words by Pyrrhus John
Lolles, music by Nat Vincent. ©
Nordyke Publishing Co., Los An-
geles; 11Jun46; EP19424.

VINCZE, ZSIGMOND.
Szép Vagy, Gyönyörü Vagy. (Magyar
Land) English lyric by Olga Paul,
music by Vincze Zsigmond, (In
Pasti, Barbara, comp. Memories of
Hungary, p. 42-45) © Edward B.
Marks Music Corp., New York;
19Nov47; on English lyric;
EP19008.

VINDIOLA, BABE.
I Think of You; words and music by
Babe Vindiola. © Nordyke Publishing Co., Los Angeles;
3Jul47; EP17514.

VINOT CHOEURS; á trois voix égales,
[by] Charles Émile Gadbois, Calixa
Lavallée, Joseph Beaulieu and
others, words by A. B. Routhier
and others] © Charles Émile
Gadbois, La Bonne Chanson,
Séminaire de St.-Hyacinthe,
Prov. Quebec, Can.; 15May47;
LP6064.

VIOTTI, GIOVANNI BATTISTA.
Seconda Sinfonia Concertante, por
due violini principali e
orchestra, [by] G. B. Viotti,
elaborazione di Felice Quaranta,
partitura. © Carisch, s.a.,
Milan; 10Sep46; on elaboration;
EP6278.

VISTA, FIDEL ARMANDO.
Alegre Canción ... letra y música
de Fidel A. Vista. © Promotora
Hispano Americana de Música,
s.a., México; 29Jul47; EP6199.
Lucerito Mañanero ... letra ©
música de Fidel A. Vista. ©
Promotora Hispano Americana de
Música, s.a., México; 29Jul47;
EP6200.

VITAK, LOUIS.
Blue Eyes Polka; [for] piano
accordion, arr. by Joseph P.
Elsnic. © Vitak-Elsnic Co.,
Chicago; 18Apr47; on arrange-
ment; EP15765.

VITALI, GIOVANNI BATTISTA.
Chaconne; [by] Giovanni Battista
Vitali ... ou son fils Tommaso
Vitali ... Éd. annotée et doigtée
par Lino Talluel. Paris,
Éditions Costallat, L. de Lacour.
© Lucien de Lacour, Paris;
2Jul45; on annotations & finger-
ing; EF6375. Score (violin and
piano) and part.

VITONE, CITTORIO, 1890-
Si e No ... [by] V. Vitone. È
Nato un Marinar ... [by] V.
Chiesa, testo di Gianipa [pseud.]
© Odeon, s.a., Milan; 17Feb47;
EP7160. Piano-conductor score
(orchestra, with words) and
parts.

VITTO, BEN.
No Name; by Ben Vitto. © Carl
Fischer, inc., New York;
19Jun47; EP15354. Condensed
score (band) and parts.

VITTORIA, LUDOVICO TOMMASO DA. See
Victoria, Tomás Luis de.

VIVALDI, ANTONIO, 1680 (ca.)-1741.
Concerti delle Stagioni ... [by]
Antonio Vivaldi, realizzazione
del basso continuo e revisione
istrumentale di Alceo Toni.
© Carisch, s.a., Milan; v. 1-4,
15Jul42; on realization of bass
& revision; EP6222, 6221,
6220, 6225. Score: violin and
string orchestra, with bass
realized for keyboard in-
strument. Contents.- 1. La
Primavera.- 2. L'Estate.- 3.
L'Autunno.- 4. L'Inverno.
Concerto alla Rustica; [by]
Antonio Vivaldi, revisione di
Alfredo Casella. © Carisch,
s.a., Milan; 10Jun40; on revision; EP6212. Score:
string orchestra and bass realized for harpsichord.
Concerto terzo (da "La Cetra");
[by] Antonio Vivaldi,
elaborazione di Alfredo
Casella. © Carisch, s.a.,
Milan; 10Jun40; on elaboration;
EP6223. Score: violin and
string orchestra.

(Concerto, violin & string
orchestra) Concerto in si
minore, per violino, archi
e cembalo, [by] Antonio
Vivaldi. [Transcribed by]
Fausto Torrefranca,
collaboratore tecnico, Mo.
Roberto Lupi. Partitura. ©
Carisch, s.a., Milan; 27May47;
on transcription & elaboration;
EF6378.
(Concerto, violin, no. 1) Con-
certo in sol minore n. 1; [by]
A. Vivaldi, [transcribed by]
Fausto Torrefranca, (collaboratore
tecnico, Roberto Lupi]
Partitura. © Carisch, s.a.,
Milan; 22Nov57; on transcription; EF6215.
Due Arie. See his Ercole sul Termodonte.
(Ercole sul Termodonte) Due Arie,
dall'Opera "Ercole sul Termodonte"
[by] Antonio Vivaldi, [rev. by]
Alfredo Casella] © Carisch,
s.a., Milan; 15Nov40; on revision;
EP6227. Score: soprano, string
orchestra and harpsichord. Con-
tents.- Chiare Onde. Dai Due Venti.
Ingrata Lidia; cantata [by] A. Vivaldi, trascrizione di V. Mortari. © Carisch s.a., Milan;
3Nov47; on transcription; EP7154.
For voice and piano.
(Olimpiade) Sinfonia, nell'
opera "Olimpiade"; [by] Antonio
Vivaldi, elaborazione di
Virgilio Mortari. © Carisch,
s.a., Milan; 15Dec39; on
elaboration; EP6213. Score:
string orchestra.
Stabat Mater; per contralto solo
e pianoforte, [by] Antonio
Vivaldi, elaborazione di
Alfredo Casella. © Carisch,
s.a., Milan; 30Aug41; on
elaboration; EP6214.

[VOETH, ZOE]
Curiosity; [words] by Joan Whitney
[pseud.] Alex Kramer and Sam
Ward, [music by Joan Whitney and
Alex Kramer] © Beaux Arts
Music, inc., New York; 5Dec47;
EP19178.

VOGEL, GILBERT.
So Ends the Night; words by
Gretchen Damon, music by Gilbert
Vogel. © Peer International
Corp., New York; 26Sep47;
EP17865.

VOLKART-SCHLAGER, KATHE, 1897-
Jahrmarkt ... The Fair ... 12
pieces for the piano ... by K.
Volkart-Schlager. © Rug & Co.,
Music-Publishers, Zurich,
Switzerland; 18Apr47; EF6842.

VOLPE, HARRY, 1906-
Bolero; guitar solo [by] Harry
Volpe. Op. 1. c1939. © Albert
Rocky Co., New York; 10Jan40;
EP20190.
Dawn; guitar solo [by] Harry Volpe.
c1939. © Albert Rocky Co., New
York; 10Jan40; EP20188.
Honey's Waltz; guitar solo [by]
Harry Volpe. c1939. © Albert
Rocky Co., New York; 10Jan40;
on arrangement; EP20209.

VON CASTELBERG, MARTHA. See
Castelberg, Martha Von.

VON KOCH, ERLAND. See
Koch, Erland von.

VON LUEHRTE, FRANK.
Gettin' Nowhere; words and music
by Frank Von Luehrte. © Nordyke Publishing Co., Los Angeles; 15Jun46; EP20367.

VOROS, WALTER J ed.
Modern Classics for the Alto Recorder; with piano acc.., comp.
and ed. by Walter J. Voros. ©
Boston Music Co., Boston; 1Dec47;
on compilation & editing; EP19806.

VOTAW, LYRAVINE V   1907-
The Rhythm Band Series for Kindergarten and Primary Grades; by
Lyravine Votaw, Ruth Laederach
and Corn Mannheimer ... Teacher's
manual. © The Raymond A. Hoffman
Co., Chicago; 12Oct29; EP15573.

VOXMAN, H
Rubank Intermediate Method for
Bassoon; to follow any elementary
method for individual or class
instruction, by H. Voxman. ©
Rubank, inc., Chicago; 1Nov47;
EP18375.

VOXMAN, H   ed.
Selected Duets; for clarinet ...
comp. and ed. by H. Voxman. ©
Rubank, inc., Chicago; v.1,
1Nov47; EP18374. Score: 2
clarinets.

W

WADE, HUGH, 1907-
I Believe in You; by Tommie Connor
and Hugh Wade. © B. Feldman &
Co., ltd., London; 5Aug47;
EP6252. For voice and piano,
with ukulele diagrams and chord
symbols. Melody also in tonic
sol-fa notation.

WADE, STUART.
Under the Hands; six characteristic
pieces for piano in the five
finger position, by Stuart Wade.
© Keith, Prowse & Co., ltd.,
London; 31Jul47; EF6242.

WADELY, F   W
Forth in Thy Name; full anthem
for treble voices, words by
C. Wesley, music by F. W.
Wadely. © Novello & Co., ltd.,
London; 30Aug47; EF6553.

The Holy Birth; a nativity play in
four scenes, words written and
selected by the Very Rev. Cyril
Mayne ... music composed and arr.
by F. W. Wadely. © Novello & Co.,
ltd., London; 24Nov47; EF7365.
For solo voices, mixed chorus and
piano.

WAGNER, JOSEPH.
Dance Divertissement; piano solo
[by] Joseph Wagner. New York,
Marks Ed. © Edward B. Marks
Music Corp., New York; 29Jul47;
EP15959.

WAGNER, JOSEPH FREDERICK, 1900-
Radio City Snapshots ... for piano
solo by Joseph Wagner. © Mills
Music, inc., New York; 8Dec47;
EP19909.

WAGNER, RICHARD, 1813-1883.
Awake! See his Die Meistersinger.

(Die Meistersinger) Awake! ...
from Die Meistersinger, [by] R.
Wagner, arr. by O.C.C. © Neil
A. Kjos Music Co., Chicago;
30Jul47; on arrangement;
EP17975. Score: chorus (SATB)
and piano or organ reduction.

WAKELY, JIMMY, 1914-
Are You Ashamed? Words and music
by Jimmy Wakely. © Leeds
Music Corp., New York; 30Jul47;
EP16098.

I Hear You Talkin'; by Jimmie
Wakely. © Mono-Music, North
Hollywood, Calif.; 28Apr47;
EP16147. For voice and piano,
with chord symbols.

Now or Never; by Bill Boyd, Fred
Stryker [and] Jimmy Wakely.
© Fairway Music Co., Hollywood,
Calif.; 26Aug47; EP16582. For
voice and piano, with chord
symbols.

Western Song Parade; [comp. by]
Jimmy Wakely, [words and music
by Jimmy Wakely and others]. ©
Mono Music, North Hollywood,
Calif.; 4Jun47; EP16213. For
voice and piano, with chord
symbols.

WAKEMAN, FRANK MERWIN, 1870-
Psalm 147 [Psalm 148, Psalm 149]
... [set to music by] F. M.
Wakeman. © Frank Merwin Wake-
man, Sherman, Conn.; 25Sep47;
EP18610.

WALDTEUFEL, EMIL.
Dolores ... by Emil Waldteufel,
[arr. by Douglas MacLean,
pseud.] © Remick Music Corp.,
New York; 18Aug47; on
arrangement; EP16434. For
piano solo.

Dolores (piano solo) [arr. by
Walter L. Rosemont] All My Life
(song) [based on Waldteufel's
"Dolores," lyrics and adaptation
by Jack Edwards and Lee Edwards]
© Edwards Music Co., New York;
6Nov47; on simplified arrangement & new lyrics; EP18672.
Includes parts for 2 instruments
or small orchestra.

Dolores ... piano solo by E.
Waldteufel, a John W. Schaum
arrangement. © Belwin, inc.,
New York; 20Nov47; on arrangement; EP18805.

The Grenadiers ... [by] Waldteufel,
arr. by Frank Wright. London,
Sole selling agents, Boosey &
Hawkes. © Hawkes & Son (London)
ltd., London; 26Nov47; on arrangement; EF7192. Parts: band.

Wings on Our Feet ... arr. from
"The skater's waltz," by E.
Waldteufel ... four-part mixed
voices (S.A.T.B.) [words by
Edith Sanford Tillotson, arr.
by Ira B. Wilson] © Lorenz
Publishing Co., Dayton, Ohio;
24Sep47; on vocal arrangement;
EP17893.

Wings on Our Feet ... arr. from
"The skater's waltz," by E.
Waldteufel ... three-part mixed
(S.A.B.) [arr. by Ira B. Wilson,
words by Edith Sanford Tillot-
son] © Lorenz Publishing Co.,
Dayton, Ohio; 24Sep47; on vocal
arrangement; EP17894.

WALKER, BEE.
Everybody's Friends with Everybody; words by Gladys Shelley.
© Rytvoc, inc., New York;
10Jul47; EP15601. For voice
and piano, with chord symbols.

I Had a Wonderful Time in Columbus;
words and music by Kermit Goell
and Bee Walker. [c1946] ©
Hudson Music Corp., New York;
17April47; EP18335.

WALKER, BERNARD.
Legend; for organ, by Bernard
Walker. © The Oxford University
Press, London; 5Dec46; EF6088.

WALKER, CINDY.
How Can It Be Wrong? Words and
music by Bob Wills and Cindy
Walker. © Bob Wills Music,
inc., Hollywood, Calif.;
15Sep47; EP17222.

My Rancho Rio Grande; words and
music by Cindy Walker, arr. by
Van Alexander. © Criterion
Music Corp., New York; 5Nov47;
on arrangement; EP18470. Piano-
conductor score (orchestra, with
words) and parts.

My Rancho Rio Grande; words and
music by Cindy Walker. New
York, Capitol Songs. © Criterion
Music Corp., New York; 29Oct47;
EP18413.

On Silver Wings to San Antone;
words and music by Cindy Walker.
© Hill and Range Songs, inc.,
Hollywood, Calif.; 29Aug47;
EP16589.

Sugar Moon; words and music by
Bob Wills and Cindy Walker.
© Bob Wills Music, inc., Holly-
wood, Calif.; 26Jun47; EP15300.

Texas Waltz; words and music by
Al Dexter and Cindy Walker.
Hollywood, Calif., Hill and
Range Songs. © Hill and Range
Songs, inc. and Al Dexter Music
Publishing Co., Hollywood, Calif.;
15Dec47; EP20132.

WALKER, ERNEST.
I Will Lift Up Mine Eyes; anthem
for alto, tenor, and bass, by
Ernest Walker. (Op.16, no.1)
Psalm CXXI. 1-4. Rev. ed. ©
Novello & Co., ltd., London;
10Nov47; EF7048.

I Will Lift up Mine Eyes; anthem
for female voices, arr. from the
original anthem for alto, tenor,
and bass, by Ernest Walker.
Op.16, no.1. [Words from] Psalm
CXXI. 1-4. Rev. ed. © Novello
& Co., ltd., London; 10Nov47;
on arrangement; EF7131.

Lord, Thou Hast Been Our Refuge;
anthem for bass solo and A.T.B.
by Ernest Walker. (Op. 16, no.
2) Rev. ed. Ps. XC. 1-6, 9.
Novello & Co., ltd., London;
16Sep47; EF6548.

Lord, Thou Hast Been Our Refuge;
anthem for bass solo and S.A.T.
B., by Ernest Walker. (Op. 16,
no. 2) Rev. ed. (Adapted to the
composer from the original
setting for male voices) Ps.
XC. 1-6, 9. © Novello & Co.,
ltd., London; 16Sep47; on
arrangement; EF6547.

WALKER, JOSEPHINE.
From Day to Day ... by Josephine
Walker [and That Is Christmas,
music by Josephine Walker, words
by Tressa Page Moore. © Josephine
Walker, Los Angeles; 1Nov46;
EF17104, 17103. For voice and
piano.

WALKER, LEE. See
Walker, Leona Redwine.

WALKER, LEONA REDWINE.
My Heart Sees Stars; words and
music by Lee Walker. © Nordyke
Publishing Co., Los Angeles;
22Aug47; EP19668.

WALKER, MARGIE. See
Walker, Marjorie Louise.

WALKER, MARJORIE LOUISE, 1918-
I Know Better Now; words and
music by Eddy Arnold, Lee
Nichols and Margie Walker.
© Adams, Vee & Abbott, inc.,
Chicago; 15May47; EP16026.

WALKER, HILLARD, 1914-
Mother and Maiden; carol for four-
part chorus of mixed voices a
cappella, [music by] Hillard
Walker, anonymous [words from]
XV century. © The Boston Music
Co., Boston; 22Aug47; EP16551.

WALKER, THOMAS STANLEY, 1902-
arr.
Folk Tunes for Solo Descant Recorder; arr. by T. S. Walker.
© Schott & Co., ltd., London;
bk. 1-3, 4Nov46; on arrangement; EF3946-3948.

WALLA, PEARL.
Will There Be Sagebrush in Heaven?
Words and music by Pearl Walla.
(In Bob Nolan's Sons of the
Pioneers, p.26-27) © Tim
Spencer Music, inc., Hollywood,
Calif.; 30Jul47; EP16030.

369

WALLACE, MINNIE, 1884-
We Don't Know Who Will Be Next on the Roll; words and music by Minnie Wallace, arr. by Clarke Tate. © Minnie Wallace, Memphis; 23Oct47; EP18283.

WALLACE, VINCENT.
The Angelus. See his Maritana.

(Maritana) The Angelus; ("Angels, that around us hover") from "Maritana"; words by E. Fitzball, music by Vincent Wallace (arr. with new piano acc., for male voices, by Purcell J. Mansfield. Op. 136, no. 3) © Ascherberg, Hopwood & Crew, ltd., London; 16Sep47; on arrangement & new piano accompaniment; EF6758.

WALLACE, WILLIAM VINCENT. See Wallace, Vincent.

WALLBANK, NEWELL.
(Chorale preludes, organ) Six Chorale Preludes for Organ, by Newell Wallbank. Op. 24. © Alfred Lengnick & Co., ltd., London; 30Apr47; EF3939.

Six Chorale Preludes for Organ. See his Chorale Preludes, organ.

WALLEN, HAROLD.
Montana, Land of Treasure; words and music by Harold (Wally) Wallen. © Nordyke Publishing Co., Los Angeles; 31Jul47; EP19687.

WALLEN, WALLY. See Wallen, Harold.

WALTER, SERGE, 1896-
Again, Again, Again; by Serge Walter ... [and] Jack Edwards, [words by] Doris Mayer. © Edwards Music Co., New York; 7Jan47; EP17793.

My Love Is What the Blues Are Made of; lyric by Doris Mayer, music by Serge Walter, [arr. by Jerry Phillips] © Crystal Music Publishers, inc., Hollywood, Calif.; 8Oct47; EP17910.

(Rattle, Rattle, Rattle) Pop Corn Sack; words by Rene Du Plessis, music by Serge Walter. © Tune Towne Tunes, Hollywood, Calif.; 25Sep47; EP17823.

WALTERS, HAROLD L   1918-
Juke Box; [music] by Harold L. Walters. © Sam Fox Publishing Co., New York; 20Nov47; EP19243. Condensed score (band) and parts. Includes part for narrator.

Popular Style Playing; by Harold L. Walters. © Rubank, inc., Chicago; 20Nov47; EP18823. Includes exercises for cornet or trumpet, and scores for 1-4 cornets or trumpets and piano.

Western Idyl; overture. © Ludwig Music Pub. Co., Cleveland; 13Aug47; EP16183. Condensed score (band) and parts.

WALTERS, RAY.
Things Like This Don't Happen; words and music by Ray Walters. © Nordyke Publishing Co., Los Angeles; 11Jul47; EP17484.

WALTON, WILLIAM.
(Henry V) Two Pieces for strings; from the film music Henry V, by William Walton. Score. © The Oxford University Press, London; 10Apr47; EF6130. Contents.—Passacaglia: Death of Falstaff.—"Touch Her Soft Lips and Part."

(Quartet, strings) String Quartet in A minor; [by] William Walton, 1947. Score. © Oxford Univ. Press, London; 14Aug47; EF6662.

Sinfonia Concertante; [by] William Walton, 1943. Rev. version. Reduction ... by Roy Douglas. © Oxford Univ. Press, London; 4Sep47; on reduction; EF6658. Score; piano 1-2.

Two Pieces for strings. See his Henry V.

Where Does the Uttered Music Go? For unacc. mixed voices, [by] William Walton, [words by] John Masefield. © The Oxford University Press, London; 23Jan47; EF6143.

WANDEWELLE, ERNEST. See Velde, Ernest van de.

VANHAL, JOHANN BAPTIST, 1739-1813. Symphonie; A-moll ... A-minor, für orchester, hrsg. von ... Fr. Kneusslin. © Hug & Co., Music Publishers, Zürich, Switzerland; 15Apr47; EF6009. Score.

WANSBOROUGH, HAROLD.
In an Oriental Market Place; by Harold Wansborough, for piano. © J. Fischer & Bro., New York; 19Sep47; EP17799.

WARD, ARDIS MAR, 1899-
Bonita Dolores ... letra de Roy A. Keech, música de Ardis Mar Ward. Plattsburg, N. Y., Musicraft Publications. © Roy Adalbert Keech, Santa Fe, N. M. & Ardis Mar Ward, San Antonio; 22Sep47; EP18358.

WARD, C   B
The Band Played On; by C. B. Ward, S.A.T.B. arr. by Frederic Fay Swift. © Belwin, inc., New York; 28Nov47; on arrangement; EP19063.

WARD, EDDIE.
Each Night at Nine; words by Opal Stohler, music by Eddie Ward. [c1946] © Nordyke Publishing Co., Los Angeles; 30Jan47; EP19647.

[WARD, JOHN J   ] 1882-
John Ward's Collection of Irish Comic Songs; [arr. by Philip D. Warner] © Ward Music Publishing Co., Chicago; 3Nov47; EP18684.

WARE, GILBERT L   1910-
A Texas Lullaby; words by Maude Reeder Lyons, music by Gilbert L. Ware. © Uhl & Ware, San Antonio; 18Nov47; EP19102.

WARLOCK, PETER, pseud. See Heseltine, Philip.

WARNER, AL.
Oh, Oh, Romeo; words and music by Al. Warner. © Nordyke Publishing Co., Los Angeles; 29Apr47; EP16832.

WARNER, CLAYTON H.
When It's Over, Over There; words & music by "Prof. Radio Rube" Clayton H. Warner. © Nordyke Publishing Co., Los Angeles; 27Sep46; EP19640.

WARNER, EDDIE.
Bahamas; paroles de Jacques Plante, musique de Eddie Warner. © Ste Ame Fse Chappell, Paris; 14Jul47; EF6541.

WARREN, BETTY.
The Seven Joys of Mary; for three-part chorus of women's voices (a cappella) Traditional words, traditional melody arr. by B. Warren. © E. C. Schirmer Music Co., Boston; 29Jul47; on arrangement; EP15974.

WARREN, ELINOR REMICK.
Mr. Nobody; for chorus of women's voices, three part, [composed and arr.] by Elinor Remick Warren. Anonymous [words] © Galaxy Music Corp., New York; 16Jul47; on arrangement; EP15756.

We Two; for voice and piano, [words by Walt Whitman, music] by Elinor Remick Warren. © G. Schirmer, inc., New York; 27Aug47; EP18736.

WARREN, HARRY.
Baby, Have You Got a Little Love To Spare? Lyric by Ted Koehler, music by Harry Warren. © Harry Warren Music, inc., New York; 25Aug47; EP16612.

The First Time I Kissed You; lyric by Ralph Blane, music by Harry Warren. © Harry Warren Music, inc., New York; 18Nov47; EP19120.

WARREN, IOLA NANCY, 1902-
I Could Be Dreaming; words and music by Iola Nancy Warren, [arrangement by Frank Furlett] © Triad Music Co., Chicago; (in notice: Iola Nancy Warren) Chicago; 19Jul47; EP17980.

There's a Rainbow over Chicago; words and music by Frank Furlett. © Triad Music Co., Chicago; 11Dec47; EP19982.

This Lovely Christmas Night; words and music by Iola Nancy Warren, [arrangement by Frank Furlett] © Triad Music Co., Chicago; 19Jul47; EP17979.

WARWICK, PEGGY.
Garden of Delight; (Oh! How I love you, garden of delight) song, lyric by Edward Teschemacher (Edward Lockton) music by Peggy Warwick. © M. Witmark & Sons, New York; 17Dec20; EP19171.

WASHBURNE, COUNTRY.
You Don't Kno' What Lonesome Is (till you git to herdin' cows); words and music by Foster Carling ... and Country Washburne. © Southern Music Publishing Co., inc., New York; 27Aug47; EP17860.

WASSIL, BRUNO.
La Vispa Teresa; raccolta di poesie per bambini a cura di Lucilla Antonelli, musicate da Bruno Wassil, illustrazioni di Lorini. © Edizioni Musicali Cora, Milan; 30Aug45; EF5765.

WATERS, HERB.
I Ain't Confessin' My Troubles to Nobody; words and music by Tony Gottuso and Herb Waters. © Bob Miller, inc., New York; 27Oct47; EP18602.

WATKINS, PAUL.
Heaven and You; words and music by Ann Douglas and Paul Watkins. © Nordyke Publishing Co., Los Angeles; 11Jul47; EP17524.

WATSON, MURIEL, 1901-
The Ivy Still Grows (on the old garden wall); words by Jack Denby, music by Muriel Watson. © Noel Gay Music Co., ltd., London; 16Jun47; EP5861.

Just because I Love You; words by Jack Denby [pseud.], music by Muriel Watson. © B. Feldman & Co., ltd., London; 14Aug47; EF8269.

WATSON, ORMSBY M
Unfair to Love; words and music by Raymond C. McCollister, Tony Ferragamo and O. M. Watson. © Raymond C. McCollister, Wichita, Kan.; 28Jul47; EP16006.

WATT, JANE C
Hymn to the Virgin; (S.A.T.B. with soprano solo and piano or organ acc.) [by] Jane C. Watt, [poem anonymous, adapted by J.C.W.] © Carl Fischer, inc., New York; 24Sep47; EP18072.

WAVERLY, JACK, 1896-
Since Them Hillbillies Moved Down
to the Holler; tale and toon
by Jack Waverly. © Jack
Waverly, Bellmore, N. Y.;
18Sep47; EP17247. For voice
and piano, with guitar
diagrams and chord symbols.

WAYNE, MABEL.
It Happened in Hawaii; lyric by
Al Dubin ... music by Mabel
Wayne, scored by Jerry Sears.
© Remick Music Corp., New York;
3Sep47; on vocal orchestration;
EP17275. Piano-conductor
score (orchestra, with words)
and parts.

WAYWORTH, WALTER GEORGE, 1901-
I'll Be Over All in Clover; music
and words by Walter Wayworth.
© Walter G. Wayworth, Hartford;
20Oct47; EP18174.

WEATHERSEED, JOHN J   1900-
Prevent Us O Lord; for four-part
chorus of mixed voices, with
organ acc. ad lib. [by] John J.
Weatherseed, [text from] prayer
of 16th century. © Boston Music
Co., Boston; 12Dec47; EP19979.

WEAVER, MARION.
I Walked into the Garden; words by
Dale White, music by Marion
Weaver ... medium [voice] ©
Lewis Music Publishing Co.,
inc., New York; 19Nov47; EP18770.

WEBER, KARL MARIA FRIEDRICH ERNST
FREIHERR VON, 1786-1826.
Freischütz Overture; [by] C. M.
von Weber, score. (Conducting
analysis by Max Rudolf] ©
Edward B. Marks Music Corp., New
York; 15Oct47; on conducting
analysis; EP18004.

Invitation to the Dance; by C. M.
von Weber, and Serenade, A. E.
Titl, arr. by M. C. Meyrelles,
arr. for modern bands with new
parts by H. R. Kent [pseud.] ©
Carl Fischer, inc., New York;
23Oct47; on arrangement for
modern band; EP18590. Condensed
score and parts.

WEBER, OLGA THERESIA, 1903-
You Say You're Sorry; by Olga
Weber. [Arr. by Thomas Alexander Phillips] © La Mar Music
Publishers, inc., Canton, Ohio;
12Nov47; EP18790. For voice
and piano.

WEBSTER, JULIAN, arr.
Joshua Fit the Battle of Jericho ...
arr. ... for men's voices by
Julian Webster and ed. [by]
George Strickling. © Broadcast
Music, inc., New York; 12Sep47;
on arrangement & editing;
EP14056.

Joshua Fit the Battle of Jericho
... arr. ... for mixed voices by
Julian Webster and ed. [by]
George Strickling. © Broadcast
Music, inc., New York; 12Sep47;
on arrangement & editing;
EP18054.

WEIGAND, MARION MARIE.
You Never Say You Love Me;
words and music by Marion
Marie Weigand. © Nordyke
Publishing Co., Los Angeles;
11Aug47; EP17472.

WEIGL, VALLY.
The Little Jesus Came to Town.
.("A Christmas folk-song") for
three-part chorus of women's
voices, [by] Vally Weigl, [words
by] Lizette Woodworth Reese.
© E. C. Schirmer Music Co.,
Boston; 29Sep47; EP18133.

Saint Francis ... [by] Vally Weigl.
© E. C. Schirmer Music Co.,
Boston; 29Sep47; EP18132.
Score (chorus (SSA), flute (or
violin) and piano) and part for
flute (or violin)

WEIGOLD, FAITH S
When the Cactus Are A-blooming;
words and music by Faith S.
Weigold. © Nordyke Publishing
Co., Los Angeles; 25Jun47;
EP17584.

WEIMER, PAUL, 1890-
I Don't Mind Your Kissing Mo;
words and music by Paul Weimer.
© Paul Weimer, New York; 29Aug47;
on additional music; EP16662.

WEINBERG, JACOB.
Canzona; [by] Jacob Weinberg.
© Transcontinental Music Corp.,
New York; 27Sep47; EP17347.
Score (violin and piano) and
part.

Five Hebrew Melodies; freely
adapted for piano [by] Jacob
Weinberg. Op. 11. © Transcontinental Music Corp., New
York; 27Sep47; EP17346.

Thirty Hymns and Songs; with organ
or piano acc. for congregation,
school, home, by Jacob Weinberg.
Op.51. © Jacob Weinberg, New
York; 17Jun47; EP15399. Part of
the words in Hebrew (transliterated), part in English.

WEINER, LAZAR.
Gele Late. The Yellow Patch. Poem
by A. Almi, music by Lazar Wei-
ner. © Transcontinental Music
Corp., New York; 18Nov47;
EP18825. Score; SATB and piano;
words in both Yiddish and
Yiddish transliterated.

WEISMAN, BENNY, 1922-
Worthy of You; by Benny Weisman.
© Ben Weisman, Los Angeles;
24Jun47; EP15414. For voice and
piano.

[WEISSHAUS, IMRE] 1904-
Quatorze Choeurs; a 4, 5, 6 et 7
voix mixtes, sur des chansons
populaires de divers pays, [by]
Paul Arma [pseud.] © Henry Lemoine & Cie, Paris; 25Mar47; on
harmonization; EP7238.

WEITZMAN, MORRIS ABBA, 1880-
Atomic Age Wife ... words and
music by Morris A. Weitzman.
© Morris A. Weitzman, Chicago;
27May47; on English translation;
EP16207.

WEITZNER, GEZA.
Gyere, Cigány. (Play Your Music,
Gypsy] English lyric by Olga
Paul, music by Weitzner Géza.
(In Pasti, Barbera, comp. Memo-
ries of Hungary. p. 50-51) ©
Edward B. Marks Music Corp., New
York; 19Nov47; on English lyric;
EP19012.

WELDON, FRANK.
Why Did It Have to End so Soon?
By Marty Symes, Dick Robertson
and Frank Weldon. © Irving
Berlin Music Corp., New York;
29Jan47; EP12256. For voice and
piano, with chord symbols.

WELK, LAWRENCE.
Waltzing in a Dream; music by
Lawrence Welk, words by Ted
Fetter. © J. J. Robbins &
Sons, inc., New York; 26Aug47;
EP16637.

WELKER, JOHN.
Pickaninny's Lullaby; words and
music by "Red" Welker. ©
Nordyke Publishing Co., Los
Angeles; 3Jul47; EP17414.

WELKER, RED. See
Welker, John.

WELLAND, JAMES, pseud. See
Woodford, Gordon Robert.

WELLER, BEN, 1890-
Weller School of Popular Piano
Playing. © Ben Weller, Kansas
City, Mo.; bk.2, 15Oct47;
EP19347.

WELLESZ, EGON, 1885-
The Leaden Echo and the Golden Echo;
cantata for high voice, violin,
clarinet, violoncello and piano,
[by] E. Wellesz. [Op.61] Words
by G. M. Hopkins. Vocal score.
© Schott & Co., ltd., London;
9Jun47; EP5793.

WELLINGTON, MARTHA.
Americans Will Always Be Americans;
by Martha Wellington. © George
F. Briegel, inc., New York;
10Oct47; EP18963. For voice and
piano.

WELLS, ERNEST.
A Joyous Carol; ([for] S.A.T.B.,
divided, a cappella) [By]
Ernest Wells, ed., by John
Finley Williamson. © Carl
Fischer, inc., New York;
11Aug47; EP16428.

WELLS, ROBERT.
Magic Town, from the ... produc-
tion "Magic Town," by Mel Tormé
... [and] Robert Wells. ©
Burke and Van Heusen, inc.,
New York; 10Jul47; EP15626.
For voice and piano, with chord
symbols.

WELSH, STUART R
My Troubles Are Gone; words by
Betty Boon, music by Stuart R.
Welsh. © Nordyke Publishing Co.,
Los Angeles; 29Apr47; EP16860.

WERNETT, EMMA D
In Dear Ohio; words and music by
Emma D. Wernett. © Emma D.
Wernett, Columbus, Ohio; 13Sep47;
EP17083. Score: SATB and piano.

WESLEY, ANNE.
Two of You; words and music by
Carrole Martin, Louisa Mohr
and Anne Wesley. © Nordyke
Publishing Co., Los Angeles;
25Jun47; EP17483.

WESLEY, SAMUEL SEBASTIAN.
Lead Me, Lord; anthem for four-
part chorus of mixed voices.
[Words from] Psalm 5:8, 4:9,
ed. by Frank B. Cookson.
© The Raymond A. Hoffman Co.,
Chicago; 23Sep38; EP15591.

WESSELLS, KATHERINE TYLER, 1897-
The Little Golden Book of Singing
Games; selected and arr. by
Katharine Tyler Wessells, illus.
by Corinne Malvern. © Simon &
Schuster, inc. & Artists and
Writers Guild, inc., New York;
15Oct47; A19679.

WEST, EUGENE.
Arizay! By Pinky Vidacovich and
Eugene West. © Rialto Music Pub.
Corp., New York; 20Aug47;
EP18983. For voice and piano,
with guitar diagrams and chord
symbols.

WEST, MARIE.
Memories of My Childhood Home;
words and music by Marie West.
© Nordyke Publishing Co., Los
Angeles; 2Jul46; EP19686.

WEST, MORGAN.
Song at Dusk; for piano [by] Mor-
gan West. © Theodore Presser
Co., Philadelphia; 29Nov47;
EP19810.

When Lights Are Low; piano solo by
Morgan West. © Theodore Presser
Co., Philadelphia; 27Sep47;
EP17730.

WEST, ROBERT HAIGHT, 1916-
"Maybe It's a Dream," [by Robert
Haight West] © Robert Haight
West, Elmira, N. Y.; 15Oct47;
EP18002. For piano solo.

WESTBERG, ERIC, 1892-1944.
Nenia; för stråkorkester, [by]
Eric Westberg. Stockholm, Ed.
Suecia. © Föreningen svenska
tonsättare, Edition Suecia,
Stockholm; 1Jan45; EF7078.
Score: string orchestra.

WESTBROOK, HELEN SEARLES, 1905-
Concert Piece; in D, for the organ by Helen Searles Westbrook.
© Neil A. Kjos Music Co., Chicago; 8Aug47; EP17978. Includes registration for Hammond
organ.

WESTENDORF, T   P
(Magic Town) My Book of Memory;
from ... "Magic Town." Based
on melody "I'll Take You Home
Again Kathleen," by T. P.
Westendorf, lyric [and arrange-
ment] by Edward Heyman. ©
Burke and Van Heusen, inc.,
New York; 25Aug47; on words and
arrangement; EP16680.

WESTLING, EJNAR.
På Myrgårds Loge; text och musik;
Ejnar Westling. © Reuter & Reuter förlags, a.-b., Stockholm;
1Jan46; EF6953.

WHEATLEY, WILLIAM D
Howdy, Buddy; music by W. D.
Wheatley, lyric by Riley W.
Geary. © Riley W. Geary,
Phoenix, Ariz.; 12Aug47;
EP16451.

WHEELER, CLARENCE E
San Gabriel Valley; by Walt
Davidson and Clarence E. Wheeler.
© Davidson & Wheeler, Hollywood,
Calif.; 16Apr47; EP16173. For
voice and piano, with chord
symbols.

WHEELER, JOHN A
Lonely Mood; words and music by
John Wheeler. © Nordyke Publish-
ing Co., Los Angeles; 13Aug47;
EP19348.

WHELDON, FREDERICK.
Calm waters; song, words and music
by Frederick Wheldon. © Chappell
& Co., ltd., London; 20Nov47;
EP7267.

WHELPLEY, BENJAMIN, d. 1946.
In Heavenly Love Abiding; [by]
Benjamin Whelpley, [words by]
Anna Letitia Waring. © The
Arthur P. Schmidt Co., Boston;
18Aug47; EP16376. Score:
soprano, chorus (SATB) and piano.

Oh How Amiable Are Thy Dwellings;
[by] Benjamin Whelpley, Psalm
LXXXIV. © The Arthur P. Schmidt
Co., Boston; 18Aug47; EP16374.
Score: SATB and piano.

WHEN CHRIST WAS BORN; a Christmas service. © Lorenz Publishing Co., Dayton, Ohio; 8Sep47; EP17919. In
part, for voice and piano; in part,
close score: SATB.

WHERRY, BERTHA.
The Yanks behind the Tanks; words
and music by Bertha Wherry.
© Nordyke Publishing Co., Los
Angeles; 15Jul46; EP20378.

WHICKER, R   LEE,
How Was I to Know? Words and
music by R. Lee Whicker. © Nordyke Publishing Co., Los Angeles; 19Jun47; EP17525.

WHISTLER, HARVEY S   1907-
Developing Double-stops; for
violin, a complete course of
study for double note and chord
development, by Harvey S.
Whistler. © Rubank, inc.,
Chicago; 9Jul47; EP15515.

From Violin to Viola; a
transitional method. © Rubank,
inc., Chicago; 5Aug47; EP16080.

Introducing the Positions ... for
cello ... by Harvey S. Whistler.
© Rubank, inc., Chicago; v.1-2,
5Aug47; EP16078-16079.

WHISTON, DON.
Tailor Made Baby; words and music
by Spade Cooley and Don Whiston.
© Hill and Range Songs, inc.,
Hollywood, Calif.; 14Nov47;
EP18767.

WHITE, CARL.
My Heart Can't Stand the Strain;
words by J. B. J., music by
Carl White. © Nordyke Publish-
ing Co., Los Angeles; 12Aug47;
EP17497.

WHITE, CLARENCE THEODORE, 1912-
Forgive and Forget; words and music
by C. "Ted" White, [piano
arrangement by Frank Mitchell]
© Kala Publications, San Diego,
Calif.; 30Sep47; EP18931.

La Presle ... words and music by
C. "Ted" White. © Kala Publications, San Diego, Calif.;
30Sep47; EP18930.

WHITE, EDWARD, 1910-
Cabana ... [by] Edward White.
London, Sole Selling Agents,
Boosey & Hawkes. © J. R.
Lafleur & Son, ltd., London;
10Sep47; EF6613. Piano-conductor
score (orchestra) and parts.

WHITE, JOHNNY.
As Sweet As You; words and music
by Johnny White. © Regent
Music Corp., New York; 20ct47;
EP17750.

WHITE, L   J
A Prayer of St. Richard of Chichester ... for treble voices,
[by] L. J. White. © The Oxford University Press, London;
5Jun47; EF6119.

WHITE, MAUDE VALERIE.
Plus Jamais, Oi Nuit sans Voiles.
(So We'll Go No More a Roving)
Texte français de Louis
Henneve, d'après le poème de
Lord Byron, musique de Maude
Valerie White. © Chappell &
Co., ltd., London; 18May47;
on new words; EF3952.

WHITE, MICHAEL.
The Ghost; song, words by Walter
De La Mare, music by Michael
White. [London] Boosey &
Hawkes. © Boosey & Co., ltd.,
London; 27Jun47; EF3988.

WHITE, STAN.
My Heart Promises; words by
Denver Bryant, music by Stan
White. © Denver McQueen
Bryant, Inyokern, Calif.;
5Feb47; EP17689.

WHITE, TED.   See
White, Clarence Theodore.

WHITEFIELD, BERNARD, 1910-
Bernard Whitefield Piano Method ...
the simplest book for the first
year. © Boston Music Co., Boston;
24Nov47; AA69118.

Psalm 101; for four-part chorus and
baritone solo, with piano or organ
accompaniment, [by] Bernard Whitefield. © The Boston Music Co.,
Boston; 25Sep47; EP17725.

WHITEHALL, ALICE.
Church Bells on Sunday Morning;
piano solo by Alice Whitehall.
© Pallma Music Products,
Chicago; 27May47; EP15669.

Toy Soldiers on Parade; piano
solo by Alice Whitehall.
© Pallma Music Products,
Chicago; 27May47; EP15664.

WHITEHEAD, ALFRED.
Sunday Morning in Norway; folk-
tune from Norway arr. by Alfred
Whitehead, the words by Staines
Franklin. © Novello & Co., ltd.,
London; 28Sep47; on arrangement;
EF6551. Score: SA and piano.

WHITEHEAD, HAROLD.
Come, Loyal Hearts; two-part song,
[by] Harold Whitehead, [words
by] Irene Gass. © The Oxford
University Press, London;
1May47; on arrangement;
EF6113.

WHITFIELD, ROBERT, 1916-
Avak Jackson; by Smoki Whitfield
and [words by] Paul Marion.
© Laura-Lea Music, Hollywood,
Calif.; 27Sep47; EP17641.

WHITFIELD, SMOKI.   See
Whitfield, Robert.

WHITING, RICHARD A   d. 1938.
Ain't We Got Fun ... Arr. by
Jerry Sears, lyric by Gus
Kahn and Raymond B. Egan,
music by Richard A. Whiting.
© Remick Music Corp., New
York; 25Aug47; on arrange-
ment; EP17155. Piano-
conductor score (orchestra,
with words) and parts.

(Dark Passage) Too Marvelous for
Words, from the ... picture
"Dark Passage"; music by Richard
A. Whiting, words by Johnny
Mercer ... scored by Jerry
Sears. © Harms, inc., New York;
25Aug47; on vocal orchestration;
EP17151. Piano-conductor score
(orchestra, with words) and
parts.

Guilty; words and music by Gus
Kahn, Harry Akst and Richard A.
Whiting, [arr. by Helmy Kresa.
Rev. ed.] © Leo Feist, inc.,
New York; 16Oct46; on arrange-
ment; EP16233.

WHITLEY, RAY.
Ages and Ages Ago; by Gene Autry,
Fred Rose and Ray Whitley.
© Western Music Publishing Co.,
Hollywood, Calif.; 12Nov47;
EP18849. For voice and piano,
with chord symbols.

I've Lived a Lifetime for You;
by Elmer Newman and Ray
Whitley. © Bourne, inc., New
York; 12Aug47; EP16178. For
voice and piano, with chord
symbols.

WHITLOCK, PERCY WILLIAM, 1903-1946.
Reflections; three quiet pieces
for organ, by Percy Whitlock.
© The Oxford University Press,
London; 5Dec46; EF6089.

Six Hymn-Preludes; for organ, by
Percy Whitlock. [c1945] ©
Oxford University Press, London;
10Jan46; on arrangement; EF6573.

WHITMAN, MERLE J   1905-
Let Me Carry You Back to Texas;
words by Bob Ferriter, music by
Merle Whitman. © Robert J.
Ferriter, Broken Bow, Neb.;
20Aug47; EP18548.

WHITMER, T   CARL.
Four Short Pieces for the Church
Service; for organ [by] T. Carl
Whitmer. © The Arthur P.
Schmidt Co., Boston; 23Sep47;
EP17323.

WHITMORE, ROBERT.
A Mansion in the Sky; music by
Robert Whitmore, words by Raymond Stoffer. © Raymond Stoffer, North Georgetown, Ohio;
19Dec47; EP20140.

WHITNEY, JOAN, pseud.   See
Voeth, Zoe.

WHITNEY, MAURICE C
Eternal God; anthem for mixed
voices. [Words by] Henry H.
Tweedy, [music by] Maurice C.
Whitney. © H. W. Gray Co.,
inc., New York; 12Sep47;
EP17373.

Roulade ... [by] Maurice C. Whitney. © Carl Fischer, inc., New
York; 10Sep47; EP18083. Score
(4 clarinets) and parts.

WHITNEY, RALPH TAYLOR, 1890-
I Don't Want to Miss Heaven, Do
You? [By] Ralph Taylor Whitney,
[words by] M.C.W. [and] R.T.W.
© Ralph Taylor Whitney, Wellas-
ton, Mass.; 18Oct47; EP18147.
Close score; SATB.

WHITTAKER, NOLA, 1907-
Utah, Home of Mine; lyrics and
music by Esther Wiltshire and
Nola Whittaker. © Esther
Wiltshire & Nola Whittaker,
Circlesville, Utah; 15Jul47;
EP16989.

WHITTINGTON, VAL.
San Francisco (we're sorry we're
saying "So long"); words and
music by Val Whittington. ©
Nordyke Publishing Co., Los
Angeles; 29Jul47; EP17406.

WIANT, BLISS, arr.
Chinese Lyrics; a collection of
twenty-seven compositions ... ed.
by T. Tertius Noble, arr. with
piano acc. by Bliss Wiant. Text
tr. by Bliss Wiant and others.
© J. Fischer & Bro., New York;
3Sep47; A16036.

WICK, FREDERICK.
The Mountaineer; Bor Jeg På Det
Høie Fjeld. Norwegian folk song;
English ... text [and] T.T.B.B.
arr. by Frederick Wick. [Minnea-
polis, Wick Music Publishing Co.]
© Frederick Wick, Minneapolis;
28Aug47; on English text &
arrangement; EP17935.

WIDÉEN, IVAR.
Det Første Møde; [by] Ivar Widéen,
ur "Portällinger," [by] Bjørn-
stjerne Bjørnson. © Nordiska
musikförlaget, a/b, Stockholm;
1Dec20; EF6948. Score: mezzo-
soprano, baritone and piano.

Hymn till Västergötland; [words
by] Paul Nilsson, [music by]
Ivar Widéen. © Nordiska musikförlaget, a.b., Stockholm;
1Jan45; EF7056. Close score:
SATB.

WIEGAND, J
Postlude; by J. Wiegand, arr. by
C. B. Righter. © Carl Fischer,
inc., New York; 19Jun47; on
arrangement; EP15541. Condensed
score (band) and parts.

WIENER, JEAN ALBERT HENRI, 1896-
Capitaine Blomet; partition cinématographique, musique de Jean Wiener. © Éditions du Coquelicot,
Paris; 24Sep47; EF7302.

Quatre Petites Pièces-Radio; pour
piano. © Jean Jobert, Éditeur,
Paris; 15May47; EF5851.

WIESNER, MORRIS.
I've Gora a Gal in Texas; words by
Morris Wiesner and Tod Hazel-
quist, music by Morris Wiesner.
© Nordyke Publishing Co., Los
Angeles; 27Mar47; EP16716.

WIKLUND, ADOLF.
Tre Stycken; för stråkorkester och
harpa [by] Adolf Wiklund. Stockholm, Ed. Suecia. © Föreningen
svenska tonsättare, Edition
Suecia, Stockholm; 1Jan45;
EF7062. Score: string orchestra
and harp.

WILBANKS, JAN, 1928-
Jesus Is the King of Glory ...
[by] Jan Wilbanks, [words by]
Frank E. Roush. © Frank E.
Roush, Lynchburg, Ohio; 1Nov47;
EP18346. Close score: SATB.

WILBURN, NORMA.
Please Be True; words and music by
Norma Wilburn. © Nordyke Publishing
Co., Los Angeles; 5Jun47; EP17573.

WILCHER, JACK.
Spring Is Really Spring This Year.
© Woodward Music, inc., New
York; 11Jul47; EP15552. For
voice and piano, with chord
symbols.

[WILCOCK, FRANK SAMUEL] 1887-
The New World over the Hill ...
Words by Frank Eyton [pseud.],
music by Alan Colville [pseud.]
© Ascherberg, Hopwood & Crew,
ltd., London; 2Jul47; EF5752.

WILCOX, VERNON LEE, 1909-
Make Me Worthy of Calvary; [by] ...
V. L. Wilcox, [words by] Mrs.
W. M. Franklin. © Mrs. W. M.
Franklin, Fargo, N. D.; 5Jul47;
EP15532. Close score: SATB.

WILKES, ROBERT W
Bring to the Lord; [by] Robert W.
Wilkes. Op. 43. Words from the
Psalms. © The Arthur P. Schmidt
Co., Boston; 18Aug47; EP16375.
Score: SATB and piano.

WILKINS, CLEMENTINE.
Sentimental Blues; words by Ur-
sula Smith, music by Clementine
Wilkins. © Nordyke Publishing
Co., Los Angeles; 27Sep46;
EP19645.

[WILKINS, ROBERT NICHOLS] 1905-
Just Look at My Baby; words and
music by Bob Nichols [pseud.]
© Robert Nichols Wilkins &
Theodore B. Yasi (Yasi-Nichols
Music Publishers), New York;
7Oct47; EP17803.

WILLAN, HEALEY.
Missa Sancti Michaelis; (Missa
brevis no. IX) for chorus of
mixed voices, by Healey Willan.
© The H. W. Gray Co., inc.,
New York; 2Jul47; EP15436.
English words.

WILLIAMS, ARNOLD, 1887-
Laus Deo; for chorus of mixed
voices, S.C.T.B. (unaccompanied)
From "The Shorter Poems of Rob-
ert Bridges," music by Arnold
Williams. London, J. Curwen,
New York, G. Schirmer, sole
agents. © Arnold Williams,
Bournemouth East, Hampshire,
Eng.; 16Sep47; EF6731. English
words.

You Gotta Get a Glory; unison song,
words American Negro, music
by Arnold Williams. London, J.
Curwen, New York: G. Schirmer,
sole agents. © Arnold Williams,
Bournemouth East, Hampshire,
Eng.; 16Sep47; EF6738.

WILLIAMS, CARL CARNELIUS, 1926-
Lord, Hold to My Hand; [words by
Carl C. Williams, music by Carl
C. Williams, jr.] © Carl C.
Williams, jr., Noblesville, Ind.;
5Jul47; EP15631. Close score:
SATB.

Wonderful Jesus; [words by Carl C.
Williams, music by Carl C.
Williams, jr.] © Carl C. Will-
iams, Noblesville, Ind.; 5Jul47;
EP15632. Close score: SATB.

WILLIAMS, CORDELIA.
Only with You; [by] Adele Becker
[and] Cordelia Williams. ©
A. Becker & C. Williams, San
Francisco; 3Dec47; EP19863. For
voice and piano, with chord
symbols.

Where? Written by Adele Becker
[and] Cordelia Williams. ©
Adele Becker and Cordelia
Williams, d. b. a. Becker-Wil-
liams, San Francisco; 3Dec47;
EP19862. For voice and piano,
with chord symbols.

WILLIAMS, DAVID WILT, 1902-
Come to Calvary's Saviour; [by]
David W. Williams, [words by]
Frank E. Roush. © Frank E.
Roush, Lynchburg, Ohio; 23Jul47;
EP15949.

I Love Him because He First Loved
Me ... [by] David W. Williams,
[words by] Frank E. Roush. ©
Frank E. Roush, Lynchburg, Ohio;
23Jul47; EP15948. Close score:
SATB.

King of My Heart; [by] David
W. Williams, [words by] Frank
E. Roush. © Frank Elgar Roush,
Lynchburg, Ohio; 2Aug47;
EP16021. Close score: SATB.

WILLIAMS, FRANCES.
Little Christ-Child, Sweet and
Holy; [for] two-part treble,
with optional descant [by]
Frances Williams, [words by]
Rhoda Newton. © Harold
Flammer, inc., New York;
28Jul47; EP16243.

Lullaby Song; [for] SSA
accompanied, words and music by
Frances Williams. © Harold
Flammer, inc., New York;
28Jul47; EP16250.

To the Dawn ... [for] SATB
accompanied, [music by] Frances
Williams, music by Rhoda Newton.
© Harold Flammer, inc., New
York; 28Jul47; EP16244.

To the Dawn ... [for] SSA
accompanied [by] Frances
Williams, words by Rhoda
Newton. © Harold Flammer, inc.,
New York; 28Jul47; on
arrangement; EP16255.

WILLIAMS, FREDDIE.
Goodbye, I'll Say It Now; words &
music by Freddie Williams.
© Nordyke Publishing Co., Los
Angeles; 11Oct46; EP19483.

WILLIAMS, GLADYS VIRGINIA, 1896-
I Heard the Bells on Christmas
Day ... Poem by Henry W. Long-
fellow, music by Gladys V.
Williams. © Hunleth Music Co.,
St. Louis; 30Jul47; EP15896.
Score: SATB and piano or organ.

WILLIAMS, HANK.
(Last Night) I Heard You Crying
in Your Sleep; by Hank Williams.
© Acuff-Rose Publications, Nashville; 16Jul47; EP15638. For
voice and piano, with guitar
diagrams and chord symbols.

Move It on Over; by Hank Williams.
© Acuff-Rose Publications, Nashville; 16Jul47; EP15637. For
voice and piano, with guitar
diagrams and chord symbols.

WILLIAMS, MRS. HOWARD, 1916-
The Great Physician of the Skies;
and Open Your Heart's Door;
words and music by Mrs. Howard
Williams. © Mrs. Howard
Williams, Mowrystown, Ohio;
29Jul47; EP17767-17768.

WILLIAMS, JEAN.
Mariner's song; piano solo by Jean
Williams. © Schroeder & Gunther,
inc., Rhinebeck, N. Y.; 21Nov47;
EP18840.

Sevillana; [by] Jean Williams. ©
Schroeder & Gunther, inc.,
Rhinebeck, N. Y.; 5Sep47;
EP16648. Two scores for piano
1-2.

Street Parade; piano solo by Jean
Williams. © Schroeder & Gunther,
inc., Rhinebeck, N. Y.; 21Nov47;
EP18841.

WILLIAMS, JOHN.
Your Smile, Your Kiss; a song
by Williams. © Nordyke
Publishing Co., Los Angeles;
24Jul47; EP17468.

WILLIAMS, JONATHAN.
Wild Orchid; words and music by
Jonathan Williams. [c1945] ©
Nordyke Publishing Co., Los An-
geles; 12Jun46; EP194088.

WILLIAMS, KATHLEEN.
Wanderlust; words by Mary Ann
Sievers, music by Kathleen
Williams. © Nordyke Publishing
Co., Los Angeles; 15Aug47;
EP20095.

WILLIAMS, LELA MACK. See
Williams-Biggers, Lela Mack.

WILLIAMS, MARY LOU.
Lonely moments; arr. by Mary Lou
Williams and Milton Orent, composed by Mary Lou Williams. ©
Harman Music, inc., New York;
26Apr47; EP14060. Piano-conductor score (orchestra) and
parts.

[WILLIAMS, RALPH]
The Four Seasons; suite for
violin and piano by Ralph
Raymond [pseud.] © The Boston
Music Co., Boston; 11Sep47;
EP17206. Score and part.

WILLIAMS, RALPH EDWIN, 1916-
Father Eternal; S.A.T.B. ...
[words by] Laurence Housman ...
[music by] Ralph E. Williams.
© Paul A. Schmitt Music Co.,
Minneapolis; 25Oct47; EP18962.

Hear My Prayer, O Lord; mixed
voices - a cappella. Text selection from Psalm 102, [music by]
Ralph E. Williams. © Paul A.
Schmitt Music Co., Minneapolis;
6Jun47; EP16055.

Take Not Thy Holy Spirit from Me;
S.A.T.B. divided, Psalm Li [by]
Ralph E. Williams. © Neil A.
Kjos Music Co., Chicago;
8Jul47; EP16132.

WILLIAMS, RALPH VAUGHAN. See
Vaughan Williams, Ralph.

WILLIAMS, ROBERT MORRIS, 1887-
Musical Composition Arranged for
Male Voices ... music composed
by Robt. M. Williams, [words
by John Mason Neale, John
Newton and others] © Robert M.
Williams, Detroit; 23May47;
EP16237. Sacred compositions.

Nine Choir Responses; (S.A.T.B.)
[by] R. M. Williams. © Hall &
McCreary Co., Chicago; 23Jul47;
EP16100.

WILLIAMS, S
In Old Bermuda; words by Albert
G. Miller, music by S.
Williams. © Chappell & Co.,
inc., New York; 14Jul47;
EP15779.

WILLIAMS, SOL.
Smoke! Smoke! Smoke! (that
cigarette) words and music
by Merle Travis and Tex
Williams. © American Music,
inc., Hollywood, Calif.;
27Jun47; EP16044.

WILLIAMS, TEX. See
Williams, Sol.

WILLIAMS-BIGGERS, LELA MACK.
Biggers Business College Song;
words [and melody] by ... Lela
M. Williams, music setting by
... Jeanette D. Dyer. ©
Biggers Business College,
Indianapolis; 21Jan47; EP16499.

WILLIAMSON, HOMER JAMES, 1886-
Make Me a Crusader Today; words
and melody [by] Homer J.
Williamson ... arr. by George M.
Turmail. © Homer J. Williamson,
Indianapolis; 29Jul47; EP17068.
Close score: SATB.

WILLIS BROTHERS.
Old Indians Never Die; words and
music by Jimmie & Leon Short
and the Willis brothers. ©
Ernest Tubb Music, inc., Hollywood, Calif.; 29Aug47; EP17929.

WILLNER, ARTHUR, 1881- arr.
Classical Album. Album Classique
... Arr. by Arthur Willner. ©
Hawkes & Son (London) ltd.,
London; 30Sep47; on arrangement;
EP6652. Score (clarinet and
piano) and part.

Classical Album. Album Classique
... Arr. by Arthur Willner. ©
Hawkes & Son (London) ltd.,
London; 30Sep47; on arrangement;
EF6653. Score (trumpet or
cornet and piano) and part.

Classical Album ... arr. by
Arthur Willner. © Hawkes &
Son (London) ltd., London;
16Oct47; on arrangement;
EF6818. Score (bassoon and
piano) and part.

Classical Album ... for horn in F
and piano ... arr. by Arthur
Willner. © Hawkes & Son
(London) ltd., London; 29Oct47;
on arrangement; EF6896. Score
and part.

Classical Album ... for oboe and
piano ... arr. by Arthur Willner.
© Hawkes & Son (London) ltd.,
London; 29Oct47; on arrangement;
EF6897. Score and part.

WILLNOR, V
Night Birds ... [By] V. Willnor,
arr. [by] Den Berry. © W.
Paxton & Co., ltd., London;
29Jul46; on arrangement;
EF5746. Piano-conductor score
(orchestra) and parts.

WILLS, BOB.
Bob Wills Boogie; by Bob Wills,
L. R. Barnard [and] M. Kelso.
© Bob Wills Music, inc., Holly-
wood, Calif.; 15Sep47; EP18545.
For piano solo, with guitar dia-
grams and chord symbols.

Punkin' Stomp; by Bob Wills.
© Bob Wills Music, inc., Hollywood, Calif.; 30Oct47; EP18542.
For piano solo, with guitar
diagrams and chord symbols.

WILLS, BOB, comp.
Songs from San Antone. © Hill and
Range Songs, inc., Hollywood,
Calif.; 24Sep46; EP5699. For
voice and piano; with guitar dia-
grams and chord symbols.

WILLSON, MEREDITH.
You and I ... words and music by
Meredith Willson, arr. by
Van Alexander. © Bourne, inc.,
New York; 25Jul47; on arrange-
ment; EP16121. Piano-conductor
score (orchestra, with words)
and parts.

WILMOT, L A
Twenty-Four Short Studies, for
technic and sight reading (with-
out octaves); for piano by L. A.
Wilmot. © Theodore Presser Co.,
Philadelphia; 18Jul47; EP15755.

WILSON, BETTY.
Flood Waters; words and music by
Betty Wilson. © Nordyke Publishing Co., Los Angeles;
12Aug47; EP19663.

WILSON, EDWARD E
Wondering; words and music by
Edward E. Wilson. © Nordyke
Publishing Co., Los Angeles;
10Sep45; EP16912.

WILSON, EDWARD KNOX, 1880-
The Ship of Eternal Life; words
and music by ... Edward Knox
Wilson. © Edward Knox Wilson,
Los Angeles; 7Jul47; EP15535.
Close score: SATB.

WILSON, FAITH CHAMBERS.
Prayer for the New Year ... [music
by] Faith Chambers Wilson,
[words by] Elizabeth B. Jones.
(In Sunshine. v.57, no.12,
p.[4]) © Nazarene Publishing
House, Kansas City, Mo.; 1Nov47;
B5-2667. For voice and piano.

Thanksgiving ... [music by] Faith
Chambers Wilson, [words by]
Elizabeth B. Jones. (In Sun-
shine. v.37, no.11, p.[4]) ©
Nazarene Publishing House, Kansas
City, Mo.; 10Oct47; B5-2666. For
voice and piano.

WILSON, HARRY ROBERT, 1901- ed.
and arr.
Choral program series; by Harry
Robert Wilson. © Silver Burdett
Co., New York; bk.3, 90Oct47;
EP18384. Contents.- bk.3. Two-,
three-, and four-part male
voices.

In His Steps; for four-part
chorus of mixed voices with
piano or organ acc. ... Words
and music by Harry Robert
Wilson. © Carl Fischer, inc.,
New York; 7Jul47; EP15698.

In His Steps; sacred song with
piano or organ accompaniment,
words and music by Harry Robert
Wilson. Medium high [voice]
© Carl Fischer, inc., New York;
21Aug47; EP16617.

In His Steps; words and music
by Harry Robert Wilson ...
[for] treble voices with
piano or organ accompaniment.
© Carl Fischer, inc., New
York; 11Aug47; on arrangement;
EP16429.

Let Us Not Forget; words and
music by Harry Robert Wilson.
© J. J. Robbins & Sons, inc.,
New York; 21Aug47; EP18244.

WILSON, HUGH.
Alas! And Did My Savior Bleed;
[by] Hugh Wilson, arr. by W. B.
Olds [for] S.A.T.B., [words by
Isaac Watts] © Hall & McCreary
Co., Chicago; 29Sep47; on ar-
rangement; EP17906.

[WILSON, IRA BISHOP] 1880-
Chimes of the Holy Night; an S.A.B.
Christmas choir cantata arr. ...
from the four-part cantata ...
bearing the same title, text by
Herman Von Berge, music by Fred
B. Holton [pseud.] © Lorenz
Publishing Co., Dayton, Ohio;
30Oct47; on arrangement; EP18910.

A Christmas Dream; a Christmas
pageant, book and lyrics by Emily
Bonaghy, music by Chas. Francis
Lane [pseud.] © Lorenz Publish-
ing Co., Dayton, Ohio; 21Jul47;
D pub 1576.

The Little Lord Jesus; a Christmas
service for younger children [by
Fred B. Holton [pseud., words
by Mildred Lewis Kerr] © Lorenz
Publishing Co., Dayton, Ohio;
8Sep47; EP17718.

Pardon Me, Santa! A Santa Claus
cantata ... text by Valeria R.
Lehman, music by Ruth Dale
[pseud.] © Lorenz Publishing
Co., Dayton, Ohio; 28Jul47;
D pub 1577.

WILSON, IRA BISHOP, 1880- acc.
Lorenz's Gospel Solos New and Old
... comp. and arr. by Ira B.
Wilson. © Lorenz Publishing Co.,
Dayton, Ohio; 20Oct47; EP18913.

WILSON, JOHNNY.
It's Music to My Ears; words and
music by Johnny Wilson.
© Nordyke Publishing Co., Los
Angeles; 29Apr47; EP16885.

WILSON, ROBERT BARCLAY.
To Spring; for piano [by] Robert
Barclay Wilson. © Augener, ltd.,
London; 20Aug47; EF7129.

[WILSON, ROGER C   ] 1912-
The Hand of God ... by Adam Cole
[pseud.], solo for medium
voice. © Lorenz Publishing
Co., Dayton, Ohio; 10ct47;
EP17884.

The Star of Peace; a Christmas
cantata-pageant, text by Elsie
Duncan Yale, music by Roger C.
Wilson. © Lorenz Publishing
Co., Dayton, Ohio; 30ct47;
EP18909. With piano acc.

WILSON, ROGER C   1912-   ed.
Piano Hymn Voluntaries ... ed. by
Roger C. Wilson. © Lorenz Publishing Co., Dayton, Ohio; no.2,
8Oct47; EP18912.

WILTSHIRE, ESTHER, 1912-
Golden October Leaves; [by] Esther
Wiltshire and Nola Whittaker. ©
Esther Wiltshire & Nola Whittaker,
Circleville, Utah; 15Jul47;
EP16990. For voice and piano.

Lilac Twilight; [by] Esther Wilt-
shire and Nola Whittaker. ©
Esther Wiltshire & Nola Whittaker,
Circleville, Utah; 15Jul47;
EP16988. For voice and piano.

WINDHAM, CORNELIUS, 1899-
I'll Reach My Home Some Day; for
choirs and chorus, by Cornelius
Windham, arr. by Perr Lee Mot-
ley. Detroit, Motley's Studio
of Gospel Music. © Cornelius
Windham, Detroit; 5Sep47;
EP18928.

WINKLER, GERHARD.
Aladins Wunderlampe ... Musik: Gerhard Winkler, Arrangement: Adolf
Steimel ... Chinesischer Strassensänger ... Musik und Arrangement:
Gerhard Mohr. © Edition Turicephon, AG., Zürich, Switzerland;
11Aug47; on 2 pieces; EF7039, 7034.
Piano-conductor score (orchestra)
and parts.

WINN, KENNETH EUGENE, 1925-
You Went Away; lyrics by Kay Law-
rence, music by Kenneth E. Winn.
© Kenneth Eugene Winn, Columbia,
Mo., & Kay Helen Lawrence, San
Diego, Calif.; 12Dec47; on words;
EP19858.

WINOGRAD, JACK, 1908-
Last Night in a Dream; (melody
adapted from Mendelssohn's con-
certo), lyrics and adaptation by
Hi Pollock, Roger Genger and Jack
Winograd, [piano score by Frank
V. Turner] © Brightlights Music
Publishing Co., New York; 13e46;
on adaptation and lyrics; EP15507.

WINSTEAD, KENNETH.
Cindy; an American folk song,
four part male voices, T.T.B.B.
a cappella, arr. by Kenneth
Winstead. © M. Witmark & Sons,
New York; 10Dec47; on arrangement; EP20466.

WINTER, DAVID LE. See
Le Winter, David.

[WINTERS, HARRY ELLSWORTH]
My Whole Life Through; [by H. E.
Winters, arr. by Richard Stock-
ton] © Harry E. Winters, Lan-
caster, Pa.; 7Oct47; EP18163.
For voice and piano.

WIREN, DAG IVAR, 1905-
(Sonatina, violoncello & piano)
Sonatin för violoncell och piano.
Op.1. [By] Dag Wirén. Stockholm,
Ed. Suecia. © Föreningen svenska
tonsättare, Edition Suecia, Stock-
holm; 1Jan45; EF7077. Score and
part.

Suite Miniature ... [by] Dag Wirén.
Op. 8 B. Stockholm, Ed. Suecia.
© Föreninger svenska tonsättare,
Edition Suecia, Stockholm;
1Jan40; EF7061. Score (violon-
cello and piano) and part.

WIRGES, WILLIAM FRANCIS.
Say a Prayer for Jim; by Maurice
Crance, Richard Maxwell and
William Wirges. © Maxwell-
Wirges Publications, inc.,
New York; 22Dec43; on words;
EP16566. For voice and piano.

WISE, FRED.
Tomorrow May Be Too Late; words
and music by Steve Nelson, Mil-
ton Leeds [pseud.] and Fred
Wise. © Bob Miller, inc., New
York; 27Oct47; EP18592.

[WISEMAN, SCOTT] 1909-
Lulu Belle and Scotty's Mountain
Melodies; [by Scott Wiseman,
Myrtle Eleanor Wiseman and
Bascomb Lamer Lunsford] ©
Lulu Belle and Scotty (Myrtle
E. Wiseman and Scott Wiseman),
Chicago; 1Jun47; EP16238.
Melody and chord symbols, with
words.

WISNIEWSKI, JOHN B
My Love; words by Peter M. Jorgen-
sen, music by John B. Wisniewski,
arr. by Lindsay McPhail. [c1946]
© Nordyke Publishing Co., Los
Angeles; 28Jan47; EP19357.

WISTER, LELAH ISABEL (MORATH) 1870-
Song of a Mountain Trail; by
Isabel Wister, [words by Lelah P.
Morath, pseud.] San Diego,
Calif., Wister Studio. © Isabel
Wister, San Diego, Calif.;
9Sep47; EP17075. For voice and
piano, with coda for SAB.

WISTERMAN, BOB.
Just to Dream of You; words and
music by Bob Wisterman. © Nordyke Publishing Co., Los Angeles;
31Jul47; EP19501.

We'll Build Our Castle on the
Rainbow; words and music by
Bob Wisterman. © Nordyke
Publishing Co., Los Angeles;
3Sep47; EP19310.

WITKOWSKI, LEO, 1908-
Hurricane Polka; by Leo Witkowski
and Jan Klocek. © Accordion
Music Publishing Co., New York;
11Aug47; EP16311. For accordion
solo.

WITT, F   X
Suscipe Domine; sop. or ten. solo
and four equal voices [by] F. X.
Witt. © McLaughlin & Reilly Co.,
Boston; 2Jun47; EP15880.

WŁODYKA, LENA WOŁOWSKA- See
Wołowska-Włodyka, Lena.

WOHLBERG, MAX, 1907-
Shirei Zimroh; a new musical
setting of the complete Sabbath
morning service ... arr. for
continuous congregational
participation for both youth and
adult services, by Max Wohlberg.
[New York, Bloch Publishing Co.]
© Max Wohlberg, Philadelphia;
25Aug47; EP17917. Melody and
Hebrew words (transliterated)

WOLF-FERRARI, ERMANNO, 1876-
(Concerto, violin) Konzert, D-dur
für Violine und Orchester ... Op.
26. [By] Ermanno Wolf-Ferrari,
Ausg. rev. von Guila Bustabo.
© Casa Musicale Sonzogno di Piero
Ostali, Milano; 31Dec46; EF6930.

Symphonia Brevis; [by] Ermanno
Wolf Ferrari. © Casa Musicale
Sonzogno di Piero Ostali, Milano;
15Jun47; EF6931. Score: orchestra.

WOLFE, JACQUES, arr.
Jacques Wolfe's American Songster;
17 American folk-songs in
arrangements for medium voice
and piano. © Carl Fischer, inc.,
New York; 8Sep47; on arrangement;
EP18081.

WOLFE, SADIE M
You're Like a Dear White Rosebud;
words and music by Sadie M.
Wolfe. [c1946] © Nordyke Publishing Co., Los Angeles;
30Oct47; EP20389.

WOLFF, S. DRUMMOND- See also
Drummond-Wolff, S.

WOLFF, S   DRUMMOND, 1916-
ed. and arr.
Metropolitan Organ Book; [comp.],
arr. and ed. by S. Drummond
Wolff. © Gordon V. Thompson,
ltd., Toronto; 8Sep47; on
arrangement & compilation;
EF6792.

WOŁOWSKA-WŁODYKA, LENA, 1921-
Piosenka z Paryża. Chanson de Paris.
Słowa i muzyka: Lena Wołowska-
Włodyka, paroles françaises de
Georges Liferman. © Éditions
musicales Nuences, Paris; 17Jul47;
EF7317.

WOOD, DALE, pseud. See
Hansen, Bill.

WOOD, GERALDENE.
Drunk on Love; words and music by
Geraldene Wood. © Nordyke Publishing Co., Los Angeles;
21Aug47; EP19637.

When the Sun Is Going Down; words
and music by Geraldene Wood.
© Nordyke Publishing Co., Los
Angeles; 14Jul47; EP17543.

WOOD, GUY.
Blow the Man Down; (There was a
young skipper) Words and music by
Sammy Gallop and Guy Wood. ©
Empire Music Co., inc., New York;
19Sep47; on words & arrangement;
EP18546.

"I'm Down to My Last Dream;"
words and music by Eddie Seiler,
music by Guy Wood.
© Rainbow Music Corp., New
York; 31Oct47; EP20158.

Music from beyond the Moon; lyric
by Jack Lawrence, music by Guy
Wood. © Robert Music Corp.,
New York; 7Nov47; EP18793.

WOOD, HAYDN.
Princess Elizabeth of England;
(arr. as a two-part song for soprano voices) words by Dr. W. E.
St. Lawrence Finny, music by
Haydn Wood. © Ascherberg, Hopwood & Crew, ltd., London;
29Sep47; on arrangement; EF7360.

Princess Elizabeth of England;
song, words by Dr. W. E. St.
Lawrence Finny, music by Haydn
Wood. © Ascherberg, Hopwood
& Crew, ltd., London; 5Aug47;
EF6253.

Princess Elizabeth of England;
words by Dr. W. E. St. Lawrence
Finny, music by Haydn Wood, arr.
for mixed voices, S. C. T. B.,
by the composer. © Ascherberg,
Hopwood & Crew, ltd., London;
14Aug47; EF6370.

A Thousand Beautiful Things; words
by Richard Corrin, music by
Haydn Wood, arr. for mixed
voices (S.A.T.B.) by the
composer. © Ascherberg, Hopwood
and Crew, ltd., London; 15Sep47;
on arrangement; EF6753.

WOOD, HAYDN. Cont'd.
Whene'er You Call; song, words by
Harry Dawson, music by Haydn Wood.
© Ascherberg, Hopwood & Crew,
ltd., London; 19Aug47; EF6361.

WOOD, HOWARD ORTON, 1889-
Hymn of Praise; for mixed voices,
words by R. Mant ... music by
Howard Orton Wood. © Howard O.
Wood, Hollis, Queen's County,
N. Y.; 16Oct47; EP18933.

WOODBURY, JOHN JEWETT, 1915-
I Can't Hit the Ground with My
Hat; words and music by Ken
Woodbury. © Dreamhouse Publications, inc.,
Hollywood, Calif.; 4Aug47;
EP16572.

WOODFORD, GORDON ROBERT, 1917-
Blue Birds in the Rain; words by
Eva Chapman, music by Gordon R.
Woodford. © Nordyke Publishing
Co., Los Angeles; 25May46;
EP19491.

Dear Pal of Long Ago; words by
James Welle Maddin, music by
James Welland [pseud.] © Nordyke Publishing Co., Los Ange-
les; 19Jun47; EP17533.

How Can You Talk about Love?
Words by Virginia Mains, music
by James Welland, music
by James Welland [pseud. c1946]
© Nordyke Publishing Co., Los
Angele; 28Jan47; EP19937.

Mary Was a Little Girl; words
by Ernest M. J. Keller, music
by James Welland [pseud.]
© Nordyke Publishing Co., Los
Angeles; 31Jul47; EP17493.

Smile; words by Ralph Burns,
music by James Welland [pseud.]
© Nordyke Publishing Co., Los
Angeles; 25Jul46; EP20325.

Sparkling Diamonds; words by Edmund
H. Hentges, music by James Well-
and [pseud.] © Nordyke Publishing Co., Los Angeles; 28Jul7;
EP20037.

There Goes My Heart Again; words by
Ruth Evans, music by James Welland
[pseud.] © Nordyke Publishing Co.,
Los Angeles; 11Jun47; EP17578.

Why Did You Tell Me a Lie?
Words by Jewell House, music by
James Welland, [pseud.] ©
Nordyke Publishing Co., Los
Angeles; 27Mar47; EP16774.

WOODGATE, HUBERT LESLIE. See
Woodgate, Leslie.

WOODGATE, LESLIE, 1902-
The Merry-Go-Rounds; two-part song
for equal voices (soprano) words
by Elizabeth Fleming, music by
Leslie Woodgate. © Ascherberg,
Hopwood & Crew, ltd., London;
15Sep47; EF6754.

The Road End; unison song, words
by Elizabeth Fleming, music by
Leslie Woodgate. © Ascherberg,
Hopwood & Crew, ltd., London;
15Sep47; EF6755.

WOODSIDE, JAMES, 1895-1945.
What Tidings Bringest Thou,
Messenger? Ancient English
Christmas carol for four-part
chorus of mixed voices with
solo or junior choir. Modern
English version adapted from the
original "Middle English" by
James Woodside ... arr. by
James Woodside. © Boston Music
Co., Boston; 17Sep47; on modern
English versions & arrangement;
EP17360.

WOOLDRIDGE, JOHN.
(Fame Is the Spur) Music for the
piano from the ... production
"Fame Is the Spur." ... The
music by John Wooldridge. © De
Wolfe (Meyer De Wolfe), London;
15Jun47; EF5788.

WOOLER, HARRY.
Show Me My Task; three part
S.S.A., [by] Harry Wooler, arr.
by Dora Flick Flood, poem by
Rev. B. V. Tippett. © Dorothea
Louise Schroeder, Flushing,
N. Y.; 5Sep47; on arrangement;
EP17774.

WOOLSON, ROBERT CALHOUN, 1922-
SAE Sweetheart; words by Robert
Petersen, music by Robert Woolson.
© Robert Calhoun Woolson,
Winnetka, Ill. and Robert James
Petersen, Waterloo, Iowa; 18Aug47;
EP16571.

WOOTEN, IRENE.
Will I Forget You? Words and
music by Irene Wooten. [c1945]©
Nordyke Publishing Co., Los
Angeles; 14Jun46; EP19474.

WORDSWORTH, WILLIAM.
Hymn of Dedication; for S.A.T.B,
with organ acc. [by] William Words-
worth, words by G. K. Chesterton.
© Alfred Lengnick & Co., ltd.,
London; 8Aug47; EF6846.

WORK, JOHN W
Listen to the Angels Shouting; for
chorus of women's voices, with
contralto solo, S.S.A. or S.A.A.
Negro spiritual, arr. by John W.
Work. © Galaxy Music Corporation, New York; 26Nov47; on
arrangement; EP19121.

WORLD WIDE RADIO SONGS; a special
collection of favorite sacred and
spiritual songs ... [by Sam. L.
Wallace, Robert E. Arnold, and
others, words by Orris A. Ferris,·
and others] comp. by the Stamps
Quartets and our editorial staff.
© Stamps Quartet Music Co., inc.,
Jasper, Ala.; 88ep47; EP17836.
Shape-note notation.

WORMAL, NELLIE E
St. Christopher's-by-the-River;
by Nellie E. Wormal. © Nellie E.
Wormal, Ashtabula, Ohio;
20Aug47; EP17086. For piano
solo.

WORTH, BOBBY, 1918-
So Far, So Wonderful; words and
music by Bobby Worth. © Hollywood
Melodies, Music Publishers; Los
Angeles; 1Jul47; EP16664.

WRAY, JOHN.
Capriccioso ... [by] John Wray.
© The Oxford University Press,
London; 17Apr47; EF6099.
Score (viola and piano) and
part.

WRIGHT, ELBERT LUTCHER, 1902-
That Old Time Religion; by E. L.
Wright. © Elbert Lutcher
Wright, Burkeville, Tex.;
9Nov47; EP18978. Close score?
SATB; shape-note notation.

WRIGHT, ELIOT.
Awake I Dream; words by Betty
Yates, music by Eliot Wright.
[c1945] © Nordyke Publishing
Co., Los Angeles; 21Jun46;
EP19472.

If Love Can Win the Way; words by
Alma Buffum, music by Eliot
Wright. © Alma Buffum, Port
Orchard, Wash.; 3Dec47; EP19861.

On the Shores of Pearl Harbor Far
Away; words by Newton A. Get-
tings, music by Eliot Wright.
[c1945] © Nordyke Publishing
Co., Los Angeles; 28Jun46;
EP19412.

WRIGHT, ELIOT HOPKINS, 1907-
Pioneer Trail; words by Charles
Croall, music by Eliot Wright.
© Charles Croall, Portland, Or.;
7Apr47; EP19207.

WRIGHT, EMMA HOUSTON, 1885-
Let the People Praise Thee;
[words] adapted from LXVII
Psalm, music by Emma Houston
Wright. © Uhl & Ware, San
Antonio; 10Jul47; EP15718.
Score: SSA and piano.

WRIGHT, FRANK, 1901-   arr.
My Lady Greensleeves; arr. for
brass band by Frank Wright. ©
Besson and Co., ltd., London;
16Oct47; on arrangement;
EF6824. Condensed score and
parts.

WRIGHT, HELEN.
Bless My Soul; words and music
by Helen Wright. © Helen
Wright, Palo Alto; Calif.;
5Jul47; EP15640.

[WRIGHT, LAWRENCE] 1893-   comp.
Wedding Album; [comp. by Lawrence
Wright] © Lawrence Wright Music
Co., ltd., London; 20Oct47;
EF6751. Principally for voice
and piano.

WRIGHT, M   SEARLE.
Magnificat and Nunc Dimittis; for
mixed voices in the key of E
minor, by M. Searle Wright. ©
The H. W. Gray Co., inc., New
York; 7Nov47; EP19262. English
words.

WRIGHT,   LOUISE, 1879-
Parade March; for piano by N.
Louise Wright. © Willis Music
Co., Cincinnati; 11Dec47;
EP19986.

Valse Débonnaire; for piano [by] N.
Louise Wright. © Theodore Presser
Co., Philadelphia; 6Dec47;
EP20443.

A Wee Little Waltz ... [by] N.
Louise Wright. (In Hirschberg,
David, ed. and comp. Pieces
Are Fun. bk. 1, p. 12-13) ©
Musicord Publications, New
York; 2Jul47; EP15930. For
piano solo.

[WRIGHT, WILLIAM JOHN]
New Songs that Will Live; [by Will
J. Wright] © William John Wright,
Mishawaka, Ind.; 21Jul47; EP15737.

WRUBEL, ALLIE.
Don't Call It Love. See his I Walk Alone

Forsaking All Others; lyric by Don
George ... music by Allie Wrubel.
© Jewel Music Publishing Co.,
inc., New York; 2Jul47; EP15371.

(I Walk Alone) Don't Call It
Love, as sung in ... "I Walk
Alone", words by Ned Washington,
music by Allie Wrubel. © Famous
Music Corp., New York; 20Oct47;
EP18530.

I'm A-Comin' A-Courtin' Corabelle;
lyric by Chas. Newman, music by
Allie Wrubel. © Famous Music
Corp., New York; 9Oct47; EP17791.

WUERTHNER, JULIUS J
Lions' Convention Song; words and
music by Julius J. Wuerthner.
© Lions Club of Great Falls,
Great Falls, Mont.; 30Jun47;
EP15513.

WULFFEN, OTTO ALBERT, 1898-
I'll Keep on Smiling; ... music
by ... Otto Wulffen, words
[by] Mary Taglioli, [arr. by
Carl Philip Gronemeyer] © Mary
J. Taglioli, Chicago; 4Jun47;
EP15534.

WURMSER, LUCIEN, 1877-
Études de concert et de concours,
[by] Lucien Wurmser. © Éditions
Ouvrières, Paris; livre 1,
21Apr47; EF5963. For piano solo.

WYRTZEN, CASPER JOHN, 1913-   comp.
Word of Life Chorus-Melodies; for
... young people's meeting, con-
ference, youth rally and Sunday
School ... comp. by Jack Wyrtzen
... Carlton Booth ... [and]
Norman Clayton. Lalverne, N. Y.,
Gospel Songs. © Norman John
Clayton, Lalverne, N. Y.; 29Aug47;
EP17773.

WYRTZEN, JACK. See
Wyrtzen, Casper John.

X

X, pseud. See
Grill, Karl Rudolf N

Y

YABLOK, OSHER ZAIV, 1875-
Vichtige Retzitativen. © Osher
Zaiv Yablok, Columbus, Ohio;
30Jun47; EP15481. Melody for
cantor; Hebrew words.

YAMIN, JAIME.
Que Importa Mi Sufrir? (You Don't
Seem to Care) ... English words
by Joe Davis, Spanish words and
music by Jaime Yamin. © Caribbean Music Co., New York;
1Dec47; EF18955.

YANKOVIC, FRANK J   1915-
Beach Polka; by Frank Yankovic,
arr. for the accordion by Joseph
Trolli, arr. for piano and Bb-Eb
instruments by Vladimir Maleckar.
[n.p.] Sole selling agent,
Trophy Products Co. © F. & J.
Publishing Co., Cleveland;
31Mar47; on piano and accordion
arrangement; EP15404.

Café Polka; by Frank Yankovic, arr.
for the accordion by Joseph
Trolli, arr. for piano and Bb-Eb
instruments by Vladimir Maleckar.
[n.p.] Sole selling agent,
Trophy Products Co. © F. & J.
Publishing Co., Cleveland;
31Mar47; on piano and accordion
arrangement; EP15405.

Happy Hour Waltz; by Frank Yankovic, arr. for the accordion by
Joseph Trolli, arr. for piano
and Bb-Eb instruments by Vladimir
Maleckar. [n.p.] Sole selling
agent, Trophy Products Co. © F.
& J. Publishing Co., Cleveland;
31Mar47; on piano and accordion
arrangement; EP15409.

Hurray Slovenes Polka; by Frank
Yankovic, arr. for the accordion
by Joseph Trolli, arr. for piano
and Bb-Eb instruments by Vladimir
Maleckar. [n.p.] Sole selling
agent, Trophy Products Co. © F.
& J. Publishing Co., Cleveland;
31Mar47; on piano and accordion
arrangement; EP15408.

Let's Go to the Green Town Waltz;
by Frank Yankovic, arr. for the
accordion by Joseph Trolli, arr.
for piano and Bb-Eb instruments
by Vladimir Maleckar. [n.p.]
Sole selling agent, Trophy Products Co. © F. & J Publishing
Co., Cleveland; 31Mar47; on piano
and accordion arrangement; EP15403.

Shanty Polka; by Frank Yankovic,
arr. for the accordion by Joseph
Trolli, arr. for piano and Bb-Eb
instruments by Vladimir Maleckar.
[n.p.] Sole selling agent,
Trophy Products Co. © F. & J.
Publishing Co., Cleveland;
31Mar47; on piano and accordion
arrangement; EP15406.

Waltz Medley; by Frank Yankovic,
arr. for the accordion by Joseph
Trolli, arr. for piano and Bb-Eb
instruments by Vladimir Maleckar.
[n.p.] Sole selling agent,
Trophy Products Co. © F. & J.
Publishing Co., Cleveland; 31Mar47;
on piano & accordion arrangement;
EP15407. Caption title: Slovenian waltz medley.

YANTZ, JACKIE.
Here Is My Heart; lyrics by Tom
Gravemeyer, music by Jackie
Yantz. Louisville, Ky., J.
Gravemeyer. © H. L.
Gravemeyer, Louisville, Ky.;
7Aug47; EP16091.

YARBROUGH, Mrs. C   C   1914-
The Old Log Cabin Song; by Mrs. C.
C. Yarbrough. © Stamps Quartet
Music Co., inc., Dallas; 25Jul47;
EP16020. For voice and piano.

YARDUMIAN, RICHARD.
Chromatic Sonata; for piano solo.
© Elkan-Vogel Co., inc., Phila-
dolphia; 17Jul47; EP15869.

YAW, RALPH.
Down in Chihuahua ... by Johnny
Richards and Ralph Yaw. ©
Leslie Music Corp., New York;
6Dec46; EP15838. For voice and
piano, with chord symbols.

Down in Chihuahua; words and music
by Johnny Richards & Ralph Yaw,
arr. by Van Alexander. New
York, Capitol Songs. © Leslie
Music Corp., New York; 30Oct47;
EP18512. Piano-conductor score
(orchestra, with words) and
parts.

YEAKEY, MARGARET, 1876-
My America; [by] Margaret Yeakey.
© Margaret Yeakey, Westcliffe,
Colo.; 30Oct47; EP18094. Close
score: SATB; shape-note nota-
tion.

YERGER, DONALD OSCAR, 1925-
I Gave My Heart to You; words and
music by Donald O. Yerger. ©
Donald O. Yerger, Lock Haven,
Pa.; 16Oct47; EP18091.

YODER, PAUL.
Eyes of Texas; arr. by Paul Yoder.
© Volkwein Bros., inc., Pittsburgh; 2Jul46; on arrangement's
score, added parts & editing;
EP16968. Piano-conductor score
(band) and parts.

Mountain Majesty ... [by] Paul
Yoder. © Belwin, inc., New
York; 90ct47; EP18146. Score
(band), condensed score and
parts.

Symphonic Series of Sacred Songs;
by Paul Yoder. Winona Lake,
Ind., Rodeheaver Hall-Mack Co.
© The Rodeheaver Co., Winona
Lake, Ind., 12Sep47; on instrumentation; EP17740. Condensed
score (band) and parts.

--- The Old Rugged Cross, All Hail
the Power, Rock of Ages, from
Symphonic Series of Sacred Songs,
by Paul Yoder, for mixed voices
in eight parts. © The Rodeheaver Co., Winona Lake, Ind.;
12Sep47; on arrangement;
EP17739. Vocal score, without
the band acc.

YODER, WALTER ELI, 1889-   ed.
Junior Hymns ... Walter E. Yoder,
editor. © Herald Press, Scott-
dale, Pa.; 15Nov47; A19159.

YOGAN, JERRY.
Colorado; by Jerry Yogan. ©
Bourne, inc., New York; 10Nov47;
EP18611. For voice and piano,
with chord symbols.

Yolson, Asa. See
Jolson, Al

YON, PIETRO, 1886-1943.
Veni Domine. (Come, O Lord) [For]
high solo and 2 or 3 part chorus
of equal voices, [by] Pietro Yon,
arr. by T.N.M. © McLaughlin &
Reilly Co., Boston; 15Nov47; on
arrangement; EP18915.

YON, S   COSTANTINO.
One Hour with Thee; (for T.T.B.B.
voices) [by] S. C. Yon. © National Headquarters of the Holy
Name Societies, New York;
12Sep47; EP17874.

Queen of the Holy Rosary; (for
T.T.B.B. voices) [by] S. C.
Yon. © National Headquarters
of Holy Name Societies, New
York; 12Sep47; EP17877.

YORK, FRED E
My Million Dollar Baby; words and
music by Fred E. York. [c1945]
© Nordyke Publishing Co., Los
Angeles; 30Oct47; EP20096.

YORK, LESLIE.
Hamtramck Mama; (song) by Leslie
York. © Dixie Music Pub. Co.,
New York; 25Aug47; EP18982.

YOUMANS, VINCENT, 1898-1946.
Carioca; two part chorus arr. by
Gus Kahn and Edward Eliscu, music by
Vincent Youmans. New York, T. B.
Harms. © Max Dreyfus & A. L. Ber-
man, as executor of the estate of
Vincent Youmans, New York; 1Dec47;
on arrangement; EP20457.

Hallelujah; [by] Vincent Youmans,
transcribed by Gregory Stone
[for] piano duet. © Harms,
inc., New York; 10Nov47; on
arrangement; EP18876.

(No No Nanette) Tea for Two. "Tú
Serás." From the musical comedy
"No No Nanette," Spanish text
by Johnnie Camacho, words by
Irving Cnesar, music by Vincent
Youmans. © Harms, inc., New
York; 9Jul47; on Spanish text;
EP15624.

Orchids in the Moonlight; words
by Gus Kahn and Edward Eliscu,
music by Vincent Youmans ...
S.A.B. arr. by William Stickles.
New York, T. B. Harms Co. ©
Max Dreyfus & A. L. Berman as
executor of the estate of Vincent Youmans, deceased, New York;
70Oct47; on arrangement; EP18277.

Orchids in the Moonlight; words by
Gus Kahn and Edward Eliscu, music
by Vincent Youmans, two part
chorus arr. by William Stickles.
New York, T. B. Harms Co. ©
Max Dreyfus and A. L. Berman as
executor of the estate of Vincent Youmans, deceased, New York;
70Oct47; EP18276.

Tea for two. See his No No Nanette.

Tú Serás. See his No No Nanette.

YOUNG, ARTHUR.
Six Shakespearian Songs; (words by
Shakespeare, and others) set to
music by Arthur Young. ©
Chappell & Co., ltd., London;
19Jul47; EF6529.

YOUNG, BILL.
Possum Trot (in Tennessee); by
Bill Young. © Campbell-Forgie,
inc., New York; 5Jun47; EP6988.
For voice and piano, with chord
symbols.

YOUNG, PETER, pseud. See
Paul, Alan.

YOUNG, VICTOR, 1900-
Golden Earrings; [from the Para-
mount picture "Golden Earrings"]
Words by Jay Livingston and Ray
Evans, music by Victor Young.
[c1946] © Famous Music Corp.,
New York; 17Jul47; EP15773.

Stella by Starlight; by Victor
Young. Piano solo arrangement
by Jack Fina, [ed. by Olin B.
Adams] © Famous Music Corp.,
New York; 9Sep47; on arrange-
ment; EP17210.

Sweet Sue, Just You ... music by
Victor Young ... [arr.] by
Charles Magnante. © Shapiro,
Bernstein & Co., inc., New
York; 14Oct47; on arrangement;
EP18025. For accordion solo.
Includes "straight version" and
"A Charles Magnante interpreta-
tion."

Waltzing in a Dream; by Victor
Young, arr. by Allan Small.
© Leeds Music Corp., New York;
16Jun47; on arrangement;
EP15349. Piano-conductor score
(orchestra) and parts.

Why Did I Leave My Home; old Irish
song, [words] collected by D. E.
Wheeler, [music] by Victor Young.
© Theodore Presser Co., Philadelphia; 22Oct47; EP18420.

[YOXSIMER, HELEN] 1914-
I'd Be a Fool Again; words ... by
Rita Paul [pseud.], music [by
Rita Paul and Mabel F. Gehring]
© Clock Publishing Co., inc.,
Santa Monica, Calif.; 15Oct47;
EP18548.

YRADIER, S
La Paloma; plectrum guitar solo,
[by] S. Yradier, arr. as played
by F. Victor. c1939. © Albert
Rocky Co., New York; 10Jan40;
on arrangement; EP20183.

YSABEL, ALBERT K
Was It You? Words and music by
Albert K. Ysabel. © Nordyke
Publishing Co., Los Angeles;
16Dec46; EP19473.

YUILL, MILDRED.
Four Out-Door Scenes; for piano
by M. Yuill. © The B. F. Wood
Music Co., Boston; 15Aug47.
Contents.- [1] Woodland Echoes
(© EP16222) - [2] Wood Nymph's
Serenade (© EP16223) - [3] Nod-
ding Buttercups (© EP16224) -
[4] Field Day (© EP16225)

YVAIN, MAURICE, 1891-
Chanson Gitane; opérette en 2 actes
et 13 tableaux ... couplets de L,
Poterat, musique de Maurice Yvain.
Paris, Choudens. © Editions
Royalty, Paris; 3. recueil,
31Mar47; EF5902.

Z

ZAHAVI, HENRY GOLD- pseud. See
Gold, Henryk.

ZAIRA, M
Call of the Soil. Adama. Melody
by M. Zaira, poem by E. Harusi,
English text adaptation by Ben M.
Edidin, setting for ... S.A.T.B.
by Erwin Jospe. © Transcontinental Music Corp., New York;
18Nov47; on arrangement & English
adaptation; EP18829.

To Zion's Shore. Pakud Adonai ...
Melody by M. Zaira, transcribed
for mixed voices (S.A.T.B.) by
Harry Coopersmith. © Trans-
continental Music Corp., New
York; 25Jul47; on arrangement;
EP15898. Hebrew words (trans-
literated)

[ZAMMATARO, SALVATORE JOSEPH]
1900-
Blond Eyelash in His Black
Mustache; words and music by
Al Zammy, [pseud.] ©
Salvatore Joseph Zammataro,
New York; 22Aug47; EP16512.

ZAMMY, AL, pseud. See
Zammataro, Salvatore Joseph.

ZANIRATO, TONY EDWARD.
With the Thoughts of You; words
and music by Tony Edward Zanirato. © Nordyke Publishing Co.,
Los Angeles; 21Aug47; EP20071.

ZARABOZO, DANIEL.
Tú Te Vas ... Letra, música y
arreglo de Daniel Zarabozo.
© Editorial Mexicana de Música
Internacional, s. a., Mexico;
30Dec46; EP5811. Condensed
score (orchestra), piano-
conductor score and parts.

ZELL, O
Little Heart-Breaker; words and
music by Harris B. Robison and
O. E. Zell. © Nordyke Publish-
ing Co., Los Angeles; 14Jun47;
EP17555.

ZELLECKER, FERRY, 1911-
Wiener Bonbons; ein musikalisches
Bilderbuch, aus dem Wien der
siebziger Jahre, in einem Vorspiel
und sechs Bildern, Buch und
Musik, von Ferry Zelwecker. ©
Ludwig Doblinger (Bernhard
Herzmansky) K.G., Music Publish-
er, Vienna; 20Sep43; EP5813.
Piano-vocal score.

ZICCARDI, FELIX STANISLAUS.
Missa in Honorem Sanctissimae
Trinitatis; (for two equal
voices); music by Rev. F. S.
Ziccardi ... a simplified and
easier arrangement of the ...
Mass in G, for four mixed
voices. Trinidad, Colo.,
Father Ziccardi's Boys Band. ©
Felix Stanislaus Ziccardi,
Trinidad, Colo.; 24Sep47; on
arrangement; EP18239.

ZIEGLER, ELMER.
The Service Musician; by Elmer
Ziegler. © Ziegler Band Music
Publishing Co., Sterling, Ill.;
30Jun47; on arrangement; EP15549.
Condensed score (band) and parts.
"Rev. and rearranged to suit
modern instrumentation."

ZIEGLER, LILY F
My Dream Is Ended; words & music
by Lily F. Ziegler. © Nordyke
Publishing Co., Los Angeles;
9Nov46; EP19777.

ZIEHLER, JACK.
Dear Diary; words and music by
Catherine Novak, Ace Pancoast
[and] Jack Ziehler. © Mardi Gras
Music Co., Buffalo; 16Jun47;
EP6991.

ZILBERTS, ZAVEL.
Vehu Rachum ... (He is Merciful);
liturgical chant, music by Zavel
Zilberts, for voice and piano.
New York, Metro Music Co.
© Henry Lefkowitch, New York;
22Apr47; EP15533. Hebrew words
(transliterated)

ZINN, LUCILLE.
Sweet Sweet; words and music by
Lucille Zinn. © Nordyke
Publishing Co., Los Angeles;
22Jul47; EP20054.

ZITA, FRANTIŠEK, 1880-1946.
Fanfárový pochod; [by] Fr. Zita.
© Jaroslav Stožický, Brno,
Czechoslovakia; 9Jun46; EP5424.
Parts: band.

ZMIGROD, ALFRED, 1905-
Meisje, Doe Me een Lol. Puerta
del Sol. Música e letras [by]
Alfredo Zmigrod, ned. tekst [by]
Han Dunk, [piano arrangement
by Ronny Luce] © Metro-Muziek,
Amsterdam, Holland; 15Apr46;
EP6922.

ZOEFER, WILLIAM.
That's Why I Love You; words and
music by William Zoffer. [c1946]
© Nordyke Publishing Co., Los
Angeles; 13Jan47; EP19478.

[ZORDAN, ANTHONY]
Brown Eyes ... for piano accordion,
[by] Anthony Zordan] © Chart
Music Publishing House, inc.,
Chicago; 17Oct47; EP18404.

Loretta ... [By] Antonio Zordan.
© Chart Music Publishing House,
inc., Chicago; 3Sep47; EP17201.
For piano accordion solo.

Lucille; polka [by] Antonio Zor-
dan. © Chart Music Publishing
House, inc.; 15Jul47; EP19128.
For accordion solo.

March of the Cavaliers. © Chart
Music Publishing House, inc.,
Chicago; 23Jul47; EP15965. For
piano accordion solo.

ZURKE, BOB.
Sugared Candy; [by] Bob Zurke.
© Leo Feist, inc., New York;
10Apr39; EP16151. Correcting
EP76316. For piano solo.

All Aboard.
. Harm, M. L.
All about doggies.
Alkire, E. H.
All about jugs.
Alkire, E. H. All about doggies.
All about stars.
Alkire, E. H., All about doggies.
All Dressed Up with a Broken Heart.
Val, J.
All Hail the Power.
Yoder, P. Symphonic Series of Sacred
Songs.
All in the Morning.
Cockshott, G.
All My Dreams.
Hall, D.
All My Dreams Come True.
Gage, H. A.
All My Hope on Earth Is Jesus.
Fillmore, F. A.
All My Life.
Waldteufel, E. Dolores.
All My Love.
Akst, H.
All Nature Is Smiling.
Bach, J. S. Weichet Nur.
All of My Life.
Clyde, T.
All of the Time.
Rinehart, J.
All on account of You.
Clark, C. van N.
All over Again.
Arthur, W.
All the Good Things Come from
Missouri.
Habing, F. F.
All the World Is Mine.
Portnoff, M. Carnegie Hall.
Alla Marcia.
Sibelius, J.
Allah.
Chadwick, G. W.
Allegro.
Rodgers, R.
Allegro Brillante. .
Carson, R. B.
Allegro da Concerto.
Botti, C. Composizioni per tromba e
piano-forte.
Allegro Symphonique.
Fleury, A.
Allegro Vigoroso.
Norden, H.
Alleluia.
Mozart, J. C. W. A. Exsultate, jubilate.
Alleluia, Lord God.
Palestrina, G. P. da, Adoramus Te.
Alleluja.
Bach, J. S. Uns ist ein Kind Geboren.
Alles Versteh'n Heisst Alles Verzeih'n.
Kreuder, P.
Allez Lui Dire que Je L'Aimé.
Cadou, A. P.
Almira.
Händel, G. F.
Almost Like Being in Love.
Loewe, F. Brigadoon.
Alone in Spring.
Novelli, S. P.
Alone in the Valley of Dreams.
Kaiser, M. M.
Alone with the Moon.
Montgomery, C. R.
Along El Camino Real.
Hamilton, A.
Along the Blue Muskingum.
Bartlett, F.
Along the Street I Hear.
Bartholomew, M.
Alto Mood at Midnite.
Hornett, S.
Alto Reverie.
Cardew, D.
Always and a Day.
Vanderburg, G. J.

Always Keep Busy.
Bartlett, F.
Always Working.
Shtreicher, L.
Am End Macht "Er" Alles Allright.
Benatzky, R.
Am I to Blame.
Paris, J. B.
Am I Wastin' My Time.
Preobrajensky, V.
Am I Wasting My Time on You.
Bibo, I.
Am I Worthy of You.
Fein, S. B.
Amapola.
Lacalle, J. M.
America.
Bond, A. J.
America for Me.
Filas, J.
America, My Native Land.
Arthur, W.
American Ballads.
Harris, R.
American Dance.
Basham, L.
American Girl.
Arthur, W.
American Patrol.
Meacham, F. W.
American Salute.
Gould, M.
American Songster.
Wolfe, J., arr.
American Symphonette no. 2.
Gould, M.
American Wings Band Book.
Hyde, A.
Americana.
Gould, M.
Americans Will Always Be Americans.
Wellington, M.
America's Favorite Radio Songs.
Easterling, M. W., comp.
Amo Solo la Fisarmonica.
Lezza, C.
Amor de Mi Vida.
Los Cuates Castilla (Musicians)
Amour à la Boogie Woogie.
Couët, J. D.
Amour de Moi.
Quilter, R. My Lady's Garden.
Amour de Ninette.
Betti, H. Mam'zelle Printemps.
Amour Est un Jeu.
Tranchant, J. H.
Amour N'est Qu'une Comédie.
Cloerec, R. Monsieur Alibi.
Amour S'Amuse.
Pipon, L.
Amours de Jupiter.
Ibert, J.
Anahuac.
Miramontes, A.
Anchors Aweigh.
Brahms, J.
And in That Day.
Mopper, I.
And Mimi.
Simon, N.
And Now I'm Lonely.
Hall, D.
And on Earth Peace.
Strickland, L. T.
And there were shepherds abiding in the
field.
Bach, J. S. Christmas Symphony.
Andalucia.
Lecuona y Casado, E.
Lecuona y Casado, E. Malagueña.
Andalucia Suite.
Lecuona y Casado, E. Gitanerias.
Andante and Finale.
Gershwin, G. Rhapsody in Blue.
Andante Religioso.
Albanese, L.
Angel in the wings.
Sigman, C.

Angel I've fallen for you.
Carter, J.
Angel o Demonio.
Curiel, G.
Angel Song.
Millard, M.
A-N-G-E-L Spells Mary.
Frisch, A.
Angels are Singing.
Blair, H. The New Born King.
Angels, that around us hover.
Wallace, V. (Maritana) The Angelus.
Angelus.
Wallace, V. Maritana.
Anges dans Nos Campagnes.
Daltry, J. S.
Animal Parade.
Stevens, E.
Anitra's Dance.
Grieg, E. H.
Grieg, E. H. Peer Gynt.
Anneau d'argent.
Chaminade. C. The Silver Ring.
Annen Polka.
Strauss, J.
Annie Get Your Gun.
Berlin, I.
Annie Laurie.
Scott, J. D., lady.
Annie Rooney.
Nolan, M.
Anniversary Song.
Chaplin, S. The Jolson Story.
Another Man's Wife.
Tobin, L.
Ansias de Amar.
Brito, A. You and Your Love.
Answer to Rainbow at Midnight.
Miller, J. A.
Anthem for a Harvest Festival.
Ley, H. G.
Antiche Intavolature.
Salfi, F., arr.
Apalachicola, Fla.
Van Heusen, J. The Road to Rio.
Aphèse Me na Philèso.
Bellas, G. G.
Apopse Th'artho na Se Klepso.
Iakobidēs, Z.
Appel.
Agosti, G. Due Liriche.
Apple Blossom Wedding.
Simon, N.
Apple Blossoms.
Antoine, brother.
Après les Devoirs.
Martin, M. C.
April and Tulip Time.
Chanslor, H.
April in Paris.
Dukelsky, V. Walk a Little Faster.
April Nosegay.
Hopkins, J. M.
April Showers.
Silvers, L.
Apurimac.
Napolitano, E. A.
Aquatennial Parade.
Starbeck, E. T.
Arab Chant.
Steiner, M.
Arab Dance.
Chaikovskiĭ, P. I.
Arabesque.
Bowen, Y.
Are You Ashamed.
Wakely, J.
Are You Hiding the Word of God.
Niswander, D. L.
Are You Kidding.
Castellanos, A. L.
Are You Listening in.
Hallett, J. C., comp. Singing Along.
Are You Satisfied Now.
Daffan, T.
Aria.
Bach, J. S.

380

Handel, G. F. Ptolemy.
Scarlatti, A.
Arise. All Nations.
Deis, C.
Arizay.
West, E.
Arizona Moon.
Richard, L.
Arizona Serenade.
Vanderburg, G. J.
Arkansas Traveler.
Glynn, B. B.
Arlésienne.
Bizet, G.
Arm in Arm.
Vandercook, H. A.
Army's Little Jeep.
Tobin, L.
Around the Throne Afterwhile.
Smith, B. L.
Arpeggietto.
Bryant, A.
Arrimate.
Moya, R. de.
Arrostēsa stē Xeniteia.
Sakellariou, A. C. Tria Phtaiximata.
Arrow and the Song.
Cain, N.
Arrulladora.
Miramontes, A.
Miramontes, A. Dos Miniaturas.
Art Songs of Soviet Russia.
Haywood, C., ed.
Sergeev, A. The Red Army Soldier's Son.
Arthur Tallman Music Features - You. See title entry in composer list.
Artistry in Bolero.
Rugolo, P.
Artistry in Boogie.
Kenton, S.
Artistry in Percussion.
Rugolo, P.
As Blue As I Am.
Lepponen, E.
As Ein Kala a Theios ap' tēn Amerikē.
Phrantzeskakēs, D. G.
As Fancy Free as a melody.
Arthur, W.
As I walked in Bethlehem.
Anderson, W. H.
As Irish as Dublin Town.
Bridges, R.
As Joseph Was A-walking.
Montgomery, R.
As Lately We Watched.
Howorth, W.
As Long As I Live.
Sawaya, J. J.
As Long As There Is Love.
Capano, T.
As Long As We Live.
Arthur, W.
As Mary Sings.
Anderson, W. H.
As on the Night.
Carr, A., arr.
As Sweet As You.
White, J.
As Time Goes By.
Arthur, W.
As We Part.
Ilgenfritz, M.
Ash Grove.
Quilter, R.
Ashira Ladonai.
Jospe, E. Sing Unto the Lord.
Ask If Yon Damask Rose Be Sweet.
Handel, G. F. Susannah.
Assurance.
Radley, J. M.
At Eventide.
Steele, M. C.
At Last.
Hennessy, H.
At Last My Dream Came True.
Lopez, T. Recuerdo de un Cocktail.

At My Teacher's Studio.
Schaum, J. W.
At the Break of Day.
James, A. W.
At the Candlelight Café.
David, M. Tisa.
At the Foot of the Hill.
Clyde, T.
At the Forest's Edge, There's Celebration.
Sas, N. Erdőszélen Nagy a Zsivaj.
At the Mercy Seat.
Bostwick, F. J.
At the Opera.
Ilgenfritz, M.
At the Tavern Ball.
Kreps, W. H.
At Thy Feet.
Stairs, L. E.
A-tish-oo.
Rendall, H.
Atoma.
Klamp, P.
Atomic Age Wife.
Weitzman, M. A.
Au Clin du Feu.
Lucchesi, R. A.
Au Pays des Cigales.
Scotto, V.
Au Petit Trot des Mules.
Rabey, R. Suite Savoyarde.
Au Pied de l'Autel.
Roparts, J. G.
Au Revoir.
Stein, S. A.
Au Revoir Again.
Josefovits, T.
Auma, the song of the wanderer.
Kuaana, D. K.
Aubade.
Granville, N.
Auf der Piazzetta, wo Caruso Sang.
Stolz, R.
A-ulf-ule.
Giacone, A. Luna Bugiarda.
Aunque Estes Lejos.
Peres Leyva, N.
Aunt Hetty Likes.
Parker, R.
Aurora.
Panizza, H.
Autumn Thoughts.
Talmadge, C. L.
Autumn's waning.
Huffman, C. H.
Autumno.
Vivaldi, A. Concerti delle Stagioni.
Aux Quatre Coins de Paris.
Lopes, F. Les Trois Cousines.
Avak Jackson.
Whitfield, R.
Ave Maria.
Clitheroe, F.
Eulalia, sister.
Gounod, C. F.
Gyldmark, H. G. S.
Schubert, F. P.
Singenberger, J. B.
Ave Verum Corpus.
Mozart, J. C. W. A.
Aventura.
Domingues, A.
Aventure de Babar.
Rousseau, P.
Avesta in Song.
Hanish, O. Z.-A.
Aveugle de Ma Rue.
Pipon, L.
Avez-vous vu Louise.
Arlys, F.
Avodath Hakodesh Shel Kehilath Anshe
Maariv.
Janowski, M.
Avril à Paris.
Dukelsky, V. (Walk a Little Faster)
April in Paris.
Avril aux Champs-Élysées.
Tabet, G.

Awake.
Wagner, R. Die Meistersinger.
Awake I Dream.
Wright, E.
Awakening Song.
Essenburg, E. Oh, To Be Like the Master.
Axel Christensen's Break Studies.
Christensen, A. W.
Azur, Re d'Ormus.
Salieri, A.
Aye. Mama.
Guglielmi, L.
Ayre for Dancing.
Norden, H.
As a Szép.
Pártos, J.
Aza Yur Olf Mir.
Ellstein, A. (Just My Luck) Such a Year on Me.
Azúcar, Malvones, Menta.
Ficher, J.
Azusa, Cucamonga and Anaheim.
Stept, S. H.

B

Baa! Baa! Black Sheep.
Richardson, C.
Baal Shem.
Bloch, E. Nigun.
Babdadu.
Landl, E.
Babe.
De Rose, P.
Babe in a Manger Born.
Schubert, F. P. Ave Maria.
The Babe in Bethlehem.
Scholin, C. A.
The Babe of Bethlehem.
Saunders, E. P.
Babes in Arms.
Rodgers, R.
Baby Ann, Lullaby.
Nolder, M.
Baby, Baby, to Love You.
Nepper, J. C.
Baby, Be Good.
Ryerson, F.
Baby, Can't You See That's Class.
Boyles, R.
Baby, Come Home.
Shaftel, Selig.
Baby, Don't You No, no Me.
Hinson, W.
Baby, Have You Got a Little Love To Spare.
Warren, H.
Baby, I Don't Cry over You.
Krouse, M.
Baby Lions' Lullaby.
Lyon, J.
Baby Sitter.
Sanders, L.
Baby, You Are Special Made.
Smith, W.
Baby, You're Mine for Keeps.
Atwood, H. G.
Baby's Lullaby.
Chadwick, L. K.
Bacancita.
Burli, A.
Baccalauréat, de l'operette.
Betti, H. Mam'zelle Printemps.
Bach for the Clarinet.
Bach, J. S.
The Bachelor and the Bobby-Soxer.
Meyer, J.
Baciagaloop makes love on da stoop.
Prima, L.
Back Home with You.
Carleton, R. L.
Back in Your Loving Arms.
Morris, G. R.
Back on the Range in My Sunny Texas Home.
Chettick, J. M.
Ba-Da-Boum.
Lucchesi, R. A.

Bagatelle.
  Beethoven, L. van.
Bahama Nights.
  Clark, Mrs. K. R.
Bahamas.
  Warner, E.
Baile Tijera.
  Inclarte Brioso, R.
The Bailiff's Daughter.
  Fuleihan, A.
Bainbridge Island Sketches.
  McKay, F. H.
Baisse un Peu l'Abat-jour.
  Bourtayre, H.
Bakony Erdön Sir a Gerle.
  Kurucz, J.
Bal des Blanchisseuses.
  Dukelsky, V.
Balalaika.
  Posford, G.
Balalaika Serenade.
  Steininger, F. Music in My Heart.
Ball and Chain Boogie.
  Horton, V.
Ballad of Pocahontas.
  Lorens, E. J.
Ballad of the People.
  Levey, H.
Ballads of B. C.
  MacMillan, E.
Ballerina.
  Lake, G.
  Roma, V. The Dancer.
Ballet in Education, Children's Examina-
    tions.
  Pitfield, T. B.
Ballet on Skates.
  Brown, A. L.
Bamba de Vera Cruz.
  Tucci, T.
Bambola.
  Colombo, J.
Banana Vendor.
  Handal, L. El Bananero.
Bananero.
  Handal, L.
Banco.
  Lopez, F. Trente et Quarante.
The Band Played On.
  Ward, C. B.
Bandit Prince.
  Coldrey, A. G. J.
Bandjive.
  Rusch, H. W.
Bandonéon.
  Betti, H. Mam'zelle Printemps.
Bands Away.
  Akey, C. N.
Bangkok.
  Labbe, A. Un Vent de Folie.
Banjo Polka.
  De Paul, L.
Baptiste.
  Kosma, J.
Barbara.
  Denes, J.
Barbara la Créole.
  Travnicek, A.
Barbe Bleue.
  Ibert, J.
Barcarolle.
  Offenbach, J.
  Rowley, A.
Barcarolle d'Automne.
  Arney, J.
Bard College Song.
  Sherman, R. M.
Barefoot boy with cheek.
  Lippman, S.
A Barn Dance Shuffle.
  Robinson, A.
Barndomshemet i Kentucky.
  Foster, S. C.
Baroque Suite.
  Bedell, R. L., ed.
Barranca.
  Bastien, A. Eldorado.

Bartered Bride.
  Smetana, B.
Bas-Bleu.
  Guentzel, G.
Bashful and Shy.
  Boddiford, E. L.
Bastien und Bastienne.
  Mozart, J. C. W. A.
Batamú.
  Blanco, J.
Bats in Your Belfry.
  Nelson, K.
Battle Hymn of the Republic.
  Ballatore, P., arr.
Battle ob Jerico.
  Roberton, H. S.
A Bayou Tale.
  Bown, P. B.
Be a Good Homemaker.
  Spillman, L.
Be an Angel.
  Fensterstock, B.
Be Careful with My Heart.
  Dudgeon, F.
Be My Beau.
  Alkire, E. H. Eddie Alkire's Be My
    Beau.
Be Not Afraid.
  Mendelssohn-Bartholdy, F., Elijah.
Be Present at Our Table, Lord.
  Purcell, E.
Be Strong.
  Sergey, J. M.
Be Strong and of a Good Courage.
  Haeseler, W.
Be Sure.
  Rolg, G.
Be Sweet to Me, Kid.
  Sawaya, J.
Be Ye Kind, One to Another.
  Davis, K. K.
Beach Polka.
  Yankovic, F. J.
Beale Street Mamma.
  Robinson, J. R.
Beanero.
  Disney (W.) Productions, Ltd. Fun
    and Fancy Free.
Beautiful, Beautiful Ohio.
  Arthur, W.
Beautiful blue Danube.
  Strauss, J. Tales of the Vienna woods.
Beautiful City.
  Essenburg, E.
Beautiful City of Gold.
  Pond, C. A.
Beautiful Dreamer.
  Foster, S. C.
  Foster, S. C. Duel in the Sun.
Beautiful Hawaiian Islands of Love.
  Tobin, L.
Beautiful Oregon, I Love You.
  Atterbury, G. A. Oregon Melody.
The Beautiful Thing That Is You.
  Arthur, W.
Beauty Shop Quartet.
  Lorens, E. J.
Because.
  Bowers, F. V.
  Spialek, H.
Because I Love You So.
  Hudson, J. T.
Because I Think of You.
  Sawaya, J.
Because I Walk With Thee, Dear Lord.
  Miller, M. C.
Because I'm in Love with You.
  Estrella, J. C.
Because I'm So in Love.
  Rae, R.
Because of You.
  Arthur, W.
  Lamkoff, P.
Because You Went Away.
  Briston, M. R.

Bed of Roses.
  Manus, J.
Bedre Sent end Aldrig.
  Jensen, H.
Bedtime Prayer.
  Spearman, F. T.
Bed-time Story.
  Thompson, J. J.
Bee.
  Schubert, F.
Beeg Palloons.
  Bibo, I.
Beer Barrel Polka.
  Vejvoda, J.
Before the Harvest Days Are Over.
  Freleigh, R. D.
Beg Your Pardon.
  Smith, B.
Beggar's Holiday.
  Ellington, D.
Beginner's Boogie.
  Allen, B.
Beginning of the Christmas Time.
  Ritter, W. S.
Behind the Eight Ball.
  Carson, J. L.
Behold the Lamb of God.
  Baker, W.
Behold, What Manner of Love.
  Fichthorn, C. L.
Bela Cumbancha.
  De Moraes, N.
Believe Me, Dear.
  Arthur, W.
Believe Me If All Those Endearing
    Young Charms.
  Ballatore, P., arr.
  Quilter, R.
Believe Me, I'll Be Leaving You.
  Melsher, I.
The Bell at the Fountain.
  Frost, B.
Bell Song.
  Delibes, L. Lakme.
Belle Genève, à Toi Nos Coeurs.
  Loponte, F.
Belle of Ball.
  Lamkoff, P.
Belle of the Monon.
  McGee, J. A. The Monon Centennial
    Show.
Bells across the meadows.
  Ketelbey, A. W.
Bells Are Ringing.
  Lupton, H. J.
Bells in the Night.
  Thal, J.
Bells of Aberdovey.
  Thomas, A.
Bells of Heaven.
  Kahn, P. B.
Beloved, Be Mine.
  Murray, C.
Beloved California.
  Clyde, T.
Belwin ... Accordion Course.
  Hazelle, E.
Belwin Method for Song Bells.
  Eybel, A, S.
Ben Jonson's Carol.
  Sellew, D. E.
Benediction Hymns for Four Men's Voices.
  See title entry in composer list.
Benedictus.
  Ferry, C. T.
Benedictus Es, Domine.
  Garabrant, M.
  Hough, B. W.
  Snow, F. W.
Bent on Love.
  Bartlett, F.
Bercelonnette.
  Mazellier, J.
Berceuse.
  Urdahl, O. N.
Berceuse for Bethlehem.
  Compagno, G. M.

Bergère des Aravis.
　Périssas, M. G. R., arr.
Berkeley Band Book.
　Keller, E. M.
Berlingot.
　Betti, H. Mam'zelle Printemps.
Bermuda.
　Keith, S.
Bern-Waltz.
　Durlak, J. P. Do Berna Chlopcy Do Berna.
Bernard Whitefield Piano Method.
　Whitefield, B.
Bernice.
　Sorna, J.
Bernice Frost's Companion Series.
　Frost, B.
Beside Thy Cradle Here I Stand.
　Bach, J. S.
The Best Known Music of Grieg.
　Grieg, E. H.
Best Known Music of Rachmaninoff.
　Rachmaninoff, S.
Best Known Music of Schumann.
　Schumann, R. A.
The Best Known Music of Tschaikowsky.
　Chaikovskii, P. I.
Best Things in Life Are Free.
　Henderson, R. Good News.
Bestiaire du Chien à Ne Pas Mettre
　Dehors.
　Petit, P. Y. M. C. Mélodies.
Bet a Yid Rosh'Hashono.
　Gailing, B.
Bethlehem.
　Barnes, E. S.
Betrothal Prayer.
　Gamauf, L. C.
Betty Blue.
　Murry, T.
Between Heaven and a Heartbreak.
　McNeil, J. C.
Beulah's Boogie.
　Hampton, L.
Big Bass Drum.
　Hopkins, H. P.
Big Bass Polka.
　Soldi, A.
Big Note Boogie.
　Rosner, B.
Big Rock Candy Mountains.
　Lorenz, E. J.
Big Show.
　Hubbell, R.
Big Sue.
　Herman, The Hermit, pseud.
Biggers Business College Song.
　Williams-Biggers, L. M.
Bill Monroe's Grand Ole Opry.
　Lee, E., comp.
Billy Boy.
　Barnes, J. E.
Bing Crosby's Favorite Hymns. See
　title entry in composer list.
Bing Crosby's Hits of the Day.
　Bradley, K., comp.
Bird Sings in May.
　Ingraham, G.
Bird Sketches.
　Gendron, J. C.
Bird Symphony.
　Caribou, J.
Birdies' First Flight.
　Day, R. E.
Birds and the Bees.
　Fain, S.
Birds in the Garden.
　Diggle, R.
Birds Will Be Singing Brightly.
　Dickason, G. M.
Birmingham Boogie.
　Revel, H.
Birmingham Jail.
　Miller, B., arr.
Birthday of a King.
　Neidlinger, W. H.
Bite Your Tongue and Say You're Sorry.
　Miller, B.
Bitter Sweet.
　Coward, N. P.

Black.
　LaFarge, G.
Black Velvet.
　Huffnagle, H.
Blackbird.
　Driver, A. New Songs for Old.
Blaue Halstuch.
　Kreuder, P.
Bless My Soul.
　Wright, H.
Bless the Bride.
　Ellis, V.
Bless'd Are They Who in Jesus Live.
　Bach, J. S. Selig, Wer an Jesum
　Denkt.
Blessed Are the Peacemakers.
　Rasley, J. M.
Blessed Are the Sons of God.
　Aufdemberge, E. H.
Blessed Art Thou, O Lord.
　Day, G. H.
Blessed Event Song.
　La Marge, J.
Blessed Hope.
　Haslett, R.
Blessed Is He Whose Unrighteousness Is
　Forgiv'n.
　Purcell, H.
Blessed Lord.
　Smith, N. O.
Blessed Virgin's Expostulation.
　Purcell, H.
Blighted Swain.
　Fulelhan, A.
Blizzard Head Blues.
　Pripps, E. R.
Blond Eyelash in His Black Mustache.
　Zammataro, S. J.
Blonde in Blue.
　Lennerts, W. J.
Blondes, Brunettes and Redheads.
　Taylor, H.
Blood So Cleansing to Me.
　Kickler, D. C.
Bloop, Bleep.
　Loesser, F.
Blow, Blow, Thou Winter Wind.
　Ilgenfritz, M.
Blow the Man Down.
　Harris, R.
　Wood, G.
Blowing Bubbles.
　Jenkins, C. W.
Blue and Sentimental.
　David, C.
Blue Beat Boogie.
　Smith, A.
Blue-Bells.
　Phillips, M. F.
Blue Birds in the Rain.
　Woodford, G. R.
Blue Darling.
　Clark, A.
Blue Eyed Mary Lou.
　Battiste, L. L.
Blue Eyes Polka.
　Vitak, J.
Blue Jacket Blues.
　Furney, A. J.
Blue Mediterranean.
　Stranks, A.
Blue Music.
　Meyer, J.
Blue Rain.
　Sendrey, A.
Blue Reminiscent Blues.
　Smith, J. C.
Blue River Waltz.
　Kessler, M. T.
Blue Rose of the Rio.
　Keefer, A. M.
Bluejay.
　Greene, J.
Bluesalamode.
　Meissner, J. J.
Bob White.
　Gendron, J. C. Bird Sketches.

Bob White Polka.
　Kogen, H.
Bob Wills Boogie.
　Wills, B.
A Bobolink in May.
　Howell, I.
Body and Soul.
　Green, J.
　Green, J. Three's a Crowd.
　Stone, G.
Boggs Boogie.
　Boggs, N.
Boin-n-n-ng.
　Stept, S. H.
Bold Pedlar.
　Pitfield, T. B.
Bolerito.
　D'Auberge.
Boléro.
　Ledrut, J. C. E.
　Volpe, H.
Bolero Triste.
　Ravasini, N.
Bonaventure.
　Curzon, F.
Bondage.
　Garman, W. M.
Bonita.
　Vandercook, H. A.
Bonita Dolores.
　Ward, A. M.
Bonne Chanson. See title entry in composer
　list.
Bonne Chanson à l'École. See title entry
　in composer list.
Bonne-Maman.
　LaFarge, G.
Bonnie Lassie.
　Cowles, C.
Bonny Earl of Moray.
　Lovatt, S. E.
Boogie Boogie Feet.
　Clyde, T.
Boogie Concerto.
　Lynch, P.
Boogie Express.
　King, H.
Boogie Man.
　Green, C. E.
Boogie Mood.
　Franks, A.
Boogie Woogie Blue Plate.
　Bushkin, J.
Boogie Woogie Yodel Song.
　Smith, C.
Book of Piano Pieces.
　Ketterer, E.
Boosey & Hawkes Band Method.
　Skornicka, J. E.
Bor Jeg På Det Höle Fjeld.
　Wick, F. The Mountaineer.
Born There ... Where the Winding Tisza.
　Doczy, J. A Kanyargó Tisza Partján
　Ott Születtem.
Botella.
　Mendoza, O.
Bottoms Up.
　Bartlett, F.
Boulevard of Memories.
　Loeb, J. J.
The Bouncing Ball.
　Adams, E. H. Two Little Etudes for
　piano-forte.
Bow Bells.
　Bernard, B. Dancing with Crime.
Boys Like to Play.
　Foster, A. H., comp. Piano Pieces.
Boys Town Victory March.
　Kapphahn, T. A. Men of Boys Town.
Brahms.
　Brahms, J.
Brahms' Cradle Song.
　Brahms, J.
Brahms' Songs of Love.
　Brahms, J.
Brahms' String Quintet in F Minor.
　Brahms, J.

Brahms' Waltz.
  Brahms, J.
Brain Cloudy Blues.
  Duncan, T.
Brand New Saddle and Silver Spurs.
  Mikeska, Mrs. E. F.
Brand New Wagon.
  Basie, C.
Brand Vin.
  Passani, È. B.
Bread of Life.
  De Lamarter, E.
Bread of the World.
  Anderson, W. H.
Break Forth into Joy.
  Hickman, R. M.
Break Studies.
  Christensen, A. W. Axel Christensen's
    Break Studies.
Breezes from the Hilltop.
  Ferry, C. T.
Breve Metodo per l'Allievo Pianista.
  Beraldi, M., comp.
Brief Maria Theresias an Friedrich
  den Grossen.
  Benatzky, R.
Brigadoon.
  Loewe, F.
Bright Star of Heaven.
  Jacobs, A. C.
Brilliant Star.
  Fama, M.
Bring Back the Sunshine.
  Sullivan, G.
Bring on the Drums.
  Rowlands, J.
Bring to the Lord.
  Wilkes, R. W.
Brinnande Ljus.
  Rangström, T.
Brisas del Mar Tropical.
  Valdés, G.
Broadcaster.
  Alpert, S. L.
Broadway Shuffle.
  Clyde, T.
Bröllopsvalsen.
  Hellström, D.
Bronco Bustin'.
  Stevenson, R. M. Texas Suite.
The Brook.
  Blake, D. G.
Brown Eyes.
  Zordan, A.
Bruder-Klausen-Marsch.
  Gogniat, J. Hymne Patriotique.
Brush Up.
  McKee, J.
Brussels Express.
  Kennedy, J.
Bub-bub-bubble.
  Elam, C. M.
Bucolique Variée.
  Pierné, P.
Bugle Call Rag.
  Pettis, J.
Bugs Bunny.
  Arthur, W.
Bulgar Song.
  Eilstein, A.
Bumble Basses.
  Rimskil-Korsakov, N. A. Tsar Saltan.
Buongiorno, Amore Mio.
  Oldrati, R. R.
Burden'd Chile.
  Mells, H. F.
Burning of the Winecoff.
  Carson, J. L. Songs.
Burning Trails.
  Karp, O.
Buscando.
  Thébault, V.
Bush Pilot.
  Hersenhoren, S.
Business in Bb.
  Handlon, J. E.
Busy Gettin' Dizzy.
  Vanderburg, G. J.

But Beautiful.
  Van Heusen, J. The Road to Rio.
But Thanks Be to God.
  Harkness, R.
By Starlight.
  Lemont, C. W.
By the Waters of Babylon.
  Coopersmith, H.
By the Waters of Minnetonka.
  Lieurance, T.
Bye and Bye.
  Evans, C.
Byli jsme a budem.
  Stellbský, J.

C

C'Est à Champ-Dominelle.
  Richepin, T.
C'est la Chanson des Accordéons.
  Ledru, J.
C'est le Bon Lever, Doux Pastoureau.
  Aubanel, G. P. P.
C'est Merveilleux.
  Monnot, M. Étoile sans Lumière.
C'est un Village.
  Coste, M.
C'Était un Grand Garçon.
  Gasté, L.
C'Était un Jour de Fête.
  Monnot, M.
C.M.A. Is Marching Onward.
  Harper, E. G.
Ca' the Yowes to the Knowes.
  Quilter, R.
Caballo Blanco.
  Lavista, R. Cuando Lloran los
    Valientes.
Caballo con Tres Frenos.
  Tintorer Sardiña, F.
Cabana.
  White, E.
Cable Car Song.
  Melvin, B.
Cadenza for the violin concerto.
  Brahms, J. Concerto, violin.
Café Polka.
  Yankovic, F. J.
Cahiers de Polyphonie Vocale.
  Couraud, M.
Cala d'Or.
  Padilla, J.
California.
  Roche, A. T.
California, Here I Come.
  Meyer, J.
California Lullaby.
  McEvoy, T.
Californy Song.
  Raynor, J.
Call Me What You Will.
  Hall, D.
Call of the Soil.
  Zaira, M.
Call to Worship.
  Mitchell, R. B.
Calle de Alcalá.
  Grant, J.
Calle Schwens Vals.
  Taube, E.
Calling to You, Sweetheart.
  Pepin, T.
Calling you.
  Bake , W.
Calm Waters.
  Wheldon, F.
Calmes aux quais Déserts.
  Mulot, A. M. Soirs.
Caminito de Belén.
  Gianneo, L.
Campanella.
  Liszt, .
Campina Cubaña.
  Sunshine, M. Cuban Countryside.
Camping Out.
  Hopkins, H. P.
Campo Junior.
  Boote, H., arr.

Can It Be True.
  Raby, W.
Can It Ever Be the Same.
  Bierman, B.
Can This Love Be Real.
  Dexter, A.
Caña y Azúcar.
  Lluis Espinol, R.
Canada, My Home.
  Brundle, J.
Canadian Boat Song.
  Oliver, H. Vesper Song.
Canadian Capers.
  Chandler, G.
Canción,
  Longás, F.
Canción de Cuna India.
  Gilardi, G.
Canción de los Andes.
  Marcelli, N. Song of the Andes.
Cancion de un Muchacho.
  Recli, G.
Cancion del Saldan.
  Napolitano, Emilio A.
Canciones Populares de las Islas
  Británicas.
  Holst, I. Folk Songs of the British Isles.
    Chansons Populaires des Iles Britanni-
    ques.
Canciones y Danzas Argentinas.
  Cabrera, Ana S. de.
Candle Talk.
  Kurth, B. Kitty's Tongue.
Candy Clock.
  Lake, G. Candy Town Tunes.
Candy Parade.
  Lake, G. Candy Town Tunes.
Candy Town Tunes.
  Lake, G.
Cannon Ball Wall.
  Scott, T. W.
Canoeing with You.
  Russell, J. W.
Can't Get the Cork out of Grandpappy's Jug.
  Erwin, L.
Can't Help Lovin' Dat Man.
  Kern, J.
Can't You Dream for Tonight.
  Reichert, F. E.
Can't You Just See Yourself.
  Styne, J. High Button Shoes.
Can't You See It My Way for a Change.
  Arthur, W.
Canta per Me.
  Casadesus, F.
Cantador.
  Castillo, N. Sueño.
Cantata Pastorale.
  Scarlatti, A.
Canti d'Amore.
  Murtari, V. Due Canti d'Amore.
Canticle.
  Diamond, D. L. 2 Pieces.
Cantico al Niño Dios.
  Niven, L. A Song for the Little Jesus.
Cantilena.
  Darnton, C.
Canto Amoroso.
  Quiroga, M.
Canto Bretone.
  Lavagnino, A. F.
Canto por Ti.
  Serão, E. In the Valley of Roses.
Canzona.
  Panel, L.
  Weinberg, J.
Canzone d'Autunno.
  Boncompagni, S. Ho un Segreto sul Cuor.
Canzone del Mare.
  Bettarini, L. Ombra della Valle.
Canzone dell'Amore.
  Bixio, C. A.
Canzone dell' Anniversario.
  Chaplin, S. The Jolson Story.
Canzone della Terra.
  Brodsky, N. A Man about the House.
Canzone della Valle.
  Bettarini, L. Ombra della Valle.

384

Canzone delle Sonagliere.
Petralia, T. Vado verso il Mio Paese.
Canzonetta.
Mendelssohn-Bartholdy, F.
Piedigrotta. 1947.
Canzoni del 1946-1947. See title entry
in composer list.
Canzoni di Napoli.
Nicolò, M.
Capinera.
Giuliani, A.
Capitaine Biomet.
Wiener, J. A. H.
Capitals, Capitals.
Thomson, V.
Capitan.
Sousa, J. P.
Capitana.
Curiel, G. Angel o Demonio.
Capotin.
Krone, B. P.
Capriccietto.
Steiner, E.
Capriccio.
Busch, W. Suite.
Scarlatti, D.
Capriccio on the Departure of a
Beloved Brother.
Bach, J. S.
Capriccioso.
Wray, J.
Caprice Espagnol.
Moszkowski, M.
Caprice no. XXIV.
Paganini, N.
Capriol.
Heseltine, P.
Captain and the Soldier.
Sendrey, A.
Captain from Castile.
Newman, A.
Cara Piccina.
Lama, G. My Dearest Darling.
Caravan.
Hyden, W.
Caravan of Dreams.
Ahlert, F.
Caravelle.
Petit, P. Y. M. C. Melodies.
Careless Love Boogie.
Carrier, C.
Careless Sweetheart.
Daffan, T.
Caribbean Melodies.
Hurston, Z. N., comp.
Caribbean Moonlight.
Lane, V.
Caribbean Night.
Faith, P. Noche Caribe.
Carida No Tá Vini.
Casamor, J.
Carillon.
Bizet, G. Arlésienne.
Carillon Heigh-Ho.
Perry, J.
Carioca.
Youmans, V.
Carioca Album of Brazilian Songs.
Flory, S.
Carlos, the Gaucho.
McNeil, J. C.
Carmel Valley.
Hitchcock, M.
Carmen.
Bizet, G.
Carmen Fantasia.
Bizet, G.
Carnaval des Animaux.
Saint-Saëns, C.
Carnegie Hall.
Levy, L., arr.
Portnoff, M.
Carnival.
Torjussen, T.
Carnival of Roses.
Olivadoti, J.
Carnival of Venice.
Eckhardt, F. G., arr. Songs of Italy.

Carnival Procession.
Lecuona y Casado, E. La Comparsa.
Carnival Suite.
Richter, C.
Carol of the New Year.
Hollis, R. S., arr.
Carolare.
Anderson, M.
Carousel.
Rodgers, R.
Carpet of Gold.
Hennessy, N.
Carrousel.
Larson, E. R.
Carry Me Back to Old Virginny.
Bland, J. A.
Casanova Cricket.
Carmichael, H.
Casi Polka.
Castro, J. J.
Cat Song.
LaMar, E. H.
Catana.
Newman, A. Captain from Castile.
Caucasian Sketches.
Ippolitov-Ivanov, M.
Cavalry Patrol.
Knipper, L. K.
Cchiù Zitto.
Anepeta, G.
Ce N'Était Pas Original.
Gaste, L.
Cello Song.
Fletcher, L.
Centennial Song.
Van Leishout, E. M.
Centennial Whiskers.
Underwood, C. G.
Cetra.
Vivaldi, A. Concerto terzo.
Cette Aimable Tourterelle.
Parrish, C. Little Turtle Dove So Lovely.
Chacarera.
Valenti Costa, P. Seis Movimientos
Corales a la Manera Popular Argentina.
Chaconne.
Fernstrom, J.
Vitali, G. B.
Chain of Daisies.
Brown, L.
Champion.
Rollins, J.
Champion Folio.
McGee, D.
Chaney's Rapid-Note-Reader.
Chaney, W. C.
Change of Position Studies.
Dounis, D. C. The Development of
Flexibility.
Changeable as the Weather.
Hall, D.
Changing Seas.
Broadhead, G. F.
Chanson de l'Etudiant.
Scotto, V.
Chanson de la Servante.
Caby, R. J. A.
Chanson de Paris.
Wojowska-Wojodyda, L. Piosenka z
Paryza.
Chanson Gitane.
Yvain, M.
Chanson Militaire.
Grechaninov, A. T.
Chanson Populaire.
Betti, A. E.
Chanson Triste.
Kalinnokov, B.
Chansonette.
Ettore, E.
Chansons de la Mer et de la Voile.
Texier, H. G., comp.
Chansons du Blé Qui Lève.
Hemmerle, J., comp.
Chansons du Jamboree.
Chailley, J., comp.
Chansons Populaires des Iles Britanniques.
Holst, I., arr. Folk Songs of the British
Isles.

Chant de l'Avenir.
Jolivet, A.
Chant des Alpes.
Maye, P.
Chant du Pirate.
Monnot, M. Étoile sans Lumière.
Chante Encore pour Moi.
Casadesus, F. Canta per Me.
Chanteur Inconnu.
Bourtayre, H.
Chants de Misère.
Milhaud, D.
Chapel in the Hills.
Taylor, H.
Chapel of Broken Dreams.
Bartlett, F.
Chapel Voluntaries.
Alphenaar, G., ed. & comp.
Charlie Is My Darling.
Quilter, R.
Charlot's Revue.
Braham, P.
Charm Waltz.
Henman, G.
Charro.
Tarver, J. L.
Chatterbox Polka.
Grill, A.
Cheatin' Women.
Taylor, H.
Checkin' on the Freedom Train.
Heyward, S.
Cheer, Cheer, Cheer for Michigan.
Tann, L.
Cheer Up!
Phillips, M. F.
Cherry Blossom Time.
Russell, K. The Nightingale.
Cheshire Cat Goes to Sleep.
Diggle, R. Alice in Wonderland Suite.
Chester.
Billings, W. Compositions.
Chevelure.
DeBussy, C.
Cheveux au Vent.
Durand, P.
Chèvre de Monsieur Seguin.
Cornille, G.
Chiapanecas.
Condaris, A. J., arr.
Chiaroscuro.
Diggle, R.
Chicago Waltz.
Elsnic, J. P.
Chickasaw Limited.
Manning, D.
Chicks Come Home To Roost.
Arthur, W.
Chidabee, Chidabee, Chidabee.
Crane, H.
Chien Qui Rapporte.
Sablon, A.
Children's Ball.
Schumann, R. A.
Children's Overture.
Quilter, R.
Children's Suite.
Lewis, U.
Chillun' Come on Home.
Cain, N.
Chimes Love Waltz.
Carpentier, J. M.
Chimes of the Holy Night.
Wilson, I. B.
Chimes of the Sabbath.
Glarum, L. S.
Chimes of Victory.
Bergeim, J.
Chinese Dance.
Hernried, R.
Chinese Lyrics.
Wiant, B., arr.
Chinese Scene.
Scher, W.
Chinesischer Strassensänger.
Winkler, G. Aladins Wunderlampe.
Chinita Chula.
Monreal, G. Ah! Les Femmes.

Chirpy Cricket.
  Hubbell, F. A.
Chismecito de Moda.
  Cairo, P.
Choclo.
  Villolda, A. G.
Chocolate Choo-Choo.
  Moore, W.
Chola Apasionada.
  Iglesias Villoud, H.
Choo Choo Baby.
  Chanslor, H.
Choo Choo Blues.
  Lee, S.
Chop-Chop Tim-m-m-m-ber.
  Cryor, J.
Choral Benediction and Amen.
  Cronham, C. R.
Choral Mass in honor of the Infant'
  Jesus.
  Marsh, W. J.
Choral program series.
  Wilson, H. R., ed. & arr.
Choral Suite.
  Starominsky, M.
Chorale March.
  Fiorillo, D.
Chris Crosses.
  Boland, C. A.
Christ Bled and Died for You and Me.
  Sands, J.
Christ Is Coming Again.
  Essenburg, E.
Christ Is Risen.
  Emery, D. R.
Christ Is the Light of the World.
  Crane, J.
Christ of Galilee.
  Steger, L.
Christ, the Answer.
  Gibson, E. L.
Christ the Lord Is Risen Today.
  Krone, B. P.
Christ Understands.
  Jones, G. J.
Christian Songs.
  Kerr, P. S.
Christmas Album.
  Schaum, J. W., comp.
Christmas at Snowbank Corners.
  Kaiser, J. The Christmas Spelling Bee.
Christmas Bells.
  Elliott, M.
  Hutchens, F.
  McCollin, F.
Christmas Bells Are Ringing.
  Runkel, K. E.
Christmas Cantata.
  Scarlatti, A. Cantata Pastorale.
Christmas Carol from Lapland.
  Dickinson, C.
Christmas Carols.
  Parke, D.
Christmas Comes But Once a Year.
  Burnett, E.
Christmas Comes Once a Year.
  Goudey, R.
Christmas Day.
  Kwong, M. D. K.
  Roberts, M.
Christmas Dream.
  Wilson, I. B.
Christmas Dreaming.
  Lee, L.
Christmas Everywhere.
  Morgan, K.
Christmas folk-song.
  Weigl, V. The Little Jesus Came to
    Town.
Christmas in Song.
  Preuss, T., arr.
Christmas in Song and Carol.
  Breck, E. S., arr.
Christmas in the Heart.
  Loveless, W. P.
Christmas Is Coming.
  Krone, B. P.

Christmas Lullaby.
  Brook, H.
Christmas Morning.
  McKay, G. F.
Christmas on the Ranch.
  Clyde, T.
Christmas Oratorio.
  Bach, J. S. Beside Thy Cradle Here
    I Stand.
Christmas Prayer.
  Barthelson, J.
Christmas Rhapsody.
  Diggle, R.
Christmas Souvenir.
  Hall, D.
Christmas Spelling Bee.
  Kaiser, J.
Christmas Spirit.
  Loes, H. D.
Christmas Story.
  George, C.
  Hedgren, V.
Christmas Symphony.
  Bach, J. S.
Christmas Together.
  Deschenes, J.
Christmas Wish.
  Luvaas, M. J.
Christmastide.
  Baines, W.
Christ's Loving Children.
  Diggle, R.
Chromatic Caprice.
  McKay, F. H.
Chromatic Sonata.
  Yardumian, R.
Church Bells on Sunday Morning.
  Fain, S.
  Whitehall, A.
Ciel Comme un Lac d'Or Pâle.
  Mulot, A. M. Soirs.
Ciel d'Espagne.
  Padilla, J.
Cinderella.
  Provost, W.
Cindy.
  Winstead, K.
Cinq Danses Rituelles.
  Jolivet, A.
Cinq Epilogues.
  Guinopoulos, M.
Cinquantaine.
  Marie, G. Golden Wedding.
Cinquième Quatuor Quasi una Fantasia.
  Ropartz, J. G. M. Quartet, strings, no. 5.
Circle 'round the Moon.
  Knowlton, E. R.
Circus Day with You.
  Stella, S. J.
Circus Parade.
  Hopkins, H. P.
Ciribiribin.
  Eckhardt, F. G., arr. Songs of Italy.
City Guardians.
  Fink, F. A.
City of Gold.
  Pond, C. A.
City of Memphis.
  Fowler, J. W.
Civilization.
  Sigman, C.
Clair de Lune.
  DeBussy, C. (Suite Bergamasque)
Clap Yo' Hands.
  Gershwin, G. (Oh, Kay)
Clarence H. Cobbs Songs of Zion.
  Frye (T. R.) Publishers, ed.
Clarinet Trios.
  Rosenthal, C. A., arr.
Clarinet Velocity.
  Gornston, D.
Clarinetina Polka.
  Plachanski, J.
Classical Album.
  Willner, A., arr.
Classics Are Fun.
  Hirschberg, D., ed. & comp.

Classiques-Albums.
  Velde, E. van de.
Clavecin Obtempérant.
  Schmitt, F.
Clavicembalisti Italiani.
  Rossi, N., ed.
Clayton's Grand March.
  Blake, C. D.
Clear Water.
  Nolan, B. Ne-Hah-Neé.
Clear Your Lines Before You Call.
  Nolan, Mrs. E. L.
Clic.
  Liferman, G.
Click Click Song.
  Rosales, M.
Clock Song.
  Sanders, G. H.
Close Now Thine Eyes.
  Bullock, E.
Clover Blossom.
  Price, F. B. March of the Beetles.
Clyde "Carolina" Moody's Song Folio.
  Moody, C.
Cobbler.
  Cockshott, G.
Cockle Shells.
  Eichhorn, H. W.
Coeur de Palmier.
  Trenet, C.
Coeur de Parisienne.
  Sablon, A. (Un Chien Qui Rapporte)
Cole Porter Selection.
  Porter, C.
Collaboration.
  Kenton, S.
Collection of Dance Airs.
  Mozart, J. C. W. A.
Collection of Irish Comic Songs.
  Ward, J. J.
Collection of Songs.
  Ellington, D. Beggar's Holiday.
Colmenar.
  Monge, J.
Color Blind.
  Hull, D.
Colorado.
  Yogan, J.
Combat de Tancrède et Clorinde.
  Monteverdi, C.
Combination to My Heart.
  Arthur, W.
Come Again, Summer.
  Hill, A.
Come Away, Death.
  Bullock, E. Three Songs from Twelfth
    Night.
Come Back to Sorrento.
  Curtis, E. de. Torno a Surriento.
Come for a Dance in the Moonlight.
  Diamond, C. S.
Come Hither, Ye Faithful.
  Norden, H.
Come Home.
  Morris, K.
  Rodgers, R. Allegro.
Come, Kindly Death.
  Bach, J. S. Komm Süsser Tod.
Come Lasses and Lads.
  Richardson, C.
Come le rose.
  Lama, G. Like April's Roses.
Come, Let Us Sing to the Lord.
  Schvedoff, C.
Come, Loyal Hearts.
  Whitehead, H.
Come My Love, Take a Ride With Me.
  Crandall, C. M.
Come, O Lord.
  Yon, P. Veni Domine.
Come On Out and Be With Me.
  Bartlett, F.
Come, Sleep.
  Clark, H. Two Songs.
Come Thou Saviour of Mankind.
  Langstroth, I. Four Chorale Preludes.
Come to Calvary's Saviour.
  Williams, D. W.

Come to Jesus.
  Cosby, R. E. Just Inside the Door.
Come to the Mardi Gras.
  Olivera, M. de.
Come to the Saviour.
  Bollck, B.
Come Up, Come In with Streamers.
  Dels, C.
Come What May.
  Bartlett, F.
Come, Ye Faithful, Raise the Strain.
  Cain, N.
Comes At Times a Stillness.
  Madeira, E. E.
Comfort Ye, My People.
  Aufdemberge, E. H.
Comin' in on the C. P. R.
  Grant, F.
Coming Then for Me.
  Tovey, H. G.
Commander.
  Vandercook, H. A.
Comme Facette Mammeta.
  Gambardella, S.
Comme une Etoile.
  Guglielmi, L. Trente et Quarante.
Commedia Espanõl.
  Kay, S. J.
Communion Anthem.
  Holsholt, M. S.
Como Gozo.
  Lopês, M. A.
Como Mé Da la Gana Soy Yo.
  Cairo, P.
Como Te Quiero.
  Mom, M. M.
Companion Series.
  Frost, B.
Comparsa.
  Lecuona y Casado, E.
Complainte Corse.
  Lucchesi, R. L'Ile d'Amour.
Complet Gris.
  Gasté, L.
Complete Nursery Song Book.
  Bertail, I., ed. & arr.
Complete Organ Works.
  Bach, J. S.
Compositions.
  Billings, W.
Composizioni per tromba e piano-forte.
  Botti, C.
Comprehensive Chordal Études.
  Arline, L. L.
Comus.
  Purcell, H.
Concert mass in four movements.
  Llemohn, E. Holy, Holy, Holy.
Concert Piece.
  Adler, S. H.
  Westbrook, H. S.
Concerti delle Stagioni.
  Vivaldi, A.
Concertino.
  Harsanyi, T. Divertimento no. 1.
  Rivier, J.
Concerto.
  Barbirolli, J.
  Barraud, H.
  Bonporti, F. A.
Concerto alla Rustica.
  Vivaldi, A.
Concerto for violoncello and orchestra.
  Moeran, E. J.
Concerto, piano, no. 1.
  Chalkovskii, P. I.
Concerto, piano, no. 2.
  Rachmaninoff, S.
Concerto en ré.
  Stravinskii, I. F. Concerto, string
    orchestra.
Concerto en ut mineur.
  Bach, J. C. Concerto, violin & piano.
Concerto for Bass.
  Safranski, E.
Concerto for 4 clarinets.
  Telemann, G. P.

Concerto for oboe and strings.
  Vaughan Williams, R. Concerto, oboe
    & string orchestra.
Concerto for organ, strings, and harp.
  Hanson, H. Concerto, organ.
Concerto for piano and orchestra.
  Khachaturian, A. L. Concerto, piano.
Concerto for Squeeze Box.
  René, H.
Concerto Grosso for string orchestra.
  Corelli, A.
Concerto in A major for pianoforte and
    orchestra.
  Händel, G. F.
Concerto in A minor.
  Grieg, E. H. Concerto piano.
Concerto in fa maggiore.
  Bonporti, F. A.
Concerto in si minore.
  Vivaldi, A. Concerto, violin & string
    orchestra.
Concerto in sol minore n. 1.
  Vivaldi, A. Concerto, violin, no. 1.
Concerto Jazz-a-nine.
  Johnson, J. P.
Concerto Petite.
  Garman, W. M.
Concerto pour violon et orchestre.
  Harsanyi, T. Concerto, violin.
Concerto terzo.
  Vivaldi, A.
Conchita.
  Ball, E.
Confesión.
  Acuña, M. S.
Confession.
  Revell, P.
Conflict Concerto.
  Kentwell, W. D. The Intimate Stranger.
Congratulation Minuet.
  Guenther, F., ed. Dances by Great Mas-
    ters.
Connecticut Yankee.
  Rodgers, R.
Connie Polka.
  Bortoli, F.
Constancy.
  Ferry, C. T.
Constant Flame.
  Murray, A.
Constructeurs.
  Durey, L.
Contemplation.
  Tardif, H. M., father. Triptique Marial.
Confredanse à la Sous-Préfecture.
  Laparcerie, M.
Cookie for Snip.
  Kurth, B.
Cool Sea.
  Driver, A. New Songs for Old.
Copacabana.
  Barro, J. de
  Flory, S. Carioca Album of Brazilian Songs.
  Ruby, H.
Copenhagen Waltz.
  Turner, E. W.
Copias.
  Juralsky, A.
Coquette.
  Thompson, J. W.
Corazoncito.
  Burli, A.
Corcovado.
  Flory, S. Carioca Album of Brazilian
    Songs.
Corinna.
  Rowley, A.
Cormorant.
  Lárchet, J. F.
Cornbread and 'Lasses, sassafrass
    tea.
  Sullivan, R.
Corner of My Heart.
  Tobin, L.
Cornered.
  Callender, C. R.
Cornish Rhapsody.
  Bath, H.

Cortege Nocturne dans la Neige
  Rabey, R. Suite Savoyarde.
Cortèges.
  Rawsthorne, A.
Cosas del Encargado.
  Días, J.
Cougar Song.
  Sandgren, C. D.
Cougars Fight.
  Fountain, F. R.
Could It Be.
  Gordon, J.
Could It Be You.
  Long, B. W.
Counterpoint Workbook.
  Kanitz, E.
Countin' Blues.
  Smith, A.
Counting Sheep.
  Rowley, A.
Counting the Falling Stars.
  Arthur, W.
Counting the Stars.
  Capano, F.
Country-dances.
  Klickmann, F. H., arr. Ed Durlacher's
    Country Dances.
Country Lane.
  Marshall, L. K.
Country Pictures.
  Gow, D. G.
Country Road.
  Pitfield, T. B.
County Antrim.
  Verrall, J. I know Where I'm Goln!
Courante.
  Händel, G. F. Suite, harpsichord.
Covered Wagon Home.
  Clyde, M. D.
Cowbell Polka.
  Cooley, D. C.
Cowboy Joe.
  Sendrey, A.
Cowboy on a Rocking Horse.
  Preston, M. L.
Cradle Song.
  Brahms, J. Anchors Aweigh.
  Reblkoff, V.
Cradled Here among the Kine.
  Lundquist, M. N.
Crawdad Song.
  Fisher, S., arr.
Crawford Quick-step Band Book.
  Leidzen, E. W. G., arr.
Crazy Summer.
  Champion, S.
Cream of Kentucky.
  Halle, F. J.
Credimi.
  Godini, A.
Credo.
  Grechaninov, A. T.
Créole Sérénade.
  Lopez, F. Mélopée Lointaine.
Crepuscolo.
  Bossi, M. E.
Crescendo for Band.
  Fiorillo, D.
Criss Cross.
  Price, F. B.
Cross of White in Picardy tonight.
  Powell, R. E.
Crosstown Stroll.
  Hopkins, E.
Crucifixus.
  Grover, R. S.
Crying 'Cause I'm Happy.
  Constantine, F.
Cuando.
  Valentí Costa, P. Seis Movimientos
    Corales a la Manera Popular Ar-
    gentina para çoros mixtos a capella.
Cuando Aprenderás.
  Camacho, J. When You Cross Your
    Heart.
Cuando Llora el Corazón.
  Alcaniz Farre, A.

Cuando Lloran los Valientes.
　Lavista, R.
Cuatro Piezas sobre Temas Infantiles.
　Castro, W.
Cuatro Preludios para Piano.
　Sebastiani, P.
Cuban Countryside.
　Sunshine, M.
Cuban Spell.
　Lambert, C.
Cuban Stew.
　Morales, O. El Sopón.
Cuckoo.
　Stone, Norman.
Cuckoo and the Cockatoo.
　Lawrence, S. Three Early Grade
　　Pieces.
Cuddle Me in the Clover.
　Barron, B.
Cueillons la Fraise et la Framboise.
　Passani, E. B.
Cumparsita.
　Rodrigues, G. H.
　Rodriguez, M.
Cup of Coffee.
　Fassone, V.
Cup of Cold Water.
　Jenkins, M. H. Inspired Hymns of the
　　Hour.
Cupid Stole My Heart.
　McNeil, J. C.
Cupid's Got Me Corralled.
　Modin, S.
Curiosity.
　Voeth, Z.
Cut the Pigeon Wing.
　Raezer, C. M.
Cutest Little Red-Headed Doll.
　Sigman, C.
Cutie, You Are a Beauty.
　Conroy, M.
Cygnes.
　Darcieux, F.
Cynthia.
　Finke, J.
　Green, J.
Czardas.
　Monti, V.
Czyja To Dziewczyna.
　Durlak, J. P.

D

D'Autres Chansons.
　Kosma, J.
Dactylo.
　Bourtayre, H.
Dad and Mother Are There.
　Potter, A. L.
Daffodil and White Dreams.
　Kurth, B.
Dagmar Revyen, 1947.
　Andersen, K. N.
Dags Visor.
　Tegner, A.
Daily Drills and Technical Studies for
　Trombone.
　Schlossberg, M.
Daisies.
　Rachmaninoff, S.
Daisy.
　Dacre, H.
Dakota Waltz.
　Goss, R.
Dal Pollice al Mignolo.
　Trecate, L. F.
Danae.
　Agosti, G. Tre Liriche.
　Perissas, M. G. R.
Dance.
　Mozart, J. C. W. A.
Dance Divertissement.
　Wagner, J.
Dance Night in the Valley.
　Simonds, W. D.
Dance of the Blessed Spirits.
　Guenther, F., ed. Dances by Great Masters.
Dance of the Rose Maidens.
　Khachaturian, A. I. Three Dances.

Dance of the Spanish Onion.
　Rose, D. The Outstanding Compositions
　　of David Rose.
Dance of the Sugar Plum Fairy.
　Chaikovskii, P. I.
Dance with me.
　Brodsky, R.
Dancer.
　Roma, V.
Dances by Great Masters.
　Guenther, F., ed.
Dancing, Dear, with You in My Arms.
　Gage, H. A.
Dancing Dewdrops.
　Baines, W.
Dancing in the Blue.
　Bartlett, F.
Dancing in the Dark.
　Schwarts, A.
Dancing on a Rainbow.
　Lake, G.
Dancing on the Keyboard.
　Bortoli, F.
Dancing on the Stars.
　Arthur, W.
Dancing Tambourine.
　Polla, W. C.
Dancing with Crime.
　Bernard, B.
Dangerous Ground.
　Nelson, E.
Danish Carol.
　Matthews, H. A.
Dans la Fumée des Cigarettes.
　Neuman, A.
Dans la Nuit J'Entends une Chanson.
　Scotto, V.
Dans le Temple d'Isis.
　Baggers, M.
Dans les Rues d'Paname.
　Pascal, L.
Dans Notre Roulotte.
　Scotto, V. Au Pays des Cigales.
Dans Tes Yeux.
　Trénet, C.
Danse des Mirlitons.
　Chaikovskii, P. I.
Danse Grotesque.
　Torjussen, T. Carnival.
Danse Macabre.
　Saint-Saëns, C.
Danseuse Est Créole.
　Guglielmi, L.
Danube Waves.
　Ivanovici, J.
　Ivanovici, J. The Wedding Waltz.
Danza.
　Rossini, G. A.
Danza de las Bailarinas Cortesanas.
　Napolitano, E. A. Apurimac.
La Danza de las Liebres.
　Gianneo, L.
Danza Espagnola No. 6.
　Granados y Campiña, E.
Danzetta.
　Eichhorn, F.
Dardanella.
　Black, J. S.
Dare I.
　Plumb, N.
Dark Eyes.
　Childe, R. S.
　Condaris, A. J., arr.
Dark of the Moon.
　Hendl, W.
Dark Passage.
　Whiting, R. A.
Darling, I Love You.
　Holstrom, E. J.
Darling, I Love You I Do.
　Arthur, W.
Darling, I Mean Them Still.
　Arthur, W.
Darling Jeanie.
　Swaynie, E. W.
Darling, Keep on Dreaming.
　Alkire, E. H.

Darling, That's My Heart.
　Prigmore, B. W.
Darling, Why Did You Leave Me.
　Bartlett, F.
Darn It, Oh Darn It! She Knows. (Heavenly
　Rose).
　Tobin, L.
Date to Be with You.
　Goslowsky, G.
Daughter of Jole Blon.
　Dawson, B.
David's lamentation.
　Billings, W. Compositions.
Dawn.
　Kalinnikoff, V.
　Volpe, H.
Day.
　Bornschein, F. C.
Day I Fell in Love with You.
　Enticknap, C. G.
Day I Left Alsace Lorraine.
　Lamarre, R.
Day in June.
　Cain, N.
Day Is Dawning This Side of Heaven.
　Davis, R. A.
Day of Freedom.
　Morales, O. Dia de Reyes.
Daybreak.
　Binge, R. Madrugado.
Daytona.
　Tryon, E. E.
De la Madeleine à l'Opéra.
　Tabet, G. Z.
De Profundis.
　Read, G.
De quién es tu corazón.
　Denegri, G.
Dear Christians, Let Us Now Rejoice.
　Bach, J. S., 1685-1750.
Dear Cowboy Santa Claus.
　Cody, W.
Dear Diary.
　Ziehler, J.
Dear Little Boy.
　Shaffer, H. L.
Dear Lord and Father of Mankind.
　Maker, F. C.
Dear Nightingale, Awake.
　Mueller, C. F.
Dear Old Mother of Mine.
　Dale, J.
Dear One.
　Arthur, W.
Dear Pal of Long Ago.
　Woodford, G. R.
Dearest Beloved.
　Burnet, W. P.
Dearest Santa.
　Dunn, M.
Death of Mamie Brown.
　D'Angelo, L.
Deb Dyer and His Gospel Singin' Bee. See
　title entry in composer list.
Debonnaire.
　Vandercook, H. A.
Dedication.
　Koppes, M. C., sister.
　Mossman, T.
　Schumann, R. A. Schumann's Songs of
　　Love.
Deep Blue Waters.
　Bandini, A.
Deep in My Heart.
　Bishop, H. R.
　Carleton, R. L.
Deep in My Heart, Dear.
　Romberg, S. The Student Prince.
Deep River.
　Gould, M.
　Howorth, W.
　Scholin, C. A., arr.
Deep Song.
　Cory, G.
Déjame Dormir, Amor.
　Ficher, J.
Déliateur.
　Velde, E. van de.

388

Delicately Tinted Are the Yellow Roses.
Sándor, J. Halvány Sárga Rózsát.
Dem Fort Worth Blues.
Samuels, W.
Départ dans la Nuit.
Richepin, T.
Der Var Li 'som Haemning.
Riis, A. Tivoli Revyen.
Descamisado.
Pizarro, M.
Descants on Eight Hymns.
Boyd, J.
Desengaño.
Moya, R. de.
Desert Dance.
Klemm, E. G.
Desert Flower.
Baker, W.
Desert night.
Brown, L.
The Desert Song.
Romberg, S.
Desfile.
Ficher, J.
Desire.
Ferry, C. T.
Tobin, L.
Destin.
Stein, S. A. Destins.
Destino y un Amor.
Díaz Altamirano, L.
Destins.
Lopez, F.
Martinet, H. A. L.
Schubert, F. P.
Scotto, V.
Stein, S. A.
Det Er Jo Ogsaa No'et Der Gør.
Andersen, K. N. Dagmar Revyen.
Det Er Saa Lidt Der Skal Til.
Evans, K.
Det Sitter en Duva pa Liljekvist.
Berg, N. Engelbrekt.
Deux Chansons de Melpomène.
Ibert, J. Barbe Bleue.
Deux Danses alla Grecque.
Guinopoulos, M. Cinq Epilogues.
Deux Manières.
Huguet-y Tagell, R. J.
Deux Pièces pour Alto.
Casadesus, F.
2ème Sonate.
Milhaud, D. Sonata, viola & piano, no. 2.
Developing Double-stops.
Whistler, H. S.
Development of Flexibility.
Doynis, D. C.
Devil's Night Out.
Federer, R.
Dey's a Ghost 'Round' de Corner.
Cain, N.
Dia de Reyes.
Morales, O.
Diabolero.
Spurgin, A. M.
Dialogue between the Innkeeper and
Joseph.
Cronham, C. R. Nativity Scenes.
Dickey-Bird Song.
Fain, S. The Birds and the Bees.
Did You Mean It.
Cerny, R. J.
Did You Mean That Last Goodbye.
Carver, Z.
Didn't you know.
Bourtayre, H. Imaginez.
Dieci Arrangiamenti per Complesso Hot.
Mobiglia, T., arr.
A Dilemma.
Senob, C.
Dime Por Que Tu Eres Así.
Tintorer Sardiña, F.
Ding-a-ling.
Thal, J.
Dirty Moon.
Arthur, W.

Disappointed.
Moya, R. de. Desengaño.
Schein, J.
Disc Jockey Jump.
Krupa, G.
Dismas.
Johnson, H. W.
Disparu.
Poulenc, F.
Diversions.
Baynon, A.
Divertimento no. 1.
Harsanyi, T.
Divorce Me C.O.D.
Stone, C.
Dixie Lee.
Friel, J. J.
Dixieland Traveller.
Blanc, M.
Dizzy Joe.
Adams, P. H.
Do Berná Chłopcy Do Berna.
Durlak, J. P.
Do Si, La Sol, Fa Mi, Ré Do.
Gabriel-Marie, J.
Do You Ever Dream.
Richter, W. B.
Do You Feel That Way Too.
Kenny, B.
Do You Love Me.
Eisemann, M. Szeret-e Még.
Do You Remember.
Cernkovich, R. Sječaš Li Se Onog Sata.
Doagie-boogie.
Post, B. H.
Dodici Ragazze.
Borgazzi, F.
Does No Mean No.
Karolevitz, B.
Does the Moon Shine over Atlanta.
Richard, L.
Doghouse Cafe.
Arthur, W.
Dollar Ain't a Dollar Anymore.
Stoner, M.
Dolly's Lullaby.
Arant, B.
Dolores.
Waldteufel, E.
Dominant Spirit.
Thomas, G. A.
Domino Polka.
Elsnic, J. P., arr. Finger Polka.
Don Giovanni.
Mozart, J. C. W. A.
Doña Bonifacia.
Claro Fumero, J.
Donauwellen.
Ivanovici, J.
Donkey Ride.
Strouse, P.
Don't Ache, My Heart.
Lamkoff, P.
Don't Ask Me Why.
Dickerhoff, D. W.
Don't Be That Way to Me.
Hollis, L. P.
Don't Believe a Thing They Say.
Dean, E.
Don't Bother to Cry.
Merrill, B.
Don't Bring Me No News.
Campbell, B.
Don't Call It Love.
Wrubel, A. I Walk Alone.
Don't Cry over Me when I'm gone.
Bailes, W.
Don't Deny It.
Arthur, W.
Don't Disturb My Day Dream.
Turner, M. M.
Don't Ever Leave Me.
Swierkos, E.
Don't Fuss.
Amstell, B.
Don't Give It Another Thought.
Hackforth, N.

Don't Keep Me Waitin' Too Long.
Dean, E.
Don't Kill the Goose that lays the golden egg.
Fain, S.
Don't Leave Me Alone.
Gilbert, F.
Don't Play around Me Anymore.
Mank, C.
Don't That Moon Look Lonesome.
Sullivan, E. T.
Don't Wait for the Sunrise Tomorrow.
Seely, N.
Don't You Care.
Hall, D.
Don't You Love Me Anymore.
Livingston, J.
Dors, Mon Amour.
Delettre, J.
Dos Amores.
Monge, J.
Dos Miniaturas.
Miramontes, A.
Douce France.
Trenet, C.
Douze Études.
Cavallini, E.
Douze Études-Caprices de Concert.
Gallois Montbrun, R.
Douze Pièces Melodiques.
Bernard, P., arr.
Dove Andrai.
Lezza, C. Amo Solo la Fisarmonica.
Dover Beach.
Johnstone, M.
Doves.
Chanler, T.
Down Beat's Styles of Famous 88'ers.
Pease, S., ed.
Down Bethlehem Way.
Koppes, M. C., sister.
Down by the Glenside.
Borguno, A.
Down in Chihuahua.
Yaw, R.
Down in Mexico.
Roberts, P.
Down in Salinas.
Alkire, E. H.
Down in the Glen.
Connor, T.
Down in the Valley.
Pollack, R.
Down South.
Dungan, O.
Down Texas Way.
LaMar, E. H.
Down the Green Hudson Valley.
Gilbert, R. Der Holunderbusch blunt.
Down the Milky Way.
David, H.
Down the Old Spanish Trail.
Smith, K. L.
Down the Sunny San Joaquin.
Miller, F.
Downbeat Boogie.
Taylor, H.
Dream after Dream.
Nurnberg, V.
Dream Girl.
Arthur, W.
Dream I Dreamed of You.
Brennan, J. A.
Dream of Love.
Liszt, F. Liebestraum no. 3.
Tafarella, P.
Dream or Two.
Perry, K.
Dream Pedlary.
Roberton, H. S.
Dream Valse.
De Page, B.
Dreamin' Time, Mah Honey.
Strickland, L. T.
Dreaming.
Laura, A.
Schumann, R. A. Träumerei.
Dreaming Is Believing.
Arthur, W.

Epitaph.
  Diamond, D. L. 5 Songs.
Epithalamium.
  Bax, A.
Era un Pajarito.
  Castro, W. Cuantro Piezas sobre
    Temas Infantiles.
Ercole sul Termodonte.
  Vivaldi, A.
Erdösszélén Nagy a Zsivaj.
  Sas, N.
Erie.
  Harley, F.
Es ist ein' Ros' Entsprungen.
  Brahms, J.
Escape Me Never.
  Korngold, E. W.
Esclave d'Amour.
  Bozi, H.
Escondido.
  Valenti Costa, P. Seis Movimientos
    Corales a la Manera Popular Argentina.
Eso Eres Tu.
  Fidanzini, V. See If I Care.
Espera y Veras.
  Sánchez Vásquez, P.
Esquisse d'une Poeme.
  Simon, W. J.
Essential Scale Studies.
  Dounis, D. C.
Estate.
  Vivaldi, A. Concerti delle Stagioni.
Estel Lee's Arizona Wildcats.
  Livernash, W., arr.
Estrellita.
  Ponce, M. M.
Estudio en fa.
  Casella, E. M.
Eterna Cansone.
  Taccani, S.
Eternal God.
  Whitney, M. C.
Éternellement.
  Durand, P.
Eternidad.
  Paes, M.
Eternity.
  Paes, M. Eternidad.

Etoile des Tropiques.
  Travnicek, A. Dans Tes Yeux.
Etoile sans Lumière.
  Monnot, M.
Étrange Mélodie.
  Lucchesi, R. Sérénade aux Nuages.
Etude for piano.
  Golz, W.
Étude-Tableau.
  Rachmaninoff, S.
Etude to Eileen.
  Lewis, V.
Études et exercises.
  Bernard, P., arr. Douze Piéces
    Melodiques.
Etudes for Every Pianist and How to Study
    Them.
  Maier, G.
Etudes Modernes.
  Jeanjean, P.
Even Tho' I'll Shed a Million Tears.
  Fox, C.
Evening Hour.
  Cole, W.
Evening Prayer.
  Gabriel, C. H.
  Hodges, E. L.
  Kinder, R.
  Richards, M. R.
Evening Prayer and Dream Pantomine.
  Humperdinck, E.
Evening Service in C.
  Smith, H. L.
Evening Service in F.
  Long, K. R.
Evening Song.
  Chajes, J. T.

Evening We Went Out to Dine.
  Stewart, C. H.
Eventail.
  Hajos, J.
Ever Lighter Grow My Slumbers.
  Brahms, J.
Ever Present Jesus.
  Mills, G. W.
Ever Since You Went Away.
Everybody's Baby.
  Greer, J. B.
Everybody's Friends with Everybody.
  Walker, B.
Everybody's Gonna Have a Wonderful
    Time Up There.
  Abernathy, L. R.
Every Cloud Would Wear a Rainbow, if
    I had you, dear, only you.
  Schoenberger, A.
Every Day Is a Rainy Day for Me.
  Clyde, T.
Every Day Is Friday to a Seal.
  Hellner, I.
Every Day's My Birthday.
  Abraham, I.
Every Night When It Is Twilight.
  Benson, R. E.
Everyone Has Their Dreams.
  Cook, J.
Everything's the Same But You.
  McCormick, B.
Every Time I See You.
  Carleton, R. L.
Evocación.
  Gonzalez, L.
Evocation.
  Samazeuilh, G.
Ev'ry Little Bug.
  Harr, B.
Ev'ry Thing'll Be All Right.
  Huston, B.
Ev'ry Time I See a Rose.
  Bartlett, F.
Ev'rybody and His Brother.
  Saxon, J.
Ev'rybody knows I Love You.
  Gindhart, T. J.
Ev'rybody's Buying My Love Song
    just to get a picture of you.
  Alexander, P.
Ev'rything Shall Pass, My Love, but You.
  Siegel, C.
Exactly like You.
  McHugh, J. F. International Revue.
Excerpts from Concertos.
  Ambroise, V., arr.
Exercises pour les cinq doigts.
  Schmitt, A. Five-finger exercises.
Experience.
  Van Heusen, J. The Road to Rio.
Exsultate, Jubilate.
  Mozart, J.C.W.A.
Eyes of Texas.
  Yoder, P.

F

F. D. Roosevelt.
  Lamhoff, P.
Fävitska Jungfrurna.
  Atterberg, K.
Facility.
  Cochran, L. T.
Fair.
  Volkart-Schlager, K.
Fair Are the Meadows.
  Buchtel, F. L., arr.
Fair Follies of '47.
  Large, D.
Fair Helen.
  Montgomery, B.
Fairest Isle.
  Purcell, H.
Fairest Lord Jesus.
  Burkhard, S. T.
Fairy Enchantment.
  Raezer, C. M.

Fairy Tale Parade.
  Sharp, D. S.
Faith of Our Fathers.
  Hemy, H. F.
Fall in Love.
  Harman, G. F.
Fame Is the Spur.
  Wooldridge, J.
Familiar Moe.
  Conniff, R.
Family Reunion in Heaven.
  Steger, I.
Famous Folio of Songs to Remember.
  See title entry in composer list.
Famous Frog-i-more Rag.
  Morton, F. J. Frog-i-More-Rag.
Fanfárový pochod.
  Zita, F.
Fantaisie.
  Bedouin, P.
Fantaisie Impromptu.
  Chopin, F. F.
Fantaisiestück.
  Martelli, H.
Fantasia.
  Purcell, H.
Fantasia in B minor.
  Milford, R.
Fantasia Mexicana.
  Copland, A. Fiesta.
Fantasia on Greensleeves.
  Vaughan Williams, R. Sir John in
    Love.
Fantasie.
  Gibbons, O.
Fantasie in F minor.
  Mozart, J. C. W. A.
Fantasie on Swedish Folk Songs.
  Gilbert, H.
Fantasy.
  Kenton, S.
  Segal, J.
Fantasy in F-sharp minor.
  Federer, R.
Fantasy on an American Air.
  Fred, H. W.
Fantasy Quartet.
  Moeran, E. J.
Far Away.
  Shank, J.
Far Away in Bethlehem.
  Bush, G. Two Christmas Songs.
Farandole en Provence.
  Betti, H. Mam'selle Printemps.
Fare-thee-well, Dear Alma Mater.
  Myrow, J. Mother Wore Tights.
Fare you well, my friends.
  Billings, W. Compositions.
Farewell.
  Shannon, I.
Farewell anthem.
  Lutkin, P. C. The Lord Bless You and
    Keep You.
Farm Is the Place for Me.
  Clyde, T.
Farmer Took a Holiday.
  Roberts, A.
Farmer's Boy.
  Richardson, C.
Farolito de Madrid.
  Bastida, R. G.
Farr Brothers' Stomp.
  Farr, C.
Father Eternal.
  Williams, R. E.
Father in heaven.
  Gounod, C. F.
  Hallett, J. C. 33 Solos and Duets.
Father Omnipotent.
  Pasquet, J.
Faubourg Saint Honoré
  Marcopoulos, J.
Faust.
  Gounod, C. F.
Favorite Cowboy and Hill-billy Songs.
  Roberts, P. Paul and Ann Roberts.
Favorite Hymns.
  Bing Crosby's Favorite Hymns.

391

Favorite Polkas.
  Frey, H., arr. Lawrence Welk's
    Favorite Polkas.
Fee-fi-fo-fum.
  Disney (W.) Productions, Ltd. Fun
    and Fancy Free.
Feet of Fish.
  Bourtayre, H. Le Pas du Hareng.
Fellow Needs a Girl.
  Rodgers, R. Allegro.
Fem Sånger.
  Lidholm, I.
  Paulson, G.
Femme Espagnole.
  Padilla, J. Mujer de España.
Femmes Vengées.
  Philidor, F. A. D.
Ferme Tes Yeux.
  Rocca-Serra, P.
Fermín Rivera.
  Domínguez B., A.
Festal March.
  James, P.
Festal March Perstare et Praestare.
  James, P.
Festival.
  Addinsell, R. Trespass.
Festival Days.
  Guentzel, G.
Festival of Love.
  D'Angelo, L.
Festival Prelude.
  McKay, F. H.
Feu Follet.
  Bourtayre, H.
Feux de Camp.
  Lucchesi, R. Le Gardian.
Fiacre.
  Simon, L. M.
Fickle You.
  Lowe, H. L.
Fiddle-Faddle.
  Anderson, L.
Fido and Me.
  Alter, L. Living in a Big Way.
Field Day.
  Yuill, M. Four Out-Door Scenes.
Fiesta.
  Copland, A.
Fiesta Brava.
  Alarcón Leal, E. Porque Te Quiero.
Fiesta de Santa Fé.
  Guizar, T. Fiesta in Santa Fé.
Fiesta in Santa Fé.
  Guizar, T.
Fiesta mexicana.
  Esperon, M. No basta ser charro.
Fifteen Fingers.
  Tate, P.
Fifteen Organ Works from the Litany
  for Organ.
  Muset, J. Litany for Organ.
50 Questions 50 Answers.
  Jacobs, D.
Fifty-seventh Session March.
  Clitheroe, F.
Figaro's Air.
  Mozart, J. C. W. A.
Fight for Jersey.
  Newton, J. W.
Fight for Ol' Missou'.
  Sweet, M.
Fight for Our Nevada.
  Teakle, B.
Fighting Marines.
  Chanslor, H.
Fill Your Community Chest.
  Rettenberg, M.
Fine and True.
  Pártos, J. Az a Szép.
Finger Polka.
  Elsnic, J. P., arr.
Finger Tricks.
  Treharne, B., comp.
Fingers, Be Nimble, Fingers, Be Quick.
  Ramsey, A.
Fingers on Fire.
  Smith, A.

Finlandia.
  Sibelius, J.
Finnes Alltid Rosor.
  Stothart, H., Mrs. Miniver.
Flor di Cempáca.
  Pisani, D.
Fire of Your Love.
  Benjamin, A.
Firebird Ballet Suite.
  Stravinskii, I. F.
Fireflies.
  Glaser, V. M.
Firefly.
  Friml, R. Giannina Mia.
  Friml, R. Sympathy Waltz.
Fireside Book of Folk Songs.
  Boni, M. B., ed.
Firmeza.
  Valenti Costa, P. Seis Movimientos Cor-
    ales.
First Christmas Candle.
  Olds, W. B.
First Collection of Waltz Classics.
  Forbes, R., arr.
First Day of Summer.
  Miller, L.
First Love Song.
  Hall, C. G.
First Noel.
  Howorth, W.
  Scholin, C. A.
First Nowell.
  Gruber, F. Silent Night.
First Robin of Spring.
  Hall, D.
First Sinfonia.
  Bach, J. S.
First Time I Kissed You.
  Warren, H.
First Tunes.
  Sheinwold, E.
Fish in the Unruffled Lakes.
  Britten, B.
Fisher of Pusilleco.
  Tagliaferri, E.
Five-finger exercises.
  Schmitt, A.
Five Greek Folk Songs.
  Bax, A.
Five Hebrew Melodies.
  Wei, e.g., J.
Five Introits and Vespers.
  Anderson, W. H.
Five Kisses Till Midnight.
  Brodsky, R.
Five Pieces for Young People.
  Smit, L.
Five Postludes for Organ.
  Harris, C.
5 Songs.
  Diamond, D. L.
Flag of Stars for Victory.
  Farmer, W. L.
Flamengo.
  Flory, S. Carioca Album of
    Brazilian Songs.
Flashlight.
  Thorne, D.
Fleur sur l'Oreille.
  Bourtayre, H.
Flibber Flabber, Jibber Jabber.
  McClellan, J. C.
Flickan och Göken.
  Fernström, J. Sex Sånger.
Flight of the Bumble Bee.
  Rimskii-Korsakov, N. A. (Tsar
    Saltan)
Flight of the Fairies.
  Hamer, G. F.
Flock of Sparrows.
  Gendron, J. C.
Flood Waters.
  Wilson, B.
Flor de Valencia.
  Harper, M.
Flora Boogie.
  Marchese, V.
Flotsam's Follies.
  Hilliam, B. C.

Flower Leis.
  Alkire, E. H.
Flower of Valencia.
  Harper, M. La Flor de Valencia.
Flowers for Heliodora.
  Clark, H. Two Songs.
Flowers for Mother.
  Forrest, S.
Flowers o' Edinburgh.
  Hartley, F.
Flow'r of Theta Chi.
  Kaye, S.
Flustered Flea.
  Hinkle, L.
Fly, Eagles, Fly.
  Sweet, M.
För Vilsna Fötter Sjunger Gråset.
  Kallstenius, E.
  Lidholm, I. Fem Sånger.
Försök Inte med Mej, Fröken.
  Lagerkrans, K. O.
Första Möde.
  Widéen, I.
Folk Overture.
  Mennin, P.
Folk Preludes.
  Bowles, P.
Folk Songs of the British Isles.
  Holst, L., arr.
Folk Tunes for Solo Descant Recorder.
  Walker, T. S., arr.
Follow Your Rainbow.
  Jackson, T. K.
Followed by Your Prayer.
  Baker, P.
Fond Memories.
  Arthur, W.
Fonder You Are to My Heart.
  Bartlett, F.
Fool Am I.
  Carleton, R. L.
Fool That I Am.
  Hunt, F.
Foolin' My Heart.
  Nelson, K. F.
Foolish Dog.
  Scarmolin, A. L.
Foolish Pride.
  Bartlett, F.
Foolish Tears.
  Carson, J. L.
For All That I Want.
  Baran, L.
For As the Rain and Snow from Heaven
  Fall.
  Bach, J. S. Gleich Wie der Regen und
    Schnee vom Himmel Fällt.
For Better, for Worse.
  Elmer, K.
For Elise.
  Beethoven, L. van.
For Hun Er Saa Ung.
  Riis, A. Tivoli Revyen.
For I Love You Dear.
  Sieger, R.
For Once in Your Life.
  Fisher, M.
For sentimental reasons.
  Best, W. I Love you.
For You a Rose in Portland grows.
  Rutherford, A.
For Your Heart Will Break, Not Mine.
  Bartlett, F.
Forest of Two Blue Skies.
  Toelle, F. B.
Forever Amber.
  Raksin, D.
Forever in My Heart.
  Braden, E.
Forever, O Jehovah, Thy Word.
  De Lamarter, E.
Forgeron.
  Delfau, R.
Forget and Forgive Me.
  Davis, R. W.
Forget Me.
  Meisher, L.

Forget Me Not.
Bach, J. S. Aria, Forget Me Not.
Forgive and Forget.
White, C. T.
Forgive Me.
Dutton, G.
Forgiven.
Rusthoi, E. K. Gospel Songs.
Forgiving You.
Manus, J.
Forgotten Melody.
Federer, R.
Forsaken.
Morales, M. T. Güe-lé-le.
Forsaking All Others.
Wrubel, A.
Fortällinger.
Widéen, I. Pörste Möde.
Forte e nova mia disavventura.
Mortari, V. Lamenti.
Forth in Thy Name.
Wadely, F. W.
Fortune Teller.
Herbert, V.
44 Original Canadian Jigs and Reels for
Square Dances.
Cormier, B.
Forward.
Collins, W.
Fount of Liberty.
Milkey, E. T.
Four Aces Polka.
Panetti, C.
Four Carols.
Mellers, W.
Four Children's Pieces.
Klein, J.
Four Chorale Preludes.
Langstroth, I.
Four Chorus Gems.
Turney, N. D.
4 Easy Etudes.
Hayes, O. L.
Four Epitaphs.
Beckhard, R. L.
Four Out-Door Scenes.
Yuill, M.
Four Pieces.
Bax, A.
Four-pointed Kiss.
Hibbeler, R. O.
Four Preludes.
Ball, E.
Four Seasons.
Williams, R.
Four Short Pieces for the Church Service.
Whitmer. T. C.
Fourth Symphony.
Antheil, G. Symphony, no. 4.
Fra le Stelle.
Borgazzi, F. Le Dodici Ragazze.
Fra lek til alvor.
Selmer, M. Praktisk Klaverskole.
Fragment Lyrique.
Arney, J.
Fragrant Malva, Pretty Flow'r.
Keller, D. Szagos Malyva, Gyöngyvirág.
Frammenti Sinfonici.
Dallapiccola, L. Marsia.
Frasquita Serenade.
Lehár, F.
Fraternal Greeting Song.
Simms, A. M. The Grand's Song.
Fraulein Rosmarie.
Landl, E.
Freckles.
Hall, D.
Free.
Saxon, D.
Free and Equal Blues.
Robinson, E.
Freedom and Brotherly Love.
Savino, D.
Freedom Train.
Berlin, I.
Heyward, S. Checkin' on the Freedom
Train.

Freischütz Overture.
Weber, K. M. F. E. freiherr v.
French Military Marching Song.
Romberg, S. Desert Song.
Fresque marine.
Tournier, M. L.
Friendly Mountains.
Lilley, J. J. The Emperor Waltz.
Fröken Johanssons Sjömansvals.
Johansson, N.
Frog.
Dunhill, T. F.
Frog-i-more Rag.
Morton, F. J.
From Afar.
Christiansen, P. J.
From an Old Sketch Book.
Sladek, P.
From Day to Day.
Walker, J.
From Easter to Advent.
Bragers, A. P., arr. Proprium de
Tempore.
From Emily's Diary.
Bacon, E.
From Glory to Glory.
Bostwick, F. J.
From My Diary.
Sessions, R.
From Now until Forever.
Sprouse, P.
From the Bottom of My Heart.
Spencer, T.
From the Chinese.
Redman, R. E.
From the New World.
Dvořák, A. Symphony, no. 5.
From the Realms of Glory.
Frazee, G. F.
From the Russian Steppes.
Eckhardt, F. G.
From This Day On.
Guerin, G. Gloria.
From Violin to Viola.
Whistler, H. S.
Fruit Song.
Driver, A. New Songs for Old.
Fuego en Panamá.
Fontanals, F.
Fuga.
Miramontes, A. (Anáhuac) Respiro.
Fugitivo.
Paz, S.
Fugue.
Fuleihan, A.
Fugue in C minor.
Bach, J. S.
Fun and Fancy Free.
Disney (W.) Productions, Ltd.
Fun in the Sun at Las Vegas.
Nord, J. S.
Funiculi-Funicula.
Denza, L.
Funny As It Seems.
Stone, A. A.
Funny Little Money Man.
Rodney, D.
Funny Old Clown.
Crosby, M.
Fusilé.
Caby, R. J. A.
Futile Frustration.
Mundy, J.
Fyra Sånger.
De Frumerie, G.

G

Gång Blir Allting Stilla.
De Frumerie, G. Fyra Sånger.
Gaily Tripping.
Cherie, E. E.
Gala Pote.
Trenet, C.
Gallo Tuerto.
Barros, J.
Gamal, G'malil.
Chajes, J. T. Song of the Camel
Driver.

Gambol of the Gnomes.
Garman, W. M.
Gamle Stol.
Riis, A. Tivoli Revyen.
Gammal Batsman.
Ahde, S. En Sjomansvisa.
Gammalswenska wijsor.
Koch, S. y.
Gamme et l'Amour.
Guglielmi, L. Trente et Quarante.
Garden City, We Love You.
Hall, W. L.-E.
Garden of Delight.
Warwick, P.
Garden of Jamshyd.
Treharne, B.
Garden of Love.
Moquin, A.
Garden of Melody.
Baxter, J. R., comp.
Garden of Mem'ries.
Blackburn, H.
Garden Talk of Flowers is what my heart
would say.
McNeil, J. C.
Gardener.
Rowley, A.
Gardenia Lady.
Ceeley, L.
Gardian.
Lucchesi, R.
Gars de la Provence.
Tomasi, H. F.
Gaudent in Caelis.
Victoria, T. L. de.
Gávea.
Flory, S. Carioca Album of Brazilian
Songs.
Gavilán.
Fergo, T.
Gavotta.
Prokof'ev, S. S.
Gavotte.
Brown, R. Sarabande.
Guenther, F., ed. Dances by Great Mas-
ters.
Gavotte Antique.
Peeters, F.
Gay Promenade.
Frost, B.
Gayne Ballet.
Khachaturian, A. I. Three Dances.
Gee, I Love You.
Gianella, P.
Gele Late.
Weiner, L.
General Grant's Grand March.
Mack, E.
Gentle Mary.
McFeeters, R.
Gentleman Is a Dope.
Rodgers, R. Allegro.
Gentleman Who Paid My Fare.
McGee, J. A. The Monon Centennial
Show.
George Gershwin Selection.
Gershwin, G.
George Gershwin's Second Prelude.
Gershwin, G.
George Washington, Abraham Lincoln,
Ulysses S., Robert E. Lee.
Hayes, C.
George Washington's Prayer.
Gaul, H. B.
Georgia Waltz.
Krise, S.
Geremia.
Luzzatto, L. M.
Gertie.
McNeil, J. C.
Get Away for a Day.
Styne, J. High Button Shoes.
Get Hep to the Lawd.
Stout, C.
Get Swing Quick.
Nelson, S.
Get up Those Stairs, Mademoiselle.
Brent, R.

Gettin' Nowhere.
 Von Luehrte, F.
Getting Acquainted with the Keyboard.
 Cobb, H.
Ghasel.
 Rangström, T.
Ghost.
 White, M.
Ghosts.
 Lang, M. R.
Gi' Agapé As Milésoume Pali.
 Gabriélidés, M. G.
Giannina Mia.
 Friml, R.
Giant Note Home Songs.
 Spivak, S., arr.
Giant-Note Hymns.
 Klickmann, F. H., arr.
 Spivak, S., arr.
Giant Note Kiddie Songs.
 Spivak, S., arr.
Giant Note Waltzes.
 Spivak, S., arr.
Gib Mir einen Abschiedskuss.
 Siegel, P. Kiss Me and Then Go Away.
Gift Divine.
 Andrew, J. F.
Gigue.
 Simmons, H.
Gilly Gilly Wish Wash.
 Katzman, H.
Girl from the Production Line.
 Porter, J. S.
Girl Has a Right To Change Her Mind.
 Hecimovich, J.
Girl in the Cream Colored Coat.
 Kippel, H.
Girl in the Picture Hat.
 Federer, R.
Girl in the Valley.
 Mings, R.
Girl That I Remember.
 Rhodes, S.
Girl with the Corn Colored Hair.
 Robinson, W.
Girl with the 3 Blue Eyes.
 Burrows, A.
Girls of Idaho.
 Arthur, W.
Gitana.
 Thegodaeva, I.
Gitanerias.
 Lecuona y Casado, E.
Give a Man a Horse He Can Ride.
 Roberton, H. S.
Give Me a Burden.
 Hulin, E. F.
Give Me a Dolly.
 Buck, R.
Give Me a Song.
 Adrian, W.
Give Me an Atom of Love.
 Drew, N. L.
Give Me Romance.
 Lewis, W.
Glad Tidings Hymnal.
 Higgins, R. B.
Glad Trumpet.
 Shure, R. D.
Glade of Tuoni.
 Sibelius, J.
Gleich Wie der Regen und Schnee vom
  Himmel Fällt.
 Bach, J. S.
Gliders.
 Lake, G.
Gloomy Rain Blues.
 McNeil, J. C.
Gloria.
 Chesnokov. Nunc Dimittis.
 Guerin, G.
 Hall, C. L.
Gloria in Excelsis Deo.
 Sifler, P. J.
Gloria Victoribus.
 Milhaud, D. Two Marches.
Glorious Old Glory.
 Barris, E. P.

Glorious Victory.
 Kendall, W. M.
Glory! Praise and Power.
 Dicks, E. A.
Glory to Christ the King.
 Eberhle.
Glory to God.
 Handel, G. F. The Messiah.
Glory to God in the Highest.
 Pergolesi, G. B.
 Ridderhof, N. L.
Glow-worm.
 Lincke, P.
Glyko Mou Agori.
 Phouskas, G. K.
Go Down, Moses.
 Morgan, H.
Go, Little Song.
 Strickland, L.
Go, Mustangs, Go!
 Sweet, M.
Go-On, Go On.
 Daffan, T.
Go, Tell It on the Mountains.
 Marryott, R. E.
Go to Sleep, My Darling Curly Head.
 The Andrews Brothers.
Go to Sleep Our Baby Boy.
 Allender, N. D.
Go! Wausau High.
 Grill, K. R. N.
Go West, Young Man.
 Ruby, H. Copacabana.
God Answers Prayer.
 Frye, T. R.
God Bless Us, Darling.
 Scholl, B.
God Came, the Holy One.
 De Lamarter, E.
God Gave Me You.
 Kaiser, R. I.
God Is a Spirit.
 Kopylov, A.
God Is, He Knows and Cares.
 Hadden, H. H. Rest at Evening.
God Lives Today.
 Combs, W. W.
God of Abraham Praise.
 Mueller, C. F.
God of Mercy, God of Grace.
 Marks, C. A.
God Our Father, Lord of Heaven.
 Beobide, J. M. Tantum Ergo.
God Rest You Merry, Gentlemen.
 Scholin, C. A.
God Walks Beside Thee.
 Sateren, L. B.
God's Afterward.
 Elwell, H. B.
God's Loving Kindness.
 Bach, J. S.
God's Star.
 Miller, M. C.
God's Time.
 Grummons, R. N. I'm So Glad That
  Jesus Found Me.
God's Word.
 Pugh, J.
Gök-Rambo.
 Jonasson, J. E.
Gök-Polka.
 Uljvén, U. H.
Goin' Home to Arizona.
 Johndrow, L.
Goin' Steady with the Moon.
 Hammitt, O.
Goin' to the Old Barn Dance.
 Blanchard, D.
Going Fishing.
 Lamkoff, P.
Going Home Today.
 Carleton, R. L.
Gold Star Mother.
 McNeil, J. C.
Golden Earrings.
 Young, V.
Golden Gate Boogie.
 Johnson, C.

Golden Glow.
 Johnson, C. W.
Golden October Leaves.
 Wiltshire, E.
Golden Sails, Silver Sails.
 Newell, R. C.
Golden Steps. See title entry in composer
 list.
Golden Wedding.
 Marie, G.
Golden Years.
 Keller, F.
Golliwogg's Dance.
 Howell, I.
Gollywog Fantasy.
 Litolf, A.
Golondrina.
 Grant, J., arr. L'Hirondelle.
Golpe Maja.
 Muñiz Perez, J.
Gomes de Santa Fé.
 Melone, M. H.
Gone.
 Pazmezoglu, P.
Gone But Not Forgotten.
 Buck, R.
Gonna Get a Girl.
 Simon, H.
Good Christian Men Rejoice.
 Mueller, C. F.
Good Is It To Thank Jehovah.
 Schubert, F. P.
Good Morning.
 Grant-Schaefer, G. A.
Good Morrow to You; Springtime.
 Roberton, H. S.
Good News.
 Blane, R.
 Henderson, R.
Goodbye.
 Hallett, J. C., comp. Singing Along.
 Tosti, F. P.
Goodbye, I'll Say It Now.
 Williams, F.
Good-bye, Mr. Czerny.
 Stevens, E.
Good-bye, Old Pal.
 Monroe, B.
Goodbye to Love.
 Hall, D.
Goodnight, Baby Mine.
 Klein, M.
Goodnight, But Not Goodbye.
 Leas, L. S.
Goodnight, Little Sweetheart.
 Johnson, N.
Good Night, Machree.
 Heaton, S.
Goodnight, My Dream, Goodnight.
 Hall, D.
Goody Goody for You.
 Tucker, E. M.
Gorgeous.
 Richardson, M. K.
Gosh Darn-It, I'm Crazy 'bout You.
 Blaine, J.
Gosh Oh Friday I wish I was free.
 Carleton, R. L.
Gospel Homestead.
 Runyan, W. M.
Gospel in Song.
 Mills, G. W.
Gospel Solos New and Old.
 Wilson, I. B., arr. Lorenz's Gospel
  Solos New and Old.
Gospel Song Service.
 Smith, A. B., comp.
Gospel Songs.
 Rusthoi, E. K.
Got a Kiss on My Mind.
 Arthur, W.
Got a Little, Give a Little Polka.
 Smital, J.
Got the West on My Mind, take me back.
 Manus, J.
Gotta Have a Place to Hang My Hat.
 Sawyer, V.

394

Gotta Have Somethin'.
Tillman, F.
Goût de Miel.
Ulmer, G.
Grace, Joy, Peace and Happiness.
Thornton, A. F. de M.
Gracie.
Lee, W. J.
Gracieuse.
Caix D'Hervelois, L. de.
Graded Melody Studies.
MacLachlan, T. R.
Granada.
Albeniz, I.
Llossas, J.
Grand Coulee Serenade.
Sevier, L.
Grand Ole Opry.
Lee, E., comp. Bill Monroe's Grand
Ole Opry.
Grande Cité.
Monnot, M.
Grandfather's Joy.
Gosz, R.
Grandma Loved a Soldier.
Strickland, L. T.
Grandma's Thanksgiving.
Simeone, H.
Grandpa, I Want to Be a Soldier.
Lamkoff, P.
Grand's Song.
Simms, A. M.
Grange Diamond Jubilee.
Kelso, H.
Grant Us Thy Care.
Campbell, W. N. M. Two Anthems
for Chorus.
Grasshopper.
Diggle, R. Summer Sketches.
Grasshoppers' Holiday.
Eckhardt, F. G.
Grav.
Jonsson, J.
Grave.
Tartini, G.
Great Is the Lord.
Mueller, C. F.
Great Judgment Day.
Beaver, G.
Great Melodies from Verdi's operas.
Verdi, G.
Great Physician of the Skies.
Williams, Mrs. H.
Great Soldier and Great Sailor.
Vincent, N. H.
Green Are the Poplar Leaves.
Várady, A. Hajlik a Jegenye.
Green Dolphin Street.
Kaper, B.
Green Field.
Driver, A. New Songs for Old.
Green Fingers.
Bawcomb, J. W.
Green Grow the Lilacs.
Segal, J.
Green Hills of Ireland.
Tollerton, N.
Green Pastures.
Arthur, W.
Green Sleeves.
Ballatore, P., arr.
Vaughan Williams, R.
Grenadiers.
Waldteufel, E.
Grey Symphony.
Close, G.
Grido d'Amore.
Fadanelli, G.
Grieve Not the Holy Spirit.
Sateren, L. B.
Grieving.
Clyde, T.
Guance rosate.
Cioffi, G. Though You Are Pretty.

Guarapo y la Melcocha.
Pozo, M. A.
Guatemala.
Laurence, R.
Gubben och Gumman Skulle mota Vall.
Nystroem, G. Två Sånger.
Güe-lê-le.
Morales, M. T.
Guilty.
Whiting, R. A.
Guilty of Being in Love.
Newton, J.
Guitar Jump.
Smith, A.
Guitar Magic of Les Paul.
Paul, L.
Guitarra Andaluza.
Padilla, J. Mujer de España.
Guitarrita.
Fragna, A.
Gyere, Cigány.
Weitzner, G.
Gypsy Carnival.
Stevens, M.
Gypsy Love Song.
Herbert, V.
Herbert, V. The Fortune Teller.
Gypsy Polka.
Agay, D.
Gypsy Rondo.
Haydn, J. Trio, piano & strings.
Gypsy Trails.
Hulin, D.
Gypsy Waltz.
Padwa, V.

H

H. M. S. Pinafore.
Sullivan, sir A. S.
Ha Elér Hozzad.
Kurucz, J.
Hárda Villkoret.
Sköld, I.
Habein Yakir li Ephrayim.
Silver, M.
Habla Mi Corazon.
Vela, E. L. Take a Tip from My Heart.
Háblame.
Castellanos, A. Talk to Me.
Haciendo Nonito.
Castro, W. Cuatro Piezas sobre Temas Infantiles.
Hälsning fran det Gamla Landet.
Kraft, A.
Händel Simplified.
Händel, G. F.
Härmedh faarväll, sköln damma.
Koch, S. v. Gammalswenska wijsor.
Hagith.
Szymanowski, K.
Hail, Holy Child.
Bush, G. Two Christmas Songs.
Hail, Holy Light.
Kastalsky, A. D.
Hail, O Virgin.
Grechaninov, A. T.
Hail to the Bells.
Barthelson, J.
Hail to the Lord's Anointed.
Stanton, W. K.
Hail to Tomorrow.
Savino, D.
Hail U. B. C.
King, H.
Hajlik a Jegenye.
Várady, A.
Hallelujah.
Youmans, V.
Hallelujah Chorus.
Händel, G. F. The Messiah.
Halvány Sárga Rózsát.
Sándor, J.
Hamtramck Mama.
York, L.
Hand in Hand.
Lawrence, J.

Hand in Hand with Jesus.
Scarborough, D.
Hand of God.
Wilson, R. C.
Hang Your Stocking and reminisce on Christmas Eve.
Vanderburg, G. J.
Hangin' Round a Country Store.
Hinman, R. E.
Hangtown Gals.
Harley, F.
Hannaker Mill.
Noble, H.
Hansel and Gretel.
Humperdinck, E. Prayer.
Happy.
Arthur, W.
Happy As a Schoolboy.
Cook, L.
Happy Birthday Song.
Parmelee, G. The Up-to-date Happy Birthday Song.
Happy Christmas Morning.
Durham, G. H.
Happy Days.
Busby, B. Holiday Camp.
Happy Days Polka.
Kogen, H.
Happy Family.
Mittler, F.
Happy Hitchy Hiker.
Arbelaez, H.
Happy Hour Waltz.
Yankovic, F. J.
Happy Songs for Children.
Caines, G.
Harbor in Moonlight.
Larson, E. R.
Harbor of Dreams.
McNeil, J. C.
Hark! Hear the Merry Bells.
Banks, H.
Hark, Ten Thousand Harps and Voices.
Neander, J.
Hark to the News, Neighbour.
Nagle, W. S.
Harlem.
Elam, C. M.
Harlem Boogie.
Penrose, B.
Harmonica.
Stein, S. A.
Harmony for False Lovers.
Addinsell, R. Trespass.
Harmony Lane.
Metcalfe, G. E.
Harp.
Bauer, M.
Harp Album.
Grandjany, M.
Harry Revel's Music out of the Moon.
Revel, H.
Harvest of Love.
Hall, D.
Has Someone Taken My Place.
Arthur, W.
Hassidic Dances.
Stutchewsky, J.
Hast Thou Not Known.
Templeton, A. A.
Hasta Cuando.
López, I.
Hasta la Vista.
Jackson, A. F.
Hasta la Vista, My Sweet.
Nurnberg, V.
Hasta que Se Rompa el Coco.
Gutierrez, B. J.
Haste Thee, Nymph.
Händel, G. F.
Haunted House.
Stevens, E. Three Piano Solos.
Haunting Melody.
Arthur, W.
Have a Go, Joe.
Jordan, J.
Have a Little Patience.
Alleva, J. J.

Have Faith in God.
Jones, G. J. Christ Understands.
Have I a Chance.
Carleton, R. L.
Have I Ever Told You.
DePaul, G.
Have I Told You.
Spoliansky, M. One, Two, Three.
Have You Ever Been Told.
Cooper, H.
Have You Found Somebody New.
Arthur, W.
Have You Got a Bad Hangover.
Berry, T. D.
Have You Seen My Colleen This Mornin'.
Kent, W.
Have You Tried My Blessed Saviour,
He's Alright.
Davis, V.
Haven't Seen the Likes of You.
Del Sesto, S.
Hawaii Will Be Paradise Once More.
Owens, H. R.
Hawaiian Memories.
Brewster, M.
Hawaiian Moon.
Campbell, C.
Hawaiian Paradise.
Fredericks, C. R.
Hay Que Inventar.
López Martin, A.
He Abideth Faithful.
Baer, C. E.
He Came Back to Me Just Like He
Used to Be.
Beach, H.
He Came to Me One Day.
Loveless, W. P.
He Can Waltz.
Loesser, F. Variety Girl.
He is Merciful.
Zilberts, Z. Vehu Rachum.
He Is Mine Today.
Lofton, T. M.
He Is My Song.
Hubbard, T. H.
He is Sweeter as the Years Roll By.
Pace, C. H.
He Is the One.
Jackson, L. M.
He Is Waiting There for Me.
Hadden, H. H. Rest at Evening.
He Loves, He Saves, He Keeps, He Satisfies.
Loveless, W. P.
He Will Say We'll Done Some Day.
Pace, C. H.
Headin' Back to West Virginia.
Bartlett, F.
Headin' for Heaven.
O'Hara, A.
Headin' West.
Roth, H. H.
Heading for the End of the Rainbow.
Arthur, W.
Health Notes.
McKinley, R. C.
Hear My Prayer, O Lord.
Williams, R. E.
Hear Our Humble Prayer.
Schubert, F. P. Ave Maria.
Heart May Break.
Coombs, G.
Heart of America.
Shepherd, L.
Heartless.
Paes, M. Maldad.
Hearts of Glasgow.
Graham, B. In Dear Old Glasgow Toon.
Heather Hare.
Blower, M.
Heaven and You.
Watkins, P.
Heaven Is My Goal.
Rusthoi, E. K. Gospel Songs.
Heaven Is My Home.
Messler, O.
Turner, E.
Heaven, Our Home.
Gaddis, R. M. Repentance.

Heaven with You.
Little, G. A.
Heavenly Father.
Schubert, F. P. Ave Maria.
Heaven's Near.
McNeil, J. C.
Heaven's Radio.
Pond, C. A. Beautiful City of Gold.
Heav'n, Heav'n.
Eckhardt, F. G., arr.
Hebrew Children.
Twyeffort, B. Theme and Six Variations
for organ.
Hebrew Traditional Cantorial Masterworks.
Malavsky, S.
Heigh-ho.
McBride, E. I.
Helen-Polka.
Carroll, J.
Hello.
Hall; D.
Lucchesi, R. Sept Jours au Paradis.
Tucker, A. F.
Hello, Ev'rybody! Let Us Get Acquainted.
Huston, F. C.
Hello, Little Darling, Hello.
Arthur, W.
Help Me to Help My Neighbor.
Berlin, I.
Help Somebody as You Go Along.
Essenburg, E.
Hembra Mala.
Gonzáles, L.
Henry before Agincourt.
Noble, H.
Henry, V.
Walton, W.
Hep Step and Jump.
Alexander, W.
Her Dreams.
Crane, J.
Her Kommer Jeg med det Lille, Jeg Har.
Andersen, K. N. Dagmar Revyen,
1947.
Her Little Green Parasol.
Richards, M. R.
Here Am I, Send Me.
Benedict, E.
Here and There.
Price, F. B.
Here Comes Santa Claus.
Haldeman, O.
Here Comes the Milkman.
Manus, J.
Here I Am, Lord.
Bugét, A. J.
Here in My Heart.
Grimstvedt, D. M.
Here in the Garden, Beloved.
Vairin, L. Songs for voice and piano.
Here Is My Heart.
Yanis, J.
Here, O My Lord.
Greenfield, A. M.
Herman's Boogie.
Mosley, S.
Herzen Träumen in der Dämmerung.
Kreuder, P.
He's a Real Gone Guy.
Lutcher, N.
He's Coming.
Grummons, R. N.
He's Engraving His Name on My Heart.
Curtis, N. G.
He's Mine, This Christ, the Nazarene.
Franklin, R. M.
He's Won My Heart Completely.
Piper, E. D. Revival Choruses.
Hey, Hey, Baby.
Tarrant, R.
Hi There, Hello.
Clyde, T.
Hialmar.
Loucheur, R.
Hiberia.
Rixner, J.

Hickory Dickory Dock.
Troup, B.
Hidden Violets.
Dellafield, H.
High Button Shoes.
Styne, J.
High Cost of Living.
Arter, W. J.
High Falutin' Mama.
Nettles, W. E.
High Hat.
Schatenstein, J.
High Sierra Home.
Hatlem, C.
High Street.
Driver, A. New Songs for Old.
Highland Air.
Hill, A.
Hillbilly.
Gould, M. Americana.
Hillbilly Hit Parade.
Lee, E.
Hills of Colorado.
Manus, J.
Hippity-Hop.
Hopkins, H. P.
Hirondelle.
Grant, J., arr.
His Fraternity Pin.
Kramer, A. C.
His Mother's Gone.
Ogle, C.
His Servants Never More than He.
Iden, R. J.
Hits of the Day.
Bradley, K., comp. Bing Crosby's Hits
of the Day.
Hjaelp Mig at Følge Dig.
Salomon, S.
Ho un Segreto sul Cuor.
Bonconpagni, S.
Hobby Horses.
Raezer, C. M.
Hobo without a Frown.
Buck, R.
Hocus Pocus.
Steadman, A.
Hodie Christus Natus Est.
Denny, W. D. Lux Fulgebit Hodie.
Höstsang.
Liljefors, I. Två Sånger.
Hogyha Olykor Éjféltájban.
Kádas, G.
Hogyha Szeretnélek.
Sas, N.
Hoja de Album.
Miramontes, R., A.
Hojas Caen.
Miramontes, A.
Hokey Joe.
Swan, B. This Time for Keeps.
Hold Me Close to You.
Richard, L.
Hold Them Up in Prayer.
Philpot, E.
Holiday.
Boland, C. A. Chris Crosses.
Holiday Camp.
Busby, J.
Holiday for Strings.
Rose, D. The Outstanding Compositions
of David Rose.
Holiday Polka.
Meretta, L. V.
Holunderbusch blunt.
Gilbert, R.
Holy Birth.
Wadely, F. W.
Holy Child.
Anderson, W. H.
Holy City.
Adams, S.
Holy, Holy, Holy.
Liemohn, E.
Holy, Holy, Holy, Lord God Almighty.
Dykes, J. B.

Holy Morn.
Gounod, C. F.
Holy Thursday.
Rowley, A. Three Songs of Innocence.
Home and Eternal Bliss.
Crane, J.
Home by the Susquehanna.
McNeil, J. C.
Home Is Where the Heart Is.
Kapp, D.
Home on the Range.
Ballatore, P., arr.
Home Run King.
Lawrence, S. Three Early Grade Pieces.
Home to My Heart.
Arthur, W.
Homeland.
Greenhalgh, M.
Homeward Road.
Rowley, A.
Hommage à Chopin.
Gradstein, A.
Honey Bunny.
Story, J.
Honey Gal.
Smith, H. H.
Honey Mine.
Cunningham, B.
Honeymoon.
Howard, J. E. I Wonder Who's Kissing Her Now.
Honeymoon Medley.
Howard, J. E. I Wonder Who's Kissing Her Now.
Honeymoon Trip to the Moon.
Gibson, H.
Honey's Waltz.
Volpe, H.
Honky Tonk Train.
Lewis, M.
Honnan Jö a Fény.
Lavotta, R.
Honolulu Lou.
Ross, B.
Hookey.
LeVeille, C.
Hooray, Hooray, I'm Goin' Away.
Shaftel, S.
Hoosier Time.
McGee, J. A. The Monon Centennial Show.
Hopak.
Musorgskii, M. P.
Hope and Pray.
Paul, A.
Hope Chest.
Seymour, S. A.
Hoping to Be Remembered.
Rickus, M. E.
Hora Staccato.
Dinicu.
— Heifetz, J. Horn Swing-cato.
Horn.
Richards, K.
Hosanna in Excelsis.
Gounod, C. F. Judex.
Hosea.
Floyd, H. A.
Hot Stuff Polka.
Hoven, G.
Hot Tamale Rose.
Fillgrove, E.
Hôtel des Artistes, de l'opérette.
Ulmer, G. On A Volé une Etoile.
Houndin' Blues.
Lee, S.
House Rent Boogie.
Basie, C.
House Shortage Blues.
Hibbard, H.
How Blest Are Shepherds.
Purcell, H. King Arthur.
How Can I Forget.
Hibbeler, R. O.
How Can I Forgive You.
Jacek, V. J.

How Can I Leave Thee.
Martin, C. T., arr.
How Can I Tell You.
Arthur, W.
How Can It Be Wrong.
Walker, C.
How Can You Talk about Love.
Woodford, G. R.
How Come the Mortgage Got Paid.
Nelson, S.
How Could You Do This to Me.
Arthur, W.
How Far Is Heaven.
Arthur, W.
How I Could Love You.
Plummer, H. A.
How Ireland Got Its Music.
Blanc, J. E.
How Long.
Hall, D.
How Long Has It Been.
Gray, T. J.
How Long Wilt Thou Forget Me.
Brown, R. J.
Pflueger, C.
How Many Kisses does it take to make you fall in love with me.
Kaufman, A. S.
How to Play the Violin.
Gordon, C.
How Uplifted My Heart.
Schubert, F. P.
How Was I to Know.
Whicker, R. L.
How You All.
Clyde, T.
How Your Love Came to Me.
Arthur, W.
How'd You Like a Honeymooning.
Tobin, L.
Howdy, Buddy.
Wheatley, W. D.
Howdy, Friends, Good Evenin', Neighbors.
Nelson, K. F.
Hrossey.
Jackson, C.
Huella.
Valenti, C. P. Seis Movimientos Corales a la Manera Popular Argentina.
Hugo and Igo in Mexico.
Fields, I.
Huit Petits Instructives Morceaux.
Martens, I.
Hulda.
Franck, C. A.
Humming Bird.
Gendron, J. C. Bird Sketches.
Humor in Vocal Music.
Herford, J. G., ed.
Humoresque.
Dvořák, A.
Mirouze, M.
Paz, H.
Humoresque Boogie.
Catlett, S.
Hundred and Sixty Acres.
Kapp, D. The Last Round-up.
Hundred Candles, Hundred Bottles.
Fráter, L. Száz Szál Gyertyát, Száz Rice Mort.
Hungry.
Nettles, W. E.
Hurdy-gurdy.
Larson, E. R.
Hurdy-gurdy Man.
Marvin, L.
Hurra pour l'Espagne.
Huguet y Tagell, R. J.
Hurrah for Dear Miami.
Rushing, R. B.
Hurray! It's All Over, Over There.
Tobin, L.
Hurray Slovenes Polka.
Yankovic, F. J.
Hurricane-Express.
Casadesus, F.
Hurricane Polka.
Witkowski, L.

Hurry on Down.
Lutcher, N.
Hush Ye, 'Tis Mary.
Cline, J. D.
Hush-A-Bye Wee Rose of Killarney.
Jerome, M. K. My Wild Irish Rose.
Hut-2-3-4.
Filas, T. J.
Huvinäytelmä-alkusoitto.
Madetoja, L. A.
Hvarföre skal iagh mig medh sorger qualia.
Koch, S. v. Gammalswenska wijsor.
Hymn.
Halinás, H.
Hymn of Affirmation.
Kelley, D. M.
Hymn of Dedication.
Wordsworth, W.
Hymn of Praise.
Wood, H. O.
Hymn of Thanksgiving.
Kelley, D. M.
Hymn of the Angels.
Daley, P. A. Hymnus Angelorum.
Hymn of Triumph.
Kelley, D. M.
Hymn till Västergötland.
Wideen, L.
Hymn to Beauty.
Oldroyd, G.
Hymn to Courage.
Beethoven, L. van.
Hymn to St. Frances Xavier Cabrini.
Mauro, B.
Hymn to the Earth.
Sibelius, J. Maan virsi.
Hymn to the Night.
Cain, N.
Hymn to the Virgin.
Watt, J. C.
Hymn-tune Anthems.
Lorenz, E. J., comp.
Hymne Patriotique.
Gogniat, J.
Hymns for the Piano Accordion.
Schuitema, A. K.
Hymnus Angelorum.
Daley, P. A.

I

I Adore Thee, Blessed Savior.
Blakeslee, S. E.
I Ain't A-Gonna Leave My Love No More.
Krieg, R. C.
I Ain't Confessin' My Troubles to Nobody.
Waters, H.
I Ain't Mad at You.
Ebbins, M.
I Always Lose.
Lockin, H.
I Am a Soldier of the U.S.A.
Tobin, L.
I Am Coming Back to You.
Clyde, T.
I Am Living in a Dream.
Carleton, R. L.
I Am Ready.
Heinz, A. S.
I Am Sure My Love.
Lovinggood, P.
I Am Waiting.
Criscuolo, J. D.
I Asked the Birds to Sing.
Arthur, W.
I Believe.
Jospe, E.
Rome, H. The Advertising Song.
I Believe in Santa Claus.
Balliett, G.
I Believe in You.
Wade, H.
I Bowed in the Shadow of the Cross.
Anderson, I. K.
I Cain't Get offa My Horse.
Amsterdam, M.
I Can Hear Church Bells Ringing.
Erhardt, J.

I Can't Fall in Love All Over Again.
Breach, M.
I Can't Forget My Sorrow.
Hibbeler, R. O.
I Can't Go on Like This.
Val, J.
I Can't Help Wondering.
Bailes, W.
I Can't Hit the Ground with My Hat.
Woodbury, J. J.
I Caught a Rainbow.
Arthur, W.
I Come to Thee.
Morris, K. Come Home.
I Could Be Dreaming.
Warren, I. N.
I Couldn't Dream a Better Dream.
Thorimbert, L.
I det Lille Grønne Land.
Riis, A. Tivoli Revyen.
I Didn't Have Time.
Covington, T.
I Done Did It.
Hunt, R. G.
I Don't Care.
Freeman, T.
I Don't Know What I'd Do without You.
Noël, A.
I Don't Know Where to Go but I'm goin'.
Higginbotham, L.
I Don't Mind Your Kissing Me.
Weiner, P.
I Don't Want To Be Adored.
Arthur, W.
I Don't Want to Leave.
Luicy, E.
I Don't Want To Live without you.
Chanslor, H.
I Don't Want to Meet any More People.
Carlone, F. N.
I Don't Want to Miss Heaven, Do You.
Whitney, R. T.
I Dream of Jeanie.
Foster, S. C.
I Dreamed.
Fox, H. C.
I Dreamed of You a thousand years ago.
Ochs, R. G.
I Drove You into Someone Else's Arms.
Davis, J.
I Feel Like Crying.
Newman, R.
I Feel So Smoochie.
Moore, P.
I Fell in Love Last Night.
Grayson, B.
I Found a Gold Mine when I found you.
Bailliett, G.
I Found a Rose in Sicily.
Lawson, J.
I Found a Star.
Van Tyle, R.
I Found the Key.
Cook, L.
I Gave My Heart to You.
Yerger, D. O.
I Gave My Life for Thee.
Schuitema, A. K., arr. Jesus, Lover of
My Soul.
I Gave You the Best of My Life.
D'Angelo, L.
I Got Lost in His Arms.
Berlin, I. Annie Get Your Gun.
I Got Shoes.
Cain, N.
I Got Shoes heaven, heaven.
Cain, N.
I Guess I'll Always Love You.
Moquin, A.
I Had a Lot of Friends.
Kowalski, J. L.
I Had a Lovely Dream.
Arthur, W.
I Had a Million Dreams Last Night.
Plumb, N.
I Had a Wonderful Time in Columbus.
Walker, B.

I Hate to Lose You I'm so used to you now.
Gottler, A.
I Have Been Here Before.
Klumpkey, J.
I Have But One Heart.
Farrow, J.
I Have Found a Friend in Jesus.
Roberson, E.
I Have Made a Fine Bouquet.
Lavotta, R. Mezei Bokréta.
I Have That Certain Feeling.
Arthur, W.
I Haven't a Heart.
Arthur, W.
I Hear You Sweetly Singing.
Lama, G.
I Hear You Talkin'.
Wakely, J.
I heard a great voice.
Billings, W. Compositions.
I Heard a Voice from Heaven.
Harris, W. H.
I Heard an Old Refrain.
Owen, Mrs. H.
I Heard the Bells on Christmas Day.
Williams, G. V.
I Heard the Voice of Jesus Say.
Marsh, C. H.
Rasley, J. M.
I Heard You Crying in Your Sleep.
Williams, H. Last Night.
I Hung a Star in My Window.
Gordon, J. H.
I Just Can't Find the Words.
Michel, A.
I Just Fell out of Love with You.
Gribbs, C.
I Just Said Good-Evening.
Bodge, P.
I Just Want to Talk about You.
Parks, F. E.
I Kärlekens Ortagard.
Sylvain, J.
Sylvain, J. Svarta Rosor.
I Kiss Your Hand, Madame.
Erwin, R.
I Knew it.
McNeil, J. C.
I Knew Some Day I'd Meet Someone Like
You.
Tobin, L.
I Knew What Heaven Could Be.
Arthur, W.
I Know a Bank.
Anderson, W. H.
I Know a Beautiful Theme.
Stoughton, R. S.
I Know a Lot of Things.
Tucker, E. M.
I Know Better Now.
Walker, M. L.
I Know He Loves Me.
Hallett, J. C., comp. Singing Along.
I Know He Will Remember Me.
Harvey, L.
I Know It.
Abraham, I.
I Know What Love Can Do.
Kuhla, G. J. T.
I Know Where I'm Goin'.
Verrall, J.
I Know Why Angels Cry.
Myers, H.
I Left Myself Wide Open.
Ellis, S.
I Like How You Look.
McMillen, H. L.
I Like Life.
Addinsell, R. Tuppence Coloured.
I Like the Way You Say Goodnight.
Crawford, J. D.
I Like to Hear the Old Songs.
Roberts, J.
I Like You, Valentine.
Parmelee, G.
I Long for the Wide Open Spaces.
Overland, E. O.

I Lost My Heart to You.
Hibbeler, R. O.
I Lost My Heartaches.
Kent, B.
I Love Him because He First Loved Me.
Williams, D. W.
I Love It When It Rains.
Pentuff, O.
I Love No One But You.
Tobin, L.
I Love Nobody Else but You, Dear.
Lajtai, L. Én Nem Szeretek Mást csak
Téged.
I Love Only You.
Snow, C. R.
I Love To Be Surprised.
Henriksen, E. G.
I Love to See You Smile.
Thompson, O. M.
I Love to Sing a Duet.
Friend, C.
I Love to Tell the Story.
Fischer, W. G.
I Love To Watch the Dancers.
De Moraes, N. Belo Cumbancha.
I Love You, Dear Jesus.
Ramont, G. M.
I love you for sentimental reasons.
Best, W.
I Love You, Sweetheart Mine.
Sendrey, A.
I Married the Girl of My Dreams.
Hammonds, R.
I May Be Wrong but, I Think you're wonder-
ful.
Sullivan, H. Wallflower.
I Met Her in the Movies.
Potter, H. H.
I Met My Dream Boy in Person.
Kloster, C.
I Miss a Little Miss in Mississippi.
Kinsey, C.
I Miss You So.
Robin, S.
Scott, B.
I Miss Your Arms.
Hantakas, G.
I Must Be Up and Doing.
Sergey, J. M.
I Must Have a Sweetheart.
Dóczy, J. Szeretöt Keresek.
I Must Have Been Dreaming of You.
Ver Bruggen, J.
I Must Join That Heavenly Choir.
Farmer, W. L.
I Must Keep Workin'.
Rushan, K. G.
I Must Tell Jesus All.
Pace, C. H.
I Need Thee, Lord.
Hulin, E. F.
I Need You.
Arthur, W.
I Never Told You.
Rose, M.
I Paid for the Kiss I Stole.
Fenerty, M. E.
I Pray You'll Remember.
Jenkins, J. L.
I Promised the Moon.
Hall, D.
I Received a Dress.
Dóczy, J. Vett a Rózsám Piros Selyem
Viganót.
I Remember You.
Kayne, B.
I See His Blood upon the Rose.
Cope, C.
I Shall Remember.
North, B.
I Sing My Songs.
Tarkowski, E.
I Sink in Deep Mire.
Goldspink, H.
I Sought the Lord.
Maltzeff, A.
I Still Get Jealous.
Styne, J. High Button Shoes.

I Still Love You.
 Arthur, W.
I Still Remember.
 Tobin, L.
I Still Say Your Name in My Prayer.
 Stoner, M.
I Stolta Städer.
 Fernström, J.
I Thank My Lucky Star.
 Carmichael, C. J.
I Theenk You Weenkj
 Fain, S.
I Think I'll Plant a Garden.
 Stairs, L. E.
I Think of You.
 Vindiola, B.
I to You and you to me.
 Mulder, H.
I Told My Heart.
 Dexter, A.
I Told Ya I Love Ya, Now Get Out.
 Ellis, H.
I Took a Chance.
 Pyper, G. R.
I Truly Love You, Darling.
 Hibbeler, R. O.
I Vantan på Jäntan.
 Ullvén, U. H.
I Waited for the Lord.
 Hopkins, J. M.
I Waited for You.
 Bláha, V.
I Waited Too Long.
 Dexter, A.
I Walk Alone.
 Wrubel, A.
I Walked into the Garden.
 Weaver, M.
I Want a Dog for Christmas.
 Michels, W.
I Want More than a Sample of Love.
 Roberts, V.
I Want My Life to Count for Jesus.
 Hulin, E. F.
I Want to Be Home on Christmas Morning.
 Easter, T.
I Want to Be Loved.
 Balles, W.
I Want to Cry.
 Pirone, H.
I Want to Make Sure of Heaven.
 Kickler, D. C.
I Want to Rise Above the World.
 Hulin, E. F.
I Want You to Be a Part of Me.
 George, D.
I Was Just Window Shopping.
 Kazel, T.
I Was Never in Love Before.
 Arthur, W.
I Was Wrong.
 Capano, F.
I Wasn't Born in Ireland but I love it
 just the same.
 Sussman, J.
I Went Down to Virginia.
 Mann, D.
I Will Bless the Lord.
 Elmore, R.
I Will Follow Jesus.
 Esters, H. V.
I Will Follow the Lord.
 Brown, C. C.
I Will Gladly Tell the Story.
 Adams, R. L.
I Will Lift up Mine Eyes.
 Walker, E.
I Will Lift Up Mine Eyes unto the Hills.
 Humphreys, D.
I Will Pour Out My Spirit.
 Cain, N.
I Will Say.
 Geroux, L.
I Will Write You a Love Song.
 Arthur, W.
I Winked at You.
 Smith, C. A.

I Wish I Could Say the Same.
 Stride, H.
I Wish You a Happy Birthday.
 Deschênes, J.
I Woke Up Crying.
 Robertson, J.
I Wonder if She'd Answer Me if I would
 say 'hello'.
 Hibbeler, R. O.
I Wonder if You Care.
 Gottuso, T.
I Wonder if You Remember.
 Bailey, M. V.
I Wonder Who's Kissing Her Now.
 Howard, J. E.
I Wonder Who's Kissing Her Now,
 Honeymoon.
 Howard, J. E.
I Won't Protest.
 Rivera, H. Sin Protestar.
I Would Have a Little Garden.
 Martin, H.
I Would Like to Have Seen Jesus.
 Hulin, E. F.
I Wouldn't Be Surprised.
 Bierman, B.
I Wouldn't Know.
 Arthur, W.
Ice Cream Song.
 Brownell, W.
Ich Kann bel Gewitter Nicht Allein Sein.
 Kreuder, P. Wege der Liebe.
Ich Nenne Alle Frauen Baby.
 Kreuder, P. Das Blaue Halstuch.
Ich Steh an Deiner Krippen Hier.
 Bach, J. S. Beside Thy Cradle Here I
 Stand.
I'd Be a Fool Again.
 Yoxsimer, H.
I'd Jump at the Chance.
 Campos, O.
I'd Like to Be a Man Like Daniel.
 Balles, W.
I'd Like to Live Forever.
 Deis, C.
I'd Rather Be a Tither.
 Ross, H. K.
I'd Rather Be in Miami.
 Bayha, C. A.
I'd Rather Look at You.
 Revel, H.
Ideas.
 Toch, E.
Idyll.
 Ingall, O.
If a Rose Could Speak.
 Jansen, D.
If at Night a Band of Gypsies.
 Kádas, G. Hogyha Olykor Éjféitájban.
If Christ Would Live and Reign in Me.
 Piper, E. D. Revival Choruses.
If Ev'ry Day Was Christmas and ev'ry
 night was New Year's Eve.
 Royal, L.
If I Can't Believe in You.
 Bergman, D.
If I Can't Have You.
 Nord, J. S.
If I Could.
 Rojo, G. Si Pudiera.
If I Could Sing.
 Fleming, A.
If I could tell you.
 Munoz, R. Si Pudiera Decirte.
If I Could write a Song about You.
 Hibbeler, R. O.
If I Owned the Moon.
 Robertson, H. Y.
If I Whisper I Love You.
 Perry, T. J.
If It Hadn't Been for You.
 Hanson, K.
If It's True.
 Bently, G.
If Love Can Win the Way.
 Wright, E.
If Love Should Come.
 Barnes, E. S.

If Now You Truly Love Me.
 Bach, J. S. Willst Du Dein Herz Mir
 Schenken.
If the Shoe Fits.
 Beverly, J. W.
If There Is Someone Lovelier Than You.
 Schwartz, A. Revenge with Music.
If, When You Hear My Song.,
 Kurucz, J. Ha Elér Hozzád.
If Winter Comes.
 Carpenter, L
If Wishes Were Fishes.
 Lake, G.
If You Are There.
 North, M.
If You Don't Love Me.
 Nelson, K. F.
If You Knew Susie.
 Idriss, R.
 McHugh, J. F.
 Meyer, J.
If You Loved.
 Bellini, G. B.
If You Only Knew.
 Kogen, H.
If You Would Know.
 Donnarumma, G.
If Your Heart Aches.
 Sergey, J. M.
If You're the Girl.
 Caron, A.
Ikke Ham.
 Riis, A. Tivoli Revyen.
Il Fait des.
 Chekler, E. E.
Il Fait Froid dans Mon Coeur.
 Petit Dutaillis, J.
Il Faudrait Faire une Chanson.
 Lemit, W.
Il N'Etait Pas Sentimental.
 Gasté, L.
Il Revait.
 Neuberger, J. B. D.
Ile d'Amour.
 Gasté, L.
 Lucchesi, R.
I'll Always Love You.
 Kropp, G. W.
I'll Be Near.
 Hankin, W.
I'll Be Over All in Clover.
 Wayworth, W. G.
I'll Be Waiting at the Chapel in the Valley.
 Lord, J. R.
I'll Be with You.
 Leiter, B.
I'll Belong to You.
 Vanderburg, G.
I'll Call it a Day.
 Samuels, W.
I'll Dance at Your Wedding.
 Oakland, B.
I'll Find You.
 Samuels, W.
I'll Follow My Secret Heart.
 Coward, N. P.
I'll Give All My Dreams to You.
 F x, T. C.
I'll Go Along.
 Bechler, M. F.
I'll Hate Myself in the Morning.
 Lawrence, J.
I'll Hold You in My Heart 'til I can
 hold you in my arms.
 Dilbeck, T. C.
I'll Keep Following the Rainbow.
 Reader, W. H. R.
I'll Keep My Faith.
 Hamilton, O.
I'll Keep on Dreaming.
 Squires, H. D.
I'll Keep on Smiling.
 Wulffen, O. A.

I'll Keep You in My Heart.
  Ridley, W.
I'll Love You Till I Die.
  Richard, L.
I'll Make Up for Ev'rything.
  Parker, R.
I'll Marry a Maid.
  Langdon, C., arr.
I'll Never Be without a Dream As Long As
  I Have You.
  Stock, L.
I'll Never Fall in Love Again.
  Lama, J.
I'll Never Forget.
  Clyde, T.
I'll Never Make the Same Mistake Again.
  Berle, M.
I'll Not Forget So Soon.
  Satra, M.
I'll Reach My Home Some Day.
  Windham, C.
I'll See You Again.
  Coward, N. Bitter Sweet.
I'll Settle for You.
  Clyde, T.
I'll Wait for You.
  Arthur, W.
I'm A-Comin' A-Courtin' Corabelle.
  Wrubel, A.
I'm a Lone Cowboy.
  Edlin, I. A.
I'm a Lucky Boy.
  Golledge, E.
I'm a Rollin'.
  Shaftel, S.
I'm a Well Adjusted Cowboy.
  Alkire, E. H.
I'm Afraid.
  Allegra, A. T.
I'm Alone.
  Hall, D.
I'm Building a Mansion.
  Dailey, P.
I'm Burning a Torch for You.
  Arthur, W.
I'm Burning Up with Love for You.
  Ochs, G.
I'm Climbing Jacob's Ladder.
  Mills, G. W.
I'm Consumed by a Flame.
  Khachaturian, A.
I'm Chocked, Boiled 'n' Toasted, I'm in love.
  Feller, S.
I'm Cryin' All over Again.
  Chavis, L.
I'm Down to My Last Dream.
  Wood, G.
I'm Dreaming of You.
  Pimperal, J. M.
I'm Dying a Sinner's Death.
  Aciff, H.
I'm Flying without Wings.
  Hibbeler, R. O.
I'm Going On with Jesus.
  Harvey, L.
I'm Going to Get a Patent.
  Arthur, W.
I'm Going to Get a Puppet.
  Hicks, J.
I'm Going to Marry Marion.
  Arthur, W.
I'm Going to Move on Up a Little Higher.
  Morris, K.
I'm Going to See You Today.
  Addinsell, R.
I'm Going to Sing Hallelujah Bye and Bye.
  Battle, B. G.
I'm Gonna Buzz-Buzz-Buzz.
  Dolan, A.
I'm Gonna Hold You in My Arms.
  Reid, D.
I'm Gonna Leave This Old Town.
  Stoner, M.
I'm Gonna Make Faces at the moon.
  Shippee, D.
I'm Gonna Marry Mary.
  Daniels, W.
I'm Gonna Miss You.
  Harmon, F.
I'm Gonna Serve My Lord.
  Prather, R. L.
I'm Gonna Wait a Little Bit Longer for
  that never-on-time baby of mine.
  MacGregor, J. C.
I'm Happy Again, It Is Spring.
  Toogood, E.

I'm Having a Lot of Fun Growing Old.
  Hueston, B.
I'm Helpless.
  Hollis, L. P.
I'm Hitch-hiking to Heaven.
  Olson, R. J.
I'm in Heaven with You.
  Arthur, W.
I'm in Love.
  Darnell, B.
I'm in Love with You.
  Arthur, W.
I'm in Love with You, Darling.
  Tobin, L.
I'm Just a Dreamer of Dreams.
  James, A. W.
I'm Laughing with a Tear in My Eye.
  Dea-rest, pseud.
I'm Living in a Dream.
  Koonts, J. C.
I'm Living in Christ, My Savior.
  Marshall, D.
I'm Lonely for You.
  Alkire, E. H.
I'm Mashuga for My Sugar.
  Connor, L.
I'm My Own Grandpaw.
  Jaffe, M.
I'm not in Love.
  Bernard, B. Night Beat.
I'm Out to Forget Tonight.
  Allen, G.
I'm Ready for Love.
  Lane, B.
I'm Recording a Memory of You in My
  Heart.
  Arthur, W.
I'm Restless.
  Kirshner, C.
I'm Saved! Saved! Saved!
  Miller, W. R.
I'm Saving My Pennies.
  Masson, L.
I'm So Glad That Jesus Found Me.
  Grummons, R. N.
I'm So Helpless in Your Arms.
  Hubbard, H.
I'm So in Love with You.
  Bonner, J.
I'm So Right Tonight.
  Shand, T. I've Been So Wrong for So
    Long.
I'm Sorry I Didn't Say I'm Sorry.
  Lee, L. When a Girl's Beautiful.
I'm Stickin' Around.
  Robertson, B. E.
I'm Tired but I Don't Want to Sleep.
  Barriteau, C. A. S.
I'm Waiting for the Sunshine in the Rain.
  Bogdan, M.
I'm Walking through Heaven with You.
  Turner, J.
I'm Wearing Last Night's Smile Tonight.
  Reilly, J.
I'm Working for My Savior.
  Adams, W. D.
Imagine, if you loved me too.
  Davis, M.
Imaginez.
  Bourtayre, H.
Imagine, S. A.
Impromptu.
  Guenzel, G.
Impromptu in Ab.
  Schubert, F. P.
Impromptu Valse.
  Margat, Y.
Improve Your Piano Playing with Jessie
  Gunn Curry Figures.
  Curry, J.
Improvisation.
  Barraine, E.
  LeVelle, C.
In a Canoe.
  Marshall, L. K.
In a Dream.
  DeMarco, J. R.
In a Honeymoon Teepee.
  Hunt, O. D.
In a Little Book Shop.
  Meyer, G.
In a Swan Boat.
  Smith, J.
In an Eighteenth Century Drawing Room.
  Scott, M.
In an Oriental Market Place.
  Wansborough, H.

In Bethlehem.
  Colborn, A. G.
In Caliente.
  Sooy, A.
In Coney Island.
  Lifson, H.
In Dear Ohio.
  Wernett, E. D.
In Dear Old Glasgow Toon.
  Graham, R.
In Deepening Faith.
  Miles, R. H.
In Fairy Land.
  Mair, E. L.
In Flanders' Field.
  Devine, W. M.
In Fond Remembrance.
  King, S.
In France They Say - Tout Jour l'Amour
  Tout Jour.
  Angeloni, J.
In Heaven It is Always Autumn.
  Holst, J.
In Heavenly Love Abiding.
  Whelpley, B.
In His Presence There is Peace.
  Reitz, A. S.
In His Steps.
  Wilson, H. R.
In June.
  Musson, E.
In Lavender Silk.
  King, S.
In Malaga.
  Vallejo, F.
In Memoriam.
  Milhaud, D. Two Marches.
In Mother's Arms.
  Barr, L. S.
In My Family.
  Spearman, F. T.
In Old Bermuda.
  Williams, S.
In Old Virginia.
  Alkire, E. H.
In One Ear and Out the Other.
  Rich, M.
In Paradisum.
  Monfred, A. de.
In Santiago, Chile 'tain't chilly at all.
  Carroll, J.
In Spite of All.
  Hill, M.
In Spite of It All.
  Sawaya, J. J.
In Te Domine.
  Händel, G. F. In Thee, O Lord, Have I
    Put My Trust.
In the Beginning.
  Copland, A.
  Prentice, W. S.
In the Cathedral.
  Pierne, G.
In the Fair Twilight Hour.
  Howell, M.
In the Meadow.
  Guentzel, G.
  Lichtner, H.
In the Mexican Cafe.
  Choisser, J. D.
In the Mood.
  Garland, J. C.
In the Moonlight.
  Haskin, V. C.
In the Secret Place of Prayer.
  Rusthoi, E. K. Gospel Songs.
In the Shade of Our New Apple Tree.
  Conrardy, H. C.
In the Shambles of My Heart.
  Kent, B.
In the Spring.
  Fleming, L.
In the Summer at These Crossroads.
  Farkas, I. Megállok a Keresztútná l.
In the Summer Land up Yonder.
  Essenburg, E.
In the Valley of Daffodils.
  Monta, F. H.
In the Valley of Roses.
  Serão, S.
In the Valleys Below.
  Loes, H. D.
In the Year That King Uzziah Died.
  McCulloch, W. C.
In Thee, O Lord, Have I Put My Trust.
  Händel, G. F.

In Tudor Days.
Geehl, H.
Incanto Brasiliano.
Taccani, S.
Incatenati.
Bianchi, R.
Independent Superintendant.
Hamilton, J. H.
Indian Boogie Woogie.
Bishop, J.
Indian Choral Chants.
Kilpatrick, J. F.
Indian Epic in Song.
Bové, J. H.
Indian Flute.
Hopkins, H. P.
Indian in Brooklyn.
Osage, T.
Indian Nocturne.
Gould, M. Americana.
The Indian Queen.
Purcell, H. The Indian Queen.
Indiana.
Hanley, J. F.
Indiana is So Rich.
McGee, J. A. The Monon Centennial Show.
Indonesia.
Dimock, C.
Infant Jesu.
Hokanson, M.
Infant Saviour.
Kemmer, G. W.
Information Please.
Morin, D. W.
Ingrata Lidia.
Vivaldi, A.
Injusticia.
Beltran Ruiz, P.
Inktaminika Honika Zunk.
Ballard, F. D.
Inno a S. Antonio.
Pacifico, A.
Inno alla SS. Vergine.
Paci ico, A.
Inquietud.
Miramontes, A. Eco.
Inspired Hymns of the Hour.
Jenkins, M. H.
Instant-Modulator.
Smith, H. M.
Instrumental Music Primer.
Rohner, T.
Instrumentalist.
Skornicka, J. E.
Interlude.
Rugolo, P.
Interlude in Waltz Time.
Hirst, R.
Intermediate Method for Bassoon.
Voxman, H. Rubank Intermediate Method for Bassoon.
Intermezzo.
Glière, R. M.
Intermezzo en la^b majeur.
Poulenc, F.
International Revue.
McHugh, J. F.
Intima Miniatyrer.
Fernström, J.
The Intimate Stranger.
Kentrell, W. D.
Intimità.
Guarino, G. M.
Into Our Garden of Love.
Fuller, F. R.
Intrada.
Honegger, A.
Mozart, J. C. W. A. Bastien und Bastienne.
Intrata y Danza Rustica.
Castro, J. J.
Intrigue.
Akst, H.
Introducing New Radio Songs.
Hallett, J. C.
Introducing the Positions.
Whistler, H. S.

Introduction and Allegro.
Reicha, A. J. Quintet, winds.
Introduction and Fugue.
Vaughan Williams, R.
Introduction and Toccata.
Jacobi, F.
Introduction to Sight Reading.
Pierce, D.
Introduzione all'opera La Villanella Rapita di F. Bianchi.
Ferrari, G. G. La Villanella Rapita.
Introspection.
Anderson, R. E.
Inverno.
Vivaldi, A. Concerti delle Stagioni.
Invitation to the Dance.
Weber, K. M. F. E. freiherr v.
Iona Boat Song.
Roberton, H. S.
Iowa Poppy Song.
Dixon, E.
Ipanema.
Flory, S. Carioca Album of Brazilian Songs.
Ireland Today.
Sanders, A.
Irish Blarney.
Cochrane, P.
Irish Slumber Song.
Remsen, A.
Irish Waltz Medley.
Sears, J. arr.
Irish Washerwomen.
Richardson, C.
Irving Berlin Waltzes.
Berlin, I.
Irving Berlin's I Got Lost in His Arms.
Berlin, I. Annie Get Your Gun.
Is Cupid Ever Stupid.
Clyde, T.
Is Everybody Happy.
Iden, R. J.
Is It Real.
Hamilton, A.
Is It True.
May, J. M.
Is This How You Treat Ev'ryone.
Sawaya, J. J.
Isle of Jamaica.
Souers, M. T.
It All Came True.
Shaftel, S.
It Can't Be Done.
Schmah, I.
It Can't Be True.
Trabucco, R. M.
It Doesn't Take the Moon.
Smith, A. D.
It Happened in Hawaii.
Wayne, M.
It Happened in Spring.
Arthur, W.
It Is Christmas in This House.
Howard, J. T.
It Is Sleepy Time Now.
Carleton, R. L.
It Mighta Been Vitamin B.
Helm, E.
It Must Have Been an Ill Wind.
Holly, A.
It Takes a Long Long Train with a Red Caboose to carry my blues away.
Krieg, R. C.
It Was a Lover and His Lass.
Chapman, E. T.
France, W.
It Was Christmas in London.
Dulmage, W.
It Was June in December.
Buck, R.
It Was the Cross.
Hallett, J. C. 33 Solos and Duets.
It Was the Good Old Parson.
Potter, H.
It Was the Month of June.
McNeil, J. C.
It Won't Be Long.
Cook, L. H.
It Wouldn't Be Christmas without you.

Sheppard, B.
Italian Dance Albums for Orchestra.
Di Bella, O.
Italian in Algiers.
Rossini, G. A.
Italiana in Algeri.
Rossini, G. A.
It's a Boy.
Ormond, R.
It's a Dirty Shame.
Sapp, P.
It's a Great Life if you don't weaken.
Tovey, C.
It's a Pleasure.
Temple, N.
It's About Time.
Arthur, W.
It's Been So Long.
Alkire, E. H.
It's Been So Long Since You Said So Long.
Alkire, E. H.
It's Better That Way.
Baum, G.
It's December Again.
Ostrowsky, A. M.
It's Easy to Fool the One Who Loves You.
Potter, H. H.
It's Forever.
Díaz Altamirano, L. Un Destino y un Amor.
It's Gonna Rain.
Baum, G.
It's Gonna Take a Long Long Time to Forget You.
Robison, C. J.
It's Jack the Bell Boy Time.
Conn, P.
It's Kind of Lonesome out Tonight.
Ellington, D.
It's Like a Trip to Tipperary.
Urbano, A.
It's Love.
Gray, T. J.
It's Love, To Be Loved by You.
De Busi, D.
It's Mad, Mad, Mad.
Higginbotham, I.
It's Me for You.
Ferry, F.
It's Meant to Be.
Gunsallus, J.
It's Music to My Ears.
Wilson, J.
It's Raining Here This Morning.
Jones, G.
It's Really My Heart That Speaks.
Hueston, B. When I Say I Love You.
It's Somebody's Birthday Today.
The Duncan Sisters.
It's Spring Again.
McNeil, J. C.
It's the Little Things.
Gold, H.
It's the Natural Thing To Do.
Helpenstell, M. H.
It's the Rage.
Savage, M.
It's the Sweet Things You Say.
McPhail, L.
It's the Waltz You Must Dance.
Beadle, W.
It's to Laugh.
Carleton, R. L.
It's Way Past My Bedtime.
Spina, H.
It's Wonderful to Live This Day.
Guthrie, C. A.
It's You, Dear.
LaMar, E. H.
I've Been a Good Girl.
Nagel, J.
I've Been Dreaming Too Long.
Arthur, W.
I've Been Lonely.
Novak, G. S.
I've Been Set Free.
Piper, E. D. Revival Choruses, Number Two.
I've Been So Wrong, for So Long.
Shand, T.
I've Changed My Mind.

Ross, H. B.
I've Chased My Blues to the Blue Horizon.
  Arthur, W.
I've Closed the Door on You.
  Arthur, W.
I've Cried My Last Time over You.
  Arthur, W.
I've Discovered Heaven.
  Arthur, W.
I've Done a Lot of Dreaming in My Day.
  Novelli, S. P.
I've Fallen for the Man in the Moon.
  Cross, S. L.
I've Fallen in Love with You.
  Fleming, L.
I've Forgotten How to Smile.
  Hibbeler, R. O.
I've Gathered All Your Tears.
  Hall, D.
I've Got a Boogie Woogie Baby.
  Kay, P.
I've Got a Dream to Share with You.
  Thomas, C.
I've Got a Feelin' Somebody's Stealin' My Darlin'.
  Nelson, E. G.
I've Got a Feeling.
  Koehler, C. A.
I've Got a Funny Feeling.
  Scheuerell, F. J.
I've Got a Gal in Texas.
  Wiesner, M.
I've Got a Heart That's Broken In Two.
  Novak, G. S.
I've Got a Saviour.
  Jackson, K. C.
I've Got My Love for You.
  Mancino, M. A.
I've had enough of your two-timin'.
  Halle, F.
I've Lived a Lifetime for You.
  Whitley, R.
L've Never Tried to Forget You.
  Arthur, W.
I've Only Myself to Blame.
  Mann, D.
I've Tried All I Can.
  Schmidt, L.
I've Tried to Forget You.
  Devey, G.
I've Waited for Years for this Moment.
  Green, H.
Ivy and Holly.
  Malin, D. F.
Ivy Still Grows on the Old Garden Wall.
  Watson, M.

J'Ai Bu.
  Roche, P.
J'Ai Deux Amours.
  Scotto, V. Two Loves Have I.
J'Ai un Beau Chapeau.
  Dumas, R.
J'Attends.
  Pesenti, J.
J'Ay Vu la Beauté Ma Mie.
  Chailley, J.
Jabberwocky Song.
  Addinsell, R. Tuppence Coloured.
Jack and Joy in Yonderland.
  Green, W.
Jack Be Nimble.
  Van Nort, I.
Jackie Robinson.
  Clark, A.
Jacques Wolfe's American Songster.
  Wolfe, J. arr.
Jag Har Bött vid en Landsväg i Hela Mitt liv. See Edvard Perssons 5 Bästa.
Jagh stoorlig bekymbrat är.
  Koch, S. v. Gammalswenska wijsor.
Jahrmarkt.
  Volkart-Schlager, K.
Jalousie.
  Gade, J.
Jamais Deux sans Trois.
  Gasté, L. F.

Jayhawk Song.
  Naramore, A. P.
Je Crois en Mon Etoile.
  Caffot, S.
Je N'y Crois Plus.
  Hess, J. Maman No Vends Pas la Maison.
Je Rêve de Vos Yeux, Madame.
  Erwin, R. I Kiss Your Hand, Madame.
Je Te Pardonne.
  Huguet y Tagell, R. J.
Je Te Pardonne.
  Huguet y Tagell, R. J. Les Deux Manières.
Je Vois Veux.
  Lopez, F. Les Trois Cousines.
Jealous Blues.
  Tyler, J.
Jeanie.
  Neilly, T. A.
Jee-Bie Hop.
  Mason, J.
Jenny Kiss'd Me.
  Herbert, L. Two Songs.
Jersey City, N. J.
  Lovick, T.
Jess Sawaya's As Long As I Live.
  Sawaya, J.J.
Jesse Cowan's a Musical Time Method.
  Cowan, J.
Jessie Gunn Curry Figures.
  Curry, J. G. Improve Your Piano Playing.
Jester.
  Hayes, O. L. Three Easy Piano Pieces.
Jesu Corona Virginum.
  Ravanello, O.
Jesu Leiden, Pein und Tod.
  Bach, J. S. Jesus suffered pain and death.
Jesu, My Lord, My God, My All.
  Norden, H.
Jesus Born in Bethlehem.
  Bryan, C. F.
Jesus Calls Us.
  Mills, G. W.
Jesus, Come and Be My Lord.
  Grummons, R. N.
Jesus, I Love Thee.
  Haslett, M.
Jesus Is a Friend of Mine.
  Piper, E. D. Revival Choruses, Number Two.
Jesus Is Calling.
  Gaddis, R. M. Repentance. Heaven, Our Home.
  Schuitema, A. K., arr. Jesus, Lover of My Soul.
Jesus Is My Sunshine.
  Runyan, W. M.
Jesus Is the King of Glory.
  Wilbanks, J.
Jesus Is the Same.
  Hulin, D. N.
Jesus' Love Just Flowing Over in My Soul.
  Famous Blue Jay Singers.
Jesus, Lover of My Soul.
  Schuitema, A. K., arr.
Jesus' Name of Wondrous Love.
  Titcomb, E.
Jesus, Oh, What a Name!
  Loveless, W. P.
Jesus, Only Jesus.
  McGuill, L.
Jesus, Rose of Sharon.
  Keene, W. H.
Jesus suffered pain and death.
  Bach, J. S.
Jesus, the Name I Love To Hear.
  Jones, G. J.
Jesus, the Very Thought of Thee.
  Marler, T. N.
Jeu de l'Amour et du Hasard.
  Petit, P. Y. M. C.
Jeune Fille Française.
  Monfred, A. de.
Jeunes Filles de Bonne Famille.
  LaFarge, G.
Jeux de Plage.
  Bozza, E.
Jingle Bell Polka.
  Dickenson, H.

Jingle, Bells.
  Pierpont, J. S.
Jingle Jungle.
  Garman, W. M.
Jinguili Jongolo.
  Castro, A.
Jitta Rumba.
  Hile, R.
Jitterbug.
  Barbic, F. S.
Jive Is Sometimes the Real McCoy.
  Richard, L.
Jivin' with Jarvis.
  Hampton, L.
Joel Joel Joel.
  Davis, J.
Johannes Oppenbarelse.
  Rosenberg, H.
John W. Schaum Christmas Album.
  Schaum, J. W. comp.
John W. Schaum March Album.
  Schaum, J. W. arr.
John Ward's Collection of Irish Comic Songs.
  Ward, J. J.
Johnnie's Blue.
  Alkire, E. H.
Johnny Appleseed.
  Lorenz, E. J.
Johnny Moore.
  Diamond, C. S.
Joie de Vivre.
  Broadhead, G. F.
Jolene.
  Leidzén, E. W. G.
Joli Moi de Mai.
  Quilter, R. Pretty Month of May.
Jolly Coppersmith.
  Peter, C.
Jolly Hay Ride.
  Crane, J.
Jolly Hollander.
  Tillery, M.
Jolly Little Playmates.
  Van Nort, I.
Jolly Mailman.
  Roberts, P.
Jolson Songs.
  Bourne, inc., comp.
Jolson Story.
  Chaplin, S.
José.
  Ramirez, A. R.
Joshua Fit de Battle ob Jericho.
  Cookson, F. B.
Joshua Fit the Battle of Jericho.
  Webster, J. arr.
Jota.
  Fuchs, L.
Joue contre Joue.
  Ferrari, L.
Journey to Bethlehem.
  Cronham, C. R. Nativity Scenes.
Journeying.
  Larson, E. R.
Joy of Heaven.
  Prichard, R. H.
Joy of Life.
  Broadhead, G. F. Joie de Vivre.
Joy Ride.
  Buck, R.
  Light, F. M.
Joyful Torah Song.
  Jospe, E.
Joyous Autumn Days.
  Locke, H.
Joyous Carol.
  Wells, E.
Joyous Christian.
  Naylor, E. A.
Jubilant Song.
  Dello Joio, N.
Jubilate Deo.
  Evans, G. Psalm 100.
  Snow, F. W. Benedictus Es, Domine.
Jubilation.
  Tardif, H. M. Triptique Marial.
Judas Maccabeus.
  Händel, G. F.

402

Judex.
 Gounod, C. F.
Judo.
 Ferrier, L.
Juegos.
 Castro, W. Cuatro Piezas sobre Temas
 Infantiles.
Jugando con el Tema.
 Sabre Marroquin, J.
Juke Box.
 Walters, H. L.
Jukebox Cannonball.
 Keefer, A.
Jukebox Heck.
 Clyde, T.
Juleo and Romiet.
 Boland, C.
Julie.
 Cooper, J.
 Kukuk, W.
Jumbo Note Folk Songs.
 Frey, H. arr.
Jumbo Note Lullabies.
 Stickles, W. arr.
Jump with Rhythm.
 Kershaw, T. R.
Jumping Jacks.
 Stevens, E. Three Piano Solos.
June Bug's Dance.
 Holst, E.
June Is Bustin' Out All Over.
 Rodgers, R. Carousel.
June Rhapsody.
 Ronald, L.
June Time and You.
 Allyn, G. F.
June's Got me.
 Carleton, R. L.
Jungfrulin.
 Lidholm, I.
Jungle Jump.
 Handlon, J. E.
Jungle King.
 Dixon, W.
Junior American Piano Concerto.
 Mittler, F.
Junior Hymns.
 Yoder, W. E. ed.
Just a Faded Picture in a dusty frame.
 Casey, T.
Just an Old Tin-type Picture of You.
 Hibbeler, R. O.
Just Another Number in Your Book.
 Arthur, W.
Just Be Sure What You Say Is All True.
 Jones, N. L.
Just Because I Care.
 Seifert, L. M.
Just Because I Love You.
 Watson, M.
Just Because We've Got no Sense.
 Cavanaugh, D. P.
Just Behind the Cloud.
 Loes, H. D.
Just by Chance.
 Anderson, D.
Just Dreaming.
 Bartlett, F.
Just for To-day.
 Seaver, B. E.
Just for Two.
 Arthur, W.
Just for You.
 Kadison, P.
 Swan, M.
Just Inside the Door.
 Cosby, R. E.
Just Leave Me Here Behind.
 Bates, W.
Just Look at My Baby.
 Wilkins, R. N.
Just Me.
 McNeil, J. C.
Just Me, Without You.
 Gaglio, J.
Just Memories.
 Tobin, L.
Just My Luck.

Ellste..., A.
Just Plain Lazy.
 Bartlett, F.
Just Pretending.
 Compton, H.
Just Show Me You Do.
 Chanslor, H.
Just the Other Day.
 McNeil, J. C.
Just to Dream of You.
 Wisterman, B.
Just to Know Him.
 Hulin, E. F.
Just to Think.
 Rusthoi, E. K. Gospel Songs.
Just Wanting You.
 Pollack, S.

K

Kärleks-Var.
 Cassel, T. M. Love in Spring.
Kahdwatah.
 Alkire, E. H.
Kalle på spången. See Edvard Perssons 5
 Bästa.
Kamennoiostrow.
 Rubinstein, A. Shine on, oh Star.
Kan Man Nu Forstaa Det.
 Andersen, K. N. Dagmar Revyen,
 1947.
Kansas City, My Home Town.
 Stern, J. E.
Karelia Suite.
 Sibelius, J. Alla Marcia.
Kassie.
 Clyde, T.
Kate, have I come too early, too late.
 Berlin, I.
Katinka.
 Rovenger, L. W.
Katuscha.
 Michaeloff, M.
Keep a Cool Head and Wear a Warm Smile.
 Tobin, L.
Keep a Little Place in Your Heart for
 Dreams.
 Hall, D.
Keep America Singing.
 Diekema, W. A.
Keep Away from Me.
 Beisler, W. E.
Keep in Stride.
 Thomas, J. J.
Keep Me in Mind.
 Rohlf, E.
Keep Surrendered.
 Rusthoi, E. K. Gospel Songs.
Keep Them Cold Icy Fingers off Me.
 Lair, J.
Keller's Berkeley Band Book.
 Keller, E. M.
Kid Stuff.
 Bartlett, F.
King and Queen Were Talking.
 Diggle, R. Alice in Wonderland Suite.
King Arthur.
 Purcell, H.
King Cups.
 Driver, A. New Songs for Old.
King Midas.
 Strong, M. A.
King of My Heart.
 Williams, D. W.
Kings of the Orient.
 Cronham, C. R.
Kiss in the Dark.
 Herbert, V. Orange Blossoms.
Kiss in Your Eyes.
 Heuberger, R. The Emperor Waltz.
Kiss-Kiss-Kissin' in the Corn.
 Davidson, E.
Kiss Me and Then Go Away.
 Siegel, P.
Kissing.
 Solomon, D. M.
Kitty-Cat.
 Garman, W. M.

Kitty O'Leary.
 May, E. G.
Kitty O'Malley.
 Richter, W. B.
Kitty's Tongue.
 Kurth, B.
Kleiner Bär mit Grossen Ohren.
 Halletz, E.
Kleinstadt Zauber.
 Benatsky, R.
Knowing You Care.
 Dale, J.
Kóbt og Betalt.
 Andersen, K. N.
Köbu u der Chrigu u der Sepp.
 Huber, W.
Kokomo, Indiana.
 Myrow, J. Mother Wore Tights.
Kol Nidre.
 Guenther, F. arr.
 Helfman, M. arr.
 Rinder, R. R., arr.
Kolhoz.
 Sherfedinov, Y.
Kolmar Grand March.
 Marvin, L.
Komm Süsser Tod.
 Bach, J. S.
Koncert-Suite.
 Schultz, S. S.
Koncertetude.
 Bentzon, N. V.
Konvaljens Avsked.
 Lindvall, O. D.
Konversation.
 Kreuder, P. Wege der Liebe.
Konsert, D-dur.
 Wolf-Ferrari, E. Concerto, violin.
Korean Folk Song.
 Sungsik, L. Students!
Kris, Kris, Krisella.
 Millan, J. C.
Kukijah.
 Lavry, M.
Kuku-Kuku.
 Durlak, J. P.

L

La la la la la la, Lena.
 Val, J.
Labios de Clavel.
 Santiago Rius, F.
Lacrime.
 Lupo, P.
Ladies Know How.
 Frydan, C.
Ladies of Leamington.
 Hilliam, B. C.
Lady in Slacks.
 Perkins, H.
Lady op a Fan.
 Chaikovskii, P. L.
Lady Pepperell Waltz.
 Johnson, Q. P.
Lady's in Love.
 Kaplin, B.
Lagrima.
 Tarrega, F.
Lake.
 Moffat, A. arr.
Lake in the Mountains.
 Vaughan Williams, R.
Lakme.
 Delibes, L.
Lamb.
 Henschel, G.
Lamb of God.
 Lotti, A. Agnus Dei.
Lambs in the Meadow.
 Adler, J.
Lament.
 Kay, S, J.
 Lourié, A.
 Trusselle, S. P.
Lamenti.
 Mortari, V.
Land of Golden Sunsets.

Cates, M. D.
Land of Lakes and Mountains.
  Price, E. L.
Land of Milk and Honey.
  Keene, W. H.
Lane County Bachelor.
  O'Hara, G.
Langey-Carl Fischer Tutors for baritone,
  bass clef, 3 valves.
  Langey, O.
Langey-Carl Fischer tutors for slide
  trombone, bass clef.
  Langey, O.
Language of Your Eyes.
  Croft, C. W.
Larghetto, from the string quartet by
  César Franck.
  Franck, C. A. Quartet, strings.
Lark Now Leaves His Wat'ry Nest.
  Roberton, H. S.
Lass Uns von der Liebe Reden.
  Kreuder, R. Das Singenden Haus.
Lasse Lucidors dryckesvijsa.
  Koch, S. v. Gammalswenska wijsor.
Lassie Come Home.
  Carson, J. L. Songs.
Lasst Mir Doch Meine Träume.
  Kreuder, P. Wege der Liebe.
Last Call for Dinner.
  McGee, J. A. The Monon Centennial
  Show.
Last Mile.
  Rose, F.
Last Night.
  Hall, D.
Last Night I Counted Sheep.
  Martin, J.
Last Night I Heard You Crying In Your
  Sleep.
  Williams, H.
Last Night in a Dream.
  Winograd, J.
Last Round-up.
  Hill, B.
  Kapp, D.
Late Evening Blues.
  Lewis, J.
Latest Popular Music Folio.
  Engel, L. K.
Latter Rain.
  Jenkins, M. H. Inspired Hymns of the
  Hour.
Laud Him.
  Pepping, E.
Laus Deo.
  Williams, A.
Lavender Dreams.
  Russell, K. The Nightingale.
Lawrence Welk's Favorite Polkas.
  Frey, H. arr.
Lay Your Burdens on Me.
  Mills, G. W.
Lazy Day.
  Edwards, H.
Lazy John.
  Boatman, H.
Lazy Little Latin.
  Alkire, E. H.
Lazy May.
  Hall, D.
Lazy Mood.
  Miller, E. Love's Got Me in a Lazy Mood.
Lazy Mood Blues.
  Meissner, J. J.
Lazy Sheep.
  Childe, M.
Léa Lili, Lola, Loulou.
  Huguet Y Tagell, R. J.
Lead Me, Lord.
  Wesley, S. S.
Lead Us, O God.
  Campbell, W. N. M. Two Anthems for
  Chorus.
Leaden Echo and the Golden Echo.
  Welless, E.
Leap Frog.
  Adams, E. H. Two Little Etudes for
  piano-forte.
Learning to Fly.
  Shannon, I.
Leave Me Alone.
  Overland, H. V.
Leblon.

Flory, S. Carioca Album of Brazilian
  Songs.
Lecons de Solfège.
  Petronio, A.
Lee and Juanita's Songs of Home and the
  Hills.
  Moore, J.
Leeds Am-Rus Album of Soviet Popular
  Songs.
  Small, A. comp. & arr.
Legend.
  Walker, B.
Legion Air.
  Beskin, G. S.
Leháriana.
  Lehár, F.
Lejos De Ti.
  Monfort, J. My Heart Is Yours.
Leksen en lek.
  Selmer, M. Praktisk Klaverskole.
Lemare's Andantino.
  Lemare, E. H.
Leme.
  Flory, S. Carioca Album of Brazilian
  Songs.
Lemon-colored Dodo.
  Mopper, I.
Lena.
  Val, J. La la la la la la la.
Lenoo.
  Bétous, L.
Lest We Forget; America's first.
  Mann, R. C.
Let All Creatures of God His Praises Sing.
  Kalinnikoff.
Let All the People Praise Thee, O God.
  Shaw, M.
Let All the World.
  Gilbert, N.
Let All Things Now Living.
  Bement, G. S. arr.
Let Jesus Fix It for You.
  Holmes, M.
Let Me Call You Sweetheart.
  Friedman, L.
Let Me Carry You Back to Texas.
  Mitman, M. J.
Let Me Die with My Boots on.
  O'Hagan, J.
Let Not Your Heart Be Troubled.
  Hopkins, M.
Let Our Gladness Know no End.
  Howorth, W.
Let the People Praise Thee.
  Wright, E. H.
Let Us Break Bread Together.
  Lawrence, W.
Let Us Have Music for Christmas.
  Eckstein, M. arr.
Let Us Have Music for singing.
  Eckstein, M. ed. and arr.
Let Us Not Forget.
  Wilson, H. R.
Let Us Praise God.
  Olds, W. B.
Let Us Pray.
  Isbell, E.
Let us romance together.
  Coldrey, A. G. J. Bandit prince.
Let Us Walk in the Spirit.
  Rasley, J. M.
Let Us With a Gladsome Mind.
  Drummond-Wolff, S.
Letargo.
  Valdes, M.
Let's Be Sweethearts Again.
  Maxwell, E.
Let's Be Twenty-one.
  Russell, K. The Nightingale.
Let's Do It Again.
  Rosetti, J. G.
Let's Fall in Love.
  Arthur, W.
Let's Get Together.
  Lord, D. A.
Let's Go Sparkin'.
  Blair, H.
Let's Go to the Green Town Waltz.
  Yankovic, F. J.
Let's Have Some Fun.

Burns, I.
Let's Just Say Au Revoir.
  Mortensen, W. F.
Let's Pick Up Where We Left Off.
  Bellin, L.
Let's Put the Moon to Bed.
  Byrne, W. L.
Let's Sit the Next One Out.
  Edwards, S.
Let's Tell the World about Jesus.
  Jenkins, M. H. Inspired Hymns of
  the Hour.
Lette Klaverstykker.
  Sark, E. T.
Letter I Forgot to Mail.
  Mills, C.
Letter That Broke My Heart.
  Taylor, M. Oh, How I Miss You since
  you went away.
Lettre Inutile.
  Petit Dutaillis, J.
Lettules.
  Darcieux, F.
Liberty.
  Anderson, W. H.
Liberty Bell Special.
  Storm, J.
Liborito.
  Grenet Sánchez, E.
Liden Vid Kanin. See Edvard Perssons 5
  Bästa.
Liebesleid.
  Kreisler, F.
Liebestraum.
  Liszt, F.
Liebestraum no. 3.
  Liszt, F.
Lieblich Ist's dem Ew'gen Danken.
  Schubert, F. P. Good Is It To Thank
  Jehovah.
Lied.
  Gianneo, L.
Life for God.
  Ellis, F. A.
Life Is a Dream.
  Arthur, W.
  Taylor, M. L.
Life, Keep a Song in My Heart.
  Bronson, M.
Life Was Beautiful only for you.
  Eisenstein, A.
Life with Father.
  Moore, R.
Lifetime with You.
  Arthur, W.
Lift Ev'ry Voice and Sing.
  Johnson, J. R.
Light of the World Is Jesus.
  Bliss, P. P.
Lightly Tread.
  Scotland, J.
Lights Above.
  Arthur, W.
Lights Are On.
  Solis, B. F.
Like a Lovely Melody.
  Carleton, R. L.
Like April's Roses.
  Lama, G.
Like He's Never Loved Before.
  Campbell, B.
Like Millions Have Done.
  Chanslor, H.
Like Reaching for the Sky.
  Curtis, D.
Lilac Time.
  Howell, L.
Lilac Twilight.
  Wiltshire, E.
Lilacs.
  Clyde, T.
Limehouse Blues.
  Braham, P. Charlot's Revue.
Linnet.
  Herbert, I.
Linstead, Market.
  Benjamin, A.
Lions' Convention Song.
  Wuerthner, J. J.

404

Lips That Lie.
  Davis, S.
Lisbon Story.
  Davies, H. P.
Listen, Sinners.
  Vestal, G. L.
Listen To Me.
  Ash, G. E.
Listen to the Angels Shouting.
  Work, J. W.
Listen to the Lambs.
  Roberton, H. S.
Liszt.
  Liszt, F.
Litany for Organ.
  Muset, J.
Litet Grann Från Ovan. See Edvard Perssons
  -δ Bästa.
Lit'le David, Play on Yo' Harp.
  Roberton, H. S.
Little Ballerina.
  Porter-Brown, R.
Little Bit Longer for that never-on-time
  baby of mine.
  MacGregor, J. C. I'm Gonna Wait.
Little Bit of Heaven A-shinin' in Your Eyes.
  Hardy, A. B.
Little Blue Lies.
  Skidmore, M. B.
Little Boy Blue.
  Nevin, E. W.
Little Boy Blue come blow your horn.
  Van Nort, I.
Little Bridget Flynn.
  French, M. P.
Little Brown Bear.
  Harris, D.
Little Chinese Dancer.
  Marsh, C. H.
Little Christ-Child, Sweet and Holy.
  Williams, F.
Little Concert Master.
  Garman, W. M.
Little Did I Know.
  Carleton, R. L.
Little Dutch Dance.
  Hirschberg, D.
  Huerter, C.
Little Fingers.
  Ball, G. S.
Little Golden Book of Singing Games.
  Wessells, K. T.
Little Goldfish.
  Ballatore, P.
  Thal, J.
Little Heart-Breaker.
  Zell, O. E.
Little Hoop of Gold.
  Culberson, C.
Little Hula Shack in Hawaii.
  Campbell, C.
Little I Care.
  Browne, L. B.
Little Jack Frost Get Lost.
  Ellis, S.
Little Jesus.
  Holler, J.
  List, G.
Little Jesus Came to Town.
  Weigl, V.
Little Joe, the Wrangler.
  Hill, C. L.
Little Lamb.
  Rowley, A. Three Songs of Innocence.
Little Lamb Polka.
  O'Donnell, W.
Little Lord Jesus.
  Wilson, I. B.
Little Love Song.
  Kennard, A.
Little Miss Jealousy.
  Toutjean, V.
Little Old Mill went 'round and 'round.
  Towers, L.
Little Ounce of Sunshine is worth a ton of
  rain.
  O'Hagan, J.
Little Picture Album.
  Olson, R. J.

Little Piggies.
  Adler, M.
Little Piggy.
  Tate, P.
Little Primrose.
  Kaiser, G. C.
Little Red Cottage.
  Harris, G. E.
Little Red Shoes.
  Ivanovici, J.
Little Road to Bethlehem.
  Head, M.
Little Rocking Horse.
  Thompson, J.
Little Sandman.
  Stickles, W. Jumbo Note Lullabies.
Little Shepherd.
  Diggle, R.
Little Songs on Big Subjects.
  Singer, L.
Little Star.
  Ponce, M. M. Estrellita.
Little Su.
  Shlimovitz, H. M.
Little Suite.
  Butler, P.
Little Sweetheart.
  Richard, L.
Little Symphony.
  Haydn, J.
Little Tattler.
  Hayes, O. L. Three Easy Piano Pieces.
Little Texas Queen.
  Pollack, R.
Little Things, My Lord.
  Conway, O. F.
Little Token.
  Lilly, A. Within My Memory.
Little Turtle Dove So Lovely.
  Parrish, C.
Little While from Now.
  Novelli, S. P.
Little White House.
  Arthur, W.
Little White Lily.
  Diggle, R. Summer Sketches.
Live in My Memory.
  Chanslor, H.
Live, Love and Laugh.
  Samuels, W.
Living Above Songs and Choruses.
  Booth, F. C. comp.
Living God.
  Como, O.
Living in a Big Way.
  Alter, L.
Living in the Land of Make Believe.
  Arthur, W.
Living with a Dream of You.
  Murtha, R. W.
Livre d'orgue (1695).
  Chaumont, L.
Livsbåten.
  De Frumerie, G. Fyra Sånger.
Llanto del Alma.
  Echavarría Ferrer, A.
Llawenydd Nef.
  Prichard, R. H. Joy of Heaven.
Llegaste Tarde.
  Barreto, J.
Lo, It's a Meadow Lark.
  Angeloni, J.
Lo Mismo Me Dá.
  Rodríguez, J.
Lo! The Angel of the Lord.
  Marth, H. J.
Loads o' Fun Band Book.
  Cheyette, I. arr.
Log Cabin Lady.
  Hibbeler, R. O.
Loin de Toi.
  Mars, R.
Londonderry Air.
  Gould, M.
Lone Star Moon.
  Franklin, D.
Lone Wayward One.
  Cox, J. J.

Loneliness in View.
  Bartlett, F.
Lonely.
  Cope, D.
Lonely and Roamin'.
  Dixon, W.
Lonely Broken Heart.
  Moody, C.
Lonely Cowboy.
  Buck, R.
Lonely Dancer.
  Federer, R.
Lonely Heart of Mine.
  Brown, W. R.
Lonely Moments .
  Williams, M. L.
Lonely Mood.
  Wheeler, J. A.
Lonely Prayer.
  Halpin, J. F.
Lonely Renfro Valley Rose.
  Japhet, C.
Lonely Souls at Sea.
  Atwood, H. G.
Lonely Trail of memory.
  Nelson, K. F.
Lonely Valley.
  Sizemore, A.
Lonesome and Blue.
  Chanslor, H.
Lonesome Blues.
  Hall, D.
Lonesome Doll.
  Brown, A. L.
Lonesome Me.
  Pinkston, Q. F.
Lonesome Pine.
  Lemont, C. W.
Lonesome Prairie.
  Stevenson, R. M. Texas Suite.
Long Live Elizabeth.
  German, Sir Merrie England.
Long Live the Future.
  Valdes, M. Letargo.
Long, Long, Ago.
  Bentley, B. B.
Long, Long Year.
  McElduff, M. P.
Long Night.
  Tiomkin, D.
Long Road Ahead.
  Rose, F.
Longing.
  Thompson, J. J.
Look into My Eyes.
  Miller, R.
Looking Down at Me.
  Oliver, H.
Lord Be with Us.
  Norden, H.
Lord Bless You and Keep You.
  Lutkin, P. C.
Lord, Build Me a Cabin.
  Tribbett, S.
Lord Hath Done Great Things for Us.
  Levenson, B.
Lord Have Pity.
  Isbell, E.
Lord, Hold Out Your Hand to Me.
  Cooper, E.
Lord, Hold to My Hand.
  Williams, C. C.
Lord, I Hear Thy Call.
  Potter, A. L. Dad and Mother Are
  There.

Lord, I'm Feeling Mighty Fine Today.
Abernathy, L. R.
Lord I'm Ready Now to Go.
Abernathy, L. R.
Lord, I'm Trying, Is My Way All Right.
Bell, M. E.
Lord, in Adoration Kneeling.
Bragdon, S. C.
Lord Is My Light.
Humphreys, D. E.
Lord Is My Shepherd.
Bridges, R.
Grummons, R. N. He's Coming.
Lord Is Our Comfort.
Francis, H.
Lord Is Our Fortress.
Brahms, J. Symphony, no. 1.
Lord of All Power and Might.
France, W. &.
Lord of Life, and King All Glorious.
Bach, J. S.
Lord, Our Dwelling Place.
De Lamarter, E.
Lord, Speak to Me.
Diggle, R.
Lord, Teach Us How to Pray.
Lang, E.
Lord, Thou Hast Been Our Refuge.
Walker, E.
Lord, We Thank Thee.
Purcell, E. Be Present at Our Table, Lord.
Lord's Prayer.
Bird, M. W.
Heys, J. A.
Malotte, A. H.
Martins, M. H. Padre Nosso.
Morel, D.
Lorenz's Gospel Solos New and Old.
Wilson, I. S.
Lorenz's Hymn-tune Anthems.
Lorenz, E. J., comp.
Lorenz's S.S.A. Concert Choruses.
Lorenz, E. J., comp.
Loretta.
Zordan, A.
Lorette.
Romby, P.
Lost Chord.
Sullivan, Sir A. S.
Lost Grave.
Robinson, A.
Lost Heart.
Dea, D. Y.
Lost in a Dream that comes from my
heart.
Livernash, W.
Lost Love.
Bartlett, F.
Lost Moment.
Amfitheatrof, D.
Louella.
Meissner, J. J.
Louis Satchmo Armstrong's Immortal
Trumpet Solos.
Armstrong, L.
Love Ain't Worryin' Me.
Sullivan, E. T. Don't That Moon Look
Lonesome.
Love All Thing's Can Do.
Keener, O. L.
Love and Hate.
Trevare, W.
Love and the Weather.
Berlin, I.
Love Came Down at Christmas.
Lapo, C. E.
Love Came Smiling Through.
Daniels, C. N.
Love Divine, from Jesus Flowing.
Hughes, R.
Love for Love.
Korngold, E. W. Escape Me Never.
Love Goes 'Round an' 'Round in this
heart of mine.
Swanson, R. W.
Love Hasn't Changed.
Arthur, W.
Love-Hungry Heart.
Tobin.
Love in Spring.
Cassel, T. M.
Love in Thy Youth, Fair Maid.
Cole, R.
Love is a Wonderful Feeling.
Bartlett, F.
Love Is Best.
Arthur, W.
Love Is Like a Checkerboard.
Clyde, T.
Love Is Like a Theme Song.
Hall, D.

Love Is Love.
Carroll, B.
Love Jumped over a Pin Ball Machine.
Bartlett, F.
Love Lanes of Yesterday.
Davis, L.
Love Lives on Little Things.
Kennedy, A.
Love Me Dear.
Geist, E. A. G.
Love Me or Let Me Go.
Tucker, E. M.
Love Mood.
Hall, D.
Love Never Comes My Way.
Isaakson, J. M.
Love Never Dies.
Arthur, W.
Love Song.
Orynski, I. W.
Steininger, F. Music in My Heart.
Love Song of Old Vienna.
Mericka, V. O.
Love Story.
Alkire, E. H.
Mossman, T.
Love, the Climax of Life.
Pendleton, C. M.
Love Thy Neighbor.
Revel, H.
Love Triangle.
Arthur, W.
Love Turned Out a Bitter Brew.
Coombs, G.
Love Waltz.
Steer, C. E.
Loved Only by You.
Mitchell, J. B.
Lovely Are Your Deep Blue Eyes.
Staab, H. B.
Lovely Dream.
Baker, J.
Lovely Dreams of Springtime.
Bodrogi, Z. Szép, Tavaszi Almok.
Lovely is the Lee.
Remsen, A.
Lovely Lady.
Garvin, M.
Lovely Little Lady.
Gay, N. There's a lovely little lady.
Lovely to Look At.
Kern, J. Roberta.
Lover Come Back to Me.
Romberg, S. The New Moon.
Lover's Dream.
Dunbar, E.
Lover's Evening.
Clyde, T.
Lover's Plea.
Carroll, B.
Lover's Serenade.
Chanslor, H.
Lover's Waltz.
Chance, G.
Goss, R.
Love's a Lovely Thing.
Furlow, B.
Love's Awakening.
Nelson, R. H.
Love's Got Me in a Lazy Mood.
Miller, C.
Love's Hope.
Cleve, F.
Love's Just a Funny Guy.
Stuart, F.
Love's Lullaby.
Clyde, T.
Love's Own Sweet Song.
Kálmán, I.
Love's Philosophy.
Ashe, J. H.
Loving Is the Thing To Do.
Murray, J. A.
Loving You.
Jones, L.
Lucerito.
Orue, J. de
Lucerito Mañanero.
Vista, F. A.

Lucie E. Campbell Superior Song Book.
Frye (T. R.) Publishers, ed.
Lucille.
Zordan, A.
Lucky Day.
Glogau, J.
Lullabies from Every Land.
Bertail, I., arr.
Lullaby.
Brahms, J.
Buren, N. J.
Hardman, C. D.
Harm, M. L.
Khachaturian, A. I. Three Dances.
Korchmaryov, K.
Lullaby for a Union Man.
Hovey, S.
Lullaby for Latins.
King, W.
Lullaby for Mary's Son.
Andersen, C. W.
Lullaby, Little Jesus.
Magney, R. T.
Lullaby of the Christ Child.
Bircsak, T.
Phelps, R. L.
Lullaby of the Raindrops.
Carr, K.
Lullaby Song.
Williams, F.
Lulu Belle and Scotty's Mountain Melodies.
Wiseman, S.
Luna Bugiarda.
Giacone, A.
Lutte de l'Hiver et du Printemps.
Franck, C. A. Hulda.
Lux Fulgebit Hodie.
Denny, W. D.
Lyckan.
Koch, M.
Lyrical Piece.
Barlow, W.

M

M'Akropol.
Ritsiardes, I. M. Naylon 'tou akropol.
Ma Bella Rumba.
Tristan, Y. E.
Ma Blushin' Rosie, Ma Posie Sweet.
Stromberg, J.
Ma Chanson N'Est Pas Commerciale.
Petit Dutaillis, J.
Ma Mère l'Oye.
Nieland, J. H. I. M.
Maa Man Godt.
Riis, A. Tivoli Revyen.
Maan Virsi.
Sibelius, J.
Macatalina.
Gelabert, J.
Macouba.
Lopez, F. Les Trois Cousines.
Madam la Chance.
Lopez, F.
Madelene, I Had a Dream.
Bell, H.
Madonnans Vaggvisa.
Lidholm, I. Fem Sånger.
Madrugado.
Binge, R.
Magdalena.
Lopez, F. Trente et Quarante.
Maggie Haubell.
Stormy Jack.
Magic Gypsy Eyes.
Jemsky, K.
Magic Hour.
Klemm, G.
Magic Moon.
Arthur, W.
Magic of October.
Hall, D.
Magic Town.
Wells, R.
Westendorf, T. P.
Magnificat and Nunc Dimittis.
Harris, W. H.
Howells, H.
Wright, M.

Magyar Land.
  Vincze, Z. Szép Vagy, Gyönyöru Vagy.
Magyarország Legszebb Dalai.
  Pasti, B. comp. Memories of
    Hungary.
Ma-ha-lani Pap-doo hoy hoy.
  Livingston, J.
The Maid of Mourne Shore.
  Dawn, M.
Mail Order Mama.
  Harper, R.
Mailu.
  Gorney, J. Ziegfeld Follies of 1931.
Main Dominée par le Coeur.
  Poulenc, F.
The Major of St. Lo.
  Roberts, P.
Majorette, on Parade.
  Brooks, i. JJ
Make Me a Crusader Today.
  Williamson, H. J.
Make Me Worthy of Calvary.
  Wilcox, V. L.
Make With the Music, bang it around.
  Hunt, B.
Make Your Honeymoon To Last.
  Cook, L. H.
Making My Best Better.
  Mays, C. B.
Mal du Pays.
  Van De Kamp, P.
Mala Mujer.
  Parra, G.
Mala-Pata.
  Burli, A.
Malagueña.
  Lecuona Y casado, E.
  Pelo, A. del.
Malambo.
  Ginastera, A. E.
Malborough's Return.
  Garcia Morillo, R.
Malbad.
  Paez, M.
Maldita Sea Mi Suerte.
  Esperón, M. Los Tres García.
Maldita Suerte.
  Valdés Hernández, P.
Male Quartet.
  Ives, D. L., comp.
Málo mám málo dám.
  Smital, J. Got a Little, Give a Little
    Polka.
Mama, Mama, Let Me Out Tonight.
  D'Angelo, L.
Maman No Vends Pas la Maison.
  Hess, J.
Mamma Mia, Che Vo Sape.
  Nutile, E. Mother Always Wants to Know.
Mam'zelle Printemps.
  Betti, H.
Man about the House.
  Brodsky, N.
Man behind the Plough.
  Quilter, R.
Man Could Be a Wonderful Thing.
  Carr, L.
Man I Love.
  Gershwin, G.
Man in the Turban.
  Noble, M.
Man on the Flying Trapeze.
  Schaum, J. W. arr.
Mandarinade.
  Betti, A. E.
Mandulinata a Napule.
  Tagliaferri, E. A Serenade to Naples.
Manger.
  Loveless, W. P.
Manger at Bethlehem.
  Elmore, R.
Manhattan Square Dance.
  Rose, D.
Manhattan Suite.
  Mittler, F.
Manisero.
  Simon Rodriguez, M. The Peanut Vendor.
Manna Mou Eimaiphthisikos.
  Sakellariou, A. C. Ta Tria Phtaiximata.

Manola.
  Coll, R.
Man's Best Friend Is a Bed.
  McKinley, R.
Mansion in the Sky.
  Whitmore, R.
Manton de Manila.
  Orue, J. de. Tierra del Sol.
Maple Leaf.
  Brad, W. R.
Maracas.
  Thompson, J.
March from Carmen.
  Bizet, G. Carmen.
March, from the Nutcracker Suite.
  Chaikovskii, P. I.
March into the Sun.
  Sullivan, G. J. E.
March Kings' Album for Piano.
  Rovenger, L. W., ed. & arr.
March of the Beetles.
  Price, F. B.
March of the Cavaliers.
  Zordan, A.
March of the Drum Majorettes.
  Kogem, H.
March of the Scouts.
  Sharpe, E.
March of the Smugglers.
  Klemm, G.
March of the Wild Geese.
  Frost, B.
March on, America.
  Elliott, M.
March, The Phoenix.
  Bliss, A.
March Way to Drumming.
  Bourquin, J. S.
March with Bells.
  Lambert, C. Two Piano Duets.
Marche du Printemps sans Amours.
  Barraine, E.
Marche Militaire.
  Schubert, F. P.
Marche Triomphale du Centenaire de
  Napoléon. 1er.
  Vierne, L.
Marches.
  Händel, G. F.
Marches for piano.
  Towsley, F. A.
Marches of Peace.
  Mueller, C. F.
Marching Away.
  Foster, A. H., comp.
Marco Polo.
  Scarmolin, A. L.
Mardi Gras.
  Dittenhaver, S. L.
Margaret O'Brien ... Favorite Songs and
  Stories.
  Foster, F.
Margareta.
  Hall, D.
Margie.
  Davis, B.
Maria.
  Vincent, J. B.
Maria Mia.
  Anzi, G. D.
Mariage.
  Monnot, M. Étoile sans Lumière.
Mariage de Ramuntcho.
  Marcland, J.
Marian Triptych.
  Tardif, H. M., father, Triptique
    Marial.
Marie.
  Grassi, A.
Marie-Laurence.
  Anzi, G. D'. Maria Mia.
Marietta.
  Storm, J.
Marina.
  Caymmi, J.
Mariner's song.
  Williams, J.
Mariposa.
  Napolitano, E. A.

Maritana.
  Wallace, V.
Maritchu.
  Marcland, J.
Marriage Blessing.
  Lewis, L. H.
Mars! Avril! Mail Juin.
  LaFarge, G.
Marsia.
  Dallapiccola, L.
Martine.
  Rabaud, H.
Marvellous Dreams.
  Bitsch, M.
Marvellous Mysteries Sublime.
  Carleton, R. L.
Mary Ann O'Toole.
  Leonard, D. R.
Mary from Maryland.
  Rogers, J.
Mary Had a Little Lamb.
  Novak, G. S.
Mary Jane.
  Erwin, L.
Mary, Marry Me.
  Manners, M.
Marry, Mary, Quite Contrary.
  Capes, D.
Mary Through a Thornwood's Gone.
  Buchanan, A. M.
Mary Was a Little Girl.
  Woodford, G. R.
The masked one.
  Rodrigues, G. H. La cumparsita.
Maskovaná milenka.
  Blahník, R.
Mass.
  Van Hulse, C.
Mass in C major.
  Ashmall, W. E. Missa Pro Pace.
Mass in D in Honor of Christ the King.
  Ostermann, J. D.
Mass in Honor of Saint Charles.
  Perosi, L.
Mass in Honor of Saint Irenaeus.
  Ravanello, O.
Mass in Honor of the Blessed Sacrament.
  Korman, J. A.
Masterpieces of organ music.
  Hennefield, N. ed.
Mater Admirabilis.
  Daniels, A. J.
Matrena and the Deacon.
  Korchmaryov, K.
Matthew, Mark, Luke and John.
  Brahe, M. H.
Matthew Satra's I'll Not Forget So Soon.
  Satra, M.
Mattinata.
  Leoncavallo, R.
Mattinata Fiorentina.
  Anzi, G. d'. E Bello Qualche Volta
    Andare a Piedi.
Mature Theme.
  Nepper, J. C.
Maulin' Marandy.
  Strange, G.
May I Come In out of the Rain.
  Myers, H.
May Morning.
  Diggle, R. Summer Sketches.
May Thy Blessed Spirit.
  Clesnokov, P.
Maybe I'm Only Dreaming.
  Hall, D.
Maybe It's a Dream.
  West, R. H. -
May-be Next Year.
  Halama, F. J.
Maytime.
  Romberg, S.
Mazurka.
  Paz, H.
Mazurka-Estudio.
  Miramontes, A.
Me, Baby, Me.
  Arthur, W.
Me Dice Palabras Tiernas.
  Ficher, J.

Me Voy Compañeros.
Burli, A.
Me Voy por "Ai".
Esperón, M. Soy Charro de Rancho Grande.
Meditation.
Hunt, R.
Medley of Christmas Carols.
Gage, A. P.
Meet Me at No Special Place, and I'll Be There at No Particular Time.
Robinson, J. R.
Meet Me in Galilee.
Lemon, S. D.
Meet Me Tonight in the Moonlight.
Chanslor, H.
Meeting in the Air.
Curran, W. J.
Megállok a Keresztútnál.
Farkas, L.
Meisje, Doe Me een Lol.
Zinigrod, A.
Meistersinger.
Wagner, R.
Mel-Bay Chord System.
Bay, M. E.
Melancholy.
Bergman, D.
Melancholy Rain.
Meyer, D. C.
Mellow Moon.
Hanson, B.
Melodía de Arrabal.
Gardel, C.
Mélodie Calme et Triste.
Binder, R.
Melodies.
Petit, P. Y. M. C.
Melodies of Christendom.
Higginson, J. V. arr.
Melodious Fundamentals.
Colin, C.
Melody.
Harris, R.
Melody in F.
Rubinstein, A.
Melody of Spring.
Green, J. Cynthia.
Mélopée Lointaine.
Lopez, F.
Memorials.
Pitfield, T. B.
Memories.
Raider, C. M.
Memories' Gardenias.
Smith, L.
Memories of Hungary.
Pasti, B. comp.
Memories of Kentucky.
Arthur, W.
Memories of Old New York.
Bartlett, F.
Memories of you.
Hall, D.
Memories of Your Love.
Van Tyle, R.
Memory Lane.
Spier, L.
Memory Melodies.
McDowell, L. L., comp.
Memory Rosé.
Teat, D. G.
Memory Waltz.
Ivanovici, I.
Memories of My Childhood Home.
West, M.
Men of Boys Town.
Kaphahn, T. A.
Men of Wisconsin.
Mesang, T. L.
Mendelssohn: Excerpts from His Greatest Works.
Mendelssohn-Bartholdy, F.
Mention My Name in Sheboygan.
Mysels, S.
Menuisier du Roi.
Chaine, J.
Mépris du Mépris.
Agosti, G. Scherzo ed Epigramma.
Mercado de las Esclavas.
Sandoval, M. The Slave Market.

Merrie England.
German, Sir E.
Merry Christmas.
D'Angelo, L.
Merry Christmas Time.
Luvaas, M. J.
Merry Christmas to You.
Gage, H. A.
Merry-go-round.
Sullivan, B.
Merry-Go-Rounds.
Woodgate, L.
Merry Heart.
Denza, L. Funiculi-Funicula.
Merry, Merry Christmas.
Spring, M. C.
Merry Tune.
Norden, H.
Merry Widow.
Lehár, F. Vilia.
Messe Basse.
Bedell, R. L.
Messe Solennelle.
Gounod, C. F. Sanctus.
Messénia, Messénia.
Sakellariou, A. C.
Messiah.
Händel, G. F.
Méthode Complète de Clarinette.
Berr, F.
Méthode Complète et Essentiellement Graduée de Clarinette.
Velde, E. Van de.
Méthode Rose.
Velde, E. Van de.
Méthode Rythmique.
Velde, E. Van de.
Metodo per lo Studio Elementaire del Pianoforte.
Calza, E.
Metodo Pratico-Popolare per Fisarmonica.
Pacifico, A.
Metropolitan Organ Book.
Wolff, S. D., ed. & arr.
Mexican Clapping Song.
Condaris, A. J. arr. Chiapanecas.
Mexican Fantasy.
Copland, A. (Fiesta) Fantasia Mexicana.
Mezei, Bokréta.
Lavotta, R.
Mezza Bottiglia d'Aria.
Mobiglia, T. Dieci Arrangiamenti per Complesso Hot.
Mi Agonía.
Rivas, W.
Mi Bayamesa.
Muñiz Pérez, J.
Mi Cariñito.
Esperon, M. Los Tres García.
Mi Casita.
Martínez, L.
Mi Changuita.
Eugenia, W.
Mi Consentida.
Esperón, M. Los Tres Garcia.
Mi Dolor.
Lambertucci, R.
Mi Esprime Verbi d'Amore.
Ficher, J. Me Dice Palabras Tiernas.
Mi Lindo Monterrey.
Lavista, R. Cuando Lloran los Valientes.
Mi Oracion.
Rojo, G.
Mi Ruego.
Abelenda, A. M.
Miami Moon.
Koss, J.
Midnight in Paris.
Magidson, H.
Midsummer Dance.
Sommerfelt, M.
Midsummer Night in June.
Rehm, I. E.
Midtsommer Dans.
Sommerfelt, M. Midsummer Dance.
Midwinter Carol.
Marryott, R. E.

Miedo.
Ruíz, G.
Mighty Fortress Is Our God.
Luther, M.
Mighty Pelicans.
Nelson, L. I.
Mighty Spirit, All Transcending.
Mozart, J. C. W. A.
Mijn derde oefenboek.
Duuren, H. J. Van. Mijn eerste-[derde] oefenboek.
Mijn eerste oefenboek.
Duuren, H. J. Van. Mijn eerste-[derde] oefenboek.
Mijn twe oefenboek.
Duuren, H. J. Van. Mijn eerste-[derde] oefenboek.
Mikado and Pinafore.
Sullivan, Sir A. S.
Military Song.
Grechaninov, A. T. Chanson Militaire.
Mill.
Jensen, A.
Mill in the Black Forest.
Eilenberg, R. Le Moulin de la Forêt Noire.
Milliardaire Américain.
LaFarge, G.
Million Dollar Polka.
Kenne, E. R.
Million Dreams.
Arthur, W.
Milonguita.
Padilla, J. Voluptuosa.
Mimaamaquim.
Honegger, A.
Mine Forever.
Sadowski, J.
Mine To Be.
Sadowski, J.
Mi-ne-ap-o-lus.
Ilong, N. R.
Minek Turbékoltok.
Hubay, J.
Miners' Song.
Cornett, A.
Minervois.
Delapierre, G. B.
Miniature Concerto for piano and orchestra.
Rowley, A.
Miniature Suite.
Barkla, N.
Minnen från Hembygden.
Rosen, A. O.
Minnesota Moon.
McPhail, L.
Minor Melody. The unfinished Dance.
Thomas, D.
Minor Riff.
Rugolo, P.
Minou, la Cancon, la Baya.
Trenet, C.
Minuet.
Loeillet, J. B.
Mozart, J. C. W. A. Don Giovanni.
Minuet from Don Juan.
Mozart, J. C. W. A.
Minuet in G.
Beethoven, L. Van.
Minuet in G minor.
Händel, G. F.
Minuet in Swing.
Paisner, B.
Minueto en fa para piano.
Miramontes, A.
Minuetto.
Miramontes, A.
Scarlatti, A. Aria.
Minute Waltz.
Chopin, F. F.
Minutes with Magnante.
Magnante, C.
Mio Diletto É Partito.
Agosti, G. Tre Liriche.
Mira Que Eres Linda.
Brito, J.
Miracle of the Bells.
Norman, P.

Miramare.
Lang, H.
Mírame Chiquilla.
Longás, F.
Miriam's song of triumph.
Jospe, E. Sing Unto the Lord.
Mish-Mash.
Castellanos, A. L.
Misirlou.
Roubanis, N.
Misma Muerte.
Marín Hernández, V.
Miss Elisabeth Brown.
Rivers, J.
Missa Exultet Orbis.
Van Hulse, C. Mass, Op. 27.
Missa in Honorem Sanctissimae
Trinitatis.
Ziccardi, F. S.
Missa in Honorem SS. Trinitatis et
Beatissimae Mariae Virginis.
Schifferli, E.
Missa Pro Pace.
Ashmall, W. E.
Missa Sancti Michaelis.
Willan, H.
Missing.
Snider, L.
Mississippi Gal.
McPeters, T.
Mist.
Hibbs, C. A.
Mr. Moon.
Chanslor, H.
Curtis, D.
Mr. Nobody.
Warren, E. R.
Mr. Police, That's Is My Gel, a-what's-a
matter you.
Paone, N.
Misterios del Hampa.
Urban, M.
Mistletoe Song.
Tobias, C.
Mrs. Miniver.
Stothart, H.
Mists of the Morning.
Fischer, I.
Mit einer Träne in der Stimme.
Kreuder, ţ . Wege der Liebe.
Mock Turtle Marches On.
Diggle, R. Alice in Wonderland Suite.
Modern Classics for the Alto Recorder.
Voros, W. J., ed.
Modern Piano in the Modern Manner.
Toutjean, V.
Mohawk Mood.
Osage, T.
Moi J'M'En Fous.
Glanzberg, N.
Moi, Je ท'Aim' Pas Ca.
Lopez, F. - Les Trois Cousines.
Moineau de Paris.
Scotto, V.
Momento Musical, no. 1.
Miramontes, R. A.
Momento Musical, no. 2.
Miramontes, R. A. Intermezzo en la.
Momento Musical, no. 3.
Miramontes, R. A. Intermezzo en la.
Moments Mystiques.
Monfred, A. de.
Mom's Baked Beans.
Hannah, P. J.
Mon Aimé.
Shean, C. L.
Money Isn't Ev'rything.
Rodgers, R. Allegro.
Money, Money, Money.
Brodsky, R.
Monody.
Diamond, D. L. 5 Songs.
Monon Centennial Show.
McGee, J. A.
Monotone.
Betti, A. E.
Monsieur Alibi.
Cloerec, R.

Monsieur Attendait.
Ulmer, G.
Montana, Land of Treasure.
Wallen, H.
Montecatini.
Sacco, T. Someday We'll Meet Again in
Montecatini.
Monticello Moon.
McGee, J. A. The Monon Centennial
Show.
Mood Indigo.
Bigard, A.
Moody Monday.
David, L.
Moon Glazing.
Tobin, L.
Moon Lullaby.
Bartlett, F.
Moon Madness.
Hall, D.
Moon Magic.
Chanslor, H.
Moon of Dawn.
Beethoven, L. Van.
Savino, D.
Moon over Montana.
Drake, O.
Moon Winks His Eye.
Arthur, W.
Moondust.
Darling, A.
Moonlight and music.
Denné, C.
Moonlight and You, Sweetheart.
Clyde, T.
Moonlight on the Purple Sage.
Klenner, J.
Moonlight over the Fields.
Cernkovich, R. Sječaš Li Se Onog Sata.
Moonlight Sonata.
Beethoven, L. Van. Sonata, piano.
Moonlight Stroll.
Dion, Y.
Moonlight through My Window.
Hibbeler, R. O.
Moon's a Magic Lantern.
Vanderburg, G. J.
Moravian Evening Hymn.
Gaul, H. B.
Mordvin Lullaby.
Seiber, M.
More I See of You.
Bartlett, F.
More Than the Stars in heaven above.
McNeil, J. C..
More Themes from the Great Concertos.
Levine, H.
Mornin', Nite and Noon.
Stromer, B. W.
Morning Hymn.
Peeters, F.
Moroccan Market.
Fields, I.
Mors et Vita.
Gounod, C. F. Judex and Hosanna in
Excelsis.
Most Wondrous Kingdom.
Sateren, L. B.
Mother.
Clyde, T.
Mother Always Wants to Know.
Nutile, E.
Mother and Maiden.
Walker, M.
Mother Dear.
Arthur, W.
Mother, Dear to Me.
Calder, G.
Mother of God.
Luneau, O. J.
Mother of Mine.
Reiter, E., sister.
Mother Read Those Stories.
Casler, C. H.
Mother Wore Tights.
Myrow, J.
Mother's Eyes.
Porter, I. H.
Motivosa.
Esperón, M. Soy Charro de Rancho Grande.

Moto Perpetuo.
Paganini, N.
Mouettes.
Lazarus, D.
Moulin de la Forêt Noire.
Ellenberg, R.
Mount Mary Motet Book.
Gisela, M., sister, comp.
Mountain Majesty.
Yoder, P.
Mountain Tune.
Sumsion, H.
Mountaineer.
Wick, F.
Mousse du Bonaventure.
Pingault, C.
Move It on Over.
Williams, H.
Moving No More.
Richard, L.
Mozart.
Mozart, J. C. W. A.
Mozart's Divertimenti.
Mozart, J. C. W. A.
Muchachita.
Frydan, C. Ladies Know How.
Ruiz, A. M.
Mujer de España.
Padilla, J.
Mujer, No Puedo Perdonarte.
Angulo Rodríguez, P.
Muñequita.
Vanner, E.
Muñequita de París.
Burli, A.
Murió como un Heroe.
Arce, J. G.
Music Box.
Stella, J. J.
Music for a While.
Purcell, H.
Music for Ballet Exercises.
Atkinson, G. H.
Music for Rhythmic Movement.
Holgate, E. D.
Music for Worship.
Osborne, S. L., ed.
Music from beyond the Moon.
Wood, G.
Music in Miniature.
Haydn, J. (Quartet, strings) Serenade.
Music in My Heart.
Steininger, F.
Music Lovers' Piano Duets.
Treharne, B. arr.
Music Magic.
Dushkin, D.
Music of the Jungle.
Carleton, R. L.
Music of the Troubadours.
Bernart De Ventadorn, 12th cent,
Music out of the Moon.
Revel, H.
Music Played for Someone Sweetly.
Balāss, A. Valakinek Muzsikálnak.
Music, When Soft Voices Die.
Anderson, W. H.
Bergh, A.
Candlyn, T. F. H.
Hurst, G.
Kramer, A. W.
Music World.
Jamack, P. J.
Musical Alphabet and Figures.
Perry, J. H.
Musical Chart.
Ferrera, J. B.
Musical Clock Polka.
Gosz, R.
Musical Composition Arranged for Male
Voices.
Williams, R. M.
Musical Powder Box.
Tonner, P.
Musical Salvantionist. See title entry
in composer list.
Musical Time Method.
Cowan, J. Jesse Cowan's Musical
Time Method.

409

Musick for the Royal Fireworks.
Händel, G. F.
Muskingum Moon.
Gary, H. M.
My Adorable One.
Murray, M.
My Alabama Rose.
Bartlett, F.
My Album of Dreams.
Higgins, R.
My America.
Yeakey, M.
My Angel.
Arthur, W.
My Atom Bomb.
Sarges, L.
My Atomic Gal.
Dale, J.
My Atomic Sensation.
Stillerman, I.
My Baby Doll.
Norton, B.
My Baby's Waiting for a Kiss.
Gardner, A. E.
My Bad Habit Is You.
Crane, J.
My Best Gale Has Gone.
Denman, J. T.
My Blessed Friend.
Mills, G. W.
My Bonnie Lass.
Buckner, H. E.
My Book of Memory.
Westendorf, T. P. Magic Town.
My Boy.
Ogle, C.
My Broken Heart and I.
Morgan, A.
My Brooklyn Love Song.
Idriss, R. If You Knew Susie.
My Charming Dream.
Buck, R.
My Corny Country Cousin.
Ricardel, J.
My Country, 'Tis of Thee.
Carey, H.
My Cousin Louella.
Manus, J.
My Daily Prayer.
Otts, P. A.
My Danny.
Hall, D.
My Darling Baby.
Strong, C. E.
My Darling Curly Head.
The Andrews Brothers. Go to Sleep,
My Darling Curly Head.
My Darling, I Miss You Tonight.
Hall, D.
My Darling Today.
Tobin, L.
My Darling's Lullaby.
Bailey, F. J.
My Date.
Samuels, W.
My Day Dreams.
Haight, J.
My Dear, Remember.
Harvey, S.
My Dearest Darling.
Lama, G.
My Dearest Dreams of You.
Clyde, T.
My Dove.
Bartlett, F.
My Dream.
Noble, W. S.
Vanbrock, F.
My Dream for Tonight.
Helpenstell, M. H.
My Dream Girl.
Carleton, R. L.
My Dream Is Ended.
Ziegler, L. F.
My Dream of Dreams.
Hall, D.
My Dream of Tomorrow Is You.
Frisque, B.

My Dream of Vienna.
Klemm, G.
My Dream World.
Richard, L.
My Dreams.
Cook, H. M.
My Dreams Are Now A Reality.
Peltier, A. J.
My Faith Looks Up to Thee.
Mason, L.
My Fallen Star.
Daffan, T.
My Favorite-Dream.
Disney, (W.) Productions, Ltd. Fun
and Fancy Free.
My First Love, My Last Love for Always.
Reid, B.
My Flame Went Out Last Night.
Newman, L.
My Flaming Heart.
Poirier, E. J.
My Flower.
Adriance, B. E.
My Fondest Hope.
Clyde, T.
My Friend, Bob White.
Klemm, G.
My Friend John.
Peloquin, C. A.
My Future Address.
Robertson, B. G.
My Future Is You.
Traina, T.
My Garden of Dreams.
Van Buren, B.
My Garden of Love.
Taulman, M. B.
My Girl.
Devey, G.
My Girl of Yesteryear.
Casey, J. D.
My Girl's an Irish Girl.
Parker, R. I'll Make Up for
Ev'rything.
Popplewell, J.
My God's Going to Get Tired After While.
Davis, V.
My Golden Dreams.
Samuels, W.
My Golden Opportunity.
Hyden, A. F.
My Grandboy.
Clyde, T.
My Guitar Is My Sweetheart.
Rhodes, D.
My Guns Are of Silver, My Bullets of
Gold.
McNeil, J. C.
My Heart Beats in Hawaii.
Hibbeler, R. O.
My Heart Beats Only for You, Dear.
Tobin, L.
My Heart Begins to Cry.
Herbert, B.
My Heart Belongs to You.
Magill, H. A.
My Heart Can't Stand the Strain.
White, C.
My Heart Depends on You.
Ahlefeld, F. W.
My Heart Ever Faithful.
Bach, J. S.
My Heart Ever Trusting.
Bach, J. S.
My Heart for You.
Bourne, P. R.
My Heart Goes Out to a Soldier.
Bell, H.
My Heart Is a Violin.
Ross, C. E.
My Heart Is Aching over You.
Arthur, W.
My Heart Is Bursting with Love.
McNeil, J. C.
My Heart Is Fenced in for You.
Van Tyle, R.
My Heart Is Yours.
Burrows, R.

Ceeley, L. Gardenia Lady.
Morfort, J.
Savino, D.
My Heart Is Yours Alone.
Snow, C. R.
My Heart Is Yours to Break.
McDermott, S.
My Heart Jumped over the Moon.
Bivens, B.
My Heart Knows Nothing Better.
Kincaid, P. E.
My Heart Promises.
White, S.
My Heart Remembers.
Craig, D.
My Heart Sees Stars.
Walker, L. R.
My Heart Stood Still.
Rodgers, R. A. Connecticut Yankee.
My Heart Will Tag Along.
Arthur, W.
My Heart's on a Strike.
Hall, D.
My Heart's on My Sleeve.
Gawthrop, A. H.
My Home.
Abernathy, L. R.
Tobin, L.
My Homestead Is Waiting.
Crane, J.
My Honey Is on the Choo-Choo.
Samuels, W.
My Honey's Back Home.
Evans, H.
My Honey's Lovin' Arms.
Meyer, I.
My, How the Time Goes by.
McHugh, J. F. If You Knew Susie.
My Irish Colleen.
Curtis, D.
My Irish Home, Sweet Home.
Smith, W.
My Isle of Golden Dreams.
Blaufuss, W.
My Jesus Knows, and I Am Satisfied.
Iden, R. J.
My Jo in Idaho.
Berk, M.
My Kansas Pawnee, Wanda Rose.
Arthur, W.
My Kitten's Always Puttin' On the Dog.
Vanderburg, G. J.
My Lady Greensleeves.
Quilter, R.
Wright, F. arr.
My Lady Walks in Loveliness.
Duncan, C.
My Lady's Garden.
Quilter, R.
My Last Days on the Ranch.
Taube, O.
My Lips Will Be Calling.
Katan, B.
My Little Boy.
Selinsky, W.
My Little Dream Girl.
Del Vecchio, T.
My Little Red-Head.
Adams, F.
My Longing Heart.
Silmon, M.
My Lord Is in the Mountains.
Cairns, C. L.
My Lord's Goin' to Rain Down Fire.
Cain, N.
My Love.
Hall, D.
Shean, C. L. Mon Aimé.
Wisniewski, J. B.
My Love For You.
Arthur, W.
Hall, D.
Tobin, L.
My Love Is What the Blues Are Made of.
Walter, S.
My Love Song.
Squires, H. D.
My Love Will Always Be the Same.
Arthur, W.
My Lovely Angel.

Dello, C.
My Lovely World and You.
  Moran, J.
My Luck Has Changed.
  Hall, D.
My Lucky Day.
  Arthur, W.
My Main Trail Is Yet to Come.
  King, F.
My Man Turned Up and turned me down.
  Mann, E.
My Mansion in Glory.
  Griswold, G. L.
My Melody.
  Gilbertson, H.
My Memories.
  King, P. R.
My Miami Gal.
  Clyde, T.
My Million Dollar Baby.
  York, F. E.
My Mistake Cost Me You.
  Dean, E.
My Mother.
  Davidenko, A.
  McNeil, J. C.
My Mother, an Angel in Disguise.
  Clark, A. A.
My Mother's Eyes.
  Deis, C.
My Mother's Song.
  Miller, M. C.
My Mountain Sweetheart.
  Clyde, T.
My! My!
  Tobin, L.
My, My, Oh Why.
  Desort, F.
My Old Kentucky Home, Good Night.
  Foster, S. C. Bardomshemmet i Kentucky.
My Old Log Cabin Home down in Virginia.
  Tallman, A.
My Old Mellow Moon.
  Tabb, J. D.
My Old Rag Doll.
  George, C.
My Old Sweet Story.
  Hall, D.
My Only Love.
  Crane, J.
  Kerr, J.
My Only One.
  McNeil, J. C.
My Own Darby and Joan.
  Kulma, L.
My Pal.
  Clyde, T.
My Peachy Packing Pal.
  Arthur, W.
My Pinto.
  Davidson, D.
My Prairie Home.
  Bartlett, F.
My Prayer.
  Ramont, G. M.
  Schooner, M.
  Tobin, L.
My Prayer for You.
  Rojo, G. Mi Oracion.
My Pretty Blue Eyes.
  Samuels, W.
My Pretty Little Eileen.
  Thompson, V. F.
My Pretty Miss.
  Stockdale, C. E.
My Quaker Queen.
  Samuels, W.
My Queen of Hearts.
  Bartlett, F.
My Rancho Rio Grande.
  Walker, C.
My Rhapsody of Love.
  Nieumere, G.
My Romance.
  Rodgers, R.
My Rose under the Lilac Tree.
  Arthur, W.
My Saddle, My Broncho and You.
  Moise, M.

My San Fer-nan-do Rose.
  Davis, S.
My Selfish Prayer.
  Tobin, L.
My Senorita.
  Bartlett, F.
My Shack out in the West.
  Brown, H. S.
My Shawnee Miss.
  Buck, R.
My Sixteen Year Old Brown-Eyed
    Young Maid.
  Szánto, M. Tizenhat Esztendos Barna
    Kis Lány.
My Song Is Still Tonight.
  Shackley, G.
My Song of Songs.
  Ramont, G. M.
My Soul Doth Magnify the Lord.
  Saxton, S. E.
My Soul, Praise the Lord.
  Vaughan, W. R.
My Southern Rose.
  King, R.
My Star of Love.
  Buck, R.
My Sweet Has Turned Sour on Me.
  Arthur, W.
My Sweetheart.
  Arthur, W.
  Canfield, R.
My Sweetheart Jane of Tennessee.
  Hibbeler, R. O.
My Tahiti Rose.
  Arthur, W.
My Town.
  Leonard, R.
My Treasure.
  Arthur, W.
My Troubles Are Gone.
  Welsh, S. R.
My Trusty Gun.
  Milyutin, Y.
My Western Home.
  Brockman, J.
My Whole Life Long.
  Clyde, T.
My Whole Life Through.
  Winters, H. E.
My Wild Irish Rose.
  Jerome, M. K.
  Olcott, C.
My Window Pane.
  Arthur, W.
My Yesterdays.
  Arthur, W.

N

Naar Man Elsker Hinanden Maa Himlen
    Vanta.
  Andersen, K. N. Dagmar Revyen, 1947.
Nancy.
  Shlimovitz, H. M.
Nancy Sue.
  Lamb, F. W.
Nanon Filhadoué.
  Delannoy, M.
Nanticoke Polka.
  Castellani, L. Pittston Polka.
Não Tenho Lagrimas.
  Oliveira, M. de.
Naples and Sorrento.
  Tagliaferri, E.
Napule e Surriento.
  Tagliaferri, E. Naples and Sorrento.
Narcissus.
  Nevin, E. W.
Natch.
  Dennis, M.
National Guard March.
  Aubuchon, C.
National W. A. R. M. A. Loyalty Song.
  Locey, M.
Nativity Miniatures.
  Taylor, A.
Nativity Scenes.
  Cronham, C. R.

Natten Er Til Bare for Os.
  Andersen, K. N. Dagmar Revyen, 1947.
Nature Spirits.
  Day, R. E.
Nautical Toccata.
  Rowley, A.
Navidad.
  Goudey, R. Christmas Comes Once a
    Year.
Navy Blues.
  Moore, B.
Naylon tou Akropol.
  Ritsiardes, I. M.
Nazarena.
  Padilla, J.
Ne Rame Pas.
  Hodeige, O. J.
Neapolitan Festival.
  O'Donnell, W.
Near the Cross.
  Schuitema, A. K. arr. Jesus, Lover
    of My Soul.
Near You.
  Craig, F.
Nearer and Dearer.
  Friml, R. Northwest Outpost.
'Neath Hawaiian Palms.
  Campbell, C.
'Neath the Cloud Lit Skies.
  Sawaya, I. J.
Nebo Je Cisto, Jasno.
  Cernkovich, R.
Nebraska.
  Arthur, W.
  Negra Martica.
  Quintero Garcerán, R.
Negro Sketches.
  Cooper, E. Silver Horn.
Ne-Hah-Nee.
  Nolan, B.
Neighbor, Have You Seen My Wife.
  Roberts, P.
Neljä suomalaista kansanlaulua.
  Kiami. U. K.
Nenia.
  Westberg, E.
Nereides.
  Petit, P. Y. M. Rome, l'Unique Objet.
Nesting.
  Shannon, J.
Neuberin.
  Benatzky, R.
Neuf Variations.
  Quiroga, M.
Never.
  Arthur, W.
Never Before.
  Hall, D.
Never Give Up Your Dreams.
  Arthur, W.
Never Have I Said I Loved You.
  Sas, N. Hogyha Szeretnelek.
Never Make Eyes at the gals with the
    guys who are bigger than you.
  Fain, S.
Never Say No' to Your Sugar Daddy.
  Speaker, M.
Never Trust a Woman.
  Carson, J. L.
Never Wander, Never Stray.
  Etoll, G. W.
Never without Him.
  Naylor, E. A.
Nevermore to Return.
  Martinez, L. Nunca Más Volvera.
New Born King.
  Blair, H.
New Day.
  Towsley, F. A. Marches for piano.
New England Is the Only Place for Me.
  Roberts, A.
New Fort Worth Rag.
  Boyd, B.
New Jersey.
  Banbury, G. E.
New Look.
  Emmel, J. C.
New Mexico Sunset.
  House, C.
New Mixmaster Song.
  Miller, I.
New Moon.
  Romberg, S.
New Moon in the Sky.
  Hauck, M. L.
New Orleans Masquerade.
  Mills, I.
New Orleans Two Beat Shuffle.
  Meissner, J. J.

New Songs for Old.
  Driver, A.
New Songs For Young People.
  See title entry in composer list.
New Songs that Will Live.
  Wright, W. J.
New Vienna.
  Schumann Poveda, E.
New World.
  Savino, D.
  Vincent, N.
New World over the Hill.
  Wilcock, F. S.
Nicolas de Flue.
  Gogniat, J. Hymne Patriotique
    a Nicolas de Flue.
Night After Night Dreaming of You.
  Gollatz, M.
Night and Morning.
  Arthur, W.
Night Beat.
  Bernard, B.
Night Birds.
  Willnor, V.
Night for Loving.
  Bartlett, F.
Night Has a Thousand Eyes.
  Bergh, A.
  Duncan, C.
Night Herder.
  Dickson, A.
Night in June.
  Brahms, J.
Night in Rio.
  Desmond, P.
Night in Vienna.
  Federer, R.
Night Is Fine.
  Cable, E. L.
Night Magic.
  Hopkins, H. P.
Night Music.
  Pitfield, T. B.
Night of Love.
  Canora, L.
Night Rose Polka.
  Skertich, N.
Night Shift Blues.
  Chanslor, H.
Night Sky.
  Suesse, D.
Night That I First Met You.
  Toyas, P.
Night Was Made for Love.
  Kern, J.
Night You Said Aloha to Me.
  Aloma, H.
Nightingale.
  Russell, K.
Nigun.
  Bloch, E.
Nina Nana.
  Criscuolo, J. D.
  George, D.
Nine Choir Responses.
  Williams, R. M.
Nine O'Clock Polka.
  Cernkovich, R.
Ninfas.
  Miramontes, A.
Niño.
  Miramontes, R. A.
No, Baby, No.
  Gardner, E.
No basta ser charro.
  Esperon, M.
No Good Woman Blues.
  Hampton, L.
No Heart at All.
  Nelson, M.
No Matter Where You Go.
  Candella, L.
No Moonlight, No Song.
  Tobin, L.
No More.
  Manley, P.
No Name.
  Vitto, B.

No No Nanette.
  Youmans, V.
No One.
  Novelli, S. P.
No One Else.
  Right, J.
No Podras Olvidarme.
  Pedreira, J. E.
No Quiero Que Me Quieras.
  Roig, G. Be Sure.
No Regrets.
  Brad, W. R.
No Romance for Him.
  Hall, D.
No Rose in San Antone.
  Edlin, I. A.
No Se Va a Poder.
  Michel, J. A.
No Second Spring.
  Rose, C.
No Sufras por Mi.
  Romberg, S. (The Student Prince)
    Deep in My Heart, Dear.
No Theme Can Be Greater.
  Nygren, D. F.
Noble Accordion Course.
  Noble, M. L.
Nobody Knows the Trouble I've Seen.
  Reisfeld, B. arr.
Nobody Loves Me Anymore.
  Arthur, W.
Nobody Will Do But You.
  Johnson, E. A.
Nobody's Fool.
  Hughes, B.
Noche Caribe.
  Faith, P.
Noëna Rufa.
  Skertich, N. Night Rose Polka.
Nocturne.
  Busch, W. Suite.
  Dieterich, M.
  Nystroem, G. Tva Sånger.
Nocturne (in D flat).
  DeBussy, C.
Nocturne no. 1-3.
  Carulli, F.
Nocturno.
  Falla, M. de.
  Pahissa, J.
Nodding Buttercups.
  Yuill, M. Four Out-Door Scenes.
Nodding Tulips.
  Van Nort, I.
Noël.
  MacMichael, M.
Noël Américain.
  Casadesus, F. Hurricane-Express.
Non Mon Amour.
  Scotto, V.
None but the Lonely Heart.
  Chaĭkovskiĭ, P. I.
  Livingston, J.
Nora.
  Coots, J. F.
Nordiskt.
  Rangström, T.
Nordiskt Capriccio.
  Koch, E. Von.
Northern Lights.
  Fischer, J. L.
Northwest Outpost.
  Friml, R.
Nostalgia.
  Peeters, F.
  Rose, D.
  Rose, D. The Outstanding Composi-
    tions of David Rose.
  Van De Kamp, P. Mal du Pays.
Nostalgic Serenade.
  Salta, M.
Not a Word.
  Pace, V. H.
Not Alone for Mighty Empire.
  Prichard, R. H.
Not for Me.
  Jorgensen, E.

Not What My Hands Have Done.
  Martin, G. W.
Notte, Divina Notte.
  Donati, P.
Notti Andaluse.
  Pisani, D. Fior di Cempàka.
Notturno.
  Gubitosi, E.
  Ralfo, C.
Notturno Napolentano.
  Dello Joio, C.
Nous Deus. Tant Mieux.
  Liferman, G.
Nous Deux.
  Gasté, L.
Now and Then.
  Neha-Neha.
Now Dawns a Glorious Day.
  Langstroth, I. Four Chorale Preludes.
Now He Tells Me.
  Brandt, A.
Now I Lay Me Down to Sleep.
  Cairns, C. I.
  Stickles, W. arr. Jumbo Note Lullabies.
Now, I'm Always Dreaming.
  Taylor, M. L.
Now Is the Hour.
  Stewart, D.
Now Is the Time.
  Jackson, L. M.
Now Is the Time for Christmas.
  Taylor, D. J.
Now Let Us Rejoice.
  Phelps, W. W.
Now, Listen to Me, Honey.
  Parks, B.
Now or Never.
  Wakely, J.
Now Thank We All Our God.
  Cruger, J.
Now You Tell Me.
  Fisher, D.
Now You're Alone and I'm Alone.
  Davis, T.
Nu Vaso e 'Na Cerasa.
  Blasio, V.
Nuit de Félicité.
  Aubanel, G. P. P.
Nuit Etend Son Voile.
  Scala, T. Sortileges.
Nuit sans Amour.
  Grassi, A. J.
Nuits de Paris.
  Ulmer, G. On A Volé une Étoile.
Number One Hit Parader.
  Arthur, W.
Nun Si' Cchiù Chella.
  Griffo, G.
Nun Turnà.
  Cardone, F.
Nunc Dimittis.
  Chesnokov.
  Harris, W. H. Magnificat.
  Howells, H. Magnificat.
  Wright, M. S. Magnificat.
Nunca Mas Volvera.
  Martinez, L.
Nuove Canzoni, 1947-1948. See title
  entry in composer list.
Nuove Canzoni di Mario Nicolò.
  Nicolò, M.
Nursery Without Rhyme.
  Rose, D. The Outstanding Composi-
    tions of David Rose.
Nurse's Song.
  Somervell, A.
Nursin' One Beer.
  Vanderburg, G. J.
Nutcracker Suite.
  Chaĭkovskiĭ, P. I. Arab Dance.
  Chaĭkovskiĭ, P. I. Danse des
    Mirlitons.
  Chaĭkovskiĭ, P. I. March.
  Chaĭkovskiĭ, P. I. Overture Miniature.
Nymäne.
  Fernström, J. Sex Sånger.
Nymphs and Goblins.
  Connell, G.

O

O Aĕtos tēs Krētēs.
  Sakellariou, A. C.
O Be Ready.
  Grummons, R. N.
O. Di Bella Italian Dance Albums for
  Orchestra.
  Di Bella, O.
O Esca Viatorum.
  Sciamanna, E.
O Ever Faithful God.
  Bach, J. S.
O Filiiet Filiae.
  Leisring, V. Ye Sons and Daughters
    of the King.
O for a Closer Walk with God.
  Bullock, E.
O Friend.
  Lubin, E.
O Gloriosa Virginum.
  Kuntz, P. E.
  Ravanello, O. Two Motets for
    Profession of Vows.
O God, Have Mercy upon Us.
  Liemohn, E.
O God, Our Help in Ages Past.
  Mueller, C. F.
O Holy Saviour.
  Hahn, R.
O Houp.
  Canteloube, J.
O Jesu Christ, Mein's Lebens Licht.
  Bach, J. S.
O Jesus Christ, My Life and Light.
  Bach, J. S.
O Jesus, Thou the Beauty Art.
  Marier, T. N.
O Lamb of God.
  Brown, A. G. Y.
O Little Town of Bethlehem.
  Gevaert, F. A. Two Christmas
    Carols.
  Miller, W. N.
O Lord, Most Holy.
  Scholin, C. A.
O Lord, Support Us.
  Margetson, E. T.
O Lord, Support Us All the Day Long.
  Matthews, H. A.
O Lord, This Grieving Spirit.
  Bach, J. S. Ach Herr, Mich Armen
    Sünder.
O Love Divine.
  Godard, B. L. P.
O Lovely Words.
  Charles, E.
'O Marenariello.
  Farrow, J. I Have But One Heart.
O Mistress Mine.
  Bullock, E. Three Songs from
    Twelfth Night.
O Mortal Folk, You May Behold and See.
  Le Fleming, C.
O Nené.
  Korngold, E. W. Escape Me Never.
O! Now You Tell Me.
  Hall, D.
O Praise the Lord, My Soul.
  Ippolitov-Ivanov, M. M.
O Promise Me.
  Owens, H. R. Hawaii Will Be Paradise
    Once More.
O Salutaris.
  Hemmerlé, J. Adoro Te.
O Sing unto the Lord.
  Hassler, H. L.
O Sinner, Give Heed.
  Jackson, L. M.
O That Men Would Praise the Lord.
  Bode, A. G. H.
O That Will Be Glory.
  Gabriel, C. H.
O Vermeland.
  Nelson, G.
O Wondrous Peace.
  Nygren, D. F.
O World! O Life! O Time.
  Ashe, J. H.

O Worship the King.
  Durant, C.
  George, G.
Oahu.
  Lombardo, C.
Oasis du Bonheur.
  Neuburger, J. B. D.
Oberek Janów.
  Plachanski, J.
Ocean City Polka.
  Hoven, G.
Ocean Echoes.
  Beyer, E.
Ocean View Waltz.
  Pulitini, J.
Och Ás Ochan Mo Chàradh.
  Hill, A. Highland Air.
Octave.
  Betti, H. Mam'zelle Printemps.
Octuor.
  Pascal, C. R. G. Octet, winds
    & brass.
Ode for St. Cecilia's Day.
  Finzi, G.
Ode to Democracy.
  Baron, M.
Ömske-wijsa.
  Koch, S. v. Gammalswenska wijsor.
O'er Bethlehem's Plains.
  Matthews, H. A. Danish Carol.
Össze Tudnék Csokolgatni.
  Balázs, Á.
O Euvres d'Orgue de Léonce de Saint-
  Martin.
  Saint-Martin, L. M. J. de.
Of Thee I Sing.
  . Gershwin, G.
Offering of the Grateful Heart.
  Hartshorn, W. C.
Officer Buzz Advises.
  Grant-Schaefer, G. A.
Official Holy Name Hymnal.
  Holy Name Society.
Official West Point March.
  Egner, P.
Ogden Nash's Musical Zoo.
  Dukelsky, V.
O'Grady's Tinwhistle Band.
  Kavanagh, P.
Oh Baby, No Baby can do that to me.
  Nieder, A.
Oh, By an' By.
  Roberton, H. S.
Oh, Come Everyone That Thirsteth.
  Mendelssohn-Bartholdy, F.
    Elijah.
Oh, for a Heart to Serve Jesus.
  Esters. H. V.
Oh, God, Thou Faithful God.
  Bach, J. S.
Oh Haste Thee, My Soul.
  Bach, J. S.
Oh How Amiable Are Thy Dwellings.
  Whelpley, B.
Oh! How I Love Him Today.
  Bonnivar, F. This Old Time
    Religion.
Oh, How I Miss You, since you want away.
  Taylor, M.
Oh, Kay.
  Gershwin, G.
Oh, Lady Be Good.
  Gershwin, G.
Oh, Minnesota Moon.
  Johnson, J. O.
Oh! My Achin' Heart.
  Palmer, J.
Oh, My Darling Rose Marie.
  Storseth, L.
Oh, Oh, I Love It So.
  Singer, G. G.
Oh, Oh, Romeo.
  Warner, A.
Oh, Professor, How Could You.
  Corlet, T.
Oh, Promise Me.
  De Koven, R.
Oh, Que C' Est Haut, le Haut des
  Montagnes.
  Lopez, F. Les Trois Cousines.

Oh, So Many Years.
  Bailes, F.
Oh, Susanna.
  Foster, S. C.
Oh, Sweet Be Your Slumber.
  Vairin, L. Songs for voice and piano.
Oh, That Memory.
  McNeil, J. C.
Oh, 'Tis Sweet to Think.
  Quilter, R.
Oh, To Be like the Master.
  Essenburg, E.
Oh, What a Lovely Evening.
  Arthur, W.
Oh, What Am I Gonna Do with You.
  Becker, H.
Oh! What I Know About You.
  Kassel, A.
Oh, What Love.
  Loveless, W. P.
Oh! Willie! I'm Waitin'.
  Mitchell, M. G.
Oh! Yes We Will.
  Mills, G. W.
Oh You Basketball.
  Chenette, E.
Ohio Valley Express.
  Storm, C. W.
Oigan Amigos.
  Mocciola, J.
Oklahoma Home.
  McAllister, D. D.
Oklahoma Pioneers.
  Ahlstrand, D.
Oklahoma's Calling.
  Guthrie, J.
Ol' Man River.
  Kern, J. Show Boat.
Old Accordion.
  Hartmann, M. M.
Old Black Steer.
  Reed, R.
Old Chaperone.
  Tibbles, G.
Old Chihuahua City.
  Turner, Z.
Old Fashioned Cowboy.
  Erwin, L.
Old Ferris Wheel.
  Kenny, C.
Old Folks at Home.
  Foster, S. C.
Old Forgotten Trails.
  Nolan, B.
Old Gaelie Rune.
  Penny, M.
Old Glory.
  Ford, F.
Old Glory Waves on Forever.
  Pitre, B.
Old Hundred.
  Hill, T. J. arr.
Old Indians Never Die.
  Willis brothers.
Old Joe Has Gone Fishing.
  Britten, B. Peter Grimes.
Old Lamp-Lighter.
  Simon, N.
Old Log Cabin Song.
  Yarbrough, Mrs. C. C.
Old Memories.
  Arthur, W.
Old Moon, Say Hello.
  Deal, J. S.
Old Oaken Bucket.
  Kiallmark, G.
Old Pals.
  Cameron, P. A.
Old Rugged Cross.
  Yoder, P. Symphonic Series of
    Sacred Songs.
Old Sombrero.
  Henderson, R.
Old Spanish Mission.
  Stevenson, R. M. Texas Suite.
Old Timers.
  Hannon, B.
Old Witch.
  Anson, G.

Oldtime religion.
  Cobb, H., arr. Sweet 'Sabbath
Ole Ark's A-Moverin'.
  Condaris, A. J. arr.
Olimpiade.
  Vivaldi, A.
Olvido.
  Thébault, V. Vagabundo.
Ombra della Valle.
  Bettarini, L.
Ombres.
  Padilla, J.
On a Holy Night.
  Hollingsworth, C. B.
On a Little Two-seat Tandem.
  Myrow, J. Mother Wore Tights.
On a Lovely Summer Evening.
  Elliott, M.
On a Nankin Plate.
  McKay, G. F.
On a Sunday by the Sea.
  Styne, J. High Button Shoes.
On A Vole une Étoile.
  Ulmer, G.
On a Winter's Night.
  Cronham, C. R.
On Again, Off Again, Gone Again.
  Arthur, W.
On Biscayne Bay, Down Miami Way.
  Bayha, C. A.
On Christmas Day.
  Krone, B. P.
On Gibbon's Angel's Song.
  Steele, D.
On Green Dolphin Street.
  Kaper, B. Green Dolphin Street.
On Ilkla Moor Baht' At.
  Richardson, C.
On My Pinto Pony.
  Allen, R. K.
On Ne Sait Pas Qui On Est.
  Emer, M.
On, On, Old Glory.
  Ahlstrand, D.
On parade.
  Skornicka, J. E. Instrumentalist.
On Se Plait.
  Peyronnin, J.
On Silver Wings to San Antone.
  Walker, C.
On the Avenue.
  Freed, F.
  Goldbaum, F.
On the Beaches of the Salt Lake Shore.
  Arthur, W.
On the Farm.
  Vanderburg, G. J.
On the Hills of Galilee.
  Nardi, N.
On the Old Spanish Trail.
  Kennedy, J.
On the Sea of Sleep.
  Fair, H.
On the Shores of Pearl Harbor
    Far Away.
  Wright, E.
On the Sunny Side of the Street.
  McHugh, J. F. International Revue.
On the Teeter.
  Allen, R. K.
On to Glory.
  Lemont, C. W.
Once.
  Bowman, H. H.
Once I Used to Love You Dearly.
  Balázs, A. Valamikor Szerettelek.
Once in a Lifetime.
  Peterson, C. F.
Once to Every Heart.
  King, A. C.
Once upon a Time.
  Steininger, F. Music in My Heart.
One Alone.
  Hall, D.
One Cloudy Night.
  De Marco, M.
One Day.
  Mills. K. M.
One Elect of Stars.
  Finney, T. M.

One Girl.
  Moore, R. E.
One Hour with Thee.
  Yon, S. C.
101 Ranch Boys.
  Howard, J. comp.
101 Unfigured Melodies & Basses for
    Harmonization.
  Foster, I. R.
121st Psalm.
  Milford, R.
One I Adore.
  Petrie, J.
One Kiss, Just This.
  Koch, C. M.
One Little Tear Is an Ocean.
  Dawes, E.
One Minute Musical Announcement.
  Dawes, E.
One More Goodbye.
  Beadle, W.
One More October.
  Arthur, W.
One O'clock Boogie.
  Basie, C.
One Sunny Day.
  Savard, H. J.
One Sweet Day.
  Carleton, R. L.
One Time, So Long Ago.
  Elliott, L. E.
One, Two, Three.
  Spoliansky, M.
One Word Is Too Often Profaned.
  Quilter, R.
Only a Dreamer.
  Arthur, W.
Only Believe.
  Elwell, H. B.
Only in Dreams.
  Shain, R. W.
Only the Thought of Her is left to me Now.
  Tobin, L.
Only with You.
  Williams, C.
Only You.
  Schlotfeldt, A.
Onward, Kermit High School.
  Copeland, H. H.
Open Mine Eyes.
  Bower, S.
Open Range A-callin'.
  Newman, M. A.
Open Sky Home.
  Anderson, J.
Open the Door.
  Clark, H. D.
Open the Door, Richard.
  McVea, J.
Open Your Eyes.
  Rayl, E. H.
Open Your Heart's Door.
  Williams, Mrs. H. The Great
    Physician of the Skies.
Orange Blossoms.
  Herbert, V.
Orchestra innamorata.
  Mobiglia, T. arr. Dieci Arrangiamenti
    per Complesso Hot.
Orchestra Pazsa.
  Mobiglia, T. arr. Dieci Arrangiamenti
    per Complesso Hot.
Orchestra Studies for Clarinet.
  Bonade, D. comp.
Orchids for Youdear Mother of mine.
  Peltier, A. J.
Orchids in the Moonlight.
  Youmans, V.
Oregon Melody.
  Atterbury, G. A.
Organ Album.
  Larson, E. R., arr.
Organ Grinder.
  Rech, L.
Organ Grinder Man.
  Richter, A.
Organ Toccata & Fugue in D minor.
  Bach, J. S. Toccata & Fugue, organ.

Organ Toccata in F.
  Bach, J. S. Toccata, organ.
Organito.
  Quaratino, P.
Organum.
  Ives, C. E. 22.
Organum ad Asperges Me et Vidi Aquam.
  See title entry in composer list.
Oriana's Romance.
  Hyden, W. Caravan.
Original Compositions.
  Samuelian, H. S.
Otan Se Blepo.
  Morakes, D. N.
Other Christmas Voices.
  Durham, G. H.
Other Side of the Hill.
  Schuman, W.
Où va la jeune Indoue.
  Delibes, L. Lakme.
Ouija.
  Finch, H. E.
Our Baby.
  Arnold, T.
Our Church Bells.
  Hartmaier, F. B.
Our Colorado.
  Lewis, E. B.
Our Dream Chalet in the Hills.
  Thiel, O. En Prästkrage i Min Hand.
Our Dreams.
  Bartlett, F.
Our Faithful Friend.
  Richardson, A. E.
Our Father Which in Heaven.art.
  Heys, J. A.
Our golden lady. See title entry in
    composer list.
Our Homeland.
  Cate, H. W.
Our Hour.
  Livingston, J.
Our Ivory Tower.
  Clyde, T.
Our Living Lord.
  Ackley, B. D.
Our Martha in Blossom Time.
  Laverty, L. S.
Our Remember Melody.
  Hall, D.
Our U.S. Army Boys.
  Crane, J.
Our Waltz.
  Rose, D. The Oustanding Compositions
    of David Rose.
Our Worship, Lo.
  Bornschein, F.
Out in Pioneertown.
  Spencer, T.
Out in the Rain Again.
  Carson, J. L.
Out of the Blue.
  Jason, W.
Out of the Depths.
  Todd, M. F.
Out of the Desert.
  Chajes, J. T. Song of the Camel
    Driver.
Out of the Mist.
  Hall, D.
Out on the Chisholm Trail.
  Brannan, W. L.
Out to Win.
  Ackley, B. D. Our Living Lord.
Outside Lookin' In.
  McKissick, E.
Outstanding Compositions of David Rose.
  Rose, D.
Ovacion.
  Travnicek, A. Barbara la Créole.
Over and Over Again.
  Jenkins, M. H. Inspired Hymns of
    the Hour.
Over Bethlehem's Town.
  Marryott, R. E.
Over the Snow.
  Keck, P.
Overnight I Made a Hit with My Baby.
  Perry. C.

414

Overture Miniature.
  Chaikovskiĭ, P. I.
Overture to a Pantomime.
  Hutchinson, V. H.
  Händel, G. F. Alcina.
Overture to Les Femmes Vengées.
  Philidor, F. A. D. Les Femmes
  Vengées.
Overture to The Messiah.
  Händel, G. F. The Messiah.
Owl Song.
  Tappin, H.
Oxford Liturgical Settings of the Holy
  Communion.
  Arnold, J. H.
Oye! Destápa la Botella.
  Casamor, E.

P

Pă Myrgårds Loge.
  Westling, E.
Pacific 1860.
  Coward, N.
Padre Nosso.
  Martins, M. H. R.
Paean.
  Filkins, G. C.
Paean of Remembrance.
  Oldroyd, G.
Paganini Suite.
  Grant-Schaefer, G. A.
Pakad Adonai.
  Zaira, M. To Zion's Shore.
Pal in Palo Alto.
  Miller, B.
Pal of My Heart.
  Tough, S.
Palestine Brigade.
  Jospe, E.
Palm Springs Californiay.
  Larson, W. V.
Palms.
  Faure, J. B.
Paloma.
  Yradier, S.
Palomino, Pal of Mine.
  Dugat, I. W.
Palomma 'E 'Stu Core.
  Mazzucchi, A.
Palomma Mia.
  Ruocco, R.
Pals of Long Ago.
  Kiecker, L.
Pam.
  Bauer, B.
Pamela Mary's Piano Album.
  Graves, R.
Pan, the Piper.
  Kleinsinger, G.
Paname.
  Maye, P.
Panis Angelicus.
  Briggs, E. F.
  Linger, A. M.
Pão de Assucar.
  Flory, S. Carioca Album of
  Brazilian Songs.
Papa Won't You Dance with Me.
  Styne, J. High Button Shoes.
Para Elvirita.
  Miramontes, R. A. Momento Musical,
  no. 1.
Para Que Volyer.
  Sánchez Vázquez, P.
Parade March.
  Wright, N. L.
Parade of the Wooden Soldiers.
  Jessel, L.
Parade of the Wooden Toys.
  Travis, B.
Paradise.
  Marchman, H.
Paradise Waltz.
  Baumgartner, M.
Parágon March.
  Galla-Rini, A.
Paraphrase on Mozart's Theme.
  Sors, F.

Pardon Me, Santa.
  Wilson, I. B.
Paris.
  Ferré, L.
Parish Organ Book.
  Kreckel, P. G.
Parlor of the Valley.
  Storm, J.
Partisan.
  Kartzev, A.
Partita.
  Reizenstein, F.
Pas des Echarpes.
  Chaminade, C.
Pas du Hareng.
  Bourtayre, H.
Pasquinade.
  Gottschalk, L. M.
Pass that Peace Pipe.
  Blane, R. Good News.
Passacaille.
  Laks, S.
Passepied.
  Delibes, L. Le Roi S'Amuse.
Passing By.
  Hess, J.
Passing Fancy.
  Mann, D.
Passion.
  Murena, A. T.
Past Three o'Clock.
  Shimmin, S.
Pastime à Good Company.
  Dunhill, T. F.
Pastoral.
  Guion, D. W.
Pastorale.
  Metcalf, L. V.
Pastorale and Burlesque.
  Seiber, M.
Pastorale for organ.
  Still, W. G.
Pastores.
  Miramontes, A.
Pastourelle à Nina.
  Bourtayre, H.
Path of the Just.
  Hulin, D. N.
Patty.
  Pour, F.
Patty McGee.
  Browne, L. B.
Paul and Ann Roberts Favorite Cowboy
  and Hillbilly Songs.
  Roberts, P.
Paul et Virginie.
  Poulenc, F.
Pauvre Laboureur.
  Quilter, R. The Man Behind the
  Plough.
Pavanne.
  Gould, M. American Symphonette
  no. 2.
Pavlova.
  Hyden, N. comp.
Pawnee Trail.
  Osage, T.
Peace.
  Barnes, E. S.
  Bornschein, F. C.
Peace and Freedom.
  Carleton, R. L.
Peace, Be Still.
  Tovey, H. G.
Peace Be to Earth.
  Cordouan, G.
Peace of Mind.
  Murray, C.
  Savino, D.
Peace, Perfect Peace.
  Pedrette, E. A.
Peanut Vendor.
  Simon Rodriguez, M.
Pearl.
  Mitchell, B. M.
Pearls.
  Bawcomb, J.
Peasant Dance.
  Hirschberg, D.

Pedro.
  Ravazza, C.
Peer Gynt.
  Grieg, E. H.
Peer Gynt Suite.
  Grieg, E. H.
Pel di Carota.
  Mobiglia, T. Dieci Arrangiamenti
  per complesso Hot.
  Hampton, L.
Penelope.
  Cimarosa, D.
Penguin at the Waldorf.
  Shuman, F.
Pennsylvania Moon
  Arthur, W.
Pennsylvania Roof Garden.
  Clark, L. A.
Pensamiento Mio.
  Torriente Pilderot, E.
Pensée Élegiaque.
  Anik, H. E.
Pentecostal Praises.
  Goss, H. A., comp.
Pepe Carmona.
  Padilla, J.
Pepita.
  Lomuto, V.
Pequeña Marcha.
  Castro, J. M.
Per Te Bambina.
  Mobiglia, T. Dieci Arrangiamenti
  per Complesso Hot.
Per una Furtiva Lagrima.
  Oldrati Rossi, R. Buongiorno,
  Amore Mio.
Per Voi, Signora.
  Ambrosio, A. d.
Perchance To Dream.
  Novello, I.
Perche Mi Sfuggi.
  Taccani, S. Eterna Canzone.
Perhaps Today or Tomorrow.
  Rüsthoi, E. K. Gospel Songs.
Perles de Cristal.
  Hamel, G. L. F.
Permelia.
  Perkins, M.
Perpetual Motion.
  Diamond, D. L. 2 Pieces.
  Paganini, N.
Pesarosa.
  Gilardi, G.
Peter and the Wolf.
  Prokof'ev, S. S.
Peter Grimes.
  Britten, B.
Peter Pan.
  Brydson, J.
Petit Bal du Sam'di Soir.
  Delettre, J.
Petit Bout de Femme.
  Ulmer, G.
Petit Cours de Morale.
  Honegger, A.
Petit Homme.
  Monnot, M.
Petit Horloger.
  Heller, F.
Petit Noël.
  LaFarge, J.
Petit Paganini.
  Velde, E. van de.
Petit Papa Noël.
  Martinet, H. A. L. Destins.
Petite Boutique.
  Hodeige, O. J.
Phedre Overture.
  Shackley, G. My Song Is Still
  Tonight.
Phil, the Fluter's Ball.
  French, P.
Phoenix.
  Bliss, A. March.
Piangono gli Occhi Miei.
  Recli, G.

415

Piano à Vendre.
  Lasry, A.
Piano concerto no. 1.
  Chaikovskii, P. I. Concerto, piano, no. 1.
Piano Hymn Voluntaries.
  Wilson, R. C., ed.
Piano Pieces Boys Like to Play.
  Foster, A. H., comp.
Piano Pieces Girls Like to play.
  Foster, A. H., comp.
Piano Play for Every Day.
  Loth, J. F.
Piano Polka.
  Pjura, W. J.
Piano Queen from Port of Spain.
  Graham, M. C.
Piano Selection.
  Russell, K. The Nightingale.
Piano Sonata no. 2.
  Kerr, H. Sonata, piano, no. 2.
Piano Works.
  Ives, C. E. 22.
Pianoforte Examinations.
  Guildhall School of Music and Drama, London.
  Toronto. Conservatory of Music.
Pianoforte Sight Playing Exercises.
  Lee, E. M.
Pianola.
  Torre, J.
Pianto del Bosco.
  Taccani, S.
Pic-a-nic-in in the park.
  Fort, E. H.
Piccadilly Panorama.
  Smart, H.
Piccadilly Polka.
  Merlin, A.
Piccola Serenata.
  Mortari, V.
Piccolo Pete.
  Nevin, M.
Pick a Peach in the Garden of Love.
  Arthur, W.
Pickaninny's Lullaby.
  Welker, J.
Pickin' Petals.
  Israel, M. L.
Pico and Sepulveda.
  Styne, J.
Picture Pointers for Piano Technic.
  Eckstein, M. ed. and arr.
Piece in Seven Movements.
  Schnabel, A.
Pieces Are Fun.
  Hirschberg, D., ed. & comp.
Piedigrotta. See title entry in composer list.
Piedigrotta Mario, 1947.
  Mario, E. A., comp.
Piedigrotta 1947. See title entry in composer list.
Piedigrotta 1947 de "La Canzonetta."
  See title entry in composer list.
Piedigrotta 1947-48.
  Consentino, M., comp.
Pieges.
  Révil.
Pieta d'Avignon.
  Rosenthal, M.
Piezas Infantiles.
  Fahissa, J.
Pig Latin Way.
  Jacoby, T.
Pigeon-toed Penguin.
  Fields, I.
Pillow Fight.
  Eckhardt, F. G.
Pim-Pum-Pa.
  Padilla, J.
Pin up the Corners of Your Mouth, My Sweet.
  McNeil, J. C.
Pinafore.
  Sullivan, Sir A. S. The Mikado.
Ping Pong.
  Strum, E.

Pingst.
  Lindberg, O.
Pioneer Trail.
  Wright, E. H.
Pioneers.
  Bampton, R.
Piosenka z Paryza.
  Wojowska-Wjodyda, L.
Pipeaux.
  Velde, E. van de.
Piping down the Valleys Wild.
  Rowley, A. Three Songs of Innocence.
Piscatore 'e Pusilleco.
  Tagliaferri, E. The Fisher of Pusilleco.
Pisnicka.f.
  Hassler, K.
Pitchin' a Little Woo.
  Hassel, M.
Pittston Polka.
  Castellani, L.
Pixie.
  Harrison, T.
Pizzicato Polka.
  Delibes, L. Sylvia.
  Strauss, J.
Place in My Heart for You.
  Van Buren, B.
Plant the Stars.
  Lutz, B. F.
Plant Ydym Eto Dan ein Hoed.
  Jones, G. J. Jesus, the Name I Love to Hear.
Play Fiddle Play.
  Deutsch, E.
Play Gypsies, Dance Gypsies.
  Kalman, E.
Play Me a Duet.
  Mopper, I.
Play Me a Mode.
  Mopper, I.
Play Songs for the Nursery School.
  Holgate, E. D.
Play Your Music, Gypsy.
  Weitzner, G. Gyere, Cigány.
Playera.
  Granados Y Campiña, E.
Playing Tag.
  Travis, B.
Please Be True.
  Wilburn, N.
Please Believe Me, Dear.
  Samuels, W.
Please Come Back.
  Mansfield, R.
Please Don't Pretend.
  Baker, E.
Please, Oh Please.
  Guthrie, J.
Please Say It's Not Good-bye.
  Chalfant, B. F.
Please Show Me the Way to the Cross.
  Chalfant, B. F.
Please Tell Me.
  Hall, D.
Il Pleurait.
  Révil, Pieges.
Plight of the Bumble Bee.
  Clark, C. V.
Ploughman.
  Rowley, A.
Ploum, Ploum, Ploum.
  Eblinger, J.
Pluies.
  Rousseau, P.
Plus Jamais, Oi Nuit sans Voiles.
  White, M. V.
Plus Jolies Mélodies.
  Marinier, P.
Plus Rien.
  Couët, J. D.
Po Gradini Mjesečina Sija Meka.
  Cernkovich, R. Sjecas Li Se Onog Sata.
Po Ka Pu, el Po Ka Pi-ya.
  Berry, E.
Pocadora.
  Lara, A.

Pochi Soldi.
  Giussani, G.
Pod Mojim Okancem.
  Cernkovich, R.
Poem.
  Khachaturian, A. I.
Poeme.
  Landowski, M.
  Poulenc, F. Le Pont.
Poemes de Guillaume Apollinaire.
  Caby, R. J. A.
Poet & Peasant.
  Suppé, F. v.
Polichinelle et Colombine.
  Pénau, R.
Polka.
  Shostakovich, D. D.
Polvo, Calden, Espintllo.
  Ficher, J.
Ponder My Words, O Lord.
  Harris, C.
Pont.
  Poulenc, F.
Poor Butterfly.
  Hubbell, R. The Big Show.
Poor Little Polliwog.
  Ross, B.
Pop Corn Sack.
  Walter, S. Rattle, Rattle, Rattle.
Poppies Are Blooming.
  Lemont, C. W.
Popping Corn.
  Anderson, W. H.
Popular Music Folio.
  Engel, L. K.
Popular Piano Playing.
  Spencer, B.
Popular Style Playing.
  Walters, H.
Por Eso Tengo Miedo.
  González Allue, J.
Por Qué Te Quieres Ir.
  Treviño, P.
Por Ti.
  Muñoz, R.
Porque.
  Miramontes, R. A.
Porque Te Quiero.
  Alarcón Leal, E.
Porque Tú Lo Quieres.
  Clavell, M. M.
Porte-Bonheur.
  Gasté, L. F.
Portrait.
  Diamond, D. L. 5 Songs.
  Larrieu, P.
Portrait of a Frontier Town.
  Gillis, D.
Pos Que Voy a Hacer.
  Parra, G.
Possum Trot in Tennessee.
  Young, B.
Postlude.
  Wiegand, J.
Postlude de Fête, Te Deum Laudamus.
  Saint-Martin, L. M. J. de © OEuvres d'Orgue de Léonce de Saint-Martin.
Pound Your Plantain in a Mortar.
  Grant, R.
Pour Vous, Madame.
  Dehette, M.
Pousse-Pousse.
  Scotto, V.
Powderhorn.
  Reed, R.
Power House Polka.
  Lash, S.
Practice Makes Perfect.
  Haywood, E.
Praeludium.
  Adler, S. H.
  Mendelssohn-Bartholdy, F.
Praeludium af Kai Rostgaard-Fröhnes Hórespil, Ave Maria.
  Gyldmark, H. G. S. Ave Maria.
Prästkrage i Min Hand.
  Thiel, O.
Prairie Du Chein.
  Beaver, W.
Prairie Flower.
  Thal, J.

Prairie Skies.
 Johnson, C. W.
Prairie Song.
 Simon, N.
Praise and Worship His Name.
 Jones, G. J.
Praise Him Forevermore.
 Clayton, N. J.
Praise the Lord of Heaven.
 Thiman, E. H.
Praise the Lord, Ye Heavens Adore
 Him.
 Malin, D. F., arr.
Praktisk Klaverskole.
 Selmer, M.
Pray About It.
 Plank, K. Y.
Prayer.
 Beethoven, L. van.
 Humperdinck, E.
 Malin, D.
Prayer for an American Sailor.
 Gaul, H. B.
Prayer for Peace.
 Matesky, R.
Prayer for the New Year.
 Wilson, F. C.
Prayer for Youth.
 Lupo, C. E.
 Purcell, E. Be Present at Our
  Table, Lord.
Prayer in Song.
 Loveday, C.
Prayer of St. Richard of Chichester.
 White, L. J.
Prayer of Thanksgiving.
 Kremser, E.
 Lewis, L. H.
 Scholin, C. A.
Prayer Response.
 Filkins, G. C.
Prayer to Saint Catherine of Sienna.
 Grubb, L. W.
Pre-classic Suite.
 Miller, F. D.
Preachin'.
 Cooper, E.
Preele.
 White, C. T.
Preliminary School for the Pianoforte.
 Beyer, F.
Prelude.
 Busch, W. Suite.
 Rachmaninoff, S. Prelude, piano,
  no. 5.
Prelude and Fugue in F minor.
 Händel, G. F. Suite, harpsichord,
  no. 8.
Prelude for Pentecost.
 Gaul, H. B.
Prelude, forlane et gigue.
 Arrieu, C.
Prelude, Fugue and Variation.
 Franck, C. A.
Prelude-offertoire pour messe
 basse.
 Bedell, R. L.
Prelude on a Benedictine Plainsong,
 Adoro Devote.
 Edmundson, G.
Prelude, Theme et Variations.
 Mirouze, M.
Prelude to a Dream.
 Richardson, C.
Prelude to Dark of the Moon.
 Hendl, W. Dark of the Moon.
Prelude to Traviata.
 Verdi, G. La Traviata.
Préludes Miniatures.
 Haskins, V. C.
Preludio.
 Chopin, F. F.
Preludio al Vespro di Monteverdi.
 Tippett, M. K.
Preludio e Fuga.
 Cortese, L.
Preludio et Fuga for Organ.
 Bossi, M. E.
Preludio, num. 1.

Miramontes, A.
Preludio, núm. 2.
 Miramontes, A.
Preludio núm. 3 en la menor.
 Miramontes, A.
Preludio y Doble Fuga.
 Hoyo, F. del.
Preludio y Fuga.
 Esposito, A. d'.
Premier Concerto.
 Quiroga, M. Concerto, violin, no. 1.
Prends en Un, Prends en Deux.
 Lopez, F. Les Trois Cousines.
Prepare Your Soul.
 Lemons, S. H.
Preparing for the Music of Bach
 and Mozart.
 Herford, J. G., ed.
President Jemison Special Song Book
 no. 2.
 Frye, (T. R.) Publishers, ed.
Presto in C major.
 Haydn, J. Quartet, strings.
Pretending.
 Arthur, W.
Pretense.
 Clokev, I. W.
Pretty Kitty Kelly.
 Nelson, E. G.
Pretty Mama Boogie.
 Halle, F. J.
Pretty Mary, that sure is a pretty dress
 you're a-wearin'.
 Haldeman, O.
Pretty Month of May.
 Quilter, R.
Pretty Rainbow.
 Hopkins, H. P.
Prevent Us O Lord.
 Weatherseed, J. J.
Previn's Boogie.
 Previn, A.
Prière d'Amour.
 Cases, M.
Primary and Junior Songs.
 Meredith, I. H., ed.
Primavera.
 Vivaldi, A. Concerti delle
  Stagioni.
Primer Amor.
 Burli, A.
Prince of Peace.
 Horst, A. G.
Princess.
 Gomez, V.
Princess Elisabeth of England.
 Wood, H.
Processionals and Postludes for Organ
 Solo.
 Ashmall, W. E., arr.
Professor Owl.
 House, L. M.
Proper of the Service.
 Christensen, A. O.
Proper of the Time.
 Bragers, A. P. arr. Proprium de
  Tempore.
Prophetic Song.
 Pond, C. A. Beautiful City of Gold.
Proposito.
 Guastavino, C.
Propre du Temps.
 Bragers, A. P., arr, Proprium de
  Tempore.
Proprium de Tempore.
 Bragers, A. P., arr.
Psalm of Thanksgiving.
 Greaves, R.
Psalm 100.
 Evans, G.
Psalm 101.
 Whitefield, B.
Psalm 147.
 Wakeman, F. M.
Psalm 148.
 Wakeman, F. M. Psalm 147.

Psalm 149.
 Wakeman, F. M. Psalm 147.
P'tit Louis.
 Lopez, F.
Ptolemy.
 Händel, G. F.
Pueblito, Mi Pueblo.
 Guastavino, C.
Puerta del Sol.
 Zmigrod, A. Meisje, Doe Me een
  Lol.
Pull You Down a Moonbeam.
 Halbardier, B. H.
Punchinello.
 Vandercook, H. A.
Punkin' Stomp.
 Wills, B.
Purgatory.
 Carson, J. L. Songs.
Purple Asters.
 Baines, W.
Purple Mountains of Colorado.
 Sandler, S.
Purple Twilight.
 McAllister, L.
Put a Rosebud on Her Lips.
 Roberts, M.
Put Me off at Baltimore.
 Hammann, F. B.
Put Your Arm Around the Sinner.
 Jenkins, M. H. Inspired Hymns of
  the Hour.
Put Yourself in a Frame for Love.
 Conn, F. V.
Put Yourself in My Place, Baby.
 Laine, F.
Putting Peas in Podzies.
 Kenneth, G.
Puzzle.
 Gilbert, R.

Q

Quand On A, Comme Vous.
 Bourtayre, H.
Quand Reviendra le Jour.
 Schubert, F. P. Destins.
Quand un Vicomte.
 Hartusch, M.
Quando Tu Vorrai.
 Lupo, P. Lacrime.
Quante Stelle.
 Mobiglia, T. Dieci Arrangiamenti per
  Complesso Hot.
Quartet for strings.
 Rainier, P. Quartet, strings.
Quartet in F, for Flute or oboe,
 clarinet, horn and bassoon.
 Rossini, G. A. Quartet, winds.
Quartet no. 2.
 Prokof'ev, S. S. Quartet, strings,
  no. 2.
Quartet, strings.
 Dumler, M. G.
 Haydn, J.
Quatorze Choeurs.
 Weisshaus, I.
Quatre Chansons.
 Honegger, A.
Quatre Lieder.
 Lesur, D. J. Y. Lieder, voice,
  flute, strings & harp.
Quatre Petites Pièces-Radio.
 Wiener, J. A. H.
Que Aparezca la Piña.
 Garnica Caballero, R.
Qué Gusto Da.
 Esperon, M. Soy Charro de Rancho
  Grande.
Que Importa Mi Sufrir.
 Yamin, J.
Que Se Vaya.
 Chappotin, F.
Quedo.
 Romberg, S. The New Moon.
Queen of San Joaquin.
 Mayo, O. W.
Queen of the Holy Rosary.
 Yon, S. C.

Riding on the Prairie.
    Alkire, E. H.
Riding the Rainbow.
    Chanslor, H.
Riff Song.
    Romberg, S. The Desert Song.
Rigaudon.
    Händel, G. F. Almira.
Right Wheel, Left Wheel.
    Furney, A. J.
Rilloby-Rill.
    Mitchell, C. J.
Rimani.
    Giuliani, V. Ti Portero.
Rincón Mágico.
    Turina, J.
Ring New, Ring New, Ring Wide.
    Barthelson, J.
Ring Out, Christmas Bells.
    Dunford, J. W.
Rio de Janeiro.
    Flory, S. Carioca Album of
        Brazilian Songs.
Rise Up Early.
    Kountz, R.
Rita.
    Maltin, B.
Ritmo Tentatore.
    Taccani, S. Il Pianto del Bosco.
Ritorna.
    Ralfo, C. Notturno.
Ritournelle de Nos Amours.
    Pichon, F.
Riverboat Shuffle.
    Parish, M.
Road End.
    Woodgate, L.
Road I Have Chosen.
    Cadman, C. W.
Road to Piano Artistry.
    Scionti, S. ed.
Road to Rio.
    Van Heusen, J.
Road to Your Heart.
    Bartlett, F.
Robe.
    Petit, P. Y. M. C. Mélodies.
Robe de Soie.
    Agosti, G. Due Liriche.
Roberta.
    Kern, J.
Robin and the Woodpecker.
    McKay, G. F.
Rock My Cradle once again.
    Bond, J.
Rock of Ages.
    Yoder, P. Symphonic Series of
        Sacred Songs.
Rock-a-bye.
    Price, F. B. Criss Cross.
Rocky Mountain Melody.
    Buck, R.
Rocky Mountain Rhythm.
    Pattison, P.
Rodeo Time in Sheridan, Wyo.
    Tynan, T. T.
Rogue River Valley.
    Beckwith, L. L.
Roi S'Amuse.

Delibes, L.
Rokoko.
    Fernström, J. Sex Sanger.
Rolige Bror.
    Fernström, J. Sex Sanger.
Roll Does Eyes Around' Honey.
    Allaire, B. L.
Roll Jordan Roll.
    Gillum, R. H.
    Lawrence, W.
    Reisfeld, B., arr.
Roller Coaster.
    Hofstad, M.
Rollin' Along.
    Kotel, M.
Rolling down Bowling Green on a Little
    Two-seat Tandem.
    Myrow, J. Mother Wore Tights.
Rolling Waves.
    Chanslor, H.
Roman Breton.
    Lantier, P.
Romance.
    Sibelius, J.
Romance d'Autrefois.
    Rubinstein, A.
Romance in the Rain.
    Nurnberg, V.
Romance Lointaine.
    Chopin, F. F. Nocturne, piano.
Romance of Chief Tecumseh.
    Richardson, D. E.
Romance Provencale et Danse.
    Casadesus, F.
Romances and Songs.
    Samuellan, H. S. Original
        Compositions.
Romanesque.
    Mayerl, B.
Romans.
    Pergament, M.
    Rangström, T.
Romantic Interlude.
    Richardson, C.
Romantic Rhapsody.
    Johnson, C. W.
Romanza.
    Botti, C. Composizioni per tromba
        e pianoforte.
    Golz, W.
Romanza Andaluza.
    Sarasate Y Navascues, P. M. M. de.
        Spanish Dance.
Rome, l'Unique Objet.
    Petit, P. Y. M.
Romeo and Juliet.
    Chaikovskii, P. I.
Ronda.
    Castro, W. Cuatro Piezas sobre
        Temas Infantiles.
Rondinello.
    Cripps, H.
Rondo.
    Richardson, A. Rondo, piano.
Rondo in E flat.
    Steibelt, D.
Rondo Lirico.
    Pitfield, T. B.
Roni, li

Stutchewsky, J.
oom for Two.
    Batistich, J.
tooster's Serenade.
    Light, F. M.
Rosamunde Air.
    Schubert, F. P.
Rosangela.
    Borgazzi, F.
Rosanna.
    Rafaelli, M.
Rose Breaks into Blossom.
    Brahms, J. Es Ist ein' Ros'
        Entsprungen.
Rose for You.
    Lockett, F. E.
Rose Time.
    Coglan, A. V.
Rosenkavalier.
    Strauss, R.
Roses from the South.
    Stoye, P. Waltz Rhapsody.
Roses I Remember.
    Hall, D.
Roses Remind Me.
    Vairin, L. Songs for voice and piano.
Rosetera Cubana.
    Taccani, S. Incanto Brasiliano.
Rossignolet du Bois.
    Delfau, R. arr.
Roulade.
    Whitney, M. C.
'Round, an' 'Round, an' 'Round.
    Green, J. Something in the Wind.
Round Dance.
    Schubert, F. P.
Roundelay.
    Nichols, J. H.
Roundup Polka.
    Merrill, R.
Rubank Advanced Method for French
    Horn.
    Gower, W.
Rubank Intermediate Method for
    Bassoon.
    Voxman, H.
Rumba d'Amour.
    Ledrut, J. C.
Rumba de Amores.
    Ferreté, L. M.
Rumba Rhapsody.
    Audinot, R.
Rumba Royal.
    De Torre, L.
Rumba Rumbero.
    Valdes, M.
Rumbolero.
    Gould, M.
Runaway Showman.
    Pitfield, T. B.
Running Arpeggios.
    Gould, M.
Russian Picnic.
    Enders, H.
Rustic Maid.
    Tobin, L.
Rythme de Paris.
    Coquatrix, B.

- S -

Så Låt Oss Öppna Snart.
  Olson, D.
SAE sweetheart.
  Woolson, R. C.
Sabre Dance.
  Khachaturian, A. I. Three Dances.
Sacred Hill.
  Sevier, M. M.
Sacred Transcriptions.
  Auld, W. J.
Sad and Blue.
  Kent, B.
  Mawhinney, E. A.
Saddle in the Sky.
  Green, S.
Saddle My Horse.
  Lamkoff, P.
Sadness.
  Tenebria, J. B.
Sadness in the Rain.
  Ponzetti, P.
Safe Now Forever in Him.
  Jackson, L. M.
Safranski.
  Rugolo, P.
Saga.
  Lidholm, I. Fem Sånger.
Sailors' Dance.
  Harris, C.
Sailor's Dream.
  McNeil, J. C.
Saint Christopher.
  Russell, K.
St. Christopher's-by-the-River.
  Wormal, N. E.
Saint Francis.
  Weigl, V.
Saint Govan.
  Roberts, M.
Saint Louis Blues.
  Smith, J. W. C. Handy's Saint Louis
    Blues.
Saint Paul "Min" and Kansas City "Moe"
  Leonard, D.
Sally and Dinny Duet.
  Grandjany, M. Two Duets.
Sally's Gone to Sante Fe.
  Blanchard, D.
Salon Mexico.
  Copland, A. (Fiesta) Fantasia Mexi-
    cana.
Salut à la Vierge.
  Saint-Martin, L. M. J. de. OEuvres
    d'Orgue de Léonce de Saint-Martin.
Salutation.
  Tardif, H. M., father. Triptique
    Marial.
Salute d'Amour.
  Elgar, Sir E. W.
Salute to Brazil.
  Flory, S. Carioca Album of Brazilian
    Songs.
Salvation Army Brass Journal. (2nd ser.)
  See title entry in composer index.
Salve Regina.
  Lotti, A.
Samaritan Songs.
  Saracinj, J. A.
Samba Exótica.
  Savino, D.
Samba Sud.
  Torch, S.
Sambe-Samba.
  Hansen, Bill.
Sambo's Banjo.
  Todd, E. C.
Same, Same Old Story.
  Arthur, W.
Sammy's Bowery Follies.
  Frey, H., comp. & arr.
San Clemente Moon.
  Arthur, W.
San Francisco by the Golden Gate.
  Hartman, S.

San Francisco we're sorry we're saying
  So long.
  Stolz, R.
  Whittington, V.
San Francisco, You're the Town for Me.
  Lancaster, R.
San Gabriel Valley.
  Wheeler, C. E.
San Ignacio de Loyola.
  Mendoza y Cortes, Q. F.
Sanctus.
  Gounod, C. F.
  Liemohn, E. Holy, Holy, Holy.
Sand in Your Shoes.
  Stedman, J. H.
Sandstorm.
  Pond, D.
Sans Day Carol.
  Cockshott, G.
Santa Catalina, island of romance.
  Spina, H.
Santa Claus for President.
  Tinturin, P.
Santa Fe Blues.
  Lester, F.
Santa Fe Tipica Orchestra Folio.
  Mares, P., arr.
Santa Lucia.
  Ballatore, P., arr.
  Passani, E. B.
Santa Lucia Lontana.
  Mario. E. A. Santa Lucia, Far Away.
Santa's on His Way.
  Moore, T. W.
Santo Dominican Way.
  Eden, A.
Sarabande.
  Bach, J. S.
  Brown, R.
  Mattheson, J.
Satisfied.
  Keller, A.
  Riggs, J.
Saturday Date.
  Brooks, J.
Saudação do Brazil.
  Flory, S. Carioca Album of Brazilian
    Songs.
Savannah.
  Barthelson, J.
Save It for Me.
  Greer, J. B.
Save Me, O God.
  Charles, E.
Save Me, O God, for Thy Name's Sake.
  Purcell, H.
Save the Bones for Henry Jones 'cause
  he don't eat no meat.
  Barker, D.
Save the Pieces for Me.
  Spencer, T.
Savior Soon Is Coming Back to Earth.
  Ajaye, H. A.
Saviour, like a Shepherd Lead Us.
  Ortlip, M.
Saxophone Velocity.
  Gornston, D.
Say a Prayer for Jim.
  Wirges, W. F.
Say It with a Flower.
  Hawthorne, M.
Say It with a slap.
  Disney (W.) productions, Ltd.
    Fun and Fancy Free.
Say Something Nice about Me.
  Stept, S. H.
Say You'll Be Mine.
  Rudy, R. L.
Scale-Time Band Book.
  Buchtel, F. L.
Scarecrows in the Night.
  Scher, W.
Scarf Dance.
  Chaminade, C. Pas des Echarpes.
Scena.
  Phillips, B.

Schade drum.
  Stolz, R.
Schade, Gestern Warst Du Süss wie Schoko-
  lade.
  Keller, R.
Schafe Können Sicher Weiden.
  Bach, J. S. (Was Mir Behagt) Sheep May
    Safely Graze.
Scheherezade.
  Rimskii-Korsakov, N. A.
Scherzo.
  Botti, C. Composizioni per tromba e
    pianoforte.
  Duruflé, M. G.
  Holst, G.
  Paz, H.
  Simon, L. M.
Scherzo ed Epigramma.
  Agosti, G.
Schicksal mit Musik.
  Stolz, R.
Schön Rosmarin.
  Kreisler, F.
School Days.
  Arthur, W.
School Pledge.
  Grill, K. R. N.
Schubert Simplified.
  Schubert, F. P.
Schumann-Schaum for piano.
  Schumann, R. A.
Schumann's Songs of Love.
  Schumann, R. A.
Schweizer Bub'.
  Leverton, B. The Swiss Boy.
Sciofàr.
  Rigacci, B.
Score Reading.
  Bernstein, M., ed.
Scotch Plaid.
  Scarmolin, A. L.
Scottish Emblem.
  Ellis, A. A.
Scottish Reel.
  Salter, L.
Scout Patrol.
  Tonner, P.
Scranton Polka.
  Castellani, L.
Se Amassi.
  Bellini, G. B. If you Loved.
Se Lo Voy a Decir.
  Santa Cruz, C.
Se Op og Smil-Vaer Optimist.
  Andersen, K. N. Dagmar Revyen, 1947.
Sé Que Te Veré.
  Coward, N. (Bitter Sweet) I'll See You
    Again.
Sea at Dusk.
  Douty, N.
Sea Idyl.
  Hayes, O. L.
Searching for a Soldier's Grave.
  Acuff, R.
Searching for Love.
  Brewster, T.
Sebago Syncopation.
  Miller, F. D.
Second Bach Book.
  Bach, J. S.
2nd Movement from Concerto for horn
  & orchestra.
  Arnold, M. Concerto, horn.
Second Organ Sonata.
  Mendelssohn-Bartholdy, F. Sonata,
    organ, no. 2.
Seconda Sinfonia Concertante.
  Viotti, G. B.
Secondo Concerto in si minore.
  Paganini, N. Concerto, violin, no. 2.
Secret to Reveal.
  Musale, E.
Secretary Song.
  Barnett, J.
See If I Care.
  Fidanzini, V.
See, the Conqu'ring Hero Comes.
  Händel, G. F. Judas Maccabeus.

Seek Ye the Lord.
Kies, R. G.
Seeking for that City.
Miller, K. M.
Seen in Paris.
Bennett, R. R. Vu.
Seguidille.
Falla, M. de.
Sei Sonate.
Schers. Sonatas, flute & bass.
Seis Canciones.
Pahissa, J.
Seis Canciones Populares Españolas.
Pahissa, J.
Seis Movimientos Corales a la Manera
Popular Argentina para coros mixtos
a "capella.
Valenti, Costa, P.
Sekstet, for piano, flauto, oboe, clarinetto in
A, corno in F og fagotto.
Koppel, H. D. Sextet, piano & winds.
Selected Dances.
Chaikovskii, P. I.
Selected Duets.
Voxman, H., ed.
Selected Second Grade Studies.
Lawton, D., comp.
Selection of Jerome Kern Songs.
Kern, J.
Selfish Me.
Hall, D.
Selig, Wer an Jesum Denkt.
Bach, J. S.
Semper Fidelis.
Sousa, J. P.
Send Down Thy Truth.
Cronham, C. R.
Send Forth the Gospel.
Bostwick, F. J.
Sentimental.
Bartlett, F.
Sentimental Bee.
Mitchell, J. B.
Sentimental Blues.
Wilkins, C.
Sentimental Gaucho.
Villoldo, A. G.
Sentimental Me.
Miller, J.
Sentimental Souvenirs.
George, D.
Sentry.
Roberts, M.
Sept Jours au Paradis.
Lucchesi, R.
Sept Vocalises.
Planel, J.
Séraphin des Soirs.
Mulot, A. M. Soirs.
Serenad för Stråkorkester.
Henneberg, A. Serenade, string orchestra.
Serenade.
Romberg, S.
Sérénade à Angélique.
Honegger, A.
Sérénade à Ma Belle.
Grant, J. Visions Iberiques.
Sérénade aux Nuages.
Lucchesi, R.
Serenade in Rhythm.
Battle, E.
Serenade of the Bells.
Urbano, A.
Serenade, string orchestra.
Chaikovskii, P. I.
Serenade to a Beautiful Day.
Gibson, H. M.
Serenade to Eileen.
Sears, E.
Serenade to Naples.
Tagliaferri, E.
Serenata.
Corelli, A.
Miramontes, A. (Anáhuac) Respiro.
Serenata Andaluza.
Falla, M. de.
Serenata Serena.
Falcocchio, E.

Serenate.
Mortari, V.
Serenity.
Lyon, J.
Seriously Speaking.
Pontarollo, M. F.
Service Music.
Noble, T. T., ed. & arr.
Service Musician.
Ziegler, E.
Set Me Aside.
Tobin, L.
Set of Five.
Fuleihan, A.
Seven Descant Carols.
Milford, R.
Seven Joys of Mary.
Warren, B.
Seven Transcriptions for organ.
Corelli, A.
17 Easy Pieces for piano.
Scarlatti, D. Siebzehn Leichte Stücke.
Severn Serenade.
Brunner, V. G.
Sevilliana.
Williams, J.
Sex Sanger.
Fernström, J.
Sextet in A major.
McKay, F. H.
Sextet, strings.
Moser, F.
Sha. Shtill.
Coopersmith, S.
Shadows.
Oliver, C.
Shadows of The Past.
Alvarez Rios, M.
Shadows on My Window.
Sturgill, C. L.
Shall We Still Remember Yet.
Crane, J.
Shanty in Ypsilanti.
Ilda, L.
Shanty Polka.
Yankovic, F. J.
Shattered Dreams.
Arthur, W.
She Is the One for Me.
Hutchison, C. B.
She Said She Loved Me.
Johnson, J.
She Walks in Beauty.
Jonas, A. H.
Sheep May Safely Graze.
Bach, J. S. Was Mir Behagt.
Shepherd Sleeps.
Stevens, E.
Shepherd Song.
Sibelius, J.
Shepherdess.
Salter, L.
Shepherds and the Heavenly Host.
Cronham, C. R. Nativity Scenes.
Shepherd's Christmas.
Carrington, O. M.
Shepherds Had an Angel.
Lapo, C. E.
Sheridan, Wyoming, U. S. A.
Schunk, P. M.
Sheriff Tom Owen's Cowboys.
Hull, R. E., comp.
She's a Rose in Old Virginia.
Arthur, W.
She's Changed.
Kabell, L.
She's Got the Cutest Eyes.
Campbell, C.
She's Like Pink Roses.
Bartlett, F.
She's My Girl Friend.
Parcell, F.
She's out of This World.
DeLoach, A. L.
Shindig.
Russell, V. A.

Shine on, Harvest Moon.
Norworth, J.
Shine on, oh Star.
Rubinstein, A.
Shining Jewels.
Mills, G. W.
Ship Ahoy.
Bentley, B. B. Two Piano Solos.
Ship of Eternal Life.
Wilson, E. K.
Shir Brigadah.
Jospe, E. Palestine Brigade.
Shirei Zimroh.
Wohlberg, M.
Shootin' Just in Fun.
Gage, H. A.
Shopping Tour.
Phillips, D.
Shores of Waikiki.
Lane, V.
Short-changed in Love.
Acuff, R.
Short Classics for Band.
Gillette, J. R., arr.
Short Pieces for the Organ.
Bach, J. S.
Short'nin Bread.
Condaris, A. J., arr.
Show boat.
Kern, J.
Show Me My Task.
Wooler, H.
Show Me the Way to Go Home.
Bates, A. E. Through the Eyes of Jesus.
Shpiel Klesmer Spiel.
Ellstein, A. Bulgar Song.
Shtarker Fun Liebe.
Ellstein, A. Just My Luck.
Shufflin' Jive.
Owers, J. A.
Shut Up and Drink Your Beer.
Newman, B.
Si e No.
Vitone, C.
Si J'Avais la Chance.
Gasté, L.
Si Pudiera.
Rojo, G.
Si Pudiera Decirte.
Munoz, R.
Si ti lascio, mio ben.
Mortari, V. Lamenti.
Si Tu Voulais.
Betti, H. Mam'zelle Printemps.
Si Volviera á Querer.
Núñez M, Antonio.
Sicilienne in the old style.
Achron, J.
Sieben Geistliche Lieder.
Castelberg, M. v.
Siebzehn Leichte Stücke.
Scarlatti, D.
Siena Victory March.
Beane, R. A.
Siento Que to Quiero.
Mendiolea, R.
Sight of Happiness.
Bartlett, F.
Sight-Reading Made Easy.
Bradley, D.
Silence Est d'Or.
Parys, G. van.
Silent Night.
Alkire, E. H.
Gruber, F.
Silent Night, Holy Night.
Gruber, F. X.
Silhouette.
Tonner, P.
Silly Little Quarrels.
Hartman, S.
Silly You.
Richards, M.
Silver and Gold.
Pressley, D.
Silver Fawn.
Tonner, P.

Silver Horn.
  Cooper, E.
Silver Lake.
  Elsnic, J. P., arr.
Silver Ring.
  Chaminade, C.
Silver Shadows.
  Aulbach, F. E.
Silver Slippers.
  Steadman, A.
Silver Threads Among the Gold.
  Danks, H. P.
Simbad le Marin.
  Melone, M. H.
Simon the Fisherman.
  Jessye, E. S.
Simple Histoire.
  Bourtayre, H.
Simple Three-Part Evening Canticles.
  Arnold, J. H.
Simplex Fingering Slide Rule.
  Brand, A. L.
Sin Protestar.
  Rivera, H.
Since First i Saw Your Face.
  Ford, T.
Since I Gave My Heart to the Lord.
  Taylor, R. W.
Since I Stopped and Listened to Jesus.
  Huston, F. C. Three New Songs.
Since the Smoke Has Cleared Away.
  Robison, W. R.
Since the Time I Saw My Darling.
  Balázs, Á. Össze Tudnék Csokolgatni.
Since Them Hillbillies Moved Down
    to the Holler.
  Waverly, J.
Since You've Gone.
  Gregory, V.
Sincere.
  Riley, H. B.
Sincerely Yours.
  Jason, W.
Sinfonia.
  Dupré, M.
Sinfonia all' Italiana.
  Gnecco, F.
Sinfonia Concertante.
  Viotti, G. B. Seconda Sinfonia Concertante.
  Walton, S.
Sinfonia Funebre per la Morte del
    Pontefice, Pio VI.
  Paisiello, G.
Sinfonia, nell' opera Olimpiade.
  Vivaldi, A. Olimpiade.
Sing, Child, Sing.
  Addinsell, R. Tuppence Coloured.
Sing, Christian, Sing.
  Hunt, E. R.
Sing, Girls Sing.
  Andersen, A. O., arr.
Sing, Joyous Bird.
  Phillips, M. F.
Sing, Little Gypsy, of Love.
  Haber, R.
Sing Me a Song Tonight.
  Jackson, T. K.
Sing, O Heavens.
  Blower, M.
Sing of Our Saviour's Love.
  Roth, S. E.
Sing, Sweet Nightingale.
  Addinsell, R. Tuppence Coloured.
Sing, Tom Kitty.
  Harris, H.
Sing Unto the Lord.
  Jospe, E.
Sing Your Blues Away.
  Brobst, H.
Singenden Haus.
  Kreuder, P.
Singin' Blues.
  Darling, R.
Singin' to the Dogies on the Range.
  Clyde, T.
Singing Along.
  Hallett, J. C., comp.

Singing Along the Way.
  Gabriel, C. A.
Singing down the road.
  Siegmeister, E., arr.
Singing Farmers.
  Farmers Educational and Cooperative
    Union of America.
Singing I Go.
  Shea, G. B., comp.
Singing to the Rhythm of the Saddle.
  Chanslor, H.
Single File.
  Glogau, J.
Sioux Serenade.
  Osage, T.
Sipping Cider by the Zuyder Zee.
  Silver, A.
Sir John in Love.
  Vaughan Williams, R.
Sista Kvällen.
  Lidholm, I. Fem Sånger.
Sister Arabella.
  Shaftel, S. Sunny Skylar's Sister
    Arabella.
Sister Mary Wore Three Lengths of Chain.
  Bartholomew, M., arr.
Sister Susie Started Swinging.
  George, C.
Sitting on Your Status Quo.
  Rome, H.
Six Chorale Preludes for Organ.
  Wallbank, N. Chorale preludes, organ.
Six Hymn-Preludes.
  Whitlock, P.
Six Organ Preludes on Chorales.
  Buxtehude, D.
Six Petites Pièces.
  Petit, P.
Six Petites Pièces Faciles.
  Hermann, R. A. J.
Six Piano Pieces.
  Dohnányi, E.
Six Pièces Brèves.
  Hermann, R.
Six Sacred Pieces.
  Clokey, J. W.
Six Shakespearian Songs.
  Young, A.
Six Sonatas.
  Frost, B., ed.
Six Sonatas, Three Preludes and Fugues.
  Mendelssohn-Bartholdy, F.
Six Songs.
  Bergsma, W.
Six Sonnets.
  Milhaud, D.
Six Spirituals.
  Bartholomew, M., arr. Sister Mary
    Wore Three Lengths of Chain.
Six Traditional Carols.
  Holst, I., arr.
Sixteen.
  Lafferty, W. H.
Sixty French Horn Duets.
  Pottag, M. P., ed.
Sjecaš Li Se Onog Sata.
  Cernkovich, R.
Sjömansvisa.
  Ahde, S.
Sjung med Oss, Mamma.
  Tegnér, A. C. S.
Skaters.
  Bentley, B. B. Two Piano Solos.
Skies.
  Sherwin, M.
Skön wijsa.
  Koch, S. v. Gammalswenska
    wijsor.
Skulle iagh sörja, da wore iagh tokot.
  Koch, S. v. Gammalswenska wijsor.
Sky Is Clear and Bright.
  Cernkovich, R. Nebo Je Cisto, Jasno.
Sky Is Grey in Loveland.
  Clyde, T.
Skymningen.
  Liljefors, I. Två Sånger.
Skyscraper Fantasy.
  Phillips, D.

Skywriter.
  Bergeim, J.
Slave Market.
  Sandoval, M.
Sleep, Dear Christ-Child.
  Francis, J. H.
Sleep, Holy Babe.
  Dykes, J. B.
Sleep, Little Child of Mine.
  Chopin, F. F.
Sleep, My Little Papoose.
  Strum, E.
Sleep My Love.
  Coslow, S.
Sleep Not, Little One.
  Sterling, E.
Sleep of the Baby Jesus.
  Gevaert, F. A. Christmas Carols.
Sleep of the Infant Jesus.
  Christy, V. A.
Sleep Weary Soldier.
  Beach, F. O.
Sleeping in the Hay.
  Bachman, A.
Sleepless Nights, My Love.
  Collins, J.
Sleepy Hollow Heaven.
  Gold, E.
Sleepy Little Town in the Brown County
    Hills.
  McGee, J. A. The Monon Centennial
    Show.
Sleepy Moon.
  Bell, H. J.
Sleepy San Benito.
  Green, P.
Sleepy Song.
  Brown, L.
Sleepy-Time.
  Holub, J.
Sleepy Trumpeter.
  Kennedy, J.
Sleigh Bells in the Snow.
  Howell, I.
Slovansky pochod.
  Obruča, N.
Slovenian waltz medley.
  Yankovic, F. J. Waltz Medley.
Slow Down.
  Darby, K. L.
Slow Train thru Arkansaw.
  Shand, T.
Slumber Song.
  Caron, A.
  Schumann, R. A. Träumerei.
Small World.
  Rome, H.
Smile.
  Woodford, G. R.
Smile, Chum, Smile.
  Hiscocks, H.
Smile Will Chase Away a Tear.
  Hayes, B. S.
Smiley.
  Darling, R.
Smiling Shadows.
  Hartmann, M. M.
Smith Brothers' Book of Selected
    Radio and Revival Songs.
  Smith, W. L., ed.
Smoke! Smoke! Smoke! that cigarette.
  Williams, S.
Smoke Stacks of Home.
  Hall, D.
Smokehouse Stomp.
  Meissner, J. J.
Smorgasbord at the Swedish Cafe.
  Mann, D.
Snap-Shots.
  Tarp, S. E.
Snaps and Snails.
  Lake, G.
Snatch and Grab It.
  Pease, S.
Snooze Your Blues Away.
  Kendrick, P. M.
Snow-bound.
  Jamack, P. J.

Snow Girl.
　Hopkins, H. P.
So Are You to My Thoughts.
　Johnstone, M.
So Blue.
　Haddox, C.
So Deep in My Heart.
　Baldwin, F. S.
So Easy.
　Ballatore, P., comp.
So Ends the Night.
　Vogel, G.
So Far.
　Rodgers, R. Allegro.
So Far, So Wonderful.
　Worth, B.
So in Love.
　Diehm, D.
So La La.
　Stolz, R.
So Like a Perfect Rose You Are.
　Van Buren, B.
So Lonely and Blue.
　Arthur, W.
So Many Dreams.
　DeMay, A.
So Many Things Have Happened.
　Manley, G. T.
So Much in Love.
　Potter, H, H.
So, Now We're Through.
　Gibson, H.
So Round, So Firm, So Fully Packed.
　Kirk, E.
So Soon.
　Luce, J.
So Sure.
　Vanderburg, G. J.
So That You May Know.
　Goulding, E.
So Thrilling.
　Tuell, M. J.
So We'll Go No More a Roving.
　White, M. V. Plus Jamais, O! Nuit sans Volles.
Søeste Børn.
　Riis, A. Tivoli Revyen.
Sømanden of Stjernen.
　Sørensen, W. G.
Soeur Monique.
　Couperin, F.
Softly.
　Arthur, W.
Softly as in a Morning Sunrise.
　Romberg, S. The New Moon.
Soir d'Idumée.
　Rousseau, P.
Soirées du Petit Juas.
　Rosenthal, M.
Soirs.
　Mulot, A. M.
Soixante Leçons de Solfege.
　Souriac, B.
Sold Down the River.
　Horton, V.
Soldier, Won't You Marry Me.
　Tate, P.
Solemn Epilogue.
　Diggle, R.
Solfège à Deux Voix.
　Souriac, B.
Solfège Populaire.
　Velde, E. van de.
Solfège scolaire.
　Chevals, M.
Solfèges de Concours.
　Favre, G.
Soliloquy.
　Rubbra, E.
Solitaire.
　Emer, M.
Solitario.
　Burll, M.
Sólo con Mi Dolor.
　Gómez Barrera, C.
Solstorm.
　Koch, E. v.

Som een slöman uthistoor fhaar.
　Koch, S. v. Gammalswenska wijsor.
Som ett Blommande Mandelträd.
　Lundvik, H.
Some Glad Happy Day.
　Morris, K.
Some Little Something.
　Arthur, W.
Some Things Will Never Change.
　Anson, B.
Somebody New.
　Scholl, B.
Somebody Nobody Loves.
　Carson, J. L. Songs.
Somebody's Knocking at Your Door.
　Reisfeld, B., arr.
Some Day.
　Taylor, G.
Someday I Knew I'd See You.
　Bartholdy, C.
Someday I'll Find My Love.
　Arthur, W.
Someday I'll Find You.
　Coward, N.
Some Day I'll See My Saviour.
　Sergey, J. M.
Someday I'll Travel Home.
　McNeil, J. C.
Some Day Let My Soul Ever Be at Rest.
　Suber-Sanders, P.
Someday We'll Meet Again in Montecatini.
　Sacco, T.
Some Day, Yes, Some Day.
　Hall, D.
Someday, You and I.
　Swerdlow, M.
Someday You'll Thank Me.
　Rose, F.
Someone.
　Muñoz, R. Por Ti.
Someone I Knew.
　Helpenstell, M. H.
Something for the Boys.
　Berry, D. A.
Something in the Wind.
　Green, J.
Something in Your Eyes.
　Arthur, W.
Something Never For Sale.
　Hall, D.
Something Tells Me That It Won't Be Long.
　Rusthoj, E. K. Gospel Songs.
Somethin's Wrong with My Heart.
　Hall, D.
Sometime, Someplace, and Somewhere.
　Hall, D.
Sometimes Dreams Come True.
　De Michelle, B.
Sometimes I Feel Like a Motherless Child.
　Reisfeld, B., arr.
Someway, Somehow.
　Blank, W. D.
Somewhere.
　Diamond, D. L. 5 Songs.
　Kurucz, J. Valahol.
Somewhere a Heart Is Breaking.
　Kirby, F.
Somewhere a Voice Is Calling.
　Tate, A. F.
Somewhere under the Stars.
　Baker, T.
Son Amour.
　Betti, H. Mam'zelle Printemps.
Son Mis Gallos.
　Sánchez Vázquez, P.
Sonata.
　Coolidge, E. P. S. Sonata, oboe and piano.
　Cowell, H. Sonata, violin & piano.
　Etler, A. D. Sonata, winds & viola.
　Stein, S.
Sonata after the quartet for oboe and strings.
　Mozart, J. C. W. A. Quartet, oboe & strings.

Sonata alla Leggenda.
　Fryklöf, H.
Sonata Allegro.
　Scarlatti, D.
Sonata Brevis.
　Helm, E.
Sonata for 'cello solo.
　Bach, J. S. Sonata, violoncello, no. 1.
Sonata for viola and piano.
　Sendrey, A. Sonata, viola & piano.
Sonata in C minor.
　Bach, W. F.
Sonata, in G minor.
　Beethoven, L. van. Sonata, violoncello.
　Purcell, H.
　Rubbra, E. Sonata, violoncello & piano.
Sonata ... per due violini.
　Rossini, G. A.
Sonata per il flauto traverso.
　Locatelli, P.
Sonata, piano.
　Beethoven, L. van.
Sonata, piano, no. 1.
　Casadesus, R.
Sonate.
　Dutilleux, H. Sonata, oboe & piano.
　Poulenc, F. Sonata, violin & piano.
Sonate en fa mineur.
　Schumann, R. A. Sonata, piano.
Sonate en ut dièse.
　Decruck, F. Sonata, saxophone & piano.
Sonatin för violoncell och piano.
　Wirén, D. I. (Sonatina, violoncello & piano)
Sonatina, for two alto recorders or flutes or recorder and oboe.
　Katz, E.
Sonatine.
　Tubin, E. Sonatina, piano.
Sonatine no. 4.
　Martinon, J. Sonatina, winds, no. 4.
Sonatines-album.
　Velde, E. van de. Sonatines Graduées.
Sonatines Graduées.
　Velde, E. van de.
Sonetto CIV del Petrarca.
　Liszt, F.
Song at Dusk.
　West, M.
Song at Evening.
　Hokanson, M.
Song Eternal.
　Hall, D.
Song for Me.
　Oliver, H.
Song for the Little Jesus.
　Niven, L.
Song for You.
　Krish, E.
Song in My Heart.
　Browne, L. B.
　Lamkoff, P.
Song in the Trees.
　Hall, D.
Song in the Wilderness.
　Vardell, C. G.
Song of a Mountain Trail.
　Wister, L. I. M.
Song of Autumn.
　MacDonald, P. W.
Song of Courage.
　Clark, P. J.
Song of Endurance.
　Symons, T.
Song of Forest Lawn.
　Cadman, C. W.
Song of Freedom.
　Ricketts, C.
Song of India.
　Rimskii-Korsakov, N. A.
Song of Love.
　Arthur, W.
Song of New Orleans.
　Shaftel, S.
Song of Peace.
　Richard, L.
Song of Robin Hood.
　Castagnetta, G., arr.

Song of Scheherezade.
Rimskii-Korsakov, N. A.
Song of Songs.
Jacobson, M.
Song of the Andes.
Marcelli, N.
Song of the Angels.
Brown, S. S.
Song of the Bluebird.
Hibbeler, R. O.
Song of the Camel Driver.
Chajes, J. T.
Song of the Chimes.
Sawyer, A.
Song of the Earth.
Brodsky, N. A Man about the House.
Song of the Fishermen.
Britten, B. Peter Grimes.
Song of the Jewish Partisens.
Chajes, J.
Song of the Mourning Doves.
Neilson, L. C.
Song of the North.
Cooke, J. F.
Song of the Tartar Maiden.
Krasev, M.
Song of the Volga Boatmen.
Simeone, H.
Song of the Voyageurs.
McKay, G. F.
Song of the Whippoorwill.
Strickland, L.
Song to Hawaii.
Pryce, B., arr.
Song to Pueblo.
Richard, L.
Song-a-log.
Fisher, D. R., arr.
Songes Merveilleux.
Bitsch, M. Marvellous Dreams.
Songs.
Carson, J. L.
Songs and Monologues.
Blain, K.
Songs by Zeb Turner and His Fireside
Boys.
Turner, Z.
Songs for Little Folks.
Selvin, B., comp.
Songs for voice and piano.
Vairin, L.
Songs for Young America.
Greene, W. Jack and Joy in Yonderland.
Songs from San Antone.
Wills, B., comp.
Songs from the Countryside.
Collinson, F. M., arr.
Songs My Mother Taught Me.
Dvořák, A.
Songs of America.
Eckhardt, F. G., arr.
Ewen, D., ed.
Songs of France.
Eckhardt, F. G., arr.
Songs of Home and the Hills.
Moore, J. Lee and Juanita's Songs of
Home and the Hills.
Songs of Italy.
Eckhardt, F. G., arr.
Songs of Love.
Brahms, J.
Henman, G.
McNeil, J. C.
Schumann, R. A.
Songs of Scotland.
Bantock, Sir G., ed.
Eckhardt, F. G., arr.
Songs of the New Age.
Owen, W.
Songs of Truth for Youth.
Murray, J., comp.
Songs of Wales.
Bantock, Sir G., ed.
Songs of Zion.
Frye (T. R.) Publishers, ed. Clarence
H. Cobbs Songs of Zion.

Sonia.
Thébault, V. Buscando.
Sonnensturm.
Koch, E. V. Solstorm.
Sonnet.
Ferry, C. T.
Sonnet XVII.
Lazarus, D.
Sonnet XXII.
Lazarus, D.
Sons and Daughters of Liberty.
Pardini, A. C.
Sont Trois Hommes Fort Sages.
Aubanel, G. P. P.
Sophia's Sofa.
Crawford, J. D.
Sophisticated Sophie.
Federer, R.
Sopón.
Morales, O.
Sorcerer's Apprentice.
Dukas, P.
Sorrentina Ricciolina.
Caslar, D. E Bello Qualche Volta
Andare a Piedi.
Sortilèges.
Scala, T.
Sou.
Petit, P. Y. M. C. Melodies.
Souls of the Righteous.
Vaughan Williams, R.
Soun Tres Ome Fort Sage.
Aubanel, G. P. P. Sont Trois Hommes
Fort Sages.
Sound Off.
Robbins (J. J.) & Sons, Inc., comp.
South American Holiday.
Florillo, D.
South Carolina, That's Home Sweet Home
to Me.
Sims, A.
South Paw Special.
Saville, T.
Southern Mountain Tune.
Stevens, E. Three Piano Solos.
Southern Solitude.
Kennedy, J. Brussels Express.
Southwind.
Oakes, R. D.
Souvenir de Chopin.
Honegger, A.
Soviet Popular Songs.
Small, A., comp. & arr. Leeds Am-
Rus Album.
Soviet Seamen.
Kompaneets, Z.
Soy Charro de Rancho Grande.
Esperon, M.
Soy Yagabundo.
Sánches Vázquez, P.
Spadella.
Cooley, D. C.
Spagnola.
Richter, C., arr.
Spangle Dance.
Story, H.
Spaniard That Blighted My Life.
Thompson, W. H.
Spanish Dance.
Sarasate y Navascues, P. M. M. de.
Spanish Jazz.
Brannon, D.
Spare the Love and Spoil the Dream.
Pavey, S.
Sparkling Diamonds.
Woodford, G. R.
Special Song Book no. 2.
Frye (T. R.) Publishers, ed. President
Jemison Special Song Book no. 2.
Speed.
Kabalevsky, D.
Spinning Song.
Ellmenreich, A.
Spirit Immortal.
Verdi, G.
Spirit of Milwaukee.
Patti, S. T.

Spitzbub.
Rixner, J.
Spooks.
Simpson, J.
Spring.
Emery, W.
Spring Has Come to Old Missouri.
Blair, H.
Spring Is a Lovely Lady.
Phillips, M. F.
Spring Is Here.
Rodgers, R.
Spring Is Really Spring This Year.
Wilcher, J.
Spring Is the Time for Love.
Allen, R.
Spring Mood.
Terry, F.
Springtime.
Lee, R. E.
Vairin, L. Songs for voice and piano.
Squirrels at Play.
Berlin, B. Two Pieces.
Stabat-Mater.
Mortari, V.
Vivaldi, A.
Staking a Claim on the Moon.
Bartlett, F.
Stand Behind the Great New U. S. A.
Rush, N.
Stand up, Shout out.
Hallett, J. C., c mp, Singing Along.
Standard Bearers.
Cherepnin, N.
Stanford Rhapsody.
Wood, H.
Star Dust.
Carmichael, H.
Star of Peace.
Wilson, R. C.
Star of the East.
Kennedy, A.
Star over Texas.
Hurtgen, L.
Stav Light.
Atterbery, L. L.
Starlight and Moonbeams.
Hall, D.
Starlight Dance.
Taylor, E.
Starlight Honeymoon.
Bunn, F. S.
Star Light, Star Bright.
Herbert, V.
Stars Fell on Alabama.
Perkins, F.
Stars over Normandy.
Brown, A. L.
Stars over Texas.
Blair, H.
Stars over the Prairie.
Easterling, G.
Stars Will Remember, so will I.
Blitz, L.
Stars Will Shine Tonight.
Bartlett, F.
Statements.
Copland, A.
Status Quo.
Rome, H. Sitting on Your Status Quo.
Stay Away from My Man.
Numsen, A.
Stay Out Of the North this year.
Hammond, H. D.
Steal a Kiss then run for your life.
Croasdale, R.
Steal Away.
Clements, J.
Delmore, H. A.
Lynn, G.
Steal Away to Jesus.
Roberton, H. S.
Steel Guitar Hop.
Campbell, C.
Stella by Starlight.
Young, V.
Step and Strut.
Raezer, C. M.

424

Stepping Stones.
  Black, M. R.
Still, Still with Thee.
  Duncan, C.
  Moore, E. A.
Still the Night with Snow So Deep.
  Sellew, D.
Stolen Kisses.
  Steininger, F. Music in My Heart.
Stop Your Fooling Me.
  Arthur, W.
Stopping by Woods on a Snowy Evening.
  Glazer, F.
Storgårdsvalsen.
  Olsson, W.
Storm King.
  Elliott, M.
Storm Shelter.
  Ramont, G. M.
Story of Sorrento.
  Cugat, X.
Story of the Two Stars.
  George, D.
Stcvka Není Nic, Láska To Je Víc.
  Gollwell, J.
Stråkkvartett.
  Kallstenius, E. Quartet, strings.
  Melchers, H. M. Quartet, strings.
Strada del Mio Quartiere.
  Guarino, G. M. Intimita.
Straight Cut Stomp.
  Kennedy, J. Sleepy Trumpeter.
Strandvialen.
  Fernström, J. Sex Sånger.
Strange.
  Jurkovich, C.
Strangeness of Heart.
  Somers, H. S.
Stranger.
  Bartlett, F.
Strasbourg.
  Levy, M. M.
Strawberry Roan.
  Fisher, D.
Streamline Polka.
  Hoven, G.
Street Parade.
  Williams, J.
Striber paa Strøget.
  Ewans, K. Tiffer Revuen 1947.
String Americana.
  Herbert, V. Victor Herbert String
    Americana.
String Quartet.
  Dumler, M. G. Quartet, strings.
  Rawsthorne, A. Quartet, strings.
String Quartet in A minor.
  Vaughan Williams, R. Quartet, strings.
  Walton, W. Quartet, strings.
String Quartet in F minor.
  Rubbra, E. Quartet, strings.
String Quartet no. 2.
  Lutyens, E. Quartet, strings, no. 2.
String Quintet in F Minor.
  Brahms, J.
Strolling in the Moonlight.
  Clyde, T.
Strolling under Magic Moon.
  Buerosse, G. J.
Stronger than Love.
  Ellstein, Abraham. (Just My Luck)
    Shtarker Fun Liebe.
Student Prince.
  Romberg, S.
Students, Korean Folk Song.
  Sungsik, L.
Study Outline for Public School Music.
  Van Peursem, J. E.
Stupid.
  Maul, G.
Styles of Famous 88'ers.
  Pease, S., ed. Down Beat's Styles of
    Famous 88'ers.
Sublime Inspiracion.
  Parra, G.
Such a Little While.
  McNeil, J. C.
Such a Year on Me.
  Ellstein, A. Just My Luck.

Suelta los pollos.
  Fergo, T. Gavilán.
Sueño.
  Castillo, N.
  Rodriguez, A.
Sugar and Spice.
  Lake, G.
Sugar Bowl.
  Tobin, L.
Sugar Loaf Mountain.
  Flory, S. Carioca Album of Brazilian
    Songs.
Sugar Moon.
  Walker, C.
Sugar Puss.
  Tobin, L.
Sugared Candy.
  Zurke, B.
Suite.
  Busch, W.
Suite Bergamasque.
  DeBussy, C.
Suite Brève.
  Langlais, J.
Suite for four equal clarinets.
  Smith, T. S.
Suite for violin and piano.
  Milhaud, D.
Suite, harpsichord, no. 8.
  Händel, G. F.
Suite in 3/4 Time.
  Mittler, F.
Suite Languedocienne.
  Kosma, J.
Suite Miniature.
  Wirén, D. I.
Suite n:r 1 ur balett-pantomimen
    Yttersta Domen.
  Rosenberg, H. C. Yttersta Domen.
Suite of Scottish Dances.
  Alwyn, W.
Suite Retica.
  Piazzi, G.
Suite Savoyarde.
  Rabey, R.
Summer.
  Harvey, V.
Summer Evening.
  Davis, K. K., arr.
  Diggle, R. Summer Sketches.
  Hayes, O. L. Three Easy Piano Pieces.
Summer Evening Serenade.
  Lillya, C.
Summer Moon.
  Stravinskii, I. F.
Summer Morning.
  Kahn, P. B.
Summer Nocturne.
  Hopkins, H. P.
Summer Reverie.
  Torjussen, T.
Summer Romance.
  Hall, D.
Summer Serenade.
  Brodsky, R.
Summer Sketches.
  Diggle, R.
Summer Song.
  Jacobson, W. J.
Summer's on a Holiday.
  Vaughn, W.
Summit Ridge Drive.
  Shaw, A.
Sun Comes over the Mountain.
  Bratton, O.
De Sun Done Rose.
  Hauser, W.
Sun of My Soul.
  Olds, W. B.
Sunbeams March.
  Brown, C.
Sunday.
  Sarony, L.
Sunday in Brooklyn.
  Siegmeister, E.
Sunday Kind of Love.
  Prima, L.

Sunday Morning in Norway.
  Whitehead, A.
Sunny Curls.
  Clyde, T.
Sunny Days.
  Hirschberg, D.
Sunny Skyler's Sister Arabella.
  Shaftel, S.
Sunrise.
  Antoine, brother.
Sunset Curls.
  Henninger, G.
Sunshine and Flowers.
  Shepherd, R.
Sunshine Blues.
  McNeil, J. C.
Superior Collection of Steel Guitar Solos.
  Awai, K. E., arr.
Superior Song Book.
  Frye (T. R.) Publishers, ed. Lucie
    E. Campbell Superior Song Book.
Supernal Praises.
Sur le Bord de la Rivière.
  Passani, E. B.
Sur le Lac Enchante.
  Rabey, R. Suite Savoyarde.
Surely God Is in This Place.
  Lang, E.
Susannah.
  Händel, G. F.
Suscipe Domine.
  Witt, F. X.
Suzanne.
  Dean, J.
Suzanne et le Pacifique.
  Honegger, A. Petit Cours de Morale.
Svarta Rosor.
  Sylvain, J.
Svensk Jul.
  Tegnér, A.
Svijklige världens oundvijklige öd'-dödli-
    gheetz sorgtröstande lijksang.
  Koch, S. v. Gammalswenska wijsor.
Swan.
  Bauer, M.
  Saint-Saëns, C. Le Carnaval des
    Animaux.
Swanee River.
  Foster, S. C.
Swaying Blossoms.
  Cecilia, sister.
Sweet Bells.
  Sawaya, J. J.
Sweet California Moon.
  Burton, S.
Sweet Corrina Blues.
  Horton, V.
Sweet Eilean.
  Tobin, L.
Sweet Kind of Love.
  Rose, F. You've Got a Sweet Kind of
    Love.
Sweet Marie.
  Moore, Raymon.
  Moore, Raymond. Life with Father.
Sweet Marie and Her Baby.
  Niles, J. J.
Sweet Refrain.
  Durham, G. H.
Sweet Sabbath.
  Cobb, H., arr.
Sweet Sue, Just You.
  Young, V.
Sweet Susabella Come under My Umbrella.
  Hardy, A. F.
Sweet Suwanee Moon.
  Markle, E. K.
Sweet Sweet.
  Zinn, L.
Sweet Was the Song the Virgin Sung.
  Rowley, A.
Sweet yesterday.
  Leslie-Smith, K.
Sweetest Smile I Know.
  Arthur, W.
Sweetheart.
  Hardy, A. B.
Sweetheart America.
  Butera, J.

Sweetheart Darlin'.
  Chatterton, T.
Sweetheart Dream with Me.
  Olson, E. C.
Sweetheart, I'll Be True.
  Boiles, E. C.
Sweetheart of Mine.
  Ramsey, S.
Sweetheart, You're a Heartache.
  Kurzen, P. C.
Sweetie Pie.
  Cook, M. E.
Swimming in the Briny Deep.
  Guthrie, C. A.
Swing à l'École.
  Bourtayre, H.
Swing Low, Sweet Chariot.
  Roberton, H. S.
Swing Low, Sweet Clarinet.
  Mourant, W. B.
Swing Session at a Seance.
  Venis, G.
Swinging Back.
  Tobin, L.
Swinging down the Road.
  Brown, A. L.
Swinging in the Same Old Swing.
  Tillia, H.
Swinging on the Range.
  Hill, C. L.
Swiss Boy.
  Leverton, B.
Swiss Lullaby.
  Ribaupierre, M. de.
Sylvan Sprites.
  Rowbottom, H.
Sylvia.
  Delibes, L.
Symbol of Love.
  Saltamach, J.
Sympathie.
  Stolz, R.
Sympathy Waltz
  Friml, R.
Symphonia Brevis.
  Wolf-Ferrari, E.
Symphonic Series of Sacred Songs.
  Yoder, P.
Symphonic Studies.
  Rawsthorne, A.
Symphonie.
  Wanhal, J. B.
Symphonie Concertante.
  Stamitz, K.
Symphonie no IV.
  Honegger, A. Symphony, no. 4.
Symphonische Suite.
  Rosenberg, H. C.
Symphony in A Major.
  Moore, D.
Symphony in Blue.
  Leliwa-Tyszkiewicz, R.
Symphony No. 1.
  Martinů, B.
Symphony, no. 2.
  Madetoja, L. A.
Symphony no. 3.
  Brahms, J.
Symphony no. 5.
  Shostakovich, D. D.
Symphony of the Seasons.
  Merritt, C. E.
Symphony, organ, no. 1.
  Orakton, E. M.
Symphony, string orchestra, no. 4.
  Rivier, J.
Symptoms of Love.
  Prester, A.
Szagos Májyva. Gyöngyvirág.
  Kellér, D.
Száz Szál Gyertyát, Száz Itce Bort.
  Fráter, L.
Szép, Tavaszi Almok.
  Bodrogi, Z.
Szép Vagy, Gyönyörü Vagy.
  Vincze, Z.

Szeret-e Még.
  Eisemann, M.
Szeretök Keresek.
  Dóczy, J.

T

T. C. U. Victory Song.
  Sweet, M.
Ta Chanson.
  Prud'Homme, E. L.
Ta Jugand.
  Castellanos, A. L. Are You Kidding.
Ta Viox N'était Plus la Même.
  Neuberger, J. B. D.
Tableau Instrumental.
  Bozza, E.
Tabo Tabo.
  Gomes, E.
Tahiti, My Tahiti.
  Kuaana, D. K.
Tailor Made Baby.
  Whiston, D.
Take a Little Chance with Me.
  Rowden, H.
Take a Little Trip Down South.
  Arthur, W.
Take a Tip from My Heart.
  Vel, E. L.
Take a Trip to Luzianne.
  Pettit, A.
Take Jesus for Your Friend.
  Turner, E. M.
Take Me Back to Oklahoma where it's
  North, South, East and West all rolled
  together.
  Morrison, A.
Take Me to Calvary.
  Steger, I.
Take Me to My Home Out on the Prairie.
  Robison, C. J.
Take Not Thy Holy Spirit from Me.
  Williams, R. E.
Take Them Cold Feet Outa My Back.
  Sullivan, R. O.
Takin' My Time, You'll Surely Be Mine.
  Beach, F.
Tale of Peter Rabbit.
  Benz, V. E.
Tales from the Vienna Woods.
  Strauss, J.
Talk to Me.
  Castellanos, A.
Talking to My Baby.
  Clinghouse, M.
Talking to Myself about You.
  Hall, D.
Talking to the Wind.
  Elam, C. M.
Tallahassee.
  Curry, J. G. Embellishments on
    Standard Tune.
Tamalero.
  Guida, P. Rica Samba.
Tanglewood Pool.
  Chase, N.
Tango.
  Torjussen, T. Carnival.
Tango du Rêve.
  Malderen, E. V.
Tango d'un Soir.
  Scotto, V. Sérénade aux Nuages.
Tango Español.
  Garman, W. M.
Tango Intime.
  Uliven, U. H.
Tango-Märchen.
  Grothe, F. Abendlied.
Tango Villerupt.
  Metzler, X.
Tant Mieux.
  Liferman, G. Nous Deus.
Tantum Ergo.
  Beobide, J. M.
Tap Dancer.
  Phillips, D.

Tappagyn Jiargey.
  Foster, A. Red Top-knots.
Tarantella.
  Busch, W. Suite.
Tarantola..
  Almángano, S.
Ta-ra-ra Boom-der-é.
  Sayers, H. J.
Tattletale.
  Goodman, B.
Tavie Boogie-woogie.
  Tavernier, F. E.
Taxi Fou.
  Schwab, A.
Te Amo.
  Reade, C.
Te Deum.
  Filkins, G. C.
  Fouser, C. E.
Te Deum Laudamus.
  Marsh, C. H.
Te Sequiré Amando.
  Valdelamar, E. E.
Tea for Two.
  Youmans, V. No No Nanette.
Teach Us Thy Ways.
  Kempiński, L. A.
Teach Yourself to Play the Piano.
  McClintock, L.
Teardrops and a Sunbeam in Your
  Eyes.
  Tietze, S.
Teardrops in My Heart.
  Horton, V.
Tears Fill My Heart.
  Alcaniz Farre, A. Cuando Ll ora
    el Corazón.
Tears, That Tell Me You're in Love.
  Moser, D.
Technicolored Garden.
  Anderson, R.
Teddy O'Neil.
  Elton, L., pseud.
Telephone Kiss from You.
  Spina, H. J.
Television.
  Fergo, T.
Tell Me.
  Hall, D.
  Newhard, D.
Tell Me His Name Again.
  Piper, E. D. Revival choruses,
    Number Two.
Tell Me, Tell Me.
  Sgambellone, G.
Tell Me That You Love Me.
  Carleton, R. L.
Tell Me, Whose Darling Are You.
  Davis, D. S.
Tell Me Why You're Always Cooing.
  Hubay, J. Minek Turbékoltok.
Tellin' Lies.
  Boyd, B.
Tempest.
  Arne, T.
10 Characteristic Dances.
  Scher, W.
Ten Commandments.
  Huntley, E. M.
Ten of the Best World Famous Piano
  Solos.
  Gordon, H. S., Inc., comp.
Ten of the Best World Famous Songs.
  Gordon, H. S., inc., comp.
Tenderly.
  Rusthoi, E. K. Gospel Songs.
Tendre Sérénade.
  Gaste, L. L'Ile d'Amour.
Tennessee.
  Merritt, B. R.
Tennessee Twilight Tune.
  Gaul, H. B.
Terra . . . À Nosa.
  Quiroga, M. Emigrantes Celtas.
Test your A. Q., arranging quotient,
  with arrange-a-grams.
  Cowen, W.
Testament Villon.
  Barraud, H. H.

Tex Williams and His Western
 Caravan Song Folio.
  Haldeman, O., comp.
Texas Lullaby.
 Ware, G. L.
Texas Red.
 Fowler, W.
Texas Sandman.
 Fisher, D. The Strawberry Roan.
Texas Skiparoo.
 Farr, C.
Texas Star.
 Bartlett, F.
Texas Suite.
 Stevenson, R. M.
Texas Tech on Parade.
 Chenette, E.
Texas Waltz.
 Walker, C.
Thank Thee, O Lord.
 Stephenson, M. E.
Thanks Be to Thee.
 Händel, G. F.
Thanksgiving.
 Lewis, L. H. Prayer of Thanks-
  giving.
 Wilson, F. C.
Thanksgiving. See title entry in
 composer list.
That Arizona Moon and You.
 Davis, J. M.
That Atomic Bomb excuse please.
 Terry, A.
That Big Physique from Martinique.
 Hunt, S.
That Country Place Where I Was
 Born.
  Brennan, J. A.
That Cute Little Usherette.
 Cotton, V. L.
That Dream of Mine.
 Sarkissian, B.
That Glorious Song of Old.
 Buckley, W. H.
That Gospel Train Is Comin'.
 Nolan, T.
That Is Christmas.
 Walker, J. From Day to Day.
That Light in Your Eyes.
 Tobin, L.
That Little Old Lady I Love.
 Elliott, L.
That Matters Much to Me.
 Carleton, R. L.
That Mother-in-law.
 Long, G.
That My Lord May Live.
 Hulin, D. N.
That Night.
 Arthur, W.
That Night of Nights.
 Gage, H. A.
That Old Time Religion.
 Wright, E. L.
That Pretty Little Face.
 Taylor, H.
That Promised Land.
 Cobb, H.
That Wild and Wicked Look in Your
 Eye.
  Nichols, S.
That Would Be Heaven for Two.
 Phillips, F.
That'll Do Me.
 Jones, A. F.
That's All I Want to Know.
 Freeman, T. I Don't Care.
That's All There Is, there is no more.
 Arthur, W.
That's How I know You Love Me.
 Pond, F. G.
That's How I Stay Happy.
 Clyde, T.
That's More to My Mind.
 Cookson, F. B.
That's My Desire.
 Kresa, H.
That's the Hawaiian Swing.
 Brobst, H.

That's the Way He Does It.
 James, I.
That's What Every Young Girl Should
 Know.
  Rodney, D.
That's What I Like about the West.
 Bergdahl, E.
That's What Ireland Means to Me.
 O'Connell, T.
That's What You Did Do.
 Arthur, W.
That's What Your Heart Is For.
 Kent, W.
That's Why I Go to the Nazarene
 Sunday School.
  Dermyer, D. D.
That's Why I Love Jesus So.
 Tyllar, G. C.
That's Why I Love Only You.
 Caza, I.
That's Why I Love You.
 Arthur, W.
That's Why I'm Dreaming of You.
 Guillory, E. J.
Their Songs We Sing.
 Sandler, S.
Theme and Six Variations for organ on
 "The Hebrew Children."
  Twyeffort, B.
Theme and Two Variations from
 Beethoven's Appassionata Sonata.
  Beethoven, L. van. Sonata, piano.
Theme & Variations.
 Scott, C.
Theme from Rhythm of the Dawn.
 Hamilton, O. Rhythm of the Dawn.
Then I Knew You Were Mine.
 Hopfield, H. F.
Theone.
 Stuart, D. G.
There Are Those Times.
 Evans, T.
There But for You Go I.
 Loewe, F. Brigadoon.
There Goes My Heart Again.
 Woodford, G. R.
There Is a Song My Heart Will
 Always Sing.
  Russell, K. The Nightingale.
There Is Glory in My Soul.
 Gabriel, C. H. O That Will Be
  Glory.
There Is No Breeze to cool the flame
 of love.
  Stein, S.
There Is Only One Sky to cover us all.
 Samuels, W.
There Is Room in Heaven for You.
 Adams, W. D.
There Is Two Living Arms Wanting You.
 Chettick, J. M.
There Must Be a Reason.
 Ostrow, A.
There She Goes.
 Lake, G.
There Was a Time.
 Arthur, W.
There Was One.
 Penry, M.
There Were Shepherds.
 Stairs, L. E.
There'll Be Another Christmas.
 Tobin, L.
There'll Be No More Crying.
 Famous Blue Jay Singers.
There'll Be Some Changes Made.
 Overstreet, W. B.
There'll Never Be a Girl Like You.
 Lynton, E.
There'll Never Be Another Sister
 McPherson.
  Gilpert, F.
There's a Bluebird in the Weeping
 Willow Tree.
  Hall, M.
There's a Dove within the Forest.
 Kurucz, J. Bakony Erdőn Sir a
  Gerle.

There's a Glad New Joy.
 Huston, F. C. Three New Songs.
There's a Great Time Coming.
 Coghlan, A. V.
There's a Heart warming Richness.
 Samuels, W.
There's a Little Church in Walpack.
 Ringle, D.
There's a Lovely Little Lady.
 Gay, N.
There's a Mansion in Heaven for Me.
 Romero, G.
There's a Moon Tonight.
 Fender, I. M.
There's a New Moon Over the Ocean.
 Lisbona, E.
There's a Rainbow in Your Tears.
 Bartlett, F.
There's a Rainbow over Chicago.
 Warren, I. N.
There's Always a First Time.
 Skómra, F.
There's an Old Fashioned Swing in
 the Garden.
  Ringle, D.
There's Been a Change.
 Bolick, B.
There's Fish in the Ocean.
 Arthur, W.
There's Music in Your Voice.
 Hibbeler, R. O.
There's No One Can Keep Out of Love.
 Klaus, H. M.
There's No Prescription for Love.
 Hall, D.
There's Nothing like a Model T.
 Styne, J. High Button Shoes.
There's Only Lonely Me.
 Baum, G.
There's Something I Want.
 Bartlett, F.
Theresy.
 Colombo, J. Bambola.
These Beautiful Things.
 Lowe, J.
These Times Will Be Old Times
 Sometime.
  Kirchgassner, P. H.
These Will Be the Best Years.
 Mann, D.
They All Look Alike to Pancho.
 Sunshine, M.
They Cry on My Shoulder over someone
 else.
  Lowell, C. R.
They Didn't Believe Me.
 Kern, J.
They Said It Wouldn't Last.
 Trevare, G.
They're Jealous.
 Silver, F.
They're Mine, They're Mine, They're
 Mine.
  Pleis, J.
Thine Alone.
 Herbert, V.
Things Are No Different Now.
 Krissel, W. D.
Things I Do for Love.
 Carr, M.
Things Like This Don't Happen.
 Walters, R.
Think! Brother.
 Caron, A.
Think It Over.
 Arthur, W.
Think of Me.
 Joler, G. A.
Thinking of You.
 Arthur, W.
Thinking Only of You.
 McNeil, J. C.
3rd Piano Concerto.
 Bartók, B. Concerto, Piano, No. 3.
Third Symphony.
 Copland, A. Symphony, no. 3.
 Ives, C. E.
Thirty-five Miniatures.
 Peeters, F.

427

Thirty Hymns and Songs.
  Weinberg, J.
33 Solos and Duets.
  Hallett, J. C.
This Can Never Happen Again.
  Clements, B.
This Can't Be Me.
  Harter, A.
This Dream of You.
  Ouellette, R.
This, I Know.
  Sawaya, J. J.
This Is a Fine Time to wanna leave me.
  Coben, C.
This Is It.
  Arthur, W.
This Is My Favorite City.
  Myrow, J. Mother Wore Tights.
This Is the American Way of Life.
  O'Neal, B.
This Is the Victory.
  Lambertson, M. W.
This Kind of Love.
  Parhalo, B.
This Little Pilgrim.
  Sellev D. E.
This Lovely Christmas Night.
  Warren, I. N.
This Must Be Love.
  McNeil, J. C.
This Night Is Mine.
  Bishop, D.
This Ol' Hammer.
  Ryder, N. F.
This Old Time Religion.
  Bonnivar, F.
This Romance.
  Fisk, D. F.
This Song.
  Ostach, M. G.
This Suspense is Killin' Me.
  Nelson, K.
This Time for Keeps.
  Swan, D.
This Time the Joke's on Me.
  Houck, C.
This Time the Torch Is on Me.
  [Henriksen, E. G.]
This World Can't Stand Long.
  Acuff, R.
This World Is Not My Home.
  Diamond, D. L. 5 Songs.
'Tho I Know.
  Saltamach, J.
Those Things Money Can't Buy.
  Goodhart, A.
Thou Art My Light at Eventide.
  Tullar, G. C.
Thou Very God and David's Son.
  Bach, J. S. Du Wahrer Gott und
    Davids Sohn.
Though You are Pretty.
  Cioffi, G.
'Though You're in Love with Some-
    body Else.
  Finn, T.
Thousand Beautiful Things.
  Wood, H.
Thousand Islands Song.
  Sigman, C. Angel in the Wings.
Thread of Scarlet.
  Santiago, Rius, F. Labios de Clavel.
Three Be-Bop Solos for piano.
  Guptill, A. L.
Three Blind Mice.
  Driver, A. New Songs for Old.
  Schaum, J. W., arr.
  Swift, F. F.
Three Chinese Songs.
  Orr, R.
Three Concert Pieces.
  Reizenstein, F.
Three Dances.
  Khachaturian, A. I.
Three Early Grade Pieces.
  Lawrence, S.
Three Easy Piano Pieces.
  Hayes, O. L.
Three Equale.
  Beethoven, L. van.

Three Etchings.
  Rapoport, E.
3 Fantastic Dances.
  Shostakovich, D. D.
Three Holy Kings.
  Glière, R. M.
Three Humming Themes.
  Swift, F. F.
Three Limericks.
  Cain, N.
Three Little Kittens.
  Huber, H. S.
Three Musketeers.
  Pollet.
Three New Songs.
  Huston, F. C.
Three Piano Solos.
  Stevens, E.
Three Pieces.
  Bach, J. S. Sonata, violoncello, no. 1.
3 Preludes.
  Parris, H.
Three Protests.
  Ives, C. E. 22.
Three Psalms.
  Rubbra, E.
Three Ravens.
  Lovatt, S. E.
Three Religious Pieces.
  Brown, A. G. Y.
Three Sixteenth Century Melodies.
  Jones, G., arr.
Three Songs from Twelfth Night.
  Bullock, E.
Three Songs of Innocence.
  Rowley, A.
Three Songs of Sister Miriam.
  Bantock, G. R.
Three's a Crowd.
  Green, J.
Thrill of Love.
  Cooper, B.
Through a Lighted Window Pane.
  Arthur, W.
Through the Day.
  Hallett, J. C., comp. Singing Along.
Through the Eyes of Jesus.
  Bates, A. E.
Through the Lonely Pines.
  Bigler, J. E.
Thrush.
  Shannon, I. Farewell.
  Shannon, I. Learning to Fly.
  Shannon, I. Nesting.
Thumbing My Way to the top of the
    world.
  Balliett, G.
Thumbs Up, Thumbs Down.
  Sawyer, V.
Thunder in My Aching Heart.
  Hall, D.
Thunderer.
  Sousa, J. P.
Thy Temple, Lord.
  Bornschein, F.
Ti Portero.
  Giuliani, V.
Ti Sogno Bambina.
  Mobiglia, T. Dieci Arrangiamenti
    per Complesso Hot.
Tick-tock Polka.
  Thaj, J.
Tickle My Heart.
  Hall, D.
Tie a String Around Your Heart.
  Sawyer, V.
Tied to My Heart.
  Bender, L. S.
Tiens Bon l'Guidon,
  Maye, P.
Tierra del Sol.
  Orue, J. de.
Tierra Linda.
  Guastavino, C.
Tiffer Revuen 1947.
  Evans, K.
Tijuca.
  Flory, S. Carioca Album of
    Brazilian Songs.
Tik-a-tee, Tik-a-tay.
  Lama, G.

Till Ole Santa Will Come.
  Sowulewski, E.
Time Goes On.
  Sendrey, A.
Time I Think of You.
  Carlson, M. E.
Time out for a Dream.
  Miller, F. D.
Times Have Changed.
  Koval, M.
Tip Top March Book.
  Mesang, T. L.
Tippie and the Hurdy-gurdie.
  Thomas, H.
Tippie's Love Song.
  Thomas, H.
Tippin' Tug-boats.
  Hibbeler, R. O.
Tip-toe to Fairyland.
  Sutherland, F. A.
Tira-Lira-Li.
  Kingsley, M.
Tired Moon.
  Kurth, B. A Cookie for Snip.
Tired of Wandering.
  Adam's, W. D.
Tiroliro.
  Grant, J.
Tisa.
  David, M.
Tivoli Revyen.
  Riis, A.
Tizenhat Esztendős Barna Kis Lany.
  Szánto, M.
To a Hill-top.
  McKinney, H. D.
To a Water-Lily.
  MacDowell, E. A.
To a Wild Rose.
  MacDowell, E. Woodland Sketches.
To God the Mighty Lord.
  Phillips, C. H.
To Have and Not to Have.
  Richard, L.
To Jane.
  Chadwick, C.
To My Beloved.
  Savino, D.
To My Gal.
  Tobin, L.
To My Jesus Do I Cling.
  Bach, J. S.
To Sin Is Human.
  Meyers, H.
To Spring.
  Wilson, R. B.
To the Chief Musician.
  Helfer, W.
To the Dawn.
  Williams, F.
To the Duck Pond.
  Cobb, H.
To the Infinite.
  Schubert, F. P. How Uplifted My
    Heart.
To the Love in My Heart.
  Perry, H.
To Zion's Shore.
  Zaira, M.
Toast to Our Love.
  Capriotti, A.
Toccata.
  Bales, G. A.
  Bentzon, N. V.
  Brero, C. J.
  Callaerts, J.
  Sark, E. T.
Toccata and Fugue.
  Bach, J. S.
Toccata & Fugue, organ.
  Bach, J. S.
Toccata Guatemala.
  Morgenstern, S.
Toccata no. 2.
  Scarlatti, A. Aria.
Toccata no. 4.
  Scarlatti, A. Aria.
Toccatina.
  Griggs, F.

Todo Me Ser.
  Green, J. Th_ee's a Crowd.
Tom Binkley's Tune.
  Cowell, H.
Tom Bowling.
  Bodin, C.
Tomahawk Dance.
  Rosner, B.
Tombe, Tombe, Pluie Légére.
  Le Grand, R. L.
Tommy Trent's Dixie Fun Barn. See
  title entry in composer list.
Tomorrow.
  Jenkins, G.
  Landry, N. P.
Tomorrow Comes the Song.
  Ambrose, P.
Tomorrow Is the Day.
  Crane, J.
Tomorrow May Be Too Late.
  Bartlett, F.
  Wise, F.
Ton Amour Est Si Beau.
  Israel, M.
Tone Tune Technic.
  Binkley, F. F.
Tonene lever.
  Selmer, M. Praktisk klaverskole.
Tonight Is the Night for Love.
  Arthur, W.
Tonight when I say goodbye.
  Gregory, B.
Too Careful.
  Russell, R. S.
Too Fat Polka.
  Richardson, A.
Too Good to Be True.
  Carson, J. L. Songs.
  Disney (W.) Productions, Ltd.
    Fun and Fancy Free.
Too Long.
  Henri, P.
Too Many Sweethearts.
  De Vol, F.
Too Many Years Too Late.
  Bond, J.
Too Marvelous for Words.
  Whiting, R. A. Dark Passage.
Too Tired.
  Bartlett, F.
Torchy.
  Barris, H.
Toreador.
  Geller, H.
Torna a Surriento.
  Curtis, E. de, Come Back to Sorrento.
Torno a Surriento.
  Curtis, E. de.
Total Pa Que.
  Terry Urrutia, S.
Totem, Teepee and Tom-Tom.
  Kadison, P.
Toujours d'Accord.
  Betti, H. Mam'zelle Printemps.
Toujours Fin Prêt.
  Travnicek, A.
Tout autour du Tour.
  Maye, P.
Tout Bleu.
  Bourtayre, H. Le Chanteur Inconnu.
Tout Cela N'est Rien sans Vous.
  Trenet, C. Douce France.
Tout Doux.
  Ferrari, L.
Tout Près de Toi, Qu'il Fait Bon.
  Lucchesi, R. Sérénade aux Nuages.
Toy Doll.
  Adams, E. H.
Toy Shop.
  Bonk, A.
Toy Soldiers on Parade.
  Whitehall, A.
Toy-Town Band.
  Garman, W. M.
Toymaker's Dream.
  Golden, E.
Träum, Kleines Baby.
  Barth, H.
Träumerel.
  Schumann, R. A.
  Segal, J. Fantasy.

Traficante Certified System.
  Traficante, E., comp. and arr.
Traficante Certified System for Piano
    Accordion.
  Traficante, E.
Trail to the Rio Grande.
  Toce, A.
Trailin' My Herd.
  Clyde, T.
De Train Am Comin' Round de Bend.
  Jacks, H. L.
Transcriptions for the Organ from the
    Works of Edward MacDowell.
  MacDowell, E. A.
Traviata.
  Verdi, G.
Tre Flaggor.
  Kraft, A. En Hälsning fran det Gamla
    Landet.
Tre Liriche.
  Agosti, G.
Tre Sånger.
  De Frumerie, G.
  Hallnäs, H.
  Haquinius, A.
Tre Stycken.
  Wiklund, A.
Tread Lightly for You're Treading on
    My Dreams.
  Arthur, W.
Treasure of Sierra Madre.
  Manning, D.
Trenchmore.
  Henry VIII, king of England.
Trente et Quarante.
  Guglielmi, L.
Tres Canciones.
  Jurafsky, A.
Tres Cariños.
  Palacios, J.
Tres Claveles Rojos.
  Longás, F.
Tres Danzas en Estilo Popular
    Argentino.
  Ficher, J.
Tres Estudios.
  Castro, J. M.
Tres Garcia.
  Esperon, M.
Tres Madrigales.
  Holzmann, R.
Tres Piezas.
  Esposito, A. d'.
Trésor des Plus Belles Mélodies de
    Tous les Temps et de Tous les Pays.
  Delfolie, V.
Trespass.
  Addinsell, R.
Tria Phtaiximata.
  Sakellariou, A. Ch.
Trial Testing Time in the Valley.
  Leiter, B.
Trio.
  Damase, J. M. Trio, flute, harp &
    violoncello.
  Martelli, H. Trio, winds.
  Martinon, J. Trio, strings.
Trio Album.
  Ostling, A. E., arr.
Trio, flute, harp & violoncello.
  Damase, J. M.
Trio II.
  Beck, C. Trio, strings, no. 2.
Triolets Dansants.
  Pipon, L. L'Aveugle de Ma Rue.
Triptique Marial.
  Tardif, H. M., father.
Triste.
  De Pace, B.
Trois Antiennes á la Sainte Vierge
    Marie.
  Busser, H.
Trois Cousines.
  Lopez, F.
Trois Impromptus.
  Auric, G.
Trois plus Trois.
  Henry, C.

Trois Trios.
  Schmitt, F. Trios, women's voices &
    orchestra.
Troisiéme quatuor en sol majeur.
  Hahn, R. Quartet, piano & strings, no. 3.
Tropical Ecstasy.
  Fisk, D. F.
Trots Allt.
  Rangström, T.
True Love.
  Clyde, T.
  Hersenhoren, S. Bush Pilot.
Trumpet Overture.
  Purcell, H. The Indian Queen.
Trumpet Tune.
  Stanley, J.
Trumpet Twosome.
  Vandercook, H. A.
Trusting My All to His Care.
  Miller, W.
Try It, It's a Lot of Fun.
  Robison, H. B.
Tsar Saltan.
  Rimskil-Korsakov, N. A.
  Chaĭkovskiĭ, P. I. Concerto, piano, no. 1.
Tschaĭkowsky's Concerto no. 1.
Tu Nada Mas.
  Seijo, R.
Tu Seras.
  Youmans, V. No No Nanette.
Tú Te Vas.
  Zarabozo, D.
Türe Müsste Aufgehn.
  Kreuder, P.
Tulip Time.
  Todd, E. C.
Tulips.
  Quilter, R.
Tulsa, Straight Ahead.
  Hall, J.
Tulsa University Alma Mater.
  Crossman, A. G.
Tune for Humming.
  Loesser, F.
Tune on the Tip of My Heart.
  Rayburn, R.
Tune-Tech Class Method.
  Baker, H. F.
Tuneful Little Tune.
  Theckston, N.
Tuppence Coloured.
  Addinsell, R.
Turkey in Swing.
  Condaris, A. J., arr.
Turmiento.
  Ferraro, A.
Turn over a New Leaf.
  Dash, I.
Turn Thy Face from My Sins.
  Michelsen, B. F.
Turn to Jesus.
  Gagnon, J. B.
Turntable Song, 'Round, an' 'Round, an'
    'Round.
  Green, J. Something in the Wind.
Tus Ojillos Negros.
  Falla, M. de.
Tva Karlekssanger.
  Henneberg, A.
Två Sånger.
  Hallnäs, H.
  Henneberg, A.
  Koch, E. v.
  Liljefors, I.
  Nystroem, G.
Två Stockholmsdikter.
  Rangström, T.
Twelfth Night.
  Bullock, E. Three Songs.
12th Street Rag.
  Bowman, E. L.
Twelve Dances and Sketches.
  Goedicke, A. F.
Twelve Duos.
  Mozart, J. C. W. A.
12 Etudes for Clarinet.
  Polatschek, V.
Twelve Grey Dwarfs.
  Haydn, J.

Twenty-five Chickens, Thirty-five cows.
De Rose, P.
Twenty-five Easy and Progressive
Melodic Studies for Piano.
Concone, G.
Twenty-four Short Studies, for technic and
sight reading without octaves.
Wilmot, L. A.
Twenty Melodic Studies.
Taylor, C. H.
Twenty Teachable Tunes.
Hayes, P. L.
Twenty Tunes for Beginners.
Palmer, E.
22.
Ives, C. E.
Twilight on the Rose.
Mayer, C. I.
Twilight Shadows.
Tobin, L.
Twilight Shadows Bring Sweet Dreams of
You.
Brown, B. F.
Twilight Trail.
Manning, R.
Twinkle-Toes.
Masters, F.
Twinkle, Twinkle, Little Star.
Flood, D. F.
Two Anthems for Chorus.
Campbell, W. N. M.
Two Blocks Down, Turn to the left on the
right hand side of the street.
Rogers, D.
Two Broken Hearts.
Marvin, F.
Ormond, R. It's a Boy.
Two Choral Preludes.
Clarke, A. W.
Two Christmas Carols.
Gevaert, F. A.
Two Christmas Offertories.
Carturan, C.
Two Christmas Songs.
Bush, G.
Two Days Ago.
Arthur, W.
Two Duets.
Grandjany, M.
Two Dwellings.
Clokey, J. W.
Two Eyes Two Lips but No Heart.
Browne, B.
Two Fantasias in Four Parts.
Banchieri, A.
Two Flutes.
Robinson, A.
Two Guitars.
Peery, R. R.
Richards, A.
Two Hearts in Love.
Sendrey, A.
Two Hearts in Summertime.
Jefferies, S.
Two Hearts Will Know.
Alkire, E. H.
Two Hymn Preludes.
Douglas, W.
Two Little Chipmunks.
Jenkins, C. W.
Two Little Etudes for pianoforte.
Adams, E. H.
Two Loves Have I.
Scotto, V.
Two Marches.
Milhaud, D.
Two Moods.
Grundman, C. E.
Two Motets for Dedication of a Church.
Ravanello, O.
Two Motets for Profession of Vows.
Ravanello, O.
Two of You.
Wesley, A.
Two Piano Duets.
Lambert, C.
Two Piano Solos.
Bentley, B. B.

Two Pieces.
Barlin, B.
Diamond, D. L.
Two Pieces for strings.
Walton, W. Henry V.
Two Preludes.
Purcell, H. Preludes, piano.
Two Quartets.
Stamitz, K. Quartets, strings.
Two Responses.
Douglas, W.
Two Robins.
Vandevere, J. L.
2 Russian Dances.
Michaeloff, M.
Two Sentences or Responses.
Maltzeff, A. G.
Two Shadows in the Moonlight.
Gonzales, A.
Two Songs.
Clark, H.
Herbert, I.
Two Songs for Medium Voice.
Hulin, D. Gypsy Trails and Rainbow
Trails.
Two Voices.
Shand, T.
Two Woods.
Ives, C. E. 22.
Two Wrongs Don't Make a Right.
Stewart, H.

U

Uam-pam-piro.
Pozo, L.
Über die Dächer der Grossen Stadt.
Schröder, F.
Ukkaa Song.
McNeil, J. C.
Ultimo Beso.
Rizzuto, J. M.
Ultimo Tango.
Urban, M. Los Misterios del Hampa.
Ultra-Modern Guitar Solos.
Thomas, E.
Umbrella Man.
Stock, L.
Uncle Will March.
Kogen, H.
Under My Window.
Cernkovich, R. Pod mojim Okancem.
Under the Hands.
Wade, S.
Under the Milky Way.
Hyde, M.
Under the Starlight. See title in composer
list.
Under the Stars.
Dellafield, H.
Underbara Ogon.
Henricson, R.
Underneath the Stars.
Arthur, W.
Underneath the Stars in Texas.
Schroeder, R. S.
Underneath the Tropical Moonlight.
Casilao, A.
Unfair to Love.
Watson, O. M.
Unfinished Dance.
Davis, D. M.
Thomas, D.
Unfinished Melody.
Phillips, L.
Unforgettable You.
Bender, A.
Ungarisches Rondo.
Haydn, J. Trio, piano & strings, no. 5.
Uniforms.
Harris, P. B.
Union Pacific Streamliner.
Lee, F.
United Nations.
Baccari, A.
Unity March.
Franko, N.
Unlock the Door to My Heart.
Clyde, T.

Unloved.
Nicoletti, L.
Uns Ist ein Kind Geboren.
Bach, J. S.
Until Now.
Brakebush, H.
Until the Mississippi Runs Dry.
Vander Bunte, O.
Until the Next Time.
Rooney, M.
Until You Came Along.
Arthur, W.
Chanslor, H.
Until You Came Last Night Sweetheart.
Roettker, D.
Unto Us a Child Is Born.
Bach, J. S. Uns Ist ein Kind Geboren.
Up and Down the Monon.
McGee, J. A. The Monon Centennial
Show.
Up Melody Lane with Schubert.
Schubert, F. P.
Up-to-date Happy Birthday Song.
Parmelee, G.
Upper Fifth Avenue.
Kent, A.
Urca.
Flory, S. Carioca Album of Brazilian
Songs.
Useful Organ Music for the Church
Service.
Loud, J. H.
Utah Centennial.
Saylor, T.
Utah, Home of Mine.
Whittaker, N.
Ute i Skären.
De Frumerie, G. Fyra Sånger.
Uvchein Yiskadash.
Silver, M.

V

V. J. Song.
Lamkoff, P.
V'la l'Bon Vent.
Peloquin, C. A. My Friend John.
Vado verso il Mio Paese.
Petralia, T.
Väll then som vidt af höga klippor.
Koch, S. v. Gammalswenska wijsor.
Väverskan.
Haquinius, A.
Vagabundo.
Thebault, V.
Vaggsäng för Humpe.
Kallstenius, E.
Vague.
Petit, P. Y. M. C. Mélodies.
Val Taro Musette.
Del Grosso, P.
Valahol.
Kurucz, J.
Valakinek Muzsikálnak.
Balázs, Á.
Valamikor Szerettelek.
Balázs, Á.
Valčik.
Mokrejs, J.
Vale of the Hudson.
Coffey, E. J.
Valentine Dance.
Rapelje, M.
Valentine's Farewell.
Gounod, C. F. Faust.
Valle Profonda.
Lassus, O. de. Valley, Deep Valley.
Valley, Deep Valley.
Lassus, O. de.
Valley of Dreams-come-true.
D'Artega, A.
Valley of the Sun.
Swanson, C. J.
Vals-Capricho.
Falla, M. de.
Vals Chinoise.
Colombo, J.
Vals Miniatura.
Castro, J. M.

430

Vals Ombord.
　　Taube, E.
Valse.
　　LaFarge, G.
Valse Bleu.
　　Margris.
Valse Bluette.
　　Drigo, R.
Valse Brilliant.
　　Edwards, A. R.
Valse d'Amour.
　　Lowry, T.
Valse Debonnaire.
　　Wright, N. L.
Valse Douce.
　　Scotto, V.　Au Pays des Cigales.
Valse Est une Câline.
　　Guillon, J.
Valse Excentrique.
　　Savino, D.
Valse Grise.
　　Louvel, J.
Valse Joyeuse.
　　Betti, H.　Mam'zelle Printemps.
Valse Lento.
　　Gomez, V.
Valse Obsedante.
　　Bozi, H.　Esclave d'Amour.
Valse Renene.
　　Dvorak, R. F.
Valse Vagabond.
　　Michaeloff, M.
Vandrande Pie___t.
　　Fernström, J.　Sex Sånger.
Variaciones 1942.
　　Garcia Morillo, R.
Variations.
　　Lesur, D. J. Y.
Variations on a Theme by Diabelli.
　　Beethoven, L. van.
Variations on The Grey Cuckoo.
　　Davies, H.
Variety Girl.
　　Loesser, F.
Vayechulu.
　　Silver, M.
Va-zap-pa.
　　Capano, F.
Vehu Rachum.
　　Zilberts, Z.
Vendemmia Overture.
　　Dante, A.
Vengo Cepillando.
　　Suares, S.
Veni Domine.
　　Yon, P.
Veni Sponsa Christi.
　　Purcell, P. E.　O Gloriosa Virginum.
Vent de Folie.
　　Labbe, A.
Vermont Infantry March.
　　Brown, R. H.
Vers des Buts Nouveaux.
　　Velde, E. van de.　Méthode Rose.
Very Great Musician.
　　Slonimsky, N.
Vesper Song.
　　Oliver, H.
Vett a Rözsám Piros Selyem Viganót.
　　Doczy, J.
Vi klarar oss nog åndå.　See Edvard
　　Perssons 5 Båsta.
Vichtige Retzitativen.
　　Yablok, O. Z.
Victor Herbert Made Easy.
　　Herbert, V.
Victor Herbert String Americana.
　　Herbert, V.
Victor Herbert Waltz Medley,
　　Herbert, V.
Victory for Liberty.
　　Patrick, B. E.
Victory Waltz.
　　Tobin, L.
Vid Granskogens Bryn.
　　Reuterskiöld, L.
Vid Medelhavet.
　　Lidholm, I.　Fem Sånger.

Vidala.
　　Valenti Costa, P.　Seis Movimientos
　　Corales a la Manera Popular
　　Argentina.
Vie en Rose.
　　Guglielmi, L.
Viejo Puerto.
　　Orlando, M.　Le Vieux Port.
Vieneme 'nzuonno.　.
　　Lama, G.　I Hear You Sweetly Singing.
Vienna, My City of Dreams.
　　Sieczynski, R.
Vienna, New York, Shanghai.
　　Siegel, P.
Vier Klavierstücke.
　　Bortkiewicz, S.
Vieux Chateau.
　　Hartusch, M.
Vieux Port.
　　Orlando, M.
Villa.
　　Lehár, F.
Villagers All, this Frosty Tide.
　　Angel, J.
Villages of England.
　　Paul, A.
Villaggio.
　　Donnarumma, G.　If You Would Know.
Villanella Rapita.
　　Ferrari, G. G.
Vingt Ans.
　　Schwab, A.
Vingt Choeurs.　See title entry in composer
　　list.
Vingt-cinq Leçons de Solfege Très
　　Difficiles.
　　Desportes, Y. B. M.
Vingt Leçons d'Harmonie.
　　Dandelot, G.
Vingt Regards sur l'Enfant-Jésus.
　　Messiaen, Q.
Vingt-trois Pièces Récréactives et
　　Progressives.
　　Gagnebin, H. D.
Vintage Time.
　　Dante, A.　La Vendemmia Overture.
Violet.
　　Clyde, T.
Violin Method for Young People.
　　Nielsen, H.
Violin School.
　　Carlson, A. P.
Violinade.
　　Fresco, J.
Violinkonsert.
　　Sköld, I.　Concerto, violin.
Virginia City Moon.
　　Blower, M. A.
Vision.
　　Ratcliffe, D.
Visions Iberiques.
　　Grant, J.
Visions in the Night.
　　Close, G.
Vispa Teresa.
　　Wassil, B.
Visual Method Class Piano.
　　Educational Methods, Inc., arr. and
　　comp.
Vitamin You.
　　Clark, £.
Vitamins and Villains.
　　Dunn, R. W.
Vivir para Soñar.
　　Dominguez B., A.
V'natan Lanu Torat Emet.
　　Jospe, E.　Joyful Torah Song.
Vocalise.
　　Rachmaninoff, S.　The Best Known
　　Music of Rachmaninoff.
Vocalise-Étude.
　　Niverd, L.
Voces Matinales.
　　Brénes Candanedo, G.
Voice and keyboard; original compositions
　　for voice and figured bass, no. 1,
　　Purcell, H.　The Blessed Virgin's
　　Expostulation.
Voice and keyboard; original compositions

for voice and figured bass, no. 2,
　　Purcell, H.　Music for a While.
Voice Is Born.
　　Lukas, P.
Voice of Praise.
　　McKinney, B. B., ed.
Voice of the Wind.
　　O'Dell, E. O.
Voice Out of the Whirlwind.
　　Vaughan Williams, R.
Vole, Mon Coeur, Vole.
　　Ferrari, L.
Voluptuosa.
　　Padilla, J.
Votre Amour, Berger.
　　Rameau, J. P.
Votre Visage.
　　Trenet, C.
Voulez-Vous Danser, Grand'mère.
　　Baltel, J. R.
Vu.
　　Bennett, R. R.
Vuela, Vuela Pajarito.
　　Catalán, M. A.
Vuelta de Mambrú.
　　Garcia Morillo, R.　Malborough's
　　Return.
Vuelve.
　　Longás, F.

W

Waiting.
　　Haslett, R.
Waiting and Yearning.
　　Chanslor, H.
Waiting for You.
　　Alkire, E. H.
　　Reth, W. D.
Waiting on Broadway.
　　Storm, J.
Waiting Up.
　　Arthur, W.
Waiting with Tears in My Heart.
　　Bartlett, F.
Wait'll I Get My Sunshine in the
　　Moonlight.
　　Olson, D.
Wake Up and Dream.
　　Porter, C.
Wake Up, You Drowsy Sleepers.
　　Miller, B.
Walk a Little Faster.
　　Dukelsky, V.
Walk Beside Me, O My Saviour.
　　Elwell, H. B.
Walking with Him.
　　Hailett, J. C.　33 Solos and Duets.
Walking with Jesus.
　　Huston, F. C.　Three New Songs.
Wallflower.
　　Sullivan, H.
Walts Bohemia.
　　Saller, A.
Waltz, from Serenade.
　　Chaikovskii, P. I.　Serenade, string
　　orchestra.
Waltz, from Serenade for Strings.
　　Chaikovskii, P. I.
Waltz Me 'round the Rainbow.
　　McMeans, J. M.
Waltz Medley.
　　Yankovic, F. J.
Waltz Melody.
　　Garman, W. M.
Waltz Moderne.
　　Hibbs, C. A.
Waltz of Spring.
　　Thomas, J. J.
Waltz of the Flowers.
　　Chaikovskii, P. I.
Waltz of the Strings.
　　Brobst, H.　Dreaming of Hawaii.
Waltz of the Wind.
　　Rose, F.
Waltz Rhapsody.
　　Stoye, P.
Waltzing in a Dream.
　　Welk, L.

431

Young, V.
Waltzing Marionettes.
  Bermont, G.
Waltzing through the Years.
  Palmer, K., arr.
Waltzing thru' My Dreams.
  Baxter, L.
Waltzing with You.
  Shedd, J. L.
Wanderin'.
  Siegmeister, E.
Wandering Around.
  Clyde, T.
Wanderlust.
  Williams, K.
Wanderlust Blues.
  Lockett, F. E.
Waning Honeymoon.
  Howard, J. E. I Wonder Who's
    Kissing Her Now.
Wanna Be Loved as only you can love.
  Arthur, W.
War Is Hell.
  Bond, J.
War Polka.
  Nasca, J.
Ward Grille Polka.
  Hoven, G.
Warner's Collection of Clarinet Ensembles.
  Hartman, C. P., arr.
Warum.
  Schumann, R. A. Why.
Was Frag' Ich nach der Welt.
  Bach, J. S.
Was It September.
  Mitchell, G.
Was It You.
  Ysabel, A. K.
Was it You and I.
  Denton, E.
Was Mir Behagt.
  Bach, J. S.
Was Still Another Thing.
  Tobin, L.
Washerwomen's Ball.
  Dukelsky, V. Le Bal des Blanchisseuses.
Washington Post.
  Sousa, J. P.
Washington Post March.
  Sousa, J. P.
Watchdog.
  Lake, G.
Watching the Moonbeams Fade.
  Brooks, W. B.
Water Faucet, Drip, Drip, Drip.
  Brodsky, R.
Water Musick.
  Händel, G. F.
Waterfall.
  Carleton, R. L.
Waukegan Cowboy.
  Roth, H. H.
Waves of the Danube.
  Ivanovici, J.
Way out West.
  Hibbeler, R. O.
Way to Music on the Accordion.
  Ronchetto, L.
Way to Music on the Guitar.
  Horacek, L.
Way you Speak.
  Clyde, T.
We All Believe in One True God.
  Mueller, C. F.
We All Have Colds.
  Strickling, G. F.
We Are Going to Build a Highway to the
  Sky.
  Tobin, L.
We Call to Thee, Oh Lord of men.
  O'Hara, G.
We Could Make Such Beautiful Music.
  Katsman, H.
We Do Worship and Praise Thee.
  Rachmaninoff, S.
We Don't Know Who Will Be Next on the
  Roll.
  Wallace, M.

We Hate to Wear Galoshes.
  Beard, C. M.
We Love and Dream.
  Luboshutz, P.
We Met in the Little White Church.
  Ross, F.
We Need a Girl and a Boy.
  Hibbeler, R. O.
We Need a Little Touch from Jesus.
  Bradford, T.
We Praise Thee, O God.
  Marsh, C. H. Te Deum Laudamus.
We Sail the Ocean Blue.
  Sullivan, Sir A. S. H,M,S, Pinafore.
We Thank Our Great Leader.
  Polovinkin, L. A.
We Thank Thee, Lord.
  Durant, C.
We Two.
  Warren, F. R.
We Want Everybody to Be Happy.
  Clarke, H. D. Open the Door.
We Want Peace.
  Rigg, J. B.
We Will Sing of Glory in Victory.
  Talbott, O.
Wearing My Heart on My Sleeve.
  Booter, R.
Wearing of the Green.
  Ballatore, P. arr.
Weasel Goes Modern.
  Todd, E. C.
Wedding Album.
  Wright, L., comp.
Wedding Bells.
  Boone, C.
Wedding Bells Are Sweetly Chiming.
  Curtis, F. E.
Wedding of the Royal Princess.
  Lynton, E.
Wedding of the Winds.
  Hall, J. T.
Wedding Ring in the Spring.
  Carleton, R. L.
Wedding Waltz.
  Ivanovici, J.
Wee Little Waltz.
  Wright, N. L.
Wege der Liebe.
  Kreuder, P.
Weichet Nur.
  Bach, J. S.
Welcome Back to My Heart.
  Miller, B.
Welcome Stranger.
  The Duncan Sisters.
Welcome to All the Pleasures.
  Purcell, H.
We'll Be Happy Day By Day.
  Le Grant, L. G.
We'll Build Our Castle on the Rainbow.
  Wisterman, B.
We'll Gather Lilacs.
  Novello, I.
We'll Just Be Friends.
  Borg, M. L.
We'll Meet Again.
  Kreitner, F.
We'll Soon Reach That Heaven.
  Turner, L.
We'll Take a Trip to Heaven.
  Tobin, L.
Weller School of Popular Piano Playing.
  Weller, B.
Welsh Cradle Song.
  Roberton, H. S.
Wenn Ich Deine Lippen Küsse.
  Kreuder, P. Wege der Liebe.
Wenn Wir Uns Wiederseh'n.
  Kreitner, F. We'll Meet Again.
We're Going on a Vacation.
  Ash, Q.
Were You There.
  Clements, J.
Were You There When They Crucified
  My Lord.
  Duncan, C.
West Is in My Soul.
  Moose, C. E.

West Point March.
  Egner, P. The Official West Point
    March.
Western Idyl.
  Walters, H. L.
Western Song Parade.
  Wakely, J.
Westward Ho.
  Wood, H. A Stanford Rhapsody.
We've Been Strangers Too Long.
  Bartlett, F.
What a Fool I Have Been.
  Monaco, J. V.
What a Fool I Was.
  René, O.
What a Friend We Have in Jesus.
  Adams, W., arr.
What a Mess We've Made.
  Greenwood, N.
What Are You Doing New Year's Eve.
  Loesser, F.
What Did I Ever Do.
  Arthur, W.
What Did You Do Last Night.
  Davis, C. E.
What Ev'ry Woman Knows.
  Osser, A.
What Goes On, comes off.
  Lucraft, H.
What Good Is Dreaming.
  Van Tyle, R.
What Good Is the Moon.
  Carleton, R. L.
What Have I Done to You.
  Richard, L.
What I Want for Christmas.
  Sapp, P.
What If There Had Never Been a
  Calvary.
  Matern, Mrs. L.
What Is Love.
  McNeil, J. C.
What Is This Fragrance.
  Manning, R.
What Is This Thing Called Love.
  Porter, C. Wake Up and Dream.
What Lovely Music.
  Polite, C. R.
What More Can Jesus Do.
  Hawkins, J. M.
What My Heart Can't Say.
  Arthur, W.
What the Blues Are Made of.
  Walter, S. My Love Is What the Blues
    Are Made of.
What Tidings Bringest Thou, Messenger.
  Woodside, J.
What Will I Do.
  Shacklett, A.
What Would It Take.
  Kramer, A.
What Would You Do.
  Corey, W. B.
What You Do to Me.
  Hall, D.
What You Don't Know Won't Hurt You.
  Ellis, S.
Whatcha' Doin' About Love.
  Hall, D.
What'll I Do.
  Bartlett, F.
What's Il to You.
  Hartmann, M. M.
What's the Meaning of That Dream.
  Milligan, U. A.
What's the Use.
  Arthur, W.
  Read, D.
What's the Use of Dreaming.
  Howard, J. E. I Wonder Who's Kissing
    Her Now.
Wheel of Progress.
  Dunhill, T. F.
When a 'Eighty One' Plays a Pun on the
  Piano.
  Jansen, D.
When a Girl's Beautiful.
  Lee, L.
When a Woman Yells Loud Enough she
  usually gets what she wants.
  Miller, B.

When All My Dreams Come True.
Smith, E. F.
When All Thy Mercies, Oh, My God.
Cain, N.
When Are You Coming Home, My Baby.
Robison, W.
When Christ Was Born. See title entry
in composer list.
When Christ Was Born of Mary Free.
Sellew, D. E.
When Day Is Done.
Katcher, R.
When de Stars Begin to Fall.
Roberton, H. S.
When Dreams Come True.
Alkire, E. H.
When I Find the Sweetheart of My Dreams.
Lupe, J.
When I Found You.
Mayer, C. L.
When I Get Back to Dayton, Will You
Be Waitin'.
Granato, L.
When I Get Home.
Pace, C. H.
When I Hear Your Lovely Voice.
Hall, D.
When I Hear Your Name.
Arthur, W.
When I Hold Your Hand in Mine.
Arthur, W.
When I Join My Mother up There.
Malmquist, T.
When I Pass before Your Window.
Fráter, L. Elmegyek Ablakod
Elött.
When I Saw You.
Hall, J. E.
When I Say I Love You, It's Really
My Heart That Speaks.
Hueston, B.
When I See Cy Press Cider.
Goble, D.
When I Set Out for Lyonnesse.
O'Brien, K. E.
When I Think of My Friend, Called
Jesus.
Kennedy, M. L.
When I Was a Young Boy.
Capozzolo, I.
When I Went to See My Nina Gal.
Oftedahl, M.
When I'm Alone with You.
Arthur, W.
When It's Love.
Caldwell, H. C.
When It's Moonlight on the Lake.
Arthur, W.
When It's Over, Over There.
Warner, C. H.
When It's Spring And You're in Love.
Dawn, M.
When Jesus Calls.
Hallett, J. C. 33 Solos and Duets.
When Johnny Strolls with Me.
Cross, S. L.
When Lights Are Low.
West, M.
When London Is Saying Goodnight.
Noel, A.
When Lovers Meet.
Hall, D.
When Moonbeams Kiss the Little Homes
of Ireland.
Carr, M.
When Morning Guilds the Skies.
Barnby, J.
When Peace Has Come.
Chanslor, H.
When Spring Is Here.
Ridenour, R. C.
When Springtime Comes.
McNeil, J. C.
When Stars Are in the Quiet Skies.
Lucas, C.
When That I Was and a Little Tiny Boy.
Bullock, E. Three Songs from
Twelfth Night.
When the Brown Bomber Goes to Town.
Richard, L.

When the Cactus Are A-blooming.
Weigold, F. S.
When the Eastern Skies Shall Open.
Bailes, W.
When the Fire Comes Down.
Harrell, T.
When the Leaves Were Young and Green.
Clark, L. A.
When the Lights Are Low.
Jones, C. W.
When the Lights Go On in My Life
Again.
Adams, W. D.
When the Man in the Moon Says Hello.
Staab, H. B.
When the Maple Leaves Change Color
in the Fall.
Lindstrom, V.
When the Moon Shines upon Sweet Roses.
Douglas, F. M.
When the Mountains Start Calling Me
Home.
Clyde, T.
When the Night Birds Are Calling You
and Me.
Richard, L.
When the One You Love, Loves You.
Lubin, J.
When the Prodigal Son Came Home.
Sergey, J. M.
When the Robins Come Again.
Morgan, O.
When the Roses Bloom Again.
Hall, D.
When the Sun Is Going Down.
Wood, G.
When the Thrill Has Gone, Will You
Still Love Me.
Leach, J.
When There's a Breeze on Lake Louise.
Revel, H.
When Time Counts.
Richard, L.
When Twilight Falls.
Federer, R.
When Two Lights Are Burning.
Perron, H.
When We Meet.
Heaps, R.
When We Meet with Christ Our King.
Essenburg, E. In the Summer Land
Up Yonder.
When Will the Sun Shine Once More for
Me.
Leeker, A.
When Will You Be Madam.
Nurnberg, V.
When You Cross Your Heart.
Camacho, J.
When You Got a Man on Your Mind.
MacGimsey, R.
When You See Those Flying Saucers.
Coben, C.
When You Smile.
Bernard, B. Night Beat.
When You Walked Out with Shoes on I
knew you were gone for good.
Tucker, J. A.
When You Were Sweet Sixteen.
Thornton, J.
When Your Someone Loves You.
Sendrey, A.
When You're Around.
Tobin, L.
Whence Comes All Our Light.
Lavotta, R. Honnan Jö a Fény.
Whence Those Sounds Symphonious.
Otis, E. C.
Whene'er You Call.
Wood, H.
Where.
Williams, C.
Where Are You.
Spencer, T.
Where Are You Now.
Penny, L.
Where Did You Get Those Charms.
Hibbeler, R. O.
Where Does the Uttered Music Go.
Walton, W.

Where Have You Been Hiding.
Brumbelow, I.
Where in the World Is Heaven.
George, D.
Where or When.
Rodgers, R.
Rodgers, R. Babes in Arms.
Where She Goes, I Go.
Pace, F.
Where the Bee Sucks.
Arne, T. The Tempest.
Where the Butterflies Fly.
Vander Bunte, O.
Where the Mississippi Begins.
Hall, D.
Where the Moon Plays Peek-a-boo
Back of the Hills.
Nelson, K. F.
Where the Old Missouri Winds Its Way.
Clark, A. A.
Where the Rio Colorado Wends Its Way.
Chettick, J. M.
Where the River Maple Flows.
Richard, L.
Where the Water Lillies Grow.
Mayer, C. I.
Where the Willow Tree Whispers
Good-Night.
McNeil, J. C.
Where Water Lilies Dream.
King, R.
Wherever You Are.
Arthur, W.
Which Way Does the Pig's Tail Curl.
Martin, R. T.
Which Way Does the Wind Blow.
Phillips, P.
While I'm in This Mood.
Spector, A. b.
While Shepherds Watched.
Schreiber, F. C.
While Shepherds Watched Their Flocks
by Night.
Bairstow, Sir E. C.
While the Desert Blossoms as a Rose.
Olsen, O. N.
Whipporwill Will Soon Be Singing.
Fein, S. B.
Whiskey Is the Devil in liquid form.
Bailes, W.
Whispering Moon.
Peacock, J. F.
Whispering Woo.
Mills, G W.
Whispers of Love.
Schwandt, W.
White Cross.
Moritz, T. L.
White Hills of St. John.
Clyde, T.
White Mice.
Hibbs, C. A.
White Rabbit Is Tired.
Diggle, R. Alice in Wonderland Suite.
White Russian Legend.
Ippolitov-Ivanov, M. M.
Whitehall Suite.
Blow, J.
Whitey and Hogan's Mountain Memories.
Bourne, Inc., comp.
Who Cares Alone for This Blind World.
Bach, J. S. Was Frag' Ich nach der
Welt.
Who Cares for I love you.
Fiedel, S. S.
Who Do You Think You're Foolin'.
Keath, R.
Who Do You Think You're Foolin' Baby.
Dale, J.
Who Put That Dream in Your Eyes.
Brown, N. P.
Who Were You Kissing when you kissed me
last night.
Goodhart, A.
Who-who-oo.
Cooper, F.
Whoa, Texas.
Carleton, R. L.
Who's Gonna Love You When I'm Gone.
Dexter, A.

433

Who's Laughing Now.
  Trams, C. H.
Whose Girl Are You.
  Durlak, J. P. Czyja To Dziewczyna.
Whoso dwelleth.
  Greaves, R. A Psalm of Thanks-
    giving.
Why.
  Cramer, H. G.
  Hall, D.
  Schumann, R. A.
Why Are You Ever So Distant.
  Spencer, V.
Why Can't We Be Sweethearts Again.
  Blair, H.
Why Can't You Wait.
  Henderson, M.
Why Couldn't I Have You.
  Greer, J. B.
Why Did I Leave My Home.
  Young, V.
Why Did It Have to Be.
  Paris, J. B.
Why Did It Have to Be Me.
  Linton, W. T.
Why Did It Have to End so Soon.
  Weldon, F.
Why Did You Say Goodbye.
  Bailes, W.
Why Did You Say You Loved Me.
  Conray, A.
Why Did You Tell Me a Lie.
  Woodford, G. R.
Why Do I.
  Arthur, W.
Why Do I Love You, Oh Why.
  Pritchard, W.
Why Do You Make Promises.
  Jansen, L. D.
Why Do You Treat Me So.
  McNeil, J. C.
Why Do You Want Me Now.
  Sullivan, W. A.
Why Does It Have to Rain on Sunday.
  Merrill, B.
Why Don't You Come Around Any More.
  Fell, F. P.
Why Don't You Get Yourself Together.
  Arthur, W.
Why Don't You Try to Remember the
    Things I Try So Hard to Forget.
  Arthur, W.
Why Dream.
  Laterra, J. L.
Why Must I Keep on Loving You.
  Arthur, W.
Why, Oh Why.
  Cook, M. E.
  Samuels, W.
Why, Oh why, Oh why.
  Chanslor, H.
Why Pretend.
  Bailes, W.
Why Should I Cry over you.
  Conn, C.
Why Should I Have a Heart for You.
  Cavi, F.
Why Shouldn't You Remember Me.
  Lawson, J.
Why Was I Born.
  Kern, J.
Wicked Woman.
  Gonzalez, L. Hembra Mala.
Widow Bird Sat Mourning.
  Ashe, J. R.
  Herbert, I. Two Songs.
Wiener Bonbons.
  Zelwecker, F.
Wild Orchid.
  Williams, J.
Wild Rose.
  George, E.
  Tobin, L.
Wilda.
  Graff, M.
Wildest Gal in Town.
  Fain, S.
Will I Forget You.
  Wooten, I.

Will There Be a Sunset Tomorrow.
  Arthur, W.
Will There Be Sagebrush in Heaven.
  Walla, P.
Will You Listen.
  Robertson, B. G. My Future Address.
Will You Meet Me in the Moonlight
    Tonight.
  Denman, J. T.
Will You Not Come.
  Sergey, J. M.
Will Your Eyes Look into Mine.
  Chanslor, H.
William Tell.
  Rossini, G. A.
Willow Song.
  Carbutt, A.
Willst Du Dein Herz Mir Schenken.
  Bach, J. S.
Wind That Blows in My Hair.
  Arthur, W.
Winding Road.
  Andrew, P.
Winding Wistaria.
  Hellard, R. A.
Windmill.
  Edmunds, C.
Window.
  Richards, K.
Windowpane.
  Trusselle, S. P.
Winds of May.
  Rowley, A.
Winds of the Rolling Prairies.
  Mitchell, R. C.
Wings on Our Feet.
  Waldteufel, E.
Winter Echoes.
  Thomas, J. J.
Winter Time.
  Brezina, W.
Winter Wonderland.
  Bernard, F.
Wir Christenleut.
  Bach, J. S. Uns Ist ein Kind Geboren.
Wise and the Foolish Virgins.
  Atterberg, K. De Favitska Jungsfrurna.
Wise May Bring Their Learning.
  Mueller, C. F.
Wishing You'd Come Back.
  Schwandt, W.
With a Hey and a Hi and a Ho Ho Ho.
  Mizzy, V.
With a Song in my Heart.
  Rodgers, R. Spring Is Here.
With a Yo Heave Ho.
  Blake, D. G.
With All My Heart.
  Lukas, P. A Voice Is Born.
With Bands and Banners.
  Rosenkrans, G.
With Him in Heaven.
  Plank, K. Y.
With My Heart I Follow You.
  Strickland, L.
With My Heart's Contentment.
  Pinto, W.
With the Roses in Her Hair.
  Spina, H.
With the Thoughts of You.
  Zanirato, T. E.
With You, I'm in Love.
  Lyle, T.
With Your Head upon My Heart.
  Arthur, W.
Within My Heart a Song.
  Meredith, I. H.
Within My Memory.
  Lilly, A.
Within My Reach.
  Arthur, W.
Within the Stable.
  Johnson, K. K.
Within Your Eyes.
  Hall, D.
Without a Doubt.
  Penny, L.
Without Fear.
  Smith, W.

Without You.
  Hall, D.
  Preader, A. A.
Without You, Dear, I'm All Alone.
  Van Sickle, R.
Witnessing for Christ.
  Holstein, B. D.
Wivallij wijsa.
  Koch, S. v. Gammalswenska wijsor.
Women's Gospel Trios.
  Lorenz, E. J., comp.
Wonder.
  Larson, E. R.
Wonder If You Know.
  Moor, S. D.
Wonderful Beautiful You.
  Arthur, W.
Wonderful Jesus.
  Jenkins, M. H. Inspired Hymns of
    The Hour.
  Williams, C. C.
Wonderful Story of Grace.
  Fillmore, F. A.
Wonderful Time Up There.
  Abernathy, L. R. Everybody's Gonna
    Have a Wonderful Time Up There.
Wondering.
  Wilson, E. E.
Won't You Believe Me.
  Hoffman, J.
Won't You Come to the Savior.
  Mills, K. M.
Won't You Pray.
  Esters, H. V.
Won't You Remember.
  Bartlett, F.
Won't You Waltz with Me.
  Hall, D.
Wood Nymph's Serenade.
  Yuill, M. Four Out-Door Scenes.
Woodland Echoes.
  Yuill, M. Four Out-Door Scenes.
Woodland Sketches.
  MacDowell, E.
Woodland Stream.
  Fischer, E.
Woodpeckers at Work.
  Lake, G.
Woodwind.
  Pond, D.
Woogie-boogie polka.
  Hoven, G.
Wooin's the Doin'.
  Harman, G. F.
Word of Life Chorus-Melodies.
  Wyrtzen, C. J., comp.
Workin' on de Railroad.
  Childe, R. S.
World Is Mine tonight.
  Posford, G.
World of Tomorrow.
  Johnson, I. M.
World upon World.
  Richard, L.
World Wide Radio Songs. See title entry
    in composer list.
World's Your Home.
  LaBastille, I.
Worthy of You.
  Weisman, B.
Would It Make Any Difference.
  Bartlett, F.
Would You mind.
  Atsell, B.
Wouldn't It Be Grand, My Dear.
  Bartlett, F.
Wouldn't You.
  Schoenberger, L.
Wounded Christ.
  Peckham, R. L.
Wrap Your Troubles in Dreams and dream
    your troubles away.
  Barris, H.
Wynken, Blynken and Nod.
  Paymer, A.

X

Xanthippe.
  Benatzky, R.

434

Y

Y A d' l'Amour.
  Scotto, V. Destins.
Y Avait Une Fois Deux Amoureux.
  Chadron, F.
  Peyronnin, J. On Se Plait.
Y Nadie Sabe Na.
  Morlote, R. L.
Ya d' l'Amour.
  Scott, V. Destins.
Ya Know What.
  Roth, H. H.
Ya para Qué.
  Palacios, J.
Ya, Sure, You Betcha, ay ban tank ay do.
  Solomon, S. H.
Ya Te Pesara.
  Rodriguez, J.
Yaller Gal.
  Arthur, W.
Yanina.
  Berlin, B. Two Pieces.
Yankee Doodle Fantasy.
  Lorenz, E. J.
Yankee Land and you.
  Burns, D.
Yanks behind the Tanks.
  Wherry, B.
Yaravi.
  Napolitano, E. A., Apurimac.
Ye Banks and Braes.
  Quilter, R.
Ye Sons and Daughters of the King.
  Leisring, V.
Years We Left Behind.
  Lafferty, W. H.
Yellow Patch.
  Weiner, L. Gele Late.
Yerra Go On.
  Blythe, B.
Yes, I Do.
  Hune, B.
Yes or No.
  King, A. F.
Yes, 'Tis Then I'll Meet You There.
  Brundle, J.
Yesterday.
  Travis, S.
Yesterday, My Thought Was Only You.
  Sales, J. A.
Yielding.
  Tovey, H. G.
Yo, Yo, Yo.
  Davis, J. Joe! Joe! Joe!
Yodeling Polka.
  Cooley, D. C.
You.
  Arthur, W.
  Chanslor, H.
You Alone.
  Mance, F.
  Seijo, R. Tu Nada Mas.
You and I.
  Alkire, E. H.
  Willson, M.
You and I Together.
  Crawford, J. D.
You and Your Love.
  Brito, A.
You Are an Angel from the Sky.
  Lerner, M.
You Are Love.
  Kern, J.
You Are Mine, All Mine.
  Kaus, O.
You Are My Dream Girl.
  Fisher, M.
You Are My Favorite Dream.
  Shaughnessy, A.
You Are My Inspiration.
  Pearson, A. J.
You Are My Sweetheart.
  Renner, E.
You Are My Temptation.
  Arthur, W.
You Are My World.
  Chanslor, H.
You Are Never Away.
  Rodgers, R. Allegro.

You Are Never Off My Mind.
  Bartlett, F.
You Are So Beautiful.
  Bartlett, F.
You Are the Dawn.
  McNeil, J. C.
You Belong to Me.
  Jackson, C. Q.
You Better Mind.
  Siegmeister, E.
You Better Watch Yourself, Bub.
  Lutcher, N.
You Bore Me.
  Lamkoff, P.
You Broke a Precious Vow.
  Hall, D.
You Came into My Heart.
  Bartlett, F.
You Can Play the Piano.
  Richter, A.
You Can't Believe Everything You Hear.
  Abernathy, L. R.
You Can't Get a Tahicab in Mehico.
  Brandt, A.
You Can't Get Along without Love.
  Arthur, W.
You Can't Go Wrong Doing Right.
  David, L.
You Can't Make Money Dreamin' or I'd be a millionaire.
  Shand, T.
You Can't Play Fair.
  Jacobson, J.
You Can't Put Out a Fire by Fanning the Flame.
  Jay, F.
You Can't Remember and I can't forget.
  Bartlett, F.
You Can't Stop Me from Loving You.
  Sedlack, J.
You Can't Tell the Depth of the Well by the Length of the Handle on the Pump.
  Bond, J.
You Charm the Night.
  Coopersmith, S.
You Cooked Your Goose.
  Nelson, K. F.
You Cut a Fancy Figure in My Heart.
  Hartley, R.
You Darling, You Angel.
  Stout, B.
You Did Your Best to Break My Heart.
  Krieg, R. C.
You Do.
  Myrow, J. Mother Wore Tights.
You Don't Have to Know the Language.
  Van Heusen, J. The Road to Rio.
You Don't Kno' What Lonesome Is till you git to herdin' cows.
  Washburne, C.
You Don't Seem to Care.
  Yamin, J. Que Importa Mi Sufrir.
You Fenced in My Heart.
  Van Tyle, M.
You Gotta Get a Glory.
  Williams, A.
You Had My Heart.
  Brooking, R. L.
You Haven't Got a Chance.
  Hall, D.
You Hit the Nail Right on the Head.
  Turner, Z.
You Kissed Me in My Dreams.
  Bartlett, F.
You Know I Still Care.
  Arthur, W.
You Laughed and I Cried.
  Hayes, B.
You Locked My Heart.
  Bartlett, F.
You Made a Fool Out of Me.
  Penniman, D. G.
You Made Me Crazy 'Bout You.
  Barret, G. F.
You Made the Sun Shine thru the Rain.
  Masonier, C.
You Make My Life All Sunshine in My Dreams.
  Johnson, J. G.

You May Be Gone Forever.
  Richard, L.
You Must Be in Love.
  Hare, M.
You Must Live Like the Bible Say.
  Cheatham, E. C.
You, My Beautiful You.
  Bartlett, F.
You Never Miss the Water Till the Well Runs Dry.
  Lucky, D.
You Never Say You Love Me.
  Weigand, M. M.
You Never Went Away.
  Blondis, M.
You Ought To Know I Miss You.
  Beer, A.
You Owe Me a Kiss.
  Clyde, T.
You Rate High with Me.
  Horst, M.
You Saw Your Soul in Mine.
  Kramer, A. W.
You Say the Sweetest Things.
  Rawson, D.
You Say You Don't Love Me.
  Roberts, P.
You Say You're Sorry.
  Weber, O. T.
You Should Live So Long.
  Horton, V.
You Smiled and Said I Love You.
  Clyde, T.
You Tell Me Your Dream, I'll tell you mine.
  Alkire, E. H.
You Think I Don't Care.
  Bender, L. S.
You Thrilled My Eyes.
  Hall, D.
You Told Me You Loved Me.
  DeMay, A.
You Took My Heart.
  McBryde, E.
You Waited Too Long.
  Tobin, L.
You Went Away.
  Winn, K. E.
You went away and left me.
  Parker, J.
You Were a Workingman, My Lord.
  Demarest, V. B.
You Were Just Seventeen.
  Fogarty, D. F.
You Were Somebody Else's Sweetheart.
  Spina, H.
You Will Be My Dream Come True.
  McPhail, L.
You with the Mona Lisa Eyes.
  Ancliffe, C.
You'd Better Be Good While I'm Gone.
  Conn, M. A.
You'll Always Be the Only One.
  Bailes, W.
You'll Always Care.
  Dorta, A.
You'll Always Have My Heart.
  Peltier, A. J.
You'll Have Your Dreams.
  Myers, M.
You'll Live to Regret It, wait and see.
  Carson, J. L.
You'll Never Break My Heart Again.
  Atwood, H. G.
You'll Never Walk Alone.
  Rodgers, R. Carousel.
You'll Regret.
  Rodriguez, J. Ya Te Pesara.
Young Fiddler.
  Trotter, G.
Young Hero.
  Antoine, brother.
Young Pan America Sings.
  Kleinsinger, G.
Young Prince and the Young Princess.
  Rimskii-Korsakov, N. A. Scheherezade.
Young Trumpeter.
  Lozano, P.

Lightning Source UK Ltd.
Milton Keynes UK
UKHW021252070119
335137UK00014B/689/P